WORLD TREATY INDEX

WORLD TREATY INDEX

MAIN ENTRY SECTION

United Nations Treaty Series: Series I, Numbers 6486–10841; Series II, Numbers 1–657
National Treaty Collections

VOLUME 3

PETER H. ROHN

Associate Professor of Political Science
University of Washington

Santa Barbara, California
Oxford, England

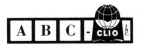

Library of Congress Catalog Card Number 73–83352
ISBN Clothbound 5-Volume Set 0–87436–125–7
ISBN Clothbound 6-Volume Set 0–87436–132–X
ISBN Clothbound Volume 3 0–87436–128–1

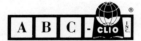

American Bibliographical Center—Clio Press, Inc.
2040 Alameda Padre Serra
Santa Barbara, California

European Bibliographical Center—Clio Press
Woodside House
Hinksey Hill
Oxford OX1 5BE, England

Designed by Barbara Monahan
Composed by Datagraphics Press
Printed and bound by Halliday Lithograph Corporation
in the United States of America

Contents

List of Abbreviations

Accept UN Charter	Unilateral declaration accepting UN Charter obligations
Admin Cooperation	Administrative Cooperation
African Coffee Org	African Coffee Organization
African Devel Bank	African Development Bank
African Insur Org	African Insurance Organization
African Tech Org	African Technical Organization
Afromalagasy Coffee	Afro-Malagasy Coffee Organization
Afromalagasy Org	Afro-Malagasy Organization
AID (Int Devel)	Agency for International Development
Allied Milit Occup	Allied Military Occupation
Anglo-Egypt Sudan	Anglo-Egyptian Sudan
Asian Devel Bank	Asian Development Bank
Asian Productivity	Asian Productivity Organization
Bel-Lux Econ Union	Belgium-Luxembourg Economic Union
BENELUX Econ Union	Belgium-Netherlands-Luxembourg Economic Union
Bnk Int Settlement	Bank for International Settlements
British Occup Germ	British Occupied Germany
Brit Solomon Is	British Solomon Islands
Brit Virgin Is	British Virgin Islands
Central Afri Power	Central African Power Company
Central Afri Rep	Central African Republic
Central Am Bank	Central American Bank
CERN (Nuc Resrch)	European Organization for Nuclear Research
China People's Rep	People's Republic of China
Cmte Industr Devel	Committee for Industrial Development
COMECON (Econ Aid)	Council for Mutual Economic Assistance
Consul/Citizenship	Consular Matters and Citizenship
Customs Coop Coun	Customs Cooperation Council
East Afri Service	East African Common Services Organization
ECSC (Coal/Steel)	European Coal and Steel Community
EEC (Econ Commnty)	European Economic Community
EFTA (Free Trade)	European Free Trade Association
EURATOM	European Atomic Energy Commission
Eur Foot Mouth Dis	European Commission for the Control of Foot and Mouth Disease
EUROCONTROL	European Organization for the Safety of Air Navigation
Eur Plant Protect	European and Mediterranean Plant Protection Organization
Eur Space Research	European Space Research Organization
Eur Space Vehicle	European Space Vehicle Launcher Development Organization
FAO (Food Agri)	Food and Agricultural Organization of the United Nations
Fed Malay States	Federation of Malay States
Fed of Malaya	Federation of Malaya
Fed Rhod/Nyasaland	Federation of Rhodesia and Nyasaland
French Occup Germ	French Occupied Germany
Fr Equatorial Afri	French Equatorial Africa
GATT (Tariff/Trade)	General Agreement on Tariffs and Trade
Gen Communications	General Communications
General HEW	General Health, Education and Welfare

General IGO	General Intergovernmental Organizations
Hague Private IL	The Hague Conference on Private International Law
IAEA (Atom Energy)	International Atomic Energy Agency
IBRD Project	International Bank for Reconstruction and Development Project
IBRD (World Bank)	International Bank for Reconstruction and Development
ICAO (Civil Aviat)	International Civil Aviation Organization
ICJ (Int Court)	International Court of Justice
ICJ Option Clause	International Court of Justice Optional Clause
	Unilateral declaration accepting ICJ optional clause, or
	Unilateral declaration regarding UN General Assembly in connection with ICJ optional clause, or
	Unilateral limited declaration regarding ICJ optional clause
IDA (Devel Assoc)	International Development Association
IFC (Finance Corp)	International Finance Corporation
IGO Establishment	Intergovernmental Organization Establishment
IGO Multilat	Three or more IGO's and no State
IGO Operations	Intergovernmental Organization Operations
IGO Status/Immunit	Intergovernmental Organizational Privileges and Immunities
ILO Labor	International Labour Organization Labor Matters
ILO (Labor Org)	International Labour Organization
IMCO (Maritime Org)	Inter-Governmental Maritime Consultative Organization
IMF (Fund)	International Monetary Fund
Indo-Pac Fish Coun	Indo-Pacific Fisheries Council
Int Bureau Educ	International Bureau of Education
Int Coffee Org	International Coffee Organization
Int Coun Expl Sea	International Council for the Exploration of the Sea
Inter-Allied Com	Inter-Allied Commission
Inter-Am Devel Bnk	Inter-American Development Bank
Inter-Am Nuc Energ	Inter-American Nuclear Energy Commission
Int Exhibit Bureau	International Exhibition Bureau
Intgov Eur Migrat	Intergovernmental Committee for European Migration
Int Org Metrology	International Organization of Legal Metrology
Int Rail Transport	Central Office for International Railway Transport
Int Relief Union	International Relief Union
Int Rice Com	International Rice Commission
Int Sugar Council	International Sugar Council
Int Whaling Com	International Whaling Commission
Int Wheat Coun	International Wheat Council
Int Wine Office	International Vine and Wine Office
IRO (Refugee Org)	International Refugees Organization
It Aegean Colonies	Italian Colonies in the Aegean
ITU (Telecommun)	International Telecommunication Union
LAFTA (Free Trade)	Latin American Free Trade Association
Lat Am Nuclear Arm	Agency for the Prohibition of Nuclear Weapons in Latin America
Medit Fish Council	Mediterranean Fisheries Council
Micronesia (US)	Micronesia (US Trust Territories in the Pacific)
Milit Assistance	Military Assistance
Milit Installation	Military Installations
Milit Occupation	Military Occupation
Milit Servic/Citiz	Military Service and Citizenship
Mostfavored Nation	Most Favored Nation
NATO (North Atlan)	North Atlantic Treaty Organization
NE Atlantic Fish	Northeast Atlantic Fisheries Commission
Netherld Antilles	Netherlands Antilles
New Hebrides Is	New Hebrides Islands
Non-IBRD Project	Non-International Bank for Reconstruction and Development Project
Non-ILO Labor	Non-International Labour Organization Labor Matters
Northern Territ	Northern Territories
NW Atlantic Fish	International Commission for the Northwest Atlantic Fisheries
OAS (Am States)	Organization of American States
OAU (Afri Unity)	Organization of African Unity
OECD (Econ Coop)	Organization for Economic Co-operation and Development
Org Ctrl Am States	Organization of Central American States
Org Rail Collabor	Soviet Railroad Organization
Other HEW	Other Health, Education and Welfare
Other Party Combin	More than one State and more than one IGO, or
	Other combination of parties

Other Unilat Decla	Other unilateral declaration
Pan Am Health Org	Pan American Health Organization
Patents/Copyrights	Patents and Copyrights
Peace/Disarmament	Peace and Disarmament
Petrol Export Org	Organization of Petroleum Exporting Countries
Portug Colonies	Portuguese Colonies
Portug East Africa	Portuguese East Africa
Portug West Africa	Portuguese West Africa
Privil/Immunities	Privileges and Immunities
Refrigeration Inst	International Institute for Refrigeration
Rhine Navigation	Central Commission for the Navigation of the Rhine
Russ Fed Sov Rep	Russian Federation of Soviet Republics
Scientific Project	Scientific Projects
SEATO (SE Asia)	Southeast Asia Treaty Organization
Serb/Croat/Slovene	The Kingdom of the Serbs, Croats and Slovenes
South Africa	Union of South Africa
South Pacific Com	South Pacific Commission
Spanish Colonies	Spanish Colonies in Africa
Special Decla ICJ	Unilateral special declaration regarding ICJ
Specif Claim/Waive	Specific Claims and Waivers
Specif Goods/Equip	Specific Goods and Equipment
State/IGO Group	One State and mixed group of IGO-State partners, or
	One State and three or more IGO's, or
	One State and two IGO's, or
	Two or more States and one IGO
States Multilat	Three or more military governments and one State, or
	Three or more States and no IGO, or
	Three or more States under FAO auspices, or
	Three or more States under IAEA auspices, or
	Three or more States under ILO auspices, or
	Three or more States under UN auspices, or
	Three or more States under UNESCO auspices, or
	Three or more States under WHO auspices
Subsahara Tech Com	Commission for Technical Cooperation in Africa South of the Sahara
Tech Assistance	Technical Assistance
Trinidad/Tobago	Trinidad and Tobago
Turk-Caicose Is	Turk-Caicose Islands
UK Great Britain	United Kingdom of Great Britain and Northern Ireland
Ukrainian SSR	Ukrainian Soviet Socialist Republic
UN Charter	United Nations Charter
UN Emergency Fund	United Nations Emergency Fund
UNESCO (Educ/Cult)	United Nations Scientific and Cultural Organization
UN Hi Com Refugees	Office of the United Nations High Commissioner for Refugees
UNICEF (Children)	United Nations Children's Fund
UNIDO (Industrial)	United Nations Industrial Development Organization
United Arab Rep	United Arab Republic
UNKRA (Korean Rec)	United Nations Commission for the Unification and Rehabilitation of Korea
UN Mission Congo	United Nations Mission to the Congo
UN Relief Palestin	United Nations Relief and Works Agency for Palestine Refugees in the Near East
UNRRA (Relief)	United Nations Relief and Rehabilitation Association
UN Special Fund	United Nations Special Fund
UNTAB (Tech Assis)	United Nations Technical Assistance Board
UPU (Postal Union)	Universal Postal Union
US Agri Commod Aid	US Agricultural Commodity Aid
USA (United States)	United States of America
US Occup Germ	United States Occupied Germany
USSR (Soviet Union)	Union of Soviet Socialist Republics
Vatican/Holy See	The Vatican and the Holy See
WEU (West Europe)	Western European Union
WHO (World Health)	World Health Organization
WMO (Meteorology)	World Meteorological Organization
W Pacif Hi Command	West Pacific High Command

MAIN ENTRY SECTION

United Nations Treaty Series: Series I, Numbers 6486–10841; Series II, Numbers 1–657
National Treaty Collections

United Nations Treaty Series:

Series I, Numbers 6486–10841; Series II, Numbers 1–657

106486 Bilateral Agreement **451 UNTS 77**
SIGNED: 20 Dec 61   FORCE: 20 Dec 61
REGISTERED: 17 Jan 63 Japan
ARTICLES: 6 LANGUAGE: English.
HEADNOTE: ZOO SANITARY AGREEMENT
TOPIC: Sanitation
CONCEPTS: General cooperation. Exchange of official publications. Exchange of information and documents. Domestic legislation. Recognition and enforcement of legal decisions. Specialists exchange. Disease control. Veterinary. Recognition of degrees. Teacher and student exchange. Vocational training. Scientific exchange. Trade procedures. General technical assistance.
PROCEDURE: Duration. Termination.
PARTIES:
 Argentina
 Japan

106487 Bilateral Exchange **451 UNTS 91**
SIGNED: 20 Dec 61   FORCE: 20 Dec 61
REGISTERED: 17 Jan 63 Japan
ARTICLES: 2 LANGUAGE: English.
HEADNOTE: TAXATION INCOME SHIPPING
TOPIC: Taxation
CONCEPTS: Definition of terms. Conformity with municipal law. Domestic legislation. Tax exemptions. Merchant vessels.
PROCEDURE: Termination.
PARTIES:
 Argentina
 Japan

106488 Bilateral Agreement **451 UNTS 97**
SIGNED: 9 Jan 62   FORCE: 11 Sep 62
REGISTERED: 17 Jan 63 Japan
ARTICLES: 7 LANGUAGE: English. Japanese.
HEADNOTE: POSTWAR ECONOMIC ASSISTANCE
TOPIC: Direct Aid
CONCEPTS: Definition of terms. General cooperation. Exchange rates and regulations. Interest rates. Payment schedules. Local currency. Claims and settlements. Economic assistance.
TREATY REF: 136UNTS45.
PARTIES:
 Japan
 USA (United States)

106489 Bilateral Agreement **451 UNTS 125**
SIGNED: 28 Mar 62   FORCE: 28 Mar 62
REGISTERED: 17 Jan 63 Japan
ARTICLES: 8 LANGUAGE: English. Portuguese.
HEADNOTE: TEXTILE TRAINING CENTER
TOPIC: Education
CONCEPTS: Definition of terms. Annex or appendix reference. Friendship and amity. Alien status. Conformity with municipal law. General cooperation. Personnel. General property. Responsibility and liability. Institute establishment. Vocational training. Research and development. Expense sharing formulae. Tax exemptions. Customs exemptions. General technical assistance. Materials, equipment and services.

PROCEDURE: Duration. Termination.
PARTIES:
 Brazil
 Japan

106490 Bilateral Agreement **451 UNTS 143**
SIGNED: 31 Mar 62   FORCE: 31 Mar 62
REGISTERED: 17 Jan 63 Japan
ARTICLES: 8 LANGUAGE: English.
HEADNOTE: MARINE PRODUCTS PROCESSING TRAINING CENTER
TOPIC: Education
CONCEPTS: Definition of terms. Annex or appendix reference. Friendship and amity. Privileges and immunities. Conformity with municipal law. General cooperation. Personnel. General property. Responsibility and liability. Institute establishment. Vocational training. Expense sharing formulae. Tax exemptions. Customs exemptions. General technical assistance. Materials, equipment and services.
PROCEDURE: Duration. Renewal or Revival.
PARTIES:
 India
 Japan

106491 Bilateral Agreement **451 UNTS 155**
SIGNED: 23 Apr 62   FORCE: 23 Apr 62
REGISTERED: 17 Jan 63 Japan
ARTICLES: 9 LANGUAGE: English.
HEADNOTE: DEMONSTRATION FARMS
TOPIC: Education
CONCEPTS: Definition of terms. Annex or appendix reference. Friendship and amity. Privileges and immunities. Conformity with municipal law. General cooperation. Operating agencies. General property. Responsibility and liability. Institute establishment. Vocational training. Expense sharing formulae. Tax exemptions. Customs exemptions. General technical assistance. Materials, equipment and services.
PROCEDURE: Duration. Renewal or Revival.
PARTIES:
 India
 Japan

106492 Bilateral Agreement **451 UNTS 167**
SIGNED: 30 Nov 61   FORCE: 2 Apr 62
REGISTERED: 18 Jan 63 USA (United States)
ARTICLES: 16 LANGUAGE: English.
HEADNOTE: EXCHANGE INTERNATIONAL MONEY ORDERS
TOPIC: Postal Service
CONCEPTS: Annex or appendix reference. Conformity with municipal law. Accounting procedures. Currency. Exchange rates and regulations. Payment schedules. Regulations. Money orders and postal checks. Rates and charges.
PROCEDURE: Duration. Termination.
PARTIES:
 Morocco
 USA (United States)

106493 Bilateral Agreement **451 UNTS 179**
SIGNED: 1 May 62   FORCE: 1 May 62
REGISTERED: 18 Jan 63 USA (United States)
ARTICLES: 6 LANGUAGE: English.
HEADNOTE: AGRI COMMOD TITLE I
TOPIC: US Agri Commod Aid
CONCEPTS: General provisions. Annex or appendix reference. Exchange of information and documents. Reexport of goods, etc.. Exchange rates and regulations. Transportation costs. Local currency. Commodities schedule. Purchase authorization. Surplus commodities. Mutual consultation.
PARTIES:
 India
 USA (United States)

106494 Bilateral Exchange **451 UNTS 197**
SIGNED: 9 May 62   FORCE: 9 May 62
REGISTERED: 18 Jan 63 USA (United States)
ARTICLES: 2 LANGUAGE: English. French.
HEADNOTE: GUARANTEE PRIVATE INVESTMENTS
TOPIC: Claims and Debts
CONCEPTS: Private investment guarantee.
PARTIES:
 Guinea
 USA (United States)

106495 Bilateral Agreement **451 UNTS 205**
SIGNED: 21 May 62   FORCE: 21 May 62
REGISTERED: 18 Jan 63 USA (United States)
ARTICLES: 5 LANGUAGE: English. Spanish.
HEADNOTE: TRADE IN AGRICULTURE
TOPIC: General Trade
CONCEPTS: Detailed regulations. General cooperation. Exchange of information and documents. Import quotas. Reexport of goods, etc.. Commodity trade. Delivery schedules. Smuggling.
PARTIES:
 Guatemala
 USA (United States)

106496 Bilateral Agreement **451 UNTS 215**
SIGNED: 8 Dec 62   FORCE: 8 Dec 62
REGISTERED: 21 Jan 63 WHO (World Health)
ARTICLES: 6 LANGUAGE: French.
HEADNOTE: TECHNICAL ADVISORY ASSISTANCE
TOPIC: Tech Assistance
CONCEPTS: Definition of terms. Privileges and immunities. General cooperation. Exchange of information and documents. Personnel. Responsibility and liability. Title and deeds. Exchange. Scholarships and grants. Vocational training. Research and development. Expense sharing formulae. Local currency. Domestic obligation. Special projects. Materials, equipment and services. IGO status. Conformity with IGO decisions.
PROCEDURE: Amendment. Termination.
PARTIES:
 Cameroon
 WHO (World Health)

3

106497 Bilateral Agreement **451 UNTS 227**
SIGNED: 2 Dec 54   FORCE: 20 May 55
REGISTERED: 24 Jan 63 Iran
ARTICLES: 5 LANGUAGE: Persian. Russian.
HEADNOTE: SETTLEMENT FRONTIER FINANCIAL
  QUESTIONS
TOPIC: Territory Boundary
CONCEPTS: Establishment of commission. Post-
  war claims settlement. Fish, wildlife, and natural
  resources. Markers and definitions.
INTL ORGS: Special Commission.
PROCEDURE: Ratification.
PARTIES:
  Iran
  USSR (Soviet Union)

106498 Bilateral Agreement **451 UNTS 269**
SIGNED: 10 Dec 62   FORCE: 10 Dec 62
REGISTERED: 24 Jan 63 United Nations
ARTICLES: 6 LANGUAGE: French.
HEADNOTE: OPERATIONAL EXECUTIVE ADMINIS-
  TRATIVE PERSONNEL
TOPIC: Tech Assistance
CONCEPTS: Treaty implementation. Annex or ap-
  pendix reference. Privileges and immunities.
  Personnel. Responsibility and liability. Arbitra-
  tion. Procedure. Negotiation. Vocational train-
  ing. Compensation. Expense sharing formulae.
  Tax exemptions. Customs exemptions. Domestic
  obligation. Special projects. Status of experts.
  Conformity with IGO decisions.
INTL ORGS: Permanent Court of Arbitration. Arbi-
  tration Commission.
PROCEDURE: Amendment. Termination.
PARTIES:
  Ivory Coast
  United Nations
                  ANNEX
608 UNTS 374. United Nations. Force 27 Oct 67.
608 UNTS 374. Ivory Coast. Termination
  27 Oct 67. Force 27 Oct 67.

106499 Bilateral Agreement **451 UNTS 281**
SIGNED: 12 Feb 62   FORCE: 12 Feb 62
REGISTERED: 24 Jan 63 USA (United States)
ARTICLES: 6 LANGUAGE: English. Spanish.
HEADNOTE: AGRI COMMOD TITLE I
TOPIC: US Agri Commod Aid
CONCEPTS: General provisions. Annex or appendix reference. Exchange of information and documents. Reexport of goods, etc.. Exchange rates
  and regulations. Payment schedules. Transportation costs. Local currency. Commodities schedule. Purchase authorization. Surplus commodities. Mutual consultation.
PARTIES:
  Bolivia
  USA (United States)
                  ANNEX
458 UNTS 368. Bolivia. Amendment 14 Jul 62.
  Force 14 Jul 62.
458 UNTS 368. USA (United States). Amendment
  14 Jul 62. Force 14 Jul 62.
462 UNTS 370. USA (United States). Amendment
  6 Dec 62. Force 6 Dec 62.
462 UNTS 370. Bolivia. Amendment 6 Dec 62.
  Force 6 Dec 62.
474 UNTS 367. Bolivia. Amendment 29 Mar 63.
  Force 29 Mar 63.
474 UNTS 367. USA (United States). Amendment
  29 Mar 63. Force 29 Mar 63.

106500 Bilateral Exchange **451 UNTS 307**
SIGNED: 13 Apr 62   FORCE: 13 Apr 62
REGISTERED: 24 Jan 63 USA (United States)
ARTICLES: 2 LANGUAGE: English. Spanish.
HEADNOTE: FURNISHING DEFENSE ARTICLES
  SERVICES
TOPIC: Milit Assistance
CONCEPTS: Non-prejudice to UN charter. Confor-
  mity with municipal law. Exchange of informa-
  tion and documents. Inspection and observation.
  Materials, equipment and services. Return of
  equipment and recapture. Security of informa-
  tion. Exchange of defense information. Restric-
  tions on transfer.
TREATY REF: 21UNTS77.
PARTIES:
  El Salvador
  USA (United States)

106501 Bilateral Exchange **452 UNTS 3**
SIGNED: 18 Apr 62   FORCE: 18 Apr 62
REGISTERED: 24 Jan 63 USA (United States)
ARTICLES: 2 LANGUAGE: English. Spanish.
HEADNOTE: ASSIGNMENT TELEVISION CHAN-
  NELS
TOPIC: Telecommunications
CONCEPTS: Previous treaty replacement. Bands
  and frequency allocation. Facilities and equip-
  ment. Telecommunications.
TREATY REF: 152UNTS27;   180UNTS378;
  445UNTS325.
PROCEDURE: Termination.
PARTIES:
  Mexico
  USA (United States)

106502 Bilateral Agreement **452 UNTS 25**
SIGNED: 27 Apr 62   FORCE: 27 Apr 62
REGISTERED: 24 Jan 63 USA (United States)
ARTICLES: 5 LANGUAGE: English. Spanish.
HEADNOTE: AGRI COMMOD TITLE I
TOPIC: US Agri Commod Aid
CONCEPTS: General provisions. Annex or appen-
  dix reference. Exchange of information and doc-
  uments. Reexport of goods, etc.. Exchange rates
  and regulations. Transportation costs. Local cur-
  rency. Commodities schedule. Purchase authori-
  zation. Surplus commodities. Mutual consulta-
  tion.
PARTIES:
  USA (United States)
  Uruguay

106503 Bilateral Agreement **452 UNTS 49**
SIGNED: 15 May 62   FORCE: 15 May 62
REGISTERED: 24 Jan 63 USA (United States)
ARTICLES: 5 LANGUAGE: English. Spanish.
HEADNOTE: TRADE IN AGRICULTURE
TOPIC: General Trade
CONCEPTS: Conditions. General cooperation. Ex-
  change of information and documents. Reexport
  of goods, etc.. Trade procedures. Financial pro-
  grams. Commodity trade. Delivery schedules.
  Smuggling. Loan and credit.
PARTIES:
  El Salvador
  USA (United States)

106504 Bilateral Agreement **452 UNTS 59**
SIGNED: 6 Jun 62   FORCE: 6 Jun 62
REGISTERED: 24 Jan 63 USA (United States)
ARTICLES: 4 LANGUAGE: English. French.
HEADNOTE: TARIFFS PURSUANT GATT AR-
  RANGEMENTS
TOPIC: General Trade
CONCEPTS: Detailed regulations. Annex or appen-
  dix reference. Tariffs. Trade procedures.
INTL ORGS: General Agreement on Tariffs and
  Trade.
TREATY REF: 278UNTS208.
PROCEDURE: Termination.
PARTIES:
  Haiti
  USA (United States)

106505 Bilateral Agreement **452 UNTS 67**
SIGNED: 30 Jun 59   FORCE: 20 Aug 59
REGISTERED: 25 Jan 63 IBRD (World Bank)
ARTICLES: 5 LANGUAGE: English. French.
HEADNOTE: GUARANTEE MANGANESE
TOPIC: IBRD Project
CONCEPTS: Definition of terms. Annex or appen-
  dix reference. Exchange of information and doc-
  uments. Inspection and observation. Bonds.
  Fees and exemptions. Tax exemptions. Domestic
  obligation. Terms of loan. Loan regulations. Loan
  guarantee. Guarantor non-interference.
PARTIES:
  France
  IBRD (World Bank)

106506 Bilateral Agreement **452 UNTS 123**
SIGNED: 30 Jun 59   FORCE: 20 Aug 59
REGISTERED: 25 Jan 63 IBRD (World Bank)
ARTICLES: 5 LANGUAGE: English.
HEADNOTE: GUARANTEE MANGANESE
TOPIC: IBRD Project
CONCEPTS: Definition of terms. Annex or appen-
  dix reference. Exchange of information and doc-
  uments. Inspection and observation. Bonds.

Fees and exemptions. Tax exemptions. Domestic
  obligation. Terms of loan. Loan regulations. Loan
  guarantee. Guarantor non-interference. Industry.
PARTIES:
  Congo (Brazzaville)
  IBRD (World Bank)

106507 Bilateral Agreement **452 UNTS 135**
SIGNED: 30 Jun 59   FORCE: 20 Aug 59
REGISTERED: 25 Jan 63 IBRD (World Bank)
ARTICLES: 5 LANGUAGE: English.
HEADNOTE: GUARANTEE MANGANESE
TOPIC: IBRD Project
CONCEPTS: Definition of terms. Annex or appen-
  dix reference. Exchange of information and doc-
  uments. Inspection and observation. Bonds.
  Fees and exemptions. Tax exemptions. Domestic
  obligation. Terms of loan. Loan regulations. Loan
  guarantee. Guarantor non-interference. Industry.
PARTIES:
  Gabon
  IBRD (World Bank)

106508 Bilateral Agreement **452 UNTS 147**
SIGNED: 17 Mar 60   FORCE: 4 Oct 60
REGISTERED: 25 Jan 63 IBRD (World Bank)
ARTICLES: 5 LANGUAGE: English. French.
HEADNOTE: GUARANTEE IRON ORE
TOPIC: IBRD Project
CONCEPTS: Definition of terms. Annex or appen-
  dix reference. Exchange of information and doc-
  uments. Inspection and observation. Bonds.
  Fees and exemptions. Tax exemptions. Domestic
  obligation. Terms of loan. Loan regulations. Loan
  guarantee. Guarantor non-interference. Industry.
PARTIES:
  France
  IBRD (World Bank)

106509 Bilateral Agreement **452 UNTS 211**
SIGNED: 17 Mar 60   FORCE: 4 Oct 60
REGISTERED: 25 Jan 63 IBRD (World Bank)
ARTICLES: 5 LANGUAGE: English.
HEADNOTE: GUARANTEE IRON ORE
TOPIC: IBRD Project
CONCEPTS: Definition of terms. Exchange of infor-
  mation and documents. Inspection and observa-
  tion. Bonds. Fees and exemptions. Tax exemp-
  tions. Domestic obligation. Terms of loan. Loan
  regulations. Loan guarantee. Guarantor non-
  interference. Industry.
PARTIES:
  Mauritania
  IBRD (World Bank)

106510 Bilateral Exchange **452 UNTS 223**
SIGNED: 31 Jul 62   FORCE: 30 Aug 62
REGISTERED: 25 Jan 63 Philippines
ARTICLES: 4 LANGUAGE: English.
HEADNOTE: ABOLITION VISA REQUIREMENTS
  WAIVER VISA FEES
TOPIC: Visas
CONCEPTS: Time limit. Visa abolition. Fees and
  exemptions.
PROCEDURE: Termination.
PARTIES:
  Malaysia
  Philippines

106511 Bilateral Exchange **452 UNTS 235**
SIGNED: 31 Jul 62   FORCE: 30 Aug 62
REGISTERED: 25 Jan 63 Philippines
ARTICLES: 2 LANGUAGE: English.
HEADNOTE: ABOLITION VISA REQUIREMENTS
  WAIVER VISA FEES
TOPIC: Visas
CONCEPTS: Emergencies. Time limit. Visa aboli-
  tion. Fees and exemptions.
PROCEDURE: Termination.
PARTIES:
  Philippines
  Thailand

106512 Bilateral Agreement **452 UNTS 243**
SIGNED: 15 Nov 62   FORCE: 15 Nov 62
REGISTERED: 29 Jan 63 United Nations
ARTICLES: 10 LANGUAGE: French.
HEADNOTE: ASSISTANCE
TOPIC: Tech Assistance
CONCEPTS: Detailed regulations. Treaty imple-
  mentation. Visas. Privileges and immunities. Ex-

change of information and documents. Inspection and observation. Operating agencies. Personnel. Responsibility and liability. Title and deeds. Use of facilities. Arbitration. Procedure. Negotiation. Reexport of goods, etc.. Accounting procedures. Exchange rates and regulations. Expense sharing formulae. Fees and exemptions. Tax exemptions. Customs exemptions. Domestic obligation. General technical assistance. Materials, equipment and services. IGO status. Conformity with IGO decisions.
INTL ORGS: International Atomic Energy Agency. International Court of Justice. United Nations. Arbitration Commission.
TREATY REF: 1UNTS15; 33UNTS261; 374UNTS147.
PROCEDURE: Amendment. Termination.
PARTIES:
Algeria
UN Special Fund

106513 Bilateral Agreement **452 UNTS 261**
SIGNED: 29 Jan 63   FORCE: 29 Jan 63
REGISTERED: 29 Jan 63 United Nations
ARTICLES: 6 LANGUAGE: English.
HEADNOTE: ARRANGEMENT VIENNA CONFERENCE CONSULAR RELATIONS
TOPIC: Consul/Citizenship
CONCEPTS: Privileges and immunities. General cooperation. Personnel. Use of facilities. Financial programs.
INTL ORGS: International Atomic Energy Agency.
TREATY REF: 452UNTS253.
PARTIES:
Austria
United Nations

106514 Bilateral Agreement **452 UNTS 271**
SIGNED: 19 Jan 63   FORCE: 31 Jan 63
REGISTERED: 31 Jan 63 United Nations
ARTICLES: 8 LANGUAGE: French.
HEADNOTE: UNICEF ACTIVITIES
TOPIC: Direct Aid
CONCEPTS: Treaty implementation. Privileges and immunities. General cooperation. Exchange of information and documents. Informational records. Public information. Responsibility and liability. Title and deeds. Attachment of funds. Tax exemptions. Customs exemptions. Domestic obligation. Assistance. General aid. Materials, equipment and services. Distribution. IGO status.
INTL ORGS: United Nations.
TREATY REF: 1UNTS15.
PROCEDURE: Amendment. Termination.
PARTIES:
Mauritania
UNICEF (Children)

106515 Bilateral Treaty **453 UNTS 3**
SIGNED: 1 Aug 62   FORCE: 1 Aug 62
REGISTERED: 1 Feb 63 New Zealand
ARTICLES: 7 LANGUAGE: English.
HEADNOTE: FRIENDSHIP
TOPIC: General Amity
CONCEPTS: Friendship and amity. Peaceful relations. Alien status. General cooperation.
PROCEDURE: Termination.
PARTIES:
New Zealand
Western Samoa
ANNEX
485 UNTS 372. Western Samoa. Implementation 8 Mar 63.
485 UNTS 372. New Zealand. Implementation 8 Mar 63.

106516 Bilateral Exchange **453 UNTS 11**
SIGNED: 2 Oct 61   FORCE: 2 Nov 61
REGISTERED: 1 Feb 63 New Zealand
ARTICLES: 2 LANGUAGE: English. Spanish.
HEADNOTE: VISAS
TOPIC: Visas
CONCEPTS: Territorial application. Time limit. Denial of admission. Resident permits. Conformity with municipal law. Fees and exemptions.
PARTIES:
New Zealand
Spain

106517 Multilateral Agreement **453 UNTS 20**
SIGNED: 21 Jan 63   FORCE: 23 Jan 63

REGISTERED: 1 Feb 63 United Nations
ARTICLES: 6 LANGUAGE: French.
HEADNOTE: TECHNICAL ASSISTANCE
TOPIC: Tech Assistance
CONCEPTS: Definition of terms. Privileges and immunities. General cooperation. Exchange of information and documents. Personnel. Responsibility and liability. Title and deeds. Use of facilities. Exchange. Scholarships and grants. Vocational training. Research and development. Exchange rates and regulations. Expense sharing formulae. Local currency. Domestic obligation. General technical assistance. Materials, equipment and services. IGO status. Conformity with IGO decisions.
INTL ORGS: United Nations Technical Assistance Board.
TREATY REF: 76UNTS132; 1UNTS15; 33UNTS261; 374UNTS147.
PROCEDURE: Amendment. Termination.
PARTIES:
Rwanda SIGNED: 23 Jan 63 FORCE: 23 Jan 63
FAO (Food Agri) SIGNED: 23 Jan 63 FORCE: 23 Jan 63
IAEA (Atom Energy) SIGNED: 23 Jan 63 FORCE: 23 Jan 63
ICAO (Civil Aviat) SIGNED: 23 Jan 63 FORCE: 23 Jan 63
ILO (Labor Org) SIGNED: 23 Jan 63 FORCE: 23 Jan 63
ITU (Telecommun) SIGNED: 23 Jan 63 FORCE: 23 Jan 63
UNESCO (Educ/Cult) SIGNED: 23 Jan 63 FORCE: 23 Jan 63
United Nations SIGNED: 23 Jan 63 FORCE: 23 Jan 63
UPU (Postal Union) SIGNED: 23 Jan 63 FORCE: 23 Jan 63
WHO (World Health) SIGNED: 23 Jan 63 FORCE: 23 Jan 63
WMO (Meteorology) SIGNED: 23 Jan 63 FORCE: 23 Jan 63
ANNEX
651 UNTS 397. IMCO (Maritime Org). Accession 18 Oct 68. Force 18 Oct 68.
651 UNTS 397. UNIDO (Industrial). Accession 18 Oct 68. Force 18 Oct 68.

106518 Multilateral Agreement **453 UNTS 36**
SIGNED: 5 Feb 63   FORCE: 5 Feb 63
REGISTERED: 5 Feb 63 United Nations
ARTICLES: 6 LANGUAGE: French.
HEADNOTE: TECHNICAL ASSISTANCE
TOPIC: Tech Assistance
CONCEPTS: Definition of terms. Privileges and immunities. General cooperation. Exchange of information and documents. Personnel. Responsibility and liability. Title and deeds. Use of facilities. Exchange. Scholarships and grants. Vocational training. Research and development. Exchange rates and regulations. Expense sharing formulae. Local currency. Domestic obligation. General technical assistance. Materials, equipment and services. IGO status. Conformity with IGO decisions.
INTL ORGS: United Nations Technical Assistance Board.
TREATY REF: 76UNTS132; 1UNTS15; 33UNTS261; 374UNTS147.
PROCEDURE: Amendment. Termination.
PARTIES:
Burundi SIGNED: 5 Feb 63 FORCE: 5 Feb 63
FAO (Food Agri) SIGNED: 5 Feb 63 FORCE: 5 Feb 63
IAEA (Atom Energy) SIGNED: 5 Feb 63 FORCE: 5 Feb 63
ICAO (Civil Aviat) SIGNED: 5 Feb 63 FORCE: 5 Feb 63
ILO (Labor Org) SIGNED: 5 Feb 63 FORCE: 5 Feb 63
ITU (Telecommun) SIGNED: 5 Feb 63 FORCE: 5 Feb 63
UNESCO (Educ/Cult) SIGNED: 5 Feb 63 FORCE: 5 Feb 63
United Nations SIGNED: 5 Feb 63 FORCE: 5 Feb 63
UPU (Postal Union) SIGNED: 5 Feb 63 FORCE: 5 Feb 63
WHO (World Health) SIGNED: 5 Feb 63 FORCE: 5 Feb 63
WMO (Meteorology) SIGNED: 5 Feb 63 FORCE: 5 Feb 63
ANNEX
651 UNTS 398. IMCO (Maritime Org). Accession

27 Nov 68. Force 27 Nov 68.
651 UNTS 398.

106519 Bilateral Agreement **453 UNTS 51**
SIGNED: 8 Nov 59   FORCE: 12 Dec 59
REGISTERED: 7 Feb 63 United Arab Rep
ARTICLES: 8 LANGUAGE: Arabic.
HEADNOTE: UTILIZATION NILE
TOPIC: Specific Resources
CONCEPTS: Annex or appendix reference. Establishment of commission. Currency. Funding procedures. Non-bank projects. Facilities and property. Regulation of natural resources.
INTL ORGS: Special Commission.
PARTIES:
Sudan
United Arab Rep

106520 Bilateral Agreement **453 UNTS 79**
SIGNED: 8 Feb 63   FORCE: 8 Feb 63
REGISTERED: 8 Feb 63 United Nations
ARTICLES: 8 LANGUAGE: Arabic.
HEADNOTE: ESTABLISHMENT REGIONAL CENTER DEMOGRAPHIC RESEARCH TRAINING AFRICA
TOPIC: Direct Aid
CONCEPTS: Visas. Privileges and immunities. General cooperation. Exchange of information and documents. Personnel. Responsibility and liability. Establishment of commission. Institute establishment. Scholarships and grants. Research and development. Claims and settlements. Domestic obligation. General technical assistance. Internal structure. Conformity with IGO decisions.
INTL ORGS: United Nations Technical Assistance Board. Special Commission.
TREATY REF: 1UNTS15.
PROCEDURE: Amendment. Duration. Renewal or Revival. Termination.
PARTIES:
United Nations
United Arab Rep
ANNEX
486 UNTS 434. United Arab Rep. Force 30 Jun 63.
486 UNTS 434. United Nations. Force 30 Jun 63.

106521 Bilateral Convention **453 UNTS 95**
SIGNED: 8 Oct 59   FORCE: 14 Sep 61
REGISTERED: 14 Feb 63 France
ARTICLES: 30 LANGUAGE: French. German.
HEADNOTE: DOUBLE TAXATION INCOME FORTUNE SUCCESSION DUTIES
TOPIC: Taxation
CONCEPTS: Definition of terms. Territorial application. Privileges and immunities. Nationality and citizenship. Conformity with municipal law. Exchange of official publications. Negotiation. Teacher and student exchange. Claims and settlements. Debts. Taxation. Death duties. Equitable taxes. Air transport. Merchant vessels.
PROCEDURE: Duration. Ratification. Termination.
PARTIES:
Austria
France

106522 Bilateral Agreement **453 UNTS 151**
SIGNED: 20 Nov 62   FORCE: 20 Nov 62
REGISTERED: 14 Feb 63 United Nations
ARTICLES: 8 LANGUAGE: French.
HEADNOTE: UNICEF ACTIVITIES
TOPIC: Direct Aid
CONCEPTS: Treaty implementation. Privileges and immunities. General cooperation. Exchange of information and documents. Informational records. Public information. Responsibility and liability. Title and deeds. Attachment of funds. Tax exemptions. Customs exemptions. Domestic obligation. Assistance. General aid. Materials, equipment and services. Distribution. IGO status.
INTL ORGS: United Nations.
TREATY REF: 1UNTS15.
PROCEDURE: Amendment. Termination.
PARTIES:
Algeria
UNICEF (Children)

106523 Bilateral Exchange **453 UNTS 161**
SIGNED: 26 Nov 62   FORCE: 26 Nov 62

5

REGISTERED: 14 Feb 63 Fed of Malaya
ARTICLES: 2 LANGUAGE: English.
HEADNOTE: EXCHANGE PLANTING MATERIAL
TOPIC: Specif Goods/Equip
CONCEPTS: Previous treaty replacement. Previous treaties adherence. Quarantine. Disease control. Export quotas. Import quotas. Agricultural commodities. Specific goods and equipment.
TREATY REF: 247UNTS400.
PARTIES:
Australia
Fed of Malaya

106524 Multilateral Agreement **453 UNTS 168**
SIGNED: 14 Feb 63   FORCE: 14 Feb 63
REGISTERED: 14 Feb 63 United Nations
ARTICLES: 6 LANGUAGE: English.
HEADNOTE: TECHNICAL ASSISTANCE
TOPIC: Tech Assistance
CONCEPTS: Definition of terms. Privileges and immunities. General cooperation. Exchange of information and documents. Personnel. Responsibility and liability. Title and deeds. Use of facilities. Exchange. Scholarships and grants. Vocational training. Research and development. Exchange rates and regulations. Expense sharing formulae. Local currency. Domestic obligation. General technical assistance. Materials, equipment and services. IGO status. Conformity with IGO decisions.
INTL ORGS: United Nations Technical Assistance Board.
TREATY   REF: 76UNTS132;   1UNTS15; 33UNTS261; 374UNTS147.
PROCEDURE: Amendment. Termination.
PARTIES:
Nepal SIGNED: 14 Feb 63 FORCE: 14 Feb 63
FAO (Food Agri) SIGNED: 14 Feb 63 FORCE: 14 Feb 63
IAEA (Atom Energy) SIGNED: 14 Feb 63 FORCE: 14 Feb 63
ICAO (Civil Aviat) SIGNED: 14 Feb 63 FORCE: 14 Feb 63
ILO (Labor Org) SIGNED: 14 Feb 63 FORCE: 14 Feb 63
ITU (Telecommun) SIGNED: 14 Feb 63 FORCE: 14 Feb 63
UNESCO (Educ/Cult) SIGNED: 14 Feb 63 FORCE: 14 Feb 63
United Nations SIGNED: 14 Feb 63 FORCE: 14 Feb 63
UPU (Postal Union) SIGNED: 14 Feb 63 FORCE: 14 Feb 63
WHO (World Health) SIGNED: 14 Feb 63 FORCE: 14 Feb 63
WMO (Meteorology) SIGNED: 14 Feb 63 FORCE: 14 Feb 63
ANNEX
552 UNTS 419. UNTAB (Tech Assis). Amendment 17 Dec 65. Force 23 Dec 65.
552 UNTS 419. Nepal. Amendment 23 Dec 65. Force 23 Dec 65.

106525 Bilateral Treaty **453 UNTS 183**
SIGNED: 28 Jan 58   FORCE: 24 Oct 59
REGISTERED: 18 Feb 63 Netherlands
ARTICLES: 22 LANGUAGE: Dutch. German.
HEADNOTE: MINING COAL
TOPIC: Specif Goods/Equip
CONCEPTS: Annex or appendix reference. Previous treaties adherence. Social security. Customs exemptions. Industry. Facilities and property. Regulation of natural resources. Raw materials.
TREATY REF: 111LTS153.
PROCEDURE: Ratification.
PARTIES:
Germany, West
Netherlands

106526 Bilateral Agreement **453 UNTS 221**
SIGNED: 9 Feb 61   FORCE: 21 Nov 61
REGISTERED: 18 Feb 63 Netherlands
ARTICLES: 14 LANGUAGE: French.
HEADNOTE: FINANCIAL CLAIMS
TOPIC: Claims and Debts
CONCEPTS: Claims, debts and assets. Claims and settlements. Debts.
PROCEDURE: Ratification.
PARTIES:
Netherlands
Yugoslavia

106527 Bilateral Exchange **453 UNTS 239**
SIGNED: 7 Apr 61   FORCE: 8 Apr 61
REGISTERED: 18 Feb 63 Netherlands
ARTICLES: 2 LANGUAGE: French. Spanish.
HEADNOTE: ABOLITION TRAVEL VISA REQUIREMENTS
TOPIC: Visas
CONCEPTS: Emergencies. Territorial application. Time limit. Previous treaty replacement. Visa abolition. Denial of admission. Resident permits. Conformity with municipal law.
TREATY REF: 292UNTS37.
PROCEDURE: Denunciation.
PARTIES:
Chile
Netherlands

106528 Bilateral Agreement **453 UNTS 249**
SIGNED: 25 Jan 63   FORCE: 25 Jan 63
REGISTERED: 19 Feb 63 United Nations
ARTICLES: 8 LANGUAGE: English.
HEADNOTE: UNICEF ACTIVITIES
TOPIC: Direct Aid
CONCEPTS: Treaty implementation. Privileges and immunities. General cooperation. Exchange of information and documents. Informational records. Public information. Responsibility and liability. Title and deeds. Attachment of funds. Tax exemptions. Customs exemptions. Domestic obligation. Assistance. General aid. Materials, equipment and services. Distribution. IGO status.
INTL ORGS: United Nations.
TREATY REF: 1UNTS115.
PROCEDURE: Amendment. Termination.
PARTIES:
UNICEF (Children)
Tanganyika
ANNEX
523 UNTS 341. United Nations. Prolongation 14 Jan 65.
523 UNTS 341. Tanzania. Prolongation 14 Jan 65.

106529 Bilateral Exchange **453 UNTS 259**
SIGNED: 16 Jul 62   FORCE: 16 Jul 62
REGISTERED: 20 Feb 63 Belgium
ARTICLES: 2 LANGUAGE: English. French.
HEADNOTE: RECOGNITION NOTARIAL ACTS
TOPIC: Admin Cooperation
CONCEPTS: Notarial acts and services.
PARTIES:
Belgium
India

106530 Bilateral Convention **453 UNTS 267**
SIGNED: 14 Jul 61   FORCE: 14 Jul 62
REGISTERED: 20 Feb 63 UK Great Britain
ARTICLES: 14 LANGUAGE: English. German.
HEADNOTE: RECOGNITION ENFORCEMENT JUDGEMENTS CIVIL COMMERCIAL MATTERS
TOPIC: Admin Cooperation
CONCEPTS: Definition of terms. Territorial application. Recognition and enforcement of legal decisions. Procedure.
PROCEDURE: Duration. Ratification. Termination.
PARTIES:
Austria
UK Great Britain

106531 Multilateral Protocol **453 UNTS 299**
SIGNED: 9 May 62   FORCE: 9 May 62
REGISTERED: 20 Feb 63 UK Great Britain
ARTICLES: 8 LANGUAGE: English. French.
HEADNOTE: ESTABLISHMENT PREPARATORY GROUP
TOPIC: IGO Establishment
CONCEPTS: Expense sharing formulae. Subsidiary organ.
PROCEDURE: Duration.
PARTIES:
Australia SIGNED: 9 May 62 FORCE: 9 May 62
Belgium SIGNED: 9 May 62 FORCE: 9 May 62
France SIGNED: 9 May 62 FORCE: 9 May 62
Germany, West SIGNED: 9 May 62 FORCE: 9 May 62
Italy SIGNED: 9 May 62 FORCE: 9 May 62
Netherlands SIGNED: 9 May 62 FORCE: 9 May 62
UK Great Britain SIGNED: 9 May 62 FORCE: 9 May 62

106532 Bilateral Exchange **453 UNTS 309**
SIGNED: 20 Aug 62   FORCE: 19 Sep 62

REGISTERED: 20 Feb 63 UK Great Britain
ARTICLES: 2 LANGUAGE: English. Spanish.
HEADNOTE: ABOLITION VISAS
TOPIC: Visas
CONCEPTS: Emergencies. Territorial application. Time limit. Visa abolition. Denial of admission. Conformity with municipal law.
PROCEDURE: Denunciation.
PARTIES:
El Salvador
UK Great Britain

106533 Bilateral Exchange **453 UNTS 317**
SIGNED: 20 Sep 62   FORCE: 20 Sep 62
REGISTERED: 20 Feb 63 UK Great Britain
ARTICLES: 2 LANGUAGE: English. German.
HEADNOTE: EXCHANGE PUBLICATIONS
TOPIC: Admin Cooperation
CONCEPTS: Exchange of official publications.
PROCEDURE: Termination.
PARTIES:
Germany, West
UK Great Britain

106534 Bilateral Agreement **453 UNTS 325**
SIGNED: 29 Nov 62   FORCE: 29 Nov 62
REGISTERED: 20 Feb 63 UK Great Britain
ARTICLES: 7 LANGUAGE: English. French.
HEADNOTE: DEVELOPMENT PRODUCTION CIVIL SUPERSONIC TRANSPORT AIRCRAFT
TOPIC: Scientific Project
CONCEPTS: Treaty implementation. Establishment of commission. Research and scientific projects. Research and development. Indemnities and reimbursements.
PARTIES:
France
UK Great Britain

106535 Bilateral Exchange **454 UNTS 3**
SIGNED: 16 Mar 62   FORCE: 16 Mar 62
REGISTERED: 20 Feb 63 USA (United States)
ARTICLES: 2 LANGUAGE: English. Spanish.
HEADNOTE: SPACE VEHICLE TRACKING STATION
TOPIC: Scientific Project
CONCEPTS: Repatriation of nationals. General cooperation. Operating agencies. General property. Use of facilities. Research cooperation. Research results. Communication satellites testing. Scientific exchange. Research and development. Tax exemptions. Economic assistance.
PROCEDURE: Duration. Renewal or Revival. Termination.
PARTIES:
Argentina
USA (United States)

106536 Bilateral Exchange **454 UNTS 13**
SIGNED: 29 Mar 62   FORCE: 29 Mar 62
REGISTERED: 20 Feb 63 USA (United States)
ARTICLES: 2 LANGUAGE: English.
HEADNOTE: USE PEACE CORPS FAO PROJECTS
TOPIC: IGO Operations
CONCEPTS: Privileges and immunities. Interagency agreements.
INTL ORGS: United Nations.
PARTIES:
FAO (Food Agri)
USA (United States)

106537 Bilateral Exchange **454 UNTS 25**
SIGNED: 25 May 62   FORCE: 25 May 62
REGISTERED: 20 Feb 63 USA (United States)
ARTICLES: 2 LANGUAGE: English. Korean.
HEADNOTE: WAIVER FEES VISAS
TOPIC: Visas
CONCEPTS: Visas. Fees and exemptions.
PROCEDURE: Termination.
PARTIES:
Korea, South
USA (United States)

106538 Bilateral Agreement **454 UNTS 31**
SIGNED: 19 Jul 62   FORCE: 19 Jul 62
REGISTERED: 20 Feb 63 USA (United States)
ARTICLES: 6 LANGUAGE: English.
HEADNOTE: AGRI COMMOD
TOPIC: US Agri Commod Aid
CONCEPTS: Currency. Agricultural commodities.
PARTIES:
Ceylon (Sri Lanka)
USA (United States)

106539 Multilateral Treaty **454 UNTS 47**
SIGNED: 10 Jun 58   FORCE: 22 Apr 60
REGISTERED: 25 Feb 63 Org Ctrl Am States
ARTICLES: 28 LANGUAGE: Spanish.
HEADNOTE: CENTRAL AMERICAN ECONOMIC IN-
TEGRATION TREATY
TOPIC: General Economic
CONCEPTS: Conditions. Exceptions and exemptions. General provisions. Treaty implementation. Treaty interpretation. Annex or appendix
reference. Informational records. Free passage
and transit. General property. Establishment of
commission. Dispute settlement. Arbitration.
Procedure. Special tribunals. Export quotas. Import quotas. Free trade. Trade procedures. Monetary and gold transfers. Non-interest rates and
fees. Quotas. Most favored nation clause. General. Customs duties. Customs declarations. Industry. General transportation. Registration certificate. Passenger transport. Navigational conditions.   General   communications.
Telecommunications.
INTL ORGS: Central American Trade Council. Organization of Central American States. United
Nations. Arbitration Commission.
PROCEDURE: Denunciation. Duration. Ratification.
Registration. Renewal or Revival.
PARTIES:
Costa Rica SIGNED: 10 Jun 58
El Salvador SIGNED: 10 Jun 58 RATIFIED:
29 Apr 59 FORCE: 2 Jun 59
Guatemala SIGNED: 10 Jun 58 RATIFIED:
2 Jun 59 FORCE: 2 Jun 59
Honduras SIGNED: 10 Jun 58 RATIFIED:
22 Apr 60 FORCE: 22 Apr 60
Nicaragua SIGNED: 10 Jun 58 RATIFIED:
17 Feb 59 FORCE: 2 Jun 59

106540 Multilateral Agreement **454 UNTS 115**
SIGNED: 10 Jun 58   FORCE: 10 Sep 62
REGISTERED: 25 Feb 63 Org Ctrl Am States
ARTICLES: 65 LANGUAGE: Spanish.
HEADNOTE: ROAD TRAFFIC
TOPIC: Land Transport
CONCEPTS: Conditions. Definition of terms. De-
tailed regulations. General provisions. Annex or
appendix reference. Registration certificate. Ag-
ricultural vehicles and construction. Driving per-
mits. Motor vehicles and combinations. Rail-
ways. Road rules.
INTL ORGS: Organization of Central American
States. United Nations.
TREATY REF: 125UNTS3; 454UNTS211.
PROCEDURE: Accession. Denunciation. Ratifica-
tion. Registration.
PARTIES:
Costa Rica SIGNED: 10 Jun 58
El Salvador SIGNED: 10 Jun 58 RATIFIED:
29 Apr 59 FORCE: 17 Dec 59
Guatemala SIGNED: 10 Jun 58 RATIFIED:
17 Nov 59 FORCE: 17 Dec 59
Honduras SIGNED: 10 Jun 58 RATIFIED:
10 Aug 62 FORCE: 10 Sep 62
Nicaragua SIGNED: 10 Jun 58 RATIFIED:
5 May 59 FORCE: 17 Dec 59

106541 Multilateral Agreement **454 UNTS 211**
SIGNED: 10 Jun 58   FORCE: 9 Apr 59
REGISTERED: 25 Feb 63 Org Ctrl Am States
ARTICLES: 57 LANGUAGE: Spanish.
HEADNOTE: UNIFORM ROAD SIGNS SIGNALS
TOPIC: Land Transport
CONCEPTS: Annex or appendix reference. Gen-
eral cooperation. Roads and highways. Road
rules.
INTL ORGS: Organization of Central American
States. United Nations.
PROCEDURE: Accession. Denunciation. Ratifica-
tion. Registration.
PARTIES:
Costa Rica SIGNED: 10 Jun 58
El Salvador SIGNED: 10 Jun 58 RATIFIED:
29 Apr 59 FORCE: 29 Apr 59
Guatemala SIGNED: 10 Jun 58 RATIFIED:
17 Nov 59 FORCE: 17 Nov 59
Honduras SIGNED: 10 Jun 58 RATIFIED:
10 Aug 62 FORCE: 10 Aug 62
Nicaragua SIGNED: 10 Jun 58 RATIFIED:
9 Apr 59 FORCE: 9 Apr 59

106542 Multilateral Agreement **454 UNTS 289**
SIGNED: 1 Sep 59   FORCE: 16 Aug 62
REGISTERED: 25 Feb 63 Org Ctrl Am States

ARTICLES: 16 LANGUAGE: Spanish.
HEADNOTE: EQUALIZATION IMPORT DUTIES
CHARGES
TOPIC: Customs
CONCEPTS: Detailed regulations. Annex or appen-
dix reference. Tariffs. Customs duties.
INTL ORGS: Central American Trade Council. Or-
ganization of Central American States.
PROCEDURE: Accession. Duration. Ratification.
Registration.
PARTIES:
Costa Rica SIGNED: 1 Sep 59
El Salvador SIGNED: 1 Sep 59 RATIFIED:
30 Jun 60 FORCE: 29 Sep 60
Guatemala SIGNED: 1 Sep 59 RATIFIED:
27 Jun 60 FORCE: 29 Sep 60
Honduras SIGNED: 1 Sep 59 RATIFIED:
16 Aug 62 FORCE: 16 Aug 62
Nicaragua SIGNED: 1 Sep 59 RATIFIED:
29 Sep 60 FORCE: 29 Sep 60
ANNEX
547 UNTS 332.   El   Salvador.   Ratification
27 Jan 64. Force 11 Oct 64.
547 UNTS 332. Guatemala. Ratification 7 Oct 63.
Force 11 Oct 64.
547 UNTS 332.   Honduras.   Implementation
29 Jan 63. Force 11 Oct 64.
547 UNTS 332.   Nicaragua.   Implementation
29 Jan 63. Force 11 Oct 64.
547 UNTS 332. Costa Rica. Ratification 2 Oct 64.
Force 11 Oct 64.

106543 Multilateral Treaty **455 UNTS 3**
SIGNED: 13 Dec 60   FORCE: 27 Apr 62
REGISTERED: 25 Feb 63 Org Ctrl Am States
ARTICLES: 33 LANGUAGE: Spanish.
HEADNOTE: CENTRAL AMERICAN ECONOMIC IN-
TEGRATION TREATY
TOPIC: General Economic
CONCEPTS: Conditions. Exceptions and exemptions. General provisions. Treaty implementation. Annex or appendix reference. Privileges
and immunities. General cooperation. Informational records. Free passage and transit. Legal
protection and assistance. Recognition and enforcement of legal decisions. Establishment of
commission. Arbitration. Procedure. Special tribunals. Export quotas. Import quotas. Free trade.
Reciprocity in trade. Export subsidies. Trade procedures. Banking. Balance of payments. Currency. Exchange rates and regulations. Non-
interest rates and fees. Quotas. General. Customs duties. Customs declarations. Loan and
credit. Industry. Routes and logistics. Decisions.
INTL ORGS: Central American Economic Council.
Organization of Central American States.
TREATY REF: 454UNTS47,289; 383UNTS3.
PROCEDURE: Accession. Denunciation. Duration.
Future Procedures Contemplated. Registration.
Renewal or Revival. Ratification.
PARTIES:
El Salvador SIGNED: 13 Dec 60 RATIFIED:
8 May 61 FORCE: 3 Jun 61
Guatemala SIGNED: 13 Dec 60 RATIFIED:
5 May 61 FORCE: 3 Jun 61
Honduras SIGNED: 13 Dec 60 RATIFIED:
27 Apr 62 FORCE: 27 Apr 62
Nicaragua SIGNED: 13 Dec 60 RATIFIED:
26 May 61 FORCE: 3 Jun 61

106544 Multilateral Agreement **455 UNTS 204**
SIGNED: 13 Dec 60   FORCE: 24 May 61
REGISTERED: 25 Feb 63 Org Ctrl Am States
ARTICLES: 42 LANGUAGE: Spanish.
HEADNOTE: CENTRAL AMERICAN BANK ECO-
NOMIC INTEGRATION
TOPIC: IGO Establishment
CONCEPTS: Treaty interpretation. Privileges and
immunities. Juridical personality. Arbitration.
Procedure. Accounting procedures. Banking.
Bonds. Currency. Investments. Exchange rates
and regulations. Funding procedures. Customs
exemptions. Agriculture. Economic assistance.
Admission. Establishment. Headquarters and fa-
cilities. Internal structure. Freedom of meeting.
IGO obligations.
INTL ORGS: Central American Bank. Organization
of Central American States.
PROCEDURE: Accession. Denunciation. Duration.
Ratification.
PARTIES:
El Salvador SIGNED: 13 Dec 60 RATIFIED:
8 May 61 FORCE: 8 May 61
Guatemala SIGNED: 13 Dec 60 RATIFIED:

5 May 61 FORCE: 8 May 61
Honduras SIGNED: 13 Dec 60 RATIFIED:
5 May 61 FORCE: 8 May 61
Nicaragua SIGNED: 13 Dec 60 RATIFIED:
24 May 61 FORCE: 24 May 61
ANNEX
491 UNTS 400. Costa Rica. Accession 23 Sep 63.

106545 Bilateral Convention **455 UNTS 241**
SIGNED: 1 Dec 59   FORCE: 17 Feb 62
REGISTERED: 25 Feb 63 Netherlands
ARTICLES: 22 LANGUAGE: French.
HEADNOTE: VETERINARY CONVENTION
TOPIC: Sanitation
CONCEPTS: Detailed regulations. Previous treaty
extension. Exchange of official publications. Ex-
change of information and documents. Estab-
lishment of commission. Procedure. Border con-
trol. Disease control. Veterinary. Trade proce-
dures.
PROCEDURE: Amendment. Denunciation. Dura-
tion. Future Procedures Contemplated. Ratifica-
tion. Renewal or Revival.
PARTIES:
Italy
Netherlands

106546 Bilateral Agreement **455 UNTS 259**
SIGNED: 6 Aug 60   FORCE: 6 Aug 60
REGISTERED: 25 Feb 63 Netherlands
ARTICLES: 22 LANGUAGE: French.
HEADNOTE: RECRUITMENT PLACEMENT WORK-
ERS
TOPIC: Non-ILO Labor
CONCEPTS: Conditions. Definition of terms. De-
tailed regulations. Exceptions and exemptions.
Exchange of information and documents. Estab-
lishment of commission. Public health. Employ-
ment regulations. Safety standards. Wages and
salaries. Non-ILO labor relations. Administrative
cooperation. Social security. Migrant worker. Ex-
pense sharing formulae.
INTL ORGS: European Economic Community.
TREATY REF: 298UNTS3.
PROCEDURE: Denunciation. Duration. Renewal or
Revival.
PARTIES:
Italy
Netherlands
ANNEX
551 UNTS 326.   Netherlands.   Amendment
6 Dec 65. Force 6 Dec 65.
551 UNTS 326.   Italy.   Amendment   6 Dec 65.
Force 6 Dec 65.

106547 Bilateral Agreement **455 UNTS 276**
SIGNED: 8 Dec 60   FORCE: 8 Aug 62
REGISTERED: 25 Feb 63 Netherlands
ARTICLES: 9 LANGUAGE: Dutch. Arabic. French.
HEADNOTE: CULTURAL AGREEMENT
TOPIC: Culture
CONCEPTS: Treaty interpretation. Friendship and
amity. Conformity with municipal law. General
cooperation. Recognition of degrees. Exchange.
Teacher and student exchange. Scholarships
and grants. Exchange. General cultural cooper-
ation. Artists. Anthropology and archeology. Re-
search results. Scientific exchange. Research
and development.
PROCEDURE: Duration. Ratification. Renewal or
Revival. Termination.
PARTIES:
Netherlands
United Arab Rep

106548 Bilateral Agreement **455 UNTS 289**
SIGNED: 5 Nov 62   FORCE: 27 Jan 63
REGISTERED: 25 Feb 63 Finland
ARTICLES: 11 LANGUAGE: Finnish. Swedish.
HEADNOTE: FRONTIER CUSTOMS COOPERATION
TOPIC: Customs
CONCEPTS: General cooperation. Juridical per-
sonality. Claims and settlements. Customs du-
ties. Frontier crossing points.
PROCEDURE: Ratification. Termination.
PARTIES:
Finland
Sweden

106549 Bilateral Convention **455 UNTS 305**
SIGNED: 4 Sep 61   FORCE: 28 Dec 62
REGISTERED: 27 Feb 63 Denmark

ARTICLES: 21 LANGUAGE: Danish. English.
HEADNOTE: DOUBLE TAXATION FISCAL EVASION TAXES INCOME
TOPIC: Taxation
CONCEPTS: Definition of terms. Territorial application. Privileges and immunities. Conformity with municipal law. Exchange of official publications. Teacher and student exchange. Claims and settlements. Taxation. Tax credits. Equitable taxes. General. Tax exemptions. Air transport.
PROCEDURE: Duration. Ratification. Termination.
PARTIES:
Denmark
Pakistan

106550 Bilateral Treaty **455 UNTS 337**
SIGNED: 10 Nov 61 FORCE: 30 Dec 62
REGISTERED: 5 Mar 63 Austria
ARTICLES: 30 LANGUAGE: German. Czechoslovakian.
HEADNOTE: COMMUNICATION LEGAL DOCUMENTS
TOPIC: Admin Cooperation
CONCEPTS: General provisions. Protection of nationals. Exchange of information and documents. Legal protection and assistance. Recognition of legal documents. Indemnities and reimbursements.
PROCEDURE: Denunciation. Duration. Ratification. Renewal or Revival.
PARTIES:
Austria
Czechoslovakia

106551 Bilateral Exchange **455 UNTS 381**
SIGNED: 13 Feb 62 FORCE: 13 Feb 62
REGISTERED: 5 Mar 63 Austria
ARTICLES: 2 LANGUAGE: German. Czechoslovakian.
HEADNOTE: SCHOOL DOCUMENTS
TOPIC: Education
CONCEPTS: General cooperation. Exchange of official publications. Informational records. Recognition of degrees.
PARTIES:
Austria
Czechoslovakia

106552 Multilateral Agreement **455 UNTS 386**
SIGNED: 6 Mar 63 FORCE: 6 Mar 63
REGISTERED: 6 Mar 63 United Nations
ARTICLES: 6 LANGUAGE: English.
HEADNOTE: TECHNICAL ASSISTANCE
TOPIC: Tech Assistance
CONCEPTS: Definition of terms. Privileges and immunities. General cooperation. Exchange of information and documents. Personnel. Responsibility and liability. Title and deeds. Use of facilities. Exchange. Scholarships and grants. Vocational training. Research and development. Exchange rates and regulations. Expense sharing formulae. Local currency. Domestic obligation. General technical assistance. Materials, equipment and services. IGO status. Conformity with IGO decisions.
INTL ORGS: United Nations.
TREATY REF: 76UNTS132; 1UNTS15; 33UNTS261; 374UNTS147.
PROCEDURE: Amendment. Termination.
PARTIES:
FAO (Food Agri) SIGNED: 6 Mar 63 FORCE: 6 Mar 63
IAEA (Atom Energy) SIGNED: 6 Mar 63 FORCE: 6 Mar 63
ICAO (Civil Aviat) SIGNED: 6 Mar 63 FORCE: 6 Mar 63
ILO (Labor Org) SIGNED: 6 Mar 63 FORCE: 6 Mar 63
ITU (Telecommun) SIGNED: 6 Mar 63 FORCE: 6 Mar 63
UNESCO (Educ/Cult) SIGNED: 6 Mar 63 FORCE: 6 Mar 63
United Nations SIGNED: 6 Mar 63 FORCE: 6 Mar 63
UPU (Postal Union) SIGNED: 6 Mar 63 FORCE: 6 Mar 63
WHO (World Health) SIGNED: 6 Mar 63 FORCE: 6 Mar 63
Tanganyika SIGNED: 6 Mar 63 FORCE: 6 Mar 63
ANNEX
530 UNTS 374. USA (United States). Amendment 30 Jun 64. Force 30 Jun 64.
530 UNTS 374. Chile. Amendment 30 Jun 64.

Force 30 Jun 64.
535 UNTS 446. UNTAB (Tech Assis). Prolongation 30 Apr 65.
535 UNTS 446. Tanzania. Prolongation 18 May 65.

106553 Multilateral Agreement **455 UNTS 402**
SIGNED: 11 Sep 62 FORCE: 11 Sep 62
REGISTERED: 7 Mar 63 United Nations
ARTICLES: 6 LANGUAGE: French. Arabic.
HEADNOTE: TECHNICAL AID PROGRAM
TOPIC: Tech Assistance
CONCEPTS: Exchange of official publications. Operating agencies. General technical assistance. Assistance. Status of experts.
INTL ORGS: United Nations.
TREATY REF: 33UNTS261; 374UNTS147; 193UNTS49; 76UNTS132; 1UNTS.
PROCEDURE: Termination.
PARTIES:
Lebanon SIGNED: 11 Sep 62 FORCE: 11 Sep 62
FAO (Food Agri) SIGNED: 11 Sep 62 FORCE: 11 Sep 62
IAEA (Atom Energy) SIGNED: 11 Sep 62 FORCE: 11 Sep 62
ICAO (Civil Aviat) SIGNED: 11 Sep 62 FORCE: 11 Sep 62
ILO (Labor Org) SIGNED: 11 Sep 62 FORCE: 11 Sep 62
UNESCO (Educ/Cult) SIGNED: 11 Sep 62 FORCE: 11 Sep 62
United Nations SIGNED: 11 Sep 62 FORCE: 11 Sep 62
WHO (World Health) SIGNED: 11 Sep 62 FORCE: 11 Sep 62
WMO (Meteorology) SIGNED: 11 Sep 62 FORCE: 11 Sep 62

106554 Bilateral Agreement **455 UNTS 429**
SIGNED: 28 Nov 62 FORCE: 28 Nov 62
REGISTERED: 7 Mar 63 Denmark
ARTICLES: 4 LANGUAGE: Danish. Spanish.
HEADNOTE: MILITARY SERVICE
TOPIC: Milit Servic/Citiz
CONCEPTS: Dual nationality. Certificates of service. Service in foreign army.
PROCEDURE: Termination.
PARTIES:
Argentina
Denmark

106555 Multilateral Protocol **456 UNTS 3**
SIGNED: 11 May 53 FORCE: 8 Mar 63
REGISTERED: 8 Mar 63 United Nations
ARTICLES: 26 LANGUAGE: English. French. Chinese. Russian. Spanish.
HEADNOTE: OPIUM CONFERENCE
TOPIC: Sanitation
CONCEPTS: Definition of terms. Exceptions and exemptions. Treaty implementation. Annex or appendix reference. Exchange of information and documents. Domestic legislation. Personnel. Narcotic drugs. Trade procedures. Agriculture. Purchase authorization.
INTL ORGS: United Nations. Special Commission.
TREATY REF: 14TH SESS(E-2332)P.28; 51LTS337; 12UNTS179; ETC..
PROCEDURE: Accession. Future Procedures Contemplated.
PARTIES:
Australia Nauru RATIFIED: 13 Jan 55 FORCE: 8 Mar 63
Australia New Guinea RATIFIED: 13 Jan 55 FORCE: 8 Mar 63
Australia Norfolk Islands RATIFIED: 13 Jan 55 FORCE: 8 Mar 63
Australia Papua RATIFIED: 13 Jan 55 FORCE: 8 Mar 63
Belgium Belgian Colonies RATIFIED: 30 Jun 58 FORCE: 8 Mar 63
Belgium Ruanda-Urundi RATIFIED: 30 Jun 58 FORCE: 8 Mar 63
Cambodia SIGNED: 29 Dec 53 RATIFIED: 22 Mar 57 FORCE: 8 Mar 63
Cameroon RATIFIED: 15 Jan 62
Canada SIGNED: 23 Dec 53 RATIFIED: 7 May 54 FORCE: 8 Mar 63
Chile SIGNED: 9 Jul 53 RATIFIED: 9 May 54 FORCE: 8 Mar 63
Taiwan SIGNED: 18 Sep 53 RATIFIED: 25 May 54 FORCE: 8 Mar 63
Central Afri Rep RATIFIED: 4 Sep 62

Congo (Brazzaville) RATIFIED: 15 Oct 52
Congo (Zaire) RATIFIED: 31 May 62
Costa Rica SIGNED: 9 Jul 53
Denmark SIGNED: 23 Jun 53 RATIFIED: 20 Jul 54 FORCE: 8 Mar 63
Dominican Republic SIGNED: 23 Jun 53 RATIFIED: 9 Jun 58 FORCE: 8 Mar 63
Ecuador SIGNED: 23 Jun 53 RATIFIED: 17 Aug 55 FORCE: 8 Mar 63
United Arab Rep SIGNED: 23 Jun 53 RATIFIED: 8 Mar 54 FORCE: 8 Mar 63
France SIGNED: 23 Jun 53 RATIFIED: 21 Apr 54 FORCE: 8 Mar 63
France All Territories RATIFIED: 21 Apr 54 FORCE: 8 Mar 63
Germany, West Berlin RATIFIED: 12 Aug 59 FORCE: 8 Mar 63
Germany, West SIGNED: 23 Jun 53 RATIFIED: 12 Aug 59 FORCE: 8 Mar 63
Greece SIGNED: 23 Jun 53 RATIFIED: 6 Feb 63 FORCE: 8 Mar 63
India SIGNED: 23 Jun 53 RATIFIED: 30 Apr 54 FORCE: 8 Mar 63
Iran SIGNED: 15 Dec 53 RATIFIED: 30 Dec 59 FORCE: 8 Mar 63
Iraq SIGNED: 29 Dec 53
Israel SIGNED: 30 Dec 53 RATIFIED: 8 Oct 57 FORCE: 8 Mar 63
Italy SIGNED: 23 Jun 53 RATIFIED: 13 Nov 57 FORCE: 8 Mar 63
Japan SIGNED: 23 Jun 53 RATIFIED: 21 Jul 54 FORCE: 8 Mar 63
Korea, South SIGNED: 23 Jun 53 RATIFIED: 29 Apr 58 FORCE: 8 Mar 63
Lebanon SIGNED: 11 Nov 63
Liechtenstein SIGNED: 23 Jun 53 RATIFIED: 24 May 61 FORCE: 8 Mar 63
Monaco SIGNED: 26 Jun 53 RATIFIED: 12 Apr 56 FORCE: 8 Mar 63
Netherlands SIGNED: 30 Dec 53
New Zealand Cook Islands RATIFIED: 2 Nov 56 FORCE: 8 Mar 63
New Zealand Niue RATIFIED: 2 Nov 56 FORCE: 8 Mar 63
New Zealand SIGNED: 28 Dec 53 RATIFIED: 2 Nov 56 FORCE: 8 Mar 63
New Zealand Tokelau Islands RATIFIED: 2 Nov 56 FORCE: 8 Mar 63
New Zealand Western Samoa RATIFIED: 2 Nov 56 FORCE: 8 Mar 63
Pakistan SIGNED: 3 Dec 53 RATIFIED: 10 Mar 55 FORCE: 8 Mar 63
Panama SIGNED: 28 Dec 53 RATIFIED: 13 Apr 54 FORCE: 8 Mar 63
Philippines SIGNED: 23 Jun 53 RATIFIED: 1 Jun 55 FORCE: 8 Mar 63
South Africa SIGNED: 29 Dec 53 RATIFIED: 9 Mar 60 FORCE: 8 Mar 63
South Africa Southwest Africa RATIFIED: 9 Mar 60 FORCE: 8 Mar 63
Spain SIGNED: 22 Oct 53 RATIFIED: 15 Jun 56 FORCE: 8 Mar 63
Switzerland SIGNED: 23 Jun 53 RATIFIED: 27 Nov 56 FORCE: 8 Mar 63
Turkey SIGNED: 28 Dec 53
UK Great Britain SIGNED: 23 Jun 53
USA (United States) SIGNED: 23 Jun 53 RATIFIED: 18 Feb 55
USA (United States) All Territories RATIFIED: 18 Feb 55
Venezuela SIGNED: 30 Dec 53
Vietnam SIGNED: 23 Jun 53
Yugoslavia SIGNED: 24 Jun 53
ANNEX
463 UNTS 369. Senegal. Succession 2 May 63.
470 UNTS 433. Turkey. Ratification 15 Jul 63. Force 14 Aug 63.
472 UNTS 399. Madagascar. Succession 31 Jul 63.
494 UNTS 328. Rwanda. Succession 30 Apr 64.
520 UNTS 432. Niger. Succession 7 Dec 64.
653 UNTS 460. New Zealand. Denunciation 17 Dec 68. Force 1 Jan 69.

106556 Bilateral Agreement **456 UNTS 185**
SIGNED: 23 Jan 63 FORCE: 23 Jan 63
REGISTERED: 12 Mar 63 Australia
ARTICLES: 3 LANGUAGE: English.
HEADNOTE: PATENTS INVENTIONS
TOPIC: Patents/Copyrights
CONCEPTS: Domestic legislation. Patents, copyrights and trademarks. Recognition. Press and wire services.

PARTIES:
Australia
India

106557 Bilateral Agreement **456 UNTS 192**
SIGNED: 15 Nov 61 FORCE: 15 Nov 61
REGISTERED: 14 Mar 63 USA (United States)
ARTICLES: 6 LANGUAGE: English. Spanish.
HEADNOTE: AGRI COMMOD TITLE I
TOPIC: US Agri Commod Aid
CONCEPTS: General provisions. Annex or appendix reference. Exchange of information and documents. Reexport of goods, etc.. Exchange rates and regulations. Transportation costs. Local currency. Commodities schedule. Purchase authorization. Surplus commodities. Mutual consultation.
PARTIES:
Bolivia
USA (United States)

106558 Bilateral Agreement **456 UNTS 209**
SIGNED: 15 Mar 62 FORCE: 15 Mar 62
REGISTERED: 14 Mar 63 USA (United States)
ARTICLES: 6 LANGUAGE: English. Portuguese.
HEADNOTE: AGRI COMMOD TITLE I
TOPIC: US Agri Commod Aid
CONCEPTS: General provisions. Annex or appendix reference. Exchange of information and documents. Reexport of goods, etc.. Exchange rates and regulations. Transportation costs. Local currency. Commodities schedule. Purchase authorization. Surplus commodities. Mutual consultation.
PARTIES:
Brazil
USA (United States)
ANNEX
479 UNTS 398. Brazil. Supplementation 15 Mar 62. Force 15 Mar 62.
479 UNTS 398. USA (United States). Supplementation 15 Mar 62. Force 15 Mar 62.
479 UNTS 420. USA (United States). Amendment 4 Oct 62. Force 4 Oct 62.
479 UNTS 420. Brazil. Amendment 4 Oct 62. Force 4 Oct 62.
488 UNTS 310. Brazil. Amendment 22 Aug 63. Force 22 Aug 63.
488 UNTS 310. USA (United States). Amendment 22 Aug 63. Force 22 Aug 63.

106559 Bilateral Exchange **456 UNTS 241**
SIGNED: 30 Mar 62 FORCE: 14 May 62
REGISTERED: 14 Mar 63 USA (United States)
ARTICLES: 2 LANGUAGE: English. Spanish.
HEADNOTE: ECONOMIC TECHNICAL RELATED ASSISTANCE
TOPIC: Tech Assistance
CONCEPTS: Change of circumstances. Exceptions and exemptions. Previous treaty replacement. Diplomatic privileges. Conformity with municipal law. Personnel. Exchange rates and regulations. Inadequacy of funds. Tax exemptions. Customs exemptions. Domestic obligation. General technical assistance. Economic assistance. Materials, equipment and services. Aid missions.
TREATY REF: 92UNTS155.
PROCEDURE: Amendment. Ratification. Termination.
PARTIES:
Nicaragua
USA (United States)

106560 Bilateral Agreement **456 UNTS 255**
SIGNED: 19 Apr 62 FORCE: 19 Apr 62
REGISTERED: 14 Mar 63 USA (United States)
ARTICLES: 5 LANGUAGE: English. Portuguese.
HEADNOTE: AGRICULTURAL TRADE
TOPIC: General Trade
CONCEPTS: Exchange of information and documents. Export quotas. Import quotas. Reciprocity in trade.
PARTIES:
Brazil
USA (United States)

106561 Bilateral Exchange **456 UNTS 265**
SIGNED: 26 May 62 FORCE: 26 May 62
REGISTERED: 14 Mar 63 USA (United States)
ARTICLES: 2 LANGUAGE: English. Romanian.
HEADNOTE: ISSUANCE VISAS

TOPIC: Visas
CONCEPTS: Time limit. Visas.
PARTIES:
Romania
USA (United States)

106562 Bilateral Agreement **456 UNTS 275**
SIGNED: 17 May 62 FORCE: 17 May 62
REGISTERED: 14 Mar 63 USA (United States)
ARTICLES: 5 LANGUAGE: English. Spanish.
HEADNOTE: AGRI COMMOD TITLE I
TOPIC: US Agri Commod Aid
CONCEPTS: General provisions. Annex or appendix reference. Exchange of information and documents. Exchange rates and regulations. Transportation costs. Local currency. Purchase authorization. Commodities schedule. Purchase authorization. Mutual consultation.
PARTIES:
USA (United States)
Venezuela
ANNEX
459 UNTS 348. Venezuela. Amendment 18 Jun 62. Force 18 Jun 62.
459 UNTS 348. USA (United States). Amendment 18 Jun 62. Force 18 Jun 62.

106563 Bilateral Exchange **456 UNTS 293**
SIGNED: 23 May 62 FORCE: 23 May 62
REGISTERED: 14 Mar 63 USA (United States)
ARTICLES: 2 LANGUAGE: English.
HEADNOTE: PEACE CORPS PROGRAM
TOPIC: General Aid
CONCEPTS: Treaty implementation. Diplomatic privileges. Conformity with municipal law. Legal protection and assistance. Personnel. Exchange rates and regulations. Fees and exemptions. Funding procedures. Tax exemptions. Customs exemptions. Domestic obligation. Materials, equipment and services. Volunteer programs.
PROCEDURE: Termination.
PARTIES:
Ethiopia
USA (United States)

106564 Multilateral Protocol **456 UNTS 302**
SIGNED: 23 Jul 62 FORCE: 23 Jul 62
REGISTERED: 14 Mar 63 UK Great Britain
ARTICLES: 1 LANGUAGE: English. Chinese. French. Laotian. Russian.
HEADNOTE: NEUTRALITY LAOS
TOPIC: Recognition
CONCEPTS: Peaceful relations. Recognition. Incorporation of treaty provisions into national law. General technical assistance. Defense and security. Withdrawal of forces.
INTL ORGS: Southeast Asia Treaty Organization.
PARTIES:
Burma SIGNED: 23 Jul 62 FORCE: 23 Jul 62
Cambodia SIGNED: 23 Jul 62 FORCE: 23 Jul 62
Canada SIGNED: 23 Jul 62 FORCE: 23 Jul 62
Taiwan SIGNED: 23 Jul 62 FORCE: 23 Jul 62
France SIGNED: 23 Jul 62 FORCE: 23 Jul 62
India SIGNED: 23 Jul 62 FORCE: 23 Jul 62
Laos SIGNED: 23 Jul 62 FORCE: 23 Jul 62
Poland SIGNED: 23 Jul 62 FORCE: 23 Jul 62
Thailand SIGNED: 23 Jul 62 FORCE: 23 Jul 62
UK Great Britain SIGNED: 23 Jul 62 FORCE: 23 Jul 62
USA (United States) SIGNED: 23 Jul 62 FORCE: 23 Jul 62
USSR (Soviet Union) SIGNED: 23 Jul 62 FORCE: 23 Jul 62
Vietnam, North SIGNED: 23 Jul 62 FORCE: 23 Jul 62
Vietnam, South SIGNED: 23 Jul 62 FORCE: 23 Jul 62

106565 Bilateral Agreement **456 UNTS 359**
SIGNED: 17 Nov 62 FORCE: 16 Mar 63
REGISTERED: 16 Mar 63 United Nations
ARTICLES: 6 LANGUAGE: English. Arabic.
HEADNOTE: ADMINISTRATIVE PERSONNEL
TOPIC: IGO Status/Immunit
CONCEPTS: Annex or appendix reference. General consular functions. Diplomatic privileges. Diplomatic missions. Privileges and immunities. Arbitration. Status of experts.
PROCEDURE: Amendment. Ratification. Termination.
PARTIES:
United Nations
Syria

106566 Bilateral Agreement **456 UNTS 379**
SIGNED: 16 Mar 62 FORCE: 16 Mar 63
REGISTERED: 16 Mar 63 United Nations
ARTICLES: 6 LANGUAGE: English. Arabic.
HEADNOTE: PROVISION UN ADMINISTRATORS
TOPIC: Tech Assistance
CONCEPTS: Annex or appendix reference. General consular functions. Diplomatic privileges. Diplomatic missions. Privileges and immunities. Arbitration. Procedure. General technical assistance. Assistance. Status of experts.
TREATY REF: 319UNTS14.
PROCEDURE: Amendment. Termination.
PARTIES:
United Nations
Saudi Arabia
ANNEX
483 UNTS 384. United Nations. Supplementation 10 Apr 63. Force 26 Sep 63.
483 UNTS 384. Saudi Arabia. Supplementation 26 Sep 63. Force 26 Sep 63.

106567 Multilateral Agreement **456 UNTS 409**
SIGNED: 15 Jan 63 FORCE: 15 Jan 63
REGISTERED: 18 Mar 63 Finland
ARTICLES: 11 LANGUAGE: Finnish. Danish. Norwegian. Swedish.
HEADNOTE: TECHNICAL COOPERATION
TOPIC: Tech Assistance
CONCEPTS: General cooperation. Personnel. Establishment of commission. Expense sharing formulae. General technical assistance. Internal structure.
INTL ORGS: United Nations. Special Commission.
PARTIES:
Denmark SIGNED: 15 Jan 63 FORCE: 15 Jan 63
Finland SIGNED: 15 Jan 63 FORCE: 15 Jan 63
Norway SIGNED: 15 Jan 63 FORCE: 15 Jan 63
Sweden SIGNED: 15 Jan 63 FORCE: 15 Jan 63

106568 Bilateral Convention **456 UNTS 425**
SIGNED: 13 Oct 62 FORCE: 1 Oct 62
REGISTERED: 19 Mar 63 Belgium
ARTICLES: 9 LANGUAGE: French.
HEADNOTE: COOPERATION TECHNICAL ASSISTANCE
TOPIC: Tech Assistance
CONCEPTS: Treaty implementation. General cooperation. Personnel. Private contracts. Arbitration. Procedure. Scholarships and grants. Vocational training. Financial programs. General technical assistance. Aid missions.
PROCEDURE: Denunciation. Future Procedures Contemplated.
PARTIES:
Belgium
Rwanda

106569 Bilateral Convention **456 UNTS 431**
SIGNED: 13 Oct 62 FORCE: 13 Oct 62
REGISTERED: 19 Mar 63 Belgium
ARTICLES: 20 LANGUAGE: French.
HEADNOTE: ASSISTANCE MATTER PERSONNEL
TOPIC: Tech Assistance
CONCEPTS: Detailed regulations. Treaty implementation. Annex type material. Peaceful relations. Privileges and immunities. Conformity with municipal law. General cooperation. Exchange of information and documents. Personnel. Establishment of commission. Scholarships and grants. Vocational training. Compensation. Expense sharing formulae. National treatment. General. Special projects.
INTL ORGS: Special Commission.
TREATY REF: 456UNTS427.
PROCEDURE: Denunciation. Duration.
PARTIES:
Belgium
Rwanda

106570 Bilateral Instrument **456 UNTS 447**
SIGNED: 20 Aug 62 FORCE: 20 Aug 62
REGISTERED: 20 Mar 63 IAEA (Atom Energy)
ARTICLES: 14 LANGUAGE: English.
HEADNOTE: MASTER CONTRACT SALE NUCLEAR MATERIALS
TOPIC: Commodity Trade
CONCEPTS: Detailed regulations. Treaty implementation. Arbitration. Procedure. Existing tribunals. Reexport of goods, etc.. Trade procedures. Currency. Interest rates. Payment schedules. Commodity trade. Delivery schedules. Transport of goods.
INTL ORGS: United Nations.

TREATY REF: 339UNTS359.
PARTIES:
IAEA (Atom Energy)
USA (United States)

106571   Bilateral Exchange   **456 UNTS 457**
SIGNED: 25 Oct 62   FORCE: 25 Oct 62
REGISTERED: 20 Mar 63 Denmark
ARTICLES: 2 LANGUAGE: French.
HEADNOTE: TAX EXEMPTION INCOME AIR NAVI-
GATION
TOPIC: Taxation
CONCEPTS: Definition of terms. Tax exemptions.
Air transport.
PARTIES:
Czechoslovakia
Denmark

106572   Bilateral Agreement   **456 UNTS 466**
SIGNED: 22 Mar 63   FORCE: 22 Mar 63
REGISTERED: 22 Mar 63 United Nations
ARTICLES: 10 LANGUAGE: English.
HEADNOTE: ASSISTANCE
TOPIC: Direct Aid
CONCEPTS: Detailed regulations. Treaty imple-
mentation. Visas. Privileges and immunities. Ex-
change of information and documents. Informa-
tional records. Inspection and observation. Oper-
ating agencies. Personnel. Public information.
Responsibility and liability. Title and deeds. Use
of facilities. Arbitration. Procedure. Negotiation.
Import quotas. Attachment of funds. Exchange
rates and regulations. Expense sharing formulae.
Financial programs. Domestic obligation. Gen-
eral technical assistance. Economic assistance.
Materials, equipment and services. IGO status.
INTL ORGS: International Court of Justice. United
Nations.
TREATY   REF: 1UNTS15;   33UNTS261;
374UNTS147.
PROCEDURE: Amendment. Termination.
PARTIES:
UN Special Fund
Uganda

106573   Bilateral Agreement   **457 UNTS 3**
SIGNED: 30 Sep 61   FORCE: 9 Apr 62
REGISTERED: 26 Mar 63 Romania
ARTICLES: 7 LANGUAGE: English.
HEADNOTE: CULTURAL COOPERATION
TOPIC: Culture
CONCEPTS: Treaty implementation. Friendship
and amity. Exchange of information and docu-
ments. Exchange. Teacher and student ex-
change. Scholarships and grants. Exchange.
General cultural cooperation. Artists. Scientific
exchange. Publications exchange. Mass media
exchange. Press and wire services.
PROCEDURE: Denunciation. Duration. Future Pro-
cedures Contemplated. Ratification. Renewal or
Revival. Termination.
PARTIES:
Ghana
Romania

106574   Bilateral Agreement   **457 UNTS 9**
SIGNED: 28 Oct 60   FORCE: 28 Oct 60
REGISTERED: 26 Mar 63 Romania
ARTICLES: 9 LANGUAGE: Romanian. Spanish.
HEADNOTE: CULTURAL COOPERATION
TOPIC: Culture
CONCEPTS: Friendship and amity. Treaty imple-
mentation. Conformity with municipal law. Ex-
change of information and documents. Public in-
formation. Exchange. Professorships. Scholar-
ships and grants. Exchange. General cultural
cooperation. Artists. Athletes. Scientific ex-
change. Research and development. Indemnities
and reimbursements. Publications exchange.
Mass media exchange. Press and wire services.
PROCEDURE: Denunciation. Duration. Future Procedures Contemplated. Ratification. Renewal or
Revival.
PARTIES:
Cuba
Romania

106575   Bilateral Treaty   **457 UNTS 22**
SIGNED: 25 Nov 59   FORCE: 28 Apr 62
REGISTERED: 26 Mar 63 Pakistan
ARTICLES: 14 LANGUAGE: English. German.
HEADNOTE: PROMOTION PROTECTION INVEST-
MENTS
TOPIC: General Economic

CONCEPTS: Definition of terms. Detailed regulations. Emergencies. Annex or appendix refer-
ence. General cooperation. Expropriation. Legal
protection and assistance. Immovable property.
General property. Arbitration. Procedure. Exist-
ing tribunals. Special tribunals. Research coop-
eration. Scientific exchange. Compensation.
Non-interest rates and fees.
INTL ORGS: International Court of Justice. Interna-
tional Monetary Fund.
TREATY   REF: 2UNTS40;   333UNTS3;
437UNTS367.
PROCEDURE: Duration. Ratification. Termination.
Application to Non-self-governing Territories.
PARTIES:
Germany, West
Pakistan

106576   Unilateral Instrument   **457 UNTS 59**
SIGNED: 20 Mar 63   FORCE: 27 Oct 61
REGISTERED: 26 Mar 63 United Nations
ARTICLES: 1 LANGUAGE: French.
HEADNOTE: ACCEPTANCE OBLIGATIONS UN
TOPIC: UN Charter
CONCEPTS: Acceptance of UN obligations.
INTL ORGS: United Nations.
PARTIES:
Mauritania

106577   Multilateral Exchange   **457 UNTS 63**
SIGNED: 29 Nov 62   FORCE: 16 Dec 62
REGISTERED: 27 Mar 63 Belgium
ARTICLES: 11 LANGUAGE: French. English.
HEADNOTE: ABOLITION PASSPORT VISA RE-
QUIREMENTS
TOPIC: Visas
CONCEPTS: Definition of terms. Emergencies.
Time limit. Denial of admission. Resident per-
mits. Conformity with municipal law.
PROCEDURE: Denunciation. Duration. Renewal or
Revival.
PARTIES:
Belgium SIGNED: 16 Nov 62 FORCE: 16 Dec 62
Cyprus SIGNED: 29 Nov 62 FORCE: 16 Dec 62
Luxembourg   SIGNED: 16 Nov 62   FORCE:
16 Dec 62
Netherlands   SIGNED: 16 Nov 62   FORCE:
16 Dec 62

106578   Multilateral Agreement   **457 UNTS 72**
SIGNED: 12 Dec 62   FORCE: 16 Mar 63
REGISTERED: 1 Apr 63 United Nations
ARTICLES: 6 LANGUAGE: English. Arabic.
HEADNOTE: TECHNICAL ASSISTANCE
TOPIC: Tech Assistance
CONCEPTS: Definition of terms. Annex or appendix reference. Previous treaty replacement. Privileges and immunities. General cooperation. Ex-
change of information and documents. Personnel. Title and deeds. Use of facilities. Exchange.
Scholarships and grants. Vocational training. Research and development. Exchange rates and
regulations. Expense sharing formulae. Local
currency. Domestic obligation. General technical assistance. Materials, equipment and services. IGO status. Conformity with IGO decisions.
TREATY   REF: 76UNTS132;   1UNTS15;
33UNTS261; 324UNTS147; ETC..
PROCEDURE: Amendment. Termination.
PARTIES:
FAO (Food Agri) SIGNED: 12 Dec 62 FORCE:
16 Mar 63
IAEA (Atom Energy) SIGNED: 12 Dec 62 FORCE:
16 Mar 63
ICAO (Civil Aviat) SIGNED: 12 Dec 62 FORCE:
16 Mar 63
ILO (Labor Org) SIGNED: 12 Dec 62 FORCE:
16 Mar 63
ITU (Telecommun) SIGNED: 12 Dec 62 FORCE:
16 Mar 63
UNESCO (Educ/Cult) SIGNED: 12 Dec 62
FORCE: 16 Mar 63
United Nations SIGNED: 12 Dec 62 FORCE:
16 Mar 63
UPU (Postal Union) SIGNED: 12 Dec 62 FORCE:
16 Mar 63
WHO (World Health) SIGNED: 12 Dec 62 FORCE:
16 Mar 63
WMO (Meteorology) SIGNED: 12 Dec 62 FORCE:
16 Mar 63
Syria SIGNED: 12 Dec 62 RATIFIED: 16 Mar 63
FORCE: 16 Mar 63

106579   Bilateral Agreement   **457 UNTS 103**
SIGNED: 1 Apr 63   FORCE: 1 Apr 63
REGISTERED: 1 Apr 63 United Nations
ARTICLES: 8 LANGUAGE: English.
HEADNOTE: UNICEF ACTIVITIES
TOPIC: IGO Operations
CONCEPTS: Annex or appendix reference. Privi-
leges and immunities. Exchange of information
and documents. Accounting procedures. Inter-
agency agreements. Mutual consultation.
TREATY REF: 15UNTS413.
PROCEDURE: Amendment. Termination.
PARTIES:
Ethiopia
UNICEF (Children)

106580   Multilateral Exchange   **457 UNTS 117**
SIGNED: 7 Aug 62   FORCE: 6 Aug 62
REGISTERED: 2 Apr 63 UK Great Britain
ARTICLES: 2 LANGUAGE: English.
HEADNOTE: INHERITANCE   INTERNATIONAL
RIGHTS OBLIGATIONS
TOPIC: Recognition
CONCEPTS: Continuity of rights and obligations.
PARTIES:
Multilateral

106581   Multilateral Exchange   **457 UNTS 123**
SIGNED: 31 Aug 62   FORCE: 31 Aug 62
REGISTERED: 2 Apr 63 UK Great Britain
ARTICLES: 2 LANGUAGE: English.
HEADNOTE: INHERITANCE   INTERNATIONAL
RIGHTS OBLIGATIONS
TOPIC: Recognition
CONCEPTS: Continuity of rights and obligations.
PARTIES:
Multilateral

106582   Multilateral Exchange   **457 UNTS 129**
SIGNED: 25 Oct 62   FORCE: 25 Oct 62
REGISTERED: 2 Apr 63 UK Great Britain
ARTICLES: 2 LANGUAGE: English.
HEADNOTE: PEACE CORPS
TOPIC: Tech Assistance
CONCEPTS: Diplomatic privileges. Conformity
with municipal law. General cooperation. Per-
sonnel. Fees and exemptions. General. Tax ex-
emptions. Customs exemptions. Domestic obli-
gation. Materials, equipment and services. Aid
missions. Volunteer programs.
PROCEDURE: Termination.
PARTIES:
Multilateral

106583   Multilateral Exchange   **457 UNTS 137**
SIGNED: 25 Oct 62   FORCE: 25 Oct 62
REGISTERED: 2 Apr 63 UK Great Britain
ARTICLES: 2 LANGUAGE: English.
HEADNOTE: PEACE CORPS
TOPIC: General Aid
CONCEPTS: Diplomatic privileges. Conformity
with municipal law. General cooperation. Per-
sonnel. Fees and exemptions. General. Tax ex-
emptions. Customs exemptions. Domestic obli-
gation. Materials, equipment and services. Aid
missions. Volunteer programs.
PROCEDURE: Termination.
PARTIES:
Multilateral

106584   Bilateral Agreement   **457 UNTS 145**
SIGNED: 6 Dec 62   FORCE: 6 Mar 63
REGISTERED: 2 Apr 63 UK Great Britain
ARTICLES: 10 LANGUAGE: English.
HEADNOTE: EXCHANGE MONEY ORDERS
TOPIC: Postal Service
CONCEPTS: Detailed regulations. Territorial appli-
cation. General cooperation. Accounting proce-
dures. Currency. Postal services. Regulations.
Money orders and postal checks.
PROCEDURE: Termination.
PARTIES:
Australia
UK Great Britain

106585   Bilateral Exchange   **457 UNTS 153**
SIGNED: 10 Jan 63   FORCE: 1 Feb 63
REGISTERED: 3 Apr 63 Belgium
ARTICLES: 2 LANGUAGE: English. Spanish.
HEADNOTE: ABOLITION TRAVEL VISAS
TOPIC: Visas
CONCEPTS: Emergencies. Time limit. Previous
treaty replacement. Visa abolition. Denial of ad-

mission. Resident permits. Conformity with municipal law.
TREATY REF: 304UNTS207.
PROCEDURE: Denunciation.
PARTIES:
Belgium
Ecuador

106586 Bilateral Treaty **457 UNTS 161**
SIGNED: 14 May 57 FORCE: 20 Dec 62
REGISTERED: 8 Apr 63 USSR (Soviet Union)
ARTICLES: 44 LANGUAGE: Russian. Persian.
HEADNOTE: PROCEDURE SETTLEMENT FRONTIER DISPUTES INCIDENTS
TOPIC: Dispute Settlement
CONCEPTS: Definition of terms. Annex or appendix reference. Previous treaty replacement. Establishment of commission. Procedure. Markers and definitions. Frontier peoples and personnel. Frontier waterways.
INTL ORGS: Special Commission.
TREATY REF: 457UNTS161(ART 42).
PROCEDURE: Duration. Ratification.
PARTIES:
Iran
USSR (Soviet Union)

106587 Bilateral Agreement **457 UNTS 263**
SIGNED: 2 Jun 61 FORCE: 10 Feb 62
REGISTERED: 8 Apr 63 USSR (Soviet Union)
ARTICLES: 12 LANGUAGE: Russian. Italian.
HEADNOTE: ECONOMIC TECHNICAL COOPERATION
TOPIC: Tech Assistance
CONCEPTS: Guarantees and safeguards. Time limit. Treaty implementation. General cooperation. Exchange of information and documents. Vocational training. Research and development. Accounting procedures. Compensation. Currency deposits. Exchange rates and regulations. Local currency. Delivery schedules. Domestic obligation. General technical assistance. Agriculture. Economic assistance. Materials, equipment and services. Loan repayment. Hydro-electric power.
PROCEDURE: Ratification.
PARTIES:
Somalia
USSR (Soviet Union)

106588 Bilateral Agreement **457 UNTS 285**
SIGNED: 19 Aug 62 FORCE: 9 Jan 63
REGISTERED: 8 Apr 63 USSR (Soviet Union)
ARTICLES: 13 LANGUAGE: Russian. Arabic.
HEADNOTE: CULTURAL COOPERATION
TOPIC: Culture
CONCEPTS: Treaty implementation. Previous treaty replacement. Friendship and amity. Conformity with municipal law. Specialists exchange. Public health. Recognition of degrees. Exchange. Teacher and student exchange. Professorships. Scholarships and grants. Exchange. General cultural cooperation. Artists. Athletes. Scientific exchange. Publications exchange. Mass media exchange.
INTL ORGS: United Nations.
TREATY REF: 274UNTS105.
PROCEDURE: Duration. Ratification. Renewal or Revival. Termination.
PARTIES:
Syria
USSR (Soviet Union)

106589 Bilateral Agreement **458 UNTS 3**
SIGNED: 11 Sep 62 FORCE: 25 Feb 63
REGISTERED: 8 Apr 63 USSR (Soviet Union)
ARTICLES: 7 LANGUAGE: Russian. Danish.
HEADNOTE: CULTURAL COOPERATION
TOPIC: Culture
CONCEPTS: Annex type material. Friendship and amity. Tourism. Non-diplomatic delegations. Specialists exchange. Exchange. Teacher and student exchange. Exchange. General cultural cooperation. Artists. Athletes. Scientific exchange. Peaceful use. Publications exchange. Mass media exchange. Press and wire services.
PROCEDURE: Duration. Ratification. Termination.
PARTIES:
Denmark
USSR (Soviet Union)

106590 Bilateral Agreement **458 UNTS 21**
SIGNED: 1 Dec 62 FORCE: 6 Feb 63

REGISTERED: 8 Apr 63 USSR (Soviet Union)
ARTICLES: 9 LANGUAGE: Russian. Laotian. French.
HEADNOTE: TRADE DEVELOPMENT
TOPIC: General Trade
CONCEPTS: General cooperation. Export quotas. Import quotas. Reciprocity in trade. Payment schedules. Customs duties.
PROCEDURE: Denunciation. Duration. Ratification. Renewal or Revival.
PARTIES:
Laos
USSR (Soviet Union)

106591 Bilateral Treaty **458 UNTS 41**
SIGNED: 11 Jul 62 FORCE: 29 Dec 62
REGISTERED: 9 Apr 63 Taiwan
ARTICLES: 9 LANGUAGE: Chinese. Spanish.
HEADNOTE: TRADE
TOPIC: General Trade
CONCEPTS: Exceptions and exemptions. General cooperation. Licenses and permits. Reciprocity in trade. Payment schedules. Most favored nation clause. Laws and formalities. Recognition. General technical assistance. Economic assistance.
PARTIES:
Taiwan
Paraguay

106592 Bilateral Agreement **458 UNTS 59**
SIGNED: 19 Nov 62 FORCE: 16 Mar 63
REGISTERED: 9 Apr 63 South Africa
ARTICLES: 18 LANGUAGE: English. Afrikaans.
HEADNOTE: EXTRADITION
TOPIC: Extradition
CONCEPTS: Extradition, deportation and repatriation. Extraditable offenses. Location of crime. Refusal of extradition. Pre-treaty crimes. Provisional detainment. Extradition postponement. Material evidence. Conformity with municipal law.
PROCEDURE: Ratification. Termination.
PARTIES:
Fed Rhod/Nyasaland
South Africa

106593 Bilateral Agreement **458 UNTS 79**
SIGNED: 8 Feb 63 FORCE: 8 Feb 63
REGISTERED: 9 Apr 63 South Africa
ARTICLES: 11 LANGUAGE: English. Afrikaans. Spanish.
HEADNOTE: MOST FAVORED NATION TRADE AGREEMENT
TOPIC: Mostfavored Nation
CONCEPTS: Exceptions and exemptions. Territorial application. General cooperation. General trade. Trade agencies. Trade procedures. Currency. Quotas. Most favored nation clause. General.
PROCEDURE: Duration. Renewal or Revival. Termination.
PARTIES:
South Africa
Spain

106594 Bilateral Agreement **458 UNTS 97**
SIGNED: 22 Jun 62 FORCE: 27 Jul 62
REGISTERED: 9 Apr 63 USA (United States)
ARTICLES: 12 LANGUAGE: English.
HEADNOTE: CIVIL USES ATOMIC ENERGY
TOPIC: Atomic Energy
CONCEPTS: Definition of terms. Previous treaty replacement. Exchange of information and documents. Inspection and observation. Responsibility and liability. Research cooperation. Research results. Establishment of trade relations. Acceptance of delivery. Nuclear materials. Non-nuclear materials. Peaceful use. Rights of supplier. Security of information.
INTL ORGS: International Atomic Energy Agency.
TREATY REF: 235UNTS121; 378UNTS376.
PROCEDURE: Duration.
PARTIES:
Argentina
USA (United States)
ANNEX
531 UNTS 387. USA (United States). Amendment 8 Jun 64. Force 29 Sep 64.
531 UNTS 387. Argentina. Amendment 8 Jun 64. Force 29 Sep 64.

106595 Bilateral Agreement **458 UNTS 123**
SIGNED: 23 Jul 62 FORCE: 27 Jul 62

REGISTERED: 9 Apr 63 USA (United States)
ARTICLES: 6 LANGUAGE: English. Spanish.
HEADNOTE: ECONOMIC TECHNICAL RELATED ASSISTANCE
TOPIC: General Aid
CONCEPTS: Change of circumstances. Treaty implementation. Previous treaty replacement. Diplomatic privileges. Privileges and immunities. Conformity with municipal law. Exchange of information and documents. Inspection and observation. Personnel. General property. Exchange rates and regulations. Funding procedures. Tax exemptions. Customs exemptions. Domestic obligation. General technical assistance. Economic assistance. Aid missions.
TREATY REF: 141UNTS15; 405UNTS55.
PROCEDURE: Amendment. Termination.
PARTIES:
Colombia
USA (United States)

106596 Bilateral Exchange **458 UNTS 137**
SIGNED: 20 Jul 62 FORCE: 20 Jul 62
REGISTERED: 9 Apr 63 USA (United States)
ARTICLES: 2 LANGUAGE: English. French.
HEADNOTE: MILITARY EQUIPMENT MATERIALS SERVICES
TOPIC: Milit Assistance
CONCEPTS: Non-prejudice to UN charter. Privileges and immunities. Inspection and observation. Materials, equipment and services. Self-defense. Military assistance. Return of equipment and recapture. Security of information. Restrictions on transfer.
INTL ORGS: United Nations.
PARTIES:
Senegal
USA (United States)

106597 Unilateral Instrument **458 UNTS 143**
SIGNED: 25 Mar 63 FORCE: 11 Apr 63
REGISTERED: 11 Apr 63 United Nations
ARTICLES: 1 LANGUAGE: English.
HEADNOTE: ACCEPTANCE ICJ JURISDICTION
TOPIC: ICJ Option Clause
CONCEPTS: Compulsory jurisdiction.
INTL ORGS: International Court of Justice. United Nations.
PROCEDURE: Amendment. Termination.
PARTIES:
Somalia

106598 Bilateral Exchange **458 UNTS 147**
SIGNED: 30 May 58 FORCE: 30 May 58
REGISTERED: 12 Apr 63 Netherlands
ARTICLES: 2 LANGUAGE: Dutch. German.
HEADNOTE: ABOLITION PASSPORTS
TOPIC: Visas
CONCEPTS: Emergencies. Time limit. Previous treaty replacement. Visa abolition. Border traffic and migration. Passports non-diplomatic. Resident permits. Non-visa travel documents. Fees and exemptions.
TREATY REF: 24MAY1951; 15JUNE1951.
PROCEDURE: Duration. Renewal or Revival. Termination.
PARTIES:
Austria
Netherlands

106599 Bilateral Exchange **458 UNTS 165**
SIGNED: 27 May 59 FORCE: 1 Jun 59
REGISTERED: 12 Apr 63 Netherlands
ARTICLES: 2 LANGUAGE: English. Spanish.
HEADNOTE: ABOLITION VISAS
TOPIC: Visas
CONCEPTS: Emergencies. Territorial application. Time limit. Visa abolition. Denial of admission. Resident permits. Conformity with municipal law. Fees and exemptions.
PROCEDURE: Denunciation. Ratification.
PARTIES:
Netherlands
Spain

106600 Bilateral Exchange **458 UNTS 173**
SIGNED: 16 Oct 59 FORCE: 27 May 60
REGISTERED: 12 Apr 63 Netherlands
ARTICLES: 2 LANGUAGE: French.
HEADNOTE: VALIDITY TREATIES CONVENTIONS
TOPIC: Admin Cooperation
CONCEPTS: Exceptions and exemptions. Annex or appendix reference. Concessions.
TREATY REF: 9LTS167; 17LTS375; 7BFSP536.

PARTIES:
Austria
Netherlands

106601 Bilateral Agreement **458 UNTS 197**
SIGNED: 21 May 62   FORCE: 21 May 62
REGISTERED: 15 Apr 63 USA (United States)
ARTICLES: 8 LANGUAGE: English. Arabic.
HEADNOTE: CULTURAL
TOPIC: Culture
CONCEPTS: Friendship and amity. Conformity with municipal law. Specialists exchange. Teacher and student exchange. Professorships. Institute establishment. Scholarships and grants. General cultural cooperation. Artists. Anthropology and archeology. Scientific exchange. Research and development. Publications exchange. Mass media exchange.
PROCEDURE: Duration. Termination.
PARTIES:
United Arab Rep
USA (United States)

106602 Bilateral Exchange **458 UNTS 209**
SIGNED: 8 Jun 62   FORCE: 8 Jun 62
REGISTERED: 15 Apr 63 USA (United States)
ARTICLES: 2 LANGUAGE: English.
HEADNOTE: LOAN VESSEL TO NEW ZEALAND
TOPIC: Loans and Credits
CONCEPTS: Responsibility and liability. Title and deeds. Indemnities and reimbursements. Terms of loan. Burial arrangements. Lease of military property. Naval vessels. Security of information.
TREATY REF: 131UNTS83.
PROCEDURE: Denunciation. Renewal or Revival.
PARTIES:
New Zealand
USA (United States)

106603 Bilateral Exchange **458 UNTS 219**
SIGNED: 13 Jun 62   FORCE: 13 Jun 62
REGISTERED: 15 Apr 63 USA (United States)
ARTICLES: 2 LANGUAGE: English. French.
HEADNOTE: FURNISHING MILITARY EQUIPMENT MATERIALS SERVICES
TOPIC: Milit Assistance
CONCEPTS: Non-prejudice to UN charter. Exchange of information and documents. Materials, equipment and services. Self-defense. Military assistance. Return of equipment and recapture. Security of information. Exchange of defense information. Restrictions on transfer.
INTL ORGS: United Nations.
PARTIES:
Dahomey
USA (United States)

106604 Bilateral Exchange **458 UNTS 225**
SIGNED: 23 May 62   FORCE: 23 May 62
REGISTERED: 15 Apr 63 USA (United States)
ARTICLES: 2 LANGUAGE: English. Spanish.
HEADNOTE: FURNISHING DEFENSE ARTICLES SERVICES
TOPIC: Milit Assistance
CONCEPTS: Non-prejudice to UN charter. Conformity with municipal law. Exchange of information and documents. Inspection and observation. Materials, equipment and services. Self-defense. Military assistance. Return of equipment and recapture. Security of information. Exchange of defense information. Restrictions on transfer.
TREATY REF: 21UNTS77.
PARTIES:
Panama
USA (United States)

106605 Bilateral Exchange **458 UNTS 233**
SIGNED: 14 Jun 62   FORCE: 14 Jun 62
REGISTERED: 15 Apr 63 USA (United States)
ARTICLES: 2 LANGUAGE: English. French.
HEADNOTE: FURNISHING MILITARY EQUIPMENT MATERIALS SERVICES
TOPIC: Milit Assistance
CONCEPTS: Non-prejudice to UN charter. Inspection and observation. Materials, equipment and services. Self-defense. Military assistance. Return of equipment and recapture. Security of information. Exchange of defense information. Restrictions on transfer.
INTL ORGS: United Nations.
PARTIES:
Niger
USA (United States)

106606 Bilateral Exchange **458 UNTS 239**
SIGNED: 19 Jun 62   FORCE: 19 Jun 62
REGISTERED: 15 Apr 63 USA (United States)
ARTICLES: 2 LANGUAGE: English. Spanish.
HEADNOTE: PEACE CORPS PROGRAM
TOPIC: General Aid
CONCEPTS: Diplomatic privileges. General cooperation. Personnel. Exchange rates and regulations. Fees and exemptions. Funding procedures. Tax exemptions. Customs exemptions. Domestic obligation. Materials, equipment and services. Aid missions. Volunteer programs.
PROCEDURE: Termination.
PARTIES:
Bolivia
USA (United States)

106607 Bilateral Exchange **458 UNTS 249**
SIGNED: 28 May 62   FORCE: 28 May 62
REGISTERED: 15 Apr 63 USA (United States)
ARTICLES: 2 LANGUAGE: English. Spanish.
HEADNOTE: PEACE CORPS PROGRAM
TOPIC: Tech Assistance
CONCEPTS: Annex type material. General cooperation. Domestic obligation. Materials, equipment and services. Aid missions. Volunteer programs.
TREATY REF: 186UNTS23.
PROCEDURE: Termination.
PARTIES:
USA (United States)
Venezuela

106608 Bilateral Exchange **458 UNTS 259**
SIGNED: 25 May 62   FORCE: 25 May 62
REGISTERED: 15 Apr 63 USA (United States)
ARTICLES: 2 LANGUAGE: English. German.
HEADNOTE: DISPOSITION DEFENSE EQUIPMENT MATERIALS
TOPIC: Milit Assistance
CONCEPTS: Reexport of goods, etc.. Payment for war supplies. Military assistance. Return of equipment and recapture.
TREATY REF: 240UNTS69.
PROCEDURE: Future Procedures Contemplated.
PARTIES:
Germany, West
USA (United States)

106609 Bilateral Exchange **459 UNTS 3**
SIGNED: 24 Apr 62   FORCE: 24 Apr 62
REGISTERED: 15 Apr 63 USA (United States)
ARTICLES: 2 LANGUAGE: English.
HEADNOTE: USE GREEK PORTS TERRITORIAL WATERS NS SAVANNAH
TOPIC: Water Transport
CONCEPTS: Conformity with municipal law. Inspection and observation. Responsibility and liability. Claims and settlements. Peaceful use. Navigational conditions. Inland and territorial waters. Ports and pilotage. Naval vessels. Ocean resources.
TREATY REF: S.EX.DOC.D 87TH CONG.2ND SESS..
PROCEDURE: Amendment. Termination.
PARTIES:
Greece
USA (United States)

106610 Bilateral Agreement **459 UNTS 17**
SIGNED: 5 Mar 62   FORCE: 18 May 62
REGISTERED: 15 Apr 63 USA (United States)
ARTICLES: 4 LANGUAGE: English.
HEADNOTE: GATT INTERIM AGREEMENT
TOPIC: Commodity Trade
CONCEPTS: Annex or appendix reference. General trade.
TREATY REF: 55UNTS187; 459UNTS18-FN__2&3; 459UNTS20-FN__2.
PROCEDURE: Ratification. Termination.
PARTIES:
Sweden
USA (United States)

106611 Bilateral Agreement **459 UNTS 31**
SIGNED: 13 Aug 62   FORCE: 13 Aug 62
REGISTERED: 15 Apr 63 USA (United States)
ARTICLES: 4 LANGUAGE: English.
HEADNOTE: AGRI COMMOD TITLE I
TOPIC: US Agri Commod Aid
CONCEPTS: General provisions. Annex or appendix reference. Exchange of information and documents. Reexport of goods, etc.. Currency. Payment schedules. Purchase authorization. Commodities schedule. Purchase authorization. Mutual consultation.
PARTIES:
Ethiopia
USA (United States)

106612 Bilateral Agreement **459 UNTS 45**
SIGNED: 29 Mar 61   FORCE: 12 Jul 62
REGISTERED: 15 Apr 63 USA (United States)
ARTICLES: 7 LANGUAGE: English. German.
HEADNOTE: EUROPEAN RECOVERY PROGRAM COUNTERPART SETTLEMENT
TOPIC: Direct Aid
CONCEPTS: Annex type material. Exchange of information and documents. Responsibility and liability. Establishment of trade relations. Financial programs. Aid and development. Domestic obligation. Economic assistance. Use restrictions. Loan and credit. Terms of loan.
PROCEDURE: Ratification.
PARTIES:
Austria
USA (United States)

106613 Bilateral Exchange **459 UNTS 79**
SIGNED: 3 Aug 62   FORCE: 3 Aug 62
REGISTERED: 15 Apr 63 USA (United States)
ARTICLES: 2 LANGUAGE: English.
HEADNOTE: INVESTMENT GUARANTIES
TOPIC: Claims and Debts
CONCEPTS: General property. Arbitration. Procedure. Existing tribunals. Negotiation. Reciprocity in financial treatment. Currency. Claims and settlements. Private investment guarantee.
PARTIES:
Ethiopia
USA (United States)

106614 Bilateral Exchange **459 UNTS 87**
SIGNED: 25 Jul 62   FORCE: 25 Jul 62
REGISTERED: 15 Apr 63 USA (United States)
ARTICLES: 2 LANGUAGE: English.
HEADNOTE: COMMITMENT FUNDS
TOPIC: Direct Aid
CONCEPTS: Aid and development. Loan and credit. Credit provisions.
PARTIES:
Pakistan
USA (United States)

106615 Bilateral Agreement **459 UNTS 95**
SIGNED: 12 Jan 62   FORCE: 1 Jul 62
REGISTERED: 15 Apr 63 USA (United States)
ARTICLES: 16 LANGUAGE: English. German.
HEADNOTE: EXCHANGE INTERNATIONAL MONEY ORDERS
TOPIC: Postal Service
CONCEPTS: Annex or appendix reference. Conformity with municipal law. Accounting procedures. Currency. Exchange rates and regulations. Postal services. Regulations. Money orders and postal checks. Rates and charges.
PROCEDURE: Duration. Termination.
PARTIES:
Thailand
USA (United States)

106616 Bilateral Exchange **459 UNTS 117**
SIGNED: 1 Sep 62   FORCE: 1 Sep 62
REGISTERED: 16 Apr 63 USA (United States)
ARTICLES: 2 LANGUAGE: English. French.
HEADNOTE: INVESTMENT GUARANTIES
TOPIC: Claims and Debts
CONCEPTS: General property. Arbitration. Procedure. Existing tribunals. Negotiation. Reciprocity in financial treatment. Currency. Claims and settlements. Private investment guarantee.
INTL ORGS: International Court of Justice.
PARTIES:
Congo (Brazzaville)
USA (United States)

106617 Bilateral Exchange **459 UNTS 123**
SIGNED: 6 Jul 62   FORCE: 6 Jul 62
REGISTERED: 16 Apr 63 USA (United States)
ARTICLES: 2 LANGUAGE: English.
HEADNOTE: EXPORTS COTTON VELVETEEN PRODUCTS
TOPIC: Commodity Trade
CONCEPTS: Previous treaty replacement. Export quotas. Bonds. Commodity trade.

TREATY REF: USA'TIAS 4884;.
PARTIES:
Italy
USA (United States)
ANNEX
529 UNTS 364. Italy. Amendment 29 Jul 64.
Force 29 Jul 64.
529 UNTS 364. USA (United States). Amendment
29 Jul 64. Force 29 Jul 64.

106618 Bilateral Exchange **459 UNTS 129**
SIGNED: 26 Apr 62 FORCE: 26 Apr 62
REGISTERED: 16 Apr 63 USA (United States)
ARTICLES: 2 LANGUAGE: English. French.
HEADNOTE: INVESTMENT GUARANTIES
TOPIC: Claims and Debts
CONCEPTS: Detailed regulations. Arbitration. Pro-
cedure. Existing tribunals. Negotiation. Reciproc-
ity in financial treatment. Currency. Claims and
settlements. Private investment guarantee.
PARTIES:
Niger
USA (United States)

106619 Bilateral Agreement **459 UNTS 135**
SIGNED: 31 May 62 FORCE: 1 Oct 62
REGISTERED: 16 Apr 63 USA (United States)
ARTICLES: 31 LANGUAGE: English.
HEADNOTE: PARCEL POST
TOPIC: Postal Service
CONCEPTS: Detailed regulations. Exchange of in-
formation and documents. Responsibility and lia-
bility. Compensation. Payment schedules. Cus-
toms duties. Postal services. Regulations. In-
sured letters and boxes. Conveyance in transit.
Parcel post. Rates and charges.
TREATY REF: 364UNTS3; 391UNTS322;
404UNTS380.
PROCEDURE: Duration. Termination.
PARTIES:
Thailand
USA (United States)

106620 Bilateral Exchange **459 UNTS 185**
SIGNED: 4 Oct 62 FORCE: 4 Oct 62
REGISTERED: 16 Apr 63 USA (United States)
ARTICLES: 2 LANGUAGE: English. French.
HEADNOTE: PEACE CORPS PROGRAM
TOPIC: General Aid
CONCEPTS: Diplomatic privileges. Conformity
with municipal law. General cooperation. Ex-
change rates and regulations. Fees and exemp-
tions. Funding procedures. Tax exemptions. Cus-
toms exemptions. Domestic obligation. Materi-
als, equipment and services. Aid missions.
Volunteer programs.
PARTIES:
Gabon
USA (United States)

106621 Bilateral Exchange **459 UNTS 191**
SIGNED: 5 Oct 62 FORCE: 5 Oct 62
REGISTERED: 16 Apr 63 USA (United States)
ARTICLES: 2 LANGUAGE: English. Spanish.
HEADNOTE: INVESTMENT GUARANTIES
TOPIC: Finance
CONCEPTS: Private investment guarantee.
PARTIES:
Colombia
USA (United States)

106622 Bilateral Exchange **459 UNTS 197**
SIGNED: 14 Nov 62 FORCE: 14 Nov 62
REGISTERED: 16 Apr 63 USA (United States)
ARTICLES: 2 LANGUAGE: English.
HEADNOTE: INTERCONTINENTAL TESTING EX-
PERIMENTAL COMMUNICATIONS SATELLITE
TOPIC: Telecommunications
CONCEPTS: Satellites.
PARTIES:
Italy
USA (United States)

106623 Bilateral Exchange **459 UNTS 203**
SIGNED: 6 Nov 62 FORCE: 6 Nov 62
REGISTERED: 16 Apr 63 USA (United States)
ARTICLES: 2 LANGUAGE: English. Japanese.
HEADNOTE: INTERCONTINENTAL TESTING EX-
PERIMENTAL COMMUNICATIONS SATELLITE
TOPIC: Telecommunications
CONCEPTS: Satellites.
PARTIES:
Japan
USA (United States)

106624 Bilateral Exchange **459 UNTS 211**
SIGNED: 24 Oct 62 FORCE: 24 Oct 62
REGISTERED: 16 Apr 63 USA (United States)
ARTICLES: 2 LANGUAGE: English. Spanish.
HEADNOTE: FURNISHING DEFENSE ARTICLES
SERVICES
TOPIC: Milit Assistance
CONCEPTS: Previous treaty amendment. Materi-
als, equipment and services. Military assistance.
Return of equipment and recapture.
TREATY REF: 21UNTS77.
PARTIES:
Honduras
USA (United States)

106625 Bilateral Exchange **459 UNTS 219**
SIGNED: 13 Oct 61 FORCE: 21 Nov 62
REGISTERED: 16 Apr 63 USA (United States)
ARTICLES: 2 LANGUAGE: English. German.
HEADNOTE: IMPORTED AIRCRAFT AIRWORTHI-
NESS CERTIFICATES
TOPIC: Air Transport
CONCEPTS: Conformity with municipal law. Gen-
eral cooperation. Exchange of information and
documents. Recognition of legal documents.
Registration certificate. Airworthiness certifi-
cates.
PROCEDURE: Ratification. Termination. Applica-
tion to Non-self-governing Territories.
PARTIES:
Switzerland
USA (United States)

106626 Bilateral Agreement **459 UNTS 231**
SIGNED: 30 Nov 62 FORCE: 30 Nov 62
REGISTERED: 16 Apr 63 USA (United States)
ARTICLES: 6 LANGUAGE: English.
HEADNOTE: AGRI COMMOD TITLE I
TOPIC: US Agri Commod Aid
CONCEPTS: General provisions. Annex or appen-
dix reference. Exchange of information and doc-
uments. Reexport of goods, etc.. Exchange rates
and regulations. Transportation costs. Local cur-
rency. Commodities schedule. Purchase authori-
zation. Surplus commodities. Mutual consulta-
tion.
PARTIES:
India
USA (United States)

106627 Bilateral Exchange **459 UNTS 247**
SIGNED: 25 Oct 62 FORCE: 25 Oct 62
REGISTERED: 16 Apr 63 USA (United States)
ARTICLES: 2 LANGUAGE: English. Spanish.
HEADNOTE: METEROLOGICAL PROGRAM
TOPIC: Scientific Project
CONCEPTS: Previous treaty extension. Exchange
of information and documents. Operating agen-
cies. General property. Responsibility and liabil-
ity. Commissions and foundations. Research and
scientific projects. Research results. Indemnities
and reimbursements. Fees and exemptions. Tax
exemptions.
TREATY REF: 263UNTS181.
PROCEDURE: Duration. Renewal or Revival. Termi-
nation.
PARTIES:
Dominican Republic
USA (United States)

106628 Bilateral Exchange **459 UNTS 259**
SIGNED: 3 Nov 62 FORCE: 3 Nov 62
REGISTERED: 16 Apr 63 USA (United States)
ARTICLES: 2 LANGUAGE: English. French.
HEADNOTE: INFORMATIONAL MEDIA GUARANTY
PROGRAM
TOPIC: Mass Media
CONCEPTS: Local currency. Media guaranty.
PARTIES:
Guinea
USA (United States)

106629 Bilateral Agreement **459 UNTS 263**
SIGNED: 19 Nov 62 FORCE: 19 Nov 62
REGISTERED: 16 Apr 63 USA (United States)
ARTICLES: 6 LANGUAGE: English. Chinese.
HEADNOTE: AGRI COMMOD TITLE I
TOPIC: US Agri Commod Aid
CONCEPTS: General provisions. Annex or appen-
dix reference. Exchange of information and doc-
uments. Reexport of goods, etc.. Exchange rates
and regulations. Transportation costs. Local cur-
rency. Commodities schedule. Purchase authori-

zation. Surplus commodities. Mutual consulta-
tion.
PARTIES:
Taiwan
USA (United States)
ANNEX
473 UNTS 372. Taiwan. Amendment 24 Jan 63.
Force 24 Jan 63.
473 UNTS 372. USA (United States). Amendment
24 Jan 63. Force 24 Jan 63.

106630 Bilateral Agreement **460 UNTS 3**
SIGNED: 8 Mar 62 FORCE: 8 Mar 62
REGISTERED: 16 Apr 63 USA (United States)
ARTICLES: 14 LANGUAGE: English. Russian.
HEADNOTE: EXCHANGE SCIENTIFIC TECHNICAL
EDUCATIONAL CULTURAL OTHER FIELDS
TOPIC: Health/Educ/Welfare
CONCEPTS: General cooperation. Exchange of in-
formation and documents. Personnel. Special-
ists exchange. Disease control. Sanitation. Rec-
ognition of degrees. Exchange. Commissions
and foundations. Teacher and student ex-
change. Professorships. Scholarships and
grants. Vocational training. Exchange. Artists.
Athletes. Meteorology. Nuclear research. Scien-
tific exchange. Research and development.
Trade procedures. Agriculture. Specific techni-
cal assistance. General. General transportation.
Navigational conditions. Publications exchange.
Mass media exchange. Press and wire services.
INTL ORGS: International Atomic Energy Agency.
PROCEDURE: Duration.
PARTIES:
USA (United States)
USSR (Soviet Union)

106631 Bilateral Exchange **460 UNTS 75**
SIGNED: 31 May 62 FORCE: 31 May 62
REGISTERED: 16 Apr 63 USA (United States)
ARTICLES: 2 LANGUAGE: English.
HEADNOTE: PEACE CORPS PROGRAM
TOPIC: General Aid
CONCEPTS: General cooperation. Exchange rates
and regulations. Fees and exemptions. Funding
procedures. General. Tax exemptions. Customs
exemptions. Domestic obligation. Materials,
equipment and services. Aid missions. Volunteer
programs.
PROCEDURE: Termination.
PARTIES:
Pakistan
USA (United States)

106632 Bilateral Exchange **460 UNTS 83**
SIGNED: 13 Jul 62 FORCE: 13 Jul 62
REGISTERED: 16 Apr 63 USA (United States)
ARTICLES: 2 LANGUAGE: English.
HEADNOTE: SUSPENSION TOLLS WELLAND CA-
NAL ST. LAWRENCE SEAWAY
TOPIC: Water Transport
CONCEPTS: Annex type material. Fees and exemp-
tions. Canal improvement.
TREATY REF: 340UNTS295.
PARTIES:
Canada
USA (United States)
ANNEX
494 UNTS 330. USA (United States). Amendment
20 Dec 63. Force 20 Dec 63.
494 UNTS 330. Canada. Amendment 19 Dec 63.
Force 19 Dec 63.
527 UNTS 318. USA (United States). Prolongation
31 Mar 64. Force 31 Mar 64.
527 UNTS 318. Canada. Prolongation 31 Mar 64.
Force 31 Mar 64.

106633 Bilateral Agreement **460 UNTS 89**
SIGNED: 30 May 53 FORCE: 13 Nov 59
REGISTERED: 18 Apr 63 USA (United States)
ARTICLES: 6 LANGUAGE: English. Portuguese.
HEADNOTE: SPECIAL TECHNICAL SERVICES
TOPIC: Tech Assistance
CONCEPTS: Treaty implementation. Annex type
material. Privileges and immunities. General co-
operation. Exchange of information and docu-
ments. Inspection and observation. Operating
agencies. Personnel. Private contracts. Voca-
tional training. Expense sharing formulae. Tax
exemptions. Customs exemptions. Assistance.
Economic assistance. Materials, equipment and
services. Aid missions.
TREATY REF: 141UNTS3.

PROCEDURE: Duration. Termination.
PARTIES:
Brazil
USA (United States)
ANNEX
511 UNTS 308. Brazil. Prolongation 30 Dec 63. Force 30 Dec 63.
511 UNTS 308. USA (United States). Prolongation 27 Jan 63. Force 30 Dec 63.

106634   Bilateral Exchange   **460 UNTS 113**
SIGNED: 15 Nov 61   FORCE: 15 Nov 61
REGISTERED: 18 Apr 63 USA (United States)
ARTICLES: 2 LANGUAGE: English. Spanish.
HEADNOTE: INDUSTRIAL PRODUCTIVITY PROGRAM
TOPIC: Non-IBRD Project
CONCEPTS: Informational records. Operating agencies. Customs exemptions. Temporary importation. General technical assistance. Industry.
TREATY REF: 141UNTS211; 200UNTS312; 233UNTS306; 263UNTS247.
PROCEDURE: Duration. Termination.
PARTIES:
Mexico
USA (United States)

106635   Bilateral Exchange   **460 UNTS 125**
SIGNED: 20 Jul 62   FORCE: 20 Jul 62
REGISTERED: 18 Apr 63 USA (United States)
ARTICLES: 2 LANGUAGE: English. Spanish.
HEADNOTE: PEACE CORPS PROGRAM
TOPIC: General Aid
CONCEPTS: Diplomatic privileges. Conformity with municipal law. General cooperation. Personnel. Exchange rates and regulations. Funding procedures. General. Tax exemptions. Customs exemptions. Domestic obligation. Materials, equipment and services. Aid missions. Volunteer programs.
PROCEDURE: Termination.
PARTIES:
Honduras
USA (United States)

106636   Bilateral Exchange   **460 UNTS 133**
SIGNED: 3 Aug 62   FORCE: 3 Aug 62
REGISTERED: 18 Apr 63 USA (United States)
ARTICLES: 2 LANGUAGE: English. Spanish.
HEADNOTE: PEACE CORPS PROGRAM
TOPIC: General Aid
CONCEPTS: Diplomatic privileges. Conformity with municipal law. Personnel. Fees and exemptions. General. Tax exemptions. Customs exemptions. Domestic obligation. Materials, equipment and services. Aid missions. Volunteer programs.
PROCEDURE: Termination.
PARTIES:
Ecuador
USA (United States)

106637   Bilateral Exchange   **460 UNTS 143**
SIGNED: 24 Aug 62   FORCE: 24 Aug 62
REGISTERED: 18 Apr 63 USA (United States)
ARTICLES: 2 LANGUAGE: English.
HEADNOTE: PEACE CORPS PROGRAM
TOPIC: General Aid
CONCEPTS: Conformity with municipal law. General cooperation. Personnel. Exchange rates and regulations. Fees and exemptions. Funding procedures. General. Tax exemptions. Customs duties. Customs exemptions. Domestic obligation. Materials, equipment and services. Volunteer programs.
PROCEDURE: Termination.
PARTIES:
Nepal
USA (United States)

106638   Bilateral Agreement   **460 UNTS 151**
SIGNED: 6 Dec 62   FORCE: 6 Dec 62
REGISTERED: 18 Apr 63 USA (United States)
ARTICLES: 6 LANGUAGE: English.
HEADNOTE: AGRI AGREE TITLE I
TOPIC: US Agri Commod Aid
CONCEPTS: General provisions. Annex or appendix reference. Exchange of information and documents. Reexport of goods, etc.. Exchange rates and regulations. Transportation costs. Local currency. Commodities schedule. Purchase authorization. Surplus commodities. Mutual consultation.
PARTIES:
Israel
USA (United States)
ANNEX
494 UNTS 334. USA (United States). Amendment 24 Dec 63. Force 30 Dec 63.
494 UNTS 334. Israel. Amendment 30 Dec 63. Force 30 Dec 63.
515 UNTS 310. USA (United States). Amendment 27 Apr 64. Force 27 Apr 64.
515 UNTS 310. Israel. Amendment 27 Apr 64. Force 27 Apr 64.
515 UNTS 314. USA (United States). Amendment 23 Jun 64. Force 23 Jun 64.
515 UNTS 314. Israel. Amendment 23 Jun 64. Force 23 Jun 64.
515 UNTS 318. USA (United States). Amendment 6 Jul 64. Force 6 Jul 64.
515 UNTS 318. Israel. Amendment 6 Jul 64. Force 6 Jul 64.
545 UNTS 352. USA (United States). Amendment 26 May 65. Force 27 May 65.
545 UNTS 352. Israel. Amendment 27 May 65. Force 27 May 65.
545 UNTS 356. USA (United States). Amendment 22 Jun 65. Force 22 Jun 66.
545 UNTS 356. Israel. Amendment 22 Jun 65. Force 22 Jun 66.

106639   Bilateral Agreement   **460 UNTS 169**
SIGNED: 29 Nov 62   FORCE: 29 Nov 62
REGISTERED: 18 Apr 63 USA (United States)
ARTICLES: 10 LANGUAGE: English. German.
HEADNOTE: USE TERRITORIAL WATERS PORTS NS SAVANNAH
TOPIC: Water Transport
CONCEPTS: Definition of terms. Exceptions and exemptions. Conformity with municipal law. Inspection and observation. Licenses and permits. Responsibility and liability. Claims and settlements. Peaceful use. Routes and logistics. Navigational conditions. Inland and territorial waters. Ports and pilotage. Naval vessels. Ocean resources.
TREATY REF: S.EX.DOC.D. 87TH CONG. 2ND SESS..
PROCEDURE: Amendment. Termination.
PARTIES:
Germany, West
USA (United States)

106640   Bilateral Agreement   **460 UNTS 185**
SIGNED: 28 Nov 62   FORCE: 28 Nov 62
REGISTERED: 18 Apr 63 USA (United States)
ARTICLES: 6 LANGUAGE: English.
HEADNOTE: AGRI COMMOD TITLE I
TOPIC: US Agri Commod Aid
CONCEPTS: General provisions. Annex or appendix reference. Union with other states. Exchange of information and documents. Reexport of goods, etc.. Exchange rates and regulations. Transportation costs. Local currency. Commodities schedule. Purchase authorization. Surplus commodities.
PARTIES:
USA (United States)
Yugoslavia
ANNEX
479 UNTS 412.   Yugoslavia.   Amendment 9 May 63. Force 9 May 63.
479 UNTS 412. USA (United States). Amendment 19 Apr 63. Force 9 May 63.
573 UNTS 336. USA (United States). Amendment 19 Aug 65. Force 3 Nov 65.
573 UNTS 336.   Yugoslavia.   Amendment 3 Nov 65. Force 3 Nov 65.

106641   Bilateral Agreement   **460 UNTS 203**
SIGNED: 26 Nov 62   FORCE: 26 Nov 62
REGISTERED: 18 Apr 63 USA (United States)
ARTICLES: 6 LANGUAGE: English.
HEADNOTE: AGRI COMMOD TITLE I
TOPIC: US Agri Commod Aid
CONCEPTS: General provisions. Annex or appendix reference. Exchange of information and documents. Reexport of goods, etc.. Exchange rates and regulations. Transportation costs. Local currency. Commodities schedule. Purchase authorization. Surplus commodities. Mutual consultation.

PARTIES:
India
USA (United States)
ANNEX
474 UNTS 372. USA (United States). Amendment 1 Apr 63. Force 1 Apr 63.
474 UNTS 372. India. Amendment 1 Apr 63. Force 1 Apr 63.
488 UNTS 314. USA (United States). Amendment 4 Sep 63. Force 4 Sep 63.
488 UNTS 314. India. Amendment 4 Sep 63. Force 4 Sep 63.
526 UNTS 326. USA (United States). Amendment 17 Apr 65. Force 17 Apr 64.
526 UNTS 326. India. Amendment 17 Apr 64. Force 17 Apr 64.

106642   Multilateral Agreement **460 UNTS 219**
SIGNED: 28 Jul 62   FORCE: 22 Feb 63
REGISTERED: 18 Apr 63 Poland
ARTICLES: 7 LANGUAGE: German. Polish. Russian.
HEADNOTE: COOPERATION MARINE FISHING
TOPIC: Specific Resources
CONCEPTS: Establishment of commission. Fisheries and fishing.
INTL ORGS: Special Commission.
PROCEDURE: Denunciation. Duration. Registration. Renewal or Revival.
PARTIES:
Germany, West SIGNED: 28 Jul 62 FORCE: 22 Feb 63
Poland SIGNED: 28 Jul 62 FORCE: 22 Feb 63
USSR (Soviet Union) SIGNED: 28 Jul 62 FORCE: 22 Feb 63
ANNEX
618 UNTS 382. Bulgaria. Accession 19 Sep 64.
618 UNTS 382. Romania. Accession 1 Sep 66.

106643   Bilateral Exchange   **460 UNTS 237**
SIGNED: 15 Aug 62   FORCE: 15 Aug 62
REGISTERED: 22 Apr 63 USA (United States)
ARTICLES: 2 LANGUAGE: English. Chinese.
HEADNOTE: LOAN VESSELS CHINA
TOPIC: Loans and Credits
CONCEPTS: Annex type material. Lease of military property. Naval vessels.
TREATY REF: 231UNTS165; 251UNTS399; 284UNTS380.
PARTIES:
Taiwan
USA (United States)

106644   Bilateral Agreement   **460 UNTS 247**
SIGNED: 31 Aug 62   FORCE: 31 Aug 62
REGISTERED: 22 Apr 63 USA (United States)
ARTICLES: 5 LANGUAGE: English. Chinese.
HEADNOTE: AGRI COMMOD TITLE IV
TOPIC: US Agri Commod Aid
CONCEPTS: General provisions. Exchange of information and documents. Reexport of goods, etc.. Payment schedules. Purchase authorization. Commodities schedule. Purchase authorization. Mutual consultation.
PARTIES:
Taiwan
USA (United States)
ANNEX
473 UNTS 380. USA (United States). Amendment 15 Jan 63. Force 15 Jan 63.
473 UNTS 380. Taiwan. Amendment 15 Jan 63. Force 15 Jan 63.
526 UNTS 330. USA (United States). Amendment 3 Jun 64. Force 3 Jun 64.
526 UNTS 330. Taiwan. Amendment 3 Jun 64. Force 3 Jun 64.

106645   Bilateral Exchange   **460 UNTS 267**
SIGNED: 28 Aug 62   FORCE: 28 Aug 62
REGISTERED: 22 Apr 63 USA (United States)
ARTICLES: 2 LANGUAGE: English. Japanese.
HEADNOTE: GRANT VESSELS TO JAPAN
TOPIC: Loans and Credits
CONCEPTS: Annex or appendix reference. Defense and security. Lease of military property. Naval vessels.
TREATY REF: 304UNTS355; 184UNTS111.
PARTIES:
Japan
USA (United States)

106646   Bilateral Agreement   **460 UNTS 277**
SIGNED: 22 Dec 61   FORCE: 7 Sep 62

REGISTERED: 22 Apr 63 USA (United States)
ARTICLES: 6 LANGUAGE: English. Spanish.
HEADNOTE: ECONOMIC TECHNICAL RELATED ASSISTANCE
TOPIC: General Aid
CONCEPTS: Change of circumstances. Treaty implementation. Previous treaty replacement. Diplomatic privileges. Privileges and immunities. Conformity with municipal law. Exchange of information and documents. Inspection and observation. Personnel. General property. Exchange rates and regulations. Funding procedures. Tax exemptions. Customs exemptions. Domestic obligation. General technical assistance. Economic assistance. Aid missions.
TREATY REF: 92UNTS179.
PROCEDURE: Ratification. Termination.
PARTIES:
Costa Rica
USA (United States)

106647 Bilateral Agreement **461 UNTS 3**
SIGNED: 17 May 62   FORCE: 5 Sep 62
REGISTERED: 22 Apr 63 USA (United States)
ARTICLES: 11 LANGUAGE: English. French.
HEADNOTE: ATOMIC ENERGY MUTUAL DEFENSE
TOPIC: Milit Assistance
CONCEPTS: Definition of terms. Conformity with municipal law. General cooperation. Exchange of information and documents. Recognition. Non-nuclear materials. Joint defense. Atomic weapons. Military training. Security of information. Exchange of defense information. Restrictions on transfer.
PROCEDURE: Ratification. Termination.
PARTIES:
Belgium
USA (United States)

106648 Bilateral Exchange **461 UNTS 15**
SIGNED: 9 Aug 60   FORCE: 29 Aug 62
REGISTERED: 22 Apr 63 USA (United States)
ARTICLES: 2 LANGUAGE: English. Spanish.
HEADNOTE: INVESTMENT GUARANTIES
TOPIC: Finance
CONCEPTS: Detailed regulations. Previous treaty replacement. Conformity with municipal law. General cooperation. Exchange of information and documents. Expropriation. Arbitration. Procedure. Existing tribunals. Negotiation. Currency. Claims and settlements. Private investment guarantee. Most favored nation clause.
INTL ORGS: International Court of Justice. Arbitration Commission.
TREATY REF: 252UNTS143.
PROCEDURE: Termination.
PARTIES:
Guatemala
USA (United States)

106649 Bilateral Agreement **461 UNTS 31**
SIGNED: 14 Sep 62   FORCE: 14 Sep 62
REGISTERED: 22 Apr 63 USA (United States)
ARTICLES: 6 LANGUAGE: English. French.
HEADNOTE: AGRI COMMOD TITLE I
TOPIC: US Agri Commod Aid
CONCEPTS: General provisions. Annex or appendix reference. Exchange of information and documents. Reexport of goods, etc.. Exchange rates and regulations. Transportation costs. Local currency. Commodities schedule. Purchase authorization. Surplus commodities. Mutual consultation.
PARTIES:
Tunisia
USA (United States)
ANNEX
488 UNTS 318. USA (United States). Amendment 13 Sep 63. Force 13 Sep 63.
488 UNTS 318. Tunisia. Amendment 13 Sep 63. Force 13 Sep 63.
494 UNTS 338. USA (United States). Amendment 19 Dec 63. Force 19 Dec 63.
494 UNTS 338. Tunisia. Amendment 19 Dec 63. Force 19 Dec 63.

106650 Bilateral Exchange **461 UNTS 47**
SIGNED: 5 Sep 62   FORCE: 5 Sep 62
REGISTERED: 22 Apr 63 USA (United States)
ARTICLES: 2 LANGUAGE: English. French.
HEADNOTE: PEACE CORPS PROGRAMS
TOPIC: General Aid
CONCEPTS: Diplomatic privileges. Conformity

with municipal law. Personnel. Exchange rates and regulations. Fees and exemptions. Funding procedures. General. Tax exemptions. Customs exemptions. Domestic obligation. Materials, equipment and services. Aid missions. Volunteer programs.
PROCEDURE: Termination.
PARTIES:
Togo
USA (United States)

106651 Bilateral Exchange **461 UNTS 55**
SIGNED: 27 Aug 62   FORCE: 27 Aug 62
REGISTERED: 22 Apr 63 USA (United States)
ARTICLES: 2 LANGUAGE: English.
HEADNOTE: PEACE CORPS PROGRAM
TOPIC: General Aid
CONCEPTS: General cooperation. Personnel. Fees and exemptions. General. Tax exemptions. Customs exemptions. Domestic obligation. Volunteer programs.
PROCEDURE: Termination.
PARTIES:
Turkey
USA (United States)

106652 Bilateral Agreement **461 UNTS 61**
SIGNED: 7 Aug 62   FORCE: 7 Aug 62
REGISTERED: 22 Apr 63 USA (United States)
ARTICLES: 5 LANGUAGE: English. Spanish.
HEADNOTE: AGRI COMMOD TITLE IV
TOPIC: US Agri Commod Aid
CONCEPTS: General provisions. Reexport of goods, etc.. Currency. Payment schedules. Purchase authorization. Commodities schedule. Purchase authorization. Mutual consultation.
PARTIES:
Chile
USA (United States)
ANNEX
469 UNTS 440. USA (United States). Amendment 29 Nov 62. Force 29 Nov 62.
469 UNTS 440. Chile. Amendment 29 Nov 62. Force 29 Nov 62.
474 UNTS 376. USA (United States). Amendment 14 Feb 63. Force 14 Feb 63.
474 UNTS 376. Chile. Amendment 14 Feb 63. Force 14 Feb 63.
476 UNTS 353. USA (United States). Amendment 1 Mar 63. Force 27 Mar 63.
476 UNTS 353. Chile. Amendment 27 Mar 63. Force 27 Mar 63.
531 UNTS 392. Chile. Amendment 17 Nov 64. Force 17 Nov 64.
531 UNTS 392. USA (United States). Amendment 17 Nov 64. Force 17 Nov 64.

106653 Bilateral Agreement **461 UNTS 91**
SIGNED: 26 Sep 61   FORCE: 26 Sep 61
REGISTERED: 22 Apr 63 USA (United States)
ARTICLES: 6 LANGUAGE: English. Spanish.
HEADNOTE: ECONOMIC TECHNICAL RELATED ASSISTANCE
TOPIC: General Aid
CONCEPTS: Change of circumstances. Exceptions and exemptions. Previous treaty replacement. Diplomatic privileges. Privileges and immunities. Conformity with municipal law. General cooperation. Personnel. Currency. Exchange rates and regulations. Funding procedures. Customs exemptions. Domestic obligation. General technical assistance. Economic assistance. Materials, equipment and services. Aid missions.
TREATY REF: 122UNTS157; 180UNTS334.
PROCEDURE: Amendment. Termination.
PARTIES:
Paraguay
USA (United States)

106654 Bilateral Exchange **461 UNTS 105**
SIGNED: 26 Apr 62   FORCE: 26 Apr 62
REGISTERED: 22 Apr 63 USA (United States)
ARTICLES: 2 LANGUAGE: English. Spanish.
HEADNOTE: FURNISHING DEFENSE ARTICLES SERVICES
TOPIC: Milit Assistance
CONCEPTS: Non-prejudice to UN charter. Conformity with municipal law. Exchange of information and documents. Inspection and observation. Materials, equipment and services. Self-defense. Military assistance. Return of equipment and recapture. Security of information. Exchange of defense information. Restrictions on transfer.

TREATY REF: 21UNTS77.
PARTIES:
Bolivia
USA (United States)

106655 Bilateral Agreement **461 UNTS 113**
SIGNED: 9 Nov 62   FORCE: 9 Nov 62
REGISTERED: 22 Apr 63 USA (United States)
ARTICLES: 6 LANGUAGE: English.
HEADNOTE: AGRI COMMOD TITLE I
TOPIC: US Agri Commod Aid
CONCEPTS: General provisions. Annex or appendix reference. Exchange of information and documents. Reexport of goods, etc.. Exchange rates and regulations. Transportation costs. Local currency. Commodities schedule. Purchase authorization. Surplus commodities. Mutual consultation.
PARTIES:
Burma
USA (United States)

106656 Bilateral Exchange **461 UNTS 129**
SIGNED: 4 Oct 62   FORCE: 4 Oct 62
REGISTERED: 22 Apr 63 USA (United States)
ARTICLES: 2 LANGUAGE: English. Spanish.
HEADNOTE: PEACE CORPS PROGRAM
TOPIC: Tech Assistance
CONCEPTS: Annex type material. Privileges and immunities. General cooperation. Personnel. Domestic obligation. Volunteer programs.
TREATY REF: 151UNTS147.
PROCEDURE: Termination.
PARTIES:
Chile
USA (United States)

106657 Bilateral Exchange **461 UNTS 137**
SIGNED: 28 Aug 62   FORCE: 28 Aug 62
REGISTERED: 24 Apr 63 USA (United States)
ARTICLES: 2 LANGUAGE: English. Italian.
HEADNOTE: CHILD FEEDING PROGRAM
TOPIC: Sanitation
CONCEPTS: Conditions. Definition of terms. Detailed regulations. Treaty implementation. Domestic legislation. Education. Vocational training. Family allowances. Financial programs. Funding procedures. General technical assistance. Grants.
TREATY REF: 258UNTS15; 389UNTS237; 355UNTS393.
PARTIES:
Italy
USA (United States)

106658 Bilateral Exchange **461 UNTS 147**
SIGNED: 23 Aug 62   FORCE: 23 Aug 62
REGISTERED: 24 Apr 63 USA (United States)
ARTICLES: 2 LANGUAGE: English.
HEADNOTE: PEACE CORPS PROGRAM
TOPIC: General Aid
CONCEPTS: Diplomatic privileges. Conformity with municipal law. General cooperation. Exchange rates and regulations. Fees and exemptions. Funding procedures. General. Tax exemptions. Customs exemptions. Domestic obligation. Materials, equipment and services. Aid missions. Volunteer programs.
PROCEDURE: Termination.
PARTIES:
Cyprus
USA (United States)

106659 Bilateral Exchange **461 UNTS 155**
SIGNED: 18 Jun 62   FORCE: 18 Jun 62
REGISTERED: 24 Apr 63 USA (United States)
ARTICLES: 2 LANGUAGE: English. Spanish.
HEADNOTE: FURNISHING DEFENSE ARTICLES SERVICES
TOPIC: Milit Assistance
CONCEPTS: Non-prejudice to UN charter. Conformity with municipal law. Exchange of information and documents. Inspection and observation. Materials, equipment and services. Self-defense. Military assistance. Return of equipment and recapture. Security of information. Exchange of defense information. Restrictions on transfer.
TREATY REF: 21UNTS77.
PARTIES:
Costa Rica
USA (United States)

106660 Bilateral Exchange **461 UNTS 163**
SIGNED: 21 Aug 62   FORCE: 21 Aug 62
REGISTERED: 24 Apr 63 USA (United States)
ARTICLES: 2 LANGUAGE: English.
HEADNOTE: DISPOSAL USS CANOPUS
TOPIC: Milit Assistance
CONCEPTS: Inspection and observation. Responsibility and liability. Title and deeds. Naval vessels.
PARTIES:
Philippines
USA (United States)

106661 Bilateral Exchange **461 UNTS 169**
SIGNED: 11 Sep 62   FORCE: 11 Sep 62
REGISTERED: 24 Apr 63 USA (United States)
ARTICLES: 2 LANGUAGE: English.
HEADNOTE: PEACE CORPS PROGRAM
TOPIC: General Aid
CONCEPTS: Diplomatic privileges. Personnel. Responsibility and liability. Reexport of goods, etc.. Funding procedures. Tax exemptions. Domestic obligation. Materials, equipment and services. Aid missions. Volunteer programs.
PROCEDURE: Termination.
PARTIES:
Afghanistan
USA (United States)

106662 Bilateral Exchange **461 UNTS 177**
SIGNED: 10 Sep 62   FORCE: 10 Sep 62
REGISTERED: 24 Apr 63 USA (United States)
ARTICLES: 2 LANGUAGE: English. French.
HEADNOTE: PEACE CORP PROGRAM
TOPIC: Tech Assistance
CONCEPTS: Assistance.
PROCEDURE: Termination.
PARTIES:
Cameroon
USA (United States)

106663 Bilateral Exchange **461 UNTS 185**
SIGNED: 5 Sep 62   FORCE: 5 Sep 62
REGISTERED: 24 Apr 63 USA (United States)
ARTICLES: 2 LANGUAGE: English. Italian.
HEADNOTE: SPACE SCIENCE RESEARCH PROGRAM
TOPIC: Scientific Project
CONCEPTS: General cooperation. Operating agencies. Responsibility and liability. Use of facilities. Vocational training. Research and scientific projects. Scientific exchange. Research and development. Economic assistance.
PARTIES:
Italy
USA (United States)

106664 Bilateral Exchange **461 UNTS 199**
SIGNED: 2 Aug 62   FORCE: 2 Aug 62
REGISTERED: 24 Apr 63 USA (United States)
ARTICLES: 2 LANGUAGE: English. Spanish.
HEADNOTE: FURNISHING DEFENSE ARTICLES SERVICES
TOPIC: Milit Assistance
CONCEPTS: Previous treaty amendment. Materials, equipment and services. Self-defense. Military assistance. Return of equipment and recapture.
TREATY REF: 262UNTS105.
PARTIES:
Guatemala
USA (United States)

106665 Bilateral Exchange **461 UNTS 207**
SIGNED: 25 Aug 62   FORCE: 25 Aug 62
REGISTERED: 24 Apr 63 USA (United States)
ARTICLES: 2 LANGUAGE: English. Spanish.
HEADNOTE: ASSISTANCE INCREASE AIR TRANSPORT CAPABILITY
TOPIC: Milit Assistance
CONCEPTS: Conformity with municipal law. Exchange of information and documents. Inspection and observation. Materials, equipment and services. Return of equipment and recapture. Security of information. Restrictions on transfer.
PARTIES:
Paraguay
USA (United States)

106666 Bilateral Exchange **462 UNTS 3**
SIGNED: 6 Aug 58   FORCE: 6 Aug 58
REGISTERED: 24 Apr 63 USA (United States)
ARTICLES: 2 LANGUAGE: English. Chinese.
HEADNOTE: CONSTRUCTION SCATTER WAVE
RADIO FACILITY
TOPIC: Milit Installation
CONCEPTS: Privileges and immunities. General cooperation. General property. Private contracts. Responsibility and liability. Use of facilities. Tax exemptions. Customs exemptions. Joint defense. Procurement and logistics. Bases and facilities.
TREATY REF: 248UNTS213.
PROCEDURE: Amendment.
PARTIES:
Taiwan
USA (United States)

106667 Bilateral Exchange **462 UNTS 19**
SIGNED: 15 Apr 60   FORCE: 15 Apr 60
REGISTERED: 24 Apr 63 USA (United States)
ARTICLES: 2 LANGUAGE: English. Chinese.
HEADNOTE: CONSTRUCTION COMMUNICATION FACILITY
TOPIC: Milit Installation
CONCEPTS: Military installations and equipment. Bases and facilities.
TREATY REF: 462UNTS3.
PROCEDURE: Future Procedures Contemplated.
PARTIES:
Taiwan
USA (United States)

106668 Bilateral Exchange **462 UNTS 25**
SIGNED: 28 Feb 62   FORCE: 28 Feb 62
REGISTERED: 24 Apr 63 USA (United States)
ARTICLES: 2 LANGUAGE: English. Chinese.
HEADNOTE: CONSTRUCTION SCATTER WAVE CONTROL FACILITY
TOPIC: Milit Installation
CONCEPTS: Military installations and equipment. Bases and facilities.
TREATY REF: 462UNTS3.
PROCEDURE: Future Procedures Contemplated.
PARTIES:
Taiwan
USA (United States)

106669 Bilateral Exchange **462 UNTS 31**
SIGNED: 4 Oct 62   FORCE: 4 Oct 62
REGISTERED: 24 Apr 63 USA (United States)
ARTICLES: 2 LANGUAGE: English.
HEADNOTE: PATENT RIGHTS TECHNICAL INFORMATION DEFENSE PURPOSES
TOPIC: Milit Assistance
CONCEPTS: Exchange of information and documents. Establishment of commission. Compensation. Patents, copyrights and trademarks. Recognition. Materials, equipment and services. Security of information. Exchange of defense information.
TREATY REF: 187UNTS3.
PROCEDURE: Future Procedures Contemplated. Termination.
PARTIES:
Sweden
USA (United States)
ANNEX
532 UNTS 378. USA (United States). Implementation 20 Oct 64. Force 17 Nov 64.
532 UNTS 378. Sweden. Implementation 17 Nov 64. Force 17 Nov 64.

106670 Bilateral Agreement **462 UNTS 39**
SIGNED: 8 Oct 62   FORCE: 8 Oct 62
REGISTERED: 24 Apr 63 USA (United States)
ARTICLES: 6 LANGUAGE: English.
HEADNOTE: AGRI COMMOD TITLE I
TOPIC: US Agri Commod Aid
CONCEPTS: General provisions. Annex or appendix reference. Exchange of information and documents. Reexport of goods, etc.. Exchange rates and regulations. Transportation costs. Local currency. Commodities schedule. Purchase authorization. Surplus commodities. Mutual consultation.
PARTIES:
United Arab Rep
USA (United States)
ANNEX
488 UNTS 322. United Arab Rep. Amendment 15 Jun 63. Force 15 Jun 63.
488 UNTS 322. USA (United States). Amendment 15 Jun 63. Force 15 Jun 63.
488 UNTS 326. USA (United States). Amendment 7 Oct 63. Force 7 Oct 63.
488 UNTS 326. United Arab Rep. Amendment 7 Oct 63. Force 7 Oct 63.

524 UNTS 330. United Arab Rep. Amendment 20 Apr 64. Force 20 Apr 64.
524 UNTS 330. USA (United States). Amendment 20 Apr 64. Force 20 Apr 64.
530 UNTS 382. USA (United States). Amendment 30 Jun 64. Force 30 Jun 64.
530 UNTS 382. United Arab Rep. Amendment 30 Jun 64. Force 30 Jun 64.
531 UNTS 396. USA (United States). Amendment 20 Jul 64. Force 20 Jul 64.
531 UNTS 396. United Arab Rep. Amendment 20 Jul 64. Force 20 Jul 64.

106671 Bilateral Exchange **462 UNTS 57**
SIGNED: 7 Feb 61   FORCE: 7 Feb 61
REGISTERED: 24 Apr 63 USA (United States)
ARTICLES: 5 LANGUAGE: English.
HEADNOTE: BALLON FLIGHTS STUDY AIR CURRENTS
TOPIC: Scientific Project
CONCEPTS: General cooperation. Operating agencies. Use of facilities. Research and scientific projects. Meteorology. Scientific exchange. Research and development. Tax exemptions. Economic assistance.
PARTIES:
India
USA (United States)

106672 Bilateral Exchange **462 UNTS 67**
SIGNED: 24 Oct 62   FORCE: 24 Oct 62
REGISTERED: 24 Apr 63 USA (United States)
ARTICLES: 2 LANGUAGE: English.
HEADNOTE: COORDINATION USE RADIO FREQUENCIES
TOPIC: Telecommunications
CONCEPTS: Annex or appendix reference. Bands and frequency allocation. Radio-telephone-telegraphic communications.
INTL ORGS: International Telecommunication Union.
PROCEDURE: Termination.
PARTIES:
Canada
USA (United States)
ANNEX
549 UNTS 300. USA (United States). Amendment 16 Jun 65. Force 24 Jun 65.
549 UNTS 300. Canada. Amendment 24 Jun 65. Force 24 Jun 65.

106673 Bilateral Exchange **462 UNTS 119**
SIGNED: 24 Oct 62   FORCE: 24 Oct 62
REGISTERED: 24 Apr 63 USA (United States)
ARTICLES: 2 LANGUAGE: English.
HEADNOTE: SANITATION SHELLFISH PROCESSING
TOPIC: Sanitation
CONCEPTS: Treaty implementation. General cooperation. Exchange of information and documents. Inspection and observation. Domestic legislation. Recognition and enforcement of legal decisions. Disease control. Public health. Sanitation. Trade procedures.
PROCEDURE: Termination.
PARTIES:
Japan
USA (United States)

106674 Bilateral Agreement **462 UNTS 129**
SIGNED: 7 Nov 62   FORCE: 7 Nov 62
REGISTERED: 24 Apr 63 USA (United States)
ARTICLES: 0 LANGUAGE: English.
HEADNOTE: AGRI COMMOD TITLE I
TOPIC: US Agri Commod Aid
CONCEPTS: General provisions. Annex or appendix reference. Exchange of information and documents. Reexport of goods, etc.. Exchange rates and regulations. Transportation costs. Local currency. Commodities schedule. Purchase authorization. Surplus commodities. Mutual consultation.
PARTIES:
Korea, South
USA (United States)
ANNEX
479 UNTS 416. USA (United States). Amendment 17 Jun 63. Force 17 Jun 63.
479 UNTS 416. Korea, South. Amendment 17 Jun 63. Force 17 Jun 63.
479 UNTS 420. Korea, South. Amendment 5 Jul 63. Force 5 Jul 63.
479 UNTS 420. USA (United States). Amendment 5 Jul 63. Force 5 Jul 63.

487 UNTS 386. USA (United States). Amendment 16 Aug 63. Force 16 Aug 63.
487 UNTS 386. Korea, South. Amendment 16 Aug 63. Force 16 Aug 63.

106675 Bilateral Exchange **462 UNTS 145**
SIGNED: 8 Oct 62 FORCE: 8 Oct 62
REGISTERED: 24 Apr 63 USA (United States)
ARTICLES: 2 LANGUAGE: English.
HEADNOTE: CARIBBEAN AREA AIR SERVICES
TOPIC: Air Transport
CONCEPTS: Previous treaty extension. Continuity of rights and obligations. Routes and logistics. Air transport. Operating authorizations and regulations.
TREATY REF: 3UNTS253; 425UNTS296.
PARTIES:
Trinidad/Tobago
USA (United States)

106676 Bilateral Agreement **462 UNTS 151**
SIGNED: 9 Jan 57 FORCE: 1 Jan 59
REGISTERED: 24 Apr 63 USA (United States)
ARTICLES: 11 LANGUAGE: English. Spanish.
HEADNOTE: EDUCATIONAL PROGRAM
TOPIC: Education
CONCEPTS: Friendship and amity. Standardization. Conformity with municipal law. General cooperation. Exchange of information and documents. Inspection and observation. Personnel. General property. Exchange. Commissions and foundations. Scholarships and grants. Accounting procedures. Currency. Exchange rates and regulations. Expense sharing formulae. Financial programs. Funding procedures. Special status.
TREATY REF: 265UNTS337; 241UNTS25; TIAS 3936.
PROCEDURE: Amendment. Ratification.
PARTIES:
Colombia
USA (United States)

106677 Bilateral Exchange **462 UNTS 180**
SIGNED: 24 Dec 62 FORCE: 24 Dec 62
REGISTERED: 24 Apr 63 USA (United States)
ARTICLES: 2 LANGUAGE: English.
HEADNOTE: INVESTMENT GUARANTIES
TOPIC: Claims and Debts
CONCEPTS: General cooperation. Exchange of information and documents. Arbitration. Procedure. Existing tribunals. Negotiation. Reciprocity in financial treatment. Currency. Financial programs. Payment schedules. Claims and settlements. Private investment guarantee.
INTL ORGS: Arbitration Commission.
PARTIES:
Nigeria
USA (United States)

106678 Bilateral Agreement **462 UNTS 187**
SIGNED: 22 Oct 62 FORCE: 22 Oct 62
REGISTERED: 24 Apr 63 USA (United States)
ARTICLES: 6 LANGUAGE: English.
HEADNOTE: AGRI COMMOD TITLE I
TOPIC: US Agri Commod Aid
CONCEPTS: General provisions. Annex or appendix reference. Exchange of information and documents. Reexport of goods, etc.. Exchange rates and regulations. Transportation costs. Local currency. Commodities schedule. Purchase authorization. Surplus commodities. Mutual consultation.
PARTIES:
Greece
USA (United States)

106679 Bilateral Exchange **462 UNTS 201**
SIGNED: 29 Oct 62 FORCE: 29 Oct 62
REGISTERED: 24 Apr 63 USA (United States)
ARTICLES: 2 LANGUAGE: English. French.
HEADNOTE: COMMITTMENT FUNDS TUNESIA THREE-YEAR PLAN
TOPIC: Direct Aid
CONCEPTS: Treaty implementation. Conformity with municipal law. Financial programs. Funding procedures. Domestic obligation. General aid. Procurement.
TREATY REF: 26MARCH1957'EXCHANGE OF NOTES US&TUNISIA;.
PROCEDURE: Renewal or Revival.
PARTIES:
Tunisia
USA (United States)

106680 Bilateral Exchange **462 UNTS 207**
SIGNED: 11 Sep 62 FORCE: 11 Sep 62
REGISTERED: 26 Apr 63 USA (United States)
ARTICLES: 2 LANGUAGE: English. French.
HEADNOTE: AGREEMENT ON AGRI COMMOD
TOPIC: US Agri Commod Aid
CONCEPTS: General provisions. Exchange of information and documents. Currency. Exchange rates and regulations. Payment schedules. Local currency. Purchase authorization. Mutual consultation.
PARTIES:
Morocco
USA (United States)

106681 Bilateral Exchange **462 UNTS 221**
SIGNED: 1 Dec 61 FORCE: 1 Dec 61
REGISTERED: 26 Apr 63 USA (United States)
ARTICLES: 2 LANGUAGE: English. French.
HEADNOTE: INVESTMENT GUARANTEES
TOPIC: Claims and Debts
CONCEPTS: Exceptions and exemptions. General cooperation. Exchange of information and documents. Arbitration. Procedure. Existing tribunals. Negotiation. Reciprocity in financial treatment. Currency. Financial programs. Payment schedules. Claims and settlements. Private investment guarantee.
INTL ORGS: International Court of Justice.
PARTIES:
Ivory Coast
USA (United States)

106682 Bilateral Exchange **462 UNTS 229**
SIGNED: 29 Nov 62 FORCE: 29 Nov 62
REGISTERED: 26 Apr 63 USA (United States)
ARTICLES: 2 LANGUAGE: English.
HEADNOTE: AIR SERVICE
TOPIC: Air Transport
CONCEPTS: Previous treaty extension. Continuity of rights and obligations. Air transport. Operating authorizations and regulations.
TREATY REF: 3UNTS253; 426UNTS296.
PARTIES:
Jamaica
USA (United States)

106683 Bilateral Exchange **462 UNTS 237**
SIGNED: 21 Nov 62 FORCE: 21 Nov 62
REGISTERED: 26 Apr 63 USA (United States)
ARTICLES: 2 LANGUAGE: English. Sinhalese.
HEADNOTE: PEACE CORPS PROGRAM
TOPIC: General Aid
CONCEPTS: Diplomatic privileges. Conformity with municipal law. General cooperation. Personnel. Specialists exchange. Reexport of goods, etc.. Exchange rates and regulations. Fees and exemptions. Funding procedures. General. Tax exemptions. Customs duties. Customs exemptions. Domestic obligation. Materials, equipment and services. Aid missions. Volunteer programs.
PROCEDURE: Termination.
PARTIES:
Ceylon (Sri Lanka)
USA (United States)

106684 Bilateral Exchange **462 UNTS 247**
SIGNED: 14 Dec 62 FORCE: 14 Dec 62
REGISTERED: 26 Apr 63 USA (United States)
ARTICLES: 2 LANGUAGE: English. French.
HEADNOTE: PEACE CORPS PROGRAM
TOPIC: General Aid
CONCEPTS: Diplomatic privileges. Conformity with municipal law. General cooperation. Personnel. Exchange rates and regulations. Fees and exemptions. Funding procedures. General. Tax exemptions. Customs exemptions. Domestic obligation. Materials, equipment and services. Aid missions. Volunteer programs.
PROCEDURE: Termination.
PARTIES:
Guinea
USA (United States)

106685 Bilateral Exchange **462 UNTS 255**
SIGNED: 21 Nov 62 FORCE: 21 Nov 62
REGISTERED: 26 Apr 63 USA (United States)
ARTICLES: 2 LANGUAGE: English.
HEADNOTE: PEACE CORPS PROGRAM
TOPIC: General Aid
CONCEPTS: Diplomatic privileges. Conformity with municipal law. Funding procedures. Tax exemptions. Customs exemptions. Domestic obli-

gation. Materials, equipment and services. Aid missions. Volunteer programs.
PROCEDURE: Termination.
PARTIES:
India
USA (United States)

106686 Bilateral Agreement **462 UNTS 263**
SIGNED: 25 Jul 61 FORCE: 30 Oct 62
REGISTERED: 29 Apr 63 Netherlands
ARTICLES: 19 LANGUAGE: Dutch.
HEADNOTE: JOINT NUCLEAR RESEARCH CENTER
TOPIC: Scientific Project
CONCEPTS: Definition of terms. Annex or appendix reference. Conformity with municipal law. Personnel. Use of facilities. Establishment of commission. Existing tribunals. Teacher and student exchange. Research and scientific projects. Research cooperation. Nuclear research. Research and development. Funding procedures. Domestic obligation. Acceptance of delivery. General. Rights of supplier. IGO obligations.
INTL ORGS: Court of Justice of the European Community. Special Commission.
TREATY REF: 298UNTS167.
PROCEDURE: Duration. Future Procedures Contemplated.
PARTIES:
Netherlands
Euratom

106687 Bilateral Exchange **462 UNTS 313**
SIGNED: 25 Jul 61 FORCE: 25 Jul 61
REGISTERED: 29 Apr 63 Netherlands
ARTICLES: 2 LANGUAGE: Dutch.
HEADNOTE: PRIVILEGES & IMMUNITIES
TOPIC: IGO Status/Immunit
CONCEPTS: Annex or appendix reference. Privileges and immunities. IGO status.
INTL ORGS: Court of Justice of the European Community. European Atomic Energy Commission.
TREATY REF: 298UNTS167.
PARTIES:
Netherlands
Euratom

106688 Multilateral Agreement **463 UNTS 3**
SIGNED: 27 Jun 62 FORCE: 27 Dec 62
REGISTERED: 30 Apr 63 IAEA (Atom Energy)
ARTICLES: 5 LANGUAGE: French.
HEADNOTE: TRANSFER TITLE ENRICHED URANIUM
TOPIC: Atomic Energy
CONCEPTS: Inspection and observation. Responsibility and liability. Title and deeds. Indemnities and reimbursements. Nuclear materials.
PROCEDURE: Amendment.
PARTIES:
Belgium SIGNED: 27 Jun 62 FORCE: 27 Jun 62
Congo (Zaire) SIGNED: 27 Jun 62 FORCE: 27 Jun 62
IAEA (Atom Energy) SIGNED: 27 Jun 62 FORCE: 27 Jun 62

106689 Multilateral Protocol **463 UNTS 11**
SIGNED: 27 Jun 62 FORCE: 27 Jun 62
REGISTERED: 30 Apr 63 IAEA (Atom Energy)
ARTICLES: 3 LANGUAGE: English. French.
HEADNOTE: PROTOCOL SIGNATURE AGREEMENTS CONCERNING TRICO REACTOR PROJECT
TOPIC: Atomic Energy
CONCEPTS: Annex type material. Atomic energy assistance.
PARTIES:
Belgium SIGNED: 27 Jun 62 FORCE: 27 Jun 62
Congo (Zaire) SIGNED: 27 Jun 62 FORCE: 27 Jun 62
IAEA (Atom Energy) SIGNED: 27 Jun 62 FORCE: 27 Jun 62
USA (United States) SIGNED: 27 Jun 62 FORCE: 27 Jun 62

106690 Multilateral Instrument **463 UNTS 17**
SIGNED: 27 Jun 62 FORCE: 27 Dec 62
REGISTERED: 30 Apr 63 IAEA (Atom Energy)
ARTICLES: 6 LANGUAGE: English. French.
HEADNOTE: TRANSFER ENRICHED URANIUM
TOPIC: Atomic Energy
CONCEPTS: Inspection and observation. Responsibility and liability. Title and deeds. Arbitration. Procedure. Negotiation. Indemnities and reimbursements. Payment schedules. Nuclear materials. Peaceful use. Transport of goods.

INTL ORGS: International Court of Justice.
PARTIES:
Congo (Zaire) SIGNED: 27 Jun 62 FORCE: 27 Jun 62
IAEA (Atom Energy) SIGNED: 27 Jun 62 FORCE: 27 Jun 62
USA (United States) SIGNED: 27 Jun 62 FORCE: 27 Jun 62

106691 Bilateral Agreement **463 UNTS 31**
SIGNED: 27 Jun 62 FORCE: 27 Dec 62
REGISTERED: 30 Apr 63 IAEA (Atom Energy)
ARTICLES: 11 LANGUAGE: French.
HEADNOTE: ASSISTANCE CONTINUATION RESEARCH REACTOR PROJECT
TOPIC: Direct Aid
CONCEPTS: Guarantees and safeguards. Annex or appendix reference. Privileges and immunities. General cooperation. Exchange of information and documents. Informational records. Licenses and permits. Personnel. Title and deeds. Arbitration. Procedure. Negotiation. Patents, copyrights and trademarks. Nuclear materials. Transport of goods.
TREATY REF: 463UNTS17; 3741NTS147.
PARTIES:
Congo (Zaire)
IAEA (Atom Energy)

106692 Multilateral Agreement **463 UNTS 44**
SIGNED: 18 Apr 62 FORCE: 18 Apr 63
REGISTERED: 1 May 63 United Nations
ARTICLES: 6 LANGUAGE: English.
HEADNOTE: TECHNICAL ASSISTANCE
TOPIC: Tech Assistance
CONCEPTS: Definition of terms. Privileges and immunities. General cooperation. Exchange of information and documents. Personnel. Responsibility and liability. Title and deeds. Use of facilities. Exchange. Scholarships and grants. Vocational training. Research and development. Exchange rates and regulations. Expense sharing formulae. Local currency. Domestic obligation. General technical assistance. Materials, equipment and services. IGO status. Conformity with IGO decisions.
TREATY REF: 76UNTS132; 1UNTS15; 33UNTS261; 374UNTS147.
PROCEDURE: Amendment. Termination.
PARTIES:
Cyprus SIGNED: 18 Apr 63 FORCE: 18 Apr 63
FAO (Food Agri) SIGNED: 18 Apr 63 FORCE: 18 Apr 63
IAEA (Atom Energy) SIGNED: 18 Apr 63 FORCE: 18 Apr 63
ICAO (Civil Aviat) SIGNED: 18 Apr 63 FORCE: 18 Apr 63
ILO (Labor Org) SIGNED: 18 Apr 63 FORCE: 18 Apr 63
ITU (Telecommun) SIGNED: 18 Apr 63 FORCE: 18 Apr 63
UNESCO (Educ/Cult) SIGNED: 18 Apr 63 FORCE: 18 Apr 63
United Nations SIGNED: 18 Apr 63 FORCE: 18 Apr 63
UPU (Postal Union) SIGNED: 18 Apr 63 FORCE: 18 Apr 63
WHO (World Health) SIGNED: 18 Apr 63 FORCE: 18 Apr 63
WMO (Meteorology) SIGNED: 18 Apr 63 FORCE: 18 Apr 63

106693 Bilateral Agreement **463 UNTS 61**
SIGNED: 13 Feb 62 FORCE: 30 Jan 63
REGISTERED: 3 May 63 Hungary
ARTICLES: 20 LANGUAGE: English.
HEADNOTE: AIR TRANSPORT
TOPIC: Air Transport
CONCEPTS: Definition of terms. Exceptions and exemptions. Representation. Conformity with municipal law. General cooperation. Exchange of information and documents. Informational records. Licenses and permits. Recognition of legal documents. Use of facilities. Procedure. Negotiation. Disease control. Humanitarian matters. Non-interest rates and fees. Tax exemptions. Customs exemptions. Competency certificate. Registration certificate. Routes and logistics. Navigational conditions. Permit designation. Air transport. Airport facilities. Airworthiness certificates. Conditions of airlines operating permission. Operating authorizations and regulations.
PROCEDURE: Amendment. Ratification. Termina-

tion.
PARTIES:
Finland
Hungary

106694 Multilateral Agreement **463 UNTS 78**
SIGNED: 6 May 63 FORCE: 6 May 63
REGISTERED: 6 May 63 United Nations
ARTICLES: 6 LANGUAGE: English.
HEADNOTE: TECHNICAL ASSISTANCE
TOPIC: Tech Assistance
CONCEPTS: Definition of terms. Privileges and immunities. General cooperation. Exchange of information and documents. Personnel. Responsibility and liability. Title and deeds. Use of facilities. Exchange. Scholarships and grants. Vocational training. Research and development. Exchange rates and regulations. Expense sharing formulae. Local currency. Domestic obligation. General technical assistance. Materials, equipment and services. IGO status. Conformity with IGO decisions.
TREATY REF: 76UNTS132; 1UNTS15; 33UNTS261; 374UNTS147.
PROCEDURE: Amendment. Termination.
PARTIES:
FAO (Food Agri) SIGNED: 6 May 63 FORCE: 6 May 63
IAEA (Atom Energy) SIGNED: 6 May 63 FORCE: 6 May 63
ICAO (Civil Aviat) SIGNED: 6 May 63 FORCE: 6 May 63
ILO (Labor Org) SIGNED: 6 May 63 FORCE: 6 May 63
ITU (Telecommun) SIGNED: 6 May 63 FORCE: 6 May 63
UNESCO (Educ/Cult) SIGNED: 6 May 63 FORCE: 6 May 63
United Nations SIGNED: 6 May 63 FORCE: 6 May 63
UPU (Postal Union) SIGNED: 6 May 63 FORCE: 6 May 63
WHO (World Health) SIGNED: 6 May 63 FORCE: 6 May 63
WMO (Meteorology) SIGNED: 6 May 63 FORCE: 6 May 63
Trinidad/Tobago SIGNED: 6 May 63 FORCE: 6 May 63

106695 Bilateral Agreement **463 UNTS 93**
SIGNED: 6 May 63 FORCE: 6 May 63
REGISTERED: 6 May 63 United Nations
ARTICLES: 10 LANGUAGE: English.
HEADNOTE: ASSISTANCE
TOPIC: Direct Aid
CONCEPTS: Diplomatic missions. Privileges and immunities. Procedure. Domestic obligation. Special status. Inter-agency agreements.
INTL ORGS: International Atomic Energy Agency. International Court of Justice. United Nations. Arbitration Commission.
PROCEDURE: Amendment. Termination.
PARTIES:
UN Special Fund
Trinidad/Tobago

106696 Bilateral Agreement **463 UNTS 109**
SIGNED: 6 May 63 FORCE: 6 May 63
REGISTERED: 6 May 63 United Nations
ARTICLES: 6 LANGUAGE: English.
HEADNOTE: PERSONNEL
TOPIC: IGO Status/Immunit
CONCEPTS: Annex or appendix reference. General consular functions. Diplomatic privileges. Inviolability. Privileges and immunities. Property. Arbitration. Procedure. Diplomatic missions. Status of experts.
PROCEDURE: Amendment. Termination.
PARTIES:
United Nations
Trinidad/Tobago

106697 Multilateral Agreement **463 UNTS 121**
SIGNED: 18 Apr 63 FORCE: 18 Apr 63
REGISTERED: 6 May 63 United Nations
ARTICLES: 6 LANGUAGE: French.
HEADNOTE: TECHNICAL ASSISTANCE
TOPIC: Tech Assistance
CONCEPTS: Definition of terms. Privileges and immunities. General cooperation. Exchange of information and documents. Personnel. Responsibility and liability. Title and deeds. Use of facilities. Exchange. Scholarships and grants. Vocational training. Research and development.

Exchange rates and regulations. Expense sharing formulae. Local currency. Domestic obligation. General technical assistance. Materials, equipment and services. IGO status. Conformity with IGO decisions.
TREATY REF: 76UNTS132; 1UNTS15; 33UNTS261; 374UNTS147.
PROCEDURE: Amendment. Termination.
PARTIES:
FAO (Food Agri) SIGNED: 8 Apr 63 FORCE: 8 Apr 63
IAEA (Atom Energy) SIGNED: 8 Apr 63 FORCE: 8 Apr 63
ICAO (Civil Aviat) SIGNED: 8 Apr 63 FORCE: 8 Apr 63
ILO (Labor Org) SIGNED: 8 Apr 63 FORCE: 8 Apr 63
ITU (Telecommun) SIGNED: 8 Apr 63 FORCE: 8 Apr 63
UNESCO (Educ/Cult) SIGNED: 8 Apr 63 FORCE: 8 Apr 63
United Nations SIGNED: 8 Apr 63 FORCE: 8 Apr 63
UPU (Postal Union) SIGNED: 8 Apr 63 FORCE: 8 Apr 63
WHO (World Health) SIGNED: 8 Apr 63 FORCE: 8 Apr 63
WMO (Meteorology) SIGNED: 8 Apr 63 FORCE: 8 Apr 63
Upper Volta SIGNED: 8 Apr 63 FORCE: 8 Apr 63

106698 Bilateral Agreement **463 UNTS 135**
SIGNED: 20 Dec 62 FORCE: 20 Dec 62
REGISTERED: 7 May 63 WHO (World Health)
ARTICLES: 6 LANGUAGE: French.
HEADNOTE: TECHNICAL ADVISORY ASSISTANCE
TOPIC: Tech Assistance
CONCEPTS: Definition of terms. Privileges and immunities. General cooperation. Exchange of information and documents. Personnel. Responsibility and liability. Title and deeds. Exchange. Scholarships and grants. Vocational training. Research and development. Expense sharing formulae. Local currency. Domestic obligation. Special projects. Materials, equipment and services. IGO status. Conformity with IGO decisions.
INTL ORGS: United Nations.
TREATY REF: 33UNTS261.
PROCEDURE: Amendment. Termination.
PARTIES:
Algeria
WHO (World Health)

106699 Bilateral Agreement **463 UNTS 147**
SIGNED: 9 May 63 FORCE: 9 May 63
REGISTERED: 9 May 63 United Nations
ARTICLES: 6 LANGUAGE: French.
HEADNOTE: PROVISION ADMINISTRATIVE PERSONNEL
TOPIC: Tech Assistance
CONCEPTS: General consular functions. Diplomatic privileges. Diplomatic missions. Privileges and immunities. Arbitration. Procedure. Assistance.
INTL ORGS: Permanent Court of Arbitration.
TREATY REF: 319UNTS15.
PROCEDURE: Amendment. Termination.
PARTIES:
Mali
United Nations

106700 Multilateral Agreement **463 UNTS 159**
SIGNED: 9 May 63 FORCE: 9 May 63
REGISTERED: 9 May 63 United Nations
ARTICLES: 6 LANGUAGE: French.
HEADNOTE: TECHNICAL ASSISTANCE
TOPIC: Tech Assistance
CONCEPTS: Definition of terms. Privileges and immunities. General cooperation. Exchange of information and documents. Personnel. Responsibility and liability. Title and deeds. Use of facilities. Exchange. Scholarships and grants. Vocational training. Research and development. Exchange rates and regulations. Expense sharing formulae. Local currency. Domestic obligation. General technical assistance. Materials, equipment and services. IGO status. Conformity with IGO decisions.
TREATY REF: 76UNTS132; 1UNTS15; 33UNTS261; 3741NTS147.
PROCEDURE: Amendment. Termination.
PARTIES:
Mali SIGNED: 9 May 63 FORCE: 9 May 63

FAO (Food Agri) SIGNED: 9 May 63 FORCE:
9 May 63
IAEA (Atom Energy) SIGNED: 9 May 63 FORCE:
9 May 63
ICAO (Civil Aviat) SIGNED: 9 May 63 FORCE:
9 May 63
ILO (Labor Org) SIGNED: 9 May 63 FORCE:
9 May 63
ITU (Telecommun) SIGNED: 9 May 63 FORCE:
9 May 63
UNESCO (Educ/Cult) SIGNED: 9 May 63 FORCE:
9 May 63
United Nations SIGNED: 9 May 63 FORCE:
9 May 63
UPU (Postal Union) SIGNED: 9 May 63 FORCE:
9 May 63
WHO (World Health) SIGNED: 9 May 63 FORCE:
9 May 63
WMO (Meteorology) SIGNED: 9 May 63 FORCE:
9 May 63
ANNEX
649 UNTS 354. IMCO (Maritime Org). Accession
31 Oct 68. Force 31 Oct 68.
649 UNTS 354. UNIDO (Industrial). Accession
31 Oct 68. Force 31 Oct 68.

106701 Bilateral Agreement **463 UNTS 173**
SIGNED: 30 Nov 62 FORCE: 1 Jan 63
REGISTERED: 13 May 63 France
ARTICLES: 8 LANGUAGE: French. German.
HEADNOTE: ACCEPTANCE PERSONS FRONTIER
TOPIC: Visas
CONCEPTS: Border traffic and migration. Pass-
ports diplomatic. Refugees and stateless per-
sons. Nationality and citizenship. Extradition, de-
portation and repatriation. General cooperation.
Indemnities and reimbursements.
PROCEDURE: Termination.
PARTIES:
Austria
France

106702 Bilateral Agreement **463 UNTS 187**
SIGNED: 13 May 63 FORCE: 13 May 63
REGISTERED: 13 May 63 United Nations
ARTICLES: 5 LANGUAGE: English.
HEADNOTE: UN SEMINAR ON HUMAN RIGHTS
TOPIC: Education
CONCEPTS: Definition of terms. Visas. Alien
status. Privileges and immunities. General coop-
eration. Personnel. Exchange. Indemnities and
reimbursements. Expense sharing formulae.
Special status.
TREATY REF: 1UNTS15,263.
PROCEDURE: Duration. Future Procedures Con-
templated.
PARTIES:
Australia
United Nations

106703 Bilateral Treaty **463 UNTS 195**
SIGNED: 4 Apr 62 FORCE: 21 Feb 63
REGISTERED: 14 May 63 Taiwan
ARTICLES: 6 LANGUAGE: French. Chinese.
HEADNOTE: FRIENDSHIP
TOPIC: General Amity
CONCEPTS: Friendship and amity. Consular rela-
tions establishment. Privileges and immunities.
Procedure. Existing tribunals.
INTL ORGS: International Court of Justice.
PROCEDURE: Ratification.
PARTIES:
Taiwan
Malagasy

106704 Bilateral Agreement **463 UNTS 207**
SIGNED: 12 May 60 FORCE: 11 Apr 63
REGISTERED: 14 May 63 Netherlands
ARTICLES: 8 LANGUAGE: French
HEADNOTE: CULTURAL
TOPIC: Culture
CONCEPTS: Territorial application. Treaty imple-
mentation. Friendship and amity. Conformity
with municipal law. Establishment of commis-
sion. Specialists exchange. Exchange. Teacher
and student exchange. Institute establishment.
Scholarships and grants. Exchange. General cul-
tural cooperation. Artists. Athletes. Scientific ex-
change. Mass media exchange.
PROCEDURE: Duration. Ratification. Renewal or
Revival. Termination.
PARTIES:
Netherlands
Turkey

106705 Unilateral Instrument **463 UNTS 213**
SIGNED: 20 Apr 63 FORCE: 14 May 63
REGISTERED: 14 May 63 United Nations
ARTICLES: 1 LANGUAGE: English.
HEADNOTE: ACCEPTANCE UN CHARTER
TOPIC: UN Charter
CONCEPTS: Acceptance of UN obligations.
INTL ORGS: United Nations.
PARTIES:
Kuwait

106706 Bilateral Agreement **463 UNTS 217**
SIGNED: 25 Feb 56 FORCE: 16 Oct 57
REGISTERED: 15 May 63 ICAO (Civil Aviat)
ARTICLES: 18 LANGUAGE: French.
HEADNOTE: SCHEDULED CIVIL AIR SERVICES
TOPIC: Air Transport
CONCEPTS: Detailed regulations. Exceptions and
exemptions. Annex or appendix reference. Non-
prejudice to third party. Conformity with municipal law. General cooperation. Licenses and permits. Recognition of legal documents. Use of facilities. Arbitration. Procedure. Existing
tribunals. Negotiation. Currency. Monetary and
gold transfers. Fees and exemptions. Non-interest rates and fees. Most favored nation clause.
National treatment. Customs exemptions. Competency certificate. Navigational conditions. Permit designation. Air transport. Airport facilities.
Airworthiness certificates. Conditions of airlines
operating permission. Overflights and technical
stops. Operating authorizations and regulations.
Licenses and certificates of nationality.
INTL ORGS: International Civil Aviation Organiza-
tion. Arbitration Commission.
PROCEDURE: Amendment. Future Procedures
Contemplated. Ratification. Registration. Termi-
nation.
PARTIES:
Norway
Syria

106707 Bilateral Agreement **463 UNTS 239**
SIGNED: 16 May 56 FORCE: 27 Apr 57
REGISTERED: 15 May 63 ICAO (Civil Aviat)
ARTICLES: 14 LANGUAGE: Portuguese. Spanish.
HEADNOTE: AIR TRANSPORT
TOPIC: Air Transport
CONCEPTS: Definition of terms. Exceptions and
exemptions. Non-prejudice to third party. Conformity with municipal law. Licenses and permits. Recognition of legal documents. Use of facilities. Procedure. Existing tribunals. Fees and
exemptions. Most favored nation clause. National treatment. Customs exemptions. Compe-
tency certificate. Routes and logistics. Navigational conditions. Permit designation. Air transport. Airport facilities. Airworthiness certificates.
Conditions of airlines operating permission. Operating authorizations and regulations. Licenses
and certificates of nationality.
INTL ORGS: International Civil Aviation Organization.
TREATY REF: 15UNTS295.
PROCEDURE: Future Procedures Contemplated.
Ratification. Registration. Termination.
PARTIES:
Portugal
Venezuela

106708 Bilateral Agreement **463 UNTS 269**
SIGNED: 10 Apr 57 FORCE: 13 Jul 59
REGISTERED: 15 May 63 ICAO (Civil Aviat)
ARTICLES: 22 LANGUAGE: German. Serbo-Croat.
HEADNOTE: AIR TRANSPORT
TOPIC: Air Transport
CONCEPTS: Definition of terms. Detailed regula-
tions. Exceptions and exemptions. Annex or ap-
pendix reference. Previous treaty replacement.
Conformity with municipal law. General cooperation. Exchange of information and documents.
Informational records. Licenses and permits.
Recognition of legal documents. Use of facilities.
Arbitration. Procedure. Special tribunals. Humanitarian matters. Fees and exemptions. Non-
interest rates and fees. National treatment. Tax
exemptions. Customs exemptions. Competency
certificate. Registration certificate. Routes and
logistics. Navigational conditions. Permit designation. Air transport. Airport facilities. Airworthiness certificates. Conditions of airlines operating permission. Operating authorizations and
regulations. Licenses and certificates of nationality.

INTL ORGS: International Civil Aviation Organiza-
tion. International Court of Justice. Arbitration
Commission.
PROCEDURE: Amendment. Ratification. Registra-
tion. Termination.
PARTIES:
Germany, West
Yugoslavia

106709 Bilateral Agreement **464 UNTS 3**
SIGNED: 17 Apr 57 FORCE: 16 Dec 58
REGISTERED: 15 May 63 ICAO (Civil Aviat)
ARTICLES: 14 LANGUAGE: French.
HEADNOTE: CIVIL AIR TRANSPORT
TOPIC: Air Transport
CONCEPTS: Definition of terms. Representation.
Annex or appendix reference. Conformity with
municipal law. General cooperation. Informa-
tional records. Licenses and permits. Personnel.
Recognition of legal documents. Use of facilities.
Procedure. Humanitarian matters. Fees and ex-
emptions. Non-interest rates and fees. Customs
exemptions. Registration certificate. Routes and
logistics. Navigational conditions. Permit designation. Air transport. Airport facilities. Airworthiness certificates. Conditions of airlines operating permission. Operating authorizations and
regulations.
PROCEDURE: Amendment. Denunciation. Ratification. Termination.
PARTIES:
Bulgaria
Sweden

106710 Bilateral Agreement **464 UNTS 21**
SIGNED: 10 Jan 58 FORCE: 9 Nov 61
REGISTERED: 15 May 63 ICAO (Civil Aviat)
ARTICLES: 13 LANGUAGE: English. French.
HEADNOTE: AIR SERVICES
TOPIC: Air Transport
CONCEPTS: Definition of terms. Detailed regula-
tions. Exceptions and exemptions. Annex or appendix reference. General cooperation. Ex-
change of information and documents. Use of
facilities. Arbitration. Procedure. Existing tribu-
nals. Negotiation. Public health. Fees and exemp-
tions. Non-interest rates and fees. Most favored
nation clause. National treatment. Customs du-
ties. Routes and logistics. Permit designation.
Airport facilities. Overflights and technical stops.
Operating authorizations and regulations.
INTL ORGS: International Civil Aviation Organization. Arbitration Commission.
TREATY REF: 15UNTS295.
PROCEDURE: Amendment. Future Procedures
Contemplated. Ratification. Registration. Termi-
nation.
PARTIES:
Canada
Switzerland

106711 Bilateral Agreement **464 UNTS 39**
SIGNED: 8 Feb 58 FORCE: 17 May 61
REGISTERED: 15 May 63 ICAO (Civil Aviat)
ARTICLES: 14 LANGUAGE: Turkish. Persian. English.
HEADNOTE: AIR TRANSPORT
TOPIC: Air Transport
CONCEPTS: Definition of terms. Detailed regulations. Annex or appendix reference. Conformity
with municipal law. General cooperation. Exchange of information and documents. Licenses
and permits. Recognition of legal documents. Arbitration. Procedure. Special tribunals. Negotiation. Expense sharing formulae. Non-interest
rates and fees. Most favored nation clause. National treatment. Customs duties. Customs exemptions. Competency certificate. Routes and
logistics. Navigational conditions. Permit designation. Air transport. Airworthiness certificates.
Conditions of airlines operating permission.
Overflights and technical stops. Operating authorizations and regulations. Licenses and certificates of nationality.
INTL ORGS: International Civil Aviation Organization. Arbitration Commission.
PROCEDURE: Amendment.
PARTIES:
Afghanistan
Turkey

106712 Bilateral Agreement **464 UNTS 71**
SIGNED: 21 Mar 58 FORCE: 7 Oct 59

REGISTERED: 15 May 63 ICAO (Civil Aviat)
ARTICLES: 15 LANGUAGE: German. Portuguese.
HEADNOTE: AIR TRANSPORT
TOPIC: Air Transport
CONCEPTS: Definition of terms. Detailed regulations. Exceptions and exemptions. Annex or appendix reference. Conformity with municipal law. General cooperation. Exchange of information and documents. Use of facilities. Arbitration. Procedure. Special tribunals. Reexport of goods, etc.. Expense sharing formulae. Fees and exemptions. Non-interest rates and fees. National treatment. Customs exemptions. Routes and logistics. Permit designation. Air transport. Airport facilities. Conditions of airlines operating permission. Overflights and technical stops. Operating authorizations and regulations.
INTL ORGS: International Civil Aviation Organization. Arbitration Commission.
TREATY REF: 15UNTS295.
PROCEDURE: Amendment. Denunciation. Future Procedures Contemplated. Ratification. Registration. Termination.
PARTIES:
Germany, West
Portugal

106713 Bilateral Agreement **464 UNTS 109**
SIGNED: 29 May 59 FORCE: 29 May 59
REGISTERED: 15 May 63 ICAO (Civil Aviat)
ARTICLES: 18 LANGUAGE: English.
HEADNOTE: RELATING AIR SERVICES
TOPIC: Air Transport
CONCEPTS: Definition of terms. Detailed regulations. Annex or appendix reference. Conformity with municipal law. General cooperation. Exchange of information and documents. Licenses and permits. Recognition of legal documents. Use of facilities. Arbitration. Procedure. Existing tribunals. Reexport of goods, etc.. Currency. Fees and exemptions. Non-interest rates and fees. Most favored nation clause. National treatment. Customs exemptions. Competency certificate. Routes and logistics. Navigational conditions. Permit designation. Airport facilities. Airworthiness certificates. Conditions of airlines operating permission. Licenses and certificates of nationality. Collision.
INTL ORGS: International Civil Aviation Organization. Arbitration Commission.
TREATY REF: 15UNTS295.
PROCEDURE: Amendment. Future Procedures Contemplated. Registration. Termination. Application to Non-self-governing Territories.
PARTIES:
Ceylon (Sri Lanka)
Sweden

106714 Bilateral Agreement **464 UNTS 129**
SIGNED: 16 Jul 59 FORCE: 12 Mar 62
REGISTERED: 15 May 63 ICAO (Civil Aviat)
ARTICLES: 14 LANGUAGE: Hindi. English. Italian.
HEADNOTE: RELATING AIR SERVICES
TOPIC: Air Transport
CONCEPTS: Definition of terms. Detailed regulations. Exceptions and exemptions. Annex or appendix reference. Conformity with municipal law. General cooperation. Exchange of information and documents. Arbitration. Procedure. Existing tribunals. Reexport of goods, etc.. Non-interest rates and fees. National treatment. Customs duties. Customs exemptions. Temporary importation. Routes and logistics. Navigational conditions. Permit designation. Conditions of airlines operating permission. Overflights and technical stops. Operating authorizations and regulations. Optional clause ICJ.
INTL ORGS: International Civil Aviation Organization. Arbitration Commission.
TREATY REF: 15UNTS295.
PROCEDURE: Amendment. Future Procedures Contemplated. Ratification. Termination.
PARTIES:
India
Italy

106715 Bilateral Agreement **464 UNTS 177**
SIGNED: 22 Jul 59 FORCE: 10 Jul 61
REGISTERED: 15 May 63 ICAO (Civil Aviat)
ARTICLES: 16 LANGUAGE: German. Persian. English.
HEADNOTE: AIR TRANSPORT
TOPIC: Air Transport
CONCEPTS: Definition of terms. Detailed regula-

tions. Treaty interpretation. Annex or appendix reference. Conformity with municipal law. General cooperation. Exchange of information and documents. Personnel. Use of facilities. Arbitration. Procedure. Special tribunals. Expense sharing formulae. Fees and exemptions. Non-interest rates and fees. National treatment. Tax exemptions. Customs exemptions. Routes and logistics. Permit designation. Air transport. Airport facilities. Conditions of airlines operating permission. Overflights and technical stops. Operating authorizations and regulations.
INTL ORGS: International Civil Aviation Organization. Arbitration Commission.
TREATY REF: 15UNTS295; 84UNTS389.
PROCEDURE: Amendment. Future Procedures Contemplated. Ratification. Registration. Termination.
PARTIES:
Afghanistan
Germany, West

106716 Bilateral Agreement **464 UNTS 219**
SIGNED: 9 Dec 59 FORCE: 9 Dec 59
REGISTERED: 15 May 63 ICAO (Civil Aviat)
ARTICLES: 10 LANGUAGE: English.
HEADNOTE: AIR SERVICES
TOPIC: Air Transport
CONCEPTS: Definition of terms. Annex or appendix reference. Conformity with municipal law. General cooperation. Arbitration. Procedure. Existing tribunals. Negotiation. Reexport of goods, etc.. Non-interest rates and fees. Customs exemptions. Routes and logistics. Permit designation. Air transport. Conditions of airlines operating permission. Overflights and technical stops. Operating authorizations and regulations. Optional clause ICJ.
INTL ORGS: International Court of Justice. Arbitration Commission.
TREATY REF: 15UNTS295; 84UNTS389.
PROCEDURE: Amendment. Ratification. Termination.
PARTIES:
Liberia
Sweden

106717 Bilateral Agreement **464 UNTS 233**
SIGNED: 16 Feb 60 FORCE: 3 Aug 62
REGISTERED: 15 May 63 ICAO (Civil Aviat)
ARTICLES: 14 LANGUAGE: German. Arabic. English.
HEADNOTE: AIR TRANSPORT
TOPIC: Air Transport
CONCEPTS: Definition of terms. Detailed regulations. Conformity with municipal law. General cooperation. Exchange of information and documents. Arbitration. Procedure. Special tribunals. Expense sharing formulae. Non-interest rates and fees. Customs exemptions. Routes and logistics. Permit designation. Air transport. Conditions of airlines operating permission. Operating authorizations and regulations.
INTL ORGS: International Civil Aviation Organization. Arbitration Commission.
TREATY REF: 15UNTS295.
PROCEDURE: Amendment. Future Procedures Contemplated. Ratification. Registration. Termination.
PARTIES:
Germany, West
United Arab Rep

106718 Bilateral Agreement **464 UNTS 267**
SIGNED: 11 Mar 60 FORCE: 22 Aug 61
REGISTERED: 15 May 63 ICAO (Civil Aviat)
ARTICLES: 11 LANGUAGE: Czechoslovakian. Arabic. English.
HEADNOTE: AIR TRANSPORT
TOPIC: Air Transport
CONCEPTS: Definition of terms. Treaty interpretation. Annex or appendix reference. Conformity with municipal law. General cooperation. Use of facilities. Procedure. Negotiation. Fees and exemptions. Most favored nation clause. Customs duties. Customs exemptions. Routes and logistics. Navigational conditions. Permit designation. Air transport. Airport facilities. Conditions of airlines operating permission. Operating authorizations and regulations.
TREATY REF: 15UNTS295.
PROCEDURE: Amendment. Ratification. Termination.
PARTIES:

Czechoslovakia
Iraq

106719 Bilateral Agreement **464 UNTS 293**
SIGNED: 9 Apr 60 FORCE: 9 Apr 60
REGISTERED: 15 May 63 ICAO (Civil Aviat)
ARTICLES: 19 LANGUAGE: French.
HEADNOTE: AIR TRANSPORT
TOPIC: Air Transport
CONCEPTS: Definition of terms. Detailed regulations. Exceptions and exemptions. Annex or appendix reference. Conformity with municipal law. General cooperation. Exchange of information and documents. Informational records. Licenses and permits. Recognition of legal documents. Use of facilities. Arbitration. Procedure. Special tribunals. Negotiation. Expense sharing formulae. Fees and exemptions. Non-interest rates and fees. Customs duties. Customs exemptions. Registration certificate. Routes and logistics. Navigational conditions. Permit designation. Air transport. Airport facilities. Airworthiness certificates. Conditions of airlines operating permission. Operating authorizations and regulations. Licenses and certificates of nationality.
INTL ORGS: International Civil Aviation Organization. Arbitration Commission.
PROCEDURE: Amendment. Ratification. Termination.
PARTIES:
Luxembourg
Yugoslavia

106720 Bilateral Agreement **465 UNTS 3**
SIGNED: 28 Apr 60 FORCE: 2 Sep 61
REGISTERED: 15 May 63 ICAO (Civil Aviat)
ARTICLES: 18 LANGUAGE: German. Spanish.
HEADNOTE: AIR TRANSPORT
TOPIC: Air Transport
CONCEPTS: Definition of terms. Detailed regulations. Previous treaty replacement. Conformity with municipal law. General cooperation. Exchange of information and documents. Personnel. Use of facilities. Arbitration. Procedure. Special tribunals. Expense sharing formulae. Fees and exemptions. Non-interest rates and fees. National treatment. Customs exemptions. Routes and logistics. Permit designation. Air transport. Airport facilities. Conditions of airlines operating permission. Overflights and technical stops. Operating authorizations and regulations.
INTL ORGS: International Civil Aviation Organization. Arbitration Commission.
TREATY REF: 15UNTS295.
PROCEDURE: Amendment. Denunciation. Future Procedures Contemplated. Ratification. Registration.
PARTIES:
Germany, West
Spain

106721 Bilateral Agreement **465 UNTS 41**
SIGNED: 20 Jul 60 FORCE: 25 Nov 61
REGISTERED: 15 May 63 ICAO (Civil Aviat)
ARTICLES: 15 LANGUAGE: German. English.
HEADNOTE: AIR TRANSPORT
TOPIC: Air Transport
CONCEPTS: Definition of terms. Detailed regulations. Annex or appendix reference. Conformity with municipal law. General cooperation. Exchange of information and documents. Use of facilities. Arbitration. Procedure. Special tribunals. Expense sharing formulae. Fees and exemptions. Non-interest rates and fees. National treatment. Tax exemptions. Customs exemptions. Routes and logistics. Permit designation. Air transport. Airport facilities. Conditions of airlines operating permission. Overflights and technical stops. Operating authorizations and regulations.
INTL ORGS: International Civil Aviation Organization. Arbitration Commission.
TREATY REF: 15UNTS295; 84UNTS389.
PROCEDURE: Amendment. Future Procedures Contemplated. Ratification. Registration. Termination.
PARTIES:
Germany, West
Pakistan

106722 Bilateral Agreement **465 UNTS 67**
SIGNED: 19 Sep 60 FORCE: 7 Jun 61

REGISTERED: 15 May 63 ICAO (Civil Aviat)
ARTICLES: 14 LANGUAGE: Hindi. Czechoslovakian. English.
HEADNOTE: RELATING AIR SERVICES
TOPIC: Air Transport
CONCEPTS: Definition of terms. Detailed regulations. Treaty interpretation. Annex or appendix
reference. Conformity with municipal law. General cooperation. Exchange of information and
documents. Personnel. Use of facilities. Procedure. Negotiation. Customs duties. Customs exemptions. Routes and logistics. Navigational
conditions. Permit designation. Airport facilities.
Conditions of airlines operating permission. Operating authorizations and regulations.
INTL ORGS: International Civil Aviation Organization.
TREATY REF: 15UNTS295.
PROCEDURE: Amendment. Ratification. Termination.
PARTIES:
Czechoslovakia
India

106723   Bilateral Agreement   **465 UNTS 97**
SIGNED: 31 Oct 60   FORCE: 20 Aug 62
REGISTERED: 15 May 63 ICAO (Civil Aviat)
ARTICLES: 17 LANGUAGE: French. English.
HEADNOTE: AIR TRANSPORT
TOPIC: Air Transport
CONCEPTS: Definition of terms. Exceptions and
exemptions. Treaty interpretation. Annex or appendix reference. Non-prejudice to third party.
Conformity with municipal law. Licenses and
permits. Recognition of legal documents. Use of
facilities. Arbitration. Procedure. Special tribunals. Competence of tribunal. Monetary and gold
transfers. Exchange rates and regulations. Expense sharing formulae. Fees and exemptions.
Non-interest rates and fees. Most favored nation
clause. National treatment. Customs exemptions. Competency certificate. Routes and logistics. Navigational conditions. Permit designation. Air transport. Airport facilities. Airworthiness certificates. Conditions of airlines
operating permission. Operating authorizations
and regulations. Licenses and certificates of nationality.
INTL ORGS: International Civil Aviation Organization.
TREATY REF: 15UNTS295.
PROCEDURE: Amendment. Future Procedures
Contemplated. Ratification. Registration. Termination.
PARTIES:
Burma
Switzerland

106724   Bilateral Agreement   **465 UNTS 115**
SIGNED: 21 Dec 60   FORCE: 21 Dec 60
REGISTERED: 15 May 63 ICAO (Civil Aviat)
ARTICLES: 15 LANGUAGE: English.
HEADNOTE: RELATING AIR SERVICES
TOPIC: Air Transport
CONCEPTS: Definition of terms. Detailed regulations. Annex or appendix reference. Conformity
with municipal law. General cooperation. Exchange of information and documents. Arbitra-
tion. Procedure. Existing tribunals. Negotiation.
Reexport of goods, etc.. Non-interest rates and
fees. Most favored nation clause. National treat-
ment. Customs duties. Customs exemptions.
Routes and logistics. Permit designation. Condi-
tions of airlines operating permission. Overflights and technical stops. Operating authorizations and regulations.
INTL ORGS: International Civil Aviation Organization. Arbitration Commission.
TREATY REF: 15UNTS295; 84UNTS389.
PROCEDURE: Amendment. Future Procedures
Contemplated. Registration. Termination. Appli-
cation to Non-self-governing Territories.
PARTIES:
Canada
Pakistan

106725   Bilateral Agreement   **465 UNTS 131**
SIGNED: 29 Dec 60   FORCE: 7 Feb 62

REGISTERED: 15 May 63 ICAO (Civil Aviat)
ARTICLES: 14 LANGUAGE: French. Thai.
HEADNOTE: AIR TRANSPORT
TOPIC: Air Transport
CONCEPTS: Definition of terms. Detailed regulations. Conformity with municipal law. General
cooperation. Exchange of information and documents. Licenses and permits. Recognition of legal documents. Use of facilities. Arbitration. Procedure. Existing tribunals. Negotiation. Fees and
exemptions. Non-interest rates and fees. Most
favored nation clause. National treatment. Customs exemptions. Competency certificate.
Routes and logistics. Navigational conditions.
Permit designation. Air transport. Airport facilities. Airworthiness certificates. Conditions of airlines operating permission. Overflights and technical stops. Operating authorizations and regulations. Licenses and certificates of nationality.
INTL ORGS: International Civil Aviation Organization. Arbitration Commission.
TREATY REF: 15UNTS295.
PROCEDURE: Amendment. Future Procedures
Contemplated. Ratification. Registration. Termi-
nation.
PARTIES:
Luxembourg
Thailand

106726   Bilateral Agreement   **465 UNTS 155**
SIGNED: 9 Jan 61   FORCE: 9 Jan 61
REGISTERED: 15 May 63 ICAO (Civil Aviat)
ARTICLES: 15 LANGUAGE: English.
HEADNOTE: AIR SERVICES
TOPIC: Air Transport
CONCEPTS: Annex or appendix reference. Confor-
mity with municipal law. General cooperation.
Arbitration. Procedure. Special tribunals. Negoti-
ation. Reexport of goods, etc.. Monetary and
gold transfers. Exchange rates and regulations.
Non-interest rates and fees. Tax exemptions.
Customs exemptions. Routes and logistics. Navi-
gational conditions. Permit designation. Condi-
tions of airlines operating permission. Over-
lights and technical stops. Operating authoriza-
tions and regulations.
INTL ORGS: International Civil Aviation Organiza-
tion. Arbitration Commission.
TREATY REF: 15UNTS295; 84UNTS389.
PROCEDURE: Amendment. Future Procedures
Contemplated. Ratification. Termination.
PARTIES:
Jordan
Sweden

106727   Bilateral Agreement   **465 UNTS 173**
SIGNED: 18 Jan 61   FORCE: 12 Jul 62
REGISTERED: 15 May 63 ICAO (Civil Aviat)
ARTICLES: 18 LANGUAGE: German. Japanese. English.
HEADNOTE: AIR SERVICES
TOPIC: Air Transport
CONCEPTS: Definition of terms. Detailed regulations. Exceptions and exemptions. Conformity
with municipal law. General cooperation. Exchange of information and documents. Use of
facilities. Arbitration. Procedure. Special tribunals. Expense sharing formulae. Fees and exemptions. Non-interest rates and fees. Most favored nation clause. National treatment. Customs exemptions. Routes and logistics. Permit
designation. Airport facilities. Conditions of airlines operating permission. Overflights and technical stops. Operating authorizations and regulations.
INTL ORGS: International Civil Aviation Organization. Arbitration Commission.
TREATY REF: 15UNTS295.
PROCEDURE: Amendment. Future Procedures
Contemplated. Ratification. Registration. Termination. Application to Non-self-governing Territories.
PARTIES:
Germany, West
Japan

106728   Bilateral Agreement   **465 UNTS 209**
SIGNED: 4 Mar 61   FORCE: 10 Jul 61
REGISTERED: 15 May 63 ICAO (Civil Aviat)
ARTICLES: 14 LANGUAGE: Spanish. Czechoslo-
vakian.
HEADNOTE: AIR TRANSPORT
TOPIC: Air Transport

CONCEPTS: Definition of terms. Annex or appendix reference. Conformity with municipal law.
General cooperation. Personnel. Use of facilities.
Procedure. Negotiation. Reexport of goods, etc..
Fees and exemptions. Non-interest rates and
fees. Most favored nation clause. Tax exemp-
tions. Customs exemptions. Routes and logistics.
Navigational conditions. Permit designation. Air
transport. Airport facilities. Conditions of airlines
operating permission. Operating authorizations
and regulations.
PROCEDURE: Amendment. Denunciation. Ratifica-
tion.
PARTIES:
Cuba
Czechoslovakia

106729   Bilateral Agreement   **465 UNTS 236**
SIGNED: 17 Jun 61   FORCE: 17 Jun 61
REGISTERED: 15 May 63 ICAO (Civil Aviat)
ARTICLES: 11 LANGUAGE: French.
HEADNOTE: AIR TRANSPORT
TOPIC: Air Transport
CONCEPTS: Annex or appendix reference. Confor-
mity with municipal law. Arbitration. Procedure.
Existing tribunals. Negotiation. Reexport of
goods, etc.. Non-interest rates and fees. Customs
exemptions. Routes and logistics. Navigational
conditions. Permit designation. Air transport.
Conditions of airlines operating permission. Op-
erating authorizations and regulations.
INTL ORGS: International Civil Aviation Organiza-
tion. International Court of Justice. Arbitration
Commission.
PROCEDURE: Amendment. Denunciation. Ratifica-
tion. Registration.
PARTIES:
Guinea
Sweden

106730   Bilateral Agreement   **465 UNTS 249**
SIGNED: 2 Aug 61   FORCE: 14 Mar 62
REGISTERED: 15 May 63 ICAO (Civil Aviat)
ARTICLES: 16 LANGUAGE: Czechoslovakian. En-
glish.
HEADNOTE: AIR SERVICES BETWEEN BEYOND
RESPECTIVE TERRIRORIES
TOPIC: Air Transport
CONCEPTS: Conditions. Definition of terms. De-
tailed regulations. Exceptions and exemptions.
Annex or appendix reference. General cooper-
ation. Exchange of information and documents.
Personnel. Arbitration. Procedure. Special tribu-
nals. Negotiation. Monetary and gold transfers.
Non-interest rates and fees. Most favored nation
clause. Customs exemptions. Routes and logis-
tics. Permit designation. Conditions of airlines
operating permission. Overflights and technical
stops. Operating authorizations and regulations.
INTL ORGS: International Civil Aviation Organiza-
tion. Arbitration Commission.
TREATY REF: 15UNTS295.
PROCEDURE: Amendment. Ratification. Registra-
tion. Termination.
PARTIES:
Czechoslovakia
Ghana

106731   Bilateral Agreement   **465 UNTS 275**
SIGNED: 21 Aug 61   FORCE: 21 Aug 61
REGISTERED: 15 May 63 ICAO (Civil Aviat)
ARTICLES: 15 LANGUAGE: English.
HEADNOTE: AIR SERVICES
TOPIC: Air Transport
CONCEPTS: Detailed regulations. Annex or appen-
dix reference. Conformity with municipal law.
General cooperation. Arbitration. Procedure.
Special tribunals. Negotiation. Reexport of
goods, etc.. Monetary and gold transfers. Non-
interest rates and fees. Claims and settlements.
Tax exemptions. Navigational conditions. Permit
designation. Conditions of airlines operating
permission. Overflights and technical stops. Op-
erating authorizations and regulations.
INTL ORGS: International Civil Aviation Organiza-
tion. Arbitration Commission.
TREATY REF: 15UNTS295; 84UNTS389.
PROCEDURE: Amendment. Future Procedures
Contemplated. Ratification. Termination.
PARTIES:
Jordan
Norway

106732 Bilateral Agreement **465 UNTS 291**
SIGNED: 24 Aug 61   FORCE: 24 Aug 61
REGISTERED: 15 May 63 ICAO (Civil Aviat)
ARTICLES: 19 LANGUAGE: Dutch. Spanish. English.
HEADNOTE: AIR TRANSPORT
TOPIC: Air Transport
CONCEPTS: Definition of terms. Detailed regulations. Annex or appendix reference. Previous treaty replacement. Conformity with municipal law. Licenses and permits. Recognition of legal documents. Use of facilities. Arbitration. Procedure. Special tribunals. Expense sharing formulae. Fees and exemptions. Non-interest rates and fees. Most favored nation clause. National treatment. Customs exemptions. Competency certificate. Routes and logistics. Navigational conditions. Permit designation. Air transport. Airport facilities. Airworthiness certificates. Conditions of airlines operating permission. Overflights and technical stops. Operating authorizations and regulations. Licenses and certificates of nationality.
INTL ORGS: International Civil Aviation Organization. Arbitration Commission.
TREATY REF: 15UNTS295; 163UNTS341.
PROCEDURE: Amendment. Duration. Future Procedures Contemplated. Ratification. Registration. Termination. Application to Non-self-governing Territories.
PARTIES:
  Mexico
  Netherlands

106733 Bilateral Agreement **466 UNTS 3**
SIGNED: 24 Aug 61   FORCE: 25 Jun 62
REGISTERED: 15 May 63 ICAO (Civil Aviat)
ARTICLES: 12 LANGUAGE: English.
HEADNOTE: AIR SERVICES
TOPIC: Air Transport
CONCEPTS: Territorial application. Annex or appendix reference. Conformity with municipal law. Arbitration. Procedure. Existing tribunals. Negotiation. Fees and exemptions. Non-interest rates and fees. Customs exemptions. Routes and logistics. Navigational conditions. Permit designation. Air transport. Conditions of airlines operating permission. Operating authorizations and regulations. Optional clause ICJ.
INTL ORGS: International Civil Aviation Organization. International Court of Justice. Arbitration Commission.
TREATY REF: 15UNTS295.
PROCEDURE: Amendment. Ratification. Registration. Termination.
PARTIES:
  Jordan
  Netherlands

106734 Bilateral Agreement **466 UNTS 17**
SIGNED: 17 Oct 61   FORCE: 12 Jul 62
REGISTERED: 15 May 63 ICAO (Civil Aviat)
ARTICLES: 15 LANGUAGE: English.
HEADNOTE: RELATING AIR SERVICES
TOPIC: Air Transport
CONCEPTS: Definition of terms. Detailed regulations. Annex or appendix reference. Conformity with municipal law. General cooperation. Exchange of information and documents. Arbitration. Procedure. Special tribunals. Negotiation. Reexport of goods, etc.. Non-interest rates and fees. Most favored nation clause. National treatment. Customs duties. Customs exemptions. Routes and logistics. Conditions of airlines operating permission. Overflights and technical stops. Operating authorizations and regulations.
INTL ORGS: International Civil Aviation Organization. Arbitration Commission.
TREATY REF: 15UNTS295; 84UNTS309.
PROCEDURE: Amendment. Future Procedures Contemplated. Ratification. Registration. Termination. Application to Non-self-governing Territories.
PARTIES:
  Japan
  Pakistan

106735 Bilateral Exchange **466 UNTS 35**
SIGNED: 14 Nov 61   FORCE: 14 Nov 61
REGISTERED: 15 May 63 ICAO (Civil Aviat)
ARTICLES: 2 LANGUAGE: English.
HEADNOTE: AIR SERVICES
TOPIC: Air Transport
CONCEPTS: Customs duties. Registration certificate. Air transport.
TREATY REF: 335UNTS23.
PARTIES:
  Australia
  UK Great Britain

106736 Bilateral Agreement **466 UNTS 41**
SIGNED: 27 Nov 61   FORCE: 27 Nov 61
REGISTERED: 15 May 63 ICAO (Civil Aviat)
ARTICLES: 14 LANGUAGE: French. Czechoslovakian.
HEADNOTE: CONCERNING AIR SERVICES
TOPIC: Air Transport
CONCEPTS: Definition of terms. Annex or appendix reference. Conformity with municipal law. General cooperation. Personnel. Use of facilities. Procedure. Negotiation. Reexport of goods, etc.. Fees and exemptions. Non-interest rates and fees. Most favored nation clause. National treatment. Tax exemptions. Customs duties. Customs exemptions. Routes and logistics. Navigational conditions. Permit designation. Air transport. Airport facilities. Conditions of airlines operating permission. Operating authorizations and regulations.
PROCEDURE: Amendment. Denunciation. Ratification.
PARTIES:
  Czechoslovakia
  Mali
                    ANNEX
486 UNTS 435.   Czechoslovakia.   Other
27 Nov 61.

106737 Bilateral Agreement **466 UNTS 65**
SIGNED: 8 Jan 62   FORCE: 8 Jan 62
REGISTERED: 15 May 63 ICAO (Civil Aviat)
ARTICLES: 12 LANGUAGE: English.
HEADNOTE: ESTABLISHMENT OPERATION AIR SERVICES
TOPIC: Air Transport
CONCEPTS: Territorial application. Annex or appendix reference. General cooperation. Arbitration. Procedure. Special tribunals. Negotiation. Reexport of goods, etc.. Monetary and gold transfers. Exchange rates and regulations. Non-interest rates and fees. Tax exemptions. Customs exemptions. Routes and logistics. Permit designation. Air transport. Conditions of airlines operating permission. Overflights and technical stops. Operating authorizations and regulations.
INTL ORGS: International Civil Aviation Organization. Arbitration Commission.
TREATY REF: 15UNTS295.
PROCEDURE: Amendment. Ratification. Termination.
PARTIES:
  Netherlands
  Sweden

106738 Bilateral Agreement **466 UNTS 81**
SIGNED: 21 Jun 62   FORCE: 21 Jun 62
REGISTERED: 15 May 63 ICAO (Civil Aviat)
ARTICLES: 11 LANGUAGE: French.
HEADNOTE: AIR TRANSPORT
TOPIC: Air Transport
CONCEPTS: Annex or appendix reference. Conformity with municipal law. Arbitration. Procedure. Existing tribunals. Negotiation. Reexport of goods, etc.. Fees and exemptions. Non-interest rates and fees. Routes and logistics. Navigational conditions. Permit designation. Air transport. Conditions of airlines operating permission. Operating authorizations and regulations. Optional clause ICJ.
INTL ORGS: International Civil Aviation Organization. International Court of Justice. Arbitration Commission.
PROCEDURE: Amendment. Denunciation.
PARTIES:
  Guinea
  Norway

106739 Bilateral Agreement **466 UNTS 95**
SIGNED: 29 Jun 62   FORCE: 29 Jun 62
REGISTERED: 15 May 63 ICAO (Civil Aviat)
ARTICLES: 10 LANGUAGE: English.
HEADNOTE: AIR SERVICES
TOPIC: Air Transport
CONCEPTS: Definition of terms. Annex or appendix reference. Conformity with municipal law. General cooperation. Arbitration. Procedure. Existing tribunals. Negotiation. Reexport of goods, etc.. Fees and exemptions. Non-interest rates

and fees. Customs exemptions. Routes and logistics. Permit designation. Air transport. Conditions of airlines operating permission. Overflights and technical stops. Operating authorizations and regulations. Optional clause ICJ.
INTL ORGS: International Court of Justice. Arbitration Commission.
TREATY REF: 15UNTS295; 84UNTS389.
PROCEDURE: Amendment. Ratification. Termination.
PARTIES:
  Liberia
  Norway

106740 Bilateral Agreement **466 UNTS 109**
SIGNED: 13 Jul 62   FORCE: 13 Jul 62
REGISTERED: 15 May 63 ICAO (Civil Aviat)
ARTICLES: 14 LANGUAGE: Dutch. Spanish.
HEADNOTE: TRADE
TOPIC: Air Transport
CONCEPTS: Exceptions and exemptions. Treaty implementation. Annex or appendix reference. Establishment of trade relations. Most favored nation clause.
INTL ORGS: International Civil Aviation Organization. Arbitration Commission.
PROCEDURE: Denunciation. Ratification. Renewal or Revival.
PARTIES:
  Chile
  Netherlands

106741 Bilateral Agreement **466 UNTS 145**
SIGNED: 18 Oct 62   FORCE: 18 Oct 62
REGISTERED: 15 May 63 ICAO (Civil Aviat)
ARTICLES: 12 LANGUAGE: English.
HEADNOTE: AIR SERVICES
TOPIC: Air Transport
CONCEPTS: Territorial application. Annex or appendix reference. General cooperation. Arbitration. Procedure. Special tribunals. Negotiation. Reexport of goods, etc.. Monetary and gold transfers. Exchange rates and regulations. Fees and exemptions. Non-interest rates and fees. Tax exemptions. Customs exemptions. Routes and logistics. Permit designation. Air transport. Conditions of airlines operating permission. Overflights and technical stops. Operating authorizations and regulations.
INTL ORGS: International Civil Aviation Organization. Arbitration Commission.
TREATY REF: 15UNTS295.
PROCEDURE: Amendment. Ratification. Termination.
PARTIES:
  Netherlands
  Norway

106742 Bilateral Agreement **466 UNTS 165**
SIGNED: 9 Jan 63   FORCE: 9 Jan 63
REGISTERED: 15 May 63 ICAO (Civil Aviat)
ARTICLES: 14 LANGUAGE: French. English.
HEADNOTE: INTERNATIONAL AIR TRANSPORT
TOPIC: Air Transport
CONCEPTS: Definition of terms. Detailed regulations. Treaty interpretation. Annex or appendix reference. General cooperation. Exchange of information and documents. Licenses and permits. Personnel. Recognition of legal documents. Arbitration. Procedure. Existing tribunals. Special tribunals. Expense sharing formulae. Fees and exemptions. Non-interest rates and fees. Tax exemptions. Customs exemptions. Competency certificate. Routes and logistics. Permit designation. Air transport. Airworthiness certificates. Conditions of airlines operating permission. Overflights and technical stops. Operating authorizations and regulations.
INTL ORGS: International Civil Aviation Organization. Arbitration Commission.
TREATY REF: 15UNTS295.
PROCEDURE: Amendment. Future Procedures Contemplated. Registration. Termination.
PARTIES:
  Ghana
  Mali

106743 Bilateral Exchange **466 UNTS 181**
SIGNED: 15 Jan 63   FORCE: 15 Jan 63
REGISTERED: 16 May 63 UK Great Britain
ARTICLES: 2 LANGUAGE: English.

HEADNOTE: HARP TROPICAL WEATHER RE-
SEARCH PROJECT
TOPIC: Scientific Project
CONCEPTS: Alien status. General cooperation.
Personnel. General property. Vocational train-
ing. Research and scientific projects.
Meteorology. Claims and settlements. Materials,
equipment and services.
TREATY REF: 409UNTS67.
PARTIES:
UK Great Britain
USA (United States)

106744   Bilateral Exchange   **466 UNTS 189**
SIGNED: 27 Nov 62   FORCE: 27 Nov 62
REGISTERED: 16 May 63 UK Great Britain
ARTICLES: 2 LANGUAGE: English.
HEADNOTE: PROVISION ARMS EQUIPMENT
TOPIC: Milit Installation
CONCEPTS: Exchange of information and docu-
ments. Inspection and observation. Use of facili-
ties. Delivery schedules. Military assistance. Re-
turn of equipment and recapture. Restrictions on
transfer.
PARTIES:
India
UK Great Britain

106745   Bilateral Convention   **466 UNTS 195**
SIGNED: 4 Jul 60   FORCE: 28 Nov 62
REGISTERED: 16 May 63 UK Great Britain
ARTICLES: 23 LANGUAGE: English. Italian.
HEADNOTE: DOUBLE TAXATION FISCAL EVA-
SION TAXES INCOME
TOPIC: Taxation
CONCEPTS: Definition of terms. Territorial applica-
tion. Conformity with municipal law. Exchange
of official publications. Teacher and student ex-
change. Taxation. Tax credits. Equitable taxes.
Tax exemptions. Air transport. Merchant vessels.
PROCEDURE: Duration. Ratification. Termination.
PARTIES:
Italy
UK Great Britain

106746   Bilateral Exchange   **466 UNTS 235**
SIGNED: 14 Jul 62   FORCE: 7 Aug 62
REGISTERED: 16 May 63 UK Great Britain
ARTICLES: 2 LANGUAGE: English. French.
HEADNOTE: ABOLITION VISAS
TOPIC: Visas
CONCEPTS: Emergencies. Territorial application.
Visa abolition. Denial of admission. Conformity
with municipal law.
PROCEDURE: Denunciation.
PARTIES:
Tunisia
UK Great Britain

106747   Bilateral Exchange   **466 UNTS 243**
SIGNED: 20 Nov 62   FORCE: 20 Nov 62
REGISTERED: 16 May 63 UK Great Britain
ARTICLES: 2 LANGUAGE: English.
HEADNOTE: PRIVILEGES COLOMBO PLAN EX-
PERTS
TOPIC: Tech Assistance
CONCEPTS: Annex type material. Alien registra-
tion. Privileges and immunities. Tax exemptions.
Customs exemptions.
TREATY REF: COLOMBO PLAN.
PARTIES:
Thailand
UK Great Britain

106748   Bilateral Agreement   **466 UNTS 249**
SIGNED: 28 Feb 62   FORCE: 1 May 62
REGISTERED: 16 May 63 UK Great Britain
ARTICLES: 26 LANGUAGE: English.
HEADNOTE: EXCHANGE MONEY ORDERS
TOPIC: Postal Service
CONCEPTS: Annex or appendix reference. Confor-
mity with municipal law. Domestic legislation.
Accounting procedures. Exchange rates and reg-
ulations. Postal services. Money orders and
postal checks. Rates and charges. Advice lists
and orders.
PROCEDURE: Denunciation. Duration.
PARTIES:
Jordan
UK Great Britain

106749   Bilateral Exchange   **466 UNTS 277**
SIGNED: 2 Nov 62   FORCE: 2 Dec 62
REGISTERED: 16 May 63 UK Great Britain

ARTICLES: 2 LANGUAGE: English. Japanese.
HEADNOTE: ABOLITION VISAS
TOPIC: Visas
CONCEPTS: Emergencies. Territorial application.
Time limit. Visa abolition. Denial of admission.
Resident permits. Conformity with municipal
law.
PROCEDURE: Termination.
PARTIES:
Japan
UK Great Britain

106750   Bilateral Agreement   **466 UNTS 289**
SIGNED: 24 May 63   FORCE: 24 May 63
REGISTERED: 16 May 63 United Nations
ARTICLES: 10 LANGUAGE: English.
HEADNOTE: ASSISTANCE
TOPIC: Direct Aid
CONCEPTS: Detailed regulations. Treaty imple-
mentation. Annex or appendix reference. Visas.
Privileges and immunities. Exchange of informa-
tion and documents. Informational records. In-
spection and observation. Operating agencies.
Personnel. Public information. Responsibility
and liability. Title and deeds. Use of facilities.
Arbitration. Procedure. Negotiation. Import
quotas. Attachment of funds. Exchange rates
and regulations. Expense sharing formulae. Fi-
nancial programs. Domestic obligation. General
technical assistance. Economic assistance. Materials, equipment and services. IGO status.
INTL ORGS: International Atomic Energy Agency.
International Court of Justice. United Nations.
Arbitration Commission.
TREATY REF: 1UNTS15;   33UNTS261;
374UNTS147.
PROCEDURE: Amendment. Termination.
PARTIES:
Netherlands
UN Special Fund
ANNEX
490 UNTS 470.   UN   Special   Fund.   Force
27 Feb 64.
490 UNTS 470. Netherlands. Force 27 Feb 64.

106751   Bilateral Agreement   **466 UNTS 311**
SIGNED: 29 May 63   FORCE: 29 May 63
REGISTERED: 29 May 63 United Nations
ARTICLES: 6 LANGUAGE: English.
HEADNOTE: UN & UGANDA
TOPIC: IGO Status/Immunit
CONCEPTS: General consular functions. Diplo-
matic privileges. Diplomatic missions. Privileges
and immunities. Arbitration. Procedure. Status
of experts.
TREATY REF: 319UNTS15.
PROCEDURE: Amendment. Termination.
PARTIES:
United Nations
Uganda
ANNEX
479 UNTS 424.   Uganda.   Supplementation
21 Aug 63. Force 1 Oct 63.
479 UNTS 424. United Nations. Supplementation
1 Oct 63. Force 1 Oct 63.

106752   Multilateral Instrument   **466 UNTS 323**
SIGNED: 22 Jun 62   FORCE: 22 May 63
REGISTERED: 31 May 63 ILO (Labor Org)
ARTICLES: 5 LANGUAGE: English. French.
HEADNOTE: AMENDMENT ILO
TOPIC: IGO Establishment
CONCEPTS: Annex type material.
INTL ORGS: International Labour Organization.
TREATY REF: 15UNTS40.
PROCEDURE: Amendment.
PARTIES:
Multilateral
ANNEX
471 UNTS 346. Argentina. Ratification 4 Jun 63.
471 UNTS 346. Ethiopia. Ratification 4 Jun 63.
471 UNTS 346. Albania. Ratification 7 Jun 63.
471 UNTS 346. Ceylon (Sri Lanka). Ratification
17 Jun 63.
471 UNTS 346. Hungary. Ratification 23 May 63.
471 UNTS 346. Thailand. Ratification 23 May 63.
471 UNTS 346.   Trinidad/Tobago.   Ratification
23 May 63.
471 UNTS 346. Burundi. Acceptance 28 May 63.
471 UNTS 346.   Romania.   Acceptance
30 May 63.
471 UNTS 346.   Luxembourg.   Ratification
31 May 63.
471 UNTS 346. Poland. Ratification 3 Jun 63.
473 UNTS 384. Senegal. Ratification 4 Jul 63.
473 UNTS 384: Guatemala. Ratification 8 Jul 63.

473 UNTS 384. Honduras. Ratification 8 Jul 63.
473 UNTS 384. Colombia. Ratification 24 Jul 63.
475 UNTS 367.   Afghanistan.   Acceptance
6 Aug 63.
475 UNTS 367. USA (United States). Acceptance
6 Aug 63.
475 UNTS 367. Chile. Ratification 20 Aug 63.
475 UNTS 367. Cuba. Ratification 26 Aug 63.
480 UNTS 444.   Switzerland.   Ratification
14 Oct 63.
485 UNTS 376. Paraguay. Ratification 5 Dec 63.

106753   Bilateral Agreement   **466 UNTS 331**
SIGNED: 13 Mar 62   FORCE: 3 Apr 63
REGISTERED: 31 May 63 IDA (Devel Assoc)
ARTICLES: 6 LANGUAGE: English.
HEADNOTE: FINANCIAL ASSISTANCE IDA
TOPIC: Direct Aid
CONCEPTS: Territorial application. Currency. Ex-
change rates and regulations. Financial pro-
grams. Funding procedures. IDA development
project.
TREATY REF: 466UNTS334.
PARTIES:
IDA (Devel Assoc)
UK Great Britain

106754   Multilateral Agreement   **466 UNTS 346**
SIGNED: 24 May 63   FORCE: 24 May 63
REGISTERED: 3 Jun 63 United Nations
ARTICLES: 6 LANGUAGE: English.
HEADNOTE: TECHNICAL ASSISTANCE
TOPIC: Tech Assistance
CONCEPTS: Definition of terms. Privileges and immunities. General cooperation. Exchange of in-
formation and documents. Personnel. Responsi-
bility and liability. Title and deeds. Use of facili-
ties. Exchange. Scholarships and grants.
Vocational training. Research and development.
Exchange rates and regulations. Expense shar-
ing formulae. Local currency. Domestic obliga-
tion. General technical assistance. Materials,
equipment and services. IGO status. Conformity
with IGO decisions.
TREATY   REF: 76UNTS132;   1UNTS15;
33UNTS261; 374UNTS147.
PARTIES:
FAO (Food Agri) SIGNED: 24 May 63 FORCE:
24 May 63
IAEA (Atom Energy) SIGNED: 24 May 63 FORCE:
24 May 63
ICAO (Civil Aviat) SIGNED: 24 May 63 FORCE:
24 May 63
ILO (Labor Org) SIGNED: 24 May 63 FORCE:
24 May 63
ITU (Telecommun) SIGNED: 24 May 63 FORCE:
24 May 63
UNESCO   (Educ/Cult)   SIGNED: 24 May 63
FORCE: 24 May 63
United Nations SIGNED: 24 May 63 FORCE:
24 May 63
UPU (Postal Union) SIGNED: 24 May 63 FORCE:
24 May 63
WHO   (World   Health)   SIGNED: 24 May 63
FORCE: 24 May 63
WMO   (Meteorology)   SIGNED: 24 May 63
FORCE: 24 May 63
Uganda SIGNED: 24 May 63 FORCE: 24 May 63

106755   Bilateral Agreement   **466 UNTS 361**
SIGNED: 31 Oct 62   FORCE: 28 Dec 62
REGISTERED: 4 Jun 63 Norway
ARTICLES: 5 LANGUAGE: Swedish. Norwegian.
HEADNOTE: DIVISION REVENUES FOR TAX PUR-
POSES
TOPIC: Claims and Debts
CONCEPTS: Detailed regulations. Taxation. Gen-
eral.
TREATY REF: 261UNTS71; 348UNTS354.
PROCEDURE: Denunciation. Ratification.
PARTIES:
Norway
Sweden

106756   Bilateral Agreement   **467 UNTS 3**
SIGNED: 13 Feb 62   FORCE: 15 Apr 63
REGISTERED: 5 Jun 63 IBRD (World Bank)
ARTICLES: 5 LANGUAGE: English.
HEADNOTE: GUARANTEE INDUSTRIAL CREDIT
TOPIC: IBRD Project
CONCEPTS: Definition of terms. Annex or appen-
dix reference. Exchange of information and doc-
uments. Inspection and observation. Bonds.

Fees and exemptions. Tax exemptions. Domestic obligation. Terms of loan. Loan regulations. Loan guarantee. Guarantor non-interference. Industry.
PARTIES:
Pakistan
IBRD (World Bank)

106757 Bilateral Agreement **467 UNTS 43**
SIGNED: 21 Dec 62   FORCE: 11 Apr 63
REGISTERED: 5 Jun 63 IBRD (World Bank)
ARTICLES: 8 LANGUAGE: English.
HEADNOTE: LOAN AGREEMENT
TOPIC: IBRD Project
CONCEPTS: Default remedies. Definition of terms. Annex or appendix reference. Exchange of information and documents. Informational records. Inspection and observation. Accounting procedures. Bonds. Fees and exemptions. Interest rates. Tax exemptions. Domestic obligation. Terms of loan. Loan regulations. Loan guarantee. Guarantor non-interference.
PARTIES:
IBRD (World Bank)
Thailand

106758 Bilateral Agreement **467 UNTS 63**
SIGNED: 21 Dec 62   FORCE: 11 Apr 63
REGISTERED: 5 Jun 63 IBRD (World Bank)
ARTICLES: 8 LANGUAGE: English.
HEADNOTE: LOAN IRRIGATION
TOPIC: IBRD Project
CONCEPTS: Default remedies. Definition of terms. Annex or appendix reference. Exchange of information and documents. Informational records. Inspection and observation. Accounting procedures. Bonds. Fees and exemptions. Interest rates. Tax exemptions. Domestic obligation. Terms of loan. Loan regulations. Loan guarantee. Guarantor non-interference. Irrigation.
PARTIES:
IBRD (World Bank)
Thailand

106759 Bilateral Agreement **467 UNTS 83**
SIGNED: 7 Mar 63   FORCE: 18 Apr 63
REGISTERED: 5 Jun 63 IBRD (World Bank)
ARTICLES: 5 LANGUAGE: English.
HEADNOTE: GUARANTEE AGREEMENT
TOPIC: IBRD Project
CONCEPTS: Annex or appendix reference. Exchange of information and documents. Inspection and observation. Bonds. Fees and exemptions. Tax exemptions. Domestic obligation. Terms of loan. Loan regulations. Loan guarantee. Guarantor non-interference.
PARTIES:
IBRD (World Bank)
Thailand

106760 Bilateral Agreement **467 UNTS 107**
SIGNED: 17 Oct 62   FORCE: 21 Dec 62
REGISTERED: 5 Jun 63 IBRD (World Bank)
ARTICLES: 7 LANGUAGE: English.
HEADNOTE: LOAN ROAD
TOPIC: IBRD Project
CONCEPTS: Default remedies. Definition of terms. Annex or appendix reference. Exchange of information and documents. Informational records. Inspection and observation. Accounting procedures. Fees and exemptions. Interest rates. Tax exemptions. Terms of loan. Loan regulations. Loan guarantee. Guarantor non-interference. Roads and highways.
PARTIES:
Israel
IBRD (World Bank)

106761 Bilateral Agreement **467 UNTS 125**
SIGNED: 14 Sep 62   FORCE: 8 Nov 62
REGISTERED: 5 Jun 63 IBRD (World Bank)
ARTICLES: 8 LANGUAGE: English.
HEADNOTE: LOAN RAILWAY
TOPIC: IBRD Project
CONCEPTS: Definition of terms. Annex or appendix reference. Exchange of information and documents. Inspection and observation. Bonds. Fees and exemptions. Tax exemptions. Domestic obligation. Terms of loan. Loan regulations. Loan guarantee. Guarantor non-interference.
PARTIES:
Pakistan
IBRD (World Bank)

106762 Bilateral Agreement **467 UNTS 152**
SIGNED: 14 Sep 62   FORCE: 8 Nov 62
REGISTERED: 5 Jun 63 IBRD (World Bank)
ARTICLES: 8 LANGUAGE: English.
HEADNOTE: LOAN RAILWAY
TOPIC: IBRD Project
CONCEPTS: Default remedies. Definition of terms. Annex or appendix reference. Exchange of information and documents. Informational records. Inspection and observation. Accounting procedures. Bonds. Fees and exemptions. Interest rates. Tax exemptions. Domestic obligation. Terms of loan. Loan regulations. Loan guarantee. Guarantor non-interference. Railways.
PARTIES:
Pakistan
IBRD (World Bank)

106763 Bilateral Agreement **467 UNTS 177**
SIGNED: 15 Aug 62   FORCE: 1 Oct 62
REGISTERED: 5 Jun 63 IBRD (World Bank)
ARTICLES: 5 LANGUAGE: English.
HEADNOTE: GUARANTEE POWER EXPANSION
TOPIC: IBRD Project
CONCEPTS: Definition of terms. Annex or appendix reference. Exchange of information and documents. Inspection and observation. Bonds. Fees and exemptions. Tax exemptions. Domestic obligation. Terms of loan. Loan regulations. Loan guarantee. Guarantor non-interference. Hydro-electric power.
PARTIES:
Finland
IBRD (World Bank)

106764 Bilateral Agreement **467 UNTS 205**
SIGNED: 20 Jun 62   FORCE: 27 Aug 62
REGISTERED: 5 Jun 63 IBRD (World Bank)
ARTICLES: 5 LANGUAGE: English.
HEADNOTE: GUARANTEE TRANSPORT FACILITIES
TOPIC: IBRD Project
CONCEPTS: Definition of terms. Annex or appendix reference. Exchange of information and documents. Inspection and observation. Bonds. Fees and exemptions. Tax exemptions. Domestic obligation. Terms of loan. Loan regulations. Loan guarantee. Guarantor non-interference. Water transport.
PARTIES:
Mexico
IBRD (World Bank)

106765 Bilateral Agreement **467 UNTS 237**
SIGNED: 31 May 62   FORCE: 18 Dec 62
REGISTERED: 5 Jun 63 IBRD (World Bank)
ARTICLES: 5 LANGUAGE: English.
HEADNOTE: GUARANTEE TELECOMMUNICATIONS
TOPIC: IBRD Project
CONCEPTS: Definition of terms. Annex or appendix reference. Exchange of information and documents. Inspection and observation. Bonds. Fees and exemptions. Tax exemptions. Domestic obligation. Terms of loan. Loan regulations. Loan guarantee. Guarantor non-interference. Telecommunications.
PARTIES:
Ethiopia
IBRD (World Bank)

106766 Bilateral Agreement **467 UNTS 265**
SIGNED: 14 Sep 62   FORCE: 1 Nov 62
REGISTERED: 5 Jun 63 IBRD (World Bank)
ARTICLES: 7 LANGUAGE: English.
HEADNOTE: DEVELOPMENT CREDIT PORT
TOPIC: IBRD Project
CONCEPTS: Definition of terms. Annex or appendix reference. Exchange of information and documents. Inspection and observation. Bonds. Fees and exemptions. Tax exemptions. Domestic obligation. Terms of loan. Loan regulations. Loan guarantee. Guarantor non-interference. Water transport.
PARTIES:
India
IDA (Devel Assoc)

106767 Bilateral Agreement **467 UNTS 293**
SIGNED: 19 Mar 53   FORCE: 20 Apr 53
REGISTERED: 6 Jun 63 Austria
ARTICLES: 8 LANGUAGE: German. Serbo-Croat.
HEADNOTE: IMMOVABLE PROPERTY AUSTRIAN DUAL OWNERS YUGOSLAV FRONTIER ZONE

TOPIC: Visas
CONCEPTS: Exceptions and exemptions. Immovable property. Title and deeds. Establishment of commission.
INTL ORGS: Special Commission.
PARTIES:
Austria
Yugoslavia

106768 Bilateral Agreement **467 UNTS 323**
SIGNED: 19 Mar 53   FORCE: 20 Apr 53
REGISTERED: 6 Jun 63 Austria
ARTICLES: 25 LANGUAGE: German. Serbo-Croat.
HEADNOTE: REGULATION MINOR FRONTIER TRAFFIC
TOPIC: Visas
CONCEPTS: Emergencies. Time limit. Treaty interpretation. Annex or appendix reference. Border traffic and migration. Resident permits. Frontier permits. Conformity with municipal law. General cooperation. Immovable property. General property. Border control. Public health. Veterinary. Customs exemptions. Pasturage in frontier zones. Frontier peoples and personnel.
PROCEDURE: Denunciation.
PARTIES:
Austria
Yugoslavia
                    ANNEX
493 UNTS 342. Austria. Amendment 18 Jul 63. Force 1 Oct 63.
493 UNTS 342. Yugoslavia. Amendment 18 Jul 63. Force 1 Oct 63.
493 UNTS 342. Yugoslavia. Supplementation 18 Jul 63.
493 UNTS 342. Austria. Supplementation 18 Jul 63.
539 UNTS 368. Yugoslavia. Amendment 27 Nov 64. Force 1 Jan 65.
539 UNTS 368. Austria. Amendment 27 Nov 64. Force 1 Jan 65.

106769 Bilateral Agreement **467 UNTS 443**
SIGNED: 30 Sep 61   FORCE: 9 Apr 62
REGISTERED: 7 Jun 63 Romania
ARTICLES: 17 LANGUAGE: English.
HEADNOTE: AIR SERVICES
TOPIC: Air Transport
CONCEPTS: Conditions. Definition of terms. Detailed regulations. Exceptions and exemptions. Annex or appendix reference. General cooperation. Exchange of information and documents. Licenses and permits. Recognition of legal documents. Use of facilities. Arbitration. Procedure. Special tribunals. Negotiation. Humanitarian matters. Monetary and gold transfers. Fees and exemptions. Non-interest rates and fees. Customs exemptions. Competency certificate. Routes and logistics. Permit designation. Airport facilities. Airworthiness certificates. Conditions of airlines operating permission. Overflights and technical stops. Operating authorizations and regulations. Licenses and certificates of nationality.
PROCEDURE: Amendment. Ratification. Termination.
PARTIES:
Ghana
Romania

106770 Bilateral Treaty **468 UNTS 3**
SIGNED: 25 Jan 62   FORCE: 6 Dec 62
REGISTERED: 7 Jun 63 Romania
ARTICLES: 84 LANGUAGE: Romanian. Polish.
HEADNOTE: LEGAL ASSISTANCE CIVIL FAMILY CRIMINAL CASES
TOPIC: Admin Cooperation
CONCEPTS: General provisions. Previous treaty replacement. Privileges and immunities. Consular functions in property. Extradition, deportation and repatriation. Refusal of extradition. Concurrent requests. Limits of prosecution. Provisional detainment. Extradition postponement. Material evidence. Family law. Exchange of information and documents. Informational records. Juridical personality. Legal protection and assistance. Recognition and enforcement of legal decisions. Succession. Recognition of legal documents. Prizes and arbitral awards. Indemnities and reimbursements. Fees and exemptions. Assets trans-

fer. Tax exemptions. Conveyance in transit.
TREATY REF: 130LTS205; 153LTS87.
PROCEDURE: Duration. Ratification. Renewal or
  Revival.
PARTIES:
  Poland
  Romania

106771   Bilateral Agreement   **468 UNTS 109**
SIGNED: 20 Jun 62   FORCE: 26 Jul 62
REGISTERED: 11 Jun 63 IBRD (World Bank)
ARTICLES: 5 LANGUAGE: English.
HEADNOTE: GUARANTEE POWER
TOPIC: IBRD Project
CONCEPTS: Definition of terms. Annex or appen-
  dix reference. Exchange of information and doc-
  uments. Inspection and observation. Bonds.
  Fees and exemptions. Tax exemptions. Domestic
  obligation. Terms of loan. Loan regulations. Loan
  guarantee. Guarantor non-interference. Hydro-
  electric power.
PARTIES:
  Mexico
  IBRD (World Bank)

106772   Bilateral Agreement   **468 UNTS 143**
SIGNED: 11 Jul 62   FORCE: 28 Nov 62
REGISTERED: 11 Jun 63 IBRD (World Bank)
ARTICLES: 5 LANGUAGE: English.
HEADNOTE: GUARANTEE POWER
TOPIC: IBRD Project
CONCEPTS: Definition of terms. Annex or appen-
  dix reference. Exchange of information and doc-
  uments. Inspection and observation. Bonds.
  Fees and exemptions. Tax exemptions. Domestic
  obligation. Loan regulations. Loan guarantee.
  Guarantor non-interference. Hydro-electric
  power.
PARTIES:
  IBRD (World Bank)
  Yugoslavia

106773   Bilateral Agreement   **468 UNTS 177**
SIGNED: 14 Feb 62   FORCE: 7 Nov 62
REGISTERED: 11 Jun 63 IDA (Devel Assoc)
ARTICLES: 7 LANGUAGE: English.
HEADNOTE: DEVELOPMENT CREDIT FOURTH
  DVC PROJECT
TOPIC: Non-IBRD Project
CONCEPTS: Definition of terms. Detailed regula-
  tions. Previous treaty amendment. Exchange of
  information and documents. Informational
  records. Accounting procedures. Interest rates.
  Tax exemptions. Credit provisions. Loan repay-
  ment. Terms of loan. Loan regulations. IDA devel-
  opment project.
TREATY REF: 155UNTS117;   201UNTS145;
  317UNTS3.
PARTIES:
  India
  IDA (Devel Assoc)

106774   Bilateral Agreement   **468 UNTS 205**
SIGNED: 2 Nov 62   FORCE: 17 Jan 63
REGISTERED: 11 Jun 63 IDA (Devel Assoc)
ARTICLES: 7 LANGUAGE: English.
HEADNOTE: DEVELOPMENT CREDIT HIGHWAY
TOPIC: Non-IBRD Project
CONCEPTS: Definition of terms. Detailed regula-
  tions. Previous treaty amendment. Exchange of
  information and documents. Informational
  records. Accounting procedures. Interest rates.
  Tax exemptions. Credit provisions. Loan repay-
  ment. Terms of loan. Loan regulations. IDA devel-
  opment project. Roads and highways.
PARTIES:
  Haiti
  IDA (Devel Assoc)

106775   Bilateral Agreement   **468 UNTS 223**
SIGNED: 1 Feb 63   FORCE: 24 Apr 63
REGISTERED: 11 Jun 63 IDA (Devel Assoc)
ARTICLES: 7 LANGUAGE: English.
HEADNOTE: CREDIT AGREEMENT
TOPIC: Non-IBRD Project
CONCEPTS: Loan and credit. Credit provisions.
  Terms of loan.
PROCEDURE: Termination.
PARTIES:
  IDA (Devel Assoc)
  Turkey

106776   Bilateral Agreement   **468 UNTS 255**
SIGNED: 10 Dec 62   FORCE: 18 Feb 63
REGISTERED: 12 Jun 63 IBRD (World Bank)
ARTICLES: 5 LANGUAGE: English.
HEADNOTE: GUARANTEE WHARF
TOPIC: IBRD Project
CONCEPTS: Annex or appendix reference. Ex-
  change of information and documents. Inspec-
  tion and observation. Bonds. Fees and exemp-
  tions. Tax exemptions. Domestic obligation.
  Terms of loan. Loan regulations. Loan guarantee.
  Guarantor non-interference. Water transport.
PARTIES:
  Nigeria
  IBRD (World Bank)

106777   Bilateral Agreement   **468 UNTS 281**
SIGNED: 7 Nov 62   FORCE: 4 Jan 63
REGISTERED: 12 Jun 63 IBRD (World Bank)
ARTICLES: 5 LANGUAGE: English.
HEADNOTE: LOAN GUARANTEE
TOPIC: Loans and Credits
CONCEPTS: Debts. Liens. Loan and credit. Credit
  provisions.
PARTIES:
  Philippines
  IBRD (World Bank)

106778   Bilateral Exchange   **468 UNTS 313**
SIGNED: 29 Mar 63   FORCE: 1 May 63
REGISTERED: 13 Jun 63 Australia
ARTICLES: 2 LANGUAGE: English.
HEADNOTE: VISAS VISA FEES
TOPIC: Visas
CONCEPTS: Time limit. Visa abolition. Resident
  permits. Visas. Conformity with municipal law.
  Fees and exemptions.
PROCEDURE: Termination.
PARTIES:
  Australia
  Portugal

106779   Bilateral Agreement   **468 UNTS 319**
SIGNED: 17 May 63   FORCE: 17 May 63
REGISTERED: 18 Jun 63 Thailand
ARTICLES: 5 LANGUAGE: English.
HEADNOTE: BORDER ARRANGEMENTS COOPER-
  ATION
TOPIC: Visas
CONCEPTS: Annex or appendix reference. Estab-
  lishment of commission. Procedure.
INTL ORGS: Special Commission.
PROCEDURE: Amendment. Termination.
PARTIES:
  Burma
  Thailand

106780   Bilateral Agreement   **468 UNTS 331**
SIGNED: 2 Nov 62   FORCE: 8 Apr 63
REGISTERED: 18 Jun 63 IDA (Devel Assoc)
ARTICLES: 7 LANGUAGE: English.
HEADNOTE: DEVELOPMENT CREDIT HIGHWAY
TOPIC: Non-IBRD Project
CONCEPTS: Detailed regulations. Previous treaty
  amendment. Exchange of information and docu-
  ments. Informational records. Accounting proce-
  dures. Interest rates. Tax exemptions. Credit pro-
  visions. Loan repayment. Terms of loan. Plans
  and standards. IDA development project. Roads
  and highways.
PARTIES:
  El Salvador
  IDA (Devel Assoc)

106781   Bilateral Agreement   **468 UNTS 351**
SIGNED: 2 Nov 62   FORCE: 15 Mar 63
REGISTERED: 18 Jun 63 IDA (Devel Assoc)
ARTICLES: 7 LANGUAGE: English.
HEADNOTE: DEVELOPMENT CREDIT INDUSTRIAL
  ESTATES
TOPIC: Non-IBRD Project
CONCEPTS: Definition of terms. Detailed regula-
  tions. Previous treaty amendment. Exchange of
  information and documents. Informational
  records. Accounting procedures. Interest rates.
  Tax exemptions. Credit provisions. Loan repay-
  ment. Terms of loan. Plans and standards. IDA
  development project. Industry.
PARTIES:
  Pakistan
  IDA (Devel Assoc)

106782   Bilateral Agreement   **469 UNTS 3**
SIGNED: 23 Nov 62   FORCE: 27 Feb 63

REGISTERED: 18 Jun 63 IDA (Devel Assoc)
ARTICLES: 8 LANGUAGE: English.
HEADNOTE: DEVELOPMENT CREDIT INDUSTRIAL
  DEVELOPMENT BANK
TOPIC: Non-IBRD Project
CONCEPTS: Definition of terms. Detailed regula-
  tions. Previous treaty amendment. Exchange of
  information and documents. Informational
  records. Accounting procedures. Interest rates.
  Tax exemptions. Credit provisions. Loan repay-
  ment. Terms of loan. Plans and standards. IDA
  development project. Industry.
PARTIES:
  IDA (Devel Assoc)
  Turkey

106783   Bilateral Agreement   **469 UNTS 33**
SIGNED: 17 Sep 62   FORCE: 28 Jan 63
REGISTERED: 18 Jun 63 IDA (Devel Assoc)
ARTICLES: 6 LANGUAGE: English.
HEADNOTE: DEVELOPMENT CREDIT EDUCATION
TOPIC: Non-IBRD Project
CONCEPTS: Detailed regulations. Previous treaty
  amendment. Exchange of information and docu-
  ments. Informational records. Education. Ac-
  counting procedures. Interest rates. Tax exemp-
  tions. Credit provisions. Loan repayment. Terms
  of loan. Plans and standards. IDA development
  project.
PARTIES:
  IDA (Devel Assoc)
  Tunisia

106784   Bilateral Agreement   **469 UNTS 55**
SIGNED: 9 May 63   FORCE: 9 May 63
REGISTERED: 20 Jun 63 Australia
ARTICLES: 24 LANGUAGE: English.
HEADNOTE: STATUS FORCES
TOPIC: Status of Forces
CONCEPTS: Definition of terms. Time limit. Annex
  or appendix reference. Frontier formalities.
  Court procedures. General cooperation. General
  property. Recognition of legal documents. Inves-
  tigation of violations. Arbitration. Procedure. In-
  demnities and reimbursements. Expense sharing
  formulae. Claims and settlements. General. Tax
  exemptions. Customs duties. Customs exemp-
  tions. Materials, equipment and services. Postal
  services. Security of information. Jurisdiction.
  Status of forces.
PROCEDURE: Duration. Termination.
PARTIES:
  Australia
  USA (United States)

106785   Bilateral Exchange   **469 UNTS 91**
SIGNED: 27 Dec 62   FORCE: 27 Dec 62
REGISTERED: 24 Jun 63 USA (United States)
ARTICLES: 2 LANGUAGE: English.
HEADNOTE: DOUBLE TAXATION SHIPS AIR-
  CRAFT
TOPIC: Taxation
CONCEPTS: Definition of terms. Previous treaty re-
  placement. Conformity with municipal law. Do-
  mestic legislation. Taxation. Air transport. Mer-
  chant vessels.
TREATY REF: 133LTS381.
PROCEDURE: Termination.
PARTIES:
  Iceland
  USA (United States)

106786   Bilateral Agreement   **469 UNTS 101**
SIGNED: 21 Nov 62   FORCE: 21 Nov 62
REGISTERED: 24 Jun 63 USA (United States)
ARTICLES: 6 LANGUAGE: English.
HEADNOTE: AGRI COMMOD
TOPIC: US Agri Commod Aid
CONCEPTS: Currency. Agricultural commodities.
PARTIES:
  USA (United States)
  Vietnam, South
                      ANNEX
488 UNTS 330. USA (United States). Amendment
  4 Apr 63. Force 4 Apr 63.
488 UNTS 330. Vietnam, South. Amendment
  4 Apr 63. Force 4 Apr 63.
488 UNTS 333. USA (United States). Amendment
  24 Jul 63. Force 24 Jul 63.
488 UNTS 333. Vietnam, South. Amendment
  24 Jul 63. Force 24 Jul 63.
505 UNTS 329. Vietnam, South. Amendment
  8 Nov 63. Force 8 Nov 63.
505 UNTS 329. USA (United States). Amendment
  8 Nov 63. Force 8 Nov 63.

106787   Bilateral Exchange   **469 UNTS 115**
SIGNED: 21 Dec 62   FORCE: 21 Dec 62

REGISTERED: 24 Jun 63 USA (United States)
ARTICLES: 2 LANGUAGE: English. Czechoslovakian.
HEADNOTE: ISSUANCE RE-ENTRY VISAS DIPLOMATIC PERSONNEL
TOPIC: Visas
CONCEPTS: Visas.
PARTIES:
Czechoslovakia
USA (United States)

106788 Bilateral Agreement **469 UNTS 121**
SIGNED: 17 Dec 62   FORCE: 17 Dec 62
REGISTERED: 24 Jun 63 USA (United States)
ARTICLES: 6 LANGUAGE: English. Spanish.
HEADNOTE: AGRI COMMOD TITLE I
TOPIC: US Agri Commod Aid
CONCEPTS: General provisions. Annex or appendix reference. Exchange of information and documents. Reexport of goods, etc.. Exchange rates and regulations. Transportation costs. Local currency. Commodities schedule. Purchase authorization. Surplus commodities. Mutual consultation.
PARTIES:
Bolivia
USA (United States)
          ANNEX
494 UNTS 341. Bolivia. Amendment 24 Jun 63. Force 24 Jun 63.
494 UNTS 341. USA (United States). Amendment 24 Jun 63. Force 24 Jun 63.

106789 Bilateral Agreement **469 UNTS 145**
SIGNED: 27 Jun 63   FORCE: 27 Jun 63
REGISTERED: 27 Jun 63 United Nations
ARTICLES: 6 LANGUAGE: English.
HEADNOTE: PERSONNEL
TOPIC: Trusteeship
CONCEPTS: Annex or appendix reference. Diplomatic privileges. Privileges and immunities. Juridical personality. Arbitration. Procedure. Assistance to United Nations. Administering authority.
PROCEDURE: Amendment. Termination.
PARTIES:
United Nations
UK Great Britain
          ANNEX
478 UNTS 440. United Nations. Supplementation 23 Aug 63. Force 27 Sep 63.
478 UNTS 440. UK Great Britain. Supplementation 27 Sep 63. Force 27 Sep 63.
490 UNTS 472. United Nations. Acknowledgement 9 Mar 64. Force 9 Mar 64.
490 UNTS 472. UK Great Britain. Northern Rhodesia. Force 9 Mar 64.
490 UNTS 472. UK Great Britain. Nyasaland. Force 9 Mar 64.

106790 Bilateral Convention **469 UNTS 163**
SIGNED: 29 Aug 60   FORCE: 29 Aug 60
REGISTERED: 28 Jun 63 Cuba
ARTICLES: 3 LANGUAGE: Spanish. Korean.
HEADNOTE: ESTABLISH DIPLOMATIC RELATIONS EXCHANGE DIPLOMATIC REPRESENTATIVES
TOPIC: Consul/Citizenship
CONCEPTS: Diplomatic relations establishment.
PROCEDURE: Ratification.
PARTIES:
Cuba
Korea, North

106791 Multilateral Agreement **469 UNTS 169**
SIGNED: 28 Sep 62   FORCE: 1 Jul 63
REGISTERED: 1 Jul 63 United Nations
ARTICLES: 74 LANGUAGE: English. French. Russian. Spanish. Portuguese.
HEADNOTE: INTERNATIONAL COFFEE
TOPIC: IGO Establishment
CONCEPTS: Definition of terms. Annex or appendix reference. Treaty violation. Exchange of information and documents. Informational records. Juridical personality. Procedure. Special tribunals. Specialists exchange. Institute establishment. Research results. Export quotas. Import quotas. Certificates of origin. Reexport of goods, etc.. Trade procedures. Accounting procedures. Currency. Funding procedures. Payment schedules. Quotas. Customs exemptions. Admission. Establishment. Headquarters and facilities. Liaison with other IGO's. Internal structure. Freedom of meeting. Conformity with IGO

decisions. Inter-agency agreements.
INTL ORGS: Inter-American Coffee Board. United Nations.
PROCEDURE: Amendment. Accession. Denunciation. Duration. Ratification. Termination.
PARTIES:
Argentina SIGNED: 28 Sep 62
Australia New Guinea RATIFIED: 23 Nov 62
Australia Papua RATIFIED: 23 Nov 62
Australia SIGNED: 23 Nov 62
Austria SIGNED: 23 Nov 62
Belgium SIGNED: 28 Sep 62
Bolivia SIGNED: 28 Sep 62
Brazil SIGNED: 28 Sep 62
Burundi SIGNED: 28 Sep 62
Cameroon SIGNED: 28 Sep 62
Canada SIGNED: 16 Oct 62
Chile SIGNED: 30 Nov 62
Central Afri Rep SIGNED: 16 Nov 62
Congo (Zaire) SIGNED: 27 Nov 62
Colombia SIGNED: 28 Sep 62
Costa Rica SIGNED: 28 Sep 62
Cuba SIGNED: 30 Nov 62
Denmark SIGNED: 29 Nov 62
Dominican Republic SIGNED: 28 Sep 62
Ecuador SIGNED: 28 Nov 62
El Salvador SIGNED: 28 Sep 62
France SIGNED: 28 Sep 62
Gabon SIGNED: 12 Oct 62
Germany, West SIGNED: 19 Nov 62
Guatemala SIGNED: 28 Sep 62
Haiti SIGNED: 28 Sep 62
Honduras SIGNED: 28 Sep 62
India SIGNED: 29 Nov 62
Indonesia SIGNED: 21 Nov 62
Italy SIGNED: 28 Sep 62
Ivory Coast SIGNED: 24 Oct 62
Japan SIGNED: 28 Sep 62
Lebanon SIGNED: 12 Oct 62
Luxembourg SIGNED: 20 Nov 62
Madagascar SIGNED: 28 Sep 62
Mexico SIGNED: 28 Sep 62
Netherlands SIGNED: 30 Nov 62
New Zealand SIGNED: 29 Nov 62
Nicaragua SIGNED: 29 Nov 62
Nigeria SIGNED: 29 Nov 62
Norway SIGNED: 30 Nov 62
Panama SIGNED: 8 Nov 62
Peru SIGNED: 28 Sep 62
Portugal SIGNED: 29 Nov 62
Rwanda SIGNED: 2 Oct 62
Sierra Leone SIGNED: 30 Nov 62
Spain SIGNED: 28 Sep 62
Sweden SIGNED: 5 Oct 62
Switzerland SIGNED: 30 Nov 62
Tanganyika SIGNED: 28 Sep 62
Trinidad/Tobago SIGNED: 30 Nov 62
Uganda SIGNED: 21 Nov 62
UK Great Britain SIGNED: 28 Sep 62
USA (United States) SIGNED: 28 Sep 62
USSR (Soviet Union) SIGNED: 23 Nov 62
Venezuela SIGNED: 28 Sep 62
          ANNEX
470 UNTS 434.
472 UNTS 400.
473 UNTS 385.
474 UNTS 381.
479 UNTS 428.
480 UNTS 466.
483 UNTS 390.
484 UNTS 416.
484 UNTS 418.
492 UNTS 370.
501 UNTS 374.
506 UNTS 382.
507 UNTS 346.
509 UNTS 305.
510 UNTS 336.
515 UNTS 322.
518 UNTS 299.
519 UNTS 402.
521 UNTS 401.
541 UNTS 350.
547 UNTS 354.
555 UNTS 258.
607 UNTS 341.
608 UNTS 375.
608 UNTS 375.
620 UNTS 323.
635 UNTS 357.

106792 Bilateral Agreement **470 UNTS 3**
SIGNED: 28 Jun 63   FORCE: 28 Jun 63
REGISTERED: 1 Jul 63 United Nations

ARTICLES: 10 LANGUAGE: English.
HEADNOTE: ASSISTANCE FROM SPECIAL FUND
TOPIC: Non-IBRD Project
CONCEPTS: Previous treaty amendment. Exchange of information and documents. Informational records. Operating agencies. Arbitration. Negotiation. Financial programs. Tax exemptions. Loan and credit. Non-bank projects. Special status. Status of experts.
INTL ORGS: International Atomic Energy Agency. International Court of Justice. United Nations. Arbitration Commission.
TREATY REF: 33UNTS261.
PROCEDURE: Duration. Termination.
PARTIES:
New Zealand
UN Special Fund

106793 Multilateral Convention **470 UNTS 25**
SIGNED: 23 Mar 62   FORCE: 1 Jul 63
REGISTERED: 1 Jul 63 Norway
ARTICLES: 7 LANGUAGE: Swedish. Danish. Finnish. Icelandic. Norwegian.
HEADNOTE: RECOVERY MAINTENANCE CONTRIBUTIONS
TOPIC: Admin Cooperation
CONCEPTS: Previous treaty replacement. General cooperation. Family law. Operating agencies. Recognition and enforcement of legal decisions. Indemnities and reimbursements.
TREATY REF: 126LTS41; 227UNTS169.
PROCEDURE: Ratification. Termination.
PARTIES:
Denmark   SIGNED: 23 Mar 62   RATIFIED: 30 Jan 63 FORCE: 1 Jul 63
Finland   SIGNED: 23 Mar 62   RATIFIED: 25 Jan 63 FORCE: 1 Jul 63
Iceland   SIGNED: 23 Mar 62   RATIFIED: 29 Jan 63 FORCE: 1 Jul 63
Norway SIGNED: 23 Mar 62 RATIFIED: 2 Jan 63 FORCE: 1 Jul 63
Sweden   SIGNED: 23 Mar 62   RATIFIED: 21 Jan 63 FORCE: 1 Jul 63

106794 Bilateral Exchange **470 UNTS 51**
SIGNED: 30 Nov 62   FORCE: 30 Nov 62
REGISTERED: 1 Jul 63 UK Great Britain
ARTICLES: 2 LANGUAGE: English.
HEADNOTE: EXCHANGE OFFICIAL PUBLICATIONS
TOPIC: Admin Cooperation
CONCEPTS: Exchange of official publications. Operating agencies. Indemnities and reimbursements.
PARTIES:
UK Great Britain
Vietnam, South

106795 Bilateral Exchange **470 UNTS 59**
SIGNED: 9 Jan 63   FORCE: 9 Jan 63
REGISTERED: 1 Jul 63 UK Great Britain
ARTICLES: 2 LANGUAGE: English.
HEADNOTE: EXCHANGE OFFICIAL PUBLICATIONS
TOPIC: Admin Cooperation
CONCEPTS: Exchange of official publications. Exchange of information and documents. Publications exchange.
PROCEDURE: Termination.
PARTIES:
Thailand
UK Great Britain

106796 Bilateral Exchange **470 UNTS 65**
SIGNED: 28 Nov 62   FORCE: 1 Jan 63
REGISTERED: 1 Jul 63 UK Great Britain
ARTICLES: 2 LANGUAGE: English.
HEADNOTE: IMPORTATION BOOKS
TOPIC: Commodity Trade
CONCEPTS: Exchange rates and regulations. Commodity trade.
TREATY REF: 431UNTS35; 360UNTS79; 404UNTS376.
PROCEDURE: Duration. Termination.
PARTIES:
UK Great Britain
Yugoslavia

106797 Bilateral Convention **470 UNTS 71**
SIGNED: 19 Jun 61   FORCE: 21 Mar 63
REGISTERED: 1 Jul 63 UK Great Britain

ARTICLES: 0 LANGUAGE: English.
HEADNOTE: CULTURAL
TOPIC: Culture
CONCEPTS: Establishment of commission. Culture. Exchange. General cultural cooperation.
PROCEDURE: Ratification.
PARTIES:
 Argentina
 UK Great Britain

106798 Bilateral Exchange **470 UNTS 87**
SIGNED: 30 Sep 59 FORCE: 30 Oct 59
REGISTERED: 8 Jul 63 Canada
ARTICLES: 2 LANGUAGE: English.
HEADNOTE: NON-IMMIGRANT VISA ARRANGEMENTS
TOPIC: Visas
CONCEPTS: Denial of admission. Visas. Conformity with municipal law. Fees and exemptions.
PROCEDURE: Termination.
PARTIES:
 Canada
 Greece

106799 Bilateral Exchange **470 UNTS 93**
SIGNED: 8 Oct 59 FORCE: 1 Nov 59
REGISTERED: 8 Jul 63 Canada
ARTICLES: 2 LANGUAGE: English. Spanish.
HEADNOTE: VISA REQUIREMENTS
TOPIC: Visas
CONCEPTS: Visas. Conformity with municipal law. Fees and exemptions.
PARTIES:
 Canada
 Venezuela

106800 Bilateral Exchange **470 UNTS 101**
SIGNED: 22 Sep 59 FORCE: 22 Sep 59
REGISTERED: 8 Jul 63 Canada
ARTICLES: 2 LANGUAGE: French.
HEADNOTE: TAXATION SHIPS AIRCRAFT
TOPIC: Taxation
CONCEPTS: Definition of terms. General. Air transport. Merchant vessels.
PROCEDURE: Duration. Termination.
PARTIES:
 Canada
 Switzerland

106801 Bilateral Exchange **470 UNTS 109**
SIGNED: 25 Apr 60 FORCE: 25 Apr 60
REGISTERED: 8 Jul 63 Canada
ARTICLES: 2 LANGUAGE: English.
HEADNOTE: SUPPLY WHEAT FLOUR WARTIME EMERGENCY STOCKPILING
TOPIC: Milit Installation
CONCEPTS: Inspection and observation. Indemnities and reimbursements. Delivery schedules. Agricultural commodities. Military installations and equipment.
INTL ORGS: North Atlantic Treaty Organization.
PARTIES:
 Canada
 Norway

106802 Bilateral Exchange **470 UNTS 117**
SIGNED: 18 Dec 59 FORCE: 25 Jan 60
REGISTERED: 8 Jul 63 Canada
ARTICLES: 2 LANGUAGE: English. Spanish.
HEADNOTE: VISA REQUIREMENTS
TOPIC: Visas
CONCEPTS: Time limit. Visa abolition. Resident permits. Visas. Conformity with municipal law. Fees and exemptions.
PARTIES:
 Canada
 Spain

106803 Bilateral Exchange **470 UNTS 125**
SIGNED: 24 May 60 FORCE: 24 May 60
REGISTERED: 8 Jul 63 Canada
ARTICLES: 2 LANGUAGE: English.
HEADNOTE: DEFENSE SCIENCE INFORMATION EXCHANGE PROJECT
TOPIC: Milit Installation
CONCEPTS: Annex or appendix reference. Military installations and equipment. Exchange of defense information.
PROCEDURE: Termination.
PARTIES:
 Canada
 Norway

106804 Bilateral Exchange **470 UNTS 133**
SIGNED: 5 Aug 60 FORCE: 5 Aug 60
REGISTERED: 8 Jul 63 Canada
ARTICLES: 2 LANGUAGE: English.
HEADNOTE: EMERGENCY STOCKPILING WHEAT FLOUR
TOPIC: Milit Installation
CONCEPTS: Inspection and observation. Indemnities and reimbursements. Delivery schedules. Agricultural commodities. Military installations and equipment.
INTL ORGS: North Atlantic Treaty Organization.
PARTIES:
 Canada
 UK Great Britain

106805 Bilateral Exchange **470 UNTS 139**
SIGNED: 10 Mar 61 FORCE: 9 Apr 61
REGISTERED: 8 Jul 63 Canada
ARTICLES: 2 LANGUAGE: English.
HEADNOTE: VISA REQUIREMENTS
TOPIC: Visas
CONCEPTS: Emergencies. Time limit. Denial of admission. Resident permits. Visas. Conformity with municipal law. Fees and exemptions.
PROCEDURE: Termination.
PARTIES:
 Canada
 Iran

106806 Bilateral Exchange **470 UNTS 148**
SIGNED: 22 Nov 61 FORCE: 22 Nov 61
REGISTERED: 8 Jul 63 Canada
ARTICLES: 2 LANGUAGE: English. Spanish.
HEADNOTE: AMATEUR RADIO STATIONS EXCHANGE MESSAGES FROM TO THIRD PARTIES
TOPIC: Telecommunications
CONCEPTS: Amateur radio. Amateur third party message. Radio-telephone-telegraphic communications.
PROCEDURE: Termination.
PARTIES:
 Canada
 Venezuela

106807 Bilateral Agreement **470 UNTS 153**
SIGNED: 18 Dec 61 FORCE: 18 Dec 61
REGISTERED: 8 Jul 63 Canada
ARTICLES: 9 LANGUAGE: English. Italian.
HEADNOTE: SALE ITALY WASTE MATERIAL SCRAP
TOPIC: Specific Resources
CONCEPTS: Export quotas. Surplus property. Raw materials.
PROCEDURE: Duration. Ratification. Registration. Renewal or Revival. Termination.
PARTIES:
 Canada
 Italy

ANNEX
528 UNTS 312. Canada. Amendment 18 Sep 63. Force 18 Sep 63.
528 UNTS 312. Italy. Amendment 18 Sep 63. Force 18 Sep 63.

106808 Bilateral Exchange **470 UNTS 163**
SIGNED: 25 May 62 FORCE: 25 May 62
REGISTERED: 8 Jul 63 Canada
ARTICLES: 2 LANGUAGE: French.
HEADNOTE: DEFENSE SERVICE INFORMATION
TOPIC: Other Military
CONCEPTS: Security of information. Exchange of defense information. Restrictions on transfer.
PARTIES:
 Canada
 France

106809 Multilateral Agreement **470 UNTS 171**
SIGNED: 8 Nov 56 FORCE: 24 Apr 57
REGISTERED: 10 Jul 63 Org Ctrl Am States
ARTICLES: 22 LANGUAGE: Spanish.
HEADNOTE: TEMPORARY IMPORTATION BOND VEHICLES
TOPIC: Commodity Trade
CONCEPTS: Definition of terms. Treaty implementation. Annex or appendix reference. Conformity with municipal law. Licenses and permits. Reexport of goods, etc.. Commodity trade. Customs declarations. Temporary importation. Land transport. Railway border crossing. Road rules.
INTL ORGS: Organization of Central American States.

PROCEDURE: Accession. Ratification. Registration. Termination.
PARTIES:
 Costa Rica SIGNED: 8 Nov 56
 El Salvador SIGNED: 8 Nov 56 FORCE: 16 May 57
 Guatemala SIGNED: 8 Nov 56 RATIFIED: 24 Apr 57 FORCE: 24 Apr 57
 Honduras SIGNED: 8 Nov 56
 Nicaragua SIGNED: 8 Nov 56 FORCE: 3 Dec 57

106810 Multilateral Agreement **470 UNTS 208**
SIGNED: 24 May 63 FORCE: 24 May 63
REGISTERED: 12 Jul 63 United Nations
ARTICLES: 6 LANGUAGE: English. Russian. Mongolian.
HEADNOTE: TECHNICAL ASSISTANCE
TOPIC: Tech Assistance
CONCEPTS: General technical assistance. Assistance.
PARTIES:
 Mongolia SIGNED: 24 May 63 FORCE: 24 May 63
 FAO (Food Agri) SIGNED: 24 May 63 FORCE: 24 May 63
 ICAO (Civil Aviat) SIGNED: 24 May 63 FORCE: 24 May 63
 ILO (Labor Org) SIGNED: 24 May 63 FORCE: 24 May 63
 ITU (Telecommun) SIGNED: 24 May 63 FORCE: 24 May 63
 UNESCO (Educ/Cult) SIGNED: 24 May 63 FORCE: 24 May 63
 United Nations SIGNED: 24 May 63 FORCE: 24 May 63
 UPU (Postal Union) SIGNED: 24 May 63 FORCE: 24 May 63
 WHO (World Health) SIGNED: 24 May 63 FORCE: 24 May 63
 WMO (Meteorology) SIGNED: 24 May 63 FORCE: 24 May 63

106811 Multilateral Agreement **470 UNTS 239**
SIGNED: 15 Apr 60 FORCE: 6 Apr 63
REGISTERED: 15 Jul 63 Belgium
ARTICLES: 13 LANGUAGE: French.
HEADNOTE: SETTLEMENT FINANCIAL CLAIMS
TOPIC: Finance
CONCEPTS: Detailed regulations. Treaty implementation. Treaty interpretation. General cooperation. Exchange of information and documents. Responsibility and liability. Procedure. Bonds. Expense sharing formulae. Payment schedules. Claims and settlements. Lump sum settlements.
PROCEDURE: Ratification.
PARTIES:
 Belgium SIGNED: 15 Apr 60 FORCE: 6 Apr 63
 Luxembourg SIGNED: 15 Apr 60 FORCE: 6 Apr 63
 Yugoslavia SIGNED: 15 Apr 60 FORCE: 6 Apr 63

106812 Bilateral Agreement **470 UNTS 259**
SIGNED: 15 May 63 FORCE: 30 Apr 63
REGISTERED: 15 Jul 63 Belgium
ARTICLES: 11 LANGUAGE: French. Dutch.
HEADNOTE: CULTURAL
TOPIC: Culture
CONCEPTS: Treaty implementation. Friendship and amity. Dispute settlement. Specialists exchange. Exchange. Teacher and student exchange. Scholarships and grants. Exchange. General cultural cooperation. Artists. Scientific exchange. Research and development. Publications exchange. Mass media exchange.
PROCEDURE: Denunciation. Duration. Ratification. Renewal or Revival.
PARTIES:
 Belgium
 Venezuela

106813 Bilateral Treaty **470 UNTS 273**
SIGNED: 17 Apr 59 FORCE: 30 Apr 60
REGISTERED: 15 Jul 63 Malaysia
ARTICLES: 10 LANGUAGE: Malay. Indonesian. English.
HEADNOTE: FRIENDSHIP
TOPIC: General Amity
CONCEPTS: Treaty interpretation. Friendship and amity. Border traffic and migration. Consular re-

lations establishment. Diplomatic relations establishment. Procedure. General cultural cooperation.
PROCEDURE: Future Procedures Contemplated. Ratification. Termination.
PARTIES:
Indonesia
Malaysia

106814 Multilateral Agreement **470 UNTS 291**
SIGNED: 16 Oct 62   FORCE: 16 Oct 62
REGISTERED: 15 Jul 63 Malaysia
ARTICLES: 41 LANGUAGE: English.
HEADNOTE: MONEY ORDER BUSINESS
TOPIC: Postal Service
CONCEPTS: Conformity with municipal law. Responsibility and liability. Accounting procedures. Payment schedules. Postal services. Regulations. Money orders and postal checks. Rates and charges. Advice lists and orders. Telegrams.
TREATY REF: INTERNATIONAL TELECOMMUNICATIONS CONVENTION.
PROCEDURE: Duration. Termination.
PARTIES:
Australia SIGNED: 16 Oct 62 FORCE: 16 Oct 62
Fed of Malaya SIGNED: 16 Oct 62 FORCE: 16 Oct 62
UK Great Britain SIGNED: 16 Oct 62 FORCE: 16 Oct 62

106815 Multilateral Agreement **470 UNTS 321**
SIGNED: 16 Oct 62   FORCE: 16 Oct 62
REGISTERED: 15 Jul 63 Malaysia
ARTICLES: 11 LANGUAGE: English.
HEADNOTE: EXCHANGE POSTAL PARCELS SUBJECT TRADE CHARGES
TOPIC: Postal Service
CONCEPTS: Detailed regulations. Accounting procedures. Currency. Postal services. Conveyance in transit. Money orders and postal checks. Parcel post. Rates and charges.
PROCEDURE: Duration. Termination. Application to Non-self-governing Territories.
PARTIES:
Australia SIGNED: 16 Oct 62 FORCE: 16 Oct 62
Fed of Malaya SIGNED: 16 Oct 62 FORCE: 16 Oct 62
UK Great Britain SIGNED: 16 Oct 62 FORCE: 16 Oct 62

106816 Multilateral Agreement **470 UNTS 336**
SIGNED: 16 Oct 62   FORCE: 16 Oct 62
REGISTERED: 15 Jul 63 Malaysia
ARTICLES: 26 LANGUAGE: English.
HEADNOTE: EXCHANGE PARCELS PARCEL POST
TOPIC: Postal Service
CONCEPTS: Definition of terms. Detailed regulations. Customs duties. Postal services. Regulations. Parcel post. Rates and charges.
PROCEDURE: Duration. Termination.
PARTIES:
Australia SIGNED: 16 Oct 62 FORCE: 16 Oct 62
Fed of Malaya SIGNED: 16 Oct 62 FORCE: 16 Oct 62
UK Great Britain SIGNED: 16 Oct 62 FORCE: 16 Oct 62

106817 Bilateral Agreement **471 UNTS 3**
SIGNED: 16 Jul 63   FORCE: 16 Jul 63
REGISTERED: 16 Jul 63 United Nations
ARTICLES: 6 LANGUAGE: English.
HEADNOTE: RIGHTS OF CHILDREN SEMINAR
TOPIC: IGO Operations
CONCEPTS: Diplomatic missions. Privileges and immunities. Funding procedures. Domestic obligation. Subsidiary organ. Internal structure. Inter-agency agreements. UN recommendations.
TREATY REF: 12UNTS46.
PROCEDURE: Amendment.
PARTIES:
Poland
United Nations

106818 Bilateral Exchange **471 UNTS 13**
SIGNED: 28 Dec 62   FORCE: 28 Dec 62
REGISTERED: 16 Jul 63 USA (United States)
ARTICLES: 2 LANGUAGE: English.
HEADNOTE: METEROLOGICAL SATELLITE SYSTEM

TOPIC: Scientific Project
CONCEPTS: Border traffic and migration. General cooperation. Operating agencies. General property. Research and scientific projects. Meteorology. Communication satellites testing. Research and development. Funding procedures. Tax exemptions. Telecommunications.
PROCEDURE: Duration. Renewal or Revival. Termination.
PARTIES:
Canada
USA (United States)

106819 Bilateral Agreement **471 UNTS 25**
SIGNED: 30 Nov 62   FORCE: 30 Nov 62
REGISTERED: 16 Jul 63 USA (United States)
ARTICLES: 5 LANGUAGE: English. Spanish.
HEADNOTE: AGRI COMMOD TITLE IV
TOPIC: US Agri Commod Aid
CONCEPTS: General provisions. Exchange of information and documents. Reexport of goods, etc.. Currency. Payment schedules. Transportation costs. Local currency. Purchase authorization. Commodities schedule. Purchase authorization.
PARTIES:
Dominican Republic
USA (United States)
ANNEX
505 UNTS 332. USA (United States). Amendment 14 Sep 63. Force 14 Sep 63.
505 UNTS 332. Dominican Republic. Amendment 14 Sep 63. Force 14 Sep 63.

106820 Bilateral Exchange **471 UNTS 39**
SIGNED: 9 Oct 62   FORCE: 9 Oct 62
REGISTERED: 16 Jul 63 USA (United States)
ARTICLES: 2 LANGUAGE: English.
HEADNOTE: INTERNATIONAL METEROLOGICAL CENTER
TOPIC: Scientific Project
CONCEPTS: Operating agencies. General cooperation. General property. Education. Teacher and student exchange. Research and scientific projects. Meteorology. Communication satellites testing. Expense sharing formulae. Tax exemptions.
PROCEDURE: Duration. Renewal or Revival. Termination.
PARTIES:
India
USA (United States)
ANNEX
476 UNTS 358. USA (United States). Supplementation 23 Apr 63. Force 23 Apr 63.
476 UNTS 358. India. Supplementation 22 Apr 63. Force 23 Apr 63.

106821 Bilateral Agreement **471 UNTS 49**
SIGNED: 24 Nov 62   FORCE: 24 Nov 62
REGISTERED: 16 Jul 63 USA (United States)
ARTICLES: 6 LANGUAGE: English. Spanish.
HEADNOTE: AGRI COMMOD TITLE I
TOPIC: US Agri Commod Aid
CONCEPTS: General provisions. Annex or appendix reference. Exchange of information and documents. Reexport of goods, etc.. Exchange rates and regulations. Transportation costs. Local currency. Commodities schedule. Purchase authorization. Surplus commodities. Mutual consultation.
PARTIES:
Paraguay
USA (United States)

106822 Bilateral Exchange **471 UNTS 75**
SIGNED: 20 Dec 62   FORCE: 20 Dec 62
REGISTERED: 16 Jul 63 USA (United States)
ARTICLES: 2 LANGUAGE: English. Spanish.
HEADNOTE: FURNISHING DEFENSE ARTICLES SERVICES
TOPIC: Milit Installation
CONCEPTS: Defense and security. Military assistance. Return of equipment and recapture.
INTL ORGS: Organization of American States.
PARTIES:
Peru
USA (United States)

106823 Bilateral Agreement **471 UNTS 83**
SIGNED: 31 Dec 62   FORCE: 31 Dec 62
REGISTERED: 16 Jul 63 USA (United States)
ARTICLES: 1 LANGUAGE: English.
HEADNOTE: SUPPLEMENTARY AGREEMENT GATT
TOPIC: Mostfavored Nation
CONCEPTS: Annex type material. Most favored nation clause.
INTL ORGS: General Agreement on Tariffs and Trade.
TREATY REF: 55UNTS187; 471UNTS84-FN__3; 471UNTS296-FN__1.
PARTIES:
Japan
USA (United States)

106824 Bilateral Agreement **471 UNTS 91**
SIGNED: 10 Dec 62   FORCE: 10 Dec 62
REGISTERED: 16 Jul 63 USA (United States)
ARTICLES: 1 LANGUAGE: English.
HEADNOTE: SUPPLEMENTARY AGREEMENT GATT
TOPIC: Mostfavored Nation
CONCEPTS: Annex type material. General trade.
INTL ORGS: General Agreement on Tariffs and Trade.
TREATY REF: 55UNTS187; 471UNTS296 FN 1; 471UNTS84 FN__3.
PARTIES:
UK Great Britain
USA (United States)

106825 Bilateral Agreement **471 UNTS 99**
SIGNED: 31 Dec 62   FORCE: 31 Dec 62
REGISTERED: 16 Jul 63 USA (United States)
ARTICLES: 1 LANGUAGE: English. French. Spanish.
HEADNOTE: INTERIM AGREEMENT TRADE TARIFFS
TOPIC: Commodity Trade
CONCEPTS: Annex or appendix reference. General cooperation. General trade. Tariffs.
INTL ORGS: General Agreement on Tariffs and Trade.
TREATY REF: GATT; 62UNTS34.
PROCEDURE: Amendment. Termination.
PARTIES:
Spain
USA (United States)

106826 Bilateral Exchange **471 UNTS 119**
SIGNED: 4 Jan 63   FORCE: 4 Jan 63
REGISTERED: 17 Jul 63 USA (United States)
ARTICLES: 2 LANGUAGE: English.
HEADNOTE: INVESTMENT GUARANTIES
TOPIC: Finance
CONCEPTS: Previous treaty amendment. General cooperation. Arbitration. Procedure. Existing tribunals. Negotiation. Reciprocity in financial treatment. Payment schedules. Claims and settlements. Private investment guarantee.
TREATY REF: 22UNTS263.
PARTIES:
Jamaica
USA (United States)

106827 Bilateral Exchange **471 UNTS 127**
SIGNED: 11 Jan 63   FORCE: 11 Jan 63
REGISTERED: 17 Jul 63 USA (United States)
ARTICLES: 2 LANGUAGE: English.
HEADNOTE: WAIVER FINGERPRINTING NON-IMMIGRANT VISAS
TOPIC: Visas
CONCEPTS: General cooperation.
PARTIES:
Cyprus
USA (United States)

106828 Bilateral Exchange **471 UNTS 133**
SIGNED: 16 Jan 63   FORCE: 16 Jan 63
REGISTERED: 17 Jul 63 USA (United States)
ARTICLES: 2 LANGUAGE: English.
HEADNOTE: VELLES LOAN
TOPIC: Milit Assistance
CONCEPTS: Time limit. Responsibility and liability. Title and deeds. Compensation. Delivery schedules. Lease of military property. Naval vessels.

Return of equipment and recapture. Restrictions on transfer.
TREATY REF: 202UNTS301.
PARTIES:
Pakistan
USA (United States)

106829 Bilateral Exchange **471 UNTS 141**
SIGNED: 15 Jan 63   FORCE: 15 Jan 63
REGISTERED: 17 Jul 63 USA (United States)
ARTICLES: 2 LANGUAGE: English.
HEADNOTE: INVESTMENT GUARANTIES
TOPIC: Finance
CONCEPTS: Previous treaty amendment. Conformity with municipal law. General cooperation. General property. Arbitration. Procedure. Existing tribunals. Negotiation. Reciprocity in financial treatment. Currency. Private investment guarantee.
INTL ORGS: International Court of Justice.
TREATY REF: 22UNTS263.
PARTIES:
Trinidad/Tobago
USA (United States)

106830 Bilateral Exchange **471 UNTS 151**
SIGNED: 21 Jan 63   FORCE: 21 Jan 63
REGISTERED: 17 Jul 63 USA (United States)
ARTICLES: 2 LANGUAGE: English. Polish.
HEADNOTE: WAIVER VISA FEES PERFORMING ARTISTS GROUPS
TOPIC: Visas
CONCEPTS: Visas. Fees and exemptions.
PARTIES:
Poland
USA (United States)

106831 Multilateral Agreement **471 UNTS 158**
SIGNED: 23 Jul 63   FORCE: 23 Jul 63
REGISTERED: 23 Jul 63 United Nations
ARTICLES: 6 LANGUAGE: English. Spanish.
HEADNOTE: TECHNICAL ASSISTANCE
TOPIC: Tech Assistance
CONCEPTS: Definition of terms. Privileges and immunities. General cooperation. Exchange of information and documents. Personnel. Responsibility and liability. Title and deeds. Use of facilities. Exchange. Scholarships and grants. Vocational training. Research and development. Exchange rates and regulations. Expense sharing formulae. Commodities and services. General technical assistance. Materials, equipment and services. IGO status. Conformity with IGO decisions.
TREATY REF: 76UNTS132; 1UNTS15; 33UNTS261; 374UNTS147.
PROCEDURE: Amendment. Termination.
PARTIES:
Mexico SIGNED: 23 Jul 63 FORCE: 23 Jul 63
FAO (Food Agri) SIGNED: 23 Jul 63 FORCE: 23 Jul 63
IAEA (Atom Energy) SIGNED: 23 Jul 63 FORCE: 23 Jul 63
ICAO (Civil Aviat) SIGNED: 23 Jul 63 FORCE: 23 Jul 63
ILO (Labor Org) SIGNED: 23 Jul 63 FORCE: 23 Jul 63
ITU (Telecommun) SIGNED: 23 Jul 63 FORCE: 23 Jul 63
UNESCO (Educ/Cult) SIGNED: 23 Jul 63 FORCE: 23 Jul 63
United Nations SIGNED: 23 Jul 63 FORCE: 23 Jul 63
UPU (Postal Union) SIGNED: 23 Jul 63 FORCE: 23 Jul 63
WHO (World Health) SIGNED: 23 Jul 63 FORCE: 23 Jul 63
WMO (Meteorology) SIGNED: 23 Jul 63 FORCE: 23 Jul 63
ANNEX
643 UNTS 397. UNTAB (Tech Assis). Amendment 31 Jul 68. Force 28 Aug 68.
643 UNTS 397. Mexico. Amendment 28 Aug 62. Force 28 Aug 68.

106832 Bilateral Agreement **471 UNTS 181**
SIGNED: 1 Dec 62   FORCE: 6 Feb 63
REGISTERED: 24 Jul 63 USSR (Soviet Union)
ARTICLES: 8 LANGUAGE: Russian. Laotian. French.

HEADNOTE: PAYMENTS
TOPIC: Finance
CONCEPTS: Accounting procedures. Banking. Currency. Exchange rates and regulations. Fees and exemptions. Interest rates. Payment schedules.
PROCEDURE: Ratification.
PARTIES:
Laos
USSR (Soviet Union)

106833 Bilateral Treaty **471 UNTS 195**
SIGNED: 24 Feb 62   FORCE: 26 May 63
REGISTERED: 24 Jul 63 USSR (Soviet Union)
ARTICLES: 78 LANGUAGE: Russian. Serbo-Croat.
HEADNOTE: LEGAL ASSISTANCE CIVIL FAMILY CRIMINAL CASES
TOPIC: Admin Cooperation
CONCEPTS: Exceptions and exemptions. General provisions. Privileges and immunities. Protection of nationals. Consular functions in property. Extradition, deportation and repatriation. Extraditable offenses. Refusal of extradition. Concurrent requests. Limits of prosecution. Provisional detainment. Extradition postponement. Material evidence. Family law. Exchange of information and documents. Informational records. Juridical personality. Legal protection and assistance. Recognition and enforcement of legal decisions. Succession. Recognition of legal documents. Procedure. Indemnities and reimbursements. Assets transfer.
PROCEDURE: Ratification. Termination.
PARTIES:
USSR (Soviet Union)
Yugoslavia

106834 Bilateral Agreement **472 UNTS 3**
SIGNED: 1 Dec 62   FORCE: 1 Dec 62
REGISTERED: 24 Jul 63 USSR (Soviet Union)
ARTICLES: 11 LANGUAGE: Russian. French.
HEADNOTE: ECONOMIC TECHNICAL ASSISTANCE
TOPIC: Direct Aid
CONCEPTS: Treaty implementation. Personnel. Vocational training. Accounting procedures. Indemnities and reimbursements. Currency. Interest rates. Domestic obligation. General technical assistance. General aid. Materials, equipment and services. Loan and credit. Loan repayment. Hydro-electric power.
TREATY REF: 458UNTS21; 471UNTS7.
PROCEDURE: Ratification.
PARTIES:
Laos
USSR (Soviet Union)

106835 Bilateral Agreement **472 UNTS 19**
SIGNED: 23 Jun 62   FORCE: 1 Jan 63
REGISTERED: 24 Jul 63 USSR (Soviet Union)
ARTICLES: 14 LANGUAGE: Russian. Arabic.
HEADNOTE: PAYMENTS
TOPIC: Finance
CONCEPTS: Detailed regulations. Treaty implementation. Conformity with municipal law. General cooperation. Accounting procedures. Banking. Currency. Monetary and gold transfers. Exchange rates and regulations. Fees and exemptions. Inadequacy of funds. Interest rates. Payment schedules. Assets transfer. Most favored nation clause. Loan and credit. Credit provisions.
PROCEDURE: Ratification.
PARTIES:
United Arab Rep
USSR (Soviet Union)

106836 Bilateral Agreement **472 UNTS 43**
SIGNED: 23 Jun 62   FORCE: 1 Jan 63
REGISTERED: 24 Jul 63 USSR (Soviet Union)
ARTICLES: 20 LANGUAGE: Russian. Arabic.
HEADNOTE: TRADE
TOPIC: General Trade
CONCEPTS: Treaty implementation. Annex or appendix reference. Previous treaty replacement.

General cooperation. Licenses and permits. Use of facilities. Establishment of commission. Export quotas. Reexport of goods, etc.. Trade agencies. Trade procedures. Banking. Payment schedules. Non-interest rates and fees. Delivery guarantees. Delivery schedules. Smuggling. Most favored nation clause. Customs exemptions.
TREATY REF: 472UNTS19.
PROCEDURE: Amendment. Denunciation. Ratification. Renewal or Revival.
PARTIES:
United Arab Rep
USSR (Soviet Union)

106837 Multilateral Agreement **472 UNTS 95**
SIGNED: 7 Jun 63   FORCE: 7 Jun 63
REGISTERED: 24 Jul 63 USA (United States)
ARTICLES: 4 LANGUAGE: Russian. German. Polish.
HEADNOTE: LOAD LINE AGREEMENT
TOPIC: Water Transport
CONCEPTS: Exceptions and exemptions. Navigational conditions. Ports and pilotage.
TREATY REF: 135LTS301.
PROCEDURE: Denunciation. Registration.
PARTIES:
Germany, West SIGNED: 7 Jun 63 FORCE: 7 Jun 63
Poland SIGNED: 7 Jun 63 FORCE: 7 Jun 63
USSR (Soviet Union) SIGNED: 7 Jun 63 FORCE: 7 Jun 63

106838 Bilateral Agreement **472 UNTS 157**
SIGNED: 6 Jun 63   FORCE: 1 Jul 63
REGISTERED: 25 Jul 63 Australia
ARTICLES: 7 LANGUAGE: English.
HEADNOTE: MEDICAL TREATMENT
TOPIC: Sanitation
CONCEPTS: Conditions. Definition of terms. Territorial application. General cooperation. Domestic legislation. Personnel. Public health. Accounting procedures. Indemnities and reimbursements. Currency. Financial programs. Funding procedures.
PROCEDURE: Amendment. Duration. Termination.
PARTIES:
Australia
UK Great Britain

106839 Bilateral Instrument **472 UNTS 163**
SIGNED: 20 Jun 63   FORCE: 20 Jun 63
REGISTERED: 29 Jul 63 USSR (Soviet Union)
ARTICLES: 1 LANGUAGE: Russian. English.
HEADNOTE: ESTABLISHMENT DIRECT COMMUNICATION LINK
TOPIC: Specif Goods/Equip
CONCEPTS: Annex or appendix reference. Communications linkage.
PARTIES:
USA (United States)
USSR (Soviet Union)

106840 Bilateral Agreement **472 UNTS 173**
SIGNED: 26 Jul 63   FORCE: 26 Jul 63
REGISTERED: 29 Jul 63 United Nations
ARTICLES: 7 LANGUAGE: English.
HEADNOTE: TRAVEL & TOURISM CONFERENCE
TOPIC: IGO Operations
CONCEPTS: Diplomatic privileges. Diplomatic missions. Privileges and immunities. Funding procedures. Domestic obligation. Special status. Conferences.
TREATY REF: 1UNTS15.
PARTIES:
Italy
United Nations

106841 Multilateral Convention **472 UNTS 185**
SIGNED: 20 Apr 59   FORCE: 12 Jun 62
REGISTERED: 30 Jul 63 Council of Europe
ARTICLES: 30 LANGUAGE: English. French.
HEADNOTE: MUTUAL ASSISTANCE CRIMINAL MATTERS
TOPIC: Admin Cooperation
CONCEPTS: Exceptions and exemptions. Territorial application. General provisions. Treaty implementation. Previous treaty replacement. Material evidence. Exchange of information and

documents. Informational records. Recognition of legal documents.
INTL ORGS: Council of Europe.
PROCEDURE: Accession. Denunciation. Ratification.
PARTIES:
Austria SIGNED: 20 Apr 59
Belgium SIGNED: 20 Apr 59
Denmark SIGNED: 20 Apr 59 RATIFIED: 13 Sep 62 FORCE: 12 Dec 62
France SIGNED: 28 Apr 61
Germany, West SIGNED: 20 Apr 59
Greece SIGNED: 20 Apr 59 RATIFIED: 23 Feb 62 FORCE: 12 Jun 62
Italy SIGNED: 20 Apr 59 RATIFIED: 23 Aug 61 FORCE: 12 Jun 62
Luxembourg SIGNED: 20 Apr 59
Norway SIGNED: 21 Apr 61 RATIFIED: 14 Mar 62 FORCE: 12 Jun 62
Sweden SIGNED: 20 Apr 59
Turkey SIGNED: 23 Oct 59
ANNEX
635 UNTS 358. Israel. Qualified Accession 27 Sep 67. Force 26 Dec 67.
648 UNTS 374. Austria. Ratification 2 Oct 68. Force 31 Dec 68.

106842 Multilateral Agreement **472 UNTS 220**
SIGNED: 31 Jul 63 FORCE: 31 Jul 63
REGISTERED: 31 Jul 63 United Nations
ARTICLES: 6 LANGUAGE: English. Spanish.
HEADNOTE: TECHNICAL ASSISTANCE
TOPIC: Tech Assistance
CONCEPTS: Definition of terms. Visas. Privileges and immunities. General cooperation. Exchange of information and documents. Licenses and permits. Personnel. Responsibility and liability. Title and deeds. Use of facilities. Exchange. Scholarships and grants. Vocational training. Research and development. Import quotas. Exchange rates and regulations. Expense sharing formulae. Local currency. Domestic obligation. General technical assistance. Materials, equipment and services. IGO status. Conformity with IGO decisions.
TREATY REF: 76UNTS32; 33UNTS261; 1UNTS15; 374UNTS147.
PARTIES:
El Salvador SIGNED: 31 Jul 63 FORCE: 31 Jul 63
FAO (Food Agri) SIGNED: 31 Jul 63 FORCE: 31 Jul 63
IAEA (Atom Energy) SIGNED: 31 Jul 63 FORCE: 31 Jul 63
ICAO (Civil Aviat) SIGNED: 31 Jul 63 FORCE: 31 Jul 63
ILO (Labor Org) SIGNED: 31 Jul 63 FORCE: 31 Jul 63
ITU (Telecommun) SIGNED: 31 Jul 63 FORCE: 31 Jul 63
UNESCO (Educ/Cult) SIGNED: 31 Jul 63 FORCE: 31 Jul 63
United Nations SIGNED: 31 Jul 63 FORCE: 31 Jul 63
UPU (Postal Union) SIGNED: 31 Jul 63 FORCE: 31 Jul 63
WHO (World Health) SIGNED: 31 Jul 63 FORCE: 31 Jul 63
WMO (Meteorology) SIGNED: 31 Jul 63 FORCE: 31 Jul 63

106843 Bilateral Convention **472 UNTS 245**
SIGNED: 24 Dec 60 FORCE: 1 Aug 61
REGISTERED: 1 Aug 63 Romania
ARTICLES: 18 LANGUAGE: Romanian. Russian.
HEADNOTE: COOPERATION FIELD SOCIAL SECURITY
TOPIC: Admin Cooperation
CONCEPTS: General provisions. General cooperation. Social security.
PROCEDURE: Denunciation. Duration. Ratification.
PARTIES:
Romania
USSR (Soviet Union)

106844 Bilateral Convention **472 UNTS 279**
SIGNED: 14 Mar 60 FORCE: 31 May 60
REGISTERED: 1 Aug 63 Romania
ARTICLES: 14 LANGUAGE: Romanian. Bulgarian.
HEADNOTE: COOPERATION FIELD SOCIAL PROBLEMS

TOPIC: Admin Cooperation
CONCEPTS: Conformity with municipal law. Procedure. Sickness and invalidity insurance. Social security.
PROCEDURE: Denunciation. Duration. Ratification.
PARTIES:
Bulgaria
Romania

106845 Bilateral Convention **472 UNTS 305**
SIGNED: 8 Nov 62 FORCE: 18 Jul 63
REGISTERED: 1 Aug 63 Romania
ARTICLES: 27 LANGUAGE: Romanian. Serbo-Croat.
HEADNOTE: CONSULAR
TOPIC: Consul/Citizenship
CONCEPTS: Definition of terms. General provisions. General consular functions. Diplomatic privileges. Consular relations establishment. Inviolability. Privileges and immunities. Diplomatic correspondence. Responsibility and liability.
PROCEDURE: Ratification. Termination.
PARTIES:
Romania
Yugoslavia

106846 Bilateral Agreement **472 UNTS 345**
SIGNED: 5 Jun 63 FORCE: 4 Aug 63
REGISTERED: 4 Aug 63 Finland
ARTICLES: 4 LANGUAGE: Finnish. English.
HEADNOTE: RECOGNITION TONNAGE CERTIFICATES MERCHANT SHIPS
TOPIC: Water Transport
CONCEPTS: Previous treaty replacement. Recognition of legal documents. Registration certificate. Merchant vessels. Tonnage.
TREATY REF: 28LTS512.
PROCEDURE: Termination.
PARTIES:
Canada
Finland

106847 Bilateral Agreement **472 UNTS 353**
SIGNED: 5 Aug 63 FORCE: 5 Aug 63
REGISTERED: 5 Aug 63 United Nations
ARTICLES: 6 LANGUAGE: Spanish.
HEADNOTE: PERSONNEL
TOPIC: IGO Status/Immunit
CONCEPTS: General consular functions. Diplomatic privileges. Diplomatic missions. Privileges and immunities. Arbitration. Procedure. Status of experts.
INTL ORGS: Permanent Court of Arbitration. Arbitration Commission.
TREATY REF: 319UNTS14.
PROCEDURE: Amendment. Termination.
PARTIES:
Dominican Republic
United Nations

106848 Bilateral Agreement **472 UNTS 373**
SIGNED: 21 Jun 63 FORCE: 11 Jul 63
REGISTERED: 5 Aug 63 WHO (World Health)
ARTICLES: 6 LANGUAGE: English.
HEADNOTE: TECHNICAL ADVISORY ASSISTANCE
TOPIC: Tech Assistance
CONCEPTS: Definition of terms. Privileges and immunities. General cooperation. Exchange of information and documents. Personnel. Responsibility and liability. Title and deeds. Exchange. Scholarships and grants. Vocational training. Research and development. Expense sharing formulae. Local currency. Domestic obligation. Special projects. Materials, equipment and services. IGO status. Conformity with IGO decisions.
TREATY REF: 33UNTS261.
PROCEDURE: Amendment. Termination.
PARTIES:
Mongolia
WHO (World Health)

106849 Bilateral Instrument **473 UNTS 3**
SIGNED: 22 Jan 63 FORCE: 22 Jan 63
REGISTERED: 6 Aug 63 USA (United States)
ARTICLES: 10 LANGUAGE: English. French.
HEADNOTE: COMPROMISE ARBITRATION RELATING 27 MAR 46 AGREEMENT
TOPIC: Dispute Settlement
CONCEPTS: Annex type material.

INTL ORGS: International Civil Aviation Organization. International Court of Justice. Arbitration Commission.
PARTIES:
France
USA (United States)

106850 Bilateral Agreement **473 UNTS 15**
SIGNED: 28 Jan 63 FORCE: 28 Jan 63
REGISTERED: 6 Aug 63 USA (United States)
ARTICLES: 11 LANGUAGE: English.
HEADNOTE: EDUCATION PROGRAM
TOPIC: Education
CONCEPTS: Definition of terms. Friendship and amity. Standardization. Conformity with municipal law. General cooperation. Exchange of information and documents. Inspection and observation. Personnel. General property. Exchange. Commissions and foundations. Scholarships and grants. Accounting procedures. Currency. Expense sharing formulae. Financial programs. Funding procedures. Special status.
INTL ORGS: Special Commission.
PROCEDURE: Amendment.
PARTIES:
Malaysia
USA (United States)

106851 Bilateral Agreement **473 UNTS 27**
SIGNED: 25 Jan 63 FORCE: 25 Jan 63
REGISTERED: 6 Aug 63 USA (United States)
ARTICLES: 10 LANGUAGE: English.
HEADNOTE: AERIAL PHOTOGRAPHY MAPPING
TOPIC: Scientific Project
CONCEPTS: General cooperation. Operating agencies. Use of facilities. Vocational training. Research and scientific projects. Scientific exchange. Research and development. Indemnities and reimbursements. Materials, equipment and services. Security of information.
PROCEDURE: Duration. Termination.
PARTIES:
Ethiopia
USA (United States)

106852 Bilateral Exchange **473 UNTS 37**
SIGNED: 1 Feb 63 FORCE: 1 Feb 63
REGISTERED: 6 Aug 63 USA (United States)
ARTICLES: 2 LANGUAGE: English.
HEADNOTE: RADIATION MEDICAL CENTER
TOPIC: Scientific Project
CONCEPTS: Responsibility and liability. Public health. Research and scientific projects. Research results. Nuclear research. Research and development. Funding procedures. Transportation costs. Special projects. Materials, equipment and services. General.
TREATY REF: 21UNTS77.
PARTIES:
India
USA (United States)

106853 Bilateral Exchange **473 UNTS 43**
SIGNED: 11 Jan 63 FORCE: 15 Jan 63
REGISTERED: 6 Aug 63 USA (United States)
ARTICLES: 2 LANGUAGE: English.
HEADNOTE: RELINQUISHMENT RADIO TRANSMITTING FACILITY
TOPIC: Specific Resources
CONCEPTS: Facilities and equipment. Return of equipment and recapture. Military installations and equipment. Facilities and property.
TREATY REF: 43UNTS271.
PARTIES:
Philippines
USA (United States)

106854 Bilateral Exchange **473 UNTS 49**
SIGNED: 1 Feb 63 FORCE: 1 Feb 63
REGISTERED: 7 Aug 63 USA (United States)
ARTICLES: 2 LANGUAGE: English.
HEADNOTE: CERTIFICATES AIRWORTHINESS
TOPIC: Air Transport
CONCEPTS: Conformity with municipal law. Exchange of information and documents. Recognition of legal documents. Export quotas. Registration certificate. Airworthiness certificates.
PROCEDURE: Termination. Application to Non-self-governing Territories.

PARTIES:
Japan
USA (United States)

106855 Bilateral Exchange **473 UNTS 57**
SIGNED: 25 Jan 62 FORCE: 25 Jan 62
REGISTERED: 7 Aug 63 USA (United States)
ARTICLES: 2 LANGUAGE: English. Spanish.
HEADNOTE: PEACE CORPS PROGRAM
TOPIC: Tech Assistance
CONCEPTS: Diplomatic privileges. Conformity with municipal law. General cooperation. Personnel. Fees and exemptions. Tax exemptions. Customs exemptions. Domestic obligation. Materials, equipment and services. Aid missions. Volunteer programs.
PROCEDURE: Termination.
PARTIES:
Peru
USA (United States)

106856 Bilateral Agreement **473 UNTS 65**
SIGNED: 4 Feb 63 FORCE: 4 Feb 63
REGISTERED: 7 Aug 63 USA (United States)
ARTICLES: 5 LANGUAGE: English. Spanish.
HEADNOTE: AGRI COMMOD TITLE IV
TOPIC: US Agri Commod Aid
CONCEPTS: General provisions. Exchange of information and documents. Currency. Payment schedules. Local currency. Purchase authorization. Commodities schedule. Purchase authorization. Merchant vessels. Mutual consultation.
PARTIES:
Bolivia
USA (United States)
ANNEX
494 UNTS 346. Bolivia. Amendment 24 Jun 63. Force 24 Jun 63.
494 UNTS 346. USA (United States). Amendment 24 Jun 63. Force 24 Jun 63.
494 UNTS 349. USA (United States). Amendment 20 Nov 63. Force 28 Nov 63.
494 UNTS 349. Bolivia. Amendment 20 Nov 63. Force 28 Nov 63.
526 UNTS 343. Bolivia. Amendment 27 Apr 64. Force 27 Apr 64.
526 UNTS 343. USA (United States). Amendment 27 Apr 64. Force 27 Apr 64.

106857 Bilateral Exchange **473 UNTS 83**
SIGNED: 10 Feb 63 FORCE: 10 Feb 63
REGISTERED: 7 Aug 63 USA (United States)
ARTICLES: 2 LANGUAGE: English. French.
HEADNOTE: ECONOMIC TECHNICAL RELATED ASSISTANCE
TOPIC: Direct Aid
CONCEPTS: Change of circumstances. Diplomatic privileges. Privileges and immunities. Conformity with municipal law. Exchange of information and documents. Inspection and observation. Operating agencies. Personnel. Accounting procedures. Attachment of funds. Currency deposits. Exchange rates and regulations. Funding procedures. Garnishment of funds. Seizure funds. Local currency. Tax exemptions. Customs exemptions. Commodities and services. Domestic obligation. General technical assistance. Economic assistance. Materials, equipment and services. Grants.
PROCEDURE: Termination.
PARTIES:
Central Afri Rep
USA (United States)

106858 Bilateral Agreement **473 UNTS 93**
SIGNED: 6 Feb 63 FORCE: 6 Feb 63
REGISTERED: 7 Aug 63 USA (United States)
ARTICLES: 6 LANGUAGE: English.
HEADNOTE: AGRI COMMOD TITLE I
TOPIC: US Agri Commod Aid
CONCEPTS: General provisions. Annex or appendix reference. Exchange of information and documents. Free trade. Exchange rates and regulations. Transportation costs. Local currency. Commodities schedule. Purchase authorization. Surplus commodities.
TREATY REF: 191UNTS59.
PARTIES:
Iceland
USA (United States)

106859 Bilateral Exchange **473 UNTS 107**
SIGNED: 19 Feb 63 FORCE: 19 Feb 63
REGISTERED: 7 Aug 63 USA (United States)
ARTICLES: 2 LANGUAGE: English. Japanese.
HEADNOTE: SETTLEMENT POSTWAR ECONOMIC ASSISTANCE
TOPIC: Direct Aid
CONCEPTS: Payment schedules. Economic assistance.
TREATY REF: 451UNTS97.
PARTIES:
Japan
USA (United States)

106860 Bilateral Agreement **473 UNTS 117**
SIGNED: 29 Aug 60 FORCE: 6 Dec 60
REGISTERED: 8 Aug 63 Cuba
ARTICLES: 10 LANGUAGE: Spanish. Korean.
HEADNOTE: CULTURAL
TOPIC: Culture
CONCEPTS: Treaty implementation. Friendship and amity. Non-diplomatic delegations. Exchange. Teacher and student exchange. Exchange. General cultural cooperation. Artists. Athletes. Scientific exchange. Publications exchange. Mass media exchange. Press and wire services.
PROCEDURE: Amendment. Ratification. Termination.
PARTIES:
Cuba
Korea, North

106861 Multilateral Convention **473 UNTS 131**
SIGNED: 6 Oct 60 FORCE: 15 Mar 62
REGISTERED: 8 Aug 63 Customs Coop Coun
ARTICLES: 22 LANGUAGE: French. English.
HEADNOTE: CUSTOMS CONVENTION PACKINGS
TOPIC: Customs
CONCEPTS: Definition of terms. Territorial application. Negotiation. Temporary importation.
INTL ORGS: Customs Co-operation Council. General Agreement on Tariffs and Trade. United Nations.
PROCEDURE: Amendment. Accession. Denunciation. Duration. Ratification. Registration.
PARTIES:
Austria SIGNED: 7 Dec 60 RATIFIED: 9 Mar 62 FORCE: 10 Jun 62
Belgium SIGNED: 6 Oct 60 RATIFIED: 27 Jun 63 FORCE: 28 Sep 63
Cambodia RATIFIED: 20 Feb 63 FORCE: 21 May 63
Central Afri Rep RATIFIED: 23 Feb 62 FORCE: 24 May 62
Cuba SIGNED: 28 Mar 61
Czechoslovakia RATIFIED: 4 May 62 FORCE: 5 Aug 62
France SIGNED: 26 Jan 61 FORCE: 15 Mar 62
Germany, West SIGNED: 7 Dec 60
Italy SIGNED: 22 Mar 61 RATIFIED: 30 May 63 FORCE: 31 Aug 63
Luxembourg SIGNED: 10 Feb 61
Sweden SIGNED: 21 Mar 61 FORCE: 15 Mar 62
Switzerland SIGNED: 31 Mar 61 RATIFIED: 30 Apr 63 FORCE: 31 Jul 63
ANNEX
483 UNTS 391. Cuba. Qualified Ratification 31 Oct 63. Force 1 Feb 64.
500 UNTS 331. Luxembourg. Ratification 12 May 64. Force 13 Aug 64.
526 UNTS 349. Spain. Qualified Accession 8 Jan 65. Force 9 Apr 65.
535 UNTS 447. Finland. Accession 23 Apr 65. Force 24 Jul 65.
541 UNTS 351. Poland. Qualified Accession 29 Jun 65. Force 30 Sep 65.
547 UNTS 355. Ireland. Accession 15 Sep 65. Force 16 Dec 65.
552 UNTS 420. Turkey. Ratification 27 Dec 65. Force 28 Mar 66.
638 UNTS 294. Iran. Accession 16 Apr 68. Force 16 Jul 68.

106862 Multilateral Convention **473 UNTS 153**
SIGNED: 8 Jun 61 FORCE: 1 Jul 62
REGISTERED: 8 Aug 63 Customs Coop Coun
ARTICLES: 22 LANGUAGE: French. English.
HEADNOTE: CUSTOMS CONVENTION
TOPIC: Customs
CONCEPTS: Definition of terms. Territorial applica-

tion. Annex or appendix reference. Responsibility and liability. Negotiation. Customs duties. Temporary importation.
INTL ORGS: Customs Co-operation Council. General Agreement on Tariffs and Trade. United Nations Educational, Scientific and Cultural Organization. United Nations.
TREATY REF: 157UNTS129.
PROCEDURE: Amendment. Accession. Denunciation. Duration. Ratification. Registration.
PARTIES:
Austria SIGNED: 30 Oct 61 RATIFIED: 5 Oct 62 FORCE: 6 Jan 63
Central Afri Rep RATIFIED: 1 Apr 62 FORCE: 2 Jul 62
Cuba SIGNED: 28 Feb 62 RATIFIED: 3 Dec 62 FORCE: 4 Mar 63
Czechoslovakia SIGNED: 28 Mar 62 FORCE: 1 Jul 62
Denmark SIGNED: 27 Mar 62
France SIGNED: 31 Mar 62 FORCE: 1 Jul 62
Germany, West SIGNED: 8 Mar 62
Hungary RATIFIED: 4 Feb 63 FORCE: 5 May 63
Iran SIGNED: 16 Feb 62
Italy SIGNED: 7 Dec 61
Madagascar RATIFIED: 12 Apr 62 FORCE: 13 Jul 62
Niger SIGNED: 14 Mar 62 FORCE: 1 Jul 62
Norway SIGNED: 30 Mar 62 FORCE: 1 Jul 62
Portugal SIGNED: 15 Mar 62 FORCE: 1 Jul 62
Spain SIGNED: 21 Feb 62 RATIFIED: 11 Feb 62 FORCE: 12 May 63
Sweden SIGNED: 30 Mar 62
Switzerland SIGNED: 7 Dec 61 RATIFIED: 30 Apr 63 FORCE: 31 Jul 63
Turkey SIGNED: 31 Mar 62
UK Great Britain Guernsey Island RATIFIED: 25 Mar 63 FORCE: 26 Jun 63
UK Great Britain Isle of Man RATIFIED: 25 Mar 63 FORCE: 26 Jun 63
UK Great Britain Jersey Island RATIFIED: 25 Mar 63 FORCE: 26 Jun 63
UK Great Britain SIGNED: 27 Feb 62 RATIFIED: 25 Mar 63 FORCE: 26 Jun 63
ANNEX
480 UNTS 448. Italy. Ratification 20 Sep 63. Force 21 Dec 63.
482 UNTS 393. Yugoslavia. Accession 5 Nov 63. Force 6 Feb 64.
489 UNTS 404. Netherlands. Netherlands Antilles. Force 18 Apr 64.
489 UNTS 404. Netherlands. Accession 17 Jan 64. Force 18 Apr 64.
489 UNTS 404. Netherlands. Surinam. Force 18 Apr 64.
494 UNTS 356. Sweden. Ratification 19 Mar 64. Force 20 Jun 64.
510 UNTS 337. Bulgaria. Accession 31 Jul 64. Force 1 Nov 64.
510 UNTS 337. Finland. Accession 1 Aug 64.
535 UNTS 448. Denmark. Ratification 14 Apr 65. Force 15 Jul 65.
535 UNTS 448. Ireland. Accession 15 Apr 65. Force 16 Jul 65.
547 UNTS 356. Belgium. Accession 7 Sep 65. Force 8 Dec 65.
555 UNTS 259. Luxembourg. Accession 28 Jan 66.
559 UNTS 355. Israel. Accession 1 Feb 66. Force 1 Mar 66.
619 UNTS 339. Australia. Accession 4 Dec 67. Force 4 Mar 68.
636 UNTS 369. Romania. Qualified Accession 26 Mar 68.
638 UNTS 295. Iran. Ratification 16 Apr 68. Force 16 Jul 68.

106863 Multilateral Convention **473 UNTS 187**
SIGNED: 8 Jun 61 FORCE: 13 Jul 62
REGISTERED: 8 Aug 63 Customs Coop Coun
ARTICLES: 25 LANGUAGE: French. English.
HEADNOTE: FACILITIES IMPORTATION GOODS CUSTOMS CONVENTION
TOPIC: Customs
CONCEPTS: Definition of terms. Investigation of violations. Negotiation. Import quotas. Temporary importation.
INTL ORGS: Customs Co-operation Council. United Nations Educational, Scientific and Cultural Organization. United Nations.
PROCEDURE: Amendment. Accession. Denunciation. Duration. Ratification. Registration.

PARTIES:
Australia SIGNED: 27 Mar 62 RATIFIED: 20 Dec 62 FORCE: 21 Mar 63
Austria SIGNED: 30 Oct 61 RATIFIED: 20 Sep 62 FORCE: 21 Dec 62
Cambodia RATIFIED: 20 Feb 63 FORCE: 21 May 63
Central Afri Rep RATIFIED: 1 Apr 62 FORCE: 13 Jul 62
Cuba SIGNED: 28 Feb 62 RATIFIED: 2 May 62 FORCE: 3 Aug 62
Czechoslovakia SIGNED: 28 Mar 62 FORCE: 13 Jul 62
Denmark SIGNED: 27 Mar 62
France SIGNED: 31 Mar 62
Germany, West SIGNED: 8 Mar 62
Hungary RATIFIED: 4 Feb 63 FORCE: 15 May 63
Iran SIGNED: 31 Mar 62
Italy SIGNED: 7 Dec 61
Madagascar RATIFIED: 12 Apr 62 FORCE: 13 Jul 62
Morocco RATIFIED: 16 Nov 62 FORCE: 17 Feb 63
Niger SIGNED: 14 Mar 62 FORCE: 13 Jul 62
Portugal SIGNED: 31 Mar 62 FORCE: 13 Jul 62
Spain SIGNED: 21 Feb 62 RATIFIED: 11 Feb 62 FORCE: 2 May 63
Sweden SIGNED: 30 Mar 62
Switzerland SIGNED: 7 Dec 61 RATIFIED: 30 Apr 63 FORCE: 31 Jul 63
Turkey SIGNED: 31 Mar 62
UK Great Britain Guernsey Island RATIFIED: 25 Mar 63 FORCE: 26 Jun 63
UK Great Britain Isle of Man RATIFIED: 25 Mar 63 FORCE: 26 Jun 63
UK Great Britain Jersey Island RATIFIED: 25 Mar 63 FORCE: 26 Jun 63
UK Great Britain SIGNED: 27 Feb 62 RATIFIED: 25 Mar 63 FORCE: 26 Jun 63
ANNEX
480 UNTS 450. Norway. Ratification 23 Sep 63. Force 24 Dec 63.
483 UNTS 392. Italy. Qualified Ratification 9 Nov 63. Force 10 Feb 64.
489 UNTS 405. Netherlands. Netherlands Antilles. Force 18 Apr 64.
489 UNTS 405. Netherlands. Accession 17 Jan 64. Force 18 Apr 64.
489 UNTS 405. Netherlands. Surinam. Force 18 Apr 64.
489 UNTS 405. Romania. Accession 15 Jan 64. Force 16 Apr 64.
494 UNTS 376. Sweden. Ratification 19 Mar 64. Force 20 Jun 64.
510 UNTS 338. Finland. Accession 1 Aug 64. Force 2 Nov 64.
510 UNTS 338. France. Ratification 22 Jun 64. Force 23 Sep 64.
510 UNTS 338. Bulgaria. Accession 31 Jul 64. Force 1 Nov 64.
523 UNTS 342. Israel. Accession 16 Dec 64. Force 17 Mar 65.
535 UNTS 449. Ireland. Accession 15 Apr 65. Force 16 Jul 65.
535 UNTS 449. Denmark. Ratification 14 Apr 65. Force 15 Jul 65.
555 UNTS 259. Yugoslavia. Accession 7 Jan 66. Force 8 Apr 66.
600 UNTS 361. Germany, West. Ratification 9 Jun 67. Force 9 Sep 67.
604 UNTS 381. Belgium. Accession 6 Jul 67. Force 6 Oct 67.
633 UNTS 414. Australia. Papua. Force 15 May 68.
633 UNTS 414. Australia. New Guinea. Force 15 May 68.
638 UNTS 296. Iran. Ratification 16 Apr 68. Force 16 Jul 68.

106864 Multilateral Convention **473 UNTS 219**
SIGNED: 6 Dec 61 FORCE: 30 Jul 63
REGISTERED: 8 Aug 63 Customs Coop Coun
ARTICLES: 28 LANGUAGE: English. French.
HEADNOTE: CUSTOMS CONVENTION TEMPORARY ADMISSION GOODS
TOPIC: Customs
CONCEPTS: Definition of terms. Territorial application. Annex or appendix reference. Inspection and observation. Responsibility and liability. Investigation of violations. Temporary importation.
INTL ORGS: Customs Co-operation Council. General Agreement on Tariffs and Trade. United Na-

tions Educational, Scientific and Cultural Organization. United Nations.
PROCEDURE: Amendment. Accession. Denunciation. Duration. Ratification. Registration.
PARTIES:
Australia SIGNED: 26 Jul 62
Austria SIGNED: 5 Jun 62 RATIFIED: 20 May 63 FORCE: 21 Aug 63
Cuba SIGNED: 20 Jul 62
Czechoslovakia RATIFIED: 21 Dec 62 FORCE: 30 Jul 63
Denmark SIGNED: 21 Jun 62
Germany, West SIGNED: 5 Jun 62
Italy SIGNED: 6 Jun 62
Ivory Coast SIGNED: 14 Jun 62 RATIFIED: 1 Jan 63 FORCE: 30 Jul 64
Portugal SIGNED: 30 Jul 62
Spain SIGNED: 11 Jul 62
Sweden SIGNED: 31 Jul 62
Switzerland SIGNED: 6 Jun 62 RATIFIED: 30 Apr 63 FORCE: 30 Jul 63
Tunisia SIGNED: 27 Jul 62
UK Great Britain Guernsey Island RATIFIED: 19 Jul 63 FORCE: 20 Oct 63
UK Great Britain Isle of Man RATIFIED: 19 Jul 63 FORCE: 20 Oct 63
UK Great Britain Jersey Island RATIFIED: 19 Jul 63 FORCE: 20 Oct 63
UK Great Britain SIGNED: 5 Jul 62 RATIFIED: 19 Jul 63 FORCE: 20 Oct 63
ANNEX
480 UNTS 452. Cuba. Ratification 24 Sep 63. Force 25 Dec 63.
489 UNTS 406. Netherlands. Netherlands Antilles. Force 18 Apr 64.
489 UNTS 406. Netherlands. Accession 17 Jan 64. Force 18 Apr 64.
494 UNTS 376. Sweden. Ratification 19 Mar 64. Force 20 Jun 64.
495 UNTS 264. Spain. Ratification 6 Apr 64. Force 7 Jul 64.
510 UNTS 339. Italy. Ratification 19 Jun 64. Force 20 Sep 64.
510 UNTS 339. Finland. Accession 1 Aug 64. Force 2 Nov 64.
510 UNTS 339. Bulgaria. Accession 31 Jul 64. Force 1 Nov 64.
516 UNTS 382. Norway. Accession 29 Oct 64. Force 30 Jan 65.
535 UNTS 450. Denmark. Ratification 14 Apr 65. Force 15 Jul 65.
535 UNTS 450. Ireland. Qualified Accession 15 Apr 65. Force 16 Jul 65.
548 UNTS 371. Germany, West. Ratification 15 Oct 65. Force 16 Jan 66.
552 UNTS 421. Hungary. Accession 22 Nov 65. Force 23 Feb 66.
555 UNTS 260. Germany, West. Berlin. Force 16 Jan 66.
559 UNTS 355. Belgium. Accession 22 Feb 66. Force 22 May 66.
561 UNTS 352. Portugal. Ratification 20 Apr 66. Force 20 Jul 66.
561 UNTS 352. Portugal. Ratification 20 Apr 66. Force 20 Jul 66.
566 UNTS 371. Luxembourg. Accession 10 Jun 66. Force 10 Sep 66.
573 UNTS 340. Israel. Accession 25 Aug 66. Force 25 Nov 66.
600 UNTS 362. Australia. Qualified Ratification 14 Jun 67.
619 UNTS 340. United Arab Rep. Accession 11 Jan 68. Force 11 Apr 68.
638 UNTS 297. Iran. Accession 16 Apr 68. Force 16 Jul 68.

106865 Bilateral Agreement **473 UNTS 281**
SIGNED: 8 Aug 63 FORCE: 8 Aug 63
REGISTERED: 8 Aug 63 United Nations
ARTICLES: 8 LANGUAGE: English.
HEADNOTE: UNICEF ACTIVITIES
TOPIC: IGO Operations
CONCEPTS: Privileges and immunities. Freedom of action. Security of the government. Special status. Inter-agency agreements. Internal travel.
INTL ORGS: United Nations.
TREATY REF: 1UNTS15.
PROCEDURE: Amendment. Termination.
PARTIES:
UNICEF (Children)
Trinidad/Tobago

106866 Bilateral Agreement **473 UNTS 291**
SIGNED: 15 Oct 62 FORCE: 15 Oct 62
REGISTERED: 12 Aug 63 USA (United States)
ARTICLES: 6 LANGUAGE: English. Persian.
HEADNOTE: AGRI COMMOD TITLE I
TOPIC: US Agri Commod Aid
CONCEPTS: General provisions. Annex or appendix reference. Exchange of information and documents. Reexport of goods, etc.. Exchange rates and regulations. Transportation costs. Local currency. Commodities schedule. Purchase authorization. Mutual consultation.
PARTIES:
Iran
USA (United States)

106867 Bilateral Agreement **473 UNTS 311**
SIGNED: 21 Feb 63 FORCE: 21 Feb 63
REGISTERED: 12 Aug 63 USA (United States)
ARTICLES: 6 LANGUAGE: English.
HEADNOTE: AGRI COMMOD TITLE I
TOPIC: US Agri Commod Aid
CONCEPTS: General provisions. Annex or appendix reference. Exchange of information and documents. Reexport of goods, etc.. Exchange rates and regulations. Transportation costs. Local currency. Commodities schedule. Purchase authorization. Surplus commodities. Mutual consultation.
PARTIES:
Turkey
USA (United States)
ANNEX
542 UNTS 392. USA (United States). Amendment 22 Jan 65. Force 22 Jan 65.
542 UNTS 392. Turkey. Amendment 22 Jan 65. Force 22 Jan 65.

106868 Bilateral Treaty **474 UNTS 3**
SIGNED: 23 Feb 62 FORCE: 28 Mar 63
REGISTERED: 12 Aug 63 USA (United States)
ARTICLES: 19 LANGUAGE: English. French.
HEADNOTE: FRIENDSHIP ESTABLISHMENT NAVIGATION
TOPIC: General Amity
CONCEPTS: Definition of terms. Territorial application. Previous treaty replacement. Alien status. Human rights. General cooperation. Juridical personality. Free passage and transit. Legal protection and assistance. General property. Private contracts. Existing tribunals. Balance of payments. Exchange rates and regulations. National treatment. Taxation. Laws and formalities.
INTL ORGS: International Court of Justice.
TREATY REF: 2'23DEMARTENS373;.
PROCEDURE: Duration. Ratification. Termination.
PARTIES:
Luxembourg
USA (United States)

106869 Bilateral Exchange **474 UNTS 31**
SIGNED: 29 Dec 62 FORCE: 29 Dec 62
REGISTERED: 12 Aug 63 USA (United States)
ARTICLES: 2 LANGUAGE: English. Spanish.
HEADNOTE: PEACE CORPS PROGRAM
TOPIC: Tech Assistance
CONCEPTS: Annex type material. Diplomatic privileges. Conformity with municipal law. General cooperation. Personnel. Customs exemptions. Domestic obligation. Materials, equipment and services. Aid missions. Volunteer programs.
TREATY REF: 199UNTS51.
PROCEDURE: Termination.
PARTIES:
Guatemala
USA (United States)

106870 Bilateral Exchange **474 UNTS 41**
SIGNED: 17 Nov 62 FORCE: 17 Nov 62
REGISTERED: 12 Aug 63 USA (United States)
ARTICLES: 2 LANGUAGE: English. French.
HEADNOTE: INVESTMENT GUARANTIES
TOPIC: Finance
CONCEPTS: General cooperation. Public information. Arbitration. Procedure. Existing tribunals. Negotiation. Reciprocity in financial treatment. Currency. Claims and settlements. Private investment guarantee.

PARTIES:
Congo (Zaire)
USA (United States)

106871 Bilateral Agreement **474 UNTS 49**
SIGNED: 6 Apr 63   FORCE: 6 Apr 63
REGISTERED: 12 Aug 63 USA (United States)
ARTICLES: 16 LANGUAGE: English.
HEADNOTE: POLARIS SALES AGREEMENT
TOPIC: Milit Installation
CONCEPTS: Definition of terms. Court procedures. General cooperation. Exchange of information and documents. Inspection and observation. Private contracts. Responsibility and liability. Use of facilities. Establishment of commission. Accounting procedures. Indemnities and reimbursements. Expense sharing formulae. Claims and settlements. Delivery schedules. Recognition. Joint defense. Atomic weapons. Payment for war supplies. Military assistance. Military training. Security of information. Exchange of defense information. Restrictions on transfer.
PROCEDURE: Future Procedures Contemplated.
PARTIES:
UK Great Britain
USA (United States)

106872 Bilateral Exchange **474 UNTS 71**
SIGNED: 14 Mar 63   FORCE: 14 Mar 63
REGISTERED: 12 Aug 63 USA (United States)
ARTICLES: 2 LANGUAGE: English. German.
HEADNOTE: SETTLEMENT CLAIMS
TOPIC: Status of Forces
CONCEPTS: Compensation. Claims and settlements. Status of military forces.
TREATY REF: 332UNTS3.
PROCEDURE: Future Procedures Contemplated.
PARTIES:
Germany, West
USA (United States)

106873 Bilateral Agreement **474 UNTS 80**
SIGNED: 23 Mar 63   FORCE: 23 Mar 63
REGISTERED: 12 Aug 63 USA (United States)
ARTICLES: 15 LANGUAGE: English.
HEADNOTE: EDUCATIONAL PROGRAM
TOPIC: Education
CONCEPTS: Definition of terms. Previous treaty replacement. Friendship and amity. Standardization. Conformity with municipal law. General cooperation. Inspection and observation. Personnel. General property. Exchange. Commissions and foundations. Teacher and student exchange. Scholarships and grants. Accounting procedures. Currency. Expense sharing formulae. Financial programs. Funding procedures.
TREATY REF: 43UNTS247.
PROCEDURE: Amendment.
PARTIES:
Philippines
USA (United States)

106874 Bilateral Exchange **474 UNTS 95**
SIGNED: 2 Apr 63   FORCE: 2 Apr 63
REGISTERED: 12 Aug 63 USA (United States)
ARTICLES: 2 LANGUAGE: English. Romanian.
HEADNOTE: CULTURAL RELATIONS
TOPIC: Culture
CONCEPTS: Tourism. Non-diplomatic delegations. Conformity with municipal law. Exchange of information and documents. Exchange. Teacher and student exchange. Vocational training. Exchange. General cultural cooperation. Artists. Athletes. Scientific exchange. Indemnities and reimbursements. Publications exchange. Mass media exchange.
PARTIES:
Romania
USA (United States)

106875 Bilateral Exchange **474 UNTS 107**
SIGNED: 29 Nov 62   FORCE: 29 Nov 62
REGISTERED: 12 Aug 63 USA (United States)
ARTICLES: 2 LANGUAGE: English. Spanish.
HEADNOTE: INVESTMENT GUARANTIES
TOPIC: Finance
CONCEPTS: General cooperation. Private investment guarantee.

PARTIES:
USA (United States)
Venezuela

106876 Bilateral Exchange **474 UNTS 113**
SIGNED: 10 Apr 63   FORCE: 10 Apr 63
REGISTERED: 12 Aug 63 USA (United States)
ARTICLES: 2 LANGUAGE: English. French.
HEADNOTE: INVESTMENT GUARANTIES
TOPIC: Finance
CONCEPTS: General cooperation. Arbitration. Procedure. Existing tribunals. Negotiation. Reciprocity in financial treatment. Currency. Payment schedules. Claims and settlements. Private investment guarantee.
PARTIES:
Gabon
USA (United States)

106877 Bilateral Agreement **474 UNTS 119**
SIGNED: 17 Jan 33   FORCE: 17 May 63
REGISTERED: 16 Aug 63 USA (United States)
ARTICLES: 6 LANGUAGE: Dutch. German.
HEADNOTE: STATIONING MILITARY UNITS
TOPIC: Status of Forces
CONCEPTS: Annex or appendix reference. Use of facilities. Procedure. Defense and security. Jurisdiction. Status of forces. Bases and facilities. Frontier crossing points.
INTL ORGS: North Atlantic Treaty Organization.
TREATY REF: 34UNTS243.
PARTIES:
Netherlands
USA (United States)

106878 Bilateral Agreement **474 UNTS 137**
SIGNED: 26 Jul 63   FORCE: 26 Jul 63
REGISTERED: 19 Aug 63 United Nations
ARTICLES: 10 LANGUAGE: English. French.
HEADNOTE: ASSISTANCE SPECIAL FUND
TOPIC: Direct Aid
CONCEPTS: Privileges and immunities. Arbitration. Economic assistance. Loan and credit.
INTL ORGS: International Atomic Energy Agency. International Court of Justice. United Nations. Arbitration Commission.
PROCEDURE: Termination.
PARTIES:
Congo (Zaire)
UN Special Fund

106879 Bilateral Exchange **474 UNTS 155**
SIGNED: 23 Aug 63   FORCE: 23 Aug 63
REGISTERED: 23 Aug 63 United Nations
ARTICLES: 2 LANGUAGE: English.
HEADNOTE: UN SAUDI ARABIA
TOPIC: IGO Status/Immunit
CONCEPTS: Diplomatic and consular relations. Privileges and immunities. Special status.
PARTIES:
United Nations
Saudi Arabia

106880 Bilateral Exchange **474 UNTS 161**
SIGNED: 24 Feb 61   FORCE: 14 Dec 62
REGISTERED: 23 Aug 63 Netherlands
ARTICLES: 2 LANGUAGE: Dutch.
HEADNOTE: CONCERNING 12 MAY 1863 TREATY 11 JAN 1873 TREATY
TOPIC: Admin Cooperation
CONCEPTS: Annex type material. Previous treaty extension.
TREATY REF: 1DEMARTENS117,123.
PARTIES:
Belgium
Netherlands

106881 Bilateral Treaty **474 UNTS 167**
SIGNED: 24 Feb 61   FORCE: 7 Sep 62
REGISTERED: 23 Aug 63 Netherlands
ARTICLES: 13 LANGUAGE: Dutch. French.
HEADNOTE: IMPROVEMENT CONNECTION JULIANA CANAL ALBERT CANAL
TOPIC: Water Transport
CONCEPTS: Detailed regulations. Annex or appendix reference. Previous treaty replacement. Conformity with municipal law. General cooperation. Exchange of information and documents. Ex-

pense sharing formulae. Fees and exemptions. Funding procedures. Payment schedules. Non-interest rates and fees. Canal improvement.
TREATY REF: 3'8DEMARTENS383;.
PROCEDURE: Ratification.
PARTIES:
Belgium
Netherlands

106882 Bilateral Agreement **474 UNTS 195**
SIGNED: 22 May 59   FORCE: 30 Aug 61
REGISTERED: 26 Aug 63 Netherlands
ARTICLES: 8 LANGUAGE: Dutch. Persian. French.
HEADNOTE: CULTURAL
TOPIC: Culture
CONCEPTS: Treaty implementation. Treaty interpretation. Friendship and amity. Conformity with municipal law. Establishment of commission. Exchange. Teacher and student exchange. Institute establishment. Scholarships and grants. General cultural cooperation. Artists. Athletes. Scientific exchange. Mass media exchange.
PROCEDURE: Duration. Ratification. Renewal or Revival. Termination.
PARTIES:
Iran
Netherlands

106883 Bilateral Convention **474 UNTS 207**
SIGNED: 17 Apr 59   FORCE: 18 May 63
REGISTERED: 26 Aug 63 Netherlands
ARTICLES: 16 LANGUAGE: French.
HEADNOTE: RECOGNITION ENFORCEMENT JUDICIAL DECISIONS CIVIL COMMERCIAL MATTERS
TOPIC: Admin Cooperation
CONCEPTS: Definition of terms. Territorial application. Exchange of information and documents. Informational records. Recognition and enforcement of legal decisions. Competence of tribunal. Indemnities and reimbursements.
TREATY REF: 92LTS301; 286UNTS265.
PROCEDURE: Denunciation. Ratification.
PARTIES:
Italy
Netherlands

106884 Bilateral Agreement **474 UNTS 221**
SIGNED: 27 Aug 63   FORCE: 27 Aug 63
REGISTERED: 27 Aug 63 United Nations
ARTICLES: 6 LANGUAGE: English.
HEADNOTE: UN PROVISION ADMINISTRATORS
TOPIC: Tech Assistance
CONCEPTS: General consular functions. Diplomatic privileges. Diplomatic missions. Privileges and immunities. Arbitration. Procedure. Assistance.
INTL ORGS: Permanent Court of Arbitration. Arbitration Commission.
TREATY REF: 319UNTS14.
PROCEDURE: Amendment. Termination.
PARTIES:
United Nations
United Arab Rep
ANNEX
529 UNTS 368. United Arab Rep. Force 13 Feb 64.

106885 Bilateral Convention **474 UNTS 233**
SIGNED: 26 Sep 62   FORCE: 13 Feb 63
REGISTERED: 27 Aug 63 UK Great Britain
ARTICLES: 24 LANGUAGE: English. Hebrew.
HEADNOTE: DOUBLE TAXATION FISCAL EVASION TAXES INCOME
TOPIC: Taxation
CONCEPTS: Definition of terms. Territorial application. Previous treaty replacement. Conformity with municipal law. Exchange of official publications. Teacher and student exchange. Taxation. Tax credits. Equitable taxes. Tax exemptions. Air transport. Merchant vessels.
TREATY REF: 86UNTS211.
PROCEDURE: Termination.
PARTIES:
Israel
UK Great Britain

106886 Bilateral Exchange **474 UNTS 295**
SIGNED: 17 Apr 63   FORCE: 17 Apr 63
REGISTERED: 27 Aug 63 UK Great Britain

ARTICLES: 2 LANGUAGE: English. French.
HEADNOTE: AMENDMENT 6 AUG 14 PROTOCOL
TOPIC: Admin Cooperation
CONCEPTS: Annex type material.
TREATY REF: 10LTS333.
PARTIES:
France
UK Great Britain

106887 Bilateral Agreement **475 UNTS 3**
SIGNED: 21 Jan 63 FORCE: 21 Jan 63
REGISTERED: 27 Aug 63 UK Great Britain
ARTICLES: 15 LANGUAGE: English. Russian.
HEADNOTE: RELATIONS SCIENTIFIC TECHNO-
LOGICAL EDUCATIONAL & CULTURAL
TOPIC: Health/Educ/Welfare
CONCEPTS: Annex or appendix reference. Gen-
eral cooperation. Exchange of information and
documents. Personnel. Specialists exchange.
Education. Teacher and student exchange.
Scholarships and grants. Vocational training. Ex-
change. Artists. Athletes. Research results.
Scientific exchange. Research and develop-
ment. General transportation. Mass media ex-
change. International organizations.
TREATY REF: 409UNTS175.
PARTIES:
UK Great Britain
USSR (Soviet Union)

106888 Bilateral Convention **475 UNTS 31**
SIGNED: 4 Sep 62 FORCE: 23 Apr 63
REGISTERED: 27 Aug 63 UK Great Britain
ARTICLES: 24 LANGUAGE: English. Japanese.
HEADNOTE: DOUBLE TAXATION FISCAL EVA-
SION TAXES INCOME
TOPIC: Taxation
CONCEPTS: Definition of terms. Territorial applica-
tion. Equitable taxes. Conformity with municipal
law. Exchange of official publications. Teacher
and student exchange. Taxation. General. Tax
exemptions. Air transport. Merchant vessels.
PROCEDURE: Ratification. Termination.
PARTIES:
Japan
UK Great Britain

106889 Multilateral Agreement **475 UNTS 121**
SIGNED: 2 Apr 63 FORCE: 2 Apr 63
REGISTERED: 27 Aug 63 UK Great Britain
ARTICLES: 4 LANGUAGE: English.
HEADNOTE: COTTON YARNS RAW COTTON
TOPIC: Commodity Trade
CONCEPTS: Treaty implementation. Annex or appendix reference. General cooperation. Export
quotas. Import quotas. Trade agencies. Trade
procedures. Banking. Compensation. Balance of
payments. Currency. Payment schedules. Non-
interest rates and fees. Commodity trade. Delivery schedules. General aid. Agricultural commodities. Purchase authorization.
PARTIES:
USA (United States) SIGNED: 27 Jun 62 FORCE:
27 Jun 62

106890 Bilateral Agreement **475 UNTS 139**
SIGNED: 2 Apr 63 FORCE: 2 Apr 63
REGISTERED: 27 Aug 63 UK Great Britain
ARTICLES: 4 LANGUAGE: English.
HEADNOTE: COTTON YARNS RAW COTTON
TOPIC: Commodity Trade
CONCEPTS: Treaty implementation. Annex or ap-
pendix reference. General cooperation. Export
quotas. Import quotas. Trade agencies. Trade
procedures. Banking. Compensation. Balance of
payments. Currency. Payment schedules. Non-
interest rates and fees. Commodity trade. Deliv-
ery schedules. General aid. Agricultural com-
modities. Purchase authorization.
TREATY REF: 461UNTS113.
PARTIES:
Burma
UK Great Britain

106891 Bilateral Exchange **475 UNTS 155**
SIGNED: 17 May 63 FORCE: 17 May 63
REGISTERED: 27 Aug 63 UK Great Britain
ARTICLES: 2 LANGUAGE: English. French.
HEADNOTE: ECONOMIC AID

TOPIC: Direct Aid
CONCEPTS: Annex or appendix reference. General cooperation. Import quotas. Accounting procedures. Indemnities and reimbursements. Financial programs. Transportation costs. Economic assistance.
PROCEDURE: Amendment.
PARTIES:
Laos
UK Great Britain
ANNEX
502 UNTS 387. Laos. Amendment 24 Dec 63.
Force 24 Dec 63.
502 UNTS 387. UK Great Britain. Amendment
24 Dec 63. Force 24 Dec 63.
534 UNTS 481. UK Great Britain. Amendment
18 Aug 64. Force 18 Aug 64.
534 UNTS 481. Laos. Amendment 18 Aug 64.
Force 18 Aug 64.

106892 Bilateral Exchange **475 UNTS 169**
SIGNED: 27 Apr 63 FORCE: 27 Apr 63
REGISTERED: 27 Aug 63 UK Great Britain
ARTICLES: 2 LANGUAGE: English. Arabic.
HEADNOTE: LOAN
TOPIC: Loans and Credits
CONCEPTS: Funding procedures. Interest rates.
Payment schedules. Loan and credit. Loan repay-
ment. Terms of loan. Airport facilities. Roads and
highways.
PARTIES:
Jordan
UK Great Britain
ANNEX
533 UNTS 359. UK Great Britain. Implementation
28 Feb 64. Force 2 Mar 64.
533 UNTS 359. Jordan. Implementation
2 Mar 64. Force 2 Mar 64.

106893 Bilateral Agreement **475 UNTS 177**
SIGNED: 10 Oct 62 FORCE: 10 Oct 62
REGISTERED: 27 Aug 63 UK Great Britain
ARTICLES: 9 LANGUAGE: English.
HEADNOTE: PUBLIC OFFICERS
TOPIC: Admin Cooperation
CONCEPTS: Definition of terms. Personnel. Social
security. Payment schedules.
PARTIES:
Uganda
UK Great Britain

106894 Bilateral Agreement **475 UNTS 187**
SIGNED: 6 Oct 59 FORCE: 18 Nov 59
REGISTERED: 28 Aug 63 Canada
ARTICLES: 15 LANGUAGE: English. French. Ger-
man. Italian. Dutch.
HEADNOTE: PEACEFUL USES ATOMIC ENERGY
TOPIC: Scientific Project
CONCEPTS: Definition of terms. Conformity with
municipal law. Exchange of information and doc-
uments. Licenses and permits. Use of facilities.
Vocational training. Nuclear research. Scientific
exchange. Trademarks. Economic assistance.
Materials, equipment and services. Acceptance
of delivery. Peaceful use. Rights of supplier.
TREATY REF: 298UNTS167.
PROCEDURE: Future Procedures Contemplated.
Renewal or Revival. Termination.
PARTIES:
Canada
Euratom

106895 Bilateral Convention **475 UNTS 233**
SIGNED: 1 Mar 63 FORCE: 24 Jul 63
REGISTERED: 4 Sep 63 Thailand
ARTICLES: 20 LANGUAGE: English.
HEADNOTE: DOUBLE TAXATION FISCAL EVA-
SION TAXES INCOME
TOPIC: Taxation
CONCEPTS: Definition of terms. Privileges and im-
munities. Conformity with municipal law. Ex-
change of official publications. Domestic legisla-
tion. Negotiation. Teacher and student ex-
change. Taxation. Equitable taxes. General. Tax
exemptions. Air transport. Merchant vessels. Ar-
mistice and peace.
PROCEDURE: Termination.
PARTIES:
Japan
Thailand

106896 Bilateral Agreement **475 UNTS 269**
SIGNED: 25 Aug 61 FORCE: 25 Jul 63
REGISTERED: 5 Sep 63 Norway
ARTICLES: 30 LANGUAGE: Norwegian. Italian.
HEADNOTE: DOUBLE TAXATION FISCAL EVA-
SION TAXES INCOME
TOPIC: Taxation
CONCEPTS: Definition of terms. Nationality and
citizenship. Conformity with municipal law. Ex-
change of official publications. Negotiation.
Teacher and student exchange. Claims and set-
tlements. Taxation. Equitable taxes. General. Tax
exemptions. Air transport. Merchant vessels.
PROCEDURE: Duration. Ratification. Termination.
PARTIES:
Italy
Norway

106897 Bilateral Agreement **475 UNTS 331**
SIGNED: 9 May 63 FORCE: 28 Jun 63
REGISTERED: 6 Sep 63 Australia
ARTICLES: 16 LANGUAGE: English.
HEADNOTE: ESTABLISHMENT NAVAL COMMUNI-
CATIONS
TOPIC: Milit Installation
CONCEPTS: Conformity with municipal law. Gen-
eral cooperation. Inspection and observation. Ti-
tle and deeds. Compensation. Indemnities and
reimbursements. Claims and settlements. Tax
exemptions. Customs exemptions. Materials,
equipment and services. Facilities and equip-
ment. Procurement and logistics. Bases and fa-
cilities.
TREATY REF: 131UNTS83.
PROCEDURE: Duration. Future Procedures Contemplated. Ratification. Termination.
PARTIES:
Australia
USA (United States)
ANNEX
660 UNTS 401. Australia. Amendment 12 Jul 68.
Force 12 Jul 68.
660 UNTS 401. USA (United States). Amendment
12 Jul 68. Force 12 Jul 68.

106898 Bilateral Exchange **476 UNTS 3**
SIGNED: 30 Nov 62 FORCE: 30 Nov 62
REGISTERED: 11 Sep 63 New Zealand
ARTICLES: 2 LANGUAGE: English.
HEADNOTE: INHERITANCE INTERNATIONAL
RIGHTS
TOPIC: Recognition
CONCEPTS: Continuity of rights and obligations.
PARTIES:
New Zealand
Western Samoa

106899 Bilateral Agreement **476 UNTS 9**
SIGNED: 9 Apr 62 FORCE: 29 Mar 63
REGISTERED: 11 Sep 63 USA (United States)
ARTICLES: 11 LANGUAGE: English.
HEADNOTE: CIVIL USES ATOMIC ENERGY
TOPIC: Scientific Project
CONCEPTS: Definition of terms. Exchange of infor-
mation and documents. Responsibility and liabil-
ity. Use of facilities. Establishment of commis-
sion. Public health. Nuclear research. Scientific
exchange. Materials, equipment and services.
Nuclear materials. Non-nuclear materials. Peace-
ful use. Rights of supplier. Samples and testing.
Security of information.
INTL ORGS: International Atomic Energy Agency.
PROCEDURE: Duration. Renewal or Revival. Termi-
nation.
PARTIES:
Colombia
USA (United States)

106900 Bilateral Agreement **476 UNTS 29**
SIGNED: 19 Apr 63 FORCE: 19 Apr 63
REGISTERED: 11 Sep 63 USA (United States)
ARTICLES: 9 LANGUAGE: English. French.
HEADNOTE: COMMUNICATIONS FACILITIES
TOPIC: Gen Communications
CONCEPTS: Personnel. General property. Facili-
ties and equipment. Telecommunications.
Status of forces.
TREATY REF: 260UNTS452; 286UNTS380;
199UNTS67; 200UNTS340.

PROCEDURE: Duration. Future Procedures Contemplated. Termination.
PARTIES:
Belgium
USA (United States)

106901 Bilateral Agreement **476 UNTS 35**
SIGNED: 7 May 63 FORCE: 7 May 63
REGISTERED: 11 Sep 63 USA (United States)
ARTICLES: 7 LANGUAGE: English. Spanish.
HEADNOTE: AGRI COMMOD
TOPIC: US Agri Commod Aid
CONCEPTS: Exchange of information and documents. Reciprocity in trade. Reexport of goods, etc.. Funding procedures. Purchase authorization. Mutual consultation.
PARTIES:
El Salvador
USA (United States)

106902 Bilateral Agreement **476 UNTS 43**
SIGNED: 9 May 63 FORCE: 9 May 63
REGISTERED: 11 Sep 63 USA (United States)
ARTICLES: 7 LANGUAGE: English.
HEADNOTE: AGRI COMMOD
TOPIC: US Agri Commod Aid
CONCEPTS: Reciprocity in trade. Reexport of goods, etc.. Transportation costs. Purchase authorization. Purchase authorization. Mutual consultation.
PARTIES:
India
USA (United States)

106903 Bilateral Agreement **476 UNTS 49**
SIGNED: 22 Aug 63 FORCE: 22 Aug 63
REGISTERED: 12 Sep 63 United Nations
ARTICLES: 10 LANGUAGE: English. French.
HEADNOTE: ASSISTANCE
TOPIC: Direct Aid
CONCEPTS: Detailed regulations. Treaty implementation. Visas. Privileges and immunities. Exchange of information and documents. Informational records. Inspection and observation. Operating agencies. Personnel. Public information. Responsibility and liability. Title and deeds. Use of facilities. Arbitration. Procedure. Negotiation. Import quotas. Attachment of funds. Exchange rates and regulations. Expense sharing formulae. Financial programs. Domestic obligation. General technical assistance. Economic assistance. Materials, equipment and services. IGO status.
INTL ORGS: International Atomic Energy Agency. International Court of Justice. United Nations. Arbitration Commission.
TREATY REF: 1UNTS15; 33UNTS261; 374UNTS147.
PROCEDURE: Amendment. Termination.
PARTIES:
Burundi
UN Special Fund

106904 Bilateral Exchange **476 UNTS 67**
SIGNED: 29 Mar 63 FORCE: 29 Mar 63
REGISTERED: 12 Sep 63 USA (United States)
ARTICLES: 2 LANGUAGE: English. Portuguese.
HEADNOTE: RADIOBIOLOGICAL EQUIPMENT
TOPIC: Scientific Project
CONCEPTS: Annex type material. Responsibility and liability. Scholarships and grants. Research and scientific projects. Research results. Nuclear research. Financial programs. Funding procedures. Transportation costs. Materials, equipment and services. General. Peaceful use.
PARTIES:
Brazil
USA (United States)

106905 Bilateral Agreement **476 UNTS 77**
SIGNED: 24 Oct 56 FORCE: 1 Jan 57
REGISTERED: 12 Sep 63 USA (United States)
ARTICLES: 17 LANGUAGE: English. Spanish.
HEADNOTE: AIR TRANSPORT
TOPIC: Air Transport
CONCEPTS: Definition of terms. Detailed regulations. Exceptions and exemptions. Annex or appendix reference. Previous treaty replacement. Conformity with municipal law. General cooperation. Licenses and permits. Recognition of legal documents. Use of facilities. Arbitration. Procedure. Special tribunals. Expense sharing formulae. Fees and exemptions. National treatment. Customs exemptions. Competency certificate. Routes and logistics. Navigational conditions. Permit designation. Air transport. Airport facilities. Airworthiness certificates. Conditions of airlines operating permission. Overflights and technical stops. Operating authorizations and regulations. Licenses and certificates of nationality.
INTL ORGS: International Civil Aviation Organization. International Court of Justice. Arbitration Commission.
TREATY REF: 15UNTS295.
PROCEDURE: Amendment. Future Procedures Contemplated. Ratification. Registration. Termination. Application to Non-self-governing Territories.
PARTIES:
Colombia
USA (United States)

106906 Bilateral Exchange **476 UNTS 115**
SIGNED: 25 Apr 63 FORCE: 25 Apr 63
REGISTERED: 12 Sep 63 USA (United States)
ARTICLES: 2 LANGUAGE: English.
HEADNOTE: GUARANTEE POWER
TOPIC: Sanitation
CONCEPTS: Definition of terms. Annex or appendix reference. Exchange of information and documents. Inspection and observation. Bonds. Fees and exemptions. Tax exemptions. Domestic obligation. Terms of loan. Loan regulations. Loan guarantee. Guarantor non-interference. Hydroelectric power.
INTL ORGS: Southeast Asia Treaty Organization.
TREATY REF: 405UNTS135.
PARTIES:
Thailand
USA (United States)

106907 Bilateral Exchange **476 UNTS 131**
SIGNED: 21 Mar 63 FORCE: 21 Mar 63
REGISTERED: 12 Sep 63 USA (United States)
ARTICLES: 2 LANGUAGE: English.
HEADNOTE: SCHOOL FEEDING PROGRAM
TOPIC: Education
CONCEPTS: Conditions. Annex or appendix reference. Conformity with municipal law. Exchange of information and documents. Inspection and observation. Responsibility and liability. Family allowances. Currency. Expense sharing formulae. Funding procedures. General technical assistance. Agricultural commodities.
PROCEDURE: Duration.
PARTIES:
Israel
USA (United States)

106908 Bilateral Agreement **476 UNTS 153**
SIGNED: 14 Sep 62 FORCE: 24 Jan 63
REGISTERED: 18 Sep 63 IBRD (World Bank)
ARTICLES: 5 LANGUAGE: English.
HEADNOTE: GUARANTEE ELECTRIFICATION
TOPIC: IBRD Project
CONCEPTS: Definition of terms. Annex or appendix reference. Exchange of information and documents. Inspection and observation. Bonds. Fees and exemptions. Tax exemptions. Domestic obligation. Terms of loan. Loan regulations. Loan guarantee. Guarantor non-interference. Hydroelectric power.
PARTIES:
Panama
IBRD (World Bank)

106909 Bilateral Agreement **476 UNTS 185**
SIGNED: 17 Apr 63 FORCE: 9 Aug 63
REGISTERED: 18 Sep 63 IBRD (World Bank)
ARTICLES: 5 LANGUAGE: English.
HEADNOTE: GUARANTEE
TOPIC: IBRD Project
CONCEPTS: Loan and credit. Credit provisions.
PARTIES:
Cyprus
IBRD (World Bank)

106910 Bilateral Agreement **476 UNTS 211**
SIGNED: 16 May 63 FORCE: 3 Jul 63

REGISTERED: 18 Sep 63 IBRD (World Bank)
ARTICLES: 5 LANGUAGE: English.
HEADNOTE: GUARANTEE POWER
TOPIC: IBRD Project
CONCEPTS: Definition of terms. Annex or appendix reference. Exchange of information and documents. Inspection and observation. Bonds. Fees and exemptions. Tax exemptions. Domestic obligation. Terms of loan. Loan regulations. Loan guarantee. Guarantor non-interference. Hydroelectric power.
PARTIES:
IBRD (World Bank)
UK Great Britain

106911 Bilateral Agreement **477 UNTS 3**
SIGNED: 22 Mar 63 FORCE: 2 May 63
REGISTERED: 18 Sep 63 IDA (Devel Assoc)
ARTICLES: 6 LANGUAGE: English.
HEADNOTE: DEVELOPMENT CREDIT RAILWAY
TOPIC: Non-IBRD Project
CONCEPTS: Detailed regulations. Previous treaty amendment. Exchange of information and documents. Informational records. Accounting procedures. Interest rates. Tax exemptions. Credit provisions. Loan repayment. Terms of loan. Plans and standards. IDA development project. Railways.
INTL ORGS: International Bank for Reconstruction and Development.
TREATY REF: 154UNTS269; 288UNTS135; 346UNTS33; 418UNTS3; ETC..
PARTIES:
India
IDA (Devel Assoc)

106912 Bilateral Exchange **477 UNTS 21**
SIGNED: 29 Jun 63 FORCE: 29 Jun 63
REGISTERED: 18 Sep 63 Finland
ARTICLES: 2 LANGUAGE: Swedish.
HEADNOTE: TORNE-AAVASAKA RIVER BRIDGE
TOPIC: Land Transport
PARTIES:
Finland
Sweden

106913 Bilateral Exchange **477 UNTS 29**
SIGNED: 6 Jun 63 FORCE: 6 Jun 63
REGISTERED: 18 Sep 63 Jamaica
ARTICLES: 2 LANGUAGE: English.
HEADNOTE: FURNISHING DEFENSE ARTICLES SERVICES
TOPIC: Milit Assistance
CONCEPTS: Non-prejudice to UN charter. Privileges and immunities. Conformity with municipal law. Exchange of information and documents. Inspection and observation. Aid missions. Self-defense. Military assistance. Return of equipment and recapture. Security of information. Exchange of defense information. Restrictions on transfer.
PARTIES:
Jamaica
USA (United States)

106914 Bilateral Exchange **477 UNTS 37**
SIGNED: 26 Apr 63 FORCE: 26 Apr 63
REGISTERED: 18 Sep 63 USA (United States)
ARTICLES: 2 LANGUAGE: English. Japanese.
HEADNOTE: MISSILE BATTALIONS AIR DEFENSE
TOPIC: Milit Installation
CONCEPTS: Time limit. Annex or appendix reference. Conformity with municipal law. Compensation. Materials, equipment and services. Defense and security. Payment for war supplies. Military training. Military installations and equipment.
TREATY REF: 232UNTS169.
PARTIES:
Japan
USA (United States)

106915 Bilateral Exchange **477 UNTS 55**
SIGNED: 15 May 63 FORCE: 15 May 63
REGISTERED: 18 Sep 63 USA (United States)
ARTICLES: 2 LANGUAGE: English.
HEADNOTE: RESEARCH AEROSPACE DISTURBANCES
TOPIC: Military Mission

CONCEPTS: Annex or appendix reference. Meteorology.
PARTIES:
New Zealand
USA (United States)

106916 Bilateral Agreement **477 UNTS 67**
SIGNED: 6 May 63   FORCE: 6 May 63
REGISTERED: 18 Sep 63 USA (United States)
ARTICLES: 8 LANGUAGE: English.
HEADNOTE: RADIO BROADCASTING FACILITIES
TOPIC: Telecommunications
CONCEPTS: Previous treaty replacement. Passports non-diplomatic. Visas. Conformity with municipal law. General property. Responsibility and liability. Teacher and student exchange. Tax exemptions. Bands and frequency allocation. Facilities and equipment. Radio-telephone-telegraphic communications.
TREATY REF: PHILIPINES&USA 1947.
PROCEDURE: Termination.
PARTIES:
Philippines
USA (United States)

106917 Bilateral Exchange **477 UNTS 101**
SIGNED: 7 Jan 63   FORCE: 7 Jan 63
REGISTERED: 18 Sep 63 USA (United States)
ARTICLES: 2 LANGUAGE: English. Spanish.
HEADNOTE: ISSUANCE NON-IMMIGRANT VISAS
TOPIC: Visas
CONCEPTS: Visas. Fees and exemptions.
PROCEDURE: Termination.
PARTIES:
Ecuador
USA (United States)

106918 Bilateral Agreement **477 UNTS 123**
SIGNED: 24 May 63   FORCE: 24 May 63
REGISTERED: 18 Sep 63 USA (United States)
ARTICLES: 12 LANGUAGE: English.
HEADNOTE: EDUCATIONAL PROGRAM
TOPIC: Education
CONCEPTS: Definition of terms. Friendship and amity. Standardization. Conformity with municipal law. General cooperation. Exchange of information and documents. Inspection and observation. Personnel. General property. Exchange. Commissions and foundations. Scholarships and grants. Accounting procedures. Currency. Expense sharing formulae. Financial programs. Funding procedures. Special status.
TREATY REF: 81UNTS61.
PROCEDURE: Amendment.
PARTIES:
Thailand
USA (United States)

106919 Bilateral Agreement **477 UNTS 135**
SIGNED: 5 Apr 63   FORCE: 5 Apr 63
REGISTERED: 18 Sep 63 USA (United States)
ARTICLES: 5 LANGUAGE: English. Spanish.
HEADNOTE: AGRI COMMOD TITLE IV
TOPIC: US Agri Commod Aid
CONCEPTS: General provisions. Reexport of goods, etc.. Payment schedules. Purchase authorization. Commodities schedule. Purchase authorization. Merchant vessels. Mutual consultation. Internal travel.
PARTIES:
Ecuador
USA (United States)
                    ANNEX
531 UNTS 400. USA (United States). Amendment 6 Oct 64. Force 6 Oct 64.
531 UNTS 400. Ecuador. Amendment 6 Oct 64. Force 6 Oct 64.

106920 Bilateral Treaty **477 UNTS 155**
SIGNED: 24 Jan 48   FORCE: 2 Jun 48
REGISTERED: 19 Sep 63 Hungary
ARTICLES: 7 LANGUAGE: Hungarian. Romanian.
HEADNOTE: FRIENDSHIP COOPERATION MUTUAL ASSISTANCE
TOPIC: General Amity
CONCEPTS: Friendship and amity. Non-prejudice to UN charter. Peaceful relations. General cooperation. Defense and security.
PROCEDURE: Ratification. Termination.

PARTIES:
Hungary
Romania

106921 Bilateral Treaty **477 UNTS 169**
SIGNED: 16 Jul 48   FORCE: 14 Mar 49
REGISTERED: 19 Sep 63 Hungary
ARTICLES: 8 LANGUAGE: Hungarian. Bulgarian.
HEADNOTE: FRIENDSHIP COOPERATION MUTUAL ASSISTANCE
TOPIC: General Amity
CONCEPTS: Non-prejudice to third party. Friendship and amity. Non-prejudice to UN charter. Peaceful relations. General cooperation. Defense and security.
PROCEDURE: Denunciation. Duration. Ratification.
PARTIES:
Bulgaria
Hungary

106922 Bilateral Treaty **477 UNTS 183**
SIGNED: 16 Apr 49   FORCE: 16 Apr 49
REGISTERED: 19 Sep 63 Hungary
ARTICLES: 7 LANGUAGE: Hungarian. Slovene.
HEADNOTE: FRIENDSHIP COOPERATION MUTUAL ASSISTANCE
TOPIC: General Amity
CONCEPTS: Friendship and amity. Peaceful relations. General cooperation. Defense and security.
PROCEDURE: Duration. Ratification. Termination.
PARTIES:
Czechoslovakia
Hungary

106923 Bilateral Agreement **477 UNTS 197**
SIGNED: 28 Apr 55   FORCE: 14 Jun 56
REGISTERED: 19 Sep 63 Hungary
ARTICLES: 13 LANGUAGE: Hungarian. Czechoslovakian.
HEADNOTE: HEALTH COOPERATION
TOPIC: Sanitation
CONCEPTS: Exchange of official publications. Exchange of information and documents. Informational records. Domestic legislation. Establishment of commission. Specialists exchange. Public health. Pharmaceuticals. Teacher and student exchange. Vocational training. Family allowances. Research results. Scientific exchange. Research and development. Indemnities and reimbursements. General technical assistance. Materials, equipment and services. Publications exchange.
PROCEDURE: Duration. Future Procedures Contemplated. Ratification. Renewal or Revival. Termination.
PARTIES:
Czechoslovakia
Hungary

106924 Bilateral Agreement **477 UNTS 219**
SIGNED: 25 May 57   FORCE: 21 Aug 58
REGISTERED: 19 Sep 63 Hungary
ARTICLES: 24 LANGUAGE: Hungarian. Serbo-Croat.
HEADNOTE: VETERINARY MATTERS
TOPIC: Sanitation
CONCEPTS: Definition of terms. Detailed regulations. Exceptions and exemptions. Border traffic and migration. General cooperation. Exchange of information and documents. Inspection and observation. Domestic legislation. Establishment of commission. Procedure. Negotiation. Specialists exchange. Border control. Disease control. Veterinary. Scientific exchange. Trade procedures.
PROCEDURE: Denunciation. Duration. Renewal or Revival.
PARTIES:
Hungary
Yugoslavia

106925 Bilateral Convention **477 UNTS 267**
SIGNED: 20 Nov 57   FORCE: 27 Nov 58
REGISTERED: 19 Sep 63 Hungary
ARTICLES: 16 LANGUAGE: Hungarian. Serbo-Croat.
HEADNOTE: CONTROL COMMUNICABLE DISEASES

TOPIC: Sanitation
CONCEPTS: Definition of terms. Detailed regulations. Exceptions and exemptions. Exchange of information and documents. Domestic legislation. Specialists exchange. Quarantine. Border control. Disease control. Public health. Research cooperation. Research results. Scientific exchange. Research and development. Indemnities and reimbursements. Publications exchange.
PROCEDURE: Denunciation. Duration. Ratification.
PARTIES:
Hungary
Yugoslavia

106926 Bilateral Agreement **477 UNTS 303**
SIGNED: 17 Dec 57   FORCE: 27 May 58
REGISTERED: 19 Sep 63 Hungary
ARTICLES: 9 LANGUAGE: Hungarian. Romanian.
HEADNOTE: HEALTH COOPERATION
TOPIC: Sanitation
CONCEPTS: General cooperation. Exchange of official publications. Exchange of information and documents. Informational records. Establishment of commission. Specialists exchange. Disease control. Public health. Pharmaceuticals. Teacher and student exchange. Research results. Scientific exchange. Research and development. Indemnities and reimbursements. General technical assistance. Materials, equipment and services. Publications exchange.
PROCEDURE: Duration. Ratification. Renewal or Revival. Termination.
PARTIES:
Hungary
Romania

106927 Bilateral Convention **477 UNTS 321**
SIGNED: 27 Jun 58   FORCE: 4 Jul 59
REGISTERED: 19 Sep 63 Hungary
ARTICLES: 13 LANGUAGE: Hungarian. Bulgarian.
HEADNOTE: REGULATING NATIONALITY PERSONS HAVING DUAL NATIONALITY
TOPIC: Consul/Citizenship
CONCEPTS: Detailed regulations. Dual citizenship. Nationality and citizenship. Procedure. Fees and exemptions.
PROCEDURE: Duration. Ratification. Termination.
PARTIES:
Czechoslovakia
Hungary

106928 Bilateral Agreement **477 UNTS 346**
SIGNED: 8 Aug 63   FORCE: 30 Aug 63
REGISTERED: 19 Sep 63 WHO (World Health)
ARTICLES: 6 LANGUAGE: French.
HEADNOTE: TECHNICAL ADVISORY ASSISTANCE
TOPIC: Tech Assistance
CONCEPTS: Definition of terms. Annex or appendix reference. Privileges and immunities. Administrative cooperation. Exchange of information and documents. Personnel. Responsibility and liability. Title and deeds. Exchange. Scholarships and grants. Vocational training. Research and development. Expense sharing formulae. Local currency. Domestic obligation. Special projects. Materials, equipment and services. IGO status. Conformity with IGO decisions.
TREATY REF: 33UNTS261.
PROCEDURE: Amendment. Termination.
PARTIES:
Burundi
WHO (World Health)

106929 Bilateral Agreement **477 UNTS 361**
SIGNED: 16 May 63   FORCE: 11 Jul 63
REGISTERED: 20 Sep 63 IBRD (World Bank)
ARTICLES: 5 LANGUAGE: English.
HEADNOTE: GUARANTEE POWER
TOPIC: IBRD Project
CONCEPTS: Definition of terms. Annex or appendix reference. Exchange of information and documents. Inspection and observation. Bonds. Fees and exemptions. Tax exemptions. Domestic obligation. Terms of loan. Loan regulations. Loan guarantee. Guarantor non-interference. Hydroelectric power.
PARTIES:
IBRD (World Bank)
UK Great Britain

106930 Bilateral Exchange **477 UNTS 405**
SIGNED: 10 Jun 63 FORCE: 10 Jun 63
REGISTERED: 20 Sep 63 Denmark
ARTICLES: 2 LANGUAGE: German. Danish.
HEADNOTE: AMENDMENT
TOPIC: Admin Cooperation
CONCEPTS: Annex type material. Previous treaty
extension.
TREATY REF: 171LTS9.
PARTIES:
Denmark
Germany, West

106931 Bilateral Exchange **478 UNTS 3**
SIGNED: 29 May 61 FORCE: 1 Jun 61
REGISTERED: 23 Sep 63 Nigeria
ARTICLES: 2 LANGUAGE: English.
HEADNOTE: INCORPORATION NORTHERN CAME-
ROONS FEDERATION OF NIGERIA
TOPIC: Recognition
CONCEPTS: Union with other states.
PARTIES:
Nigeria
UK Great Britain

106932 Bilateral Agreement **478 UNTS 9**
SIGNED: 1 Jun 61 FORCE: 2 Jun 61
REGISTERED: 23 Sep 63 UK Great Britain
ARTICLES: 8 LANGUAGE: English.
HEADNOTE: PUBLIC OFFICERS
TOPIC: Recognition
CONCEPTS: Definition of terms. Personnel. Holi-
days and rest periods.
PARTIES:
Jamaica
UK Great Britain

106933 Bilateral Exchange **478 UNTS 23**
SIGNED: 3 Apr 63 FORCE: 3 Apr 63
REGISTERED: 23 Sep 63 UK Great Britain
ARTICLES: 2 LANGUAGE: English.
HEADNOTE: APPEAL
TOPIC: Admin Cooperation
CONCEPTS: Competence of tribunal.
PARTIES:
Tanganyika
UK Great Britain

106934 Bilateral Treaty **478 UNTS 29**
SIGNED: 14 Nov 62 FORCE: 4 May 63
REGISTERED: 23 Sep 63 UK Great Britain
ARTICLES: 33 LANGUAGE: English. Japanese.
HEADNOTE: COMMERCE NAVIGATION
TOPIC: General Trade
CONCEPTS: Definition of terms. Detailed regula-
tions. Emergencies. Exceptions and exemptions.
Territorial application. Treaty implementation.
Treaty interpretation. Privileges and immunities.
Court procedures. General cooperation. Juridical personality. Expropriation. Legal protection
and assistance. Licenses and permits. Immovable property. General property. Public information. Investigation of violations. Arbitration. Existing tribunals. Export quotas. Import quotas. Indemnities and reimbursements. Payment
schedules. Transportation costs. Commodity
trade. Quotas. National treatment. Equitable
taxes. General. Tax exemptions. Customs duties.
Passenger transport. Routes and logistics. Navigational conditions. Transport of goods. Merchant vessels. Inland and territorial waters. Shipwreck and salvage. Foreign nationals.
INTL ORGS: International Court of Justice. Inter-
Governmental Maritime Consultative Organiza-
tion. International Monetary Fund.
TREATY REF: 30LTS371; 1UNTS269; 192LTS17;
ETC..
PROCEDURE: Ratification. Termination.
PARTIES:
Japan
UK Great Britain

106935 Bilateral Agreement **478 UNTS 148**
SIGNED: 29 Jul 63 FORCE: 29 Jul 63
REGISTERED: 23 Sep 63 UK Great Britain
ARTICLES: 10 LANGUAGE: English. French.
HEADNOTE: ECONOMIC COOPERATION ENCOUR-
AGING INVESTMENT
TOPIC: General Economic

CONCEPTS: Annex or appendix reference. Conformity with municipal law. Exchange of information and documents. Expropriation. General
property. Establishment of commission. Arbitration. Existing tribunals. Special tribunals. Establishment of trade relations. Quotas. Water transport.
INTL ORGS: International Court of Justice. Arbitration Commission. Special Commission.
PROCEDURE: Duration. Termination.
PARTIES:
Cameroon
UK Great Britain

106936 Bilateral Agreement **478 UNTS 161**
SIGNED: 15 Feb 63 FORCE: 13 Jul 63
REGISTERED: 24 Sep 63 IBRD (World Bank)
ARTICLES: 5 LANGUAGE: English.
HEADNOTE: GUARANTEE
TOPIC: IBRD Project
CONCEPTS: Definition of terms. Annex or appen-
dix reference. Exchange of information and doc-
uments. Inspection and observation. Bonds.
Fees and exemptions. Tax exemptions. Domestic
obligation. Terms of loan. Loan regulations. Loan
guarantee. Guarantor non-interference.
PARTIES:
Philippines
IBRD (World Bank)

106937 Bilateral Agreement **478 UNTS 205**
SIGNED: 21 Dec 62 FORCE: 15 Jan 63
REGISTERED: 24 Sep 63 IBRD (World Bank)
ARTICLES: 5 LANGUAGE: English.
HEADNOTE: GUARANTEE AGREEMENT
TOPIC: IBRD Project
CONCEPTS: Definition of terms. Annex or appen-
dix reference. Exchange of information and doc-
uments. Inspection and observation. Bonds.
Fees and exemptions. Tax exemptions. Domestic
obligation. Terms of loan. Loan regulations. Loan
guarantee. Guarantor non-interference.
PARTIES:
Morocco
IBRD (World Bank)

106938 Bilateral Agreement **478 UNTS 245**
SIGNED: 13 Mar 63 FORCE: 26 Aug 63
REGISTERED: 24 Sep 63 IBRD (World Bank)
ARTICLES: 5 LANGUAGE: English.
HEADNOTE: GUARANTEE RAILWAY
TOPIC: IBRD Project
CONCEPTS: Annex or appendix reference. Ex-
change of information and documents. Inspec-
tion and observation. Bonds. Fees and exemp-
tions. Tax exemptions. Domestic obligation.
Terms of loan. Loan regulations. Loan guarantee.
Guarantor non-interference. Railways.
PARTIES:
Peru
IBRD (World Bank)

106939 Bilateral Agreement **478 UNTS 289**
SIGNED: 27 Feb 63 FORCE: 27 Aug 63
REGISTERED: 24 Sep 63 IDA (Devel Assoc)
ARTICLES: 7 LANGUAGE: English.
HEADNOTE: DEVELOPMENT CREDIT HIGHWAY
TOPIC: Non-IBRD Project
CONCEPTS: Detailed regulations. Previous treaty
amendment. Exchange of information and docu-
ments. Informational records. Accounting proce-
dures. Interest rates. Tax exemptions. Credit pro-
visions. Loan repayment. Terms of loan. Plans
and standards. IDA development project.
INTL ORGS: International Bank for Reconstruction
and Development.
PARTIES:
Ethiopia
IDA (Devel Assoc)

106940 Bilateral Agreement **478 UNTS 313**
SIGNED: 7 Sep 62 FORCE: 10 Jul 63
REGISTERED: 24 Sep 63 IDA (Devel Assoc)
ARTICLES: 7 LANGUAGE: English.
HEADNOTE: DEVELOPMENT CREDIT WATER SUP-
PLY
TOPIC: Non-IBRD Project
CONCEPTS: Detailed regulations. Previous treaty
amendment. Exchange of information and docu-

ments. Informational records. Accounting procedures. Interest rates. Tax exemptions. Credit provisions. Loan repayment. Terms of loan. Plans
and standards. IDA development project. Natural
resources.
PARTIES:
Nicaragua
IDA (Devel Assoc)

106941 Bilateral Agreement **478 UNTS 335**
SIGNED: 8 Aug 62 FORCE: 24 Oct 62
REGISTERED: 24 Sep 63 IDA (Devel Assoc)
ARTICLES: 7 LANGUAGE: English.
HEADNOTE: CREDIT DEVELOPMENT
TOPIC: Non-IBRD Project
CONCEPTS: Loan and credit. Credit provisions.
INTL ORGS: International Bank for Reconstruction
and Development.
PROCEDURE: Termination.
PARTIES:
India
IDA (Devel Assoc)

106942 Bilateral Exchange **478 UNTS 363**
SIGNED: 31 Jul 63 FORCE: 30 Sep 63
REGISTERED: 30 Sep 63 Australia
ARTICLES: 2 LANGUAGE: English.
HEADNOTE: MUTUAL RECOGNITION CERTIFI-
CATES REGISTRY OTHER NATIONAL DOCU-
MENTS
TOPIC: Admin Cooperation
CONCEPTS: Recognition of legal documents.
PARTIES:
Australia
Finland

106943 Multilateral Protocol **478 UNTS 371**
SIGNED: 28 Sep 55 FORCE: 1 Aug 63
REGISTERED: 30 Sep 63 Poland
ARTICLES: 27 LANGUAGE: French. English. Span-
ish.
HEADNOTE: AMEND CONVENTION
TOPIC: Air Transport
CONCEPTS: Exceptions and exemptions. Treaty in-
terpretation. Annex type material. Air transport.
TREATY REF: 137LTS11.
PROCEDURE: Accession. Denunciation. Ratifica-
tion. Registration. Application to Non-self-gov-
erning Territories.
PARTIES:
Australia SIGNED: 12 Jul 56
Belgium SIGNED: 28 Sep 55
Brazil SIGNED: 28 Sep 55
Byelorussia SIGNED: 9 Apr 60 RATIFIED:
17 Jan 61 FORCE: 1 Aug 63
Cameroon RATIFIED: 21 Aug 61 FORCE:
1 Aug 63
Canada SIGNED: 16 Aug 56 RATIFIED:
23 Jun 56 FORCE: 1 Aug 63
Congo (Brazzaville) RATIFIED: 5 Jan 62 FORCE:
1 Aug 63
Czechoslovakia SIGNED: 28 Sep 55 RATIFIED:
23 Nov 57 FORCE: 1 Aug 63
Dahomey RATIFIED: 9 Jan 62 FORCE: 1 Aug 63
Denmark SIGNED: 16 Mar 57 FORCE: 1 Aug 63
United Arab Rep SIGNED: 28 Sep 55 RATIFIED:
26 Apr 56 FORCE: 1 Aug 63
El Salvador SIGNED: 28 Sep 55 RATIFIED:
9 May 56 FORCE: 1 Aug 63
France SIGNED: 28 Sep 55 RATIFIED:
19 May 59 FORCE: 1 Aug 63
Germany, East SIGNED: 11 Dec 57 RATIFIED:
19 May 56 FORCE: 1 Aug 63
Germany, West SIGNED: 28 Sep 55 RATIFIED:
27 Oct 60 FORCE: 1 Aug 63
Greece SIGNED: 28 Sep 55
Hungary SIGNED: 28 Sep 55 RATIFIED:
4 Oct 57
Iceland SIGNED: 3 May 63 RATIFIED: 3 May 63
FORCE: 1 Aug 63
Ireland SIGNED: 28 Sep 55 RATIFIED: 12 Oct 59
Israel SIGNED: 28 Sep 55
Italy SIGNED: 28 Sep 55 RATIFIED: 4 May 63
FORCE: 1 Aug 63
Ivory Coast RATIFIED: 2 Feb 62 FORCE:
1 Aug 63
Japan SIGNED: 2 May 56
Laos SIGNED: 28 Sep 55 RATIFIED: 9 May 56
FORCE: 1 Aug 63
Liechtenstein SIGNED: 28 Sep 55

Luxembourg SIGNED: 28 Sep 55 RATIFIED: 13 Feb 57 FORCE: 1 Aug 63
Madagascar RATIFIED: 17 Aug 62 FORCE: 1 Aug 63
Mali SIGNED: 16 Aug 62
Mexico SIGNED: 28 Sep 55 RATIFIED: 24 May 57 FORCE: 1 Aug 63
Morocco SIGNED: 31 May 63
Netherlands SIGNED: 28 Sep 55 RATIFIED: 21 Sep 60 FORCE: 1 Aug 63
New Zealand SIGNED: 19 Mar 58
Niger RATIFIED: 20 Feb 62 FORCE: 1 Aug 63
Norway SIGNED: 28 Sep 55 RATIFIED: 3 May 63 FORCE: 1 Aug 63
Pakistan SIGNED: 8 Aug 60 RATIFIED: 16 Jan 61 FORCE: 1 Aug 63
Philippines SIGNED: 28 Sep 55
Poland SIGNED: 28 Sep 55 RATIFIED: 23 Apr 56 FORCE: 1 Aug 63
Portugal SIGNED: 28 Sep 55
Romania SIGNED: 28 Sep 55 RATIFIED: 3 Dec 58 FORCE: 1 Aug 63
Sweden SIGNED: 28 Sep 55 RATIFIED: 3 May 63 FORCE: 1 Aug 63
Switzerland SIGNED: 28 Sep 55 RATIFIED: 3 May 63 FORCE: 1 Aug 63
UK Great Britain SIGNED: 23 Mar 56
USA (United States) SIGNED: 28 Jun 56
Ukrainian SSR SIGNED: 15 Jan 60 RATIFIED: 23 Jun 63 FORCE: 1 Aug 63
USSR (Soviet Union) SIGNED: 28 Sep 55 RATIFIED: 25 Mar 57 FORCE: 1 Aug 63
Venezuela SIGNED: 28 Sep 55 RATIFIED: 26 Aug 60 FORCE: 1 Aug 63
Yugoslavia SIGNED: 3 Dec 58 RATIFIED: 16 Apr 59 FORCE: 1 Aug 63

106944 Bilateral Agreement **479 UNTS 3**
SIGNED: 1 Jun 62 FORCE: 1 Jun 62
REGISTERED: 1 Oct 63 United Nations
ARTICLES: 6 LANGUAGE: English.
HEADNOTE: UN PROVISION ADMINISTRATORS
TOPIC: Tech Assistance
CONCEPTS: General consular functions. Diplomatic privileges. Diplomatic missions. Privileges and immunities. Arbitration. Procedure. Assistance.
INTL ORGS: Permanent Court of Arbitration. Arbitration Commission.
PROCEDURE: Amendment. Termination.
PARTIES:
United Nations
Tanganyika
ANNEX
480 UNTS 454. Tanganyika. Interpretation 18 Oct 63. Force 18 Oct 63.
480 UNTS 454. United Nations. Interpretation 16 Oct 63. Force 18 Oct 63.
550 UNTS 409. Tanzania. Force 14 May 65.
550 UNTS 409. United Nations. Force 14 May 65.

106945 Bilateral Agreement **479 UNTS 19**
SIGNED: 22 May 63 FORCE: 22 May 63
REGISTERED: 2 Oct 63 United Nations
ARTICLES: 6 LANGUAGE: English.
HEADNOTE: PERSONNEL
TOPIC: IGO Status/Immunit
CONCEPTS: General consular functions. Diplomatic privileges. Diplomatic missions. Privileges and immunities. Arbitration. Procedure. Status of experts.
INTL ORGS: Permanent Court of Arbitration. Arbitration Commission.
PROCEDURE: Amendment. Termination.
PARTIES:
Jamaica
United Nations

106946 Unilateral Instrument **479 UNTS 35**
SIGNED: 3 Oct 63 FORCE: 3 Oct 63
REGISTERED: 3 Oct 63 United Nations
ARTICLES: 1 LANGUAGE: English.
HEADNOTE: ACCEPTANCE ICJ JURISDICTION
TOPIC: ICJ Option Clause
CONCEPTS: Compulsory jurisdiction.
INTL ORGS: International Court of Justice.
PARTIES:
Uganda

106947 Multilateral Instrument **479 UNTS 39**
SIGNED: 25 May 63 FORCE: 13 Sep 63
REGISTERED: 4 Oct 63 Ethiopia
ARTICLES: 33 LANGUAGE: Amharic. Arabic. English. French.
HEADNOTE: CHARTER ORGANIZATION AFRICAN UNITY
TOPIC: IGO Establishment
CONCEPTS: Arbitration. Subsidiary organ. Establishment. Internal structure. Conformity with IGO decisions. Acceptance of UN obligations.
INTL ORGS: Organization of African Unity. United Nations. Arbitration Commission.
PROCEDURE: Ratification.
PARTIES:
Algeria SIGNED: 25 May 63
Burundi SIGNED: 25 May 63
Cameroon SIGNED: 25 May 63 RATIFIED: 26 Aug 63 FORCE: 13 Sep 63
Chad SIGNED: 25 May 63 RATIFIED: 7 Aug 63 FORCE: 13 Sep 63
Central Afri Rep SIGNED: 25 May 63
Congo (Brazzaville) SIGNED: 25 May 63 RATIFIED: 12 Jul 63 FORCE: 13 Sep 63
Congo (Zaire) SIGNED: 25 May 63 RATIFIED: 13 Sep 63 FORCE: 13 Sep 63
Dahomey SIGNED: 25 May 63 RATIFIED: 7 Sep 63 FORCE: 13 Sep 63
Ethiopia SIGNED: 25 May 63 RATIFIED: 9 Jun 63 FORCE: 13 Sep 63
Gabon SIGNED: 25 May 63 RATIFIED: 6 Jul 63 FORCE: 13 Sep 63
Ghana SIGNED: 25 May 63 RATIFIED: 15 Jul 63 FORCE: 13 Sep 63
Guinea SIGNED: 25 May 63 RATIFIED: 24 Jun 63 FORCE: 13 Sep 63
Ivory Coast SIGNED: 25 May 63 RATIFIED: 8 Jun 63 FORCE: 13 Sep 63
Liberia SIGNED: 25 May 63 RATIFIED: 29 Aug 63 FORCE: 13 Sep 63
Libya SIGNED: 25 May 63 RATIFIED: 11 Sep 63 FORCE: 13 Sep 63
Madagascar SIGNED: 25 May 63 RATIFIED: 10 Aug 63 FORCE: 13 Sep 63
Mali SIGNED: 25 May 63 RATIFIED: 24 Jul 63 FORCE: 13 Sep 63
Mauritania SIGNED: 25 May 63 RATIFIED: 26 Aug 63 FORCE: 13 Sep 63
Morocco SIGNED: 19 Sep 63
Nigeria SIGNED: 25 May 63 RATIFIED: 14 Nov 63 FORCE: 14 Nov 63
Niger SIGNED: 25 May 63 RATIFIED: 26 Jul 63 FORCE: 13 Sep 63
Rwanda SIGNED: 25 May 63 RATIFIED: 5 Aug 63 FORCE: 14 Nov 63
Senegal SIGNED: 25 May 63 RATIFIED: 2 Jul 63 FORCE: 14 Nov 63
Sierra Leone SIGNED: 25 May 63 RATIFIED: 11 Sep 63 FORCE: 13 Sep 63
Somalia SIGNED: 25 May 63
Sudan SIGNED: 25 May 63 RATIFIED: 19 Jul 63 FORCE: 14 Nov 63
Tanganyika SIGNED: 25 May 63 RATIFIED: 14 Sep 63 FORCE: 14 Sep 63
Tunisia SIGNED: 25 May 63 RATIFIED: 1 Oct 63 FORCE: 1 Oct 63
United Arab Rep SIGNED: 25 May 63 RATIFIED: 27 Jul 63 FORCE: 13 Sep 63
Uganda SIGNED: 25 May 63 RATIFIED: 3 Aug 63 FORCE: 13 Sep 63
Upper Volta SIGNED: 25 May 63 RATIFIED: 29 Oct 63 FORCE: 29 Oct 63

106948 Bilateral Protocol **479 UNTS 91**
SIGNED: 30 Sep 60 FORCE: 30 Jun 61
REGISTERED: 4 Oct 63 Netherlands
ARTICLES: 8 LANGUAGE: French.
HEADNOTE: SETTLEMENT FINANCIAL QUESTIONS
TOPIC: General Economic
CONCEPTS: Territorial application. Annex or appendix reference. Accounting procedures. Banking. Currency. Payment schedules.
PARTIES:
Netherlands
Romania
ANNEX
607 UNTS 342. Netherlands. Abrogation 31 Jul 67.
607 UNTS 342. Romania. Abrogation 31 Jul 67.

106949 Bilateral Agreement **479 UNTS 99**
SIGNED: 27 Sep 62 FORCE: 27 Aug 63
REGISTERED: 7 Oct 63 Finland
ARTICLES: 19 LANGUAGE: Finnish. Russian.
HEADNOTE: LEASE SOVIET PART OF SAIMAA CANAL AND VYOTSKY ISLAND
TOPIC: Territory Boundary
CONCEPTS: Conformity with municipal law. General cooperation. Inspection and observation. Free passage and transit. Responsibility and liability. Establishment of commission. Payment schedules. Materials, equipment and services. Navigational conditions. Canal improvement. Inland and territorial waters. Ports and pilotage. Frontier peoples and personnel. Frontier waterways.
INTL ORGS: Arbitration Commission. Special Commission.
TREATY REF: 258UNTS89.
PROCEDURE: Duration. Ratification.
PARTIES:
Finland
USSR (Soviet Union)
ANNEX
528 UNTS 320. USSR (Soviet Union). Signature 11 Aug 64. Force 18 Sep 64.
528 UNTS 320. Finland. Signature 11 Aug 64. Force 18 Sep 64.

106950 Bilateral Agreement **479 UNTS 145**
SIGNED: 24 Jun 59 FORCE: 27 Jun 63
REGISTERED: 8 Oct 63 USA (United States)
ARTICLES: 11 LANGUAGE: English. Spanish.
HEADNOTE: CIVIL USES ATOMIC ENERGY
TOPIC: Scientific Project
CONCEPTS: Definition of terms. Exchange of information and documents. Responsibility and liability. Use of facilities. Establishment of commission. Public health. Nuclear research. Scientific exchange. Materials, equipment and services. Nuclear materials. Non-nuclear materials. Peaceful use. Rights of supplier. Samples and testing. Security of information.
PROCEDURE: Duration. Renewal or Revival. Termination.
PARTIES:
Panama
USA (United States)

106951 Bilateral Exchange **479 UNTS 165**
SIGNED: 14 Jun 63 FORCE: 14 Jun 63
REGISTERED: 8 Oct 63 USA (United States)
ARTICLES: 2 LANGUAGE: English. Japanese.
HEADNOTE: USE AGRICULTURE COMMODITIES SALE INCOME FOR DEBT PAYMENT
TOPIC: Finance
CONCEPTS: Payment schedules. Agricultural commodities. Payment for war supplies.
TREATY REF: 241UNTS197.
PARTIES:
Japan
USA (United States)

106952 Bilateral Agreement **479 UNTS 175**
SIGNED: 19 Jun 63 FORCE: 19 Jun 63
REGISTERED: 8 Oct 63 USA (United States)
ARTICLES: 15 LANGUAGE: English.
HEADNOTE: EDUCATIONAL PROGRAM
TOPIC: Education
CONCEPTS: Definition of terms. Previous treaty replacement. Friendship and amity. Alien status. Standardization. Conformity with municipal law. General cooperation. Exchange of information and documents. Inspection and observation. Personnel. General property. Exchange. Commissions and foundations. Scholarships and grants. Accounting procedures. Currency. Expense sharing formulae. Financial programs. Funding procedures.
TREATY REF: 89UNTS127.
PROCEDURE: Amendment.
PARTIES:
India
USA (United States)

106953 Bilateral Agreement **479 UNTS 191**
SIGNED: 18 Jun 63 FORCE: 18 Jun 63
REGISTERED: 8 Oct 63 USA (United States)
ARTICLES: 6 LANGUAGE: English.
HEADNOTE: AGRI COMMOD TITLE I

TOPIC: US Agri Commod Aid
CONCEPTS: General provisions. Annex or appendix reference. Exchange of information and documents. Reexport of goods, etc.. Exchange rates and regulations. Transportation costs. Local currency. Commodities schedule. Purchase authorization. Surplus commodities. Mutual consultation.
PARTIES:
Cyprus
USA (United States)

106954 Bilateral Exchange **479 UNTS 207**
SIGNED: 29 Jun 63   FORCE: 29 Jun 63
REGISTERED: 8 Oct 63 USA (United States)
ARTICLES: 2 LANGUAGE: English.
HEADNOTE: INVESTMENT GUARANTIES
TOPIC: Finance
CONCEPTS: General cooperation. Arbitration. Procedure. Existing tribunals. Negotiation. Reciprocity in financial treatment. Currency. Payment schedules. Claims and settlements. Private investment guarantee.
PARTIES:
United Arab Rep
USA (United States)

106955 Bilateral Agreement **479 UNTS 215**
SIGNED: 27 Jun 63   FORCE: 27 Jun 63
REGISTERED: 8 Oct 63 USA (United States)
ARTICLES: 9 LANGUAGE: English.
HEADNOTE: AGRI TRADE TITLE III
TOPIC: US Agri Commod Aid
CONCEPTS: Reciprocity in trade. Currency. Payment schedules. Transportation costs. Agricultural commodities assistance.
PARTIES:
India
USA (United States)
ANNEX
494 UNTS 358. India. Amendment 20 Dec 63. Force 20 Nov 63.
494 UNTS 358. USA (United States). Amendment 9 Dec 63. Force 20 Dec 63.

106956 Bilateral Agreement **479 UNTS 223**
SIGNED: 25 Jun 63   FORCE: 25 Jun 63
REGISTERED: 8 Oct 63 USA (United States)
ARTICLES: 12 LANGUAGE: English. German.
HEADNOTE: EDUCATION CULTURE PROGRAM
TOPIC: Education
CONCEPTS: Previous treaty replacement. Privileges and immunities. Standardization. Conformity with municipal law. General cooperation. Inspection and observation. Personnel. General property. Exchange. Commissions and foundations. Teacher and student exchange. Scholarships and grants. Exchange. Research and development. Accounting procedures. Financial programs. Funding procedures.
INTL ORGS: Special Commission.
TREATY REF: 92UNTS201; 261UNTS468; 435UNTS316; 459UNTS45.
PROCEDURE: Amendment.
PARTIES:
Austria
USA (United States)

106957 Bilateral Agreement **479 UNTS 245**
SIGNED: 2 Jul 63   FORCE: 2 Jul 63
REGISTERED: 8 Oct 63 USA (United States)
ARTICLES: 5 LANGUAGE: English. Bulgarian.
HEADNOTE: CLAIMS
TOPIC: Claims and Debts
CONCEPTS: Conformity with municipal law. Expropriation. Compensation. Financial programs. Assets. Claims and settlements. Lump sum settlements.
PARTIES:
Bulgaria
USA (United States)

106958 Bilateral Exchange **479 UNTS 263**
SIGNED: 17 Jul 63   FORCE: 17 Jul 63
REGISTERED: 9 Oct 63 Denmark
ARTICLES: 2 LANGUAGE: Danish. German.
HEADNOTE: EXCHANGE NATURALIZATION NOTICES
TOPIC: Consul/Citizenship

CONCEPTS: Definition of terms. Annex or appendix reference. Exchange of information and documents.
PROCEDURE: Denunciation. Termination.
PARTIES:
Austria
Denmark

106959 Bilateral Agreement **479 UNTS 277**
SIGNED: 19 Oct 60   FORCE: 31 Jul 63
REGISTERED: 11 Oct 63 Belgium
ARTICLES: 12 LANGUAGE: English.
HEADNOTE: ESTABLISHMENT SCHEDULED AIR SERVICES
TOPIC: Air Transport
CONCEPTS: Definition of terms. Annex or appendix reference. Conformity with municipal law. Arbitration. Procedure. Existing tribunals. Negotiation. Reexport of goods, etc.. Fees and exemptions. Non-interest rates and fees. Customs exemptions. Routes and logistics. Navigational conditions. Permit designation. Air transport. Conditions of airlines operating permission. Operating authorizations and regulations.
INTL ORGS: International Civil Aviation Organization. International Court of Justice. Arbitration Commission.
TREATY REF: 15UNTS295.
PROCEDURE: Amendment. Ratification. Registration. Termination.
PARTIES:
Belgium
Jordan

106960 Bilateral Agreement **479 UNTS 291**
SIGNED: 4 Jun 61   FORCE: 4 Jul 63
REGISTERED: 11 Oct 63 Czechoslovakia
ARTICLES: 12 LANGUAGE: Czechoslovakian. English.
HEADNOTE: CULTURAL COOPERATION
TOPIC: Culture
CONCEPTS: Friendship and amity. Non-diplomatic delegations. Conformity with municipal law. Exchange of information and documents. Specialists exchange. Public health. Exchange. Scholarships and grants. Vocational training. Exchange. General cultural cooperation. Artists. Athletes. Scientific exchange. Publications exchange. Mass media exchange.
PROCEDURE: Denunciation. Duration. Ratification.
PARTIES:
Czechoslovakia
Somalia

106961 Bilateral Agreement **479 UNTS 301**
SIGNED: 16 Oct 62   FORCE: 8 Jul 63
REGISTERED: 11 Oct 63 Czechoslovakia
ARTICLES: 21 LANGUAGE: Czechoslovakian. Hungarian.
HEADNOTE: REGULATION FRONTIER TRAFFIC
TOPIC: Visas
CONCEPTS: Detailed regulations. General provisions. Border traffic and migration. Frontier permits. Conformity with municipal law. Immovable property. General property. Customs exemptions. Markers and definitions. Frontier peoples and personnel.
PROCEDURE: Denunciation. Duration. Renewal or Revival.
PARTIES:
Czechoslovakia
Hungary

106962 Bilateral Treaty **479 UNTS 337**
SIGNED: 29 May 61   FORCE: 10 Jan 63
REGISTERED: 11 Oct 63 Czechoslovakia
ARTICLES: 7 LANGUAGE: Czechoslovakian. Indonesian. English.
HEADNOTE: FRIENDSHIP & COOPERATION
TOPIC: General Amity
CONCEPTS: Friendship and amity. Peaceful relations. General cooperation. Procedure.
PROCEDURE: Denunciation. Ratification.
PARTIES:
Czechoslovakia
Indonesia

106963 Bilateral Agreement **480 UNTS 3**
SIGNED: 5 Apr 63   FORCE: 1 Apr 63

REGISTERED: 15 Oct 63 Austria
ARTICLES: 13 LANGUAGE: German. Bulgarian.
HEADNOTE: LONG-TERM REGULATION TRADE
TOPIC: General Trade
CONCEPTS: Detailed regulations. General provisions. Annex or appendix reference. Previous treaty replacement. Conformity with municipal law. General cooperation. Exchange of information and documents. Licenses and permits. Establishment of commission. Payment schedules. Smuggling. Customs declarations.
INTL ORGS: Special Commission.
TREATY REF: 27JULY60 TRADE AGREEMENT; 16OCT48 PAYMENTS AGREEME.
PROCEDURE: Denunciation. Duration.
PARTIES:
Austria
Bulgaria

106964 Multilateral Treaty **480 UNTS 43**
SIGNED: 5 Aug 63   FORCE: 10 Oct 63
REGISTERED: 15 Oct 63 USSR (Soviet Union)
ARTICLES: 5 LANGUAGE: English. Russian.
HEADNOTE: NUCLEAR TEST BAN TREATY
TOPIC: Sanitation
CONCEPTS: Definition of terms. Detailed regulations. General. Nuclear materials. Peaceful use. Samples and testing. Arms limitations.
PROCEDURE: Amendment. Accession. Duration. Ratification. Termination.
PARTIES:
Afghanistan SIGNED: 9 Aug 63
Algeria SIGNED: 19 Aug 63
Argentina SIGNED: 9 Aug 63
Australia SIGNED: 8 Aug 63
Austria SIGNED: 11 Sep 63
Belgium SIGNED: 8 Aug 63
Bolivia SIGNED: 20 Sep 63
Brazil SIGNED: 9 Aug 63
Bulgaria SIGNED: 8 Aug 63
Burma SIGNED: 14 Aug 63
Burundi SIGNED: 4 Oct 63
Byelorussia SIGNED: 8 Oct 63
Cameroon SIGNED: 27 Aug 63
Canada SIGNED: 8 Aug 63
Ceylon (Sri Lanka) SIGNED: 23 Aug 63
Chad SIGNED: 26 Aug 63
Chile SIGNED: 9 Aug 63
Taiwan SIGNED: 23 Aug 63
Congo (Zaire) SIGNED: 12 Aug 63
Colombia SIGNED: 16 Aug 63
Costa Rica SIGNED: 23 Aug 63
Cyprus SIGNED: 8 Aug 63
Czechoslovakia SIGNED: 8 Aug 63
Dahomey SIGNED: 9 Oct 63
Denmark SIGNED: 9 Aug 63
Dominican Republic SIGNED: 19 Sep 63
Ecuador SIGNED: 1 Oct 63
El Salvador SIGNED: 23 Aug 63
Ethiopia SIGNED: 19 Sep 63
Finland SIGNED: 8 Aug 63
Fed of Malaya SIGNED: 21 Aug 63
Gabon SIGNED: 10 Sep 63
Germany, East SIGNED: 8 Aug 63
Germany, West SIGNED: 19 Aug 63
Ghana SIGNED: 8 Aug 63
Greece SIGNED: 9 Aug 63
Guatemala SIGNED: 23 Sep 63
Haiti SIGNED: 9 Oct 63
Honduras SIGNED: 16 Aug 63
Hungary SIGNED: 8 Aug 63
Iceland SIGNED: 12 Aug 63
India SIGNED: 8 Aug 63
Indonesia SIGNED: 23 Aug 63
Iran SIGNED: 8 Aug 63
Iraq SIGNED: 12 Aug 63
Ireland SIGNED: 8 Aug 63
Israel SIGNED: 8 Aug 63
Italy SIGNED: 8 Aug 63
Ivory Coast SIGNED: 5 Sep 63
Jamaica SIGNED: 13 Aug 63
Japan SIGNED: 14 Aug 63
Jordan SIGNED: 19 Aug 63
Korea, South SIGNED: 30 Aug 63
Kuwait SIGNED: 20 Aug 63
Laos SIGNED: 8 Aug 63
Lebanon SIGNED: 13 Aug 63
Liberia SIGNED: 27 Aug 63
Libya SIGNED: 16 Aug 63
Luxembourg SIGNED: 13 Sep 63
Malagasy SIGNED: 23 Sep 63
Mali SIGNED: 23 Aug 63
Mauritania SIGNED: 8 Oct 63

Mexico SIGNED: 8 Aug 63
Mongolia SIGNED: 8 Aug 63
Morocco SIGNED: 27 Aug 63
Nepal SIGNED: 26 Aug 63
Netherlands SIGNED: 9 Aug 63
New Zealand SIGNED: 8 Aug 63 RATIFIED: 10 Oct 63 FORCE: 10 Oct 63
Nicaragua SIGNED: 16 Aug 63
Nigeria SIGNED: 30 Aug 63
Niger SIGNED: 24 Sep 63
Norway SIGNED: 9 Aug 63
Pakistan SIGNED: 14 Aug 63
Panama SIGNED: 20 Sep 63
Paraguay SIGNED: 21 Aug 63
Peru SIGNED: 23 Aug 63
Philippines SIGNED: 14 Aug 63
Poland SIGNED: 8 Aug 63 RATIFIED: 14 Oct 63 FORCE: 14 Oct 63
Portugal SIGNED: 9 Oct 63
Romania SIGNED: 8 Aug 63
Rwanda SIGNED: 19 Sep 63
San Marino SIGNED: 24 Sep 63
Senegal SIGNED: 9 Oct 63
Sierra Leone SIGNED: 9 Sep 63
South Africa RATIFIED: 10 Oct 63 FORCE: 10 Oct 63
Somalia SIGNED: 19 Aug 63
Spain SIGNED: 13 Aug 63
Sudan SIGNED: 9 Aug 63
Sweden SIGNED: 12 Aug 63
Switzerland SIGNED: 26 Aug 63
Syria SIGNED: 13 Aug 63
Tanganyika SIGNED: 20 Sep 63
Thailand SIGNED: 8 Aug 63
Togo SIGNED: 18 Sep 63
Trinidad/Tobago SIGNED: 13 Aug 63
Tunisia SIGNED: 13 Aug 63
Turkey SIGNED: 9 Aug 63
United Arab Rep SIGNED: 8 Aug 63
Uganda SIGNED: 29 Aug 63
UK Great Britain SIGNED: 5 Aug 63 RATIFIED: 10 Oct 63 FORCE: 10 Oct 63
USA (United States) SIGNED: 5 Aug 63 RATIFIED: 10 Oct 63 FORCE: 10 Oct 63
Ukrainian SSR SIGNED: 8 Oct 63
Upper Volta SIGNED: 30 Aug 63
Uruguay SIGNED: 27 Sep 63
USSR (Soviet Union) SIGNED: 5 Aug 63 RATIFIED: 10 Oct 63 FORCE: 10 Oct 63
Venezuela SIGNED: 16 Aug 63
Vietnam SIGNED: 1 Oct 63
Western Samoa SIGNED: 6 Sep 63
Yemen SIGNED: 12 Aug 63
Yugoslavia SIGNED: 8 Aug 63
ANNEX
485 UNTS 377.
486 UNTS 437.
489 UNTS 407.
492 UNTS 371.
500 UNTS 332.
510 UNTS 340.
529 UNTS 370.
533 UNTS 365.
533 UNTS 367.
535 UNTS 452.
541 UNTS 352.
545 UNTS 360.
572 UNTS 362.
604 UNTS 382.
614 UNTS 319.
639 UNTS 334.
639 UNTS 335.
639 UNTS 336.
649 UNTS 356.

106965 Multilateral Agreement **480 UNTS 100**
SIGNED: 10 Sep 63   FORCE: 10 Sep 63
REGISTERED: 16 Oct 63 United Nations
ARTICLES: 6 LANGUAGE: English. Arabic.
HEADNOTE: TECHNICAL ASSISTANCE
TOPIC: Tech Assistance
CONCEPTS: Definition of terms. Previous treaty replacement. Privileges and immunities. General cooperation. Exchange of information and documents. Personnel. Responsibility and liability. Title and deeds. Use of facilities. Exchange. Scholarships and grants. Vocational training. Research and development. Exchange rates and regulations. Expense sharing formulae. Local currency. Domestic obligation. General technical assistance. Materials, equipment and services. IGO status. Conformity with IGO decisions.

TREATY REF: 76UNTS132; 1UNTS15; 33UNTS261; 374UNTS147; 141UNTS.
PROCEDURE: Amendment. Termination.
PARTIES:
  FAO (Food Agri) SIGNED: 10 Sep 63 FORCE: 10 Sep 63
  IAEA (Atom Energy) SIGNED: 10 Sep 63 FORCE: 10 Sep 63
  ICAO (Civil Aviat) SIGNED: 10 Sep 63 FORCE: 10 Sep 63
  ILO (Labor Org) SIGNED: 10 Sep 63 FORCE: 10 Sep 63
  ITU (Telecommun) SIGNED: 10 Sep 63 FORCE: 10 Sep 63
  UNESCO (Educ/Cult) SIGNED: 10 Sep 63 FORCE: 10 Sep 63
  United Nations SIGNED: 10 Sep 63 FORCE: 10 Sep 63
  UPU (Postal Union) SIGNED: 10 Sep 63 FORCE: 10 Sep 63
  WHO (World Health) SIGNED: 10 Sep 63 FORCE: 10 Sep 63
  WMO (Meteorology) SIGNED: 10 Sep 63 FORCE: 10 Sep 63
  United Arab Rep SIGNED: 10 Sep 63 FORCE: 10 Sep 63

106966 Bilateral Agreement **480 UNTS 127**
SIGNED: 31 May 63   FORCE: 4 Sep 63
REGISTERED: 24 Oct 63 IDA (Devel Assoc)
ARTICLES: 6 LANGUAGE: English.
HEADNOTE: DEVELOPMENT CREDIT IRRIGATION
TOPIC: Non-IBRD Project
CONCEPTS: Definition of terms. Detailed regulations. Previous treaty amendment. Exchange of information and documents. Informational records. Accounting procedures. Currency. Interest rates. Tax exemptions. Credit provisions. Loan repayment. Terms of loan. Plans and standards. IDA development project. Irrigation.
PARTIES:
  IDA (Devel Assoc)
  Turkey

106967 Bilateral Treaty **480 UNTS 149**
SIGNED: 21 Feb 61   FORCE: 3 Oct 63
REGISTERED: 25 Oct 63 Belgium
ARTICLES: 21 LANGUAGE: French. English.
HEADNOTE: FRIENDSHIP ESTABLISHMENT NAVIGATION
TOPIC: General Amity
CONCEPTS: Definition of terms. Exceptions and exemptions. Territorial application. Previous treaty replacement. Alien status. General cooperation. Juridical personality. Expropriation. Free passage and transit. Legal protection and assistance. Private contracts. Procedure. Existing tribunals. Exchange rates and regulations. Fees and exemptions. Most favored nation clause. National treatment. Taxation. Navigational conditions. Inland and territorial waters. Shipwreck and salvage.
INTL ORGS: General Agreement on Tariffs and Trade. International Court of Justice.
TREATY REF: 2'1DEMARTENS54; 2'11DEMARTENS794;NA.
PROCEDURE: Duration. Ratification. Termination.
PARTIES:
  Belgium
  USA (United States)

106968 Multilateral Agreement **480 UNTS 180**
SIGNED: 30 Oct 63   FORCE: 30 Oct 63
REGISTERED: 1 Nov 63 United Nations
ARTICLES: 6 LANGUAGE: French.
HEADNOTE: TECHNICAL ASSISTANCE
TOPIC: Tech Assistance
CONCEPTS: Definition of terms. Privileges and immunities. General cooperation. Exchange of information and documents. Personnel. Responsibility and liability. Title and deeds. Use of facilities. Exchange. Scholarships and grants. Vocational training. Research and development. Exchange rates and regulations. Expense sharing formulae. Local currency. Domestic obligation. General technical assistance. Materials, equipment and services. IGO status. Conformity with IGO decisions.
TREATY REF: 76UNTS132; 33UNTS261; 1UNTS15; 374UNTS147.
PROCEDURE: Amendment. Termination.

PARTIES:
  FAO (Food Agri) SIGNED: 30 Oct 63 FORCE: 30 Oct 63
  IAEA (Atom Energy) SIGNED: 30 Oct 63 FORCE: 30 Oct 63
  ICAO (Civil Aviat) SIGNED: 30 Oct 63 FORCE: 30 Oct 63
  ILO (Labor Org) SIGNED: 30 Oct 63 FORCE: 30 Oct 63
  ITU (Telecommun) SIGNED: 30 Oct 63 FORCE: 30 Oct 63
  UNESCO (Educ/Cult) SIGNED: 30 Oct 63 FORCE: 30 Oct 63
  United Nations SIGNED: 30 Oct 63 FORCE: 30 Oct 63
  UPU (Postal Union) SIGNED: 30 Oct 63 FORCE: 30 Oct 63
  WHO (World Health) SIGNED: 30 Oct 63 FORCE: 30 Oct 63
  WMO (Meteorology) SIGNED: 30 Oct 63 FORCE: 30 Oct 63
  South Africa SIGNED: 30 Oct 63 FORCE: 30 Oct 63

106969 Multilateral Agreement **480 UNTS 197**
SIGNED: 21 Oct 63   FORCE: 21 Oct 63
REGISTERED: 1 Nov 63 United Nations
ARTICLES: 7 LANGUAGE: Spanish.
HEADNOTE: CENTRAL AMERICAN PUBLIC ADMINISTRATION SCHOOL
TOPIC: Tech Assistance
CONCEPTS: Time limit. Annex type material. Personnel. Teacher and student exchange. Scholarships and grants. Compensation. Expense sharing formulae. Domestic obligation. General technical assistance.
TREATY REF: 345UNTS251.
PROCEDURE: Amendment. Termination.
PARTIES:
  Costa Rica SIGNED: 21 Oct 63 FORCE: 21 Oct 63
  El Salvador SIGNED: 21 Oct 63 FORCE: 21 Oct 63
  Guatemala SIGNED: 21 Oct 63 FORCE: 21 Oct 63
  Honduras SIGNED: 21 Oct 63 FORCE: 21 Oct 63
  Nicaragua SIGNED: 21 Oct 63 FORCE: 21 Oct 63
  Panama SIGNED: 21 Oct 63 FORCE: 21 Oct 63
  United Nations SIGNED: 21 Oct 63 FORCE: 21 Oct 63

106970 Bilateral Agreement **480 UNTS 209**
SIGNED: 3 Jul 63   FORCE: 6 Sep 63
REGISTERED: 6 Nov 63 IBRD (World Bank)
ARTICLES: 6 LANGUAGE: English.
HEADNOTE: MASTER AGREEMENT EDUCATION
TOPIC: IBRD Project
CONCEPTS: Annex or appendix reference. Visa abolition. Exchange of information and documents. Informational records. Inspection and observation. Use of facilities. Arbitration. Exchange. Research results. Accounting procedures. Indemnities and reimbursements. Financial programs. Tax exemptions. Customs exemptions.
INTL ORGS: International Development Association. Arbitration Commission.
PARTIES:
  IBRD (World Bank)
  Tunisia

106971 Multilateral Agreement **480 UNTS 232**
SIGNED: 7 Nov 63   FORCE: 7 Nov 63
REGISTERED: 7 Nov 63 United Nations
ARTICLES: 6 LANGUAGE: French.
HEADNOTE: TECHNICAL ASSISTANCE
TOPIC: Tech Assistance
CONCEPTS: Definition of terms. Privileges and immunities. General cooperation. Exchange of information and documents. Personnel. Responsibility and liability. Title and deeds. Use of facilities. Exchange. Scholarships and grants. Vocational training. Research and development. Exchange rates and regulations. Local currency. Domestic obligation. General technical assistance. Materials, equipment and services. IGO status. Conformity with IGO decisions.
TREATY REF: 76UNTS132; 1UNTS15; 33UNTS261; 374UNTS147.

PROCEDURE: Amendment. Termination.
PARTIES:
Congo (Brazzaville) SIGNED: 7 Nov 63 FORCE: 7 Nov 63
FAO (Food Agri) SIGNED: 7 Nov 63 FORCE: 7 Nov 63
IAEA (Atom Energy) SIGNED: 7 Nov 63 FORCE: 7 Nov 63
ICAO (Civil Aviat) SIGNED: 7 Nov 63 FORCE: 7 Nov 63
ILO (Labor Org) SIGNED: 7 Nov 63 FORCE: 7 Nov 63
ITU (Telecommun) SIGNED: 7 Nov 63 FORCE: 7 Nov 63
UNESCO (Educ/Cult) SIGNED: 7 Nov 63 FORCE: 7 Nov 63
United Nations SIGNED: 7 Nov 63 FORCE: 7 Nov 63
UPU (Postal Union) SIGNED: 7 Nov 63 FORCE: 7 Nov 63
WHO (World Health) SIGNED: 7 Nov 63 FORCE: 7 Nov 63
WMO (Meteorology) SIGNED: 7 Nov 63 FORCE: 7 Nov 63

106972 Bilateral Agreement **480 UNTS 249**
SIGNED: 18 Nov 62   FORCE: 22 Sep 63
REGISTERED: 11 Nov 63 WHO (World Health)
ARTICLES: 6 LANGUAGE: French.
HEADNOTE: TECHNICAL ADVISORY ASSISTANCE
TOPIC: Tech Assistance
CONCEPTS: Definition of terms. Previous treaty replacement. Privileges and immunities. General cooperation. Exchange of information and documents. Personnel. Responsibility and liability. Title and deeds. Exchange. Scholarships and grants. Vocational training. Research and development. Expense sharing formulae. Local currency. Domestic obligation. Special projects. Materials, equipment and services. IGO status. Conformity with IGO decisions.
TREATY REF: 33UNTS261; 385UNTS3.
PROCEDURE: Amendment. Termination.
PARTIES:
WHO (World Health)
Syria

106973 Bilateral Agreement **480 UNTS 261**
SIGNED: 4 Jun 61   FORCE: 4 Jul 63
REGISTERED: 13 Nov 63 Czechoslovakia
ARTICLES: 9 LANGUAGE: English.
HEADNOTE: SCIENTIFIC TECHNICAL COOPERATION
TOPIC: Tech Assistance
CONCEPTS: Exceptions and exemptions. Guarantees and safeguards. Treaty implementation. General cooperation. Use of facilities. Research and scientific projects. Scientific exchange. General technical assistance.
PROCEDURE: Denunciation. Termination.
PARTIES:
Czechoslovakia
Somalia

106974 Bilateral Agreement **480 UNTS 267**
SIGNED: 22 Oct 62   FORCE: 12 Jul 63
REGISTERED: 13 Nov 63 Czechoslovakia
ARTICLES: 28 LANGUAGE: Czechoslovakian. Serbo-Croat.
HEADNOTE: INTERNATIONAL ROAD TRANSPORT
TOPIC: Land Transport
CONCEPTS: Exceptions and exemptions. General provisions. Annex or appendix reference. Visas. Conformity with municipal law. Exchange of information and documents. Licenses and permits. Personnel. Investigation of violations. Establishment of commission. Reexport of goods, etc.. Payment schedules. Tax exemptions. Customs exemptions. Temporary importation. Special projects. Passenger transport. Goods in transit. Transport of goods. Commercial road vehicles. Road rules.
PROCEDURE: Denunciation. Duration. Ratification. Renewal or Revival.
PARTIES:
Czechoslovakia
Yugoslavia

106975 Bilateral Agreement **481 UNTS 3**
SIGNED: 27 Aug 63   FORCE: 27 Aug 63

REGISTERED: 14 Nov 63 United Nations
ARTICLES: 5 LANGUAGE: Spanish.
HEADNOTE: SEMINAR (UN) WOMEN IN FAMILY LAW
TOPIC: Education
CONCEPTS: Definition of terms. Visas. Alien status. Human rights. Privileges and immunities. General cooperation. Family law. Personnel. Exchange. Special status.
INTL ORGS: Organization of American States.
TREATY REF: 1UNTS15,263; 33UNTS261.
PARTIES:
Colombia
United Nations

106976 Bilateral Agreement **481 UNTS 15**
SIGNED: 1 Mar 63   FORCE: 3 Oct 63
REGISTERED: 15 Nov 63 IBRD (World Bank)
ARTICLES: 8 LANGUAGE: English.
HEADNOTE: LOAN IMMIGRATION
TOPIC: IBRD Project
CONCEPTS: Default remedies. Definition of terms. Annex or appendix reference. Exchange of information and documents. Informational records. Inspection and observation. Accounting procedures. Bonds. Fees and exemptions. Interest rates. Tax exemptions. Domestic obligation. Terms of loan. Loan regulations. Loan guarantee. Guarantor non-interference. Irrigation.
PARTIES:
Nicaragua
IBRD (World Bank)

106977 Bilateral Agreement **481 UNTS 39**
SIGNED: 26 Oct 62   FORCE: 26 Oct 63
REGISTERED: 15 Nov 63 IBRD (World Bank)
ARTICLES: 8 LANGUAGE: English.
HEADNOTE: LOAN HIGHWAY
TOPIC: IBRD Project
CONCEPTS: Default remedies. Definition of terms. Annex or appendix reference. Exchange of information and documents. Informational records. Inspection and observation. Accounting procedures. Bonds. Fees and exemptions. Interest rates. Tax exemptions. Domestic obligation. Terms of loan. Loan regulations. Loan guarantee. Guarantor non-interference. Roads and highways.
PARTIES:
IBRD (World Bank)
Uruguay

106978 Bilateral Agreement **481 UNTS 59**
SIGNED: 19 Jun 63   FORCE: 16 Oct 63
REGISTERED: 15 Nov 63 IBRD (World Bank)
ARTICLES: 5 LANGUAGE: English.
HEADNOTE: GUARANTEE POWER
TOPIC: IBRD Project
CONCEPTS: Annex or appendix reference. Exchange of information and documents. Inspection and observation. Bonds. Compensation. Tax exemptions. Domestic obligation. Terms of loan. Loan regulations. Loan guarantee. Guarantor non-interference. Industry.
PARTIES:
El Salvador
IBRD (World Bank)

106979 Bilateral Agreement **481 UNTS 85**
SIGNED: 22 Dec 61   FORCE: 17 Sep 63
REGISTERED: 15 Nov 63 IBRD (World Bank)
ARTICLES: 5 LANGUAGE: English.
HEADNOTE: GUARANTEE IRON & STEEL
TOPIC: IBRD Project
CONCEPTS: Definition of terms. Annex or appendix reference. Exchange of information and documents. Bonds. Fees and exemptions. Tax exemptions. Domestic obligation. Loan regulations. Loan guarantee. Guarantor non-interference. Industry.
PARTIES:
India
IBRD (World Bank)

106980 Bilateral Agreement **481 UNTS 125**
SIGNED: 25 Sep 63   FORCE: 25 Sep 63
REGISTERED: 15 Nov 63 WHO (World Health)
ARTICLES: 6 LANGUAGE: English.
HEADNOTE: TECHNICAL ADVISORY ASSISTANCE

TOPIC: Tech Assistance
CONCEPTS: Definition of terms. Treaty implementation. Privileges and immunities. General cooperation. Exchange of information and documents. Personnel. Responsibility and liability. Title and deeds. Scholarships and grants. Vocational training. Research and development. Expense sharing formulae. Local currency. Domestic obligation. Special projects. Materials, equipment and services. IGO status. Conformity with IGO decisions.
TREATY REF: 14UNTS185; 33UNTS261.
PROCEDURE: Amendment. Termination.
PARTIES:
Jamaica
WHO (World Health)

106981 Bilateral Convention **481 UNTS 137**
SIGNED: 6 Oct 61   FORCE: 20 Aug 63
REGISTERED: 15 Nov 63 Greece
ARTICLES: 31 LANGUAGE: English.
HEADNOTE: DOUBLE TAXATION FISCAL EVASION TAXES INCOME
TOPIC: Taxation
CONCEPTS: Exceptions and exemptions. Previous treaty renunciation. Privileges and immunities. Conformity with municipal law. Exchange of official publications. Negotiation. Teacher and student exchange. Taxation. Death duties. Tax credits. Equitable taxes. Tax exemptions. Air transport. Merchant vessels.
TREATY REF: 126LTS411; 219UNTS147.
PROCEDURE: Duration. Ratification. Termination.
PARTIES:
Greece
Sweden

106982 Bilateral Agreement **481 UNTS 171**
SIGNED: 24 Jul 63   FORCE: 7 Oct 63
REGISTERED: 18 Nov 63 IBRD (World Bank)
ARTICLES: 8 LANGUAGE: English.
HEADNOTE: LOAN POWER
TOPIC: IBRD Project
CONCEPTS: Default remedies. Definition of terms. Annex or appendix reference. Exchange of information and documents. Informational records. Inspection and observation. Accounting procedures. Bonds. Fees and exemptions. Interest rates. Tax exemptions. Domestic obligation. Terms of loan. Loan regulations. Loan guarantee. Guarantor non-interference. Hydro-electric power.
PARTIES:
Denmark
IBRD (World Bank)

106983 Bilateral Agreement **481 UNTS 191**
SIGNED: 5 Jun 63   FORCE: 17 Sep 63
REGISTERED: 18 Nov 63 IBRD (World Bank)
ARTICLES: 5 LANGUAGE: English.
HEADNOTE: GUARANTEE INDUSTRIAL CREDIT & INVESTMENT
TOPIC: IBRD Project
CONCEPTS: Definition of terms. Annex or appendix reference. Exchange of information and documents. Inspection and observation. Bonds. Fees and exemptions. Tax exemptions. Domestic obligation. Terms of loan. Loan regulations. Loan guarantee. Guarantor non-interference.
PARTIES:
India
IBRD (World Bank)

106984 Bilateral Agreement **481 UNTS 227**
SIGNED: 11 Jun 63   FORCE: 23 Jul 63
REGISTERED: 18 Nov 63 IBRD (World Bank)
ARTICLES: 8 LANGUAGE: English.
HEADNOTE: LOAN HIGHWAY
TOPIC: IBRD Project
CONCEPTS: Default remedies. Definition of terms. Annex or appendix reference. Exchange of information and documents. Informational records. Accounting procedures. Bonds. Fees and exemptions. Tax exemptions. Domestic obligation. Terms of loan. Loan regulations. Loan guarantee. Guarantor non-interference. Roads and highways.
PARTIES:
IBRD (World Bank)
Thailand

106985 Bilateral Agreement **481 UNTS 247**
SIGNED: 30 Oct 63 FORCE: 30 Oct 63
REGISTERED: 18 Nov 63 United Nations
ARTICLES: 10 LANGUAGE: French.
HEADNOTE: ASSISTANCE
TOPIC: Direct Aid
CONCEPTS: Detailed regulations. Treaty implementation. Visas. Privileges and immunities. Exchange of information and documents. Informational records. Inspection and observation. Operating agencies. Personnel. Public information. Responsibility and liability. Title and deeds. Use of facilities. Arbitration. Procedure. Negotiation. Import quotas. Attachment of funds. Exchange rates and regulations. Expense sharing formulae. Financial programs. Domestic obligation. General technical assistance. Economic assistance. Materials, equipment and services. IGO status.
INTL ORGS: International Atomic Energy Agency. International Court of Justice. United Nations. Arbitration Commission.
TREATY REF: 1UNTS15; 33UNTS261; 374UNTS147.
PROCEDURE: Amendment. Termination.
PARTIES:
Central Afri Rep
UN Special Fund

106986 Multilateral Agreement **481 UNTS 262**
SIGNED: 3 Aug 59 FORCE: 1 Jul 63
REGISTERED: 19 Nov 63 USA (United States)
ARTICLES: 83 LANGUAGE: English. French. German.
HEADNOTE: STATUS OF FORCES
TOPIC: Status of Forces
CONCEPTS: Annex type material.
INTL ORGS: International Civil Aviation Organization. North Atlantic Treaty Organization. Arbitration Commission. Special Commission.
PARTIES:
Belgium SIGNED: 3 Aug 59 RATIFIED: 15 May 63 FORCE: 1 Jul 63
Canada SIGNED: 3 Aug 59 RATIFIED: 11 Dec 63 FORCE: 1 Jul 63
France SIGNED: 3 Aug 59 RATIFIED: 11 Jan 62 FORCE: 1 Jul 63
Germany, West SIGNED: 3 Aug 59 RATIFIED: 1 Jun 63 FORCE: 1 Jul 63
Netherlands SIGNED: 3 Aug 59 RATIFIED: 10 Sep 62 FORCE: 1 Jul 63
UK Great Britain SIGNED: 3 Aug 59 RATIFIED: 9 Jul 62 FORCE: 1 Jul 63
USA (United States) SIGNED: 3 Aug 59 RATIFIED: 28 Jul 61 FORCE: 1 Jul 63

106987 Bilateral Agreement **482 UNTS 3**
SIGNED: 21 Dec 62 FORCE: 21 Oct 63
REGISTERED: 19 Nov 63 Belgium
ARTICLES: 14 LANGUAGE: French. Dutch. Arabic.
HEADNOTE: CULTURAL CONVENTION
TOPIC: Culture
CONCEPTS: Treaty implementation. Friendship and amity. Conformity with municipal law. Establishment of commission. Specialists exchange. Recognition of degrees. Exchange. Teacher and student exchange. Scholarships and grants. Vocational training. Exchange. General cultural cooperation. Artists. Athletes. Scientific exchange. Research and development. Publications exchange. Mass media exchange.
PROCEDURE: Denunciation. Duration. Ratification.
PARTIES:
Belgium
Tunisia

106988 Multilateral Exchange **482 UNTS 19**
SIGNED: 19 Jun 63 FORCE: 19 Jul 63
REGISTERED: 21 Nov 63 Belgium
ARTICLES: 2 LANGUAGE: French. Spanish.
HEADNOTE: MOVEMENT SEAMEN
TOPIC: Visas
CONCEPTS: Definition of terms. Border traffic and migration. Denial of admission. Non-visa travel documents. Conformity with municipal law. Indemnities and reimbursements.
PROCEDURE: Denunciation. Duration. Renewal or Revival.
PARTIES:
Belgium SIGNED: 19 Jun 63 FORCE: 19 Jul 63
Luxembourg SIGNED: 19 Jun 63 FORCE: 19 Jul 63

Netherlands SIGNED: 19 Jun 63 FORCE: 19 Jul 63
Spain SIGNED: 19 Jun 63 FORCE: 19 Jul 63

106989 Bilateral Agreement **482 UNTS 29**
SIGNED: 9 Jul 63 FORCE: 9 Aug 63
REGISTERED: 21 Nov 63 Hungary
ARTICLES: 8 LANGUAGE: Hungarian. German.
HEADNOTE: COOPERATION PLANT PROTECTION
TOPIC: Sanitation
CONCEPTS: General cooperation. Disease control.
PROCEDURE: Denunciation. Duration.
PARTIES:
Austria
Hungary

106990 Bilateral Agreement **482 UNTS 43**
SIGNED: 21 Jun 63 FORCE: 1 Nov 63
REGISTERED: 22 Nov 63 IBRD (World Bank)
ARTICLES: 5 LANGUAGE: English.
HEADNOTE: GUARANTEE POWER & TELECOMMUNICATIONS
TOPIC: IBRD Project
CONCEPTS: Definition of terms. Annex or appendix reference. Exchange of information and documents. Inspection and observation. Bonds. Fees and exemptions. Tax exemptions. Domestic obligation. Terms of loan. Loan regulations. Loan guarantee. Guarantor non-interference. Roads and highways.
PARTIES:
IBRD (World Bank)
Yugoslavia

106991 Bilateral Agreement **482 UNTS 69**
SIGNED: 10 Jul 63 FORCE: 17 Oct 63
REGISTERED: 22 Nov 63 IBRD (World Bank)
ARTICLES: 5 LANGUAGE: English.
HEADNOTE: GUARANTEE AGREEMENT - POWER AND TELECOMMUNICATION PROJECT
TOPIC: IBRD Project
CONCEPTS: Definition of terms. Annex or appendix reference. Exchange of information and documents. Inspection and observation. Fees and exemptions. Tax exemptions. Domestic obligation. Terms of loan. Loan regulations. Loan guarantee. Guarantor non-interference. Hydroelectric power. Telecommunications.
PARTIES:
Costa Rica
IBRD (World Bank)

106992 Bilateral Agreement **482 UNTS 103**
SIGNED: 15 Oct 63 FORCE: 6 Nov 63
REGISTERED: 22 Nov 63 IBRD (World Bank)
ARTICLES: 7 LANGUAGE: English.
HEADNOTE: LOAN AGREEMENT
TOPIC: IBRD Project
CONCEPTS: Default remedies. Definition of terms. Annex or appendix reference. Exchange of information and documents. Informational records. Inspection and observation. Accounting procedures. Bonds. Fees and exemptions. Interest rates. Tax exemptions. Domestic obligation. Terms of loan. Loan regulations. Loan guarantee.
PARTIES:
Norway
IBRD (World Bank)

106993 Bilateral Agreement **482 UNTS 123**
SIGNED: 15 Jul 63 FORCE: 8 Oct 63
REGISTERED: 22 Nov 63 IBRD (World Bank)
ARTICLES: 5 LANGUAGE: English.
HEADNOTE: GUARANTEE DEVELOPMENT BANK
TOPIC: IBRD Project
CONCEPTS: Definition of terms. Annex or appendix reference. Exchange of information and documents. Inspection and observation. Bonds. Fees and exemptions. Tax exemptions. Domestic obligation. Terms of loan. Loan regulations. Loan guarantee. Guarantor non-interference.
PARTIES:
Malaysia
IBRD (World Bank)
ANNEX
549 UNTS 342. IBRD (World Bank). Amendment 2 Sep 65. Force 2 Sep 65.
549 UNTS 342. Malaysia. Amendment 2 Sep 65. Force 2 Sep 65.

106994 Bilateral Agreement **482 UNTS 159**
SIGNED: 21 Jun 63 FORCE: 7 Aug 63
REGISTERED: 26 Nov 63 IBRD (World Bank)
ARTICLES: 5 LANGUAGE: English.
HEADNOTE: GUARANTEE RAILROAD
TOPIC: IBRD Project
CONCEPTS: Definition of terms. Annex or appendix reference. Exchange of information and documents. Inspection and observation. Bonds. Fees and exemptions. Tax exemptions. Domestic obligation. Terms of loan. Loan regulations. Loan guarantee. Guarantor non-interference. Railways.
PARTIES:
Colombia
IBRD (World Bank)

106995 Unilateral Instrument **482 UNTS 187**
SIGNED: 27 Nov 63 FORCE: 27 Nov 63
REGISTERED: 26 Nov 63 United Nations
ARTICLES: 1 LANGUAGE: English.
HEADNOTE: ACCEPTANCE ICJ JURISDICTION
TOPIC: ICJ Option Clause
CONCEPTS: Exceptions and exemptions. Compulsory jurisdiction.
INTL ORGS: International Court of Justice. United Nations.
PROCEDURE: Amendment. Denunciation. Termination.
PARTIES:
UK Great Britain
ANNEX
654 UNTS 381. UK Great Britain. Termination 1 Jan 69.

106996 Bilateral Agreement **482 UNTS 193**
SIGNED: 8 Apr 61 FORCE: 8 Apr 61
REGISTERED: 26 Nov 63 Netherlands
ARTICLES: 23 LANGUAGE: Dutch. Spanish.
HEADNOTE: IMMIGRANT RECRUITMENT PLACEMENT
TOPIC: Non-ILO Labor
CONCEPTS: Definition of terms. Detailed regulations. General provisions. Annex or appendix reference. Border traffic and migration. Resident permits. Repatriation of nationals. Private contracts. Establishment of commission. Safety standards. Wages and salaries. Non-ILO labor relations. Administrative cooperation. Migrant worker. Indemnities and reimbursements. Monetary and gold transfers.
PROCEDURE: Denunciation. Duration. Renewal or Revival.
PARTIES:
Netherlands
Spain

106997 Bilateral Agreement **482 UNTS 227**
SIGNED: 20 Sep 63 FORCE: 7 Oct 63
REGISTERED: 27 Nov 63 IBRD (World Bank)
ARTICLES: 5 LANGUAGE: English.
HEADNOTE: GUARANTEE HYDROELECTRIC PROJECT
TOPIC: IBRD Project
CONCEPTS: Definition of terms. Annex or appendix reference. Exchange of information and documents. Inspection and observation. Bonds. Fees and exemptions. Tax exemptions. Domestic obligation. Terms of loan. Loan regulations. Loan guarantee. Guarantor non-interference. Hydroelectric power.
PARTIES:
IBRD (World Bank)
Venezuela

106998 Bilateral Agreement **482 UNTS 256**
SIGNED: 16 Jul 63 FORCE: 5 Nov 63
REGISTERED: 29 Nov 63 IBRD (World Bank)
ARTICLES: 5 LANGUAGE: English.
HEADNOTE: GUARANTEE POWER
TOPIC: IBRD Project
CONCEPTS: Definition of terms. Annex or appendix reference. Exchange of information and documents. Inspection and observation. Bonds. Fees and exemptions. Tax exemptions. Domestic obligation. Terms of loan. Loan regulations. Loan guarantee. Guarantor non-interference. Hydroelectric power.

PARTIES:
Colombia
IBRD (World Bank)

106999 Multilateral Agreement **482 UNTS 286**
SIGNED: 8 Nov 63   FORCE: 8 Nov 63
REGISTERED: 1 Dec 63 United Nations
ARTICLES: 6 LANGUAGE: English. Spanish.
HEADNOTE: TECHNICAL ASSISTANCE
TOPIC: Tech Assistance
CONCEPTS: Definition of terms. Previous treaty replacement. Visas. Privileges and immunities. General cooperation. Exchange of information and documents. Licenses and permits. Personnel. Responsibility and liability. Title and deeds. Use of facilities. Exchange. Scholarships and grants. Vocational training. Research and development. Import quotas. Exchange rates and regulations. Expense sharing formulae. Local currency. Domestic obligation. General technical assistance. Materials, equipment and services. IGO status. Conformity with IGO decisions.
TREATY REF: 76UNTS32; 33UNTS261; 1UNTS15; 374UNTS147.
PROCEDURE: Amendment. Termination.
PARTIES:
Honduras SIGNED: 8 Nov 63 FORCE: 8 Nov 63
FAO (Food Agri) SIGNED: 8 Nov 63 FORCE: 8 Nov 63
IAEA (Atom Energy) SIGNED: 8 Nov 63 FORCE: 8 Nov 63
ICAO (Civil Aviat) SIGNED: 8 Nov 63 FORCE: 8 Nov 63
ILO (Labor Org) SIGNED: 8 Nov 63 FORCE: 8 Nov 63
ITU (Telecommun) SIGNED: 8 Nov 63 FORCE: 8 Nov 63
UNESCO (Educ/Cult) SIGNED: 8 Nov 63 FORCE: 8 Nov 63
United Nations SIGNED: 8 Nov 63 FORCE: 8 Nov 63
UPU (Postal Union) SIGNED: 8 Nov 63 FORCE: 8 Nov 63
WHO (World Health) SIGNED: 8 Nov 63 FORCE: 8 Nov 63
WMO (Meteorology) SIGNED: 8 Nov 63 FORCE: 8 Nov 63

107000 Bilateral Agreement **482 UNTS 309**
SIGNED: 8 May 63   FORCE: 5 Nov 63
REGISTERED: 2 Dec 63 Finland
ARTICLES: 4 LANGUAGE: Finnish. Spanish.
HEADNOTE: MILITARY SERVICE
TOPIC: Milit Servic/Citiz
CONCEPTS: Dual nationality. Certificates of service. Service in foreign army.
PROCEDURE: Denunciation. Ratification.
PARTIES:
Argentina
Finland

107001 Bilateral Agreement **482 UNTS 319**
SIGNED: 3 Dec 63   FORCE: 3 Dec 63
REGISTERED: 3 Dec 63 United Nations
ARTICLES: 8 LANGUAGE: English.
HEADNOTE: UNICEF ACTIVITIES
TOPIC: IGO Operations
CONCEPTS: Privileges and immunities. Exchange of information and documents. Accounting procedures. Liaison with other IGO's. Security of the government. Inter-agency agreements.
INTL ORGS: United Nations.
TREATY REF: 42UNTS354.
PROCEDURE: Amendment. Termination.
PARTIES:
Iraq
UNICEF (Children)

107002 Bilateral Agreement **482 UNTS 329**
SIGNED: 3 Dec 63   FORCE: 3 Dec 63
REGISTERED: 3 Dec 63 United Nations
ARTICLES: 6 LANGUAGE: Spanish.
HEADNOTE: EXECUTIVE ADMINISTRATIVE PERSONNEL
TOPIC: IGO Status/Immunit
CONCEPTS: Annex or appendix reference. Diplomatic missions. Privileges and immunities. Diplomatic correspondence. Notarial acts and services. Responsibility and liability. Arbitration. Special tribunals. Customs duties. Status of experts. IGO obligations.
INTL ORGS: Permanent Court of Arbitration. Arbitration Commission.
TREATY REF: 319UNTS14.
PROCEDURE: Amendment.
PARTIES:
Nicaragua
United Nations

107003 Bilateral Exchange **482 UNTS 347**
SIGNED: 13 Mar 63   FORCE: 13 Mar 63
REGISTERED: 4 Dec 63 UK Great Britain
ARTICLES: 2 LANGUAGE: English.
HEADNOTE: SUPPLY URANIUM
TOPIC: Atomic Energy
CONCEPTS: Atomic energy assistance. General. Nuclear materials.
PARTIES:
Pakistan
UK Great Britain

107004 Bilateral Agreement **482 UNTS 353**
SIGNED: 5 Jun 63   FORCE: 5 Jun 63
REGISTERED: 4 Dec 63 UK Great Britain
ARTICLES: 9 LANGUAGE: English. Spanish.
HEADNOTE: LOAN
TOPIC: Loans and Credits
CONCEPTS: Definition of terms. Annex or appendix reference. Currency. Interest rates. Payment schedules. Economic assistance. Loan and credit. Loan repayment. Refinance of loan.
PARTIES:
Argentina
UK Great Britain

107005 Bilateral Agreement **483 UNTS 3**
SIGNED: 11 Oct 63   FORCE: 11 Oct 63
REGISTERED: 4 Dec 63 UK Great Britain
ARTICLES: 21 LANGUAGE: English.
HEADNOTE: ATLANTIC UNDERSEA TEST EVALUATION CENTER
TOPIC: Scientific Project
CONCEPTS: Definition of terms. Annex or appendix reference. Visas. Privileges and immunities. Incorporation of treaty provisions into national law. Personnel. General property. Private contracts. Use of facilities. Public health. Employment regulations. Research and scientific projects. Research and development. Currency. Local currency. Claims and settlements. Tax exemptions. Special projects. Aid missions. Navigational conditions. Navigational equipment. Facilities and equipment. Postal services. Security of information. Jurisdiction. Status of forces.
PROCEDURE: Duration.
PARTIES:
UK Great Britain
USA (United States)

107006 Bilateral Agreement **483 UNTS 39**
SIGNED: 23 Sep 63   FORCE: 1 Oct 63
REGISTERED: 4 Dec 63 UK Great Britain
ARTICLES: 23 LANGUAGE: English.
HEADNOTE: EXCHANGE MONEY ORDERS
TOPIC: Postal Service
CONCEPTS: Detailed regulations. Conformity with municipal law. Accounting procedures. Currency. Payment schedules. Regulations. Money orders and postal checks. Rates and charges. Advice lists and orders. Telegrams.
PROCEDURE: Duration. Termination. Application to Non-self-governing Territories.
PARTIES:
Australia
UK Great Britain

107007 Multilateral Agreement **483 UNTS 72**
SIGNED: 22 May 63   FORCE: 22 May 63
REGISTERED: 6 Dec 63 United Nations
ARTICLES: 6 LANGUAGE: English.
HEADNOTE: TECHNICAL ASSISTANCE
TOPIC: Tech Assistance
CONCEPTS: Definition of terms. Privileges and immunities. General cooperation. Exchange of information and documents. Personnel. Responsibility and liability. Title and deeds. Use of facilities. Exchange. Scholarships and grants. Vocational training. Research and development. Exchange rates and regulations. Expense sharing formulae. Local currency. Domestic obligation. General technical assistance. Materials, equipment and services. IGO status. Conformity with IGO decisions.
TREATY REF: 76UNTS132; 1UNTS15; 33UNTS261; 374UNTS147.
PARTIES:
Jamaica SIGNED: 22 May 63 FORCE: 22 May 63
FAO (Food Agri) SIGNED: 22 May 63 FORCE: 22 May 63
IAEA (Atom Energy) SIGNED: 22 May 63 FORCE: 22 May 63
ICAO (Civil Aviat) SIGNED: 22 May 63 FORCE: 22 May 63
ILO (Labor Org) SIGNED: 22 May 63 FORCE: 22 May 63
ITU (Telecommun) SIGNED: 22 May 63 FORCE: 22 May 63
UNESCO (Educ/Cult) SIGNED: 22 May 63 FORCE: 22 May 63
United Nations SIGNED: 22 May 63 FORCE: 22 May 63
UPU (Postal Union) SIGNED: 22 May 63 FORCE: 22 May 63
WHO (World Health) SIGNED: 22 May 63 FORCE: 22 May 63
WMO (Meteorology) SIGNED: 22 May 63 FORCE: 22 May 63

107008 Bilateral Agreement **483 UNTS 89**
SIGNED: 2 Mar 60   FORCE: 2 Mar 60
REGISTERED: 9 Dec 63 Greece
ARTICLES: 11 LANGUAGE: French.
HEADNOTE: TRADE
TOPIC: General Trade
CONCEPTS: Annex or appendix reference. General cooperation. Inspection and observation. Licenses and permits. Establishment of commission. Export quotas. Import quotas. Reciprocity in trade. Trade procedures. Payment schedules. Smuggling. Most favored nation clause. General transportation.
INTL ORGS: Organization for Economic Co-operation and Development.
PARTIES:
Greece
Tunisia

107009 Bilateral Agreement **483 UNTS 113**
SIGNED: 1 Nov 61   FORCE: 1 Nov 61
REGISTERED: 9 Dec 63 Greece
ARTICLES: 9 LANGUAGE: French.
HEADNOTE: TRADE
TOPIC: General Trade
CONCEPTS: Definition of terms. Annex or appendix reference. Licenses and permits. Establishment of commission. Trade procedures. Currency. Smuggling. Most favored nation clause. Customs declarations.
INTL ORGS: Organization for Economic Co-operation and Development. Special Commission.
PROCEDURE: Duration. Renewal or Revival. Termination.
PARTIES:
Greece
Morocco

107010 Bilateral Agreement **483 UNTS 127**
SIGNED: 8 Nov 60   FORCE: 1 Oct 60
REGISTERED: 9 Dec 63 Greece
ARTICLES: 8 LANGUAGE: French.
HEADNOTE: LONG-TERM TRADE
TOPIC: General Trade
CONCEPTS: Annex or appendix reference. Previous treaty replacement. General cooperation. Licenses and permits. Establishment of commission. Export quotas. Import quotas. Currency. Payment schedules. Quotas.
INTL ORGS: Special Commission.
TREATY REF: 30JULY56 PLUS 22OCT58.
PROCEDURE: Duration. Renewal or Revival. Termination.
PARTIES:
Greece
Poland

107011 Bilateral Agreement **483 UNTS 141**
SIGNED: 8 Nov 60   FORCE: 1 Oct 60
REGISTERED: 9 Dec 63 Greece

ARTICLES: 9 LANGUAGE: French.
HEADNOTE: PAYMENTS
TOPIC: Finance
CONCEPTS: Detailed regulations. General cooper-
ation. General trade. Accounting procedures. At-
tachment of funds. Banking. Balance of pay-
ments. Exchange rates and regulations. Fees and
exemptions. Financial programs. Payment
schedules. Assets transfer.
TREATY REF: 483UNTS127.
PROCEDURE: Denunciation. Duration.
PARTIES:
 Greece
 Poland

107012　Bilateral Agreement　**483 UNTS 151**
SIGNED: 27 Sep 63　　　FORCE: 22 Nov 63
REGISTERED: 10 Dec 63 IBRD (World Bank)
ARTICLES: 8 LANGUAGE: English.
HEADNOTE: LOAN DEEP SEA FISHERIES
TOPIC: IBRD Project
CONCEPTS: Default remedies. Definition of terms.
Annex or appendix reference. Exchange of infor-
mation and documents. Informational records.
Inspection and observation. Accounting proce-
dures. Bonds. Fees and exemptions. Interest
rates. Tax exemptions. Domestic obligation.
Terms of loan. Loan regulations. Loan guarantee.
Guarantor non-interference. Ocean resources.
PARTIES:
 Taiwan
 IBRD (World Bank)

107013　Bilateral Agreement　**483 UNTS 173**
SIGNED: 6 Sep 63　　　FORCE: 4 Dec 63
REGISTERED: 11 Dec 63 IBRD (World Bank)
ARTICLES: 5 LANGUAGE: English.
HEADNOTE: GUARANTEE ELECTRICITY BOOD
PROJECT
TOPIC: IBRD Project
CONCEPTS: Definition of terms. Annex or appen-
dix reference. Exchange of information and docu-
ments. Inspection and observation. Bonds.
Fees and exemptions. Tax exemptions. Domestic
obligation. Terms of loan. Loan regulations. Loan
guarantee. Guarantor non-interference. Hydro-
electric power.
PARTIES:
 IBRD (World Bank)
 UK Great Britain

107014　Bilateral Agreement　**483 UNTS 205**
SIGNED: 24 May 63　　　FORCE: 3 Jul 63
REGISTERED: 12 Dec 63 IDA (Devel Assoc)
ARTICLES: 7 LANGUAGE: English.
HEADNOTE: DEVELOPMENT CREDIT POWER
TOPIC: Non-IBRD Project
CONCEPTS: Definition of terms. Detailed regula-
tions. Previous treaty amendment. Exchange of
information and documents. Informational
records. Accounting procedures. Currency. In-
terest rates. Tax exemptions. Credit provisions.
Loan repayment. Terms of loan. Plans and stan-
dards. IDA development project. Hydro-electric
power.
PARTIES:
 India
 IDA (Devel Assoc)

107015　Unilateral Instrument　**483 UNTS 233**
SIGNED: 12 Dec 63　　　FORCE: 16 Dec 63
REGISTERED: 16 Dec 63 United Nations
ARTICLES: 1 LANGUAGE: English.
HEADNOTE: ACCEPTANCE OBLIGATIONS UN
TOPIC: UN Charter
CONCEPTS: Acceptance of UN obligations. Adher-
ence to UN charter.
INTL ORGS: United Nations.
PARTIES:
 Kenya

107016　Unilateral Instrument　**483 UNTS 237**
SIGNED: 10 Dec 63　　　FORCE: 16 Dec 63
REGISTERED: 16 Dec 63 United Nations
ARTICLES: 1 LANGUAGE: English.
HEADNOTE: ACCEPTANCE OBLIGATIONS UN
TOPIC: UN Charter
CONCEPTS: Acceptance of UN obligations. Adher-
ence to UN charter.

INTL ORGS: United Nations.
PARTIES:
 Zanzibar

107017　Bilateral Exchange　**483 UNTS 241**
SIGNED: 29 Apr 63　　　FORCE: 29 Apr 63
REGISTERED: 23 Dec 63 New Zealand
ARTICLES: 2 LANGUAGE: English.
HEADNOTE: ANTI-DUMPING PROCEDURES
TOPIC: Customs
CONCEPTS: Import quotas. Export subsidies.
PARTIES:
 Australia
 New Zealand

107018　Bilateral Convention　**483 UNTS 249**
SIGNED: 19 Sep 61　　　FORCE: 14 Feb 63
REGISTERED: 23 Dec 63 Poland
ARTICLES: 31 LANGUAGE: Polish. German.
HEADNOTE: CONSULAR
TOPIC: Consul/Citizenship
CONCEPTS: Definition of terms. General provi-
sions. Previous treaty replacement. General con-
sular functions. Diplomatic privileges. Consular
relations establishment. Inviolability. Privileges
and immunities. Diplomatic correspondence. Re-
sponsibility and liability. Procedure. Most fa-
vored nation clause.
TREATY REF: 159LTS265.
PROCEDURE: Denunciation. Ratification.
PARTIES:
 Bulgaria
 Poland

107019　Bilateral Treaty　**484 UNTS 3**
SIGNED: 4 Dec 61　　　FORCE: 19 Apr 63
REGISTERED: 23 Dec 63 Poland
ARTICLES: 92 LANGUAGE: Polish. Bulgarian.
HEADNOTE: LEGAL ASSISTANCE CIVIL FAMILY
CRIMINAL CASES
TOPIC: Admin Cooperation
CONCEPTS: General provisions. Extradition, deportation and repatriation. Refusal of extradition.
Concurrent requests. Limits of prosecution. Ex-
tradition postponement. Material evidence. Gen-
eral cooperation. Family law. Exchange of infor-
mation and documents. Juridical personality. Le-
gal protection and assistance. Recognition and
enforcement of legal decisions. Immovable
property. General property. Succession. Recognition of legal documents. Prizes and arbitral
awards. Indemnities and reimbursements. Assets transfer. Conveyance in transit.
PROCEDURE: Denunciation. Duration. Ratification.
PARTIES:
 Bulgaria
 Poland

107020　Bilateral Agreement　**484 UNTS 123**
SIGNED: 6 Mar 61　　　FORCE: 10 Oct 62
REGISTERED: 23 Dec 63 Poland
ARTICLES: 9 LANGUAGE: Polish. Spanish.
HEADNOTE: CULTURAL COOPERATION
TOPIC: Culture
CONCEPTS: Treaty implementation. Friendship
and amity. Conformity with municipal law. Spe-
cialists exchange. Exchange. Teacher and stu-
dent exchange. Scholarships and grants. Voca-
tional training. Exchange. General cultural coop-
eration. Artists. Athletes. Scientific exchange.
Research and development. Publications ex-
change. Mass media exchange. Press and wire
services.
PROCEDURE: Denunciation. Duration. Ratification.
Renewal or Revival.
PARTIES:
 Cuba
 Poland

107021　Bilateral Exchange　**484 UNTS 137**
SIGNED: 6 Jun 63　　　FORCE: 6 Jun 63
REGISTERED: 31 Dec 63 Denmark
ARTICLES: 2 LANGUAGE: English.
HEADNOTE: SECRECY PATENTS
TOPIC: Patents/Copyrights
CONCEPTS: Territorial application. Previous trea-
ties adherence. Press and wire services. Security
of information. Exchange of defense informa-
tion.

TREATY REF: 394UNTS3.
PROCEDURE: Renewal or Revival.
PARTIES:
 Denmark
 Netherlands

107022　Bilateral Exchange　**484 UNTS 143**
SIGNED: 14 Feb 62　　　FORCE: 15 May 62
REGISTERED: 2 Jan 64 Israel
ARTICLES: 2 LANGUAGE: French.
HEADNOTE: ABOLITION VISAS
TOPIC: Visas
CONCEPTS: Time limit. Visa abolition. Resident
permits.
PROCEDURE: Denunciation.
PARTIES:
 Central Afri Rep
 Israel

107023　Bilateral Exchange　**484 UNTS 149**
SIGNED: 21 Dec 62　　　FORCE: 21 Mar 63
REGISTERED: 2 Jan 64 Israel
ARTICLES: 2 LANGUAGE: Spanish.
HEADNOTE: ABOLITION VISAS
TOPIC: Visas
CONCEPTS: Exceptions and exemptions. Time
limit. Visa abolition. Conformity with municipal
law.
PROCEDURE: Denunciation.
PARTIES:
 Colombia
 Israel

107024　Bilateral Convention　**484 UNTS 155**
SIGNED: 31 Jul 62　　　FORCE: 14 May 63
REGISTERED: 2 Jan 64 Israel
ARTICLES: 8 LANGUAGE: Hebrew. Spanish.
HEADNOTE: CULTURAL EXCHANGE
TOPIC: Education
CONCEPTS: Tourism. General cooperation.
Teacher and student exchange. Exchange. Art-
ists. Research results. Scientific exchange. In-
demnities and reimbursements. Publications ex-
change. Mass media exchange.
PROCEDURE: Denunciation. Ratification.
PARTIES:
 Costa Rica
 Israel

107025　Bilateral Exchange　**484 UNTS 169**
SIGNED: 17 Aug 61　　　FORCE: 1 Sep 61
REGISTERED: 2 Jan 64 Israel
ARTICLES: 2 LANGUAGE: English.
HEADNOTE: ABOLITION VISA FEES
TOPIC: Visas
CONCEPTS: Visas. Fees and exemptions.
PROCEDURE: Denunciation.
PARTIES:
 Cyprus
 Israel

107026　Bilateral Exchange　**484 UNTS 175**
SIGNED: 10 Oct 62　　　FORCE: 9 Dec 62
REGISTERED: 2 Jan 64 Israel
ARTICLES: 2 LANGUAGE: French.
HEADNOTE: EXEMPTION VISAS
TOPIC: Visas
CONCEPTS: Time limit. Visa abolition. Denial of
admission.
PROCEDURE: Denunciation.
PARTIES:
 Gabon
 Israel

107027　Bilateral Treaty　**484 UNTS 181**
SIGNED: 15 May 62　　　FORCE: 21 Aug 62
REGISTERED: 2 Jan 64 Israel
ARTICLES: 2 LANGUAGE: Hebrew. French.
HEADNOTE: FRIENDSHIP
TOPIC: General Amity
CONCEPTS: Friendship and amity. Consular rela-
tions establishment. Diplomatic relations estab-
lishment. Privileges and immunities. Procedure.
PROCEDURE: Ratification. Registration.
PARTIES:
 Gabon
 Israel

107028 Bilateral Exchange **484 UNTS 189**
SIGNED: 10 Oct 62   FORCE: 10 Jan 63
REGISTERED: 2 Jan 64 Israel
ARTICLES: 2 LANGUAGE: Spanish.
HEADNOTE: ABOLITION VISAS
TOPIC: Visas
CONCEPTS: Time limit. Visa abolition. Resident permits.
PROCEDURE: Termination.
PARTIES:
  Honduras
  Israel

107029 Bilateral Exchange **484 UNTS 197**
SIGNED: 30 Aug 61   FORCE: 1 Nov 61
REGISTERED: 2 Jan 64 Israel
ARTICLES: 2 LANGUAGE: French.
HEADNOTE: ABOLITION VISAS
TOPIC: Visas
CONCEPTS: Visa abolition.
PARTIES:
  Israel
  Italy

107030 Bilateral Exchange **484 UNTS 203**
SIGNED: 3 Aug 61   FORCE: 1 Nov 61
REGISTERED: 2 Jan 64 Israel
ARTICLES: 2 LANGUAGE: English.
HEADNOTE: ABOLITION VISAS
TOPIC: Visas
CONCEPTS: Time limit. Visa abolition. Resident permits.
PROCEDURE: Termination.
PARTIES:
  Israel
  Liberia

107031 Bilateral Agreement **484 UNTS 209**
SIGNED: 18 Sep 62   FORCE: 1 Nov 62
REGISTERED: 2 Jan 64 Israel
ARTICLES: 10 LANGUAGE: English.
HEADNOTE: POSTAL PARCELS
TOPIC: Postal Service
CONCEPTS: Parcel post. Rates and charges.
INTL ORGS: Universal Postal Union.
PROCEDURE: Termination.
PARTIES:
  Israel
  Liberia

107032 Bilateral Treaty **484 UNTS 217**
SIGNED: 27 Aug 61   FORCE: 26 Jan 63
REGISTERED: 2 Jan 64 Israel
ARTICLES: 5 LANGUAGE: Hebrew. French.
HEADNOTE: FRIENDSHIP
TOPIC: General Amity
CONCEPTS: Friendship and amity. Consular relations establishment. Diplomatic relations establishment. Privileges and immunities. Procedure.
PROCEDURE: Ratification. Registration.
PARTIES:
  Israel
  Malagasy

107033 Bilateral Exchange **484 UNTS 225**
SIGNED: 4 May 63   FORCE: 2 Aug 63
REGISTERED: 2 Jan 64 Israel
ARTICLES: 2 LANGUAGE: French.
HEADNOTE: ABOLITION VISAS
TOPIC: Visas
CONCEPTS: Time limit. Visa abolition. Resident permits.
PROCEDURE: Denunciation.
PARTIES:
  Israel
  Malagasy

107034 Bilateral Agreement **484 UNTS 231**
SIGNED: 25 Apr 63   FORCE: 1 Nov 63
REGISTERED: 2 Jan 64 Israel
ARTICLES: 6 LANGUAGE: English.
HEADNOTE: PAYMENT OLD-AGE PENSIONS
TOPIC: Admin Cooperation
CONCEPTS: Territorial application. Old age insurance. Social security.
PROCEDURE: Duration.

PARTIES:
  Israel
  Netherlands

107035 Bilateral Exchange **484 UNTS 241**
SIGNED: 11 Oct 62   FORCE: 11 Oct 62
REGISTERED: 2 Jan 64 Israel
ARTICLES: 2 LANGUAGE: English.
HEADNOTE: AGREEMENT CONCERNING TECHNICAL COOPERATION ARRANGEMENTS
TOPIC: Tech Assistance
CONCEPTS: Treaty implementation. Annex or appendix reference. Inspection and observation. Responsibility and liability. Scholarships and grants. Compensation. Financial programs. General technical assistance.
PROCEDURE: Amendment.
PARTIES:
  Israel
  OAS (Am States)

107036 Bilateral Agreement **484 UNTS 261**
SIGNED: 15 May 62   FORCE: 7 Feb 63
REGISTERED: 2 Jan 64 Israel
ARTICLES: 17 LANGUAGE: English.
HEADNOTE: DOUBLE TAXATION DEATH DUTIES
TOPIC: Taxation
CONCEPTS: Definition of terms. Privileges and immunities. Exchange of official publications. Claims and settlements. Debts. Taxation. Death duties.
PROCEDURE: Duration. Ratification. Termination.
PARTIES:
  Israel
  Sweden

107037 Bilateral Agreement **484 UNTS 273**
SIGNED: 4 Feb 63   FORCE: 4 Feb 63
REGISTERED: 2 Jan 64 Israel
ARTICLES: 4 LANGUAGE: Hebrew. English.
HEADNOTE: TECHNICAL COOPERATION
TOPIC: Tech Assistance
CONCEPTS: Treaty implementation. Personnel. Public health. Education. Scholarships and grants. Vocational training. General technical assistance. Agriculture. Non-bank projects. General transportation. General communications.
PARTIES:
  Israel
  Uganda

107038 Bilateral Convention **484 UNTS 283**
SIGNED: 10 Dec 62   FORCE: 5 Dec 63
REGISTERED: 2 Jan 64 Israel
ARTICLES: 9 LANGUAGE: Hebrew. English.
HEADNOTE: EXTRADITION
TOPIC: Extradition
CONCEPTS: Definition of terms. Time limit. Extradition, deportation and repatriation. Extradition requests. Extraditable offenses. Location of crime. Refusal of extradition. Concurrent requests. Provisional detainment. Extradition postponement. Indemnities and reimbursements. Conveyance in transit.
PROCEDURE: Ratification. Termination.
PARTIES:
  Israel
  USA (United States)

107039 Bilateral Agreement **484 UNTS 309**
SIGNED: 8 Dec 59   FORCE: 1 Mar 61
REGISTERED: 2 Jan 64 Netherlands
ARTICLES: 12 LANGUAGE: French.
HEADNOTE: ROAD TRANSPORT
TOPIC: Land Transport
CONCEPTS: Default remedies. Territorial application. General provisions. Remedies. Conformity with municipal law. Exchange of information and documents. Licenses and permits. Passenger transport. Transport of goods. Operating authorizations and regulations. Roads and highways. Road rules.
INTL ORGS: United Nations.
PROCEDURE: Denunciation. Ratification.
PARTIES:
  Italy
  Netherlands

107040 Bilateral Agreement **484 UNTS 319**
SIGNED: 6 Apr 63   FORCE: 1 Oct 63
REGISTERED: 3 Jan 64 South Africa
ARTICLES: 23 LANGUAGE: English. Japanese.
HEADNOTE: PARCEL POST
TOPIC: Postal Service
CONCEPTS: Responsibility and liability. Customs duties. Customs declarations. Customs exemptions. Air transport. Water transport. Postal services. Regulations. Conveyance in transit. Parcel post. Rates and charges.
INTL ORGS: Universal Postal Union.
PROCEDURE: Duration. Termination.
PARTIES:
  Japan
  South Africa

107041 Multilateral Convention **484 UNTS 349**
SIGNED: 21 Apr 61   FORCE: 7 Jan 64
REGISTERED: 7 Jan 64 United Nations
ARTICLES: 10 LANGUAGE: English. French. Russian.
HEADNOTE: INTERNATIONAL COMMERCIAL ARBITRATION
TOPIC: IGO Establishment
CONCEPTS: Annex type material. Arbitration. Compulsory jurisdiction.
INTL ORGS: United Nations. Arbitration Commission.
TREATY REF: TRADE-96.
PARTIES:
  Austria SIGNED: 21 Apr 61
  Belgium SIGNED: 21 Apr 61
  Bulgaria SIGNED: 21 Apr 61
  Byelorussia SIGNED: 21 Apr 61
  Czechoslovakia SIGNED: 21 Apr 61
  Denmark SIGNED: 21 Apr 61
  Finland SIGNED: 21 Apr 61
  France SIGNED: 21 Apr 61
  Germany, West SIGNED: 21 Apr 61
  Hungary SIGNED: 21 Apr 61
  Italy SIGNED: 21 Apr 61
  Poland SIGNED: 21 Apr 61
  Romania   SIGNED: 21 Apr 61   RATIFIED: 16 Aug 63 FORCE: 7 Jan 64
  Spain SIGNED: 21 Apr 61
  Ukrainian SSR SIGNED: 21 Apr 61 RATIFIED: 18 Mar 63 FORCE: 7 Jan 64
  USSR (Soviet Union) SIGNED: 21 Apr 61 RATIFIED: 27 Jun 62 FORCE: 7 Jan 64
  Yugoslavia   SIGNED: 21 Apr 61   RATIFIED: 25 Sep 63 FORCE: 7 Jan 64
                    ANNEX
  490 UNTS 476. Austria. Ratification 6 Mar 64. Force 4 Jun 64.
  495 UNTS 265. Bulgaria. Ratification 13 May 64. Force 11 Aug 64.
  510 UNTS 341. Poland. Ratification 15 Sep 64. Force 14 Sep 64.
  514 UNTS 295. Germany, West. Ratification 27 Oct 64. Force 25 Jan 65.
  514 UNTS 295. Germany, West. Berlin. Force 25 Jan 65.
  523 UNTS 343.   Upper   Volta.   Accession 26 Jan 65. Force 26 Apr 65.
  544 UNTS 376. Cuba. Accession 1 Sep 65. Force 30 Nov 65.

107042 Multilateral Convention **485 UNTS 3**
SIGNED: 28 Jul 60   FORCE: 14 Nov 63
REGISTERED: 7 Jan 64 Spain
ARTICLES: 8 LANGUAGE: Spanish.
HEADNOTE: SPANISH LANGUAGE ACADEMICS
TOPIC: IGO Establishment
CONCEPTS: Juridical personality. Commissions and foundations. General cultural cooperation. Accounting procedures. Establishment. Headquarters and facilities.
INTL ORGS: United Nations.
PROCEDURE: Accession. Denunciation. Duration. Ratification. Registration.
PARTIES:
  Argentina   SIGNED: 28 Jul 60   RATIFIED: 25 Mar 63 FORCE: 14 Nov 63
  Bolivia SIGNED: 28 Jul 60
  Chile SIGNED: 28 Jul 60
  Colombia SIGNED: 28 Jul 60
  Costa Rica   SIGNED: 28 Jul 60   RATIFIED: 22 Oct 63 FORCE: 14 Nov 63
  Ecuador SIGNED: 28 Jul 60
  El Salvador SIGNED: 28 Jul 60

Guatemala SIGNED: 28 Jul 60 RATIFIED:
14 Nov 63 FORCE: 14 Nov 63
Honduras SIGNED: 28 Jul 60 RATIFIED:
13 Dec 62 FORCE: 14 Nov 63
Nicaragua SIGNED: 28 Jul 60
Panama SIGNED: 28 Jul 60 RATIFIED:
18 Dec 62 FORCE: 14 Nov 63
Paraguay SIGNED: 28 Jul 60 RATIFIED:
18 Oct 63 FORCE: 14 Nov 63
Peru SIGNED: 28 Jul 60
Spain SIGNED: 28 Jul 60 RATIFIED: 17 Jul 63
FORCE: 14 Nov 63
Uruguay SIGNED: 28 Jul 60
Venezuela SIGNED: 6 Aug 60

107043 Bilateral Agreement **485 UNTS 17**
SIGNED: 2 May 60 FORCE: 2 May 60
REGISTERED: 7 Jan 64 Greece
ARTICLES: 16 LANGUAGE: French.
HEADNOTE: SCHEDULED COMMERCIAL AIR SER-
VICES
TOPIC: Air Transport
CONCEPTS: Definition of terms. Detailed regulations. Representation. Annex or appendix reference. Conformity with municipal law. General
cooperation. Exchange of information and documents. Licenses and permits. Recognition of legal documents. Use of facilities. Procedure. Negotiation. Humanitarian matters. Fees and exemptions. Non-interest rates and fees. Customs
exemptions. Competency certificate. Registration certificate. Routes and logistics. Navigational conditions. Permit designation. Airport facilities. Airworthiness certificates. Conditions of
airlines operating permission. Operating authorizations and regulations. Licenses and certificates of nationality.
PROCEDURE: Amendment. Denunciation. Ratification. Registration. Termination.
PARTIES:
Greece
Romania

107044 Bilateral Agreement **485 UNTS 35**
SIGNED: 21 Nov 63 FORCE: 21 Nov 63
REGISTERED: 8 Jan 64 United Nations
ARTICLES: 8 LANGUAGE: English.
HEADNOTE: UNICEF ACTIVITIES
TOPIC: IGO Operations
CONCEPTS: Privileges and immunities. Exchange
of information and documents. Accounting pro-
cedures. Materials, equipment and services. In-
ter-agency agreements.
INTL ORGS: United Nations.
TREATY REF: 1UNTS5; 14UNTS461;
247UNTS11.
PROCEDURE: Amendment. Termination.
PARTIES:
Iran
UNICEF (Children)

107045 Bilateral Agreement **485 UNTS 45**
SIGNED: 8 Jan 64 FORCE: 8 Jan 64
REGISTERED: 8 Jan 64 United Nations
ARTICLES: 8 LANGUAGE: French.
HEADNOTE: UNICEF ACTIVITIES
TOPIC: IGO Operations
CONCEPTS: Privileges and immunities. Exchange
of information and documents. Accounting pro-
cedures. Inter-agency agreements.
INTL ORGS: United Nations.
PROCEDURE: Amendment. Termination.
PARTIES:
Burundi
UNICEF (Children)

107046 Bilateral Treaty **485 UNTS 55**
SIGNED: 14 Nov 53 FORCE: 4 Dec 56
REGISTERED: 8 Jan 64 Pakistan
ARTICLES: 8 LANGUAGE: English. Arabic.
HEADNOTE: CULTURAL TREATY
TOPIC: Culture
CONCEPTS: Friendship and amity. Conformity
with municipal law. Recognition of degrees.
Commissions and foundations. Teacher and stu-
dent exchange. Professorships. Culture. Ex-
change. Artists. Athletes. Scientific exchange.
Publications exchange.
PROCEDURE: Denunciation. Duration. Ratification.

PARTIES:
Pakistan
United Arab Rep

107047 Bilateral Agreement **485 UNTS 67**
SIGNED: 24 Jan 57 FORCE: 18 Nov 60
REGISTERED: 9 Jan 64 Netherlands
ARTICLES: 26 LANGUAGE: Dutch. Italian.
HEADNOTE: DOUBLE TAXATION INCOME FOR-
TUNE
TOPIC: Taxation
CONCEPTS: Definition of terms. Conformity with
municipal law. Negotiation. Teacher and student
exchange. Claims and settlements. Taxation. Tax
credits. Tax exemptions.
PROCEDURE: Duration. Ratification. Termination.
PARTIES:
Italy
Netherlands

107048 Bilateral Exchange **485 UNTS 117**
SIGNED: 19 Mar 59 FORCE: 18 Apr 59
REGISTERED: 9 Jan 64 Netherlands
ARTICLES: 2 LANGUAGE: Dutch. German.
HEADNOTE: RECIPROCAL RECOGNITION DRIV-
ING PERMITS
TOPIC: Admin Cooperation
CONCEPTS: Licenses and permits. Driving per-
mits.
PARTIES:
Austria
Netherlands

107049 Bilateral Exchange **485 UNTS 123**
SIGNED: 28 Apr 59 FORCE: 28 Apr 59
REGISTERED: 9 Jan 64 Netherlands
ARTICLES: 2 LANGUAGE: Dutch.
HEADNOTE: AMORTIZATION
TOPIC: Finance
CONCEPTS: Banking. Financial programs. Interest
rates. Payment schedules. Lump sum settle-
ments.
INTL ORGS: European Payments Union. Organiza-
tion for Economic Co-operation and Develop-
ment.
PARTIES:
Belgium
Netherlands

107050 Bilateral Agreement **485 UNTS 129**
SIGNED: 30 Apr 59 FORCE: 30 Apr 59
REGISTERED: 9 Jan 64 Netherlands
ARTICLES: 8 LANGUAGE: French.
HEADNOTE: AMORTIZATION
TOPIC: Finance
CONCEPTS: Banking. Fees and exemptions. Finan-
cial programs. Interest rates. Payment sched-
ules. Debt settlement. Loan repayment.
INTL ORGS: European Payments Union. Organiza-
tion for Economic Co-operation and Develop-
ment.
PARTIES:
Netherlands
Portugal

107051 Bilateral Agreement **485 UNTS 135**
SIGNED: 30 Apr 59 FORCE: 30 Apr 59
REGISTERED: 9 Jan 64 Netherlands
ARTICLES: 6 LANGUAGE: French.
HEADNOTE: AMORTIZATION
TOPIC: Finance
CONCEPTS: Fees and exemptions. Interest rates.
Payment schedules. Lump sum settlements. Ma-
terials, equipment and services.
INTL ORGS: European Payments Union. Organiza-
tion for Economic Co-operation and Develop-
ment.
PARTIES:
Greece
Netherlands

107052 Bilateral Agreement **485 UNTS 141**
SIGNED: 30 Apr 59 FORCE: 30 Apr 59
REGISTERED: 9 Jan 64 Netherlands
ARTICLES: 7 LANGUAGE: French.
HEADNOTE: AMORTIZATION
TOPIC: Finance
CONCEPTS: Banking. Currency. Financial pro-

grams. Interest rates. Payment schedules. Debt
settlement. Loan repayment.
INTL ORGS: European Payments Union. Organiza-
tion for Economic Co-operation and Develop-
ment.
PARTIES:
Germany, West
Netherlands

107053 Bilateral Agreement **485 UNTS 147**
SIGNED: 30 Apr 59 FORCE: 30 Apr 59
REGISTERED: 9 Jan 64 Netherlands
ARTICLES: 7 LANGUAGE: French.
HEADNOTE: AMORTIZATION
TOPIC: Finance
CONCEPTS: Banking. Currency. Fees and exemp-
tions. Interest rates. Payment schedules. Lump
sum settlements.
INTL ORGS: European Payments Union. Organiza-
tion for Economic Co-operation and Develop-
ment.
PROCEDURE: Ratification.
PARTIES:
Netherlands
Sweden

107054 Bilateral Agreement **485 UNTS 153**
SIGNED: 6 May 59 FORCE: 1 Jan 60
REGISTERED: 9 Jan 64 Netherlands
ARTICLES: 15 LANGUAGE: Dutch. German.
HEADNOTE: COMMERCIAL TRANSPORT TRANS-
PORT OWN ACCOUNT ROAD
TOPIC: Land Transport
CONCEPTS: Exceptions and exemptions. Territo-
rial application. Conformity with municipal law.
General cooperation. Exchange of information
and documents. Informational records. Licenses
and permits. Commercial road vehicles. Driving
permits. Road rules.
PROCEDURE: Denunciation. Ratification.
PARTIES:
Austria
Netherlands

107055 Bilateral Agreement **485 UNTS 175**
SIGNED: 6 May 59 FORCE: 1 Jan 60
REGISTERED: 9 Jan 64 Netherlands
ARTICLES: 5 LANGUAGE: Dutch. German.
HEADNOTE: BUS SERVICES
TOPIC: Land Transport
CONCEPTS: Definition of terms. Territorial applica-
tion. General provisions. General cooperation.
Exchange of information and documents. Li-
censes and permits. Operating authorizations
and regulations. Commercial road vehicles.
PROCEDURE: Denunciation. Ratification.
PARTIES:
Austria
Netherlands

107056 Bilateral Agreement **485 UNTS 185**
SIGNED: 9 Mar 61 FORCE: 4 Jul 62
REGISTERED: 9 Jan 64 Netherlands
ARTICLES: 15 LANGUAGE: Dutch. German.
HEADNOTE: APPLICATION NETHERLANDS LEGIS-
LATION OLD-AGE INSURANCE
TOPIC: Admin Cooperation
CONCEPTS: Detailed regulations. Domestic legis-
lation. Old age insurance.
PROCEDURE: Denunciation. Duration. Ratification.
Renewal or Revival.
PARTIES:
Germany, West
Netherlands

107057 Bilateral Exchange **485 UNTS 219**
SIGNED: 12 Feb 62 FORCE: 14 Mar 62
REGISTERED: 9 Jan 64 Netherlands
ARTICLES: 2 LANGUAGE: French.
HEADNOTE: ABOLITION VISAS
TOPIC: Visas
CONCEPTS: Emergencies. Territorial application.
Visa abolition. Denial of admission.
PROCEDURE: Denunciation. Duration.
PARTIES:
Ivory Coast
Netherlands

107058   Bilateral Exchange   **485 UNTS 225**
SIGNED: 3 Aug 62   FORCE: 3 Sep 62
REGISTERED: 9 Jan 64 Netherlands
ARTICLES: 2 LANGUAGE: Dutch. Spanish.
HEADNOTE: ABOLITION TRAVEL VISAS
TOPIC: Visas
CONCEPTS: Emergencies. Territorial application.
Time limit. Visa abolition. Denial of admission.
Resident permits. Conformity with municipal
law.
PROCEDURE: Denunciation. Duration.
PARTIES:
Colombia
Netherlands

107059   Bilateral Agreement   **485 UNTS 233**
SIGNED: 12 Nov 63   FORCE: 20 Nov 63
REGISTERED: 9 Jan 64 IBRD (World Bank)
ARTICLES: 7 LANGUAGE: English.
HEADNOTE: LOAN HARBOR
TOPIC: IBRD Project
CONCEPTS: Default remedies. Definition of terms.
Annex or appendix reference. Exchange of infor-
mation and documents. Informational records.
Inspection and observation. Accounting proce-
dures. Bonds. Fees and exemptions. Interest
rates. Tax exemptions. Domestic obligation.
Terms of loan. Loan regulations. Loan guarantee.
Guarantor non-interference. Water transport.
PARTIES:
New Zealand
IBRD (World Bank)

107060   Bilateral Agreement   **485 UNTS 253**
SIGNED: 7 Aug 63   FORCE: 25 Oct 63
REGISTERED: 9 Jan 64 IBRD (World Bank)
ARTICLES: 5 LANGUAGE: English.
HEADNOTE: GUARANTEE AGREEMENT
TOPIC: IBRD Project
CONCEPTS: Definition of terms. Annex or appen-
dix reference. Exchange of information and doc-
uments. Inspection and observation. Bonds.
Fees and exemptions. Tax exemptions. Domestic
obligation. Terms of loan. Loan regulations. Loan
guarantee. Guarantor non-interference.
PARTIES:
Malaysia
IBRD (World Bank)

107061   Bilateral Agreement   **485 UNTS 283**
SIGNED: 27 Sep 63   FORCE: 21 Nov 63
REGISTERED: 9 Jan 64 IBRD (World Bank)
ARTICLES: 5 LANGUAGE: English.
HEADNOTE: GUARANTEE EXPRESSWAY
TOPIC: IBRD Project
CONCEPTS: Definition of terms. Annex or appen-
dix reference. Exchange of information and doc-
uments. Inspection and observation. Bonds.
Fees and exemptions. Tax exemptions. Domestic
obligation. Terms of loan. Loan regulations. Loan
guarantee. Guarantor non-interference. Roads
and highways.
PARTIES:
Japan
IBRD (World Bank)

107062   Bilateral Agreement   **485 UNTS 313**
SIGNED: 30 Aug 62   FORCE: 1 Sep 62
REGISTERED: 10 Jan 64 Belgium
ARTICLES: 6 LANGUAGE: French.
HEADNOTE: DOUBLE TAXATION TAXES FOOT-
BALL POOLS
TOPIC: Taxation
CONCEPTS: Nationality and citizenship. Taxation.
General.
PROCEDURE: Ratification.
PARTIES:
Belgium
Luxembourg

107063   Bilateral Instrument   **485 UNTS 321**
SIGNED: 4 Oct 63   FORCE: 4 Oct 63
REGISTERED: 10 Jan 64 Kuwait
ARTICLES: 1 LANGUAGE: Arabic.
HEADNOTE: RESTORATION FRIENDLY RELA-
TIONS
TOPIC: Visas
CONCEPTS: Friendship and amity. Peaceful rela-
tions. Diplomatic relations establishment.

PARTIES:
Iraq
Kuwait

107064   Bilateral Agreement   **485 UNTS 331**
SIGNED: 12 Nov 62   FORCE: 10 Jan 63
REGISTERED: 14 Jan 64 New Zealand
ARTICLES: 5 LANGUAGE: English. Finnish.
HEADNOTE: RECOGNITION TONNAGE CERTIFI-
CATES MERCHANT SHIPS
TOPIC: Water Transport
CONCEPTS: Territorial application. Previous treaty
replacement. Recognition of legal documents.
Registration certificate. Merchant vessels. Ton-
nage.
TREATY REF: 28LTS512.
PROCEDURE: Termination.
PARTIES:
Finland
New Zealand

107065   Bilateral Exchange   **485 UNTS 339**
SIGNED: 9 Mar 62   FORCE: 9 Mar 62
REGISTERED: 14 Jan 64 New Zealand
ARTICLES: 2 LANGUAGE: English. Japanese.
HEADNOTE: TRADE
TOPIC: General Trade
CONCEPTS: Treaty interpretation. Annex type ma-
terial. General cooperation. Trade procedures.
INTL ORGS: General Agreement on Tariffs and
Trade.
TREATY REF: 55UNTS187; 325UNTS119.
PROCEDURE: Amendment.
PARTIES:
Japan
New Zealand

107066   Bilateral Exchange   **485 UNTS 351**
SIGNED: 9 Mar 62   FORCE: 9 Mar 62
REGISTERED: 14 Jan 64 New Zealand
ARTICLES: 2 LANGUAGE: English. Japanese.
HEADNOTE: TARIFF NEGOTIATIONS
TOPIC: General Trade
CONCEPTS: Treaty interpretation. Annex type ma-
terial. Tariffs. Trade procedures. Commodity
trade. Customs duties.
PARTIES:
Japan
New Zealand

107067   Bilateral Exchange   **486 UNTS 3**
SIGNED: 6 Dec 61   FORCE: 6 Jan 62
REGISTERED: 14 Jan 64 New Zealand
ARTICLES: 2 LANGUAGE: English.
HEADNOTE: VISAS
TOPIC: Visas
CONCEPTS: Territorial application. Time limit. De-
nial of admission. Resident permits. Visas. Con-
formity with municipal law. Fees and exemp-
tions.
PROCEDURE: Termination.
PARTIES:
Greece
New Zealand

107068   Bilateral Exchange   **486 UNTS 11**
SIGNED: 15 May 63   FORCE: 15 May 63
REGISTERED: 14 Jan 64 New Zealand
ARTICLES: 2 LANGUAGE: English.
HEADNOTE: IMPORTATION BUTTER
TOPIC: Commodity Trade
CONCEPTS: Conformity with municipal law. Gen-
eral cooperation. Tariffs. Commodity trade.
Quotas.
TREATY REF: 354UNTS161.
PARTIES:
New Zealand
UK Great Britain

107069   Bilateral Agreement   **486 UNTS 19**
SIGNED: 22 Feb 63   FORCE: 22 Feb 63
REGISTERED: 14 Jan 64 New Zealand
ARTICLES: 4 LANGUAGE: English.
HEADNOTE: CREDIT PURCHASE AUTHORIZATION
WOOL
TOPIC: Loans and Credits
CONCEPTS: Annex type material. Accounting pro-
cedures. Currency. Interest rates. Payment

schedules. Loan and credit. Credit provisions.
Purchase authorization. Loan repayment. Terms
of loan.
PARTIES:
India
New Zealand

107070   Bilateral Agreement   **486 UNTS 27**
SIGNED: 1 Aug 63   FORCE: 1 Aug 63
REGISTERED: 14 Jan 64 New Zealand
ARTICLES: 8 LANGUAGE: English. Russian.
HEADNOTE: TRADE
TOPIC: General Trade
CONCEPTS: Exceptions and exemptions. General
cooperation. Licenses and permits. Reciprocity
in trade. Currency. Payment schedules. Quotas.
Most favored nation clause. Water transport.
PROCEDURE: Duration. Termination.
PARTIES:
New Zealand
USSR (Soviet Union)

107071   Bilateral Convention   **486 UNTS 37**
SIGNED: 29 Nov 61   FORCE: 1 Jan 64
REGISTERED: 17 Jan 64 Belgium
ARTICLES: 29 LANGUAGE: French.
HEADNOTE: EXAMINATION BELGIAN-LUXEM-
BOURG FRONTIER
TOPIC: Visas
CONCEPTS: Definition of terms. Detailed regulations. General provisions. Border traffic and migration. Denial of admission Provisional detainment. Conformity with municipal law. General
cooperation. Inspection and observation. Use of
facilities. Dangerous goods. Railway border
crossing. Markers and definitions. Frontier peoples and personnel.
PROCEDURE: Denunciation. Ratification. Termination.
PARTIES:
Belgium
Luxembourg
                          ANNEX
521 UNTS 402.   Belgium.   Implementation
   1 Oct 64. Force 19 Oct 64.
521 UNTS 402.   Luxembourg.   Implementation
   1 Oct 64. Force 19 Oct 64.
560 UNTS 289.   Belgium.   Supplementation
   25 Jan 66. Force 1 Feb 66.
560 UNTS 289.   Luxembourg.   Supplementation
   31 Jan 66. Force 1 Feb 66.
566 UNTS 372.   Belgium.   Implementation
   27 May 66. Force 1 Jun 66.
566 UNTS 372.   Luxembourg.   Implementation
   6 Jun 66. Force 1 Jun 66.
605 UNTS 362. Belgium. Force 1 Jul 67. Implementation 30 Jun 67.
605 UNTS 362. Luxembourg. Force 1 Jul 67. Implementation 30 Jun 67.
649 UNTS 357. Belgium. Force 15 Oct 68.
649 UNTS 357. Luxembourg. Force 15 Oct 68.

107072   Bilateral Agreement   **486 UNTS 57**
SIGNED: 18 Dec 63   FORCE: 18 Dec 63
REGISTERED: 17 Jan 64 Finland
ARTICLES: 13 LANGUAGE: English.
HEADNOTE: EXCHANGE TRAINEES
TOPIC: Non-ILO Labor
CONCEPTS: Conditions. Definition of terms. Resi-
dent permits. Operating agencies. Professor-
ships. Employment regulations. Non-ILO labor re-
lations. Administrative cooperation. Unemploy-
ment. Migrant worker.
PROCEDURE: Denunciation. Duration. Renewal or
Revival.
PARTIES:
Finland
Poland

107073   Bilateral Agreement   **486 UNTS 65**
SIGNED: 9 May 60   FORCE: 2 Aug 60
REGISTERED: 20 Jan 64 Philippines
ARTICLES: 18 LANGUAGE: English.
HEADNOTE: PARCEL POST
TOPIC: Postal Service

CONCEPTS: Detailed regulations. Conformity with municipal law. Customs duties. Postal services. Regulations. Parcel post. Rates and charges.
TREATY REF: 364UNTS3; 391UNTS322; 404UNTS380.
PROCEDURE: Duration. Termination.
PARTIES:
New Zealand
Philippines

107074 Bilateral Agreement **486 UNTS 91**
SIGNED: 22 Jan 64 FORCE: 22 Jan 64
REGISTERED: 22 Jan 64 United Nations
ARTICLES: 8 LANGUAGE: French.
HEADNOTE: HEADQUARTERS AGREEMENT
TOPIC: IGO Operations
CONCEPTS: Privileges and immunities. Regional offices.
INTL ORGS: United Nations.
TREATY REF: 1UNTS15.
PROCEDURE: Termination.
PARTIES:
UNICEF (Children)
Senegal
ANNEX
541 UNTS 353. Senegal. Ratification 31 Jul 65.

107075 Multilateral Convention **486 UNTS 103**
SIGNED: 25 May 62 FORCE: 13 Apr 63
REGISTERED: 22 Jan 64 Mali
ARTICLES: 10 LANGUAGE: English. French. ·
HEADNOTE: CONVENTION ON MIGRATORY LOCUST
TOPIC: IGO Establishment
CONCEPTS: Detailed regulations. Exchange of information and documents. Research and scientific projects. Monetary and gold transfers. Funding procedures. Special projects. Establishment. Headquarters and facilities. Internal structure. Recognition of specialized agency.
INTL ORGS: International Red Locust Control Service. Food and Agricultural Organization of the United Nations. United Nations.
PROCEDURE: Ratification. Registration.
PARTIES:
Chad RATIFIED: 4 Aug 62 FORCE: 13 Apr 63
Dahomey SIGNED: 25 May 62 RATIFIED: 3 Mar 63 FORCE: 13 Apr 63
Guinea SIGNED: 25 May 62
Ivory Coast SIGNED: 25 May 62 RATIFIED: 21 Feb 63 FORCE: 13 Apr 63
Kenya SIGNED: 25 May 62
Mali SIGNED: 25 May 62 RATIFIED: 11 Jan 63 FORCE: 16 Apr 63
Niger SIGNED: 25 May 62 RATIFIED: 16 Jan 63 FORCE: 16 Apr 63
Upper Volta RATIFIED: 13 Apr 63 FORCE: 13 Apr 63
ANNEX
496 UNTS 363. Senegal. Ratification 13 Nov 63.
496 UNTS 363. Kenya. Ratification 29 Nov 63.

107076 Multilateral Agreement **486 UNTS 119**
SIGNED: 17 Dec 62 FORCE: 27 Dec 63
REGISTERED: 3 Feb 64 Council of Europe
ARTICLES: 9 LANGUAGE: English. French.
HEADNOTE: HEALTH APPLIANCES CONVENTION
TOPIC: Sanitation
CONCEPTS: Detailed regulations. Privileges and immunities. Recognition and enforcement of legal decisions. Public health. Sickness and invalidity insurance. Research cooperation. Indemnities and reimbursements. Materials, equipment and services.
INTL ORGS: Council of Europe.
TREATY REF: 87UNTS103; 196UNTS347; 218UNTS211,153; ETC.
PROCEDURE: Amendment. Accession. Denunciation. Duration. Ratification.
PARTIES:
Austria SIGNED: 17 Dec 62
Belgium SIGNED: 11 Feb 63 RATIFIED: 26 Nov 63 FORCE: 27 Dec 63
Denmark SIGNED: 17 Dec 63
France SIGNED: 17 Dec 63 RATIFIED: 8 Nov 63 FORCE: 27 Dec 63
Germany, West SIGNED: 17 Dec 63
Italy SIGNED: 17 Dec 63
Luxembourg SIGNED: 17 Dec 63
Netherlands SIGNED: 15 Nov 63

UK Great Britain SIGNED: 17 Dec 63 RATIFIED: 17 Oct 63 FORCE: 27 Dec 63
ANNEX
560 UNTS 290. Netherlands. Ratification 22 May 64. Force 23 Jun 64.
560 UNTS 290. Netherlands. Surinam. Force 23 Jun 64.
560 UNTS 290. Luxembourg. Ratification 7 Apr 65. Force 8 May 65.
560 UNTS 290. Germany, West. Qualified Ratification 28 Jun 65. Force 29 Jul 65.
635 UNTS 364. Ireland. Signature 21 Sep 67. Force 22 Oct 67.

107077 Bilateral Treaty **486 UNTS 143**
SIGNED: 10 Feb 47 FORCE: 5 Oct 63
REGISTERED: 3 Feb 64 Taiwan
ARTICLES: 9 LANGUAGE: Chinese. Spanish. English.
HEADNOTE: AMITY
TOPIC: General Amity
CONCEPTS: Treaty interpretation. Friendship and amity. Peaceful relations. Alien status. Consular relations establishment. Diplomatic relations establishment. Privileges and immunities. Legal protection and assistance.
PROCEDURE: Future Procedures Contemplated. Ratification.
PARTIES:
Argentina
Taiwan

107078 Multilateral Convention **486 UNTS 157**
SIGNED: 24 Jan 59 FORCE: 27 Jun 63
REGISTERED: 3 Feb 64 UK Great Britain
ARTICLES: 17 LANGUAGE: English. French.
HEADNOTE: FISHERIES
TOPIC: IGO Establishment
CONCEPTS: Establishment. Ocean resources.
INTL ORGS: Northeast Atlantic Fisheries Commission.
PARTIES:
Belgium SIGNED: 24 Jan 59 RATIFIED: 15 Sep 61 FORCE: 27 Jun 63
Denmark SIGNED: 24 Jan 59 RATIFIED: 14 Jul 60 FORCE: 27 Jun 63
France SIGNED: 24 Jan 59 RATIFIED: 20 Mar 62 FORCE: 27 Jun 63
Germany, West SIGNED: 24 Jan 59 RATIFIED: 27 Jun 63 FORCE: 27 Jun 63
Iceland SIGNED: 24 Jan 59 RATIFIED: 12 Apr 60 FORCE: 27 Jun 63
Ireland SIGNED: 24 Jan 59 RATIFIED: 2 Oct 62 FORCE: 27 Jun 63
Netherlands SIGNED: 24 Jan 59 RATIFIED: 21 Apr 60 FORCE: 27 Jun 63
Norway SIGNED: 24 Jan 59 RATIFIED: 12 Jan 60 FORCE: 27 Jun 63
Poland SIGNED: 24 Jan 59 RATIFIED: 13 Dec 62 FORCE: 27 Jun 63
Spain SIGNED: 24 Jan 59 RATIFIED: 7 Nov 60 FORCE: 27 Jun 63
Sweden SIGNED: 24 Jan 59 RATIFIED: 31 Mar 60 FORCE: 27 Jun 63
UK Great Britain SIGNED: 24 Jan 59 RATIFIED: 27 Aug 59 FORCE: 27 Jun 63
USSR (Soviet Union) SIGNED: 24 Jan 59 RATIFIED: 25 Aug 60 FORCE: 27 Jun 63

107079 Bilateral Exchange **486 UNTS 183**
SIGNED: 27 Aug 63 FORCE: 1 Oct 63
REGISTERED: 3 Feb 64 UK Great Britain
ARTICLES: 2 LANGUAGE: English. French.
HEADNOTE: TRAVEL
TOPIC: General Transport
CONCEPTS: Change of circumstances. Exceptions and exemptions. Time limit. Annex or appendix reference. Previous treaty replacement. Frontier formalities. Passports non-diplomatic. Non-visa travel documents. Tourism. Conformity with municipal law.
TREATY REF: 11UNTS217.
PROCEDURE: Denunciation. Termination. Application to Non-self-governing Territories.
PARTIES:
Switzerland
UK Great Britain
ANNEX
560 UNTS 292. UK Great Britain. Southern Rhodesia.

107080 Multilateral Instrument **486 UNTS 263**
SIGNED: 6 Jun 62 FORCE: 13 Apr 63
REGISTERED: 3 Feb 64 UK Great Britain
ARTICLES: 7 LANGUAGE: English.
HEADNOTE: REGULATION ANTARCTIC PELAGIC WHALING
TOPIC: Privil/Immunities
CONCEPTS: Definition of terms. Time limit. Quotas.
PROCEDURE: Accession.
PARTIES:
Japan SIGNED: 6 Jun 62 RATIFIED: 5 Nov 62 FORCE: 13 Apr 63
Netherlands SIGNED: 6 Jun 62 RATIFIED: 22 Feb 63 FORCE: 13 Apr 63
Norway SIGNED: 6 Jun 62 RATIFIED: 25 Oct 62 FORCE: 13 Apr 63
UK Great Britain SIGNED: 6 Jun 62 RATIFIED: 27 Nov 62 FORCE: 13 Apr 63
USSR (Soviet Union) SIGNED: 6 Jun 62 RATIFIED: 13 Apr 63 FORCE: 13 Apr 63

107081 Multilateral Instrument **486 UNTS 271**
SIGNED: 6 Jun 62 FORCE: 22 Feb 63
REGISTERED: 3 Feb 64 UK Great Britain
ARTICLES: 5 LANGUAGE: English.
HEADNOTE: SUPPLEMENTARY ARRANGEMENTS
TOPIC: Privil/Immunities
CONCEPTS: Annex type material.
PARTIES:
Japan SIGNED: 6 Jun 62 RATIFIED: 5 Nov 62 FORCE: 22 Feb 63
Netherlands SIGNED: 6 Jun 62 RATIFIED: 22 Feb 63 FORCE: 22 Feb 63
Norway SIGNED: 6 Jun 62 RATIFIED: 25 Oct 62 FORCE: 22 Feb 63
UK Great Britain SIGNED: 6 Jun 62 RATIFIED: 27 Nov 62 FORCE: 22 Feb 63

107082 Bilateral Exchange **486 UNTS 279**
SIGNED: 3 Dec 63 FORCE: 3 Dec 63
REGISTERED: 4 Feb 64 Australia
ARTICLES: 2 LANGUAGE: English.
HEADNOTE: DEFENSE AID
TOPIC: Milit Assistance
CONCEPTS: Inspection and observation. Use of facilities. Indemnities and reimbursements. Military assistance. Restrictions on transfer.
PARTIES:
Australia
India

107083 Bilateral Convention **486 UNTS 285**
SIGNED: 16 Feb 63 FORCE: 8 Oct 63
REGISTERED: 4 Feb 64 Denmark
ARTICLES: 20 LANGUAGE: Danish. Sinhalese. English.
HEADNOTE: DOUBLE TAXATION FISCAL EVASION TAXES INCOME PROPERTY
TOPIC: Taxation
CONCEPTS: Definition of terms. Territorial application. Conformity with municipal law. Exchange of official publications. Teacher and student exchange. Claims and settlements. Taxation. Equitable taxes. Tax exemptions. Air transport. Merchant vessels.
PROCEDURE: Duration. Ratification. Termination.
PARTIES:
Ceylon (Sri Lanka)
Denmark

107084 Bilateral Exchange **486 UNTS 331**
SIGNED: 16 Apr 58 FORCE: 1 Nov 59
REGISTERED: 4 Feb 64 Netherlands
ARTICLES: 2 LANGUAGE: Dutch. German.
HEADNOTE: VETERINARY CONTROL
TOPIC: Sanitation
CONCEPTS: Definition of terms. Detailed regulations. Exchange of information and documents. Personnel. Border control. Disease control. Veterinary.
PROCEDURE: Amendment. Denunciation. Termination.
PARTIES:
Germany, West
Netherlands

107085 Bilateral Convention **486 UNTS 345**
SIGNED: 10 Oct 58 FORCE: 19 Aug 59

REGISTERED: 4 Feb 64 Netherlands
ARTICLES: 2 LANGUAGE: Dutch. German.
HEADNOTE: FACILITATE ACCEPTANCE PERSONS
FRONTIER
TOPIC: Visas
CONCEPTS: Border traffic and migration. Refugees. Nationality and citizenship. Extradition, deportation and repatriation. General cooperation. Frontier crossing points.
PROCEDURE: Denunciation.
PARTIES:
  Germany, West
  Netherlands
ANNEX
571 UNTS 327. Germany, West. Force 1 Jul 66.
571 UNTS 327. Netherlands. Force 1 Jul 66.

107086   Bilateral Agreement   **486 UNTS 367**
SIGNED: 14 Apr 59   FORCE: 26 Oct 59
REGISTERED: 4 Feb 64 Netherlands
ARTICLES: 7 LANGUAGE: French.
HEADNOTE: AMORTIZATION
TOPIC: Finance
CONCEPTS: Territorial application. Banking. Fees and exemptions. Financial programs. Interest rates. Payment schedules. Local currency. Lump sum settlements. Debts.
INTL ORGS: European Payments Union. Organization for Economic Co-operation and Development.
PROCEDURE: Ratification.
PARTIES:
  Netherlands
  Switzerland

107087   Bilateral Exchange   **486 UNTS 373**
SIGNED: 29 Apr 59   FORCE: 29 Apr 59
REGISTERED: 4 Feb 64 Netherlands
ARTICLES: 2 LANGUAGE: French.
HEADNOTE: AMORTIZATION
TOPIC: Finance
CONCEPTS: Territorial application. Financial programs. Interest rates. Payment schedules. Lump sum settlements. Debt settlement.
INTL ORGS: European Payments Union. Organization for Economic Co-operation and Development.
PARTIES:
  Austria
  Netherlands

107088   Bilateral Agreement   **486 UNTS 379**
SIGNED: 29 Apr 59   FORCE: 29 Apr 59
REGISTERED: 4 Feb 64 Netherlands
ARTICLES: 8 LANGUAGE: French.
HEADNOTE: AMORTIZATION
TOPIC: Finance
CONCEPTS: Definition of terms. Previous treaty replacement. Banking. Exchange rates and regulations. Fees and exemptions. Financial programs. Payment schedules. Lump sum settlements. Debts. Loan repayment.
INTL ORGS: European Payments Union. Organization for Economic Co-operation and Development.
TREATY REF: 9JULY54 PAYMENT AGREEMENT.
PARTIES:
  France
  Netherlands

107089   Bilateral Exchange   **486 UNTS 387**
SIGNED: 29 Apr 59   FORCE: 29 Apr 59
REGISTERED: 4 Feb 64 Netherlands
ARTICLES: 2 LANGUAGE: French.
HEADNOTE: AMORTIZATION
TOPIC: Finance
CONCEPTS: Financial programs. Interest rates. Payment schedules. Lump sum settlements. Debt settlement.
INTL ORGS: European Payments Union. Organization for Economic Co-operation and Development.
TREATY REF: 287UNTS193,421.
PARTIES:
  Italy
  Netherlands

107090   Bilateral Agreement   **487 UNTS 3**
SIGNED: 30 Apr 59   FORCE: 30 Apr 59

REGISTERED: 4 Feb 64 Netherlands
ARTICLES: 8 LANGUAGE: French.
HEADNOTE: AMORTIZATION
TOPIC: Finance
CONCEPTS: Previous treaty replacement. Banking. Bonds. Fees and exemptions. Financial programs. Interest rates. Payment schedules. Local currency. Lump sum settlements. Loan repayment.
INTL ORGS: European Payments Union. Organization for Economic Co-operation and Development.
TREATY REF: 9JULY54 & 29JUNE56 PAYMENTS AGREEMENTS.
PARTIES:
  Netherlands
  Norway

107091   Bilateral Agreement   **487 UNTS 13**
SIGNED: 30 Apr 59   FORCE: 30 Apr 59
REGISTERED: 4 Feb 64 Netherlands
ARTICLES: 8 LANGUAGE: French.
HEADNOTE: AMORTIZATION
TOPIC: Finance
CONCEPTS: Territorial application. Previous treaty replacement. Banking. Bonds. Fees and exemptions. Financial programs. Interest rates. Payment schedules. Local currency. Lump sum settlements. Debts. Loan repayment.
INTL ORGS: European Payments Union. Organization for Economic Co-operation and Development.
TREATY REF: 28DEC54 PAYMENTS AGREEMENTS.
PARTIES:
  Iceland
  Netherlands

107092   Bilateral Agreement   **487 UNTS 23**
SIGNED: 30 Apr 59   FORCE: 30 Apr 59
REGISTERED: 4 Feb 64 Netherlands
ARTICLES: 7 LANGUAGE: French.
HEADNOTE: AMORTIZATION
TOPIC: Finance
CONCEPTS: Previous treaty replacement. Financial programs. Payment schedules. Lump sum settlements. Debts. Interest rates.
INTL ORGS: European Payments Union. Organization for Economic Co-operation and Development.
TREATY REF: 31JAN56 PAYMENTS AGREEMENTS.
PARTIES:
  Denmark
  Netherlands

107093   Bilateral Exchange   **487 UNTS 29**
SIGNED: 20 Oct 59   FORCE: 30 Oct 59
REGISTERED: 4 Feb 64 Netherlands
ARTICLES: 2 LANGUAGE: French.
HEADNOTE: RECOGNITION TRAVEL DOCUMENTS
TOPIC: Visas
CONCEPTS: Time limit. Border traffic and migration. Resident permits. Non-visa travel documents.
PROCEDURE: Termination.
PARTIES:
  Monaco
  Netherlands

107094   Bilateral Agreement   **487 UNTS 37**
SIGNED: 3 Jun 60   FORCE: 1 Jul 61
REGISTERED: 4 Feb 64 Netherlands
ARTICLES: 20 LANGUAGE: Dutch. German.
HEADNOTE: MINOR FRONTIER TRAFFIC
TOPIC: Visas
CONCEPTS: General provisions. Annex or appendix reference. Denial of admission. Frontier permits. Markers and definitions. Frontier peoples and personnel. Frontier crossing points.
PROCEDURE: Termination.
PARTIES:
  Germany, West
  Netherlands

107095   Bilateral Agreement   **487 UNTS 77**
SIGNED: 27 Apr 61   FORCE: 21 Apr 62
REGISTERED: 4 Feb 64 Netherlands
ARTICLES: 18 LANGUAGE: Dutch. German.

HEADNOTE: CULTURAL
TOPIC: Culture
CONCEPTS: Definition of terms. Territorial application. Treaty implementation. Friendship and amity. Conformity with municipal law. Establishment of commission. Specialists exchange. Recognition of degrees. Teacher and student exchange. Institute establishment. Scholarships and grants. General cultural cooperation. Artists. Publications exchange. Mass media exchange.
INTL ORGS: Special Commission.
PROCEDURE: Denunciation. Duration. Ratification.
PARTIES:
  Germany, West
  Netherlands

107096   Bilateral Exchange   **487 UNTS 95**
SIGNED: 18 Jul 61   FORCE: 20 Jul 61
REGISTERED: 4 Feb 64 Netherlands
ARTICLES: 2 LANGUAGE: Dutch. German.
HEADNOTE: MENTAL PATIENTS
TOPIC: Sanitation
CONCEPTS: Detailed regulations. Territorial application. Annex or appendix reference. Exchange of information and documents. Public health.
PROCEDURE: Denunciation. Duration. Renewal or Revival.
PARTIES:
  Germany, West
  Netherlands

107097   Bilateral Exchange   **487 UNTS 105**
SIGNED: 30 Sep 61   FORCE: 1 Oct 61
REGISTERED: 4 Feb 64 Netherlands
ARTICLES: 2 LANGUAGE: French. Spanish.
HEADNOTE: ABOLITION TRAVEL VISA REQUIREMENT
TOPIC: Visas
CONCEPTS: Emergencies. Time limit. Visa abolition. Denial of admission. Resident permits. Conformity with municipal law.
PROCEDURE: Denunciation.
PARTIES:
  Bolivia
  Netherlands
ANNEX
539 UNTS 380. Netherlands. Surinam. Force 1 Apr 64.
539 UNTS 380. Netherlands. Netherlands Antilles. Force 1 Apr 64.

107098   Bilateral Agreement   **487 UNTS 113**
SIGNED: 6 Feb 63   FORCE: 22 May 63
REGISTERED: 4 Feb 64 Netherlands
ARTICLES: 11 LANGUAGE: Dutch. English.
HEADNOTE: PUBLIC LIABILITY DAMAGE CAUSED NS SAVANNAH
TOPIC: Status of Forces
CONCEPTS: Definition of terms. Territorial application. Annex or appendix reference. Responsibility and liability. Claims and settlements. Merchant vessels. Disposition of particulars.
PROCEDURE: Amendment. Future Procedures Contemplated. Ratification. Termination.
PARTIES:
  Netherlands
  USA (United States)

107099   Bilateral Agreement   **487 UNTS 123**
SIGNED: 20 May 63   FORCE: 22 May 63
REGISTERED: 4 Feb 64 Netherlands
ARTICLES: 29 LANGUAGE: Dutch. English.
HEADNOTE: VISIT NS SAVANNAH
TOPIC: Specif Goods/Equip
CONCEPTS: General cooperation. Inspection and observation. Private contracts. Merchant vessels. Inland and territorial waters. Ports and pilotage. Facilities and property.
PARTIES:
  Netherlands
  USA (United States)

107100   Bilateral Agreement   **487 UNTS 143**
SIGNED: 1 Feb 63   FORCE: 1 Feb 63
REGISTERED: 5 Feb 64 USA (United States)
ARTICLES: 6 LANGUAGE: English. Polish.
HEADNOTE: AGRI COMMOD TITLE I
TOPIC: US Agri Commod Aid
CONCEPTS: General provisions. Annex or appen-

dix reference. Exchange of information and documents. Reexport of goods, etc.. Exchange rates and regulations. Transportation costs. Local currency. Commodities schedule. Purchase authorization. Surplus commodities. Mutual consultation.
PARTIES:
Poland
USA (United States)

107101   Bilateral Exchange   **487 UNTS 169**
SIGNED: 22 Apr 63   FORCE: 22 May 63
REGISTERED: 5 Feb 64 USA (United States)
ARTICLES: 2 LANGUAGE: English. Spanish.
HEADNOTE: RADIO COMMUNICATIONS AMATEUR STATIONS BEHALF THIRD PARTIES
TOPIC: Telecommunications
CONCEPTS: Amateur radio. Amateur third party message. Radio-telephone-telegraphic communications.
PROCEDURE: Termination.
PARTIES:
Dominican Republic
USA (United States)

107102   Bilateral Exchange   **487 UNTS 177**
SIGNED: 11 Jul 63   FORCE: 11 Jul 63
REGISTERED: 5 Feb 64 USA (United States)
ARTICLES: 2 LANGUAGE: English.
HEADNOTE: US SCHEDULES TRADE AGREEMENTS 1936 & 1955
TOPIC: General Trade
CONCEPTS: Detailed regulations. Annex type material. Tariffs.
TREATY   REF: 171LTS231;   133UNTS53;
239UNTS362.
PARTIES:
Switzerland
USA (United States)

107103   Bilateral Exchange   **487 UNTS 183**
SIGNED: 24 Jul 63   FORCE: 24 Jul 63
REGISTERED: 5 Feb 64 USA (United States)
ARTICLES: 2 LANGUAGE: English. Spanish.
HEADNOTE: US SCHEDULES TRADE AGREEMENT 1941
TOPIC: General Trade
CONCEPTS: Detailed regulations. Annex type material. Negotiation. Tariffs.
TREATY REF: 119UNTS193.
PARTIES:
Argentina
USA (United States)

107104   Bilateral Exchange   **487 UNTS 189**
SIGNED: 26 Jul 63   FORCE: 26 Jul 63
REGISTERED: 5 Feb 64 USA (United States)
ARTICLES: 2 LANGUAGE: English. French.
HEADNOTE: INVESTMENT GUARANTIES
TOPIC: Finance
CONCEPTS: General cooperation. General property. Arbitration. Procedure. Existing tribunals. Negotiation. Reciprocity in financial treatment. Currency. Claims and settlements. Private investment guarantee.
PARTIES:
Malagasy
USA (United States)

107105   Bilateral Exchange   **487 UNTS 197**
SIGNED: 27 Aug 63   FORCE: 27 Aug 63
REGISTERED: 5 Feb 64 USA (United States)
ARTICLES: 2 LANGUAGE: English.
HEADNOTE: COTTON TEXTILE TRADE
TOPIC: Commodity Trade
CONCEPTS: Commodity trade.
TREATY REF: 471UNTS296.
PARTIES:
Japan
USA (United States)
ANNEX
545 UNTS 362. Japan. Amendment 19 May 65. Force 19 May 65.
545 UNTS 362. USA (United States). Amendment 19 May 65. Force 19 May 65.

107106   Bilateral Exchange   **487 UNTS 237**
SIGNED: 28 Aug 63   FORCE: 28 Aug 63

REGISTERED: 5 Feb 64 USA (United States)
ARTICLES: 2 LANGUAGE: English.
HEADNOTE: ZIPPEN CHAIN EXPORTS
TOPIC: Commodity Trade
CONCEPTS: General cooperation. Licenses and permits. Commodity trade.
PARTIES:
Japan
USA (United States)

107107   Bilateral Exchange   **487 UNTS 243**
SIGNED: 29 Jun 63   FORCE: 29 Jun 63
REGISTERED: 5 Feb 64 USA (United States)
ARTICLES: 2 LANGUAGE: English.
HEADNOTE: LOAN VESSEL PAKISTAN
TOPIC: Milit Assistance
CONCEPTS: Annex type material. Lease of military property. Naval vessels.
TREATY REF: 471UNTS133.
PARTIES:
Pakistan
USA (United States)

107108   Bilateral Agreement   **487 UNTS 251**
SIGNED: 22 May 63   FORCE: 22 May 63
REGISTERED: 6 Feb 64 USA (United States)
ARTICLES: 6 LANGUAGE: English. French.
HEADNOTE: AGRI COMMOD TITLE I
TOPIC: US Agri Commod Aid
CONCEPTS: General provisions. Annex or appendix reference. Exchange of information and documents. Reexport of goods, etc.. Exchange rates and regulations. Transportation costs. Local currency. Commodities schedule. Purchase authorization. Surplus commodities. Mutual consultation.
PARTIES:
Guinea
USA (United States)
ANNEX
494 UNTS 362. Guinea. Amendment 2 Nov 63. Force 2 Nov 63.
494 UNTS 362. USA (United States). Amendment 2 Nov 63. Force 2 Nov 63.
531 UNTS 408. USA (United States). Amendment 1 Jul 64. Force 11 Jul 64.
531 UNTS 408. Guinea. Amendment 11 Jul 64. Force 11 Jul 64.

107109   Bilateral Agreement   **487 UNTS 269**
SIGNED: 11 Jun 63   FORCE: 11 Jun 63
REGISTERED: 6 Feb 64 USA (United States)
ARTICLES: 6 LANGUAGE: English.
HEADNOTE: AGRI COMMOD TITLE I
TOPIC: US Agri Commod Aid
CONCEPTS: General provisions. Exchange of information and documents. Free trade. Exchange rates and regulations. Payment schedules. Transportation costs. Local currency. Commodities schedule. Purchase authorization. Surplus commodities. Mutual consultation.
PARTIES:
Ethiopia
USA (United States)

107110   Bilateral Exchange   **487 UNTS 283**
SIGNED: 29 May 63   FORCE: 29 May 63
REGISTERED: 6 Feb 64 USA (United States)
ARTICLES: 2 LANGUAGE: English.
HEADNOTE: INVESTMENT GUARANTIES
TOPIC: Finance
CONCEPTS: General cooperation. General property. Arbitration. Procedure. Existing tribunals. Negotiation. Reciprocity in financial treatment. Currency. Claims and settlements. Private investment guarantee.
PARTIES:
Cyprus
USA (United States)

107111   Bilateral Exchange   **487 UNTS 291**
SIGNED: 23 Apr 63   FORCE: 23 Apr 63
REGISTERED: 6 Feb 64 USA (United States)
ARTICLES: 2 LANGUAGE: English. French.
HEADNOTE: RADIO COMMUNICATION FACILITIES
TOPIC: Telecommunications
CONCEPTS: Commercial and public radio. Radio-telephone-telegraphic communications.

PARTIES:
Cyprus
USA (United States)

107112   Bilateral Agreement   **487 UNTS 297**
SIGNED: 18 Jun 63   FORCE: 18 Jun 63
REGISTERED: 6 Feb 64 USA (United States)
ARTICLES: 13 LANGUAGE: English. Korean.
HEADNOTE: EDUCATION PROGRAM
TOPIC: Education
CONCEPTS: Definition of terms. Previous treaty replacement. Friendship and amity. Alien status. Standardization. Conformity with municipal law. General cooperation. Exchange of information and documents. Inspection and observation. Personnel. General property. Exchange. Commissions and foundations. Scholarships and grants. Accounting procedures. Currency. Expense sharing formulae. Financial programs. Funding procedures.
TREATY REF: 93UNTS21.
PROCEDURE: Amendment.
PARTIES:
Korea, South
USA (United States)

107113   Bilateral Exchange   **487 UNTS 319**
SIGNED: 21 May 63   FORCE: 21 May 63
REGISTERED: 6 Feb 64 USA (United States)
ARTICLES: 2 LANGUAGE: English.
HEADNOTE: RADIO COMMUNICATION FACILITIES
TOPIC: Telecommunications
CONCEPTS: Commercial and public radio. Radio-telephone-telegraphic communications.
PARTIES:
Israel
USA (United States)

107114   Bilateral Exchange   **487 UNTS 325**
SIGNED: 23 Jul 62   FORCE: 23 Jul 62
REGISTERED: 6 Feb 64 USA (United States)
ARTICLES: 2 LANGUAGE: English. French.
HEADNOTE: PEACE CORPS
TOPIC: Tech Assistance
CONCEPTS: Diplomatic privileges. Conformity with municipal law. General cooperation. Personnel. Exchange rates and regulations. Fees and exemptions. Funding procedures. General. Tax exemptions. Customs exemptions. Domestic obligation. Materials, equipment and services. Aid missions. Volunteer programs.
PROCEDURE: Termination.
PARTIES:
Niger
USA (United States)

107115   Bilateral Exchange   **488 UNTS 3**
SIGNED: 31 Jul 63   FORCE: 31 Jul 63
REGISTERED: 7 Feb 64 USA (United States)
ARTICLES: 2 LANGUAGE: English. Spanish.
HEADNOTE: PEACE CORPS PROGRAM
TOPIC: Tech Assistance
CONCEPTS: Annex type material. Conformity with municipal law. Personnel. Fees and exemptions. Funding procedures. General. Tax exemptions. Customs exemptions. Domestic obligation. Materials, equipment and services. Aid missions. Volunteer programs.
TREATY REF: 376UNTS311.
PROCEDURE: Termination.
PARTIES:
USA (United States)
Uruguay

107116   Bilateral Exchange   **488 UNTS 11**
SIGNED: 30 Aug 63   FORCE: 30 Aug 63
REGISTERED: 7 Feb 64 USA (United States)
ARTICLES: 2 LANGUAGE: English. Spanish.
HEADNOTE: WITHHOLDING INCOME TAX
TOPIC: Taxation
CONCEPTS: Taxation. Tax credits.
PARTIES:
Panama
USA (United States)

107117   Bilateral Agreement   **488 UNTS 21**
SIGNED: 8 Aug 63   FORCE: 25 Oct 63

REGISTERED: 7 Feb 64 USA (United States)
ARTICLES: 10 LANGUAGE: English.
HEADNOTE: CIVIL USES ATOMIC ENERGY
TOPIC: Scientific Project
CONCEPTS: Definition of terms. Exchange of information and documents. Responsibility and liability. Use of facilities. Establishment of commission. Public health. Nuclear research. Scientific exchange. Materials, equipment and services. Nuclear materials. Non-nuclear materials. Peaceful use. Rights of supplier. Samples and testing. Security of information.
INTL ORGS: International Atomic Energy Agency.
PROCEDURE: Duration. Renewal or Revival. Termination.
PARTIES:
India
USA (United States)

107118　Bilateral Agreement　488 UNTS 41
SIGNED: 20 Aug 63　　FORCE: 20 Aug 63
REGISTERED: 7 Feb 64 USA (United States)
ARTICLES: 11 LANGUAGE: English. Afghan.
HEADNOTE: EDUCATIONAL PROGRAM
TOPIC: Education
CONCEPTS: Friendship and amity. Alien status. Standardization. Conformity with municipal law. General cooperation. Exchange of information and documents. Inspection and observation. Personnel. General property. Exchange. Commissions and foundations. Teacher and student exchange. Scholarships and grants. Research and development. Accounting procedures. Currency. Financial programs. Funding procedures.
TREATY REF: 461UNTS169.
PROCEDURE: Amendment.
PARTIES:
Afghanistan
USA (United States)

107119　Bilateral Agreement　488 UNTS 61
SIGNED: 21 Aug 63　　FORCE: 21 Aug 63
REGISTERED: 7 Feb 64 USA (United States)
ARTICLES: 11 LANGUAGE: English. Spanish.
HEADNOTE: EDUCATION PROGRAM
TOPIC: Education
CONCEPTS: Previous treaty replacement. Friendship and amity. Standardization. Conformity with municipal law. General cooperation. Exchange of information and documents. Inspection and observation. Personnel. General property. Exchange. Commissions and foundations. Teacher and student exchange. Professorships. Research and development. Accounting procedures. Financial programs. Funding procedures.
TREATY REF: 187LTS125;　　277UNTS143;
307UNTS320; 410UNTS321.
PROCEDURE: Amendment.
PARTIES:
Argentina
USA (United States)

107120　Bilateral Exchange　488 UNTS 77
SIGNED: 16 Jul 63　　FORCE: 16 Jul 63
REGISTERED: 7 Feb 64 USA (United States)
ARTICLES: 2 LANGUAGE: English.
HEADNOTE: TRADE COTTON TEXTILES
TOPIC: Commodity Trade
CONCEPTS: Detailed regulations. Annex or appendix reference. General cooperation. Exchange of information and documents. Export quotas. Commodity trade. Delivery schedules.
TREATY REF: 471UNTS296; USA'TIAS 4884;.
PROCEDURE: Termination.
PARTIES:
Spain
USA (United States)
ANNEX
527 UNTS 322. USA (United States). Amendment 15 Jun 64. Force 17 Jun 65.
527 UNTS 322. Spain. Amendment 17 Jun 64. Force 17 Jun 65.
533 UNTS 368. USA (United States). Amendment 30 Oct 64. Force 30 Oct 64.
533 UNTS 368. Spain. Amendment 30 Oct 64. Force 30 Oct 64.
541 UNTS 354. Spain. Amendment 22 Jan 65. Force 3 Feb 65.
541 UNTS 354. USA (United States). Amendment 3 Feb 65. Force 3 Feb 65.

107121　Bilateral Agreement　488 UNTS 91
SIGNED: 23 Sep 63　　FORCE: 23 Sep 63
REGISTERED: 7 Feb 64 USA (United States)
ARTICLES: 7 LANGUAGE: English. Spanish.
HEADNOTE: AGRI COMMOD
TOPIC: US Agri Commod Aid
CONCEPTS: Exchange of information and documents. Reciprocity in trade. Reexport of goods, etc.. Purchase authorization. Mutual consultation.
PARTIES:
Peru
USA (United States)

107122　Multilateral Agreement　488 UNTS 99
SIGNED: 23 Sep 63　　FORCE: 1 Nov 63
REGISTERED: 7 Feb 64 USA (United States)
ARTICLES: 8 LANGUAGE: English.
HEADNOTE: SAFEGUARDS CIVIL USE ATOMIC ENERGY
TOPIC: Atomic Energy
CONCEPTS: Definition of terms. Detailed regulations. Exceptions and exemptions. Annex or appendix reference. Informational records. Inspection and observation. Procedure. Indemnities and reimbursements. Materials, equipment and services. Privileges and immunities. General. Nuclear materials. Peaceful use. Rights of supplier. Samples and testing.
INTL ORGS: International Court of Justice. Arbitration Commission.
TREATY　REF:　325UNTS143;　276UNTS3;
293UNTS359; 374UNTS147.
PROCEDURE: Duration. Termination.
PARTIES:
Japan SIGNED: 23 Sep 63 FORCE: 1 Nov 63
IAEA (Atom Energy) SIGNED: 23 Sep 63 FORCE: 1 Nov 63
USA (United States) SIGNED: 23 Sep 63 FORCE: 1 Nov 63

107123　Multilateral Exchange　488 UNTS 121
SIGNED: 14 Sep 63　　FORCE: 14 Sep 63
REGISTERED: 11 Feb 64 USA (United States)
ARTICLES: 2 LANGUAGE: English.
HEADNOTE: COMMUNICATIONS SATELLITES TESTING
TOPIC: Telecommunications
CONCEPTS: Satellites.
PARTIES:
Denmark　SIGNED:　14 Sep 63　FORCE: 14 Sep 63
Norway SIGNED: 11 Sep 63 FORCE: 14 Sep 63
Sweden SIGNED: 25 Jul 63 FORCE: 14 Sep 63
USA (United States) SIGNED: 5 Jul 63 FORCE: 14 Sep 63

107124　Bilateral Exchange　488 UNTS 133
SIGNED: 1 Oct 63　　FORCE: 1 Oct 63
REGISTERED: 11 Feb 64 USA (United States)
ARTICLES: 2 LANGUAGE: English.
HEADNOTE: COTTON TEXTILE TRADE
TOPIC: Commodity Trade
CONCEPTS: Detailed regulations. General cooperation. Exchange of information and documents. Export quotas. Commodity trade. Delivery schedules. Quotas.
TREATY REF: 471UNTS296; USA'TIAS 4884;'.
PROCEDURE: Amendment.
PARTIES:
Jamaica
USA (United States)
ANNEX
526 UNTS 350. USA (United States). Amendment 31 Mar 64. Force 17 Apr 64.
526 UNTS 350. Jamaica. Amendment 17 Apr 64. Force 17 Apr 64.

107125　Bilateral Agreement　488 UNTS 147
SIGNED: 20 Sep 63　　FORCE: 20 Sep 63
REGISTERED: 11 Feb 64 USA (United States)
ARTICLES: 11 LANGUAGE: English. Spanish.
HEADNOTE: EDUCATION PROGRAM
TOPIC: Education
CONCEPTS: Previous treaty replacement. Friendship and amity. Standardization. Conformity with municipal law. General cooperation. Exchange of information and documents. Inspection and observation. Personnel. General property. Exchange. Commissions and foundations.

Teacher and student exchange. Professorships. Research and development. Accounting procedures. Financial programs. Funding procedures.
TREATY REF: TIAS 3936; 283UNTS151.
PARTIES:
Ecuador
USA (United States)

107126　Bilateral Agreement　488 UNTS 163
SIGNED: 23 Jan 63　　FORCE: 13 Aug 63
REGISTERED: 11 Feb 64 USA (United States)
ARTICLES: 11 LANGUAGE: English. Arabic.
HEADNOTE: CULTURAL
TOPIC: Culture
CONCEPTS: Friendship and amity. Conformity with municipal law. General cooperation. Specialists exchange. Exchange. Teacher and student exchange. Professorships. Scholarships and grants. Exchange. General cultural cooperation. Artists. Anthropology and archeology. Research and development. Publications exchange. Mass media exchange.
PROCEDURE: Duration. Ratification. Termination.
PARTIES:
Iraq
USA (United States)

107127　Bilateral Exchange　488 UNTS 175
SIGNED: 13 Nov 62　　FORCE: 13 Nov 62
REGISTERED: 11 Feb 64 USA (United States)
ARTICLES: 2 LANGUAGE: English. Arabic.
HEADNOTE: LOAN AIRCRAFT
TOPIC: Loans and Credits
CONCEPTS: Annex or appendix reference. General property. Responsibility and liability. Use of facilities. Indemnities and reimbursements. Terms of loan. Plans and standards. Defense and security. Lease of military property. Naval vessels.
TREATY REF: 102UNTS73.
PARTIES:
Saudi Arabia
USA (United States)

107128　Bilateral Exchange　488 UNTS 189
SIGNED: 1 Aug 63　　FORCE: 1 Aug 63
REGISTERED: 11 Feb 64 USA (United States)
ARTICLES: 2 LANGUAGE: English. Arabic.
HEADNOTE: ABOLITION VISA FEES
TOPIC: Visas
CONCEPTS: Visas. Fees and exemptions.
PARTIES:
United Arab Rep
USA (United States)

107129　Bilateral Exchange　488 UNTS 197
SIGNED: 31 Jan 64　　FORCE: 1 Feb 64
REGISTERED: 11 Feb 64 Australia
ARTICLES: 2 LANGUAGE: English.
HEADNOTE: ASSISTED MIGRATION
TOPIC: Non-ILO Labor
CONCEPTS: Annex type material. Border traffic and migration. Non-ILO labor relations.
TREATY REF: 131UNTS187.
PARTIES:
Australia
Italy

107130　Bilateral Agreement　488 UNTS 203
SIGNED: 19 Mar 62　　FORCE: 13 Dec 63
REGISTERED: 12 Feb 64 Australia
ARTICLES: 21 LANGUAGE: English. German.
HEADNOTE: EXCHANGE POSTAL PARCELS
TOPIC: Postal Service
CONCEPTS: Conformity with municipal law. Responsibility and liability. Accounting procedures. Postal services. Regulations. Insured letters and boxes. Parcel post. Rates and charges.
TREATY　REF:　365UNTS3;　391UNTS327;
404UNTS381; 412UNTS352.
PROCEDURE: Ratification.
PARTIES:
Australia
Germany, West

107131　Bilateral Treaty　489 UNTS 3
SIGNED: 24 Oct 57　　FORCE: 17 Sep 59
REGISTERED: 14 Feb 64 Netherlands

ARTICLES: 2 LANGUAGE: Dutch. French.
HEADNOTE: AMENDING
TOPIC: Water Transport
CONCEPTS: Annex type material. Fees and exemptions. Customs exemptions. Navigational conditions. Canal improvement. Ports and pilotage.
TREATY REF: 3'3DEMARTENS613; 3'16DEMARTENS773;.
PROCEDURE: Ratification.
PARTIES:
  Belgium
  Netherlands

107132 Bilateral Agreement **489 UNTS 11**
SIGNED: 24 Oct 57   FORCE: 17 Sep 59
REGISTERED: 14 Feb 64 Netherlands
ARTICLES: 7 LANGUAGE: Dutch. French.
HEADNOTE: PILOTAGE TERNEUZEN CANAL
TOPIC: Water Transport
CONCEPTS: Annex or appendix reference. Fees and exemptions. Non-interest rates and fees. Customs exemptions. Navigational conditions. Canal improvement. Ports and pilotage.
TREATY REF: 3'5DEMARTENS294,307,367; 489UNTS3 ETC.3.
PARTIES:
  Belgium
  Netherlands

107133 Bilateral Agreement **489 UNTS 21**
SIGNED: 7 Jul 61   FORCE: 1 Jul 62
REGISTERED: 14 Feb 64 Netherlands
ARTICLES: 9 LANGUAGE: French.
HEADNOTE: SETTLEMENT FINANCIAL QUESTIONS
TOPIC: Finance
CONCEPTS: Detailed regulations. Territorial application. General cooperation. Exchange of information and documents. Expropriation. Responsibility and liability. Currency. Exchange rates and regulations. Payment schedules. Local currency. Claims and settlements. Loan repayment.
TREATY REF: 41UNTS21.
PROCEDURE: Ratification.
PARTIES:
  Bulgaria
  Netherlands

107134 Bilateral Agreement **489 UNTS 45**
SIGNED: 3 Nov 61   FORCE: 20 Dec 61
REGISTERED: 14 Feb 64 Syria
ARTICLES: 15 LANGUAGE: Arabic.
HEADNOTE: ECONOMIC INTEGRATION
TOPIC: General Trade
CONCEPTS: Detailed regulations. Exceptions and exemptions. General provisions. Annex or appendix reference. Visa abolition. Licenses and permits. General property. Use of facilities. Establishment of commission. Export quotas. Import quotas. Certificates of origin. Reexport of goods, etc.. Accounting procedures. Banking. Currency. Monetary and gold transfers. Financial programs. Payment schedules. Transportation costs. Customs declarations. Customs exemptions. Transport of goods. Commercial road vehicles. Motor vehicles and combinations.
PROCEDURE: Amendment. Duration. Ratification. Renewal or Revival. Termination.
PARTIES:
  Iraq
  Syria

107135 Bilateral Agreement **489 UNTS 71**
SIGNED: 25 Jun 62   FORCE: 25 Jul 62
REGISTERED: 18 Feb 64 Syria
ARTICLES: 3 LANGUAGE: Arabic. German.
HEADNOTE: TECHNICAL ASSISTANCE DEVELOPMENT EXPERIMENTAL STOCK FARM
TOPIC: Tech Assistance
CONCEPTS: Time limit. Resident permits. Privileges and immunities. General cooperation. Exchange of information and documents. Personnel. Establishment of commission. Research and development. Expense sharing formulae. Tax exemptions. Customs exemptions. Domestic obligation. General technical assistance. Agriculture. Materials, equipment and services.
PARTIES:
  Germany, West
  Syria

107136 Bilateral Agreement **489 UNTS 91**
SIGNED: 19 Feb 64   FORCE: 19 Feb 64
REGISTERED: 19 Feb 64 United Nations
ARTICLES: 6 LANGUAGE: English.
HEADNOTE: PERSONNEL
TOPIC: IGO Status/Immunit
CONCEPTS: Annex or appendix reference. General consular functions. Diplomatic privileges. Diplomatic missions. Privileges and immunities. Arbitration. Procedure.
INTL ORGS: Permanent Court of Arbitration.
PROCEDURE: Amendment. Termination.
PARTIES:
  United Nations
  Sierra Leone

107137 Bilateral Agreement **489 UNTS 113**
SIGNED: 28 Jun 63   FORCE: 3 Jan 64
REGISTERED: 21 Feb 64 IBRD (World Bank)
ARTICLES: 5 LANGUAGE: English.
HEADNOTE: GUARANTEE AGREEMENT
TOPIC: IBRD Project
CONCEPTS: Definition of terms. Annex or appendix reference. Exchange of information and documents. Inspection and observation. Bonds. Fees and exemptions. Tax exemptions. Domestic obligation. Terms of loan. Loan regulations. Loan guarantee. Guarantor non-interference.
PARTIES:
  Colombia
  IBRD (World Bank)

107138 Bilateral Agreement **489 UNTS 151**
SIGNED: 29 Apr 63   FORCE: 3 Jan 64
REGISTERED: 21 Feb 64 IBRD (World Bank)
ARTICLES: 5 LANGUAGE: English.
HEADNOTE: GUARANTEE IRRIGATION
TOPIC: IBRD Project
CONCEPTS: Definition of terms. Annex or appendix reference. Exchange of information and documents. Informational records. Inspection and observation. Bonds. Fees and exemptions. Tax exemptions. Domestic obligation. Terms of loan. Loan regulations. Loan guarantee. Guarantor non-interference. Irrigation.
PARTIES:
  Mexico
  IBRD (World Bank)

107139 Bilateral Agreement **489 UNTS 179**
SIGNED: 26 Feb 64   FORCE: 26 Feb 64
REGISTERED: 26 Feb 64 United Nations
ARTICLES: 6 LANGUAGE: French.
HEADNOTE: PERSONNEL
TOPIC: IGO Status/Immunit
CONCEPTS: Annex or appendix reference. General consular functions. Diplomatic privileges. Diplomatic missions. Privileges and immunities. Arbitration. Procedure.
INTL ORGS: Permanent Court of Arbitration. Arbitration Commission.
PROCEDURE: Amendment. Termination.
PARTIES:
  United Nations
  Upper Volta

107140 Bilateral Agreement **489 UNTS 191**
SIGNED: 22 May 63   FORCE: 22 May 63
REGISTERED: 26 Feb 64 United Nations
ARTICLES: 10 LANGUAGE: English.
HEADNOTE: ASSISTANCE
TOPIC: Direct Aid
CONCEPTS: Detailed regulations. Treaty implementation. Visas. Privileges and immunities. Exchange of information and documents. Informational records. Inspection and observation. Operating agencies. Personnel. Public information. Responsibility and liability. Title and deeds. Use of facilities. Arbitration. Procedure. Negotiation. Import quotas. Attachment of funds. Exchange rates and regulations. Expense sharing formulae. Financial programs. Domestic obligation. General technical assistance. Economic assistance. Materials, equipment and services. IGO status.
INTL ORGS: International Atomic Energy Agency. International Court of Justice. United Nations. Arbitration Commission.
TREATY REF: 1UNTS15; 33UNTS261; 374UNTS147.
PROCEDURE: Amendment. Termination.

PARTIES:
  Jamaica
  UN Special Fund

107141 Multilateral Agreement **489 UNTS 209**
SIGNED: 9 Nov 63   FORCE: 9 Nov 63
REGISTERED: 27 Feb 64 UNESCO (Educ/Cult)
ARTICLES: 8 LANGUAGE: English. French. Russian. Spanish.
HEADNOTE: CONTRIBUTIONS GIVEN EXECUTION PROJECT SAVE ABU SIMBEL TEMPLES
TOPIC: Direct Aid
CONCEPTS: Annex or appendix reference. Exchange of information and documents. Monetary and gold transfers. Financial programs. Payment schedules. Domestic obligation.
INTL ORGS: United Nations Educational, Scientific and Cultural Organization. United Nations.
PROCEDURE: Ratification. Registration.
PARTIES:
  Austria SIGNED: 18 Nov 63 FORCE: 18 Nov 63
  Cameroon SIGNED: 9 Jan 64 FORCE: 9 Jan 64
  Cuba SIGNED: 18 Feb 64 FORCE: 18 Feb 64
  France SIGNED: 9 Nov 63 FORCE: 9 Nov 63
  Greece SIGNED: 24 Feb 64 FORCE: 24 Feb 64
  India SIGNED: 9 Nov 63 FORCE: 9 Nov 63
  Italy SIGNED: 9 Nov 63 FORCE: 9 Nov 63
  Libya SIGNED: 14 Nov 63 FORCE: 14 Nov 63
  Mali SIGNED: 9 Nov 63 FORCE: 9 Nov 63
  Philippines SIGNED: 20 Feb 64 FORCE: 20 Feb 64
  UNESCO (Educ/Cult) SIGNED: 9 Nov 63 FORCE: 9 Nov 63
  Spain SIGNED: 9 Nov 63
  UK Great Britain SIGNED: 9 Nov 63 FORCE: 9 Nov 63
  Yugoslavia SIGNED: 9 Nov 63 FORCE: 9 Nov 63
  ANNEX
490 UNTS 478. Japan. Signature without Reservation as to Approval 3 Mar 64.
490 UNTS 478. Nigeria. Signature without Reservation as to Approval 6 Mar 64.
511 UNTS 312. Malaysia. Signature without Reservation as to Approval 1 Oct 64.
528 UNTS 328. Spain. Ratification 5 Mar 65.
528 UNTS 328. Sweden. Signature 12 Mar 63.
559 UNTS 356. Netherlands. Ratification 25 Feb 66.

107142 Bilateral Agreement **489 UNTS 233**
SIGNED: 9 Nov 63   FORCE: 9 Nov 63
REGISTERED: 27 Feb 64 UNESCO (Educ/Cult)
ARTICLES: 8 LANGUAGE: English. French. Arabic.
HEADNOTE: SALVAGE ABU SIMBEL TEMPLES
TOPIC: Culture
CONCEPTS: Private contracts. Programs. Anthropology and archeology. Research and development. Currency. Financial programs. Funding procedures. Conformity with IGO decisions.
TREATY REF: 4UNTS275; 15UNTS383.
PROCEDURE: Denunciation.
PARTIES:
  UNESCO (Educ/Cult)
  United Arab Rep

107143 Bilateral Agreement **489 UNTS 257**
SIGNED: 27 Feb 64   FORCE: 27 Feb 64
REGISTERED: 27 Feb 64 United Nations
ARTICLES: 9 LANGUAGE: English.
HEADNOTE: WORLD POPULATION CONFERENCE
TOPIC: IGO Operations
CONCEPTS: Friendship and amity. Privileges and immunities. General cooperation. Personnel. Responsibility and liability. Exchange. Scientific exchange. Indemnities and reimbursements. Expense sharing formulae. Tax exemptions. Customs exemptions. General transportation. Special status. Conferences.
TREATY REF: 1UNTS15; UN31SESS SUPP.1(E-3499)P.2 ETC..
PROCEDURE: Duration.
PARTIES:
  UNESCO (Educ/Cult)
  Yugoslavia

107144 Bilateral Agreement **489 UNTS 271**
SIGNED: 27 Aug 63   FORCE: 27 Aug 63
REGISTERED: 28 Feb 64 USA (United States)
ARTICLES: 5 LANGUAGE: English. Arabic.
HEADNOTE: AGRI COMMOD TITLE IV

TOPIC: US Agri Commod Aid
CONCEPTS: General provisions. Annex or appendix reference. Exchange of information and documents. Reciprocity in trade. Reexport of goods, etc.. Payment schedules. Transportation costs. Purchase authorization. Commodities schedule. Purchase authorization. Mutual consultation.
PARTIES:
  Iraq
  USA (United States)
ANNEX
494 UNTS 365. Iraq. Amendment 5 Dec 63. Force 5 Dec 63.
494 UNTS 365. USA (United States). Amendment 5 Dec 63. Force 5 Dec 63.

107145 Bilateral Agreement **489 UNTS 289**
SIGNED: 27 Mar 63   FORCE: 27 Mar 63
REGISTERED: 28 Feb 64 USA (United States)
ARTICLES: 4 LANGUAGE: English. Spanish.
HEADNOTE: AGRI COMMOD TITLE IV
TOPIC: US Agri Commod Aid
CONCEPTS: General provisions. Exchange of information and documents. Reexport of goods, etc.. Currency. Payment schedules. Transportation costs. Purchase authorization. Commodities schedule. Purchase authorization. Mutual consultation.
PARTIES:
  Colombia
  USA (United States)
ANNEX
511 UNTS 313. USA (United States). Amendment 11 Oct 63. Force 25 Oct 63.
511 UNTS 313. Colombia. Amendment 25 Oct 63. Force 25 Oct 63.

107146 Bilateral Agreement **489 UNTS 303**
SIGNED: 24 Oct 63   FORCE: 24 Oct 63
REGISTERED: 28 Feb 64 USA (United States)
ARTICLES: 12 LANGUAGE: English. Persian.
HEADNOTE: EDUCATION EXCHANGE PROGRAM
TOPIC: Culture
CONCEPTS: Definition of terms. Previous treaty replacement. Friendship and amity. Alien status. Standardization. Conformity with municipal law. General cooperation. Inspection and observation. Personnel. General property. Responsibility and liability. Establishment of commission. Exchange. Teacher and student exchange. Scholarships and grants. Accounting procedures. Currency. Financial programs. Funding procedures. Most favored nation clause. Tax exemptions. Customs exemptions.
TREATY REF: 79UNTS155; 303UNTS308.
PROCEDURE: Amendment.
PARTIES:
  Iran
  USA (United States)

107147 Bilateral Exchange **489 UNTS 323**
SIGNED: 30 Aug 63   FORCE: 30 Aug 63
REGISTERED: 28 Feb 64 USA (United States)
ARTICLES: 2 LANGUAGE: English.
HEADNOTE: SOCIAL SECURITY COVERAGE NON-US CITIZEN EMPLOYEES
TOPIC: Non-ILO Labor
CONCEPTS: Social security.
TREATY REF: 43UNTS271.
PARTIES:
  Philippines
  USA (United States)

107148 Bilateral Agreement **489 UNTS 337**
SIGNED: 24 Oct 63   FORCE: 24 Oct 63
REGISTERED: 28 Feb 64 USA (United States)
ARTICLES: 6 LANGUAGE: English.
HEADNOTE: ECONOMIC TECHNICAL RELATED ASSISTANCE
TOPIC: General Aid
CONCEPTS: Change of circumstances. Conditions. Exceptions and exemptions. Diplomatic privileges. Conformity with municipal law. General cooperation. Personnel. Import quotas. Exchange rates and regulations. Funding procedures. Tax exemptions. Customs declarations. Customs exemptions. Domestic obligation. General technical assistance. Economic assistance. Materials, equipment and services. Aid missions.
TREATY REF: 122UNTS263; 105UNTS74.

PROCEDURE: Amendment. Termination.
PARTIES:
  Jamaica
  USA (United States)

107149 Bilateral Exchange **489 UNTS 347**
SIGNED: 22 Feb 63   FORCE: 22 Feb 63
REGISTERED: 28 Feb 64 USA (United States)
ARTICLES: 2 LANGUAGE: English.
HEADNOTE: ILO US PEACE CORPS VOLUNTEERS
TOPIC: IGO Operations
CONCEPTS: Natural resources. Assistance to United Nations.
PROCEDURE: Termination.
PARTIES:
  ILO (Labor Org)
  USA (United States)

107150 Bilateral Exchange **490 UNTS 3**
SIGNED: 27 Aug 63   FORCE: 19 Nov 63
REGISTERED: 2 Mar 64 UK Great Britain
ARTICLES: 2 LANGUAGE: English.
HEADNOTE: WAR GRAVES
TOPIC: Other Military
CONCEPTS: Annex or appendix reference. Burial arrangements. Upkeep of war graves. Establishment of war cemeteries.
PARTIES:
  Netherlands
  UK Great Britain

107151 Bilateral Exchange **490 UNTS 11**
SIGNED: 30 Oct 63   FORCE: 30 Oct 63
REGISTERED: 2 Mar 64 UK Great Britain
ARTICLES: 2 LANGUAGE: English.
HEADNOTE: SECRECY INVENTIONS RELATING DEFENSE
TOPIC: Other Military
CONCEPTS: Recognition. Security of information. Exchange of defense information.
TREATY REF: 394UNTS3.
PROCEDURE: Denunciation.
PARTIES:
  Netherlands
  UK Great Britain

107152 Bilateral Exchange **490 UNTS 19**
SIGNED: 13 Sep 63   FORCE: 13 Oct 63
REGISTERED: 2 Mar 64 UK Great Britain
ARTICLES: 2 LANGUAGE: English. Spanish.
HEADNOTE: ABOLITION VISAS
TOPIC: Visas
CONCEPTS: Territorial application. Visa abolition. Denial of admission. Resident permits.
PROCEDURE: Termination.
PARTIES:
  Ecuador
  UK Great Britain

107153 Bilateral Agreement **490 UNTS 28**
SIGNED: 3 Aug 59   FORCE: 3 Aug 59
REGISTERED: 2 Mar 64 USA (United States)
ARTICLES: 5 LANGUAGE: English. German.
HEADNOTE: STATUS FORCES
TOPIC: Status of Forces
CONCEPTS: Status of military forces. Procurement and logistics. Status of forces.
TREATY REF: 481UNTS262.
PROCEDURE: Ratification.
PARTIES:
  Germany, West
  USA (United States)

107154 Bilateral Agreement **490 UNTS 187**
SIGNED: 3 Mar 64   FORCE: 3 Mar 64
REGISTERED: 2 Mar 64 United Nations
ARTICLES: 6 LANGUAGE: French.
HEADNOTE: PERSONNEL
TOPIC: IGO Status/Immunit
CONCEPTS: Annex or appendix reference. General consular functions. Diplomatic privileges. Diplomatic missions. Privileges and immunities. Arbitration. Procedure.
INTL ORGS: Permanent Court of Arbitration. Arbitration Commission.
PROCEDURE: Amendment. Termination.

PARTIES:
  Morocco
  United Nations

107155 Bilateral Agreement **490 UNTS 199**
SIGNED: 3 Jun 63   FORCE: 31 Oct 63
REGISTERED: 5 Mar 64 IBRD (World Bank)
ARTICLES: 5 LANGUAGE: English.
HEADNOTE: GUARANTEE POWER
TOPIC: IBRD Project
CONCEPTS: Definition of terms. Annex or appendix reference. Exchange of information and documents. Inspection and observation. Bonds. Fees and exemptions. Tax exemptions. Domestic obligation. Terms of loan. Loan regulations. Loan guarantee. Guarantor non-interference. Hydroelectric power.
PARTIES:
  Colombia
  IBRD (World Bank)

107156 Bilateral Exchange **490 UNTS 231**
SIGNED: 22 Feb 63   FORCE: 1 Feb 63
REGISTERED: 5 Mar 64 Philippines
ARTICLES: 2 LANGUAGE: Spanish.
HEADNOTE: ABOLITION VISAS
TOPIC: Visas
CONCEPTS: Time limit. Visa abolition. Visas. Fees and exemptions.
PROCEDURE: Amendment. Termination.
PARTIES:
  Bolivia
  Philippines

107157 Bilateral Exchange **490 UNTS 237**
SIGNED: 14 Jul 59   FORCE: 30 Jul 59
REGISTERED: 5 Mar 64 Philippines
ARTICLES: 2 LANGUAGE: English.
HEADNOTE: ABOLITION VISAS
TOPIC: Visas
CONCEPTS: Time limit. Visas. Fees and exemptions.
PROCEDURE: Amendment. Termination.
PARTIES:
  Italy
  Philippines

107158 Bilateral Exchange **490 UNTS 243**
SIGNED: 4 Jul 62   FORCE: 1 Aug 62
REGISTERED: 5 Mar 64 Philippines
ARTICLES: 2 LANGUAGE: Spanish.
HEADNOTE: ABOLITION VISAS
TOPIC: Visas
CONCEPTS: Time limit. Visa abolition. Visas. Fees and exemptions.
PROCEDURE: Amendment. Termination.
PARTIES:
  Philippines
  Spain

107159 Bilateral Exchange **490 UNTS 249**
SIGNED: 11 Nov 60   FORCE: 11 Nov 60
REGISTERED: 5 Mar 64 Philippines
ARTICLES: 2 LANGUAGE: English.
HEADNOTE: RECIPROCAL WAIVER PASSPORT VISA FEES
TOPIC: Visas
CONCEPTS: Time limit. Visas. Fees and exemptions.
PARTIES:
  Korea, South
  Philippines

107160 Bilateral Agreement **490 UNTS 255**
SIGNED: 8 Oct 63   FORCE: 29 Jan 64
REGISTERED: 6 Mar 64 Finland
ARTICLES: 30 LANGUAGE: Finnish. German.
HEADNOTE: DOUBLE TAXATION INCOME FORTUNE
TOPIC: Taxation
CONCEPTS: Definition of terms. Privileges and immunities. Nationality and citizenship. Exchange of official publications. Negotiation. Teacher and student exchange. Claims and settlements. Taxation. Tax credits. Equitable taxes. Tax exemptions.
PROCEDURE: Duration. Ratification. Termination.

PARTIES:
Austria
Finland
ANNEX
525 UNTS 322. Finland. Implementation 4 Jul 64. Force 23 Jul 64.
525 UNTS 322. Austria. Implementation 23 Jul 64. Force 23 Jul 64.

107161 Bilateral Convention **490 UNTS 317**
SIGNED: 6 Apr 62   FORCE: 13 Feb 64
REGISTERED: 9 Mar 64 Belgium
ARTICLES: 19 LANGUAGE: English.
HEADNOTE: RECOGNITION ENFORCEMENT JUDICIAL DECISIONS
TOPIC: Admin Cooperation
CONCEPTS: Exchange of information and documents. Recognition and enforcement of legal decisions.
PROCEDURE: Denunciation. Ratification.
PARTIES:
Belgium
Italy

107162 Bilateral Agreement **490 UNTS 333**
SIGNED: 4 Mar 63   FORCE: 5 Mar 63
REGISTERED: 10 Mar 64 IAEA (Atom Energy)
ARTICLES: 1 LANGUAGE: English.
HEADNOTE: ASSISTANCE ESTABLISHING RESEARCH PROJECT
TOPIC: Atomic Energy
CONCEPTS: Annex or appendix reference. Exchange of information and documents. Inspection and observation. Procedure. Negotiation. Research cooperation. Research results. Nuclear materials. Peaceful use. Security of information.
TREATY REF: 412UNTS225.
PARTIES:
IAEA (Atom Energy)
Yugoslavia

107163 Bilateral Agreement **490 UNTS 343**
SIGNED: 4 Jun 63   FORCE: 26 Jul 63
REGISTERED: 10 Mar 64 IAEA (Atom Energy)
ARTICLES: 1 LANGUAGE: English.
HEADNOTE: ESTABLISHING RESEARCH PROJECT
TOPIC: Atomic Energy
CONCEPTS: Annex or appendix reference. Exchange of information and documents. Inspection and observation. Procedure. Negotiation. Research cooperation. Research results. Acceptance of delivery. Nuclear materials. Peaceful use. Transport of goods. Security of information.
TREATY REF: 412UNTS225.
PARTIES:
IAEA (Atom Energy)
Yugoslavia

107164 Bilateral Agreement **490 UNTS 351**
SIGNED: 21 Jun 63   FORCE: 27 Jun 63
REGISTERED: 10 Mar 64 IAEA (Atom Energy)
ARTICLES: 1 LANGUAGE: English.
HEADNOTE: FURTHERING RESEARCH PROJECT
TOPIC: Atomic Energy
CONCEPTS: Annex or appendix reference. Exchange of information and documents. Inspection and observation. Arbitration. Special tribunals. Negotiation. Research cooperation. Research results. Payment schedules. Nuclear materials. Peaceful use. Transport of goods. Security of information.
TREATY REF: 456UNTS447.
PARTIES:
Austria
IAEA (Atom Energy)

107165 Bilateral Agreement **490 UNTS 361**
SIGNED: 18 Dec 63   FORCE: 18 Dec 63
REGISTERED: 10 Mar 64 IAEA (Atom Energy)
ARTICLES: 11 LANGUAGE: English. Spanish.
HEADNOTE: ESTABLISHING RESEARCH REACTOR PROJECT
TOPIC: Atomic Energy
CONCEPTS: Annex or appendix reference. Exchange of information and documents. Inspection and observation. Procedure. Research cooperation. Research results. Nuclear research. Nuclear materials. Transport of goods. Security of information. Special status. Status of experts.

TREATY REF: 329UNTS359; 374UNTS147.
PARTIES:
Mexico
IAEA (Atom Energy)

107166 Multilateral Instrument **490 UNTS 383**
SIGNED: 18 Dec 63   FORCE: 18 Dec 63
REGISTERED: 10 Mar 64 IAEA (Atom Energy)
ARTICLES: 6 LANGUAGE: English. Spanish.
HEADNOTE: TRANSFER ENRICHED URANIUM RESEARCH REACTOR
TOPIC: Atomic Energy
CONCEPTS: Annex or appendix reference. Licenses and permits. Responsibility and liability. Arbitration. Special tribunals. Negotiation. Currency. Payment schedules. Nuclear materials. Transport of goods.
INTL ORGS: International Court of Justice. Arbitration Commission.
TREATY REF: 339UNTS359.
PARTIES:
Mexico SIGNED: 18 Dec 63 FORCE: 18 Dec 63
IAEA (Atom Energy) SIGNED: 18 Dec 63 FORCE: 18 Dec 63
USA (United States) SIGNED: 18 Dec 63 FORCE: 18 Dec 63

107167 Bilateral Agreement **490 UNTS 403**
SIGNED: 2 Jul 63   FORCE: 30 Sep 63
REGISTERED: 10 Mar 64 IAEA (Atom Energy)
ARTICLES: 1 LANGUAGE: English.
HEADNOTE: FURTHERING RESEARCH PROJECT
TOPIC: Atomic Energy
CONCEPTS: Annex or appendix reference. Exchange of information and documents. Inspection and observation. Arbitration. Special tribunals. Public health. Research cooperation. Research results. Currency. Payment schedules. Nuclear materials. Peaceful use. Transport of goods.
INTL ORGS: International Court of Justice. Arbitration Commission.
TREATY REF: 456UNTS447.
PARTIES:
Finland
IAEA (Atom Energy)

107168 Bilateral Agreement **490 UNTS 413**
SIGNED: 30 Jul 63   FORCE: 30 Jul 63
REGISTERED: 10 Mar 64 IAEA (Atom Energy)
ARTICLES: 10 LANGUAGE: English.
HEADNOTE: ESTABLISHING SUB-CRITICAL ASSEMBLIES PROJECT
TOPIC: Atomic Energy
CONCEPTS: Annex or appendix reference. Exchange of information and documents. Negotiation. Public health. Research cooperation. Research results. Nuclear materials. Peaceful use. Transport of goods.
TREATY REF: 339UNTS341; 395UNTS257.
PARTIES:
Finland
IAEA (Atom Energy)

107169 Bilateral Agreement **490 UNTS 423**
SIGNED: 30 Aug 63   FORCE: 19 Sep 63
REGISTERED: 16 Mar 64 WHO (World Health)
ARTICLES: 6 LANGUAGE: French.
HEADNOTE: SERVICES OPERATIONAL OFFICERS
TOPIC: IGO Operations
CONCEPTS: Arbitration. Status of experts.
INTL ORGS: Permanent Court of Arbitration. Arbitration Commission.
PROCEDURE: Termination.
PARTIES:
Burundi
WHO (World Health)

107170 Bilateral Agreement **491 UNTS 3**
SIGNED: 18 Mar 64   FORCE: 18 Mar 64
REGISTERED: 18 Mar 64 UN Special Fund
ARTICLES: 10 LANGUAGE: English. French.
HEADNOTE: SPECIAL FUND
TOPIC: Direct Aid
CONCEPTS: Frontier formalities. Privileges and immunities. Economic assistance.
INTL ORGS: International Atomic Energy Agency. International Court of Justice. United Nations. Arbitration Commission.

PARTIES:
Rwanda
UN Special Fund

107171 Bilateral Agreement **491 UNTS 21**
SIGNED: 18 Mar 64   FORCE: 18 Mar 64
REGISTERED: 18 Mar 64 United Nations
ARTICLES: 7 LANGUAGE: English.
HEADNOTE: SEMINAR FREEDOM INFORMATION
TOPIC: Education
CONCEPTS: Definition of terms. Friendship and amity. Visas. Alien status. Human rights. Privileges and immunities. General cooperation. Exchange of information and documents. Personnel. Indemnities and reimbursements. Expense sharing formulae. Funding procedures. General transportation.
INTL ORGS: Food and Agricultural Organization of the United Nations.
TREATY REF: UN10SESS SUPP.19(A-3116)P.13; 33UNTS261; ETC..
PROCEDURE: Amendment. Duration.
PARTIES:
Italy
United Nations

107172 Multilateral Agreement **491 UNTS 30**
SIGNED: 20 Feb 64   FORCE: 20 Feb 64
REGISTERED: 19 Mar 64 United Nations
ARTICLES: 6 LANGUAGE: English. Spanish.
HEADNOTE: TECHNICAL ASSISTANCE
TOPIC: Tech Assistance
CONCEPTS: Definition of terms. Previous treaty replacement. Privileges and immunities. General cooperation. Exchange of information and documents. Personnel. Responsibility and liability. Title and deeds. Use of facilities. Exchange. Scholarships and grants. Vocational training. Research and development. Exchange rates and regulations. Expense sharing formulae. Local currency. Domestic obligation. General technical assistance. Materials, equipment and services. IGO status. Conformity with IGO decisions.
TREATY REF: 76UNTS132; 33UNTS261; 25UNTS245;374UNTS147; ETC..
PROCEDURE: Amendment. Termination.
PARTIES:
Dominican Republic SIGNED: 20 Feb 64 FORCE: 20 Feb 64
FAO (Food Agri) SIGNED: 20 Feb 64 FORCE: 20 Feb 64
IAEA (Atom Energy) SIGNED: 20 Feb 64 FORCE: 20 Feb 64
ICAO (Civil Aviat) SIGNED: 20 Feb 64 FORCE: 20 Feb 64
ILO (Labor Org) SIGNED: 20 Feb 64 FORCE: 20 Feb 64
ITU (Telecommun) SIGNED: 20 Feb 64 FORCE: 20 Feb 64
UNESCO (Educ/Cult) SIGNED: 20 Feb 64 FORCE: 20 Feb 64
United Nations SIGNED: 20 Feb 64 FORCE: 20 Feb 64
UPU (Postal Union) SIGNED: 20 Feb 64 FORCE: 20 Feb 64
WHO (World Health) SIGNED: 20 Feb 64 FORCE: 20 Feb 64
WMO (Meteorology) SIGNED: 20 Feb 64 FORCE: 20 Feb 64
ANNEX
649 UNTS 358. IMCO (Maritime Org). Accession 9 Sep 68. Force 9 Sep 68.
649 UNTS 358. UNIDO (Industrial). Accession 9 Sep 68. Force 9 Sep 68.

107173 Bilateral Exchange **491 UNTS 53**
SIGNED: 22 Apr 63   FORCE: 22 May 63
REGISTERED: 20 Mar 64 Austria
ARTICLES: 2 LANGUAGE: German. Italian.
HEADNOTE: ACCEPTANCE PERSONS FRONTIER
TOPIC: Visas
CONCEPTS: Previous treaty replacement. Border traffic and migration. Nationality and citizenship.
PROCEDURE: Denunciation.
PARTIES:
Austria
Italy

107174 Bilateral Convention **491 UNTS 63**
SIGNED: 16 Oct 62   FORCE: 28 Oct 63
REGISTERED: 20 Mar 64 Austria
ARTICLES: 27 LANGUAGE: English.
HEADNOTE: DOUBLE TAXATION FISCAL EVASION TAXES INCOME CAPITAL
TOPIC: Taxation

CONCEPTS: Definition of terms. Conformity with municipal law. Exchange of official publications. Domestic legislation. Negotiation. Teacher and student exchange. Taxation. Equitable taxes. Tax exemptions. Air transport. Merchant vessels.
PROCEDURE: Duration. Ratification. Termination.
PARTIES:
Austria
United Arab Rep

107175 Bilateral Agreement **491 UNTS 101**
SIGNED: 22 Nov 63   FORCE: 20 Dec 63
REGISTERED: 23 Mar 64 IBRD (World Bank)
ARTICLES: 5 LANGUAGE: English.
HEADNOTE: GUARANTEE AGREEMENT
TOPIC: IBRD Project
CONCEPTS: Definition of terms. Annex or appendix reference. Exchange of information and documents. Inspection and observation. Bonds. Fees and exemptions. Tax exemptions. Domestic obligation. Terms of loan. Loan regulations. Loan guarantee. Guarantor non-interference.
PARTIES:
Peru
IBRD (World Bank)

107176 Bilateral Agreement **491 UNTS 137**
SIGNED: 6 Nov 63   FORCE: 10 Feb 64
REGISTERED: 23 Mar 64 IBRD (World Bank)
ARTICLES: 5 LANGUAGE: English.
HEADNOTE: GUARANTEE THERMOELECTRIC POWER
TOPIC: IBRD Project
CONCEPTS: Definition of terms. Annex or appendix reference. Exchange of information and documents. Inspection and observation. Bonds. Fees and exemptions. Tax exemptions. Domestic obligation. Terms of loan. Loan regulations. Loan guarantee. Guarantor non-interference. Hydroelectric power.
PARTIES:
Portugal
IBRD (World Bank)

107177 Bilateral Agreement **491 UNTS 163**
SIGNED: 16 Nov 61   FORCE: 10 Nov 62
REGISTERED: 24 Mar 64 Syria
ARTICLES: 13 LANGUAGE: Arabic.
HEADNOTE: ECONOMIC COOPERATION
TOPIC: General Economic
CONCEPTS: Previous treaty replacement.
TREATY REF: 30JAN61 TRADE AGREEMENT.
PARTIES:
Saudi Arabia
Syria

107178 Bilateral Agreement **491 UNTS 209**
SIGNED: 18 Oct 62   FORCE: 22 May 63
REGISTERED: 24 Mar 64 Syria
ARTICLES: 18 LANGUAGE: French.
HEADNOTE: CIVIL AIR TRANSPORT
TOPIC: Air Transport
CONCEPTS: Exceptions and exemptions. Representation. Annex or appendix reference. Conformity with municipal law. General cooperation. Exchange of information and documents. Informational records. Licenses and permits. Recognition of legal documents. Use of facilities. Procedure. Negotiation. Humanitarian matters. Fees and exemptions. Non-interest rates and fees. Most favored nation clause. General. Customs duties. Customs exemptions. Registration certificate. Routes and logistics. Navigational conditions. Permit designation. Air transport. Airport facilities. Airworthiness certificates. Conditions of airlines operating permission. Operating authorizations and regulations. Licenses and certificates of nationality.
PROCEDURE: Amendment. Ratification. Termination.
PARTIES:
Hungary
Syria

107179 Bilateral Agreement **491 UNTS 228**
SIGNED: 10 Nov 62   FORCE: 10 Jun 63
REGISTERED: 24 Mar 64 Syria
ARTICLES: 19 LANGUAGE: French.
HEADNOTE: SCHEDULED CIVIL AIR SERVICES

TOPIC: Air Transport
CONCEPTS: Definition of terms. Annex or appendix reference. Non-prejudice to third party. Conformity with municipal law. General cooperation. Exchange of information and documents. Use of facilities. Procedure. Negotiation. Reexport of goods, etc.. Fees and exemptions. Non-interest rates and fees. Most favored nation clause. National treatment. Tax exemptions. Customs duties. Customs exemptions. Routes and logistics. Navigational conditions. Permit designation. Air transport. Airport facilities. Conditions of airlines operating permission. Overflights and technical stops. Operating authorizations and regulations.
TREATY REF: 15UNTS295.
PROCEDURE: Amendment. Denunciation. Ratification. Termination.
PARTIES:
Poland
Syria

107180 Bilateral Agreement **491 UNTS 245**
SIGNED: 27 Dec 62   FORCE: 2 Apr 63
REGISTERED: 24 Mar 64 Syria
ARTICLES: 15 LANGUAGE: Arabic. Russian. French.
HEADNOTE: SCHEDULED CIVIL AIR SERVICES
TOPIC: Air Transport
CONCEPTS: Representation. Annex or appendix reference. Conformity with municipal law. General cooperation. Exchange of information and documents. Informational records. Licenses and permits. Recognition of legal documents. Use of facilities. Procedure. Negotiation. Humanitarian matters. Reexport of goods, etc.. Monetary and gold transfers. Fees and exemptions. Tax exemptions. Customs exemptions. Registration certificate. Routes and logistics. Navigational conditions. Permit designation. Airworthiness certificates. Conditions of airlines operating permission. Operating authorizations and regulations. Licenses and certificates of nationality.
PROCEDURE: Amendment. Denunciation. Ratification. Termination.
PARTIES:
Syria
United Arab Rep

107181 Bilateral Agreement **491 UNTS 297**
SIGNED: 25 Oct 63   FORCE: 11 Mar 64
REGISTERED: 24 Mar 64 IBRD (World Bank)
ARTICLES: 8 LANGUAGE: English.
HEADNOTE: LOAN ROAD
TOPIC: IBRD Project
CONCEPTS: Default remedies. Definition of terms. Annex or appendix reference. Exchange of information and documents. Inspection and observation. Accounting procedures. Bonds. Fees and exemptions. Interest rates. Tax exemptions. Domestic obligation. Terms of loan. Loan regulations. Loan guarantee. Guarantor non-interference. Roads and highways.
PARTIES:
IBRD (World Bank)
Spain

107182 Bilateral Agreement **491 UNTS 317**
SIGNED: 20 Sep 63   FORCE: 8 Jan 64
REGISTERED: 24 Mar 64 IBRD (World Bank)
ARTICLES: 5 LANGUAGE: English.
HEADNOTE: GUARANTEE ROAD
TOPIC: IBRD Project
CONCEPTS: Definition of terms. Annex or appendix reference. Exchange of information and documents. Inspection and observation. Bonds. Fees and exemptions. Tax exemptions. Domestic obligation. Terms of loan. Loan regulations. Loan guarantee. Guarantor non-interference. Roads and highways.
PARTIES:
Mexico
IBRD (World Bank)

107183 Bilateral Agreement **491 UNTS 345**
SIGNED: 18 Sep 63   FORCE: 17 Dec 63
REGISTERED: 25 Mar 64 IBRD (World Bank)
ARTICLES: 5 LANGUAGE: English.
HEADNOTE: GUARANTEE AGREEMENT
TOPIC: IBRD Project
CONCEPTS: Definition of terms. Annex or appen-

dix reference. Exchange of information and documents. Inspection and observation. Bonds. Fees and exemptions. Financial programs. Tax exemptions. Domestic obligation. Terms of loan. Loan regulations. Loan guarantee. Guarantor non-interference.
PARTIES:
Finland
IBRD (World Bank)

107184 Bilateral Agreement **492 UNTS 3**
SIGNED: 12 Dec 63   FORCE: 5 Mar 64
REGISTERED: 26 Mar 64 IDA (Devel Assoc)
ARTICLES: 7 LANGUAGE: English.
HEADNOTE: DEVELOPMENT CREDIT AGRICULTURAL
TOPIC: Non-IBRD Project
CONCEPTS: Definition of terms. Detailed regulations. Previous treaty amendment. Exchange of information and documents. Informational records. Accounting procedures. Currency. Interest rates. Tax exemptions. Agricultural commodities. Credit provisions. Loan repayment. Terms of loan. Plans and standards. IDA development project.
PARTIES:
Jordan
IDA (Devel Assoc)

107185 Bilateral Agreement **492 UNTS 31**
SIGNED: 22 Nov 63   FORCE: 22 Nov 63
REGISTERED: 27 Mar 64 Netherlands
ARTICLES: 22 LANGUAGE: French.
HEADNOTE: RECRUITMENT PLACEMENT WORKERS
TOPIC: Non-ILO Labor
CONCEPTS: Definition of terms. Detailed regulations. Border traffic and migration. Resident permits. Repatriation of nationals. Private contracts. Dispute settlement. Holidays and rest periods. Safety standards. Wages and salaries. Non-ILO labor relations. Administrative cooperation. Migrant worker. Indemnities and reimbursements. Monetary and gold transfers. National treatment.
INTL ORGS: Special Commission.
PROCEDURE: Duration. Renewal or Revival. Termination.
PARTIES:
Netherlands
Portugal

107186 Bilateral Agreement **492 UNTS 47**
SIGNED: 12 Jun 62   FORCE: 6 Nov 63
REGISTERED: 30 Mar 64 Greece
ARTICLES: 6 LANGUAGE: Greek. French.
HEADNOTE: DOUBLE TAXATION SHIPS AIRCRAFT
TOPIC: Taxation
CONCEPTS: Definition of terms. Previous treaty replacement. Taxation. Air transport. Merchant vessels.
TREATY REF: 19JUNE; 4JULY1950.
PROCEDURE: Duration. Ratification. Termination.
PARTIES:
Greece
Switzerland

107187 Bilateral Exchange **492 UNTS 57**
SIGNED: 31 Mar 64   FORCE: 14 Mar 64
REGISTERED: 31 Mar 64 United Nations
ARTICLES: 2 LANGUAGE: English.
HEADNOTE: STATUS OF FORCES
TOPIC: IGO Status/Immunit
CONCEPTS: Definition of terms. Non-visa travel documents. Diplomatic privileges. Diplomatic missions. Privileges and immunities. Diplomatic correspondence. Conformity with municipal law. Procedure. Special tribunals. Local currency. Payment for war supplies. Return of equipment and recapture. Jurisdiction. Procurement and logistics. Status of forces. Certificates of service. Responsibility for war dead. Special status. Status of experts.
INTL ORGS: International Court of Justice. Arbitration Commission.
PROCEDURE: Duration. Ratification.
PARTIES:
Cyprus
United Nations

555 UNTS 261. Cyprus. Ratification 25 Jun 54.
Force 25 Jun 54.

107188 Bilateral Agreement **492 UNTS 89**
SIGNED: 6 Nov 63 FORCE: 23 Mar 64
REGISTERED: 2 Apr 64 IBRD (World Bank)
ARTICLES: 5 LANGUAGE: English.
HEADNOTE: GUARANTEE HYDROELECTRIC
POWER
TOPIC: IBRD Project
CONCEPTS: Definition of terms. Annex or appendix reference. Exchange of information and documents. Inspection and observation. Bonds. Fees and exemptions. Tax exemptions. Domestic obligation. Terms of loan. Loan regulations. Loan guarantee. Guarantor non-interference. Hydroelectric power.
PARTIES:
Portugal
IBRD (World Bank)

107189 Bilateral Agreement **492 UNTS 115**
SIGNED: 26 Jun 63 FORCE: 31 Jan 64
REGISTERED: 2 Apr 64 IDA (Devel Assoc)
ARTICLES: 7 LANGUAGE: English.
HEADNOTE: DEVELOPMENT CREDIT FLOOD EMBANKMENT
TOPIC: Non-IBRD Project
CONCEPTS: Definition of terms. Detailed regulations. Previous treaty amendment. Exchange of information and documents. Informational records. Accounting procedures. Currency. Interest rates. Tax exemptions. Credit provisions. Loan repayment. Terms of loan. Plans and standards. IDA development project. Irrigation.
PARTIES:
Pakistan
IDA (Devel Assoc)

107190 Bilateral Agreement **492 UNTS 143**
SIGNED: 26 Jul 63 FORCE: 31 Jan 64
REGISTERED: 2 Apr 64 IDA (Devel Assoc)
ARTICLES: 7 LANGUAGE: English.
HEADNOTE: DEVELOPMENT CREDIT IRRIGATION
TOPIC: Non-IBRD Project
CONCEPTS: Definition of terms. Detailed regulations. Previous treaty amendment. Exchange of information and documents. Informational records. Accounting procedures. Currency. Interest rates. Tax exemptions. Credit provisions. Loan repayment. Terms of loan. Plans and standards. IDA development project. Irrigation.
PARTIES:
Pakistan
IDA (Devel Assoc)

107191 Bilateral Agreement **492 UNTS 171**
SIGNED: 16 Aug 63 FORCE: 6 Mar 64
REGISTERED: 2 Apr 64 IDA (Devel Assoc)
ARTICLES: 7 LANGUAGE: English.
HEADNOTE: DEVELOPMENT CREDIT WATER SUPPLY SEWERAGE
TOPIC: Non-IBRD Project
CONCEPTS: Definition of terms. Detailed regulations. Previous treaty amendment. Exchange of information and documents. Informational records. Accounting procedures. Currency. Interest rates. Tax exemptions. Credit provisions. Loan repayment. Terms of loan. Plans and standards. IDA development project. Natural resources.
PARTIES:
Pakistan
IDA (Devel Assoc)

107192 Bilateral Agreement **492 UNTS 205**
SIGNED: 16 Aug 63 FORCE: 4 Feb 64
REGISTERED: 2 Apr 64 IDA (Devel Assoc)
ARTICLES: 7 LANGUAGE: English.
HEADNOTE: DEVELOPMENT CREDIT WATER SUPPLY SEWERAGE
TOPIC: Non-IBRD Project
CONCEPTS: Definition of terms. Detailed regulations. Previous treaty amendment. Exchange of information and documents. Informational records. Accounting procedures. Currency. Interest rates. Tax exemptions. Credit provisions. Loan repayment. Terms of loan. Plans and stan-

dards. IDA development project. Natural resources.
PARTIES:
Pakistan
IDA (Devel Assoc)

107193 Bilateral Agreement **492 UNTS 241**
SIGNED: 19 Dec 63 FORCE: 4 Mar 64
REGISTERED: 2 Apr 64 IDA (Devel Assoc)
ARTICLES: 6 LANGUAGE: English.
HEADNOTE: DEVELOPMENT CREDIT
TOPIC: Non-IBRD Project
CONCEPTS: Credit provisions.
PARTIES:
IDA (Devel Assoc)
Tanganyika

107194 Bilateral Exchange **492 UNTS 261**
SIGNED: 30 Mar 64 FORCE: 30 Mar 64
REGISTERED: 3 Apr 64 United Nations
ARTICLES: 2 LANGUAGE: English.
HEADNOTE: PRIVILEGES IMMUNITIES & FACILITIES
TOPIC: IGO Status/Immunit
CONCEPTS: Privileges and immunities. Status of experts.
PARTIES:
Cyprus
United Nations
ANNEX
514 UNTS 296. Cyprus. Implementation 6 Oct 64.
514 UNTS 296. Greece. Implementation 6 Oct 64.
514 UNTS 296. United Nations. Implementation 10 Oct 64.
514 UNTS 296. Turkey. Implementation 6 Oct 64.
514 UNTS 296. United Nations. Implementation 15 Oct 64.
514 UNTS 296. UK Great Britain. Implementation 6 Oct 64.
514 UNTS 296. United Nations. Implementation 14 Oct 64.
514 UNTS 296. United Nations. Implementation 22 Oct 64.

107195 Bilateral Exchange **492 UNTS 267**
SIGNED: 31 Mar 64 FORCE: 31 Mar 64
REGISTERED: 3 Apr 64 United Nations
ARTICLES: 2 LANGUAGE: English.
HEADNOTE: PRIVILEGES IMMUNITIES & FACILITIES
TOPIC: IGO Status/Immunit
CONCEPTS: Privileges and immunities. Status of experts.
PARTIES:
Greece
United Nations
ANNEX
514 UNTS 296. Cyprus. Implementation 6 Oct 64.
514 UNTS 296. United Nations. Implementation 22 Oct 64.
514 UNTS 296. Greece. Implementation 6 Oct 64.
514 UNTS 296. United Nations. Implementation 10 Oct 64.
514 UNTS 296. Turkey. Implementation 6 Oct 64.
514 UNTS 296. United Nations. Implementation 15 Oct 64.
514 UNTS 296. UK Great Britain. Implementation 6 Oct 64.
514 UNTS 296. United Nations. Implementation 14 Oct 64.

107196 Bilateral Exchange **492 UNTS 273**
SIGNED: 31 Mar 64 FORCE: 31 Mar 64
REGISTERED: 3 Apr 64 United Nations
ARTICLES: 2 LANGUAGE: English.
HEADNOTE: PRIVILEGES IMMUNITIES & FACILITIES
TOPIC: IGO Status/Immunit
CONCEPTS: Privileges and immunities. Status of experts.
PARTIES:
United Nations
Turkey
ANNEX
514 UNTS 296. Greece. Implementation 6 Oct 64.

514 UNTS 296. Turkey. Implementation 6 Oct 64.
514 UNTS 296. United Nations. Implementation 15 Oct 64.
514 UNTS 296. UK Great Britain. Implementation 6 Oct 64.
514 UNTS 296. United Nations. Implementation 14 Oct 64.
514 UNTS 296. Cyprus. Implementation 6 Oct 64.
514 UNTS 296. United Nations. Implementation 22 Oct 64.

107197 Bilateral Exchange **492 UNTS 279**
SIGNED: 2 Apr 64 FORCE: 2 Apr 64
REGISTERED: 3 Apr 64 United Nations
ARTICLES: 2 LANGUAGE: English.
HEADNOTE: PRIVILEGES IMMUNITIES & FACILITIES
TOPIC: IGO Status/Immunit
CONCEPTS: Privileges and immunities. Status of experts.
PARTIES:
United Nations
UK Great Britain
ANNEX
514 UNTS 296. Cyprus. Implementation 6 Oct 64.
514 UNTS 296. United Nations. Implementation 22 Oct 64.
514 UNTS 296. Greece. Implementation 6 Oct 64.
514 UNTS 296. United Nations. Implementation 10 Oct 64.
514 UNTS 296. Turkey. Implementation 6 Oct 64.
514 UNTS 296. United Nations. Implementation 15 Oct 64.
514 UNTS 296. UK Great Britain. Implementation 6 Oct 64.
514 UNTS 296. United Nations. Implementation 14 Oct 64.

107198 Bilateral Agreement **492 UNTS 285**
SIGNED: 8 Jan 64 FORCE: 8 Mar 64
REGISTERED: 3 Apr 64 Finland
ARTICLES: 4 LANGUAGE: English. Finnish. Sinhalese.
HEADNOTE: RECOGNITION TONNAGE CERTIFICATES MERCHANT SHIPS
TOPIC: Water Transport
CONCEPTS: Previous treaty replacement. Recognition of legal documents. Registration certificate. Merchant vessels. Tonnage.
TREATY REF: 28LTS511; 104LTS29.
PROCEDURE: Termination.
PARTIES:
Ceylon (Sri Lanka)
Finland

107199 Bilateral Exchange **492 UNTS 295**
SIGNED: 31 Jan 52 FORCE: 31 Jan 52
REGISTERED: 9 Apr 64 Netherlands
ARTICLES: 2 LANGUAGE: Dutch. German.
HEADNOTE: APPLICABILITY TREATIES
TOPIC: Admin Cooperation
CONCEPTS: Revival of treaties.
TREATY REF: 492UNTS298-FN1,2,3; 492UNTS299-FN1,2,3,4,5,6.
PARTIES:
Germany, West
Netherlands

107200 Bilateral Exchange **492 UNTS 305**
SIGNED: 13 Aug 54 FORCE: 15 Nov 54
REGISTERED: 9 Apr 64 Netherlands
ARTICLES: 2 LANGUAGE: Dutch. German.
HEADNOTE: APPLICABILITY TREATIES
TOPIC: Admin Cooperation
CONCEPTS: Revival of treaties.
TREATY REF: 492UNTS314-FN1&2;492UNTS312-FN1-4; 492UNTS313-FN1-.
PARTIES:
Germany, West
Netherlands

107201 Bilateral Exchange **492 UNTS 321**
SIGNED: 3 Aug 61 FORCE: 15 Jan 62
REGISTERED: 9 Apr 64 Netherlands
ARTICLES: 2 LANGUAGE: Dutch. German.

HEADNOTE: APPLICABILITY TREATIES
TOPIC: Admin Cooperation
CONCEPTS: Revival of treaties.
PARTIES:
    Germany, West
    Netherlands

107202   Bilateral Agreement   **492 UNTS 327**
SIGNED: 13 Aug 63   FORCE: 13 Aug 63
REGISTERED: 13 Apr 64 USA (United States)
ARTICLES: 7 LANGUAGE: English. Spanish.
HEADNOTE: AGRI COMMOD AGREE
TOPIC: US Agri Commod Aid
CONCEPTS: General provisions. Exchange of information and documents. Reciprocity in trade. Reexport of goods, etc.. Mutual consultation.
PARTIES:
    Dominican Republic
    USA (United States)

107203   Bilateral Agreement   **493 UNTS 3**
SIGNED: 23 Feb 63   FORCE: 23 Feb 63
REGISTERED: 13 Apr 64 USA (United States)
ARTICLES: 6 LANGUAGE: English. French.
HEADNOTE: AGRI COMMOD TITLE I
TOPIC: US Agri Commod Aid
CONCEPTS: General provisions. Exchange of information and documents. Reexport of goods, etc.. Currency. Exchange rates and regulations. Transportation costs. Local currency. Commodities schedule. Purchase authorization. Surplus commodities. Mutual consultation.
INTL ORGS: United Nations.
PARTIES:
    Congo (Zaire)
    USA (United States)
ANNEX
531 UNTS 411. Congo (Zaire). Amendment 4 Sep 64. Force 4 Sep 64.
531 UNTS 411. USA (United States). Amendment 28 Aug 64. Force 4 Sep 64.

107204   Bilateral Agreement   **493 UNTS 17**
SIGNED: 23 Feb 63   FORCE: 23 Feb 63
REGISTERED: 13 Apr 64 USA (United States)
ARTICLES: 6 LANGUAGE: English. French.
HEADNOTE: AGRI COMMOD TITLE I
TOPIC: US Agri Commod Aid
CONCEPTS: General provisions. Annex or appendix reference. Exchange of information and documents. Reexport of goods, etc.. Exchange rates and regulations. Transportation costs. Local currency. Commodities schedule. Purchase authorization. Surplus commodities.
INTL ORGS: United Nations.
PARTIES:
    Congo (Zaire)
    USA (United States)
ANNEX
505 UNTS 338. Congo (Zaire). Amendment 19 Dec 63. Force 19 Dec 63.
505 UNTS 338. USA (United States). Amendment 18 Dec 63. Force 19 Dec 63.
531 UNTS 412. Congo (Zaire). Amendment 4 Sep 64. Force 4 Sep 64.
531 UNTS 412. USA (United States). Amendment 28 Aug 64. Force 4 Sep 64.
531 UNTS 413. USA (United States). Amendment 9 Dec 64. Force 9 Dec 64.
531 UNTS 413. Congo (Zaire). Amendment 9 Dec 64. Force 9 Dec 64.

107205   Bilateral Agreement   **493 UNTS 29**
SIGNED: 30 Oct 63   FORCE: 30 Oct 63
REGISTERED: 13 Apr 64 USA (United States)
ARTICLES: 6 LANGUAGE: English.
HEADNOTE: AGRI COMMOD TITLE I
TOPIC: US Agri Commod Aid
CONCEPTS: General provisions. Annex or appendix reference. Exchange of information and documents. Reexport of goods, etc.. Exchange rates and regulations. Transportation costs. Local currency. Commodities schedule. Purchase authorization. Surplus commodities. Mutual consultation.
PARTIES:
    Greece
    USA (United States)

ANNEX
529 UNTS 372. USA (United States). Amendment 14 Jul 64. Force 16 Jul 64.
529 UNTS 372. Greece. Amendment 16 Jul 64. Force 16 Jul 64.
532 UNTS 390. USA (United States). Amendment 16 Nov 64. Force 16 Nov 64.
532 UNTS 390. Greece. Amendment 16 Nov 64. Force 16 Nov 64.

107206   Bilateral Exchange   **493 UNTS 45**
SIGNED: 3 Oct 63   FORCE: 3 Oct 63
REGISTERED: 13 Apr 64 USA (United States)
ARTICLES: 2 LANGUAGE: English. Spanish.
HEADNOTE: COOPERATION CONSTRUCTION INTER-AMERICAN HIGHWAY
TOPIC: Direct Aid
CONCEPTS: Tax exemptions. Customs exemptions. General technical assistance. Plans and standards. Non-bank projects.
TREATY REF: 6OCT1954'USA&GUATEMALA;.
PARTIES:
    Guatemala
    USA (United States)

107207   Bilateral Exchange   **493 UNTS 67**
SIGNED: 15 Nov 63   FORCE: 15 Nov 63
REGISTERED: 13 Apr 64 USA (United States)
ARTICLES: 2 LANGUAGE: English.
HEADNOTE: CIVIL EMERGENCY PLANNING
TOPIC: Other Military
CONCEPTS: Previous treaty replacement. Establishment of commission. Joint defense. Defense and security. Exchange of defense information.
TREATY REF: 132UNTS333.
PARTIES:
    Canada
    USA (United States)

107208   Bilateral Exchange   **493 UNTS 75**
SIGNED: 14 Nov 63   FORCE: 14 Nov 63
REGISTERED: 13 Apr 64 USA (United States)
ARTICLES: 2 LANGUAGE: English.
HEADNOTE: INVESTMENT GUARANTIES
TOPIC: Claims and Debts
CONCEPTS: General cooperation. General property. Arbitration. Procedure. Existing tribunals. Negotiation. Reciprocity in financial treatment. Currency. Claims and settlements. Private investment guarantee.
PARTIES:
    Tanganyika
    USA (United States)

107209   Bilateral Agreement   **493 UNTS 83**
SIGNED: 19 Apr 63   FORCE: 27 Nov 63
REGISTERED: 13 Apr 64 USA (United States)
ARTICLES: 16 LANGUAGE: English. French.
HEADNOTE: VISIT NS SAVANNAH BELGIAN PORTS
TOPIC: Water Transport
CONCEPTS: Treaty interpretation. Conformity with municipal law. Inspection and observation. Personnel. Responsibility and liability. Compensation. Payment schedules. Peaceful use. Navigational conditions. Inland and territorial waters. Ports and pilotage. Naval vessels. Ocean resources.
TREATY REF: INTL CONFERENCE LIFE AT SEA SAFETY 1960 P.20.
PROCEDURE: Amendment. Future Procedures Contemplated. Ratification. Termination.
PARTIES:
    Belgium
    USA (United States)

107210   Bilateral Exchange   **493 UNTS 97**
SIGNED: 17 Jan 63   FORCE: 17 Jan 63
REGISTERED: 13 Apr 64 USA (United States)
ARTICLES: 2 LANGUAGE: English. French.
HEADNOTE: PEACE CORPS PROGRAM
TOPIC: General Aid
CONCEPTS: Treaty implementation. Diplomatic privileges. Conformity with municipal law. Personnel. Tax exemptions. Customs exemptions. Domestic obligation. Materials, equipment and services. Aid missions. Volunteer programs.
PROCEDURE: Termination.

PARTIES:
    Senegal
    USA (United States)

107211   Bilateral Convention   **493 UNTS 105**
SIGNED: 8 Jan 63   FORCE: 19 Dec 63
REGISTERED: 13 Apr 64 USA (United States)
ARTICLES: 18 LANGUAGE: English. Korean.
HEADNOTE: CONSULAR
TOPIC: Consul/Citizenship
CONCEPTS: Exceptions and exemptions. Territorial application. Diplomatic privileges. Consular relations establishment. Inviolability. Privileges and immunities. Protection of nationals. Diplomatic correspondence. Consular functions in shipping. Consular functions in property. Notarial acts and services. Procedure. Social security. Headquarters and facilities.
INTL ORGS: International Court of Justice.
PROCEDURE: Duration. Ratification. Termination.
PARTIES:
    Korea, South
    USA (United States)

107212   Bilateral Exchange   **493 UNTS 147**
SIGNED: 20 Jan 59   FORCE: 5 Mar 60
REGISTERED: 14 Apr 64 Netherlands
ARTICLES: 2 LANGUAGE: English.
HEADNOTE: ABOLITION PASSPORT VISAS
TOPIC: Visas
CONCEPTS: Emergencies. Visa abolition. Denial of admission. Conformity with municipal law.
PROCEDURE: Denunciation.
PARTIES:
    Malaysia
    Netherlands

107213   Bilateral Agreement   **493 UNTS 155**
SIGNED: 9 Jun 62   FORCE: 28 Oct 63
REGISTERED: 14 Apr 64 USSR (Soviet Union)
ARTICLES: 13 LANGUAGE: Russian. Turkish. French.
HEADNOTE: WIRE TELEPHONE & RADIO TELEGRAPH COMMUNICATIONS
TOPIC: Telecommunications
CONCEPTS: Radio-telephone-telegraphic communications.
TREATY REF: INTERNATIONAL TELECOMMUNICATION CONVENTION.
PARTIES:
    Turkey
    USSR (Soviet Union)

107214   Bilateral Agreement   **493 UNTS 173**
SIGNED: 2 Jun 61   FORCE: 10 Feb 62
REGISTERED: 14 Apr 64 USSR (Soviet Union)
ARTICLES: 13 LANGUAGE: Russian. Italian.
HEADNOTE: ECONOMIC TRADE RELATIONS
TOPIC: General Trade
CONCEPTS: Exceptions and exemptions. Treaty implementation. Annex or appendix reference. General cooperation. Licenses and permits. Establishment of commission. Export quotas. Import quotas. Accounting procedures. Banking. Currency. Monetary and gold transfers. Payment schedules. Most favored nation clause. Credit provisions. Navigational conditions. Transport of goods.
INTL ORGS: Special Commission.
PROCEDURE: Denunciation. Duration. Ratification. Renewal or Revival.
PARTIES:
    Somalia
    USSR (Soviet Union)

107215   Bilateral Agreement   **493 UNTS 195**
SIGNED: 14 Aug 63   FORCE: 2 Dec 63
REGISTERED: 14 Apr 64 USSR (Soviet Union)
ARTICLES: 15 LANGUAGE: Russian. English.
HEADNOTE: TRADE DEVELOPMENT
TOPIC: General Trade
CONCEPTS: Definition of terms. Exceptions and exemptions. Treaty implementation. Annex or appendix reference. Conformity with municipal law. General cooperation. Licenses and permits. Establishment of trade relations. Export quotas. Import quotas. Certificates of origin. Reciprocity in trade. Reexport of goods, etc.. Balance of payments. Currency. Payment schedules. Non-inter-

est rates and fees. Transportation costs. Most favored nation clause. Equitable taxes. Customs duties. Temporary importation. Navigational conditions. Transport of goods. Merchant vessels. Inland and territorial waters. Ports and pilotage.
PROCEDURE: Ratification. Termination.
PARTIES:
Tanganyika
USSR (Soviet Union)

107216   Bilateral Agreement   **493 UNTS 219**
SIGNED: 10 Oct 62   FORCE: 5 Feb 64
REGISTERED: 14 Apr 64 USSR (Soviet Union)
ARTICLES: 5 LANGUAGE: Russian. French.
HEADNOTE: ECONOMIC & AGRICULTURAL TECHNICAL ASSISTANCE
TOPIC: Tech Assistance
CONCEPTS: Treaty implementation. Personnel. Compensation. Taxation. Customs duties. Domestic obligation. General technical assistance. Agriculture. Economic assistance. Materials, equipment and services. Credit provisions.
TREATY REF: USSR-MALI ECON AND TECH COOP 18MAR61.
PROCEDURE: Ratification.
PARTIES:
Mali
USSR (Soviet Union)

107217   Bilateral Agreement   **493 UNTS 229**
SIGNED: 22 Apr 63   FORCE: 14 Nov 63
REGISTERED: 14 Apr 64 USSR (Soviet Union)
ARTICLES: 10 LANGUAGE: Russian. Polish.
HEADNOTE: POLISH TRAIN TRAFFIC SECTION RAILWAYS SOVIET SOCIALIST REPUBLICS
TOPIC: Land Transport
CONCEPTS: Frontier formalities. Conformity with municipal law. Informational records. Personnel. Responsibility and liability. Investigation of violations. Payment schedules. Claims and settlements. Customs exemptions. Passenger transport. Routes and logistics. Transport of goods. Operating authorizations and regulations. Railway border crossing. Railways.
PROCEDURE: Denunciation. Ratification.
PARTIES:
Poland
USSR (Soviet Union)

107218   Bilateral Agreement   **493 UNTS 243**
SIGNED: 8 Nov 63   FORCE: 23 Nov 63
REGISTERED: 16 Apr 64 WHO (World Health)
ARTICLES: 6 LANGUAGE: English.
HEADNOTE: OPERATIONAL ASSISTANCE
TOPIC: IGO Operations
CONCEPTS: Annex or appendix reference. Diplomatic missions. Private contracts. Procedure. Domestic obligation. IGO obligations.
INTL ORGS: Permanent Court of Arbitration. Arbitration Commission.
TREATY REF: 490UNTS.
PROCEDURE: Amendment. Termination.
PARTIES:
WHO (World Health)
Somalia
ANNEX
529 UNTS 376. Somalia. Prolongation 7 Jan 65.
529 UNTS 376. WHO (World Health). Prolongation 30 Dec 64.

107219   Bilateral Agreement   **493 UNTS 255**
SIGNED: 22 Nov 63   FORCE: 12 Dec 63
REGISTERED: 20 Apr 64 WHO (World Health)
ARTICLES: 6 LANGUAGE: English.
HEADNOTE: OPERATIONAL ASSISTANCE
TOPIC: IGO Operations
CONCEPTS: Annex or appendix reference. Diplomatic missions. Private contracts. Procedure. Domestic obligation. IGO obligations.
INTL ORGS: Permanent Court of Arbitration. Arbitration Commission.
TREATY REF: 490UNTS.
PROCEDURE: Amendment. Termination.
PARTIES:
WHO (World Health)
Sierra Leone

107220   Bilateral Agreement   **493 UNTS 267**
SIGNED: 11 Sep 63   FORCE: 11 Sep 63
REGISTERED: 22 Apr 64 USA (United States)
ARTICLES: 6 LANGUAGE: English. Portuguese.
HEADNOTE: AGRI COMMOD TITLE I
TOPIC: US Agri Commod Aid
CONCEPTS: General provisions. Annex or appendix reference. Exchange of information and documents. Reexport of goods, etc.. Exchange rates and regulations. Transportation costs. Local currency. Commodities schedule. Purchase authorization. Surplus commodities. Mutual consultation.
PARTIES:
Brazil
USA (United States)
ANNEX
526 UNTS 354. USA (United States). Amendment 15 May 64. Force 15 May 64.
526 UNTS 354. Brazil. Amendment 15 May 64. Force 15 May 64.

107221   Bilateral Exchange   **494 UNTS 3**
SIGNED: 7 Oct 63   FORCE: 7 Oct 63
REGISTERED: 22 Apr 64 USA (United States)
ARTICLES: 2 LANGUAGE: English. French.
HEADNOTE: SPACE VEHICLE TRACKING COMMUNICATIONS STATION
TOPIC: Scientific Project
CONCEPTS: Alien status. Conformity with municipal law. General property. Research cooperation. Communication satellites testing. Tax exemptions. Facilities and equipment. Interference of broadcasts. Satellites. Facilities and property.
PARTIES:
Malagasy
USA (United States)

107222   Bilateral Exchange   **494 UNTS 13**
SIGNED: 23 Aug 63   FORCE: 23 Aug 63
REGISTERED: 22 Apr 64 USA (United States)
ARTICLES: 2 LANGUAGE: English.
HEADNOTE: TESTING EXPERIMENTAL COMMUNICATIONS SATELLITES
TOPIC: Telecommunications
CONCEPTS: Annex or appendix reference. Satellites.
PARTIES:
Canada
USA (United States)

107223   Bilateral Exchange   **494 UNTS 21**
SIGNED: 27 Dec 63   FORCE: 27 Dec 63
REGISTERED: 22 Apr 64 USA (United States)
ARTICLES: 2 LANGUAGE: English.
HEADNOTE: AIR TRAFFIC CONTROL
TOPIC: Air Transport
CONCEPTS: Treaty implementation. Conformity with municipal law. Exchange of information and documents. Navigational conditions. Air transport. Operating authorizations and regulations. Boundaries of territory.
PARTIES:
Canada
USA (United States)

107224   Bilateral Exchange   **494 UNTS 27**
SIGNED: 19 Oct 63   FORCE: 19 Oct 63
REGISTERED: 22 Apr 64 USA (United States)
ARTICLES: 2 LANGUAGE: English.
HEADNOTE: TRADE COTTON TEXTILES
TOPIC: Commodity Trade
CONCEPTS: Detailed regulations. Time limit. Annex or appendix reference. General cooperation. Exchange of information and documents. Export quotas. Commodity trade. Quotas.
TREATY REF: 471UNTS296.
PROCEDURE: Amendment. Termination.
PARTIES:
Taiwan
USA (United States)
ANNEX
524 UNTS 336. Taiwan. Amendment 3 Feb 64. Force 18 Mar 64.
524 UNTS 336. USA (United States). Amendment 3 Feb 64. Force 18 Mar 64.
541 UNTS 358. USA (United States). Amendment 13 Jan 65. Force 13 Jan 65.
541 UNTS 358. Taiwan. Amendment 13 Jan 65. Force 13 Jan 65.

550 UNTS 410. USA (United States). Amendment 22 Jun 65. Force 22 Jun 65.
550 UNTS 410. Taiwan. Acknowledgement 22 Jun 65. Force 22 Jun 65.

107225   Bilateral Exchange   **494 UNTS 49**
SIGNED: 29 Nov 63   FORCE: 29 Dec 63
REGISTERED: 22 Apr 64 USA (United States)
ARTICLES: 2 LANGUAGE: English. Spanish.
HEADNOTE: RADIO COMMUNICATIONS AMATEUR STATIONS BEHALF THIRD PARTIES
TOPIC: Gen Communications
CONCEPTS: Amateur radio. Amateur third party message. Radio-telephone-telegraphic communications.
PARTIES:
Colombia
USA (United States)

107226   Bilateral Agreement   **494 UNTS 55**
SIGNED: 13 Dec 63   FORCE: 13 Dec 63
REGISTERED: 22 Apr 64 USA (United States)
ARTICLES: 16 LANGUAGE: English. Greek.
HEADNOTE: EDUCATIONAL PROGRAM
TOPIC: Education
CONCEPTS: Previous treaty replacement. Border traffic and migration. Alien status. Standardization. Conformity with municipal law. Exchange of information and documents. Inspection and observation. Personnel. General property. Exchange. Commissions and foundations. Teacher and student exchange. Professorships. Scientific exchange. Accounting procedures. Currency. Exchange rates and regulations. Financial programs. Funding procedures. Tax exemptions. Customs exemptions.
TREATY REF: 74UNTS107; 223UNTS320,332; 261UNTS392; 406UNTS292.
PROCEDURE: Amendment.
PARTIES:
Greece
USA (United States)

107227   Bilateral Agreement   **494 UNTS 77**
SIGNED: 28 Apr 64   FORCE: 28 Apr 64
REGISTERED: 28 Apr 64 United Nations
ARTICLES: 6 LANGUAGE: English.
HEADNOTE: UN SEMINAR HUMAN RIGHTS
TOPIC: Education
CONCEPTS: Visas. Alien status. Privileges and immunities. General cooperation. Personnel. Exchange. Indemnities and reimbursements. Expense sharing formulae. General transportation. Conferences.
TREATY REF: 1UNTS15; 33UNTS261; UN10-SESS. SUPP19(A-3116)13.
PROCEDURE: Amendment. Duration.
PARTIES:
Afghanistan
United Nations

107228   Bilateral Exchange   **494 UNTS 89**
SIGNED: 22 Nov 63   FORCE: 22 Nov 63
REGISTERED: 28 Apr 64 USA (United States)
ARTICLES: 2 LANGUAGE: English.
HEADNOTE: TRADE COTTON TEXTILES
TOPIC: Commodity Trade
CONCEPTS: Detailed regulations. Time limit. Annex or appendix reference. General cooperation. Exchange of information and documents. Export quotas. Commodity trade. Quotas.
PROCEDURE: Amendment. Termination.
PARTIES:
Israel
USA (United States)

107229   Bilateral Agreement   **494 UNTS 101**
SIGNED: 16 Sep 63   FORCE: 16 Sep 63
REGISTERED: 28 Apr 64 USA (United States)
ARTICLES: 5 LANGUAGE: English. Spanish.
HEADNOTE: AGRI COMMOD TITLE IV
TOPIC: US Agri Commod Aid
CONCEPTS: General provisions. Annex or appendix reference. Reciprocity in trade. Reexport of goods, etc.. Payment schedules. Transportation costs. Purchase authorization. Commodities schedule. Purchase authorization. Mutual consultation. Internal travel.

107235 Bilateral Instrument **494 UNTS 213**
SIGNED: 18 Nov 61   FORCE: 13 Feb 62
REGISTERED: 30 Apr 64 United Nations
ARTICLES: 5 LANGUAGE: English.
HEADNOTE: AGRI COMMOD
TOPIC: US Agri Commod Aid
CONCEPTS: Exchange of information and documents. Accounting procedures. Currency deposits. Payment schedules. Commodities schedule. Purchase authorization.
TREATY REF: 433UNTS207.
PROCEDURE: Duration.
PARTIES:
  United Nations
  USA (United States)
                    ANNEX
529 UNTS 378. USA (United States). Amendment 25 Aug 64. Force 26 Aug 64.
529 UNTS 378. United Nations. Amendment 26 Aug 64. Force 26 Aug 64.

107236 Multilateral Agreement **494 UNTS 219**
SIGNED: 14 Sep 62   FORCE: 29 Jan 63
REGISTERED: 30 Apr 64 United Arab Rep
ARTICLES: 17 LANGUAGE: English. French.
HEADNOTE: ARAB REGIONAL RADIOISOTOPE CENTRE
TOPIC: IGO Status/Immunit
CONCEPTS: Arbitration. Procedure. International circulation. Specialists exchange. Medical assistance and/or facilities. Regional offices.
INTL ORGS: International Court of Justice.
PROCEDURE: Amendment. Duration. Termination.
PARTIES:
  Iraq RATIFIED: 24 Dec 63 FORCE: 24 Dec 63
  Kuwait RATIFIED: 27 May 63 FORCE: 27 May 63
  Lebanon RATIFIED: 28 Aug 63 FORCE: 29 Jan 63
  Libya RATIFIED: 22 Dec 63 FORCE: 29 Jan 63
  Tunisia RATIFIED: 31 Dec 63 FORCE: 29 Jan 63
  United Arab Rep RATIFIED: 29 Jan 63 FORCE: 29 Jan 63
  Yemen RATIFIED: 29 Jul 63 FORCE: 29 Jan 63

107237 Multilateral Convention **494 UNTS 249**
SIGNED: 22 Jun 62   FORCE: 23 Apr 64
REGISTERED: 4 May 64 ILO (Labor Org)
ARTICLES: 25 LANGUAGE: English. French.
HEADNOTE: BASIC AIMS STANDARDS SOCIAL POLICY
TOPIC: ILO Labor
CONCEPTS: Incorporation of treaty provisions into national law. Commissions and foundations. Vocational training. ILO conventions. Anti-discrimination. Wages and salaries. Social security. Migrant worker. Economic assistance. Socio-economic development.
INTL ORGS: United Nations.
TREATY REF: 218UNTS345.
PROCEDURE: Amendment. Denunciation. Duration. Ratification. Registration. Renewal or Revival.
PARTIES:
  Israel RATIFIED: 15 Jan 64
  Jordan RATIFIED: 7 Mar 63
  Kuwait RATIFIED: 23 Apr 63
                    ANNEX
504 UNTS 371. Ghana. Ratification 18 Jun 64. Force 18 Jun 65.
504 UNTS 371. Madagascar. Ratification 1 Jun 64. Force 1 Jun 65.
504 UNTS 371. Central Afri Rep. Ratification 9 Jun 64. Force 9 Jun 65.
521 UNTS 429. Niger. Ratification 23 Nov 64. Force 23 Nov 65.
522 UNTS 392. Zambia. Ratification 2 Dec 64. Force 2 Dec 64.
522 UNTS 392. Taiwan. Ratification 10 Dec 64. Force 10 Dec 65.
522 UNTS 392. Syria. Ratification 11 Dec 64. Force 11 Dec 65.
553 UNTS 346. Costa Rica. Ratification 27 Jan 66. Force 27 Jan 67.
553 UNTS 346. Jamaica. Ratification 4 Jan 66. Force 4 Jan 67.
607 UNTS 368. Congo (Zaire). Ratification 5 Sep 67. Force 5 Sep 68.
613 UNTS 427. Senegal. Ratification 13 Nov 67. Force 13 Nov 68.
660 UNTS 431. Paraguay. Ratification 20 Feb 69. Force 20 Feb 69.

PARTIES:
  Paraguay
  USA (United States)

107230 Bilateral Agreement **494 UNTS 119**
SIGNED: 31 Jan 63   FORCE: 31 Jan 63
REGISTERED: 28 Apr 64 USA (United States)
ARTICLES: 6 LANGUAGE: English. Arabic.
HEADNOTE: AGRI COMMOD TITLE I
TOPIC: US Agri Commod Aid
CONCEPTS: General provisions. Annex or appendix reference. Exchange of information and documents. Reexport of goods, etc.. Exchange rates and regulations. Transportation costs. Local currency. Commodities schedule. Purchase authorization. Surplus commodities. Mutual consultation.
PARTIES:
  Sudan
  USA (United States)

107231 Bilateral Convention **494 UNTS 141**
SIGNED: 24 Oct 61   FORCE: 3 Dec 63
REGISTERED: 28 Apr 64 USA (United States)
ARTICLES: 16 LANGUAGE: English. Swedish.
HEADNOTE: EXTRADITION
TOPIC: Extradition
CONCEPTS: Definition of terms. Extradition, deportation and repatriation. Extradition requests. Extraditable offenses. Location of crime. Refusal of extradition. Limits of prosecution. Extradition postponement. Conformity with municipal law. Indemnities and reimbursements. Conveyance in transit.
PROCEDURE: Ratification. Termination.
PARTIES:
  Sweden
  USA (United States)

107232 Bilateral Agreement **494 UNTS 169**
SIGNED: 18 Nov 63   FORCE: 18 Nov 63
REGISTERED: 28 Apr 64 USA (United States)
ARTICLES: 5 LANGUAGE: English. Arabic.
HEADNOTE: AGRI COMMOD TITLE IV
TOPIC: US Agri Commod Aid
CONCEPTS: General provisions. Exchange of information and documents. Reexport of goods, etc.. Currency. Payment schedules. Purchase authorization. Commodities schedule. Purchase authorization. Mutual consultation.
PARTIES:
  Syria
  USA (United States)

107233 Bilateral Agreement **494 UNTS 193**
SIGNED: 18 Nov 63   FORCE: 18 Nov 63
REGISTERED: 28 Apr 64 USA (United States)
ARTICLES: 12 LANGUAGE: English. French.
HEADNOTE: EDUCATION PROGRAM
TOPIC: Education
CONCEPTS: Border traffic and migration. Alien status. Standardization. Conformity with municipal law. Exchange of information and documents. Inspection and observation. Personnel. General property. Exchange. Teacher and student exchange. Professorships. Exchange rates and regulations. Accounting procedures. Currency. Financial programs. Funding procedures. Tax exemptions.
PARTIES:
  Tunisia
  USA (United States)

107234 Bilateral Agreement **494 UNTS 205**
SIGNED: 12 Jun 61   FORCE: 12 Jun 61
REGISTERED: 30 Apr 64 United Nations
ARTICLES: 12 LANGUAGE: French.
HEADNOTE: ECONOMIC FINANCIAL ASSISTANCE
TOPIC: General Aid
CONCEPTS: General cooperation. Exchange of information and documents. Operating agencies. Accounting procedures. Currency deposits. Financial programs. Funding procedures. Internal finance. Local currency. Assets. General. Economic assistance.
PROCEDURE: Registration.
PARTIES:
  Congo (Zaire)
  United Nations

107238 Multilateral Convention **494 UNTS 271**
SIGNED: 28 Jun 62   FORCE: 25 Apr 64
REGISTERED: 4 May 64 ILO (Labor Org)
ARTICLES: 21 LANGUAGE: English. French.
HEADNOTE: EQUAL TREATMENT SOCIAL SECURITY
TOPIC: ILO Labor
CONCEPTS: Conditions. Definition of terms. Detailed regulations. Refugees. Stateless persons. General cooperation. Incorporation of treaty provisions into national law. Establishment of commission. ILO conventions. Anti-discrimination. Old age and invalidity insurance. Sickness and invalidity insurance. Social security. Unemployment. National treatment.
INTL ORGS: United Nations.
TREATY REF: 40UNTS73.
PROCEDURE: Amendment. Denunciation. Duration. Ratification. Registration. Renewal or Revival.
PARTIES:
  Guatemala RATIFIED: 4 Nov 63
  Jordan RATIFIED: 7 Mar 63
  Norway RATIFIED: 28 Aug 63
  Sweden RATIFIED: 25 Apr 63
  Syria RATIFIED: 18 Nov 63
                    ANNEX
504 UNTS 372. Madagascar. Ratification 22 Jun 64. Force 1 Jun 65.
504 UNTS 372. Netherlands. Ratification 3 Jul 64. Force 3 Jul 65.
504 UNTS 372. Netherlands. Netherlands Antilles.
510 UNTS 368. India. Ratification 19 Aug 64. Force 19 Aug 65.
515 UNTS 346. Central Afri Rep. Qualified Ratification 8 Oct 64. Force 8 Oct 64.
521 UNTS 430. Ireland. Ratification 26 Nov 64. Force 26 Nov 65.
524 UNTS 372. Taiwan. Ratification 4 Jan 65. Force 4 Jan 66.
530 UNTS 368. Netherlands. Surinam.
541 UNTS 382. Israel. Ratification 9 Jun 65. Force 9 Jun 66.
547 UNTS 370. Tunisia. Ratification 20 Sep 65.
607 UNTS 369. Guinea. Ratification 11 Aug 68. Force 11 Aug 68.
613 UNTS 428. Congo (Brazzaville). Ratification 1 Nov 67. Force 1 Nov 68.
642 UNTS 397. Mauritania. Ratification 15 Jul 68. Force 15 Jul 69.

107239 Multilateral Agreement **495 UNTS 3**
SIGNED: 20 Apr 63   FORCE: 17 Mar 64
REGISTERED: 5 May 64 Spain
ARTICLES: 42 LANGUAGE: English. French. Spanish.
HEADNOTE: OLIVE OIL AGREEMENT
TOPIC: IGO Establishment
CONCEPTS: Definition of terms. Annex or appendix reference. Privileges and immunities. Conformity with municipal law. Exchange of information and documents. Informational records. Procedure. Existing tribunals. Employment regulations. Accounting procedures. Funding procedures. Economic assistance. Admission. Decisions. Establishment. Liaison with other IGO's. Internal structure.
INTL ORGS: International Olive Oil Council. Food and Agricultural Organization of the United Nations. International Court of Justice. United Nations.
PROCEDURE: Amendment. Accession. Denunciation. Duration. Ratification. Registration. Renewal or Revival.
PARTIES:
  Algeria SIGNED: 29 Jun 63 RATIFIED: 28 Oct 63 FORCE: 17 Mar 64
  Belgium SIGNED: 28 Jun 63
  France SIGNED: 29 Jun 63 RATIFIED: 28 Jun 63 FORCE: 17 Mar 64
  Greece SIGNED: 29 Jun 63
  Israel SIGNED: 25 Jun 63 RATIFIED: 28 Sep 63 FORCE: 17 Mar 64
  Italy SIGNED: 21 Jun 63
  Libya RATIFIED: 13 Aug 63 FORCE: 17 Mar 64
  Morocco SIGNED: 20 Jun 63 RATIFIED: 30 Sep 63 FORCE: 17 Mar 64
  Portugal SIGNED: 28 Jun 63
  Spain SIGNED: 28 Jun 63
  Tunisia SIGNED: 22 Jun 63
  Turkey SIGNED: 28 Jun 63 RATIFIED: 26 Oct 63 FORCE: 17 Mar 64

UK Great Britain Guernsey Island RATIFIED: 17 Mar 64 FORCE: 17 Mar 64
UK Great Britain Isle of Man RATIFIED: 17 Mar 64 FORCE: 17 Mar 64
UK Great Britain Jersey Island RATIFIED: 17 Mar 64 FORCE: 17 Mar 64
UK Great Britain SIGNED: 28 Jun 63 RATIFIED: 17 Mar 64 FORCE: 17 Mar 64
ANNEX
501 UNTS 375. Spain. Ratification 27 May 64.
501 UNTS 375. United Arab Rep. Qualified Accession 21 May 64.
502 UNTS 389. Portugal. Ratification 13 Jun 64.
533 UNTS 384. Italy. Qualified Ratification 25 Mar 65.
533 UNTS 384. Italy. Ratification 6 Apr 65.
636 UNTS 370. UK Great Britain. Signature 27 Jun 67. Force 25 Nov 67.
636 UNTS 370. Belgium. Signature 15 Jun 67.
636 UNTS 370. Morocco. Supplementation 27 Jun 67.
636 UNTS 370. Dominican Republic. Accession 21 Dec 67. Force 21 Dec 67.
636 UNTS 370. Tunisia. Signature 30 May 67. Ratification 21 Dec 67.
636 UNTS 370. Greece. Supplementation 23 Jun 67.
636 UNTS 370. Luxembourg. Signature 15 Jun 67.
636 UNTS 370. Israel. Signature 31 May 67. Force 25 Nov 67.
636 UNTS 370. France. Signature 28 Jun 67. Force 25 Nov 67.
636 UNTS 370. Italy. Supplementation 5 Jun 67.
636 UNTS 370. Portugal. Signature 23 Jun 67. Ratification 20 Nov 67.
636 UNTS 370. Turkey. Signature 13 Jun 67. Ratification 1 Mar 68.
636 UNTS 370. Algeria. Signature 27 Jun 67. Force 25 Nov 67.
636 UNTS 370. Argentina. Signature 30 Jun 67. Ratification 25 Apr 68.
636 UNTS 370. Libya. Signature 7 Jun 67. Force 25 Nov 67.
636 UNTS 370. United Arab Rep. Signature 30 Mar 67. Ratification 20 Mar 68.
636 UNTS 370. Spain. Signature 10 Jun 67. Ratification 25 Nov 67.
646 UNTS 406. Syria. Accession 30 Jul 68.

107240   Bilateral Agreement   **495 UNTS 85**
SIGNED: 30 Mar 50   FORCE: 30 Mar 50
REGISTERED: 13 May 64 Czechoslovakia
ARTICLES: 10 LANGUAGE: Czechoslovakian. German.
HEADNOTE: PLANT PROTECTION
TOPIC: Sanitation
CONCEPTS: Definition of terms. Non-prejudice to third party. Exchange of information and documents. Informational records. Inspection and observation. Domestic legislation. Border control. Disease control. Insect control. Education. Scientific exchange. Reexport of goods, etc.. Trade procedures. Agriculture. Conferences.
PROCEDURE: Denunciation. Duration. Renewal or Revival.
PARTIES:
Austria
Czechoslovakia

107241   Bilateral Agreement   **495 UNTS 99**
SIGNED: 23 Jan 60   FORCE: 23 Jan 60
REGISTERED: 13 May 64 Czechoslovakia
ARTICLES: 11 LANGUAGE: Czechoslovakian. German.
HEADNOTE: GEOLOGICAL COOPERATION
TOPIC: Scientific Project
CONCEPTS: Definition of terms. Border traffic and migration. General cooperation. Operating agencies. Programs. Research and scientific projects. Scientific exchange. Indemnities and reimbursements. Conferences. Regulation of natural resources.
PROCEDURE: Denunciation. Duration. Renewal or Revival.
PARTIES:
Austria
Czechoslovakia

107242   Bilateral Agreement   **495 UNTS 125**
SIGNED: 23 Jan 60   FORCE: 23 Jan 60
REGISTERED: 13 May 64 Czechoslovakia
ARTICLES: 9 LANGUAGE: Czechoslovakian. German.
HEADNOTE: WORKING DEPOSITS NATURAL GAS PETROLEUM
TOPIC: Specific Resources
CONCEPTS: Exchange of official publications. Exchange of information and documents. Establishment of commission. Arbitration. Negotiation. Raw materials.
INTL ORGS: Special Commission.
PARTIES:
Austria
Czechoslovakia

107243   Bilateral Agreement   **495 UNTS 143**
SIGNED: 14 Sep 60   FORCE: 14 Nov 60
REGISTERED: 13 May 64 Czechoslovakia
ARTICLES: 10 LANGUAGE: Czechoslovakian. German.
HEADNOTE: CINEMATOGRAPHIC FILMS
TOPIC: Commodity Trade
CONCEPTS: Treaty implementation. General cooperation. Licenses and permits. Establishment of commission. Certificates of origin. Payment schedules. Commodity trade. Quotas.
INTL ORGS: Special Commission.
PROCEDURE: Denunciation. Duration. Renewal or Revival.
PARTIES:
Austria
Czechoslovakia

107244   Bilateral Agreement   **495 UNTS 157**
SIGNED: 22 Sep 62   FORCE: 2 Mar 64
REGISTERED: 13 May 64 Czechoslovakia
ARTICLES: 26 LANGUAGE: Czechoslovakian. German.
HEADNOTE: REGULATION RAILWAY TRAFFIC ACROSS FRONTIER
TOPIC: Land Transport
CONCEPTS: Definition of terms. General provisions. Treaty implementation. Annex or appendix reference. Passports non-diplomatic. Non-visa travel documents. Visas. Conformity with municipal law. Personnel. Recognition of legal documents. Responsibility and liability. Investigation of violations. Arbitration. Procedure. Special tribunals. Competence of tribunal. Humanitarian matters. Compensation. Indemnities and reimbursements. Fees and exemptions. Funding procedures. Claims and settlements. National treatment. Tax exemptions. Customs exemptions. Routes and logistics. Operating authorizations and regulations. Railway border crossing. Railways. Regulations. Services.
INTL ORGS: Arbitration Commission.
TREATY REF: 364UNTS3,331;SCOTT;1907 HAGUE CONF.P81DOC,ETC..
PROCEDURE: Denunciation. Ratification.
PARTIES:
Austria
Czechoslovakia
ANNEX
617 UNTS 370. Czechoslovakia. Amendment 3 Jan 67. Force 4 Nov 67.
617 UNTS 370. Austria. Amendment 3 Jan 67. Force 4 Nov 67.

107245   Bilateral Treaty   **495 UNTS 219**
SIGNED: 8 Mar 63   FORCE: 16 Nov 63
REGISTERED: 13 May 64 Czechoslovakia
ARTICLES: 17 LANGUAGE: Czechoslovakian. Bulgarian.
HEADNOTE: TRADE NAVIGATION
TOPIC: General Economic
CONCEPTS: Detailed regulations. Exceptions and exemptions. General provisions. Conformity with municipal law. Exchange of information and documents. Juridical personality. Legal protection and assistance. Recognition and enforcement of legal decisions. Recognition of legal documents. Arbitration. Procedure. Export quotas. Import quotas. Reciprocity in trade. Reexport of goods, etc.. Transportation costs. Most favored nation clause. Temporary importation. General technical assistance. Economic assistance. Registration certificate. Navigational conditions. Inland and territorial waters. Shipwreck and salvage.
INTL ORGS: Arbitration Commission.

PROCEDURE: Ratification. Termination.
PARTIES:
Austria
Czechoslovakia

107246   Bilateral Convention   **496 UNTS 3**
SIGNED: 24 Jun 63   FORCE: 21 Feb 64
REGISTERED: 13 May 64 Czechoslovakia
ARTICLES: 34 LANGUAGE: Czechoslovakian. Serbo-Croat.
HEADNOTE: CONSULAR RELATIONS
TOPIC: Consul/Citizenship
CONCEPTS: Definition of terms. General provisions. Previous treaty replacement. General consular functions. Diplomatic privileges. Consular relations establishment. Inviolability. Privileges and immunities. Diplomatic correspondence. Responsibility and liability.
TREATY REF: 98LTS297.
PROCEDURE: Denunciation. Ratification.
PARTIES:
Czechoslovakia
Yugoslavia

107247   Multilateral Convention   **496 UNTS 43**
SIGNED: 26 Oct 61   FORCE: 18 May 64
REGISTERED: 18 May 64 United Nations
ARTICLES: 34 LANGUAGE: English. French. Spanish.
HEADNOTE: PROTECTION PERFORMERS PHONOGRAPH PRODUCERS BROADCASTERS
TOPIC: Patents/Copyrights
CONCEPTS: Definition of terms. Alien status. Conformity with municipal law. Exchange. Laws and formalities.
INTL ORGS: International Court of Justice. International Labour Organization. United Nations Educational, Scientific and Cultural Organization. United Nations.
TREATY REF: 216UNTS133.
PROCEDURE: Accession. Denunciation. Ratification. Registration.
PARTIES:
Argentina SIGNED: 26 Oct 61
Austria SIGNED: 26 Oct 61
Belgium SIGNED: 26 Oct 61
Brazil SIGNED: 26 Oct 61
Cambodia SIGNED: 26 Oct 61
Chile SIGNED: 26 Oct 61
Denmark SIGNED: 26 Oct 61
Ecuador SIGNED: 26 Jun 62 RATIFIED: 19 Dec 63 FORCE: 18 May 64
Finland SIGNED: 21 Jun 62
France SIGNED: 26 Oct 61
Germany, West SIGNED: 26 Oct 61
Iceland SIGNED: 26 Oct 61
India SIGNED: 26 Oct 61
Ireland SIGNED: 30 Jun 62
Israel SIGNED: 7 Feb 62
Italy SIGNED: 26 Oct 61
Lebanon SIGNED: 26 Jun 63
Mexico SIGNED: 26 Oct 61 RATIFIED: 17 Feb 64 FORCE: 18 May 64
Monaco SIGNED: 22 Jun 62
Paraguay SIGNED: 30 Jun 62
Spain SIGNED: 26 Oct 61
Sweden SIGNED: 26 Oct 61 RATIFIED: 13 Jul 62 FORCE: 18 May 64
UK Great Britain SIGNED: 26 Oct 61 RATIFIED: 30 Oct 63 FORCE: 18 May 64
Vatican/Holy See SIGNED: 26 Oct 61
Yugoslavia SIGNED: 26 Oct 61
ANNEX
540 UNTS 338. Denmark. Qualified Ratification 23 Jun 65. Force 23 Sep 65.
540 UNTS 338. Brazil. Ratification 29 Jun 65. Force 29 Sep 65.
568 UNTS 362. Germany, West. Qualified Ratification 21 Jul 66. Force 21 Oct 66.

107248   Bilateral Agreement   **496 UNTS 97**
SIGNED: 18 Oct 62   FORCE: 7 Feb 64
REGISTERED: 19 May 64 Austria
ARTICLES: 29 LANGUAGE: German.
HEADNOTE: DOUBLE TAXATION INCOME FORTUNE
TOPIC: Taxation
CONCEPTS: Definition of terms. Privileges and immunities. Nationality and citizenship. Conformity with municipal law. Exchange of official publications. Negotiation. Teacher and student ex-

change. Taxation. Equitable taxes. Air transport. Merchant vessels.
PROCEDURE: Duration. Ratification. Termination.
PARTIES:
Austria
Luxembourg

107249 Multilateral Exchange **496 UNTS 151**
SIGNED: 10 Feb 64 FORCE: 1 Mar 64
REGISTERED: 19 May 64 Belgium
ARTICLES: 2 LANGUAGE: French.
HEADNOTE: USE SEAMENS BOOKS TRAVEL DOCUMENTS
TOPIC: Visas
CONCEPTS: Definition of terms. Previous treaty replacement. Visa abolition. Border traffic and migration. Denial of admission. Non-visa travel documents.
TREATY REF: 173UNTS53; 292UNTS23.
PROCEDURE: Denunciation.
PARTIES:
Belgium SIGNED: 7 Feb 64 FORCE: 1 Mar 64
Greece SIGNED: 10 Feb 64 FORCE: 1 Mar 64
Luxembourg SIGNED: 7 Feb 64 FORCE: 1 Mar 64
Netherlands SIGNED: 7 Feb 64 FORCE: 1 Mar 64

107250 Bilateral Protocol **496 UNTS 161**
SIGNED: 27 Nov 63 FORCE: 10 Dec 63
REGISTERED: 21 May 64 USSR (Soviet Union)
ARTICLES: 2 LANGUAGE: Russian. Czechoslovakian.
HEADNOTE: RENEWING TREATY FRIENDSHIP MUTUAL ASSISTANCE POST-WAR COOPERATION
TOPIC: General Amity
CONCEPTS: Annex type material. Previous treaty extension.
TREATY REF: FRIENDSHIP AND COOP TREATY, 12DEC43.
PROCEDURE: Denunciation. Ratification.
PARTIES:
Czechoslovakia
USSR (Soviet Union)

107251 Bilateral Agreement **496 UNTS 171**
SIGNED: 15 Jul 63 FORCE: 15 Jul 63
REGISTERED: 25 May 64 Mongolia
ARTICLES: 6 LANGUAGE: Mongolian. German. English.
HEADNOTE: TRADE PAYMENTS AGREEMENT
TOPIC: General Trade
CONCEPTS: Annex or appendix reference. Conformity with municipal law. Licenses and permits. Establishment of commission. General trade. Currency. Payment schedules. General transportation.
PROCEDURE: Duration. Renewal or Revival. Termination.
PARTIES:
Austria
Mongolia

107252 Bilateral Agreement **496 UNTS 193**
SIGNED: 5 Nov 63 FORCE: 5 Nov 63
REGISTERED: 2 Jun 64 WHO (World Health)
ARTICLES: 6 LANGUAGE: English.
HEADNOTE: TECHNICAL ADVISORY ASSISTANCE
TOPIC: Tech Assistance
CONCEPTS: Definition of terms. Privileges and immunities. General cooperation. Exchange of information and documents. Personnel. Responsibility and liability. Title and deeds. Exchange. Scholarships and grants. Vocational training. Research and development. Expense sharing formulae. Local currency. Domestic obligation. Special projects. Materials, equipment and services. IGO status. Conformity with IGO decisions.
TREATY REF: 33UNTS261.
PARTIES:
WHO (World Health)
Tanganyika

107253 Bilateral Agreement **496 UNTS 205**
SIGNED: 3 Jun 64 FORCE: 3 Jun 64
REGISTERED: 3 Jun 64 United Nations
ARTICLES: 10 LANGUAGE: English.
HEADNOTE: ASSISTANCE
TOPIC: Direct Aid
CONCEPTS: Detailed regulations. Treaty imple-

mentation. Visas. Privileges and immunities. Extraditable offenses. Exchange of information and documents. Informational records. Inspection and observation. Operating agencies. Personnel. Public information. Responsibility and liability. Title and deeds. Use of facilities. Arbitration. Negotiation. Import quotas. Attachment of funds. Exchange rates and regulations. Expense sharing formulae. Financial programs. Domestic obligation. General technical assistance. Economic assistance. Materials, equipment and services. IGO status.
INTL ORGS: International Atomic Energy Agency. International Court of Justice. United Nations.
TREATY REF: 1UNTS15; 33UNTS261; 3741NTS147.
PROCEDURE: Amendment. Termination.
PARTIES:
Ireland
UN Special Fund

107254 Bilateral Exchange **496 UNTS 223**
SIGNED: 28 Nov 63 FORCE: 28 Nov 63
REGISTERED: 3 Jun 64 Denmark
ARTICLES: 2 LANGUAGE: English.
HEADNOTE: GREENLAND AIR TRAFFIC CONTROL
TOPIC: Air Transport
CONCEPTS: Exceptions and exemptions. Annex or appendix reference. Fees and exemptions. Navigational conditions. Air transport. Operating authorizations and regulations.
INTL ORGS: International Civil Aviation Organization.
TREATY REF: 15UNTS295.
PROCEDURE: Termination.
PARTIES:
Canada
Denmark

107255 Bilateral Exchange **496 UNTS 233**
SIGNED: 14 Apr 64 FORCE: 15 May 64
REGISTERED: 4 Jun 64 Australia
ARTICLES: 2 LANGUAGE: English.
HEADNOTE: VISAS VISA FEES
TOPIC: Visas
CONCEPTS: Time limit. Denial of admission. Visas. Conformity with municipal law. Fees and exemptions.
PROCEDURE: Termination.
PARTIES:
Australia
Israel

107256 Bilateral Exchange **496 UNTS 239**
SIGNED: 20 Feb 64 FORCE: 1 Dec 63
REGISTERED: 5 Jun 64 Jamaica
ARTICLES: 2 LANGUAGE: English.
HEADNOTE: STAFFING ADMINISTRATION TRAINING
TOPIC: Military Mission
CONCEPTS: Annex or appendix reference. Military training. Airforce-army-navy personnel ratio.
PARTIES:
Jamaica
UK Great Britain

107257 Bilateral Agreement **496 UNTS 273**
SIGNED: 27 May 54 FORCE: 15 Apr 58
REGISTERED: 8 Jun 64 ICAO (Civil Aviat)
ARTICLES: 16 LANGUAGE: French.
HEADNOTE: COMMERCIAL AIR SERVICES
TOPIC: Air Transport
CONCEPTS: Definition of terms. Detailed regulations. Exceptions and exemptions. Non-prejudice to third party. Conformity with municipal law. Exchange of information and documents. Arbitration. Procedure. Existing tribunals. Non-interest rates and fees. Permit designation. Conditions of airlines operating permission. Overflights and technical stops. Operating authorizations and regulations.
INTL ORGS: International Civil Aviation Organization.
TREATY REF: 15UNTS295.
PROCEDURE: Amendment. Denunciation. Future Procedures Contemplated. Ratification. Registration. Termination.
PARTIES:
Iran
Switzerland

107258 Bilateral Agreement **496 UNTS 301**
SIGNED: 26 May 56 FORCE: 1 Apr 61
REGISTERED: 8 Jun 64 ICAO (Civil Aviat)
ARTICLES: 14 LANGUAGE: French.
HEADNOTE: AIR SERVICES
TOPIC: Air Transport
CONCEPTS: Definition of terms. Detailed regulations. Annex or appendix reference. Conformity with municipal law. General cooperation. Exchange of information and documents. Licenses and permits. Recognition of legal documents. Use of facilities. Arbitration. Procedure. Special tribunals. Reexport of goods, etc.. Fees and exemptions. Non-interest rates and fees. National treatment. Customs exemptions. Competency certificate. Routes and logistics. Navigational conditions. Permit designation. Air transport. Airport facilities. Airworthiness certificates. Conditions of airlines operating permission. Operating authorizations and regulations. Licenses and certificates of nationality.
INTL ORGS: International Civil Aviation Organization. Arbitration Commission.
TREATY REF: 15UNTS295.
PROCEDURE: Future Procedures Contemplated. Ratification. Registration. Termination.
PARTIES:
Greece
Italy

107259 Bilateral Agreement **497 UNTS 3**
SIGNED: 20 Dec 56 FORCE: 20 Dec 56
REGISTERED: 8 Jun 64 ICAO (Civil Aviat)
ARTICLES: 4 LANGUAGE: Spanish.
HEADNOTE: REGIONAL OFFICE
TOPIC: IGO Operations
CONCEPTS: Treaty implementation. Annex or appendix reference. Non-visa travel documents. Diplomatic privileges. Diplomatic missions. Privileges and immunities. Diplomatic correspondence. Juridical personality. Arbitration. Domestic obligation. Special status. Status of experts.
INTL ORGS: International Court of Justice. United Nations.
PROCEDURE: Amendment. Duration. Termination.
PARTIES:
Mexico
ICAO (Civil Aviat)

107260 Bilateral Exchange **497 UNTS 29**
SIGNED: 30 Dec 57 FORCE: 26 Nov 57
REGISTERED: 8 Jun 64 ICAO (Civil Aviat)
ARTICLES: 2 LANGUAGE: English.
HEADNOTE: AIR TRANSPORT
TOPIC: Air Transport
CONCEPTS: Detailed regulations. Conformity with municipal law. General cooperation. Exchange of information and documents. Procedure. Special tribunals. Negotiation. Fees and exemptions. Non-interest rates and fees. Customs exemptions. Routes and logistics. Permit designation. Air transport. Conditions of airlines operating permission. Overflights and technical stops. Operating authorizations and regulations.
INTL ORGS: International Civil Aviation Organization. Arbitration Commission.
TREATY REF: 15UNTS295.
PROCEDURE: Amendment. Future Procedures Contemplated. Registration. Termination.
PARTIES:
Australia
Ireland

107261 Bilateral Agreement **497 UNTS 43**
SIGNED: 19 Mar 59 FORCE: 19 Mar 59
REGISTERED: 8 Jun 64 ICAO (Civil Aviat)
ARTICLES: 13 LANGUAGE: French.
HEADNOTE: AIR TRANSPORT
TOPIC: Air Transport
CONCEPTS: Detailed regulations. Annex or appendix reference. Conformity with municipal law. Licenses and permits. Recognition of legal documents. Use of facilities. Arbitration. Procedure. Negotiation. Reexport of goods, etc.. Fees and exemptions. Non-interest rates and fees. Most favored nation clause. National treatment. Customs duties. Customs exemptions. Competency certificate. Routes and logistics. Navigational conditions. Permit designation. Air transport. Airport facilities. Airworthiness certificates. Conditions of airlines operating permission. Overf-

lights and technical stops. Operating authorizations and regulations. Licenses and certificates of nationality.
INTL ORGS: International Civil Aviation Organization. Arbitration Commission.
TREATY REF: 15UNTS295.
PROCEDURE: Future Procedures Contemplated. Termination.
PARTIES:
Sweden
Tunisia

107262   Bilateral Agreement   **497 UNTS 61**
SIGNED: 19 Mar 59   FORCE: 19 Mar 59
REGISTERED: 8 Jun 64 ICAO (Civil Aviat)
ARTICLES: 12 LANGUAGE: French.
HEADNOTE: AIR TRANSPORT
TOPIC: Air Transport
CONCEPTS: Detailed regulations. Territorial application. Annex or appendix reference. Conformity with municipal law. General cooperation. Use of facilities. Procedure. Negotiation. Reexport of goods, etc.. Fees and exemptions. Non-interest rates and fees. Most favored nation clause. National treatment. Customs duties. Customs exemptions. Routes and logistics. Navigational conditions. Permit designation. Air transport. Airport facilities. Conditions of airlines operating permission. Overflights and technical stops. Operating authorizations and regulations.
INTL ORGS: International Civil Aviation Organization.
TREATY REF: 15UNTS295.
PROCEDURE: Amendment. Ratification. Registration. Termination.
PARTIES:
Netherlands
Tunisia

107263   Bilateral Agreement   **497 UNTS 77**
SIGNED: 28 Mar 59   FORCE: 28 Mar 59
REGISTERED: 8 Jun 64 ICAO (Civil Aviat)
ARTICLES: 13 LANGUAGE: French.
HEADNOTE: AIR TRANSPORT
TOPIC: Air Transport
CONCEPTS: Detailed regulations. Annex or appendix reference. Conformity with municipal law. Licenses and permits. Recognition of legal documents. Use of facilities. Arbitration. Procedure. Negotiation. Reexport of goods, etc.. Fees and exemptions. Non-interest rates and fees. Most favored nation clause. National treatment. Customs duties. Customs exemptions. Competency certificate. Routes and logistics. Navigational conditions. Permit designation. Air transport. Airport facilities. Airworthiness certificates. Conditions of airlines operating permission. Overflights and technical stops. Operating authorizations and regulations. Licenses and certificates of nationality.
INTL ORGS: International Civil Aviation Organization. Arbitration Commission.
TREATY REF: 15UNTS295.
PROCEDURE: Future Procedures Contemplated. Termination.
PARTIES:
Norway
Tunisia

107264   Bilateral Agreement   **497 UNTS 95**
SIGNED: 10 Mar 60   FORCE: 10 Mar 60
REGISTERED: 8 Jun 64 ICAO (Civil Aviat)
ARTICLES: 13 LANGUAGE: Swedish.
HEADNOTE: AIR TRANSPORT
TOPIC: Air Transport
CONCEPTS: Annex or appendix reference. Conformity with municipal law. General cooperation. Licenses and permits. Recognition of legal documents. Use of facilities. Arbitration. Procedure. Special tribunals. Negotiation. Expense sharing formulae. Fees and exemptions. Most favored nation clause. National treatment. General. Customs duties. Customs exemptions. Competency certificate. Navigational conditions. Permit designation. Air transport. Airport facilities. Airworthiness certificates. Conditions of airlines operating permission. Operating authorizations and regulations. Licenses and certificates of nationality.
INTL ORGS: International Civil Aviation Organization. Arbitration Commission.

PROCEDURE: Amendment. Future Procedures Contemplated. Registration. Termination.
PARTIES:
Finland
Iceland

107265   Bilateral Agreement   **497 UNTS 109**
SIGNED: 21 May 60   FORCE: 21 May 60
REGISTERED: 8 Jun 64 ICAO (Civil Aviat)
ARTICLES: 15 LANGUAGE: French.
HEADNOTE: AIR TRANSPORT
TOPIC: Air Transport
CONCEPTS: Detailed regulations. Annex or appendix reference. Conformity with municipal law. General cooperation. Exchange of information and documents. Licenses and permits. Recognition of legal documents. Use of facilities. Arbitration. Procedure. Negotiation. Monetary and gold transfers. Fees and exemptions. Non-interest rates and fees. Most favored nation clause. National treatment. Customs duties. Customs exemptions. Competency certificate. Routes and logistics. Navigational conditions. Permit designation. Air transport. Airport facilities. Conditions of airlines operating permission. Overflights and technical stops. Operating authorizations and regulations. Licenses and certificates of nationality.
INTL ORGS: International Civil Aviation Organization. Arbitration Commission.
TREATY REF: 15UNTS295.
PROCEDURE: Future Procedures Contemplated. Ratification. Registration. Termination.
PARTIES:
Switzerland
Tunisia

107266   Bilateral Agreement   **497 UNTS 129**
SIGNED: 28 May 60   FORCE: 28 May 60
REGISTERED: 8 Jun 64 ICAO (Civil Aviat)
ARTICLES: 14 LANGUAGE: English.
HEADNOTE: AIR TRANSPORT
TOPIC: Air Transport
CONCEPTS: Definition of terms. Annex or appendix reference. Conformity with municipal law. General cooperation. Licenses and permits. Personnel. Recognition of legal documents. Use of facilities. Procedure. Negotiation. Reexport of goods, etc.. Fees and exemptions. Non-interest rates and fees. Most favored nation clause. National treatment. Tax exemptions. Customs duties. Customs exemptions. Competency certificate. Routes and logistics. Navigational conditions. Permit designation. Air transport. Airport facilities. Airworthiness certificates. Conditions of airlines operating permission. Operating authorizations and regulations. Licenses and certificates of nationality.
PROCEDURE: Amendment. Ratification. Termination.
PARTIES:
Afghanistan
Czechoslovakia

107267   Bilateral Agreement   **497 UNTS 143**
SIGNED: 13 Jun 60   FORCE: 13 Jun 60
REGISTERED: 8 Jun 64 ICAO (Civil Aviat)
ARTICLES: 12 LANGUAGE: French.
HEADNOTE: AIR TRANSPORT
TOPIC: Air Transport
CONCEPTS: Definition of terms. Annex or appendix reference. Conformity with municipal law. General cooperation. Licenses and permits. Recognition of legal documents. Use of facilities. Procedure. Negotiation. Fees and exemptions. Non-interest rates and fees. National treatment. Customs exemptions. Competency certificate. Routes and logistics. Navigational conditions. Permit designation. Air transport. Airport facilities. Airworthiness certificates. Conditions of airlines operating permission. Overflights and technical stops. Operating authorizations and regulations. Licenses and certificates of nationality.
INTL ORGS: International Civil Aviation Organization.
TREATY REF: 15UNTS295.
PROCEDURE: Amendment. Future Procedures Contemplated. Ratification. Registration. Termination.

PARTIES:
Luxembourg
Tunisia

107268   Bilateral Agreement   **497 UNTS 161**
SIGNED: 14 Jul 60   FORCE: 30 Apr 62
REGISTERED: 8 Jun 64 ICAO (Civil Aviat)
ARTICLES: 19 LANGUAGE: French. Arabic.
HEADNOTE: SCHEDULED AIR TRANSPORT
TOPIC: Air Transport
CONCEPTS: Detailed regulations. Exceptions and exemptions. Annex or appendix reference. Alien registration. General cooperation. Exchange of information and documents. Arbitration. Procedure. Existing tribunals. Negotiation. Indemnities and reimbursements. Non-interest rates and fees. Customs exemptions. Routes and logistics. Navigational conditions. Permit designation. Air transport. Conditions of airlines operating permission. Operating authorizations and regulations.
INTL ORGS: International Civil Aviation Organization. Arbitration Commission.
TREATY REF: 15UNTS295.
PROCEDURE: Denunciation. Future Procedures Contemplated. Ratification. Registration.
PARTIES:
Switzerland
United Arab Rep

107269   Bilateral Agreement   **497 UNTS 189**
SIGNED: 21 Jul 60   FORCE: 21 Jul 60
REGISTERED: 8 Jun 64 ICAO (Civil Aviat)
ARTICLES: 15 LANGUAGE: French.
HEADNOTE: AIR TRANSPORT
TOPIC: Air Transport
CONCEPTS: Airport facilities. Airworthiness certificates. Conditions of airlines operating permission. Overflights and technical stops. Operating authorizations and regulations. Licenses and certificates of nationality.
PROCEDURE: Denunciation. Termination.
PARTIES:
Netherlands
Poland

107270   Bilateral Agreement   **497 UNTS 207**
SIGNED: 2 Nov 60   FORCE: 2 Nov 60
REGISTERED: 8 Jun 64 ICAO (Civil Aviat)
ARTICLES: 12 LANGUAGE: Spanish. Norwegian.
HEADNOTE: AIR TRANSPORT
TOPIC: Air Transport
CONCEPTS: Definition of terms. Exceptions and exemptions. Treaty interpretation. Annex or appendix reference. Conformity with municipal law. General cooperation. Licenses and permits. Recognition of legal documents. Use of facilities. Arbitration. Procedure. Existing tribunals. Negotiation. Reexport of goods, etc.. Fees and exemptions. Most favored nation clause. National treatment. Customs duties. Customs exemptions. Competency certificate. Routes and logistics. Navigational conditions. Permit designation. Air transport. Airport facilities. Airworthiness certificates. Conditions of airlines operating permission. Operating authorizations and regulations. Licenses and certificates of nationality.
INTL ORGS: International Civil Aviation Organization. Arbitration Commission.
TREATY REF: 15UNTS295.
PROCEDURE: Ratification. Registration. Termination.
PARTIES:
Norway
Peru

107271   Bilateral Agreement   **497 UNTS 247**
SIGNED: 10 Nov 60   FORCE: 10 May 63
REGISTERED: 8 Jun 64 ICAO (Civil Aviat)
ARTICLES: 15 LANGUAGE: English. Italian.
HEADNOTE: AIR SERVICES
TOPIC: Air Transport
CONCEPTS: Definition of terms. Detailed regulations. Annex or appendix reference. Conformity with municipal law. General cooperation. Exchange of information and documents. Arbitration. Procedure. Special tribunals. Negotiation. Fees and exemptions. Non-interest rates and fees. Customs exemptions. Routes and logistics. Permit designation. Air transport. Conditions of

airlines operating permission. Overflights and technical stops. Operating authorizations and regulations.
INTL ORGS: International Civil Aviation Organization. Arbitration Commission.
TREATY REF: 15UNTS295.
PROCEDURE: Amendment. Future Procedures Contemplated. Ratification. Registration. Termination.
PARTIES:
Australia
Italy

107272 Bilateral Agreement **497 UNTS 275**
SIGNED: 8 Jun 61   FORCE: 19 Oct 62
REGISTERED: 8 Jun 64 ICAO (Civil Aviat)
ARTICLES: 21 LANGUAGE: French.
HEADNOTE: AIR TRANSPORT
TOPIC: Air Transport
CONCEPTS: Definition of terms. Detailed regulations. Annex or appendix reference. Conformity with municipal law. General cooperation. Licenses and permits. Personnel. Recognition of legal documents. Use of facilities. Arbitration. Procedure. Special tribunals. Reexport of goods, etc.. Expense sharing formulae. Fees and exemptions. Non-interest rates and fees. Equitable taxes. Customs exemptions. Competency certificate. Routes and logistics. Navigational conditions. Permit designation. Air transport. Airport facilities. Airworthiness certificates. Conditions of airlines operating permission. Operating authorizations and regulations. Licenses and certificates of nationality.
INTL ORGS: International Civil Aviation Organization. Arbitration Commission.
TREATY REF: 15UNTS295.
PROCEDURE: Amendment. Future Procedures Contemplated. Ratification. Registration. Termination.
PARTIES:
Czechoslovakia
Morocco

107273 Bilateral Agreement **497 UNTS 293**
SIGNED: 13 Jun 61   FORCE: 13 Jun 61
REGISTERED: 8 Jun 64 ICAO (Civil Aviat)
ARTICLES: 17 LANGUAGE: English.
HEADNOTE: AIR SERVICES
TOPIC: Air Transport
CONCEPTS: Conditions. Definition of terms. Detailed regulations. Exceptions and exemptions. Annex or appendix reference. General cooperation. Exchange of information and documents. Arbitration. Procedure. Special tribunals. Negotiation. Reexport of goods, etc.. Monetary and gold transfers. Fees and exemptions. Non-interest rates and fees. Customs exemptions. Routes and logistics. Permit designation. Conditions of airlines operating permission. Overflights and technical stops. Operating authorizations and regulations.
INTL ORGS: International Civil Aviation Organization. Arbitration Commission.
TREATY REF: 15UNTS295.
PROCEDURE: Amendment. Future Procedures Contemplated. Termination. Application to Non-self-governing Territories.
PARTIES:
New Zealand
UK Great Britain

107274 Bilateral Agreement **497 UNTS 311**
SIGNED: 23 Nov 61   FORCE: 20 Jul 63
REGISTERED: 8 Jun 64 ICAO (Civil Aviat)
ARTICLES: 19 LANGUAGE: Greek.
HEADNOTE: COMMERCIAL SCHEDULED AIR TRANSPORT
TOPIC: Air Transport
CONCEPTS: Definition of terms. Detailed regulations. Exceptions and exemptions. Annex or appendix reference. Previous treaty replacement. General cooperation. Exchange of information and documents. Use of facilities. Arbitration. Procedure. Special tribunals. Negotiation. Reexport of goods, etc.. Expense sharing formulae. Fees and exemptions. Non-interest rates and fees. Tax exemptions. Customs exemptions. Routes and logistics. Permit designation. Air transport. Airport facilities. Conditions of airlines operating

permission. Overflights and technical stops. Operating authorizations and regulations.
INTL ORGS: International Civil Aviation Organization. Arbitration Commission.
TREATY REF: 15UNTS295.
PROCEDURE: Amendment. Future Procedures Contemplated. Ratification. Registration. Termination.
PARTIES:
Cyprus
Greece

107275 Bilateral Agreement **498 UNTS 3**
SIGNED: 15 Jan 62   FORCE: 15 Jan 62
REGISTERED: 8 Jun 64 ICAO (Civil Aviat)
ARTICLES: 18 LANGUAGE: English.
HEADNOTE: COMMERCIAL SCHEDULED AIR TRANSPORT
TOPIC: Air Transport
CONCEPTS: Definition of terms. Detailed regulations. Exceptions and exemptions. Annex or appendix reference. General cooperation. Exchange of information and documents. Use of facilities. Arbitration. Procedure. Special tribunals. Negotiation. Reexport of goods, etc.. Expense sharing formulae. Fees and exemptions. Non-interest rates and fees. National treatment. Tax exemptions. Customs exemptions. Routes and logistics. Permit designation. Air transport. Airport facilities. Conditions of airlines operating permission. Overflights and technical stops. Operating authorizations and regulations.
INTL ORGS: International Civil Aviation Organization. Arbitration Commission.
TREATY REF: 15UNTS295.
PROCEDURE: Amendment. Future Procedures Contemplated. Ratification. Registration. Termination.
PARTIES:
Austria
Greece

107276 Bilateral Agreement **498 UNTS 23**
SIGNED: 31 Jan 62   FORCE: 26 Jul 63
REGISTERED: 8 Jun 64 ICAO (Civil Aviat)
ARTICLES: 18 LANGUAGE: English.
HEADNOTE: AIR SERVICES
TOPIC: Air Transport
CONCEPTS: Definition of terms. Detailed regulations. Exceptions and exemptions. Annex or appendix reference. Conformity with municipal law. General cooperation. Exchange of information and documents. Arbitration. Procedure. Special tribunals. Negotiation. Reexport of goods, etc.. Fees and exemptions. Non-interest rates and fees. Customs exemptions. Routes and logistics. Permit designation. Conditions of airlines operating permission. Overflights and technical stops. Operating authorizations and regulations.
INTL ORGS: International Civil Aviation Organization. Arbitration Commission.
TREATY REF: 15UNTS295.
PROCEDURE: Amendment. Future Procedures Contemplated. Ratification. Registration. Termination. Application to Non-self-governing Territories.
PARTIES:
Italy
Japan

107277 Bilateral Agreement **498 UNTS 41**
SIGNED: 6 Apr 62   FORCE: 6 Apr 62
REGISTERED: 8 Jun 64 ICAO (Civil Aviat)
ARTICLES: 17 LANGUAGE: English. Russian.
HEADNOTE: AIR TRANSPORT
TOPIC: Air Transport
CONCEPTS: Representation. Annex or appendix reference. Conformity with municipal law. General cooperation. Exchange of information and documents. Recognition of legal documents. Use of facilities. Procedure. Negotiation. Humanitarian matters. Accounting procedures. Fees and exemptions. Non-interest rates and fees. Tax exemptions. Customs exemptions. Registration certificate. Routes and logistics. Navigational conditions. Permit designation. Air transport. Airworthiness certificates. Conditions of airlines operating permission. Operating authorizations and regulations.
PROCEDURE: Denunciation.

PARTIES:
Ghana
USSR (Soviet Union)

107278 Bilateral Agreement **498 UNTS 69**
SIGNED: 10 May 62   FORCE: 6 Jun 63
REGISTERED: 8 Jun 64 ICAO (Civil Aviat)
ARTICLES: 18 LANGUAGE: Japanese. Arabic. English.
HEADNOTE: AIR SERVICES
TOPIC: Air Transport
CONCEPTS: Definition of terms. Detailed regulations. Exceptions and exemptions. Treaty interpretation. Annex or appendix reference. Conformity with municipal law. General cooperation. Exchange of information and documents. Arbitration. Procedure. Special tribunals. Negotiation. Fees and exemptions. Non-interest rates and fees. Customs exemptions. Routes and logistics. Permit designation. Conditions of airlines operating permission. Overflights and technical stops. Operating authorizations and regulations.
INTL ORGS: International Civil Aviation Organization. International Court of Justice. Arbitration Commission.
TREATY REF: 15UNTS295.
PROCEDURE: Amendment. Future Procedures Contemplated. Ratification. Registration. Termination.
PARTIES:
Japan
United Arab Rep

107279 Bilateral Agreement **498 UNTS 115**
SIGNED: 18 May 62   FORCE: 18 May 62
REGISTERED: 8 Jun 64 ICAO (Civil Aviat)
ARTICLES: 17 LANGUAGE: French. Romanian.
HEADNOTE: AIR TRANSPORT
TOPIC: Air Transport
CONCEPTS: Definition of terms. Detailed regulations. Representation. Annex or appendix reference. Conformity with municipal law. General cooperation. Exchange of information and documents. Licenses and permits. Personnel. Recognition of legal documents. Use of facilities. Procedure. Humanitarian matters. Reexport of goods, etc.. Fees and exemptions. Payment schedules. Non-interest rates and fees. Customs exemptions. Registration certificate. Routes and logistics. Navigational conditions. Permit designation. Air transport. Airport facilities. Airworthiness certificates. Conditions of airlines operating permission. Operating authorizations and regulations. Licenses and certificates of nationality.
PROCEDURE: Amendment. Denunciation. Ratification.
PARTIES:
France
Romania

107280 Bilateral Agreement **498 UNTS 145**
SIGNED: 20 Jun 62   FORCE: 20 Jun 62
REGISTERED: 8 Jun 64 ICAO (Civil Aviat)
ARTICLES: 21 LANGUAGE: French. Czechoslovakian.
HEADNOTE: AIR TRANSPORT
TOPIC: Air Transport
CONCEPTS: Definition of terms. Detailed regulations. Annex or appendix reference. Conformity with municipal law. General cooperation. Exchange of information and documents. Personnel. Arbitration. Procedure. Special tribunals. Negotiation. Reexport of goods, etc.. Monetary and gold transfers. Fees and exemptions. Non-interest rates and fees. Customs exemptions. Routes and logistics. Navigational conditions. Permit designation. Air transport. Conditions of airlines operating permission. Operating authorizations and regulations.
INTL ORGS: International Civil Aviation Organization. Arbitration Commission.
TREATY REF: 15UNTS295.
PROCEDURE: Amendment. Denunciation. Ratification. Registration.
PARTIES:
Czechoslovakia
Senegal

107281 Bilateral Agreement **498 UNTS 171**
SIGNED: 5 Jul 62   FORCE: 19 Mar 64
REGISTERED: 8 Jun 64 ICAO (Civil Aviat)
ARTICLES: 16 LANGUAGE: French.
HEADNOTE: AIR SERVICES
TOPIC: Air Transport
CONCEPTS: Definition of terms. Detailed regulations. Annex or appendix reference. Conformity with municipal law. General cooperation. Exchange of information and documents. Licenses and permits. Recognition of legal documents. Use of facilities. Arbitration. Procedure. Special tribunals. Reexport of goods, etc.. Expense sharing formulae. Fees and exemptions. Non-interest rates and fees. Most favored nation clause. National treatment. Equitable taxes. Tax exemptions. Customs exemptions. Competency certificate. Routes and logistics. Navigational conditions. Permit designation. Air transport. Airport facilities. Airworthiness certificates. Conditions of airlines operating permission. Overflights and technical stops. Operating authorizations and regulations. Licenses and certificates of nationality.
INTL ORGS: International Civil Aviation Organization. Arbitration Commission.
TREATY REF: 15UNTS295.
PROCEDURE: Amendment. Denunciation. Future Procedures Contemplated. Ratification. Registration.
PARTIES:
  Morocco
  Switzerland

              ANNEX
602 UNTS 350.   Switzerland.   Modification
10 Jun 65.
602 UNTS 350.   Morocco.   Modification
10 Jun 65.

107282 Bilateral Agreement **498 UNTS 189**
SIGNED: 5 Jul 62   FORCE: 19 Mar 64
REGISTERED: 8 Jun 64 ICAO (Civil Aviat)
ARTICLES: 7 LANGUAGE: French.
HEADNOTE: NON-SCHEDULED AIR SERVICES
TOPIC: Air Transport
CONCEPTS: Detailed regulations. Exchange of information and documents. Arbitration. Procedure. Special tribunals. Humanitarian matters. Expense sharing formulae. Passenger transport. Transport of goods. Conditions of airlines operating permission. Operating authorizations and regulations.
INTL ORGS: International Civil Aviation Organization. Arbitration Commission.
TREATY REF: 15UNTS295.
PROCEDURE: Denunciation. Ratification.
PARTIES:
  Morocco
  Switzerland

107283 Bilateral Agreement **498 UNTS 199**
SIGNED: 20 Sep 62   FORCE: 21 Dec 63
REGISTERED: 8 Jun 64 ICAO (Civil Aviat)
ARTICLES: 16 LANGUAGE: Spanish. German.
HEADNOTE: AIR SERVICES
TOPIC: Air Transport
CONCEPTS: Definition of terms. Detailed regulations. Conformity with municipal law. General cooperation. Exchange of information and documents. Personnel. Use of facilities. Arbitration. Procedure. Special tribunals. Reexport of goods, etc.. Expense sharing formulae. Fees and exemptions. Non-interest rates and fees. National treatment. Tax exemptions. Customs exemptions. Routes and logistics. Permit designation. Airport facilities. Conditions of airlines operating permission. Overflights and technical stops. Operating authorizations and regulations.
INTL ORGS: International Civil Aviation Organization. Arbitration Commission.
TREATY REF: 15UNTS295.
PROCEDURE: Amendment. Denunciation. Future Procedures Contemplated. Ratification. Registration.
PARTIES:
  Ecuador
  Germany, West

107284 Bilateral Agreement **498 UNTS 235**
SIGNED: 6 Oct 62   FORCE: 20 Jun 63
REGISTERED: 8 Jun 64 ICAO (Civil Aviat)

ARTICLES: 16 LANGUAGE: English. Arabic. Japanese.
HEADNOTE: AIR SERVICES
TOPIC: Air Transport
CONCEPTS: Conditions. Definition of terms. Detailed regulations. Exceptions and exemptions. Treaty interpretation. Annex or appendix reference. Conformity with municipal law. General cooperation. Exchange of information and documents. Use of facilities. Arbitration. Procedure. Special tribunals. Negotiation. Fees and exemptions. Non-interest rates and fees. Most favored nation clause. National treatment. Customs exemptions. Routes and logistics. Permit designation. Airport facilities. Conditions of airlines operating permission. Overflights and technical stops. Operating authorizations and regulations.
INTL ORGS: International Civil Aviation Organization. International Court of Justice. Arbitration Commission.
TREATY REF: 15UNTS295.
PROCEDURE: Amendment. Future Procedures Contemplated. Ratification. Registration. Termination. Application to Non-self-governing Territories.
PARTIES:
  Japan
  Kuwait

107285 Bilateral Agreement **498 UNTS 299**
SIGNED: 12 Oct 62   FORCE: 8 Jul 63
REGISTERED: 8 Jun 64 ICAO (Civil Aviat)
ARTICLES: 18 LANGUAGE: French.
HEADNOTE: AIR TRANSPORT
TOPIC: Air Transport
CONCEPTS: Definition of terms. Detailed regulations. Exceptions and exemptions. Annex or appendix reference. Conformity with municipal law. General cooperation. Licenses and permits. Recognition of legal documents. Arbitration. Procedure. Special tribunals. Reexport of goods, etc.. Expense sharing formulae. Fees and exemptions. Non-interest rates and fees. Customs exemptions. Competency certificate. Routes and logistics. Navigational conditions. Permit designation. Air transport. Airport facilities. Airworthiness certificates. Conditions of airlines operating permission. Overflights and technical stops. Operating authorizations and regulations. Licenses and certificates of nationality.
INTL ORGS: International Civil Aviation Organization. Arbitration Commission.
TREATY REF: 15UNTS295.
PROCEDURE: Amendment. Denunciation. Ratification. Registration.
PARTIES:
  Finland
  France

107286 Bilateral Agreement **498 UNTS 317**
SIGNED: 19 Oct 62   FORCE: 19 Oct 62
REGISTERED: 8 Jun 64 ICAO (Civil Aviat)
ARTICLES: 20 LANGUAGE: French.
HEADNOTE: AIR TRANSPORT
TOPIC: Air Transport
CONCEPTS: Definition of terms. Detailed regulations. Annex or appendix reference. Conformity with municipal law. General cooperation. Exchange of information and documents. Licenses and permits. Recognition of legal documents. Arbitration. Procedure. Special tribunals. Reexport of goods, etc.. Expense sharing formulae. Fees and exemptions. Non-interest rates and fees. Customs exemptions. Competency certificate. Routes and logistics. Navigational conditions. Permit designation. Air transport. Airworthiness certificates. Conditions of airlines operating permission. Operating authorizations and regulations. Licenses and certificates of nationality.
INTL ORGS: International Civil Aviation Organization. Arbitration Commission.
TREATY REF: 15UNTS295.
PROCEDURE: Amendment. Denunciation. Registration.
PARTIES:
  France
  Ivory Coast

107287 Bilateral Exchange **498 UNTS 335**
SIGNED: 25 Oct 62   FORCE: 25 Oct 62
REGISTERED: 8 Jun 64 ICAO (Civil Aviat)

ARTICLES: 2 LANGUAGE: French.
HEADNOTE: EXEMPTION TAXES PROFITS INCOME PROPERTY AIR TRANSPORT
TOPIC: Taxation
CONCEPTS: Definition of terms. Conformity with municipal law. Tax exemptions. Navigational conditions. Air transport.
PROCEDURE: Termination.
PARTIES:
  Czechoslovakia
  Norway

107288 Bilateral Exchange **498 UNTS 343**
SIGNED: 25 Oct 62   FORCE: 25 Oct 62
REGISTERED: 8 Jun 64 ICAO (Civil Aviat)
ARTICLES: 2 LANGUAGE: French.
HEADNOTE: EXEMPTION TAXES PROFITS INCOME PROPERTY AIR TRANSPORT
TOPIC: Air Transport
CONCEPTS: Definition of terms. Conformity with municipal law. Tax exemptions. Navigational conditions. Air transport.
PROCEDURE: Termination.
PARTIES:
  Czechoslovakia
  Sweden

107289 Bilateral Agreement **499 UNTS 3**
SIGNED: 17 Nov 62   FORCE: 21 Dec 63
REGISTERED: 8 Jun 64 ICAO (Civil Aviat)
ARTICLES: 20 LANGUAGE: French.
HEADNOTE: AIR TRANSPORT
TOPIC: Air Transport
CONCEPTS: Definition of terms. Detailed regulations. Annex or appendix reference. Conformity with municipal law. General cooperation. Exchange of information and documents. Licenses and permits. Recognition of legal documents. Arbitration. Procedure. Special tribunals. Reexport of goods, etc.. Expense sharing formulae. Fees and exemptions. Non-interest rates and fees. National treatment. Customs exemptions. Competency certificate. Routes and logistics. Navigational conditions. Permit designation. Air transport. Airworthiness certificates. Overflights and technical stops. Operating authorizations and regulations. Licenses and certificates of nationality.
INTL ORGS: International Civil Aviation Organization. International Court of Justice. Arbitration Commission.
TREATY REF: 15UNTS295.
PROCEDURE: Amendment. Denunciation. Ratification. Registration.
PARTIES:
  Ivory Coast
  Switzerland

107290 Bilateral Agreement **499 UNTS 21**
SIGNED: 24 Jan 63   FORCE: 1 Jan 62
REGISTERED: 8 Jun 64 ICAO (Civil Aviat)
ARTICLES: 9 LANGUAGE: English.
HEADNOTE: CIVIL AVIATION
TOPIC: Air Transport
CONCEPTS: Definition of terms. Annex or appendix reference. Conformity with municipal law. General cooperation. Personnel. General property. Vocational training. Indemnities and reimbursements. Financial programs. Customs exemptions. Domestic obligation. Assistance. Materials, equipment and services. Navigational conditions. Navigational equipment. Air transport. Airport facilities. Facilities and equipment.
TREATY REF: 15UNTS295.
PROCEDURE: Duration. Renewal or Revival. Termination.
PARTIES:
  New Zealand
  Western Samoa
              ANNEX
646 UNTS 407. New Zealand. Prolongation
30 Dec 66. Force 30 Dec 66.
646 UNTS 407. Western Samoa. Prolongation
30 Dec 66. Force 30 Dec 66.

107291 Bilateral Agreement **499 UNTS 35**
SIGNED: 1 Feb 63   FORCE: 18 Jan 64
REGISTERED: 8 Jun 64 ICAO (Civil Aviat)
ARTICLES: 16 LANGUAGE: French.
HEADNOTE: AIR SERVICES

TOPIC: Air Transport

CONCEPTS: Detailed regulations. Conformity with municipal law. General cooperation. Exchange of information and documents. Arbitration. Procedure. Special tribunals. Exchange rates and regulations. Expense sharing formulae. Non-interest rates and fees. National treatment. Customs exemptions. Navigational conditions. Permit designation. Air transport. Conditions of airlines operating permission. Overflights and technical stops. Operating authorizations and regulations.

INTL ORGS: International Civil Aviation Organization. Arbitration Commission.

PROCEDURE: Future Procedures Contemplated. Ratification. Registration. Termination.

PARTIES:
Guinea
Switzerland

107292   Bilateral Agreement   **499 UNTS 49**
SIGNED: 7 May 63   FORCE: 7 May 63
REGISTERED: 8 Jun 64 ICAO (Civil Aviat)
ARTICLES: 9 LANGUAGE: English. Portuguese.
HEADNOTE: AIR SERVICES
TOPIC: Air Transport

CONCEPTS: Definition of terms. Annex or appendix reference. Previous treaty replacement. Conformity with municipal law. General cooperation. Non-interest rates and fees. Routes and logistics. Permit designation. Conditions of airlines operating permission. Operating authorizations and regulations.

INTL ORGS: International Civil Aviation Organization.

TREATY REF: 189LTS121.

PROCEDURE: Amendment. Termination. Application to Non-self-governing Territories.

PARTIES:
Portugal
South Africa

107293   Bilateral Agreement   **499 UNTS 71**
SIGNED: 26 Jun 63   FORCE: 26 Jun 63
REGISTERED: 8 Jun 64 ICAO (Civil Aviat)
ARTICLES: 20 LANGUAGE: French.
HEADNOTE: AIR TRANSPORT
TOPIC: Air Transport

CONCEPTS: Definition of terms. Detailed regulations. Annex or appendix reference. Conformity with municipal law. General cooperation. Exchange of information and documents. Licenses and permits. Recognition of legal documents. Arbitration. Procedure. Special tribunals. Reexport of goods, etc.. Expense sharing formulae. Fees and exemptions. Non-interest rates and fees. Customs exemptions. Competency certificate. Routes and logistics. Navigational conditions. Permit designation. Air transport. Airworthiness certificates. Conditions of airlines operating permission. Operating authorizations and regulations. Licenses and certificates of nationality.

INTL ORGS: International Civil Aviation Organization. Arbitration Commission.

TREATY REF: 15UNTS295.

PROCEDURE: Amendment. Denunciation. Ratification. Registration.

PARTIES:
Guinea
Ivory Coast

107294   Bilateral Agreement   **499 UNTS 91**
SIGNED: 12 Jul 63   FORCE: 26 Jul 63
REGISTERED: 8 Jun 64 ICAO (Civil Aviat)
ARTICLES: 16 LANGUAGE: French. German.
HEADNOTE: AIR TRANSPORT
TOPIC: Air Transport

CONCEPTS: Definition of terms. Detailed regulations. General cooperation. Exchange of information and documents. Arbitration. Procedure. Special tribunals. Reexport of goods, etc.. Expense sharing formulae. Fees and exemptions. Non-interest rates and fees. Customs exemptions. Routes and logistics. Permit designation. Air transport. Conditions of airlines operating permission. Overflights and technical stops. Operating authorizations and regulations.

INTL ORGS: International Civil Aviation Organization. Arbitration Commission.

TREATY REF: 15UNTS295.

PROCEDURE: Amendment. Denunciation. Future Procedures Contemplated. Registration.

PARTIES:
Austria
France

107295   Bilateral Agreement   **499 UNTS 121**
SIGNED: 9 Aug 63   FORCE: 9 Aug 63
REGISTERED: 8 Jun 64 ICAO (Civil Aviat)
ARTICLES: 20 LANGUAGE: French.
HEADNOTE: AIR TRANSPORT
TOPIC: Air Transport

CONCEPTS: Definition of terms. Detailed regulations. Annex or appendix reference. Conformity with municipal law. General cooperation. Exchange of information and documents. Licenses and permits. Recognition of legal documents. Arbitration. Procedure. Special tribunals. Negotiation. Reexport of goods, etc.. Expense sharing formulae. Fees and exemptions. Non-interest rates and fees. Customs exemptions. Competency certificate. Routes and logistics. Navigational conditions. Permit designation. Air transport. Airworthiness certificates. Conditions of airlines operating permission. Operating authorizations and regulations. Licenses and certificates of nationality.

INTL ORGS: International Civil Aviation Organization. Arbitration Commission.

TREATY REF: 15UNTS295.

PROCEDURE: Amendment. Ratification. Registration. Termination.

PARTIES:
Cameroon
Israel

107296   Bilateral Agreement   **499 UNTS 141**
SIGNED: 9 Oct 63   FORCE: 9 Oct 63
REGISTERED: 8 Jun 64 ICAO (Civil Aviat)
ARTICLES: 20 LANGUAGE: French.
HEADNOTE: AIR TRANSPORT
TOPIC: Air Transport

CONCEPTS: Definition of terms. Detailed regulations. Annex or appendix reference. Conformity with municipal law. General cooperation. Exchange of information and documents. Licenses and permits. Recognition of legal documents. Arbitration. Procedure. Special tribunals. Reexport of goods, etc.. Expense sharing formulae. Fees and exemptions. Non-interest rates and fees. Customs exemptions. Competency certificate. Routes and logistics. Navigational conditions. Permit designation. Air transport. Airworthiness certificates. Conditions of airlines operating permission. Operating authorizations and regulations. Licenses and certificates of nationality.

INTL ORGS: International Civil Aviation Organization. Arbitration Commission.

TREATY REF: 15UNTS295.

PROCEDURE: Amendment. Ratification. Registration. Termination.

PARTIES:
Ivory Coast
Netherlands

107297   Bilateral Agreement   **499 UNTS 161**
SIGNED: 7 Oct 63   FORCE: 7 Oct 63
REGISTERED: 8 Jun 64 ICAO (Civil Aviat)
ARTICLES: 22 LANGUAGE: English. Russian.
HEADNOTE: AIR SERVICES
TOPIC: Air Transport

CONCEPTS: Definition of terms. Detailed regulations. Treaty implementation. Annex or appendix reference. Visas. Conformity with municipal law. General cooperation. Exchange of information and documents. Informational records. Licenses and permits. Personnel. Recognition of legal documents. Responsibility and liability. Use of facilities. Procedure. Negotiation. International circulation. Humanitarian matters. Reexport of goods, etc.. Accounting procedures. Fees and exemptions. Non-interest rates and fees. Tax exemptions. Customs exemptions. Registration certificate. Routes and logistics. Navigational equipment. Permit designation. Airport facilities. Airworthiness certificates. Conditions of airlines operating permission. Operating authorizations and regulations.

TREATY REF: 138LTS11; 478UNTS371.

PROCEDURE: Amendment. Future Procedures Contemplated. Termination.

PARTIES:
Pakistan
USSR (Soviet Union)

                    ANNEX
522 UNTS 345.   USSR (Soviet Union). Amendment 7 Oct 63.
522 UNTS 345. Pakistan. Amendment 7 Oct 63.

107298   Bilateral Exchange   **499 UNTS 191**
SIGNED: 27 Feb 64   FORCE: 27 Feb 64
REGISTERED: 8 Jun 64 ICAO (Civil Aviat)
ARTICLES: 2 LANGUAGE: English. French.
HEADNOTE: AIR SERVICES NOUMEA AUCKLAND
TOPIC: Air Transport

CONCEPTS: Routes and logistics. Permit designation. Air transport. Operating authorizations and regulations.

PROCEDURE: Termination.

PARTIES:
France
New Zealand

107299   Bilateral Agreement   **499 UNTS 197**
SIGNED: 15 Jan 64   FORCE: 15 Jan 64
REGISTERED: 8 Jun 64 ICAO (Civil Aviat)
ARTICLES: 21 LANGUAGE: French.
HEADNOTE: AIR TRANSPORT
TOPIC: Air Transport

CONCEPTS: Definition of terms. Detailed regulations. Annex or appendix reference. Conformity with municipal law. General cooperation. Exchange of information and documents. Licenses and permits. Personnel. Recognition of legal documents. Arbitration. Procedure. Special tribunals. Reexport of goods, etc.. Expense sharing formulae. Fees and exemptions. Non-interest rates and fees. Equitable taxes. Customs exemptions. Competency certificate. Routes and logistics. Navigational conditions. Permit designation. Air transport. Airworthiness certificates. Conditions of airlines operating permission. Operating authorizations and regulations. Licenses and certificates of nationality.

INTL ORGS: International Civil Aviation Organization. Arbitration Commission.

TREATY REF: 15UNTS295.

PROCEDURE: Amendment. Future Procedures Contemplated. Ratification. Registration. Termination.

PARTIES:
Mali
Niger

107300   Bilateral Convention   **499 UNTS 219**
SIGNED: 16 Mar 59   FORCE: 30 Apr 64
REGISTERED: 8 Jun 64 Netherlands
ARTICLES: 7 LANGUAGE: French.
HEADNOTE: FREE LEGAL AID
TOPIC: Admin Cooperation

CONCEPTS: General cooperation. Exchange of information and documents. Legal protection and assistance. Fees and exemptions.

PROCEDURE: Denunciation. Ratification.

PARTIES:
Brazil
Netherlands

107301   Bilateral Convention   **499 UNTS 227**
SIGNED: 17 Dec 62   FORCE: 1 Nov 63
REGISTERED: 8 Jun 64 Netherlands
ARTICLES: 47 LANGUAGE: Dutch. Spanish.
HEADNOTE: CONVENTION SOCIAL SECURITY
TOPIC: Health/Educ/Welfare

CONCEPTS: Alien status. Nationality and citizenship. General cooperation. Legal protection and assistance. Personnel. Responsibility and liability. Holidays and rest periods. Family allowances. Administrative cooperation. Old age insurance. Sickness and invalidity insurance. Social security. Unemployment.

INTL ORGS: Arbitration Commission.

PROCEDURE: Ratification. Termination.

PARTIES:
Netherlands
Spain

107302 Multilateral Convention **499 UNTS 311**
SIGNED: 29 Apr 58   FORCE: 10 Jun 64
REGISTERED: 10 Jun 64 United Nations

ARTICLES: 15 LANGUAGE: English. French. Chinese. Russian. Spanish.
HEADNOTE: CONTINENTAL SHELF
TOPIC: Territory Boundary
CONCEPTS: Exceptions and exemptions. Fish, wildlife, and natural resources. Continental shelf.
INTL ORGS: United Nations.
PROCEDURE: Amendment. Accession. Ratification.
PARTIES:
Afghanistan SIGNED: 30 Oct 58
Argentina SIGNED: 29 Apr 58
Australia SIGNED: 30 Oct 58 RATIFIED: 14 May 63 FORCE: 10 Jun 64
Bolivia SIGNED: 17 Oct 58
Byelorussia SIGNED: 31 Nov 58 RATIFIED: 27 Feb 61 FORCE: 10 Jun 64
Canada SIGNED: 29 Apr 58
Ceylon (Sri Lanka) SIGNED: 30 Nov 58
Chile SIGNED: 31 Oct 58
Taiwan SIGNED: 29 Apr 58
Colombia SIGNED: 29 Apr 58 RATIFIED: 8 Jun 62 FORCE: 10 Jun 64
Costa Rica SIGNED: 29 Apr 58
Cuba SIGNED: 29 Apr 58
Czechoslovakia SIGNED: 31 Oct 58 RATIFIED: 31 Aug 61 FORCE: 10 Jun 64
Denmark SIGNED: 29 Apr 58 RATIFIED: 12 Jun 63 FORCE: 10 Jun 64
Dominican Republic SIGNED: 29 Apr 58
Ecuador SIGNED: 31 Oct 58
Finland SIGNED: 27 Oct 58
Germany, West SIGNED: 30 Oct 58
Ghana SIGNED: 29 Apr 58
Guatemala SIGNED: 29 Apr 58 RATIFIED: 27 Nov 61 FORCE: 10 Jun 64
Haiti SIGNED: 29 Apr 58 RATIFIED: 29 Mar 60 FORCE: 10 Jun 64
Iceland SIGNED: 29 Apr 58
Indonesia SIGNED: 8 May 58
Iran SIGNED: 28 May 58
Ireland SIGNED: 2 Nov 58
Israel SIGNED: 29 Apr 58 RATIFIED: 6 Sep 61 FORCE: 10 Jun 64
Lebanon SIGNED: 29 May 58
Liberia SIGNED: 27 May 58
Madagascar RATIFIED: 31 Jul 62 FORCE: 10 Jun 64
Malaysia RATIFIED: 21 Dec 60 FORCE: 10 Jun 64
Nepal SIGNED: 29 Apr 58
Netherlands SIGNED: 31 Oct 58
New Zealand SIGNED: 29 Oct 58
Pakistan SIGNED: 31 Oct 58
Panama SIGNED: 2 May 58
Peru SIGNED: 31 Oct 58
Poland SIGNED: 31 Oct 58 RATIFIED: 29 Jun 62 FORCE: 10 Jun 64
Portugal SIGNED: 28 Oct 58 RATIFIED: 8 Jan 63 FORCE: 10 Jun 64
Senegal RATIFIED: 25 Apr 61 FORCE: 10 Jun 64
Switzerland SIGNED: 22 Oct 58
Thailand SIGNED: 29 Apr 58
Tunisia SIGNED: 30 Oct 58
UK Great Britain SIGNED: 9 Sep 58 RATIFIED: 22 Nov 60 FORCE: 10 Jun 64
USA (United States) SIGNED: 15 Sep 58 RATIFIED: 12 Apr 61 FORCE: 10 Jun 64
Ukrainian SSR SIGNED: 31 Oct 58 RATIFIED: 12 Jan 61 FORCE: 10 Jun 64
Uruguay SIGNED: 29 Apr 58
USSR (Soviet Union) SIGNED: 31 Oct 58 RATIFIED: 22 Nov 60 FORCE: 10 Jun 64
Venezuela SIGNED: 30 Oct 58 RATIFIED: 13 Aug 61 FORCE: 10 Jun 64
Yugoslavia SIGNED: 29 Apr 58
ANNEX
505 UNTS 348. Dominican Republic. Ratification 11 Aug 64. Force 10 Sep 64.
510 UNTS 341. Uganda. Accession 14 Sep 64. Force 14 Oct 64.
520 UNTS 433. Albania. Accession 7 Dec 64. Force 6 Jan 65.
523 UNTS 344. New Zealand. Ratification 18 Jan 65. Force 17 Feb 65.
525 UNTS 338. Finland. Ratification 16 Feb 65. Force 18 Mar 65.
538 UNTS 336. France. Qualified Accession 14 Jun 65. Force 14 Jul 65.
538 UNTS 338. France. Objection 14 Jun 65.
544 UNTS 377. USA (United States). Objection 9 Sep 65.

547 UNTS 357. Malawi. Accession 3 Nov 65. Force 3 Dec 65.
547 UNTS 357. Yugoslavia. Objection 29 Sep 65.
547 UNTS 357. Jamaica. Accession 8 Oct 65. Force 3 Dec 65.
551 UNTS 334. UK Great Britain. Objection 14 Jan 66.
552 UNTS 422. Yugoslavia. Qualified Ratification 28 Jan 66. Force 27 Feb 66.
555 UNTS 262. Netherlands. Qualified Ratification 18 Feb 66. Force 20 Mar 66.
563 UNTS 364. Sweden. Accession 1 Jun 66. Force 1 Jul 66.
639 UNTS 337. Thailand. Declaration 2 Jul 68.
639 UNTS 337. Thailand. Ratification 2 Jul 68. Force 1 Aug 68.
640 UNTS 372. Trinidad/Tobago. Accession 11 Jul 68. Force 10 Aug 68.

107303   Bilateral Treaty   **500 UNTS 3**
SIGNED: 30 Aug 62   FORCE: 3 May 64
REGISTERED: 10 Jun 64 Netherlands
ARTICLES: 17 LANGUAGE: Dutch. German.
HEADNOTE: SIMPLIFICATION JUDICIAL RELATIONS
TOPIC: Admin Cooperation
CONCEPTS: Territorial application. Treaty interpretation. General cooperation. Exchange of information and documents. Legal protection and assistance. Procedure. Indemnities and reimbursements. Fees and exemptions.
TREATY REF: 31JULY1909 AGREEMENT.
PROCEDURE: Denunciation. Ratification.
PARTIES:
Germany, West
Netherlands

107304 Multilateral Agreement **500 UNTS 25**
SIGNED: 26 Nov 60   FORCE: 12 Dec 60
REGISTERED: 12 Jun 64 Australia
ARTICLES: 3 LANGUAGE: English.
HEADNOTE: TAX EXEMPTION CONTRIBUTION DEVELOPMENT WATER RESOURCES
TOPIC: Taxation
CONCEPTS: Tax exemptions. Non-bank projects. Irrigation.
PARTIES:
Australia SIGNED: 12 Dec 60 FORCE: 12 Dec 60
Cambodia SIGNED: 26 Nov 60 FORCE: 12 Dec 60
Laos SIGNED: 26 Nov 60 FORCE: 12 Dec 60
Thailand SIGNED: 26 Nov 60 FORCE: 12 Dec 60
Vietnam, South SIGNED: 26 Nov 60 FORCE: 12 Dec 60

107305 Multilateral Convention **500 UNTS 31**
SIGNED: 18 Sep 61   FORCE: 1 May 64
REGISTERED: 15 Jun 64 Mexico
ARTICLES: 18 LANGUAGE: English. French. Spanish.
HEADNOTE: SUPPLEMENTARY WARSAW CONVENTION
TOPIC: Air Transport
CONCEPTS: Definition of terms. Exceptions and exemptions. Territorial application. Treaty interpretation. Responsibility and liability. Arbitration. Claims and settlements. Air transport. Operating authorizations and regulations.
INTL ORGS: International Civil Aviation Organization. United Nations.
TREATY REF: 138LTS11; 478UNTS371.
PROCEDURE: Accession. Denunciation. Ratification. Registration.
PARTIES:

107306   Bilateral Agreement **500 UNTS 49**
SIGNED: 8 Apr 64   FORCE: 12 May 64
REGISTERED: 18 Jun 64 United Nations
ARTICLES: 8 LANGUAGE: English.
HEADNOTE: UNICEF ACTIVITIES
TOPIC: IGO Operations
CONCEPTS: Diplomatic missions. Privileges and immunities. Exchange of information and documents. Labor statistics. Accounting procedures. Domestic obligation. Economic assistance. Special status. Assistance to United Nations. Inter-agency agreements.
INTL ORGS: United Nations Educational, Scientific and Cultural Organization.
TREATY REF: 15UNTS94.

PROCEDURE: Amendment. Termination.
PARTIES:
Taiwan
UNICEF (Children)

107307   Bilateral Agreement **500 UNTS 61**
SIGNED: 28 Dec 62   FORCE: 21 Mar 64
REGISTERED: 18 Jun 64 Taiwan
ARTICLES: 9 LANGUAGE: Chinese. Portuguese. English.
HEADNOTE: COMMERCE TRADE
TOPIC: General Trade
CONCEPTS: Exceptions and exemptions. Conformity with municipal law. Licenses and permits. Investigation of violations. Export quotas. Import quotas. Certificates of origin. Trade procedures. Currency. Payment schedules. Most favored nation clause.
PROCEDURE: Duration. Ratification. Termination.
PARTIES:
Brazil
Taiwan

107308   Bilateral Agreement **500 UNTS 75**
SIGNED: 19 May 64   FORCE: 19 May 64
REGISTERED: 21 Jun 64 United Nations
ARTICLES: 8 LANGUAGE: English.
HEADNOTE: UNICEF ACTIVITIES
TOPIC: IGO Operations
CONCEPTS: Diplomatic missions. Privileges and immunities. Exchange of information and documents. Accounting procedures. Freedom of meeting. Special status. Assistance to United Nations. Inter-agency agreements.
INTL ORGS: International Civil Aviation Organization.
PROCEDURE: Amendment. Termination.
PARTIES:
Jamaica
UNICEF (Children)

107309   Bilateral Agreement **500 UNTS 85**
SIGNED: 11 Jun 64   FORCE: 11 Jun 64
REGISTERED: 23 Jun 64 United Nations
ARTICLES: 5 LANGUAGE: English.
HEADNOTE: UN TECHNICAL ASSISTANCE COMMITTEE
TOPIC: IGO Status/Immunit
CONCEPTS: Non-visa travel documents. Diplomatic missions. Privileges and immunities. Funding procedures. Subsidiary organ. Status of experts.
INTL ORGS: International Atomic Energy Agency.
PARTIES:
Austria
United Nations

107310 Multilateral Convention **500 UNTS 95**
SIGNED: 18 Apr 61   FORCE: 24 Apr 64
REGISTERED: 24 Jun 64 United Nations
ARTICLES: 53 LANGUAGE: English. French. Chinese. Russian. Spanish.
HEADNOTE: VIENNA CONVENTION DIPLOMATIC RELATIONS
TOPIC: Consul/Citizenship
CONCEPTS: Definition of terms. Emergencies. Exceptions and exemptions. Denial of admission. General consular functions. Diplomatic privileges. Consular relations establishment. Diplomatic relations establishment. Inviolability. Privileges and immunities. Proxy diplomacy. Diplomatic correspondence. Conformity with municipal law. Personnel. Use of facilities. Social security.
INTL ORGS: United Nations.
PROCEDURE: Amendment. Ratification.
PARTIES:
Albania SIGNED: 18 Apr 61
Algeria RATIFIED: 14 Apr 64 FORCE: 24 Apr 64
Argentina SIGNED: 18 Apr 61 RATIFIED: 10 Oct 63 FORCE: 24 Apr 64
Australia SIGNED: 30 Mar 62
Austria SIGNED: 18 Apr 61
Belgium SIGNED: 23 Oct 61
Brazil SIGNED: 18 Apr 61
Bulgaria SIGNED: 18 Apr 61
Byelorussia SIGNED: 18 Apr 61 RATIFIED: 14 May 64 FORCE: 24 Apr 64
Canada SIGNED: 5 Feb 62
Ceylon (Sri Lanka) SIGNED: 18 Apr 61

Chile SIGNED: 18 Apr 61
Taiwan SIGNED: 18 Apr 61
Central Afri Rep SIGNED: 28 Mar 62
Congo (Zaire) SIGNED: 18 Apr 61
Colombia SIGNED: 18 Apr 61
Costa Rica SIGNED: 14 Feb 62
Cuba SIGNED: 16 Jan 62 RATIFIED: 26 Sep 63
   FORCE: 24 Apr 64
Czechoslovakia SIGNED: 18 Apr 61 RATIFIED:
   24 May 63 FORCE: 24 Apr 64
Denmark SIGNED: 18 Apr 61
Dominican Republic SIGNED: 30 Mar 62 RATI-
   FIED: 14 Jan 64 FORCE: 24 Apr 64
Ecuador SIGNED: 18 Apr 61
Finland SIGNED: 20 Oct 61
France SIGNED: 30 Mar 62
Germany, West SIGNED: 18 Apr 61
Ghana SIGNED: 18 Apr 61 RATIFIED: 28 Jun 63
   FORCE: 24 Apr 64
Greece SIGNED: 29 Mar 62
Guatemala SIGNED: 18 Apr 61 RATIFIED:
   28 Jun 63 FORCE: 24 Apr 64
Hungary SIGNED: 18 Apr 61
Iran SIGNED: 27 May 61
Iraq SIGNED: 20 Feb 64 RATIFIED: 15 Oct 63
   FORCE: 24 Apr 64
Ireland SIGNED: 18 Apr 61
Israel SIGNED: 18 Apr 61
Italy SIGNED: 13 Mar 62
Jamaica RATIFIED: 5 Jun 63 FORCE: 24 Apr 64
Japan SIGNED: 26 Mar 62 RATIFIED: 8 Jun 64
   FORCE: 24 Apr 64
Korea, South SIGNED: 28 Mar 62
Lebanon SIGNED: 18 Apr 61
Liberia SIGNED: 18 Apr 61 RATIFIED:
   15 May 62 FORCE: 24 Apr 64
Liechtenstein SIGNED: 18 Apr 61 RATIFIED:
   8 May 64 FORCE: 24 Apr 64
Luxembourg SIGNED: 2 Feb 62
Mauritania RATIFIED: 16 Jul 62 FORCE:
   24 Apr 64
Mexico SIGNED: 18 Apr 61
New Zealand SIGNED: 28 Mar 62
Nigeria SIGNED: 31 Mar 62
Norway SIGNED: 18 Apr 61
Pakistan SIGNED: 29 Mar 62 RATIFIED:
   29 Mar 62 FORCE: 24 Apr 64
Panama SIGNED: 18 Apr 61 RATIFIED: 4 Dec 63
   FORCE: 24 Apr 64
Philippines SIGNED: 20 Oct 61
Poland SIGNED: 18 Apr 61
Romania SIGNED: 18 Apr 61
Rwanda RATIFIED: 15 Apr 64 FORCE: 24 Apr 64
San Marino SIGNED: 25 Oct 61
Senegal SIGNED: 18 Apr 61
Sierra Leone RATIFIED: 13 Aug 62 FORCE:
   24 Apr 64
South Africa SIGNED: 28 Mar 62
Sweden SIGNED: 18 Apr 61
Switzerland SIGNED: 18 Apr 61 RATIFIED:
   30 Oct 63 FORCE: 24 Apr 64
Tanganyika SIGNED: 27 Feb 62 RATIFIED:
   5 Nov 62 FORCE: 24 Apr 64
Thailand SIGNED: 30 Oct 61
UK Great Britain SIGNED: 11 Dec 61
USA (United States) SIGNED: 29 Jun 61
Ukrainian SSR SIGNED: 18 Apr 61 RATIFIED:
   12 Jun 64 FORCE: 24 Apr 64
Uruguay SIGNED: 18 Apr 61
USSR (Soviet Union) SIGNED: 18 Apr 61 RATI-
   FIED: 25 Mar 64 FORCE: 24 Apr 64
Vatican/Holy See SIGNED: 18 Apr 61 RATIFIED:
   17 Apr 64 FORCE: 24 Apr 64
Venezuela SIGNED: 18 Apr 61
Yugoslavia SIGNED: 18 Apr 61 RATIFIED:
   1 Apr 63 FORCE: 24 Apr 64
         ANNEX
507 UNTS 347. UK Great Britain. Ratification
   1 Jun 64. Force 1 Oct 64.
507 UNTS 347. UK Great Britain. Objection
   1 Sep 64.
510 UNTS 342. Ecuador. Ratification 21 Sep 64.
   Force 21 Oct 64.
515 UNTS 328. Germany, West. Qualified Ratification 11 Nov 64. Force 11 Nov 64.
515 UNTS 328. Costa Rica. Ratification 9 Nov 64.
   Force 9 Nov 64.
523 UNTS 345. Luxembourg. Objection
   18 Jan 65.
523 UNTS 345. Iran. Ratification 3 Feb 65. Force
   5 Mar 65.
528 UNTS 330. Venezuela. Qualified Ratification
   16 Mar 65. Force 24 Apr 65.

528 UNTS 330. Brazil. Qualified Ratification
   25 Mar 65. Force 24 Apr 65.
531 UNTS 416. Uganda. Accession 15 Apr 65.
   Force 15 May 65.
531 UNTS 416. Poland. Ratification 19 Apr 65.
   Force 19 May 65.
535 UNTS 454. Malawi. Accession 19 May 65.
   Force 18 Jun 65.
539 UNTS 381. Mexico. Ratification 16 Jun 65.
   Force 16 Jun 65.
540 UNTS 340. Kenya. Accession 1 Jul 65. Force
   31 Jul 65.
541 UNTS 362. Congo (Zaire). Ratification
   19 Jul 65. Force 18 Aug 65.
544 UNTS 378. San Marino. Ratification
   8 Sep 65. Force 8 Oct 65.
544 UNTS 378. Cambodia. Qualified Accession
   31 Aug 65.
545 UNTS 368. Hungary. Qualified Ratification
   14 Sep 65. Force 24 Oct 65.
547 UNTS 358. Nepal. Qualified Accession
   28 Sep 65.
547 UNTS 358. Afghanistan. Accession 6 Oct 65.
   Force 5 Nov 65.
547 UNTS 358. India. Accession 15 Oct 65. Force
   14 Nov 65.
547 UNTS 358. Trinidad/Tobago. Accession
   19 Oct 65. Force 18 Nov 65.
547 UNTS 358. Luxembourg. Objection
   25 Oct 65.
548 UNTS 372. Malaysia. Accession 9 Nov 65.
   Force 9 Dec 65.
548 UNTS 372. Philippines. Ratification
   15 Nov 65. Force 15 Dec 65.
550 UNTS 414. El Salvador. Accession 9 Dec 65.
   Force 8 Jan 66.
561 UNTS 353. Austria. Ratification 28 Apr 66.
   Force 28 May 66.
561 UNTS 353. Austria. Ratification 28 Apr 66.
   Force 28 May 66.
562 UNTS 337. Canada. Qualified Ratification
   26 May 66. Force 25 Jun 66.
571 UNTS 328. Luxembourg. Ratification
   17 Aug 66. Force 16 Sep 66.
608 UNTS 376. Norway. Ratification 24 Oct 67.
   Force 23 Nov 67.
616 UNTS 501. Chile. Ratification 9 Jan 68. Force
   8 Feb 68.
616 UNTS 501. Guinea. Accession 10 Jan 68.
   Force 9 Feb 68.
618 UNTS 383. Bulgaria. Ratification 17 Jan 68.
   Reservation 17 Jan 68.
618 UNTS 383. Bulgaria. Declaration 17 Jan 68.
619 UNTS 341. Australia. Ratification 26 Jan 68.
   Force 25 Feb 68.
619 UNTS 341. Tunisia. Accession 24 Jan 68.
   Force 23 Feb 68.
630 UNTS 408. Honduras. Accession 13 Feb 68.
   Force 14 Mar 68.
633 UNTS 416. Mali. Accession 28 Mar 68. Force
   27 Apr 68.
633 UNTS 416. Somalia. Accession 29 Mar 68.
   Force 28 Apr 68.
633 UNTS 416. UK Great Britain. Declaration
   29 Mar 68.
635 UNTS 365. Belgium. Accession 2 May 68.
   Force 1 Jun 68.
635 UNTS 365. Burundi. Ratification 1 May 68.
   Force 31 May 68.
638 UNTS 298. Morocco. Objection 19 Jun 68.
638 UNTS 298. Morocco. Accession 19 Jun 68.
   Reservation 19 Jun 68.
640 UNTS 373. Germany, West. Objection
   9 Jul 68.
643 UNTS 398. UK Great Britain. Objection
   23 Aug 68.
645 UNTS 372. Cyprus. Accession 10 Sep 68.
   Force 10 Oct 68.
645 UNTS 372. Portugal. Accession 11 Sep 68.
   Force 10 Oct 68.
648 UNTS 376. Denmark. Ratification 2 Oct 68.
   Force 1 Nov 68.
649 UNTS 359. Romania. Declaration 15 Nov 68.
   Ratification 15 Nov 68.
653 UNTS 461. Peru. Accession 18 Dec 68. Force
   17 Jan 69.
653 UNTS 461. Germany, West. Objection
   23 Dec 68.
668 UNTS 369. Botswana. Accession 11 Apr 69.
   Reservation 11 Apr 69.

107311   Multilateral Protocol   **500 UNTS 223**
SIGNED: 18 Apr 61   FORCE: 24 Apr 64

REGISTERED: 24 Jun 64 United Nations
ARTICLES: 8 LANGUAGE: English. French. Chi-
   nese. Russian. Spanish.
HEADNOTE: DIPLOMATIC RELATIONS CONCERN-
   ING ACQUISITION NATIONALITY
TOPIC: Consul/Citizenship
CONCEPTS: Acquisition of nationality.
INTL ORGS: United Nations.
PROCEDURE: Accession. Ratification.
PARTIES:
   Argentina SIGNED: 25 Oct 61 RATIFIED:
      10 Oct 63 FORCE: 24 Apr 64
   Taiwan SIGNED: 18 Apr 61
   Central Afri Rep SIGNED: 28 Mar 62
   Denmark SIGNED: 18 Apr 61
   Dominican Republic SIGNED: 30 Mar 62 RATI-
      FIED: 14 Jan 64 FORCE: 24 Apr 64
   Finland SIGNED: 20 Oct 61
   Gabon RATIFIED: 2 Apr 64 FORCE: 2 May 64
   Germany, West SIGNED: 28 Mar 62
   Ghana SIGNED: 18 Apr 61
   Iran SIGNED: 27 May 61
   Iraq SIGNED: 20 Feb 62 RATIFIED: 15 Oct 63
      FORCE: 24 Apr 64
   Italy SIGNED: 13 Mar 62
   Korea, South SIGNED: 30 Mar 62
   Laos RATIFIED: 3 Dec 62 FORCE: 24 Apr 64
   Lebanon SIGNED: 18 Apr 61
   Madagascar RATIFIED: 31 Jul 63 FORCE:
      24 Apr 64
   Norway SIGNED: 18 Apr 61
   Panama RATIFIED: 4 Dec 63 FORCE: 24 Apr 64
   Philippines SIGNED: 20 Oct 61
   Senegal SIGNED: 18 Apr 61
   Sweden SIGNED: 18 Apr 61
   Tanganyika SIGNED: 27 Feb 62 RATIFIED:
      5 Nov 62 FORCE: 24 Apr 64
   Thailand SIGNED: 30 Oct 61
   United Arab Rep RATIFIED: 9 Jun 64 FORCE:
      9 Jun 64
   Yugoslavia SIGNED: 18 Apr 61 RATIFIED:
      1 Apr 63 FORCE: 24 Apr 64
         ANNEX
515 UNTS 330. Germany, West. Qualified Ratification 11 Nov 64. Force 11 Nov 64.
523 UNTS 346. Iran. Ratification 3 Feb 65. Force
   5 Mar 65.
540 UNTS 340. Kenya. Accession 1 Jul 65. Force
   31 Jul 65.
544 UNTS 379. Cambodia. Accession 31 Aug 65.
547 UNTS 360. Nepal. Accession 28 Sep 65.
547 UNTS 360. India. Accession 15 Oct 65. Force
   14 Nov 65.
548 UNTS 372. Malaysia. Accession 9 Nov 65.
   Force 9 Dec 65.
548 UNTS 372. Philippines. Ratification
   15 Nov 65. Force 15 Dec 65.
560 UNTS 293. Niger. Accession 28 Mar 66.
   Force 27 Apr 66.
608 UNTS 376. Norway. Ratification 24 Oct 67.
   Force 23 Nov 67.
616 UNTS 502. Guinea. Accession 10 Jan 68.
   Force 9 Feb 68.
619 UNTS 342. Tunisia. Accession 24 Jan 68.
   Force 23 Feb 68.
635 UNTS 366. Belgium. Accession 2 May 68.
   Force 1 Jun 68.
648 UNTS 376. Denmark. Ratification 2 Oct 68.
   Force 1 Nov 68.
668 UNTS 370. Botswana. Accession 11 Apr 69.

107312   Multilateral Protocol   **500 UNTS 243**
SIGNED: 18 Apr 61   FORCE: 24 Apr 64
REGISTERED: 24 Jun 64 United Nations
ARTICLES: 10 LANGUAGE: English. French. Chi-
   nese. Russian. Spanish.
HEADNOTE: COMPULSORY SETTLEMENT DIS-
   PUTES
TOPIC: Dispute Settlement
CONCEPTS: Time limit. Treaty interpretation. Pro-
   cedure. Existing tribunals. Conciliation.
INTL ORGS: International Court of Justice. United
   Nations. Arbitration Commission.
PROCEDURE: Accession. Ratification.
PARTIES:
   Austria SIGNED: 18 Apr 61
   Belgium SIGNED: 23 Oct 61
   Taiwan SIGNED: 18 Apr 61
   Central Afri Rep SIGNED: 28 Mar 62
   Colombia SIGNED: 18 Apr 61
   Denmark SIGNED: 18 Apr 61
   Dominican Republic SIGNED: 30 Mar 62 RATI-
      FIED: 13 Feb 64 FORCE: 24 Apr 64

Ecuador SIGNED: 18 Apr 61
Finland SIGNED: 20 Oct 61
France SIGNED: 30 Mar 62.
Gabon RATIFIED: 2 Apr 64 FORCE: 2 May 64
Germany, West SIGNED: 18 Apr 61
Ghana SIGNED: 18 Apr 61
Iran SIGNED: 27 May 61
Iraq SIGNED: 20 Feb 62 RATIFIED: 15 Oct 63 FORCE: 24 Apr 64
Ireland SIGNED: 18 Apr 61
Israel SIGNED: 18 Apr 61
Italy SIGNED: 13 Mar 62
Japan SIGNED: 26 Mar 62 RATIFIED: 8 Jun 64 FORCE: 8 Jul 64
Korea, South SIGNED: 30 Mar 62
Laos RATIFIED: 3 Dec 62 FORCE: 24 Apr 64
Lebanon SIGNED: 18 Apr 61
Liechtenstein SIGNED: 18 Apr 61 RATIFIED: 8 May 64 FORCE: 7 Jun 64
Luxembourg SIGNED: 2 Feb 62
Madagascar RATIFIED: 31 Jul 63 FORCE: 24 Apr 64
New Zealand SIGNED: 28 Mar 62
Norway SIGNED: 18 Apr 61
Panama RATIFIED: 4 Dec 63 FORCE: 24 Apr 64
Philippines SIGNED: 20 Oct 61
Sweden SIGNED: 18 Apr 61
Switzerland SIGNED: 18 Apr 61 RATIFIED: 22 Nov 63 FORCE: 24 Apr 64
Tanganyika SIGNED: 27 Feb 62 RATIFIED: 5 Nov 62 FORCE: 24 Apr 64
UK Great Britain SIGNED: 11 Dec 61
USA (United States) SIGNED: 29 Jun 61
Yugoslavia SIGNED: 18 Apr 61 RATIFIED: 1 Apr 63 FORCE: 24 Apr 64
ANNEX
507 UNTS 348. UK Great Britain. Ratification 1 Sep 64. Force 1 Oct 64.
510 UNTS 342. Ecuador. Ratification 21 Sep 64. Force 21 Oct 64.
515 UNTS 331. Costa Rica. Accession 9 Nov 64. Force 9 Nov 64.
515 UNTS 331. Germany, West. Qualified Ratification 11 Nov 64. Force 11 Nov 64.
523 UNTS 347. Iran. Ratification 3 Feb 65. Force 5 Mar 65.
540 UNTS 341. Kenya. Accession 1 Jul 65. Force 31 Jul 65.
541 UNTS 363. Congo (Zaire). Accession 19 Jul 65. Force 18 Aug 65.
544 UNTS 379. Cambodia. Accession 31 Aug 65.
547 UNTS 360. Nepal. Accession 28 Sep 65.
547 UNTS 360. India. Accession 15 Oct 65. Force 14 Nov 65.
548 UNTS 372. Malaysia. Accession 9 Nov 65. Force 9 Dec 65.
548 UNTS 372. Philippines. Ratification 15 Nov 65. Force 15 Dec 65.
561 UNTS 354. Niger. Accession 26 Apr 66. Force 26 May 66.
561 UNTS 354. Austria. Ratification 28 Apr 66. Force 28 May 66.
561 UNTS 354. Austria. Ratification 28 Apr 66. Force 28 May 66.
561 UNTS 354. Niger. Accession 26 Apr 66. Force 26 May 66.
571 UNTS 328. Luxembourg. Ratification 17 Aug 66. Force 16 Sep 66.
608 UNTS 376. Norway. Ratification 24 Oct 67. Force 23 Nov 67.
616 UNTS 503. Guinea. Accession 10 Jan 68. Force 9 Feb 68.
619 UNTS 342. Australia. Accession 25 Jan 68. Force 25 Feb 68.
635 UNTS 367. Belgium. Ratification 2 May 68. Force 1 Jun 68.
668 UNTS 370. Botswana. Accession 11 Apr 69. Ratification 2 Oct 68.

107313 Multilateral Agreement **500 UNTS 267**
SIGNED: 11 May 48   FORCE: 18 Sep 57
REGISTERED: 24 Jun 64 UK Great Britain
ARTICLES: 5 LANGUAGE: English.
HEADNOTE: TELEGRAPHS
TOPIC: Telecommunications
CONCEPTS: Detailed regulations. Accounting procedures. Assets transfer. Telegrams. IGO constitution. Subsidiary organ. Establishment. Extension of functions. Internal structure.
INTL ORGS: Commonwealth Telecommunications Board.
PROCEDURE: Accession.

PARTIES:
Australia SIGNED: 25 Jul 63 FORCE: 25 Jul 63
Canada SIGNED: 25 Jul 63 FORCE: 25 Jul 63
Ceylon (Sri Lanka) SIGNED: 25 Jul 63 FORCE: 25 Jul 63
Cyprus SIGNED: 25 Jul 63 FORCE: 25 Jul 63
Fed of Malaya SIGNED: 25 Jul 63 FORCE: 25 Jul 63
Fed Rhod/Nyasaland SIGNED: 25 Jul 63 FORCE: 25 Jul 63
Ghana SIGNED: 25 Jul 63 FORCE: 25 Jul 63
India SIGNED: 25 Jul 63 FORCE: 25 Jul 63
New Zealand SIGNED: 25 Jul 63 FORCE: 25 Jul 63
Nigeria SIGNED: 25 Jul 63 FORCE: 25 Jul 63
UK Great Britain SIGNED: 25 Jul 63 FORCE: 25 Jul 63

107314 Bilateral Treaty **501 UNTS 3**
SIGNED: 13 Apr 54   FORCE: 16 Dec 54
REGISTERED: 24 Jun 64 Czechoslovakia
ARTICLES: 91 LANGUAGE: Czechoslovakian. Bulgarian.
HEADNOTE: LEGAL ASSISTANCE CIVIL CRIMINAL CASES
TOPIC: Admin Cooperation
CONCEPTS: General provisions. Previous treaty replacement. Extradition, deportation and repatriation. Extradition requests. Extraditable offenses. Concurrent requests. Provisional detainment. Extradition postponement. Witnesses and experts. Material evidence. Family law. Exchange of information and documents. Juridical personality. Legal protection and assistance. Recognition and enforcement of legal decisions. Succession. Recognition of legal documents. Indemnities and reimbursements. Fees and exemptions. Conveyance in transit.
TREATY REF: 60LTS203; 60LTS169.
PROCEDURE: Denunciation. Ratification. Termination.
PARTIES:
Bulgaria
Czechoslovakia

107315 Bilateral Convention **501 UNTS 109**
SIGNED: 6 Oct 56   FORCE: 20 Dec 56
REGISTERED: 24 Jun 64 Czechoslovakia
ARTICLES: 7 LANGUAGE: Czechoslovakian. German.
HEADNOTE: ASSISTANCE EVENT NATURAL DISASTER
TOPIC: Humanitarian
CONCEPTS: Detailed regulations. Frontier permits. General cooperation. Humanitarian matters. Indemnities and reimbursements. Customs exemptions. Materials, equipment and services. Frontier peoples and personnel.
PROCEDURE: Duration. Ratification. Termination.
PARTIES:
Czechoslovakia
Germany, East

107316 Bilateral Agreement **501 UNTS 149**
SIGNED: 25 Jan 57   FORCE: 1 Aug 57
REGISTERED: 24 Jun 64 Czechoslovakia
ARTICLES: 17 LANGUAGE: Czechoslovakian. Bulgarian.
HEADNOTE: COOPERATION FIELD SOCIAL POLICY
TOPIC: Non-ILO Labor
CONCEPTS: Time limit. General cooperation. Legal protection and assistance. Social security. Unemployment. Payment schedules.
PROCEDURE: Denunciation. Ratification. Termination.
PARTIES:
Bulgaria
Czechoslovakia

107317 Bilateral Treaty **501 UNTS 171**
SIGNED: 8 Apr 57   FORCE: 1 Aug 57
REGISTERED: 24 Jun 64 Czechoslovakia
ARTICLES: 4 LANGUAGE: Czechoslovakian. Mongolian.
HEADNOTE: FRIENDSHIP COOPERATION
TOPIC: General Amity
CONCEPTS: Peaceful relations. General cultural cooperation. Economic assistance.
PROCEDURE: Denunciation. Duration. Ratification.

PARTIES:
Czechoslovakia
Mongolia

107318 Bilateral Convention **501 UNTS 181**
SIGNED: 14 Jan 63   FORCE: 8 Apr 64
REGISTERED: 24 Jun 64 Czechoslovakia
ARTICLES: 26 LANGUAGE: Czechoslovakian. Vietnamese.
HEADNOTE: CONSULAR CONVENTION
TOPIC: Consul/Citizenship
CONCEPTS: General consular functions. Diplomatic privileges. Consular relations establishment. Inviolability. Privileges and immunities. Diplomatic correspondence. Responsibility and liability.
PROCEDURE: Duration. Ratification. Termination.
PARTIES:
Czechoslovakia
Vietnam, North

107319 Bilateral Agreement **501 UNTS 213**
SIGNED: 27 Jan 64   FORCE: 31 Jan 64
REGISTERED: 26 Jun 64 IAEA (Atom Energy)
ARTICLES: 1 LANGUAGE: English.
HEADNOTE: RESEARCH REACTOR PROJECT
TOPIC: Scientific Project
CONCEPTS: Definition of terms. Research and development. Indemnities and reimbursements. Payment schedules. Transportation costs. Special projects. General. Nuclear materials. Peaceful use. Samples and testing.
TREATY REF: 395UNTS258; 456UNTS447.
PARTIES:
Finland
IAEA (Atom Energy)

107320 Multilateral Instrument **501 UNTS 221**
SIGNED: 8 Apr 64   FORCE: 8 Apr 64
REGISTERED: 26 Jun 64 IAEA (Atom Energy)
ARTICLES: 7 LANGUAGE: English.
HEADNOTE: LEASE URANIUM
TOPIC: Loans and Credits
CONCEPTS: Annex or appendix reference. Previous treaty extension. Responsibility and liability. Title and deeds. Dispute settlement. Research results. Nuclear research. Indemnities and reimbursements. Payment schedules. Atomic energy assistance. Acceptance of delivery. Nuclear materials. Peaceful use. Rights of supplier. Samples and testing.
INTL ORGS: Arbitration Commission.
TREATY REF: 402UNTS255; 501UNTS360; 339UNTS359; 276UNTS3; ETC..
PROCEDURE: Duration.
PARTIES:
Norway SIGNED: 8 Apr 64 FORCE: 8 Apr 64
IAEA (Atom Energy) SIGNED: 8 Apr 64 FORCE: 8 Apr 64
USA (United States) SIGNED: 8 Apr 64 FORCE: 8 Apr 64

107321 Multilateral Agreement **501 UNTS 245**
SIGNED: 28 Feb 64   FORCE: 10 Apr 64
REGISTERED: 26 Jun 64 IAEA (Atom Energy)
ARTICLES: 8 LANGUAGE: English.
HEADNOTE: COOPERATIVE RESEARCH REACTOR PHYSICS
TOPIC: Atomic Energy
CONCEPTS: Definition of terms. Annex or appendix reference. Operating agencies. Personnel. Responsibility and liability. Use of facilities. Establishment of commission. Dispute settlement. Existing tribunals. Specialists exchange. Public health. Teacher and student exchange. Scholarships and grants. Research and development. Indemnities and reimbursements. Expense sharing formulae. Tax exemptions. Recognition. Atomic energy assistance. Nuclear materials. Nonnuclear materials. Peaceful use.
INTL ORGS: Arbitration Commission. Special Commission.
TREATY REF: 402UNTS255; 501UNTS245.
PROCEDURE: Duration. Termination.
PARTIES:
Norway SIGNED: 10 Apr 64 FORCE: 10 Apr 64
Poland SIGNED: 28 Feb 64 FORCE: 10 Apr 64
IAEA (Atom Energy) SIGNED: 10 Apr 64 FORCE: 10 Apr 64

Yugoslavia   SIGNED: 28 Feb 64   FORCE:
   10 Apr 64
ANNEX
603 UNTS 338. Norway. Prolongation 24 Apr 67.
   Force 24 Apr 67.
603 UNTS 338. IAEA (Atom Energy). Prolongation
   24 Apr 67. Force 24 Apr 67.
603 UNTS 338. Poland. Prolongation 24 Apr 67.
   Force 24 Apr 67.
603 UNTS 338.   Yugoslavia.   Prolongation
   24 Apr 67. Force 24 Apr 67.

107322   Bilateral Agreement   **501 UNTS 273**
SIGNED: 7 Dec 63   FORCE: 2 Jan 64
REGISTERED: 26 Jun 64 IAEA (Atom Energy)
ARTICLES: 1 LANGUAGE: English.
HEADNOTE: ATOMIC   ENERGY   RESEARCH
   PROJECTS
TOPIC: Scientific Project
CONCEPTS: Definition of terms. Annex or appen-
   dix reference. Existing tribunals. Public health.
   Nuclear research. Research and development.
   Indemnities   and   reimbursements.   Payment
   schedules. Quotas. Trademarks. Technical edu-
   cation. General. Nuclear materials.
INTL ORGS: International Court of Justice. Arbitra-
   tion Commission.
TREATY REF: 456UNTS447; 412UNTS225.
PARTIES:
   IAEA (Atom Energy)
   Yugoslavia

107323   Multilateral Agreement   **502 UNTS 3**
SIGNED: 10 Sep 62   FORCE: 19 Apr 64
REGISTERED: 30 Jun 64 Australia
ARTICLES: 7 LANGUAGE: English. Indonesian.
HEADNOTE: WAR CEMETERIES GRAVES MEMORI-
   ALS
TOPIC: Other Military
CONCEPTS: Customs exemptions. Burial arrange-
   ments. Responsibility for war dead. Upkeep of
   war graves. Establishment of war cemeteries.
INTL ORGS: Special Commission.
PARTIES:
   Australia SIGNED: 10 Sep 62 FORCE: 19 Apr 64
   Canada SIGNED: 10 Sep 62 FORCE: 19 Apr 64
   India SIGNED: 10 Sep 62 FORCE: 19 Apr 64
   Indonesia   SIGNED: 10 Sep 62   RATIFIED:
      19 Mar 64 FORCE: 19 Apr 64
   New Zealand SIGNED: 10 Sep 62 FORCE:
      19 Apr 64
   Pakistan SIGNED: 10 Sep 62 FORCE: 19 Apr 64
   UK Great Britain SIGNED: 10 Sep 62 FORCE:
      19 Apr 64

107324   Bilateral Agreement   **502 UNTS 17**
SIGNED: 4 Aug 59   FORCE: 17 Aug 60
REGISTERED: 30 Jun 64 Romania
ARTICLES: 11 LANGUAGE: Romanian. Arabic. En-
   glish.
HEADNOTE: CULTURAL COOPERATION
TOPIC: Culture
CONCEPTS: Treaty implementation. Treaty inter-
   pretation. Friendship and amity. Non-diplomatic
   delegations. Specialists exchange. Recognition
   of degrees. Teacher and student exchange.
   Professorships. Scholarships and grants. Gen-
   eral cultural cooperation. Artists. Athletes. Scien-
   tific exchange. Publications exchange. Mass me-
   dia exchange. Press and wire services.
PROCEDURE: Amendment. Ratification. Termination.
PARTIES:
   Iraq *
   Romania

107325   Bilateral Convention   **502 UNTS 31**
SIGNED: 12 Oct 62   FORCE: 13 Nov 63
REGISTERED: 30 Jun 64 Iraq
ARTICLES: 22 LANGUAGE: Romanian. French.
HEADNOTE: VETERINARY HEALTH
TOPIC: Sanitation
CONCEPTS: Detailed regulations. General cooper-
   ation. Exchange of information and documents.
   Inspection and observation. Domestic legisla-
   tion. Establishment of commission. Border con-
   trol. Veterinary. Reexport of goods, etc.. Trade
   procedures.
INTL ORGS: Special Commission.

PROCEDURE: Amendment. Denunciation. Dura-
   tion. Ratification. Renewal or Revival.
PARTIES:
   Belgium
   Romania

107326   Bilateral Treaty   **502 UNTS 63**
SIGNED: 21 Sep 62   FORCE: 1 Apr 64
REGISTERED: 30 Jun 64 Belgium
ARTICLES: 12 LANGUAGE: French. German.
HEADNOTE: COMPENSATION WAR VICTIMS
TOPIC: Reparations
CONCEPTS: Territorial application.   Arbitration.
   Procedure. Compensation. Payment schedules.
   Loss and/or damage. Post-war claims settle-
   ment.
INTL ORGS: Arbitration Commission.
PROCEDURE: Ratification.
PARTIES:
   Belgium
   Germany, West

107327   Bilateral Convention   **502 UNTS 79**
SIGNED: 24 Jun 60   FORCE: 26 Dec 63
REGISTERED: 2 Jul 64 UK Great Britain
ARTICLES: 47 LANGUAGE: English. German.
HEADNOTE: CONSULAR
TOPIC: Consul/Citizenship
CONCEPTS: Definition of terms. Territorial applica-
   tion. General provisions. Annex or appendix ref-
   erence. General consular functions. Diplomatic
   privileges. Consular relations establishment. In-
   violability. Privileges and immunities. Diplomatic
   correspondence. Consular functions in shipping.
   Consular functions in property. Conformity with
   municipal law. Responsibility and liability. Exist-
   ing tribunals.
INTL ORGS: International Court of Justice.
PROCEDURE: Amendment. Ratification. Termination.
PARTIES:
   Austria
   UK Great Britain

107328   Bilateral Exchange   **502 UNTS 177**
SIGNED: 18 Dec 63   FORCE: 1 Jan 64
REGISTERED: 2 Jul 64 UK Great Britain
ARTICLES: 2 LANGUAGE: English.
HEADNOTE: IMPORTATION BOOKS FILMS
TOPIC: Commodity Trade
CONCEPTS: Commodity trade.
TREATY   REF: 470UNTS65;   360UNTS79;
   404UNTS376.
PROCEDURE: Duration. Termination.
PARTIES:
   UK Great Britain
   Yugoslavia

107329   Bilateral Exchange   **502 UNTS 183**
SIGNED: 6 Jan 64   FORCE: 6 Jan 64
REGISTERED: 2 Jul 64 UK Great Britain
ARTICLES: 2 LANGUAGE: English.
HEADNOTE: TRANSFER   UNITED   KINGDOM
   QUOTA
TOPIC: Specific Resources
CONCEPTS: Assets transfer. Ocean resources.
   Fisheries and fishing.
TREATY REF: 486UNTS.
PARTIES:
   Japan
   UK Great Britain

107330   Bilateral Exchange   **502 UNTS 189**
SIGNED: 24 Dec 63   FORCE: 24 Dec 63
REGISTERED: 2 Jul 64 UK Great Britain
ARTICLES: 2 LANGUAGE: English. French.
HEADNOTE: CREATION FOREIGN EXCHANGE OP-
   ERATIONS FUND
TOPIC: Finance
CONCEPTS: Personnel. Financial programs. Inter-
   nal finance.
INTL ORGS: Special Commission.
PROCEDURE: Amendment. Termination.
PARTIES:
   Laos
   UK Great Britain
ANNEX
551 UNTS 336.   Laos.   Amendment   7 Apr 65.
   Force 7 Apr 65.

551 UNTS 336. UK Great Britain. Amendment
   7 Apr 65. Force 7 Apr 65.
565 UNTS 320. UK Great Britain. Amendment
   29 Jan 66. Force 29 Jan 66.
565 UNTS 320. Laos. Amendment 29 Jan 66.
   Force 29 Jan 66.
605 UNTS 364. UK Great Britain. Amendment
   11 Jan 67. Force 11 Jan 67.
605 UNTS 364. Laos. Force 11 Jan 67. Amendment 11 Jan 67.
649 UNTS 360. UK Great Britain. Amendment
   7 Jun 68. Force 7 Jun 68.
649 UNTS 360. Laos. Amendment 7 Jun 68.
   Force 7 Jun 68.

107331   Bilateral Agreement   **502 UNTS 197**
SIGNED: 3 Aug 59   FORCE: 1 Jul 63
REGISTERED: 2 Jul 64 UK Great Britain
ARTICLES: 11 LANGUAGE: English. German.
HEADNOTE: SETTLEMENT DISPUTES ARISING DI-
   RECT PROCUREMENT
TOPIC: Dispute Settlement
CONCEPTS: Recognition and enforcement of legal
   decisions. Mediation and good offices. Proce-
   dure. Existing tribunals. Indemnities and reim-
   bursements. Currency deposits.
INTL ORGS: Arbitration Commission.
PROCEDURE: Ratification.
PARTIES:
   Germany, West
   UK Great Britain

107332   Bilateral Agreement   **502 UNTS 213**
SIGNED: 16 Jan 64   FORCE: 16 Jan 64
REGISTERED: 2 Jul 64 UK Great Britain
ARTICLES: 10 LANGUAGE: English.
HEADNOTE: PUBLIC OFFICERS
TOPIC: Admin Cooperation
CONCEPTS: Definition of terms. Social security.
   Payment schedules.
PARTIES:
   Kenya
   UK Great Britain

107333 Multilateral Convention **502 UNTS 225**
SIGNED: 5 Oct 62   FORCE: 24 Dec 63
REGISTERED: 2 Jul 64 France
ARTICLES: 16 LANGUAGE: French. German.
   Dutch. Swedish.
HEADNOTE: EUROPEAN   ORGANIZATION   AS-
   TRONOMICAL RESEARCH SOUTH HEMISPHERE
TOPIC: IGO Establishment
CONCEPTS: Annex or appendix reference. Ex-
   change of official publications. Funding proce-
   dures. Admission. Establishment. Headquarters
   and facilities. Internal structure.
INTL ORGS: Permanent Court of Arbitration. Eu-
   ropean Organization for Astronomical Research.
   United Nations.
PROCEDURE: Amendment. Accession. Ratifica-
   tion. Registration. Termination.
PARTIES:
   Belgium SIGNED: 5 Oct 62
   France SIGNED: 5 Oct 62 RATIFIED: 24 Dec 63
      FORCE: 24 Dec 63
   Germany, West SIGNED: 5 Oct 62 RATIFIED:
      5 Dec 63 FORCE: 24 Dec 63
   Netherlands   SIGNED: 5 Oct 62   RATIFIED:
      12 Jun 63 FORCE: 24 Dec 63
   Sweden SIGNED: 5 Oct 62 RATIFIED: 5 Oct 63
      FORCE: 24 Dec 63
ANNEX
608 UNTS 377. Belgium. Ratification 2 Oct 67.

107334   Bilateral Agreement   **502 UNTS 287**
SIGNED: 3 Jul 64   FORCE: 3 Jul 64
REGISTERED: 3 Jul 64 United Nations
ARTICLES: 6 LANGUAGE: French.
HEADNOTE: SEMINAR WOMEN FAMILY LAW
TOPIC: Education
CONCEPTS: Definition of terms. Visas. Alien
   status. Human rights. Privileges and immunities.
   General cooperation. Family law. Personnel. Ex-
   change. Indemnities and reimbursements. Ex-
   pense sharing formulae. Conferences.
TREATY REF: 1UNTS15; 33UNTS261.
PROCEDURE: Amendment.
PARTIES:
   United Nations
   Togo

107335 Bilateral Convention **502 UNTS 297**
SIGNED: 30 Mar 62   FORCE: 1 May 64
REGISTERED: 3 Jul 64 Belgium
ARTICLES: 33 LANGUAGE: French.
HEADNOTE: CONTROL FRONTIER
TOPIC: Visas
CONCEPTS: Definition of terms. General provisions. Denial of admission. Conformity with municipal law. General cooperation. Inspection and observation. Personnel. Use of facilities. Railway border crossing. Markers and definitions. Frontier crossing points.
PARTIES:
Belgium
France

	ANNEX	
544 UNTS 380.	France.	Implementation
30 Jul 65. Force 1 Aug 65.		
544 UNTS 380.	Belgium.	Implementation
16 Jul 65. Force 1 Aug 65.		
605 UNTS 368.	France.	Implementation
30 Mar 62.		
605 UNTS 368.	Belgium.	Implementation
30 Mar 62.		
631 UNTS 354.	Belgium.	Implementation
13 Nov 67.		
631 UNTS 354.	France.	Implementation
13 Nov 67.		
651 UNTS 399.	Belgium.	Confirmation
20 Sep 68. Force 1 Oct 68.		
651 UNTS 399. France. Confirmation 20 Sep 68. Force 1 Oct 68.		

107336 Multilateral Agreement **502 UNTS 321**
SIGNED: 28 Jan 64   FORCE: 10 Jul 64
REGISTERED: 10 Jul 64 United Nations
ARTICLES: 6 LANGUAGE: English. Spanish.
HEADNOTE: TECHNICAL ASSISTANCE
TOPIC: Tech Assistance
CONCEPTS: Definition of terms. Previous treaty replacement. Visas. Privileges and immunities. General cooperation. Exchange of information and documents. Licenses and permits. Personnel. Responsibility and liability. Title and deeds. Use of facilities. Exchange. Scholarships and grants. Vocational training. Research and development. Import quotas. Exchange rates and regulations. Expense sharing formulae. Local currency. Domestic obligation. General technical assistance. Materials, equipment and services. IGO status. Conformity with IGO decisions.
INTL ORGS: United Nations Technical Assistance Board.
TREATY REF: 76UNTS132; 1UNTS15; 374UNTS147; 191UNTS271; ETC..
PROCEDURE: Amendment. Termination.
PARTIES:
Guatemala SIGNED: 28 Jan 64 FORCE: 10 Jul 64
FAO (Food Agri) SIGNED: 28 Jan 64 FORCE: 10 Jul 64
IAEA (Atom Energy) SIGNED: 28 Jan 64 FORCE: 10 Jul 64
ICAO (Civil Aviat) SIGNED: 28 Jan 64 FORCE: 10 Jul 64
ILO (Labor Org) SIGNED: 28 Jan 64 FORCE: 10 Jul 64
ITU (Telecommun) SIGNED: 28 Jan 64 FORCE: 10 Jul 64
UNESCO (Educ/Cult) SIGNED: 28 Jan 64 FORCE: 10 Jul 64
United Nations SIGNED: 28 Jan 64 FORCE: 10 Jul 64
UPU (Postal Union) SIGNED: 28 Jan 64 FORCE: 10 Jul 64
WHO (World Health) SIGNED: 28 Jan 64 FORCE: 10 Jul 64
WMO (Meteorology) SIGNED: 28 Jan 64 FORCE: 10 Jul 64

107337 Bilateral Agreement **502 UNTS 343**
SIGNED: 10 Jul 64   FORCE: 10 Jul 64
REGISTERED: 10 Jul 64 United Nations
ARTICLES: 10 LANGUAGE: English.
HEADNOTE: ASSISTANCE
TOPIC: IGO Operations
CONCEPTS: Non-visa travel documents. Diplomatic privileges. Diplomatic missions. Privileges and immunities. Exchange of information and documents. Procedure. Accounting procedures. Domestic obligation. Special status.

INTL ORGS: International Atomic Energy Agency. United Nations. Arbitration Commission.
PROCEDURE: Amendment. Termination.
PARTIES:
Iceland
UN Special Fund

107338 Bilateral Agreement **503 UNTS 3**
SIGNED: 2 Apr 64   FORCE: 2 Apr 64
REGISTERED: 16 Jul 64 Thailand
ARTICLES: 10 LANGUAGE: German. Thai. English.
HEADNOTE: TECHNICAL COOPERATION
TOPIC: Tech Assistance
CONCEPTS: Territorial application. Treaty implementation. Treaty interpretation. Privileges and immunities. Exchange of information and documents. Personnel. Use of facilities. Teacher and student exchange. Institute establishment. Vocational training. Compensation. Tax exemptions. Customs exemptions. Domestic obligation. General technical assistance. Materials, equipment and services.
PROCEDURE: Duration. Future Procedures Contemplated.
PARTIES:
Germany, West
Thailand

107339 Bilateral Exchange **503 UNTS 25**
SIGNED: 18 Apr 63   FORCE: 18 Apr 63
REGISTERED: 20 Jul 64 United Nations
ARTICLES: 2 LANGUAGE: English.
HEADNOTE: UN SECURITY FORCE WEST IRIAN
TOPIC: IGO Operations
CONCEPTS: Treaty implementation. Privileges and immunities. Conformity with municipal law. Ranks and privileges. Jurisdiction. Regional offices. Special status.
TREATY REF: 437UNTS273.
PARTIES:
Pakistan
United Nations

107340 Bilateral Agreement **503 UNTS 41**
SIGNED: 25 Apr 63   FORCE: 24 May 64
REGISTERED: 21 Jul 64 Norway
ARTICLES: 30 LANGUAGE: Norwegian. Spanish.
HEADNOTE: DOUBLE TAXATION INCOME FORTUNE
TOPIC: Taxation
CONCEPTS: Definition of terms. Privileges and immunities. Nationality and citizenship. Exchange of official publications. Negotiation. Teacher and student exchange. Taxation. Equitable taxes. Taxation of immovable property. Tax exemptions. Air transport. Merchant vessels.
PROCEDURE: Duration. Ratification. Termination.
PARTIES:
Norway
Spain

107341 Bilateral Convention **503 UNTS 125**
SIGNED: 8 Nov 63   FORCE: 10 Apr 64
REGISTERED: 21 Jul 64 Czechoslovakia
ARTICLES: 27 LANGUAGE: Czechoslovakian. Mongolian. Russian.
HEADNOTE: CONSULAR
TOPIC: Consul/Citizenship
CONCEPTS: Definition of terms. General consular functions. Diplomatic privileges. Consular relations establishment. Inviolability. Privileges and immunities.
PROCEDURE: Duration. Ratification. Termination.
PARTIES:
Czechoslovakia
Mongolia

107342 Bilateral Agreement **503 UNTS 167**
SIGNED: 23 Jun 64   FORCE: 23 Jun 64
REGISTERED: 21 Jul 64 WHO (World Health)
ARTICLES: 6 LANGUAGE: English.
HEADNOTE: TECHNICAL ADVISORY ASSISTANCE
TOPIC: Tech Assistance
CONCEPTS: Definition of terms. Privileges and immunities. General cooperation. Exchange of information and documents. Personnel. Responsibility and liability. Title and deeds. Exchange. Scholarships and grants. Vocational training. Research and development. Expense sharing for-

mulae. Local currency. Domestic obligation. Special projects. Materials, equipment and services. IGO status. Conformity with IGO decisions.
TREATY REF: 33UNTS261.
PROCEDURE: Amendment. Termination.
PARTIES:
WHO (World Health)
Trinidad/Tobago

107343 Bilateral Agreement **503 UNTS 179**
SIGNED: 10 Jun 63   FORCE: 15 May 64
REGISTERED: 24 Jul 64 Finland
ARTICLES: 16 LANGUAGE: English.
HEADNOTE: CIVIL AIR TRANSPORT
TOPIC: Air Transport
CONCEPTS: Definition of terms. Detailed regulations. Annex or appendix reference. Conformity with municipal law. General cooperation. Procedure. Negotiation. Reexport of goods, etc.. Accounting procedures. Fees and exemptions. Payment schedules. Non-interest rates and fees. Tax exemptions. Customs exemptions. Routes and logistics. Navigational conditions. Permit designation. Air transport. Conditions of airlines operating permission. Overflights and technical stops. Operating authorizations and regulations.
TREATY REF: 15UNTS295.
PROCEDURE: Amendment. Ratification. Termination.
PARTIES:
Finland
Poland

107344 Bilateral Agreement **503 UNTS 195**
SIGNED: 5 Dec 62   FORCE: 22 May 64
REGISTERED: 28 Jul 64 United Nations
ARTICLES: 8 LANGUAGE: French.
HEADNOTE: UNICEF ACTIVITIES
TOPIC: IGO Operations
CONCEPTS: Diplomatic privileges. Privileges and immunities. Exchange of information and documents. Accounting procedures. Freedom of meeting. Assistance to United Nations. Inter-agency agreements.
INTL ORGS: United Nations.
TREATY REF: 1UNTS15.
PROCEDURE: Amendment. Termination.
PARTIES:
Niger
UNICEF (Children)

107345 Bilateral Agreement **503 UNTS 205**
SIGNED: 9 Jun 64   FORCE: 9 Jun 64
REGISTERED: 31 Jul 64 Finland
ARTICLES: 7 LANGUAGE: Finnish. Norwegian.
HEADNOTE: REGARDING FISHING FISHING AREA NAATAMO WATER COURSE
TOPIC: Specific Resources
CONCEPTS: Detailed regulations. Time limit. Fish, wildlife, and natural resources.
PROCEDURE: Denunciation.
PARTIES:
Finland
Norway

107346 Bilateral Agreement **503 UNTS 229**
SIGNED: 1 Jul 64   FORCE: 1 Jul 64
REGISTERED: 1 Aug 64 United Nations
ARTICLES: 8 LANGUAGE: English.
HEADNOTE: UNICEF ACTIVITIES
TOPIC: IGO Operations
CONCEPTS: Diplomatic privileges. Privileges and immunities. Exchange of information and documents. Accounting procedures. Economic assistance. Assistance to United Nations. Inter-agency agreements.
INTL ORGS: United Nations.
TREATY REF: 1UNTS15.
PROCEDURE: Amendment. Termination.
PARTIES:
Malaysia
UNICEF (Children)

107347 Multilateral Exchange **503 UNTS 239**
SIGNED: 3 Aug 64   FORCE: 3 Aug 64
REGISTERED: 3 Aug 64 United Nations
ARTICLES: 2 LANGUAGE: English. Arabic.
HEADNOTE: AMENDING REVISED STANDARD AGREEMENT

TOPIC: Tech Assistance
CONCEPTS: Annex type material.
TREATY REF: 212UNTS263; 274UNTS147.
PARTIES:
　Jordan SIGNED: 3 Aug 64 FORCE: 3 Aug 64
　FAO (Food Agri) SIGNED: 3 Aug 64 FORCE:
　　3 Aug 64
　IAEA (Atom Energy) SIGNED: 3 Aug 64 FORCE:
　　3 Aug 64
　ICAO (Civil Aviat) SIGNED: 3 Aug 64 FORCE:
　　3 Aug 64
　ILO (Labor Org) SIGNED: 3 Aug 64 FORCE:
　　3 Aug 64
　ITU (Telecommun) SIGNED: 3 Aug 64 FORCE:
　　3 Aug 64
　UNESCO (Educ/Cult) SIGNED: 3 Aug 64 FORCE:
　　3 Aug 64
　United Nations SIGNED: 3 Aug 64 FORCE:
　　3 Aug 64
　UPU (Postal Union) SIGNED: 3 Aug 64 FORCE:
　　3 Aug 64
　WHO (World Health) SIGNED: 3 Aug 64 FORCE:
　　3 Aug 64
　WMO (Meteorology) SIGNED: 3 Aug 64 FORCE:
　　3 Aug 64
ANNEX
651 UNTS 400. IMCO (Maritime Org). Accession
19 Nov 68. Force 19 Nov 68.
651 UNTS 400. UNIDO (Industrial). Accession
19 Nov 68. Force 19 Nov 68.

107348　Bilateral Agreement　**503 UNTS 247**
SIGNED: 23 Sep 63　　　FORCE: 6 Apr 64
REGISTERED: 4 Aug 64 IBRD (World Bank)
ARTICLES: 5 LANGUAGE: English.
HEADNOTE: GUARANTEE POWER
TOPIC: IBRD Project
CONCEPTS: Definition of terms. Annex or appen-
dix reference. Exchange of information and doc-
uments. Inspection and observation. Bonds.
Fees and exemptions. Tax exemptions. Domestic
obligation. Terms of loan. Loan regulations. Loan
guarantee. Guarantor non-interference. Hydro-
electric power.
PARTIES:
　IBRD (World Bank)
　UK Great Britain

107349　Bilateral Agreement　**503 UNTS 289**
SIGNED: 28 Oct 63　　　FORCE: 7 Jan 64
REGISTERED: 4 Aug 64 IBRD (World Bank)
ARTICLES: 5 LANGUAGE: English.
HEADNOTE: GUARANTEE RAILWAY
TOPIC: IBRD Project
CONCEPTS: Definition of terms. Annex or appen-
dix reference. Exchange of information and doc-
uments. Inspection and observation. Bonds.
Fees and exemptions. Tax exemptions. Domestic
obligation. Terms of loan. Loan regulations. Loan
guarantee. Railways.
PARTIES:
　IBRD (World Bank)
　Yugoslavia

107350　Bilateral Exchange　**503 UNTS 315**
SIGNED: 24 Dec 63　　　FORCE: 24 Dec 63
REGISTERED: 5 Aug 64 Australia
ARTICLES: 2 LANGUAGE: English. French.
HEADNOTE: FOREIGN EXCHANGE OPERATIONS
FUND
TOPIC: Finance
CONCEPTS: Establishment of commission. Ex-
change rates and regulations. Domestic obliga-
tion.
INTL ORGS: Special Commission.
PROCEDURE: Amendment. Termination.
PARTIES:
　Australia
　Laos
ANNEX
538 UNTS 340. Australia. Amendment 7 Apr 65.
Force 7 Apr 65.

107351　Bilateral Agreement　**504 UNTS 3**
SIGNED: 18 Dec 63　　　FORCE: 2 Jul 64
REGISTERED: 5 Aug 64 IBRD (World Bank)
ARTICLES: 5 LANGUAGE: English.
HEADNOTE: GUARANTEE LIVESTOCK DEVELOP-
MENT
TOPIC: IBRD Project

CONCEPTS: Definition of terms. Annex or appendix reference. Exchange of information and documents. Inspection and observation. Bonds.
Fees and exemptions. Tax exemptions. Domestic
obligation. Agriculture. Terms of loan. Loan regulations. Loan guarantee. Guarantor non-interference.
PARTIES:
　Chile
　IBRD (World Bank)

107352　Bilateral Agreement　**504 UNTS 29**
SIGNED: 18 Dec 63　　　FORCE: 2 Jul 64
REGISTERED: 5 Aug 64 IBRD (World Bank)
ARTICLES: 5 LANGUAGE: English.
HEADNOTE: MILK & MEAT PROCESSING
TOPIC: IBRD Project
CONCEPTS: Conditions. Definition of terms. Ex-
change of information and documents. Inspec-
tion and observation. General property. Public
health. Financial programs. Indemnities and re-
imbursements. Funding procedures. Interest
rates. Tax exemptions. Loan repayment. Terms
of loan. World Bank projects. Loan regulations.
Loan guarantee. Guarantor non-interference.
Plans and standards.
PARTIES:
　Chile
　IBRD (World Bank)

107353　Bilateral Agreement　**504 UNTS 53**
SIGNED: 8 Jan 64　　　FORCE: 3 Apr 64
REGISTERED: 5 Aug 64 IBRD (World Bank)
ARTICLES: 7 LANGUAGE: English.
HEADNOTE: LOAN ROAD
TOPIC: IBRD Project
CONCEPTS: Default remedies. Definition of terms.
Annex or appendix reference. Exchange of infor-
mation and documents. Informational records.
Inspection and observation. Accounting proce-
dures. Bonds. Fees and exemptions. Interest
rates. Tax exemptions. Domestic obligation.
Terms of loan. Loan regulations. Loan guarantee.
Guarantor non-interference. Roads and high-
ways.
PARTIES:
　Liberia
　IBRD (World Bank)
ANNEX
549 UNTS 348. IBRD (World Bank). Amendment
24 Aug 65. Force 14 Oct 65.
549 UNTS 348. Liberia. Amendment 24 Aug 65.
Force 14 Oct 65.

107354　Bilateral Agreement　**504 UNTS 73**
SIGNED: 11 Mar 64　　　FORCE: 3 Apr 64
REGISTERED: 5 Aug 64 IBRD (World Bank)
ARTICLES: 5 LANGUAGE: English.
HEADNOTE: GUARANTEE AGREEMENT
TOPIC: IBRD Project
CONCEPTS: Definition of terms. Annex or appen-
dix reference. Exchange of information and doc-
uments. Inspection and observation. Bonds.
Fees and exemptions. Tax exemptions. Domestic
obligation. Terms of loan. Loan regulations. Loan
guarantee. Guarantor non-interference.
PARTIES:
　IBRD (World Bank)
　Thailand

107355　Bilateral Agreement　**504 UNTS 107**
SIGNED: 11 Jun 57　　　FORCE: 1 Apr 58
REGISTERED: 6 Aug 64 Czechoslovakia
ARTICLES: 27 LANGUAGE: Czechoslovakian. Serbo-Croat.
HEADNOTE: VETERINARY COOPERATION
TOPIC: Sanitation
CONCEPTS: Definition of terms. Detailed regulations. Exceptions and exemptions. General cooperation. Exchange of information and documents. Domestic legislation. Negotiation. Specialists exchange. Border control. Disease
control. Insect control. Veterinary. Teacher and
student exchange. Vocational training. Research
results. Scientific exchange. Research and development. Trade procedures. Currency. General
technical assistance. Materials, equipment and
services. Publications exchange. Conferences.
PROCEDURE: Denunciation. Duration. Renewal or
Revival.

PARTIES:
　Czechoslovakia
　Yugoslavia

107356　Bilateral Agreement　**504 UNTS 151**
SIGNED: 5 Oct 63　　　FORCE: 13 Mar 64
REGISTERED: 6 Aug 64 Czechoslovakia
ARTICLES: 5 LANGUAGE: Czechoslovakian. Ser-
bo-Croat.
HEADNOTE: PUBLIC HEALTH
TOPIC: Sanitation
CONCEPTS: Detailed regulations. General cooper-
ation. Exchange of official publications. Ex-
change of information and documents. Informa-
tional records. Domestic legislation. Establish-
ment of commission. Specialists exchange.
Public health. Exchange. Teacher and student
exchange. Scientific exchange. Research and
development. Indemnities and reimbursements.
INTL ORGS: Special Commission.
PROCEDURE: Duration. Ratification. Renewal or
Revival. Termination.
PARTIES:
　Czechoslovakia
　Yugoslavia

107357　Bilateral Instrument　**504 UNTS 163**
SIGNED: 23 Jun 50　　　FORCE: 23 Jun 50
REGISTERED: 6 Aug 64 Czechoslovakia
ARTICLES: 1 LANGUAGE: Czechoslovakian. Ger-
man.
HEADNOTE: AIMS PURPOSES POLICY TWO
COUNTRIES
TOPIC: General Amity
CONCEPTS: Peaceful relations.
PARTIES:
　Czechoslovakia
　Germany, East

107358　Bilateral Agreement　**504 UNTS 173**
SIGNED: 24 Oct 55　　　FORCE: 15 Feb 56
REGISTERED: 6 Aug 64 Czechoslovakia
ARTICLES: 26 LANGUAGE: Czechoslovakian. German.
HEADNOTE: RAILWAY TRAFFIC
TOPIC: Land Transport
CONCEPTS: Treaty implementation. Frontier formalities. Passports non-diplomatic. Non-visa
travel documents. Conformity with municipal
law. General cooperation. Inspection and obser-
vation. Personnel. Responsibility and liability.
Use of facilities. Humanitarian matters. Compen-
sation. Indemnities and reimbursements. Cur-
rency. Fees and exemptions. National treatment.
Tax exemptions. Customs duties. Customs exemptions. Routes and logistics. Operating authorizations and regulations. Railway border crossing. Railways. Regulations. Services. Telegrams.
Markers and definitions.
PROCEDURE: Denunciation. Ratification.
PARTIES:
　Czechoslovakia
　Germany, East

107359　Bilateral Agreement　**504 UNTS 221**
SIGNED: 26 Jun 58　　　FORCE: 16 Dec 58
REGISTERED: 6 Aug 64 Czechoslovakia
ARTICLES: 6 LANGUAGE: Czechoslovakian. Ger-
man.
HEADNOTE: INVENTIONS TRADEMARKS
TOPIC: Patents/Copyrights
CONCEPTS: Non-prejudice to third party. Confor-
mity with municipal law. Trademarks. Laws and
formalities.
INTL ORGS: International Union for the Protection
of Industrial Property.
TREATY REF: 74LTS289.
PARTIES:
　Czechoslovakia
　Germany, East

107360　Bilateral Agreement　**504 UNTS 231**
SIGNED: 16 Apr 54　　　FORCE: 16 May 54
REGISTERED: 6 Aug 64 Czechoslovakia
ARTICLES: 35 LANGUAGE: Slovak. Hungarian.
HEADNOTE: FRONTIER WATERCOURSES
TOPIC: Specific Resources
CONCEPTS: Definition of terms. Previous treaty re-
placement. Previous treaties adherence. Ex-

change of official publications. Inspection and observation. Establishment of commission. Indemnities and reimbursements. Payment schedules. Debt settlement. Customs exemptions. Materials, equipment and services. Plans and standards. Hydro-electric power. Frontier waterways.
INTL ORGS: Special Commission.
TREATY REF: 41UNTS135; 26UNTS119; 189LTS403.
PROCEDURE: Denunciation.
PARTIES:
Czechoslovakia
Hungary

107361   Bilateral Agreement   **504 UNTS 279**
SIGNED: 30 Aug 55   FORCE: 28 Dec 55
REGISTERED: 6 Aug 64 Czechoslovakia
ARTICLES: 8 LANGUAGE: Czechoslovakian. German.
HEADNOTE: VETERINARY MEDICINE
TOPIC: Sanitation
CONCEPTS: Standardization. General cooperation. Exchange of information and documents. Informational records. Domestic legislation. Border control. Disease control. Veterinary. Exchange. Teacher and student exchange. Vocational training. Scientific exchange. Indemnities and reimbursements. Materials, equipment and services. Publications exchange.
PROCEDURE: Denunciation. Duration. Future Procedures Contemplated. Ratification. Renewal or Revival.
PARTIES:
Czechoslovakia
Germany, East

107362   Bilateral Agreement   **505 UNTS 3**
SIGNED: 12 Mar 64   FORCE: 20 Apr 64
REGISTERED: 7 Aug 64 IBRD (World Bank)
ARTICLES: 7 LANGUAGE: English.
HEADNOTE: LOAN TRANSMISSION PROJECT
TOPIC: IBRD Project
CONCEPTS: Default remedies. Definition of terms. Annex or appendix reference. Exchange of information and documents. Informational records. Inspection and observation. Accounting procedures. Bonds. Fees and exemptions. Interest rates. Tax exemptions. Domestic obligation. Terms of loan. Loan regulations. Loan guarantee. Guarantor non-interference. Hydro-electric power.
PARTIES:
New Zealand
IBRD (World Bank)

107363   Bilateral Agreement   **505 UNTS 21**
SIGNED: 22 Apr 64   FORCE: 24 Jun 64
REGISTERED: 7 Aug 64 IBRD (World Bank)
ARTICLES: 5 LANGUAGE: English.
HEADNOTE: GUARANTEE EXPRESSWAY
TOPIC: IBRD Project
CONCEPTS: Definition of terms. Annex or appendix reference. Exchange of information and documents. Inspection and observation. Bonds. Fees and exemptions. Tax exemptions. Domestic obligation. Terms of loan. Loan regulations. Loan guarantee. Guarantor non-interference. Roads and highways.
PARTIES:
Japan
IBRD (World Bank)

107364   Bilateral Agreement   **505 UNTS 51**
SIGNED: 8 May 64   FORCE: 3 Jul 64
REGISTERED: 7 Aug 64 IBRD (World Bank)
ARTICLES: 5 LANGUAGE: English.
HEADNOTE: GUARANTEE POWER
TOPIC: IBRD Project
CONCEPTS: Definition of terms. Annex or appendix reference. Exchange of information and documents. Inspection and observation. Bonds. Fees and exemptions. Tax exemptions. Domestic obligation. Terms of loan. Loan regulations. Loan guarantee. Guarantor non-interference. Hydro-electric power.
PARTIES:
Ethiopia
IBRD (World Bank)

107365   Bilateral Exchange   **505 UNTS 79**
SIGNED: 14 Mar 63   FORCE: 14 Mar 63
REGISTERED: 10 Aug 64 USA (United States)
ARTICLES: 2 LANGUAGE: English. Indonesian.
HEADNOTE: PEACE CORPS PROGRAM
TOPIC: General Aid
CONCEPTS: Privileges and immunities. General cooperation. Personnel. General cultural cooperation. Import quotas. Banking. Financial programs. Aid missions. Volunteer programs.
PARTIES:
Indonesia
USA (United States)

107366   Bilateral Agreement   **505 UNTS 87**
SIGNED: 14 Nov 63   FORCE: 14 Nov 63
REGISTERED: 10 Aug 64 USA (United States)
ARTICLES: 6 LANGUAGE: English. Spanish.
HEADNOTE: AGRI COMMOD TITLE I
TOPIC: US Agri Commod Aid
CONCEPTS: General provisions. Annex or appendix reference. Exchange of information and documents. Reexport of goods, etc.. Exchange rates and regulations. Transportation costs. Local currency. Commodities schedule. Purchase authorization. Surplus commodities. Mutual consultation.
PARTIES:
Paraguay
USA (United States)

107367   Bilateral Agreement   **505 UNTS 107**
SIGNED: 12 Jun 64   FORCE: 11 Aug 64
REGISTERED: 11 Aug 64 Finland
ARTICLES: 5 LANGUAGE: Finnish. English. Afrikaans.
HEADNOTE: RECOGNITION TONNAGE CERTIFICATES MERCHANT SHIPS
TOPIC: Water Transport
CONCEPTS: Territorial application. Previous treaty replacement. Recognition of legal documents. Registration certificate. Merchant vessels. Tonnage.
TREATY REF: 28LTS511; 230UNTS121.
PROCEDURE: Termination.
PARTIES:
Finland
South Africa

107368   Bilateral Exchange   **505 UNTS 117**
SIGNED: 4 Dec 63   FORCE: 4 Dec 63
REGISTERED: 11 Aug 64 USA (United States)
ARTICLES: 2 LANGUAGE: English.
HEADNOTE: TRADE COTTON TEXTILES
TOPIC: Commodity Trade
CONCEPTS: Detailed regulations. Treaty implementation. Annex or appendix reference. General cooperation. Exchange of information and documents. Trade agencies. Commodity trade. Delivery schedules. Quotas.
TREATY REF: 471UNTS296.
PROCEDURE: Amendment. Duration. Termination.
PARTIES:
United Arab Rep
USA (United States)

107369   Bilateral Exchange   **505 UNTS 131**
SIGNED: 30 Nov 63   FORCE: 30 Nov 63
REGISTERED: 11 Aug 64 USA (United States)
ARTICLES: 2 LANGUAGE: English. Spanish.
HEADNOTE: RESEARCH TRAINING PROGRAM SOLID PHYSICS
TOPIC: Scientific Project
CONCEPTS: Responsibility and liability. Research and scientific projects. Research results. Nuclear research. Research and development. Payment schedules. Transportation costs. Materials, equipment and services. Peaceful use.
PARTIES:
Argentina
USA (United States)

107370   Bilateral Agreement   **505 UNTS 139**
SIGNED: 29 Sep 48   FORCE: 4 Nov 48
REGISTERED: 11 Aug 64 USA (United States)
ARTICLES: 12 LANGUAGE: English. Spanish.
HEADNOTE: AIR TRANSPORT SERVICES
TOPIC: Air Transport
CONCEPTS: Exceptions and exemptions. Annex or

appendix reference. Non-prejudice to third party. Conformity with municipal law. Licenses and permits. Recognition of legal documents. Use of facilities. Arbitration. Procedure. Special tribunals. Competence of tribunal. Expense sharing formulae. Fees and exemptions. Most favored nation clause. National treatment. Customs duties. Customs exemptions. Competency certificate. Routes and logistics. Navigational conditions. Permit designation. Air transport. Airport facilities. Airworthiness certificates. Conditions of airlines operating permission. Operating authorizations and regulations. Licenses and certificates of nationality.
INTL ORGS: International Civil Aviation Organization. Arbitration Commission.
TREATY REF: INTL CIVIL AIR CONF, CHICAGO,-NOV-DEC44,DOC.2187.
PROCEDURE: Amendment. Future Procedures Contemplated. Ratification. Registration. Termination.
PARTIES:
Bolivia
USA (United States)

107371   Bilateral Exchange   **505 UNTS 159**
SIGNED: 3 Jan 64   FORCE: 3 Jan 64
REGISTERED: 11 Aug 64 USA (United States)
ARTICLES: 2 LANGUAGE: English.
HEADNOTE: RADIO COMMUNICATIONS
TOPIC: Gen Communications
CONCEPTS: Exchange of information and documents. Personnel. Facilities and equipment. Services.
PARTIES:
Australia
USA (United States)
                    ANNEX
545 UNTS 370. Australia. Amendment 12 Apr 65. Force 12 Apr 65.
545 UNTS 370. USA (United States). Amendment 12 Apr 65. Force 12 Apr 65.

107372   Bilateral Exchange   **505 UNTS 165**
SIGNED: 8 Jan 64   FORCE: 8 Jan 64
REGISTERED: 11 Aug 64 USA (United States)
ARTICLES: 2 LANGUAGE: English.
HEADNOTE: INVESTMENT GUARANTIES
TOPIC: Claims and Debts
CONCEPTS: General cooperation. Public information. Arbitration. Procedure. Existing tribunals. Negotiation. Currency. Claims and settlements. Private investment guarantee.
INTL ORGS: International Court of Justice. Arbitration Commission.
PARTIES:
Somalia
USA (United States)

107373   Bilateral Agreement   **505 UNTS 173**
SIGNED: 9 Jan 64   FORCE: 9 Jan 64
REGISTERED: 11 Aug 64 USA (United States)
ARTICLES: 6 LANGUAGE: English. French.
HEADNOTE: AGRI COMMOD TITLE I
TOPIC: US Agri Commod Aid
CONCEPTS: General provisions. Annex or appendix reference. Exchange of information and documents. Reexport of goods, etc.. Exchange rates and regulations. Transportation costs. Local currency. Commodities schedule. Purchase authorization. Surplus commodities. Mutual consultation.
PARTIES:
USA (United States)
Vietnam, South
                    ANNEX
526 UNTS 369. USA (United States). Amendment 14 Apr 64. Force 14 Apr 64.
526 UNTS 369. Vietnam, South. Amendment 14 Apr 64. Force 14 Apr 64.
529 UNTS 384. USA (United States). Amendment 24 Jul 64. Force 24 Jul 64.
529 UNTS 384. Vietnam, South. Amendment 24 Jul 64. Force 24 Jul 64.
531 UNTS 417. Vietnam, South. Amendment 30 Nov 64. Force 30 Nov 64.
531 UNTS 417. USA (United States). Amendment 30 Nov 64. Force 30 Nov 64.

107374 Bilateral Convention **505 UNTS 185**
SIGNED: 29 Aug 63 FORCE: 14 Jan 64
REGISTERED: 11 Aug 64 USA (United States)
ARTICLES: 12 LANGUAGE: English. Spanish.
HEADNOTE: PROBLEM CHAMIZAL
TOPIC: Territory Boundary
CONCEPTS: Annex or appendix reference. Title
and deeds. Indemnities and reimbursements. Financial programs. Markers and definitions. Frontier waterways.
INTL ORGS: Special Commission.
TREATY REF: 3UNTS313.
PROCEDURE: Ratification.
PARTIES:
Mexico
USA (United States)

107375 Bilateral Agreement **505 UNTS 215**
SIGNED: 3 Feb 64 FORCE: 3 Feb 64
REGISTERED: 11 Aug 64 USA (United States)
ARTICLES: 6 LANGUAGE: English. Polish.
HEADNOTE: AGRI COMMOD TITLE I
TOPIC: US Agri Commod Aid
CONCEPTS: General provisions. Annex or appendix reference. Exchange of information and documents. Reexport of goods, etc.. Exchange rates and regulations. Transportation costs. Local currency. Commodities schedule. Purchase authorization. Surplus commodities. Mutual consultation.
PARTIES:
Poland
USA (United States)

107376 Bilateral Agreement **505 UNTS 245**
SIGNED: 3 Feb 64 FORCE: 3 Feb 64
REGISTERED: 11 Aug 64 USA (United States)
ARTICLES: 6 LANGUAGE: English. Polish.
HEADNOTE: AGRI COMMOD TITLE I
TOPIC: US Agri Commod Aid
CONCEPTS: General provisions. Annex or appendix reference. Exchange of information and documents. Reexport of goods, etc.. Exchange rates and regulations. Transportation costs. Local currency. Commodities schedule. Purchase authorization. Surplus commodities. Mutual consultation.
PARTIES:
Poland
USA (United States)

107377 Bilateral Agreement **505 UNTS 263**
SIGNED: 20 Nov 62 FORCE: 24 Jan 64
REGISTERED: 11 Aug 64 USA (United States)
ARTICLES: 13 LANGUAGE: English. German.
HEADNOTE: EDUCATIONAL PROGRAM
TOPIC: Education
CONCEPTS: Previous treaty replacement. Friendship and amity. Privileges and immunities. Standardization. Conformity with municipal law. Inspection and observation. Personnel. Exchange. Commissions and foundations. Teacher and student exchange. Professorships. Research and development. Currency. Exchange rates and regulations. Expense sharing formulae. Financial programs. Funding procedures. Special status. Status of experts.
INTL ORGS: Special Commission.
TREATY REF: 33UNTS261; 165UNTS167.
PROCEDURE: Amendment.
PARTIES:
Germany, West
USA (United States)

107378 Bilateral Exchange **505 UNTS 283**
SIGNED: 24 Feb 64 FORCE: 24 Feb 64
REGISTERED: 11 Aug 64 USA (United States)
ARTICLES: 2 LANGUAGE: English.
HEADNOTE: TRADE COTTON TEXTILES
TOPIC: Commodity Trade
CONCEPTS: Detailed regulations. General cooperation. Exchange of information and documents. Trade agencies. Commodity trade. Delivery schedules. Quotas.
PROCEDURE: Amendment. Duration. Termination.
PARTIES:
Philippines
USA (United States)

ANNEX
573 UNTS 342. USA (United States). Amendment
5 Oct 65. Force 5 Oct 65.
573 UNTS 342. Philippines. Amendment
5 Oct 65. Force 5 Oct 65.

107379 Bilateral Agreement **506 UNTS 3**
SIGNED: 11 Jun 64 FORCE: 27 Jul 64
REGISTERED: 12 Aug 64 IDA (Devel Assoc)
ARTICLES: 7 LANGUAGE: English.
HEADNOTE: DEVELOPMENT CREDIT HIGHWAY
TOPIC: Non-IBRD Project
CONCEPTS: Definition of terms. Detailed regulations. Previous treaty amendment. Exchange of information and documents. Informational records. Accounting procedures. Currency. Interest rates. Tax exemptions. Credit provisions. Loan repayment. Terms of loan. Plans and standards. IDA development project. Roads and highways.
PARTIES:
Pakistan
IDA (Devel Assoc)

107380 Bilateral Agreement **506 UNTS 31**
SIGNED: 9 Jun 64 FORCE: 16 Jul 64
REGISTERED: 12 Aug 64 IDA (Devel Assoc)
ARTICLES: 6 LANGUAGE: English.
HEADNOTE: DEVELOPMENT CREDIT INDUSTRIAL IMPORTS
TOPIC: Non-IBRD Project
CONCEPTS: Definition of terms. Detailed regulations. Previous treaty amendment. Exchange of information and documents. Informational records. Accounting procedures. Currency. Interest rates. Tax exemptions. Credit provisions. Loan repayment. Terms of loan. Plans and standards. IDA development project. Industry.
PARTIES:
India
IDA (Devel Assoc)

107381 Bilateral Agreement **506 UNTS 51**
SIGNED: 12 Dec 63 FORCE: 17 Apr 64
REGISTERED: 12 Aug 64 IDA (Devel Assoc)
ARTICLES: 7 LANGUAGE: English.
HEADNOTE: DEVELOPMENT CREDIT WATER SUPPLY
TOPIC: Non-IBRD Project
CONCEPTS: Definition of terms. Detailed regulations. Previous treaty amendment. Exchange of information and documents. Informational records. Accounting procedures. Interest rates. Tax exemptions. Credit provisions. Loan repayment. Terms of loan. Plans and standards. IDA development project. Natural resources.
PARTIES:
Jordan
IDA (Devel Assoc)

107382 Bilateral Agreement **506 UNTS 91**
SIGNED: 5 Feb 64 FORCE: 16 Apr 64
REGISTERED: 12 Aug 64 IDA (Devel Assoc)
ARTICLES: 6 LANGUAGE: English.
HEADNOTE: DEVELOPMENT CREDIT HIGHWAY
TOPIC: Non-IBRD Project
CONCEPTS: Detailed regulations. Previous treaty amendment. Exchange of information and documents. Informational records. Accounting procedures. Currency. Interest rates. Tax exemptions. Credit provisions. Loan repayment. Terms of loan. Plans and standards. IDA development project. Roads and highways.
PARTIES:
IDA (Devel Assoc)
Tanganyika

107383 Multilateral Agreement **506 UNTS 108**
SIGNED: 23 Jun 64 FORCE: 23 Jun 64
REGISTERED: 14 Aug 64 United Nations
ARTICLES: 6 LANGUAGE: English.
HEADNOTE: TECHNICAL ASSISTANCE
TOPIC: Tech Assistance
CONCEPTS: Definition of terms. Privileges and immunities. General cooperation. Exchange of information and documents. Personnel. Responsibility and liability. Title and deeds. Use of facilities. Exchange. Scholarships and grants. Vocational training. Research and development.

Exchange rates and regulations. Expense sharing formulae. Local currency. Domestic obligation. General technical assistance. Materials, equipment and services. IGO status. Conformity with IGO decisions.
TREATY REF: 76UNTS132; 1UNTS15; 33UNTS261; 374UNTS147.
PROCEDURE: Amendment. Termination.
PARTIES:
State/IGO Group
Nigeria
FAO (Food Agri)
IAEA (Atom Energy)
ICAO (Civil Aviat)
ILO (Labor Org)
IMCO (Maritime Org)
ITU (Telecommun)
UNESCO (Educ/Cult)
United Nations
UPU (Postal Union)
WHO (World Health)
WMO (Meteorology)
ANNEX
608 UNTS 378. IMCO (Maritime Org). Accession
25 Aug 67. Force 25 Aug 67.

107384 Multilateral Agreement **506 UNTS 125**
SIGNED: 23 Nov 57 FORCE: 27 Dec 61
REGISTERED: 20 Aug 64 Netherlands
ARTICLES: 21 LANGUAGE: English. French.
HEADNOTE: REFUGEE SEAMEN
TOPIC: Refugees
CONCEPTS: Definition of terms. Emergencies. Territorial application. Resident permits. Non-visa travel documents. Assistance. Refugees. Procedure. Existing tribunals.
INTL ORGS: International Court of Justice. Office of the United Nations High Commissioner for Refugees.
PROCEDURE: Accession. Denunciation. Ratification.
PARTIES:
Belgium SIGNED: 27 Nov 57 RATIFIED: 16 May 60 FORCE: 27 Dec 61
Denmark SIGNED: 23 Nov 57 RATIFIED: 2 Sep 59 FORCE: 27 Dec 61
France SIGNED: 23 Nov 57 RATIFIED: 20 Jun 58 FORCE: 27 Dec 61
Germany, West Berlin RATIFIED: 28 Sep 61 FORCE: 27 Dec 61
Germany, West SIGNED: 25 Nov 57 RATIFIED: 28 Sep 61 FORCE: 27 Dec 61
Ireland RATIFIED: 21 Apr 64 FORCE: 20 Jul 64
Monaco RATIFIED: 11 Apr 60 FORCE: 27 Dec 61
Morocco RATIFIED: 20 May 59 FORCE: 27 Dec 61
Netherlands SIGNED: 23 Nov 57 RATIFIED: 27 Aug 59 FORCE: 27 Dec 61
Norway SIGNED: 23 Nov 57 RATIFIED: 28 May 59 FORCE: 27 Dec 61
Sweden SIGNED: 10 Feb 58 RATIFIED: 28 May 59 FORCE: 27 Dec 61
Switzerland RATIFIED: 12 Dec 62 FORCE: 12 Mar 63
UK Great Britain Antigua RATIFIED: 17 Jan 64 FORCE: 16 Apr 64
UK Great Britain British Guiana RATIFIED: 17 Jan 61 FORCE: 16 Apr 64
UK Great Britain British Honduras RATIFIED: 24 Jul 61 FORCE: 27 Dec 61
UK Great Britain Brit Solomon Is RATIFIED: 24 Jul 61 FORCE: 27 Dec 61
UK Great Britain Brit Virgin Islands RATIFIED: 8 Jul 64 FORCE: 6 Oct 64
UK Great Britain Brunei RATIFIED: 17 Jan 64 FORCE: 16 Apr 64
UK Great Britain Dominican Republic RATIFIED: 24 Jul 61 FORCE: 27 Dec 61
UK Great Britain Falkland Islands RATIFIED: 24 Jul 61 FORCE: 27 Dec 61
UK Great Britain Fiji Islands RATIFIED: 24 Jul 61 FORCE. 27 Dec 61
UK Great Britain Gambia RATIFIED: 24 Jul 61 FORCE: 27 Dec 61
UK Great Britain Gilbert Islands RATIFIED: 24 Jul 61 FORCE: 27 Dec 61
UK Great Britain Grenada RATIFIED: 24 Jul 61 FORCE: 27 Dec 61
UK Great Britain Guernsey Island RATIFIED: 14 Oct 59 FORCE: 27 Dec 61
UK Great Britain Jamaica RATIFIED: 24 Jul 61 FORCE: 27 Dec 61

UK Great Britain Jersey Island RATIFIED:
14 Oct 59 FORCE: 27 Dec 61
UK Great Britain Martinique RATIFIED:
17 Jan 61 FORCE: 16 Apr 64
UK Great Britain Mauritius RATIFIED: 24 Jul 61
FORCE: 27 Dec 61
UK Great Britain SIGNED: 23 Nov 57 RATIFIED:
9 Aug 58 FORCE: 27 Dec 61
UK Great Britain Isle of Man RATIFIED: 14 Oct 59
FORCE: 27 Dec 61
UK Great Britain Seychelles RATIFIED: 24 Jul 61
FORCE: 27 Dec 61
UK Great Britain St. Christopher RATIFIED:
17 Jan 61 FORCE: 16 Apr 64
UK Great Britain St. Helena RATIFIED: 24 Jul 61
FORCE: 27 Dec 61
UK Great Britain St. Lucia RATIFIED: 17 Jan 61
FORCE: 16 Apr 64
UK Great Britain St. Vincent RATIFIED: 24 Jul 61
FORCE: 27 Dec 61
Yugoslavia   RATIFIED: 4 Dec 63   FORCE:
3 Mar 64

107385   Bilateral Exchange   **506 UNTS 141**
SIGNED: 27 Apr 59   FORCE: 18 Oct 60
REGISTERED: 20 Aug 64 Netherlands
ARTICLES: 2 LANGUAGE: English.
HEADNOTE: TECHNICAL FINANCIAL ASSIS-
TANCE DESALINIZATION SALE SOILS
TOPIC: Tech Assistance
CONCEPTS: Annex or appendix reference. Finan-
cial programs. General technical assistance. Ag-
riculture. Special projects.
PARTIES:
India
Netherlands

107386   Bilateral Exchange   **506 UNTS 153**
SIGNED: 16 Jan 59   FORCE: 19 Oct 60
REGISTERED: 20 Aug 64 Netherlands
ARTICLES: 2 LANGUAGE: English.
HEADNOTE: ESTABLISHMENT TRAINING CENTER
TOPIC: Tech Assistance
CONCEPTS: Annex or appendix reference. Insti-
tute establishment.
INTL ORGS: Food and Agricultural Organization of
the United Nations.
PARTIES:
India
Netherlands

107387 Multilateral Agreement **506 UNTS 177**
SIGNED: 25 Jul 62   FORCE: 25 Jul 62
REGISTERED: 20 Aug 64 COMECON (Econ Aid)
ARTICLES: 13 LANGUAGE: Russian.
HEADNOTE: ESTABLISHMENT CENTRAL CON-
TROL OFFICE COMBINED POWER SYSTEMS
TOPIC: Specific Property
CONCEPTS: Privileges and immunities. Operating
agencies. Accounting procedures. Indemnities
and reimbursements. Hydro-electric power. Fa-
cilities and property.
INTL ORGS: Council for Mutual Economic Assis-
tance. Central Control Office for Electric Power
Systems.
TREATY REF: 368UNTS237.
PROCEDURE: Amendment. Accession. Registra-
tion.
PARTIES:
Bulgaria SIGNED: 25 Jul 62 FORCE: 25 Jul 62
Czechoslovakia   SIGNED: 25 Jul 62   FORCE:
25 Jul 62
Germany, East SIGNED: 25 Jul 62 FORCE:
25 Jul 62
Hungary SIGNED: 25 Jul 62 FORCE: 25 Jul 62
Poland SIGNED: 25 Jul 62 FORCE: 25 Jul 62
Romania SIGNED: 25 Jul 62 FORCE: 25 Jul 62
USSR (Soviet Union) SIGNED: 25 Jul 62 FORCE:
25 Jul 62

107388 Multilateral Agreement **506 UNTS 197**
SIGNED: 23 Oct 63   FORCE: 18 May 64
REGISTERED: 20 Aug 64 COMECON (Econ Aid)
ARTICLES: 16 LANGUAGE: Russian.
HEADNOTE: STRENGTHENING COMMERCIAL &
ECONOMIC TIES FINANCIAL ETC. FACTOR
TOPIC: IGO Establishment
CONCEPTS: Detailed regulations. Treaty imple-
mentation. Previous treaty replacement. Privi-
leges and immunities. General cooperation. Ex-

change of information and documents. Informational records. Legal protection and assistance.
Establishment of trade relations. Import quotas.
Accounting procedures. Banking. Balance of
payments. Currency. Monetary and gold transfers. Currency deposits. Funding procedures. Interest rates. Payment schedules. Credit provisions. Loan repayment. Subsidiary organ. Procedure. Headquarters and facilities. Extension of
functions.
INTL ORGS: International Bank for Economic Cooperation. Council for Mutual Economic Assistance.
TREATY REF: MULTILATERAL CLEARING 20JU-
NE57.
PROCEDURE: Amendment. Accession. Denunciation. Ratification.
PARTIES:
Bulgaria   SIGNED: 22 Oct 63   RATIFIED:
10 Jan 64 FORCE: 18 May 64
Czechoslovakia SIGNED: 22 Oct 63 RATIFIED:
12 Mar 64 FORCE: 18 May 64
Germany, East SIGNED: 22 Oct 63 RATIFIED:
27 Mar 64 FORCE: 18 May 64
Hungary SIGNED: 22 Oct 63 RATIFIED: 4 Dec 63
FORCE: 18 May 64
Mongolia   SIGNED: 22 Oct 63   RATIFIED:
28 Dec 63 FORCE: 18 May 64
Poland   SIGNED: 22 Oct 63   RATIFIED:
23 May 64 FORCE: 18 May 64
Romania   SIGNED: 22 Oct 63   RATIFIED:
18 May 64 FORCE: 18 May 64
USSR (Soviet Union) SIGNED: 22 Oct 63 RATI-
FIED: 5 Feb 64 FORCE: 18 May 64

107389   Bilateral Agreement   **506 UNTS 257**
SIGNED: 30 Mar 63   FORCE: 26 Oct 63
REGISTERED: 20 Aug 64 COMECON (Econ Aid)
ARTICLES: 8 LANGUAGE: Russian. Bulgarian.
HEADNOTE: OFFICES FUNCTIONS COUNCIL MU-
TUAL ECONOMIC ASSISTANCE
TOPIC: IGO Operations
CONCEPTS: Economic assistance. Headquarters
and facilities. Special status.
PARTIES:
Bulgaria
COMECON (Econ Aid)

107390   Bilateral Agreement   **506 UNTS 281**
SIGNED: 28 Feb 63   FORCE: 10 Jun 63
REGISTERED: 20 Aug 64 COMECON (Econ Aid)
ARTICLES: 8 LANGUAGE: Russian. Hungarian.
HEADNOTE: COUNCIL   MUTUAL   ASSISTANCE
HUNGARY
TOPIC: IGO Operations
CONCEPTS: Definition of terms. Annex or appen-
dix reference. Non-visa travel documents. Privi-
leges and immunities. Exchange of official publi-
cations. Juridical personality. Procedure. Fund-
ing procedures. Domestic obligation. IGO
obligations.
TREATY REF: 328UNTS253.
PROCEDURE: Amendment.
PARTIES:
Hungary
COMECON (Econ Aid)

107391   Bilateral Agreement   **506 UNTS 303**
SIGNED: 22 Feb 63   FORCE: 1 Aug 63
REGISTERED: 20 Aug 64 COMECON (Econ Aid)
ARTICLES: 8 LANGUAGE: Russian. Polish.
HEADNOTE: COUNCIL MUTUAL ECONOMIC AS-
SISTANCE POLAND
TOPIC: IGO Operations
CONCEPTS: Definition of terms. Annex or appen-
dix reference. Non-visa travel documents. Privi-
leges and immunities. Exchange of official publi-
cations. Juridical personality. Procedure. Fund-
ing procedures. Domestic obligation. Regional
offices. Mutual consultation.
TREATY REF: 368UNTS253.
PROCEDURE: Amendment. Denunciation.
PARTIES:
Poland
COMECON (Econ Aid)

107392   Bilateral Agreement   **506 UNTS 325**
SIGNED: 7 Dec 61   FORCE: 5 Mar 62
REGISTERED: 20 Aug 64 COMECON (Econ Aid)
ARTICLES: 9 LANGUAGE: Russian.

HEADNOTE: LOCATION INSTITUTIONS
TOPIC: IGO Operations
CONCEPTS: Definition of terms. Non-visa travel
documents. Privileges and immunities. Ex-
change of official publications. Exchange of in-
formation and documents. Procedure. Funding
procedures. Domestic obligation. Regional of-
fices. Mutual consultation.
TREATY REF: 368UNTS253.
PROCEDURE: Amendment.
PARTIES:
COMECON (Econ Aid)
USSR (Soviet Union)

107393   Bilateral Agreement   **506 UNTS 345**
SIGNED: 20 Jul 62   FORCE: 3 Nov 62
REGISTERED: 20 Aug 64 COMECON (Econ Aid)
ARTICLES: 8 LANGUAGE: Russian. Czechoslo-
vakian.
HEADNOTE: COUNCIL MUTUAL ECONOMIC AS-
SISTANCE CZECHOSLOVAKIA
TOPIC: IGO Operations
CONCEPTS: Definition of terms. Privileges and im-
munities. Exchange of official publications. Proce-
dure. Funding procedures. Domestic obligation.
Regional offices. Mutual consultation.
PROCEDURE: Amendment.
PARTIES:
Czechoslovakia
COMECON (Econ Aid)

107394   Bilateral Agreement   **507 UNTS 3**
SIGNED: 26 Dec 63   FORCE: 4 Jun 64
REGISTERED: 24 Aug 64 IDA (Devel Assoc)
ARTICLES: 8 LANGUAGE: English.
HEADNOTE: DEVELOPMENT CREDIT CATTLE
TOPIC: Non-IBRD Project
CONCEPTS: Definition of terms. Detailed regula-
tions. Previous treaty amendment. Exchange of
information and documents. Informational
records. Accounting procedures. Currency. In-
terest rates. Tax exemptions. Credit provisions.
Loan repayment. Terms of loan. Plans and stan-
dards. IDA development project.
PARTIES:
Paraguay
IDA (Devel Assoc)

107395   Bilateral Exchange   **507 UNTS 25**
SIGNED: 3 Jul 62   FORCE: 3 Jul 62
REGISTERED: 24 Aug 64 France
ARTICLES: 2 LANGUAGE: French.
HEADNOTE: EVIAN TALKS
TOPIC: Recognition
CONCEPTS: Repatriation of nationals. Status of
state. Democratic institutions. Transition period.
Recognition. Arbitration. Conciliation. Culture.
Establishment of trade relations. Balance of pay-
ments. Currency. General technical assistance.
Economic assistance. Jurisdiction. Withdrawal
of forces. Bases and facilities. Optional clause
ICJ. Raw materials.
PARTIES:
Algeria
France

107396   Bilateral Agreement   **507 UNTS 101**
SIGNED: 28 Aug 63   FORCE: 6 Dec 63
REGISTERED: 25 Aug 64 United Nations
ARTICLES: 8 LANGUAGE: French.
HEADNOTE: UNICEF ACTIVITIES
TOPIC: IGO Operations
CONCEPTS: Privileges and immunities. Exchange
of information and documents. Accounting pro-
cedures. Economic assistance. Assistance to
United Nations. Inter-agency agreements.
TREATY REF: 1UNTS15.
PROCEDURE: Amendment. Termination.
PARTIES:
Dahomey
UNICEF (Children)

107397   Bilateral Agreement   **507 UNTS 111**
SIGNED: 30 Sep 59   FORCE: 18 May 60
REGISTERED: 26 Aug 64 Netherlands
ARTICLES: 3 LANGUAGE: Dutch. German.
HEADNOTE: SETTLEMENT MATTERS RELATING
TO PROPERTY RIGHTS

TOPIC: Specific Property
CONCEPTS: Annex or appendix reference. Conformity with municipal law. General property. Currency. Claims and settlements. Assets transfer.
TREATY REF: 217UNTS223.
PARTIES:
Austria
Netherlands

107398 Bilateral Treaty **507 UNTS 135**
SIGNED: 26 Feb 58　　　　FORCE: 18 Dec 63
REGISTERED: 27 Aug 64 Philippines
ARTICLES: 8 LANGUAGE: English. Hebrew.
HEADNOTE: FRIENDSHIP
TOPIC: General Amity
CONCEPTS: Friendship and amity. Alien status. Consular relations establishment. Diplomatic relations establishment. Privileges and immunities. Exchange of official publications. Procedure.
PROCEDURE: Future Procedures Contemplated. Ratification.
PARTIES:
Israel
Philippines

107399 Multilateral Agreement **507 UNTS 149**
SIGNED: 14 Dec 63　　　　FORCE: 18 May 64
REGISTERED: 28 Aug 64 Guatemala
ARTICLES: 26 LANGUAGE: Spanish.
HEADNOTE: CENTRAL AMERICAN DEFENSE
TOPIC: IGO Establishment
CONCEPTS: Conformity with municipal law. Joint defense. Defense and security. Admission. Establishment. Headquarters and facilities. Internal structure.
INTL ORGS: Organization of Central American States. United Nations.
TREATY REF: 119UNTS3.
PROCEDURE: Accession. Denunciation. Duration. Ratification. Registration.
PARTIES:
Costa Rica SIGNED: 14 Dec 63
Guatemala　SIGNED:　14 Dec 63　RATIFIED: 24 Jan 64 FORCE: 18 May 64
Honduras　SIGNED:　14 Dec 63　RATIFIED: 18 May 64 FORCE: 18 May 64
Nicaragua　SIGNED:　14 Dec 63　RATIFIED: 7 Apr 64 FORCE: 18 May 64
Panama SIGNED: 14 Dec 63

107400 Bilateral Exchange **507 UNTS 171**
SIGNED: 16 Feb 63　　　　FORCE: 16 Feb 63
REGISTERED: 31 Aug 64 UK Great Britain
ARTICLES: 2 LANGUAGE: English.
HEADNOTE: ABOLISHMENT REQUIREMENT PRESENTATION AIRCRAFT PASSENGER MANIFESTS
TOPIC: Air Transport
CONCEPTS: Exceptions and exemptions. Exchange of information and documents. Air transport. Operating authorizations and regulations.
PARTIES:
UK Great Britain
Yugoslavia

107401 Multilateral Convention **507 UNTS 177**
SIGNED: 29 Mar 62　　　　FORCE: 29 Feb 64
REGISTERED: 31 Aug 64 UK Great Britain
ARTICLES: 30 LANGUAGE: English. French.
HEADNOTE: DEVELOPMENT SPACE VEHICLES
TOPIC: IGO Establishment
CONCEPTS: Definition of terms. Annex or appendix reference. Exchange of information and documents. Juridical personality. Arbitration. Procedure. Scientific exchange. Accounting procedures. Funding procedures. Special projects. Economic assistance. Admission. Establishment. Headquarters and facilities. Liaison with other IGO's. Conformity with IGO decisions.
INTL ORGS: Court of Justice of the European Community. European Space Launcher Development Organization. United Nations. Arbitration Commission.
PROCEDURE: Amendment. Accession. Denunciation. Duration. Ratification. Registration. Termination.
PARTIES:
Australia　SIGNED:　29 Mar 62　RATIFIED: 15 Jan 63 FORCE: 29 Feb 64

Belgium SIGNED: 29 Mar 62 RATIFIED: 2 Apr 64 FORCE: 2 Apr 64
France SIGNED: 29 Mar 62 RATIFIED: 30 Jan 64 FORCE: 29 Feb 64
Germany, West SIGNED: 29 Mar 62 RATIFIED: 29 Feb 64 FORCE: 29 Feb 64
Italy SIGNED: 29 Mar 62
Netherlands　SIGNED:　29 Mar 62　RATIFIED: 12 Jun 63 FORCE: 28 Feb 64
UK Great Britain SIGNED: 29 Mar 62 RATIFIED: 28 Mar 63 FORCE: 29 Feb 64
ANNEX
605 UNTS 370. Australia. Force 26 Jan 67. Implementation 29 Jun 64.
605 UNTS 370. Australia. Reservation 29 Jun 64.
605 UNTS 370. Belgium. Force 26 Jan 67. Implementation 29 Jun 64.
605 UNTS 370. Germany, West. Force 26 Jan 67. Implementation 29 Jun 64.
605 UNTS 370. Italy. Force 26 Jan 67. Implementation 29 Jun 64.
605 UNTS 370. Netherlands. Force 26 Jan 67. Implementation 29 Jun 64.
605 UNTS 370. UK Great Britain. Force 26 Jan 67. Implementation 29 Jun 64.
605 UNTS 370. France. Force 26 Oct 67. Implementation 29 Jun 64.

107402 Bilateral Agreement **507 UNTS 245**
SIGNED: 24 Jun 59　　　　FORCE: 24 Jun 59
REGISTERED: 1 Sep 64 United Nations
ARTICLES: 6 LANGUAGE: Spanish.
HEADNOTE: OPERATIONAL EXECUTIVE ADMINISTRATIVE PERSONNEL
TOPIC: IGO Operations
CONCEPTS: Annex or appendix reference. Diplomatic missions. Procedure. Domestic obligation. Assistance to United Nations. Mutual consultation.
INTL ORGS: Permanent Court of Arbitration. Arbitration Commission.
TREATY REF: 274UNTS172.
PROCEDURE: Amendment. Termination.
PARTIES:
Panama
United Nations

107403 Bilateral Agreement **508 UNTS 3**
SIGNED: 18 Aug 58　　　　FORCE: 18 Aug 58
REGISTERED: 3 Sep 64 United Nations
ARTICLES: 6 LANGUAGE: English.
HEADNOTE: PERSONNEL
TOPIC: Admin Cooperation
CONCEPTS: Diplomatic missions. Procedure. Domestic obligation. Assistance to United Nations. Inter-agency agreements. Mutual consultation.
INTL ORGS: Permanent Court of Arbitration. Arbitration Commission.
PROCEDURE: Amendment. Termination.
PARTIES:
Nepal
United Nations
ANNEX
535 UNTS 455. United Nations. Force 25 May 65.
535 UNTS 455. Nepal. Force 25 May 65.

107404 Bilateral Treaty **508 UNTS 14**
SIGNED: 8 Apr 60　　　　FORCE: 1 Aug 63
REGISTERED: 3 Sep 64 Netherlands
ARTICLES: 4 LANGUAGE: Dutch. German.
HEADNOTE: SETTLEMENT FRONTIER QUESTIONS
TOPIC: Territory Boundary
CONCEPTS: Treaty implementation. Annex or appendix reference. Visa abolition. Border traffic and migration. Acquisition of nationality. Alien status. General cooperation. Exchange of information and documents. Informational records. Licenses and permits. Recognition and enforcement of legal decisions. Responsibility and liability. Establishment of commission. Arbitration. Procedure. Special tribunals. Competence of tribunal. Veterinary. Expense sharing formulae. Tax exemptions. Railway border crossing. Railways. Reparations and restrictions. International organizations. Changes of territory. Markers and definitions. Frontier waterways. Frontier crossing points. Regulation of natural resources.
INTL ORGS: International Court of Justice.
TREATY REF: 509UNTS64.
PROCEDURE: Ratification.

PARTIES:
Germany, West
Netherlands

107405 Bilateral Exchange **509 UNTS 269**
SIGNED: 20 Sep 56　　　　FORCE: 24 Aug 57
REGISTERED: 4 Sep 64 Netherlands
ARTICLES: 2 LANGUAGE: Dutch. German.
HEADNOTE: LIGHTHOUSES
TOPIC: Specific Property
CONCEPTS: Previous treaty replacement. Navigational conditions. Inland and territorial waters. Facilities and property.
TREATY REF: 30NOV191.
PARTIES:
Germany, West
Netherlands

107406 Bilateral Agreement **509 UNTS 275**
SIGNED: 20 Jan 64　　　　FORCE: 20 Jan 64
REGISTERED: 9 Sep 64 Belgium
ARTICLES: 6 LANGUAGE: French. German.
HEADNOTE: CERTAIN CATEGORIES INTERNATIONAL PASSENGER TRANSPORT ROAD
TOPIC: Land Transport
CONCEPTS: Conditions. Detailed regulations. Remedies. Conformity with municipal law. Passenger transport. Commercial road vehicles. Roads and highways. Road rules.
PROCEDURE: Duration. Renewal or Revival.
PARTIES:
Austria
Belgium

107407 Bilateral Agreement **509 UNTS 285**
SIGNED: 27 Feb 64　　　　FORCE: 27 Feb 64
REGISTERED: 9 Sep 64 Denmark
ARTICLES: 7 LANGUAGE: Danish. Russian.
HEADNOTE: SETTLEMENT RECIPROCAL FINANCIAL PROPERTY OTHER CLAIMS
TOPIC: Specif Claim/Waive
CONCEPTS: Exchange of information and documents. Payment schedules. Claims and settlements. Lump sum settlements. Specific claims or waivers.
PARTIES:
Denmark
USSR (Soviet Union)

107408 Multilateral Agreement **510 UNTS 3**
SIGNED: 4 Aug 63　　　　FORCE: 10 Sep 64
REGISTERED: 10 Sep 64 United Nations
ARTICLES: 66 LANGUAGE: English. French.
HEADNOTE: ESTABLISHMENT DEVELOPMENT BANK
TOPIC: IGO Establishment
CONCEPTS: Subsidiary organ.
INTL ORGS: African Development Bank.
PARTIES:
Algeria SIGNED: 4 Aug 63 RATIFIED: 10 Sep 64 FORCE: 10 Sep 64
Burundi SIGNED: 4 Aug 63
Cameroon　SIGNED:　8 Oct 63　RATIFIED: 7 May 64 FORCE: 10 Sep 64
Central Afri Rep SIGNED: 4 Aug 63
Congo (Brazzaville) SIGNED: 29 Nov 63
Congo (Zaire) SIGNED: 4 Aug 63 RATIFIED: 5 Jun 64 FORCE: 10 Sep 64
Dahomey　SIGNED:　8 Oct 63　RATIFIED: 25 Aug 64 FORCE: 10 Sep 64
Ethiopia SIGNED: 4 Aug 63 RATIFIED: 14 Jul 64 FORCE: 10 Sep 64
Ghana SIGNED: 4 Aug 63 RATIFIED: 30 Jun 64 FORCE: 10 Sep 64
Guinea SIGNED: 4 Aug 63 RATIFIED: 21 May 64 FORCE: 10 Sep 64
Ivory Coast　SIGNED:　4 Aug 63　RATIFIED: 20 Mar 64 FORCE: 10 Sep 64
Kenya SIGNED: 4 Aug 63 RATIFIED: 24 Jan 64 FORCE: 10 Sep 64
Liberia SIGNED: 4 Aug 63 RATIFIED: 23 Jun 64 FORCE: 10 Sep 64
Libya SIGNED: 4 Aug 63
Mali　SIGNED:　4 Aug 63　RATIFIED: 23 Apr 64 FORCE: 10 Sep 64
Mauritania　SIGNED:　4 Aug 63　RATIFIED: 9 Sep 64 FORCE: 10 Sep 64
Mauritius SIGNED: 4 Aug 63
Morocco SIGNED: 4 Aug 63 RATIFIED: 2 Jun 64 FORCE: 10 Sep 64

Nigeria SIGNED: 4 Aug 63 RATIFIED: 12 Mar 64
FORCE: 10 Sep 64
Niger SIGNED: 25 Oct 63 RATIFIED: 29 Jul 64
FORCE: 10 Sep 64
Nyasaland SIGNED: 4 Aug 63
Rwanda SIGNED: 18 Dec 63
Senegal SIGNED: 17 Dec 63 RATIFIED:
11 Dec 64
Sierra Leone SIGNED: 4 Aug 63 RATIFIED:
18 Feb 64 FORCE: 10 Sep 64
Somalia SIGNED: 4 Aug 63
Sudan SIGNED: 4 Aug 63 RATIFIED: 9 Sep 63
FORCE: 10 Sep 64
Tanganyika SIGNED: 4 Aug 63 RATIFIED:
27 Nov 63 FORCE: 10 Sep 64
Togo SIGNED: 18 Oct 63 RATIFIED: 3 Jul 64
FORCE: 10 Sep 63
Tunisia SIGNED: 4 Aug 63
United Arab Rep SIGNED: 4 Aug 63 RATIFIED:
14 Sep 64
Uganda SIGNED: 4 Aug 63 RATIFIED: 16 Dec 63
FORCE: 10 Sep 63
Upper Volta SIGNED: 21 Nov 63 RATIFIED:
22 Sep 64
Zanzibar SIGNED: 4 Aug 63
ANNEX
514 UNTS 298. Somalia. Ratification 22 Oct 64.
514 UNTS 298. Tunisia. Ratification 29 Oct 64.
523 UNTS 348. Rwanda. Ratification 18 Jan 65.
525 UNTS 339. Congo (Brazzaville). Ratification
10 Feb 65.
572 UNTS 363. Zambia. Accession 1 Sep 66.
616 UNTS 504. Brunei. Accession 2 Jan 68.
643 UNTS 399. Chad. Accession 26 Aug 68.

107409 Bilateral Agreement **510 UNTS 127**
SIGNED: 11 Sep 64 FORCE: 11 Sep 64
REGISTERED: 11 Sep 64 United Nations
ARTICLES: 8 LANGUAGE: French.
HEADNOTE: UNICEF ACTIVITIES
TOPIC: IGO Operations
CONCEPTS: Privileges and immunities. Accounting procedures. Economic assistance. Special status. Assistance to United Nations. Interagency agreements. Internal travel.
TREATY REF: 1UNTS15.
PROCEDURE: Amendment. Termination.
PARTIES:
Rwanda
UNICEF (Children)

107410 Bilateral Agreement **510 UNTS 137**
SIGNED: 15 Sep 64 FORCE: 15 Sep 64
REGISTERED: 15 Sep 64 United Nations
ARTICLES: 7 LANGUAGE: English.
HEADNOTE: FOURTH UN REG CARDIOGRAPHIC
CONVENTION
TOPIC: IGO Operations
CONCEPTS: Non-visa travel documents. Diplomatic missions. Privileges and immunities. Personnel. Domestic obligation. Regional offices.
TREATY REF: 1UNTS15; 33UNTS261.
PARTIES:
Philippines
United Nations

107411 Multilateral Convention **510 UNTS 147**
SIGNED: 15 Sep 64 FORCE: 1 Sep 64
REGISTERED: 15 Sep 64 Netherlands
ARTICLES: 12 LANGUAGE: French.
HEADNOTE: COMMON LAW SALE GOODS
TOPIC: General Trade
CONCEPTS: Definition of terms. Exceptions and exemptions. Territorial application. Conformity with municipal law. Inspection and observation. Incorporation of treaty provisions into national law.
PROCEDURE: Accession. Denunciation. Duration. Ratification. Renewal or Revival.
PARTIES:
Belgium SIGNED: 1 Aug 55 RATIFIED: 29 Oct 62
FORCE: 1 Sep 64
Denmark SIGNED: 23 Oct 56 RATIFIED: 3 Jul 64
FORCE: 1 Sep 64
Finland SIGNED: 12 Apr 57 RATIFIED: 3 Jul 64
FORCE: 1 Sep 64
France SIGNED: 25 Jul 55 RATIFIED: 30 Jul 63
FORCE: 1 Sep 64
Italy SIGNED: 13 Apr 56 RATIFIED: 17 Mar 58
FORCE: 1 Sep 64
Luxembourg SIGNED: 15 Jun 55

Netherlands SIGNED: 15 Jun 55
Norway SIGNED: 24 Oct 56 RATIFIED: 3 Jul 64
FORCE: 1 Sep 64
Spain SIGNED: 12 Apr 57
Sweden SIGNED: 23 Oct 56 RATIFIED: 8 Jul 64
FORCE: 6 Sep 64

107412 Multilateral Convention **510 UNTS 161**
SIGNED: 24 Oct 56 FORCE: 1 Jan 62
REGISTERED: 15 Sep 64 Netherlands
ARTICLES: 12 LANGUAGE: French.
HEADNOTE: LAW APPLICABLE MAINTENANCE OBLIGATIONS TOWARDS CHILDREN
TOPIC: Admin Cooperation
CONCEPTS: Exceptions and exemptions. Territorial application. General cooperation.
PROCEDURE: Accession. Denunciation. Duration. Ratification. Renewal or Revival.
PARTIES:
Austria SIGNED: 24 Oct 56 RATIFIED: 24 Jun 59
FORCE: 1 Jan 62
France SIGNED: 24 Oct 56 RATIFIED: 2 May 63
FORCE: 1 Jul 63
Germany, West SIGNED: 23 Aug 59 RATIFIED:
2 Nov 61 FORCE: 1 Jan 62
Greece SIGNED: 24 Oct 56
Italy SIGNED: 8 Oct 58 RATIFIED: 22 Feb 61
FORCE: 1 Jan 62
Luxembourg SIGNED: 24 Oct 56 RATIFIED:
27 Aug 58 FORCE: 1 Jan 62
Netherlands SIGNED: 24 Oct 56 RATIFIED:
15 Oct 52 FORCE: 14 Dec 62
Norway SIGNED: 24 Oct 56
Portugal SIGNED: 7 Jan 58
Spain SIGNED: 24 Oct 56
Switzerland SIGNED: 4 Jul 63

107413 Multilateral Convention **510 UNTS 175**
SIGNED: 5 Oct 61 FORCE: 5 Jan 64
REGISTERED: 15 Sep 64 Netherlands
ARTICLES: 20 LANGUAGE: French. English.
HEADNOTE: CONFLICTS LAWS FORM TESTAMENTARY DISPOSITIONS
TOPIC: Dispute Settlement
CONCEPTS: Exceptions and exemptions. Territorial application. Conformity with municipal law. Succession. Procedure.
PROCEDURE: Accession. Denunciation. Duration. Ratification.
PARTIES:
Austria SIGNED: 5 Oct 61 RATIFIED: 28 Oct 63
FORCE: 5 Jan 64
Denmark SIGNED: 5 Oct 61
Finland SIGNED: 13 Mar 62
France SIGNED: 9 Oct 61
Germany, West SIGNED: 5 Oct 61
Greece SIGNED: 5 Oct 61
Italy SIGNED: 15 Dec 61
Japan SIGNED: 30 Jan 64 RATIFIED: 3 Jun 64
FORCE: 2 Aug 64
Norway SIGNED: 5 Oct 61
Sweden SIGNED: 5 Oct 61
UK Great Britain SIGNED: 5 Oct 61 RATIFIED:
6 Nov 63 FORCE: 5 Jan 64
Yugoslavia SIGNED: 5 Oct 61 RATIFIED:
25 Sep 62 FORCE: 5 Jan 64

107414 Bilateral Exchange **510 UNTS 191**
SIGNED: 1 Dec 59 FORCE: 1 Dec 59
REGISTERED: 15 Sep 64 Netherlands
ARTICLES: 2 LANGUAGE: French.
HEADNOTE: PRIVILIGES IMMUNITIES
TOPIC: IGO Status/Immunit
CONCEPTS: Privileges and immunities. IGO status.
TREATY REF: 220UNTS121.
PROCEDURE: Denunciation.
PARTIES:
Hague Private IL
Netherlands

107415 Bilateral Agreement **510 UNTS 201**
SIGNED: 28 Aug 64 FORCE: 28 Aug 64
REGISTERED: 16 Sep 64 Australia
ARTICLES: 15 LANGUAGE: English.
HEADNOTE: EDUCATIONAL PROGRAM
TOPIC: Education
CONCEPTS: Previous treaty replacement. Friendship and amity. Standardization. Conformity with municipal law. Exchange of information and documents. Personnel. General property. Ex-

change. Commissions and foundations. Teacher and student exchange. Professorships. Research and development. Accounting procedures. Expense sharing formulae. Funding procedures. Tax exemptions. Customs exemptions. Establishment.
INTL ORGS: Special Commission.
TREATY REF: 45UNTS133.
PROCEDURE: Amendment. Termination.
PARTIES:
Australia
USA (United States)
ANNEX
638 UNTS 300. Australia. Amendment
12 May 67. Force 12 May 67.
638 UNTS 300. USA (United States). Amendment
12 May 67. Force 12 May 67.

107416 Bilateral Agreement **510 UNTS 217**
SIGNED: 23 Sep 64 FORCE: 23 Sep 64
REGISTERED: 23 Sep 64 United Nations
ARTICLES: 6 LANGUAGE: French.
HEADNOTE: PERSONNEL
TOPIC: IGO Operations
CONCEPTS: Annex or appendix reference. Diplomatic missions. Personnel. Arbitration. Procedure. Domestic obligation. IGO obligations.
INTL ORGS: Permanent Court of Arbitration. Arbitration Commission.
TREATY REF: 489UNTS102.
PROCEDURE: Accession. Termination.
PARTIES:
Algeria
United Nations

107417 Bilateral Exchange **510 UNTS 229**
SIGNED: 16 Jul 64 FORCE: 16 Jul 64
REGISTERED: 24 Sep 64 Norway
ARTICLES: 2 LANGUAGE: French.
HEADNOTE: LITERARY ARTISTIC WORKS
TOPIC: Patents/Copyrights
CONCEPTS: Previous treaty extension. Domestic legislation. Meteorology. Press and wire services.
TREATY REF: 2'9DEMARTENS173,177;
2'18DEMARTENS122;DE.
PARTIES:
France
Norway

107418 Multilateral Agreement **510 UNTS 235**
SIGNED: 8 Dec 62 FORCE: 29 May 64
REGISTERED: 28 Sep 64 Italy
ARTICLES: 15 LANGUAGE: French.
HEADNOTE: SOUTHERN RAILWAY COMPANY BONDS
TOPIC: Finance
CONCEPTS: Definition of terms. Detailed regulations. Previous treaty amendment. Treaty implementation. Annex or appendix reference. Conformity with municipal law. General cooperation. Exchange of information and documents. Informational records. Legal protection and assistance. Public information. Negotiation. Accounting procedures. Banking. Bonds. Currency. Inadequacy of funds. Payment schedules. Claims and settlements. Debts. Debt settlement. General. Railways.
TREATY REF: 41UNTS135; 49UNTS50;
217UNTS233; 23LTS255; 23LTS37.
PROCEDURE: Ratification.
PARTIES:
Austria SIGNED: 8 Dec 62 RATIFIED: 1 Feb 64
FORCE: 29 May 64
Hungary SIGNED: 8 Dec 62 RATIFIED:
22 Nov 63 FORCE: 29 May 64
Italy SIGNED: 8 Dec 62 RATIFIED: 29 May 64
FORCE: 29 May 64
Yugoslavia SIGNED: 8 Dec 62 RATIFIED:
21 Feb 64 FORCE: 29 May 64

107419 Bilateral Agreement **510 UNTS 277**
SIGNED: 30 Sep 64 FORCE: 30 Sep 64
REGISTERED: 30 Sep 64 United Nations
ARTICLES: 10 LANGUAGE: English.
HEADNOTE: RESEARCH COCONUT RHINOCEROS BEETLE
TOPIC: Scientific Project
CONCEPTS: General cooperation. Exchange of information and documents. General property.

Use of facilities. Existing tribunals. Insect control. Research and scientific projects. Research results. Research and development. Financial programs. Funding procedures. Domestic obligation. Materials, equipment and services. Conformity with IGO decisions. IGO obligations.
INTL ORGS: International Court of Justice. United Nations. Arbitration Commission.
TREATY REF: 97UNTS221; 124UNTS320.
PROCEDURE: Amendment. Duration. Future Procedures Contemplated. Renewal or Revival. Termination.
PARTIES:
  Australia
  UN Special Fund

107420 Bilateral Agreement **510 UNTS 295**
SIGNED: 13 Feb 64   FORCE: 13 Feb 64
REGISTERED: 30 Sep 64 USA (United States)
ARTICLES: 6 LANGUAGE: English.
HEADNOTE: AGRI COMMOD TITLE I
TOPIC: US Agri Commod Aid
CONCEPTS: General provisions. Annex or appendix reference. Exchange of information and documents. Reexport of goods, etc.. Exchange rates and regulations. Transportation costs. Local currency. Commodities schedule. Purchase authorization. Surplus commodities. Mutual consultation.
PARTIES:
  Iceland
  USA (United States)

107421 Bilateral Agreement **511 UNTS 3**
SIGNED: 13 Feb 64   FORCE: 13 Feb 64
REGISTERED: 30 Sep 64 USA (United States)
ARTICLES: 5 LANGUAGE: English.
HEADNOTE: AGRI COMMOD TITLE IV
TOPIC: US Agri Commod Aid
CONCEPTS: General provisions. Exchange of information and documents. Free trade. Currency. Payment schedules. Purchase authorization. Commodities schedule. Purchase authorization. Mutual consultation.
PARTIES:
  Iceland
  USA (United States)

107422 Bilateral Exchange **511 UNTS 17**
SIGNED: 17 Feb 64   FORCE: 17 Feb 64
REGISTERED: 30 Sep 64 USA (United States)
ARTICLES: 2 LANGUAGE: English.
HEADNOTE: TRADE BEEF VEAL MUTTON
TOPIC: Commodity Trade
CONCEPTS: Detailed regulations. General cooperation. Trade agencies. Commodity trade. Quotas.
INTL ORGS: General Agreement on Tariffs and Trade.
TREATY REF: 55UNTS187.
PROCEDURE: Termination.
PARTIES:
  Australia
  USA (United States)

107423 Bilateral Exchange **511 UNTS 27**
SIGNED: 25 Feb 64   FORCE: 25 Feb 64
REGISTERED: 30 Sep 64 USA (United States)
ARTICLES: 2 LANGUAGE: English.
HEADNOTE: TRADE BEEF VEAL
TOPIC: Commodity Trade
CONCEPTS: Detailed regulations. General cooperation. Commodity trade. Quotas.
PROCEDURE: Termination.
PARTIES:
  Ireland
  USA (United States)

107424 Bilateral Exchange **511 UNTS 37**
SIGNED: 17 Feb 64   FORCE: 17 Feb 64
REGISTERED: 30 Sep 64 USA (United States)
ARTICLES: 2 LANGUAGE: English.
HEADNOTE: TRADE BEEF VEAL
TOPIC: Commodity Trade
CONCEPTS: Detailed regulations. General cooperation. Commodity trade. Quotas.
INTL ORGS: General Agreement on Tariffs and Trade.

PARTIES:
  New Zealand
  USA (United States)

107425 Bilateral Exchange **511 UNTS 47**
SIGNED: 19 Jul 63   FORCE: 19 Jul 63
REGISTERED: 30 Sep 64 USA (United States)
ARTICLES: 2 LANGUAGE: English. French.
HEADNOTE: FURNISHING MILITARY EQUIPMENT SURPLUS SERVICES
TOPIC: Milit Installation
CONCEPTS: Non-prejudice to UN charter. Tax exemptions. Customs exemptions. Postal services. Self-defense. Military assistance. Return of equipment and recapture. Security of information. Military assistance missions. Airforce-army-navy personnel ratio. Ranks and privileges. Restrictions on transfer.
TREATY REF: 500UNTS7310.
PARTIES:
  Congo (Zaire)
  USA (United States)

107426 Bilateral Exchange **511 UNTS 53**
SIGNED: 10 Feb 64   FORCE: 10 Feb 64
REGISTERED: 30 Sep 64 USA (United States)
ARTICLES: 2 LANGUAGE: English. Spanish.
HEADNOTE: INCREASING ROAD CONSTRUCTION MAINTENANCE CAPABILITY
TOPIC: Milit Assistance
CONCEPTS: Conformity with municipal law. Exchange of information and documents. Inspection and observation. Materials, equipment and services. Military assistance. Return of equipment and recapture. Security of information. Restrictions on transfer.
PARTIES:
  Paraguay
  USA (United States)

107427 Bilateral Exchange **511 UNTS 61**
SIGNED: 29 Jan 64   FORCE: 29 Jan 64
REGISTERED: 30 Sep 64 USA (United States)
ARTICLES: 2 LANGUAGE: English. Spanish.
HEADNOTE: TRACKING STATIONS
TOPIC: Specific Property
CONCEPTS: Testing ranges and sites. Facilities and property.
PARTIES:
  Spain
  USA (United States)

107428 Bilateral Exchange **511 UNTS 77**
SIGNED: 30 Jan 64   FORCE: 30 Jan 64
REGISTERED: 30 Sep 64 USA (United States)
ARTICLES: 2 LANGUAGE: English. Portuguese.
HEADNOTE: MILITARY ASSISTANCE
TOPIC: Milit Assistance
CONCEPTS: Joint defense. Defense and security. Military assistance.
TREATY REF: 199UNTS221.
PROCEDURE: Future Procedures Contemplated.
PARTIES:
  Brazil
  USA (United States)

107429 Bilateral Agreement **511 UNTS 85**
SIGNED: 11 Feb 64   FORCE: 11 Feb 64
REGISTERED: 30 Sep 64 USA (United States)
ARTICLES: 6 LANGUAGE: English. Arabic.
HEADNOTE: AGRI COMMOD TITLE I
TOPIC: US Agri Commod Aid
CONCEPTS: General provisions. Annex or appendix reference. Exchange of information and documents. Reexport of goods, etc.. Exchange rates and regulations. Transportation costs. Local currency. Commodities schedule. Purchase authorization. Surplus commodities. Mutual consultation.
PARTIES:
  Jordan
  USA (United States)

107430 Bilateral Exchange **511 UNTS 103**
SIGNED: 5 Feb 64   FORCE: 5 Feb 64
REGISTERED: 30 Sep 64 USA (United States)
ARTICLES: 2 LANGUAGE: English.
HEADNOTE: SETTLEMENT LOGISTICAL SUPPORT

TOPIC: Status of Forces
CONCEPTS: Time limit. Annex or appendix reference. Interest rates. Payment schedules. Lump sum settlements.
PARTIES:
  Australia
  USA (United States)

107431 Bilateral Agreement **511 UNTS 119**
SIGNED: 13 Feb 64   FORCE: 13 Feb 64
REGISTERED: 30 Sep 64 USA (United States)
ARTICLES: 6 LANGUAGE: English.
HEADNOTE: AGRI COMMOD TITLE I
TOPIC: US Agri Commod Aid
CONCEPTS: General provisions. Annex or appendix reference. Exchange of information and documents. Reexport of goods, etc.. Exchange rates and regulations. Transportation costs. Local currency. Commodities schedule. Purchase authorization. Surplus commodities. Mutual consultation.
PARTIES:
  Peru
  USA (United States)

107432 Bilateral Agreement **511 UNTS 145**
SIGNED: 30 Jan 59   FORCE: 19 May 64
REGISTERED: 30 Sep 64 USA (United States)
ARTICLES: 7 LANGUAGE: English. German.
HEADNOTE: RETURN PROPERTY
TOPIC: Claims and Debts
CONCEPTS: Detailed regulations. Exceptions and exemptions. Annex or appendix reference. General property. Responsibility and liability. Assessment procedures. Assets transfer.
TREATY REF: 217UNTS223.
PROCEDURE: Ratification.
PARTIES:
  Austria
  USA (United States)

107433 Bilateral Agreement **511 UNTS 181**
SIGNED: 1 Oct 64   FORCE: 1 Oct 64
REGISTERED: 1 Oct 64 United Nations
ARTICLES: 10 LANGUAGE: English.
HEADNOTE: ASSISTANCE
TOPIC: IGO Operations
CONCEPTS: Diplomatic missions. Exchange of information and documents. Procedure. Domestic obligation. General technical assistance. Economic assistance. Assistance to United Nations.
INTL ORGS: International Court of Justice. United Nations. Arbitration Commission.
TREATY REF: 1UNTS15; 33UNTS261; 374UNTS147.
PROCEDURE: Amendment. Termination.
PARTIES:
  Kenya
  UN Special Fund

107434 Bilateral Agreement **511 UNTS 199**
SIGNED: 1 Oct 64   FORCE: 1 Oct 64
REGISTERED: 1 Oct 64 United Nations
ARTICLES: 6 LANGUAGE: English.
HEADNOTE: PERSONNEL
TOPIC: IGO Operations
CONCEPTS: Annex or appendix reference. Diplomatic missions. Property. Arbitration. Procedure. Domestic obligation. IGO obligations.
INTL ORGS: Permanent Court of Arbitration. Arbitration Commission.
TREATY REF: 489UNTS102.
PROCEDURE: Amendment. Termination.
PARTIES:
  Kenya
  United Nations
                ANNEX
533 UNTS 385. United Nations. Force 26 Apr 65.
533 UNTS 385. Kenya. Force 26 Apr 65.

107435 Multilateral Agreement **511 UNTS 210**
SIGNED: 27 Aug 63   FORCE: 8 Oct 64
REGISTERED: 8 Oct 64 United Nations
ARTICLES: 6 LANGUAGE: English. Spanish.
HEADNOTE: TECHNICAL ASSISTANCE
TOPIC: Tech Assistance
CONCEPTS: Visas. Privileges and immunities. General cooperation. Exchange of information and documents. Licenses and permits. Personnel.

Responsibility and liability. Title and deeds. Use of facilities. Exchange. Scholarships and grants. Vocational training. Research and development. Import quotas. Exchange rates and regulations. Expense sharing formulae. Local currency. Domestic obligation. General technical assistance. Materials, equipment and services. IGO status. Conformity with IGO decisions.
TREATY REF: 76UNTS132; 1UNTS15; 33UNTS261; 374UNTS147.
PROCEDURE: Amendment. Termination.
PARTIES:
Costa Rica SIGNED: 27 Aug 63 RATIFIED: 8 Oct 64 FORCE: 8 Oct 64
FAO (Food Agri) SIGNED: 27 Aug 63 FORCE: 8 Oct 64
IAEA (Atom Energy) SIGNED: 27 Aug 63 FORCE: 8 Oct 64
ICAO (Civil Aviat) SIGNED: 27 Aug 63 FORCE: 8 Oct 64
ILO (Labor Org) SIGNED: 27 Aug 63 FORCE: 8 Oct 64
ITU (Telecommun) SIGNED: 27 Aug 63 FORCE: 8 Oct 64
UNESCO (Educ/Cult) SIGNED: 27 Aug 63 FORCE: 8 Oct 64
United Nations SIGNED: 27 Aug 63 FORCE: 8 Oct 64
UPU (Postal Union) SIGNED: 27 Aug 63 FORCE: 8 Oct 64
WHO (World Health) SIGNED: 27 Aug 63 FORCE: 8 Oct 64
WMO (Meteorology) SIGNED: 27 Aug 63 FORCE: 8 Oct 64

107436 Bilateral Agreement **511 UNTS 233**
SIGNED: 25 Aug 64 FORCE: 25 Aug 64
REGISTERED: 8 Oct 64 Philippines
ARTICLES: 7 LANGUAGE: English.
HEADNOTE: TECHNICAL COOPERATION
TOPIC: Tech Assistance
CONCEPTS: Treaty implementation. Frontier formalities. Privileges and immunities. Personnel. Institute establishment. Vocational training. Expense sharing formulae. General technical assistance. Agriculture.
PROCEDURE: Duration. Termination.
PARTIES:
Taiwan
Philippines

107437 Bilateral Agreement **511 UNTS 241**
SIGNED: 11 Feb 64 FORCE: 31 Jul 64
REGISTERED: 15 Oct 64 Denmark
ARTICLES: 19 LANGUAGE: French.
HEADNOTE: AIR TRANSPORT
TOPIC: Air Transport
CONCEPTS: Definition of terms. Exceptions and exemptions. Annex or appendix reference. Nonprejudice to third party. Conformity with municipal law. General cooperation. Exchange of information and documents. Informational records. Licenses and permits. Recognition of legal documents. Use of facilities. Arbitration. Procedure. Special tribunals. Negotiation. Humanitarian matters. Expense sharing formulae. Fees and exemptions. Non-interest rates and fees. Most favored nation clause. National treatment. Customs duties. Customs exemptions. Registration certificate. Routes and logistics. Permit designation. Air transport. Airport facilities. Airworthiness certificates. Conditions of airlines operating permission. Operating authorizations and regulations. Licenses and certificates of nationality.
INTL ORGS: International Civil Aviation Organization. International Court of Justice. Arbitration Commission.
PROCEDURE: Amendment. Denunciation. Ratification.
PARTIES:
Denmark
Yugoslavia

107438 Bilateral Agreement **512 UNTS 2**
SIGNED: 30 Nov 63 FORCE: 16 Jul 64
REGISTERED: 19 Oct 64 Yugoslavia
ARTICLES: 23 LANGUAGE: Serbo-Croat. Romanian.
HEADNOTE: ESTABLISHMENT IRON GATES WATER POWER & NAVIGATION SYSTEMS

TOPIC: Specific Property
CONCEPTS: Inspection and observation. Operating agencies. Responsibility and liability. Establishment of commission. Arbitration. Negotiation. Accounting procedures. Indemnities and reimbursements. Investments. Funding procedures. Interest rates. Hydro-electric power. Frontier waterways. Frontier crossing points.
INTL ORGS: Arbitration Commission. Special Commission.
TREATY REF: 33UNTS181; 513UNTS56.
PROCEDURE: Duration. Ratification.
PARTIES:
Romania
Yugoslavia
ANNEX
559 UNTS 358. Yugoslavia. Amendment 29 Sep 64. Force 6 Feb 65.
559 UNTS 358. Romania. Amendment 29 Sep 64. Force 6 Feb 65.

107439 Bilateral Exchange **514 UNTS 3**
SIGNED: 20 May 64 FORCE: 21 Jul 64
REGISTERED: 19 Oct 64 Yugoslavia
ARTICLES: 2 LANGUAGE: German. Serbo-Croat.
HEADNOTE: REPATRIATION INDIGENT PERSONS
TOPIC: Extradition
CONCEPTS: Extradition, deportation and repatriation. Expense sharing formulae.
PROCEDURE: Termination.
PARTIES:
Austria
Yugoslavia

107440 Bilateral Agreement **514 UNTS 11**
SIGNED: 22 Jun 64 FORCE: 22 Jun 64
REGISTERED: 19 Oct 64 WHO (World Health)
ARTICLES: 6 LANGUAGE: French.
HEADNOTE: TECHNICAL ADVISORY ASSISTANCE
TOPIC: Tech Assistance
CONCEPTS: Definition of terms. Annex or appendix reference. Privileges and immunities. General cooperation. Exchange of information and documents. Personnel. Responsibility and liability. Title and deeds. Exchange. Scholarships and grants. Vocational training. Research and development. Expense sharing formulae. Local currency. Domestic obligation. Special projects. Materials, equipment and services. IGO status. Conformity with IGO decisions.
TREATY REF: 33UNTS261.
PROCEDURE: Amendment. Termination.
PARTIES:
Rwanda
WHO (World Health)

107441 Multilateral Agreement **514 UNTS 25**
SIGNED: 20 Aug 64 FORCE: 20 Aug 64
REGISTERED: 20 Oct 64 USA (United States)
ARTICLES: 15 LANGUAGE: English. French.
HEADNOTE: PRODUCTION TRADE POLICIES CEREALS
TOPIC: Telecommunications
CONCEPTS: Detailed regulations. Annex or appendix reference. General cooperation. Balance of payments. Fees and exemptions. Non-interest rates and fees. Commodity trade.
INTL ORGS: United Nations. Arbitration Commission.
PROCEDURE: Termination.
PARTIES:
Australia SIGNED: 20 Aug 64 FORCE: 24 Aug 64
Belgium SIGNED: 28 Sep 64
Canada SIGNED: 20 Aug 64 FORCE: 20 Aug 64
Denmark SIGNED: 20 Aug 64
France SIGNED: 20 Aug 64
Germany, West SIGNED: 21 Sep 64 FORCE: 21 Sep 64
Ireland SIGNED: 5 Oct 64 FORCE: 5 Oct 64
Italy SIGNED: 20 Aug 64
Japan SIGNED: 20 Aug 64
Netherlands SIGNED: 20 Aug 64 FORCE: 20 Aug 64
Norway SIGNED: 31 Aug 64 FORCE: 31 Aug 64
Spain SIGNED: 20 Aug 64 FORCE: 20 Aug 64
Sweden SIGNED: 20 Aug 64
Switzerland SIGNED: 16 Sep 64 FORCE: 16 Sep 64
UK Great Britain SIGNED: 20 Aug 64 FORCE: 20 Aug 64

USA (United States) SIGNED: 20 Aug 64 FORCE: 20 Aug 64
Vatican/Holy See SIGNED: 20 Aug 64 FORCE: 20 Aug 64
ANNEX
535 UNTS 456. Israel. Signature 30 Nov 64. Force 30 Nov 64.
535 UNTS 456. Syria. Signature 12 Feb 65. Force 12 Feb 65.
535 UNTS 456. United Arab Rep. Signature 19 Feb 65. Force 19 Feb 65.
535 UNTS 456. Colombia. Signature 19 Feb 65. Force 19 Feb 65.
535 UNTS 456. Italy. Approval 10 Mar 65. Force 10 Mar 65.
535 UNTS 456. Jordan. Signature 12 Feb 65. Force 12 Feb 65.
535 UNTS 456. Kuwait. Signature 12 Feb 65. Force 12 Feb 65.
535 UNTS 456. Taiwan. Signature 17 Feb 65. Force 17 Feb 65.
535 UNTS 456. Lebanon. Signature 12 Feb 65. Force 12 Feb 65.
535 UNTS 456. Tunisia. Signature 19 Feb 65. Force 19 Feb 65.
535 UNTS 456. Ethiopia. Signature 19 Feb 65. Force 19 Feb 65.
535 UNTS 456. Saudi Arabia. Signature 19 Feb 65. Force 19 Feb 65.
535 UNTS 456. Denmark. Approval 3 Mar 65. Force 3 Mar 65.
535 UNTS 456. Libya. Signature 12 Feb 65. Force 12 Feb 65.
535 UNTS 456. New Zealand. Signature 12 Feb 65. Force 12 Feb 65.
535 UNTS 456. Belgium. Implementation 10 Feb 65. Force 10 Feb 65.
535 UNTS 456. France. Approval 18 Jan 65. Force 18 Jan 65.
535 UNTS 456. Indonesia. Signature 19 Feb 65. Force 19 Feb 65.
535 UNTS 456. Algeria. Signature 19 Feb 65. Force 19 Feb 65.
535 UNTS 456. Sudan. Signature 12 Feb 65. Force 12 Feb 65.
535 UNTS 456. Iraq. Signature 17 Feb 65. Force 17 Feb 65.
535 UNTS 456. South Africa. Signature 8 Feb 65. Force 8 Feb 65.
535 UNTS 456. Sweden. Approval 18 Jan 65. Force 18 Jan 65.
535 UNTS 456. Portugal. Approval 14 Jan 65. Force 14 Jan 65.
535 UNTS 456. Ceylon (Sri Lanka). Signature 17 Feb 65. Force 17 Feb 65.
535 UNTS 456. Monaco. Signature 18 Feb 65. Force 18 Feb 65.
535 UNTS 458. Lebanon. Signature 12 Feb 65. Force 12 Feb 65.
535 UNTS 458. Syria. Signature 12 Feb 65. Force 12 Feb 65.
535 UNTS 458. Italy. Signature 17 Feb 64. Force 10 Mar 65.
535 UNTS 458. Sudan. Signature 5 Apr 65. Force 12 Feb 65.
535 UNTS 458. Algeria. Signature 19 Feb 65. Force 19 Feb 65.
535 UNTS 458. Ceylon (Sri Lanka). Signature 17 Feb 65. Force 17 Feb 65.
535 UNTS 458. Denmark. Approval 3 Mar 65. Force 3 Mar 65.
535 UNTS 458. Ethiopia. Signature 19 Feb 65. Force 19 Feb 65.
535 UNTS 458. France. Approval 18 Jan 65. Force 18 Jan 65.
535 UNTS 458. Belgium. Implementation 10 Feb 65. Force 10 Feb 65.
535 UNTS 458. Colombia. Signature 19 Feb 65. Force 19 Feb 65.
535 UNTS 458. Saudi Arabia. Signature 19 Feb 65. Force 19 Feb 65.
535 UNTS 458. Indonesia. Signature 19 Feb 65. Force 19 Feb 65.
535 UNTS 458. Iraq. Signature 17 Feb 65. Force 17 Feb 65.
535 UNTS 458. Israel. Signature 30 Nov 64. Force 30 Nov 64.
535 UNTS 458. Jordan. Signature 12 Feb 65. Force 12 Feb 65.
535 UNTS 458. Kuwait. Signature 12 Feb 65. Force 12 Feb 65.
535 UNTS 458. Portugal. Approval 14 Jan 65. Force 14 Jan 65.

535 UNTS 458. Sweden. Acceptance 18 Jan 65. Force 18 Jan 65.
535 UNTS 458. Tunisia. Signature 19 Feb 65. Force 19 Feb 65.
535 UNTS 458. Libya. Signature 12 Feb 65. Force 12 Feb 65.
535 UNTS 458. United Arab Rep. Signature 19 Feb 65. Force 19 Feb 65.
535 UNTS 458. Monaco. Signature 18 Feb 65. Force 18 Feb 65.
535 UNTS 458. New Zealand. Signature 12 Feb 65. Force 12 Feb 65.
535 UNTS 458. Taiwan. Signature 17 Feb 65. Force 17 Feb 65.
535 UNTS 458. South Africa. Signature 8 Feb 65. Force 8 Feb 65.

107442 Multilateral Agreement **514 UNTS 71**
SIGNED: 6 May 64   FORCE: 6 May 64
REGISTERED: 21 Oct 64 Eur Space Vehicle
ARTICLES: 11 LANGUAGE: English. French.
HEADNOTE: INTERIM AGREEMENT MISSILE FIRING
TOPIC: IGO Operations
CONCEPTS: Default remedies. Arbitration. Procedure.
INTL ORGS: International Court of Justice. United Nations. Arbitration Commission.
PARTIES:
  Australia SIGNED: 6 May 64 FORCE: 6 May 64
  Eur Space Vehicle SIGNED: 6 May 64 FORCE: 6 May 64
  UK Great Britain SIGNED: 6 May 64 FORCE: 6 May 64
            ANNEX
543 UNTS 374. Australia. Supplementation 13 Jul 65. Force 13 Jul 65.
543 UNTS 374. UK Great Britain. Supplementation 13 Jul 65. Force 13 Jul 65.
543 UNTS 374. Eur Space Vehicle. Supplementation 13 Jul 65. Force 13 Jul 65.

107443 Bilateral Exchange **514 UNTS 87**
SIGNED: 21 Jan 63   FORCE: 5 Jun 64
REGISTERED: 21 Oct 64 Netherlands
ARTICLES: 2 LANGUAGE: French. Spanish.
HEADNOTE: ELIMINATE VISA REQUIREMENT
TOPIC: Visas
CONCEPTS: Emergencies. Time limit. Visa abolition. Denial of admission. Resident permits. Conformity with municipal law.
PROCEDURE: Denunciation.
PARTIES:
  Ecuador
  Netherlands

107444 Bilateral Agreement **514 UNTS 95**
SIGNED: 22 Oct 63   FORCE: 23 May 64
REGISTERED: 27 Oct 64 Czechoslovakia
ARTICLES: 31 LANGUAGE: Czechoslovakian. Hungarian.
HEADNOTE: RAIL TRAFFIC BETWEEN TWO COUNTRIES
TOPIC: Land Transport
CONCEPTS: Definition of terms. General provisions. Treaty implementation. Previous treaty replacement. Passports non-diplomatic. Non-visa travel documents. Visas. Conformity with municipal law. General cooperation. Inspection and observation. Legal protection and assistance. Licenses and permits. Personnel. Responsibility and liability. Use of facilities. Compensation. Indemnities and reimbursements. Fees and exemptions. Funding procedures. Claims and settlements. National treatment. Tax exemptions. Customs duties. Customs exemptions. Routes and logistics. Railway border crossing. Railways. Facilities and equipment. Regulations. Services. Markers and definitions.
TREATY REF: 351UNTS3.
PROCEDURE: Denunciation. Duration. Ratification. Renewal or Revival.
PARTIES:
  Czechoslovakia
  Hungary

107445 Bilateral Agreement **514 UNTS 157**
SIGNED: 23 Jun 64   FORCE: 23 Jun 64
REGISTERED: 28 Oct 64 WHO (World Health)
ARTICLES: 6 LANGUAGE: English.

HEADNOTE: TECHNICAL ADVISORY ASSISTANCE
TOPIC: Tech Assistance
CONCEPTS: Definition of terms. Privileges and immunities. General cooperation. Exchange of information and documents. Personnel. Responsibility and liability. Title and deeds. Exchange. Scholarships and grants. Vocational training. Research and development. Expense sharing formulae. Local currency. Domestic obligation. Special projects. Materials, equipment and services. IGO status. Conformity with IGO decisions.
TREATY REF: 33UNTS261.
PROCEDURE: Amendment. Termination.
PARTIES:
  Kenya
  WHO (World Health)
            ANNEX
540 UNTS 342. Kenya. Correction 19 May 65.
540 UNTS 342. WHO (World Health). Correction 25 Mar 65.

107446 Bilateral Agreement **514 UNTS 169**
SIGNED: 20 Dec 63   FORCE: 10 Jul 64
REGISTERED: 29 Oct 64 Netherlands
ARTICLES: 9 LANGUAGE: French.
HEADNOTE: COMPENSATION INTEREST
TOPIC: Claims and Debts
CONCEPTS: Exceptions and exemptions. Territorial application. Time limit. Exchange of information and documents. Expropriation. Responsibility and liability. Accounting procedures. Banking. Bonds. Compensation. Currency. Financial programs. Payment schedules. Claims and settlements. Lump sum settlements.
PROCEDURE: Ratification.
PARTIES:
  Netherlands
  Poland

107447 Bilateral Exchange **514 UNTS 187**
SIGNED: 7 Oct 64   FORCE: 7 Oct 64
REGISTERED: 30 Oct 64 Jamaica
ARTICLES: 2 LANGUAGE: English. German.
HEADNOTE: AIR TRANSPORT RELATIONS
TOPIC: Air Transport
CONCEPTS: Detailed regulations. Exchange of information and documents. Routes and logistics. Air transport. Operating authorizations and regulations.
PARTIES:
  Germany, West
  Jamaica

107448 Bilateral Agreement **514 UNTS 195**
SIGNED: 9 Dec 63   FORCE: 31 Jul 64
REGISTERED: 2 Nov 64 Belgium
ARTICLES: 5 LANGUAGE: French. Dutch. Polish.
HEADNOTE: CULTURAL
TOPIC: Culture
CONCEPTS: Treaty implementation. Friendship and amity. Conformity with municipal law. Establishment of commission. Specialists exchange. Recognition of degrees. Teacher and student exchange. Scholarships and grants. Exchange. General cultural cooperation. Artists. Scientific exchange. Research and development. Publications exchange. Mass media exchange.
INTL ORGS: Special Commission.
PROCEDURE: Denunciation. Duration. Ratification. Renewal or Revival.
PARTIES:
  Belgium
  Poland

107449 Multilateral Protocol **514 UNTS 209**
SIGNED: 21 Jun 61   FORCE: 17 Jul 62
REGISTERED: 4 Nov 64 ICAO (Civil Aviat)
ARTICLES: 1 LANGUAGE: English. French. Spanish.
HEADNOTE: INTERNATIONAL AVIATION
TOPIC: IGO Establishment
CONCEPTS: Annex type material. Admission.
INTL ORGS: International Civil Aviation Organization.
TREATY REF: 15UNTS295.
PARTIES:
  Argentina RATIFIED: 19 Nov 63 FORCE: 19 Nov 63
  Australia RATIFIED: 19 Jan 62 FORCE: 17 Jul 62
  Austria RATIFIED: 17 Jul 62 FORCE: 17 Jul 62

Belgium RATIFIED: 15 Feb 62 FORCE: 17 Jul 62
Cameroon RATIFIED: 14 Nov 61 FORCE: 17 Jul 62
Canada RATIFIED: 17 Oct 61 FORCE: 17 Jul 62
Ceylon (Sri Lanka) RATIFIED: 28 May 62 FORCE: 17 Jul 62
Chad RATIFIED: 28 Aug 64 FORCE: 28 Aug 64
Taiwan RATIFIED: 10 Aug 62 FORCE: 10 Aug 62
Central Afri Rep RATIFIED: 22 May 62 FORCE: 17 Jul 62
Congo (Brazzaville) RATIFIED: 26 May 62 FORCE: 17 Jul 62
Costa Rica RATIFIED: 9 Jan 64 FORCE: 9 Jan 64
Cuba RATIFIED: 29 Oct 62 FORCE: 29 Oct 62
Cyprus RATIFIED: 31 Jul 62 FORCE: 31 Jul 62
Czechoslovakia RATIFIED: 9 Mar 62 FORCE: 17 Jul 62
Dahomey RATIFIED: 30 Mar 62 FORCE: 17 Jul 62
Denmark RATIFIED: 15 May 62 FORCE: 17 Jul 62
Dominican Republic RATIFIED: 24 Oct 61 FORCE: 17 Jul 62
El Salvador RATIFIED: 22 Jan 63 FORCE: 22 Jan 63
Ethiopia RATIFIED: 23 Jan 63 FORCE: 23 Jan 63
Finland RATIFIED: 18 Sep 61 FORCE: 17 Jul 62
Fed of Malaya RATIFIED: 3 Oct 61 FORCE: 17 Jul 62
France RATIFIED: 20 Nov 62 FORCE: 20 Nov 62
Germany, West RATIFIED: 16 Aug 62 FORCE: 16 Aug 62
Ghana RATIFIED: 13 Apr 62 FORCE: 17 Jul 62
Guinea RATIFIED: 21 Aug 61 FORCE: 17 Jul 62
Honduras RATIFIED: 20 Dec 62 FORCE: 20 Dec 62
India RATIFIED: 18 Dec 61 FORCE: 17 Jul 62
Indonesia RATIFIED: 28 Jul 61 FORCE: 17 Jul 62
Ireland RATIFIED: 9 Apr 62 FORCE: 17 Jul 62
Israel RATIFIED: 12 Feb 62 FORCE: 17 Jul 62
Italy RATIFIED: 17 May 63 FORCE: 17 May 63
Ivory Coast RATIFIED: 14 Nov 61 FORCE: 17 Jul 62
Jamaica RATIFIED: 18 Oct 63 FORCE: 18 Oct 63
Japan RATIFIED: 4 Jun 62 FORCE: 17 Jul 62
Jordan RATIFIED: 27 Jul 61 FORCE: 17 Jul 62
Kenya RATIFIED: 31 May 64 FORCE: 31 May 64
Korea, South RATIFIED: 16 Feb 62 FORCE: 17 Jul 62
Kuwait RATIFIED: 3 Jul 62 FORCE: 17 Jul 62
Laos RATIFIED: 7 Mar 62 FORCE: 17 Jul 62
Lebanon RATIFIED: 18 Jun 62 FORCE: 17 Jul 62
Libya RATIFIED: 17 Aug 62 FORCE: 17 Aug 62
Malagasy RATIFIED: 7 Dec 62 FORCE: 7 Dec 62
Mali RATIFIED: 12 Jul 61 FORCE: 17 Jul 62
Mauritania RATIFIED: 2 Apr 62 FORCE: 17 Jul 62
Mexico RATIFIED: 9 Apr 62 FORCE: 17 Jul 62
Netherlands RATIFIED: 8 May 62 FORCE: 17 Jul 62
New Zealand RATIFIED: 14 May 62 FORCE: 17 Jul 62
Nicaragua RATIFIED: 17 Nov 61 FORCE: 17 Jul 62
Nigeria RATIFIED: 7 Mar 62 FORCE: 17 Jul 62
Niger RATIFIED: 14 Sep 61 FORCE: 17 Jul 62
Norway RATIFIED: 10 Oct 61 FORCE: 17 Jul 62
Pakistan RATIFIED: 30 Apr 62 FORCE: 17 Jul 62
Panama RATIFIED: 9 Jul 62 FORCE: 17 Jul 62
Peru RATIFIED: 12 Mar 64 FORCE: 12 Mar 64
Philippines RATIFIED: 12 Nov 62 FORCE: 12 Nov 62
Poland RATIFIED: 23 May 62 FORCE: 17 Jul 62
Portugal RATIFIED: 29 May 62 FORCE: 17 Jul 62
Senegal RATIFIED: 5 Mar 62 FORCE: 17 Jul 62
Sierra Leone RATIFIED: 15 May 62 FORCE: 17 Jul 62
South Africa RATIFIED: 13 Feb 62 FORCE: 17 Jul 62
Somalia RATIFIED: 30 Sep 64 FORCE: 30 Sep 64
Spain RATIFIED: 2 Apr 62 FORCE: 17 Jul 62
Sudan RATIFIED: 31 May 62 FORCE: 17 Jul 62
Sweden RATIFIED: 28 Dec 61 FORCE: 17 Jul 62
Switzerland RATIFIED: 22 May 62 FORCE: 17 Jul 62
Syria RATIFIED: 16 Jul 62 FORCE: 17 Jul 62
Tanganyika RATIFIED: 10 Apr 63 FORCE: 10 Apr 63
Thailand RATIFIED: 17 Jan 62 FORCE: 17 Jul 62
Tunisia RATIFIED: 27 Dec 61 FORCE: 17 Jul 62
United Arab Rep RATIFIED: 27 Feb 62 FORCE: 17 Jul 62

UK Great Britain RATIFIED: 4 Jan 62 FORCE:
17 Jul 62
USA (United States) RATIFIED: 23 Mar 62
FORCE: 17 Jul 62
Venezuela RATIFIED: 6 Feb 62 FORCE: 17 Jul 62
Vietnam, South RATIFIED: 13 Apr 62 FORCE:
17 Jul 62
Yugoslavia RATIFIED: 5 Mar 62 FORCE:
17 Jul 62

107450 Bilateral Exchange **515 UNTS 3**
SIGNED: 15 Apr 64 FORCE: 15 Apr 64
REGISTERED: 4 Nov 64 UK Great Britain
ARTICLES: 2 LANGUAGE: English. Spanish.
HEADNOTE: PRODUCTION TRADE POLICIES CE-
REALS
TOPIC: Commodity Trade
CONCEPTS: Detailed regulations. Annex or appen-
dix reference. General cooperation. Balance of
payments. Fees and exemptions. Non-interest
rates and fees. Commodity trade.
INTL ORGS: General Agreement on Tariffs and
Trade.
TREATY REF: 55UNTS187; 60UNTS131;
138UNTS398.
PROCEDURE: Termination.
PARTIES:
Argentina
UK Great Britain

107451 Bilateral Exchange **515 UNTS 23**
SIGNED: 15 Apr 64 FORCE: 15 Apr 64
REGISTERED: 4 Nov 64 UK Great Britain
ARTICLES: 2 LANGUAGE: English.
HEADNOTE: PRODUCTION TRADE POLICIES CE-
REALS
TOPIC: Commodity Trade
CONCEPTS: Detailed regulations. Annex or appen-
dix reference. General cooperation. Balance of
payments. Fees and exemptions. Non-interest
rates and fees. Commodity trade.
INTL ORGS: General Agreement on Tariffs and
Trade.
TREATY REF: 515UNTS3; 265UNTS197.
PROCEDURE: Termination.
PARTIES:
Australia
UK Great Britain

107452 Bilateral Exchange **515 UNTS 39**
SIGNED: 15 Apr 64 FORCE: 15 Apr 64
REGISTERED: 4 Nov 64 UK Great Britain
ARTICLES: 2 LANGUAGE: English.
HEADNOTE: PRODUCTION TRADE POLICIES CE-
REALS
TOPIC: Commodity Trade
CONCEPTS: Detailed regulations. Annex or appen-
dix reference. General cooperation. Balance of
payments. Fees and exemptions. Non-interest
rates and fees. Commodity trade.
INTL ORGS: General Agreement on Tariffs and
Trade.
TREATY REF: 55UNTS187; 515UNTS4.
PROCEDURE: Termination.
PARTIES:
Canada
UK Great Britain

107453 Bilateral Exchange **515 UNTS 55**
SIGNED: 15 Apr 64 FORCE: 15 Apr 64
REGISTERED: 4 Nov 64 UK Great Britain
ARTICLES: 2 LANGUAGE: English.
HEADNOTE: PRODUCTION TRADE POLICIES CE-
REALS
TOPIC: Commodity Trade
CONCEPTS: Detailed regulations. Annex or appen-
dix reference. General cooperation. Balance of
payments. Fees and exemptions. Non-interest
rates and fees. Commodity trade.
INTL ORGS: General Agreement on Tariffs and
Trade.
TREATY REF: 55UNTS187; 515UNTS4.
PROCEDURE: Termination.
PARTIES:
UK Great Britain
USA (United States)

107454 Bilateral Exchange **515 UNTS 71**
SIGNED: 22 Jun 64 FORCE: 22 Jun 64

REGISTERED: 4 Nov 64 UK Great Britain
ARTICLES: 2 LANGUAGE: English.
HEADNOTE: PRODUCTION TRADE POLICIES CE-
REALS
TOPIC: Commodity Trade
CONCEPTS: Detailed regulations. Annex or appen-
dix reference. General cooperation. Balance of
payments. Fees and exemptions. Non-interest
rates and fees. Commodity trade.
INTL ORGS: General Agreement on Tariffs and
Trade.
TREATY REF: 55UNTS187; 515UNTS4.
PROCEDURE: Termination.
PARTIES:
South Africa
UK Great Britain

107455 Bilateral Exchange **515 UNTS 83**
SIGNED: 30 Jun 64 FORCE: 30 Jun 64
REGISTERED: 4 Nov 64 UK Great Britain
ARTICLES: 2 LANGUAGE: English.
HEADNOTE: PRODUCTION TRADE POLICIES CE-
REALS
TOPIC: Commodity Trade
CONCEPTS: Detailed regulations. Annex or appen-
dix reference. General cooperation. Balance of
payments. Fees and exemptions. Non-interest
rates and fees. Commodity trade.
INTL ORGS: General Agreement on Tariffs and
Trade.
TREATY REF: 55UNTS187; 515UNTS.
PROCEDURE: Termination.
PARTIES:
Sweden
UK Great Britain

107456 Multilateral Agreement **515 UNTS 94**
SIGNED: 11 Nov 64 FORCE: 11 Nov 64
REGISTERED: 11 Nov 64 United Nations
ARTICLES: 6 LANGUAGE: English.
HEADNOTE: TECHNICAL ASSISTANCE
TOPIC: Tech Assistance
CONCEPTS: Definition of terms. Privileges and im-
munities. General cooperation. Exchange of in-
formation and documents. Personnel. Responsi-
bility and liability. Title and deeds. Use of facili-
ties. Exchange. Scholarships and grants.
Vocational training. Research and development.
Exchange rates and regulations. Expense shar-
ing formulae. Local currency. Domestic obliga-
tion. General technical assistance. Materials,
equipment and services. IGO status. Conformity
with IGO decisions.
TREATY REF: 76UNTS132; 1UNTS15;
33UNTS261; 374UNTS147.
PROCEDURE: Amendment. Termination.
PARTIES:
Kenya SIGNED: 11 Nov 64 FORCE: 11 Nov 64
FAO (Food Agri) SIGNED: 11 Nov 64 FORCE:
11 Nov 64
IAEA (Atom Energy) SIGNED: 11 Nov 64 FORCE:
11 Nov 64
ICAO (Civil Aviat) SIGNED: 11 Nov 64 FORCE:
11 Nov 64
ILO (Labor Org) SIGNED: 11 Nov 64 FORCE:
11 Nov 64
ITU (Telecommun) SIGNED: 11 Nov 64 FORCE:
11 Nov 64
UNESCO (Educ/Cult) SIGNED: 11 Nov 64
FORCE: 11 Nov 64
United Nations SIGNED: 11 Nov 64 FORCE:
11 Nov 64
UPU (Postal Union) SIGNED: 11 Nov 64 FORCE:
11 Nov 64
WHO (World Health) SIGNED: 11 Nov 64 FORCE:
11 Nov 64
WMO (Meteorology) SIGNED: 11 Nov 64 FORCE:
11 Nov 64

107457 Bilateral Agreement **515 UNTS 109**
SIGNED: 15 May 64 FORCE: 15 May 64
REGISTERED: 12 Nov 64 Austria
ARTICLES: 17 LANGUAGE: German. Turkish.
HEADNOTE: RECRUITMENT EMPLOYMENT
WORKERS
TOPIC: Non-ILO Labor
CONCEPTS: Definition of terms. Annex or appen-
dix reference. Resident permits. Conformity with
municipal law. Operating agencies. Private con-
tracts. Technical and commercial staff. Estab-
lishment of commission. Employment regula-

tions. Non-ILO labor relations. Administrative co-
operation. Migrant worker. Monetary and gold
transfers. Transportation costs. National treat-
ment.
INTL ORGS: Special Commission.
PROCEDURE: Denunciation. Duration. Termina-
tion.
PARTIES:
Austria
Turkey

107458 Bilateral Agreement **515 UNTS 151**
SIGNED: 24 Jun 59 FORCE: 6 Apr 64
REGISTERED: 18 Nov 64 Israel
ARTICLES: 13 LANGUAGE: Hebrew. Portuguese.
French.
HEADNOTE: CULTURAL
TOPIC: Culture
CONCEPTS: Treaty implementation. Treaty inter-
pretation. Friendship and amity. Tourism. Con-
formity with municipal law. Specialists ex-
change. Teacher and student exchange. Profes-
sorships. Institute establishment. Scholarships
and grants. Vocational training. Exchange. Gen-
eral cultural cooperation. Artists. Athletes. Scien-
tific exchange. Publications exchange. Mass me-
dia exchange. Press and wire services.
PROCEDURE: Denunciation. Ratification.
PARTIES:
Brazil
Israel

107459 Bilateral Exchange **515 UNTS 165**
SIGNED: 20 Dec 63 FORCE: 2 Dec 63
REGISTERED: 18 Nov 64 Israel
ARTICLES: 3 LANGUAGE: French.
HEADNOTE: EXEMPTION DEATH DUTIES
TOPIC: Customs
CONCEPTS: Conformity with municipal law. Cus-
toms exemptions.
PARTIES:
France
Israel

107460 Bilateral Convention **515 UNTS 173**
SIGNED: 20 Aug 63 FORCE: 1 Sep 64
REGISTERED: 18 Nov 64 Israel
ARTICLES: 28 LANGUAGE: Hebrew. French.
HEADNOTE: DOUBLE TAXATION INCOME
TOPIC: Taxation
CONCEPTS: Definition of terms. Territorial applica-
tion. Previous treaty replacement. Conformity
with municipal law. Exchange of official publica-
tions. Domestic legislation. Negotiation. Teacher
and student exchange. Taxation. Tax credits. Eq-
uitable taxes. General. Tax exemptions. Air trans-
port. Merchant vessels.
TREATY REF: 220UNTS55.
PROCEDURE: Duration. Termination.
PARTIES:
France
Israel

107461 Bilateral Agreement **515 UNTS 237**
SIGNED: 25 May 62 FORCE: 17 Jun 63
REGISTERED: 18 Nov 64 Israel
ARTICLES: 7 LANGUAGE: Hebrew. English.
HEADNOTE: TECHNICAL COOPERATION
TOPIC: Tech Assistance
CONCEPTS: Detailed regulations. Personnel. Use
of facilities. Scholarships and grants. Expense
sharing formulae. General technical assistance.
PROCEDURE: Ratification. Registration.
PARTIES:
Ghana
Israel

107462 Bilateral Exchange **515 UNTS 251**
SIGNED: 26 Oct 61 FORCE: 24 Jan 62
REGISTERED: 18 Nov 64 Israel
ARTICLES: 2 LANGUAGE: French.
HEADNOTE: ABOLITION VISAS
TOPIC: Visas
CONCEPTS: Time limit. Visa abolition. Resident
permits.
PROCEDURE: Termination.
PARTIES:
Israel
Ivory Coast

107463   Bilateral Exchange   **515 UNTS 257**
SIGNED: 23 Jul 63   FORCE: 21 Oct 63
REGISTERED: 18 Nov 64 Israel
ARTICLES: 2 LANGUAGE: French.
HEADNOTE: ABOLITION VISAS
TOPIC: Visas
CONCEPTS: Time limit. Visa abolition. Resident
  permits.
PARTIES:
  Israel
  Niger

107464   Bilateral Convention   **515 UNTS 263**
SIGNED: 25 Jun 62   FORCE: 11 Sep 63
REGISTERED: 18 Nov 64 Israel
ARTICLES: 3 LANGUAGE: Hebrew. Spanish.
HEADNOTE: CULTURAL CONVENTION
TOPIC: Culture
CONCEPTS: Friendship and amity. Conformity
  with municipal law. Exchange of official publica-
  tions. Exchange of information and documents.
  Teacher and student exchange. Professorships.
  Institute establishment. Exchange. General cul-
  tural cooperation. Artists. Athletes. An-
  thropology and archeology. Scientific exchange.
  Research and development. Recognition. Publi-
  cations exchange. Mass media exchange. Press
  and wire services.
PROCEDURE: Denunciation. Ratification.
PARTIES:
  Israel
  Peru

107465   Bilateral Convention   **515 UNTS 279**
SIGNED: 2 Apr 63   FORCE: 11 Sep 63
REGISTERED: 18 Nov 64 Israel
ARTICLES: 5 LANGUAGE: Hebrew. Spanish.
HEADNOTE: TECHNICAL COOPERATION
TOPIC: Tech Assistance
CONCEPTS: General technical assistance.
PARTIES:
  Israel
  Peru

107466   Bilateral Agreement   **515 UNTS 291**
SIGNED: 23 Oct 62   FORCE: 9 Jun 64
REGISTERED: 18 Nov 64 Israel
ARTICLES: 4 LANGUAGE: Hebrew. French.
HEADNOTE: TECHNICAL COOPERATION
TOPIC: Tech Assistance
CONCEPTS: General cooperation. Personnel. Pub-
  lic health. Education. Scholarships and grants.
  Vocational training. Research and development.
  Expense sharing formulae. General technical as-
  sistance. Agriculture. General transportation.
PROCEDURE: Ratification.
PARTIES:
  Israel
  Rwanda

107467   Bilateral Agreement   **516 UNTS 3**
SIGNED: 10 Sep 63   FORCE: 2 Sep 64
REGISTERED: 18 Nov 64 Israel
ARTICLES: 23 LANGUAGE: Hebrew. Swedish. En-
  glish.
HEADNOTE: RECIPROCAL EXTRADITION CRIMI-
  NALS
TOPIC: Extradition
CONCEPTS: Time limit. Extradition, deportation
  and repatriation. Extradition requests. Extradita-
  ble offenses. Location of crime. Special factors.
  Refusal of extradition. Concurrent requests. Pre-
  treaty crimes. Limits of prosecution. Provisional
  detainment. Material evidence.
PROCEDURE: Ratification. Termination.
PARTIES:
  Israel
  Sweden

107468   Bilateral Agreement   **516 UNTS 39**
SIGNED: 28 Jan 63   FORCE: 28 Jan 63
REGISTERED: 18 Nov 64 Israel
ARTICLES: 4 LANGUAGE: Hebrew. English.
HEADNOTE: TECHNICAL COOPERATION
TOPIC: Tech Assistance
CONCEPTS: Treaty implementation. Personnel.
  Public health. Education. Scholarships and
  grants. Vocational training. Research and devel-

opment. General technical assistance. Agricul-
ture. General transportation.
PROCEDURE: Amendment.
PARTIES:
  Israel
  Tanganyika

107469   Bilateral Exchange   **516 UNTS 47**
SIGNED: 17 Sep 63   FORCE: 17 Sep 63
REGISTERED: 18 Nov 64 Israel
ARTICLES: 2 LANGUAGE: English.
HEADNOTE: ABOLITION VISAS
TOPIC: Visas
CONCEPTS: Time limit. Visa abolition. Passports
  diplomatic. Resident permits.
PROCEDURE: Termination.
PARTIES:
  Israel
  Tanganyika

107470   Multilateral Exchange   **516 UNTS 53**
SIGNED: 3 Mar 64   FORCE: 12 Mar 64
REGISTERED: 18 Nov 64 Israel
ARTICLES: 2 LANGUAGE: English. Russian.
HEADNOTE: ABOLITION FEES CONSULAR SER-
  VICE
TOPIC: Consul/Citizenship
CONCEPTS: General consular functions. Notarial
  acts and services. Fees and exemptions.
PARTIES:
  Israel
  USSR (Soviet Union)

107471   Bilateral Agreement   **516 UNTS 59**
SIGNED: 7 Oct 64   FORCE: 7 Oct 64
REGISTERED: 18 Nov 64 Israel
ARTICLES: 6 LANGUAGE: Hebrew. Russian.
HEADNOTE: SALE PROPERTY
TOPIC: Specific Property
CONCEPTS: Annex or appendix reference. Gen-
  eral property. Indemnities and reimbursements.
  Interest rates. Payment schedules. Local cur-
  rency. Assets transfer.
PARTIES:
  Israel
  USSR (Soviet Union)

107472   Bilateral Exchange   **516 UNTS 91**
SIGNED: 13 Jun 64   FORCE: 15 Jul 64
REGISTERED: 18 Nov 64 Israel
ARTICLES: 2 LANGUAGE: French.
HEADNOTE: ABOLITION VISA FEES
TOPIC: Visas
CONCEPTS: Visas. Fees and exemptions.
PROCEDURE: Termination.
PARTIES:
  Israel
  Yugoslavia

107473   Bilateral Agreement   **516 UNTS 99**
SIGNED: 7 Feb 64   FORCE: 4 Aug 64
REGISTERED: 20 Nov 64 IBRD (World Bank)
ARTICLES: 5 LANGUAGE: English.
HEADNOTE: GUARANTEE AGREEMENT
TOPIC: IBRD Project
CONCEPTS: Definition of terms. Annex or appen-
  dix reference. Exchange of information and doc-
  uments. Inspection and observation. Bonds.
  Fees and exemptions. Tax exemptions. Domestic
  obligation. Terms of loan. Loan regulations. Loan
  guarantee. Guarantor non-interference.
PARTIES:
  Colombia
  IBRD (World Bank)
                     ANNEX
639 UNTS 338. IBRD (World Bank). Amendment
  22 Dec 67. Force 29 Mar 68.
639 UNTS 338.   Colombia.   Amendment
  22 Dec 67. Force 29 Mar 68.

107474   Bilateral Agreement   **516 UNTS 125**
SIGNED: 10 Jul 64   FORCE: 21 Aug 64
REGISTERED: 20 Nov 64 IBRD (World Bank)
ARTICLES: 7 LANGUAGE: English.
HEADNOTE: LOAN ROAD
TOPIC: IBRD Project
CONCEPTS: Default remedies. Definition of terms.
  Annex or appendix reference. Exchange of infor-

mation and documents. Informational records.
Inspection and observation. Accounting proce-
dures. Bonds. Fees and exemptions. Interest
rates. Tax exemptions. Domestic obligation.
Terms of loan. Loan regulations. Loan guarantee.
Guarantor non-interference. Roads and high-
ways.
PARTIES:
  Finland
  IBRD (World Bank)

107475   Bilateral Agreement   **516 UNTS 145**
SIGNED: 14 May 64   FORCE: 10 Aug 64
REGISTERED: 20 Nov 64 IBRD (World Bank)
ARTICLES: 5 LANGUAGE: English.
HEADNOTE: GUARANTEE POST
TOPIC: IBRD Project
CONCEPTS: Definition of terms. Annex or appen-
  dix reference. Exchange of information and doc-
  uments. Inspection and observation. Bonds.
  Fees and exemptions. Tax exemptions. Domestic
  obligation. Terms of loan. Loan regulations. Loan
  guarantee. Guarantor non-interference. Water
  transport.
PARTIES:
  Pakistan
  IBRD (World Bank)

107476   Bilateral Agreement   **516 UNTS 171**
SIGNED: 22 Jul 64   FORCE: 4 Nov 64
REGISTERED: 20 Nov 64 IBRD (World Bank)
ARTICLES: 6 LANGUAGE: English.
HEADNOTE: GUARANTEE WATER
TOPIC: IBRD Project
CONCEPTS: Definition of terms. Annex or appen-
  dix reference. Exchange of information and doc-
  uments. Inspection and observation. Sanitation.
  Bonds. Fees and exemptions. Tax exemptions.
  Domestic obligation. Terms of loan. Loan regula-
  tions. Loan guarantee. Guarantor non-interfer-
  ence.
PARTIES:
  Philippines
  IBRD (World Bank)

107477   Multilateral Convention **516 UNTS 205**
SIGNED: 29 Apr 58   FORCE: 10 Sep 64
REGISTERED: 22 Nov 64 United Nations
ARTICLES: 32 LANGUAGE: English. French. Chi-
  nese. Russian. Spanish.
HEADNOTE: TERRITORIAL SEA CONTIGUOUS
  ZONE
TOPIC: Territory Boundary
CONCEPTS: Juridical personality. Innocent pas-
  sage. Merchant vessels. Naval vessels. Markers
  and definitions. Frontier waterways.
INTL ORGS: United Nations.
PROCEDURE: Accession. Duration. Ratification.
  Registration.
PARTIES:
  Afghanistan SIGNED: 30 Oct 58
  Argentina SIGNED: 29 Apr 58
  Australia   SIGNED: 30 Oct 58   RATIFIED:
    14 May 64 FORCE: 10 Sep 64
  Austria SIGNED: 27 Oct 58
  Bolivia SIGNED: 17 Oct 58
  Bulgaria   SIGNED: 31 Oct 58   RATIFIED:
    31 Aug 62 FORCE: 10 Sep 64
  Canada SIGNED: 29 Apr 58
  Ceylon (Sri Lanka) SIGNED: 30 Oct 58
  Taiwan SIGNED: 29 Apr 58
  Colombia SIGNED: 29 Apr 58
  Costa Rica SIGNED: 29 Apr 58
  Cuba SIGNED: 29 Apr 58
  Czechoslovakia SIGNED: 30 Oct 58 RATIFIED:
    31 Aug 61 FORCE: 10 Sep 64
  Denmark SIGNED: 29 Apr 58
  Dominican Republic SIGNED: 29 Apr 58 RATI-
    FIED: 11 Aug 64 FORCE: 10 Sep 64
  Finland SIGNED: 27 Oct 58
  Ghana SIGNED: 29 Apr 58
  Guatemala SIGNED: 29 Apr 58
  Haiti SIGNED: 29 Apr 58 RATIFIED: 29 Mar 60
    FORCE: 10 Sep 64
  Hungary SIGNED: 31 Oct 58 RATIFIED: 6 Dec 61
    FORCE: 10 Sep 64
  Iceland SIGNED: 29 Apr 58
  Iran SIGNED: 28 May 58
  Ireland SIGNED: 2 Sep 58
  Israel SIGNED: 29 Apr 58 RATIFIED: 6 Sep 61
    FORCE: 10 Sep 64

Liberia SIGNED: 27 May 58
Madagascar RATIFIED: 31 Jul 62 FORCE: 10 Sep 64
Malaysia RATIFIED: 21 Dec 60 FORCE: 10 Sep 64
Nepal SIGNED: 29 Apr 58
Netherlands SIGNED: 31 Oct 58
New Zealand SIGNED: 29 Oct 58
Niger RATIFIED: 26 Jun 61 FORCE: 10 Sep 64
Pakistan SIGNED: 31 Oct 58
Panama SIGNED: 2 May 58
Portugal SIGNED: 28 Oct 58 RATIFIED: 8 Jan 63 FORCE: 10 Sep 64
Romania SIGNED: 31 Oct 58 RATIFIED: 12 Dec 61 FORCE: 10 Sep 64
Senegal RATIFIED: 25 Apr 61 FORCE: 10 Sep 64
Sierra Leone RATIFIED: 13 Mar 62 FORCE: 10 Sep 64
Switzerland SIGNED: 22 Oct 58
Thailand SIGNED: 29 Apr 58
Tunisia SIGNED: 30 Oct 58
Uganda RATIFIED: 14 Sep 64 FORCE: 27 Sep 64
UK Great Britain SIGNED: 9 Sep 58 RATIFIED: 14 Mar 60 FORCE: 10 Sep 64
USA (United States) SIGNED: 15 Sep 58 RATIFIED: 12 Apr 61 FORCE: 10 Sep 64
Ukrainian SSR SIGNED: 30 Oct 58 RATIFIED: 12 Jan 61 FORCE: 10 Sep 64
Uruguay SIGNED: 29 Apr 58
USSR (Soviet Union) SIGNED: 30 Oct 58 RATIFIED: 22 Nov 60 FORCE: 10 Sep 64
Vatican/Holy See SIGNED: 30 Oct 58
Venezuela SIGNED: 30 Oct 58 RATIFIED: 15 Apr 61 FORCE: 10 Sep 64
Yugoslavia SIGNED: 29 Apr 58
ANNEX
521 UNTS 404. Italy. Qualified Accession 17 Dec 64.
525 UNTS 340. Finland. Ratification 16 Feb 65. Force 18 Mar 65.
539 UNTS 382. USA (United States). Objection 17 Jun 65.
547 UNTS 361. Jamaica. Succession 8 Oct 65.
547 UNTS 361. Malawi. Accession 3 Nov 65. Force 3 Dec 65.
552 UNTS 422. Yugoslavia. Ratification 28 Jan 66. Force 27 Feb 66.
555 UNTS 262. Netherlands. Qualified Ratification 18 Feb 66. Force 20 Mar 66.
560 UNTS 294. Trinidad/Tobago. Succession 11 Apr 66.
562 UNTS 338. Switzerland. Ratification 18 May 66. Force 17 Jun 66.
562 UNTS 338. Malta. Succession 19 May 66. Force 21 Sep 64.
573 UNTS 346. USA (United States). Objection 27 Sep 66.
638 UNTS 304. Japan. Declaration 10 Jun 68.
638 UNTS 304. Japan. Accession 10 Jun 68. Force 10 Jul 68.
639 UNTS 350. Thailand. Declaration 2 Jul 68. Force 1 Aug 68.
639 UNTS 350. Thailand. Ratification 2 Jul 68. Force 1 Aug 68.
646 UNTS 408. Denmark. Signature Subject to Ratification 26 Sep 68. Force 26 Oct 68.

107478 Bilateral Exchange 516 UNTS 283
SIGNED: 12 Sep 61 FORCE: 20 Dec 63
REGISTERED: 23 Nov 64 Denmark
ARTICLES: 2 LANGUAGE: German.
HEADNOTE: STUDENT EMPLOYEES
TOPIC: Non-ILO Labor
CONCEPTS: Territorial application. Resident permits. Conformity with municipal law. Professorships. Employment regulations. Wages and salaries. Non-ILO labor relations. Administrative cooperation. Migrant worker. Fees and exemptions. Transportation costs. Quotas. National treatment.
PROCEDURE: Denunciation. Duration. Renewal or Revival.
PARTIES:
Denmark
Germany, West

107479 Bilateral Agreement 516 UNTS 295
SIGNED: 18 Aug 64 FORCE: 26 Oct 64
REGISTERED: 25 Nov 64 IBRD (World Bank)
ARTICLES: 5 LANGUAGE: English.

HEADNOTE: GUARANTEE POWER
TOPIC: IBRD Project
CONCEPTS: Definition of terms. Annex or appendix reference. Exchange of information and documents. Inspection and observation. Bonds. Fees and exemptions. Tax exemptions. Domestic obligation. Terms of loan. Loan regulations. Loan guarantee. Guarantor non-interference. Hydroelectric power.
PARTIES:
IBRD (World Bank)
Sierra Leone

107480 Bilateral Agreement 516 UNTS 325
SIGNED: 12 Mar 64 FORCE: 10 Aug 64
REGISTERED: 25 Nov 64 IBRD (World Bank)
ARTICLES: 5 LANGUAGE: English.
HEADNOTE: GUARANTEE TRANSMISSION PROJECT
TOPIC: IBRD Project
CONCEPTS: Definition of terms. Annex or appendix reference. Exchange of information and documents. Inspection and observation. Bonds. Fees and exemptions. Tax exemptions. Domestic obligation. Terms of loan. Loan regulations. Loan guarantee. Guarantor non-interference. Facilities and equipment.
PARTIES:
Nigeria
IBRD (World Bank)

107481 Bilateral Agreement 517 UNTS 3
SIGNED: 1 Oct 63 FORCE: 11 Sep 64
REGISTERED: 25 Nov 64 IBRD (World Bank)
ARTICLES: 8 LANGUAGE: English.
HEADNOTE: GUARANTEE TELECOMMUNICATION PROJECT
TOPIC: IBRD Project
CONCEPTS: Definition of terms. Annex or appendix reference. Exchange of information and documents. Inspection and observation. Bonds. Fees and exemptions. Tax exemptions. Domestic obligation. Terms of loan. Loan regulations. Loan guarantee. Guarantor non-interference. Telecommunications.
PARTIES:
El Salvador
IBRD (World Bank)

107482 Bilateral Agreement 517 UNTS 33
SIGNED: 20 Mar 56 FORCE: 1 Jul 56
REGISTERED: 25 Nov 64 Japan
ARTICLES: 24 LANGUAGE: English. Japanese.
HEADNOTE: PARCEL POST
TOPIC: Postal Service
CONCEPTS: Previous treaty replacement. Responsibility and liability. Accounting procedures. Customs declarations. Postal services. Regulations. Insured letters and boxes. Parcel post. Rates and charges.
INTL ORGS: Universal Postal Union.
TREATY REF: JAPAN-CANADA.
PROCEDURE: Duration. Termination.
PARTIES:
Canada
Japan

107483 Bilateral Agreement 517 UNTS 81
SIGNED: 1 Mar 62 FORCE: 1 Oct 62
REGISTERED: 25 Nov 64 Japan
ARTICLES: 18 LANGUAGE: Japanese. English.
HEADNOTE: PARCEL POST
TOPIC: Postal Service
CONCEPTS: Previous treaty replacement. Responsibility and liability. Accounting procedures. Postal services. Regulations. Insured letters and boxes. Conveyance in transit. Parcel post. Rates and charges.
INTL ORGS: Universal Postal Union.
TREATY REF: JAPAN-AUSTRALIA 1906; 365UNTS3.
PROCEDURE: Duration. Termination.
PARTIES:
Australia
Japan

107484 Bilateral Treaty 517 UNTS 107
SIGNED: 1 Jul 61 FORCE: 8 Mar 63
REGISTERED: 25 Nov 64 Japan

ARTICLES: 12 LANGUAGE: Japanese. Indonesian. English.
HEADNOTE: AMITY COMMERCE
TOPIC: General Amity
CONCEPTS: Exceptions and exemptions. Alien status. General cooperation. Expropriation. Legal protection and assistance. Export quotas. Import quotas. Balance of payments. Monetary and gold transfers. Payment schedules. Most favored nation clause. Taxation. Customs duties. Service in foreign army.
INTL ORGS: General Agreement on Tariffs and Trade. International Monetary Fund.
TREATY REF: GATT.
PROCEDURE: Duration. Ratification. Termination.
PARTIES:
Indonesia
Japan

107485 Bilateral Convention 517 UNTS 155
SIGNED: 20 Dec 61 FORCE: 4 Apr 63
REGISTERED: 25 Nov 64 Japan
ARTICLES: 25 LANGUAGE: English.
HEADNOTE: DOUBLE TAXATION INCOME
TOPIC: Taxation
CONCEPTS: Definition of terms. Conformity with municipal law. Exchange of official publications. Negotiation. Teacher and student exchange. Taxation. Tax credits. Equitable taxes. General. Tax exemptions. Air transport. Merchant vessels.
PROCEDURE: Duration. Ratification. Termination.
PARTIES:
Austria
Japan

107486 Bilateral Convention 517 UNTS 183
SIGNED: 30 Jan 63 FORCE: 19 Apr 63
REGISTERED: 25 Nov 64 Japan
ARTICLES: 19 LANGUAGE: Japanese. English.
HEADNOTE: DOUBLE TAXATION INCOME
TOPIC: Taxation
CONCEPTS: Definition of terms. Privileges and immunities. Conformity with municipal law. Exchange of official publications. Negotiation. Teacher and student exchange. Claims and settlements. Taxation. Tax credits. General. Tax exemptions. Air transport. Merchant vessels.
PROCEDURE: Ratification. Termination.
PARTIES:
Japan
New Zealand
ANNEX
614 UNTS 324. New Zealand. Amendment 30 Jan 63. Force 30 Sep 67.
614 UNTS 324. Japan. Amendment 30 Jan 63. Force 30 Sep 67.

107487 Bilateral Agreement 517 UNTS 229
SIGNED: 15 Mar 63 FORCE: 1 Aug 63
REGISTERED: 25 Nov 64 Japan
ARTICLES: 11 LANGUAGE: Japanese. English.
HEADNOTE: PARCEL POST
TOPIC: Postal Service
CONCEPTS: Postal services. Regulations. Insured letters and boxes. Conveyance in transit. Parcel post. Rates and charges.
INTL ORGS: Universal Postal Union.
TREATY REF: 365UNTS3.
PROCEDURE: Duration. Termination.
PARTIES:
Japan
New Zealand

107488 Bilateral Convention 517 UNTS 245
SIGNED: 4 Jun 63 FORCE: 21 Aug 63
REGISTERED: 25 Nov 64 Japan
ARTICLES: 18 LANGUAGE: English.
HEADNOTE: DOUBLE TAXATION INCOME
TOPIC: Taxation
CONCEPTS: Definition of terms. Conformity with municipal law. Exchange of official publications. Domestic legislation. Negotiation. Teacher and student exchange. Taxation. Tax credits. Equitable taxes. Tax exemptions. Air transport. Merchant vessels.
PROCEDURE: Ratification. Termination.
PARTIES:
Japan
Malaysia

107489 Bilateral Agreement **517 UNTS 281**
SIGNED: 19 Jan 63 FORCE: 1 Sep 63
REGISTERED: 25 Nov 64 Japan
ARTICLES: 20 LANGUAGE: Japanese. Philippine. English.
HEADNOTE: PARCEL POST
TOPIC: Postal Service
CONCEPTS: Detailed regulations. Conformity with municipal law. Claims and settlements. Customs duties. Postal services. Regulations. Parcel post. Rates and charges.
PROCEDURE: Duration. Termination.
PARTIES:
 Japan
 Philippines

107490 Bilateral Agreement **518 UNTS 3**
SIGNED: 29 Mar 63 FORCE: 25 Oct 63
REGISTERED: 25 Nov 64 Japan
ARTICLES: 11 LANGUAGE: English.
HEADNOTE: ECONOMIC TECHNICAL COOPERATION
TOPIC: General Aid
CONCEPTS: Treaty implementation. Annex or appendix reference. Annex type material. Inviolability. Privileges and immunities. General cooperation. Private contracts. Use of facilities. Establishment of commission. Arbitration. Procedure. Reexport of goods, etc.. Payment schedules. Tax exemptions. Customs exemptions. Commodities and services. General technical assistance. Economic assistance. Aid missions. Grants.
INTL ORGS: International Court of Justice. Arbitration Commission. Special Commission.
PROCEDURE: Ratification.
PARTIES:
 Burma
 Japan

107491 Bilateral Agreement **518 UNTS 29**
SIGNED: 14 Nov 60 FORCE: 29 Oct 63
REGISTERED: 25 Nov 64 Japan
ARTICLES: 50 LANGUAGE: Japanese. Portuguese.
HEADNOTE: MIGRATION SETTLEMENT
TOPIC: Consul/Citizenship
CONCEPTS: Detailed regulations. Border traffic and migration. Visas. Conformity with municipal law. General cooperation. Establishment of commission. Sickness and invalidity insurance. Financial programs. Customs exemptions.
INTL ORGS: Special Commission.
PROCEDURE: Amendment. Ratification. Termination.
PARTIES:
 Brazil
 Japan

107492 Bilateral Agreement **518 UNTS 91**
SIGNED: 17 Dec 58 FORCE: 31 Oct 63
REGISTERED: 25 Nov 64 Japan
ARTICLES: 7 LANGUAGE: Japanese. French.
HEADNOTE: DEVELOPMENT COMMERCIAL RELATIONS
TOPIC: General Economic
CONCEPTS: Exceptions and exemptions. Annex or appendix reference. Scientific exchange. Establishment of trade relations. Reciprocity in trade. Balance of payments. Most favored nation clause. Water transport. Merchant vessels.
PROCEDURE: Duration. Ratification. Termination.
PARTIES:
 Haiti
 Japan

107493 Bilateral Agreement **518 UNTS 111**
SIGNED: 14 May 63 FORCE: 10 Jan 64
REGISTERED: 25 Nov 64 Japan
ARTICLES: 7 LANGUAGE: Japanese. French.
HEADNOTE: AGREEMENT COMMERCE
TOPIC: General Economic
CONCEPTS: Exceptions and exemptions. Territorial application. Annex or appendix reference. General cooperation. Reciprocity in trade. Equitable taxes.
INTL ORGS: European Economic Community. General Agreement on Tariffs and Trade. International Monetary Fund.
TREATY REF: GATT;IMF;EEC;55UNTS187;1-36UNTS45;2UNTS39.

PROCEDURE: Amendment. Denunciation. Duration. Future Procedures Contemplated.
PARTIES:
 France
 Japan

107494 Bilateral Agreement **518 UNTS 135**
SIGNED: 19 Jul 63 FORCE: 1 Jul 64
REGISTERED: 25 Nov 64 Japan
ARTICLES: 10 LANGUAGE: Japanese. Spanish. English.
HEADNOTE: AGREEMENT COMMERCE
TOPIC: General Economic
CONCEPTS: Exceptions and exemptions. Annex or appendix reference. General cooperation. Expropriation. Legal protection and assistance. General property. Private contracts. Export quotas. Import quotas. Reciprocity in trade. Most favored nation clause. Equitable taxes. Recognition. Passenger transport. Transport of goods. Merchant vessels. Ports and pilotage.
INTL ORGS: International Monetary Fund.
TREATY REF: IMF.
PROCEDURE: Duration. Ratification. Renewal or Revival. Termination.
PARTIES:
 El Salvador
 Japan

107495 Bilateral Convention **518 UNTS 179**
SIGNED: 22 Mar 63 FORCE: 1 Aug 64
REGISTERED: 25 Nov 64 Japan
ARTICLES: 27 LANGUAGE: Japanese. English.
HEADNOTE: CONSULAR
TOPIC: Consul/Citizenship
CONCEPTS: Definition of terms. Territorial application. General consular functions. Diplomatic privileges. Consular relations establishment. Inviolability. Privileges and immunities. Diplomatic correspondence. Consular functions in shipping. Consular functions in property. Responsibility and liability.
PROCEDURE: Duration. Ratification. Termination.
PARTIES:
 Japan
 USA (United States)

107496 Unilateral Instrument **519 UNTS 3**
SIGNED: 4 Aug 64 FORCE: 1 Dec 64
REGISTERED: 1 Dec 64 United Nations
ARTICLES: 1 LANGUAGE: English.
HEADNOTE: ACCEPTANCE OBLIGATIONS UN
TOPIC: UN Charter
CONCEPTS: Acceptance of UN obligations. Adherence to UN charter.
INTL ORGS: United Nations.
PARTIES:
 Malawi

107497 Unilateral Instrument **519 UNTS 7**
SIGNED: 29 Sep 64 FORCE: 1 Dec 64
REGISTERED: 1 Dec 64 United Nations
ARTICLES: 1 LANGUAGE: English.
HEADNOTE: ACCEPTANCE OBLIGATIONS UN
TOPIC: UN Charter
CONCEPTS: Acceptance of UN obligations.
INTL ORGS: United Nations.
PARTIES:
 Malta

107498 Unilateral Instrument **519 UNTS 11**
SIGNED: 26 Oct 64 FORCE: 1 Dec 64
REGISTERED: 1 Dec 64 United Nations
ARTICLES: 1 LANGUAGE: English.
HEADNOTE: ACCEPTANCE OBLIGATIONS UN
TOPIC: UN Charter
CONCEPTS: Acceptance of UN obligations. Adherence to UN charter.
INTL ORGS: United Nations.
PARTIES:
 Zambia

107499 Multilateral Agreement **519 UNTS 14**
SIGNED: 28 Jun 64 FORCE: 28 Jun 64
REGISTERED: 1 Dec 64 United Nations
ARTICLES: 6 LANGUAGE: English.
HEADNOTE: TECHNICAL ASSISTANCE
TOPIC: Tech Assistance

CONCEPTS: Definition of terms. Previous treaty replacement. Privileges and immunities. General cooperation. Exchange of information and documents. Personnel. Responsibility and liability. Title and deeds. Use of facilities. Exchange. Scholarships and grants. Vocational training. Research and development. Exchange rates and regulations. Expense sharing formulae. Local currency. Domestic obligation. General technical assistance. Materials, equipment and services. IGO status. Conformity with IGO decisions.
TREATY REF: 76UNTS132; 1UNTS15; 33UNTS261; 374UNTS.
PROCEDURE: Amendment. Termination.
PARTIES:
 Libya SIGNED: 28 Jun 64 FORCE: 28 Jun 64
 FAO (Food Agri) SIGNED: 28 Jun 64 FORCE: 28 Jun 64
 IAEA (Atom Energy) SIGNED: 28 Jun 64 FORCE: 28 Jun 64
 ICAO (Civil Aviat) SIGNED: 28 Jun 64 FORCE: 28 Jun 64
 ILO (Labor Org) SIGNED: 28 Jun 64 FORCE: 28 Jun 64
 ITU (Telecommun) SIGNED: 28 Jun 64 FORCE: 28 Jun 64
 UNESCO (Educ/Cult) SIGNED: 28 Jun 64 FORCE: 28 Jun 64
 United Nations SIGNED: 28 Jun 64 FORCE: 28 Jun 64
 UPU (Postal Union) SIGNED: 28 Jun 64 FORCE: 28 Jun 64
 WHO (World Health) SIGNED: 28 Jun 64 FORCE: 28 Jun 64
 WMO (Meteorology) SIGNED: 28 Jun 64 FORCE: 28 Jun 64
 ANNEX
651 UNTS 401. UNIDO (Industrial). Accession 23 Nov 68. Force 23 Nov 68.
651 UNTS 401. IMCO (Maritime Org). Accession 23 Nov 68. Force 23 Nov 68.

107500 Bilateral Agreement **519 UNTS 29**
SIGNED: 24 Oct 64 FORCE: 24 Oct 64
REGISTERED: 1 Dec 64 United Nations
ARTICLES: 10 LANGUAGE: English. French.
HEADNOTE: ASSISTANCE
TOPIC: IGO Operations
CONCEPTS: Diplomatic missions. Privileges and immunities. Exchange of information and documents. Procedure. Domestic obligation. General technical assistance. IGO obligations.
INTL ORGS: International Atomic Energy Agency. International Court of Justice. United Nations. Arbitration Commission.
TREATY REF: 1UNTS15; 30UNTS261.
PROCEDURE: Amendment. Termination.
PARTIES:
 Romania
 UN Special Fund

107501 Bilateral Agreement **519 UNTS 47**
SIGNED: 25 Nov 64 FORCE: 25 Nov 64
REGISTERED: 1 Dec 64 United Nations
ARTICLES: 8 LANGUAGE: English.
HEADNOTE: DEMOGRAPHIC TRAINING RESEARCH CENTER
TOPIC: Scientific Project
CONCEPTS: Definition of terms. Previous treaty replacement. Privileges and immunities. General cooperation. Use of facilities. Establishment of commission. Specialists exchange. Scholarships and grants. Vocational training. Research and scientific projects. Research cooperation. Research results. Research and development. Domestic obligation. Materials, equipment and services. IGO obligations.
INTL ORGS: Asia Economic Development Organization. Demographic Centre.
TREATY REF: 450UNTS3.
PROCEDURE: Duration. Renewal or Revival. Termination.
PARTIES:
 India
 United Nations
 ANNEX
540 UNTS 344. United Nations. Prolongation 8 May 65. Force 29 Jun 65.
540 UNTS 344. India. Prolongation 29 Jun 65. Force 29 Jun 65.
634 UNTS 436. India. Prolongation 1 Jul 67. Force 1 Jul 68.

634 UNTS 436. United Nations. Prolongation 1 Jul 67. Force 1 Jul 68.

107502 Bilateral Agreement **519 UNTS 57**
SIGNED: 30 Jun 64   FORCE: 18 Sep 64
REGISTERED: 1 Dec 64 IBRD (World Bank)
ARTICLES: 7 LANGUAGE: English.
HEADNOTE: GUARANTEE
TOPIC: IBRD Project
CONCEPTS: Credit provisions.
PARTIES:
  Pakistan
  IBRD (World Bank)

107503 Bilateral Agreement **519 UNTS 95**
SIGNED: 22 Apr 64   FORCE: 28 Jul 64
REGISTERED: 1 Dec 64 IBRD (World Bank)
ARTICLES: 7 LANGUAGE: English.
HEADNOTE: LOAN AGREEMENT
TOPIC: IBRD Project
CONCEPTS: Exchange of information and documents. Informational records. Inspection and observation. Loan regulations. Loan guarantee. Guarantor non-interference. Domestic obligation. Accounting procedures. Bonds. Fees and exemptions. Tax exemptions. Interest rates. Default remedies. Definition of terms.
PARTIES:
  Peru
  IBRD (World Bank)

107504 Bilateral Agreement **519 UNTS 119**
SIGNED: 30 Mar 62   FORCE: 25 Apr 63
REGISTERED: 3 Dec 64 Hungary
ARTICLES: 5 LANGUAGE: Polish. Hindi. English.
HEADNOTE: CULTURAL
TOPIC: Culture
CONCEPTS: Treaty interpretation. Friendship and amity. Conformity with municipal law. Specialists exchange. Recognition of degrees. Exchange. Teacher and student exchange. Institute establishment. Exchange. General cultural cooperation. Artists. Athletes. Scientific exchange. Publications exchange. Mass media exchange.
PROCEDURE: Duration. Ratification. Renewal or Revival. Termination.
PARTIES:
  Hungary
  India

107505 Bilateral Agreement **519 UNTS 131**
SIGNED: 12 Jan 60   FORCE: 10 Nov 60
REGISTERED: 3 Dec 64 Hungary
ARTICLES: 7 LANGUAGE: Polish. French.
HEADNOTE: CULTURAL RELATIONS
TOPIC: Culture
CONCEPTS: Treaty implementation. Friendship and amity. Non-diplomatic delegations. Conformity with municipal law. Exchange of information and documents. Public information. Recognition of degrees. Professorships. Scholarships and grants. General cultural cooperation. Artists. Athletes. Scientific exchange. Publications exchange. Mass media exchange. Press and wire services.
PROCEDURE: Duration. Ratification. Renewal or Revival. Termination.
PARTIES:
  Guinea
  Hungary

107506 Bilateral Agreement **519 UNTS 141**
SIGNED: 7 Sep 61   FORCE: 25 Nov 61
REGISTERED: 3 Dec 64 Hungary
ARTICLES: 15 LANGUAGE: Polish. Romanian.
HEADNOTE: COOPERATION MATTERS SOCIAL POLICY
TOPIC: Non-ILO Labor
CONCEPTS: Definition of terms. General cooperation. Old age and invalidity insurance. Social security. Indemnities and reimbursements. Payment schedules. National treatment.
PROCEDURE: Denunciation. Duration. Ratification.
PARTIES:
  Hungary
  Romania

107507 Bilateral Treaty **519 UNTS 163**
SIGNED: 23 Aug 61   FORCE: 2 Nov 62
REGISTERED: 3 Dec 64 Hungary
ARTICLES: 7 LANGUAGE: Polish. Indonesian. English.
HEADNOTE: FRIENDSHIP COOPERATION
TOPIC: General Amity
CONCEPTS: Peaceful relations. General cooperation. Procedure.
PROCEDURE: Ratification. Termination.
PARTIES:
  Hungary
  Indonesia

107508 Bilateral Convention **519 UNTS 173**
SIGNED: 10 Jul 63   FORCE: 28 Dec 63
REGISTERED: 3 Dec 64 Hungary
ARTICLES: 25 LANGUAGE: Polish. Mongolian. Russian.
HEADNOTE: CONSULAR CONVENTION
TOPIC: Consul/Citizenship
CONCEPTS: Definition of terms. Detailed regulations. Exceptions and exemptions. Treaty interpretation. Friendship and amity. Visas. Legal status. Alien status. Diplomatic privileges. Consular relations establishment. Diplomatic missions. Inviolability. Privileges and immunities. Property. Diplomatic correspondence. Conformity with municipal law. General cooperation. Informational records. Legal protection and assistance. General property. Death duties. Overflights and technical stops.
PROCEDURE: Denunciation. Duration. Ratification. Renewal or Revival.
PARTIES:
  Hungary
  Mongolia

107509 Bilateral Agreement **519 UNTS 215**
SIGNED: 6 Dec 57   FORCE: 6 Aug 59
REGISTERED: 3 Dec 64 Hungary
ARTICLES: 12 LANGUAGE: Polish. Serbo-Croat.
HEADNOTE: PLANT PROTECTION
TOPIC: Sanitation
CONCEPTS: Definition of terms. Detailed regulations. General cooperation. Exchange of information and documents. Domestic legislation. Dispute settlement. Specialists exchange. Quarantine. Border control. Disease control. Insect control. Scientific exchange. Trade procedures. Indemnities and reimbursements. Agriculture. Materials, equipment and services. Publications exchange. Conferences.
PROCEDURE: Amendment. Denunciation. Duration. Renewal or Revival.
PARTIES:
  Hungary
  Yugoslavia

107510 Bilateral Treaty **519 UNTS 237**
SIGNED: 7 May 60   FORCE: 13 Feb 61
REGISTERED: 3 Dec 64 Hungary
ARTICLES: 96 LANGUAGE: Polish. Serbo-Croat.
HEADNOTE: MUTUAL LEGAL ASSISTANCE
TOPIC: Admin Cooperation
CONCEPTS: Exceptions and exemptions. General provisions. Previous treaty replacement. Extradition, deportation and repatriation. Family law. Exchange of information and documents. Juridical personality. Legal protection and assistance. Recognition and enforcement of legal decisions. Succession. Recognition of legal documents. Procedure. Fees and exemptions. Conveyance in transit.
TREATY REF: 101LTS197; 187LTS363.
PROCEDURE: Ratification. Termination.
PARTIES:
  Hungary
  Yugoslavia

107511 Bilateral Treaty **520 UNTS 3**
SIGNED: 12 Jan 60   FORCE: 28 Oct 60
REGISTERED: 3 Dec 64 Hungary
ARTICLES: 78 LANGUAGE: Polish. German.
HEADNOTE: LEGAL ASSISTANCE CIVIL FAMILY CRIMINAL
TOPIC: Admin Cooperation
CONCEPTS: Exceptions and exemptions. Consular functions in property. Extradition, deportation and repatriation. Extradition requests. Refusal of extradition. Concurrent requests. Limits of prosecution. Provisional detainment. Extradition postponement. Material evidence. General cooperation. Family law. Exchange of information and documents. Juridical personality. Legal protection and assistance. Recognition and enforcement of legal decisions. Immovable property. General property. Succession. Recognition of legal documents. Indemnities and reimbursements. Fees and exemptions. Assets transfer. Conveyance in transit.
PROCEDURE: Ratification. Termination.
PARTIES:
  Albania
  Hungary

107512 Bilateral Agreement **520 UNTS 97**
SIGNED: 28 Aug 64   FORCE: 30 Oct 64
REGISTERED: 7 Dec 64 IBRD (World Bank)
ARTICLES: 7 LANGUAGE: English. Spanish.
HEADNOTE: LOAN HIGHWAY
TOPIC: IBRD Project
CONCEPTS: Default remedies. Definition of terms. Annex or appendix reference. Exchange of information and documents. Informational records. Inspection and observation. Accounting procedures. Bonds. Currency deposits. Fees and exemptions. Domestic obligation. Terms of loan. Loan regulations. Loan guarantee. Guarantor non-interference. Roads and highways.
PARTIES:
  IBRD (World Bank)
  Venezuela

107513 Bilateral Agreement **520 UNTS 119**
SIGNED: 13 Nov 63   FORCE: 14 Jul 64
REGISTERED: 7 Dec 64 Belgium
ARTICLES: 11 LANGUAGE: French. Dutch. Romanian.
HEADNOTE: CULTURAL COOPERATION
TOPIC: Culture
CONCEPTS: Exchange of information and documents. Responsibility and liability. Establishment of commission. Specialists exchange. Recognition of degrees. Exchange. Teacher and student exchange. Scholarships and grants. Exchange. General cultural cooperation. Artists. Athletes. Research results. Scientific exchange. Research and development. Finances and payments. Publications exchange. Mass media exchange.
INTL ORGS: Special Commission.
PROCEDURE: Denunciation. Duration. Ratification. Renewal or Revival.
PARTIES:
  Belgium
  Romania

107514 Bilateral Agreement **520 UNTS 133**
SIGNED: 9 Dec 63   FORCE: 1 Nov 64
REGISTERED: 8 Dec 64 Austria
ARTICLES: 4 LANGUAGE: German. Danish.
HEADNOTE: ABOLITION NOBILITY CERTIFICATES
TOPIC: Admin Cooperation
CONCEPTS: General cooperation.
PROCEDURE: Denunciation. Duration.
PARTIES:
  Austria
  Denmark

107515 Multilateral Convention **520 UNTS 151**
SIGNED: 30 Mar 61   FORCE: 13 Dec 64
REGISTERED: 13 Dec 64 United Nations
ARTICLES: 51 LANGUAGE: English. French. Spanish. Chinese. Russian.
HEADNOTE: NARCOTIC DRUGS CONVENTION
TOPIC: Sanitation
CONCEPTS: Definition of terms. Exceptions and exemptions. Territorial application. Annex or appendix reference. Treaty violation. Previous treaty replacement. General cooperation. Exchange of official publications. Informational records. Domestic legislation. Licenses and permits. Establishment of commission. Narcotic drugs. WHO used as agency. Research and scientific projects. Reexport of goods, etc.. Trade procedures. Indemnities and reimbursements. Agriculture.

INTL ORGS: International Court of Justice. United Nations. World Health Organization.
TREATY REF: 7LTS187;50LTS337;81LTS317.
PROCEDURE: Amendment. Accession. Ratification. Termination.
PARTIES:
Afghanistan SIGNED: 30 Mar 61 RATIFIED: 19 Mar 63 FORCE: 13 Dec 64
Argentina SIGNED: 31 Jul 64 FORCE: 13 Dec 64
Austria SIGNED: 30 Mar 61
Belgium SIGNED: 28 Jul 61
Brazil SIGNED: 30 Mar 61 RATIFIED: 18 Jun 64 FORCE: 13 Dec 64
Bulgaria SIGNED: 31 Jul 61
Burma SIGNED: 30 Mar 61 RATIFIED: 29 Jul 63 FORCE: 13 Dec 64
Byelorussia SIGNED: 31 Jul 61 RATIFIED: 20 Feb 64 FORCE: 13 Dec 64
Cambodia SIGNED: 30 Mar 61
Canada SIGNED: 30 Mar 61 RATIFIED: 11 Oct 61 FORCE: 13 Dec 64
Chad SIGNED: 30 Mar 61 RATIFIED: 29 Jan 63 FORCE: 13 Dec 64
Chile SIGNED: 30 Mar 61
Taiwan SIGNED: 30 Mar 61
Congo (Brazzaville) SIGNED: 30 Mar 61
Congo (Zaire) SIGNED: 28 Apr 61
Costa Rica SIGNED: 30 Mar 61
Czechoslovakia SIGNED: 31 Jul 61 RATIFIED: 20 Mar 64 FORCE: 13 Dec 64
Dahomey SIGNED: 30 Mar 61 RATIFIED: 27 Apr 62 FORCE: 13 Dec 64
Denmark SIGNED: 30 Mar 61 RATIFIED: 15 Sep 64 FORCE: 13 Dec 64
El Salvador SIGNED: 30 Mar 61
Finland SIGNED: 30 Mar 61
Germany, West SIGNED: 31 Jul 64
Ghana SIGNED: 30 Mar 61 RATIFIED: 15 Jan 64 FORCE: 13 Dec 64
Guatemala SIGNED: 26 Jul 61
Haiti SIGNED: 3 Apr 61
Hungary SIGNED: 31 Jul 61 RATIFIED: 24 Apr 64 FORCE: 13 Dec 64
India SIGNED: 30 Mar 61 RATIFIED: 13 Dec 64 FORCE: 12 Jan 65
Indonesia SIGNED: 28 Jul 61
Iran SIGNED: 30 Mar 61
Iraq SIGNED: 30 Mar 61 RATIFIED: 29 Aug 62 FORCE: 13 Dec 64
Italy SIGNED: 4 Apr 61
Jamaica RATIFIED: 29 Apr 64 FORCE: 13 Dec 64
Japan SIGNED: 26 Jul 61 RATIFIED: 13 Jul 64 FORCE: 13 Dec 64
Jordan SIGNED: 30 Mar 61 RATIFIED: 15 Nov 62 FORCE: 13 Dec 64
Kenya RATIFIED: 13 Nov 64 FORCE: 13 Dec 64
Korea, South SIGNED: 31 Mar 61 RATIFIED: 13 Feb 62 FORCE: 13 Dec 64
Lebanon SIGNED: 30 Mar 61
Liberia SIGNED: 30 Mar 61
Liechtenstein SIGNED: 14 Jul 61
Luxembourg SIGNED: 28 Jul 61
Madagascar SIGNED: 30 Mar 61
Mexico SIGNED: 24 Jul 61
Netherlands SIGNED: 31 Jul 61
New Zealand SIGNED: 30 Mar 61 RATIFIED: 26 Mar 63 FORCE: 13 Dec 64
New Zealand Cook Islands RATIFIED: 26 Mar 63 FORCE: 13 Dec 64
New Zealand Niue RATIFIED: 26 Mar 63 FORCE: 13 Dec 64
New Zealand Tokelau Islands RATIFIED: 26 Mar 63 FORCE: 13 Dec 64
Nicaragua SIGNED: 30 Mar 61
Nigeria SIGNED: 30 Mar 61
Norway SIGNED: 30 Mar 61
Pakistan SIGNED: 30 Mar 61
Panama SIGNED: 30 Mar 61 RATIFIED: 4 Dec 63 FORCE: 13 Dec 64
Paraguay SIGNED: 30 Mar 61
Peru SIGNED: 30 Mar 61 RATIFIED: 22 Jul 64 FORCE: 13 Dec 64
Philippines SIGNED: 30 Mar 61
Poland SIGNED: 31 Jul 61
Portugal SIGNED: 31 Mar 61
Spain SIGNED: 27 Jul 61
Sweden SIGNED: 3 Apr 61 RATIFIED: 18 Dec 64 FORCE: 17 Jan 65
Switzerland SIGNED: 20 Apr 61
Syria RATIFIED: 22 Aug 62 FORCE: 13 Dec 64
Thailand SIGNED: 24 Jul 61 RATIFIED: 31 Oct 61 FORCE: 13 Dec 64

Trinidad/Tobago RATIFIED: 22 Jun 64 FORCE: 13 Dec 64
Tunisia SIGNED: 30 Mar 61 RATIFIED: 8 Sep 64 FORCE: 13 Dec 64
United Arab Rep SIGNED: 30 Mar 61
UK Great Britain SIGNED: 30 Mar 61 RATIFIED: 2 Sep 64 FORCE: 13 Dec 64
Ukrainian SSR SIGNED: 31 Jul 61 RATIFIED: 15 Apr 64 FORCE: 13 Dec 64
USSR (Soviet Union) SIGNED: 31 Jul 61 RATIFIED: 20 Feb 64 FORCE: 13 Dec 64
Vatican/Holy See SIGNED: 30 Mar 61
Venezuela SIGNED: 30 Mar 61
Yugoslavia SIGNED: 30 Mar 61 RATIFIED: 27 Aug 63 FORCE: 13 Dec 64
ANNEX
523 UNTS 349.
530 UNTS 390.
531 UNTS 420.
533 UNTS 385.
535 UNTS 460.
538 UNTS 345.
540 UNTS 348.
541 UNTS 364.
542 UNTS 396.
557 UNTS 280.
559 UNTS 370.
561 UNTS 355.
568 UNTS 364.
573 UNTS 347.
600 UNTS 363. Malaysia. Accession 11 Jul 67. Force 10 Aug 67.
604 UNTS 383.
606 UNTS 400.
613 UNTS 416. Guatemala. Ratification 1 Dec 67. Force 31 Dec 67.
613 UNTS 416. Australia. All Territories. Ratification 1 Dec 67. Force 31 Dec 67.
620 UNTS 324. Chile. Ratification 7 Feb 68.
648 UNTS 378.
649 UNTS 362.
657 UNTS 402.

107516 Bilateral Convention **521 UNTS 3**
SIGNED: 5 Oct 62 FORCE: 31 Aug 63
REGISTERED: 14 Dec 64 Poland
ARTICLES: 29 LANGUAGE: Polish. Romanian.
HEADNOTE: CONSULAR
TOPIC: Consul/Citizenship
CONCEPTS: Definition of terms. Previous treaty replacement. General consular functions. Diplomatic privileges. Consular relations establishment. Inviolability. Privileges and immunities. Responsibility and liability.
PROCEDURE: Duration. Ratification. Renewal or Revival. Termination.
PARTIES:
Poland
Romania

107517 Bilateral Treaty **521 UNTS 37**
SIGNED: 6 Feb 60 FORCE: 5 Jun 63
REGISTERED: 14 Dec 64 Poland
ARTICLES: 96 LANGUAGE: Polish. Serbo-Croat.
HEADNOTE: LEGAL RELATIONS CIVIL CRIMINAL CASES
TOPIC: Admin Cooperation
CONCEPTS: Exceptions and exemptions. General provisions. Previous treaty replacement. Extradition, deportation and repatriation. General cooperation. Family law. Exchange of information and documents. Juridical personality. Legal protection and assistance. Recognition and enforcement of legal decisions. General property. Succession. Recognition of legal documents. Procedure. Indemnities and reimbursements. Conveyance in transit.
TREATY REF: 85LTS455.
PROCEDURE: Ratification. Termination.
PARTIES:
Poland
Yugoslavia

107518 Bilateral Exchange **521 UNTS 157**
SIGNED: 11 Jun 64 FORCE: 11 Jun 64
REGISTERED: 17 Dec 64 Belgium
ARTICLES: 2 LANGUAGE: French.
HEADNOTE: DOUBLE TAXATION AIR TRANSPORT
TOPIC: Taxation
CONCEPTS: Taxation. Air transport.

PARTIES:
Austria
Belgium

107519 Bilateral Exchange **521 UNTS 163**
SIGNED: 31 Dec 63 FORCE: 31 Dec 63
REGISTERED: 17 Dec 64 New Zealand
ARTICLES: 2 LANGUAGE: English.
HEADNOTE: METEROLOGICAL GEOPHYSICAL PROGRAMS
TOPIC: Scientific Project
CONCEPTS: General cooperation. General property. Responsibility and liability. Use of facilities. Research and scientific projects. Meteorology. Research and development. Indemnities and reimbursements. Expense sharing formulae. Domestic obligation. Materials, equipment and services.
PARTIES:
New Zealand
Western Samoa

107520 Bilateral Exchange **521 UNTS 173**
SIGNED: 23 Jul 64 FORCE: 23 Jul 64
REGISTERED: 17 Dec 64 New Zealand
ARTICLES: 2 LANGUAGE: English.
HEADNOTE: LOAN HARBORS DEVELOPMENT
TOPIC: Non-IBRD Project
CONCEPTS: Interest rates. Loan repayment. Terms of loan. Agricultural development/credit.
PARTIES:
New Zealand
Western Samoa

107521 Bilateral Exchange **521 UNTS 181**
SIGNED: 3 Nov 64 FORCE: 3 Nov 64
REGISTERED: 18 Dec 64 Western Samoa
ARTICLES: 2 LANGUAGE: English.
HEADNOTE: METEROLOGICAL PROGRAM
TOPIC: Scientific Project
CONCEPTS: Annex type material. Research and scientific projects. Meteorology.
TREATY REF: 338UNTS281; 371UNTS356.
PARTIES:
USA (United States)
Western Samoa

107522 Bilateral Exchange **521 UNTS 191**
SIGNED: 28 May 64 FORCE: 1 Jun 64
REGISTERED: 21 Dec 64 Netherlands
ARTICLES: 3 LANGUAGE: French.
HEADNOTE: ABOLITION VISA FEES
TOPIC: Visas
CONCEPTS: Visas. Fees and exemptions.
PARTIES:
Netherlands
Yugoslavia

107523 Bilateral Agreement **521 UNTS 197**
SIGNED: 19 Aug 64 FORCE: 19 Aug 64
REGISTERED: 21 Dec 64 Netherlands
ARTICLES: 25 LANGUAGE: French.
HEADNOTE: IMMIGRATION RECRUITMENT PLACEMENT WORKERS
TOPIC: Non-ILO Labor
CONCEPTS: General provisions. Annex or appendix reference. Border traffic and migration. Repatriation of nationals. Non-diplomatic delegations. Conformity with municipal law. Exchange of information and documents. Dispute settlement. Public health. Employment regulations. Non-ILO labor relations. Administrative cooperation. Migrant worker. Indemnities and reimbursements. Transportation costs.
INTL ORGS: Special Commission.
PROCEDURE: Denunciation. Duration. Renewal or Revival.
PARTIES:
Netherlands
Turkey

107524 Bilateral Agreement **521 UNTS 217**
SIGNED: 10 Dec 64 FORCE: 10 Dec 64
REGISTERED: 22 Dec 64 ILO (Labor Org)
ARTICLES: 9 LANGUAGE: English.
HEADNOTE: ACCEPTING COMPULSORY ICJ
TOPIC: IGO Establishment

CONCEPTS: Acceptance of UN obligations. Compulsory jurisdiction.
INTL ORGS: International Court of Justice. United Nations. Arbitration Commission.
PARTIES:
Ethiopia
ILO (Labor Org)

107525 Multilateral Convention **521 UNTS 231**
SIGNED: 10 Dec 62   FORCE: 9 Dec 64
REGISTERED: 23 Dec 64 United Nations
ARTICLES: 10 LANGUAGE: English. French. Chinese. Russian. Spanish.
HEADNOTE: CONVENTION MARRIAGE
TOPIC: Culture
CONCEPTS: Detailed regulations. Treaty interpretation. Human rights. Refusal of extradition. Family law. Negotiation. Administering authority.
INTL ORGS: International Court of Justice. United Nations.
PROCEDURE: Accession. Denunciation. Ratification.
PARTIES:
Ceylon (Sri Lanka) SIGNED: 12 Dec 62
Chile SIGNED: 10 Dec 62
Taiwan SIGNED: 4 Apr 63
Cuba SIGNED: 17 Oct 63
Czechoslovakia SIGNED: 8 Oct 63
Denmark   SIGNED: 31 Oct 63   RATIFIED: 8 Sep 64 FORCE: 9 Dec 64
France SIGNED: 10 Dec 62
Greece SIGNED: 3 Jan 63
Guinea SIGNED: 10 Dec 62
Israel SIGNED: 10 Dec 62
Italy SIGNED: 20 Dec 63
Netherlands SIGNED: 10 Dec 62
New Zealand SIGNED: 23 Dec 63 RATIFIED: 12 Jun 64 FORCE: 9 Dec 64
Philippines SIGNED: 5 Feb 63
Poland SIGNED: 17 Dec 62
Romania SIGNED: 27 Dec 63
Sweden   SIGNED: 10 Dec 62   RATIFIED: 16 Jun 64 FORCE: 9 Dec 64
USA (United States) SIGNED: 10 Dec 62
Yugoslavia   SIGNED: 10 Dec 62   RATIFIED: 19 Jun 64 FORCE: 9 Dec 64
ANNEX
522 UNTS 356. Poland. Ratification 8 Jan 65.
523 UNTS 350.   Philippines.   Ratification 21 Jan 65.
527 UNTS 328.   Czechoslovakia.   Ratification 5 Mar 65. Force 3 Jun 65.
540 UNTS 349.   Netherlands.   Netherlands Antilles. Force 30 Sep 65.
540 UNTS 349. Netherlands. Surinam. Force 30 Sep 65.
540 UNTS 349.   Netherlands.   Ratification 2 Jul 65.
543 UNTS 378. Cuba. Force 18 Nov 65.
547 UNTS 362. Dahomey. Accession 19 Oct 65. Force 17 Jan 66.
619 UNTS 343. Tunisia. Accession 24 Jan 68. Force 23 Apr 68.
619 UNTS 343. Tunisia. Accession 24 Jan 68. Force 23 Apr 68.
668 UNTS 371. Spain. Accession 15 Apr 69. Force 14 Jul 69.

107526 Bilateral Agreement **521 UNTS 281**
SIGNED: 25 Nov 54   FORCE: 1 Jun 63
REGISTERED: 23 Dec 64 Australia
ARTICLES: 17 LANGUAGE: English. Polish.
HEADNOTE: EXCHANGE POSTAL PARCELS
TOPIC: Postal Service
CONCEPTS: Responsibility and liability. Accounting procedures. Postal services. Regulations. Insured letters and boxes. Conveyance in transit. Parcel post. Rates and charges.
INTL ORGS: Universal Postal Union.
TREATY REF: 365UNTS3.
PROCEDURE: Duration. Termination.
PARTIES:
Australia
Poland

107527 Bilateral Agreement **521 UNTS 303**
SIGNED: 18 Dec 63   FORCE: 22 Sep 64
REGISTERED: 23 Dec 64 Netherlands
ARTICLES: 8 LANGUAGE: English. French.
HEADNOTE: EMPLOYMENT VOLUNTEERS
TOPIC: General Aid

CONCEPTS: Privileges and immunities. General cooperation. Inspection and observation. Personnel. Vocational training. Export quotas. Import quotas. Exchange rates and regulations. Financial programs. Funding procedures. Tax exemptions. Domestic obligation. Materials, equipment and services. Volunteer programs.
PROCEDURE: Duration. Renewal or Revival. Termination.
PARTIES:
Cameroon
Netherlands

107528 Bilateral Agreement **521 UNTS 311**
SIGNED: 28 Oct 64   FORCE: 28 Oct 64
REGISTERED: 28 Dec 64 Thailand
ARTICLES: 9 LANGUAGE: Thai. German. English.
HEADNOTE: FINANCIAL ASSISTANCE YANHEE POWER DISTRIBUTION SYSTEM
TOPIC: Non-IBRD Project
CONCEPTS: Non-visa travel documents. Conformity with municipal law. Tax exemptions. Loan and credit. Terms of loan. Hydro-electric power.
PARTIES:
Germany, West
Thailand

107529 Bilateral Agreement **521 UNTS 333**
SIGNED: 28 Oct 64   FORCE: 28 Oct 64
REGISTERED: 28 Dec 64 Thailand
ARTICLES: 9 LANGUAGE: Thai. German. English.
HEADNOTE: FINANCIAL ASSISTANCE NORTH-SOUTH TELECOMMUNICATION PROJECT
TOPIC: Loans and Credits
CONCEPTS: Tax exemptions. Loan and credit. Terms of loan.
PARTIES:
Germany, West
Thailand

107530 Bilateral Treaty **521 UNTS 351**
SIGNED: 22 Aug 57   FORCE: 5 Mar 58
REGISTERED: 30 Dec 64 Mongolia
ARTICLES: 6 LANGUAGE: Mongolian. German.
HEADNOTE: FRIENDSHIP COOPERATION
TOPIC: General Amity
CONCEPTS: Peaceful relations.
PROCEDURE: Amendment. Duration. Future Procedures Contemplated. Ratification. Termination.
PARTIES:
Germany, East
Mongolia

107531 Bilateral Convention **521 UNTS 361**
SIGNED: 15 Jun 63   FORCE: 8 Jul 64
REGISTERED: 31 Dec 64 Taiwan
ARTICLES: 7 LANGUAGE: Chinese. English.
HEADNOTE: CULTURAL CONVENTION
TOPIC: Culture
CONCEPTS: Exchange. General cultural cooperation. Artists.
PROCEDURE: Ratification.
PARTIES:
Taiwan
Liberia

107532 Bilateral Agreement **522 UNTS 3**
SIGNED: 15 Dec 64   FORCE: 15 Dec 64
REGISTERED: 1 Jan 65 United Nations
ARTICLES: 10 LANGUAGE: English.
HEADNOTE: ASSISTANCE
TOPIC: Direct Aid
CONCEPTS: Diplomatic privileges. Diplomatic missions. Privileges and immunities. Exchange of information and documents. Procedure. Domestic obligation. General technical assistance. IGO obligations.
INTL ORGS: International Court of Justice. United Nations. Arbitration Commission.
TREATY REF: 1UNTS15; 33UNTS261.
PROCEDURE: Amendment. Termination.
PARTIES:
UN Special Fund
Zambia

107533 Multilateral Agreement **522 UNTS 20**
SIGNED: 15 Dec 64   FORCE: 15 Dec 64
REGISTERED: 1 Jan 65 United Nations

ARTICLES: 6 LANGUAGE: English.
HEADNOTE: TECHNICAL ASSISTANCE
TOPIC: Tech Assistance
CONCEPTS: Privileges and immunities. General technical assistance. Assistance.
PROCEDURE: Termination.
PARTIES:
Malta SIGNED: 15 Dec 64 FORCE: 15 Dec 64
FAO (Food Agri) SIGNED: 15 Dec 64 FORCE: 15 Dec 64
IAEA (Atom Energy) SIGNED: 15 Dec 64 FORCE: 15 Dec 64
ICAO (Civil Aviat) SIGNED: 15 Dec 64 FORCE: 15 Dec 64
ILO (Labor Org) SIGNED: 15 Dec 64 FORCE: 15 Dec 64
ITU (Telecommun) SIGNED: 15 Dec 64 FORCE: 15 Dec 64
UNESCO (Educ/Cult) SIGNED: 15 Dec 64 FORCE: 15 Dec 64
United Nations SIGNED: 15 Dec 64 FORCE: 15 Dec 64
UPU (Postal Union) SIGNED: 15 Dec 64 FORCE: 15 Dec 64
WHO (World Health) SIGNED: 15 Dec 64 FORCE: 15 Dec 64
WMO (Meteorology) SIGNED: 15 Dec 64 FORCE: 15 Dec 64
ANNEX
649 UNTS 364. IMCO (Maritime Org). Accession 15 Oct 68. Force 15 Oct 68.
649 UNTS 364. UNIDO (Industrial). Accession 15 Oct 68. Force 15 Oct 68.

107534 Bilateral Agreement **522 UNTS 35**
SIGNED: 15 Aug 61   FORCE: 14 Oct 64
REGISTERED: 4 Jan 65 Philippines
ARTICLES: 13 LANGUAGE: English.
HEADNOTE: CULTURAL
TOPIC: Culture
CONCEPTS: Definition of terms. Friendship and amity. Conformity with municipal law. Responsibility and liability. Establishment of commission. Recognition of degrees. Exchange. Teacher and student exchange. Institute establishment. Scholarships and grants. Vocational training. Exchange. General cultural cooperation. Artists. Athletes. Anthropology and archeology. Publications exchange. Mass media exchange.
PROCEDURE: Denunciation. Duration. Ratification.
PARTIES:
Pakistan
Philippines

107535 Bilateral Agreement **522 UNTS 45**
SIGNED: 6 Jan 65   FORCE: 6 Jan 65
REGISTERED: 6 Jan 65 United Nations
ARTICLES: 6 LANGUAGE: English.
HEADNOTE: HUMAN RIGHTS SEMINAR HELD ULAN BATOR
TOPIC: IGO Operations
CONCEPTS: Privileges and immunities. Use of facilities. Domestic obligation. Conferences. IGO obligations.
PROCEDURE: Amendment.
PARTIES:
Mongolia
United Nations

107536 Bilateral Agreement **522 UNTS 55**
SIGNED: 7 Jan 65   FORCE: 7 Jan 65
REGISTERED: 7 Jan 65 United Nations
ARTICLES: 6 LANGUAGE: English.
HEADNOTE: HUMAN RIGHTS SEMINAR HELD BELGRADE
TOPIC: IGO Operations
CONCEPTS: Privileges and immunities. Use of facilities. Domestic obligation. Conferences. IGO obligations.
PROCEDURE: Amendment.
PARTIES:
United Nations
Yugoslavia

107537 Bilateral Convention **522 UNTS 65**
SIGNED: 9 Jan 64   FORCE: 31 Dec 64
REGISTERED: 11 Jan 65 Thailand
ARTICLES: 29 LANGUAGE: English.
HEADNOTE: DOUBLE TAXATION FISCAL EVASION INCOME CAPITAL

TOPIC: Taxation
CONCEPTS: Definition of terms. Privileges and immunities. Nationality and citizenship. Exchange of official publications. Negotiation. Teacher and student exchange. Taxation. Tax credits. Equitable taxes. Tax exemptions. Air transport. Merchant vessels.
PROCEDURE: Duration. Ratification. Termination.
PARTIES:
Norway
Thailand

107538 Bilateral Exchange **522 UNTS 99**
SIGNED: 11 Sep 64   FORCE: 11 Sep 64
REGISTERED: 13 Jan 65 UK Great Britain
ARTICLES: 2 LANGUAGE: English.
HEADNOTE: STATUS FORCES
TOPIC: Status of Forces
CONCEPTS: Annex or appendix reference. Status of military forces.
PARTIES:
Canada
UK Great Britain

107539 Bilateral Exchange **522 UNTS 117**
SIGNED: 1 Sep 64   FORCE: 1 Sep 64
REGISTERED: 13 Jan 65 UK Great Britain
ARTICLES: 2 LANGUAGE: English.
HEADNOTE: PRODUCTION TRADE POLICIES CEREALS
TOPIC: Commodity Trade
CONCEPTS: Annex or appendix reference. General cooperation. Balance of payments. Fees and exemptions. Non-interest rates and fees. Commodity trade.
INTL ORGS: General Agreement on Tariffs and Trade.
TREATY REF: 60UNTS131;138UNTS398;5-22UNTS122;55UNTS187.
PROCEDURE: Termination.
PARTIES:
Malawi
UK Great Britain

107540 Bilateral Exchange **522 UNTS 129**
SIGNED: 2 Jul 64   FORCE: 2 Jul 64
REGISTERED: 13 Jan 65 UK Great Britain
ARTICLES: 2 LANGUAGE: English.
HEADNOTE: PRODUCTION TRADE POLICIES CEREALS
TOPIC: Commodity Trade
CONCEPTS: Detailed regulations. Annex or appendix reference. General cooperation. Balance of payments. Fees and exemptions. Non-interest rates and fees. Commodity trade.
INTL ORGS: General Agreement on Tariffs and Trade.
TREATY REF: 55UNTS187.
PROCEDURE: Termination.
PARTIES:
Cyprus
UK Great Britain

107541 Bilateral Exchange **522 UNTS 141**
SIGNED: 30 Jun 64   FORCE: 30 Jun 64
REGISTERED: 13 Jan 65 UK Great Britain
ARTICLES: 2 LANGUAGE: English.
HEADNOTE: PRODUCTION TRADE POLICIES
TOPIC: Commodity Trade
CONCEPTS: Export subsidies. Trade procedures.
INTL ORGS: General Agreement on Tariffs and Trade.
PARTIES:
Ireland
UK Great Britain

107542 Bilateral Exchange **522 UNTS 153**
SIGNED: 31 Jul 64   FORCE: 31 Jul 64
REGISTERED: 13 Jan 65 UK Great Britain
ARTICLES: 2 LANGUAGE: English.
HEADNOTE: PRODUCTION TRADE POLICIES CEREALS
TOPIC: Commodity Trade
CONCEPTS: Detailed regulations. Annex or appendix reference. General cooperation. Balance of payments. Fees and exemptions. Non-interest rates and fees. Commodity trade.
INTL ORGS: General Agreement on Tariffs and Trade.

TREATY REF: 55UNTS187.
PARTIES:
India
UK Great Britain

107543 Bilateral Exchange **522 UNTS 165**
SIGNED: 25 Aug 64   FORCE: 25 Aug 64
REGISTERED: 13 Jan 65 UK Great Britain
ARTICLES: 2 LANGUAGE: English.
HEADNOTE: PRODUCTION TRADE POLICIES CEREALS
TOPIC: Commodity Trade
CONCEPTS: Detailed regulations. Annex or appendix reference. General cooperation. Balance of payments. Fees and exemptions. Non-interest rates and fees. Commodity trade.
INTL ORGS: General Agreement on Tariffs and Trade.
TREATY REF: 55UNTS187.
PARTIES:
Kenya
UK Great Britain

107544 Bilateral Exchange **522 UNTS 177**
SIGNED: 2 Sep 64   FORCE: 2 Sep 64
REGISTERED: 13 Jan 65 UK Great Britain
ARTICLES: 2 LANGUAGE: English.
HEADNOTE: PRODUCTION TRADE POLICIES CEREALS
TOPIC: Commodity Trade
CONCEPTS: Detailed regulations. Annex or appendix reference. General cooperation. Balance of payments. Fees and exemptions. Non-interest rates and fees. Commodity trade.
INTL ORGS: General Agreement on Tariffs and Trade.
TREATY REF: 55UNTS187.
PARTIES:
Tanganyika
UK Great Britain

107545 Bilateral Agreement **522 UNTS 189**
SIGNED: 9 Jul 64   FORCE: 9 Jul 64
REGISTERED: 13 Jan 65 UK Great Britain
ARTICLES: 10 LANGUAGE: English.
HEADNOTE: PUBLIC OFFICERS
TOPIC: Consul/Citizenship
CONCEPTS: Conditions. Definition of terms. Social security. Payment schedules.
PARTIES:
Malaysia
UK Great Britain

107546 Bilateral Agreement **522 UNTS 201**
SIGNED: 9 Jul 64   FORCE: 9 Jul 64
REGISTERED: 13 Jan 65 UK Great Britain
ARTICLES: 10 LANGUAGE: English.
HEADNOTE: PUBLIC OFFICERS
TOPIC: Consul/Citizenship
CONCEPTS: Conditions. Definition of terms. Social security. Payment schedules.
PARTIES:
Malaysia
UK Great Britain

107547 Bilateral Agreement **522 UNTS 213**
SIGNED: 9 Jul 64   FORCE: 9 Jul 64
REGISTERED: 13 Jan 65 UK Great Britain
ARTICLES: 9 LANGUAGE: English.
HEADNOTE: PUBLIC OFFICERS
TOPIC: Consul/Citizenship
CONCEPTS: Conditions. Definition of terms. Social security. Payment schedules.
PARTIES:
Malaysia
UK Great Britain

107548 Bilateral Agreement **522 UNTS 223**
SIGNED: 28 Aug 64   FORCE: 28 Aug 64
REGISTERED: 13 Jan 65 UK Great Britain
ARTICLES: 10 LANGUAGE: English.
HEADNOTE: PUBLIC OFFICERS SUPPLEMENTARY AGREEMENT
TOPIC: Consul/Citizenship
CONCEPTS: Annex type material.
TREATY REF: 522UNTS226.

PARTIES:
Malawi
UK Great Britain

107549 Bilateral Convention **522 UNTS 237**
SIGNED: 14 Nov 63   FORCE: 25 Dec 64
REGISTERED: 13 Jan 65 Belgium
ARTICLES: 3 LANGUAGE: French. English.
HEADNOTE: SUPPLEMENTARY CONVENTION
TOPIC: Extradition
CONCEPTS: Annex type material.
TREATY REF: 94BFSP610; 164LTS205.
PARTIES:
Belgium
USA (United States)

107550 Bilateral Exchange **522 UNTS 243**
SIGNED: 11 Jan 64   FORCE: 11 Jan 64
REGISTERED: 13 Jan 65 Netherlands
ARTICLES: 2 LANGUAGE: French.
HEADNOTE: EXEMPTION MOTOR VEHICLES TAXATION
TOPIC: Taxation
CONCEPTS: Tax exemptions. Commercial road vehicles. Motor vehicles and combinations.
PROCEDURE: Denunciation. Renewal or Revival.
PARTIES:
Hungary
Netherlands

107551 Bilateral Agreement **522 UNTS 249**
SIGNED: 14 May 60   FORCE: 19 Nov 64
REGISTERED: 13 Jan 65 Belgium
ARTICLES: 12 LANGUAGE: French. Dutch. Persian.
HEADNOTE: CULTURAL
TOPIC: Culture
CONCEPTS: Treaty implementation. Treaty interpretation. Friendship and amity. Exchange. Scholarships and grants. Exchange. General cultural cooperation. Artists. Publications exchange. Mass media exchange.
PROCEDURE: Denunciation. Duration. Ratification. Renewal or Revival.
PARTIES:
Belgium
Iran

107552 Bilateral Agreement **522 UNTS 265**
SIGNED: 14 May 64   FORCE: 29 Jul 64
REGISTERED: 14 Jan 65 IBRD (World Bank)
ARTICLES: 5 LANGUAGE: English.
HEADNOTE: GUARANTEE LIQUIFY GAS
TOPIC: IBRD Project
CONCEPTS: Definition of terms. Annex or appendix reference. Exchange of information and documents. Bonds. Fees and exemptions. Tax exemptions. Domestic obligation. Terms of loan. Loan regulations. Loan guarantee. Guarantor non-interference. Natural resources.
PARTIES:
Algeria
IBRD (World Bank)

107553 Multilateral Agreement **523 UNTS 3**
SIGNED: 19 Nov 64   FORCE: 1 Jan 65
REGISTERED: 15 Jan 65 Belgium
ARTICLES: 10 LANGUAGE: French. Dutch. Persian.
HEADNOTE: ABOLITION VISAS
TOPIC: Visas
CONCEPTS: Emergencies. Time limit. Visa abolition. Denial of admission. Resident permits. Nationality and citizenship. Conformity with municipal law.
PROCEDURE: Denunciation.
PARTIES:
Belgium SIGNED: 19 Nov 64 FORCE: 1 Jan 65
Iran SIGNED: 19 Nov 64 FORCE: 1 Jan 65
Luxembourg SIGNED: 19 Nov 64 FORCE: 1 Jan 65
Netherlands SIGNED: 19 Nov 64 FORCE: 1 Jan 65

107554 Bilateral Convention **523 UNTS 17**
SIGNED: 8 Mar 61   FORCE: 1 Oct 64
REGISTERED: 20 Jan 65 Belgium
ARTICLES: 46 LANGUAGE: French. English.
HEADNOTE: CONSULAR
TOPIC: Consul/Citizenship

CONCEPTS: Definition of terms. Territorial application. Previous treaty replacement. General consular functions. Diplomatic privileges. Consular relations establishment. Privileges and immunities. Consular functions in shipping. Procedure. Existing tribunals.
INTL ORGS: International Court of Justice.
TREATY REF: 51BFSP913; U.K.'CMD. 6908;.
PROCEDURE: Ratification. Termination.
PARTIES:
  Belgium
  UK Great Britain

107555 Multilateral Agreement **523 UNTS 93**
SIGNED: 17 Dec 62   FORCE: 25 Jan 65
REGISTERED: 25 Jan 65 Council of Europe
ARTICLES: 6 LANGUAGE: English. French.
HEADNOTE: APPLICATION EUROPEAN CONVENTION COMMERCIAL ARBITRATION
TOPIC: General Economic
CONCEPTS: Annex type material. Procedure.
INTL ORGS: Council of Europe.
TREATY REF: 484UNTS349;490UNTS479;4-95UNTS265;510UNTS341.
PROCEDURE: Accession. Denunciation. Ratification. Registration.
PARTIES:
  Austria SIGNED: 17 Dec 62 FORCE: 20 Jan 65
  Belgium SIGNED: 11 Feb 63
  France SIGNED: 17 Dec 62
  Germany, West SIGNED: 17 Dec 62 RATIFIED: 19 Oct 64 FORCE: 25 Jan 65
  Germany, West Berlin RATIFIED: 25 Jan 65
  Italy SIGNED: 17 Dec 62

107556 Multilateral Agreement **523 UNTS 102**
SIGNED: 27 Jan 65   FORCE: 27 Jan 65
REGISTERED: 27 Jan 65 United Nations
ARTICLES: 6 LANGUAGE: English. French.
HEADNOTE: TECHNICAL ASSISTANCE
TOPIC: Tech Assistance
CONCEPTS: Definition of terms. Privileges and immunities. General cooperation. Exchange of information and documents. Personnel. Responsibility and liability. Title and deeds. Use of facilities. Exchange. Scholarships and grants. Vocational training. Research and development. Exchange rates and regulations. Expense sharing formulae. Local currency. Domestic obligation. General technical assistance. Materials, equipment and services. IGO status. Conformity with IGO decisions.
TREATY REF: 374UNTS147; 76UNTS132; 1UNTS15; 33UNTS261.
PROCEDURE: Amendment. Termination.
PARTIES:
  Romania SIGNED: 27 Jan 65 FORCE: 27 Jan 65
  FAO (Food Agri) SIGNED: 27 Jan 65 FORCE: 27 Jan 65
  IAEA (Atom Energy) SIGNED: 27 Jan 65 FORCE: 27 Jan 65
  ICAO (Civil Aviat) SIGNED: 27 Jan 65 FORCE: 27 Jan 65
  ILO (Labor Org) SIGNED: 27 Jan 65 FORCE: 27 Jan 65
  ITU (Telecommun) SIGNED: 27 Jan 65 FORCE: 27 Jan 65
  UNESCO (Educ/Cult) SIGNED: 27 Jan 65 FORCE: 27 Jan 65
  United Nations SIGNED: 27 Jan 65 FORCE: 27 Jan 65
  UPU (Postal Union) SIGNED: 27 Jan 65 FORCE: 27 Jan 65
  WHO (World Health) SIGNED: 27 Jan 65 FORCE: 27 Jan 65
  WMO (Meteorology) SIGNED: 27 Jan 65 FORCE: 27 Jan 65
ANNEX
654 UNTS 382. UNIDO (Industrial). Accession 24 Dec 68. Force 24 Dec 68.
654 UNTS 382. IMCO (Maritime Org). Accession 24 Dec 68. Force 24 Dec 68.

107557 Multilateral Convention **523 UNTS 117**
SIGNED: 13 Dec 60   FORCE: 1 Mar 63
REGISTERED: 28 Jan 65 Belgium
ARTICLES: 42 LANGUAGE: English. French. German. Dutch.
HEADNOTE: EUROCONTROL SAFETY AIR NAVIGATION
TOPIC: Air Transport

CONCEPTS: Definition of terms. Detailed regulations. Emergencies. Territorial application. Treaty implementation. Treaty interpretation. Annex or appendix reference. Diplomatic privileges. Inviolability. Standardization. Conformity with municipal law. General cooperation. Exchange of information and documents. Juridical personality. Expropriation. Personnel. Immovable property. General property. Responsibility and liability. Use of facilities. Investigation of violations. Arbitration. Procedure. Special tribunals. Negotiation. Vocational training. Humanitarian matters. Indemnities and reimbursements. Currency. Monetary and gold transfers. Fees and exemptions. Financial programs. Non-interest rates and fees. Seizure funds. Tax exemptions. Customs exemptions. Loan and credit. Routes and logistics. Navigational conditions. Navigational equipment. Air transport. Bands and frequency allocation. Admission. Decisions. Subsidiary organ. Establishment. Procedure. Headquarters and facilities. Special status. Status of experts.
INTL ORGS: International Civil Aviation Organization. Arbitration Commission.
TREATY REF: 7306.
PROCEDURE: Accession. Denunciation. Duration. Ratification. Registration. Renewal or Revival. Application to Non-self-governing Territories.
PARTIES:
  Belgium SIGNED: 13 Dec 60 RATIFIED: 13 Mar 63 FORCE: 1 Mar 63
  France SIGNED: 13 Dec 60 RATIFIED: 28 Feb 63 FORCE: 1 Mar 63
  Germany, West SIGNED: 13 Dec 60 RATIFIED: 8 Feb 63 FORCE: 1 Mar 63
  Israel RATIFIED: 23 Dec 64 FORCE: 1 Jan 65
  Luxembourg SIGNED: 13 Dec 60 RATIFIED: 6 Feb 62 FORCE: 1 Mar 63
  Netherlands SIGNED: 13 Dec 60 RATIFIED: 10 Oct 62 FORCE: 1 Mar 63
  UK Great Britain SIGNED: 13 Dec 60 RATIFIED: 3 Aug 62 FORCE: 1 Mar 63

107558 Bilateral Convention **523 UNTS 237**
SIGNED: 23 May 63   FORCE: 19 Dec 64
REGISTERED: 29 Jan 65 Netherlands
ARTICLES: 8 LANGUAGE: French.
HEADNOTE: ENCOURAGEMENT CAPITAL INVESTMENT PROTECTION PROPERTY
TOPIC: Finance
CONCEPTS: Detailed regulations. General provisions. Conformity with municipal law. Expropriation. Legal protection and assistance. General property. Arbitration. Procedure. Existing tribunals. Compensation. Investments. Assets transfer. National treatment.
INTL ORGS: International Court of Justice. Arbitration Commission.
PROCEDURE: Duration. Ratification. Termination.
PARTIES:
  Netherlands
  Tunisia

107559 Multilateral Agreement **523 UNTS 249**
SIGNED: 19 Oct 63   FORCE: 19 Oct 63
REGISTERED: 29 Jan 65 Netherlands
ARTICLES: 7 LANGUAGE: English. French.
HEADNOTE: NETHERLANDS CONTRIBUTION TO MEKONG BASIN INVESTIGATING COMMITTEE
TOPIC: Direct Aid
CONCEPTS: Payment schedules. Customs exemptions. Materials, equipment and services. IGO operations.
INTL ORGS: Mekong Commission.
PARTIES:
  Cambodia SIGNED: 18 Oct 63 FORCE: 19 Oct 63
  Laos SIGNED: 5 Oct 63 FORCE: 19 Oct 63
  Netherlands SIGNED: 6 Sep 63 FORCE: 19 Oct 63
  Thailand SIGNED: 18 Sep 63 FORCE: 19 Oct 63
  Vietnam, South SIGNED: 19 Oct 63 FORCE: 19 Oct 63

107560 Multilateral Agreement **523 UNTS 256**
SIGNED: 2 Feb 65   FORCE: 2 Feb 65
REGISTERED: 2 Feb 65 United Nations
ARTICLES: 6 LANGUAGE: English.
HEADNOTE: TECHNICAL ASSISTANCE
TOPIC: Tech Assistance
CONCEPTS: Definition of terms. Privileges and im-

munities. General cooperation. Exchange of information and documents. Personnel. Responsibility and liability. Title and deeds. Use of facilities. Exchange. Scholarships and grants. Vocational training. Research and development. Exchange rates and regulations. Expense sharing formulae. Local currency. Domestic obligation. General technical assistance. Materials, equipment and services. IGO status. Conformity with IGO decisions.
TREATY REF: 374UNTS147; 76UNTS132; 1UNTS15; 33UNTS261.
PROCEDURE: Amendment. Termination.
PARTIES:
  Poland SIGNED: 2 Feb 65 FORCE: 2 Feb 65
  FAO (Food Agri) SIGNED: 2 Feb 65 FORCE: 2 Feb 65
  IAEA (Atom Energy) SIGNED: 2 Feb 65 FORCE: 2 Feb 65
  ICAO (Civil Aviat) SIGNED: 2 Feb 65 FORCE: 2 Feb 65
  ILO (Labor Org) SIGNED: 2 Feb 65 FORCE: 2 Feb 65
  ITU (Telecommun) SIGNED: 2 Feb 65 FORCE: 2 Feb 65
  UNESCO (Educ/Cult) SIGNED: 2 Feb 65 FORCE: 2 Feb 65
  United Nations SIGNED: 2 Feb 65 FORCE: 2 Feb 65
  UPU (Postal Union) SIGNED: 2 Feb 65 FORCE: 2 Feb 65
  WHO (World Health) SIGNED: 2 Feb 65 FORCE: 2 Feb 65
  WMO (Meteorology) SIGNED: 2 Feb 65 FORCE: 2 Feb 65
ANNEX
643 UNTS 400. UNTAB (Tech Assis). Amendment 31 Jul 68. Force 29 Aug 68.
643 UNTS 400. Poland. Amendment 29 Aug 68. Force 29 Aug 68.

107561 Bilateral Agreement **523 UNTS 271**
SIGNED: 25 Jul 61   FORCE: 25 Jul 61
REGISTERED: 3 Feb 65 ICAO (Civil Aviat)
ARTICLES: 16 LANGUAGE: English.
HEADNOTE: AIR SERVICES
TOPIC: Air Transport
CONCEPTS: Arbitration. Air transport. Airport facilities. Airport equipment. Conditions of airlines operating permission. Overflights and technical stops.
INTL ORGS: International Civil Aviation Organization. Arbitration Commission.
PROCEDURE: Termination.
PARTIES:
  Australia
  New Zealand

107562 Bilateral Agreement **523 UNTS 289**
SIGNED: 12 Oct 61   FORCE: 23 Aug 63
REGISTERED: 3 Feb 65 ICAO (Civil Aviat)
ARTICLES: 16 LANGUAGE: German. French.
HEADNOTE: AIR TRANSPORT
TOPIC: Air Transport
CONCEPTS: Definition of terms. Detailed regulations. Conformity with municipal law. General cooperation. Exchange of information and documents. Personnel. Use of facilities. Arbitration. Procedure. Special tribunals. Expense sharing formulae. Fees and exemptions. Non-interest rates and fees. National treatment. Customs exemptions. Routes and logistics. Permit designation. Air transport. Airport facilities. Conditions of airlines operating permission. Overflights and technical stops. Operating authorizations and regulations.
INTL ORGS: International Civil Aviation Organization. Arbitration Commission.
TREATY REF: 15UNTS295.
PROCEDURE: Amendment. Denunciation. Future Procedures Contemplated. Ratification. Registration.
PARTIES:
  Germany, West
  Morocco

107563 Bilateral Agreement **524 UNTS 3**
SIGNED: 15 Jun 62   FORCE: 15 Jun 62
REGISTERED: 3 Feb 65 ICAO (Civil Aviat)
ARTICLES: 20 LANGUAGE: French.
HEADNOTE: AIR TRANSPORT

TOPIC: Air Transport
CONCEPTS: Definition of terms. Detailed regulations. Annex or appendix reference. Conformity with municipal law. General cooperation. Exchange of information and documents. Licenses and permits. Recognition of legal documents. Arbitration. Procedure. Special tribunals. Reexport of goods, etc.. Expense sharing formulae. Fees and exemptions. Non-interest rates and fees. Tax exemptions. Customs exemptions. Competency certificate. Routes and logistics. Navigational conditions. Permit designation. Air transport. Airworthiness certificates. Conditions of airlines operating permission. Operating authorizations and regulations. Licenses and certificates of nationality.
INTL ORGS: International Civil Aviation Organization. Arbitration Commission.
TREATY REF: 15UNTS295.
PROCEDURE: Amendment. Registration. Termination.
PARTIES:
France
Senegal

107564   Bilateral Agreement   **524 UNTS 23**
SIGNED: 23 Jan 63   FORCE: 7 Sep 64
REGISTERED: 3 Feb 65 ICAO (Civil Aviat)
ARTICLES: 22 LANGUAGE: French.
HEADNOTE: AIR TRANSPORT
TOPIC: Air Transport
CONCEPTS: Definition of terms. Detailed regulations. Annex or appendix reference. Conformity with municipal law. General cooperation. Exchange of information and documents. Licenses and permits. Recognition of legal documents. Arbitration. Procedure. Special tribunals. Reexport of goods, etc.. Monetary and gold transfers. Currency deposits. Expense sharing formulae. Non-interest rates and fees. National treatment. Customs exemptions. Competency certificate. Routes and logistics. Navigational conditions. Permit designation. Air transport. Airworthiness certificates. Conditions of airlines operating permission. Overflights and technical stops. Operating authorizations and regulations. Licenses and certificates of nationality.
INTL ORGS: International Civil Aviation Organization. Arbitration Commission.
TREATY REF: 15UNTS295.
PROCEDURE: Amendment. Ratification. Termination.
PARTIES:
Senegal
Switzerland

107565   Bilateral Agreement   **524 UNTS 41**
SIGNED: 7 Feb 63   FORCE: 7 Feb 63
REGISTERED: 3 Feb 65 ICAO (Civil Aviat)
ARTICLES: 21 LANGUAGE: French.
HEADNOTE: AIR TRANSPORT
TOPIC: Air Transport
CONCEPTS: Definition of terms. Detailed regulations. Annex or appendix reference. Conformity with municipal law. General cooperation. Exchange of information and documents. Licenses and permits. Personnel. Recognition of legal documents. Arbitration. Procedure. Special tribunals. Reexport of goods, etc.. Expense sharing formulae. Fees and exemptions. Non-interest rates and fees. Customs exemptions. Competency certificate. Routes and logistics. Navigational conditions. Permit designation. Air transport. Airport facilities. Airworthiness certificates. Conditions of airlines operating permission. Operating authorizations and regulations. Licenses and certificates of nationality.
INTL ORGS: International Civil Aviation Organization. Arbitration Commission.
TREATY REF: 15UNTS295.
PROCEDURE: Amendment. Registration. Termination.
PARTIES:
Mali
Senegal

107566   Bilateral Agreement   **524 UNTS 61**
SIGNED: 17 Mar 64   FORCE: 17 Mar 64
REGISTERED: 3 Feb 65 ICAO (Civil Aviat)
ARTICLES: 19 LANGUAGE: French.
HEADNOTE: AIR TRANSPORT

TOPIC: Air Transport
CONCEPTS: Definition of terms. Detailed regulations. Annex or appendix reference. General cooperation. Exchange of official publications. Exchange of information and documents. Licenses and permits. Recognition of legal documents. Use of facilities. Arbitration. Procedure. Special tribunals. Reexport of goods, etc.. Expense sharing formulae. Fees and exemptions. Non-interest rates and fees. National treatment. Customs exemptions. Competency certificate. Routes and logistics. Navigational conditions. Permit designation. Air transport. Airworthiness certificates. Conditions of airlines operating permission. Operating authorizations and regulations. Licenses and certificates of nationality.
INTL ORGS: International Civil Aviation Organization. Arbitration Commission.
PROCEDURE: Amendment. Future Procedures Contemplated. Registration. Termination.
PARTIES:
Cameroon
Mali

107567   Bilateral Agreement   **524 UNTS 81**
SIGNED: 7 Apr 64   FORCE: 7 Apr 64
REGISTERED: 3 Feb 65 ICAO (Civil Aviat)
ARTICLES: 15 LANGUAGE: English.
HEADNOTE: AIR SERVICES
TOPIC: Air Transport
CONCEPTS: Conditions. Definition of terms. Detailed regulations. Exceptions and exemptions. Territorial application. Annex or appendix reference. General cooperation. Exchange of information and documents. Arbitration. Procedure. Existing tribunals. Negotiation. Reexport of goods, etc.. Currency. Monetary and gold transfers. Exchange rates and regulations. Fees and exemptions. Non-interest rates and fees. Most favored nation clause. National treatment. Tax exemptions. Customs exemptions. Routes and logistics. Permit designation. Conditions of airlines operating permission. Overflights and technical stops. Operating authorizations and regulations.
INTL ORGS: International Civil Aviation Organization. Arbitration Commission.
TREATY REF: 15UNTS295.
PROCEDURE: Amendment. Future Procedures Contemplated. Ratification. Registration. Termination. Application to Non-self-governing Territories.
PARTIES:
Malaysia
Netherlands

107568   Bilateral Agreement   **524 UNTS 101**
SIGNED: 24 Jun 64   FORCE: 24 Jun 64
REGISTERED: 3 Feb 65 ICAO (Civil Aviat)
ARTICLES: 18 LANGUAGE: English.
HEADNOTE: AIR TRANSPORT
TOPIC: Air Transport
CONCEPTS: Definition of terms. Detailed regulations. Annex or appendix reference. Previous treaty replacement. Conformity with municipal law. General cooperation. Licenses and permits. Recognition of legal documents. Use of facilities. Arbitration. Procedure. Special tribunals. Competence of tribunal. Expense sharing formulae. Fees and exemptions. Non-interest rates and fees. National treatment. Customs exemptions. Competency certificate. Routes and logistics. Navigational conditions. Permit designation. Air transport. Airport facilities. Airworthiness certificates. Conditions of airlines operating permission. Overflights and technical stops. Operating authorizations and regulations. Licenses and certificates of nationality.
INTL ORGS: International Civil Aviation Organization. International Court of Justice. Arbitration Commission.
TREATY REF: 7UNTS175.
PROCEDURE: Amendment. Future Procedures Contemplated. Registration. Termination. Application to Non-self-governing Territories.
PARTIES:
New Zealand
USA (United States)

107569   Bilateral Agreement   **524 UNTS 121**
SIGNED: 9 Jul 64   FORCE: 9 Jul 64
REGISTERED: 3 Feb 65 ICAO (Civil Aviat)

ARTICLES: 21 LANGUAGE: French.
HEADNOTE: AIR TRANSPORT
TOPIC: Air Transport
CONCEPTS: Definition of terms. Detailed regulations. Annex or appendix reference. Conformity with municipal law. General cooperation. Exchange of information and documents. Licenses and permits. Recognition of legal documents. Use of facilities. Arbitration. Procedure. Special tribunals. Reexport of goods, etc.. Expense sharing formulae. Fees and exemptions. Non-interest rates and fees. National treatment. Customs exemptions. Competency certificate. Routes and logistics. Navigational conditions. Permit designation. Air transport. Airworthiness certificates. Conditions of airlines operating permission. Operating authorizations and regulations. Licenses and certificates of nationality.
INTL ORGS: International Civil Aviation Organization. Arbitration Commission.
TREATY REF: 15UNTS295.
PROCEDURE: Amendment. Registration. Termination.
PARTIES:
Ivory Coast
Mali

107570   Bilateral Agreement   **524 UNTS 141**
SIGNED: 23 Apr 64   FORCE: 23 Apr 64
REGISTERED: 3 Feb 65 USA (United States)
ARTICLES: 14 LANGUAGE: English. Chinese.
HEADNOTE: FINANCING EDUCATIONAL CULTURAL EXCHANGE PROGRAMS
TOPIC: Health/Educ/Welfare
CONCEPTS: Legal protection and assistance. Personnel. Immovable property. Specialists exchange. Exchange. Commissions and foundations. Teacher and student exchange. Scholarships and grants. Exchange. Currency. Customs duties.
TREATY REF: 12UNTS39;   303UNTS286;   404UNTS284.
PARTIES:
Taiwan
USA (United States)

107571   Bilateral Exchange   **524 UNTS 165**
SIGNED: 20 Apr 64   FORCE: 20 Apr 64
REGISTERED: 3 Feb 65 USA (United States)
ARTICLES: 2 LANGUAGE: English.
HEADNOTE: INVESTMENT GUARANTIES
TOPIC: Claims and Debts
CONCEPTS: General cooperation. General property. Arbitration. Procedure. Existing tribunals. Negotiation. Reciprocity in financial treatment. Currency. Claims and settlements. Private investment guarantee.
INTL ORGS: Special Commission.
PARTIES:
Kenya
USA (United States)

107572   Bilateral Exchange   **524 UNTS 173**
SIGNED: 6 May 64   FORCE: 6 May 64
REGISTERED: 3 Feb 65 USA (United States)
ARTICLES: 2 LANGUAGE: English.
HEADNOTE: IONOSPHERIC RESEARCH SATELLITE
TOPIC: Scientific Project
CONCEPTS: General cooperation. Operating agencies. Licenses and permits. Research and scientific projects. Research results. Communication satellites testing. Scientific exchange. Research and development. Fees and exemptions. Domestic obligation. Materials, equipment and services.
PROCEDURE: Termination.
PARTIES:
Canada
USA (United States)

107573   Bilateral Agreement   **524 UNTS 185**
SIGNED: 1 Mar 63   FORCE: 8 May 64
REGISTERED: 3 Feb 65 USA (United States)
ARTICLES: 13 LANGUAGE: English.
HEADNOTE: NORWEGIAN PORTS TERRITORIAL WATERS BY NS SAVANNAH
TOPIC: Water Transport
CONCEPTS: Conformity with municipal law. Inspection and observation. Personnel. Responsi-

bility and liability. Compensation. Claims and settlements. Peaceful use. Navigational conditions. Inland and territorial waters. Ports and pilotage. Naval vessels. Ocean resources.
TREATY REF: S.EX.DOC.K, 87TH CONG. 1ST SESS..
PROCEDURE: Termination.
PARTIES:
Norway
USA (United States)

107574 Bilateral Exchange **524 UNTS 197**
SIGNED: 14 Feb 64 FORCE: 14 Feb 64
REGISTERED: 5 Feb 65 USA (United States)
ARTICLES: 2 LANGUAGE: English. Spanish.
HEADNOTE: METEOROLOGICAL PROGRAM
TOPIC: Scientific Project
CONCEPTS: Annex type material. Previous treaty replacement. Operating agencies. General property. Responsibility and liability. Research and scientific projects. Meteorology. Indemnities and reimbursements. Fees and exemptions. Tax exemptions. Domestic obligation. Special projects. Materials, equipment and services. Facilities and equipment. Facilities and equipment.
TREATY REF: 290UNTS286; 458UNTS278; 473UNTS333.
PROCEDURE: Amendment. Duration. Renewal or Revival. Termination.
PARTIES:
Mexico
USA (United States)

107575 Bilateral Agreement **524 UNTS 217**
SIGNED: 2 Mar 64 FORCE: 2 Mar 64
REGISTERED: 5 Feb 65 USA (United States)
ARTICLES: 6 LANGUAGE: English.
HEADNOTE: AGRI COMMOD TITLE I
TOPIC: US Agri Commod Aid
CONCEPTS: General provisions. Annex or appendix reference. Exchange of information and documents. Reexport of goods, etc.. Exchange rates and regulations. Transportation costs. Local currency. Commodities schedule. Purchase authorization. Surplus commodities. Mutual consultation.
PARTIES:
Sudan
USA (United States)

107576 Bilateral Agreement **524 UNTS 235**
SIGNED: 13 Feb 64 FORCE: 13 Feb 64
REGISTERED: 5 Feb 65 USA (United States)
ARTICLES: 12 LANGUAGE: English. Icelandic.
HEADNOTE: EDUCATIONAL PROGRAM
TOPIC: Education
CONCEPTS: Previous treaty replacement. Friendship and amity. Privileges and immunities. Standardization. Conformity with municipal law. Inspection and observation. Personnel. Exchange. Commissions and foundations. Teacher and student exchange. Professorships. Vocational training. Currency. Exchange rates and regulations. Expense sharing formulae. Financial programs. Funding procedures. Special status.
INTL ORGS: Special Commission.
TREATY REF: 283UNTS73.
PROCEDURE: Amendment.
PARTIES:
Iceland
USA (United States)

107577 Bilateral Exchange **524 UNTS 255**
SIGNED: 6 Mar 64 FORCE: 6 Mar 64
REGISTERED: 5 Feb 65 USA (United States)
ARTICLES: 2 LANGUAGE: English.
HEADNOTE: WINTER MAINTENANCE HAINES ROAD
TOPIC: Specific Property
CONCEPTS: Indemnities and reimbursements. Roads and highways. Boundaries of territory.
TREATY REF: 2661NTS109.
PARTIES:
Canada
USA (United States)
ANNEX
531 UNTS 422. USA (United States). Prolongation 27 Nov 64. Force 27 Nov 64.
531 UNTS 422. Canada. Prolongation 27 Nov 64. Force 27 Nov 64.

573 UNTS 348. Canada. Prolongation 17 Nov 65. Force 17 Nov 65.
573 UNTS 348. USA (United States). Prolongation 17 Nov 65. Force 17 Nov 65.

107578 Bilateral Agreement **524 UNTS 263**
SIGNED: 18 Mar 64 FORCE: 18 Mar 64
REGISTERED: 5 Feb 65 USA (United States)
ARTICLES: 6 LANGUAGE: English.
HEADNOTE: AGRICULTURAL TRADE
TOPIC: US Agri Commod Aid
CONCEPTS: General trade. Currency. Agricultural commodities.
PARTIES:
Korea, South
USA (United States)

107579 Bilateral Agreement **524 UNTS 281**
SIGNED: 8 Jan 65 FORCE: 8 Jan 65
REGISTERED: 5 Feb 65 WHO (World Health)
ARTICLES: 6 LANGUAGE: English.
HEADNOTE: TECHNICAL ADVISORY ASSISTANCE
TOPIC: Tech Assistance
CONCEPTS: Definition of terms. Privileges and immunities. General cooperation. Exchange of information and documents. Personnel. Responsibility and liability. Title and deeds. Exchange. Scholarships and grants. Vocational training. Research and development. Expense sharing formulae. Local currency. Domestic obligation. Special projects. Materials, equipment and services. IGO status. Conformity with IGO decisions.
TREATY REF: 33UNTS261.
PROCEDURE: Amendment. Termination.
PARTIES:
Malawi
WHO (World Health)
ANNEX
540 UNTS 350. WHO (World Health). Correction 25 Mar 65.
540 UNTS 350. Malawi. Correction 3 May 65.

107580 Bilateral Agreement **525 UNTS 3**
SIGNED: 15 Jun 64 FORCE: 1 Aug 64
REGISTERED: 8 Feb 65 IAEA (Atom Energy)
ARTICLES: 8 LANGUAGE: English.
HEADNOTE: APPLICATION SAFEGUARDS REACTOR FACILITIES
TOPIC: Atomic Energy
CONCEPTS: Definition of terms. Exchange of information and documents. Inspection and observation. Arbitration. Special tribunals. Indemnities and reimbursements. Nuclear materials. Peaceful use. Security of information. Special status.
TREATY REF: 276UNTS3; 471UNTS334.
PROCEDURE: Amendment. Duration. Renewal or Revival. Termination.
PARTIES:
IAEA (Atom Energy)
USA (United States)

107581 Bilateral Agreement **525 UNTS 19**
SIGNED: 17 Sep 64 FORCE: 17 Sep 64
REGISTERED: 8 Feb 65 IAEA (Atom Energy)
ARTICLES: 9 LANGUAGE: English.
HEADNOTE: FURTHERING RESEARCH PROJECT
TOPIC: Atomic Energy
CONCEPTS: Inspection and observation. Arbitration. Special tribunals. Negotiation. Public health. Research cooperation. Research results. Nuclear materials. Peaceful use. Transport of goods. Security of information. Special status.
INTL ORGS: International Court of Justice.
TREATY REF: 374UNTS147; 276UNTS3; 417UNTS334.
PARTIES:
IAEA (Atom Energy)
United Arab Rep

107582 Bilateral Agreement **525 UNTS 29**
SIGNED: 2 Dec 64 FORCE: 2 Dec 64
REGISTERED: 8 Feb 65 IAEA (Atom Energy)
ARTICLES: 10 LANGUAGE: English. Spanish.
HEADNOTE: ESTABLISHING RESEARCH & ISOTOPE PRODUCTION REACTOR PROJECT
TOPIC: Atomic Energy
CONCEPTS: Annex or appendix reference. Exchange of information and documents. Inspection and observation. Arbitration. Special tribu-

nals. Research cooperation. Research results. Nuclear materials. Peaceful use. Special status. Status of experts.
INTL ORGS: International Court of Justice.
TREATY REF: 276UNTS3; 471UNTS334.
PARTIES:
Argentina
IAEA (Atom Energy)

107583 Multilateral Instrument **525 UNTS 51**
SIGNED: 2 Dec 64 FORCE: 2 Dec 64
REGISTERED: 8 Feb 65 IAEA (Atom Energy)
ARTICLES: 4 LANGUAGE: English. Spanish.
HEADNOTE: TRANSFER TITLE ENRICHED URANIUM RESEARCH ISOTOPE PRODUCTION REACTOR
TOPIC: Atomic Energy
CONCEPTS: Licenses and permits. Responsibility and liability. Nuclear materials.
INTL ORGS: International Court of Justice.
PARTIES:
Argentina SIGNED: 2 Dec 64 FORCE: 2 Dec 64
IAEA (Atom Energy) SIGNED: 2 Dec 64 FORCE: 2 Dec 64
USA (United States) SIGNED: 2 Dec 64 FORCE: 2 Dec 64

107584 Multilateral Agreement **525 UNTS 61**
SIGNED: 11 Jun 64 FORCE: 31 Aug 64
REGISTERED: 8 Feb 65 IAEA (Atom Energy)
ARTICLES: 10 LANGUAGE: English.
HEADNOTE: REGIONAL JOINT TRAINING RESEARCH PROGRAM
TOPIC: Atomic Energy
CONCEPTS: Territorial application. Annex or appendix reference. Exchange of information and documents. Responsibility and liability. Establishment of commission. Arbitration. Special tribunals. Public health. Scholarships and grants. Research cooperation. Research results. Scientific exchange. Peaceful use.
INTL ORGS: International Court of Justice.
TREATY REF: 201UNTS95; 374UNTS147.
PROCEDURE: Duration.
PARTIES:
India RATIFIED: 31 Aug 64 FORCE: 31 Aug 64
Philippines RATIFIED: 19 Aug 64 FORCE: 31 Aug 64
IAEA (Atom Energy) RATIFIED: 11 Jun 64 FORCE: 31 Aug 64

107585 Multilateral Agreement **525 UNTS 75**
SIGNED: 17 Oct 63 FORCE: 19 Jun 64
REGISTERED: 8 Feb 65 IAEA (Atom Energy)
ARTICLES: 12 LANGUAGE: English.
HEADNOTE: RADIATION ACCIDENTS
TOPIC: Atomic Energy
CONCEPTS: Annex or appendix reference. Inspection and observation. Operating agencies. Responsibility and liability. Arbitration. Special tribunals. Public health. Research cooperation. Communication satellites testing. Compensation. Indemnities and reimbursements. Peaceful use. Security of information. Paragraph 2, Article 36.
TREATY REF: 374UNTS147.
PROCEDURE: Ratification.
PARTIES:
Denmark SIGNED: 17 Oct 63 RATIFIED: 17 Aug 64 FORCE: 17 Aug 64
Finland SIGNED: 17 Oct 63
Norway SIGNED: 17 Oct 63 RATIFIED: 19 Jun 64 FORCE: 19 Jun 64
IAEA (Atom Energy) SIGNED: 17 Oct 63 FORCE: 19 Jun 64
Sweden SIGNED: 17 Oct 63 FORCE: 19 Jun 64
ANNEX
556 UNTS 202. Finland. Ratification 16 Jun 65.

107586 Bilateral Agreement **525 UNTS 89**
SIGNED: 7 Apr 64 FORCE: 13 Jan 65
REGISTERED: 8 Feb 65 Finland
ARTICLES: 32 LANGUAGE: Finnish. Danish.
HEADNOTE: DOUBLE TAXATION FISCAL EVASION INCOME CAPITAL
TOPIC: Taxation
CONCEPTS: Definition of terms. Territorial application. Privileges and immunities. Exchange of official publications. Negotiation. Teacher and student exchange. Taxation. Death duties. Tax cred-

its. Equitable taxes. Tax exemptions. Air transport. Merchant vessels.
TREATY REF: 76UNTS132;1UNTS15;-33UNTS261;374UNTS147.
PROCEDURE: Duration. Ratification. Termination.
PARTIES:
Denmark
Finland

107587 Multilateral Agreement **525 UNTS 148**
SIGNED: 12 Feb 65   FORCE: 12 Feb 65
REGISTERED: 12 Feb 65 United Nations
ARTICLES: 6 LANGUAGE: English.
HEADNOTE: TECHNICAL ASSISTANCE
TOPIC: Tech Assistance
CONCEPTS: Definition of terms. Previous treaty replacement. Privileges and immunities. General cooperation. Exchange of information and documents. Personnel. Responsibility and liability. Title and deeds. Use of facilities. Exchange. Scholarships and grants. Vocational training. Research and development. Exchange rates and regulations. Expense sharing formulae. Local currency. Domestic obligation. General technical assistance. Materials, equipment and services. IGO status. Conformity with IGO decisions.
TREATY REF: 76UNTS132;   1UNTS15;
33UNTS261; 374UNTS147.
PROCEDURE: Amendment. Termination.
PARTIES:
Liberia SIGNED: 12 Feb 65 FORCE: 12 Feb 65
FAO (Food Agri) SIGNED: 12 Feb 65 FORCE: 12 Feb 65
IAEA (Atom Energy) SIGNED: 12 Feb 65 FORCE: 12 Feb 65
ICAO (Civil Aviat) SIGNED: 12 Feb 65 FORCE: 12 Feb 65
ILO (Labor Org) SIGNED: 12 Feb 65 FORCE: 12 Feb 65
ITU (Telecommun) SIGNED: 12 Feb 65 FORCE: 12 Feb 65
UNESCO (Educ/Cult) SIGNED: 12 Feb 65 FORCE: 12 Feb 65
United Nations SIGNED: 12 Feb 65 FORCE: 12 Feb 65
UPU (Postal Union) SIGNED: 12 Feb 65 FORCE: 12 Feb 65
WHO (World Health) SIGNED: 12 Feb 65 FORCE: 12 Feb 65
WMO (Meteorology) SIGNED: 12 Feb 65 FORCE: 12 Feb 65

107588 Bilateral Agreement **525 UNTS 165**
SIGNED: 6 Jan 65   FORCE: 6 Jan 65
REGISTERED: 12 Feb 65 WHO (World Health)
ARTICLES: 6 LANGUAGE: English.
HEADNOTE: TECHNICAL ADVISORY ASSISTANCE
TOPIC: Tech Assistance
CONCEPTS: Definition of terms. Privileges and immunities. General cooperation. Exchange of information and documents. Personnel. Responsibility and liability. Title and deeds. Exchange. Scholarships and grants. Vocational training. Research and development. Expense sharing formulae. Local currency. Domestic obligation. Special projects. Materials, equipment and services. IGO status. Conformity with IGO decisions.
TREATY REF: 33UNTS261.
PROCEDURE: Amendment. Termination.
PARTIES:
Zambia
WHO (World Health)
                    ANNEX
538 UNTS 346. Zambia. Correction 10 Apr 65.
538 UNTS 346. WHO (World Health). Correction 25 Mar 65.

107589 Bilateral Exchange **525 UNTS 177**
SIGNED: 23 Dec 64   FORCE: 23 Dec 64
REGISTERED: 15 Feb 65 Thailand
ARTICLES: 2 LANGUAGE: English.
HEADNOTE: WOOD RESEARCH INSTITUTE
TOPIC: Scientific Project
CONCEPTS: Use of facilities. Specialists exchange. Scholarships and grants. Vocational training. Research and scientific projects. Research and development. Indemnities and reimbursements. Domestic obligation. General technical assistance. Materials, equipment and services.
TREATY REF: 503UNTS3.

PARTIES:
Germany, West
Thailand

107590 Bilateral Exchange **525 UNTS 185**
SIGNED: 23 Dec 64   FORCE: 23 Dec 64
REGISTERED: 15 Feb 65 Thailand
ARTICLES: 2 LANGUAGE: English.
HEADNOTE: ASSIGNMENT EXPERT VEHICLE TESTING
TOPIC: Tech Assistance
CONCEPTS: Time limit. Annex type material. Personnel. Title and deeds. Domestic obligation. Special projects. Materials, equipment and services.
TREATY REF: GERM.W, THAILAND;2APR1964 ON TECHNICAL COOPERATION.
PARTIES:
Germany, West
Thailand

107591 Bilateral Exchange **525 UNTS 193**
SIGNED: 23 Dec 64   FORCE: 23 Dec 64
REGISTERED: 15 Feb 65 Thailand
ARTICLES: 2 LANGUAGE: English.
HEADNOTE: SARABURI SETTLEMENT PROJECT
TOPIC: Non-IBRD Project
CONCEPTS: Assistance. Materials, equipment and services. Withdrawal conditions. Non-bank projects.
TREATY REF: 503UNTS3.
PARTIES:
Germany, West
Thailand

107592 Bilateral Exchange **525 UNTS 201**
SIGNED: 23 Dec 64   FORCE: 23 Dec 64
REGISTERED: 15 Feb 65 Thailand
ARTICLES: 2 LANGUAGE: English.
HEADNOTE: EXPERIMENTAL CENTER
TOPIC: Sanitation
CONCEPTS: General property. Veterinary. Scholarships and grants. Research cooperation. Research and development. Indemnities and reimbursements. Expense sharing formulae. Agriculture. Special projects.
TREATY REF: 503UNTS3.
PARTIES:
Germany, West
Thailand

107593 Bilateral Agreement **525 UNTS 211**
SIGNED: 16 Feb 65   FORCE: 16 Feb 65
REGISTERED: 16 Feb 65 United Nations
ARTICLES: 6 LANGUAGE: English.
HEADNOTE: 18 SESSION UN COMMISSION STATUS OF WOMEN
TOPIC: Admin Cooperation
CONCEPTS: Privileges and immunities. General cooperation. Personnel. Use of facilities. Financial programs. Conferences.
PARTIES:
Iran
United Nations

107594 Bilateral Exchange **525 UNTS 221**
SIGNED: 31 Dec 64   FORCE: 31 Dec 64
REGISTERED: 19 Feb 65 Malta
ARTICLES: 2 LANGUAGE: English.
HEADNOTE: MALTESE ASSUMPTION PRE-INDEPENDENCE INTERNATIONAL RIGHTS & OBLIGATIONS
TOPIC: Admin Cooperation
CONCEPTS: Continuity of rights and obligations.
PARTIES:
Malta
UK Great Britain

107595 Bilateral Exchange **525 UNTS 227**
SIGNED: 15 Oct 64   FORCE: 14 Dec 64
REGISTERED: 19 Feb 65 Denmark
ARTICLES: 2 LANGUAGE: English.
HEADNOTE: RECOGNITION MERCHANT SHIP TONNAGE CERTIFICATES
TOPIC: Water Transport
CONCEPTS: Recognition of legal documents. Registration certificate. Merchant vessels. Tonnage.
PROCEDURE: Termination.

PARTIES:
Canada
Denmark

107596 Bilateral Convention **525 UNTS 233**
SIGNED: 4 Feb 64   FORCE: 5 Jan 65
REGISTERED: 19 Feb 65 Denmark
ARTICLES: 30
HEADNOTE: DOUBLE TAXATION
TOPIC: Taxation
CONCEPTS: Taxation. Equitable taxes. Tax exemptions.
PROCEDURE: Termination.
PARTIES:
Denmark
Ireland

107597 Bilateral Agreement **526 UNTS 3**
SIGNED: 16 Nov 62   FORCE: 22 Sep 64
REGISTERED: 23 Feb 65 Czechoslovakia
ARTICLES: 26 LANGUAGE: Czechoslovakian. Polish.
HEADNOTE: RAILWAY LINE TRANSIT TRAFFIC
TOPIC: Land Transport
CONCEPTS: General provisions. Treaty implementation. Previous treaty replacement. Non-visa travel documents. Conformity with municipal law. General cooperation. Exchange of information and documents. Free passage and transit. Recognition of legal documents. Responsibility and liability. Investigation of violations. Humanitarian matters. Compensation. Indemnities and reimbursements. Fees and exemptions. Funding procedures. Payment schedules. Claims and settlements. Customs exemptions. Passenger transport. Routes and logistics. Transport of goods. Operating authorizations and regulations. Railway border crossing. Railways. Facilities and equipment. Regulations. Services.
TREATY REF: 431UNTS99; 260UNTS179.
PROCEDURE: Denunciation. Ratification.
PARTIES:
Czechoslovakia
Poland

107598 Bilateral Exchange **526 UNTS 39**
SIGNED: 21 Apr 62   FORCE: 21 Apr 62
REGISTERED: 25 Feb 65 USA (United States)
ARTICLES: 2 LANGUAGE: English. French.
HEADNOTE: PEACE CORPS
TOPIC: General Aid
CONCEPTS: Diplomatic privileges. General cooperation. Personnel. Exchange rates and regulations. Funding procedures. Tax exemptions. Aid missions. Volunteer programs.
PROCEDURE: Termination.
PARTIES:
Ivory Coast
USA (United States)

107599 Bilateral Exchange **526 UNTS 47**
SIGNED: 4 Apr 64   FORCE: 15 Apr 64
REGISTERED: 25 Feb 65 USA (United States)
ARTICLES: 3 LANGUAGE: English.
HEADNOTE: ABOLITION VISA FEES
TOPIC: Visas
CONCEPTS: Visas. Fees and exemptions.
PROCEDURE: Termination.
PARTIES:
USA (United States)
Yugoslavia

107600 Bilateral Agreement **526 UNTS 55**
SIGNED: 28 Apr 64   FORCE: 28 Apr 64
REGISTERED: 25 Feb 65 USA (United States)
ARTICLES: 6 LANGUAGE: English. French.
HEADNOTE: AGRI COMMOD TITLE I
TOPIC: US Agri Commod Aid
CONCEPTS: General provisions. Annex or appendix reference. Exchange of information and documents. Reexport of goods, etc.. Exchange rates and regulations. Transportation costs. Local currency. Commodities schedule. Surplus commodities. Mutual consultation.
PARTIES:
Congo (Zaire)
USA (United States)

ANNEX

531 UNTS 426. USA (United States). Amendment 25 Aug 64. Force 25 Aug 64.

531 UNTS 426. Congo (Zaire). Amendment 25 Aug 64. Force 25 Aug 64.

531 UNTS 429. Congo (Zaire). Amendment 9 Dec 65. Force 9 Dec 64.

531 UNTS 429. Congo (Zaire). Amendment 9 Dec 65. Force 9 Dec 64.

546 UNTS 393. Congo (Zaire). Amendment 29 Apr 65. Force 29 Apr 65.

546 UNTS 393. USA (United States). Amendment 29 Apr 65. Force 29 Apr 65.

107601 Bilateral Agreement **526 UNTS 73**
SIGNED: 27 Apr 64 FORCE: 27 Apr 64
REGISTERED: 25 Feb 65 USA (United States)
ARTICLES: 6 LANGUAGE: English.
HEADNOTE: AGRI COMMOD TITLE I
TOPIC: US Agri Commod Aid
CONCEPTS: General provisions. Annex or appendix reference. Exchange of information and documents. Reexport of goods, etc.. Currency. Exchange rates and regulations. Payment schedules. Transportation costs. Local currency. Commodities schedule. Purchase authorization. Surplus commodities. Merchant vessels. Mutual consultation.
PARTIES:
USA (United States)
Yugoslavia

107602 Bilateral Agreement **526 UNTS 89**
SIGNED: 27 Apr 64 FORCE: 27 Apr 64
REGISTERED: 25 Feb 65 USA (United States)
ARTICLES: 5 LANGUAGE: English.
HEADNOTE: AGRI COMMOD TITLE IV
TOPIC: US Agri Commod Aid
CONCEPTS: General provisions. Annex or appendix reference. Exchange of information and documents. Reexport of goods, etc.. Payment schedules. Transportation costs. Purchase authorization. Commodities schedule. Purchase authorization. Mutual consultation.
PARTIES:
USA (United States)
Yugoslavia

107603 Bilateral Agreement **526 UNTS 103**
SIGNED: 28 Apr 64 FORCE: 28 Apr 64
REGISTERED: 25 Feb 65 USA (United States)
ARTICLES: 5 LANGUAGE: English.
HEADNOTE: AGRI COMMOD TITLE IV
TOPIC: US Agri Commod Aid
CONCEPTS: General provisions. Exchange of information and documents. Reexport of goods, etc.. Payment schedules. Transportation costs. Purchase authorization. Commodities schedule. Purchase authorization. Mutual consultation.
PARTIES:
USA (United States)
Yugoslavia

107604 Bilateral Agreement **526 UNTS 113**
SIGNED: 14 May 64 FORCE: 14 May 64
REGISTERED: 25 Feb 65 USA (United States)
ARTICLES: 6 LANGUAGE: English.
HEADNOTE: AGRI COMMOD TITLE I
TOPIC: US Agri Commod Aid
CONCEPTS: General provisions. Annex or appendix reference. Exchange of information and documents. Reexport of goods, etc.. Exchange rates and regulations. Transportation costs. Local currency. Commodities schedule. Purchase authorization. Surplus commodities. Mutual consultation.
PARTIES:
Philippines
USA (United States)

107605 Bilateral Agreement **526 UNTS 131**
SIGNED: 22 Feb 64 FORCE: 22 Feb 64
REGISTERED: 25 Feb 65 USA (United States)
ARTICLES: 14 LANGUAGE: English. Russian.
HEADNOTE: EXCHANGE SCIENTIFIC TECHNICAL EDUCATIONAL CULTURAL & OTHER FIELDS
TOPIC: Health/Educ/Welfare
CONCEPTS: General cooperation. Exchange of information and documents. Personnel. Special-

ists exchange. Disease control. Insect control. Sanitation. Recognition of degrees. Exchange. Commissions and foundations. Teacher and student exchange. Professorships. Scholarships and grants. Vocational training. Exchange. Artists. Athletes. Meteorology. Nuclear research. Scientific exchange. Research and development. Trade procedures. Agriculture. Specific technical assistance. General. General transportation. Navigational conditions. Publications exchange. Mass media exchange. Press and wire services.
PROCEDURE: Duration.
PARTIES:
USA (United States)
USSR (Soviet Union)

107606 Bilateral Exchange **526 UNTS 221**
SIGNED: 14 Apr 64 FORCE: 14 Apr 64
REGISTERED: 25 Feb 65 USA (United States)
ARTICLES: 2 LANGUAGE: English.
HEADNOTE: TRANSFER LIBERIA TITLE PORT OF MONROVIA
TOPIC: Specific Property
CONCEPTS: Title and deeds. Currency. Payment schedules. Ports and pilotage. Facilities and property.
TREATY REF: 106UNTS199.
PARTIES:
Liberia
USA (United States)

107607 Bilateral Exchange **526 UNTS 228**
SIGNED: 14 May 64 FORCE: 14 May 64
REGISTERED: 25 Feb 65 USA (United States)
ARTICLES: 2 LANGUAGE: English. Spanish.
HEADNOTE: TRADE BEEF VEAL
TOPIC: Commodity Trade
CONCEPTS: Detailed regulations. General cooperation. Trade agencies. Commodity trade. Quotas.
PARTIES:
Mexico
USA (United States)

107608 Bilateral Agreement **526 UNTS 239**
SIGNED: 8 May 64 FORCE: 8 May 64
REGISTERED: 25 Feb 65 USA (United States)
ARTICLES: 11 LANGUAGE: English.
HEADNOTE: EDUCATION CULTURAL PROGRAM
TOPIC: Education
CONCEPTS: Friendship and amity. Alien status. Standardization. Conformity with municipal law. Exchange of information and documents. Inspection and observation. Personnel. General property. Exchange. Commissions and foundations. Teacher and student exchange. Scholarships and grants. Accounting procedures. Currency. Expense sharing formulae. Financial programs. Funding procedures.
INTL ORGS: Special Commission.
TREATY REF: 526UNTS221.
PROCEDURE: Amendment.
PARTIES:
Liberia
USA (United States)

107609 Bilateral Exchange **526 UNTS 251**
SIGNED: 25 May 64 FORCE: 25 May 64
REGISTERED: 25 Feb 65 USA (United States)
ARTICLES: 2 LANGUAGE: English.
HEADNOTE: PHASING OUT CERTAIN RADAR STATIONS
TOPIC: Milit Installation
CONCEPTS: Bases and facilities.
TREATY REF: 233UNTS109.
PARTIES:
Canada
USA (United States)

107610 Bilateral Agreement **526 UNTS 257**
SIGNED: 3 Jun 64 FORCE: 3 Jun 64
REGISTERED: 25 Feb 65 USA (United States)
ARTICLES: 6 LANGUAGE: English. Chinese.
HEADNOTE: AGRI COMMOD TITLE I
TOPIC: US Agri Commod Aid
CONCEPTS: General provisions. Annex or appendix reference. Exchange of information and documents. Free trade. Exchange rates and regulations. Transportation costs. Local currency. Com-

modities schedule. Purchase authorization. Surplus commodities. Mutual consultation.
PARTIES:
Taiwan
USA (United States)

107611 Bilateral Agreement **526 UNTS 285**
SIGNED: 10 Mar 64 FORCE: 10 Mar 64
REGISTERED: 26 Feb 65 USA (United States)
ARTICLES: 6 LANGUAGE: English. French.
HEADNOTE: AGRI COMMOD TITLE I
TOPIC: US Agri Commod Aid
CONCEPTS: General provisions. Annex or appendix reference. Exchange of information and documents. Reexport of goods, etc.. Exchange rates and regulations. Transportation costs. Local currency. Commodities schedule. Purchase authorization. Surplus commodities. Mutual consultation.
PARTIES:
Ivory Coast
USA (United States)

107612 Bilateral Exchange **526 UNTS 301**
SIGNED: 9 Dec 63 FORCE: 9 Dec 63
REGISTERED: 26 Feb 65 USA (United States)
ARTICLES: 2 LANGUAGE: English.
HEADNOTE: TECHNICAL COOPERATION
TOPIC: Tech Assistance
CONCEPTS: Previous treaty extension. General technical assistance.
TREATY REF: 103UNTS71.
PARTIES:
Tanganyika
USA (United States)

107613 Bilateral Agreement **527 UNTS 3**
SIGNED: 7 Apr 64 FORCE: 7 Apr 64
REGISTERED: 26 Feb 65 USA (United States)
ARTICLES: 6 LANGUAGE: English. French.
HEADNOTE: AGRI COMMOD TITLE I
TOPIC: US Agri Commod Aid
CONCEPTS: General provisions. Annex or appendix reference. Exchange of information and documents. Reexport of goods, etc.. Exchange rates and regulations. Transportation costs. Local currency. Commodities schedule. Purchase authorization. Surplus commodities. Mutual consultation.
PARTIES:
Tunisia
USA (United States)
ANNEX

529 UNTS 387. USA (United States). Amendment 7 Jul 64. Force 7 Jul 64.

529 UNTS 387. Tunisia. Amendment 7 Jul 64. Force 7 Jul 64.

107614 Bilateral Exchange **527 UNTS 19**
SIGNED: 15 Apr 64 FORCE: 15 Apr 64
REGISTERED: 26 Feb 65 USA (United States)
ARTICLES: 2 LANGUAGE: English.
HEADNOTE: TRADE COTTON TEXTILES
TOPIC: Commodity Trade
CONCEPTS: Treaty implementation. Annex or appendix reference. General cooperation. Commodity trade. Quotas.
INTL ORGS: General Agreement on Tariffs and Trade.
TREATY REF: 55UNTS187; 471UNTSI96.
PROCEDURE: Amendment. Duration. Termination.
PARTIES:
India
USA (United States)
ANNEX

531 UNTS 430. USA (United States). Amendment 15 Sep 64. Force 15 Sep 64.

531 UNTS 430. India. Amendment 15 Sep 64. Force 15 Sep 64.

107615 Bilateral Agreement **527 UNTS 29**
SIGNED: 8 Mar 62 FORCE: 10 Jun 64
REGISTERED: 26 Feb 65 USA (United States)
ARTICLES: 9 LANGUAGE: English. Spanish.
HEADNOTE: MILITARY ASSISTANCE AGREEMENT
TOPIC: Milit Assistance
CONCEPTS: Exceptions and exemptions. Guarantees and safeguards. Non-prejudice to UN charter. Peaceful relations. Privileges and immuni-

ties. Conformity with municipal law. Inspection and observation. Public information. Use of facilities. Garnishment of funds. Claims and settlements. Most favored nation clause. Tax exemptions. Recognition. Customs exemptions. Domestic obligation. Materials, equipment and services. Aid missions. Self-defense. Return of equipment and recapture. Security of information. Exchange of defense information. Restrictions on transfer.
INTL ORGS: United Nations.
TREATY REF: 21UNTS77.
PROCEDURE: Amendment. Future Procedures Contemplated. Ratification. Registration. Termination.
PARTIES:
Dominican Republic
USA (United States)

107616 Bilateral Exchange **527 UNTS 45**
SIGNED: 15 Jul 63 FORCE: 15 Jul 63
REGISTERED: 26 Feb 65 USA (United States)
ARTICLES: 2 LANGUAGE: English. Icelandic.
HEADNOTE: TRADE
TOPIC: General Trade
CONCEPTS: Annex or appendix reference. Annex type material. Tariffs.
TREATY REF: 29UNTS317.
PARTIES:
Iceland
USA (United States)

107617 Bilateral Exchange **527 UNTS 69**
SIGNED: 19 Dec 63 FORCE: 19 Dec 63
REGISTERED: 26 Feb 65 USA (United States)
ARTICLES: 2 LANGUAGE: English.
HEADNOTE: COMBINED MILITARY EXERCISES
TOPIC: Status of Forces
CONCEPTS: Privileges and immunities. Responsibility and liability. Joint defense. Defense and security. Status of military forces.
TREATY REF: 132UNTS273.
PARTIES:
Taiwan
USA (United States)

107618 Bilateral Exchange **527 UNTS 77**
SIGNED: 10 May 64 FORCE: 10 May 64
REGISTERED: 26 Feb 65 USA (United States)
ARTICLES: 2 LANGUAGE: English. Spanish.
HEADNOTE: MILITARY ASSISTANCE
TOPIC: Milit Assistance
CONCEPTS: Annex or appendix reference. Materials, equipment and services. Military assistance.
INTL ORGS: Organization of American States.
PARTIES:
Argentina
USA (United States)

107619 Bilateral Exchange **527 UNTS 89**
SIGNED: 1 Aug 63 FORCE: 1 Aug 63
REGISTERED: 26 Feb 65 USA (United States)
ARTICLES: 2 LANGUAGE: English. French.
HEADNOTE: ELECTRICITY TAX SURPLUS COMMODITY HOUSING
TOPIC: Taxation
CONCEPTS: Payment schedules. General.
PARTIES:
France
USA (United States)

107620 Bilateral Agreement **527 UNTS 95**
SIGNED: 3 Jul 63 FORCE: 3 Jul 63
REGISTERED: 26 Feb 65 USA (United States)
ARTICLES: 6 LANGUAGE: English. French.
HEADNOTE: AGRI COMMOD
TOPIC: US Agri Commod Aid
CONCEPTS: Annex or appendix reference. Exchange of information and documents. Reexport of goods, etc.. Currency. Exchange rates and regulations. Payment schedules. Local currency. Purchase authorization. Commodities schedule. Purchase authorization. Mutual consultation.
PARTIES:
Senegal
USA (United States)

107621 Bilateral Exchange **527 UNTS 115**
SIGNED: 4 Feb 65 FORCE: 4 Feb 65
REGISTERED: 1 Mar 65 United Nations
ARTICLES: 2 LANGUAGE: English.
HEADNOTE: ZAMBIA ASSUMPTION OBLIGATIONS
TOPIC: Admin Cooperation
CONCEPTS: Responsibility and liability. Domestic obligation.
TREATY REF: 348UNTS177.
PARTIES:
UN Special Fund
Zambia

107622 Multilateral Agreement **527 UNTS 120**
SIGNED: 23 Feb 65 FORCE: 23 Feb 65
REGISTERED: 1 Mar 65 United Nations
ARTICLES: 6 LANGUAGE: English.
HEADNOTE: OPERATIONAL ASSISTANCE
TOPIC: IGO Operations
CONCEPTS: Annex or appendix reference. Previous treaty replacement. Diplomatic privileges. Diplomatic missions. Privileges and immunities. Arbitration. Procedure. Existing tribunals. Domestic obligation. Liaison with other IGO's. Interagency agreements. IGO obligations.
INTL ORGS: Permanent Court of Arbitration. United Nations Technical Assistance Board. Arbitration Commission.
TREATY REF: 243UNTS103; 397UNTS187.
PROCEDURE: Amendment. Termination.
PARTIES:
Afghanistan SIGNED: 23 Feb 65 FORCE: 23 Feb 65
FAO (Food Agri) SIGNED: 23 Feb 65 FORCE: 23 Feb 65
IAEA (Atom Energy) SIGNED: 23 Feb 65 FORCE: 23 Feb 65
ICAO (Civil Aviat) SIGNED: 23 Feb 65 FORCE: 23 Feb 65
ILO (Labor Org) SIGNED: 23 Feb 65 FORCE: 23 Feb 65
ITU (Telecommun) SIGNED: 23 Feb 65 FORCE: 23 Feb 65
UNESCO (Educ/Cult) SIGNED: 23 Feb 65 FORCE: 23 Feb 65
United Nations SIGNED: 23 Feb 65 FORCE: 23 Feb 65
UPU (Postal Union) SIGNED: 23 Feb 65 FORCE: 23 Feb 65
WHO (World Health) SIGNED: 23 Feb 65 FORCE: 23 Feb 65
WMO (Meteorology) SIGNED: 23 Feb 65 FORCE: 23 Feb 65
ANNEX
540 UNTS 352. Afghanistan. Termination 13 Jun 65.
540 UNTS 352. UNTAB (Tech Assis). Termination 13 Jun 65.
651 UNTS 402. IMCO (Maritime Org). Accession 2 Dec 68. Force 2 Dec 68.
651 UNTS 402. UNIDO (Industrial). Accession 2 Dec 68. Force 2 Dec 68.

107623 Multilateral Agreement **527 UNTS 145**
SIGNED: 11 May 59 FORCE: 11 May 59
REGISTERED: 1 Mar 65 Netherlands
ARTICLES: 16 LANGUAGE: French. English.
HEADNOTE: COMMERCIAL DEBTS
TOPIC: Claims and Debts
CONCEPTS: Definition of terms. Exceptions and exemptions. General provisions. Treaty implementation. Exchange of information and documents. Informational records. Responsibility and liability. Banking. Currency. Financial programs. Interest rates. Payment schedules. Debts. Assets transfer. Conferences.
INTL ORGS: International Monetary Fund. Organization for Economic Co-operation and Development.
TREATY REF: 527UNTS180.
PROCEDURE: Ratification. Termination.
PARTIES:
Austria SIGNED: 11 May 59 RATIFIED: 2 Dec 59 FORCE: 16 Nov 62
Belgium SIGNED: 11 May 59 RATIFIED: 8 Jul 60 FORCE: 16 Nov 62
Denmark SIGNED: 11 May 59 RATIFIED: 6 Oct 59 FORCE: 16 Nov 62
France SIGNED: 11 May 59 RATIFIED: 10 Aug 59 FORCE: 16 Nov 62
Germany, West SIGNED: 11 May 59 RATIFIED: 21 Apr 60 FORCE: 16 Nov 62
Italy SIGNED: 11 May 59 RATIFIED: 11 Apr 60 FORCE: 16 Nov 62
Luxembourg SIGNED: 11 May 59 RATIFIED: 16 Aug 61 FORCE: 16 Nov 62
Netherlands Netherlands Antilles RATIFIED: 26 Nov 59 FORCE: 16 Nov 62
Netherlands Dutch New Guinea RATIFIED: 26 Nov 59 FORCE: 16 Nov 62
Netherlands SIGNED: 11 May 59 RATIFIED: 26 Nov 59 FORCE: 16 Nov 62
Netherlands Surinam RATIFIED: 26 Nov 59 FORCE: 16 Nov 62
Norway SIGNED: 11 May 59 RATIFIED: 24 Nov 59 FORCE: 16 Nov 62
Portugal SIGNED: 11 May 59 RATIFIED: 3 Apr 62 FORCE: 16 Nov 62
Sweden SIGNED: 11 May 59 RATIFIED: 17 Mar 60 FORCE: 16 Nov 62
Switzerland SIGNED: 11 May 59 RATIFIED: 7 Dec 59 FORCE: 16 Nov 62
Turkey SIGNED: 11 May 59 RATIFIED: 16 Nov 62 FORCE: 16 Nov 62
UK Great Britain SIGNED: 11 May 59 RATIFIED: 6 May 60 FORCE: 16 Nov 62

107624 Bilateral Agreement **527 UNTS 181**
SIGNED: 12 Aug 59 FORCE: 28 Nov 59
REGISTERED: 1 Mar 65 Netherlands
ARTICLES: 8 LANGUAGE: French.
HEADNOTE: TECHNICAL RULES APPLICATION COMMERCIAL DEBTS
TOPIC: Admin Cooperation
CONCEPTS: Detailed regulations. Time limit. Treaty interpretation. Previous treaty replacement. Banking. Currency. Interest rates. Claims and settlements. Debts. Assessment procedures.
TREATY REF: 34UNTS243; 126UNTS350; 243UNTS308; 243UNTS313.
PROCEDURE: Ratification.
PARTIES:
Netherlands
Turkey

107625 Multilateral Convention **527 UNTS 181**
SIGNED: 5 Oct 61 FORCE: 24 Jan 65
REGISTERED: 1 Mar 65 Netherlands
ARTICLES: 15 LANGUAGE: French. English.
HEADNOTE: LEGALIZATION/FOREIGN PUBLIC DOCUMENTS
TOPIC: Patents/Copyrights
CONCEPTS: Exchange of official publications. Exchange of information and documents. Laws and formalities.
PROCEDURE: Duration. Ratification.
PARTIES:
Austria SIGNED: 5 Oct 61
Finland SIGNED: 13 Mar 62
France All Territories RATIFIED: 25 Nov 64
France SIGNED: 9 Oct 61 FORCE: 24 Jan 65
Germany, West SIGNED: 5 Oct 61
Greece SIGNED: 5 Oct 61
Italy SIGNED: 15 Dec 61
Liechtenstein SIGNED: 18 Apr 62
Luxembourg SIGNED: 5 Oct 61
Netherlands SIGNED: 30 Nov 62
Switzerland SIGNED: 5 Oct 61
Turkey SIGNED: 8 May 62
UK Great Britain Guernsey Island RATIFIED: 21 Aug 64 FORCE: 24 Jan 65
UK Great Britain Isle of Man RATIFIED: 21 Aug 64 FORCE: 24 Jan 65
UK Great Britain Jersey Island RATIFIED: 21 Aug 64 FORCE: 24 Jan 65
UK Great Britain SIGNED: 19 Oct 61 RATIFIED: 21 Aug 64 FORCE: 24 Jan 65
Yugoslavia SIGNED: 5 Oct 61 RATIFIED: 25 Sep 62 FORCE: 24 Jan 65
ANNEX
604 UNTS 384. Netherlands. Netherlands Antilles. Force 30 Apr 67.
604 UNTS 384. Netherlands. Surinam. Force 15 Jul 67.
613 UNTS 417. Malawi. Accession 24 Feb 67. Force 1 Dec 67.

107626 Bilateral Agreement **527 UNTS 205**
SIGNED: 3 Jun 64 FORCE: 28 Sep 64
REGISTERED: 2 Mar 65 Cuba

ARTICLES: 9 LANGUAGE: Spanish. Czechoslovakian.
HEADNOTE: VETERINARY MATTERS
TOPIC: Sanitation
CONCEPTS: General cooperation. Informational records. Domestic legislation. Specialists exchange. Quarantine. Disease control. Insect control. Pharmaceuticals. Veterinary. Exchange. Vocational training. Scientific exchange. Research and development. Trade procedures. Indemnities and reimbursements. General technical assistance. Materials, equipment and services. Publications exchange.
PROCEDURE: Duration. Future Procedures Contemplated. Ratification. Renewal or Revival. Termination.
PARTIES:
Cuba
Czechoslovakia

107627 Multilateral Agreement **527 UNTS 221**
SIGNED: 5 Mar 65   FORCE: 5 Mar 65
REGISTERED: 5 Mar 65 United Nations
ARTICLES: 6 LANGUAGE: English.
HEADNOTE: OPERATIONAL ASSISTANCE
TOPIC: IGO Operations
CONCEPTS: Annex or appendix reference. Previous treaty replacement. Diplomatic privileges. Diplomatic missions. Privileges and immunities. Arbitration. Procedure. Existing tribunals. Liaison with other IGO's. Inter-agency agreements. IGO obligations.
INTL ORGS: Permanent Court of Arbitration. United Nations Technical Assistance Board. Arbitration Commission.
PROCEDURE: Amendment. Termination.
PARTIES:
Cyprus SIGNED: 5 Mar 65 FORCE: 5 Mar 65
FAO (Food Agri) SIGNED: 5 Mar 65 FORCE: 5 Mar 65
IAEA (Atom Energy) SIGNED: 5 Mar 65 FORCE: 5 Mar 65
ICAO (Civil Aviat) SIGNED: 5 Mar 65 FORCE: 5 Mar 65
ILO (Labor Org) SIGNED: 5 Mar 65 FORCE: 5 Mar 65
ITU (Telecommun) SIGNED: 5 Mar 65 FORCE: 5 Mar 65
UNESCO (Educ/Cult) SIGNED: 5 Mar 65 FORCE: 5 Mar 65
United Nations SIGNED: 5 Mar 65 FORCE: 5 Mar 65
UPU (Postal Union) SIGNED: 5 Mar 65 FORCE: 5 Mar 65
WHO (World Health) SIGNED: 5 Mar 65 FORCE: 5 Mar 65
WMO (Meteorology) SIGNED: 5 Mar 65 FORCE: 5 Mar 65
ANNEX
645 UNTS 373. Cyprus. Acceptance 7 Sep 68. Force 7 Sep 68.
645 UNTS 373. ITU (Telecommun). Acceptance 7 Sep 68. Force 7 Sep 68.
645 UNTS 373. ILO (Labor Org). Acceptance 7 Sep 68. Force 7 Sep 68.
645 UNTS 373. UNESCO (Educ/Cult). Acceptance 7 Sep 68. Force 7 Sep 68.
645 UNTS 373. ICAO (Civil Aviat). Acceptance 7 Sep 68. Force 7 Sep 68.
645 UNTS 373. WHO (World Health). Acceptance 7 Sep 68. Force 7 Sep 68.
645 UNTS 373. WMO (Meteorology). Acceptance 7 Sep 68. Force 7 Sep 68.
645 UNTS 373. IAEA (Atom Energy). Acceptance 7 Sep 68. Force 7 Sep 68.
645 UNTS 373. FAO (Food Agri). Acceptance 7 Sep 68. Force 7 Sep 68.
645 UNTS 373. UPU (Postal Union). Acceptance 7 Sep 68. Force 7 Sep 68.
645 UNTS 373. United Nations. Acceptance 7 Sep 68. Force 7 Sep 68.

107628 Bilateral Agreement **527 UNTS 239**
SIGNED: 30 Sep 64   FORCE: 30 Sep 64
REGISTERED: 9 Mar 64 Thailand
ARTICLES: 6 LANGUAGE: English.
HEADNOTE: TRADE
TOPIC: General Trade
CONCEPTS: Conformity with municipal law. General cooperation. Licenses and permits. Export quotas. Import quotas. Trade agencies.
PROCEDURE: Amendment. Duration. Termination.

PARTIES:
Austria
Thailand

107629 Bilateral Agreement **527 UNTS 245**
SIGNED: 20 Dec 63   FORCE: 6 Oct 64
REGISTERED: 10 Mar 65 Romania
ARTICLES: 21 LANGUAGE: Romanian. Serbo-Croat.
HEADNOTE: ROMANIAN-YUGOSLAV FRONTIER
TOPIC: Visas
CONCEPTS: Privileges and immunities. Use of facilities. Establishment of commission. Decisions. Markers and definitions. Frontier peoples and personnel.
INTL ORGS: Special Commission.
PROCEDURE: Denunciation. Duration. Ratification.
PARTIES:
Romania
Yugoslavia

107630 Bilateral Treaty **527 UNTS 285**
SIGNED: 16 Dec 63   FORCE: 2 Jul 64
REGISTERED: 10 Mar 65 Romania
ARTICLES: 15 LANGUAGE: Romanian. Czechoslovakian.
HEADNOTE: EXPAND ECONOMIC TRADE RELATIONS
TOPIC: General Trade
CONCEPTS: Exceptions and exemptions. Conformity with municipal law. Informational records. Juridical personality. Free passage and transit. Legal protection and assistance. Arbitration. Procedure. Domestic jurisdiction. Existing tribunals. Export quotas. Import quotas. Certificates of origin. Reciprocity in trade. Most favored nation clause. Customs duties. Customs exemptions. Economic assistance. Licenses and certificates of nationality. Merchant vessels. Inland and territorial waters. Tonnage. Ports and pilotage. Shipwreck and salvage.
INTL ORGS: Danube Commission.
TREATY REF: 33UNTS181.
PROCEDURE: Ratification. Termination.
PARTIES:
Czechoslovakia
Romania

107631 Multilateral Exchange **528 UNTS 3**
SIGNED: 14 May 64   FORCE: 15 Jun 64
REGISTERED: 10 Mar 65 Netherlands
ARTICLES: 2 LANGUAGE: French.
HEADNOTE: SEAMANS BOOK TRAVEL DOCUMENT
TOPIC: Visas
CONCEPTS: Denial of admission. Non-visa travel documents.
TREATY REF: 374UNTS3.
PROCEDURE: Denunciation.
PARTIES:
Belgium SIGNED: 14 May 64 FORCE: 15 Jun 64
Luxembourg SIGNED: 14 May 64 FORCE: 15 Jun 64
Netherlands SIGNED: 14 May 64 FORCE: 15 Jun 64
Switzerland SIGNED: 14 May 64 FORCE: 15 Jun 64

107632 Multilateral Exchange **528 UNTS 13**
SIGNED: 14 May 64   FORCE: 15 Jun 64
REGISTERED: 10 Mar 65 Netherlands
ARTICLES: 2 LANGUAGE: French.
HEADNOTE: MOVEMENT REFUGEES
TOPIC: Refugees
CONCEPTS: Emergencies. Time limit. Visa abolition. Denial of admission. Resident permits. Non-visa travel documents. Frontier crossing points.
TREATY REF: 374UNTS3; 189UNTS17.
PROCEDURE: Denunciation. Renewal or Revival.
PARTIES:
Belgium SIGNED: 14 May 64 FORCE: 15 Jun 64
Luxembourg SIGNED: 14 May 64 FORCE: 15 Jun 64
Netherlands SIGNED: 14 May 64 FORCE: 15 Jun 64
Switzerland SIGNED: 14 May 64 FORCE: 15 Jun 64

107633 Multilateral Exchange **528 UNTS 23**
SIGNED: 14 May 64   FORCE: 15 Jun 64
REGISTERED: 10 Mar 65 Netherlands
ARTICLES: 2 LANGUAGE: French.
HEADNOTE: RIGHT OF RETURN REFUGEE WORKERS
TOPIC: Refugees
CONCEPTS: Resident permits. Non-visa travel documents.
INTL ORGS: Organization for Economic Co-operation and Development.
TREATY REF: 374UNTS3; 189UNTS137.
PROCEDURE: Denunciation. Renewal or Revival.
PARTIES:
Belgium SIGNED: 14 May 64 FORCE: 15 Jun 64
Luxembourg SIGNED: 14 May 64 FORCE: 15 Jun 64
Netherlands SIGNED: 14 May 64 FORCE: 15 Jun 64
Switzerland SIGNED: 14 May 64 FORCE: 15 Jun 64

107634 Multilateral Convention **528 UNTS 33**
SIGNED: 14 Jun 62   FORCE: 20 Mar 64
REGISTERED: 11 Mar 65 France
ARTICLES: 24 LANGUAGE: French. English.
HEADNOTE: EUROPEAN SPACE RESEARCH
TOPIC: IGO Establishment
CONCEPTS: Default remedies. Annex or appendix reference. Privileges and immunities. Exchange of official publications. Exchange of information and documents. Informational records. Juridical personality. Procedure. Existing tribunals. Specialists exchange. Research cooperation. Accounting procedures. Funding procedures. Recognition. General technical assistance. Admission. Subsidiary organ. Establishment. Headquarters and facilities. Internal structure. Special status. Status of experts.
INTL ORGS: European Space Research Organization. International Court of Justice. United Nations.
TREATY REF: 414UNTS109.
PROCEDURE: Amendment. Accession. Denunciation. Ratification. Registration. Termination.
PARTIES:
Belgium SIGNED: 19 Jun 62 RATIFIED: 21 Mar 64 FORCE: 21 Mar 64
Denmark SIGNED: 20 Dec 62 RATIFIED: 13 Mar 64 FORCE: 20 Mar 64
France SIGNED: 14 Jun 62 RATIFIED: 17 Jan 64 FORCE: 20 Mar 64
Germany, West SIGNED: 19 Jun 62 RATIFIED: 24 Feb 64 FORCE: 20 Mar 64
Italy SIGNED: 14 Jun 62
Netherlands SIGNED: 14 Jun 62 RATIFIED: 12 Jun 63 FORCE: 20 Mar 64
Spain SIGNED: 14 Jun 62 RATIFIED: 18 Jan 64 FORCE: 20 Mar 64
Sweden SIGNED: 14 Jun 62 RATIFIED: 7 Mar 64 FORCE: 20 Mar 64
Switzerland SIGNED: 14 Jun 62 RATIFIED: 16 Apr 63 FORCE: 20 Mar 64
UK Great Britain SIGNED: 14 Jun 62 RATIFIED: 30 Aug 63 FORCE: 20 Mar 64
ANNEX
537 UNTS 374. Italy. Ratification 8 Mar 65.

107635 Bilateral Agreement **528 UNTS 75**
SIGNED: 23 May 64   FORCE: 23 May 64
REGISTERED: 11 Mar 65 Eur Space Research
ARTICLES: 5 LANGUAGE: French. English.
HEADNOTE: COOPERATION SPACE RESEARCH
TOPIC: IGO Operations
CONCEPTS: Previous treaty extension. Internal structure.
PROCEDURE: Amendment. Denunciation. Duration. Termination.
PARTIES:
Italy
Eur Space Research
ANNEX
533 UNTS 386. Italy. Prolongation 19 Jan 65. Force 19 Jan 65.
533 UNTS 386. Eur Space Research. Prolongation 19 Jan 65. Force 19 Jan 65.

107636 Bilateral Agreement **528 UNTS 81**
SIGNED: 29 Jul 64   FORCE: 29 Jul 64
REGISTERED: 11 Mar 65 Eur Space Research

ARTICLES: 28 LANGUAGE: French. English. Swedish.
HEADNOTE: KIRUNA LAUNCHING RANGE
TOPIC: IGO Operations
CONCEPTS: Default remedies. Annex or appendix reference. Arbitration. Procedure. Special tribunals. Compensation.
INTL ORGS: International Court of Justice. Arbitration Commission. Special Commission.
PROCEDURE: Duration.
PARTIES:
Eur Space Research
Sweden

107637 Bilateral Exchange **528 UNTS 135**
SIGNED: 10 Aug 64 FORCE: 15 Aug 64
REGISTERED: 11 Mar 65 Eur Space Research
ARTICLES: 2 LANGUAGE: French.
HEADNOTE: ROCKET FIRING
TOPIC: IGO Operations
CONCEPTS: Annex or appendix reference. Diplomatic missions. Privileges and immunities. Conformity with municipal law. Arbitration. Procedure. Labor statistics. Compensation. Economic assistance.
INTL ORGS: International Court of Justice. Arbitration Commission.
PROCEDURE: Duration.
PARTIES:
France
Eur Space Research

107638 Bilateral Agreement **528 UNTS 147**
SIGNED: 2 Jun 61 FORCE: 13 Sep 62
REGISTERED: 12 Mar 65 USSR (Soviet Union)
ARTICLES: 13 LANGUAGE: Russian. English.
HEADNOTE: CULTURAL
TOPIC: Culture
CONCEPTS: Friendship and amity. Conformity with municipal law. Exchange of information and documents. Public health. Exchange. Teacher and student exchange. Scholarships and grants. Exchange. General cultural cooperation. Artists. Athletes. Scientific exchange. Publications exchange. Mass media exchange.
PROCEDURE: Duration. Ratification. Termination.
PARTIES:
Somalia
USSR (Soviet Union)

107639 Bilateral Agreement **528 UNTS 157**
SIGNED: 6 Nov 63 FORCE: 18 Mar 64
REGISTERED: 12 Mar 65 USSR (Soviet Union)
ARTICLES: 13 LANGUAGE: Russian. English.
HEADNOTE: CULTURAL COOPERATION
TOPIC: Culture
CONCEPTS: Friendship and amity. Conformity with municipal law. Exchange of information and documents. Public health. Exchange. Teacher and student exchange. Scholarships and grants. Exchange. General cultural cooperation. Artists. Athletes. Scientific exchange. Publications exchange. Mass media exchange.
PROCEDURE: Duration. Ratification. Termination.
PARTIES:
Tanganyika
USSR (Soviet Union)

107640 Bilateral Agreement **528 UNTS 167**
SIGNED: 10 Jul 63 FORCE: 2 Aug 64
REGISTERED: 12 Mar 65 USSR (Soviet Union)
ARTICLES: 10 LANGUAGE: Russian. French.
HEADNOTE: TRADE
TOPIC: General Trade
CONCEPTS: Establishment of trade relations. National treatment.
INTL ORGS: Special Commission.
PROCEDURE: Ratification.
PARTIES:
Dahomey
USSR (Soviet Union)

107641 Bilateral Agreement **528 UNTS 181**
SIGNED: 20 Mar 63 FORCE: 17 Jul 64
REGISTERED: 12 Mar 65 USSR (Soviet Union)
ARTICLES: 15 LANGUAGE: Russian. French.
HEADNOTE: CULTURAL SCIENTIFIC COOPERATION
TOPIC: Culture

CONCEPTS: Friendship and amity. Tourism. Public health. Recognition of degrees. Exchange. Teacher and student exchange. Scholarships and grants. Vocational training. Exchange. General cultural cooperation. Artists. Athletes. Scientific exchange. Publications exchange. Mass media exchange.
PROCEDURE: Amendment. Denunciation. Duration. Future Procedures Contemplated. Ratification. Renewal or Revival.
PARTIES:
Dahomey
USSR (Soviet Union)

107642 Bilateral Agreement **528 UNTS 193**
SIGNED: 26 Sep 63 FORCE: 21 Aug 64
REGISTERED: 17 Mar 65 Romania
ARTICLES: 6 LANGUAGE: Romanian. French.
HEADNOTE: CULTURAL SCIENTIFIC COOPERATION
TOPIC: Culture
CONCEPTS: Friendship and amity. Exchange of information and documents. Exchange. Scholarships and grants. General cultural cooperation. Artists. Athletes. Scientific exchange. Publications exchange. Press and wire services.
PROCEDURE: Denunciation. Duration. Ratification. Renewal or Revival.
PARTIES:
Mali
Romania

107643 Bilateral Exchange **528 UNTS 201**
SIGNED: 6 Jan 65 FORCE: 6 Jan 65
REGISTERED: 22 Mar 65 Denmark
ARTICLES: 2 LANGUAGE: Danish. German.
HEADNOTE: EXCHANGE OFFICIAL PUBLICATIONS
TOPIC: Admin Cooperation
CONCEPTS: Exchange of official publications.
PARTIES:
Denmark
Germany, West

107644 Bilateral Agreement **528 UNTS 209**
SIGNED: 27 Jan 65 FORCE: 27 Jan 65
REGISTERED: 25 Mar 65 WHO (World Health)
ARTICLES: 6 LANGUAGE: French.
HEADNOTE: ADVISORY ASSISTANCE
TOPIC: IGO Operations
CONCEPTS: Previous treaty replacement. Diplomatic privileges. Diplomatic missions. Privileges and immunities. Funding procedures. General technical assistance. Materials, equipment and services. Inter-agency agreements. IGO obligations.
TREATY REF: 33UNTS261.
PROCEDURE: Termination.
PARTIES:
WHO (World Health)
Tunisia

107645 Bilateral Agreement **528 UNTS 221**
SIGNED: 8 Jan 62 FORCE: 8 Jan 62
REGISTERED: 25 Mar 65 Canada
ARTICLES: 32 LANGUAGE: English.
HEADNOTE: MILITARY ASSISTANCE
TOPIC: Military Mission
CONCEPTS: Claims and settlements. General. Military assistance missions. Airforce-army-navy personnel ratio. Jurisdiction. Procurement and logistics. Status of forces.
PROCEDURE: Termination.
PARTIES:
Canada
Ghana

107646 Bilateral Exchange **528 UNTS 257**
SIGNED: 30 Jul 62 FORCE: 29 Aug 62
REGISTERED: 25 Mar 65 Canada
ARTICLES: 2 LANGUAGE: English. Spanish.
HEADNOTE: AMATEUR RADIO STATIONS
TOPIC: Gen Communications
CONCEPTS: Amateur radio. Amateur third party message.
PROCEDURE: Termination.
PARTIES:
Canada
Mexico

107647 Bilateral Exchange **528 UNTS 265**
SIGNED: 18 Jul 62 FORCE: 18 Aug 62
REGISTERED: 25 Mar 65 Canada
ARTICLES: 2 LANGUAGE: English.
HEADNOTE: EXCHANGE DEFENSE SCIENCE INFORMATION
TOPIC: General Military
CONCEPTS: Annex or appendix reference. General property. Recognition. Defense and security. Military assistance. Lend lease. Security of information. Exchange of defense information. Restrictions on transfer.
PARTIES:
Canada
Greece

107648 Bilateral Exchange **528 UNTS 273**
SIGNED: 14 Oct 62 FORCE: 14 Oct 62
REGISTERED: 25 Mar 65 Canada
ARTICLES: 2 LANGUAGE: English. Spanish.
HEADNOTE: AMATEUR RADIO STATIONS
TOPIC: Gen Communications
CONCEPTS: Amateur radio. Amateur third party message.
PROCEDURE: Termination.
PARTIES:
Canada
Chile

107649 Bilateral Exchange **528 UNTS 281**
SIGNED: 17 Oct 62 FORCE: 1 Nov 62
REGISTERED: 25 Mar 65 Canada
ARTICLES: 2 LANGUAGE: English.
HEADNOTE: VISA ARRANGEMENTS NON-IMMIGRANT TRAVELLERS
TOPIC: Visas
CONCEPTS: Time limit. Visa abolition. Denial of admission. Conformity with municipal law.
PROCEDURE: Termination.
PARTIES:
Canada
Iceland

107650 Bilateral Exchange **529 UNTS 3**
SIGNED: 16 Oct 62 FORCE: 15 Nov 62
REGISTERED: 25 Mar 65 Canada
ARTICLES: 2 LANGUAGE: French.
HEADNOTE: VISA REQUIREMENTS NON-IMMIGRANT TRAVELLERS
TOPIC: Visas
CONCEPTS: Time limit. Visa abolition. Resident permits. Visas. Conformity with municipal law. Fees and exemptions.
PROCEDURE: Termination.
PARTIES:
Canada
San Marino

107651 Bilateral Agreement **529 UNTS 9**
SIGNED: 11 Sep 62 FORCE: 6 Dec 62
REGISTERED: 25 Mar 65 Canada
ARTICLES: 7 LANGUAGE: English. French.
HEADNOTE: COOPERATION PEACEFUL USES ATOMIC ENERGY
TOPIC: Atomic Energy
CONCEPTS: Definition of terms. Exchange of information and documents. Inspection and observation. Nuclear materials. Peaceful use. Security of information.
INTL ORGS: International Atomic Energy Agency.
TREATY REF: 276UNTS3.
PROCEDURE: Duration. Ratification. Termination.
PARTIES:
Canada
Sweden

107652 Bilateral Exchange **529 UNTS 25**
SIGNED: 11 Mar 63 FORCE: 9 Apr 63
REGISTERED: 25 Mar 65 Canada
ARTICLES: 2 LANGUAGE: English. Spanish.
HEADNOTE: AMATEUR RADIO
TOPIC: Gen Communications
CONCEPTS: Amateur radio.
PARTIES:
Canada
El Salvador

107653 Bilateral Agreement **529 UNTS 31**
SIGNED: 14 May 63 FORCE: 14 May 63
REGISTERED: 25 Mar 65 Canada
ARTICLES: 1 LANGUAGE: English.
HEADNOTE: FINANCES
TOPIC: Loans and Credits
CONCEPTS: Detailed regulations. Treaty implementation. Currency. Financial programs. Interest rates. Loan and credit. Loan repayment. Terms of loan. Air transport.
PARTIES:
Canada
India

107654 Bilateral Exchange **529 UNTS 37**
SIGNED: 31 May 63 FORCE: 31 May 63
REGISTERED: 25 Mar 65 Canada
ARTICLES: 2 LANGUAGE: English. Spanish.
HEADNOTE: AMATEUR RADIO STATIONS
TOPIC: Gen Communications
CONCEPTS: Amateur radio. Amateur third party message.
PROCEDURE: Termination. Termination.
PARTIES:
Bolivia
Canada

107655 Bilateral Agreement **529 UNTS 45**
SIGNED: 16 Dec 63 FORCE: 16 Dec 63
REGISTERED: 25 Mar 65 Canada
ARTICLES: 18 LANGUAGE: English.
HEADNOTE: RAJASTHAN ATOMIC POWER STATION DOUGLAS POINT STATION
TOPIC: Atomic Energy
CONCEPTS: Definition of terms. Exchange of information and documents. National treatment. Credit provisions. Nuclear materials. Nonnuclear materials. Peaceful use. Plans and standards. Hydro-electric power.
INTL ORGS: International Atomic Energy Agency.
PARTIES:
Canada
India

107656 Bilateral Agreement **529 UNTS 57**
SIGNED: 3 Jul 63 FORCE: 3 Jul 63
REGISTERED: 25 Mar 65 Canada
ARTICLES: 21 LANGUAGE: English.
HEADNOTE: TRAINING PERSONNEL
TOPIC: Milit Assistance
CONCEPTS: Definition of terms. Alien status. Responsibility and liability. Indemnities and reimbursements. Expense sharing formulae. Claims and settlements. Military assistance. Military training. Security of information.
PROCEDURE: Amendment. Termination.
PARTIES:
Canada
Nigeria

107657 Bilateral Agreement **529 UNTS 71**
SIGNED: 11 Oct 63 FORCE: 11 Oct 63
REGISTERED: 25 Mar 65 Canada
ARTICLES: 3 LANGUAGE: French. English.
HEADNOTE: FILMS PRODUCTION
TOPIC: Mass Media
CONCEPTS: Detailed regulations. Treaty implementation. Annex or appendix reference. Privileges and immunities. Conformity with municipal law. General cooperation. Exchange of information and documents. General property. Establishment of commission. Export quotas. Free trade. Accounting procedures. Expense sharing formulae. Financial programs. Mass media exchange.
INTL ORGS: Special Commission.
PROCEDURE: Duration. Renewal or Revival. Termination.
PARTIES:
Canada
France

107658 Bilateral Agreement **529 UNTS 81**
SIGNED: 5 Nov 63 FORCE: 5 Nov 63
REGISTERED: 25 Mar 65 Canada
ARTICLES: 4 LANGUAGE: English. Polish.
HEADNOTE: WHEAT
TOPIC: Commodity Trade

CONCEPTS: Trade agencies. Commodity trade. Quotas. Loan and credit.
PARTIES:
Canada
Poland

107659 Multilateral Instrument **529 UNTS 89**
SIGNED: 18 Oct 61 FORCE: 26 Feb 65
REGISTERED: 30 Mar 65 Council of Europe
ARTICLES: 38 LANGUAGE: English. French.
HEADNOTE: EUROPEAN SOCIAL CHARTER
TOPIC: IGO Establishment
CONCEPTS: Exceptions and exemptions. Treaty implementation. Annex or appendix reference. Visa abolition. Exchange of information and documents. Specialists exchange. Sanitation. Public health. Vocational training. Anti-discrimination. Employment regulations. Old age and invalidity insurance. Right to organize. Old age insurance. Sickness and invalidity insurance. Social security. Unemployment. Migrant worker. Establishment. Conformity with IGO decisions. UN administrative tribunal. Basic freedoms.
INTL ORGS: Council of Europe. International Labour Organization. Special Commission.
PROCEDURE: Amendment. Denunciation. Ratification.
PARTIES:
Austria SIGNED: 22 Jul 63
Belgium SIGNED: 18 Oct 61
Denmark SIGNED: 18 Oct 61 RATIFIED: 3 Mar 65 FORCE: 2 Apr 65
France SIGNED: 18 Oct 61
Germany, West SIGNED: 18 Oct 61 RATIFIED: 27 Jan 65 FORCE: 26 Feb 65
Germany, West Berlin RATIFIED: 27 Jan 65 FORCE: 26 Feb 65
Greece SIGNED: 18 Oct 61
Ireland SIGNED: 18 Oct 61 RATIFIED: 7 Oct 64 FORCE: 26 Feb 65
Italy SIGNED: 18 Oct 61
Luxembourg SIGNED: 18 Oct 61
Netherlands SIGNED: 18 Oct 61
Norway SIGNED: 18 Oct 61 RATIFIED: 26 Oct 62 FORCE: 26 Feb 65
Sweden SIGNED: 18 Oct 61 RATIFIED: 17 Dec 62 FORCE: 26 Feb 65
Turkey SIGNED: 18 Oct 61
UK Great Britain SIGNED: 18 Oct 61 RATIFIED: 11 Jul 62 FORCE: 26 Feb 65
ANNEX
560 UNTS 295. Italy. Qualified Ratification 22 Oct 65. Force 21 Nov 65.
635 UNTS 368. Cyprus. Ratification 7 Mar 68. Force 6 Apr 68.

107660 Multilateral Convention **529 UNTS 141**
SIGNED: 13 Dec 55 FORCE: 23 Feb 65
REGISTERED: 30 Mar 65 Council of Europe
ARTICLES: 34 LANGUAGE: English. French.
HEADNOTE: CONVENTION ON ESTABLISHMENT
TOPIC: IGO Operations
CONCEPTS: Definition of terms. Annex or appendix reference. Non-visa travel documents. Alien status. Standardization. Procedure. General technical assistance. Economic assistance. Subsidiary organ. Conformity with IGO decisions.
INTL ORGS: Council of Europe. International Court of Justice. Special Commission.
TREATY REF: 218UNTS153; 320UNTS243.
PROCEDURE: Accession. Denunciation. Ratification.
PARTIES:
Austria SIGNED: 13 Dec 57 FORCE: 23 Feb 65
Belgium SIGNED: 13 Dec 55 RATIFIED: 12 Jan 62 FORCE: 23 Feb 65
Denmark SIGNED: 13 Dec 55 RATIFIED: 9 Mar 61 FORCE: 23 Feb 65
France SIGNED: 13 Dec 55 FORCE: 23 Feb 65
Germany, West SIGNED: 13 Dec 55 RATIFIED: 23 Feb 65 FORCE: 2 Mar 65
Greece SIGNED: 13 Dec 55 RATIFIED: 2 Mar 65 FORCE: 2 Mar 65
Iceland SIGNED: 13 Dec 55 FORCE: 23 Feb 65
Italy SIGNED: 13 Dec 55 RATIFIED: 13 Oct 63 FORCE: 23 Feb 65
Luxembourg SIGNED: 13 Dec 55 FORCE: 23 Feb 65
Netherlands SIGNED: 13 Dec 55 FORCE: 23 Feb 65
Norway SIGNED: 13 Dec 55 RATIFIED: 20 Nov 57 FORCE: 23 Feb 65

Saar SIGNED: 13 Dec 55 FORCE: 23 Feb 65
Sweden SIGNED: 13 Dec 55 FORCE: 23 Feb 65
Turkey SIGNED: 13 Dec 55 FORCE: 23 Feb 65
UK Great Britain SIGNED: 24 Feb 56 FORCE: 23 Feb 65
ANNEX
572 UNTS 364. Ireland. Signature 1 Sep 66. Qualified Ratification 1 Sep 66.

107661 Bilateral Exchange **529 UNTS 187**
SIGNED: 16 Jul 64 FORCE: 16 Jul 64
REGISTERED: 31 Mar 65 USA (United States)
ARTICLES: 2 LANGUAGE: English. Spanish.
HEADNOTE: USE SPANISH PORTS TERRITORIAL WATERS NS SAVANNAH
TOPIC: Water Transport
CONCEPTS: Annex or appendix reference. Conformity with municipal law. Inspection and observation. Personnel. Responsibility and liability. Negotiation. Compensation. Claims and settlements. Peaceful use. Navigational conditions. Inland and territorial waters. Ports and pilotage. Naval vessels. Ocean resources.
TREATY REF: S.EX.DOC.K. 87TH CONG. 1ST SESS. PP.370-444.
PROCEDURE: Amendment. Future Procedures Contemplated. Termination.
PARTIES:
Spain
USA (United States)

107662 Bilateral Exchange **529 UNTS 205**
SIGNED: 4 Aug 64 FORCE: 4 Aug 64
REGISTERED: 31 Mar 65 USA (United States)
ARTICLES: 2 LANGUAGE: English. Italian.
HEADNOTE: SAFEGUARDING CLASSIFIED INFORMATION
TOPIC: General Military
CONCEPTS: Definition of terms. Exceptions and exemptions. Guarantees and safeguards. Annex or appendix reference. General property. Compliance with domestic patent and copyright laws. Recognition. Defense and security. Security of information. Exchange of defense information. Restrictions on transfer.
INTL ORGS: North Atlantic Treaty Organization.
TREATY REF: 34UNTS243.
PROCEDURE: Future Procedures Contemplated.
PARTIES:
Italy
USA (United States)

107663 Multilateral Agreement **529 UNTS 217**
SIGNED: 3 Dec 63 FORCE: 15 Dec 64
REGISTERED: 2 Apr 65 FAO (Food Agri)
ARTICLES: 21 LANGUAGE: English. French. Spanish.
HEADNOTE: CENTRAL LOCUS COMMISSION
TOPIC: IGO Establishment
CONCEPTS: Detailed regulations. Treaty violation. Exchange of information and documents. Procedure. Existing tribunals. Research cooperation. Research results. Scientific exchange. Research and development. Funding procedures. General technical assistance. Admission. Establishment. Headquarters and facilities. Liaison with other IGO's. Internal structure.
INTL ORGS: International Court of Justice. Special Commission.
PROCEDURE: Amendment. Accession. Denunciation. Termination.
PARTIES:
Afghanistan RATIFIED: 14 Jul 64 FORCE: 15 Dec 64
India RATIFIED: 15 Dec 64 FORCE: 15 Dec 64
Iran RATIFIED: 19 Nov 64 FORCE: 15 Dec 64
FAO (Food Agri) SIGNED: 15 Dec 63
ANNEX
541 UNTS 365. Pakistan. Acceptance 12 Jul 65.

107664 Bilateral Agreement **529 UNTS 255**
SIGNED: 27 Apr 63 FORCE: 16 Dec 64
REGISTERED: 2 Apr 65 Denmark
ARTICLES: 19 LANGUAGE: English.
HEADNOTE: COMMERCIAL SCHEDULED AIR TRANSPORT
TOPIC: Air Transport
CONCEPTS: Definition of terms. Detailed regulations. Exceptions and exemptions. Annex or appendix reference. General cooperation. Ex-

change of information and documents. Arbitration. Procedure. Special tribunals. Negotiation. Reexport of goods, etc.. Monetary and gold transfers. Exchange rates and regulations. Expense sharing formulae. Fees and exemptions. Non-interest rates and fees. National treatment. Tax exemptions. Customs exemptions. Routes and logistics. Navigational equipment. Permit designation. Air transport. Airport facilities. Conditions of airlines operating permission. Overflights and technical stops. Operating authorizations and regulations.
INTL ORGS: International Civil Aviation Organization. Arbitration Commission.
TREATY REF: 15UNTS295.
PROCEDURE: Amendment. Future Procedures Contemplated. Registration. Termination.
PARTIES:
Cyprus
Denmark

107665   Bilateral Agreement   **529 UNTS 277**
SIGNED: 2 Jul 64   FORCE: 2 Jul 64
REGISTERED: 6 Apr 65 USA (United States)
ARTICLES: 12 LANGUAGE: English.
HEADNOTE: VISITS NS SAVANNAH
TOPIC: Water Transport
CONCEPTS: Definition of terms. Conformity with municipal law. Inspection and observation. Responsibility and liability. Claims and settlements. Peaceful use. Navigational conditions. Inland and territorial waters. Ports and pilotage. Naval vessels. Ocean resources.
TREATY REF: S.EX.DOC.K.87TH CONG. 1ST SESS. PP.370-444.
PROCEDURE: Amendment. Future Procedures Contemplated. Termination.
PARTIES:
Denmark
USA (United States)

107666   Bilateral Exchange   **529 UNTS 287**
SIGNED: 6 Jul 64   FORCE: 6 Jul 64
REGISTERED: 6 Apr 65 USA (United States)
ARTICLES: 2 LANGUAGE: English.
HEADNOTE: USE SWEDISH PORTS WATERS BY NS SAVANNAH
TOPIC: Water Transport
CONCEPTS: Definition of terms. Conformity with municipal law. Licenses and permits. Responsibility and liability. Compensation. Currency. Claims and settlements. Peaceful use. Operating authorizations and regulations. Inland and territorial waters. Ports and pilotage. Naval vessels.
PROCEDURE: Future Procedures Contemplated. Termination.
PARTIES:
Sweden
USA (United States)

107667   Bilateral Agreement   **529 UNTS 299**
SIGNED: 12 May 64   FORCE: 3 Sep 64
REGISTERED: 6 Apr 65 USA (United States)
ARTICLES: 10 LANGUAGE: English.
HEADNOTE: PETROLEUM AGREEMENT
TOPIC: Commodity Trade
CONCEPTS: Treaty implementation. Previous treaty replacement. Use of facilities. Establishment of commission. Payment schedules. Claims and settlements. Commodity trade. Self-defense.
INTL ORGS: Special Commission.
TREATY REF: 179UNTS23;   405UNTS37; 413UNTS392.
PROCEDURE: Amendment. Ratification. Termination.
PARTIES:
Korea, South
USA (United States)

107668   Bilateral Exchange   **530 UNTS 3**
SIGNED: 30 Oct 63   FORCE: 6 Jul 64
REGISTERED: 6 Apr 65 USA (United States)
ARTICLES: 2 LANGUAGE: English. Spanish.
HEADNOTE: PEACE CORPS
TOPIC: General Aid
CONCEPTS: Diplomatic privileges. Privileges and immunities. Non-diplomatic delegations. General cooperation. Personnel. Funding procedures. Tax exemptions. Customs exemptions. Materials, equipment and services. Aid missions.
PROCEDURE: Termination.
PARTIES:
Panama
USA (United States)

107669   Bilateral Exchange   **530 UNTS 13**
SIGNED: 17 Jul 64   FORCE: 17 Jul 64
REGISTERED: 6 Apr 65 USA (United States)
ARTICLES: 2 LANGUAGE: English.
HEADNOTE: TRADE COTTON TEXTILES
TOPIC: Commodity Trade
CONCEPTS: General cooperation. Exchange of information and documents. Export quotas. Trade agencies. Commodity trade. Quotas.
TREATY REF: 471UNTS296.
PROCEDURE: Amendment. Duration. Termination.
PARTIES:
Greece
USA (United States)

107670   Bilateral Exchange   **530 UNTS 25**
SIGNED: 17 Jul 64   FORCE: 17 Jul 64
REGISTERED: 6 Apr 65 USA (United States)
ARTICLES: 2 LANGUAGE: English.
HEADNOTE: TRADE COTTON TEXTILES
TOPIC: Commodity Trade
CONCEPTS: General cooperation. Exchange of information and documents. Export quotas. Trade agencies. Commodity trade.
TREATY REF: 471UNTS296.
PROCEDURE: Amendment. Duration. Termination.
PARTIES:
Turkey
USA (United States)

107671   Bilateral Agreement   **530 UNTS 41**
SIGNED: 17 Nov 63   FORCE: 17 Nov 63
REGISTERED: 6 Apr 65 USA (United States)
ARTICLES: 6 LANGUAGE: English. Persian.
HEADNOTE: AGRI COMMOD
TOPIC: US Agri Commod Aid
CONCEPTS: Currency. Agricultural commodities. Use restrictions.
PARTIES:
Iran
USA (United States)

107672   Bilateral Exchange   **530 UNTS 61**
SIGNED: 25 Apr 64   FORCE: 24 Apr 64
REGISTERED: 6 Apr 65 USA (United States)
ARTICLES: 2 LANGUAGE: English. Japanese.
HEADNOTE: PRECISE ARRANGEMENTS ECONOMIC COOPERATION
TOPIC: General Economic
CONCEPTS: Annex or appendix reference. General cooperation. Establishment of commission. Economic assistance. Materials, equipment and services.
INTL ORGS: Special Commission.
TREATY REF: 136UNTS45;163UNTS385;1-84UNTS358;199UNTS344.
PARTIES:
Japan
USA (United States)
ANNEX
546 UNTS 397. USA (United States). Amendment 2 Apr 65. Force 2 Apr 65.
546 UNTS 397. Japan. Amendment 2 Apr 65. Force 2 Apr 65.

107673   Bilateral Exchange   **530 UNTS 77**
SIGNED: 13 May 64   FORCE: 13 May 64
REGISTERED: 6 Apr 65 USA (United States)
ARTICLES: 2 LANGUAGE: English. Spanish.
HEADNOTE: METEOROLOGICAL PROGRAM
TOPIC: Scientific Project
CONCEPTS: Annex type material. Previous treaty extension.
TREATY REF: 271UNTS303; 344UNTS193.
PARTIES:
Colombia
USA (United States)

107674   Bilateral Agreement   **530 UNTS 89**
SIGNED: 22 Jan 64   FORCE: 14 Aug 64
REGISTERED: 7 Apr 65 USA (United States)
ARTICLES: 12 LANGUAGE: English.
HEADNOTE: ESTABLISHMENT ROOSEVELT CAMPOBELLO INTERNATIONAL PARK
TOPIC: Specific Property
CONCEPTS: Conformity with municipal law. Juridical personality. General property. Establishment of commission. Indemnities and reimbursements. Assets. Tax exemptions. Customs exemptions. Facilities and property.
INTL ORGS: Special Commission.
PARTIES:
Canada
USA (United States)

107675   Bilateral Exchange   **530 UNTS 99**
SIGNED: 19 Jun 64   FORCE: 19 Jun 64
REGISTERED: 7 Apr 65 USA (United States)
ARTICLES: 2 LANGUAGE: English.
HEADNOTE: USE UK PORTS TERRITORIAL WATERS NS SAVANNAH
TOPIC: Water Transport
CONCEPTS: Territorial application. Conformity with municipal law. Exchange of information and documents. Inspection and observation. Personnel. Responsibility and liability. Compensation. Payment schedules. Claims and settlements. Samples and testing. Routes and logistics. Navigational conditions. Inland and territorial waters. Ports and pilotage. Naval vessels. Ocean resources.
TREATY REF: 191UNTS3;   164UNTS113; 135LTS301; 205LTS33.
PROCEDURE: Amendment. Termination.
PARTIES:
UK Great Britain
USA (United States)

107676   Bilateral Exchange   **530 UNTS 113**
SIGNED: 7 Jul 64   FORCE: 7 Jul 64
REGISTERED: 7 Apr 65 USA (United States)
ARTICLES: 2 LANGUAGE: English. Spanish.
HEADNOTE: METEOROLOGICAL PROGRAM
TOPIC: Scientific Project
CONCEPTS: Annex type material. Research and scientific projects. Meteorology.
TREATY REF: 283UNTS3;   340UNTS388; 371UNTS310.
PARTIES:
Peru
USA (United States)

107677   Bilateral Exchange   **530 UNTS 123**
SIGNED: 7 Aug 64   FORCE: 7 Aug 64
REGISTERED: 7 Apr 65 USA (United States)
ARTICLES: 2 LANGUAGE: English. Spanish.
HEADNOTE: DOUBLE TAXATION SHIPS AIRCRAFT
TOPIC: Taxation
CONCEPTS: Definition of terms. Conformity with municipal law. Domestic legislation. Taxation. Tax exemptions. Air transport. Merchant vessels.
PROCEDURE: Termination.
PARTIES:
Mexico
USA (United States)

107678   Bilateral Exchange   **530 UNTS 133**
SIGNED: 9 Jun 64   FORCE: 9 Jun 64
REGISTERED: 7 Apr 65 USA (United States)
ARTICLES: 2 LANGUAGE: French.
HEADNOTE: INVESTMENT GUARANTIES
TOPIC: Claims and Debts
CONCEPTS: General cooperation. General property. Arbitration. Procedure. Existing tribunals. Negotiation. Reciprocity in financial treatment. Currency. Claims and settlements. Private investment guarantee.
INTL ORGS: International Court of Justice. Arbitration Commission.
PARTIES:
Mali
USA (United States)

107679 Multilateral Convention **530 UNTS 141**
SIGNED: 23 Jan 61   FORCE: 1 Apr 62
REGISTERED: 8 Apr 65 Philippines
ARTICLES: 24 LANGUAGE: English.
HEADNOTE: POSTAL CONVENTION
TOPIC: Postal Service

CONCEPTS: Detailed regulations. Incorporation of treaty provisions into national law. Arbitration. Postal services. Rates and charges. Admission. Establishment. Headquarters and facilities. Internal structure. Conformity with IGO decisions.
INTL ORGS: Asia Oceania Postal Union. United Nations. Universal Postal Union.
TREATY REF: 364UNTS3.
PROCEDURE: Ratification.
PARTIES:
Australia SIGNED: 23 Jan 61
Taiwan   SIGNED: 23 Jan 61   RATIFIED: 29 Mar 62 FORCE: 1 Apr 62
Korea, South SIGNED: 23 Jan 61   RATIFIED: 12 Apr 62 FORCE: 1 Apr 62
New Zealand SIGNED: 23 Jan 61
Philippines   SIGNED: 23 Jan 61   RATIFIED: 1 Apr 62 FORCE: 1 Apr 62
Thailand   SIGNED: 23 Jan 61   RATIFIED: 11 May 62 FORCE: 1 Apr 62

107680   Bilateral Agreement   **530 UNTS 173**
SIGNED: 25 Jan 65   FORCE: 25 Jan 65
REGISTERED: 4 Sep 65 Thailand
ARTICLES: 10 LANGUAGE: English.
HEADNOTE: TECHNICAL COOPERATION GENETICS SILVER CULTURE
TOPIC: Tech Assistance
CONCEPTS: Treaty implementation. General cooperation. Use of facilities. Establishment of commission. Scholarships and grants. Research and development. Expense sharing formulae. Tax exemptions. Customs exemptions. General technical assistance. Materials, equipment and services.
INTL ORGS: Special Commission.
PARTIES:
Denmark
Thailand

107681   Bilateral Agreement   **530 UNTS 181**
SIGNED: 19 Oct 57   FORCE: 24 Mar 58
REGISTERED: 13 Apr 65 Czechoslovakia
ARTICLES: 7 LANGUAGE: Czechoslovakian. Arabic. English.
HEADNOTE: CULTURAL COOPERATION
TOPIC: Culture
CONCEPTS: Treaty interpretation. Friendship and amity. Exchange of information and documents. International circulation. Recognition of degrees. Exchange. Teacher and student exchange. Scholarships and grants. General cultural cooperation. Athletes. Scientific exchange. Recognition. Publications exchange. Mass media exchange.
PROCEDURE: Denunciation. Ratification.
PARTIES:
Czechoslovakia
United Arab Rep

107682   Bilateral Agreement   **530 UNTS 195**
SIGNED: 17 Nov 50   FORCE: 9 Mar 51
REGISTERED: 13 Apr 65 Czechoslovakia
ARTICLES: 9 LANGUAGE: Czechoslovakian. Polish.
HEADNOTE: HEALTH COOPERATION
TOPIC: Sanitation
CONCEPTS: Definition of terms. General cooperation. Exchange of information and documents. Domestic legislation. Establishment of commission. Specialists exchange. Insect control. Exchange. Teacher and student exchange. Vocational training. Scientific exchange. Research and development. Materials, equipment and services. Canal improvement.
INTL ORGS: Special Commission.
PROCEDURE: Duration. Ratification. Renewal or Revival. Termination.
PARTIES:
Czechoslovakia
Poland

107683   Bilateral Exchange   **530 UNTS 209**
SIGNED: 17 Aug 64   FORCE: 17 Aug 64
REGISTERED: 14 Apr 65 USA (United States)
ARTICLES: 2 LANGUAGE: English.
HEADNOTE: SPECTROMETRIC RESEARCH
TOPIC: Scientific Project
CONCEPTS: Privileges and immunities. Responsibility and liability. Specialists exchange. Wages and salaries. Research and scientific projects. Research results. Scientific exchange. Research and development.
PROCEDURE: Duration. Renewal or Revival. Termination.
PARTIES:
Australia
USA (United States)

107684   Bilateral Exchange   **530 UNTS 217**
SIGNED: 18 Jun 64   FORCE: 18 Jun 64
REGISTERED: 14 Apr 65 USA (United States)
ARTICLES: 2 LANGUAGE: English.
HEADNOTE: PUBLIC LIABILITY DAMAGE CAUSED BY NS SAVANNAH
TOPIC: Water Transport
CONCEPTS: General cooperation. Responsibility and liability. Compensation. Payment schedules. Claims and settlements. Merchant vessels. Naval vessels.
PROCEDURE: Termination.
PARTIES:
Ireland
USA (United States)

107685   Bilateral Agreement   **530 UNTS 225**
SIGNED: 5 Sep 64   FORCE: 5 Sep 64
REGISTERED: 14 Apr 65 USA (United States)
ARTICLES: 6 LANGUAGE: English. Spanish.
HEADNOTE: AGRI COMMOD TITLE I
TOPIC: US Agri Commod Aid
CONCEPTS: General provisions. Annex or appendix reference. Exchange of information and documents. Reexport of goods, etc.. Exchange rates and regulations. Transportation costs. Local currency. Commodities schedule. Purchase authorization. Surplus commodities. Mutual consultation.
PARTIES:
Paraguay
USA (United States)

107686   Bilateral Convention   **530 UNTS 247**
SIGNED: 22 Oct 63   FORCE: 11 Sep 64
REGISTERED: 14 Apr 65 USA (United States)
ARTICLES: 3 LANGUAGE: English. Swedish.
HEADNOTE: INCOME TAXES
TOPIC: Taxation
CONCEPTS: Previous treaty amendment. Treaty violation. General.
PROCEDURE: Ratification.
PARTIES:
Sweden
USA (United States)

107687   Bilateral Exchange   **530 UNTS 267**
SIGNED: 16 Sep 64   FORCE: 16 Sep 64
REGISTERED: 14 Apr 65 USA (United States)
ARTICLES: 2 LANGUAGE: English.
HEADNOTE: ESTABLISHMENT LORAN-C STATION
TOPIC: Gen Communications
CONCEPTS: Annex or appendix reference. Facilities and equipment.
PROCEDURE: Duration. Termination.
PARTIES:
Canada
USA (United States)

107688   Bilateral Agreement   **530 UNTS 281**
SIGNED: 21 Oct 63   FORCE: 16 Sep 64
REGISTERED: 14 Apr 65 USA (United States)
ARTICLES: 30 LANGUAGE: English.
HEADNOTE: PARCEL POST
TOPIC: Postal Service
CONCEPTS: Detailed regulations. Responsibility and liability. Currency. Customs duties. Customs exemptions. Postal services. Regulations. Insured letters and boxes. Conveyance in transit. Parcel post.
INTL ORGS: Universal Postal Union.
TREATY REF: 364UNTS3.
PROCEDURE: Duration. Termination.
PARTIES:
Kuwait
USA (United States)

107689   Bilateral Exchange   **531 UNTS 3**
SIGNED: 6 Jan 64   FORCE: 6 Jan 64
REGISTERED: 14 Apr 65 USA (United States)
ARTICLES: 2 LANGUAGE: English. Arabic.
HEADNOTE: ESTABLISHMENT TELEVISION SYSTEM
TOPIC: Telecommunications
CONCEPTS: Alien status. Conformity with municipal law. Tax exemptions. Customs exemptions. Commercial and public radio. Telecommunications.
PARTIES:
Saudi Arabia
USA (United States)
                    ANNEX
601 UNTS 357. Saudi Arabia. Prolongation 30 Jul 66. Force 30 Jul 66.
601 UNTS 357. USA (United States). Prolongation 30 Jul 66. Force 30 Jul 66.

107690   Bilateral Agreement   **531 UNTS 23**
SIGNED: 6 Feb 65   FORCE: 7 Apr 65
REGISTERED: 14 Apr 65 Denmark
ARTICLES: 5 LANGUAGE: Danish. Hindi. English.
HEADNOTE: RECOGNITION TONNAGE CERTIFICATES MERCHANT SHIPS
TOPIC: Water Transport
CONCEPTS: Recognition of legal documents. Registration certificate. Merchant vessels. Tonnage.
PROCEDURE: Termination.
PARTIES:
Denmark
India

107691   Bilateral Agreement   **531 UNTS 35**
SIGNED: 28 Aug 64   FORCE: 28 Aug 64
REGISTERED: 15 Apr 65 USA (United States)
ARTICLES: 8 LANGUAGE: English. Spanish.
HEADNOTE: MAPPING CHARTING GEODESY
TOPIC: Scientific Project
CONCEPTS: Visas. Privileges and immunities. Personnel. Use of facilities. Social security. Research and scientific projects. Scientific exchange. Research and development. Fees and exemptions. Tax exemptions. Domestic obligation. Materials, equipment and services. Security of information.
INTL ORGS: Pan-American Institute of Geography and History.
TREATY REF: 119UNTS3;134UNTS388.
PROCEDURE: Amendment. Duration. Termination.
PARTIES:
Dominican Republic
USA (United States)

107692   Bilateral Exchange   **531 UNTS 51**
SIGNED: 26 Aug 64   FORCE: 26 Aug 64
REGISTERED: 15 Apr 65 USA (United States)
ARTICLES: 2 LANGUAGE: English.
HEADNOTE: PEACE CORPS
TOPIC: General Aid
CONCEPTS: Exceptions and exemptions. Privileges and immunities. General cooperation. Personnel. Taxable items. Tax exemptions. Customs duties. Customs exemptions. Materials, equipment and services. Aid missions. Volunteer programs.
PROCEDURE: Termination.
PARTIES:
Kenya
USA (United States)

107693   Bilateral Exchange   **531 UNTS 63**
SIGNED: 5 Oct 64   FORCE: 1 Jan 65
REGISTERED: 15 Apr 65 USA (United States)
ARTICLES: 4 LANGUAGE: English.
HEADNOTE: TRADE COTTON TEXTILES
TOPIC: Commodity Trade
CONCEPTS: Detailed regulations. General cooperation. Exchange of information and documents. Export quotas. Trade agencies. Commodity trade. Delivery schedules. Quotas.
TREATY REF: 471UNTS296.
PROCEDURE: Amendment. Duration. Termination.
PARTIES:
USA (United States)
Yugoslavia

107694   Bilateral Exchange   **531 UNTS 85**
SIGNED: 20 Aug 64   FORCE: 20 Aug 64
REGISTERED: 15 Apr 65 USA (United States)

ARTICLES: 2 LANGUAGE: English.
HEADNOTE: USE BEANE FIELD
TOPIC: Specific Property
CONCEPTS: Use of facilities. Facilities and property.
TREATY REF: 409UNTS67.
PARTIES:
UK Great Britain
USA (United States)

107695   Bilateral Agreement   **531 UNTS 93**
SIGNED: 29 Aug 64   FORCE: 29 Aug 64
REGISTERED: 15 Apr 65 USA (United States)
ARTICLES: 13 LANGUAGE: English.
HEADNOTE: EDUCATION PROGRAM
TOPIC: Education
CONCEPTS: Previous treaty replacement. Friendship and amity. Alien status. Standardization. Conformity with municipal law. General cooperation. Inspection and observation. Personnel. General property. Exchange. Commissions and foundations. Teacher and student exchange. Professorships. Currency. Financial programs. Funding procedures. Tax exemptions. Customs exemptions.
INTL ORGS: Special Commission.
TREATY REF: 180UNTS207.
PARTIES:
Ceylon (Sri Lanka)
USA (United States)

107696   Bilateral Exchange   **531 UNTS 107**
SIGNED: 24 Aug 64   FORCE: 24 Aug 64
REGISTERED: 15 Apr 65 USA (United States)
ARTICLES: 2 LANGUAGE: English. Spanish.
HEADNOTE: ALIEN AMATEUR RADIO OPERATORS
TOPIC: Gen Communications
CONCEPTS: Conformity with municipal law. Licenses and permits. Amateur radio.
TREATY REF: USA'TIAS 4893;.
PROCEDURE: Termination.
PARTIES:
Costa Rica
USA (United States)

107697   Bilateral Instrument   **531 UNTS 113**
SIGNED: 12 Apr 65   FORCE: 19 Apr 65
REGISTERED: 19 Apr 65 United Nations
ARTICLES: 1 LANGUAGE: English.
HEADNOTE: ACCEPTANCE ICJ JURISDICTION
TOPIC: ICJ Option Clause
CONCEPTS: Exceptions and exemptions. Compulsory jurisdiction.
INTL ORGS: International Court of Justice. United Nations.
PARTIES:
Kenya

107698   Bilateral Agreement   **531 UNTS 119**
SIGNED: 6 Jan 64   FORCE: 4 Mar 65
REGISTERED: 19 Apr 65 Belgium
ARTICLES: 7 LANGUAGE: French. Dutch.
HEADNOTE: SETTLEMENT FINANCIAL DISPUTES
TOPIC: Reparations
CONCEPTS: Territorial application. Compensation. Lump sum settlements. Post-war claims settlement.
PROCEDURE: Ratification.
PARTIES:
Belgium
Netherlands

107699   Bilateral Agreement   **531 UNTS 129**
SIGNED: 16 Dec 64   FORCE: 16 Dec 64
REGISTERED: 21 Apr 65 Jamaica
ARTICLES: 11 LANGUAGE: English. German.
HEADNOTE: TECHNICAL COOPERATION
TOPIC: Tech Assistance
CONCEPTS: Treaty implementation. Resident permits. Non-visa travel documents. Privileges and immunities. General cooperation. Exchange of information and documents. Personnel. Responsibility and liability. Use of facilities. Institute establishment. Vocational training. Expense sharing formulae. Tax exemptions. Customs exemptions. General technical assistance.
PROCEDURE: Duration. Future Procedures Contemplated.

PARTIES:
Germany, West
Jamaica

107700   Bilateral Exchange   **531 UNTS 143**
SIGNED: 3 Feb 65   FORCE: 3 Feb 65
REGISTERED: 21 Apr 65 Jamaica
ARTICLES: 2 LANGUAGE: English. German.
HEADNOTE: CERAMIST EXPERT
TOPIC: Scientific Project
CONCEPTS: General cooperation. Specialists exchange. Vocational training. Research and scientific projects. Research and development. Indemnies and reimbursements. General technical assistance.
TREATY REF: 531UNTS129.
PARTIES:
Germany, West
Jamaica

107701   Bilateral Agreement   **531 UNTS 149**
SIGNED: 6 Jan 60   FORCE: 17 Apr 65
REGISTERED: 22 Apr 65 Belgium
ARTICLES: 10 LANGUAGE: Dutch. French. Portuguese.
HEADNOTE: CULTURAL
TOPIC: Culture
CONCEPTS: Treaty implementation. Treaty interpretation. Friendship and amity. Exchange of information and documents. Specialists exchange. Exchange. Teacher and student exchange. Scholarships and grants. Exchange. General cultural cooperation. Artists. Scientific exchange. Research and development. Publications exchange. Mass media exchange.
PROCEDURE: Denunciation. Ratification.
PARTIES:
Belgium
Brazil

107702   Bilateral Agreement   **531 UNTS 163**
SIGNED: 29 Sep 64   FORCE: 29 Sep 64
REGISTERED: 23 Apr 65 USA (United States)
ARTICLES: 6 LANGUAGE: English.
HEADNOTE: AGRI COMMOD TITLE I
TOPIC: US Agri Commod Aid
CONCEPTS: General provisions. Annex or appendix reference. Exchange of information and documents. Maritime products and equipment. Exchange rates and regulations. Transportation costs. Local currency. Commodities schedule. Purchase authorization. Surplus commodities. Mutual consultation.
PARTIES:
Iran
USA (United States)

107703   Bilateral Agreement   **531 UNTS 183**
SIGNED: 29 Sep 64   FORCE: 29 Sep 64
REGISTERED: 23 Apr 65 USA (United States)
ARTICLES: 6 LANGUAGE: English. French.
HEADNOTE: AGRI COMMOD TITLE I
TOPIC: US Agri Commod Aid
CONCEPTS: General provisions. Annex or appendix reference. Exchange of information and documents. Reexport of goods, etc.. Exchange rates and regulations. Transportation costs. Local currency. Commodities schedule. Purchase authorization. Surplus commodities. Mutual consultation.
PARTIES:
USA (United States)
Vietnam, South

107704   Bilateral Agreement   **531 UNTS 197**
SIGNED: 20 Aug 63   FORCE: 1 Oct 64
REGISTERED: 23 Apr 65 USA (United States)
ARTICLES: 11 LANGUAGE: English. Spanish.
HEADNOTE: EDUCATIONAL PROGRAM
TOPIC: Education
CONCEPTS: Definition of terms. Friendship and amity. Standardization. Conformity with municipal law. General cooperation. Exchange of information and documents. Inspection and observation. Personnel. General property. Specialists exchange. Exchange. Commissions and foundations. Teacher and student exchange. Professorships. Accounting procedures. Financial programs. Funding procedures.

INTL ORGS: Special Commission.
TREATY REF: 284UNTS161.
PARTIES:
Paraguay
USA (United States)

107705   Bilateral Agreement   **531 UNTS 213**
SIGNED: 14 Dec 64   FORCE: 14 Dec 64
REGISTERED: 23 Apr 65 USA (United States)
ARTICLES: 8 LANGUAGE: English. Russian.
HEADNOTE: FISHING OPERATIONS
TOPIC: Specific Property
CONCEPTS: Bands and frequency allocation. Facilities and property. Ocean resources.
PROCEDURE: Duration. Renewal or Revival. Termination.
PARTIES:
USA (United States)
USSR (Soviet Union)

107706   Bilateral Agreement   **531 UNTS 229**
SIGNED: 5 May 64   FORCE: 7 Apr 65
REGISTERED: 23 Apr 65 USA (United States)
ARTICLES: 13 LANGUAGE: English.
HEADNOTE: AIR TRANSPORT
TOPIC: Air Transport
CONCEPTS: Definition of terms. Detailed regulations. Annex or appendix reference. Previous treaty replacement. Conformity with municipal law. General cooperation. Licenses and permits. Recognition of legal documents. Use of facilities. Arbitration. Procedure. Special tribunals. Competence of tribunal. Expense sharing formulae. Fees and exemptions. Non-interest rates and fees. National treatment. Tax exemptions. Customs exemptions. Competency certificate. Routes and logistics. Navigational conditions. Permit designation. Air transport. Airport facilities. Airworthiness certificates. Conditions of airlines operating permission. Overflights and technical stops. Operating authorizations and regulations. Licenses and certificates of nationality.
INTL ORGS: International Civil Aviation Organization. International Court of Justice. Arbitration Commission.
TREATY REF: 15UNTS295; 71UNTS157.
PROCEDURE: Amendment. Future Procedures Contemplated. Ratification. Registration. Termination. Application to Non-self-governing Territories.
PARTIES:
United Arab Rep
USA (United States)

107707   Bilateral Agreement   **531 UNTS 249**
SIGNED: 9 Dec 64   FORCE: 9 Dec 64
REGISTERED: 23 Apr 65 USA (United States)
ARTICLES: 6 LANGUAGE: English. French.
HEADNOTE: AGRI COMMOD TITLE I
TOPIC: US Agri Commod Aid
CONCEPTS: General provisions. Annex or appendix reference. Exchange of information and documents. Reexport of goods, etc.. Exchange rates and regulations. Transportation costs. Local currency. Commodities schedule. Purchase authorization. Surplus commodities. Mutual consultation.
PARTIES:
Congo (Zaire)
USA (United States)

107708   Bilateral Agreement   **531 UNTS 263**
SIGNED: 13 Jun 64   FORCE: 13 Jun 64
REGISTERED: 26 Apr 65 USA (United States)
ARTICLES: 6 LANGUAGE: English. French.
HEADNOTE: AGRI COMMOD
TOPIC: US Agri Commod Aid
CONCEPTS: Currency. Agricultural commodities. Use restrictions.
PARTIES:
Guinea
USA (United States)

107709   Bilateral Agreement   **531 UNTS 287**
SIGNED: 30 Dec 64   FORCE: 30 Dec 64
REGISTERED: 26 Apr 65 USA (United States)
ARTICLES: 5 LANGUAGE: English.
HEADNOTE: AGRI COMMOD TITLE IV
TOPIC: US Agri Commod Aid

CONCEPTS: General provisions. Annex or appendix reference. Exchange of information and documents. Reexport of goods, etc.. Payment schedules. Purchase authorization. Commodities schedule. Purchase authorization. Merchant vessels. Mutual consultation.
PARTIES:
Iceland
USA (United States)

107710 Bilateral Agreement **532 UNTS 3**
SIGNED: 25 Mar 64   FORCE: 25 Mar 64
REGISTERED: 26 Apr 65 USA (United States)
ARTICLES: 6 LANGUAGE: English. Spanish.
HEADNOTE: AGRI COMMOD TITLE I
TOPIC: US Agri Commod Aid
CONCEPTS: General provisions. Annex or appendix reference. Exchange of information and documents. Reexport of goods, etc.. Exchange rates and regulations. Transportation costs. Local currency. Commodities schedule. Purchase authorization. Surplus commodities. Mutual consultation.
PARTIES:
Bolivia
USA (United States)

107711 Bilateral Agreement **532 UNTS 29**
SIGNED: 31 Dec 64   FORCE: 31 Dec 64
REGISTERED: 26 Apr 65 USA (United States)
ARTICLES: 6 LANGUAGE: English. Chinese.
HEADNOTE: AGRI COMMOD TITTLE I
TOPIC: US Agri Commod Aid
CONCEPTS: General provisions. Annex or appendix reference. Exchange of information and documents. Reexport of goods, etc.. Exchange rates and regulations. Transportation costs. Local currency. Commodities schedule. Purchase authorization. Surplus commodities. Mutual consultation.
PARTIES:
Taiwan
USA (United States)

107712 Bilateral Agreement **532 UNTS 59**
SIGNED: 31 Dec 64   FORCE: 31 Dec 64
REGISTERED: 26 Apr 65 USA (United States)
ARTICLES: 5 LANGUAGE: English. Chinese.
HEADNOTE: AGRI COMMOD TITLE IV
TOPIC: US Agri Commod Aid
CONCEPTS: General provisions. Annex or appendix reference. Exchange of information and documents. Reexport of goods, etc.. Payment schedules. Transportation costs. Purchase authorization. Commodities schedule. Purchase authorization. Mutual consultation.
PARTIES:
Taiwan
USA (United States)

107713 Bilateral Agreement **532 UNTS 87**
SIGNED: 14 Dec 46   FORCE: 14 Dec 46
REGISTERED: 26 Apr 65 USA (United States)
ARTICLES: 12 LANGUAGE: English. Spanish.
HEADNOTE: AIR TRANSPORT
TOPIC: Air Transport
CONCEPTS: Exceptions and exemptions. Annex or appendix reference. Non-prejudice to third party. Conformity with municipal law. Licenses and permits. Recognition of legal documents. Use of facilities. Arbitration. Procedure. Existing tribunals. Competence of tribunal. Fees and exemptions. Most favored nation clause. National treatment. Customs duties. Customs exemptions. Competency certificate. Routes and logistics. Navigational conditions. Permit designation. Air transport. Airport facilities. Airworthiness certificates. Conditions of airlines operating permission. Operating authorizations and regulations. Licenses and certificates of nationality.
INTL ORGS: International Civil Aviation Organization.
TREATY REF: 171UNTS345; 532UNTS88 FN__2.
PROCEDURE: Amendment. Ratification. Registration. Termination.
PARTIES:
USA (United States)
Uruguay

107714 Bilateral Agreement **532 UNTS 107**
SIGNED: 17 Nov 64   FORCE: 17 Nov 64
REGISTERED: 26 Apr 65 USA (United States)
ARTICLES: 5 LANGUAGE: English.
HEADNOTE: AGRI COMMOD TITLE IV
TOPIC: US Agri Commod Aid
CONCEPTS: General provisions. Annex or appendix reference. Exchange of information and documents. Reexport of goods, etc.. Payment schedules. Transportation costs. Purchase authorization. Commodities schedule. Purchase authorization. Mutual consultation.
PARTIES:
Greece
USA (United States)
ANNEX
546 UNTS 404. USA (United States). Amendment 9 Apr 65. Force 27 Apr 65.
546 UNTS 404. Greece. Amendment 27 Apr 65. Force 24 Jul 65.

107715 Bilateral Exchange **532 UNTS 125**
SIGNED: 25 Nov 64   FORCE: 25 Nov 64
REGISTERED: 26 Apr 65 USA (United States)
ARTICLES: 2 LANGUAGE: English.
HEADNOTE: EXCHANGE OFFICIAL PUBLICATIONS
TOPIC: Mass Media
CONCEPTS: Indemnities and reimbursements. Publications exchange.
PARTIES:
Ethiopia
USA (United States)

107716 Bilateral Agreement **532 UNTS 133**
SIGNED: 23 Nov 64   FORCE: 23 Nov 64
REGISTERED: 26 Apr 65 USA (United States)
ARTICLES: 11 LANGUAGE: English. Italian.
HEADNOTE: ITALIAN PORTS
TOPIC: Milit Assistance
CONCEPTS: Annex or appendix reference. Conformity with municipal law. Inspection and observation. Private contracts. Responsibility and liability. Compensation. Peaceful use. Operating authorizations and regulations. Ports and pilotage. Naval vessels. Ocean resources.
TREATY REF: S.EX.DOC.K. 87TH CONG. 1ST SESS. PP.370-444.
PROCEDURE: Future Procedures Contemplated. Termination.
PARTIES:
Italy
USA (United States)

107717 Multilateral Convention **532 UNTS 159**
SIGNED: 25 Jun 63   FORCE: 21 Apr 65
REGISTERED: 26 Apr 65 ILO (Labor Org)
ARTICLES: 25 LANGUAGE: English. French.
HEADNOTE: GUARDING MACHINERY
TOPIC: ILO Labor
CONCEPTS: Definition of terms. Detailed regulations. Exceptions and exemptions. Domestic legislation. Incorporation of treaty provisions into national law. Use of facilities. Investigation of violations. ILO conventions. Safety standards.
INTL ORGS: International Labour Organization. United Nations.
PROCEDURE: Amendment. Denunciation. Duration. Ratification. Registration. Renewal or Revival.
PARTIES:
Multilateral
ANNEX
541 UNTS 383. Syria. Ratification 10 Jun 65. Force 10 Jun 66.
559 UNTS 386. Taiwan. Ratification 22 Feb 66. Force 22 Feb 67.
603 UNTS 357. Paraguay. Ratification 10 Jul 67. Force 10 Jul 67.
607 UNTS 370. Congo (Zaire). Ratification 5 Sep 67. Force 5 Sep 68.
613 UNTS 429. Turkey. Ratification 13 Nov 67. Force 13 Nov 63.

107718 Bilateral Treaty **532 UNTS 177**
SIGNED: 13 Jan 61   FORCE: 17 Dec 64
REGISTERED: 27 Apr 65 USA (United States)
ARTICLES: 22 LANGUAGE: English. Portuguese.
HEADNOTE: EXTRADITION
TOPIC: Extradition

CONCEPTS: Definition of terms. Time limit. Extradition, deportation and repatriation. Extraditable offenses. Location of crime. Refusal of extradition. Limits of prosecution. Provisional detainment. Extradition postponement. Conformity with municipal law. General cooperation. Conveyance in transit.
PROCEDURE: Ratification. Termination.
PARTIES:
Brazil
USA (United States)

107719 Bilateral Agreement **532 UNTS 213**
SIGNED: 16 Nov 64   FORCE: 16 Nov 64
REGISTERED: 27 Apr 65 USA (United States)
ARTICLES: 5 LANGUAGE: English.
HEADNOTE: AGRI COMMOD TITLE IV
TOPIC: US Agri Commod Aid
CONCEPTS: General provisions. Annex or appendix reference. Exchange of information and documents. Reexport of goods, etc.. Payment schedules. Transportation costs. Purchase authorization. Commodities schedule. Purchase authorization. Mutual consultation.
PARTIES:
Iran
USA (United States)
ANNEX
546 UNTS 408. USA (United States). Amendment 28 Apr 65. Force 28 Apr 65.
546 UNTS 408. Iran. Amendment 28 Apr 65. Force 28 Apr 65.

107720 Bilateral Agreement **532 UNTS 231**
SIGNED: 22 Dec 64   FORCE: 22 Dec 64
REGISTERED: 27 Apr 65 USA (United States)
ARTICLES: 6 LANGUAGE: English.
HEADNOTE: AGRI COMMOD TITLE I
TOPIC: US Agri Commod Aid
CONCEPTS: General provisions. Annex or appendix reference. Exchange of information and documents. Reexport of goods, etc.. Exchange rates and regulations. Transportation costs. Local currency. Commodities schedule. Purchase authorization. Surplus commodities. Mutual consultation.
PARTIES:
Israel
USA (United States)

107721 Bilateral Exchange **532 UNTS 249**
SIGNED: 4 Dec 64   FORCE: 4 Dec 64
REGISTERED: 27 Apr 65 USA (United States)
ARTICLES: 2 LANGUAGE: English. Japanese.
HEADNOTE: MUTUAL DEFENSE ASSISTANCE EQUIPMENT MATERIALS SERVICES
TOPIC: Milit Installation
CONCEPTS: Conformity with municipal law. Expense sharing formulae. Tax exemptions. Recognition. Customs exemptions. Materials, equipment and services. Joint defense. Defense and security. Bases and facilities.
TREATY REF: 232UNTS169.
PROCEDURE: Future Procedures Contemplated.
PARTIES:
Japan
USA (United States)
ANNEX
550 UNTS 415. USA (United States). Supplementation 18 Jun 65. Force 18 Jun 65.
550 UNTS 415. Japan. Acknowledgement 18 Jun 65. Force 18 Jun 65.

107722 Bilateral Agreement **532 UNTS 263**
SIGNED: 7 Dec 64   FORCE: 7 Dec 64
REGISTERED: 27 Apr 65 USA (United States)
ARTICLES: 5 LANGUAGE: English.
HEADNOTE: AGRI COMMOD TITLE IV
TOPIC: US Agri Commod Aid
CONCEPTS: General provisions. Annex or appendix reference. Exchange of information and documents. Reexport of goods, etc.. Exchange rates and regulations. Transportation costs. Local currency. Purchase authorization. Commodities schedule. Purchase authorization. Surplus commodities. Mutual consultation.
PARTIES:
Kenya
USA (United States)

ANNEX
542 UNTS 398. USA (United States). Amendment 15 Feb 65. Force 15 Feb 65.
542 UNTS 398. Kenya. Amendment 15 Feb 65. Force 15 Feb 65.

107723 Bilateral Convention **532 UNTS 277**
SIGNED: 18 Dec 62   FORCE: 22 Dec 64
REGISTERED: 27 Apr 65 USA (United States)
ARTICLES: 22 LANGUAGE: English. French.
HEADNOTE: TAXES INCOME PROPERTY
TOPIC: Taxation
CONCEPTS: Definition of terms. Privileges and immunities. Conformity with municipal law. Exchange of official publications. Domestic legislation. Teacher and student exchange. Claims and settlements. Taxation. Tax credits. General. Tax exemptions. Air transport. Merchant vessels.
PROCEDURE: Duration. Ratification. Termination.
PARTIES:
Luxembourg
USA (United States)

107724 Bilateral Exchange **532 UNTS 307**
SIGNED: 3 Jul 64   FORCE: 3 Jul 64
REGISTERED: 27 Apr 65 USA (United States)
ARTICLES: 2 LANGUAGE: English. French.
HEADNOTE: GUARANTY/PRIVATE INVESTMENT
TOPIC: Finance
CONCEPTS: Arbitration. Currency. Private investment guarantee.
INTL ORGS: International Court of Justice. Arbitration Commission.
PARTIES:
Mauritania
USA (United States)

107725 Bilateral Exchange **532 UNTS 313**
SIGNED: 19 Dec 64   FORCE: 19 Dec 64
REGISTERED: 27 Apr 65 USA (United States)
ARTICLES: 2 LANGUAGE: English.
HEADNOTE: COMBINED MILITARY EXERCISES
TOPIC: Status of Forces
CONCEPTS: Privileges and immunities. Claims and settlements. Defense and security. Status of military forces.
TREATY REF: 132UNTS273.
PARTIES:
Taiwan
USA (United States)

107726 Bilateral Agreement **532 UNTS 321**
SIGNED: 30 Sep 64   FORCE: 30 Sep 64
REGISTERED: 27 Apr 65 USA (United States)
ARTICLES: 6 LANGUAGE: English.
HEADNOTE: AGRI COMMOD TITLE I
TOPIC: US Agri Commod Aid
CONCEPTS: General provisions. Annex or appendix reference. Exchange of information and documents. Reexport of goods, etc.. Exchange rates and regulations. Transportation costs. Local currency. Commodities schedule. Purchase authorization. Surplus commodities. Mutual consultation. Internal travel.
PARTIES:
India
USA (United States)
ANNEX
546 UNTS 412. USA (United States). Amendment 21 Apr 65. Force 21 Apr 65.
546 UNTS 412. India. Acceptance 21 Apr 65. Force 21 Apr 65.
607 UNTS 348. USA (United States). Amendment 14 Oct 66. Force 14 Oct 66.
607 UNTS 348. India. Amendment 14 Oct 66. Force 14 Oct 66.

107727 Bilateral Exchange **532 UNTS 347**
SIGNED: 27 Oct 64   FORCE: 27 Oct 64
REGISTERED: 27 Apr 65 USA (United States)
ARTICLES: 2 LANGUAGE: English. Spanish.
HEADNOTE: UNITING REPLACING AIR FORCE NAVAL ARMY MISSION AGREEMENTS
TOPIC: Military Mission
CONCEPTS: Definition of terms. Previous treaty extension. Use of facilities. Compensation. Indemnities and reimbursements. Exchange rates and regulations. Expense sharing formulae. Tax exemptions. Customs exemptions. Military assis-

tance. Military training. Security of information. Airforce-army-navy personnel ratio. Ranks and privileges. Conditions for assistance missions. Status of forces.
TREATY REF: 133UNTS95.
PROCEDURE: Termination.
PARTIES:
Chile
USA (United States)

107728 Bilateral Agreement **533 UNTS 3**
SIGNED: 28 Oct 64   FORCE: 28 Oct 64
REGISTERED: 27 Apr 65 USA (United States)
ARTICLES: 5 LANGUAGE: English.
HEADNOTE: AGRI COMMOD TITLE IV
TOPIC: US Agri Commod Aid
CONCEPTS: General provisions. Annex or appendix reference. Exchange of information and documents. Reexport of goods, etc.. Payment schedules. Transportation costs. Purchase authorization. Commodities schedule. Purchase authorization. Mutual consultation.
PARTIES:
USA (United States)
Yugoslavia

107729 Bilateral Agreement **533 UNTS 17**
SIGNED: 29 Oct 64   FORCE: 29 Oct 64
REGISTERED: 27 Apr 65 USA (United States)
ARTICLES: 5 LANGUAGE: English.
HEADNOTE: AGRI COMMOD TITLE IV
TOPIC: US Agri Commod Aid
CONCEPTS: General provisions. Annex or appendix reference. Exchange of information and documents. Reexport of goods, etc.. Payment schedules. Transportation costs. Purchase authorization. Commodities schedule. Purchase authorization.
PARTIES:
USA (United States)
Yugoslavia

107730 Bilateral Exchange **533 UNTS 31**
SIGNED: 25 Nov 64   FORCE: 25 Nov 64
REGISTERED: 27 Apr 65 USA (United States)
ARTICLES: 2 LANGUAGE: English.
HEADNOTE: KING CRAB FISHERY
TOPIC: Specific Property
CONCEPTS: Annex or appendix reference. Research cooperation. Research results. Wildlife.
INTL ORGS: International North Pacific Fisheries Commission.
TREATY REF: 205UNTS65.
PARTIES:
Japan
USA (United States)

107731 Bilateral Agreement **533 UNTS 39**
SIGNED: 9 Nov 64   FORCE: 9 Nov 64
REGISTERED: 27 Apr 65 USA (United States)
ARTICLES: 12 LANGUAGE: English.
HEADNOTE: FINANCING EDUCATIONAL EXCHANGE
TOPIC: Education
CONCEPTS: Definition of terms. Friendship and amity. Standardization. Conformity with municipal law. General cooperation. Exchange of information and documents. Inspection and observation. Personnel. General property. Exchange. Commissions and foundations. Teacher and student exchange. Professorships. Accounting procedures. Currency. Financial programs. Funding procedures.
INTL ORGS: Special Commission.
PROCEDURE: Amendment.
PARTIES:
USA (United States)
Yugoslavia

107732 Multilateral Agreement **533 UNTS 50**
SIGNED: 26 Apr 65   FORCE: 26 Apr 65
REGISTERED: 26 Apr 65 United Nations
ARTICLES: 6 LANGUAGE: English.
HEADNOTE: OPERATIONAL ASSISTANCE
TOPIC: IGO Operations
CONCEPTS: Annex or appendix reference. Previous treaty replacement. Diplomatic privileges. Diplomatic missions. Privileges and immunities. Arbitration. Procedure. Special tribunals. Burial

arrangements. Mutual consultation. Special status.
INTL ORGS: Permanent Court of Arbitration. United Nations Technical Assistance Board. Arbitration Commission.
TREATY REF: 515UNTS94; 511UNTS199.
PROCEDURE: Amendment. Termination.
PARTIES:
Kenya SIGNED: 26 Apr 65 FORCE: 26 Apr 65
FAO (Food Agri) SIGNED: 26 Apr 65 FORCE: 26 Apr 65
IAEA (Atom Energy) SIGNED: 26 Apr 65 FORCE: 26 Apr 65
ICAO (Civil Aviat) SIGNED: 26 Apr 65 FORCE: 26 Apr 65
ILO (Labor Org) SIGNED: 26 Apr 65 FORCE: 26 Apr 65
ITU (Telecommun) SIGNED: 26 Apr 65 FORCE: 26 Apr 65
UNESCO (Educ/Cult) SIGNED: 26 Apr 65 FORCE: 26 Apr 65
United Nations SIGNED: 26 Apr 65 FORCE: 26 Apr 65
UPU (Postal Union) SIGNED: 26 Apr 65 FORCE: 26 Apr 65
WHO (World Health) SIGNED: 26 Apr 65 FORCE: 26 Apr 65
WMO (Meteorology) SIGNED: 26 Apr 65 FORCE: 26 Apr 65

107733 Multilateral Agreement **533 UNTS 66**
SIGNED: 8 Apr 65   FORCE: 8 Apr 65
REGISTERED: 1 May 65 United Nations
ARTICLES: 6 LANGUAGE: French.
HEADNOTE: OPERATIONAL ASSISTANCE
TOPIC: IGO Operations
CONCEPTS: Annex or appendix reference. Previous treaty replacement. Diplomatic privileges. Diplomatic missions. Privileges and immunities. Arbitration. Procedure. Existing tribunals. Domestic obligation. Special status. Mutual consultation.
INTL ORGS: Permanent Court of Arbitration. United Nations Technical Assistance Board. Arbitration Commission.
TREATY REF: 359UNTS322; 321UNTS3.
PROCEDURE: Amendment. Termination.
PARTIES:
FAO (Food Agri) SIGNED: 8 Apr 65 FORCE: 8 Apr 65
IAEA (Atom Energy) SIGNED: 8 Apr 65 FORCE: 8 Apr 65
ICAO (Civil Aviat) SIGNED: 8 Apr 65 FORCE: 8 Apr 65
ILO (Labor Org) SIGNED: 8 Apr 65 FORCE: 8 Apr 65
ITU (Telecommun) SIGNED: 8 Apr 65 FORCE: 8 Apr 65
UNESCO (Educ/Cult) SIGNED: 8 Apr 65 FORCE: 8 Apr 65
United Nations SIGNED: 8 Apr 65 FORCE: 8 Apr 65
UPU (Postal Union) SIGNED: 8 Apr 65 FORCE: 8 Apr 65
WHO (World Health) SIGNED: 8 Apr 65 FORCE: 8 Apr 65
WMO (Meteorology) SIGNED: 8 Apr 65 FORCE: 8 Apr 65
Tunisia SIGNED: 8 Apr 65 FORCE: 8 Apr 65

107734 Bilateral Exchange **533 UNTS 83**
SIGNED: 20 Mar 64   FORCE: 2 Mar 64
REGISTERED: 1 May 65 United Nations
ARTICLES: 2 LANGUAGE: French.
HEADNOTE: TRANSFER BASES
TOPIC: Milit Installation
CONCEPTS: Annex or appendix reference. Bases and facilities.
INTL ORGS: Special Commission.
PROCEDURE: Future Procedures Contemplated.
PARTIES:
Belgium
United Nations

107735 Bilateral Exchange **533 UNTS 93**
SIGNED: 2 Mar 64   FORCE: 2 Mar 64
REGISTERED: 1 May 65 United Nations
ARTICLES: 2 LANGUAGE: French.
HEADNOTE: ADMINISTRATION BASES
TOPIC: Milit Installation

CONCEPTS: General cooperation. Bases and facilities.
INTL ORGS: United Nations Mission to the Congo.
TREATY REF: 533UNTS83.
PARTIES:
Congo (Zaire)
United Nations

107736 Multilateral Agreement **533 UNTS 98**
SIGNED: 15 Feb 64   FORCE: 15 Feb 64
REGISTERED: 1 May 65 United Nations
ARTICLES: 1 LANGUAGE: French.
HEADNOTE: COMMENCEMENT HAND-OVER OPERATIONS BASE
TOPIC: Milit Installation
CONCEPTS: Bases and facilities.
INTL ORGS: United Nations Mission to the Congo.
TREATY REF: 533UNTS83.
PARTIES:
Belgium SIGNED: 15 Feb 64 FORCE: 15 Feb 64
Congo (Zaire) SIGNED: 15 Feb 64 FORCE: 15 Feb 64
UN Mission Congo SIGNED: 15 Feb 64 FORCE: 15 Feb 64

107737 Bilateral Agreement **533 UNTS 107**
SIGNED: 22 Apr 65   FORCE: 22 Apr 65
REGISTERED: 1 May 65 United Nations
ARTICLES: 8 LANGUAGE: English.
HEADNOTE: ACTIVITIES MALAWI
TOPIC: IGO Operations
CONCEPTS: Diplomatic privileges. Privileges and immunities. Exchange of information and documents. Accounting procedures. Materials, equipment and services. Terms of loan. Assistance to United Nations.
INTL ORGS: United Nations.
TREATY REF: 1UNTS15.
PROCEDURE: Amendment. Termination.
PARTIES:
Malta
UNICEF (Children)

107738 Bilateral Exchange **533 UNTS 117**
SIGNED: 17 Jul 64   FORCE: 17 Jul 64
REGISTERED: 1 May 65 United Nations
ARTICLES: 2 LANGUAGE: English. Spanish.
HEADNOTE: PRINCIPLES INTERNATIONAL LAW
TOPIC: IGO Operations
CONCEPTS: Default remedies. Non-visa travel documents. Diplomatic missions. Privileges and immunities. Funding procedures. Subsidiary organ.
TREATY REF: 1UNTS15.
PARTIES:
Mexico
United Nations

107739 Bilateral Agreement **533 UNTS 133**
SIGNED: 3 Mar 64   FORCE: 5 Oct 64
REGISTERED: 4 May 65 Netherlands
ARTICLES: 6 LANGUAGE: French.
HEADNOTE: ESTABLISHMENT ANIMAL HUSBANDRY TRAINING CENTER
TOPIC: Tech Assistance
CONCEPTS: Time limit. Treaty implementation. General cooperation. Personnel. Responsibility and liability. Institute establishment. Reexport of goods, etc.. Customs exemptions. Agriculture. Materials, equipment and services.
PROCEDURE: Denunciation. Duration.
PARTIES:
Netherlands
Tunisia

107740 Bilateral Agreement **533 UNTS 141**
SIGNED: 17 Jun 64   FORCE: 11 Feb 65
REGISTERED: 4 May 65 Taiwan
ARTICLES: 11 LANGUAGE: Chinese. Spanish. English.
HEADNOTE: TRADE
TOPIC: General Trade
CONCEPTS: Exceptions and exemptions. Conformity with municipal law. Licenses and permits. Investigation of violations. Establishment of trade relations. Export quotas. Import quotas. Certificates of origin. Reciprocity in trade. Currency. Payment schedules. Most favored nation clause.
PROCEDURE: Duration. Ratification. Termination.

PARTIES:
Taiwan
Ecuador

107741 Bilateral Instrument **533 UNTS 157**
SIGNED: 11 Jan 65   FORCE: 11 Jan 65
REGISTERED: 6 May 65 Belgium
ARTICLES: 1 LANGUAGE: French. Dutch.
HEADNOTE: EDUCATION SCIENCE ART COOPERATION
TOPIC: Education
CONCEPTS: Annex or appendix reference. Exchange of information and documents. Exchange. Teacher and student exchange. Professorships. General cultural cooperation. Artists. Scientific exchange. Indemnities and reimbursements. Publications exchange. Mass media exchange.
PROCEDURE: Amendment.
PARTIES:
Belgium
Sweden

107742 Bilateral Agreement **533 UNTS 165**
SIGNED: 24 Jun 64   FORCE: 10 Aug 64
REGISTERED: 7 May 65 IDA (Devel Assoc)
ARTICLES: 7 LANGUAGE: English.
HEADNOTE: DEVELOPMENT CREDIT HIGHWAY
TOPIC: Non-IBRD Project
CONCEPTS: Definition of terms. Detailed regulations. Previous treaty amendment. Exchange of information and documents. Informational records. Accounting procedures. Currency. Interest rates. Tax exemptions. Credit provisions. Loan repayment. Terms of loan. Plans and standards. IDA development project. Roads and highways.
PARTIES:
Pakistan
IDA (Devel Assoc)

107743 Bilateral Agreement **533 UNTS 191**
SIGNED: 24 Jun 64   FORCE: 27 Aug 64
REGISTERED: 7 May 65 IDA (Devel Assoc)
ARTICLES: 7 LANGUAGE: English.
HEADNOTE: DEVELOPMENT CREDIT RAILWAY
TOPIC: Non-IBRD Project
CONCEPTS: Definition of terms. Detailed regulations. Previous treaty amendment. Exchange of information and documents. Informational records. Accounting procedures. Currency. Interest rates. Tax exemptions. Credit provisions. Loan repayment. Terms of loan. Plans and standards. IDA development project. Railways.
PARTIES:
Pakistan
IDA (Devel Assoc)

107744 Bilateral Instrument **533 UNTS 217**
SIGNED: 2 Aug 57   FORCE: 4 Dec 57
REGISTERED: 10 May 65 Greece
ARTICLES: 2 LANGUAGE: English.
HEADNOTE: SAR SERVICES
TOPIC: Air Transport
CONCEPTS: Definition of terms. Detailed regulations. Annex or appendix reference. Conformity with municipal law. General cooperation. Licenses and permits. Recognition of legal documents. Arbitration. Procedure. Special tribunals. Vocational training. Reexport of goods, etc.. Expense sharing formulae. Fees and exemptions. Non-interest rates and fees. Tax exemptions. Customs exemptions. Competency certificate. Routes and logistics. Navigational conditions. Permit designation. Air transport. Airport facilities. Airworthiness certificates. Conditions of airlines operating permission. Operating authorizations and regulations. Licenses and certificates of nationality. Facilities and equipment. Military installations and equipment.
INTL ORGS: International Civil Aviation Organization.
PROCEDURE: Amendment. Termination.
PARTIES:
Greece
Italy

107745 Bilateral Agreement **533 UNTS 227**
SIGNED: 25 Jul 60   FORCE: 25 Jul 60

REGISTERED: 10 May 65 Greece
ARTICLES: 14 LANGUAGE: French.
HEADNOTE: TECHNICAL SCIENTIFIC COOPERATION
TOPIC: General Aid
CONCEPTS: Treaty implementation. General cooperation. Exchange of information and documents. Personnel. Use of facilities. Establishment of commission. Exchange. Scholarships and grants. Vocational training. Research and scientific projects. Research results. General technical assistance.
INTL ORGS: Special Commission.
PROCEDURE: Amendment. Termination.
PARTIES:
France
Greece

107746 Bilateral Convention **533 UNTS 235**
SIGNED: 21 Aug 63   FORCE: 31 Jan 65
REGISTERED: 10 May 65 Greece
ARTICLES: 31 LANGUAGE: French.
HEADNOTE: DOUBLE TAXATION INCOME
TOPIC: Taxation
CONCEPTS: Definition of terms. Territorial application. Conformity with municipal law. Exchange of official publications. Domestic legislation. Teacher and student exchange. Claims and settlements. Debts. Taxation. Tax credits. Equitable taxes. Tax exemptions. Air transport. Merchant vessels.
PROCEDURE: Denunciation. Duration. Ratification.
PARTIES:
France
Greece

107747 Bilateral Agreement **533 UNTS 269**
SIGNED: 8 Mar 62   FORCE: 1 May 62
REGISTERED: 10 May 65 Greece
ARTICLES: 15 LANGUAGE: Greek. German.
HEADNOTE: INTERNATIONAL CARRIAGE GOODS ROAD
TOPIC: Land Transport
CONCEPTS: Detailed regulations. Exceptions and exemptions. General provisions. Remedies. Conformity with municipal law. General cooperation. Exchange of information and documents. Licenses and permits. Reexport of goods, etc.. Transport of goods. Commercial road vehicles. Driving permits. Motor vehicles and combinations. Roads and highways. Road rules.
PROCEDURE: Termination. Application to Non-self-governing Territories.
PARTIES:
Germany, West
Greece

107748 Bilateral Exchange **533 UNTS 303**
SIGNED: 27 Jan 53   FORCE: 27 Jan 53
REGISTERED: 10 May 65 Greece
ARTICLES: 2 LANGUAGE: English.
HEADNOTE: MOST FAVORED NATION TREATMENT
TOPIC: Mostfavored Nation
CONCEPTS: Most favored nation clause. Navigational conditions.
PARTIES:
Greece
South Africa

107749 Bilateral Agreement **533 UNTS 309**
SIGNED: 21 Jan 64   FORCE: 24 Nov 64
REGISTERED: 10 May 65 Greece
ARTICLES: 3 LANGUAGE: French.
HEADNOTE: TAXATION SEA AIR TRANSPORT
TOPIC: Taxation
CONCEPTS: Tax exemptions. Air transport. Merchant vessels.
PROCEDURE: Termination.
PARTIES:
Greece
Poland

107750 Bilateral Agreement **534 UNTS 3**
SIGNED: 27 Apr 63   FORCE: 27 Apr 63
REGISTERED: 10 May 65 Greece
ARTICLES: 15 LANGUAGE: English.
HEADNOTE: CIVIL AVIATION
TOPIC: Air Transport

CONCEPTS: Definition of terms. Detailed regulations. Representation. Annex or appendix reference. Conformity with municipal law. General cooperation. Exchange of information and documents. Informational records. Licenses and permits. Recognition of legal documents. Procedure. Negotiation. Humanitarian matters. Non-interest rates and fees. General. Tax exemptions. Customs exemptions. Registration certificate. Routes and logistics. Navigational conditions. Permit designation. Air transport. Airport facilities. Airworthiness certificates. Conditions of airlines operating permission. Operating authorizations and regulations. Licenses and certificates of nationality.
INTL ORGS: United Nations.
PROCEDURE: Amendment. Denunciation. Ratification. Registration. Termination.
PARTIES:
Greece
Hungary
        ANNEX
552 UNTS 423. Greece. Ratification 16 Dec 65. Force 16 Dec 65.
552 UNTS 423. Hungary. Ratification 16 Dec 65. Force 16 Dec 65.

107751 Bilateral Agreement **534 UNTS 23**
SIGNED: 30 Sep 63   FORCE: 1 Oct 63
REGISTERED: 10 May 65 Greece
ARTICLES: 8 LANGUAGE: French.
HEADNOTE: NEW LONG-TERM TRADE AGREEMENT
TOPIC: General Trade
CONCEPTS: Annex type material. Previous treaty replacement. Licenses and permits. Establishment of commission. Export quotas. Import quotas. Reexport of goods, etc.. Trade procedures. Currency. Payment schedules. Delivery schedules. Quotas.
INTL ORGS: Special Commission.
TREATY REF: 483UNTS127; 483UNTS141.
PROCEDURE: Duration. Renewal or Revival. Termination.
PARTIES:
Greece
Poland

107752 Bilateral Exchange **534 UNTS 43**
SIGNED: 26 Sep 63   FORCE: 25 Aug 63
REGISTERED: 10 May 65 Greece
ARTICLES: 2 LANGUAGE: French.
HEADNOTE: TRADE DURING LIMITED PERIOD
TOPIC: General Trade
CONCEPTS: Annex or appendix reference. Trade procedures. Quotas.
PARTIES:
Denmark
Greece

107753 Bilateral Agreement **534 UNTS 49**
SIGNED: 6 Jul 64   FORCE: 4 Aug 64
REGISTERED: 10 May 65 IDA (Devel Assoc)
ARTICLES: 7 LANGUAGE: English.
HEADNOTE: DEVELOPMENT CREDIT TELECOMMUNICATIONS
TOPIC: Non-IBRD Project
CONCEPTS: Definition of terms. Detailed regulations. Previous treaty amendment. Exchange of information and documents. Informational records. Accounting procedures. Currency. Interest rates. Tax exemptions. Credit provisions. Loan repayment. Terms of loan. Plans and standards. IDA development project. Telecommunications.
PARTIES:
India
IDA (Devel Assoc)

107754 Bilateral Exchange **534 UNTS 71**
SIGNED: 13 Oct 64   FORCE: 13 Oct 64
REGISTERED: 10 May 65 UK Great Britain
ARTICLES: 2 LANGUAGE: English.
HEADNOTE: SUPPLY USE NUCLEAR MATERIAL PEACEFUL RESEARCH PURPOSES
TOPIC: Atomic Energy
CONCEPTS: Nuclear materials. Peaceful use.
PARTIES:
Pakistan
UK Great Britain

107755 Bilateral Agreement **534 UNTS 77**
SIGNED: 20 Oct 64   FORCE: 20 Oct 64
REGISTERED: 10 May 65 UK Great Britain
ARTICLES: 2 LANGUAGE: English.
HEADNOTE: DUTY-FREE ENTRY RELIEF SUPPLIES
TOPIC: Customs
CONCEPTS: Definition of terms. Transportation costs. Customs exemptions. Relief supplies.
PROCEDURE: Termination.
PARTIES:
India
UK Great Britain

107756 Bilateral Exchange **534 UNTS 85**
SIGNED: 20 Nov 64   FORCE: 20 Nov 64
REGISTERED: 10 May 65 UK Great Britain
ARTICLES: 2 LANGUAGE: English.
HEADNOTE: SPECIAL DEFENSE CREDIT
TOPIC: Milit Assistance
CONCEPTS: Private contracts. Interest rates. Payment schedules. Payment for war supplies.
PARTIES:
India
UK Great Britain

107757 Bilateral Agreement **534 UNTS 93**
SIGNED: 26 May 64   FORCE: 24 Dec 64
REGISTERED: 10 May 65 IDA (Devel Assoc)
ARTICLES: 7 LANGUAGE: English.
HEADNOTE: DEVELOPMENT CREDIT HIGHWAY
TOPIC: Non-IBRD Project
CONCEPTS: Definition of terms. Detailed regulations. Exchange of information and documents. Informational records. Accounting procedures. Interest rates. Tax exemptions. Credit provisions. Loan repayment. Terms of loan. Plans and standards. IDA development project. Railways.
INTL ORGS: International Bank for Reconstruction and Development.
PARTIES:
Ecuador
IDA (Devel Assoc)

107758 Bilateral Agreement **534 UNTS 113**
SIGNED: 26 May 64   FORCE: 24 Dec 64
REGISTERED: 10 May 65 IBRD (World Bank)
ARTICLES: 8 LANGUAGE: English.
HEADNOTE: LOAN HIGHWAY
TOPIC: IBRD Project
CONCEPTS: Default remedies. Definition of terms. Exchange of information and documents. Informational records. Inspection and observation. Accounting procedures. Bonds. Fees and exemptions. Tax exemptions. Domestic obligation. Terms of loan. Loan regulations. Loan guarantee. Guarantor non-interference. Roads and highways.
INTL ORGS: Inter-American Bank. International Development Association. Special Commission.
PARTIES:
Ecuador
IBRD (World Bank)

107759 Bilateral Agreement **534 UNTS 147**
SIGNED: 22 Jun 59   FORCE: 22 Jun 59
REGISTERED: 10 May 65 Greece
ARTICLES: 8 LANGUAGE: English.
HEADNOTE: DEVELOPING COMMERCIAL RELATIONS
TOPIC: General Economic
CONCEPTS: Exceptions and exemptions. Annex or appendix reference. Licenses and permits. Payment schedules. Most favored nation clause.
PROCEDURE: Denunciation. Duration.
PARTIES:
Ethiopia
Greece

107760 Bilateral Agreement **534 UNTS 157**
SIGNED: 4 Mar 61   FORCE: 14 Apr 65
REGISTERED: 10 May 65 Greece
ARTICLES: 4 LANGUAGE: French.
HEADNOTE: TAXES MARITIME AIR TRANSPORT
TOPIC: Taxation
CONCEPTS: Tax exemptions. Air transport. Merchant vessels.
INTL ORGS: United Nations.
PROCEDURE: Denunciation. Ratification. Registration.

PARTIES:
Denmark
Greece

107761 Bilateral Agreement **534 UNTS 163**
SIGNED: 26 May 62   FORCE: 26 May 62
REGISTERED: 10 May 65 Greece
ARTICLES: 6 LANGUAGE: French.
HEADNOTE: ECONOMIC TECHNICAL SCIENTIFIC COOPERATION
TOPIC: General Aid
CONCEPTS: Treaty implementation. General cooperation. Exchange of information and documents. Personnel. Scholarships and grants. Vocational training. Research and scientific projects. Investments. Most favored nation clause. Tax exemptions. Customs exemptions. General technical assistance. Economic assistance. Materials, equipment and services.
PROCEDURE: Denunciation. Duration. Renewal or Revival.
PARTIES:
Greece
Tunisia

107762 Bilateral Agreement **534 UNTS 171**
SIGNED: 24 Jul 64   FORCE: 25 Aug 64
REGISTERED: 11 May 65 IDA (Devel Assoc)
ARTICLES: 7 LANGUAGE: English.
HEADNOTE: DEVELOPMENT CREDIT BPC POWER PROJECT
TOPIC: Non-IBRD Project
CONCEPTS: Definition of terms. Detailed regulations. Previous treaty amendment. Exchange of information and documents. Informational records. Accounting procedures. Currency. Interest rates. Tax exemptions. Credit provisions. Loan repayment. Terms of loan. Plans and standards. IDA development project. Hydro-electric power.
PARTIES:
Bolivia
IDA (Devel Assoc)

107763 Bilateral Agreement **534 UNTS 203**
SIGNED: 24 Jul 64   FORCE: 25 Aug 64
REGISTERED: 11 May 65 IDA (Devel Assoc)
ARTICLES: 7 LANGUAGE: English.
HEADNOTE: DEVELOPMENT CREDIT ENDE POWER PROJECT
TOPIC: Non-IBRD Project
CONCEPTS: Definition of terms. Detailed regulations. Previous treaty amendment. Accounting procedures. Exchange of information and documents. Informational records. Currency. Interest rates. Tax exemptions. Credit provisions. Loan repayment. Terms of loan. Plans and standards. IDA development project. Hydro-electric power.
INTL ORGS: Inter-American Bank.
PARTIES:
Bolivia
IDA (Devel Assoc)

107764 Bilateral Agreement **534 UNTS 253**
SIGNED: 24 Dec 63   FORCE: 16 Mar 65
REGISTERED: 11 May 65 IDA (Devel Assoc)
ARTICLES: 7 LANGUAGE: English.
HEADNOTE: DEVELOPMENT CREDIT HIGHWAY
TOPIC: Non-IBRD Project
CONCEPTS: Definition of terms. Detailed regulations. Previous treaty amendment. Exchange of information and documents. Informational records. Accounting procedures. Currency. Interest rates. Tax exemptions. Credit provisions. Loan repayment. Terms of loan. Plans and standards. IDA development project. Roads and highways.
PARTIES:
IDA (Devel Assoc)
Syria

107765 Bilateral Agreement **534 UNTS 275**
SIGNED: 25 Mar 64   FORCE: 13 Aug 64
REGISTERED: 11 May 65 IDA (Devel Assoc)
ARTICLES: 7 LANGUAGE: English.
HEADNOTE: DEVELOPMENT CREDIT EDUCATION
TOPIC: Non-IBRD Project
CONCEPTS: Definition of terms. Detailed regulations. Previous treaty amendment. Exchange of

information and documents. Informational records. Education. Accounting procedures. Currency. Interest rates. Tax exemptions. Credit provisions. Loan repayment. Terms of loan. Plans and standards. IDA development project.
PARTIES:
Pakistan
IDA (Devel Assoc)

107766 Bilateral Agreement **534 UNTS 309**
SIGNED: 11 Jun 64 FORCE: 10 Aug 64
REGISTERED: 11 May 65 IDA (Devel Assoc)
ARTICLES: 7 LANGUAGE: English.
HEADNOTE: DEVELOPMENT CREDIT HIGHWAY
TOPIC: Non-IBRD Project
CONCEPTS: Definition of terms. Detailed regulations. Previous treaty amendment. Exchange of information and documents. Informational records. Accounting procedures. Currency. Interest rates. Tax exemptions. Credit provisions. Loan repayment. Terms of loan. Plans and standards. IDA development project. Roads and highways.
PARTIES:
Pakistan
IDA (Devel Assoc)

107767 Bilateral Agreement **534 UNTS 339**
SIGNED: 14 Jul 64 FORCE: 16 Oct 64
REGISTERED: 11 May 65 IDA (Devel Assoc)
ARTICLES: 7 LANGUAGE: English.
HEADNOTE: DEVELOPMENT CREDIT POWER
TOPIC: Non-IBRD Project
CONCEPTS: Definition of terms. Detailed regulations. Previous treaty amendment. Exchange of information and documents. Informational records. Accounting procedures. Currency. Interest rates. Tax exemptions. Credit provisions. Loan repayment. Terms of loan. Plans and standards. IDA development project. Hydro-electric power.
PARTIES:
IDA (Devel Assoc)
Turkey

107768 Bilateral Agreement **534 UNTS 373**
SIGNED: 21 Jul 64 FORCE: 14 Sep 64
REGISTERED: 11 May 65 IDA (Devel Assoc)
ARTICLES: 6 LANGUAGE: English.
HEADNOTE: DEVELOPMENT CREDIT INDUS BASIN PROJECT
TOPIC: Non-IBRD Project
CONCEPTS: Definition of terms. Detailed regulations. Previous treaty amendment. Exchange of information and documents. Informational records. Accounting procedures. Currency. Interest rates. Tax exemptions. Credit provisions. Loan repayment. Terms of loan. Plans and standards. IDA development project. Natural resources.
INTL ORGS: International Bank for Reconstruction and Development. Special Commission.
PARTIES:
Pakistan
IDA (Devel Assoc)

107769 Multilateral Agreement **534 UNTS 390**
SIGNED: 12 May 65 FORCE: 12 May 65
REGISTERED: 12 May 65 United Nations
ARTICLES: 6 LANGUAGE: Spanish.
HEADNOTE: OPERATIONAL ASSISTANCE
TOPIC: IGO Operations
CONCEPTS: Annex or appendix reference. Previous treaty replacement. Diplomatic privileges. Diplomatic missions. Privileges and immunities. Arbitration. Procedure. Domestic obligation. Special status. Assistance to United Nations. Inter-agency agreements. IGO obligations.
INTL ORGS: Permanent Court of Arbitration. United Nations Technical Assistance Board. Arbitration Commission.
TREATY REF: 382UNTS283.
PROCEDURE: Amendment. Termination.
PARTIES:
Bolivia SIGNED: 12 May 65 FORCE: 12 May 65
FAO (Food Agri) SIGNED: 12 May 65 FORCE: 12 May 65
IAEA (Atom Energy) SIGNED: 12 May 65 FORCE: 12 May 65

ICAO (Civil Aviat) SIGNED: 12 May 65 FORCE: 12 May 65
ILO (Labor Org) SIGNED: 12 May 65 FORCE: 12 May 65
IMCO (Maritime Org) SIGNED: 12 May 65 FORCE: 12 May 65
ITU (Telecommun) SIGNED: 12 May 65 FORCE: 12 May 65
UNESCO (Educ/Cult) SIGNED: 12 May 65 FORCE: 12 May 65
United Nations SIGNED: 12 May 65 FORCE: 12 May 65
UPU (Postal Union) SIGNED: 12 May 65 FORCE: 12 May 65
WHO (World Health) SIGNED: 12 May 65 FORCE: 12 May 65
WMO (Meteorology) SIGNED: 12 May 65 FORCE: 12 May 65
ANNEX
659 UNTS 376. UNIDO (Industrial). Accession 13 Jan 69. Force 13 Jan 69.

107770 Bilateral Exchange **534 UNTS 417**
SIGNED: 3 Jan 64 FORCE: 3 Jan 64
REGISTERED: 12 May 65 UK Great Britain
ARTICLES: 2 LANGUAGE: French.
HEADNOTE: LOAN
TOPIC: Loans and Credits
CONCEPTS: Annex or appendix reference. Licenses and permits. Accounting procedures. Currency. Quotas. Loan and credit. Purchase authorization. Terms of loan. Plans and standards.
PROCEDURE: Amendment.
PARTIES:
Congo (Zaire)
UK Great Britain

107771 Bilateral Exchange **534 UNTS 427**
SIGNED: 16 Sep 64 FORCE: 16 Sep 64
REGISTERED: 12 May 65 UK Great Britain
ARTICLES: 2 LANGUAGE: English.
HEADNOTE: TRADE POLICIES CEREALS
TOPIC: Commodity Trade
CONCEPTS: Annex or appendix reference. General cooperation. Export quotas. Fees and exemptions. Non-interest rates and fees. Commodity trade.
INTL ORGS: General Agreement on Tariffs and Trade.
TREATY REF: 55UNTS187;374UNTS233;470UNTS420;371UNTS3.
PROCEDURE: Termination.
PARTIES:
Denmark
UK Great Britain

107772 Bilateral Exchange **535 UNTS 3**
SIGNED: 24 Oct 63 FORCE: 2 Sep 64
REGISTERED: 12 May 65 UK Great Britain
ARTICLES: 2 LANGUAGE: English. Arabic.
HEADNOTE: DOUBLE TAXATION SHIPPING AIR TRANSPORT
TOPIC: Taxation
CONCEPTS: Definition of terms. Territorial application. Domestic legislation. Taxation. Tax exemptions. Air transport. Merchant vessels.
PROCEDURE: Termination.
PARTIES:
Lebanon
UK Great Britain

107773 Bilateral Exchange **535 UNTS 13**
SIGNED: 12 Sep 64 FORCE: 12 Sep 64
REGISTERED: 12 May 65 UK Great Britain
ARTICLES: 2 LANGUAGE: English.
HEADNOTE: PRODUCTION TRADE POLICIES CEREALS
TOPIC: Commodity Trade
CONCEPTS: Annex or appendix reference. General cooperation. Export quotas. Fees and exemptions. Non-interest rates and fees. Commodity trade.
INTL ORGS: General Agreement on Tariffs and Trade.
TREATY REF: 55UNTS187; 60UNTS131; 138UNTS398.
PARTIES:
Finland
UK Great Britain

107774 Bilateral Agreement **535 UNTS 25**
SIGNED: 12 Oct 64 FORCE: 12 Oct 64
REGISTERED: 12 May 65 Trinidad/Tobago
ARTICLES: 17 LANGUAGE: English. French.
HEADNOTE: AIR SERVICES
TOPIC: Air Transport
CONCEPTS: Air transport. Airport facilities. Airport equipment. Airworthiness certificates. Conditions of airlines operating permission. Overflights and technical stops. Operating authorizations and regulations.
INTL ORGS: International Civil Aviation Organization. Arbitration Commission.
PARTIES:
France
Trinidad/Tobago

107775 Bilateral Agreement **535 UNTS 43**
SIGNED: 25 Mar 64 FORCE: 10 Sep 64
REGISTERED: 13 May 65 IDA (Devel Assoc)
ARTICLES: 7 LANGUAGE: English.
HEADNOTE: DEVELOPMENT CREDIT EDUCATION
TOPIC: Non-IBRD Project
CONCEPTS: Definition of terms. Detailed regulations. Previous treaty amendment. Exchange of information and documents. Informational records. Education. Accounting procedures. Currency. Interest rates. Tax exemptions. Credit provisions. Loan repayment. Terms of loan. IDA development project.
PARTIES:
Pakistan
IDA (Devel Assoc)

107776 Bilateral Agreement **535 UNTS 79**
SIGNED: 17 Aug 64 FORCE: 23 Sep 64
REGISTERED: 14 May 65 IDA (Devel Assoc)
ARTICLES: 7 LANGUAGE: English.
HEADNOTE: DEVELOPMENT CREDIT TEA DEVELOPMENT AUTHORITY
TOPIC: Non-IBRD Project
CONCEPTS: Definition of terms. Detailed regulations. Previous treaty amendment. Exchange of information and documents. Informational records. Accounting procedures. Currency. Interest rates. Tax exemptions. Agricultural commodities. Credit provisions. Loan repayment. Terms of loan. Plans and standards. IDA development project.
PARTIES:
Kenya
IDA (Devel Assoc)

107777 Bilateral Agreement **535 UNTS 111**
SIGNED: 31 Aug 64 FORCE: 1 Dec 64
REGISTERED: 14 May 65 IDA (Devel Assoc)
ARTICLES: 9 LANGUAGE: English.
HEADNOTE: DEVELOPMENT CREDIT INDUSTRIAL DEVELOPMENT BANK
TOPIC: Non-IBRD Project
CONCEPTS: Definition of terms. Detailed regulations. Previous treaty amendment. Exchange of information and documents. Informational records. Accounting procedures. Banking. Currency. Interest rates. Tax exemptions. Credit provisions. Loan repayment. Terms of loan. Plans and standards. IDA development project.
PARTIES:
IDA (Devel Assoc)
Turkey

107778 Bilateral Treaty **535 UNTS 143**
SIGNED: 2 May 63 FORCE: 18 Jun 64
REGISTERED: 14 May 65 Austria
ARTICLES: 10 LANGUAGE: German. Bulgarian.
HEADNOTE: SETTLEMENT FINANCIAL QUESTIONS
TOPIC: Finance
CONCEPTS: Treaty implementation. General cooperation. Exchange of information and documents. Informational records. Juridical personality. Expropriation. General property. Responsibility and liability. General trade. Accounting procedures. Banking. Bonds. Interest rates. Payment schedules. Claims and settlements. Debts.

Debt settlement. Assets transfer. Loan and credit.
PROCEDURE: Ratification.
PARTIES:
Austria
Bulgaria

107779   Bilateral Exchange   **535 UNTS 191**
SIGNED: 20 Feb 65   FORCE: 20 Feb 65
REGISTERED: 17 May 65 United Nations
ARTICLES: 2 LANGUAGE: French.
HEADNOTE: SETTLING FINANCIAL QUESTION CONCERNING CONGO BASES
TOPIC: Finance
CONCEPTS: Accounting procedures. Expense sharing formulae. Claims and settlements. Materials, equipment and services.
PARTIES:
Belgium
United Nations

107780   Bilateral Exchange   **535 UNTS 197**
SIGNED: 20 Feb 65   FORCE: 17 May 65
REGISTERED: 17 May 65 United Nations
ARTICLES: 2 LANGUAGE: French.
HEADNOTE: CLAIM SETTLEMENT
TOPIC: Claims and Debts
CONCEPTS: Privileges and immunities. Exchange of information and documents. Financial programs. Payment schedules. Claims and settlements. Peace-keeping force.
PROCEDURE: Future Procedures Contemplated.
PARTIES:
Belgium
United Nations

107781   Bilateral Agreement   **535 UNTS 205**
SIGNED: 31 Jul 64   FORCE: 24 Dec 64
REGISTERED: 18 May 65 IDA (Devel Assoc)
ARTICLES: 6 LANGUAGE: English.
HEADNOTE: ROAD PROJECT
TOPIC: Non-IBRD Project
CONCEPTS: Annex or appendix reference. Financial programs. IDA development project. Roads and highways.
PARTIES:
IDA (Devel Assoc)
UK Great Britain

107782   Bilateral Agreement   **535 UNTS 225**
SIGNED: 29 Dec 64   FORCE: 30 Mar 65
REGISTERED: 18 May 65 IDA (Devel Assoc)
ARTICLES: 6 LANGUAGE: English.
HEADNOTE: DEVELOPMENT CREDIT HIGHWAY
TOPIC: Non-IBRD Project
CONCEPTS: Detailed regulations. Previous treaty amendment. Exchange of information and documents. Informational records. Accounting procedures. Currency. Interest rates. Tax exemptions. Credit provisions. Loan repayment. Terms of loan. Plans and standards. IDA development project. Roads and highways.
PARTIES:
Kenya
IDA (Devel Assoc)

107783   Bilateral Agreement   **535 UNTS 245**
SIGNED: 26 Oct 64   FORCE: 19 Nov 64
REGISTERED: 18 May 65 IDA (Devel Assoc)
ARTICLES: 6 LANGUAGE: English.
HEADNOTE: DEVELOPMENT CREDIT RAILWAY
TOPIC: Non-IBRD Project
CONCEPTS: Detailed regulations. Previous treaty amendment. Exchange of information and documents. Informational records. Accounting procedures. Currency. Interest rates. Tax exemptions. Credit provisions. Loan repayment. Terms of loan. Plans and standards. IDA development project.
PARTIES:
India
IDA (Devel Assoc)

107784   Bilateral Agreement   **535 UNTS 263**
SIGNED: 26 Aug 64   FORCE: 22 Oct 64
REGISTERED: 18 May 65 IDA (Devel Assoc)
ARTICLES: 7 LANGUAGE: English.

HEADNOTE: DEVELOPMENT CREDIT WATER TRANSPORT
TOPIC: Non-IBRD Project
CONCEPTS: Detailed regulations. Previous treaty amendment. Exchange of information and documents. Informational records. Accounting procedures. Currency. Interest rates. Tax exemptions. Credit provisions. Loan repayment. Terms of loan. Plans and standards. IDA development project. Natural resources.
PARTIES:
Pakistan
IDA (Devel Assoc)

107785   Bilateral Treaty   **535 UNTS 293**
SIGNED: 12 Feb 60   FORCE: 25 Mar 65
REGISTERED: 18 May 65 Philippines
ARTICLES: 15 LANGUAGE: English. Spanish.
HEADNOTE: FRIENDSHIP CULTURAL RELATIONS
TOPIC: General Amity
CONCEPTS: Friendship and amity. Alien status. Consular relations establishment. Diplomatic relations establishment. Privileges and immunities. Legal protection and assistance. Mediation and good offices. Procedure. Negotiation. Conciliation. General cultural cooperation.
PROCEDURE: Future Procedures Contemplated. Ratification.
PARTIES:
Argentina
Philippines

107786   Bilateral Agreement   **535 UNTS 307**
SIGNED: 18 Nov 64   FORCE: 18 Nov 64
REGISTERED: 21 May 65 USA (United States)
ARTICLES: 8 LANGUAGE: English. Russian.
HEADNOTE: COOPERATION FIELD DESALINATION INCLUDING USE ATOMIC ENERGY
TOPIC: Atomic Energy
CONCEPTS: Exchange of information and documents. Research cooperation. Research results. Nuclear research. Scientific exchange. Peaceful use.
INTL ORGS: International Atomic Energy Agency.
TREATY REF: 526UNTS131.
PROCEDURE: Duration. Renewal or Revival.
PARTIES:
USA (United States)
USSR (Soviet Union)

107787   Bilateral Agreement   **535 UNTS 315**
SIGNED: 31 Dec 64   FORCE: 31 Dec 64
REGISTERED: 21 May 65 USA (United States)
ARTICLES: 6 LANGUAGE: English.
HEADNOTE: AGRI COMMOD TITLE I
TOPIC: US Agri Commod Aid
CONCEPTS: General provisions. Annex or appendix reference. Exchange of information and documents. Reexport of goods, etc.. Exchange rates and regulations. Transportation costs. Local currency. Commodities schedule. Purchase authorization. Surplus commodities. Mutual consultation.
PARTIES:
Korea, South
USA (United States)

107788   Bilateral Exchange   **535 UNTS 331**
SIGNED: 5 Dec 64   FORCE: 5 Dec 64
REGISTERED: 21 May 65 USA (United States)
ARTICLES: 2 LANGUAGE: English.
HEADNOTE: RELEASE DRY DOCK FACILITIES
TOPIC: Milit Installation
CONCEPTS: Definition of terms. Treaty implementation. Inspection and observation. Responsibility and liability. Use of facilities. Compensation. Indemnities and reimbursements. Security of information. Bases and facilities.
PARTIES:
Trinidad/Tobago
USA (United States)

107789   Bilateral Exchange   **535 UNTS 343**
SIGNED: 18 Mar 64   FORCE: 18 Mar 64
REGISTERED: 21 May 65 USA (United States)
ARTICLES: 2 LANGUAGE: English. Spanish.
HEADNOTE: CULTURAL EXCHANGE FINANCING THEREOF
TOPIC: Culture

CONCEPTS: Conditions. Definition of terms. Previous treaty amendment. Previous treaty replacement. Conformity with municipal law. General cooperation. Inspection and observation. Operating agencies. General property. Responsibility and liability. Establishment of commission. Recognition of degrees. Exchange. Teacher and student exchange. General cultural cooperation. Research and development. Accounting procedures. Financial programs. Funding procedures. Local currency.
TREATY REF: 336UNTS153; 400UNTS405.
PROCEDURE: Amendment.
PARTIES:
Spain
USA (United States)

107790   Bilateral Exchange   **535 UNTS 359**
SIGNED: 23 Dec 64   FORCE: 23 Dec 64
REGISTERED: 21 May 65 USA (United States)
ARTICLES: 2 LANGUAGE: English. Romanian.
HEADNOTE: CULTURAL EDUCATIONAL SCIENTIFIC
TOPIC: Health/Educ/Welfare
CONCEPTS: International circulation. Specialists exchange. Exchange. General cultural cooperation. Artists. Athletes.
PARTIES:
Romania
USA (United States)

107791 Multilateral Agreement **535 UNTS 374**
SIGNED: 25 May 65   FORCE: 25 May 65
REGISTERED: 25 May 65 United Nations
ARTICLES: 6 LANGUAGE: English.
HEADNOTE: OPERATIONAL ASSISTANCE
TOPIC: IGO Operations
CONCEPTS: Previous treaty replacement. Diplomatic privileges. Diplomatic missions. Privileges and immunities. Arbitration. Procedure. Domestic obligation. Special status. Assistance to United Nations. Inter-agency agreements. IGO obligations.
INTL ORGS: Permanent Court of Arbitration. Arbitration Commission.
TREATY REF: 508UNTS.
PROCEDURE: Amendment. Termination.
PARTIES:
Nepal SIGNED: 25 May 65 FORCE: 25 May 65
FAO (Food Agri) SIGNED: 25 May 65 FORCE: 25 May 65
IAEA (Atom Energy) SIGNED: 25 May 65 FORCE: 25 May 65
ICAO (Civil Aviat) SIGNED: 25 May 65 FORCE: 25 May 65
ILO (Labor Org) SIGNED: 25 May 65 FORCE: 25 May 65
ITU (Telecommun) SIGNED: 25 May 65 FORCE: 25 May 65
UNESCO (Educ/Cult) SIGNED: 25 May 65 FORCE: 25 May 65
United Nations SIGNED: 25 May 65 FORCE: 25 May 65
UPU (Postal Union) SIGNED: 25 May 65 FORCE: 25 May 65
WHO (World Health) SIGNED: 25 May 65 FORCE: 25 May 65
WMO (Meteorology) SIGNED: 25 May 65 FORCE: 25 May 65
ANNEX
552 UNTS 424. UNTAB (Tech Assis). Amendment 17 Dec 65. Force 23 Dec 65.
552 UNTS 424. Nepal. Amendment 23 Dec 65. Force 23 Dec 65.

107792   Bilateral Agreement   **535 UNTS 393**
SIGNED: 14 Nov 63   FORCE: 14 Feb 65
REGISTERED: 26 May 65 Belgium
ARTICLES: 14 LANGUAGE: French. Dutch. English.
HEADNOTE: CULTURAL
TOPIC: Culture
CONCEPTS: Definition of terms. Friendship and amity. Conformity with municipal law. Specialists exchange. Recognition of degrees. Exchange. Teacher and student exchange. Institute establishment. Scholarships and grants. Vocational training. Exchange. General cultural cooperation. Artists. Athletes. Scientific exchange. Publications exchange. Mass media exchange.
PROCEDURE: Denunciation. Ratification.

PARTIES:
Belgium
Pakistan

107793 Bilateral Agreement **536 UNTS 3**
SIGNED: 20 Nov 63   FORCE: 2 Jun 64
REGISTERED: 1 Jun 65 United Nations
ARTICLES: 15 LANGUAGE: French.
HEADNOTE: SUB-REGIONAL OFFICE UNIECA
TOPIC: IGO Establishment
CONCEPTS: Default remedies. Treaty interpretation. Annex or appendix reference. Visa abolition. Inviolability. Privileges and immunities. Diplomatic correspondence. Exchange of information and documents. Dispute settlement. Existing tribunals. Customs exemptions. Commodities and services. Domestic obligation. Regional offices. Status of experts.
INTL ORGS: International Telecommunication Union.
PROCEDURE: Termination.
PARTIES:
Niger
United Nations

107794 Multilateral Convention **536 UNTS 27**
SIGNED: 17 Jun 60   FORCE: 17 Jun 60
REGISTERED: 2 Jun 65 IMCO (Maritime Org)
ARTICLES: 14 LANGUAGE: English. French.
HEADNOTE: SAFETY LIFE SEA
TOPIC: Humanitarian
CONCEPTS: Emergencies. Territorial application. Previous treaty replacement. Privileges and immunities. Exchange of information and documents. Humanitarian matters. Registration certificate. Navigational conditions. Merchant vessels. Repatriation of civilians.
INTL ORGS: Inter-Governmental Maritime Consultative Organization. United Nations.
TREATY REF: 164UNTS113.
PROCEDURE: Amendment. Accession. Denunciation. Registration.
PARTIES:
Algeria RATIFIED: 20 Jun 64 FORCE: 26 May 65
Argentina SIGNED: 17 Jun 60
Austria SIGNED: 17 Jun 60
Belgium SIGNED: 17 Jun 60
Brazil SIGNED: 17 Jun 60
Bulgaria SIGNED: 17 Jun 60
Cameroon SIGNED: 17 Jun 60
Canada   SIGNED: 17 Jun 60   RATIFIED: 26 May 65 FORCE: 26 May 65
Taiwan   SIGNED: 17 Jun 60   RATIFIED: 23 Feb 65 FORCE: 26 May 65
Denmark   SIGNED: 17 Jun 60   RATIFIED: 1 Dec 64 FORCE: 26 May 65
Dominican Republic SIGNED: 17 Jun 60
Finland   SIGNED: 17 Jun 60   RATIFIED: 11 May 65 FORCE: 26 May 65
France SIGNED: 17 Jun 60 RATIFIED: 16 Oct 61 FORCE: 26 May 65
Germany, West SIGNED: 17 Jun 60 RATIFIED: 25 May 65 FORCE: 26 May 65
Ghana RATIFIED: 22 Mar 62 FORCE: 26 May 65
Greece   SIGNED: 17 Jun 60   RATIFIED: 13 Feb 63 FORCE: 26 May 65
Haiti RATIFIED: 17 Mar 61 FORCE: 26 May 65
Hungary SIGNED: 17 Jun 60
Iceland   SIGNED: 17 Jun 60   RATIFIED: 11 Dec 64 FORCE: 26 May 65
India SIGNED: 17 Jun 60
Ireland SIGNED: 17 Jun 60
Israel SIGNED: 17 Jun 60
Italy SIGNED: 17 Jun 60
Japan SIGNED: 17 Jun 60 RATIFIED: 23 Apr 63 FORCE: 26 May 65
Korea, South SIGNED: 17 Jun 60 RATIFIED: 21 May 65 FORCE: 26 May 65
Kuwait   SIGNED: 17 Jun 60   RATIFIED: 14 May 65 FORCE: 26 May 65
Liberia   SIGNED: 17 Jun 60   RATIFIED: 23 May 65 FORCE: 26 May 65
Malagasy   RATIFIED: 13 Sep 62   FORCE: 26 May 65
Morocco   RATIFIED: 28 Nov 62   FORCE: 26 May 65
Netherlands SIGNED: 17 Jun 60 RATIFIED: 16 Oct 64 FORCE: 26 May 65
New Zealand SIGNED: 17 Jun 60
Norway   SIGNED: 17 Jun 60   RATIFIED: 23 Aug 61 FORCE: 26 May 65
Pakistan SIGNED: 17 Jun 60

Panama SIGNED: 17 Jun 60
Paraguay   RATIFIED: 11 Sep 63   FORCE: 26 May 65
Peru SIGNED: 17 Jun 60 RATIFIED: 25 Jul 62 FORCE: 26 May 65
Philippines SIGNED: 17 Jun 60
Portugal SIGNED: 17 Jun 60
Saudi Arabia RATIFIED: 3 May 65 FORCE: 26 May 65
Sweden SIGNED: 17 Jun 60
Switzerland SIGNED: 17 Jun 60
Tunisia RATIFIED: 20 May 63 FORCE: 26 May 65
United Arab Rep SIGNED: 17 Jun 60
UK Great Britain SIGNED: 17 Jun 60 RATIFIED: 11 Jun 64 FORCE: 26 May 65
USA (United States) SIGNED: 17 Jun 60 RATIFIED: 2 Aug 62 FORCE: 26 May 65
USSR (Soviet Union) SIGNED: 17 Jun 60
Venezuela SIGNED: 17 Jun 60
Vietnam, South RATIFIED: 8 Jan 62 FORCE: 26 May 65
Yugoslavia   SIGNED: 17 Jun 60   RATIFIED: 23 Feb 65 FORCE: 26 May 65
ANNEX
541 UNTS 366. Burma. Acceptance 12 Jul 65. Force 12 Oct 65.
543 UNTS 379. Malaysia. Acceptance 16 Aug 65. Force 16 Nov 65.
543 UNTS 379. United Arab Rep. Qualified Acceptance 27 Jul 65. Force 27 Oct 65.
543 UNTS 379. Philippines. Acceptance 11 Aug 65. Force 11 Nov 65.
543 UNTS 379. Cyprus. Acceptance 26 Jul 65. Force 26 Oct 65.
544 UNTS 386. USSR (Soviet Union). Acceptance 4 Aug 65. Force 4 Nov 65.
547 UNTS 363. Panama. Acceptance 12 Oct 65. Force 12 Jan 66.
547 UNTS 363. Israel. Acceptance 5 Oct 65. Force 5 Jan 66.
547 UNTS 363. Ivory Coast. Acceptance 2 Nov 65. Force 2 Feb 66.
548 UNTS 373. Ivory Coast. Acceptance 2 Nov 65. Force 2 Feb 66.
549 UNTS 354. Nigeria. Acceptance 30 Nov 65. Force 28 Feb 66.
552 UNTS 425. Sweden. Acceptance 23 Dec 65. Force 23 Mar 66.
552 UNTS 425. Switzerland. Acceptance 12 Jan 66. Force 12 Apr 66.
556 UNTS 203. New Zealand. Acceptance 14 Feb 66. Force 14 May 66.
556 UNTS 203. Belgium. Acceptance 10 Feb 66. Force 10 May 66.
559 UNTS 372. India. Acceptance 28 Feb 66. Force 28 May 66.
559 UNTS 372. Pakistan. Qualified Acceptance 24 Feb 66. Force 24 May 66.
561 UNTS 356. Lebanon. Acceptance 27 Apr 66. Force 27 Jul 66.
561 UNTS 356. Poland. Acceptance 29 Apr 66. Force 29 Jul 66.
561 UNTS 356. Argentina. Acceptance 27 Apr 66. Force 27 Jul 66.
561 UNTS 356. Lebanon. Acceptance 27 Apr 66. Force 27 Jul 66.
561 UNTS 356. Poland. Acceptance 29 Apr 66. Force 29 Jul 66.
561 UNTS 356. Argentina. Acceptance 27 Apr 66. Force 27 Jul 66.
565 UNTS 324. Mexico. Acceptance 22 Jun 66. Force 22 Sep 66.
565 UNTS 324. Portugal. Qualified Acceptance 14 Jun 66. Force 14 Sep 66.
572 UNTS 366. Chile. Acceptance 7 Sep 66. Force 7 Dec 66.
572 UNTS 366. Trinidad/Tobago. Acceptance 6 Sep 66. Force 6 Dec 66.
601 UNTS 361. Czechoslovakia. Acceptance 5 Jul 67. Force 5 Oct 67.
607 UNTS 352. Nicaragua. Acceptance 9 Oct 67. Force 9 Jan 68.
609 UNTS 327. Bulgaria. Acceptance 16 Oct 67. Force 16 Jan 68.
614 UNTS 330. Mauritania. Acceptance 4 Dec 67. Force 4 Mar 68.
614 UNTS 330. South Africa. Acceptance 13 Dec 67. Force 13 Mar 68.
616 UNTS 505. Australia. Acceptance 20 Dec 67. Force 20 Mar 68.
620 UNTS 325. Maldive Islands. Acceptance 29 Jan 68. Force 29 Apr 68.
645 UNTS 374. Guinea. Signature 17 Jun 60. Force 19 Dec 68.

646 UNTS 410. Uruguay. Acceptance 19 Sep 68. Force 19 Dec 68.
659 UNTS 378. Singapore. Acceptance 12 Feb 69. Force 12 May 69.
659 UNTS 378. Venezuela. Acceptance 23 Jan 69. Force 23 Apr 69.
659 UNTS 378. Honduras. Acceptance 18 Feb 69. Force 18 May 69.

107795 Bilateral Agreement **537 UNTS 3**
SIGNED: 7 Jul 64   FORCE: 19 Jan 65
REGISTERED: 2 Jun 65 IBRD (World Bank)
ARTICLES: 5 LANGUAGE: English.
HEADNOTE: GUARANTEE AGREEMENT
TOPIC: IBRD Project
CONCEPTS: Definition of terms. Annex or appendix reference. Exchange of information and documents. Inspection and observation. Bonds. Fees and exemptions. Tax exemptions. Domestic obligation. Terms of loan. Loan regulations. Loan guarantee. Guarantor non-interference.
PARTIES:
Nigeria
IBRD (World Bank)

107796 Bilateral Agreement **537 UNTS 35**
SIGNED: 12 Feb 65   FORCE: 23 Apr 65
REGISTERED: 2 Jun 65 IBRD (World Bank)
ARTICLES: 5 LANGUAGE: English.
HEADNOTE: GUARANTEE POWER
TOPIC: IBRD Project
CONCEPTS: Definition of terms. Annex or appendix reference. Exchange of information and documents. Inspection and observation. Bonds. Fees and exemptions. Tax exemptions. Domestic obligation. Terms of loan. Loan regulations. Loan guarantee. Guarantor non-interference. Hydroelectric power.
PARTIES:
Chile
IBRD (World Bank)

107797 Bilateral Agreement **537 UNTS 63**
SIGNED: 10 Jul 64   FORCE: 9 Feb 65
REGISTERED: 2 Jun 65 IBRD (World Bank)
ARTICLES: 7 LANGUAGE: English.
HEADNOTE: LOAN ROAD
TOPIC: IBRD Project
CONCEPTS: Default remedies. Definition of terms. Annex or appendix reference. Exchange of information and documents. Informational records. Inspection and observation. Accounting procedures. Bonds. Fees and exemptions. Interest rates. Tax exemptions. Domestic obligation. Terms of loan. Loan regulations. Loan guarantee. Guarantor non-interference. Roads and highways.
PARTIES:
Gabon
IBRD (World Bank)

107798 Bilateral Agreement **537 UNTS 81**
SIGNED: 31 Jul 64   FORCE: 25 Feb 65
REGISTERED: 2 Jun 65 IBRD (World Bank)
ARTICLES: 5 LANGUAGE: English.
HEADNOTE: GUARANTEE RAILWAY
TOPIC: IBRD Project
CONCEPTS: Definition of terms. Annex or appendix reference. Exchange of information and documents. Inspection and observation. Bonds. Fees and exemptions. Liens. Domestic obligation. Terms of loan. Loan regulations. Loan guarantee. Guarantor non-interference. Railways.
PARTIES:
IBRD (World Bank)
Spain

107799 Bilateral Agreement **537 UNTS 111**
SIGNED: 10 Jun 64   FORCE: 11 May 65
REGISTERED: 2 Jun 65 IBRD (World Bank)
ARTICLES: 7 LANGUAGE: English.
HEADNOTE: LOAN ROAD
TOPIC: IBRD Project
CONCEPTS: Default remedies. Definition of terms. Annex or appendix reference. Exchange of information and documents. Informational records. Inspection and observation. Accounting procedures. Bonds. Fees and exemptions. Tax exemptions. Domestic obligation. Terms of loan. Loan

regulations. Loan guarantee. Guarantor non-interference. Roads and highways.
TREATY REF: 348UNTS103.
PARTIES:
Iran
IBRD (World Bank)

107800 Bilateral Agreement **537 UNTS 135**
SIGNED: 28 Aug 64   FORCE: 24 Dec 64
REGISTERED: 2 Jun 65 IBRD (World Bank)
ARTICLES: 5 LANGUAGE: English.
HEADNOTE: GUARANTEE POWER TRANSMISSION
TOPIC: IBRD Project
CONCEPTS: Definition of terms. Annex or appendix reference. Exchange of information and documents. Inspection and observation. Bonds. Fees and exemptions. Tax exemptions. Domestic obligation. Terms of loan. Loan regulations. Loan guarantee. Guarantor non-interference. Hydroelectric power.
PARTIES:
IBRD (World Bank)
Venezuela

107801 Bilateral Agreement **537 UNTS 165**
SIGNED: 28 Oct 64   FORCE: 1 Feb 65
REGISTERED: 2 Jun 65 IBRD (World Bank)
ARTICLES: 8 LANGUAGE: English.
HEADNOTE: LOAN EDUCATION
TOPIC: IBRD Project
CONCEPTS: Default remedies. Definition of terms. Annex or appendix reference. Exchange of information and documents. Informational records. Inspection and observation. Exchange. Accounting procedures. Bonds. Fees and exemptions. Interest rates. Tax exemptions. Domestic obligation. Terms of loan. Loan regulations. Loan guarantee. Guarantor non-interference.
PARTIES:
Philippines
IBRD (World Bank)

107802 Bilateral Agreement **537 UNTS 193**
SIGNED: 26 Aug 64   FORCE: 9 Apr 65
REGISTERED: 2 Jun 65 IBRD (World Bank)
ARTICLES: 7 LANGUAGE: English.
HEADNOTE: LOAN AGRICULTURE DEVELOPMENT
TOPIC: IBRD Project
CONCEPTS: Default remedies. Definition of terms. Annex or appendix reference. Exchange of information and documents. Informational records. Inspection and observation. Accounting procedures. Bonds. Fees and exemptions. Interest rates. Tax exemptions. Domestic obligation. Agriculture. Terms of loan. Loan regulations. Loan guarantee. Guarantor non-interference.
PARTIES:
Morocco
IBRD (World Bank)

107803 Multilateral Agreement **537 UNTS 214**
SIGNED: 19 Jun 60   FORCE: 9 Aug 60
REGISTERED: 4 Jun 65 United Nations
ARTICLES: 6 LANGUAGE: English.
HEADNOTE: TECHNICAL ASSISTANCE
TOPIC: IGO Operations
CONCEPTS: Definition of terms. Previous treaty replacement. Privileges and immunities. Specialists exchange. Scholarships and grants. Funding procedures. Domestic obligation. General technical assistance. IGO obligations. Inter-agency agreements. Vocational training.
TREATY REF: 15NTS15; 33UNTSI61.
PROCEDURE: Amendment. Termination.
PARTIES:
Iraq SIGNED: 19 Jun 60 RATIFIED: 9 Aug 60
  FORCE: 9 Aug 60
FAO (Food Agri) SIGNED: 19 Jun 60 FORCE: 9 Aug 60
IAEA (Atom Energy) SIGNED: 19 Jun 60 FORCE: 9 Aug 60
ICAO (Civil Aviat) SIGNED: 19 Jun 60 FORCE: 9 Aug 60
ILO (Labor Org) SIGNED: 19 Jun 60 FORCE: 9 Aug 60
ITU (Telecommun) SIGNED: 19 Jun 60 FORCE: 9 Aug 60
UNESCO (Educ/Cult) SIGNED: 19 Jun 60 FORCE: 9 Aug 60

United Nations SIGNED: 19 Jun 60 FORCE: 9 Aug 60
WHO (World Health) SIGNED: 19 Jun 60 FORCE: 9 Aug 60
WMO (Meteorology) SIGNED: 19 Jun 60 FORCE: 9 Aug 60
ANNEX
550 UNTS 424. Iraq. Amendment 1 Dec 65. Force 1 Dec 65.
550 UNTS 424. United Nations. Amendment 14 Jul 65. Force 1 Dec 65.

107804 Bilateral Agreement **537 UNTS 231**
SIGNED: 24 Apr 64   FORCE: 6 May 65
REGISTERED: 4 Jun 65 Finland
ARTICLES: 22 LANGUAGE: Finnish. Russian.
HEADNOTE: CONCERNING FRONTIER WATERCOURSES
TOPIC: Territory Boundary
CONCEPTS: Previous treaty replacement. Inspection and observation. Establishment of commission. Procedure. Customs exemptions. Reparations and restrictions. Fish, wildlife, and natural resources. Frontier waterways. Regulation of natural resources.
INTL ORGS: Special Commission.
TREATY REF: 379UNTS277; 19LTS183.
PROCEDURE: Duration. Ratification. Renewal or Revival. Termination.
PARTIES:
Finland
USSR (Soviet Union)

107805 Bilateral Agreement **537 UNTS 273**
SIGNED: 25 Nov 64   FORCE: 3 Feb 65
REGISTERED: 7 Jun 65 IBRD (World Bank)
ARTICLES: 8 LANGUAGE: English.
HEADNOTE: LOAN IRRIGATION
TOPIC: IBRD Project
CONCEPTS: Default remedies. Definition of terms. Annex or appendix reference. Exchange of information and documents. Informational records. Inspection and observation. Accounting procedures. Bonds. Fees and exemptions. Interest rates. Tax exemptions. Domestic obligation. Terms of loan. Loan regulations. Loan guarantee. Guarantor non-interference. Irrigation.
PARTIES:
IBRD (World Bank)
Thailand

107806 Bilateral Agreement **537 UNTS 293**
SIGNED: 13 Jan 65   FORCE: 26 Mar 65
REGISTERED: 7 Jun 65 IBRD (World Bank)
ARTICLES: 5 LANGUAGE: English.
HEADNOTE: GUARANTEE AGREEMENT
TOPIC: IBRD Project
CONCEPTS: Definition of terms. Annex or appendix reference. Exchange of information and documents. Inspection and observation. Bonds. Fees and exemptions. Tax exemptions. Domestic obligation. Terms of loan. Loan regulations. Loan guarantee. Guarantor non-interference.
PARTIES:
Japan
IBRD (World Bank)

107807 Bilateral Agreement **537 UNTS 321**
SIGNED: 11 Dec 64   FORCE: 12 Feb 65
REGISTERED: 7 Jun 65 IBRD (World Bank)
ARTICLES: 5 LANGUAGE: English.
HEADNOTE: GUARANTEE RAILWAY
TOPIC: IBRD Project
CONCEPTS: Definition of terms. Exchange of information and documents. Inspection and observation. Bonds. Fees and exemptions. Tax exemptions. Domestic obligation. Terms of loan. Loan regulations. Loan guarantee. Guarantor non-interference. Railways.
PARTIES:
IBRD (World Bank)
Yugoslavia

107808 Bilateral Agreement **538 UNTS 3**
SIGNED: 17 Dec 64   FORCE: 17 Feb 65
REGISTERED: 7 Jun 65 IBRD (World Bank)
ARTICLES: 5 LANGUAGE: English.
HEADNOTE: GUARANTEE AGREEMENT
TOPIC: IBRD Project

CONCEPTS: Definition of terms. Annex or appendix reference. Exchange of information and documents. Inspection and observation. Bonds. Fees and exemptions. Tax exemptions. Domestic obligation. Terms of loan. Loan regulations. Loan guarantee. Guarantor non-interference.
PARTIES:
Taiwan
IBRD (World Bank)

107809 Bilateral Agreement **538 UNTS 37**
SIGNED: 23 Dec 64   FORCE: 25 Feb 65
REGISTERED: 7 Jun 65 IBRD (World Bank)
ARTICLES: 5 LANGUAGE: English.
HEADNOTE: GUARANTEE EXPRESSWAY
TOPIC: IBRD Project
CONCEPTS: Definition of terms. Annex or appendix reference. Exchange of information and documents. Inspection and observation. Bonds. Fees and exemptions. Tax exemptions. Domestic obligation. Terms of loan. Loan regulations. Loan guarantee. Guarantor non-interference. Roads and highways.
PARTIES:
Japan
IBRD (World Bank)

107810 Bilateral Agreement **538 UNTS 63**
SIGNED: 22 Mar 65   FORCE: 27 Apr 65
REGISTERED: 7 Jun 65 IBRD (World Bank)
ARTICLES: 5 LANGUAGE: English.
HEADNOTE: GUARANTEE AGREEMENT
TOPIC: IBRD Project
CONCEPTS: Definition of terms. Annex or appendix reference. Exchange of information and documents. Inspection and observation. Bonds. Fees and exemptions. Tax exemptions. Domestic obligation. Terms of loan. Loan regulations. Loan guarantee. Guarantor non-interference.
PARTIES:
IBRD (World Bank)
Thailand

107811 Bilateral Agreement **538 UNTS 89**
SIGNED: 21 Mar 58   FORCE: 7 Aug 58
REGISTERED: 11 Jun 65 Czechoslovakia
ARTICLES: 15 LANGUAGE: Czechoslovakian. Polish.
HEADNOTE: USE WATER RESOURCES FRONTIER WATERS
TOPIC: Specific Resources
CONCEPTS: Definition of terms. Annex or appendix reference. Previous treaty replacement. General cooperation. Operating agencies. Customs exemptions. Materials, equipment and services. Frontier waterways. Regulation of natural resources.
TREATY REF: 100LTS273.
PROCEDURE: Denunciation. Duration. Renewal or Revival.
PARTIES:
Czechoslovakia
Poland

107812 Bilateral Treaty **538 UNTS 127**
SIGNED: 20 Dec 63   FORCE: 25 Oct 64
REGISTERED: 11 Jun 65 Czechoslovakia
ARTICLES: 23 LANGUAGE: Czechoslovakian. Hungarian.
HEADNOTE: TRADE NAVIGATION
TOPIC: General Economic
CONCEPTS: Detailed regulations. General provisions. Privileges and immunities. Conformity with municipal law. Juridical personality. Free passage and transit. Legal protection and assistance. Licenses and permits. Recognition of legal documents. Certificates of origin. Non-interest rates and fees. Most favored nation clause. National treatment. General. Patents, copyrights and trademarks. Recognition. Customs duties. Customs declarations. Customs exemptions. General technical assistance. Aid missions. Licenses and certificates of nationality. Inland and territorial waters. Shipwreck and salvage.
PROCEDURE: Denunciation. Duration. Ratification.
PARTIES:
Czechoslovakia
Hungary

107813 Bilateral Agreement **538 UNTS 155**
SIGNED: 21 Dec 63 FORCE: 21 Dec 63
REGISTERED: 14 Jun 65 Greece
ARTICLES: 19 LANGUAGE: English.
HEADNOTE: TRADE
TOPIC: Air Transport
CONCEPTS: Exceptions and exemptions. Treaty implementation. Annex or appendix reference. Conformity with municipal law. General cooperation. Licenses and permits. Export quotas. Import quotas. Trade agencies. Currency. Payment schedules. Non-interest rates and fees. Most favored nation clause. Merchant vessels.
INTL ORGS: International Civil Aviation Organization.
TREATY REF: 15UNTSI95.
PROCEDURE: Denunciation. Duration. Renewal or Revival.
PARTIES:
Greece
Poland

107814 Bilateral Agreement **538 UNTS 175**
SIGNED: 17 Jan 63 FORCE: 17 Jan 63
REGISTERED: 14 Jun 65 Greece
ARTICLES: 9 LANGUAGE: English.
HEADNOTE: TRADE
TOPIC: General Trade
CONCEPTS: Exceptions and exemptions. Annex or appendix reference. General cooperation. Licenses and permits. Export quotas. Import quotas. Trade procedures. Currency. Payment schedules. Most favored nation clause. Merchant vessels. Ports and pilotage.
INTL ORGS: General Agreement on Tariffs and Trade.
TREATY REF: 55UNTS187.
PROCEDURE: Duration.
PARTIES:
Greece
Pakistan

107815 Bilateral Agreement **538 UNTS 185**
SIGNED: 29 Oct 62 FORCE: 29 Oct 62
REGISTERED: 14 Jun 65 Greece
ARTICLES: 11 LANGUAGE: French.
HEADNOTE: TRADE
TOPIC: General Trade
CONCEPTS: Establishment of trade relations. Export quotas. Import quotas. Currency. National treatment.
PROCEDURE: Denunciation. Duration.
PARTIES:
Cameroon
Greece

107816 Bilateral Treaty **538 UNTS 197**
SIGNED: 20 Jan 64 FORCE: 2 Aug 64
REGISTERED: 14 Jun 65 Czechoslovakia
ARTICLES: 85 LANGUAGE: Czechoslovakian. Serbo-Croat.
HEADNOTE: LEGAL RELATIONS CIVIL FAMILY CRIMINAL CASES
TOPIC: Admin Cooperation
CONCEPTS: Previous treaty replacement. Privileges and immunities. Consular functions in property. Extradition requests. Refusal of extradition. Concurrent requests. Limits of prosecution. Provisional detainment. Extradition postponement. Witnesses and experts. Material evidence. Family law. Exchange of information and documents. Juridical personality. Legal protection and assistance. Recognition and enforcement of legal decisions. General property. Succession. Recognition of legal documents. Indemnities and reimbursements. Fees and exemptions. Assets transfer. Conveyance in transit.
TREATY REF: 45LTS107.
PROCEDURE: Denunciation. Duration. Ratification.
PARTIES:
Czechoslovakia
Yugoslavia

107817 Bilateral Agreement **538 UNTS 301**
SIGNED: 14 May 64 FORCE: 15 Sep 64
REGISTERED: 14 Jun 65 Czechoslovakia
ARTICLES: 14 LANGUAGE: French.
HEADNOTE: CULTURAL COOPERATION
TOPIC: Culture
CONCEPTS: Treaty implementation. Friendship and amity. Dispute settlement. Specialists exchange. Recognition of degrees. Exchange. Teacher and student exchange. Scholarships and grants. Exchange. General cultural cooperation. Artists. Athletes. Scientific exchange. Recognition. Publications exchange. Mass media exchange. Press and wire services.
PROCEDURE: Denunciation. Duration. Ratification.
PARTIES:
Algeria
Czechoslovakia

107818 Multilateral Agreement **538 UNTS 309**
SIGNED: 9 Jun 63 FORCE: 25 Jun 63
REGISTERED: 14 Jun 65 Greece
ARTICLES: 17 LANGUAGE: English.
HEADNOTE: STABILIZATION RAISIN MARKETS
TOPIC: General Economic
CONCEPTS: Establishment of commission. Arbitration. Procedure. Trade procedures. Commodity trade. Quotas.
INTL ORGS: Food and Agricultural Organization of the United Nations. Arbitration Commission. Special Commission.
PROCEDURE: Duration. Renewal or Revival.
PARTIES:
Australia SIGNED: 9 Jun 63 FORCE: 25 Jun 63
Greece SIGNED: 9 Jun 63 FORCE: 25 Jun 63
Turkey SIGNED: 9 Jun 63 FORCE: 25 Jun 63

107819 Multilateral Agreement **539 UNTS 3**
SIGNED: 20 Jun 64 FORCE: 15 Jul 64
REGISTERED: 14 Jun 65 Greece
ARTICLES: 16 LANGUAGE: English.
HEADNOTE: STABILIZATION RAISIN MARKETS
TOPIC: General Economic
CONCEPTS: Previous treaty replacement. Establishment of commission. Arbitration. Procedure. Reexport of goods, etc.. Trade procedures. Non-interest rates and fees. Commodity trade.
INTL ORGS: Special Commission.
TREATY REF: 538UNTS.
PROCEDURE: Duration. Renewal or Revival.
PARTIES:
Australia SIGNED: 20 Jun 64 FORCE: 15 Jul 64
Greece SIGNED: 20 Jun 64 FORCE: 15 Jul 64
Turkey SIGNED: 20 Jun 64 FORCE: 15 Jul 64

107820 Bilateral Agreement **539 UNTS 13**
SIGNED: 5 Nov 64 FORCE: 12 Apr 65
REGISTERED: 14 Jun 65 Greece
ARTICLES: 7 LANGUAGE: French.
HEADNOTE: EXCHANGE LAND HOLDING ACROSS FRONTIER
TOPIC: Territory Boundary
CONCEPTS: Previous treaties adherence. Currency. Payment schedules. Changes of territory.
TREATY REF: 388UNTS3; 483UNTS355.
PARTIES:
Greece
Yugoslavia

107821 Bilateral Agreement **539 UNTS 19**
SIGNED: 5 Nov 64 FORCE: 12 Apr 65
REGISTERED: 14 Jun 65 Greece
ARTICLES: 8 LANGUAGE: French.
HEADNOTE: CERTAIN QUESTIONS ROAD TRANSPORT
TOPIC: Land Transport
CONCEPTS: Frontier formalities. Tax exemptions. Customs exemptions. Routes and logistics. Transport of goods. Operating authorizations and regulations. Commercial road vehicles. Roads and highways. Road rules.
TREATY REF: 368UNTS27; 327UNTS123; 338UNTS103; 348UNTS13.
PROCEDURE: Denunciation. Duration. Ratification. Renewal or Revival.
PARTIES:
Greece
Yugoslavia

107822 Multilateral Convention **539 UNTS 27**
SIGNED: 15 Apr 58 FORCE: 1 Jan 62
REGISTERED: 16 Jun 65 Netherlands
ARTICLES: 19 LANGUAGE: French.
HEADNOTE: MAINTENANCE OBLIGATIONS TOWARD CHILDREN
TOPIC: Health/Educ/Welfare
CONCEPTS: Territorial application. Exchange of information and documents. Domestic legislation. Recognition and enforcement of legal decisions. Responsibility and liability. Investigation of violations.
PROCEDURE: Accession. Denunciation. Duration. Ratification. Renewal or Revival.
PARTIES:
Austria SIGNED: 15 Apr 58 RATIFIED: 5 Sep 60 FORCE: 1 Jan 62
Belgium SIGNED: 11 Jul 58 RATIFIED: 15 Sep 61 FORCE: 1 Jan 62
France SIGNED: 6 Jan 65
Germany, East SIGNED: 8 Oct 58 RATIFIED: 2 Nov 61 FORCE: 1 Jan 62
Greece SIGNED: 15 Apr 58
Hungary RATIFIED: 20 Oct 64 FORCE: 19 Dec 64
Italy SIGNED: 8 Oct 58 FORCE: 1 Jan 62
Luxembourg SIGNED: 14 Mar 62
Netherlands Netherlands Antilles RATIFIED: 28 Feb 64 FORCE: 15 Jun 64
Netherlands SIGNED: 25 May 59 RATIFIED: 28 Feb 64 FORCE: 28 Apr 64
Netherlands Surinam RATIFIED: 27 May 64 FORCE: 1 Sep 64
Norway SIGNED: 19 May 58
Switzerland SIGNED: 4 Jul 63 RATIFIED: 18 Nov 64 FORCE: 17 Jan 65
ANNEX
659 UNTS 380.
659 UNTS 380. Denmark. Acceptance 7 Nov 66. Force 5 Jan 67.
659 UNTS 380. Sweden. Acceptance 5 Jun 68. Force 3 Aug 68.
659 UNTS 380. Austria. Acceptance 11 Jun 68. Force 9 Aug 68.
659 UNTS 380. Netherlands. Netherlands Antilles. Acceptance 3 Jan 68. Force 2 Mar 68.
659 UNTS 380. Austria. Acceptance 13 Aug 68. Force 11 Oct 68.
659 UNTS 380. Netherlands. Surinam. Acceptance 3 Jan 68. Force 2 Mar 69.

107823 Bilateral Agreement **539 UNTS 45**
SIGNED: 16 Jun 65 FORCE: 16 Jun 65
REGISTERED: 16 Jun 65 United Nations
ARTICLES: 10 LANGUAGE: English.
HEADNOTE: PREVENTION CRIME CONGRESS
TOPIC: Admin Cooperation
CONCEPTS: Succession. Subsidiary organ.
PARTIES:
United Nations
Sweden

107824 Bilateral Exchange **539 UNTS 59**
SIGNED: 31 Mar 65 FORCE: 14 Apr 65
REGISTERED: 16 Jun 65 Jamaica
ARTICLES: 2 LANGUAGE: English.
HEADNOTE: PERSONNEL ASSIST TRAINING DEVELOPMENT
TOPIC: Military Mission
CONCEPTS: Annex or appendix reference. Military assistance. Military training. Airforce-army-navy personnel ratio. Ranks and privileges. Conditions for assistance missions.
PARTIES:
Jamaica
UK Great Britain

107825 Multilateral Agreement **539 UNTS 67**
SIGNED: 26 Mar 62 FORCE: 10 Jun 65
REGISTERED: 18 Jun 65 UNESCO (Educ/Cult)
ARTICLES: 14 LANGUAGE: Spanish. French. Portuguese.
HEADNOTE: LATIN AMERICA PHYSICS CENTER
TOPIC: IGO Establishment
CONCEPTS: Juridical personality. Commissions and foundations. Teacher and student exchange. Research and scientific projects. Research cooperation. Scientific exchange. Admission. Establishment. Headquarters and facilities. Internal structure. Special status.
INTL ORGS: United Nations Educational, Scientific and Cultural Organization.
PROCEDURE: Amendment. Accession. Denunciation. Registration.
PARTIES:
Argentina SIGNED: 9 Apr 64 FORCE: 10 Jun 65
Bolivia SIGNED: 26 Mar 62 FORCE: 10 Jun 65

Brazil SIGNED: 26 Mar 62 RATIFIED: 11 Aug 64
FORCE: 10 Jun 65
Chile SIGNED: 26 Mar 62 FORCE: 10 Jun 65
Colombia SIGNED: 26 Mar 62 FORCE:
10 Jun 65
Cuba SIGNED: 26 Mar 62 RATIFIED: 26 Mar 62
FORCE: 10 Jun 65
Ecuador SIGNED: 26 Mar 62 RATIFIED:
24 Jan 64 FORCE: 10 Jun 65
Haiti SIGNED: 26 Mar 62 FORCE: 10 Jun 65
Honduras SIGNED: 26 Mar 62 FORCE:
10 Jun 65
Mexico SIGNED: 26 Mar 62 RATIFIED: 28 Jul 64
FORCE: 10 Jun 65
Nicaragua SIGNED: 26 Mar 62 RATIFIED:
10 Jun 65 FORCE: 10 Jun 65
Panama SIGNED: 26 Mar 62 FORCE: 10 Jun 65
Paraguay SIGNED: 26 Mar 62 FORCE: 10 Jun 65
Peru SIGNED: 26 Mar 62 RATIFIED: 25 Nov 64
FORCE: 10 Jun 65
Uruguay SIGNED: 26 Mar 62 FORCE: 10 Jun 65
Venezuela SIGNED: 26 Mar 62 FORCE:
10 Jun 65
ANNEX
631 UNTS 356. Chile. Acceptance 7 Feb 68.
657 UNTS 403.

107826 Bilateral Agreement **539 UNTS 103**
SIGNED: 25 Mar 65 FORCE: 25 Mar 65
REGISTERED: 18 Jun 65 Finland
ARTICLES: 16 LANGUAGE: Finnish. English.
HEADNOTE: AIR SERVICES
TOPIC: Air Transport
CONCEPTS: Definition of terms. Detailed regulations. Exceptions and exemptions. Annex or appendix reference. General cooperation. Exchange of information and documents. Arbitra-
tion. Procedure. Special tribunals. Negotiation.
Reexport of goods, etc.. Monetary and gold
transfers. Exchange rates and regulations. Fees
and exemptions. Non-interest rates and fees.
Customs exemptions. Routes and logistics. Per-
mit designation. Conditions of airlines operating
permission. Overflights and technical stops. Operating authorizations and regulations.
INTL ORGS: Inter-Governmental Maritime Consultative Organization. Arbitration Commission.
TREATY REF: 15UNTS295.
PROCEDURE: Amendment. Future Procedures
Contemplated. Termination. Application to Non-
self-governing Territories.
PARTIES:
Finland
UK Great Britain

107827 Bilateral Agreement **539 UNTS 129**
SIGNED: 5 Jun 64 FORCE: 9 Jun 65
REGISTERED: 18 Jun 65 IBRD (World Bank)
ARTICLES: 8 LANGUAGE: English.
HEADNOTE: LOAN POST
TOPIC: IBRD Project
CONCEPTS: Default remedies. Definition of terms.
Annex or appendix reference. Exchange of infor-
mation and documents. Informational records.
Inspection and observation. Bonds. Currency de-
posits. Fees and exemptions. Tax exemptions.
Domestic obligation. Terms of loan. Loan regula-
tions. Loan guarantee. Guarantor non-interfer-
ence. Water transport.
PARTIES:
IBRD (World Bank)
Tunisia

107828 Bilateral Exchange **539 UNTS 153**
SIGNED: 26 Sep 64 FORCE: 30 Sep 64
REGISTERED: 18 Jun 65 UK Great Britain
ARTICLES: 2 LANGUAGE: English. Polish.
HEADNOTE: RIGHTS POLISH VESSELS WITHIN
BRITISH FISHERY LIMITS
TOPIC: Specific Property
CONCEPTS: Visa abolition. Facilities and property.
Fish, wildlife, and natural resources. Wildlife.
PARTIES:
Poland
UK Great Britain

107829 Bilateral Exchange **539 UNTS 159**
SIGNED: 30 Sep 64 FORCE: 30 Sep 64
REGISTERED: 18 Jun 65 UK Great Britain
ARTICLES: 2 LANGUAGE: English. Russian.

HEADNOTE: ESTABLISHMENT FISHERY REGIME
TOPIC: Specific Property
CONCEPTS: Facilities and property. Fish, wildlife,
and natural resources. Frontier crossing points.
PROCEDURE: Duration. Termination.
PARTIES:
UK Great Britain
USSR (Soviet Union)

107830 Bilateral Convention **539 UNTS 167**
SIGNED: 7 Apr 64 FORCE: 7 Apr 64
REGISTERED: 18 Jun 65 UK Great Britain
ARTICLES: 13 LANGUAGE: English. Portuguese.
HEADNOTE: CONSTRUCTION CONNECTING RAIL-
WAYS BETWEEN SWAZILAND MOZAMBIQUE
TOPIC: Land Transport
CONCEPTS: Change of circumstances. Time limit.
Treaty implementation. Arbitration. Procedure.
Competence of tribunal. Reexport of goods, etc..
Fees and exemptions. Non-interest rates and
fees. Tax exemptions. Materials, equipment and
services. Routes and logistics. Operating authori-
zations and regulations. Ports and pilotage. Rail-
ways.
INTL ORGS: Arbitration Commission.
PROCEDURE: Amendment. Denunciation. Dura-
tion. Termination.
PARTIES:
Portugal
UK Great Britain

107831 Bilateral Agreement **539 UNTS 187**
SIGNED: 9 Jun 64 FORCE: 9 Jun 64
REGISTERED: 18 Jun 65 UK Great Britain
ARTICLES: 5 LANGUAGE: English. German.
HEADNOTE: AGREEMENT COMPENSATION
TOPIC: Reparations
CONCEPTS: Territorial application. Lump sum set-
tlements. Loss and/or damage. Reparations and
restrictions. Post-war claims settlement.
PARTIES:
Germany, West
UK Great Britain

107832 Bilateral Exchange **539 UNTS 197**
SIGNED: 13 Apr 64 FORCE: 13 Apr 64
REGISTERED: 18 Jun 65 UK Great Britain
ARTICLES: 2 LANGUAGE: English. Russian.
HEADNOTE: MUTUAL ABOLITION VISA FEES
TOPIC: Visas
CONCEPTS: Visas. Fees and exemptions.
PROCEDURE: Denunciation.
PARTIES:
UK Great Britain
USSR (Soviet Union)

107833 Bilateral Exchange **539 UNTS 203**
SIGNED: 30 Jun 64 FORCE: 30 Jun 64
REGISTERED: 18 Jun 65 UK Great Britain
ARTICLES: 2 LANGUAGE: English. Danish.
HEADNOTE: TESTING RULES STRUCTURAL FIRE
PROTECTION SHIPS
TOPIC: Water Transport
CONCEPTS: Merchant vessels. Shipwreck and sal-
vage.
TREATY REF: 536UNTS7794.
PARTIES:
Denmark
UK Great Britain

107834 Bilateral Agreement **539 UNTS 233**
SIGNED: 20 Aug 63 FORCE: 15 Jul 64
REGISTERED: 18 Jun 65 UK Great Britain
ARTICLES: 13 LANGUAGE: English. French.
HEADNOTE: CULTURAL COOPERATION
TOPIC: Culture
CONCEPTS: Friendship and amity. Tourism. Privi-
leges and immunities. Conformity with munici-
pal law. Establishment of commission. Recogni-
tion of degrees. Exchange. Teacher and student
exchange. Institute establishment. Scholarships
and grants. Exchange. General cultural cooper-
ation. Artists. Athletes. Research and develop-
ment. Mass media exchange.
PROCEDURE: Duration.
PARTIES:
Cameroon
UK Great Britain

107835 Bilateral Agreement **539 UNTS 243**
SIGNED: 27 Jul 64 FORCE: 27 Jul 64
REGISTERED: 18 Jun 65 UK Great Britain
ARTICLES: 7 LANGUAGE: English. German.
HEADNOTE: OFF-SETTING FOREIGN EXCHANGE
EXPENDITURE
TOPIC: Status of Forces
CONCEPTS: Annex or appendix reference. Estab-
lishment of commission. Balance of payments.
Payment schedules.
INTL ORGS: Special Commission.
PARTIES:
Germany, West
UK Great Britain
ANNEX
548 UNTS 374. UK Great Britain. Extension and
Amendment 20 Jul 65. Force 20 Jul 65.
548 UNTS 374. Germany, West. Extension and
Amendment 20 Jul 65. Force 20 Jul 65.

107836 Bilateral Exchange **539 UNTS 253**
SIGNED: 3 Jun 64 FORCE: 3 Jun 64
REGISTERED: 18 Jun 65 UK Great Britain
ARTICLES: 4 LANGUAGE: English. French.
HEADNOTE: GEOLOGICAL SURVEY CHANNEL
TUNNEL PROJECT
TOPIC: Scientific Project
CONCEPTS: General cooperation. Informational
records. Operating agencies. Responsibility and
liability. Establishment of commission. Research
and scientific projects. Research and develop-
ment.
INTL ORGS: Special Commission.
PARTIES:
France
UK Great Britain

107837 Bilateral Exchange **539 UNTS 259**
SIGNED: 31 Aug 64 FORCE: 31 Aug 64
REGISTERED: 18 Jun 65 UK Great Britain
ARTICLES: 2 LANGUAGE: English. Arabic.
HEADNOTE: PRODUCTION TRADE POLICIES CE-
REALS
TOPIC: Commodity Trade
CONCEPTS: Annex or appendix reference. Gen-
eral cooperation. Export quotas. Fees and ex-
emptions. Non-interest rates and fees. Commod-
ity trade.
INTL ORGS: General Agreement on Tariffs and
Trade.
TREATY REF: 55UNTS187; 539UNTS260 FN__2.
PROCEDURE: Termination.
PARTIES:
Syria
UK Great Britain

107838 Bilateral Exchange **539 UNTS 277**
SIGNED: 5 Nov 63 FORCE: 1 Jul 64
REGISTERED: 18 Jun 65 UK Great Britain
ARTICLES: 2 LANGUAGE: English. French.
HEADNOTE: DOUBLE TAXATION SEA AIR TRANS-
PORT
TOPIC: Taxation
CONCEPTS: Definition of terms. Conformity with
municipal law. Taxation. Tax exemptions. Air
transport. Merchant vessels.
PROCEDURE: Termination.
PARTIES:
France
UK Great Britain

107839 Bilateral Exchange **539 UNTS 283**
SIGNED: 15 Sep 64 FORCE: 15 Sep 64
REGISTERED: 18 Jun 65 UK Great Britain
ARTICLES: 2 LANGUAGE: English.
HEADNOTE: TRADE COTTON YARN
TOPIC: Taxation
CONCEPTS: Commodity trade. Quotas.
TREATY REF: 471UNTS296.
PARTIES:
Israel
UK Great Britain

107840 Bilateral Agreement **539 UNTS 289**
SIGNED: 14 Oct 64 FORCE: 14 Oct 64
REGISTERED: 18 Jun 65 UK Great Britain
ARTICLES: 8 LANGUAGE: English. Portuguese.
HEADNOTE: LOAN
TOPIC: Loans and Credits

CONCEPTS: Definition of terms. Currency. Interest rates. Payment schedules. Loan and credit. Loan repayment. Refinance of loan. Terms of loan.
PARTIES:
Brazil
UK Great Britain

107841 Bilateral Agreement **539 UNTS 303**
SIGNED: 8 Apr 65　　　　FORCE: 9 Jun 65
REGISTERED: 22 Jun 65 IBRD (World Bank)
ARTICLES: 5 LANGUAGE: English.
HEADNOTE: LOAN-HIGHWAY PROJECT
TOPIC: IBRD Project
CONCEPTS: General cooperation. Exchange of information and documents. Accounting procedures. Bonds. Currency. Interest rates. Non-interest rates and fees. Debt settlement. Terms of loan. World Bank projects. Loan regulations. Plans and standards. Roads and highways.
PARTIES:
Jamaica
IBRD (World Bank)

107842　　Bilateral Treaty　　**539 UNTS 321**
SIGNED: 24 Dec 53　　　　FORCE: 16 Apr 65
REGISTERED: 22 Jun 65 Belgium
ARTICLES: 20 LANGUAGE: French. Arabic.
HEADNOTE: EXTRADITION
TOPIC: Extradition
CONCEPTS: Time limit. Extradition, deportation and repatriation. Extradition requests. Extraditable offenses. Location of crime. Refusal of extradition. Concurrent requests. Pre-treaty crimes. Limits of prosecution. Provisional detainment. Extradition postponement. Material evidence. Informational records. Public information. Indemnities and reimbursements.
PROCEDURE: Denunciation. Ratification.
PARTIES:
Belgium
Lebanon

107843　　Bilateral Treaty　　**540 UNTS 3**
SIGNED: 13 May 63　　　　FORCE: 23 Apr 65
REGISTERED: 22 Jun 65 Netherlands
ARTICLES: 51 LANGUAGE: Dutch. French.
HEADNOTE: CONNECTION BETWEEN SCHELDT AND RHINE
TOPIC: Territory Boundary
CONCEPTS: Definition of terms. Annex or appendix reference. Previous treaty replacement. Inspection and observation. Operating agencies. Arbitration. Indemnities and reimbursements. Currency. Financial programs. Payment schedules. National treatment. Canal improvement. Inland and territorial waters. Frontier waterways. Ocean resources. Regulation of natural resources.
INTL ORGS: European Atomic Energy Commission.
TREATY REF: 381UNTS165; 480UNTS432; 298UNTS167.
PROCEDURE: Ratification.
PARTIES:
Belgium
Netherlands

107844　　Bilateral Agreement　　**540 UNTS 83**
SIGNED: 23 Jun 65　　　　FORCE: 23 Jun 65
REGISTERED: 23 Jun 65 United Nations
ARTICLES: 8 LANGUAGE: English. Mongolian.
HEADNOTE: ACTIVITIES
TOPIC: IGO Operations
CONCEPTS: Privileges and immunities. Exchange of information and documents. Accounting procedures. Materials, equipment and services. Assistance to United Nations. Inter-agency agreements.
TREATY REF: 1UNTS15; 429UNTS246.
PROCEDURE: Amendment. Termination.
PARTIES:
Mongolia
UNICEF (Children)

107845　　Bilateral Treaty　　**540 UNTS 97**
SIGNED: 8 Apr 65　　　　FORCE: 21 Apr 65
REGISTERED: 30 Jun 65 Poland
ARTICLES: 9 LANGUAGE: Polish. Russian.

HEADNOTE: FRIENDSHIP COOPERATION MUTUAL ASSISTANCE
TOPIC: General Amity
CONCEPTS: Peaceful relations. General cooperation. General cultural cooperation. Defense and security.
INTL ORGS: United Nations. Council for Mutual Economic Assistance.
TREATY REF: 219UNTS3.
PROCEDURE: Denunciation. Duration. Ratification. Renewal or Revival.
PARTIES:
Poland
USSR (Soviet Union)

107846 Multilateral Agreement **540 UNTS 110**
SIGNED: 2 Jul 56　　　　FORCE: 2 Jul 56
REGISTERED: 30 Jun 65 United Nations
ARTICLES: 6 LANGUAGE: English.
HEADNOTE: TECHNICAL ASSISTANCE
TOPIC: Tech Assistance
CONCEPTS: Definition of terms. Annex or appendix reference. Previous treaty replacement. Privileges and immunities. General cooperation. Exchange of information and documents. Personnel. Responsibility and liability. Title and deeds. Use of facilities. Exchange. Scholarships and grants. Vocational training. Research and development. Exchange rates and regulations. Expense sharing formulae. Local currency. Domestic obligation. General technical assistance. Materials, equipment and services. IGO status. Conformity with IGO decisions.
TREATY REF: 76UNTS132; 1UNTS15; 33UNTS261; 128UNTS191.
PROCEDURE: Amendment. Termination.
PARTIES:
Pakistan SIGNED: 2 Jul 56 FORCE: 2 Jul 56
FAO (Food Agri) SIGNED: 2 Jul 56 FORCE: 2 Jul 56
ICAO (Civil Aviat) SIGNED: 2 Jul 56 FORCE: 2 Jul 56
ILO (Labor Org) SIGNED: 2 Jul 56 FORCE: 2 Jul 56
ITU (Telecommun) SIGNED: 2 Jul 56 FORCE: 2 Jul 56
UNESCO (Educ/Cult) SIGNED: 2 Jul 56 FORCE: 2 Jul 56
United Nations SIGNED: 2 Jul 56 FORCE: 2 Jul 56
WHO (World Health) SIGNED: 2 Jul 56 FORCE: 2 Jul 56
WMO (Meteorology) SIGNED: 2 Jul 56 FORCE: 2 Jul 56

107847　　Bilateral Agreement　　**540 UNTS 135**
SIGNED: 27 Jun 63　　　　FORCE: 21 May 64
REGISTERED: 1 Jul 65 United Nations
ARTICLES: 8 LANGUAGE: French.
HEADNOTE: ACTIVITIES
TOPIC: IGO Operations
CONCEPTS: Privileges and immunities. Exchange of information and documents. Accounting procedures. Materials, equipment and services. Assistance to United Nations. Inter-agency agreements. IGO obligations.
INTL ORGS: United Nations.
TREATY REF: 1UNTS15; 423UNTS276.
PROCEDURE: Amendment. Termination.
PARTIES:
UNICEF (Children)
Togo

107848 Multilateral Agreement **540 UNTS 145**
SIGNED: 29 Mar 65　　　　FORCE: 29 Mar 65
REGISTERED: 1 Jul 65 IDA (Devel Assoc)
ARTICLES: 6 LANGUAGE: English.
HEADNOTE: DEVELOPMENT CREDIT AGREEMENT
TOPIC: Non-IBRD Project
CONCEPTS: Definition of terms. Informational records. Currency. Credit provisions. Terms of loan. IDA development project.
PARTIES:
Mauritania SIGNED: 29 Mar 65 FORCE: 29 Mar 65
EEC (Econ Commnty) SIGNED: 29 Mar 65 FORCE: 29 Mar 65
IDA (Devel Assoc) SIGNED: 29 Mar 65 FORCE: 29 Mar 65

107849 Bilateral Agreement **540 UNTS 163**
SIGNED: 28 Dec 64　　　　FORCE: 3 Mar 65
REGISTERED: 1 Jul 65 IDA (Devel Assoc)
ARTICLES: 6 LANGUAGE: English.
HEADNOTE: DEVELOPMENT CREDIT ROAD
TOPIC: Non-IBRD Project
CONCEPTS: Detailed regulations. Previous treaty amendment. Exchange of information and documents. Informational records. Accounting procedures. Currency. Interest rates. Tax exemptions. Credit provisions. Loan repayment. Terms of loan. Plans and standards. IDA development project. Roads and highways.
INTL ORGS: European Economic Community.
PARTIES:
Mauritania
IDA (Devel Assoc)

107850 Bilateral Agreement **540 UNTS 185**
SIGNED: 17 Aug 60　　　　FORCE: 30 Jul 64
REGISTERED: 5 Jul 65 Belgium
ARTICLES: 17 LANGUAGE: English.
HEADNOTE: AIR TRANSPORT
TOPIC: Air Transport
CONCEPTS: Definition of terms. Exceptions and exemptions. Annex or appendix reference. Non-prejudice to third party. Conformity with municipal law. Licenses and permits. Recognition of legal documents. Use of facilities. Arbitration. Procedure. Special tribunals. Competence of tribunal. Monetary and gold transfers. Exchange rates and regulations. Expense sharing formulae. Fees and exemptions. Non-interest rates and fees. Most favored nation clause. National treatment. Customs exemptions. Competency certificate. Routes and logistics. Navigational conditions. Permit designation. Air transport. Airport facilities. Airworthiness certificates. Conditions of airlines operating permission. Operating authorizations and regulations. Licenses and certificates of nationality.
INTL ORGS: International Civil Aviation Organization.
TREATY REF: 15UNTS295.
PROCEDURE: Amendment. Future Procedures Contemplated. Ratification. Registration. Termination.
PARTIES:
Belgium
Burma

107851　　Bilateral Agreement　　**540 UNTS 205**
SIGNED: 26 Mar 65　　　　FORCE: 26 Mar 65
REGISTERED: 5 Jul 65 Denmark
ARTICLES: 15 LANGUAGE: English.
HEADNOTE: AIR SERVICES
TOPIC: Air Transport
CONCEPTS: Conditions. Definition of terms. Detailed regulations. Exceptions and exemptions. Annex or appendix reference. Conformity with municipal law. General cooperation. Exchange of information and documents. Arbitration. Procedure. Existing tribunals. Negotiation. Currency. Monetary and gold transfers. Exchange rates and regulations. Fees and exemptions. Non-interest rates and fees. Most favored nation clause. National treatment. Customs duties. Customs exemptions. Routes and logistics. Permit designation. Conditions of airlines operating permission. Overflights and technical stops. Operating authorizations and regulations.
INTL ORGS: International Civil Aviation Organization.
TREATY REF: 15UNTS295.
PROCEDURE: Amendment. Future Procedures Contemplated. Registration. Termination. Application to Non-self-governing Territories.
PARTIES:
Denmark
Malaysia

107852　Bilateral Convention　**540 UNTS 227**
SIGNED: 6 Feb 65　　　　FORCE: 11 May 65
REGISTERED: 8 Jul 65 Belgium
ARTICLES: 20 LANGUAGE: French.
HEADNOTE: SETTLEMENT PUBLIC DEBT
TOPIC: Claims and Debts
CONCEPTS: Definition of terms. Detailed regulations. Annex or appendix reference. Conformity with municipal law. Responsibility and liability. Arbitration. Procedure. Special tribunals. Ac-

counting procedures. Banking. Bonds. Currency. Debts. Assets transfer. Terms of loan. World Bank projects.
INTL ORGS: International Bank for Reconstruction and Development. International Court of Justice.
PROCEDURE: Ratification.
PARTIES:
Belgium
Congo (Zaire)

107853 Bilateral Convention **540 UNTS 275**
SIGNED: 6 Feb 65　　　FORCE: 11 May 65
REGISTERED: 8 Jul 65 Belgium
ARTICLES: 28 LANGUAGE: French.
HEADNOTE: BELGO-CONGOLESE AMORTIZATION AND ADMINISTRATION FUND
TOPIC: Finance
CONCEPTS: Diplomatic privileges. Juridical personality. Operating agencies. Personnel. Responsibility and liability. Establishment of commission. Accounting procedures. Banking. Bonds. Funding procedures. Tax exemptions.
PROCEDURE: Ratification.
PARTIES:
Belgium
Congo (Zaire)

107854 Bilateral Exchange **540 UNTS 297**
SIGNED: 11 Mar 65　　　FORCE: 11 May 65
REGISTERED: 8 Jul 65 Belgium
ARTICLES: 2 LANGUAGE: French. Dutch.
HEADNOTE: DOUBLE TAXATION DIRECT TAXES
TOPIC: Taxation
CONCEPTS: Previous treaty amendment. Conformity with municipal law. Domestic legislation. Taxation. General.
TREATY REF: 127LTS267; 147UNTS3.
PARTIES:
Belgium
Luxembourg
　　　　　　ANNEX
552 UNTS 426. Belgium. Amendment 16 Nov 65. Force 14 Dec 65.
552 UNTS 426.　Luxembourg.　Amendment 14 Dec 65. Force 14 Dec 65.

107855 Bilateral Convention **540 UNTS 311**
SIGNED: 21 Jun 63　　　FORCE: 30 Jun 64
REGISTERED: 14 Jul 65 UK Great Britain
ARTICLES: 12 LANGUAGE: English. French.
HEADNOTE: DOUBLE TAXATION ESTATES DECEASED PERSONS
TOPIC: Taxation
CONCEPTS: Definition of terms. Territorial application. Nationality and citizenship. Conformity with municipal law. Exchange of official publications. Claims and settlements. Taxation. Death duties.
PROCEDURE: Duration. Termination.
PARTIES:
France
UK Great Britain

107856 Bilateral Exchange **541 UNTS 3**
SIGNED: 31 Aug 64　　　FORCE: 31 Aug 64
REGISTERED: 14 Jul 65 USA (United States)
ARTICLES: 2 LANGUAGE: English. Arabic.
HEADNOTE: LOAN
TOPIC: Loans and Credits
CONCEPTS: Veterinary. Interest rates. Payment schedules. Loan and credit. Loan repayment. Terms of loan. Irrigation. Natural resources.
INTL ORGS: Food and Agricultural Organization of the United Nations.
PARTIES:
Jordan
UK Great Britain
　　　　　　ANNEX
551 UNTS 341. UK Great Britain. Supplementation 27 Feb 65. Force 1 Mar 65.
551 UNTS 341.　Jordan.　Supplementation 1 Mar 65. Force 1 Mar 65.

107857 Multilateral Agreement **541 UNTS 12**
SIGNED: 20 Jul 65　　　FORCE: 20 Jul 65
REGISTERED: 20 Jul 65 United Nations
ARTICLES: 6 LANGUAGE: English.
HEADNOTE: OPERATIONAL ASSISTANCE
TOPIC: IGO Operations
CONCEPTS: Annex or appendix reference. Diplo-

matic privileges. Diplomatic missions. Privileges and immunities. Arbitration. Procedure. Domestic obligation. Assistance to United Nations. Inter-agency agreements. IGO obligations.
TREATY REF: 514UNTS220.
PROCEDURE: Amendment. Termination.
PARTIES:
Malawi SIGNED: 20 Jul 65 FORCE: 20 Jul 65
FAO (Food Agri) SIGNED: 20 Jul 65 FORCE: 20 Jul 65
IAEA (Atom Energy) SIGNED: 20 Jul 65 FORCE: 20 Jul 65
ICAO (Civil Aviat) SIGNED: 20 Jul 65 FORCE: 20 Jul 65
ILO (Labor Org) SIGNED: 20 Jul 65 FORCE: 20 Jul 65
IMCO (Maritime Org) SIGNED: 20 Jul 65 FORCE: 20 Jul 65
ITU (Telecommun) SIGNED: 20 Jul 65 FORCE: 20 Jul 65
UNESCO (Educ/Cult) SIGNED: 20 Jul 65 FORCE: 20 Jul 65
United Nations SIGNED: 20 Jul 65 FORCE: 20 Jul 65
UPU (Postal Union) SIGNED: 20 Jul 65 FORCE: 20 Jul 65
WHO (World Health) SIGNED: 20 Jul 65 FORCE: 20 Jul 65
WMO (Meteorology) SIGNED: 20 Jul 65 FORCE: 20 Jul 65

107858 Bilateral Agreement **541 UNTS 31**
SIGNED: 16 Jun 65　　　FORCE: 16 Jun 65
REGISTERED: 21 Jul 65 Philippines
ARTICLES: 9 LANGUAGE: English.
HEADNOTE: COMMERCE
TOPIC: General Trade
CONCEPTS: Exceptions and exemptions. General provisions. Conformity with municipal law. General cooperation. Tariffs. Reciprocity in trade. Most favored nation clause.
INTL ORGS: General Agreement on Tariffs and Trade. United Nations.
PROCEDURE: Amendment. Duration. Termination.
PARTIES:
Australia
Philippines

107859 Bilateral Agreement **541 UNTS 45**
SIGNED: 15 Aug 61　　　FORCE: 20 May 65
REGISTERED: 21 Jul 65 Finland
ARTICLES: 15 LANGUAGE: English.
HEADNOTE: AIR TRANSPORT
TOPIC: Air Transport
CONCEPTS: Definition of terms. Annex or appendix reference. Conformity with municipal law. General cooperation. Licenses and permits. Recognition of legal documents. Use of facilities. Arbitration. Procedure. Existing tribunals. Negotiation. Fees and exemptions. Non-interest rates and fees. Most favored nation clause. National treatment. Customs duties. Customs exemptions. Competency certificate. Navigational conditions. Permit designation. Air transport. Airport facilities. Airworthiness certificates. Conditions of airlines operating permission. Licenses and certificates of nationality.
INTL ORGS: International Civil Aviation Organization.
TREATY REF: 15UNTSI95.
PROCEDURE: Amendment. Future Procedures Contemplated. Ratification. Registration. Termination.
PARTIES:
Finland
Luxembourg

107860 Bilateral Protocol **541 UNTS 57**
SIGNED: 18 Oct 56　　　FORCE: 18 Oct 56
REGISTERED: 21 Jul 65 Philippines
ARTICLES: 1 LANGUAGE: English.
HEADNOTE: COMMERCE TRADE
TOPIC: General Trade
CONCEPTS: Exceptions and exemptions. Annex or appendix reference. Reciprocity in trade. Quotas.
PARTIES:
Taiwan
Philippines

107861 Bilateral Exchange **541 UNTS 67**
SIGNED: 23 Nov 62　　　FORCE: 11 Aug 64
REGISTERED: 27 Jul 65 USA (United States)
ARTICLES: 2 LANGUAGE: English. Spanish.
HEADNOTE: PEACE CORPS
TOPIC: General Aid
CONCEPTS: Diplomatic privileges. Privileges and immunities. General cooperation. Personnel. Exchange rates and regulations. Funding procedures. Tax exemptions. Customs exemptions. Materials, equipment and services. Aid missions. Volunteer programs.
PROCEDURE: Termination.
PARTIES:
Costa Rica
USA (United States)

107862 Bilateral Exchange **541 UNTS 77**
SIGNED: 26 Jan 65　　　FORCE: 26 Jan 65
REGISTERED: 27 Jul 65 USA (United States)
ARTICLES: 4 LANGUAGE: English.
HEADNOTE: TRADE COTTON TEXTILES
TOPIC: Commodity Trade
CONCEPTS: Detailed regulations. General cooperation. Exchange of information and documents. Export quotas. Trade agencies. Commodity trade. Delivery schedules. Quotas.
TREATY REF: 471UNTS296.
PARTIES:
Korea, South
USA (United States)

107863 Bilateral Agreement **541 UNTS 97**
SIGNED: 5 Feb 65　　　FORCE: 5 Feb 65
REGISTERED: 27 Jul 65 USA (United States)
ARTICLES: 5 LANGUAGE: English. Russian.
HEADNOTE: FISHING KING CRAB
TOPIC: Specific Resources
CONCEPTS: Annex or appendix reference. Exchange of information and documents. Inspection and observation. Scientific exchange. Ocean resources. Fisheries and fishing.
TREATY REF: 499UNTS311.
PARTIES:
USA (United States)
USSR (Soviet Union)

107864 Bilateral Exchange **541 UNTS 107**
SIGNED: 13 Jan 65　　　FORCE: 13 Jan 65
REGISTERED: 27 Jul 65 USA (United States)
ARTICLES: 2 LANGUAGE: English.
HEADNOTE: MILITARY ASSISTANCE
TOPIC: Milit Assistance
CONCEPTS: Annex or appendix reference. Title and deeds. Use of facilities. Expense sharing formulae. Local currency. Self-defense. Military assistance.
TREATY REF: 141UNTS47.
PROCEDURE: Future Procedures Contemplated.
PARTIES:
India
USA (United States)

107865 Bilateral Agreement **541 UNTS 117**
SIGNED: 31 Dec 64　　　FORCE: 31 Dec 64
REGISTERED: 27 Jul 65 USA (United States)
ARTICLES: 6 LANGUAGE: English. French.
HEADNOTE: AGRI COMMOD TITLE I
TOPIC: US Agri Commod Aid
CONCEPTS: General provisions. Annex or appendix reference. Exchange of information and documents. Free trade. Exchange rates and regulations. Transportation costs. Local currency. Mutual consultation. Commodities schedule. Purchase authorization. Surplus commodities.
PARTIES:
Dahomey
USA (United States)

107866 Bilateral Agreement **541 UNTS 135**
SIGNED: 27 Jan 65　　　FORCE: 27 Jan 65
REGISTERED: 2 Aug 65 WHO (World Health)
ARTICLES: 6 LANGUAGE: English.
HEADNOTE: OPERATIONAL ASSISTANCE
TOPIC: IGO Operations
CONCEPTS: Diplomatic privileges. Diplomatic missions. Privileges and immunities. Arbitration. Procedure. Domestic obligation. Assistance to United Nations. IGO obligations.

INTL ORGS: Permanent Court of Arbitration.
TREATY REF: 490UNTS435.
PROCEDURE: Amendment. Termination.
PARTIES:
Ethiopia
WHO (World Health)
ANNEX
552 UNTS 431. Ethiopia. Amendment 24 Nov 65.
Force 24 Nov 65.
552 UNTS 431. WHO (World Health). Amendment
7 Oct 65. Force 24 Nov 65.

107867   Bilateral Exchange   **541 UNTS 147**
SIGNED: 29 May 64   FORCE: 29 May 64
REGISTERED: 2 Aug 65 Italy
ARTICLES: 2 LANGUAGE: French.
HEADNOTE: SAFEGUARDING DEFENSE SECRETS
TOPIC: Other Military
CONCEPTS: Territorial application. Recognition.
Security of information. Exchange of defense in-
formation. Restrictions on transfer.
INTL ORGS: North Atlantic Treaty Organization.
TREATY REF: 394UNTS3.
PROCEDURE: Denunciation.
PARTIES:
Italy
Netherlands

107868   Bilateral Exchange   **541 UNTS 155**
SIGNED: 25 Jun 65   FORCE: 25 Jun 65
REGISTERED: 2 Aug 65 Australia
ARTICLES: 2 LANGUAGE: English.
HEADNOTE: AMATEUR RADIO OPERATORS
TOPIC: Gen Communications
CONCEPTS: Conformity with municipal law. Li-
censes and permits. Amateur radio.
TREATY REF: USA'TIAS 4893;.
PROCEDURE: Termination.
PARTIES:
Australia
USA (United States)

107869   Bilateral Agreement   **541 UNTS 163**
SIGNED: 4 May 65   FORCE: 4 May 65
REGISTERED: 2 Aug 65 Malawi
ARTICLES: 13 LANGUAGE: English.
HEADNOTE: INTERNATIONAL TRANSPORT
TOPIC: Air Transport
CONCEPTS: Definition of terms. Detailed regulations. Annex or appendix reference. General cooperation. Exchange of information and documents. Arbitration. Procedure. Existing tribunals.
Special tribunals. Reexport of goods, etc.. Monetary and gold transfers. Exchange rates and regu-
lations. Expense sharing formulae. Fees and ex-
emptions. Non-interest rates and fees. Tax exemptions. Customs exemptions. Routes and
logistics. Permit designation. Air transport. Conditions of airlines operating permission. Overflights and technical stops. Operating authorizations and regulations.
INTL ORGS: International Civil Aviation Organization.
TREATY REF: 15UNTS295.
PROCEDURE: Amendment. Future Procedures
Contemplated. Registration. Termination.
PARTIES:
Ghana
Malawi

107870   Bilateral Treaty   **541 UNTS 181**
SIGNED: 13 Dec 61   FORCE: 10 Apr 65
REGISTERED: 4 Aug 65 Thailand
ARTICLES: 14 LANGUAGE: English. Thai. German.
HEADNOTE: PROMOTION RECIPROCAL PROTEC-
TION INVESTMENTS
TOPIC: Claims and Debts
CONCEPTS: Conditions. Definition of terms. De-
tailed regulations. Exceptions and exemptions.
Territorial application. Licenses and permits. Ar-
bitration. Procedure. Existing tribunals. Reci-
procity in financial treatment. Exchange rates
and regulations. Financial programs. Claims and
settlements. Private investment guarantee. As-
sets transfer. Most favored nation clause. National treatment.
INTL ORGS: International Court of Justice. International Monetary Fund.
TREATY REF: 2UNTS39.

PROCEDURE: Duration. Ratification. Renewal or
Revival. Termination.
PARTIES:
Germany, West
Thailand

107871   Bilateral Agreement   **541 UNTS 217**
SIGNED: 24 Oct 64   FORCE: 28 Jun 65
REGISTERED: 6 Aug 65 ILO (Labor Org)
ARTICLES: 8 LANGUAGE: French.
HEADNOTE: INTERNATIONAL CENTER AD-
VANCED TECHNICAL VOCATIONAL TRAINING
TOPIC: IGO Establishment
CONCEPTS: Annex or appendix reference. Border
traffic and migration. Alien status. Juridical per-
sonality. General property. Dispute settlement.
Procedure. Institute establishment. Scholarships
and grants. Vocational training. Financial pro-
grams.
INTL ORGS: International Court of Justice.
TREATY REF: 33UNTS261.
PROCEDURE: Amendment. Future Procedures
Contemplated.
PARTIES:
Italy
ILO (Labor Org)

107872   Bilateral Agreement   **541 UNTS 235**
SIGNED: 28 Oct 64   FORCE: 24 Feb 65
REGISTERED: 10 Aug 65 Netherlands
ARTICLES: 6 LANGUAGE: English.
HEADNOTE: TECHNICAL COOPERATION PUBLIC
HEALTH
TOPIC: Tech Assistance
CONCEPTS: Treaty implementation. Legal protec-
tion and assistance. Personnel. Responsibility
and liability. Public health. Compensation. Tax
exemptions. Customs exemptions. Domestic ob-
ligation. General technical assistance. Materials,
equipment and services.
PROCEDURE: Duration.
PARTIES:
Ethiopia
Netherlands

107873   Bilateral Agreement   **541 UNTS 243**
SIGNED: 30 Oct 64   FORCE: 9 Mar 65
REGISTERED: 10 Aug 65 Netherlands
ARTICLES: 6 LANGUAGE: English.
HEADNOTE: ESTABLISHMENT   TECHNICAL
TRAINING CENTER
TOPIC: Tech Assistance
CONCEPTS: Treaty implementation. Privileges and
immunities. General cooperation. Personnel. Re-
sponsibility and liability. Use of facilities. Insti-
tute establishment. Scholarships and grants.
Compensation. Tax exemptions. Customs ex-
emptions. Domestic obligation. General techni-
cal assistance. Materials, equipment and ser-
vices.
PROCEDURE: Duration.
PARTIES:
Netherlands
Pakistan

107874   Bilateral Exchange   **541 UNTS 251**
SIGNED: 12 Nov 64   FORCE: 12 Nov 64
REGISTERED: 10 Aug 65 USA (United States)
ARTICLES: 2 LANGUAGE: English. Portuguese.
HEADNOTE: USE PORTUGUESE PORTS USS SA-
VANNAH
TOPIC: Specific Property
CONCEPTS: Annex or appendix reference. Ports
and pilotage. Facilities and property.
PARTIES:
Portugal
USA (United States)

107875   Bilateral Exchange   **542 UNTS 3**
SIGNED: 12 Mar 64   FORCE: 12 Mar 64
REGISTERED: 10 Aug 65 USA (United States)
ARTICLES: 2 LANGUAGE: English.
HEADNOTE: TRADE COTTON TEXTILES
TOPIC: Commodity Trade
CONCEPTS: Detailed regulations. Treaty interpre-
tation. General cooperation. Exchange of infor-
mation and documents. Trade agencies. Com-
modity trade. Quotas.
TREATY REF: 471UNTS296.

PROCEDURE: Amendment. Duration.
PARTIES:
Portugal
USA (United States)
ANNEX
601 UNTS 362. USA (United States). Amendment
17 Aug 66. Force 17 Aug 66.
601 UNTS 362. Portugal. Amendment 17 Aug 66.
Force 17 Aug 66.

107876   Bilateral Exchange   **542 UNTS 23**
SIGNED: 29 Dec 64   FORCE: 29 Dec 64
REGISTERED: 10 Aug 65 USA (United States)
ARTICLES: 2 LANGUAGE: English. French.
HEADNOTE: INVESTMENT GUARANTIES
TOPIC: Claims and Debts
CONCEPTS: General cooperation. General prop-
erty. Arbitration. Procedure. Existing tribunals.
Negotiation. Reciprocity in financial treatment.
Currency. Claims and settlements. Private invest-
ment guarantee.
INTL ORGS: International Court of Justice.
PARTIES:
Laos
USA (United States)

107877   Bilateral Exchange   **542 UNTS 29**
SIGNED: 31 Dec 64   FORCE: 1 Jan 65
REGISTERED: 10 Aug 65 USA (United States)
ARTICLES: 2 LANGUAGE: English. French.
HEADNOTE: INVESTMENT GUARANTIES
TOPIC: Claims and Debts
CONCEPTS: General cooperation. General prop-
erty. Arbitration. Procedure. Existing tribunals.
Negotiation. Reciprocity in financial treatment.
Currency. Claims and settlements. Private invest-
ment guarantee.
PARTIES:
Central Afri Rep
USA (United States)

107878   Bilateral Agreement   **542 UNTS 37**
SIGNED: 30 Dec 64   FORCE: 30 Dec 64
REGISTERED: 10 Aug 65 USA (United States)
ARTICLES: 6 LANGUAGE: English.
HEADNOTE: AGRI COMMOD TITLE I
TOPIC: US Agri Commod Aid
CONCEPTS: General provisions. Annex or appen-
dix reference. Exchange of information and doc-
uments. Reexport of goods, etc.. Exchange rates
and regulations. Payment schedules. Transporta-
tion costs. Local currency. Commodities sched-
ule. Purchase authorization. Mutual consultation.
PARTIES:
Iceland
USA (United States)

107879   Bilateral Agreement   **542 UNTS 53**
SIGNED: 21 Jun 65   FORCE: 29 Aug 62
REGISTERED: 12 Aug 65 Australia
ARTICLES: 13 LANGUAGE: English. German.
HEADNOTE: ASSISTED MIGRATION
TOPIC: Visas
CONCEPTS: Definition of terms. Detailed regula-
tions. Territorial application. Border traffic and
migration. Repatriation of nationals. Extradition,
deportation and repatriation. General cooper-
ation. Employment regulations. Sickness and in-
validity insurance. Migrant worker. Fees and ex-
emptions. Domestic obligation.
PROCEDURE: Future Procedures Contemplated.
Termination.
PARTIES:
Australia
Germany, West

107880   Bilateral Exchange   **542 UNTS 75**
SIGNED: 21 Jun 65   FORCE: 21 Jun 65
REGISTERED: 12 Aug 65 Australia
ARTICLES: 2 LANGUAGE: English.
HEADNOTE: TREATMENT ASIAN RESIDENTS
CHRISTMAS ISLAND
TOPIC: Humanitarian
CONCEPTS: Treaty interpretation. Public health.
TREATY REF: 472UNTS157.
PROCEDURE: Amendment. Termination.
PARTIES:
Australia
Malaysia

107881 Bilateral Exchange **542 UNTS 81**
SIGNED: 26 Jan 65 FORCE: 26 Jan 65
REGISTERED: 12 Aug 65 USA (United States)
ARTICLES: 2 LANGUAGE: English. Spanish.
HEADNOTE: COMMUNICATION SATELLITES
TOPIC: Scientific Project
CONCEPTS: General cooperation. Communication
satellites testing. Research and development.
PARTIES:
Spain
USA (United States)

107882 Bilateral Agreement **542 UNTS 87**
SIGNED: 29 Jan 65 FORCE: 29 Jan 65
REGISTERED: 12 Aug 65 USA (United States)
ARTICLES: 5 LANGUAGE: English.
HEADNOTE: AGRI COMMOD TITLE IV
TOPIC: US Agri Commod Aid
CONCEPTS: Annex or appendix reference. Ex-
change of information and documents. Reexport
of goods, etc.. Payment schedules. Transporta-
tion costs. Purchase authorization. Commodities
schedule. Purchase authorization. Mutual con-
sultation.
PARTIES:
Sierra Leone
USA (United States)
ANNEX
549 UNTS 356. Sierra Leone. Amendment
5 May 65. Force 5 May 65.
549 UNTS 356. USA (United States). Amendment
5 May 65. Force 5 May 65.

107883 Bilateral Exchange **542 UNTS 103**
SIGNED: 26 Feb 65 FORCE: 26 Feb 65
REGISTERED: 12 Aug 65 USA (United States)
ARTICLES: 2 LANGUAGE: English.
HEADNOTE: TRADE COTTON TEXTILES
TOPIC: Commodity Trade
CONCEPTS: Detailed regulations. Time limit.
Treaty implementation. General cooperation. Ex-
change of information and documents. Export
quotas. Commodity trade.
TREATY REF: 471UNTS296.
PROCEDURE: Amendment. Duration. Termination.
PARTIES:
Pakistan
USA (United States)

107884 Bilateral Exchange **542 UNTS 117**
SIGNED: 2 Feb 65 FORCE: 2 Feb 65
REGISTERED: 12 Aug 65 USA (United States)
ARTICLES: 2 LANGUAGE: English. Spanish.
HEADNOTE: ALIEN AMATEUR RADIO OPERATORS
TOPIC: Gen Communications
CONCEPTS: Conformity with municipal law. Li-
censes and permits. Amateur radio.
TREATY REF: USA'TIAS 4893;.
PROCEDURE: Termination.
PARTIES:
Dominican Republic
USA (United States)

107885 Bilateral Agreement **542 UNTS 125**
SIGNED: 17 Feb 65 FORCE: 17 Feb 65
REGISTERED: 12 Aug 65 USA (United States)
ARTICLES: 6 LANGUAGE: English.
HEADNOTE: AGRI COMMOD TITLE I
TOPIC: US Agri Commod Aid
CONCEPTS: General provisions. Annex or appen-
dix reference. Exchange of information and doc-
uments. Reexport of goods, etc.. Exchange rates
and regulations. Transportation costs. Local cur-
rency. Commodities schedule. Purchase authori-
zation. Mutual consultation.
PARTIES:
Tunisia
USA (United States)
ANNEX
573 UNTS 352. USA (United States). Amendment
29 Nov 65. Force 29 Nov 65.
573 UNTS 352. Tunisia. Amendment 29 Nov 65.
Force 29 Nov 65.

107886 Multilateral Agreement **542 UNTS 145**
SIGNED: 18 Jun 64 FORCE: 12 Mar 65
REGISTERED: 12 Aug 65 USA (United States)
ARTICLES: 12 LANGUAGE: English. French.

HEADNOTE: COOPERATION REGARDING ATOMIC
INFORMATION
TOPIC: Atomic Energy
CONCEPTS: Definition of terms. Previous treaties
adherence. Exchange of information and docu-
ments. Research results. Scientific exchange.
Atomic energy assistance. Security of informa-
tion.
INTL ORGS: North Atlantic Treaty Organization.
TREATY REF: 249UNTS3,371.
PROCEDURE: Duration. Registration. Termination.
PARTIES:
Belgium SIGNED: 18 Jun 64 RATIFIED:
13 Nov 64 FORCE: 12 Mar 65
Canada SIGNED: 30 Jun 64 RATIFIED:
12 Oct 64 FORCE: 12 Mar 65
Denmark SIGNED: 25 Jun 64 RATIFIED:
29 Jul 64 FORCE: 12 Mar 65
France SIGNED: 18 Jun 64 RATIFIED: 27 Oct 64
FORCE: 12 Mar 65
Germany, West SIGNED: 18 Jun 64 RATIFIED:
12 Mar 65 FORCE: 12 Mar 65
Greece SIGNED: 18 Jun 64 RATIFIED:
20 Nov 64 FORCE: 12 Mar 65
Iceland SIGNED: 18 Jun 64 RATIFIED:
20 Nov 64 FORCE: 12 Mar 65
Italy SIGNED: 22 Jun 64 RATIFIED: 14 Sep 64
FORCE: 12 Mar 65
Luxembourg SIGNED: 18 Jun 64 RATIFIED:
21 Dec 64 FORCE: 12 Mar 65
Netherlands SIGNED: 18 Jun 64 RATIFIED:
11 Dec 64 FORCE: 12 Mar 65
Norway SIGNED: 24 Jul 64 RATIFIED:
20 Aug 64 FORCE: 12 Mar 65
Portugal SIGNED: 9 Jul 64 RATIFIED: 24 Aug 64
FORCE: 12 Mar 65
Turkey SIGNED: 18 Jun 64 RATIFIED: 18 Sep 64
FORCE: 12 Mar 65
UK Great Britain SIGNED: 18 Jun 64 RATIFIED:
9 Nov 64 FORCE: 12 Mar 65
USA (United States) SIGNED: 18 Jun 64 RATI-
FIED: 25 Sep 64 FORCE: 12 Mar 65

107887 Bilateral Agreement **542 UNTS 161**
SIGNED: 16 Mar 65 FORCE: 16 Mar 65
REGISTERED: 12 Aug 65 USA (United States)
ARTICLES: 5 LANGUAGE: English.
HEADNOTE: AGRI COMMOD TITLE IV
TOPIC: US Agri Commod Aid
CONCEPTS: General provisions. Annex or appen-
dix reference. Exchange of information and doc-
uments. Reexport of goods, etc.. Payment sched-
ules. Transportation costs. Purchase authoriza-
tion. Surplus commodities. Mutual consultation.
PARTIES:
USA (United States)
Yugoslavia

107888 Bilateral Exchange **542 UNTS 175**
SIGNED: 9 Feb 65 FORCE: 9 Feb 65
REGISTERED: 12 Aug 65 USA (United States)
ARTICLES: 2 LANGUAGE: English.
HEADNOTE: WAIVER CERTAIN CLAIMS
TOPIC: Claims and Debts
CONCEPTS: Claims and settlements.
PARTIES:
USA (United States)
Vietnam, South

107889 Bilateral Exchange **542 UNTS 181**
SIGNED: 27 Feb 65 FORCE: 27 Feb 65
REGISTERED: 12 Aug 65 USA (United States)
ARTICLES: 2 LANGUAGE: English. Spanish.
HEADNOTE: USE TRACKING COMMUNICATION
STATION
TOPIC: Scientific Project
CONCEPTS: Previous treaty replacement. Person-
nel. Title and deeds. Establishment of commis-
sion. Research cooperation. Research results. In-
demnities and reimbursements. Financial pro-
grams. Customs exemptions. Bands and
frequency allocation. Facilities and equipment.
TREATY REF: 372UNTS47; 479UNTS379;
541UNTS NO.5287.
PROCEDURE: Termination.
PARTIES:
Mexico
USA (United States)

107890 Bilateral Exchange **542 UNTS 199**
SIGNED: 16 Mar 65 FORCE: 16 Mar 65
REGISTERED: 12 Aug 65 USA (United States)
ARTICLES: 2 LANGUAGE: English.
HEADNOTE: MILITARY COMMUNICATIONS FA-
CILITY
TOPIC: Status of Forces
CONCEPTS: Jurisdiction. Bases and facilities.
PARTIES:
Philippines
USA (United States)

107891 Bilateral Exchange **542 UNTS 209**
SIGNED: 16 Mar 65 FORCE: 15 Apr 65
REGISTERED: 12 Aug 65 USA (United States)
ARTICLES: 2 LANGUAGE: English. Spanish.
HEADNOTE: AMATEUR RADIO OPERATORS
TOPIC: Gen Communications
CONCEPTS: Conformity with municipal law. Li-
censes and permits. Amateur radio.
TREATY REF: USA'TIAS 4893;.
PROCEDURE: Termination.
PARTIES:
Bolivia
USA (United States)

107892 Bilateral Agreement **542 UNTS 215**
SIGNED: 18 Mar 65 FORCE: 18 Mar 65
REGISTERED: 12 Aug 65 USA (United States)
ARTICLES: 5 LANGUAGE: English. Spanish.
HEADNOTE: AGRI COMMOD TITLE IV
TOPIC: US Agri Commod Aid
CONCEPTS: General provisions. Annex or appen-
dix reference. Exchange of information and doc-
uments. Reexport of goods, etc.. Transportation
costs. Payment schedules. Commodities sched-
ule. Purchase authorization. Mutual consultation.
PARTIES:
Dominican Republic
USA (United States)

107893 Bilateral Agreement **542 UNTS 237**
SIGNED: 26 Mar 65 FORCE: 26 Mar 65
REGISTERED: 12 Aug 65 USA (United States)
ARTICLES: 2 LANGUAGE: English. Spanish.
HEADNOTE: AMATEUR RADIO OPERATORS
TOPIC: Gen Communications
CONCEPTS: Conformity with municipal law. Li-
censes and permits. Amateur radio.
TREATY REF: USA'TIAS 4893;.
PROCEDURE: Termination.
PARTIES:
Ecuador
USA (United States)

107894 Bilateral Treaty **542 UNTS 224**
SIGNED: 17 Jan 61 FORCE: 16 Sep 64
REGISTERED: 13 Aug 65 Canada
ARTICLES: 21 LANGUAGE: English.
HEADNOTE: COOPERATIVE DEVELOPMENT WA-
TER RESOURCES
TOPIC: Specific Resources
CONCEPTS: Definition of terms. Annex or appen-
dix reference. Previous treaties adherence. Oper-
ating agencies. Responsibility and liability. Es-
tablishment of commission. Arbitration. Existing
tribunals. Payment schedules. Hydro-electric
power. Facilities and property. Frontier water-
ways. Regulation of natural resources.
INTL ORGS: International Court of Justice. United
States-Canadian Defense Organization.
TREATY REF: TREATIES&AGREEMENT AFFECTING
CANADA-1814,1825 P.31.
PROCEDURE: Duration. Ratification. Registration.
Termination.
PARTIES:
Canada
USA (United States)

107895 Bilateral Convention **543 UNTS 3**
SIGNED: 20 Oct 64 FORCE: 29 Jul 65
REGISTERED: 16 Aug 65 Norway
ARTICLES: 29 LANGUAGE: English.
HEADNOTE: DOUBLE TAXATION FISCAL EVA-
SION TAXES INCOME
TOPIC: Taxation
CONCEPTS: Definition of terms. Privileges and im-
munities. Nationality and citizenship. Conformity
with municipal law. Exchange of official publica-

tions. Negotiation. Teacher and student exchange. Taxation. Tax credits. Equitable taxes. Tax exemptions. Air transport. Merchant vessels.
PROCEDURE: Denunciation. Duration. Ratification. Termination.
PARTIES:
Norway
United Arab Rep

107896 Bilateral Agreement **543 UNTS 43**
SIGNED: 13 Feb 65　　　FORCE: 13 Feb 65
REGISTERED: 18 Aug 65 UK Great Britain
ARTICLES: 14 LANGUAGE: English. Russian.
HEADNOTE: RELATIONS SCIENTIFIC TECHNOLOGICAL EDUCATIONAL CULTURAL FIELDS
TOPIC: Health/Educ/Welfare
CONCEPTS: General cooperation. Exchange of information and documents. Personnel. Technical and commercial staff. Specialists exchange. Education. Exchange. Teacher and student exchange. Exchange. General cultural cooperation. Artists. Athletes. Scientific exchange. Research and development. General transportation. Publications exchange. Mass media exchange.
TREATY REF: 475UNTS3.
PROCEDURE: Duration.
PARTIES:
UK Great Britain
USSR (Soviet Union)

107897 Bilateral Instrument **543 UNTS 77**
SIGNED: 6 Jan 65　　　FORCE: 6 Jan 65
REGISTERED: 18 Aug 65 UK Great Britain
ARTICLES: 8 LANGUAGE: English. Russian.
HEADNOTE: AGRICULTURAL RESEARCH
TOPIC: Scientific Project
CONCEPTS: Friendship and amity. General cooperation. Establishment of commission. Specialists exchange. Research and scientific projects. Research results. Scientific exchange. Research and development. Indemnities and reimbursements. Agriculture. Conferences.
PROCEDURE: Amendment. Duration. Renewal or Revival. Termination.
PARTIES:
UK Great Britain
USSR (Soviet Union)

107898 Bilateral Convention **543 UNTS 135**
SIGNED: 14 Oct 64　　　FORCE: 10 Mar 65
REGISTERED: 18 Aug 65 UK Great Britain
ARTICLES: 12 LANGUAGE: English. Swedish.
HEADNOTE: DOUBLE TAXATION FISCAL EVASION
TOPIC: Taxation
CONCEPTS: Definition of terms. Territorial application. Previous treaty replacement. Conformity with municipal law. Exchange of official publications. Claims and settlements. Taxation. Death duties. Tax credits.
TREATY REF: 404UNTS113.
PROCEDURE: Duration. Ratification. Termination.
PARTIES:
Sweden
UK Great Britain

107899 Bilateral Exchange **543 UNTS 157**
SIGNED: 25 Feb 65　　　FORCE: 1 Mar 65
REGISTERED: 18 Aug 65 UK Great Britain
ARTICLES: 2 LANGUAGE: English. French.
HEADNOTE: PAYMENT FAMILY ALLOWANCES MIGRANT WORKERS
TOPIC: Non-ILO Labor
CONCEPTS: Definition of terms. Detailed regulations. Conformity with municipal law. Exchange of information and documents. Wages and salaries. Non-ILO labor relations. Family allowances. Administrative cooperation. Migrant worker. Payment schedules.
PARTIES:
France
UK Great Britain

107900 Bilateral Exchange **543 UNTS 165**
SIGNED: 18 Jun 52　　　FORCE: 18 Jun 52
REGISTERED: 20 Aug 65 Philippines
ARTICLES: 2 LANGUAGE: English.
HEADNOTE: MILITARY VICARIATE ARMED FORCES

TOPIC: Status of Forces
CONCEPTS: Diplomatic and consular relations. General military.
PARTIES:
Philippines
Vatican/Holy See

107901 Bilateral Treaty **543 UNTS 175**
SIGNED: 2 Nov 52　　　FORCE: 9 Sep 54
REGISTERED: 20 Aug 65 Philippines
ARTICLES: 7 LANGUAGE: English. Spanish.
HEADNOTE: FRIENDSHIP
TOPIC: General Amity
CONCEPTS: Friendship and amity. Alien status. Consular relations establishment. Diplomatic relations establishment. Privileges and immunities.
PROCEDURE: Future Procedures Contemplated. Ratification. Termination.
PARTIES:
Dominican Republic
Philippines

107902 Bilateral Agreement **543 UNTS 183**
SIGNED: 13 Jul 65　　　FORCE: 13 Jul 65
REGISTERED: 24 Aug 65 Eur Space Vehicle
ARTICLES: 15 LANGUAGE: English. French.
HEADNOTE: CONSTRUCTION SPACE VEHICLES
TOPIC: IGO Operations
CONCEPTS: Default remedies. Definition of terms. Arbitration. Procedure. Inter-agency agreements. IGO obligations.
INTL ORGS: International Court of Justice.
TREATY REF: 507UNTS177.
PROCEDURE: Amendment.
PARTIES:
Australia
Eur Space Vehicle

107903 Bilateral Agreement **543 UNTS 227**
SIGNED: 8 Nov 64　　　FORCE: 18 Jan 65
REGISTERED: 24 Aug 65 Taiwan
ARTICLES: 9 LANGUAGE: Chinese. Spanish. English.
HEADNOTE: TRADE
TOPIC: General Trade
CONCEPTS: Exceptions and exemptions. Treaty implementation. Conformity with municipal law. Licenses and permits. Certificates of origin. Currency. Payment schedules. Most favored nation clause.
PROCEDURE: Duration. Ratification. Renewal or Revival. Termination.
PARTIES:
Taiwan
Guatemala

107904 Bilateral Agreement **543 UNTS 241**
SIGNED: 23 Oct 64　　　FORCE: 25 Jun 65
REGISTERED: 24 Aug 65 Taiwan
ARTICLES: 9 LANGUAGE: Chinese. Spanish. English.
HEADNOTE: TRADE
TOPIC: General Trade
CONCEPTS: Exceptions and exemptions. Treaty implementation. Conformity with municipal law. Licenses and permits. Investigation of violations. Certificates of origin. Currency. Payment schedules. Most favored nation clause.
PROCEDURE: Duration. Ratification. Termination.
PARTIES:
Taiwan
Ecuador

107905 Bilateral Agreement **543 UNTS 255**
SIGNED: 5 May 65　　　FORCE: 5 May 65
REGISTERED: 24 Aug 65 Denmark
ARTICLES: 18 LANGUAGE: English. Spanish.
HEADNOTE: AIR SERVICES
TOPIC: Air Transport
CONCEPTS: Definition of terms. Detailed regulations. Annex or appendix reference. General cooperation. Use of facilities. Arbitration. Procedure. Special tribunals. Negotiation. Reexport of goods, etc.. Monetary and gold transfers. Exchange rates and regulations. Fees and exemptions. Non-interest rates and fees. Tax exemptions. Customs exemptions. Routes and logistics. Permit designation. Airport facilities. Conditions

of airlines operating permission. Overflights and technical stops. Operating authorizations and regulations.
INTL ORGS: International Civil Aviation Organization.
TREATY REF: 15UNTS295; 84UNTS389.
PROCEDURE: Amendment. Future Procedures Contemplated. Registration. Termination.
PARTIES:
Denmark
Spain

107906 Bilateral Agreement **543 UNTS 289**
SIGNED: 6 Jul 64　　　FORCE: 27 Jan 65
REGISTERED: 25 Aug 65 Netherlands
ARTICLES: 8 LANGUAGE: Dutch. Spanish.
HEADNOTE: PROVISION VOLUNTEERS WORK
TOPIC: General Aid
CONCEPTS: Exceptions and exemptions. Privileges and immunities. General cooperation. Inspection and observation. Personnel. Establishment of commission. Import quotas. Reexport of goods, etc.. Exchange rates and regulations. Financial programs. Funding procedures. Tax exemptions. Customs exemptions. Domestic obligation. Economic assistance. Materials, equipment and services. Volunteer programs.
PROCEDURE: Duration. Renewal or Revival. Termination.
PARTIES:
Colombia
Netherlands

107907 Bilateral Agreement **543 UNTS 305**
SIGNED: 8 Jul 65　　　FORCE: 8 Jul 65
REGISTERED: 25 Aug 65 Australia
ARTICLES: 22 LANGUAGE: English. German.
HEADNOTE: EXCHANGE MONEY ORDERS
TOPIC: Postal Service
CONCEPTS: Accounting procedures. Compensation. Payment schedules. Money orders and postal checks. Rates and charges. Advice lists and orders.
PROCEDURE: Duration. Termination.
PARTIES:
Australia
Germany, West

107908 Bilateral Agreement **544 UNTS 3**
SIGNED: 11 Feb 65　　　FORCE: 30 Jul 65
REGISTERED: 30 Aug 65 Belgium
ARTICLES: 15 LANGUAGE: French. Dutch. Hungarian.
HEADNOTE: CULTURAL COOPERATION
TOPIC: Culture
CONCEPTS: Conformity with municipal law. Exchange of information and documents. Establishment of commission. Recognition of degrees. Exchange. Teacher and student exchange. Scholarships and grants. Exchange. General cultural cooperation. Artists. Athletes. Scientific exchange. Publications exchange. Mass media exchange. Press and wire services.
PROCEDURE: Denunciation. Duration. Ratification. Renewal or Revival.
PARTIES:
Belgium
Hungary

107909 Multilateral Agreement **544 UNTS 19**
SIGNED: 16 Dec 61　　　FORCE: 16 Jan 62
REGISTERED: 30 Aug 65 Council of Europe
ARTICLES: 18 LANGUAGE: English. French.
HEADNOTE: COLLECTIVE PASSPORTS TRAVEL YOUNG PERSONS
TOPIC: Visas
CONCEPTS: Detailed regulations. Time limit. Passports non-diplomatic. Nationality and citizenship.
INTL ORGS: Council of Europe.
PROCEDURE: Accession. Ratification. Termination.
PARTIES:
Belgium SIGNED: 16 Dec 61 FORCE: 16 Jan 61
France SIGNED: 16 Dec 61 FORCE: 16 Jan 61
Greece SIGNED: 16 Dec 61 FORCE: 16 Jan 61
Ireland SIGNED: 14 May 62 FORCE: 15 Jun 61
Italy SIGNED: 16 Dec 61 RATIFIED: 6 Aug 63
　FORCE: 7 Sep 63
Luxembourg SIGNED: 16 Dec 61

Netherlands SIGNED: 16 Dec 61 RATIFIED: 4 Jul 63 FORCE: 5 Aug 63
Turkey SIGNED: 14 Sep 62 FORCE: 15 Oct 62
UK Great Britain SIGNED: 16 Dec 61 RATIFIED: 22 Jun 64 FORCE: 23 Jul 64
ANNEX
560 UNTS 296. Luxembourg. Qualified Ratification 27 Oct 65. Force 28 Nov 65.
648 UNTS 380. Norway. Reservation 29 May 68. Force 29 May 68.
648 UNTS 380. Sweden. Signature 27 May 68. Reservation 27 May 68.
648 UNTS 380. Denmark. Signature 27 May 68. Reservation 29 May 68.

107910 Multilateral Agreement **544 UNTS 39**
SIGNED: 14 May 62 FORCE: 14 Oct 62
REGISTERED: 2 Sep 65 Council of Europe
ARTICLES: 11 LANGUAGE: English. French.
HEADNOTE: BLOOD-GROUPING REAGENTS
TOPIC: Scientific Project
CONCEPTS: Definition of terms. Exceptions and exemptions. Annex or appendix reference. Standardization. Exchange of information and documents. International circulation. Public health. Research and scientific projects. Research and development. Indemnities and reimbursements. Fees and exemptions.
INTL ORGS: Council of Europe.
TREATY REF: 351UNTS159.
PROCEDURE: Amendment. Accession. Duration. Ratification. Termination.
PARTIES:
Belgium SIGNED: 14 May 62
Denmark SIGNED: 13 Sep 62 FORCE: 14 Oct 62
France SIGNED: 14 May 62 RATIFIED: 5 Feb 64 FORCE: 21 Jan 64
Germany, West SIGNED: 26 Jun 62
Greece SIGNED: 14 May 62
Italy SIGNED: 14 May 62
Luxembourg SIGNED: 14 May 62
Netherlands SIGNED: 15 Jul 64 RATIFIED: 20 May 65 FORCE: 21 Jun 65
Norway SIGNED: 14 May 62 FORCE: 14 Oct 62
Sweden SIGNED: 14 May 62 FORCE: 14 Oct 62
Switzerland SIGNED: 15 Apr 64
Turkey SIGNED: 14 May 62 RATIFIED: 27 Nov 64 FORCE: 28 Dec 64
UK Great Britain SIGNED: 21 Nov 63 RATIFIED: 8 Dec 64 FORCE: 9 Jan 65
ANNEX
560 UNTS 298. Switzerland. Ratification 29 Nov 65. Force 30 Dec 65.
560 UNTS 298. Italy. Ratification 24 Mar 66. Force 25 Apr 66.

107911 Multilateral Agreement **544 UNTS 81**
SIGNED: 14 May 62 FORCE: 15 Jun 62
REGISTERED: 2 Sep 65 Council of Europe
ARTICLES: 14 LANGUAGE: English. French.
HEADNOTE: SPECIAL MEDICAL TREATMENTS
TOPIC: Sanitation
CONCEPTS: Detailed regulations. Exceptions and exemptions. Standardization. Conformity with municipal law. General cooperation. Domestic legislation. Insect control. Sickness and invalidity insurance. Social security. Research cooperation. Indemnities and reimbursements. Expense sharing formulae.
INTL ORGS: Council of Europe. European Economic Community.
PROCEDURE: Amendment. Accession. Duration. Ratification. Termination.
PARTIES:
Belgium SIGNED: 14 May 62 RATIFIED: 20 Jan 64 FORCE: 20 Feb 64
Denmark SIGNED: 13 Sep 62 FORCE: 14 Oct 62
Germany, West SIGNED: 26 Jun 62
Greece SIGNED: 14 May 62
Ireland SIGNED: 14 May 62 FORCE: 15 Jun 62
Italy SIGNED: 14 May 62
Luxembourg SIGNED: 14 May 62
Norway SIGNED: 25 Jun 63 RATIFIED: 12 Jun 64 FORCE: 13 Jul 64
Sweden SIGNED: 14 May 62 FORCE: 15 Jun 62
Turkey SIGNED: 14 May 62 RATIFIED: 27 Nov 64 FORCE: 28 Dec 64
UK Great Britain SIGNED: 14 May 62 FORCE: 15 Jun 62

107912 Bilateral Convention **544 UNTS 97**
SIGNED: 14 Nov 63 FORCE: 11 Jul 65
REGISTERED: 2 Sep 65 Belgium
ARTICLES: 4 LANGUAGE: French. German.
HEADNOTE: SETTLEMENT PROBLEMS PROPERTY RIGHTS INTERESTS
TOPIC: Specific Property
CONCEPTS: General property. Claims and settlements. Assets transfer. Changes of territory.
TREATY REF: 217UNTS223.
PROCEDURE: Ratification.
PARTIES:
Austria
Belgium

107913 Unilateral Instrument **544 UNTS 113**
SIGNED: 14 Aug 65 FORCE: 3 Sep 65
REGISTERED: 3 Sep 65 United Nations
ARTICLES: 1 LANGUAGE: English.
HEADNOTE: ACCEPTANCE ICJ JURISDICTION
TOPIC: ICJ Option Clause
CONCEPTS: Compulsory jurisdiction.
PARTIES:
Nigeria

107914 Bilateral Exchange **544 UNTS 117**
SIGNED: 4 Aug 64 FORCE: 4 Aug 64
REGISTERED: 3 Sep 65 Denmark
ARTICLES: 2 LANGUAGE: English.
HEADNOTE: DOUBLE TAXATION FISCAL EVASION TAXES INCOME
TOPIC: Taxation
CONCEPTS: Previous treaty extension. Taxation.
INTL ORGS: United Nations.
TREATY REF: 68UNTS117.
PARTIES:
Denmark
Tanganyika

107915 Bilateral Exchange **544 UNTS 123**
SIGNED: 4 Aug 64 FORCE: 4 Aug 64
REGISTERED: 3 Sep 65 Denmark
ARTICLES: 2 LANGUAGE: English.
HEADNOTE: MAINTAINING FORCE CONVENTION 29 NOV 32
TOPIC: Dispute Settlement
CONCEPTS: Previous treaty extension.
INTL ORGS: United Nations.
TREATY REF: 139LTS9.
PARTIES:
Denmark
Tanganyika

107916 Bilateral Agreement **544 UNTS 129**
SIGNED: 8 Oct 64 FORCE: 1 Feb 65
REGISTERED: 3 Sep 65 Czechoslovakia
ARTICLES: 14 LANGUAGE: Czechoslovakian. Serbo-Croat.
HEADNOTE: ABOLITION VISA REQUIREMENT
TOPIC: Visas
CONCEPTS: Visa abolition. Denial of admission. Conformity with municipal law. Exchange of information and documents. Most favored nation clause. Frontier crossing points.
PROCEDURE: Denunciation.
PARTIES:
Czechoslovakia
Yugoslavia

107917 Bilateral Agreement **544 UNTS 147**
SIGNED: 14 Mar 64 FORCE: 3 Jul 64
REGISTERED: 3 Sep 65 Czechoslovakia
ARTICLES: 11 LANGUAGE: Czechoslovakian. Serbo-Croat.
HEADNOTE: COOPERATION TOURISM
TOPIC: Visas
CONCEPTS: Border traffic and migration. Tourism. Conformity with municipal law. General cooperation. Exchange of information and documents. Programs. Specialists exchange.
PROCEDURE: Denunciation. Duration. Ratification. Renewal or Revival.
PARTIES:
Czechoslovakia
Yugoslavia

107918 Bilateral Agreement **544 UNTS 159**
SIGNED: 30 Jun 65 FORCE: 30 Jun 65

REGISTERED: 13 Sep 65 United Nations
ARTICLES: 10 LANGUAGE: English. Spanish.
HEADNOTE: ASSISTANCE
TOPIC: Direct Aid
CONCEPTS: Detailed regulations. Treaty implementation. Annex or appendix reference. Visas. Privileges and immunities. Exchange of information and documents. Informational records. Inspection and observation. Operating agencies. Personnel. Public information. Responsibility and liability. Title and deeds. Use of facilities. Arbitration. Procedure. Negotiation. Import quotas. Attachment of funds. Exchange rates and regulations. Expense sharing formulae. Financial programs. Domestic obligation. General technical assistance. Economic assistance. Materials, equipment and services. IGO status.
INTL ORGS: International Court of Justice. United Nations.
TREATY REF: 1UNTS15; 33UNTS261; 374UNTS147.
PROCEDURE: Amendment. Termination.
PARTIES:
UN Special Fund
Spain

107919 Bilateral Agreement **544 UNTS 193**
SIGNED: 7 Jun 63 FORCE: 13 Aug 65
REGISTERED: 13 Sep 65 Greece
ARTICLES: 18 LANGUAGE: Greek. German. English.
HEADNOTE: COMMERCIAL SCHEDULED AIR TRANSPORT
TOPIC: Air Transport
INTL ORGS: International Civil Aviation Organization.
TREATY REF: 15UNTS295.
PROCEDURE: Amendment. Future Procedures Contemplated. Ratification. Registration. Termination.
PARTIES:
Germany, West
Greece

107920 Bilateral Agreement **544 UNTS 237**
SIGNED: 25 May 64 FORCE: 13 Apr 65
REGISTERED: 15 Sep 65 Netherlands
ARTICLES: 14 LANGUAGE: Dutch. English. French.
HEADNOTE: ESTABLISHMENT OPERATION INTERNATIONAL MILITARY HEADQUARTERS
TOPIC: Status of Forces
CONCEPTS: Definition of terms. Treaty interpretation. Annex or appendix reference. Inviolability. Legal protection and assistance. Use of facilities. Negotiation. Indemnities and reimbursements. National treatment. Tax exemptions. Customs duties. Customs exemptions. Facilities and equipment. Joint defense. Conditions for assistance missions. Procurement and logistics. Bases and facilities.
PROCEDURE: Amendment. Future Procedures Contemplated. Termination.
PARTIES:
Netherlands
NATO (North Atlan)

107921 Bilateral Treaty **544 UNTS 265**
SIGNED: 23 Jul 64 FORCE: 10 Sep 65
REGISTERED: 15 Sep 65 Netherlands
ARTICLES: 14 LANGUAGE: Dutch. German.
HEADNOTE: SIMPLIFICATION LEGAL RELATIONS
TOPIC: Admin Cooperation
CONCEPTS: Territorial application. General cooperation. Exchange of information and documents. Indemnities and reimbursements.
PROCEDURE: Denunciation. Ratification.
PARTIES:
Austria
Netherlands

107922 Bilateral Exchange **545 UNTS 3**
SIGNED: 10 Feb 65 FORCE: 15 Mar 65
REGISTERED: 15 Sep 65 Netherlands
ARTICLES: 2 LANGUAGE: Dutch. Spanish.
HEADNOTE: RECOGNITION SEAMANS BOOK TRAVEL DOCUMENT
TOPIC: Visas
CONCEPTS: Territorial application. Denial of admission. Non-visa travel documents. Conformity with municipal law.

TREATY REF: 482UNTS19.
PROCEDURE: Denunciation.
PARTIES:
Netherlands
Spain

107923 Bilateral Convention **545 UNTS 11**
SIGNED: 26 Nov 64 FORCE: 26 Nov 64
REGISTERED: 16 Sep 65 Czechoslovakia
ARTICLES: 13 LANGUAGE: English.
HEADNOTE: PUBLIC HEALTH
TOPIC: Sanitation
CONCEPTS: Non-diplomatic delegations. General
cooperation. Exchange of information and docu-
ments. Specialists exchange. Insect control. Ex-
change. Teacher and student exchange. Voca-
tional training. Research cooperation. Scientific
exchange. Accounting procedures. Indemnities
and reimbursements. Materials, equipment and
services. Publications exchange.
PROCEDURE: Denunciation. Duration. Renewal or
Revival.
PARTIES:
Czechoslovakia
United Arab Rep

107924 Bilateral Agreement **545 UNTS 21**
SIGNED: 17 Oct 64 FORCE: 19 Mar 65
REGISTERED: 16 Sep 65 Czechoslovakia
ARTICLES: 35 LANGUAGE: Czechoslovakian. Hun-
garian.
HEADNOTE: INTERNATIONAL ROAD TRANSPORT
TOPIC: Land Transport
CONCEPTS: Exceptions and exemptions. General
provisions. Conformity with municipal law. Gen-
eral cooperation. Exchange of information and
documents. Informational records. Investigation
of violations. Reexport of goods, etc.. Payment
schedules. Tax exemptions. Customs exemp-
tions. Temporary importation. Passenger trans-
port. Routes and logistics. Transport of goods.
Commercial road vehicles. Roads and highways.
Road rules.
TREATY REF: 348UNTS13.
PROCEDURE: Denunciation. Duration. Ratification.
Renewal or Revival.
PARTIES:
Czechoslovakia
Hungary

107925 Bilateral Agreement **545 UNTS 65**
SIGNED: 22 May 65 FORCE: 22 May 65
REGISTERED: 16 Sep 65 Czechoslovakia
ARTICLES: 16 LANGUAGE: Czechoslovakian. Bulgarian.
HEADNOTE: CULTURAL COOPERATION
TOPIC: Culture
CONCEPTS: Treaty implementation. Previous
treaty replacement. Friendship and amity. Conformity with municipal law. Exchange of informa-
tion and documents. Public information. Special-
ists exchange. Recognition of degrees. Ex-
change. Teacher and student exchange.
Professorships. Exchange. General cultural co-
operation. Artists. Athletes. Research and development. Export quotas. Finances and payments.
Recognition. Publications exchange. Mass media exchange. Press and wire services. Conferences.
TREATY REF: 46UNTS15.
PROCEDURE: Denunciation. Duration. Future Procedures Contemplated. Renewal or Revival.
PARTIES:
Bulgaria
Czechoslovakia

107926 Bilateral Agreement **545 UNTS 91**
SIGNED: 21 Oct 64 FORCE: 26 Feb 65
REGISTERED: 16 Sep 65 Czechoslovakia
ARTICLES: 9 LANGUAGE: Czechoslovakian. Mongolian. Russian.
HEADNOTE: VETERINARY MATTERS
TOPIC: Sanitation
CONCEPTS: Conformity with municipal law. Exchange of information and documents. Domestic legislation. Specialists exchange. Disease
control. Veterinary. Exchange. Vocational training. Scientific exchange. Research and development. Trade procedures. Indemnities and reim-

bursements. Funding procedures. Materials,
equipment and services. Publications exchange.
PROCEDURE: Duration. Ratification. Renewal or
Revival. Termination.
PARTIES:
Czechoslovakia
Mongolia

107927 Bilateral Agreement **545 UNTS 113**
SIGNED: 6 Oct 64 FORCE: 19 Feb 65
REGISTERED: 16 Sep 65 Czechoslovakia
ARTICLES: 16 LANGUAGE: Czechoslovakian. Ger-
man.
HEADNOTE: CULTURAL COOPERATION
TOPIC: Culture
CONCEPTS: Treaty implementation. Friendship
and amity. Tourism. Conformity with municipal
law. Exchange of information and documents.
Specialists exchange. Recognition of degrees.
Exchange. Teacher and student exchange.
Professorships. Exchange. General cultural co-
operation. Artists. Athletes. Scientific exchange.
Export quotas. Finances and payments. Recogni-
tion. Publications exchange. Mass media ex-
change. Press and wire services. Conferences.
PROCEDURE: Denunciation. Duration. Ratification.
Renewal or Revival.
PARTIES:
Czechoslovakia
Germany, East

107928 Unilateral Instrument **545 UNTS 143**
SIGNED: 18 Feb 65 FORCE: 21 Sep 65
REGISTERED: 21 Sep 65 United Nations
ARTICLES: 1 LANGUAGE: English.
HEADNOTE: ACCEPTANCE UN CHARTER
TOPIC: UN Charter
CONCEPTS: Acceptance of UN obligations. Accep-
tance of obligations upon admittance to UN.
INTL ORGS: United Nations.
PARTIES:
Gambia

107929 Unilateral Instrument **545 UNTS 147**
SIGNED: 26 Aug 65 FORCE: 21 Sep 65
REGISTERED: 21 Sep 65 United Nations
ARTICLES: 1 LANGUAGE: English.
HEADNOTE: ACCEPTANCE OBLIGATIONS UN
TOPIC: UN Charter
CONCEPTS: Acceptance of UN obligations.
INTL ORGS: United Nations.
PARTIES:
Maldive Islands

107930 Unilateral Instrument **545 UNTS 151**
SIGNED: 4 Sep 65 FORCE: 21 Sep 65
REGISTERED: 21 Sep 65 United Nations
ARTICLES: 1 LANGUAGE: English.
HEADNOTE: ACCEPTANCE OBLIGATIONS UN
TOPIC: UN Charter
CONCEPTS: Acceptance of UN obligations.
INTL ORGS: United Nations.
PARTIES:
Singapore

107931 Bilateral Agreement **545 UNTS 155**
SIGNED: 4 Dec 64 FORCE: 6 May 65
REGISTERED: 21 Sep 65 Netherlands
ARTICLES: 6 LANGUAGE: English.
HEADNOTE: DEVELOPING FACULTY ENGINEER-
ING UNIVERSITY NIGERIA
TOPIC: Education
CONCEPTS: Definition of terms. Friendship and
amity. Alien status. General cooperation. Re-
sponsibility and liability. Exchange. Teacher and
student exchange. Professorships. Indemnities
and reimbursements. Tax exemptions. Customs
exemptions. Materials, equipment and services.
PROCEDURE: Duration. Future Procedures Con-
templated. Renewal or Revival. Termination.
PARTIES:
Netherlands
Nigeria

107932 Bilateral Exchange **545 UNTS 163**
SIGNED: 4 May 65 FORCE: 4 May 65
REGISTERED: 21 Sep 65 USA (United States)
ARTICLES: 2 LANGUAGE: English. Spanish.

HEADNOTE: STATUS PERSONNEL
TOPIC: Status of Forces
CONCEPTS: Privileges and immunities. Jurisdic-
tion. Status of forces.
TREATY REF: 262UNTS105.
PROCEDURE: Future Procedures Contemplated.
PARTIES:
Guatemala
USA (United States)

107933 Bilateral Exchange **545 UNTS 169**
SIGNED: 12 May 65 FORCE: 12 May 65
REGISTERED: 21 Sep 65 USA (United States)
ARTICLES: 2 LANGUAGE: English.
HEADNOTE: ESTABLISHMENT OPERATION MAIN-
TENANCE TORPEDO TEST RANGE
TOPIC: Milit Installation
CONCEPTS: Annex or appendix reference. Proce-
dure. Testing ranges and sites. Bases and facili-
ties.
PROCEDURE: Duration. Termination.
PARTIES:
Canada
USA (United States)

107934 Bilateral Agreement **545 UNTS 181**
SIGNED: 10 May 65 FORCE: 10 May 65
REGISTERED: 21 Sep 65 USA (United States)
ARTICLES: 17 LANGUAGE: English.
HEADNOTE: EDUCATIONAL CULTURAL EX-
CHANGE
TOPIC: Education
CONCEPTS: Definition of terms. Standardization.
Conformity with municipal law. Inspection and
observation. Personnel. General property. Ex-
change. Commissions and foundations. Teacher
and student exchange. Professorships. Ex-
change. Research and development. Accounting
procedures. Currency. Exchange rates and regu-
lations. Expense sharing formulae. Funding pro-
cedures. Tax exemptions.
TREATY REF: 71UNTS64; 4UNTS92;
134UNTS266; 284UNTS362.
PROCEDURE: Amendment. Termination.
PARTIES:
UK Great Britain
USA (United States)
ANNEX
605 UNTS 394. USA (United States). Force
16 Jan 67. Amendment 16 Feb 67.

107935 Bilateral Convention **545 UNTS 199**
SIGNED: 24 Sep 63 FORCE: 5 Apr 65
REGISTERED: 23 Sep 65 Austria
ARTICLES: 22 LANGUAGE: English.
HEADNOTE: DOUBLE TAXATION TAXES INCOME
TOPIC: Taxation
CONCEPTS: Definition of terms. Conformity with
municipal law. Exchange of official publications.
Teacher and student exchange. Claims and set-
tlements. Taxation. Air transport.
PROCEDURE: Duration. Ratification. Termination.
PARTIES:
Austria
India

107936 Bilateral Treaty **545 UNTS 223**
SIGNED: 31 Oct 64 FORCE: 9 Apr 65
REGISTERED: 23 Sep 65 Austria
ARTICLES: 12 LANGUAGE: German. Hungarian.
HEADNOTE: INVESTIGATION FRONTIER INCI-
DENTS
TOPIC: Visas
CONCEPTS: Privileges and immunities. Establish-
ment of commission.
PROCEDURE: Denunciation. Ratification.
PARTIES:
Austria
Hungary

107937 Bilateral Treaty **545 UNTS 241**
SIGNED: 31 Oct 64 FORCE: 9 Apr 65
REGISTERED: 24 Sep 65 Austria
ARTICLES: 31 LANGUAGE: German. Hungarian.
HEADNOTE: KEEPING COMMON STATE FRON-
TIER VISIBLE
TOPIC: Visas

CONCEPTS: Frontier permits. General cooperation. Establishment of commission. Fish, wildlife, and natural resources. Markers and definitions. Frontier peoples and personnel. Frontier waterways.
INTL ORGS: League of Nations.
TREATY   REF:
6LTS187;2LTS35;9LTS103;41UNTS135;217-
UNTS223.
PROCEDURE: Denunciation. Ratification.
PARTIES:
  Austria
  Hungary

107938   Bilateral Convention   **546 UNTS 3**
SIGNED: 11 Dec 62   FORCE: 22 Apr 65
REGISTERED: 24 Sep 65 Austria
ARTICLES: 30 LANGUAGE: German. Serbo-Croat.
HEADNOTE: REGULATION RAILWAY TRAFFIC ACROSS FRONTIER
TOPIC: Land Transport
CONCEPTS: Definition of terms. General provisions. Treaty implementation. Annex or appendix reference. Frontier formalities. Non-visa travel documents. Visas. Conformity with municipal law. General cooperation. Legal protection and assistance. Personnel. Recognition of legal documents. Responsibility and liability. Investigation of violations. Arbitration. Procedure. Special tribunals. Competence of tribunal. Humanitarian matters. Reexport of goods, etc.. Compensation. Indemnities and reimbursements. Expense sharing formulae. Fees and exemptions. Payment schedules. Claims and settlements. National treatment. General. Tax exemptions. Customs exemptions. Passenger transport. Routes and logistics. Operating authorizations and regulations. Railway border crossing. Railways. Regulations. Services.
INTL ORGS: International Court of Justice.
PROCEDURE: Denunciation. Ratification.
PARTIES:
  Austria
  Yugoslavia
                    ANNEX
644 UNTS 462. Austria. Ratification 22 Apr 68. Force 22 Jul 68.
644 UNTS 462.   Yugoslavia   Ratification 22 Apr 68. Force 22 Jul 68.

107939   Bilateral Exchange   **546 UNTS 81**
SIGNED: 9 Apr 65   FORCE: 1 Jul 65
REGISTERED: 24 Sep 65 USA (United States)
ARTICLES: 2 LANGUAGE: English. Chinese.
HEADNOTE: ESTABLISHMENT OF ECONOMIC SOCIAL DEVELOPMENT FUND
TOPIC: General Economic
CONCEPTS: Annex or appendix reference. Inspection and observation. Establishment of commission. Trade agencies. Accounting procedures. Banking. Aid and development. Loan and credit. Purchase authorization.
TREATY   REF: 17UNTS119;45UNTS326;-
76UNTS245;76UNTS235,354.
PROCEDURE: Future Procedures Contemplated.
PARTIES:
  Taiwan
  USA (United States)

107940   Bilateral Exchange   **546 UNTS 135**
SIGNED: 27 Feb 65   FORCE: 27 Feb 65
REGISTERED: 24 Sep 65 USA (United States)
ARTICLES: 2 LANGUAGE: English. Spanish.
HEADNOTE: SPACE RESEARCH PROGRAM
TOPIC: Scientific Project
CONCEPTS: General cooperation. Vocational training. Research and scientific projects. Research cooperation. Meteorology. Research and development. Indemnities and reimbursements.
PROCEDURE: Future Procedures Contemplated.
PARTIES:
  Mexico
  USA (United States)

107941   Bilateral Agreement   **546 UNTS 143**
SIGNED: 5 Apr 65   FORCE: 5 Apr 65
REGISTERED: 24 Sep 65 USA (United States)
ARTICLES: 5 LANGUAGE: English. French.
HEADNOTE: AGRI COMMOD TITLE IV
TOPIC: US Agri Commod Aid

CONCEPTS: General provisions. Annex or appendix reference. Exchange of information and documents. Reexport of goods, etc.. Payment schedules. Purchase authorization. Commodities schedule. Purchase authorization. Mutual consultation.
PARTIES:
  Ivory Coast
  USA (United States)

107942   Bilateral Agreement   **546 UNTS 157**
SIGNED: 23 Apr 65   FORCE: 23 Apr 65
REGISTERED: 24 Sep 65 USA (United States)
ARTICLES: 6 LANGUAGE: English.
HEADNOTE: AGRI COMMOD TITLE I
TOPIC: US Agri Commod Aid
CONCEPTS: General provisions. Annex or appendix reference. Exchange of information and documents. Reexport of goods, etc.. Currency. Currency deposits. Payment schedules. Transportation costs. Local currency. Purchase authorization. Commodities schedule. Purchase authorization. Mutual consultation.
PARTIES:
  Philippines
  USA (United States)

107943   Bilateral Exchange   **546 UNTS 175**
SIGNED: 20 Apr 65   FORCE: 20 Apr 65
REGISTERED: 24 Sep 65 USA (United States)
ARTICLES: 2 LANGUAGE: English.
HEADNOTE: PEACE CORPS
TOPIC: General Aid
CONCEPTS: Diplomatic privileges. Privileges and immunities. General cooperation. Personnel. Exchange rates and regulations. Funding procedures. Tax exemptions. Customs exemptions. Materials, equipment and services. Aid missions. Volunteer programs.
PROCEDURE: Termination.
PARTIES:
  Malawi
  USA (United States)

107944   Bilateral Exchange   **546 UNTS 183**
SIGNED: 12 May 65   FORCE: 12 May 65
REGISTERED: 24 Sep 65 USA (United States)
ARTICLES: 2 LANGUAGE: English. French.
HEADNOTE: INVESTMENT GUARANTIES
TOPIC: Finance
CONCEPTS: General cooperation. General property. Arbitration. Procedure. Existing tribunals. Negotiation. Reciprocity in financial treatment. Currency. Claims and settlements. Private investment guarantee.
PARTIES:
  Chad
  USA (United States)

107945   Bilateral Exchange   **546 UNTS 189**
SIGNED: 26 May 65   FORCE: 26 May 65
REGISTERED: 24 Sep 65 USA (United States)
ARTICLES: 2 LANGUAGE: English. Portuguese.
HEADNOTE: ALIEN AMATEUR RADIO OPERATORS
TOPIC: Gen Communications
CONCEPTS: Conformity with municipal law. Licenses and permits. Amateur radio.
TREATY REF: USA'TIAS 4893;.
PARTIES:
  Portugal
  USA (United States)

107946   Bilateral Exchange   **546 UNTS 195**
SIGNED: 1 Jun 65   FORCE: 1 Jun 65
REGISTERED: 24 Sep 65 USA (United States)
ARTICLES: 2 LANGUAGE: English. Portuguese.
HEADNOTE: RADIO COMMUNICATIONS BETWEEN AMATEUR STATIONS
TOPIC: Gen Communications
CONCEPTS: Amateur radio. Amateur third party message.
PROCEDURE: Termination.
PARTIES:
  Brazil
  USA (United States)

107947   Bilateral Exchange   **546 UNTS 201**
SIGNED: 8 Jun 65   FORCE: 8 Jun 65

REGISTERED: 24 Sep 65 USA (United States)
ARTICLES: 2 LANGUAGE: English.
HEADNOTE: LOAN LONG RANGE AID NAVIGATION EQUIPMENT
TOPIC: Gen Communications
CONCEPTS: Conformity with municipal law. Claims and settlements. Customs exemptions. General technical assistance. Materials, equipment and services. Navigational equipment.
PROCEDURE: Future Procedures Contemplated. Termination.
PARTIES:
  Canada
  USA (United States)
                    ANNEX
601 UNTS 366. USA (United States). Interpretation 28 Jul 66. Force 28 Jul 66.
601 UNTS 366. Canada. Interpretation 28 Jul 66. Force 28 Jul 66.

107948   Bilateral Exchange   **546 UNTS 209**
SIGNED: 29 May 65   FORCE: 29 May 65
REGISTERED: 24 Sep 65 USA (United States)
ARTICLES: 2 LANGUAGE: English.
HEADNOTE: INVESTMENT GUARANTIES
TOPIC: Claims and Debts
CONCEPTS: General cooperation. General property. Arbitration. Procedure. Existing tribunals. Negotiation. Reciprocity in financial treatment. Currency. Claims and settlements. Private investment guarantee.
INTL ORGS: International Court of Justice.
PROCEDURE: Amendment. Termination.
PARTIES:
  Uganda
  USA (United States)

107949   Bilateral Agreement   **546 UNTS 217**
SIGNED: 19 Nov 64   FORCE: 2 Sep 65
REGISTERED: 24 Sep 65 Belgium
ARTICLES: 12 LANGUAGE: French. Dutch. Spanish.
HEADNOTE: CULTURAL
TOPIC: Culture
CONCEPTS: Treaty implementation. Friendship and amity. Conformity with municipal law. Programs. Specialists exchange. Recognition of degrees. Exchange. Teacher and student exchange. Institute establishment. Scholarships and grants. General cultural cooperation. Artists. Research and development. Publications exchange. Mass media exchange.
PROCEDURE: Denunciation. Duration. Future Procedures Contemplated. Ratification. Renewal or Revival. Termination.
PARTIES:
  Belgium
  Mexico

107950 Multilateral Agreement **546 UNTS 235**
SIGNED: 15 Dec 58   FORCE: 1 Jul 61
REGISTERED: 27 Sep 65 Council of Europe
ARTICLES: 12 LANGUAGE: English. French.
HEADNOTE: PROGRAMME EXCHANGES MEANS TELEVISION FILMS
TOPIC: Mass Media
CONCEPTS: Recognition. Publications exchange. Mass media exchange.
INTL ORGS: Council of Europe. International Union for the Protection of Literary and Artistic Works.
PROCEDURE: Accession. Denunciation. Duration. Ratification.
PARTIES:
  Austria SIGNED: 5 Dec 58
  Belgium SIGNED: 5 Dec 58 RATIFIED: 9 Mar 62 FORCE: 8 Apr 62
  Denmark   SIGNED: 5 Dec 58   RATIFIED: 26 Oct 61 FORCE: 25 Nov 61
  France SIGNED: 5 Dec 58 FORCE: 1 Jul 61
  Greece SIGNED: 5 Dec 58 RATIFIED: 10 Jan 62 FORCE: 9 Feb 62
  Ireland SIGNED: 5 Mar 65 RATIFIED: 5 Mar 65 FORCE: 4 Apr 65
  Italy SIGNED: 5 Dec 58
  Luxembourg SIGNED: 5 Dec 58
  Netherlands   SIGNED: 7 Oct 64   FORCE: 13 Oct 63
  Norway   SIGNED: 17 Nov 59   RATIFIED: 13 Feb 63 FORCE: 15 Mar 63
  Sweden SIGNED: 5 Dec 58 FORCE: 1 Jul 61
  Turkey SIGNED: 5 Dec 58 FORCE: 28 Mar 64

UK Great Britain SIGNED: 5 Dec 58 FORCE:
1 Jul 61

107951 Multilateral Agreement **546 UNTS 247**
SIGNED: 22 Jun 60   FORCE: 1 Jul 61
REGISTERED: 27 Sep 65 Council of Europe
ARTICLES: 14 LANGUAGE: English. French.
HEADNOTE: PROTECTION TELEVISION BROAD-
CASTS
TOPIC: Mass Media
CONCEPTS: Conformity with municipal law. Tele-
communications.
INTL ORGS: Council of Europe. International Union
for the Protection of Literary and Artistic Works.
PROCEDURE: Accession. Denunciation. Duration.
Ratification.
PARTIES:
Belgium SIGNED: 13 Sep 60
Denmark SIGNED: 22 Jun 60 RATIFIED:
26 Oct 61 FORCE: 27 Nov 61
France SIGNED: 22 Jun 60 FORCE: 1 Jul 61
Germany, West SIGNED: 11 Jul 60 FORCE:
1 Jul 61
Greece SIGNED: 22 Jun 60 FORCE: 1 Jul 61
Ireland SIGNED: 22 Jun 60
Italy SIGNED: 22 Jun 60
Luxembourg SIGNED: 13 Sep 60
Netherlands SIGNED: 7 Oct 64
Norway SIGNED: 29 Jun 65
Sweden SIGNED: 3 Aug 60 RATIFIED:
31 May 61 FORCE: 1 Jul 61
Turkey SIGNED: 22 Jun 60
UK Great Britain SIGNED: 13 Jul 60 .RATIFIED:
9 Mar 61 FORCE: 1 Jul 61
ANNEX
635 UNTS 370. Germany, West. Qualified Ratifi-
cation 8 Sep 67. Force 9 Oct 67.
635 UNTS 370. Belgium. Qualified Ratification
7 Feb 68. Force 8 Mar 68.
645 UNTS 375. Norway. Ratification 9 Jul 68.
Force 10 Aug 68.

107952 Multilateral Agreement **546 UNTS 277**
SIGNED: 15 Feb 65   FORCE: 1 Apr 65
REGISTERED: 28 Sep 65 Austria
ARTICLES: 8 LANGUAGE: German. French. Dutch.
HEADNOTE: RESIDENCE REFUGEES
TOPIC: Refugees
CONCEPTS: Territorial application. Resident per-
mits. Non-visa travel documents.
TREATY REF: 189UNTS137; 374UNTS3.
PROCEDURE: Denunciation. Duration.
PARTIES:
Austria SIGNED: 15 Feb 65 FORCE: 1 Apr 65
Belgium SIGNED: 15 Feb 65 FORCE: 1 Apr 65
Luxembourg SIGNED: 15 Feb 65 FORCE:
1 Apr 65
Netherlands SIGNED: 15 Feb 65 FORCE:
1 Apr 65
ANNEX
573 UNTS 356. Austria. Acknowledgement
19 Oct 65. Force 21 Jan 66.
573 UNTS 356. Netherlands. Surinam.

107953 Multilateral Agreement **547 UNTS 3**
SIGNED: 15 Feb 65   FORCE: 1 Apr 65
REGISTERED: 28 Sep 65 Austria
ARTICLES: 9 LANGUAGE: German. French. Dutch.
HEADNOTE: ACCEPTANCE PERSONS FRONTIER
TOPIC: Visas
CONCEPTS: Passports diplomatic. Resident per-
mits. Nationality and citizenship. Extradition, de-
portation and repatriation. General cooperation.
PROCEDURE: Denunciation. Duration. Renewal or
Revival.
PARTIES:
Austria SIGNED: 15 Feb 65 FORCE: 1 Apr 65
Belgium SIGNED: 15 Feb 65 FORCE: 1 Apr 65
Luxembourg SIGNED: 15 Feb 65 FORCE:
1 Apr 65
Netherlands SIGNED: 15 Feb 65 FORCE:
1 Apr 65
ANNEX
573 UNTS 356. Austria. Acknowledgement
19 Oct 65. Force 21 Jan 66.
573 UNTS 356. Netherlands. Surinam.

107954 Bilateral Agreement **547 UNTS 29**
SIGNED: 29 May 65   FORCE: 29 May 65
REGISTERED: 1 Oct 65 United Nations

ARTICLES: 8 LANGUAGE: English.
HEADNOTE: ACTIVITIES
TOPIC: IGO Operations
CONCEPTS: Previous treaty replacement. Diplo-
matic privileges. Privileges and immunities. Ex-
change of information and documents. Account-
ing procedures. Materials, equipment and ser-
vices. Assistance to United Nations. Inter-agency
agreements.
TREATY REF: 1UNTS15; 180UNTS59.
PROCEDURE: Amendment. Termination.
PARTIES:
Gambia
UNICEF (Children)

107955 Bilateral Exchange **547 UNTS 39**
SIGNED: 29 Jan 63   FORCE: 1 Aug 65
REGISTERED: 11 Oct 65 Belgium
ARTICLES: 26 LANGUAGE: French. Dutch.
HEADNOTE: AMENDING PROTOCOL BELGO-LUX-
EMBOURG ECONOMIC UNION
TOPIC: IGO Establishment
CONCEPTS: Annex type material.
INTL ORGS: Benelux Economic Union.
PARTIES:
Belgium
Luxembourg

107956 Bilateral Agreement **547 UNTS 165**
SIGNED: 17 Feb 65   FORCE: 26 May 65
REGISTERED: 13 Oct 65 Belgium
ARTICLES: 10 LANGUAGE: French.
HEADNOTE: DEVELOPMENT ECONOMIC INDUS-
TRIAL TECHNICAL COOPERATION
TOPIC: General Economic
CONCEPTS: Treaty implementation. General coop-
eration. Exchange of official publications. Estab-
lishment of commission. Exchange. Vocational
training. Administrative cooperation. Payment
schedules. Delivery schedules. Economic assis-
tance.
INTL ORGS: Benelux Economic Union.
PROCEDURE: Denunciation. Duration.
PARTIES:
Benelux Econ Union
Poland

107957 Bilateral Treaty **547 UNTS 173**
SIGNED: 30 Aug 62   FORCE: 15 Sep 65
REGISTERED: 13 Oct 65 Netherlands
ARTICLES: 23 LANGUAGE: Dutch. German.
HEADNOTE: RECOGNITION ENFORCEMENT JUDI-
CIAL DECISIONS
TOPIC: Admin Cooperation
CONCEPTS: Definition of terms. Territorial applica-
tion. General provisions. General cooperation.
Recognition and enforcement of legal decisions.
Competence of tribunal.
PROCEDURE: Denunciation. Ratification.
PARTIES:
Germany, West
Netherlands

107958 Bilateral Convention **547 UNTS 209**
SIGNED: 12 Aug 65   FORCE: 12 Aug 65
REGISTERED: 15 Oct 65 Laos
ARTICLES: 8 LANGUAGE: English. French.
HEADNOTE: SUPPLY POWER
TOPIC: Specific Property
CONCEPTS: Non-interest rates and fees. Materials,
equipment and services. Hydro-electric power.
Facilities and property.
PARTIES:
Laos
Thailand

107959 Multilateral Agreement **547 UNTS 216**
SIGNED: 21 Oct 65   FORCE: 21 Oct 65
REGISTERED: 21 Oct 65 United Nations
ARTICLES: 6 LANGUAGE: English.
HEADNOTE: TECHNICAL ASSISTANCE
TOPIC: Tech Assistance
CONCEPTS: Definition of terms. Previous treaty replacement. Privileges and immunities. General
cooperation. Exchange of information and documents. Personnel. Responsibility and liability. Title and deeds. Use of facilities. Exchange. Professorships. Scholarships and grants. Research and
development. Exchange rates and regulations.

Expense sharing formulae. Local currency. Do-
mestic obligation. General technical assistance.
Materials, equipment and services. IGO status.
Conformity with IGO decisions.
TREATY REF: 76UNTS132; 1UNTS15;
33UNTS261; 374UNTS147.
PROCEDURE: Amendment. Termination.
PARTIES:
State/IGO Group
FAO (Food Agri)
IAEA (Atom Energy)
ICAO (Civil Aviat)
ILO (Labor Org)
IMCO (Maritime Org)
ITU (Telecommun)
UNESCO (Educ/Cult)
United Nations
UPU (Postal Union)
WHO (World Health)
WMO (Meteorology)
Turkey
ANNEX
668 UNTS 372.

107960 Bilateral Agreement **547 UNTS 233**
SIGNED: 25 Sep 64   FORCE: 1 Sep 65
REGISTERED: 22 Oct 65 Taiwan
ARTICLES: 8 LANGUAGE: Chinese. Spanish.
HEADNOTE: TRADE
TOPIC: General Trade
CONCEPTS: Exceptions and exemptions. Treaty
implementation. Conformity with municipal law.
Export quotas. Import quotas. Currency. Pay-
ment schedules. Most favored nation clause.
Customs duties.
PROCEDURE: Amendment. Duration. Ratification.
Termination.
PARTIES:
Taiwan
Mexico

107961 Multilateral Agreement **547 UNTS 248**
SIGNED: 13 Sep 65   FORCE: 13 Sep 65
REGISTERED: 2 Nov 65 United Nations
ARTICLES: 6 LANGUAGE: English.
HEADNOTE: OPERATIONAL ASSISTANCE
TOPIC: IGO Operations
CONCEPTS: Annex or appendix reference. Previ-
ous treaty replacement. Diplomatic privileges.
Diplomatic missions. Privileges and immunities.
Arbitration. Procedure. Domestic obligation. As-
sistance to United Nations. Inter-agency agree-
ments. IGO obligations.
INTL ORGS: Permanent Court of Arbitration.
TREATY REF: 527UNTS121; 327UNTS95.
PROCEDURE: Amendment. Termination.
PARTIES:
FAO (Food Agri) SIGNED: 13 Sep 65 FORCE:
13 Sep 65
IAEA (Atom Energy) SIGNED: 13 Sep 65 FORCE:
13 Sep 65
ICAO (Civil Aviat) SIGNED: 13 Sep 65 FORCE:
13 Sep 65
ILO (Labor Org) SIGNED: 13 Sep 65 FORCE:
13 Sep 65
IMCO (Maritime Org) SIGNED: 13 Sep 65
FORCE: 13 Sep 65
ITU (Telecommun) SIGNED: 13 Sep 65 FORCE:
13 Sep 65
UNESCO (Educ/Cult) SIGNED: 13 Sep 65
FORCE: 13 Sep 65
United Nations SIGNED: 13 Sep 65 FORCE:
13 Sep 65
UPU (Postal Union) SIGNED: 13 Sep 65 FORCE:
13 Sep 65
WHO (World Health) SIGNED: 13 Sep 65 FORCE:
13 Sep 65
WMO (Meteorology) SIGNED: 13 Sep 65 FORCE:
13 Sep 65
Sudan SIGNED: 13 Sep 65 FORCE: 13 Sep 65
ANNEX
659 UNTS 384. UNIDO (Industrial). Accession
15 Feb 69. Force 15 Feb 69.

107962 Multilateral Agreement **547 UNTS 264**
SIGNED: 13 Sep 65   FORCE: 13 Sep 65
REGISTERED: 2 Nov 65 United Nations
ARTICLES: 6 LANGUAGE: English.
HEADNOTE: TECHNICAL ASSISTANCE
TOPIC: Tech Assistance
CONCEPTS: Definition of terms. Previous treaty re-

placement. Privileges and immunities. General cooperation. Exchange of information and documents. Personnel. Responsibility and liability. Title and deeds. Use of facilities. Exchange. Scholarships and grants. Vocational training. Research and development. Exchange rates and regulations. Expense sharing formulae. Local currency. Domestic obligation. General technical assistance. Materials, equipment and services. IGO status. Conformity with IGO decisions.
TREATY REF: 76UNTS132; 1UNTS15; 33UNTS261; 374UNTS147.
PROCEDURE: Amendment. Termination.
PARTIES:
FAO (Food Agri) SIGNED: 13 Sep 65 FORCE: 13 Sep 65
IAEA (Atom Energy) SIGNED: 13 Sep 65 FORCE: 13 Sep 65
ICAO (Civil Aviat) SIGNED: 13 Sep 65 FORCE: 13 Sep 65
ILO (Labor Org) SIGNED: 13 Sep 65 FORCE: 13 Sep 65
IMCO (Maritime Org) SIGNED: 13 Sep 65 FORCE: 13 Sep 65
ITU (Telecommun) SIGNED: 13 Sep 65 FORCE: 13 Sep 65
UNESCO (Educ/Cult) SIGNED: 13 Sep 65 FORCE: 13 Sep 65
United Nations SIGNED: 13 Sep 65 FORCE: 13 Sep 65
UPU (Postal Union) SIGNED: 13 Sep 65 FORCE: 13 Sep 65
WHO (World Health) SIGNED: 13 Sep 65 FORCE: 13 Sep 65
WMO (Meteorology) SIGNED: 13 Sep 65 FORCE: 13 Sep 65
Sudan SIGNED: 13 Sep 65 FORCE: 13 Sep 65
ANNEX
659 UNTS 386. UNIDO (Industrial). Accession 15 Feb 69. Force 15 Feb 69.

107963 Multilateral Agreement **547 UNTS 280**
SIGNED: 21 Sep 65 FORCE: 21 Sep 65
REGISTERED: 3 Nov 65 United Nations
ARTICLES: 6 LANGUAGE: English.
HEADNOTE: OPERATIONAL ASSISTANCE
TOPIC: IGO Operations
CONCEPTS: Annex or appendix reference. Previous treaty replacement. Diplomatic privileges. Diplomatic missions. Diplomatic correspondence. Arbitration. Procedure. Domestic obligation. Assistance to United Nations. Inter-agency agreements. IGO obligations.
INTL ORGS: Permanent Court of Arbitration.
TREATY REF: 387UNTS202; 500UNTS322; 327UNTS120; 420UNTS133.
PROCEDURE: Amendment. Termination.
PARTIES:
FAO (Food Agri) SIGNED: 21 Sep 65 FORCE: 21 Sep 65
IAEA (Atom Energy) SIGNED: 21 Sep 65 FORCE: 21 Sep 65
ICAO (Civil Aviat) SIGNED: 21 Sep 65 FORCE: 21 Sep 65
ILO (Labor Org) SIGNED: 21 Sep 65 FORCE: 21 Sep 65
IMCO (Maritime Org) SIGNED: 21 Sep 65 FORCE: 21 Sep 65
ITU (Telecommun) SIGNED: 21 Sep 65 FORCE: 21 Sep 65
UNESCO (Educ/Cult) SIGNED: 21 Sep 65 FORCE: 21 Sep 65
United Nations SIGNED: 21 Sep 65 FORCE: 21 Sep 65
UPU (Postal Union) SIGNED: 21 Sep 65 FORCE: 21 Sep 65
WHO (World Health) SIGNED: 21 Sep 65 FORCE: 21 Sep 65
WMO (Meteorology) SIGNED: 21 Sep 65 FORCE: 21 Sep 65
Somalia SIGNED: 21 Sep 65 FORCE: 21 Sep 65
ANNEX
649 UNTS 366. UNIDO (Industrial). Accession 2 Nov 68. Force 2 Nov 68.

107964 Multilateral Agreement **547 UNTS 297**
SIGNED: 11 Dec 64 FORCE: 11 Dec 64
REGISTERED: 4 Nov 65 United Nations
ARTICLES: 6 LANGUAGE: English.
HEADNOTE: ECONOMIC COMMISSION
TOPIC: IGO Operations
CONCEPTS: Diplomatic missions. Privileges and

immunities. Diplomatic correspondence. Personnel. Subsidiary organ. Status of experts.
PARTIES:
Kenya
FAO (Food Agri)
IAEA (Atom Energy)
ICAO (Civil Aviat)
ILO (Labor Org)
IMCO (Maritime Org)
UNESCO (Educ/Cult)
United Nations
UPU (Postal Union)
WHO (World Health)
WMO (Meteorology)

107965 Multilateral Agreement **548 UNTS 3**
SIGNED: 7 Nov 64 FORCE: 7 Nov 64
REGISTERED: 4 Nov 65 New Zealand
ARTICLES: 14 LANGUAGE: English.
HEADNOTE: SOUTH PACIFIC HEALTH SERVICE
TOPIC: Sanitation
CONCEPTS: Definition of terms. Detailed regulations. Territorial application. Annex or appendix reference. Previous treaty extension. Previous treaty replacement. Standardization. General cooperation. Exchange of information and documents. Personnel. Responsibility and liability. Quarantine. Disease control. Public health. Nursing. Sanitation. WHO used as agency. Vocational training. Research and development. Accounting procedures. Indemnities and reimbursements. Expense sharing formulae. Conferences.
INTL ORGS: World Health Organization. South Pacific Health Service.
TREATY REF: 287UNTS104.
PROCEDURE: Duration. Renewal or Revival. Termination.
PARTIES:
Fiji Islands SIGNED: 7 Oct 64 FORCE: 7 Nov 64
New Zealand SIGNED: 18 Aug 64 FORCE: 7 Nov 64
New Zealand Cook Islands RATIFIED: 18 Aug 64 FORCE: 7 Nov 64
New Zealand Tokelau Islands RATIFIED: 18 Aug 64 FORCE: 7 Nov 64
Tonga SIGNED: 23 Oct 64 FORCE: 7 Nov 64
W Pacif Hi Command SIGNED: 7 Nov 64 FORCE: 7 Nov 64
Western Samoa SIGNED: 14 Sep 64 FORCE: 7 Nov 64

107966 Bilateral Agreement **548 UNTS 19**
SIGNED: 7 Jul 65 FORCE: 7 Jul 65
REGISTERED: 4 Nov 65 New Zealand
ARTICLES: 7 LANGUAGE: English.
HEADNOTE: TRADE
TOPIC: General Trade
CONCEPTS: Exceptions and exemptions. General cooperation. Balance of payments. Currency. Payment schedules. Most favored nation clause. Customs duties.
INTL ORGS: Council for Mutual Economic Assistance.
PROCEDURE: Amendment. Duration. Termination.
PARTIES:
New Zealand
Poland

107967 Multilateral Agreement **548 UNTS 27**
SIGNED: 16 Apr 64 FORCE: 16 May 64
REGISTERED: 5 Nov 65 Netherlands
ARTICLES: 15 LANGUAGE: French.
HEADNOTE: COMMON FRONTIERS
TOPIC: Visas
CONCEPTS: Visa abolition. Non-visa travel documents. Frontier permits. Immigration and emigration.
PROCEDURE: Denunciation. Termination.
PARTIES:
Belgium SIGNED: 16 Apr 64 FORCE: 16 May 64
France SIGNED: 16 Apr 64 FORCE: 16 May 64
Luxembourg SIGNED: 16 Apr 64 FORCE: 16 May 64
Netherlands SIGNED: 16 Apr 64 FORCE: 16 May 64

107968 Multilateral Exchange **548 UNTS 47**
SIGNED: 27 Nov 64 FORCE: 8 Dec 64
REGISTERED: 5 Nov 65 Netherlands
ARTICLES: 2 LANGUAGE: French.

HEADNOTE: ABOLITION VISA REQUIREMENT
TOPIC: Visas
CONCEPTS: Emergencies. Territorial application. Time limit. Visa abolition. Denial of admission. Resident permits. Conformity with municipal law.
TREATY REF: 196UNTS245; 226UNTS247; 220UNTS93; 220UNTS99.
PROCEDURE: Denunciation. Duration.
PARTIES:
Belgium SIGNED: 27 Nov 64 FORCE: 8 Dec 64
Israel SIGNED: 27 Nov 64 FORCE: 8 Dec 64
Luxembourg SIGNED: 27 Nov 64 FORCE: 8 Dec 64
Netherlands SIGNED: 27 Nov 64 FORCE: 8 Dec 64

107969 Bilateral Exchange **548 UNTS 57**
SIGNED: 16 Dec 64 FORCE: 16 Dec 64
REGISTERED: 8 Nov 65 UK Great Britain
ARTICLES: 2 LANGUAGE: English.
HEADNOTE: PROVISION UN METEOROLOGICAL PERSONNEL
TOPIC: Tech Assistance
CONCEPTS: Resident permits. Nationality and citizenship. Extradition, deportation and repatriation. General cooperation. Assistance.
TREATY REF: 469UNTS145.
PROCEDURE: Duration. Renewal or Revival. Termination.
PARTIES:
WMO (Meteorology)
UK Great Britain

107970 Bilateral Agreement **548 UNTS 63**
SIGNED: 28 Sep 64 FORCE: 11 Mar 65
REGISTERED: 8 Nov 65 UK Great Britain
ARTICLES: 8 LANGUAGE: English. Norwegian.
HEADNOTE: FISHING NORWEGIAN VESSELS
TOPIC: Specific Property
CONCEPTS: Visa abolition. Facilities and property. Fish, wildlife, and natural resources. Ocean resources.
TREATY REF: 398UNTS189.
PROCEDURE: Ratification.
PARTIES:
Norway
UK Great Britain

107971 Bilateral Agreement **548 UNTS 79**
SIGNED: 27 May 64 FORCE: 27 May 64
REGISTERED: 8 Nov 65 United Nations
ARTICLES: 7 LANGUAGE: English.
HEADNOTE: PRIVILEGES & IMMUNITIES SPECIAL FUND GOVERNING SESSION
TOPIC: IGO Status/Immunit
CONCEPTS: Non-visa travel documents. Diplomatic privileges. Privileges and immunities. IGO status. Special status. Conferences.
PARTIES:
Netherlands
United Nations

107972 Bilateral Exchange **548 UNTS 85**
SIGNED: 1 Mar 65 FORCE: 1 Jan 65
REGISTERED: 8 Nov 65 UK Great Britain
ARTICLES: 2 LANGUAGE: English.
HEADNOTE: IMPORTATION BOOKS FILMS
TOPIC: General Trade
CONCEPTS: Previous treaty replacement.
TREATY REF: 502UNTS177; 360UNTS79; 404UNTS376.
PROCEDURE: Duration. Termination.
PARTIES:
UK Great Britain
Yugoslavia

107973 Bilateral Convention **548 UNTS 91**
SIGNED: 2 Sep 63 FORCE: 14 Jan 65
REGISTERED: 16 Nov 65 Austria
ARTICLES: 25 LANGUAGE: German.
HEADNOTE: ESTABLISHMENT FRONTIER CLEARANCE OFFICES
TOPIC: Visas
CONCEPTS: Definition of terms. Establishment of commission. Customs declarations. Boundaries of territory. Markers and definitions. Frontier peoples and personnel.
PROCEDURE: Denunciation. Ratification.

PARTIES:
Austria
Switzerland
ANNEX
636 UNTS 396.   Austria.   Supplementation
24 Oct 67. Force 24 Jan 68.
636 UNTS 396.   Austria.   Supplementation
24 Oct 67. Force 24 Jan 68.

107974   Multilateral Protocol   **548 UNTS 129**
SIGNED: 2 Sep 63   FORCE: 14 Jan 65
REGISTERED: 16 Nov 65 Austria.
ARTICLES: 5 LANGUAGE: German.
HEADNOTE: APPLICATION AUSTRIAN-SWISS
FRONTIER CONVENTION
TOPIC: General Transport
CONCEPTS: Annex type material. Previous treaty
extension. Border traffic and migration. Stan-
dardization. Conformity with municipal law.
Routes and logistics.
TREATY REF: 548UNTS104.
PROCEDURE: Ratification.
PARTIES:
Austria SIGNED: 2 Sep 63 RATIFIED: 14 Dec 64
FORCE: 14 Jan 65
Liechtenstein SIGNED: 2 Sep 63 RATIFIED:
14 Dec 64 FORCE: 14 Jan 65
Switzerland SIGNED: 2 Sep 63 RATIFIED:
14 Dec 64 FORCE: 14 Jan 65
ANNEX
636 UNTS 410. Liechtenstein. Supplementation
24 Oct 67. Force 24 Jan 68.
636 UNTS 410. Switzerland. Supplementation
24 Oct 67. Force 24 Jan 68.

107975   Bilateral Treaty   **548 UNTS 137**
SIGNED: 24 Mar 64   FORCE: 8 Oct 65
REGISTERED: 17 Nov 65 Netherlands
ARTICLES: 13 LANGUAGE: Dutch. French.
HEADNOTE: COOPERATION DIPLOMATIC REPRE-
SENTATION
TOPIC: Consul/Citizenship
CONCEPTS: Non-prejudice to third party. Proxy di-
plomacy.
PROCEDURE: Denunciation. Ratification.
PARTIES:
Luxembourg
Netherlands

107976   Bilateral Agreement   **548 UNTS 151**
SIGNED: 8 Jun 64   FORCE: 10 Sep 65
REGISTERED: 17 Nov 65 Taiwan
ARTICLES: 6 LANGUAGE: Chinese. Spanish. En-
glish.
HEADNOTE: COMMERCE
TOPIC: General Trade
CONCEPTS: Treaty implementation. Conformity
with municipal law. Establishment of trade rela-
tions. Certificates of origin. Currency.
PROCEDURE: Denunciation. Duration. Renewal or
Revival.
PARTIES:
Taiwan
Peru

107977   Bilateral Agreement   **548 UNTS 163**
SIGNED: 21 Sep 65   FORCE: 21 Sep 65
REGISTERED: 17 Nov 65 Australia
ARTICLES: 11 LANGUAGE: English. Korean.
HEADNOTE: TRADE
TOPIC: General Trade
CONCEPTS: Exceptions and exemptions. Territo-
rial application. General provisions. Annex or ap-
pendix reference. Privileges and immunities.
General cooperation. Export quotas. Import
quotas. Trade agencies. Trade procedures. Pay-
ment schedules. Most favored nation clause.
Customs duties.
INTL ORGS: General Agreement on Tariffs and
Trade. United Nations.
PROCEDURE: Amendment. Duration. Termination.
PARTIES:
Australia
Korea, South

107978   Bilateral Agreement   **548 UNTS 193**
SIGNED: 20 Jan 65   FORCE: 23 Feb 65
REGISTERED: 23 Nov 65 Malta
ARTICLES: 9 LANGUAGE: English. French.

HEADNOTE: DEVELOPING TRADE TECHNICAL CO-
OPERATION
TOPIC: General Trade
CONCEPTS: Exceptions and exemptions. Treaty
implementation. Expropriation. General prop-
erty. Arbitration. Procedure. Special tribunals.
Negotiation. Export quotas. Balance of pay-
ments. Payment schedules. Assets transfer.
Most favored nation clause. National treatment.
General technical assistance. Economic assis-
tance.
INTL ORGS: International Court of Justice.
PROCEDURE: Duration. Renewal or Revival. Termi-
nation.
PARTIES:
Malta
Switzerland

107979   Bilateral Agreement   **548 UNTS 203**
SIGNED: 28 Apr 65   FORCE: 1 Jul 65
REGISTERED: 23 Nov 65 Malta
ARTICLES: 23 LANGUAGE: English.
HEADNOTE: ASSISTED MIGRATION
TOPIC: Non-ILO Labor
CONCEPTS: General provisions. Border traffic and
migration. General cooperation. Financial pro-
grams.
PROCEDURE: Duration. Renewal or Revival.
PARTIES:
Australia
Malta

107980   Bilateral Agreement   **548 UNTS 223**
SIGNED: 26 Jul 65   FORCE: 26 Jul 65
REGISTERED: 24 Nov 65 UK Great Britain
ARTICLES: 6 LANGUAGE: English.
HEADNOTE: AGREEMENT
TOPIC: General Amity
CONCEPTS: Peaceful relations.
TREATY REF: UK CMB.948.
PARTIES:
Maldive Islands
UK Great Britain

107981 Multilateral Agreement **548 UNTS 241**
SIGNED: 23 Jun 65   FORCE: 23 Jun 65
REGISTERED: 24 Nov 65 UK Great Britain
ARTICLES: 32 LANGUAGE: English.
HEADNOTE: APPLICATION SAFEGUARDS
TOPIC: Atomic Energy
CONCEPTS: Definition of terms. Treaty interpreta-
tion. Exchange of information and documents.
Inspection and observation. Establishment of
commission. Special tribunals. Accounting pro-
cedures. Indemnities and reimbursements. Nu-
clear materials. Peaceful use. Security of infor-
mation. Special status. Status of experts.
INTL ORGS: International Court of Justice.
TREATY REF: 374UNTS245; 276UNTS3.
PROCEDURE: Amendment. Duration. Renewal or
Revival. Termination.
PARTIES:
Denmark SIGNED: 23 Jun 65 FORCE: 23 Jun 65
IAEA (Atom Energy) SIGNED: 23 Jun 65 FORCE:
23 Jun 65
UK Great Britain SIGNED: 23 Jun 65 FORCE:
23 Jun 65

107982   Bilateral Exchange   **548 UNTS 265**
SIGNED: 16 Jul 65   FORCE: 9 Sep 64
REGISTERED: 25 Nov 65 Jamaica
ARTICLES: 2 LANGUAGE: English.
HEADNOTE: TRAINING MILITARY PERSONNEL
TOPIC: Milit Assistance
CONCEPTS: Non-visa travel documents. Immigra-
tion and emigration. Military training. Jurisdic-
tion. Specific claims or waivers.
PROCEDURE: Termination.
PARTIES:
Canada
Jamaica

107983   Bilateral Agreement   **548 UNTS 277**
SIGNED: 30 Jun 65   FORCE: 30 Jun 65
REGISTERED: 29 Nov 65 India
ARTICLES: 3 LANGUAGE: English.
HEADNOTE: ARRANGEMENTS DETERMINATION
BORDER
TOPIC: Territory Boundary

CONCEPTS: Special tribunals. Armistice and
peace. Markers and definitions.
INTL ORGS: United Nations.
TREATY REF: 375UNTS199; 362UNTS24.
PARTIES:
India
Pakistan

107984   Bilateral Exchange   **548 UNTS 285**
SIGNED: 5 Jun 65   FORCE: 5 Jun 65
REGISTERED: 30 Nov 65 USA (United States)
ARTICLES: 2 LANGUAGE: English. Arabic.
HEADNOTE: CONSTRUCTION MILITARY FACILI-
TIES
TOPIC: Milit Installation
CONCEPTS: Conformity with municipal law. Gen-
eral cooperation. Private contracts. Responsibil-
ity and liability. Procedure. Accounting proce-
dures. Indemnities and reimbursements. Claims
and settlements. Tax exemptions. Customs ex-
emptions. Special projects. Overflights and tech-
nical stops. Facilities and equipment. Airforce-
army-navy personnel ratio. Ranks and privileges.
Conditions for assistance missions. Jurisdiction.
Procurement and logistics. Status of forces.
Bases and facilities.
PROCEDURE: Duration. Future Procedures Contemplated. Renewal or Revival. Termination.
PARTIES:
Saudi Arabia
USA (United States)

107985   Bilateral Exchange   **549 UNTS 3**
SIGNED: 9 Jun 65   FORCE: 9 Jun 65
REGISTERED: 30 Nov 65 USA (United States)
ARTICLES: 2 LANGUAGE: English. Spanish.
HEADNOTE: TRADE COTTON TEXTILES
TOPIC: Commodity Trade
CONCEPTS: Detailed regulations. Commodity
trade. Quotas.
TREATY REF: 471UNTS296.
PROCEDURE: Duration. Termination.
PARTIES:
Colombia
USA (United States)

107986   Bilateral Agreement   **549 UNTS 23**
SIGNED: 25 Jun 65   FORCE: 25 Jun 65
REGISTERED: 30 Nov 65 USA (United States)
ARTICLES: 5 LANGUAGE: English. Spanish.
HEADNOTE: AGRI COMMOD TITLE IV
TOPIC: US Agri Commod Aid
CONCEPTS: General provisions. Annex or appen-
dix reference. Exchange of information and doc-
uments. Reexport of goods, etc.. Payment sched-
ules. Transportation costs. Purchase authoriza-
tion. Commodities schedule. Purchase
authorization. Merchant vessels. Mutual consul-
tation.
PARTIES:
Ecuador
USA (United States)

107987   Bilateral Exchange   **549 UNTS 43**
SIGNED: 13 Mar 65   FORCE: 13 Mar 65
REGISTERED: 30 Nov 65 USA (United States)
ARTICLES: 2 LANGUAGE: English. French.
HEADNOTE: INVESTMENT GUARANTIES
TOPIC: Claims and Debts
CONCEPTS: General cooperation. General prop-
erty. Arbitration. Procedure. Existing tribunals.
Negotiation. Reciprocity in financial treatment.
Currency. Claims and settlements. Private invest-
ment guarantee.
PARTIES:
Dahomey
USA (United States)

107988   Bilateral Exchange   **549 UNTS 49**
SIGNED: 26 Jul 65   FORCE: 26 Jul 65
REGISTERED: 30 Nov 65 USA (United States)
ARTICLES: 2 LANGUAGE: English.
HEADNOTE: PROCUREMENT US DEPARTMENT
DEFENSE
TOPIC: Status of Forces
CONCEPTS: Currency. Payment schedules. Pro-
curement and logistics.

PARTIES:
Israel
USA (United States)

107989   Bilateral Exchange   **549 UNTS 55**
SIGNED: 20 Jul 65   FORCE: 20 Jul 65
REGISTERED: 30 Nov 65 USA (United States)
ARTICLES: 2 LANGUAGE: English.
HEADNOTE: PROCUREMENT GOODS SERVICES
DEFENSE
TOPIC: Milit Assistance
CONCEPTS: Annex or appendix reference. Inspec-
tion and observation. Private contracts. Export
quotas. Accounting procedures. Local currency.
Materials, equipment and services. Payment for
war supplies.
PROCEDURE: Termination.
PARTIES:
Israel
USA (United States)

107990   Bilateral Convention   **549 UNTS 63**
SIGNED: 20 Sep 65   FORCE: 1 Oct 65
REGISTERED: 30 Nov 65 Denmark
ARTICLES: 4 LANGUAGE: French.
HEADNOTE: TAXATION MOTOR VEHICLES
TOPIC: Taxation
CONCEPTS: General. Tax exemptions. Customs
duties. Motor vehicles and combinations. Con-
formity with IGO decisions.
PROCEDURE: Denunciation.
PARTIES:
Belgium
Denmark

107991   Bilateral Agreement   **549 UNTS 69**
SIGNED: 29 Apr 65   FORCE: 28 Jun 65
REGISTERED: 30 Nov 65 IBRD (World Bank)
ARTICLES: 5 LANGUAGE: English.
HEADNOTE: GUARANTEE POWER
TOPIC: IBRD Project
CONCEPTS: Definition of terms. Annex or appen-
dix reference. Exchange of information and doc-
uments. Inspection and observation. Bonds.
Fees and exemptions. Tax exemptions. Domestic
obligation. Terms of loan. Loan regulations. Loan
guarantee. Guarantor non-interference. Hydro-
electric power.
PARTIES:
Portugal
IBRD (World Bank)

107992   Bilateral Exchange   **549 UNTS 95**
SIGNED: 18 Jun 65   FORCE: 18 Jun 65
REGISTERED: 30 Nov 65 Belgium
ARTICLES: 2 LANGUAGE: English.
HEADNOTE: AMATEUR RADIO OPERATORS
TOPIC: Gen Communications
CONCEPTS: Conformity with municipal law. Li-
censes and permits. Amateur radio. Amateur
third party message.
TREATY REF: USA'TIAS 4893;.
PROCEDURE: Termination.
PARTIES:
Belgium
USA (United States)

107993   Bilateral Agreement   **549 UNTS 101**
SIGNED: 23 Oct 65   FORCE: 23 Oct 65
REGISTERED: 1 Dec 65 United Nations
ARTICLES: 6 LANGUAGE: English.
HEADNOTE: AFRICAN INDUSTRIAL DEVELOP-
MENT CONFERENCE
TOPIC: IGO Operations
CONCEPTS: Frontier formalities. Privileges and im-
munities. Headquarters and facilities. IGO status.
Conferences.
INTL ORGS: United Nations.
TREATY REF: 549UNTS106 FN__1&2.
PARTIES:
United Nations
Zambia

107994   Bilateral Agreement   **549 UNTS 111**
SIGNED: 16 Jul 65   FORCE: 16 Jul 65
REGISTERED: 1 Dec 65 USA (United States)
ARTICLES: 5 LANGUAGE: English.
HEADNOTE: AGRI COMMOD TITLE I

TOPIC: US Agri Commod Aid
CONCEPTS: General provisions. Annex or appendix reference. Exchange of information and documents. Reexport of goods, etc.. Payment schedules. Transportation costs. Purchase authorization. Commodities schedule. Purchase
authorization. Mutual consultation.
PARTIES:
USA (United States)
Yugoslavia

107995   Bilateral Exchange   **549 UNTS 125**
SIGNED: 26 May 65   FORCE: 25 Jul 65
REGISTERED: 1 Dec 65 USA (United States)
ARTICLES: 2 LANGUAGE: English. Portuguese.
HEADNOTE: WAIVER NON-IMMIGRANT VISA
FEES
TOPIC: Visas
CONCEPTS: Time limit. Visas. Fees and exemp-
tions.
PARTIES:
Brazil
USA (United States)

107996   Bilateral Exchange   **549 UNTS 133**
SIGNED: 18 Jun 65   FORCE: 18 Jun 65
REGISTERED: 1 Dec 65 USA (United States)
ARTICLES: 2 LANGUAGE: English. French.
HEADNOTE: INVESTMENT GUARANTIES
TOPIC: Finance
CONCEPTS: General cooperation. General prop-
erty. Arbitration. Procedure. Existing tribunals.
Negotiation. Reciprocity in financial treatment.
Currency. Claims and settlements. Private invest-
ment guarantee.
INTL ORGS: International Court of Justice.
PARTIES:
USA (United States)
Upper Volta

107997   Bilateral Exchange   **549 UNTS 139**
SIGNED: 29 Jun 65   FORCE: 29 Jun 65
REGISTERED: 1 Dec 65 USA (United States)
ARTICLES: 2 LANGUAGE: English. French.
HEADNOTE: DEFENSE EQUIPMENT MATERIALS
SERVICES
TOPIC: Milit Installation
CONCEPTS: Conformity with municipal law. In-
spection and observation. Tax exemptions. Cus-
toms exemptions. Materials, equipment and ser-
vices. Military assistance. Return of equipment
and recapture. Security of information. Military
assistance missions. Bases and facilities. Restric-
tions on transfer.
PARTIES:
Guinea
USA (United States)

107998   Bilateral Agreement   **549 UNTS 145**
SIGNED: 28 Apr 65   FORCE: 25 Jun 65
REGISTERED: 3 Dec 65 IBRD (World Bank)
ARTICLES: 8 LANGUAGE: English.
HEADNOTE: LOAN RAILWAY
TOPIC: IBRD Project
CONCEPTS: Default remedies. Definition of terms.
Annex or appendix reference. Exchange of infor-
mation and documents. Informational records.
Inspection and observation. Accounting proce-
dures. Bonds. Fees and exemptions. Interest
rates. Tax exemptions. Domestic obligation.
Terms of loan. Loan regulations. Loan guarantee.
Guarantor non-interference. Railways.
INTL ORGS: International Development Associa-
tion.
PARTIES:
Taiwan
IBRD (World Bank)

107999   Bilateral Agreement   **549 UNTS 173**
SIGNED: 16 Dec 64   FORCE: 9 Sep 65
REGISTERED: 3 Dec 65 IBRD (World Bank)
ARTICLES: 7 LANGUAGE: English.
HEADNOTE: LOAN ROAD
TOPIC: IBRD Project
CONCEPTS: Definition of terms. Annex or appen-
dix reference. Exchange of information and doc-
uments. Inspection and observation. Bonds.
Fees and exemptions. Tax exemptions. Domestic
obligation. Terms of loan. Loan regulations. Loan

guarantee. Guarantor non-interference. Roads
and highways.
INTL ORGS: International Development Associa-
tion.
PARTIES:
Paraguay
IBRD (World Bank)

108000   Bilateral Agreement   **549 UNTS 189**
SIGNED: 4 Feb 65   FORCE: 11 May 65
REGISTERED: 6 Dec 65 IBRD (World Bank)
ARTICLES: 5 LANGUAGE: English.
HEADNOTE: GUARANTEE AGREEMENT
TOPIC: IBRD Project
CONCEPTS: Definition of terms. Annex or appen-
dix reference. Exchange of information and doc-
uments. Inspection and observation. Bonds.
Fees and exemptions. Tax exemptions. Domestic
obligation. Terms of loan. Loan regulations. Loan
guarantee. Guarantor non-interference.
PARTIES:
Mexico
IBRD (World Bank)

108001   Bilateral Protocol   **549 UNTS 221**
SIGNED: 17 Sep 65   FORCE: 17 Sep 65
REGISTERED: 6 Dec 65 Czechoslovakia
ARTICLES: 17 LANGUAGE: Czechoslovakian. Rus-
sian.
HEADNOTE: EXEMPTION VISA REQUIREMENTS
TOPIC: Visas
CONCEPTS: Time limit. Previous treaty replace-
ment. Visa abolition. Denial of admission. Resi-
dent permits. Non-visa travel documents.
PROCEDURE: Denunciation.
PARTIES:
Czechoslovakia
USSR (Soviet Union)

108002   Bilateral Agreement   **549 UNTS 239**
SIGNED: 26 Feb 65   FORCE: 11 May 65
REGISTERED: 8 Dec 65 IBRD (World Bank)
ARTICLES: 5 LANGUAGE: English.
HEADNOTE: GUARANTEE RIVER WATER
TOPIC: IBRD Project
CONCEPTS: Definition of terms. Annex or appen-
dix reference. Exchange of information and doc-
uments. Inspection and observation. Bonds.
Fees and exemptions. Tax exemptions. Domestic
obligation. Terms of loan. Loan regulations. Loan
guarantee. Guarantor non-interference. Irriga-
tion.
PARTIES:
Malaysia
IBRD (World Bank)

108003   Bilateral Exchange   **549 UNTS 273**
SIGNED: 29 Jun 65   FORCE: 29 Jun 65
REGISTERED: 8 Dec 65 USA (United States)
ARTICLES: 3 LANGUAGE: English.
HEADNOTE: SEISMIC OBSERVATIONS PROJECT
VELA UNIFORM
TOPIC: Scientific Project
CONCEPTS: Previous treaty extension. General
property. Research and scientific projects. Re-
search results. Nuclear research. Research and
development. Materials, equipment and ser-
vices.
PROCEDURE: Duration.
PARTIES:
Canada
USA (United States)

108004   Bilateral Exchange   **549 UNTS 281**
SIGNED: 7 Jul 65   FORCE: 6 Aug 65
REGISTERED: 8 Dec 65 USA (United States)
ARTICLES: 2 LANGUAGE: English.
HEADNOTE: RADIO COMMUNICATIONS AMA-
TEUR STATIONS
TOPIC: Gen Communications
CONCEPTS: Amateur radio. Amateur third party
message.
PROCEDURE: Termination.
PARTIES:
Israel
USA (United States)

108005 Bilateral Agreement **550 UNTS 3**
SIGNED: 26 May 65   FORCE: 26 May 65
REGISTERED: 8 Dec 65 USA (United States)
ARTICLES: 6 LANGUAGE: English. French.
HEADNOTE: AGRI COMMOD TITLE I
TOPIC: US Agri Commod Aid
CONCEPTS: General provisions. Annex or appendix reference. Exchange of information and documents. Reexport of goods, etc.. Exchange rates and regulations. Transportation costs. Local currency. Commodities schedule. Purchase authorization. Mutual consultation.
PARTIES:
USA (United States)
Vietnam, South

108006 Bilateral Exchange **550 UNTS 23**
SIGNED: 16 Oct 64   FORCE: 16 Oct 64
REGISTERED: 8 Dec 65 USA (United States)
ARTICLES: 2 LANGUAGE: English.
HEADNOTE: PRESERVATION TEMPLES FROM INUNDATION
TOPIC: Specific Property
CONCEPTS: Exchange of official publications. Indemnities and reimbursements. Facilities and property.
PARTIES:
UNESCO (Educ/Cult)
USA (United States)

108007 Bilateral Agreement **550 UNTS 31**
SIGNED: 5 Nov 64   FORCE: 20 Jan 65
REGISTERED: 8 Dec 65 USA (United States)
ARTICLES: 5 LANGUAGE: English. Serbo-Croat.
HEADNOTE: CLAIMS
TOPIC: Claims and Debts
CONCEPTS: Exchange of information and documents. Expropriation. Currency. Payment schedules. Claims and settlements.
PROCEDURE: Ratification.
PARTIES:
USA (United States)
Yugoslavia

108008 Multilateral Agreement **550 UNTS 45**
SIGNED: 15 Jun 57   FORCE: 8 Apr 61
REGISTERED: 17 Dec 65 France
ARTICLES: 11 LANGUAGE: French.
HEADNOTE: UNION REGISTRATION TRADE-MARKS ETC.
TOPIC: General Trade
CONCEPTS: Detailed regulations. Treaty implementation. General cooperation. Informational records. Public information. Indemnities and reimbursements. Trademarks. Recognition.
INTL ORGS: International Union for the Protection of Industrial Property.
PROCEDURE: Amendment. Accession. Denunciation. Duration. Ratification.
PARTIES:
Australia SIGNED: 15 Jun 57
Belgium SIGNED: 15 Jun 57 RATIFIED: 6 Mar 62 FORCE: 6 Jun 62
Czechoslovakia SIGNED: 15 Jun 57 RATIFIED: 21 Oct 60 FORCE: 8 Apr 61
Denmark SIGNED: 15 Jun 57 RATIFIED: 30 Oct 61 FORCE: 30 Nov 61
France SIGNED: 15 Jun 57 RATIFIED: 9 Nov 59 FORCE: 8 Apr 61
Germany, West SIGNED: 15 Jun 57 RATIFIED: 29 Dec 61 FORCE: 29 Jan 62
Hungary SIGNED: 15 Jun 57
Italy SIGNED: 15 Jun 57 RATIFIED: 25 Jul 60 FORCE: 8 Apr 61
Lebanon SIGNED: 15 Jun 57 RATIFIED: 30 May 60 FORCE: 8 Apr 61
Liechtenstein SIGNED: 15 Jun 57
Luxembourg SIGNED: 15 Jun 57
Monaco SIGNED: 15 Jun 57 RATIFIED: 8 Mar 61 FORCE: 8 Apr 61
Morocco SIGNED: 15 Jun 57
Netherlands SIGNED: 15 Jun 57 RATIFIED: 21 May 62 FORCE: 20 Aug 62
Norway SIGNED: 15 Jun 57 RATIFIED: 28 Jun 61 FORCE: 28 Jul 61
Poland SIGNED: 15 Jun 57 RATIFIED: 25 Mar 58 FORCE: 8 Apr 61
Portugal Azores RATIFIED: 2 Apr 59 FORCE: 8 Apr 61
Portugal Madeira RATIFIED: 2 Apr 59 FORCE: 8 Apr 61
Portugal SIGNED: 15 Jun 57 RATIFIED: 2 Apr 59 FORCE: 8 Apr 61
Romania SIGNED: 31 Dec 58
Spain SIGNED: 15 Jun 57 RATIFIED: 25 Mar 58 FORCE: 8 Apr 61
Sweden SIGNED: 15 Jun 57 RATIFIED: 28 Jun 61 FORCE: 28 Jul 61
Switzerland SIGNED: 15 Jun 57 RATIFIED: 20 Jul 62 FORCE: 20 Aug 62
Tunisia SIGNED: 15 Jun 57
Turkey SIGNED: 31 Dec 58
UK Great Britain SIGNED: 15 Jun 57 RATIFIED: 30 Oct 62 FORCE: 15 Apr 63
Yugoslavia SIGNED: 15 Jun 57

108009 Bilateral Agreement **550 UNTS 63**
SIGNED: 30 Jun 65   FORCE: 20 Jul 65
REGISTERED: 20 Dec 65 IBRD (World Bank)
ARTICLES: 5 LANGUAGE: English.
HEADNOTE: GUARANTEE DEVELOPMENT BORB PROJECT
TOPIC: IBRD Project
CONCEPTS: Definition of terms. Annex or appendix reference. Exchange of information and documents. Inspection and observation. Bonds. Fees and exemptions. Financial programs. Tax exemptions. Domestic obligation. Terms of loan. Loan regulations. Loan guarantee. Guarantor non-interference.
TREATY REF: 491UNTS345.
PARTIES:
Finland
IBRD (World Bank)

108010 Bilateral Agreement **550 UNTS 95**
SIGNED: 26 May 65   FORCE: 20 Jul 65
REGISTERED: 21 Dec 65 IBRD (World Bank)
ARTICLES: 5 LANGUAGE: English.
HEADNOTE: GUARANTEE EXPRESSWAY
TOPIC: IBRD Project
CONCEPTS: Definition of terms. Annex or appendix reference. Exchange of information and documents. Inspection and observation. Bonds. Fees and exemptions. Tax exemptions. Domestic obligation. Terms of loan. Loan regulations. Loan guarantee. Guarantor non-interference. Roads and highways.
PARTIES:
Japan
IBRD (World Bank)

108011 Bilateral Treaty **550 UNTS 123**
SIGNED: 1 Dec 64   FORCE: 18 Sep 65
REGISTERED: 22 Dec 65 Netherlands
ARTICLES: 4 LANGUAGE: Dutch. German.
HEADNOTE: LATERAL DELIMITATION CONTINENTAL SHELF
TOPIC: Territory Boundary
CONCEPTS: Previous treaties adherence. Markers and definitions. Continental shelf.
TREATY REF: 509UNTS2.
PROCEDURE: Ratification.
PARTIES:
Germany, West
Netherlands

108012 Multilateral Convention **550 UNTS 133**
SIGNED: 1 Dec 64   FORCE: 11 Dec 65
REGISTERED: 23 Dec 65 Customs Coop Coun
ARTICLES: 19 LANGUAGE: English. French.
HEADNOTE: CUSTOMS WELFARE MATERIALS SEAFARERS
TOPIC: Water Transport
CONCEPTS: Definition of terms. Privileges and immunities. Legal protection and assistance. Arbitration. Mediation and good offices. Procedure. Customs exemptions. Merchant vessels. Ports and pilotage.
INTL ORGS: International Labour Organization. United Nations.
PROCEDURE: Amendment. Accession. Denunciation. Duration. Ratification.
PARTIES:
Australia SIGNED: 28 Sep 65
Denmark SIGNED: 31 Aug 65
Germany, West SIGNED: 2 Jun 65
Ivory Coast SIGNED: 11 Jun 65
Japan SIGNED: 16 Sep 65
Lebanon SIGNED: 31 Aug 65 FORCE: 11 Dec 65
Madagascar SIGNED: 12 Jul 65

New Zealand SIGNED: 3 Jun 65 FORCE: 11 Dec 65
New Zealand Cook Islands RATIFIED: 3 Jun 65 FORCE: 11 Dec 65
New Zealand Niue RATIFIED: 3 Jun 65 FORCE: 11 Dec 65
New Zealand Tokelau Islands RATIFIED: 3 Jun 65 FORCE: 11 Dec 65
Niger SIGNED: 8 Jul 65 FORCE: 11 Dec 65
Norway SIGNED: 10 Sep 65 FORCE: 11 Dec 65
Poland SIGNED: 28 Sep 65
Romania SIGNED: 30 Sep 65
South Africa SIGNED: 27 Sep 65 FORCE: 28 Dec 65
Spain SIGNED: 27 Sep 65
Sweden SIGNED: 28 Sep 65
Switzerland SIGNED: 28 Sep 65
Tunisia SIGNED: 14 Jul 65 FORCE: 11 Dec 65
UK Great Britain SIGNED: 4 Jun 65
ANNEX
559 UNTS 374. Sweden. Ratification 15 Feb 66. Force 15 May 66.
561 UNTS 357. Yugoslavia. Accession 15 Apr 66. Force 15 Jul 66.
561 UNTS 357. Yugoslavia. Accession 15 Apr 66. Force 15 Jul 66.
565 UNTS 326. UK Great Britain. Qualified Ratification 25 May 66.
565 UNTS 326. UK Great Britain. Jersey Island.
565 UNTS 326. UK Great Britain. Isle of Man.
565 UNTS 326. UK Great Britain. Guernsey Island.
566 UNTS 373. Belgium. Accession 20 Jun 66. Force 20 Sep 66.
573 UNTS 358. Sierra Leone. Accession 7 Sep 66. Force 7 Dec 66.
600 UNTS 364. Uganda. Qualified Accession 19 Jun 67. Force 19 Sep 67.
606 UNTS 401. Denmark. Faroe Islands. Force 2 Nov 67.
635 UNTS 374. Italy. Accession 26 Mar 68. Force 26 Jun 68.
638 UNTS 306. Finland. Accession 17 May 68. Force 17 Aug 68.
640 UNTS 374. Japan. Ratification 15 Jun 68.
642 UNTS 378. UK Great Britain. Brit Solomon Is. Force 26 Nov 66.
642 UNTS 378. UK Great Britain. Dominican Republic. Force 26 Nov 66.
642 UNTS 378. UK Great Britain. Gibralter. Force 26 Nov 66.
642 UNTS 378. UK Great Britain. Montserrat. Force 26 Nov 66.
642 UNTS 378. UK Great Britain. Seychelles. Force 26 Nov 66.
642 UNTS 378. UK Great Britain. Cayman Island. Force 26 Nov 66.
642 UNTS 378. UK Great Britain. Fiji Islands. Force 26 Nov 66.
642 UNTS 378. UK Great Britain. Gilbert Islands. Force 26 Nov 66.
645 UNTS 376. Switzerland. Ratification 22 Aug 68. Force 22 Nov 68.

108013 Multilateral Agreement **550 UNTS 160**
SIGNED: 12 Nov 65   FORCE: 12 Nov 65
REGISTERED: 27 Dec 65 United Nations
ARTICLES: 6 LANGUAGE: English.
HEADNOTE: OPERATIONAL ASSISTANCE
TOPIC: IGO Operations
CONCEPTS: Previous treaty extension. Diplomatic privileges. Diplomatic missions. Privileges and immunities. Arbitration. Procedure. Domestic obligation. Assistance to United Nations. Interagency agreements. IGO obligations.
INTL ORGS: Permanent Court of Arbitration.
TREATY REF: 292UNTS272; 527UNTS136; 368UNTS143.
PROCEDURE: Amendment. Termination.
PARTIES:
Ethiopia SIGNED: 12 Nov 65 FORCE: 12 Nov 65
FAO (Food Agri) SIGNED: 12 Nov 65 FORCE: 12 Nov 65
IAEA (Atom Energy) SIGNED: 12 Nov 65 FORCE: 12 Nov 65
ICAO (Civil Aviat) SIGNED: 12 Nov 65 FORCE: 12 Nov 65
ILO (Labor Org) SIGNED: 12 Nov 65 FORCE: 12 Nov 65
IMCO (Maritime Org) SIGNED: 12 Nov 65 FORCE: 12 Nov 65
ITU (Telecommun) SIGNED: 12 Nov 65 FORCE: 12 Nov 65

UNESCO (Educ/Cult) SIGNED: 12 Nov 65
FORCE: 12 Nov 65
United Nations SIGNED: 12 Nov 65 FORCE:
12 Nov 65
UPU (Postal Union) SIGNED: 12 Nov 65 FORCE:
12 Nov 65
WHO (World Health) SIGNED: 12 Nov 65 FORCE:
12 Nov 65
WMO (Meteorology) SIGNED: 12 Nov 65 FORCE:
12 Nov 65
ANNEX
655 UNTS 396. UNIDO (Industrial). Accession
14 Jan 69. Force 14 Jan 69.

108014   Bilateral Exchange   **550 UNTS 179**
SIGNED: 7 Nov 62   FORCE: 7 Nov 62
REGISTERED: 29 Dec 65 Greece
ARTICLES: 4 LANGUAGE: English.
HEADNOTE: TAX EXEMPTION MARITIME SHIP-
PING
TOPIC: Taxation
CONCEPTS: Definition of terms. Conformity with
municipal law. Domestic legislation. Tax exemp-
tions. Merchant vessels.
PROCEDURE: Duration. Termination.
PARTIES:
Ethiopia
Greece

108015   Bilateral Exchange   **550 UNTS 189**
SIGNED: 7 Nov 62   FORCE: 7 Nov 62
REGISTERED: 29 Dec 65 Greece
ARTICLES: 2 LANGUAGE: English.
HEADNOTE: TAX EXEMPTION AIR TRANSPORT
TOPIC: Taxation
CONCEPTS: Definition of terms. Domestic legisla-
tion. Taxation. Air transport.
PROCEDURE: Duration. Termination.
PARTIES:
Ethiopia
Greece

108016   Bilateral Agreement   **550 UNTS 197**
SIGNED: 27 Apr 63   FORCE: 19 Oct 65
REGISTERED: 29 Dec 65 Greece
ARTICLES: 7 LANGUAGE: French.
HEADNOTE: SETTLEMENT FINANCIAL QUES-
TIONS
TOPIC: Finance
CONCEPTS: Treaty implementation. Exchange of
information and documents. Informational
records. Juridical personality. General property.
Accounting procedures. Bonds. Payment sched-
ules. Claims and settlements. Debt settlement.
Loan repayment. Post-war claims settlement.
PROCEDURE: Ratification.
PARTIES:
Greece
Hungary

108017   Bilateral Agreement   **550 UNTS 203**
SIGNED: 26 Sep 63   FORCE: 12 Oct 65
REGISTERED: 29 Dec 65 Greece
ARTICLES: 13 LANGUAGE: Greek. German.
HEADNOTE: WAR GRAVES
TOPIC: Other Military
CONCEPTS: Definition of terms. Treaty implemen-
tation. Exchange of information and documents.
Indemnities and reimbursements. Tax exemp-
tions. Customs exemptions. Burial arrange-
ments. Responsibility for war dead. Upkeep of
war graves. Establishment of war cemeteries.
PROCEDURE: Ratification.
PARTIES:
Germany, West
Greece

108018   Bilateral Agreement   **550 UNTS 221**
SIGNED: 25 Dec 63   FORCE: 5 May 65
REGISTERED: 29 Dec 65 Israel
ARTICLES: 3 LANGUAGE: Hebrew. Spanish.
HEADNOTE: TECHNICAL COOPERATION
TOPIC: Tech Assistance
CONCEPTS: Treaty implementation. General tech-
nical assistance. Agriculture.
PROCEDURE: Denunciation. Ratification.
PARTIES:
Dominican Republic
Israel

108019   Bilateral Agreement   **550 UNTS 231**
SIGNED: 30 Nov 64   FORCE: 30 Nov 64
REGISTERED: 29 Dec 65 Israel
ARTICLES: 16 LANGUAGE: English.
HEADNOTE: COOPERATION AGRICULTURE
TOPIC: Tech Assistance
CONCEPTS: General cooperation. Operating agen-
cies. Personnel. Vocational training. Accounting
procedures. Domestic obligation. Agriculture.
Materials, equipment and services.
TREATY REF: 515UNTS237.
PROCEDURE: Duration. Renewal or Revival. Termi-
nation.
PARTIES:
Ghana
Israel

108020   Bilateral Convention   **550 UNTS 239**
SIGNED: 26 Jul 56   FORCE: 29 Apr 65
REGISTERED: 29 Dec 65 Israel
ARTICLES: 20 LANGUAGE: Hebrew. French.
HEADNOTE: EXTRADITION
TOPIC: Extradition
CONCEPTS: Time limit. Extradition, deportation
and repatriation. Extradition requests. Extradita-
ble offenses. Location of crime. Refusal of extra-
dition. Concurrent requests. Limits of prosecu-
tion. Provisional detainment. Extradition post-
ponement. Witnesses and experts. Material
evidence. Legal protection and assistance. In-
demnities and reimbursements. Conveyance in
transit.
PROCEDURE: Ratification. Termination.
PARTIES:
Israel
Luxembourg

108021   Bilateral Agreement   **550 UNTS 269**
SIGNED: 16 Mar 64   FORCE: 16 Mar 64
REGISTERED: 29 Dec 65 Israel
ARTICLES: 4 LANGUAGE: English.
HEADNOTE: TECHNICAL ASSISTANCE
TOPIC: Tech Assistance
CONCEPTS: Personnel. Expense sharing formulae.
General technical assistance. Assistance.
PARTIES:
Israel
Philippines

108022   Bilateral Agreement   **550 UNTS 275**
SIGNED: 22 Aug 65   FORCE: 22 Aug 65
REGISTERED: 29 Dec 65 Israel
ARTICLES: 8 LANGUAGE: Hebrew. English.
HEADNOTE: CULTURAL
TOPIC: Culture
CONCEPTS: Friendship and amity. Tourism. Con-
formity with municipal law. Teacher and student
exchange. Exchange. General cultural cooper-
ation. Artists. Scientific exchange. Publications
exchange. Mass media exchange.
PROCEDURE: Amendment. Duration. Termination.
PARTIES:
Israel
Sierra Leone

108023   Bilateral Agreement   **550 UNTS 285**
SIGNED: 22 Aug 65   FORCE: 22 Aug 65
REGISTERED: 29 Dec 65 Israel
ARTICLES: 5 LANGUAGE: Hebrew. English.
HEADNOTE: TECHNICAL COOPERATION
TOPIC: Tech Assistance
CONCEPTS: Treaty implementation. Personnel.
Public health. Education. Scholarships and
grants. Vocational training. Research and devel-
opment. General technical assistance. Agricul-
ture.
PROCEDURE: Amendment. Termination.
PARTIES:
Israel
Sierra Leone

108024   Bilateral Exchange   **550 UNTS 297**
SIGNED: 9 Feb 65   FORCE: 10 May 65
REGISTERED: 29 Dec 65 Israel
ARTICLES: 2 LANGUAGE: French.
HEADNOTE: ABOLITION VISAS
TOPIC: Visas
CONCEPTS: Time limit. Visa abolition.

PARTIES:
Israel
Togo

108025   Bilateral Exchange   **550 UNTS 303**
SIGNED: 13 Nov 64   FORCE: 15 Nov 64
REGISTERED: 29 Dec 65 Israel
ARTICLES: 2 LANGUAGE: English.
HEADNOTE: TECHNICAL COOPERATION RURAL
PLANNING & DEVELOPMENT
TOPIC: Tech Assistance
CONCEPTS: Personnel. Vocational training. Ex-
pense sharing formulae. General technical assis-
tance. Assistance.
PROCEDURE: Duration. Future Procedures Con-
templated.
PARTIES:
Israel
Turkey

108026 Multilateral Agreement **550 UNTS 310**
SIGNED: 14 May 65   FORCE: 14 May 65
REGISTERED: 29 Dec 65 United Nations
ARTICLES: 6 LANGUAGE: English.
HEADNOTE: OPERATIONAL ASSISTANCE
TOPIC: IGO Operations
CONCEPTS: Annex or appendix reference. Diplo-
matic privileges. Diplomatic missions. Privileges
and immunities. Procedure. Existing tribunals.
Domestic obligation. Assistance to United Na-
tions. Conferences. IGO obligations.
INTL ORGS: Permanent Court of Arbitration.
TREATY REF: 45KUNTS389; 537UNTS136.
PROCEDURE: Amendment. Termination.
PARTIES:
FAO (Food Agri) SIGNED: 14 May 65 FORCE:
14 May 65
IAEA (Atom Energy) SIGNED: 14 May 65 FORCE:
14 May 65
ICAO (Civil Aviat) SIGNED: 14 May 65 FORCE:
14 May 65
ILO (Labor Org) SIGNED: 14 May 65 FORCE:
14 May 65
ITU (Telecommun) SIGNED: 14 May 65 FORCE:
14 May 65
UNESCO (Educ/Cult) SIGNED: 14 May 65
FORCE: 14 May 65
United Nations SIGNED: 14 May 65 FORCE:
14 May 65
UPU (Postal Union) SIGNED: 14 May 65 FORCE:
14 May 65
WHO (World Health) SIGNED: 14 May 65
FORCE: 14 May 65
WMO (Meteorology) SIGNED: 14 May 65
FORCE: 14 May 65
Tanzania SIGNED: 14 May 65 FORCE:
14 May 65

108027   Bilateral Exchange   **550 UNTS 329**
SIGNED: 1 Oct 65   FORCE: 1 Oct 65
REGISTERED: 30 Dec 65 Malta
ARTICLES: 2 LANGUAGE: English.
HEADNOTE: VISA ABOLITION
TOPIC: Visas
CONCEPTS: Time limit. Visa abolition. Denial of
admission. Conformity with municipal law.
PROCEDURE: Denunciation.
PARTIES:
Greece
Malta

108028   Bilateral Exchange   **550 UNTS 337**
SIGNED: 23 Oct 65   FORCE: 1 Dec 65
REGISTERED: 30 Dec 65 Malta
ARTICLES: 2 LANGUAGE: English. Italian.
HEADNOTE: IDENTITY CARDS TRAVEL DOCU-
MENTS
TOPIC: Visas
CONCEPTS: Non-visa travel documents.
PARTIES:
Italy
Malta

108029 Multilateral Instrument **550 UNTS 343**
SIGNED: 31 Jul 63   FORCE: 31 Jul 63
REGISTERED: 30 Dec 65 Philippines
ARTICLES: 4 LANGUAGE: English.
HEADNOTE: MANILA ACCORD
TOPIC: General Amity

CONCEPTS: Peaceful relations. Self-determination. General cooperation. Claims and settlements.
INTL ORGS: United Nations.
PARTIES:
Fed of Malaya SIGNED: 31 Jul 60 FORCE: 31 Jul 60
Indonesia SIGNED: 31 Jul 60 FORCE: 31 Jul 60
Philippines SIGNED: 31 Jul 60 FORCE: 31 Jul 60

108030 Multilateral Agreement **551 UNTS 2**
SIGNED: 2 Jun 65 FORCE: 2 Jun 65
REGISTERED: 1 Jan 65 United Nations
ARTICLES: 6 LANGUAGE: English.
HEADNOTE: OPERATIONAL ASSISTANCE
TOPIC: Tech Assistance
CONCEPTS: General provisions. Treaty implementation. Annex or appendix reference. Annex type material. Privileges and immunities. General cooperation. Personnel. Responsibility and liability. Arbitration. Procedure. Negotiation. Vocational training. Compensation. Indemnities and reimbursements. Exchange rates and regulations. Expense sharing formulae. Tax exemptions. Customs exemptions. Domestic obligation. General technical assistance. Assistance. Status of experts.
TREATY REF: 537UNTS348.
PROCEDURE: Amendment. Termination.
PARTIES:
Gambia SIGNED: 2 Jun 65 FORCE: 2 Jun 65
FAO (Food Agri) SIGNED: 2 Jun 65 FORCE: 2 Jun 65
IAEA (Atom Energy) SIGNED: 2 Jun 65 FORCE: 2 Jun 65
ICAO (Civil Aviat) SIGNED: 2 Jun 65 FORCE: 2 Jun 65
ILO (Labor Org) SIGNED: 2 Jun 65 FORCE: 2 Jun 65
IMCO (Maritime Org) SIGNED: 2 Jun 65 FORCE: 2 Jun 65
ITU (Telecommun) SIGNED: 2 Jun 65 FORCE: 2 Jun 65
UNESCO (Educ/Cult) SIGNED: 2 Jun 65 FORCE: 2 Jun 65
United Nations SIGNED: 2 Jun 65 FORCE: 2 Jun 65
UPU (Postal Union) SIGNED: 2 Jun 65 FORCE: 2 Jun 65
WHO (World Health) SIGNED: 2 Jun 65 FORCE: 2 Jun 65
WMO (Meteorology) SIGNED: 2 Jun 65 FORCE: 2 Jun 65

108031 Bilateral Exchange **551 UNTS 19**
SIGNED: 15 Apr 65 FORCE: 15 Apr 65
REGISTERED: 5 Jan 66 UK Great Britain
ARTICLES: 18 LANGUAGE: English.
HEADNOTE: FINANCE
TOPIC: Finance
CONCEPTS: Informational records. Use of facilities. Payment schedules. Claims and settlements. Lump sum settlements. Trusteeship.
PARTIES:
Israel
UK Great Britain

108032 Bilateral Exchange **551 UNTS 53**
SIGNED: 29 Mar 65 FORCE: 28 Apr 65
REGISTERED: 5 Jan 66 UK Great Britain
ARTICLES: 2 LANGUAGE: English. French.
HEADNOTE: ABOLITION VISAS
TOPIC: Visas
CONCEPTS: Emergencies. Territorial application. Time limit. Visa abolition. Denial of admission.
PROCEDURE: Denunciation.
PARTIES:
Ivory Coast
UK Great Britain

108033 Bilateral Agreement **551 UNTS 59**
SIGNED: 13 Jun 59 FORCE: 13 Jun 59
REGISTERED: 5 Jan 66 UK Great Britain
ARTICLES: 8 LANGUAGE: English.
HEADNOTE: COMMERCIAL DEBTS
TOPIC: Claims and Debts
CONCEPTS: Detailed regulations. Annex or appendix reference. Banking. Balance of payments. Financial programs. Interest rates. Payment schedules. Debts. Assessment procedures.
INTL ORGS: North Atlantic Treaty Organization.
TREATY REF: 52MUNTS145; 34UNTS243; 12LUNTS350; 243UNTS308.
PARTIES:
Turkey
UK Great Britain

108034 Bilateral Exchange **551 UNTS 69**
SIGNED: 20 Apr 65 FORCE: 1 Sep 65
REGISTERED: 5 Jan 66 UK Great Britain
ARTICLES: 2 LANGUAGE: English.
HEADNOTE: WAIVER VISA FEES
TOPIC: Visas
CONCEPTS: Territorial application. Visas. Fees and exemptions.
PROCEDURE: Termination.
PARTIES:
UK Great Britain
Yugoslavia

108035 Multilateral Agreement **551 UNTS 75**
SIGNED: 30 Dec 63 FORCE: 1 Jan 64
REGISTERED: 10 Jan 66 IBRD (World Bank)
ARTICLES: 5 LANGUAGE: English.
HEADNOTE: LOAN ASSUMPTION AGREEMENT
TOPIC: IBRD Project
CONCEPTS: Default remedies. Definition of terms. Previous treaty amendment. Bonds. Tax exemptions. Loan regulations. Loan guarantee.
PARTIES:
Central Afri Power SIGNED: 30 Dec 63 FORCE: 1 Jan 64
IBRD (World Bank) SIGNED: 30 Dec 63 FORCE: 1 Jan 64
UK Great Britain SIGNED: 30 Dec 63 FORCE: 1 Jan 64

108036 Multilateral Agreement **551 UNTS 105**
SIGNED: 30 Dec 63 FORCE: 1 Jan 64
REGISTERED: 10 Jan 66 IBRD (World Bank)
ARTICLES: 6 LANGUAGE: English.
HEADNOTE: GUARANTEE AGREEMENT
TOPIC: IBRD Project
CONCEPTS: Definition of terms. Annex or appendix reference. Exchange of information and documents. Inspection and observation. Bonds. Fees and exemptions. Tax exemptions. Domestic obligation. Terms of loan. Loan regulations. Loan guarantee. Guarantor non-interference.
PARTIES:
IBRD (World Bank) SIGNED: 30 Dec 63 FORCE: 1 Jan 64
Southern Rhodesia SIGNED: 30 Dec 63 FORCE: 1 Jan 64
UK Great Britain SIGNED: 30 Dec 63 FORCE: 1 Jan 64

108037 Multilateral Agreement **551 UNTS 119**
SIGNED: 30 Dec 63 FORCE: 1 Jan 64
REGISTERED: 10 Jan 66 IBRD (World Bank)
ARTICLES: 6 LANGUAGE: English.
HEADNOTE: GUARANTEE AGREEMENT
TOPIC: IBRD Project
CONCEPTS: Definition of terms. Annex or appendix reference. Exchange of information and documents. Inspection and observation. Bonds. Fees and exemptions. Tax exemptions. Domestic obligation. Terms of loan. Loan regulations. Loan guarantee. Guarantor non-interference.
TREATY REF: 285UNTS326.
PARTIES:
Northern Rhodesia SIGNED: 30 Dec 63 FORCE: 1 Jan 64
IBRD (World Bank) SIGNED: 30 Dec 63 FORCE: 1 Jan 64
UK Great Britain SIGNED: 30 Dec 63 FORCE: 1 Jan 64

108038 Bilateral Agreement **551 UNTS 129**
SIGNED: 14 Jan 65 FORCE: 8 Oct 65
REGISTERED: 10 Jan 66 Netherlands
ARTICLES: 6 LANGUAGE: Dutch. Spanish.
HEADNOTE: DAIRY FARMING TRAINING CENTER & SLAUGHTERING TECHNIQUE
TOPIC: Health/Educ/Welfare
CONCEPTS: Personnel. Specialists exchange. Veterinary. Vocational training. Research cooperation. Research and development. Tax exemptions. Customs exemptions. Specific technical assistance. Technical cooperation.
INTL ORGS: United Nations.
PROCEDURE: Duration. Termination.
PARTIES:
Ecuador
Netherlands

108039 Bilateral Agreement **551 UNTS 147**
SIGNED: 12 Jan 66 FORCE: 12 Jan 66
REGISTERED: 12 Jan 66 United Nations
ARTICLES: 6 LANGUAGE: French.
HEADNOTE: S N SEMINAR HUMAN RIGHTS DEVELOPING AREAS
TOPIC: Health/Educ/Welfare
CONCEPTS: Visas. Privileges and immunities. General cooperation. Exchange of information and documents. Personnel. Exchange. Postal services. Press and wire services. Status of experts. Conferences.
PROCEDURE: Duration. Termination.
PARTIES:
United Nations
Senegal

108040 Bilateral Convention **551 UNTS 157**
SIGNED: 1 Jun 65 FORCE: 23 Dec 65
REGISTERED: 13 Jan 66 Thailand
ARTICLES: 30 LANGUAGE: English.
HEADNOTE: DOUBLE TAXATION FISCAL EVASION TAXES INCOME & CAPITAL
TOPIC: Taxation
CONCEPTS: Definition of terms. Territorial application. Privileges and immunities. Nationality and citizenship. Conformity with municipal law. Exchange of official publications. Negotiation. Teacher and student exchange. Claims and settlements. Taxation. Tax credits. Equitable taxes. Tax exemptions. Air transport. Merchant vessels.
PROCEDURE: Duration. Ratification. Termination.
PARTIES:
Denmark
Thailand

108041 Bilateral Agreement **551 UNTS 193**
SIGNED: 5 Jun 65 FORCE: 22 Feb 65
REGISTERED: 14 Jan 66 UK Great Britain
ARTICLES: 10 LANGUAGE: English.
HEADNOTE: PUBLIC OFFICERS
TOPIC: Admin Cooperation
CONCEPTS: Definition of terms. Social security. Payment schedules.
PARTIES:
Gambia
UK Great Britain

108042 Bilateral Exchange **551 UNTS 205**
SIGNED: 8 Jun 65 FORCE: 8 Jul 65
REGISTERED: 14 Jan 66 UK Great Britain
ARTICLES: 2 LANGUAGE: English.
HEADNOTE: RECIPROCAL ABOLITION VISAS
TOPIC: Visas
CONCEPTS: Annex or appendix reference. Visa abolition. Denial of admission. Conformity with municipal law.
TREATY REF: 172UNTS265.
PROCEDURE: Denunciation.
PARTIES:
Greece
UK Great Britain

108043 Bilateral Agreement **551 UNTS 213**
SIGNED: 10 Mar 65 FORCE: 29 Jun 65
REGISTERED: 14 Jan 66 UK Great Britain
ARTICLES: 6 LANGUAGE: English. Norwegian.
HEADNOTE: DELIMITATION CONTINENTAL SHELF
TOPIC: Territory Boundary
CONCEPTS: Markers and definitions. Continental shelf.
PROCEDURE: Ratification.
PARTIES:
Norway
UK Great Britain

108044 Bilateral Exchange **551 UNTS 221**
SIGNED: 7 Jul 65 FORCE: 7 Jul 65

REGISTERED: 14 Jan 66 UK Great Britain
ARTICLES: 2 LANGUAGE: English.
HEADNOTE: ESTABLISHMENT FACILITY FOR NASA
TOPIC: Specific Property
CONCEPTS: Facilities and property.
TREATY REF: 249UNTS91; 351UNTS438.
PARTIES:
UK Great Britain
USA (United States)

108045 Bilateral Agreement **551 UNTS 227**
SIGNED: 3 Jun 65   FORCE: 22 Jul 65
REGISTERED: 17 Jan 66 IBRD (World Bank)
ARTICLES: 5 LANGUAGE: English.
HEADNOTE: GUARANTEE AGRICULTURAL CREDIT
TOPIC: IBRD Project
CONCEPTS: Definition of terms. Annex or appendix reference. Exchange of information and documents. Inspection and observation. Bonds. Fees and exemptions. Tax exemptions. Domestic obligation. Agriculture. Terms of loan. Loan regulations. Loan guarantee. Guarantor non-interference.
PARTIES:
Peru
IBRD (World Bank)

108046 Bilateral Agreement **551 UNTS 253**
SIGNED: 26 Nov 65   FORCE: 26 Nov 65
REGISTERED: 21 Jan 66 United Nations
ARTICLES: 6 LANGUAGE: English.
HEADNOTE: ARRANGEMENTS SYMPOSIUM ON INDUSTRIAL DEVELOPMENT AFRICA
TOPIC: IGO Operations
CONCEPTS: Frontier formalities. Border traffic and migration. Visas. Privileges and immunities. Personnel. Responsibility and liability. Use of facilities. Claims and settlements. General transportation. Security of information. Conferences.
INTL ORGS: Other United Nations Organizations. International Atomic Energy Agency.
TREATY REF: 1UNTS15; 18UNTS382; 33UNTS261; 199UNTS314.
PARTIES:
United Nations
United Arab Rep

108047 Bilateral Agreement **552 UNTS 3**
SIGNED: 26 Aug 65   FORCE: 26 Aug 65
REGISTERED: 21 Jan 66 WHO (World Health)
ARTICLES: 6 LANGUAGE: French.
HEADNOTE: TECHNICAL ADVISORY ASSISTANCE
TOPIC: Tech Assistance
CONCEPTS: Definition of terms. Privileges and immunities. General cooperation. Exchange of information and documents. Personnel. Responsibility and liability. Title and deeds. Exchange. Scholarships and grants. Vocational training. Research and development. Expense sharing formulae. Local currency. Domestic obligation. Special projects. Materials, equipment and services. IGO status. Conformity with IGO decisions.
TREATY REF: 33UNTS261.
PROCEDURE: Amendment. Termination.
PARTIES:
Poland
WHO (World Health)

108048 Multilateral Instrument **552 UNTS 15**
SIGNED: 12 Dec 62   FORCE: 30 Mar 65
REGISTERED: 24 Jan 66 Org Ctrl Am States
ARTICLES: 35 LANGUAGE: Spanish.
HEADNOTE: OCAS
TOPIC: IGO Establishment
CONCEPTS: Exchange of information and documents. Special tribunals. Exchange. Scientific exchange. Attachment of funds. Funding procedures. Economic assistance. Defense and security. Admission. Establishment. Headquarters and facilities. Internal structure. Conformity with IGO decisions.
INTL ORGS: United Nations.
PROCEDURE: Accession.
PARTIES:
Costa Rica SIGNED: 12 Dec 62   RATIFIED: 30 Mar 65 FORCE: 30 Mar 65
El Salvador SIGNED: 12 Dec 62   RATIFIED: 23 Aug 63 FORCE: 30 Mar 65
Honduras SIGNED: 12 Dec 62   RATIFIED: 23 Aug 63 FORCE: 30 Mar 65
Nicaragua SIGNED: 12 Dec 62   RATIFIED: 19 Nov 63 FORCE: 30 Mar 65

108049 Bilateral Agreement **552 UNTS 39**
SIGNED: 28 May 65   FORCE: 20 Aug 65
REGISTERED: 25 Jan 66 IBRD (World Bank)
ARTICLES: 5 LANGUAGE: English.
HEADNOTE: GUARANTEE INDUSTRIAL CREDIT
TOPIC: Loans and Credits
CONCEPTS: Definition of terms. Guarantees and safeguards. Annex or appendix reference. Exchange of information and documents. Currency. Interest rates. Payment schedules. Liens. Tax exemptions. Loan repayment. World Bank projects. Loan regulations.
PROCEDURE: Amendment. Termination.
PARTIES:
India
IBRD (World Bank)

108050 Bilateral Agreement **552 UNTS 75**
SIGNED: 19 Oct 61   FORCE: 2 Dec 64
REGISTERED: 25 Jan 66 Poland
ARTICLES: 8 LANGUAGE: Polish. Portuguese.
HEADNOTE: CULTURAL
TOPIC: Culture
CONCEPTS: Treaty implementation. Friendship and amity. Exchange of information and documents. Exchange. Teacher and student exchange. Scholarships and grants. Exchange. General cultural cooperation. Artists. Scientific exchange. Research and development. Finances and payments. Mass media exchange. Press and wire services.
INTL ORGS: United Nations.
PROCEDURE: Denunciation. Duration. Ratification.
PARTIES:
Brazil
Poland

108051 Bilateral Agreement **552 UNTS 89**
SIGNED: 6 Oct 64   FORCE: 11 May 65
REGISTERED: 25 Jan 66 Poland
ARTICLES: 15 LANGUAGE: Polish. German.
HEADNOTE: CULTURAL COOPERATION
TOPIC: Culture
CONCEPTS: Previous treaty replacement. Friendship and amity. Tourism. General cooperation. Exchange of information and documents. Public information. Specialists exchange. Exchange. Teacher and student exchange. Institute establishment. General cultural cooperation. Artists. Athletes. Scientific exchange. Finances and payments. Recognition. Publications exchange. Mass media exchange. Press and wire services.
TREATY REF: 304UNTS113.
PROCEDURE: Denunciation. Duration. Future Procedures Contemplated. Ratification. Renewal or Revival.
PARTIES:
Germany, East
Poland

108052 Bilateral Convention **552 UNTS 115**
SIGNED: 28 Oct 64   FORCE: 27 Jun 65
REGISTERED: 25 Jan 66 Poland
ARTICLES: 25 LANGUAGE: Polish. Mongolian. Russian.
HEADNOTE: CONSULAR
TOPIC: Consul/Citizenship
CONCEPTS: Definition of terms. General consular functions. Consular relations establishment. Privileges and immunities.
PROCEDURE: Ratification. Termination.
PARTIES:
Mongolia
Poland

108053 Bilateral Agreement **552 UNTS 157**
SIGNED: 26 Nov 64   FORCE: 10 Aug 65
REGISTERED: 25 Jan 66 Poland
ARTICLES: 13 LANGUAGE: Polish. Romanian.
HEADNOTE: CULTURAL SCIENTIFIC COOPERATION
TOPIC: Health/Educ/Welfare
CONCEPTS: Exchange of information and documents. Establishment of commission. Special-
ists exchange. Teacher and student exchange. Professorships. Vocational training. Exchange. Artists. Athletes. Research results. Scientific exchange. Mass media exchange.
PROCEDURE: Denunciation. Duration. Ratification. Renewal or Revival.
PARTIES:
Poland
Romania

108054 Bilateral Agreement **552 UNTS 175**
SIGNED: 17 Jul 64   FORCE: 16 Feb 65
REGISTERED: 25 Jan 66 Poland
ARTICLES: 16 LANGUAGE: Polish. Russian.
HEADNOTE: USE WATER RESOURCES FRONTIER WATER
TOPIC: Specific Resources
CONCEPTS: Definition of terms. Previous treaties adherence. General cooperation. Exchange of information and documents. Operating agencies. Frontier waterways. Regulation of natural resources.
TREATY REF: 420UNTS282.
PROCEDURE: Denunciation. Duration. Ratification. Renewal or Revival.
PARTIES:
Poland
USSR (Soviet Union)

108055 Bilateral Agreement **552 UNTS 201**
SIGNED: 26 Jan 66   FORCE: 26 Jan 66
REGISTERED: 26 Jan 66 United Nations
ARTICLES: 10 LANGUAGE: English.
HEADNOTE: ASSISTANCE
TOPIC: Direct Aid
CONCEPTS: Detailed regulations. Treaty implementation. Visas. Privileges and immunities. Exchange of information and documents. Informational records. Inspection and observation. Operating agencies. Personnel. Public information. Responsibility and liability. Title and deeds. Use of facilities. Arbitration. Procedure. Negotiation. Import quotas. Attachment of funds. Exchange rates and regulations. Expense sharing formulae. Financial programs. Domestic obligation. General technical assistance. Economic assistance. Materials, equipment and services. IGO status.
INTL ORGS: International Atomic Energy Agency. International Court of Justice. United Nations.
TREATY REF: 1UNTS15; 33UNTS261; 374UNTS147.
PROCEDURE: Amendment. Termination.
PARTIES:
Mongolia
UN Special Fund

108056 Bilateral Agreement **552 UNTS 219**
SIGNED: 2 Apr 65   FORCE: 3 Aug 65
REGISTERED: 28 Jan 66 UK Great Britain
ARTICLES: 24 LANGUAGE: English.
HEADNOTE: DOUBLE TAXATION FISCAL EVASION TAXES INCOME
TOPIC: Taxation
CONCEPTS: Definition of terms. Territorial application. Conformity with municipal law. Exchange of official publications. Domestic legislation. Teacher and student exchange. Taxation. Tax credits. Air transport. Merchant vessels.
PROCEDURE: Duration. Termination.
PARTIES:
Jamaica
UK Great Britain

108057 Bilateral Exchange **552 UNTS 251**
SIGNED: 8 Jun 65   FORCE: 8 Jun 65
REGISTERED: 28 Jan 66 UK Great Britain
ARTICLES: 2 LANGUAGE: English. Arabic.
HEADNOTE: INTEREST FREE LOAN
TOPIC: Loans and Credits
CONCEPTS: Payment schedules. Agriculture. Loan and credit. Loan repayment. Terms of loan. Natural resources. Roads and highways.
PARTIES:
Jordan
UK Great Britain
ANNEX
560 UNTS 300. UK Great Britain. Supplementation 18 Sep 65. Force 18 Sep 65.
560 UNTS 300. Jordan. Supplementation 18 Sep 65. Force 18 Sep 65.

108058   Bilateral Agreement   **552 UNTS 259**
SIGNED: 7 May 65   FORCE: 1 Jan 64
REGISTERED: 28 Jan 66 UK Great Britain
ARTICLES: 10 LANGUAGE: English.
HEADNOTE: OVERSEAS OFFICERS SERVING
  SABAH SARAWAK
TOPIC: Admin Cooperation
CONCEPTS: Definition of terms. Informational
  records. Bonds. General.
PROCEDURE: Duration. Termination.
PARTIES:
  Malaysia
  UK Great Britain

108059   Bilateral Agreement   **552 UNTS 271**
SIGNED: 11 Aug 64   FORCE: 5 Aug 65
REGISTERED: 28 Jan 66 UK Great Britain
ARTICLES: 12 LANGUAGE: English. French.
HEADNOTE: COOPERATION PEACEFUL USES
  ATOMIC ENERGY
TOPIC: Atomic Energy
CONCEPTS: Definition of terms. Non-prejudice to
  third party. Exchange of information and docu-
  ments. Inspection and observation. Research co-
  operation. Research results. Scientific ex-
  change. Nuclear materials. Peaceful use. Secu-
  rity of information.
INTL ORGS: International Atomic Energy Agency.
PROCEDURE: Duration. Ratification. Termination.
PARTIES:
  Switzerland
  UK Great Britain

108060   Multilateral Exchange   **552 UNTS 292**
SIGNED: 31 Dec 65   FORCE: 31 Dec 65
REGISTERED: 1 Feb 66 United Nations
ARTICLES: 2 LANGUAGE: English.
HEADNOTE: OBLIGATIONS IN PROVISION TECH-
  NICAL PERSONNEL
TOPIC: Recognition
CONCEPTS: Continuity of rights and obligations.
  Personnel. General technical assistance.
PARTIES:
  FAO (Food Agri) SIGNED: 31 Dec 65 FORCE:
    31 Dec 65
  IAEA (Atom Energy) SIGNED. 31 Dec 65 FORCE:
    31 Dec 65
  ICAO (Civil Aviat) SIGNED: 31 Dec 65 FORCE:
    31 Dec 65
  ILO (Labor Org) SIGNED: 31 Dec 65 FORCE:
    31 Dec 65
  ITU (Telecommun) SIGNED: 31 Dec 65 FORCE:
    31 Dec 65
  UNESCO (Educ/Cult) SIGNED: 31 Dec 65
    FORCE: 31 Dec 65
  United Nations SIGNED: 31 Dec 65 FORCE:
    31 Dec 65
  UPU (Postal Union) SIGNED: 31 Dec 65 FORCE:
    31 Dec 65
  WHO (World Health) SIGNED: 31 Dec 65 FORCE:
    31 Dec 65
  WMO (Meteorology) SIGNED: 31 Dec 65 FORCE:
    31 Dec 65
  Singapore   SIGNED: 13 Dec 65   FORCE:
    31 Dec 65

108061   Bilateral Exchange   **552 UNTS 299**
SIGNED: 31 Dec 65   FORCE: 31 Dec 65
REGISTERED: 1 Feb 66 United Nations
ARTICLES: 2 LANGUAGE: English.
HEADNOTE: ASSUMPTION OBLIGATIONS IN-
  CURRED SPECIAL FUND PROJECTS
TOPIC: Admin Cooperation
CONCEPTS: Continuity of rights and obligations.
  Responsibility and liability.
TREATY REF: 401UNTS159.
PARTIES:
  UN Special Fund
  Singapore

108062   Bilateral Exchange   **552 UNTS 305**
SIGNED: 14 Apr 64   FORCE: 28 Jul 65
REGISTERED: 1 Feb 66 Israel
ARTICLES: 2 LANGUAGE: French.
HEADNOTE: ABOLITION VISAS
TOPIC: Visas
CONCEPTS: Time limit. Visa abolition. Resident
  permits.
PROCEDURE: Denunciation.

PARTIES:
  Congo (Zaire)
  Israel

108063   Bilateral Convention   **552 UNTS 311**
SIGNED: 11 Sep 56   FORCE: 14 Dec 65
REGISTERED: 3 Feb 66 Greece
ARTICLES: 16 LANGUAGE: French.
HEADNOTE: PLANT PROTECTION
TOPIC: Health/Educ/Welfare
CONCEPTS: General cooperation. Exchange of in-
  formation and documents. Specialists ex-
  change. Quarantine. Border control. Disease
  control. Insect control. Research results. Spe-
  cific technical assistance.
PROCEDURE: Denunciation. Duration. Future Pro-
  cedures Contemplated. Renewal or Revival.
PARTIES:
  Greece
  Yugoslavia

108064   Bilateral Agreement   **552 UNTS 325**
SIGNED: 16 Jun 56   FORCE: 2 Dec 65
REGISTERED: 7 Feb 66 Czechoslovakia
ARTICLES: 14 LANGUAGE: Czechoslovakian. Ser-
  bo-Croat.
HEADNOTE: PLANT PROTECTION
TOPIC: Health/Educ/Welfare
CONCEPTS: General cooperation. Exchange of in-
  formation and documents. Specialists ex-
  change. Border control. Disease control. Insect
  control. Research results. Scientific exchange.
  Research and development. Specific technical
  assistance.
PROCEDURE: Denunciation. Duration. Renewal or
  Revival.
PARTIES:
  Czechoslovakia
  Yugoslavia

108065   Bilateral Agreement   **553 UNTS 3**
SIGNED: 26 Feb 65   FORCE: 8 Jul 65
REGISTERED: 7 Feb 66 IBRD (World Bank)
ARTICLES: 5 LANGUAGE: English.
HEADNOTE: GUARANTEE   HYDROELECTRIC
  PROJECT
TOPIC: IBRD Project
CONCEPTS: Definition of terms. Annex or appen-
  dix reference. Exchange of information and doc-
  uments. Inspection and observation. Bonds.
  Fees and exemptions. Tax exemptions. Domestic
  obligation. Terms of loan. Loan regulations. Loan
  guarantee. Guarantor non-interference. Hydro-
  electric power.
PARTIES:
  Brazil
  IBRD (World Bank)
                 ANNEX
600 UNTS 366. IBRD (World Bank). Amendment
  19 Dec 66.
600 UNTS 366. Brazil. Amendment 19 Dec 66.
668 UNTS 374.

108066   Bilateral Exchange   **553 UNTS 37**
SIGNED: 13 May 47   FORCE: 15 May 47
REGISTERED: 7 Feb 66 Ireland
ARTICLES: 2 LANGUAGE: English.
HEADNOTE: MUTUAL ABOLITION VISAS
TOPIC: Visas
CONCEPTS: Time limit. Visa abolition. Denial of
  admission. Resident permits. Conformity with
  municipal law.
PARTIES:
  Denmark
  Ireland

108067   Bilateral Exchange   **553 UNTS 45**
SIGNED: 1 Feb 55   FORCE: 1 Feb 55
REGISTERED: 7 Feb 66 Ireland
ARTICLES: 2 LANGUAGE: English.
HEADNOTE: MUTUAL ABOLITION VISAS
TOPIC: Visas
CONCEPTS: Emergencies. Time limit. Visa aboli-
  tion. Denial of admission. Conformity with mu-
  nicipal law.
PARTIES:
  Finland
  Ireland

108068   Bilateral Agreement   **553 UNTS 51**
SIGNED: 22 Apr 47   FORCE: 1 May 47
REGISTERED: 7 Feb 66 Ireland
ARTICLES: 2 LANGUAGE: French.
HEADNOTE: MUTUAL ABOLITION VISAS
TOPIC: Visas
CONCEPTS: Territorial application. Time limit. Visa
  abolition. Conformity with municipal law.
PARTIES:
  France
  Ireland

108069   Bilateral Agreement   **553 UNTS 59**
SIGNED: 21 Nov 49   FORCE: 21 Nov 49
REGISTERED: 7 Feb 66 Ireland
ARTICLES: 11 LANGUAGE: French.
HEADNOTE: STUDENT EMPLOYEES
TOPIC: Non-ILO Labor
CONCEPTS: Definition of terms. Visas. Exchange
  of information and documents. Vocational train-
  ing. Employment regulations. Wages and sala-
  ries. Non-ILO labor relations. Administrative co-
  operation. Migrant worker. Quotas.
PROCEDURE: Denunciation. Duration. Renewal or
  Revival.
PARTIES:
  France
  Ireland

108070   Bilateral Agreement   **553 UNTS 69**
SIGNED: 11 May 60   FORCE: 1 Jan 62
REGISTERED: 7 Feb 66 Ireland
ARTICLES: 10 LANGUAGE: Irish. German.
HEADNOTE: STUDENT EMPLOYEES
TOPIC: Non-ILO Labor
CONCEPTS: Territorial application. Conformity
  with municipal law. Exchange of information and
  documents. Legal protection and assistance.
  Employment regulations. Wages and salaries.
  Non-ILO labor relations. Administrative cooper-
  ation. Migrant worker. Fees and exemptions.
  Quotas. National treatment.
PROCEDURE: Duration. Ratification. Renewal or
  Revival. Termination.
PARTIES:
  Germany, West
  Ireland

108071   Bilateral Exchange   **553 UNTS 87**
SIGNED: 13 May 64   FORCE: 13 May 64
REGISTERED: 7 Feb 66 Ireland
ARTICLES: 2 LANGUAGE: Irish. German.
HEADNOTE: WAR GRAVES
TOPIC: Other Military
CONCEPTS: Indemnities and reimbursements. Tax
  exemptions. Customs exemptions. Burial ar-
  rangements. Responsibility for war dead. Up-
  keep of war graves. Establishment of war ceme-
  teries.
PARTIES:
  Germany, West
  Ireland

108072   Bilateral Exchange   **553 UNTS 93**
SIGNED: 5 Jun 56   FORCE: 15 Jun 56
REGISTERED: 7 Feb 66 Ireland
ARTICLES: 2 LANGUAGE: English.
HEADNOTE: MUTUAL ABOLITION VISAS
TOPIC: Visas
CONCEPTS: Visa abolition. Denial of admission
  Conformity with municipal law.
PROCEDURE: Amendment. Termination.
PARTIES:
  Greece
  Ireland

108073   Bilateral Exchange   **553 UNTS 99**
SIGNED: 20 May 49   FORCE: 1 Jun 49
REGISTERED: 7 Feb 66 Ireland
ARTICLES: 2 LANGUAGE: English.
HEADNOTE: MUTUAL ABOLITION VISAS
TOPIC: Visas
CONCEPTS: Visa abolition. Denial of admission
  Conformity with municipal law.
PARTIES:
  Iceland
  Ireland

108074 Bilateral Exchange 553 UNTS 105
SIGNED: 28 Nov 49 FORCE: 25 Dec 49
REGISTERED: 7 Feb 66 Ireland
ARTICLES: 2 LANGUAGE: English.
HEADNOTE: MUTUAL ABOLITION VISAS
TOPIC: Visas
CONCEPTS: Time limit. Visa abolition. Denial of
admission. Conformity with municipal law.
PROCEDURE: Amendment. Termination.
PARTIES:
Ireland
Italy

108075 Bilateral Exchange 553 UNTS 111
SIGNED: 1 Dec 48 FORCE: 1 Jan 49
REGISTERED: 7 Feb 66 Ireland
ARTICLES: 2 LANGUAGE: French.
HEADNOTE: MUTUAL ABOLITION VISAS
TOPIC: Visas
CONCEPTS: Visa abolition. Denial of admission.
Conformity with municipal law.
PARTIES:
Ireland
Luxembourg

108076 Bilateral Exchange 553 UNTS 117
SIGNED: 6 Jul 54 FORCE: 15 Jul 54
REGISTERED: 7 Feb 66 Ireland
ARTICLES: 2 LANGUAGE: French.
HEADNOTE: MUTUAL ABOLITION VISAS
TOPIC: Visas
CONCEPTS: Visa abolition. Denial of admission.
Conformity with municipal law.
PARTIES:
Ireland
Monaco

108077 Bilateral Agreement 553 UNTS 123
SIGNED: 18 Oct 54 FORCE: 31 May 55
REGISTERED: 7 Feb 66 Ireland
ARTICLES: 4 LANGUAGE: English.
HEADNOTE: DOUBLE TAXATION SEA AIR TRANS-
PORT
TOPIC: Taxation
CONCEPTS: Definition of terms. Taxation. Tax ex-
emptions. Air transport. Merchant vessels.
TREATY REF: 109LTS77.
PROCEDURE: Ratification. Termination.
PARTIES:
Ireland
Norway

108078 Bilateral Agreement 553 UNTS 129
SIGNED: 2 Apr 64 FORCE: 1 Dec 64
REGISTERED: 7 Feb 66 Ireland
ARTICLES: 4 LANGUAGE: English.
HEADNOTE: CULTURAL
TOPIC: Culture
CONCEPTS: Treaty implementation. Friendship
and amity. Exchange. Exchange. General cultural
cooperation. Artists. Scientific exchange.
PROCEDURE: Duration. Future Procedures Con-
templated. Ratification. Renewal or Revival. Ter-
mination.
PARTIES:
Ireland
Norway

108079 Bilateral Exchange 553 UNTS 135
SIGNED: 29 Jul 55 FORCE: 15 Aug 55
REGISTERED: 7 Feb 66 Ireland
ARTICLES: 2 LANGUAGE: English. Portuguese.
HEADNOTE: MUTUAL ABOLITION VISAS
TOPIC: Visas
CONCEPTS: Emergencies. Time limit. Visa aboli-
tion. Denial of admission. Resident permits.
PROCEDURE: Denunciation.
PARTIES:
Ireland
Portugal

108080 Bilateral Exchange 553 UNTS 141
SIGNED: 11 Nov 57 FORCE: 11 Nov 57
REGISTERED: 7 Feb 66 Ireland
ARTICLES: 2 LANGUAGE: English. Portuguese.
HEADNOTE: MOST FAVORED NATION SHIPPING
TOPIC: Mostfavored Nation

CONCEPTS: Territorial application. Most favored
nation clause. Navigational conditions.
TREATY REF: 131LTS145.
PROCEDURE: Termination.
PARTIES:
Ireland
Portugal

108081 Bilateral Agreement 553 UNTS 147
SIGNED: 11 May 50 FORCE: 11 May 50
REGISTERED: 7 Feb 66 Ireland
ARTICLES: 5 LANGUAGE: English. Spanish.
HEADNOTE: MUTUAL AID EXCHANGE METEORO-
LOGICAL INFORMATION
TOPIC: Scientific Project
CONCEPTS: Exchange of information and docu-
ments. Meteorology.
PROCEDURE: Denunciation.
PARTIES:
Ireland
Spain

108082 Bilateral Exchange 553 UNTS 157
SIGNED: 17 Apr 59 FORCE: 17 Apr 59
REGISTERED: 7 Feb 66 Ireland
ARTICLES: 2 LANGUAGE: Spanish.
HEADNOTE: MUTUAL ABOLITION VISAS
TOPIC: Visas
CONCEPTS: Visa abolition. Denial of admission.
Resident permits.
PROCEDURE: Denunciation.
PARTIES:
Ireland
Spain

108083 Bilateral Exchange 553 UNTS 163
SIGNED: 19 Mar 47 FORCE: 1 Apr 47
REGISTERED: 7 Feb 66 Ireland
ARTICLES: 2 LANGUAGE: English.
HEADNOTE: MUTUAL ABOLITION VISAS
TOPIC: Visas
CONCEPTS: Time limit. Visa abolition. Denial of
admission. Conformity with municipal law.
PARTIES:
Ireland
Sweden

108084 Bilateral Exchange 553 UNTS 169
SIGNED: 9 Jun 47 FORCE: 20 Jun 47
REGISTERED: 7 Feb 66 Ireland
ARTICLES: 2 LANGUAGE: French.
HEADNOTE: MUTUAL ABOLITION VISAS
TOPIC: Visas
CONCEPTS: Visa abolition. Denial of admission.
Conformity with municipal law.
PARTIES:
Ireland
Switzerland

108085 Bilateral Exchange 553 UNTS 175
SIGNED: 14 Mar 49 FORCE: 14 Mar 49
REGISTERED: 7 Feb 66 Ireland
ARTICLES: 9 LANGUAGE: English. French.
HEADNOTE: EXCHANGE EMPLOYMENT FACILI-
TIES
TOPIC: Non-ILO Labor
CONCEPTS: Administrative cooperation. Migrant
worker.
PROCEDURE: Denunciation. Renewal or Revival.
PARTIES:
Ireland
Switzerland

108086 Bilateral Agreement 553 UNTS 183
SIGNED: 18 Jun 58 FORCE: 26 Aug 60
REGISTERED: 7 Feb 66 Ireland
ARTICLES: 4 LANGUAGE: Irish. German.
HEADNOTE: TAXATION SHIPS AIRCRAFT
TOPIC: Taxation
CONCEPTS: Definition of terms. Domestic legisla-
tion. Taxation. Tax exemptions. Air transport.
Merchant vessels.
PROCEDURE: Duration. Termination.
PARTIES:
Ireland
Switzerland

108087 Bilateral Exchange 553 UNTS 193
SIGNED: 27 Sep 55 FORCE: 20 Oct 55
REGISTERED: 7 Feb 66 Ireland
ARTICLES: 2 LANGUAGE: English. French.
HEADNOTE: MUTUAL ABOLITION VISAS
TOPIC: Visas
CONCEPTS: Visa abolition. Denial of admission.
Resident permits. Conformity with municipal
law.
PROCEDURE: Denunciation.
PARTIES:
Ireland
Turkey

108088 Bilateral Agreement 553 UNTS 197
SIGNED: 6 Apr 54 FORCE: 6 Apr 54
REGISTERED: 7 Feb 66 Ireland
ARTICLES: 10 LANGUAGE: English.
HEADNOTE: VETERINARY SURGEONS
TOPIC: Sanitation
CONCEPTS: Definition of terms. General cooper-
ation. Recognition of degrees. Exchange. Voca-
tional training. Fees and exemptions.
PROCEDURE: Termination.
PARTIES:
Ireland
UK Great Britain

108089 Bilateral Agreement 553 UNTS 209
SIGNED: 18 May 49 FORCE: 28 Jul 49
REGISTERED: 7 Feb 66 Ireland
ARTICLES: 10 LANGUAGE: English.
HEADNOTE: DOUBLE TAXATION CORPORATION
PROFITS TAX
TOPIC: Taxation
CONCEPTS: Definition of terms. Frontier formali-
ties. Conformity with municipal law. Exchange of
official publications. Taxation. Tax credits. Equi-
table taxes. Tax exemptions. Merchant vessels.
PROCEDURE: Duration. Termination.
PARTIES:
Ireland
UK Great Britain

108090 Bilateral Agreement 553 UNTS 221
SIGNED: 25 Jun 64 FORCE: 27 Jun 63
REGISTERED: 7 Feb 66 Ireland
ARTICLES: 13 LANGUAGE: English.
HEADNOTE: PURCHASE SUGAR
TOPIC: Commodity Trade
CONCEPTS: Treaty implementation. Trade agen-
cies. Payment schedules. Non-interest rates and
fees. Commodity trade.
PROCEDURE: Duration. Renewal or Revival. Termi-
nation.
PARTIES:
Ireland
UK Great Britain
ANNEX
655 UNTS 398. Ireland. Signature 1 Jul 67. Force
1 Jul 67.
655 UNTS 398.

108091 Bilateral Exchange 553 UNTS 233
SIGNED: 1 Dec 64 FORCE: 1 Dec 64
REGISTERED: 7 Feb 66 Ireland
ARTICLES: 2 LANGUAGE: English.
HEADNOTE: TRADE
TOPIC: General Trade
CONCEPTS: Exceptions and exemptions. Tariffs.
Most favored nation clause.
PROCEDURE: Duration. Renewal or Revival. Termi-
nation.
PARTIES:
Ireland
Vietnam, South

108092 Bilateral Agreement 553 UNTS 239
SIGNED: 15 Oct 65 FORCE: 15 Oct 65
REGISTERED: 8 Feb 66 USSR (Soviet Union)
ARTICLES: 7 LANGUAGE: Russian. English.
HEADNOTE: TRADE
TOPIC: General Trade
CONCEPTS: Exceptions and exemptions. General
cooperation. Export quotas. Import quotas. Reci-
procity in trade. Balance of payments. Currency.
Payment schedules. Most favored nation clause.
Customs duties.
PROCEDURE: Duration. Termination.

PARTIES:
Australia
USSR (Soviet Union)

108093 Bilateral Treaty **553 UNTS 249**
SIGNED: 12 Jun 64 FORCE: 29 Sep 64
REGISTERED: 8 Feb 66 USSR (Soviet Union)
ARTICLES: 11 LANGUAGE: Russian. German.
HEADNOTE: FRIENDSHIP MUTUAL ASSISTANCE
COOPERATION
TOPIC: General Amity
CONCEPTS: Non-prejudice to UN charter. Peaceful
relations. Re-establishment. Defense and secu-
rity.
INTL ORGS: United Nations. Council for Mutual
Economic Assistance.
PROCEDURE: Duration. Ratification. Renewal or
Revival.
PARTIES:
Germany, East
USSR (Soviet Union)

108094 Bilateral Treaty **553 UNTS 267**
SIGNED: 21 Mar 64 FORCE: 20 Oct 64
REGISTERED: 8 Feb 66 USSR (Soviet Union)
ARTICLES: 6 LANGUAGE: Russian. Arabic.
HEADNOTE: FRIENDSHIP
TOPIC: General Amity
CONCEPTS: Treaty interpretation. Friendship and
amity. Peaceful relations. Alien status. Proce-
dure. Establishment of trade relations.
INTL ORGS: United Nations.
PROCEDURE: Amendment. Denunciation. Dura-
tion. Renewal or Revival.
PARTIES:
USSR (Soviet Union)
Yemen

108095 Bilateral Agreement **554 UNTS 3**
SIGNED: 12 Jul 65 FORCE: 14 Sep 65
REGISTERED: 9 Feb 66 IBRD (World Bank)
ARTICLES: 5 LANGUAGE: English.
HEADNOTE: GUARANTEE AGREEMENT
TOPIC: IBRD Project
CONCEPTS: Definition of terms. Annex or appen-
dix reference. Exchange of information and doc-
uments. Inspection and observation. Bonds.
Fees and exemptions. Tax exemptions. Domestic
obligation. Terms of loan. Loan regulations. Loan
guarantee. Guarantor non-interference.
PARTIES:
Iran
IBRD (World Bank)

108096 Bilateral Agreement **554 UNTS 39**
SIGNED: 9 Jul 65 FORCE: 2 Sep 65
REGISTERED: 9 Feb 66 IBRD (World Bank)
ARTICLES: 5 LANGUAGE: English.
HEADNOTE: GUARANTEE AGREEMENT
TOPIC: IBRD Project
CONCEPTS: Definition of terms. Annex or appen-
dix reference. Exchange of information and doc-
uments. Informational records. Inspection and
observation. Bonds. Fees and exemptions. Tax
exemptions. Domestic obligation. Terms of loan.
Loan regulations. Loan guarantee. Guarantor
non-interference.
PARTIES:
Pakistan
IBRD (World Bank)

108097 Bilateral Agreement **554 UNTS 75**
SIGNED: 30 Jun 65 FORCE: 16 Sep 65
REGISTERED: 9 Feb 66 IDA (Devel Assoc)
ARTICLES: 6 LANGUAGE: English.
HEADNOTE: DEVELOPMENT CREDIT TEA ROAD
TOPIC: Non-IBRD Project
CONCEPTS: Detailed regulations. Previous treaty
amendment. Informational records. Accounting
procedures. Currency. Interest rates. Tax exemp-
tions. Credit provisions. Loan repayment. Terms
of loan. Plans and standards. IDA development
project. Roads and highways.
PARTIES:
Kenya
IDA (Devel Assoc)

108098 Bilateral Agreement **554 UNTS 93**
SIGNED: 24 Jun 64 FORCE: 8 Jul 65
REGISTERED: 9 Feb 66 IDA (Devel Assoc)
ARTICLES: 7 LANGUAGE: English.
HEADNOTE: DEVELOPMENT CREDIT ROAD
TOPIC: Non-IBRD Project
CONCEPTS: Detailed regulations. Previous treaty
amendment. Informational records. Accounting
procedures. Currency. Interest rates. Tax exemp-
tions. Credit provisions. Loan repayment. Terms
of loan. Plans and standards. IDA development
project. Roads and highways.
PARTIES:
Niger
IDA (Devel Assoc)

108099 Bilateral Agreement **554 UNTS 111**
SIGNED: 30 Jun 65 FORCE: 3 Sep 65
REGISTERED: 9 Feb 66 IDA (Devel Assoc)
ARTICLES: 7 LANGUAGE: English.
HEADNOTE: DEVELOPMENT CREDIT AGRICUL-
TURAL BANK
TOPIC: Non-IBRD Project
CONCEPTS: Definition of terms. Detailed regula-
tions. Previous treaty amendment. Informational
records. Athletes. Accounting procedures. Bank-
ing. Currency. Interest rates. Tax exemptions.
Loan repayment. Terms of loan. Plans and stan-
dards. IDA development project.
PARTIES:
Pakistan
IDA (Devel Assoc)

108100 Bilateral Agreement **554 UNTS 137**
SIGNED: 1 Apr 65 FORCE: 9 Jul 65
REGISTERED: 9 Feb 66 IDA (Devel Assoc)
ARTICLES: 9 LANGUAGE: English.
HEADNOTE: DEVELOPMENT BANK PROJECT IN-
DUSTRIAL DEVELOPMENT BANK
TOPIC: Non-IBRD Project
CONCEPTS: Definition of terms. Detailed regula-
tions. Previous treaty amendment. Informational
records. Accounting procedures. Banking. Cur-
rency. Interest rates. Tax exemptions. Credit pro-
visions. Loan repayment. Terms of loan. Plans
and standards. IDA development project.
TREATY REF: 469UNTS3; 535UNTS111.
PARTIES:
IDA (Devel Assoc)
Turkey

108101 Bilateral Agreement **554 UNTS 169**
SIGNED: 31 Aug 65 FORCE: 1 Jan 66
REGISTERED: 11 Feb 66 New Zealand
ARTICLES: 17 LANGUAGE: English.
HEADNOTE: STRENGTHENING COMMERCIAL &
ECONOMIC TIES
TOPIC: General Trade
CONCEPTS: Definition of terms. Detailed regula-
tions. Exceptions and exemptions. Territorial ap-
plication. General provisions. Annex or appendix
reference. General cooperation. Export quotas.
Import quotas. Tariffs. Reexport of goods, etc..
Export subsidies. Trade procedures. Balance of
payments. Smuggling. General. Customs duties.
TREATY REF: 48OUNTS241;5SEPT33 TRADE
AGREEMENTS; GATT.
PARTIES:
Australia
New Zealand

108102 Bilateral Treaty **555 UNTS 3**
SIGNED: 27 Nov 64 FORCE: 3 Dec 65
REGISTERED: 14 Feb 66 Taiwan
ARTICLES: 9 LANGUAGE: Chinese. Korean. En-
glish.
HEADNOTE: AMITY
TOPIC: General Amity
CONCEPTS: Friendship and amity. Peaceful rela-
tions. Alien status. Consular relations establish-
ment. Diplomatic relations establishment. Privi-
leges and immunities.
PROCEDURE: Future Procedures Contemplated.
Ratification.
PARTIES:
Taiwan
Korea, South

108103 Bilateral Agreement **555 UNTS 21**
SIGNED: 28 Apr 65 FORCE: 9 Sep 65
REGISTERED: 14 Feb 66 IBRD (World Bank)
ARTICLES: 7 LANGUAGE: English.
HEADNOTE: LOAN ROAD
TOPIC: IBRD Project
CONCEPTS: Default remedies. Definition of terms.
Annex or appendix reference. Exchange of infor-
mation and documents. Informational records.
Inspection and observation. Accounting proce-
dures. Bonds. Fees and exemptions. Interest
rates. Tax exemptions. Domestic obligation.
Terms of loan. Loan regulations. Loan guarantee.
Guarantor non-interference. Roads and high-
ways.
PARTIES:
Iran
IBRD (World Bank)

108104 Bilateral Agreement **555 UNTS 45**
SIGNED: 28 Apr 65 FORCE: 9 Sep 65
REGISTERED: 14 Feb 66 IBRD (World Bank)
ARTICLES: 7 LANGUAGE: English.
HEADNOTE: LOAN ROAD
TOPIC: IBRD Project
CONCEPTS: Default remedies. Definition of terms.
Annex or appendix reference. Exchange of infor-
mation and documents. Informational records.
Inspection and observation. Accounting proce-
dures. Bonds. Currency deposits. Fees and ex-
emptions. Tax exemptions. Domestic obligation.
Terms of loan. Loan regulations. Loan guarantee.
Guarantor non-interference. Roads and high-
ways.
INTL ORGS: United Nations.
PARTIES:
Iran
IBRD (World Bank)

108105 Multilateral Agreement **555 UNTS 69**
SIGNED: 14 Jan 46 FORCE: 24 Jan 46
REGISTERED: 15 Feb 66 France
ARTICLES: 26 LANGUAGE: English.
HEADNOTE: REPARATION RESTITUTION MONE-
TARY GOLD
TOPIC: Reparations
CONCEPTS: Territorial application. Treaty imple-
mentation. Annex or appendix reference. Assis-
tance. Repatriation of nationals. General cooper-
ation. Exchange of information and documents.
Establishment of commission. Arbitration. Proce-
dure. Accounting procedures. Attachment of
funds. Indemnities and reimbursements. Mer-
chant vessels. Loss and/or damage. Enemy fi-
nancial interests. Reparations and restrictions.
Internal structure. Status of experts.
INTL ORGS: Inter-Allied Reparations Agency. Inter-
national Refugees Organization. United Nations.
PROCEDURE: Application to Non-self-governing
Territories.
PARTIES:
Albania SIGNED: 14 Mar 46 FORCE: 14 Mar 46
Australia SIGNED: 25 Feb 46 FORCE: 25 Feb 46
Belgium SIGNED: 14 Jan 46 FORCE: 24 Jan 46
Canada SIGNED: 30 Jan 46 FORCE: 30 Jan 46
Czechoslovakia SIGNED: 27 Feb 46 FORCE:
27 Feb 46
Denmark SIGNED: 20 Feb 46 FORCE: 20 Feb 46
United Arab Rep SIGNED: 8 Mar 46 FORCE:
8 Mar 46
France SIGNED: 14 Jan 46 FORCE: 14 Jan 46
Greece SIGNED: 24 Jan 46 FORCE: 14 Jan 46
India SIGNED: 25 Feb 46 FORCE: 25 Feb 46
Italy RATIFIED: 16 Dec 47 FORCE: 15 Sep 47
Luxembourg SIGNED: 14 Jan 46 FORCE:
14 Jan 46
Netherlands SIGNED: 14 Jan 46 FORCE:
14 Jan 46
New Zealand SIGNED: 20 Feb 46 FORCE:
20 Feb 46
Norway SIGNED: 6 Feb 46 FORCE: 6 Feb 46
South Africa SIGNED: 28 Feb 46 FORCE:
28 Feb 46
UK Great Britain SIGNED: 14 Jan 46 FORCE:
14 Jan 46
USA (United States) SIGNED: 14 Mar 46 FORCE:
24 Jan 46
Yugoslavia SIGNED: 4 Feb 46 FORCE: 4 Feb 46

108106 Bilateral Agreement **555 UNTS 111**
SIGNED: 6 Apr 63 FORCE: 5 Jul 64

REGISTERED: 16 Feb 66 Tunisia
ARTICLES: 11 LANGUAGE: French.
HEADNOTE: CULTURAL COOPERATION
TOPIC: Culture
CONCEPTS: Treaty implementation. Friendship and amity. Specialists exchange. Exchange. Teacher and student exchange. Scholarships and grants. General cultural cooperation. Artists. Scientific exchange. Recognition. Publications exchange. Mass media exchange. Press and wire services.
PROCEDURE: Denunciation. Duration. Ratification. Renewal or Revival.
PARTIES:
Czechoslovakia
Tunisia

108107   Bilateral Exchange   **555 UNTS 119**
SIGNED: 21 Feb 66   FORCE: 13 Mar 64
REGISTERED: 21 Feb 66 United Nations
ARTICLES: 2 LANGUAGE: English.
HEADNOTE: PEACE KEEPING FORCE
TOPIC: IGO Operations
CONCEPTS: Annex or appendix reference. Privileges and immunities. Procedure. Ranks and privileges. Jurisdiction. Withdrawal of occupation. Status of experts.
INTL ORGS: International Court of Justice. United Nations Educational, Scientific and Cultural Organization. United Nations Forces on Cyprus. Arbitration Commission.
TREATY REF: 492UNTS57; 75UNTS31; 249UNTS215.
PARTIES:
Canada
United Nations

108108   Bilateral Exchange   **555 UNTS 151**
SIGNED: 21 Feb 66   FORCE: 14 May 64
REGISTERED: 21 Feb 66 United Nations
ARTICLES: 2 LANGUAGE: English.
HEADNOTE: UN PEACE KEEPING FORCE
TOPIC: IGO Operations
CONCEPTS: Annex or appendix reference. Privileges and immunities. Procedure. Ranks and privileges. Jurisdiction. Withdrawal of occupation. Status of experts.
INTL ORGS: United Nations Forces on Cyprus.
TREATY REF: 492UNTS57; 75UNTS31; 249UNTS215.
PARTIES:
Denmark
United Nations

108109   Bilateral Exchange   **555 UNTS 157**
SIGNED: 21 Feb 66   FORCE: 28 Mar 64
REGISTERED: 21 Feb 66 United Nations
ARTICLES: 2 LANGUAGE: English.
HEADNOTE: UN PEACE KEEPING FORCE
TOPIC: IGO Operations
CONCEPTS: Annex or appendix reference. Privileges and immunities. Procedure. Ranks and privileges. Jurisdiction. Withdrawal of occupation. Status of experts.
INTL ORGS: United Nations Forces on Cyprus.
TREATY REF: 492UNTS57; 75UNTS31; 249UNTS215.
PARTIES:
Finland
United Nations

108110   Bilateral Exchange   **555 UNTS 163**
SIGNED: 21 Feb 66   FORCE: 14 May 64
REGISTERED: 21 Feb 66 United Nations
ARTICLES: 2 LANGUAGE: English.
HEADNOTE: UN PEACE KEEPING FORCE
TOPIC: IGO Operations
CONCEPTS: Annex or appendix reference. Privileges and immunities. Procedure. Ranks and privileges. Jurisdiction. Withdrawal of occupation. Status of experts.
INTL ORGS: United Nations Forces on Cyprus.
TREATY REF: 492UNTS57; 75UNTS31; 249UNTS215.
PARTIES:
New Zealand
United Nations

108111   Bilateral Exchange   **555 UNTS 169**
SIGNED: 21 Feb 66   FORCE: 26 Mar 64
REGISTERED: 21 Feb 66 United Nations
ARTICLES: 2 LANGUAGE: English.
HEADNOTE: UN PEACE KEEPING FORCE
TOPIC: IGO Operations
CONCEPTS: Annex or appendix reference. Privileges and immunities. Procedure. Ranks and privileges. Jurisdiction. Withdrawal of occupation.
INTL ORGS: United Nations Forces on Cyprus.
TREATY REF: 492UNTS57; 75UNTS31; 249UNTS215.
PARTIES:
United Nations
Sweden

108112   Bilateral Exchange   **555 UNTS 177**
SIGNED: 21 Feb 66   FORCE: 27 Mar 64
REGISTERED: 21 Feb 66 United Nations
ARTICLES: 2 LANGUAGE: English.
HEADNOTE: PEACE KEEPING FORCES CYPRUS
TOPIC: General Economic
CONCEPTS: Annex type material. Procedure. Existing tribunals. Special tribunals. Status of forces. Peace-keeping force.
INTL ORGS: United Nations Forces on Cyprus.
TREATY REF: 492UNTS57; 75UNTS31; 249UNTS215; 75UNTS85,135.
PARTIES:
United Nations
UK Great Britain

108113   Multilateral Agreement   **555 UNTS 183**
SIGNED: 28 Jul 64   FORCE: 13 Dec 65
REGISTERED: 21 Feb 66 IAEA (Atom Energy)
ARTICLES: 8 LANGUAGE: English.
HEADNOTE: SAFEGUARDS
TOPIC: IGO Operations
CONCEPTS: Annex or appendix reference. Exchange of information and documents. Arbitration. Procedure. Accounting procedures. Funding procedures. Materials, equipment and services. Atomic energy assistance. Acceptance of delivery. General. Nuclear materials. Non-nuclear materials. Peaceful use. Conformity with IGO decisions.
INTL ORGS: International Court of Justice.
TREATY REF: 374UNTS147.
PROCEDURE: Amendment. Duration.
PARTIES:
Austria SIGNED: 28 Jul 64 FORCE: 13 Dec 65
IAEA (Atom Energy) SIGNED: 28 Jul 64 FORCE: 13 Dec 65
USA (United States) SIGNED: 15 Jun 64 FORCE: 13 Dec 65

108114   Multilateral Agreement   **555 UNTS 205**
SIGNED: 18 Sep 64   FORCE: 24 Sep 65
REGISTERED: 21 Feb 66 IAEA (Atom Energy)
ARTICLES: 8 LANGUAGE: English.
HEADNOTE: SAFEGUARDS
TOPIC: IGO Operations
CONCEPTS: Definition of terms. Annex or appendix reference. Exchange of information and documents. Arbitration. Procedure. Accounting procedures. Funding procedures. Materials, equipment and services. Atomic energy assistance. Acceptance of delivery. General. Nuclear materials. Non-nuclear materials. Peaceful use. Conformity with IGO decisions.
INTL ORGS: International Court of Justice.
PARTIES:
Philippines SIGNED: 18 Sep 64 FORCE: 24 Sep 65
IAEA (Atom Energy) SIGNED: 18 Sep 64 FORCE: 24 Sep 65
USA (United States) SIGNED: 15 Jun 54 FORCE: 24 Sep 65

108115   Multilateral Agreement   **555 UNTS 227**
SIGNED: 21 Sep 64   FORCE: 29 Oct 65
REGISTERED: 21 Feb 66 IAEA (Atom Energy)
ARTICLES: 8 LANGUAGE: English.
HEADNOTE: SAFEGUARDS
TOPIC: IGO Operations
CONCEPTS: Definition of terms. Annex or appendix reference. Exchange of information and documents. Arbitration. Procedure. Funding procedures. Materials, equipment and services.

Atomic energy assistance. Acceptance of delivery. General. Nuclear materials. Non-nuclear materials. Peaceful use. Conformity with IGO decisions.
INTL ORGS: International Court of Justice.
PARTIES:
Taiwan SIGNED: 21 Sep 64 FORCE: 29 Oct 65
IAEA (Atom Energy) SIGNED: 21 Sep 64 FORCE: 29 Oct 65
USA (United States) SIGNED: 21 Sep 64 FORCE: 29 Oct 65

108116   Multilateral Agreement   **556 UNTS 3**
SIGNED: 30 Sep 64   FORCE: 10 Sep 65
REGISTERED: 21 Feb 66 IAEA (Atom Energy)
ARTICLES: 8 LANGUAGE: English.
HEADNOTE: SAFEGUARDS
TOPIC: IGO Operations
CONCEPTS: Definition of terms. Annex or appendix reference. Exchange of information and documents. Arbitration. Accounting procedures. Funding procedures. Materials, equipment and services. Atomic energy assistance. Acceptance of delivery. General. Nuclear materials. Non-nuclear materials. Peaceful use. Conformity with IGO decisions.
INTL ORGS: International Court of Justice.
PROCEDURE: Amendment. Duration.
PARTIES:
IAEA (Atom Energy) SIGNED: 30 Sep 64 FORCE: 10 Sep 65
Thailand SIGNED: 30 Sep 64 FORCE: 10 Sep 65
USA (United States) SIGNED: 30 Sep 64 FORCE: 10 Sep 65

108117   Multilateral Agreement   **556 UNTS 25**
SIGNED: 18 Sep 64   FORCE: 25 Oct 65
REGISTERED: 21 Feb 66 IAEA (Atom Energy)
ARTICLES: 8 LANGUAGE: English.
HEADNOTE: SAFEGUARDS
TOPIC: IGO Operations
CONCEPTS: Definition of terms. Annex or appendix reference. Exchange of information and documents. Arbitration. Accounting procedures. Funding procedures. Materials, equipment and services. Atomic energy assistance. Acceptance of delivery. General. Non-nuclear materials. Peaceful use. Conformity with IGO decisions.
INTL ORGS: International Court of Justice. Arbitration Commission.
TREATY REF: 347UNTS113; 529UNTS356; 276UNTS3.
PROCEDURE: Amendment. Duration.
PARTIES:
IAEA (Atom Energy) SIGNED: 25 Nov 64 FORCE: 25 Oct 65
USA (United States) SIGNED: 25 Nov 64 FORCE: 25 Oct 65
Vietnam, South SIGNED: 25 Nov 64 FORCE: 25 Oct 65

108118   Multilateral Agreement   **556 UNTS 47**
SIGNED: 24 Feb 65   FORCE: 15 Dec 65
REGISTERED: 21 Feb 66 IAEA (Atom Energy)
ARTICLES: 8 LANGUAGE: English. French.
HEADNOTE: SAFEGUARDS
TOPIC: IGO Operations
CONCEPTS: Default remedies. Definition of terms. Annex or appendix reference. Exchange of information and documents. Arbitration. Procedure. Accounting procedures. Funding procedures. Materials, equipment and services. Atomic energy assistance. Acceptance of delivery. General. Nuclear materials. Non-nuclear materials. Peaceful use. Conformity with IGO decisions.
INTL ORGS: International Court of Justice. Arbitration Commission.
TREATY REF: 556UNTS48 FN__2&3; 374UNTS147.
PROCEDURE: Amendment. Duration.
PARTIES:
Portugal SIGNED: 24 Feb 65 FORCE: 15 Dec 65
IAEA (Atom Energy) SIGNED: 24 Feb 65 FORCE: 15 Dec 65
USA (United States) SIGNED: 24 Feb 65 FORCE: 15 Dec 65

108119   Multilateral Agreement   **556 UNTS 69**
SIGNED: 26 Feb 65   FORCE: 8 Oct 65
REGISTERED: 21 Feb 66 IAEA (Atom Energy)

ARTICLES: 8 LANGUAGE: English.
HEADNOTE: SAFEGUARDS
TOPIC: IGO Operations
CONCEPTS: Definition of terms. Annex or appendix reference. Exchange of information and documents. Arbitration. Procedure. Accounting procedures. Funding procedures. Materials, equipment and services. Atomic energy assistance. Acceptance of delivery. General. Nuclear materials. Non-nuclear materials. Peaceful use. Conformity with IGO decisions.
INTL ORGS: Permanent Court of Arbitration. International Court of Justice.
TREATY REF: 556UNTS70 FN 2,3,&4; 374UNTS147.
PROCEDURE: Amendment. Duration.
PARTIES:
  IAEA (Atom Energy) SIGNED: 26 Feb 65 FORCE: 8 Oct 65
  South Africa SIGNED: 26 Feb 65 FORCE: 8 Oct 65
  USA (United States) SIGNED: 26 Feb 65 FORCE: 8 Oct 65

108120 Bilateral Agreement **556 UNTS 89**
SIGNED: 11 Jun 64 FORCE: 10 Dec 64
REGISTERED: 21 Feb 66 Netherlands
ARTICLES: 8 LANGUAGE: English.
HEADNOTE: FINANCE
TOPIC: Claims and Debts
CONCEPTS: Detailed regulations. Exchange of information and documents. Expropriation. General property. Responsibility and liability. Accounting procedures. Assets. Claims and settlements. Lump sum settlements. General. Loan repayment.
PROCEDURE: Ratification.
PARTIES:
  Czechoslovakia
  Netherlands

108121 Bilateral Agreement **556 UNTS 101**
SIGNED: 24 Sep 65 FORCE: 24 Sep 65
REGISTERED: 21 Feb 66 IAEA (Atom Energy)
ARTICLES: 1 LANGUAGE: English.
HEADNOTE: TRANSFER THERAPEUTIC IRRADIATION EQUIPMENT
TOPIC: Atomic Energy
CONCEPTS: Exchange of information and documents. Inspection and observation. Special tribunals. Public health. Research results. Non-nuclear materials. Peaceful use. Transport of goods. Special status. Status of experts.
INTL ORGS: International Court of Justice.
TREATY REF: 374UNTS147; 276UNTS3; 471UNTS334.
PARTIES:
  Afghanistan
  IAEA (Atom Energy)

108122 Bilateral Agreement **556 UNTS 109**
SIGNED: 24 Sep 65 FORCE: 24 Sep 65
REGISTERED: 21 Feb 66 IAEA (Atom Energy)
ARTICLES: 8 LANGUAGE: French.
HEADNOTE: DELIVERY RADIO THERAPY EQUIPMENT
TOPIC: Atomic Energy
CONCEPTS: Annex or appendix reference. Exchange of information and documents. Inspection and observation. Responsibility and liability. Special tribunals. Public health. Research results. Acceptance of delivery. Non-nuclear materials. Peaceful use. Transport of goods. Special status. Status of experts.
INTL ORGS: International Court of Justice.
TREATY REF: 374UNTS147.
PARTIES:
  Morocco
  IAEA (Atom Energy)

108123 Bilateral Agreement **556 UNTS 117**
SIGNED: 24 Sep 65 FORCE: 24 Sep 65
REGISTERED: 21 Feb 66 IAEA (Atom Energy)
ARTICLES: 10 LANGUAGE: English. Spanish.
HEADNOTE: ASSISTANCE ESTABLISHING REACTOR PROJECT
TOPIC: Atomic Energy
CONCEPTS: Annex or appendix reference. Non-prejudice to third party. Exchange of information and documents. Inspection and observation. Re-

sponsibility and liability. Procedure. Public health. Research cooperation. Research results. Nuclear research. Nuclear materials. Peaceful use. Transport of goods. Special status. Status of experts.
PARTIES:
  IAEA (Atom Energy)
  Uruguay

108124 Multilateral Instrument **556 UNTS 141**
SIGNED: 24 Sep 65 FORCE: 24 Sep 65
REGISTERED: 21 Feb 66 IAEA (Atom Energy)
ARTICLES: 15 LANGUAGE: English. Spanish.
HEADNOTE: LEASE ENRICHED URANIUM TRANSFER SPECIAL FISSIONABLE MATERIAL
TOPIC: Atomic Energy
CONCEPTS: Exchange of information and documents. Responsibility and liability. Title and deeds. Special tribunals. Negotiation. Indemnities and reimbursements. Interest rates. Payment schedules. Assets transfer. Nuclear materials. Non-nuclear materials. Transport of goods.
INTL ORGS: International Court of Justice. Arbitration Commission.
PARTIES:
  IAEA (Atom Energy) SIGNED: 24 Sep 65 FORCE: 24 Sep 65
  USA (United States) SIGNED: 24 Sep 65 FORCE: 24 Sep 65
  Uruguay SIGNED: 24 Sep 65 FORCE: 24 Sep 65

108125 Multilateral Agreement **556 UNTS 175**
SIGNED: 7 Oct 65 FORCE: 7 Oct 65
REGISTERED: 21 Feb 66 IAEA (Atom Energy)
ARTICLES: 12 LANGUAGE: English. Spanish.
HEADNOTE: NUCLEAR ELECTRIC POWER DESALTING PLANT
TOPIC: Atomic Energy
CONCEPTS: Establishment of commission. Research cooperation. General. Hydro-electric power.
PARTIES:
  Mexico SIGNED: 7 Oct 65 FORCE: 7 Oct 65
  IAEA (Atom Energy) SIGNED: 7 Oct 65 FORCE: 7 Oct 65
  USA (United States) SIGNED: 7 Oct 65 FORCE: 7 Oct 65

108126 Multilateral Agreement **557 UNTS 3**
SIGNED: 30 Dec 65 FORCE: 30 Dec 65
REGISTERED: 21 Feb 66 IAEA (Atom Energy)
ARTICLES: 5 LANGUAGE: English. Spanish.
HEADNOTE: CONTRACT TRANSFER TITLE ENRICHED URANIUM
TOPIC: Atomic Energy
CONCEPTS: Title and deeds. Establishment of commission. Nuclear materials.
TREATY REF: 339UNTS359; 276UNTS3; 471UNTS334.
PARTIES:
  Argentina SIGNED: 13 Dec 65 FORCE: 30 Dec 65
  IAEA (Atom Energy) SIGNED: 30 Dec 65 FORCE: 30 Dec 65
  USA (United States) SIGNED: 13 Dec 65 FORCE: 30 Dec 65

108127 Bilateral Convention **557 UNTS 13**
SIGNED: 10 Mar 64 FORCE: 17 Jun 65
REGISTERED: 23 Feb 66 Belgium
ARTICLES: 28 LANGUAGE: French.
HEADNOTE: DOUBLE TAXATION INCOME
TOPIC: Taxation
CONCEPTS: Definition of terms. Territorial application. Previous treaty replacement. Conformity with municipal law. Exchange of official publications. Negotiation. Teacher and student exchange. Debts. Taxation. Tax credits. Equitable taxes. General. Tax exemptions.
TREATY REF: 111LTS43; 231UNTS101.
PROCEDURE: Duration. Ratification. Termination.
PARTIES:
  Belgium
  France

108128 Bilateral Agreement **557 UNTS 59**
SIGNED: 11 Jun 65 FORCE: 27 Jul 65
REGISTERED: 24 Feb 66 IBRD (World Bank)
ARTICLES: 8 LANGUAGE: English.

HEADNOTE: LOAN POWER TRANSMISSION
TOPIC: IBRD Project
CONCEPTS: Default remedies. Definition of terms. Annex or appendix reference. Exchange of information and documents. Informational records. Inspection and observation. Accounting procedures. Bonds. Fees and exemptions. Interest rates. Tax exemptions. Domestic obligation. Terms of loan. Loan regulations. Loan guarantee. Guarantor non-interference. Hydro-electric power.
PARTIES:
  India
  IBRD (World Bank)

108129 Bilateral Exchange **557 UNTS 85**
SIGNED: 25 Feb 66 FORCE: 14 May 64
REGISTERED: 25 Feb 66 United Nations
ARTICLES: 3 LANGUAGE: English.
HEADNOTE: PEACE KEEPING
TOPIC: IGO Operations
CONCEPTS: Annex or appendix reference. Privileges and immunities. Juridical personality. Arbitration. Procedure. Jurisdiction. Foreign nationals. Control and occupation machinery.
TREATY REF: 497UNTS57; 75UNTS3; 249UNTS215.
PARTIES:
  Australia
  United Nations

108130 Bilateral Agreement **557 UNTS 101**
SIGNED: 11 Jun 65 FORCE: 3 Aug 65
REGISTERED: 25 Feb 66 IBRD (World Bank)
ARTICLES: 8 LANGUAGE: English.
HEADNOTE: LOAN POWER
TOPIC: IBRD Project
CONCEPTS: Definition of terms. Emergencies. Annex or appendix reference. Exchange of information and documents. Informational records. Inspection and observation. Accounting procedures. Bonds. Fees and exemptions. Interest rates. Tax exemptions. Domestic obligation. Terms of loan. Loan regulations. Loan guarantee. Guarantor non-interference. Hydro-electric power.
PARTIES:
  India
  IBRD (World Bank)

108131 Bilateral Exchange **557 UNTS 129**
SIGNED: 24 Feb 66 FORCE: 28 Feb 66
REGISTERED: 28 Feb 66 United Nations
ARTICLES: 2 LANGUAGE: English.
HEADNOTE: UN PEACE KEEPING FORCE
TOPIC: IGO Operations
CONCEPTS: Annex or appendix reference. Privileges and immunities. Juridical personality. Arbitration. Procedure. Jurisdiction. Foreign nationals. Control and occupation machinery.
INTL ORGS: International Court of Justice. United Nations Educational, Scientific and Cultural Organization.
TREATY REF: 492UNTS57; 75UNTS31; 249UNTS215.
PARTIES:
  Austria
  United Nations
                          ANNEX
606 UNTS 402. Austria. Supplementation 28 Sep 67. Force 28 Sep 67.
606 UNTS 402. United Nations. Supplementation 28 Sep 67. Force 28 Sep 67.

108132 Unilateral Instrument **557 UNTS 143**
SIGNED: 31 Aug 65 FORCE: 31 Aug 65
REGISTERED: 1 Mar 66 United Nations
ARTICLES: 1 LANGUAGE: English. French. Chinese. Russian. Spanish.
HEADNOTE: AMENDMENT UN CHARTER
TOPIC: IGO Establishment
CONCEPTS: Annex or appendix reference. Annex type material. IGO constitution. Internal structure.
PROCEDURE: Amendment.
PARTIES:
  United Nations
                          ANNEX
638 UNTS 308. United Nations. Force 12 Jun 68.
643 UNTS 401. Chile. Ratification 22 Aug 68.

645 UNTS 377. Maldive Islands. Ratification
5 Sep 68.
648 UNTS 384. Honduras. Ratification 9 Oct 68.
653 UNTS 462. Gabon. Ratification 24 Dec 68.
668 UNTS 388. Uganda. Ratification 15 Apr 69.
668 UNTS 388. Mongolia. Ratification 17 Apr 69.

108133 Bilateral Exchange **557 UNTS 173**
SIGNED: 6 Oct 50 FORCE: 6 Oct 50
REGISTERED: 1 Mar 66 Ireland
ARTICLES: 2 LANGUAGE: English.
HEADNOTE: TRADE
TOPIC: General Trade
CONCEPTS: General cooperation. Import quotas.
Trade procedures. Payment schedules.
TREATY REF: UKTS NO.59(1949) CMD.7546.
PARTIES:
Austria
Ireland

108134 Bilateral Exchange **557 UNTS 180**
SIGNED: 23 Sep 60 FORCE: 1 Jul 52
REGISTERED: 1 Mar 66 Ireland
ARTICLES: 14 LANGUAGE: English.
HEADNOTE: CATTLE TRADE
TOPIC: Commodity Trade
CONCEPTS: Time limit. Licenses and permits. Use
of facilities. Trade agencies. Commodity trade.
Quotas.
PARTIES:
Belgium
Ireland

108135 Multilateral Agreement **557 UNTS 211**
SIGNED: 22 Jul 49 FORCE: 22 Jul 49
REGISTERED: 1 Mar 66 Ireland
ARTICLES: 6 LANGUAGE: English. French.
HEADNOTE: TRADE DEVELOPMENT
TOPIC: General Trade
CONCEPTS: Annex or appendix reference. Gen-
eral cooperation. Licenses and permits. Estab-
lishment of trade relations. Payment schedules.
Most favored nation clause.
PROCEDURE: Duration.
PARTIES:
France SIGNED: 22 Jul 49 FORCE: 22 Jul 49
UK Great Britain SIGNED: 22 Jul 49 FORCE:
22 Jul 49
USA (United States) SIGNED: 22 Jul 49 FORCE:
22 Jul 49

108136 Bilateral Agreement **557 UNTS 221**
SIGNED: 12 Jul 50 FORCE: 12 Jul 50
REGISTERED: 1 Mar 66 Ireland
ARTICLES: 8 LANGUAGE: English. German.
HEADNOTE: EXCHANGE COMMODITIES
TOPIC: Exchange Trade
CONCEPTS: Detailed regulations. Exceptions and
exemptions. Treaty implementation. Annex or
appendix reference. General cooperation. Li-
censes and permits. Payment schedules. Quotas.
Most favored nation clause. Navigational condi-
tions. Merchant vessels. Inland and territorial
waters. Ports and pilotage.
PARTIES:
Germany, West
Ireland

108137 Bilateral Exchange **558 UNTS 3**
SIGNED: 23 Jul 51 FORCE: 1 Jul 51
REGISTERED: 1 Mar 66 Ireland
ARTICLES: 2 LANGUAGE: English. German.
HEADNOTE: TRADE
TOPIC: General Trade
CONCEPTS: Treaty implementation. Annex or ap-
pendix reference. General cooperation. Licenses
and permits. Import quotas. Trade procedures.
Quotas.
PARTIES:
Germany, West
Ireland

108138 Bilateral Agreement **558 UNTS 27**
SIGNED: 26 Sep 52 FORCE: 1 Oct 52
REGISTERED: 1 Mar 66 Ireland
ARTICLES: 1 LANGUAGE: English. German.
HEADNOTE: TRADE
TOPIC: General Trade

CONCEPTS: General provisions. General cooper-
ation. Use of facilities. Import quotas. Trade
agencies. Trade procedures. Payment sched-
ules. Commodity trade.
PROCEDURE: Duration.
PARTIES:
Germany, West
Ireland

108139 Bilateral Agreement **558 UNTS 38**
SIGNED: 2 Dec 53 FORCE: 1 Oct 53
REGISTERED: 1 Mar 66 Ireland
ARTICLES: 11 LANGUAGE: Irish. German. English.
HEADNOTE: TRADE
TOPIC: General Trade
CONCEPTS: Annex or appendix reference. Estab-
lishment of trade relations. Currency.
PARTIES:
Germany, West
Ireland
ANNEX
609 UNTS 328. Ireland. Implementation
1 Sep 66. Force 1 Sep 66.
609 UNTS 328. Germany, West. Implementation
1 Sep 66. Force 1 Sep 66.

108140 Bilateral Exchange **558 UNTS 120**
SIGNED: 6 Jan 51 FORCE: 1 Jun 51
REGISTERED: 1 Mar 66 Ireland
ARTICLES: 23 LANGUAGE: English.
HEADNOTE: ECONOMIC COMMERCIAL RELA-
TIONS
TOPIC: General Trade
CONCEPTS: Territorial application. General provi-
sions. Annex or appendix reference. General cooperation. Informational records. Licenses and
permits. Export quotas. Import quotas. Trade
agencies. Trade procedures. Currency. Payment
schedules. Commodity trade. Transport of
goods. Water transport.
PROCEDURE: Duration. Termination.
PARTIES:
Finland
Ireland
ANNEX
604 UNTS 386. Ireland. Supplementation
28 May 65. Force 28 May 65.
604 UNTS 386. Finland. Ireland. Supplementation 28 May 65. Force 28 May 65.
614 UNTS 332. Finland. Supplementation
7 Dec 65. Force 1 Jan 66.
614 UNTS 332. Ireland. Supplementation
7 Dec 65. Force 1 Jan 66.

108141 Bilateral Exchange **558 UNTS 170**
SIGNED: 6 May 48 FORCE: 5 Jun 48
REGISTERED: 1 Mar 66 Ireland
ARTICLES: 15 LANGUAGE: English. French.
HEADNOTE: TRADE
TOPIC: General Trade
CONCEPTS: Use of facilities. Import quotas. Bal-
ance of payments. Commodity trade. Agricul-
ture.
INTL ORGS: Organization for Economic Co-opera-
tion and Development.
PARTIES:
France
Ireland

108142 Bilateral Agreement **558 UNTS 217**
SIGNED: 7 Jun 55 FORCE: 1 Apr 55
REGISTERED: 1 Mar 66 Ireland
ARTICLES: 7 LANGUAGE: Irish. French.
HEADNOTE: TRADE
TOPIC: General Trade
CONCEPTS: Territorial application. Annex or ap-
pendix reference. General cooperation. Licenses
and permits. Import quotas. Trade procedures.
Payment schedules. Commodity trade. Quotas.
Raw materials.
PROCEDURE: Duration.
PARTIES:
France
Ireland

108143 Bilateral Exchange **558 UNTS 231**
SIGNED: 2 Dec 50 FORCE: 2 Dec 50
REGISTERED: 1 Mar 66 Ireland
ARTICLES: 2 LANGUAGE: English.

HEADNOTE: TRADE
TOPIC: General Trade
CONCEPTS: General cooperation. Informational
records. Licenses and permits. Import quotas.
Trade procedures. Transport of goods. Merchant
vessels.
INTL ORGS: Organization for Economic Co-opera-
tion and Development.
PARTIES:
Iceland
Ireland

108144 Bilateral Agreement **558 UNTS 237**
SIGNED: 27 Jul 53 FORCE: 27 Jul 53
REGISTERED: 1 Mar 66 Ireland
ARTICLES: 10 LANGUAGE: Irish. Italian.
HEADNOTE: ECONOMIC COMMERCIAL RELA-
TIONS
TOPIC: General Trade
CONCEPTS: General provisions. General cooper-
ation. Licenses and permits. Import quotas.
Trade agencies. Trade procedures. Payment
schedules. Commodity trade. Transport of
goods. Merchant vessels.
INTL ORGS: Organization for Economic Co-opera-
tion and Development.
PROCEDURE: Duration. Termination. Duration.
Termination.
PARTIES:
Ireland
Italy

108145 Bilateral Exchange **558 UNTS 249**
SIGNED: 2 Sep 48 FORCE: 2 Sep 48
REGISTERED: 1 Mar 66 Ireland
ARTICLES: 2 LANGUAGE: English.
HEADNOTE: TRADE
TOPIC: General Trade
CONCEPTS: General provisions. Licenses and per-
mits. Use of facilities. Trade procedures. Balance
of payments. Payment schedules. Commodity
trade. Quotas.
INTL ORGS: Organization for Economic Co-opera-
tion and Development.
PARTIES:
Ireland
Netherlands

108146 Bilateral Exchange **558 UNTS 256**
SIGNED: 25 Nov 49 FORCE: 25 Nov 49
REGISTERED: 1 Mar 66 Ireland
ARTICLES: 12 LANGUAGE: English.
HEADNOTE: TRADE
TOPIC: General Trade
CONCEPTS: Annex type material. General cooper-
ation. Licenses and permits. Export quotas. Im-
port quotas. Commodity trade.
INTL ORGS: Organization for Economic Co-opera-
tion and Development.
PARTIES:
Ireland
Netherlands

108147 Bilateral Exchange **558 UNTS 289**
SIGNED: 6 Feb 52 FORCE: 6 Feb 52
REGISTERED: 1 Mar 66 Ireland
ARTICLES: 2 LANGUAGE: Irish. Portuguese.
HEADNOTE: TRADE
TOPIC: General Trade
CONCEPTS: Definition of terms. Annex type mate-
rial. General cooperation. Licenses and permits.
Use of facilities. Import quotas. Trade agencies.
Trade procedures. Payment schedules. Trans-
port of goods. Merchant vessels.
INTL ORGS: Organization for Economic Co-opera-
tion and Development.
PROCEDURE: Duration. Termination.
PARTIES:
Ireland
Portugal

108148 Bilateral Exchange **558 UNTS 299**
SIGNED: 25 Jun 49 FORCE: 25 Jun 49
REGISTERED: 1 Mar 66 Ireland
ARTICLES: 2 LANGUAGE: English.
HEADNOTE: TRADE
TOPIC: General Trade
CONCEPTS: General cooperation. Informational

records. Licenses and permits. Establishment of commission. Export quotas. Trade procedures.
INTL ORGS: Organization for Economic Co-operation and Development.
PARTIES:
Ireland
Sweden

108149 Bilateral Exchange **558 UNTS 305**
SIGNED: 26 Dec 51 FORCE: 26 Dec 51
REGISTERED: 1 Mar 66 Ireland
ARTICLES: 2 LANGUAGE: Irish. English.
HEADNOTE: TRADE
TOPIC: General Trade
CONCEPTS: General cooperation. Informational records. Licenses and permits. Establishment of commission. Export quotas. Trade agencies. Trade procedures. Payment schedules. Transport of goods. Merchant vessels.
INTL ORGS: Organization for Economic Co-operation and Development.
PROCEDURE: Duration. Termination.
PARTIES:
Ireland
Switzerland

108150 Bilateral Agreement **558 UNTS 313**
SIGNED: 16 Jun 64 FORCE: 30 Mar 65
REGISTERED: 2 Mar 66 Romania
ARTICLES: 5 LANGUAGE: Romanian. Italian.
HEADNOTE: TECHNICAL SCIENTIFIC COOPERATION
TOPIC: Scientific Project
CONCEPTS: General cooperation. Exchange of information and documents. Operating agencies. Licenses and permits. Establishment of commission. Specialists exchange. Scholarships and grants. Research results. Scientific exchange. Trademarks. General technical assistance.
PROCEDURE: Denunciation. Duration. Ratification. Renewal or Revival.
PARTIES:
Italy
Romania

108151 Bilateral Agreement **559 UNTS 3**
SIGNED: 4 Mar 66 FORCE: 4 Mar 66
REGISTERED: 4 Mar 66 United Nations
ARTICLES: 6 LANGUAGE: English.
HEADNOTE: SEMINAR LOCAL ADMINISTRATION
TOPIC: IGO Operations
CONCEPTS: Diplomatic privileges. Diplomatic missions. Privileges and immunities. Domestic obligation. Admission. Assistance to United Nations. Inter-agency agreements. IGO obligations.
TREATY REF: 1UNTS15; 33UNTS261.
PROCEDURE: Amendment. Duration.
PARTIES:
Hungary
United Nations

108152 Bilateral Agreement **559 UNTS 13**
SIGNED: 10 Mar 66 FORCE: 10 Mar 66
REGISTERED: 10 Mar 66 United Nations
ARTICLES: 8 LANGUAGE: French.
HEADNOTE: ACTIVITIES
TOPIC: IGO Operations
CONCEPTS: Privileges and immunities. Exchange of information and documents. Accounting procedures. Materials, equipment and services. Special status. Assistance to United Nations. Inter-agency agreements.
PROCEDURE: Amendment. Termination.
PARTIES:
Bulgaria
UNICEF (Children)

108153 Bilateral Convention **559 UNTS 23**
SIGNED: 11 Jun 64 FORCE: 16 Jan 66
REGISTERED: 11 Mar 66 Norway
ARTICLES: 24 LANGUAGE: English.
HEADNOTE: DOUBLE TAXATION FISCAL EVASION INCOME PROPERTY
TOPIC: Taxation
CONCEPTS: Definition of terms. Privileges and immunities. Conformity with municipal law. Exchange of official publications. Negotiation. Claims and settlements. Taxation. Equitable

taxes. Tax exemptions. Air transport. Merchant vessels.
PROCEDURE: Duration. Ratification. Termination.
PARTIES:
Ceylon (Sri Lanka)
Norway

108154 Bilateral Agreement **559 UNTS 49**
SIGNED: 16 Dec 61 FORCE: 18 Jan 64
REGISTERED: 15 Mar 66 ICAO (Civil Aviat)
ARTICLES: 17 LANGUAGE: French. Czechoslovakian.
HEADNOTE: AIR SERVICES
TOPIC: Air Transport
CONCEPTS: Definition of terms. Detailed regulations. Annex or appendix reference. Conformity with municipal law. General cooperation. Personnel. Use of facilities. Arbitration. Procedure. Special tribunals. Negotiation. Reexport of goods, etc.. Monetary and gold transfers. Fees and exemptions. Non-interest rates and fees. Most favored nation clause. Customs duties. Customs exemptions. Routes and logistics. Navigational conditions. Permit designation. Air transport. Airport facilities. Conditions of airlines operating permission. Overflights and technical stops. Operating authorizations and regulations.
INTL ORGS: International Civil Aviation Organization.
TREATY REF: 15UNTS295.
PROCEDURE: Amendment. Ratification. Registration. Termination.
PARTIES:
Czechoslovakia
Guinea

108155 Bilateral Agreement **559 UNTS 77**
SIGNED: 23 Jan 62 FORCE: 3 Sep 63
REGISTERED: 15 Mar 66 ICAO (Civil Aviat)
ARTICLES: 17 LANGUAGE: English.
HEADNOTE: AIR SERVICES
TOPIC: Air Transport
CONCEPTS: Definition of terms. Detailed regulations. Exceptions and exemptions. Annex or appendix reference. Conformity with municipal law. Exchange of information and documents. Use of facilities. Arbitration. Procedure. Special tribunals. Negotiation. Fees and exemptions. Non-interest rates and fees. Most favored nation clause. National treatment. Customs exemptions. Routes and logistics. Permit designation. Air transport. Airport facilities. Conditions of airlines operating permission. Overflights and technical stops. Operating authorizations and regulations.
INTL ORGS: International Civil Aviation Organization.
TREATY REF: 15UNTS295.
PROCEDURE: Amendment. Future Procedures Contemplated. Ratification. Registration.
PARTIES:
Indonesia
Japan

ANNEX
602 UNTS 352. Japan. Amendment 24 Feb 65. Force 24 Feb 65.
602 UNTS 352. Indonesia. Amendment 24 Feb 65. Force 24 Feb 65.

108156 Bilateral Agreement **559 UNTS 95**
SIGNED: 25 Oct 57 FORCE: 13 Dec 58
REGISTERED: 15 Mar 66 ICAO (Civil Aviat)
ARTICLES: 20 LANGUAGE: French.
HEADNOTE: AIR TRANSPORT
TOPIC: Air Transport
CONCEPTS: Detailed regulations. Annex or appendix reference. Conformity with municipal law. General cooperation. Licenses and permits. Recognition of legal documents. Arbitration. Procedure. Special tribunals. Expense sharing formulae. Fees and exemptions. Non-interest rates and fees. National treatment. General. Tax exemptions. Customs exemptions. Competency certificate. Routes and logistics. Navigational conditions. Permit designation. Air transport. Airport facilities. Airworthiness certificates. Conditions of airlines operating permission. Operating authorizations and regulations. Licenses and certificates of nationality.
INTL ORGS: International Civil Aviation Organization.

TREATY REF: 15UNTS295.
PROCEDURE: Amendment. Denunciation. Ratification. Registration. Application to Non-self-governing Territories.
PARTIES:
France
Morocco

108157 Bilateral Agreement **559 UNTS 121**
SIGNED: 25 Jan 56 FORCE: 7 Feb 63
REGISTERED: 15 Mar 66 ICAO (Civil Aviat)
ARTICLES: 19 LANGUAGE: French. Spanish.
HEADNOTE: SCHEDULED AIR TRANSPORT SERVICES
TOPIC: Air Transport
CONCEPTS: Definition of terms. Annex or appendix reference. Conformity with municipal law. Licenses and permits. Recognition of legal documents. Responsibility and liability. Use of facilities. Investigation of violations. Arbitration. Procedure. Special tribunals. Reexport of goods, etc.. Fees and exemptions. Most favored nation clause. National treatment. General. Customs duties. Customs exemptions. Competency certificate. Navigational conditions. Permit designation. Air transport. Airport facilities. Airworthiness certificates. Conditions of airlines operating permission. Operating authorizations and regulations. Licenses and certificates of nationality.
INTL ORGS: International Civil Aviation Organization.
TREATY REF: 15UNTS295.
PROCEDURE: Amendment. Denunciation. Future Procedures Contemplated. Ratification. Registration. Termination.
PARTIES:
Argentina
Switzerland

ANNEX
602 UNTS 356. Argentina. Modification 12 May 65.
602 UNTS 356. Switzerland. Modification 12 May 65.

108158 Bilateral Agreement **559 UNTS 157**
SIGNED: 2 May 56 FORCE: 2 Jun 57
REGISTERED: 15 Mar 66 ICAO (Civil Aviat)
ARTICLES: 20 LANGUAGE: German.
HEADNOTE: AIR TRANSPORT
TOPIC: Air Transport
CONCEPTS: Definition of terms. Detailed regulations. Previous treaty replacement. Conformity with municipal law. General cooperation. Exchange of information and documents. Licenses and permits. Personnel. Recognition of legal documents. Use of facilities. Arbitration. Procedure. Special tribunals. Expense sharing formulae. Fees and exemptions. Non-interest rates and fees. National treatment. Tax exemptions. Customs exemptions. Competency certificate. Routes and logistics. Air transport. Airport facilities. Airworthiness certificates. Conditions of airlines operating permission. Overflights and technical stops. Licenses and certificates of nationality.
INTL ORGS: International Civil Aviation Organization. Arbitration Commission.
TREATY REF: 15UNTS295; 2LTS331.
PROCEDURE: Amendment. Future Procedures Contemplated. Ratification. Registration. Termination.
PARTIES:
Germany, West
Switzerland

108159 Bilateral Agreement **559 UNTS 193**
SIGNED: 17 May 61 FORCE: 12 Oct 63
REGISTERED: 15 Mar 66 ICAO (Civil Aviat)
ARTICLES: 16 LANGUAGE: French. English.
HEADNOTE: FINANCIAL ASSISTANCE
TOPIC: Air Transport
CONCEPTS: Time limit. Annex or appendix reference. Responsibility and liability. Import quotas. Financial programs. Commodities and services. Grants. Loan and credit.
INTL ORGS: International Civil Aviation Organization.
TREATY REF: 15UNTS295.

PARTIES:
Ghana
Switzerland

108160 Bilateral Agreement **559 UNTS 215**
SIGNED: 31 Aug 61   FORCE: 25 Jul 63
REGISTERED: 15 Mar 66 ICAO (Civil Aviat)
ARTICLES: 17 LANGUAGE: French. English.
HEADNOTE: ESTABLISHMENT OPERATION AIR
SERVICES
TOPIC: Air Transport
CONCEPTS: Definition of terms. Detailed regulations. Annex or appendix reference. Border traffic and migration. Visas. Conformity with municipal law. General cooperation. Exchange of information and documents. Inspection and
observation. Licenses and permits. Recognition
of legal documents. Arbitration. Procedure. Existing tribunals. Negotiation. Humanitarian matters. Indemnities and reimbursements. Monetary
and gold transfers. Non-interest rates and fees.
National treatment. Customs exemptions. Competency certificate. Routes and logistics. Navigational conditions. Permit designation. Air transport. Airworthiness certificates. Conditions of
airlines operating permission. Operating authorizations and regulations. Licenses and certificates of nationality.
INTL ORGS: International Civil Aviation Organization. International Court of Justice. Arbitration
Commission.
TREATY REF: 15UNTS295; 84UNTS389.
PROCEDURE: Amendment. Future Procedures
Contemplated. Ratification. Registration. Termi-
nation.
PARTIES:
Liberia
Switzerland

108161 Bilateral Agreement **559 UNTS 233**
SIGNED: 18 May 61   FORCE: 13 May 63
REGISTERED: 15 Mar 66 ICAO (Civil Aviat)
ARTICLES: 15 LANGUAGE: French. Polish.
HEADNOTE: CIVIL AIR TRANSPORT
TOPIC: Air Transport
CONCEPTS: Definition of terms. Annex or appen-
dix reference. Conformity with municipal law.
Procedure. Negotiation. Reexport of goods, etc..
Fees and exemptions. Non-interest rates and
fees. Customs exemptions. Routes and logistics.
Navigational conditions. Permit designation. Air
transport. Conditions of airlines operating per-
mission. Overflights and technical stops. Operat-
ing authorizations and regulations.
TREATY REF: 15UNTS295.
PROCEDURE: Amendment. Denunciation. Ratifica-
tion. Termination.
PARTIES:
Poland
Switzerland
                    ANNEX
646 UNTS 411. Poland. Amendment 5 Dec 66.
Force 5 Dec 66.
646 UNTS 411.   Switzerland.   Amendment
5 Dec 66. Force 5 Dec 66.

108162 Bilateral Agreement **559 UNTS 257**
SIGNED: 19 Oct 59   FORCE: 19 Sep 61
REGISTERED: 15 Mar 66 ICAO (Civil Aviat)
ARTICLES: 11 LANGUAGE: French. English.
HEADNOTE: AIR SERVICES
TOPIC: Air Transport
CONCEPTS: Definition of terms. Annex or appen-
dix reference. Previous treaty replacement. Con-
formity with municipal law. General cooperation.
Exchange of information and documents. Non-
interest rates and fees. National treatment. Cus-
toms exemptions. Routes and logistics. Naviga-
tional conditions. Permit designation. Air trans-
port. Conditions of airlines operating
permission. Operating authorizations and regu-
lations.
INTL ORGS: International Civil Aviation Organization.
TREATY REF: 15UNTS295; 216UNTS19.
PROCEDURE: Amendment. Future Procedures
Contemplated. Ratification. Application to Non-
self-governing Territories.
PARTIES:
South Africa
Switzerland

108163 Multilateral Agreement **559 UNTS 273**
SIGNED: 28 May 65   FORCE: 28 May 65
REGISTERED: 18 Mar 66 Sierra Leone
ARTICLES: 17 LANGUAGE: English. French.
HEADNOTE: WEST AFRICA ECONOMIC COOPER-
ATION
TOPIC: IGO Establishment
CONCEPTS: Exchange of official publications.
General trade. Accounting procedures. Customs
duties. Economic assistance. Establishment.
Headquarters and facilities. Internal structure.
INTL ORGS: Organization of African Unity.
PARTIES:
Guinea SIGNED: 28 May 65 FORCE: 28 May 65
Ivory Coast SIGNED: 28 May 65 FORCE:
28 May 65
Liberia SIGNED: 28 May 65 FORCE: 28 May 65
Sierra Leone SIGNED: 28 May 65 FORCE:
28 May 65

108164 Multilateral Convention **559 UNTS 285**
SIGNED: 29 Apr 58   FORCE: 20 Mar 66
REGISTERED: 20 Mar 66 United Nations
ARTICLES: 22 LANGUAGE: English. French. Chi-
nese. Russian. Spanish.
HEADNOTE: FISHING CONSERVATION LIVING RE-
SOURCES HIGH SEAS
TOPIC: Specific Resources
CONCEPTS: Definition of terms. Establishment of
commission. Procedure. National treatment.
Fish, wildlife, and natural resources. Ocean re-
sources. Fisheries and fishing.
INTL ORGS: Food and Agricultural Organization of
the United Nations. International Court of Jus-
tice.
PROCEDURE: Accession. Ratification. Registra-
tion.
PARTIES:
Afghanistan SIGNED: 30 Oct 58
Argentina SIGNED: 29 Apr 58
Australia   SIGNED: 30 Oct 58   RATIFIED:
14 May 63 FORCE: 20 Mar 66
Bolivia SIGNED: 17 Oct 58
Canada SIGNED: 29 Apr 58
Ceylon (Sri Lanka) SIGNED: 30 Oct 58
Taiwan SIGNED: 29 Apr 58
Colombia   SIGNED: 29 Apr 58   RATIFIED:
3 Jan 63 FORCE: 20 Mar 66
Costa Rica SIGNED: 29 Apr 58
Cuba SIGNED: 29 Apr 58
Denmark SIGNED: 29 Apr 58
Dominican Republic SIGNED: 29 Apr 58 RATI-
FIED: 11 Aug 64 FORCE: 20 Mar 66
Finland   SIGNED: 27 Oct 58   RATIFIED:
16 Feb 65 FORCE: 20 Mar 66
France SIGNED: 30 Oct 58
Ghana SIGNED: 29 Apr 58
Haiti SIGNED: 29 Apr 58 RATIFIED: 29 Mar 60
FORCE: 20 Mar 66
Iceland SIGNED: 29 Apr 58
Indonesia SIGNED: 8 May 58
Iran SIGNED: 28 May 58
Ireland SIGNED: 2 Oct 58
Israel SIGNED: 29 Apr 58
Jamaica   RATIFIED: 16 Apr 64   FORCE:
20 Mar 66
Lebanon SIGNED: 29 May 58
Liberia SIGNED: 27 May 58
Madagascar   RATIFIED: 31 Jul 62   FORCE:
20 Mar 66
Malawi RATIFIED: 3 Nov 65 FORCE: 20 Mar 66
Malaysia   RATIFIED: 21 Dec 60   FORCE:
20 Mar 66
Nepal SIGNED: 29 Apr 58
Netherlands   SIGNED: 31 Oct 58   RATIFIED:
18 Feb 66 FORCE: 20 Mar 66
New Zealand SIGNED: 29 Oct 58
Nigeria RATIFIED: 26 Jun 61 FORCE: 20 Mar 66
Pakistan SIGNED: 31 Oct 58
Panama SIGNED: 2 May 58
Portugal SIGNED: 28 Oct 58 RATIFIED: 8 Jan 63
FORCE: 20 Mar 66
Senegal   RATIFIED: 25 Apr 61   FORCE:
20 Mar 66
Sierra Leone   RATIFIED: 13 Mar 62   FORCE:
20 Mar 66
Switzerland SIGNED: 22 Oct 58
Thailand SIGNED: 29 Apr 58
Tunisia SIGNED: 30 Oct 58
Uganda   RATIFIED: 14 Sep 64   FORCE:
20 Mar 66
UK Great Britain SIGNED: 9 Sep 58 RATIFIED:
14 Mar 60 FORCE: 20 Mar 66

USA (United States) SIGNED: 13 Sep 58 RATI-
FIED: 12 Apr 61 FORCE: 20 Mar 66
Upper Volta   RATIFIED: 14 Oct 65   FORCE:
20 Mar 66
Uruguay SIGNED: 29 Apr 58
Venezuela   SIGNED: 30 Oct 58   RATIFIED:
10 Jul 63 FORCE: 20 Mar 66
Yugoslavia   SIGNED: 29 Apr 58   RATIFIED:
28 Jan 66 FORCE: 20 Mar 66
                    ANNEX
560 UNTS 307.   Trinidad/Tobago.   Succession
11 Apr 66.
562 UNTS 339.   Switzerland.   Ratification
18 May 66. Force 17 Jun 66.
639 UNTS 351. Thailand. Ratification 2 Jul 68.
Force 1 Aug 68.
646 UNTS 412. Denmark. Ratification 26 Sep 68.
Force 26 Oct 68.

108165 Multilateral Convention **560 UNTS 3**
SIGNED: 12 Oct 55   FORCE: 28 May 58
REGISTERED: 22 Mar 66 France
ARTICLES: 40 LANGUAGE: French.
HEADNOTE: INTERNATION ORGANIZATION LE-
GAL METROLOGY
TOPIC: IGO Establishment
CONCEPTS: Default remedies. Treaty interpreta-
tion. Privileges and immunities. Exchange of in-
formation and documents. Dispute settlement.
Arbitration. Existing tribunals. Research cooper-
ation. Research and development. Currency. In-
vestments. Funding procedures. Customs ex-
emptions. Admission. Establishment. Headquar-
ters and facilities. Internal structure. Special
status. Status of experts.
PROCEDURE: Amendment. Accession. Denuncia-
tion. Duration. Ratification. Termination.
PARTIES:
Australia   RATIFIED: 18 Aug 59   FORCE:
17 Sep 59
Austria   SIGNED: 21 Dec 55   RATIFIED:
27 Jun 56 FORCE: 28 May 58
Belgium   SIGNED: 21 Dec 55   RATIFIED:
10 Nov 59 FORCE: 28 May 58
Bulgaria RATIFIED: 4 Jun 56 FORCE: 28 May 58
Cuba SIGNED: 31 Mar 56 RATIFIED: 30 Oct 62
FORCE: 29 Nov 62
Czechoslovakia SIGNED: 27 Dec 55 RATIFIED:
27 Oct 56 FORCE: 28 May 58
Denmark   SIGNED: 27 Dec 55   FORCE:
28 May 58
Dominican Republic SIGNED: 8 Dec 55
Finland SIGNED: 22 Dec 55 FORCE: 28 May 58
France SIGNED: 12 Oct 55 RATIFIED: 23 Apr 58
FORCE: 28 May 58
Germany, West SIGNED: 20 Jan 56 RATIFIED:
8 Dec 59 FORCE: 7 Jan 60
Guinea RATIFIED: 5 Mar 60 FORCE: 4 Apr 60
Hungary   SIGNED: 6 Jan 56   RATIFIED:
19 Sep 56 FORCE: 28 May 58
India SIGNED: 31 Mar 56 RATIFIED: 27 Oct 56
FORCE: 28 May 58
Indonesia   RATIFIED: 30 Sep 60   FORCE:
30 Oct 60
Iran SIGNED: 19 Nov 55 RATIFIED: 30 Sep 59
FORCE: 30 Oct 59
Italy RATIFIED: 28 Oct 58 FORCE: 27 Nov 58
Japan RATIFIED: 16 May 61 FORCE: 15 Jun 61
Lebanon RATIFIED: 6 Nov 62 FORCE: 6 Dec 62
Monaco   SIGNED: 27 Mar 56   RATIFIED:
9 Aug 56 FORCE: 28 May 58
Morocco   RATIFIED: 16 Sep 58   FORCE:
16 Oct 58
Netherlands   SIGNED: 23 Jan 56   RATIFIED:
12 Jun 58 FORCE: 12 Jul 58
New Zealand   RATIFIED: 20 Jan 59   FORCE:
19 Feb 59
Norway   SIGNED: 28 Mar 56   RATIFIED:
28 Apr 58 FORCE: 28 May 58
Pakistan RATIFIED: 2 Feb 62 FORCE: 4 Mar 62
Poland SIGNED: 15 Oct 55 RATIFIED: 16 Jul 57
FORCE: 28 May 58
Romania   SIGNED: 31 Mar 56   RATIFIED:
17 Oct 56 FORCE: 28 May 58
Spain SIGNED: 27 Dec 55 RATIFIED: 14 May 57
FORCE: 28 May 58
Sweden   SIGNED: 29 Mar 56   RATIFIED:
11 Jul 58 FORCE: 10 Aug 58
Switzerland   SIGNED: 21 Dec 55   RATIFIED:
9 Oct 56 FORCE: 28 May 58
Turkey RATIFIED: 22 Mar 62 FORCE: 21 Apr 62
United Arab Rep RATIFIED: 28 Jul 61 FORCE:
27 Aug 61

UK Great Britain RATIFIED: 11 May 62 FORCE: 10 Jun 62

USSR (Soviet Union) SIGNED: 31 Dec 55 RATIFIED: 18 Dec 56 FORCE: 28 May 58

Venezuela RATIFIED: 25 Jul 60 FORCE: 24 Aug 60

Yugoslavia SIGNED: 24 Jan 56 RATIFIED: 7 May 57 FORCE: 28 May 58

ANNEX

634 UNTS 444. Ceylon (Sri Lanka). Accession 15 Mar 68. Force 17 Apr 68.

108166 Bilateral Instrument **560 UNTS 39**
SIGNED: 10 Jan 66 FORCE: 10 Jan 66
REGISTERED: 22 Mar 66 India
ARTICLES: 9 LANGUAGE: English.
HEADNOTE: TASHKENT DECLARATION
TOPIC: General Amity
CONCEPTS: Peaceful relations. Repatriation of nationals. Consular relations establishment. Diplomatic relations establishment. General cooperation. Withdrawal of forces.
TREATY REF: 500UNTS295.
PARTIES:
India
Pakistan

108167 Bilateral Agreement **560 UNTS 47**
SIGNED: 24 Mar 66 FORCE: 24 Mar 66
REGISTERED: 24 Mar 66 United Nations
ARTICLES: 6 LANGUAGE: English.
HEADNOTE: SEMINAR ON APARTHEID
TOPIC: IGO Establishment
CONCEPTS: Privileges and immunities. Decisions. Subsidiary organ.
PARTIES:
Brazil
United Nations

108168 Bilateral Convention **560 UNTS 57**
SIGNED: 15 Jul 64 FORCE: 15 Jul 64
REGISTERED: 24 Mar 66 Belgium
ARTICLES: 9 LANGUAGE: French.
HEADNOTE: TECHNICAL COOPERATION
TOPIC: Tech Assistance
CONCEPTS: Personnel. Establishment of commission. Scholarships and grants. Investments. Expense sharing formulae. Tax exemptions. Customs exemptions. Domestic obligation. General technical assistance. Materials, equipment and services.
PROCEDURE: Denunciation.
PARTIES:
Belgium
Tunisia

108169 Bilateral Instrument **560 UNTS 65**
SIGNED: 15 Jul 64 FORCE: 15 Jul 64
REGISTERED: 24 Mar 66 Belgium
ARTICLES: 5 LANGUAGE: French.
HEADNOTE: PERSONNEL
TOPIC: Tech Assistance
CONCEPTS: Treaty implementation. Annex or appendix reference. Privileges and immunities. Conformity with municipal law. Personnel. Financial programs. General. Assistance.
PROCEDURE: Amendment. Denunciation.
PARTIES:
Belgium
Tunisia

108170 Bilateral Agreement **560 UNTS 85**
SIGNED: 1 Jun 65 FORCE: 30 Dec 65
REGISTERED: 29 Mar 66 Netherlands
ARTICLES: 12 LANGUAGE: Dutch. English.
HEADNOTE: MIGRATION SETTLEMENT
TOPIC: Consul/Citizenship
CONCEPTS: Border traffic and migration. Conformity with municipal law. General cooperation. Legal protection and assistance. Administrative cooperation. National treatment.
PROCEDURE: Duration. Ratification.
PARTIES:
Australia
Netherlands

108171 Bilateral Agreement **560 UNTS 123**
SIGNED: 22 Feb 65 FORCE: 1 Oct 65

REGISTERED: 30 Mar 66 UK Great Britain
ARTICLES: 16 LANGUAGE: English. Japanese.
HEADNOTE: EXCHANGE MONEY ORDER
TOPIC: Finance
CONCEPTS: Definition of terms. Previous treaty replacement. Accounting procedures. Currency. Exchange rates and regulations. Mail and money orders. Postal services. Regulations. Money orders and postal checks. Rates and charges.
TREATY REF: UKTS 74(1961) CMB.1484.
PROCEDURE: Ratification. Termination.
PARTIES:
Japan
UK Great Britain

108172 Bilateral Agreement **560 UNTS 143**
SIGNED: 15 Sep 51 FORCE: 26 Aug 65
REGISTERED: 30 Mar 66 UK Great Britain
ARTICLES: 13 LANGUAGE: English. Spanish.
HEADNOTE: AVIATION
TOPIC: Air Transport
CONCEPTS: Definition of terms. Exceptions and exemptions. Annex or appendix reference. Conformity with municipal law. Licenses and permits. Recognition of legal documents. Use of facilities. Arbitration. Procedure. Special tribunals. Negotiation. Competence of tribunal. Expense sharing formulae. Fees and exemptions. Most favored nation clause. National treatment. Customs exemptions. Competency certificate. Routes and logistics. Navigational conditions. Permit designation. Airport facilities. Airworthiness certificates. Conditions of airlines operating permission. Operating authorizations and regulations. Licenses and certificates of nationality.
INTL ORGS: International Civil Aviation Organization.
PROCEDURE: Amendment. Future Procedures Contemplated. Ratification. Registration. Termination. Application to Non-self-governing Territories.
PARTIES:
Panama
UK Great Britain

108173 Bilateral Agreement **560 UNTS 169**
SIGNED: 4 Jun 65 FORCE: 12 Mar 66
REGISTERED: 4 Apr 66 Finland
ARTICLES: 12 LANGUAGE: Finnish. Russian.
HEADNOTE: REINDEER
TOPIC: Specific Resources
CONCEPTS: Exchange of information and documents. Operating agencies. Indemnities and reimbursements. Payment schedules. Fish, wildlife, and natural resources. Wildlife.
TREATY REF: 48UNTS149; 379UNTS277.
PROCEDURE: Denunciation. Duration. Ratification. Renewal or Revival.
PARTIES:
Finland
USSR (Soviet Union)

108174 Bilateral Agreement **560 UNTS 191**
SIGNED: 5 Apr 66 FORCE: 5 Apr 66
REGISTERED: 5 Apr 66 United Nations
ARTICLES: 6 LANGUAGE: English.
HEADNOTE: UN SEMINAR ADVANCEMENT WOMEN
TOPIC: Health/Educ/Welfare
CONCEPTS: Definition of terms. Visas. Consular relations establishment. Privileges and immunities. General cooperation. Programs. Research results. Financial programs. General transportation. Radio-telephone-telegraphic communications. Press and wire services.
PROCEDURE: Duration.
PARTIES:
Philippines
United Nations

108175 Multilateral Convention **560 UNTS 201**
SIGNED: 8 Jul 64 FORCE: 29 Mar 66
REGISTERED: 5 Apr 66 ILO (Labor Org)
ARTICLES: 27 LANGUAGE: English. French.
HEADNOTE: HYGIENE COMMERCE OFFICES
TOPIC: ILO Labor
CONCEPTS: Detailed regulations. Inspection and observation. Domestic legislation. Operating agencies. Incorporation of treaty provisions into

national law. Public health. ILO conventions. Safety standards.
PROCEDURE: Amendment. Denunciation. Duration. Ratification. Registration. Renewal or Revival.
PARTIES:
Multilateral

ANNEX

561 UNTS 366. Senegal. Ratification 25 Apr 66. Force 25 Apr 67.
561 UNTS 366. Senegal. Ratification 25 Apr 66. Force 25 Apr 67.
567 UNTS 360. Norway. Ratification 6 Jun 66. Force 6 Jun 67.
603 UNTS 357. Paraguay. Ratification 10 Jul 67. Force 10 Jul 67.
607 UNTS 370. Congo (Zaire). Ratification 5 Sep 67. Force 5 Sep 68.
607 UNTS 370. USSR (Soviet Union). Ratification 5 Sep 67. Force 22 Sep 68.
630 UNTS 410. UK Great Britain. Declaration 11 Jan 68.
630 UNTS 411. UK Great Britain. Declaration 11 Jan 68.
636 UNTS 426. UK Great Britain. Declaration 9 Apr 68.
640 UNTS 390. Mexico. Ratification 18 Jun 68. Force 18 Jun 69.
640 UNTS 390. Poland. Ratification 26 Jun 68. Force 26 Jun 69.
640 UNTS 390. Ukrainian SSR. Ratification 19 Jun 68. Force 19 Jun 69.
648 UNTS 390. Finland. Ratification 23 Sep 68. Force 23 Sep 69.
649 UNTS 385. UK Great Britain. Declaration 9 Oct 68.

108176 Bilateral Agreement **560 UNTS 215**
SIGNED: 23 Nov 65 FORCE: 23 Nov 65
REGISTERED: 15 Apr 66 UK Great Britain
ARTICLES: 9 LANGUAGE: English. Spanish.
HEADNOTE: LOAN
TOPIC: Loans and Credits
CONCEPTS: Definition of terms. Currency. Interest rates. Payment schedules. Loan and credit. Loan repayment. Refinance of loan. Terms of loan.
PARTIES:
Chile
UK Great Britain

108177 Bilateral Agreement **561 UNTS 3**
SIGNED: 21 Sep 65 FORCE: 6 Nov 65
REGISTERED: 15 Apr 66 UK Great Britain
ARTICLES: 9 LANGUAGE: English. French.
HEADNOTE: FILM COPRODUCTION
TOPIC: Culture
CONCEPTS: Definition of terms. Annex or appendix reference. Resident permits. Privileges and immunities. Conformity with municipal law. General cooperation. Use of facilities. Establishment of commission. Mass media exchange.
TREATY REF: 473UNTS153.
PROCEDURE: Amendment. Duration. Renewal or Revival. Termination.
PARTIES:
France
UK Great Britain

108178 Bilateral Exchange **561 UNTS 19**
SIGNED: 19 Nov 65 FORCE: 1 Dec 65
REGISTERED: 15 Apr 66 UK Great Britain
ARTICLES: 2 LANGUAGE: English. French.
HEADNOTE: FAMILY ALLOWANCES MIGRANT WORKERS
TOPIC: Non-ILO Labor
CONCEPTS: Definition of terms. Conformity with municipal law. Wages and salaries. Non-ILO labor relations. Family allowances. Migrant worker. Indemnities and reimbursements.
PROCEDURE: Denunciation. Duration. Renewal or Revival.
PARTIES:
France
UK Great Britain

108179 Bilateral Convention **561 UNTS 25**
SIGNED: 4 May 64 FORCE: 10 Oct 65
REGISTERED: 15 Apr 66 UK Great Britain
ARTICLES: 41 LANGUAGE: English. Japanese.
HEADNOTE: CONSULAR

TOPIC: Consul/Citizenship
CONCEPTS: Definition of terms. Exceptions and exemptions. Territorial application. General provisions. General consular functions. Consular relations establishment. Privileges and immunities. Consular functions in shipping. Consular functions in property. Procedure. Existing tribunals.
PROCEDURE: Duration. Ratification. Termination.
PARTIES:
Japan
UK Great Britain

108180 Bilateral Agreement **561 UNTS 185**
SIGNED: 21 Oct 65 FORCE: 21 Oct 65
REGISTERED: 15 Apr 66 UK Great Britain
ARTICLES: 6 LANGUAGE: English.
HEADNOTE: LOAN
TOPIC: Loans and Credits
CONCEPTS: Definition of terms. Currency. Interest rates. Payment schedules. Economic assistance. Loan and credit. Loan repayment. Refinance of loan.
TREATY REF: 527UNTS145; 551UNTS59.
PARTIES:
Turkey
UK Great Britain

108181 Bilateral Exchange **561 UNTS 193**
SIGNED: 26 Nov 65 FORCE: 26 Nov 65
REGISTERED: 15 Apr 66 UK Great Britain
ARTICLES: 2 LANGUAGE: English.
HEADNOTE: AMATEUR RADIO OPERATORS
TOPIC: Gen Communications
CONCEPTS: Licenses and permits. Amateur radio. Amateur third party message.
TREATY REF: TOIA 4893.
PROCEDURE: Termination.
PARTIES:
UK Great Britain
USA (United States)

108182 Bilateral Exchange **561 UNTS 199**
SIGNED: 30 Dec 65 FORCE: 1 Jan 66
REGISTERED: 19 Apr 66 Malta
ARTICLES: 2 LANGUAGE: English.
HEADNOTE: ARRANGEMENTS FACILITATE TRAVEL
TOPIC: Visas
CONCEPTS: Emergencies. Time limit. Visa abolition. Denial of admission. Conformity with municipal law.
TREATY REF: 322UNTS245.
PROCEDURE: Denunciation.
PARTIES:
Denmark
Malta

108183 Bilateral Exchange **561 UNTS 205**
SIGNED: 8 Dec 65 FORCE: 1 Jan 66
REGISTERED: 19 Apr 66 Malta
ARTICLES: 2 LANGUAGE: English.
HEADNOTE: ARRANGEMENTS FACILITATE TRAVEL
TOPIC: Visas
CONCEPTS: Emergencies. Time limit. Visa abolition. Denial of admission. Conformity with municipal law.
TREATY REF: 322UNTS245.
PROCEDURE: Denunciation.
PARTIES:
Finland
Malta

108184 Bilateral Exchange **561 UNTS 211**
SIGNED: 29 Dec 65 FORCE: 1 Jan 66
REGISTERED: 19 Apr 66 Malta
ARTICLES: 2 LANGUAGE: English.
HEADNOTE: FACILITATE TRAVEL
TOPIC: Visas
CONCEPTS: Emergencies. Time limit. Visa abolition. Denial of admission. Conformity with municipal law.
TREATY REF: 322UNTS245.
PROCEDURE: Denunciation.
PARTIES:
Malta
Norway

108185 Bilateral Exchange **561 UNTS 217**
SIGNED: 29 Dec 65 FORCE: 1 Jan 66
REGISTERED: 19 Apr 66 Malta
ARTICLES: 2 LANGUAGE: English.
HEADNOTE: FACILITATE TRAVEL
TOPIC: Visas
CONCEPTS: Emergencies. Time limit. Visa abolition. Denial of admission. Conformity with municipal law.
TREATY REF: 322UNTS245.
PROCEDURE: Denunciation.
PARTIES:
Malta
Sweden

108186 Bilateral Agreement **561 UNTS 223**
SIGNED: 15 Jul 65 FORCE: 18 Dec 66
REGISTERED: 19 Apr 66 Malta
ARTICLES: 9 LANGUAGE: English.
HEADNOTE: TRADE
TOPIC: General Trade
CONCEPTS: Exceptions and exemptions. Conformity with municipal law. Establishment of commission. Currency. Payment schedules. Most favored nation clause. Customs duties. Customs exemptions. Navigational equipment. Merchant vessels. Ports and pilotage.
TREATY REF: 58LTS285.
PROCEDURE: Duration. Ratification. Renewal or Revival. Termination.
PARTIES:
Malta
Yugoslavia

108187 Bilateral Agreement **561 UNTS 233**
SIGNED: 4 Feb 66 FORCE: 4 Feb 66
REGISTERED: 21 Apr 66 Denmark
ARTICLES: 21 LANGUAGE: French.
HEADNOTE: ROAD TRANSPORT PASSENGERS GOODS COMMERCIAL VEHICLES
TOPIC: Land Transport
CONCEPTS: Conditions. Default remedies. Exceptions and exemptions. General provisions. Annex or appendix reference. Conformity with municipal law. Exchange of information and documents. Licenses and permits. Establishment of commission. Fees and exemptions. Passenger transport. Routes and logistics. Transport of goods. Commercial road vehicles. Driving permits. Road rules.
PARTIES:
Belgium
Denmark

108188 Bilateral Agreement **561 UNTS 255**
SIGNED: 2 Feb 65 FORCE: 1 Feb 66
REGISTERED: 28 Apr 66 IBRD (World Bank)
ARTICLES: 8 LANGUAGE: English.
HEADNOTE: LOAN ROAD
TOPIC: IBRD Project
CONCEPTS: Default remedies. Definition of terms. Annex or appendix reference. Exchange of information and documents. Informational records. Inspection and observation. Accounting procedures. Fees and exemptions. Interest rates. Tax exemptions. Domestic obligation. Terms of loan. Loan regulations. Loan guarantee. Guarantor non-interference. Roads and highways.
INTL ORGS: Inter-American Bank.
PARTIES:
Honduras
IBRD (World Bank)

108189 Bilateral Agreement **561 UNTS 279**
SIGNED: 2 Feb 65 FORCE: 1 Feb 66
REGISTERED: 28 Apr 66 IDA (Devel Assoc)
ARTICLES: 7 LANGUAGE: English.
HEADNOTE: DEVELOPMENT CREDIT ROAD
TOPIC: Non-IBRD Project
CONCEPTS: Definition of terms. Detailed regulations. Previous treaty amendment. Informational records. Accounting procedures. Currency. Interest rates. Tax exemptions. Credit provisions. Loan repayment. Terms of loan. Plans and standards. IDA development project. Roads and highways.
INTL ORGS: International Bank for Reconstruction and Development.

PARTIES:
Honduras
IDA (Devel Assoc)

108190 Bilateral Convention **561 UNTS 297**
SIGNED: 15 Jul 64 FORCE: 9 Apr 66
REGISTERED: 2 May 66 Belgium
ARTICLES: 7 LANGUAGE: French.
HEADNOTE: ENCOURGEMENT CAPITAL INVESTMENT PROTECTION PROPERTY
TOPIC: General Economic
CONCEPTS: Exceptions and exemptions. Alien status. Privileges and immunities. General cooperation. General property. Arbitration. Procedure. Special tribunals. Investments. Most favored nation clause.
INTL ORGS: International Court of Justice. Arbitration Commission.
PROCEDURE: Duration. Ratification. Renewal or Revival. Termination.
PARTIES:
Belgium
Tunisia

108191 Bilateral Exchange **561 UNTS 313**
SIGNED: 12 Mar 65 FORCE: 26 Apr 65
REGISTERED: 5 May 66 UK Great Britain
ARTICLES: 2 LANGUAGE: English.
HEADNOTE: PRIVILEGES & IMMUNITIES
TOPIC: IGO Status/Immunit
CONCEPTS: Annex or appendix reference. Privileges and immunities.
PARTIES:
SEATO (SE Asia)
UK Great Britain

108192 Bilateral Agreement **561 UNTS 321**
SIGNED: 17 Feb 66 FORCE: 17 Feb 66
REGISTERED: 5 May 66 Venezuela
ARTICLES: 8 LANGUAGE: Spanish. English.
HEADNOTE: CONTROVERSY OVER FRONTIER
TOPIC: Territory Boundary
CONCEPTS: Establishment of commission. Acceptance of obligations upon admittance to UN. Markers and definitions.
INTL ORGS: United Nations.
TREATY REF: 92BFSP160.
PARTIES:
UK Great Britain
Venezuela

108193 Bilateral Convention **562 UNTS 3**
SIGNED: 1 Apr 65 FORCE: 2 Apr 66
REGISTERED: 11 May 66 Finland
ARTICLES: 29 LANGUAGE: English.
HEADNOTE: DOUBLE TAXATION FISCAL EVASION TAXES INCOME
TOPIC: Taxation
CONCEPTS: Definition of terms. Privileges and immunities. Nationality and citizenship. Conformity with municipal law. Exchange of official publications. Domestic legislation. Negotiation. Teacher and student exchange. Taxation. Tax credits. Equitable taxes. Tax exemptions. Air transport. Merchant vessels.
PROCEDURE: Denunciation. Duration. Ratification. Termination.
PARTIES:
Finland
United Arab Rep

108194 Bilateral Treaty **562 UNTS 43**
SIGNED: 15 Jan 66 FORCE: 25 Feb 66
REGISTERED: 16 May 66 USSR (Soviet Union)
ARTICLES: 10 LANGUAGE: Mongolian. Russian.
HEADNOTE: FRIENDSHIP COOPERATION MUTUAL ASSISTANCE
TOPIC: General Amity
CONCEPTS: Peaceful relations. General cooperation. Defense and security.
INTL ORGS: Council for Mutual Economic Assistance.
PROCEDURE: Duration. Future Procedures Contemplated. Ratification.
PARTIES:
Mongolia
USSR (Soviet Union)

108195 Bilateral Agreement **562 UNTS 59**
SIGNED: 28 Mar 66   FORCE: 28 May 66
REGISTERED: 19 May 66 WHO (World Health)
ARTICLES: 6 LANGUAGE: English.
HEADNOTE: TECHNICAL ADVISORY ASSISTANCE
TOPIC: Tech Assistance
CONCEPTS: Definition of terms. Privileges and immunities. General cooperation. Exchange of information and documents. Personnel. Responsibility and liability. Title and deeds. Exchange. Scholarships and grants. Vocational training. Research and development. Expense sharing formulae. Local currency. Domestic obligation. Special projects. Materials, equipment and services. IGO status. Conformity with IGO decisions.
INTL ORGS: United Nations.
TREATY REF: 33UNTS261.
PROCEDURE: Amendment. Termination.
PARTIES:
WHO (World Health)
Singapore

108196 Unilateral Instrument **562 UNTS 299**
SIGNED: 16 May 66   FORCE: 20 May 66
REGISTERED: 20 May 66 United Nations
ARTICLES: 1 LANGUAGE: French.
HEADNOTE: ACCEPTANCE ICJ JURISDICTION
TOPIC: ICJ Option Clause
CONCEPTS: Exceptions and exemptions. Compulsory jurisdiction.
INTL ORGS: International Court of Justice.
TREATY REF: 337UNTS65.
PROCEDURE: Termination.
PARTIES:
France

108197 Bilateral Convention **562 UNTS 75**
SIGNED: 27 Jun 62   FORCE: 23 Mar 63
REGISTERED: 20 May 66 UK Great Britain
ARTICLES: 39 LANGUAGE: English. Danish.
HEADNOTE: CONSULAR
TOPIC: Consul/Citizenship
CONCEPTS: Definition of terms. Territorial application. General provisions. Previous treaty replacement. General consular functions. Diplomatic privileges. Consular relations establishment. Privileges and immunities. Consular functions in shipping. Consular functions in property. Existing tribunals.
TREATY REF: 2'8DEMARTENS694; 3'14DEMARTENS476;.
PROCEDURE: Ratification.
PARTIES:
Denmark
UK Great Britain

108198 Bilateral Convention **562 UNTS 169**
SIGNED: 30 May 61   FORCE: 12 Apr 63
REGISTERED: 20 May 66 UK Great Britain
ARTICLES: 56 LANGUAGE: English. Spanish.
HEADNOTE: CONSULAR
TOPIC: Consul/Citizenship
CONCEPTS: Definition of terms. Territorial application. Previous treaty replacement. General consular functions. Diplomatic privileges. Consular relations establishment. Privileges and immunities. Protection of nationals. Consular functions in shipping. Consular functions in property. Existing tribunals.
TREATY REF: 28LTS339; 117LTS56.
PROCEDURE: Ratification. Termination.
PARTIES:
Spain
UK Great Britain

108199 Bilateral Agreement **562 UNTS 277**
SIGNED: 11 Aug 65   FORCE: 10 Sep 65
REGISTERED: 26 May 66 IDA (Devel Assoc)
ARTICLES: 6 LANGUAGE: English.
HEADNOTE: DEVELOPMENT CREDIT INDUSTRIAL IMPORTS
TOPIC: Non-IBRD Project
CONCEPTS: Definition of terms. Detailed regulations. Previous treaty amendment. Informational records. Accounting procedures. Currency. Interest rates. Tax exemptions. Credit provisions. Loan repayment. Terms of loan. Plans and standards. IDA development project. Industry.

PARTIES:
India
IDA (Devel Assoc)

108200 Bilateral Agreement **562 UNTS 299**
SIGNED: 11 Oct 65   FORCE: 28 Dec 65
REGISTERED: 26 May 66 IDA (Devel Assoc)
ARTICLES: 7 LANGUAGE: English.
HEADNOTE: DEVELOPMENT CREDIT EDUCATION
TOPIC: Non-IBRD Project
CONCEPTS: Detailed regulations. Previous treaty amendment. Informational records. Education. Accounting procedures. Currency. Interest rates. Tax exemptions. Credit provisions. Loan repayment. Terms of loan. Plans and standards. IDA development project.
PARTIES:
Morocco
IDA (Devel Assoc)

108201 Bilateral Agreement **563 UNTS 3**
SIGNED: 1 Mar 65   FORCE: 31 Aug 65
REGISTERED: 26 May 66 IDA (Devel Assoc)
ARTICLES: 7 LANGUAGE: English.
HEADNOTE: DEVELOPMENT CREDIT ROAD
TOPIC: Non-IBRD Project
CONCEPTS: Definition of terms. Detailed regulations. Previous treaty amendment. Exchange of information and documents. Informational records. Accounting procedures. Currency. Tax exemptions. Interest rates. Credit provisions. Loan repayment. Terms of loan. Plans and standards. IDA development project. Roads and highways.
PARTIES:
Nigeria
IDA (Devel Assoc)

108202 Bilateral Convention **563 UNTS 31**
SIGNED: 11 Nov 57   FORCE: 19 Mar 66
REGISTERED: 26 May 66 Taiwan
ARTICLES: 9 LANGUAGE: Chinese. Persian. English.
HEADNOTE: CULTURAL CONVENTION
TOPIC: Culture
CONCEPTS: Treaty interpretation. Friendship and amity. General cooperation. Use of facilities. Exchange. Teacher and student exchange. Scholarships and grants. General cultural cooperation. Artists. Athletes. Scientific exchange. Mass media exchange.
PROCEDURE: Duration. Ratification. Renewal or Revival. Termination.
PARTIES:
Taiwan
Iran

108203 Bilateral Agreement **563 UNTS 45**
SIGNED: 21 May 64   FORCE: 5 Apr 66
REGISTERED: 21 May 66 Norway
ARTICLES: 7 LANGUAGE: English. Romanian.
HEADNOTE: FINANCE
TOPIC: Claims and Debts
CONCEPTS: Exchange of information and documents. Informational records. Expropriation. Responsibility and liability. Payment schedules. Claims and settlements. Lump sum settlements. Debts.
PROCEDURE: Ratification.
PARTIES:
Norway
Romania

108204 Multilateral Agreement **563 UNTS 54**
SIGNED: 12 May 66   FORCE: 12 May 66
REGISTERED: 1 Jun 66 United Nations
ARTICLES: 6 LANGUAGE: English.
HEADNOTE: OPERATIONAL ASSISTANCE
TOPIC: General Aid
CONCEPTS: Arbitration. Special projects. Admission. Procedure. Liaison with other IGO's. Internal structure. IGO obligations.
PROCEDURE: Termination.
PARTIES:
Malta SIGNED: 12 May 66 FORCE: 12 May 66
FAO (Food Agri) SIGNED: 12 May 66 FORCE: 12 May 66
IAEA (Atom Energy) SIGNED: 12 May 66 FORCE: 12 May 66

ICAO (Civil Aviat) SIGNED: 12 May 66 FORCE: 12 May 66
ILO (Labor Org) SIGNED: 12 May 66 FORCE: 12 May 66
IMCO (Maritime Org) SIGNED: 12 May 66 FORCE: 12 May 66
ITU (Telecommun) SIGNED: 12 May 66 FORCE: 12 May 66
UNESCO (Educ/Cult) SIGNED: 12 May 66 FORCE: 12 May 66
United Nations SIGNED: 12 May 66 FORCE: 12 May 66
UPU (Postal Union) SIGNED: 12 May 66 FORCE: 12 May 66
WHO (World Health) SIGNED: 12 May 66 FORCE: 12 May 66
WMO (Meteorology) SIGNED: 12 May 66 FORCE: 12 May 66
ANNEX
649 UNTS 368. UNIDO (Industrial). Accession 15 Oct 68. Force 15 Oct 68.

108205 Bilateral Agreement **563 UNTS 71**
SIGNED: 26 May 66   FORCE: 26 May 66
REGISTERED: 1 Jun 66 United Nations
ARTICLES: 10 LANGUAGE: English. French.
HEADNOTE: DEVELOPMENT PROGRAM (UN SPECIAL FUND)
TOPIC: General Aid
CONCEPTS: Conditions. Exceptions and exemptions. General cooperation. Exchange of information and documents. Informational records. Inspection and observation. Operating agencies. Personnel. Responsibility and liability. Title and deeds. Arbitration. Procedure. Research results. Accounting procedures. Financial programs. Claims and settlements. Tax exemptions. Customs exemptions. Assistance. Materials, equipment and services. IGO status.
INTL ORGS: International Atomic Energy Agency. International Court of Justice. United Nations. Arbitration Commission.
TREATY REF: 1UNTS15; 33UNTS261; 374UNTS147.
PROCEDURE: Amendment. Termination.
PARTIES:
Bulgaria
UN Special Fund

108206 Bilateral Agreement **563 UNTS 89**
SIGNED: 7 Aug 65   FORCE: 9 Aug 65
REGISTERED: 1 Jun 66 Singapore
ARTICLES: 8 LANGUAGE: English.
HEADNOTE: SINGAPORE SOVEREIGNTY FROM MALAYSIA
TOPIC: Recognition
CONCEPTS: Annex or appendix reference. Status of state. Recognition. Responsibility and liability.
PROCEDURE: Future Procedures Contemplated.
PARTIES:
Malaysia
Singapore

108207 Multilateral Agreement **563 UNTS 104**
SIGNED: 5 Jul 65   FORCE: 5 Jul 65
REGISTERED: 3 Jun 66 United Nations
ARTICLES: 6 LANGUAGE: French.
HEADNOTE: OPERATIONAL ASSISTANCE
TOPIC: General Aid
CONCEPTS: Exceptions and exemptions. Annex or appendix reference. Privileges and immunities. General cooperation. Personnel. Private contracts. Arbitration. Procedure. Negotiation. Compensation. Financial programs. Claims and settlements. Tax exemptions. Customs exemptions. Domestic obligation. Assistance. Expense sharing formulae.
TREATY REF: 480UNTS232.
PROCEDURE: Amendment. Termination.
PARTIES:
Congo (Brazzaville) SIGNED: 5 Jul 65 FORCE: 5 Jul 65
FAO (Food Agri) SIGNED: 5 Jul 65 FORCE: 5 Jul 65
IAEA (Atom Energy) SIGNED: 5 Jul 65 FORCE: 5 Jul 65
ICAO (Civil Aviat) SIGNED: 5 Jul 65 FORCE: 5 Jul 65
ILO (Labor Org) SIGNED: 5 Jul 65 FORCE: 5 Jul 65

IMCO (Maritime Org) SIGNED: 5 Jul 65 FORCE: 5 Jul 65
ITU (Telecommun) SIGNED: 5 Jul 65 FORCE: 5 Jul 65
UNESCO (Educ/Cult) SIGNED: 5 Jul 65 FORCE: 5 Jul 65
United Nations SIGNED: 5 Jul 65 FORCE: 5 Jul 65
UPU (Postal Union) SIGNED: 5 Jul 65 FORCE: 5 Jul 65
WHO (World Health) SIGNED: 5 Jul 65 FORCE: 5 Jul 65
WMO (Meteorology) SIGNED: 5 Jul 65 FORCE: 5 Jul 65

108208   Bilateral Agreement   **563 UNTS 121**
SIGNED: 19 May 60   FORCE: 26 Dec 65
REGISTERED: 3 Jun 66 ICAO (Civil Aviat)
ARTICLES: 19 LANGUAGE: French. Arabic.
HEADNOTE: AIR TRANSPORT
TOPIC: Air Transport
CONCEPTS: Definition of terms. Detailed regulations. Annex or appendix reference. Conformity with municipal law. General cooperation. Exchange of information and documents. Licenses and permits. Personnel. Recognition of legal documents. Use of facilities. Arbitration. Procedure. Special tribunals. Reexport of goods, etc.. Expense sharing formulae. Fees and exemptions. Non-interest rates and fees. General. Tax exemptions. Customs exemptions. Competency certificate. Routes and logistics. Navigational conditions. Permit designation. Air transport. Airport facilities. Airworthiness certificates. Conditions of airlines operating permission. Operating authorizations and regulations.
INTL ORGS: International Civil Aviation Organization. Arbitration Commission.
TREATY REF: 15UNTS295.
PROCEDURE: Amendment. Future Procedures Contemplated. Ratification. Registration. Termination.
PARTIES:
Morocco
United Arab Rep

108209   Bilateral Agreement   **563 UNTS 153**
SIGNED: 31 Jan 62   FORCE: 1 Feb 62
REGISTERED: 3 Jun 66 ICAO (Civil Aviat)
ARTICLES: 10 LANGUAGE: English.
HEADNOTE: AIR SERVICES
TOPIC: Air Transport
CONCEPTS: Definition of terms. Annex or appendix reference. Conformity with municipal law. General cooperation. Exchange of information and documents. Fees and exemptions. Non-interest rates and fees. National treatment. Customs exemptions. Routes and logistics. Navigational conditions. Permit designation. Conditions of airlines operating permission.
TREATY REF: 15UNTS295.
PROCEDURE: Amendment. Termination. Application to Non-self-governing Territories.
PARTIES:
Luxembourg
South Africa

108210   Bilateral Agreement   **563 UNTS 165**
SIGNED: 5 Mar 62   FORCE: 2 Sep 65
REGISTERED: 3 Jun 66 ICAO (Civil Aviat)
ARTICLES: 15 LANGUAGE: Thai. German. English.
HEADNOTE: AIR TRANSPORT
TOPIC: Air Transport
CONCEPTS: Definition of terms. Detailed regulations. Treaty interpretation. Annex or appendix reference. Conformity with municipal law. General cooperation. Exchange of information and documents. Use of facilities. Arbitration. Procedure. Special tribunals. Expense sharing formulae. Fees and exemptions. Non-interest rates and fees. National treatment. Customs exemptions. Routes and logistics. Permit designation. Air transport. Airport facilities. Conditions of airlines operating permission. Overflights and technical stops. Operating authorizations and regulations.
INTL ORGS: International Civil Aviation Organization. Arbitration Commission.
TREATY REF: 15UNTS295.
PROCEDURE: Amendment. Future Procedures Contemplated. Ratification. Registration. Termination.

PARTIES:
Germany, West
Thailand

108211   Bilateral Agreement   **563 UNTS 205**
SIGNED: 26 Mar 62   FORCE: 2 Jun 65
REGISTERED: 3 Jun 66 ICAO (Civil Aviat)
ARTICLES: 15 LANGUAGE: French. Spanish.
HEADNOTE: AIR TRANSPORT
TOPIC: Air Transport
CONCEPTS: Detailed regulations. Annex or appendix reference. General cooperation. Arbitration. Procedure. Special tribunals. Negotiation. Reexport of goods, etc.. Monetary and gold transfers. Fees and exemptions. Non-interest rates and fees. Customs exemptions. Routes and logistics. Permit designation. Air transport. Conditions of airlines operating permission. Overflights and technical stops. Operating authorizations and regulations.
INTL ORGS: International Civil Aviation Organization. Arbitration Commission.
TREATY REF: 15UNTS295.
PROCEDURE: Amendment. Denunciation. Future Procedures Contemplated. Ratification. Termination.
PARTIES:
Luxembourg
Spain

108212   Bilateral Agreement   **563 UNTS 227**
SIGNED: 29 Mar 62   FORCE: 27 Apr 65
REGISTERED: 3 Jun 66 ICAO (Civil Aviat)
ARTICLES: 14 LANGUAGE: French.
HEADNOTE: AIR TRANSPORT
TOPIC: Air Transport
CONCEPTS: Detailed regulations. Annex or appendix reference. Conformity with municipal law. General cooperation. Arbitration. Procedure. Special tribunals. Negotiation. Reexport of goods, etc.. Monetary and gold transfers. Fees and exemptions. Non-interest rates and fees. Customs exemptions. Routes and logistics. Permit designation. Air transport. Conditions of airlines operating permission. Overflights and technical stops. Operating authorizations and regulations.
INTL ORGS: International Civil Aviation Organization. Arbitration Commission.
TREATY REF: 15UNTS295.
PROCEDURE: Amendment. Denunciation. Future Procedures Contemplated. Ratification. Termination.
PARTIES:
France
Luxembourg

108213   Bilateral Agreement   **563 UNTS 243**
SIGNED: 11 Dec 62   FORCE: 11 Dec 62
REGISTERED: 3 Jun 66 ICAO (Civil Aviat)
ARTICLES: 21 LANGUAGE: English.
HEADNOTE: AIR TRANSPORT
TOPIC: Air Transport
CONCEPTS: Conditions. Definition of terms. Detailed regulations. Annex or appendix reference. Conformity with municipal law. General cooperation. Recognition of legal documents. Use of facilities. Procedure. Existing tribunals. Reexport of goods, etc.. Monetary and gold transfers. Exchange rates and regulations. Expense sharing formulae. Non-interest rates and fees. National treatment. General. Tax exemptions. Customs exemptions. Competency certificate. Routes and logistics. Permit designation. Air transport. Airworthiness certificates. Conditions of airlines operating permission. Overflights and technical stops.
INTL ORGS: International Civil Aviation Organization. Arbitration Commission.
TREATY REF: 15UNTS295.
PROCEDURE: Amendment. Future Procedures Contemplated. Ratification. Registration. Termination.
PARTIES:
Ghana
Tunisia

108214   Bilateral Agreement   **563 UNTS 263**
SIGNED: 18 Feb 63   FORCE: 18 Feb 63
REGISTERED: 3 Jun 66 ICAO (Civil Aviat)

ARTICLES: 23 LANGUAGE: French.
HEADNOTE: AIR TRANSPORT
TOPIC: Air Transport
CONCEPTS: Definition of terms. Detailed regulations. Annex or appendix reference. Conformity with municipal law. Exchange of information and documents. Licenses and permits. Recognition of legal documents. Arbitration. Procedure. Special tribunals. Negotiation. Reexport of goods, etc.. Expense sharing formulae. Fees and exemptions. Non-interest rates and fees. Tax exemptions. Customs exemptions. Competency certificate. Routes and logistics. Navigational conditions. Permit designation. Air transport. Airworthiness certificates. Conditions of airlines operating permission. Operating authorizations and regulations. Licenses and certificates of nationality.
INTL ORGS: International Civil Aviation Organization. Arbitration Commission.
TREATY REF: 15UNTS295.
PROCEDURE: Amendment. Ratification. Registration. Termination.
PARTIES:
Algeria
France

108215   Bilateral Agreement   **563 UNTS 281**
SIGNED: 18 Feb 63   FORCE: 21 Sep 64
REGISTERED: 3 Jun 66 ICAO (Civil Aviat)
ARTICLES: 13 LANGUAGE: French. Arabic.
HEADNOTE: AIR SERVICES
TOPIC: Air Transport
CONCEPTS: Definition of terms. Detailed regulations. Exceptions and exemptions. Treaty interpretation. Annex or appendix reference. General cooperation. Exchange of information and documents. Arbitration. Procedure. Special tribunals. Negotiation. Fees and exemptions. Non-interest rates and fees. Most favored nation clause. National treatment. Customs exemptions. Routes and logistics. Permit designation. Conditions of airlines operating permission. Overflights and technical stops. Operating authorizations and regulations.
INTL ORGS: International Civil Aviation Organization. International Court of Justice. Arbitration Commission.
TREATY REF: 15UNTS295.
PROCEDURE: Amendment. Future Procedures Contemplated. Ratification. Registration. Termination.
PARTIES:
Sudan
Switzerland

108216   Bilateral Agreement   **563 UNTS 305**
SIGNED: 5 Mar 63   FORCE: 30 Oct 64
REGISTERED: 3 Jun 66 ICAO (Civil Aviat)
ARTICLES: 19 LANGUAGE: English.
HEADNOTE: AIR TRANSPORT
TOPIC: Air Transport
CONCEPTS: Airport equipment. Airworthiness certificates. Conditions of airlines operating permission. Overflights and technical stops. Operating authorizations and regulations.
INTL ORGS: International Civil Aviation Organization. Arbitration Commission.
TREATY REF: 15UNTS295.
PARTIES:
Cyprus
Norway

108217   Bilateral Agreement   **564 UNTS 3**
SIGNED: 30 Apr 63   FORCE: 30 Apr 63
REGISTERED: 3 Jun 66 ICAO (Civil Aviat)
ARTICLES: 25 LANGUAGE: French.
HEADNOTE: AIR TRANSPORT
TOPIC: Air Transport
CONCEPTS: Definition of terms. Detailed regulations. General provisions. Annex or appendix reference. Conformity with municipal law. General cooperation. Exchange of information and documents. Licenses and permits. Personnel. Recognition of legal documents. Arbitration. Procedure. Special tribunals. Competence of tribunal. Reexport of goods, etc.. Fees and exemptions. Funding procedures. Non-interest rates and fees. Tax exemptions. Customs exemptions. Competency certificate. Routes and logistics. Navigational conditions. Permit designation. Air trans-

port. Airport facilities. Airworthiness certificates. Conditions of airlines operating permission. Operating authorizations and regulations. Licenses and certificates of nationality.
INTL ORGS: International Civil Aviation Organization. Arbitration Commission.
TREATY REF: 15UNTS295.
PROCEDURE: Amendment. Future Procedures Contemplated. Ratification. Registration. Termination.
PARTIES:
Algeria
Morocco

108218　Bilateral Exchange　**564 UNTS 23**
SIGNED: 19 Jul 63　　　　FORCE: 19 Jul 63
REGISTERED: 3 Jun 66 ICAO (Civil Aviat)
ARTICLES: 2 LANGUAGE: French.
HEADNOTE: CIVIL AIR TRANSPORT
TOPIC: Air Transport
CONCEPTS: Routes and logistics. Permit designation. Air transport. Operating authorizations and regulations.
TREATY REF: 15UNTS295.
PROCEDURE: Duration. Renewal or Revival. Termination.
PARTIES:
Taiwan
Luxembourg

108219　Bilateral Agreement　**564 UNTS 29**
SIGNED: 22 Jul 63　　　　FORCE: 22 Jul 63
REGISTERED: 3 Jun 66 ICAO (Civil Aviat)
ARTICLES: 20 LANGUAGE: French.
HEADNOTE: AIR TRANSPORT
TOPIC: Air Transport
CONCEPTS: Definition of terms. Detailed regulations. General provisions. Annex or appendix reference. Conformity with municipal law. General cooperation. Exchange of information and documents. Licenses and permits. Personnel. Recognition of legal documents. Arbitration. Procedure. Special tribunals. Competence of tribunal. Reexport of goods, etc.. Fees and exemptions. Funding procedures. Non-interest rates and fees. Tax exemptions. Customs exemptions. Competency certificate. Routes and logistics. Navigational conditions. Permit designation. Air transport. Airport facilities. Airworthiness certificates. Conditions of airlines operating permission. Operating authorizations and regulations. Licenses and certificates of nationality.
INTL ORGS: International Civil Aviation Organization. Arbitration Commission.
TREATY REF: 15UNTS295.
PROCEDURE: Amendment. Ratification. Registration. Termination.
PARTIES:
Algeria
Mali

108220　Bilateral Agreement　**564 UNTS 49**
SIGNED: 2 Jul 65　　　　FORCE: 28 Feb 66
REGISTERED: 8 Jun 66 Netherlands
ARTICLES: 7 LANGUAGE: French.
HEADNOTE: FINANCIAL QUESTIONS
TOPIC: Finance
CONCEPTS: Claims and settlements.
PARTIES:
Hungary
Netherlands

108221　Bilateral Exchange　**564 UNTS 69**
SIGNED: 17 May 65　　　　FORCE: 17 May 65
REGISTERED: 9 Jun 66 USA (United States)
ARTICLES: 2 LANGUAGE: English. Spanish.
HEADNOTE: EDUCATION COMMISSION PROGRAM
TOPIC: Education
CONCEPTS: Previous treaty replacement. Operating agencies. General property. Establishment of commission. Education. Exchange. Commissions and foundations. Teacher and student exchange. Scholarships and grants. Research and development. Exchange rates and regulations. Local currency. Tax exemptions. Surplus commodities.
TREATY REF: 341UNTS201; 346UNTS358; 388UNTS315.
PROCEDURE: Termination.

PARTIES:
USA (United States)
Uruguay

108222　Bilateral Exchange　**564 UNTS 83**
SIGNED: 11 Jun 65　　　　FORCE: 1 Jan 66
REGISTERED: 9 Jun 66 USA (United States)
ARTICLES: 2 LANGUAGE: English.
HEADNOTE: ATMOSPHERIC RESEARCH FACILITIES
TOPIC: Scientific Project
CONCEPTS: Annex or appendix reference. Previous treaty replacement. Responsibility and liability. Research and scientific projects. Research cooperation. Meteorology.
TREATY REF: 377UNTS365; 546UNTS376.
PARTIES:
Canada
USA (United States)

108223　Bilateral Agreement　**564 UNTS 101**
SIGNED: 14 Jul 65　　　　FORCE: 14 Jul 65
REGISTERED: 9 Jun 66 USA (United States)
ARTICLES: 6 LANGUAGE: English. French.
HEADNOTE: AGRI COMMOD TITLE I
TOPIC: US Agri Commod Aid
CONCEPTS: General provisions. Annex or appendix reference. Exchange of information and documents. Reexport of goods, etc.. Currency. Exchange rates and regulations. Transportation costs. Local currency. Commodities schedule. Purchase authorization. Mutual consultation.
PARTIES:
Mali
USA (United States)
ANNEX
573 UNTS 359. USA (United States). Amendment 8 Dec 65. Force 15 Dec 65.
573 UNTS 359. Mali. Amendment 15 Dec 65. Force 15 Dec 65.

108224　Bilateral Agreement　**564 UNTS 119**
SIGNED: 17 Aug 65　　　　FORCE: 17 Aug 65
REGISTERED: 9 Jun 66 USA (United States)
ARTICLES: 5 LANGUAGE: English.
HEADNOTE: AGRI COMMOD TITLE IV
TOPIC: US Agri Commod Aid
CONCEPTS: General provisions. Annex or appendix reference. Exchange of information and documents. Reexport of goods, etc.. Payment schedules. Transportation costs. Purchase authorization. Commodities schedule. Purchase authorization. Mutual consultation.
PARTIES:
Ethiopia
USA (United States)

108225　Bilateral Exchange　**564 UNTS 135**
SIGNED: 11 Aug 65　　　　FORCE: 11 Aug 65
REGISTERED: 9 Jun 66 USA (United States)
ARTICLES: 2 LANGUAGE: English. Spanish.
HEADNOTE: ALIEN AMATEUR RADIO OPERATORS
TOPIC: Gen Communications
CONCEPTS: Conformity with municipal law. Licenses and permits. Amateur radio. Amateur third party message.
TREATY REF: USA'TIAS 4893;.
PROCEDURE: Termination.
PARTIES:
Peru
USA (United States)

108226　Bilateral Agreement　**564 UNTS 143**
SIGNED: 12 May 65　　　　FORCE: 12 May 65
REGISTERED: 9 Jun 66 USA (United States)
ARTICLES: 6 LANGUAGE: English. Spanish.
HEADNOTE: AGRI COMMOD TITLE I
TOPIC: US Agri Commod Aid
CONCEPTS: General provisions. Annex or appendix reference. Exchange of information and documents. Reexport of goods, etc.. Currency. Exchange rates and regulations. Transportation costs. Commodities schedule. Purchase authorization. Surplus commodities. Mutual consultation.
PARTIES:
Bolivia
USA (United States)

108227　Bilateral Exchange　**564 UNTS 169**
SIGNED: 27 Sep 65　　　　FORCE: 27 Sep 65
REGISTERED: 9 Jun 66 USA (United States)
ARTICLES: 2 LANGUAGE: English.
HEADNOTE: CERTIFICATES AIRWORTHINESS IMPORTED CIVIL GLIDER AIRCRAFT
TOPIC: Air Transport
CONCEPTS: General cooperation. Export quotas. Import quotas. Airworthiness certificates.
PARTIES:
Poland
USA (United States)

108228　Bilateral Exchange　**564 UNTS 179**
SIGNED: 9 Apr 65　　　　FORCE: 1 May 65
REGISTERED: 10 Jun 66 Austria
ARTICLES: 2 LANGUAGE: German. Hungarian.
HEADNOTE: MUTUAL ABOLITION VISAS
TOPIC: Visas
CONCEPTS: Time limit. Visa abolition.
PARTIES:
Austria
Hungary

108229　Bilateral Exchange　**564 UNTS 185**
SIGNED: 17 Nov 65　　　　FORCE: 1 Jan 66
REGISTERED: 15 Jun 66 Austria
ARTICLES: 2 LANGUAGE: German. Romanian.
HEADNOTE: MUTUAL ABOLITION VISAS
TOPIC: Visas
CONCEPTS: Time limit. Visa abolition.
PARTIES:
Austria
Romania

108230　Bilateral Exchange　**565 UNTS 3**
SIGNED: 20 Jun 66　　　　FORCE: 20 Jun 66
REGISTERED: 20 Jun 66 United Nations
ARTICLES: 2 LANGUAGE: French.
HEADNOTE: CLAIM SETTLEMENT
TOPIC: Claims and Debts
CONCEPTS: Privileges and immunities. Responsibility and liability. Payment schedules. Claims and settlements. Assessment procedures. Peace-keeping force.
PARTIES:
Greece
United Nations

108231　Bilateral Agreement　**565 UNTS 11**
SIGNED: 23 May 66　　　　FORCE: 23 May 66
REGISTERED: 20 Jun 66 United Nations
ARTICLES: 7 LANGUAGE: English.
HEADNOTE: COUNCIL DEVELOPMENT PROGRAM
TOPIC: IGO Operations
CONCEPTS: Diplomatic privileges. Diplomatic missions. Privileges and immunities. Personnel. Funding procedures. Subsidiary organ.
TREATY REF: 1UNTS15; 286UNTS329.
PARTIES:
Italy
United Nations

108232　Unilateral Instrument　**565 UNTS 21**
SIGNED: 14 Jun 66　　　　FORCE: 22 Jun 66
REGISTERED: 22 Jun 66 United Nations
ARTICLES: 1 LANGUAGE: English.
HEADNOTE: ACCEPTANCE ICJ JURISDICTION
TOPIC: ICJ Option Clause
CONCEPTS: Compulsory jurisdiction.
INTL ORGS: International Court of Justice.
PARTIES:
Gambia

108233　Bilateral Exchange　**565 UNTS 25**
SIGNED: 7 Jan 66　　　　FORCE: 6 Feb 66
REGISTERED: 27 Jun 66 UK Great Britain
ARTICLES: 2 LANGUAGE: English. Spanish.
HEADNOTE: ABOLITION VISAS
TOPIC: Visas
CONCEPTS: Emergencies. Time limit. Visa abolition. Denial of admission. Conformity with municipal law.
PROCEDURE: Termination.
PARTIES:
Panama
UK Great Britain

108234 Bilateral Agreement **565 UNTS 33**
SIGNED: 28 Feb 66 FORCE: 4 Apr 66
REGISTERED: 27 Jun 66 UK Great Britain
ARTICLES: 14 LANGUAGE: English.
HEADNOTE: SOCIAL SECURITY
TOPIC: Health/Educ/Welfare
CONCEPTS: Conditions. Definition of terms. Legal
protection and assistance. Domestic legislation.
General property. Responsibility and liability.
Family allowances. Administrative cooperation.
Old age insurance. Sickness and invalidity insur-
ance. Social security. Unemployment. Migrant
worker.
PROCEDURE: Duration. Termination.
PARTIES:
Ireland
UK Great Britain

108235 Bilateral Agreement **565 UNTS 58**
SIGNED: 14 Dec 65 FORCE: 1 Jul 66
REGISTERED: 1 Jul 66 Ireland
ARTICLES: 27 LANGUAGE: English.
HEADNOTE: EXPANDING TRADE ELIMINATING
DUTIES
TOPIC: General Trade
CONCEPTS: Definition of terms. Detailed regula-
tions. Exceptions and exemptions. Territorial ap-
plication. Treaty implementation. Treaty inter-
pretation. Annex or appendix reference. Previ-
ous treaty replacement. General cooperation.
Unemployment. Export quotas. Import quotas.
Free trade. Tariffs. Reciprocity in trade. Reexport
of goods, etc.. Trade procedures. Balance of payments. Commodity trade. Quotas. General. Customs duties. Customs declarations. Raw materials.
TREATY REF: 2UNTS40; 552UNTS362;-
86UNTS37;55UNTS187.
PARTIES:
Ireland
UK Great Britain
ANNEX
643 UNTS 402. Ireland. Supplementation
11 Mar 68. Force 11 Mar 68.
643 UNTS 402. UK Great Britain. Supplementation 11 Mar 68. Force 11 Mar 68.

108236 Bilateral Agreement **566 UNTS 2**
SIGNED: 17 Jan 61 FORCE: 17 Jan 61
REGISTERED: 1 Jul 66 UK Great Britain
ARTICLES: 0 LANGUAGE: French.
HEADNOTE: TRADE
TOPIC: General Trade
CONCEPTS: Establishment of trade relations. Ex-
port quotas. Import quotas. Reciprocity in trade.
Quotas.
PARTIES:
Tunisia
UK Great Britain

108237 Bilateral Agreement **566 UNTS 19**
SIGNED: 23 May 66 FORCE: 23 May 66
REGISTERED: 5 Jul 66 WHO (World Health)
ARTICLES: 6 LANGUAGE: English.
HEADNOTE: TECHNICAL ADVISORY ASSISTANCE
TOPIC: Tech Assistance
CONCEPTS: Privileges and immunities. General
technical assistance. Assistance.
TREATY REF: 33UNTS261,71UNTS318,-
79UNTS326,ETC.
PROCEDURE: Termination.
PARTIES:
Maldive Islands
WHO (World Health)

108238 Bilateral Agreement **566 UNTS 31**
SIGNED: 20 May 65 FORCE: 25 May 66
REGISTERED: 6 Jul 66 Finland
ARTICLES: 7 LANGUAGE: Finnish. Russian.
HEADNOTE: EXPANDING TRADE ELIMINATING
DUTIES
TOPIC: Territory Boundary
CONCEPTS: Fish, wildlife, and natural resources.
Markers and definitions.
TREATY REF: 48UNTS149,226UNTS338,5-
16UNTS205,48UNTS203.
PARTIES:
Finland
USSR (Soviet Union)

108239 Bilateral Agreement **566 UNTS 45**
SIGNED: 3 Apr 64 FORCE: 17 Nov 64
REGISTERED: 7 Jul 66 Netherlands
ARTICLES: 7 LANGUAGE: English.
HEADNOTE: TECHNICAL COOPERATION
TOPIC: Tech Assistance
CONCEPTS: General technical assistance. Assis-
tance. Specific technical assistance.
PROCEDURE: Duration.
PARTIES:
Indonesia
Netherlands

108240 Bilateral Agreement **566 UNTS 51**
SIGNED: 30 Mar 66 FORCE: 10 Jun 66
REGISTERED: 7 Jul 66 Norway
ARTICLES: 32 LANGUAGE: Norwegian. Icelandic.
HEADNOTE: AVOIDANCE DOUBLE TAXATION
TOPIC: Taxation
CONCEPTS: Taxation. Equitable taxes. General.
Tax exemptions.
PROCEDURE: Denunciation. Termination.
PARTIES:
Iceland
Norway

108241 Bilateral Agreement **566 UNTS 129**
SIGNED: 2 May 60 FORCE: 27 Jan 66
REGISTERED: 7 Jul 66 UK Great Britain
ARTICLES: 0 LANGUAGE: English. Persian.
HEADNOTE: AIR SERVICES
TOPIC: Air Transport
CONCEPTS: Customs exemptions. Airport facili-
ties. Airport equipment. Airworthiness certifi-
cates. Conditions of airlines operating permis-
sion. Overflights and technical stops. Operating
authorizations and regulations. Licenses and cer-
tificates of nationality.
TREATY REF: 15UNTS295,320UNTS209,4-
18UNTS161,514UNTS209.
PROCEDURE: Ratification.
PARTIES:
Iran
UK Great Britain

108242 Bilateral Agreement **566 UNTS 159**
SIGNED: 23 Apr 66 FORCE: 23 Apr 66
REGISTERED: 11 Jul 66 USSR (Soviet Union)
ARTICLES: 23 LANGUAGE: Russian. Czechoslo-
vakian.
HEADNOTE: CULTURAL SCIENTIFIC COOPER-
ATION
TOPIC: Culture
CONCEPTS: Culture. Exchange. General cultural
cooperation. Artists. Athletes. Research cooper-
ation. Scientific exchange.
TREATY REF: 145BFSP238,496UNTS161,2-
59UNTS341,313UNTS291.
PROCEDURE: Duration. Termination.
PARTIES:
Czechoslovakia
USSR (Soviet Union)

108243 Bilateral Exchange **566 UNTS 187**
SIGNED: 26 Apr 66 FORCE: 26 Apr 66
REGISTERED: 12 Jul 66 Belgium
ARTICLES: 3 LANGUAGE: French.
HEADNOTE: FREE COPY CIVIL REGISTRATION
TOPIC: Admin Cooperation
CONCEPTS: Administrative cooperation. Ex-
change of information and documents. Juridical
personality.
PROCEDURE: Denunciation.
PARTIES:
Belgium
Israel

108244 Bilateral Agreement **566 UNTS 195**
SIGNED: 23 Sep 63 FORCE: 14 Jan 64
REGISTERED: 12 Jul 66 Belgium
ARTICLES: 8 LANGUAGE: French.
HEADNOTE: FINANCIAL ASSISTANCE
TOPIC: Direct Aid
CONCEPTS: Loan and credit. Credit provisions.
PROCEDURE: Ratification.
PARTIES:
Belgium
Turkey

108245 Bilateral Agreement **566 UNTS 212**
SIGNED: 16 Sep 65 FORCE: 17 Nov 65
REGISTERED: 12 Jul 66 IBRD (World Bank)
ARTICLES: 5 LANGUAGE: English.
HEADNOTE: GUARANTEE INDUSTRIAL FINANCE
TOPIC: Claims and Debts
CONCEPTS: Debts. Loan and credit. Credit provi-
sions. Loan repayment.
PROCEDURE: Termination.
PARTIES:
Israel
IBRD (World Bank)

108246 Bilateral Agreement **566 UNTS 249**
SIGNED: 10 Sep 65 FORCE: 4 Nov 65
REGISTERED: IBRD (World Bank)
ARTICLES: 5 LANGUAGE: English.
HEADNOTE: GUARANTEE KOBE EXPRESSWAY
TOPIC: Claims and Debts
CONCEPTS: Debts. Loan and credit. Credit provi-
sions. Loan repayment.
PROCEDURE: Termination.
PARTIES:
Japan
IBRD (World Bank)

108247 Bilateral Agreement **566 UNTS 279**
SIGNED: 8 Nov 65 FORCE: 17 Feb 66
REGISTERED: 12 Jul 66 IBRD (World Bank)
ARTICLES: 5 LANGUAGE: English.
HEADNOTE: GUARANTEE AGRICULTURAL
CREDIT
TOPIC: Claims and Debts
CONCEPTS: Debts. Loan and credit. Credit provi-
sions. Loan repayment.
PROCEDURE: Termination.
PARTIES:
Morocco
IBRD (World Bank)

108248 Bilateral Agreement **566 UNTS 311**
SIGNED: 17 Sep 65 FORCE: 30 Nov 65
REGISTERED: 12 Jul 66 IBRD (World Bank)
ARTICLES: 6 LANGUAGE: English.
HEADNOTE: LOAN LA OROYA-AGUAYTIA ROAD
TOPIC: Loans and Credits
CONCEPTS: Loan and credit. Credit provisions.
World Bank projects. Loan regulations. Plans
and standards.
PARTIES:
Peru
IBRD (World Bank)

108249 Bilateral Agreement **567 UNTS 3**
SIGNED: 2 Nov 65 FORCE: 27 Jan 66
REGISTERED: 12 Jul 66 IBRD (World Bank)
ARTICLES: 5 LANGUAGE: English.
HEADNOTE: GUARANTEE RURAL CREDIT
TOPIC: IBRD Project
CONCEPTS: Definition of terms. Annex or appen-
dix reference. Exchange of information and doc-
uments. Inspection and observation. Bonds.
Fees and exemptions. Tax exemptions. Domestic
obligation. Loan and credit. Terms of loan. Loan
regulations. Loan guarantee. Guarantor non-
interference.
PARTIES:
Philippines
IBRD (World Bank)

108250 Bilateral Agreement **567 UNTS 27**
SIGNED: 27 Dec 65 FORCE: 10 Mar 66
REGISTERED: 12 Jul 66 IBRD (World Bank)
ARTICLES: 7 LANGUAGE: English.
HEADNOTE: RAILWAY CAPITAL DEVELOPMENT
LOAN
TOPIC: IBRD Project
CONCEPTS: Definition of terms. Annex or appen-
dix reference. Loan guarantee. Railways. Guar-
antor non-interference. Domestic obligation.
Terms of loan. Exchange of information and doc-
uments. Informational records. Inspection and
observation. Accounting procedures. Bonds.
Fees and exemptions. Tax exemptions. Interest
rates. Default remedies.
PARTIES:
IBRD (World Bank)
Sudan

108251 Bilateral Agreement **567 UNTS 45**
SIGNED: 30 Mar 65 FORCE: 28 Dec 65
REGISTERED: 12 Jul 66 IBRD (World Bank)
ARTICLES: 9 LANGUAGE: English.
HEADNOTE: LOAN LIVESTOCK
TOPIC: IBRD Project
CONCEPTS: Default remedies. Definition of terms.
Annex or appendix reference. Exchange of information and documents. Informational records.
Inspection and observation. Bonds. Fees and exemptions. Interest rates. Domestic obligation.
Agriculture. Terms of loan. Loan regulations.
Loan guarantee. Guarantor non-interference.
PARTIES:
IBRD (World Bank)
Uruguay

108252 Bilateral Agreement **567 UNTS 67**
SIGNED: 13 Jan 66 FORCE: 10 Feb 66
REGISTERED: 12 Jul 66 IDA (Devel Assoc)
ARTICLES: 6 LANGUAGE: English.
HEADNOTE: DEVELOPMENT CREDIT ROAD VEHICLES
TOPIC: Non-IBRD Project
CONCEPTS: Definition of terms. Detailed regulations. Previous treaty amendment. Exchange of information and documents. Informational records. Accounting procedures. Currency. Interest rates. Tax exemptions. Credit provisions.
Loan repayment. Terms of loan. Plans and standards. IDA development project. Commercial road vehicles.
PARTIES:
Pakistan
IDA (Devel Assoc)

108253 Bilateral Agreement **567 UNTS 91**
SIGNED: 26 Feb 65 FORCE: 7 Apr 66
REGISTERED: 13 Jul 66 IBRD (World Bank)
ARTICLES: 5 LANGUAGE: English.
HEADNOTE: GUARANTEE HYDROELECTRIC
PROJECT
TOPIC: IBRD Project
CONCEPTS: Definition of terms. Annex or appendix reference. Definition of terms. Exchange of information and documents. Inspection and observation. Fees and exemptions. Tax exemptions. Domestic obligation. Terms of loan. Loan regulations. Loan guarantee. Guarantor non-interference. Hydro-electric power.
PARTIES:
Brazil
IBRD (World Bank)
ANNEX
599 UNTS 372. IBRD (World Bank). Interpretation
26 Apr 67.
599 UNTS 372. Brazil. Interpretation 26 Apr 67.

108254 Bilateral Agreement **567 UNTS 127**
SIGNED: 28 Jun 65 FORCE: 3 Sep 65
REGISTERED: 13 Jul 66 IBRD (World Bank)
ARTICLES: 6 LANGUAGE: English.
HEADNOTE: GUARANTEE INDUSTRIAL
TOPIC: IBRD Project
CONCEPTS: Definition of terms. Annex or appendix reference. Exchange of information and documents. Inspection and observation. Bonds.
Fees and exemptions. Tax exemptions. Domestic obligation. Terms of loan. Loan regulations. Loan guarantee. Guarantor non-interference. Hydro-electric power.
PARTIES:
Italy
IBRD (World Bank)

108255 Bilateral Agreement **567 UNTS 155**
SIGNED: 23 Nov 64 FORCE: 2 Mar 66
REGISTERED: 13 Jul 66 IDA (Devel Assoc)
ARTICLES: 7 LANGUAGE: English.
HEADNOTE: DEVELOPMENT CREDIT EDUCATION
TOPIC: Non-IBRD Project
CONCEPTS: Definition of terms. Detailed regulations. Previous treaty amendment. Exchange of information and documents. Informational records. Education. Accounting procedures. Currency. Interest rates. Tax exemptions. Credit provisions. Loan repayment. Terms of loan. Plans and standards. IDA development project.
INTL ORGS: United Nations Educational, Scientific

and Cultural Organization. United Nations Children's Fund.
PARTIES:
Afghanistan
IDA (Devel Assoc)

108256 Bilateral Agreement **567 UNTS 177**
SIGNED: 13 Jan 66 FORCE: 4 Mar 66
REGISTERED: 13 Jul 66 IDA (Devel Assoc)
ARTICLES: 7 LANGUAGE: English.
HEADNOTE: DEVELOPMENT CREDIT AGRICULTURAL CREDIT
TOPIC: Non-IBRD Project
CONCEPTS: Definition of terms. Detailed regulations. Previous treaty amendment. Exchange of information and documents. Informational records. Accounting procedures. Currency. Interest rates. Tax exemptions. Agriculture. Credit provisions. Loan repayment. Terms of loan. Plans and standards. IDA development project.
PROCEDURE: Termination.
PARTIES:
IDA (Devel Assoc)
Tanzania

108257 Bilateral Exchange **567 UNTS 207**
SIGNED: 8 Feb 66 FORCE: 24 Feb 66
REGISTERED: 13 Jul 66 IDA (Devel Assoc)
ARTICLES: 2 LANGUAGE: English.
HEADNOTE: ROAD PROJECT
TOPIC: Non-IBRD Project
CONCEPTS: Treaty implementation. Annex or appendix reference. Currency. Financial programs.
Funding procedures. Non-bank projects. Roads and highways.
TREATY REF: 439UNTS249; 480UNTS438;
528UNTS310.
PARTIES:
IDA (Devel Assoc)
UK Great Britain

108258 Bilateral Agreement **567 UNTS 229**
SIGNED: 28 Dec 65 FORCE: 2 May 66
REGISTERED: 18 Jul 66 IBRD (World Bank)
ARTICLES: 5 LANGUAGE: English.
HEADNOTE: GUARANTEE THIRD TELECOMMUNICATIONS PROJECT
TOPIC: IBRD Project
CONCEPTS: Definition of terms. Annex or appendix reference. Exchange of information and documents. Inspection and observation. Bonds.
Fees and exemptions. Tax exemptions. Domestic obligation. Terms of loan. Loan regulations. Loan guarantee. Guarantor non-interference. Telecommunications.
PARTIES:
Ethiopia
IBRD (World Bank)

108259 Bilateral Agreement **567 UNTS 255**
SIGNED: 17 Dec 65 FORCE: 15 Feb 66
REGISTERED: 18 Jul 66 IBRD (World Bank)
ARTICLES: 7 LANGUAGE: English.
HEADNOTE: LOAN MARSDEN POINT POWER
PROJECT
TOPIC: IBRD Project
CONCEPTS: Default remedies. Annex or appendix reference. Exchange of information and documents. Informational records. Inspection and observation. Accounting procedures. Bonds. Fees and exemptions. Interest rates. Tax exemptions.
Domestic obligation. Terms of loan. Loan regulations. Loan guarantee. Guarantor non-interference. Hydro-electric power.
PARTIES:
New Zealand
IBRD (World Bank)

108260 Bilateral Agreement **567 UNTS 275**
SIGNED: 17 Dec 65 FORCE: 15 Feb 66
REGISTERED: 18 Jul 66 IBRD (World Bank)
ARTICLES: 7 LANGUAGE: English.
HEADNOTE: LOAN RAILWAY
TOPIC: IBRD Project
CONCEPTS: Default remedies. Definition of terms.
Annex or appendix reference. Exchange of information and documents. Informational records.
Inspection and observation. Accounting procedures. Bonds. Fees and exemptions. Interest

rates. Tax exemptions. Domestic obligation.
Terms of loan. Loan regulations. Loan guarantee.
Guarantor non-interference. Railways.
PARTIES:
New Zealand
IBRD (World Bank)

108261 Bilateral Agreement **567 UNTS 293**
SIGNED: 6 Oct 65 FORCE: 23 Dec 65
REGISTERED: 19 Jul 66 IBRD (World Bank)
ARTICLES: 5 LANGUAGE: English.
HEADNOTE: GUARANTEE VOCATIONAL TRAINING
TOPIC: IBRD Project
CONCEPTS: Definition of terms. Annex or appendix reference. Exchange of information and documents. Vocational training. Bonds. Fees and exemptions. Tax exemptions. Domestic obligation.
Terms of loan. Loan regulations. Loan guarantee.
Guarantor non-interference.
PARTIES:
Chile
IBRD (World Bank)

108262 Bilateral Agreement **568 UNTS 3**
SIGNED: 30 Mar 66 FORCE: 18 May 66
REGISTERED: 19 Jul 66 IBRD (World Bank)
ARTICLES: 6 LANGUAGE: English.
HEADNOTE: LOAN ENGINEERING
TOPIC: IBRD Project
CONCEPTS: Default remedies. Definition of terms.
Annex or appendix reference. Exchange of information and documents. Informational records.
Inspection and observation. Accounting procedures. Bonds. Fees and exemptions. Interest rates. Tax exemptions. Domestic obligation.
General technical assistance. Terms of loan.
Loan regulations. Loan guarantee. Guarantor non-interference.
PARTIES:
Guinea
IBRD (World Bank)

108263 Bilateral Agreement **568 UNTS 23**
SIGNED: 17 Nov 65 FORCE: 1 Feb 66
REGISTERED: 19 Jul 66 IBRD (World Bank)
ARTICLES: 8 LANGUAGE: English.
HEADNOTE: LOAN IRRIGATION
TOPIC: IBRD Project
CONCEPTS: Default remedies. Definition of terms.
Annex or appendix reference. Exchange of information and documents. Informational records.
Inspection and observation. Accounting procedures. Bonds. Fees and exemptions. Tax exemptions. Domestic obligation. Terms of loan. Loan regulations. Loan guarantee. Guarantor non-interference. Irrigation.
PARTIES:
Malaysia
IBRD (World Bank)

108264 Bilateral Agreement **568 UNTS 49**
SIGNED: 29 Sep 65 FORCE: 31 Jan 66
REGISTERED: 19 Jul 66 IBRD (World Bank)
ARTICLES: 8 LANGUAGE: English.
HEADNOTE: LOAN PARTS
TOPIC: IBRD Project
CONCEPTS: Default remedies. Definition of terms.
Annex or appendix reference. Exchange of information and documents. Informational records.
Inspection and observation. Accounting procedures. Bonds. Fees and exemptions. Interest rates. Tax exemptions. Domestic obligation.
Terms of loan. Loan regulations. Loan guarantee.
Guarantor non-interference. Water transport.
PARTIES:
IBRD (World Bank)
Spain

108265 Bilateral Agreement **568 UNTS 77**
SIGNED: 13 Dec 65 FORCE: 1 Feb 66
REGISTERED: 20 Jul 66 IBRD (World Bank)
ARTICLES: 5 LANGUAGE: English.
HEADNOTE: GUARANTEE TELECOMMUNICATIONS
TOPIC: IBRD Project
CONCEPTS: Definition of terms. Annex or appendix reference. Exchange of information and documents. Inspection and observation. Bonds.

Fees and exemptions. Tax exemptions. Domestic obligation. Terms of loan. Loan regulations. Loan guarantee. Guarantor non-interference. Telecommunications.
PARTIES:
IBRD (World Bank)
Venezuela

108266 Bilateral Agreement **568 UNTS 107**
SIGNED: 27 Apr 66   FORCE: 16 Jun 66
REGISTERED: 21 Jul 66 IBRD (World Bank)
ARTICLES: 7 LANGUAGE: English.
HEADNOTE: LOAN ROAD
TOPIC: IBRD Project
CONCEPTS: Default remedies. Definition of terms. Annex or appendix reference. Exchange of information and documents. Informational records. Inspection and observation. Accounting procedures. Bonds. Fees and exemptions. Interest rates. Tax exemptions. Domestic obligation. Terms of loan. Loan regulations. Loan guarantee. Guarantor non-interference. Roads and highways.
PARTIES:
Finland
IBRD (World Bank)

108267 Bilateral Agreement **568 UNTS 125**
SIGNED: 15 Dec 65   FORCE: 17 Jan 66
REGISTERED: 21 Jul 66 IBRD (World Bank)
ARTICLES: 5 LANGUAGE: English.
HEADNOTE: GUARANTEE POWER SECTOR
TOPIC: IBRD Project
CONCEPTS: Definition of terms. Annex or appendix reference. Exchange of information and documents. Inspection and observation. Bonds. Fees and exemptions. Tax exemptions. Domestic obligation. Terms of loan. Loan regulations. Loan guarantee. Guarantor non-interference. Hydroelectric power.
PARTIES:
Mexico
IBRD (World Bank)
ANNEX
639 UNTS 352. IBRD (World Bank). Amendment 15 Nov 67. Force 26 Jan 68.
639 UNTS 352. Mexico. Amendment 15 Nov 67. Force 26 Jan 68.

108268 Bilateral Agreement **568 UNTS 165**
SIGNED: 16 Dec 65   FORCE: 30 Jun 66
REGISTERED: 21 Jul 66 IBRD (World Bank)
ARTICLES: 5 LANGUAGE: English.
HEADNOTE: GUARANTEE PORT
TOPIC: IBRD Project
CONCEPTS: Definition of terms. Annex or appendix reference. Exchange of information and documents. Inspection and observation. Bonds. Fees and exemptions. Tax exemptions. Domestic obligation. Terms of loan. Loan regulations. Loan guarantee. Guarantor non-interference. Water transport.
PARTIES:
Paraguay
IBRD (World Bank)

108269 Bilateral Agreement **568 UNTS 191**
SIGNED: 18 Jun 65   FORCE: 24 Nov 65
REGISTERED: 21 Jul 66 IBRD (World Bank)
ARTICLES: 9 LANGUAGE: English.
HEADNOTE: LOAN AGREEMENT
TOPIC: IBRD Project
CONCEPTS: Default remedies. Definition of terms. Annex or appendix reference. Exchange of information and documents. Informational records. Inspection and observation. Accounting procedures. Bonds. Fees and exemptions. Interest rates. Tax exemptions. Domestic obligation. Terms of loan. Loan regulations. Loan guarantee. Guarantor non-interference.
TREATY REF: 211UNTS115.
PARTIES:
Peru
IBRD (World Bank)

108270 Multilateral Agreement **568 UNTS 215**
SIGNED: 30 Dec 63   FORCE: 1 Jan 64
REGISTERED: 21 Jul 66 IBRD (World Bank)
ARTICLES: 6 LANGUAGE: English.

HEADNOTE: LOAN RAILWAYS
TOPIC: IBRD Project
CONCEPTS: Default remedies. Definition of terms. Annex or appendix reference. Exchange of information and documents. Informational records. Inspection and observation. Accounting procedures. Bonds. Fees and exemptions. Interest rates. Tax exemptions. Domestic obligation. Terms of loan. Loan regulations. Loan guarantee. Guarantor non-interference. Railways.
TREATY REF: 260UNTS376.
PARTIES:
Northern Rhodesia SIGNED: 30 Dec 63 FORCE: 1 Jan 64
Rhone Railroad SIGNED: 30 Dec 63 FORCE: 1 Jan 64
IBRD (World Bank) SIGNED: 30 Dec 63 FORCE: 1 Jan 64
UK Great Britain SIGNED: 30 Dec 63 FORCE: 1 Jan 64

108271 Multilateral Agreement **568 UNTS 233**
SIGNED: 30 Dec 63   FORCE: 1 Jan 64
REGISTERED: 21 Jul 66 IBRD (World Bank)
ARTICLES: 6 LANGUAGE: English.
HEADNOTE: LOAN ASSUMPTION RAILWAY
TOPIC: IBRD Project
CONCEPTS: Default remedies. Definition of terms. Annex or appendix reference. Exchange of information and documents. Informational records. Accounting procedures. Bonds. Fees and exemptions. Interest rates. Tax exemptions. Domestic obligation. Terms of loan. Loan regulations. Loan guarantee. Guarantor non-interference. Railways.
TREATY REF: 309UNTS35.
PARTIES:
Rhone Railroad SIGNED: 30 Dec 63 FORCE: 1 Jan 64
IBRD (World Bank) SIGNED: 30 Dec 63 FORCE: 1 Jan 64
Southern Rhodesia SIGNED: 30 Dec 63 FORCE: 1 Jan 64
UK Great Britain SIGNED: 30 Dec 63 FORCE: 1 Jan 64

108272 Multilateral Agreement **568 UNTS 243**
SIGNED: 30 Dec 63   FORCE: 1 Jan 64
REGISTERED: 21 Jul 66 IBRD (World Bank)
ARTICLES: 6 LANGUAGE: English.
HEADNOTE: LOAN AGRICULTURE
TOPIC: IBRD Project
CONCEPTS: Default remedies. Annex or appendix reference. Continuity of rights and obligations. Exchange of information and documents. Informational records. Inspection and observation. Accounting procedures. Bonds. Fees and exemptions. Interest rates. Tax exemptions. Domestic obligation. Agriculture. Terms of loan. Loan regulations. Loan guarantee. Guarantor non-interference.
TREATY REF: 379UNTS397.
PARTIES:
IBRD (World Bank) SIGNED: 30 Dec 63 FORCE: 1 Jan 64
Southern Rhodesia SIGNED: 30 Dec 63 FORCE: 1 Jan 64
UK Great Britain SIGNED: 30 Dec 63 FORCE: 1 Jan 64

108273 Bilateral Agreement **568 UNTS 257**
SIGNED: 21 Apr 66   FORCE: 26 May 66
REGISTERED: 21 Jul 66 IBRD (World Bank)
ARTICLES: 5 LANGUAGE: English.
HEADNOTE: GUARANTEE WATER SUPPLY
TOPIC: IBRD Project
CONCEPTS: Definition of terms. Annex or appendix reference. Exchange of information and documents. Inspection and observation. Sanitation. Bonds. Fees and exemptions. Tax exemptions. Domestic obligation. Terms of loan. Loan regulations. Loan guarantee. Guarantor non-interference.
PARTIES:
IBRD (World Bank)
Venezuela

108274 Bilateral Agreement **568 UNTS 289**
SIGNED: 29 Sep 65   FORCE: 20 Apr 66
REGISTERED: 21 Jul 66 IBRD (World Bank)

ARTICLES: 5 LANGUAGE: English.
HEADNOTE: GUARANTEE RAILWAYS HARBORS
TOPIC: IBRD Project
CONCEPTS: Definition of terms. Annex or appendix reference. Exchange of information and documents. Inspection and observation. Bonds. Fees and exemptions. Tax exemptions. Domestic obligation. Terms of loan. Loan regulations. Loan guarantee. Guarantor non-interference. Water transport. Railways.
TREATY REF: 568UNTS327.
PARTIES:
Kenya
IBRD (World Bank)

108275 Bilateral Agreement **568 UNTS 309**
SIGNED: 29 Sep 65   FORCE: 20 Apr 66
REGISTERED: 21 Jul 66 IBRD (World Bank)
ARTICLES: 5 LANGUAGE: English.
HEADNOTE: GUARANTEE RAILWAYS HARBORS
TOPIC: IBRD Project
CONCEPTS: Definition of terms. Annex or appendix reference. Exchange of information and documents. Inspection and observation. Bonds. Fees and exemptions. Tax exemptions. Domestic obligation. Terms of loan. Loan regulations. Loan guarantee. Guarantor non-interference. Water transport. Railways.
TREATY REF: 568UNTSI89.
PARTIES:
IBRD (World Bank)
Tanzania

108276 Bilateral Agreement **568 UNTS 317**
SIGNED: 29 Sep 65   FORCE: 20 Apr 66
REGISTERED: 21 Jul 66 IBRD (World Bank)
ARTICLES: 5 LANGUAGE: English.
HEADNOTE: GUARANTEE RAILWAYS HARBORS
TOPIC: IBRD Project
CONCEPTS: Definition of terms. Annex or appendix reference. Exchange of information and documents. Inspection and observation. Bonds. Fees and exemptions. Tax exemptions. Domestic obligation. Terms of loan. Loan regulations. Loan guarantee. Guarantor non-interference. Water transport. Railways.
TREATY REF: 568UNTS327.
PARTIES:
IBRD (World Bank)
Uganda

108277 Bilateral Agreement **569 UNTS 3**
SIGNED: 31 Mar 66   FORCE: 28 Jun 66
REGISTERED: 21 Jul 66 IDA (Devel Assoc)
ARTICLES: 7 LANGUAGE: English.
HEADNOTE: DEVELOPMENT CREDIT BUJUMBURA WATER SUPPLY
TOPIC: Loans and Credits
CONCEPTS: Loan and credit. Credit provisions. Loan repayment.
PROCEDURE: Termination.
PARTIES:
Burundi
IDA (Devel Assoc)

108278 Bilateral Agreement **569 UNTS 43**
SIGNED: 16 Feb 66   FORCE: 22 Jun 66
REGISTERED: 21 Jul 66 IDA (Devel Assoc)
ARTICLES: 6 LANGUAGE: English.
HEADNOTE: DEVELOPMENT CREDIT EDUCATION
TOPIC: Loans and Credits
CONCEPTS: Loan and credit. Credit provisions. Loan repayment.
PROCEDURE: Termination.
PARTIES:
Ethiopia
IDA (Devel Assoc)

108279 Multilateral Convention **569 UNTS 65**
SIGNED: 13 Jul 64   FORCE: 15 Jul 66
REGISTERED: 22 Jul 66 ILO (Labor Org)
ARTICLES: 11 LANGUAGE: English. French.
HEADNOTE: EMPLOYMENT POLICY
TOPIC: ILO Labor
CONCEPTS: General provisions. Establishment of commission. ILO conventions. Anti-discrimination. Employment regulations. Socio-economic development.
PROCEDURE: Amendment. Denunciation. Dura-

tion. Ratification. Registration. Renewal or Revival.
PARTIES:
Costa Rica RATIFIED: 27 Jan 65 FORCE: 27 Jan 67
Jordan RATIFIED: 10 Mar 66 FORCE: 10 Mar 67
New Zealand RATIFIED: 15 Jul 65 FORCE: 15 Jul 65
Norway RATIFIED: 6 Jun 66 FORCE: 6 Jun 67
Senegal RATIFIED: 25 Apr 66 FORCE: 25 Apr 67
Sweden RATIFIED: 11 Jun 65 FORCE: 15 Jul 66
Tunisia RATIFIED: 17 Feb 66 FORCE: 17 Feb 67
UK Great Britain RATIFIED: 27 Jun 66 FORCE: 27 Jun 67
ANNEX
571 UNTS 332. Cyprus. Ratification 28 Jul 66. Force 28 Jul 67.
600 UNTS 412. Uganda. Ratification 23 Jun 67. Force 23 Jun 68.
600 UNTS 412. Ireland. Ratification 20 Jun 66. Force 20 Jun 67.
603 UNTS 358. Peru. Ratification 27 Jul 67. Force 27 Jul 68.
607 UNTS 371. USSR (Soviet Union). Ratification 22 Sep 67. Force 22 Sep 68.
609 UNTS 341. UK Great Britain. British Honduras.
640 UNTS 391. Ukrainian SSR. Ratification 19 Jun 68. Force 19 Jun 69.
648 UNTS 390. Finland. Ratification 23 Sep 68. Force 23 Sep 69.
649 UNTS 386. Chile. Ratification 24 Oct 68. Declaration 9 Oct 68.
655 UNTS 414. UK Great Britain. Declaration 10 Dec 68.
660 UNTS 432. Paraguay. Ratification 20 Feb 69. Force 20 Feb 69.
660 UNTS 432. Thailand. Ratification 26 Feb 69. Force 26 Feb 69.

108280   Bilateral Exchange   **569 UNTS 77**
SIGNED: 8 Mar 63   FORCE: 1 Jun 63
REGISTERED: 22 Jul 66 Philippines
ARTICLES: 1 LANGUAGE: English. French.
HEADNOTE: WAIVER VISAS DIPLOMATIC PASSPORTS
TOPIC: Visas
CONCEPTS: Visa abolition. Passports diplomatic.
PARTIES:
France
Philippines

108281   Bilateral Agreement   **569 UNTS 81**
SIGNED: 23 Jan 61   FORCE: 17 Nov 64
REGISTERED: 28 Jul 66 Japan
ARTICLES: 11 LANGUAGE: Japanese. Portuguese. English.
HEADNOTE: CULTURAL
TOPIC: Culture
CONCEPTS: Culture. Exchange. General cultural cooperation. Artists. Athletes.
PROCEDURE: Duration. Ratification. Termination.
PARTIES:
Brazil
Japan

108282   Bilateral Convention   **569 UNTS 99**
SIGNED: 5 Sep 64   FORCE: 30 Apr 65
REGISTERED: 28 Jul 66 Japan
ARTICLES: 19 LANGUAGE: Japanese. English.
HEADNOTE: AVOIDANCE DOUBLE TAXATION
TOPIC: Taxation
CONCEPTS: Privileges and immunities. Procedure. Teacher and student exchange. Taxation. Equitable taxes. General. Tax exemptions.
PROCEDURE: Ratification. Termination.
PARTIES:
Canada
Japan

108283   Bilateral Convention   **569 UNTS 157**
SIGNED: 27 Nov 64   FORCE: 22 Aug 65
REGISTERED: 28 Jul 66 Japan
ARTICLES: 31 LANGUAGE: Japanese. French.
HEADNOTE: AVOIDANCE DOUBLE TAXATION
TOPIC: Taxation
CONCEPTS: Privileges and immunities. Procedure. Teacher and student exchange. Taxation. Equitable taxes. General. Tax exemptions.
PROCEDURE: Denunciation. Termination.

PARTIES:
France
Japan

108284   Bilateral Agreement   **570 UNTS 3**
SIGNED: 24 Feb 65   FORCE: 2 Sep 65
REGISTERED: 28 Jul 66 Japan
ARTICLES: 26 LANGUAGE: Japanese. English.
HEADNOTE: MONEY ORDERS
TOPIC: Postal Service
CONCEPTS: Mail and money orders. Regulations. Money orders and postal checks.
PROCEDURE: Termination.
PARTIES:
India
Japan

108285   Multilateral Protocol   **570 UNTS 23**
SIGNED: 30 Apr 63   FORCE: 21 Oct 64
REGISTERED: 28 Jul 66 Japan
ARTICLES: 7 LANGUAGE: English.
HEADNOTE: TRADE RELATIONS
TOPIC: General Trade
CONCEPTS: Establishment of trade relations. Export quotas. Import quotas.
PROCEDURE: Termination.
PARTIES:
Bel-Lux Econ Union SIGNED: 30 Apr 63 FORCE: 21 Oct 64
Japan SIGNED: 30 Apr 63 FORCE: 21 Oct 64
Netherlands SIGNED: 30 Apr 63 FORCE: 21 Oct 64

108286   Bilateral Protocol   **570 UNTS 31**
SIGNED: 8 Jun 66   FORCE: 8 Jun 66
REGISTERED: 1 Sep 66 United Nations
ARTICLES: 8 LANGUAGE: English.
HEADNOTE: UNICEF ACTIVITIES
TOPIC: General Amity
CONCEPTS: Privileges and immunities. Claims and settlements. Subsidiary organ. Assistance to United Nations. Mutual consultation.
INTL ORGS: United Nations.
PROCEDURE: Termination.
PARTIES:
Liberia
UNICEF (Children)

108287   Bilateral Agreement   **570 UNTS 41**
SIGNED: 4 Apr 66   FORCE: 20 Jul 66
REGISTERED: 1 Sep 66 IBRD (World Bank)
ARTICLES: 7 LANGUAGE: English.
HEADNOTE: LOAN ROAD
TOPIC: IBRD Project
CONCEPTS: Default remedies. Definition of terms. Annex or appendix reference. Exchange of information and documents. Informational records. Inspection and observation. Accounting procedures. Bonds. Fees and exemptions. Interest rates. Tax exemptions. Domestic obligation. Terms of loan. Loan regulations. Loan guarantee. Guarantor non-interference. Roads and highways.
PARTIES:
Paraguay
IBRD (World Bank)

108288   Bilateral Agreement   **570 UNTS 61**
SIGNED: 13 May 66   FORCE: 15 Jul 66
REGISTERED: 1 Sep 66 IBRD (World Bank)
ARTICLES: 7 LANGUAGE: English.
HEADNOTE: LOAN PORT
TOPIC: IBRD Project
CONCEPTS: Default remedies. Definition of terms. Annex or appendix reference. Exchange of information and documents. Informational records. Inspection and observation. Accounting procedures. Bonds. Fees and exemptions. Interest rates. Tax exemptions. Domestic obligation. Terms of loan. Loan regulations. Loan guarantee. Guarantor non-interference. Water transport.
PARTIES:
Peru
IBRD (World Bank)

108289   Bilateral Agreement   **570 UNTS 91**
SIGNED: 9 Jun 65   FORCE: 27 May 66
REGISTERED: 3 Sep 66 Denmark

ARTICLES: 3 LANGUAGE: Danish. German.
HEADNOTE: DELIMITATIONS CONTINENTAL SHELF
TOPIC: Territory Boundary
CONCEPTS: Markers and definitions. Continental shelf.
PROCEDURE: Ratification.
PARTIES:
Denmark
Germany, West

108290   Bilateral Treaty   **570 UNTS 101**
SIGNED: 6 Feb 63   FORCE: 30 Apr 66
REGISTERED: 5 Sep 66 Netherlands
ARTICLES: 14 LANGUAGE: Dutch. German.
HEADNOTE: RECOGNITION ENFORCEMENT JUDICIAL DECISIONS
TOPIC: Admin Cooperation
CONCEPTS: Definition of terms. Territorial application. General cooperation. Exchange of information and documents. Recognition and enforcement of legal decisions. Competence of tribunal. Claims and settlements.
PROCEDURE: Denunciation. Ratification.
PARTIES:
Austria
Netherlands

108291   Bilateral Agreement   **570 UNTS 127**
SIGNED: 30 May 58   FORCE: 28 Sep 60
REGISTERED: 5 Sep 66 Netherlands
ARTICLES: 26 LANGUAGE: Dutch. German.
HEADNOTE: FRONTIER CONTROL
TOPIC: Visas
CONCEPTS: Border traffic and migration. Frontier permits. Customs declarations. Railway border crossing.
PROCEDURE: Ratification. Termination.
PARTIES:
Germany, West
Netherlands
ANNEX
645 UNTS 378. Netherlands. Force 4 Jun 68.
645 UNTS 378. Germany. Force 4 Jun 68.

108292   Bilateral Agreement   **570 UNTS 165**
SIGNED: 11 Dec 64   FORCE: 8 Mar 66
REGISTERED: 5 Sep 66 Netherlands
ARTICLES: 7 LANGUAGE: English.
HEADNOTE: AERIAL PHOTOGRAPHY INTERPRETATION INSTITUTE
TOPIC: Scientific Project
CONCEPTS: Friendship and amity. Privileges and immunities. General cooperation. Exchange of information and documents. Personnel. Responsibility and liability. Institute establishment. Scholarships and grants. Research and scientific projects. Meteorology. Fees and exemptions. Transportation costs. Tax exemptions. Materials, equipment and services.
PROCEDURE: Amendment. Duration. Renewal or Revival. Termination.
PARTIES:
India
Netherlands

108293   Bilateral Agreement   **570 UNTS 173**
SIGNED: 11 Feb 64   FORCE: 20 Jan 66
REGISTERED: 5 Sep 66 Netherlands
ARTICLES: 7 LANGUAGE: French.
HEADNOTE: CULTURAL
TOPIC: Culture
CONCEPTS: Friendship and amity. Conformity with municipal law. Recognition of degrees. Exchange. Teacher and student exchange. Scholarships and grants. General cultural cooperation. Athletes. Research cooperation. Anthropology and archeology. Scientific exchange.
PROCEDURE: Duration. Ratification. Renewal or Revival. Termination.
PARTIES:
Netherlands
Tunisia

108294   Multilateral Agreement   **570 UNTS 178**
SIGNED: 6 Aug 66   FORCE: 6 Aug 66
REGISTERED: 6 Aug 66 United Nations
ARTICLES: 4 LANGUAGE: French.
HEADNOTE: TECHNICAL ASSISTANCE

TOPIC: Tech Assistance
CONCEPTS: Privileges and immunities. Assistance.
PROCEDURE: Termination.
PARTIES:
Congo (Zaire) SIGNED: 6 Aug 66 FORCE: 6 Aug 66
FAO (Food Agri) SIGNED: 6 Aug 66 FORCE: 6 Aug 66
IAEA (Atom Energy) SIGNED: 6 Aug 66 FORCE: 6 Aug 66
ICAO (Civil Aviat) SIGNED: 6 Aug 66 FORCE: 6 Aug 66
ILO (Labor Org) SIGNED: 6 Aug 66 FORCE: 6 Aug 66
IMCO (Maritime Org) SIGNED: 6 Aug 66 FORCE: 6 Aug 66
ITU (Telecommun) SIGNED: 6 Aug 66 FORCE: 6 Aug 66
UNESCO (Educ/Cult) SIGNED: 6 Aug 66 FORCE: 6 Aug 66
United Nations SIGNED: 6 Aug 66 FORCE: 6 Aug 66
UPU (Postal Union) SIGNED: 6 Aug 66 FORCE: 6 Aug 66
WHO (World Health) SIGNED: 6 Aug 66 FORCE: 6 Aug 66
WMO (Meteorology) SIGNED: 6 Aug 66 FORCE: 6 Aug 66
ANNEX
651 UNTS 403. UNIDO (Industrial). Accession 4 Nov 68. Force 4 Nov 68.

108295 Multilateral Convention **570 UNTS 201**
SIGNED: 16 Dec 65 FORCE: 1 Jul 66
REGISTERED: 10 Aug 66 Philippines
ARTICLES: 25 LANGUAGE: English.
HEADNOTE: POSTAL CONVENTION
TOPIC: Postal Service
CONCEPTS: Arbitration. Postal services. Regulations. Insured letters and boxes. Conveyance in transit. Money orders and postal checks. Rates and charges. Advice lists and orders.
PARTIES:
Taiwan SIGNED: 16 Dec 65 FORCE: 1 Jul 66
Korea, South SIGNED: 16 Dec 65 FORCE: 1 Jul 66
Philippines SIGNED: 16 Dec 65 FORCE: 1 Jul 66
Thailand SIGNED: 16 Dec 65 FORCE: 1 Jul 66

108296 Bilateral Agreement **570 UNTS 233**
SIGNED: 26 Sep 65 FORCE: 29 Mar 66
REGISTERED: 16 Sep 66 IBRD (World Bank)
ARTICLES: 8 LANGUAGE: English.
HEADNOTE: LOAN ROAD
TOPIC: IBRD Project
CONCEPTS: Default remedies. Definition of terms. Annex or appendix reference. Exchange of information and documents. Informational records. Inspection and observation. Accounting procedures. Bonds. Fees and exemptions. Interest rates. Tax exemptions. Domestic obligation. Terms of loan. Loan regulations. Loan guarantee. Guarantor non-interference. Roads and highways.
PARTIES:
Nigeria
IBRD (World Bank)

108297 Bilateral Agreement **571 UNTS 3**
SIGNED: 1 Mar 65 FORCE: 10 May 66
REGISTERED: 16 Aug 66 IDA (Devel Assoc)
ARTICLES: 8 LANGUAGE: English.
HEADNOTE: DEVELOPMENT CREDIT EDUCATION
TOPIC: Non-IBRD Project
CONCEPTS: Definition of terms. Detailed regulations. Previous treaty amendment. Exchange of information and documents. Informational records. Education. Accounting procedures. Currency. Interest rates. Tax exemptions. Credit provisions. Loan repayment. Terms of loan. Plans and standards. IDA development project.
PARTIES:
Nigeria
IDA (Devel Assoc)

108298 Bilateral Agreement **571 UNTS 39**
SIGNED: 26 Sep 65 FORCE: 23 Feb 66
REGISTERED: 16 Aug 66 IBRD (World Bank)
ARTICLES: 7 LANGUAGE: English.

HEADNOTE: LOAN ROAD
TOPIC: IBRD Project
CONCEPTS: Default remedies. Definition of terms. Annex or appendix reference. Exchange of information and documents. Informational records. Inspection and observation. Accounting procedures. Bonds. Fees and exemptions. Interest rates. Tax exemptions. Domestic obligation. Terms of loan. Loan regulations. Loan guarantee. Guarantor non-interference. Roads and highways.
PARTIES:
Nigeria
IBRD (World Bank)

108299 Bilateral Agreement **571 UNTS 63**
SIGNED: 6 Jul 65 FORCE: 7 May 66
REGISTERED: 17 Aug 66 Netherlands
ARTICLES: 14 LANGUAGE: French.
HEADNOTE: TECHNICAL COOPERATION
TOPIC: Tech Assistance
CONCEPTS: Assistance. Special projects.
INTL ORGS: International Court of Justice.
PROCEDURE: Ratification.
PARTIES:
Cameroon
Netherlands

108300 Bilateral Agreement **571 UNTS 75**
SIGNED: 6 Jul 65 FORCE: 7 May 66
REGISTERED: 17 Aug 66 Netherlands
ARTICLES: 6 LANGUAGE: French.
HEADNOTE: ESTABLISHMENT AGRICULTURAL TRAINING CENTERS
TOPIC: Tech Assistance
CONCEPTS: Treaty implementation. Responsibility and liability. Institute establishment. Tax exemptions. Customs exemptions. Agriculture. Materials, equipment and services.
PROCEDURE: Denunciation. Duration.
PARTIES:
Cameroon
Netherlands

108301 Bilateral Exchange **571 UNTS 83**
SIGNED: 8 Dec 65 FORCE: 29 Apr 66
REGISTERED: 17 Aug 66 Netherlands
ARTICLES: 2 LANGUAGE: English.
HEADNOTE: PATENTS TRADEMARKS
TOPIC: Patents/Copyrights
CONCEPTS: Conformity with municipal law. Trademarks. Laws and formalities.
PROCEDURE: Termination.
PARTIES:
Korea, South
Netherlands

108302 Multilateral Agreement **571 UNTS 89**
SIGNED: 17 May 66 FORCE: 1 Jul 66
REGISTERED: 17 Aug 66 Netherlands
ARTICLES: 18 LANGUAGE: Dutch. German. French.
HEADNOTE: ACCEPTANCE PERSONS FRONTIER
TOPIC: Visas
CONCEPTS: Territorial application. Visa abolition. Legal status. Refugees. Nationality and citizenship. Refusal of extradition. Conformity with municipal law. Legal protection and assistance. Indemnities and reimbursements.
PROCEDURE: Denunciation. Duration.
PARTIES:
Belgium SIGNED: 17 May 66 FORCE: 1 Jul 66
Germany, West SIGNED: 17 May 66 FORCE: 1 Jul 66
Luxembourg SIGNED: 17 May 66 FORCE: 1 Jul 66
Netherlands SIGNED: 17 May 66 FORCE: 1 Jul 66

108303 Multilateral Agreement **571 UNTS 123**
SIGNED: 4 Dec 65 FORCE: 22 Aug 66
REGISTERED: 22 Aug 66 United Nations
ARTICLES: 66 LANGUAGE: English.
HEADNOTE: ASIAN DEVELOPMENT BANK
TOPIC: IGO Establishment
CONCEPTS: Default remedies. Treaty implementation. Treaty interpretation. Annex or appendix reference. Treaty violation. Diplomatic privileges. Privileges and immunities. Diplomatic cor-

respondence. Juridical personality. Arbitration. Accounting procedures. Currency. Monetary and gold transfers. Currency deposits. Expense sharing formulae. Funding procedures. General technical assistance. Hydro-electric power. Admission. Establishment. Internal structure.
INTL ORGS: International Court of Justice. International Monetary Fund.
PROCEDURE: Amendment. Ratification.
PARTIES:
Afghanistan SIGNED: 4 Dec 65 RATIFIED: 22 Aug 66 FORCE: 22 Aug 66
Australia SIGNED: 4 Dec 65
Austria SIGNED: 31 Jan 66
Belgium SIGNED: 31 Jan 66 RATIFIED: 16 Aug 66 FORCE: 22 Aug 66
Cambodia SIGNED: 4 Dec 65
Canada SIGNED: 4 Dec 65 RATIFIED: 22 Aug 66 FORCE: 22 Aug 66
Ceylon (Sri Lanka) SIGNED: 4 Dec 65
Taiwan SIGNED: 4 Dec 65
Denmark SIGNED: 28 Jan 66 RATIFIED: 16 Aug 66 FORCE: 22 Aug 66
Finland SIGNED: 28 Jan 66 RATIFIED: 22 Aug 66 FORCE: 22 Aug 66
Germany, West SIGNED: 4 Dec 65 RATIFIED: 30 Aug 66 FORCE: 30 Aug 66
India SIGNED: 4 Dec 65 RATIFIED: 20 Jul 66 FORCE: 22 Aug 66
Iran SIGNED: 4 Dec 65
Italy SIGNED: 31 Jan 66
Japan SIGNED: 4 Dec 65 RATIFIED: 16 Aug 66 FORCE: 22 Aug 66
Korea, South SIGNED: 4 Dec 65 RATIFIED: 16 Aug 66 FORCE: 22 Aug 66
Laos SIGNED: 4 Dec 65 RATIFIED: 30 Aug 66 FORCE: 30 Aug 66
Malaysia SIGNED: 4 Dec 65 RATIFIED: 16 Aug 66 FORCE: 22 Aug 66
Nepal SIGNED: 4 Dec 65 RATIFIED: 21 Jun 66 FORCE: 22 Aug 66
Netherlands SIGNED: 4 Dec 65 RATIFIED: 29 Aug 66 FORCE: 29 Aug 66
New Zealand SIGNED: 4 Dec 65
Norway SIGNED: 28 Jan 66 RATIFIED: 14 Jul 66 FORCE: 22 Aug 66
Pakistan SIGNED: 4 Dec 65 RATIFIED: 12 May 66 FORCE: 22 Aug 66
Philippines SIGNED: 4 Dec 65 RATIFIED: 5 Jul 66 FORCE: 22 Aug 66
Singapore SIGNED: 28 Jan 66
Sweden SIGNED: 31 Jan 66
Thailand SIGNED: 4 Dec 65 RATIFIED: 16 Aug 66 FORCE: 22 Aug 66
UK Great Britain SIGNED: 4 Dec 65
USA (United States) SIGNED: 4 Dec 65 RATIFIED: 16 Aug 66 FORCE: 22 Aug 66
Vietnam, South SIGNED: 28 Jan 66
Western Samoa SIGNED: 4 Dec 65 RATIFIED: 23 Jun 66 FORCE: 22 Aug 66
ANNEX
572 UNTS 368. Australia. Qualified Ratification 19 Sep 66.
573 UNTS 0. UK Great Britain. Qualified Ratification 26 Sep 66.
573 UNTS 360. Singapore. Qualified Ratification 21 Sep 66.
573 UNTS 360. Taiwan. Ratification 22 Sep 66.
573 UNTS 360. Vietnam, South. Ratification 22 Sep 66.
608 UNTS 380. Asian Devel Bank. Amendment 2 Nov 67.

108304 Bilateral Convention **571 UNTS 217**
SIGNED: 31 Mar 65 FORCE: 30 Jan 66
REGISTERED: 25 Aug 66 USSR (Soviet Union)
ARTICLES: 11 LANGUAGE: Russian. Polish.
HEADNOTE: AVOIDANCE CASES DUAL NATIONALITY
TOPIC: Consul/Citizenship
CONCEPTS: Detailed regulations. Treaty interpretation. Acquisition of nationality. Dual citizenship. Public information. Tax exemptions.
PROCEDURE: Denunciation. Ratification.
PARTIES:
Poland
USSR (Soviet Union)

108305 Bilateral Convention **571 UNTS 239**
SIGNED: 12 Feb 65 FORCE: 1 Jul 66
REGISTERED: 29 Aug 66 Luxembourg
ARTICLES: 40 LANGUAGE: French.

HEADNOTE: SOCIAL SECURITY
TOPIC: Non-ILO Labor
CONCEPTS: Definition of terms. Exceptions and exemptions. General provisions. Annex or appendix reference. Conformity with municipal law. Exchange of information and documents. Domestic legislation. Incorporation of treaty provisions into national law. Old age and invalidity insurance. Wages and salaries. Family allowances. Old age insurance. Sickness and invalidity insurance. Social security. Unemployment.
PROCEDURE: Duration. Ratification. Renewal or Revival. Termination.
PARTIES:
Luxembourg
Portugal

108306 Bilateral Exchange **571 UNTS 275**
SIGNED: 2 Feb 66   FORCE: 1 Jan 66
REGISTERED: 29 Aug 66 UK Great Britain
ARTICLES: 2 LANGUAGE: English.
HEADNOTE: IMPORTATION BOOKS FILMS
TOPIC: Commodity Trade
CONCEPTS: Conditions. Commodity trade.
TREATY REF: 548UNTS585; 360UNTS79; 565UNTSI96.
PARTIES:
UK Great Britain
Yugoslavia

108307 Bilateral Exchange **571 UNTS 281**
SIGNED: 22 Mar 66   FORCE: 22 Mar 66
REGISTERED: 29 Aug 66 UK Great Britain
ARTICLES: 2 LANGUAGE: English. Romanian.
HEADNOTE: PRODUCTION TRADE POLICIES CEREALS
TOPIC: Commodity Trade
CONCEPTS: Annex or appendix reference. General cooperation. Export quotas. Non-interest rates and fees. Commodity trade.
TREATY REF: 655UNTS187; 571UNTS282 FN__2&3.
PROCEDURE: Termination.
PARTIES:
Romania
UK Great Britain

108308 Bilateral Agreement **572 UNTS 3**
SIGNED: 31 Aug 65   FORCE: 12 Apr 66
REGISTERED: 1 Sep 66 China
ARTICLES: 20 LANGUAGE: Chinese. English.
HEADNOTE: STATUS OF FORCES
TOPIC: Status of Forces
CONCEPTS: Claims and settlements. Status of military forces. Jurisdiction. Procurement and logistics. Withdrawal of forces. Status of forces. Bases and facilities.
TREATY REF: 248UNTS213.
PROCEDURE: Duration. Termination.
PARTIES:
China
USA (United States)

108309 Multilateral Agreement **572 UNTS 105**
SIGNED: 3 Dec 65   FORCE: 12 Sep 66
REGISTERED: 12 Sep 66 Denmark
ARTICLES: 11 LANGUAGE: Danish. Finnish.
HEADNOTE: TRANSIT OF DEPORTED PERSONS
TOPIC: Admin Cooperation
CONCEPTS: Definition of terms. Extradition, deportation and repatriation. Conformity with municipal law. General cooperation. Conveyance in transit.
PARTIES:
Denmark SIGNED: 3 Dec 65 RATIFIED: 24 Feb 66 FORCE: 21 Apr 66
Finland SIGNED: 3 Dec 65 RATIFIED: 28 Mar 66 FORCE: 21 Apr 66
Iceland SIGNED: 3 Dec 65 RATIFIED: 12 Jan 66 FORCE: 21 Apr 66
Norway SIGNED: 3 Dec 65 RATIFIED: 21 Apr 66 FORCE: 21 Apr 66
Sweden SIGNED: 3 Dec 65 RATIFIED: 12 Jan 66 FORCE: 21 Apr 66

108310 Multilateral Convention **572 UNTS 133**
SIGNED: 15 Mar 60   FORCE: 13 Sep 66
REGISTERED: 13 Sep 66 United Nations
ARTICLES: 20 LANGUAGE: French. Russian.

HEADNOTE: UNIFICATION RULES COLLISIONS INLAND NAVIGATION
TOPIC: Water Transport
CONCEPTS: Definition of terms. Exceptions and exemptions. Time limit. Treaty interpretation. Responsibility and liability. Procedure. Negotiation. Compensation. Payment schedules. Dangerous goods. Optional clause ICJ.
PROCEDURE: Amendment. Accession. Denunciation. Ratification. Termination.
PARTIES:
Austria   SIGNED: 14 Jun 60   RATIFIED: 27 Sep 62 FORCE: 13 Sep 66
Belgium SIGNED: 15 Jun 60
France SIGNED: 15 Jun 60 RATIFIED: 12 Mar 62 FORCE: 13 Sep 66
Germany, West SIGNED: 14 Jun 60
Netherlands SIGNED: 14 Jun 60 RATIFIED: 15 Jun 66 FORCE: 13 Sep 66
Netherlands Surinam RATIFIED: 15 Jun 66 FORCE: 13 Sep 66
USSR (Soviet Union) RATIFIED: 26 Jan 62 FORCE: 13 Sep 66
Yugoslavia   RATIFIED: 14 Feb 62   FORCE: 13 Sep 66

108311 Bilateral Agreement **572 UNTS 161**
SIGNED: 6 Dec 65   FORCE: 12 May 66
REGISTERED: 15 Sep 66 UK Great Britain
ARTICLES: 11
HEADNOTE: AVOIDANCE DOUBLE TAXATION
TOPIC: Taxation
CONCEPTS: Taxation. General. Tax exemptions.
TREATY REF: 27UNTS207,304UNTS336,345UNTS326.
PROCEDURE: Termination.
PARTIES:
Canada
UK Great Britain

108312 Bilateral Convention **572 UNTS 181**
SIGNED: 17 May 65   FORCE: 20 May 66
REGISTERED: 19 Sep 66 Poland
ARTICLES: 1 LANGUAGE: Polish. Czechoslovakian.
HEADNOTE: DUAL NATIONALITY
TOPIC: Consul/Citizenship
CONCEPTS: Acquisition of nationality. Alien status. Dual citizenship.
PROCEDURE: Denunciation. Ratification.
PARTIES:
Czechoslovakia
Poland

108313 Bilateral Protocol **572 UNTS 203**
SIGNED: 29 Jul 65   FORCE: 24 Mar 66
REGISTERED: 19 Sep 66 Poland
ARTICLES: 2 LANGUAGE: Polish. Czechoslovakian.
HEADNOTE: TERMINATION TREATY CONCILIATION ARBITRATION
TOPIC: Dispute Settlement
CONCEPTS: Annex type material.
TREATY REF: 158LTS383,154LTS285.
PARTIES:
Czechoslovakia
Poland

108314 Bilateral Agreement **572 UNTS 209**
SIGNED: 17 Jan 61   FORCE: 18 Oct 65
REGISTERED: 19 Sep 66 Poland
ARTICLES: 10 LANGUAGE: Polish. English.
HEADNOTE: CULTURAL COOPERATION
TOPIC: Culture
CONCEPTS: Culture. Exchange. General cultural cooperation. Artists. Athletes.
PROCEDURE: Amendment. Ratification. Termination.
PARTIES:
Ghana
Poland

108315 Bilateral Agreement **572 UNTS 219**
SIGNED: 2 Nov 62   FORCE: 15 Aug 64
REGISTERED: 19 Sep 66 Poland
ARTICLES: 9 LANGUAGE: French.
HEADNOTE: CULTURAL COOPERATION
TOPIC: Culture

CONCEPTS: Culture. Exchange. General cultural cooperation. Artists. Athletes.
PROCEDURE: Denunciation. Termination.
PARTIES:
Mali
Poland

108316 Unilateral Instrument **572 UNTS 225**
SIGNED: 4 Jun 66   FORCE: 4 Jun 66
REGISTERED: 20 Sep 66 United Nations
ARTICLES: 1 LANGUAGE: English.
HEADNOTE: ACCEPTANCE UN CHARTER OBLIGATIONS
TOPIC: UN Charter
CONCEPTS: Acceptance of UN obligations.
PARTIES:
Guyana

108317 Multilateral Agreement **572 UNTS 229**
SIGNED: 2 Dec 64   FORCE: 1 Mar 66
REGISTERED: 20 Sep 66 IAEA (Atom Energy)
ARTICLES: 8 LANGUAGE: English. Spanish.
HEADNOTE: SAFEGUARDS
TOPIC: Scientific Project
CONCEPTS: Default remedies. Definition of terms. Annex or appendix reference. Exchange of information and documents. Arbitration. Procedure. Accounting procedures. Funding procedures. Materials, equipment and services. Acceptance of delivery. General. Nuclear materials. Non-nuclear materials. Peaceful use. Conformity with IGO decisions.
TREATY REF: 458UNTS97; 531UNTS387; 276UNTS39.
PROCEDURE: Amendment. Duration.
PARTIES:
Argentina SIGNED: 2 Dec 64 FORCE: 1 Mar 66
IAEA (Atom Energy) SIGNED: 2 Dec 64 FORCE: 1 Mar 66
USA (United States) SIGNED: 2 Dec 64 FORCE: 1 Mar 66

108318 Multilateral Agreement **572 UNTS 263**
SIGNED: 20 Jun 66   FORCE: 20 Jun 66
REGISTERED: 20 Sep 66 IAEA (Atom Energy)
ARTICLES: 7 LANGUAGE: English. Spanish.
HEADNOTE: SAFEGUARDS
TOPIC: Scientific Project
CONCEPTS: Default remedies. Definition of terms. Annex or appendix reference. Exchange of information and documents. Arbitration. Procedure. Accounting procedures. Funding procedures. Materials, equipment and services. Acceptance of delivery. General. Nuclear materials. Non-nuclear materials. Peaceful use. Conformity with IGO decisions.
TREATY REF: 383UNTS243; 276UNTS3.
PARTIES:
Canada SIGNED: 20 Jun 66 FORCE: 20 Jun 66
Japan SIGNED: 20 Jun 66 FORCE: 20 Jun 66
IAEA (Atom Energy) SIGNED: 20 Jun 66 FORCE: 20 Jun 66

108319 Multilateral Instrument **572 UNTS 283**
SIGNED: 8 Jul 66   FORCE: 8 Jul 66
REGISTERED: 20 Sep 66 IAEA (Atom Energy)
ARTICLES: 1 LANGUAGE: English.
HEADNOTE: TRANSFER ENRICHED URANIUM
TOPIC: Atomic Energy
CONCEPTS: Non-nuclear materials.
PARTIES:
Finland SIGNED: 8 Jul 66 FORCE: 6 Jul 66
IAEA (Atom Energy) SIGNED: 8 Jul 66 FORCE: 8 Jul 66
USA (United States) SIGNED: 8 Jul 66 FORCE: 8 Jul 66

108320 Multilateral Agreement **573 UNTS 3**
SIGNED: 18 Jun 65   FORCE: 15 Jun 66
REGISTERED: 20 Sep 66 IAEA (Atom Energy)
ARTICLES: 8 LANGUAGE: English.
HEADNOTE: APPLICATION SAFEGUARDS
TOPIC: Atomic Energy
CONCEPTS: Definition of terms. Annex or appendix reference. Exchange of information and documents. Inspection and observation. Investigation of violations. Special tribunals. Research results. Indemnities and reimbursements. Nuclear materials. Non-nuclear materials. Peaceful use.

Security of information. Special status. Status of experts.
INTL ORGS: International Court of Justice. Arbitration Commission.
TREATY REF: 219UNTS185.
PARTIES:
Israel SIGNED: 18 Jun 65 FORCE: 15 Jun 66
IAEA (Atom Energy) SIGNED: 18 Jun 65 FORCE: 15 Jun 66
USA (United States) SIGNED: 18 Jun 65 FORCE: 15 Jun 66

108321 Bilateral Agreement **573 UNTS 25**
SIGNED: 20 Jun 66 FORCE: 20 Jun 66
REGISTERED: 20 Sep 66 IAEA (Atom Energy)
ARTICLES: 9 LANGUAGE: English. Spanish.
HEADNOTE: SUB-CRITICAL ASSEMBLY PROJECT
TOPIC: Atomic Energy
CONCEPTS: Annex or appendix reference. Exchange of information and documents. Licenses and permits. Procedure. Negotiation. Public health. Research cooperation. Research results. Nuclear materials. Transport of goods. Security of information.
TREATY REF: 339UNTS359; 276UNTS3; 471UNTS334.
PARTIES:
Mexico
IAEA (Atom Energy)

108322 Multilateral Instrument **573 UNTS 41**
SIGNED: 20 Jun 66 FORCE: 20 Jun 66
REGISTERED: 20 Sep 66 IAEA (Atom Energy)
ARTICLES: 15 LANGUAGE: English. Spanish.
HEADNOTE: LEASE NATURAL URANIUM TRANSFER PLUTONIUM
TOPIC: Atomic Energy
CONCEPTS: Annex or appendix reference. Title and deeds. Establishment of commission. Special tribunals. Negotiation. Research cooperation. Nuclear research. Indemnities and reimbursements. Currency. Interest rates. Payment schedules. Nuclear materials. Non-nuclear materials. Transport of goods.
INTL ORGS: International Court of Justice. Arbitration Commission.
TREATY REF: 339UNTS359; 276UNTS3; 471UNTS334.
PARTIES:
Mexico SIGNED: 20 Jun 66 FORCE: 20 Jun 66
IAEA (Atom Energy) SIGNED: 20 Jun 66 FORCE: 20 Jun 66
USA (United States) SIGNED: 20 Jun 66 FORCE: 20 Jun 66

108323 Bilateral Agreement **573 UNTS 75**
SIGNED: 8 Feb 66 FORCE: 8 Feb 66
REGISTERED: 20 Sep 66 IAEA (Atom Energy)
ARTICLES: 1 LANGUAGE: English.
HEADNOTE: FURTHERING PROJECTS SUPPLY MATERIALS
TOPIC: Atomic Energy
CONCEPTS: Exchange of information and documents. Title and deeds. Special tribunals. Negotiation. Public health. Research results. Payment schedules. Acceptance of delivery. Nuclear materials. Peaceful use. Transport of goods. Security of information. Special status. Status of experts.
INTL ORGS: International Court of Justice. Arbitration Commission.
TREATY REF: 339UNTS359; 276UNTS3; 471UNTS334.
PARTIES:
IAEA (Atom Energy)
Turkey

108324 Multilateral Agreement **573 UNTS 85**
SIGNED: 15 Jun 64 FORCE: 13 Jan 66
REGISTERED: 20 Sep 66 IAEA (Atom Energy)
ARTICLES: 8 LANGUAGE: English.
HEADNOTE: APPLICATION SAFEGUARDS
TOPIC: Atomic Energy
CONCEPTS: Definition of terms. Annex or appendix reference. Exchange of information and documents. Inspection and observation. Investigation of violations. Special tribunals. Negotiation. Research results. Indemnities and reimbursements. Nuclear materials. Non-nuclear materials.

Peaceful use. Transport of goods. Security of information. Special status. Status of experts.
INTL ORGS: International Court of Justice. Arbitration Commission.
TREATY REF: 235UNTS57.
PROCEDURE: Amendment. Duration. Termination.
PARTIES:
Greece SIGNED: 15 Jun 64 FORCE: 13 Jan 66
IAEA (Atom Energy) SIGNED: 15 Jun 64 FORCE: 13 Jan 66
USA (United States) SIGNED: 15 Jun 64 FORCE: 13 Jan 66

108325 Bilateral Agreement **573 UNTS 107**
SIGNED: 26 Jun 64 FORCE: 26 Jun 64
REGISTERED: 21 Sep 66 Denmark
ARTICLES: 11 LANGUAGE: English.
HEADNOTE: EDUCATIONAL EXCHANGE
TOPIC: Education
CONCEPTS: Education. Exchange.
PARTIES:
Denmark
Kenya

108326 Bilateral Agreement **573 UNTS 115**
SIGNED: 23 Sep 66 FORCE: 23 Sep 66
REGISTERED: 23 Sep 66 United Nations
ARTICLES: 10 LANGUAGE: English.
HEADNOTE: UN SPECIAL FUND AID TO SINGAPORE
TOPIC: General Aid
CONCEPTS: General aid. Materials, equipment and services. Status of experts.
INTL ORGS: International Atomic Energy Agency. International Court of Justice. Arbitration Commission.
PARTIES:
UN Special Fund
Singapore

108327 Multilateral Agreement **573 UNTS 132**
SIGNED: 23 Sep 66 FORCE: 23 Sep 66
REGISTERED: 23 Sep 66 United Nations
ARTICLES: 6 LANGUAGE: English.
HEADNOTE: TECHNICAL ASSISTANCE
TOPIC: IGO Operations
CONCEPTS: Diplomatic privileges. Diplomatic missions. Privileges and immunities. Specialists exchange. Commissions and foundations. Institute establishment. Scholarships and grants. Vocational training. Funding procedures. Domestic obligation. General technical assistance. Mutual consultation. IGO obligations.
TREATY REF: 76UNTS137; 1UNTS15; 33UNTS261; 374UNTS147.
PROCEDURE: Amendment. Termination.
PARTIES:
FAO (Food Agri) SIGNED: 23 Sep 66 FORCE: 23 Sep 66
IAEA (Atom Energy) SIGNED: 23 Sep 66 FORCE: 23 Sep 66
ICAO (Civil Aviat) SIGNED: 23 Sep 66 FORCE: 23 Sep 66
ILO (Labor Org) SIGNED: 23 Sep 66 FORCE: 23 Sep 66
IMCO (Maritime Org) SIGNED: 23 Sep 66 FORCE: 23 Sep 66
ITU (Telecommun) SIGNED: 23 Sep 66 FORCE: 23 Sep 66
UNESCO (Educ/Cult) SIGNED: 23 Sep 66 FORCE: 23 Sep 66
United Nations SIGNED: 23 Sep 66 FORCE: 23 Sep 66
UPU (Postal Union) SIGNED: 23 Sep 66 FORCE: 23 Sep 66
WHO (World Health) SIGNED: 23 Sep 66 FORCE: 23 Sep 66
WMO (Meteorology) SIGNED: 23 Sep 66 FORCE: 23 Sep 66
Singapore SIGNED: 23 Sep 66 FORCE: 23 Sep 66
ANNEX
645 UNTS 382. IAEA (Atom Energy). Acceptance 12 Sep 68. Force 12 Sep 68.
645 UNTS 382. Singapore. Acceptance 12 Sep 68. Force 12 Sep 68.
645 UNTS 382. WHO (World Health). Acceptance 12 Sep 68. Force 12 Sep 68.
645 UNTS 382. United Nations. Acceptance 12 Sep 68. Force 12 Sep 68.

645 UNTS 382. ILO (Labor Org). Acceptance 12 Sep 68. Force 12 Sep 68.
645 UNTS 382. FAO (Food Agri). Acceptance 12 Sep 68. Force 12 Sep 68.
645 UNTS 382. UNESCO (Educ/Cult). Acceptance 12 Sep 68. Force 12 Sep 68.
645 UNTS 382. ICAO (Civil Aviat). Acceptance 12 Sep 68. Force 12 Sep 68.
645 UNTS 382. ITU (Telecommun). Acceptance 12 Sep 68. Force 12 Sep 68.
645 UNTS 382. IMCO (Maritime Org). Acceptance 12 Sep 68. Force 12 Sep 68.
645 UNTS 382. UPU (Postal Union). Acceptance 12 Sep 68. Force 12 Sep 68.
645 UNTS 382. WMO (Meteorology). Force 12 Sep 68.

108328 Multilateral Agreement **573 UNTS 148**
SIGNED: 23 Sep 66 FORCE: 23 Sep 66
REGISTERED: 23 Sep 66 United Nations
ARTICLES: 6 LANGUAGE: English.
HEADNOTE: STANDARD OPERATIONAL AID AGREEMENT
TOPIC: General Aid
CONCEPTS: Aid and development. General technical assistance. Assistance.
INTL ORGS: Permanent Court of Arbitration.
PARTIES:
FAO (Food Agri) SIGNED: 23 Sep 66 FORCE: 23 Sep 66
IAEA (Atom Energy) SIGNED: 23 Sep 66 FORCE: 23 Sep 66
ICAO (Civil Aviat) SIGNED: 23 Sep 66 FORCE: 23 Sep 66
ILO (Labor Org) SIGNED: 23 Sep 66 FORCE: 23 Sep 66
IMCO (Maritime Org) SIGNED: 23 Sep 66 FORCE: 23 Sep 66
ITU (Telecommun) SIGNED: 23 Sep 66 FORCE: 23 Sep 66
UNESCO (Educ/Cult) SIGNED: 23 Sep 66 FORCE: 23 Sep 66
United Nations SIGNED: 23 Sep 66 FORCE: 23 Sep 66
UPU (Postal Union) SIGNED: 23 Sep 66 FORCE: 23 Sep 66
WHO (World Health) SIGNED: 23 Sep 66 FORCE: 23 Sep 66
WMO (Meteorology) SIGNED: 23 Sep 66 FORCE: 23 Sep 66
Singapore SIGNED: 23 Sep 66 FORCE: 23 Sep 66
ANNEX
645 UNTS 383. IAEA (Atom Energy). Force 12 Sep 68.
645 UNTS 383. UPU (Postal Union). Force 12 Sep 68.
645 UNTS 383. IDA (Devel Assoc). Accession 12 Sep 68. Force 12 Sep 68.
645 UNTS 383. UNESCO (Educ/Cult). Force 12 Sep 68.
645 UNTS 383. WHO (World Health). Force 12 Sep 68.
645 UNTS 383. ITU (Telecommun). Force 12 Sep 68.
645 UNTS 383. WMO (Meteorology). Force 12 Sep 68.
645 UNTS 383. IMCO (Maritime Org). Force 12 Sep 68.
645 UNTS 383. ILO (Labor Org). Force 12 Sep 68.
645 UNTS 383. FAO (Food Agri). Force 12 Sep 68.
645 UNTS 383. United Nations. Force 12 Sep 68.
645 UNTS 383. Singapore. Force 12 Sep 68.
645 UNTS 383. ICAO (Civil Aviat). Force 12 Sep 68.

108329 Bilateral Agreement **573 UNTS 165**
SIGNED: 20 Dec 65 FORCE: 21 Dec 65
REGISTERED: 23 Sep 66 Austria
ARTICLES: 7 LANGUAGE: German. Serbo-Croat.
HEADNOTE: ABOLITION VISAS
TOPIC: Visas
CONCEPTS: Emergencies. Visa abolition. Denial of admission. Resident permits. Non-visa travel documents. Visas. Fees and exemptions.
PROCEDURE: Denunciation.
PARTIES:
Austria
Yugoslavia

108330   Bilateral Exchange   **573 UNTS 175**
SIGNED: 3 Nov 65   FORCE: 3 Nov 65
REGISTERED: 26 Sep 66 USA (United States)
ARTICLES: 2 LANGUAGE: English.
HEADNOTE: CERTIFICATES AIRWORTHINESS IMPORTED CIVIL GLIDER AIRCRAFT
TOPIC: Air Transport
CONCEPTS: General cooperation. Export quotas. Import quotas. Airworthiness certificates.
PROCEDURE: Termination.
PARTIES:
   Finland
   USA (United States)

108331   Bilateral Agreement   **573 UNTS 183**
SIGNED: 7 May 65   FORCE: 28 May 65
REGISTERED: 26 Sep 66 USA (United States)
ARTICLES: 13 LANGUAGE: English. French.
HEADNOTE: ACADEMIC & CULTURAL EXCHANGE
TOPIC: Education
CONCEPTS: Education. Exchange. Teacher and student exchange. Professorships.
PARTIES:
   France
   USA (United States)

108332   Bilateral Exchange   **573 UNTS 197**
SIGNED: 29 Jul 65   FORCE: 29 Jul 65
REGISTERED: 26 Sep 66 USA (United States)
ARTICLES: 2 LANGUAGE: English. French.
HEADNOTE: ALIEN AMATEUR RADIO OPERATORS
TOPIC: Gen Communications
CONCEPTS: Conformity with municipal law. Licenses and permits. Amateur radio. Amateur third party message.
TREATY REF: USA'TIAS 4893;.
PROCEDURE: Termination.
PARTIES:
   Luxembourg
   USA (United States)

108333   Bilateral Exchange   **573 UNTS 203**
SIGNED: 20 Jun 66   FORCE: 20 Jun 66
REGISTERED: 27 Sep 66 UK Great Britain
ARTICLES: 2 LANGUAGE: English.
HEADNOTE: INHERITANCE INTERNATIONAL RIGHTS & OBLIGATIONS
TOPIC: Recognition
CONCEPTS: Continuity of rights and obligations.
PARTIES:
   Gambia
   UK Great Britain

108334   Bilateral Agreement   **573 UNTS 209**
SIGNED: 18 Apr 66   FORCE: 18 Apr 66
REGISTERED: 28 Sep 66 UK Great Britain
ARTICLES: 15 LANGUAGE: English.
HEADNOTE: ADMINISTRATION FUNDS ECONOMIC ASSISTANCE
TOPIC: IGO Operations
CONCEPTS: Detailed regulations. Annex or appendix reference. Private contracts. Accounting procedures.
PROCEDURE: Amendment. Termination.
PARTIES:
   IBRD (World Bank)
   UK Great Britain

108335   Bilateral Exchange   **573 UNTS 223**
SIGNED: 17 Apr 66   FORCE: 17 Apr 66
REGISTERED: 27 Sep 66 UK Great Britain
ARTICLES: 2 LANGUAGE: English. Portuguese.
HEADNOTE: ESTABLISHMENT LOCAL AIR SERVICE MATSAPA LOURENCO MARQUE
TOPIC: Air Transport
CONCEPTS: Routes and logistics. Permit designation. Air transport. Operating authorizations and regulations.
TREATY REF: 5UNTS67.
PROCEDURE: Application to Non-self-governing Territories.
PARTIES:
   Portugal
   UK Great Britain

108336   Bilateral Agreement   **573 UNTS 229**
SIGNED: 2 Jun 66   FORCE: 15 Jul 66
REGISTERED: 27 Sep 66 UK Great Britain

ARTICLES: 10 LANGUAGE: English.
HEADNOTE: COOPERATION CIVIL POWER APPLICATIONS ATOMIC ENERGY
TOPIC: Atomic Energy
CONCEPTS: Definition of terms. Exchange of information and documents. Establishment of commission. Nuclear materials. Peaceful use. Hydroelectric power. Transport of goods. Security of information.
PROCEDURE: Duration.
PARTIES:
   UK Great Britain
   USA (United States)

108337   Bilateral Convention   **573 UNTS 243**
SIGNED: 27 Jan 66   FORCE: 1 Jun 66
REGISTERED: 27 Sep 66 UK Great Britain
ARTICLES: 12 LANGUAGE: English. Serbo-Croat.
HEADNOTE: CULTURAL CONVENTION
TOPIC: Culture
CONCEPTS: Definition of terms. Treaty implementation. Friendship and amity. Conformity with municipal law. Exchange of information and documents. Use of facilities. Specialists exchange. Teacher and student exchange. Professorships. Institute establishment. Scholarships and grants. General cultural cooperation. Artists. Research cooperation. Scientific exchange. Mass media exchange.
PROCEDURE: Denunciation. Duration. Future Procedures Contemplated. Ratification. Renewal or Revival.
PARTIES:
   UK Great Britain
   Yugoslavia

108338   Bilateral Agreement   **574 UNTS 3**
SIGNED: 28 Jun 66   FORCE: 28 Jun 66
REGISTERED: 27 Sep 66 Denmark
ARTICLES: 15 LANGUAGE: English.
HEADNOTE: LOAN
TOPIC: Loans and Credits
CONCEPTS: Annex or appendix reference. Friendship and amity. Conformity with municipal law. Exchange of information and documents. Dispute settlement. Family allowances. Accounting procedures. Interest rates. Payment schedules. Debt settlement. Tax exemptions. Loan and credit. Purchase authorization. Loan repayment. Plans and standards.
TREATY REF: 552UNTS292; 330UNTS109.
PROCEDURE: Duration. Termination.
PARTIES:
   Denmark
   Jordan

108339   Bilateral Agreement   **574 UNTS 21**
SIGNED: 12 Dec 65   FORCE: 12 Dec 65
REGISTERED: 29 Sep 66 Denmark
ARTICLES: 14 LANGUAGE: English.
HEADNOTE: TECHNICAL COOPERATION
TOPIC: Tech Assistance
CONCEPTS: Assistance.
PROCEDURE: Termination.
PARTIES:
   Denmark
   Zambia

108340   Bilateral Exchange   **574 UNTS 37**
SIGNED: 1 Dec 65   FORCE: 1 Dec 65
REGISTERED: 29 Sep 66 USA (United States)
ARTICLES: 2 LANGUAGE: English.
HEADNOTE: COMMUNICATIONS FACILITIES DEFENSE
TOPIC: Milit Installation
CONCEPTS: Annex type material. Joint defense. Defense and security. Bases and facilities.
TREATY REF: 233UNTS109.
PROCEDURE: Duration. Future Procedures Contemplated. Termination.
PARTIES:
   Canada
   USA (United States)

108341   Bilateral Agreement   **574 UNTS 49**
SIGNED: 17 Dec 65   FORCE: 17 Dec 65
REGISTERED: 29 Sep 66 USA (United States)
ARTICLES: 2 LANGUAGE: English. French.
HEADNOTE: TARIFFS TRADE

TOPIC: General Trade
CONCEPTS: Tariffs. Trade procedures.
PROCEDURE: Termination.
PARTIES:
   Canada
   USA (United States)

108342   Bilateral Agreement   **574 UNTS 83**
SIGNED: 27 Jul 65   FORCE: 23 Sep 65
REGISTERED: 29 Sep 66 USA (United States)
ARTICLES: 6 LANGUAGE: English. Spanish.
HEADNOTE: AGRI COMMOD TITLE I
TOPIC: US Agri Commod Aid
CONCEPTS: General provisions. Annex or appendix reference. Exchange of information and documents. Reexport of goods, etc.. Exchange rates and regulations. Transportation costs. Local currency. Commodities schedule. Purchase authorization. Mutual consultation.
PARTIES:
   Chile
   USA (United States)

108343   Bilateral Exchange   **574 UNTS 109**
SIGNED: 28 Oct 65   FORCE: 28 Nov 65
REGISTERED: 29 Sep 66 USA (United States)
ARTICLES: 2 LANGUAGE: Spanish. English.
HEADNOTE: ALIEN AMATEUR RADIO OPERATORS
TOPIC: Telecommunications
CONCEPTS: Amateur radio. Radio-telephone-telegraphic communications.
PROCEDURE: Termination.
PARTIES:
   Colombia
   USA (United States)

108344   Bilateral Agreement   **574 UNTS 115**
SIGNED: 14 Dec 65   FORCE: 14 Dec 65
REGISTERED: 29 Sep 66 USA (United States)
ARTICLES: 5 LANGUAGE: English.
HEADNOTE: AGRI COMMOD TITLE IV
TOPIC: US Agri Commod Aid
CONCEPTS: General provisions. Annex or appendix reference. Exchange of information and documents. Reexport of goods, etc.. Transportation costs. Payment schedules. Purchase authorization. Commodities schedule. Purchase authorization. Mutual consultation.
PARTIES:
   Ethiopia
   USA (United States)

108345   Bilateral Agreement   **574 UNTS 129**
SIGNED: 30 Dec 65   FORCE: 30 Dec 65
REGISTERED: 29 Sep 66 USA (United States)
ARTICLES: 11 LANGUAGE: English.
HEADNOTE: ESTABLISHMENT NAVAL MEDICAL RESEARCH UNIT
TOPIC: Milit Installation
CONCEPTS: Informational records. Use of facilities. Public health. Research cooperation. Research results. Customs exemptions. Materials, equipment and services. Bases and facilities.
TREATY REF: 191UNTS59.
PROCEDURE: Termination.
PARTIES:
   Ethiopia
   USA (United States)

108346   Bilateral Exchange   **574 UNTS 139**
SIGNED: 16 Dec 65   FORCE: 16 Dec 65
REGISTERED: 29 Sep 66 USA (United States)
ARTICLES: 2 LANGUAGE: English. Italian.
HEADNOTE: US LIABILITY DAMAGE FROM NS SAVANNAH VISIT
TOPIC: Specif Claim/Waive
CONCEPTS: Claims and settlements. Merchant vessels. Specific claims or waivers.
PROCEDURE: Termination.
PARTIES:
   Italy
   USA (United States)

108347   Bilateral Exchange   **574 UNTS 145**
SIGNED: 27 Dec 65   FORCE: 27 Dec 65
REGISTERED: 29 Sep 66 USA (United States)
ARTICLES: 2 LANGUAGE: English. Italian.
HEADNOTE: LOAN VESSELS

TOPIC: Specific Property
CONCEPTS: Annex or appendix reference. Indemnities and reimbursements. Currency. Terms of loan. Merchant vessels.
PARTIES:
Italy
USA (United States)

108348 Bilateral Exchange **574 UNTS 153**
SIGNED: 19 Aug 65   FORCE: 19 Aug 65
REGISTERED: 29 Sep 66 USA (United States)
ARTICLES: 2 LANGUAGE: English.
HEADNOTE: EXTRADITION
TOPIC: Extradition
CONCEPTS: Extradition requests.
INTL ORGS: United Nations.
PARTIES:
Kenya
USA (United States)

108349 Bilateral Agreement **574 UNTS 159**
SIGNED: 12 Nov 64   FORCE: 1 Nov 65
REGISTERED: 29 Sep 66 USA (United States)
ARTICLES: 31 LANGUAGE: English.
HEADNOTE: PARCEL POST
TOPIC: Postal Service
CONCEPTS: Postal services. Regulations. Insured letters and boxes. Money orders and postal checks. Parcel post. Advice lists and orders.
PROCEDURE: Termination.
PARTIES:
Philippines
USA (United States)

108350 Bilateral Exchange **574 UNTS 205**
SIGNED: 15 Nov 65   FORCE: 15 Nov 65
REGISTERED: 29 Sep 66 USA (United States)
ARTICLES: 2 LANGUAGE: English.
HEADNOTE: ESTABLISHMENT BANKING FACILITIES
TOPIC: Milit Assistance
CONCEPTS: Conformity with municipal law. Banking. Bases and facilities.
TREATY REF: 43UNTS271.
PARTIES:
Philippines
USA (United States)

108351 Bilateral Agreement **574 UNTS 211**
SIGNED: 22 Nov 65   FORCE: 22 Nov 65
REGISTERED: 29 Sep 66 USA (United States)
ARTICLES: 4 LANGUAGE: English.
HEADNOTE: AGRI COMMOD TITLE IV
TOPIC: US Agri Commod Aid
CONCEPTS: General provisions. Annex or appendix reference. Exchange of information and documents. Reexport of goods, etc.. Payment schedules. Transportation costs. Purchase authorization. Commodities schedule. Purchase authorization. Mutual consultation.
PARTIES:
USA (United States)
Yugoslavia

108352 Bilateral Agreement **575 UNTS 3**
SIGNED: 19 Jul 66   FORCE: 1 Oct 66
REGISTERED: 1 Oct 66 Belgium
ARTICLES: 21 LANGUAGE: French. Dutch. Spanish.
HEADNOTE: ROAD TRANSPORT
TOPIC: Land Transport
CONCEPTS: Establishment of commission. General. Competency certificate. Registration certificate. Passenger transport. Transport of goods. Land transport. Agricultural vehicles and construction. Commercial road vehicles. Motor vehicles and combinations. Road rules.
PROCEDURE: Denunciation. Duration.
PARTIES:
Belgium
Spain

108353 Bilateral Treaty **575 UNTS 35**
SIGNED: 8 Apr 64   FORCE: 21 Jul 66
REGISTERED: 6 Oct 66 Netherlands
ARTICLES: 9 LANGUAGE: Dutch. Spanish.
HEADNOTE: CULTURAL RELATIONS
TOPIC: Culture

CONCEPTS: Territorial application. Friendship and amity. Exchange of information and documents. Establishment of commission. Exchange. Teacher and student exchange. Professorships. Scholarships and grants. General cultural cooperation. Artists. Research cooperation. Scientific exchange. Publications exchange. Mass media exchange.
PROCEDURE: Duration. Ratification. Renewal or Revival. Termination.
PARTIES:
Mexico
Netherlands

108354 Multilateral Agreement **575 UNTS 49**
SIGNED: 4 May 66   FORCE: 29 Aug 66
REGISTERED: 7 Oct 66 IBRD (World Bank)
ARTICLES: 14 LANGUAGE: English. French.
HEADNOTE: DEVELOPMENT FUND AGREEMENT
TOPIC: IBRD Project
CONCEPTS: Default remedies. Definition of terms. Annex or appendix reference. Exchange of information and documents. Informational records. Arbitration. Negotiation. Accounting procedures. Indemnities and reimbursements. Financial programs. Payment schedules. Domestic obligation. Loan regulations. Loan guarantee.
PROCEDURE: Accession. Termination.
PARTIES:
Australia SIGNED: 4 May 66 FORCE: 29 Aug 66
Canada SIGNED: 4 May 66 FORCE: 29 Aug 66
Denmark SIGNED: 4 May 66 FORCE: 29 Aug 66
Japan SIGNED: 4 May 66 FORCE: 29 Aug 66
Laos SIGNED: 4 May 66 FORCE: 29 Aug 66
Netherlands SIGNED: 4 May 66 RATIFIED: 29 Aug 66 FORCE: 29 Aug 66
New Zealand SIGNED: 4 May 66 FORCE: 29 Aug 66
IBRD (World Bank) SIGNED: 4 May 66 FORCE: 29 Aug 66
Thailand SIGNED: 4 May 66 FORCE: 29 Aug 66
USA (United States) SIGNED: 4 May 66 FORCE: 29 Aug 66

108355 Bilateral Agreement **575 UNTS 89**
SIGNED: 10 Feb 66   FORCE: 19 Apr 66
REGISTERED: 11 Oct 66 IDA (Devel Assoc)
ARTICLES: 7 LANGUAGE: English.
HEADNOTE: DEVELOPMENT CREDIT FOODGRAIN STORAGE
TOPIC: Non-IBRD Project
CONCEPTS: Definition of terms. Detailed regulations. Previous treaty amendment. Exchange of information and documents. Informational records. Bonds. Currency. Interest rates. Tax exemptions. Agricultural commodities. Credit provisions. Loan repayment. Terms of loan. Plans and standards. Non-bank projects.
PARTIES:
Pakistan
IDA (Devel Assoc)

108356 Multilateral Agreement **575 UNTS 129**
SIGNED: 10 Feb 66   FORCE: 19 Apr 66
REGISTERED: 11 Oct 66 IDA (Devel Assoc)
ARTICLES: 5 LANGUAGE: English.
HEADNOTE: IDA CREDIT AGREEMENT FOODGRAIN STORAGE
TOPIC: Loans and Credits
CONCEPTS: Definition of terms. Annex or appendix reference. General cooperation. Exchange of information and documents. Currency. Interest rates. Payment schedules. Credit provisions. Loan repayment. Terms of loan. Plans and standards. IDA development project.
PARTIES:
Pakistan SIGNED: 10 Feb 66 FORCE: 19 Apr 66
IDA (Devel Assoc) SIGNED: 10 Feb 66 FORCE: 19 Apr 66
Sweden SIGNED: 10 Feb 66 FORCE: 19 Apr 66

108357 Unilateral Instrument **575 UNTS 151**
SIGNED: 30 Sep 66   FORCE: 30 Sep 66
REGISTERED: 17 Oct 66 United Nations
ARTICLES: 1 LANGUAGE: English.
HEADNOTE: ACCEPT OBLIGATIONS UN CHARTER
TOPIC: UN Charter
CONCEPTS: Acceptance of UN obligations.
INTL ORGS: United Nations.

PARTIES:
Botswana

108358 Bilateral Instrument **575 UNTS 155**
SIGNED: 4 Oct 66   FORCE: 17 Oct 66
REGISTERED: 17 Oct 66 United Nations
ARTICLES: 1 LANGUAGE: English.
HEADNOTE: ACCEPT OBLIGATIONS UN CHARTER
TOPIC: UN Charter
CONCEPTS: Acceptance of UN obligations.
INTL ORGS: United Nations.
PARTIES:
Lesotho

108359 Multilateral Convention **575 UNTS 159**
SIGNED: 18 Mar 65   FORCE: 15 Oct 66
REGISTERED: 18 Mar 66 IBRD (World Bank)
ARTICLES: 75 LANGUAGE: English. French. Spanish.
HEADNOTE: SETTLEMENT INVESTMENT DISPUTES
TOPIC: Dispute Settlement
CONCEPTS: Territorial application. Privileges and immunities. Domestic legislation. Recognition and enforcement of legal decisions. Personnel. Jurisdiction. Prizes and arbitral awards. Establishment of commission. Arbitration. Procedure. Special tribunals. Conciliation. Competence of tribunal. Indemnities and reimbursements. Financial programs. Internal structure.
PROCEDURE: Amendment. Denunciation. Ratification.
PARTIES:
Afghanistan SIGNED: 30 Sep 66 FORCE: 14 Oct 66
Austria SIGNED: 17 May 66 FORCE: 14 Oct 66
Belgium SIGNED: 15 Dec 65 FORCE: 14 Oct 66
Cameroon SIGNED: 23 Sep 65 FORCE: 14 Oct 66
Chad SIGNED: 12 May 66 RATIFIED: 29 Aug 66 FORCE: 14 Oct 66
Taiwan SIGNED: 13 Jan 66 FORCE: 14 Oct 66
Central Afri Rep SIGNED: 27 Aug 65 RATIFIED: 23 Feb 66 FORCE: 14 Oct 66
Congo (Brazzaville) SIGNED: 27 Dec 65 RATIFIED: 23 Jun 66 FORCE: 14 Oct 66
Cyprus SIGNED: 9 Mar 66 FORCE: 14 Oct 66
Dahomey SIGNED: 3 Sep 65 RATIFIED: 6 Sep 66 FORCE: 14 Oct 66
Denmark SIGNED: 11 Oct 65 FORCE: 14 Oct 66
Ethiopia SIGNED: 21 Sep 65 FORCE: 14 Oct 66
France SIGNED: 22 Dec 65 FORCE: 14 Oct 66
Gabon SIGNED: 21 Sep 65 RATIFIED: 4 Apr 66 FORCE: 14 Oct 66
Germany, West SIGNED: 27 Jan 66 FORCE: 14 Oct 66
Ghana SIGNED: 26 Nov 65 RATIFIED: 13 Jul 66 FORCE: 14 Oct 66
Greece SIGNED: 16 Mar 66 FORCE: 14 Oct 66
Iceland SIGNED: 25 Jul 66 RATIFIED: 25 Jul 66 FORCE: 14 Oct 66
Ireland SIGNED: 30 Aug 66 FORCE: 14 Oct 66
Italy SIGNED: 18 Nov 65 FORCE: 14 Oct 66
Ivory Coast SIGNED: 30 Jun 65 RATIFIED: 16 Feb 66 FORCE: 14 Oct 66
Jamaica SIGNED: 23 Jun 65 RATIFIED: 9 Sep 66 FORCE: 14 Oct 66
Japan SIGNED: 23 Sep 65 FORCE: 14 Oct 66
Kenya SIGNED: 24 May 66 FORCE: 14 Oct 66
Korea, South SIGNED: 18 Apr 66 FORCE: 14 Oct 66
Liberia SIGNED: 3 Sep 65 FORCE: 14 Oct 66
Luxembourg SIGNED: 28 Sep 65 FORCE: 14 Oct 66
Madagascar SIGNED: 1 Jun 66 RATIFIED: 6 Sep 66 FORCE: 14 Oct 66
Malawi SIGNED: 9 Jun 66 RATIFIED: 23 Aug 66 FORCE: 14 Oct 66
Malaysia SIGNED: 22 Oct 65 RATIFIED: 8 Aug 66 FORCE: 14 Oct 66
Mauritania SIGNED: 30 Jul 65 RATIFIED: 11 Jan 66 FORCE: 14 Oct 66
Morocco SIGNED: 11 Oct 65 FORCE: 14 Oct 66
Nepal SIGNED: 28 Sep 65 FORCE: 14 Oct 66
Netherlands SIGNED: 25 May 66 RATIFIED: 14 Sep 66 FORCE: 14 Oct 66
Nigeria SIGNED: 13 Jul 65 RATIFIED: 25 Aug 65 FORCE: 14 Oct 66
Niger SIGNED: 26 Aug 65 FORCE: 14 Oct 66
Norway SIGNED: 24 Jun 66 FORCE: 14 Oct 66
Pakistan SIGNED: 6 Jul 65 RATIFIED: 15 Sep 66 FORCE: 15 Oct 66

IBRD (World Bank) SIGNED: 18 Mar 65 FORCE:
14 Oct 66
Senegal SIGNED: 26 Sep 66 FORCE: 14 Oct 66
Sierra Leone SIGNED: 27 Sep 65 RATIFIED:
2 Aug 66 FORCE: 14 Oct 66
Somalia SIGNED: 27 Sep 65 FORCE: 14 Oct 66
Sweden SIGNED: 25 Sep 65 FORCE: 14 Oct 66
Togo SIGNED: 24 Jan 66 FORCE: 14 Oct 66
Trinidad/Tobago SIGNED: 5 Oct 66 FORCE:
14 Oct 66
Tunisia SIGNED: 5 May 65 RATIFIED: 22 Jun 66
FORCE: 14 Oct 66
Uganda SIGNED: 7 Jun 66 RATIFIED: 6 Jun 66
FORCE: 14 Oct 66
UK Great Britain SIGNED: 26 May 65 FORCE:
14 Oct 66
USA (United States) SIGNED: 27 Aug 65 RATI-
FIED: 10 Jun 66 FORCE: 14 Oct 66
Upper Volta SIGNED: 16 Sep 65 RATIFIED:
29 Aug 66 FORCE: 14 Oct 66
ANNEX
608 UNTS 384. Norway. Ratification 16 Aug 67.
Force 15 Sep 67.
608 UNTS 384. France. Ratification 21 Aug 67.
Force 20 Sep 67.
608 UNTS 384. Togo. Ratification 11 Aug 67.
Force 10 Sep 67.
608 UNTS 384. Japan. Ratification 17 Aug 67.
Force 16 Sep 67.
614 UNTS 336. Ceylon (Sri Lanka). Signature
30 Aug 67. Force 11 Nov 67.
614 UNTS 336. Ceylon (Sri Lanka). Ratification
12 Oct 67. Force 11 Nov 67.
638 UNTS 327. Denmark. Declaration
15 May 68.
638 UNTS 327. Denmark. Ratification 24 Apr 68.
Force 24 May 68.
638 UNTS 327. Somalia. Ratification 29 Feb 68.
Force 30 Mar 68.
639 UNTS 366. Switzerland. Force 14 Jun 68.
639 UNTS 366. Switzerland. Ratification
15 May 68. Signature 22 Sep 67.
642 UNTS 379. Afghanistan. Ratification
25 Jun 68. Force 25 Jul 68.
649 UNTS 370. Indonesia. Signature 16 Feb 68.
Ratification 28 Sep 68.
659 UNTS 388. Taiwan. Ratification 10 Dec 68.
Force 9 Jan 69.
659 UNTS 388. Nepal. Ratification 7 Jan 69.
Force 6 Feb 69.
659 UNTS 388. Finland. Ratification 9 Jan 69.
Force 8 Feb 69.

108360 Bilateral Exchange **576 UNTS 3**
SIGNED: 30 Sep 66 FORCE: 30 Sep 66
REGISTERED: 1 Nov 66 United Nations
ARTICLES: 2 LANGUAGE: English.
HEADNOTE: APPLICATION ASSISTANCE
TOPIC: IGO Operations
CONCEPTS: Volunteer programs. Assistance to
United Nations. Inter-agency agreements.
TREATY REF: 348UNTS177.
PARTIES:
Botswana
UN Special Fund

108361 Multilateral Exchange **576 UNTS 8**
SIGNED: 30 Sep 66 FORCE: 30 Sep 66
REGISTERED: 1 Nov 66 United Nations
ARTICLES: 2 LANGUAGE: English.
HEADNOTE: TECHNICAL ASSISTANCE
TOPIC: IGO Operations
CONCEPTS: General technical assistance. IGO op-
erations.
TREATY REF: 366UNTS311.
PARTIES:
Botswana SIGNED: 30 Sep 66 FORCE:
30 Sep 66
FAO (Food Agri) SIGNED: 30 Sep 66 FORCE:
30 Sep 66
IAEA (Atom Energy) SIGNED: 30 Sep 66 FORCE:
30 Sep 66
ICAO (Civil Aviat) SIGNED: 30 Sep 66 FORCE:
30 Sep 66
ILO (Labor Org) SIGNED: 30 Sep 66 FORCE:
30 Sep 66
ITU (Telecommun) SIGNED: 30 Sep 66 FORCE:
30 Sep 66
UNESCO (Educ/Cult) SIGNED: 30 Sep 66
FORCE: 30 Sep 66
United Nations SIGNED: 30 Sep 66 FORCE:
30 Sep 66

UPU (Postal Union) SIGNED: 30 Sep 66 FORCE:
30 Sep 66
WHO (World Health) SIGNED: 30 Sep 66 FORCE:
30 Sep 66
WMO (Meteorology) SIGNED: 30 Sep 66 FORCE:
30 Sep 66
ANNEX
607 UNTS 354. Botswana. Termination
12 Oct 67.
607 UNTS 354. UNTAB (Tech Assis). Termination
12 Oct 67.

108362 Bilateral Exchange **576 UNTS 17**
SIGNED: 30 Sep 66 FORCE: 30 Sep 66
REGISTERED: 1 Nov 66 United Nations
ARTICLES: 2 LANGUAGE: English.
HEADNOTE: EXECUTIVE ADMINISTRATIVE PER-
SONNEL
TOPIC: Tech Assistance
CONCEPTS: General cooperation. Personnel. As-
sistance.
INTL ORGS: United Nations Special Fund.
TREATY REF: 469UNTS145; 478UNTS440.
PARTIES:
Botswana
United Nations

108363 Bilateral Agreement **576 UNTS 23**
SIGNED: 4 Aug 66 FORCE: 4 Aug 66
REGISTERED: 1 Nov 66 United Nations
ARTICLES: 8 LANGUAGE: French.
HEADNOTE: NATION REGIONAL CARTOGRAPHIC
CONFERENCE
TOPIC: IGO Operations
CONCEPTS: Diplomatic privileges. Diplomatic mis-
sions. Privileges and immunities. Personnel.
Funding procedures. Admission. Subsidiary or-
gan.
TREATY REF: 1UNTS15; 33UNTS261.
PARTIES:
United Nations
Tunisia

108364 Bilateral Convention **576 UNTS 35**
SIGNED: 24 Jan 66 FORCE: 14 Oct 66
REGISTERED: 7 Nov 66 Finland
ARTICLES: 35 LANGUAGE: Finnish. Russian.
HEADNOTE: CONSULAR
TOPIC: Consul/Citizenship
CONCEPTS: Definition of terms. General consular
functions. Consular relations establishment.
Privileges and immunities. Personnel.
PROCEDURE: Ratification. Termination.
PARTIES:
Finland
USSR (Soviet Union)

108365 Bilateral Agreement **576 UNTS 85**
SIGNED: 8 Nov 66 FORCE: 8 Nov 66
REGISTERED: 8 Nov 66 United Nations
ARTICLES: 5 LANGUAGE: English.
HEADNOTE: PILOT COURSE PHOTO-PROCESSING
PHOTOGRAMMETRY
TOPIC: Scientific Project
CONCEPTS: Privileges and immunities. General
cooperation. Personnel. Responsibility and liabil-
ity. Use of facilities. Specialists exchange.
Teacher and student exchange. Professorships.
Scholarships and grants. Research and scientific
projects. Research and development. Domestic
obligation. IGO obligations.
TREATY REF: 1UNTS15; 93UNTS327.
PROCEDURE: Amendment. Duration.
PARTIES:
United Nations
Sudan

108366 Bilateral Agreement **576 UNTS 95**
SIGNED: 25 Dec 63 FORCE: 14 May 64
REGISTERED: 8 Nov 66 Romania
ARTICLES: 28 LANGUAGE: Romanian. Serbo-
Croat.
HEADNOTE: INTERNATIONAL ROAD TRANSPORT
TOPIC: Land Transport
CONCEPTS: Exceptions and exemptions. General
provisions. Remedies. Annex or appendix refer-
ence. Passports non-diplomatic. Visas. Confor-
mity with municipal law. Exchange of informa-
tion and documents. Investigation of violations.

Establishment of commission. Payment sched-
ules. Customs duties. Customs exemptions. Tem-
porary importation. Registration certificate. Pas-
senger transport. Routes and logistics. Transport
of goods. Commercial road vehicles. Driving per-
mits. Motor vehicles and combinations. Roads
and highways. Road rules.
INTL ORGS: Arbitration Commission.
TREATY REF: 348UNTS13.
PROCEDURE: Denunciation. Duration. Ratification.
Renewal or Revival.
PARTIES:
Romania
Yugoslavia

108367 Bilateral Agreement **576 UNTS 145**
SIGNED: 25 May 65 FORCE: 16 Feb 66
REGISTERED: 25 May 65 Hungary
ARTICLES: 12 LANGUAGE: Hungarian. Serbo-
Croat.
HEADNOTE: CUSTOMS MATTERS
TOPIC: Customs
CONCEPTS: Customs duties. Commercial road ve-
hicles. Frontier crossing points.
PROCEDURE: Duration. Ratification. Renewal or
Revival. Termination.
PARTIES:
Hungary
Yugoslavia

108368 Bilateral Agreement **576 UNTS 163**
SIGNED: 11 Nov 64 FORCE: 11 Jan 65
REGISTERED: 9 Nov 66 Hungary
ARTICLES: 28 LANGUAGE: Hungarian. German.
HEADNOTE: VETERINARY AGREEMENT
TOPIC: Sanitation
CONCEPTS: Definition of terms. Detailed regula-
tions. Exceptions and exemptions. Annex or ap-
pendix reference. Previous treaty extension.
Conformity with municipal law. Exchange of in-
formation and documents. Inspection and obser-
vation. Domestic legislation. Establishment of
commission. Dispute settlement. Specialists ex-
change. Quarantine. Border control. Disease
control. Veterinary. Trade procedures.
INTL ORGS: Arbitration Commission.
PROCEDURE: Denunciation. Duration. Renewal or
Revival.
PARTIES:
Austria
Hungary

108369 Bilateral Treaty **576 UNTS 275**
SIGNED: 13 Jun 63 FORCE: 4 Jun 64
REGISTERED: 9 Nov 66 Hungary
ARTICLES: 61 LANGUAGE: Hungarian. Romanian.
HEADNOTE: REGIME HUNGARIAN-ROMANIAN
STATE FRONTIER
TOPIC: Territory Boundary
CONCEPTS: Annex or appendix reference. Inspec-
tion and observation. Operating agencies.
Claims and settlements. Inland and territorial
waters. Fish, wildlife, and natural resources.
Markers and definitions. Frontier peoples and
personnel. Frontier waterways. Frontier crossing
points. Wildlife. Regulation of natural resources.
TREATY REF: 41UNTS135.
PROCEDURE: Duration. Ratification. Renewal or
Revival. Termination.
PARTIES:
Hungary
Romania

108370 Bilateral Agreement **577 UNTS 3**
SIGNED: 9 Feb 62 FORCE: 11 Feb 63
REGISTERED: 9 Nov 66 Hungary
ARTICLES: 28 LANGUAGE: Hungarian. Serbo-
Croat.
HEADNOTE: MOTOR VEHICLE CUSTOMS PROCE-
DURE
TOPIC: Land Transport
CONCEPTS: Exceptions and exemptions. Reme-
dies. Annex or appendix reference. Passports
non-diplomatic. Visas. Conformity with munici-
pal law. General cooperation. Exchange of infor-
mation and documents. Informational records.
Inspection and observation. Recognition of legal
documents. Establishment of commission. Cur-
rency. Payment schedules. Tax exemptions. Customs duties. Customs exemptions. Transport of

goods. Motor vehicles and combinations. Roads and highways. Road rules.
TREATY REF: 327UNTS13; 348UNTS13; 338UNTS103.
PROCEDURE: Denunciation. Duration. Ratification. Renewal or Revival.
PARTIES:
Hungary
Yugoslavia

108371 Bilateral Treaty **577 UNTS 39**
SIGNED: 30 May 64   FORCE: 20 Oct 64
REGISTERED: 9 Nov 66 Hungary
ARTICLES: 6 LANGUAGE: Hungarian. Arabic.
HEADNOTE: FRIENDSHIP COOPERATION
TOPIC: General Amity
CONCEPTS: Peaceful relations. Procedure.
PROCEDURE: Duration. Ratification. Termination.
PARTIES:
Hungary
Yemen

108372 Bilateral Convention **577 UNTS 49**
SIGNED: 15 Oct 63   FORCE: 29 May 64
REGISTERED: 9 Nov 66 Hungary
ARTICLES: 12 LANGUAGE: Hungarian. Serbo-Croat.
HEADNOTE: SCIENTIFIC EDUCATIONAL CULTURAL COOPERATION
TOPIC: Health/Educ/Welfare
CONCEPTS: Friendship and amity. Non-diplomatic delegations. General cooperation. Exchange of information and documents. Personnel. Specialists exchange. Exchange. Commissions and foundations. Teacher and student exchange. Professorships. Scholarships and grants. Vocational training. Exchange. Artists. Athletes. Research results. Scientific exchange. Research and development. Funding procedures. Recognition. Publications exchange. Mass media exchange.
PROCEDURE: Duration. Ratification. Renewal or Revival. Termination. Denunciation.
PARTIES:
Hungary
Yugoslavia

108373 Bilateral Agreement **577 UNTS 67**
SIGNED: 19 Aug 65   FORCE: 19 Aug 65
REGISTERED: 9 Nov 66 Hungary
ARTICLES: 14 LANGUAGE: Hungarian. Bulgarian.
HEADNOTE: SCIENTIFIC CULTURAL COOPERATION
TOPIC: Culture
CONCEPTS: Treaty implementation. Previous treaty replacement. Institute establishment. Athletes. Recognition. Press and wire services.
PROCEDURE: Denunciation. Duration. Renewal or Revival.
PARTIES:
Bulgaria
Hungary

108374 Bilateral Agreement **577 UNTS 89**
SIGNED: 23 Nov 65   FORCE: 15 Feb 66
REGISTERED: 9 Nov 66 Hungary
ARTICLES: 10 LANGUAGE: Hungarian. Serbo-Croat.
HEADNOTE: ABOLITION VISAS
TOPIC: Visas
CONCEPTS: Time limit. Previous treaty replacement. Visa abolition. Resident permits. Non-visa travel documents. Conformity with municipal law. Fees and exemptions. Frontier crossing points.
PROCEDURE: Denunciation. Ratification.
PARTIES:
Hungary
Yugoslavia

108375 Bilateral Agreement **577 UNTS 103**
SIGNED: 9 Aug 65   FORCE: 28 Dec 65
REGISTERED: 9 Nov 66 Hungary
ARTICLES: 9 LANGUAGE: Hungarian. Slovene.
HEADNOTE: REGULATION MINOR FRONTIER TRAFFIC
TOPIC: Visas
CONCEPTS: Annex or appendix reference. Frontier permits. Establishment of commission. Markers and definitions. Frontier peoples and personnel.
INTL ORGS: Arbitration Commission.
PROCEDURE: Denunciation. Duration. Ratification.
PARTIES:
Hungary
Yugoslavia

108376 Bilateral Agreement **577 UNTS 161**
SIGNED: 18 Jul 65   FORCE: 19 Nov 65
REGISTERED: 9 Nov 66 Hungary
ARTICLES: 29 LANGUAGE: Hungarian. Polish.
HEADNOTE: INTERNATIONAL MOTOR TRANSPORT
TOPIC: Land Transport
CONCEPTS: Exceptions and exemptions. General provisions. Treaty implementation. Frontier formalities. Conformity with municipal law. General cooperation. Informational records. Responsibility and liability. Investigation of violations. Payment schedules. Customs duties. Temporary importation. Passenger transport. Routes and logistics. Transport of goods. Motor vehicles and combinations. Roads and highways. Road rules.
TREATY REF: 399UNTS189; 348UNTS13.
PROCEDURE: Denunciation. Ratification.
PARTIES:
Hungary
Poland

108377 Bilateral Agreement **577 UNTS 193**
SIGNED: 25 May 65   FORCE: 8 Jul 66
REGISTERED: 9 Nov 66 Hungary
ARTICLES: 10 LANGUAGE: English.
HEADNOTE: CULTURAL & SCIENTIFIC EDUCATIONAL COOPERATION
TOPIC: Health/Educ/Welfare
CONCEPTS: Friendship and amity. Exchange of information and documents. Establishment of commission. Specialists exchange. Exchange. Scholarships and grants. Exchange. Artists. Athletes. Research results. Scientific exchange. Mass media exchange.
PROCEDURE: Duration. Ratification. Renewal or Revival. Termination.
PARTIES:
Ethiopia
Hungary

108378 Bilateral Agreement **577 UNTS 201**
SIGNED: 21 Jan 63   FORCE: 19 Aug 63
REGISTERED: 9 Nov 66 Hungary
ARTICLES: 13 LANGUAGE: Hungarian. Russian.
HEADNOTE: AVOIDANCE CASES DUAL CITIZENSHIP
TOPIC: Consul/Citizenship
CONCEPTS: Detailed regulations. Acquisition of nationality. Dual citizenship.
PROCEDURE: Denunciation. Duration. Ratification. Renewal or Revival.
PARTIES:
Hungary
USSR (Soviet Union)

108379 Bilateral Agreement **577 UNTS 219**
SIGNED: 29 Mar 63   FORCE: 29 Mar 63
REGISTERED: 9 Nov 66 Hungary
ARTICLES: 5 LANGUAGE: Hungarian. Korean
HEADNOTE: HEALTH COOPERATION
TOPIC: Sanitation
CONCEPTS: General cooperation. Exchange of information and documents. Informational records. Domestic legislation. Responsibility and liability. Specialists exchange. Disease control. Public health. Exchange. Vocational training. Scientific exchange. Indemnities and reimbursements. Expense sharing formulae. Publications exchange.
PROCEDURE: Denunciation. Duration. Renewal or Revival.
PARTIES:
Hungary
Korea, North

108380 Bilateral Agreement **577 UNTS 231**
SIGNED: 11 Oct 61   FORCE: 9 Apr 62
REGISTERED: 9 Nov 66 Hungary
ARTICLES: 10 LANGUAGE: Hungarian. Arabic.
HEADNOTE: COOPERATION RADIO TV ETC.
TOPIC: Gen Communications
CONCEPTS: Mass media exchange.
PROCEDURE: Duration. Ratification. Termination.
PARTIES:
Hungary
Iraq

108381 Bilateral Agreement **577 UNTS 245**
SIGNED: 20 Dec 62   FORCE: 1 Jul 63
REGISTERED: 9 Nov 66 Hungary
ARTICLES: 21 LANGUAGE: Hungarian. Russian.
HEADNOTE: COOPERATION FIELD SOCIAL SECURITY
TOPIC: Non-ILO Labor
CONCEPTS: General provisions. General consular functions. Notarial acts and services. General cooperation. Exchange of information and documents. Domestic legislation. Operating agencies. Procedure. Sickness and invalidity insurance. Social security. Payment schedules.
PROCEDURE: Denunciation. Duration. Ratification. Renewal or Revival.
PARTIES:
Hungary
USSR (Soviet Union)

108382 Multilateral Exchange **578 UNTS 3**
SIGNED: 8 Sep 65   FORCE: 1 Oct 65
REGISTERED: 10 Nov 66 Netherlands
ARTICLES: 2 LANGUAGE: French. Italian.
HEADNOTE: RECOGNITION SEAMANS BOOK TRAVEL DOCUMENT
TOPIC: Visas
CONCEPTS: Denial of admission. Non-visa travel documents.
PARTIES:
Belgium SIGNED: 12 Mar 65 FORCE: 1 Oct 65
Italy SIGNED: 12 Mar 65 FORCE: 1 Oct 65
Luxembourg SIGNED: 12 Mar 65 FORCE: 1 Oct 65
Netherlands SIGNED: 12 Mar 65 FORCE: 1 Oct 65

108383 Bilateral Agreement **578 UNTS 15**
SIGNED: 28 Oct 65   FORCE: 11 Aug 66
REGISTERED: 10 Nov 66 Netherlands
ARTICLES: 7 LANGUAGE: English.
HEADNOTE: FACULTY VETERINARY SCIENCE
TOPIC: Scientific Project
CONCEPTS: Privileges and immunities. Responsibility and liability. Education. Scholarships and grants. Veterinary. Fees and exemptions. Transportation costs. Tax exemptions. Materials, equipment and services.
PROCEDURE: Amendment. Duration. Renewal or Revival. Termination.
PARTIES:
Netherlands
Nigeria

108384 Multilateral Agreement **578 UNTS 23**
SIGNED: 12 Jul 66   FORCE: 1 Aug 66
REGISTERED: 10 Nov 66 Netherlands
ARTICLES: 13 LANGUAGE: French.
HEADNOTE: ABOLITION VISAS
TOPIC: Visas
CONCEPTS: Emergencies. Territorial application. Time limit. Visa abolition. Denial of admission. Resident permits. Conformity with municipal law.
PROCEDURE: Denunciation.
PARTIES:
Belgium SIGNED: 12 Jul 66 FORCE: 1 Aug 66
Luxembourg SIGNED: 12 Jul 66 FORCE: 1 Aug 66
Netherlands SIGNED: 12 Jul 66 FORCE: 1 Aug 66
Niger SIGNED: 12 Jul 66 FORCE: 1 Aug 66

108385 Bilateral Exchange **578 UNTS 33**
SIGNED: 12 Oct 66   FORCE: 19 Feb 66
REGISTERED: 15 Nov 66 UK Great Britain
ARTICLES: 2 LANGUAGE: English. French.
HEADNOTE: RESTORATION LAND WAR CEMETERY
TOPIC: Other Military
CONCEPTS: Annex or appendix reference. General property. Indemnities and reimbursements.

Burial arrangements. Responsibility for war dead.
PARTIES:
Greece
UK Great Britain

108386   Bilateral Agreement   **578 UNTS 47**
SIGNED: 17 Nov 66   FORCE: 17 Nov 66
REGISTERED: 17 Nov 66 United Nations
ARTICLES: 8 LANGUAGE: English.
HEADNOTE: ACTIVITIES
TOPIC: IGO Operations
CONCEPTS: Diplomatic privileges. Privileges and immunities. Exchange of information and documents. Accounting procedures. Materials, equipment and services. Assistance to United Nations. Inter-agency agreements.
INTL ORGS: United Nations.
PROCEDURE: Amendment. Termination.
PARTIES:
Indonesia
UNICEF (Children)

108387   Multilateral Agreement   **578 UNTS 57**
SIGNED: 4 Mar 66   FORCE: 4 Mar 66
REGISTERED: 21 Nov 66 USA (United States)
ARTICLES: 5 LANGUAGE: English.
HEADNOTE: AGRI COMMOD TITLE IV
TOPIC: US Agri Commod Aid
CONCEPTS: Territorial application. Annex or appendix reference. General cooperation. Exchange of information and documents. Reexport of goods, etc.. Exchange rates and regulations. Payment schedules. Purchase authorization. Commodities schedule. Purchase authorization.
PARTIES:
East Afri Service SIGNED: 19 Feb 66 FORCE: 4 Mar 66
Kenya SIGNED: 22 Feb 66 FORCE: 4 Mar 66
Tanzania SIGNED: 18 Feb 66 FORCE: 4 Mar 66
Uganda SIGNED: 4 Mar 66 FORCE: 4 Mar 66
USA (United States) SIGNED: 19 Feb 66 FORCE: 4 Mar 66

108388   Bilateral Agreement   **578 UNTS 73**
SIGNED: 22 Apr 66   FORCE: 22 Apr 66
REGISTERED: 21 Nov 66 USA (United States)
ARTICLES: 6 LANGUAGE: English. Spanish.
HEADNOTE: AGRI COMMOD
TOPIC: US Agri Commod Aid
CONCEPTS: General provisions. Annex or appendix reference. Exchange of information and documents. Reexport of goods, etc.. Exchange rates and regulations. Transportation costs. Local currency. Commodities schedule. Purchase authorization. Mutual consultation.
PARTIES:
Bolivia
USA (United States)

108389   Bilateral Exchange   **578 UNTS 99**
SIGNED: 11 Apr 66   FORCE: 11 Apr 66
REGISTERED: 21 Nov 66 USA (United States)
ARTICLES: 2 LANGUAGE: English. Spanish.
HEADNOTE: ADDITIONAL MILITARY ASSISTANCE
TOPIC: Milit Assistance
CONCEPTS: Conformity with municipal law. Exchange of information and documents. Inspection and observation. Military assistance. Security of information. Restrictions on transfer.
PARTIES:
Paraguay
USA (United States)

108390   Bilateral Agreement   **578 UNTS 106**
SIGNED: 18 Apr 66   FORCE: 18 Apr 66
REGISTERED: 21 Nov 66 USA (United States)
ARTICLES: 5 LANGUAGE: English.
HEADNOTE: AGRI COMMOD TITLE IV
TOPIC: US Agri Commod Aid
CONCEPTS: General provisions. Annex or appendix reference. Exchange of information and documents. Reexport of goods, etc.. Payment schedules. Purchase authorization. Commodities schedule.
PARTIES:
Indonesia
USA (United States)

108391   Bilateral Agreement   **578 UNTS 121**
SIGNED: 27 Apr 66   FORCE: 27 Apr 66
REGISTERED: 21 Nov 66 USA (United States)
ARTICLES: 5 LANGUAGE: English. Spanish.
HEADNOTE: AGRI COMMOD TITLE IV
TOPIC: US Agri Commod Aid
CONCEPTS: General provisions. Annex or appendix reference. General cooperation. Exchange of information and documents. Reexport of goods, etc.. Payment schedules. Agricultural commodities. Purchase authorization.
PARTIES:
Paraguay
USA (United States)

108392   Bilateral Agreement   **578 UNTS 143**
SIGNED: 6 Jun 66   FORCE: 6 Jun 66
REGISTERED: 21 Nov 66 USA (United States)
ARTICLES: 5 LANGUAGE: English.
HEADNOTE: AMATEUR RADIO OPERATORS
TOPIC: US Agri Commod Aid
CONCEPTS: Currency. Agricultural commodities. Credit provisions.
PARTIES:
Israel
USA (United States)

108393   Bilateral Exchange   **578 UNTS 159**
SIGNED: 15 Jun 66   FORCE: 15 Jun 66
REGISTERED: 21 Nov 66 USA (United States)
ARTICLES: 2 LANGUAGE: English.
HEADNOTE: AMATEUR RADIO OPERATORS
TOPIC: Telecommunications
CONCEPTS: Amateur radio.
TREATY REF: USA'TIAS 4893;$.
PARTIES:
Israel
USA (United States)

108394   Bilateral Agreement   **578 UNTS 165**
SIGNED: 21 Mar 66   FORCE: 21 Mar 66
REGISTERED: 21 Nov 66 USA (United States)
ARTICLES: 6 LANGUAGE: English.
HEADNOTE: AGRI COMMOD
TOPIC: US Agri Commod Aid
CONCEPTS: Currency. Agricultural commodities. Economic assistance. Use restrictions. Grants.
PARTIES:
USA (United States)
Vietnam, South

108395   Bilateral Agreement   **579 UNTS 3**
SIGNED: 8 Oct 64   FORCE: 8 Oct 64
REGISTERED: 21 Nov 66 USA (United States)
ARTICLES: 6 LANGUAGE: English. Spanish.
HEADNOTE: AGRI COMMOD TITLE I
TOPIC: US Agri Commod Aid
CONCEPTS: General provisions. Annex or appendix reference. General cooperation. Exchange of information and documents. Reexport of goods, etc.. Exchange rates and regulations. Transportation costs. Local currency. Commodities schedule. Purchase authorization.
PARTIES:
Colombia
USA (United States)

108396   Bilateral Agreement   **579 UNTS 29**
SIGNED: 22 May 65   FORCE: 22 May 65
REGISTERED: 21 Nov 66 USA (United States)
ARTICLES: 6 LANGUAGE: English.
HEADNOTE: AGRI COMMOD TITLE I
TOPIC: US Agri Commod Aid
CONCEPTS: General provisions. Annex or appendix reference. General cooperation. Exchange of information and documents. Reexport of goods, etc.. Exchange rates and regulations. Transportation costs. Local currency. Purchase authorization.
PARTIES:
Afghanistan
USA (United States)

108397   Bilateral Exchange   **579 UNTS 47**
SIGNED: 12 Aug 65   FORCE: 12 Aug 65
REGISTERED: 21 Nov 66 USA (United States)
ARTICLES: 2 LANGUAGE: English.

HEADNOTE: CONSTRUCTION INSTALLATION CABLE COMMUNICATIONS FACILITIES DEFENSE
TOPIC: Milit Installation
CONCEPTS: Annex or appendix reference. Use of facilities. Bases and facilities. Restrictions on transfer.
TREATY REF: 43UNTS271.
PROCEDURE: Future Procedures Contemplated. Termination.
PARTIES:
Philippines
USA (United States)

108398   Bilateral Exchange   **579 UNTS 55**
SIGNED: 16 Aug 65   FORCE: 16 Aug 65
REGISTERED: 21 Nov 66 USA (United States)
ARTICLES: 2 LANGUAGE: English.
HEADNOTE: ALIEN AMATEUR RADIO OPERATORS
TOPIC: Telecommunications
CONCEPTS: Amateur radio. Radio-telephone-telegraphic communications.
TREATY REF: USA'TIAS 4893;0.
PROCEDURE: Termination.
PARTIES:
Sierra Leone
USA (United States)

108399   Bilateral Agreement   **579 UNTS 63**
SIGNED: 3 Jan 66   FORCE: 3 Jan 66
REGISTERED: 21 Nov 66 USA (United States)
ARTICLES: 6 LANGUAGE: English.
HEADNOTE: AGRI COMMOD TITLE I
TOPIC: US Agri Commod Aid
CONCEPTS: General provisions. Annex or appendix reference. General cooperation. Exchange of information and documents. Reexport of goods, etc.. Exchange rates and regulations. Transportation costs. Local currency. Commodities schedule. Purchase authorization.
PARTIES:
United Arab Rep
USA (United States)

108400   Bilateral Agreement   **579 UNTS 83**
SIGNED: 3 Jan 66   FORCE: 3 Jan 66
REGISTERED: 21 Nov 66 USA (United States)
ARTICLES: 5 LANGUAGE: English.
HEADNOTE: AGRI COMMOD TITLE IV
TOPIC: US Agri Commod Aid
CONCEPTS: General provisions. Annex or appendix reference. General cooperation. Exchange of information and documents. Payment schedules. Local currency. Purchase authorization. Commodities schedule.
PARTIES:
United Arab Rep
USA (United States)

108401   Bilateral Exchange   **579 UNTS 99**
SIGNED: 3 Jan 66   FORCE: 3 Jan 66
REGISTERED: 21 Nov 66 USA (United States)
ARTICLES: 2 LANGUAGE: English.
HEADNOTE: TELEVISION BROADCASTING VIETNAM
TOPIC: Mass Media
CONCEPTS: Customs exemptions. Commercial and public radio. Facilities and equipment. Telecommunications.
TREATY REF: UKTS NO.74 (1961) CMD.1484; USA'TIAS 4893;0.
PARTIES:
USA (United States)
Vietnam, South

108402   Bilateral Exchange   **579 UNTS 109**
SIGNED: 15 Jan 66   FORCE: 15 Jan 66
REGISTERED: 21 Nov 66 USA (United States)
ARTICLES: 2 LANGUAGE: English.
HEADNOTE: DEPLOYMENT VESSELS MALTA REPAIR SERVICES
TOPIC: Specif Goods/Equip
CONCEPTS: Previous treaties adherence. Visa abolition. Claims and settlements. Customs exemptions. Naval vessels. Specific goods and equipment.
PARTIES:
Malta
USA (United States)

108403 Bilateral Agreement **579 UNTS 117**
SIGNED: 12 Mar 66 FORCE: 12 Mar 66
REGISTERED: 21 Nov 66 USA (United States)
ARTICLES: 6 LANGUAGE: English.
HEADNOTE: AGRI COMMOD TITLE I
TOPIC: US Agri Commod Aid
CONCEPTS: General provisions. Annex or appendix reference. General cooperation. Exchange of information and documents. Reexport of goods, etc.. Exchange rates and regulations. Transportation costs. Local currency. Commodities schedule. Purchase authorization.
PARTIES:
Ceylon (Sri Lanka)
USA (United States)
ANNEX
603 UNTS 342. USA (United States). Amendment 25 Aug 66. Force 25 Aug 66.
603 UNTS 342. Ceylon (Sri Lanka). Amendment 25 Aug 66. Force 25 Aug 66.

108404 Bilateral Agreement **579 UNTS 137**
SIGNED: 7 Mar 66 FORCE: 7 Mar 66
REGISTERED: 21 Nov 66 USA (United States)
ARTICLES: 6 LANGUAGE: English.
HEADNOTE: AGRI COMMOD TITLE I
TOPIC: US Agri Commod Aid
CONCEPTS: General provisions. Annex or appendix reference. General cooperation. Exchange of information and documents. Reexport of goods, etc.. Exchange rates and regulations. Transportation costs. Local currency. Commodities schedule. Purchase authorization.
PARTIES:
Korea, South
USA (United States)

108405 Bilateral Agreement **579 UNTS 157**
SIGNED: 1 Apr 66 FORCE: 1 Apr 66
REGISTERED: 21 Nov 66 USA (United States)
ARTICLES: 6 LANGUAGE: English.
HEADNOTE: AGRI COMMOD TITLE I
TOPIC: US Agri Commod Aid
CONCEPTS: General provisions. Annex or appendix reference. General cooperation. Exchange of information and documents. Reexport of goods, etc.. Exchange rates and regulations. Transportation costs. Local currency. Commodities schedule. Purchase authorization.
PARTIES:
Ghana
USA (United States)

108406 Bilateral Exchange **579 UNTS 173**
SIGNED: 14 Apr 66 FORCE: 14 Apr 66
REGISTERED: 21 Nov 66 USA (United States)
ARTICLES: 2 LANGUAGE: English. Spanish.
HEADNOTE: OPERATION EXPANSION TRACKING STATION
TOPIC: Specific Property
CONCEPTS: Previous treaty replacement. Nationality and citizenship. Operating agencies. Personnel. Title and deeds. Research cooperation. Indemnities and reimbursements. Tax exemptions. Customs exemptions. Bands and frequency allocation. Facilities and equipment. Facilities and property.
INTL ORGS: International Telecommunication Union.
TREATY REF: 74UKTS(1961)CMD.1484; US-TIAS4893; 487UNTS370; ETC..
PROCEDURE: Duration.
PARTIES:
Spain
USA (United States)

108407 Bilateral Agreement **579 UNTS 193**
SIGNED: 18 Dec 65 FORCE: 18 Dec 65
REGISTERED: 21 Nov 66 USA (United States)
ARTICLES: 6 LANGUAGE: English. German.
HEADNOTE: SUPPORT PERSONNEL DURING EMERGENCIES
TOPIC: Status of Forces
CONCEPTS: Definition of terms. Use of facilities. Indemnities and reimbursements. Military assistance. Status of military forces.
INTL ORGS: North Atlantic Treaty Organization.
TREATY REF: 199UNTS67.
PROCEDURE: Termination.

PARTIES:
Germany, West
USA (United States)

108408 Bilateral Exchange **579 UNTS 203**
SIGNED: 22 Dec 66 FORCE: 22 Dec 65
REGISTERED: 21 Nov 66 USA (United States)
ARTICLES: 2 LANGUAGE: English.
HEADNOTE: CONSTRUCTION MAINTANANCE MEMORIAL
TOPIC: Other Military
CONCEPTS: Annex or appendix reference. Establishment of war cemeteries.
PARTIES:
Philippines
USA (United States)

108409 Bilateral Agreement **579 UNTS 213**
SIGNED: 4 Feb 66 FORCE: 4 Feb 66
REGISTERED: 21 Nov 66 USA (United States)
ARTICLES: 6 LANGUAGE: English. French.
HEADNOTE: AGRI COMMOD TITLE I
TOPIC: US Agri Commod Aid
CONCEPTS: General provisions. Annex or appendix reference. General cooperation. Exchange of information and documents. Reexport of goods, etc.. Exchange rates and regulations. Transportation costs. Local currency. Commodities schedule. Purchase authorization.
PARTIES:
Guinea
USA (United States)

108410 Bilateral Exchange **579 UNTS 231**
SIGNED: 1 Sep 66 FORCE: 1 Oct 66
REGISTERED: 23 Nov 66 Malta
ARTICLES: 2 LANGUAGE: English.
HEADNOTE: FACILITATE TRAVEL
TOPIC: Visas
CONCEPTS: Territorial application. Time limit. Visa abolition. Denial of admission. Conformity with municipal law.
PROCEDURE: Denunciation.
PARTIES:
Malta
Portugal

108411 Bilateral Exchange **579 UNTS 237**
SIGNED: 6 Jun 66 FORCE: 6 Jul 66
REGISTERED: 23 Nov 66 Malta
ARTICLES: 2 LANGUAGE: English.
HEADNOTE: FACILITATE TRAVEL
TOPIC: Visas
CONCEPTS: Time limit. Visa abolition. Denial of admission. Conformity with municipal law.
PROCEDURE: Denunciation.
PARTIES:
Malta
Turkey

108412 Bilateral Exchange **579 UNTS 243**
SIGNED: 17 Nov 64 FORCE: 1 Jun 66
REGISTERED: 28 Nov 66 Netherlands
ARTICLES: 2 LANGUAGE: English.
HEADNOTE: HEALTH CENTER
TOPIC: Sanitation
CONCEPTS: Detailed regulations. Inspection and observation. Recognition and enforcement of legal decisions. Personnel. Public health. WHO used as agency. Aid missions.
INTL ORGS: World Health Organization.
TREATY REF: 175UNTS215.
PROCEDURE: Duration. Ratification. Renewal or Revival. Termination.
PARTIES:
Netherlands
Norway

108413 Bilateral Agreement **579 UNTS 251**
SIGNED: 21 Sep 65 FORCE: 21 Sep 65
REGISTERED: 28 Nov 66 Eur Space Research
ARTICLES: 5 LANGUAGE: English. French.
HEADNOTE: TELEMETRY STATION
TOPIC: IGO Operations
CONCEPTS: Non-visa travel documents. General technical assistance. Headquarters and facilities.
TREATY REF: 528UNTS33.

PARTIES:
Norway
Eur Space Research

108414 Bilateral Agreement **580 UNTS 3**
SIGNED: 31 Jan 66 FORCE: 31 Jan 66
REGISTERED: 28 Nov 66 Eur Space Research
ARTICLES: 6 LANGUAGE: English. French.
HEADNOTE: LAUNCHING SOUNDING ROCKETS
TOPIC: Specific Property
CONCEPTS: Exchange of information and documents. Negotiation. Research cooperation. Tax exemptions. Customs exemptions. Facilities and property.
TREATY REF: 348UNTS177.
PARTIES:
Norway
Eur Space Research

108415 Bilateral Exchange **580 UNTS 9**
SIGNED: 18 Jun 66 FORCE: 20 Jun 66
REGISTERED: 30 Nov 66 Norway
ARTICLES: 2 LANGUAGE: English.
HEADNOTE: DOUBLE TAXATION AIR MARITIME NAVIGATION
TOPIC: Taxation
CONCEPTS: Definition of terms. Taxation. Air transport. Merchant vessels.
PARTIES:
Fed Rhod/Nyasaland
Norway

108416 Bilateral Exchange **580 UNTS 17**
SIGNED: 17 Nov 66 FORCE: 17 Nov 66
REGISTERED: 1 Dec 66 United Nations
ARTICLES: 2 LANGUAGE: English.
HEADNOTE: ASSUMPTION SPECIAL FUND PROJECT RIGHTS & OBLIGATIONS
TOPIC: Recognition
CONCEPTS: Continuity of rights and obligations. General aid.
PARTIES:
Lesotho
UN Special Fund

108417 Multilateral Exchange **580 UNTS 22**
SIGNED: 17 Nov 66 FORCE: 17 Nov 66
REGISTERED: 1 Dec 66 United Nations
ARTICLES: 2 LANGUAGE: English.
HEADNOTE: PARTIES MUTUALLY BOUND BY REVISED TREATY
TOPIC: IGO Operations
CONCEPTS: Previous treaty extension. General technical assistance.
TREATY REF: 366UNTS310.
PARTIES:
Lesotho SIGNED: 17 Nov 66 FORCE: 17 Nov 66
FAO (Food Agri) SIGNED: 17 Nov 66 FORCE: 17 Nov 66
IAEA (Atom Energy) SIGNED: 17 Nov 66 FORCE: 17 Nov 66
ICAO (Civil Aviat) SIGNED: 17 Nov 66 FORCE: 17 Nov 66
ILO (Labor Org) SIGNED: 17 Nov 66 FORCE: 17 Nov 66
UNESCO (Educ/Cult) SIGNED: 17 Nov 66 FORCE: 17 Nov 66
United Nations SIGNED: 17 Nov 66 FORCE: 17 Nov 66
UPU (Postal Union) SIGNED: 17 Nov 66 FORCE: 17 Nov 66
WHO (World Health) SIGNED: 17 Nov 66 FORCE: 17 Nov 66
WMO (Meteorology) SIGNED: 17 Nov 66 FORCE: 17 Nov 66

108418 Bilateral Exchange **580 UNTS 29**
SIGNED: 17 Nov 66 FORCE: 17 Nov 66
REGISTERED: 1 Dec 66 United Nations
ARTICLES: 2 LANGUAGE: English.
HEADNOTE: APPLICATION UN-BRITISH AGREEMENT EXECUTIVE ADMINISTRATIVE PERSONNEL
TOPIC: IGO Operations
CONCEPTS: Previous treaty extension. General cooperation.
INTL ORGS: United Nations Special Fund.
TREATY REF: 469UNTS145.

PARTIES:
Lesotho
United Nations

108419   Bilateral Exchange   **580 UNTS 35**
SIGNED: 19 Nov 65   FORCE: 19 Nov 65
REGISTERED: 1 Dec 66 USA (United States)
ARTICLES: 2 LANGUAGE: English. Arabic.
HEADNOTE: CONSTRUCTION WATER DESALT-
ING ELECTRIC POWER PLANT
TOPIC: Non-IBRD Project
CONCEPTS: Accounting procedures. Financial
programs. Claims and settlements. General.
Laws and formalities. Customs exemptions. Ma-
terials, equipment and services. Credit provi-
sions. Non-bank projects. Natural resources.
PROCEDURE: Termination.
PARTIES:
Saudi Arabia
USA (United States)

108420   Bilateral Exchange   **580 UNTS 181**
SIGNED: 9 Aug 65   FORCE: 9 Aug 65
REGISTERED: 1 Dec 66 USA (United States)
ARTICLES: 2 LANGUAGE: English.
HEADNOTE: PEACE CORPS
TOPIC: General Aid
CONCEPTS: General. Assistance.
PROCEDURE: Termination.
PARTIES:
UK Great Britain
USA (United States)

108421   Bilateral Exchange   **580 UNTS 189**
SIGNED: 15 Aug 62   FORCE: 15 Aug 62
REGISTERED: 1 Dec 66 USA (United States)
ARTICLES: 2 LANGUAGE: English.
HEADNOTE: PEACE CORPS
TOPIC: General Aid
CONCEPTS: General. Assistance.
PROCEDURE: Termination.
PARTIES:
UK Great Britain
USA (United States)

108422   Bilateral Exchange   **580 UNTS 197**
SIGNED: 10 Nov 65   FORCE: 10 Nov 65
REGISTERED: 1 Dec 66 USA (United States)
ARTICLES: 2 LANGUAGE: English.
HEADNOTE: PEACE CORPS
TOPIC: General Aid
CONCEPTS: General. Assistance.
PROCEDURE: Termination.
PARTIES:
UK Great Britain
USA (United States)

108423   Unilateral Instrument   **580 UNTS 205**
SIGNED: 29 Nov 66   FORCE: 29 Nov 66
REGISTERED: 6 Dec 66 United Nations
ARTICLES: 1 LANGUAGE: English.
HEADNOTE: COMPULSORY ICJ
TOPIC: ICJ Option Clause
CONCEPTS: Exceptions and exemptions. Compul-
sory jurisdiction.
INTL ORGS: United Nations.
PROCEDURE: Amendment. Termination.
PARTIES:
Malta

108424   Bilateral Agreement   **580 UNTS 211**
SIGNED: 6 Dec 66   FORCE: 6 Dec 66
REGISTERED: 6 Dec 66 United Nations
ARTICLES: 6 LANGUAGE: English.
HEADNOTE: UN SEMINAR
TOPIC: IGO Operations
CONCEPTS: Privileges and immunities. Procedure.
Headquarters and facilities. Conferences.
PARTIES:
Jamaica
United Nations

108425   Bilateral Exchange   **580 UNTS 221**
SIGNED: 25 Mar 66   FORCE: 25 Mar 66
REGISTERED: 6 Dec 66 USA (United States)
ARTICLES: 2 LANGUAGE: English.
HEADNOTE: INVESTMENT GUARANTIES

TOPIC: Finance
CONCEPTS: Currency. Private investment guaran-
tee.
TREATY REF: U.S.-MALAYA AGREEMENT 1959.
PROCEDURE: Denunciation.
PARTIES:
Singapore
USA (United States)

108426   Bilateral Exchange   **580 UNTS 231**
SIGNED: 21 Apr 66   FORCE: 21 Apr 66
REGISTERED: 6 Dec 66 USA (United States)
ARTICLES: 2 LANGUAGE: Spanish. English.
HEADNOTE: LOAN NAVAL VESSEL
TOPIC: Milit Assistance
CONCEPTS: Treaty implementation. Conformity
with municipal law. Indemnities and reimburse-
ments. Lease of military property. Naval vessels.
Return of equipment and recapture.
PARTIES:
Spain
USA (United States)

108427   Bilateral Agreement   **580 UNTS 239**
SIGNED: 11 Apr 66   FORCE: 11 Apr 66
REGISTERED: 6 Dec 66 USA (United States)
ARTICLES: 5 LANGUAGE: English.
HEADNOTE: AGRI COMMOD TITLE IV
TOPIC: US Agri Commod Aid
CONCEPTS: General provisions. Annex or appen-
dix reference. General cooperation. Exchange of
information and documents. Reexport of goods,
etc.. Exchange rates and regulations. Transporta-
tion costs. Local currency. Commodities sched-
ule. Purchase authorization.
PARTIES:
USA (United States)
Yugoslavia

108428   Bilateral Agreement   **580 UNTS 253**
SIGNED: 1 Jun 66   FORCE: 1 Jun 66
REGISTERED: 6 Dec 66 USA (United States)
ARTICLES: 8 LANGUAGE: English.
HEADNOTE: USE US GOVERNMENT-OWNED BUR-
MESE KYATS
TOPIC: Loans and Credits
CONCEPTS: Education. Interest rates. Payment
schedules. Local currency. Loan and credit. Fa-
cilities and property.
TREATY REF: 268UNTS__17N.
PARTIES:
Burma
USA (United States)

108429   Bilateral Exchange   **580 UNTS 263**
SIGNED: 9 Jun 66   FORCE: 9 Jun 66
REGISTERED: 6 Dec 66 USA (United States)
ARTICLES: 22 LANGUAGE: English.
HEADNOTE: CONSTRUCTION SEWAGE DIS-
POSAL SYSTEM
TOPIC: Non-IBRD Project
CONCEPTS: Financial programs. Non-bank
projects.
PARTIES:
Canada
USA (United States)

108430   Bilateral Agreement   **581 UNTS 3**
SIGNED: 14 Jun 66   FORCE: 12 Aug 66
REGISTERED: 6 Dec 66 IBRD (World Bank)
ARTICLES: 5 LANGUAGE: English.
HEADNOTE: GUARANTEE POWER
TOPIC: IBRD Project
CONCEPTS: Definition of terms. Annex or appen-
dix reference. Exchange of information and doc-
uments. Inspection and observation. Bonds.
Fees and exemptions. Tax exemptions. Domestic
obligation. Terms of loan. Loan regulations. Loan
guarantee. Guarantor non-interference. Hydro-
electric power.
TREATY REF: 400UNTS212.
PARTIES:
Portugal
IBRD (World Bank)

108431   Bilateral Agreement   **581 UNTS 29**
SIGNED: 14 Jun 66   FORCE: 31 Aug 66
REGISTERED: 6 Dec 66 IBRD (World Bank)

ARTICLES: 5 LANGUAGE: English.
HEADNOTE: GUARANTEE POWER
TOPIC: IBRD Project
CONCEPTS: Definition of terms. Annex or appen-
dix reference. Exchange of information and doc-
uments. Inspection and observation. Bonds.
Fees and exemptions. Tax exemptions. Domestic
obligation. Terms of loan. Loan regulations. Loan
guarantee. Guarantor non-interference. Hydro-
electric power.
PARTIES:
Portugal
IBRD (World Bank)

108432   Multilateral Convention   **581 UNTS 57**
SIGNED: 9 Mar 64   FORCE: 11 Sep 64
REGISTERED: 6 Dec 66 UK Great Britain
ARTICLES: 15 LANGUAGE: English. French.
HEADNOTE: FISHERIES
TOPIC: Specific Resources
CONCEPTS: Annex or appendix reference. Arbitra-
tion. Markers and definitions. Ocean resources.
Fisheries and fishing. Regulation of natural re-
sources.
TREATY REF: GENEVA CONVENTION ON THE TER-
RITORIAL SEA.
PROCEDURE: Amendment. Accession. Denuncia-
tion. Duration. Ratification.
PARTIES:
Austria SIGNED: 9 Mar 64
Belgium SIGNED: 1 Apr 64 RATIFIED: 10 Feb 66
Denmark   SIGNED: 31 Mar 64   RATIFIED:
9 Oct 64
France SIGNED: 9 Apr 64 RATIFIED: 5 Jul 65
Germany, West SIGNED: 10 Apr 64
Ireland   SIGNED: 18 Mar 64   RATIFIED:
20 Sep 65 FORCE: 1 Oct 65
Italy SIGNED: 10 Apr 64
Luxembourg SIGNED: 10 Apr 64
Netherlands SIGNED: 7 Apr 64
Portugal SIGNED: 7 Apr 64
Spain SIGNED: 8 Apr 64 RATIFIED: 15 Sep 65
Sweden SIGNED: 8 Apr 64 RATIFIED: 16 Feb 66
UK Great Britain SIGNED: 9 Mar 64 RATIFIED:
11 Sep 64 FORCE: 11 Sep 64

108433   Multilateral Agreement   **581 UNTS 83**
SIGNED: 9 Mar 64   FORCE: 18 Mar 64
REGISTERED: 6 Dec 66 UK Great Britain
ARTICLES: 3 LANGUAGE: English. French.
HEADNOTE: TRANSITIONAL RIGHTS
TOPIC: Specific Resources
CONCEPTS: Annex type material. Fisheries and
fishing.
PROCEDURE: Registration.
PARTIES:
Belgium SIGNED: 1 Apr 64 FORCE: 1 Apr 64
France SIGNED: 10 Apr 64 FORCE: 10 Apr 64
Germany, West SIGNED: 9 Apr 64 FORCE:
9 Apr 64
Ireland SIGNED: 18 Mar 64 FORCE: 18 Mar 64
Netherlands SIGNED: 7 Apr 64 FORCE: 7 Apr 64
UK Great Britain SIGNED: 9 Mar 64 FORCE:
9 Mar 64

108434   Multilateral Agreement   **581 UNTS 89**
SIGNED: 9 Mar 64   FORCE: 18 Mar 64
REGISTERED: 6 Dec 66 UK Great Britain
ARTICLES: 3 LANGUAGE: English. French.
HEADNOTE: TRANSITIONAL RIGHTS
TOPIC: Specific Resources
CONCEPTS: Annex type material. Fisheries and
fishing.
PROCEDURE: Registration.
PARTIES:
Belgium SIGNED: 1 Apr 64 FORCE: 1 Apr 64
France SIGNED: 10 Apr 64 FORCE: 10 Apr 64
Germany, West SIGNED: 9 Apr 64 FORCE:
9 Apr 64
Ireland SIGNED: 18 Mar 64 FORCE: 18 Mar 64
Netherlands SIGNED: 7 Apr 64 FORCE: 7 Apr 64
Spain SIGNED: 8 Apr 64 FORCE: 8 Apr 64
UK Great Britain SIGNED: 9 Mar 64 FORCE:
18 Mar 64

108435   Bilateral Agreement   **581 UNTS 95**
SIGNED: 8 Jul 66   FORCE: 8 Jul 66
REGISTERED: 7 Dec 66 Denmark
ARTICLES: 15 LANGUAGE: English. Portuguese.
HEADNOTE: LOAN

TOPIC: Loans and Credits
CONCEPTS: Conformity with municipal law. Dispute settlement. Accounting procedures. Currency. Interest rates. Payment schedules. Debt settlement. Tax exemptions. Loan and credit. Credit provisions. Purchase authorization. Loan repayment. Terms of loan. Plans and standards.
INTL ORGS: International Court of Justice. Arbitration Commission.
PROCEDURE: Duration. Termination.
PARTIES:
Brazil
Denmark

108436 Bilateral Agreement **581 UNTS 125**
SIGNED: 23 Nov 66   FORCE: 23 Nov 66
REGISTERED: 8 Dec 66 Thailand
ARTICLES: 6 LANGUAGE: English.
HEADNOTE: TRADE
TOPIC: General Trade
CONCEPTS: Establishment of trade relations.
PROCEDURE: Termination.
PARTIES:
Taiwan
Thailand

108437 Unilateral Instrument **581 UNTS 131**
SIGNED: 30 Nov 66   FORCE: 30 Nov 66
REGISTERED: 9 Dec 66 United Nations
ARTICLES: 1 LANGUAGE: English.
HEADNOTE: ACCEPT OBLIGATIONS UN CHARTER
TOPIC: UN Charter
CONCEPTS: Acceptance of UN obligations.
PARTIES:
United Arab Rep

108438 Bilateral Instrument **581 UNTS 135**
SIGNED: 22 Nov 66
REGISTERED: 9 Dec 66 United Nations
ARTICLES: 1 LANGUAGE: English.
HEADNOTE: ACCEPTING COMPULSORY ICJ
TOPIC: ICJ Option Clause
CONCEPTS: Exceptions and exemptions. Compulsory jurisdiction.
PROCEDURE: Amendment. Termination.
PARTIES:
Malawi

108439 Bilateral Agreement **581 UNTS 141**
SIGNED: 9 Jun 65   FORCE: 2 Dec 66
REGISTERED: 13 Dec 66 Denmark
ARTICLES: 13 LANGUAGE: Danish. German.
HEADNOTE: NAVIGATION WATERWAYS
TOPIC: Water Transport
CONCEPTS: Inland and territorial waters.
PARTIES:
Denmark
Germany, West

108440 Bilateral Exchange **581 UNTS 167**
SIGNED: 12 Sep 66   FORCE: 12 Sep 66
REGISTERED: 14 Dec 66 Israel
ARTICLES: 2 LANGUAGE: English.
HEADNOTE: AMATEUR RADIO
TOPIC: Telecommunications
CONCEPTS: Amateur radio.
PARTIES:
Canada
Israel

108441 Bilateral Agreement **581 UNTS 173**
SIGNED: 15 Jan 65   FORCE: 25 Oct 65
REGISTERED: 14 Dec 66 Israel
ARTICLES: 6 LANGUAGE: Spanish.
HEADNOTE: TECHNICAL COOPERATION
TOPIC: Tech Assistance
CONCEPTS: General technical assistance. Assistance.
PROCEDURE: Denunciation. Duration.
PARTIES:
Colombia
Israel

108442 Bilateral Exchange **581 UNTS 181**
SIGNED: 12 Jul 66   FORCE: 10 Oct 66
REGISTERED: 14 Dec 66 Israel
ARTICLES: 2 LANGUAGE: Spanish.

HEADNOTE: ABOLITION VISAS
TOPIC: Visas
CONCEPTS: Visa abolition.
PROCEDURE: Denunciation.
PARTIES:
Colombia
Israel

108443 Bilateral Exchange **581 UNTS 187**
SIGNED: 23 Feb 66   FORCE: 1 Apr 66
REGISTERED: 14 Dec 66 Israel
ARTICLES: 2 LANGUAGE: English.
HEADNOTE: ABOLITION VISAS
TOPIC: Visas
CONCEPTS: Visa abolition.
PARTIES:
Denmark
Israel

108444 Bilateral Exchange **581 UNTS 195**
SIGNED: 23 Feb 66   FORCE: 1 Apr 66
REGISTERED: 14 Dec 66 Israel
ARTICLES: 2 LANGUAGE: English.
HEADNOTE: ABOLITION VISAS
TOPIC: Visas
CONCEPTS: Visa abolition.
PROCEDURE: Termination.
PARTIES:
Israel
Sweden

108445 Bilateral Exchange **581 UNTS 203**
SIGNED: 23 Feb 66   FORCE: 1 Apr 66
REGISTERED: 14 Dec 66 Israel
ARTICLES: 2 LANGUAGE: English.
HEADNOTE: ABOLITION VISAS
TOPIC: Visas
CONCEPTS: Visa abolition.
PROCEDURE: Termination.
PARTIES:
Israel
Norway

108446 Bilateral Exchange **581 UNTS 211**
SIGNED: 23 Feb 66   FORCE: 1 Apr 66
REGISTERED: 14 Dec 66 Israel
ARTICLES: 2 LANGUAGE: English.
HEADNOTE: ABOLITION VISAS
TOPIC: Visas
CONCEPTS: Visa abolition.
PROCEDURE: Termination.
PARTIES:
Iceland
Israel

108447 Bilateral Exchange **581 UNTS 219**
SIGNED: 23 Feb 66   FORCE: 1 Apr 66
REGISTERED: 14 Dec 66 Israel
ARTICLES: 2 LANGUAGE: English.
HEADNOTE: ABOLITION VISAS
TOPIC: Visas
CONCEPTS: Visa abolition.
PROCEDURE: Termination.
PARTIES:
Finland
Israel

108448 Bilateral Convention **581 UNTS 227**
SIGNED: 27 Jun 66   FORCE: 31 Oct 66
REGISTERED: 14 Dec 66 Israel
ARTICLES: 32 LANGUAGE: English.
HEADNOTE: DOUBLE TAXATION FISCAL EVASION TAXES INCOME CAPITAL
TOPIC: Taxation
CONCEPTS: Definition of terms. Territorial application. Privileges and immunities. Nationality and citizenship. Conformity with municipal law. Exchange of official publications. Negotiation. Teacher and student exchange. Taxation. Tax credits. Equitable taxes. Tax exemptions. Air transport. Merchant vessels.
PROCEDURE: Denunciation. Duration. Ratification. Termination.
PARTIES:
Denmark
Israel

108449 Bilateral Agreement **581 UNTS 265**
SIGNED: 20 Jun 66   FORCE: 17 Sep 66
REGISTERED: 14 Dec 66 Israel
ARTICLES: 1 LANGUAGE: Hebrew. Spanish.
HEADNOTE: ABOLITION VISAS
TOPIC: Visas
CONCEPTS: Visa abolition.
PROCEDURE: Termination.
PARTIES:
Ecuador
Israel

108450 Bilateral Convention **581 UNTS 275**
SIGNED: 21 Jan 65   FORCE: 23 Feb 66
REGISTERED: 14 Dec 66 Israel
ARTICLES: 30 LANGUAGE: English.
HEADNOTE: DOUBLE TAXATION FISCAL EVASION TAXES INCOME CAPITAL
TOPIC: Taxation
CONCEPTS: Definition of terms. Privileges and immunities. Nationality and citizenship. Conformity with municipal law. Exchange of official publications. Negotiation. Teacher and student exchange. Taxation. Equitable taxes. Tax exemptions. Air transport. Merchant vessels. Armistice and peace.
PROCEDURE: Denunciation. Duration. Ratification. Termination.
PARTIES:
Finland
Israel

108451 Bilateral Convention **581 UNTS 311**
SIGNED: 17 Dec 65   FORCE: 1 Oct 66
REGISTERED: 14 Dec 66 Israel
ARTICLES: 29 LANGUAGE: Hebrew. French.
HEADNOTE: SOCIAL SECURITY
TOPIC: Non-ILO Labor
CONCEPTS: Definition of terms. Territorial application. General provisions. General cooperation. Old age insurance. Sickness and invalidity insurance. Social security. Fees and exemptions. Payment schedules.
PROCEDURE: Denunciation. Duration. Ratification.
PARTIES:
France
Israel

108452 Bilateral Protocol **582 UNTS 3**
SIGNED: 17 Dec 65   FORCE: 1 Oct 66
REGISTERED: 14 Dec 66 Israel
ARTICLES: 4 LANGUAGE: Hebrew. French.
HEADNOTE: SOCIAL INSURANCE ARRANGEMENTS STUDENTS
TOPIC: Non-ILO Labor
CONCEPTS: General cooperation. Social security.
PROCEDURE: Denunciation. Duration.
PARTIES:
France
Israel

108453 Bilateral Exchange **582 UNTS 11**
SIGNED: 11 Jul 66   FORCE: 1 Aug 66
REGISTERED: 14 Dec 66 Israel
ARTICLES: 2 LANGUAGE: English.
HEADNOTE: ABOLITION VISAS
TOPIC: Visas
CONCEPTS: Emergencies. Visa abolition. Resident permits.
PROCEDURE: Denunciation.
PARTIES:
Gambia
Israel

108454 Bilateral Exchange **582 UNTS 17**
SIGNED: 12 Sep 66   FORCE: 12 Sep 66
REGISTERED: 14 Dec 66 Israel
ARTICLES: 2 LANGUAGE: English.
HEADNOTE: EXCHANGE OFFICIAL PRINTED MATTER
TOPIC: Education
CONCEPTS: Definition of terms. Exchange of official publications. Accounting procedures.
PROCEDURE: Termination.
PARTIES:
Germany, West
Israel

108455 Bilateral Agreement **582 UNTS 23**
SIGNED: 25 Feb 66   FORCE: 25 Feb 66
REGISTERED: 14 Dec 66 Israel
ARTICLES: 17 LANGUAGE: English. Hebrew.
HEADNOTE: TECHNICAL SCIENTIFIC COOPER-
ATION
TOPIC: Tech Assistance
CONCEPTS: Change of circumstances. Privileges
and immunities. General cooperation. Person-
nel. Vocational training. Research and scientific
projects. Research and development. Expense
sharing formulae. National treatment. Tax ex-
emptions. Customs exemptions. Domestic obli-
gation. General technical assistance.
PROCEDURE: Amendment. Duration. Renewal or
Revival. Termination.
PARTIES:
  Israel
  Kenya

108456 Bilateral Exchange **582 UNTS 53**
SIGNED: 3 Aug 66   FORCE: 1 Nov 66
REGISTERED: 14 Dec 66 Israel
ARTICLES: 2 LANGUAGE: English.
HEADNOTE: ABOLITION VISAS
TOPIC: Visas
CONCEPTS: Visa abolition. Resident permits.
PROCEDURE: Denunciation. Termination.
PARTIES:
  Israel
  Malawi

108457 Multilateral Agreement **582 UNTS 59**
SIGNED: 2 Aug 66   FORCE: 2 Aug 66
REGISTERED: 14 Dec 66 Israel
ARTICLES: 6 LANGUAGE: English.
HEADNOTE: COOPERATION RURAL DEVELOP-
MENT
TOPIC: Tech Assistance
CONCEPTS: Specialists exchange. Agriculture.
PARTIES:
  Inter-Am Devel Bnk SIGNED: 2 Aug 66 FORCE:
    2 Aug 66
  Israel SIGNED: 2 Aug 66 FORCE: 2 Aug 66
  OAS (Am States) SIGNED: 2 Aug 66 FORCE:
    2 Aug 66

108458 Bilateral Exchange **582 UNTS 65**
SIGNED: 21 Nov 65   FORCE: 19 Feb 66
REGISTERED: 14 Dec 66 Israel
ARTICLES: 2 LANGUAGE: Spanish.
HEADNOTE: ABOLITION VISAS
TOPIC: Visas
CONCEPTS: Emergencies. Time limit. Visa aboli-
tion. Denial of admission. Conformity with mu-
nicipal law.
PROCEDURE: Denunciation.
PARTIES:
  Israel
  Paraguay

108459 Bilateral Exchange **582 UNTS 73**
SIGNED: 3 Apr 66   FORCE: 2 Jul 66
REGISTERED: 14 Dec 66 Israel
ARTICLES: 2 LANGUAGE: Spanish.
HEADNOTE: ABOLITION VISAS
TOPIC: Visas
CONCEPTS: Exceptions and exemptions. Time
limit. Visa abolition.
PROCEDURE: Denunciation.
PARTIES:
  Israel
  Uruguay

108460 Bilateral Agreement **582 UNTS 79**
SIGNED: 25 Aug 66   FORCE: 7 Nov 66
REGISTERED: 14 Dec 66 IBRD (World Bank)
ARTICLES: 8 LANGUAGE: English.
HEADNOTE: GUARANTEE AGREEMENT
TOPIC: IBRD Project
CONCEPTS: Definition of terms. Annex or appen-
dix reference. Exchange of information and doc-
uments. Inspection and observation. Bonds.
Fees and exemptions. Tax exemptions. Domestic
obligation. Terms of loan. Loan regulations. Loan
guarantee. Guarantor non-interference.
PARTIES:
  Honduras
  IBRD (World Bank)

108461 Bilateral Agreement **582 UNTS 107**
SIGNED: 26 Jul 66   FORCE: 30 Aug 66
REGISTERED: 14 Dec 66 IBRD (World Bank)
ARTICLES: 5 LANGUAGE: English.
HEADNOTE: GUARANTEE AGREEMENT
TOPIC: IBRD Project
CONCEPTS: Definition of terms. Annex or appen-
dix reference. Exchange of information and doc-
uments. Inspection and observation. Bonds.
Fees and exemptions. Tax exemptions. Domestic
obligation. Terms of loan. Loan regulations. Loan
guarantee. Guarantor non-interference.
PARTIES:
  Iran
  IBRD (World Bank)

108462 Bilateral Agreement **582 UNTS 145**
SIGNED: 20 Jun 66   FORCE: 9 Aug 66
REGISTERED: 14 Dec 66 IBRD (World Bank)
ARTICLES: 5 LANGUAGE: English.
HEADNOTE: GUARANTEE POWER
TOPIC: IBRD Project
CONCEPTS: Definition of terms. Annex or appen-
dix reference. Exchange of information and doc-
uments. Inspection and observation. Bonds.
Fees and exemptions. Tax exemptions. Domestic
obligation. Terms of loan. Loan regulations. Loan
guarantee. Guarantor non-interference. Hydro-
electric power.
PARTIES:
  Jamaica
  IBRD (World Bank)

108463 Bilateral Agreement **582 UNTS 179**
SIGNED: 30 Sep 66   FORCE: 25 Oct 66
REGISTERED: 14 Dec 66 IBRD (World Bank)
ARTICLES: 7 LANGUAGE: English.
HEADNOTE: LOAN EDUCATION
TOPIC: IBRD Project
CONCEPTS: Default remedies. Definition of terms.
Annex or appendix reference. Exchange of infor-
mation and documents. Informational records.
Inspection and observation. Exchange. Account-
ing procedures. Bonds. Fees and exemptions. In-
terest rates. Tax exemptions. Domestic obliga-
tion. Terms of loan. Loan regulations. Loan guar-
antee. Guarantor non-interference.
PARTIES:
  Jamaica
  IBRD (World Bank)

108464 Bilateral Agreement **582 UNTS 209**
SIGNED: 29 Jul 66   FORCE: 20 Aug 66
REGISTERED: 14 Dec 66 IBRD (World Bank)
ARTICLES: 2 LANGUAGE: English.
HEADNOTE: GUARANTEE EXPRESSWAY
TOPIC: IBRD Project
CONCEPTS: Annex or appendix reference. Loan
regulations. Roads and highways.
TREATY REF: 485UNTS283.
PARTIES:
  Japan
  IBRD (World Bank)

108465 Bilateral Agreement **582 UNTS 231**
SIGNED: 5 Oct 66   FORCE: 25 Oct 66
REGISTERED: 14 Dec 66 IBRD (World Bank)
ARTICLES: 5 LANGUAGE: English.
HEADNOTE: GUARANTEE POWER
TOPIC: IBRD Project
CONCEPTS: Definition of terms. Annex or appen-
dix reference. Exchange of information and doc-
uments. Inspection and observation. Bonds.
Fees and exemptions. Tax exemptions. Domestic
obligation. Terms of loan. Loan regulations. Loan
guarantee. Guarantor non-interference. Hydro-
electric power.
PARTIES:
  Nicaragua
  IBRD (World Bank)

108466 Bilateral Agreement **582 UNTS 259**
SIGNED: 24 Jun 66   FORCE: 23 Aug 66
REGISTERED: 14 Dec 66 IBRD (World Bank)
ARTICLES: 7 LANGUAGE: English.
HEADNOTE: LOAN HIGHWAY
TOPIC: IBRD Project
CONCEPTS: Default remedies. Definition of terms.
Annex or appendix reference. Self-determina-

tion. Exchange of information and documents.
Informational records. Accounting procedures.
Bonds. Fees and exemptions. Interest rates. Tax
exemptions. Domestic obligation. Terms of loan.
Loan regulations. Loan guarantee. Guarantor
non-interference. Roads and highways.
PARTIES:
  IBRD (World Bank)
  Thailand

108467 Bilateral Agreement **582 UNTS 277**
SIGNED: 29 Jun 66   FORCE: 3 Aug 66
REGISTERED: 14 Dec 66 IDA (Devel Assoc)
ARTICLES: 6 LANGUAGE: English.
HEADNOTE: DEVELOPMENT CREDIT RAILWAY
TOPIC: Non-IBRD Project
CONCEPTS: Definition of terms. Detailed regula-
tions. Previous treaty amendment. Exchange of
information and documents. Informational
records. Accounting procedures. Currency. In-
terest rates. Tax exemptions. Credit provisions.
Loan repayment. Terms of loan. Plans and stan-
dards. IDA development project. Railways.
TREATY REF: 154UNTS269; 323UNTS235;
535UNTS245; ETC..
PARTIES:
  India
  IDA (Devel Assoc)

108468 Bilateral Agreement **582 UNTS 297**
SIGNED: 17 Jun 66   FORCE: 28 Jul 66
REGISTERED: 14 Dec 66 IDA (Devel Assoc)
ARTICLES: 7 LANGUAGE: English.
HEADNOTE: DEVELOPMENT CREDIT EDUCATION
TOPIC: Non-IBRD Project
CONCEPTS: Definition of terms. Detailed regula-
tions. Previous treaty amendment. Exchange of
information and documents. Informational
records. Accounting procedures. Currency. In-
ternal finance. Interest rates. Tax exemptions.
Credit provisions. Loan repayment. Terms of
loan. Plans and standards. IDA development
project.
PARTIES:
  Pakistan
  IDA (Devel Assoc)

108469 Bilateral Agreement **582 UNTS 331**
SIGNED: 4 Apr 66   FORCE: 28 Jul 66
REGISTERED: 14 Dec 66 IDA (Devel Assoc)
ARTICLES: 7 LANGUAGE: English.
HEADNOTE: DEVELOPMENT CREDIT LIVESTOCK
TOPIC: Non-IBRD Project
CONCEPTS: Definition of terms. Detailed regula-
tions. Previous treaty amendment. Exchange of
information and documents. Informational
records. Accounting procedures. Currency. In-
terest rates. Tax exemptions. Agricultural com-
modities. Credit provisions. Loan repayment.
Terms of loan. Plans and standards. IDA develop-
ment project.
PARTIES:
  Paraguay
  IDA (Devel Assoc)

108470 Multilateral Agreement **583 UNTS 3**
SIGNED: 15 Jun 57   FORCE: 15 Dec 66
REGISTERED: 15 Dec 66 France
ARTICLES: 12 LANGUAGE: French.
HEADNOTE: TRADEMARKS
TOPIC: Patents/Copyrights
CONCEPTS: Fees and exemptions. Information
agency.
TREATY REF: 1UNTS269; 92LTS17.
PROCEDURE: Accession. Denunciation. Ratifica-
tion.
PARTIES:
  Austria SIGNED: 15 Jun 57
  Belgium SIGNED: 15 Jun 57 RATIFIED: 8 Mar 62
    FORCE: 15 Dec 66
  Czechoslovakia SIGNED: 15 Jun 57 RATIFIED:
    21 Oct 60 FORCE: 15 Dec 66
  France SIGNED: 15 Jun 57 RATIFIED: 9 Nov 59
    FORCE: 15 Dec 66
  Germany, East RATIFIED: 23 Sep 64 FORCE:
    15 Dec 66
  Germany, West SIGNED: 15 Jun 57 RATIFIED:
    8 Oct 64 FORCE: 15 Dec 66
  Hungary SIGNED: 15 Jun 57

Italy SIGNED: 15 Jun 57 RATIFIED: 25 Jun 60
  FORCE: 15 Dec 66
Liechtenstein SIGNED: 15 Jun 57
Luxembourg SIGNED: 15 Jun 57 RATIFIED:
  20 Jan 64 FORCE: 15 Dec 66
Monaco SIGNED: 15 Jun 57 RATIFIED: 8 Mar 61
  FORCE: 15 Dec 66
Morocco SIGNED: 15 Jun 57
Netherlands SIGNED: 15 Jun 57 RATIFIED:
  11 May 62 FORCE: 15 Dec 66
Portugal SIGNED: 15 Jun 57 RATIFIED:
  2 Mar 59 FORCE: 15 Dec 66
Romania RATIFIED: 9 Feb 59 FORCE: 15 Dec 66
Spain SIGNED: 15 Jun 57 RATIFIED: 13 Nov 58
  FORCE: 15 Dec 66
Switzerland SIGNED: 15 Jun 57 RATIFIED:
  2 Oct 62 FORCE: 15 Dec 66
United Arab Rep RATIFIED: 4 Aug 65 FORCE:
  15 Dec 66
Yugoslavia SIGNED: 15 Jun 57 RATIFIED:
  23 Sep 66 FORCE: 15 Dec 66

108471 Bilateral Treaty **583 UNTS 33**
SIGNED: 22 Jun 65 FORCE: 18 Dec 65
REGISTERED: 15 Dec 66 Japan
ARTICLES: 7 LANGUAGE: Japanese. Korean.
HEADNOTE: BASIC RELATIONS
TOPIC: General Amity
CONCEPTS: Diplomatic relations establishment.
  Diplomatic relations resumption. Establishment
  of trade relations. Acceptance of UN obligations.
TREATY REF: TREATY PEACE, SAN FRANCISCO
  SEPT. 8, 1951.
PROCEDURE: Ratification.
PARTIES:
  Japan
  Korea, South

108472 Bilateral Agreement **583 UNTS 51**
SIGNED: 22 Jun 65 FORCE: 18 Dec 65
REGISTERED: 15 Dec 66 Japan
ARTICLES: 10 LANGUAGE: Japanese. Korean.
HEADNOTE: FISHERIES
TOPIC: Specific Resources
CONCEPTS: Annex or appendix reference. Estab-
  lishment of commission. Arbitration. Markers
  and definitions. Ocean resources. Fisheries and
  fishing. Regulation of natural resources.
INTL ORGS: Arbitration Commission.
PROCEDURE: Duration. Ratification. Termination.
PARTIES:
  Japan
  Korea, South

108473 Bilateral Agreement **583 UNTS 173**
SIGNED: 22 Jun 65 FORCE: 18 Dec 65
REGISTERED: 15 Dec 66 Japan
ARTICLES: 4 LANGUAGE: Japanese. Korean.
HEADNOTE: CLAIM SETTLEMENT
TOPIC: Claims and Debts
CONCEPTS: Arbitration. Claims and settlements.
  Post-war claims settlement.
INTL ORGS: Arbitration Commission.
PROCEDURE: Ratification.
PARTIES:
  Japan
  Korea, South

108474 Bilateral Agreement **584 UNTS 3**
SIGNED: 22 Jun 65 FORCE: 17 Jan 66
REGISTERED: 15 Dec 66 Japan
ARTICLES: 4 LANGUAGE: Japanese. Korean.
HEADNOTE: LEGAL STATUS TREATMENT NA-
TIONALS ROK RESIDING JAPAN
TOPIC: Consul/Citizenship
CONCEPTS: Resident permits. Extradition, depor-
  tation and repatriation. Conformity with munici-
  pal law. General property. Domestic obligation.
PROCEDURE: Ratification.
PARTIES:
  Japan
  Korea, South

108475 Bilateral Agreement **584 UNTS 49**
SIGNED: 22 Jun 65 FORCE: 18 Dec 65
REGISTERED: 15 Dec 66 Japan
ARTICLES: 4 LANGUAGE: Japanese. Korean.
HEADNOTE: CULTURAL COOPERATION ART OB-
JECTS
TOPIC: Culture
CONCEPTS: Annex or appendix reference. Gen-
  eral cultural cooperation. Artists. Anthropology
  and archeology.
PROCEDURE: Ratification.
PARTIES:
  Japan
  Korea, South

108476 Bilateral Exchange **584 UNTS 147**
SIGNED: 22 Jun 65 FORCE: 18 Dec 65
REGISTERED: 15 Dec 66 Japan
ARTICLES: 2 LANGUAGE: Japanese. Korean.
HEADNOTE: SETTLEMENT DISPUTES
TOPIC: Dispute Settlement
CONCEPTS: Mediation and good offices. Proce-
  dure. Conciliation.
INTL ORGS: Arbitration Commission.
PARTIES:
  Japan
  Korea, South

108477 Bilateral Agreement **584 UNTS 155**
SIGNED: 16 May 66 FORCE: 11 Jul 66
REGISTERED: 20 Dec 66 IBRD (World Bank)
ARTICLES: 5 LANGUAGE: English. French.
HEADNOTE: GUARANTEE AGREEMENT
TOPIC: IBRD Project
CONCEPTS: Definition of terms. Annex or appen-
  dix reference. Exchange of information and doc-
  uments. Inspection and observation. Bonds.
  Fees and exemptions. Tax exemptions. Domestic
  obligation. Terms of loan. Loan regulations. Loan
  guarantee. Guarantor non-interference.
PARTIES:
  IBRD (World Bank)
  Tunisia

108478 Bilateral Agreement **584 UNTS 193**
SIGNED: 19 Aug 66 FORCE: 3 Oct 66
REGISTERED: 20 Dec 66 IDA (Devel Assoc)
ARTICLES: 6 LANGUAGE: English.
HEADNOTE: DEVELOPMENT CREDIT INDUSTRIAL
IMPORTS
TOPIC: Non-IBRD Project
CONCEPTS: Definition of terms. Detailed regula-
  tions. Previous treaty amendment. Exchange of
  information and documents. Informational
  records. Bonds. Currency. Interest rates. Tax ex-
  emptions. Credit provisions. Loan repayment.
  Terms of loan. Plans and standards. IDA develop-
  ment project. Industry.
PARTIES:
  India
  IDA (Devel Assoc)

108479 Bilateral Agreement **584 UNTS 215**
SIGNED: 4 Oct 66 FORCE: 4 Nov 66
REGISTERED: 20 Dec 66 IDA (Devel Assoc)
ARTICLES: 5 LANGUAGE: English.
HEADNOTE: DEVELOPMENT CREDIT HIGHWAY
TOPIC: Non-IBRD Project
CONCEPTS: Definition of terms. Detailed regula-
  tions. Previous treaty amendment. Exchange of
  information and documents. Informational
  records. Accounting procedures. Currency. In-
  terest rates. Tax exemptions. Credit provisions.
  Loan repayment. Terms of loan. Plans and stan-
  dards. IDA development project. Roads and high-
  ways.
PARTIES:
  Malawi
  IDA (Devel Assoc)

108480 Bilateral Agreement **584 UNTS 233**
SIGNED: 22 Jul 66 FORCE: 20 Sep 66
REGISTERED: 21 Dec 66 IBRD (World Bank)
ARTICLES: 7 LANGUAGE: English.
HEADNOTE: LOAN ROAD
TOPIC: IBRD Project
CONCEPTS: Default remedies. Definition of terms.
  Annex or appendix reference. Exchange of infor-
  mation and documents. Informational records.
  Inspection and observation. Accounting proce-
  dures. Bonds. Fees and exemptions. Interest
  rates. Tax exemptions. Domestic obligation.
  Terms of loan. Loan regulations. Loan guarantee.
  Guarantor non-interference. Roads and high-
  ways.

PARTIES:
  Iraq
  IBRD (World Bank)

108481 Bilateral Agreement **585 UNTS 3**
SIGNED: 7 Sep 66 FORCE: 22 Sep 66
REGISTERED: 21 Dec 66 IBRD (World Bank)
ARTICLES: 5 LANGUAGE: English.
HEADNOTE: GUARANTEE POWER DISTRIBUTION
TOPIC: IBRD Project
CONCEPTS: Definition of terms. Annex or appen-
  dix reference. Exchange of information and doc-
  uments. Inspection and observation. Bonds.
  Fees and exemptions. Tax exemptions. Domestic
  obligation. Terms of loan. Loan regulations. Loan
  guarantee. Guarantor non-interference. Hydro-
  electric power.
PARTIES:
  Peru
  IBRD (World Bank)

108482 Bilateral Agreement **585 UNTS 39**
SIGNED: 11 Aug 66 FORCE: 22 Sep 66
REGISTERED: 21 Dec 66 IBRD (World Bank)
ARTICLES: 5 LANGUAGE: English.
HEADNOTE: GUARANTEE PORT
TOPIC: IBRD Project
CONCEPTS: Definition of terms. Annex or appen-
  dix reference. Exchange of information and doc-
  uments. Inspection and observation. Bonds.
  Fees and exemptions. Tax exemptions. Domestic
  obligation. Terms of loan. Loan regulations. Loan
  guarantee. Guarantor non-interference. Water
  transport.
PARTIES:
  IBRD (World Bank)
  Singapore

108483 Bilateral Agreement **585 UNTS 71**
SIGNED: 8 Sep 66 FORCE: 27 Oct 66
REGISTERED: 21 Dec 66 IBRD (World Bank)
ARTICLES: 5 LANGUAGE: English.
HEADNOTE: GUARANTEE AGREEMENT
TOPIC: IBRD Project
CONCEPTS: Definition of terms. Annex or appen-
  dix reference. Exchange of information and doc-
  uments. Inspection and observation. Bonds.
  Fees and exemptions. Tax exemptions. Domestic
  obligation. Terms of loan. Loan regulations. Loan
  guarantee. Guarantor non-interference.
PARTIES:
  IBRD (World Bank)
  South Africa

108484 Bilateral Agreement **585 UNTS 101**
SIGNED: 29 Jun 66 FORCE: 31 Oct 66
REGISTERED: 21 Dec 66 IDA (Devel Assoc)
ARTICLES: 7 LANGUAGE: English.
HEADNOTE: DEVELOPMENT CREDIT BEAS EQUIP-
MENT
TOPIC: Non-IBRD Project
CONCEPTS: Definition of terms. Detailed regula-
  tions. Previous treaty amendment. Exchange of
  information and documents. Informational
  records. Accounting procedures. Currency. In-
  terest rates. Tax exemptions. Credit provisions.
  Loan repayment. Terms of loan. Plans and stan-
  dards. IDA development project.
PARTIES:
  India
  IDA (Devel Assoc)

108485 Bilateral Agreement **585 UNTS 119**
SIGNED: 19 Aug 66 FORCE: 3 Oct 66
REGISTERED: 21 Dec 66 IDA (Devel Assoc)
ARTICLES: 6 LANGUAGE: English.
HEADNOTE: DEVELOPMENT CREDIT EDUCATION
TOPIC: Non-IBRD Project
CONCEPTS: Detailed regulations. Previous treaty
  amendment. Exchange of information and docu-
  ments. Informational records. Education. Ac-
  counting procedures. Currency. Interest rates.
  Tax exemptions. Credit provisions. Loan repay-
  ment. Terms of loan. Plans and standards. IDA
  development project.
PARTIES:
  Kenya
  IDA (Devel Assoc)

108486 Bilateral Agreement **585 UNTS 137**
SIGNED: 22 Dec 66   FORCE: 22 Dec 66
REGISTERED: 22 Dec 66 United Nations
ARTICLES: 8 LANGUAGE: French.
HEADNOTE: UNICEF ACTIVITIES
TOPIC: IGO Operations
CONCEPTS: Privileges and immunities. Claims and
settlements. Extension of functions.
PROCEDURE: Termination.
PARTIES:
Guinea
UNICEF (Children)

108487 Bilateral Exchange **585 UNTS 147**
SIGNED: 28 Dec 66   FORCE: 28 Dec 66
REGISTERED: 28 Dec 66 United Nations
ARTICLES: 2 LANGUAGE: French.
HEADNOTE: SETTLEMENT CLAIMS
TOPIC: Claims and Debts
CONCEPTS: Claims and settlements.
PARTIES:
Luxembourg
United Nations

108488 Bilateral Agreement **585 UNTS 155**
SIGNED: 4 Nov 66   FORCE: 28 Nov 66
REGISTERED: 28 Dec 66 IBRD (World Bank)
ARTICLES: 5 LANGUAGE: English.
HEADNOTE: GUARANTEE POWER
TOPIC: IBRD Project
CONCEPTS: Definition of terms. Annex or appen-
dix reference. Exchange of information and doc-
uments. Inspection and observation. Bonds.
Fees and exemptions. Tax exemptions. Domestic
obligation. Terms of loan. Loan regulations. Loan
guarantee. Guarantor non-interference. Hydro-
electric power.
PARTIES:
IBRD (World Bank)
Singapore

108489 Bilateral Agreement **585 UNTS 181**
SIGNED: 4 Oct 66   FORCE: 23 Nov 66
REGISTERED: 28 Dec 66 IBRD (World Bank)
ARTICLES: 7 LANGUAGE: English.
HEADNOTE: LOAN HIGHWAY
TOPIC: IBRD Project
CONCEPTS: Default remedies. Definition of terms.
Annex or appendix reference. Exchange of infor-
mation and documents. Informational records.
Inspection and observation. Accounting proce-
dures. Bonds. Fees and exemptions. Interest
rates. Tax exemptions. Domestic obligation.
Terms of loan. Loan regulations. Loan guarantee.
Guarantor non-interference. Roads and high-
ways.
PARTIES:
IBRD (World Bank)
Zambia

108490 Bilateral Agreement **585 UNTS 199**
SIGNED: 10 Aug 66   FORCE: 10 Nov 66
REGISTERED: 28 Dec 66 IBRD (World Bank)
ARTICLES: 5 LANGUAGE: English.
HEADNOTE: GUARANTEE AGREEMENT
TOPIC: IBRD Project
CONCEPTS: Definition of terms. Annex or appen-
dix reference. Exchange of information and doc-
uments. Inspection and observation. Bonds.
Fees and exemptions. Tax exemptions. Domestic
obligation. Terms of loan. Loan regulations. Loan
guarantee. Guarantor non-interference.
PARTIES:
IBRD (World Bank)
Turkey

108491 Bilateral Agreement **585 UNTS 237**
SIGNED: 10 Aug 66   FORCE: 10 Nov 66
REGISTERED: 28 Dec 66 IDA (Devel Assoc)
ARTICLES: 8 LANGUAGE: English.
HEADNOTE: DEVELOPMENT CREDIT INDUSTRIAL
DEVELOPMENT BANK
TOPIC: Non-IBRD Project
CONCEPTS: Definition of terms. Detailed regula-
tions. Previous treaty amendment. Exchange of
information and documents. Informational
records. Accounting procedures. Currency. In-
terest rates. Tax exemptions. Credit provisions.

Loan repayment. Terms of loan. Plans and stan-
dards. IDA development project. Industry.
PARTIES:
IDA (Devel Assoc)
Turkey

108492 Bilateral Agreement **585 UNTS 271**
SIGNED: 2 Aug 66   FORCE: 11 Oct 66
REGISTERED: 28 Dec 66 IDA (Devel Assoc)
ARTICLES: 6 LANGUAGE: English.
HEADNOTE: DEVELOPMENT CREDIT ROAD
TOPIC: Non-IBRD Project
CONCEPTS: Detailed regulations. Previous treaty
amendment. Exchange of information and docu-
ments. Informational records. Accounting proce-
dures. Currency. Interest rates. Tax exemptions.
Credit provisions. Loan repayment. Terms of
loan. Plans and standards. IDA development
project. Roads and highways.
PARTIES:
IDA (Devel Assoc)
Siam

108493 Bilateral Agreement **586 UNTS 3**
SIGNED: 1 Sep 66   FORCE: 1 Sep 66
REGISTERED: 28 Dec 66 Denmark
ARTICLES: 15 LANGUAGE: English.
HEADNOTE: LOAN
TOPIC: Loans and Credits
CONCEPTS: Conformity with municipal law. Dis-
pute settlement. Accounting procedures. Cur-
rency. Interest rates. Payment schedules. Debt
settlement. Tax exemptions. Loan and credit.
Credit provisions. Purchase authorization. Loan
repayment. Terms of loan. Plans and standards.
INTL ORGS: International Court of Justice.
PROCEDURE: Duration. Termination.
PARTIES:
Denmark
Malawi

108494 Bilateral Exchange **586 UNTS 27**
SIGNED: 15 Feb 66   FORCE: 15 Feb 67
REGISTERED: 30 Dec 66 USA (United States)
ARTICLES: 3 LANGUAGE: English. Spanish.
HEADNOTE: SEA LEVEL CANAL SITE
TOPIC: Scientific Project
CONCEPTS: Consular functions in property. Gen-
eral cooperation. Personnel. General property.
Establishment of commission. Research and
scientific projects. Research and development.
Indemnities and reimbursements. Claims and
settlements. Special projects. Materials, equip-
ment and services.
PARTIES:
Panama
USA (United States)

108495 Bilateral Agreement **586 UNTS 39**
SIGNED: 13 Apr 66   FORCE: 13 Apr 66
REGISTERED: 30 Dec 66 USA (United States)
ARTICLES: 6 LANGUAGE: English.
HEADNOTE: AGRI COMMOD TITLE I
TOPIC: US Agri Commod Aid
CONCEPTS: General provisions. Annex or appen-
dix reference. General cooperation. Exchange of
information and documents. Reexport of goods,
etc.. Exchange rates and regulations. Transporta-
tion costs. Local currency. Commodities sched-
ule. Purchase authorization.
PARTIES:
Sudan
USA (United States)

108496 Bilateral Exchange **586 UNTS 57**
SIGNED: 4 Feb 60   FORCE: 4 Feb 66
REGISTERED: 30 Dec 66 USA (United States)
ARTICLES: 2 LANGUAGE: English. Spanish.
HEADNOTE: METEOROLOGICAL PROGRAM
TOPIC: Scientific Project
CONCEPTS: Annex type material. Previous treaty
extension. Research and scientific projects.
Meteorology.
TREATY REF: 524UNTS197.
PARTIES:
Mexico
USA (United States)

108497 Bilateral Exchange **586 UNTS 79**
SIGNED: 14 Apr 66   FORCE: 14 Apr 66
REGISTERED: 30 Dec 66 USA (United States)
ARTICLES: 2 LANGUAGE: English. Spanish.
HEADNOTE: SPACE RESEARCH PROJECTS
TOPIC: Scientific Project
CONCEPTS: Annex or appendix reference. Gen-
eral cooperation. Research and scientific
projects. Meteorology. Research and develop-
ment.
PARTIES:
Spain
USA (United States)

108498 Bilateral Exchange **586 UNTS 91**
SIGNED: 23 Feb 66   FORCE: 23 Feb 66
REGISTERED: 30 Dec 66 USA (United States)
ARTICLES: 2 LANGUAGE: English.
HEADNOTE: INVESTMENT GUARANTEES
TOPIC: Finance
CONCEPTS: Arbitration. Claims and settlements.
Private investment guarantee.
PARTIES:
Ceylon (Sri Lanka)
USA (United States)

108499 Bilateral Agreement **586 UNTS 101**
SIGNED: 29 Mar 65   FORCE: 16 Sep 66
REGISTERED: 30 Dec 66 IDA (Devel Assoc)
ARTICLES: 7 LANGUAGE: English.
HEADNOTE: DEVELOPMENT CREDIT ROAD
TOPIC: Non-IBRD Project
CONCEPTS: Detailed regulations. Previous treaty
amendment. Exchange of information and docu-
ments. Informational records. Accounting proce-
dures. Currency. Interest rates. Tax exemptions.
Credit provisions. Loan repayment. Terms of
loan. Plans and standards. IDA development
project. Roads and highways.
PARTIES:
IDA (Devel Assoc)
Somalia

108500 Multilateral Agreement **586 UNTS 123**
SIGNED: 29 Apr 65   FORCE: 16 Sep 66
REGISTERED: 30 Dec 66 IDA (Devel Assoc)
ARTICLES: 6 LANGUAGE: English.
HEADNOTE: ADMINISTRATION ROAD
TOPIC: Non-IBRD Project
CONCEPTS: Definition of terms. Exchange of infor-
mation and documents. Informational records.
Financial programs. Credit provisions. Terms of
loan. IDA development project. Roads and high-
ways.
PARTIES:
EEC (Econ Commnty) SIGNED: 29 Mar 65
FORCE: 16 Sep 66
IDA (Devel Assoc) SIGNED: 29 Mar 65 FORCE:
16 Sep 66
Somalia SIGNED: 29 Mar 65 FORCE: 16 Sep 66

108501 Bilateral Exchange **586 UNTS 143**
SIGNED: 16 Nov 64   FORCE: 16 Nov 64
REGISTERED: 30 Dec 66 USA (United States)
ARTICLES: 2 LANGUAGE: English.
HEADNOTE: PEACE CORPS
TOPIC: General Aid
CONCEPTS: Assistance. Volunteer programs.
PROCEDURE: Termination.
PARTIES:
Uganda
USA (United States)

108502 Bilateral Agreement **586 UNTS 151**
SIGNED: 17 Jan 66   FORCE: 17 Jun 66
REGISTERED: 30 Dec 66 USA (United States)
ARTICLES: 20 LANGUAGE: English. French.
HEADNOTE: AIR TRANSPORT
TOPIC: Air Transport
CONCEPTS: Air transport. Airport facilities. Airport
equipment. Airworthiness certificates. Condi-
tions of airlines operating permission. Over-
flights and technical stops. Operating authoriza-
tions and regulations. Licenses and certificates
of nationality.
INTL ORGS: International Civil Aviation Organiza-
tion.
PROCEDURE: Termination.

PARTIES:
Canada
USA (United States)

108503 Bilateral Exchange **586 UNTS 189**
SIGNED: 18 Apr 66　　　　FORCE: 18 Apr 66
REGISTERED: 30 Dec 66 USA (United States)
ARTICLES: 2 LANGUAGE: English. Spanish.
HEADNOTE: ALIEN AMATEUR RADIO OPERATORS
TOPIC: Gen Communications
CONCEPTS: Amateur radio.
PROCEDURE: Termination.
PARTIES:
Paraguay
USA (United States)

108504 Bilateral Agreement **586 UNTS 195**
SIGNED: 26 Jul 66　　　　FORCE: 30 Sep 66
REGISTERED: 30 Dec 66 IBRD (World Bank)
ARTICLES: 5 LANGUAGE: English.
HEADNOTE: GUARANTEE ELECTRICITY BOARD
TOPIC: IBRD Project
CONCEPTS: Definition of terms. Annex or appendix reference. Exchange of information and documents. Inspection and observation. Bonds. Fees and exemptions. Tax exemptions. Domestic obligation. Terms of loan. Loan regulations. Loan guarantee. Guarantor non-interference. Hydroelectric power.
PARTIES:
Malaysia
IBRD (World Bank)

108505 Bilateral Exchange **587 UNTS 3**
SIGNED: 11 Nov 66　　　　FORCE: 1 Jan 67
REGISTERED: 1 Jan 67 Philippines
ARTICLES: 2 LANGUAGE: English.
HEADNOTE: ABOLITION VISAS
TOPIC: Visas
CONCEPTS: Emergencies. Time limit. Visa abolition. Denial of admission. Conformity with municipal law.
PROCEDURE: Denunciation.
PARTIES:
Philippines
Sweden

108506 Multilateral Instrument **587 UNTS 9**
SIGNED: 26 Oct 63　　　　FORCE: 1 Feb 66
REGISTERED: 4 Jan 67 Niger
ARTICLES: 9 LANGUAGE: English. French.
HEADNOTE: NAVIGATION ECONOMIC COOPERATION
TOPIC: Water Transport
CONCEPTS: Arbitration. Procedure. Existing tribunals. Inland and territorial waters. Establishment.
INTL ORGS: International Court of Justice. Organization of African Unity. United Nations.
PROCEDURE: Ratification. Registration.
PARTIES:
Cameroon　SIGNED:　26 Oct 63　RATIFIED: 24 Dec 65 FORCE: 1 Feb 66
Chad SIGNED: 26 Oct 63 RATIFIED: 1 Feb 66 FORCE: 1 Feb 66
Dahomey　SIGNED:　26 Oct 63　RATIFIED: 11 Jan 66 FORCE: 1 Feb 66
Guinea SIGNED: 26 Oct 63 RATIFIED: 7 Dec 64 FORCE: 1 Feb 66
Ivory　Coast　SIGNED:　26 Oct 63　RATIFIED: 21 Sep 65 FORCE: 1 Feb 66
Mali SIGNED: 26 Oct 63 RATIFIED: 6 Nov 64 FORCE: 1 Feb 66
Nigeria SIGNED: 26 Oct 63 RATIFIED: 7 Apr 65 FORCE: 1 Feb 66
Niger SIGNED: 26 Oct 63 RATIFIED: 26 Dec 63 FORCE: 1 Feb 66
Upper Volta SIGNED: 26 Oct 63 RATIFIED: 20 Aug 65 FORCE: 1 Feb 66

108507 Multilateral Agreement **587 UNTS 19**
SIGNED: 25 Nov 64　　　　FORCE: 12 Apr 66
REGISTERED: 4 Jan 67 Niger
ARTICLES: 19 LANGUAGE: English. French.
HEADNOTE: NIGER RIVER COMMISSION NAVIGATION TRANSPORT RIVER NIGER
TOPIC: Water Transport
CONCEPTS: Detailed regulations. General cooperation. Exchange of information and documents. Personnel. Fees and exemptions. Funding proce-

dures. General. Customs duties. Navigational conditions. Canal improvement. Railways. Roads and highways. Establishment. Procedure. Headquarters and facilities. Special status. Conservation of specific resources.
INTL ORGS: Niger River Commission. Organization of African Unity. United Nations.
TREATY REF: 587UNTS9.
PROCEDURE: Amendment. Denunciation. Ratification. Registration.
PARTIES:
Cameroon　SIGNED:　25 Nov 64　RATIFIED: 24 Dec 65 FORCE: 12 Apr 66
Chad SIGNED: 25 Nov 64 RATIFIED: 1 Feb 66 FORCE: 12 Apr 66
Dahomey　SIGNED:　25 Nov 64　RATIFIED: 11 Jan 66 FORCE: 12 Apr 66
Guinea　SIGNED:　25 Nov 64　RATIFIED: 20 Dec 65 FORCE: 12 Apr 66
Ivory　Coast　SIGNED:　25 Nov 64　RATIFIED: 21 Sep 65 FORCE: 12 Apr 66
Mali SIGNED: 25 Nov 64 RATIFIED: 13 Oct 65 FORCE: 12 Apr 66
Nigeria SIGNED: 25 Nov 64 RATIFIED: 8 Jul 65 FORCE: 12 Apr 66
Niger SIGNED: 25 Nov 64 RATIFIED: 9 Feb 65 FORCE: 12 Apr 66
Upper Volta SIGNED: 25 Nov 64 RATIFIED: 12 Apr 66 FORCE: 12 Apr 66
ANNEX
636 UNTS 418. Multilateral. Correction 3 Jan 68.

108508 Bilateral Treaty **587 UNTS 35**
SIGNED: 2 Oct 65　　　　FORCE: 1 Dec 65
REGISTERED: 2 Oct 65 Hungary
ARTICLES: 6 LANGUAGE: Hungarian. Mongolian.
HEADNOTE: FRIENDSHIP COOPERATION
TOPIC: General Amity
CONCEPTS: Peaceful relations. General cooperation.
PROCEDURE: Ratification.
PARTIES:
Hungary
Mongolia

108509 Bilateral Exchange **587 UNTS 45**
SIGNED: 12 Jul 65　　　　FORCE: 1 Aug 65
REGISTERED: 9 Jan 67 Austria
ARTICLES: 2 LANGUAGE: German. Bulgarian.
HEADNOTE: ABOLITION VISAS
TOPIC: Visas
CONCEPTS: Visa abolition.
PARTIES:
Austria
Bulgaria

ANNEX
614 UNTS 337. Austria. Termination 21 May 67.
614 UNTS 337. Bulgaria. Termination 21 May 67.

108510 Bilateral Agreement **587 UNTS 51**
SIGNED: 12 Jul 65　　　　FORCE: 10 Sep 65
REGISTERED: 9 Jan 67 Austria
ARTICLES: 27 LANGUAGE: German. Bulgarian.
HEADNOTE: VETERINARY AGREEMENT
TOPIC: Sanitation
CONCEPTS: Definition of terms. Detailed regulations. Exceptions and exemptions. Annex or appendix reference. General cooperation. Exchange of information and documents. Informational records. Inspection and observation. Domestic legislation. Establishment of commission. Specialists exchange. Quarantine. Border control. Disease control. Veterinary. Trade procedures. Conferences.
PROCEDURE: Denunciation. Duration. Future Procedures Contemplated.
PARTIES:
Austria
Bulgaria

108511 Bilateral Treaty **587 UNTS 169**
SIGNED: 8 Apr 65　　　　FORCE: 20 Oct 66
REGISTERED: 9 Jan 67 Austria
ARTICLES: 40 LANGUAGE: German. Serbo-Croat.
HEADNOTE: CONCERNING COMMON STATE FRONTIER
TOPIC: Territory Boundary
CONCEPTS: Annex or appendix reference. Frontier permits. Inspection and observation. Operating agencies. Establishment of commission. Ar-

bitration. Tax exemptions. Customs exemptions. Materials, equipment and services. Road rules. Markers and definitions. Frontier waterways. Frontier crossing points.
INTL ORGS: Arbitration Commission.
TREATY REF: 217UNTS233; 125UNTS3.
PROCEDURE: Denunciation. Duration. Ratification.
PARTIES:
Hungary
Yugoslavia

108512 Bilateral Agreement **587 UNTS 239**
SIGNED: 19 Nov 65　　　　FORCE: 3 Apr 66
REGISTERED: 9 Jan 67 Austria
ARTICLES: 17 LANGUAGE: German. Serbo-Croat.
HEADNOTE: EMPLOYMENT REGULATIONS
TOPIC: Non-ILO Labor
CONCEPTS: Annex or appendix reference. Resident permits. Exchange of information and documents. Operating agencies. Private contracts. Technical and commercial staff. Establishment of commission. Employment regulations. Safety standards. Non-ILO labor relations. Social security. Unemployment. Migrant worker. Transportation costs. National treatment.
INTL ORGS: Arbitration Commission.
PROCEDURE: Duration. Termination.
PARTIES:
Austria
Yugoslavia

108513 Bilateral Agreement **587 UNTS 273**
SIGNED: 28 Jan 65　　　　FORCE: 25 Aug 65
REGISTERED: 10 Jan 67 USA (United States)
ARTICLES: 12 LANGUAGE: English. Spanish.
HEADNOTE: EDUCATION PROGRAM
TOPIC: Education
CONCEPTS: Definition of terms. Friendship and amity. Standardization. Conformity with municipal law. General cooperation. Exchange of information and documents. Inspection and observation. Personnel. General property. Specialists exchange. Exchange. Commissions and foundations. Teacher and student exchange. Professorships. Accounting procedures. Financial programs. Funding procedures.
TREATY REF: 272UNTS59.
PROCEDURE: Amendment. Termination.
PARTIES:
Peru
USA (United States)

108514 Bilateral Agreement **587 UNTS 289**
SIGNED: 17 Aug 65　　　　FORCE: 17 Aug 65
REGISTERED: 10 Jan 67 USA (United States)
ARTICLES: 5 LANGUAGE: English. Spanish.
HEADNOTE: AGRI COMMOD TITLE IV
TOPIC: US Agri Commod Aid
CONCEPTS: General provisions. Annex or appendix reference. General cooperation. Reexport of goods, etc.. Payment schedules. Local currency. Agricultural commodities. Purchase authorization.
PARTIES:
Bolivia
USA (United States)

108515 Bilateral Exchange **587 UNTS 309**
SIGNED: 12 Jan 66　　　　FORCE: 12 Jan 66
REGISTERED: 10 Jan 67 USA (United States)
ARTICLES: 2 LANGUAGE: English. Italian.
HEADNOTE: TRANSFER TREATY CLAIM FUNDS
TOPIC: Reparations
CONCEPTS: Exchange. Accounting procedures. Post-war claims settlement.
TREATY REF: 299UNTS157.
PARTIES:
Italy
USA (United States)

108516 Bilateral Agreement **588 UNTS 3**
SIGNED: 3 Jul 63　　　　FORCE: 27 Apr 65
REGISTERED: 12 Jan 67 Romania
ARTICLES: 9 LANGUAGE: German. Romanian.
HEADNOTE: FINANCE
TOPIC: Claims and Debts
CONCEPTS: Treaty implementation. General cooperation. Informational records. Inspection and observation. Expropriation. General property.

Responsibility and liability. Accounting procedures. Banking. Balance of payments. Interest rates. Non-interest rates and fees. Claims and settlements. Lump sum settlements.
PROCEDURE: Ratification.
PARTIES:
Austria
Romania

108517 Bilateral Agreement **588 UNTS 29**
SIGNED: 27 May 64   FORCE: 21 Jul 64
REGISTERED: 12 Jan 67 Romania
ARTICLES: 9 LANGUAGE: German. Romanian.
HEADNOTE: INTERNATIONAL TRANSPORT GOODS ROAD
TOPIC: Land Transport
CONCEPTS: Detailed regulations. Exceptions and exemptions. Remedies. General cooperation. Licenses and permits. Investigation of violations. Transport of goods. Driving permits. Roads and highways. Road rules.
PROCEDURE: Denunciation. Duration. Ratification. Renewal or Revival.
PARTIES:
Austria
Romania

108518 Bilateral Agreement **588 UNTS 55**
SIGNED: 21 Sep 64   FORCE: 21 Sep 64
REGISTERED: 13 Jan 67 UK Great Britain
ARTICLES: 10 LANGUAGE: English.
HEADNOTE: MUTUAL DEFENSE ASSISTANCE
TOPIC: Military Mission
CONCEPTS: Change of circumstances. Annex or appendix reference. Non-prejudice to UN charter. General cooperation. Use of facilities. Defense and security. Military assistance. Military training. Airforce-army-navy personnel ratio. Bases and facilities.
PROCEDURE: Duration.
PARTIES:
Malta
UK Great Britain

108519 Bilateral Agreement **588 UNTS 125**
SIGNED: 21 Sep 64   FORCE: 21 Sep 64
REGISTERED: 13 Jan 67 UK Great Britain
ARTICLES: 7 LANGUAGE: English.
HEADNOTE: FINANCIAL ASSISTANCE
TOPIC: Direct Aid
CONCEPTS: Economic assistance. Use restrictions. Procurement. Loan and credit.
PARTIES:
Malta
UK Great Britain

108520 Bilateral Exchange **588 UNTS 137**
SIGNED: 6 Jul 66   FORCE: 1 Aug 66
REGISTERED: 13 Jan 67 UK Great Britain
ARTICLES: 2 LANGUAGE: English.
HEADNOTE: EXTENDING TONGA PROVISIONS EXTRADITION TREATY
TOPIC: Extradition
CONCEPTS: Territorial application.
TREATY REF: 163LTS59; 193LTS353; 204LTS464.
PARTIES:
UK Great Britain
USA (United States)

108521 Bilateral Agreement **588 UNTS 143**
SIGNED: 26 May 66   FORCE: 26 May 66
REGISTERED: 13 Jan 67 UK Great Britain
ARTICLES: 10 LANGUAGE: English.
HEADNOTE: PUBLIC OFFICERS
TOPIC: Admin Cooperation
CONCEPTS: Definition of terms. Treaty interpretation. Social security. Payment schedules.
PARTIES:
Guyana
UK Great Britain

108522 Bilateral Agreement **588 UNTS 153**
SIGNED: 16 Jan 67   FORCE: 16 Jan 67
REGISTERED: 16 Jan 67 United Nations
ARTICLES: 6 LANGUAGE: English.
HEADNOTE: UN SEMINAR EDUCATION WOMEN
TOPIC: Education

CONCEPTS: Visas. Alien status. Human rights. Privileges and immunities. General cooperation. Personnel. Exchange. Indemnities and reimbursements. Expense sharing formulae. General transportation. Postal services. Status of experts. Conferences.
TREATY REF: 1UNTS15; 33UNTS261.
PROCEDURE: Amendment. Duration.
PARTIES:
Finland
United Nations

108523 Bilateral Agreement **588 UNTS 163**
SIGNED: 28 Dec 65   FORCE: 28 Dec 65
REGISTERED: 16 Jan 67 Denmark
ARTICLES: 10 LANGUAGE: French. Arabic.
HEADNOTE: SEED POTATO CULTIVATION CENTER
TOPIC: Tech Assistance
CONCEPTS: Tax exemptions. Customs exemptions. Domestic obligation. Agriculture. Assistance. Economic assistance. Materials, equipment and services.
PROCEDURE: Ratification.
PARTIES:
Denmark
Syria

108524 Bilateral Agreement **588 UNTS 175**
SIGNED: 22 Jan 66   FORCE: 9 Jul 66
REGISTERED: 17 Jan 67 Poland
ARTICLES: 17 LANGUAGE: Polish. Czechoslovakian.
HEADNOTE: CULTURAL COOPERATION
TOPIC: Culture
CONCEPTS: Treaty implementation. Previous treaty replacement. Friendship and amity. Non-diplomatic delegations. Conformity with municipal law. Exchange of information and documents. Use of facilities. Specialists exchange. Exchange. Professorships. General cultural cooperation. Artists. Athletes. Scientific exchange. Trade procedures. Payment schedules. Recognition. Publications exchange. Mass media exchange. Press and wire services.
PROCEDURE: Denunciation. Duration. Ratification. Renewal or Revival.
PARTIES:
Czechoslovakia
Poland

108525 Bilateral Exchange **588 UNTS 197**
SIGNED: 18 Jan 67   FORCE: 18 Jan 67
REGISTERED: 18 Jan 67 United Nations
ARTICLES: 2 LANGUAGE: English.
HEADNOTE: SETTLEMENT CLAIMS
TOPIC: Specif Claim/Waive
CONCEPTS: Exchange of information and documents. Claims and settlements. Lump sum settlements. Specific claims or waivers.
PARTIES:
Italy
United Nations

108526 Bilateral Agreement **588 UNTS 205**
SIGNED: 10 Jan 63   FORCE: 11 Jun 63
REGISTERED: 19 Jan 67 Philippines
ARTICLES: 1 LANGUAGE: English.
HEADNOTE: COOPERATION PEACEFUL USES ATOMIC ENERGY
TOPIC: Atomic Energy
CONCEPTS: Exchange of information and documents. Research cooperation. Scientific exchange. Peaceful use.
PROCEDURE: Duration. Renewal or Revival.
PARTIES:
Israel
Philippines

108527 Multilateral Exchange **588 UNTS 212**
SIGNED: 25 Jan 67   FORCE: 17 Nov 66
REGISTERED: 25 Jan 67 United Nations
ARTICLES: 3 LANGUAGE: English.
HEADNOTE: ASSISTANCE
TOPIC: IGO Operations
CONCEPTS: Previous treaty extension. Diplomatic missions. Privileges and immunities. Funding procedures. General technical assistance. Liai-

son with other IGO's. Special status. Status of experts.
TREATY REF: 378UNTS141; 201UNTS115; 378UNTS141; 201UNTS115.
PROCEDURE: Amendment.
PARTIES:
Indonesia SIGNED: 17 Nov 66 FORCE: 17 Nov 66
FAO (Food Agri) SIGNED: 1 Nov 66 FORCE: 17 Nov 66
IAEA (Atom Energy) SIGNED: 1 Nov 66 FORCE: 17 Nov 66
ICAO (Civil Aviat) SIGNED: 1 Nov 66 FORCE: 17 Nov 66
IMCO (Maritime Org) SIGNED: 1 Nov 66 FORCE: 17 Nov 66
ITU (Telecommun) SIGNED: 1 Nov 66 FORCE: 17 Nov 66
UNESCO (Educ/Cult) SIGNED: 1 Nov 66 FORCE: 17 Nov 66
United Nations SIGNED: 1 Nov 66 FORCE: 17 Nov 66
UN Special Fund SIGNED: 1 Nov 66 FORCE: 17 Nov 66
UPU (Postal Union) SIGNED: 1 Nov 66 FORCE: 17 Nov 66
WHO (World Health) SIGNED: 1 Nov 66 FORCE: 17 Nov 66
WMO (Meteorology) SIGNED: 1 Nov 66 FORCE: 17 Nov 66
ANNEX
646 UNTS 414. Indonesia. Amendment 25 Sep 68. Force 25 Sep 68.
646 UNTS 414. WHO (World Health). Amendment 25 Sep 68. Force 25 Sep 68.
646 UNTS 414. WMO (Meteorology). Amendment 25 Sep 68. Force 25 Sep 68.
646 UNTS 414. ICAO (Civil Aviat). Amendment 25 Sep 68. Force 25 Sep 68.
646 UNTS 414. UN Special Fund. Amendment 25 Sep 68. Force 25 Sep 68.
646 UNTS 414. United Nations. Amendment 25 Sep 68. Force 25 Sep 68.
646 UNTS 414. FAO (Food Agri). Amendment 25 Sep 68. Force 25 Sep 68.
646 UNTS 414. ILO (Labor Org). Amendment 25 Sep 68. Force 25 Sep 68.
646 UNTS 414. UNESCO (Educ/Cult). Amendment 25 Sep 68. Force 25 Sep 68.
646 UNTS 414. IAEA (Atom Energy). Amendment 25 Sep 68. Force 25 Sep 68.
646 UNTS 414. UPU (Postal Union). Amendment 25 Sep 68. Force 25 Sep 68.
646 UNTS 414. IMCO (Maritime Org). Amendment 25 Sep 68. Force 25 Sep 68.
646 UNTS 414. ITU (Telecommun). Amendment 25 Sep 68. Force 25 Sep 68.

108528 Bilateral Convention **588 UNTS 227**
SIGNED: 23 Sep 66   FORCE: 23 Sep 66
REGISTERED: 25 Jan 67 Belgium
ARTICLES: 7 LANGUAGE: French.
HEADNOTE: RADIOLOGICAL PROTECTION
TOPIC: Atomic Energy
CONCEPTS: Annex or appendix reference. Exchange of information and documents. Establishment of commission. Public health. Frontier crossing points. Ocean resources.
PROCEDURE: Duration.
PARTIES:
Belgium
France

108529 Bilateral Agreement **588 UNTS 243**
SIGNED: 18 Nov 56   FORCE: 18 Nov 66
REGISTERED: 1 Feb 67 United Nations
ARTICLES: 17 LANGUAGE: Spanish.
HEADNOTE: UN ECONOMIC COUNCIL AT CARACAS
TOPIC: IGO Operations
CONCEPTS: Non-visa travel documents. Diplomatic privileges. Diplomatic missions. Privileges and immunities. Diplomatic correspondence. Personnel. Funding procedures. Subsidiary organ.
PROCEDURE: Duration.
PARTIES:
United Nations
Venezuela

108530 Bilateral Agreement **588 UNTS 261**
SIGNED: 15 Mar 66   FORCE: 15 Mar 66
REGISTERED: 1 Feb 67 IAEA (Atom Energy)
ARTICLES: 8 LANGUAGE: English.
HEADNOTE: TRANSFER THERAPEUTIC IRRADIA-
TION EQUIPMENT
TOPIC: Claims and Debts
CONCEPTS: Arbitration. Procedure. Assets trans-
fer. Non-nuclear materials. Peaceful use.
INTL ORGS: International Court of Justice. Arbitra-
tion Commission.
TREATY REF: 374UNTS147.
PARTIES:
Pakistan
IAEA (Atom Energy)

108531 Bilateral Agreement **588 UNTS 269**
SIGNED: 20 Jun 66   FORCE: 1 Sep 66
REGISTERED: 1 Feb 67 IAEA (Atom Energy)
ARTICLES: 9 LANGUAGE: English.
HEADNOTE: NUCLEAR POWER STATION SAFE-
GUARDS
TOPIC: IGO Operations
CONCEPTS: Arbitration. Nuclear research. IGO op-
erations.
INTL ORGS: International Court of Justice. Arbitra-
tion Commission.
PROCEDURE: Duration. Termination.
PARTIES:
IAEA (Atom Energy)
UK Great Britain

108532 Bilateral Agreement **589 UNTS 3**
SIGNED: 26 Sep 66   FORCE: 26 Sep 66
REGISTERED: 1 Feb 67 IAEA (Atom Energy)
ARTICLES: 8 LANGUAGE: English.
HEADNOTE: APPLICATION SAFEGUARDS
TOPIC: Atomic Energy
CONCEPTS: Definition of terms. Non-prejudice to
third party. Exchange of information and docu-
ments. Responsibility and liability. Special tribu-
nals. Negotiation. Indemnities and reimburse-
ments. Peaceful use. Security of information.
Special status. Status of experts.
INTL ORGS: International Court of Justice. Arbitra-
tion Commission.
TREATY REF: 283UNTS275.
PROCEDURE: Amendment. Duration. Renewal or
Revival. Termination.
PARTIES:
IAEA (Atom Energy)
USA (United States)

108533 Bilateral Agreement **589 UNTS 25**
SIGNED: 28 Sep 66   FORCE: 28 Sep 66
REGISTERED: 1 Feb 67 IAEA (Atom Energy)
ARTICLES: 10 LANGUAGE: English.
HEADNOTE: ASSISTANCE CONTINUING REAC-
TOR PROJECT
TOPIC: Atomic Energy
CONCEPTS: Annex or appendix reference. Non-
prejudice to third party. Exchange of information
and documents. Inspection and observation. Re-
sponsibility and liability. Procedure. Public
health. Research cooperation. Research results.
Nuclear materials. Transport of goods. Security
of information. Special status. Status of experts.
TREATY REF: 339UNTS359.
PARTIES:
Philippines
IAEA (Atom Energy)

108534 Multilateral Instrument **589 UNTS 41**
SIGNED: 28 Sep 66   FORCE: 28 Sep 66
REGISTERED: 1 Feb 67 IAEA (Atom Energy)
ARTICLES: 6 LANGUAGE: English.
HEADNOTE: TRANSFER ENRICHED URANIUM RE-
SEARCH REACTOR
TOPIC: Specif Goods/Equip
CONCEPTS: Annex or appendix reference. Re-
sponsibility and liability. Arbitration. Procedure.
Special tribunals. Payment schedules. Accep-
tance of delivery. General. Nuclear materials.
INTL ORGS: International Court of Justice. Arbitra-
tion Commission.
TREATY REF: 339UNTS359; 276UNTS3;
471UNTS334.
PARTIES:
Philippines
IAEA (Atom Energy)

USA (United States)

108535 Bilateral Agreement **589 UNTS 55**
SIGNED: 9 Dec 66   FORCE: 9 Dec 66
REGISTERED: 1 Feb 67 IAEA (Atom Energy)
ARTICLES: 8 LANGUAGE: English. Spanish.
HEADNOTE: APPLICATION SAFEGUARDS
TOPIC: Atomic Energy
CONCEPTS: Definition of terms. Non-prejudice to
third party. Inspection and observation. Respon-
sibility and liability. Investigation of violations.
Negotiation. Indemnities and reimbursements.
Nuclear materials. Non-nuclear materials. Peace-
ful use. Security of information. Special status.
Status of experts.
INTL ORGS: International Court of Justice. Arbitra-
tion Commission.
TREATY REF: 307UNTS169; 586UNTS260;
276UNTS3; 471UNTS335.
PROCEDURE: Amendment. Duration. Renewal or
Revival. Termination.
PARTIES:
IAEA (Atom Energy)
USA (United States)

108536 Bilateral Agreement **589 UNTS 89**
SIGNED: 2 Feb 67   FORCE: 2 Feb 67
REGISTERED: 2 Feb 67 United Nations
ARTICLES: 8 LANGUAGE: English.
HEADNOTE: ACTIVITIES
TOPIC: IGO Operations
CONCEPTS: Privileges and immunities. Exchange
of information and documents. Accounting pro-
cedures. Domestic obligation. Materials, equip-
ment and services. Assistance to United Nations.
IGO obligations.
INTL ORGS: United Nations.
PROCEDURE: Amendment. Termination.
PARTIES:
UNICEF (Children)
Zambia

108537 Bilateral Agreement **589 UNTS 99**
SIGNED: 30 Jun 66   FORCE: 25 Aug 66
REGISTERED: 2 Feb 67 USSR (Soviet Union)
ARTICLES: 7 LANGUAGE: Russian. French.
HEADNOTE: SPACE EXPLORATION
TOPIC: Scientific Project
CONCEPTS: Friendship and amity. General coop-
eration. Research and scientific projects.
Meteorology. Research results. Communication
satellites testing. Scientific exchange. Research
and development.
PROCEDURE: Amendment. Denunciation. Dura-
tion. Future Procedures Contemplated. Ratifica-
tion. Renewal or Revival.
PARTIES:
France
USSR (Soviet Union)

108538 Bilateral Agreement **589 UNTS 109**
SIGNED: 30 Jun 66   FORCE: 25 Aug 66
REGISTERED: 2 Feb 67 USSR (Soviet Union)
ARTICLES: 7 LANGUAGE: Russian. French.
HEADNOTE: SCIENTIFIC TECHNICAL ECONOMIC
COOPERATION
TOPIC: Culture
CONCEPTS: Establishment of commission. Re-
search cooperation. General technical assis-
tance. Economic assistance.
PROCEDURE: Denunciation.
PARTIES:
France
USSR (Soviet Union)

108539 Bilateral Agreement **589 UNTS 119**
SIGNED: 30 Dec 65   FORCE: 30 Dec 65
REGISTERED: 3 Feb 67 Austria
ARTICLES: 7 LANGUAGE: German. French.
HEADNOTE: TECHNICAL COOPERATION CROP
PROTECTION
TOPIC: Tech Assistance
CONCEPTS: Annex or appendix reference. Non-
visa travel documents. Visas. Personnel. Ex-
pense sharing formulae. Tax exemptions. Cus-
toms exemptions. Agriculture. Materials, equip-
ment and services.

PARTIES:
Austria
Tunisia

108540 Bilateral Agreement **589 UNTS 135**
SIGNED: 24 Jun 65   FORCE: 30 Dec 65
REGISTERED: 3 Feb 67 Austria
ARTICLES: 27 LANGUAGE: German. English.
HEADNOTE: HEADQUATERS
TOPIC: IGO Operations
CONCEPTS: Definition of terms. Diplomatic privi-
leges. Privileges and immunities. Diplomatic cor-
respondence. Juridical personality. Private con-
tracts. Arbitration. Social security. Currency.
Headquarters and facilities. Status of experts.
Special status.
INTL ORGS: International Court of Justice. Arbitra-
tion Commission.
PROCEDURE: Amendment.
PARTIES:
Austria
Petrol Export Org

108541 Bilateral Agreement **589 UNTS 169**
SIGNED: 15 Jul 64   FORCE: 1 Feb 66
REGISTERED: 3 Feb 67 Austria
ARTICLES: 46 LANGUAGE: German. Spanish.
HEADNOTE: SOCIAL SECURITY
TOPIC: Non-ILO Labor
CONCEPTS: Definition of terms. Exceptions and
exemptions. Annex or appendix reference. Do-
mestic legislation. Incorporation of treaty provi-
sions into national law. Dispute settlement. Old
age and invalidity insurance. Wages and sala-
ries. Non-ILO labor relations. Family allowances.
Old age insurance. Sickness and invalidity insur-
ance. Social security. Unemployment. Payment
schedules.
INTL ORGS: Arbitration Commission.
PROCEDURE: Duration. Ratification. Renewal or
Revival. Termination.
PARTIES:
Austria
Spain

108542 Bilateral Agreement **589 UNTS 339**
SIGNED: 1 Oct 65   FORCE: 8 Dec 65
REGISTERED: 3 Feb 67 IBRD (World Bank)
ARTICLES: 5 LANGUAGE: English.
HEADNOTE: GUARANTEE AGRICULTURAL
CREDIT
TOPIC: IBRD Project
CONCEPTS: Definition of terms. Annex or appen-
dix reference. Exchange of information and doc-
uments. Inspection and observation. Bonds.
Fees and exemptions. Tax exemptions. Domestic
obligation. Agriculture. Terms of loan. Loan regu-
lations. Loan guarantee. Guarantor non-interfer-
ence.
PARTIES:
Mexico
IBRD (World Bank)

108543 Bilateral Agreement **590 UNTS 3**
SIGNED: 6 Feb 67   FORCE: 6 Feb 67
REGISTERED: 6 Feb 67 United Nations
ARTICLES: 10 LANGUAGE: English.
HEADNOTE: ASSISTANCE
TOPIC: IGO Operations
CONCEPTS: Annex or appendix reference. Diplo-
matic missions. Privileges and immunities. Ex-
change of official publications. Exchange of in-
formation and documents. Informational
records. Procedure. Accounting procedures. Do-
mestic obligation. Passports diplomatic.
INTL ORGS: International Atomic Energy Agency.
International Court of Justice. United Nations.
Arbitration Commission.
TREATY REF: 1UNTS15; 33UNTS261.
PROCEDURE: Amendment. Termination.
PARTIES:
Australia
UN Special Fund

108544 Bilateral Agreement **590 UNTS 25**
SIGNED: 7 Feb 67   FORCE: 7 Feb 67
REGISTERED: 7 Feb 67 United Nations
ARTICLES: 7 LANGUAGE: English.

HEADNOTE: ARRANGEMENTS ECONOMIC COM-
MISSION AFRICA
TOPIC: IGO Operations
CONCEPTS: Privileges and immunities. Subsidiary
organ. Status of experts. Facilities and property.
PARTIES:
Nigeria
United Nations

108545   Bilateral Convention   **590 UNTS 35**
SIGNED: 30 Sep 65   FORCE: 1 Feb 67
REGISTERED: 9 Feb 67 Belgium
ARTICLES: 16 LANGUAGE: French. Dutch.
HEADNOTE: COOPERATION CONSULAR MAT-
TERS
TOPIC: Consul/Citizenship
CONCEPTS: General consular functions.
INTL ORGS: Benelux Economic Union.
PROCEDURE: Ratification.
PARTIES:
Belgium
Luxembourg

108546   Bilateral Agreement   **590 UNTS 51**
SIGNED: 4 Jan 67   FORCE: 4 Jan 67
REGISTERED: 16 Feb 67 Philippines
ARTICLES: 9 LANGUAGE: English.
HEADNOTE: CUSTOMS ADMINISTRATION
TOPIC: Customs
CONCEPTS: Annex or appendix reference. Gen-
eral cooperation. Exchange of official publica-
tions. Customs duties.
PARTIES:
Philippines
USA (United States)

108547   Bilateral Agreement   **590 UNTS 71**
SIGNED: 20 Feb 67   FORCE: 29 Feb 67
REGISTERED: 20 Feb 67 United Nations
ARTICLES: 6 LANGUAGE: English.
HEADNOTE: ECONOMIC SOCIAL RIGHTS
TOPIC: IGO Operations
CONCEPTS: Diplomatic missions. Privileges and
immunities. Commissions and foundations. Do-
mestic obligation. IGO obligations.
TREATY REF: 33UNTS261; 1UNTS15.
PROCEDURE: Amendment.
PARTIES:
Poland
United Nations

108548 Multilateral Convention **590 UNTS 81**
SIGNED: 17 Dec 62   FORCE: 15 Feb 67
REGISTERED: 20 Feb 67 Council of Europe
ARTICLES: 7 LANGUAGE: English. French.
HEADNOTE: LIABILITY HOTEL KEEPERS CON-
CERNING PROPERTY GUESTS
TOPIC: Admin Cooperation
CONCEPTS: Territorial application. Annex or ap-
pendix reference. Domestic legislation. Respon-
sibility and liability.
INTL ORGS: Council of Europe.
PROCEDURE: Accession. Denunciation. Ratifica-
tion.
PARTIES:
Austria SIGNED: 17 Dec 62
Belgium SIGNED: 17 Dec 62
Denmark
France SIGNED: 17 Dec 62
Germany, West SIGNED: 17 Dec 62 RATIFIED:
14 Nov 66 FORCE: 15 Feb 67
Greece SIGNED: 17 Dec 62
Ireland RATIFIED: 7 May 63 FORCE: 15 Feb 67
Malta SIGNED: 17 Dec 62
Turkey SIGNED: 17 Dec 62
UK Great Britain SIGNED: 17 Dec 62 RATIFIED:
12 Jul 63 FORCE: 15 Feb 67
ANNEX
635 UNTS 375.   France.   Approval   18 Sep 67.
Force 19 Dec 67.

108549   Bilateral Agreement   **590 UNTS 95**
SIGNED: 25 Feb 66   FORCE: 30 Dec 66
REGISTERED: 21 Feb 67 Denmark
ARTICLES: 12 LANGUAGE: English. Portuguese.
HEADNOTE: TECHNICAL COOPERATION
TOPIC: Tech Assistance
CONCEPTS: Treaty implementation. General coop-
eration. Exchange of information and docu-

ments. Personnel. Exchange. Scholarships and
grants. Research and development. Reexport of
goods, etc.. Expense sharing formulae. Tax exemptions. Customs exemptions. Materials,
equipment and services.
PROCEDURE: Amendment. Termination.
PARTIES:
Brazil
Denmark

108550   Bilateral Exchange   **590 UNTS 109**
SIGNED: 22 Jun 66   FORCE: 21 Dec 66
REGISTERED: 24 Feb 67 Netherlands
ARTICLES: 2 LANGUAGE: English.
HEADNOTE: AUTHORIZATIONS AMATEUR RADIO
OPERATORS
TOPIC: Gen Communications
CONCEPTS: Territorial application. Amateur radio.
Radio-telephone-telegraphic communications.
PROCEDURE: Duration. Termination.
PARTIES:
Netherlands
USA (United States)
ANNEX
651 UNTS 404.   Netherlands.   Surinam.   Force
23 Aug 68.

108551   Bilateral Treaty   **590 UNTS 117**
SIGNED: 26 Apr 63   FORCE: 29 Mar 66
REGISTERED: 27 Feb 67 UK Great Britain
ARTICLES: 21 LANGUAGE: English. Swedish.
HEADNOTE: EXTRADITION
TOPIC: Extradition
CONCEPTS: Territorial application. Extradition, de-
portation and repatriation. Extradition requests.
Extraditable offenses. Location of crime. Refusal
of extradition. Pre-treaty crimes. Limits of prose-
cution. Extradition postponement. Witnesses
and experts. Indemnities and reimbursements.
PROCEDURE: Ratification. Termination.
PARTIES:
Sweden
UK Great Britain

108552 Multilateral Agreement **590 UNTS 156**
SIGNED: 27 Feb 67   FORCE: 27 Feb 67
REGISTERED: 1 Mar 67 United Nations
ARTICLES: 6 LANGUAGE: English.
HEADNOTE: OPERATIONAL ASSISTANCE
TOPIC: IGO Operations
CONCEPTS: Previous treaty replacement. Privi-
leges and immunities. Arbitration. Procedure.
Domestic obligation. Internal structure. Assis-
tance to United Nations. Inter-agency agree-
ments. IGO obligations.
TREATY REF: 466UNTS346.
PROCEDURE: Amendment. Termination.
PARTIES:
FAO (Food Agri) SIGNED: 27 May 67
IAEA (Atom Energy) SIGNED: 27 May 67
ICAO (Civil Aviat) SIGNED: 27 May 67
ILO (Labor Org) SIGNED: 27 May 67
IMCO (Maritime Org) SIGNED: 27 May 67
ITU (Telecommun) SIGNED: 27 May 67
UNESCO (Educ/Cult) SIGNED: 27 May 67
United Nations SIGNED: 27 May 67
UPU (Postal Union) SIGNED: 27 May 67
WHO (World Health) SIGNED: 27 May 67
WMO (Meteorology) SIGNED: 27 May 67
Uganda SIGNED: 27 May 67

108553   Bilateral Agreement   **590 UNTS 173**
SIGNED: 30 Jan 62   FORCE: 1 Apr 61
REGISTERED: 1 Mar 67 Zambia
ARTICLES: 8 LANGUAGE: English.
HEADNOTE: EMPLOY BRITISH OFFICERS
TOPIC: Non-ILO Labor
CONCEPTS: Definition of terms. Detailed regula-
tions. Exchange of information and documents.
Employment regulations. Wages and salaries.
Non-ILO labor relations. Indemnities and reim-
bursements. Payment schedules. Tax exemp-
tions.
PROCEDURE: Duration. Renewal or Revival. Termi-
nation.
PARTIES:
UK Great Britain
Zambia

108554   Bilateral Exchange   **590 UNTS 191**
SIGNED: 28 Jul 66   FORCE: 28 Jul 66
REGISTERED: 1 Mar 67 Zambia
ARTICLES: 11 LANGUAGE: English.
HEADNOTE: BRITISH AIDED CONDITIONS SER-
VICE
TOPIC: Non-ILO Labor
CONCEPTS: Definition of terms. General cooper-
ation. Social security. Payment schedules.
PROCEDURE: Termination.
PARTIES:
UK Great Britain
Zambia

108555   Bilateral Instrument   **590 UNTS 203**
SIGNED: 24 Mar 66   FORCE: 1 Jul 66
REGISTERED: 3 Mar 67 Austria
ARTICLES: 10 LANGUAGE: German. Spanish.
HEADNOTE: TRANSPORT GOODS ROAD
TOPIC: Land Transport
CONCEPTS: Remedies. Conformity with municipal
law. Exchange of information and documents.
Investigation of violations. Establishment of
commission. Transport of goods. Agricultural ve-
hicles and construction. Commercial road vehi-
cles. Motor vehicles and combinations. Road
rules.
PROCEDURE: Duration. Renewal or Revival.
PARTIES:
Austria
Spain

108556   Bilateral Convention   **591 UNTS 3**
SIGNED: 19 Nov 65   FORCE: 1 Jan 67
REGISTERED: 3 Mar 67 Austria
ARTICLES: 49 LANGUAGE: Serbo-Croat. German.
HEADNOTE: SOCIAL SECURITY
TOPIC: Non-ILO Labor
CONCEPTS: Definition of terms. General provi-
sions. Domestic legislation. Responsibility and
liability. Arbitration. Procedure. Sickness and in-
validity insurance. Social security. Unemploy-
ment. Indemnities and reimbursements. Fees
and exemptions. Payment schedules.
PROCEDURE: Denunciation. Ratification.
PARTIES:
Austria
Yugoslavia

108557   Bilateral Agreement   **591 UNTS 177**
SIGNED: 8 Sep 66   FORCE: 8 Sep 66
REGISTERED: 3 Mar 67 Denmark
ARTICLES: 16 LANGUAGE: English.
HEADNOTE: AIR SERVICES
TOPIC: Air Transport
CONCEPTS: Air transport. Airport facilities. Airport
equipment. Airworthiness certificates. Condi-
tions of airlines operating permission. Over-
flights and technical stops. Operating authoriza-
tions and regulations. Licenses and certificates
of nationality.
INTL ORGS: International Civil Aviation Organiza-
tion.
TREATY REF: INTERNAT. CIVIL AVIATION CONV.
7DEC44.
PARTIES:
Denmark
Nigeria

108558   Bilateral Agreement   **591 UNTS 201**
SIGNED: 19 Jul 66   FORCE: 11 Aug 66
REGISTERED: 3 Mar 67 Netherlands
ARTICLES: 10 LANGUAGE: Dutch. Spanish.
HEADNOTE: TECHNICAL COOPERATION
TOPIC: Tech Assistance
CONCEPTS: Juridical personality. General techni-
cal assistance. Assistance.
TREATY REF: VOLUNTEER WORKERS,BOGOTA
6JULY64.
PROCEDURE: Denunciation. Duration. Renewal or
Revival.
PARTIES:
Colombia
Netherlands

108559   Bilateral Agreement   **591 UNTS 219**
SIGNED: 22 Dec 66   FORCE: 22 Dec 66
REGISTERED: 6 Mar 67 Philippines
ARTICLES: 5 LANGUAGE: English.

HEADNOTE: AGRI COMMOD TITLE IV
TOPIC: US Agri Commod Aid
CONCEPTS: Annex or appendix reference. General cooperation. Exchange of information and documents. Reexport of goods, etc.. Interest rates. Payment schedules. Transportation costs. Credit provisions. Purchase authorization. Commodities schedule. Surplus commodities.
PARTIES:
    Philippines
    USA (United States)

108560   Bilateral Convention   **591 UNTS 235**
SIGNED: 8 Jul 66   FORCE: 11 Jan 67
REGISTERED: 6 Mar 67 Netherlands
ARTICLES: 8 LANGUAGE: French.
HEADNOTE: TECHNICAL COOPERATION
TOPIC: Tech Assistance
CONCEPTS: Juridical personality. General technical assistance. Assistance.
PROCEDURE: Denunciation. Duration.
PARTIES:
    Netherlands
    Tunisia

108561   Bilateral Agreement   **591 UNTS 245**
SIGNED: 1 Aug 66   FORCE: 20 Oct 66
REGISTERED: 6 Mar 67 Netherlands
ARTICLES: 6 LANGUAGE: French.
HEADNOTE: RURAL EDUCATION CENTER
TOPIC: Education
CONCEPTS: General cooperation. Responsibility and liability. Education. Exchange. Professorships. Export quotas. Import quotas. Tax exemptions. Domestic obligation. General technical assistance. Materials, equipment and services.
PROCEDURE: Denunciation. Duration. Future Procedures Contemplated. Ratification.
PARTIES:
    Ivory Coast
    Netherlands

108562   Bilateral Exchange   **591 UNTS 253**
SIGNED: 14 Dec 66   FORCE: 1 Jan 67
REGISTERED: 7 Mar 67 Philippines
ARTICLES: 2 LANGUAGE: English.
HEADNOTE: VISAS
TOPIC: Visas
CONCEPTS: Visa abolition.
PROCEDURE: Denunciation.
PARTIES:
    Norway
    Philippines

108563   Bilateral Exchange   **591 UNTS 259**
SIGNED: 20 Dec 66   FORCE: 1 Jan 67
REGISTERED: 7 Mar 67 Philippines
ARTICLES: 2 LANGUAGE: English.
HEADNOTE: VISAS
TOPIC: Visas
CONCEPTS: Visa abolition.
PARTIES:
    Denmark
    Philippines

108564 Multilateral Convention **591 UNTS 265**
SIGNED: 9 Apr 65   FORCE: 5 Mar 67
REGISTERED: 9 Mar 67 IMCO (Maritime Org)
ARTICLES: 16 LANGUAGE: English. French.
HEADNOTE: INTERNATIONAL MARITIME TRAFFIC
TOPIC: Water Transport
CONCEPTS: Merchant vessels.
INTL ORGS: International Atomic Energy Agency. International Court of Justice. Inter-Governmental Maritime Consultative Organization. United Nations.
PROCEDURE: Accession. Denunciation.
PARTIES:
    Algeria SIGNED: 9 Apr 65
    Argentina SIGNED: 9 Apr 65
    Belgium SIGNED: 9 Apr 65 RATIFIED: 4 Jan 67 FORCE: 5 Mar 67
    Brazil SIGNED: 9 Apr 65
    Canada SIGNED: 9 Apr 65
    Taiwan SIGNED: 9 Apr 65
    Czechoslovakia SIGNED: 9 Apr 65 RATIFIED: 19 Dec 66 FORCE: 5 Mar 67
    Denmark SIGNED: 9 Apr 65

Dominican Republic SIGNED: 9 Apr 65 RATIFIED: 11 Jul 66 FORCE: 5 Mar 67
Ecuador SIGNED: 9 Apr 65
Finland SIGNED: 9 Apr 65
Germany, West SIGNED: 9 Apr 65
Ghana SIGNED: 9 Apr 65 RATIFIED: 5 Nov 65 FORCE: 5 Mar 67
Greece SIGNED: 9 Apr 65
Hungary SIGNED: 9 Apr 65
Iceland RATIFIED: 24 Jan 67 FORCE: 25 Mar 67
Ivory Coast RATIFIED: 16 Feb 67 FORCE: 17 Apr 67
Japan SIGNED: 9 Apr 65
Korea, South SIGNED: 9 Apr 65
Monaco SIGNED: 9 Apr 65 RATIFIED: 9 Apr 65 FORCE: 5 Mar 67
Netherlands SIGNED: 9 Apr 65
Nicaragua SIGNED: 9 Apr 65
Nigeria RATIFIED: 24 Jan 67 FORCE: 25 Mar 67
Norway SIGNED: 9 Apr 65 RATIFIED: 8 Sep 66 FORCE: 5 Mar 67
Philippines SIGNED: 9 Apr 65
Poland SIGNED: 9 Apr 65
Senegal SIGNED: 9 Apr 65
Togo SIGNED: 9 Apr 65
UK Great Britain SIGNED: 24 Feb 66
Ukrainian SSR SIGNED: 9 Apr 65
USSR (Soviet Union) SIGNED: 9 Apr 65 RATIFIED: 25 Oct 66 FORCE: 5 Mar 67
Yugoslavia SIGNED: 9 Apr 65 RATIFIED: 18 Jul 66 FORCE: 5 Mar 67
Zambia RATIFIED: 14 Dec 65 FORCE: 5 Mar 67
                    ANNEX
601 UNTS 370. Canada. Ratification 18 Jul 67. Force 16 Sep 67.
603 UNTS 346. Sweden. Acceptance 28 Jul 67.
603 UNTS 346. Germany, West. Acceptance 26 Jul 67.
606 UNTS 406. Netherlands. Netherlands Antilles. Force 20 Nov 67.
606 UNTS 406. Netherlands. Acceptance 21 Sep 67. Force 20 Nov 67.
606 UNTS 406. Netherlands. Surinam. Force 20 Nov 67.
613 UNTS 418. France. Acceptance 29 Nov 67. Force 28 Jan 68.
617 UNTS 376. Denmark. Acceptance 9 Jan 68. Force 9 Mar 68.
635 UNTS 376. Switzerland. Acceptance 23 Apr 68. Force 22 Jun 68.
640 UNTS 375. Taiwan. Acceptance 19 Jul 68. Force 17 Sep 68.

108565   Bilateral Convention   **591 UNTS 327**
SIGNED: 4 Mar 66   FORCE: 23 Jun 66
REGISTERED: 10 Mar 67 Romania
ARTICLES: 14 LANGUAGE: Russian. Romanian.
HEADNOTE: ABOLITION VISAS
TOPIC: Visas
CONCEPTS: Visa abolition.
PROCEDURE: Denunciation.
PARTIES:
    Romania
    USSR (Soviet Union)

108566   Bilateral Treaty   **592 UNTS 3**
SIGNED: 27 May 65   FORCE: 13 Aug 65
REGISTERED: 10 Mar 67 Romania
ARTICLES: 13 LANGUAGE: Romanian. Chinese.
HEADNOTE: CULTURAL COOPERATION
TOPIC: Culture
CONCEPTS: Treaty implementation. Friendship and amity. Non-diplomatic delegations. Conformity with municipal law. Exchange of information and documents. Public information. Public health. Recognition of degrees. Exchange. Teacher and student exchange. Scholarships and grants. General cultural cooperation. Artists. Athletes. Scientific exchange. Publications exchange. Mass media exchange. Press and wire services.
PROCEDURE: Denunciation. Duration. Ratification. Renewal or Revival.
PARTIES:
    China People's Rep
    Romania

108567   Bilateral Convention   **592 UNTS 21**
SIGNED: 3 May 61   FORCE: 3 Jan 63
REGISTERED: 10 Mar 67 Romania
ARTICLES: 18 LANGUAGE: Romanian. Albanian.

HEADNOTE: COOPERATION SOCIAL PROBLEMS
TOPIC: Non-ILO Labor
CONCEPTS: General provisions. General cooperation. Social security.
PROCEDURE: Denunciation. Duration. Ratification.
PARTIES:
    Albania
    Romania

108568   Bilateral Exchange   **592 UNTS 51**
SIGNED: 6 Dec 65   FORCE: 6 Dec 65
REGISTERED: 13 Mar 67 USA (United States)
ARTICLES: 2 LANGUAGE: English.
HEADNOTE: CONTINUED APPLICATION TANZANIA 1931 EXTRADITION TREATY
TOPIC: Consul/Citizenship
CONCEPTS: Previous treaty extension.
TREATY REF: 163LTS59; 197LTS353; 204LTS264; 165UNTS121.
PARTIES:
    Tanzania
    USA (United States)

108569   Bilateral Agreement   **592 UNTS 61**
SIGNED: 5 Apr 66   FORCE: 5 Apr 66
REGISTERED: 13 Mar 67 USA (United States)
ARTICLES: 3 LANGUAGE: English.
HEADNOTE: INTERIM TARIFF AGREEMENT HONG GATT LINES
TOPIC: General Trade
CONCEPTS: Detailed regulations. Negotiation. Tariffs. Trade procedures.
INTL ORGS: General Agreement on Tariffs and Trade.
TREATY REF: 61UNTS1; 55UNTS187.
PROCEDURE: Duration. Termination.
PARTIES:
    UK Great Britain
    USA (United States)

108570   Bilateral Agreement   **592 UNTS 101**
SIGNED: 6 Jan 66   FORCE: 6 Jan 66
REGISTERED: 13 Mar 67 USA (United States)
ARTICLES: 5 LANGUAGE: English.
HEADNOTE: AGRI COMMOD TITLE IV
TOPIC: US Agri Commod Aid
CONCEPTS: Annex or appendix reference. General cooperation. Exchange of information and documents. Reexport of goods, etc.. Interest rates. Payment schedules. Transportation costs. Credit provisions. Purchase authorization. Commodities schedule. Surplus commodities.
PARTIES:
    Liberia
    USA (United States)

108571   Bilateral Agreement   **592 UNTS 117**
SIGNED: 23 Feb 66   FORCE: 23 Feb 66
REGISTERED: 13 Mar 67 USA (United States)
ARTICLES: 5 LANGUAGE: English. French.
HEADNOTE: AGRI COMMOD TITLE IV
TOPIC: Direct Aid
CONCEPTS: General cooperation. Exchange of information and documents. Reexport of goods, etc.. Interest rates. Payment schedules. Transportation costs. Credit provisions. Purchase authorization. Commodities schedule. Surplus commodities.
PARTIES:
    Algeria
    USA (United States)

108572 Multilateral Agreement **592 UNTS 139**
SIGNED: 13 Aug 63   FORCE: 13 Feb 67
REGISTERED: 16 Mar 67 Belgium
ARTICLES: 21 LANGUAGE: French. Dutch.
HEADNOTE: TRADE & NAVIGATION
TOPIC: General Trade
CONCEPTS: Establishment of trade relations. Export quotas. Import quotas. Certificates of origin. Reciprocity in trade. Trade procedures. Banking.
INTL ORGS: Benelux Economic Union. European Economic Community.
PROCEDURE: Denunciation. Ratification.
PARTIES:
    Benelux Econ Union SIGNED: 13 Aug 63 RATIFIED: 13 Feb 67 FORCE: 13 Feb 67
    Netherlands SIGNED: 13 Aug 63 RATIFIED: 5 Feb 66 FORCE: 13 Feb 67

Netherlands Netherlands Antilles RATIFIED:
13 Aug 63
Netherlands Surinam RATIFIED: 13 Aug 63
Paraguay SIGNED: 13 Aug 63 RATIFIED:
25 Aug 66 FORCE: 13 Feb 67

108573 Multilateral Agreement **592 UNTS 101**
SIGNED: 17 Jan 66 FORCE: 23 Feb 66
REGISTERED: 16 Mar 67 USA (United States)
ARTICLES: 9 LANGUAGE: English.
HEADNOTE: COTTON INSTITUTE
TOPIC: IGO Establishment
CONCEPTS: Privileges and immunities. Procedure.
Finances and payments. Currency. Assessment
procedures. Tax exemptions. Subsidiary organ.
INTL ORGS: International Cotton Institute. Food
and Agricultural Organization of the United Na-
tions. United Nations. Arbitration Commission.
PROCEDURE: Acession. Ratification.
PARTIES:
India SIGNED: 28 Jan 66 RATIFIED: 3 Feb 67
FORCE: 23 Feb 66
Mexico SIGNED: 17 Jun 66 RATIFIED:
30 Dec 66 FORCE: 23 Feb 66
Spain SIGNED: 28 Jan 66 FORCE: 23 Feb 66
Sudan SIGNED: 18 Feb 66 FORCE: 23 Feb 66
Tanzania RATIFIED: 8 Aug 66
United Arab Rep SIGNED: 28 Jan 66 FORCE:
23 Feb 66
Uganda RATIFIED: 24 Jun 66
USA (United States) SIGNED: 24 Jan 66 RATI-
FIED: 23 Feb 66 FORCE: 23 Feb 66

108574 Bilateral Agreement **592 UNTS 207**
SIGNED: 3 Mar 66 FORCE: 6 Feb 67
REGISTERED: 17 Mar 67 Denmark
ARTICLES: 5 LANGUAGE: English. Danish.
HEADNOTE: DELIMITATION CONTINENTAL
SHELF
TOPIC: Territory Boundary
CONCEPTS: Continental shelf.
PROCEDURE: Ratification.
PARTIES:
Denmark
UK Great Britain

108575 Multilateral Agreement **592 UNTS 215**
SIGNED: 2 Jul 65 FORCE: 21 Feb 67
REGISTERED: 17 Mar 67 FAO (Food Agri)
ARTICLES: 20 LANGUAGE: English. French.
HEADNOTE: DESERT LOCUST CONTROL
TOPIC: Sanitation
CONCEPTS: Definition of terms. Territorial application. General cooperation. Exchange of information and documents. Inspection and observation.
Dispute settlement. Specialists exchange. Insect
control. Vocational training. Research cooperation. Research results. Research and development. Accounting procedures. Indemnities and
reimbursements. Expense sharing formulae.
Customs exemptions. General technical assistance. Materials, equipment and services. Admission. Subsidiary organ. Establishment. Procedure. Assistance to United Nations.
INTL ORGS: Food and Agricultural Organization of
the United Nations. International Court of Justice. United Nations.
PROCEDURE: Amendment. Accession. Ratification. Termination.
PARTIES:
Multilateral
ANNEX
601 UNTS 371. United Arab Rep. Acceptance
6 Jul 67.
605 UNTS 398. Kuwait. Acceptance 10 Aug 64.
653 UNTS 463. Syria. Acceptance 3 Dec 68.
660 UNTS 402. Bahrain. Acceptance 24 Feb 69.

108576 Bilateral Agreement **593 UNTS 3**
SIGNED: 16 Jun 59 FORCE: 18 Sep 60
REGISTERED: 22 Mar 67 Netherlands
ARTICLES: 29 LANGUAGE: Dutch. German.
HEADNOTE: DOUBLE TAXATION INCOME FOR-
TUNE
TOPIC: Taxation
CONCEPTS: Definition of terms. Territorial applica-
tion. Privileges and immunities. Nationality and
citizenship. Conformity with municipal law. Ex-
change of official publications. Teacher and stu-
dent exchange. Claims and settlements. Taxa-

tion. General. Tax exemptions. Air transport.
Merchant vessels.
PROCEDURE: Duration. Ratification. Termination.
PARTIES:
Germany, West
Netherlands

108577 Bilateral Agreement **593 UNTS 85**
SIGNED: 13 Apr 57 FORCE: 15 Apr 57
REGISTERED: 22 Mar 67 Netherlands
ARTICLES: 4 LANGUAGE: Dutch. Spanish.
HEADNOTE: PAYMENTS
TOPIC: Finance
CONCEPTS: Previous treaty replacement. General
cooperation. Accounting procedures. Banking.
Currency. Exchange rates and regulations. Inter-
est rates. Payment schedules. Local currency.
TREATY REF: 30JAN50 PAYMENTS AGREEMENT.
PROCEDURE: Denunciation. Duration. Renewal or
Revival.
PARTIES:
Netherlands
Paraguay

108578 Bilateral Exchange **593 UNTS 109**
SIGNED: 21 Feb 67 FORCE: 21 Feb 67
REGISTERED: 22 Mar 67 Philippines
ARTICLES: 2 LANGUAGE: English.
HEADNOTE: RADIO COMMUNICATION SYSTEM
TOPIC: Gen Communications
CONCEPTS: Facilities and equipment. Communi-
cations linkage.
PARTIES:
Indonesia
Philippines

108579 Bilateral Agreement **593 UNTS 115**
SIGNED: 5 Jun 65 FORCE: 13 May 66
REGISTERED: 23 Mar 67 USSR (Soviet Union)
ARTICLES: 13 LANGUAGE: English. Russian.
HEADNOTE: CULTURAL SCIENTIFIC COOPER-
ATION
TOPIC: Culture
CONCEPTS: Treaty implementation. Tourism. Non-
diplomatic delegations. Conformity with munici-
pal law. Exchange of information and docu-
ments. Specialists exchange. Public health. Rec-
ognition of degrees. Exchange. Teacher and
student exchange. Vocational training. General
cultural cooperation. Artists. Athletes. Scientific
exchange. Publications exchange. Mass media
exchange.
PROCEDURE: Amendment. Duration. Future Procedures Contemplated. Ratification. Termination.
PARTIES:
Pakistan
USSR (Soviet Union)

108580 Bilateral Agreement **593 UNTS 125**
SIGNED: 20 Dec 66 FORCE: 20 Dec 66
REGISTERED: 24 Mar 67 Denmark
ARTICLES: 17 LANGUAGE: English.
HEADNOTE: AIR SERVICES
TOPIC: Air Transport
CONCEPTS: Conditions. Definition of terms. Detailed regulations. Exceptions and exemptions.
Annex or appendix reference. Conformity with
municipal law. General cooperation. Exchange
of information and documents. Licenses and permits. Recognition of legal documents. Use of facilities. Arbitration. Procedure. Existing tribunals. Negotiation. Reexport of goods, etc.. Monetary and gold transfers. Exchange rates and
regulations. Fees and exemptions. Non-interest
rates and fees. Most favored nation clause. National treatment. Tax exemptions. Customs exemptions. Competency certificate. Routes and
logistics. Navigational conditions. Permit designation. Airport facilities. Airworthiness certificates. Conditions of airlines operating permission. Overflights and technical stops. Operating
authorizations and regulations. Licenses and certificates of nationality.
INTL ORGS: International Civil Aviation Organization.
TREATY REF: 15UNTS295.
PROCEDURE: Amendment. Future Procedures
Contemplated. Registration. Termination. Application to Non-self-governing Territories.

PARTIES:
Denmark
Singapore

108581 Bilateral Exchange **593 UNTS 147**
SIGNED: 24 Jun 65 FORCE: 24 Jun 65
REGISTERED: 28 Mar 67 USA (United States)
ARTICLES: 2 LANGUAGE: English.
HEADNOTE: TRADE COTTON TEXTILES
TOPIC: Commodity Trade
CONCEPTS: Treaty interpretation. Annex type ma-
terial. Commodity trade. Quotas.
TREATY REF: 471UNTS295.
PARTIES:
Poland
USA (United States)

108582 Bilateral Exchange **593 UNTS 157**
SIGNED: 25 May 66 FORCE: 25 May 66
REGISTERED: 28 Mar 67 USA (United States)
ARTICLES: 2 LANGUAGE: English.
HEADNOTE: ALIEN AMATEUR RADIO OPERATORS
TOPIC: Gen Communications
CONCEPTS: Amateur radio.
PARTIES:
India
USA (United States)

108583 Bilateral Agreement **593 UNTS 165**
SIGNED: 6 Jun 66 FORCE: 6 Jun 66
REGISTERED: 28 Mar 67 USA (United States)
ARTICLES: 4 LANGUAGE: English.
HEADNOTE: AGRI COMMOD AGREE
TOPIC: US Agri Commod Aid
CONCEPTS: General provisions. Guarantees and
safeguards. Annex or appendix reference. Gen-
eral cooperation. Exchange of information and
documents. Currency deposits. Exchange rates
and regulations. Transportation costs. Local cur-
rency. Agricultural commodities assistance.
Commodities schedule. Purchase authorization.
Surplus commodities.
PARTIES:
Israel
USA (United States)

108584 Bilateral Exchange **593 UNTS 185**
SIGNED: 29 Dec 64 FORCE: 29 Dec 64
REGISTERED: 28 Mar 67 USA (United States)
ARTICLES: 6 LANGUAGE: English. French.
HEADNOTE: AGRI COMMOD
TOPIC: Commodity Trade
CONCEPTS: Detailed regulations. General cooper-
ation. Exchange of information and documents.
General trade. Trade agencies. Finances and
payments. Currency. Non-interest rates and fees.
Transportation costs. Commodity trade. General
aid. Agricultural commodities. Loan and credit.
Purchase authorization.
PARTIES:
Morocco
USA (United States)

108585 Bilateral Agreement **593 UNTS 201**
SIGNED: 28 Jun 66 FORCE: 28 Jun 66
REGISTERED: 28 Mar 67 USA (United States)
ARTICLES: 5 LANGUAGE: English.
HEADNOTE: AGRI COMMOD TITLE IV
TOPIC: US Agri Commod Aid
CONCEPTS: Annex or appendix reference. Gen-
eral cooperation. Exchange of information and
documents. Reexport of goods, etc.. Interest
rates. Payment schedules. Transportation costs.
Credit provisions. Purchase authorization. Com-
modities schedule. Surplus commodities.
PARTIES:
Indonesia
USA (United States)

108586 Bilateral Agreement **593 UNTS 215**
SIGNED: 19 Jul 65 FORCE: 19 Jul 65
REGISTERED: 28 Mar 67 USA (United States)
ARTICLES: 6 LANGUAGE: English.
HEADNOTE: AGRI COMMOD TITLE I
TOPIC: Direct Aid
CONCEPTS: Annex or appendix reference. Gen-
eral cooperation. Exchange of information and
documents. Reexport of goods, etc.. Currency

deposits. Exchange rates and regulations. Purchase authorizations. Transportation costs. Local currency. Commodities schedule. Surplus commodities.
PARTIES:
Congo (Zaire)
USA (United States)

108587 Bilateral Agreement **593 UNTS 239**
SIGNED: 5 Apr 66   FORCE: 5 Apr 66
REGISTERED: 28 Mar 67 USA (United States)
ARTICLES: 6 LANGUAGE: English.
HEADNOTE: AGRI COMMOD TITLE I
TOPIC: Direct Aid
CONCEPTS: Annex or appendix reference. General cooperation. Exchange of information and documents. Reexport of goods, etc.. Currency deposits. Exchange rates and regulations. Purchase authorizations. Transportation costs. Local currency. Commodities schedule. Surplus commodities.
PARTIES:
Jordan
USA (United States)

108588 Multilateral Instrument **593 UNTS 261**
SIGNED: 30 Mar 66   FORCE: 30 Mar 66
REGISTERED: 28 Mar 67 USA (United States)
ARTICLES: 6 LANGUAGE: English.
HEADNOTE: RE-ENTRY EXPERIMENTS COOPERATION
TOPIC: Scientific Project
CONCEPTS: Research cooperation. Nuclear research. Tax exemptions.
PROCEDURE: Duration. Termination.
PARTIES:
Australia SIGNED: 30 Mar 66 FORCE: 30 Mar 66
UK Great Britain SIGNED: 30 Mar 66 FORCE: 30 Mar 66
USA (United States) SIGNED: 30 Mar 66 FORCE: 30 Mar 66

108589 Bilateral Exchange **593 UNTS 279**
SIGNED: 5 May 66   FORCE: 1 Jul 66
REGISTERED: 28 Mar 67 USA (United States)
ARTICLES: 2 LANGUAGE: English. French.
HEADNOTE: ALIEN AMATEUR RADIO OPERATORS
TOPIC: Admin Cooperation
CONCEPTS: Licenses and permits. Amateur radio.
PARTIES:
France
USA (United States)

108590 Bilateral Exchange **593 UNTS 289**
SIGNED: 24 Jul 66   FORCE: 19 Jul 66
REGISTERED: 28 Mar 67 USA (United States)
ARTICLES: 2 LANGUAGE: English.
HEADNOTE: ALIEN AMATEUR RADIO OPERATORS
TOPIC: Gen Communications
CONCEPTS: Amateur radio.
PARTIES:
Kuwait
USA (United States)

108591 Bilateral Exchange **594 UNTS 3**
SIGNED: 23 Apr 65   FORCE: 23 Apr 65
REGISTERED: 28 Mar 67 USA (United States)
ARTICLES: 10 LANGUAGE: English. French.
HEADNOTE: AGRI COMMOD TITLE I
TOPIC: US Agri Commod Aid
CONCEPTS: Annex or appendix reference. General cooperation. Exchange of information and documents. Reexport of goods, etc.. Currency deposits. Exchange rates and regulations. Purchase authorizations. Transportation costs. Local currency. Commodities schedule. Surplus commodities.
PARTIES:
Morocco
USA (United States)

108592 Bilateral Agreement **594 UNTS 27**
SIGNED: 26 May 66   FORCE: 26 May 66
REGISTERED: 28 Mar 67 USA (United States)
ARTICLES: 6 LANGUAGE: English.
HEADNOTE: AGRI COMMOD
TOPIC: US Agri Commod Aid
CONCEPTS: Annex or appendix reference. General cooperation. Exchange of information and documents. Reexport of goods, etc.. Currency deposits. Exchange rates and regulations. Purchase authorizations. Transportation costs. Local currency. Commodities schedule. Surplus commodities.
PARTIES:
Pakistan
USA (United States)
                    ANNEX
603 UNTS 348.   Pakistan.   Amendment 10 Aug 66. Force 10 Aug 66.
603 UNTS 348. USA (United States). Amendment 10 Aug 66. Force 10 Aug 66.

108593 Bilateral Exchange **594 UNTS 47**
SIGNED: 6 May 66   FORCE: 6 May 66
REGISTERED: 28 Mar 67 USA (United States)
ARTICLES: 2 LANGUAGE: English.
HEADNOTE: JUDICIAL PROCEDURE
TOPIC: Admin Cooperation
CONCEPTS: General cooperation. Domestic legislation. Competence of tribunal.
PROCEDURE: Termination.
PARTIES:
Sierra Leone
USA (United States)

108594 Bilateral Agreement **594 UNTS 55**
SIGNED: 30 Jan 65   FORCE: 8 Aug 66
REGISTERED: 28 Mar 67 USA (United States)
ARTICLES: 13 LANGUAGE: English. French.
HEADNOTE: CIVIL USES ATOMIC ENERGY
TOPIC: Atomic Energy
CONCEPTS: Definition of terms. Exchange of information and documents. Research cooperation. Research results. Nuclear materials. Non-nuclear materials. Peaceful use. Security of information.
TREATY REF: 279UNTS4; 346UNTS346; 400UNTS396.
PROCEDURE: Duration.
PARTIES:
Switzerland
USA (United States)

108595 Bilateral Exchange **594 UNTS 83**
SIGNED: 15 Jun 66   FORCE: 15 Jun 66
REGISTERED: 28 Mar 67 USA (United States)
ARTICLES: 2 LANGUAGE: English.
HEADNOTE: USE LAND
TOPIC: Milit Installation
CONCEPTS: Procedure. Bases and facilities.
TREATY REF: 233UNTS109.
PROCEDURE: Duration. Termination.
PARTIES:
Canada
USA (United States)

108596 Bilateral Exchange **594 UNTS 91**
SIGNED: 3 Mar 67   FORCE: 3 Mar 67
REGISTERED: 1 Apr 67 United Nations
ARTICLES: 2 LANGUAGE: English.
HEADNOTE: SPECIAL FUND PROJECTS
TOPIC: Tech Assistance
CONCEPTS: Continuity of rights and obligations. Assistance.
TREATY REF: 348UNTS177.
PARTIES:
Barbados
UN Special Fund

108597 Multilateral Exchange **594 UNTS 96**
SIGNED: 3 Mar 67   FORCE: 3 Mar 67
REGISTERED: 1 Apr 67 United Nations
ARTICLES: 2 LANGUAGE: English.
HEADNOTE: CONSENT BOUND BY REVISED STANDARD AGREEMENT
TOPIC: Tech Assistance
CONCEPTS: Annex type material.
INTL ORGS: United Nations Special Fund.
TREATY REF: 366UNTS311,463UNTS356,490UNTS464.
PARTIES:
Barbados SIGNED: 20 Dec 66
IAEA (Atom Energy) SIGNED: 20 Dec 66
ICAO (Civil Aviat) SIGNED: 20 Dec 66
ILO (Labor Org) SIGNED: 20 Dec 66
ITU (Telecommun) SIGNED: 20 Dec 66
UNESCO (Educ/Cult) SIGNED: 20 Dec 66
United Nations SIGNED: 20 Dec 66
UPU (Postal Union) SIGNED: 20 Dec 66
WHO (World Health) SIGNED: 20 Dec 66
WMO (Meteorology) SIGNED: 20 Dec 66

108598 Multilateral Agreement **594 UNTS 105**
SIGNED: 17 Mar 67   FORCE: 1 Apr 67
REGISTERED: 1 Apr 67 United Nations
ARTICLES: 5 LANGUAGE: English.
HEADNOTE: DEVELOPMENT OF FISHERIES
TOPIC: Non-IBRD Project
CONCEPTS: Annex or appendix reference. Operating agencies. Financial programs. Funding procedures. Assistance. Materials, equipment and services. Natural resources.
PROCEDURE: Termination.
PARTIES:
India SIGNED: 17 Mar 67 FORCE: 1 Apr 67
Norway SIGNED: 17 Mar 67 FORCE: 1 Apr 67
United Nations SIGNED: 17 Mar 67 FORCE: 1 Apr 67

108599 Bilateral Agreement **594 UNTS 123**
SIGNED: 27 Apr 65   FORCE: 15 Feb 67
REGISTERED: 5 Apr 67 Netherlands
ARTICLES: 7 LANGUAGE: English.
HEADNOTE: TECHNICAL COOPERATION
TOPIC: Tech Assistance
CONCEPTS: Privileges and immunities. General cooperation. Exchange of information and documents. Personnel. Import quotas. Reexport of goods, etc.. General technical assistance. Materials, equipment and services.
PROCEDURE: Duration. Renewal or Revival.
PARTIES:
Netherlands
Tanzania

108600 Bilateral Convention **594 UNTS 131**
SIGNED: 19 Apr 56   FORCE: 5 Feb 67
REGISTERED: 7 Apr 67 Greece
ARTICLES: 13 LANGUAGE: French.
HEADNOTE: PROTECTION OF PLANTS
TOPIC: Sanitation
CONCEPTS: Definition of terms. Annex or appendix reference. Standardization. General cooperation. Exchange of information and documents. Inspection and observation. Domestic legislation. Dispute settlement. Specialists exchange. Quarantine. Border control. Disease control. Insect control. Scientific exchange. Trade procedures. Indemnities and reimbursements. Agriculture. Materials, equipment and services. Publications exchange.
PROCEDURE: Denunciation. Duration. Ratification. Renewal or Revival.
PARTIES:
Bulgaria
Greece

108601 Bilateral Agreement **594 UNTS 149**
SIGNED: 8 Apr 67   FORCE: 8 Apr 67
REGISTERED: 8 Apr 67 United Nations
ARTICLES: 7 LANGUAGE: English.
HEADNOTE: MEETING MINISTERS ECONOMIC COMMUNITY WEST AFRICA
TOPIC: IGO Operations
CONCEPTS: Diplomatic missions. Privileges and immunities. Personnel. Funding procedures. Conferences.
TREATY REF: 1UNTS15; 33UNTS261.
PARTIES:
Ghana
United Nations

108602 Bilateral Exchange **594 UNTS 159**
SIGNED: 8 Apr 67   FORCE: 8 Apr 67
REGISTERED: 8 Apr 67 United Nations
ARTICLES: 3 LANGUAGE: English.
HEADNOTE: PRIVILEGES IMMUNITIES APPLIED JOINT MEETINGS UNESCO
TOPIC: Privil/Immunities
CONCEPTS: Visas. Privileges and immunities. Fees and exemptions. IGO operations. Conferences.
PARTIES:
Romania
United Nations

108603 Bilateral Agreement **594 UNTS 165**
SIGNED: 23 Dec 66   FORCE: 26 Jan 67
REGISTERED: 10 Apr 67 IDA (Devel Assoc)
ARTICLES: 6 LANGUAGE: English.
HEADNOTE: DEVELOPMENT CREDIT INDUSTRIAL IMPORTS
TOPIC: Non-IBRD Project
CONCEPTS: Definition of terms. Detailed regulations. Previous treaty amendment. Exchange of information and documents. Informational records. Accounting procedures. Currency. Interest rates. Tax exemptions. Credit provisions. Loan repayment. Terms of loan. Plans and standards. IDA development project. Industry.
PARTIES:
India
IDA (Devel Assoc)

108604 Bilateral Agreement **594 UNTS 187**
SIGNED: 29 Sep 64   FORCE: 25 Jan 67
REGISTERED: 10 Apr 67 IDA (Devel Assoc)
ARTICLES: 7 LANGUAGE: English.
HEADNOTE: DEVELOPMENT CREDIT RAILWAY
TOPIC: Non-IBRD Project
CONCEPTS: Definition of terms. Detailed regulations. Previous treaty amendment. Exchange of information and documents. Informational records. Accounting procedures. Currency. Interest rates. Tax exemptions. Credit provisions. Loan repayment. Terms of loan. Plans and standards. IDA development project. Railways.
PARTIES:
Mali
IDA (Devel Assoc)

108605 Bilateral Agreement **594 UNTS 225**
SIGNED: 22 Sep 64   FORCE: 21 Oct 66
REGISTERED: 10 Apr 67 IDA (Devel Assoc)
ARTICLES: 7 LANGUAGE: English.
HEADNOTE: DEVELOPMENT CREDIT HIGHWAY ENGINEERING
TOPIC: Non-IBRD Project
CONCEPTS: Definition of terms. Detailed regulations. Previous treaty amendment. Exchange of information and documents. Informational records. Accounting procedures. Currency. Interest rates. Tax exemptions. Credit provisions. Loan repayment. Terms of loan. Plans and standards. IDA development project. Roads and highways.
PARTIES:
Pakistan
IDA (Devel Assoc)

108606 Bilateral Agreement **594 UNTS 255**
SIGNED: 23 Dec 66   FORCE: 21 Feb 67
REGISTERED: 10 Apr 67 IDA (Devel Assoc)
ARTICLES: 6 LANGUAGE: English.
HEADNOTE: DEVELOPMENT CREDIT INDUSTRIAL IMPORTS
TOPIC: Non-IBRD Project
CONCEPTS: Definition of terms. Detailed regulations. Previous treaty amendment. Exchange of information and documents. Informational records. Accounting procedures. Currency. Interest rates. Tax exemptions. Credit provisions. Loan repayment. Terms of loan. Plans and standards. IDA development project. Industry.
PARTIES:
Pakistan
IDA (Devel Assoc)

108607 Bilateral Agreement **594 UNTS 277**
SIGNED: 29 Sep 66   FORCE: 25 Jan 67
REGISTERED: 10 Apr 67 IDA (Devel Assoc)
ARTICLES: 7 LANGUAGE: English.
HEADNOTE: DEVELOPMENT CREDIT RAILWAY
TOPIC: Non-IBRD Project
CONCEPTS: Definition of terms. Detailed regulations. Previous treaty amendment. Exchange of information and documents. Informational records. Accounting procedures. Currency. Interest rates. Tax exemptions. Credit provisions. Loan repayment. Terms of loan. Plans and standards. IDA development project. Railways.
PARTIES:
IDA (Devel Assoc)
Senegal

108608 Bilateral Agreement **594 UNTS 311**
SIGNED: 23 Jan 67   FORCE: 17 Feb 67
REGISTERED: 10 Apr 67 IBRD (World Bank)
ARTICLES: 5 LANGUAGE: English.
HEADNOTE: GUARANTEE TELECOMMUNICA-TIONS
TOPIC: IBRD Project
CONCEPTS: Definition of terms. Annex or appendix reference. Exchange of information and documents. Inspection and observation. Bonds. Fees and exemptions. Tax exemptions. Domestic obligation. Terms of loan. Loan regulations. Loan guarantee. Guarantor non-interference. Telecommunications.
PARTIES:
Jamaica
IBRD (World Bank)

108609 Bilateral Agreement **594 UNTS 347**
SIGNED: 19 Oct 66   FORCE: 19 Dec 66
REGISTERED: 10 Apr 67 IBRD (World Bank)
ARTICLES: 7 LANGUAGE: English.
HEADNOTE: LOAN
TOPIC: IBRD Project
CONCEPTS: Loan and credit. Credit provisions. Loan repayment. Terms of loan.
INTL ORGS: International Development Association.
PROCEDURE: Termination.
PARTIES:
IBRD (World Bank)
Thailand

108610 Bilateral Agreement **595 UNTS 3**
SIGNED: 7 Jul 66   FORCE: 16 Mar 67
REGISTERED: 12 Apr 67 IBRD (World Bank)
ARTICLES: 5 LANGUAGE: English.
HEADNOTE: GUARANTEE STEEL
TOPIC: IBRD Project
CONCEPTS: Definition of terms. Annex or appendix reference. Exchange of information and documents. Inspection and observation. Bonds. Fees and exemptions. Tax exemptions. Domestic obligation. Terms of loan. Loan regulations. Loan guarantee. Guarantor non-interference. Industry.
PARTIES:
India
IBRD (World Bank)

108611 Bilateral Agreement **595 UNTS 47**
SIGNED: 30 Dec 64   FORCE: 27 Jan 65
REGISTERED: 12 Apr 67 Denmark
ARTICLES: 9 LANGUAGE: Danish. Spanish.
HEADNOTE: TECHNICAL SCIENTIFIC COOPER-ATION
TOPIC: Tech Assistance
CONCEPTS: General technical assistance.
INTL ORGS: United Nations.
PROCEDURE: Denunciation. Duration.
PARTIES:
Denmark
Peru
ANNEX
634 UNTS 446. Peru. Supplementation 20 Apr 66. Force 7 Sep 66.
634 UNTS 446. Denmark. Supplementation 20 Apr 66. Force 7 Sep 66.
660 UNTS 404. Peru. Signature 22 Nov 68. Force 22 Nov 68.
660 UNTS 404. Denmark. Signature 22 Nov 68. Force 22 Nov 68.

108612 Multilateral Agreement **595 UNTS 60**
SIGNED: 13 Apr 67   FORCE: 13 Apr 67
REGISTERED: 13 Apr 67 United Nations
ARTICLES: 6 LANGUAGE: English. Spanish.
HEADNOTE: STANDARD AGREEMENT OPERA-TION ASSISTANCE
TOPIC: IGO Operations
CONCEPTS: Diplomatic missions. Privileges and immunities. General cooperation. Responsibility and liability. Dispute settlement. Arbitration. Labor statistics. IGO obligations.
PROCEDURE: Amendment. Termination.
PARTIES:
Costa Rica SIGNED: 13 Apr 67 FORCE: 13 Apr 67
FAO (Food Agri) SIGNED: 13 Apr 67 FORCE: 13 Apr 67
IAEA (Atom Energy) SIGNED: 13 Apr 67 FORCE: 13 Apr 67
ICAO (Civil Aviat) SIGNED: 13 Apr 67 FORCE: 13 Apr 67
ILO (Labor Org) SIGNED: 13 Apr 67 FORCE: 13 Apr 67
IMCO (Maritime Org) SIGNED: 13 Apr 67 FORCE: 13 Apr 67
ITU (Telecommun) SIGNED: 13 Apr 67 FORCE: 13 Apr 67
UNESCO (Educ/Cult) SIGNED: 13 Apr 67 FORCE: 13 Apr 67
United Nations SIGNED: 13 Apr 67 FORCE: 13 Apr 67
WHO (World Health) SIGNED: 13 Apr 67 FORCE: 13 Apr 67
WMO (Meteorology) SIGNED: 13 Apr 67 FORCE: 13 Apr 67

108613 Bilateral Agreement **595 UNTS 83**
SIGNED: 14 Apr 67   FORCE: 14 Apr 67
REGISTERED: 14 Apr 67 United Nations
ARTICLES: 15 LANGUAGE: English.
HEADNOTE: ARRANGEMENTS SYMPOSIUM
TOPIC: IGO Operations
CONCEPTS: Default remedies. Diplomatic privileges. Diplomatic missions. Privileges and immunities. Diplomatic correspondence. Responsibility and liability. Dispute settlement. Existing tribunals. Specialists exchange. Financial programs. Special status. Status of experts.
PARTIES:
Greece
United Nations

108614 Bilateral Agreement **595 UNTS 99**
SIGNED: 6 Apr 67   FORCE: 6 Apr 67
REGISTERED: 17 Apr 67 ILO (Labor Org)
ARTICLES: 5 LANGUAGE: French.
HEADNOTE: ESTABLISHING OFFICE ILO
TOPIC: IGO Establishment
CONCEPTS: Passports diplomatic. Diplomatic missions. Privileges and immunities. Regional offices.
TREATY REF: 71UNTS318.
PROCEDURE: Amendment. Duration.
PARTIES:
Algeria
ILO (Labor Org)

108615 Bilateral Agreement **595 UNTS 105**
SIGNED: 6 Oct 65   FORCE: 23 Dec 66
REGISTERED: 17 Apr 67 Netherlands
ARTICLES: 4 LANGUAGE: Dutch. English.
HEADNOTE: CONTINENTAL SHELF
TOPIC: Territory Boundary
CONCEPTS: Arbitration. Continental shelf. Regulation of natural resources.
PROCEDURE: Ratification. Termination.
PARTIES:
Netherlands
UK Great Britain

108616 Bilateral Agreement **595 UNTS 113**
SIGNED: 6 Oct 65   FORCE: 23 Dec 66
REGISTERED: 17 Apr 67 Netherlands
ARTICLES: 4 LANGUAGE: Dutch. English.
HEADNOTE: DELIMITATION CONTINENTAL SHELF
TOPIC: Territory Boundary
CONCEPTS: Negotiation. Continental shelf.
PROCEDURE: Ratification.
PARTIES:
Netherlands
UK Great Britain

108617 Multilateral Agreement **595 UNTS 120**
SIGNED: 19 Apr 67   FORCE: 19 Apr 67
REGISTERED: 19 Apr 67 United Nations
ARTICLES: 7 LANGUAGE: English.
HEADNOTE: TECHNICAL ASSISTANCE
TOPIC: Tech Assistance
CONCEPTS: Privileges and immunities. Arbitration. Assistance. Loan and credit.
PROCEDURE: Termination.
PARTIES:
Netherlands SIGNED: 19 Apr 67
FAO (Food Agri) SIGNED: 19 Apr 67
IAEA (Atom Energy) SIGNED: 19 Apr 67

ICAO (Civil Aviat) SIGNED: 19 Apr 67
ILO (Labor Org) SIGNED: 19 Apr 67
IMCO (Maritime Org) SIGNED: 19 Apr 67
ITU (Telecommun) SIGNED: 19 Apr 67
UNESCO (Educ/Cult) SIGNED: 19 Apr 67
United Nations SIGNED: 19 Apr 67
UPU (Postal Union) SIGNED: 19 Apr 67
WHO (World Health) SIGNED: 19 Apr 67
WMO (Meteorology) SIGNED: 19 Apr 67

108618   Bilateral Agreement   **595 UNTS 141**
SIGNED: 23 Dec 66   FORCE: 17 Feb 67
REGISTERED: 27 Apr 67 IBRD (World Bank)
ARTICLES: 5 LANGUAGE: English.
HEADNOTE: GUARANTEE POWER
TOPIC: IBRD Project
CONCEPTS: Definition of terms. Annex or appen-
dix reference. Exchange of information and doc-
uments. Inspection and observation. Bonds.
Fees and exemptions. Tax exemptions. Domestic
obligation. Terms of loan. Loan regulations. Loan
guarantee. Guarantor non-interference. Hydro-
electric power.
PARTIES:
Chile
IBRD (World Bank)

108619   Bilateral Agreement   **595 UNTS 171**
SIGNED: 28 Apr 67   FORCE: 28 Apr 67
REGISTERED: 28 Apr 67 United Nations
ARTICLES: 10 LANGUAGE: English.
HEADNOTE: ASSISTANCE DEVELOPMENT PRO-
GRAM
TOPIC: General Aid
CONCEPTS: Privileges and immunities. Arbitra-
tion. Loan and credit. Credit provisions.
INTL ORGS: International Atomic Energy Agency.
International Court of Justice. United Nations.
PROCEDURE: Termination.
PARTIES:
Hungary
UN Special Fund

108620   Bilateral Convention   **595 UNTS 189**
SIGNED: 21 Apr 65   FORCE: 5 May 66
REGISTERED: 1 May 67 UK Great Britain
ARTICLES: 48 LANGUAGE: English.
HEADNOTE: CONSULAR
TOPIC: Consul/Citizenship
CONCEPTS: General consular functions. Diplo-
matic privileges. Consular relations establish-
ment. Diplomatic missions. Inviolability. Privi-
leges and immunities. Property. Nationality and
citizenship. Diplomatic correspondence. Con-
sular functions in shipping. Consular functions in
property.
INTL ORGS: International Court of Justice.
PROCEDURE: Ratification.
PARTIES:
UK Great Britain
Yugoslavia

108621   Bilateral Agreement   **595 UNTS 255**
SIGNED: 26 May 66   FORCE: 26 May 66
REGISTERED: 1 May 67 UK Great Britain
ARTICLES: 13 LANGUAGE: English.
HEADNOTE: STATUS FORCES
TOPIC: Status of Forces
CONCEPTS: Definition of terms. Visa abolition. In-
violability. Conformity with municipal law. Legal
protection and assistance. Recognition of legal
documents. Responsibility and liability. Investi-
gation of violations. Claims and settlements. Tax
exemptions. Customs exemptions. Postal ser-
vices. Airforce-army-navy personnel ratio. Condi-
tions for assistance missions. Jurisdiction.
Status of forces. Bases and facilities.
PARTIES:
Guyana
UK Great Britain

108622   Bilateral Agreement   **595 UNTS 273**
SIGNED: 10 Oct 66   FORCE: 1 Jan 67
REGISTERED: 2 May 67 Yugoslavia
ARTICLES: 8 LANGUAGE: German. Serbo-Croat.
HEADNOTE: TOURIST TRAFFIC FRONTIER REGION
TOPIC: Visas
CONCEPTS: Tourism. Frontier peoples and person-
nel.

PROCEDURE: Denunciation.
PARTIES:
Austria
Yugoslavia

108623   Multilateral Instrument   **595 UNTS 287**
SIGNED: 4 May 67   FORCE: 4 May 67
REGISTERED: 4 May 67 United Nations
ARTICLES: 7 LANGUAGE: English. French.
HEADNOTE: ARTICLES ASSOCIATION ECONOMIC
COMMUNITY WEST AFRICA
TOPIC: IGO Establishment
CONCEPTS: Treaty implementation. Exchange of
information and documents. Customs exemp-
tions. Temporary importation. Economic assis-
tance. Admission. Establishment. Internal struc-
ture. Inter-agency agreements.
PARTIES:
Dahomey SIGNED: 4 May 67 FORCE: 4 May 67
Ghana SIGNED: 4 May 67 FORCE: 4 May 67
Ivory Coast RATIFIED: 4 May 67
Liberia SIGNED: 4 May 67 FORCE: 4 May 67
Mali SIGNED: 4 May 67 FORCE: 4 May 67
Mauritania SIGNED: 4 May 67 FORCE: 4 May 67
Nigeria SIGNED: 4 May 67 FORCE: 4 May 67
Niger SIGNED: 4 May 67 FORCE: 4 May 67
Senegal SIGNED: 4 May 67 FORCE: 4 May 67
Sierra Leone SIGNED: 4 May 67 FORCE:
4 May 67
Togo SIGNED: 4 May 67 FORCE: 4 May 67
Upper Volta SIGNED: 4 May 67 FORCE:
4 May 67

108624   Bilateral Exchange   **595 UNTS 299**
SIGNED: 21 Dec 65   FORCE: 21 Dec 65
REGISTERED: 4 May 67 Austria
ARTICLES: 2 LANGUAGE: German. Portuguese.
HEADNOTE: EXTENSION PERIOD PROTECTION
LITERARY ARTISTIC WORKS
TOPIC: Admin Cooperation
CONCEPTS: Domestic legislation. General cultural
cooperation.
PARTIES:
Austria
Brazil

108625   Bilateral Exchange   **595 UNTS 307**
SIGNED: 21 Dec 66   FORCE: 21 Jan 67
REGISTERED: 4 May 67 Malta
ARTICLES: 2 LANGUAGE: English.
HEADNOTE: FACILITATE TRAVEL
TOPIC: Visas
CONCEPTS: Visa abolition.
PARTIES:
Austria
Malta

108626   Bilateral Agreement   **595 UNTS 313**
SIGNED: 7 Jun 66   FORCE: 8 Mar 67
REGISTERED: 5 May 67 Denmark
ARTICLES: 20 LANGUAGE: French.
HEADNOTE: AIR TRANSPORT
TOPIC: Air Transport
CONCEPTS: Airport facilities. Airport equipment.
Airworthiness certificates. Conditions of airlines
operating permission. Overflights and technical
stops. Operating authorizations and regulations.
Licenses and certificates of nationality.
INTL ORGS: International Civil Aviation Organiza-
tion.
PARTIES:
Denmark
Ivory Coast

108627   Bilateral Agreement   **596 UNTS 3**
SIGNED: 25 May 66   FORCE: 30 Dec 66
REGISTERED: 9 May 67 IBRD (World Bank)
ARTICLES: 5 LANGUAGE: English.
HEADNOTE: GUARANTEE IRRIGATION
TOPIC: IBRD Project
CONCEPTS: Definition of terms. Annex or appen-
dix reference. Exchange of information and doc-
uments. Inspection and observation. Bonds.
Fees and exemptions. Tax exemptions. Domestic
obligation. Terms of loan. Loan regulations. Loan
guarantee. Guarantor non-interference. Irriga-
tion.

PARTIES:
Mexico
IBRD (World Bank)

108628   Bilateral Agreement   **596 UNTS 35**
SIGNED: 26 Jan 67   FORCE: 3 May 67
REGISTERED: 9 May 67 IBRD (World Bank)
ARTICLES: 5 LANGUAGE: English.
HEADNOTE: GUARANTEE EXTRA HIGH VOLTAGE
TOPIC: IBRD Project
CONCEPTS: Definition of terms. Annex or appen-
dix reference. Exchange of information and doc-
uments. Inspection and observation. Bonds.
Fees and exemptions. Tax exemptions. Domestic
obligation. Terms of loan. Loan regulations. Loan
guarantee. Guarantor non-interference. Hydro-
electric power.
PARTIES:
IBRD (World Bank)
Venezuela

108629   Bilateral Agreement   **596 UNTS 71**
SIGNED: 23 Sep 66   FORCE: 22 Dec 66
REGISTERED: 11 May 67 IBRD (World Bank)
ARTICLES: 5 LANGUAGE: English.
HEADNOTE: LOAN
TOPIC: IBRD Project
CONCEPTS: Interest rates. Liens. Loan guarantee.
PARTIES:
Philippines
IBRD (World Bank)

108630   Bilateral Convention   **596 UNTS 121**
SIGNED: 3 May 61   FORCE: 6 Feb 67
REGISTERED: 15 May 67 Taiwan
ARTICLES: 8 LANGUAGE: Chinese. Spanish.
HEADNOTE: CULTURAL CONVENTION
TOPIC: Culture
CONCEPTS: Friendship and amity. Exchange.
Teacher and student exchange. General cultural
cooperation. Artists. Athletes. Publications ex-
change. Mass media exchange.
PROCEDURE: Duration. Ratification. Renewal or
Revival. Termination.
PARTIES:
Taiwan
Uruguay

108631   Multilateral Agreement   **596 UNTS 133**
SIGNED: 24 Feb 67   FORCE: 1 Apr 67
REGISTERED: 17 May 67 Denmark
ARTICLES: 16 LANGUAGE: Danish. Finnish.
HEADNOTE: SICKNESS INSURANCE
TOPIC: Health/Educ/Welfare
CONCEPTS: Old age and invalidity insurance.
PARTIES:
Denmark SIGNED: 24 Feb 67 FORCE: 1 Apr 67
Finland SIGNED: 24 Feb 67 FORCE: 1 Apr 67
Iceland SIGNED: 24 Feb 67 FORCE: 1 Apr 67
Norway SIGNED: 24 Feb 67 FORCE: 1 Apr 67
Sweden SIGNED: 24 Feb 67 FORCE: 1 Apr 67

108632   Bilateral Convention   **596 UNTS 177**
SIGNED: 6 Jul 66   FORCE: 20 Jan 67
REGISTERED: 22 May 67 USSR (Soviet Union)
ARTICLES: 11 LANGUAGE: Bulgarian. Russian.
HEADNOTE: DUAL CITIZENSHIP
TOPIC: Consul/Citizenship
CONCEPTS: Dual citizenship.
PROCEDURE: Denunciation. Duration. Ratification.
PARTIES:
Bulgaria
USSR (Soviet Union)

108633   Bilateral Agreement   **596 UNTS 199**
SIGNED: 24 Jul 65   FORCE: 11 Jan 67
REGISTERED: 22 May 67 USSR (Soviet Union)
ARTICLES: 12 LANGUAGE: English. Russian.
HEADNOTE: CULTURAL SCIENTIFIC COOPER-
ATION
TOPIC: Culture
CONCEPTS: Friendship and amity. Conformity
with municipal law. Public health. Recognition of
degrees. Exchange. Teacher and student ex-
change. Scholarships and grants. Vocational
training. General cultural cooperation. Artists.
Athletes. Scientific exchange. Publications ex-

change. Mass media exchange. Press and wire services.
PROCEDURE: Ratification. Termination.
PARTIES:
Uganda
USSR (Soviet Union)

108634 Bilateral Agreement **596 UNTS 209**
SIGNED: 7 May 67   FORCE: 7 May 67
REGISTERED: 23 May 67 ILO (Labor Org)
ARTICLES: 6 LANGUAGE: English.
HEADNOTE: ESTABLISHING OFFICE
TOPIC: IGO Operations
CONCEPTS: Passports diplomatic. Diplomatic missions. Privileges and immunities. Regional offices.
TREATY REF: 71UNTS318.
PROCEDURE: Amendment. Duration.
PARTIES:
Cameroon
ILO (Labor Org)

108635 Bilateral Agreement **596 UNTS 215**
SIGNED: 30 Nov 65   FORCE: 5 Jun 67
REGISTERED: 5 Jun 67 United Nations
ARTICLES: 9 LANGUAGE: Spanish.
HEADNOTE: CONDITIONS OPERATE CHILE
TOPIC: IGO Operations
CONCEPTS: Definition of terms. Previous treaty extension. Diplomatic privileges. Privileges and immunities. Nationality and citizenship. Diplomatic correspondence. Responsibility and liability. Status of experts.
TREATY REF: 126UNTS119; 354UNTS398; 1UNTS15.
PROCEDURE: Amendment. Duration.
PARTIES:
Chile
UNICEF (Children)

108636 Bilateral Treaty **596 UNTS 235**
SIGNED: 27 Apr 65   FORCE: 23 Mar 67
REGISTERED: 5 Jun 67 Netherlands
ARTICLES: 5 LANGUAGE: Dutch. French.
HEADNOTE: MINING COAL
TOPIC: Specific Resources
CONCEPTS: Raw materials.
TREATY REF: 136UNTS31; 507UNTS270.
PROCEDURE: Ratification.
PARTIES:
Belgium
Netherlands

108637 Bilateral Agreement **596 UNTS 245**
SIGNED: 13 Sep 66   FORCE: 1 Nov 66
REGISTERED: 5 Jun 67 Netherlands
ARTICLES: 20 LANGUAGE: French.
HEADNOTE: SICKNESS MATERNITY INSURANCE
TOPIC: Non-ILO Labor
CONCEPTS: Definition of terms. Territorial application. General provisions. Time limit. Extraditable offenses. General cooperation. Sickness and invalidity insurance. Unemployment. Fees and exemptions.
PROCEDURE: Denunciation. Duration.
PARTIES:
Greece
Netherlands

108638 Multilateral Convention **596 UNTS 261**
SIGNED: 24 Apr 63   FORCE: 19 Mar 67
REGISTERED: 8 Jun 67 United Nations
ARTICLES: 79 LANGUAGE: English. French.
HEADNOTE: CONSULAR RELATIONS
TOPIC: Consul/Citizenship
CONCEPTS: General consular functions. Diplomatic privileges. Consular relations establishment. Diplomatic missions. Inviolability. Privileges and immunities. Property. Diplomatic correspondence. Taxation of professional services.
INTL ORGS: International Court of Justice. United Nations.
PROCEDURE: Accession. Ratification.
PARTIES:
Albania RATIFIED: 14 Apr 64 FORCE: 19 Mar 67
Argentina   SIGNED: 24 Apr 63   RATIFIED:
7 Mar 67 FORCE: 19 Mar 67
Australia SIGNED: 31 Mar 64
Austria SIGNED: 24 Apr 63

Belgium SIGNED: 24 Apr 63
Bolivia SIGNED: 6 Aug 63
Brazil SIGNED: 24 Apr 63 RATIFIED: 11 May 67 FORCE: 19 Mar 67
Cameroon   SIGNED: 21 Aug 63   RATIFIED: 22 May 67 FORCE: 19 Mar 67
Chile SIGNED: 24 Apr 63
China SIGNED: 24 Apr 63
Central Afri Rep SIGNED: 24 Apr 63
Congo (Brazzaville) SIGNED: 24 Apr 63
Congo (Zaire) SIGNED: 24 Apr 63
Colombia SIGNED: 24 Apr 63
Costa Rica   SIGNED: 6 Jun 63   RATIFIED: 29 Dec 66 FORCE: 19 Mar 67
Cuba SIGNED: 31 Mar 64 RATIFIED: 15 Oct 65 FORCE: 19 Mar 67
Czechoslovakia SIGNED: 31 Mar 64
Dahomey SIGNED: 24 Apr 63
Denmark SIGNED: 24 Apr 63
Dominican Republic SIGNED: 24 Apr 63 RATIFIED: 4 Mar 64 FORCE: 19 Mar 67
Ecuador   SIGNED: 25 Mar 64   RATIFIED: 11 Mar 65 FORCE: 19 Mar 67
Finland SIGNED: 28 Oct 63
France SIGNED: 24 Apr 63
Gabon SIGNED: 24 Apr 63 RATIFIED: 23 Feb 65 FORCE: 19 Mar 67
Germany, West SIGNED: 24 Apr 63
Ghana SIGNED: 24 Apr 63 RATIFIED: 4 Oct 63 FORCE: 19 Mar 67
Iran SIGNED: 24 Apr 63
Ireland   SIGNED: 24 Apr 63   RATIFIED: 10 May 67 FORCE: 19 Mar 67
Israel SIGNED: 25 Feb 64
Italy SIGNED: 22 Nov 63
Ivory Coast SIGNED: 24 Apr 63
Kenya RATIFIED: 1 Jul 65 FORCE: 19 Mar 67
Kuwait SIGNED: 10 Jan 64
Lebanon SIGNED: 24 Apr 63
Liberia SIGNED: 24 Apr 63
Liechtenstein   SIGNED: 24 Apr 63   RATIFIED: 18 May 66 FORCE: 19 Mar 67
Luxembourg SIGNED: 24 Mar 64
Madagascar   RATIFIED: 17 Feb 67   FORCE: 19 Mar 67
Mexico SIGNED: 7 Oct 63 RATIFIED: 16 Jun 65 FORCE: 19 Mar 67
Nepal RATIFIED: 28 Sep 65 FORCE: 19 Mar 67
Norway SIGNED: 24 Apr 63
Panama SIGNED: 4 Dec 63
Peru SIGNED: 24 Apr 63
Philippines   SIGNED: 24 Apr 63   RATIFIED: 15 Nov 65 FORCE: 19 Mar 67
Poland SIGNED: 20 Mar 64
Saudi Arabia   RATIFIED: 29 Apr 66   FORCE: 19 Mar 67
Sweden SIGNED: 8 Oct 63
Switzerland   SIGNED: 23 Oct 63   RATIFIED: 3 May 65 FORCE: 19 Mar 67
Trinidad/Tobago RATIFIED: 19 Oct 65 FORCE: 19 Mar 67
Tunisia RATIFIED: 8 Jul 64 FORCE: 19 Mar 67
United Arab Rep RATIFIED: 21 Jun 65 FORCE: 19 Mar 67
UK Great Britain SIGNED: 17 Mar 64
USA (United States) SIGNED: 24 Apr 63
Upper Volta   SIGNED: 24 Apr 63   RATIFIED: 11 Aug 64 FORCE: 19 Mar 67
Uruguay SIGNED: 24 Apr 63
Vatican/Holy See SIGNED: 24 Apr 63
Venezuela   SIGNED: 24 Apr 63   RATIFIED: 27 Oct 65 FORCE: 19 Mar 67
Yugoslavia   SIGNED: 24 Apr 63   RATIFIED: 8 Feb 65 FORCE: 19 Mar 67
ANNEX
604 UNTS 390. Panama. Ratification 28 Aug 67. Force 27 Sep 67.
616 UNTS 506. Chile. Ratification 9 Jan 68. Force 8 Feb 68.
619 UNTS 344. Nigeria. Accession 22 Jan 68. Force 21 Feb 68.
630 UNTS 409. Honduras. Accession 13 Feb 68. Force 14 Mar 68.
633 UNTS 417. Mali. Accession 28 Mar 68. Force 27 Apr 68.
633 UNTS 417. Somalia. Accession 29 Mar 68. Force 28 Apr 68.
668 UNTS 389. Pakistan. Accession 14 Apr 69. Force 14 May 69.

108639 Multilateral Protocol **596 UNTS 469**
SIGNED: 24 Apr 63   FORCE: 19 Mar 67
REGISTERED: 8 Jun 67 United Nations

ARTICLES: 8 LANGUAGE: English. French.
HEADNOTE: CONSULAR RELATIONS AQUISITION NATIONALITY
TOPIC: Consul/Citizenship
CONCEPTS: Nationality and citizenship.
INTL ORGS: International Court of Justice. United Nations.
PROCEDURE: Accession.
PARTIES:
Multilateral
ANNEX
604 UNTS 390. Panama. Ratification 28 Aug 67. Force 27 Sep 67.
619 UNTS 344. Tunisia. Accession 24 Jan 68. Force 23 Feb 68.

108640 Multilateral Protocol **596 UNTS 487**
SIGNED: 24 Apr 63   FORCE: 19 Mar 67
REGISTERED: 8 Jun 67 United Nations
ARTICLES: 10 LANGUAGE: English. French.
HEADNOTE: COMPULSORY SETTLEMENT DISPUTES
TOPIC: Consul/Citizenship
CONCEPTS: Dispute settlement. Procedure.
INTL ORGS: International Court of Justice. United Nations.
PROCEDURE: Ratification.
PARTIES:
Argentina SIGNED: 24 Apr 63
Austria SIGNED: 24 Apr 63
Belgium SIGNED: 31 Mar 64
Cameroon SIGNED: 21 Aug 63
Chile SIGNED: 24 Apr 63
Taiwan SIGNED: 24 Apr 63
Central Afri Rep SIGNED: 24 Apr 63
Congo (Brazzaville) SIGNED: 24 Apr 63
Congo (Zaire) SIGNED: 24 Apr 63
Colombia SIGNED: 24 Apr 63
Dahomey SIGNED: 24 Apr 63
Denmark SIGNED: 24 Apr 63
Dominican Republic SIGNED: 24 Apr 63 RATIFIED: 4 Mar 64 FORCE: 19 Mar 67
Finland SIGNED: 28 Oct 63
France SIGNED: 24 Apr 63
Gabon RATIFIED: 23 Feb 65 FORCE: 19 Mar 67
Germany, West SIGNED: 31 Oct 63
Ghana SIGNED: 24 Apr 63
Ireland SIGNED: 24 Apr 63
Italy SIGNED: 24 Apr 63
Ivory Coast SIGNED: 24 Apr 63
Kenya RATIFIED: 1 Jul 65 FORCE: 19 Mar 67
Kuwait SIGNED: 10 Jan 64
Lebanon SIGNED: 24 Apr 63
Liberia SIGNED: 24 Apr 63
Liechtenstein   SIGNED: 24 Apr 63   RATIFIED: 18 May 66 FORCE: 19 Mar 67
Luxembourg SIGNED: 24 Mar 63
Madagascar   RATIFIED: 17 Feb 67   FORCE: 19 Mar 67
Nepal RATIFIED: 28 Sep 65 FORCE: 19 Mar 67
Niger SIGNED: 24 Apr 63
Norway SIGNED: 24 Apr 63
Panama SIGNED: 24 Apr 63
Panama SIGNED: 4 Dec 63
Peru SIGNED: 24 Apr 63
Philippines   SIGNED: 24 Apr 63   RATIFIED: 15 Nov 65 FORCE: 19 Mar 67
Senegal   RATIFIED: 29 Apr 66   FORCE: 19 Mar 67
Sweden SIGNED: 8 Oct 63
Switzerland   SIGNED: 23 Oct 63   RATIFIED: 3 May 65 FORCE: 19 Mar 67
UK Great Britain SIGNED: 27 Mar 64
USA (United States) SIGNED: 24 Apr 63
Upper Volta   SIGNED: 24 Apr 63   RATIFIED: 11 Aug 64 FORCE: 19 Mar 67
Uruguay SIGNED: 24 Apr 63
Yugoslavia SIGNED: 24 Apr 63
ANNEX
604 UNTS 390. Panama. Ratification 28 Aug 67. Force 27 Sep 67.

108641 Multilateral Convention **597 UNTS 3**
SIGNED: 8 Jul 65   FORCE: 9 Jun 67
REGISTERED: 9 Jun 67 ICAO (Civil Aviat)
ARTICLES: 23 LANGUAGE: English. French.
HEADNOTE: TRANSIT TRADE LAND-LOCKED COUNTRIES
TOPIC: General Trade
CONCEPTS: Annex type material. General trade.
INTL ORGS: International Court of Justice. United Nations.

PARTIES:
  Afghanistan
  Argentina
  Austria
  Belgium
  Bolivia
  Brazil
  Burundi
  Byelorussia
  Cameroon
  Chad
  Chile
  Central Afri Rep
  Congo (Brazzaville)
  Czechoslovakia
  France
  Germany, West
  Greece
  Hungary
  India
  Italy
  Ivory Coast
  Japan
  Kenya
  Korea, South
  Laos
  Liberia
  Luxembourg
  Malawi
  Mali
  Mongolia
  Nepal
  Netherlands
  Nigeria
  Niger
  Norway
  Pakistan
  Paraguay
  Poland
  Portugal
  Romania
  Rwanda
  San Marino
  Senegal
  South Africa
  Spain
  Sudan
  Switzerland
  Tanzania
  Thailand
  Turkey
  Uganda
  UK Great Britain
  USA (United States)
  Ukrainian SSR
  Upper Volta
  USSR (Soviet Union)
  Vatican/Holy See
  Vietnam, South
  Yugoslavia
  Zambia
             ANNEX
603 UNTS 352. Czechoslovakia. Ratification
  8 Aug 67.
605 UNTS 399. Hungary. Ratification 20 Sep 67.
  Reservation 20 Sep 67.
607 UNTS 357. Mali. Accession 11 Oct 67. Force
  10 Nov 67.
615 UNTS 412. Laos. Ratification 29 Dec 67.
  Force 28 Jan 68.
635 UNTS 377. Burundi. Accession 1 May 68.
638 UNTS 328. San Marino. Accession
  12 Jun 68. Force 12 Jul 68.
642 UNTS 379. Rwanda. Ratification 13 Aug 68.
  Force 12 Sep 68.
645 UNTS 384. Norway. Accession 17 Sep 68.
  Force 17 Oct 68.
649 UNTS 371. USA (United States). Ratification
  29 Oct 68. Force 28 Nov 68.

108642 Bilateral Exchange **597 UNTS 139**
SIGNED: 20 Feb 67   FORCE: 11 Jul 67
REGISTERED: 11 Jul 67 Philippines
ARTICLES: 3 LANGUAGE: English.
HEADNOTE: COOPERATION PEACEFUL USES
  ATOMIC ENERGY
TOPIC: Atomic Energy
CONCEPTS: Exchange. Research cooperation. Re-
  search results. Nuclear research. Scientific ex-
  change. General. Peaceful use.
PROCEDURE: Duration. Renewal or Revival.

PARTIES:
  Israel
  Philippines

108643 Bilateral Agreement **597 UNTS 147**
SIGNED: 8 Sep 66   FORCE: 4 Apr 67
REGISTERED: 12 Jul 67 Netherlands
ARTICLES: 19 LANGUAGE: French.
HEADNOTE: INTERNATIONAL ROAD TRANSPORT
TOPIC: Land Transport
CONCEPTS: Exceptions and exemptions. Territo-
  rial application. General provisions. Remedies.
  Conformity with municipal law. Exchange of in-
  formation and documents. Investigation of viola-
  tions. Establishment of commission. Tax exemp-
  tions. Customs exemptions. Passenger trans-
  port. Routes and logistics. Transport of goods.
  Commercial road vehicles. Roads and highways.
  Road rules.
PROCEDURE: Denunciation. Duration. Ratification.
  Renewal or Revival.
PARTIES:
  Netherlands
  Yugoslavia

108644 Multilateral Agreement **597 UNTS 159**
SIGNED: 20 Feb 62   FORCE: 28 Oct 66
REGISTERED: 15 Jun 67 UK Great Britain
ARTICLES: 12 LANGUAGE: English. French.
HEADNOTE: MAINTENANCE CERTAIN RIGHTS
  RED SEA
TOPIC: Water Transport
CONCEPTS: Change of circumstances. Default
  remedies. Definition of terms. Treaty interpreta-
  tion. Exchange of information and documents.
  Responsibility and liability. Abolition of extrater-
  ritorial rights. Indemnities and reimbursements.
  Fees and exemptions. Funding procedures. Pay-
  ment schedules. Navigational conditions. Navi-
  gational equipment. Water transport. Tonnage.
TREATY   REF: 28LTS11;   UK   MISC-
  .NO.1(1931)CMD.3755.
PROCEDURE: Amendment. Denunciation.
PARTIES:
  Denmark SIGNED: 3 Aug 62 RATIFIED: 3 Aug 62
    FORCE: 28 Oct 66
  Germany, West SIGNED: 16 Aug 62 RATIFIED:
    14 Sep 65 FORCE: 28 Oct 66
  Italy SIGNED: 14 Aug 62 RATIFIED: 26 Oct 66
    FORCE: 28 Oct 66
  Netherlands SIGNED: 16 Aug 62 RATIFIED:
    15 Jan 64 FORCE: 28 Oct 66
  Norway   SIGNED: 17 Aug 62   RATIFIED:
    25 Oct 66 FORCE: 28 Oct 66
  Pakistan RATIFIED: 27 Oct 65 FORCE: 28 Oct 66
  Sweden SIGNED: 2 Aug 62 RATIFIED: 2 Aug 62
    FORCE: 28 Oct 66
  United Arab Rep RATIFIED: 3 Oct 63 FORCE:
    28 Oct 66
  UK Great Britain SIGNED: 20 Feb 62 RATIFIED:
    2 Feb 62 FORCE: 28 Oct 66
  USA (United States) SIGNED: 2 Mar 62 RATI-
    FIED: 6 Apr 64 FORCE: 28 Oct 66
  USSR (Soviet Union) RATIFIED: 16 Dec 66
    FORCE: 28 Oct 66

108645 Bilateral Agreement **597 UNTS 177**
SIGNED: 12 Jan 65   FORCE: 7 Oct 66
REGISTERED: 15 Jun 67 UK Great Britain
ARTICLES: 17 LANGUAGE: English. Spanish.
HEADNOTE: AIR SERVICES
TOPIC: Air Transport
CONCEPTS: Definition of terms. Detailed regula-
  tions. Representation. Annex or appendix reference. Conformity with municipal law. General
  cooperation. Exchange of information and docu-
  ments. Use of facilities. Investigation of viola-
  tions. Arbitration. Procedure. Special tribunals.
  Reexport of goods, etc.. Expense sharing formulae. Fees and exemptions. Non-interest rates and
  fees. Most favored nation clause. National treatment. Customs duties. Customs exemptions.
  Routes and logistics. Navigational conditions.
  Permit designation. Air transport. Airport facilities. Conditions of airlines operating permission.
  Overflights and technical stops. Operating authorizations and regulations.
INTL ORGS: International Civil Aviation Organization.
TREATY REF: 15UNTS295.

PROCEDURE: Amendment. Future Procedures
  Contemplated. Ratification. Termination.
PARTIES:
  Argentina
  UK Great Britain

108646 Bilateral Agreement **597 UNTS 211**
SIGNED: 30 Sep 66   FORCE: 30 Sep 66
REGISTERED: 15 Jun 67 UK Great Britain
ARTICLES: 8 LANGUAGE: English.
HEADNOTE: STATUS ARMED FORCES
TOPIC: Status of Forces
CONCEPTS: Definition of terms. Visa abolition.
  Court procedures. Legal protection and assis-
  tance. Compensation. Tax exemptions. Customs
  exemptions. Jurisdiction. Status of forces.
PARTIES:
  Botswana
  UK Great Britain

108647 Bilateral Exchange **597 UNTS 219**
SIGNED: 26 Jul 66   FORCE: 26 Jul 66
REGISTERED: 15 Jun 67 UK Great Britain
ARTICLES: 2 LANGUAGE: English. Arabic.
HEADNOTE: INTEREST FREE LOAN
TOPIC: Loans and Credits
CONCEPTS: Interest rates. Payment schedules.
  Loan and credit. Loan repayment. Terms of loan.
  Industry. Irrigation. Hydro-electric power.
PARTIES:
  Jordan
  UK Great Britain

108648 Bilateral Exchange **597 UNTS 229**
SIGNED: 27 Oct 66   FORCE: 27 Nov 66
REGISTERED: 15 Jun 67 UK Great Britain
ARTICLES: 2 LANGUAGE: English. Spanish.
HEADNOTE: ABOLITION VISAS
TOPIC: Visas
CONCEPTS: Emergencies. Territorial application.
  Visa abolition. Denial of admission. Conformity
  with municipal law.
PROCEDURE: Denunciation.
PARTIES:
  Paraguay
  UK Great Britain

108649 Bilateral Exchange **597 UNTS 241**
SIGNED: 29 Jul 66   FORCE: 29 Jul 66
REGISTERED: 15 Jun 67 UK Great Britain
ARTICLES: 2 LANGUAGE: English.
HEADNOTE: INTEREST FREE LOAN DEVELOPE-
  MENT
TOPIC: Loans and Credits
CONCEPTS: Definition of terms. Detailed regula-
  tions. Annex or appendix reference. Accounting
  procedures. Currency. Payment schedules. Eco-
  nomic assistance. Loan and credit. Purchase au-
  thorization. Loan repayment. Terms of loan.
PARTIES:
  Turkey
  UK Great Britain

108650 Bilateral Exchange **597 UNTS 265**
SIGNED: 27 Oct 66   FORCE: 27 Nov 66
REGISTERED: 15 Jun 67 UK Great Britain
ARTICLES: 2 LANGUAGE: English.
HEADNOTE: INDEMNIFICATION THIRD PARTY LIA-
  BILITY
TOPIC: Claims and Debts
CONCEPTS: Conformity with municipal law. Re-
  sponsibility and liability. Payment schedules.
  Claims and settlements. Restrictions on transfer.
TREATY REF: 199UNTS67; 34UNTS243.
PROCEDURE: Duration. Termination.
PARTIES:
  UK Great Britain
  USA (United States)

108651 Bilateral Treaty **597 UNTS 273**
SIGNED: 21 Feb 66   FORCE: 24 Apr 67
REGISTERED: 19 Jun 67 Austria
ARTICLES: 6 LANGUAGE: German. Finnish.
HEADNOTE: FINANCE PROPERTY
TOPIC: Claims and Debts
CONCEPTS: Treaty implementation. Exchange of
  information and documents. Informational

records. Responsibility and liability. Banking. Claims and settlements. Lump sum settlements.
PROCEDURE: Ratification.
PARTIES:
Austria
Finland

108652 Bilateral Agreement **597 UNTS 283**
SIGNED: 14 Jun 66　　　FORCE: 14 Jul 66
REGISTERED: 20 Jul 67 Denmark
ARTICLES: 11 LANGUAGE: English.
HEADNOTE: AGRICULTURAL RESEARCH CENTER
TOPIC: Tech Assistance
CONCEPTS: Definition of terms. Annex or appendix reference. Friendship and amity. Privileges and immunities. General property. Exchange. Commissions and foundations. Scholarships and grants. Vocational training. Research cooperation. Research and development. Indemnities and reimbursements. Expense sharing formulae. Tax exemptions. Customs exemptions. Agriculture. Economic assistance.
PROCEDURE: Duration.
PARTIES:
Denmark
Iran

108653 Multilateral Agreement **598 UNTS 2**
SIGNED: 21 Jun 67　　　FORCE: 21 Jul 67
REGISTERED: 21 Jul 67 United Nations
ARTICLES: 6 LANGUAGE: English. Spanish.
HEADNOTE: OPERATIONAL ASSISTANCE
TOPIC: Tech Assistance
CONCEPTS: General provisions. Treaty implementation. Treaty interpretation. Annex or appendix reference. Privileges and immunities. General cooperation. Personnel. Responsibility and liability. Arbitration. Procedure. Negotiation. Vocational training. Compensation. Indemnities and reimbursements. Exchange rates and regulations. Expense sharing formulae. Tax exemptions. Customs exemptions. Domestic obligation. General technical assistance. Assistance. Status of experts.
TREATY REF: 482UNTS286.
PROCEDURE: Amendment. Termination.
PARTIES:
Honduras　SIGNED: 21 Jun 67　FORCE: 21 Jun 67
FAO (Food Agri) SIGNED: 21 Jun 67 FORCE: 21 Jun 67
IAEA (Atom Energy) SIGNED: 21 Jun 67 FORCE: 21 Jun 67
ICAO (Civil Aviat) SIGNED: 21 Jun 67 FORCE: 21 Jun 67
ILO (Labor Org) SIGNED: 21 Jun 67 FORCE: 21 Jun 67
IMCO (Maritime Org) SIGNED: 21 Jun 67 FORCE: 21 Jun 67
ITU (Telecommun) SIGNED: 21 Jun 67 FORCE: 21 Jun 67
UNESCO (Educ/Cult) SIGNED: 21 Jun 67 FORCE: 21 Jun 67
United Nations SIGNED: 21 Jun 67 FORCE: 21 Jun 67
UPU (Postal Union) SIGNED: 21 Jun 67 FORCE: 21 Jun 67
WHO (World Health) SIGNED: 21 Jun 67 FORCE: 21 Jun 67
WMO (Meteorology) SIGNED: 21 Jun 67 FORCE: 21 Jun 67

108654 Bilateral Treaty **598 UNTS 25**
SIGNED: 21 Apr 65　　　FORCE: 30 Jan 66
REGISTERED: 22 Jul 67 Australia
ARTICLES: 16 LANGUAGE: English. German.
HEADNOTE: COMPENSATION PROPERTY
TOPIC: Claims and Debts
CONCEPTS: Detailed regulations. Territorial application. Acquisition of nationality. General property. Compensation. Indemnities and reimbursements. Payment schedules. Claims and settlements.
PROCEDURE: Ratification.
PARTIES:
Australia
Germany, West

108655 Multilateral Agreement **598 UNTS 81**
SIGNED: 26 Nov 65　　　FORCE: 26 Nov 65

REGISTERED: 27 Jul 67 Australia
ARTICLES: 8 LANGUAGE: English.
HEADNOTE: TERRITORY NAURU
TOPIC: Recognition
CONCEPTS: Definition of terms. Exceptions and exemptions. Democratic institutions. Governor-general functions. Self-government. General cooperation.
TREATY REF: 113BFSP151.
PARTIES:
Australia SIGNED: 26 Nov 65 FORCE: 26 Nov 65
New Zealand SIGNED: 26 Nov 65 FORCE: 26 Nov 65
UK Great Britain SIGNED: 26 Nov 65 FORCE: 26 Nov 65

108656 Bilateral Agreement **598 UNTS 91**
SIGNED: 31 Jan 67　　　FORCE: 31 Jan 67
REGISTERED: 22 Jul 67 New Zealand
ARTICLES: 9 LANGUAGE: English. Korean.
HEADNOTE: TRADE ECONOMIC RELATIONS
TOPIC: General Trade
CONCEPTS: Exceptions and exemptions. Territorial application. General cooperation. Negotiation. Export quotas. Import quotas. Reciprocity in trade. Trade procedures. Balance of payments. Currency. Payment schedules. Most favored nation clause. National treatment.
PROCEDURE: Amendment. Duration. Termination.
PARTIES:
Korea, South
New Zealand

108657 Bilateral Exchange **598 UNTS 115**
SIGNED: 29 Jul 66　　　FORCE: 27 Jul 66
REGISTERED: 22 Jul 67 New Zealand
ARTICLES: 2 LANGUAGE: English.
HEADNOTE: FINANCIAL ASSISTANCE PLANTATIONS RESTORATION
TOPIC: Direct Aid
CONCEPTS: General cooperation. General aid. Relief supplies. Grants. Loan and credit. Loan repayment. Terms of loan.
PARTIES:
New Zealand
Western Samoa

108658 Bilateral Agreement **598 UNTS 121**
SIGNED: 13 Jul 66　　　FORCE: 11 Sep 66
REGISTERED: 22 Jun 67 New Zealand
ARTICLES: 24 LANGUAGE: English.
HEADNOTE: DOUBLE TAXATION
TOPIC: Taxation
CONCEPTS: Taxation. Tax credits. General. Tax exemptions.
PROCEDURE: Termination.
PARTIES:
New Zealand
UK Great Britain

108659 Bilateral Agreement **598 UNTS 161**
SIGNED: 9 Jan 67　　　FORCE: 7 Mar 67
REGISTERED: 23 Jun 67 IBRD (World Bank)
ARTICLES: 5 LANGUAGE: English.
HEADNOTE: POTASH PROJECT
TOPIC: IBRD Project
CONCEPTS: Loan and credit. Credit provisions.
PARTIES:
Congo (Brazzaville)
IBRD (World Bank)

108660 Bilateral Agreement **598 UNTS 223**
SIGNED: 14 Sep 66　　　FORCE: 20 Sep 66
REGISTERED: 23 Jun 67 IBRD (World Bank)
ARTICLES: 5 LANGUAGE: English.
HEADNOTE: GUARANTEE
TOPIC: IBRD Project
CONCEPTS: Loan and credit. Credit provisions.
PARTIES:
Iceland
IBRD (World Bank)

108661 Bilateral Agreement **598 UNTS 261**
SIGNED: 5 Apr 67　　　FORCE: 12 Jun 67
REGISTERED: 23 Jun 67 IBRD (World Bank)
ARTICLES: 6 LANGUAGE: English.
HEADNOTE: GUARANTEE
TOPIC: IBRD Project

CONCEPTS: Credit provisions.
PARTIES:
Philippines
IBRD (World Bank)

108662 Bilateral Agreement **599 UNTS 3**
SIGNED: 10 Mar 67　　　FORCE: 26 Apr 67
REGISTERED: 23 Jun 67 IBRD (World Bank)
ARTICLES: 5 LANGUAGE: English.
HEADNOTE: LOAN AGREEMENT
TOPIC: IBRD Project
CONCEPTS: Definition of terms. Treaty implementation. Annex or appendix reference. Bonds. Financial programs. Interest rates. Credit provisions. Loan repayment. Terms of loan. Loan regulations.
PARTIES:
IBRD (World Bank)
Trinidad/Tobago

108663 Bilateral Agreement **599 UNTS 27**
SIGNED: 24 Feb 67　　　FORCE: 26 May 67
REGISTERED: 23 Jun 67 IBRD (World Bank)
ARTICLES: 5 LANGUAGE: English.
HEADNOTE: GUARANTEE AGREEMENT
TOPIC: IBRD Project
CONCEPTS: Definition of terms. Annex or appendix reference. Exchange of information and documents. Bonds. Interest rates. Debts. General. Loan repayment. Terms of loan. Loan regulations. Loan guarantee.
PARTIES:
IBRD (World Bank)
Yugoslavia

108664 Bilateral Agreement **599 UNTS 52**
SIGNED: 15 Mar 66　　　FORCE: 29 May 67
REGISTERED: 26 Jun 67 IBRD (World Bank)
ARTICLES: 5 LANGUAGE: English.
HEADNOTE: GUARANTEE AGREEMENT
TOPIC: IBRD Project
CONCEPTS: Definition of terms. Annex or appendix reference. Exchange of information and documents. Bonds. Interest rates. Debts. General. Loan repayment. Terms of loan. Loan regulations. Loan guarantee. Plans and standards.
PARTIES:
Brazil
IBRD (World Bank)

108665 Bilateral Agreement **599 UNTS 107**
SIGNED: 19 Dec 66　　　FORCE: 1 Jun 67
REGISTERED: 26 Jun 67 IBRD (World Bank)
ARTICLES: 5 LANGUAGE: English.
HEADNOTE: GUARANTEE
TOPIC: IBRD Project
CONCEPTS: Definition of terms. Annex or appendix reference. Exchange of information and documents. Inspection and observation. Bonds. Interest rates. Liens. General. Loan regulations. Loan guarantee.
PARTIES:
Brazil
IBRD (World Bank)

108666 Bilateral Agreement **599 UNTS 149**
SIGNED: 19 Dec 66　　　FORCE: 1 Jun 67
REGISTERED: 26 Jun 67 IBRD (World Bank)
ARTICLES: 8 LANGUAGE: English.
HEADNOTE: GUARANTEE
TOPIC: IBRD Project
CONCEPTS: Definition of terms. Annex or appendix reference. Exchange of information and documents. Inspection and observation. Bonds. Interest rates. Liens. General. Loan regulations. Loan guarantee.
PARTIES:
Brazil
IBRD (World Bank)

108667 Bilateral Agreement **599 UNTS 177**
SIGNED: 19 Dec 66　　　FORCE: 1 Jun 67
REGISTERED: 26 Jun 67 IBRD (World Bank)
ARTICLES: 8 LANGUAGE: English.
HEADNOTE: GUARANTEE
TOPIC: IBRD Project
CONCEPTS: Definition of terms. Annex or appendix reference. Exchange of information and doc-

uments. Inspection and observation. Bonds. Interest rates. Liens. General. Loan regulations. Loan guarantee.
PARTIES:
Brazil
IBRD (World Bank)

108668 Bilateral Agreement **599 UNTS 205**
SIGNED: 19 Dec 66　　　FORCE: 1 Jun 67
REGISTERED: 26 Jun 67 IBRD (World Bank)
ARTICLES: 8 LANGUAGE: English.
HEADNOTE: GUARANTEE
TOPIC: IBRD Project
CONCEPTS: Definition of terms. Annex or appendix reference. Exchange of information and documents. Inspection and observation. Bonds. Interest rates. Liens. General. Loan regulations. Loan guarantee.
PARTIES:
Brazil
IBRD (World Bank)

108669 Bilateral Agreement **599 UNTS 233**
SIGNED: 17 Feb 67　　　FORCE: 12 May 67
REGISTERED: 26 Jun 67 IBRD (World Bank)
ARTICLES: 5 LANGUAGE: English.
HEADNOTE: GUARANTEE
TOPIC: IBRD Project
CONCEPTS: Definition of terms. Annex or appendix reference. Exchange of information and documents. Inspection and observation. Assets. Liens. General. Credit provisions. Loan repayment. Loan regulations. Loan guarantee.
PARTIES:
Kenya
IBRD (World Bank)

108670 Bilateral Agreement **599 UNTS 245**
SIGNED: 15 Mar 67　　　FORCE: 10 May 67
REGISTERED: 26 Jun 67 IBRD (World Bank)
ARTICLES: 5 LANGUAGE: English.
HEADNOTE: GUARANTEE
TOPIC: IBRD Project
CONCEPTS: Definition of terms. Annex or appendix reference. Exchange of information and documents. Inspection and observation. Assets. Liens. General. Loan regulations. Loan guarantee.
PARTIES:
Pakistan
IBRD (World Bank)

108671 Bilateral Agreement **599 UNTS 287**
SIGNED: 17 Feb 67　　　FORCE: 12 May 67
REGISTERED: 26 Jun 67 IBRD (World Bank)
ARTICLES: 5 LANGUAGE: English.
HEADNOTE: GUARANTEE
TOPIC: IBRD Project
CONCEPTS: Definition of terms. Exchange of information and documents. Inspection and observation. Bonds. Interest rates. Assets. Liens. General. Tax exemptions. Credit provisions. Loan regulations. Loan guarantee.
PARTIES:
IBRD (World Bank)
Tanzania

108672 Bilateral Agreement **599 UNTS 299**
SIGNED: 24 Mar 67　　　FORCE: 23 May 67
REGISTERED: 26 Jun 67 IBRD (World Bank)
ARTICLES: 5 LANGUAGE: English.
HEADNOTE: GUARANTEE
TOPIC: IBRD Project
CONCEPTS: Definition of terms. Annex or appendix reference. Exchange of information and documents. Inspection and observation. Interest rates. Assets. Liens. Tax exemptions. Credit provisions. Loan regulations. Loan guarantee.
PARTIES:
IBRD (World Bank)
Thailand

108673 Bilateral Agreement **599 UNTS 321**
SIGNED: 17 Feb 67　　　FORCE: 12 May 67
REGISTERED: 26 Jun 67 IBRD (World Bank)
ARTICLES: 5 LANGUAGE: English.
HEADNOTE: GUARANTEE
TOPIC: IBRD Project

CONCEPTS: Definition of terms. Annex or appendix reference. Exchange of information and documents. Inspection and observation. Interest rates. Assets. Liens. Tax exemptions. Credit provisions. Loan regulations. Loan guarantee.
PARTIES:
IBRD (World Bank)
Uganda

108674 Bilateral Agreement **600 UNTS 3**
SIGNED: 24 Apr 67　　　FORCE: 26 May 67
REGISTERED: 26 Jun 67 IBRD (World Bank)
ARTICLES: 5 LANGUAGE: English.
HEADNOTE: LOAN BETWEEN SWAZILAND & ELECTRICAL COMPANY
TOPIC: IBRD Project
CONCEPTS: General cooperation. Bonds. Interest rates. Claims and settlements. Debts. Loan repayment. Services.
PARTIES:
IBRD (World Bank)
UK Great Britain

108675 Multilateral Agreement **600 UNTS 49**
SIGNED: 16 Jul 65　　　FORCE: 31 Jan 67
REGISTERED: 28 Jun 67 Netherlands
ARTICLES: 11 LANGUAGE: French.
HEADNOTE: LONG-TERM TRADE
TOPIC: General Trade
CONCEPTS: Establishment of commission. Export quotas. Import quotas. Balance of payments.
TREATY REF: 381 UNTS 165.
PARTIES:
Belgium　　SIGNED:　　16 Jul 65　　RATIFIED: 25 Oct 65 FORCE: 31 Jan 67
Bulgaria　　SIGNED:　　16 Jul 65　　RATIFIED: 31 Jan 67 FORCE: 31 Jan 67
Luxembourg　SIGNED:　　16 Jul 65　　RATIFIED: 25 Oct 65 FORCE: 31 Jan 67
Netherlands　SIGNED:　　16 Jul 65　　RATIFIED: 17 May 66 FORCE: 31 Jan 67

108676 Bilateral Agreement **600 UNTS 69**
SIGNED: 14 May 66　　　FORCE: 14 May 66
REGISTERED: 29 Jun 67 ILO (Labor Org)
ARTICLES: 6 LANGUAGE: French.
HEADNOTE: ESTABLISH OFFICE OF ORGANIZATION
TOPIC: IGO Establishment
CONCEPTS: General cooperation. Operating agencies. Regional offices.
PARTIES:
Lebanon
ILO (Labor Org)

108677 Bilateral Agreement **600 UNTS 75**
SIGNED: 9 Feb 67　　　FORCE: 9 Feb 67
REGISTERED: 29 Jun 67 ILO (Labor Org)
ARTICLES: 6 LANGUAGE: French.
HEADNOTE: ESTABLISH OFFICE OF ORGANIZATION
TOPIC: IGO Establishment
CONCEPTS: General cooperation. Operating agencies. Regional offices.
PARTIES:
ILO (Labor Org)
Senegal

108678 Bilateral Agreement **600 UNTS 81**
SIGNED: 6 Jul 67　　　FORCE: 6 Jul 67
REGISTERED: 6 Jul 67 United Nations
ARTICLES: 10 LANGUAGE: English.
HEADNOTE: INTERNATIONAL SEMINAR APARTHEID
TOPIC: IGO Operations
CONCEPTS: General cooperation. Informational records. Legal protection and assistance. Conferences.
PARTIES:
United Nations
Zambia

108679 Bilateral Agreement **600 UNTS 93**
SIGNED: 13 Apr 67　　　FORCE: 7 Jul 67
REGISTERED: 7 Jul 67 United Nations
ARTICLES: 47 LANGUAGE: English. German.
HEADNOTE: HEADQUARTERS UNIPO
TOPIC: IGO Establishment

CONCEPTS: Privileges and immunities. Dispute settlement. Social security. Finances and payments. Tax exemptions. General transportation. Radio-telephone-telegraphic communications. Publications exchange. Headquarters and facilities.
PARTIES:
Austria
United Nations

108680 Multilateral Agreement **600 UNTS 161**
SIGNED: 8 Dec 65　　　FORCE: 2 Apr 66
REGISTERED: 12 Jul 67 Trinidad/Tobago
ARTICLES: 14 LANGUAGE: English.
HEADNOTE: CARIBBEAN METEOROLOGICAL SERVICE
TOPIC: IGO Establishment
CONCEPTS: General cooperation. Responsibility and liability. Arbitration. Meteorology. Finances and payments. Headquarters and facilities. Internal structure.
PARTIES:
Jamaica SIGNED: 14 Dec 65 FORCE: 2 Apr 66
Trinidad/Tobago SIGNED: 8 Dec 65 FORCE: 2 Apr 66
UK Great Britain Antigua RATIFIED: 30 Mar 66 FORCE: 2 Apr 66
UK Great Britain Barbados RATIFIED: 8 Dec 65 FORCE: 2 Apr 66
UK Great Britain British Guiana RATIFIED: 8 Dec 65 FORCE: 2 Apr 66
UK Great Britain British Honduras RATIFIED: 14 Mar 66 FORCE: 2 Apr 66
UK Great Britain Brit Virgin Islands RATIFIED: 1 Apr 66 FORCE: 2 Apr 66
UK Great Britain Cayman Island RATIFIED: 8 Dec 65 FORCE: 2 Apr 66
UK Great Britain Dominican Republic RATIFIED: 29 Mar 66 FORCE: 2 Apr 66
UK Great Britain Grenada RATIFIED: 23 Dec 65 FORCE: 2 Apr 66
UK Great Britain Montserrat RATIFIED: 8 Dec 65 FORCE: 2 Apr 66
UK Great Britain St. Lucia RATIFIED: 8 Dec 65 FORCE: 2 Apr 66
UK Great Britain St. Vincent RATIFIED: 28 Mar 66 FORCE: 2 Apr 66

108681 Bilateral Agreement **600 UNTS 189**
SIGNED: 27 Feb 67　　　FORCE: 27 Feb 67
REGISTERED: 12 Jul 67 Denmark
ARTICLES: 20 LANGUAGE: French.
HEADNOTE: SCHEDULED AIR TRANSPORT
TOPIC: Air Transport
CONCEPTS: Special tribunals. Tariffs. Airport facilities. Airport equipment. Airworthiness certificates. Conditions of airlines operating permission. Operating authorizations and regulations.
PARTIES:
Congo (Brazzaville)
Denmark

108682 Bilateral Convention **600 UNTS 213**
SIGNED: 6 Jun 63　　　FORCE: 3 Feb 65
REGISTERED: 12 Jul 67 Denmark
ARTICLES: 11 LANGUAGE: French.
HEADNOTE: MILITARY SERVICE DUAL NATIONALITY
TOPIC: Milit Servic/Citiz
CONCEPTS: Dual nationality. Foreign nationals. Service in foreign army.
PARTIES:
Denmark
France

108683 Bilateral Agreement **600 UNTS 227**
SIGNED: 22 Sep 66　　　FORCE: 6 Jun 67
REGISTERED: 12 Jul 67 Norway
ARTICLES: 36 LANGUAGE: Dutch. Norwegian.
HEADNOTE: DOUBLE TAXATION TAX EVASION
TOPIC: Taxation
CONCEPTS: General consular functions. Exchange of information and documents. Immovable property. Revival of treaties. Social security. Financial programs. Interest rates. Non-interest rates and fees. Assets. Taxation. Equitable taxes. Air transport.
PARTIES:
Netherlands
Norway

108684 Bilateral Agreement **601 UNTS 3**
SIGNED: 9 Jun 65 FORCE: 10 May 67
REGISTERED: 12 Jul 67 Yugoslavia
ARTICLES: 10 LANGUAGE: Serbo-Croat. Spanish.
HEADNOTE: TRADE
TOPIC: General Trade
CONCEPTS: Exceptions and exemptions. Previous treaty replacement. Establishment of commission. General trade. Export quotas. Import quotas. Reciprocity in trade. Trade agencies. Trade procedures. Finances and payments. Reciprocity in financial treatment. Non-interest rates and fees. Claims, debts and assets. Most favored nation clause. Customs duties. Water transport. Merchant vessels.
PROCEDURE: Ratification. Renewal or Revival. Termination.
PARTIES:
Argentina
Yugoslavia

108685 Bilateral Agreement **601 UNTS 21**
SIGNED: 26 Sep 66 FORCE: 28 Apr 67
REGISTERED: 12 Jul 67 Yugoslavia
ARTICLES: 8 LANGUAGE: Serbo-Croat. Hungarian.
HEADNOTE: COOPERATION HEALTH MATTERS
TOPIC: Sanitation
CONCEPTS: General cooperation. Exchange of information and documents. International circulation. Specialists exchange. Sanitation. Public health. Pharmaceuticals. Medical assistance and/or facilities. Teacher and student exchange. Professorships. Research and scientific projects. Scientific exchange.
PROCEDURE: Denunciation. Ratification.
PARTIES:
Hungary
Yugoslavia

108686 Bilateral Agreement **601 UNTS 37**
SIGNED: 20 Mar 67 FORCE: 20 Mar 67
REGISTERED: 19 Jul 67 Belgium
ARTICLES: 21 LANGUAGE: French.
HEADNOTE: ROAD TRANSPORT GOODS PASSENGERS
TOPIC: Land Transport
CONCEPTS: General provisions. Visas. Exchange of information and documents. Establishment of commission. General. Passenger transport. Permit designation. Transport of goods. Merchant vessels. Commercial road vehicles.
PROCEDURE: Denunciation. Renewal or Revival.
PARTIES:
Belgium
Hungary

108687 Bilateral Agreement **601 UNTS 51**
SIGNED: 23 Jun 66 FORCE: 23 Jul 66
REGISTERED: 19 Jul 67 USA (United States)
ARTICLES: 20 LANGUAGE: English. German.
HEADNOTE: AIR TRANSPORT
TOPIC: Air Transport
CONCEPTS: Definition of terms. General cooperation. Exchange of information and documents. Procedure. Special tribunals. Negotiation. Tariffs. Customs duties. Routes and logistics. Air transport. Conditions of airlines operating permission. Operating authorizations and regulations.
TREATY REF: 15 UNTS 295, ETC.; 25 UNTS 3.
PARTIES:
Austria
USA (United States)

108688 Bilateral Exchange **601 UNTS 81**
SIGNED: 6 Nov 65 FORCE: 6 Nov 65
REGISTERED: 19 Jul 67 USA (United States)
ARTICLES: 18 LANGUAGE: Spanish.
HEADNOTE: CUBAN REFUGEES
TOPIC: Refugees
CONCEPTS: Refugees and stateless persons. Assistance. Refugees. Procedure. Water transport.
PARTIES:
Cuba
USA (United States)

108689 Bilateral Exchange **601 UNTS 107**
SIGNED: 30 Jun 66 FORCE: 30 Jun 66
REGISTERED: 19 Jul 67 USA (United States)

ARTICLES: 2 LANGUAGE: English. German.
HEADNOTE: AMATEUR RADIO OPERATIONS
TOPIC: Gen Communications
CONCEPTS: Territorial application. Amateur radio.
TREATY REF: USA' TREATIES ANN OTHER INTL ACTS SERIES 4893;$.
PROCEDURE: Termination.
PARTIES:
Germany, West
USA (United States)

108690 Bilateral Exchange **601 UNTS 113**
SIGNED: 17 Jun 66 FORCE: 17 Jun 66
REGISTERED: 19 Jul 67 USA (United States)
ARTICLES: 2 LANGUAGE: English. French.
HEADNOTE: COOPERATION SPACE MATTERS
TOPIC: Scientific Project
CONCEPTS: Research and scientific projects. Research cooperation. Meteorology.
PARTIES:
France
USA (United States)

108691 Bilateral Exchange **601 UNTS 125**
SIGNED: 3 Aug 66 FORCE: 3 Aug 66
REGISTERED: 19 Jul 67 USA (United States)
ARTICLES: 10 LANGUAGE: English.
HEADNOTE: DEPLOYMENT SHIP
TOPIC: Milit Assistance
CONCEPTS: Use of facilities. Lease of military property. Naval vessels. Procurement and logistics.
PARTIES:
Malta
USA (United States)

108692 Bilateral Agreement **601 UNTS 133**
SIGNED: 30 Jul 66 FORCE: 30 Jul 66
REGISTERED: 19 Jul 67 USA (United States)
ARTICLES: 6 LANGUAGE: English.
HEADNOTE: AGRICULTURAL COMMODITIES AGREEMENT
TOPIC: US Agri Commod Aid
CONCEPTS: General provisions. General cooperation. Currency. Agricultural commodities assistance. Purchase authorization.
PARTIES:
Tunisia
USA (United States)
ANNEX
606 UNTS 408. USA (United States). Amendment 19 Sep 66. Force 19 Sep 66.
606 UNTS 408. Tunisia. Amendment 19 Sep 66. Force 19 Sep 66.

108693 Bilateral Agreement **601 UNTS 153**
SIGNED: 24 May 67 FORCE: 1 Jul 67
REGISTERED: 24 Jul 67 Belgium
ARTICLES: 11 LANGUAGE: Portuguese. French. Dutch.
HEADNOTE: SEAMANS BOOK TRAVEL DOCUMENT
TOPIC: Visas
CONCEPTS: Definition of terms. Territorial application. Frontier formalities. Border traffic and migration. Non-visa travel documents.
TREATY REF: 374 UNTS 3.
PROCEDURE: Denunciation. Duration.
PARTIES:
Benelux Econ Union
Portugal

108694 Bilateral Agreement **601 UNTS 167**
SIGNED: 14 Jun 66 FORCE: 4 Dec 66
REGISTERED: 24 Jul 67 Belgium
ARTICLES: 11 LANGUAGE: French.
HEADNOTE: ECONOMIC INDUSTRIAL TECHNICAL COOPERATION
TOPIC: General Economic
CONCEPTS: Establishment of commission. Research and scientific projects. General economics. Payment schedules. Transport of goods.
TREATY REF: 600 UNTS.
PROCEDURE: Denunciation. Ratification.
PARTIES:
Bel-Lux Econ Union
Bulgaria

108695 Bilateral Agreement **601 UNTS 175**
SIGNED: 30 Oct 64 FORCE: 10 May 67
REGISTERED: 28 Jul 67 Argentina
ARTICLES: 7 LANGUAGE: Spanish.
HEADNOTE: CULTURE
TOPIC: Culture
CONCEPTS: Establishment of commission. Institute establishment. Scholarships and grants. Culture. Exchange. Attachment of funds.
PROCEDURE: Denunciation. Ratification. Renewal or Revival.
PARTIES:
Argentina
Guatemala

108696 Bilateral Agreement **601 UNTS 187**
SIGNED: 10 Oct 66 FORCE: 28 Jan 67
REGISTERED: 28 Jul 67 Argentina
ARTICLES: 7 LANGUAGE: Spanish. Italian.
HEADNOTE: AGREEMENT
TOPIC: Consul/Citizenship
CONCEPTS: Peaceful relations. Privileges and immunities. General cooperation. Procedure.
PROCEDURE: Ratification.
PARTIES:
Argentina
Vatican/Holy See

108697 Bilateral Agreement **601 UNTS 201**
SIGNED: 26 Mar 66 FORCE: 26 May 67
REGISTERED: 28 Jul 67 Argentina
ARTICLES: 9 LANGUAGE: Spanish. English.
HEADNOTE: TRADE
TOPIC: General Trade
CONCEPTS: General cooperation. General trade. Export quotas. Import quotas. Non-interest rates and fees. Commodity trade. Most favored nation clause. Customs duties. Water transport.
TREATY REF: TATT.
PROCEDURE: Ratification. Termination.
PARTIES:
Argentina
India

108698 Bilateral Agreement **601 UNTS 213**
SIGNED: 12 Sep 63 FORCE: 22 Mar 67
REGISTERED: 28 Jul 67 Argentina
ARTICLES: 7 LANGUAGE: Spanish. English.
HEADNOTE: MILITARY SERVICE
TOPIC: Milit Servic/Citiz
CONCEPTS: Military service and citizenship. Certificates of service. Foreign nationals.
PROCEDURE: Ratification. Termination.
PARTIES:
Argentina
UK Great Britain
ANNEX
633 UNTS 418. UK Great Britain. Jersey Island. Force 27 Nov 67.
633 UNTS 418. UK Great Britain. Isle of Man. Force 27 Nov 67.

108699 Bilateral Protocol **601 UNTS 229**
SIGNED: 6 Jan 64 FORCE: 6 Jan 64
REGISTERED: 28 Jul 67 South Africa
ARTICLES: 14 LANGUAGE: English. Afrikaans. French.
HEADNOTE: SPACE TRACKING STATION
TOPIC: Scientific Project
CONCEPTS: General property. Arbitration. Procedure. Research and scientific projects. Research cooperation. Tax exemptions. Customs duties. Customs exemptions.
PROCEDURE: Future Procedures Contemplated. Ratification.
PARTIES:
France
South Africa

108700 Bilateral Agreement **601 UNTS 247**
SIGNED: 9 Mar 64 FORCE: 16 Sep 64
REGISTERED: 31 Jul 64 ICAO (Civil Aviat)
ARTICLES: 24 LANGUAGE: French. Czechoslovakian.
HEADNOTE: AIR TRANSPORT
TOPIC: Air Transport
CONCEPTS: Definition of terms. Treaty implementation. Treaty interpretation. Procedure. Air

transport. Operating authorizations and regulations.
PROCEDURE: Amendment. Future Procedures Contemplated. Termination.
PARTIES:
Algeria
Czechoslovakia

108701   Bilateral Agreement   **601 UNTS 275**
SIGNED: 1 Sep 63   FORCE: 1 Sep 63
REGISTERED: 31 Jul 64 ICAO (Civil Aviat)
ARTICLES: 19 LANGUAGE: French.
HEADNOTE: AIR TRANSPORT
TOPIC: Air Transport
CONCEPTS: Definition of terms. Detailed regulations. Treaty implementation. Treaty interpretation. IGO reference. General cooperation. Licenses and permits. Arbitration. Procedure. Special tribunals. Negotiation. Finances and payments. Customs duties. Competency certificate. Passenger transport. Transport of goods. Air transport. Airport equipment. Overflights and technical stops. Operating authorizations and regulations.
INTL ORGS: International Civil Aviation Organization.
TREATY REF: 15 UNTS 295; 320 UNTS 209,217; 418 UNTS 161.
PROCEDURE: Amendment. Termination.
PARTIES:
Algeria
Tunisia

108702   Bilateral Agreement   **601 UNTS 293**
SIGNED: 13 Apr 65   FORCE: 13 Apr 65
REGISTERED: 31 Jul 64 ICAO (Civil Aviat)
ARTICLES: 16 LANGUAGE: French. English.
HEADNOTE: AIR TRANSPORT
TOPIC: Air Transport
CONCEPTS: Definition of terms. Detailed regulations. Treaty implementation. Treaty interpretation. Annex or appendix reference. IGO reference. Licenses and permits. Arbitration. Procedure. Special tribunals. Negotiation. Finances and payments. Customs duties. Competency certificate. Passenger transport. Air transport. Airport equipment. Overflights and technical stops. Operating authorizations and regulations.
INTL ORGS: International Civil Aviation Organization.
TREATY REF: 15 UNTS 295; 320 UNTS 209,217; 418 UNTS 161.
PROCEDURE: Termination.
PARTIES:
Australia
France

108703   Bilateral Agreement   **601 UNTS 311**
SIGNED: 8 Jun 63   FORCE: 16 Jun 66
REGISTERED: 31 Jul 64 ICAO (Civil Aviat)
ARTICLES: 19 LANGUAGE: English.
HEADNOTE: AIR TRANSPORT
TOPIC: Air Transport
CONCEPTS: Definition of terms. Detailed regulations. Treaty implementation. Treaty interpretation. Annex or appendix reference. Previous treaty replacement. IGO reference. General cooperation. Licenses and permits. Arbitration. Procedure. Special tribunals. Negotiation. Tariffs. Finances and payments. Taxation of immovable property. Competency certificate. Passenger transport. Air transport. Airport equipment. Overflights and technical stops. Operating authorizations and regulations.
INTL ORGS: International Civil Aviation Organization.
TREATY REF: 15 UNTS 295; 320 UNTS 209, 217; 418 UNTS 161.
PROCEDURE: Amendment. Ratification.
PARTIES:
Belgium
Cyprus

108704   Bilateral Agreement   **602 UNTS 3**
SIGNED: 2 Jun 64   FORCE: 24 May 66
REGISTERED: 31 Jul 67 ICAO (Civil Aviat)
ARTICLES: 24 LANGUAGE: English.
HEADNOTE: AIR TRANSPORT
TOPIC: Air Transport
CONCEPTS: Definition of terms. Detailed regula-

tions. Treaty implementation. Treaty interpretation. Annex or appendix reference. Previous treaty replacement. IGO reference. General cooperation. Licenses and permits. Arbitration. Procedure. Special tribunals. Negotiation. Tariffs. Finances and payments. Taxation of immovable property. Competency certificate. Passenger transport. Air transport. Airport equipment. Airworthiness certificates. Overflights and technical stops. Operating authorizations and regulations.
INTL ORGS: International Civil Aviation Organization.
PARTIES:
Cyprus
Hungary

108705   Bilateral Agreement   **602 UNTS 25**
SIGNED: 22 Dec 64   FORCE: 16 May 65
REGISTERED: 31 Jul 67 ICAO (Civil Aviat)
ARTICLES: 21 LANGUAGE: English.
HEADNOTE: AIR TRANSPORT
TOPIC: Air Transport
CONCEPTS: Definition of terms. Detailed regulations. Treaty implementation. Treaty interpretation. Annex or appendix reference. Previous treaty replacement. IGO reference. General cooperation. Licenses and permits. Arbitration. Procedure. Special tribunals. Negotiation. Finances and payments. Taxation of immovable property. Customs duties. Competency certificate. Passenger transport. Air transport. Airport equipment. Airworthiness certificates. Overflights and technical stops. Operating authorizations and regulations.
INTL ORGS: International Civil Aviation Organization.
TREATY REF: 15 UNTS 295; 320 UNTS 209, 217; 418 UNTS 161.
PARTIES:
Cyprus
Syria

108706   Bilateral Agreement   **602 UNTS 45**
SIGNED: 29 Feb 64   FORCE: 29 Apr 65
REGISTERED: 31 Jul 67 ICAO (Civil Aviat)
ARTICLES: 11 LANGUAGE: English. Russian.
HEADNOTE: AIR TRANSPORT
TOPIC: Air Transport
CONCEPTS: Annex or appendix reference. General cooperation. Exchange of information and documents. Accounting procedures. Fees and exemptions. Air transport. Airport equipment. Conditions of airlines operating permission. Overflights and technical stops. Operating authorizations and regulations. Licenses and certificates of nationality.
PROCEDURE: Termination.
PARTIES:
Cyprus
USSR (Soviet Union)

108707   Bilateral Agreement   **602 UNTS 71**
SIGNED: 15 Dec 65   FORCE: 15 Dec 65
REGISTERED: 31 Jul 67 ICAO (Civil Aviat)
ARTICLES: 17 LANGUAGE: English.
HEADNOTE: AIR TRANSPORT
TOPIC: Air Transport
CONCEPTS: Definition of terms. Detailed regulations. Time limit. Treaty implementation. Treaty interpretation. IGO reference. Licenses and permits. Tariffs. Customs duties. Competency certificate. Passenger transport. Routes and logistics. Transport of goods. Air transport. Airport equipment. Airworthiness certificates. Operating authorizations and regulations.
INTL ORGS: International Civil Aviation Organization.
PROCEDURE: Amendment. Registration. Termination.
PARTIES:
Burma
Czechoslovakia

108708   Bilateral Agreement   **602 UNTS 91**
SIGNED: 24 Jul 63   FORCE: 24 Jul 63
REGISTERED: 31 Jul 67 ICAO (Civil Aviat)
ARTICLES: 21 LANGUAGE: French.
HEADNOTE: AIR SERVICES
TOPIC: Air Transport

CONCEPTS: Definition of terms. Detailed regulations. General provisions. Time limit. IGO reference. General cooperation. Arbitration. Procedure. Special tribunals. Negotiation. Currency. Payment schedules. Non-interest rates and fees. Routes and logistics. Air transport. Overflights and technical stops.
INTL ORGS: International Civil Aviation Organization.
TREATY REF: 15 UNTS 295; 320 UNTS 209, 217; 418 UNTS 161.
PROCEDURE: Termination. Amendment.
PARTIES:
Mali
Tunisia

108709   Bilateral Agreement   **602 UNTS 111**
SIGNED: 11 May 65   FORCE: 11 May 65
REGISTERED: 31 Jul 67 ICAO (Civil Aviat)
ARTICLES: 16 LANGUAGE: French. Spanish.
HEADNOTE: AIR TRANSPORT
TOPIC: Air Transport
CONCEPTS: Definition of terms. IGO reference. General cooperation. Exchange of information and documents. Arbitration. Procedure. Special tribunals. Tariffs. Customs duties. Competency certificate. Air transport. Airworthiness certificates. Conditions of airlines operating permission. Overflights and technical stops. Licenses and certificates of nationality. Tonnage.
INTL ORGS: International Civil Aviation Organization.
TREATY REF: 15 UNTS 295; 320 UNTS 209, 217; 418 UNTS 161.
PROCEDURE: Amendment. Denunciation. Ratification. Registration.
PARTIES:
Mauritania
Spain

108710   Bilateral Agreement   **602 UNTS 137**
SIGNED: 11 Oct 65   FORCE: 11 Oct 65
REGISTERED: 31 Jul 67 ICAO (Civil Aviat)
ARTICLES: 16 LANGUAGE: French. English.
HEADNOTE: AIR SERVICES
TOPIC: Air Transport
CONCEPTS: Definition of terms. Time limit. IGO reference. General cooperation. Exchange of information and documents. Arbitration. Procedure. Special tribunals. Tariffs. Customs duties. Competency certificate. Air transport. Airworthiness certificates. Conditions of airlines operating permission. Overflights and technical stops. Licenses and certificates of nationality. Tonnage.
INTL ORGS: International Civil Aviation Organization.
TREATY REF: 15 UNTS 295.
PROCEDURE: Ratification. Termination.
PARTIES:
Nigeria
Switzerland

108711   Bilateral Agreement   **602 UNTS 157**
SIGNED: 26 May 65   FORCE: 26 May 65
REGISTERED: 31 Jul 67 ICAO (Civil Aviat)
ARTICLES: 15 LANGUAGE: English.
HEADNOTE: AIR SERVICES
TOPIC: Air Transport
CONCEPTS: Definition of terms. Time limit. IGO reference. General cooperation. Exchange of information and documents. Arbitration. Procedure. Special tribunals. Tariffs. Customs duties. Competency certificate. Airworthiness certificates. Conditions of airlines operating permission. Overflights and technical stops. Licenses and certificates of nationality. Tonnage.
INTL ORGS: International Civil Aviation Organization.
PROCEDURE: Amendment. Termination.
PARTIES:
Malaysia
Norway

108712   Bilateral Agreement   **602 UNTS 177**
SIGNED: 15 Apr 64   FORCE: 15 Apr 64
REGISTERED: 31 Jul 67 ICAO (Civil Aviat)
ARTICLES: 19 LANGUAGE: French.
HEADNOTE: AIR TRANSPORT
TOPIC: Air Transport

CONCEPTS: Definition of terms. Time limit. IGO reference. General cooperation. Exchange of information and documents. Arbitration. Procedure. Existing tribunals. Special tribunals. Negotiation. Tariffs. Indemnities and reimbursements. Registration certificate. Air transport. Airport facilities. Airport equipment. Airworthiness certificates. Conditions of airlines operating permission. Licenses and certificates of nationality.
INTL ORGS: International Civil Aviation Organization. International Court of Justice.
PROCEDURE: Amendment. Denunciation. Termination. Denunciation. Ratification.
PARTIES:
Norway
Yugoslavia

108713 Bilateral Agreement **602 UNTS 199**
SIGNED: 17 Apr 54   FORCE: 4 May 64
REGISTERED: 31 Jul 67 ICAO (Civil Aviat)
ARTICLES: 16 LANGUAGE: French.
HEADNOTE: AIR SERVICES
TOPIC: Air Transport
CONCEPTS: Time limit. General cooperation. Exchange of information and documents. Arbitration. Procedure. Negotiation. Tariffs. Indemnities and reimbursements. Registration certificate. Air transport. Airport facilities. Airport equipment. Airworthiness certificates. Conditions of airlines operating permission. Licenses and certificates of nationality.
PARTIES:
Lebanon
Yugoslavia

108714 Multilateral Agreement **602 UNTS 212**
SIGNED: 10 Jun 67   FORCE: 10 Jun 67
REGISTERED: 31 Jul 67 United Nations
ARTICLES: 6 LANGUAGE: English.
HEADNOTE: OPERATIONAL ASSISTANCE
TOPIC: Direct Aid
CONCEPTS: General provisions. Previous treaty replacement. Arbitration. Procedure. Existing tribunals. Aid and development. Domestic obligation.
TREATY REF: 204 UNTS 323; 527 UNTS 136.
PROCEDURE: Amendment. Termination.
PARTIES:
Ceylon (Sri Lanka) SIGNED: 10 Jun 67 FORCE: 10 Jun 67
FAO (Food Agri) SIGNED: 10 Jun 67 FORCE: 10 Jun 67
IAEA (Atom Energy) SIGNED: 10 Jun 67 FORCE: 10 Jun 67
ICAO (Civil Aviat) SIGNED: 10 Jun 67 FORCE: 10 Jun 67
ILO (Labor Org) SIGNED: 10 Jun 67 FORCE: 10 Jun 67
IMCO (Maritime Org) SIGNED: 10 Jun 67 FORCE: 10 Jun 67
ITU (Telecommun) SIGNED: 10 Jun 67 FORCE: 10 Jun 67
UNESCO (Educ/Cult) SIGNED: 10 Jun 67 FORCE: 10 Jun 67
United Nations SIGNED: 10 Jun 67 FORCE: 10 Jun 67
UPU (Postal Union) SIGNED: 10 Jun 67 FORCE: 10 Jun 67
WHO (World Health) SIGNED: 10 Jun 67 FORCE: 10 Jun 67
WMO (Meteorology) SIGNED: 10 Jun 67 FORCE: 10 Jun 67

108715 Bilateral Agreement **602 UNTS 231**
SIGNED: 12 Jun 65   FORCE: 23 May 67
REGISTERED: 1 Aug 67 Netherlands
ARTICLES: 15 LANGUAGE: French.
HEADNOTE: ECONOMIC TECHNICAL COOPERATION
TOPIC: General Economic
CONCEPTS: Establishment of commission. Arbitration. Procedure. Existing tribunals. Special tribunals. National treatment. General. General technical assistance. Assistance. Special projects. Materials, equipment and services. General transportation. Air transport.
PROCEDURE: Denunciation. Ratification. Renewal or Revival.
PARTIES:
Netherlands
Senegal

108716 Bilateral Agreement **602 UNTS 243**
SIGNED: 11 Aug 66   FORCE: 29 May 67
REGISTERED: 1 Aug 67 Netherlands
ARTICLES: 8 LANGUAGE: English.
HEADNOTE: CULTURE
TOPIC: Culture
CONCEPTS: General cooperation. Education. Teacher and student exchange. Professorships. Culture. Exchange. General cultural cooperation. Artists.
PROCEDURE: Denunciation. Ratification.
PARTIES:
Netherlands
Yugoslavia

108717 Bilateral Exchange **602 UNTS 251**
SIGNED: 29 Mar 67   FORCE: 29 May 67
REGISTERED: 4 Aug 67 Denmark
ARTICLES: 2 LANGUAGE: French.
HEADNOTE: DOUBLE TAXATION
TOPIC: Taxation
CONCEPTS: Definition of terms. Taxation. Tax exemptions. General transportation.
PROCEDURE: Denunciation.
PARTIES:
Denmark
Lebanon

108718 Multilateral Convention **602 UNTS 259**
SIGNED: 8 Jul 64   FORCE: 28 Jul 67
REGISTERED: 7 Aug 67 ILO (Labor Org)
ARTICLES: 39 LANGUAGE: English. French.
HEADNOTE: EMPLOYMENT INJURY ILO
TOPIC: ILO Labor
CONCEPTS: Definition of terms. General provisions. Public health. ILO conventions. Anti-discrimination. Employment regulations. Old age and invalidity insurance. Sickness and invalidity insurance. National treatment.
TREATY REF: ILO.
PROCEDURE: Amendment. Denunciation. Ratification. Registration.
PARTIES:
Multilateral
ANNEX
648 UNTS 391. Finland. Ratification 23 Sep 68. Force 23 Sep 69.

108719 Multilateral Agreement **603 UNTS 2**
SIGNED: 14 Jun 67   FORCE: 14 Jun 67
REGISTERED: 8 Aug 67 United Nations
ARTICLES: 6 LANGUAGE: French. English.
HEADNOTE: OPERATIONAL ASSISTANCE
TOPIC: Direct Aid
CONCEPTS: General provisions. Previous treaty replacement. Personnel. Procedure. Domestic obligation. General technical assistance. IGO obligations.
PROCEDURE: Termination.
PARTIES:
Laos SIGNED: 14 Jun 67 FORCE: 14 Jun 67
FAO (Food Agri) SIGNED: 14 Jun 67 FORCE: 14 Jun 67
IAEA (Atom Energy) SIGNED: 14 Jun 67 FORCE: 14 Jun 67
ICAO (Civil Aviat) SIGNED: 14 Jun 67 FORCE: 14 Jun 67
ILO (Labor Org) SIGNED: 14 Jun 67 FORCE: 14 Jun 67
IMCO (Maritime Org) SIGNED: 14 Jun 67 FORCE: 14 Jun 67
ITU (Telecommun) SIGNED: 14 Jun 67 FORCE: 14 Jun 67
UNESCO (Educ/Cult) SIGNED: 14 Jun 67 FORCE: 14 Jun 67
United Nations SIGNED: 14 Jun 67 FORCE: 14 Jun 67
UPU (Postal Union) SIGNED: 14 Jun 67 FORCE: 14 Jun 67
WHO (World Health) SIGNED: 14 Jun 67 FORCE: 14 Jun 67
WMO (Meteorology) SIGNED: 14 Jun 67 FORCE: 14 Jun 67
ANNEX
655 UNTS 402. UNIDO (Industrial). Accession 9 Jan 69. Force 9 Jan 69.

108720 Bilateral Exchange **603 UNTS 19**
SIGNED: 5 Aug 61   FORCE: 5 Aug 61
REGISTERED: 10 Aug 67 USA (United States)

ARTICLES: 2 LANGUAGE: French. English.
HEADNOTE: CONTINUED APPLICATION TREATIES
TOPIC: Admin Cooperation
CONCEPTS: Previous treaty extension. Revival of treaties.
PARTIES:
Congo (Brazzaville)
USA (United States)

108721 Bilateral Agreement **603 UNTS 23**
SIGNED: 22 Apr 66   FORCE: 22 Apr 66
REGISTERED: 11 Aug 67 IAEA (Atom Energy)
ARTICLES: 14 LANGUAGE: French.
HEADNOTE: ASSISTANCE SUPPLY MATERIALS
TOPIC: Atomic Energy
CONCEPTS: Annex or appendix reference. IGO reference. Exchange of information and documents. Title and deeds. Arbitration. Conciliation. Domestic obligation. Atomic energy assistance. Nuclear materials. Non-nuclear materials. Transport of goods.
INTL ORGS: International Court of Justice.
PARTIES:
Romania
IAEA (Atom Energy)

108722 Bilateral Agreement **603 UNTS 35**
SIGNED: 9 Dec 66   FORCE: 9 Dec 66
REGISTERED: 11 Aug 67 IAEA (Atom Energy)
ARTICLES: 14 LANGUAGE: English.
HEADNOTE: ASSISTANCE SUPPLY MATERIALS
TOPIC: Atomic Energy
CONCEPTS: Guarantees and safeguards. Annex or appendix reference. IGO reference. Exchange of information and documents. Title and deeds. Arbitration. Conciliation. Payment schedules. Domestic obligation. Peaceful use. Transport of goods. IGO obligations.
INTL ORGS: International Court of Justice.
PARTIES:
India
IAEA (Atom Energy)

108723 Bilateral Agreement **603 UNTS 45**
SIGNED: 14 Jan 65   FORCE: 1 May 67
REGISTERED: 11 Aug 67 IAEA (Atom Energy)
ARTICLES: 9 LANGUAGE: English.
HEADNOTE: ASSISTANCE TRAINING MEDICAL APPLICATIONS
TOPIC: Atomic Energy
CONCEPTS: IGO reference. Exchange of information and documents. Arbitration. Conciliation. Public health. Assistance. Peaceful use.
INTL ORGS: International Court of Justice.
PROCEDURE: Ratification.
PARTIES:
IAEA (Atom Energy)
United Arab Rep

108724 Bilateral Agreement **603 UNTS 53**
SIGNED: 18 Oct 66   FORCE: 15 May 67
REGISTERED: 11 Aug 67 Netherlands
ARTICLES: 6 LANGUAGE: English.
HEADNOTE: DEVELOPMENT PHOTOGRAMMETRIC BRANCH
TOPIC: Education
CONCEPTS: General cooperation. Scientific exchange. Assistance. Materials, equipment and services.
PROCEDURE: Duration. Termination.
PARTIES:
Netherlands
Nigeria

108725 Bilateral Agreement **603 UNTS 61**
SIGNED: 28 Jul 66   FORCE: 15 Sep 66
REGISTERED: 14 Aug 67 USA (United States)
ARTICLES: 14 LANGUAGE: English.
HEADNOTE: CIVIL USES ATOMIC ENERGY
TOPIC: Atomic Energy
CONCEPTS: Definition of terms. Guarantees and safeguards. Previous treaty replacement. Exchange of information and documents. Responsibility and liability. Use restrictions. Nuclear materials. Non-nuclear materials. Peaceful use.
TREATY REF: 240 UNTS 413.
PROCEDURE: Duration. Ratification.

PARTIES:
Sweden
USA (United States)

108726 Bilateral Agreement **603 UNTS 87**
SIGNED: 18 Jul 67   FORCE: 18 Jul 67
REGISTERED: 16 Aug 67 WHO (World Health)
ARTICLES: 6 LANGUAGE: English.
HEADNOTE: TECHNICAL ADVISORY ASSISTANCE
TOPIC: Tech Assistance
CONCEPTS: General provisions. Privileges and immunities. Use of facilities. Domestic obligation. General technical assistance. IGO obligations.
PROCEDURE: Amendment. Termination.
PARTIES:
Barbados
WHO (World Health)

108727 Bilateral Agreement **603 UNTS 99**
SIGNED: 10 May 67   FORCE: 10 May 67
REGISTERED: 16 Aug 67 WHO (World Health)
ARTICLES: 6 LANGUAGE: English.
HEADNOTE: TECHNICAL ADVISORY ASSISTANCE
TOPIC: Tech Assistance
CONCEPTS: General provisions. Privileges and immunities. Use of facilities. Domestic obligation. General technical assistance. IGO obligations.
PROCEDURE: Amendment. Termination.
PARTIES:
Malta
WHO (World Health)

108728 Bilateral Agreement **603 UNTS 111**
SIGNED: 5 Apr 67   FORCE: 5 Apr 67
REGISTERED: 17 Aug 67 Denmark
ARTICLES: 12 LANGUAGE: English.
HEADNOTE: VOLUNTEERS
TOPIC: Tech Assistance
CONCEPTS: Time limit. Personnel. Domestic obligation. Use restrictions. Volunteer programs.
PROCEDURE: Termination.
PARTIES:
Denmark
Tanzania

108729 Bilateral Agreement **603 UNTS 121**
SIGNED: 21 Apr 67   FORCE: 21 May 67
REGISTERED: 22 Aug 67 Austria
ARTICLES: 9 LANGUAGE: German. Bulgarian.
HEADNOTE: ABOLITION VISA REQUIREMENT
TOPIC: Visas
CONCEPTS: Change of circumstances. Time limit. Visa abolition. Border traffic and migration. Conformity with municipal law. Fees and exemptions.
PROCEDURE: Denunciation.
PARTIES:
Austria
Bulgaria

108730 Multilateral Exchange **603 UNTS 135**
SIGNED: 9 Mar 67   FORCE: 9 Mar 67
REGISTERED: 22 Aug 67 Austria
ARTICLES: 2 LANGUAGE: German. English.
HEADNOTE: COMMONWEALTH WAR CEMETARY KLAGENFURT
TOPIC: Other Military
CONCEPTS: General cooperation. Upkeep of war graves.
PARTIES:
Austria SIGNED: 9 Mar 67 FORCE: 9 Mar 67
New Zealand SIGNED: 9 Mar 67 FORCE: 9 Mar 67
UK Great Britain SIGNED: 9 Mar 67 FORCE: 9 Mar 67

108731 Bilateral Exchange **603 UNTS 143**
SIGNED: 26 Apr 67   FORCE: 26 May 67
REGISTERED: 22 Aug 67 Austria
ARTICLES: 2 LANGUAGE: German. Serbo-Croat.
HEADNOTE: ACCESS CHURCH ST. PANCRAS
TOPIC: Admin Cooperation
CONCEPTS: Border traffic and migration. General cooperation. Transport of goods.
PARTIES:
Austria
Yugoslavia

108732 Bilateral Agreement **603 UNTS 151**
SIGNED: 15 Sep 66   FORCE: 15 Sep 66
REGISTERED: 22 Aug 67 UK Great Britain
ARTICLES: 8 LANGUAGE: English. Spanish.
HEADNOTE: LOAN
TOPIC: Loans and Credits
CONCEPTS: Definition of terms. Interest rates. Payment schedules. Loan and credit. Credit provisions. Loan repayment.
PARTIES:
Argentina
UK Great Britain

108733 Bilateral Exchange **603 UNTS 167**
SIGNED: 7 Oct 66   FORCE: 7 Oct 66
REGISTERED: 22 Aug 67 UK Great Britain
ARTICLES: 2 LANGUAGE: English. Spanish.
HEADNOTE: TECHNICAL COOPERATION PROGRAM
TOPIC: Tech Assistance
CONCEPTS: Annex or appendix reference. Operating agencies. General technical assistance. Assistance.
PARTIES:
Chile
UK Great Britain

108734 Bilateral Convention **603 UNTS 183**
SIGNED: 26 Nov 64   FORCE: 30 Jan 67
REGISTERED: 22 Aug 67 UK Great Britain
ARTICLES: 24 LANGUAGE: English. German.
HEADNOTE: AVOIDANCE DOUBLE TAXATION PREVENTION FISCAL EVASION
TOPIC: Taxation
CONCEPTS: Definition of terms. Territorial application. Previous treaty replacement. Conformity with municipal law. General property. Succession. Equitable taxes. General. Tax exemptions.
TREATY REF: 218 UNTS 301.
PROCEDURE: Ratification. Termination.
PARTIES:
Germany, West
UK Great Britain

108735 Bilateral Exchange **603 UNTS 235**
SIGNED: 12 Dec 66   FORCE: 12 Dec 66
REGISTERED: 22 Aug 67 UK Great Britain
ARTICLES: 2 LANGUAGE: English.
HEADNOTE: CONTINUED OPERATION HURRICANE RESEARCH CENTERS
TOPIC: Scientific Project
CONCEPTS: Annex type material.
TREATY REF: 338 UNTS 281; 371 UNTS 356.
PARTIES:
UK Great Britain
USA (United States)

108736 Bilateral Exchange **603 UNTS 245**
SIGNED: 30 Dec 66   FORCE: 30 Dec 66
REGISTERED: 22 Aug 67 UK Great Britain
ARTICLES: 2 LANGUAGE: English.
HEADNOTE: TRACKING TELEMETRY FACILITIES
TOPIC: Scientific Project
CONCEPTS: Time limit. General cooperation. Licenses and permits. General property. Jurisdiction. Use of facilities. Border control. Research cooperation. Indemnities and reimbursements. Claims and settlements. Taxation. Customs duties. Transport of goods. Postal services. Joint defense.
PROCEDURE: Duration.
PARTIES:
UK Great Britain
USA (United States)

108737 Bilateral Exchange **603 UNTS 273**
SIGNED: 30 Dec 66   FORCE: 30 Dec 66
REGISTERED: 22 Aug 67 UK Great Britain
ARTICLES: 2 LANGUAGE: English.
HEADNOTE: DEFENSE PURPOSES BRITISH INDIAN OCEAN TERRITORY
TOPIC: General Military
CONCEPTS: Definition of terms. Annex or appendix reference. Non-prejudice to third party. Title and deeds. Indemnities and reimbursements. Self-defense. Boundaries of territory.
PARTIES:
UK Great Britain
USA (United States)

108738 Bilateral Exchange **604 UNTS 3**
SIGNED: 1 Jan 67   FORCE: 1 Jan 67
REGISTERED: 22 Aug 67 UK Great Britain
ARTICLES: 14 LANGUAGE: English.
HEADNOTE: SPACE VEHICLE TRACKING STATIONS
TOPIC: Scientific Project
CONCEPTS: Definition of terms. Treaty implementation. Annex type material. Previous treaty replacement. Personnel. General property. Research cooperation. Indemnities and reimbursements. Customs duties. Satellites.
TREATY REF: 402 UNTS 153; 565 UNTS 318; 588 UNTS 332.
PROCEDURE: Duration. Termination.
PARTIES:
UK Great Britain
USA (United States)

108739 Bilateral Exchange **604 UNTS 13**
SIGNED: 5 Jan 67   FORCE: 1 Jan 67
REGISTERED: 22 Aug 67 UK Great Britain
ARTICLES: 2 LANGUAGE: English.
HEADNOTE: IMPORTS BOOKS FILMS
TOPIC: Mass Media
CONCEPTS: Annex type material. Commodity trade.
TREATY REF: 571 UNTS 275; 360 UNTS 79; 404 UNTS 376;.
PROCEDURE: Termination.
PARTIES:
UK Great Britain
Yugoslavia

108740 Bilateral Agreement **604 UNTS 19**
SIGNED: 5 Apr 67   FORCE: 5 Apr 67
REGISTERED: 24 Aug 67 Denmark
ARTICLES: 10 LANGUAGE: English.
HEADNOTE: SCIENTIFIC TECHNICAL COOPERATION
TOPIC: Scientific Project
CONCEPTS: Definition of terms. Visas. General cooperation. Legal protection and assistance. Personnel. General property. Responsibility and liability. Indemnities and reimbursements. Tax exemptions. Customs duties. General technical assistance. Special projects.
PROCEDURE: Duration. Future Procedures Contemplated. Termination.
PARTIES:
Denmark
Tanzania

108741 Bilateral Agreement **604 UNTS 33**
SIGNED: 14 Mar 66   FORCE: 1 May 66
REGISTERED: 24 Aug 67 Romania
ARTICLES: 23 LANGUAGE: Romanian. French.
HEADNOTE: GOODS TRANSPORT
TOPIC: Land Transport
CONCEPTS: General provisions. Treaty implementation. Inspection and observation. Recognition and enforcement of legal decisions. Establishment of commission. Commodity trade. Quotas. Customs duties. Registration certificate. Transport of goods. Land transport. Motor vehicles and combinations.
PROCEDURE: Denunciation. Duration.
PARTIES:
France
Romania

108742 Bilateral Agreement **604 UNTS 49**
SIGNED: 6 Sep 65   FORCE: 10 Mar 66
REGISTERED: 24 Aug 67 Romania
ARTICLES: 7 LANGUAGE: French.
HEADNOTE: ECONOMIC INDUSTRIAL TECHNICAL COLLABORATION
TOPIC: General Economic
CONCEPTS: General cooperation. Establishment of commission. General economics. General trade.
PROCEDURE: Termination.
PARTIES:
Italy
Romania

108743 Bilateral Agreement **604 UNTS 57**
SIGNED: 21 Apr 66   FORCE: 8 Sep 66
REGISTERED: 24 Aug 67 Romania

ARTICLES: 12 LANGUAGE: French.
HEADNOTE: CULTURE COOPERATION
TOPIC: Culture
CONCEPTS: Treaty implementation. IGO reference. Exchange. Teacher and student exchange. Scholarships and grants. Exchange. General cultural cooperation. Artists. Athletes.
PROCEDURE: Denunciation. Duration. Future Procedures Contemplated. Renewal or Revival.
PARTIES:
Romania
Tunisia

108744   Bilateral Agreement   **604 UNTS 65**
SIGNED: 21 Apr 66   FORCE: 17 Feb 67
REGISTERED: 24 Aug 67 Romania
ARTICLES: 9 LANGUAGE: French.
HEADNOTE: SCIENTIFIC TECHNICAL COOPERATION
TOPIC: Scientific Project
CONCEPTS: Establishment of commission. Exchange. Teacher and student exchange. Scholarships and grants. Scientific exchange. Indemnities and reimbursements. General technical assistance.
PROCEDURE: Denunciation. Renewal or Revival. Termination.
PARTIES:
Romania
Tunisia

108745   Bilateral Protocol   **604 UNTS 73**
SIGNED: 3 Sep 66   FORCE: 17 Apr 67
REGISTERED: 24 Aug 67 Romania
ARTICLES: 8 LANGUAGE: English.
HEADNOTE: TECHNICAL SCIENTIFIC COOPERATION AGRICULTURE
TOPIC: Direct Aid
CONCEPTS: General cooperation. Exchange of information and documents. Dispute settlement. Disease control. Education. Exchange. Scholarships and grants. General technical assistance. Agriculture.
PROCEDURE: Denunciation. Ratification.
PARTIES:
Romania
United Arab Rep

108746   Bilateral Agreement   **604 UNTS 81**
SIGNED: 21 Jun 66   FORCE: 9 Dec 66
REGISTERED: 24 Aug 67 Romania
ARTICLES: 17 LANGUAGE: Romanian. Russian.
HEADNOTE: TRANSPORT GOODS ROAD
TOPIC: Land Transport
CONCEPTS: Procedure. Finances and payments. Payment schedules. Customs duties. Routes and logistics. Permit designation. Transport of goods. Land transport. Motor vehicles and combinations.
PROCEDURE: Future Procedures Contemplated. Renewal or Revival.
PARTIES:
Romania
USSR (Soviet Union)

108747   Bilateral Agreement   **604 UNTS 103**
SIGNED: 20 Apr 67   FORCE: 10 Jul 67
REGISTERED: 29 Aug 67 Denmark
ARTICLES: 4 LANGUAGE: Danish. Norwegian.
HEADNOTE: FISHERIES
TOPIC: Specific Resources
CONCEPTS: Procedure. Fisheries and fishing.
PROCEDURE: Ratification. Termination.
PARTIES:
Denmark
Norway

108748 Multilateral Agreement **604 UNTS 114**
SIGNED: 30 Mar 56   FORCE: 30 Mar 56
REGISTERED: 29 Aug 67 United Nations
ARTICLES: 6 LANGUAGE: Spanish.
HEADNOTE: TECHNICAL ASSISTANCE
TOPIC: IGO Operations
CONCEPTS: General provisions. Privileges and immunities. Finances and payments. Domestic obligation. General technical assistance.
TREATY REF: 76 UNTS 132; 1 UNTS 15; 9OUNTS 327; 33 UNTS 261;E.

PARTIES:
Peru SIGNED: 30 Mar 56 FORCE: 30 Mar 56
FAO (Food Agri) SIGNED: 30 Mar 56 FORCE: 30 Mar 56
ICAO (Civil Aviat) SIGNED: 30 Mar 56 FORCE: 30 Mar 56
ILO (Labor Org) SIGNED: 30 Mar 56 FORCE: 30 Mar 56
ITU (Telecommun) SIGNED: 30 Mar 56 FORCE: 30 Mar 56
UNESCO (Educ/Cult) SIGNED: 30 Mar 56 FORCE: 30 Mar 56
United Nations SIGNED: 30 Mar 56 FORCE: 30 Mar 56
WHO (World Health) SIGNED: 30 Mar 56 FORCE: 30 Mar 56
WMO (Meteorology) SIGNED: 30 Mar 56 FORCE: 30 Mar 56
ANNEX
654 UNTS 383. UNIDO (Industrial). Accession 16 Oct 68. Force 16 Oct 68.

108749   Bilateral Convention   **604 UNTS 135**
SIGNED: 17 Oct 62   FORCE: 2 Apr 64
REGISTERED: 29 Aug 67 Ireland
ARTICLES: 28 LANGUAGE: Irish. English. German.
HEADNOTE: AVOIDANCE DOUBLE TAXATION
TOPIC: Taxation
CONCEPTS: Definition of terms. Nationality and citizenship. General property. Corporations. Procedure. Interest rates. Payment schedules. Non-interest rates and fees. Assets. Assessment procedures. Taxation. General. Tax exemptions.
PROCEDURE: Ratification. Termination.
PARTIES:
Germany, West
Ireland

108750   Bilateral Agreement   **604 UNTS 199**
SIGNED: 15 Sep 65   FORCE: 15 Nov 65
REGISTERED: 29 Aug 67 Ireland
ARTICLES: 4 LANGUAGE: Irish. English. Finnish.
HEADNOTE: TONNAGE CERTIFICATES SHIPS
TOPIC: Water Transport
CONCEPTS: Registration certificate. Water transport. Merchant vessels. Tonnage.
TREATY REF: 28 LNTS 511;$.
PROCEDURE: Termination.
PARTIES:
Finland
Ireland

108751   Bilateral Agreement   **604 UNTS 209**
SIGNED: 31 Mar 66   FORCE: 1 Aug 67
REGISTERED: 29 Aug 67 Netherlands
ARTICLES: 3 LANGUAGE: Dutch. Danish.
HEADNOTE: DELIMITATION   CONTINENTAL SHELF
TOPIC: Territory Boundary
CONCEPTS: Definition of terms. Immovable property. Corporations. Procedure. Finances and payments. Banking. Interest rates. Assessment procedures. Taxation. Equitable taxes. General. Tax exemptions. Air transport. Water transport. Boundaries of territory. Markers and definitions.
PROCEDURE: Ratification.
PARTIES:
Denmark
Netherlands

108752 Multilateral Agreement **604 UNTS 219**
SIGNED: 28 Apr 66   FORCE: 1 Aug 67
REGISTERED: 29 Aug 67 Netherlands
ARTICLES: 13 LANGUAGE: French.
HEADNOTE: SOCIAL SECURITY EMPLOYMENT
TOPIC: Non-ILO Labor
CONCEPTS: Definition of terms. Time limit. General cooperation. Procedure. Sickness and invalidity insurance. Migrant worker. Balance of payments.
TREATY REF: 01 UNTS 609, 495 UNTS 249; 295 UNTS 351.
PROCEDURE: Denunciation. Ratification.
PARTIES:
France SIGNED: 28 Apr 66 FORCE: 1 Aug 66
Netherlands SIGNED: 28 Apr 66 FORCE: 1 Aug 66
Poland SIGNED: 28 Apr 66 FORCE: 1 Aug 66

108753   Bilateral Exchange   **604 UNTS 231**
SIGNED: 14 Jun 67   FORCE: 14 Jun 67
REGISTERED: 31 Aug 67 USA (United States)
ARTICLES: 17 LANGUAGE: English.
HEADNOTE: EXPORT COTTON TEXTILES
TOPIC: Commodity Trade
CONCEPTS: Definition of terms. General cooperation. Exchange of information and documents. Procedure. Export quotas. Import quotas. Tariffs. Commodity trade. Delivery schedules. Quotas.
TREATY REF: 471 UNTS 296; 596 UNTS 524;$.
PROCEDURE: Termination.
PARTIES:
Malta
USA (United States)

108754   Bilateral Agreement   **604 UNTS 247**
SIGNED: 15 Feb 67   FORCE: 10 Jun 67
REGISTERED: 5 Sep 67 Denmark
ARTICLES: 16 LANGUAGE: Danish. French.
HEADNOTE: CULTURE
TOPIC: Culture
CONCEPTS: Establishment   of   commission. Teacher and student exchange. Scholarships and grants. Culture. General cultural cooperation. Artists. Indemnities and reimbursements. Customs exemptions.
TREATY REF: 473 UNTS 187.
PROCEDURE: Denunciation. Ratification. Renewal or Revival.
PARTIES:
Denmark
France

108755   Bilateral Convention   **604 UNTS 265**
SIGNED: 15 Jul 66   FORCE: 13 Aug 67
REGISTERED: 7 Sep 67 Austria
ARTICLES: 23 LANGUAGE: German. French.
HEADNOTE: CIVIL COMMERCIAL MATTERS ENFORCEMENT RECOGNITION
TOPIC: Admin Cooperation
CONCEPTS: Definition of terms. Conformity with municipal law. General cooperation. Exchange of information and documents. Recognition and enforcement of legal decisions. General property. Recognition of legal documents. Responsibility and liability. Corporations. Procedure.
PROCEDURE: Denunciation. Ratification.
PARTIES:
Austria
France

108756   Bilateral Agreement   **604 UNTS 287**
SIGNED: 13 Feb 67   FORCE: 20 Jul 67
REGISTERED: 8 Sep 67 Netherlands
ARTICLES: 8 LANGUAGE: English.
HEADNOTE: CULTURE
TOPIC: Culture
CONCEPTS: Definition of terms. Exchange of information and documents. Recognition of degrees. Commissions and foundations. Scholarships and grants. Culture. General cultural cooperation. Artists. Athletes.
PROCEDURE: Denunciation. Ratification. Termination.
PARTIES:
Netherlands
Romania

108757   Bilateral Convention   **604 UNTS 295**
SIGNED: 23 Nov 66   FORCE: 24 Aug 67
REGISTERED: 11 Sep 67 Norway
ARTICLES: 28 LANGUAGE: Norwegian. English. French.
HEADNOTE: DOUBLE TAXATION
TOPIC: Taxation
CONCEPTS: General consular functions. Exchange of information and documents. Taxation.
PROCEDURE: Ratification. Termination.
PARTIES:
Canada
Norway

108758   Bilateral Treaty   **605 UNTS 3**
SIGNED: 31 Oct 64   FORCE: 18 Aug 64
REGISTERED: 18 Sep 64 Austria
ARTICLES: 8 LANGUAGE: German. Hungarian.
HEADNOTE: SETTLEMENT FINANCIAL QUESTIONS

TOPIC: Finance
CONCEPTS: Expropriation. Finances and payments. Bonds. Payment schedules. Lump sum settlements.
PROCEDURE: Ratification.
PARTIES:
Austria
Hungary

108759 Bilateral Agreement **605 UNTS 63**
SIGNED: 31 Oct 64 FORCE: 18 Aug 67
REGISTERED: 18 Sep 67 Austria
ARTICLES: 7 LANGUAGE: German. Hungarian.
HEADNOTE: SETTLEMENT QUESTIONS DANUBE STEAM NAVIGATION COMPANY
TOPIC: Claims and Debts
CONCEPTS: Exchange of information and documents. Responsibility and liability. Banking. Payment schedules. Claims and settlements. Lump sum settlements.
PARTIES:
Austria
Hungary

108760 Bilateral Agreement **605 UNTS 77**
SIGNED: 31 Oct 64 FORCE: 18 Aug 67
REGISTERED: 18 Sep 67 Austria
ARTICLES: 6 LANGUAGE: German. Hungarian.
HEADNOTE: CLAIM SETTLEMENT
TOPIC: Claims and Debts
CONCEPTS: Claims and settlements. Lump sum settlements.
PARTIES:
Austria
Hungary

108761 Bilateral Agreement **605 UNTS 87**
SIGNED: 29 May 65 FORCE: 18 Aug 65
REGISTERED: 19 Sep 67 USA (United States)
ARTICLES: 8 LANGUAGE: English.
HEADNOTE: INVESTMENT GUARANTY AGREEMENT
TOPIC: Loans and Credits
CONCEPTS: IGO reference. Procedure. Special tribunals. Negotiation. Competence of tribunal. Finances and payments. Investments. Expense sharing formulae.
INTL ORGS: International Court of Justice.
PROCEDURE: Denunciation. Ratification.
PARTIES:
British Guiana
USA (United States)

108762 Bilateral Agreement **605 UNTS 95**
SIGNED: 9 Jun 65 FORCE: 11 Sep 65
REGISTERED: 20 Sep 67 Denmark
ARTICLES: 33 LANGUAGE: Danish. German.
HEADNOTE: FRONTIER CONTROL OPERATIONS
TOPIC: Territory Boundary
CONCEPTS: Definition of terms. Territorial application. Frontier formalities. Border traffic and migration. Customs declarations. General transportation. Water transport. Land transport. Railway border crossing. Railways.
PROCEDURE: Denunciation. Ratification.
PARTIES:
Denmark
Germany, West

108763 Bilateral Agreement **605 UNTS 153**
SIGNED: 1 Dec 66 FORCE: 23 Mar 67
REGISTERED: 21 Sep 67 UK Great Britain
ARTICLES: 24 LANGUAGE: English.
HEADNOTE: DOUBLE TAXATION
TOPIC: Taxation
CONCEPTS: Definition of terms. General consular functions. Exchange of information and documents. Immovable property. Corporations. Finances and payments. Interest rates. Assessment procedures. Taxation. Equitable taxes. General. Tax exemptions. Air transport. Water transport.
PROCEDURE: Termination.
PARTIES:
Singapore
UK Great Britain

108764 Bilateral Agreement **605 UNTS 195**
SIGNED: 9 Mar 67 FORCE: 9 Mar 67
REGISTERED: 21 Sep 67 UK Great Britain
ARTICLES: 6 LANGUAGE: English. Romanian.
HEADNOTE: SCIENTIFIC TECHNICAL COOPERATION
TOPIC: Scientific Project
CONCEPTS: General cooperation. Exchange of information and documents. Licenses and permits. Specialists exchange. Exchange.
PROCEDURE: Future Procedures Contemplated. Termination.
PARTIES:
Romania
UK Great Britain

108765 Bilateral Treaty **605 UNTS 205**
SIGNED: 7 Jul 65 FORCE: 9 Feb 67
REGISTERED: 21 Sep 67 UK Great Britain
ARTICLES: 40 LANGUAGE: English. French.
HEADNOTE: CONCILIATION JUDICIAL SETTLEMENT ARBITRATION
TOPIC: Dispute Settlement
CONCEPTS: IGO reference. Dispute settlement. Arbitration. Procedure. Existing tribunals. Special tribunals. Conciliation. Competence of tribunal.
INTL ORGS: International Court of Justice.
PROCEDURE: Denunciation. Ratification.
PARTIES:
Switzerland
UK Great Britain

108766 Bilateral Agreement **605 UNTS 237**
SIGNED: 29 Dec 66 FORCE: 23 Mar 67
REGISTERED: 21 Sep 67 UK Great Britain
ARTICLES: 27 LANGUAGE: English.
HEADNOTE: DOUBLE TAXATION
TOPIC: Taxation
CONCEPTS: Definition of terms. General consular functions. Exchange of information and documents. Immovable property. Corporations. Finances and payments. Interest rates. Assessment procedures. Taxation. Equitable taxes. General. Tax exemptions. Air transport. Water transport.
PROCEDURE: Amendment. Renewal or Revival. Termination.
PARTIES:
Trinidad/Tobago
UK Great Britain

108767 Bilateral Exchange **605 UNTS 277**
SIGNED: 23 Jan 67 FORCE: 23 Jan 67
REGISTERED: 21 Sep 67 UK Great Britain
ARTICLES: 19 LANGUAGE: English.
HEADNOTE: SPACE VEHICLE TRACKING
TOPIC: Telecommunications
CONCEPTS: Definition of terms. Privileges and immunities. Legal protection and assistance. Use of facilities. Research and scientific projects. Research cooperation. Finances and payments. Indemnities and reimbursements. Currency. Claims and settlements. Customs duties. Customs exemptions. Procurement. Driving permits.
TREATY REF: 409 UNTS 67; 531 UNTS 368.
PROCEDURE: Termination.
PARTIES:
Trinidad/Tobago
UK Great Britain

108768 Multilateral Convention **605 UNTS 295**
SIGNED: 18 Jun 49 FORCE: 14 Sep 67
REGISTERED: 26 Sep 67 ILO (Labor Org)
ARTICLES: 19 LANGUAGE: English. French.
HEADNOTE: ILO VACATION PAY SEAFARERS
TOPIC: ILO Labor
CONCEPTS: ILO conventions. Employment regulations. Holidays and rest periods. Wages and salaries. Water transport.
PROCEDURE: Denunciation. Future Procedures Contemplated. Ratification. Registration.
PARTIES:
Algeria RATIFIED: 19 Oct 62 FORCE: 14 Sep 67
Belgium RATIFIED: 30 Aug 62 FORCE: 14 Sep 67
Brazil RATIFIED: 18 Jun 65 FORCE: 14 Sep 67
China RATIFIED: 14 Mar 67 FORCE: 14 Sep 67
Cuba RATIFIED: 29 Apr 52 FORCE: 14 Sep 67
Finland RATIFIED: 22 Dec 51 FORCE: 14 Sep 67
France RATIFIED: 26 Oct 51 FORCE: 14 Sep 67

Iceland RATIFIED: 15 Jul 52 FORCE: 14 Sep 67
Israel RATIFIED: 30 Mar 53 FORCE: 14 Sep 67
Mauritania RATIFIED: 8 Nov 63 FORCE: 14 Sep 67
Netherlands RATIFIED: 22 Dec 61 FORCE: 14 Sep 67
Norway RATIFIED: 29 Jun 50 FORCE: 14 Sep 67
Poland RATIFIED: 8 Oct 56 FORCE: 14 Sep 67
Portugal RATIFIED: 29 Apr 52 FORCE: 14 Sep 67
Yugoslavia RATIFIED: 11 Aug 67 FORCE: 11 Feb 68

108769 Multilateral Agreement **605 UNTS 313**
SIGNED: 19 Dec 66 FORCE: 7 Aug 67
REGISTERED: 27 Sep 67 Denmark
ARTICLES: 3 LANGUAGE: Danish. Norwegian. Swedish.
HEADNOTE: RECIPROCAL ACCESS TO FISHING
TOPIC: Specific Resources
CONCEPTS: Markers and definitions. Conservation of specific resources. Fisheries and fishing.
PARTIES:
Denmark SIGNED: 19 Dec 66 FORCE: 7 Aug 67
Norway SIGNED: 19 Dec 66 FORCE: 7 Aug 67
Sweden SIGNED: 19 Dec 66 FORCE: 7 Aug 67

108770 Bilateral Exchange **606 UNTS 3**
SIGNED: 19 Dec 66 FORCE: 7 Aug 67
REGISTERED: 27 Sep 67 Denmark
ARTICLES: 2 LANGUAGE: Danish.
HEADNOTE: FISHING
TOPIC: Specific Resources
CONCEPTS: Markers and definitions. Conservation of specific resources. Fisheries and fishing.
TREATY REF: 605 UNTS.
PARTIES:
Denmark
Norway

108771 Bilateral Agreement **606 UNTS 9**
SIGNED: 11 Feb 65 FORCE: 17 Mar 67
REGISTERED: 27 Sep 67 India
ARTICLES: 21 LANGUAGE: English.
HEADNOTE: DOUBLE TAXATION
TOPIC: Taxation
CONCEPTS: Definition of terms. General consular functions. Exchange of information and documents. Immovable property. Corporations. Finances and payments. Interest rates. Assessment procedures. Taxation. Equitable taxes. General. Tax exemptions. Air transport. Water transport.
PARTIES:
Greece
India

108772 Bilateral Agreement **606 UNTS 31**
SIGNED: 16 Jan 65 FORCE: 16 Sep 66
REGISTERED: 29 Sep 67 USA (United States)
ARTICLES: 7 LANGUAGE: English. French.
HEADNOTE: AUTOMOTIVE PRODUCTS
TOPIC: Commodity Trade
CONCEPTS: Export quotas. Import quotas. Tariffs. Commodity trade. Customs duties. Customs exemptions.
TREATY REF: GATT.
PROCEDURE: Ratification. Termination.
PARTIES:
Canada
USA (United States)

108773 Bilateral Exchange **606 UNTS 47**
SIGNED: 31 Aug 66 FORCE: 31 Aug 66
REGISTERED: 29 Sep 67 USA (United States)
ARTICLES: 4 LANGUAGE: English. French.
HEADNOTE: PEACE CORPS
TOPIC: Direct Aid
CONCEPTS: Privileges and immunities. General cooperation. Volunteer programs.
PROCEDURE: Termination.
PARTIES:
Chad
USA (United States)

108774 Bilateral Exchange **606 UNTS 55**
SIGNED: 14 Sep 66 FORCE: 14 Sep 66
REGISTERED: 29 Sep 67 USA (United States)

ARTICLES: 5 LANGUAGE: English.
HEADNOTE: PEACE CORPS
TOPIC: Direct Aid
CONCEPTS: Privileges and immunities. General cooperation. Volunteer programs.
PROCEDURE: Termination.
PARTIES:
    Korea, South
    USA (United States)

108775   Bilateral Exchange   **606 UNTS 65**
SIGNED: 11 Nov 65   FORCE: 11 Nov 65
REGISTERED: 29 Sep 67 USA (United States)
ARTICLES: 2 LANGUAGE: English. Arabic.
HEADNOTE: TRANSFER OF AIRCRAFT EQUIPMENT LOAN
TOPIC: Milit Installation
CONCEPTS: Annex type material.
TREATY REF: 488 UNTS 175.
PARTIES:
    Saudi Arabia
    USA (United States)

108776   Bilateral Agreement   **606 UNTS 71**
SIGNED: 13 Jul 67   FORCE: 13 Jul 67
REGISTERED: 1 Oct 67 United Nations
ARTICLES: 10 LANGUAGE: English. French.
HEADNOTE: ASSISTANCE SPECIAL FUND
TOPIC: Non-IBRD Project
CONCEPTS: IGO reference. Privileges and immunities. Arbitration. Procedure. Domestic obligation. Withdrawal conditions. Plans and standards. Non-bank projects.
INTL ORGS: Permanent Court of Arbitration.
PROCEDURE: Amendment. Termination.
PARTIES:
    Czechoslovakia
    UN Special Fund

108777   Multilateral Protocol   **606 UNTS 89**
SIGNED: 2 Feb 67   FORCE: 2 Feb 67
REGISTERED: 2 Oct 67 Denmark
ARTICLES: 1 LANGUAGE: Danish. Dutch. German.
HEADNOTE: SUBMIT CONTINENTAL SHELF CASE ICJ
TOPIC: Dispute Settlement
CONCEPTS: Territorial application. Dispute settlement. Existing tribunals. Markers and definitions. Continental shelf.
TREATY REF: 606 UNTS 98; 606 UNTS 106;$.
PARTIES:
    Denmark SIGNED: 2 Feb 67 FORCE: 2 Feb 67
    Germany, West SIGNED: 2 Feb 67 FORCE: 2 Feb 67
    Netherlands SIGNED: 2 Feb 67 FORCE: 2 Feb 67

108778   Bilateral Agreement   **606 UNTS 97**
SIGNED: 2 Feb 67   FORCE: 2 Feb 67
REGISTERED: 2 Oct 67 Denmark
ARTICLES: 3 LANGUAGE: English.
HEADNOTE: SUBMIT CONTINENTAL SHELF CASE ICJ
TOPIC: Dispute Settlement
CONCEPTS: Territorial application. Dispute settlement. Existing tribunals. Markers and definitions. Continental shelf.
TREATY REF: 570 UNTS 91; 61 LNTS 325; 320 UNTS 243;$.
PARTIES:
    Denmark
    Germany, West

108779   Bilateral Agreement   **606 UNTS 105**
SIGNED: 2 Feb 67   FORCE: 2 Feb 67
REGISTERED: 2 Oct 67 Denmark
ARTICLES: 3 LANGUAGE: English.
HEADNOTE: SUBMIT CONTINENTAL SHELF CASE ICJ
TOPIC: Dispute Settlement
CONCEPTS: Territorial application. Dispute settlement. Existing tribunals. Markers and definitions. Continental shelf.
TREATY REF: 550 UNTS 123; 66 LNTS 103; 320 UNTS 243;$.
PARTIES:
    Germany, West
    Netherlands

108780   Bilateral Exchange   **606 UNTS 113**
SIGNED: 29 Jun 67   FORCE: 1 Jul 67
REGISTERED: 3 Oct 67 Denmark
ARTICLES: 2 LANGUAGE: French.
HEADNOTE: FISHERY RIGHTS ZONES
TOPIC: Specific Resources
CONCEPTS: Markers and definitions. Fisheries and fishing.
TREATY REF: 581 UNTS 57.
PARTIES:
    Belgium
    Denmark

108781   Bilateral Exchange   **606 UNTS 119**
SIGNED: 15 Feb 67   FORCE: 15 Feb 67
REGISTERED: 3 Oct 67 UK Great Britain
ARTICLES: 2 LANGUAGE: English. French.
HEADNOTE: AMENDING CIVIC MATTERS
TOPIC: Admin Cooperation
CONCEPTS: Annex type material.
TREATY REF: 10 LNTS 333;$.
PARTIES:
    France
    UK Great Britain

108782   Bilateral Exchange   **606 UNTS 125**
SIGNED: 1 Dec 66   FORCE: 1 Dec 66
REGISTERED: 3 Oct 67 UK Great Britain
ARTICLES: 4 LANGUAGE: English.
HEADNOTE: LOSSES DISTURBANCES
TOPIC: Claims and Debts
CONCEPTS: Claims, debts and assets. Claims and settlements.
PARTIES:
    Indonesia
    UK Great Britain

108783   Bilateral Agreement   **606 UNTS 133**
SIGNED: 27 Feb 67   FORCE: 28 Feb 67
REGISTERED: 3 Oct 67 UK Great Britain
ARTICLES: 11 LANGUAGE: English.
HEADNOTE: COMMERCIAL DEBTS
TOPIC: Claims and Debts
CONCEPTS: Definition of terms. Detailed regulations. Exchange of information and documents. Banking. Interest rates. Payment schedules. Claims, debts and assets. Lump sum settlements. Debt settlement.
PROCEDURE: Termination.
PARTIES:
    Ghana
    UK Great Britain

108784   Bilateral Agreement   **606 UNTS 149**
SIGNED: 1 Mar 67   FORCE: 1 Mar 67
REGISTERED: 3 Oct 67 UK Great Britain
ARTICLES: 17 LANGUAGE: English.
HEADNOTE: AIR SERVICES
TOPIC: Air Transport
CONCEPTS: Definition of terms. IGO reference. General cooperation. Exchange of information and documents. Procedure. Special tribunals. Negotiation. Competence of tribunal. Tariffs. Customs duties. Routes and logistics. Air transport. Conditions of airlines operating permission. Operating authorizations and regulations.
INTL ORGS: International Civil Aviation Organization.
TREATY REF: 15 UNTS 295; 320 UNTS 299, 217; 418 UNTS 161.
PROCEDURE: Amendment. Termination.
PARTIES:
    Trinidad/Tobago
    UK Great Britain

108785   Bilateral Agreement   **606 UNTS 171**
SIGNED: 24 Feb 67   FORCE: 24 Feb 67
REGISTERED: 3 Oct 67 UK Great Britain
ARTICLES: 14 LANGUAGE: English. Russian.
HEADNOTE: SCIENTIFIC TECHNOLOGICAL EDUCATIONAL CULTURAL RELATIONS
TOPIC: Scientific Project
CONCEPTS: Treaty implementation. Tourism. General cooperation. General health, education, culture, welfare and labor. Public health. Education. Teacher and student exchange. Culture. Artists. Athletes. Research and scientific projects. Scientific exchange. Agriculture. General communications. Communications linkage. Fisheries and fishing.
TREATY REF: 543 UNTS 43.
PROCEDURE: Future Procedures Contemplated.
PARTIES:
    UK Great Britain
    USSR (Soviet Union)

108786   Bilateral Exchange   **606 UNTS 209**
SIGNED: 8 Aug 66   FORCE: 8 Aug 66
REGISTERED: 3 Oct 67 USA (United States)
ARTICLES: 2 LANGUAGE: English. Spanish.
HEADNOTE: TARIFFS TRADE
TOPIC: Admin Cooperation
CONCEPTS: Annex type material. General trade. Tariffs.
TREATY REF: 119 UNTS 193.
PARTIES:
    Argentina
    USA (United States)

108787   Bilateral Exchange   **606 UNTS 219**
SIGNED: 23 Aug 66   FORCE: 22 Sep 66
REGISTERED: 3 Oct 67 USA (United States)
ARTICLES: 4 LANGUAGE: English. Japanese.
HEADNOTE: NON-IMMIGRANT VISA FEES
TOPIC: Visas
CONCEPTS: Definition of terms. Visas. Fees and exemptions.
TREATY REF: 288 UNTS 201.
PARTIES:
    Japan
    USA (United States)

108788   Bilateral Agreement   **606 UNTS 237**
SIGNED: 25 Aug 66   FORCE: 25 Aug 66
REGISTERED: 3 Oct 67 USA (United States)
ARTICLES: 5 LANGUAGE: English.
HEADNOTE: US AGRI COMMOD AGREE
TOPIC: US Agri Commod Aid
CONCEPTS: General provisions. General cooperation. Agricultural commodities assistance. Purchase authorization. Surplus commodities.
PARTIES:
    Jordan
    USA (United States)

108789   Bilateral Exchange   **606 UNTS 251**
SIGNED: 24 Aug 66   FORCE: 24 Aug 66
REGISTERED: 3 Oct 67 USA (United States)
ARTICLES: 5 LANGUAGE: English. Spanish.
HEADNOTE: LOAN OF WATERS IRRIGATION
TOPIC: Non-IBRD Project
CONCEPTS: Materials, equipment and services. Irrigation. Frontier waterways. Regulation of natural resources.
TREATY REF: 3 UNTS 313.
PARTIES:
    Mexico
    USA (United States)

108790   Bilateral Exchange   **606 UNTS 259**
SIGNED: 26 Aug 66   FORCE: 26 Aug 66
REGISTERED: 3 Oct 67 USA (United States)
ARTICLES: 11 LANGUAGE: English.
HEADNOTE: PETROLEUM PIPELINE OPERATION DEFENSE
TOPIC: Milit Installation
CONCEPTS: General cooperation. Security of information. Raw materials.
TREATY REF: 43 UNTS 271, ETC;$.
PROCEDURE: Termination.
PARTIES:
    Philippines
    USA (United States)

108791   Multilateral Protocol   **606 UNTS 267**
SIGNED: 31 Jan 67   FORCE: 4 Oct 67
REGISTERED: 4 Oct 67 United Nations
ARTICLES: 11 LANGUAGE: French. Chinese. Russian. Spanish.
HEADNOTE: REFUGEE STATUS
TOPIC: Refugees
CONCEPTS: Extradiction, deportation and repatriation.
TREATY REF: 189 UNTS 137.

PARTIES:
Cameroon RATIFIED: 19 Sep 67 FORCE:
4 Oct 67
Central Afri Rep RATIFIED: 30 Aug 67 FORCE:
4 Oct 67
Gambia RATIFIED: 29 Sep 67 FORCE: 4 Oct 67
Senegal RATIFIED: 3 Oct 67 FORCE: 4 Oct 67
Sweden RATIFIED: 4 Oct 67 FORCE: 4 Oct 67
Vatican/Holy See RATIFIED: 8 Jun 67 FORCE:
4 Oct 67

ANNEX
617 UNTS 377. Yugoslavia. Accession
15 Jan 68.
619 UNTS 345. Denmark. Accession 29 Jan 68.
640 UNTS 376. Cyprus. Accession 9 Jul 68.
640 UNTS 376. Turkey. Accession 31 Jul 68.
642 UNTS 381. Greece. Accession 7 Aug 68.
645 UNTS 385. UK Great Britain. Accession
4 Sep 68.
645 UNTS 385. Tanzania. Reservation 4 Sep 68.
648 UNTS 385. Finland. Accession 10 Oct 68.
649 UNTS 372. USA (United States). Accession
1 Nov 68. Reservation 28 Jul 51.
649 UNTS 372. Ireland. Accession 6 Nov 68.
649 UNTS 372. Tunisia. Accession 16 Oct 68.
649 UNTS 372. Ghana. Accession 30 Oct 68.
Reservation 30 Oct 68.
651 UNTS 405. Netherlands. Accession
29 Nov 68.
655 UNTS 404. Botswana. Accession 6 Jan 69.
660 UNTS 412. Ecuador. Accession 6 Mar 69.

108792 Multilateral Agreement **607 UNTS 2**
SIGNED: 12 Oct 67 FORCE: 12 Oct 67
REGISTERED: 12 Oct 67 United Nations
ARTICLES: 6 LANGUAGE: English.
HEADNOTE: OPERATIONAL ASSISTANCE
TOPIC: Direct Aid
CONCEPTS: General provisions. Previous treaty re-
placement. IGO reference. Personnel. Arbitra-
tion. Conciliation. Domestic obligation. General
technical assistance. IGO obligations.
INTL ORGS: International Court of Justice.
TREATY REF: 576 UNTS 17; 469 UNTS 145.
PROCEDURE: Amendment. Termination.
PARTIES:
Botswana SIGNED: 12 Oct 67 FORCE: 12 Oct 67
FAO (Food Agri) SIGNED: 12 Oct 67 FORCE:
12 Oct 67
IAEA (Atom Energy) SIGNED: 12 Oct 67 FORCE:
12 Oct 67
ICAO (Civil Aviat) SIGNED: 12 Oct 67 FORCE:
12 Oct 67
ILO (Labor Org) SIGNED: 12 Oct 67 FORCE:
12 Oct 67
IMCO (Maritime Org) SIGNED: 12 Oct 67 FORCE:
12 Oct 67
ITU (Telecommun) SIGNED: 12 Oct 67 FORCE:
12 Oct 67
UNESCO (Educ/Cult) SIGNED: 12 Oct 67 FORCE:
12 Oct 67
United Nations SIGNED: 12 Oct 67 FORCE:
12 Oct 67
UPU (Postal Union) SIGNED: 12 Oct 67 FORCE:
12 Oct 67
WHO (World Health) SIGNED: 12 Oct 67 FORCE:
12 Oct 67
WMO (Meteorology) SIGNED: 12 Oct 67 FORCE:
12 Oct 67

108793 Multilateral Agreement **607 UNTS 20**
SIGNED: 12 Oct 67 FORCE: 12 Oct 67
REGISTERED: 12 Oct 67 United Nations
ARTICLES: 6 LANGUAGE: English.
HEADNOTE: REVISED STANDARD
TOPIC: Direct Aid
CONCEPTS: General provisions. Previous treaty re-
placement. Privileges and immunities. Title and
deeds. Financial programs. Domestic obligation.
General technical assistance. IGO obligations.
TREATY REF: 1 UNTS 15; 33 UNTS 261; 374
UNTS 147; 576 UNTS3.
PROCEDURE: Amendment. Termination.
PARTIES:
Botswana SIGNED: 12 Oct 67 FORCE: 12 Oct 67
FAO (Food Agri) SIGNED: 12 Oct 67 FORCE:
12 Oct 67
IAEA (Atom Energy) SIGNED: 12 Oct 67 FORCE:
12 Oct 67
ICAO (Civil Aviat) SIGNED: 12 Oct 67 FORCE:
12 Oct 67

ILO (Labor Org) SIGNED: 12 Oct 67 FORCE:
12 Oct 67
IMCO (Maritime Org) SIGNED: 12 Oct 67 FORCE:
12 Oct 67
ITU (Telecommun) SIGNED: 12 Oct 67 FORCE:
12 Oct 67
UNESCO (Educ/Cult) SIGNED: 12 Oct 67 FORCE:
12 Oct 67
United Nations SIGNED: 12 Oct 67 FORCE:
12 Oct 67
UPU (Postal Union) SIGNED: 12 Oct 67 FORCE:
12 Oct 67
WHO (World Health) SIGNED: 12 Oct 67 FORCE:
12 Oct 67
WMO (Meteorology) SIGNED: 12 Oct 67 FORCE:
12 Oct 67

108794 Bilateral Agreement **607 UNTS 37**
SIGNED: 12 Oct 67 FORCE: 12 Oct 67
REGISTERED: 12 Oct 67 United Nations
ARTICLES: 10 LANGUAGE: English.
HEADNOTE: ASSISTANCE
TOPIC: Direct Aid
CONCEPTS: IGO reference. Privileges and immuni-
ties. Exchange of information and documents.
Title and deeds. Arbitration. Conciliation. Do-
mestic obligation. General technical assistance.
Use restrictions. Plans and standards.
INTL ORGS: International Court of Justice.
PARTIES:
Botswana
UN Special Fund

108795 Bilateral Agreement **607 UNTS 57**
SIGNED: 29 Aug 67 FORCE: 29 Aug 67
REGISTERED: 17 Oct 67 WHO (World Health)
ARTICLES: 7 LANGUAGE: English.
HEADNOTE: TECHNICAL ADVISORY ASSISTANCE
TOPIC: Direct Aid
CONCEPTS: Definition of terms. Privileges and im-
munities. Title and deeds. Financial programs.
Domestic obligation. General technical assis-
tance. IGO obligations.
PROCEDURE: Amendment. Termination.
PARTIES:
New Zealand
WHO (World Health)

108796 Bilateral Agreement **607 UNTS 69**
SIGNED: 22 Jun 66 FORCE: 22 Jun 66
REGISTERED: 18 Oct 67 Australia
ARTICLES: 7 LANGUAGE: English.
HEADNOTE: TRADE
TOPIC: General Trade
CONCEPTS: Exceptions and exemptions. General
cooperation. Establishment of trade relations.
Trade procedures. Payment schedules. Most fa-
vored nation clause.
PROCEDURE: Duration.
PARTIES:
Australia
Bulgaria

108797 Bilateral Exchange **607 UNTS 77**
SIGNED: 13 Jan 67 FORCE: 1 Feb 67
REGISTERED: 18 Oct 67 Australia
ARTICLES: 2 LANGUAGE: English. Spanish.
HEADNOTE: ABOLITION VISA FEES
TOPIC: Visas
CONCEPTS: Visa abolition. Denial of admission.
Conformity with municipal law. Fees and exemp-
tions.
PARTIES:
Australia
Mexico

108798 Bilateral Agreement **607 UNTS 83**
SIGNED: 9 Dec 66 FORCE: 9 Dec 66
REGISTERED: 18 Oct 67 Australia
ARTICLES: 13 LANGUAGE: English.
HEADNOTE: ESTABLISHMENT JOINT DEFENSE
SPACE RESEARCH FACILITY
TOPIC: Scientific Project
CONCEPTS: Operating agencies. Research coop-
eration. Tax exemptions. Domestic obligation.
Materials, equipment and services. Self-defense.
Research cooperation.
TREATY REF: 131 UNTS 83; 469 UNTS 55.
PROCEDURE: Duration. Termination.

PARTIES:
Australia
USA (United States)

108799 Multilateral Exchange **607 UNTS 97**
SIGNED: 20 Jun 67 FORCE: 1 Jul 67
REGISTERED: 18 Oct 67 Netherlands
ARTICLES: 10 LANGUAGE: English. French.
HEADNOTE: USE SEAMENS BOOKS TRAVEL DOC-
UMENTS
TOPIC: Visas
CONCEPTS: Non-visa travel documents.
PROCEDURE: Denunciation.
PARTIES:
Belgium SIGNED: 20 Jun 67 FORCE: 31 Jul 67
Luxembourg SIGNED: 20 Jul 67 FORCE:
31 Jul 67
Netherlands SIGNED: 20 Jun 67 FORCE:
31 Jul 67
Pakistan SIGNED: 20 Jul 67 FORCE: 31 Jul 67

108800 Bilateral Agreement **607 UNTS 105**
SIGNED: 8 May 67 FORCE: 31 Jul 67
REGISTERED: 18 Oct 67 Netherlands
ARTICLES: 10 LANGUAGE: French.
HEADNOTE: SETTLEMENT OUTSTANDING FINAN-
CIAL PROBLEMS
TOPIC: Finance
CONCEPTS: Previous treaty replacement. General
property. Payment schedules. Claims and settle-
ments. Lump sum settlements.
TREATY REF: 479 UNTS 91.
PROCEDURE: Ratification.
PARTIES:
Netherlands
Romania

108801 Bilateral Agreement **607 UNTS 117**
SIGNED: 23 Apr 66 FORCE: 23 Apr 66
REGISTERED: 18 Oct 67 USA (United States)
ARTICLES: 5 LANGUAGE: English. Portuguese.
HEADNOTE: AGRI COMMOD TITLE IV
TOPIC: US Agri Commod Aid
CONCEPTS: General provisions. General cooper-
ation. Agricultural commodities. Credit provi-
sions.
PARTIES:
Brazil
USA (United States)

108802 Bilateral Agreement **607 UNTS 141**
SIGNED: 25 Mar 65 FORCE: 11 Oct 66
REGISTERED: 18 Oct 67 USA (United States)
ARTICLES: 16 LANGUAGE: English.
HEADNOTE: ESTABLISHMENT ARBITRAL TRIBU-
NAL DISPOSE US CLAIMS GUT DAM
TOPIC: Dispute Settlement
CONCEPTS: Informational records. Operating
agencies. Jurisdiction. Prizes and arbitral
awards. Special tribunals. Indemnities and reim-
bursements. Claims and settlements.
PROCEDURE: Ratification.
PARTIES:
Canada
USA (United States)

108803 Bilateral Exchange **607 UNTS 157**
SIGNED: 24 Sep 66 FORCE: 24 Sep 66
REGISTERED: 18 Oct 67 USA (United States)
ARTICLES: 1 LANGUAGE: English. Korean.
HEADNOTE: EXCHANGE OFFICIAL PUBLICA-
TIONS
TOPIC: Admin Cooperation
CONCEPTS: Exchange of official publications. Op-
erating agencies. Indemnities and reimburse-
ments.
PARTIES:
Korea, South
USA (United States)

108804 Bilateral Exchange **607 UNTS 167**
SIGNED: 20 Sep 66 FORCE: 20 Sep 66
REGISTERED: 18 Oct 67 USA (United States)
ARTICLES: 2 LANGUAGE: English. Spanish.
HEADNOTE: AUTHORIZATION AMATEUR RADIO
OPERATORS
TOPIC: Gen Communications
CONCEPTS: Amateur radio.

TREATY REF: TIAS 4893.
PARTIES:
  Nicaragua
  USA (United States)

108805   Bilateral Exchange   **607 UNTS 175**
SIGNED: 12 Sep 61   FORCE: 26 Sep 66
REGISTERED: 18 Oct 67 USA (United States)
ARTICLES: 2 LANGUAGE: English. Spanish.
HEADNOTE: RADIO COMMUNICATIONS AMA-
  TEUR STATIONS THIRD PARTY
TOPIC: Gen Communications
CONCEPTS: Exchange of information and docu-
  ments. Amateur radio. Amateur third party mes-
  sage.
PARTIES:
  USA (United States)
  Uruguay

108806   Bilateral Convention   **607 UNTS 183**
SIGNED: 14 Jun 66   FORCE: 31 May 67
REGISTERED: 19 Oct 67 Belgium
ARTICLES: 34 LANGUAGE: French. Dutch. Bul-
  garian.
HEADNOTE: VETERINARY HEALTH
TOPIC: Other HEW
CONCEPTS: Definition of terms. Detailed regula-
  tions. Exceptions and exemptions. Establish-
  ment of commission. Public health. Sanitation.
  Veterinary. Establishment of trade relations. Ex-
  port quotas. Export subsidies. Transport of
  goods.
PROCEDURE: Amendment. Denunciation. Dura-
  tion. Ratification. Renewal or Revival.
PARTIES:
  Belgium
  Bulgaria

108807   Bilateral Agreement   **607 UNTS 235**
SIGNED: 28 Mar 66   FORCE: 23 Oct 67
REGISTERED: 23 Oct 67 United Nations
ARTICLES: 8 LANGUAGE: English.
HEADNOTE: ACTIVITIES UNICEF BRAZIL
TOPIC: IGO Operations
CONCEPTS: General provisions. Previous treaty re-
  placement. Privileges and immunities. General
  cooperation. Informational records. Public infor-
  mation. Title and deeds. Claims and settlements.
  Domestic obligation. Materials, equipment and
  services. Mutual consultation.
TREATY REF: 1 UNTS 15; 66 UNTS 75.
PROCEDURE: Amendment. Termination.
PARTIES:
  Brazil
  UNICEF (Children)

108808   Bilateral Exchange   **607 UNTS 245**
SIGNED: 30 Jul 60   FORCE: 30 Jun 60
REGISTERED: 23 Oct 67 Greece
ARTICLES: 12 LANGUAGE: French.
HEADNOTE: PROVISIONAL TRADE PAYMENTS
TOPIC: General Trade
CONCEPTS: Establishment of trade relations. Pay-
  ment schedules.
PARTIES:
  Brazil
  Greece
ANNEX
654 UNTS 384. Brazil. Prolongation 31 Jan 68.
654 UNTS 384. Greece. Prolongation 31 Jan 68.

108809   Bilateral Exchange   **608 UNTS 3**
SIGNED: 7 Feb 66   FORCE: 7 Feb 66
REGISTERED: 24 Oct 67 Philippines
ARTICLES: 1 LANGUAGE: English.
HEADNOTE: UN IMPLEMENTATION MANILA AC-
  CORD
TOPIC: Admin Cooperation
CONCEPTS: Friendship and amity. Claims and set-
  tlements.
PARTIES:
  Malaysia
  Philippines

108810   Bilateral Agreement   **608 UNTS 13**
SIGNED: 1 Sep 67   FORCE: 1 Dec 67
REGISTERED: 24 Oct 67 Philippines
ARTICLES: 1 LANGUAGE: English.

HEADNOTE: ANTI-SMUGGLING COOPERATION
TOPIC: Commodity Trade
CONCEPTS: General cooperation. Trade proce-
  dures. Customs declarations. Ports and pilotage.
PARTIES:
  Malaysia
  Philippines

108811   Multilateral Agreement   **608 UNTS 37**
SIGNED: 27 Oct 67   FORCE: 27 Oct 67
REGISTERED: 27 Oct 67 United Nations
ARTICLES: 1 LANGUAGE: French.
HEADNOTE: OPERATIONAL ASSISTANCE
TOPIC: General Aid
CONCEPTS: Procedure. Assistance. Economic as-
  sistance. Internal structure. Status of experts.
  IGO obligations.
PARTIES:
  Ivory   Coast   SIGNED: 27 Oct 67   FORCE:
    27 Oct 67
  FAO (Food Agri) SIGNED: 27 Oct 67 FORCE:
    27 Oct 67
  IAEA (Atom Energy) SIGNED: 27 Oct 67 FORCE:
    27 Oct 67
  ICAO (Civil Aviat) SIGNED: 27 Oct 67 FORCE:
    27 Oct 67
  ILO (Labor Org) SIGNED: 27 Oct 67 FORCE:
    27 Oct 67
  IMCO (Maritime Org) SIGNED: 27 Oct 67 FORCE:
    27 Oct 67
  ITU (Telecommun) SIGNED: 27 Oct 67 FORCE:
    27 Oct 67
  UNESCO (Educ/Cult) SIGNED: 27 Oct 67 FORCE:
    27 Oct 67
  UPU (Postal Union) SIGNED: 27 Oct 67 FORCE:
    27 Oct 67
  WHO (World Health) SIGNED: 27 Oct 67 FORCE:
    27 Oct 67
  WMO (Meteorology) SIGNED: 27 Oct 67 FORCE:
    27 Oct 67
ANNEX
649 UNTS 374. UNIDO (Industrial). Accession
18 Oct 68. Force 18 Oct 68.

108812   Bilateral Agreement   **608 UNTS 55**
SIGNED: 3 May 67   FORCE: 30 Jun 67
REGISTERED: 27 Oct 67 Denmark
ARTICLES: 1 LANGUAGE: Danish. Spanish.
HEADNOTE: COMMERCE & NAVIGATION
TOPIC: General Trade
CONCEPTS: General trade. Trade procedures.
  Debt settlement. Most favored nation clause.
  Customs duties.
PARTIES:
  Denmark
  Paraguay

108813   Bilateral Agreement   **608 UNTS 69**
SIGNED: 8 Dec 66   FORCE: 8 Dec 66
REGISTERED: 27 Oct 67 Turkey
ARTICLES: 11 LANGUAGE: English.
HEADNOTE: INTER-REGIONAL TRAINING ISO-
  TOPE TECHNIQUE HYDROLOGY
TOPIC: Atomic Energy
CONCEPTS: Procedure. Exchange. Teacher and
  student exchange. Research cooperation. Scien-
  tific exchange. Peaceful use. Procedure. IGO ob-
  ligations.
PARTIES:
  IAEA (Atom Energy)
  Turkey

108814   Bilateral Agreement   **608 UNTS 79**
SIGNED: 16 May 67   FORCE: 16 May 67
REGISTERED: 27 Oct 67 USSR (Soviet Union)
ARTICLES: 9 LANGUAGE: Russian. Italian.
HEADNOTE: COOPERATION IN TOURISM
TOPIC: Admin Cooperation
CONCEPTS: Visas. Tourism. Frontier permits. Gen-
  eral cooperation. Exchange of information and
  documents. Payment schedules.
PARTIES:
  Italy
  USSR (Soviet Union)

108815   Bilateral Convention   **608 UNTS 93**
SIGNED: 29 Jul 66
REGISTERED: 27 Oct 67 USSR (Soviet Union)
ARTICLES: 43 LANGUAGE: Russian. Japanese.

HEADNOTE: CONSUL
TOPIC: Consul/Citizenship
CONCEPTS: General consular functions. Consular
  relations establishment. Privileges and immuni-
  ties. Consular functions in shipping. Consular
  functions in property.
PARTIES:
  Japan
  USSR (Soviet Union)

108816   Bilateral Agreement   **608 UNTS 197**
SIGNED: 27 Oct 66   FORCE: 27 Oct 66
REGISTERED: 27 Oct 67 USSR (Soviet Union)
ARTICLES: 7 LANGUAGE: Russian. French.
HEADNOTE: SCIENTIFIC & TECHNICAL COOPER-
  ATION
TOPIC: Scientific Project
CONCEPTS: General cooperation. Scientific ex-
  change. Research and development. Laws and
  formalities.
PARTIES:
  Morocco
  USSR (Soviet Union)

108817   Bilateral Agreement   **608 UNTS 207**
SIGNED: 27 Oct 66   FORCE: 27 Oct 66
REGISTERED: 27 Oct 67 USSR (Soviet Union)
ARTICLES: 1 LANGUAGE: Russian. French.
HEADNOTE: COOPERATION RADIO & TELEVISION
TOPIC: Mass Media
CONCEPTS: Mass media exchange. Press and wire
  services.
PARTIES:
  Morocco
  USSR (Soviet Union)

108818   Bilateral Agreement   **608 UNTS 219**
SIGNED: 29 Sep 66   FORCE: 10 Apr 67
REGISTERED: 27 Oct 67 USSR (Soviet Union)
ARTICLES: 1 LANGUAGE: Russian. Serbo-Croat.
HEADNOTE: ECONOMIC & TECHNICAL ASSIS-
  TANCE
TOPIC: General Aid
CONCEPTS: Exchange of information and docu-
  ments. Accounting procedures. Banking. Inter-
  est rates. Payment schedules. Economic assis-
  tance. Loan guarantee.
PARTIES:
  USSR (Soviet Union)
  Yugoslavia

108819   Bilateral Agreement   **608 UNTS 249**
SIGNED: 16 May 66   FORCE: 16 Nov 66
REGISTERED: 1 Nov 67 IBRD (World Bank)
ARTICLES: 8 LANGUAGE: English.
HEADNOTE: LOAN
TOPIC: Loans and Credits
CONCEPTS: Bonds. Loan repayment. Loan regula-
  tions.
PARTIES:
  Colombia
  IBRD (World Bank)

108820   Bilateral Agreement   **608 UNTS 279**
SIGNED: 31 May 66   FORCE: 13 Oct 66
REGISTERED: 1 Nov 67 IBRD (World Bank)
ARTICLES: 5 LANGUAGE: English.
HEADNOTE: GUARANTEE
TOPIC: Loans and Credits
CONCEPTS: Loan guarantee.
PARTIES:
  Colombia
  IBRD (World Bank)

108821   Bilateral Agreement   **608 UNTS 327**
SIGNED: 7 Oct 67   FORCE: 7 Oct 67
REGISTERED: 1 Nov 67 WHO (World Health)
ARTICLES: 6 LANGUAGE: English.
HEADNOTE: TECHNICAL ADVISORY ASSISTANCE
TOPIC: Direct Aid
CONCEPTS: General cooperation. General techni-
  cal assistance. Headquarters and facilities. IGO
  status. IGO obligations.
PARTIES:
  Cyprus
  WHO (World Health)

108822 Bilateral Exchange **608 UNTS 339**
SIGNED: 1 Sep 66   FORCE: 1 Sep 66
REGISTERED: 3 Nov 67 Ireland
ARTICLES: 2 LANGUAGE: English.
HEADNOTE: RECIPROCAL WAIVING PASSPORT
  VISAS
TOPIC: Visas
CONCEPTS: Visa abolition.
PARTIES:
  Ireland
  Japan

108823 Bilateral Exchange **608 UNTS 345**
SIGNED: 27 Jan 67
REGISTERED: 3 Nov 67 Netherlands
ARTICLES: 2 LANGUAGE: English.
HEADNOTE: EXTRADITION
TOPIC: Extradition
CONCEPTS: Extradition, deportation and repatria-
  tion.
TREATY REF: 90 BFSP 51, 108 BFSP 366.
PARTIES:
  Netherlands
  Uganda

108824 Bilateral Agreement **609 UNTS 3**
SIGNED: 4 Nov 67   FORCE: 4 Nov 67
REGISTERED: 4 Nov 67 United Nations
ARTICLES: 7 LANGUAGE: English.
HEADNOTE: ARRANGEMENTS SECOND UN CON-
  FERENCE TRADE DEVELOPMENT
TOPIC: IGO Operations
CONCEPTS: Privileges and immunities. Legal pro-
  tection and assistance. Personnel. Title and
  deeds. Financial programs. Materials, equipment
  and services. Passenger transport. Conferences.
TREATY REF: 1 UNTS 15; 33 UNTS 261.
PARTIES:
  India
  United Nations

108825 Bilateral Agreement **609 UNTS 15**
SIGNED: 23 Aug 62   FORCE: 23 Aug 62
REGISTERED: 6 Nov 67 Greece
ARTICLES: 11 LANGUAGE: Greek.
HEADNOTE: TRADE
TOPIC: General Trade
CONCEPTS: Definition of terms. Exceptions and
  exemptions. Tourism. General cooperation. Es-
  tablishment of commission. Export quotas. Im-
  port quotas. Reciprocity in trade. Payment
  schedules. Most favored nation clause. Patents,
  copyrights and trademarks. Merchant vessels.
PROCEDURE: Denunciation. Duration. Renewal or
  Revival.
PARTIES:
  Cyprus
  Greece

108826 Bilateral Agreement **609 UNTS 27**
SIGNED: 16 Apr 64   FORCE: 1 Apr 67
REGISTERED: 6 Nov 67 Greece
ARTICLES: 13 LANGUAGE: Greek. German.
HEADNOTE: PROTECTION MARKS DESIGNATION
  ORIGIN
TOPIC: Other Economic
CONCEPTS: Detailed regulations. Annex or appen-
  dix reference. Legal protection and assistance.
  Establishment of commission. Claims and settle-
  ments. Patents, copyrights and trademarks.
PROCEDURE: Amendment. Denunciation. Ratifica-
  tion.
PARTIES:
  Germany, West
  Greece

108827 Bilateral Agreement **609 UNTS 94**
SIGNED: 14 Feb 58   FORCE: 14 Feb 58
REGISTERED: 6 Nov 67 Greece
ARTICLES: 7 LANGUAGE: English.
HEADNOTE: TRADE
TOPIC: General Trade
CONCEPTS: General cooperation. Export quotas.
  Import quotas. Exchange rates and regulations.
  Payment schedules. Transport of goods.
PROCEDURE: Amendment. Duration. Renewal or
  Revival.

PARTIES:
  Greece
  India
              ANNEX
654 UNTS 388. India. Prolongation 3 Apr 67.
  Force 3 Apr 67.
654 UNTS 388. Greece. Prolongation 3 Apr 67.
  Force 3 Apr 67.

108828 Bilateral Agreement **609 UNTS 103**
SIGNED: 20 Sep 66   FORCE: 20 Sep 66
REGISTERED: 6 Nov 67 Greece
ARTICLES: 5 LANGUAGE: English.
HEADNOTE: SETTLEMENT CERTAIN GREEK
  CLAIMS
TOPIC: Claims and Debts
CONCEPTS: Claims and settlements. Lump sum
  settlements.
TREATY REF: 136 UNTS 45.
PARTIES:
  Greece
  Japan

108829 Bilateral Agreement **609 UNTS 109**
SIGNED: 20 Jul 63   FORCE: 17 Jun 67
REGISTERED: 6 Nov 67 Greece
ARTICLES: 4 LANGUAGE: French.
HEADNOTE: EXEMPTION TAXES INCOME MARI-
  TIME AIR TRANSPORT OPERATIONS
TOPIC: Taxation
CONCEPTS: Tax exemptions. Air transport. Water
  transport.
PROCEDURE: Denunciation. Ratification. Registra-
  tion.
PARTIES:
  Greece
  Romania

108830 Multilateral Convention **609 UNTS 115**
SIGNED: 18 Nov 65   FORCE: 17 Feb 66
REGISTERED: 15 Nov 67 Czechoslovakia
ARTICLES: 20 LANGUAGE: Russian.
HEADNOTE: CUSTOMS CLEARANCE INTERNA-
  TIONAL TRANSPORT GOODS ROAD VEHICLE
TOPIC: Customs
CONCEPTS: Definition of terms. Detailed regula-
  tions. Annex or appendix reference. Claims and
  settlements. Customs duties. Transport of
  goods.
PROCEDURE: Amendment. Accession. Denuncia-
  tion. Ratification.
PARTIES:
  Bulgaria SIGNED: 18 Nov 65 FORCE: 14 Sep 66
  Czechoslovakia SIGNED: 18 Nov 65 FORCE:
    17 Feb 66
  Germany, West SIGNED: 18 Nov 65 FORCE:
    17 Feb 66
  Hungary SIGNED: 18 Nov 65 FORCE: 17 Feb 66
  Poland SIGNED: 18 Nov 65 FORCE: 28 Jul 66
  USSR (Soviet Union) SIGNED: 18 Nov 65
    FORCE: 17 Feb 66

108831 Bilateral Treaty **609 UNTS 187**
SIGNED: 17 Mar 67   FORCE: 26 Jun 67
REGISTERED: 15 Nov 67 Czechoslovakia
ARTICLES: 12 LANGUAGE: Czechoslovakian. Ger-
  man.
HEADNOTE: FRIENDSHIP COOPERATION MU-
  TUAL ASSISTANCE
TOPIC: General Amity
CONCEPTS: IGO reference. Peaceful relations. Ex-
  change of information and documents. General
  trade. Attachment of funds. Defense and secu-
  rity.
TREATY REF: 504 UNTS 163; 145 BFSP 852; 219
  UNTS 3 142 AFSP 4.
PROCEDURE: Denunciation. Duration. Registra-
  tion. Renewal or Revival.
PARTIES:
  Czechoslovakia
  Germany, East

108832 Bilateral Agreement **610 UNTS 0**
SIGNED: 26 Apr 67   FORCE: 8 Sep 67
REGISTERED: 15 Nov 67 Czechoslovakia
ARTICLES: 0 LANGUAGE: Czechoslovakian. Pol-
  ish.
HEADNOTE: EXCHANGE STUDENTS
TOPIC: Education

CONCEPTS: Exchange. Teacher and student ex-
  change.
PROCEDURE: Duration. Ratification.
PARTIES:
  Czechoslovakia
  Poland

108833 Bilateral Agreement **610 UNTS 0**
SIGNED: 9 Feb 67   FORCE: 30 Sep 67
REGISTERED: 16 Nov 67 Netherlands
ARTICLES: 0 LANGUAGE: English.
HEADNOTE: EMPLOYMENT VOLUNTEERS
TOPIC: Non-ILO Labor
CONCEPTS: Migrant worker. Materials, equipment
  and services. Volunteer programs.
PROCEDURE: Duration. Termination.
PARTIES:
  Kenya
  Netherlands

108834 Bilateral Exchange **610 UNTS 0**
SIGNED: 24 Mar 67   FORCE: 24 Mar 67
REGISTERED: 16 Nov 67 Netherlands
ARTICLES: 0 LANGUAGE: French.
HEADNOTE: ANTI-TUBERCULOSIS CAMPAIGN
TOPIC: Sanitation
CONCEPTS: Disease control. Public health. Assis-
  tance. Materials, equipment and services.
PARTIES:
  Netherlands
  Vietnam, South

108835 Bilateral Protocol **610 UNTS 0**
SIGNED: 25 Sep 64   FORCE: 1 Jan 65
REGISTERED: 17 Nov 67 Greece
ARTICLES: 0 LANGUAGE: French.
HEADNOTE: RECIPROCAL GRANT IMPORT-
  EXPORT LICENSES
TOPIC: General Economic
CONCEPTS: Export quotas. Import quotas. Reci-
  procity in trade. Trade procedures.
TREATY REF: 30UNTS161,178UNTS384,2-
  30UNTS428.
PROCEDURE: Duration.
PARTIES:
  Greece
  Norway

108836 Multilateral Convention **610 UNTS 0**
SIGNED: 22 Jun 65   FORCE: 10 Nov 67
REGISTERED: 21 Nov 67 ILO (Labor Org)
ARTICLES: 0 LANGUAGE: English. French.
HEADNOTE: MINIMUM AGE EMPLOYMENT UN-
  DERGROUND MINES
TOPIC: ILO Labor
CONCEPTS: Employment regulations. Safety stan-
  dards.
PROCEDURE: Denunciation. Ratification.
PARTIES:
  Multilateral
              ANNEX
636 UNTS 427. Thailand. Ratification 5 Apr 68.
  Force 5 Apr 69.
640 UNTS 392. Czechoslovakia. Ratification
  7 Jun 68. Force 7 Jun 69.
640 UNTS 392. Hungary. Ratification 8 Jun 68.
  Force 8 Jun 69.
640 UNTS 392. Kenya. Ratification 20 Jun 68.
  Force 20 Jun 68.
645 UNTS 390. Mexico. Ratification 29 Aug 68.
  Force 29 Aug 69.
649 UNTS 387. Paraguay. Ratification 10 Oct 68.
  Force 10 Oct 69.
649 UNTS 387. Gabon. Ratification 18 Oct 68.
  Force 18 Oct 69.

108837 Bilateral Exchange **610 UNTS 0**
SIGNED: 2 May 67   FORCE: 2 May 67
REGISTERED: 21 Nov 67 UK Great Britain
ARTICLES: 0 LANGUAGE: English. Arabic.
HEADNOTE: CONSOLIDATION FINANCIAL AGREE-
  MENTS
TOPIC: Finance
CONCEPTS: Finances and payments. Loan and
  credit.
TREATY   REF: 310UNTS340,27UNTS77,1-
  17UNTS19,ETC.

PARTIES:
Jordan
UK Great Britain

108838 Bilateral Exchange **610 UNTS 0**
SIGNED: 21 Apr 67   FORCE: 21 Apr 67
REGISTERED: 21 Nov 67 UK Great Britain
ARTICLES: 0 LANGUAGE: English.
HEADNOTE: INTEREST FREE DEVELOPMENT
LOAN
TOPIC: Loans and Credits
CONCEPTS: Loan and credit. Loan repayment.
Terms of loan.
PARTIES:
Turkey
UK Great Britain

108839 Bilateral Treaty **610 UNTS 0**
SIGNED: 21 Jul 67   FORCE: 13 Sep 67
REGISTERED: 22 Nov 67 Mongolia
ARTICLES: 0 LANGUAGE: Mongolian. Bulgarian.
HEADNOTE: FRIENDSHIP COOPERATION
TOPIC: General Amity
CONCEPTS: Friendship and amity. Peaceful rela-
tions. General cultural cooperation.
PROCEDURE: Ratification. Termination.
PARTIES:
Bulgaria
Mongolia

108840 Multilateral Agreement **610 UNTS 143**
SIGNED: 15 Jul 64   FORCE: 2 Nov 64
REGISTERED: 22 Nov 67 Hungary.
ARTICLES: 0 LANGUAGE: Russian.
HEADNOTE: COOPERATION, IRON & STEEL IN-
DUSTRY
TOPIC: IGO Establishment
CONCEPTS: Research and scientific projects.
Scientific exchange. General technical assis-
tance. Establishment.
PARTIES:
Czechoslovakia SIGNED: 15 Jul 64 FORCE:
2 Nov 64
Hungary SIGNED: 15 Jul 64 FORCE: 2 Nov 64
Poland SIGNED: 15 Jul 64 FORCE: 2 Nov 64

108841 Multilateral Agreement **610 UNTS 169**
SIGNED: 3 Oct 66   FORCE: 1 Jul 67
REGISTERED: 27 Nov 67 Denmark
ARTICLES: 0 LANGUAGE: Danish.
HEADNOTE: NORDIC CULTURAL FUND
TOPIC: Culture
CONCEPTS: Exchange. General cultural cooper-
ation.
TREATY REF: 434UNTS145.
PROCEDURE: Denunciation. Ratification. Termina-
tion.
PARTIES:
Denmark SIGNED: 3 Oct 66 RATIFIED:
29 Mar 67 FORCE: 1 Jul 67
Finland SIGNED: 3 Oct 66 RATIFIED: 23 May 67
FORCE: 1 Jul 67
Iceland SIGNED: 3 Oct 66 RATIFIED: 19 Dec 66
FORCE: 1 Jul 67
Norway SIGNED: 3 Oct 66 RATIFIED: 27 Jan 67
FORCE: 1 Jul 67
Sweden SIGNED: 3 Oct 66 RATIFIED: 30 Jun 67
FORCE: 1 Jul 67

108842 Bilateral Agreement **610 UNTS 0**
SIGNED: 9 Aug 67   FORCE: 9 Aug 67
REGISTERED: 27 Nov 67 Denmark
ARTICLES: 0 LANGUAGE: English.
HEADNOTE: GOVERNMENT LOAN
TOPIC: Loans and Credits
CONCEPTS: Procedure. Loan and credit. Credit
provisions. Terms of loan.
PROCEDURE: Duration. Termination.
PARTIES:
Denmark
Ghana

108843 Multilateral Treaty **610 UNTS 205**
SIGNED: 27 Jan 67   FORCE: 10 Oct 67
REGISTERED: 30 Nov 67 USSR (Soviet Union)
ARTICLES: 0 LANGUAGE: Chinese. English.
HEADNOTE: PRINCIPLES GOVERNING EXPLORA-
TION USE OUTER SPACE

TOPIC: Scientific Project
CONCEPTS: Humanitarian matters. Research and
scientific projects. Atomic weapons.
PROCEDURE: Accession. Ratification.
PARTIES:
Afghanistan   SIGNED: 30 Jan 67   FORCE:
10 Oct 67
Argentina   SIGNED: 27 Jan 67   FORCE:
10 Oct 67
Australia   SIGNED: 27 Jan 67   RATIFIED:
10 Oct 67 FORCE: 10 Oct 67
Brazil SIGNED: 2 Feb 67 FORCE: 10 Oct 67
Bulgaria   SIGNED: 27 Jan 67   RATIFIED:
11 Apr 67 FORCE: 10 Oct 67
Burma SIGNED: 22 May 67 FORCE: 10 Oct 67
Canada   SIGNED: 27 Jan 67   RATIFIED:
10 Oct 67 FORCE: 10 Oct 67
Congo (Brazzaville) SIGNED: 4 May 67 FORCE:
10 Oct 67
Czechoslovakia SIGNED: 27 Jan 67 RATIFIED:
22 May 67 FORCE: 10 Oct 67
Ecuador SIGNED: 7 Jun 67 FORCE: 10 Oct 67
France SIGNED: 25 Sep 67 FORCE: 10 Oct 67
Germany, East SIGNED: 27 Jan 67 RATIFIED:
2 Feb 67 FORCE: 10 Oct 67
India SIGNED: 3 Mar 67 FORCE: 10 Oct 67
Indonesia SIGNED: 14 Feb 67 FORCE: 10 Oct 67
Iraq SIGNED: 9 Mar 67 FORCE: 10 Oct 67
Israel SIGNED: 27 Jan 67 FORCE: 10 Oct 67
Italy SIGNED: 27 Jan 67 FORCE: 10 Oct 67
Jamaica SIGNED: 29 Jun 67 FORCE: 10 Oct 67
Jordan SIGNED: 2 Feb 67 FORCE: 10 Oct 67
Laos SIGNED: 2 Feb 67 FORCE: 10 Oct 67
Lebanon SIGNED: 23 Feb 67 FORCE: 10 Oct 67
Luxembourg   SIGNED: 27 Jan 67   FORCE:
10 Oct 67
Malaysia SIGNED: 3 May 67 FORCE: 10 Oct 67
Mexico SIGNED: 27 Jan 67 FORCE: 10 Oct 67
Niger SIGNED: 1 Feb 67 FORCE: 10 Oct 67
Pakistan SIGNED: 12 Sep 67 FORCE: 10 Oct 67
Panama SIGNED: 27 Jan 67 FORCE: 10 Oct 67
Peru SIGNED: 30 Jun 67 FORCE: 10 Oct 67
Philippines   SIGNED: 27 Jan 67   FORCE:
10 Oct 67
Philippines   SIGNED: 29 Apr 67   FORCE:
10 Oct 67
Poland SIGNED: 27 Jan 67 FORCE: 10 Oct 67
Poland SIGNED: 27 Jan 67 FORCE: 10 Oct 67
Romania SIGNED: 27 Jan 67 FORCE: 10 Oct 67
Rwanda SIGNED: 27 Jan 67 FORCE: 10 Oct 67
San   Marino   SIGNED: 6 Jun 67   FORCE:
10 Oct 67
South   Africa   SIGNED: 1 Mar 67   FORCE:
10 Oct 67
Somalia SIGNED: 2 Feb 67 FORCE: 10 Oct 67
Sweden SIGNED: 27 Jan 67 FORCE: 10 Oct 67
Switzerland   SIGNED: 27 Jan 67   FORCE:
10 Oct 67
Thailand SIGNED: 27 Jan 67 FORCE: 10 Oct 67
Togo SIGNED: 27 Jan 67 FORCE: 10 Oct 67
Trinidad/Tobago SIGNED: 28 Sep 67 FORCE:
10 Oct 67
United Arab Rep SIGNED: 27 Jan 67 FORCE:
10 Oct 67
UK Great Britain SIGNED: 27 Jan 67 RATIFIED:
10 Oct 67 FORCE: 10 Oct 67
USA (United States) SIGNED: 27 Jan 67 RATI-
FIED: 10 Oct 67 FORCE: 10 Oct 67
Upper   Volta   SIGNED: 3 Mar 67   FORCE:
10 Oct 67
Uruguay SIGNED: 27 Jan 67 FORCE: 10 Oct 67
USSR (Soviet Union) SIGNED: 27 Jan 67 RATI-
FIED: 10 Oct 67 FORCE: 10 Oct 67
Venezuela   SIGNED: 27 Jan 67   FORCE:
10 Oct 67
Yugoslavia   SIGNED: 27 Jan 67   FORCE:
10 Oct 67

ANNEX
639 UNTS 367. Australia. Ratification 26 Feb 68.
639 UNTS 367. Iceland. Ratification 5 Feb 68.
639 UNTS 367. Mexico. Ratification 31 Jan 68.
639 UNTS 367. Morocco. Accession 21 Dec 67.
639 UNTS 367. Pakistan. Ratification 8 Apr 68.
639 UNTS 367. Poland. Ratification 30 Jan 68.
639 UNTS 367. Tunisia. Ratification 4 Apr 68.
639 UNTS 367. Turkey. Ratification 27 Mar 68.
639 UNTS 367. United Arab Rep. Ratification
23 Jan 68.
639 UNTS 367. Romania. Ratification 9 Apr 68.
649 UNTS 376.   New   Zealand.   Ratification
31 May 68.
649 UNTS 376. Morocco. Accession 21 Dec 67.
649 UNTS 376. Poland. Ratification 10 Jan 68.
649 UNTS 376. Nigeria. Accession 14 Nov 67.

649 UNTS 376. Thailand. Ratification 5 Sep 68.
649 UNTS 376. Romania. Ratification 9 Apr 68.
649 UNTS 376. Pakistan. Ratification 8 Apr 68.
649 UNTS 376. Tunisia. Ratification 28 Mar 68.
649 UNTS 376. Turkey. Ratification 27 Mar 68.
649 UNTS 376. Iceland. Ratification 5 Feb 68.
649 UNTS 376. Mexico. Ratification 31 Jan 68.
649 UNTS 376.   South   Africa.   Ratification
8 Oct 68.
649 UNTS 376. Austria. Ratification 26 Feb 68.
649 UNTS 376. Ireland. Ratification 19 Jul 68.

108844 Multilateral Instrument **611 UNTS 7**
SIGNED: 10 Jul 64   FORCE: 1 Jan 66
REGISTERED: 1 Dec 67 Austria
ARTICLES: 33 LANGUAGE: French.
HEADNOTE: CONSTITUTION UPU
TOPIC: Postal Service
CONCEPTS: General provisions. Procedure. Finan-
cial programs. Internal structure.
PROCEDURE: Amendment. Accession. Denuncia-
tion. Ratification.
PARTIES:
Afghanistan   SIGNED: 10 Jul 64   FORCE:
1 Jan 66
Albania SIGNED: 10 Jul 64 FORCE: 1 Jan 66
Algeria SIGNED: 10 Jul 64 FORCE: 1 Jan 66
Argentina   SIGNED: 10 Jul 64   RATIFIED:
23 Jun 67 FORCE: 1 Jan 66
Australia All Territories RATIFIED: 23 Dec 65
FORCE: 1 Jan 66
Australia   SIGNED: 10 Jul 64   RATIFIED:
23 Dec 65 FORCE: 1 Jan 66
Austria SIGNED: 10 Jul 64 RATIFIED: 23 Dec 65
FORCE: 1 Jan 66
Barbados   RATIFIED: 11 Nov 67   FORCE:
11 Nov 67
Belgium SIGNED: 10 Jul 64 RATIFIED: 4 Nov 65
FORCE: 1 Jan 66
Bolivia SIGNED: 10 Jul 64 FORCE: 1 Jan 66
Brazil SIGNED: 10 Jul 64 FORCE: 1 Jan 66
Bulgaria SIGNED: 10 Jul 64 FORCE: 1 Jan 66
Burma SIGNED: 10 Jul 64 FORCE: 1 Jan 66
Burundi SIGNED: 10 Jul 64 FORCE: 1 Jan 66
Byelorussia SIGNED: 10 Jul 64 FORCE: 1 Jan 66
Cambodia SIGNED: 10 Jul 64 FORCE: 1 Jan 66
Cameroon SIGNED: 10 Jul 64 FORCE: 1 Jan 66
Canada SIGNED: 10 Jul 64 RATIFIED: 8 Mar 66
FORCE: 1 Jan 66
Ceylon (Sri Lanka) SIGNED: 10 Jul 64 RATIFIED:
14 Mar 67 FORCE: 1 Jan 66
Chad SIGNED: 10 Jul 64 FORCE: 1 Jan 66
Chile SIGNED: 10 Jul 64 FORCE: 1 Jan 66
Taiwan SIGNED: 10 Jul 64 RATIFIED: 6 Sep 66
FORCE: 1 Jan 66
Central   Afri   Rep   SIGNED: 10 Jul 64   FORCE:
1 Jan 66
Congo (Brazzaville) SIGNED: 10 Jul 64 RATI-
FIED: 7 Sep 66 FORCE: 1 Jan 66
Congo   (Zaire)   SIGNED: 10 Jul 64   FORCE:
1 Jan 66
Colombia SIGNED: 10 Jul 64 FORCE: 1 Jan 66
Costa Rica SIGNED: 10 Jul 64 FORCE: 1 Jan 66
Cuba SIGNED: 10 Jul 64 FORCE: 1 Jan 66
Cyprus SIGNED: 10 Jul 64 FORCE: 1 Jan 66
Czechoslovakia SIGNED: 10 Jul 64 RATIFIED:
20 May 66 FORCE: 1 Jan 66
Dahomey   SIGNED: 10 Jul 64   RATIFIED:
13 Jan 67 FORCE: 1 Jan 66
Denmark SIGNED: 10 Jul 64 FORCE: 1 Jan 66
Dominican Republic SIGNED: 10 Jul 64 FORCE:
1 Jan 66
Ecuador SIGNED: 10 Jul 64 FORCE: 1 Jan 66
El Salvador SIGNED: 10 Jul 64 FORCE: 1 Jan 66
Ethiopia SIGNED: 10 Jul 64 FORCE: 1 Jan 66
Finland SIGNED: 10 Jul 64 RATIFIED: 17 Dec 65
FORCE: 1 Jan 66
France   All   Territories   RATIFIED: 10 Jul 64
FORCE: 1 Jan 66
France SIGNED: 10 Jul 64 RATIFIED: 21 Dec 65
FORCE: 1 Jan 66
Gabon SIGNED: 10 Jul 64 RATIFIED: 27 Jan 67
FORCE: 1 Jan 66
Germany, West SIGNED: 10 Jul 64 RATIFIED:
27 Jun 66 FORCE: 1 Jan 66
Ghana SIGNED: 10 Jul 64 RATIFIED: 16 Nov 66
FORCE: 1 Jan 66
Greece SIGNED: 10 Jul 64 FORCE: 1 Jan 66
Guatemala SIGNED: 10 Jul 64 FORCE: 1 Jan 66
Guinea SIGNED: 10 Jul 64 RATIFIED: 12 Dec 66
FORCE: 1 Jan 66
Guyana RATIFIED: 22 Mar 67 FORCE: 22 Mar 67
Haiti SIGNED: 10 Jul 64 FORCE: 1 Jan 66

Honduras SIGNED: 10 Jul 64 FORCE: 1 Jan 66
Hungary SIGNED: 10 Jul 64 RATIFIED: 2 May 67 FORCE: 1 Jan 66
Iceland SIGNED: 10 Jul 64 RATIFIED: 10 Aug 65 FORCE: 1 Jan 66
India SIGNED: 10 Jul 64 RATIFIED: 8 Nov 66 FORCE: 1 Jan 66
Indonesia SIGNED: 10 Jul 64 FORCE: 1 Jan 66
Iran SIGNED: 10 Jul 64 FORCE: 1 Jan 66
Iraq SIGNED: 10 Jul 64 RATIFIED: 22 Sep 67 FORCE: 1 Jan 66
Ireland SIGNED: 10 Jul 64 RATIFIED: 4 Mar 66 FORCE: 1 Jan 66
Israel SIGNED: 10 Jul 64 FORCE: 1 Jan 66
Italy SIGNED: 10 Jul 64 FORCE: 1 Jan 66
Ivory Coast SIGNED: 10 Jul 64 RATIFIED: 17 Sep 65 FORCE: 1 Jan 66
Jamaica SIGNED: 10 Jul 64 FORCE: 1 Jan 66
Japan SIGNED: 10 Jul 64 RATIFIED: 22 Jul 65 FORCE: 1 Jan 66
Jordan SIGNED: 10 Jul 64 FORCE: 1 Jan 66
Korea, South SIGNED: 10 Jul 64 RATIFIED: 20 May 66 FORCE: 1 Jan 66
Kuwait SIGNED: 10 Jul 64 RATIFIED: 16 Aug 67 FORCE: 1 Jan 66
Laos SIGNED: 10 Jul 64 RATIFIED: 25 Sep 67 FORCE: 1 Jan 66
Lebanon SIGNED: 10 Jul 64 FORCE: 1 Jan 66
Lesotho RATIFIED: 6 Sep 67 FORCE: 6 Sep 67
Liberia SIGNED: 10 Jul 64 FORCE: 1 Jan 66
Libya SIGNED: 10 Jul 64 FORCE: 1 Jan 66
Liechtenstein SIGNED: 10 Jul 64 RATIFIED: 5 Oct 67 FORCE: 1 Jan 66
Luxembourg SIGNED: 10 Jul 64 RATIFIED: 29 Dec 65 FORCE: 1 Jan 66
Madagascar RATIFIED: 25 Aug 65 FORCE: 1 Jan 66
Malagasy SIGNED: 10 Jul 64 FORCE: 1 Jan 66
Malawi RATIFIED: 25 Oct 65 FORCE: 1 Jan 66
Malaysia SIGNED: 10 Jul 64 FORCE: 1 Jan 66
Maldive Islands RATIFIED: 15 Aug 67 FORCE: 15 Aug 67
Mali SIGNED: 10 Jul 64 RATIFIED: 18 Dec 65 FORCE: 1 Jan 66
Mauritania RATIFIED: 22 Mar 67 FORCE: 22 Mar 67
Mexico SIGNED: 10 Jul 64 FORCE: 1 Jan 66
Monaco SIGNED: 10 Jul 64 FORCE: 1 Jan 66
Mongolia SIGNED: 10 Jul 64 FORCE: 1 Jan 66
Morocco SIGNED: 10 Jul 64 RATIFIED: 7 Apr 65 FORCE: 1 Jan 66
Nepal SIGNED: 10 Jul 64 FORCE: 1 Jan 66
Netherlands SIGNED: 10 Jul 64 FORCE: 1 Jan 66
Netherlands Netherlands Antilles RATIFIED: 10 Jul 64 FORCE: 1 Jan 66
Netherlands Surinam RATIFIED: 10 Jul 64 FORCE: 1 Jan 66
New Zealand All Territories RATIFIED: 10 Jul 64 FORCE: 1 Jan 66
New Zealand SIGNED: 10 Jul 64 RATIFIED: 21 Oct 66 FORCE: 1 Jan 66
Nicaragua SIGNED: 10 Jul 64 FORCE: 1 Jan 66
Nigeria SIGNED: 10 Jul 64 RATIFIED: 10 Jan 67 FORCE: 1 Jan 66
Niger SIGNED: 10 Jul 64 RATIFIED: 28 Feb 66 FORCE: 1 Jan 66
Norway SIGNED: 10 Jul 64 RATIFIED: 1 Dec 67 FORCE: 1 Jan 66
Pakistan SIGNED: 10 Jul 64 RATIFIED: 19 Dec 66 FORCE: 1 Jan 66
Panama SIGNED: 10 Jul 64 FORCE: 1 Jan 66
Paraguay SIGNED: 10 Jul 64 FORCE: 1 Jan 66
Peru SIGNED: 10 Jul 64 FORCE: 1 Jan 66
Philippines SIGNED: 10 Jul 64 FORCE: 1 Jan 66
Poland SIGNED: 10 Jul 64 RATIFIED: 12 Sep 66 FORCE: 1 Jan 66
Portugal SIGNED: 10 Jul 64 FORCE: 1 Jan 66
Romania SIGNED: 10 Jul 64 FORCE: 1 Jan 66
Rwanda SIGNED: 10 Jul 64 FORCE: 1 Jan 66
San Marino SIGNED: 10 Jul 64 RATIFIED: 11 Oct 67 FORCE: 1 Jan 66
Saudi Arabia SIGNED: 10 Jul 64 FORCE: 1 Jan 66
Senegal SIGNED: 10 Jul 64 RATIFIED: 26 Sep 67 FORCE: 1 Jan 66
Sierra Leone SIGNED: 10 Jul 64 RATIFIED: 24 Aug 67 FORCE: 1 Jan 66
Singapore RATIFIED: 8 Jan 66 FORCE: 8 Jan 66
South Africa RATIFIED: 7 Oct 64 FORCE: 1 Jan 66
Somalia SIGNED: 10 Jul 64 FORCE: 1 Jan 66
Spain All Territories RATIFIED: 10 Jul 64 FORCE: 1 Jan 66

Spain SIGNED: 10 Jul 64 RATIFIED: 9 Nov 66 FORCE: 1 Jan 66
Sudan SIGNED: 10 Jul 64 FORCE: 1 Jan 66
Sweden SIGNED: 10 Jul 64 RATIFIED: 13 Dec 66 FORCE: 1 Jan 66
Switzerland SIGNED: 10 Jul 64 RATIFIED: 4 Feb 66 FORCE: 1 Jan 66
Syria SIGNED: 10 Jul 64 RATIFIED: 18 Nov 66 FORCE: 1 Jan 66
Tanzania SIGNED: 10 Jul 64 RATIFIED: 26 Sep 67 FORCE: 1 Jan 66
Thailand SIGNED: 10 Jul 64 RATIFIED: 7 Feb 66 FORCE: 1 Jan 66
Togo SIGNED: 10 Jul 64 RATIFIED: 28 Aug 67 FORCE: 1 Jan 66
Trinidad/Tobago SIGNED: 10 Jul 64 FORCE: 1 Jan 66
Tunisia SIGNED: 10 Jul 64 RATIFIED: 13 Sep 66 FORCE: 1 Jan 66
Turkey SIGNED: 10 Jul 64 FORCE: 1 Jan 66
United Arab Rep SIGNED: 10 Jul 64 RATIFIED: 30 Jun 67 FORCE: 1 Jan 66
Uganda SIGNED: 10 Jul 64 RATIFIED: 29 Dec 65 FORCE: 1 Jan 66
UK Great Britain SIGNED: 10 Jul 64 RATIFIED: 2 Aug 66
UK Great Britain All Territories RATIFIED: 10 Jul 64 FORCE: 1 Jan 66
USA (United States) All Territories RATIFIED: 10 Jul 64 FORCE: 1 Jan 66
USA (United States) SIGNED: 10 Jul 64 RATIFIED: 22 Jun 66 FORCE: 1 Jan 66
Ukrainian SSR SIGNED: 10 Jul 44 FORCE: 1 Jan 66
Upper Volta SIGNED: 10 Jul 64 RATIFIED: 24 Apr 67 FORCE: 1 Jan 66
Uruguay SIGNED: 10 Jul 64 FORCE: 1 Jan 66
USSR (Soviet Union) SIGNED: 10 Jul 64 FORCE: 1 Jan 66
Vatican/Holy See SIGNED: 10 Jul 64 FORCE: 1 Jan 66
Venezuela SIGNED: 10 Jul 64 FORCE: 1 Jan 66
Vietnam, South SIGNED: 10 Jul 64 RATIFIED: 5 Jun 67 FORCE: 1 Jan 66
Yemen SIGNED: 10 Jul 64 FORCE: 1 Jan 66
Yugoslavia SIGNED: 10 Jul 64 RATIFIED: 15 Nov 66 FORCE: 1 Jan 66
Zambia RATIFIED: 22 Mar 67 FORCE: 22 Mar 67
ANNEX
619 UNTS 346. Botswana. Accession 12 Jan 68.
633 UNTS 422. Jordan. Ratification 2 Feb 67. Approval 3 Jan 68.
634 UNTS 466. UK Great Britain. Mauritius.
634 UNTS 466. UK Great Britain. New Hebrides Is.
634 UNTS 466. UK Great Britain. Pitcairn Island.
634 UNTS 466. UK Great Britain. Falkland Islands.
634 UNTS 466. UK Great Britain. Antigua.
634 UNTS 466. UK Great Britain. Brit Virgin Islands.
634 UNTS 466. UK Great Britain. Cayman Island.
634 UNTS 466. UK Great Britain. Fiji Islands.
634 UNTS 466. UK Great Britain. Gibralter.
634 UNTS 466. UK Great Britain. Montserrat.
634 UNTS 466. UK Great Britain. St. Helena.
634 UNTS 466. UK Great Britain. St. Vincent.
634 UNTS 466. UK Great Britain. Seychelles.
634 UNTS 466. UK Great Britain. Southern Rhodesia.
634 UNTS 466. UK Great Britain. Brit Solomon Is.
634 UNTS 466. UK Great Britain. Gilbert Islands.
634 UNTS 466. Israel. Ratification 29 Feb 68.
634 UNTS 466. UK Great Britain. Dominican Republic.
634 UNTS 466. UK Great Britain. Grenada.
634 UNTS 466. UK Great Britain. St. Christopher.
634 UNTS 466. UK Great Britain. Nevis.
634 UNTS 466. UK Great Britain. St. Lucia.
634 UNTS 466. UK Great Britain. Brunei.
634 UNTS 466. UK Great Britain. Hong Kong.
634 UNTS 466. UK Great Britain. Swaziland.
634 UNTS 466. UK Great Britain. Tonga.
634 UNTS 466. UK Great Britain. Bahamas.
634 UNTS 466. UK Great Britain. Bermuda.
634 UNTS 466. UK Great Britain. British Honduras.
634 UNTS 466. UK Great Britain. British India.
639 UNTS 367. Kenya. Accession 26 Apr 68.
639 UNTS 368. Vatican/Holy See. Ratification 22 Apr 68.
639 UNTS 368. Greece. Ratification 8 May 68.
640 UNTS 378. Somalia. Ratification 27 May 68.
640 UNTS 378. Malta. Accession 4 Jun 68.

640 UNTS 378. Southern Yemen. Accession 28 Jun 68.
643 UNTS 410. Algeria. Ratification 12 Jun 68.
643 UNTS 410. Italy. Ratification 12 Jul 68.
646 UNTS 416. Trinidad/Tobago. Ratification 14 Jun 68.
646 UNTS 416. Central Afri Rep. Ratification 26 Jul 68.
651 UNTS 406. Monaco. Ratification 30 Sep 68.
651 UNTS 406. Iran. Ratification 28 Aug 68.
655 UNTS 406. Mongolia. Ratification 8 Apr 68.
655 UNTS 406. Albania. Ratification 4 Nov 68.
658 UNTS 440. Cameroon. Ratification 23 Dec 68.
658 UNTS 440. Yemen. Ratification 10 Jan 69.
658 UNTS 440. Qatar. Accession 31 Jan 69. Declaration 31 Jan 69.

108845 Multilateral Convention **611 UNTS 105**
SIGNED: 10 Jul 64 FORCE: 1 Jan 66
REGISTERED: 1 Dec 67 Austria
ARTICLES: 70 LANGUAGE: French.
HEADNOTE: POSTAL CONVENTION
TOPIC: Postal Service
CONCEPTS: Mail and money orders. Postal services.
PARTIES:
Afghanistan SIGNED: 10 Jul 64 FORCE: 1 Jan 66
Albania SIGNED: 10 Jul 64 FORCE: 1 Jan 66
Algeria SIGNED: 10 Jul 64 FORCE: 1 Jan 66
Argentina SIGNED: 10 Jul 64 RATIFIED: 23 Jul 67 FORCE: 1 Jan 66
Australia SIGNED: 10 Jul 64 RATIFIED: 23 Dec 65 FORCE: 1 Jan 66
Australia All Territories RATIFIED: 23 Dec 65 FORCE: 1 Jan 67
Austria SIGNED: 10 Jul 64 RATIFIED: 23 Dec 65 FORCE: 1 Jan 66
Barbados RATIFIED: 11 Nov 67 FORCE: 1 Jan 67
Belgium SIGNED: 10 Jul 64 RATIFIED: 4 Nov 65 FORCE: 1 Jan 66
Bolivia SIGNED: 10 Jul 64 FORCE: 1 Jan 66
Brazil SIGNED: 10 Jul 64 FORCE: 1 Jan 66
Bulgaria SIGNED: 10 Jul 64 FORCE: 1 Jan 66
Burma SIGNED: 10 Jul 64 FORCE: 1 Jan 66
Burundi SIGNED: 10 Jul 64 FORCE: 1 Jan 66
Byelorussia SIGNED: 10 Jul 64 FORCE: 1 Jan 66
Cambodia SIGNED: 10 Jul 64 FORCE: 1 Jan 66
Cameroon SIGNED: 10 Jul 64 FORCE: 1 Jan 66
Canada SIGNED: 10 Jul 64 RATIFIED: 8 Mar 66 FORCE: 1 Jan 66
Ceylon (Sri Lanka) SIGNED: 10 Jul 64 RATIFIED: 14 Mar 67 FORCE: 1 Jan 66
Chad SIGNED: 10 Jul 64 FORCE: 1 Jan 66
Chile SIGNED: 10 Jul 64 FORCE: 1 Jan 66
Taiwan SIGNED: 10 Jul 64 RATIFIED: 6 Sep 66 FORCE: 1 Jan 66
Central Afri Rep SIGNED: 10 Jul 64 FORCE: 1 Jan 66
Congo (Brazzaville) SIGNED: 10 Jul 64 RATIFIED: 7 Sep 66 FORCE: 1 Jan 66
Congo (Zaire) SIGNED: 10 Jul 64 FORCE: 1 Jan 66
Colombia SIGNED: 10 Jul 64 FORCE: 1 Jan 66
Costa Rica SIGNED: 10 Jul 64 FORCE: 1 Jan 66
Cuba SIGNED: 10 Jul 64 FORCE: 1 Jan 66
Cyprus SIGNED: 10 Jul 64 FORCE: 1 Jan 66
Czechoslovakia SIGNED: 10 Jul 64 RATIFIED: 20 May 66 FORCE: 1 Jan 66
Dahomey SIGNED: 10 Jul 64 RATIFIED: 13 Jan 67 FORCE: 1 Jan 66
Denmark SIGNED: 10 Jul 64 RATIFIED: 23 Dec 65 FORCE: 1 Jan 66
Dominican Republic SIGNED: 10 Jul 64 FORCE: 1 Jan 66
Ecuador SIGNED: 10 Jul 64 FORCE: 1 Jan 66
El Salvador SIGNED: 10 Jul 64 FORCE: 1 Jan 66
Ethiopia SIGNED: 10 Jul 64 FORCE: 1 Jan 66
Finland SIGNED: 10 Jul 64 RATIFIED: 17 Dec 65 FORCE: 1 Jan 66
France All Territories RATIFIED: 10 Jul 64 FORCE: 1 Jan 66
France SIGNED: 10 Jul 64 RATIFIED: 22 Jan 66 FORCE: 1 Jan 66
Gabon SIGNED: 10 Jul 64 RATIFIED: 27 Jan 67 FORCE: 1 Jan 66
Germany, West SIGNED: 10 Jul 64 RATIFIED: 27 Jun 66 FORCE: 1 Jan 66
Germany, West Berlin RATIFIED: 27 Jun 66 FORCE: 1 Jan 67
Ghana SIGNED: 10 Jul 64 RATIFIED: 17 Nov 66 FORCE: 1 Jan 66

Greece SIGNED: 10 Jul 64 FORCE: 1 Jan 66
Guatemala SIGNED: 10 Jul 64 FORCE: 1 Jan 66
Guinea SIGNED: 10 Jul 64 RATIFIED: 5 Sep 66
  FORCE: 1 Jan 66
Guyana RATIFIED: 22 Mar 67 FORCE: 1 Jan 67
Haiti SIGNED: 10 Jul 64 FORCE: 1 Jan 66
Honduras SIGNED: 10 Jul 64 RATIFIED:
  2 May 67 FORCE: 1 Jan 66
Hungary SIGNED: 10 Jul 64 FORCE: 1 Jan 66
Iceland SIGNED: 10 Jul 64 RATIFIED: 10 Aug 65
  FORCE: 1 Jan 66
India SIGNED: 10 Jul 64 RATIFIED: 8 Nov 66
  FORCE: 1 Jan 66
Indonesia SIGNED: 10 Jul 64 FORCE: 1 Jan 66
Iran SIGNED: 10 Jul 64 FORCE: 1 Jan 66
Iraq SIGNED: 10 Jul 64 RATIFIED: 22 Sep 67
  FORCE: 1 Jan 66
Ireland SIGNED: 10 Jul 64 RATIFIED: 4 Mar 66
  FORCE: 1 Jan 66
Israel SIGNED: 10 Jul 64 FORCE: 1 Jan 67
Italy SIGNED: 10 Jul 64 FORCE: 1 Jan 67
Ivory Coast SIGNED: 10 Jul 64 RATIFIED:
  28 Oct 65 FORCE: 1 Jan 66
Jamaica SIGNED: 10 Jul 64 FORCE: 1 Jan 67
Japan SIGNED: 10 Jul 64 RATIFIED: 22 Jul 67
  FORCE: 1 Jan 67
Jordan SIGNED: 10 Jul 64 FORCE: 1 Jan 67
Korea, South SIGNED: 10 Jul 64 RATIFIED:
  20 May 66 FORCE: 1 Jan 66
Kuwait SIGNED: 10 Jul 64 RATIFIED: 16 Aug 67
  FORCE: 1 Jan 66
Laos SIGNED: 10 Jul 64 RATIFIED: 25 Sep 67
  FORCE: 1 Jan 67
Lebanon SIGNED: 10 Jul 64 FORCE: 1 Jan 67
Lesotho RATIFIED: 6 Sep 67 FORCE: 1 Jan 66
Liberia SIGNED: 10 Jul 64 FORCE: 1 Jan 67
Libya SIGNED: 10 Jul 64 FORCE: 1 Jan 67
Liechtenstein SIGNED: 10 Jul 64 RATIFIED:
  5 Oct 67 FORCE: 1 Jan 67
Luxembourg SIGNED: 10 Jul 64 RATIFIED:
  29 Dec 65 FORCE: 1 Jan 67
Madagascar RATIFIED: 25 Aug 65 FORCE:
  1 Jan 66
Malagasy SIGNED: 10 Jul 64 FORCE: 1 Jan 67
Malawi RATIFIED: 25 Oct 66 FORCE: 25 Oct 66
Malaysia SIGNED: 10 Jul 64 FORCE: 1 Jan 67
Maldive Islands RATIFIED: 15 Aug 67 FORCE:
  15 Aug 67
Mali SIGNED: 10 Jul 64 RATIFIED: 18 Dec 65
  FORCE: 1 Jan 66
Mauritania RATIFIED: 22 Mar 67 FORCE:
  22 Mar 67
Mexico SIGNED: 10 Jul 64 FORCE: 1 Jan 67
Monaco SIGNED: 10 Jul 64 FORCE: 1 Jan 67
Mongolia SIGNED: 10 Jul 64 FORCE: 1 Jan 67
Morocco SIGNED: 10 Jul 64 RATIFIED: 7 Apr 67
  FORCE: 1 Jan 67
Nepal SIGNED: 10 Jul 64 FORCE: 1 Jan 67
Netherlands SIGNED: 10 Jul 64 FORCE:
  1 Jan 66
Netherlands Netherlands Antilles RATIFIED:
  10 Jul 64 FORCE: 1 Jan 66
Netherlands Surinam RATIFIED: 10 Jul 64
  FORCE: 1 Jan 66
New Zealand All Territories RATIFIED: 10 Jul 64
  FORCE: 1 Jan 66
New Zealand SIGNED: 10 Jul 64 RATIFIED:
  21 Oct 66 FORCE: 1 Jan 66
Nicaragua SIGNED: 10 Jul 64 FORCE: 1 Jan 67
Nigeria SIGNED: 10 Jul 64 RATIFIED: 18 Jan 67
  FORCE: 1 Jan 67
Niger SIGNED: 10 Jul 64 RATIFIED: 8 Feb 66
  FORCE: 1 Jan 67
Norway SIGNED: 10 Jul 64 RATIFIED: 1 Dec 65
  FORCE: 1 Jan 67
Pakistan SIGNED: 10 Jul 64 RATIFIED:
  19 Dec 66 FORCE: 1 Jan 67
Panama SIGNED: 10 Jul 64 FORCE: 1 Jan 67
Paraguay SIGNED: 10 Jul 64 FORCE: 1 Jan 67
Peru SIGNED: 10 Jul 64 FORCE: 1 Jan 66
Philippines SIGNED: 10 Jul 64 FORCE: 1 Jan 66
Poland SIGNED: 10 Jul 64 RATIFIED: 14 Sep 66
  FORCE: 1 Jan 66
Portugal SIGNED: 10 Jul 64 FORCE: 1 Jan 66
Romania SIGNED: 10 Jul 64 FORCE: 1 Jan 66
Rwanda SIGNED: 10 Jul 64 FORCE: 1 Jan 66
San Marino SIGNED: 10 Jul 64 RATIFIED:
  11 Oct 67 FORCE: 1 Jan 66
Saudi Arabia SIGNED: 10 Jul 64 FORCE:
  1 Jan 66
Senegal SIGNED: 10 Jul 64 RATIFIED:
  26 Sep 67 FORCE: 1 Jan 66
Sierra Leone SIGNED: 10 Jul 64 RATIFIED:
  24 Aug 67 FORCE: 1 Jan 66

Singapore RATIFIED: 8 Jan 66 FORCE: 8 Jan 66
South Africa RATIFIED: 7 Oct 64 FORCE:
  7 Oct 64
Somalia SIGNED: 10 Jul 64 FORCE: 1 Jan 66
Spain All Territories RATIFIED: 10 Jul 64 FORCE:
  1 Jan 66
Spain SIGNED: 10 Jul 64 RATIFIED: 9 Nov 66
  FORCE: 1 Jan 66
Sudan SIGNED: 10 Jul 64 FORCE: 1 Jan 66
Sweden SIGNED: 10 Jul 64 RATIFIED:
  13 Dec 66 FORCE: 1 Jan 66
Switzerland SIGNED: 10 Jul 64 RATIFIED:
  4 Feb 66 FORCE: 1 Jan 66
Syria SIGNED: 10 Jul 64 RATIFIED: 18 Nov 66
  FORCE: 1 Jan 66
Tanzania SIGNED: 10 Jul 64 RATIFIED: 2 Sep 67
  FORCE: 1 Jan 66
Thailand SIGNED: 10 Jul 64 RATIFIED:
  10 May 66 FORCE: 1 Jan 66
Togo SIGNED: 10 Jul 64 RATIFIED: 28 Aug 67
  FORCE: 1 Jan 66
Trinidad/Tobago SIGNED: 10 Jul 64 FORCE:
  1 Jan 66
Tunisia SIGNED: 10 Jul 64 RATIFIED: 13 Sep 66
  FORCE: 1 Jan 66
Turkey SIGNED: 10 Jul 64 FORCE: 1 Jan 66
United Arab Rep SIGNED: 10 Jul 64 RATIFIED:
  30 Jun 67 FORCE: 1 Jan 66
Uganda SIGNED: 10 Jul 64 RATIFIED:
  29 Dec 65 FORCE: 1 Jan 67
UK Great Britain SIGNED: 10 Jul 64 RATIFIED:
  2 Aug 66 FORCE: 1 Jan 66
UK Great Britain All Territories RATIFIED:
  10 Jul 64 FORCE: 1 Jan 66
USA (United States) All Territories RATIFIED:
  10 Jul 64 FORCE: 1 Jan 66
USA (United States) SIGNED: 10 Jul 64 RATI-
  FIED: 22 Apr 66 FORCE: 1 Jan 66
Ukrainian SSR SIGNED: 10 Jul 64 FORCE:
  1 Jan 67
Upper Volta SIGNED: 10 Jul 64 RATIFIED:
  4 Feb 67 FORCE: 1 Jan 66
Uruguay SIGNED: 10 Jul 64 FORCE: 1 Jan 67
USSR (Soviet Union) SIGNED: 10 Jul 64 FORCE:
  1 Jan 67
Vatican/Holy See SIGNED: 10 Jul 64 FORCE:
  1 Jan 67
Venezuela SIGNED: 10 Jul 64 FORCE: 1 Jan 67
Vietnam, South SIGNED: 10 Jul 64 RATIFIED:
  5 Jun 67 FORCE: 1 Jan 67
Yemen SIGNED: 10 Jul 64 FORCE: 1 Jan 67
Yugoslavia SIGNED: 10 Jul 64 RATIFIED:
  15 Nov 66 FORCE: 1 Jan 66
Zambia RATIFIED: 22 Mar 67 FORCE: 22 Mar 67
ANNEX
619 UNTS 347. Botswana. Accession 12 Jan 68.
  Reservation 12 Jan 68.
633 UNTS 422. Jordan. Approval 3 Jan 68.
634 UNTS 470. UK Great Britain. New Hebrides
  Is.
634 UNTS 470. UK Great Britain. Pitcairn Island.
634 UNTS 470. UK Great Britain. Montserrat.
634 UNTS 470. UK Great Britain. Cayman Island.
634 UNTS 470. UK Great Britain. Brunei.
634 UNTS 470. UK Great Britain. St. Christopher.
634 UNTS 470. UK Great Britain. St. Helena.
634 UNTS 470. UK Great Britain. Southern
  Rhodesia.
634 UNTS 470. UK Great Britain. British Honduras.
634 UNTS 470. UK Great Britain. Tonga.
634 UNTS 470. UK Great Britain. Bahamas.
634 UNTS 470. UK Great Britain. Bermuda.
634 UNTS 470. UK Great Britain. British India.
634 UNTS 470. UK Great Britain. Brit Virgin Islands.
634 UNTS 470. UK Great Britain. Falkland Islands.
634 UNTS 470. UK Great Britain. Fiji Islands.
634 UNTS 470. UK Great Britain. Gibralter.
634 UNTS 470. UK Great Britain. Hong Kong.
634 UNTS 470. UK Great Britain. Gilbert Islands.
634 UNTS 470. UK Great Britain. St. Vincent.
634 UNTS 470. UK Great Britain. Seychelles.
634 UNTS 470. UK Great Britain. Antigua.
634 UNTS 470. UK Great Britain. Dominican
  Republic.
634 UNTS 470. UK Great Britain. Nevis.
634 UNTS 470. UK Great Britain. Grenada.
634 UNTS 470. UK Great Britain. Mauritius.
634 UNTS 470. UK Great Britain. St. Lucia.
634 UNTS 470. Israel. Ratification 29 Feb 68.
634 UNTS 470. UK Great Britain. Swaziland.
634 UNTS 470. UK Great Britain. Brit Solomon Is.

639 UNTS 368. Greece. Ratification 8 May 68.
639 UNTS 368. Vatican/Holy See. Ratification
  22 Apr 68.
639 UNTS 368. Kenya. Accession 26 Apr 68.
640 UNTS 378. Malta. Accession 4 Jun 68.
640 UNTS 378. Somalia. Ratification 27 May 68.
640 UNTS 378. Southern Yemen. Accession
  28 Jun 68.
643 UNTS 410. Italy. Ratification 12 Jul 68.
643 UNTS 410. Algeria. Ratification 12 Jun 68.
651 UNTS 406. Iran. Ratification 28 Aug 68.
651 UNTS 406. Monaco. Ratification 30 Sep 68.
655 UNTS 406. Albania. Ratification 4 Nov 68.
655 UNTS 406. Mongolia. Ratification 8 Apr 68.
658 UNTS 440. Yemen. Ratification 10 Jan 69.
658 UNTS 440. Qatar. Accession 31 Jan 69. Declaration 31 Jan 69.
658 UNTS 440. Cameroon. Ratification
  23 Dec 68.

108846 Multilateral Agreement **611 UNTS 387**
SIGNED: 10 Jul 64   FORCE: 1 Jan 66
REGISTERED: 1 Dec 67 Austria
ARTICLES: 18 LANGUAGE: French.
HEADNOTE: INSURED LETTERS BOXES
TOPIC: Postal Service
CONCEPTS: General provisions. Annex or appen-
  dix reference. Responsibility and liability. Regu-
  lations. Rates and charges.
PROCEDURE: Duration.
PARTIES:
Albania SIGNED: 10 Jul 64 FORCE: 1 Jan 66
Algeria SIGNED: 10 Jul 64 FORCE: 1 Jan 66
Argentina SIGNED: 10 Jul 64 RATIFIED:
  23 Jun 67 FORCE: 1 Jan 66
Austria SIGNED: 10 Jul 64 RATIFIED: 23 Dec 65
  FORCE: 1 Jan 66
Barbados RATIFIED: 11 Nov 67 FORCE:
  11 Nov 67
Belgium SIGNED: 10 Jul 64 RATIFIED: 4 Nov 65
  FORCE: 1 Jan 66
Bolivia SIGNED: 10 Jul 64 FORCE: 1 Jan 66
Brazil SIGNED: 10 Jul 64 FORCE: 1 Jan 66
Bulgaria SIGNED: 10 Jul 64 FORCE: 1 Jan 66
Burma SIGNED: 10 Jul 64 FORCE: 1 Jan 66
Burundi SIGNED: 10 Jul 64 FORCE: 1 Jan 66
Byelorussia SIGNED: 10 Jul 64 FORCE: 1 Jan 66
Cambodia SIGNED: 10 Jul 64 FORCE: 1 Jan 66
Cameroon SIGNED: 10 Jul 64 FORCE: 1 Jan 66
Ceylon (Sri Lanka) SIGNED: 10 Jul 64 RATIFIED:
  14 Mar 67 FORCE: 1 Jan 66
Chad SIGNED: 10 Jul 64 FORCE: 1 Jan 66
Chile SIGNED: 10 Jul 64 FORCE: 1 Jan 66
Taiwan SIGNED: 10 Jul 64 RATIFIED: 6 Sep 66
  FORCE: 1 Jan 66
Central Afri Rep SIGNED: 10 Jul 64 FORCE:
  1 Jan 66
Congo (Brazzaville) SIGNED: 10 Jul 64 RATI-
  FIED: 7 Sep 66 FORCE: 1 Jan 66
Congo (Zaire) SIGNED: 10 Jul 64 FORCE:
  1 Jan 66
Colombia SIGNED: 10 Jul 64 FORCE: 1 Jan 66
Costa Rica SIGNED: 10 Jul 64 FORCE: 1 Jan 66
Cuba SIGNED: 10 Jul 64 FORCE: 1 Jan 66
Cyprus SIGNED: 10 Jul 64 FORCE: 1 Jan 66
Czechoslovakia SIGNED: 10 Jul 64 RATIFIED:
  20 May 66 FORCE: 1 Jan 66
Dahomey SIGNED: 10 Jul 64 RATIFIED:
  13 Jan 67 FORCE: 1 Jan 66
Denmark SIGNED: 10 Jul 64 RATIFIED:
  23 Dec 65 FORCE: 1 Jan 66
El Salvador SIGNED: 10 Jul 64 FORCE: 1 Jan 66
Finland SIGNED: 10 Jul 64 RATIFIED: 17 Dec 65
  FORCE: 1 Jan 66
France All Territories RATIFIED: 10 Jul 64
  FORCE: 1 Jan 66
France SIGNED: 10 Jul 64 RATIFIED: 22 Jan 66
  FORCE: 1 Jan 66
Gabon SIGNED: 10 Jul 64 RATIFIED: 21 Oct 67
  FORCE: 1 Jan 66
Germany, West Berlin RATIFIED: 27 Jun 66
  FORCE: 1 Jan 66
Germany, West SIGNED: 10 Jul 64 RATIFIED:
  27 Jun 66 FORCE: 1 Jan 66
Ghana SIGNED: 10 Jul 64 RATIFIED: 17 Nov 66
  FORCE: 1 Jan 66
Greece SIGNED: 10 Jul 64 FORCE: 1 Jan 66
Guinea SIGNED: 10 Jul 64 RATIFIED: 5 Sep 66
  FORCE: 1 Jan 66
Guyana RATIFIED: 22 Mar 67 FORCE: 22 Mar 67
Hungary SIGNED: 10 Jul 64 RATIFIED: 2 May 67
  FORCE: 1 Jan 66

Iceland SIGNED: 10 Jul 64 RATIFIED: 10 Aug 65 FORCE: 1 Jan 66

India SIGNED: 10 Jul 64 RATIFIED: 8 Nov 66 FORCE: 1 Jan 66

Indonesia SIGNED: 10 Jul 64 FORCE: 1 Jan 66

Iran SIGNED: 10 Jul 64 FORCE: 1 Jan 66

Iraq SIGNED: 10 Jul 64 RATIFIED: 22 Sep 67 FORCE: 1 Jan 66

Ireland SIGNED: 10 Jul 64 RATIFIED: 4 Mar 66 FORCE: 1 Jan 66

Italy SIGNED: 10 Jul 64 FORCE: 1 Jan 66

Ivory Coast SIGNED: 10 Jul 64 RATIFIED: 28 Oct 65 FORCE: 1 Jan 66

Jamaica SIGNED: 10 Jul 64 FORCE: 1 Jan 66

Japan SIGNED: 10 Jul 64 RATIFIED: 22 Jul 65 FORCE: 1 Jan 66

Jordan SIGNED: 10 Jul 64 FORCE: 1 Jan 66

Kuwait SIGNED: 10 Jul 64 RATIFIED: 16 Aug 67 FORCE: 1 Jan 66

Laos SIGNED: 10 Jul 65 RATIFIED: 25 Sep 67 FORCE: 1 Jan 66

Lebanon SIGNED: 10 Jul 64 FORCE: 1 Jan 66

Libya SIGNED: 10 Jul 64 FORCE: 1 Jan 66

Liechtenstein SIGNED: 10 Jul 64 RATIFIED: 5 Oct 67 FORCE: 1 Jan 66

Luxembourg SIGNED: 10 Jul 64 RATIFIED: 29 Dec 65 FORCE: 1 Jan 66

Madagascar RATIFIED: 25 Aug 66 FORCE: 1 Jan 66

Malagasy SIGNED: 10 Jul 64 FORCE: 1 Jan 66

Malawi RATIFIED: 25 Oct 66 FORCE: 25 Oct 66

Malaysia SIGNED: 10 Jul 64 FORCE: 1 Jan 66

Mali SIGNED: 10 Jul 64 RATIFIED: 18 Dec 65 FORCE: 1 Jan 66

Mauritania RATIFIED: 22 Mar 67 FORCE: 22 Mar 67

Monaco SIGNED: 10 Jul 64 FORCE: 1 Jan 66

Mongolia SIGNED: 10 Jul 64 FORCE: 1 Jan 66

Morocco SIGNED: 10 Jul 64 RATIFIED: 7 Apr 67 FORCE: 1 Jan 66

Netherlands SIGNED: 10 Jul 64 FORCE: 1 Jan 66

Netherlands Netherlands Antilles RATIFIED: 10 Jul 64 FORCE: 1 Jan 66

Netherlands Surinam RATIFIED: 10 Jul 64 FORCE: 1 Jan 66

New Zealand SIGNED: 10 Jul 64 RATIFIED: 21 Oct 66 FORCE: 1 Jan 66

New Zealand All Territories RATIFIED: 21 Oct 66 FORCE: 1 Jan 66

Nicaragua SIGNED: 10 Jul 64 FORCE: 1 Jan 66

Nigeria SIGNED: 10 Jul 64 RATIFIED: 18 Jan 67 FORCE: 1 Jan 66

Niger SIGNED: 10 Jul 64 RATIFIED: 8 Feb 66 FORCE: 1 Jan 66

Norway SIGNED: 10 Jul 64 RATIFIED: 1 Dec 65 FORCE: 1 Jan 66

Pakistan SIGNED: 10 Jul 64 RATIFIED: 19 Dec 66 FORCE: 1 Jan 66

Paraguay SIGNED: 10 Jul 64 FORCE: 1 Jan 66

Poland SIGNED: 10 Jul 64 RATIFIED: 14 Sep 66 FORCE: 1 Jan 66

Portugal SIGNED: 10 Jul 64 FORCE: 1 Jan 66

Romania SIGNED: 10 Jul 64 FORCE: 1 Jan 66

Rwanda SIGNED: 10 Jul 64 FORCE: 1 Jan 66

San Marino SIGNED: 10 Jul 64 RATIFIED: 11 Oct 67 FORCE: 1 Jan 66

Saudi Arabia SIGNED: 10 Jul 64 FORCE: 1 Jan 66

Senegal SIGNED: 10 Jul 64 RATIFIED: 26 Sep 67 FORCE: 1 Jan 66

Sierra Leone SIGNED: 10 Jul 64 RATIFIED: 24 Aug 67 FORCE: 1 Jan 66

Singapore RATIFIED: 8 Jan 66 FORCE: 8 Jan 66

Somalia SIGNED: 10 Jul 64 FORCE: 1 Jan 66

Spain SIGNED: 10 Jul 64 RATIFIED: 9 Nov 66 FORCE: 1 Jan 66

Spain All Territories RATIFIED: 10 Jul 64 FORCE: 1 Jan 66

Sudan SIGNED: 10 Jul 64 FORCE: 1 Jan 66

Sweden SIGNED: 10 Jul 64 RATIFIED: 13 Dec 66 FORCE: 1 Jan 66

Switzerland SIGNED: 10 Jul 64 RATIFIED: 4 Feb 66 FORCE: 1 Jan 66

Syria SIGNED: 10 Jul 64 RATIFIED: 18 Nov 66 FORCE: 1 Jan 66

Tanzania SIGNED: 10 Jul 64 RATIFIED: 26 Sep 67 FORCE: 1 Jan 66

Thailand SIGNED: 10 Jul 64 RATIFIED: 10 May 66 FORCE: 1 Jan 66

Togo SIGNED: 10 Jul 64 RATIFIED: 28 Aug 67 FORCE: 1 Jan 66

Trinidad/Tobago SIGNED: 10 Jul 64 FORCE: 1 Jan 66

Tunisia SIGNED: 10 Jul 64 RATIFIED: 13 Sep 66 FORCE: 1 Jan 66

Turkey SIGNED: 10 Jul 64 FORCE: 1 Jan 66

United Arab Rep SIGNED: 10 Jul 64 RATIFIED: 30 Jun 67 FORCE: 1 Jan 66

Uganda SIGNED: 10 Jul 64 RATIFIED: 29 Dec 65 FORCE: 1 Jan 66

UK Great Britain All Territories RATIFIED: 10 Jul 64 FORCE: 1 Jan 66

UK Great Britain SIGNED: 10 Jul 64 RATIFIED: 2 Aug 66 FORCE: 1 Jan 66

Ukrainian SSR SIGNED: 10 Jul 64 FORCE: 1 Jan 66

Upper Volta SIGNED: 10 Jul 64 RATIFIED: 4 Feb 67 FORCE: 1 Jan 66

Uruguay SIGNED: 10 Jul 64 FORCE: 1 Jan 66

USSR (Soviet Union) SIGNED: 10 Jul 64 FORCE: 1 Jan 66

Vatican/Holy See SIGNED: 10 Jul 64 FORCE: 1 Jan 66

Venezuela SIGNED: 10 Jul 64 FORCE: 1 Jan 66

Vietnam, South SIGNED: 10 Jul 64 RATIFIED: 5 Jun 67 FORCE: 1 Jan 66

Yemen SIGNED: 10 Jul 64 FORCE: 1 Jan 66

Yugoslavia SIGNED: 10 Jul 64 RATIFIED: 15 Nov 66 FORCE: 1 Jan 66

ANNEX

634 UNTS 471. UK Great Britain. Nevis.
634 UNTS 471. UK Great Britain. St. Lucia.
634 UNTS 471. UK Great Britain. New Hebrides Is.
634 UNTS 471. UK Great Britain. Pitcairn Island.
634 UNTS 471. UK Great Britain. Falkland Islands.
634 UNTS 471. UK Great Britain. Bermuda.
634 UNTS 471. UK Great Britain. Brit Solomon Is.
634 UNTS 471. UK Great Britain. Gilbert Islands.
634 UNTS 471. UK Great Britain. Dominican Republic.
634 UNTS 471. UK Great Britain. Grenada.
634 UNTS 471. UK Great Britain. British Honduras.
634 UNTS 471. UK Great Britain. St. Christopher.
634 UNTS 471. UK Great Britain. Antigua.
634 UNTS 471. UK Great Britain. Brit Virgin Islands.
634 UNTS 471. UK Great Britain. Brunei.
634 UNTS 471. UK Great Britain. Tonga.
634 UNTS 471. UK Great Britain. Cayman Island.
634 UNTS 471. UK Great Britain. Fiji Islands.
634 UNTS 471. UK Great Britain. Gibralter.
634 UNTS 471. UK Great Britain. Hong Kong.
634 UNTS 471. UK Great Britain. Mauritius.
634 UNTS 471. UK Great Britain. Montserrat.
634 UNTS 471. UK Great Britain. St. Helena.
634 UNTS 471. UK Great Britain. St. Vincent.
634 UNTS 471. UK Great Britain. Seychelles.
639 UNTS 369. Kenya. Accession 26 Apr 68.
639 UNTS 369. Vatican/Holy See. Ratification 22 Apr 68.
639 UNTS 369. Greece. Ratification 8 May 68.
640 UNTS 378. Southern Yemen. Accession 28 Jun 68.
640 UNTS 378. Somalia. Ratification 27 May 68.
640 UNTS 378. Malta. Accession 4 Jun 68.
643 UNTS 410. Algeria. Ratification 12 Jun 68.
643 UNTS 410. Italy. Ratification 12 Jul 68.
646 UNTS 417. Trinidad/Tobago. Ratification 14 Jun 68.
646 UNTS 417. Central Afri Rep. Ratification 14 Jun 68.
651 UNTS 406. Monaco. Ratification 30 Sep 68.
651 UNTS 406. Iran. Ratification 28 Aug 68.
655 UNTS 408. Mongolia. Ratification 8 Apr 68.
658 UNTS 442. Qatar. Accession 31 Jan 69.
658 UNTS 442. Cameroon. Ratification 23 Dec 68.

108847 Multilateral Agreement **612 UNTS 3**
SIGNED: 10 Jul 64 FORCE: 1 Jan 66
REGISTERED: 1 Dec 67 Austria
ARTICLES: 0 LANGUAGE: French. English.
HEADNOTE: PARCEL POST
TOPIC: Postal Service
CONCEPTS: Postal services. Parcel post.
PARTIES:
Afghanistan SIGNED: 10 Jul 64
Albania SIGNED: 10 Jul 64
Algeria SIGNED: 10 Jul 64
Argentina SIGNED: 10 Jul 64 RATIFIED: 23 Jun 67 FORCE: 23 Jun 67
Australia SIGNED: 10 Jul 64 RATIFIED: 23 Dec 65 FORCE: 1 Jan 66

Australia All Territories RATIFIED: 10 Jul 64 FORCE: 1 Jan 66

Austria SIGNED: 10 Jul 64 RATIFIED: 23 Dec 65 FORCE: 1 Jan 66

Barbados RATIFIED: 11 Nov 67 FORCE: 11 Nov 67

Belgium SIGNED: 10 Jul 64 RATIFIED: 4 Nov 65 FORCE: 1 Jan 66

Bolivia SIGNED: 10 Jul 64
Brazil SIGNED: 10 Jul 64
Bulgaria SIGNED: 10 Jul 64
Burma SIGNED: 10 Jul 64
Burundi SIGNED: 10 Jul 64
Byelorussia SIGNED: 10 Jul 64
Cambodia SIGNED: 10 Jul 64
Ceylon (Sri Lanka) SIGNED: 10 Jul 64 RATIFIED: 14 Mar 67 FORCE: 14 Mar 67

Chad SIGNED: 10 Jul 64
Chile SIGNED: 10 Jul 64
Taiwan SIGNED: 10 Jul 64 RATIFIED: 6 Sep 66 FORCE: 6 Sep 66

Congo (Brazzaville) SIGNED: 10 Jul 64
Congo (Zaire) SIGNED: 10 Jul 64 RATIFIED: 7 Sep 66 FORCE: 7 Sep 66

Colombia SIGNED: 10 Jul 64
Costa Rica SIGNED: 10 Jul 64
Cuba SIGNED: 10 Jul 64
Cyprus SIGNED: 10 Jul 64
Czechoslovakia SIGNED: 10 Jul 64 RATIFIED: 20 May 66 FORCE: 20 May 66

Dahomey SIGNED: 10 Jul 64 RATIFIED: 13 Jan 67 FORCE: 13 Jan 67

Denmark SIGNED: 10 Jul 64 RATIFIED: 20 May 66 FORCE: 1 Jan 66

Dominican Republic SIGNED: 10 Jul 64
Ecuador SIGNED: 10 Jul 64
El Salvador SIGNED: 10 Jul 64
Ethiopia SIGNED: 10 Jul 64
Finland SIGNED: 10 Jul 64 RATIFIED: 17 Dec 65 FORCE: 1 Jan 66

France All Territories RATIFIED: 10 Jul 64 FORCE: 22 Jan 66

France SIGNED: 10 Jul 64 RATIFIED: 22 Jan 66 FORCE: 22 Jan 66

Gabon SIGNED: 10 Jul 64 RATIFIED: 27 Jan 67 FORCE: 27 Jan 67

Germany, West SIGNED: 10 Jul 64 RATIFIED: 27 Jun 66 FORCE: 27 Jun 66

Ghana SIGNED: 10 Jul 64 RATIFIED: 17 Nov 66 FORCE: 17 Nov 66

Greece SIGNED: 10 Jul 64
Guatemala SIGNED: 10 Jul 64
Guinea SIGNED: 10 Jul 64 RATIFIED: 5 Sep 66 FORCE: 5 Sep 66

Guyana RATIFIED: 22 Mar 67 FORCE: 22 Mar 67
Honduras SIGNED: 10 Jul 64
Hungary SIGNED: 10 Jul 64 RATIFIED: 2 May 67 FORCE: 2 May 67

Iceland SIGNED: 10 Jul 64 RATIFIED: 10 Aug 65 FORCE: 1 Jan 66

India SIGNED: 10 Jul 64 RATIFIED: 8 Nov 66 FORCE: 8 Nov 66

Indonesia SIGNED: 10 Jul 64
Iran SIGNED: 10 Jul 64
Iraq SIGNED: 10 Jul 64 RATIFIED: 22 Sep 67 FORCE: 22 Sep 67

Ireland SIGNED: 10 Jul 64 RATIFIED: 4 Mar 66 FORCE: 4 Mar 66

Israel SIGNED: 10 Jul 64
Italy SIGNED: 10 Jul 64
Ivory Coast SIGNED: 10 Jul 64 RATIFIED: 28 Oct 65 FORCE: 1 Jan 66

Jamaica SIGNED: 10 Jul 64
Japan SIGNED: 10 Jul 64 RATIFIED: 22 Jul 65 FORCE: 1 Jan 66

Jordan SIGNED: 10 Jul 64
Korea, South SIGNED: 10 Jul 64 RATIFIED: 20 May 66 FORCE: 20 May 66

Kuwait SIGNED: 10 Jul 64 RATIFIED: 16 Aug 67 FORCE: 16 Aug 67

Laos SIGNED: 10 Jul 64 RATIFIED: 25 Sep 67 FORCE: 25 Sep 67

Lebanon SIGNED: 10 Jul 64
Liberia SIGNED: 10 Jul 64
Libya SIGNED: 10 Jul 64
Liechtenstein SIGNED: 10 Jul 64 RATIFIED: 5 Oct 67 FORCE: 5 Oct 67

Luxembourg SIGNED: 10 Jul 64 RATIFIED: 29 Dec 65 FORCE: 1 Jan 66

Madagascar SIGNED: 10 Jul 64 RATIFIED: 25 Aug 65 FORCE: 1 Jan 66

Malagasy SIGNED: 10 Jul 64
Malawi RATIFIED: 25 Oct 66 FORCE: 25 Oct 66
Malaysia SIGNED: 10 Jul 64

Mali SIGNED: 10 Jul 64 RATIFIED: 18 Dec 65 FORCE: 1 Jan 66

Mauritania RATIFIED: 22 Mar 67 FORCE: 22 Mar 67

Mexico SIGNED: 10 Jul 64

Monaco SIGNED: 10 Jul 64

Mongolia SIGNED: 10 Jul 64

Morocco SIGNED: 10 Jul 64 RATIFIED: 7 Apr 67 FORCE: 7 Apr 67

Netherlands Netherlands Antilles RATIFIED: 10 Jul 64

Netherlands SIGNED: 10 Jul 64

Netherlands Surinam RATIFIED: 10 Jul 64

New Zealand All Territories RATIFIED: 21 Oct 66 FORCE: 21 Oct 66

New Zealand SIGNED: 10 Jul 64 RATIFIED: 21 Oct 66 FORCE: 21 Oct 66

Nicaragua SIGNED: 10 Jul 64

Nigeria SIGNED: 10 Jul 64 RATIFIED: 18 Jan 67 FORCE: 18 Jan 67

Niger SIGNED: 10 Jul 64 RATIFIED: 8 Feb 66 FORCE: 8 Feb 66

Norway SIGNED: 10 Jul 64 RATIFIED: 1 Dec 65 FORCE: 1 Jan 66

Pakistan SIGNED: 10 Jul 64 RATIFIED: 19 Dec 66 FORCE: 19 Dec 66

Paraguay SIGNED: 10 Jul 64

Peru SIGNED: 10 Jul 64

Poland SIGNED: 10 Jul 64 RATIFIED: 14 Sep 66 FORCE: 14 Sep 66

Portugal SIGNED: 10 Jul 64

Romania SIGNED: 10 Jul 64

Rwanda SIGNED: 10 Jul 64

San Marino SIGNED: 10 Jul 64 RATIFIED: 11 Oct 67 FORCE: 11 Oct 67

Saudi Arabia SIGNED: 10 Jul 64

Senegal SIGNED: 10 Jul 64 RATIFIED: 26 Sep 67 FORCE: 26 Sep 67

Sierra Leone SIGNED: 10 Jul 64 RATIFIED: 24 Aug 67 FORCE: 24 Aug 67

Singapore RATIFIED: 8 Jan 66 FORCE: 8 Jan 66

South Africa RATIFIED: 7 Oct 64 FORCE: 1 Jan 66

Somalia SIGNED: 10 Jul 64

Spain SIGNED: 10 Jul 64 RATIFIED: 9 Nov 66 FORCE: 9 Nov 66

Spain Spanish Colonies RATIFIED: 10 Jul 64 FORCE: 9 Nov 66

Sudan SIGNED: 10 Jul 64

Sweden SIGNED: 10 Jul 64 RATIFIED: 13 Dec 66 FORCE: 13 Dec 66

Switzerland SIGNED: 10 Jul 64 RATIFIED: 4 Feb 66 FORCE: 4 Feb 66

Syria SIGNED: 10 Jul 64 RATIFIED: 18 Nov 66 FORCE: 18 Nov 66

Tanzania SIGNED: 10 Jul 64 RATIFIED: 26 Sep 67 FORCE: 26 Sep 67

Thailand SIGNED: 10 Jul 64 RATIFIED: 10 May 66 FORCE: 10 May 66

Togo SIGNED: 10 Jul 64 RATIFIED: 28 Aug 67 FORCE: 28 Aug 67

Trinidad/Tobago SIGNED: 10 Jul 64

Tunisia SIGNED: 10 Jul 64 RATIFIED: 13 Sep 66 FORCE: 13 Sep 66

Turkey SIGNED: 10 Jul 64

United Arab Rep SIGNED: 10 Jul 64

Uganda RATIFIED: 29 Dec 65 FORCE: 1 Jan 66

UK Great Britain SIGNED: 10 Jul 64 RATIFIED: 2 Aug 66 FORCE: 2 Aug 66

Ukrainian SSR SIGNED: 10 Jul 64

Upper Volta SIGNED: 10 Jul 64 RATIFIED: 4 Feb 67 FORCE: 4 Feb 67

Uruguay SIGNED: 10 Jul 64

USSR (Soviet Union) SIGNED: 10 Jul 64

Venezuela SIGNED: 10 Jul 64

Vietnam, South SIGNED: 10 Jul 64 RATIFIED: 5 Jun 67 FORCE: 5 Jun 67

Yemen SIGNED: 10 Jul 64

Yugoslavia SIGNED: 10 Jul 64 RATIFIED: 15 Nov 66 FORCE: 15 Nov 66

Zambia RATIFIED: 22 Mar 67 FORCE: 22 Mar 67

ANNEX

6 19 UNTS 348. Botswana. Declaration 12 Jan 68.

633 UNTS 422. Jordan. Approval 3 Jan 68.

634 UNTS 472. UK Great Britain. St. Lucia.

634 UNTS 472. UK Great Britain. New Hebrides Is.

634 UNTS 472. UK Great Britain. Pitcairn Island.

634 UNTS 472. UK Great Britain. Falkland Islands.

634 UNTS 472. UK Great Britain. Hong Kong.

634 UNTS 472. UK Great Britain. Brunei.

634 UNTS 472. UK Great Britain. Tonga.

634 UNTS 472. UK Great Britain. Bahamas.

634 UNTS 472. UK Great Britain. Bermuda.

634 UNTS 472. UK Great Britain. British Honduras.

634 UNTS 472. UK Great Britain. Mauritius.

634 UNTS 472. UK Great Britain. Cayman Island.

634 UNTS 472. UK Great Britain. Gibralter.

634 UNTS 472. UK Great Britain. Montserrat.

634 UNTS 472. UK Great Britain. Dominican Republic.

634 UNTS 472. UK Great Britain. Grenada.

634 UNTS 472. UK Great Britain. Nevis.

634 UNTS 472. UK Great Britain. St. Helena.

634 UNTS 472. UK Great Britain. St. Vincent.

634 UNTS 472. UK Great Britain. St. Christopher.

634 UNTS 472. UK Great Britain. Fiji Islands.

634 UNTS 472. UK Great Britain. British India.

634 UNTS 472. UK Great Britain. Brit Virgin Islands.

634 UNTS 472. UK Great Britain. Seychelles.

634 UNTS 472. UK Great Britain. Southern Rhodesia.

634 UNTS 472. UK Great Britain. Brit Solomon Is.

634 UNTS 472. UK Great Britain. Gilbert Islands.

634 UNTS 472. Israel. Ratification 29 Feb 68.

634 UNTS 472. UK Great Britain. Antigua.

639 UNTS 369. Kenya. Accession 26 Apr 68.

639 UNTS 369. Greece. Ratification 8 May 68.

639 UNTS 369. Vatican/Holy See. Ratification 22 Apr 68.

639 UNTS 370. Vatican/Holy See. Ratification 22 Apr 68.

639 UNTS 370. Greece. Ratification 8 May 68.

643 UNTS 411. Algeria. Ratification 12 Jun 68.

643 UNTS 411. Italy. Ratification 12 Jul 68.

651 UNTS 406. Iran. Ratification 28 Aug 68.

651 UNTS 406. Monaco. Ratification 30 Sep 68.

655 UNTS 408. Mongolia. Ratification 8 Apr 68.

655 UNTS 408. Albania. Ratification 4 Nov 68.

658 UNTS 442. Yemen. Ratification 10 Jan 69.

658 UNTS 442. Qatar. Accession 31 Jan 69. Declaration 31 Jan 69.

658 UNTS 442. Cameroon. Ratification 23 Dec 68.

108848 Multilateral Agreement **612 UNTS 233**
SIGNED: 10 Jul 64 FORCE: 1 Jan 66
REGISTERED: 1 Dec 67 Austria
ARTICLES: 0 LANGUAGE: French. English.
HEADNOTE: POSTAL MONEY ORDERS & TRAVELERS CHEQUES
TOPIC: Postal Service
CONCEPTS: Mail and money orders. Money orders and postal checks.
PARTIES:

Albania SIGNED: 10 Jul 64

Algeria SIGNED: 10 Jul 64

Argentina SIGNED: 10 Jul 64 RATIFIED: 23 Jun 67 FORCE: 23 Jun 67

Austria SIGNED: 10 Jul 64 RATIFIED: 23 Dec 65 FORCE: 1 Jan 66

Belgium SIGNED: 10 Jul 64 RATIFIED: 4 Nov 65 FORCE: 1 Jan 66

Bolivia SIGNED: 10 Jul 64

Bulgaria SIGNED: 10 Jul 64

Burundi SIGNED: 10 Jul 64

Cambodia SIGNED: 10 Jul 64

Cameroon SIGNED: 10 Jul 64

Chad SIGNED: 10 Jul 64

Chile SIGNED: 10 Jul 64

Taiwan SIGNED: 10 Jul 64 RATIFIED: 6 Sep 66 FORCE: 6 Sep 66

Central Afri Rep SIGNED: 10 Jul 64

Congo (Brazzaville) SIGNED: 10 Jul 64

Congo (Zaire) SIGNED: 10 Jul 64 RATIFIED: 7 Sep 66 FORCE: 7 Sep 66

Colombia SIGNED: 10 Jul 64

Costa Rica SIGNED: 10 Jul 64

Cuba SIGNED: 10 Jul 64

Czechoslovakia SIGNED: 10 Jul 66 RATIFIED: 20 May 66 FORCE: 20 May 66

Dahomey SIGNED: 10 Jul 64 RATIFIED: 13 Jan 67 FORCE: 13 Jan 67

Denmark SIGNED: 10 Jul 64 RATIFIED: 23 Dec 65 FORCE: 1 Jan 66

El Salvador SIGNED: 10 Jul 64

Finland SIGNED: 10 Jul 64 RATIFIED: 17 Dec 65 FORCE: 1 Jan 66

France All Territories RATIFIED: 10 Jul 64 FORCE: 22 Jan 66

France SIGNED: 10 Jul 64 RATIFIED: 22 Jan 66 FORCE: 22 Jan 66

Gabon SIGNED: 10 Jul 64 RATIFIED: 21 Jan 67 FORCE: 21 Jan 67

Germany, West SIGNED: 10 Jul 64 RATIFIED: 27 Jun 66 FORCE: 27 Jun 66

Ghana SIGNED: 10 Jul 64 RATIFIED: 17 Nov 66 FORCE: 17 Nov 66

Greece SIGNED: 10 Jul 64

Guinea SIGNED: 10 Jul 64 RATIFIED: 5 Sep 66 FORCE: 5 Sep 66

Hungary SIGNED: 10 Jul 64 RATIFIED: 2 May 67 FORCE: 2 May 67

Iceland SIGNED: 10 Jul 64 RATIFIED: 10 Aug 65 FORCE: 1 Jan 66

Indonesia SIGNED: 10 Jul 64

Italy SIGNED: 10 Jul 64

Ivory Coast SIGNED: 10 Jul 64 RATIFIED: 28 Oct 65 FORCE: 1 Jan 66

Japan SIGNED: 10 Jul 64 RATIFIED: 22 Jul 65 FORCE: 1 Jan 66

Korea, South SIGNED: 10 Jul 64 RATIFIED: 20 May 66 FORCE: 20 May 66

Laos SIGNED: 10 Jul 64 RATIFIED: 25 Sep 67 FORCE: 25 Sep 67

Lebanon SIGNED: 10 Jul 64

Libya SIGNED: 10 Jul 64

Liechtenstein SIGNED: 10 Jul 64 RATIFIED: 5 Oct 67 FORCE: 5 Oct 67

Luxembourg SIGNED: 10 Jul 64 RATIFIED: 29 Dec 65 FORCE: 1 Jan 66

Madagascar SIGNED: 10 Jul 64 RATIFIED: 25 Aug 65 FORCE: 1 Jan 66

Malagasy SIGNED: 10 Jul 64

Mali SIGNED: 10 Jul 64 RATIFIED: 18 Dec 65 FORCE: 1 Jan 66

Mauritania RATIFIED: 22 Mar 67 FORCE: 22 Mar 67

Mexico SIGNED: 10 Jul 64

Monaco SIGNED: 10 Jul 64

Morocco SIGNED: 10 Jul 64 RATIFIED: 7 Apr 67 FORCE: 7 Apr 67

Netherlands SIGNED: 10 Jul 64

Netherlands Netherlands Antilles RATIFIED: 10 Jul 64

Netherlands Surinam RATIFIED: 10 Jul 64

Nicaragua SIGNED: 10 Jul 64

Niger SIGNED: 10 Jul 64 RATIFIED: 8 Feb 66 FORCE: 8 Feb 66

Norway SIGNED: 10 Jul 64 RATIFIED: 1 Dec 65 FORCE: 1 Jan 66

Paraguay SIGNED: 10 Jul 64

Poland SIGNED: 10 Jul 64 RATIFIED: 14 Sep 66 FORCE: 14 Sep 66

Portugal SIGNED: 10 Jul 64

Romania SIGNED: 10 Jul 64

San Marino SIGNED: 10 Jul 64 RATIFIED: 11 Oct 67 FORCE: 11 Oct 67

Saudi Arabia SIGNED: 10 Jul 64

Senegal SIGNED: 10 Jul 64 RATIFIED: 26 Sep 67 FORCE: 26 Sep 67

Somalia SIGNED: 10 Jul 64

Spain SIGNED: 10 Jul 64 RATIFIED: 9 Nov 66 FORCE: 9 Nov 66

Spain Spanish Colonies RATIFIED: 10 Jul 64 FORCE: 9 Nov 66

Sudan SIGNED: 10 Jul 64

Sweden SIGNED: 10 Jul 64 RATIFIED: 13 Dec 66 FORCE: 13 Dec 66

Switzerland SIGNED: 10 Jul 64 RATIFIED: 4 Feb 66 FORCE: 4 Feb 66

Syria SIGNED: 10 Jul 64 RATIFIED: 18 Nov 66 FORCE: 18 Nov 66

Thailand SIGNED: 10 Jul 64 RATIFIED: 10 May 66 FORCE: 10 May 66

Togo SIGNED: 10 Jul 64 RATIFIED: 28 Aug 67 FORCE: 28 Aug 67

Tunisia SIGNED: 10 Jul 64 RATIFIED: 13 Sep 66 FORCE: 13 Sep 66

Turkey SIGNED: 10 Jul 64

United Arab Rep SIGNED: 10 Jul 64 RATIFIED: 30 Jun 67 FORCE: 30 Jun 67

Upper Volta SIGNED: 10 Jul 64 RATIFIED: 4 Feb 67 FORCE: 4 Feb 67

Uruguay SIGNED: 10 Jul 64

Venezuela SIGNED: 10 Jul 64

Vietnam, South SIGNED: 10 Jul 64 RATIFIED: 5 Jun 67 FORCE: 5 Jun 67

Yemen SIGNED: 10 Jul 64

Yugoslavia SIGNED: 10 Jul 64 RATIFIED: 15 Nov 66 FORCE: 15 Nov 66

ANNEX

639 UNTS 370. Vatican/Holy See. Ratification 22 Apr 68.

639 UNTS 370. Greece. Ratification 8 May 68.

643 UNTS 411. Italy. Ratification 12 Jul 68.

643 UNTS 411. Algeria. Ratification 12 Jun 68.

646 UNTS 418. Central Afri Rep. Ratification 26 Jul 68.

651 UNTS 408. Monaco. Ratification 30 Sep 68.
658 UNTS 444. Cameroon. Ratification 23 Dec 68.

108849 Multilateral Agreement **612 UNTS 361**
SIGNED: 10 Jul 64   FORCE: 1 Jan 66
REGISTERED: 1 Dec 67 Austria
ARTICLES: 0 LANGUAGE: French. English.
HEADNOTE: TRANSFERS TO FROM POSTAL CHECKING ACCOUNTS
TOPIC: Postal Service
CONCEPTS: Mail and money orders. Money orders and postal checks.
PARTIES:
Albania SIGNED: 10 Jul 64
Algeria SIGNED: 10 Jul 64
Argentina SIGNED: 10 Jul 64 RATIFIED: 23 Jun 67 FORCE: 23 Jun 67
Australia SIGNED: 10 Jul 64 RATIFIED: 23 Dec 65 FORCE: 1 Jan 66
Austria SIGNED: 10 Jul 64 RATIFIED: 23 Dec 65 FORCE: 1 Jan 66
Belgium SIGNED: 10 Jul 64 RATIFIED: 4 Nov 65 FORCE: 1 Jan 66
Bolivia SIGNED: 10 Jul 64
Burundi SIGNED: 10 Jul 64
Cameroon SIGNED: 10 Jul 64
Chad SIGNED: 10 Jul 64
Chile SIGNED: 10 Jul 64
Central Afri Rep SIGNED: 10 Jul 64
Congo (Brazzaville) SIGNED: 10 Jul 64
Congo (Zaire) SIGNED: 10 Jul 64 RATIFIED: 7 Sep 66 FORCE: 7 Sep 66
Colombia SIGNED: 10 Jul 64
Cuba SIGNED: 10 Jul 64
Dahomey SIGNED: 10 Jul 64 RATIFIED: 13 Jan 67 FORCE: 13 Jan 67
Denmark SIGNED: 10 Jul 64 RATIFIED: 23 Dec 65 FORCE: 1 Jan 66
Finland SIGNED: 10 Jul 64 RATIFIED: 17 Dec 65 FORCE: 1 Jan 66
France All Territories RATIFIED: 10 Jul 64 FORCE: 22 Jan 66
France SIGNED: 10 Jul 64 RATIFIED: 22 Jan 66 FORCE: 22 Jan 66
Gabon SIGNED: 10 Jul 64 RATIFIED: 21 Jan 67 FORCE: 21 Jan 67
Germany, West SIGNED: 10 Jul 64 RATIFIED: 27 Jun 66 FORCE: 27 Jun 66
Greece SIGNED: 10 Jul 64
Guinea SIGNED: 10 Jul 64 RATIFIED: 5 Sep 66 FORCE: 5 Sep 66
Indonesia SIGNED: 10 Jul 64
Italy SIGNED: 10 Jul 64
Ivory Coast SIGNED: 10 Jul 64 RATIFIED: 28 Oct 65 FORCE: 1 Jan 66
Japan SIGNED: 10 Jul 64 RATIFIED: 22 Jul 65 FORCE: 1 Jan 66
Laos SIGNED: 10 Jul 64 RATIFIED: 25 Sep 67 FORCE: 25 Sep 67
Lebanon SIGNED: 10 Jul 64
Liechtenstein SIGNED: 10 Jul 64 RATIFIED: 5 Oct 67 FORCE: 5 Oct 67
Luxembourg SIGNED: 10 Jul 64 RATIFIED: 29 Dec 65 FORCE: 1 Jan 66
Madagascar SIGNED: 10 Jul 64 RATIFIED: 25 Aug 65 FORCE: 1 Jan 66
Malagasy SIGNED: 10 Jul 64
Mali SIGNED: 10 Jul 64 RATIFIED: 18 Dec 65 FORCE: 1 Jan 66
Mauritania RATIFIED: 22 Mar 67 FORCE: 22 Mar 67
Monaco SIGNED: 10 Jul 64
Morocco SIGNED: 10 Jul 64 RATIFIED: 7 Apr 67 FORCE: 7 Apr 67
Netherlands SIGNED: 10 Jul 64
Nicaragua SIGNED: 10 Jul 64
Niger SIGNED: 10 Jul 64 RATIFIED: 8 Feb 66 FORCE: 8 Feb 66
Norway SIGNED: 10 Jul 64 RATIFIED: 1 Dec 65 FORCE: 1 Jan 66
Paraguay SIGNED: 10 Jul 64
Romania SIGNED: 10 Jul 64
San Marino SIGNED: 10 Jul 64 RATIFIED: 11 Oct 67 FORCE: 11 Oct 67
Senegal SIGNED: 10 Jul 64 RATIFIED: 26 Sep 67 FORCE: 26 Sep 67
Somalia SIGNED: 10 Jul 64
Spain SIGNED: 10 Jul 64 RATIFIED: 9 Nov 66 FORCE: 9 Nov 66
Spain Spanish Colonies RATIFIED: 10 Jul 64 FORCE: 9 Nov 66
Sweden SIGNED: 10 Jul 64 RATIFIED: 13 Dec 66 FORCE: 13 Dec 66
Switzerland SIGNED: 10 Jul 64 RATIFIED: 4 Feb 66 FORCE: 4 Feb 66
Togo SIGNED: 10 Jul 64 RATIFIED: 28 Aug 67 FORCE: 28 Aug 67
Tunisia SIGNED: 10 Jul 64 RATIFIED: 13 Sep 66 FORCE: 13 Sep 66
Turkey SIGNED: 10 Jul 64
United Arab Rep SIGNED: 10 Jul 64 RATIFIED: 30 Jun 67 FORCE: 30 Jun 67
Upper Volta SIGNED: 10 Jul 64 RATIFIED: 4 Feb 67 FORCE: 4 Feb 67
Uruguay SIGNED: 10 Jul 64
Vatican/Holy See SIGNED: 10 Jul 64
Venezuela SIGNED: 10 Jul 64
Yemen SIGNED: 10 Jul 64
Yugoslavia SIGNED: 10 Jul 64
ANNEX
643 UNTS 411. Italy. Ratification 12 Jul 68.
643 UNTS 411. Algeria. Ratification 12 Jun 68.
646 UNTS 418. Central Afri Rep. Ratification 29 Jul 68.
651 UNTS 408. Monaco. Ratification 30 Sep 68.
658 UNTS 444. Cameroon. Ratification 23 Dec 68.

108850 Multilateral Agreement **613 UNTS 3**
SIGNED: 10 Jul 64   FORCE: 1 Jan 66
REGISTERED: 1 Dec 67 Austria
ARTICLES: 21 LANGUAGE: French.
HEADNOTE: CASH-ON-DELIVERY ITEMS
TOPIC: Postal Service
CONCEPTS: General provisions. Responsibility and liability. Payment schedules. Rates and charges.
PROCEDURE: Duration.
PARTIES:
Albania SIGNED: 10 Jul 64 FORCE: 1 Jan 66
Algeria SIGNED: 10 Jul 64 FORCE: 1 Jan 66
Argentina SIGNED: 10 Jul 64 RATIFIED: 23 Jun 67 FORCE: 1 Jan 66
Austria SIGNED: 10 Jul 64 RATIFIED: 23 Dec 65 FORCE: 1 Jan 66
Belgium SIGNED: 10 Jul 64 RATIFIED: 4 Nov 65 FORCE: 1 Jan 66
Bolivia SIGNED: 10 Jul 64 FORCE: 1 Jan 66
Burundi SIGNED: 10 Jul 64 FORCE: 1 Jan 66
Cambodia SIGNED: 10 Jul 64 FORCE: 1 Jan 66
Cameroon SIGNED: 10 Jul 64 FORCE: 1 Jan 66
Chad SIGNED: 10 Jul 64 FORCE: 1 Jan 66
Chile SIGNED: 10 Jul 64 FORCE: 1 Jan 66
China SIGNED: 10 Jul 64 RATIFIED: 6 Sep 66 FORCE: 1 Jan 66
Central Afri Rep SIGNED: 10 Jul 64 FORCE: 1 Jan 66
Congo (Brazzaville) SIGNED: 10 Jul 64 RATIFIED: 7 Sep 66 FORCE: 1 Jan 66
Congo (Zaire) SIGNED: 10 Jul 64 RATIFIED: 7 Sep 66 FORCE: 1 Jan 66
Colombia SIGNED: 10 Jul 64 FORCE: 1 Jan 66
Cuba SIGNED: 10 Jul 64 FORCE: 1 Jan 66
Czechoslovakia SIGNED: 10 Jul 64 FORCE: 1 Jan 66
Denmark SIGNED: 10 Jul 64 RATIFIED: 23 Dec 65 FORCE: 1 Jan 66
Dominican Republic SIGNED: 10 Jul 64 FORCE: 1 Jan 66
Finland SIGNED: 10 Jul 64 RATIFIED: 17 Dec 65 FORCE: 1 Jan 66
France All Territories RATIFIED: 10 Jul 64
France SIGNED: 10 Jul 64 RATIFIED: 22 Jan 66 FORCE: 1 Jan 66
Gabon SIGNED: 10 Jul 64 RATIFIED: 27 Jan 67 FORCE: 1 Jan 66
Germany, West SIGNED: 10 Jul 64 RATIFIED: 27 Jun 66 FORCE: 1 Jan 66
Greece SIGNED: 10 Jul 64 FORCE: 1 Jan 66
Hungary SIGNED: 10 Jul 64 RATIFIED: 2 May 67 FORCE: 1 Jan 66
Iceland SIGNED: 10 Jul 64 RATIFIED: 10 Aug 65 FORCE: 1 Jan 66
Indonesia SIGNED: 10 Jul 64 FORCE: 1 Jan 66
Iraq SIGNED: 10 Jul 64 FORCE: 1 Jan 66
Italy SIGNED: 10 Jul 64 FORCE: 1 Jan 66
Ivory Coast SIGNED: 10 Jul 64 RATIFIED: 28 Oct 65 FORCE: 1 Jan 66
Japan SIGNED: 10 Jul 64 RATIFIED: 22 Jul 65 FORCE: 1 Jan 66
Laos SIGNED: 10 Jul 64 RATIFIED: 25 Sep 67 FORCE: 1 Jan 66
Lebanon SIGNED: 10 Jul 64 FORCE: 1 Jan 66
Libya SIGNED: 10 Jul 64 FORCE: 1 Jan 66
Liechtenstein SIGNED: 10 Jul 64 RATIFIED: 5 Oct 67 FORCE: 1 Jan 66
Luxembourg SIGNED: 10 Jul 64 RATIFIED: 29 Dec 65 FORCE: 1 Jan 66
Madagascar RATIFIED: 25 Aug 65
Malagasy SIGNED: 10 Jul 64 FORCE: 1 Jan 66
Mali SIGNED: 10 Jul 64 RATIFIED: 18 Dec 65 FORCE: 1 Jan 66
Mauritania RATIFIED: 22 Mar 67
Monaco SIGNED: 10 Jul 64 FORCE: 1 Jan 66
Morocco SIGNED: 10 Jul 64 RATIFIED: 7 Apr 67 FORCE: 1 Jan 66
Netherlands Netherlands Antilles RATIFIED: 10 Jul 64
Netherlands SIGNED: 10 Jul 64 FORCE: 1 Jan 66
Netherlands Surinam RATIFIED: 10 Jul 64 FORCE: 1 Jan 66
Nicaragua SIGNED: 10 Jul 64 FORCE: 1 Jan 66
Niger SIGNED: 10 Jul 64 RATIFIED: 8 Feb 66 FORCE: 1 Jan 66
Norway SIGNED: 10 Jul 64 RATIFIED: 1 Dec 65 FORCE: 1 Jan 66
Paraguay SIGNED: 10 Jul 64 FORCE: 1 Jan 66
Poland SIGNED: 10 Jul 64 FORCE: 1 Jan 66
Portugal SIGNED: 10 Jul 64 FORCE: 1 Jan 66
Romania SIGNED: 10 Jul 64 FORCE: 1 Jan 66
San Marino SIGNED: 10 Jul 64 RATIFIED: 11 Oct 67 FORCE: 1 Jan 66
Senegal SIGNED: 10 Jul 64 RATIFIED: 26 Sep 67 FORCE: 1 Jan 66
Somalia SIGNED: 10 Jul 64 FORCE: 1 Jan 66
Spain SIGNED: 10 Jul 64 RATIFIED: 9 Nov 66 FORCE: 1 Jan 66
Spain All Territories RATIFIED: 10 Jul 64
Sweden SIGNED: 10 Jul 64 RATIFIED: 13 Dec 66 FORCE: 1 Jan 66
Switzerland SIGNED: 10 Jul 64 RATIFIED: 4 Feb 66 FORCE: 1 Jan 66
Syria SIGNED: 10 Jul 64 RATIFIED: 18 Nov 66 FORCE: 1 Jan 66
Thailand SIGNED: 10 Jul 64 RATIFIED: 10 May 66 FORCE: 1 Jan 66
Togo SIGNED: 10 Jul 64 RATIFIED: 28 Aug 67 FORCE: 1 Jan 66
Tunisia SIGNED: 10 Jul 64 RATIFIED: 13 Sep 66 FORCE: 1 Jan 66
Turkey SIGNED: 10 Jul 64 FORCE: 1 Jan 66
United Arab Rep SIGNED: 10 Jul 64 RATIFIED: 30 Jun 67 FORCE: 1 Jan 66
Upper Volta SIGNED: 10 Jul 64 RATIFIED: 4 Feb 67 FORCE: 1 Jan 66
Uruguay SIGNED: 10 Jul 64 FORCE: 1 Jan 66
Vatican/Holy See SIGNED: 10 Jul 64 FORCE: 1 Jan 66
Venezuela SIGNED: 10 Jul 64 FORCE: 1 Jan 66
Vietnam SIGNED: 10 Jul 64 FORCE: 1 Jan 66
Yemen SIGNED: 10 Jul 64 FORCE: 1 Jan 66
Yugoslavia SIGNED: 10 Jul 64 FORCE: 1 Jan 66
ANNEX
639 UNTS 371. Greece. Ratification 8 May 68.
639 UNTS 371. Vatican/Holy See. Ratification 22 Apr 68.
643 UNTS 412. Italy. Ratification 12 Jul 68.
643 UNTS 412. Algeria. Ratification 12 Jun 68.
651 UNTS 408. Monaco. Ratification 30 Sep 68.
658 UNTS 444. Cameroon. Ratification 23 Dec 68.

108851 Multilateral Agreement **613 UNTS 3**
SIGNED: 10 Jul 64   FORCE: 1 Jan 66
REGISTERED: 1 Dec 67 Austria
ARTICLES: 25 LANGUAGE: French.
HEADNOTE: COLLECTION BILLS DRAFTS
TOPIC: Postal Service
CONCEPTS: Informational records. Legal protection and assistance. Currency. Postal services. Regulations.
TREATY REF: 611UNTS17.
PROCEDURE: Duration.
PARTIES:
Albania SIGNED: 10 Jul 64 FORCE: 1 Jan 66
Algeria SIGNED: 10 Jul 64 FORCE: 1 Jan 66
Argentina SIGNED: 10 Jul 64 RATIFIED: 23 Jun 67 FORCE: 1 Jan 66
Austria SIGNED: 10 Jul 64 RATIFIED: 23 Dec 65 FORCE: 1 Jan 66
Belgium SIGNED: 10 Jul 64 RATIFIED: 4 Nov 65 FORCE: 1 Jan 66
Bolivia SIGNED: 10 Jul 64 FORCE: 1 Jan 66
Cambodia SIGNED: 10 Jul 64 FORCE: 1 Jan 66
Cameroon SIGNED: 10 Jul 64 FORCE: 1 Jan 66
Chile SIGNED: 10 Jul 64 FORCE: 1 Jan 66
Central Afri Rep SIGNED: 10 Jul 64 FORCE: 1 Jan 66

Congo (Brazzaville) SIGNED: 10 Jul 64 RATI-
FIED: 7 Sep 66 FORCE: 1 Jan 66
Colombia SIGNED: 10 Jul 64 FORCE: 1 Jan 66
Cuba SIGNED: 10 Jul 64 FORCE: 1 Jan 66
Dahomey SIGNED: 10 Jul 64 FORCE: 1 Jan 66
Denmark SIGNED: 10 Jul 64 RATIFIED:
23 Dec 65 FORCE: 1 Jan 66
Dominican Republic SIGNED: 10 Jul 64 FORCE:
1 Jan 66
France All Territories RATIFIED: 10 Jul 64
Germany, West SIGNED: 10 Jul 64 RATIFIED:
27 Jun 66 FORCE: 1 Jan 66
Ivory Coast SIGNED: 10 Jul 64 RATIFIED:
28 Oct 65 FORCE: 1 Jan 66
Madagascar RATIFIED: 25 Aug 65 FORCE:
1 Jan 66
Mauritania RATIFIED: 22 Mar 67 FORCE:
1 Jan 66
Netherlands Netherlands Antilles RATIFIED:
10 Jul 64
Spain All Territories RATIFIED: 10 Jul 64
ANNEX
639 UNTS 371. Greece.
639 UNTS 371. Vatican/Holy See. Ratification
22 Apr 68.
643 UNTS 412. Algeria. Ratification 12 Jun 68.
643 UNTS 412. Italy. Ratification 12 Jul 68.
646 UNTS 419. Central Afri Rep. Ratification
26 Jul 68.
651 UNTS 408. Monaco. Ratification 30 Sep 68.
658 UNTS 444. Cameroon. Ratification
23 Dec 68.

108852 Multilateral Agreement **613 UNTS 193**
SIGNED: 10 Jul 64   FORCE: 1 Jan 66
REGISTERED: 1 Dec 67 Austria
ARTICLES: 18 LANGUAGE: French.
HEADNOTE: INTERNATIONAL BANK SERVICE
TOPIC: Postal Service
CONCEPTS: General provisions. Responsibility
and liability. Banking. Payment schedules. Postal
services.
TREATY REF: 611UNTS68.
PROCEDURE: Duration.
PARTIES:
Albania SIGNED: 10 Jul 64 FORCE: 1 Jan 66
Algeria SIGNED: 10 Jul 64 FORCE: 1 Jan 66
Argentina SIGNED: 10 Jul 64 RATIFIED:
23 Jun 67 FORCE: 1 Jan 66
Austria SIGNED: 10 Jul 64 RATIFIED: 23 Dec 65
FORCE: 1 Jan 66
Belgium SIGNED: 10 Jul 64 RATIFIED: 4 Nov 65
FORCE: 1 Jan 66
Bolivia SIGNED: 10 Jul 64 FORCE: 1 Jan 66
Bulgaria SIGNED: 10 Jul 64 FORCE: 1 Jan 66
Cambodia SIGNED: 10 Jul 64 FORCE: 1 Jan 66
Cameroon SIGNED: 10 Jul 64 FORCE: 1 Jan 66
Chile SIGNED: 10 Jul 64 FORCE: 1 Jan 66
China RATIFIED: 6 Sep 66
Colombia SIGNED: 10 Jul 64 FORCE: 1 Jan 66
Cuba SIGNED: 10 Jul 64 FORCE: 1 Jan 66
Dahomey SIGNED: 10 Jul 64 RATIFIED:
13 Jan 67 FORCE: 1 Jan 66
Denmark SIGNED: 10 Jul 64 RATIFIED:
23 Dec 65 FORCE: 1 Jan 66
Dominican Republic SIGNED: 10 Jul 64 FORCE:
1 Jan 66
Ecuador SIGNED: 10 Jul 64 FORCE: 1 Jan 66
Finland SIGNED: 10 Jul 64 RATIFIED: 17 Dec 65
FORCE: 1 Jan 66
France SIGNED: 10 Jul 64 RATIFIED: 22 Jan 66
FORCE: 1 Jan 66
Germany, West SIGNED: 10 Jul 64 RATIFIED:
27 Jun 66 FORCE: 1 Jan 66
Greece SIGNED: 10 Jul 64 FORCE: 1 Jan 66
Hungary SIGNED: 10 Jul 64 RATIFIED: 2 May 67
FORCE: 1 Jan 66
Italy SIGNED: 10 Jul 64 FORCE: 1 Jan 66
Laos SIGNED: 10 Jul 64 RATIFIED: 25 Sep 67
FORCE: 1 Jan 66
Liechtenstein SIGNED: 10 Jul 64 RATIFIED:
5 Oct 67 FORCE: 1 Jan 66
Luxembourg SIGNED: 10 Jul 64 RATIFIED:
29 Dec 65 FORCE: 1 Jan 66
Mali SIGNED: 10 Jul 64 RATIFIED: 18 Dec 65
FORCE: 1 Jan 66
Mauritania RATIFIED: 22 Mar 67
Monaco SIGNED: 10 Jul 64 FORCE: 1 Jan 66
Morocco SIGNED: 10 Jul 64 RATIFIED: 7 Apr 67
FORCE: 1 Jan 66
Netherlands SIGNED: 10 Jul 64 FORCE:
1 Jan 66
Nicaragua SIGNED: 10 Jul 64 FORCE: 1 Jan 66

Niger SIGNED: 10 Jul 64 RATIFIED: 8 Feb 66
FORCE: 1 Jan 66
Norway SIGNED: 10 Jul 64 RATIFIED: 1 Dec 65
FORCE: 1 Jan 66
Paraguay SIGNED: 10 Jul 64 FORCE: 1 Jan 66
Poland SIGNED: 10 Jul 64 FORCE: 1 Jan 66
Portugal SIGNED: 10 Jul 64 FORCE: 1 Jan 66
Romania SIGNED: 10 Jul 64 FORCE: 1 Jan 66
Somalia SIGNED: 10 Jul 64 FORCE: 1 Jan 66
Spain SIGNED: 10 Jul 64 RATIFIED: 9 Nov 66
FORCE: 1 Jan 66
Spain All Territories RATIFIED: 10 Jul 64
Sweden SIGNED: 10 Jul 64 RATIFIED:
13 Dec 66 FORCE: 1 Jan 66
Switzerland SIGNED: 10 Jul 64 RATIFIED:
4 Feb 66 FORCE: 1 Jan 66
Thailand SIGNED: 10 Jul 64 RATIFIED:
10 May 66 FORCE: 1 Jan 66
Togo SIGNED: 10 Jul 64 RATIFIED: 28 Aug 67
FORCE: 1 Jan 66
Tunisia SIGNED: 10 Jul 64 RATIFIED: 13 Sep 66
FORCE: 1 Jan 66
Turkey SIGNED: 10 Jul 64 FORCE: 1 Jan 66
United Arab Rep SIGNED: 10 Jul 64 RATIFIED:
30 Jun 67 FORCE: 1 Jan 66
Upper Volta SIGNED: 10 Jul 64 RATIFIED:
4 Feb 67 FORCE: 1 Jan 66
Uruguay SIGNED: 10 Jul 64 FORCE: 1 Jan 66
Vatican/Holy See SIGNED: 10 Jul 64 FORCE:
1 Jan 66
Venezuela SIGNED: 10 Jul 64 FORCE: 1 Jan 66
Vietnam SIGNED: 10 Jul 64 FORCE: 1 Jan 66
Yemen SIGNED: 10 Jul 64 FORCE: 1 Jan 66
Yugoslavia SIGNED: 10 Jul 64 FORCE: 1 Jan 66
ANNEX
643 UNTS 413. Italy. Ratification 12 Jul 68.

108853 Multilateral Agreement **613 UNTS 127**
SIGNED: 10 Jul 64   FORCE: 1 Jan 66
REGISTERED: 1 Dec 67 Austria
ARTICLES: 24 LANGUAGE: French.
HEADNOTE: SUBSCRIPTIONS NEWSPAPERS PE-
RIODICALS
TOPIC: Postal Service
CONCEPTS: General provisions. Employment reg-
ulations. Indemnities and reimbursements. Pub-
lications exchange.
TREATY REF: 611UNTS68.
PROCEDURE: Duration.
PARTIES:
Belgium SIGNED: 10 Jul 64 RATIFIED: 4 Nov 65
FORCE: 1 Jan 66
Cameroon SIGNED: 10 Jul 64 FORCE: 1 Jan 66
Chile SIGNED: 10 Jul 64 FORCE: 1 Jan 66
Colombia SIGNED: 10 Jul 64 FORCE: 1 Jan 66
Dahomey SIGNED: 10 Jul 64 RATIFIED:
13 Jan 67 FORCE: 1 Jan 66
Finland SIGNED: 10 Jul 64 RATIFIED: 17 Dec 65
FORCE: 1 Jan 66
France SIGNED: 10 Jul 64 RATIFIED: 22 Jan 66
FORCE: 1 Jan 66
Germany, West SIGNED: 10 Jul 64 RATIFIED:
27 Jun 66 FORCE: 1 Jan 66
Italy SIGNED: 10 Jul 64 FORCE: 1 Jan 66
Japan SIGNED: 10 Jul 64 RATIFIED: 22 Jul 65
FORCE: 1 Jan 66
Mali SIGNED: 10 Jul 64 RATIFIED: 18 Dec 65
FORCE: 1 Jan 66
Niger SIGNED: 10 Jul 64 RATIFIED: 8 Feb 66
FORCE: 1 Jan 66
Norway SIGNED: 10 Jul 64 RATIFIED: 1 Dec 65
FORCE: 1 Jan 66
Paraguay SIGNED: 10 Jul 64 FORCE: 1 Jan 66
San Marino SIGNED: 10 Jul 64 RATIFIED:
11 Oct 67 FORCE: 1 Jan 66
Spain All Territories RATIFIED: 13 Dec 66
Spain SIGNED: 10 Jul 64 RATIFIED: 9 Nov 66
FORCE: 1 Jan 66
Sweden SIGNED: 10 Jul 64 RATIFIED:
13 Dec 66 FORCE: 1 Jan 66
Togo SIGNED: 10 Jul 64 FORCE: 1 Jan 66
Turkey SIGNED: 10 Jul 64 FORCE: 1 Jan 66
United Arab Rep SIGNED: 10 Jul 64 RATIFIED:
30 Jun 67 FORCE: 1 Jan 66
Vietnam SIGNED: 10 Jul 64 FORCE: 1 Jan 66
Yugoslavia SIGNED: 10 Jul 64 FORCE: 1 Jan 66
ANNEX
639 UNTS 371. Vatican/Holy See. Ratification
22 Apr 68.
639 UNTS 371. Greece. Ratification 8 May 68.
643 UNTS 413. Italy. Ratification 12 Jul 68.
643 UNTS 413. Algeria. Ratification 12 Jun 68.

646 UNTS 419. Central Afri Rep. Ratification
26 Jul 68.
651 UNTS 408. Monaco. Ratification 30 Sep 68.

108854 Bilateral Agreement **613 UNTS 255**
SIGNED: 8 Nov 67   FORCE: 8 Nov 67
REGISTERED: 1 Dec 67 United Nations
ARTICLES: 7 LANGUAGE: French.
HEADNOTE: MEETING MINISTERS ARRANGE-
MENTS
TOPIC: Admin Cooperation
CONCEPTS: Privileges and immunities. Legal pro-
tection and assistance. Personnel. Use of facili-
ties. Financial programs. Materials, equipment
and services. Passenger transport. Assistance to
United Nations.
TREATY REF: 1 UNTS 15.
PARTIES:
United Nations
Senegal

108855 Bilateral Exchange **613 UNTS 265**
SIGNED: 23 Dec 66   FORCE: 1 Jan 67
REGISTERED: 1 Dec 67 Denmark
ARTICLES: 2 LANGUAGE: Danish. Norwegian.
HEADNOTE: TRADE AGRICULTURAL GOODS
TOPIC: General Trade
CONCEPTS: IGO reference. Tariffs. Commodity
trade. Temporary importation. Agricultural com-
modities.
INTL ORGS: European Free Trade Association.
PARTIES:
Denmark
Norway

108856 Bilateral Agreement **613 UNTS 271**
SIGNED: 11 May 63   FORCE: 1 Jul 63
REGISTERED: 1 Dec 67 Denmark
ARTICLES: 11 LANGUAGE: Danish. Norwegian.
HEADNOTE: TRADE AGRICULTURAL GOODS
TOPIC: General Trade
CONCEPTS: IGO reference. Establishment of com-
mission. Export quotas. Import quotas. Export
subsidies. Commodity trade. Agricultural com-
modities.
INTL ORGS: European Free Trade Association.
PROCEDURE: Future Procedures Contemplated.
PARTIES:
Denmark
Norway

108857 Bilateral Agreement **613 UNTS 289**
SIGNED: 12 Sep 63   FORCE: 25 Jan 64
REGISTERED: 1 Dec 67 Denmark
ARTICLES: 9 LANGUAGE: Danish. Norwegian.
HEADNOTE: OFFSETTING FOREIGN EXCHANGE
EXPENDITURE
TOPIC: General Trade
CONCEPTS: Annex or appendix reference. Previ-
ous treaty replacement. IGO reference. General
cooperation. Establishment of commission. Ac-
counting procedures. Balance of payments. Ex-
change rates and regulations. Payment sched-
ules. Commodity trade. Agricultural commodi-
ties.
INTL ORGS: European Free Trade Association.
TREATY REF: 539 UNTS 243; 548 UNTS 374.
PROCEDURE: Future Procedures Contemplated.
Ratification.
PARTIES:
Denmark
Norway

108858 Bilateral Agreement **613 UNTS 313**
SIGNED: 5 May 67   FORCE: 5 May 67
REGISTERED: 1 Dec 67 UK Great Britain
ARTICLES: 1 LANGUAGE: English. German.
HEADNOTE: OFFSET FOREIGN EXCHANGE
SPENDING BRITISH FORCES IN GERMANY
TOPIC: Finance
CONCEPTS: Finances and payments. Balance of
payments. Currency.
PARTIES:
Germany, West
UK Great Britain

108859 Bilateral Agreement **613 UNTS 323**
SIGNED: 20 Dec 61   FORCE: 25 Sep 67

REGISTERED: 12 Dec 67 Japan
ARTICLES: 15 LANGUAGE: Japanese. Spanish. English.
HEADNOTE: FRIENDSHIP COMMERCE NAVIGATION
TOPIC: General Amity
CONCEPTS: Exceptions and exemptions. Previous treaty replacement. IGO reference. Friendship and amity. Alien status. General cooperation. Private contracts. Establishment of trade relations. Reciprocity in trade. Most favored nation clause. National treatment. Navigational conditions. Merchant vessels.
INTL ORGS: General Agreement on Tariffs and Trade. International Monetary Fund.
TREATY REF: 3 FEB 1898.
PROCEDURE: Duration. Ratification. Renewal or Revival.
PARTIES:
Argentina
Japan

108860 Multilateral Agreement **614 UNTS 2**
SIGNED: 14 Nov 67   FORCE: 14 Nov 67
REGISTERED: 12 Dec 67 United Nations
ARTICLES: 6 LANGUAGE: English.
HEADNOTE: OPERATIONAL ASSISTANCE
TOPIC: Admin Cooperation
CONCEPTS: Previous treaty replacement. Personnel. Arbitration. Procedure. Existing tribunals. Conciliation. Domestic obligation. Assistance. IGO obligations.
TREATY REF: 783 UNST 72; JM. UNTS 19.
PROCEDURE: Amendment. Termination.
PARTIES:
Jamaica
FAO (Food Agri)
IAEA (Atom Energy)
ICAO (Civil Aviat)
ILO (Labor Org)
IMCO (Maritime Org)
ITU (Telecommun)
UNESCO (Educ/Cult)
United Nations
UPU (Postal Union)
WHO (World Health)
WMO (Meteorology)

108861 Bilateral Agreement **614 UNTS 21**
SIGNED: 30 Nov 67   FORCE: 1 Dec 67
REGISTERED: 14 Dec 67 United Nations
ARTICLES: 1 LANGUAGE: English.
HEADNOTE: ACCEPTANCE OBLIGATIONS UN CHARTER
TOPIC: UN Charter
CONCEPTS: Acceptance of UN obligations.
PARTIES:
Southern Yemen

108862 Bilateral Agreement **614 UNTS 26**
SIGNED: 14 Dec 67   FORCE: 19 Oct 67
REGISTERED: 14 Dec 67 Denmark
ARTICLES: 14 LANGUAGE: English. Malay.
HEADNOTE: AIR SERVICES
TOPIC: Air Transport
CONCEPTS: Annex or appendix reference. IGO reference. General cooperation. Exchange of information and documents. Arbitration. Conciliation. Tariffs. Monetary and gold transfers. Routes and logistics. Navigational conditions. Airport facilities. Airport equipment. Conditions of airlines operating permission. Operating authorizations and regulations.
INTL ORGS: International Civil Aviation Organization.
PROCEDURE: Amendment. Registration. Termination.
PARTIES:
Denmark
Malaysia

108863 Bilateral Agreement **614 UNTS 55**
SIGNED: 4 Feb 64   FORCE: 17 Dec 65
REGISTERED: 18 Dec 67 ICAO (Civil Aviat)
ARTICLES: 15 LANGUAGE: Arabic. English.
HEADNOTE: AIR SERVICES
TOPIC: Air Transport
CONCEPTS: Definition of terms. Annex or appendix reference. IGO reference. Exchange of information and documents. Arbitration. Conciliation. Tariffs. Routes and logistics. Airport facilities. Airport equipment. Conditions of airlines operating permission. Operating authorizations and regulations.
INTL ORGS: International Civil Aviation Organization.
PROCEDURE: Ratification. Termination.
PARTIES:
Lebanon
Pakistan

108864 Bilateral Agreement **614 UNTS 83**
SIGNED: 21 Dec 67   FORCE: 21 Dec 67
REGISTERED: 21 Dec 67 United Nations
ARTICLES: 8 LANGUAGE: English.
HEADNOTE: ACTIVITIES UNICEF
TOPIC: IGO Operations
CONCEPTS: IGO reference. Privileges and immunities. General cooperation. Public information. Accounting procedures. Claims and settlements. Assistance. Materials, equipment and services.
INTL ORGS: United Nations.
TREATY REF: 1 UNTS 15.
PROCEDURE: Amendment. Termination.
PARTIES:
Australia
UNICEF (Children)

108865 Bilateral Agreement **614 UNTS 93**
SIGNED: 10 May 67   FORCE: 10 May 67
REGISTERED: 22 Dec 67 IAEA (Atom Energy)
ARTICLES: 10 LANGUAGE: English.
HEADNOTE: ASSISTANCE RESEARCH REACTOR PROJECT
TOPIC: IGO Operations
CONCEPTS: Definition of terms. Guarantees and safeguards. Annex or appendix reference. Exchange of information and documents. Inspection and observation. Procedure. Conciliation. Assistance. Nuclear materials. Transport of goods.
TREATY REF: 374 UNTS 147.
PARTIES:
Iran
IAEA (Atom Energy)

108866 Bilateral Agreement **614 UNTS 109**
SIGNED: 7 Jun 67   FORCE: 7 Jun 67
REGISTERED: 22 Dec 67 IAEA (Atom Energy)
ARTICLES: 6 LANGUAGE: English.
HEADNOTE: TRANSFER URANIUM PLUTONIUM RESEARCH REACTOR IRAN
TOPIC: IGO Operations
CONCEPTS: IGO reference. Responsibility and liability. Arbitration. Procedure. Conciliation. Payment schedules. Nuclear materials. Transport of goods.
INTL ORGS: International Court of Justice.
TREATY REF: 339 UNTS 359; 276 UNTS 3.
PARTIES:
IAEA (Atom Energy)
USA (United States)

108867 Bilateral Agreement **614 UNTS 123**
SIGNED: 18 Aug 67   FORCE: 18 Aug 67
REGISTERED: 22 Dec 67 IAEA (Atom Energy)
ARTICLES: 8 LANGUAGE: English.
HEADNOTE: TRANSFER RADIODIAGNOSTIC EQUIPMENT
TOPIC: IGO Operations
CONCEPTS: IGO reference. Arbitration. Conciliation. Non-nuclear materials. Transport of goods.
INTL ORGS: International Court of Justice.
PARTIES:
Mexico
IAEA (Atom Energy)

108868 Bilateral Agreement **614 UNTS 133**
SIGNED: 23 Aug 67   FORCE: 23 Aug 67
REGISTERED: 22 Dec 67 IAEA (Atom Energy)
ARTICLES: 9 LANGUAGE: English.
HEADNOTE: ESTABLISHING SUB-CRITICAL ASSEMBLY PROJECT
TOPIC: IGO Operations
CONCEPTS: Definition of terms. Guarantees and safeguards. Exchange of information and documents. Conciliation. Assistance. Nuclear materials. Transport of goods.

TREATY REF: 339 UNTS 359; 276 UNTS 3 614 UNTS 145.
PARTIES:
Mexico
IAEA (Atom Energy)

108869 Multilateral Instrument **614 UNTS 145**
SIGNED: 23 Aug 67   FORCE: 23 Aug 67
REGISTERED: 22 Dec 67 IAEA (Atom Energy)
ARTICLES: 15 LANGUAGE: English.
HEADNOTE: LEASE URANIUM TRANSFER PLUTONIUM
TOPIC: IGO Operations
CONCEPTS: Exceptions and exemptions. IGO reference. Responsibility and liability. Title and deeds. Arbitration. Conciliation. Payment schedules. Acceptance of delivery. Nuclear materials.
INTL ORGS: International Court of Justice.
TREATY REF: 339 UNTS 359; 276 UNTS 3.
PARTIES:
Mexico SIGNED: 23 Aug 67 FORCE: 23 Aug 67
IAEA (Atom Energy) SIGNED: 23 Aug 67 FORCE: 23 Aug 67
USA (United States) SIGNED: 23 Aug 67 FORCE: 23 Aug 67

108870 Bilateral Agreement **614 UNTS 169**
SIGNED: 23 Jun 67   FORCE: 23 Jun 67
REGISTERED: 22 Dec 67 IAEA (Atom Energy)
ARTICLES: 10 LANGUAGE: English.
HEADNOTE: ASSISTANCE ESTABLISHMENT ZERO ENERGY FAST REACTOR PROJECT
TOPIC: IGO Operations
CONCEPTS: Definition of terms. Guarantees and safeguards. Annex or appendix reference. Exchange of information and documents. Inspection and observation. Procedure. Assistance. Nuclear materials.
TREATY REF: 339 UNTS 359; 276 UNTS 3 614 UNTS 185.
PARTIES:
IAEA (Atom Energy)
Spain

108871 Multilateral Instrument **614 UNTS 185**
SIGNED: 23 Jun 67   FORCE: 23 Jun 67
REGISTERED: 22 Dec 67 IAEA (Atom Energy)
ARTICLES: 22 LANGUAGE: English.
HEADNOTE: LEASE URANIUM RESEARCH REACTOR
TOPIC: IGO Operations
CONCEPTS: Conditions. Definition of terms. Exceptions and exemptions. IGO reference. Responsibility and liability. Penal sanctions. Arbitration. Procedure. Conciliation. Accounting procedures. Payment schedules. Non-interest rates and fees. Acceptance of delivery. Nuclear materials.
INTL ORGS: International Court of Justice.
PROCEDURE: Termination.
PARTIES:
IAEA (Atom Energy) SIGNED: 23 Jun 67 FORCE: 23 Jun 67
Spain SIGNED: 23 Jun 67 FORCE: 23 Jun 67
USA (United States) SIGNED: 23 Jun 67 FORCE: 23 Jun 67

108872 Multilateral Agreement **614 UNTS 217**
SIGNED: 26 Jul 67   FORCE: 26 Jul 67
REGISTERED: 22 Dec 67 IAEA (Atom Energy)
ARTICLES: 8 LANGUAGE: English.
HEADNOTE: APPLICATION SAFEGUARDS
TOPIC: IGO Operations
CONCEPTS: Definition of terms. Guarantees and safeguards. IGO reference. Exchange of information and documents. Inspection and observation. Arbitration. Conciliation. Financial programs. Domestic obligation. IGO obligations.
INTL ORGS: International Court of Justice.
TREATY REF: 374 UNTS 147; 290 UNTS 147; 458 UNTS 328.
PROCEDURE: Amendment. Duration. Termination.
PARTIES:
IAEA (Atom Energy) SIGNED: 26 Jul 67 FORCE: 26 Jul 67
South Africa SIGNED: 26 Jul 67 FORCE: 26 Jul 67
USA (United States) SIGNED: 26 Jul 67 FORCE: 26 Jul 67

108873 Multilateral Convention **614 UNTS 239**
SIGNED: 23 Jun 65   FORCE: 13 Dec 67
REGISTERED: 27 Dec 67 ILO (Labor Org)
ARTICLES: 13 LANGUAGE: English. French.
HEADNOTE: MEDICAL EXAMINATION YOUNG
  PERSONS EMPLOYMENT MINES
TOPIC: General IGO
CONCEPTS: Definition of terms. IGO reference.
  General cooperation. Public health. Medical as-
  sistance and/or facilities.
INTL ORGS: United Nations.
PROCEDURE: Denunciation. Ratification. Registra-
  tion.
PARTIES:
  China SIGNED: 23 Jun 65 RATIFIED: 19 Apr 67
    FORCE: 13 Dec 67
  Cyprus SIGNED: 23 Jun 65 RATIFIED: 18 Jan 67
    FORCE: 13 Dec 67
  Jordan SIGNED: 23 Jun 65 RATIFIED: 6 Jun 66
    FORCE: 13 Dec 67
  Madagascar SIGNED: 23 Jun 65 RATIFIED:
    23 Oct 67 FORCE: 13 Dec 67
  Paraguay   SIGNED: 23 Jun 65   RATIFIED:
    10 Jul 67 FORCE: 13 Dec 67
  Tunisia SIGNED: 23 Jun 65 RATIFIED: 3 May 67
    FORCE: 13 Dec 67
  Uganda   SIGNED: 23 Jun 65   RATIFIED:
    23 Jun 67 FORCE: 13 Dec 67
  UK Great Britain SIGNED: 23 Jun 65 RATIFIED:
    13 Dec 66 FORCE: 13 Dec 67
  Zambia   SIGNED: 23 Jun 65   RATIFIED:
    10 Mar 67 FORCE: 13 Dec 67
                    ANNEX
  640 UNTS 393. Poland. Ratification 26 Jun 68.
    Force 26 Jun 69.
  640 UNTS 393. Hungary. Ratification 8 Jun 68.
    Force 8 Jun 69.
  642 UNTS 398. UK Great Britain. Declaration
    12 Jul 68.
  645 UNTS 390. Mexico. Ratification 29 Aug 68.
    Force 29 Aug 69.
  648 UNTS 391. Finland. Ratification 23 Sep 68.
    Force 23 Sep 69.
  649 UNTS 387. Gabon. Ratification 18 Oct 68.
    Force 18 Oct 69.

108874   Bilateral Treaty   **614 UNTS 251**
SIGNED: 2 Feb 67   FORCE: 5 Sep 67
REGISTERED: 27 Dec 67 Thailand
ARTICLES: 6 LANGUAGE: Thai. Persian. English.
HEADNOTE: FRIENDSHIP
TOPIC: General Amity
CONCEPTS: Peaceful relations. Consular relations
  establishment. Diplomatic relations establish-
  ment. Procedure.
PROCEDURE: Future Procedures Contemplated.
  Ratification. Termination.
PARTIES:
  Iran
  Thailand

108875   Bilateral Treaty   **614 UNTS 263**
SIGNED: 17 Feb 66   FORCE: 1 Nov 67
REGISTERED: 28 Dec 67 Austria
ARTICLES: 27 LANGUAGE: German.
HEADNOTE: TRANSIT TRAFFIC ROSSFELD ROAD
TOPIC: Land Transport
CONCEPTS: Annex or appendix reference. Legal
  protection and assistance. Licenses and permits.
  Arbitration. Conciliation. Export quotas. Import
  quotas. Fees and exemptions. Claims and settle-
  ments. Tax exemptions. Customs exemptions.
  Passenger transport. Railway border crossing.
  Roads and highways. Road rules.
PROCEDURE: Amendment. Denunciation. Ratifica-
  tion.
PARTIES:
  Austria
  Germany, West

108876   Bilateral Treaty   **615 UNTS 3**
SIGNED: 17 Feb 66   FORCE: 1 Nov 67
REGISTERED: 28 Dec 67 Austria
ARTICLES: 38 LANGUAGE: German.
HEADNOTE: TRANSIT TRAFFIC WALCHEN ACHE,
  PITTENBACH, BACHENTAL, RISSTAL
TOPIC: Land Transport
CONCEPTS: General provisions. Annex or appen-
  dix reference. Arbitration. Conciliation. Motor ve-
  hicles and combinations. Roads and highways.
  Road rules.

PROCEDURE: Denunciation. Ratification.
PARTIES:
  Austria
  Germany, West

108877   Bilateral Agreement   **615 UNTS 47**
SIGNED: 15 Jun 67   FORCE: 14 Sep 67
REGISTERED: 29 Dec 67 IBRD (World Bank)
ARTICLES: 5 LANGUAGE: English.
HEADNOTE: GUARANTEE
TOPIC: Gen Communications
CONCEPTS: Annex or appendix reference. Bonds.
  Loan regulations. Loan guarantee. Guarantor
  non-interference.
PARTIES:
  Colombia
  IBRD (World Bank)

108878   Bilateral Agreement   **615 UNTS 75**
SIGNED: 19 Jun 67   FORCE: 4 Dec 67
REGISTERED: 29 Dec 67 IBRD (World Bank)
ARTICLES: 8 LANGUAGE: English.
HEADNOTE: LOAN BY IBRD TO BANCO CENTRAL
  DEL ECUADOR
TOPIC: IGO Operations
CONCEPTS: Definition of terms. Detailed regula-
  tions. Remedies. Annex or appendix reference.
  Bonds. Use restrictions. Terms of loan. Loan reg-
  ulations.
PROCEDURE: Termination.
PARTIES:
  Other Party Combin
  Ecuador

108879   Bilateral Agreement   **615 UNTS 145**
SIGNED: 26 May 67   FORCE: 15 Sep 67
REGISTERED: 29 Dec 67 IBRD (World Bank)
ARTICLES: 8 LANGUAGE: English.
HEADNOTE: LOAN
TOPIC: IGO Operations
CONCEPTS: Detailed regulations. Remedies. An-
  nex or appendix reference. Bonds. Use restric-
  tions. Terms of loan. Loan regulations.
PROCEDURE: Termination.
PARTIES:
  Honduras
  IBRD (World Bank)

108880   Bilateral Agreement   **615 UNTS 165**
SIGNED: 19 Sep 67   FORCE: 14 Nov 67
REGISTERED: 29 Dec 67 IBRD (World Bank)
ARTICLES: 5 LANGUAGE: English.
HEADNOTE: GUARANTEE
TOPIC: IGO Operations
CONCEPTS: Annex or appendix reference. Bonds.
  Loan regulations. Loan guarantee. Guarantor
  non-interference.
PARTIES:
  India
  IBRD (World Bank)

108881   Bilateral Agreement   **615 UNTS 205**
SIGNED: 13 Jun 66   FORCE: 2 Aug 66
REGISTERED: 29 Dec 67 IBRD (World Bank)
ARTICLES: 5 LANGUAGE: English.
HEADNOTE: GUARANTEE
TOPIC: IGO Operations
CONCEPTS: Annex or appendix reference. Bonds.
  Loan regulations. Loan guarantee. Guarantor
  non-interference.
TREATY REF: 339 UNTS 359; 276 UNTS 3.
PARTIES:
  Morocco
  IBRD (World Bank)

108882   Bilateral Agreement   **615 UNTS 243**
SIGNED: 14 Jun 67   FORCE: 8 Aug 67
REGISTERED: 29 Dec 67 IBRD (World Bank)
ARTICLES: 8 LANGUAGE: English.
HEADNOTE: LOAN
TOPIC: IGO Operations
CONCEPTS: Definition of terms. Detailed regula-
  tions. Remedies. Annex or appendix reference.

Bonds. Use restrictions. Terms of loan. Loan reg-
  ulations.
PROCEDURE: Termination.
PARTIES:
  China
  IBRD (World Bank)

108883   Bilateral Agreement   **615 UNTS 267**
SIGNED: 1 May 67   FORCE: 12 Sep 67
REGISTERED: 29 Dec 67 IBRD (World Bank)
ARTICLES: 5 LANGUAGE: English.
HEADNOTE: GUARANTEE
TOPIC: IGO Operations
CONCEPTS: Annex or appendix reference. Bonds.
  Loan regulations. Loan guarantee. Guarantor
  non-interference.
PARTIES:
  IBRD (World Bank)
  Senegal

108884   Bilateral Agreement   **615 UNTS 295**
SIGNED: 15 Sep 67   FORCE: 27 Oct 67
REGISTERED: 29 Dec 67 IBRD (World Bank)
ARTICLES: 5 LANGUAGE: English.
HEADNOTE: GUARANTEE
TOPIC: IGO Operations
CONCEPTS: Annex or appendix reference. Bonds.
  Loan regulations. Loan guarantee. Guarantor
  non-interference.
PARTIES:
  IBRD (World Bank)
  Singapore

108885 Multilateral Agreement **615 UNTS 321**
SIGNED: 12 Jun 67   FORCE: 27 Jul 67
REGISTERED: 29 Dec 67 IBRD (World Bank)
ARTICLES: 7 LANGUAGE: English.
HEADNOTE: LOAN
TOPIC: IGO Operations
CONCEPTS: Definition of terms. Detailed regula-
  tions. Remedies. Annex or appendix reference.
  Bonds. Use restrictions. Terms of loan. Loan reg-
  ulations.
PROCEDURE: Termination.
PARTIES:
  IBRD (World Bank) SIGNED: 12 Jun 67 FORCE:
    27 Jul 67
  Tobago SIGNED: 12 Jun 67 FORCE: 27 Jul 67
  Trinidad SIGNED: 12 Jun 67 FORCE: 27 Jul 67

108886   Bilateral Agreement   **615 UNTS 343**
SIGNED: 18 Jul 67   FORCE: 14 Nov 67
REGISTERED: 29 Dec 67 IBRD (World Bank)
ARTICLES: 5 LANGUAGE: English.
HEADNOTE: GUARANTEE
TOPIC: IGO Operations
CONCEPTS: Annex or appendix reference. Bonds.
  Loan regulations. Loan guarantee. Guarantor
  non-interference.
PARTIES:
  IBRD (World Bank)
  Yugoslavia

108887   Bilateral Agreement   **615 UNTS 375**
SIGNED: 22 Dec 66   FORCE: 28 Jul 67
REGISTERED: 29 Dec 67 Philippines
ARTICLES: 15 LANGUAGE: English.
HEADNOTE: HEADQUARTERS
TOPIC: IGO Establishment
CONCEPTS: Definition of terms. General provi-
  sions. IGO reference. Inviolability. Privileges and
  immunities. General cooperation. Juridical per-
  sonality. General property. Arbitration. Concilia-
  tion. Financial programs. General. Facilities and
  equipment. Headquarters and facilities.
INTL ORGS: International Court of Justice. United
  Nations.
PROCEDURE: Ratification. Registration.
PARTIES:
  Asian Devel Bank
  Philippines

108888   Bilateral Agreement   **616 UNTS 3**
SIGNED: 12 Jul 63   FORCE: 12 Jul 63
REGISTERED: 1 Jan 68 Denmark
ARTICLES: 5 LANGUAGE: Danish. English.
HEADNOTE: LOAN
TOPIC: Loans and Credits

CONCEPTS: Procedure. Interest rates. Loan repayment. Terms of loan.
PARTIES:
Denmark
India

108889 Bilateral Agreement **616 UNTS 23**
SIGNED: 15 May 63 FORCE: 15 May 63
REGISTERED: 1 Jan 68 Denmark
ARTICLES: 11 LANGUAGE: English.
HEADNOTE: ESTABLISHMENT AGRICULTURAL TECHNICAL COOPERATION PROJECT
TOPIC: Direct Aid
CONCEPTS: Privileges and immunities. General cooperation. Title and deeds. Vocational training. Indemnities and reimbursements. Financial programs. Customs exemptions. Plans and standards.
PROCEDURE: Amendment. Duration. Termination.
PARTIES:
Denmark
India

108890 Bilateral Agreement **616 UNTS 39**
SIGNED: 15 May 63 FORCE: 15 May 63
REGISTERED: 1 Jan 68 Denmark
ARTICLES: 9 LANGUAGE: English.
HEADNOTE: CONTINUATION EXPANSION TECHNICAL COOPERATION PROJECT
TOPIC: Direct Aid
CONCEPTS: Privileges and immunities. Title and deeds. Programs. Wages and salaries. Indemnities and reimbursements. Customs exemptions. Economic assistance.
PROCEDURE: Duration. Termination.
PARTIES:
Denmark
India

108891 Bilateral Agreement **616 UNTS 49**
SIGNED: 15 May 63 FORCE: 2 Aug 66
REGISTERED: 1 Jan 68 Denmark
ARTICLES: 10 LANGUAGE: English.
HEADNOTE: LEPROSY CONTROL WORK
TOPIC: Tech Assistance
CONCEPTS: IGO reference. Privileges and immunities. Personnel. Disease control. Indemnities and reimbursements.
INTL ORGS: United Nations Children's Fund. World Health Organization.
PROCEDURE: Duration. Termination.
PARTIES:
Denmark
India

108892 Bilateral Agreement **616 UNTS 69**
SIGNED: 1 Sep 67 FORCE: 1 Aug 67
REGISTERED: 1 Aug 67 Denmark
ARTICLES: 11 LANGUAGE: English.
HEADNOTE: VOLUNTEERS
TOPIC: Direct Aid
CONCEPTS: Time limit. General cooperation. Use of facilities. Volunteer programs.
PROCEDURE: Termination.
PARTIES:
Denmark
India

108893 Multilateral Treaty **616 UNTS 79**
SIGNED: 27 Jun 62 FORCE: 11 Dec 67
REGISTERED: 2 Jan 68 Belgium
ARTICLES: 50 LANGUAGE: French. Dutch.
HEADNOTE: EXTRADITION MUTUAL ASSISTANCE CRIMINAL MATTERS
TOPIC: Extradition
CONCEPTS: Definition of terms. Territorial application. Time limit. Previous treaty replacement. Extradition, deportation and repatriation. Extradition requests. Extraditable offenses. Location of crime. Special factors. Concurrent requests. Pretreaty crimes. Provisional detainment. Extradition postponement. Material evidence. Legal protection and assistance. Conveyance in transit.
PROCEDURE: Denunciation. Ratification.
PARTIES:
Belgium SIGNED: 27 Jun 62 RATIFIED: 2 Jan 68 FORCE: 30 Jul 64

Luxembourg SIGNED: 27 Jun 62 RATIFIED: 2 Jan 68 FORCE: 23 Aug 65
Netherlands SIGNED: 27 Jun 62 RATIFIED: 2 Jan 68 FORCE: 11 Oct 67

108894 Bilateral Agreement **616 UNTS 139**
SIGNED: 10 Mar 67 FORCE: 14 Nov 67
REGISTERED: 2 Jan 68 IBRD (World Bank)
ARTICLES: 8 LANGUAGE: English.
HEADNOTE: GUARANTEE POWER
TOPIC: Loans and Credits
CONCEPTS: Remedies. Bonds. Payment schedules. Tax exemptions. Loan regulations. Loan guarantee. Guarantor non-interference. Plans and standards.
PARTIES:
Guatemala
IBRD (World Bank)

108895 Bilateral Agreement **616 UNTS 167**
SIGNED: 26 May 67 FORCE: 14 Jul 67
REGISTERED: 2 Jan 68 IBRD (World Bank)
ARTICLES: 8 LANGUAGE: English.
HEADNOTE: LOAN RAILWAY
TOPIC: Loans and Credits
CONCEPTS: Definition of terms. Detailed regulations. Bonds. Loan regulations.
PROCEDURE: Ratification. Termination.
PARTIES:
Pakistan
IBRD (World Bank)

108896 Bilateral Exchange **616 UNTS 193**
SIGNED: 30 Sep 66 FORCE: 30 Sep 66
REGISTERED: 3 Jan 68 USA (United States)
ARTICLES: 2 LANGUAGE: English.
HEADNOTE: PHASING OUT RADAR STATIONS
TOPIC: Milit Installation
CONCEPTS: Return of equipment and recapture.
TREATY REF: 233 UNTS 109; 410 UNTS 21; 421 UNTS 199.
PARTIES:
Canada
USA (United States)

108897 Bilateral Agreement **616 UNTS 199**
SIGNED: 30 Sep 66 FORCE: 30 Sep 66
REGISTERED: 3 Jan 68 USA (United States)
ARTICLES: 5 LANGUAGE: English.
HEADNOTE: AGRI COMMOD TITLE IV
TOPIC: US Agri Commod Aid
CONCEPTS: General provisions. General cooperation. Funding procedures. Credit provisions.
PARTIES:
Indonesia
USA (United States)

108898 Bilateral Agreement **616 UNTS 215**
SIGNED: 6 Sep 66 FORCE: 6 Sep 66
REGISTERED: 3 Jan 68 USA (United States)
ARTICLES: 3 LANGUAGE: English.
HEADNOTE: RENEGOTIATION SCHEDULE XX GATT
TOPIC: General Trade
CONCEPTS: Annex or appendix reference. Concessions. General trade.
PROCEDURE: Termination.
PARTIES:
Japan
USA (United States)

108899 Bilateral Exchange **616 UNTS 242**
SIGNED: 30 Aug 66 FORCE: 30 Aug 66
REGISTERED: 3 Jan 68 USA (United States)
ARTICLES: 1 LANGUAGE: English.
HEADNOTE: TRADE COTTON TEXTILES
TOPIC: General Trade
CONCEPTS: Annex or appendix reference. Reciprocity in trade. Commodity trade.
PARTIES:
Singapore
USA (United States)

108900 Bilateral Exchange **616 UNTS 259**
SIGNED: 26 Sep 66 FORCE: 26 Sep 66
REGISTERED: 3 Jan 68 USA (United States)
ARTICLES: 1 LANGUAGE: English.

HEADNOTE: ESTABLISHMENT OPERATION MEDITERRANEAN MARINE SORTING CENTER
TOPIC: Scientific Project
CONCEPTS: Privileges and immunities. Personnel. Use of facilities. Recognition of degrees. Research cooperation. Indemnities and reimbursements. Tax exemptions. Customs exemptions.
PARTIES:
Tunisia
USA (United States)

108901 Bilateral Exchange **616 UNTS 267**
SIGNED: 11 Aug 66 FORCE: 11 Aug 66
REGISTERED: 3 Jan 68 USA (United States)
ARTICLES: 1 LANGUAGE: English.
HEADNOTE: INVESTMENT GUARANTIES
TOPIC: Finance
CONCEPTS: Exceptions and exemptions. Treaty interpretation. Conformity with municipal law. Currency. Investments. Claims and settlements.
PROCEDURE: Duration.
PARTIES:
USA (United States)
Zambia

108902 Bilateral Agreement **616 UNTS 277**
SIGNED: 15 Nov 67 FORCE: 15 Nov 67
REGISTERED: 4 Jan 68 South Africa
ARTICLES: 2 LANGUAGE: English.
HEADNOTE: CONSULAR PRIVILEGES
TOPIC: Consul/Citizenship
CONCEPTS: Definition of terms. Exceptions and exemptions. Territorial application. Diplomatic privileges.
PARTIES:
South Africa
UK Great Britain

108903 Bilateral Agreement **616 UNTS 285**
SIGNED: 16 Sep 66 FORCE: 20 Dec 66
REGISTERED: 9 Jan 68 IDA (Devel Assoc)
ARTICLES: 6 LANGUAGE: English.
HEADNOTE: DEVELOPMENT CREDIT EDUCATION
TOPIC: Loans and Credits
CONCEPTS: Detailed regulations. Remedies. Annex or appendix reference. Use restrictions. Loan and credit. Credit provisions.
PROCEDURE: Termination.
PARTIES:
IDA (Devel Assoc)
Tunisia

108904 Multilateral Agreement **616 UNTS 317**
SIGNED: 31 Dec 65 FORCE: 1 Jul 66
REGISTERED: 10 Jan 68 UK Great Britain
ARTICLES: 28 LANGUAGE: English. French. Spanish.
HEADNOTE: TIN
TOPIC: Specific Resources
CONCEPTS: Change of circumstances. Definition of terms. Exceptions and exemptions. Treaty interpretation. Annex or appendix reference. Privileges and immunities. Procedure. Export quotas. Export subsidies. Trade procedures. Currency. Internal finance. Subsidiary organ. Internal structure. Conferences. Membership.
PROCEDURE: Amendment. Accession. Duration. Ratification. Registration. Renewal or Revival. Termination.
PARTIES:
Australia SIGNED: 31 Dec 65 FORCE: 1 Jul 66
Austria SIGNED: 31 Dec 65 FORCE: 1 Jul 66
Belgium SIGNED: 31 Dec 65 FORCE: 1 Jul 66
Bolivia SIGNED: 31 Dec 65 FORCE: 1 Jul 66
Canada SIGNED: 31 Dec 65 FORCE: 1 Jul 66
Congo (Zaire) SIGNED: 31 Dec 65 FORCE: 1 Jul 66
Czechoslovakia SIGNED: 31 Dec 65 FORCE: 1 Jul 66
Denmark SIGNED: 31 Dec 65 FORCE: 1 Jul 66
France SIGNED: 31 Dec 65 FORCE: 1 Jul 66
Indonesia SIGNED: 31 Dec 65 FORCE: 1 Jul 66
Israel SIGNED: 31 Dec 65 FORCE: 1 Jul 66
Italy SIGNED: 31 Dec 65 FORCE: 1 Jul 66
Japan SIGNED: 31 Dec 65 FORCE: 1 Jul 66
Korea, South SIGNED: 31 Dec 65 FORCE: 1 Jul 66
Malaysia SIGNED: 31 Dec 65 FORCE: 1 Jul 66
Mexico SIGNED: 31 Dec 65 FORCE: 1 Jul 66

Netherlands SIGNED: 31 Dec 65 FORCE:
1 Jul 66
Nigeria SIGNED: 31 Dec 65 FORCE: 1 Jul 66
Rwanda SIGNED: 31 Dec 65 FORCE: 1 Jul 66
Spain SIGNED: 31 Dec 65 FORCE: 1 Jul 66
Thailand SIGNED: 31 Dec 65 FORCE: 1 Jul 66
Turkey SIGNED: 31 Dec 65 FORCE: 1 Jul 66
UK Great Britain SIGNED: 31 Dec 65 FORCE:
1 Jul 66

108905 Bilateral Treaty **617 UNTS 3**
SIGNED: 18 May 67 FORCE: 25 Sep 67
REGISTERED: 10 Jan 68 Hungary
ARTICLES: 12 LANGUAGE: Hungarian. German.
HEADNOTE: FRIENDSHIP COOPERATION MU-
TUAL ASSISTANCE
TOPIC: General Amity
CONCEPTS: Non-prejudice to UN charter. Peaceful
relations. General cooperation. Culture. General
trade. Self-defense.
TREATY REF: WARSAW TREATY 14-5-55.
PROCEDURE: Duration. Ratification. Registration.
Renewal or Revival.
PARTIES:
Germany, East
Hungary

108906 Bilateral Agreement **617 UNTS 21**
SIGNED: 16 May 67 FORCE: 11 Jul 67
REGISTERED: 10 Jan 68 IBRD (World Bank)
ARTICLES: 4 LANGUAGE: English.
HEADNOTE: GUARANTEE POWER
TOPIC: Loans and Credits
CONCEPTS: Detailed regulations. Bonds. Loan
regulations. Loan guarantee.
PARTIES:
Cyprus
IBRD (World Bank)

108907 Bilateral Agreement **617 UNTS 47**
SIGNED: 9 May 67 FORCE: 3 Oct 67
REGISTERED: 10 Jan 68 IDA (Devel Assoc)
ARTICLES: 7 LANGUAGE: English.
HEADNOTE: DEVELOPMENT CREDIT
TOPIC: Loans and Credits
CONCEPTS: Conditions. Definition of terms. Reme-
dies. Annex or appendix reference. Use restric-
tions. Loan and credit. Credit provisions.
PROCEDURE: Termination.
PARTIES:
Jordan
IDA (Devel Assoc)

108908 Bilateral Agreement **617 UNTS 91**
SIGNED: 11 May 67 FORCE: 19 Jun 67
REGISTERED: 10 Jan 68 IDA (Devel Assoc)
ARTICLES: 6 LANGUAGE: English.
HEADNOTE: DEVELOPMENT CREDIT
TOPIC: General Aid
CONCEPTS: Conditions. Definition of terms. Reme-
dies. Annex or appendix reference. Use restric-
tions. Loan and credit. Credit provisions.
PROCEDURE: Termination.
PARTIES:
Kenya
IDA (Devel Assoc)

108909 Bilateral Agreement **617 UNTS 111**
SIGNED: 11 May 67 FORCE: 30 Jun 67
REGISTERED: 10 Jan 68 IDA (Devel Assoc)
ARTICLES: 7 LANGUAGE: English.
HEADNOTE: DEVELOPMENT CREDIT
TOPIC: General Aid
CONCEPTS: Conditions. Definition of terms. Reme-
dies. Annex or appendix reference. Use restric-
tions. Loan and credit. Credit provisions.
PARTIES:
Kenya
IDA (Devel Assoc)

108910 Bilateral Agreement **617 UNTS 141**
SIGNED: 4 May 67 FORCE: 3 Jul 67
REGISTERED: 10 Jan 68 IDA (Devel Assoc)
ARTICLES: 6 LANGUAGE: English.
HEADNOTE: DEVELOPMENT CREDIT
TOPIC: Loans and Credits
CONCEPTS: Conditions. Definition of terms. Reme-

dies. Annex or appendix reference. Use restric-
tions. Loan and credit. Credit provisions.
PARTIES:
Malawi
IDA (Devel Assoc)

108911 Bilateral Agreement **617 UNTS 161**
SIGNED: 21 Apr 67 FORCE: 24 May 67
REGISTERED: 10 Jan 68 IDA (Devel Assoc)
ARTICLES: 6 LANGUAGE: English.
HEADNOTE: DEVELOPMENT CREDIT
TOPIC: General Aid
CONCEPTS: Conditions. Remedies. Annex or ap-
pendix reference. Use restrictions. Loan and
credit. Credit provisions.
PARTIES:
IDA (Devel Assoc)
Uganda

108912 Bilateral Agreement **617 UNTS 177**
SIGNED: 28 Jul 67 FORCE: 10 Aug 67
REGISTERED: 10 Jan 68 IDA (Devel Assoc)
ARTICLES: 6 LANGUAGE: English.
HEADNOTE: DEVELOPMENT CREDIT
TOPIC: General Aid
CONCEPTS: Conditions. Remedies. Annex or ap-
pendix reference. Use restrictions. Loan and
credit. Credit provisions.
PARTIES:
IDA (Devel Assoc)
Uganda

108913 Bilateral Exchange **617 UNTS 193**
SIGNED: 17 Feb 67 FORCE: 19 Mar 67
REGISTERED: 10 Jan 68 UK Great Britain
ARTICLES: 2 LANGUAGE: English. Spanish.
HEADNOTE: ABOLITION VISAS
TOPIC: Visas
CONCEPTS: Territorial application. Visa abolition.
Conformity with municipal law.
PARTIES:
Argentina
UK Great Britain

108914 Bilateral Agreement **617 UNTS 203**
SIGNED: 29 Dec 66 FORCE: 1 Jan 67
REGISTERED: 10 Jan 68 UK Great Britain
ARTICLES: 27 LANGUAGE: English.
HEADNOTE: EXCHANGE MONEY ORDERS
TOPIC: Postal Service
CONCEPTS: Definition of terms. Annex or appen-
dix reference. Exchange of information and doc-
uments. Payment schedules. Non-interest rates
and fees. Regulations. Money orders and postal
checks. Advice lists and orders.
PROCEDURE: Termination.
PARTIES:
Kuwait
UK Great Britain

108915 Bilateral Exchange **617 UNTS 231**
SIGNED: 3 Dec 66 FORCE: 3 Dec 67
REGISTERED: 10 Jan 68 UK Great Britain
ARTICLES: 2 LANGUAGE: English. Spanish.
HEADNOTE: LOAN
TOPIC: Loans and Credits
CONCEPTS: Annex or appendix reference. Private
contracts. Accounting procedures. Use restric-
tions. Loan and credit. Loan repayment.
PARTIES:
Peru
UK Great Britain

108916 Bilateral Exchange **617 UNTS 261**
SIGNED: 29 Jun 67 FORCE: 29 Jun 67
REGISTERED: 10 Jan 68 UK Great Britain
ARTICLES: 3 LANGUAGE: English. French.
HEADNOTE: LICENSES AMATEUR RADIO OPERA-
TORS
TOPIC: Gen Communications
CONCEPTS: Licenses and permits. Amateur radio.
TREATY REF: TIAS 4893.
PARTIES:
Switzerland
UK Great Britain

108917 Bilateral Agreement **617 UNTS 267**
SIGNED: 3 Feb 67 FORCE: 5 May 67
REGISTERED: 11 Jan 68 Czechoslovakia
ARTICLES: 25 LANGUAGE: Czechoslovakian. Rus-
sian.
HEADNOTE: ROAD TRANSPORT
TOPIC: Land Transport
CONCEPTS: General provisions. Previous treaties
adherence. Frontier formalities. Conformity with
municipal law. Exchange of information and doc-
uments. Procedure. Payment schedules. Trans-
port of goods. Land transport. Driving permits.
Motor vehicles and combinations. Road rules.
PROCEDURE: Denunciation. Ratification.
PARTIES:
Czechoslovakia
USSR (Soviet Union)

108918 Bilateral Agreement **617 UNTS 305**
SIGNED: 17 May 67 FORCE: 4 Oct 67
REGISTERED: 11 Jan 68 Czechoslovakia
ARTICLES: 8 LANGUAGE: Czechoslovakian. Ser-
bo-Croat.
HEADNOTE: CUSTOMS MATTERS
TOPIC: Customs
CONCEPTS: Definition of terms. Standardization.
General cooperation. Exchange of information
and documents. Recognition of legal docu-
ments. Establishment of commission. Customs
duties.
PROCEDURE: Denunciation. Duration. Ratification.
Renewal or Revival.
PARTIES:
Czechoslovakia
Yugoslavia

108919 Bilateral Treaty **617 UNTS 319**
SIGNED: 15 Nov 67 FORCE: 15 Nov 67
REGISTERED: 13 Jan 68 UK Great Britain
ARTICLES: 3 LANGUAGE: English. Arabic.
HEADNOTE: CESSION KURIA MURIA ISLANDS
TOPIC: Territory Boundary
CONCEPTS: Status of state. Boundaries of terri-
tory. Changes of territory.
PARTIES:
Muscat and Oman
UK Great Britain

108920 Bilateral Treaty **617 UNTS 327**
SIGNED: 6 Apr 67 FORCE: 24 Aug 67
REGISTERED: 17 Jan 68 Bulgaria
ARTICLES: 9 LANGUAGE: Bulgarian. Polish.
HEADNOTE: FRIENDSHIP COOPERATION MU-
TUAL ASSISTANCE
TOPIC: General Amity
CONCEPTS: Non-prejudice to UN charter. Peaceful
relations. General cooperation. Sanitation. Edu-
cation. Culture. Defense and security.
TREATY REF: 219 UNTS 3; 26 UNTS 213 WAR-
SAW 14-5-55.
PROCEDURE: Duration. Ratification. Renewal or
Revival.
PARTIES:
Bulgaria
Poland

108921 Bilateral Agreement **618 UNTS 3**
SIGNED: 3 Oct 66 FORCE: 24 Aug 67
REGISTERED: 17 Jan 68 Poland
ARTICLES: 10 LANGUAGE: Polish. Bulgarian.
HEADNOTE: CULTURAL COOPERATION
TOPIC: Culture
CONCEPTS: Previous treaty replacement. Recogni-
tion of degrees. Exchange. Teacher and student
exchange. General cultural cooperation. Publica-
tions exchange. Scientific exchange.
TREATY REF: 15 UNTS 123.
PROCEDURE: Denunciation. Duration. Future Pro-
cedures Contemplated. Ratification.
PARTIES:
Bulgaria
Poland

108922 Bilateral Treaty **618 UNTS 21**
SIGNED: 15 Mar 67 FORCE: 26 Jun 67
REGISTERED: 17 Jan 68 Poland
ARTICLES: 12 LANGUAGE: Polish. German.
HEADNOTE: FRIENDSHIP COOPERATION MU-
TUAL ASSISTANCE

TOPIC: General Amity
CONCEPTS: IGO reference. Peaceful relations. Education. General cultural cooperation. Defense and security.
INTL ORGS: Council for Mutual Economic Assistance.
TREATY REF: 219 UNTS 3; 319 UNTS 93; 145 BFSP 852.
PROCEDURE: Duration. Future Procedures Contemplated. Ratification. Registration. Renewal or Revival.
PARTIES:
Germany, East
Poland

108923 Bilateral Agreement **618 UNTS 39**
SIGNED: 21 Feb 67 FORCE: 3 Jul 67
REGISTERED: 17 Jan 68 IBRD (World Bank)
ARTICLES: 8 LANGUAGE: English.
HEADNOTE: LOAN
TOPIC: IBRD Project
CONCEPTS: Conditions. Definition of terms. Remedies. Annex or appendix reference. Bonds. Use restrictions. Loan and credit. Loan regulations.
PROCEDURE: Termination.
PARTIES:
IBRD (World Bank)
Tunisia

108924 Bilateral Agreement **618 UNTS 69**
SIGNED: 21 Feb 67 FORCE: 3 Jul 67
REGISTERED: 17 Jan 68 IDA (Devel Assoc)
ARTICLES: 7 LANGUAGE: English.
HEADNOTE: DEVELOPMENT CREDIT
TOPIC: Non-IBRD Project
CONCEPTS: Conditions. Definition of terms. Remedies. Annex or appendix reference. Use restrictions. Loan and credit. Credit provisions.
PROCEDURE: Termination.
PARTIES:
IDA (Devel Assoc)
Tunisia

108925 Bilateral Agreement **618 UNTS 89**
SIGNED: 28 Mar 67 FORCE: 7 Jul 67
REGISTERED: 17 Jan 68 IBRD (World Bank)
ARTICLES: 5 LANGUAGE: English.
HEADNOTE: GUARANTEE
TOPIC: IBRD Project
CONCEPTS: Annex or appendix reference. Bonds. Loan regulations. Loan guarantee. Guarantor non-interference.
PARTIES:
Cameroon
IBRD (World Bank)

108926 Bilateral Agreement **618 UNTS 133**
SIGNED: 28 Mar 67 FORCE: 7 Jul 67
REGISTERED: 17 Jan 68 IDA (Devel Assoc)
ARTICLES: 7 LANGUAGE: English.
HEADNOTE: DEVELOPMENT CREDIT
TOPIC: Non-IBRD Project
CONCEPTS: Conditions. Definition of terms. Remedies. Annex or appendix reference. Use restrictions. Loan and credit. Credit provisions.
PROCEDURE: Termination.
PARTIES:
Cameroon
IDA (Devel Assoc)

108927 Bilateral Agreement **618 UNTS 159**
SIGNED: 26 May 67 FORCE: 12 Dec 67
REGISTERED: 17 Jan 68 IDA (Devel Assoc)
ARTICLES: 7 LANGUAGE: English.
HEADNOTE: DEVELOPMENT CREDIT
TOPIC: Non-IBRD Project
CONCEPTS: Conditions. Definition of terms. Remedies. Annex or appendix reference. Use restrictions. Loan and credit. Credit provisions.
PARTIES:
Bolivia
IDA (Devel Assoc)

108928 Bilateral Agreement **618 UNTS 189**
SIGNED: 5 Jul 67 FORCE: 26 Jul 67
REGISTERED: 17 Jan 68 IBRD (World Bank)
ARTICLES: 5 LANGUAGE: English.
HEADNOTE: GUARANTEE

TOPIC: IBRD Project
CONCEPTS: Detailed regulations. Annex or appendix reference. Bonds. Loan regulations. Loan guarantee. Guarantor non-interference.
PARTIES:
IBRD (World Bank)
Singapore

108929 Bilateral Agreement **618 UNTS 215**
SIGNED: 23 Aug 67 FORCE: 24 Oct 67
REGISTERED: 19 Jan 68 IBRD (World Bank)
ARTICLES: 7 LANGUAGE: English.
HEADNOTE: LOAN
TOPIC: IBRD Project
CONCEPTS: Conditions. Remedies. Annex or appendix reference. Bonds. Use restrictions. Loan and credit. Loan regulations.
PROCEDURE: Termination.
PARTIES:
Madagascar
IBRD (World Bank)

108930 Bilateral Agreement **618 UNTS 235**
SIGNED: 15 Jun 67 FORCE: 31 Oct 67
REGISTERED: 19 Jan 68 IBRD (World Bank)
ARTICLES: 8 LANGUAGE: English.
HEADNOTE: LOAN
TOPIC: IBRD Project
CONCEPTS: Conditions. Definition of terms. Remedies. Annex or appendix reference. Bonds. Use restrictions. Loan and credit. Loan regulations.
PROCEDURE: Termination.
PARTIES:
Malaysia
IBRD (World Bank)

108931 Bilateral Agreement **618 UNTS 261**
SIGNED: 10 Aug 67 FORCE: 11 Oct 67
REGISTERED: 19 Jan 68 IBRD (World Bank)
ARTICLES: 5 LANGUAGE: English.
HEADNOTE: GUARANTEE
TOPIC: IBRD Project
CONCEPTS: Detailed regulations. Annex or appendix reference. Bonds. Loan regulations. Loan guarantee. Guarantor non-interference.
PARTIES:
Pakistan
IBRD (World Bank)

108932 Bilateral Agreement **618 UNTS 301**
SIGNED: 2 Aug 67 FORCE: 29 Sep 67
REGISTERED: 19 Jan 68 IBRD (World Bank)
ARTICLES: 5 LANGUAGE: English.
HEADNOTE: GUARANTEE
TOPIC: IBRD Project
CONCEPTS: Detailed regulations. Annex or appendix reference. Bonds. Loan regulations. Loan guarantee. Guarantor non-interference.
PARTIES:
Taiwan
IBRD (World Bank)

108933 Bilateral Exchange **618 UNTS 329**
SIGNED: 16 Jun 67 FORCE: 16 Jun 67
REGISTERED: 22 Jan 68 UK Great Britain
ARTICLES: 11 LANGUAGE: English.
HEADNOTE: CAMEROON DEVELOPMENT CORPORATION
TOPIC: Loans and Credits
CONCEPTS: Annex or appendix reference. Exchange of information and documents. Personnel. Accounting procedures. Payment schedules. Debt settlement. Use restrictions. Loan and credit.
PARTIES:
Cameroon
UK Great Britain

108934 Bilateral Agreement **618 UNTS 353**
SIGNED: 31 Jul 54 FORCE: 29 Sep 59
REGISTERED: 22 Jan 68 UK Great Britain
ARTICLES: 16 LANGUAGE: English. Spanish.
HEADNOTE: CAMEROON DEVELOPMENT CORPORATION
TOPIC: Milit Servic/Citiz
CONCEPTS: Emergencies. Exceptions and exemptions. Previous treaty replacement. General cooperation. Exchange of information and docu-

ments. Recognition of legal documents. Procedure. Dual nationality. Certificates of service. Service in foreign army.
TREATY REF: 82 UNTS 209.
PROCEDURE: Ratification. Termination.
PARTIES:
Chile
UK Great Britain

108935 Bilateral Exchange **619 UNTS 3**
SIGNED: 20 Jun 67 FORCE: 20 Jun 67
REGISTERED: 22 Jan 68 UK Great Britain
ARTICLES: 2 LANGUAGE: English. Spanish.
HEADNOTE: ABOLITION VISAS
TOPIC: Visas
CONCEPTS: Exceptions and exemptions. Territorial application. Visa abolition. Denial of admission. Visas. Conformity with municipal law. General cooperation. Exchange of information and documents.
PARTIES:
Dominican Republic
UK Great Britain

108936 Bilateral Agreement **619 UNTS 11**
SIGNED: 10 Jul 67 FORCE: 10 Jul 67
REGISTERED: 22 Jan 68 UK Great Britain
ARTICLES: 15 LANGUAGE: English.
HEADNOTE: AIR SERVICES
TOPIC: Air Transport
CONCEPTS: Definition of terms. Annex or appendix reference. IGO reference. General cooperation. Exchange of information and documents. Arbitration. Negotiation. Tariffs. Exchange rates and regulations. Customs exemptions. Routes and logistics. Conditions of airlines operating permission. Operating authorizations and regulations.
INTL ORGS: International Civil Aviation Organization. International Court of Justice.
PROCEDURE: Amendment. Termination.
PARTIES:
Malta
UK Great Britain

108937 Bilateral Agreement **619 UNTS 29**
SIGNED: 1 Aug 67 FORCE: 1 Aug 67
REGISTERED: 22 Jan 68 UK Great Britain
ARTICLES: 15 LANGUAGE: English.
HEADNOTE: AIR SERVICES
TOPIC: Air Transport
CONCEPTS: Definition of terms. IGO reference. General cooperation. Exchange of information and documents. Arbitration. Negotiation. Tariffs. Exchange rates and regulations. Routes and logistics. Airport facilities. Airport equipment. Operating authorizations and regulations.
INTL ORGS: International Civil Aviation Organization.
PROCEDURE: Registration.
PARTIES:
Singapore
UK Great Britain

108938 Bilateral Agreement **619 UNTS 47**
SIGNED: 1 Nov 67 FORCE: 1 Nov 67
REGISTERED: 24 Jan 68 Denmark
ARTICLES: 12 LANGUAGE: English.
HEADNOTE: LOAN
TOPIC: Loans and Credits
CONCEPTS: Conditions. Conformity with municipal law. Accounting procedures. Interest rates. Payment schedules. Use restrictions. Loan and credit.
PROCEDURE: Termination.
PARTIES:
Denmark
Tanzania

108939 Bilateral Agreement **619 UNTS 67**
SIGNED: 20 Jun 67 FORCE: 20 Jun 67
REGISTERED: 24 Jan 68 Netherlands
ARTICLES: 14 LANGUAGE: French.
HEADNOTE: STUDENT EMPLOYEES
TOPIC: Non-ILO Labor
CONCEPTS: Territorial application. Conformity with municipal law. Licenses and permits. Arbitration. Negotiation. Employment regulations.

Wages and salaries. Delivery schedules. Tax exemptions. Internal travel.
PROCEDURE: Denunciation. Renewal or Revival.
PARTIES:
Denmark
Netherlands

108940 Multilateral Agreement **619 UNTS 77**
SIGNED: 30 Sep 57   FORCE: 29 Jan 68
REGISTERED: 29 Jan 68 United Nations
ARTICLES: 17 LANGUAGE: French. English.
HEADNOTE: CARRIAGE DANGEROUS GOODS ROAD
TOPIC: General Transport
CONCEPTS: Definition of terms. Exceptions and exemptions. Annex or appendix reference. Previous treaties adherence. IGO reference. Conformity with municipal law. Arbitration. Negotiation. Dangerous goods. Transport of goods. Operating authorizations and regulations.
INTL ORGS: Council of Europe.
PROCEDURE: Amendment. Accession. Denunciation. Duration. Future Procedures Contemplated. Ratification. Registration. Termination.
PARTIES:
Austria SIGNED: 13 Dec 57
Belgium   SIGNED: 18 Oct 57   RATIFIED: 25 Aug 60 FORCE: 29 Jan 68
France SIGNED: 13 Dec 57 RATIFIED: 2 Feb 60 FORCE: 29 Jan 68
Germany, West SIGNED: 13 Dec 57
Italy SIGNED: 13 Dec 57 RATIFIED: 3 Jun 63 FORCE: 29 Jan 68
Netherlands SIGNED: 13 Dec 57   RATIFIED: 1 Nov 63 FORCE: 29 Jan 68
Portugal   RATIFIED: 29 Dec 67   FORCE: 29 Jan 68
Switzerland SIGNED: 6 Nov 57
UK Great Britain SIGNED: 1 Oct 57
                    ANNEX
639 UNTS 372. UK Great Britain. Ratification 29 Jun 68. Force 29 Jul 68.

108941   Bilateral Agreement   **619 UNTS 99**
SIGNED: 29 Jun 67   FORCE: 2 Nov 67
REGISTERED: 29 Jan 68 IBRD (World Bank)
ARTICLES: 5 LANGUAGE: English.
HEADNOTE: GUARANTEE
TOPIC: IBRD Project
CONCEPTS: Annex or appendix reference. Bonds. Terms of loan. Loan regulations. Loan guarantee. Guarantor non-interference.
PARTIES:
Colombia
IBRD (World Bank)

108942   Bilateral Agreement   **619 UNTS 129**
SIGNED: 15 Nov 67   FORCE: 26 Dec 67
REGISTERED: 29 Jan 68 IBRD (World Bank)
ARTICLES: 5 LANGUAGE: English.
HEADNOTE: GUARANTEE
TOPIC: IBRD Project
CONCEPTS: Annex or appendix reference. Bonds. Terms of loan. Loan regulations. Loan guarantee. Guarantor non-interference.
PARTIES:
Israel
IBRD (World Bank)

108943   Bilateral Agreement   **619 UNTS 171**
SIGNED: 11 Sep 67   FORCE: 28 Dec 67
REGISTERED: 29 Jan 68 IBRD (World Bank)
ARTICLES: 5 LANGUAGE: English.
HEADNOTE: GUARANTEE
TOPIC: IBRD Project
CONCEPTS: Annex or appendix reference. Bonds. Terms of loan. Loan regulations. Loan guarantee. Guarantor non-interference.
PARTIES:
Peru
IBRD (World Bank)

108944   Bilateral Agreement   **619 UNTS 209**
SIGNED: 4 Aug 67   FORCE: 15 Dec 67
REGISTERED: 29 Jan 68 IBRD (World Bank)
ARTICLES: 5 LANGUAGE: English.
HEADNOTE: GUARANTEE
TOPIC: IBRD Project
CONCEPTS: Annex or appendix reference. Bonds.

Terms of loan. Loan regulations. Loan guarantee. Guarantor non-interference.
PARTIES:
IBRD (World Bank)
Spain

108945   Bilateral Agreement   **619 UNTS 239**
SIGNED: 13 Dec 67   FORCE: 27 Dec 67
REGISTERED: 29 Jan 68 IBRD (World Bank)
ARTICLES: 5 LANGUAGE: English.
HEADNOTE: GUARANTEE
TOPIC: IBRD Project
CONCEPTS: Annex or appendix reference. Bonds. Terms of loan. Loan regulations. Loan guarantee. Guarantor non-interference.
PARTIES:
IBRD (World Bank)
Tanzania

108946   Bilateral Agreement   **619 UNTS 275**
SIGNED: 19 Sep 67   FORCE: 14 Nov 67
REGISTERED: 29 Jan 68 IBRD (World Bank)
ARTICLES: 5 LANGUAGE: English.
HEADNOTE: LOAN
TOPIC: IBRD Project
CONCEPTS: Conditions. Remedies. Annex or appendix reference. Bonds. Use restrictions. Loan and credit. Credit provisions.
PROCEDURE: Termination.
PARTIES:
IBRD (World Bank)
Thailand

108947   Bilateral Agreement   **619 UNTS 293**
SIGNED: 20 Dec 67   FORCE: 20 Dec 67
REGISTERED: 29 Jan 68 ILO (Labor Org)
ARTICLES: 6 LANGUAGE: English.
HEADNOTE: ESTABLISHMENT ILO OFFICE LUSAKA
TOPIC: IGO Operations
CONCEPTS: Border traffic and migration. Privileges and immunities. Domestic obligation. Regional offices.
PROCEDURE: Amendment.
PARTIES:
ILO (Labor Org)
Zambia

108948 Multilateral Agreement **619 UNTS 299**
SIGNED: 14 Nov 63   FORCE: 21 Nov 67
REGISTERED: 30 Jan 68 Belgium
ARTICLES: 12 LANGUAGE: French. Polish.
HEADNOTE: COMPENSATION BELGIUM LUXEMBOURG INTEREST POLAND
TOPIC: Finance
CONCEPTS: Exceptions and exemptions. Annex or appendix reference. Immovable property. General property. Compensation. Payment schedules. Claims and settlements. Lump sum settlements.
PROCEDURE: Ratification.
PARTIES:
Belgium
Luxembourg
Poland

108949   Bilateral Agreement   **620 UNTS 3**
SIGNED: 14 Jan 65   FORCE: 23 May 67
REGISTERED: 30 Jan 68 Belgium
ARTICLES: 11 LANGUAGE: French. Dutch.
HEADNOTE: COMPENSATION BELGIUM LUXEMBOURG INTEREST POLAND
TOPIC: Claims and Debts
CONCEPTS: General cooperation. Establishment of commission. Compensation. Indemnities and reimbursements. Claims and settlements. Internal structure.
PROCEDURE: Ratification.
PARTIES:
Belgium
Luxembourg

108950   Bilateral Convention   **620 UNTS 13**
SIGNED: 26 Nov 65   FORCE: 1 Oct 67
REGISTERED: 30 Jan 68 Belgium
ARTICLES: 42 LANGUAGE: French. Dutch.
HEADNOTE: SOCIAL SECURITY
TOPIC: Non-ILO Labor

CONCEPTS: Conditions. General provisions. General cooperation. Old age and invalidity insurance. Family allowances. Old age insurance. Social security.
PROCEDURE: Termination.
PARTIES:
Belgium
Poland

108951   Bilateral Agreement   **620 UNTS 77**
SIGNED: 23 Sep 67   FORCE: 28 Dec 67
REGISTERED: 30 Jan 68 IBRD (World Bank)
ARTICLES: 8 LANGUAGE: English.
HEADNOTE: LOAN
TOPIC: IBRD Project
CONCEPTS: Conditions. Definition of terms. Remedies. Annex or appendix reference. Bonds. Use restrictions. Loan and credit. Credit provisions.
PROCEDURE: Termination.
PARTIES:
Brazil
IBRD (World Bank)

108952   Bilateral Agreement   **620 UNTS 113**
SIGNED: 7 Aug 67   FORCE: 2 Nov 67
REGISTERED: 30 Jan 68 IBRD (World Bank)
ARTICLES: 5 LANGUAGE: English.
HEADNOTE: GUARANTEE
TOPIC: IBRD Project
CONCEPTS: Annex or appendix reference. Bonds. Terms of loan. Loan regulations. Loan guarantee.
PARTIES:
Taiwan
IBRD (World Bank)

108953 Multilateral Convention **620 UNTS 149**
SIGNED: 25 May 64   FORCE: 1 Dec 66
REGISTERED: 30 Jan 68 Netherlands
ARTICLES: 15 LANGUAGE: Dutch. French.
HEADNOTE: MUTUAL ASSISTANCE COLLECTION TURNOVER TAX PURCHASE TAX
TOPIC: Taxation
CONCEPTS: Definition of terms. General cooperation. Exchange of information and documents. Informational records. Legal protection and assistance. Operating agencies. Indemnities and reimbursements. General. Tax exemptions.
PROCEDURE: Denunciation. Ratification.
PARTIES:
Belgium   SIGNED: 25 May 64   RATIFIED: 2 Mar 66 FORCE: 1 Dec 66
Luxembourg SIGNED: 25 May 64   RATIFIED: 27 Oct 66 FORCE: 1 Dec 66
Netherlands SIGNED: 25 May 64   RATIFIED: 9 Jun 66 FORCE: 1 Dec 66

108954   Bilateral Convention   **620 UNTS 171**
SIGNED: 28 Apr 65   FORCE: 18 Oct 67
REGISTERED: 30 Jan 68 Belgium
ARTICLES: 8 LANGUAGE: French.
HEADNOTE: CAPITAL INVESTMENT PROTECTION PROPERTY
TOPIC: General Economic
CONCEPTS: Detailed regulations. Previous treaties adherence. Conformity with municipal law. Recognition and enforcement of legal decisions. Arbitration. Special tribunals. Negotiation. Wages and salaries. Investments. Assets transfer.
PROCEDURE: Duration. Ratification. Termination.
PARTIES:
Bel-Lux Econ Union
Morocco

108955   Bilateral Exchange   **620 UNTS 183**
SIGNED: 14 Jun 67   FORCE: 14 Jun 67
REGISTERED: 31 Jan 68 United Nations
ARTICLES: 2 LANGUAGE: English.
HEADNOTE: ASSISTANCE PALESTINE REFUGEES
TOPIC: Direct Aid
CONCEPTS: Assistance. Domestic obligation.
TREATY REF: 1 UNTS 15; 90 UNTS 327.
PARTIES:
Israel
UN Relief Palestin

108956 Multilateral Agreement **620 UNTS 191**
SIGNED: 30 Apr 66   FORCE: 25 Nov 67

REGISTERED: 5 Feb 68 Austria
ARTICLES: 13 LANGUAGE: German.
HEADNOTE: WITHDRAWAL WATER LAKE CON-
STANCE
TOPIC: Specific Resources
CONCEPTS: General cooperation. Exchange of in-
formation and documents. Establishment of
commission. Arbitration. Existing tribunals. Ne-
gotiation. Reparations and restrictions. Frontier
waterways.
PROCEDURE: Denunciation. Ratification.
PARTIES:
Austria   SIGNED: 30 Apr 66   RATIFIED:
24 May 67 FORCE: 25 Nov 67
Germany, West SIGNED: 30 Apr 66 FORCE:
25 Nov 67
Switzerland   SIGNED: 30 Apr 66   RATIFIED:
28 Dec 66 FORCE: 25 Nov 67

108957   Bilateral Exchange   **620 UNTS 211**
SIGNED: 14 Feb 67   FORCE: 14 Feb 67
REGISTERED: 6 Feb 68 Denmark
ARTICLES: 2 LANGUAGE: English.
HEADNOTE: LANGUAGE DOCUMENTS LEGAL
MATTERS
TOPIC: Admin Cooperation
CONCEPTS: General cooperation.
PARTIES:
Denmark
Israel

108958   Bilateral Agreement   **620 UNTS 217**
SIGNED: 1 Jun 67   FORCE: 31 Jul 67
REGISTERED: 6 Feb 68 Denmark
ARTICLES: 4 LANGUAGE: English. Danish.
HEADNOTE: RECOGNITION TONNAGE CERTIFI-
CATES MERCHANT SHIPS
TOPIC: Water Transport
CONCEPTS: Registration certificate. Tonnage.
PROCEDURE: Termination.
PARTIES:
Denmark
Pakistan

108959 Multilateral Agreement **620 UNTS 225**
SIGNED: 8 Dec 67   FORCE: 8 Jan 68
REGISTERED: 6 Feb 68 Denmark
ARTICLES: 8 LANGUAGE: Danish. Finnish.
HEADNOTE: COMPLIANCE REGULATIONS PRE-
VENTING POLLUTION SEA BY OIL
TOPIC: Specific Resources
CONCEPTS: Exchange of information and docu-
ments. Inspection and observation. Ocean re-
sources. Regulation of natural resources.
PROCEDURE: Denunciation.
PARTIES:
Denmark SIGNED: 8 Dec 67 FORCE: 8 Jan 68
Finland SIGNED: 8 Dec 67 FORCE: 8 Jan 68
Norway SIGNED: 8 Dec 67 FORCE: 8 Jan 68
Sweden SIGNED: 8 Dec 67 FORCE: 8 Jan 68

108960   Bilateral Agreement   **620 UNTS 239**
SIGNED: 17 Oct 67   FORCE: 17 Oct 67
REGISTERED: 8 Feb 68 Denmark
ARTICLES: 9 LANGUAGE: English.
HEADNOTE: TECHNICAL COOPERATION TRAIN-
ING SCHEME
TOPIC: Tech Assistance
CONCEPTS: Privileges and immunities. Procedure.
Vocational training. Wages and salaries. Indem-
nities and reimbursements. Assistance.
PROCEDURE: Duration. Renewal or Revival.
PARTIES:
Denmark
Zambia

108961   Bilateral Agreement   **630 UNTS 3**
SIGNED: 27 Mar 61   FORCE: 26 Jun 61
REGISTERED: 9 Feb 68 Denmark
ARTICLES: 4 LANGUAGE: Danish. Finnish.
HEADNOTE: TRADE AGRICULTURE PRODUCTS
TOPIC: Commodity Trade
CONCEPTS: IGO reference. General cooperation.
Concessions. Commodity trade.
INTL ORGS: European Free Trade Association.
PROCEDURE: Ratification.
PARTIES:
Denmark
Finland

108962   Bilateral Protocol   **630 UNTS 29**
SIGNED: 14 Nov 59   FORCE: 28 Dec 59
REGISTERED: 12 Feb 68 Denmark
ARTICLES: 8 LANGUAGE: German.
HEADNOTE: AGRI CONNECTION ESTABLISH-
MENT EUROPEAN FREE TRADE ASSOCIATION
(EFTA)
TOPIC: Commodity Trade
CONCEPTS: IGO reference. Establishment of com-
mission. Export subsidies. Commodity trade.
INTL ORGS: European Free Trade Association.
PROCEDURE: Ratification.
PARTIES:
Austria
Denmark

108963   Bilateral Agreement   **630 UNTS 41**
SIGNED: 21 Sep 67   FORCE: 21 Sep 67
REGISTERED: 13 Feb 68 IAEA (Atom Energy)
ARTICLES: 8 LANGUAGE: English.
HEADNOTE: TRANSFER RADIO THERAPY EQUIP-
MENT
TOPIC: Atomic Energy
CONCEPTS: Responsibility and liability. Title and
deeds. Arbitration. Existing tribunals. Negotia-
tion. Atomic energy assistance. Acceptance of
delivery.
PARTIES:
Iraq
IAEA (Atom Energy)

108964   Bilateral Agreement   **630 UNTS 49**
SIGNED: 11 Oct 67   FORCE: 11 Oct 67
REGISTERED: 13 Feb 68 IAEA (Atom Energy)
ARTICLES: 8 LANGUAGE: English.
HEADNOTE: TRANSFER RADIO THERAPY EQUIP-
MENT
TOPIC: Atomic Energy
CONCEPTS: Responsibility and iiability. Title and
deeds. Arbitration. Existing tribunals. Negotia-
tion. Atomic energy assistance. Acceptance of
delivery.
PARTIES:
Burma
IAEA (Atom Energy)

108965   Bilateral Instrument   **630 UNTS 57**
SIGNED: 16 Oct 67   FORCE: 16 Oct 67
REGISTERED: 13 Feb 68 IAEA (Atom Energy)
ARTICLES: 12 LANGUAGE: English. French.
HEADNOTE: TRANSFER ENRICHED URANIUM
TOPIC: Atomic Energy
CONCEPTS: Responsibility and liability. Proce-
dure. Payment schedules. Nuclear materials.
PARTIES:
IAEA (Atom Energy)
USA (United States)

108966 Multilateral Instrument **630 UNTS 69**
SIGNED: 19 Oct 67   FORCE: 19 Oct 67
REGISTERED: 13 Feb 68 IAEA (Atom Energy)
ARTICLES: 5 LANGUAGE: English.
HEADNOTE: TRANSFER ENRICHED URANIUM
TOPIC: Atomic Energy
CONCEPTS: Detailed regulations. Payment sched-
ules. Nuclear materials.
PROCEDURE: Amendment.
PARTIES:
Pakistan SIGNED: 19 Oct 67 FORCE: 19 Oct 67
IAEA (Atom Energy) SIGNED: 19 Oct 67 FORCE:
19 Oct 67
USA (United States) SIGNED: 19 Oct 67 FORCE:
19 Oct 67

108967 Multilateral Instrument **630 UNTS 77**
SIGNED: 5 Nov 67   FORCE: 5 Nov 67
REGISTERED: 13 Feb 68 IAEA (Atom Energy)
ARTICLES: 5 LANGUAGE: English.
HEADNOTE: TRANSFER ENRICHED URANIUM
TOPIC: Atomic Energy
CONCEPTS: Detailed regulations. Payment sched-
ules. Nuclear materials.
PROCEDURE: Amendment.
PARTIES:
Finland SIGNED: 5 Nov 67 FORCE: 5 Nov 67
IAEA (Atom Energy) SIGNED: 5 Nov 67 FORCE:
5 Nov 67
USA (United States) SIGNED: 5 Nov 67 FORCE:
5 Nov 67

108968   Bilateral Convention   **630 UNTS 87**
SIGNED: 9 Jul 62   FORCE: 21 Aug 66
REGISTERED: 13 Feb 68 Israel
ARTICLES: 26 LANGUAGE: Hebrew. German. En-
glish.
HEADNOTE: AVOIDANCE DOUBLE TAXATION
TOPIC: Taxation
CONCEPTS: Definition of terms. Territorial applica-
tion. Immovable property. General property.
Wages and salaries. Seizure funds. Taxation.
General. Tax exemptions. Air transport. Water
transport.
PROCEDURE: Ratification. Termination.
PARTIES:
Germany, West
Israel

108969   Bilateral Agreement   **630 UNTS 175**
SIGNED: 7 Oct 64   FORCE: 24 Apr 66
REGISTERED: 13 Feb 68 Israel
ARTICLES: 2 LANGUAGE: Hebrew. French.
HEADNOTE: TECHNICAL COOPERATION
TOPIC: Tech Assistance
CONCEPTS: IGO reference. Scholarships and
grants. Wages and salaries. Scientific exchange.
Indemnities and reimbursements. General tech-
nical assistance.
INTL ORGS: United Nations.
PROCEDURE: Ratification. Registration.
PARTIES:
Chad
Israel

108971   Bilateral Convention   **630 UNTS 189**
SIGNED: 5 Jul 66   FORCE: 16 Nov 67
REGISTERED: 13 Feb 68 Israel
ARTICLES: 18 LANGUAGE: Hebrew. English.
HEADNOTE: LEGAL PROCEEDINGS CIVIL COM-
MERCIAL MATTERS
TOPIC: Admin Cooperation
CONCEPTS: Definition of terms. Detailed regula-
tions. Territorial application. Material evidence.
Exchange of information and documents. Legal
protection and assistance. Negotiation. Indemni-
ties and reimbursements. Debts.
PROCEDURE: Ratification. Termination.
PARTIES:
Israel
UK Great Britain

108972   Bilateral Convention   **630 UNTS 225**
SIGNED: 2 Nov 66   FORCE: 11 Jan 68
REGISTERED: 13 Feb 68 Israel
ARTICLES: 32 LANGUAGE: English.
HEADNOTE: AVOIDANCE DOUBLE TAXATION
TOPIC: Taxation
CONCEPTS: Definition of terms. Territorial applica-
tion. Previous treaty replacement. Diplomatic
privileges. Exchange of information and docu-
ments. General property. Taxation. General. Tax
exemptions. Air transport. Water transport.
TREATY REF: 220 UNTS 71.
PROCEDURE: Ratification. Termination.
PARTIES:
Israel
Norway

108973   Bilateral Exchange   **630 UNTS 267**
SIGNED: 30 Nov 66   FORCE: 30 Nov 66
REGISTERED: 13 Feb 68 Israel
ARTICLES: 6 LANGUAGE: English. French.
HEADNOTE: AVOIDANCE DOUBLE TAXATION
SHIPS AIRCRAFT
TOPIC: Taxation
CONCEPTS: Definition of terms. Taxation. Tax ex-
emptions. Air transport. Water transport.
PROCEDURE: Termination.
PARTIES:
Canada
Israel

108974   Bilateral Agreement   **630 UNTS 275**
SIGNED: 23 Mar 67   FORCE: 21 Jan 67
REGISTERED: 13 Feb 68 Israel
ARTICLES: 15 LANGUAGE: Hebrew. French.
Dutch.
HEADNOTE: CULTURAL
TOPIC: Culture
CONCEPTS: Exchange of information and docu-

ments. Establishment of commission. Recognition of degrees. Exchange. Teacher and student exchange. Scholarships and grants. Publications exchange.
PROCEDURE: Ratification. Termination.
PARTIES:
  Belgium
  Israel

108975   Bilateral Treaty   **630 UNTS 293**
SIGNED: 28 Mar 67   FORCE: 28 Mar 67
REGISTERED: 13 Feb 68 Israel
ARTICLES: 11 LANGUAGE: French.
HEADNOTE: FRIENDSHIP COMMERCE NAVIGATION
TOPIC: General Amity
CONCEPTS: Border traffic and migration. Alien status. Conformity with municipal law. Legal protection and assistance. Certificates of origin. Payment schedules. Most favored nation clause. Tax exemptions. Navigational conditions.
TREATY REF: 55 UNTS 187.
PROCEDURE: Duration.
PARTIES:
  Haiti
  Israel

108976   Bilateral Exchange   **630 UNTS 301**
SIGNED: 3 Apr 67   FORCE: 3 Apr 67
REGISTERED: 13 Feb 68 Israel
ARTICLES: 2 LANGUAGE: English.
HEADNOTE: ALIEN AMATEUR RADIO OPERATORS
TOPIC: Gen Communications
CONCEPTS: Amateur radio.
PARTIES:
  Austria
  Israel

108977   Bilateral Exchange   **630 UNTS 307**
SIGNED: 18 Apr 67   FORCE: 18 Apr 67
REGISTERED: 13 Feb 68 Israel
ARTICLES: 2 LANGUAGE: English.
HEADNOTE: LANGUAGES DOCUMENTS LEGAL MATTERS
TOPIC: Admin Cooperation
CONCEPTS: General cooperation.
PARTIES:
  Israel
  Norway

108978   Bilateral Exchange   **630 UNTS 313**
SIGNED: 1 May 67   FORCE: 1 Jun 67
REGISTERED: 13 Feb 68 Israel
ARTICLES: 11 LANGUAGE: French.
HEADNOTE: VISAS
TOPIC: Visas
CONCEPTS: Territorial application. Time limit. Visa abolition. Denial of admission. Visas. Conformity with municipal law.
PROCEDURE: Denunciation.
PARTIES:
  Israel
  Switzerland

108979   Bilateral Exchange   **630 UNTS 319**
SIGNED: 9 Aug 67   FORCE: 7 Nov 67
REGISTERED: 13 Feb 68 Israel
ARTICLES: 7 LANGUAGE: Spanish.
HEADNOTE: ABOLITION VISAS
TOPIC: Visas
CONCEPTS: Change of circumstances. Time limit. Visa abolition. Denial of admission. Conformity with municipal law.
PROCEDURE: Denunciation. Duration.
PARTIES:
  Ecuador
  Israel

108980   Bilateral Agreement   **630 UNTS 325**
SIGNED: 29 Aug 66   FORCE: 1 Nov 67
REGISTERED: 14 Feb 68 Bulgaria
ARTICLES: 33 LANGUAGE: English.
HEADNOTE: VETERINARY
TOPIC: Sanitation
CONCEPTS: Definition of terms. Exchange of information and documents. Inspection and observation. Public information. Recognition of legal documents. Establishment of commission. Vet-

erinary. Export quotas. Import quotas. Transport of goods.
PROCEDURE: Denunciation. Duration. Ratification. Renewal or Revival.
PARTIES:
  Bulgaria
  United Arab Rep

108981   Bilateral Agreement   **630 UNTS 353**
SIGNED: 12 Feb 67   FORCE: 12 Feb 67
REGISTERED: 14 Feb 68 Bulgaria
ARTICLES: 11 LANGUAGE: Bulgarian. Arabic. English.
HEADNOTE: COOPERATION BROADCASTING
TOPIC: Gen Communications
CONCEPTS: Exchange of information and documents. Exchange. General technical assistance. General communications.
TREATY REF: 292 UNTS 151.
PROCEDURE: Amendment. Denunciation. Duration.
PARTIES:
  Bulgaria
  United Arab Rep

108982   Bilateral Agreement   **630 UNTS 363**
SIGNED: 12 Feb 67   FORCE: 12 Feb 67
REGISTERED: 14 Feb 68 Bulgaria
ARTICLES: 12 LANGUAGE: Bulgarian. Arabic. English.
HEADNOTE: COOPERATION BROADCASTING
TOPIC: Telecommunications
CONCEPTS: General cooperation. Exchange of information and documents. General technical assistance. General communications.
TREATY REF: 292 UNTS 151.
PROCEDURE: Amendment. Duration. Renewal or Revival.
PARTIES:
  Bulgaria
  United Arab Rep

108983   Bilateral Agreement   **631 UNTS 3**
SIGNED: 27 Apr 67   FORCE: 27 Apr 67
REGISTERED: 14 Feb 68 Bulgaria
ARTICLES: 11 LANGUAGE: Bulgarian. Russian.
HEADNOTE: COOPERATION PEACEFUL USES ATOMIC ENERGY
TOPIC: Atomic Energy
CONCEPTS: Annex or appendix reference. Conformity with municipal law. General cooperation. Exchange of information and documents. Establishment of commission. Research cooperation. Scientific exchange. Establishment of trade relations. Export quotas. Import quotas. Trade agencies. Payment schedules. Most favored nation clause. Peaceful use. Merchant vessels.
PROCEDURE: Termination.
PARTIES:
  Bulgaria
  USSR (Soviet Union)

108984   Bilateral Convention   **631 UNTS 19**
SIGNED: 30 May 67   FORCE: 1 Dec 67
REGISTERED: 14 Dec 68 Bulgaria
ARTICLES: 9 LANGUAGE: French.
HEADNOTE: PLANT PROTECTION
TOPIC: Sanitation
CONCEPTS: Annex or appendix reference. Exchange of information and documents. Domestic legislation. Establishment of commission. Negotiation. Border control. Disease control. Scientific exchange. Trade procedures.
PROCEDURE: Denunciation. Duration. Ratification. Renewal or Revival.
PARTIES:
  Bulgaria
  Turkey

108985   Bilateral Agreement   **631 UNTS 33**
SIGNED: 29 Jul 67   FORCE: 29 Jul 67
REGISTERED: 14 Feb 68 Bulgaria
ARTICLES: 13 LANGUAGE: Bulgarian. Italian.
HEADNOTE: FILMS COPRODUCTION
TOPIC: Mass Media
CONCEPTS: Detailed regulations. Nationality and citizenship. Establishment of commission. Financial programs.

PROCEDURE: Denunciation. Duration. Renewal or Revival.
PARTIES:
  Bulgaria
  Italy

108986   Bilateral Agreement   **631 UNTS 49**
SIGNED: 22 Aug 67   FORCE: 10 Dec 67
REGISTERED: 14 Feb 68 Bulgaria
ARTICLES: 16 LANGUAGE: Bulgarian. Romanian.
HEADNOTE: ABOLITION ENTRY EXIT VISAS
TOPIC: Visas
CONCEPTS: Time limit. Annex or appendix reference. Previous treaty replacement. Visa abolition. Border traffic and migration. Resident permits. Non-visa travel documents. Visas. Tourism. Conformity with municipal law. General cooperation.
PROCEDURE: Denunciation. Duration. Ratification.
PARTIES:
  Bulgaria
  Romania

108987   Bilateral Agreement   **631 UNTS 71**
SIGNED: 2 Sep 67   FORCE: 1 Jan 68
REGISTERED: 14 Feb 68 Bulgaria
ARTICLES: 7 LANGUAGE: Bulgarian. Danish.
HEADNOTE: ABOLITION VISAS
TOPIC: Visas
CONCEPTS: Change of circumstances. Visa abolition. Denial of admission. Conformity with municipal law.
TREATY REF: 322 UNTS 245.
PROCEDURE: Denunciation.
PARTIES:
  Bulgaria
  Denmark

108988   Bilateral Treaty   **631 UNTS 81**
SIGNED: 7 Sep 67   FORCE: 13 Nov 67
REGISTERED: 14 Feb 68 Bulgaria
ARTICLES: 11 LANGUAGE: Bulgarian. German.
HEADNOTE: FRIENDSHIP COOPERATION MUTUAL ASSISTANCE
TOPIC: General Amity
CONCEPTS: IGO reference. Friendship and amity. Peaceful relations. General cooperation. General cultural cooperation. General technical assistance. Repatriation of combatants. Defense and security.
INTL ORGS: United Nations.
TREATY REF: 719 UNTS 3.
PROCEDURE: Denunciation. Duration. Ratification. Registration. Renewal or Revival.
PARTIES:
  Bulgaria
  Germany, East

108989   Bilateral Agreement   **631 UNTS 99**
SIGNED: 11 Dec 67   FORCE: 9 Feb 68
REGISTERED: 14 Feb 68 Finland
ARTICLES: 4 LANGUAGE: Finnish. English.
HEADNOTE: RECOGNITION TONNAGE CERTIFICATES MERCHANT SHIPS
TOPIC: Water Transport
CONCEPTS: Merchant vessels. Tonnage.
PROCEDURE: Termination.
PARTIES:
  Finland
  Pakistan

108990   Bilateral Agreement   **631 UNTS 103**
SIGNED: 15 Feb 68   FORCE: 15 Feb 68
REGISTERED: 15 Feb 68 United Nations
ARTICLES: 16 LANGUAGE: English.
HEADNOTE: ARRANGEMENTS CONFERENCE HUMAN RIGHTS
TOPIC: Consul/Citizenship
CONCEPTS: Privileges and immunities. Exchange of information and documents. Legal protection and assistance. Personnel. Responsibility and liability. Use of facilities. Arbitration. Negotiation. Indemnities and reimbursements. Financial programs. Claims and settlements. Passenger transport. Conferences.
PROCEDURE: Duration.
PARTIES:
  Iran
  United Nations

108991 Bilateral Exchange **631 UNTS 119**
SIGNED: 1 Jun 67   FORCE: 1 Jun 67
REGISTERED: 15 Feb 68 Norway
ARTICLES: 3 LANGUAGE: English.
HEADNOTE: AUTHORIZATION AMATEUR RADIO
  OPERATORS
TOPIC: Gen Communications
CONCEPTS: Licenses and permits. Amateur radio.
TREATY REF: TIAS 4893.
PARTIES:
  Norway
  USA (United States)

108992 Bilateral Agreement **631 UNTS 125**
SIGNED: 2 Apr 66   FORCE: 2 Apr 66
REGISTERED: 15 Feb 68 Singapore
ARTICLES: 22 LANGUAGE: English. Russian.
HEADNOTE: TRADE
TOPIC: General Trade
CONCEPTS: Annex or appendix reference. General cooperation. Free passage and transit. Arbitration. Procedure. Establishment of trade relations. Export quotas. Import quotas. Trade agencies. Payment schedules. Most favored nation clause. Merchant vessels.
PROCEDURE: Duration. Renewal or Revival. Termination.
PARTIES:
  Singapore
  USSR (Soviet Union)
                    ANNEX
642 UNTS 382.   Singapore.   Supplementation
2 Apr 68. Force 2 Apr 68.
642 UNTS 382. USSR (Soviet Union). Supplementation 2 Apr 68. Force 2 Apr 68.

108993 Bilateral Agreement **631 UNTS 165**
SIGNED: 5 May 66   FORCE: 5 May 66
REGISTERED: 15 Feb 68 Singapore
ARTICLES: 14 LANGUAGE: English.
HEADNOTE: TRADE
TOPIC: General Trade
CONCEPTS: General trade.
PROCEDURE: Duration. Renewal or Revival. Termination.
PARTIES:
  Bulgaria
  Singapore

108994 Bilateral Agreement **631 UNTS 189**
SIGNED: 7 Jun 66   FORCE: 7 Jun 66
REGISTERED: 15 Feb 68 Singapore
ARTICLES: 13 LANGUAGE: English.
HEADNOTE: TRADE ECONOMIC
TOPIC: General Trade
CONCEPTS: Annex or appendix reference. Conformity with municipal law. Establishment of trade relations. Export quotas. Import quotas. Trade agencies. Payment schedules. Most favored nation clause. Merchant vessels.
PROCEDURE: Duration. Renewal or Revival. Termination.
PARTIES:
  Poland
  Singapore

108995 Bilateral Agreement **631 UNTS 215**
SIGNED: 17 May 67   FORCE: 15 Nov 67
REGISTERED: 16 Feb 68 Belgium
ARTICLES: 12 LANGUAGE: French. Dutch. Bulgarian.
HEADNOTE: CULTURAL COOPERATION
TOPIC: Culture
CONCEPTS: Exchange of information and documents. Establishment of commission. Exchange. General cultural cooperation. Artists. Athletes. Scientific exchange. Publications exchange.
PROCEDURE: Denunciation. Ratification.
PARTIES:
  Belgium
  Bulgaria

108996 Bilateral Convention **631 UNTS 229**
SIGNED: 17 Dec 64   FORCE: 1 Apr 67
REGISTERED: 16 Feb 68 Belgium
ARTICLES: 6 LANGUAGE: French. Dutch. German.
HEADNOTE: TAXATION MOTOR VEHICLES
TOPIC: Land Transport
CONCEPTS: Exceptions and exemptions. Territo-

rial application. Previous treaty replacement. Tax exemptions. Motor vehicles and combinations.
TREATY REF: 159 LTS 9.
PROCEDURE: Denunciation. Ratification.
PARTIES:
  Belgium
  Germany, West

108997 Bilateral Treaty **631 UNTS 239**
SIGNED: 12 May 67   FORCE: 4 Aug 67
REGISTERED: 20 Feb 68 Bulgaria
ARTICLES: 10 LANGUAGE: Bulgarian. Russian.
HEADNOTE: FRIENDSHIP COOPERATION MUTUAL ASSISTANCE
TOPIC: General Amity
CONCEPTS: IGO reference. Friendship and amity. Peaceful relations. General cooperation. Reciprocity in trade. General technical assistance. Defense and security.
INTL ORGS: United Nations.
TREATY REF: 48 UNTS 135; 219 UNTS 3.
PROCEDURE: Denunciation. Duration. Ratification.
PARTIES:
  Bulgaria
  USSR (Soviet Union)

108998 Bilateral Exchange **631 UNTS 257**
SIGNED: 5 Dec 67   FORCE: 5 Dec 67
REGISTERED: 20 Feb 68 Denmark
ARTICLES: 4 LANGUAGE: Swedish. Danish.
HEADNOTE: DIRECT LANDINGS FISH
TOPIC: Specific Resources
CONCEPTS: Annex type material. Ocean resources.
PARTIES:
  Denmark
  Sweden

108999 Bilateral Agreement **631 UNTS 263**
SIGNED: 18 Apr 66   FORCE: 24 Jun 67
REGISTERED: 26 Feb 68 Bulgaria
ARTICLES: 21 LANGUAGE: Bulgarian. Turkish. English.
HEADNOTE: AIR TRANSPORT
TOPIC: Air Transport
CONCEPTS: Definition of terms. Annex or appendix reference. IGO reference. General cooperation. Negotiation. Tariffs. Payment schedules. Tax exemptions. Passenger transport. Routes and logistics. Airport facilities. Airport equipment. Airworthiness certificates. Conditions of airlines operating permission. Overflights and technical stops. Operating authorizations and regulations.
INTL ORGS: United Nations.
PROCEDURE: Amendment. Duration. Registration. Renewal or Revival.
PARTIES:
  Bulgaria
  Turkey

109000 Bilateral Agreement **631 UNTS 311**
SIGNED: 17 Dec 65   FORCE: 19 Oct 67
REGISTERED: 27 Feb 68 Netherlands
ARTICLES: 10 LANGUAGE: English.
HEADNOTE: EMPLOYMENT VOLUNTEERS
TOPIC: Non-ILO Labor
CONCEPTS: Alien status. General cooperation. Migrant worker. Indemnities and reimbursements. Volunteer programs.
PROCEDURE: Ratification. Termination.
PARTIES:
  Netherlands
  Zambia

109001 Bilateral Agreement **631 UNTS 319**
SIGNED: 11 Nov 64   FORCE: 3 Nov 67
REGISTERED: 27 Feb 68 South Africa
ARTICLES: 5 LANGUAGE: English.
HEADNOTE: EXEMPTION TAXES SHIPS AIRCRAFT
TOPIC: Taxation
CONCEPTS: Definition of terms. Tax exemptions. Air transport. Water transport.
PROCEDURE: Ratification. Termination.
PARTIES:
  Greece
  South Africa

109002 Bilateral Agreement **631 UNTS 325**
SIGNED: 2 Mar 66   FORCE: 5 Oct 67
REGISTERED: 27 Feb 68 Netherlands
ARTICLES: 5 LANGUAGE: English.
HEADNOTE: ESTABLISHMENT TRAINING INSTITUTE
TOPIC: Tech Assistance
CONCEPTS: General property. Institute establishment. Scientific exchange. Assistance.
PROCEDURE: Duration. Future Procedures Contemplated. Ratification.
PARTIES:
  Netherlands
  Philippines

109003 Bilateral Agreement **631 UNTS 333**
SIGNED: 7 Dec 61   FORCE: 7 Dec 61
REGISTERED: 29 Feb 68 Denmark
ARTICLES: 15 LANGUAGE: English.
HEADNOTE: AIR SERVICES
TOPIC: Air Transport
CONCEPTS: Definition of terms. Annex or appendix reference. IGO reference. General cooperation. Arbitration. Negotiation. Tariffs. Currency. Routes and logistics. Airport facilities. Airport equipment. Conditions of airlines operating permission. Overflights and technical stops. Operating authorizations and regulations.
INTL ORGS: International Civil Aviation Organization.
PROCEDURE: Amendment. Ratification.
PARTIES:
  Denmark
  Jordan

109004 Bilateral Agreement **632 UNTS 3**
SIGNED: 17 Feb 67   FORCE: 17 Feb 67
REGISTERED: 29 Feb 68 UK Great Britain
ARTICLES: 0 LANGUAGE: English.
HEADNOTE: PUBLIC OFFICERS AGREEMENT
TOPIC: Admin Cooperation
CONCEPTS: Post-colonial administration.
PARTIES:
  Lesotho
  UK Great Britain

109005 Bilateral Exchange **632 UNTS 15**
SIGNED: 15 Jun 67   FORCE: 26 May 66
REGISTERED: 29 Feb 68 UK Great Britain
ARTICLES: 0 LANGUAGE: English.
HEADNOTE: TRAINING ASSISTANCE PERSONNEL
TOPIC: Military Mission
CONCEPTS: Military training. Airforce-army-navy personnel ratio.
PARTIES:
  Guyana
  UK Great Britain

109006 Bilateral Agreement **632 UNTS 39**
SIGNED: 9 Aug 67   FORCE: 9 Aug 67
REGISTERED: 29 Feb 68 UK Great Britain
ARTICLES: 0 LANGUAGE: English.
HEADNOTE: COOPERATION SCIENCE & TECHNOLOGY
TOPIC: Scientific Project
CONCEPTS: Research cooperation. Scientific exchange.
PROCEDURE: Duration. Termination.
PARTIES:
  Hungary
  UK Great Britain

109007 Bilateral Agreement **632 UNTS 49**
SIGNED: 25 Aug 67   FORCE: 25 Aug 67
REGISTERED: 29 Feb 68 UK Great Britain
ARTICLES: 0 LANGUAGE: English. Russian.
HEADNOTE: DIRECT COMMUNICATIONS LINK, PRIME MINISTER TO KREMLIN
TOPIC: Gen Communications
CONCEPTS: Services. Radio-telephone-telegraphic communications.
PARTIES:
  UK Great Britain
  USSR (Soviet Union)

109008 Bilateral Exchange **632 UNTS 61**
SIGNED: 9 Apr 65   FORCE: 9 Apr 65
REGISTERED: 1 Mar 68 Greece

ARTICLES: 0 LANGUAGE: English.
HEADNOTE: TRADE ARRANGEMENT
TOPIC: General Trade
CONCEPTS: General trade. Trade procedures.
PROCEDURE: Termination.
PARTIES:
Greece
Japan

109009 Bilateral Agreement **632 UNTS 66**
SIGNED: 3 Apr 68 FORCE: 3 Apr 68
REGISTERED: 3 Apr 68 United Nations
ARTICLES: 0 LANGUAGE: English.
HEADNOTE: OPERATIONAL ASSISTANCE
TOPIC: Direct Aid
CONCEPTS: Privileges and immunities. Procedure.
General aid. International organizations.
PROCEDURE: Termination.
PARTIES:
State/IGO Group
Jordan

109010 Bilateral Exchange **632 UNTS 83**
SIGNED: 5 Dec 67 FORCE: 4 Mar 68
REGISTERED: 4 Mar 68 Jamaica
ARTICLES: 0 LANGUAGE: English.
HEADNOTE: ELIMINATION VISAS
TOPIC: Visas
CONCEPTS: Visa abolition.
PARTIES:
Israel
Jamaica

109011 Bilateral Treaty **632 UNTS 89**
SIGNED: 7 Sep 67 FORCE: 28 Nov 67
REGISTERED: 5 Mar 68 Hungary
ARTICLES: 0 LANGUAGE: Hungarian. Russian.
HEADNOTE: FRIENDSHIP COOPERATION MU-
TUAL ASSISTANCE
TOPIC: General Amity
CONCEPTS: Friendship and amity. Non-prejudice
to UN charter. Peaceful relations.
TREATY REF: 48UNTS163,219UNTS3.
PROCEDURE: Duration. Ratification.
PARTIES:
Hungary
USSR (Soviet Union)

109012 Bilateral Agreement **632 UNTS 105**
SIGNED: 21 Oct 67 FORCE: 21 Oct 67
REGISTERED: 5 Mar 68 Denmark
ARTICLES: 0 LANGUAGE: English.
HEADNOTE: TECHNICAL COOPERATION
TOPIC: Tech Assistance
CONCEPTS: General technical assistance. Assis-
tance. Special projects. Materials, equipment
and services.
PARTIES:
Denmark
Pakistan

109013 Bilateral Exchange **632 UNTS 113**
SIGNED: 16 Oct 67 FORCE: 16 Oct 67
REGISTERED: 7 Mar 68 Philippines
ARTICLES: 0 LANGUAGE: English.
HEADNOTE: EXCHANGE PORTIONS NAVAL RES-
ERVATION
TOPIC: General Military
CONCEPTS: Military installations and equipment.
Bases and facilities. Changes of territory. Mark-
ers and definitions.
PARTIES:
Philippines
USA (United States)

109014 Bilateral Agreement **632 UNTS 121**
SIGNED: 12 Mar 68 FORCE: 12 Mar 68
REGISTERED: 12 Mar 68 United Nations
ARTICLES: 0 LANGUAGE: English.
HEADNOTE: SEMINAR FREEDOM OF ASSOCIA-
TION
TOPIC: IGO Operations
CONCEPTS: Privileges and immunities. Subsidiary
organ.
PARTIES:
United Nations
UK Great Britain

109015 Bilateral Agreement **632 UNTS 131**
SIGNED: 12 Mar 68 FORCE: 12 Mar 68
REGISTERED: 12 Mar 68 United Nations
ARTICLES: 0 LANGUAGE: English.
HEADNOTE: UN CONFERENCE LAW OF TREATIES
TOPIC: IGO Operations
CONCEPTS: Privileges and immunities. IGO consti-
tution. Subsidiary organ.
PARTIES:
Austria
United Nations
ANNEX
660 UNTS 414. United Nations. Signature
14 Mar 69. Force 14 Mar 69.
660 UNTS 414.

109016 Bilateral Agreement **632 UNTS 143**
SIGNED: 7 Nov 67 FORCE: 11 Dec 67
REGISTERED: 12 Mar 68 WHO (World Health)
ARTICLES: 0 LANGUAGE: English.
HEADNOTE: TECHNICAL ASSISTANCE
TOPIC: Tech Assistance
CONCEPTS: Privileges and immunities. General
technical assistance. Assistance.
TREATY REF: 33UNTS2618 71UNTS318,
79UNTS326, ETC..
PROCEDURE: Termination.
PARTIES:
Lesotho
WHO (World Health)

109017 Bilateral Exchange **632 UNTS 153**
SIGNED: 30 Nov 67 FORCE: 30 Nov 67
REGISTERED: 12 Mar 68 Denmark
ARTICLES: 0 LANGUAGE: Danish.
HEADNOTE: FISHING RIGHTS
TOPIC: Specific Resources
CONCEPTS: Fish, wildlife, and natural resources.
Markers and definitions.
TREATY REF: 581UNTS57, 570UNTS91.
PARTIES:
Denmark
Germany, West

109018 Bilateral Agreement **632 UNTS 161**
SIGNED: 13 Mar 68 FORCE: 13 Mar 68
REGISTERED: 13 Mar 68 United Nations
ARTICLES: 0 LANGUAGE: French.
HEADNOTE: MEETING ENERGY FOR CENTRAL
AFRICA
TOPIC: IGO Operations
CONCEPTS: Privileges and immunities. Subsidiary
organ. Procedure.
PARTIES:
Congo (Brazzaville)
United Nations

109019 Bilateral Agreement **632 UNTS 171**
SIGNED: 22 Nov 66 FORCE: 22 Nov 66
REGISTERED: 13 Mar 68 IBRD (World Bank)
ARTICLES: 0 LANGUAGE: English.
HEADNOTE: TECHNICAL ASSISTANCE HIGHWAY
MAINTENANCE
TOPIC: IBRD Project
CONCEPTS: General technical assistance. Assis-
tance. Plans and standards.
PARTIES:
Afghanistan
IBRD (World Bank)

109020 Bilateral Agreement **632 UNTS 177**
SIGNED: 13 Mar 67 FORCE: 12 Apr 67
REGISTERED: 13 Mar 68 IBRD (World Bank)
ARTICLES: 0 LANGUAGE: English.
HEADNOTE: TECHNICAL ASSISTANCE PORT EX-
PANSION
TOPIC: IBRD Project
CONCEPTS: General technical assistance. Assis-
tance. Special projects. Plans and standards.
PARTIES:
Nicaragua
IBRD (World Bank)

109021 Bilateral Agreement **632 UNTS 185**
SIGNED: 10 May 67 FORCE: 13 Apr 67
REGISTERED: 13 Mar 68 IBRD (World Bank)
ARTICLES: 0 LANGUAGE: English.

HEADNOTE: TECHNICAL ASSISTANCE ROAD
STUDY
TOPIC: IBRD Project
CONCEPTS: General technical assistance. Assis-
tance. Special projects. Plans and standards.
PARTIES:
Congo (Brazzaville)
IBRD (World Bank)

109022 Bilateral Agreement **632 UNTS 193**
SIGNED: 11 May 67 FORCE: 11 May 67
REGISTERED: 13 Mar 68 IBRD (World Bank)
ARTICLES: 0 LANGUAGE: English.
HEADNOTE: TECHNICAL ASSISTANCE ELECTRIC
POWER INDUSTRY
TOPIC: IBRD Project
CONCEPTS: General technical assistance. Assis-
tance. Special projects. Plans and standards. Hy-
dro-electric power.
PARTIES:
IBRD (World Bank)
Turkey

109023 Bilateral Agreement **632 UNTS 201**
SIGNED: 26 Aug 64 FORCE: 26 Aug 64
REGISTERED: 14 Mar 68 IBRD (World Bank)
ARTICLES: 0 LANGUAGE: English.
HEADNOTE: TECHNICAL ASSISTANCE PORT SUR-
VEYS
TOPIC: IBRD Project
CONCEPTS: General technical assistance. Assis-
tance. Special projects. Plans and standards.
TREATY REF: 535UNTS263.
PARTIES:
Pakistan
IBRD (World Bank)

109024 Bilateral Agreement **632 UNTS 209**
SIGNED: 15 Mar 65 FORCE: 24 Aug 65
REGISTERED: 14 Mar 68 IBRD (World Bank)
ARTICLES: 0 LANGUAGE: English.
HEADNOTE: TECHNICAL ASSISTANCE HIGHWAY
FEASIBILITY STUDIES
TOPIC: IBRD Project
CONCEPTS: General technical assistance. Assis-
tance. Special projects. Plans and standards.
PARTIES:
Peru
IBRD (World Bank)

109025 Bilateral Agreement **632 UNTS 217**
SIGNED: 24 Aug 67 FORCE: 12 Oct 67
REGISTERED: 14 Mar 68 IBRD (World Bank)
ARTICLES: 0 LANGUAGE: English.
HEADNOTE: TECHNICAL ASSISTANCE HIGHWAY
STUDY
TOPIC: IBRD Project
CONCEPTS: Procedure. General technical assis-
tance. Assistance. Special projects. Plans and
standards.
PROCEDURE: Termination.
PARTIES:
Ceylon (Sri Lanka)
IBRD (World Bank)

109026 Bilateral Agreement **632 UNTS 237**
SIGNED: 30 Mar 66 FORCE: 1 Mar 67
REGISTERED: 14 Mar 68 Belgium
ARTICLES: 0 LANGUAGE: French.
HEADNOTE: RESTORATION BELGIAN PROPERTY
TOPIC: Claims and Debts
CONCEPTS: Claims and settlements.
PARTIES:
Belgium
United Arab Rep

109027 Bilateral Treaty **632 UNTS 255**
SIGNED: 1 Mar 67 FORCE: 12 Mar 67
REGISTERED: 15 Mar 68 Czechoslovakia
ARTICLES: 0 LANGUAGE: Czechoslovakian. Pol-
ish.
HEADNOTE: FRIENDSHIP COOPERATION ASSIS-
TANCE
TOPIC: General Amity
CONCEPTS: IGO reference. General relations and
amity. Friendship and amity. Peaceful relations.
INTL ORGS: United Nations.

TREATY REF: 145BFSP852, 219UNTS3, 25UNTS231.
PROCEDURE: Duration. Ratification.
PARTIES:
Czechoslovakia
Poland

109028 Bilateral Exchange **632 UNTS 269**
SIGNED: 15 Aug 67   FORCE: 15 Aug 67
REGISTERED: 15 Mar 68 UK Great Britain
ARTICLES: 0 LANGUAGE: English.
HEADNOTE: DEVELOPMENT LOAN
TOPIC: Loans and Credits
CONCEPTS: Loan and credit. Loan repayment. Terms of loan.
PARTIES:
Jordan
UK Great Britain

109029 Bilateral Agreement **632 UNTS 277**
SIGNED: 26 Oct 67   FORCE: 26 Oct 67
REGISTERED: 15 Mar 68 UK Great Britain
ARTICLES: 0 LANGUAGE: English.
HEADNOTE: INTERCHANGE INVENTIONS DEFENSE PURPOSES
TOPIC: Milit Assistance
CONCEPTS: Security of information. Exchange of defense information.
PROCEDURE: Termination.
PARTIES:
Sweden
UK Great Britain

109030 Bilateral Agreement **633 UNTS 3**
SIGNED: 18 Mar 68   FORCE: 18 Mar 68
REGISTERED: 18 Mar 68 United Nations
ARTICLES: 7 LANGUAGE: French.
HEADNOTE: SEMINAR MANAGEMENT PUBLIC ENTERPRISES
TOPIC: IGO Operations
CONCEPTS: Privileges and immunities. Legal protection and assistance. Personnel. Use of facilities. Financial programs. Domestic obligation. Passenger transport. Conferences.
TREATY REF: 1 UNTS 15; 90 UNTS 327; 33 UNTS 261.
PARTIES:
United Nations
Tunisia

109031 Bilateral Agreement **633 UNTS 13**
SIGNED: 5 Jun 67   FORCE: 14 Sep 67
REGISTERED: 18 Mar 68 IBRD (World Bank)
ARTICLES: 5 LANGUAGE: English.
HEADNOTE: TECHNICAL ASSISTANCE
TOPIC: Tech Assistance
CONCEPTS: Annex or appendix reference. Conformity with municipal law. Exchange of information and documents. Responsibility and liability. Payment schedules. General technical assistance. Natural resources.
PROCEDURE: Amendment. Duration.
PARTIES:
Liberia
IBRD (World Bank)

109032 Bilateral Agreement **633 UNTS 21**
SIGNED: 20 Jul 67   FORCE: 9 Mar 68
REGISTERED: 18 Mar 68 Netherlands
ARTICLES: 27 LANGUAGE: French.
HEADNOTE: VETERINARY
TOPIC: Sanitation
CONCEPTS: Detailed regulations. Territorial application. Time limit. Treaty implementation. Exchange of official publications. Exchange of information and documents. Establishment of commission. Border control. Disease control. Veterinary. Research cooperation. Export quotas. Import quotas. Certificates of origin. Indemnities and reimbursements.
PROCEDURE: Denunciation. Ratification.
PARTIES:
Netherlands
Romania

109033 Bilateral Convention **633 UNTS 45**
SIGNED: 19 Apr 65   FORCE: 30 Nov 67
REGISTERED: 18 Mar 68 UK Great Britain

ARTICLES: 12 LANGUAGE: English. Persian.
HEADNOTE: CULTURAL
TOPIC: Culture
CONCEPTS: Definition of terms. Conformity with municipal law. General cooperation. Exchange of information and documents. Public information. Use of facilities. General cultural cooperation. Athletes.
PROCEDURE: Denunciation. Duration. Ratification.
PARTIES:
Afghanistan
UK Great Britain

109034 Bilateral Agreement **633 UNTS 58**
SIGNED: 26 Nov 66   FORCE: 23 Nov 67
REGISTERED: 18 Mar 68 UK Great Britain
ARTICLES: 11 LANGUAGE: English.
HEADNOTE: CULTURAL
TOPIC: Culture
CONCEPTS: Definition of terms. Conformity with municipal law. General cooperation. Exchange of information and documents. Public information. Use of facilities. Teacher and student exchange. Exchange. General cultural cooperation.
PROCEDURE: Duration. Ratification. Renewal or Revival. Termination.
PARTIES:
Kuwait
UK Great Britain

109035 Multilateral Agreement **633 UNTS 73**
SIGNED: 26 Sep 67   FORCE: 26 Sep 67
REGISTERED: 18 Mar 68 IAEA (Atom Energy)
ARTICLES: 7 LANGUAGE: English.
HEADNOTE: ATOMIC ENERGY COOPERATION SAFEGUARDS
TOPIC: Atomic Energy
CONCEPTS: Detailed regulations. Atomic energy assistance. Peaceful use.
PARTIES:
Japan SIGNED: 26 Sep 67 FORCE: 26 Sep 67
IAEA (Atom Energy) SIGNED: 26 Sep 67 FORCE: 26 Sep 67
UK Great Britain SIGNED: 26 Sep 67 FORCE: 26 Sep 67

109036 Bilateral Agreement **633 UNTS 93**
SIGNED: 1 Aug 67   FORCE: 1 Aug 67
REGISTERED: 18 Mar 68 UK Great Britain
ARTICLES: 15 LANGUAGE: English. Malay.
HEADNOTE: AIR SERVICES
TOPIC: Air Transport
CONCEPTS: Definition of terms. Annex or appendix reference. IGO reference. General cooperation. Procedure. Negotiation. Tariffs. Routes and logistics. Airport facilities. Airport equipment. Airworthiness certificates. Conditions of airlines operating permission. Overflights and technical stops. Operating authorizations and regulations.
INTL ORGS: International Air Transport Association. International Civil Aviation Organization.
PROCEDURE: Registration. Termination.
PARTIES:
Malaysia
UK Great Britain

109037 Bilateral Agreement **633 UNTS 123**
SIGNED: 13 Jan 66   FORCE: 29 Jun 66
REGISTERED: 19 Mar 68 USSR (Soviet Union)
ARTICLES: 19 LANGUAGE: Russian. Persian.
HEADNOTE: CONSTRUCTION INDUSTRIAL OTHER PROJECTS
TOPIC: Non-IBRD Project
CONCEPTS: Change of circumstances. Guarantees and safeguards. Annex or appendix reference. General cooperation. Exchange of information and documents. Procedure. Payment schedules. Assistance. Materials, equipment and services. Loan and credit. Industry.
PROCEDURE: Ratification.
PARTIES:
Iran
USSR (Soviet Union)

109038 Bilateral Agreement **633 UNTS 165**
SIGNED: 21 Jan 66   FORCE: 21 Jun 66
REGISTERED: 19 Mar 68 USSR (Soviet Union)
ARTICLES: 10 LANGUAGE: Russian. Japanese.

HEADNOTE: TRADE PAYMENTS
TOPIC: General Trade
CONCEPTS: Annex or appendix reference. Conformity with municipal law. Licenses and permits. Arbitration. Procedure. Export quotas. Import quotas. Trade agencies. Currency. Payment schedules.
PROCEDURE: Duration.
PARTIES:
Japan
USSR (Soviet Union)

109039 Bilateral Agreement **633 UNTS 217**
SIGNED: 6 May 66   FORCE: 23 Mar 67
REGISTERED: 19 Mar 68 USSR (Soviet Union)
ARTICLES: 16 LANGUAGE: Russian. French.
HEADNOTE: CULTURAL SCIENTIFIC COOPERATION
TOPIC: Culture
CONCEPTS: Tourism. Exchange of information and documents. Exchange. Teacher and student exchange. Scholarships and grants. General cultural cooperation. Athletes. Scientific exchange. Financial programs. Publications exchange. Mass media exchange.
PROCEDURE: Amendment. Ratification. Termination.
PARTIES:
Rwanda
USSR (Soviet Union)

109040 Bilateral Agreement **633 UNTS 231**
SIGNED: 17 Oct 66   FORCE: 18 Mar 67
REGISTERED: 19 Mar 68 USSR (Soviet Union)
ARTICLES: 13 LANGUAGE: Russian. French.
HEADNOTE: TRADE
TOPIC: General Trade
CONCEPTS: Annex or appendix reference. General cooperation. Juridical personality. Export quotas. Import quotas. Reexport of goods, etc.. Trade agencies. Trade procedures. Payment schedules. Most favored nation clause. Tax exemptions. Customs exemptions. Merchant vessels.
PROCEDURE: Amendment. Ratification. Registration. Renewal or Revival. Termination.
PARTIES:
Mauritania
USSR (Soviet Union)

109041 Bilateral Agreement **633 UNTS 247**
SIGNED: 18 Dec 66   FORCE: 19 May 67
REGISTERED: 19 Mar 68 USSR (Soviet Union)
ARTICLES: 16 LANGUAGE: Russian. Arabic.
HEADNOTE: ECONOMIC TECHNICAL COOPERATION
TOPIC: Non-IBRD Project
CONCEPTS: General cooperation. Exchange of information and documents. Responsibility and liability. Scientific exchange. Accounting procedures. Interest rates. Payment schedules. General technical assistance. Use restrictions. Materials, equipment and services. Loan and credit. Terms of loan. Hydro-electric power.
PROCEDURE: Ratification.
PARTIES:
Syria
USSR (Soviet Union)

109042 Bilateral Agreement **633 UNTS 289**
SIGNED: 31 Jul 67   FORCE: 30 Oct 67
REGISTERED: 19 Mar 68 IBRD (World Bank)
ARTICLES: 8 LANGUAGE: English.
HEADNOTE: LOAN
TOPIC: IBRD Project
CONCEPTS: Conditions. Definition of terms. Remedies. Annex or appendix reference. Bonds. Use restrictions. Loan and credit. Terms of loan. Loan regulations. Loan guarantee.
PROCEDURE: Termination.
PARTIES:
Argentina
IBRD (World Bank)

109043 Bilateral Exchange **633 UNTS 327**
SIGNED: 9 May 64   FORCE: 9 May 64
REGISTERED: 21 Mar 68 UK Great Britain
ARTICLES: 2 LANGUAGE: English.

HEADNOTE: AMENDING PUBLIC OFFICERS
  AGREEMENT
TOPIC: Admin Cooperation
CONCEPTS: Annex type material.
PARTIES:
  Trinidad/Tobago
  UK Great Britain

109044   Bilateral Agreement   **633 UNTS 339**
SIGNED: 30 Sep 66   FORCE: 30 Sep 66
REGISTERED: 22 Mar 68 UK Great Britain
ARTICLES: 10 LANGUAGE: English.
HEADNOTE: PUBLIC OFFICERS
TOPIC: Consul/Citizenship
CONCEPTS: Conditions. Definition of terms. Per-
  sonnel. Wages and salaries. Old age insurance.
  Social security. Payment schedules.
PARTIES:
  Botswana
  UK Great Britain
              ANNEX
642 UNTS 388. UK Great Britain. Amendment
  1 Dec 67. Force 18 Dec 67.
642 UNTS 388.   Botswana.   Amendment
  18 Dec 67. Force 18 Dec 67.

109045   Bilateral Agreement   **633 UNTS 351**
SIGNED: 21 Dec 59   FORCE: 1 Jul 60
REGISTERED: 22 Mar 68 Denmark
ARTICLES: 13 LANGUAGE: German.
HEADNOTE: IMPORTATION   AGRICULTURAL
  PRODUCTS FOODSTUFF
TOPIC: Commodity Trade
CONCEPTS: Annex or appendix reference. IGO ref-
  erence. Establishment of commission. Export
  quotas. Import quotas. Commodity trade.
  Quotas.
INTL ORGS: European Free Trade Association.
PARTIES:
  Denmark
  Switzerland

109046   Bilateral Agreement   **633 UNTS 373**
SIGNED: 15 Apr 67   FORCE: 14 Mar 68
REGISTERED: 29 Mar 68 Greece
ARTICLES: 4 LANGUAGE: French.
HEADNOTE: TAX PROFITS MARITIME AIR TRANS-
  PORT
TOPIC: Taxation
CONCEPTS: IGO reference. Tax exemptions. Air
  transport. Water transport.
INTL ORGS: United Nations.
PROCEDURE: Denunciation. Ratification. Registra-
  tion.
PARTIES:
  Greece
  Yugoslavia

109047   Bilateral Convention   **634 UNTS 3**
SIGNED: 15 Jul 66   FORCE: 13 Aug 67
REGISTERED: 3 Apr 68 Austria
ARTICLES: 13 LANGUAGE: German. French.
HEADNOTE: SUPPLEMENTARY HAGUE CONVEN-
  TION
TOPIC: Admin Cooperation
CONCEPTS: Annex type material.
TREATY REF: 286 UNTS 265.
PARTIES:
  Austria
  France

109048   Bilateral Agreement   **634 UNTS 19**
SIGNED: 19 Oct 67   FORCE: 1 Jan 68
REGISTERED: 3 Apr 68 Austria
ARTICLES: 17 LANGUAGE: German. Czechoslo-
  vakian.
HEADNOTE: PASSENGER TRANSPORT
TOPIC: Land Transport
CONCEPTS: General provisions. Passenger trans-
  port. Transport of goods.
PROCEDURE: Denunciation.
PARTIES:
  Austria
  Czechoslovakia

109049   Bilateral Agreement   **634 UNTS 43**
SIGNED: 21 Nov 67   FORCE: 21 Dec 67
REGISTERED: 3 Apr 68 Austria

ARTICLES: 4 LANGUAGE: German. English.
HEADNOTE: OPERATION AMATEUR RADIO STA-
  TIONS
TOPIC: Gen Communications
CONCEPTS: Conformity with municipal law. Li-
  censes and permits. Amateur radio.
TREATY REF: TIAS 4893.
PROCEDURE: Termination.
PARTIES:
  Austria
  USA (United States)

109050   Bilateral Exchange   **634 UNTS 51**
SIGNED: 14 Dec 67   FORCE: 20 Dec 67
REGISTERED: 3 Apr 68 Austria
ARTICLES: 2 LANGUAGE: German. Czechoslo-
  vakian.
HEADNOTE: ABOLITION VISAS
TOPIC: Visas
CONCEPTS: Visa abolition.
PARTIES:
  Austria
  Czechoslovakia

109051   Bilateral Agreement   **634 UNTS 57**
SIGNED: 15 Jun 67   FORCE: 25 Aug 67
REGISTERED: 3 Apr 68 Bulgaria
ARTICLES: 12 LANGUAGE: Bulgarian. Romanian.
HEADNOTE: TOURISM
TOPIC: Visas
CONCEPTS: Non-prejudice to third party. Border
  traffic and migration. Tourism. Exchange of in-
  formation and documents.
PROCEDURE: Denunciation. Duration. Ratification.
  Renewal or Revival.
PARTIES:
  Bulgaria
  Romania

109052   Bilateral Agreement   **634 UNTS 71**
SIGNED: 8 Dec 65   FORCE: 22 Jun 66
REGISTERED: 4 Apr 68 Denmark
ARTICLES: 5 LANGUAGE: Danish. Norwegian.
HEADNOTE: DELIMITATION   CONTINENTAL
  SHELF
TOPIC: Territory Boundary
CONCEPTS: Markers and definitions. Continental
  shelf.
PARTIES:
  Denmark
  Norway
              ANNEX
643 UNTS 414.   Denmark.   Amendment
  24 Apr 68.
643 UNTS 414. Norway. Amendment 24 Apr 68.

109053   Bilateral Agreement   **634 UNTS 81**
SIGNED: 26 Apr 65   FORCE: 8 Sep 66
REGISTERED: 11 Apr 68 Netherlands
ARTICLES: 15 LANGUAGE: French.
HEADNOTE: ECONOMIC TECHNICAL COOPER-
  ATION
TOPIC: General Economic
CONCEPTS: Territorial application. IGO reference.
  Expropriation. Domestic legislation. Establish-
  ment of commission. Arbitration. Procedure.
  General economics. Compensation. Invest-
  ments. National treatment. Laws and formalities.
  General technical assistance. Air transport.
INTL ORGS: International Court of Justice.
TREATY REF: 499 UNTS 141.
PROCEDURE: Denunciation. Ratification. Renewal
  or Revival.
PARTIES:
  Ivory Coast
  Netherlands

109054   Bilateral Agreement   **634 UNTS 95**
SIGNED: 3 Jun 65   FORCE: 27 Jan 68
REGISTERED: 11 Apr 68 Netherlands
ARTICLES: 9 LANGUAGE: French.
HEADNOTE: EMPLOYMENT VOLUNTEERS
TOPIC: Non-ILO Labor
CONCEPTS: General cooperation. Personnel. Mi-
  grant worker. Tax exemptions. Customs exemp-
  tions. Volunteer programs.
PROCEDURE: Duration. Renewal or Revival. Termi-
  nation.

PARTIES:
  Ivory Coast
  Netherlands

109055   Bilateral Treaty   **634 UNTS 105**
SIGNED: 15 Sep 66   FORCE: 15 Sep 66
REGISTERED: 11 Apr 68 Morocco
ARTICLES: 8 LANGUAGE: French. Arabic.
HEADNOTE: FRIENDSHIP SOLIDARITY
TOPIC: General Amity
CONCEPTS: IGO reference. Friendship and amity.
  General cooperation. Establishment of commis-
  sion.
INTL ORGS: Organization of African Unity. United
  Nations.
TREATY REF: 479 UNTS 39.
PARTIES:
  Morocco
  Senegal

109056   Bilateral Agreement   **634 UNTS 117**
SIGNED: 2 Jun 64   FORCE: 4 Oct 67
REGISTERED: 16 Apr 68 France
ARTICLES: 9 LANGUAGE: French.
HEADNOTE: REPAYMENT ITALIAN BONDS
TOPIC: Finance
CONCEPTS: Bonds. Payment schedules.
PROCEDURE: Ratification.
PARTIES:
  France
  Italy

109057   Bilateral Agreement   **634 UNTS 127**
SIGNED: 7 Feb 64   FORCE: 14 Apr 67
REGISTERED: 17 Apr 68 Argentina
ARTICLES: 21 LANGUAGE: Spanish.
HEADNOTE: AIR SERVICES
TOPIC: Air Transport
CONCEPTS: Definition of terms. IGO reference.
  Conformity with municipal law. General cooper-
  ation. Exchange of information and documents.
  Arbitration. Tariffs. Routes and logistics. Airport
  facilities. Airport equipment. Conditions of air-
  lines operating permission. Overflights and tech-
  nical stops.
INTL ORGS: International Civil Aviation Organiza-
  tion.
TREATY REF: 15 UNTS 295.
PROCEDURE: Denunciation. Ratification.
PARTIES:
  Argentina
  Paraguay

109058   Bilateral Agreement   **634 UNTS 161**
SIGNED: 21 Jun 65   FORCE: 11 May 67
REGISTERED: 17 Apr 68 Argentina
ARTICLES: 13 LANGUAGE: Spanish. English.
HEADNOTE: COMMERCIAL
TOPIC: General Economic
CONCEPTS: Conformity with municipal law. Estab-
  lishment of commission. Export quotas. Reci-
  procity in trade. Most favored nation clause.
PROCEDURE: Ratification. Renewal or Revival. Ter-
  mination.
PARTIES:
  Argentina
  United Arab Rep

109059   Bilateral Exchange   **634 UNTS 177**
SIGNED: 21 Jun 65   FORCE: 21 Jun 65
REGISTERED: 17 Apr 68 Argentina
ARTICLES: 2 LANGUAGE: Spanish. English.
HEADNOTE: PURCHASE WHEAT
TOPIC: Commodity Trade
CONCEPTS: Commodity trade.
PARTIES:
  Argentina
  United Arab Rep

109060   Bilateral Treaty   **634 UNTS 181**
SIGNED: 23 Jan 67   FORCE: 14 Mar 67
REGISTERED: 17 Apr 68 Argentina
ARTICLES: 6 LANGUAGE: Spanish.
HEADNOTE: NAVIGATION
TOPIC: Water Transport
CONCEPTS: Definition of terms. Exceptions and
  exemptions. Negotiation. Inland and territorial
  waters.

TREATY REF: 68 BFSP 91.
PROCEDURE: Ratification.
PARTIES:
 Argentina
 Paraguay

109061 Bilateral Exchange   **634 UNTS 193**
SIGNED: 23 Jan 67   FORCE: 23 Jan 67
REGISTERED: 17 Apr 68 Argentina
ARTICLES: 6 LANGUAGE: Spanish.
HEADNOTE: IMPROVEMENT TRADE RELATIONS
TOPIC: General Trade
CONCEPTS: IGO reference. Establishment of com-
mission.
INTL ORGS: Latin American Free Trade Associa-
tion.
PARTIES:
 Argentina
 Paraguay

109062 Multilateral Exchange   **634 UNTS 199**
SIGNED: 8 Mar 68   FORCE: 7 Apr 68
REGISTERED: 17 Apr 68 Jamaica
ARTICLES: 7 LANGUAGE: English.
HEADNOTE: SUPPRESSION VISAS
TOPIC: Visas
CONCEPTS: Change of circumstances. Time limit.
Visa abolition. Visas. Conformity with municipal
law.
PROCEDURE: Termination.
PARTIES:
 Jamaica SIGNED: 8 Mar 68 FORCE: 7 Apr 68
 Liechtenstein   SIGNED: 8 Mar 68   FORCE:
 7 Apr 68
 Switzerland SIGNED: 8 Mar 68 FORCE: 7 Apr 68

109063 Bilateral Agreement   **634 UNTS 207**
SIGNED: 22 Apr 68   FORCE: 22 Apr 68
REGISTERED: 22 Apr 68 United Nations
ARTICLES: 8 LANGUAGE: English.
HEADNOTE: ACTIVITIES UNICEF
TOPIC: IGO Operations
CONCEPTS: Previous treaty replacement. IGO ref-
erence. Privileges and immunities. General coop-
eration. Exchange of information and docu-
ments. Public information. Claims and settle-
ments. Materials, equipment and services.
Non-bank projects.
INTL ORGS: United Nations.
TREATY REF: 1UNTS15.
PROCEDURE: Amendment. Termination.
PARTIES:
 UN Special Fund
 Syria

109064 Unilateral Instrument   **634 UNTS 217**
SIGNED: 12 Mar 68   FORCE: 13 Mar 68
REGISTERED: 24 Apr 68 United Nations
ARTICLES: 1 LANGUAGE: English.
HEADNOTE: ACCEPTANCE OBLIGATION UN
CHARTER
TOPIC: UN Charter
CONCEPTS: Adherence to UN Charter.
PARTIES:
 Mauritius

109065 Multilateral Convention   **634 UNTS 221**
SIGNED: 6 May 63   FORCE: 28 Mar 68
REGISTERED: 24 Apr 68 Council of Europe
ARTICLES: 13 LANGUAGE: English. French.
HEADNOTE: REDUCTION CASES MULTIPLE NA-
TIONALITY MILITARY OBLIGATIONS
TOPIC: Consul/Citizenship
CONCEPTS: Definition of terms. General provi-
sions. Treaty implementation. Annex or appen-
dix reference. Nationality and citizenship. Dual
nationality.
PROCEDURE: Accession. Denunciation. Ratifica-
tion.
PARTIES:
 Austria SIGNED: 6 May 63
 Belgium SIGNED: 6 May 63
 France SIGNED: 6 May 63 RATIFIED: 26 Jan 65
 FORCE: 28 Mar 68

Italy SIGNED: 6 May 63 RATIFIED: 26 Jan 65
 FORCE: 28 Mar 68
Netherlands SIGNED: 6 May 63
Norway SIGNED: 6 May 63
UK Great Britain SIGNED: 6 May 63

109066 Multilateral Agreement   **634 UNTS 239**
SIGNED: 22 Jan 65   FORCE: 19 Oct 67
REGISTERED: 24 Apr 68 Council of Europe
ARTICLES: 13 LANGUAGE: English. French.
HEADNOTE: PREVENTION BROADCASTS STA-
TIONS OUTSIDE NATIONAL TERRITORIES
TOPIC: Gen Communications
CONCEPTS: Territorial application. IGO reference.
Conformity with municipal law. Penal sanctions.
Bands and frequency allocation.
INTL ORGS: International Telecommunication
Union.
PROCEDURE: Accession. Ratification.
PARTIES:
 Belgium   SIGNED: 22 Jan 65   RATIFIED:
 18 Sep 67 FORCE: 19 Oct 67
 Denmark   SIGNED: 22 Jan 65   RATIFIED:
 22 Sep 65 FORCE: 19 Oct 67
 France SIGNED: 22 Jan 65 RATIFIED: 5 Mar 68
 FORCE: 6 Apr 68
 Germany, West SIGNED: 22 Jan 65
 Greece SIGNED: 22 Jan 65
 Ireland SIGNED: 9 Mar 65
 Italy SIGNED: 17 Feb 65
 Luxembourg SIGNED: 22 Jan 65
 Netherlands SIGNED: 13 Jul 65
 Norway SIGNED: 3 Mar 65
 Sweden   SIGNED: 22 Jan 65   RATIFIED:
 15 Jun 66 FORCE: 19 Oct 67
 UK Great Britain SIGNED: 22 Jan 65 RATIFIED:
 2 Nov 67 FORCE: 3 Dec 67

109067 Multilateral Convention   **634 UNTS 255**
SIGNED: 24 Apr 67   FORCE: 26 Apr 68
REGISTERED: 24 Apr 68 Council of Europe
ARTICLES: 28 LANGUAGE: English. French.
HEADNOTE: ADOPTION CHILDREN
TOPIC: Humanitarian
CONCEPTS: General provisions. Treaty implemen-
tation. Family law.
PROCEDURE: Accession. Denunciation. Ratifica-
tion.
PARTIES:
 Denmark SIGNED: 24 Apr 67
 France SIGNED: 24 Apr 67
 Germany, West SIGNED: 24 Apr 67
 Greece SIGNED: 24 Apr 67
 Ireland SIGNED: 25 Jan 68 RATIFIED: 25 Jan 68
 FORCE: 26 Apr 68
 Italy SIGNED: 24 Apr 67
 Luxembourg SIGNED: 24 Apr 67
 Malta SIGNED: 24 Apr 67 RATIFIED: 22 Sep 67
 FORCE: 26 Apr 68
 Norway SIGNED: 24 Apr 67
 Sweden SIGNED: 24 Apr 67
 UK Great Britain SIGNED: 24 Apr 67 RATIFIED:
 21 Dec 67 FORCE: 26 Apr 68

109068 Multilateral Treaty   **634 UNTS 281**
SIGNED: 14 Feb 67   FORCE: 22 Apr 68
REGISTERED: 26 Apr 68 Mexico
ARTICLES: 31 LANGUAGE: Spanish. French. En-
glish. Portuguese. Chinese.
HEADNOTE: PROHIBITION NUCLEAR WEAPONS
LATIN AMERICA
TOPIC: General Military
CONCEPTS: Definition of terms. Exceptions and
exemptions. Remedies. Treaty implementation.
Annex or appendix reference. IGO reference.
Privileges and immunities. General cooperation.
Exchange of information and documents. In-
spection and observation. Existing tribunals.
Peaceful use. Atomic weapons. Subsidiary or-
gan. Internal structure. Conferences.
INTL ORGS: International Atomic Energy Agency.
International Court of Justice. United Nations.
PROCEDURE: Amendment. Denunciation. Dura-
tion. Ratification. Registration.
PARTIES:
 Bolivia SIGNED: 14 Feb 67
 Brazil SIGNED: 9 May 67 RATIFIED: 29 Jan 68
 FORCE: 22 Apr 68
 Chile SIGNED: 14 Feb 67
 Colombia SIGNED: 14 Feb 67
 Costa Rica SIGNED: 14 Feb 67

Dominican Republic SIGNED: 28 Jul 67
Ecuador SIGNED: 14 Feb 67
El Salvador   SIGNED: 14 Feb 67   RATIFIED:
 22 Apr 68 FORCE: 22 Apr 68
Guatemala SIGNED: 14 Feb 67
Haiti SIGNED: 14 Feb 67
Honduras SIGNED: 14 Feb 67
Jamaica SIGNED: 26 Oct 67
Mexico   SIGNED: 14 Feb 67   RATIFIED:
 20 Sep 67 FORCE: 22 Apr 68
Nicaragua SIGNED: 15 Feb 67
Panama SIGNED: 14 Feb 67
Paraguay SIGNED: 26 Apr 67
Peru SIGNED: 14 Feb 67
Trinidad/Tobago SIGNED: 27 Jun 67
Uruguay SIGNED: 14 Feb 67
Venezuela SIGNED: 14 Feb 67
                    ANNEX
639 UNTS 373. Dominican Republic. Ratification
 14 Jun 68. Declaration 14 Jun 68.
649 UNTS 377.   Nicaragua.   Ratification
 24 Oct 68. Force 24 Oct 68.
659 UNTS 390. Ecuador. Ratification 11 Feb 69.
 Declaration 11 Feb 69.
659 UNTS 390. Bolivia. Ratification 18 Feb 69.
 Declaration 18 Feb 69.

109069 Bilateral Agreement   **635 UNTS 3**
SIGNED: 29 Nov 66   FORCE: 29 Nov 66
REGISTERED: 30 Apr 68 Czechoslovakia
ARTICLES: 9   LANGUAGE: Czechoslovakian.
French.
HEADNOTE: CULTURAL COOPERATION
TOPIC: Culture
CONCEPTS: Exchange of information and docu-
ments. Scholarships and grants. Exchange. Gen-
eral cultural cooperation. Athletes.
PROCEDURE: Denunciation. Duration. Future Pro-
cedures Contemplated. Renewal or Revival.
PARTIES:
 Congo (Brazzaville)
 Czechoslovakia

109070 Bilateral Exchange   **635 UNTS 11**
SIGNED: 15 Jan 68   FORCE: 6 May 68
REGISTERED: 6 May 68 United Nations
ARTICLES: 2 LANGUAGE: French.
HEADNOTE: ESTABLISHMENT UN SOCIAL DE-
FENCE RESEARCH INSTITUTE
TOPIC: Scientific Project
CONCEPTS: Annex or appendix reference. Privi-
leges and immunities. Payment schedules. Sub-
sidiary organ. Internal structure.
TREATY REF: 1 UNTS 15;.
PROCEDURE: Amendment. Denunciation. Dura-
tion. Future Procedures Contemplated. Ratifica-
tion.
PARTIES:
 Italy
 United Nations

109071 Bilateral Agreement   **635 UNTS 21**
SIGNED: 14 Dec 48   FORCE: 17 Jan 67
REGISTERED: 6 May 68 Argentina
ARTICLES: 16 LANGUAGE: Spanish.
HEADNOTE: AIR TRANSPORT
TOPIC: Air Transport
CONCEPTS: Default remedies. Definition of terms.
Annex or appendix reference. IGO reference.
Conformity with municipal law. General cooper-
ation. Licenses and permits. Existing tribunals.
Competency certificate. Routes and logistics. Air
transport. Airport facilities. Airport equipment.
Airworthiness certificates. Conditions of airlines
operating permission. Operating authorizations
and regulations.
INTL ORGS: International Civil Aviation Organiza-
tion.
PROCEDURE: Amendment. Ratification. Registra-
tion. Termination.
PARTIES:
 Argentina
 Chile

109072 Bilateral Agreement   **635 UNTS 69**
SIGNED: 27 Apr 57   FORCE: 17 Oct 67
REGISTERED: 6 May 68 Argentina
ARTICLES: 7 LANGUAGE: Spanish.
HEADNOTE: SOCIAL SECURITY
TOPIC: Non-ILO Labor
CONCEPTS: Establishment of commission. Social
security. Payment schedules.
PROCEDURE: Denunciation. Ratification.

PARTIES:
Argentina
Uruguay

109073   Bilateral Agreement   **635 UNTS 79**
SIGNED: 26 Jan 60   FORCE: 23 Dec 67
REGISTERED: 6 May 68 Argentina
ARTICLES: 8 LANGUAGE: Spanish.
HEADNOTE: CULTURAL
TOPIC: Culture
CONCEPTS: Establishment of commission. Professorships. Exchange. General cultural cooperation. Recognition. Passenger transport.
PROCEDURE: Ratification.
PARTIES:
Argentina
Mexico

109074   Bilateral Treaty   **635 UNTS 91**
SIGNED: 7 Apr 61   FORCE: 19 Jan 66
REGISTERED: 6 May 68 Argentina
ARTICLES: 11 LANGUAGE: Spanish.
HEADNOTE: BOUNDARY RIVER URUGUAY
TOPIC: Territory Boundary
CONCEPTS: Establishment of commission. Navigational conditions. Navigational equipment. Markers and definitions. Frontier peoples and personnel. Regulation of natural resources.
PROCEDURE: Ratification.
PARTIES:
Argentina
Uruguay

109075   Bilateral Agreement   **635 UNTS 111**
SIGNED: 29 Dec 61   FORCE: 29 Mar 67
REGISTERED: 6 May 68 Argentina
ARTICLES: 11 LANGUAGE: Spanish.
HEADNOTE: PROTECTION FRONTIER FORESTS
TOPIC: Territory Boundary
CONCEPTS: Detailed regulations. General cooperation. Fish, wildlife, and natural resources. Markers and definitions.
PROCEDURE: Denunciation.
PARTIES:
Argentina
Chile

109076   Bilateral Exchange   **635 UNTS 125**
SIGNED: 12 Feb 67   FORCE: 12 Feb 67
REGISTERED: 6 May 68 Argentina
ARTICLES: 2 LANGUAGE: Spanish.
HEADNOTE: RIVER TRAFFIC
TOPIC: Water Transport
CONCEPTS: Exceptions and exemptions. IGO reference. Conformity with municipal law. Most favored nation clause. Passenger transport. Transport of goods. Water transport. Inland and territorial waters. Ports and pilotage. Shipwreck and salvage.
INTL ORGS: Latin American Free Trade Association.
TREATY REF: TREATY OF MONTEUJDEN.
PARTIES:
Argentina
Uruguay

109077   Bilateral Convention   **635 UNTS 135**
SIGNED: 11 Jun 63   FORCE: 2 Aug 67
REGISTERED: 6 May 68 Argentina
ARTICLES: 6 LANGUAGE: Spanish. French.
HEADNOTE: MILITARY SERVICE
TOPIC: Milit Servic/Citiz
CONCEPTS: Exceptions and exemptions. Nationality and citizenship. Foreign nationals.
PROCEDURE: Denunciation. Ratification.
PARTIES:
Argentina
Belgium

109078   Bilateral Agreement   **635 UNTS 153**
SIGNED: 21 Mar 64   FORCE: 23 May 67
REGISTERED: 6 May 68 Argentina
ARTICLES: 6 LANGUAGE: French.
HEADNOTE: COMPENSATION ARGENTINE PROPERTY RIGHTS INTEREST NATIONALIZED
TOPIC: Claims and Debts
CONCEPTS: Conformity with municipal law. Expro-

priation. Compensation. Claims and settlements. Lump sum settlements.
PARTIES:
Argentina
Yugoslavia

109079   Bilateral Exchange   **635 UNTS 149**
SIGNED: 12 Sep 64   FORCE: 12 Sep 64
REGISTERED: 6 May 68 Argentina
ARTICLES: 2 LANGUAGE: Spanish.
HEADNOTE: ABOLITION VISAS
TOPIC: Visas
CONCEPTS: Exceptions and exemptions. Visa abolition. Conformity with municipal law.
PARTIES:
Argentina
Colombia

109080   Bilateral Agreement   **635 UNTS 155**
SIGNED: 3 Oct 64   FORCE: 4 Jan 67
REGISTERED: 6 May 68 Argentina
ARTICLES: 26 LANGUAGE: Spanish. French.
HEADNOTE: CULTURAL SCIENTIFIC TECHNICAL COOPERATION
TOPIC: Culture
CONCEPTS: General provisions. Establishment of commission. Exchange. Professorships. Scholarships and grants. General cultural cooperation. Artists. General. Customs declarations. General technical assistance. Mass media exchange. Television.
PROCEDURE: Duration. Renewal or Revival.
PARTIES:
Argentina
France

109081   Bilateral Agreement   **635 UNTS 177**
SIGNED: 21 Oct 64   FORCE: 20 Jul 67
REGISTERED: 6 May 68 Argentina
ARTICLES: 6 LANGUAGE: Spanish.
HEADNOTE: CONSTRUCTION BRIDGE PILCOMAYO RIVER
TOPIC: Specific Property
CONCEPTS: Personnel. Establishment of commission. Indemnities and reimbursements. Markers and definitions. Frontier waterways.
PROCEDURE: Ratification.
PARTIES:
Argentina
Paraguay

109082   Bilateral Agreement   **635 UNTS 189**
SIGNED: 21 Oct 64   FORCE: 20 Jul 67
REGISTERED: 6 May 68 Argentina
ARTICLES: 13 LANGUAGE: Spanish.
HEADNOTE: CONSTRUCTION BRIDGE RIVER PARAGUAY
TOPIC: Specific Property
CONCEPTS: Establishment of commission. Customs exemptions. Frontier waterways.
PROCEDURE: Ratification.
PARTIES:
Argentina
Paraguay

109083   Bilateral Agreement   **635 UNTS 205**
SIGNED: 21 Nov 64   FORCE: 25 Aug 67
REGISTERED: 6 May 68 Argentina
ARTICLES: 9 LANGUAGE: Spanish.
HEADNOTE: CULTURAL
TOPIC: Culture
CONCEPTS: Exchange of information and documents. Establishment of commission. Recognition of degrees. Exchange. Scholarships and grants. Exchange. General cultural cooperation.
PROCEDURE: Ratification. Termination.
PARTIES:
Argentina
Panama

109084   Bilateral Agreement   **635 UNTS 213**
SIGNED: 23 Nov 64   FORCE: 24 Jun 67
REGISTERED: 6 May 68 Argentina
ARTICLES: 9 LANGUAGE: Spanish.
HEADNOTE: CULTURAL
TOPIC: Culture
CONCEPTS: Exchange of information and documents. Establishment of commission. Recogni-

tion of degrees. Exchange. Scholarships and grants. Exchange. General cultural cooperation.
PROCEDURE: Ratification. Termination.
PARTIES:
Argentina
Costa Rica

109085   Bilateral Exchange   **635 UNTS 221**
SIGNED: 12 Oct 65   FORCE: 12 Oct 65
REGISTERED: 6 May 68 Argentina
ARTICLES: 6 LANGUAGE: Spanish.
HEADNOTE: ABOLITION TOURIST VISAS
TOPIC: Visas
CONCEPTS: Exceptions and exemptions. Territorial application. Time limit. Visa abolition. Denial of admission. Conformity with municipal law.
PARTIES:
Argentina
Spain

109086   Bilateral Agreement   **635 UNTS 229**
SIGNED: 5 Nov 65   FORCE: 18 Jul 67
REGISTERED: 6 May 68 Argentina
ARTICLES: 14 LANGUAGE: Spanish. French. Dutch.
HEADNOTE: CULTURAL
TOPIC: Culture
CONCEPTS: Treaty interpretation. Exchange of information and documents. Establishment of commission. Recognition of degrees. Exchange. Scholarships and grants. General cultural cooperation. Artists. Scientific exchange. Mass media exchange.
PROCEDURE: Denunciation. Ratification.
PARTIES:
Argentina
Belgium

109087   Bilateral Agreement   **635 UNTS 247**
SIGNED: 1 Mar 66   FORCE: 25 Aug 67
REGISTERED: 6 May 68 Argentina
ARTICLES: 11 LANGUAGE: Spanish. German.
HEADNOTE: TECHNICAL ECONOMIC COOPERATION
TOPIC: Tech Assistance
CONCEPTS: Use of facilities. Exchange. General economics. Tax exemptions. Customs exemptions. General technical assistance.
PROCEDURE: Duration. Renewal or Revival.
PARTIES:
Argentina
Germany, West

109088   Bilateral Exchange   **635 UNTS 275**
SIGNED: 7 Mar 66   FORCE: 7 Mar 66
REGISTERED: 6 May 68 Argentina
ARTICLES: 2 LANGUAGE: Spanish.
HEADNOTE: MIXED COMMISSION
TOPIC: General Trade
CONCEPTS: Annex type material. Accounting procedures. Claims and settlements.
PARTIES:
Argentina
Uruguay

109089   Bilateral Convention   **635 UNTS 281**
SIGNED: 19 Mar 66   FORCE: 10 Oct 67
REGISTERED: 6 May 68 Argentina
ARTICLES: 15 LANGUAGE: Spanish. Chinese. English.
HEADNOTE: CULTURAL
TOPIC: Culture
CONCEPTS: Treaty interpretation. Tourism. Exchange of information and documents. Legal protection and assistance. Establishment of commission. Recognition of degrees. Professorships. Institute establishment. Exchange. General cultural cooperation. Athletes. Mass media exchange.
PROCEDURE: Ratification. Termination.
PARTIES:
Argentina
Taiwan

109090   Bilateral Agreement   **635 UNTS 301**
SIGNED: 20 May 66   FORCE: 27 Oct 67
REGISTERED: 6 May 68 Argentina
ARTICLES: 31 LANGUAGE: Spanish. Portuguese.

HEADNOTE: SOCIAL SECURITY
TOPIC: Non-ILO Labor
CONCEPTS: Definition of terms. Exceptions and
exemptions. General provisions. Protection of
nationals. General cooperation. Domestic legis-
lation. Old age and invalidity insurance. Old age
insurance. Sickness and invalidity insurance. So-
cial security. Claims and settlements.
PROCEDURE: Amendment. Duration. Ratification.
Renewal or Revival. Termination.
PARTIES:
Argentina
Portugal

109091   Bilateral Agreement   **636 UNTS 3**
SIGNED: 13 Jul 66   FORCE: 19 Oct 67
REGISTERED: 6 May 68 Argentina
ARTICLES: 28 LANGUAGE: Spanish. German.
HEADNOTE: AVOIDANCE DOUBLE TAXATION IN-
COME FORTUNE
TOPIC: Taxation
CONCEPTS: Definition of terms. Immovable prop-
erty. General property. Wages and salaries. Inter-
est rates. Most favored nation clause. General.
Tax exemptions.
PROCEDURE: Ratification. Termination.
PARTIES:
Argentina
Germany, West

109092   Bilateral Exchange   **636 UNTS 75**
SIGNED: 19 Dec 66   FORCE: 19 Dec 66
REGISTERED: 6 May 68 Argentina
ARTICLES: 3 LANGUAGE: Spanish.
HEADNOTE: REGIONAL INTEGRATION PROJECTS
TOPIC: Tech Assistance
CONCEPTS: Veterinary. Vocational training. Gen-
eral technical assistance.
PARTIES:
Argentina
Bolivia

109093   Bilateral Exchange   **636 UNTS 83**
SIGNED: 19 Dec 66   FORCE: 19 Dec 66
REGISTERED: 6 May 68 Argentina
ARTICLES: 2 LANGUAGE: Spanish.
HEADNOTE: DEVELOPMENT FUNDAMENTAL ED-
UCATION PROGRAMS
TOPIC: Education
CONCEPTS: Exchange.
PARTIES:
Argentina
Bolivia

109094   Bilateral Exchange   **636 UNTS 89**
SIGNED: 19 Dec 66   FORCE: 19 Dec 66
REGISTERED: 6 May 68 Argentina
ARTICLES: 2 LANGUAGE: Spanish.
HEADNOTE: LINKING TELECOMMUNICATIONS
SYSTEMS
TOPIC: Telecommunications
CONCEPTS: Domestic legislation. Communica-
tions linkage.
PARTIES:
Argentina
Bolivia

109095   Bilateral Exchange   **636 UNTS 95**
SIGNED: 31 Mar 67   FORCE: 29 Apr 67
REGISTERED: 6 May 68 Argentina
ARTICLES: 3 LANGUAGE: Spanish. English.
HEADNOTE: AMATEUR RADIO OPERATOR AU-
THORIZATIONS
TOPIC: Gen Communications
CONCEPTS: Licenses and permits. Amateur radio.
PARTIES:
Argentina
USA (United States)

109096   Bilateral Exchange   **636 UNTS 103**
SIGNED: 31 Mar 67   FORCE: 29 Apr 67
REGISTERED: 6 May 68 Argentina
ARTICLES: 4 LANGUAGE: Spanish. English.
HEADNOTE: EXCHANGE THIRD PARTY MES-
SAGES
TOPIC: Gen Communications
CONCEPTS: Amateur radio. Amateur third party
message.

PARTIES:
Argentina
USA (United States)

109097   Bilateral Exchange   **636 UNTS 111**
SIGNED: 6 Nov 67   FORCE: 6 Nov 67
REGISTERED: 6 May 68 Argentina
ARTICLES: 2 LANGUAGE: Spanish.
HEADNOTE: DOUBLE TAXATION CONCES-
SIONAIRE DINING CARS
TOPIC: Taxation
CONCEPTS: Taxation. General.
PARTIES:
Argentina
Chile

109098   Bilateral Exchange   **636 UNTS 117**
SIGNED: 5 Jul 67   FORCE: 5 Jul 67
REGISTERED: 6 May 68 Austria
ARTICLES: 3 LANGUAGE: English. German.
HEADNOTE: COMMONWEALTH WAR CEMETERY
KLAGENFURT
TOPIC: Other Military
CONCEPTS: General cooperation. War graves. Up-
keep of war graves.
TREATY REF: 217 UNTS 223.
PARTIES:
Australia
Austria

109099   Bilateral Exchange   **636 UNTS 125**
SIGNED: 8 Nov 67   FORCE: 8 Nov 67
REGISTERED: 8 May 68 Austria
ARTICLES: 3 LANGUAGE: English. German.
HEADNOTE: COMMONWEALTH WAR CEMETERY
KLAGENFURT
TOPIC: Other Military
CONCEPTS: General cooperation. War graves. Up-
keep of war graves.
PARTIES:
Austria
South Africa

109100   Bilateral Exchange   **636 UNTS 133**
SIGNED: 10 Jan 68   FORCE: 10 Jan 68
REGISTERED: 8 May 68 Austria
ARTICLES: 3 LANGUAGE: English. German.
HEADNOTE: COMMONWEALTH WAR CEMETERY
KLAGENFURT
TOPIC: Other Military
CONCEPTS: General cooperation. War graves. Up-
keep of war graves.
PARTIES:
Austria
Pakistan

109101   Bilateral Exchange   **636 UNTS 141**
SIGNED: 28 Feb 68   FORCE: 28 Feb 68
REGISTERED: 8 May 68 Austria
ARTICLES: 3 LANGUAGE: English. German.
HEADNOTE: COMMONWEALTH WAR CEMETERY
KLAGENFURT
TOPIC: Other Military
CONCEPTS: General cooperation. General eco-
nomics. Interest rates. Payment schedules. Do-
mestic obligation. General technical assistance.
War graves. Upkeep of war graves.
PROCEDURE: Ratification.
PARTIES:
Austria
Canada

109102   Bilateral Convention   **636 UNTS 149**
SIGNED: 24 May 66   FORCE: 5 Jan 68
REGISTERED: 8 May 68 Austria
ARTICLES: 27 LANGUAGE: English. German.
HEADNOTE: AVOIDANCE DOUBLE TAXATION IN-
COME
TOPIC: Taxation
CONCEPTS: Definition of terms. Conformity with
municipal law. Exchange of information and doc-
uments. Immovable property. General property.
Wages and salaries. General. Tax exemptions.
PROCEDURE: Ratification. Termination.
PARTIES:
Austria
Ireland

109103   Bilateral Agreement   **636 UNTS 197**
SIGNED: 20 Dec 66   FORCE: 1 Jan 68
REGISTERED: 8 May 68 Austria
ARTICLES: 30 LANGUAGE: German. Spanish.
HEADNOTE: AVOIDANCE DOUBLE TAXATION IN-
COME FORTUNE
TOPIC: Taxation
CONCEPTS: Definition of terms. Immovable prop-
erty. General property. Wages and salaries. Tax-
ation. General. Tax exemptions.
PROCEDURE: Denunciation. Ratification. Termina-
tion.
PARTIES:
Austria
Spain

109104   Bilateral Exchange   **636 UNTS 267**
SIGNED: 14 Dec 67   FORCE: 13 Jan 68
REGISTERED: 9 May 68 Austria
ARTICLES: 6 LANGUAGE: English. German.
HEADNOTE: MUTUAL ABOLITION VISAS
TOPIC: Visas
CONCEPTS: Change of circumstances. Annex type
material. Visa abolition. Denial of admission.
Visas.
PROCEDURE: Termination.
PARTIES:
Austria
Cyprus

109105   Bilateral Agreement   **636 UNTS 276**
SIGNED: 10 May 68   FORCE: 10 May 68
REGISTERED: 10 May 68 United Nations
ARTICLES: 6 LANGUAGE: English.
HEADNOTE: OPERATIONAL ASSISTANCE
TOPIC: IGO Operations
CONCEPTS: General provisions. Annex or appen-
dix reference. Previous treaty replacement. Per-
sonnel. Procedure. Domestic obligation. General
technical assistance. General aid. IGO obliga-
tions.
TREATY REF: 423 UNTS 122; 330 UNTS 109.
PROCEDURE: Amendment. Termination.
PARTIES:
State/IGO Group
Malaysia

109106   Bilateral Agreement   **636 UNTS 294**
SIGNED: 20 Apr 68   FORCE: 20 Apr 68
REGISTERED: 13 May 68 United Nations
ARTICLES: 6 LANGUAGE: English.
HEADNOTE: OPERATIONAL ASSISTANCE
TOPIC: IGO Operations
CONCEPTS: General provisions. Annex or appen-
dix reference. Previous treaty replacement. Per-
sonnel. Procedure. Domestic obligation. General
technical assistance. General aid. IGO obliga-
tions.
TREATY REF: 435 UNTS 167.
PROCEDURE: Amendment. Termination.
PARTIES:
State/IGO Group
Nigeria

109107   Bilateral Agreement   **636 UNTS 313**
SIGNED: 12 Dec 64   FORCE: 12 Dec 64
REGISTERED: 20 May 68 Denmark
ARTICLES: 8 LANGUAGE: English.
HEADNOTE: TECHNICAL COOPERATION
TOPIC: Tech Assistance
CONCEPTS: Indemnities and reimbursements. Tax
exemptions. Domestic obligation. General tech-
nical assistance. Assistance.
PARTIES:
Denmark
Pakistan

109108   Bilateral Agreement   **636 UNTS 326**
SIGNED: 21 May 68   FORCE: 21 May 68
REGISTERED: 21 May 68 United Nations
ARTICLES: 6 LANGUAGE: English.
HEADNOTE: PROVISION TECHNICAL ASSIS-
TANCE
TOPIC: Tech Assistance
CONCEPTS: Exceptions and exemptions. General
provisions. IGO reference. Privileges and immu-
nities. Use of facilities. Domestic obligation. Gen-
eral technical assistance. Financial programs.
IGO obligations.

INTL ORGS: United Nations Special Fund.
TREATY REF: 1 UNTS 15; 33 UNTS 261; 374
UNTS 147.
PROCEDURE: Amendment. Termination.
PARTIES:
State/IGO Group
Australia

109109   Bilateral Agreement   **637 UNTS 0**
SIGNED: 22 Sep 67   FORCE: 8 Apr 68
REGISTERED: 21 May 68 Belgium
ARTICLES: 0 LANGUAGE: French. Dutch.
HEADNOTE: COMMERCIAL ROAD TRANSPORT
TOPIC: Land Transport
CONCEPTS: Visas. Exchange of information and
documents. Commercial road vehicles. Driving
permits. Motor vehicles and combinations.
PROCEDURE: Duration.
PARTIES:
Belgium
Romania

109110   Bilateral Agreement   **637 UNTS 0**
SIGNED: 2 May 68   FORCE: 2 May 68
REGISTERED: 21 May 68 IBRD (World Bank)
ARTICLES: 0 LANGUAGE: English.
HEADNOTE: TARBELA DEVELOPMENT FUND
TOPIC: Direct Aid
CONCEPTS: IGO reference. Procedure. World
Bank projects. Loan regulations. Plans and stan-
dards.
INTL ORGS: United Nations.
TREATY REF: 444UNTS259, 503UNTS388.
PROCEDURE: Termination.
PARTIES:
State/IGO Group
IBRD (World Bank)

109111   Bilateral Agreement   **637 UNTS 0**
SIGNED: 4 Dec 64   FORCE: 4 Dec 64
REGISTERED: 21 May 68 IAEA (Atom Energy)
ARTICLES: 0 LANGUAGE: English.
HEADNOTE: SAFEGUARDS
TOPIC: Atomic Energy
CONCEPTS: Procedure. Atomic energy assistance.
Nuclear materials. Peaceful use.
TREATY REF: 342UNTS29.
PROCEDURE: Amendment. Duration. Termination.
PARTIES:
State/IGO Group
IAEA (Atom Energy)

109112   Bilateral Agreement   **637 UNTS 0**
SIGNED: 19 Jun 67   FORCE: 6 Dec 67
REGISTERED: 21 May 68 IAEA (Atom Energy)
ARTICLES: 0 LANGUAGE: English.
HEADNOTE: SAFEGUARDS
TOPIC: Atomic Energy
CONCEPTS: Procedure. Atomic energy assistance.
Nuclear materials. Peaceful use.
TREATY   REF: 388UNTS287,   276UNTS3,
471UNTS334, 374UNTS147.
PROCEDURE: Amendment. Duration.
PARTIES:
State/IGO Group
IAEA (Atom Energy)

109113   Bilateral Agreement   **637 UNTS 0**
SIGNED: 26 Sep 67   FORCE: 26 Sep 67
REGISTERED: 21 May 68 IAEA (Atom Energy)
ARTICLES: 0 LANGUAGE: English.
HEADNOTE: IAEA SAFEGUARDS ON ATOMIC AC-
TIVITY
TOPIC: Atomic Energy
TREATY REF: 633UNTS73, 325UNTS185.
PARTIES:
Japan
IAEA (Atom Energy)

109114   Bilateral Agreement   **637 UNTS 0**
SIGNED: 5 Jan 68   FORCE: 5 Jan 68
REGISTERED: 21 May 68 IAEA (Atom Energy)
ARTICLES: 0 LANGUAGE: English.
HEADNOTE: SAFEGUARDS
TOPIC: Atomic Energy
CONCEPTS: Procedure. Atomic energy assistance.
Nuclear materials. Peaceful use.

TREATY   REF: 240UNTS129,   316UNTS358,
578UNTS268, ETC..
PARTIES:
State/IGO Group
IAEA (Atom Energy)

109115   Bilateral Agreement   **637 UNTS 0**
SIGNED: 28 Feb 68   FORCE: 29 Feb 68
REGISTERED: 21 May 68 IAEA (Atom Energy)
ARTICLES: 0 LANGUAGE: English.
HEADNOTE: SAFEGUARDS
TOPIC: Atomic Energy
CONCEPTS: Procedure. Atomic energy assistance.
Nuclear materials. Peaceful use.
TREATY   REF: 235UNTS245,   280UNTS378,
335UNTS310, ETC..
PROCEDURE: Amendment. Duration. Termination.
PARTIES:
State/IGO Group
IAEA (Atom Energy)

109116   Bilateral Agreement   **637 UNTS 0**
SIGNED: 18 Oct 67   FORCE: 23 Dec 67
REGISTERED: 23 May 68 Denmark
ARTICLES: 0 LANGUAGE: English.
HEADNOTE: LOAN
TOPIC: Loans and Credits
CONCEPTS: Loan and credit. Credit provisions.
Purchase authorization. Loan repayment. Terms
of loan.
PROCEDURE: Duration. Termination.
PARTIES:
Denmark
Zambia

109117   Bilateral Agreement   **637 UNTS 0**
SIGNED: 25 May 68   FORCE: 25 May 68
REGISTERED: 25 May 68 United Nations
ARTICLES: 0 LANGUAGE: English.
HEADNOTE: UN   CONFERENCE   EXPLORATION
PEACEFUL USE OUTER SPACE
TOPIC: IGO Operations
CONCEPTS: IGO reference. Privileges and immuni-
ties. Status of experts. Conferences.
INTL ORGS: United Nations.
PROCEDURE: Amendment. Duration.
PARTIES:
Austria
United Nations

109118   Bilateral Agreement   **637 UNTS 0**
SIGNED: 25 May 68   FORCE: 25 May 68
REGISTERED: 25 May 68 United Nations
ARTICLES: 0 LANGUAGE: English.
HEADNOTE: ARRANGEMENTS UN DEVELOPMENT
PROGRAM GOVERNING COUNCIL
TOPIC: IGO Operations
CONCEPTS: Status of experts. Conferences.
TREATY   REF: 1UNTS15,   90UNTS327,
600UNTS93.
PROCEDURE: Amendment. Duration.
PARTIES:
Austria
United Nations

109119   Bilateral Agreement   **637 UNTS 0**
SIGNED: 8 May 67   FORCE: 5 May 68
REGISTERED: 27 May 68 Belgium
ARTICLES: 0 LANGUAGE: Dutch. English.
HEADNOTE: CULTURAL
TOPIC: Culture
CONCEPTS: Teacher and student exchange. Cul-
ture. Exchange. General cultural cooperation.
PROCEDURE: Denunciation. Ratification.
PARTIES:
Belgium
Canada

109120   Bilateral Agreement   **637 UNTS 0**
SIGNED: 29 May 68   FORCE: 29 May 68
REGISTERED: 29 May 68 United Nations
ARTICLES: 0 LANGUAGE: English.
HEADNOTE: OPERATIONAL ASSISTANCE
TOPIC: Direct Aid
CONCEPTS: Procedure. Assistance. Procedure. Ex-
tension of functions. Special status. IGO opera-
tions.
TREATY REF: 410UNTS240, 489UNTS91,400.

PROCEDURE: Termination.
PARTIES:
State/IGO Group
Sierra Leone

109121   Multilateral Instrument   **637 UNTS 0**
SIGNED: 27 May 66   FORCE: 28 Dec 67
REGISTERED: 29 May 68 Cameroon
ARTICLES: 0 LANGUAGE: French.
HEADNOTE: AFRICAN MALAGASY COMMON OR-
GANIZATION
TOPIC: IGO Establishment
CONCEPTS: IGO reference. Establishment. Proce-
dure. Headquarters and facilities. Liaison with
other IGO's. Internal structure.
INTL ORGS: Organization of African Unity. United
Nations.
TREATY REF: 479UNTS39.
PROCEDURE: Amendment.
PARTIES:
Cameroon
Chad
Central Afri Rep
Congo (Zaire)
Dahomey
Gabon
Ivory Coast
Malagasy
Niger
Senegal
Togo
Upper Volta

109122   Bilateral Agreement   **637 UNTS 0**
SIGNED: 29 Mar 68   FORCE: 29 Mar 68
REGISTERED: 29 May 68 Thailand
ARTICLES: 0 LANGUAGE: Thai. German.
HEADNOTE: FINANCIAL ASSISTANCE YANHEE
POWER SYSTEM
TOPIC: Direct Aid
CONCEPTS: Assistance. Loan and credit. Credit
provisions. Internal loans. Passenger transport.
PARTIES:
Germany, West
Thailand

109123   Bilateral Agreement   **637 UNTS 0**
SIGNED: 30 Mar 68   FORCE: 30 Mar 68
REGISTERED: 30 Mar 68 United Nations
ARTICLES: 0 LANGUAGE: English.
HEADNOTE: UNICEF ACTIVITIES
TOPIC: IGO Operations
CONCEPTS: Claims and settlements. Extension of
functions. IGO status. Special status. Status of
experts. Socio-economic development.
TREATY REF: 1UNTS15, 90UNTS327.
PROCEDURE: Amendment. Termination.
PARTIES:
Barbados
UNICEF (Children)

109124   Bilateral Agreement   **637 UNTS 0**
SIGNED: 9 Dec 66   FORCE: 10 Nov 67
REGISTERED: 4 Jun 68 Czechoslovakia
ARTICLES: 0 LANGUAGE: Russian.
HEADNOTE: QUARANTINE PLANTS
TOPIC: Sanitation
CONCEPTS: Quarantine. Border control. Insect
control.
PROCEDURE: Denunciation.
PARTIES:
Czechoslovakia
Mongolia

109125   Bilateral Exchange   **637 UNTS 0**
SIGNED: 19 Jul 66   FORCE: 19 Jul 66
REGISTERED: 4 Jun 68 UK Great Britain
ARTICLES: 0 LANGUAGE: English.
HEADNOTE: EMOLUMENTS PUBLIC SERVICE OF-
FICERS
TOPIC: Admin Cooperation
CONCEPTS: Personnel. Economic assistance.
PROCEDURE: Termination.
PARTIES:
Malawi
UK Great Britain

109126 Bilateral Exchange **637 UNTS 0**
SIGNED: 21 Nov 66 FORCE: 21 Nov 66
REGISTERED: 4 Jun 68 UK Great Britain
ARTICLES: 0 LANGUAGE: English.
HEADNOTE: CONDITIONS OF SERVICE BRITISH OFFICERS
TOPIC: Admin Cooperation
CONCEPTS: Personnel. General technical assistance. Assistance. Special projects.
PROCEDURE: Termination.
PARTIES:
Malawi
UK Great Britain

109127 Bilateral Agreement **637 UNTS 0**
SIGNED: 17 Jul 67 FORCE: 21 Dec 67
REGISTERED: 4 Jun 68 UK Great Britain
ARTICLES: 0 LANGUAGE: English.
HEADNOTE: AVOIDANCE DOUBLE TAXATION
TOPIC: Taxation
CONCEPTS: Taxation. General. Tax exemptions.
PARTIES:
Malaysia
UK Great Britain

109128 Bilateral Agreement **638 UNTS 3**
SIGNED: 1 Aug 67 FORCE: 1 Aug 67
REGISTERED: 4 Jun 68 UK Great Britain
ARTICLES: 11 LANGUAGE: English.
HEADNOTE: COMMERCIAL DEBTS
TOPIC: Claims and Debts
CONCEPTS: Exchange of information and documents. Responsibility and liability. Artists. Interest rates. Claims and settlements. Debts.
PARTIES:
Indonesia
UK Great Britain

109129 Bilateral Agreement **638 UNTS 17**
SIGNED: 24 Nov 67 FORCE: 24 Nov 67
REGISTERED: 4 Jun 68 UK Great Britain
ARTICLES: 18 LANGUAGE: English. French.
HEADNOTE: ESTABLISHMENT USE TELEMETRY STATIONS FALKLAND ISLANDS
TOPIC: Gen Communications
CONCEPTS: General provisions. Annex or appendix reference. Privileges and immunities. Exchange of information and documents. Use of facilities. Arbitration. Existing tribunals. Recognition of degrees. Financial programs. Special projects. Transport of goods. Satellites. Services. Headquarters and facilities.
PROCEDURE: Amendment. Duration. Renewal or Revival. Termination.
PARTIES:
Eur Space Research
UK Great Britain

109130 Bilateral Agreement **638 UNTS 41**
SIGNED: 5 Jan 68 FORCE: 5 Jan 68
REGISTERED: 4 Jun 68 UK Great Britain
ARTICLES: 7 LANGUAGE: English. Russian.
HEADNOTE: SETTLEMENT FINANCIAL PROPERTY CLAIMS
TOPIC: Claims and Debts
CONCEPTS: Accounting procedures. Claims and settlements. Lump sum settlements.
PARTIES:
UK Great Britain
USSR (Soviet Union)

109131 Bilateral Agreement **638 UNTS 53**
SIGNED: 9 Apr 65 FORCE: 28 Aug 67
REGISTERED: 6 Jun 68 Hungary
ARTICLES: 24 LANGUAGE: Hungarian. German.
HEADNOTE: PASSPORT CUSTOMS CONTROL
TOPIC: Visas
CONCEPTS: Definition of terms. General provisions. Previous treaty replacement. Border traffic and migration. Personnel. Conciliation. Land transport. Frontier waterways. Frontier crossing points.
TREATY REF: 122 LTS 69.
PROCEDURE: Denunciation. Ratification.
PARTIES:
Austria
Hungary

109132 Bilateral Treaty **638 UNTS 105**
SIGNED: 9 Apr 65 FORCE: 26 Sep 67
REGISTERED: 6 Jun 68 Hungary
ARTICLES: 19 LANGUAGE: Hungarian. German.
HEADNOTE: MATTERS SUCCESSION
TOPIC: Recognition
CONCEPTS: General provisions. Conformity with municipal law. Recognition and enforcement of legal decisions. Immovable property. General property. Succession. Jurisdiction. Recognition of legal documents.
PROCEDURE: Denunciation. Duration. Ratification.
PARTIES:
Austria
Hungary

109133 Bilateral Treaty **638 UNTS 135**
SIGNED: 9 Apr 65 FORCE: 26 Sep 67
REGISTERED: 6 Jun 68 Hungary
ARTICLES: 31 LANGUAGE: Hungarian. German.
HEADNOTE: LEGAL RELATIONS CIVIL CASES OFFICAL DOCUMENTS
TOPIC: Admin Cooperation
CONCEPTS: Conditions. Notarial acts and services. Exchange of information and documents. Legal protection and assistance. Recognition of legal documents. Indemnities and reimbursements.
PROCEDURE: Denunciation. Duration. Ratification.
PARTIES:
Austria
Hungary

109134 Multilateral Convention **638 UNTS 185**
SIGNED: 18 Oct 50 FORCE: 17 Jan 63
REGISTERED: 7 Jun 68 France
ARTICLES: 11 LANGUAGE: French.
HEADNOTE: PROTECTION BIRDS
TOPIC: Specific Resources
CONCEPTS: Exceptions and exemptions. Previous treaty replacement. Wildlife.
TREATY REF: 1902 INTL CONVENTION.
PROCEDURE: Accession. Denunciation. Duration. Ratification.
PARTIES:
Austria SIGNED: 18 Oct 50
Belgium SIGNED: 18 Oct 50 RATIFIED: 17 Jan 55 FORCE: 17 Jan 63
Bulgaria SIGNED: 18 Oct 50
France SIGNED: 18 Oct 50
Greece SIGNED: 18 Oct 50
Iceland RATIFIED: 29 Oct 55 FORCE: 17 Jan 63
Luxembourg RATIFIED: 19 Oct 62 FORCE: 17 Jan 63
Monaco SIGNED: 18 Oct 50
Netherlands SIGNED: 31 May 54 RATIFIED: 30 Jan 55 FORCE: 17 Jan 63
Portugal SIGNED: 18 Oct 50
Spain SIGNED: 18 Oct 50 RATIFIED: 24 Aug 55 FORCE: 17 Jan 63
Sweden SIGNED: 18 Oct 50
Switzerland SIGNED: 18 Oct 50 RATIFIED: 26 Oct 55 FORCE: 17 Jan 63
Turkey SIGNED: 18 Oct 50

109136 Bilateral Agreement **638 UNTS 201**
SIGNED: 20 Jun 66 FORCE: 20 Jun 66
REGISTERED: 12 Jun 68 Australia
ARTICLES: 7 LANGUAGE: English.
HEADNOTE: TRADE
TOPIC: General Trade
CONCEPTS: Exceptions and exemptions. Conformity with municipal law. General cooperation. General trade. Export quotas. Import quotas. Payment schedules. Most favored nation clause.
PROCEDURE: Duration. Termination.
PARTIES:
Australia
Poland

109137 Bilateral Agreement **638 UNTS 209**
SIGNED: 5 Dec 67 FORCE: 5 Dec 67
REGISTERED: 12 Jun 68 Australia
ARTICLES: 8 LANGUAGE: English.
HEADNOTE: TRADE
TOPIC: General Trade
CONCEPTS: Exceptions and exemptions. Conformity with municipal law. General cooperation. General trade. Export quotas. Import quotas. Payment schedules. Most favored nation clause.
PROCEDURE: Duration. Termination.
PARTIES:
Australia
Hungary

109138 Bilateral Agreement **638 UNTS 217**
SIGNED: 2 Nov 67 FORCE: 8 Feb 68
REGISTERED: 17 Jun 68 Denmark
ARTICLES: 14 LANGUAGE: English.
HEADNOTE: LOAN
TOPIC: Loans and Credits
CONCEPTS: Change of circumstances. Conditions. General provisions. Remedies. IGO reference. Conformity with municipal law. Arbitration. Conciliation. Accounting procedures. Interest rates. Payment schedules. Use restrictions. Loan and credit.
INTL ORGS: International Court of Justice.
PROCEDURE: Ratification. Termination.
PARTIES:
Denmark
Iran

109139 Multilateral Convention **638 UNTS 235**
SIGNED: 16 Mar 61 FORCE: 26 Jan 68
REGISTERED: 17 Jun 68 Belgium
ARTICLES: 27 LANGUAGE: French. Dutch.
HEADNOTE: REGULATION IMPORTS EXPORTS TRANSIT TRAFFIC
TOPIC: General Trade
CONCEPTS: Territorial application. General provisions. Conformity with municipal law. General cooperation. Legal protection and assistance. Export quotas. Import quotas. Trade procedures. Land transport.
PROCEDURE: Ratification.
PARTIES:
Belgium SIGNED: 26 Jan 68 FORCE: 26 Jan 68
Luxembourg SIGNED: 26 Jan 68 FORCE: 26 Jan 68
Netherlands SIGNED: 26 Jan 68 FORCE: 26 Jan 68

109140 Bilateral Agreement **639 UNTS 3**
SIGNED: 22 Feb 67 FORCE: 14 Jun 68
REGISTERED: 21 Jun 68 Belgium
ARTICLES: 10 LANGUAGE: French. Dutch.
HEADNOTE: CULTURAL
TOPIC: Culture
CONCEPTS: Establishment of commission. Exchange. General cultural cooperation. Research cooperation.
PROCEDURE: Denunciation. Ratification.
PARTIES:
Belgium
Luxembourg

109141 Bilateral Exchange **639 UNTS 13**
SIGNED: 10 Jun 66 FORCE: 10 Jun 66
REGISTERED: 24 Jun 68 USA (United States)
ARTICLES: 2 LANGUAGE: English.
HEADNOTE: FACILITATE ESTABLISHMENT FERRY SERVICE
TOPIC: Water Transport
CONCEPTS: Water transport.
TREATY REF: 204 LTS 15; 66 UNTS 277.
PARTIES:
Canada
USA (United States)

109142 Bilateral Agreement **639 UNTS 25**
SIGNED: 11 Oct 63 FORCE: 5 Feb 68
REGISTERED: 24 Jun 68 IAEA (Atom Energy)
ARTICLES: 10 LANGUAGE: French.
HEADNOTE: ESTABLISHMENT INTERNATIONAL CENTER THEORETICAL PHYSICS
TOPIC: IGO Establishment
CONCEPTS: IGO reference. Privileges and immunities. Personnel. Arbitration. Conciliation. Institute establishment. Payment schedules. Domestic obligation. IGO obligations.
INTL ORGS: International Court of Justice.
PROCEDURE: Amendment. Duration. Renewal or Revival.
PARTIES:
Italy
IAEA (Atom Energy)

109143 Bilateral Agreement **639 UNTS 43**
SIGNED: 20 Feb 65 FORCE: 1 Jan 68
REGISTERED: 27 Jun 68 Denmark
ARTICLES: 8 LANGUAGE: English.
HEADNOTE: TRADE AGRICULTURAL GOODS
TOPIC: Commodity Trade
CONCEPTS: IGO reference. Technical and commercial staff. Commodity trade. Agricultural commodities.
INTL ORGS: European Economic Community. European Free Trade Association.
PARTIES:
Denmark
Portugal

109144 Bilateral Agreement **639 UNTS 61**
SIGNED: 25 Jun 68 FORCE: 25 Jun 68
REGISTERED: 1 Jul 68 United Nations
ARTICLES: 8 LANGUAGE: English.
HEADNOTE: ACTIVITIES UNICEF
TOPIC: IGO Operations
CONCEPTS: IGO reference. Privileges and immunities. General cooperation. Exchange of information and documents. Public information. Claims and settlements. Assistance. Materials, equipment and services.
INTL ORGS: United Nations.
TREATY REF: 1 UNTS 15.
PARTIES:
Botswana
UNICEF (Children)

109145 Bilateral Agreement **639 UNTS 71**
SIGNED: 7 May 68 FORCE: 7 May 68
REGISTERED: 1 Jul 68 United Nations
ARTICLES: 6 LANGUAGE: French.
HEADNOTE: ARRANGEMENTS REGIONAL MEETING YOUTH EMPLOYMENT NATIONAL DEVELOPMENT
TOPIC: IGO Operations
CONCEPTS: Privileges and immunities. Legal protection and assistance. Personnel. Use of facilities. Materials, equipment and services. Passenger transport. Conferences.
TREATY REF: 1 UNTS 15; 33 UNTS 261.
PARTIES:
Niger
United Nations

109146 Bilateral Instrument **639 UNTS 81**
SIGNED: 2 Jul 68 FORCE: 2 Jul 68
REGISTERED: 2 Jul 68 United Nations
ARTICLES: 3 LANGUAGE: English.
HEADNOTE: STUDIES ECONOMIC COOPERATION
TOPIC: General Economic
CONCEPTS: Detailed regulations. Annex or appendix reference. Assistance.
PARTIES:
Nigeria
United Nations

109147 Bilateral Exchange **639 UNTS 99**
SIGNED: 11 Jul 66 FORCE: 11 Jul 66
REGISTERED: 3 Jul 68 UK Great Britain
ARTICLES: 4 LANGUAGE: English.
HEADNOTE: SETTLEMENT DISPUTE TAXATION LIABILITY EURATOM EMPLOYEES
TOPIC: Taxation
CONCEPTS: Annex or appendix reference. Arbitration.
PARTIES:
Euratom
UK Great Britain

109148 Bilateral Agreement **639 UNTS 115**
SIGNED: 15 Sep 67 FORCE: 31 Jan 68
REGISTERED: 5 Jul 68 IDA (Devel Assoc)
ARTICLES: 7 LANGUAGE: English.
HEADNOTE: DEVELOPMENT CREDIT
TOPIC: Non-IBRD Project
CONCEPTS: Definition of terms. Detailed regulations. Remedies. Annex or appendix reference. Use restrictions. Loan and credit. Credit provisions.
PROCEDURE: Termination.
PARTIES:
IDA (Devel Assoc)
Uganda

109149 Bilateral Agreement **639 UNTS 147**
SIGNED: 14 Sep 67 FORCE: 4 Jun 68
REGISTERED: 5 Jul 68 IBRD (World Bank)
ARTICLES: 5 LANGUAGE: English.
HEADNOTE: GUARANTEE
TOPIC: IBRD Project
CONCEPTS: Annex or appendix reference. Bonds. Loan regulations. Loan guarantee. Guarantor non-interference.
PARTIES:
IBRD (World Bank)
Tunisia

109150 Bilateral Agreement **639 UNTS 187**
SIGNED: 25 Jan 68 FORCE: 2 Mar 68
REGISTERED: 5 Jul 68 IBRD (World Bank)
ARTICLES: 5 LANGUAGE: English.
HEADNOTE: GUARANTEE
TOPIC: IBRD Project
CONCEPTS: Annex or appendix reference. Bonds. Loan regulations. Loan guarantee. Guarantor non-interference.
PARTIES:
Argentina
IBRD (World Bank)

109151 Bilateral Agreement **639 UNTS 221**
SIGNED: 22 Nov 67 FORCE: 26 Feb 68
REGISTERED: 5 Jul 68 IBRD (World Bank)
ARTICLES: 5 LANGUAGE: English.
HEADNOTE: GUARANTEE
TOPIC: IBRD Project
CONCEPTS: Annex or appendix reference. Bonds. Loan regulations. Loan guarantee. Guarantor non-interference.
PARTIES:
Ceylon (Sri Lanka)
IBRD (World Bank)

109152 Bilateral Agreement **640 UNTS 3**
SIGNED: 26 Jan 68 FORCE: 25 Apr 68
REGISTERED: 5 Jul 68 IBRD (World Bank)
ARTICLES: 5 LANGUAGE: English.
HEADNOTE: GUARANTEE
TOPIC: IBRD Project
CONCEPTS: Annex or appendix reference. Bonds. Terms of loan. Loan regulations. Loan guarantee. Guarantor non-interference.
PARTIES:
Mexico
IBRD (World Bank)

109153 Bilateral Agreement **640 UNTS 29**
SIGNED: 29 Feb 68 FORCE: 29 Feb 68
REGISTERED: 9 Jul 68 Denmark
ARTICLES: 12 LANGUAGE: English.
HEADNOTE: LOAN
TOPIC: Loans and Credits
CONCEPTS: Detailed regulations. Annex or appendix reference. Accounting procedures. Interest rates. Payment schedules. Use restrictions. Loan and credit.
PROCEDURE: Duration.
PARTIES:
Denmark
Malaysia

109154 Bilateral Agreement **640 UNTS 49**
SIGNED: 27 Feb 68 FORCE: 27 Feb 68
REGISTERED: 15 Jul 68 Czechoslovakia
ARTICLES: 22 LANGUAGE: Slovak. Hungarian.
HEADNOTE: ESTABLISHMENT RIVER ADMINISTRATION RAJKA-GONYU SECTOR DANUBE
TOPIC: IGO Establishment
CONCEPTS: Definition of terms. IGO reference. Border traffic and migration. Exchange of information and documents. Juridical personality. Jurisdiction. Procedure. Indemnities and reimbursements. Hydro-electric power. Navigational conditions. Headquarters and facilities. Liaison with other IGO's. Internal structure.
INTL ORGS: Danube Commission.
PROCEDURE: Denunciation. Duration.
PARTIES:
Czechoslovakia
Hungary

109155 Multilateral Agreement **640 UNTS 87**
SIGNED: 6 Nov 67 FORCE: 6 Nov 67
REGISTERED: 17 Jul 68 Ethiopia
ARTICLES: 8 LANGUAGE: English. Amharic.
HEADNOTE: WAR CEMETERIES GRAVES MEMORIALS ETHIOPIA
TOPIC: Other Military
CONCEPTS: War graves. Responsibility for war dead. Upkeep of war graves. Establishment of war cemeteries.
PARTIES:
Australia SIGNED: 18 May 67 FORCE: 6 Nov 67
Canada SIGNED: 12 Apr 67 FORCE: 6 Nov 67
Ethiopia SIGNED: 6 Nov 67 FORCE: 6 Nov 67
India SIGNED: 12 Apr 67 FORCE: 6 Nov 67
New Zealand SIGNED: 12 Apr 67 FORCE: 6 Nov 67
Pakistan SIGNED: 6 Nov 67 FORCE: 6 Nov 67
UK Great Britain SIGNED: 12 Apr 67 FORCE: 6 Nov 67

109156 Bilateral Treaty **640 UNTS 101**
SIGNED: 19 Apr 67 FORCE: 31 Jan 68
REGISTERED: 17 Jul 68 Gambia
ARTICLES: 9 LANGUAGE: English. French.
HEADNOTE: ASSOCIATION & EXECUTIVE SECRETARIAT
TOPIC: General Amity
CONCEPTS: IGO reference. Peaceful relations. General cooperation. Establishment of commission.
INTL ORGS: Organization of African Unity. United Nations.
PROCEDURE: Ratification.
PARTIES:
Gambia
Senegal

109157 Bilateral Agreement **640 UNTS 111**
SIGNED: 5 May 67 FORCE: 15 Mar 68
REGISTERED: 18 Jul 68 Finland
ARTICLES: 3 LANGUAGE: Finnish. Russian.
HEADNOTE: BOUNDARY CONTINENTAL SHELF
TOPIC: Specific Resources
CONCEPTS: Markers and definitions. Continental shelf.
PROCEDURE: Ratification.
PARTIES:
Finland
USSR (Soviet Union)

109158 Bilateral Agreement **640 UNTS 121**
SIGNED: 22 Jul 68 FORCE: 22 Jul 68
REGISTERED: 22 Jul 68 United Nations
ARTICLES: 7 LANGUAGE: English.
HEADNOTE: SEMINAR ELIMINATION RACIAL DISCRIMINATION
TOPIC: IGO Operations
CONCEPTS: General provisions. Privileges and immunities. Responsibility and liability. Use of facilities. Domestic obligation. Conferences. IGO obligations.
PARTIES:
India
United Nations

109159 Multilateral Convention **640 UNTS 133**
SIGNED: 5 Apr 66 FORCE: 21 Jul 68
REGISTERED: 30 Jul 68 IMCO (Maritime Org)
ARTICLES: 34 LANGUAGE: English. French.
HEADNOTE: LOAD LINES
TOPIC: Water Transport
CONCEPTS: Change of circumstances. Definition of terms. Exceptions and exemptions. Territorial application. General provisions. Treaty implementation. Annex or appendix reference. IGO reference. Privileges and immunities. Exchange of information and documents. Recognition of legal documents. Registration certificate. Navigational conditions. Tonnage.
INTL ORGS: United Nations.
PROCEDURE: Amendment. Accession. Denunciation. Ratification. Registration.
PARTIES:
Argentina SIGNED: 5 Apr 66
Australia SIGNED: 4 Jul 66
Belgium SIGNED: 5 Apr 66
Brazil SIGNED: 5 Apr 66
Bulgaria SIGNED: 5 Apr 66
Canada SIGNED: 5 Apr 66

Taiwan SIGNED: 5 Apr 66 RATIFIED: 24 Jul 68
FORCE: 24 Oct 68
Congo (Zaire) RATIFIED: 20 May 68 FORCE:
20 Aug 68
France SIGNED: 5 Apr 66 RATIFIED: 30 Nov 66
FORCE: 21 Jul 68
Ghana SIGNED: 5 Apr 66
Greece SIGNED: 5 Apr 66 RATIFIED: 12 Jul 68
FORCE: 21 Jul 68
Iceland SIGNED: 5 Apr 66
India SIGNED: 5 Apr 66 RATIFIED: 19 Apr 68
FORCE: 21 Jul 68
Ireland SIGNED: 5 Apr 66
Israel SIGNED: 5 Apr 66 RATIFIED: 5 Jul 67
FORCE: 21 Jul 68
Italy SIGNED: 5 Apr 66 RATIFIED: 19 Apr 68
FORCE: 21 Jul 68
Ivory Coast SIGNED: 5 Apr 66
Japan SIGNED: 5 Apr 66 RATIFIED: 15 May 68
FORCE: 15 Aug 68
Korea, South SIGNED: 5 Apr 66
Kuwait SIGNED: 5 Apr 66
Liberia SIGNED: 5 Apr 66 RATIFIED: 8 May 67
FORCE: 21 Jul 68
Madagascar RATIFIED: 16 Jan 67 FORCE:
21 Jul 68
Malagasy SIGNED: 5 Apr 66
Maldive Islands RATIFIED: 29 Jan 68 FORCE:
21 Jul 68
Mauritania RATIFIED: 4 Dec 67 FORCE:
21 Jul 68
Morocco RATIFIED: 19 Jan 68 FORCE: 21 Jul 68
Netherlands Netherlands Antilles RATIFIED:
21 Jul 67 FORCE: 21 Jul 67
Netherlands SIGNED: 4 Jul 66 RATIFIED:
21 Jul 67 FORCE: 21 Jul 68
Netherlands Surinam RATIFIED: 21 Jul 67
FORCE: 21 Jul 67
New Zealand SIGNED: 30 Jun 66
Norway SIGNED: 1 Jul 66 RATIFIED: 18 Mar 68
FORCE: 21 Jul 68
Pakistan SIGNED: 5 Apr 66
Panama SIGNED: 13 May 66 FORCE: 21 Jul 68
Peru SIGNED: 5 Apr 66 RATIFIED: 18 Jan 67
FORCE: 21 Jul 68
Philippines SIGNED: 1 Jul 66
Poland SIGNED: 5 Apr 66
South Africa SIGNED: 5 Apr 66 RATIFIED:
14 Dec 66 FORCE: 21 Jul 68
Somalia RATIFIED: 30 Mar 67 FORCE: 21 Jul 68
Spain SIGNED: 5 Apr 66 RATIFIED: 1 Jul 68
FORCE: 1 Oct 68
Sweden RATIFIED: 28 Jul 67 FORCE: 21 Jul 68
Switzerland SIGNED: 11 May 66 RATIFIED:
23 Apr 68 FORCE: 23 Jul 68
Trinidad/Tobago SIGNED: 5 Apr 66 RATIFIED:
24 Aug 66 FORCE: 21 Jul 68
Tunisia SIGNED: 5 Jul 66 RATIFIED: 23 Aug 66
FORCE: 21 Jul 68
United Arab Rep SIGNED: 5 Apr 66
UK Great Britain SIGNED: 5 Apr 66 RATIFIED:
11 Jul 67 FORCE: 21 Jul 68
USA (United States) SIGNED: 5 Apr 66 RATI-
FIED: 17 Nov 66 FORCE: 21 Jul 68
USSR (Soviet Union) SIGNED: 4 Jul 66 FORCE:
21 Jul 68
Venezuela SIGNED: 5 Apr 66
Vietnam, South RATIFIED: 14 Jul 68 FORCE:
14 Sep 68
Yugoslavia SIGNED: 5 Apr 66
ANNEX
642 UNTS 390. Turkey. Accession 5 Aug 68.
Force 5 Nov 68.
642 UNTS 390. Australia. Acceptance 29 Jul 68.
Force 29 Oct 68.
645 UNTS 388. Kuwait. Acceptance 28 Aug 68.
Force 28 Nov 68.
645 UNTS 388. Ireland. Acceptance 28 Aug 68.
Force 28 Nov 68.
649 UNTS 379. Ghana. Acceptance 25 Sep 68.
Force 25 Dec 68.
651 UNTS 408. Nigeria. Accession 14 Nov 68.
Force 14 Feb 69.
657 UNTS 404. Cuba. Accession 6 Feb 69. Force
6 May 69.

109160 Bilateral Agreement **642 UNTS 3**
SIGNED: 26 Jan 67 FORCE: 23 Feb 67
REGISTERED: 31 Jul 68 IBRD (World Bank)
ARTICLES: 1 LANGUAGE: English.
HEADNOTE: TECHNICAL ASSISTANCE STUDY
TOPIC: IBRD Project

CONCEPTS: Exchange of information and docu-
ments. Plans and standards.
PARTIES:
Morocco
IBRD (World Bank)

109161 Bilateral Agreement **642 UNTS 13**
SIGNED: 3 Jul 68 FORCE: 3 Jul 68
REGISTERED: 31 Jul 68 WHO (World Health)
ARTICLES: 6 LANGUAGE: English.
HEADNOTE: TECHNICAL ADVISORY ASSISTANCE
TOPIC: Direct Aid
CONCEPTS: General provisions. Privileges and im-
munities. Use of facilities. Payment schedules.
Assistance. IGO obligations.
TREATY REF: 33 UNTS 261.
PROCEDURE: Amendment. Termination.
PARTIES:
Guyana
WHO (World Health)

109162 Bilateral Agreement **642 UNTS 25**
SIGNED: 18 May 67 FORCE: 18 May 67
REGISTERED: 2 Aug 68 Romania
ARTICLES: 7 LANGUAGE: English.
HEADNOTE: TRADE
TOPIC: General Trade
CONCEPTS: Exceptions and exemptions. General
cooperation. General trade. Reciprocity in trade.
Trade procedures. Purchase authorizations.
Most favored nation clause.
PROCEDURE: Duration. Termination.
PARTIES:
Australia
Romania

109163 Bilateral Agreement **642 UNTS 33**
SIGNED: 10 Oct 67 FORCE: 14 Dec 67
REGISTERED: 2 Aug 68 Romania
ARTICLES: 8 LANGUAGE: English.
HEADNOTE: TRADE
TOPIC: General Trade
CONCEPTS: Annex or appendix reference. Estab-
lishment of commission. Arbitration. General
trade. Export quotas. Import quotas. Trade proce-
dures. Currency. Most favored nation clause.
PROCEDURE: Duration. Ratification. Renewal or
Revival. Termination.
PARTIES:
Ecuador
Romania

109164 Bilateral Agreement **642 UNTS 47**
SIGNED: 3 Aug 67 FORCE: 25 Oct 67
REGISTERED: 2 Aug 68 Romania
ARTICLES: 6 LANGUAGE: Romanian. German.
HEADNOTE: TECHNICAL ECONOMIC COOPER-
ATION
TOPIC: General Economic
CONCEPTS: Previous treaty replacement. Domes-
tic legislation. Establishment of commission.
General economics. General technical assis-
tance.
PROCEDURE: Denunciation.
PARTIES:
Germany, West
Romania

109165 Bilateral Agreement **642 UNTS 63**
SIGNED: 23 Nov 66 FORCE: 26 Oct 67
REGISTERED: 2 Aug 68 Romania
ARTICLES: 16 LANGUAGE: English.
HEADNOTE: LONG-TERM TRADE
TOPIC: General Trade
CONCEPTS: Exceptions and exemptions. Annex or
appendix reference. Previous treaty replace-
ment. Conformity with municipal law. General
cooperation. Private contracts. Establishment of
commission. General trade. Reciprocity in trade.
Trade agencies. Payment schedules. Most fa-
vored nation clause. Customs exemptions.
PROCEDURE: Duration. Ratification. Renewal or
Revival. Termination.
PARTIES:
Ghana
Romania

109166 Bilateral Agreement **642 UNTS 79**
SIGNED: 23 Nov 66 FORCE: 26 Oct 67
REGISTERED: 2 Aug 68 Romania
ARTICLES: 9 LANGUAGE: English.
HEADNOTE: LONG-TERM PAYMENTS
TOPIC: Loans and Credits
CONCEPTS: Previous treaty replacement. Estab-
lishment of commission. Accounting proce-
dures. Payment schedules.
PROCEDURE: Duration. Ratification. Renewal or
Revival. Termination.
PARTIES:
Ghana
Romania

109167 Bilateral Agreement **642 UNTS 89**
SIGNED: 1 Dec 66 FORCE: 21 Jul 67
REGISTERED: 2 Aug 68 Romania
ARTICLES: 16 LANGUAGE: French.
HEADNOTE: TRADE PAYMENTS
TOPIC: General Trade
CONCEPTS: Annex or appendix reference. Confor-
mity with municipal law. General trade. Export
quotas. Import quotas. Trade procedures. Ac-
counting procedures. Currency. Payment sched-
ules. Most favored nation clause.
PROCEDURE: Duration. Ratification. Renewal or
Revival. Termination.
PARTIES:
Guinea
Romania

109168 Bilateral Agreement **642 UNTS 103**
SIGNED: 5 Jan 67 FORCE: 5 Jan 67
REGISTERED: 2 Aug 68 Romania
ARTICLES: 16 LANGUAGE: Romanian. Spanish.
HEADNOTE: ESTABLISHMENT CONSULAR TRADE
MISSIONS
TOPIC: Consul/Citizenship
CONCEPTS: Definition of terms. Consular relations
establishment. Inviolability. Privileges and im-
munities. Diplomatic correspondence. Non-
diplomatic delegations. Use of facilities. Trade
agencies. Customs exemptions.
PROCEDURE: Denunciation.
PARTIES:
Romania
Spain

109169 Bilateral Agreement **642 UNTS 129**
SIGNED: 14 Nov 66 FORCE: 30 Aug 67
REGISTERED: 2 Aug 68 Romania
ARTICLES: 20 LANGUAGE: English.
HEADNOTE: LONG-TERM TRADE
TOPIC: General Trade
CONCEPTS: Annex or appendix reference. Previ-
ous treaty replacement. General cooperation.
Private contracts. Establishment of commission.
General trade. Export quotas. Import quotas.
Trade procedures. Payment schedules. Quotas.
Most favored nation clause. Customs exemp-
tions.
PROCEDURE: Amendment. Duration. Ratification.
Renewal or Revival. Termination.
PARTIES:
Romania
United Arab Rep

109170 Bilateral Agreement **642 UNTS 141**
SIGNED: 14 Nov 66 FORCE: 30 Aug 67
REGISTERED: 2 Aug 68 Romania
ARTICLES: 14 LANGUAGE: English.
HEADNOTE: LONG-TERM PAYMENTS
TOPIC: Finance
CONCEPTS: Previous treaty replacement. Private
contracts. Accounting procedures. Currency.
Payment schedules.
PROCEDURE: Amendment. Duration. Ratification.
Renewal or Revival. Termination.
PARTIES:
Romania
United Arab Rep

109171 Bilateral Agreement **642 UNTS 155**
SIGNED: 20 Apr 67 FORCE: 17 Dec 67
REGISTERED: 2 Aug 68 Romania
ARTICLES: 9 LANGUAGE: English.
HEADNOTE: TECHNICAL SCIENTIFIC COOPER-
ATION

TOPIC: Scientific Project
CONCEPTS: Exchange of information and documents. Use of facilities. Research cooperation. Scientific exchange. General technical assistance. Assistance.
PROCEDURE: Denunciation. Duration. Ratification. Renewal or Revival.
PARTIES:
　Romania
　Somalia

109172　Bilateral Agreement　**642 UNTS 163**
SIGNED: 1 Mar 67　　　FORCE: 12 Sep 67
REGISTERED: 2 Aug 68 Romania
ARTICLES: 18 LANGUAGE: French.
HEADNOTE: TRANSPORT GOODS ROAD
TOPIC: General Transport
CONCEPTS: Definition of terms. Visas. General cooperation. Exchange of information and documents. Domestic legislation. Licenses and permits. Conciliation. Trade procedures. Tax exemptions. Customs exemptions. Registration certificate. Transport of goods.
PROCEDURE: Denunciation. Duration. Renewal or Revival.
PARTIES:
　Romania
　Sweden

109173　Bilateral Agreement　**642 UNTS 181**
SIGNED: 26 Jun 67　　　FORCE: 19 Oct 67
REGISTERED: 2 Aug 68 Romania
ARTICLES: 2 LANGUAGE: French. Romanian.
HEADNOTE: COOPERATION PHYSICAL CULTURE SPORTS YOUTH
TOPIC: Culture
CONCEPTS: Athletes.
PROCEDURE: Duration. Ratification. Termination.
PARTIES:
　France
　Romania

109174　Bilateral Agreement　**642 UNTS 191**
SIGNED: 8 Aug 67　　　FORCE: 8 Feb 67
REGISTERED: 2 Aug 68 Romania
ARTICLES: 17 LANGUAGE: Romanian. Italian.
HEADNOTE: CULTURAL
TOPIC: Culture
CONCEPTS: Tourism. General cooperation. Establishment of commission. Exchange. Scholarships and grants. Exchange. General cultural cooperation. Athletes. Research cooperation. Publications exchange.
PROCEDURE: Denunciation. Duration. Ratification. Renewal or Revival.
PARTIES:
　Italy
　Romania

109175　Bilateral Agreement　**642 UNTS 213**
SIGNED: 8 Aug 67　　　FORCE: 7 Dec 67
REGISTERED: 2 Aug 68 Romania
ARTICLES: 16 LANGUAGE: Romanian. Italian.
HEADNOTE: FILMS COPRODUCTION
TOPIC: Culture
CONCEPTS: Detailed regulations. Personnel. Establishment of commission. Indemnities and reimbursements. Mass media exchange.
PROCEDURE: Denunciation. Duration. Ratification. Renewal or Revival.
PARTIES:
　Italy
　Romania

109176　Bilateral Agreement　**642 UNTS 235**
SIGNED: 24 Apr 68　　　FORCE: 24 Apr 68
REGISTERED: 5 Aug 68 Singapore
ARTICLES: 9 LANGUAGE: English.
HEADNOTE: TRADE
TOPIC: General Trade
CONCEPTS: General cooperation. Establishment of commission. Establishment of trade relations. Export quotas. Import quotas. Trade agencies. Trade procedures. Payment schedules. Most favored nation clause.
PROCEDURE: Duration. Renewal or Revival. Termination.

PARTIES:
　Israel
　Singapore

109177　Bilateral Exchange　**642 UNTS 245**
SIGNED: 24 Apr 58　　　FORCE: 24 Apr 58
REGISTERED: 8 Aug 68 UK Great Britain
ARTICLES: 2 LANGUAGE: English.
HEADNOTE: ESTABLISHING INTERNATIONAL DESERT LOCUST INFORMATION SERVICE
TOPIC: IGO Operations
CONCEPTS: Institute establishment. Research cooperation. Subsidiary organ.
PARTIES:
　FAO (Food Agri)
　UK Great Britain

109178　Bilateral Exchange　**642 UNTS 253**
SIGNED: 20 Feb 61　　　FORCE: 20 Feb 61
REGISTERED: 8 Aug 68 UK Great Britain
ARTICLES: 2 LANGUAGE: English.
HEADNOTE: DESERT LOCUST INFORMATION SERVICE
TOPIC: IGO Operations
CONCEPTS: General cooperation. Exchange of information and documents. Subsidiary organ.
TREATY REF: 642 UNTS 245.
PARTIES:
　FAO (Food Agri)
　UK Great Britain

109179　Bilateral Exchange　**642 UNTS 263**
SIGNED: 13 Jul 67　　　FORCE: 13 Jul 67
REGISTERED: 8 Aug 68 UK Great Britain
ARTICLES: 2 LANGUAGE: English.
HEADNOTE: DESERT LOCUST INFORMATION SERVICE
TOPIC: IGO Operations
CONCEPTS: General cooperation. Exchange of information and documents. IGO operations.
TREATY REF: 642 UNTS 253.
PARTIES:
　FAO (Food Agri)
　UK Great Britain

109180　Bilateral Agreement　**642 UNTS 271**
SIGNED: 30 Sep 67　　　FORCE: 25 Nov 67
REGISTERED: 8 Aug 68 UK Great Britain
ARTICLES: 9 LANGUAGE: English. Italian.
HEADNOTE: FILMS COPRODUCTION
TOPIC: Culture
CONCEPTS: Definition of terms. Annex or appendix reference. Use of facilities. Establishment of commission. Mass media.
TREATY REF: 473 UNTS 153.
PROCEDURE: Amendment. Denunciation. Duration. Renewal or Revival.
PARTIES:
　Italy
　UK Great Britain

109181　Bilateral Exchange　**642 UNTS 293**
SIGNED: 5 Dec 67　　　FORCE: 5 Dec 67
REGISTERED: 8 Aug 68 UK Great Britain
ARTICLES: 2 LANGUAGE: English.
HEADNOTE: PERSONNEL TRAINING ARMED FORCES MALAYSIA
TOPIC: Military Mission
CONCEPTS: Annex or appendix reference. Military assistance missions. Airforce-army-navy personnel ratio.
TREATY REF: 785 UNTS 59.
PARTIES:
　Malaysia
　UK Great Britain

109182　Bilateral Agreement　**642 UNTS 325**
SIGNED: 30 Jun 67　　　FORCE: 30 Jun 67
REGISTERED: 8 Aug 68 UK Great Britain
ARTICLES: 27 LANGUAGE: English. French.
HEADNOTE: EXCHANGE MONEY ORDERS
TOPIC: Postal Service
CONCEPTS: Annex or appendix reference. Previous treaty replacement. Conformity with municipal law. Exchange of information and documents. Accounting procedures. Exchange rates and regulations. Payment schedules. Money or-

ders and postal checks. Rates and charges. Advice lists and orders.
TREATY REF: 88 UNTS 287.
PROCEDURE: Denunciation.
PARTIES:
　UK Great Britain
　Yugoslavia

109183　Bilateral Agreement　**642 UNTS 357**
SIGNED: 29 Aug 67　　　FORCE: 11 Mar 68
REGISTERED: 8 Aug 68 Denmark
ARTICLES: 11 LANGUAGE: French.
HEADNOTE: CULTURAL
TOPIC: Culture
CONCEPTS: Tourism. Establishment of commission. Exchange. Scholarships and grants. General cultural cooperation. Artists. Athletes. Research cooperation.
PROCEDURE: Duration. Ratification. Termination.
PARTIES:
　Denmark
　Romania

109184　Bilateral Convention　**643 UNTS 3**
SIGNED: 3 Jul 67　　　FORCE: 11 Jul 68
REGISTERED: 14 Aug 68 South Africa
ARTICLES: 28 LANGUAGE: English. Afrikaans. German.
HEADNOTE: DOUBLE TAXATION
TOPIC: Taxation
CONCEPTS: Definition of terms. Territorial application. General consular functions. Personnel. Immovable property. Taxation. General. Air transport. Water transport.
PROCEDURE: Ratification. Termination.
PARTIES:
　South Africa
　Switzerland

109185　Bilateral Agreement　**643 UNTS 75**
SIGNED: 27 Oct 67　　　FORCE: 15 May 68
REGISTERED: 15 Aug 68 Finland
ARTICLES: 25 LANGUAGE: Finnish. French.
HEADNOTE: INTERNATIONAL ROAD TRANSPORT
TOPIC: General Transport
CONCEPTS: Exceptions and exemptions. General provisions. Conformity with municipal law. Establishment of commission. Claims and settlements. Quotas. Registration certificate. Passenger transport. Transport of goods.
PROCEDURE: Denunciation. Ratification.
PARTIES:
　Finland
　France

109186　Bilateral Agreement　**643 UNTS 95**
SIGNED: 10 Nov 67　　　FORCE: 4 Jun 68
REGISTERED: 15 Aug 68 Finland
ARTICLES: 19 LANGUAGE: English.
HEADNOTE: INTERNATIONAL TRANSPORT ROAD
TOPIC: Land Transport
CONCEPTS: Licenses and permits. Payment schedules. Passenger transport. Transport of goods. Road rules.
PROCEDURE: Denunciation. Duration. Renewal or Revival.
PARTIES:
　Finland
　Hungary

109187　Bilateral Agreement　**643 UNTS 107**
SIGNED: 7 Mar 68　　　FORCE: 16 May 68
REGISTERED: 15 Aug 68 Finland
ARTICLES: 7 LANGUAGE: Finnish. Russian.
HEADNOTE: PASSENGER TRAFFIC
TOPIC: General Transport
CONCEPTS: Passenger transport. Navigational conditions. Water transport.
TREATY REF: 48 UNTS 149.
PROCEDURE: Ratification.
PARTIES:
　Finland
　USSR (Soviet Union)

109188　Bilateral Agreement　**643 UNTS 121**
SIGNED: 22 Jun 67　　　FORCE: 22 Jun 67
REGISTERED: 20 Aug 68 USSR (Soviet Union)
ARTICLES: 10 LANGUAGE: Russian. French.

HEADNOTE: TRADE
TOPIC: Mostfavored Nation
CONCEPTS: Annex or appendix reference. Establishment of trade relations. Export quotas. Import quotas. Most favored nation clause.
PROCEDURE: Denunciation. Duration. Renewal or Revival.
PARTIES:
Chad
USSR (Soviet Union)

109189 Bilateral Agreement **643 UNTS 135**
SIGNED: 27 Mar 67   FORCE: 11 Oct 67
REGISTERED: 20 Aug 68 USSR (Soviet Union)
ARTICLES: 10 LANGUAGE: Russian. Arabic. English.
HEADNOTE: CULTURAL
TOPIC: Culture
CONCEPTS: Exchange. Exchange. General cultural cooperation. Research cooperation.
PROCEDURE: Duration. Ratification. Termination.
PARTIES:
Kuwait
USSR (Soviet Union)

109190 Bilateral Agreement **643 UNTS 153**
SIGNED: 24 Feb 67   FORCE: 31 Aug 67
REGISTERED: 20 Aug 68 USSR (Soviet Union)
ARTICLES: 7 LANGUAGE: Russian. Turkish.
HEADNOTE: VETERINARY
TOPIC: Scientific Project
CONCEPTS: Disease control. Liaison with other IGO's. Pasturage in frontier zones.
PROCEDURE: Ratification. Termination.
PARTIES:
Turkey
USSR (Soviet Union)

109191 Bilateral Agreement **643 UNTS 179**
SIGNED: 26 May 67   FORCE: 26 May 67
REGISTERED: 20 Aug 68 USSR (Soviet Union)
ARTICLES: 12 LANGUAGE: Russian. English.
HEADNOTE: ECONOMIC TECHNICAL COOPERATION
TOPIC: General Economic
CONCEPTS: General cooperation. General economics. Interest rates. Payment schedules. Domestic obligation. General technical assistance.
PROCEDURE: Ratification.
PARTIES:
USSR (Soviet Union)
Zambia

109192 Bilateral Agreement **643 UNTS 203**
SIGNED: 22 Aug 66   FORCE: 31 Mar 68
REGISTERED: 20 Aug 68 USSR (Soviet Union)
ARTICLES: 10 LANGUAGE: Russian. Persian.
HEADNOTE: CULTURAL RELATIONS
TOPIC: Culture
CONCEPTS: Peaceful relations. Private contracts. Exchange. General cultural cooperation. Athletes.
PROCEDURE: Duration. Ratification. Termination.
PARTIES:
Iran
USSR (Soviet Union)

109193 Bilateral Exchange **643 UNTS 217**
SIGNED: 29 Dec 67   FORCE: 29 Dec 67
REGISTERED: 21 Aug 68 UK Great Britain
ARTICLES: 2 LANGUAGE: English. Portuguese.
HEADNOTE: AVOIDANCE DOUBLE TAXATION PROFITS SHIPPING AIR TRANSPORT
TOPIC: Taxation
CONCEPTS: Taxation. Tax exemptions. Air transport. Water transport.
PARTIES:
Brazil
UK Great Britain

109194 Bilateral Exchange **643 UNTS 225**
SIGNED: 22 Nov 67   FORCE: 1 Jan 68
REGISTERED: 21 Aug 68 UK Great Britain
ARTICLES: 2 LANGUAGE: English. French.
HEADNOTE: GRANTING LICENSES AMATEUR RADIO OPERATORS
TOPIC: Gen Communications
CONCEPTS: Licenses and permits. Amateur radio.

PARTIES:
France
UK Great Britain

109195 Bilateral Exchange **643 UNTS 231**
SIGNED: 14 Jul 67   FORCE: 14 Jul 67
REGISTERED: 21 Aug 68 UK Great Britain
ARTICLES: 1 LANGUAGE: English.
HEADNOTE: STATUS FORCES
TOPIC: Status of Forces
CONCEPTS: Annex or appendix reference. Status of military forces.
PARTIES:
Kenya
UK Great Britain

109196 Bilateral Exchange **643 UNTS 254**
SIGNED: 14 Jul 67   FORCE: 14 Jul 67
REGISTERED: 21 Aug 68 UK Great Britain
ARTICLES: 2 LANGUAGE: English.
HEADNOTE: ESTABLISHING BRITISH TRAINING TEAM
TOPIC: Military Mission
CONCEPTS: Annex or appendix reference. Military training.
PARTIES:
Kenya
UK Great Britain

109197 Bilateral Agreement **643 UNTS 271**
SIGNED: 12 Oct 66   FORCE: 29 May 68
REGISTERED: 21 Aug 68 Netherlands
ARTICLES: 9 LANGUAGE: Dutch. Portuguese.
HEADNOTE: CULTURAL
TOPIC: Culture
CONCEPTS: Territorial application. Establishment of commission. Exchange. Professorships. General cultural cooperation. Research cooperation.
PROCEDURE: Duration. Ratification. Renewal or Revival. Termination.
PARTIES:
Brazil
Netherlands

109198 Bilateral Exchange **643 UNTS 285**
SIGNED: 19 Nov 66   FORCE: 25 Jan 68
REGISTERED: 21 Aug 68 Netherlands
ARTICLES: 2 LANGUAGE: English.
HEADNOTE: TREATY APPLICATION
TOPIC: Admin Cooperation
CONCEPTS: Annex type material.
TREATY REF: 197 UNTS 341.
PARTIES:
Kenya
Netherlands

109199 Bilateral Agreement **643 UNTS 293**
SIGNED: 15 Dec 67   FORCE: 28 Dec 65
REGISTERED: 22 Aug 68 Denmark
ARTICLES: 8 LANGUAGE: Danish. Spanish.
HEADNOTE: SCIENTIFIC TECHNICAL COOPERATION
TOPIC: Scientific Project
CONCEPTS: Annex or appendix reference. Personnel. Research cooperation. Financial programs. General technical assistance.
PROCEDURE: Denunciation. Ratification.
PARTIES:
Chile
Denmark

109200 Bilateral Exchange **643 UNTS 343**
SIGNED: 27 Mar 68   FORCE: 27 Mar 68
REGISTERED: 22 Aug 68 South Africa
ARTICLES: 2 LANGUAGE: English. French.
HEADNOTE: LAUNCHING EOLE BALLOONS
TOPIC: Scientific Project
CONCEPTS: Research cooperation.
PARTIES:
France
South Africa

109201 Bilateral Convention **643 UNTS 349**
SIGNED: 10 Mar 66   FORCE: 9 Jul 68
REGISTERED: 29 Aug 68 Denmark
ARTICLES: 12 LANGUAGE: Danish. Italian. English.

HEADNOTE: AVOIDANCE DOUBLE TAXATION ESTATES
TOPIC: Taxation
CONCEPTS: Definition of terms. Territorial application. Diplomatic privileges. Immovable property. General property. Debts. General.
PROCEDURE: Denunciation. Ratification.
PARTIES:
Denmark
Italy

109202 Bilateral Agreement **643 UNTS 371**
SIGNED: 26 Feb 68   FORCE: 10 Jun 68
REGISTERED: 29 Aug 68 Denmark
ARTICLES: 10 LANGUAGE: English.
HEADNOTE: SALVAGE OPERATIONS
TOPIC: Water Transport
CONCEPTS: Navigational conditions. Inland and territorial waters. Shipwreck and salvage.
PROCEDURE: Denunciation. Duration. Ratification. Renewal or Revival.
PARTIES:
Denmark
Poland

109203 Bilateral Agreement **643 UNTS 383**
SIGNED: 15 Nov 67   FORCE: 31 May 68
REGISTERED: 29 Aug 68 Denmark
ARTICLES: 5 LANGUAGE: English.
HEADNOTE: ECONOMIC INDUSTRIAL TECHNICAL COOPERATION
TOPIC: General Economic
CONCEPTS: Establishment of commission. General economics. General technical assistance.
PROCEDURE: Denunciation. Termination.
PARTIES:
Denmark
Poland

109204 Bilateral Convention **0 UNTS 0**
SIGNED: 5 Apr 66   FORCE: 1 Feb 68
REGISTERED: 29 Aug 68 Netherlands
ARTICLES: 0
HEADNOTE: SOCIAL SECURITY
TOPIC: Non-ILO Labor
CONCEPTS: Old age insurance. Sickness and invalidity insurance. Social security. Unemployment.
PROCEDURE: Duration. Termination.
PARTIES:
Netherlands
Turkey

109205 Bilateral Exchange **0 UNTS 0**
SIGNED: 21 Jun 67   FORCE: 21 Jun 67
REGISTERED: 29 Aug 68 New Zealand
ARTICLES: 0
HEADNOTE: OPERATION AMATEUR RADIO
TOPIC: Gen Communications
CONCEPTS: Amateur radio.
TREATY REF: TIAS 4893.
PARTIES:
New Zealand
USA (United States)

109206 Bilateral Exchange **0 UNTS 0**
SIGNED: 2 Apr 68   FORCE: 2 Apr 68
REGISTERED: 29 Aug 68 New Zealand
ARTICLES: 0
HEADNOTE: FINANCIAL ARRANGEMENTS DEFENSE FIJI
TOPIC: General Military
CONCEPTS: Economic assistance. Military assistance. Bases and facilities.
TREATY REF: 401UNTS51, 521UNTS397.
PARTIES:
New Zealand
UK Great Britain

109207 Bilateral Agreement **0 UNTS 0**
SIGNED: 3 Nov 67   FORCE: 7 Mar 68
REGISTERED: 29 Aug 68 New Zealand
ARTICLES: 0
HEADNOTE: TRADE AGREEMENT
TOPIC: General Trade
CONCEPTS: Establishment of trade relations. Export quotas. Import quotas. Reciprocity in trade. Banking. Balance of payments. National treatment.

PROCEDURE: Ratification.
PARTIES:
  Bulgaria
  New Zealand

109208   Bilateral Exchange   **0 UNTS 0**
SIGNED: 9 Jul 68   FORCE: 9 Jul 68
REGISTERED: 29 Aug 68 New Zealand
ARTICLES: 0
HEADNOTE: SPACE VEHICLE TRACKING FACILITY
TOPIC: Scientific Project
CONCEPTS: Research and scientific projects. Research cooperation. Research and development.
PARTIES:
  New Zealand
  USA (United States)

109209   Bilateral Agreement   **0 UNTS 0**
SIGNED: 1 Apr 68   FORCE: 8 May 68
REGISTERED: 29 Aug 68 Denmark
ARTICLES: 0
HEADNOTE: GOVERNMENT LOAN
TOPIC: Loans and Credits
CONCEPTS: Loan and credit. Credit provisions. Purchase authorization. Loan repayment. Terms of loan.
PROCEDURE: Duration. Termination.
PARTIES:
  Denmark
  Uganda

109210   Bilateral Agreement   **0 UNTS 0**
SIGNED: 26 Jun 68   FORCE: 26 Jun 68
REGISTERED: 29 Aug 68 Denmark
ARTICLES: 0
HEADNOTE: GOVERNMENT LOAN
TOPIC: Loans and Credits
CONCEPTS: Loan and credit. Purchase authorization. Loan repayment. Terms of loan.
PROCEDURE: Duration. Termination.
PARTIES:
  Denmark
  Kenya

109211   Bilateral Exchange   **0 UNTS 0**
SIGNED: 26 Apr 68   FORCE: 26 Apr 68
REGISTERED: 29 Aug 68 Denmark
ARTICLES: 0
HEADNOTE: FISHING RIGHTS
TOPIC: Specific Resources
CONCEPTS: Fish, wildlife, and natural resources.
PARTIES:
  Denmark
  Norway

109212   Bilateral Exchange   **0 UNTS 0**
SIGNED: 7 Feb 68   FORCE: 8 Mar 68
REGISTERED: 30 Aug 68 Austria
ARTICLES: 0
HEADNOTE: ABOLITION VISAS
TOPIC: Visas
CONCEPTS: Visa abolition. Visas.
PARTIES:
  Austria
  Ecuador

109213   Bilateral Agreement   **0 UNTS 0**
SIGNED: 5 Feb 68   FORCE: 1 Apr 68
REGISTERED: 30 Aug 68 Austria
ARTICLES: 0
HEADNOTE: TAX TREATMENT INTERNATIONAL ROAD GOODS
TOPIC: Taxation
CONCEPTS: General. Road rules.
PARTIES:
  Austria
  Poland

109214   Bilateral Exchange   **0 UNTS 0**
SIGNED: 3 Apr 68   FORCE: 3 May 68
REGISTERED: 30 Aug 68 Austria
ARTICLES: 0
HEADNOTE: ABOLITION VISAS
TOPIC: Visas
CONCEPTS: Visa abolition. Visas.

PARTIES:
  Austria
  UK Great Britain

109215   Bilateral Exchange   **0 UNTS 0**
SIGNED: 21 Feb 68   FORCE: 22 Mar 68
REGISTERED: 30 Aug 68 Austria
ARTICLES: 0
HEADNOTE: ABOLITION VISAS
TOPIC: Visas
CONCEPTS: Visa abolition. Visas.
PARTIES:
  Austria
  Dominican Republic

109216   Bilateral Exchange   **0 UNTS 0**
SIGNED: 8 Apr 67   FORCE: 22 May 68
REGISTERED: 30 Aug 68 Austria
ARTICLES: 0
HEADNOTE: FRONTIER CLEARANCE RAILWAY PASSENGERS
TOPIC: Visas
CONCEPTS: Arbitration. Procedure. Railway border crossing. Railways.
PROCEDURE: Ratification.
PARTIES:
  Austria
  Yugoslavia

109217   Bilateral Convention   **0 UNTS 0**
SIGNED: 10 Mar 66   FORCE: 9 Jul 68
REGISTERED: 3 Sep 68 Denmark
ARTICLES: 0
HEADNOTE: AVOIDANCE DOUBLE TAXATION
TOPIC: Taxation
CONCEPTS: Taxation. Equitable taxes. General. Tax exemptions.
PROCEDURE: Denunciation. Ratification. Termination.
PARTIES:
  Denmark
  Italy

109218   Bilateral Agreement   **0 UNTS 0**
SIGNED: 22 Apr 68   FORCE: 22 Apr 68
REGISTERED: 3 Sep 68 Denmark
ARTICLES: 0
HEADNOTE: FORESTRY COOPERATION
TOPIC: Tech Assistance
CONCEPTS: General technical assistance. Assistance.
PROCEDURE: Amendment.
PARTIES:
  Denmark
  Morocco

109219   Bilateral Agreement   **0 UNTS 0**
SIGNED: 10 Jun 68   FORCE: 10 Jun 68
REGISTERED: 3 Sep 68 Denmark
ARTICLES: 0
HEADNOTE: ORAL CANCER CONTROL
TOPIC: Sanitation
CONCEPTS: Disease control. Medical assistance and/or facilities. General technical assistance. Assistance.
PROCEDURE: Termination.
PARTIES:
  Denmark
  India

109220   Bilateral Agreement   **0 UNTS 0**
SIGNED: 13 May 64   FORCE: 13 May 64
REGISTERED: 14 Sep 68 UNESCO (Educ/Cult)
ARTICLES: 0
HEADNOTE: AFRICAN TRAINING & RESEARCH CENTER ESTABLISHMENT
TOPIC: Tech Assistance
CONCEPTS: General technical assistance. Assistance. Special projects.
PARTIES:
  Morocco
  UNESCO (Educ/Cult)

109221   Bilateral Agreement   **0 UNTS 0**
SIGNED: 18 Dec 67   FORCE: 18 Dec 67
REGISTERED: 4 Sep 68 UNESCO (Educ/Cult)
ARTICLES: 0

HEADNOTE: ESTABLISHMENT DEVELOPMENT ADMINISTRATION RESEARCH CENTER
TOPIC: IGO Operations
CONCEPTS: Subsidiary organ. Headquarters and facilities. Liaison with other IGO's. Internal structure. Special status.
PROCEDURE: Ratification.
PARTIES:
  Morocco
  UNESCO (Educ/Cult)

109222   Bilateral Convention   **0 UNTS 0**
SIGNED: 31 Oct 67   FORCE: 14 Apr 68
REGISTERED: 4 Sep 68 Netherlands
ARTICLES: 0
HEADNOTE: AVOIDANCE DOUBLE TAXATION
TOPIC: Taxation
CONCEPTS: Taxation. Equitable taxes. General. Tax exemptions.
PROCEDURE: Termination.
PARTIES:
  Netherlands
  UK Great Britain

109223   Bilateral Agreement   **0 UNTS 0**
SIGNED: 15 Nov 67   FORCE: 20 Mar 68
REGISTERED: 4 Sep 68 Czechoslovakia
ARTICLES: 0
HEADNOTE: INTERNATIONAL ROAD TRANSPORT
TOPIC: Land Transport
CONCEPTS: Land transport. Commercial road vehicles. Driving permits. Motor vehicles and combinations. Roads and highways.
PROCEDURE: Denunciation. Duration. Ratification.
PARTIES:
  Czechoslovakia
  Netherlands

109224   Bilateral Agreement   **0 UNTS 0**
SIGNED: 23 Nov 67   FORCE: 23 Nov 67
REGISTERED: 4 Sep 68 Czechoslovakia
ARTICLES: 0
HEADNOTE: COMMUNICATIONS COOPERATION
TOPIC: Gen Communications
CONCEPTS: General technical assistance. Mail and money orders. Postal services. Conveyance in transit. Rates and charges. Telecommunications. Services. Telegrams. Radio-telephone-telegraphic communications.
PROCEDURE: Denunciation. Duration.
PARTIES:
  Czechoslovakia
  USSR (Soviet Union)

109225   Bilateral Agreement   **0 UNTS 0**
SIGNED: 16 Jul 64   FORCE: 16 Sep 65
REGISTERED: 5 Sep 68 France
ARTICLES: 0
HEADNOTE: RECTIFICATION FRANCO-LUXEMBOURG FRONTIER
TOPIC: Territory Boundary
CONCEPTS: Markers and definitions.
PARTIES:
  France
  Luxembourg

109226   Bilateral Treaty   **0 UNTS 0**
SIGNED: 22 Sep 66   FORCE: 12 Jul 68
REGISTERED: 6 Sep 68 Netherlands
ARTICLES: 0
HEADNOTE: RAILWAY FRONTIER CROSSINGS
TOPIC: Land Transport
CONCEPTS: Railway border crossing. Frontier crossing points.
TREATY REF: 570UNTS127; 578UNTS282; 592UNTS282; ETC..
PROCEDURE: Denunciation. Ratification.
PARTIES:
  Germany, West
  Netherlands

109227   Bilateral Exchange   **0 UNTS 0**
SIGNED: 10 Jul 68   FORCE: 10 Jul 68
REGISTERED: 6 Sep 68 Austria
ARTICLES: 0
HEADNOTE: WAR CEMETERY
TOPIC: Other Military

CONCEPTS: War graves. Responsibility for war dead. Establishment of war cemeteries.
TREATY REF: 217UNTS223.
PARTIES:
 Austria
 India

109228 Bilateral Agreement **0 UNTS 0**
SIGNED: 19 Dec 51 FORCE: 19 Dec 51
REGISTERED: 9 Sep 68 Ireland
ARTICLES: 0
HEADNOTE: TRADE AGREEMENT
TOPIC: General Trade
CONCEPTS: Establishment of trade relations. Reciprocity in trade. Trade procedures. Delivery guarantees.
PROCEDURE: Duration. Termination.
PARTIES:
 Ireland
 Spain

109229 Bilateral Agreement **0 UNTS 0**
SIGNED: 25 Mar 68 FORCE: 25 Mar 68
REGISTERED: 9 Sep 68 Denmark
ARTICLES: 0
HEADNOTE: GOVERNMENT FOOD LOAN
TOPIC: Direct Aid
CONCEPTS: Procedure. Currency. Loan and credit. Credit provisions. Purchase authorization. Loan repayment. Terms of loan.
PROCEDURE: Duration. Termination.
PARTIES:
 Denmark
 India

109230 Bilateral Agreement **0 UNTS 0**
SIGNED: 29 Apr 68 FORCE: 29 Apr 68
REGISTERED: 9 Sep 68 Denmark
ARTICLES: 0
HEADNOTE: GOVERNMENT LOAN
TOPIC: Direct Aid
CONCEPTS: Procedure. Currency. Loan and credit. Credit provisions. Purchase authorization. Loan repayment. Terms of loan.
PROCEDURE: Duration. Termination.
PARTIES:
 Denmark
 India

109231 Bilateral Agreement **0 UNTS 0**
SIGNED: 29 Aug 67 FORCE: 10 Apr 68
REGISTERED: 12 Sep 68 Denmark
ARTICLES: 0
HEADNOTE: INTERNATIONAL TRANSPORT ROAD GOODS
TOPIC: Land Transport
CONCEPTS: Transport of goods. Commercial road vehicles. Motor vehicles and combinations. Roads and highways.
PROCEDURE: Denunciation.
PARTIES:
 Denmark
 Romania

109232 Bilateral Exchange **0 UNTS 0**
SIGNED: 10 Nov 67 FORCE: 15 May 68
REGISTERED: 12 Sep 68 Netherlands
ARTICLES: 0
HEADNOTE: EXTRADITION
TOPIC: Extradition
CONCEPTS: Extradiction, deportation and repatriation.
TREATY REF: 90BFSP51; 108BFSP366.
PARTIES:
 Kenya
 Netherlands

109233 Bilateral Exchange **0 UNTS 0**
SIGNED: 30 May 68 FORCE: 30 May 68
REGISTERED: 16 Sep 68 Denmark
ARTICLES: 0
HEADNOTE: FISHING RIGHTS
TOPIC: Specific Resources
CONCEPTS: Fish, wildlife, and natural resources.
TREATY REF: 581UNTS57.
PARTIES:
 Denmark
 Netherlands

109234 Multilateral Agreement **0 UNTS 0**
SIGNED: 30 Jan 59 FORCE: 28 May 60
REGISTERED: 18 Sep 68 Netherlands
ARTICLES: 0
HEADNOTE: TRADE AGREEMENT
TOPIC: General Trade
CONCEPTS: Establishment of trade relations. Most favored nation clause.
TREATY REF: 249UNTS197; 261UNTS141.
PROCEDURE: Duration.
PARTIES:
 Belgium SIGNED: 30 Jan 59 RATIFIED: 25 May 60 FORCE: 28 May 60
 Honduras SIGNED: 30 Jan 59 RATIFIED: 28 May 60 FORCE: 28 May 60
 Luxembourg SIGNED: 30 Jan 59 RATIFIED: 25 May 60 FORCE: 28 May 60
 Netherlands SIGNED: 30 Jan 59 RATIFIED: 25 Feb 60 FORCE: 28 May 60

109235 Bilateral Exchange **0 UNTS 0**
SIGNED: 15 Mar 68 FORCE: 14 May 68
REGISTERED: 18 Sep 68 Jamaica
ARTICLES: 0
HEADNOTE: ABOLISHMENT VISAS
TOPIC: Visas
CONCEPTS: Visa abolition.
PARTIES:
 Jamaica
 Mexico

109236 Bilateral Agreement **0 UNTS 0**
SIGNED: 21 Jul 58 FORCE: 11 Jul 59
REGISTERED: 18 Sep 68 ICAO (Civil Aviat)
ARTICLES: 0
HEADNOTE: AIR SERVICES
TOPIC: Air Transport
CONCEPTS: Procedure. Air transport. Airport facilities. Airport equipment. Airworthiness certificates. Conditions of airlines operating permission. Overflights and technical stops. Operating authorizations and regulations.
TREATY REF: 15UNTS295; 320UNTS209,217; 418UNTS161; ETC..
PROCEDURE: Ratification.
PARTIES:
 Afghanistan
 Austria

109237 Bilateral Agreement **0 UNTS 0**
SIGNED: 17 Jul 59 FORCE: 6 Aug 59
REGISTERED: 18 Sep 68 ICAO (Civil Aviat)
ARTICLES: 0
HEADNOTE: AIR TRANSPORT
TOPIC: Air Transport
CONCEPTS: Procedure. Customs duties. Air transport. Airport facilities. Airport equipment. Airworthiness certificates. Conditions of airlines operating permission. Overflights and technical stops. Operating authorizations and regulations.
PROCEDURE: Amendment. Termination.
PARTIES:
 Austria
 Hungary

109238 Bilateral Agreement **0 UNTS 0**
SIGNED: 19 Feb 62 FORCE: 11 May 62
REGISTERED: 18 Sep 68 ICAO (Civil Aviat)
ARTICLES: 0
HEADNOTE: AIR TRANSPORT
TOPIC: Air Transport
CONCEPTS: Procedure. Customs duties. Air transport. Airport facilities. Airport equipment. Airworthiness certificates. Conditions of airlines operating permission. Overflights and technical stops. Operating authorizations and regulations.
TREATY REF: 15UNTS295; 320UNTS209,217; 418UNTS161; ETC..
PROCEDURE: Amendment. Denunciation.
PARTIES:
 Austria
 Spain

109239 Bilateral Agreement **0 UNTS 0**
SIGNED: 5 May 65 FORCE: 5 May 65
REGISTERED: 18 Sep 68 ICAO (Civil Aviat)
ARTICLES: 0
HEADNOTE: AIR SERVICES
TOPIC: Air Transport

CONCEPTS: Customs exemptions. Airport facilities. Airport equipment. Airworthiness certificates. Conditions of airlines operating permission. Overflights and technical stops. Operating authorizations and regulations.
TREATY REF: 15UNTS295; 320UNTS209,217; 418UNTS161; ETC..
PROCEDURE: Amendment.
PARTIES:
 Spain
 Sweden

109240 Bilateral Agreement **0 UNTS 0**
SIGNED: 7 Jun 65 FORCE: 8 Mar 67
REGISTERED: 18 Sep 68 ICAO (Civil Aviat)
ARTICLES: 0
HEADNOTE: AIR TRANSPORT
TOPIC: Air Transport
CONCEPTS: IGO reference. Procedure. Customs exemptions. Airport facilities. Airport equipment. Airworthiness certificates. Conditions of airlines operating permission. Overflights and technical stops. Operating authorizations and regulations.
INTL ORGS: International Civil Aviation Organization.
TREATY REF: 15UNTS295; 320UNTS209,217; 418UNTS161; ETC..
PROCEDURE: Ratification.
PARTIES:
 Ivory Coast
 Sweden

109241 Bilateral Exchange **0 UNTS 0**
SIGNED: 19 Aug 66 FORCE: 19 Aug 66
REGISTERED: 18 Sep 68 ICAO (Civil Aviat)
ARTICLES: 0
HEADNOTE: AIR SERVICES
TOPIC: Air Transport
CONCEPTS: Air transport. Conditions of airlines operating permission. Operating authorizations and regulations.
TREATY REF: 15UNTS295; 320UNTS209,217; 418UNTS161; ETC..
PARTIES:
 Taiwan
 Vietnam, South

109242 Bilateral Agreement **0 UNTS 0**
SIGNED: 20 Dec 66 FORCE: 20 Dec 66
REGISTERED: 18 Sep 68 ICAO (Civil Aviat)
ARTICLES: 0
HEADNOTE: AIR SERVICES
TOPIC: Air Transport
CONCEPTS: Procedure. Customs exemptions. Airport facilities. Airport equipment. Airworthiness certificates. Conditions of airlines operating permission. Overflights and technical stops. Operating authorizations and regulations.
TREATY REF: 15UNTS295; 320UNTS209,217; 418UNTS161; ETC..
PROCEDURE: Amendment. Termination.
PARTIES:
 Norway
 Singapore

109243 Bilateral Agreement **0 UNTS 0**
SIGNED: 20 Dec 66 FORCE: 20 Dec 66
REGISTERED: 18 Sep 68 ICAO (Civil Aviat)
ARTICLES: 0
HEADNOTE: AIR SERVICES
TOPIC: Air Transport
CONCEPTS: Conditions of airlines operating permission. Operating authorizations and regulations.
PARTIES:
 Singapore
 Sweden

109244 Bilateral Agreement **0 UNTS 0**
SIGNED: 14 Feb 67 FORCE: 1 Aug 67
REGISTERED: 18 Sep 68 ICAO (Civil Aviat)
ARTICLES: 0
HEADNOTE: AIR SERVICES
TOPIC: Air Transport
CONCEPTS: Procedure. Customs exemptions. Airport facilities. Airport equipment. Airworthiness certificates. Conditions of airlines operating permission. Overflights and technical stops. Operat-

ing authorizations and regulations. Licenses and certificates of nationality.
PROCEDURE: Amendment. Ratification.
PARTIES:
  Japan
  Singapore

109245   Bilateral Agreement   **0 UNTS 0**
SIGNED: 16 Feb 67   FORCE: 16 Feb 67
REGISTERED: 18 Sep 68 ICAO (Civil Aviat)
ARTICLES: 0
HEADNOTE: AIR TRANSPORT
TOPIC: Air Transport
CONCEPTS: Procedure. Customs exemptions. Airport facilities. Airport equipment. Airworthiness certificates. Conditions of airlines operating permission. Overflights and technical stops. Operating authorizations and regulations. Licenses and certificates of nationality.
TREATY REF: 15UNTS295; 320UNTS209,217; 418UNTS161; ETC..
PARTIES:
  Algeria
  Ivory Coast

109246   Bilateral Agreement   **0 UNTS 0**
SIGNED: 22 Mar 67   FORCE: 22 Mar 67
REGISTERED: 18 Sep 68 ICAO (Civil Aviat)
ARTICLES: 0
HEADNOTE: AIR SERVICES
TOPIC: Air Transport
CONCEPTS: Procedure. Customs exemptions. Airport facilities. Airport equipment. Airworthiness certificates. Conditions of airlines operating permission. Overflights and technical stops. Operating authorizations and regulations. Licenses and certificates of nationality.
TREATY REF: 15UNTS295; 320UNTS209,217; 418UNTS161; ETC..
PROCEDURE: Termination.
PARTIES:
  Australia
  Austria

109247   Bilateral Agreement   **0 UNTS 0**
SIGNED: 13 Jun 67   FORCE: 13 Jun 67
REGISTERED: 18 Sep 68 ICAO (Civil Aviat)
ARTICLES: 0
HEADNOTE: AIR SERVICES
TOPIC: Air Transport
CONCEPTS: Procedure. Customs exemptions. Airport facilities. Airport equipment. Airworthiness certificates. Conditions of airlines operating permission. Overflights and technical stops. Operating authorizations and regulations. Licenses and certificates of nationality.
TREATY REF: 15UNTS295; 320UNTS209,217; 418UNTS161; ETC..
PARTIES:
  Netherlands
  Sierra Leone

109248   Multilateral Agreement   **0 UNTS 0**
SIGNED: 3 Jul 67   FORCE: 3 Jul 67
REGISTERED: 18 Sep 68 ICAO (Civil Aviat)
ARTICLES: 0
HEADNOTE: AIR SERVICES
TOPIC: Air Transport
CONCEPTS: Procedure. Customs exemptions. Airport facilities. Airport equipment. Airworthiness certificates. Conditions of airlines operating permission. Overflights and technical stops. Operating authorizations and regulations. Licenses and certificates of nationality.
TREATY REF: 15UNTS295; 320UNTS209,217; 418UNTS161; ETC..
PARTIES:
  Netherlands SIGNED: 3 Jul 67 FORCE: 3 Jul 67
  Trinidad/Tobago SIGNED: 3 Jul 67 FORCE: 3 Jul 67

109249   Bilateral Agreement   **0 UNTS 0**
SIGNED: 7 Jun 66   FORCE: 8 Mar 67
REGISTERED: 18 Sep 68 ICAO (Civil Aviat)
ARTICLES: 0
HEADNOTE: AIR TRANSPORT
TOPIC: Air Transport
CONCEPTS: Procedure. Customs exemptions. Airport facilities. Airport equipment. Airworthiness

certificates. Conditions of airlines operating permission. Overflights and technical stops. Operating authorizations and regulations. Licenses and certificates of nationality.
TREATY REF: 15UNTS295; 320UNTS209,217; 418UNTS161; ETC..
PROCEDURE: Ratification.
PARTIES:
  Ivory Coast
  Norway

109250   Bilateral Agreement   **0 UNTS 0**
SIGNED: 19 Sep 68   FORCE: 19 Sep 68
REGISTERED: 19 Sep 68 United Nations
ARTICLES: 0
HEADNOTE: UN SEMINAR WOMENS CIVIL-POLITICAL EDUCATION
TOPIC: IGO Operations
CONCEPTS: Subsidiary organ. Status of experts. Conferences.
PROCEDURE: Amendment.
PARTIES:
  Ghana
  United Nations
                    ANNEX
651 UNTS 412. United Nations. Amendment 4 Dec 68. Force 4 Dec 68.
651 UNTS 412. Ghana. Amendment 4 Dec 68. Force 4 Dec 68.

109251   Bilateral Instrument   **0 UNTS 0**
SIGNED: 23 Sep 68
REGISTERED: 23 Sep 68 United Nations
ARTICLES: 0
HEADNOTE: COMPULSORY JURISDICTION ICJ
TOPIC: ICJ Option Clause
CONCEPTS: IGO reference. Optional clause ICJ. Compulsory jurisdiction.
INTL ORGS: International Court of Justice.
PARTIES:
  Mauritius

109252   Bilateral Instrument   **0 UNTS 0**
SIGNED: 6 Sep 68
REGISTERED: 24 Sep 68 United Nations
ARTICLES: 0
HEADNOTE: ACCEPTANCE UN CHARTER OBLIGATIONS
TOPIC: UN Charter
CONCEPTS: IGO reference. Adherence to UN Charter. Acceptance of UN obligations.
INTL ORGS: United Nations.
PARTIES:
  Swaziland

109253   Bilateral Agreement   **0 UNTS 0**
SIGNED: 24 Sep 68   FORCE: 24 Sep 68
REGISTERED: 24 Sep 68 United Nations
ARTICLES: 0
HEADNOTE: ARRANGEMENTS UN CONFERENCE ON ROAD TRAFFIC
TOPIC: IGO Operations
CONCEPTS: Subsidiary organ. Status of experts. Conferences.
PARTIES:
  Austria
  United Nations

109254   Bilateral Agreement   **0 UNTS 0**
SIGNED: 17 Oct 55   FORCE: 17 Feb 56
REGISTERED: 25 Sep 68 USSR (Soviet Union)
ARTICLES: 0
HEADNOTE: LOAN SECOND RAILWAY PROJECT
TOPIC: Non-IBRD Project
CONCEPTS: Credit provisions. World Bank projects. Loan regulations. Loan guarantee. Guarantor non-interference. Plans and standards.
PROCEDURE: Termination.
PARTIES:
  Austria
  USSR (Soviet Union)

109255   Bilateral Agreement   **0 UNTS 0**
SIGNED: 17 Oct 55   FORCE: 17 Oct 55
REGISTERED: 25 Sep 68 USSR (Soviet Union)
ARTICLES: 0
HEADNOTE: PAYMENTS

TOPIC: Finance
CONCEPTS: Accounting procedures. Currency. Monetary and gold transfers. Debts. Debt settlement.
PROCEDURE: Duration. Termination.
PARTIES:
  Austria
  USSR (Soviet Union)

109256   Bilateral Agreement   **0 UNTS 0**
SIGNED: 20 Apr 63   FORCE: 14 Apr 65
REGISTERED: 25 Sep 68 USSR (Soviet Union)
ARTICLES: 0
HEADNOTE: TRADE AND PAYMENTS AGREEMENT
TOPIC: General Trade
CONCEPTS: Establishment of trade relations. Maritime products and equipment. Reciprocity in trade. Trade agencies. Trade procedures. Accounting procedures. Banking. Balance of payments. Currency. Payment schedules. Most favored nation clause.
PROCEDURE: Denunciation. Ratification.
PARTIES:
  Brazil
  USSR (Soviet Union)

109257   Bilateral Protocol   **0 UNTS 0**
SIGNED: 20 Apr 63   FORCE: 20 Apr 63
REGISTERED: 25 Sep 68 USSR (Soviet Union)
ARTICLES: 0
HEADNOTE: REORGANIZATION TRADE MISSION AS TRADE DELEGATION
TOPIC: General Trade
CONCEPTS: Procedure. Establishment of trade relations. Export quotas. Import quotas. Reciprocity in trade. Trade agencies. Trade procedures. Currency.
PARTIES:
  Brazil
  USSR (Soviet Union)

109258   Multilateral Agreement   **0 UNTS 0**
SIGNED: 22 Sep 67
REGISTERED: 26 Sep 68 Netherlands
ARTICLES: 0
HEADNOTE: STUDY NAVIGABILITY NIGER RIVER
TOPIC: Non-IBRD Project
CONCEPTS: Research cooperation. General technical assistance. Assistance. Special projects. Inland and territorial waters.
PROCEDURE: Duration. Termination.
PARTIES:
  Dahomey
  Mali
  Netherlands
  Nigeria
  Niger
  Romania

109259   Multilateral Agreement   **0 UNTS 0**
SIGNED: 20 Jul 67   FORCE: 17 May 68
REGISTERED: Netherlands
ARTICLES: 0
HEADNOTE: ECONOMIC INDUSTRIAL TECHNICAL COOPERATION
TOPIC: General Economic
CONCEPTS: Exchange of information and documents. Research and scientific projects. Research cooperation. General economics. General technical assistance.
PROCEDURE: Denunciation.
PARTIES:
  Dahomey   SIGNED: 22 Sep 67   FORCE: 22 Sep 67
  Mali SIGNED: 22 Sep 67 FORCE: 22 Sep 67
  Netherlands   SIGNED: 22 Sep 67   FORCE: 22 Sep 67
  Nigeria SIGNED: 22 Sep 67 FORCE: 22 Sep 67
  Niger SIGNED: 22 Sep 67 FORCE: 22 Sep 67

109260   Bilateral Exchange   **0 UNTS 0**
SIGNED: 16 May 68   FORCE: 16 May 68
REGISTERED: 27 Sep 68 Netherlands
ARTICLES: 0
HEADNOTE: AERIAL PHOTO SURVEY PROJECT
TOPIC: Non-IBRD Project
CONCEPTS: General technical assistance. Assistance. Special projects.

PARTIES:
Korea, South
Netherlands

109261 Bilateral Convention **0 UNTS 0**
SIGNED: 25 Feb 67　　　　FORCE: 1 Mar 67
REGISTERED: 30 Sep 68 France
ARTICLES: 0
HEADNOTE: COOPERATION RADIO BROADCAST-
ING
TOPIC: Mass Media
CONCEPTS: General technical assistance. Assis-
tance. Special projects. Mass media exchange.
PROCEDURE: Duration. Termination.
PARTIES:
France
Niger

109262 Multilateral Agreement **0 UNTS 0**
SIGNED: 18 Mar 68　　　　FORCE: 1 Oct 68
REGISTERED: 1 Oct 68 United Nations
ARTICLES: 0
HEADNOTE: INTERNATIONAL COFFEE AGREE-
MENT
TOPIC: Commodity Trade
CONCEPTS: IGO reference. Procedure. IGO consti-
tution. Admission. Constitutional amendment.
Decisions. Subsidiary organ. Establishment. Pro-
cedure. Liaison with other IGO's. Internal struc-
ture.
INTL ORGS: United Nations.
PROCEDURE: Amendment. Accession. Ratifica-
tion. Termination.
PARTIES:
Australia RATIFIED: 26 Sep 68 FORCE: 1 Oct 68
Belgium RATIFIED: 26 Sep 68 FORCE: 1 Oct 68
Bolivia RATIFIED: 27 Sep 68 FORCE: 1 Oct 68
Brazil RATIFIED: 11 Oct 68 FORCE: 11 Oct 68
Burundi RATIFIED: 17 Sep 68 FORCE: 1 Oct 68
Cameroon RATIFIED: 30 Sep 68 FORCE:
1 Oct 68
Canada RATIFIED: 21 Aug 68 FORCE: 1 Oct 68
Central Afri Rep RATIFIED: 30 Sep 68 FORCE:
1 Oct 68
Congo (Brazzaville) RATIFIED: 30 Sep 68 FORCE:
1 Oct 68
Congo (Zaire) RATIFIED: 23 Sep 68 FORCE:
1 Oct 68
Colombia RATIFIED: 26 Sep 68 FORCE: 1 Oct 68
Costa Rica RATIFIED: 27 Sep 68 FORCE:
1 Oct 68
Cyprus RATIFIED: 26 Sep 68 FORCE: 1 Oct 68
Czechoslovakia RATIFIED: 4 Sep 68 FORCE:
1 Oct 68
Dahomey RATIFIED: 12 Sep 68 FORCE: 1 Oct 68
Denmark RATIFIED: 27 Sep 68 FORCE: 1 Oct 68
Dominican Republic RATIFIED: 30 Sep 68
FORCE: 1 Oct 68
Ecuador RATIFIED: 11 Sep 68 FORCE: 1 Oct 68
El Salvador RATIFIED: 27 Sep 68 FORCE:
1 Oct 68
Ethiopia RATIFIED: 24 Sep 68 FORCE: 1 Oct 68
Finland RATIFIED: 30 Sep 68 FORCE: 1 Oct 68
France RATIFIED: 19 Aug 68 FORCE: 1 Oct 68
Gabon RATIFIED: 30 Sep 68 FORCE: 1 Oct 68
Germany, West RATIFIED: 11 Sep 68 FORCE:
1 Oct 68
Ghana RATIFIED: 30 Sep 68 FORCE: 1 Oct 68
Guatemala RATIFIED: 30 Sep 68 FORCE:
1 Oct 68
Guinea RATIFIED: 30 Sep 68 FORCE: 1 Oct 68
Haiti RATIFIED: 25 Sep 68 FORCE: 1 Oct 68
Honduras RATIFIED: 27 Sep 68 FORCE:
1 Oct 68
India RATIFIED: 27 Sep 68 FORCE: 1 Oct 68
Indonesia RATIFIED: 26 Sep 68 FORCE:
1 Oct 68
Israel RATIFIED: 26 Sep 68 FORCE: 1 Oct 68
Italy RATIFIED: 22 Aug 68 FORCE: 1 Oct 68
Ivory Coast RATIFIED: 27 Sep 68 FORCE:
1 Oct 68
Jamaica RATIFIED: 17 Sep 68 FORCE: 1 Oct 68
Japan RATIFIED: 6 Sep 68 FORCE: 1 Oct 68
Kenya RATIFIED: 6 Sep 68 FORCE: 1 Oct 68
Liberia RATIFIED: 18 Jun 68 FORCE: 1 Oct 68
Madagascar RATIFIED: 8 Aug 68 FORCE:
1 Oct 68
Mexico RATIFIED: 21 Aug 68 FORCE: 1 Oct 68
Netherlands RATIFIED: 16 Sep 68 FORCE:
1 Oct 68
New Zealand RATIFIED: 7 Aug 68 FORCE:
1 Oct 68

Nicaragua RATIFIED: 30 Sep 68 FORCE:
1 Oct 68
Nigeria RATIFIED: 18 Jun 68 FORCE: 1 Oct 68
Norway RATIFIED: 26 Sep 68 FORCE: 1 Oct 68
Paraguay RATIFIED: 13 Sep 68 FORCE: 1 Oct 68
Peru RATIFIED: 25 Oct 68 FORCE: 25 Oct 68
Portugal RATIFIED: 30 Oct 68 FORCE: 30 Oct 68
Rwanda RATIFIED: 30 Sep 68 FORCE: 1 Oct 68
Sierra Leone RATIFIED: 17 Sep 68 FORCE:
1 Oct 68
Spain RATIFIED: 15 Aug 68 FORCE: 1 Oct 68
Sweden RATIFIED: 30 Sep 68 FORCE: 1 Oct 68
Switzerland RATIFIED: 30 Sep 68 FORCE:
1 Oct 68
Tanzania RATIFIED: 1 Oct 68 FORCE: 1 Oct 68
Togo RATIFIED: 30 Sep 68 FORCE: 1 Oct 68
Trinidad/Tobago RATIFIED: 10 Jul 68 FORCE:
1 Oct 68
Uganda RATIFIED: 14 Oct 68 FORCE: 14 Oct 68
UK Great Britain RATIFIED: 27 Sep 68 FORCE:
1 Oct 68
USA (United States) RATIFIED: 30 Sep 68
FORCE: 1 Oct 68
Venezuela RATIFIED: 30 Sep 68 FORCE:
1 Oct 68
ANNEX
648 UNTS 387. Uganda. Ratification 14 Oct 68.
648 UNTS 387. Cameroon. Ratification 9 Oct 68.
648 UNTS 387. Brazil. Ratification 11 Oct 68.
649 UNTS 380. Portugal. Ratification 30 Oct 68.
649 UNTS 380. USA (United States). Ratification
1 Nov 68.
649 UNTS 380. Peru. Ratification 25 Oct 68.
651 UNTS 414. Togo. Ratification 29 Nov 68.
653 UNTS 464. Jamaica. Ratification 17 Sep 68.
Force 30 Dec 68.
653 UNTS 464. El Salvador. Ratification
16 Dec 68. Force 30 Dec 68.
653 UNTS 464. Costa Rica. Ratification
30 Dec 68. Force 30 Dec 68.
653 UNTS 464. Ivory Coast. Ratification
27 Sep 68. Force 30 Dec 68.
653 UNTS 464. Mexico. Ratification 13 Dec 68.
Force 30 Dec 68.
653 UNTS 464. Nicaragua. Ratification
30 Sep 68. Force 30 Dec 68.
653 UNTS 464. Nigeria. Ratification 18 Jun 68.
Force 30 Dec 68.
653 UNTS 464. Peru. Ratification 25 Oct 68.
Force 30 Dec 68.
653 UNTS 464. Bolivia. Ratification 30 Dec 68.
Force 30 Dec 68.
653 UNTS 464. Brazil. Ratification 11 Oct 68.
Force 30 Dec 68.
653 UNTS 464. Norway. Ratification 23 Dec 68.
Force 30 Dec 68.
653 UNTS 464. Finland. Ratification 30 Dec 68.
Force 30 Dec 68.
653 UNTS 464. Ghana. Ratification 23 Dec 68.
Force 30 Dec 68.
653 UNTS 464. Portugal. Ratification 30 Oct 68.
Force 30 Dec 68.
653 UNTS 464. Rwanda. Ratification 31 Dec 68.
Force 31 Dec 68.
653 UNTS 464. Sierra Leone. Ratification
11 Dec 68. Force 30 Dec 68.
653 UNTS 464. Togo. Ratification 29 Nov 68.
Force 30 Dec 68.
653 UNTS 464. Trinidad/Tobago. Ratification
10 Jul 68. Force 30 Dec 68.
653 UNTS 464. Uganda. Ratification 14 Oct 68.
Force 30 Dec 68.
653 UNTS 464. Tanzania. Ratification 1 Oct 68.
Force 30 Dec 68.
653 UNTS 464. Venezuela. Ratification
18 Dec 68. Force 30 Dec 68.
653 UNTS 464. Congo (Zaire). Ratification
20 Dec 68. Force 30 Dec 68.
653 UNTS 464. Central Afri Rep. Ratification
20 Dec 68. Force 30 Dec 68.
653 UNTS 464. Bolivia. Ratification 30 Dec 68.
Force 30 Dec 68.
653 UNTS 464. Burundi. Ratification 11 Oct 68.
Force 30 Dec 68.
653 UNTS 464. Cameroon. Ratification 9 Oct 68.
Force 30 Dec 68.
653 UNTS 464. Colombia. Ratification
26 Sep 68. Force 30 Dec 68.
653 UNTS 464. Ecuador. Ratification 16 Dec 68.
Force 30 Dec 38.
653 UNTS 464. Paraguay. Ratification 27 Dec 68.
Force 30 Dec 68.
653 UNTS 464. Ecuador. Ratification 16 Dec 68.
Force 30 Dec 68.

653 UNTS 464. Panama. Accession 21 Dec 68.
Force 30 Dec 68.
653 UNTS 464. Dahomey. Ratification
12 Sep 68. Force 30 Dec 68.
653 UNTS 464. Dominican Republic. Ratification
30 Sep 68. Force 30 Dec 68.
653 UNTS 464. Gabon. Ratification 30 Sep 68.
Force 30 Dec 68.
653 UNTS 464. Guatemala. Ratification
30 Sep 68. Force 30 Dec 68.
653 UNTS 464. Congo (Brazzaville). Ratification
20 Dec 68. Force 30 Dec 68.
653 UNTS 464. Honduras. Ratification
16 Dec 68. Force 30 Dec 68.
653 UNTS 464. Guinea. Ratification 30 Dec 68.
Force 30 Dec 68.
653 UNTS 464. Haiti. Ratification 25 Sep 68.
Force 30 Dec 68.
653 UNTS 464. Netherlands. Reservation
30 Dec 68. Ratification 30 Dec 68.
653 UNTS 464. India. Ratification 31 Dec 68.
Force 31 Dec 68.
653 UNTS 464. Ethiopia. Ratification 24 Sep 68.
Force 30 Dec 68.
653 UNTS 464. Kenya. Ratification 10 Dec 68.
Force 30 Dec 68.
653 UNTS 464. Liberia. Ratification 18 Jun 68.
Force 30 Dec 68.
653 UNTS 464. Madagascar. Ratification
8 Aug 68. Force 30 Dec 68.
653 UNTS 464. Indonesia. Acceptance
26 Sep 68. Force 30 Dec 68.

109263 Bilateral Convention **0 UNTS 0**
SIGNED: 15 Sep 68　　　　FORCE: 9 Feb 68
REGISTERED: 1 Oct 68 UK Great Britain
ARTICLES: 0
HEADNOTE: AVOIDANCE DOUBLE TAXATION
TOPIC: Taxation
CONCEPTS: Taxation. Equitable taxes. General.
Tax exemptions.
PROCEDURE: Ratification.
PARTIES:
Italy
UK Great Britain

109264 Bilateral Exchange **0 UNTS 0**
SIGNED: 21 Feb 68　　　　FORCE: 21 Feb 68
REGISTERED: 1 Oct 68 UK Great Britain
ARTICLES: 0
HEADNOTE: TRAINING TEAM
TOPIC: Military Mission
CONCEPTS: Claims and settlements. Military as-
sistance missions. Airforce-army-navy personnel
ratio. Ranks and privileges. Conditions for assis-
tance missions.
PROCEDURE: Termination.
PARTIES:
UK Great Britain
Zambia

109265 Bilateral Exchange **0 UNTS 0**
SIGNED: 4 Mar 68　　　　FORCE: 4 Mar 68
REGISTERED: 1 Oct 68 UK Great Britain
ARTICLES: 0
HEADNOTE: INTEREST-FREE DEVELOPMENT
LOAN
TOPIC: Loans and Credits
CONCEPTS: Loan and credit. Credit provisions.
Loan repayment. Terms of loan.
PARTIES:
Turkey
UK Great Britain

109266 Bilateral Exchange **0 UNTS 0**
SIGNED: 4 Mar 68　　　　FORCE: 4 Mar 68
REGISTERED: 1 Oct 68 UK Great Britain
ARTICLES: 0
HEADNOTE: COMMERCIAL CREDIT AGREEMENT
TOPIC: Loans and Credits
CONCEPTS: Economic assistance. Credit provi-
sions. Purchase authorization.
PARTIES:
Turkey
UK Great Britain

109267 Bilateral Agreement **0 UNTS 0**
SIGNED: 12 Mar 68　　　　FORCE: 12 Mar 68
REGISTERED: 1 Oct 68 UK Great Britain

ARTICLES: 0
HEADNOTE: MUTUAL DEFENSE AND ASSISTANCE
TOPIC: Milit Assistance
CONCEPTS: Defense and security. Self-defense.
PROCEDURE: Termination.
PARTIES:
 Mauritius
 UK Great Britain

109268   Bilateral Exchange   **0 UNTS 0**
SIGNED: 12 Mar 68   FORCE: 12 Mar 68
REGISTERED: 1 Oct 68 UK Great Britain
ARTICLES: 0
HEADNOTE: ASSISTANCE POLICE FORCES OF MAURITIUS
TOPIC: Tech Assistance
CONCEPTS: General technical assistance. Assistance. Special projects.
PARTIES:
 Mauritius
 UK Great Britain

109269   Bilateral Agreement   **0 UNTS 0**
SIGNED: 12 Mar 68   FORCE: 12 Mar 68
REGISTERED: 1 Oct 68 UK Great Britain
ARTICLES: 0
HEADNOTE: PUBLIC OFFICERS AGREEMENT
TOPIC: Admin Cooperation
CONCEPTS: Privileges and immunities. Assistance.
PARTIES:
 Mauritius
 UK Great Britain

109270   Bilateral Agreement   **0 UNTS 0**
SIGNED: 12 Mar 68   FORCE: 12 Mar 68
REGISTERED: 1 Oct 68 UK Great Britain
ARTICLES: 0
HEADNOTE: FACILITIES FOR DETECTION STATION
TOPIC: Scientific Project
CONCEPTS: Research cooperation. General technical assistance. Special projects.
TREATY REF: 480UNTS43.
PROCEDURE: Duration.
PARTIES:
 Mauritius
 UK Great Britain

109271   Bilateral Exchange   **0 UNTS 0**
SIGNED: 25 Jun 68   FORCE: 25 Jun 68
REGISTERED: 1 Oct 68 UK Great Britain
ARTICLES: 0
HEADNOTE: PEACE CORPS OPERATIONS
TOPIC: Direct Aid
CONCEPTS: Assistance. Volunteer programs.
PROCEDURE: Termination.
PARTIES:
 UK Great Britain
 USA (United States)

109272   Bilateral Exchange   **0 UNTS 0**
SIGNED: 10 Apr 64   FORCE: 10 Apr 64
REGISTERED: 3 Oct 68 UK Great Britain
ARTICLES: 0
HEADNOTE: FISHERIES AGREEMENT
TOPIC: Specific Resources
CONCEPTS: Ocean resources.
TREATY REF: 27BFSP983; 31BFSP165; 27BFSP983; ETC..
PARTIES:
 France
 UK Great Britain

109273   Bilateral Convention   **0 UNTS 0**
SIGNED: 12 Oct 66   FORCE: 1 Jun 68
REGISTERED: 3 Oct 68 Netherlands
ARTICLES: 0
HEADNOTE: SOCIAL SECURITY
TOPIC: Non-ILO Labor
CONCEPTS: Family allowances. Administrative cooperation. Old age insurance. Sickness and invalidity insurance. Social security. Unemployment.
PROCEDURE: Duration. Ratification. Termination.
PARTIES:
 Netherlands
 Portugal

109274   Bilateral Agreement   **0 UNTS 0**
SIGNED: 13 Dec 66   FORCE: 13 Dec 66
REGISTERED: 3 Oct 68 UK Great Britain
ARTICLES: 0
HEADNOTE: PENSIONABLE EMPLOYMENT
TOPIC: Non-ILO Labor
CONCEPTS: Old age insurance.
PROCEDURE: Amendment. Duration. Termination.
PARTIES:
 Canada
 UK Great Britain

109275   Bilateral Agreement   **0 UNTS 0**
SIGNED: 22 Aug 67   FORCE: 8 May 68
REGISTERED: 3 Oct 68 Netherlands
ARTICLES: 0
HEADNOTE: CULTURAL AGREEMENT
TOPIC: Culture
CONCEPTS: Professorships. Exchange. General cultural cooperation.
PROCEDURE: Duration. Ratification.
PARTIES:
 Netherlands
 Poland

109276   Bilateral Agreement   **0 UNTS 0**
SIGNED: 22 Aug 67   FORCE: 16 May 68
REGISTERED: 3 Oct 68 Netherlands
ARTICLES: 0
HEADNOTE: ECONOMIC INDUSTRIAL & TECHNICAL COOPERATION
TOPIC: General Economic
CONCEPTS: General economics. General technical assistance.
PROCEDURE: Denunciation. Duration.
PARTIES:
 Netherlands
 Poland

109277   Bilateral Agreement   **0 UNTS 0**
SIGNED: 19 Jan 68   FORCE: 19 Jan 68
REGISTERED: 3 Oct 68 UK Great Britain
ARTICLES: 0
HEADNOTE: SCIENCE & TECHNOLOGY
TOPIC: Scientific Project
CONCEPTS: Research cooperation.
PROCEDURE: Amendment. Duration.
PARTIES:
 UK Great Britain
 USSR (Soviet Union)

109278   Bilateral Agreement   **0 UNTS 0**
SIGNED: 26 Mar 68   FORCE: 26 Mar 68
REGISTERED: 3 Oct 68 UK Great Britain
ARTICLES: 0
HEADNOTE: COOPERATION SCIENCE & TECHNOLOGY
TOPIC: Scientific Project
CONCEPTS: Scientific exchange. General technical assistance.
PROCEDURE: Duration. Termination.
PARTIES:
 Czechoslovakia
 UK Great Britain

109279   Bilateral Agreement   **0 UNTS 0**
SIGNED: 31 Mar 68   FORCE: 31 Mar 68
REGISTERED: 3 Oct 68 Czechoslovakia
ARTICLES: 0
HEADNOTE: HEALTH COOPERATION
TOPIC: Sanitation
CONCEPTS: Specialists exchange. Medical assistance and/or facilities. Teacher and student exchange.
PROCEDURE: Denunciation. Termination.
PARTIES:
 Czechoslovakia
 Mongolia

109280   Bilateral Agreement   **0 UNTS 0**
SIGNED: 17 Nov 67   FORCE: 21 Jun 68
REGISTERED: 7 Oct 68 Czechoslovakia
ARTICLES: 0
HEADNOTE: COOPERATION PLANT PROTECTION
TOPIC: Sanitation
CONCEPTS: Border control. Public health.
PROCEDURE: Denunciation. Duration.

PARTIES:
 Czechoslovakia
 Romania

109281   Multilateral Protocol   **0 UNTS 0**
SIGNED: 16 Aug 68   FORCE: 17 Mar 68
REGISTERED: 14 Oct 68 Council of Europe
ARTICLES: 0
HEADNOTE: SOCIAL SECURITY
TOPIC: Non-ILO Labor
CONCEPTS: Annex type material.
TREATY REF: 210UNTS131.
PARTIES:
 Luxembourg RATIFIED: 3 Apr 68 FORCE: 4 Apr 69
 Netherlands RATIFIED: 16 Mar 67 FORCE: 17 Mar 68
 Norway RATIFIED: 25 Mar 66 FORCE: 17 Mar 68
 Sweden RATIFIED: 25 Sep 65 FORCE: 17 Mar 68
 UK Great Britain RATIFIED: 12 Jan 68 FORCE: 13 Jan 69

109282   Bilateral Instrument   **0 UNTS 0**
SIGNED: 3 Aug 68   FORCE: 30 Apr 68
REGISTERED: 17 Oct 68 Denmark
ARTICLES: 0
HEADNOTE: GOVERNMENT LOAN
TOPIC: Loans and Credits
CONCEPTS: Procedure. Credit provisions. Purchase authorization. Loan repayment. Terms of loan.
PROCEDURE: Termination.
PARTIES:
 Denmark
 Senegal

109283   Bilateral Exchange   **0 UNTS 0**
SIGNED: 1 Sep 65   FORCE: 23 Apr 68
REGISTERED: 23 Oct 68 UK Great Britain
ARTICLES: 0
HEADNOTE: CUSTOMS EXEMPTIONS CULTURAL INSTITUTES
TOPIC: Customs
CONCEPTS: Customs exemptions.
TREATY REF: 172UNTS27.
PARTIES:
 Italy
 UK Great Britain

109284   Bilateral Exchange   **0 UNTS 0**
SIGNED: 1 Sep 65   FORCE: 23 Apr 68
REGISTERED: 23 Oct 68 UK Great Britain
ARTICLES: 0
HEADNOTE: TAX EXEMPTION CULTURAL INSTITUTES
TOPIC: Taxation
CONCEPTS: Customs exemptions.
TREATY REF: 172UNTS27.
PROCEDURE: Termination.
PARTIES:
 Italy
 UK Great Britain

109285   Bilateral Exchange   **0 UNTS 0**
SIGNED: 11 Mar 68   FORCE: 11 Mar 68
REGISTERED: 11 Mar 68 UK Great Britain
ARTICLES: 0
HEADNOTE: TRAINING TEAM
TOPIC: Military Mission
CONCEPTS: General technical assistance. Special projects. Military training. Conditions for assistance missions.
TREATY REF: 382UNTS8.
PARTIES:
 Cyprus
 UK Great Britain

109286   Bilateral Exchange   **0 UNTS 0**
SIGNED: 29 Mar 68   FORCE: 29 Mar 68
REGISTERED: 11 Mar 68 UK Great Britain
ARTICLES: 0
HEADNOTE: INTEREST-FREE DEVELOPMENT LOAN
TOPIC: Loans and Credits
CONCEPTS: Loan and credit. Credit provisions. Loan repayment. Terms of loan.

PARTIES:
Turkey
UK Great Britain

109287   Bilateral Exchange   **0 UNTS 0**
SIGNED: 22 May 68   FORCE: 22 May 68
REGISTERED: 11 Mar 68 UK Great Britain
ARTICLES: 0
HEADNOTE: INTEREST-FREE   DEVELOPMENT
LOAN
TOPIC: Loans and Credits
CONCEPTS: Credit provisions. Purchase authoriza-
tion. Loan repayment. Terms of loan.
PARTIES:
Turkey
UK Great Britain

109288   Bilateral Agreement   **0 UNTS 0**
SIGNED: 11 Apr 68   FORCE: 11 Apr 68
REGISTERED: 11 Mar 68 UK Great Britain
ARTICLES: 0
HEADNOTE: OFF-SETTING FOREIGN EXCHANGE
EXPENDITURE
TOPIC: Finance
CONCEPTS: Balance of payments. Currency. Pay-
ment for war supplies.
TREATY   REF: 613UNTS316;   539UNTS243;
548UNTS374; ETC..
PARTIES:
Germany, West
UK Great Britain

109289   Bilateral Agreement   **0 UNTS 0**
SIGNED: 25 May 68   FORCE: 5 Jul 68
REGISTERED: 11 Mar 68 Denmark
ARTICLES: 0
HEADNOTE: PUBLIC HEALTH TECHNICAL COOP-
ERATION
TOPIC: Tech Assistance
CONCEPTS: IGO reference. Public health. Phar-
maceuticals. General technical assistance. As-
sistance.
INTL ORGS: World Health Organization.
PROCEDURE: Denunciation. Duration.
PARTIES:
Congo (Zaire)
Denmark

109290   Multilateral Agreement   **0 UNTS 0**
SIGNED: 20 Jun 67   FORCE: 20 Jun 67
REGISTERED: 24 Oct 68
ARTICLES: 0
HEADNOTE: TECHNICAL ASSISTANCE
TOPIC: Tech Assistance
CONCEPTS: Personnel. Scholarships and grants.
General technical assistance. Assistance. Status
of experts.
PARTIES:
Bulgaria
FAO (Food Agri)
IAEA (Atom Energy)
ICAO (Civil Aviat)
ILO (Labor Org)
IMCO (Maritime Org)
ITU (Telecommun)
UNESCO (Educ/Cult)
UPU (Postal Union)
WHO (World Health)
WMO (Meteorology)

109291   Bilateral Agreement   **0 UNTS 0**
SIGNED: 4 Nov 67   FORCE: 7 Dec 67
REGISTERED: 5 Sep 68 Ireland
ARTICLES: 0
HEADNOTE: CULTURAL AGREEMENT
TOPIC: Culture
CONCEPTS: Culture. General cultural cooperation.
Artists. Athletes. Archives and objects.
PROCEDURE: Duration. Termination.
PARTIES:
France
Ireland

109292   Bilateral Treaty   **0 UNTS 0**
SIGNED: 16 May 68   FORCE: 28 Jun 68
REGISTERED: 28 Oct 68 Hungary
ARTICLES: 0

HEADNOTE: FRIENDSHIP COOPERATION MU-
TUAL ASSISTANCE
TOPIC: General Amity
CONCEPTS: Friendship and amity. Peaceful rela-
tions. Culture. General trade. General technical
assistance.
TREATY REF: 219UNTS3; 25UNTS319.
PROCEDURE: Denunciation. Duration. Ratification.
PARTIES:
Hungary
Poland

109293   Multilateral Agreement   **0 UNTS 0**
SIGNED: 27 Mar 68   FORCE: 1 May 68
REGISTERED: 29 Oct 68 Netherlands
ARTICLES: 0
HEADNOTE: ABOLITION VISAS
TOPIC: Visas
CONCEPTS: Visa abolition. Border traffic and mi-
gration. Non-visa travel documents.
TREATY REF: 374UNTS3.
PROCEDURE: Termination.
PARTIES:
Belgium SIGNED: 27 Mar 68 FORCE: 1 May 68
Gambia SIGNED: 27 Mar 68 FORCE: 1 May 68
Luxembourg   SIGNED: 27 Mar 68   FORCE:
1 May 68
Netherlands   SIGNED: 27 Mar 68   FORCE:
1 May 68

109294   Bilateral Agreement   **0 UNTS 0**
SIGNED: 23 Jan 58   FORCE: 15 Jun 58
REGISTERED: 4 Nov 68 Argentina
ARTICLES: 0
HEADNOTE: STUDY WATERPOWER APIPE FALLS
TOPIC: Scientific Project
CONCEPTS: Research and scientific projects. Re-
search cooperation. Scientific exchange. Re-
search and development.
PROCEDURE: Ratification.
PARTIES:
Argentina
Paraguay

109295   Bilateral Instrument   **0 UNTS 0**
SIGNED: 25 Oct 68   FORCE: 25 Oct 68
REGISTERED: 12 Nov 68 United Nations
ARTICLES: 0
HEADNOTE: ACCEPTANCE   OBLIGATIONS   UN
CHARTER
TOPIC: UN Charter
CONCEPTS: Acceptance of obligations upon ad-
mittance to UN.
PROCEDURE: Ratification.
PARTIES:
Guinea

109296   Multilateral Agreement   **0 UNTS 0**
SIGNED: 28 Sep 68   FORCE: 13 Nov 68
REGISTERED: 13 Nov 68 United Nations
ARTICLES: 0
HEADNOTE: ARRANGEMENT–PREK THNOT DE-
VELOPMENT PROJECT
TOPIC: Tech Assistance
CONCEPTS: Procedure. Aid and development. As-
sistance. Special projects. Economic assistance.
PROCEDURE: Termination.
PARTIES:
Australia SIGNED: 13 Nov 68 FORCE: 13 Nov 68
Cambodia   SIGNED: 13 Nov 68   FORCE:
13 Nov 68
Canada SIGNED: 13 Nov 68 FORCE: 13 Nov 68
Germany, West SIGNED: 13 Nov 68 FORCE:
13 Nov 68
India SIGNED: 13 Nov 68 FORCE: 13 Nov 68
Italy SIGNED: 13 Nov 68 FORCE: 13 Nov 68
Japan SIGNED: 13 Nov 68 FORCE: 13 Nov 68
Netherlands   SIGNED: 13 Nov 68   FORCE:
13 Nov 68
Pakistan SIGNED: 13 Nov 68 FORCE: 13 Nov 68
Philippines   SIGNED: 13 Nov 68   FORCE:
13 Nov 68
UK Great Britain SIGNED: 13 Nov 68 FORCE:
13 Nov 68
ANNEX
668 UNTS 390.
668 UNTS 390.   France.   Signature   9 Apr 69.
Force 9 Apr 69.

109297   Bilateral Agreement   **0 UNTS 0**
SIGNED: 13 Mar 68   FORCE: 2 Aug 68
REGISTERED: 13 Nov 68 Netherlands
ARTICLES: 0
HEADNOTE: ECONOMIC INDUSTRIAL TECHNICAL
COOPERATION
TOPIC: General Economic
CONCEPTS: Research cooperation. General eco-
nomics. General technical assistance.
PROCEDURE: Denunciation. Ratification.
PARTIES:
Netherlands
Yugoslavia

109298   Multilateral Convention   **0 UNTS 0**
SIGNED: 21 Jun 66   FORCE: 6 Nov 68
REGISTERED: 14 Nov 68 ILO (Labor Org)
ARTICLES: 0
HEADNOTE: CREW LIVING CONDITIONS ON VES-
SELS
TOPIC: Non-ILO Labor
CONCEPTS: ILO conventions. Safety standards.
PROCEDURE: Ratification.
PARTIES:
Norway SIGNED: 21 Jun 66 RATIFIED: 6 Jul 67
FORCE: 6 Nov 68
Sierra Leone SIGNED: 21 Jun 66 RATIFIED:
6 Nov 67 FORCE: 6 Nov 68
Spain SIGNED: 21 Jun 66 RATIFIED: 8 Nov 68
FORCE: 6 Nov 68

109299   Bilateral Agreement   **0 UNTS 0**
SIGNED: 7 Dec 67   FORCE: 1 Jul 68
REGISTERED: 18 Nov 68 IBRD (World Bank)
ARTICLES: 0
HEADNOTE: LOAN THIRD HIGHWAY PROJECT
TOPIC: Loans and Credits
CONCEPTS: Loan and credit. Credit provisions.
Loan repayment. Terms of loan.
TREATY REF: 468UNTS331.
PROCEDURE: Termination.
PARTIES:
El Salvador
IBRD (World Bank)

109300   Bilateral Agreement   **0 UNTS 0**
SIGNED: 10 Apr 68   FORCE: 25 Jun 68
REGISTERED: 18 Nov 68 IBRD (World Bank)
ARTICLES: 0
HEADNOTE: LOAN EDUCATION
TOPIC: Loans and Credits
CONCEPTS: Loan and credit. Credit provisions.
Loan repayment. Terms of loan.
PROCEDURE: Termination.
PARTIES:
Nicaragua
IBRD (World Bank)

109301   Bilateral Agreement   **0 UNTS 0**
SIGNED: 22 Mar 68   FORCE: 1 Aug 68
REGISTERED: 18 Nov 68 IBRD (World Bank)
ARTICLES: 0
HEADNOTE: GUARANTEE BELGRADE BAR RAIL-
WAY
TOPIC: Loans and Credits
PARTIES:
IBRD (World Bank)
Yugoslavia

109302   Bilateral Agreement   **0 UNTS 0**
SIGNED: 10 Jul 68   FORCE: 2 Aug 68
REGISTERED: 18 Nov 68 IBRD (World Bank)
ARTICLES: 0
HEADNOTE: LOAN TARBELA
TOPIC: IBRD Project
PARTIES:
Pakistan
IBRD (World Bank)

109303   Bilateral Agreement   **0 UNTS 0**
SIGNED: 14 Jun 68   FORCE: 20 Sep 68
REGISTERED: 18 Nov 68 IDA (Devel Assoc)
ARTICLES: 0
HEADNOTE: CREDIT POWER DISTRIBUTION
TOPIC: Non-IBRD Project
PARTIES:
Ghana
IDA (Devel Assoc)

109304   Bilateral Agreement   0 UNTS 0
SIGNED: 17 Jun 68   FORCE: 5 Aug 68
REGISTERED: 18 Nov 68 IDA (Devel Assoc)
ARTICLES: 0
HEADNOTE: CREDIT SECOND HIGHWAY
TOPIC: Non-IBRD Project
PARTIES:
  Kenya
  IDA (Devel Assoc)

109305   Bilateral Agreement   0 UNTS 0
SIGNED: 3 Jul 68   FORCE: 3 Jul 68
REGISTERED: 19 Nov 68 Denmark
ARTICLES: 0
HEADNOTE: VOLUNTEERS FROM DENMARK
TOPIC: Direct Aid
PARTIES:
  Denmark
  Uganda

109306   Bilateral Agreement   0 UNTS 0
SIGNED: 11 Jul 68   FORCE: 11 Jul 68
REGISTERED: 19 Nov 68 Denmark
ARTICLES: 0
HEADNOTE: VOLUNTEERS FROM DENMARK
TOPIC: Direct Aid
PARTIES:
  Denmark
  Zambia

109307   Bilateral Agreement   0 UNTS 0
SIGNED: 5 Feb 68   FORCE: 15 Mar 68
REGISTERED: 20 Nov 68 IDA (Devel Assoc)
ARTICLES: 0
HEADNOTE: CREDIT HIGHWAY PROJECT
TOPIC: Non-IBRD Project
PARTIES:
  Malawi
  IDA (Devel Assoc)

109308   Bilateral Agreement   0 UNTS 0
SIGNED: 5 Feb 68   FORCE: 15 Mar 68
REGISTERED: 20 Nov 68 IDA (Devel Assoc)
ARTICLES: 0
HEADNOTE: CREDIT LILONGWE AGRICULTURE
TOPIC: Non-IBRD Project
PARTIES:
  Malawi
  IDA (Devel Assoc)

109309   Bilateral Agreement   0 UNTS 0
SIGNED: 5 Feb 68   FORCE: 15 Mar 68
REGISTERED: 20 Nov 68 IDA (Devel Assoc)
ARTICLES: 0
HEADNOTE: CREDIT SHIRE VALLEY AGRICUL-
TURE
TOPIC: Non-IBRD Project
PARTIES:
  Malawi
  IDA (Devel Assoc)

109310   Bilateral Agreement   0 UNTS 0
SIGNED: 31 Aug 67   FORCE: 31 Aug 67
REGISTERED: 20 Nov 68 IAEA (Atom Energy)
ARTICLES: 0
HEADNOTE: TRANSFER IRRADIATION EQUIP-
MENT
TOPIC: Atomic Energy
PARTIES:
  Israel
  IAEA (Atom Energy)

109311   Bilateral Agreement   0 UNTS 0
SIGNED: 12 Feb 68   FORCE: 20 Feb 68
REGISTERED: 20 Nov 68 IAEA (Atom Energy)
ARTICLES: 0
HEADNOTE: TRANSFER ENRICHED URANIUM
TOPIC: Atomic Energy
PARTIES:
  State/IGO Group
  IAEA (Atom Energy)

109312   Bilateral Agreement   0 UNTS 0
SIGNED: 27 Mar 68   FORCE: 27 Mar 68
REGISTERED: 20 Nov 68 IAEA (Atom Energy)
ARTICLES: 0

HEADNOTE: SAFEGUARDS
TOPIC: Atomic Energy
PARTIES:
  State/IGO Group
  IAEA (Atom Energy)

109313   Bilateral Agreement   0 UNTS 0
SIGNED: 17 Jun 68   FORCE: 17 Jun 68
REGISTERED: 20 Nov 68 IAEA (Atom Energy)
ARTICLES: 0
HEADNOTE: TRANSFER ENRICHED URANIUM
TOPIC: Atomic Energy
PARTIES:
  State/IGO Group
  IAEA (Atom Energy)

109314   Bilateral Agreement   0 UNTS 0
SIGNED: 17 Jun 68   FORCE: 17 Jun 68
REGISTERED: 20 Nov 68 IAEA (Atom Energy)
ARTICLES: 0
HEADNOTE: NUCLEAR REACTOR
TOPIC: Atomic Energy
PARTIES:
  Pakistan
  IAEA (Atom Energy)

109315   Bilateral Agreement   0 UNTS 0
SIGNED: 27 Jun 68   FORCE: 27 Jun 68
REGISTERED: 20 Nov 68 IAEA (Atom Energy)
ARTICLES: 0
HEADNOTE: SAFEGUARDS
TOPIC: Atomic Energy
PARTIES:
  Romania
  IAEA (Atom Energy)

109316   Bilateral Agreement   0 UNTS 0
SIGNED: 10 Jul 68   FORCE: 10 Jul 68
REGISTERED: 20 Nov 68 IAEA (Atom Energy)
ARTICLES: 0
HEADNOTE: SAFEGUARDS
TOPIC: Atomic Energy
PARTIES:
  State/IGO Group
  IAEA (Atom Energy)

109317   Bilateral Agreement   0 UNTS 0
SIGNED: 15 Jul 68   FORCE: 19 Jul 68
REGISTERED: 20 Nov 68 IAEA (Atom Energy)
ARTICLES: 0
HEADNOTE: SAFEGUARDS
TOPIC: Atomic Energy
PARTIES:
  State/IGO Group
  IAEA (Atom Energy)

109318   Bilateral Agreement   0 UNTS 0
SIGNED: 6 Sep 68   FORCE: 6 Sep 68
REGISTERED: 20 Nov 68 IAEA (Atom Energy)
ARTICLES: 0
HEADNOTE: SAFEGUARDS
TOPIC: Atomic Energy
PARTIES:
  Mexico
  IAEA (Atom Energy)

109319   Bilateral Agreement   0 UNTS 0
SIGNED: 15 Jul 68   FORCE: 23 Jul 68
REGISTERED: 21 Nov 68 IBRD (World Bank)
ARTICLES: 0
HEADNOTE: GUARANTEE POWER PROJECT
TOPIC: IBRD Project
PARTIES:
  IBRD (World Bank)
  Sudan

109320   Bilateral Agreement   0 UNTS 0
SIGNED: 17 Jun 68   FORCE: 23 Oct 68
REGISTERED: 21 Nov 68 IDA (Devel Assoc)
ARTICLES: 0
HEADNOTE: CREDIT SECOND KENYA TEA
TOPIC: Non-IBRD Project
PARTIES:
  Kenya
  IDA (Devel Assoc)

109321   Bilateral Agreement   0 UNTS 0
SIGNED: 27 Jun 68   FORCE: 30 Aug 68
REGISTERED: 21 Nov 68 IDA (Devel Assoc)
ARTICLES: 0
HEADNOTE: CREDIT EDUCATION PROJECT
TOPIC: Non-IBRD Project
CONCEPTS: Loan and credit. Credit provisions.
  Purchase authorization. Terms of loan.
PROCEDURE: Termination.
PARTIES:
  Ecuador
  IDA (Devel Assoc)

109322   Multilateral Agreement   0 UNTS 0
SIGNED: 28 Dec 67   FORCE: 28 Dec 67
REGISTERED: 21 Nov 68 Thailand
ARTICLES: 0
HEADNOTE: SOUTHEAST ASIAN FISHERIES DE-
VELOPMENT
TOPIC: Scientific Project
CONCEPTS: Research and scientific projects. Re-
  search cooperation. Research and development.
PROCEDURE: Amendment. Accession. Duration.
  Termination.
PARTIES:
  Japan SIGNED: 28 Dec 67 FORCE: 28 Dec 67
  Malaysia SIGNED: 26 Jan 68 FORCE: 26 Jan 68
  Philippines   SIGNED: 16 Jan 68   FORCE:
    16 Jan 68
  Singapore   SIGNED: 28 Dec 67   FORCE:
    28 Dec 67
  Thailand SIGNED: 28 Dec 67 FORCE: 28 Dec 67
  Vietnam, South SIGNED: 26 Jan 68 FORCE:
    26 Jan 68

109323   Bilateral Agreement   0 UNTS 0
SIGNED: 5 Dec 51   FORCE: 13 Oct 53
REGISTERED: 25 Nov 68 Netherlands
ARTICLES: 0
HEADNOTE: CULTURE
TOPIC: Culture
CONCEPTS: Teacher and student exchange. Ex-
  change. General cultural cooperation. Artists.
  Athletes.
PROCEDURE: Duration. Ratification. Termination.
PARTIES:
  Italy
  Netherlands

109324   Bilateral Exchange   0 UNTS 0
SIGNED: 30 Apr 68   FORCE: 13 Sep 68
REGISTERED: 27 Nov 68 Austria
ARTICLES: 0
HEADNOTE: ABOLITION VISAS
TOPIC: Visas
CONCEPTS: Visa abolition.
PARTIES:
  Austria
  Costa Rica

109325   Bilateral Agreement   0 UNTS 0
SIGNED: 29 Jan 68   FORCE: 19 Mar 68
REGISTERED: 29 Nov 68 IDA (Devel Assoc)
ARTICLES: 0
HEADNOTE: CREDIT HIGHWAY ENGINEER
TOPIC: Non-IBRD Project
CONCEPTS: Loan and credit. Credit provisions.
  Purchase authorization. Terms of loan.
PROCEDURE: Termination.
PARTIES:
  Cameroon
  IDA (Devel Assoc)

109326   Bilateral Agreement   0 UNTS 0
SIGNED: 18 Mar 68   FORCE: 11 Jul 68
REGISTERED: 29 Nov 68 IBRD (World Bank)
ARTICLES: 0
HEADNOTE: GUARANTEE DEVELOPMENT FI-
NANCE CORPORATION
TOPIC: IBRD Project
CONCEPTS: World Bank projects. Loan regula-
  tions. Loan guarantee. Plans and standards.
PARTIES:
  Greece
  IBRD (World Bank)

109327   Bilateral Agreement   0 UNTS 0
SIGNED: 21 Mar 68   FORCE: 10 May 68

REGISTERED: 29 Nov 68 IDA (Devel Assoc)
ARTICLES: 0
HEADNOTE: CREDIT HIGHWAY PROJECT SUPPLE-
MENT
TOPIC: Non-IBRD Project
CONCEPTS: Loan and credit. Credit provisions.
Purchase authorization. Loan repayment. Terms
of loan.
TREATY REF: 506UNTS91.
PROCEDURE: Termination.
PARTIES:
IDA (Devel Assoc)
Tanzania

109329 Bilateral Convention **0 UNTS 0**
SIGNED: 22 Jul 65 FORCE: 1 Feb 67
REGISTERED: 2 Dec 68 France
ARTICLES: 0
HEADNOTE: SOCIAL SECURITY
TOPIC: Non-ILO Labor
CONCEPTS: Arbitration. Procedure. Family allow-
ances. Administrative cooperation. Old age in-
surance. Sickness and invalidity insurance. So-
cial security. Unemployment.
PROCEDURE: Denunciation. Duration.
PARTIES:
France
Mauritania

109330 Bilateral Exchange **0 UNTS 0**
SIGNED: 14 Mar 67 FORCE: 1 Feb 68
REGISTERED: 5 Dec 68 France
ARTICLES: 0
HEADNOTE: PATENT TAX
TOPIC: Taxation
CONCEPTS: Taxation. Tax exemptions.
PARTIES:
France
USSR (Soviet Union)

109331 Bilateral Agreement **0 UNTS 0**
SIGNED: 17 Oct 67 FORCE: 24 Jan 68
REGISTERED: 5 Dec 68 IBRD (World Bank)
ARTICLES: 0
HEADNOTE: LOAN GHAZWIN DEVELOPMENT
TOPIC: IBRD Project
CONCEPTS: Loan and credit. Credit provisions.
Purchase authorization. Loan repayment. Terms
of loan. Loan regulations. Loan guarantee. Guar-
antor non-interference. Plans and standards.
PARTIES:
Iran
IBRD (World Bank)

109332 Bilateral Agreement **0 UNTS 0**
SIGNED: 23 May 68 FORCE: 30 Jul 68
REGISTERED: 5 Dec 68 IBRD (World Bank)
ARTICLES: 0
HEADNOTE: LOAN THIRD HIGHWAY
TOPIC: IBRD Project
CONCEPTS: Loan and credit. Credit provisions.
Loan repayment. Loan regulations. Loan guaran-
tee. Guarantor non-interference. Plans and stan-
dards.
PARTIES:
IBRD (World Bank)
Thailand

109333 Bilateral Agreement **0 UNTS 0**
SIGNED: 3 Jun 68 FORCE: 3 Aug 68
REGISTERED: 5 Dec 68 IBRD (World Bank)
ARTICLES: 0
HEADNOTE: GUARANTEE THIRD EXPANSION
TOPIC: IBRD Project
CONCEPTS: Loan and credit. Credit provisions.
Loan repayment. Loan regulations. Loan guaran-
tee. Guarantor non-interference. Plans and stan-
dards.
TREATY REF: 375UNTS49; 447UNTS39.
PARTIES:
Colombia
IBRD (World Bank)

109334 Bilateral Agreement **0 UNTS 0**
SIGNED: 3 Jun 68 FORCE: 7 Aug 68
REGISTERED: 5 Dec 68 IBRD (World Bank)
ARTICLES: 0

HEADNOTE: GUARANTEE BOGOTA WATER SUP-
PLY
TOPIC: IBRD Project
CONCEPTS: Loan and credit. Credit provisions.
Loan repayment. Loan regulations. Loan guaran-
tee. Guarantor non-interference. Plans and stan-
dards.
PARTIES:
Colombia
IBRD (World Bank)

109335 Bilateral Agreement **0 UNTS 0**
SIGNED: 28 Jun 68 FORCE: 30 Aug 68
REGISTERED: 9 Dec 68 IBRD (World Bank)
ARTICLES: 0
HEADNOTE: GUARANTEE SECOND POWER SEC-
TOR
TOPIC: IBRD Project
PARTIES:
Mexico
IBRD (World Bank)

109336 Bilateral Exchange **0 UNTS 0**
SIGNED: 24 Sep 68 FORCE: 24 Oct 68
REGISTERED: 9 Dec 68 Jamaica
ARTICLES: 0
HEADNOTE: VISA SUPPRESSION
TOPIC: Visas
PARTIES:
France
Jamaica

109337 Bilateral Agreement **0 UNTS 0**
SIGNED: 25 Oct 67 FORCE: 8 Nov 68
REGISTERED: 10 Dec 68 United Nations
ARTICLES: 0
HEADNOTE: UNICEF LOCAL ACTIVITIES
TOPIC: IGO Operations
PARTIES:
UNICEF (Children)
Venezuela

109338 Bilateral Agreement **0 UNTS 0**
SIGNED: 21 Nov 67 FORCE: 5 Sep 68
REGISTERED: 10 Dec 68 UK Great Britain
ARTICLES: 0
HEADNOTE: GOODS CARRIAGE BY ROAD
TOPIC: Land Transport
PARTIES:
Sweden
UK Great Britain

109339 Bilateral Exchange **0 UNTS 0**
SIGNED: 2 Dec 67 FORCE: 2 Dec 67
REGISTERED: 10 Dec 68 UK Great Britain
ARTICLES: 0
HEADNOTE: INTEREST-FREE LOAN
TOPIC: Loans and Credits
PARTIES:
Indonesia
UK Great Britain

109340 Bilateral Exchange **0 UNTS 0**
SIGNED: 6 May 68 FORCE: 6 May 68
REGISTERED: 10 Dec 68 UK Great Britain
ARTICLES: 0
HEADNOTE: INTEREST-FREE LOAN
TOPIC: Loans and Credits
PARTIES:
Indonesia
UK Great Britain

109341 Bilateral Convention **0 UNTS 0**
SIGNED: 24 May 67 FORCE: 3 Jul 68
REGISTERED: 10 Dec 68 UK Great Britain
ARTICLES: 0
HEADNOTE: DOUBLE TAX FISCAL EVASION
TOPIC: Taxation
PARTIES:
Luxembourg
UK Great Britain

109342 Bilateral Agreement **0 UNTS 0**
SIGNED: 7 Mar 68 FORCE: 12 Jul 68
REGISTERED: 10 Dec 68 UK Great Britain
ARTICLES: 0

HEADNOTE: DOUBLE TAX FISCAL EVASION
TOPIC: Taxation
PARTIES:
Cyprus
UK Great Britain

109343 Multilateral Agreement **0 UNTS 0**
SIGNED: 9 Sep 66 FORCE: 20 Aug 67
REGISTERED: 12 Dec 68 Poland
ARTICLES: 0
HEADNOTE: STATUS PRIVILEGES INTERNA-
TIONAL ORGANS
TOPIC: IGO Status/Immunit
PARTIES:
Bulgaria SIGNED: 9 Sep 66 RATIFIED:
27 May 67 FORCE: 20 Aug 67
Czechoslovakia SIGNED: 9 Sep 66 RATIFIED:
2 Jun 67 FORCE: 20 Aug 67
Germany, East SIGNED: 9 Sep 66 RATIFIED:
21 Feb 67 FORCE: 20 Aug 67
Hungary SIGNED: 9 Sep 66 RATIFIED: 1 Feb 67
FORCE: 20 Aug 67
Poland SIGNED: 9 Sep 66 RATIFIED: 23 May 67
FORCE: 20 Aug 67
USSR (Soviet Union) SIGNED: 9 Sep 66 RATI-
FIED: 21 Jul 67 FORCE: 20 Aug 67

109344 Multilateral Convention **0 UNTS 0**
SIGNED: 12 Sep 64 FORCE: 22 Jul 68
REGISTERED: 13 Dec 68 Denmark
ARTICLES: 0
HEADNOTE: INTERNATIONAL COUNCIL EXPLO-
RATION SEA
TOPIC: Specific Resources
PARTIES:
Belgium SIGNED: 12 Sep 64 RATIFIED:
20 Jul 67 FORCE: 22 Jul 68
Canada SIGNED: 12 Sep 64 RATIFIED:
20 Jul 68 FORCE: 22 Jul 68
Denmark SIGNED: 12 Sep 64 RATIFIED:
20 Apr 65 FORCE: 22 Jul 68
Finland SIGNED: 12 Sep 64 RATIFIED:
10 Jun 65 FORCE: 22 Jul 68
France SIGNED: 12 Sep 64 RATIFIED: 19 Jan 65
FORCE: 22 Jul 68
Germany, West SIGNED: 12 Sep 64 RATIFIED:
13 May 65 FORCE: 22 Jul 68
Iceland SIGNED: 12 Sep 64 RATIFIED: 4 Dec 64
FORCE: 22 Jul 68
Ireland SIGNED: 12 Sep 64 RATIFIED:
10 Jun 65 FORCE: 22 Jul 68
Italy SIGNED: 12 Sep 64 RATIFIED: 28 Dec 67
FORCE: 22 Jul 68
Netherlands SIGNED: 12 Sep 64 RATIFIED:
13 Feb 67 FORCE: 22 Jul 68
Norway SIGNED: 12 Sep 64 RATIFIED:
26 May 65 FORCE: 22 Jul 68
Poland SIGNED: 12 Sep 64 RATIFIED:
25 Nov 66 FORCE: 22 Jul 68
Portugal SIGNED: 12 Sep 64 RATIFIED:
18 Feb 66 FORCE: 22 Jul 68
Spain SIGNED: 12 Sep 64 RATIFIED: 9 Sep 65
FORCE: 22 Jul 68
Sweden SIGNED: 12 Sep 64 RATIFIED:
30 Nov 64 FORCE: 22 Jul 68
UK Great Britain SIGNED: 12 Sep 64 RATIFIED:
4 May 65 FORCE: 22 Jul 68
USSR (Soviet Union) SIGNED: 12 Sep 64 RATI-
FIED: 28 Oct 65 FORCE: 22 Jul 68

109345 Bilateral Treaty **0 UNTS 0**
SIGNED: 29 May 66 FORCE: 8 Jun 68
REGISTERED: 16 Dec 68 Thailand
ARTICLES: 0
HEADNOTE: AMITY ECONOMIC RELATIONS
TOPIC: General Amity
PARTIES:
Thailand
USA (United States)

109346 Bilateral Convention **0 UNTS 0**
SIGNED: 6 Jun 66 FORCE: 25 Sep 68
REGISTERED: 16 Dec 68 Israel
ARTICLES: 0
HEADNOTE: LEGAL ASSISTANCE CRIMINAL MAT-
TERS
TOPIC: Admin Cooperation
CONCEPTS: Administrative cooperation. General
cooperation. Exchange of information and docu-
ments.

PROCEDURE: Denunciation. Ratification.
PARTIES:
Austria
Israel

109347   Bilateral Convention   **0 UNTS 0**
SIGNED: 6 Jun 66   FORCE: 25 Oct 68
REGISTERED: 16 Dec 68 Israel
ARTICLES: 0
HEADNOTE: JUDGMENTS CIVIL COMMERCIAL
TOPIC: Admin Cooperation
CONCEPTS: Administrative cooperation. General
cooperation. Recognition and enforcement of le-
gal decisions. Recognition of legal documents.
PROCEDURE: Denunciation. Ratification.
PARTIES:
Austria
Israel

109348   Bilateral Convention   **0 UNTS 0**
SIGNED: 11 Jul 66   FORCE: 17 Jun 68
REGISTERED: 16 Dec 68 Israel
ARTICLES: 0
HEADNOTE: TECHNICAL COOPERATION
TOPIC: Tech Assistance
CONCEPTS: General technical assistance. Conser-
vation.
PROCEDURE: Ratification.
PARTIES:
Israel
Mexico

109349   Bilateral Exchange   **0 UNTS 0**
SIGNED: 9 Feb 67   FORCE: 15 Mar 67
REGISTERED: 16 Dec 68 Israel
ARTICLES: 0
HEADNOTE: VISAS
TOPIC: Visas
CONCEPTS: Frontier formalities. Visa abolition.
Passports non-diplomatic.
PARTIES:
Israel
UK Great Britain

109350   Bilateral Exchange   **0 UNTS 0**
SIGNED: 5 Apr 67   FORCE: 5 Apr 67
REGISTERED: 16 Dec 68 Israel
ARTICLES: 0
HEADNOTE: LICENSING RADIO AMATEURS
TOPIC: Gen Communications
CONCEPTS: General communications. Amateur ra-
dio.
PARTIES:
Canada
Israel

109351   Bilateral Agreement   **0 UNTS 0**
SIGNED: 4 Aug 67   FORCE: 4 Aug 68
REGISTERED: 16 Dec 68 Israel
ARTICLES: 0
HEADNOTE: AGRI COMMOD
TOPIC: US Agri Commod Aid
CONCEPTS: Export quotas. Import quotas. Trade
procedures. Banking. Balance of payments.
Monetary and gold transfers. Expense sharing
formulae. Payment schedules. Transportation
costs. Commodity trade. Surplus commodities.
PROCEDURE: Termination.
PARTIES:
Israel
USA (United States)

109352   Bilateral Agreement   **0 UNTS 0**
SIGNED: 29 Mar 68   FORCE: 29 Mar 68
REGISTERED: 16 Dec 68 Israel
ARTICLES: 0
HEADNOTE: AGRI COMMOD
TOPIC: US Agri Commod Aid
CONCEPTS: Reexport of goods, etc.. Export subsi-
dies. Trade procedures. Commodity trade. Sur-
plus commodities.
PARTIES:
Israel
USA (United States)

109354   Bilateral Exchange   **0 UNTS 0**
SIGNED: 1 Apr 68   FORCE: 1 May 68

REGISTERED: 16 Dec 68 Israel
ARTICLES: 0
HEADNOTE: VISAS
TOPIC: Visas
CONCEPTS: Visa abolition. Passports non-
diplomatic. Visas.
PROCEDURE: Termination.
PARTIES:
Israel
Peru

109355   Bilateral Exchange   **0 UNTS 0**
SIGNED: 6 Apr 68   FORCE: 5 Jul 68
REGISTERED: 16 Dec 68 Israel
ARTICLES: 0
HEADNOTE: VISAS
TOPIC: Visas
CONCEPTS: Visa abolition. Passports non-
diplomatic. Visas.
PARTIES:
Costa Rica
Israel

109356   Bilateral Exchange   **0 UNTS 0**
SIGNED: 22 May 68   FORCE: 22 May 68
REGISTERED: 16 Dec 68 Israel
ARTICLES: 0
HEADNOTE: METEOROLOGIC RAWINSONDE STA-
TION
TOPIC: Scientific Project
CONCEPTS: IGO reference. Research and scien-
tific projects. Research cooperation.
Meteorology.
INTL ORGS: World Meteorological Organization.
PROCEDURE: Termination.
PARTIES:
Israel
USA (United States)

109357   Bilateral Exchange   **0 UNTS 0**
SIGNED: 2 May 68   FORCE: 31 Jul 68
REGISTERED: 16 Dec 68 Israel
ARTICLES: 0
HEADNOTE: VISAS
TOPIC: Visas
CONCEPTS: Visa abolition. Passports non-
diplomatic. Visas.
PARTIES:
Dominican Republic
Israel

109358   Bilateral Exchange   **0 UNTS 0**
SIGNED: 23 Jul 68   FORCE: 23 Jul 68
REGISTERED: 16 Dec 68 Israel
ARTICLES: 0
HEADNOTE: AIRWORTHINESS CERTIFICATE
TOPIC: Air Transport
CONCEPTS: Airworthiness certificates.
PARTIES:
Israel
USA (United States)

109359   Bilateral Exchange   **0 UNTS 0**
SIGNED: 25 Sep 68   FORCE: 25 Sep 68
REGISTERED: 16 Dec 68 Israel
ARTICLES: 0
HEADNOTE: CONSULAR FUNCTIONS
TOPIC: Consul/Citizenship
CONCEPTS: Diplomatic and consular relations.
General consular functions.
TREATY REF: 590UNTS35.
PARTIES:
Belgium
Israel

109360   Bilateral Agreement   **0 UNTS 0**
SIGNED: 17 Apr 68   FORCE: 12 Aug 68
REGISTERED: 18 Dec 68 IBRD (World Bank)
ARTICLES: 0
HEADNOTE: LOAN JENGKA TRIANGLE
TOPIC: IBRD Project
CONCEPTS: Credit provisions. Loan repayment.
Terms of loan. World Bank projects. Loan regula-
tions. Loan guarantee.
PROCEDURE: Termination.
PARTIES:
Malaysia
IBRD (World Bank)

109361   Bilateral Agreement   **0 UNTS 0**
SIGNED: 7 Jul 68   FORCE: 20 Sep 68
REGISTERED: 18 Dec 68 IBRD (World Bank)
ARTICLES: 0
HEADNOTE: LOAN EDUCATION
TOPIC: IBRD Project
CONCEPTS: Credit provisions. Loan repayment.
Terms of loan. World Bank projects. Loan regula-
tions. Loan guarantee.
PROCEDURE: Termination.
PARTIES:
Gabon
IBRD (World Bank)

109362   Bilateral Agreement   **0 UNTS 0**
SIGNED: 10 Oct 67   FORCE: 3 May 68
REGISTERED: 19 Dec 68 Belgium
ARTICLES: 0
HEADNOTE: INDUSTRIAL TECHNOLOGICAL CO-
OPERATION
TOPIC: Tech Assistance
CONCEPTS: Exchange rates and regulations. De-
livery guarantees. General technical assistance.
PROCEDURE: Denunciation. Duration.
PARTIES:
Bel-Lux Econ Union
Czechoslovakia

109363   Bilateral Agreement   **0 UNTS 0**
SIGNED: 21 Mar 68   FORCE: 15 Sep 68
REGISTERED: 21 Dec 68 Netherlands
ARTICLES: 0
HEADNOTE: SOCIAL SECURITY COLLECTION
TOPIC: Non-ILO Labor
CONCEPTS: Social security. Unemployment.
PROCEDURE: Duration.
PARTIES:
Belgium
Netherlands

109364   Bilateral Agreement   **0 UNTS 0**
SIGNED: 3 Jul 68   FORCE: 20 Aug 68
REGISTERED: 21 Dec 68 IBRD (World Bank)
ARTICLES: 0
HEADNOTE: LOAN SINGAPORE SEWERAGE
TOPIC: IBRD Project
CONCEPTS: Credit provisions. Loan repayment.
Terms of loan. World Bank projects. Loan regula-
tions. Loan guarantee.
PARTIES:
IBRD (World Bank)
Singapore

109365   Bilateral Agreement   **0 UNTS 0**
SIGNED: 5 Jun 68   FORCE: 2 Dec 68
REGISTERED: 27 Dec 68 IBRD (World Bank)
ARTICLES: 0
HEADNOTE: GUARANTEE AGRICULTURAL
CREDIT
TOPIC: IBRD Project
CONCEPTS: Loan guarantee. Guarantor non-inter-
ference.
PARTIES:
Costa Rica
IBRD (World Bank)

109366   Bilateral Agreement   **0 UNTS 0**
SIGNED: 21 Jun 68   FORCE: 21 Aug 68
REGISTERED: 27 Dec 68 IBRD (World Bank)
ARTICLES: 0
HEADNOTE: GUARANTEE SEVENTH POWER
TOPIC: IBRD Project
CONCEPTS: Loan guarantee. Guarantor non-inter-
ference.
PARTIES:
Nicaragua
IBRD (World Bank)

109367   Bilateral Convention   **0 UNTS 0**
SIGNED: 2 Jul 65   FORCE: 11 Jan 68
REGISTERED: 27 Dec 68 Belgium
ARTICLES: 0
HEADNOTE: DOUBLE TAX INCOME CAPITAL
TOPIC: Taxation
CONCEPTS: Taxation. Tax credits. Equitable taxes.
Tax exemptions.
PROCEDURE: Duration. Ratification. Termination.

PARTIES:
Belgium
Sweden

109368 Multilateral Agreement **0 UNTS 0**
SIGNED: 1 Aug 68 FORCE: 1 Aug 68
REGISTERED: 31 Dec 68 Korea, South
ARTICLES: 0
HEADNOTE: CULTURAL SOCIAL CENTER ASIA PACIFIC
TOPIC: Culture
CONCEPTS: Culture. General cultural cooperation. Subsidiary organ. Internal structure.
PROCEDURE: Amendment. Termination.
PARTIES:
Australia SIGNED: 1 Aug 68 FORCE: 1 Aug 68
Taiwan SIGNED: 1 Aug 68 FORCE: 1 Aug 68
Japan SIGNED: 1 Aug 68 FORCE: 1 Aug 68
Korea, South SIGNED: 1 Aug 68 FORCE: 1 Aug 68
Malaysia SIGNED: 1 Aug 68 FORCE: 1 Aug 68
New Zealand SIGNED: 1 Aug 68 FORCE: 1 Aug 68
Philippines SIGNED: 1 Aug 68 FORCE: 1 Aug 68
Thailand SIGNED: 1 Aug 68 FORCE: 1 Aug 68
Vietnam, South SIGNED: 1 Aug 68 FORCE: 1 Aug 68

109369 Multilateral Agreement **0 UNTS 0**
SIGNED: 24 Dec 68 FORCE: 1 Jan 69
REGISTERED: 1 Jan 69 United Nations
ARTICLES: 0
HEADNOTE: INTERNATIONAL SUGAR AGREEMENT
TOPIC: Commodity Trade
CONCEPTS: IGO reference. Privileges and immunities. Procedure. Safety standards. Establishment of trade relations. Tariffs. Reexport of goods, etc.. Export subsidies. Trade agencies. Trade procedures. Quotas. Admission. Decisions. Subsidiary organ. Procedure. Extension of functions. Liaison with other IGO's. IGO status. Status of experts.
INTL ORGS: Food and Agricultural Organization of the United Nations.
PROCEDURE: Amendment. Accession. Duration. Ratification.
PARTIES:
Argentina SIGNED: 29 Dec 68 RATIFIED: 31 Dec 68 FORCE: 1 Jan 69
Australia New Guinea RATIFIED: 24 Dec 68 FORCE: 1 Jan 69
Australia Papua RATIFIED: 20 Dec 68 FORCE: 1 Jan 69
Australia SIGNED: 24 Dec 68 RATIFIED: 31 Dec 68 FORCE: 1 Jan 69
Canada SIGNED: 24 Dec 68 RATIFIED: 23 Dec 68 FORCE: 1 Jan 69
Taiwan SIGNED: 24 Dec 68 RATIFIED: 16 Dec 68 FORCE: 1 Jan 69
Colombia SIGNED: 24 Dec 68 RATIFIED: 31 Dec 68 FORCE: 1 Jan 69
Cuba SIGNED: 24 Dec 68 RATIFIED: 18 Dec 68 FORCE: 1 Jan 69
Czechoslovakia SIGNED: 24 Dec 68 RATIFIED: 31 Dec 68 FORCE: 1 Jan 69
Denmark SIGNED: 24 Dec 68 RATIFIED: 23 Dec 68 FORCE: 1 Jan 69
Dominican Republic SIGNED: 24 Dec 68 RATIFIED: 30 Dec 68 FORCE: 1 Jan 69
Guatemala SIGNED: 24 Dec 68 RATIFIED: 20 Dec 68 FORCE: 1 Jan 69
Guyana SIGNED: 24 Dec 68 RATIFIED: 24 Dec 68 FORCE: 1 Jan 69
Hungary SIGNED: 24 Dec 68 RATIFIED: 15 Jan 69 FORCE: 15 Jan 69
Indonesia SIGNED: 24 Dec 68 RATIFIED: 30 Dec 68 FORCE: 1 Jan 69
Jamaica SIGNED: 24 Dec 68 RATIFIED: 27 Dec 68 FORCE: 1 Jan 69
Japan SIGNED: 24 Dec 68 RATIFIED: 23 Dec 68 FORCE: 1 Jan 69
Kenya SIGNED: 24 Dec 68 RATIFIED: 30 Dec 68 FORCE: 1 Jan 69
Madagascar SIGNED: 24 Dec 68 RATIFIED: 31 Dec 68 FORCE: 1 Jan 69
Mauritius SIGNED: 24 Dec 68 RATIFIED: 23 Dec 68 FORCE: 1 Jan 69
Mexico SIGNED: 24 Dec 68 RATIFIED: 27 Dec 68 FORCE: 1 Jan 69
New Zealand SIGNED: 24 Dec 68 RATIFIED: 23 Dec 68 FORCE: 1 Jan 69

Nicaragua SIGNED: 24 Dec 68 RATIFIED: 30 Dec 68 FORCE: 1 Jan 69
Peru. SIGNED: 24 Dec 68 RATIFIED: 31 Dec 68 FORCE: 1 Jan 69
Philippines SIGNED: 24 Dec 68 RATIFIED: 29 Jan 69 FORCE: 29 Jan 69
Poland SIGNED: 24 Dec 68 RATIFIED: 23 Dec 68 FORCE: 1 Jan 69
Portugal SIGNED: 24 Dec 68 RATIFIED: 31 Dec 68 FORCE: 1 Jan 69
South Africa SIGNED: 24 Dec 68 RATIFIED: 24 Dec 68 FORCE: 1 Jan 69
Swaziland SIGNED: 24 Dec 68 RATIFIED: 23 Dec 68 FORCE: 1 Jan 69
Sweden SIGNED: 24 Dec 68 RATIFIED: 14 Jan 69 FORCE: 14 Jan 69
Trinidad/Tobago SIGNED: 24 Dec 68 RATIFIED: 23 Dec 68 FORCE: 1 Jan 69
UK Great Britain Anguilla FORCE: 16 Jan 69
UK Great Britain Antigua RATIFIED: 20 Dec 68 FORCE: 1 Jan 69
UK Great Britain Bahamas RATIFIED: 20 Dec 68 FORCE: 27 Jan 69
UK Great Britain Fiji Islands RATIFIED: 20 Dec 68 FORCE: 1 Jan 69
UK Great Britain Gibralter RATIFIED: 23 Dec 68 FORCE: 1 Jan 69
UK Great Britain Gilbert Islands RATIFIED: 20 Dec 68 FORCE: 1 Jan 69
UK Great Britain Montserrat RATIFIED: 20 Dec 68 FORCE: 1 Jan 69
UK Great Britain SIGNED: 24 Dec 68 RATIFIED: 20 Dec 68 FORCE: 1 Jan 69
UK Great Britain British Honduras RATIFIED: 20 Dec 68 FORCE: 1 Jan 69
UK Great Britain Nevis RATIFIED: 20 Dec 68 FORCE: 16 Jan 69
UK Great Britain Seychelles RATIFIED: 20 Dec 68 FORCE: 1 Jan 69
UK Great Britain Solomon Islands RATIFIED: 20 Dec 68 FORCE: 16 Jan 69
UK Great Britain St. Helena RATIFIED: 20 Dec 68 FORCE: 1 Jan 69
UK Great Britain St. Kitts RATIFIED: 20 Dec 68 FORCE: 16 Jan 69
UK Great Britain Turk-Caicose Is RATIFIED: 20 Dec 68 FORCE: 27 Jan 69
USSR (Soviet Union) SIGNED: 24 Dec 68 RATIFIED: 30 Dec 68 FORCE: 1 Jan 69
ANNEX
655 UNTS 410. Hungary. Application for Membership 15 Jan 69.
655 UNTS 410. Sweden. Application for Membership 14 Jan 69.
657 UNTS 405. Swaziland. Ratification 18 Feb 69.
657 UNTS 405. Honduras. Ratification 17 Feb 69.
660 UNTS 422. Peru. Withdrawal of Reservation 10 Mar 69.
660 UNTS 422. China. Declaration 5 Mar 69.
660 UNTS 422. British Honduras. Accession 7 Mar 69.
660 UNTS 422. Guyana. Ratification 7 Mar 69.
660 UNTS 422. UK Great Britain. Ratification 12 Mar 69.
660 UNTS 422. S.Kit/Nevis/Anguil. Accession 7 Mar 69.
660 UNTS 422. Antigua. Accession 7 Mar 69.
660 UNTS 422. UK Great Britain. Bermuda.
660 UNTS 422. UK Great Britain. Tonga.
660 UNTS 422. Fiji Islands. Accession 7 Mar 69.
660 UNTS 422. Czechoslovakia. Ratification 7 Mar 69.
668 UNTS 391. UK Great Britain. Brunei.
668 UNTS 391. UK Great Britain. Dominican Republic.

109370 Bilateral Instrument **0 UNTS 0**
SIGNED: 1 Jan 69
REGISTERED: 1 Jan 69 United Nations
ARTICLES: 0
HEADNOTE: RECOGNITION COMPULSORY JURISDICTION, ICJ
TOPIC: ICJ Option Clause
CONCEPTS: IGO reference. Optional clause ICJ. Compulsory jurisdiction.
INTL ORGS: International Court of Justice. United Nations.
PARTIES:
UK Great Britain

109371 Bilateral Agreement **0 UNTS 0**
SIGNED: 14 Nov 68 FORCE: 14 Nov 68
REGISTERED: 1 Jan 69 United Nations
ARTICLES: 0
HEADNOTE: ESTABLISHMENT DEMOGRAPHIC RESEARCH CENTER
TOPIC: IGO Operations
CONCEPTS: Research and scientific projects. Research cooperation. Scientific exchange. Subsidiary organ. Special status. Status of experts.
TREATY REF: 453UNTS79.
PROCEDURE: Amendment. Termination.
PARTIES:
United Nations
United Arab Rep

109372 Bilateral Agreement **0 UNTS 0**
SIGNED: 15 Sep 65 FORCE: 10 Apr 68
REGISTERED: 2 Jan 68 Ireland
ARTICLES: 0
HEADNOTE: AVOIDANCE DOUBLE TAXATION
TOPIC: Taxation
CONCEPTS: Taxation. Equitable taxes. General.
PROCEDURE: Ratification. Termination.
PARTIES:
Finland
Ireland

109373 Bilateral Agreement **0 UNTS 0**
SIGNED: 5 Jun 68 FORCE: 26 Aug 68
REGISTERED: 4 Jan 68 IBRD (World Bank)
ARTICLES: 0
HEADNOTE: GUARANTEE-FOURTH DEVELOPMENT FINANCE CORP. PROJECT
TOPIC: IBRD Project
CONCEPTS: Credit provisions. Loan repayment. World Bank projects. Loan guarantee. Guarantor non-interference.
TREATY REF: 380UNTS245; 554UNTS3; 582UNTS107.
PARTIES:
Iran
IBRD (World Bank)

109374 Bilateral Exchange **0 UNTS 0**
SIGNED: 23 Sep 68 FORCE: 25 Sep 68
REGISTERED: 8 Jan 68 Ireland
ARTICLES: 0
HEADNOTE: GUARANTEE BY UNITED KINGDOM
TOPIC: Finance
CONCEPTS: Balance of payments. Currency. Currency deposits. Loan guarantee.
PROCEDURE: Duration.
PARTIES:
Ireland
UK Great Britain

109375 Bilateral Agreement **0 UNTS 0**
SIGNED: 15 Nov 67 FORCE: 30 Oct 68
REGISTERED: 9 Jan 69 Finland
ARTICLES: 0
HEADNOTE: AVOIDANCE DOUBLE TAXATION
TOPIC: Taxation
CONCEPTS: Taxation. Equitable taxes. General.
PROCEDURE: Termination.
PARTIES:
Finland
Spain

109376 Bilateral Exchange **0 UNTS 0**
SIGNED: 7 Oct 68 FORCE: 31 Oct 68
REGISTERED: 9 Jan 69 Finland
ARTICLES: 0
HEADNOTE: TORNE RIVER BRIDGE
TOPIC: General Ad Hoc
CONCEPTS: Routes and logistics. Frontier waterways. Frontier crossing points.
PARTIES:
Finland
Sweden

109377 Bilateral Agreement **0 UNTS 0**
SIGNED: 28 Apr 68 FORCE: 1 Dec 68
REGISTERED: 10 Jan 69 Austria
ARTICLES: 0
HEADNOTE: PREFERENTIAL CUSTOMS DUTES
TOPIC: Customs
CONCEPTS: Tariffs. Trade procedures.

PROCEDURE: Denunciation. Ratification.
PARTIES:
  Austria
  Romania

109378   Bilateral Agreement   **0 UNTS 0**
SIGNED: 8 Jul 67   FORCE: 16 Mar 68
REGISTERED: 13 Jan 69 France
ARTICLES: 0
HEADNOTE: MOTION PICTURE COOPERATION
TOPIC: Mass Media
CONCEPTS: Culture. Exchange. General cultural
  cooperation. Mass media exchange.
PROCEDURE: Denunciation. Renewal or Revival.
PARTIES:
  France
  USSR (Soviet Union)

109379   Bilateral Agreement   **0 UNTS 0**
SIGNED: 6 Mar 68   FORCE: 19 Jul 68
REGISTERED: 13 Jan 69 France
ARTICLES: 0
HEADNOTE: CO-PRODUCTION,   EXCHANGE
  FILMS
TOPIC: Mass Media
CONCEPTS: Culture. Exchange. General cultural
  cooperation. Mass media exchange.
PROCEDURE: Denunciation. Duration.
PARTIES:
  Czechoslovakia
  France

109380   Bilateral Protocol   **0 UNTS 0**
SIGNED: 2 Jul 61   FORCE: 2 Jul 61
REGISTERED: 15 Jan 69 USSR (Soviet Union)
ARTICLES: 0
HEADNOTE: TRADE REPRESENTATION
TOPIC: General Trade
CONCEPTS: Establishment of trade relations.
  Trade agencies. Trade procedures.
TREATY REF: 421UNTS27.
PARTIES:
  Ghana
  USSR (Soviet Union)

109381   Bilateral Agreement   **0 UNTS 0**
SIGNED: 4 Nov 61   FORCE: 1 Feb 62
REGISTERED: 15 Jan 69 USSR (Soviet Union)
ARTICLES: 0
HEADNOTE: LONG TERM PAYMENTS AGREE-
  MENT
TOPIC: Finance
CONCEPTS: Payment schedules. Loan and credit.
  Loan repayment. Terms of loan.
PROCEDURE: Ratification.
PARTIES:
  Ghana
  USSR (Soviet Union)

109382   Bilateral Agreement   **0 UNTS 0**
SIGNED: 10 Jun 63   FORCE: 1 Jan 64
REGISTERED: 15 Jan 69 USSR (Soviet Union)
ARTICLES: 0
HEADNOTE: TRADE AGREEMENT
TOPIC: General Trade
CONCEPTS: Establishment of trade relations. Ex-
  port quotas. Import quotas. Reciprocity in trade.
  Trade agencies. Trade procedures.
PROCEDURE: Duration.
PARTIES:
  India
  USSR (Soviet Union)

109383   Bilateral Convention   **0 UNTS 0**
SIGNED: 1 Jun 64   FORCE: 12 Jul 68
REGISTERED: 15 Jan 69 USSR (Soviet Union)
ARTICLES: 0
HEADNOTE: CONSULAR CONVENTION
TOPIC: Consul/Citizenship
CONCEPTS: General consular functions. Diplo-
  matic privileges. Consular relations establish-
  ment. Diplomatic missions. Privileges and immu-
  nities. Consular functions in shipping. Consular
  functions in property.
PARTIES:
  USA (United States)
  USSR (Soviet Union)

109384   Bilateral Convention   **0 UNTS 0**
SIGNED: 2 Dec 65   FORCE: 21 Sep 68
REGISTERED: 15 Jan 69 USSR (Soviet Union)
ARTICLES: 0
HEADNOTE: CONSULAR CONVENTION
TOPIC: Consul/Citizenship
CONCEPTS: Diplomatic and consular relations.
  General consular functions. Consular relations
  establishment. Diplomatic missions. Inviolabil-
  ity. Privileges and immunities. Property. Nation-
  ality and citizenship. Protection of nationals.
  Consular functions in shipping. Consular func-
  tions in property.
PROCEDURE: Duration. Ratification. Termination.
PARTIES:
  UK Great Britain
  USSR (Soviet Union)

109385   Bilateral Convention   **0 UNTS 0**
SIGNED: 30 Nov 67   FORCE: 9 Aug 68
REGISTERED: 15 Jan 69 USSR (Soviet Union)
ARTICLES: 0
HEADNOTE: CONSULAR CONVENTION
TOPIC: Consul/Citizenship
CONCEPTS: Diplomatic and consular relations.
  General consular functions. Consular relations
  establishment. Diplomatic missions. Inviolabil-
  ity. Privileges and immunities. Property. Nation-
  ality and citizenship. Protection of nationals.
  Consular functions in shipping. Consular func-
  tions in property.
PROCEDURE: Ratification. Termination.
PARTIES:
  Sweden
  USSR (Soviet Union)

109386   Bilateral Agreement   **0 UNTS 0**
SIGNED: 13 Dec 68   FORCE: 13 Dec 68
REGISTERED: 20 Jan 69 Thailand
ARTICLES: 0
HEADNOTE: TRADE
TOPIC: General Trade
PARTIES:
  India
  Thailand

109387   Multilateral Agreement   **0 UNTS 0**
SIGNED: 10 Dec 68   FORCE: 1 Jan 69
REGISTERED: 22 Jan 69 Belgium
ARTICLES: 0
HEADNOTE: VISA ABOLITION
TOPIC: Visas
PARTIES:
  Belgium SIGNED: 10 Dec 68 FORCE: 1 Jan 69
  Luxembourg SIGNED: 10 Dec 68 FORCE:
    1 Jan 69
  Netherlands SIGNED: 10 Dec 68 FORCE:
    1 Jan 69
  Upper Volta SIGNED: 10 Dec 68 FORCE:
    1 Jan 69

109388   Bilateral Exchange   **0 UNTS 0**
SIGNED: 22 Nov 68   FORCE: 22 Dec 68
REGISTERED: 23 Jan 69 Austria
ARTICLES: 0
HEADNOTE: VISA ABOLITION
TOPIC: Visas
PARTIES:
  Austria
  Israel

109389   Bilateral Exchange   **0 UNTS 0**
SIGNED: 17 Feb 67   FORCE: 17 Feb 67
REGISTERED: 24 Jan 69 Netherlands
ARTICLES: 0
HEADNOTE: FERTILIZERS MAHARASHTA STATE
TOPIC: Direct Aid
PARTIES:
  India
  Netherlands

109390   Bilateral Exchange   **0 UNTS 0**
SIGNED: 21 Dec 67   FORCE: 21 Dec 67
REGISTERED: 24 Jan 69 Netherlands
ARTICLES: 0
HEADNOTE: LYSINE
TOPIC: Direct Aid

PARTIES:
  India
  Netherlands

109391   Bilateral Agreement   **0 UNTS 0**
SIGNED: 20 Oct 67   FORCE: 12 Dec 68
REGISTERED: 24 Jan 69 Netherlands
ARTICLES: 0
HEADNOTE: FINANCIAL PROPERTY CLAIMS
TOPIC: Claims and Debts
PARTIES:
  Netherlands
  USSR (Soviet Union)

109392   Bilateral Agreement   **0 UNTS 0**
SIGNED: 1 Apr 68   FORCE: 2 Oct 68
REGISTERED: 24 Jan 69 Finland
ARTICLES: 0
HEADNOTE: ROAD TRANSPORT
TOPIC: Land Transport
PARTIES:
  Finland
  Romania

109393   Bilateral Agreement   **0 UNTS 0**
SIGNED: 28 Jun 68   FORCE: 28 Jun 68
REGISTERED: 24 Jan 69 Denmark
ARTICLES: 0
HEADNOTE: DANISH VOLUNTEERS
TOPIC: Direct Aid
PARTIES:
  Denmark
  Kenya

109394   Bilateral Agreement   **0 UNTS 0**
SIGNED: 27 Jan 69   FORCE: 27 Jan 69
REGISTERED: 27 Jan 69 United Nations
ARTICLES: 0
HEADNOTE: UNICEF ACTIVITIES
TOPIC: IGO Operations
PARTIES:
  Ceylon (Sri Lanka)
  UNICEF (Children)

109395   Bilateral Agreement   **0 UNTS 0**
SIGNED: 18 Apr 66   FORCE: 8 Dec 67
REGISTERED: 28 Jan 68 Greece
ARTICLES: 0
HEADNOTE: DOUBLE TAX CAPITAL TRADE
TOPIC: Taxation
PARTIES:
  Germany, West
  Greece

109396   Bilateral Agreement   **0 UNTS 0**
SIGNED: 5 Sep 68   FORCE: 5 Sep 68
REGISTERED: 28 Jan 68 Denmark
ARTICLES: 0
HEADNOTE: TECHNICAL COOPERATION
TOPIC: Tech Assistance
PARTIES:
  Denmark
  Pakistan

109397   Bilateral Convention   **0 UNTS 0**
SIGNED: 4 Jul 66   FORCE: 1 May 68
REGISTERED: 17 Jul 68 Belgium
ARTICLES: 0
HEADNOTE: SOCIAL SECURITY
TOPIC: Non-ILO Labor
PARTIES:
  Belgium
  Turkey

109398   Bilateral Agreement   **0 UNTS 0**
SIGNED: 18 Dec 56   FORCE: 18 Jan 69
REGISTERED: 1 Feb 69 United Nations
ARTICLES: 0
HEADNOTE: UNICEF ACTIVITIES
TOPIC: IGO Operations
PARTIES:
  UNICEF (Children)
  Uruguay

109404   Bilateral Agreement   **0 UNTS 0**
SIGNED: 29 Aug 67   FORCE: 31 May 68
REGISTERED: 7 Feb 69 Denmark
ARTICLES: 0
HEADNOTE: ECONOMIC INDUSTRIAL TECHNICAL
    COOPERATION
TOPIC: General Economic
PARTIES:
    Denmark
    Romania

109405   Bilateral Convention   **0 UNTS 0**
SIGNED: 3 Feb 68   FORCE: 26 Jul 68
REGISTERED: 14 Feb 69 Denmark
ARTICLES: 0
HEADNOTE: AVOIDANCE DOUBLE TAXATION
TOPIC: Taxation
CONCEPTS: Taxation. Tax credits. Equitable taxes.
    General. Tax exemptions.
TREATY REF: 341UNTS55.
PROCEDURE: Ratification.
PARTIES:
    Denmark
    Japan

109406   Bilateral Exchange   **0 UNTS 0**
SIGNED: 11 Apr 68   FORCE: 11 Apr 68
REGISTERED: 14 Feb 69 Denmark
ARTICLES: 0
HEADNOTE: AVOIDANCE DOUBLE TAXATION, AIR
    AND MARITIME TRAFFIC
TOPIC: Taxation
CONCEPTS: Taxation. Death duties. Tax credits.
    Equitable taxes. General. Tax exemptions.
TREATY REF: 341UNTS55.
PARTIES:
    Denmark
    Yugoslavia

109407   Bilateral Agreement   **0 UNTS 0**
SIGNED: 7 Jun 68   FORCE: 7 Jun 68
REGISTERED: 14 Feb 69 Denmark
ARTICLES: 0
HEADNOTE: LOAN
TOPIC: Loans and Credits
CONCEPTS: Procedure. Loan and credit. Credit
    provisions. Purchase authorization. Loan repay-
    ment.
PROCEDURE: Termination.
PARTIES:
    Denmark
    Tunisia

109408   Bilateral Agreement   **0 UNTS 0**
SIGNED: 12 Jul 68   FORCE: 13 Sep 68
REGISTERED: 14 Feb 69 IBRD (World Bank)
ARTICLES: 0
HEADNOTE: LOAN, RIO LINDO HYDROELECTRIC
    PROJECT
TOPIC: IBRD Project
CONCEPTS: Loan and credit. Credit provisions.
    Purchase authorization. Loan repayment.
TREATY REF: 657UNTS99,379,96.
PARTIES:
    Honduras
    IBRD (World Bank)

109409   Bilateral Agreement   **0 UNTS 0**
SIGNED: 12 Jun 68   FORCE: 13 Sep 68
REGISTERED: 14 Feb 69 IDA (Devel Assoc)
ARTICLES: 0
HEADNOTE: DEVELOPMENT CREDIT, RIO LINDO
    HYDROELECTRIC PROJECT
TOPIC: Non-IBRD Project
CONCEPTS: Procedure. Loan and credit. Credit
    provisions. Terms of loan.
TREATY REF: 657UNTS25,379,114.
PROCEDURE: Termination.
PARTIES:
    Honduras
    IDA (Devel Assoc)

109410   Bilateral Exchange   **0 UNTS 0**
SIGNED: 6 Jul 61   FORCE: 6 Jul 61
REGISTERED: 14 Feb 69 Brazil
ARTICLES: 0
HEADNOTE: EXCHANGE OFFICIAL MAIL IN DIPLO-
    MATIC POUCHES

TOPIC: Postal Service
CONCEPTS: Exchange of information and docu-
    ments. Use of facilities. Conveyance in transit.
PROCEDURE: Denunciation.
PARTIES:
    Argentina
    Brazil

109411   Bilateral Exchange   **0 UNTS 0**
SIGNED: 23 Apr 65   FORCE: 23 Apr 65
REGISTERED: 17 Dec 68 Brazil
ARTICLES: 0
HEADNOTE: ESTABLISHMENT SPECIAL COMMI-
    SION ON CO-ORDINATION
TOPIC: IGO Establishment
CONCEPTS: General trade. Trade procedures. Pro-
    cedure.
TREATY REF: 374UNTS57; 657UNTS236.
PARTIES:
    Argentina
    Brazil

109412   Bilateral Agreement   **0 UNTS 0**
SIGNED: 21 Jun 68   FORCE: 2 Dec 68
REGISTERED: 17 Feb 68 IBRD (World Bank)
ARTICLES: 0
HEADNOTE: LOAN-HIGHWAY PROJECT
TOPIC: IBRD Project
CONCEPTS: Credit provisions. Loan repayment.
    Non-nuclear materials.
PROCEDURE: Termination.
PARTIES:
    Ivory Coast
    IBRD (World Bank)

109413   Bilateral Agreement   **0 UNTS 0**
SIGNED: 24 Jul 68   FORCE: 24 Jul 68
REGISTERED: 19 Feb 68 Denmark
ARTICLES: 0
HEADNOTE: FACILITIES; INTERNATIONAL COUN-
    CIL SEA EXPLORATION
TOPIC: IGO Status/Immunit
CONCEPTS: Visas. Procedure. Subsidiary organ.
    Procedure.
PROCEDURE: Denunciation.
PARTIES:
    Denmark
    Int Coun Expl Sea

109414   Bilateral Agreement   **0 UNTS 0**
SIGNED: 3 Sep 68   FORCE: 3 Sep 68
REGISTERED: 19 Feb 69 Denmark
ARTICLES: 0
HEADNOTE: TECHNICAL TRAINING CENTER
TOPIC: Education
CONCEPTS: Institute establishment. General tech-
    nical assistance. Assistance.
PROCEDURE: Duration. Termination.
PARTIES:
    Denmark
    Malawi

109415   Bilateral Agreement   **0 UNTS 0**
SIGNED: 5 Nov 68   FORCE: 5 Nov 68
REGISTERED: 19 Feb 69 Denmark
ARTICLES: 0
HEADNOTE: LOAN
TOPIC: Loans and Credits
CONCEPTS: Procedure. Loan and credit. Credit
    provisions. Loan repayment. Terms of loan.
PARTIES:
    Denmark
    Morocco

109416   Bilateral Exchange   **0 UNTS 0**
SIGNED: 13 Oct 60   FORCE: 1 Nov 60
REGISTERED: 21 Feb 69 Brazil
ARTICLES: 0
HEADNOTE: ABOLITION VISAS AND SPECIAL
    PASSPORTS
TOPIC: Visas
CONCEPTS: Frontier formalities. Visa abolition.
PARTIES:
    Brazil
    Spain

109417   Bilateral Agreement   **0 UNTS 0**
SIGNED: 11 Aug 64   FORCE: 29 Apr 66
REGISTERED: 21 Feb 69 Brazil
ARTICLES: 0
HEADNOTE: SOCIAL COOPERATION
TOPIC: Health/Educ/Welfare
CONCEPTS: Non-ILO labor relations. Administra-
    tive cooperation. Social security. Unemploy-
    ment. Migrant worker.
TREATY REF: 658UNTS39.
PARTIES:
    Brazil
    Spain

109418   Bilateral Exchange   **0 UNTS 0**
SIGNED: 18 Mar 66   FORCE: 18 Mar 66
REGISTERED: 21 Feb 69 Brazil
ARTICLES: 0
HEADNOTE: FILM CO-PRODUCTION
TOPIC: Mass Media
CONCEPTS: Culture. General cultural cooperation.
    Artists. Mass media exchange.
PARTIES:
    Brazil
    Chile

109419   Bilateral Exchange   **0 UNTS 0**
SIGNED: 19 May 65   FORCE: 19 Aug 65
REGISTERED: 21 Feb 69 Brazil
ARTICLES: 0
HEADNOTE: ABOLITION VISAS IN DIPLOMATIC,
    SPECIAL, OFFICIAL PASSPORTS
TOPIC: Visas
CONCEPTS: Frontier formalities. Visa abolition.
PARTIES:
    Brazil
    Ecuador

109420   Bilateral Agreement   **0 UNTS 0**
SIGNED: 27 Sep 68   FORCE: 27 Sep 68
REGISTERED: 21 Feb 69 Brazil
ARTICLES: 0
HEADNOTE: MARITIME TRANSPORT
TOPIC: Water Transport
CONCEPTS: Water transport. Merchant vessels. In-
    land and territorial waters. Ports and pilotage.
PARTIES:
    Argentina
    Brazil

109421   Bilateral Agreement   **0 UNTS 0**
SIGNED: 30 Nov 63   FORCE: 25 May 65
REGISTERED: 21 Feb 69 Brazil
ARTICLES: 0
HEADNOTE: TECHNICAL CO-OPERATION
TOPIC: Tech Assistance
CONCEPTS: General technical assistance. Assis-
    tance.
PROCEDURE: Denunciation.
PARTIES:
    Brazil
    Germany, West

109422   Bilateral Exchange   **0 UNTS 0**
SIGNED: 2 Aug 62   FORCE: 24 Jul 62
REGISTERED: 22 Feb 69 Brazil
ARTICLES: 0
HEADNOTE: ABOLITION VISAS DIPLOMATIC,-
    SPECIAL,PASSPORTS
TOPIC: Visas
CONCEPTS: Frontier formalities. Visa abolition.
    Passports diplomatic. Visas.
PARTIES:
    Brazil
    Colombia

109423   Bilateral Agreement   **0 UNTS 0**
SIGNED: 30 Nov 63   FORCE: 26 Mar 66
REGISTERED: 22 Feb 69 Brazil
ARTICLES: 0
HEADNOTE: CUSTOMS PRIVILEGES CAREER
    CONSULATES, OFFICIALS
TOPIC: Consul/Citizenship
CONCEPTS: Diplomatic missions. Privileges and
    immunities. Customs declarations. Customs ex-
    emptions.
PROCEDURE: Denunciation. Ratification.

PARTIES:
Brazil
Germany, West

109424   Bilateral Treaty   **0 UNTS 0**
SIGNED: 15 Nov 61   FORCE: 7 Jul 68
REGISTERED: 22 Feb 69 Brazil
ARTICLES: 0
HEADNOTE: EXTRADITION
TOPIC: Extradition
CONCEPTS: Extradition, deportation and repatriation. Court procedures. Extradition requests. Extraditable offenses. Special factors. Refusal of extradition. Pre-treaty crimes. Limits of prosecution. Provisional detainment. Material evidence. Procedure.
PROCEDURE: Denunciation. Ratification.
PARTIES:
Argentina
Brazil

109425   Bilateral Protocol   **0 UNTS 0**
SIGNED: 30 Nov 63   FORCE: 30 Nov 63
REGISTERED: 22 Feb 69 Brazil
ARTICLES: 0
HEADNOTE: FINANCIAL CO-OPERATION
TOPIC: Finance
CONCEPTS: Investments. Purchase authorizations. Transportation costs. Loan and credit.
PARTIES:
Brazil
Germany, West

109426   Bilateral Protocol   **0 UNTS 0**
SIGNED: 30 Nov 63   FORCE: 30 Nov 63
REGISTERED: 24 Feb 69 Brazil
ARTICLES: 0
HEADNOTE: MARITIME TRANSPORT
TOPIC: Water Transport
CONCEPTS: Transport of goods. Merchant vessels.
PARTIES:
Brazil
Germany, West

109427   Bilateral Agreement   **0 UNTS 0**
SIGNED: 25 Jun 60   FORCE: 1 Jun 65
REGISTERED: 24 Feb 69 Brazil
ARTICLES: 0
HEADNOTE: CULTURAL AGREEMENT
TOPIC: Culture
CONCEPTS: Culture. Exchange. General cultural cooperation.
PROCEDURE: Denunciation. Ratification.
PARTIES:
Brazil
Spain

109428   Bilateral Agreement   **0 UNTS 0**
SIGNED: 27 Dec 60   FORCE: 10 Jun 64
REGISTERED: 24 Feb 69 Brazil
ARTICLES: 0
HEADNOTE: MIGRATION
TOPIC: Visas
CONCEPTS: Immigration and emigration.
PROCEDURE: Ratification. Termination.
PARTIES:
Brazil
Spain

109429   Bilateral Agreement   **0 UNTS 0**
SIGNED: 19 Nov 64   FORCE: 18 Sep 66
REGISTERED: 26 Feb 69 Brazil
ARTICLES: 0
HEADNOTE: CULTURAL EXCHANGES
TOPIC: Culture
CONCEPTS: Culture. Exchange. General cultural cooperation.
PROCEDURE: Denunciation. Ratification.
PARTIES:
Brazil
Costa Rica

109430   Bilateral Agreement   **0 UNTS 0**
SIGNED: 30 Nov 65   FORCE: 4 Apr 68
REGISTERED: 26 Feb 69 Brazil
ARTICLES: 0

HEADNOTE: CULTURAL EXCHANGES
TOPIC: Culture
CONCEPTS: Exchange. Teacher and student exchange. Culture. Exchange. General cultural cooperation.
PROCEDURE: Ratification.
PARTIES:
Brazil
El Salvador

109431   Multilateral Convention   **0 UNTS 0**
SIGNED: 5 Oct 61   FORCE: 4 Feb 69
REGISTERED: 26 Feb 69 Netherlands
ARTICLES: 0
HEADNOTE: LAWS FOR THE PROTECTION OF INFANTS
TOPIC: Admin Cooperation
CONCEPTS: Administrative cooperation. Family law. Legal protection and assistance. General health, education, culture, welfare and labor. International circulation. Social security.
TREATY REF: 95BFSP421.
PROCEDURE: Duration. Ratification.
PARTIES:
Luxembourg   RATIFIED: 13 Oct 67   FORCE: 4 Feb 69
Portugal RATIFIED: 6 Dec 68 FORCE: 4 Feb 69
Switzerland   RATIFIED: 9 Dec 66   FORCE: 4 Feb 69

109432   Multilateral Convention   **0 UNTS 0**
SIGNED: 15 Nov 65   FORCE: 10 Feb 69
REGISTERED: 26 Feb 69 Netherlands
ARTICLES: 0
HEADNOTE: JUDICIAL, EXTRAJUDICIAL DOCUMENTS CIVIL COMMERCIAL MATTERS
TOPIC: Admin Cooperation
CONCEPTS: Administrative cooperation. General cooperation. Exchange of official publications. Exchange of information and documents. Informational records. Inspection and observation. Juridical personality. Domestic legislation. Recognition and enforcement of legal decisions. General property. Recognition of legal documents. Investigation of violations. Programs.
TREATY REF: 99BFSP990; 286UNTS265.
PROCEDURE: Accession. Ratification.
PARTIES:
United Arab Rep RATIFIED: 12 Oct 68 FORCE: 10 Feb 69
UK Great Britain RATIFIED: 17 Nov 67 FORCE: 10 Feb 69
USA (United States) RATIFIED: 24 Aug 67 FORCE: 10 Feb 69

109433   Bilateral Convention   **0 UNTS 0**
SIGNED: 10 Jul 65   FORCE: 25 Nov 67
REGISTERED: 26 Feb 69 France
ARTICLES: 0
HEADNOTE: TAX AGREEMENT
TOPIC: Taxation
CONCEPTS: Procedure. Taxation. Death duties. Tax credits. Equitable taxes. General. Tax exemptions.
PARTIES:
Cameroon
France

109434   Bilateral Agreement   **0 UNTS 0**
SIGNED: 15 Nov 67   FORCE: 1 Jan 69
REGISTERED: 26 Feb 69 Austria
ARTICLES: 0
HEADNOTE: SOCIAL SECURITY
TOPIC: Non-ILO Labor
CONCEPTS: Legal protection and assistance. Procedure. General health, education, culture, welfare and labor. Family allowances. Administrative cooperation. Old age insurance. Sickness and invalidity insurance. Social security. Unemployment.
PROCEDURE: Denunciation. Ratification.
PARTIES:
Austria
Switzerland

109435   Bilateral Agreement   **0 UNTS 0**
SIGNED: 27 May 68   FORCE: 27 May 68
REGISTERED: 26 Feb 69 Philippines
ARTICLES: 0

HEADNOTE: EMPLOYMENT PHILIPPINE NATIONALS ON U.S. MILITARY BASES
TOPIC: Non-ILO Labor
CONCEPTS: Employment regulations. Holidays and rest periods. Safety standards. Right to organize. Wages and salaries.
TREATY REF: 43UNTS271; 68UNTS272; 185UNTS334; ETC..
PARTIES:
Philippines
USA (United States)

109436   Bilateral Agreement   **0 UNTS 0**
SIGNED: 28 Dec 68   FORCE: 28 Dec 68
REGISTERED: 26 Feb 69 Philippines
ARTICLES: 0
HEADNOTE: RECRUITMENT-EMPLOYMENT PHILIPPINE CITIZENS ON U.S. MILITARY BASES
TOPIC: Milit Installation
CONCEPTS: Holidays and rest periods. Safety standards. Wages and salaries. Military installations and equipment.
TREATY REF: 280UNTS177.
PARTIES:
Philippines
USA (United States)

109437   Bilateral Agreement   **0 UNTS 0**
SIGNED: 14 Jan 69   FORCE: 14 Jan 69
REGISTERED: 26 Feb 69 Philippines
ARTICLES: 0
HEADNOTE: CO-OPERATION PEACEFUL USES ATOMIC ENERGY
TOPIC: Atomic Energy
CONCEPTS: Atomic energy assistance. General. Nuclear materials. Peaceful use. Rights of supplier.
PROCEDURE: Termination.
PARTIES:
Israel
Philippines

109438   Bilateral Convention   **0 UNTS 0**
SIGNED: 18 May 63   FORCE: 1 Sep 63
REGISTERED: 26 Feb 69 France
ARTICLES: 0
HEADNOTE: TAXATION
TOPIC: Taxation
CONCEPTS: Taxation. Tax credits. Equitable taxes. General. Tax exemptions.
PROCEDURE: Denunciation.
PARTIES:
France
Monaco

109439   Bilateral Exchange   **0 UNTS 0**
SIGNED: 9 Dec 66   FORCE: 23 Jan 68
REGISTERED: 26 Feb 69 France
ARTICLES: 0
HEADNOTE: TAX STATUS, MONEGASQUE COMPANIES
TOPIC: Finance
CONCEPTS: Taxation. General. Tax exemptions.
PROCEDURE: Denunciation.
PARTIES:
France
Monaco

109440   Bilateral Agreement   **0 UNTS 0**
SIGNED: 19 May 64   FORCE: 19 May 64
REGISTERED: 3 Mar 69 France
ARTICLES: 0
HEADNOTE: ESTABLISHMENT FRANCO-CHAD MIXED COMMISION
TOPIC: IGO Establishment
CONCEPTS: Establishment of commission. Subsidiary organ.
PARTIES:
Chad
France

109441   Bilateral Convention   **0 UNTS 0**
SIGNED: 19 May 64   FORCE: 30 Jul 66
REGISTERED: 3 Mar 69 France
ARTICLES: 0
HEADNOTE: PROVISION PERSONNEL TO ASSIST IN THE OPERATION OF PUBLIC SERV
TOPIC: General Aid

CONCEPTS: General technical assistance. Assistance.
PROCEDURE: Ratification.
PARTIES:
Chad
France

109442 Bilateral Agreement **0 UNTS 0**
SIGNED: 19 May 64 FORCE: 1 Oct 66
REGISTERED: 3 Mar 69 France
ARTICLES: 0
HEADNOTE: CULTURAL CO-OPERATION
TOPIC: Culture
CONCEPTS: Culture. Exchange. General cultural cooperation.
PARTIES:
Chad
France

109443 Bilateral Agreement **0 UNTS 0**
SIGNED: 19 May 64 FORCE: 1 Oct 66
REGISTERED: 3 Mar 69 France
ARTICLES: 0
HEADNOTE: TECHNICAL MILITARY ASSISTANCE
TOPIC: Milit Assistance
CONCEPTS: Military assistance. Military assistance. Surplus war property. Airforce-army-navy personnel ratio. Ranks and privileges. Bases and facilities.
PARTIES:
Chad
France

109444 Bilateral Convention **0 UNTS 0**
SIGNED: 29 Sep 65 FORCE: 31 Oct 68
REGISTERED: 3 Mar 69 UK Great Britain
ARTICLES: 0
HEADNOTE: CULTURAL
TOPIC: Culture
CONCEPTS: Teacher and student exchange. Culture. General cultural cooperation.
PROCEDURE: Denunciation.
PARTIES:
United Arab Rep
UK Great Britain

109445 Bilateral Convention **0 UNTS 0**
SIGNED: 29 Oct 65 FORCE: 15 Nov 67
REGISTERED: 3 Mar 69 France
ARTICLES: 0
HEADNOTE: AVOIDANCE DOUBLE TAXATION
TOPIC: Taxation
CONCEPTS: Taxation. Equitable taxes. General. Tax exemptions.
TREATY REF: 144LTS115.
PROCEDURE: Denunciation.
PARTIES:
France
Italy

109446 Bilateral Agreement **0 UNTS 0**
SIGNED: 20 Jun 67 FORCE: 14 Jan 69
REGISTERED: 3 Mar 69 Denmark
ARTICLES: 0
HEADNOTE: GOVERNMENT LOAN
TOPIC: Loans and Credits
CONCEPTS: IGO reference. Procedure. Loan and credit. Credit provisions. Loan repayment. Terms of loan.
INTL ORGS: International Court of Justice.
PROCEDURE: Duration.
PARTIES:
Denmark
Peru

109447 Bilateral Exchange **0 UNTS 0**
SIGNED: 19 Dec 67 FORCE: 19 Dec 67
REGISTERED: 3 Mar 69 UK Great Britain
ARTICLES: 0
HEADNOTE: GOVERNMENT LOAN
TOPIC: Loans and Credits
CONCEPTS: Loan and credit. Credit provisions. Purchase authorization. Terms of loan.
PARTIES:
Peru
UK Great Britain

109448 Bilateral Exchange **0 UNTS 0**
SIGNED: 21 Dec 67 FORCE: 21 Dec 67
REGISTERED: 3 Mar 69 Ireland
ARTICLES: 0
HEADNOTE: MODIFICATION TRADE AGREEMENT
TOPIC: General Trade
CONCEPTS: Annex type material.
PARTIES:
Canada
Ireland

109449 Bilateral Agreement **0 UNTS 0**
SIGNED: 12 Feb 68 FORCE: 5 Sep 68
REGISTERED: 3 Mar 69 UK Great Britain
ARTICLES: 0
HEADNOTE: REGULATION TAXATION ROAD VEHICLES
TOPIC: Taxation
CONCEPTS: Tax exemptions. Commercial road vehicles. Motor vehicles and combinations.
PROCEDURE: Duration. Ratification.
PARTIES:
Sweden
UK Great Britain

109450 Bilateral Agreement **0 UNTS 0**
SIGNED: 2 Apr 68 FORCE: 13 Sep 68
REGISTERED: 3 Mar 69 UK Great Britain
ARTICLES: 0
HEADNOTE: SUPPLEMENT AGREEMENT AVOIDANCE DOUBLE TAXATION
TOPIC: Taxation
CONCEPTS: Taxation. Equitable taxes.
PROCEDURE: Ratification.
PARTIES:
Malawi
UK Great Britain

109451 Bilateral Exchange **0 UNTS 0**
SIGNED: 6 Aug 68 FORCE: 6 Aug 68
REGISTERED: 3 Mar 69 UK Great Britain
ARTICLES: 0
HEADNOTE: DEVELOPMENT LOAN
TOPIC: Loans and Credits
CONCEPTS: Loan and credit. Credit provisions. Loan repayment. Terms of loan.
PARTIES:
Turkey
UK Great Britain

109452 Bilateral Exchange **0 UNTS 0**
SIGNED: 2 Apr 68 FORCE: 5 Sep 68
REGISTERED: 3 Mar 69 UK Great Britain
ARTICLES: 0
HEADNOTE: EXEMPTION OF GOODS VEHICLES FROM TAXATION
TOPIC: Taxation
CONCEPTS: Taxation. Tax exemptions.
PROCEDURE: Termination.
PARTIES:
Turkey
UK Great Britain

109453 Bilateral Treaty **0 UNTS 0**
SIGNED: 12 Sep 68 FORCE: 18 Dec 68
REGISTERED: 3 Mar 69 Mongolia
ARTICLES: 0
HEADNOTE: FRIENDSHIP AND COOPERATION
TOPIC: General Amity
CONCEPTS: Non-prejudice to third party. Friendship and amity. Non-prejudice to UN charter. Peaceful relations.
TREATY REF: 521UNTS351.
PROCEDURE: Denunciation. Duration. Ratification.
PARTIES:
Germany, East
Mongolia

109454 Bilateral Agreement **0 UNTS 0**
SIGNED: 4 Apr 69 FORCE: 4 Apr 69
REGISTERED: 4 Mar 69 United Nations
ARTICLES: 0
HEADNOTE: OPERATIONAL ASSISTANCE
TOPIC: Direct Aid
CONCEPTS: IGO reference. Arbitration. Procedure. Claims and settlements. Aid and development. General technical assistance.
INTL ORGS: United Nations.

PROCEDURE: Termination.
PARTIES:
State/IGO Group
Southern Yemen

109455 Bilateral Agreement **0 UNTS 0**
SIGNED: 4 Apr 69 FORCE: 4 Apr 69
REGISTERED: 4 Mar 69 United Nations
ARTICLES: 0
HEADNOTE: TECHNICAL ASSISTANCE
TOPIC: Direct Aid
CONCEPTS: IGO reference. Privileges and immunities. Arbitration. Procedure. Claims and settlements. Aid and development. General technical assistance.
INTL ORGS: United Nations.
TREATY REF: 1UNTS15; 90UNTS327.
PROCEDURE: Amendment. Termination.
PARTIES:
State/IGO Group
Southern Yemen

109456 Bilateral Agreement **0 UNTS 0**
SIGNED: 4 Apr 69 FORCE: 4 Apr 69
REGISTERED: 4 Mar 69 United Nations
ARTICLES: 0
HEADNOTE: ASSISTANCE FROM UN DEVELOPMENT PROGRAM
TOPIC: Direct Aid
CONCEPTS: IGO reference. Privileges and immunities. Arbitration. Procedure. Aid and development. General technical assistance. Assistance.
INTL ORGS: United Nations.
TREATY REF: 1UNTS15; 90UNTS327.
PROCEDURE: Amendment. Termination.
PARTIES:
UN Special Fund
Southern Yemen

109457 Bilateral Agreement **0 UNTS 0**
SIGNED: 5 Oct 67 FORCE: 5 Oct 67
REGISTERED: 6 Mar 69 Australia
ARTICLES: 0
HEADNOTE: RESIDENCE, EMPLOYMENT TURKISH CITIZENS
TOPIC: Visas
CONCEPTS: Alien status. Nationality and citizenship. Social security. Migrant worker.
PROCEDURE: Termination.
PARTIES:
Australia
Turkey

109458 Bilateral Agreement **0 UNTS 0**
SIGNED: 7 Dec 67 FORCE: 8 May 68
REGISTERED: 6 Mar 69 Australia
ARTICLES: 0
HEADNOTE: AVOIDANCE DOUBLE TAXATION
TOPIC: Taxation
CONCEPTS: Taxation. Tax credits. Equitable taxes. General. Tax exemptions.
TREATY REF: 17UNTS182.
PROCEDURE: Ratification. Termination.
PARTIES:
Australia
UK Great Britain

109459 Bilateral Agreement **0 UNTS 0**
SIGNED: 16 Oct 68 FORCE: 16 Oct 68
REGISTERED: 6 Mar 69 Australia
ARTICLES: 0
HEADNOTE: SCIENTIFIC, TECHNICAL COOPERATION
TOPIC: Scientific Project
CONCEPTS: Research cooperation. Research results. General technical assistance.
PROCEDURE: Duration. Termination.
PARTIES:
Australia
UK Great Britain

109460 Bilateral Exchange **0 UNTS 0**
SIGNED: 13 Jan 69 FORCE: 13 Jan 69
REGISTERED: 6 Mar 69 Australia
ARTICLES: 0
HEADNOTE: ESTABLISHMENT IONOSPHERIC FACILITIES
TOPIC: Scientific Project

CONCEPTS: Research and scientific projects. Research cooperation. Meteorology. Research results. Research and development.
TREATY REF: 475UNTS332.
PARTIES:
Australia
USA (United States)

109461   Bilateral Agreement   **0 UNTS 0**
SIGNED: 16 Dec 68   FORCE: 16 Dec 68
REGISTERED: 6 Mar 69 Denmark
ARTICLES: 0
HEADNOTE: SECOND DANISH LOAN
TOPIC: Loans and Credits
CONCEPTS: Arbitration. Procedure. Loan and credit. Credit provisions. Purchase authorization. Loan repayment. Terms of loan.
TREATY REF: 586UNTS3.
PROCEDURE: Duration. Termination.
PARTIES:
Denmark
Malawi

109462   Bilateral Agreement   **0 UNTS 0**
SIGNED: 9 Dec 65   FORCE: 1 Jan 69
REGISTERED: 7 Mar 69 Finland
ARTICLES: 0
HEADNOTE: EQUIVALENCE OF DIPLOMAS
TOPIC: Education
CONCEPTS: Recognition of degrees. Teacher and student exchange.
PROCEDURE: Ratification. Termination.
PARTIES:
Austria
Finland

109463   Bilateral Agreement   **0 UNTS 0**
SIGNED: 16 Oct 68   FORCE: 16 Oct 68
REGISTERED: 10 Mar 69 Denmark
ARTICLES: 0
HEADNOTE: CO-OPERATION IN MARINE BIOLOGY
TOPIC: Scientific Project
CONCEPTS: Exchange. Research cooperation. General technical assistance. Assistance. Special projects.
PROCEDURE: Termination.
PARTIES:
Denmark
Thailand

109464   Multilateral Convention   **0 UNTS 0**
SIGNED: 7 Mar 66   FORCE: 4 Jan 69
REGISTERED: 12 Mar 69 United Nations
ARTICLES: 0
HEADNOTE: ELIMINATION RACIAL DISCRIMINATION
TOPIC: Humanitarian
CONCEPTS: Anti-discrimination. Conformity with IGO decisions.
TREATY REF: 362UNTS31; 429UNTS93.
PARTIES:
Argentina RATIFIED: 2 Oct 68 FORCE: 4 Jan 69
Brazil RATIFIED: 27 Mar 68 FORCE: 4 Jan 69
Bulgaria RATIFIED: 8 Aug 66 FORCE: 4 Jan 69
Costa Rica RATIFIED: 16 Jan 67 FORCE: 4 Jan 69
Cyprus RATIFIED: 21 Apr 67 FORCE: 4 Jan 69
Czechoslovakia RATIFIED: 29 Dec 66 FORCE: 4 Jan 69
Ecuador RATIFIED: 22 Sep 66 FORCE: 4 Jan 69
Ghana RATIFIED: 8 Sep 66 FORCE: 4 Jan 69
Hungary RATIFIED: 4 May 67 FORCE: 4 Jan 69
Iceland RATIFIED: 13 Mar 67 FORCE: 4 Jan 69
India RATIFIED: 3 Dec 68 FORCE: 4 Jan 69
Iran RATIFIED: 29 Aug 68 FORCE: 4 Jan 69
Kuwait RATIFIED: 15 Oct 68 FORCE: 4 Jan 69
Libya RATIFIED: 3 Jul 68 FORCE: 4 Jan 69
Madagascar RATIFIED: 7 Feb 69 FORCE: 7 Feb 69
Nigeria RATIFIED: 16 Oct 67 FORCE: 4 Jan 69
Niger RATIFIED: 27 Apr 67 FORCE: 4 Jan 69
Pakistan RATIFIED: 21 Sep 66 FORCE: 4 Jan 69
Panama RATIFIED: 16 Aug 67 FORCE: 4 Jan 69
Philippines RATIFIED: 15 Sep 67 FORCE: 4 Jan 69
Poland RATIFIED: 5 Dec 68 FORCE: 4 Jan 69
Sierra Leone FORCE: 4 Jan 69
Spain RATIFIED: 13 Sep 68 FORCE: 4 Jan 69
Tunisia RATIFIED: 13 Jan 67 FORCE: 4 Jan 69

United Arab Rep RATIFIED: 1 May 67 FORCE: 4 Jan 69
UK Great Britain RATIFIED: 7 Mar 69 FORCE: 7 Mar 69
Ukrainian SSR RATIFIED: 7 Mar 69 FORCE: 7 Mar 69
Uruguay RATIFIED: 30 Aug 68 FORCE: 4 Jan 69
USSR (Soviet Union) RATIFIED: 4 Feb 69 FORCE: 4 Feb 69
Venezuela RATIFIED: 10 Oct 67 FORCE: 4 Jan 69
Yugoslavia RATIFIED: 2 Oct 67 FORCE: 4 Jan 69

109465   Bilateral Convention   **0 UNTS 0**
SIGNED: 30 Mar 68   FORCE: 16 Jan 69
REGISTERED: 14 Mar 69 Greece
ARTICLES: 0
HEADNOTE: AVOIDANCE DOUBLE TAXATION
TOPIC: Taxation
CONCEPTS: Taxation. Equitable taxes. General. Tax exemptions.
PROCEDURE: Denunciation. Ratification. Termination.
PARTIES:
Cyprus
Greece

109466   Bilateral Agreement   **0 UNTS 0**
SIGNED: 3 Jul 68   FORCE: 3 Jul 68
REGISTERED: 14 Mar 69 Denmark
ARTICLES: 0
HEADNOTE: TECHNICAL CO-OPERATION
TOPIC: Tech Assistance
CONCEPTS: General technical assistance. Assistance.
PROCEDURE: Termination.
PARTIES:
Denmark
Uganda

109467   Bilateral Agreement   **0 UNTS 0**
SIGNED: 3 Jul 68   FORCE: 3 Jul 68
REGISTERED: 14 Mar 69 Denmark
ARTICLES: 0
HEADNOTE: ESTABLISHMENT OF A DAIRY SCHOOL
TOPIC: Non-IBRD Project
CONCEPTS: Institute establishment. General technical assistance. Assistance. Special projects.
TREATY REF: 466UNTS348.
PARTIES:
Denmark
Uganda

109468   Bilateral Agreement   **0 UNTS 0**
SIGNED: 17 Dec 68   FORCE: 16 Jan 68
REGISTERED: 14 Mar 69 Austria
ARTICLES: 0
HEADNOTE: VISA ABOLITION
TOPIC: Visas
PARTIES:
Austria
Romania

109469   Bilateral Agreement   **0 UNTS 0**
SIGNED: 21 Jan 69   FORCE: 21 Jan 69
REGISTERED: 14 Mar 69 Denmark
ARTICLES: 0
HEADNOTE: ROAD TRANSPORT
TOPIC: Land Transport
PARTIES:
Czechoslovakia
Denmark

109471   Bilateral Agreement   **0 UNTS 0**
SIGNED: 20 Jun 67   FORCE: 27 Jun 68
REGISTERED: 17 Mar 69 UK Great Britain
ARTICLES: 0
HEADNOTE: TECHNICAL COOPERATION
TOPIC: Tech Assistance
PARTIES:
El Salvador
UK Great Britain

109472   Bilateral Agreement   **0 UNTS 0**
SIGNED: 18 Jan 68   FORCE: 5 Sep 68
REGISTERED: 17 Mar 69 UK Great Britain

ARTICLES: 0
HEADNOTE: TECHNICAL COOPERATION
TOPIC: Tech Assistance
PARTIES:
Brazil
UK Great Britain

109473   Bilateral Exchange   **0 UNTS 0**
SIGNED: 15 Aug 68   FORCE: 15 Aug 68
REGISTERED: 17 Mar 69 UK Great Britain
ARTICLES: 0
HEADNOTE: VISA ABOLITION BEA AEROFLOT CREWS
TOPIC: Visas
PARTIES:
UK Great Britain
USSR (Soviet Union)

109474   Bilateral Agreement   **0 UNTS 0**
SIGNED: 8 Sep 68   FORCE: 8 Sep 68
REGISTERED: 17 Mar 69 UK Great Britain
ARTICLES: 0
HEADNOTE: PUBLIC OFFICERS
TOPIC: Admin Cooperation
PARTIES:
Swaziland
UK Great Britain

109475   Bilateral Exchange   **0 UNTS 0**
SIGNED: 30 Aug 68   FORCE: 30 Aug 68
REGISTERED: 19 Mar 69 Netherlands
ARTICLES: 0
HEADNOTE: WATER DEVELOPMENT BIHAR
TOPIC: Non-IBRD Project
PARTIES:
India
Netherlands

109476   Bilateral Agreement   **0 UNTS 0**
SIGNED: 30 Apr 64   FORCE: 17 Feb 68
REGISTERED: 24 Mar 69 ICAO (Civil Aviat)
ARTICLES: 0
HEADNOTE: AIR TRANSPORT
TOPIC: Air Transport
PARTIES:
Chile
Germany, West

109477   Bilateral Agreement   **0 UNTS 0**
SIGNED: 11 Feb 65   FORCE: 4 Nov 65
REGISTERED: 24 Mar 69 ICAO (Civil Aviat)
ARTICLES: 0
HEADNOTE: AIR SERVICES
TOPIC: Air Transport
PARTIES:
Japan
Malaysia

109478   Bilateral Agreement   **0 UNTS 0**
SIGNED: 15 Mar 65   FORCE: 30 Jun 66
REGISTERED: 24 Mar 69 ICAO (Civil Aviat)
ARTICLES: 0
HEADNOTE: AIR TRANSPORT
TOPIC: Air Transport
PARTIES:
Austria
Germany, West

109479   Bilateral Agreement   **0 UNTS 0**
SIGNED: 16 May 67   FORCE: 30 Aug 67
REGISTERED: 24 Mar 69 ICAO (Civil Aviat)
ARTICLES: 0
HEADNOTE: AIR SERVICES
TOPIC: Air Transport
PARTIES:
Japan
Korea, South

109480   Bilateral Agreement   **0 UNTS 0**
SIGNED: 4 Apr 68   FORCE: 4 Apr 68
REGISTERED: 24 Mar 69 ICAO (Civil Aviat)
ARTICLES: 0
HEADNOTE: AIR SERVICES
TOPIC: Air Transport

PARTIES:
New Zealand
Singapore

109481 Bilateral Agreement **0 UNTS 0**
SIGNED: 23 Apr 68 FORCE: 12 Dec 68
REGISTERED: 25 Mar 69 Netherlands
ARTICLES: 0
HEADNOTE: ROAD TRANSPORT GOODS
TOPIC: Land Transport
PARTIES:
Netherlands
Romania

109482 Bilateral Agreement **0 UNTS 0**
SIGNED: 28 Jun 68 FORCE: 11 Dec 68
REGISTERED: 27 Mar 69 IBRD (World Bank)
ARTICLES: 0
HEADNOTE: GUARANTEE GUACALATE POWER
TOPIC: IBRD Project
PARTIES:
Guatemala
IBRD (World Bank)

109483 Bilateral Agreement **0 UNTS 0**
SIGNED: 28 Jun 68 FORCE: 15 Nov 68
REGISTERED: 27 Mar 69 IBRD (World Bank)
ARTICLES: 0
HEADNOTE: GUARANTEE PAPUA NEW GUINEA
TELECOMMUNICATIONS
TOPIC: IBRD Project
PARTIES:
Australia
IBRD (World Bank)

109484 Bilateral Agreement **0 UNTS 0**
SIGNED: 25 Jul 68 FORCE: 20 Sep 68
REGISTERED: 27 Mar 69 IBRD (World Bank)
ARTICLES: 0
HEADNOTE: GUARANTEE FIFTH RAILROAD
TOPIC: IBRD Project
PARTIES:
Colombia
IBRD (World Bank)

109485 Bilateral Agreement **0 UNTS 0**
SIGNED: 27 Jul 68 FORCE: 25 Sep 68
REGISTERED: 27 Mar 69 IBRD (World Bank)
ARTICLES: 0
HEADNOTE: LOAN FIFTH HIGHWAY
TOPIC: IBRD Project
PARTIES:
Colombia
IBRD (World Bank)

109486 Bilateral Exchange **0 UNTS 0**
SIGNED: 12 Aug 65 FORCE: 12 Oct 65
REGISTERED: 31 Mar 69 Brazil
ARTICLES: 0
HEADNOTE: VISA ABOLITION
TOPIC: Visas
PARTIES:
Brazil
Spain

109487 Bilateral Agreement **0 UNTS 0**
SIGNED: 5 Aug 68 FORCE: 23 Sep 68
REGISTERED: 31 Mar 69 IBRD (World Bank)
ARTICLES: 0
HEADNOTE: GUARANTEE SECOND POWER
TOPIC: IBRD Project
PARTIES:
IBRD (World Bank)
Sierra Leone

109488 Bilateral Agreement **0 UNTS 0**
SIGNED: 24 Mar 69 FORCE: 24 Mar 69
REGISTERED: 24 Mar 69 United Nations
ARTICLES: 0
HEADNOTE: UNICEF ACTIVITIES
TOPIC: IGO Operations
PARTIES:
Jordan
UNICEF (Children)

109489 Bilateral Convention **0 UNTS 0**
SIGNED: 3 May 65 FORCE: 4 Sep 68
REGISTERED: 1 Apr 69 France
ARTICLES: 0
HEADNOTE: TAXATION
TOPIC: General Economic
PARTIES:
France
Senegal

109490 Bilateral Agreement **0 UNTS 0**
SIGNED: 28 Dec 68 FORCE: 28 Dec 68
REGISTERED: 3 Apr 69 Denmark
ARTICLES: 0
HEADNOTE: LOAN
TOPIC: Loans and Credits
PARTIES:
Ceylon (Sri Lanka)
Denmark

109491 Multilateral Agreement **0 UNTS 0**
SIGNED: 15 Jan 69 FORCE: 15 Jan 69
REGISTERED: 3 Apr 69 Denmark
ARTICLES: 0
HEADNOTE: NATIONALITY
TOPIC: Consul/Citizenship
PARTIES:
Denmark SIGNED: 15 Jan 69 FORCE: 1 Jan 69
Finland SIGNED: 15 Jan 69 FORCE: 1 Jan 69
Norway SIGNED: 15 Jan 69 FORCE: 1 Jan 69
Sweden SIGNED: 15 Jan 69 FORCE: 1 Jan 69

109492 Bilateral Agreement **0 UNTS 0**
SIGNED: 26 Sep 68 FORCE: 1 Mar 69
REGISTERED: 7 Apr 69 Austria
ARTICLES: 0
HEADNOTE: SOCIAL SECURITY
TOPIC: Non-ILO Labor
PARTIES:
Austria
Liechtenstein

109493 Bilateral Exchange **0 UNTS 0**
SIGNED: 14 Feb 67 FORCE: 14 Feb 67
REGISTERED: 8 Apr 69 UK Great Britain
ARTICLES: 0
HEADNOTE: AMEND NEW HEBRIDES PROTOCOL
TOPIC: Non-ILO Labor
PARTIES:
France
UK Great Britain

109494 Bilateral Agreement **0 UNTS 0**
SIGNED: 6 Mar 68 FORCE: 15 Oct 68
REGISTERED: 8 Apr 69 UK Great Britain
ARTICLES: 0
HEADNOTE: PEACEFUL USE ATOMIC ENERGY
TOPIC: Atomic Energy
PARTIES:
Japan
UK Great Britain

109495 Bilateral Exchange **0 UNTS 0**
SIGNED: 12 Aug 68 FORCE: 12 Aug 68
REGISTERED: 8 Apr 69 UK Great Britain
ARTICLES: 0
HEADNOTE: INTEREST-FREE DEVELOPMENT
LOAN
TOPIC: Loans and Credits
PARTIES:
Turkey
UK Great Britain

109496 Bilateral Exchange **0 UNTS 0**
SIGNED: 10 Oct 67 FORCE: 29 Mar 68
REGISTERED: 8 Apr 69 UK Great Britain
ARTICLES: 0
HEADNOTE: COOPERATION APPLIED SCIENCE
TECHNOLOGY
TOPIC: Scientific Project
PARTIES:
Poland
UK Great Britain

109497 Bilateral Agreement **0 UNTS 0**
SIGNED: 31 Oct 67 FORCE: 31 Oct 67

REGISTERED: 8 Apr 69 UK Great Britain
ARTICLES: 0
HEADNOTE: CERTAIN COMMERCIAL DEBTS
TOPIC: Claims and Debts
PARTIES:
Indonesia
UK Great Britain

109498 Bilateral Agreement **0 UNTS 0**
SIGNED: 28 Nov 68 FORCE: 28 Nov 68
REGISTERED: 8 Apr 69 UK Great Britain
ARTICLES: 0
HEADNOTE: HEADQUARTERS AGREEMENT
TOPIC: General IGO
CONCEPTS: Privileges and immunities. Institute
establishment. Subsidiary organ. Headquarters
and facilities.
TREATY REF: 727UNTS.
PROCEDURE: Termination.
PARTIES:
Int Wheat Coun
UK Great Britain

109499 Bilateral Convention **0 UNTS 0**
SIGNED: 8 Nov 66 FORCE: 16 Feb 68
REGISTERED: 10 Apr 69 Ireland
ARTICLES: 0
HEADNOTE: AVOID DOUBLE TAXATION
TOPIC: Taxation
CONCEPTS: Taxation. Tax credits. Equitable taxes.
General. Tax exemptions.
TREATY REF: 553UNTS183.
PROCEDURE: Denunciation. Ratification. Termina-
tion.
PARTIES:
Ireland
Switzerland

109500 Bilateral Agreement **0 UNTS 0**
SIGNED: 14 Mar 69 FORCE: 14 Mar 69
REGISTERED: 10 Apr 69 ILO (Labor Org)
ARTICLES: 0
HEADNOTE: ESTABLISHMENT OF AN OFFICE
TOPIC: IGO Operations
CONCEPTS: Privileges and immunities. Institute
establishment. Regional offices.
TREATY REF: 33UNTS261; 33UNTS290.
PARTIES:
ILO (Labor Org)
Trinidad/Tobago

109501 Bilateral Agreement **0 UNTS 0**
SIGNED: 17 May 67 FORCE: 17 Jan 68
REGISTERED: 14 Apr 69 Belgium
ARTICLES: 0
HEADNOTE: CULTURAL AGREEMENT
TOPIC: Culture
CONCEPTS: Culture. Exchange. General cultural
cooperation.
PROCEDURE: Denunciation. Ratification.
PARTIES:
Belgium
United Arab Rep

109502 Bilateral Convention **0 UNTS 0**
SIGNED: 5 Jan 50 FORCE: 1 Apr 51
REGISTERED: 15 Apr 69 France
ARTICLES: 0
HEADNOTE: SOCIAL SECURITY
TOPIC: Non-ILO Labor
CONCEPTS: Family allowances. Administrative co-
operation. Old age insurance. Sickness and inva-
lidity insurance. Social security. Unemployment.
PROCEDURE: Denunciation. Ratification.
PARTIES:
France
Yugoslavia

109503 Bilateral Protocol **0 UNTS 0**
SIGNED: 8 Feb 66 FORCE: 1 Feb 67
REGISTERED: 15 Apr 69 France
ARTICLES: 0
HEADNOTE: HEALTH SERVICES FOR STUDENTS
TOPIC: Sanitation
CONCEPTS: Teacher and student exchange. Sick-
ness and invalidity insurance.

PARTIES:
France
Yugoslavia

109504   Bilateral Exchange   **0 UNTS 0**
SIGNED: 28 Jun 68   FORCE: 8 Jan 69
REGISTERED: 15 Apr 69 Netherlands
ARTICLES: 0
HEADNOTE: APPLICATION EXTRADITION TREATY
TOPIC: Extradition
CONCEPTS: Annex type material.
TREATY   REF: 90BFSP51;   122LTS368;
    108BFSP366.
PARTIES:
Malawi
Netherlands

109505   Bilateral Agreement   **0 UNTS 0**
SIGNED: 27 Sep 68   FORCE: 8 Nov 68
REGISTERED: 15 Apr 69 IBRD (World Bank)
ARTICLES: 0
HEADNOTE: LOAN AGREEMENT
TOPIC: IBRD Project
CONCEPTS: World Bank projects. Loan regula-
    tions. Loan guarantee. Hydro-electric power.
TREATY REF: 668UNTS188.
PROCEDURE: Termination.
PARTIES:
Malaysia
IBRD (World Bank)

109506   Bilateral Agreement   **0 UNTS 0**
SIGNED: 27 Sep 68   FORCE: 15 Jan 69
REGISTERED: 15 Apr 69 IBRD (World Bank)
ARTICLES: 0
HEADNOTE: LOAN AGREEMENT-KUALA LUMPUR
    WATER SUPPLY PROJECT
TOPIC: IBRD Project
CONCEPTS: World Bank projects. Loan regula-
    tions. Loan guarantee.
TREATY REF: 668UNTS210.
PROCEDURE: Termination.
PARTIES:
Malaysia
IBRD (World Bank)

109507   Bilateral Protocol   **0 UNTS 0**
SIGNED: 24 Sep 62   FORCE: 24 Sep 62
REGISTERED: 16 Apr 69 France
ARTICLES: 0
HEADNOTE: TECHNICAL CO-OPERATION
TOPIC: Tech Assistance
CONCEPTS: General technical assistance. Assis-
    tance. Special projects.
TREATY REF: 507UNTS80,75,57.
PARTIES:
Algeria
France

109508   Bilateral Convention   **0 UNTS 0**
SIGNED: 8 Apr 66   FORCE: 1 Sep 66
REGISTERED: 16 Apr 69 France
ARTICLES: 0
HEADNOTE: TECHNICAL, CULTURAL COOPER-
    ATION
TOPIC: Tech Assistance
CONCEPTS: Culture. Exchange. General cultural
    cooperation. General technical assistance. As-
    sistance.
TREATY REF: 668UNTS223.
PROCEDURE: Termination.
PARTIES:
Algeria
France

109509   Bilateral Protocol   **0 UNTS 0**
SIGNED: 26 Dec 67   FORCE: 26 Dec 67
REGISTERED: 16 Apr 69 France
ARTICLES: 0
HEADNOTE: ALGERIAN TAKEOVER OF THE AERO-
    NAUTICAL ADMINISTRATION AND SAFTEY
    ORG
TOPIC: Admin Cooperation
CONCEPTS: Operating agencies. Post-colonial ad-
    ministration. Conditions of airlines operating
    permission. Operating authorizations and regu-
    lations.

TREATY   REF: 668UNTS241;   668UNTS229;
    15UNTS295.
PARTIES:
Algeria
France

109510   Bilateral Agreement   **0 UNTS 0**
SIGNED: 5 Apr 67   FORCE: 1 Feb 69
REGISTERED: 17 Apr 69 France
ARTICLES: 0
HEADNOTE: FACILITATE APPLICATION HAGUE
    CONVENTION
TOPIC: Admin Cooperation
CONCEPTS: Annex type material.
TREATY   REF: 286UNTS265;   95LTS233;
    48LTS139.
PARTIES:
France
Poland

109511   Bilateral Agreement   **0 UNTS 0**
SIGNED: 26 Jan 68   FORCE: 20 Sep 68
REGISTERED: 17 Apr 69 IBRD (World Bank)
ARTICLES: 0
HEADNOTE: GUARANTEE-RIO COLORADO-IRRI-
    GATION PROJECT
TOPIC: IBRD Project
CONCEPTS: Loan and credit. Credit provisions.
    Loan repayment. Terms of loan.
TREATY   REF: 422UNTS203;   489UNTS151;
    596UNTS3.
PARTIES:
Mexico
IBRD (World Bank)

109512   Bilateral Agreement   **0 UNTS 0**
SIGNED: 31 Jul 68   FORCE: 31 Oct 68
REGISTERED: 17 Apr 69 IBRD (World Bank)
ARTICLES: 0
HEADNOTE: LOAN   AGREEMENT-EDUCATION
    PROJECT
TOPIC: IBRD Project
CONCEPTS: World Bank projects. Loan regula-
    tions. Loan guarantee.
PROCEDURE: Termination.
PARTIES:
Colombia
IBRD (World Bank)

109513   Multilateral Instrument   **0 UNTS 0**
SIGNED: 7 Feb 68   FORCE: 6 Apr 69
REGISTERED: 21 Apr 69 Thailand
ARTICLES: 0
HEADNOTE: CHARTER-SOUTH EAST ASIAN MIN-
    ISTERS OF EDUCATION ORGANIZATION
TOPIC: IGO Establishment
CONCEPTS: Commissions and foundations. Sub-
    sidiary organ. Procedure.
PROCEDURE: Ratification.
PARTIES:
Indonesia RATIFIED: 6 Mar 69 FORCE: 6 Mar 69

109514   Bilateral Agreement   **0 UNTS 0**
SIGNED: 23 Apr 69   FORCE: 23 Apr 69
REGISTERED: 23 Apr 69 United Nations
ARTICLES: 0
HEADNOTE: OPERATIONAL ASSISTANCE
TOPIC: Direct Aid
CONCEPTS: IGO reference. Arbitration. Procedure.
    Claims and settlements. Aid and development.
    General technical assistance.
INTL ORGS: United Nations.
TREATY REF: 251UNTS181; 466UNTSO93.
PROCEDURE: Termination.
PARTIES:
State/IGO Group
Yemen

109515   Bilateral Agreement   **0 UNTS 0**
SIGNED: 2 Jun 48   FORCE: 29 Nov 66
REGISTERED: 28 Apr 69 Argentina
ARTICLES: 0
HEADNOTE: AIR TRANSPORT
TOPIC: Air Transport
CONCEPTS: Air transport. Airworthiness certifi-
    cates. Conditions of airlines operating permis-
    sion. Overflights and technical stops. Operating
    authorizations and regulations.

TREATY REF: 15UNTS295.
PROCEDURE: Ratification.
PARTIES:
Argentina
Brazil

109516   Bilateral Exchange   **0 UNTS 0**
SIGNED: 7 Sep 60   FORCE: 7 Sep 60
REGISTERED: 28 Apr 69 Argentina
ARTICLES: 0
HEADNOTE: RAILWAY AND PAYMENT PROB-
    LEMS
TOPIC: Land Transport
CONCEPTS: Monetary and gold transfers. Pay-
    ment schedules. Railways.
PARTIES:
Argentina
Bolivia

109517   Bilateral Exchange   **0 UNTS 0**
SIGNED: 2 Aug 63   FORCE: 2 Aug 63
REGISTERED: 28 Apr 69 Argentina
ARTICLES: 0
HEADNOTE: PAYMENTS, BOLIVIAN DEBT
TOPIC: Claims and Debts
CONCEPTS: Payment schedules. Debts.
TREATY REF: 669UNTS117.
PARTIES:
Argentina
Bolivia

109518   Bilateral Exchange   **0 UNTS 0**
SIGNED: 15 Jun 66   FORCE: 15 Jun 66
REGISTERED: 28 Apr 69 Argentina
ARTICLES: 0
HEADNOTE: BASIC WORKS BUDGET, YACUIBA-
    SANTA CRUZ RAILWAY
TOPIC: Finance
CONCEPTS: Indemnities and reimbursements.
    Loan repayment. Refinance of loan.
TREATY REF: 669UNTS117.
PARTIES:
Argentina
Bolivia

109519   Bilateral Exchange   **0 UNTS 0**
SIGNED: 23 Nov 60   FORCE: 23 Nov 60
REGISTERED: 28 Apr 69 Argentina
ARTICLES: 0
HEADNOTE: BRIDGE CONSTRUCTION, URUGUAY
    RIVER
TOPIC: Non-IBRD Project
CONCEPTS: Indemnities and reimbursements.
    Special projects.
PARTIES:
Argentina
Uruguay

109520   Bilateral Exchange   **0 UNTS 0**
SIGNED: 12 Feb 66   FORCE: 12 Feb 66
REGISTERED: 28 Apr 69 Argentina
ARTICLES: 0
HEADNOTE: ACCELERATION,   BRIDGE   CON-
    STRUCTION
TOPIC: Non-IBRD Project
CONCEPTS: Special projects.
PARTIES:
Argentina
Uruguay

109521   Bilateral Agreement   **0 UNTS 0**
SIGNED: 30 May 67   FORCE: 17 Oct 67
REGISTERED: 28 Apr 69 Argentina
ARTICLES: 0
HEADNOTE: BRIDGE CONSTRUCTION, URUGUAY
    RIVER
TOPIC: Non-IBRD Project
CONCEPTS: Indemnities and reimbursements.
    Special projects. Loan repayment. Refinance of
    loan.
TREATY REF: 669UNTS153; 167UNTS167.
PROCEDURE: Ratification.
PARTIES:
Argentina
Uruguay

109522 Bilateral Convention **0 UNTS 0**
SIGNED: 12 Apr 61 FORCE: 1 Jan 64
REGISTERED: 28 Apr 69 Argentina
ARTICLES: 0
HEADNOTE: SOCIAL SECURITY CONVENTION .
TOPIC: Non-ILO Labor
CONCEPTS: Family allowances. Administrative co-
operation. Old age insurance. Sickness and inva-
lidity insurance. Social security. Unemployment.
TREATY REF: 2UNTS104; 2UNTS39.
PROCEDURE: Duration. Ratification. Termination.
PARTIES:
Argentina
Italy

109523 Bilateral Exchange **0 UNTS 0**
SIGNED: 25 Jun 65 FORCE: 25 Jun 65
REGISTERED: 28 Apr 69 Argentina
ARTICLES: 0
HEADNOTE: ABOLITION TOURIST VISA
TOPIC: Visas
PARTIES:
Argentina
Ireland

109524 Bilateral Agreement **0 UNTS 0**
SIGNED: 7 Feb 66 FORCE: 20 Oct 67
REGISTERED: 28 Apr 69 Brazil
ARTICLES: 0
HEADNOTE: CULTURE
TOPIC: Culture
PARTIES:
Brazil
Korea, South

109525 Bilateral Convention **0 UNTS 0**
SIGNED: 28 May 66 FORCE: 1 Sep 67
REGISTERED: 28 Apr 69 Argentina
ARTICLES: 0
HEADNOTE: SOCIAL SECURITY
TOPIC: Non-ILO Labor
PARTIES:
Argentina
Spain

109526 Bilateral Agreement **0 UNTS 0**
SIGNED: 10 Mar 67 FORCE: 31 Oct 68
REGISTERED: 28 Apr 69 IAEA (Atom Energy)
ARTICLES: 0
HEADNOTE: SAFEGUARDS
TOPIC: Atomic Energy
PARTIES:
State/IGO Group
IAEA (Atom Energy)

109527 Bilateral Convention **0 UNTS 0**
SIGNED: 25 May 67 FORCE: 19 Feb 69
REGISTERED: 28 Apr 69 France
ARTICLES: 0
HEADNOTE: LEGAL & EXECUTION JUDGMENTS
TOPIC: Admin Cooperation
PARTIES:
France
San Marino

109528 Bilateral Exchange **0 UNTS 0**
SIGNED: 22 Aug 67 FORCE: 22 Oct 67
REGISTERED: 28 Apr 69 Brazil
ARTICLES: 0
HEADNOTE: VISA ABOLITION
TOPIC: Visas
PARTIES:
Austria
Brazil

109529 Bilateral Exchange **0 UNTS 0**
SIGNED: 15 Sep 67 FORCE: 1 Jan 67
REGISTERED: 28 Apr 69 Argentina
ARTICLES: 0
HEADNOTE: DOUBLE TAX SHIPS PLANES
TOPIC: Taxation
PARTIES:
Argentina
Colombia

109530 Bilateral Agreement **0 UNTS 0**
SIGNED: 13 Jan 68 FORCE: 19 Jul 68
REGISTERED: 28 Apr 69 France
ARTICLES: 0
HEADNOTE: CULTURAL TECHNICAL COOPER-
ATION
TOPIC: Culture
PARTIES:
France
Honduras

109531 Bilateral Agreement **0 UNTS 0**
SIGNED: 12 Jan 68 FORCE: 6 Sep 68
REGISTERED: 28 Apr 69 France
ARTICLES: 0
HEADNOTE: SCIENTIFIC TECHNICAL COOPER-
ATION
TOPIC: Scientific Project
PARTIES:
Austria
France

109532 Bilateral Agreement **0 UNTS 0**
SIGNED: 19 Mar 68 FORCE: 1 Sep 68
REGISTERED: 28 Apr 69 France
ARTICLES: 0
HEADNOTE: APPLY 1954 CONVENTION CIVIL
PROCEDURE
TOPIC: Admin Cooperation
PARTIES:
France
Hungary

109533 Bilateral Agreement **0 UNTS 0**
SIGNED: 15 Oct 68 FORCE: 15 Oct 68
REGISTERED: 28 Apr 69 IAEA (Atom Energy)
ARTICLES: 0
HEADNOTE: AGENCY SAFEGUARDS
TOPIC: Atomic Energy
PARTIES:
State/IGO Group
IAEA (Atom Energy)

109534 Bilateral Agreement **0 UNTS 0**
SIGNED: 3 May 69 FORCE: 3 May 69
REGISTERED: 3 May 69 United Nations
ARTICLES: 0
HEADNOTE: TECHNICAL ASSISTANCE
TOPIC: Tech Assistance
PARTIES:
State/IGO Group
Spain

109535 Bilateral Agreement **0 UNTS 0**
SIGNED: 16 Feb 66 FORCE: 29 Jan 69
REGISTERED: 5 May 69 United Arab Rep
ARTICLES: 0
HEADNOTE: TRADE
TOPIC: General Trade
PARTIES:
United Arab Rep
Zambia

109536 Bilateral Convention **0 UNTS 0**
SIGNED: 19 May 67 FORCE: 25 Apr 68
REGISTERED: 7 May 69 Romania
ARTICLES: 0
HEADNOTE: PLANT PROTECTION
TOPIC: Sanitation
PARTIES:
Romania
Turkey

109537 Bilateral Agreement **0 UNTS 0**
SIGNED: 6 Dec 67 FORCE: 9 Apr 68
REGISTERED: 7 May 69 Romania
ARTICLES: 0
HEADNOTE: ROAD TRANSPORT
TOPIC: Land Transport
PARTIES:
Czechoslovakia
Romania

109538 Bilateral Agreement **0 UNTS 0**
SIGNED: 29 Jan 68 FORCE: 31 May 68
REGISTERED: 7 May 69 Romania

ARTICLES: 0
HEADNOTE: ROAD TRANSPORT
TOPIC: Land Transport
PARTIES:
Poland
Romania

109539 Bilateral Agreement **0 UNTS 0**
SIGNED: 17 Apr 68 FORCE: 31 Oct 68
REGISTERED: 7 May 69 Belgium
ARTICLES: 0
HEADNOTE: ROAD TRANSPORT
TOPIC: Land Transport
PARTIES:
Belgium
Czechoslovakia

109540 Bilateral Agreement **0 UNTS 0**
SIGNED: 30 Dec 46 FORCE: 28 Jan 47
REGISTERED: 14 May 69 Argentina
ARTICLES: 0
HEADNOTE: URUGUAY RIVER RAPIDS SALTO
GRANDE
TOPIC: Specific Resources
PARTIES:
Argentina
Uruguay

109541 Bilateral Exchange **0 UNTS 0**
SIGNED: 4 Sep 63 FORCE: 4 Sep 63
REGISTERED: 14 May 69 Argentina
ARTICLES: 0
HEADNOTE: SALTO GRANDE ECONOMIC FI-
NANCE PLAN
TOPIC: General Economic
PARTIES:
Argentina
Uruguay

109542 Bilateral Exchange **0 UNTS 0**
SIGNED: 8 Jul 68 FORCE: 8 Jul 68
REGISTERED: 14 May 69 Argentina
ARTICLES: 0
HEADNOTE: SALTO GRANDE WORKS OPERA-
TION
TOPIC: Non-IBRD Project
PARTIES:
Argentina
Uruguay

109543 Bilateral Protocol **0 UNTS 0**
SIGNED: 16 Oct 68 FORCE: 16 Oct 68
REGISTERED: 14 May 69 Argentina
ARTICLES: 0
HEADNOTE: URUGUAY RIVER FRONTIER
TOPIC: Territory Boundary
PARTIES:
Argentina
Uruguay

109544 Bilateral Exchange **0 UNTS 0**
SIGNED: 8 Jul 68 FORCE: 8 Jul 68
REGISTERED: 14 May 69 Argentina
ARTICLES: 0
HEADNOTE: TOURISM
TOPIC: Visas
PARTIES:
Argentina
Uruguay

109545 Bilateral Exchange **0 UNTS 0**
SIGNED: 22 Dec 58 FORCE: 22 Dec 58
REGISTERED: 14 May 69 Argentina
ARTICLES: 0
HEADNOTE: MERCHANT MARINE DEVELOPMENT
TOPIC: Water Transport
PARTIES:
Argentina
Brazil

109546 Bilateral Convention **0 UNTS 0**
SIGNED: 15 Nov 61 FORCE: 7 Jun 68
REGISTERED: 14 May 69 Argentina
ARTICLES: 0
HEADNOTE: FREEJUDICIAL ASSISTANCE
TOPIC: Admin Cooperation

PARTIES:
  Argentina
  Brazil

109547   Bilateral Agreement   **0 UNTS 0**
SIGNED: 25 Jan 68   FORCE: 23 Feb 69
REGISTERED: 14 May 69 Argentina
ARTICLES: 0
HEADNOTE: CULTURAL EXCHANGE
TOPIC: Culture
PARTIES:
  Argentina
  Brazil

109548   Bilateral Exchange   **0 UNTS 0**
SIGNED: 24 Jan 69   FORCE: 24 Jan 69
REGISTERED: 14 May 69 Argentina
ARTICLES: 0
HEADNOTE: PLATA FRONTIER TELECOMMUNICA-
  TIONS
TOPIC: Telecommunications
PARTIES:
  Argentina
  Brazil

109549   Bilateral Exchange   **0 UNTS 0**
SIGNED: 9 Dec 60   FORCE: 9 Dec 60
REGISTERED: 14 May 69 Argentina
ARTICLES: 0
HEADNOTE: PRICES STATE-OWNED HYDROCAR-
  BONS
TOPIC: General Trade
PARTIES:
  Argentina
  Bolivia

109550   Bilateral Exchange   **0 UNTS 0**
SIGNED: 26 Oct 67   FORCE: 26 Oct 67
REGISTERED: 14 May 69 Argentina
ARTICLES: 0
HEADNOTE: ROLLING STOCK YACUIBA RAILWAY
TOPIC: Land Transport
PARTIES:
  Argentina
  Bolivia

109551   Bilateral Exchange   **0 UNTS 0**
SIGNED: 18 Apr 68   FORCE: 18 Apr 68
REGISTERED: 14 May 69 Argentina
ARTICLES: 0
HEADNOTE: CATTLE EXPORT CREDIT
TOPIC: Commodity Trade
PARTIES:
  Argentina
  Bolivia

109552   Bilateral Exchange   **0 UNTS 0**
SIGNED: 9 Jul 68   FORCE: 9 Jul 68
REGISTERED: 14 May 69 Argentina
ARTICLES: 0
HEADNOTE: RATIFICATION SALTA ACT TELE-
  COMMUNICATIONS
TOPIC: Telecommunications
PARTIES:
  Argentina
  Bolivia

109553   Bilateral Exchange   **0 UNTS 0**
SIGNED: 5 Aug 68   FORCE: 5 Aug 68
REGISTERED: 14 May 69 Argentina
ARTICLES: 0
HEADNOTE: NATURAL GAS
TOPIC: Specific Resources
PARTIES:
  Argentina
  Bolivia

109554   Bilateral Exchange   **0 UNTS 0**
SIGNED: 11 Dec 68   FORCE: 11 Dec 68
REGISTERED: 14 May 69 Argentina
ARTICLES: 0
HEADNOTE: ROSARIO FREE TRADE ZONE
TOPIC: General Trade
PARTIES:
  Argentina
  Bolivia

109555   Bilateral Exchange   **0 UNTS 0**
SIGNED: 3 Oct 64   FORCE: 3 Oct 64
REGISTERED: 14 May 69 Argentina
ARTICLES: 0
HEADNOTE: PRIVILEGES FOR ARGENTINE SPE-
  CIALISTS
TOPIC: Culture
PARTIES:
  Argentina
  France

109556   Bilateral Agreement   **0 UNTS 0**
SIGNED: 25 Nov 64   FORCE: 22 Mar 68
REGISTERED: 14 May 69 Argentina
ARTICLES: 0
HEADNOTE: CULTURE
TOPIC: Culture
PARTIES:
  Argentina
  Nicaragua

109557   Bilateral Agreement   **0 UNTS 0**
SIGNED: 26 Nov 64   FORCE: 22 Nov 68
REGISTERED: 14 May 69 Argentina
ARTICLES: 0
HEADNOTE: CULTURE
TOPIC: Culture
PARTIES:
  Argentina
  Honduras

109558   Bilateral Agreement   **0 UNTS 0**
SIGNED: 19 Aug 65   FORCE: 10 Mar 69
REGISTERED: 14 May 69 Argentina
ARTICLES: 0
HEADNOTE: CULTURE
TOPIC: Culture
PARTIES:
  Argentina
  Turkey

109559   Bilateral Agreement   **0 UNTS 0**
SIGNED: 10 Nov 65   FORCE: 14 Apr 69
REGISTERED: 14 May 69 Argentina
ARTICLES: 0
HEADNOTE: SOCIAL COOPERATION
TOPIC: Culture
PARTIES:
  Argentina
  Spain

109560   Bilateral Agreement   **0 UNTS 0**
SIGNED: 12 Sep 67   FORCE: 19 Sep 67
REGISTERED: 14 May 69 Argentina
ARTICLES: 0
HEADNOTE: CULTURE
TOPIC: Culture
PARTIES:
  Argentina
  Dominican Republic

109561   Bilateral Agreement   **0 UNTS 0**
SIGNED: 6 Nov 67   FORCE: 10 Mar 69
REGISTERED: 14 May 69 Argentina
ARTICLES: 0
HEADNOTE: TRADE
TOPIC: General Trade
PARTIES:
  Argentina
  Hungary

109562   Bilateral Exchange   **0 UNTS 0**
SIGNED: 21 Feb 68   FORCE: 21 May 68
REGISTERED: 14 May 69 Argentina
ARTICLES: 0
HEADNOTE: TOURIST VISA ABOLITION
TOPIC: Visas
PARTIES:
  Argentina
  Italy

109563   Bilateral Exchange   **0 UNTS 0**
SIGNED: 21 Mar 68   FORCE: 21 Mar 68
REGISTERED: 14 May 69 Argentina
ARTICLES: 0
HEADNOTE: WEIGHTS MEASURES SYSTEM

TOPIC: Admin Cooperation
PARTIES:
  Argentina
  Germany, West

109564   Bilateral Exchange   **0 UNTS 0**
SIGNED: 29 Aug 68   FORCE: 29 Aug 68
REGISTERED: 14 May 69 Argentina
ARTICLES: 0
HEADNOTE: STUDIES TECHNICAL ASSISTANCE
TOPIC: Tech Assistance
PARTIES:
  Argentina
  Germany, West

109565   Bilateral Exchange   **0 UNTS 0**
SIGNED: 23 Dec 68   FORCE: 23 Dec 68
REGISTERED: 14 May 69 Argentina
ARTICLES: 0
HEADNOTE: TECHNICAL ASSISTANCE SUBSOIL
  PAMPA PLAIN
TOPIC: Tech Assistance
PARTIES:
  Argentina
  Germany, West

109566   Bilateral Exchange   **0 UNTS 0**
SIGNED: 9 Apr 68   FORCE: 9 Apr 68
REGISTERED: 14 May 69 Argentina
ARTICLES: 0
HEADNOTE: MILITARY AIRMAIL SERVICE
TOPIC: General Military
PARTIES:
  Argentina
  Colombia

109567   Bilateral Exchange   **0 UNTS 0**
SIGNED: 27 Mar 69   FORCE: 27 Mar 69
REGISTERED: 14 May 69 Argentina
ARTICLES: 0
HEADNOTE: TOURIST VISA ABOLITION
TOPIC: Visas
PARTIES:
  Argentina
  Colombia

109568   Bilateral Exchange   **0 UNTS 0**
SIGNED: 27 Mar 69   FORCE: 27 Mar 69
REGISTERED: 14 May 69 Argentina
ARTICLES: 0
HEADNOTE: CULTURAL TRAVELS
TOPIC: Culture
PARTIES:
  Argentina
  Colombia

109569   Bilateral Agreement   **0 UNTS 0**
SIGNED: 4 Dec 68   FORCE: 4 Dec 68
REGISTERED: 14 May 69 Argentina
ARTICLES: 0
HEADNOTE: CAPITAL ASSISTANCE
TOPIC: Direct Aid
PARTIES:
  Argentina
  Germany, West

109570   Bilateral Exchange   **0 UNTS 0**
SIGNED: 31 Jul 68   FORCE: 31 Jul 68
REGISTERED: 14 May 69 Argentina
ARTICLES: 0
HEADNOTE: TRANS-ANDEAN RAILWAY
TOPIC: Land Transport
PARTIES:
  Argentina
  Chile

109571   Bilateral Exchange   **0 UNTS 0**
SIGNED: 4 Sep 68   FORCE: 1 Oct 68
REGISTERED: 14 May 69 Argentina
ARTICLES: 0
HEADNOTE: VISA FEE EXEMPTION
TOPIC: Visas
PARTIES:
  Argentina
  India

109572 Bilateral Exchange **0 UNTS 0**
SIGNED: 5 Sep 68   FORCE: 5 Sep 68
REGISTERED: 14 May 69 Argentina
ARTICLES: 0
HEADNOTE: EQUIPMENT IMPORT
TOPIC: Loans and Credits
PARTIES:
 Argentina
 Switzerland

109573 Bilateral Agreement **0 UNTS 0**
SIGNED: 5 Nov 68   FORCE: 3 May 69
REGISTERED: 14 May 69 Argentina
ARTICLES: 0
HEADNOTE: CULTURAL COOPERATION
TOPIC: Culture
PARTIES:
 Argentina
 Romania

109574 Multilateral Agreement **0 UNTS 0**
SIGNED: 22 Apr 68   FORCE: 3 Dec 68
REGISTERED: 15 May 69 USSR (Soviet Union)
ARTICLES: 0
HEADNOTE: RESCUE RETURN ASTRONAUTS OB-
JECTS
TOPIC: Scientific Project
PARTIES:
 Argentina   RATIFIED: 26 Mar 69   FORCE:
  26 Mar 69
 Barbados   RATIFIED: 20 Feb 69   FORCE:
  20 Feb 69
 Botswana   RATIFIED: 18 Apr 69   FORCE:
  18 Apr 69
 Bulgaria RATIFIED: 2 Apr 69 FORCE: 2 Apr 69
 Byelorussia   RATIFIED: 2 Dec 68   FORCE:
  3 Dec 68
 Cameroon   RATIFIED: 10 Jan 69   FORCE:
  10 Jan 69
 Czechoslovakia RATIFIED: 18 Feb 69 FORCE:
  18 Feb 69
 Denmark RATIFIED: 6 May 69 FORCE: 6 May 69
 Ecuador RATIFIED: 7 Mar 69 FORCE: 7 Mar 69
 Gabon RATIFIED: 2 Apr 69 FORCE: 2 Apr 69
 Gambia RATIFIED: 26 Jul 68 FORCE: 3 Dec 68
 Germany, East RATIFIED: 11 Dec 68 FORCE:
  11 Dec 68
 Ireland RATIFIED: 29 Aug 68 FORCE: 3 Dec 68
 Korea, South RATIFIED: 4 Apr 69 FORCE:
  4 Apr 69
 Lebanon RATIFIED: 31 Mar 69 FORCE: 3 Dec 68
 Madagascar   RATIFIED: 11 Feb 69   FORCE:
  11 Feb 69
 Mauritania   RATIFIED: 16 Apr 69   FORCE:
  16 Apr 69
 Mexico RATIFIED: 11 Mar 69 FORCE: 11 Mar 69
 Mongolia   RATIFIED: 31 Jan 69   FORCE:
  31 Jan 69
 Nepal RATIFIED: 11 Jul 68 FORCE: 3 Dec 68
 Niger RATIFIED: 15 Jan 69 FORCE: 15 Jan 69
 Poland RATIFIED: 14 Feb 69 FORCE: 14 Feb 69
 United Arab Rep RATIFIED: 11 Dec 68 FORCE:
  3 Dec 68
 UK Great Britain RATIFIED: 3 Dec 68 FORCE:
  3 Dec 68
 USA (United States) RATIFIED: 3 Dec 68 FORCE:
  3 Dec 68
 Ukrainian SSR RATIFIED: 16 Jan 69 FORCE:
  16 Jan 69
 Uruguay RATIFIED: 3 Dec 68 FORCE: 3 Dec 68
 USSR (Soviet Union) RATIFIED: 3 Dec 68 FORCE:
  3 Dec 68

109575 Bilateral Agreement **0 UNTS 0**
SIGNED: 24 May 68   FORCE: 20 Feb 69
REGISTERED: 17 May 69 Finland
ARTICLES: 0
HEADNOTE: PEACEFUL USE ATOMIC ENERGY
TOPIC: Atomic Energy
PARTIES:
 Finland
 UK Great Britain

109576 Bilateral Agreement **0 UNTS 0**
SIGNED: 11 Dec 48   FORCE: 11 Dec 48
REGISTERED: 19 May 69 USSR (Soviet Union)
ARTICLES: 0
HEADNOTE: TRADE
TOPIC: General Trade

PARTIES:
 Italy
 USSR (Soviet Union)

109577 Multilateral Instrument **0 UNTS 0**
SIGNED: 24 Mar 68   FORCE: 1 Mar 69
REGISTERED: 19 May 69 Senegal
ARTICLES: 0
HEADNOTE: STATUTE SENEGAL RIVER RIPARI-
ANS
TOPIC: IGO Establishment
PARTIES:
 Guinea FORCE: 1 Mar 69
 Mali FORCE: 1 Mar 69
 Mauritania FORCE: 1 Mar 69
 Senegal FORCE: 1 Mar 69

109578 Bilateral Agreement **0 UNTS 0**
SIGNED: 25 Apr 57   FORCE: 25 Oct 62
REGISTERED: 19 May 69 USSR (Soviet Union)
ARTICLES: 0
HEADNOTE: TRANSIT
TOPIC: Land Transport
PARTIES:
 Iran
 USSR (Soviet Union)

109579 Bilateral Agreement **0 UNTS 0**
SIGNED: 28 Dec 57   FORCE: 11 Jan 58
REGISTERED: 19 May 69 USSR (Soviet Union)
ARTICLES: 0
HEADNOTE: PAYMENTS
TOPIC: Finance
PARTIES:
 Italy
 USSR (Soviet Union)

109580 Bilateral Agreement **0 UNTS 0**
SIGNED: 24 Sep 62   FORCE: 24 Sep 62
REGISTERED: 19 May 69 USSR (Soviet Union)
ARTICLES: 0
HEADNOTE: TRADE
TOPIC: General Trade
PARTIES:
 Cameroon
 USSR (Soviet Union)

109581 Bilateral Protocol **0 UNTS 0**
SIGNED: 19 Mar 63   FORCE: 19 Mar 63
REGISTERED: 19 May 69 USSR (Soviet Union)
ARTICLES: 0
HEADNOTE: TRADE
TOPIC: General Trade
PARTIES:
 USSR (Soviet Union)
 Yemen

109582 Bilateral Agreement **0 UNTS 0**
SIGNED: 26 May 64   FORCE: 26 May 64
REGISTERED: 19 May 69 USSR (Soviet Union)
ARTICLES: 0
HEADNOTE: TRADE
TOPIC: General Trade
PARTIES:
 Congo (Zaire)
 USSR (Soviet Union)

109583 Bilateral Agreement **0 UNTS 0**
SIGNED: 17 Feb 65   FORCE: 6 Jul 66
REGISTERED: 19 May 69 USSR (Soviet Union)
ARTICLES: 0
HEADNOTE: TRADE
TOPIC: General Trade
PARTIES:
 Cuba
 USSR (Soviet Union)

109584 Bilateral Protocol **0 UNTS 0**
SIGNED: 22 Feb 65   FORCE: 22 Feb 65
REGISTERED: 19 May 69 USSR (Soviet Union)
ARTICLES: 0
HEADNOTE: TRADE
TOPIC: General Trade
PARTIES:
 Cyprus
 USSR (Soviet Union)

109585 Bilateral Convention **0 UNTS 0**
SIGNED: 13 Mar 68   FORCE: 20 Jan 69
REGISTERED: 19 May 69 UK Great Britain
ARTICLES: 0
HEADNOTE: MEDICAL SERVICES
TOPIC: Sanitation
PARTIES:
 Bulgaria
 UK Great Britain

109586 Bilateral Exchange **0 UNTS 0**
SIGNED: 11 Dec 68   FORCE: 11 Dec 68
REGISTERED: 19 May 69 UK Great Britain
ARTICLES: 0
HEADNOTE: DRIVING LICENSES
TOPIC: Land Transport
PARTIES:
 Belgium
 UK Great Britain

109587 Multilateral Convention **0 UNTS 0**
SIGNED: 14 May 66   FORCE: 21 Mar 69
REGISTERED: 20 May 69 FAO (Food Agri)
ARTICLES: 0
HEADNOTE: CONSERVATION ATLANTIC TUNAS
TOPIC: Specific Resources
PARTIES:
 Brazil RATIFIED: 1 Apr 69 FORCE: 1 Apr 69
 Canada RATIFIED: 20 Aug 68 FORCE: 21 Mar 69
 France RATIFIED: 7 Nov 68 FORCE: 21 Mar 69
 Ghana RATIFIED: 17 Apr 68 FORCE: 21 Mar 69
 Japan RATIFIED: 24 Aug 67 FORCE: 21 Mar 69
 South Africa RATIFIED: 17 Oct 67 FORCE:
  21 Mar 69
 Spain RATIFIED: 21 Mar 69 FORCE: 21 Mar 69
 USA (United States) RATIFIED: 18 May 67
  FORCE: 21 Mar 69

109588 Bilateral Agreement **0 UNTS 0**
SIGNED: 10 Jul 68   FORCE: 31 Jan 69
REGISTERED: 23 May 69 IBRD (World Bank)
ARTICLES: 0
HEADNOTE: GUARANTEE DAWOOD HERCULES
FERTILIZER
TOPIC: IBRD Project
PARTIES:
 Pakistan
 IBRD (World Bank)

109589 Bilateral Instrument **0 UNTS 0**
SIGNED: 9 May 69
REGISTERED: 26 May 69 United Nations
ARTICLES: 0
HEADNOTE: ICJ COMPULSORY JURISDICTION
TOPIC: ICJ Option Clause
PARTIES:
 Swaziland

109590 Bilateral Agreement **0 UNTS 0**
SIGNED: 19 Sep 68   FORCE: 25 Apr 69
REGISTERED: 30 May 69 IBRD (World Bank)
ARTICLES: 0
HEADNOTE: LOAN SECOND HIGHWAY MAINTE-
NANCE
TOPIC: IBRD Project
PARTIES:
 Chile
 IBRD (World Bank)

109591 Bilateral Agreement **0 UNTS 0**
SIGNED: 27 Nov 68   FORCE: 14 Jan 69
REGISTERED: 30 May 69 IBRD (World Bank)
ARTICLES: 0
HEADNOTE: GUARANTEE KAINJI SUPPLEMENT
TOPIC: IBRD Project
PARTIES:
 Nigeria
 IBRD (World Bank)

109592 Bilateral Agreement **0 UNTS 0**
SIGNED: 2 Dec 68   FORCE: 25 Feb 69
REGISTERED: 31 May 69 IBRD (World Bank)
ARTICLES: 0
HEADNOTE: GUARANTEE POWER INTERCONNEC-
TION
TOPIC: IBRD Project

PARTIES:
Colombia
IBRD (World Bank)

109593 Bilateral Agreement **0 UNTS 0**
SIGNED: 20 Dec 68   FORCE: 27 Feb 69
REGISTERED: 30 May 69 IBRD (World Bank)
ARTICLES: 0
HEADNOTE: LOAN SECOND WEST PAKISTAN
  HIGHWAY
TOPIC: IBRD Project
PARTIES:
Pakistan
IBRD (World Bank)

109594 Bilateral Agreement **0 UNTS 0**
SIGNED: 9 Jan 69   FORCE: 4 Mar 69
REGISTERED: 30 May 69 IBRD (World Bank)
ARTICLES: 0
HEADNOTE: GUARANTEE FOURTH POWER
TOPIC: IBRD Project
PARTIES:
Malaysia
IBRD (World Bank)

109595 Bilateral Agreement **0 UNTS 0**
SIGNED: 15 Aug 68   FORCE: 2 Feb 69
REGISTERED: 4 Jun 69 IBRD (World Bank)
ARTICLES: 0
HEADNOTE: GUARANTEE 1968 INDUSTRIAL
  PROJECTS
TOPIC: IBRD Project
PARTIES:
IBRD (World Bank)
Yugoslavia

109596 Bilateral Agreement **0 UNTS 0**
SIGNED: 24 Jan 69   FORCE: 5 Mar 69
REGISTERED: 4 Jun 69 IBRD (World Bank)
ARTICLES: 0
HEADNOTE: GUARANTEE-THIRD DEVELOPMENT
  BANK PROJECT
TOPIC: IBRD Project
CONCEPTS: Loan and credit. Credit provisions.
  Loan repayment. Terms of loan.
TREATY REF: 491UNTS345.
PARTIES:
Finland
IBRD (World Bank)

109597 Bilateral Agreement **0 UNTS 0**
SIGNED: 30 Oct 68   FORCE: 16 Jan 69
REGISTERED: 5 Jun 69 Belgium
ARTICLES: 0
HEADNOTE: INTERNATIONAL ROAD TRANSPORT
TOPIC: Land Transport
CONCEPTS: Passenger transport. Transport of
  goods. Road rules.
PROCEDURE: Denunciation. Duration. Ratification.
PARTIES:
Belgium
Poland

109598 Bilateral Agreement **0 UNTS 0**
SIGNED: 27 Feb 51   FORCE: 27 Feb 51
REGISTERED: 6 Jun 69 USA (United States)
ARTICLES: 0
HEADNOTE: ESTABLISHMENT, AIR DEPOT
TOPIC: Milit Installation
CONCEPTS: Joint defense. Bases and facilities.
  Equipment and supplies.
TREATY REF: 34UNTS243; 80UNTS171.
PARTIES:
France
USA (United States)

109599 Bilateral Agreement **0 UNTS 0**
SIGNED: 4 Oct 52   FORCE: 4 Oct 52
REGISTERED: 6 Jun 69 USA (United States)
ARTICLES: 0
HEADNOTE: AIR BASES AND FACILITIES
TOPIC: Milit Installation
CONCEPTS: Joint defense. Defense and security.
  Status of forces. Bases and facilities.
TREATY REF: 34UNTS243; 181UNTS3;
  265UNTS356.
PROCEDURE: Termination.

PARTIES:
France
USA (United States)

109600 Bilateral Exchange **0 UNTS 0**
SIGNED: 17 Jun 53   FORCE: 17 Jun 53
REGISTERED: 6 Jun 69 USA (United States)
ARTICLES: 0
HEADNOTE: INSTALLATION, OPERATION MILI-
  TARY HEADQUARTERS
TOPIC: Milit Installation
CONCEPTS: Status of forces. Bases and facilities.
TREATY REF: 34UNTS243; 199UNTS67.
PARTIES:
France
USA (United States)

109601 Bilateral Agreement **0 UNTS 0**
SIGNED: 30 Jun 53   FORCE: 30 Jun 53
REGISTERED: 6 Jun 69 USA (United States)
ARTICLES: 0
HEADNOTE: CONSTRUCTION, OPERATION, MAIN-
  TENANCE PIPELINE
TOPIC: Milit Installation
CONCEPTS: Military installations and equipment.
  Bases and facilities.
TREATY REF: 34UNTS243; 181UNTS3;
  265UNTS356.
PROCEDURE: Termination.
PARTIES:
France
USA (United States)

109602 Bilateral Agreement **0 UNTS 0**
SIGNED: 8 Dec 58   FORCE: 8 Dec 58
REGISTERED: 6 Jun 69 USA (United States)
ARTICLES: 0
HEADNOTE: COMMUNICATIONS, DEPOTS U.S.
  ARMY
TOPIC: Milit Installation
CONCEPTS: Procurement and logistics. Status of
  forces. Military installations and equipment.
  Bases and facilities.
TREATY REF: 34UNTS243; 199UNTS67.
PROCEDURE: Denunciation. Duration.
PARTIES:
France
USA (United States)

109603 Bilateral Agreement **0 UNTS 0**
SIGNED: 8 Jul 65   FORCE: 9 Nov 66
REGISTERED: 6 Jun 69 USA (United States)
ARTICLES: 0
HEADNOTE: CIVIL USE, ATOMIC ENERGY
TOPIC: Atomic Energy
CONCEPTS: IGO reference. Atomic energy assis-
  tance. Acceptance of delivery. General. Nuclear
  materials. Non-nuclear materials. Peaceful use.
  Rights of supplier.
INTL ORGS: International Atomic Energy Agency.
PROCEDURE: Duration.
PARTIES:
Brazil
USA (United States)

109604 Bilateral Agreement **0 UNTS 0**
SIGNED: 10 Mar 66   FORCE: 10 Mar 66
REGISTERED: 6 Jun 69 USA (United States)
ARTICLES: 0
HEADNOTE: AGRICULTURAL COMMODITIES
TOPIC: US Agri Commod Aid
CONCEPTS: Currency. Agricultural commodities
  assistance. Commodities schedule. Surplus
  commodities.
PARTIES:
Colombia
USA (United States)

109605 Bilateral Agreement **0 UNTS 0**
SIGNED: 9 Feb 67   FORCE: 9 Jul 66
REGISTERED: 6 Jun 69 USA (United States)
ARTICLES: 0
HEADNOTE: MUTUAL DEFENSE
TOPIC: Milit Installation
CONCEPTS: Non-ILO labor relations. Exchange
  rates and regulations. Claims, debts and assets.
  General. Customs duties. Mail and money or-
  ders. Status of military forces. Jurisdiction. Pro-

curement and logistics. Withdrawal of forces.
  Status of forces.
TREATY REF: 238UNTS199;   178UNTS97;
  400UNTS386; ETC..
PROCEDURE: Amendment. Duration. Ratification.
PARTIES:
Korea, South
USA (United States)

109606 Bilateral Agreement **0 UNTS 0**
SIGNED: 4 Nov 66   FORCE: 4 Nov 66
REGISTERED: 6 Jun 69 USA (United States)
ARTICLES: 0
HEADNOTE: CIVIL AIR TRANSPORT
TOPIC: Air Transport
PARTIES:
USA (United States)
USSR (Soviet Union)

109607 Bilateral Exchange **0 UNTS 0**
SIGNED: 6 Oct 66   FORCE: 6 Oct 66
REGISTERED: 6 Jun 69 USA (United States)
ARTICLES: 0
HEADNOTE: METEOROLOGIC RESEARCH COLD
  LAKE
TOPIC: Scientific Project
PARTIES:
Canada
USA (United States)

109608 Bilateral Agreement **0 UNTS 0**
SIGNED: 5 Oct 68   FORCE: 11 Nov 68
REGISTERED: 6 Jun 69 IBRD (World Bank)
ARTICLES: 0
HEADNOTE: LOAN SECOND HIGHWAY
TOPIC: IBRD Project
PARTIES:
IBRD (World Bank)
Zambia

109609 Bilateral Agreement **0 UNTS 0**
SIGNED: 18 Oct 68   FORCE: 13 Feb 69
REGISTERED: 6 Jun 69 Finland
ARTICLES: 0
HEADNOTE: AUTO TRAFFIC
TOPIC: Land Transport
PARTIES:
Finland
USSR (Soviet Union)

109610 Bilateral Agreement **0 UNTS 0**
SIGNED: 13 Jan 69   FORCE: 1 Apr 69
REGISTERED: 6 Jun 69 IDA (Devel Assoc)
ARTICLES: 0
HEADNOTE: CREDIT TECHNICAL ASSISTANCE
TOPIC: Non-IBRD Project
PARTIES:
Pakistan
IDA (Devel Assoc)

109611 Bilateral Agreement **0 UNTS 0**
SIGNED: 22 Jan 69   FORCE: 26 Feb 69
REGISTERED: 6 Jun 69 IDA (Devel Assoc)
ARTICLES: 0
HEADNOTE: CREDIT FIFTH INDUSTRIAL IMPORTS
TOPIC: Non-IBRD Project
PARTIES:
India
IDA (Devel Assoc)

109612 Bilateral Agreement **0 UNTS 0**
SIGNED: 27 Sep 68   FORCE: 1 Apr 68
REGISTERED: 6 Jun 69 IBRD (World Bank)
ARTICLES: 0
HEADNOTE: LOAN SEA DEFENSE
TOPIC: IBRD Project
PARTIES:
Guyana
IBRD (World Bank)

109613 Bilateral Agreement **0 UNTS 0**
SIGNED: 26 Jan 68   FORCE: 1 Aug 68
REGISTERED: 7 Jun 69 IBRD (World Bank)
ARTICLES: 0
HEADNOTE: GUARANTEE ALUMINUM
TOPIC: IBRD Project

PARTIES:
  Brazil
  IBRD (World Bank)

109614   Bilateral Agreement   **0 UNTS 0**
SIGNED: 22 May 68   FORCE: 30 Sep 68
REGISTERED: 7 Jun 69 IBRD (World Bank)
ARTICLES: 0
HEADNOTE: GUARANTEE SECOND DFC PROJECT
TOPIC: IBRD Project
PARTIES:
  Colombia
  IBRD (World Bank)

109615   Bilateral Exchange   **0 UNTS 0**
SIGNED: 10 Dec 68   FORCE: 10 Dec 68
REGISTERED: 7 Jun 69 Norway
ARTICLES: 0
HEADNOTE: TAX EXEMPTION SHIP AIR
TOPIC: Taxation
PARTIES:
  Norway
  Sweden

109616   Bilateral Exchange   **0 UNTS 0**
SIGNED: 12 Aug 66   FORCE: 12 Aug 66
REGISTERED: 10 Jun 69 USA (United States)
ARTICLES: 0
HEADNOTE: AGRI COMMOD
TOPIC: US Agri Commod Aid
PARTIES:
  Morocco
  USA (United States)

109617   Bilateral Exchange   **0 UNTS 0**
SIGNED: 19 Mar 66   FORCE: 19 Mar 66
REGISTERED: 10 Jun 69 USA (United States)
ARTICLES: 0
HEADNOTE: SCIENTIFIC & OTHER EXCHANGES
TOPIC: Scientific Project
PARTIES:
  USA (United States)
  USSR (Soviet Union)

109618   Bilateral Exchange   **0 UNTS 0**
SIGNED: 17 Oct 66   FORCE: 10 Oct 66
REGISTERED: 10 Jun 69 USA (United States)
ARTICLES: 0
HEADNOTE: PEACE CORPS
TOPIC: Direct Aid
PARTIES:
  Mauritania
  USA (United States)

109619   Bilateral Exchange   **0 UNTS 0**
SIGNED: 26 Oct 66   FORCE: 25 Oct 66
REGISTERED: 10 Jun 69 USA (United States)
ARTICLES: 0
HEADNOTE: JOINT COMMISSION SCHOLAR-
SHIPS
TOPIC: Education
PARTIES:
  Mexico
  USA (United States)

109620   Bilateral Exchange   **0 UNTS 0**
SIGNED: 4 Nov 66   FORCE: 4 Nov 66
REGISTERED: 10 Jun 69 USA (United States)
ARTICLES: 0
HEADNOTE: PEACE CORPS
TOPIC: Direct Aid
PARTIES:
  Paraguay
  USA (United States)

109621   Bilateral Exchange   **0 UNTS 0**
SIGNED: 9 May 68   FORCE: 27 Dec 68
REGISTERED: 11 Jun 69 Netherlands
ARTICLES: 0
HEADNOTE: BRITISH-DUTCH EXTRADITION
TREATY
TOPIC: Extradition
PARTIES:
  Netherlands
  Tanzania

109622   Bilateral Agreement   **0 UNTS 0**
SIGNED: 19 Jun 68   FORCE: 5 Aug 68
REGISTERED: 11 Jun 69 IDA (Devel Assoc)
ARTICLES: 0
HEADNOTE: CREDIT LIFT IRRIGATION
TOPIC: Non-IBRD Project
PARTIES:
  Ceylon (Sri Lanka)
  IDA (Devel Assoc)

109623   Bilateral Agreement   **0 UNTS 0**
SIGNED: 12 Nov 68   FORCE: 12 Feb 69
REGISTERED: 11 Jun 69 IBRD (World Bank)
ARTICLES: 0
HEADNOTE: LOAN HIGHWAY
TOPIC: IBRD Project
PARTIES:
  Ceylon (Sri Lanka)
  IBRD (World Bank)

109624   Bilateral Agreement   **0 UNTS 0**
SIGNED: 12 Nov 68   FORCE: 12 Feb 69
REGISTERED: 11 Jun 69 IDA (Devel Assoc)
ARTICLES: 0
HEADNOTE: CREDIT HIGHWAY
TOPIC: Non-IBRD Project
PARTIES:
  Ceylon (Sri Lanka)
  IDA (Devel Assoc)

109625   Bilateral Treaty   **0 UNTS 0**
SIGNED: 17 Nov 65   FORCE: 25 Apr 69
REGISTERED: 13 Jun 69 Austria
ARTICLES: 0
HEADNOTE: LEGAL ASSISTANCE CIVIL
TOPIC: Admin Cooperation
PARTIES:
  Austria
  Romania

109626   Bilateral Agreement   **0 UNTS 0**
SIGNED: 6 Sep 68   FORCE: 25 Mar 69
REGISTERED: 13 Jun 69 IDA (Devel Assoc)
ARTICLES: 0
HEADNOTE: CREDIT IRRIGATION REHABILITA-
TION
TOPIC: Non-IBRD Project
PARTIES:
  Indonesia
  IDA (Devel Assoc)

109627   Bilateral Agreement   **0 UNTS 0**
SIGNED: 23 Sep 68   FORCE: 3 Jan 69
REGISTERED: 13 Jun 69 IDA (Devel Assoc)
ARTICLES: 0
HEADNOTE: CREDIT HIGHWAY MAINTENANCE
TOPIC: Non-IBRD Project
PARTIES:
  Niger
  IDA (Devel Assoc)

109628   Bilateral Agreement   **0 UNTS 0**
SIGNED: 23 Oct 68   FORCE: 27 Feb 69
REGISTERED: 13 Jun 69 IBRD (World Bank)
ARTICLES: 0
HEADNOTE: GUARANTEE VOLTA GRANDE HY-
DROELECTRIC
TOPIC: IBRD Project
PARTIES:
  Brazil
  IBRD (World Bank)

109629   Bilateral Agreement   **0 UNTS 0**
SIGNED: 23 Oct 68   FORCE: 18 Feb 68
REGISTERED: 13 Jun 69 IBRD (World Bank)
ARTICLES: 0
HEADNOTE: GUARANTEE PORTO COLOMBIA
TOPIC: IBRD Project
PARTIES:
  Brazil
  IBRD (World Bank)

109630   Bilateral Agreement   **0 UNTS 0**
SIGNED: 31 Oct 61   FORCE: 6 Jan 69
REGISTERED: 13 Jun 69 IBRD (World Bank)
ARTICLES: 0
HEADNOTE: LOAN KEBAN TRANSMISSION
TOPIC: IBRD Project
PARTIES:
  IBRD (World Bank)
  Turkey

109631   Bilateral Agreement   **0 UNTS 0**
SIGNED: 19 Dec 68   FORCE: 21 Mar 69
REGISTERED: 13 Jun 69 IBRD (World Bank)
ARTICLES: 0
HEADNOTE: GUARANTEE EL CHOCON POWER
TOPIC: IBRD Project
PARTIES:
  Argentina
  IBRD (World Bank)

109632   Bilateral Agreement   **0 UNTS 0**
SIGNED: 28 Nov 68   FORCE: 28 Nov 68
REGISTERED: 16 Jun 69 UK Great Britain
ARTICLES: 0
HEADNOTE: IMCO HEADQUARTERS
TOPIC: IGO Operations
PARTIES:
  IMCO (Maritime Org)
  UK Great Britain

109633   Bilateral Treaty   **0 UNTS 0**
SIGNED: 27 Nov 68   FORCE: 10 Mar 69
REGISTERED: 16 Jun 69 Mongolia
ARTICLES: 0
HEADNOTE: LEGAL ASSISTANCE, CIVIL FAMILY
TOPIC: Admin Cooperation
PARTIES:
  Bulgaria
  Mongolia

109634   Bilateral Agreement   **0 UNTS 0**
SIGNED: 26 Jun 68   FORCE: 25 Feb 69
REGISTERED: 17 Jun 69 IDA (Devel Assoc)
ARTICLES: 0
HEADNOTE: CREDIT ROAD SUPPLEMENTARY
TOPIC: Non-IBRD Project
PARTIES:
  IDA (Devel Assoc)
  Somalia

109635   Bilateral Agreement   **0 UNTS 0**
SIGNED: 5 Oct 68   FORCE: 21 Jan 69
REGISTERED: 17 Jun 69 IDA (Devel Assoc)
ARTICLES: 0
HEADNOTE: CREDIT BEEF RANCHING
TOPIC: Non-IBRD Project
PARTIES:
  IDA (Devel Assoc)
  Uganda

109636   Bilateral Convention   **0 UNTS 0**
SIGNED: 5 Apr 67   FORCE: 1 Mar 69
REGISTERED: 18 Jun 69 France
ARTICLES: 0
HEADNOTE: PERSONAL, FAMILY STATUS LAW
TOPIC: Admin Cooperation
PARTIES:
  France
  Poland

109637   Bilateral Agreement   **0 UNTS 0**
SIGNED: 8 Oct 68   FORCE: 8 Oct 68
REGISTERED: 18 Jun 69 Thailand
ARTICLES: 0
HEADNOTE: FINANCIAL ASSISTANCE
TOPIC: Loans and Credits
PARTIES:
  Germany, West
  Thailand

109638   Bilateral Agreement   **0 UNTS 0**
SIGNED: 4 Dec 68   FORCE: 4 Dec 68
REGISTERED: 18 Jun 69 Thailand
ARTICLES: 0
HEADNOTE: FINANCIAL ASSISTANCE INVEST-
MENTS
TOPIC: Loans and Credits
PARTIES:
  Germany, West
  Thailand

109639   Bilateral Agreement   **0 UNTS 0**
SIGNED: 2 Dec 68   FORCE: 29 May 69
REGISTERED: 18 Jun 69 IBRD (World Bank)
ARTICLES: 0
HEADNOTE: GUARANTEE TACHIEN POWER
TOPIC: IBRD Project
PARTIES:
  Taiwan
  IBRD (World Bank)

109640   Bilateral Agreement   **0 UNTS 0**
SIGNED: 27 Dec 68   FORCE: 27 Dec 58
REGISTERED: 18 Jun 69 France
ARTICLES: 0
HEADNOTE: ALGERIAN NATIONALS IN FRANCE
TOPIC: Privil/Immunities
PARTIES:
  Algeria
  France

109641   Bilateral Agreement   **0 UNTS 0**
SIGNED: 14 Aug 68   FORCE: 11 Feb 69
REGISTERED: 19 Jun 69 IDA (Devel Assoc)
ARTICLES: 0
HEADNOTE: CREDIT HIGHWAY MAINTENANCE
TOPIC: Non-IBRD Project
PARTIES:
  Chad
  IDA (Devel Assoc)

109642   Bilateral Agreement   **0 UNTS 0**
SIGNED: 29 Aug 68   FORCE: 14 Jan 69
REGISTERED: 19 Jun 69 IDA (Devel Assoc)
ARTICLES: 0
HEADNOTE: CREDIT EDUCATION
TOPIC: Non-IBRD Project
PARTIES:
  Chad
  IDA (Devel Assoc)

109643   Bilateral Agreement   **0 UNTS 0**
SIGNED: 10 Oct 68   FORCE: 14 Jan 69
REGISTERED: 19 Jun 69 IDA (Devel Assoc)
ARTICLES: 0
HEADNOTE: CREDIT HIGHWAY MAINTENANCE
TOPIC: Non-IBRD Project
PARTIES:
  IDA (Devel Assoc)
  Togo

109644   Bilateral Agreement   **0 UNTS 0**
SIGNED: 5 Mar 69   FORCE: 27 May 69
REGISTERED: 19 Jun 69 IBRD (World Bank)
ARTICLES: 0
HEADNOTE: GUARANTEE INDUSTRIAL DEVELOP-
  MENT BANK
TOPIC: IBRD Project
PARTIES:
  Nigeria
  IBRD (World Bank)

109645   Bilateral Treaty   **0 UNTS 0**
SIGNED: 14 Jun 68   FORCE: 11 Apr 69
REGISTERED: 20 Jun 69 Hungary
ARTICLES: 0
HEADNOTE: FRIENDSHIP ASSISTANCE COOPER-
  ATION
TOPIC: General Amity
PARTIES:
  Czechoslovakia
  Hungary

109646   Bilateral Treaty   **0 UNTS 0**
SIGNED: 22 Nov 68   FORCE: 28 Apr 69
REGISTERED: 20 Jun 69 Hungary
ARTICLES: 0
HEADNOTE: LEGAL ASSISTANCE, CIVIL CRIMI-
  NAL
TOPIC: Admin Cooperation
PARTIES:
  Hungary
  Mongolia

109647   Bilateral Convention   **0 UNTS 0**
SIGNED: 22 Apr 66   FORCE: 7 Mar 69
REGISTERED: 23 Jun 69 France

ARTICLES: 0
HEADNOTE: TAXATION
TOPIC: Taxation
PARTIES:
  France
  Gabon

109648   Bilateral Convention   **0 UNTS 0**
SIGNED: 22 Jul 66   FORCE: 13 Feb 69
REGISTERED: 23 Jun 69 France
ARTICLES: 0
HEADNOTE: DOUBLE TAXATION INCOME
TOPIC: Taxation
PARTIES:
  France
  Pakistan

109649   Bilateral Agreement   **0 UNTS 0**
SIGNED: 24 Jun 68   FORCE: 24 Jan 69
REGISTERED: 23 Jun 69 IDA (Devel Assoc)
ARTICLES: 0
HEADNOTE: CREDIT EDUCATION
TOPIC: Non-IBRD Project
PARTIES:
  IDA (Devel Assoc)
  Sudan

109650   Bilateral Agreement   **0 UNTS 0**
SIGNED: 5 Oct 68   FORCE: 15 Nov 68
REGISTERED: 23 Jun 69 IBRD (World Bank)
ARTICLES: 0
HEADNOTE: LOAN INDUSTRIAL FORESTRY
TOPIC: IBRD Project
PARTIES:
  IBRD (World Bank)
  Zambia

109651   Bilateral Agreement   **0 UNTS 0**
SIGNED: 16 Oct 68   FORCE: 26 Mar 69
REGISTERED: 23 Jun 69 IBRD (World Bank)
ARTICLES: 0
HEADNOTE: LOAN EDUCATION
TOPIC: IBRD Project
PARTIES:
  IBRD (World Bank)
  Trinidad/Tobago

109652   Bilateral Agreement   **0 UNTS 0**
SIGNED: 31 Oct 68   FORCE: 15 Jan 69
REGISTERED: 23 Jun 69 IDA (Devel Assoc)
ARTICLES: 0
HEADNOTE: CREDIT BEEF RANCHING
TOPIC: Non-IBRD Project
PARTIES:
  IDA (Devel Assoc)
  Tanzania

109653   Bilateral Agreement   **0 UNTS 0**
SIGNED: 27 Dec 68   FORCE: 17 Mar 69
REGISTERED: 23 Jun 69 IDA (Devel Assoc)
ARTICLES: 0
HEADNOTE: CREDIT TECHNICAL ASSISTANCE
TOPIC: Non-IBRD Project
PARTIES:
  Indonesia
  IDA (Devel Assoc)

109654   Bilateral Agreement   **0 UNTS 0**
SIGNED: 10 Jan 69   FORCE: 11 Apr 69
REGISTERED: 23 Jun 69 IBRD (World Bank)
ARTICLES: 0
HEADNOTE: LOAN SECOND HIGHWAY
TOPIC: IBRD Project
PARTIES:
  Gabon
  IBRD (World Bank)

109655   Bilateral Agreement   **0 UNTS 0**
SIGNED: 18 Mar 68   FORCE: 16 Jan 69
REGISTERED: 24 Jun 69 UK Great Britain
ARTICLES: 0
HEADNOTE: DOUBLE TAX INCOME
TOPIC: Taxation
PARTIES:
  Sierra Leone
  UK Great Britain

109656   Bilateral Convention   **0 UNTS 0**
SIGNED: 27 Mar 68   FORCE: 17 Jan 69
REGISTERED: 24 Jun 69 UK Great Britain
ARTICLES: 0
HEADNOTE: DOUBLE TAX INCOME
TOPIC: Taxation
PARTIES:
  Portugal
  UK Great Britain

109657   Bilateral Agreement   **0 UNTS 0**
SIGNED: 19 Apr 68   FORCE: 13 Jan 69
REGISTERED: 24 Jun 69 UK Great Britain
ARTICLES: 0
HEADNOTE: APPLIED SCIENCE TECHNOLOGY
TOPIC: Scientific Project
PARTIES:
  UK Great Britain
  Yugoslavia

109658   Bilateral Agreement   **0 UNTS 0**
SIGNED: 17 Feb 68   FORCE: 17 Feb 68
REGISTERED: 24 Jun 69 UK Great Britain
ARTICLES: 0
HEADNOTE: STANDARD OPERATIONAL ASSIS-
  TANCE
TOPIC: Direct Aid
PARTIES:
  State/IGO Group
  Chad

109659   Bilateral Exchange   **0 UNTS 0**
SIGNED: 11 Nov 68   FORCE: 11 Nov 68
REGISTERED: 24 Jun 69 UK Great Britain
ARTICLES: 0
HEADNOTE: INTEREST-FREE LOAN
TOPIC: Loans and Credits
PARTIES:
  Indonesia
  UK Great Britain

109660   Bilateral Exchange   **0 UNTS 0**
SIGNED: 16 Jan 69   FORCE: 16 Jan 69
REGISTERED: 24 Jun 69 UK Great Britain
ARTICLES: 0
HEADNOTE: INTEREST-FREE LOAN
TOPIC: Loans and Credits
PARTIES:
  Indonesia
  UK Great Britain

109661   Bilateral Exchange   **0 UNTS 0**
SIGNED: 19 Nov 68   FORCE: 19 Dec 68
REGISTERED: 24 Jun 69 UK Great Britain
ARTICLES: 0
HEADNOTE: VISA ABOLITION
TOPIC: Visas
PARTIES:
  Costa Rica
  UK Great Britain

109662   Bilateral Agreement   **0 UNTS 0**
SIGNED: 26 Nov 68   FORCE: 18 Mar 68
REGISTERED: 24 Jun 69 UK Great Britain
ARTICLES: 0
HEADNOTE: DOUBLE TAX INCOME
TOPIC: Taxation
PARTIES:
  Switzerland
  UK Great Britain

109663   Bilateral Exchange   **0 UNTS 0**
SIGNED: 21 Dec 68   FORCE: 21 Dec 68
REGISTERED: 24 Jun 69 UK Great Britain
ARTICLES: 0
HEADNOTE: DOUBLE TAX AIR TRANSPORT
TOPIC: Taxation
PARTIES:
  Spain
  UK Great Britain

109664   Multilateral Agreement   **0 UNTS 0**
SIGNED: 27 Jan 69   FORCE: 1 Apr 69
REGISTERED: 24 Jun 69 UK Great Britain
ARTICLES: 0

HEADNOTE: COMMONWEALTH TELECOMMUNI-
CATIONS ORGANIZATION FINANCE
TOPIC: Telecommunications
PARTIES:
  Australia SIGNED: 27 Jan 69 FORCE: 1 Apr 69
  Barbados SIGNED: 27 Jan 69 FORCE: 1 Apr 69
  Botswana SIGNED: 27 Jan 69 FORCE: 1 Apr 69
  Canada SIGNED: 27 Jan 69 FORCE: 1 Apr 69
  Ceylon (Sri Lanka) SIGNED: 27 Jan 69 FORCE:
    1 Apr 69
  Cyprus SIGNED: 27 Jan 69 FORCE: 1 Apr 69
  Gambia SIGNED: 27 Jan 69 FORCE: 1 Apr 69
  Ghana SIGNED: 27 Jan 69 FORCE: 1 Apr 69
  Guyana SIGNED: 27 Jan 69 FORCE: 1 Apr 69
  India SIGNED: 27 Jan 69 FORCE: 1 Apr 69
  Jamaica SIGNED: 27 Jan 69 FORCE: 1 Apr 69
  Kenya SIGNED: 27 Jan 69 FORCE: 1 Apr 69
  Malawi SIGNED: 27 Jan 69 FORCE: 1 Apr 69
  Malaysia SIGNED: 27 Jan 69 FORCE: 1 Apr 69
  New Zealand SIGNED: 27 Jan 69 FORCE:
    1 Apr 69
  Nigeria SIGNED: 27 Jan 69 FORCE: 1 Apr 69
  Sierra Leone SIGNED: 27 Jan 69 FORCE:
    1 Apr 69
  Singapore SIGNED: 27 Jan 69 FORCE: 1 Apr 69
  Tanzania SIGNED: 27 Jan 69 FORCE: 1 Apr 69
  Trinidad/Tobago SIGNED: 27 Jan 69 FORCE:
    1 Apr 69
  Uganda SIGNED: 27 Jan 69 FORCE: 1 Apr 69
  UK Great Britain SIGNED: 27 Jan 69 FORCE:
    1 Apr 69

109665   Bilateral Exchange   **0 UNTS 0**
SIGNED: 30 Jan 69   FORCE: 30 Jan 69
REGISTERED: 24 Jun 69 UK Great Britain
ARTICLES: 0
HEADNOTE: SPECIAL PROJECT
TOPIC: Scientific Project
PARTIES:
  Eur Space Research
  UK Great Britain

109666   Bilateral Exchange   **0 UNTS 0**
SIGNED: 5 Feb 69   FORCE: 7 Mar 69
REGISTERED: 24 Jun 69 UK Great Britain
ARTICLES: 0
HEADNOTE: VISA ABOLITION
TOPIC: Visas
PARTIES:
  Nicaragua
  UK Great Britain

109667   Bilateral Agreement   **0 UNTS 0**
SIGNED: 6 Mar 69   FORCE: 11 Apr 69
REGISTERED: 25 Jun 69 IDA (Devel Assoc)
ARTICLES: 0
HEADNOTE: CREDIT TELECOMMUNICATIONS
TOPIC: Non-IBRD Project
PARTIES:
  Pakistan
  IDA (Devel Assoc)

109668   Bilateral Exchange   **0 UNTS 0**
SIGNED: 8 Nov 67   FORCE: 8 Nov 67
REGISTERED: 26 Jun 69 Australia
ARTICLES: 0
HEADNOTE: HIGH ALTITUDE BALLOON
TOPIC: Scientific Project
PARTIES:
  Australia
  France

109669   Bilateral Agreement   **0 UNTS 0**
SIGNED: 27 Jun 68   FORCE: 27 Jun 67
REGISTERED: 26 Jun 69 Australia
ARTICLES: 0
HEADNOTE: HOSPITALS CHRISTMAS ISLANDS
RESIDENTS
TOPIC: Health/Educ/Welfare
PARTIES:
  Australia
  Singapore

109670   Bilateral Agreement   **0 UNTS 0**
SIGNED: 12 Nov 68   FORCE: 1 Apr 69
REGISTERED: 26 Jun 69 IBRD (World Bank)
ARTICLES: 0
HEADNOTE: LOAN SECOND HIGHWAY

TOPIC: IBRD Project
PARTIES:
  Madagascar
  IBRD (World Bank)

109671   Bilateral Agreement   **0 UNTS 0**
SIGNED: 12 Nov 68   FORCE: 1 Apr 69
REGISTERED: 26 Jun 69 IDA (Devel Assoc)
ARTICLES: 0
HEADNOTE: CREDIT SECOND HIGHWAY
TOPIC: Non-IBRD Project
PARTIES:
  Madagascar
  IDA (Devel Assoc)

109672   Bilateral Agreement   **0 UNTS 0**
SIGNED: 21 Mar 69   FORCE: 21 May 69
REGISTERED: 26 Jun 69 IBRD (World Bank)
ARTICLES: 0
HEADNOTE: GUARANTEE EIGHTH INDUSTRIAL
TOPIC: IBRD Project
PARTIES:
  Pakistan
  IBRD (World Bank)

109673   Bilateral Agreement   **0 UNTS 0**
SIGNED: 15 Nov 68   FORCE: 9 Feb 69
REGISTERED: 1 Jul 69 Finland
ARTICLES: 0
HEADNOTE: ROAD TRANSPORT
TOPIC: Land Transport
PARTIES:
  Belgium
  Finland

109674   Bilateral Agreement   **0 UNTS 0**
SIGNED: 25 Nov 68   FORCE: 25 Dec 68
REGISTERED: 1 Jul 69 Finland
ARTICLES: 0
HEADNOTE: TECHNICAL COOPERATION
TOPIC: Tech Assistance
PARTIES:
  Ethiopia
  Finland

109675   Bilateral Exchange   **0 UNTS 0**
SIGNED: 27 Apr 69   FORCE: 22 Apr 69
REGISTERED: 1 Jul 69 Thailand
ARTICLES: 0
HEADNOTE: COMMERCIAL MODUS VIVENDI
TOPIC: General Economic
PARTIES:
  Canada
  Thailand

109676   Bilateral Agreement   **0 UNTS 0**
SIGNED: 28 May 64   FORCE: 5 Nov 66
REGISTERED: 2 Jul 69 USA (United States)
ARTICLES: 0
HEADNOTE: REFUND INDEBTEDNESS
TOPIC: Claims and Debts
PARTIES:
  Greece
  USA (United States)

109677   Bilateral Treaty   **0 UNTS 0**
SIGNED: 8 Feb 66   FORCE: 5 Feb 67
REGISTERED: 2 Jul 69 USA (United States)
ARTICLES: 0
HEADNOTE: AMITY ECONOMIC RELATIONS
TOPIC: General Amity
PARTIES:
  Togo
  USA (United States)

109678   Bilateral Agreement   **0 UNTS 0**
SIGNED: 2 Apr 66   FORCE: 2 Apr 66
REGISTERED: 2 Jul 69 USA (United States)
ARTICLES: 0
HEADNOTE: AGRI COMMOD
TOPIC: US Agri Commod Aid
PARTIES:
  Turkey
  USA (United States)

109679   Bilateral Exchange   **0 UNTS 0**
SIGNED: 21 Apr 66   FORCE: 21 Apr 66
REGISTERED: 2 Jul 69 USA (United States)
ARTICLES: 0
HEADNOTE: AGRI COMMOD
TOPIC: US Agri Commod Aid
PARTIES:
  Morocco
  USA (United States)

109680   Bilateral Exchange   **0 UNTS 0**
SIGNED: 21 Jul 66   FORCE: 21 Jul 66
REGISTERED: 2 Jul 69 USA (United States)
ARTICLES: 0
HEADNOTE: METEOROLOGICAL
TOPIC: Scientific Project
PARTIES:
  Dominican Republic
  USA (United States)

109681   Bilateral Exchange   **0 UNTS 0**
SIGNED: 19 Sep 66   FORCE: 19 Sep 66
REGISTERED: 2 Jul 69 USA (United States)
ARTICLES: 0
HEADNOTE: GEODETIC SATELLITE OBSERVA-
TION
TOPIC: Scientific Project
PARTIES:
  Japan
  USA (United States)

109682   Bilateral Exchange   **0 UNTS 0**
SIGNED: 30 Sep 66   FORCE: 30 Sep 66
REGISTERED: 2 Jul 69 USA (United States)
ARTICLES: 0
HEADNOTE: CONTINUE TREATIES
TOPIC: Admin Cooperation
PARTIES:
  Botswana
  USA (United States)

109683   Bilateral Agreement   **0 UNTS 0**
SIGNED: 3 Oct 66   FORCE: 3 Oct 66
REGISTERED: 2 Jul 69 USA (United States)
ARTICLES: 0
HEADNOTE: AGRI COMMOD
TOPIC: US Agri Commod Aid
PARTIES:
  Congo (Zaire)
  USA (United States)

109684   Bilateral Exchange   **0 UNTS 0**
SIGNED: 4 Oct 66   FORCE: 4 Oct 66
REGISTERED: 2 Jul 69 USA (United States)
ARTICLES: 0
HEADNOTE: CONTINUE CERTAIN UK TREATIES
TOPIC: Admin Cooperation
PARTIES:
  Lesotho
  USA (United States)

109685   Bilateral Exchange   **0 UNTS 0**
SIGNED: 19 Oct 66   FORCE: 19 Oct 66
REGISTERED: 2 Jul 69 USA (United States)
ARTICLES: 0
HEADNOTE: ESTABLISH COMMISSION EDUCA-
TION EXCHANGE
TOPIC: Education
PARTIES:
  Brazil
  USA (United States)

109686   Bilateral Exchange   **0 UNTS 0**
SIGNED: 19 Oct 66   FORCE: 19 Oct 66
REGISTERED: 2 Jul 69 USA (United States)
ARTICLES: 0
HEADNOTE: EXPORT COTTON VELVETEEN FAB-
RICS
TOPIC: Commodity Trade
PARTIES:
  Italy
  USA (United States)

109687   Bilateral Exchange   **0 UNTS 0**
SIGNED: 25 Oct 66   FORCE: 25 Oct 66
REGISTERED: 2 Jul 69 USA (United States)

ARTICLES: 0
HEADNOTE: FEASIBILITY INTER-OCEAN CANAL
TOPIC: Tech Assistance
PARTIES:
  Colombia
  USA (United States)

109688   Bilateral Exchange   **0 UNTS 0**
SIGNED: 16 Nov 66   FORCE: 16 Nov 66
REGISTERED: 2 Jul 69 USA (United States)
ARTICLES: 0
HEADNOTE: AMATEUR RADIO
TOPIC: Gen Communications
PARTIES:
  Panama
  USA (United States)

109689   Bilateral Exchange   **0 UNTS 0**
SIGNED: 21 Nov 66   FORCE: 21 Nov 66
REGISTERED: 2 Jul 69 USA (United States)
ARTICLES: 0
HEADNOTE: COTTON TEXTILES
TOPIC: Commodity Trade
PARTIES:
  Pakistan
  USA (United States)

109690   Bilateral Exchange   **0 UNTS 0**
SIGNED: 24 Nov 66   FORCE: 24 Nov 66
REGISTERED: 2 Jul 69 USA (United States)
ARTICLES: 0
HEADNOTE: PEACE CORPS
TOPIC: Direct Aid
PARTIES:
  Central Afri Rep
  USA (United States)

109691   Bilateral Exchange   **0 UNTS 0**
SIGNED: 28 Nov 66   FORCE: 28 Nov 66
REGISTERED: 2 Jul 69 USA (United States)
ARTICLES: 0
HEADNOTE: SATELLITE TELEMETRY ALASKA
TOPIC: Scientific Project
PARTIES:
  Eur Space Research
  USA (United States)

109692   Bilateral Exchange   **0 UNTS 0**
SIGNED: 3 Dec 66   FORCE: 3 Dec 66
REGISTERED: 2 Jul 69 USA (United States)
ARTICLES: 0
HEADNOTE: JOINT COMMISSION DEVELOP BOR-
  DER AREA
TOPIC: Admin Cooperation
PARTIES:
  Mexico
  USA (United States)

109693   Bilateral Exchange   **0 UNTS 0**
SIGNED: 5 Dec 66   FORCE: 5 Dec 66
REGISTERED: 2 Jul 69 USA (United States)
ARTICLES: 0
HEADNOTE: PEACE CORPS
TOPIC: Direct Aid
PARTIES:
  Gambia
  USA (United States)

109694   Bilateral Exchange   **0 UNTS 0**
SIGNED: 16 Dec 66   FORCE: 16 Dec 66
REGISTERED: 2 Jul 69 USA (United States)
ARTICLES: 0
HEADNOTE: PAINTINGS WEIMAR MUSEUM
TOPIC: Culture
PARTIES:
  Germany, West
  USA (United States)

109695   Bilateral Agreement   **0 UNTS 0**
SIGNED: 15 Dec 66   FORCE: 15 Dec 66
REGISTERED: 2 Jul 69 USA (United States)
ARTICLES: 0
HEADNOTE: AGRI COMMOD
TOPIC: US Agri Commod Aid

PARTIES:
  USA (United States)
  Vietnam, South

109696   Bilateral Agreement   **0 UNTS 0**
SIGNED: 19 Dec 66   FORCE: 19 Dec 66
REGISTERED: 2 Jul 69 USA (United States)
ARTICLES: 0
HEADNOTE: AGRI COMMOD
TOPIC: US Agri Commod Aid
PARTIES:
  Iran
  USA (United States)

109697   Bilateral Agreement   **0 UNTS 0**
SIGNED: 20 Dec 66   FORCE: 20 Dec 66
REGISTERED: 2 Jul 69 USA (United States)
ARTICLES: 0
HEADNOTE: AGRI COMMOD
TOPIC: US Agri Commod Aid
PARTIES:
  Iran
  USA (United States)

109698   Bilateral Exchange   **0 UNTS 0**
SIGNED: 20 Dec 66   FORCE: 20 Dec 66
REGISTERED: 2 Jul 69 USA (United States)
ARTICLES: 0
HEADNOTE: EXCHANGE OFFICIAL PUBLICA-
  TIONS
TOPIC: Admin Cooperation
PARTIES:
  Jamaica
  USA (United States)

109699   Bilateral Agreement   **0 UNTS 0**
SIGNED: 20 Dec 66   FORCE: 20 Dec 66
REGISTERED: 2 Jul 69 USA (United States)
ARTICLES: 0
HEADNOTE: AGRI COMMOD
TOPIC: US Agri Commod Aid
PARTIES:
  Afghanistan
  USA (United States)

109700   Bilateral Exchange   **0 UNTS 0**
SIGNED: 28 Dec 66   FORCE: 28 Dec 66
REGISTERED: 2 Jul 69 USA (United States)
ARTICLES: 0
HEADNOTE: PEACE CORPS ANTIGUA
TOPIC: Direct Aid
PARTIES:
  UK Great Britain
  USA (United States)

109701   Bilateral Exchange   **0 UNTS 0**
SIGNED: 25 Jul 68   FORCE: 25 Jul 68
REGISTERED: 2 Jul 69 Denmark
ARTICLES: 0
HEADNOTE: INFORMATION DEFENSE SCIENCE
TOPIC: Admin Cooperation
PARTIES:
  Canada
  Denmark

109702   Bilateral Exchange   **0 UNTS 0**
SIGNED: 5 Feb 69   FORCE: 5 Feb 69
REGISTERED: 2 Jul 69 Denmark
ARTICLES: 0
HEADNOTE: DANISH GRANT
TOPIC: Loans and Credits
PARTIES:
  Asian Devel Bank
  Denmark

109703   Multilateral Agreement   **0 UNTS 0**
SIGNED: 15 Nov 67   FORCE: 20 Dec 68
REGISTERED: 3 Jul 69 Czechoslovakia
ARTICLES: 0
HEADNOTE: LONG-TERM TRADE
TOPIC: General Trade
PARTIES:
  Belgium FORCE: 1 Jan 67
  Czechoslovakia FORCE: 1 Jan 67
  Luxembourg FORCE: 1 Jan 67
  Netherlands FORCE: 1 Jan 67

109704   Bilateral Convention   **0 UNTS 0**
SIGNED: 1 Feb 68   FORCE: 17 Sep 68
REGISTERED: 3 Jul 69 Romania
ARTICLES: 0
HEADNOTE: CUSTOMS COOPERATION
TOPIC: Customs
PARTIES:
  Hungary
  Romania

109705   Bilateral Agreement   **0 UNTS 0**
SIGNED: 29 Nov 68   FORCE: 24 Feb 69
REGISTERED: 3 Jul 69 Romania
ARTICLES: 0
HEADNOTE: ECONOMIC INDUSTRIAL TECHNICAL
  COOPERATION
TOPIC: General Economic
PARTIES:
  Norway
  Romania

109706   Bilateral Agreement   **0 UNTS 0**
SIGNED: 17 Mar 67   FORCE: 7 Nov 68
REGISTERED: 8 Jul 69 UK Great Britain
ARTICLES: 0
HEADNOTE: AIR SERVICES
TOPIC: Air Transport
PARTIES:
  Romania
  UK Great Britain

109707   Multilateral Agreement   **0 UNTS 0**
SIGNED: 9 Jan 68   FORCE: 1 Sep 68
REGISTERED: 8 Jul 69 Kuwait
ARTICLES: 0
HEADNOTE: ORGANIZATION ARAB PETROLEUM
  EXPORT COUNTRIES
TOPIC: IGO Establishment
PARTIES:
  Kuwait SIGNED: 9 Jan 68 RATIFIED: 16 Jun 68
    FORCE: 1 Sep 68
  Libya SIGNED: 9 Jan 68 RATIFIED: 28 Jul 68
    FORCE: 1 Sep 68
  Saudi Arabia SIGNED: 9 Jan 68 RATIFIED:
    4 Aug 68 FORCE: 1 Sep 68

109708   Bilateral Convention   **0 UNTS 0**
SIGNED: 13 Mar 68   FORCE: 21 Dec 68
REGISTERED: 8 Jul 69 UK Great Britain
ARTICLES: 0
HEADNOTE: CONSULAR
TOPIC: Consul/Citizenship
PARTIES:
  Bulgaria
  UK Great Britain

109709   Bilateral Agreement   **0 UNTS 0**
SIGNED: 1 Apr 68   FORCE: 12 Jul 68
REGISTERED: 11 Jul 69 UK Great Britain
ARTICLES: 0
HEADNOTE: AMEND 1947 ARRANGEMENT DOU-
  BLE TAX
TOPIC: Taxation
PARTIES:
  Gambia
  UK Great Britain

109710   Bilateral Exchange   **0 UNTS 0**
SIGNED: 16 Jul 68   FORCE: 16 Jul 68
REGISTERED: 8 Jul 69 UK Great Britain
ARTICLES: 0
HEADNOTE: NUCLEAR RESEARCH MATERIAL
TOPIC: Atomic Energy
PARTIES:
  Romania
  UK Great Britain

109711   Bilateral Exchange   **0 UNTS 0**
SIGNED: 9 Oct 68   FORCE: 9 Oct 68
REGISTERED: 8 Jul 69 UK Great Britain
ARTICLES: 0
HEADNOTE: TRAINING BOTSWANA POLICE
TOPIC: Military Mission
PARTIES:
  Botswana
  UK Great Britain

109712 Bilateral Agreement **0 UNTS 0**
SIGNED: 17 Dec 68 FORCE: 1 Jan 69
REGISTERED: 8 Jul 69 UK Great Britain
ARTICLES: 0
HEADNOTE: MEDIUM-TERM DEBTS
TOPIC: Claims and Debts
PARTIES:
Ghana
UK Great Britain

109713 Bilateral Agreement **0 UNTS 0**
SIGNED: 27 Sep 68 FORCE: 27 Sep 68
REGISTERED: 11 Jul 69 UK Great Britain
ARTICLES: 0
HEADNOTE: AIR SERVICES
TOPIC: Air Transport
PARTIES:
Malawi
UK Great Britain

109714 Bilateral Agreement **0 UNTS 0**
SIGNED: 4 Feb 69 FORCE: 27 Jun 69
REGISTERED: 11 Jul 69 Belgium
ARTICLES: 0
HEADNOTE: SOCIAL SECURITY OVERSEAS
TOPIC: Non-ILO Labor
PARTIES:
Belgium
Netherlands

109715 Bilateral Agreement **0 UNTS 0**
SIGNED: 22 Apr 66 FORCE: 9 Jun 67
REGISTERED: 16 Jul 69 Japan
ARTICLES: 0
HEADNOTE: DOUBLE TAX INCOME OTHER
TOPIC: Taxation
PARTIES:
Germany, West
Japan

109716 Bilateral Convention **0 UNTS 0**
SIGNED: 24 Jan 67 FORCE: 31 Dec 67
REGISTERED: 16 Jul 69 Japan
ARTICLES: 0
HEADNOTE: DOUBLE TAX INCOME
TOPIC: Taxation
PARTIES:
Brazil
Japan

109717 Bilateral Convention **0 UNTS 0**
SIGNED: 11 May 67 FORCE: 25 Oct 68
REGISTERED: 16 Jul 69 Japan
ARTICLES: 0
HEADNOTE: DOUBLE TAX INCOME
TOPIC: Taxation
PARTIES:
Japan
Norway

109718 Bilateral Agreement **0 UNTS 0**
SIGNED: 12 Jul 67 FORCE: 26 Jul 68
REGISTERED: 16 Jul 69 Japan
ARTICLES: 0
HEADNOTE: FISHERIES
TOPIC: Specific Resources
PARTIES:
Japan
New Zealand

109719 Bilateral Agreement **0 UNTS 0**
SIGNED: 21 Sep 67 FORCE: 7 May 68
REGISTERED: 16 Jul 69 Japan
ARTICLES: 0
HEADNOTE: AGREEMENT (SIC)
TOPIC: General Economic
PARTIES:
Japan
Malaysia

109720 Bilateral Agreement **0 UNTS 0**
SIGNED: 21 Sep 67 FORCE: 7 May 68
REGISTERED: 16 Jul 69 Japan
ARTICLES: 0
HEADNOTE: AGREEMENT (SIC)
TOPIC: Reparations

PARTIES:
Japan
Singapore

109721 Bilateral Convention **0 UNTS 0**
SIGNED: 12 Dec 67 FORCE: 22 Sep 68
REGISTERED: 16 Jul 69 Japan
ARTICLES: 0
HEADNOTE: DOUBLE TAX INCOME
TOPIC: Taxation
PARTIES:
Ceylon (Sri Lanka)
Japan

109722 Bilateral Agreement **0 UNTS 0**
SIGNED: 26 Feb 68 FORCE: 10 Jul 68
REGISTERED: 16 Jul 69 Japan
ARTICLES: 0
HEADNOTE: CIVIL USES ATOMIC ENERGY
TOPIC: Atomic Energy
PARTIES:
Japan
USA (United States)

109723 Bilateral Agreement **0 UNTS 0**
SIGNED: 7 Mar 68 FORCE: 10 Jun 68
REGISTERED: 16 Jul 69 Japan
ARTICLES: 0
HEADNOTE: FISHING NEAR MEXICO
TOPIC: Water Transport
PARTIES:
Japan
Mexico

109724 Bilateral Agreement **0 UNTS 0**
SIGNED: 5 Apr 68 FORCE: 26 Jul 68
REGISTERED: 16 Jul 69 Japan
ARTICLES: 0
HEADNOTE: NAMPO SHOTO & OTHER ISLANDS
TOPIC: Territory Boundary
PARTIES:
Japan
USA (United States)

109725 Bilateral Treaty **0 UNTS 0**
SIGNED: 23 Oct 57 FORCE: 15 Jul 59
REGISTERED: 22 Jul 69 Netherlands
ARTICLES: 0
HEADNOTE: LIGHT BEACON WEST SCHELDT
TOPIC: Water Transport
PARTIES:
Belgium
Netherlands

109726 Bilateral Agreement **0 UNTS 0**
SIGNED: 2 Sep 67 FORCE: 25 Feb 69
REGISTERED: 23 Jul 69 Denmark
ARTICLES: 0
HEADNOTE: ECONOMIC INDUSTRIAL TECHNICAL
COOPERATION
TOPIC: General Economic
PARTIES:
Bulgaria
Denmark

109727 Bilateral Agreement **0 UNTS 0**
SIGNED: 13 May 68 FORCE: 19 May 69
REGISTERED: 23 Jul 69 Denmark
ARTICLES: 0
HEADNOTE: ROAD TRANSPORT
TOPIC: Land Transport
PARTIES:
Denmark
Yugoslavia

109728 Multilateral Convention **0 UNTS 0**
SIGNED: 21 Jun 66 FORCE: 15 Jul 69
REGISTERED: 24 Jul 69 ILO (Labor Org)
ARTICLES: 0
HEADNOTE: NO. 125 FISHERMEN CERTIFICATES
TOPIC: ILO Labor
PARTIES:
ILO (Labor Org) RATIFIED: 21 Jun 66 FORCE:
15 Jul 69
Senegal SIGNED: 21 Jun 66 RATIFIED:
15 Jul 68 FORCE: 15 Jul 69

Sierra Leone SIGNED: 21 Jun 66 RATIFIED:
6 Nov 67 FORCE: 15 Jul 69
Syria SIGNED: 21 Jun 66 RATIFIED: 6 May 69
FORCE: 15 Jul 69

109729 Multilateral Agreement **0 UNTS 0**
SIGNED: 17 Jul 69 FORCE: 3 Jul 69
REGISTERED: 24 Jul 69 Belgium
ARTICLES: 0
HEADNOTE: VISA ABOLITION
TOPIC: Visas
PARTIES:
Belgium SIGNED: 17 Jun 69 FORCE: 3 Jul 69
Luxembourg SIGNED: 17 Jun 69 FORCE:
3 Jul 69
Netherlands SIGNED: 17 Jun 69 FORCE:
3 Jul 69
Yugoslavia SIGNED: 17 Jun 69 FORCE: 3 Jul 69

109730 Bilateral Agreement **0 UNTS 0**
SIGNED: 26 Jul 69 FORCE: 26 Jul 69
REGISTERED: 26 Jul 69 United Nations
ARTICLES: 0
HEADNOTE: UNICEF ACTIVITIES
TOPIC: IGO Operations
PARTIES:
UNICEF (Children)
Southern Yemen

109731 Bilateral Agreement **0 UNTS 0**
SIGNED: 29 May 58 FORCE: 1 Jan 60
REGISTERED: 26 Jul 69 Denmark
ARTICLES: 0
HEADNOTE: FISHERIES FLENSBORG FJORD
TOPIC: Specific Resources
PARTIES:
Denmark
Germany, West

109732 Bilateral Agreement **0 UNTS 0**
SIGNED: 12 Jan 65 FORCE: 12 Jan 65
REGISTERED: 29 Jul 69 Denmark
ARTICLES: 0
HEADNOTE: AUDIOLOGICAL CLINIC CAIRO
TOPIC: Sanitation
PARTIES:
Denmark
United Arab Rep

109733 Multilateral Agreement **0 UNTS 0**
SIGNED: 12 Dec 68 FORCE: 30 Jul 69
REGISTERED: 30 Jul 69 United Nations
ARTICLES: 0
HEADNOTE: ESTABLISH ASIAN COCONUT COM-
MUNITY
TOPIC: IGO Establishment
PARTIES:
Ceylon (Sri Lanka) RATIFIED: 25 Apr 69 FORCE:
30 Jul 69
India RATIFIED: 18 Jun 69 FORCE: 30 Jul 69
Indonesia RATIFIED: 30 Jul 69 FORCE:
30 Jul 69

109734 Bilateral Agreement **0 UNTS 0**
SIGNED: 22 Apr 68 FORCE: 22 Apr 68
REGISTERED: 30 Jul 69 Australia
ARTICLES: 0
HEADNOTE: TRADE
TOPIC: General Trade
PARTIES:
Australia
Taiwan

109735 Bilateral Agreement **0 UNTS 0**
SIGNED: 7 Mar 69 FORCE: 7 Mar 69
REGISTERED: 30 Jul 69 Australia
ARTICLES: 0
HEADNOTE: AIR SERVICES
TOPIC: Air Transport
PARTIES:
Australia
Indonesia

109736 Bilateral Agreement **0 UNTS 0**
SIGNED: 31 Jul 69 FORCE: 31 Jul 69
REGISTERED: 31 Jul 69 United Nations

ARTICLES: 0
HEADNOTE: UNICEF ACTIVITIES
TOPIC: IGO Operations
PARTIES:
　UNICEF (Children)
　Singapore

109737　　Bilateral Agreement　　**0 UNTS 0**
SIGNED: 3 Sep 68　　　　FORCE: 3 Sep 68
REGISTERED: 31 Jul 69 USA (United States)
ARTICLES: 0
HEADNOTE: USAF CRAFT PLAISANCE AIRFIELD
TOPIC: Milit Installation
PARTIES:
　Mauritius
　USA (United States)

109738　　Multilateral Agreement　　**0 UNTS 0**
SIGNED: 29 Dec 64　　　　FORCE: 5 May 66
REGISTERED: 1 Aug 69 United Nations
ARTICLES: 0
HEADNOTE: REVISED STANDARD
TOPIC: IGO Operations
PARTIES:
　Brazil SIGNED: 29 Dec 64 RATIFIED: 5 May 66
　　FORCE: 5 May 66
　FAO (Food Agri) SIGNED: 29 Dec 64 FORCE:
　　5 May 66
　IAEA (Atom Energy) SIGNED: 29 Dec 64 FORCE:
　　5 May 66
　ICAO (Civil Aviat) SIGNED: 29 Dec 64 FORCE:
　　5 May 66
　ILO (Labor Org) SIGNED: 29 Dec 64 FORCE:
　　5 May 66
　UNESCO (Educ/Cult) SIGNED: 29 Dec 64
　　FORCE: 5 May 66
　United Nations SIGNED: 29 Dec 64 FORCE:
　　5 May 66
　UPU (Postal Union) SIGNED: 29 Dec 64 FORCE:
　　5 May 66
　WHO (World Health) SIGNED: 29 Dec 64 FORCE:
　　5 May 66

109739　　Bilateral Exchange　　**0 UNTS 0**
SIGNED: 13 Dec 68　　　　FORCE: 8 May 69
REGISTERED: 1 Aug 69 Netherlands
ARTICLES: 0
HEADNOTE: TONNAGE CERTIFICATES
TOPIC: Water Transport
PARTIES:
　Netherlands
　Pakistan

109740　　Multilateral Agreement　　**0 UNTS 0**
SIGNED: 18 Jun 69　　　　FORCE: 18 Jun 69
REGISTERED: 1 Aug 69 United Nations
ARTICLES: 0
HEADNOTE: TECHNICAL ASSISTANCE
TOPIC: IGO Operations
PARTIES:
　Guinea SIGNED: 18 Jun 69 FORCE: 18 Jun 69
　FAO (Food Agri) SIGNED: 18 Jun 69 FORCE:
　　18 Jun 69
　IAEA (Atom Energy) SIGNED: 18 Jun 69 FORCE:
　　18 Jun 69
　ICAO (Civil Aviat) SIGNED: 18 Jun 69 FORCE:
　　18 Jun 69
　IDA (Devel Assoc) SIGNED: 18 Jun 69 FORCE:
　　18 Jun 69
　ILO (Labor Org) SIGNED: 18 Jun 69 FORCE:
　　18 Jun 69
　IMCO (Maritime Org) SIGNED: 18 Jun 69 FORCE:
　　18 Jun 69
　ITU (Telecommun) SIGNED: 18 Jun 69 FORCE:
　　18 Jun 69
　UNESCO (Educ/Cult) SIGNED: 18 Jun 69
　　FORCE: 18 Jun 69
　United Nations SIGNED: 18 Jun 69 FORCE:
　　18 Jun 69
　UPU (Postal Union) SIGNED: 18 Jun 69 FORCE:
　　18 Jun 69
　WHO (World Health) SIGNED: 18 Jun 69 FORCE:
　　18 Jun 69
　WMO (Meteorology) SIGNED: 18 Jun 69 FORCE:
　　18 Jun 69

109741　　Multilateral Agreement　　**0 UNTS 0**
SIGNED: 18 Jun 69　　　　FORCE: 18 Jun 69
REGISTERED: 1 Aug 69 United Nations

ARTICLES: 0
HEADNOTE: EXECUTIVE MANAGERIAL ASSIS-
　TANCE
TOPIC: IGO Operations
PARTIES:
　Guinea SIGNED: 18 Jun 69 FORCE: 18 Jun 69
　FAO (Food Agri) SIGNED: 18 Jun 69 FORCE:
　　18 Jun 69
　IAEA (Atom Energy) SIGNED: 18 Jun 69 FORCE:
　　18 Jun 69
　ICAO (Civil Aviat) SIGNED: 18 Jun 69 FORCE:
　　18 Jun 69
　IDA (Devel Assoc) SIGNED: 18 Jun 69 FORCE:
　　18 Jun 69
　ILO (Labor Org) SIGNED: 18 Jun 69 FORCE:
　　18 Jun 69
　IMCO (Maritime Org) SIGNED: 18 Jun 69 FORCE:
　　18 Jun 69
　ITU (Telecommun) SIGNED: 18 Jun 69 FORCE:
　　18 Jun 69
　UNESCO (Educ/Cult) SIGNED: 18 Jun 69
　　FORCE: 18 Jun 69
　United Nations SIGNED: 18 Jun 69 FORCE:
　　18 Jun 69
　UPU (Postal Union) SIGNED: 18 Jun 69 FORCE:
　　18 Jun 69
　WHO (World Health) SIGNED: 18 Jun 69 FORCE:
　　18 Jun 69
　WMO (Meteorology) SIGNED: 18 Jun 69 FORCE:
　　18 Jun 69

109742　　Bilateral Agreement　　**0 UNTS 0**
SIGNED: 18 Jun 69　　　　FORCE: 18 Jun 69
REGISTERED: 1 Aug 69 United Nations
ARTICLES: 0
HEADNOTE: SPECIAL FUND ASSISTANCE
TOPIC: General Aid
PARTIES:
　Guinea
　UN Special Fund

109743　　Multilateral Agreement　　**0 UNTS 0**
SIGNED: 24 Jun 69　　　　FORCE: 24 Jun 69
REGISTERED: 1 Aug 69 United Nations
ARTICLES: 0
HEADNOTE: OPERATIONAL ASSISTANCE SURI-
　NAM
TOPIC: IGO Operations
PARTIES:
　Netherlands SIGNED: 24 Jun 69 FORCE:
　　24 Jun 69
　Netherlands Netherlands Antilles SIGNED:
　　24 Jun 69 FORCE: 24 Jun 69
　Netherlands Surinam SIGNED: 24 Jun 69
　　FORCE: 24 Jun 69
　FAO (Food Agri) SIGNED: 24 Jun 69 FORCE:
　　24 Jun 69
　IAEA (Atom Energy) SIGNED: 24 Jun 69 FORCE:
　　24 Jun 69
　ICAO (Civil Aviat) SIGNED: 24 Jun 69 FORCE:
　　24 Jun 69
　IDA (Devel Assoc) SIGNED: 24 Jun 69 FORCE:
　　24 Jun 69
　ILO (Labor Org) SIGNED: 24 Jun 69 FORCE:
　　24 Jun 69
　IMCO (Maritime Org) SIGNED: 24 Jun 69 FORCE:
　　24 Jun 69
　ITU (Telecommun) SIGNED: 24 Jun 69 FORCE:
　　24 Jun 69
　UNESCO (Educ/Cult) SIGNED: 24 Jun 69
　　FORCE: 24 Jun 69
　United Nations SIGNED: 24 Jun 69 FORCE:
　　24 Jun 69
　UPU (Postal Union) SIGNED: 24 Jun 69 FORCE:
　　24 Jun 69
　WHO (World Health) SIGNED: 24 Jun 69 FORCE:
　　24 Jun 69
　WMO (Meteorology) SIGNED: 24 Jun 69 FORCE:
　　24 Jun 69

109744　　Bilateral Agreement　　**0 UNTS 0**
SIGNED: 2 Jul 69　　　　FORCE: 2 Jul 69
REGISTERED: 1 Aug 69 United Nations
ARTICLES: 0
HEADNOTE: UNICEF ACTIVITIES
TOPIC: IGO Operations
PARTIES:
　Guyana
　UNICEF (Children)

109745　　Bilateral Agreement　　**0 UNTS 0**
SIGNED: 30 Jun 67　　　　FORCE: 1 Apr 68
REGISTERED: 4 Aug 69 Denmark
ARTICLES: 0
HEADNOTE: CATTLE FOR PROCESSING
TOPIC: General Trade
PARTIES:
　Denmark
　EEC (Econ Commnty)

109746　　Bilateral Agreement　　**0 UNTS 0**
SIGNED: 30 Jun 67　　　　FORCE: 30 Jun 67
REGISTERED: 4 Aug 69 Denmark
ARTICLES: 0
HEADNOTE: IMPORT TILSIT CHEESE
TOPIC: General Trade
PARTIES:
　Denmark
　EEC (Econ Commnty)

109747　　Bilateral Exchange　　**0 UNTS 0**
SIGNED: 30 Jun 67　　　　FORCE: 1 Jul 67
REGISTERED: 4 Aug 69 Denmark
ARTICLES: 0
HEADNOTE: EEC CONCESSIONS ON HERRING
TOPIC: General Trade
PARTIES:
　Denmark
　EEC (Econ Commnty)

109748　　Bilateral Exchange　　**0 UNTS 0**
SIGNED: 30 Jun 67　　　　FORCE: 1 Jul 67
REGISTERED: 4 Aug 69 Denmark
ARTICLES: 0
HEADNOTE: EEC CONCESSIONS ON TUNA
TOPIC: General Trade
PARTIES:
　Denmark
　EEC (Econ Commnty)

109749　　Bilateral Exchange　　**0 UNTS 0**
SIGNED: 16 Nov 64　　　　FORCE: 16 Nov 64
REGISTERED: 6 Aug 69 USA (United States)
ARTICLES: 0
HEADNOTE: HONGKONG COTTON TEXTILES
TOPIC: General Trade
PARTIES:
　UK Great Britain
　USA (United States)

109750　　Bilateral Agreement　　**0 UNTS 0**
SIGNED: 22 Apr 65　　　　FORCE: 1 Jul 65
REGISTERED: 6 Aug 69 USA (United States)
ARTICLES: 0
HEADNOTE: FIJI PARCEL POST
TOPIC: Postal Service
PARTIES:
　UK Great Britain
　USA (United States)

109751　　Bilateral Agreement　　**0 UNTS 0**
SIGNED: 8 Feb 66　　　　FORCE: 8 Feb 66
REGISTERED: 6 Aug 69 USA (United States)
ARTICLES: 0
HEADNOTE: BRITISH HONDURAS INVESTMENT
　GUARANTY
TOPIC: Finance
PARTIES:
　UK Great Britain
　USA (United States)

109752　　Bilateral Agreement　　**0 UNTS 0**
SIGNED: 14 Feb 67　　　　FORCE: 14 Feb 67
REGISTERED: 6 Aug 69 USA (United States)
ARTICLES: 0
HEADNOTE: EXCHANGE SCIENTISTS ENGINEERS
TOPIC: Scientific Project
PARTIES:
　India
　USA (United States)

109753　　Bilateral Agreement　　**0 UNTS 0**
SIGNED: 6 Mar 67　　　　FORCE: 6 Mar 67
REGISTERED: 6 Aug 69 USA (United States)
ARTICLES: 0
HEADNOTE: LOAN VESSELS USS KLEINSMITH

TOPIC: Water Transport
PARTIES:
  Taiwan
  USA (United States)

109754   Bilateral Agreement   **0 UNTS 0**
SIGNED: 13 Mar 67   FORCE: 13 Mar 67
REGISTERED: 6 Aug 69 USA (United States)
ARTICLES: 0
HEADNOTE: AGRI COMMOD
TOPIC: US Agri Commod Aid
PARTIES:
  USA (United States)
  Vietnam, South

109755   Multilateral Exchange   **0 UNTS 0**
SIGNED: 16 Mar 67   FORCE: 16 Mar 67
REGISTERED: 6 Aug 69 USA (United States)
ARTICLES: 0
HEADNOTE: AMATEUR RADIO
TOPIC: Gen Communications
PARTIES:
  Trinidad/Tobago
  USA (United States)

109756   Bilateral Agreement   **0 UNTS 0**
SIGNED: 25 Mar 67   FORCE: 25 Mar 67
REGISTERED: 6 Aug 69 USA (United States)
ARTICLES: 0
HEADNOTE: AGRI COMMOD
TOPIC: US Agri Commod Aid
PARTIES:
  Korea, South
  USA (United States)

109757   Bilateral Exchange   **0 UNTS 0**
SIGNED: 28 Mar 67   FORCE: 28 Mar 67
REGISTERED: 6 Aug 69 USA (United States)
ARTICLES: 0
HEADNOTE: LOAN VESSEL
TOPIC: Water Transport
PARTIES:
  Philippines
  USA (United States)

109758   Bilateral Exchange   **0 UNTS 0**
SIGNED: 1 Apr 67   FORCE: 1 Apr 67
REGISTERED: 6 Aug 69 USA (United States)
ARTICLES: 0
HEADNOTE: LOAN VESSEL
TOPIC: Water Transport
PARTIES:
  Taiwan
  USA (United States)

109759   Bilateral Exchange   **0 UNTS 0**
SIGNED: 13 Apr 67   FORCE: 13 Apr 67
REGISTERED: 6 Aug 69 USA (United States)
ARTICLES: 0
HEADNOTE: PILOTAGE GREAT LAKES ST. LAW-
  RENCE
TOPIC: Water Transport
PARTIES:
  Canada
  USA (United States)

109760   Bilateral Exchange   **0 UNTS 0**
SIGNED: 17 Apr 67   FORCE: 17 Apr 67
REGISTERED: 6 Aug 69 USA (United States)
ARTICLES: 0
HEADNOTE: AMATEUR RADIO
TOPIC: Gen Communications
PARTIES:
  Honduras
  USA (United States)

109761   Bilateral Agreement   **0 UNTS 0**
SIGNED: 20 Apr 67   FORCE: 20 Apr 67
REGISTERED: 6 Aug 69 USA (United States)
ARTICLES: 0
HEADNOTE: AGRI COMMOD
TOPIC: US Agri Commod Aid
PARTIES:
  Morocco
  USA (United States)

109762   Bilateral Exchange   **0 UNTS 0**
SIGNED: 3 May 67   FORCE: 3 May 67
REGISTERED: 6 Aug 69 USA (United States)
ARTICLES: 0
HEADNOTE: INCOME TAX US GOVERNMENT EM-
  PLOYEES
TOPIC: Taxation
PARTIES:
  USA (United States)
  Vietnam, South

109763   Bilateral Agreement   **0 UNTS 0**
SIGNED: 4 May 67   FORCE: 8 Jun 68
REGISTERED: 6 Aug 69 USA (United States)
ARTICLES: 0
HEADNOTE: CIVIL USES ATOMIC ENERGY
TOPIC: Atomic Energy
PARTIES:
  Norway
  USA (United States)

109764   Bilateral Agreement   **0 UNTS 0**
SIGNED: 5 May 67   FORCE: 1 Jan 67
REGISTERED: 6 Aug 69 USA (United States)
ARTICLES: 0
HEADNOTE: CANADA PENSION PLAN
TOPIC: Non-ILO Labor
PARTIES:
  Canada
  USA (United States)

109765   Bilateral Exchange   **0 UNTS 0**
SIGNED: 9 May 67   FORCE: 9 May 67
REGISTERED: 6 Aug 69 USA (United States)
ARTICLES: 0
HEADNOTE: FISHERIES NEAR US COAST
TOPIC: Specific Resources
PARTIES:
  Japan
  USA (United States)

109766   Bilateral Exchange   **0 UNTS 0**
SIGNED: 9 May 67   FORCE: 9 May 67
REGISTERED: 6 Aug 69 USA (United States)
ARTICLES: 0
HEADNOTE: SALMON FISHERY
TOPIC: Specific Resources
PARTIES:
  Japan
  USA (United States)

109767   Bilateral Agreement   **0 UNTS 0**
SIGNED: 11 May 67   FORCE: 11 May 67
REGISTERED: 6 Aug 69 USA (United States)
ARTICLES: 0
HEADNOTE: AGRI COMMOD
TOPIC: US Agri Commod Aid
PARTIES:
  Pakistan
  USA (United States)

109768   Bilateral Exchange   **0 UNTS 0**
SIGNED: 16 May 67   FORCE: 16 May 67
REGISTERED: 6 Aug 69 USA (United States)
ARTICLES: 0
HEADNOTE: AMATEUR RADIO
TOPIC: Gen Communications
PARTIES:
  Switzerland
  USA (United States)

109769   Bilateral Exchange   **0 UNTS 0**
SIGNED: 26 Aug 66   FORCE: 26 Aug 66
REGISTERED: 6 Aug 69 USA (United States)
ARTICLES: 0
HEADNOTE: HONGKONG COTTON TEXTILES
TOPIC: General Trade
PARTIES:
  UK Great Britain
  USA (United States)

109770   Bilateral Exchange   **0 UNTS 0**
SIGNED: 2 Jun 67   FORCE: 2 Jun 67
REGISTERED: 6 Aug 69 USA (United States)
ARTICLES: 0
HEADNOTE: COTTON TEXTILES

TOPIC: General Trade
PARTIES:
  Mexico
  USA (United States)

109771   Bilateral Exchange   **0 UNTS 0**
SIGNED: 7 Jun 67   FORCE: 7 Jun 67
REGISTERED: 6 Aug 69 USA (United States)
ARTICLES: 0
HEADNOTE: PEACE CORPS
TOPIC: Admin Cooperation
PARTIES:
  Guyana
  USA (United States)

109772   Bilateral Exchange   **0 UNTS 0**
SIGNED: 12 Jun 67   FORCE: 12 Jun 67
REGISTERED: 6 Aug 69 USA (United States)
ARTICLES: 0
HEADNOTE: PRESUNRISE BROADCASTING
TOPIC: Gen Communications
PARTIES:
  Canada
  USA (United States)

109773   Bilateral Agreement   **0 UNTS 0**
SIGNED: 19 Jun 67   FORCE: 19 Jun 67
REGISTERED: 6 Aug 69 USA (United States)
ARTICLES: 0
HEADNOTE: SCIENTIFIC COOPERATION
TOPIC: Scientific Project
PARTIES:
  Italy
  USA (United States)

109774   Bilateral Exchange   **0 UNTS 0**
SIGNED: 28 Jun 67   FORCE: 28 Jun 67
REGISTERED: 6 Aug 69 USA (United States)
ARTICLES: 0
HEADNOTE: LOAN VESSEL
TOPIC: Water Transport
PARTIES:
  Brazil
  USA (United States)

109775   Bilateral Exchange   **0 UNTS 0**
SIGNED: 28 Jun 67   FORCE: 28 Jun 67
REGISTERED: 6 Aug 69 USA (United States)
ARTICLES: 0
HEADNOTE: LOAN VESSEL
TOPIC: Water Transport
PARTIES:
  Brazil
  USA (United States)

109776   Bilateral Agreement   **0 UNTS 0**
SIGNED: 29 Jun 67   FORCE: 29 Jun 67
REGISTERED: 6 Aug 69 USA (United States)
ARTICLES: 0
HEADNOTE: PAY CLAIMS GUERRILLAS VETER-
  ANS
TOPIC: Claims and Debts
PARTIES:
  Philippines
  USA (United States)

109777   Bilateral Exchange   **0 UNTS 0**
SIGNED: 3 Jul 67   FORCE: 1 Jul 66
REGISTERED: 6 Aug 69 USA (United States)
ARTICLES: 0
HEADNOTE: COTTON TEXTILES
TOPIC: General Trade
PARTIES:
  Pakistan
  USA (United States)

109778   Bilateral Exchange   **0 UNTS 0**
SIGNED: 13 Jul 67   FORCE: 1 Oct 66
REGISTERED: 6 Aug 69 USA (United States)
ARTICLES: 0
HEADNOTE: COTTON TEXTILES
TOPIC: General Trade
PARTIES:
  Israel
  USA (United States)

109779 Bilateral Agreement **0 UNTS 0**
SIGNED: 7 Sep 66 FORCE: 21 May 69
REGISTERED: 6 Aug 69 USA (United States)
ARTICLES: 0
HEADNOTE: OUTSTANDING FINANCIAL PROB-
LEMS
TOPIC: Finance
PARTIES:
 Indonesia
 Netherlands

109780 Bilateral Agreement **0 UNTS 0**
SIGNED: 9 Feb 67 FORCE: 9 Feb 67
REGISTERED: 7 Aug 69 Netherlands
ARTICLES: 0
HEADNOTE: IRRIGATION GALOLE
TOPIC: General Aid
PARTIES:
 Kenya
 Netherlands

109781 Bilateral Convention **0 UNTS 0**
SIGNED: 14 May 69 FORCE: 14 May 69
REGISTERED: 7 Aug 69 Netherlands
ARTICLES: 0
HEADNOTE: RECRUIT PLACE MOROCCAN WORK-
ERS
TOPIC: Non-ILO Labor
PARTIES:
 Morocco
 Netherlands

109782 Bilateral Exchange **0 UNTS 0**
SIGNED: 15 Apr 68 FORCE: 15 Apr 68
REGISTERED: 8 Aug 69 UK Great Britain
ARTICLES: 0
HEADNOTE: ATOMIC FACILITY
TOPIC: Atomic Energy
PARTIES:
 Greece
 UK Great Britain

109783 Bilateral Agreement **0 UNTS 0**
SIGNED: 3 Jul 68 FORCE: 28 Mar 69
REGISTERED: 8 Aug 69 UK Great Britain
ARTICLES: 0
HEADNOTE: DOUBLE TAX INCOME
TOPIC: Taxation
PARTIES:
 Lesotho
 UK Great Britain

109784 Bilateral Exchange **0 UNTS 0**
SIGNED: 30 Jul 68 FORCE: 30 Jul 68
REGISTERED: 8 Aug 69 UK Great Britain
ARTICLES: 0
HEADNOTE: INTEREST-FREE LOAN
TOPIC: Loans and Credits
PARTIES:
 Jordan
 UK Great Britain

109785 Bilateral Exchange **0 UNTS 0**
SIGNED: 14 Jan 69 FORCE: 14 Jan 69
REGISTERED: 8 Aug 69 UK Great Britain
ARTICLES: 0
HEADNOTE: INTEREST-FREE LOAN
TOPIC: Loans and Credits
PARTIES:
 Jordan
 UK Great Britain

109786 Bilateral Exchange **0 UNTS 0**
SIGNED: 11 Dec 68 FORCE: 11 Dec 68
REGISTERED: 8 Aug 69 UK Great Britain
ARTICLES: 0
HEADNOTE: INTEREST-FREE LOAN
TOPIC: Loans and Credits
PARTIES:
 Sudan
 UK Great Britain

109787 Bilateral Exchange **0 UNTS 0**
SIGNED: 12 Dec 68 FORCE: 12 Dec 68
REGISTERED: 8 Aug 69 UK Great Britain
ARTICLES: 0

HEADNOTE: TRANSFER NUCLEAR MATERIAL
SWEDEN
TOPIC: Atomic Energy
PARTIES:
 Switzerland
 UK Great Britain

109788 Bilateral Agreement **0 UNTS 0**
SIGNED: 13 Feb 69 FORCE: 13 Feb 69
REGISTERED: 8 Aug 69 UK Great Britain
ARTICLES: 0
HEADNOTE: BRITISH COUNCIL
TOPIC: Admin Cooperation
PARTIES:
 Ethiopia
 UK Great Britain

109789 Bilateral Agreement **0 UNTS 0**
SIGNED: 28 Feb 69 FORCE: 28 Feb 69
REGISTERED: 8 Aug 69 UK Great Britain
ARTICLES: 0
HEADNOTE: APPLIED SCIENCE TECHNOLOGY
TOPIC: Scientific Project
PARTIES:
 Bulgaria
 UK Great Britain

109790 Bilateral Agreement **0 UNTS 0**
SIGNED: 13 Mar 69 FORCE: 13 Mar 69
REGISTERED: 8 Aug 69 UK Great Britain
ARTICLES: 0
HEADNOTE: CERTAIN COMMERCIAL DEBTS
TOPIC: Claims and Debts
PARTIES:
 Indonesia
 UK Great Britain

109791 Bilateral Agreement **0 UNTS 0**
SIGNED: 1 Jun 68 FORCE: 25 Jun 68
REGISTERED: 13 Aug 69 Finland
ARTICLES: 0
HEADNOTE: FINNISH VOLUNTEERS
TOPIC: Non-ILO Labor
PARTIES:
 Finland
 Tanzania

109792 Bilateral Agreement **0 UNTS 0**
SIGNED: 26 Jan 69 FORCE: 13 Aug 69
REGISTERED: 13 Aug 69 United Nations
ARTICLES: 0
HEADNOTE: UNICEF ACTIVITIES
TOPIC: IGO Operations
PARTIES:
 Kuwait
 UNICEF (Children)

109793 Bilateral Convention **0 UNTS 0**
SIGNED: 12 Dec 68 FORCE: 1 Jul 69
REGISTERED: 18 Aug 69 Netherlands
ARTICLES: 0
HEADNOTE: PILOTAGE SCHELDT TERNEUZEN
TOPIC: Water Transport
PARTIES:
 Belgium
 Netherlands

109794 Bilateral Agreement **0 UNTS 0**
SIGNED: 16 Jun 69 FORCE: 16 Jun 69
REGISTERED: 21 Aug 69 Thailand
ARTICLES: 0
HEADNOTE: SILVICULTURE
TOPIC: Scientific Project
PARTIES:
 Denmark
 Thailand

109795 Bilateral Agreement **0 UNTS 0**
SIGNED: 20 Mar 67 FORCE: 20 Mar 67
REGISTERED: 22 Aug 69 Belgium
ARTICLES: 0
HEADNOTE: ROAD TRANSPORT GOODS
TOPIC: Land Transport
PARTIES:
 Belgium
 Sweden

109796 Bilateral Agreement **0 UNTS 0**
SIGNED: 14 Mar 69 FORCE: 14 Mar 69
REGISTERED: 25 Aug 69 Philippines
ARTICLES: 0
HEADNOTE: PEACEFUL USES ATOMIC ENERGY
TOPIC: Atomic Energy
PARTIES:
 India
 Philippines

109797 Bilateral Exchange **0 UNTS 0**
SIGNED: 16 Sep 68 FORCE: 25 Sep 68
REGISTERED: 26 Aug 69 UK Great Britain
ARTICLES: 0
HEADNOTE: MINIMUM STERLING PROPORTION
TOPIC: Finance
PARTIES:
 Mauritius
 UK Great Britain

109798 Bilateral Exchange **0 UNTS 0**
SIGNED: 18 Sep 68 FORCE: 25 Sep 68
REGISTERED: 26 Aug 69 UK Great Britain
ARTICLES: 0
HEADNOTE: MINIMUM STERLING PROPORTION
TOPIC: Finance
PARTIES:
 Ceylon (Sri Lanka)
 UK Great Britain

109799 Bilateral Exchange **0 UNTS 0**
SIGNED: 19 Sep 68 FORCE: 25 Sep 68
REGISTERED: 26 Aug 69 UK Great Britain
ARTICLES: 0
HEADNOTE: MINIMUM STERLING PROPORTION
TOPIC: Finance
CONCEPTS: Taxation.
PARTIES:
 Gambia
 UK Great Britain

109800 Bilateral Exchange **0 UNTS 0**
SIGNED: 19 Sep 68 FORCE: 25 Sep 68
REGISTERED: 26 Aug 69 UK Great Britain
ARTICLES: 0
HEADNOTE: MINIMUM STERLING PROPORTION
TOPIC: Finance
PARTIES:
 Iceland
 UK Great Britain

109801 Bilateral Exchange **0 UNTS 0**
SIGNED: 19 Sep 68 FORCE: 25 Sep 68
REGISTERED: 26 Aug 69 UK Great Britain
ARTICLES: 0
HEADNOTE: MINIMUM STERLING PROPORTION
TOPIC: Finance
PARTIES:
 Singapore
 UK Great Britain

109802 Bilateral Exchange **0 UNTS 0**
SIGNED: 25 Sep 68 FORCE: 25 Sep 68
REGISTERED: 26 Aug 69 UK Great Britain
ARTICLES: 0
HEADNOTE: MINIMUM STERLING PROPORTION
TOPIC: Finance
PARTIES:
 Barbados
 UK Great Britain

109803 Bilateral Exchange **0 UNTS 0**
SIGNED: 20 Sep 68 FORCE: 25 Sep 68
REGISTERED: 26 Aug 69 UK Great Britain
ARTICLES: 0
HEADNOTE: MINIMUM STERLING PROPORTION
TOPIC: Finance
PARTIES:
 Guyana
 UK Great Britain

109804 Bilateral Exchange **0 UNTS 0**
SIGNED: 20 Sep 68 FORCE: 25 Sep 68
REGISTERED: 26 Aug 69 UK Great Britain
ARTICLES: 0
HEADNOTE: MINIMUM STERLING PROPORTION

TOPIC: Finance
PARTIES:
  Jamaica
  UK Great Britain

109805   Bilateral Exchange   **0 UNTS 0**
SIGNED: 20 Sep 68   FORCE: 25 Sep 68
REGISTERED: 26 Aug 69 UK Great Britain
ARTICLES: 0
HEADNOTE: MINIMUM STERLING PROPORTION
TOPIC: Finance
PARTIES:
  Kenya
  UK Great Britain

109806   Bilateral Exchange   **0 UNTS 0**
SIGNED: 20 Sep 68   FORCE: 25 Sep 68
REGISTERED: 26 Aug 69 UK Great Britain
ARTICLES: 0
HEADNOTE: MINIMUM STERLING PROPORTION
TOPIC: Finance
PARTIES:
  Sierra Leone
  UK Great Britain

109807   Bilateral Exchange   **0 UNTS 0**
SIGNED: 21 Sep 68   FORCE: 25 Sep 68
REGISTERED: 26 Aug 69 UK Great Britain
ARTICLES: 0
HEADNOTE: MINIMUM STERLING PROPORTION
TOPIC: Finance
PARTIES:
  Ghana
  UK Great Britain

109808   Bilateral Exchange   **0 UNTS 0**
SIGNED: 21 Sep 68   FORCE: 25 Sep 68
REGISTERED: 26 Aug 69 UK Great Britain
ARTICLES: 0
HEADNOTE: MINIMUM STERLING PROPORTION
TOPIC: Finance
PARTIES:
  Cyprus
  UK Great Britain

109809   Bilateral Exchange   **0 UNTS 0**
SIGNED: 21 Sep 68   FORCE: 25 Sep 68
REGISTERED: 26 Aug 69 UK Great Britain
ARTICLES: 0
HEADNOTE: MINIMUM STERLING PROPORTION
TOPIC: Finance
PARTIES:
  India
  UK Great Britain

109810   Bilateral Exchange   **0 UNTS 0**
SIGNED: 21 Sep 68   FORCE: 25 Sep 68
REGISTERED: 26 Aug 69 UK Great Britain
ARTICLES: 0
HEADNOTE: MINIMUM STERLING PROPORTION
TOPIC: Finance
PARTIES:
  Uganda
  UK Great Britain

109811   Bilateral Exchange   **0 UNTS 0**
SIGNED: 22 Sep 68   FORCE: 25 Sep 68
REGISTERED: 26 Aug 69 UK Great Britain
ARTICLES: 0
HEADNOTE: MINIMUM STERLING PROPORTION
TOPIC: Finance
PARTIES:
  Jordan
  UK Great Britain

109812   Bilateral Exchange   **0 UNTS 0**
SIGNED: 22 Sep 68   FORCE: 25 Sep 68
REGISTERED: 26 Aug 69 UK Great Britain
ARTICLES: 0
HEADNOTE: MINIMUM STERLING PROPORTION
TOPIC: Finance
PARTIES:
  Malta
  UK Great Britain

109813   Bilateral Exchange   **0 UNTS 0**
SIGNED: 23 Sep 68   FORCE: 25 Sep 68
REGISTERED: 26 Aug 69 UK Great Britain
ARTICLES: 0
HEADNOTE: MINIMUM STERLING PROPORTION
TOPIC: Finance
PARTIES:
  Tanzania
  UK Great Britain

109814   Bilateral Exchange   **0 UNTS 0**
SIGNED: 23 Sep 68   FORCE: 25 Sep 68
REGISTERED: 26 Aug 69 UK Great Britain
ARTICLES: 0
HEADNOTE: MINIMUM STERLING PROPORTION
TOPIC: Finance
PARTIES:
  UK Great Britain
  Zambia

109815   Bilateral Exchange   **0 UNTS 0**
SIGNED: 24 Sep 68   FORCE: 25 Sep 68
REGISTERED: 26 Aug 69 UK Great Britain
ARTICLES: 0
HEADNOTE: MINIMUM STERLING PROPORTION
TOPIC: Finance
PARTIES:
  Libya
  UK Great Britain

109816   Bilateral Exchange   **0 UNTS 0**
SIGNED: 24 Sep 68   FORCE: 25 Sep 68
REGISTERED: 26 Aug 69 UK Great Britain
ARTICLES: 0
HEADNOTE: MINIMUM STERLING PROPORTION
TOPIC: Finance
PARTIES:
  Malawi
  UK Great Britain

109817   Bilateral Exchange   **0 UNTS 0**
SIGNED: 24 Sep 68   FORCE: 25 Sep 68
REGISTERED: 26 Aug 69 UK Great Britain
ARTICLES: 0
HEADNOTE: MINIMUM STERLING PROPORTION
TOPIC: Finance
PARTIES:
  Malaysia
  UK Great Britain

109818   Bilateral Exchange   **0 UNTS 0**
SIGNED: 24 Sep 68   FORCE: 25 Sep 68
REGISTERED: 26 Aug 69 UK Great Britain
ARTICLES: 0
HEADNOTE: MINIMUM STERLING PROPORTION
TOPIC: Finance
PARTIES:
  New Zealand
  UK Great Britain

109819   Bilateral Exchange   **0 UNTS 0**
SIGNED: 24 Sep 68   FORCE: 25 Sep 68
REGISTERED: 26 Aug 69 UK Great Britain
ARTICLES: 0
HEADNOTE: MINIMUM STERLING PROPORTION
TOPIC: Finance
PARTIES:
  Nigeria
  UK Great Britain

109820   Bilateral Exchange   **0 UNTS 0**
SIGNED: 25 Sep 68   FORCE: 25 Sep 68
REGISTERED: 26 Aug 69 UK Great Britain
ARTICLES: 0
HEADNOTE: MINIMUM STERLING PROPORTION
TOPIC: Finance
PARTIES:
  Pakistan
  UK Great Britain

109821   Bilateral Exchange   **0 UNTS 0**
SIGNED: 3 Oct 68   FORCE: 25 Sep 68
REGISTERED: 26 Aug 69 UK Great Britain
ARTICLES: 0
HEADNOTE: MINIMUM STERLING PROPORTION
TOPIC: Finance

PARTIES:
  Australia
  UK Great Britain

109822   Multilateral Exchange   **0 UNTS 0**
SIGNED: 9 Oct 68   FORCE: 25 Sep 68
REGISTERED: 26 Aug 69 UK Great Britain
ARTICLES: 0
HEADNOTE: MINIMUM STERLING PROPORTION
TOPIC: Finance
PARTIES:
  Trinidad/Tobago
  UK Great Britain

109823   Bilateral Agreement   **0 UNTS 0**
SIGNED: 27 Jun 57   FORCE: 3 Sep 56
REGISTERED: 30 Aug 69 USSR (Soviet Union)
ARTICLES: 0
HEADNOTE: TRADE
TOPIC: General Trade
PARTIES:
  Pakistan
  USSR (Soviet Union)

109824   Bilateral Protocol   **0 UNTS 0**
SIGNED: 15 Jul 56   FORCE: 15 Jul 56
REGISTERED: 30 Aug 69 USSR (Soviet Union)
ARTICLES: 0
HEADNOTE: TRADE REPRESENTATION
TOPIC: General Trade
PARTIES:
  United Arab Rep
  USSR (Soviet Union)

109825   Bilateral Agreement   **0 UNTS 0**
SIGNED: 17 Dec 67   FORCE: 30 Apr 68
REGISTERED: 30 Aug 69 USSR (Soviet Union)
ARTICLES: 0
HEADNOTE: TRADE
TOPIC: General Trade
PARTIES:
  Mongolia
  USSR (Soviet Union)

109826   Bilateral Agreement   **0 UNTS 0**
SIGNED: 18 Mar 61   FORCE: 18 Mar 61
REGISTERED: 30 Aug 69 USSR (Soviet Union)
ARTICLES: 0
HEADNOTE: TRADE
TOPIC: General Trade
PARTIES:
  Mali
  USSR (Soviet Union)

109827   Bilateral Agreement   **0 UNTS 0**
SIGNED: 1 Nov 61   FORCE: 1 Nov 61
REGISTERED: 30 Aug 69 USSR (Soviet Union)
ARTICLES: 0
HEADNOTE: LONG-TERM TRADE
TOPIC: General Trade
PARTIES:
  Sudan
  USSR (Soviet Union)

109828   Bilateral Agreement   **0 UNTS 0**
SIGNED: 22 Dec 61   FORCE: 22 Dec 61
REGISTERED: 30 Aug 69 USSR (Soviet Union)
ARTICLES: 0
HEADNOTE: TRADE & PAYMENTS
TOPIC: General Trade
PARTIES:
  Cyprus
  USSR (Soviet Union)

109829   Bilateral Agreement   **0 UNTS 0**
SIGNED: 23 Oct 64   FORCE: 23 Oct 64
REGISTERED: 30 Aug 69 USSR (Soviet Union)
ARTICLES: 0
HEADNOTE: TRADE
TOPIC: General Trade
PARTIES:
  Madagascar
  USSR (Soviet Union)

109830 Bilateral Agreement **0 UNTS 0**
SIGNED: 17 Feb 65 FORCE: 17 Feb 65
REGISTERED: 30 Aug 69 USSR (Soviet Union)
ARTICLES: 0
HEADNOTE: PAYMENT
TOPIC: Finance
PARTIES:
 Cuba
 USSR (Soviet Union)

109831 Bilateral Agreement **0 UNTS 0**
SIGNED: 26 Apr 65 FORCE: 26 Apr 65
REGISTERED: 30 Aug 69 USSR (Soviet Union)
ARTICLES: 0
HEADNOTE: TRADE
TOPIC: General Trade
PARTIES:
 Sierra Leone
 USSR (Soviet Union)

109832 Bilateral Agreement **0 UNTS 0**
SIGNED: 3 Apr 67 FORCE: 3 Apr 67
REGISTERED: 30 Aug 69 USSR (Soviet Union)
ARTICLES: 0
HEADNOTE: TRADE
TOPiC: General Trade
PARTIES:
 Malaysia
 USSR (Soviet Union)

109833 Bilateral Agreement **0 UNTS 0**
SIGNED: 13 Sep 66 FORCE: 13 Sep 66
REGISTERED: 30 Aug 69 Netherlands
ARTICLES: 0
HEADNOTE: RECRUIT EMPLOY GREEK WORKERS
TOPIC: Non-ILO Labor
PARTIES:
 Greece
 Netherlands

109834 Bilateral Agreement **0 UNTS 0**
SIGNED: 8 Aug 68 FORCE: 1 Aug 69
REGISTERED: 30 Aug 69 Philippines
ARTICLES: 0
HEADNOTE: MONEY ORDERS
TOPIC: Postal Service
PARTIES:
 Japan
 Philippines

109835 Bilateral Exchange **0 UNTS 0**
SIGNED: 25 Aug 68 FORCE: 25 Aug 68
REGISTERED: 30 Aug 69 Netherlands
ARTICLES: 0
HEADNOTE: CONSULAR RELATIONS
TOPIC: Consul/Citizenship
PARTIES:
 Muscat and Oman
 Netherlands

109836 Bilateral Exchange **0 UNTS 0**
SIGNED: 18 Aug 64 FORCE: 26 Mar 66
REGISTERED: 2 Sep 69 USA (United States)
ARTICLES: 0
HEADNOTE: MARRIAGE DOCUMENTS
TOPIC: Admin Cooperation
PARTIES:
 Italy
 USA (United States)

109837 Bilateral Agreement **0 UNTS 0**
SIGNED: 16 Nov 66 FORCE: 26 Jan 67
REGISTERED: 2 Sep 69 USA (United States)
ARTICLES: 0
HEADNOTE: INVESTMENT GUARANTY
TOPIC: Finance
PARTIES:
 Malta
 USA (United States)

109838 Bilateral Exchange **0 UNTS 0**
SIGNED: 28 Dec 66 FORCE: 28 Dec 66
REGISTERED: 2 Sep 69 USA (United States)
ARTICLES: 0
HEADNOTE: DEPLOY USS CASCADE
TOPIC: General Military
PARTIES:
 Malta
 USA (United States)

109839 Bilateral Exchange **0 UNTS 0**
SIGNED: 29 Dec 66 FORCE: 29 Dec 66
REGISTERED: 2 Sep 69 USA (United States)
ARTICLES: 0
HEADNOTE: US CLAIM POSTWAR ECONOMIC AS-
SISTANCE
TOPIC: General Aid
PARTIES:
 Germany, West
 USA (United States)

109840 Bilateral Exchange **0 UNTS 0**
SIGNED: 10 Jan 67 FORCE: 10 Jan 67
REGISTERED: 2 Sep 69 USA (United States)
ARTICLES: 0
HEADNOTE: PEACE CORPS ANGUILLA
TOPIC: General Aid
PARTIES:
 UK Great Britain
 USA (United States)

109841 Bilateral Exchange **0 UNTS 0**
SIGNED: 11 Jan 67 FORCE: 11 Jan 67
REGISTERED: 2 Sep 69 USA (United States)
ARTICLES: 0
HEADNOTE: PEACE CORPS DOMINICA
TOPIC: General Aid
PARTIES:
 UK Great Britain
 USA (United States)

109842 Bilateral Exchange **0 UNTS 0**
SIGNED: 12 Jan 67 FORCE: 12 Jan 67
REGISTERED: 2 Sep 69 USA (United States)
ARTICLES: 0
HEADNOTE: LIABILITY NS SAVANNAH
TOPIC: General Military
PARTIES:
 Greece
 USA (United States)

109843 Bilateral Exchange **0 UNTS 0**
SIGNED: 18 Jan 67 FORCE: 18 Jan 67
REGISTERED: 2 Sep 69 USA (United States)
ARTICLES: 0
HEADNOTE: PEACE CORPS ST. VINCENT
TOPIC: General Aid
PARTIES:
 UK Great Britain
 USA (United States)

109844 Bilateral Exchange **0 UNTS 0**
SIGNED: 27 Jan 67 FORCE: 27 Jan 67
REGISTERED: 2 Sep 69 USA (United States)
ARTICLES: 0
HEADNOTE: DEFENSE EQUIPMENT
TOPIC: Milit Installation
PARTIES:
 Brazil
 USA (United States)

109845 Bilateral Exchange **0 UNTS 0**
SIGNED: 27 Jan 67 FORCE: 27 Jan 67
REGISTERED: 2 Sep 69 USA (United States)
ARTICLES: 0
HEADNOTE: COTTON TEXTILES
TOPIC: Commodity Trade
PARTIES:
 Brazil
 Israel

109846 Bilateral Exchange **0 UNTS 0**
SIGNED: 28 Jan 67 FORCE: 28 Jan 67
REGISTERED: 2 Sep 69 USA (United States)
ARTICLES: 0
HEADNOTE: GEODETIC SATELLITE STATION
TOPIC: Scientific Project
PARTIES:
 Israel
 Mexico

109847 Bilateral Agreement **0 UNTS 0**
SIGNED: 10 Feb 67 FORCE: 10 Feb 67
REGISTERED: 2 Sep 69 USA (United States)
ARTICLES: 0
HEADNOTE: CULTURE
TOPIC: Culture
PARTIES:
 Morocco
 USA (United States)

109848 Bilateral Agreement **0 UNTS 0**
SIGNED: 13 Feb 67 FORCE: 13 Feb 67
REGISTERED: 2 Sep 69 USA (United States)
ARTICLES: 0
HEADNOTE: FISHERY NE PACIFIC NEAR USA
TOPIC: Specific Resources
PARTIES:
 USA (United States)
 USSR (Soviet Union)

109849 Bilateral Exchange **0 UNTS 0**
SIGNED: 18 Feb 67 FORCE: 18 Feb 67
REGISTERED: 2 Sep 69 USA (United States)
ARTICLES: 0
HEADNOTE: CULTURAL, OTHER EXCHANGES
TOPIC: Tech Assistance
PARTIES:
 Romania
 USA (United States)

109850 Bilateral Agreement **0 UNTS 0**
SIGNED: 20 Feb 67 FORCE: 20 Feb 67
REGISTERED: 2 Sep 69 USA (United States)
ARTICLES: 0
HEADNOTE: AGRI COMMOD
TOPIC: US Agri Commod Aid
PARTIES:
 India
 USA (United States)

109851 Bilateral Exchange **0 UNTS 0**
SIGNED: 21 Feb 67 FORCE: 21 Feb 67
REGISTERED: 2 Sep 69 USA (United States)
ARTICLES: 0
HEADNOTE: EDUCATIONAL CULTURAL EX-
CHANGE COMMISSION
TOPIC: Culture
PARTIES:
 United Arab Rep
 USA (United States)

109852 Bilateral Agreement **0 UNTS 0**
SIGNED: 23 Feb 67 FORCE: 10 Mar 67
REGISTERED: 2 Sep 69 USA (United States)
ARTICLES: 0
HEADNOTE: STATUS KOREAN SERVICES CORPS
TOPIC: General Aid
PARTIES:
 Korea, South
 USA (United States)

109853 Bilateral Agreement **0 UNTS 0**
SIGNED: 24 Feb 67 FORCE: 10 Mar 67
REGISTERED: 2 Sep 69 USA (United States)
ARTICLES: 0
HEADNOTE: INVESTMENT GUARANTY
TOPIC: Finance
PARTIES:
 Lesotho
 USA (United States)

109854 Bilateral Agreement **0 UNTS 0**
SIGNED: 3 Mar 67 FORCE: 3 Mar 67
REGISTERED: 2 Sep 69 USA (United States)
ARTICLES: 0
HEADNOTE: AGRI COMMOD
TOPIC: US Agri Commod Aid
PARTIES:
 Ghana
 USA (United States)

109855 Bilateral Exchange **0 UNTS 0**
SIGNED: 7 Mar 67 FORCE: 7 Mar 67
REGISTERED: 2 Sep 69 USA (United States)
ARTICLES: 0
HEADNOTE: INVESTMENT GUARANTY

PARTIES:
 Malta
 USA (United States)

TOPIC: Finance
PARTIES:
  Cameroon
  USA (United States)

109856   Bilateral Exchange   **0 UNTS 0**
SIGNED: 15 Mar 67   FORCE: 15 Mar 67
REGISTERED: 2 Sep 69 USA (United States)
ARTICLES: 0
HEADNOTE: COTTON TEXTILES
TOPIC: Commodity Trade
PARTIES:
  Poland
  USA (United States)

109857   Bilateral Exchange   **0 UNTS 0**
SIGNED: 23 Mar 67   FORCE: 23 Mar 67
REGISTERED: 2 Sep 69 USA (United States)
ARTICLES: 0
HEADNOTE: COTTON TEXTILES
TOPIC: Commodity Trade
PARTIES:
  Portugal
  USA (United States)

109858   Bilateral Agreement   **0 UNTS 0**
SIGNED: 24 Mar 67   FORCE: 1 Apr 67
REGISTERED: 2 Sep 69 USA (United States)
ARTICLES: 0
HEADNOTE: DONGES-METZ PIPELINE SYSTEM
TOPIC: Specific Property
PARTIES:
  France
  USA (United States)

109859   Bilateral Exchange   **0 UNTS 0**
SIGNED: 14 Apr 67   FORCE: 14 Apr 67
REGISTERED: 2 Sep 69 USA (United States)
ARTICLES: 0
HEADNOTE: MILITARY ASSISTANCE CIVIC ACTION
TOPIC: Milit Assistance
PARTIES:
  Indonesia
  USA (United States)

109860   Bilateral Agreement   **0 UNTS 0**
SIGNED: 25 Apr 67   FORCE: 25 Apr 67
REGISTERED: 2 Sep 69 USA (United States)
ARTICLES: 0
HEADNOTE: VETERAN MEDICAL CARE GRANT
TOPIC: Tech Assistance
PARTIES:
  Philippines
  USA (United States)

109861   Multilateral Convention   **0 UNTS 0**
SIGNED: 27 Oct 67   FORCE: 27 Oct 67
REGISTERED: 3 Sep 69 Netherlands
ARTICLES: 0
HEADNOTE: TELELINE KAMPALA KIGALI
TOPIC: Telecommunications
PARTIES:
  Netherlands   SIGNED: 27 Oct 67   FORCE:
    12 Jun 69
  Rwanda   SIGNED: 27 Oct 67   RATIFIED:
    12 Jun 69 FORCE: 12 Jun 69
  Uganda   SIGNED: 27 Oct 67   RATIFIED:
    12 Jun 69 FORCE: 12 Jun 69

109862   Bilateral Agreement   **0 UNTS 0**
SIGNED: 13 Sep 65   FORCE: 14 Jan 67
REGISTERED: 4 Sep 69 France
ARTICLES: 0
HEADNOTE: LEGAL STATUS EONR
TOPIC: Atomic Energy
PARTIES:
  France
  CERN (Nuc Resrch)

109863   Bilateral Convention   **0 UNTS 0**
SIGNED: 13 Sep 65   FORCE: 5 Mar 68
REGISTERED: 4 Sep 69 France
ARTICLES: 0
HEADNOTE: ORGANIZATION NUCLEAR RESEARCH SITE

TOPIC: Atomic Energy
PARTIES:
  France
  Switzerland

109864   Multilateral Agreement   **0 UNTS 0**
SIGNED: 30 Jun 67   FORCE: 1 Jul 68
REGISTERED: 4 Sep 69 Ireland
ARTICLES: 0
HEADNOTE: CEREALS
TOPIC: Commodity Trade
PARTIES:
  Australia SIGNED: 30 Jun 67 FORCE: 1 Jul 68
  Canada SIGNED: 30 Jun 67 FORCE: 1 Jul 68
  UK Great Britain SIGNED: 30 Jun 67 FORCE:
    1 Jul 68
  USA (United States) SIGNED: 30 Jun 67 FORCE:
    1 Jul 68

109865   Bilateral Agreement   **0 UNTS 0**
SIGNED: 16 Dec 68   FORCE: 1 Sep 69
REGISTERED: 4 Sep 69 France
ARTICLES: 0
HEADNOTE: ROAD TRANSPORT
TOPIC: Land Transport
PARTIES:
  France
  Sweden

109866   Bilateral Agreement   **0 UNTS 0**
SIGNED: 8 May 69   FORCE: 30 May 69
REGISTERED: 4 Sep 69 Philippines
ARTICLES: 0
HEADNOTE: AIR TRANSPORT
TOPIC: Air Transport
PARTIES:
  Denmark
  Philippines

109867   Bilateral Agreement   **0 UNTS 0**
SIGNED: 8 May 69   FORCE: 30 May 69
REGISTERED: 4 Sep 69 Philippines
ARTICLES: 0
HEADNOTE: AIR TRANSPORT
TOPIC: Air Transport
PARTIES:
  Norway
  Philippines

109868   Bilateral Agreement   **0 UNTS 0**
SIGNED: 8 May 69   FORCE: 30 May 69
REGISTERED: 4 Sep 69 Philippines
ARTICLES: 0
HEADNOTE: AIR TRANSPORT
TOPIC: Air Transport
PARTIES:
  Philippines
  Sweden

109869   Bilateral Agreement   **0 UNTS 0**
SIGNED: 16 Jul 69   FORCE: 16 Jul 69
REGISTERED: 4 Sep 69 Belgium
ARTICLES: 0
HEADNOTE: ROAD TRANSPORT PASSENGERS GOODS
TOPIC: General Transport
PARTIES:
  Belgium
  Greece

109870   Bilateral Agreement   **0 UNTS 0**
SIGNED: 31 Jul 69   FORCE: 31 Jul 69
REGISTERED: 4 Sep 69 Belgium
ARTICLES: 0
HEADNOTE: ROAD TRANSPORT
TOPIC: Land Transport
PARTIES:
  Belgium
  Bulgaria

109871   Bilateral Agreement   **0 UNTS 0**
SIGNED: 20 Feb 50   FORCE: 11 Jul 58
REGISTERED: 5 Sep 69 Bulgaria
ARTICLES: 0
HEADNOTE: SOCIAL POLICY
TOPIC: Health/Educ/Welfare

PARTIES:
  Bulgaria
  Germany, West

109872   Bilateral Convention   **0 UNTS 0**
SIGNED: 18 Apr 58   FORCE: 17 Oct 58
REGISTERED: 5 Sep 69 Bulgaria
ARTICLES: 0
HEADNOTE: CONSULAR
TOPIC: Consul/Citizenship
PARTIES:
  Bulgaria
  Germany, West

109873   Bilateral Agreement   **0 UNTS 0**
SIGNED: 29 Jun 63   FORCE: 24 Nov 63
REGISTERED: 5 Sep 69 Bulgaria
ARTICLES: 0
HEADNOTE: CULTURE
TOPIC: Culture
PARTIES:
  Afghanistan
  Bulgaria

109874   Bilateral Exchange   **0 UNTS 0**
SIGNED: 30 Nov 66   FORCE: 30 Nov 66
REGISTERED: 5 Sep 69 Bulgaria
ARTICLES: 0
HEADNOTE: ABOLITION AUTHENTICATION FEES
TOPIC: Finance
PARTIES:
  Brazil
  Bulgaria

109875   Bilateral Agreement   **0 UNTS 0**
SIGNED: 6 May 68   FORCE: 6 May 68
REGISTERED: 5 Sep 69 Bulgaria
ARTICLES: 0
HEADNOTE: ECONOMIC INDUSTRIAL TECHNICAL COOPERATION
TOPIC: Tech Assistance
PARTIES:
  Austria
  Bulgaria

109876   Bilateral Agreement   **0 UNTS 0**
SIGNED: 25 Oct 68   FORCE: 25 Oct 68
REGISTERED: 5 Sep 69 Denmark
ARTICLES: 0
HEADNOTE: ROAD TRANSPORT
TOPIC: Land Transport
PARTIES:
  Bulgaria
  Denmark

109877   Bilateral Agreement   **0 UNTS 0**
SIGNED: 1 Apr 69   FORCE: 1 Apr 69
REGISTERED: 5 Sep 69 Denmark
ARTICLES: 0
HEADNOTE: CONTRIBUTION
TOPIC: Loans and Credits
PARTIES:
  Asian Devel Bank
  Denmark

109878   Bilateral Exchange   **0 UNTS 0**
SIGNED: 16 Aug 65   FORCE: 16 Aug 65
REGISTERED: 9 Sep 69 UK Great Britain
ARTICLES: 0
HEADNOTE: CEREALS
TOPIC: Commodity Trade
PARTIES:
  Iraq
  UK Great Britain

109879   Bilateral Exchange   **0 UNTS 0**
SIGNED: 13 Mar 69   FORCE: 13 Mar 69
REGISTERED: 9 Sep 69 UK Great Britain
ARTICLES: 0
HEADNOTE: INTEREST-FREE LOAN
TOPIC: Loans and Credits
PARTIES:
  Indonesia
  UK Great Britain

109880   Bilateral Agreement   **0 UNTS 0**
SIGNED: 28 Mar 69   FORCE: 28 Mar 69
REGISTERED: 9 Sep 69 UK Great Britain
ARTICLES: 0
HEADNOTE: SCIENTIFIC EDUCATIONAL CUL-
TURAL RELATIONS
TOPIC: Scientific Project
PARTIES:
   UK Great Britain
   USSR (Soviet Union)

109881   Bilateral Exchange   **0 UNTS 0**
SIGNED: 31 Mar 69   FORCE: 31 Mar 69
REGISTERED: 9 Sep 69 UK Great Britain
ARTICLES: 0
HEADNOTE: ASSISTANCE EAST-WEST HIGHWAY
TOPIC: Loans and Credits
PARTIES:
   Nepal
   UK Great Britain

109882   Bilateral Agreement   **0 UNTS 0**
SIGNED: 25 Sep 68   FORCE: 20 Dec 68
REGISTERED: 10 Sep 69 India
ARTICLES: 0
HEADNOTE: DOUBLE TAX AIR SHIP
TOPIC: Taxation
PARTIES:
   India
   Romania

109883   Bilateral Exchange   **0 UNTS 0**
SIGNED: 27 May 68   FORCE: 27 May 68
REGISTERED: 11 Sep 69 USA (United States)
ARTICLES: 0
HEADNOTE: SCIENTIFIC COOPERATION
TOPIC: Scientific Project
PARTIES:
   Iran
   USA (United States)

109884   Multilateral Convention   **0 UNTS 0**
SIGNED: 11 Jun 68   FORCE: 5 Sep 68
REGISTERED: 11 Sep 69 Customs Coop Coun
ARTICLES: 0
HEADNOTE: TEMPORARY IMPORT SCIENTIFIC
EQUIPMENT
TOPIC: Scientific Project
PARTIES:
   Algeria RATIFIED: 5 Aug 69 FORCE: 5 Nov 69
   Australia SIGNED: 30 Jun 69 FORCE: 30 Sep 69
   Chad SIGNED: 30 Jun 69 FORCE: 30 Sep 69
   Customs Coop Coun SIGNED: 11 Jun 68 FORCE:
    5 Sep 69
   Dahomey SIGNED: 16 Jan 69 FORCE: 5 Sep 69
   Denmark SIGNED: 5 Jun 69 FORCE: 5 Sep 69
   France SIGNED: 22 May 69 FORCE: 5 Sep 69
   Gabon RATIFIED: 25 Aug 69 FORCE: 25 Nov 69
   Germany, West SIGNED: 10 Jun 69 FORCE:
    10 Sep 69
   Ghana SIGNED: 15 Jan 69 FORCE: 5 Sep 69
   Libya SIGNED: 18 Jun 69 FORCE: 18 Sep 69
   Niger SIGNED: 22 Feb 69 FORCE: 5 Sep 69
   Singapore RATIFIED: 8 Sep 69 FORCE: 8 Dec 69
   UK Great Britain SIGNED: 30 Jun 69 FORCE:
    30 Sep 69

109885   Bilateral Convention   **0 UNTS 0**
SIGNED: 27 Nov 68   FORCE: 9 Apr 69
REGISTERED: 11 Sep 69 Bulgaria
ARTICLES: 0
HEADNOTE: LEGAL ASSISTANCE CIVIL CRIMINAL
TOPIC: Admin Cooperation
PARTIES:
   Bulgaria
   Mongolia

109886   Bilateral Agreement   **0 UNTS 0**
SIGNED: 4 Jun 69   FORCE: 4 Jul 69
REGISTERED: 16 Sep 69 Finland
ARTICLES: 0
HEADNOTE: AIR SERVICES
TOPIC: Air Transport
PARTIES:
   Austria
   Finland

109887   Bilateral Exchange   **0 UNTS 0**
SIGNED: 8 May 69   FORCE: 8 May 69
REGISTERED: 19 Sep 69 Denmark
ARTICLES: 0
HEADNOTE: DANISH WHEAT GRANT
TOPIC: General Aid
PARTIES:
   Denmark
   India

109888   Bilateral Exchange   **643 UNTS 121**
SIGNED: 22 Jun 67   FORCE: 22 Jun 67
REGISTERED: 20 Aug 68 USSR (Soviet Union)
ARTICLES: 10 LANGUAGE: Russian. French.
HEADNOTE: BOUVETOYA WEATHER STATION
TOPIC: Scientific Project
PARTIES:
   Norway
   South Africa

109889   Bilateral Agreement   **0 UNTS 0**
SIGNED: 14 May 69   FORCE: 25 Jun 69
REGISTERED: 25 Sep 69 IBRD (World Bank)
ARTICLES: 0
HEADNOTE: GUARANTEE KINGSTON WATER
SUPPLY
TOPIC: IBRD Project
PARTIES:
   Jamaica
   IBRD (World Bank)

109890   Multilateral Agreement   **0 UNTS 0**
SIGNED: 26 Apr 67   FORCE: 12 Dec 68
REGISTERED: 25 Sep 69 Netherlands
ARTICLES: 0
HEADNOTE: LONG-TERM TRADE
TOPIC: General Trade
PARTIES:
   Belgium   SIGNED: 26 Apr 67   RATIFIED:
    12 Dec 68 FORCE: 12 Dec 68
   Hungary   SIGNED: 26 Apr 67   RATIFIED:
    12 Dec 68 FORCE: 12 Dec 68
   Luxembourg   SIGNED: 26 Apr 67   RATIFIED:
    12 Dec 68 FORCE: 12 Dec 68
   Netherlands   SIGNED: 26 Apr 67   RATIFIED:
    12 Dec 68 FORCE: 12 Dec 68

109891   Bilateral Agreement   **0 UNTS 0**
SIGNED: 11 Apr 69   FORCE: 15 Jul 69
REGISTERED: 27 Sep 69 IBRD (World Bank)
ARTICLES: 0
HEADNOTE: LOAN EDUCATION
TOPIC: IBRD Project
PARTIES:
   IBRD (World Bank)
   Zambia

109892   Bilateral Agreement   **0 UNTS 0**
SIGNED: 29 May 69   FORCE: 22 Aug 69
REGISTERED: 27 Sep 69 IBRD (World Bank)
ARTICLES: 0
HEADNOTE: LOAN THIRD RAILWAY
TOPIC: IBRD Project
PARTIES:
   Taiwan
   IBRD (World Bank)

109893   Bilateral Agreement   **0 UNTS 0**
SIGNED: 4 Jun 69   FORCE: 14 Aug 69
REGISTERED: 27 Sep 69 IBRD (World Bank)
ARTICLES: 0
HEADNOTE: GUARANTEE SECOND RURAL
CREDIT
TOPIC: IBRD Project
PARTIES:
   Philippines
   IBRD (World Bank)

109894   Bilateral Agreement   **0 UNTS 0**
SIGNED: 18 Jun 69   FORCE: 12 Sep 69
REGISTERED: 27 Sep 69 IBRD (World Bank)
ARTICLES: 0
HEADNOTE: LOAN TARAI SEEDS
TOPIC: IBRD Project
PARTIES:
   India
   IBRD (World Bank)

109895   Bilateral Exchange   **0 UNTS 0**
SIGNED: 9 Aug 65   FORCE: 27 Apr 67
REGISTERED: 1 Oct 69 USA (United States)
ARTICLES: 0
HEADNOTE: INVESTMENT GUARANTY
TOPIC: Finance
PARTIES:
   Rwanda
   USA (United States)

109896   Bilateral Exchange   **0 UNTS 0**
SIGNED: 7 Jan 67   FORCE: 22 Aug 67
REGISTERED: 1 Oct 69 USA (United States)
ARTICLES: 0
HEADNOTE: INVESTMENT GUARANTY
TOPIC: Finance
PARTIES:
   Indonesia
   USA (United States)

109897   Bilateral Agreement   **0 UNTS 0**
SIGNED: 15 Mar 67   FORCE: 15 Mar 67
REGISTERED: 1 Oct 69 USA (United States)
ARTICLES: 0
HEADNOTE: AGRI COMMOD
TOPIC: US Agri Commod Aid
PARTIES:
   Congo (Zaire)
   USA (United States)

109898   Bilateral Agreement   **0 UNTS 0**
SIGNED: 17 Mar 67   FORCE: 17 Mar 67
REGISTERED: 1 Oct 69 USA (United States)
ARTICLES: 0
HEADNOTE: AGRI COMMOD
TOPIC: US Agri Commod Aid
PARTIES:
   Tunisia
   USA (United States)

109899   Bilateral Exchange   **0 UNTS 0**
SIGNED: 4 Apr 67   FORCE: 4 Apr 67
REGISTERED: 1 Oct 69 USA (United States)
ARTICLES: 0
HEADNOTE: CONTINUE CERTAIN UK TREATIES
TOPIC: Recognition
PARTIES:
   Malawi
   USA (United States)

109900   Bilateral Exchange   **0 UNTS 0**
SIGNED: 24 Apr 67   FORCE: 24 Apr 67
REGISTERED: 1 Oct 69 USA (United States)
ARTICLES: 0
HEADNOTE: LIABILITY NS SAVANNAH
TOPIC: Finance
PARTIES:
   USA (United States)
   Yugoslavia

109901   Bilateral Exchange   **0 UNTS 0**
SIGNED: 26 May 67   FORCE: 26 May 67
REGISTERED: 1 Oct 69 USA (United States)
ARTICLES: 0
HEADNOTE: OFFSHORE FISHERY DEVELOPMENT
TOPIC: Direct Aid
PARTIES:
   FAO (Food Agri)
   USA (United States)

109902   Bilateral Exchange   **0 UNTS 0**
SIGNED: 5 Jun 67   FORCE: 5 Jun 67
REGISTERED: 1 Oct 69 USA (United States)
ARTICLES: 0
HEADNOTE: AMATEUR RADIO
TOPIC: Gen Communications
PARTIES:
   El Salvador
   USA (United States)

109903   Bilateral Agreement   **0 UNTS 0**
SIGNED: 5 Jun 67   FORCE: 5 Jun 67
REGISTERED: 1 Oct 69 USA (United States)
ARTICLES: 0
HEADNOTE: AGRI COMMOD
TOPIC: US Agri Commod Aid

PARTIES:
Iceland
USA (United States)

109904   Bilateral Exchange   **0 UNTS 0**
SIGNED: 8 Jun 67   FORCE: 8 Jun 67
REGISTERED: 1 Oct 69 USA (United States)
ARTICLES: 0
HEADNOTE: LIABILITY NS SAVANNAH
TOPIC: Water Transport
PARTIES:
Taiwan
USA (United States)

109905   Bilateral Agreement   **0 UNTS 0**
SIGNED: 15 Jun 67   FORCE: 1 Sep 67
REGISTERED: 1 Oct 69 USA (United States)
ARTICLES: 0
HEADNOTE: PARCEL POST
TOPIC: Postal Service
PARTIES:
Ethiopia
USA (United States)

109906   Bilateral Instrument   **0 UNTS 0**
SIGNED: 24 Jun 67   FORCE: 24 Jun 67
REGISTERED: 1 Oct 69 USA (United States)
ARTICLES: 0
HEADNOTE: SUPPLEMENT AGRI COMMOD
TOPIC: US Agri Commod Aid
PARTIES:
India
USA (United States)

109907   Bilateral Exchange   **0 UNTS 0**
SIGNED: 3 Jul 67   FORCE: 3 Jul 67
REGISTERED: 1 Oct 69 USA (United States)
ARTICLES: 0
HEADNOTE: PEACE CORPS
TOPIC: Direct Aid
PARTIES:
Dahomey
USA (United States)

109908   Bilateral Exchange   **0 UNTS 0**
SIGNED: 12 Jul 67   FORCE: 12 Jul 67
REGISTERED: 1 Oct 69 USA (United States)
ARTICLES: 0
HEADNOTE: US COPYRIGHT, TIME EXTENSION
TOPIC: Patents/Copyrights
PARTIES:
Germany, West
USA (United States)

109909   Bilateral Agreement   **0 UNTS 0**
SIGNED: 19 Jul 67   FORCE: 19 Jul 67
REGISTERED: 1 Oct 69 USA (United States)
ARTICLES: 0
HEADNOTE: AGRI COMMOD
TOPIC: US Agri Commod Aid
PARTIES:
Afghanistan
USA (United States)

109910   Bilateral Exchange   **0 UNTS 0**
SIGNED: 21 Jul 67   FORCE: 21 Jul 67
REGISTERED: 1 Oct 69 USA (United States)
ARTICLES: 0
HEADNOTE: INVESTMENT GUARANTY
TOPIC: Finance
PARTIES:
Malawi
USA (United States)

109911   Bilateral Exchange   **0 UNTS 0**
SIGNED: 25 Jul 67   FORCE: 25 Jul 67
REGISTERED: 1 Oct 69 USA (United States)
ARTICLES: 0
HEADNOTE: DEPLOY USS YELLOWSTONE
TOPIC: General Military
PARTIES:
Malta
USA (United States)

109912   Bilateral Instrument   **0 UNTS 0**
SIGNED: 3 Aug 67   FORCE: 3 Aug 67
REGISTERED: 1 Oct 69 USA (United States)
ARTICLES: 0
HEADNOTE: SUPPLEMENT AGRI COMMOD
TOPIC: US Agri Commod Aid
PARTIES:
Pakistan
USA (United States)

109913   Bilateral Exchange   **0 UNTS 0**
SIGNED: 8 Aug 67   FORCE: 8 Aug 67
REGISTERED: 1 Oct 69 USA (United States)
ARTICLES: 0
HEADNOTE: CIVIL EMERGENCY PLANNING
TOPIC: Scientific Project
PARTIES:
Canada
USA (United States)

109914   Bilateral Exchange   **0 UNTS 0**
SIGNED: 11 Aug 67   FORCE: 11 Aug 67
REGISTERED: 1 Oct 69 USA (United States)
ARTICLES: 0
HEADNOTE: STUDY POLAR CAP IONOSPHERE
TOPIC: Scientific Project
PARTIES:
Canada
USA (United States)

109915   Bilateral Exchange   **0 UNTS 0**
SIGNED: 24 Aug 67   FORCE: 24 Aug 67
REGISTERED: 1 Oct 69 USA (United States)
ARTICLES: 0
HEADNOTE: RESOURCES WITHIN US MILITARY
BASES
TOPIC: General Military
PARTIES:
Philippines
USA (United States)

109916   Bilateral Exchange   **0 UNTS 0**
SIGNED: 31 Aug 67   FORCE: 31 Aug 67
REGISTERED: 1 Oct 69 USA (United States)
ARTICLES: 0
HEADNOTE: TRADE COTTON TEXTILES
TOPIC: Commodity Trade
PARTIES:
India
USA (United States)

109917   Bilateral Instrument   **0 UNTS 0**
SIGNED: 12 Sep 67   FORCE: 12 Sep 67
REGISTERED: 1 Oct 69 USA (United States)
ARTICLES: 0
HEADNOTE: SUPPLEMENT AGRI COMMOD
TOPIC: US Agri Commod Aid
PARTIES:
India
USA (United States)

109918   Bilateral Agreement   **0 UNTS 0**
SIGNED: 15 Sep 67   FORCE: 15 Sep 67
REGISTERED: 1 Oct 69 USA (United States)
ARTICLES: 0
HEADNOTE: AGRI COMMOD
TOPIC: US Agri Commod Aid
PARTIES:
Indonesia
USA (United States)

109919   Bilateral Exchange   **0 UNTS 0**
SIGNED: 18 Sep 67   FORCE: 3 Oct 67
REGISTERED: 1 Oct 69 USA (United States)
ARTICLES: 0
HEADNOTE: AMATEUR RADIO
TOPIC: Gen Communications
PARTIES:
USA (United States)
Venezuela

109920   Bilateral Instrument   **0 UNTS 0**
SIGNED: 21 Sep 67   FORCE: 21 Sep 67
REGISTERED: 1 Oct 69 USA (United States)
ARTICLES: 0
HEADNOTE: SUPPLEMENT AGRI COMMOD
TOPIC: US Agri Commod Aid
PARTIES:
USA (United States)
Vietnam, South

109921   Bilateral Exchange   **0 UNTS 0**
SIGNED: 21 Sep 67   FORCE: 1 Jan 68
REGISTERED: 1 Oct 69 USA (United States)
ARTICLES: 0
HEADNOTE: COTTON TEXTILES
TOPIC: Commodity Trade
PARTIES:
Philippines
USA (United States)

109922   Bilateral Exchange   **0 UNTS 0**
SIGNED: 22 Sep 67   FORCE: 22 Sep 67
REGISTERED: 1 Oct 69 USA (United States)
ARTICLES: 0
HEADNOTE: PEACE CORPS
TOPIC: Direct Aid
PARTIES:
Lesotho
USA (United States)

109923   Bilateral Exchange   **0 UNTS 0**
SIGNED: 29 Sep 67   FORCE: 29 Sep 67
REGISTERED: 1 Oct 69 USA (United States)
ARTICLES: 0
HEADNOTE: COTTON TEXTILES
TOPIC: Commodity Trade
PARTIES:
Jamaica
USA (United States)

109924   Bilateral Agreement   **0 UNTS 0**
SIGNED: 29 Sep 67   FORCE: 29 Sep 67
REGISTERED: 1 Oct 69 USA (United States)
ARTICLES: 0
HEADNOTE: INVESTMENT GUARANTY
TOPIC: Finance
PARTIES:
Swaziland
USA (United States)

109925   Bilateral Exchange   **0 UNTS 0**
SIGNED: 27 Oct 67   FORCE: 1 Jan 68
REGISTERED: 1 Oct 69 USA (United States)
ARTICLES: 0
HEADNOTE: FISHERY ZONES CONTIGUOUS
TOPIC: Specific Resources
PARTIES:
Mexico
USA (United States)

109926   Bilateral Exchange   **0 UNTS 0**
SIGNED: 28 Mar 68   FORCE: 27 Apr 38
REGISTERED: 1 Oct 69 USA (United States)
ARTICLES: 0
HEADNOTE: WAIVER VISA FEES
TOPIC: Visas
PARTIES:
Korea, South
USA (United States)

109927   Bilateral Agreement   **0 UNTS 0**
SIGNED: 18 Aug 69   FORCE: 18 Aug 69
REGISTERED: 1 Oct 69 United Nations
ARTICLES: 0
HEADNOTE: REVISED STANDARD TECHNICAL
ASSISTANCE
TOPIC: Tech Assistance
PARTIES:
State/IGO Group
Swaziland

109928   Bilateral Agreement   **0 UNTS 0**
SIGNED: 18 Aug 69   FORCE: 18 Aug 69
REGISTERED: 1 Oct 69 United Nations
ARTICLES: 0
HEADNOTE: STANDARD OPERATIONAL ASSIS-
TANCE
TOPIC: IGO Operations
PARTIES:
State/IGO Group
Swaziland

109929   Bilateral Agreement   **0 UNTS 0**
SIGNED: 18 Aug 69   FORCE: 18 Aug 69
REGISTERED: 1 Oct 69 United Nations
ARTICLES: 0
HEADNOTE: SPECIAL FUND ASSISTANCE
TOPIC: Direct Aid
PARTIES:
  UN Special Fund
  Swaziland

109930   Bilateral Agreement   **0 UNTS 0**
SIGNED: 9 Sep 69   FORCE: 9 Sep 69
REGISTERED: 1 Oct 69 United Nations
ARTICLES: 0
HEADNOTE: ASSIST ASIAN STATISTICAL INSTI-
TUTE
TOPIC: Education
PARTIES:
  Japan
  UN Special Fund

109931   Bilateral Agreement   **0 UNTS 0**
SIGNED: 6 May 69   FORCE: 6 May 69
REGISTERED: 3 Oct 69 Denmark
ARTICLES: 0
HEADNOTE: AIR SERVICES
TOPIC: Air Transport
PARTIES:
  Denmark
  Malta

109932   Bilateral Agreement   **0 UNTS 0**
SIGNED: 20 Jun 69   FORCE: 20 Jun 69
REGISTERED: 3 Oct 69 Denmark
ARTICLES: 0
HEADNOTE: PUBLIC HEALTH DENTAL SCHOOL
TOPIC: Education
PARTIES:
  Denmark
  Uganda

109933   Bilateral Convention   **0 UNTS 0**
SIGNED: 6 Feb 57   FORCE: 15 Feb 57
REGISTERED: 8 Oct 69 France
ARTICLES: 0
HEADNOTE: ADMINISTRATIVE TECHNICAL COOP-
ERATION
TOPIC: Admin Cooperation
PARTIES:
  France
  Morocco

109934   Bilateral Exchange   **0 UNTS 0**
SIGNED: 23 Jul 63   FORCE: 23 Jul 63
REGISTERED: 8 Oct 69 France
ARTICLES: 0
HEADNOTE: FRENCH CIVIL SERVICE PENSION
TOPIC: Non-ILO Labor
PARTIES:
  France
  Morocco

109935   Bilateral Exchange   **0 UNTS 0**
SIGNED: 17 Oct 64   FORCE: 17 Oct 64
REGISTERED: 8 Oct 69 France
ARTICLES: 0
HEADNOTE: COMMON PENSION FUND
TOPIC: Non-ILO Labor
PARTIES:
  France
  Morocco

109936   Bilateral Convention   **0 UNTS 0**
SIGNED: 9 Jul 65   FORCE: 1 Jan 67
REGISTERED: 8 Oct 69 France
ARTICLES: 0
HEADNOTE: SOCIAL SECURITY
TOPIC: Non-ILO Labor
PARTIES:
  France
  Morocco

109937   Bilateral Exchange   **0 UNTS 0**
SIGNED: 15 Aug 68   FORCE: 14 Oct 68
REGISTERED: 8 Oct 69 Ireland
ARTICLES: 0

HEADNOTE: WAIVING VISAS
TOPIC: Visas
PARTIES:
  Ireland
  Mexico

109938   Bilateral Exchange   **0 UNTS 0**
SIGNED: 10 Oct 68   FORCE: 10 Oct 68
REGISTERED: 8 Oct 69 Ireland
ARTICLES: 0
HEADNOTE: AMATEUR RADIO
TOPIC: Gen Communications
PARTIES:
  Ireland
  USA (United States)

109940   Bilateral Exchange   **0 UNTS 0**
SIGNED: 25 Mar 69   FORCE: 1 Apr 69
REGISTERED: 9 Oct 69 Jamaica
ARTICLES: 0
HEADNOTE: VISA SUPPRESSION
TOPIC: Visas
PARTIES:
  Denmark
  Jamaica

109941   Bilateral Exchange   **0 UNTS 0**
SIGNED: 31 Mar 69   FORCE: 1 Apr 69
REGISTERED: 9 Oct 69 Jamaica
ARTICLES: 0
HEADNOTE: VISA SUPPRESSION
TOPIC: Visas
PARTIES:
  Jamaica
  Norway

109942   Bilateral Exchange   **0 UNTS 0**
SIGNED: 1 Apr 69   FORCE: 1 Apr 69
REGISTERED: 9 Oct 69 Jamaica
ARTICLES: 0
HEADNOTE: VISA SUPPRESSION
TOPIC: Visas
PARTIES:
  Jamaica
  Sweden

109943   Bilateral Exchange   **0 UNTS 0**
SIGNED: 2 Jul 69   FORCE: 1 Aug 69
REGISTERED: 9 Oct 69 Jamaica
ARTICLES: 0
HEADNOTE: VISA SUPPRESSION
TOPIC: Visas
PARTIES:
  Iceland
  Jamaica

109944   Bilateral Agreement   **0 UNTS 0**
SIGNED: 30 Sep 68   FORCE: 5 Jun 69
REGISTERED: 13 Oct 69 IAEA (Atom Energy)
ARTICLES: 0
HEADNOTE: SAFEGUARDS
TOPIC: Atomic Energy
PARTIES:
  IAEA (Atom Energy)
  USA (United States)

109945   Bilateral Agreement   **0 UNTS 0**
SIGNED: 4 Mar 69   FORCE: 20 Aug 69
REGISTERED: 13 Oct 69 IAEA (Atom Energy)
ARTICLES: 0
HEADNOTE: SAFEGUARDS
TOPIC: Atomic Energy
PARTIES:
  IAEA (Atom Energy)
  USA (United States)

109946   Bilateral Agreement   **0 UNTS 0**
SIGNED: 25 Apr 69   FORCE: 17 Jun 69
REGISTERED: 13 Oct 69 IBRD (World Bank)
ARTICLES: 0
HEADNOTE: GUARANTEE SECOND POWER DIS-
TRIBUTION
TOPIC: IBRD Project
PARTIES:
  IBRD (World Bank)
  Singapore

109947   Bilateral Agreement   **0 UNTS 0**
SIGNED: 3 Jun 69   FORCE: 3 Jun 69
REGISTERED: 13 Oct 69 IAEA (Atom Energy)
ARTICLES: 0
HEADNOTE: IRRADIATION EQUIPMENT
TOPIC: Atomic Energy
PARTIES:
  Argentina
  IAEA (Atom Energy)

109948   Bilateral Agreement   **0 UNTS 0**
SIGNED: 13 Jun 69   FORCE: 25 Jul 69
REGISTERED: 13 Oct 69 IAEA (Atom Energy)
ARTICLES: 0
HEADNOTE: SAFEGUARDS
TOPIC: Atomic Energy
PARTIES:
  State/IGO Group
  IAEA (Atom Energy)

109949   Bilateral Agreement   **0 UNTS 0**
SIGNED: 20 Jun 69   FORCE: 10 Jul 69
REGISTERED: 13 Oct 69 IBRD (World Bank)
ARTICLES: 0
HEADNOTE: LOAN MONROVIA PORT DREDGING
TOPIC: IBRD Project
PARTIES:
  Liberia
  IBRD (World Bank)

109950   Bilateral Agreement   **0 UNTS 0**
SIGNED: 11 Jul 69   FORCE: 19 Jul 69
REGISTERED: 13 Oct 69 IAEA (Atom Energy)
ARTICLES: 0
HEADNOTE: SAFEGUARDS
TOPIC: Atomic Energy
PARTIES:
  State/IGO Group
  IAEA (Atom Energy)

109951   Bilateral Agreement   **0 UNTS 0**
SIGNED: 24 May 67   FORCE: 1 Apr 69
REGISTERED: 16 Oct 69 Denmark
ARTICLES: 0
HEADNOTE: AIR SERVICES
TOPIC: Air Transport
PARTIES:
  Afghanistan
  Denmark

109952   Multilateral Agreement   **0 UNTS 0**
SIGNED: 5 Dec 68   FORCE: 1 Oct 69
REGISTERED: 16 Oct 69 Norway
ARTICLES: 0
HEADNOTE: RECORDING POPULATION DATA
TOPIC: Scientific Project
PARTIES:
  Denmark SIGNED: 5 Dec 68 FORCE: 1 Oct 69
  Finland SIGNED: 5 Dec 68 FORCE: 1 Oct 69
  Iceland SIGNED: 5 Dec 68 FORCE: 1 Oct 69
  Norway SIGNED: 5 Dec 68 FORCE: 1 Oct 69
  Sweden SIGNED: 5 Dec 68 FORCE: 1 Oct 69

109953   Bilateral Agreement   **0 UNTS 0**
SIGNED: 12 Apr 69   FORCE: 5 Jun 69
REGISTERED: 17 Oct 69 Denmark
ARTICLES: 0
HEADNOTE: DANISH LOAN
TOPIC: Loans and Credits
PARTIES:
  Denmark
  United Arab Rep

109954   Bilateral Agreement   **0 UNTS 0**
SIGNED: 28 Jun 62   FORCE: 10 Feb 64
REGISTERED: 20 Oct 69 Bulgaria
ARTICLES: 0
HEADNOTE: CULTURE
TOPIC: Culture
PARTIES:
  Bulgaria
  Syria

109955   Bilateral Agreement   **0 UNTS 0**
SIGNED: 20 Feb 63   FORCE: 28 Aug 63
REGISTERED: 20 Oct 69 Bulgaria

ARTICLES: 0
HEADNOTE: CULTURAL RELATIONS
TOPIC: Culture
PARTIES:
  Bulgaria
  India

109956   Bilateral Agreement   **0 UNTS 0**
SIGNED: 13 Dec 64   FORCE: 13 Dec 64
REGISTERED: 20 Oct 69 Bulgaria
ARTICLES: 0
HEADNOTE: AIR TRANSPORT
TOPIC: Air Transport
PARTIES:
  Bulgaria
  Syria

109957   Bilateral Agreement   **0 UNTS 0**
SIGNED: 8 May 65   FORCE: 8 May 65
REGISTERED: 20 Oct 69 Bulgaria
ARTICLES: 0
HEADNOTE: COMMERCIAL SCHEDULED SER-
VICES
TOPIC: Air Transport
PARTIES:
  Bulgaria
  Cyprus

109958   Bilateral Agreement   **0 UNTS 0**
SIGNED: 4 Aug 65   FORCE: 4 Aug 65
REGISTERED: 20 Oct 69 Bulgaria
ARTICLES: 0
HEADNOTE: AIR TRANSPORT
TOPIC: Air Transport
PARTIES:
  Bulgaria
  France

109959   Bilateral Agreement   **0 UNTS 0**
SIGNED: 8 Nov 65   FORCE: 29 Dec 66
REGISTERED: 20 Oct 69 Bulgaria
ARTICLES: 0
HEADNOTE: SCIENTIFIC TECHNICAL COOPER-
ATION
TOPIC: Scientific Project
PARTIES:
  Bulgaria
  Syria

109960   Bilateral Agreement   **0 UNTS 0**
SIGNED: 17 Nov 65   FORCE: 25 Jul 66
REGISTERED: 20 Oct 69 Bulgaria
ARTICLES: 0
HEADNOTE: TOURISM
TOPIC: Visas
PARTIES:
  Bulgaria
  United Arab Rep

109961   Bilateral Agreement   **0 UNTS 0**
SIGNED: 12 Jun 66   FORCE: 29 Dec 68
REGISTERED: 20 Oct 69 Bulgaria
ARTICLES: 0
HEADNOTE: TOURISM
TOPIC: Visas
PARTIES:
  Bulgaria
  Syria

109962   Bilateral Agreement   **0 UNTS 0**
SIGNED: 15 Jul 66   FORCE: 15 Jul 66
REGISTERED: 20 Oct 69 Bulgaria
ARTICLES: 0
HEADNOTE: SCIENTIFIC TECHNICAL COOPER-
ATION
TOPIC: Scientific Project
PARTIES:
  Bulgaria
  Tanzania

109963   Bilateral Agreement   **0 UNTS 0**
SIGNED: 29 Aug 66   FORCE: 22 Aug 68
REGISTERED: 20 Oct 69 Bulgaria
ARTICLES: 0
HEADNOTE: PLANT PROTECTION
TOPIC: Sanitation

PARTIES:
  Bulgaria
  United Arab Rep

109964   Bilateral Agreement   **0 UNTS 0**
SIGNED: 20 Sep 66   FORCE: 24 Dec 66
REGISTERED: 20 Oct 69 Bulgaria
ARTICLES: 0
HEADNOTE: ECONOMIC INDUSTRIAL TECHNICAL
COOPERATION
TOPIC: General Economic
PARTIES:
  Bulgaria
  Italy

109965   Bilateral Agreement   **0 UNTS 0**
SIGNED: 15 Nov 66   FORCE: 23 Dec 67
REGISTERED: 20 Oct 69 Bulgaria
ARTICLES: 0
HEADNOTE: AIR TRANSPORT
TOPIC: Air Transport
PARTIES:
  Bulgaria
  Iraq

109966   Bilateral Agreement   **0 UNTS 0**
SIGNED: 6 Mar 67   FORCE: 10 Oct 68
REGISTERED: 20 Oct 69 Bulgaria
ARTICLES: 0
HEADNOTE: SCIENTIFIC TECHNICAL COOPER-
ATION
TOPIC: Scientific Project
PARTIES:
  Bulgaria
  Sudan

109967   Bilateral Convention   **0 UNTS 0**
SIGNED: 30 May 67   FORCE: 7 Jun 68
REGISTERED: 20 Oct 69 Bulgaria
ARTICLES: 0
HEADNOTE: VETERINARY
TOPIC: Sanitation
PARTIES:
  Bulgaria
  Turkey

109968   Bilateral Agreement   **0 UNTS 0**
SIGNED: 19 Oct 67   FORCE: 19 Oct 67
REGISTERED: 20 Oct 69 Bulgaria
ARTICLES: 0
HEADNOTE: BULGARIAN PHYSICIANS IN SWE-
DEN
TOPIC: Education
PARTIES:
  Bulgaria
  Sweden

109969   Bilateral Exchange   **0 UNTS 0**
SIGNED: 14 Dec 67   FORCE: 1 Jan 68
REGISTERED: 20 Oct 69 Bulgaria
ARTICLES: 0
HEADNOTE: VISA ABOLITION
TOPIC: Visas
PARTIES:
  Bulgaria
  Finland

109970   Bilateral Convention   **0 UNTS 0**
SIGNED: 19 Mar 68   FORCE: 22 Nov 68
REGISTERED: 20 Oct 69 Bulgaria
ARTICLES: 0
HEADNOTE: PLANT PROTECTION
TOPIC: Sanitation
PARTIES:
  Bulgaria
  Finland

109971   Multilateral Agreement   **0 UNTS 0**
SIGNED: 10 Jul 67   FORCE: 30 May 68
REGISTERED: 21 Oct 69 ICAO (Civil Aviat)
ARTICLES: 0
HEADNOTE: ICAO TARIFFS
TOPIC: Air Transport
PARTIES:
  Finland SIGNED: 10 Jul 67 RATIFIED: 30 Apr 68
    FORCE: 30 May 68

France SIGNED: 10 Jul 67 RATIFIED: 4 Aug 67
    FORCE: 30 May 68
Ireland SIGNED: 10 Jul 67 RATIFIED: 15 Mar 68
    FORCE: 30 May 68
Portugal SIGNED: 10 Jul 67 RATIFIED: 8 Mar 68
    FORCE: 30 May 68
ICAO (Civil Aviat) SIGNED: 10 Jul 67 FORCE:
    30 May 68
Spain SIGNED: 10 Jul 67 RATIFIED: 16 Feb 67
    FORCE: 16 Mar 69
UK Great Britain SIGNED: 10 Jul 67 RATIFIED:
    4 Apr 68 FORCE: 30 May 68

109972   Bilateral Agreement   **0 UNTS 0**
SIGNED: 29 Oct 68   FORCE: 30 Sep 69
REGISTERED: 22 Oct 69 Philippines
ARTICLES: 0
HEADNOTE: AIR TRANSPORT
TOPIC: Air Transport
PARTIES:
  France
  Philippines

109973   Bilateral Convention   **0 UNTS 0**
SIGNED: 7 Aug 69   FORCE: 7 Aug 69
REGISTERED: 22 Oct 69 Belgium
ARTICLES: 0
HEADNOTE: TUNISIAN WORKERS IN BELGIUM
TOPIC: Non-ILO Labor
PARTIES:
  Belgium
  Tunisia

109974   Bilateral Agreement   **0 UNTS 0**
SIGNED: 7 Aug 69   FORCE: 7 Aug 69
REGISTERED: 22 Oct 69 Belgium
ARTICLES: 0
HEADNOTE: TRAINEES ADMISSION
TOPIC: Education
PARTIES:
  Belgium
  Tunisia

109975   Bilateral Agreement   **0 UNTS 0**
SIGNED: 30 Mar 67   FORCE: 1 Sep 69
REGISTERED: 27 Oct 69 Denmark
ARTICLES: 0
HEADNOTE: FRONTIER TRAFFIC CUSTOMS
TOPIC: Customs
PARTIES:
  Denmark
  Germany, West

109976   Bilateral Agreement   **0 UNTS 0**
SIGNED: 24 Oct 68   FORCE: 29 Jan 69
REGISTERED: 27 Oct 69 Saudi Arabia
ARTICLES: 0
HEADNOTE: ARABIYAH FARSI ISLANDS BOUND-
ARY
TOPIC: Territory Boundary
PARTIES:
  Iran
  Saudi Arabia

109977   Bilateral Agreement   **0 UNTS 0**
SIGNED: 10 Dec 68   FORCE: 25 Sep 69
REGISTERED: 27 Oct 69 Finland
ARTICLES: 0
HEADNOTE: FRONTIER CUSTOMS COOPERATION
TOPIC: Territory Boundary
PARTIES:
  Finland
  Norway

109978   Bilateral Agreement   **0 UNTS 0**
SIGNED: 15 Aug 69   FORCE: 29 Aug 69
REGISTERED: 30 Oct 69 Burma
ARTICLES: 0
HEADNOTE: AIR TRANSPORT
TOPIC: Air Transport
PARTIES:
  Burma
  Thailand

109979   Bilateral Agreement   **0 UNTS 0**
SIGNED: 12 Jun 63   FORCE: 12 Jun 63

REGISTERED: 1 Nov 69 USA (United States)
ARTICLES: 0
HEADNOTE: INVESTMENT GUARANTY
TOPIC: Finance
PARTIES:
 Senegal
 USA (United States)

109980 Multilateral Convention **0 UNTS 0**
SIGNED: 22 Dec 66 FORCE: 19 Dec 67
REGISTERED: 1 Nov 69 USA (United States)
ARTICLES: 0
HEADNOTE: DOUBLE TAX INCOME, TRADE
TOPIC: Taxation
PARTIES:
 Trinidad/Tobago
 USA (United States)

109981 Bilateral Exchange **0 UNTS 0**
SIGNED: 4 Jul 67 FORCE: 4 Jul 67
REGISTERED: 1 Nov 69 USA (United States)
ARTICLES: 0
HEADNOTE: AUSTRIAN VEHICLE TAX
TOPIC: Taxation
PARTIES:
 Austria
 USA (United States)

109982 Bilateral Exchange **0 UNTS 0**
SIGNED: 1 Aug 67 FORCE: 1 Aug 67
REGISTERED: 1 Nov 69 USA (United States)
ARTICLES: 0
HEADNOTE: SETTLEMENT CLAIM PIOUS FUND
 CALIFORNIA
TOPIC: Claims and Debts
PARTIES:
 Mexico
 USA (United States)

109983 Bilateral Agreement **0 UNTS 0**
SIGNED: 24 Oct 67 FORCE: 24 Oct 67
REGISTERED: 1 Nov 69 USA (United States)
ARTICLES: 0
HEADNOTE: AGRI COMMOD
TOPIC: US Agri Commod Aid
PARTIES:
 USA (United States)
 Vietnam, South

109984 Bilateral Agreement **0 UNTS 0**
SIGNED: 24 Oct 67 FORCE: 24 Oct 67
REGISTERED: 1 Nov 69 USA (United States)
ARTICLES: 0
HEADNOTE: AGRI COMMOD
TOPIC: US Agri Commod Aid
PARTIES:
 Ceylon (Sri Lanka)
 USA (United States)

109985 Bilateral Agreement **0 UNTS 0**
SIGNED: 24 Oct 67 FORCE: 24 Oct 67
REGISTERED: 1 Nov 69 USA (United States)
ARTICLES: 0
HEADNOTE: AGRI COMMOD
TOPIC: US Agri Commod Aid
PARTIES:
 Ghana
 USA (United States)

109986 Bilateral Agreement **0 UNTS 0**
SIGNED: 3 Jan 68 FORCE: 3 Jan 68
REGISTERED: 1 Nov 69 USA (United States)
ARTICLES: 0
HEADNOTE: AGRI COMMOD
TOPIC: US Agri Commod Aid
PARTIES:
 Ghana
 USA (United States)

109987 Bilateral Agreement **0 UNTS 0**
SIGNED: 22 Nov 67 FORCE: 22 Nov 67
REGISTERED: 1 Nov 69 USA (United States)
ARTICLES: 0
HEADNOTE: AGRI COMMOD
TOPIC: US Agri Commod Aid

PARTIES:
 Indonesia
 USA (United States)

109988 Bilateral Agreement **0 UNTS 0**
SIGNED: 15 Feb 68 FORCE: 15 Feb 68
REGISTERED: 1 Nov 69 USA (United States)
ARTICLES: 0
HEADNOTE: AGRI COMMOD
TOPIC: US Agri Commod Aid
PARTIES:
 Indonesia
 USA (United States)

109989 Bilateral Exchange **0 UNTS 0**
SIGNED: 15 Dec 67 FORCE: 15 Dec 67
REGISTERED: 1 Nov 69 USA (United States)
ARTICLES: 0
HEADNOTE: LOAN NAVAL VESSEL
TOPIC: Loans and Credits
PARTIES:
 Taiwan
 USA (United States)

109990 Bilateral Agreement **0 UNTS 0**
SIGNED: 26 Dec 67 FORCE: 15 Dec 67
REGISTERED: 1 Nov 69 USA (United States)
ARTICLES: 0
HEADNOTE: AGRI COMMOD
TOPIC: US Agri Commod Aid
PARTIES:
 Pakistan
 USA (United States)

109991 Bilateral Exchange **0 UNTS 0**
SIGNED: 27 Dec 67 FORCE: 27 Dec 67
REGISTERED: 1 Nov 69 USA (United States)
ARTICLES: 0
HEADNOTE: AMATEUR RADIO
TOPIC: Gen Communications
PARTIES:
 Finland
 USA (United States)

109992 Bilateral Agreement **0 UNTS 0**
SIGNED: 29 Dec 67 FORCE: 29 Dec 67
REGISTERED: 1 Nov 69 USA (United States)
ARTICLES: 0
HEADNOTE: AGRI COMMOD
TOPIC: US Agri Commod Aid
PARTIES:
 Chile
 USA (United States)

109993 Bilateral Agreement **0 UNTS 0**
SIGNED: 30 Dec 67 FORCE: 30 Dec 67
REGISTERED: 1 Nov 69 USA (United States)
ARTICLES: 0
HEADNOTE: AGRI COMMOD, THIRD SUPPLE-
MENT
TOPIC: US Agri Commod Aid
PARTIES:
 India
 USA (United States)

109994 Bilateral Agreement **0 UNTS 0**
SIGNED: 30 Dec 67 FORCE: 30 Dec 67
REGISTERED: 1 Nov 69 USA (United States)
ARTICLES: 0
HEADNOTE: PAYMENTS SURPLUS PROPERTY
TOPIC: Finance
PARTIES:
 Indonesia
 USA (United States)

109995 Bilateral Agreement **0 UNTS 0**
SIGNED: 6 Jan 68 FORCE: 6 Jan 68
REGISTERED: 1 Nov 69 USA (United States)
ARTICLES: 0
HEADNOTE: AGRI COMMOD
TOPIC: US Agri Commod Aid
PARTIES:
 USA (United States)
 Vietnam, South

109996 Bilateral Agreement **0 UNTS 0**
SIGNED: 16 May 68 FORCE: 16 May 68
REGISTERED: 1 Nov 69 USA (United States)
ARTICLES: 0
HEADNOTE: AGRI COMMOD
TOPIC: US Agri Commod Aid
PARTIES:
 Pakistan
 USA (United States)

109997 Bilateral Agreement **0 UNTS 0**
SIGNED: 12 Jan 68 FORCE: 12 Jan 68
REGISTERED: 1 Nov 69 USA (United States)
ARTICLES: 0
HEADNOTE: INVESTMENT GUARANTY
TOPIC: Finance
PARTIES:
 Botswana
 USA (United States)

109998 Bilateral Agreement **0 UNTS 0**
SIGNED: 12 Jan 68 FORCE: 12 Jan 68
REGISTERED: 1 Nov 69 USA (United States)
ARTICLES: 0
HEADNOTE: COTTON TEXTILES
TOPIC: General Trade
PARTIES:
 Japan
 USA (United States)

109999 Bilateral Agreement **0 UNTS 0**
SIGNED: 15 Dec 68 FORCE: 15 Dec 68
REGISTERED: 1 Nov 69 USA (United States)
ARTICLES: 0
HEADNOTE: AIR TRANSPORT
TOPIC: Air Transport
PARTIES:
 Indonesia
 USA (United States)

110000 Bilateral Agreement **0 UNTS 0**
SIGNED: 17 Jan 68 FORCE: 17 Jan 68
REGISTERED: 1 Nov 69 USA (United States)
ARTICLES: 0
HEADNOTE: GEODETIC SURVEY
TOPIC: Scientific Project
PARTIES:
 Mali
 USA (United States)

110001 Bilateral Exchange **0 UNTS 0**
SIGNED: 19 Jan 68 FORCE: 19 Jan 68
REGISTERED: 1 Nov 69 USA (United States)
ARTICLES: 0
HEADNOTE: NAHA ADVISORY COMMISSION
RYUKYU
TOPIC: Admin Cooperation
PARTIES:
 Japan
 USA (United States)

110002 Bilateral Agreement **0 UNTS 0**
SIGNED: 19 Jan 68 FORCE: 19 Jan 68
REGISTERED: 1 Nov 69 USA (United States)
ARTICLES: 0
HEADNOTE: AGRI COMMOD
TOPIC: US Agri Commod Aid
PARTIES:
 USA (United States)
 Uruguay

110003 Bilateral Exchange **0 UNTS 0**
SIGNED: 23 Jan 68 FORCE: 23 Jan 68
REGISTERED: 1 Nov 69 USA (United States)
ARTICLES: 0
HEADNOTE: PHILIPPINE BANK CLARK AIR BASE
TOPIC: Finance
PARTIES:
 Philippines
 USA (United States)

110004 Bilateral Agreement **0 UNTS 0**
SIGNED: 23 Jan 68 FORCE: 23 Jan 68
REGISTERED: 1 Nov 69 USA (United States)
ARTICLES: 0
HEADNOTE: AGRI COMMOD

TOPIC: US Agri Commod Aid
PARTIES:
  Sierra Leone
  USA (United States)

110005   Bilateral Exchange   **0 UNTS 0**
SIGNED: 8 Feb 68   FORCE: 8 Feb 68
REGISTERED: 1 Nov 69 USA (United States)
ARTICLES: 0
HEADNOTE: ECONOMIC TECHNICAL COOPER-
  ATION
TOPIC: General Economic
PARTIES:
  Tanzania
  USA (United States)

110006   Bilateral Exchange   **0 UNTS 0**
SIGNED: 22 Feb 68   FORCE: 22 Feb 68
REGISTERED: 1 Nov 69 USA (United States)
ARTICLES: 0
HEADNOTE: SPECIAL AIR NAVIGATION AIDS
TOPIC: Air Transport
PARTIES:
  Panama
  USA (United States)

110007   Bilateral Agreement   **0 UNTS 0**
SIGNED: 11 Mar 68   FORCE: 11 Mar 68
REGISTERED: 1 Nov 69 USA (United States)
ARTICLES: 0
HEADNOTE: INVESTMENT GUARANTY
TOPIC: Finance
PARTIES:
  Barbados
  USA (United States)

110008   Bilateral Agreement   **0 UNTS 0**
SIGNED: 15 Mar 68   FORCE: 15 Mar 68
REGISTERED: 1 Nov 69 USA (United States)
ARTICLES: 0
HEADNOTE: AGRI COMMOD
TOPIC: US Agri Commod Aid
PARTIES:
  Somalia
  USA (United States)

110009   Multilateral Agreement   **0 UNTS 0**
SIGNED: 18 Mar 68   FORCE: 1 May 68
REGISTERED: 1 Nov 69 USA (United States)
ARTICLES: 0
HEADNOTE: PARCEL POST
TOPIC: Postal Service
PARTIES:
  Trinidad/Tobago
  USA (United States)

110010   Bilateral Agreement   **0 UNTS 0**
SIGNED: 19 Mar 68   FORCE: 19 Mar 68
REGISTERED: 1 Nov 69 USA (United States)
ARTICLES: 0
HEADNOTE: DEVELOP WATER RESOURCES
TOPIC: Specific Resources
PARTIES:
  Iran
  USA (United States)

110011   Bilateral Agreement   **0 UNTS 0**
SIGNED: 4 Apr 68   FORCE: 4 Apr 68
REGISTERED: 1 Nov 69 USA (United States)
ARTICLES: 0
HEADNOTE: AGRI COMMOD
TOPIC: US Agri Commod Aid
PARTIES:
  Jordan
  USA (United States)

110012   Bilateral Exchange   **0 UNTS 0**
SIGNED: 16 Apr 68   FORCE: 16 Apr 68
REGISTERED: 1 Nov 69 USA (United States)
ARTICLES: 0
HEADNOTE: DEPLOY USS SHENANDOAH
TOPIC: Military Mission
PARTIES:
  Malta
  USA (United States)

110013   Bilateral Exchange   **0 UNTS 0**
SIGNED: 2 May 68   FORCE: 2 May 68
REGISTERED: 1 Nov 69 USA (United States)
ARTICLES: 0
HEADNOTE: AGRI COMMOD
TOPIC: US Agri Commod Aid
PARTIES:
  Morocco
  USA (United States)

110014   Bilateral Exchange   **0 UNTS 0**
SIGNED: 3 May 68   FORCE: 3 May 68
REGISTERED: 1 Nov 69 USA (United States)
ARTICLES: 0
HEADNOTE: ASSIST IN NATURAL DISASTERS
TOPIC: Admin Cooperation
PARTIES:
  Mexico
  USA (United States)

110015   Bilateral Agreement   **0 UNTS 0**
SIGNED: 7 May 68   FORCE: 7 May 68
REGISTERED: 1 Nov 69 USA (United States)
ARTICLES: 0
HEADNOTE: AGRI COMMOD
TOPIC: US Agri Commod Aid
PARTIES:
  USA (United States)
  Uruguay

110016   Bilateral Exchange   **0 UNTS 0**
SIGNED: 10 May 68   FORCE: 10 May 68
REGISTERED: 1 Nov 69 USA (United States)
ARTICLES: 0
HEADNOTE: CUSTOMS FREE ENTRY CONSULS
TOPIC: Customs
PARTIES:
  Colombia
  USA (United States)

110017   Bilateral Exchange   **0 UNTS 0**
SIGNED: 13 May 68   FORCE: 13 May 68
REGISTERED: 1 Nov 69 USA (United States)
ARTICLES: 0
HEADNOTE: AMATEUR RADIO
TOPIC: Gen Communications
PARTIES:
  Guyana
  USA (United States)

110018   Bilateral Agreement   **0 UNTS 0**
SIGNED: 16 May 68   FORCE: 16 May 68
REGISTERED: 1 Nov 69 USA (United States)
ARTICLES: 0
HEADNOTE: PEACE CORPS MONTSERRAT
TOPIC: Admin Cooperation
PARTIES:
  UK Great Britain
  USA (United States)

110019   Bilateral Agreement   **0 UNTS 0**
SIGNED: 17 May 68   FORCE: 17 May 68
REGISTERED: 1 Nov 69 USA (United States)
ARTICLES: 0
HEADNOTE: AGRI COMMOD
TOPIC: US Agri Commod Aid
PARTIES:
  Tunisia
  USA (United States)

110020   Bilateral Convention   **0 UNTS 0**
SIGNED: 30 Jun 67   FORCE: 25 Oct 69
REGISTERED: 4 Nov 69 Belgium
ARTICLES: 0
HEADNOTE: DOUBLE TAX INCOME CAPITAL
TOPIC: Taxation
PARTIES:
  Belgium
  Norway

110021   Bilateral Agreement   **0 UNTS 0**
SIGNED: 22 Jun 67   FORCE: 22 Jun 67
REGISTERED: 7 Nov 69 USA (United States)
ARTICLES: 0
HEADNOTE: AIR TRANSPORT US GOVERNMENT
  CRAFT

TOPIC: Air Transport
PARTIES:
  Ascension Island
  USA (United States)

110022   Bilateral Convention   **0 UNTS 0**
SIGNED: 17 Nov 67   FORCE: 21 Sep 69
REGISTERED: 11 Nov 69 UK Great Britain
ARTICLES: 0
HEADNOTE: CIVIL JUDGMENTS RECOGNITION
TOPIC: Dispute Settlement
PARTIES:
  Netherlands
  UK Great Britain

110023   Bilateral Convention   **0 UNTS 0**
SIGNED: 21 Nov 68   FORCE: 29 Jun 69
REGISTERED: 11 Nov 69 UK Great Britain
ARTICLES: 0
HEADNOTE: DOUBLE TAX INCOME CAPITAL
TOPIC: Taxation
PARTIES:
  South Africa
  UK Great Britain

110024   Bilateral Exchange   **0 UNTS 0**
SIGNED: 29 Apr 69   FORCE: 14 May 69
REGISTERED: 11 Nov 69 UK Great Britain
ARTICLES: 0
HEADNOTE: VISA ABOLITION
TOPIC: Visas
PARTIES:
  UK Great Britain
  Yugoslavia

110025   Bilateral Exchange   **0 UNTS 0**
SIGNED: 19 May 69   FORCE: 19 May 69
REGISTERED: 11 Nov 69 UK Great Britain
ARTICLES: 0
HEADNOTE: OFFSET EXPENSES BRITISH FORCES
TOPIC: Finance
PARTIES:
  Germany, West
  UK Great Britain

110026   Bilateral Agreement   **0 UNTS 0**
SIGNED: 3 Jun 69   FORCE: 1 Jul 69
REGISTERED: 11 Nov 69 UK Great Britain
ARTICLES: 0
HEADNOTE: LONG-TERM TRADE
TOPIC: General Trade
PARTIES:
  UK Great Britain
  USSR (Soviet Union)

110027   Bilateral Exchange   **0 UNTS 0**
SIGNED: 23 Jun 69   FORCE: 23 Jun 69
REGISTERED: 11 Nov 69 UK Great Britain
ARTICLES: 0
HEADNOTE: INTEREST-FREE LOAN
TOPIC: Loans and Credits
PARTIES:
  Turkey
  UK Great Britain

110028   Bilateral Exchange   **0 UNTS 0**
SIGNED: 11 Jun 68   FORCE: 11 Jun 68
REGISTERED: 14 Nov 69 France
ARTICLES: 0
HEADNOTE: FORTALEZA TELEMETRY STATION
TOPIC: Gen Communications
PARTIES:
  Eur Space Vehicle
  France

110029   Bilateral Convention   **0 UNTS 0**
SIGNED: 28 May 62   FORCE: 30 Jul 68
REGISTERED: 17 Nov 69 Netherlands
ARTICLES: 0
HEADNOTE: MIGRATION
TOPIC: Admin Cooperation
PARTIES:
  Chile
  Netherlands

110030   Multilateral Convention   **0 UNTS 0**
SIGNED: 29 Jun 67   FORCE: 1 Nov 69
REGISTERED: 17 Nov 69 ILO (Labor Org)
ARTICLES: 0
HEADNOTE: NO. 128 INVALIDITY OLD-AGE BENE-
   FITS
TOPIC: Non-ILO Labor
PARTIES:
   Austria SIGNED: 29 Jun 67 RATIFIED: 4 Nov 69
      FORCE: 1 Nov 69
   Cyprus SIGNED: 29 Jun 67 RATIFIED: 7 Jan 69
      FORCE: 1 Nov 69
   Netherlands   SIGNED: 29 Jun 67   RATIFIED:
      27 Oct 69 FORCE: 1 Nov 69
   Norway SIGNED: 29 Jun 67 RATIFIED: 1 Nov 68
      FORCE: 1 Nov 69
   Sweden   SIGNED: 29 Jun 67   RATIFIED:
      26 Jul 68 FORCE: 1 Nov 69

110031   Bilateral Convention   **0 UNTS 0**
SIGNED: 8 Dec 66   FORCE: 19 Sep 69
REGISTERED: 19 Nov 69 France
ARTICLES: 0
HEADNOTE: CONSULAR
TOPIC: Consul/Citizenship
PARTIES:
   France
   USSR (Soviet Union)

110032   Bilateral Convention   **0 UNTS 0**
SIGNED: 17 Oct 68   FORCE: 4 Aug 69
REGISTERED: 19 Nov 69 Greece
ARTICLES: 0
HEADNOTE: DOUBLE TAX SEA AIR TRANSPORT
TOPIC: Taxation
PARTIES:
   Greece
   Syria

110033   Bilateral Agreement   **0 UNTS 0**
SIGNED: 25 Jul 69   FORCE: 1 Aug 69
REGISTERED: 19 Nov 69 France
ARTICLES: 0
HEADNOTE: ROAD TRANSPORT GOODS
TOPIC: Land Transport
PARTIES:
   Denmark
   France

110034   Bilateral Convention   **0 UNTS 0**
SIGNED: 21 Feb 68   FORCE: 1 Apr 69
REGISTERED: 24 Nov 69 UK Great Britain
ARTICLES: 0
HEADNOTE: SOCIAL SECURITY
TOPIC: Non-ILO Labor
PARTIES:
   Switzerland
   UK Great Britain

110035   Bilateral Exchange   **0 UNTS 0**
SIGNED: 31 Mar 69   FORCE: 20 Aug 69
REGISTERED: 24 Nov 69 Finland
ARTICLES: 0
HEADNOTE: TAX RELIEF INTERNATIONAL TRANS-
   PORT VEHICLES
TOPIC: Taxation
PARTIES:
   Finland
   France

110036   Bilateral Exchange   **0 UNTS 0**
SIGNED: 29 Apr 69   FORCE: 29 Apr 69
REGISTERED: 24 Nov 69 UK Great Britain
ARTICLES: 0
HEADNOTE: INTEREST-FREE LOAN
TOPIC: Loans and Credits
PARTIES:
   Indonesia
   UK Great Britain

110037   Bilateral Agreement   **0 UNTS 0**
SIGNED: 29 May 69   FORCE: 29 May 69
REGISTERED: 24 Nov 69 UK Great Britain
ARTICLES: 0
HEADNOTE: HEADQUARTERS
TOPIC: IGO Operations

PARTIES:
   Int Coffee Org
   UK Great Britain

110038   Bilateral Agreement   **0 UNTS 0**
SIGNED: 29 May 69   FORCE: 29 May 69
REGISTERED: 24 Nov 69 UK Great Britain
ARTICLES: 0
HEADNOTE: HEADQUARTERS
TOPIC: IGO Operations
PARTIES:
   Int Sugar Council
   UK Great Britain

110039   Bilateral Exchange   **0 UNTS 0**
SIGNED: 27 Nov 64   FORCE: 1 Apr 64
REGISTERED: 26 Nov 69 UK Great Britain
ARTICLES: 0
HEADNOTE: TRAINING ARMED FORCES
TOPIC: Milit Assistance
PARTIES:
   Kenya
   UK Great Britain

110040   Bilateral Agreement   **0 UNTS 0**
SIGNED: 14 May 69   FORCE: 28 Sep 69
REGISTERED: 26 Nov 69 Finland
ARTICLES: 0
HEADNOTE: PEACEFUL USES ATOMIC ENERGY
TOPIC: Atomic Energy
PARTIES:
   Finland
   USSR (Soviet Union)

110041   Bilateral Protocol   **0 UNTS 0**
SIGNED: 30 May 69   FORCE: 30 May 69
REGISTERED: 26 Nov 69 Finland
ARTICLES: 0
HEADNOTE: EXCHANGE TEACHERS STUDENTS
TOPIC: Education
PARTIES:
   Finland
   USSR (Soviet Union)

110042   Bilateral Agreement   **0 UNTS 0**
SIGNED: 16 Sep 68   FORCE: 18 Jan 69
REGISTERED: 28 Nov 69 Belgium
ARTICLES: 0
HEADNOTE: ECONOMIC INDUSTRIAL TECHNICAL
   COOPERATION
TOPIC: General Economic
PARTIES:
   Bel-Lux Econ Union
   Romania

110043   Bilateral Exchange   **0 UNTS 0**
SIGNED: 9 May 66   FORCE: 21 Sep 68
REGISTERED: 1 Dec 69 USA (United States)
ARTICLES: 0
HEADNOTE: INVESTMENT GUARANTY
TOPIC: Finance
PARTIES:
   Nicaragua
   USA (United States)

110044   Bilateral Convention   **0 UNTS 0**
SIGNED: 18 Jul 66   FORCE: 7 Jan 68
REGISTERED: 1 Dec 69 USA (United States)
ARTICLES: 0
HEADNOTE: CONSULAR
TOPIC: Consul/Citizenship
PARTIES:
   France
   USA (United States)

110045   Bilateral Exchange   **0 UNTS 0**
SIGNED: 21 Aug 67   FORCE: 21 Aug 67
REGISTERED: 1 Dec 69 USA (United States)
ARTICLES: 0
HEADNOTE: GEODETIC SURVEY
TOPIC: Scientific Project
PARTIES:
   USA (United States)
   Upper Volta

110046   Bilateral Exchange   **0 UNTS 0**
SIGNED: 26 Sep 67   FORCE: 1 Jan 68
REGISTERED: 1 Dec 69 USA (United States)
ARTICLES: 0
HEADNOTE: COTTON TEXTILES
TOPIC: Commodity Trade
PARTIES:
   USA (United States)
   Yugoslavia

110047   Bilateral Exchange   **0 UNTS 0**
SIGNED: 12 Oct 67   FORCE: 12 Oct 67
REGISTERED: 1 Dec 69 USA (United States)
ARTICLES: 0
HEADNOTE: COTTON TEXTILES
TOPIC: Commodity Trade
PARTIES:
   Taiwan
   USA (United States)

110048   Bilateral Exchange   **0 UNTS 0**
SIGNED: 13 Oct 67   FORCE: 13 Oct 67
REGISTERED: 1 Dec 69 USA (United States)
ARTICLES: 0
HEADNOTE: MUTUAL DEFENSE ASSISTANCE
TOPIC: General Military
PARTIES:
   Japan
   USA (United States)

110049   Bilateral Exchange   **0 UNTS 0**
SIGNED: 13 Oct 67   FORCE: 13 Oct 67
REGISTERED: 1 Dec 69 USA (United States)
ARTICLES: 0
HEADNOTE: COTTON TEXTILES
TOPIC: Commodity Trade
PARTIES:
   Spain
   USA (United States)

110050   Bilateral Agreement   **0 UNTS 0**
SIGNED: 18 Oct 67   FORCE: 18 Oct 67
REGISTERED: 1 Dec 69 USA (United States)
ARTICLES: 0
HEADNOTE: AGRI COMMOD
TOPIC: US Agri Commod Aid
PARTIES:
   Guinea
   USA (United States)

110051   Bilateral Agreement   **0 UNTS 0**
SIGNED: 23 Oct 67   FORCE: 23 Oct 67
REGISTERED: 1 Dec 69 USA (United States)
ARTICLES: 0
HEADNOTE: AGRI COMMOD
TOPIC: US Agri Commod Aid
PARTIES:
   Liberia
   USA (United States)

110052   Bilateral Exchange   **0 UNTS 0**
SIGNED: 25 Oct 67   FORCE: 25 Oct 67
REGISTERED: 1 Dec 69 USA (United States)
ARTICLES: 0
HEADNOTE: LORAN-A NAVIGATION EQUIPMENT
TOPIC: Scientific Project
PARTIES:
   Canada
   USA (United States)

110053   Bilateral Agreement   **0 UNTS 0**
SIGNED: 27 Oct 67   FORCE: 27 Oct 67
REGISTERED: 1 Dec 69 USA (United States)
ARTICLES: 0
HEADNOTE: AGRI COMMOD
TOPIC: US Agri Commod Aid
PARTIES:
   Morocco
   USA (United States)

110054   Bilateral Instrument   **0 UNTS 0**
SIGNED: 1 Nov 67   FORCE: 1 Nov 67
REGISTERED: 1 Dec 69 USA (United States)
ARTICLES: 0
HEADNOTE: AGRI COMMOD
TOPIC: US Agri Commod Aid

PARTIES:
Indonesia
USA (United States)

110055   Bilateral Exchange   0 UNTS 0
SIGNED: 4 Nov 67   FORCE: 4 Nov 67
REGISTERED: 1 Dec 69 USA (United States)
ARTICLES: 0
HEADNOTE: INVESTMENT GUARANTY
TOPIC: Finance
PARTIES:
Gambia
USA (United States)

110056   Bilateral Agreement   0 UNTS 0
SIGNED: 6 Nov 67   FORCE: 6 Nov 67
REGISTERED: 1 Dec 69 USA (United States)
ARTICLES: 0
HEADNOTE: AGRI COMMOD
TOPIC: US Agri Commod Aid
PARTIES:
Tunisia
USA (United States)

110057   Bilateral Agreement   0 UNTS 0
SIGNED: 25 Nov 67   FORCE: 25 Nov 67
REGISTERED: 1 Dec 69 USA (United States)
ARTICLES: 0
HEADNOTE: FISHERY WEST MIDDLE ATLANTIC
TOPIC: Specific Resources
PARTIES:
USA (United States)
USSR (Soviet Union)

110058   Bilateral Exchange   0 UNTS 0
SIGNED: 30 Nov 67   FORCE: 30 Dec 67
REGISTERED: 1 Dec 69 USA (United States)
ARTICLES: 0
HEADNOTE: AMATEUR RADIO
TOPIC: Gen Communications
PARTIES:
Chile
USA (United States)

110059   Bilateral Agreement   0 UNTS 0
SIGNED: 11 Dec 67   FORCE: 11 Dec 67
REGISTERED: 1 Dec 69 USA (United States)
ARTICLES: 0
HEADNOTE: AGRI COMMOD
TOPIC: US Agri Commod Aid
PARTIES:
Congo (Zaire)
USA (United States)

110060   Bilateral Exchange   0 UNTS 0
SIGNED: 11 Dec 67   FORCE: 11 Dec 67
REGISTERED: 1 Dec 69 USA (United States)
ARTICLES: 0
HEADNOTE: COTTON TEXTILES
TOPIC: Commodity Trade
PARTIES:
Korea, South
USA (United States)

110061   Bilateral Agreement   0 UNTS 0
SIGNED: 12 Dec 67   FORCE: 12 Dec 67
REGISTERED: 1 Dec 69 USA (United States)
ARTICLES: 0
HEADNOTE: AGRI COMMOD
TOPIC: US Agri Commod Aid
PARTIES:
Taiwan
USA (United States)

110062   Bilateral Agreement   0 UNTS 0
SIGNED: 12 Dec 67   FORCE: 12 Dec 67
REGISTERED: 1 Dec 69 USA (United States)
ARTICLES: 0
HEADNOTE: US GOVERNMENT-OWNED TAIWAN
DOLLARS
TOPIC: US Agri Commod Aid
PARTIES:
Taiwan
USA (United States)

110063   Bilateral Exchange   0 UNTS 0
SIGNED: 16 Dec 67   FORCE: 16 Dec 67
REGISTERED: 1 Dec 69 USA (United States)
ARTICLES: 0
HEADNOTE: PEACE CORPS GRENADA
TOPIC: Direct Aid
PARTIES:
UK Great Britain
USA (United States)

110064   Bilateral Agreement   0 UNTS 0
SIGNED: 16 Jan 68   FORCE: 16 Jan 68
REGISTERED: 1 Dec 69 USA (United States)
ARTICLES: 0
HEADNOTE: AGRI COMMOD
TOPIC: US Agri Commod Aid
PARTIES:
Bolivia
USA (United States)

110065   Bilateral Instrument   0 UNTS 0
SIGNED: 16 Jan 68   FORCE: 16 Jan 68
REGISTERED: 1 Dec 69 USA (United States)
ARTICLES: 0
HEADNOTE: AGRI COMMOD, SUPPLEMENT
TOPIC: US Agri Commod Aid
PARTIES:
Bolivia
USA (United States)

110066   Bilateral Agreement   0 UNTS 0
SIGNED: 29 May 68   FORCE: 29 May 68
REGISTERED: 1 Dec 69 USA (United States)
ARTICLES: 0
HEADNOTE: AGRI COMMOD
TOPIC: US Agri Commod Aid
PARTIES:
Iceland
USA (United States)

110067   Bilateral Agreement   0 UNTS 0
SIGNED: 31 May 68   FORCE: 31 May 68
REGISTERED: 1 Dec 69 USA (United States)
ARTICLES: 0
HEADNOTE: AGRI COMMOD
TOPIC: US Agri Commod Aid
PARTIES:
Colombia
USA (United States)

110068   Bilateral Exchange   0 UNTS 0
SIGNED: 9 Jul 68   FORCE: 9 Jul 68
REGISTERED: 1 Dec 69 USA (United States)
ARTICLES: 0
HEADNOTE: BOMEX   OCEANOGRAPHIC
METEOROLOGIC
TOPIC: Scientific Project
PARTIES:
Barbados
USA (United States)

110069   Bilateral Agreement   0 UNTS 0
SIGNED: 15 Jul 68   FORCE: 15 Jul 68
REGISTERED: 1 Dec 69 USA (United States)
ARTICLES: 0
HEADNOTE: SCIENTIFIC TECHNICAL CULTURAL
EXCHANGES
TOPIC: Scientific Project
PARTIES:
USA (United States)
USSR (Soviet Union)

110070   Bilateral Instrument   0 UNTS 0
SIGNED: 5 Aug 68   FORCE: 5 Aug 68
REGISTERED: 1 Dec 69 USA (United States)
ARTICLES: 0
HEADNOTE: AGRI COMMOD
TOPIC: US Agri Commod Aid
PARTIES:
Indonesia
USA (United States)

110071   Bilateral Instrument   0 UNTS 0
SIGNED: 16 Aug 68   FORCE: 16 Aug 68
REGISTERED: 1 Dec 69 USA (United States)
ARTICLES: 0

HEADNOTE: AGRI COMMOD
TOPIC: US Agri Commod Aid
PARTIES:
Indonesia
USA (United States)

110072   Bilateral Instrument   0 UNTS 0
SIGNED: 5 Sep 68   FORCE: 5 Sep 68
REGISTERED: 1 Dec 69 USA (United States)
ARTICLES: 0
HEADNOTE: AGRI COMMOD
TOPIC: US Agri Commod Aid
PARTIES:
Indonesia
USA (United States)

110073   Bilateral Exchange   0 UNTS 0
SIGNED: 2 Sep 68   FORCE: 2 Sep 68
REGISTERED: 1 Dec 69 USA (United States)
ARTICLES: 0
HEADNOTE: SATELLITE TRACKING STATION
TOPIC: Scientific Project
PARTIES:
Japan
USA (United States)

110074   Bilateral Exchange   0 UNTS 0
SIGNED: 10 Sep 68   FORCE: 10 Sep 68
REGISTERED: 1 Dec 69 USA (United States)
ARTICLES: 0
HEADNOTE: REMOTE SENSING EARTH SURVEYS
TOPIC: Scientific Project
PARTIES:
Brazil
USA (United States)

110075   Bilateral Exchange   0 UNTS 0
SIGNED: 12 Sep 68   FORCE: 12 Sep 68
REGISTERED: 1 Dec 69 USA (United States)
ARTICLES: 0
HEADNOTE: AMATEUR RADIO
TOPIC: Gen Communications
PARTIES:
Barbados
USA (United States)

110076   Bilateral Agreement   0 UNTS 0
SIGNED: 17 Sep 68   FORCE: 17 Sep 68
REGISTERED: 1 Dec 69 USA (United States)
ARTICLES: 0
HEADNOTE: AGRI COMMOD
TOPIC: US Agri Commod Aid
PARTIES:
Guyana
USA (United States)

110077   Bilateral Exchange   0 UNTS 0
SIGNED: 18 Sep 68   FORCE: 18 Sep 68
REGISTERED: 1 Dec 69 USA (United States)
ARTICLES: 0
HEADNOTE: COTTON TEXTILES
TOPIC: Commodity Trade
PARTIES:
Colombia
USA (United States)

110078   Bilateral Exchange   0 UNTS 0
SIGNED: 20 Sep 68   FORCE: 20 Sep 68
REGISTERED: 1 Dec 69 USA (United States)
ARTICLES: 0
HEADNOTE: DIRECT   COMMUNICATION   SEA
TRANSPORT
TOPIC: Gen Communications
PARTIES:
Brazil
USA (United States)

110079   Bilateral Exchange   0 UNTS 0
SIGNED: 24 Sep 68   FORCE: 24 Sep 68
REGISTERED: 1 Dec 69 USA (United States)
ARTICLES: 0
HEADNOTE: DUTY   CERTIFICATES   STATUS
FORCES
TOPIC: Status of Forces

PARTIES:
Turkey
USA (United States)

110080   Bilateral Exchange   **0 UNTS 0**
SIGNED: 30 Sep 68   FORCE: 30 Sep 68
REGISTERED: 1 Dec 69 USA (United States)
ARTICLES: 0
HEADNOTE: DEPLOY USS EVERGLADES
TOPIC: Military Mission
PARTIES:
Malta
USA (United States)

110081   Bilateral Agreement   **0 UNTS 0**
SIGNED: 9 Oct 68   FORCE: 9 Oct 68
REGISTERED: 1 Dec 69 USA (United States)
ARTICLES: 0
HEADNOTE: INVESTMENT GUARANTY ANTIGUA
TOPIC: Finance
PARTIES:
UK Great Britain
USA (United States)

110082   Bilateral Exchange   **0 UNTS 0**
SIGNED: 10 Oct 68   FORCE: 10 Oct 68
REGISTERED: 1 Dec 69 USA (United States)
ARTICLES: 0
HEADNOTE: AMATEUR RADIO
TOPIC: Gen Communications
PARTIES:
Ireland
USA (United States)

110083   Bilateral Agreement   **0 UNTS 0**
SIGNED: 11 Oct 68   FORCE: 11 Oct 68
REGISTERED: 1 Dec 69 USA (United States)
ARTICLES: 0
HEADNOTE: INVESTMENT GUARANTY DOMINICA
TOPIC: Finance
PARTIES:
UK Great Britain
USA (United States)

110084   Bilateral Exchange   **0 UNTS 0**
SIGNED: 28 Oct 68   FORCE: 31 Dec 68
REGISTERED: 1 Dec 69 USA (United States)
ARTICLES: 0
HEADNOTE: TERMINATING 1936 COMMERCIAL
AGREEMENT
TOPIC: General Economic
PARTIES:
Switzerland
USA (United States)

110085   Bilateral Exchange   **0 UNTS 0**
SIGNED: 8 Nov 68   FORCE: 8 Nov 68
REGISTERED: 1 Dec 69 USA (United States)
ARTICLES: 0
HEADNOTE: ESTABLISH COMMITTEE CULTURAL
EDUCATIONAL COOPERATION
TOPIC: Culture
PARTIES:
Japan
USA (United States)

110086   Bilateral Exchange   **0 UNTS 0**
SIGNED: 9 Nov 68   FORCE: 9 Nov 68
REGISTERED: 1 Dec 69 USA (United States)
ARTICLES: 0
HEADNOTE: DISPOSAL PERSONAL PROPERTY US
MILITARY
TOPIC: Milit Servic/Citiz
PARTIES:
USA (United States)
Vietnam, South

110087   Bilateral Exchange   **0 UNTS 0**
SIGNED: 12 Nov 68   FORCE: 12 Nov 68
REGISTERED: 1 Dec 69 USA (United States)
ARTICLES: 0
HEADNOTE: LOAN USS BERGALL
TOPIC: Milit Installation
PARTIES:
Turkey
USA (United States)

110088   Bilateral Agreement   **0 UNTS 0**
SIGNED: 21 Nov 68   FORCE: 21 Nov 68
REGISTERED: 1 Dec 69 USA (United States)
ARTICLES: 0
HEADNOTE: INVESTMENT GUARANTY ST. CHRIS-
TOPHER
TOPIC: Finance
PARTIES:
UK Great Britain
USA (United States)

110089   Bilateral Convention   **0 UNTS 0**
SIGNED: 8 May 68   FORCE: 20 Oct 69
REGISTERED: 1 Dec 69 Netherlands
ARTICLES: 0
HEADNOTE: DOUBLE TAX INCOME CAPITAL
TOPIC: Taxation
PARTIES:
Luxembourg
Netherlands

110090   Bilateral Agreement   **0 UNTS 0**
SIGNED: 22 Dec 66   FORCE: 1 Nov 69
REGISTERED: 8 Dec 69 Austria
ARTICLES: 0
HEADNOTE: SOCIAL SECURITY
TOPIC: Non-ILO Labor
PARTIES:
Austria
Germany, West

110091   Bilateral Agreement   **0 UNTS 0**
SIGNED: 28 Feb 69   FORCE: 17 Jun 69
REGISTERED: 11 Dec 69 IBRD (World Bank)
ARTICLES: 0
HEADNOTE: LOAN SEYHAN IRRIGATION
TOPIC: IBRD Project
PARTIES:
IBRD (World Bank)
Turkey

110092   Bilateral Agreement   **0 UNTS 0**
SIGNED: 28 Feb 69   FORCE: 17 Jun 69
REGISTERED: 11 Dec 69 IDA (Devel Assoc)
ARTICLES: 0
HEADNOTE: CREDIT SEYHAN IRRIGATION
TOPIC: Non-IBRD Project
PARTIES:
IDA (Devel Assoc)
Turkey

110093   Bilateral Agreement   **0 UNTS 0**
SIGNED: 18 Jun 69   FORCE: 14 Jul 69
REGISTERED: 11 Dec 69 IBRD (World Bank)
ARTICLES: 0
HEADNOTE: LOAN THIRD TELECOMMUNICA-
TIONS
TOPIC: IBRD Project
PARTIES:
India
IBRD (World Bank)

110094   Bilateral Agreement   **0 UNTS 0**
SIGNED: 18 Jun 69   FORCE: 14 Jul 69
REGISTERED: 11 Dec 69 IDA (Devel Assoc)
ARTICLES: 0
HEADNOTE: CREDIT THIRD TELECOMMUNICA-
TIONS
TOPIC: Non-IBRD Project
PARTIES:
India
IDA (Devel Assoc)

110095   Bilateral Treaty   **0 UNTS 0**
SIGNED: 15 Jan 69   FORCE: 15 Jan 69
REGISTERED: 12 Dec 69 Morocco
ARTICLES: 0
HEADNOTE: BROTHERHOOD GOOD NEIGHBOR
COOPERATION
TOPIC: General Amity
PARTIES:
Algeria
Morocco

110096   Bilateral Agreement   **0 UNTS 0**
SIGNED: 31 Jan 69   FORCE: 23 Jul 69

REGISTERED: 15 Dec 69 IBRD (World Bank)
ARTICLES: 0
HEADNOTE: LOAN EDUCATION
TOPIC: IBRD Project
PARTIES:
Guyana
IBRD (World Bank)

110097   Bilateral Agreement   **0 UNTS 0**
SIGNED: 31 Jan 69   FORCE: 23 Jul 69
REGISTERED: 15 Dec 69 IDA (Devel Assoc)
ARTICLES: 0
HEADNOTE: CREDIT EDUCATION
TOPIC: Non-IBRD Project
PARTIES:
Guyana
IDA (Devel Assoc)

110098   Bilateral Agreement   **0 UNTS 0**
SIGNED: 13 May 69   FORCE: 29 Sep 69
REGISTERED: 15 Dec 69 IBRD (World Bank)
ARTICLES: 0
HEADNOTE: GUARANTEE SECOND SUI NORTH-
ERN GAS
TOPIC: IBRD Project
PARTIES:
Pakistan
IBRD (World Bank)

110099   Multilateral Agreement   **0 UNTS 0**
SIGNED: 9 Jun 69   FORCE: 9 Aug 69
REGISTERED: 17 Dec 69 Germany, West
ARTICLES: 0
HEADNOTE: NORTH SEA OIL POLLUTION
TOPIC: Specific Resources
PARTIES:
Belgium SIGNED: 9 Jun 69 FORCE: 9 Aug 69
Denmark SIGNED: 9 Jun 69 FORCE: 9 Aug 69
France SIGNED: 9 Jun 69 FORCE: 9 Aug 69
Germany, West SIGNED: 9 Jun 69 FORCE:
9 Aug 69
Netherlands SIGNED: 9 Jun 69
Norway SIGNED: 9 Jun 69
Sweden SIGNED: 9 Jun 69 FORCE: 9 Aug 69
UK Great Britain SIGNED: 9 Jun 69 FORCE:
9 Aug 69

110100   Multilateral Agreement   **0 UNTS 0**
SIGNED: 11 Jun 69   FORCE: 11 Jun 69
REGISTERED: 17 Dec 69 Taiwan
ARTICLES: 0
HEADNOTE: FOOD FERTILIZER CENTER ASIA
PACIFIC
TOPIC: Scientific Project
PARTIES:
Australia SIGNED: 11 Jun 69 FORCE: 11 Jun 69
Taiwan SIGNED: 11 Jun 69 FORCE: 11 Jun 69
Japan SIGNED: 11 Jun 69 FORCE: 11 Jun 69
Korea, South SIGNED: 11 Jun 69 FORCE:
11 Jun 69
Malaysia SIGNED: 11 Jun 69 FORCE: 11 Jun 69
New Zealand SIGNED: 11 Jun 69 FORCE:
11 Jun 69
Philippines SIGNED: 11 Jun 69 FORCE:
11 Jun 69
Thailand SIGNED: 11 Jun 69 FORCE: 11 Jun 69
Vietnam, South SIGNED: 11 Jun 69 FORCE:
11 Jun 69

110101   Bilateral Agreement   **0 UNTS 0**
SIGNED: 19 Mar 68   FORCE: 19 Mar 68
REGISTERED: 19 Dec 69 France
ARTICLES: 0
HEADNOTE: CULTURAL TECHNICAL SCIENTIFIC
COOPERATION
TOPIC: Culture
PARTIES:
France
United Arab Rep

110102   Bilateral Protocol   **0 UNTS 0**
SIGNED: 19 Mar 68   FORCE: 19 Mar 68
REGISTERED: 19 Dec 69 France
ARTICLES: 0
HEADNOTE: INSTITUT FRANCAIS ARCHEOLOGIE
TOPIC: Education

PARTIES:
France
United Arab Rep

110103   Bilateral Agreement   **0 UNTS 0**
SIGNED: 14 Feb 69   FORCE: 28 Oct 69
REGISTERED: 19 Dec 69 IBRD (World Bank)
ARTICLES: 0
HEADNOTE: LOAN BEEF CATTLE DEVELOPMENT
TOPIC: IBRD Project
PARTIES:
Madagascar
IBRD (World Bank)

110104   Bilateral Agreement   **0 UNTS 0**
SIGNED: 27 Jun 69   FORCE: 3 Nov 69
REGISTERED: 19 Dec 69 IBRD (World Bank)
ARTICLES: 0
HEADNOTE: LOAN AGRICULTURE CREDIT
TOPIC: IBRD Project
PARTIES:
Colombia
IBRD (World Bank)

110105   Bilateral Agreement   **0 UNTS 0**
SIGNED: 10 Jul 69   FORCE: 6 Oct 69
REGISTERED: 19 Dec 69 IBRD (World Bank)
ARTICLES: 0
HEADNOTE: GUARANTEE THIRD DEVELOPMENT
TOPIC: IBRD Project
PARTIES:
Philippines
IBRD (World Bank)

110106   Multilateral Convention   **0 UNTS 0**
SIGNED: 14 Sep 63   FORCE: 4 Dec 69
REGISTERED: 22 Dec 69 ICAO (Civil Aviat)
ARTICLES: 0
HEADNOTE: ICAO OFFENSES ON BOARD AIR-
CRAFT
TOPIC: Air Transport
PARTIES:
Taiwan   SIGNED: 14 Sep 63   RATIFIED:
28 Feb 66 FORCE: 4 Dec 69
Denmark   SIGNED: 14 Sep 63   RATIFIED:
17 Jan 67 FORCE: 4 Dec 69
Italy SIGNED: 14 Sep 63 RATIFIED: 18 Oct 68
FORCE: 4 Dec 69
Mexico   SIGNED: 14 Sep 63   RATIFIED:
18 Mar 69 FORCE: 4 Dec 69
Niger SIGNED: 14 Sep 63 RATIFIED: 27 Jun 69
FORCE: 4 Dec 69
Norway   SIGNED: 14 Sep 63   RATIFIED:
17 Jan 67 FORCE: 4 Dec 69
Philippines   SIGNED: 14 Sep 63   RATIFIED:
26 Nov 65 FORCE: 4 Dec 69
Portugal   SIGNED: 14 Sep 63   RATIFIED:
25 Nov 64 FORCE: 4 Dec 69
Sweden   SIGNED: 14 Sep 63   RATIFIED:
17 Jan 67 FORCE: 4 Dec 69
UK Great Britain SIGNED: 14 Sep 63 RATIFIED:
29 Nov 68 FORCE: 4 Dec 69
USA (United States) SIGNED: 14 Sep 63 RATI-
FIED: 5 Sep 69 FORCE: 4 Dec 69
Upper Volta SIGNED: 14 Sep 63 RATIFIED:
6 Jun 69 FORCE: 4 Dec 69

110107   Bilateral Agreement   **0 UNTS 0**
SIGNED: 23 Jun 69   FORCE: 1 Oct 69
REGISTERED: 22 Dec 69 IBRD (World Bank)
ARTICLES: 0
HEADNOTE: GUARANTEE VOLTA EXPANSION
TOPIC: IBRD Project
PARTIES:
Ghana
IBRD (World Bank)

110108   Multilateral Convention   **0 UNTS 0**
SIGNED: 19 Mar 62   FORCE: 1 Jul 69
REGISTERED: 23 Dec 69 Belgium
ARTICLES: 0
HEADNOTE: BENELUX TRADEMARKS
TOPIC: Patents/Copyrights
PARTIES:
Belgium   SIGNED: 19 Mar 62   RATIFIED:
30 Jun 69 FORCE: 1 Jul 69
Luxembourg   SIGNED: 19 Mar 62   RATIFIED:
19 Aug 68 FORCE: 1 Jul 69

Netherlands   SIGNED: 19 Mar 62   RATIFIED:
30 Sep 63 FORCE: 1 Jul 69

110109   Bilateral Convention   **0 UNTS 0**
SIGNED: 11 Apr 67   FORCE: 30 Jul 69
REGISTERED: 23 Dec 69 Belgium
ARTICLES: 0
HEADNOTE: DOUBLE TAX INCOME FORTUNE
TOPIC: Taxation
PARTIES:
Belgium
Germany, West

110110   Bilateral Convention   **0 UNTS 0**
SIGNED: 27 Feb 68   FORCE: 1 Oct 69
REGISTERED: 23 Dec 69 Belgium
ARTICLES: 0
HEADNOTE: SOCIAL SECURITY
TOPIC: Non-ILO Labor
PARTIES:
Algeria
Belgium

110111   Bilateral Treaty   **0 UNTS 0**
SIGNED: 10 Jul 69   FORCE: 8 Sep 69
REGISTERED: 23 Dec 69 Hungary
ARTICLES: 0
HEADNOTE: FRIENDSHIP COOPERATION MU-
TUAL ASSISTANCE
TOPIC: General Amity
PARTIES:
Bulgaria
Hungary

110112   Bilateral Agreement   **0 UNTS 0**
SIGNED: 5 Sep 68   FORCE: 14 Sep 69
REGISTERED: 30 Dec 69 IBRD (World Bank)
ARTICLES: 0
HEADNOTE: LOAN FISHERIES
TOPIC: IBRD Project
PARTIES:
Ecuador
IBRD (World Bank)

110113   Bilateral Agreement   **0 UNTS 0**
SIGNED: 12 Mar 69   FORCE: 29 May 69
REGISTERED: 30 Dec 69 IBRD (World Bank)
ARTICLES: 0
HEADNOTE: GUARANTEE FIFTH INDUSTRIAL DE-
VELOPMENT
TOPIC: IBRD Project
PARTIES:
IBRD (World Bank)
Turkey

110114   Bilateral Exchange   **0 UNTS 0**
SIGNED: 27 Mar 69   FORCE: 27 Mar 69
REGISTERED: 30 Dec 69 UK Great Britain
ARTICLES: 0
HEADNOTE: INTEREST-FREE LOAN
TOPIC: Loans and Credits
PARTIES:
Jordan
UK Great Britain

110115   Bilateral Exchange   **0 UNTS 0**
SIGNED: 24 May 69   FORCE: 24 May 69
REGISTERED: 30 Dec 69 UK Great Britain
ARTICLES: 0
HEADNOTE: INTEREST-FREE LOAN
TOPIC: Loans and Credits
PARTIES:
Jordan
UK Great Britain

110116   Bilateral Exchange   **0 UNTS 0**
SIGNED: 25 Jun 69   FORCE: 25 Jun 69
REGISTERED: 30 Dec 69 UK Great Britain
ARTICLES: 0
HEADNOTE: INTEREST-FREE LOAN
TOPIC: Loans and Credits
PARTIES:
Indonesia
UK Great Britain

110117   Bilateral Exchange   **0 UNTS 0**
SIGNED: 9 Jul 69   FORCE: 9 Jul 69
REGISTERED: 30 Dec 69 UK Great Britain
ARTICLES: 0
HEADNOTE: INTEREST-FREE LOAN
TOPIC: Loans and Credits
PARTIES:
Cambodia
UK Great Britain

110118   Bilateral Exchange   **0 UNTS 0**
SIGNED: 23 Jul 69   FORCE: 23 Jul 69
REGISTERED: 30 Dec 69 UK Great Britain
ARTICLES: 0
HEADNOTE: MINIMUM STERLING PROPORTION
TOPIC: Finance
PARTIES:
UK Great Britain
Western Samoa

110119   Bilateral Agreement   **0 UNTS 0**
SIGNED: 23 Oct 68   FORCE: 16 May 69
REGISTERED: 31 Dec 69 IBRD (World Bank)
ARTICLES: 0
HEADNOTE: LOAN HIGHWAY CONSTRUCTION
TOPIC: IBRD Project
PARTIES:
Brazil
IBRD (World Bank)

110120   Bilateral Agreement   **0 UNTS 0**
SIGNED: 10 Feb 69   FORCE: 25 Jun 69
REGISTERED: 31 Dec 69 IBRD (World Bank)
ARTICLES: 0
HEADNOTE: LOAN AGRICULTURE CREDIT
TOPIC: IBRD Project
PARTIES:
IBRD (World Bank)
Senegal

110121   Bilateral Agreement   **0 UNTS 0**
SIGNED: 10 Feb 69   FORCE: 25 Jun 69
REGISTERED: 31 Dec 69 IDA (Devel Assoc)
ARTICLES: 0
HEADNOTE: CREDIT AGRICULTURE CREDIT
TOPIC: Non-IBRD Project
PARTIES:
IDA (Devel Assoc)
Senegal

110122   Bilateral Agreement   **0 UNTS 0**
SIGNED: 2 Jun 69   FORCE: 4 Nov 69
REGISTERED: 31 Dec 69 IBRD (World Bank)
ARTICLES: 0
HEADNOTE: CREDIT DOUALA YAOUNDE WATER
TOPIC: IBRD Project
PARTIES:
Cameroon
IBRD (World Bank)

110123   Bilateral Agreement   **0 UNTS 0**
SIGNED: 17 Jul 62   FORCE: 17 Jul 62
REGISTERED: 5 Jan 70 ICAO (Civil Aviat)
ARTICLES: 0
HEADNOTE: AIR SERVICES
TOPIC: Air Transport
PARTIES:
Cuba
USSR (Soviet Union)

110124   Bilateral Exchange   **0 UNTS 0**
SIGNED: 10 Mar 65   FORCE: 10 Mar 65
REGISTERED: 5 Jan 70 USA (United States)
ARTICLES: 0
HEADNOTE: SOCIAL SECURITY AID EMPLOYEES
TOPIC: Non-IBRD Project
PARTIES:
Philippines
USA (United States)

110125   Bilateral Exchange   **0 UNTS 0**
SIGNED: 15 Jul 65   FORCE: 15 Jul 65
REGISTERED: 5 Jan 70 USA (United States)
ARTICLES: 0
HEADNOTE: SOCIAL SECURITY PEACE CORPS
TOPIC: Non-IBRD Project

PARTIES:
  Philippines
  USA (United States)

110126   Bilateral Exchange   **0 UNTS 0**
SIGNED: 18 May 67   FORCE: 18 May 67
REGISTERED: 5 Jan 70 USA (United States)
ARTICLES: 0
HEADNOTE: SCHOOL CONSTRUCTION SPECIAL
  FUND
TOPIC: Non-IBRD Project
PARTIES:
  Philippines
  USA (United States)

110127   Bilateral Exchange   **0 UNTS 0**
SIGNED: 26 Jun 67   FORCE: 26 Jun 67
REGISTERED: 5 Jan 70 USA (United States)
ARTICLES: 0
HEADNOTE: TEXTBOOK PRODUCTION SPECIAL
  FUND
TOPIC: Non-IBRD Project
PARTIES:
  Philippines
  USA (United States)

110128   Bilateral Exchange   **0 UNTS 0**
SIGNED: 11 Aug 67   FORCE: 11 Aug 67
REGISTERED: 5 Jan 70 USA (United States)
ARTICLES: 0
HEADNOTE: CULTURAL DEVELOPMENT
TOPIC: Non-IBRD Project
PARTIES:
  Philippines
  USA (United States)

110129   Bilateral Exchange   **0 UNTS 0**
SIGNED: 30 Apr 68   FORCE: 30 Apr 68
REGISTERED: 5 Jan 70 USA (United States)
ARTICLES: 0
HEADNOTE: RELINQUISH CERTAIN US BASE
  LAND
TOPIC: Milit Installation
PARTIES:
  Philippines
  USA (United States)

110130   Bilateral Exchange   **0 UNTS 0**
SIGNED: 11 Jun 68   FORCE: 11 Jun 68
REGISTERED: 5 Jan 70 USA (United States)
ARTICLES: 0
HEADNOTE: PRIVATE EDUCATION SPECIAL FUND
TOPIC: Non-IBRD Project
PARTIES:
  Philippines
  USA (United States)

110131   Bilateral Agreement   **0 UNTS 0**
SIGNED: 13 Jun 68   FORCE: 19 Jul 68
REGISTERED: 5 Jan 70 USA (United States)
ARTICLES: 0
HEADNOTE: CIVIL USE ATOMIC ENERGY
TOPIC: Atomic Energy
PARTIES:
  Philippines
  USA (United States)

110132   Bilateral Exchange   **0 UNTS 0**
SIGNED: 24 Apr 69   FORCE: 24 Apr 69
REGISTERED: 5 Jan 70 USA (United States)
ARTICLES: 0
HEADNOTE: ASSIST ARTIFICIAL RAIN
TOPIC: Non-IBRD Project
PARTIES:
  Philippines
  USA (United States)

110133   Bilateral Agreement   **0 UNTS 0**
SIGNED: 22 Dec 67   FORCE: 22 Dec 67
REGISTERED: 5 Jan 70 USA (United States)
ARTICLES: 0
HEADNOTE: AGRI COMMOD
TOPIC: US Agri Commod Aid
PARTIES:
  Philippines
  USA (United States)

110134   Bilateral Exchange   **0 UNTS 0**
SIGNED: 27 Feb 68   FORCE: 27 Jan 68
REGISTERED: 5 Jan 70 USA (United States)
ARTICLES: 0
HEADNOTE: TRANSFER USS CHARLES AUS-
  BURNE
TOPIC: Admin Cooperation
PARTIES:
  Germany, West
  USA (United States)

110135   Bilateral Agreement   **0 UNTS 0**
SIGNED: 11 Mar 68   FORCE: 11 Mar 68
REGISTERED: 5 Jan 70 USA (United States)
ARTICLES: 0
HEADNOTE: AGRI COMMOD
TOPIC: US Agri Commod Aid
PARTIES:
  USA (United States)
  Vietnam, South

110136   Bilateral Agreement   **0 UNTS 0**
SIGNED: 14 Jan 69   FORCE: 14 Jan 69
REGISTERED: 5 Jan 70 USA (United States)
ARTICLES: 0
HEADNOTE: AGRI COMMOD, SUPPLEMENT
TOPIC: US Agri Commod Aid
PARTIES:
  USA (United States)
  Vietnam, South

110137   Bilateral Agreement   **0 UNTS 0**
SIGNED: 5 Feb 69   FORCE: 5 Feb 69
REGISTERED: 5 Jan 70 USA (United States)
ARTICLES: 0
HEADNOTE: AGRI COMMOD, SUPPLEMENT
TOPIC: US Agri Commod Aid
PARTIES:
  USA (United States)
  Vietnam, South

110138   Bilateral Exchange   **0 UNTS 0**
SIGNED: 12 Mar 68   FORCE: 12 Mar 68
REGISTERED: 5 Jan 70 USA (United States)
ARTICLES: 0
HEADNOTE: NETWORK RAWISONDE STATION
TOPIC: Scientific Project
PARTIES:
  Brazil
  USA (United States)

110139   Bilateral Agreement   **0 UNTS 0**
SIGNED: 10 May 68   FORCE: 10 May 68
REGISTERED: 5 Jan 70 USA (United States)
ARTICLES: 0
HEADNOTE: AGRI COMMOD, SUPPLEMENT
TOPIC: US Agri Commod Aid
PARTIES:
  Korea, South
  USA (United States)

110140   Bilateral Agreement   **0 UNTS 0**
SIGNED: 23 Oct 68   FORCE: 23 Oct 68
REGISTERED: 5 Jan 70 USA (United States)
ARTICLES: 0
HEADNOTE: AGRI COMMOD, SUPPLEMENT
TOPIC: US Agri Commod Aid
PARTIES:
  Korea, South
  USA (United States)

110141   Bilateral Agreement   **0 UNTS 0**
SIGNED: 26 Feb 69   FORCE: 26 Feb 69
REGISTERED: 5 Jan 70 USA (United States)
ARTICLES: 0
HEADNOTE: AGRI COMMOD
TOPIC: US Agri Commod Aid
PARTIES:
  Korea, South
  USA (United States)

110142   Bilateral Agreement   **0 UNTS 0**
SIGNED: 8 Apr 69   FORCE: 8 Apr 69
REGISTERED: 5 Jan 70 USA (United States)
ARTICLES: 0
HEADNOTE: AGRI COMMOD, SUPPLEMENT

TOPIC: US Agri Commod Aid
PARTIES:
  Korea, South
  USA (United States)

110143   Bilateral Exchange   **0 UNTS 0**
SIGNED: 25 May 68   FORCE: 25 May 68
REGISTERED: 5 Jan 70 USA (United States)
ARTICLES: 0
HEADNOTE: PEACE CORPS
TOPIC: General Aid
PARTIES:
  Nicaragua
  USA (United States)

110144   Bilateral Exchange   **0 UNTS 0**
SIGNED: 27 May 68   FORCE: 27 May 68
REGISTERED: 5 Jan 70 USA (United States)
ARTICLES: 0
HEADNOTE: PEACE CORPS TONGA
TOPIC: General Aid
PARTIES:
  UK Great Britain
  USA (United States)

110145   Bilateral Exchange   **0 UNTS 0**
SIGNED: 15 Jun 68   FORCE: 15 Jun 68
REGISTERED: 5 Jan 70 USA (United States)
ARTICLES: 0
HEADNOTE: SEISMIC ARRAY RESEARCH, FACIL-
  ITY
TOPIC: Scientific Project
PARTIES:
  Norway
  USA (United States)

110146   Bilateral Exchange   **0 UNTS 0**
SIGNED: 18 Jun 68   FORCE: 18 Jun 68
REGISTERED: 5 Jan 70 USA (United States)
ARTICLES: 0
HEADNOTE: LOAN USS YARNALL
TOPIC: Milit Assistance
PARTIES:
  Taiwan
  USA (United States)

110147   Bilateral Exchange   **0 UNTS 0**
SIGNED: 25 Jun 68   FORCE: 25 Jun 68
REGISTERED: 5 Jan 70 USA (United States)
ARTICLES: 0
HEADNOTE: PRODUCING POTABLE WATER
TOPIC: Non-IBRD Project
PARTIES:
  Spain
  USA (United States)

110148   Bilateral Agreement   **0 UNTS 0**
SIGNED: 2 Jul 68   FORCE: 2 Jul 68
REGISTERED: 5 Jan 70 USA (United States)
ARTICLES: 0
HEADNOTE: AGRI COMMOD, SUPPLEMENT
TOPIC: US Agri Commod Aid
PARTIES:
  Afghanistan
  USA (United States)

110149   Bilateral Exchange   **0 UNTS 0**
SIGNED: 17 Jul 68   FORCE: 17 Jul 68
REGISTERED: 5 Jan 70 USA (United States)
ARTICLES: 0
HEADNOTE: SCIENTIFIC COOPERATION
TOPIC: Scientific Project
PARTIES:
  Tunisia
  USA (United States)

110150   Bilateral Agreement   **0 UNTS 0**
SIGNED: 12 Aug 68   FORCE: 12 Aug 68
REGISTERED: 5 Jan 70 USA (United States)
ARTICLES: 0
HEADNOTE: AGRI COMMOD
TOPIC: US Agri Commod Aid
PARTIES:
  Congo (Zaire)
  USA (United States)

110151　　Bilateral Exchange　　0 UNTS 0
SIGNED: 10 Dec 68　　　　FORCE: 10 Dec 68
REGISTERED: 5 Jan 70 USA (United States)
ARTICLES: 0
HEADNOTE: AMATEUR RADIO
TOPIC: Gen Communications
PARTIES:
　Indonesia
　USA (United States)

110152　　Bilateral Agreement　　0 UNTS 0
SIGNED: 19 Feb 69　　　　FORCE: 19 Feb 69
REGISTERED: 5 Jan 70 USA (United States)
ARTICLES: 0
HEADNOTE: AGRI COMMOD
TOPIC: US Agri Commod Aid
PARTIES:
　Ceylon (Sri Lanka)
　USA (United States)

110153　　Bilateral Agreement　　0 UNTS 0
SIGNED: 7 Mar 69　　　　FORCE: 7 Mar 69
REGISTERED: 5 Jan 70 USA (United States)
ARTICLES: 0
HEADNOTE: AGRI COMMOD
TOPIC: US Agri Commod Aid
PARTIES:
　Bolivia
　USA (United States)

110154　　Bilateral Agreement　　0 UNTS 0
SIGNED: 7 Mar 69　　　　FORCE: 7 Mar 69
REGISTERED: 5 Jan 70 USA (United States)
ARTICLES: 0
HEADNOTE: AGRI COMMOD
TOPIC: US Agri Commod Aid
PARTIES:
　Bolivia
　USA (United States)

110155　　Bilateral Exchange　　0 UNTS 0
SIGNED: 20 Mar 69　　　　FORCE: 20 Mar 69
REGISTERED: 5 Jan 70 USA (United States)
ARTICLES: 0
HEADNOTE: STUDIES SEA LEVEL CANAL SITE
TOPIC: Scientific Project
PARTIES:
　Panama
　USA (United States)

110156　　Bilateral Exchange　　0 UNTS 0
SIGNED: 4 Apr 69　　　　FORCE: 4 Apr 69
REGISTERED: 5 Jan 70 USA (United States)
ARTICLES: 0
HEADNOTE: PRODUCTION F-4EJ AIRCRAFT
TOPIC: Milit Assistance
PARTIES:
　Japan
　USA (United States)

110157　　Bilateral Exchange　　0 UNTS 0
SIGNED: 8 Apr 69　　　　FORCE: 8 Apr 69
REGISTERED: 5 Jan 70 USA (United States)
ARTICLES: 0
HEADNOTE: COTTON TEXTILES
TOPIC: Commodity Trade
PARTIES:
　Greece
　USA (United States)

110158　　Bilateral Agreement　　0 UNTS 0
SIGNED: 8 Apr 69　　　　FORCE: 8 Apr 69
REGISTERED: 5 Jan 70 USA (United States)
ARTICLES: 0
HEADNOTE: AGRI COMMOD
TOPIC: US Agri Commod Aid
PARTIES:
　Sierra Leone
　USA (United States)

110159　　Bilateral Exchange　　0 UNTS 0
SIGNED: 11 Apr 69　　　　FORCE: 11 Apr 69
REGISTERED: 5 Jan 70 USA (United States)
ARTICLES: 0
HEADNOTE: RAWINSONDE SANTO DOMINGO
TOPIC: Scientific Project

PARTIES:
　Dominican Republic
　USA (United States)

110160　　Bilateral Agreement　　0 UNTS 0
SIGNED: 21 Apr 69　　　　FORCE: 21 Apr 69
REGISTERED: 5 Jan 70 USA (United States)
ARTICLES: 0
HEADNOTE: AGRI COMMOD, SUPPLEMENT
TOPIC: US Agri Commod Aid
PARTIES:
　Jordan
　USA (United States)

110161　　Bilateral Agreement　　0 UNTS 0
SIGNED: 5 Aug 65　　　　FORCE: 5 Aug 65
REGISTERED: 5 Jan 70 ICAO (Civil Aviat)
ARTICLES: 0
HEADNOTE: AIR SERVICES
TOPIC: Air Transport
PARTIES:
　Netherlands
　United Arab Rep

110162　　Bilateral Agreement　　0 UNTS 0
SIGNED: 18 Oct 65　　　　FORCE: 24 Nov 65
REGISTERED: 5 Jan 70 ICAO (Civil Aviat)
ARTICLES: 0
HEADNOTE: ICAO OFFICE
TOPIC: Air Transport
PARTIES:
　ICAO (Civil Aviat)
　Thailand

110163　　Bilateral Agreement　　0 UNTS 0
SIGNED: 17 Jan 66　　　　FORCE: 1 Jan 70
REGISTERED: 1 Jan 70 Austria
ARTICLES: 0
HEADNOTE: SOCIAL & JUVENILE WELFARE
TOPIC: Health/Educ/Welfare
PARTIES:
　Austria
　Germany, West

110164　　Bilateral Agreement　　0 UNTS 0
SIGNED: 12 Jul 66　　　　FORCE: 12 Jul 66
REGISTERED: 5 Jan 70 ICAO (Civil Aviat)
ARTICLES: 0
HEADNOTE: AIR SERVICES
TOPIC: Air Transport
PARTIES:
　Indonesia
　Netherlands

110165　　Bilateral Agreement　　0 UNTS 0
SIGNED: 17 Jul 66　　　　FORCE: 17 Jul 66
REGISTERED: 5 Jan 70 ICAO (Civil Aviat)
ARTICLES: 0
HEADNOTE: AIR SERVICES
TOPIC: Air Transport
PARTIES:
　Syria
　Yugoslavia

110166　　Bilateral Agreement　　0 UNTS 0
SIGNED: 28 Sep 67　　　　FORCE: 1 Aug 67
REGISTERED: 5 Jan 70 ICAO (Civil Aviat)
ARTICLES: 0
HEADNOTE: AIR SERVICES
TOPIC: Air Transport
PARTIES:
　Lesotho
　South Africa

110167　　Bilateral Agreement　　0 UNTS 0
SIGNED: 3 Nov 67　　　　FORCE: 3 Nov 67
REGISTERED: 5 Jan 70 ICAO (Civil Aviat)
ARTICLES: 0
HEADNOTE: AIR SERVICES
TOPIC: Air Transport
PARTIES:
　Australia
　Singapore

110168　　Bilateral Agreement　　0 UNTS 0
SIGNED: 13 Nov 67　　　　FORCE: 13 Nov 67
REGISTERED: 5 Jan 70 ICAO (Civil Aviat)
ARTICLES: 0
HEADNOTE: AIR SERVICES
TOPIC: Air Transport
PARTIES:
　Belgium
　South Africa

110169　　Bilateral Agreement　　0 UNTS 0
SIGNED: 23 May 69　　　　FORCE: 16 Sep 69
REGISTERED: 7 Jan 70 IBRD (World Bank)
ARTICLES: 0
HEADNOTE: EDUCATION PROJECT LOAN
TOPIC: IBRD Project
PARTIES:
　Malaysia
　IBRD (World Bank)

110170　　Bilateral Agreement　　0 UNTS 0
SIGNED: 15 Apr 69　　　　FORCE: 15 Apr 69
REGISTERED: 9 Jan 70 United Nations
ARTICLES: 0
HEADNOTE: PROVIDE PERSONNEL
TOPIC: IGO Operations
PARTIES:
　Dahomey
　United Nations

110171　　Bilateral Agreement　　0 UNTS 0
SIGNED: 15 Apr 69　　　　FORCE: 14 Aug 69
REGISTERED: 9 Jan 70 IBRD (World Bank)
ARTICLES: 0
HEADNOTE: OIL PALM PROJECT LOAN & GUAR-
　ANTEE
TOPIC: IBRD Project
PARTIES:
　Cameroon
　IBRD (World Bank)

110172　　Bilateral Treaty　　0 UNTS 0
SIGNED: 2 Apr 68　　　　FORCE: 27 Sep 66
REGISTERED: 12 Jan 70 Czechoslovakia
ARTICLES: 0
HEADNOTE: FRIENDSHIP & COOPERATION
TOPIC: General Amity
PARTIES:
　Czechoslovakia
　Yemen

110173　　Bilateral Agreement　　0 UNTS 0
SIGNED: 14 Jun 68　　　　FORCE: 14 Jun 66
REGISTERED: 12 Jan 70 Australia
ARTICLES: 0
HEADNOTE: CULTURE
TOPIC: Culture
PARTIES:
　Australia
　Indonesia

110174　　Bilateral Agreement　　0 UNTS 0
SIGNED: 27 Nov 68　　　　FORCE: 24 Aug 69
REGISTERED: 12 Jan 70 Australia
ARTICLES: 0
HEADNOTE: FISHERIES
TOPIC: Specific Resources
PARTIES:
　Australia
　Japan

110175　　Bilateral Agreement　　0 UNTS 0
SIGNED: 11 Feb 69　　　　FORCE: 4 Jun 69
REGISTERED: 12 Jan 70 Australia
ARTICLES: 0
HEADNOTE: DOUBLE TAXATION FISCAL EVA-
　SION
TOPIC: Taxation
PARTIES:
　Australia
　Singapore

110176　　Bilateral Exchange　　0 UNTS 0
SIGNED: 29 Apr 69　　　　FORCE: 1 May 69
REGISTERED: 12 Jan 70 Australia
ARTICLES: 0

HEADNOTE: VISAS & VISA FEES
TOPIC: Visas
PARTIES:
 Australia
 Iceland

110177 Bilateral Exchange **0 UNTS 0**
SIGNED: 15 Aug 69 FORCE: 15 Aug 69
REGISTERED: 12 Jan 70 Australia
ARTICLES: 0
HEADNOTE: GRATIS VISAS
TOPIC: Visas
PARTIES:
 Australia
 Brazil

110178 Bilateral Agreement **0 UNTS 0**
SIGNED: 23 Dec 68 FORCE: 11 Feb 69
REGISTERED: 12 Jan 70 Denmark
ARTICLES: 0
HEADNOTE: LOAN
TOPIC: Loans and Credits
PARTIES:
 Denmark
 Ivory Coast

110179 Bilateral Agreement **0 UNTS 0**
SIGNED: 10 Nov 64 FORCE: 21 Oct 69
REGISTERED: 14 Jan 70 Argentina
ARTICLES: 0
HEADNOTE: CULTURE
TOPIC: Culture
PARTIES:
 Argentina
 Morocco

110180 Bilateral Agreement **0 UNTS 0**
SIGNED: 19 Dec 66 FORCE: 14 Jun 69
REGISTERED: 14 Jan 70 Argentina
ARTICLES: 0
HEADNOTE: SCHEDULED AIR TRANSPORT
TOPIC: Air Transport
PARTIES:
 Argentina
 Bolivia

110181 Bilateral Agreement **0 UNTS 0**
SIGNED: 14 Jul 67 FORCE: 19 Nov 69
REGISTERED: 14 Jan 70 Argentina
ARTICLES: 0
HEADNOTE: CULTURE
TOPIC: Culture
PARTIES:
 Argentina
 Paraguay

110182 Bilateral Agreement **0 UNTS 0**
SIGNED: 20 Jul 67 FORCE: 20 Dec 69
REGISTERED: 14 Jan 70 Argentina
ARTICLES: 0
HEADNOTE: NUCLEAR ENERGY COOPERATION
TOPIC: Atomic Energy
PARTIES:
 Argentina
 Paraguay

110183 Bilateral Agreement **0 UNTS 0**
SIGNED: 20 Jul 67 FORCE: 3 Oct 69
REGISTERED: 14 Jan 70 Argentina
ARTICLES: 0
HEADNOTE: INDUSTRIAL INVESTMENTS & COOP-
 ERATION
TOPIC: Tech Assistance
PARTIES:
 Argentina
 Paraguay

110184 Bilateral Agreement **0 UNTS 0**
SIGNED: 25 May 68 FORCE: 14 Jul 69
REGISTERED: 14 Jan 70 Argentina
ARTICLES: 0
HEADNOTE: NUCLEAR ENERGY COOPERATION
TOPIC: Atomic Energy
PARTIES:
 Argentina
 Peru

110185 Bilateral Agreement **0 UNTS 0**
SIGNED: 8 Jul 68 FORCE: 30 Oct 69
REGISTERED: 14 Jan 70 Argentina
HEADNOTE: PAYSANDU-COLON BRIDGE
TOPIC: Territory Boundary
PARTIES:
 Argentina
 Uruguay

110186 Bilateral Agreement **0 UNTS 0**
SIGNED: 8 Jul 68 FORCE: 4 Jan 70
REGISTERED: 14 Jan 70 Argentina
ARTICLES: 0
HEADNOTE: CULTURE
TOPIC: Culture
PARTIES:
 Argentina
 Korea, South

110187 Bilateral Exchange **0 UNTS 0**
SIGNED: 21 Mar 69 FORCE: 21 Mar 69
REGISTERED: 14 Jan 70 Argentina
ARTICLES: 0
HEADNOTE: ESTABLISH CULTURAL FOUNDA-
 TION
TOPIC: Culture
PARTIES:
 Argentina
 France

110188 Bilateral Agreement **0 UNTS 0**
SIGNED: 31 Mar 69 FORCE: 22 Oct 69
REGISTERED: 14 Jan 70 Argentina
ARTICLES: 0
HEADNOTE: SCIENTIFIC & TECHNICAL COOPER-
 ATION
TOPIC: Scientific Project
PARTIES:
 Argentina
 Germany, West

110189 Bilateral Agreement **0 UNTS 0**
SIGNED: 3 Apr 69 FORCE: 22 Dec 69
REGISTERED: 14 Jan 70 Argentina
ARTICLES: 0
HEADNOTE: TRADE
TOPIC: General Trade
PARTIES:
 Argentina
 Romania

110190 Bilateral Exchange **0 UNTS 0**
SIGNED: 19 May 69 FORCE: 19 May 69
REGISTERED: 14 Jan 70 Argentina
ARTICLES: 0
HEADNOTE: ELECTRICAL SERVICES STUDIES
TOPIC: Non-IBRD Project
PARTIES:
 Argentina
 Germany, West

110191 Bilateral Exchange **0 UNTS 0**
SIGNED: 27 Jun 69 FORCE: 27 Jun 69
REGISTERED: 14 Jan 70 Argentina
ARTICLES: 0
HEADNOTE: MEAT MARKETING COORDINATION
TOPIC: Commodity Trade
PARTIES:
 Argentina
 Uruguay

110192 Bilateral Exchange **0 UNTS 0**
SIGNED: 18 Sep 69 FORCE: 18 Sep 69
REGISTERED: 14 Jan 70 Argentina
ARTICLES: 0
HEADNOTE: CREDIT FOR BEEF
TOPIC: Commodity Trade
PARTIES:
 Argentina
 Uruguay

110193 Bilateral Agreement **0 UNTS 0**
SIGNED: 15 Jul 69 FORCE: 18 Nov 69
REGISTERED: 14 Jan 70 Argentina
ARTICLES: 0

HEADNOTE: PARAGUAY RIVER MAINTENANCE
TOPIC: Territory Boundary
PARTIES:
 Argentina
 Paraguay

110194 Bilateral Agreement **0 UNTS 0**
SIGNED: 28 Aug 69 FORCE: 28 Aug 69
REGISTERED: 14 Jan 70 Argentina
ARTICLES: 0
HEADNOTE: FILM RELATIONS
TOPIC: Culture
PARTIES:
 Argentina
 Spain

110195 Bilateral Agreement **0 UNTS 0**
SIGNED: 23 Oct 69 FORCE: 23 Oct 69
REGISTERED: 14 Jan 70 Argentina
ARTICLES: 0
HEADNOTE: AID FOR IBERA SYSTEM STUDY
TOPIC: Non-IBRD Project
PARTIES:
 Argentina
 Germany, West

110196 Bilateral Exchange **0 UNTS 0**
SIGNED: 27 Jul 65 FORCE: 10 May 66
REGISTERED: 14 Jan 70 Netherlands
ARTICLES: 0
HEADNOTE: DUTCH VOLUNTEERS
TOPIC: Direct Aid
PARTIES:
 India
 Netherlands

110197 Bilateral Convention **0 UNTS 0**
SIGNED: 12 Apr 66 FORCE: 1 Jan 70
REGISTERED: 14 Jan 70 Philippines
ARTICLES: 0
HEADNOTE: DOUBLE TAXATION FISCAL EVA-
 SION
TOPIC: Taxation
PARTIES:
 Philippines
 Sweden

110198 Bilateral Agreement **0 UNTS 0**
SIGNED: 18 Apr 69 FORCE: 8 Aug 69
REGISTERED: 14 Jan 70 IBRD (World Bank)
ARTICLES: 0
HEADNOTE: DEZ IRRIGATION LOAN
TOPIC: IBRD Project
PARTIES:
 Iran
 IBRD (World Bank)

110199 Bilateral Agreement **0 UNTS 0**
SIGNED: 22 Jul 69 FORCE: 11 Aug 69
REGISTERED: 14 Jan 70 Philippines
ARTICLES: 0
HEADNOTE: AIR TRANSPORT
TOPIC: Air Transport
PARTIES:
 Korea, South
 Philippines

110200 Bilateral Agreement **0 UNTS 0**
SIGNED: 15 Apr 69 FORCE: 15 Apr 69
REGISTERED: 15 Jan 70 Denmark
ARTICLES: 0
HEADNOTE: LOAN
TOPIC: Loans and Credits
PARTIES:
 Dahomey
 Denmark

110201 Bilateral Agreement **0 UNTS 0**
SIGNED: 31 Jul 69 FORCE: 31 Jul 69
REGISTERED: 15 Jan 70 Denmark
ARTICLES: 0
HEADNOTE: LOAN
TOPIC: Loans and Credits
PARTIES:
 Chad
 Denmark

110202   Bilateral Agreement   **0 UNTS 0**
SIGNED: 15 Jan 70   FORCE: 15 Jan 70
REGISTERED: 15 Jan 70 United Nations
ARTICLES: 0
HEADNOTE: OPERATIONAL ASSISTANCE
TOPIC: Tech Assistance
PARTIES:
   State/IGO Group
   Mongolia

110203   Bilateral Agreement   **0 UNTS 0**
SIGNED: 29 Sep 69   FORCE: 29 Sep 69
REGISTERED: 16 Jan 70 Belgium
ARTICLES: 0
HEADNOTE: PROPERTY & FACILITIES
TOPIC: IGO Operations
PARTIES:
   Belgium
   Eur Space Vehicle

110204   Bilateral Convention   **0 UNTS 0**
SIGNED: 29 Apr 67   FORCE: 31 Oct 68
REGISTERED: 20 Jan 70 Romania
ARTICLES: 0
HEADNOTE: CONSULAR
TOPIC: Consul/Citizenship
PARTIES:
   Mongolia
   Romania

110205   Bilateral Agreement   **0 UNTS 0**
SIGNED: 23 Dec 67   FORCE: 29 Mar 69
REGISTERED: 20 Jan 70 Romania
ARTICLES: 0
HEADNOTE: ROAD TRANSPORT
TOPIC: Land Transport
PARTIES:
   Mongolia
   Romania

110206   Bilateral Agreement   **0 UNTS 0**
SIGNED: 17 Jun 68   FORCE: 7 Oct 68
REGISTERED: 20 Jan 70 Romania
ARTICLES: 0
HEADNOTE: TRADE & ECONOMY
TOPIC: General Trade
PARTIES:
   Romania
   Southern Yemen

110207   Bilateral Agreement   **0 UNTS 0**
SIGNED: 16 Jul 68   FORCE: 18 Feb 69
REGISTERED: 20 Jan 70 Romania
ARTICLES: 0
HEADNOTE: ROAD TRANSPORT
TOPIC: Land Transport
PARTIES:
   Germany, West
   Romania

110208   Bilateral Agreement   **0 UNTS 0**
SIGNED: 13 Sep 68   FORCE: 13 Sep 68
REGISTERED: 20 Jan 70 Romania
ARTICLES: 0
HEADNOTE: LONG-TERM TRADE
TOPIC: General Trade
PARTIES:
   Central Afri Rep
   Romania

110209   Bilateral Agreement   **0 UNTS 0**
SIGNED: 13 Sep 68   FORCE: 11 Jun 69
REGISTERED: 20 Jan 70 Romania
ARTICLES: 0
HEADNOTE: CULTURAL & SCIENTIFIC COOPER-
   ATION
TOPIC: Tech Assistance
PARTIES:
   Central Afri Rep
   Romania

110210   Bilateral Agreement   **0 UNTS 0**
SIGNED: 18 Oct 68   FORCE: 18 Oct 68
REGISTERED: 20 Jan 70 Romania
ARTICLES: 0
HEADNOTE: TRADE

TOPIC: General Trade
PARTIES:
   Romania
   UK Great Britain

110211   Bilateral Agreement   **0 UNTS 0**
SIGNED: 23 Nov 68   FORCE: 17 Mar 69
REGISTERED: 20 Jan 70 Romania
ARTICLES: 0
HEADNOTE: CULTURE
TOPIC: Culture
PARTIES:
   Czechoslovakia
   Romania

110212   Bilateral Agreement   **0 UNTS 0**
SIGNED: 16 Sep 68   FORCE: 18 Jan 69
REGISTERED: 20 Jan 70 Romania
ARTICLES: 0
HEADNOTE: ECONOMIC INDUSTRIAL TECHNICAL
   COOPERATION
TOPIC: Tech Assistance
PARTIES:
   Bel-Lux Econ Union
   Romania

110213   Bilateral Convention   **0 UNTS 0**
SIGNED: 10 Feb 69   FORCE: 9 Aug 69
REGISTERED: 20 Jan 70 Romania
ARTICLES: 0
HEADNOTE: PHYTOSANITARY QUARANTINE
TOPIC: Specific Resources
PARTIES:
   Poland
   Romania

110214   Bilateral Agreement   **0 UNTS 0**
SIGNED: 16 Dec 68   FORCE: 15 Aug 69
REGISTERED: 20 Jan 70 IBRD (World Bank)
ARTICLES: 0
HEADNOTE: EDUCATION LOAN
TOPIC: IBRD Project
PARTIES:
   Guatemala
   IBRD (World Bank)

110215   Bilateral Agreement   **0 UNTS 0**
SIGNED: 18 Feb 69   FORCE: 11 Jul 69
REGISTERED: 20 Jan 70 IDA (Devel Assoc)
ARTICLES: 0
HEADNOTE: TELECOMMUNICATIONS CREDIT
TOPIC: Non-IBRD Project
PARTIES:
   IDA (Devel Assoc)
   Upper Volta

110216   Bilateral Agreement   **0 UNTS 0**
SIGNED: 5 Mar 69   FORCE: 5 Aug 69
REGISTERED: 20 Jan 70 IDA (Devel Assoc)
ARTICLES: 0
HEADNOTE: HINVI AGRICULTURE DEVELOPMENT
   CREDIT
TOPIC: Non-IBRD Project
PARTIES:
   Dahomey
   IDA (Devel Assoc)

110217   Bilateral Instrument   **0 UNTS 0**
SIGNED: 5 Mar 69   FORCE: 5 Mar 69
REGISTERED: 20 Jan 70 IDA (Devel Assoc)
ARTICLES: 0
HEADNOTE: HINVI AGRICULTURE DEVELOPMENT
TOPIC: Non-IBRD Project
PARTIES:
   France
   IDA (Devel Assoc)

110218   Bilateral Agreement   **0 UNTS 0**
SIGNED: 11 Apr 69   FORCE: 11 Jul 69
REGISTERED: 20 Jan 70 IDA (Devel Assoc)
ARTICLES: 0
HEADNOTE: COFFEE IMPROVEMENT CREDIT
TOPIC: Non-IBRD Project
PARTIES:
   Burundi
   IDA (Devel Assoc)

110219   Bilateral Agreement   **0 UNTS 0**
SIGNED: 9 May 69   FORCE: 8 Aug 69
REGISTERED: 20 Jan 70 IBRD (World Bank)
ARTICLES: 0
HEADNOTE: FINCHAA HYDROELECTRIC LOAN
TOPIC: IBRD Project
PARTIES:
   Ethiopia
   IBRD (World Bank)

110220   Bilateral Agreement   **0 UNTS 0**
SIGNED: 28 May 69   FORCE: 2 Sep 69
REGISTERED: 20 Jan 70 IBRD (World Bank)
ARTICLES: 0
HEADNOTE: POWER TRANSPORT & DISTRIBU-
   TION LOAN
TOPIC: IBRD Project
PARTIES:
   IBRD (World Bank)
   Trinidad/Tobago

110221   Bilateral Agreement   **0 UNTS 0**
SIGNED: 18 Jun 69   FORCE: 29 Aug 69
REGISTERED: 20 Jan 70 IBRD (World Bank)
ARTICLES: 0
HEADNOTE: HIGHWAY PROJECT LOAN
TOPIC: IBRD Project
PARTIES:
   IBRD (World Bank)
   Venezuela

110222   Bilateral Agreement   **0 UNTS 0**
SIGNED: 24 Mar 69   FORCE: 21 May 69
REGISTERED: 26 Jan 70 IBRD (World Bank)
ARTICLES: 0
HEADNOTE: PUMPED STORAGE POWER LOAN
TOPIC: IBRD Project
PARTIES:
   Ireland
   IBRD (World Bank)

110224   Bilateral Agreement   **0 UNTS 0**
SIGNED: 29 May 69   FORCE: 19 Jun 69
REGISTERED: 26 Jan 70 IDA (Devel Assoc)
ARTICLES: 0
HEADNOTE: EDUCATION CREDIT
TOPIC: Non-IBRD Project
PARTIES:
   IDA (Devel Assoc)
   Tanzania

110225   Bilateral Agreement   **0 UNTS 0**
SIGNED: 25 Jun 69   FORCE: 24 Dec 69
REGISTERED: 26 Jan 70 IBRD (World Bank)
ARTICLES: 0
HEADNOTE: LIVESTOCK LOAN
TOPIC: IBRD Project
PARTIES:
   Paraguay
   IBRD (World Bank)

110226   Bilateral Agreement   **0 UNTS 0**
SIGNED: 25 Jun 69   FORCE: 24 Dec 69
REGISTERED: 26 Jan 70 IDA (Devel Assoc)
ARTICLES: 0
HEADNOTE: LIVESTOCK CREDIT
TOPIC: Non-IBRD Project
PARTIES:
   Paraguay
   IDA (Devel Assoc)

110227   Bilateral Agreement   **0 UNTS 0**
SIGNED: 26 Jun 69   FORCE: 23 Sep 69
REGISTERED: 26 Jan 70 IDA (Devel Assoc)
ARTICLES: 0
HEADNOTE: AGRICULTURE DEVELOPMENT BANK
   CREDIT
TOPIC: Non-IBRD Project
PARTIES:
   Pakistan
   IDA (Devel Assoc)

110228   Bilateral Agreement   **0 UNTS 0**
SIGNED: 6 Dec 46   FORCE: 31 Oct 50
REGISTERED: 26 Jan 70 France
ARTICLES: 0

HEADNOTE: CULTURE
TOPIC: Culture
PARTIES:
  Brazil
  France

110229   Bilateral Exchange   **0 UNTS 0**
SIGNED: 22 Jan 63   FORCE: 22 Jan 63
REGISTERED: 26 Jan 70 France
ARTICLES: 0
HEADNOTE: COOPERATION PERSONNEL PRIVI-
  LEGES
TOPIC: Privil/Immunities
PARTIES:
  Brazil
  France

110230   Bilateral Agreement   **0 UNTS 0**
SIGNED: 16 Jan 67   FORCE: 3 Aug 68
REGISTERED: 26 Jan 70 France
ARTICLES: 0
HEADNOTE: TECHNICAL & SCIENTIFIC COOPER-
  ATION
TOPIC: Tech Assistance
PARTIES:
  Brazil
  France

110231   Bilateral Exchange   **0 UNTS 0**
SIGNED: 20 Jun 68   FORCE: 20 Jun 68
REGISTERED: 26 Jan 70 France
ARTICLES: 0
HEADNOTE: TELEMETRY STATION INSTALLA-
  TION
TOPIC: Scientific Project
PARTIES:
  Brazil
  France

110232   Multilateral Instrument   **0 UNTS 0**
SIGNED: 18 Oct 69   FORCE: 26 Jan 70
REGISTERED: 26 Jan 70 United Nations
ARTICLES: 0
HEADNOTE: CARIBBEAN DEVELOPMENT BANK
TOPIC: IGO Establishment
PARTIES:
  Antigua   SIGNED: 18 Oct 69   RATIFIED:
    30 Jan 70 FORCE: 30 Jan 70
  Bahamas   SIGNED: 18 Oct 69   RATIFIED:
    28 Jan 70 FORCE: 28 Jan 70
  Barbados   SIGNED: 18 Oct 69   RATIFIED:
    16 Jan 70 FORCE: 26 Jan 70
  British Honduras SIGNED: 18 Oct 69 RATIFIED:
    26 Jan 70 FORCE: 26 Jan 70
  Canada   SIGNED: 18 Oct 69   RATIFIED:
    22 Jan 70 FORCE: 26 Jan 70
  Cayman Island SIGNED: 18 Oct 69 RATIFIED:
    27 Jan 70 FORCE: 27 Jan 70
  Dominican Republic SIGNED: 18 Oct 69 RATI-
    FIED: 26 Jan 70 FORCE: 26 Jan 70
  Grenada   SIGNED: 18 Oct 69   RATIFIED:
    26 Jan 70 FORCE: 26 Jan 70
  Guyana   SIGNED: 18 Oct 69   RATIFIED:
    23 Jan 70 FORCE: 26 Jan 70
  Jamaica SIGNED: 18 Oct 69 RATIFIED: 9 Jan 70
    FORCE: 26 Jan 70
  Montserrat   SIGNED: 18 Oct 69   RATIFIED:
    28 Jan 70 FORCE: 28 Jan 70
  St. Christopher SIGNED: 18 Oct 69 RATIFIED:
    26 Jan 70 FORCE: 26 Jan 70
  St. Lucia   SIGNED: 18 Oct 69   RATIFIED:
    26 Jan 70 FORCE: 26 Jan 70
  St. Vincent SIGNED: 18 Oct 69   RATIFIED:
    26 Jan 70 FORCE: 26 Jan 70
  Trinidad/Tobago SIGNED: 18 Oct 69 RATIFIED:
    20 Jan 70 FORCE: 26 Jan 70
  Turk-Caicose Is SIGNED: 18 Oct 69 RATIFIED:
    5 Jan 70 FORCE: 26 Jan 70
  UK Great Britain SIGNED: 18 Oct 69 RATIFIED:
    23 Jan 70 FORCE: 26 Jan 70
  Virgin Islands SIGNED: 18 Oct 69 RATIFIED:
    30 Jan 70 FORCE: 30 Jan 70

110233   Multilateral Agreement   **0 UNTS 0**
SIGNED: 3 Mar 69   FORCE: 11 Jun 69
REGISTERED: 26 Jan 70 IDA (Devel Assoc)
ARTICLES: 0
HEADNOTE: PROTECTION MARKS OF ORIGIN
TOPIC: Commodity Trade

PARTIES:
  Central Afri Rep
  France
  Italy
  IDA (Devel Assoc)

110234   Bilateral Exchange   **0 UNTS 0**
SIGNED: 20 Mar 67   FORCE: 20 Mar 67
REGISTERED: 27 Jan 70 France
ARTICLES: 0
HEADNOTE: FISHERIES
TOPIC: Specific Resources
PARTIES:
  France
  Spain

110235   Bilateral Agreement   **0 UNTS 0**
SIGNED: 28 Apr 69   FORCE: 14 Oct 69
REGISTERED: 27 Jan 70 IDA (Devel Assoc)
ARTICLES: 0
HEADNOTE: ENDE POWER CREDIT
TOPIC: Non-IBRD Project
PARTIES:
  Bolivia
  IDA (Devel Assoc)

110236   Bilateral Agreement   **0 UNTS 0**
SIGNED: 18 Nov 68   FORCE: 22 Oct 69
REGISTERED: 29 Jan 70 UK Great Britain
ARTICLES: 0
HEADNOTE: ATOMIC ENERGY COOPERATION
TOPIC: Atomic Energy
PARTIES:
  Chile
  UK Great Britain

110237   Bilateral Exchange   **0 UNTS 0**
SIGNED: 8 Aug 69   FORCE: 8 Aug 69
REGISTERED: 29 Jan 70 UK Great Britain
ARTICLES: 0
HEADNOTE: FINANCIAL ASSISTANCE SCHOOL
  CONSTRUCTION
TOPIC: Direct Aid
PARTIES:
  Nepal
  UK Great Britain

110238   Bilateral Exchange   **0 UNTS 0**
SIGNED: 9 Aug 69   FORCE: 9 Aug 69
REGISTERED: 29 Jan 70 UK Great Britain
ARTICLES: 0
HEADNOTE: FOREIGN EXCHANGE OPERATIONS
  FUND
TOPIC: Finance
PARTIES:
  Laos
  UK Great Britain

110239   Bilateral Exchange   **0 UNTS 0**
SIGNED: 12 Aug 69   FORCE: 12 Aug 69
REGISTERED: 29 Jan 70 UK Great Britain
ARTICLES: 0
HEADNOTE: CEREALS
TOPIC: Commodity Trade
PARTIES:
  Hungary
  UK Great Britain

110240   Bilateral Exchange   **0 UNTS 0**
SIGNED: 1 Sep 69   FORCE: 1 Sep 69
REGISTERED: 29 Jan 70 UK Great Britain
ARTICLES: 0
HEADNOTE: STERLING RESERVES GUARANTEE
TOPIC: Finance
PARTIES:
  Botswana
  UK Great Britain

110241   Bilateral Agreement   **0 UNTS 0**
SIGNED: 1 Sep 69   FORCE: 1 Sep 69
REGISTERED: 29 Jan 70 UK Great Britain
ARTICLES: 0
HEADNOTE: FOREIGN EXCHANGE EXPENSES UK
  FORCES
TOPIC: Finance

PARTIES:
  Germany, West
  UK Great Britain

110242   Bilateral Exchange   **0 UNTS 0**
SIGNED: 15 Sep 69   FORCE: 15 Sep 69
REGISTERED: 29 Jan 70 UK Great Britain
ARTICLES: 0
HEADNOTE: DEVELOPMENT LOAN
TOPIC: Loans and Credits
PARTIES:
  Turkey
  UK Great Britain

110243   Bilateral Exchange   **0 UNTS 0**
SIGNED: 25 Sep 69   FORCE: 25 Sep 69
REGISTERED: 29 Jan 70 UK Great Britain
ARTICLES: 0
HEADNOTE: SOCIAL SECURITY PENSIONS
TOPIC: Finance
PARTIES:
  UK Great Britain
  USA (United States)

110244   Bilateral Convention   **0 UNTS 0**
SIGNED: 15 Nov 67   FORCE: 1 Mar 69
REGISTERED: 30 Jan 70 France
ARTICLES: 0
HEADNOTE: TAXATION
TOPIC: Taxation
PARTIES:
  France
  Mauritania

110245   Bilateral Exchange   **0 UNTS 0**
SIGNED: 29 Aug 69   FORCE: 29 Aug 69
REGISTERED: 1 Feb 70
ARTICLES: 0 LANGUAGE: English.
HEADNOTE: TECHNICAL ASSISTANCE UK TRUST
  TERRITORIES
TOPIC: Tech Assistance
PARTIES:
  Mauritius
  United Nations

110246   Bilateral Exchange   **0 UNTS 0**
SIGNED: 29 Aug 69   FORCE: 29 Aug 69
REGISTERED: 1 Feb 70
ARTICLES: 0 LANGUAGE: English.
HEADNOTE: ADMINISTRATIVE PERSONNEL UK
  TRUST TERRITORIES
TOPIC: Tech Assistance
PARTIES:
  Mauritius
  United Nations

110247   Bilateral Exchange   **0 UNTS 0**
SIGNED: 29 Aug 69   FORCE: 29 Aug 69
REGISTERED: 1 Feb 70
ARTICLES: 0 LANGUAGE: English.
HEADNOTE: ASSISTANCE
TOPIC: General Aid
PARTIES:
  Mauritius
  United Nations

110248   Bilateral Exchange   **0 UNTS 0**
SIGNED: 28 May 65   FORCE: 28 May 65
REGISTERED: 3 Feb 70
ARTICLES: 0 LANGUAGE: English.
HEADNOTE: FREE ENTRY DEPENDENTS US PER-
  SONNEL
TOPIC: Visas
PARTIES:
  Philippines
  USA (United States)

110249   Bilateral Agreement   **0 UNTS 0**
SIGNED: 1 Apr 68   FORCE: 1 Apr 68
REGISTERED: 3 Feb 70
ARTICLES: 0 LANGUAGE: English. Spanish.
HEADNOTE: AGRI COMMOD
TOPIC: General Aid
PARTIES:
  Dominican Republic
  USA (United States)

110250   Bilateral Agreement   **0 UNTS 0**
SIGNED: 11 Jun 68   FORCE: 11 Jun 68
REGISTERED: 3 Feb 70
ARTICLES: 0 LANGUAGE: English. Spanish.
HEADNOTE: AGRI COMMOD
TOPIC: General Aid
PARTIES:
  Dominican Republic
  USA (United States)

110251   Bilateral Agreement   **0 UNTS 0**
SIGNED: 28 Mar 69   FORCE: 28 Mar 69
REGISTERED: 3 Feb 70
ARTICLES: 0 LANGUAGE: English.
HEADNOTE: AGRI COMMOD
TOPIC: General Aid
PARTIES:
  Dominican Republic
  USA (United States)

110252   Bilateral Exchange   **0 UNTS 0**
SIGNED: 15 Jul 68   FORCE: 15 Jul 68
REGISTERED: 3 Feb 70
ARTICLES: 0 LANGUAGE: English. Spanish.
HEADNOTE: ECONOMIC RELATIONS
TOPIC: General Economic
PARTIES:
  Spain
  USA (United States)

110253   Bilateral Agreement   **0 UNTS 0**
SIGNED: 5 Dec 68   FORCE: 5 Dec 68
REGISTERED: 3 Feb 70
ARTICLES: 0 LANGUAGE: English.
HEADNOTE: VOLUNTARY AGENCY SUPPLIES
TOPIC: Customs
PARTIES:
  India
  USA (United States)

110254   Bilateral Agreement   **0 UNTS 0**
SIGNED: 10 Dec 68   FORCE: 10 Dec 68
REGISTERED: 3 Feb 70
ARTICLES: 0 LANGUAGE: English.
HEADNOTE: AGRI COMMOD
TOPIC: General Aid
PARTIES:
  Ghana
  USA (United States)

110255   Bilateral Agreement   **0 UNTS 0**
SIGNED: 9 Jun 69   FORCE: 9 Jun 69
REGISTERED: 3 Feb 70
ARTICLES: 0 LANGUAGE: English.
HEADNOTE: AGRI COMMOD
TOPIC: General Aid
PARTIES:
  Ghana
  USA (United States)

110256   Bilateral Exchange   **0 UNTS 0**
SIGNED: 16 Dec 68   FORCE: 16 Dec 68
REGISTERED: 3 Feb 70
ARTICLES: 0 LANGUAGE: English. Chinese.
HEADNOTE: TRANSFER USS GERONIMO
TOPIC: Milit Assistance
PARTIES:
  Taiwan
  USA (United States)

110257   Bilateral Exchange   **0 UNTS 0**
SIGNED: 19 Dec 68   FORCE: 19 Dec 68
REGISTERED: 3 Feb 70
ARTICLES: 0 LANGUAGE: English. Spanish.
HEADNOTE: BOGOTA SAN ANDRES RAWIN-
  SONDE
TOPIC: Scientific Project
PARTIES:
  Colombia
  USA (United States)

110258   Bilateral Exchange   **0 UNTS 0**
SIGNED: 20 Dec 68   FORCE: 20 Dec 68
REGISTERED: 3 Feb 70
ARTICLES: 0 LANGUAGE: English. Spanish.
HEADNOTE: RESEARCH EARTH SURVEYS

TOPIC: Scientific Project
PARTIES:
  Mexico
  USA (United States)

110259   Bilateral Agreement   **0 UNTS 0**
SIGNED: 23 Dec 68   FORCE: 23 Dec 68
REGISTERED: 3 Feb 70
ARTICLES: 0 LANGUAGE: English.
HEADNOTE: AGRI COMMOD
TOPIC: General Aid
PARTIES:
  India
  USA (United States)

110260   Bilateral Exchange   **0 UNTS 0**
SIGNED: 23 Dec 68   FORCE: 23 Dec 68
REGISTERED: 3 Feb 70
ARTICLES: 0 LANGUAGE: English.
HEADNOTE: COTTON TEXTILES
TOPIC: Commodity Trade
PARTIES:
  India
  USA (United States)

110261   Bilateral Agreement   **0 UNTS 0**
SIGNED: 24 Dec 68   FORCE: 24 Dec 68
REGISTERED: 3 Feb 70
ARTICLES: 0 LANGUAGE: English.
HEADNOTE: AGRI COMMOD
TOPIC: Commodity Trade
PARTIES:
  Tunisia
  USA (United States)

110262   Bilateral Exchange   **0 UNTS 0**
SIGNED: 13 Jan 69   FORCE: 13 Jan 69
REGISTERED: 3 Feb 70
ARTICLES: 0 LANGUAGE: English.
HEADNOTE: NORFOLK ISLAND IONOSPHERIC RA-
  DIO
TOPIC: Scientific Project
PARTIES:
  Australia
  USA (United States)

110263   Bilateral Agreement   **0 UNTS 0**
SIGNED: 17 Jan 69   FORCE: 17 Jan 69
REGISTERED: 3 Feb 70
ARTICLES: 0 LANGUAGE: English.
HEADNOTE: AGRI COMMOD
TOPIC: Commodity Trade
PARTIES:
  Israel
  USA (United States)

110264   Bilateral Exchange   **0 UNTS 0**
SIGNED: 23 Jan 69   FORCE: 23 Jan 69
REGISTERED: 3 Feb 70
ARTICLES: 0 LANGUAGE: English. Chinese.
HEADNOTE: SCIENTIFIC SCHOLARLY COOPER-
  ATION
TOPIC: Scientific Project
PARTIES:
  Taiwan
  USA (United States)

110265   Bilateral Exchange   **0 UNTS 0**
SIGNED: 30 Jan 69   FORCE: 30 Jan 69
REGISTERED: 3 Feb 70
ARTICLES: 0 LANGUAGE: English. French.
HEADNOTE: SAFEGUARDS NATURAL URANIUM
TOPIC: Sanitation
PARTIES:
  Canada
  USA (United States)

110266   Bilateral Agreement   **0 UNTS 0**
SIGNED: 3 Feb 69   FORCE: 3 Feb 69
REGISTERED: 3 Feb 70
ARTICLES: 0 LANGUAGE: English. French.
HEADNOTE: AGRI COMMOD
TOPIC: Commodity Trade
PARTIES:
  Guinea
  USA (United States)

110267   Bilateral Agreement   **0 UNTS 0**
SIGNED: 6 Feb 69   FORCE: 6 Feb 68
REGISTERED: 3 Feb 70
ARTICLES: 0 LANGUAGE: English.
HEADNOTE: AGRI COMMOD
TOPIC: Commodity Trade
PARTIES:
  Turkey
  USA (United States)

110268   Bilateral Agreement   **0 UNTS 0**
SIGNED: 25 Feb 69   FORCE: 25 Feb 69
REGISTERED: 3 Feb 70
ARTICLES: 0 LANGUAGE: English.
HEADNOTE: AGRI COMMOD
TOPIC: Commodity Trade
PARTIES:
  Morocco
  USA (United States)

110269   Bilateral Agreement   **0 UNTS 0**
SIGNED: 28 Feb 69   FORCE: 28 Feb 69
REGISTERED: 3 Feb 70
ARTICLES: 0 LANGUAGE: English. Czechoslo-
  vakian.
HEADNOTE: AIR TRANSPORT
TOPIC: Air Transport
PARTIES:
  Czechoslovakia
  USA (United States)

110270   Bilateral Exchange   **0 UNTS 0**
SIGNED: 21 Mar 69   FORCE: 21 Mar 69
REGISTERED: 3 Feb 70
ARTICLES: 0 LANGUAGE: English. French.
HEADNOTE: TEMPORARY COFFERDAM CON-
  STRUCTION
TOPIC: Other Ad Hoc
PARTIES:
  Canada
  USA (United States)

110271   Bilateral Exchange   **0 UNTS 0**
SIGNED: 21 Mar 69   FORCE: 20 May 69
REGISTERED: 3 Feb 70
ARTICLES: 0 LANGUAGE: English. French.
HEADNOTE: TEMPORARY DIVERSION WATER
TOPIC: Other Ad Hoc
PARTIES:
  Canada
  USA (United States)

110272   Bilateral Exchange   **0 UNTS 0**
SIGNED: 25 Apr 69   FORCE: 1 May 69
REGISTERED: 3 Feb 70
ARTICLES: 0 LANGUAGE: English. Romanian.
HEADNOTE: VISA FEES
TOPIC: Visas
PARTIES:
  Romania
  USA (United States)

110273   Bilateral Agreement   **0 UNTS 0**
SIGNED: 29 Apr 69   FORCE: 29 Apr 69
REGISTERED: 3 Feb 70
ARTICLES: 0 LANGUAGE: English. Spanish.
HEADNOTE: AGRI COMMOD
TOPIC: Commodity Trade
PARTIES:
  Chile
  USA (United States)

110274   Bilateral Agreement   **0 UNTS 0**
SIGNED: 14 May 69   FORCE: 14 May 69
REGISTERED: 3 Feb 70
ARTICLES: 0 LANGUAGE: English. French.
HEADNOTE: AGRI COMMOD
TOPIC: Commodity Trade
PARTIES:
  Congo (Brazzaville)
  USA (United States)

110275   Bilateral Agreement   **0 UNTS 0**
SIGNED: 16 May 69   FORCE: 16 May 69
REGISTERED: 3 Feb 70
ARTICLES: 0 LANGUAGE: English. Russian.

HEADNOTE: RECIPROCAL ALLOCATION LAND
  PLOTS
TOPIC: Consul/Citizenship
PARTIES:
  USA (United States)
  USSR (Soviet Union)

110276   Bilateral Agreement   **0 UNTS 0**
SIGNED: 23 May 69   FORCE: 23 May 69
REGISTERED: 3 Feb 70
ARTICLES: 0 LANGUAGE: English.
HEADNOTE: AGRI COMMOD
TOPIC: Commodity Trade
PARTIES:
  Iceland
  USA (United States)

110277   Bilateral Exchange   **0 UNTS 0**
SIGNED: 2 Jun 69   FORCE: 2 Jun 69
REGISTERED: 3 Feb 70
ARTICLES: 0 LANGUAGE: English.
HEADNOTE: AMATEUR RADIO
TOPIC: Telecommunications
PARTIES:
  Sweden
  USA (United States)

110278   Bilateral Agreement   **0 UNTS 0**
SIGNED: 4 Oct 67   FORCE: 6 Dec 68
REGISTERED: 3 Feb 70
ARTICLES: 0 LANGUAGE: Russian. Arabic.
HEADNOTE: CULTURAL SCIENTIFIC COOPER-
  ATION
TOPIC: Culture
PARTIES:
  Jordan
  USSR (Soviet Union)

110279   Bilateral Agreement   **0 UNTS 0**
SIGNED: 6 Feb 68   FORCE: 18 Mar 69
REGISTERED: 3 Feb 70
ARTICLES: 0 LANGUAGE: Russian. Persian.
HEADNOTE: ECONOMIC TECHNICAL COOPER-
  ATION
TOPIC: Tech Assistance
PARTIES:
  Afghanistan
  USSR (Soviet Union)

110280   Bilateral Agreement   **0 UNTS 0**
SIGNED: 8 Mar 68   FORCE: 29 Apr 69
REGISTERED: 3 Feb 70
ARTICLES: 0 LANGUAGE: Russian. French.
HEADNOTE: TRADE
TOPIC: General Trade
PARTIES:
  Upper Volta
  USSR (Soviet Union)

110281   Bilateral Agreement   **0 UNTS 0**
SIGNED: 22 Mar 68   FORCE: 6 Jun 69
REGISTERED: 3 Feb 70
ARTICLES: 0 LANGUAGE: Russian. German.
HEADNOTE: CULTURAL SCIENTIFIC COOPER-
  ATION
TOPIC: Culture
PARTIES:
  Austria
  USSR (Soviet Union)

110282   Bilateral Agreement   **0 UNTS 0**
SIGNED: 28 May 68   FORCE: 11 Apr 69
REGISTERED: 3 Feb 70
ARTICLES: 0 LANGUAGE: Russian. Spanish.
HEADNOTE: CULTURAL SCIENTIFIC EXCHANGES
TOPIC: Culture
PARTIES:
  Mexico
  USSR (Soviet Union)

110283   Bilateral Agreement   **0 UNTS 0**
SIGNED: 16 Nov 68   FORCE: 11 Apr 69
REGISTERED: 3 Feb 70
ARTICLES: 0 LANGUAGE: Russian. Hungarian.
HEADNOTE: CULTURAL SCIENTIFIC COOPER-
  ATION

TOPIC: Culture
PARTIES:
  Hungary
  USSR (Soviet Union)

110284   Bilateral Agreement   **0 UNTS 0**
SIGNED: 3 Apr 69   FORCE: 6 Jan 70
REGISTERED: 3 Feb 70
ARTICLES: 0 LANGUAGE: English.
HEADNOTE: CREDIT ENGINEER ACCOUNT ASSIS-
  TANCE
TOPIC: Loans and Credits
PARTIES:
  IDA (Devel Assoc)
  Somalia

110285   Bilateral Agreement   **0 UNTS 0**
SIGNED: 26 May 69   FORCE: 15 Aug 69
REGISTERED: 3 Feb 70
ARTICLES: 0 LANGUAGE: English.
HEADNOTE: CREDIT HIGHWAY ENGINEERING
TOPIC: Loans and Credits
PARTIES:
  Congo (Zaire)
  IDA (Devel Assoc)

110286   Bilateral Agreement   **0 UNTS 0**
SIGNED: 4 Jun 69   FORCE: 16 Sep 69
REGISTERED: 3 Feb 70
ARTICLES: 0 LANGUAGE: English.
HEADNOTE: GUARANTEE RAILWAY
TOPIC: IBRD Project
PARTIES:
  IBRD (World Bank)
  Tunisia

110287   Bilateral Agreement   **0 UNTS 0**
SIGNED: 4 Jun 69   FORCE: 16 Sep 69
REGISTERED: 3 Feb 70
ARTICLES: 0 LANGUAGE: English.
HEADNOTE: CREDIT RAILWAY
TOPIC: IBRD Project
PARTIES:
  IDA (Devel Assoc)
  Tunisia

110288   Bilateral Agreement   **0 UNTS 0**
SIGNED: 11 Jun 69   FORCE: 25 Sep 69
REGISTERED: 3 Feb 70
ARTICLES: 0 LANGUAGE: English.
HEADNOTE: LOAN EDUCATION
TOPIC: IBRD Project
PARTIES:
  El Salvador
  IBRD (World Bank)

110289   Bilateral Agreement   **0 UNTS 0**
SIGNED: 12 Jun 69   FORCE: 19 Sep 69
REGISTERED: 3 Feb 70
ARTICLES: 0 LANGUAGE: English.
HEADNOTE: GUARANTEE LIVESTOCK AGRICUL-
  TURE DEVELOPMENT
TOPIC: IBRD Project
PARTIES:
  Mexico
  IBRD (World Bank)

110290   Bilateral Agreement   **0 UNTS 0**
SIGNED: 24 Jun 69   FORCE: 12 Jan 70
REGISTERED: 3 Feb 70
ARTICLES: 0 LANGUAGE: English.
HEADNOTE: LOAN SECOND ROAD
TOPIC: IBRD Project
PARTIES:
  Argentina
  IBRD (World Bank)

110291   Bilateral Agreement   **0 UNTS 0**
SIGNED: 29 Jul 69   FORCE: 1 Oct 69
REGISTERED: 3 Feb 70
ARTICLES: 0 LANGUAGE: English.
HEADNOTE: CREDIT HIGHWAY ENGINEERING
TOPIC: Loans and Credits
PARTIES:
  Ghana
  IDA (Devel Assoc)

110292   Bilateral Agreement   **0 UNTS 0**
SIGNED: 8 Apr 64   FORCE: 13 Oct 64
REGISTERED: 6 Feb 70
ARTICLES: 0 LANGUAGE: Bulgarian. Arabic.
HEADNOTE: FRIENDSHIP COOPERATION
TOPIC: General Amity
PARTIES:
  Bulgaria
  Yemen

110293   Bilateral Agreement   **0 UNTS 0**
SIGNED: 8 Apr 64   FORCE: 8 Apr 64
REGISTERED: 6 Feb 70
ARTICLES: 0 LANGUAGE: Bulgarian. Arabic.
HEADNOTE: CULTURE
TOPIC: Culture
PARTIES:
  Bulgaria
  Yemen

110294   Bilateral Agreement   **0 UNTS 0**
SIGNED: 9 Jul 64   FORCE: 9 Jul 64
REGISTERED: 6 Feb 70
ARTICLES: 0 LANGUAGE: Bulgarian. Greek.
HEADNOTE: TELECOMMUNICATIONS
TOPIC: Postal Service
PARTIES:
  Bulgaria
  Greece

110295   Bilateral Agreement   **0 UNTS 0**
SIGNED: 9 Jul 64   FORCE: 9 Jul 64
REGISTERED: 6 Feb 70
ARTICLES: 0 LANGUAGE: Bulgarian. Greek.
HEADNOTE: ROAD TRANSPORT GOODS PASSEN-
  GERS
TOPIC: Land Transport
PARTIES:
  Bulgaria
  Greece

110296   Bilateral Agreement   **0 UNTS 0**
SIGNED: 9 Jul 64   FORCE: 9 Jul 64
REGISTERED: 6 Feb 70
ARTICLES: 0 LANGUAGE: Bulgarian. Greek.
HEADNOTE: COOPERATION TOURISM
TOPIC: Visas
PARTIES:
  Bulgaria
  Greece

110297   Bilateral Agreement   **0 UNTS 0**
SIGNED: 9 Jul 64   FORCE: 9 Jul 64
REGISTERED: 6 Feb 70
ARTICLES: 0 LANGUAGE: Bulgarian. Greek.
HEADNOTE: ESTABLISH AIR ROUTE
TOPIC: Air Transport
PARTIES:
  Bulgaria
  Greece

110298   Bilateral Agreement   **0 UNTS 0**
SIGNED: 31 May 65   FORCE: 20 Nov 65
REGISTERED: 6 Feb 70
ARTICLES: 0 LANGUAGE: Bulgarian. Spanish.
HEADNOTE: AIR TRANSPORT
TOPIC: Air Transport
PARTIES:
  Bulgaria
  Cuba

110299   Bilateral Agreement   **0 UNTS 0**
SIGNED: 31 May 65   FORCE: 31 May 65
REGISTERED: 6 Feb 70
ARTICLES: 0 LANGUAGE: Bulgarian. Spanish.
HEADNOTE: COOPERATION TOURISM
TOPIC: Visas
PARTIES:
  Bulgaria
  Cuba

110300   Bilateral Agreement   **0 UNTS 0**
SIGNED: 8 Jun 65   FORCE: 21 Jul 65
REGISTERED: 6 Feb 70
ARTICLES: 0 LANGUAGE: Bulgarian. Polish.
HEADNOTE: ABOLITION VISAS

TOPIC: Visas
PARTIES:
Bulgaria
Poland

110301 Bilateral Agreement **0 UNTS 0**
SIGNED: 18 Oct 66 FORCE: 27 Apr 67
REGISTERED: 6 Feb 70
ARTICLES: 0 LANGUAGE: Bulgarian. Mongolian.
HEADNOTE: VISAS
TOPIC: Visas
PARTIES:
Bulgaria
Mongolia

110302 Bilateral Agreement **0 UNTS 0**
SIGNED: 28 Oct 67 FORCE: 1 Jan 68
REGISTERED: 6 Feb 70
ARTICLES: 0 LANGUAGE: Bulgarian. Norwegian.
HEADNOTE: VISAS
TOPIC: Visas
PARTIES:
Bulgaria
Norway

110303 Bilateral Agreement **0 UNTS 0**
SIGNED: 11 Jan 68 FORCE: 1 Jun 68
REGISTERED: 6 Feb 70
ARTICLES: 0 LANGUAGE: Bulgarian. Italian.
HEADNOTE: ROAD TRANSPORT
TOPIC: Land Transport
PARTIES:
Bulgaria
Italy

110304 Bilateral Agreement **0 UNTS 0**
SIGNED: 10 Apr 68 FORCE: 1 Jul 68
REGISTERED: 6 Feb 70
ARTICLES: 0 LANGUAGE: Bulgarian. Icelandic.
HEADNOTE: VISAS
TOPIC: Visas
PARTIES:
Bulgaria
Iceland

110305 Multilateral Exchange **0 UNTS 0**
SIGNED: 12 Jun 69 FORCE: 12 Jun 69
REGISTERED: 6 Feb 70
ARTICLES: 0 LANGUAGE: French.
HEADNOTE: FACILITATION TRAVEL
TOPIC: Visas
PARTIES:
Belgium
Luxembourg
Netherlands
San Marino

110306 Multilateral Agreement **0 UNTS 0**
SIGNED: 13 Feb 61 FORCE: 1 Feb 70
REGISTERED: 9 Feb 70
ARTICLES: 0 LANGUAGE: German. French. Dutch.
HEADNOTE: SOCIAL SECURITY
TOPIC: ILO Labor
PARTIES:
Belgium SIGNED: 13 Feb 61 RATIFIED: 4 Jun 63 FORCE: 1 Feb 70
France SIGNED: 13 Feb 61 RATIFIED: 20 Nov 62 FORCE: 1 Feb 70
Germany, West SIGNED: 13 Feb 61 RATIFIED: 12 Nov 69 FORCE: 1 Feb 70
Luxembourg SIGNED: 13 Feb 61 RATIFIED: 25 Nov 63 FORCE: 1 Feb 70
Netherlands SIGNED: 13 Feb 61 RATIFIED: 23 Jan 63 FORCE: 1 Feb 70
Switzerland SIGNED: 13 Feb 61 RATIFIED: 22 Nov 66 FORCE: 1 Feb 70

110307 Bilateral Agreement **0 UNTS 0**
SIGNED: 9 May 69 FORCE: 9 May 69
REGISTERED: 9 Feb 70
ARTICLES: 0 LANGUAGE: Spanish.
HEADNOTE: ESTABLISH ILO OFFICE SAN JOSE
TOPIC: IGO Establishment
PARTIES:
Costa Rica
ILO (Labor Org)

110308 Bilateral Agreement **0 UNTS 0**
SIGNED: 28 May 69 FORCE: 4 Aug 69
REGISTERED: 9 Feb 70
ARTICLES: 0 LANGUAGE: English.
HEADNOTE: GUARANTEE FIFTH DEVELOPMENT FINANCE
TOPIC: IBRD Project
PARTIES:
Iran
IBRD (World Bank)

110309 Bilateral Agreement **0 UNTS 0**
SIGNED: 30 Jun 69 FORCE: 1 Oct 69
REGISTERED: 10 Feb 70
ARTICLES: 0 LANGUAGE: English.
HEADNOTE: LOAN CYPRUS PORTS
TOPIC: IBRD Project
PARTIES:
Cyprus
IBRD (World Bank)

110310 Bilateral Agreement **0 UNTS 0**
SIGNED: 30 Jun 69 FORCE: 10 Oct 69
REGISTERED: 10 Feb 70
ARTICLES: 0 LANGUAGE: English.
HEADNOTE: LOAN LIVESTOCK DEVELOPMENT
TOPIC: IBRD Project
PARTIES:
IBRD (World Bank)
Zambia

110311 Bilateral Agreement **0 UNTS 0**
SIGNED: 27 Jun 69 FORCE: 29 Sep 69
REGISTERED: 12 Feb 70
ARTICLES: 0 LANGUAGE: English.
HEADNOTE: LOAN FOURTH HIGHWAY
TOPIC: IBRD Project
PARTIES:
IBRD (World Bank)
Thailand

110312 Bilateral Agreement **0 UNTS 0**
SIGNED: 14 Apr 67 FORCE: 18 Jan 69
REGISTERED: 16 Feb 70
ARTICLES: 0 LANGUAGE: French.
HEADNOTE: PRIVILEGES IMMUNITIES HEAD-QUARTERS
TOPIC: IGO Establishment
PARTIES:
African Coffee Org
France

110313 Bilateral Agreement **0 UNTS 0**
SIGNED: 8 Jan 70 FORCE: 8 Jan 70
REGISTERED: 16 Feb 70
ARTICLES: 0 LANGUAGE: French.
HEADNOTE: ADMISSION TRAINEES
TOPIC: Tech Assistance
PARTIES:
Algeria
Belgium

110314 Bilateral Convention **0 UNTS 0**
SIGNED: 8 Jan 70 FORCE: 8 Jan 70
REGISTERED: 16 Feb 70
ARTICLES: 0 LANGUAGE: French.
HEADNOTE: EMPLOYMENT ALGERIAN WORKERS
TOPIC: Non-ILO Labor
PARTIES:
Algeria
Belgium

110315 Bilateral Convention **0 UNTS 0**
SIGNED: 13 Nov 67 FORCE: 1 Dec 69
REGISTERED: 19 Feb 70
ARTICLES: 0 LANGUAGE: French.
HEADNOTE: TAXATION
TOPIC: Taxation
PARTIES:
Congo (Brazzaville)
France

110316 Bilateral Protocol **0 UNTS 0**
SIGNED: 14 Feb 69 FORCE: 1 Oct 69
REGISTERED: 19 Feb 70
ARTICLES: 0 LANGUAGE: French.

HEADNOTE: CULTURAL COOPERATION
TOPIC: Culture
PARTIES:
France
Tunisia

110317 Bilateral Protocol **0 UNTS 0**
SIGNED: 5 Jun 69 FORCE: 5 Jun 69
REGISTERED: 19 Feb 70
ARTICLES: 0 LANGUAGE: French.
HEADNOTE: TECHNICAL COOPERATION
TOPIC: Tech Assistance
PARTIES:
France
Tunisia

110318 Bilateral Exchange **0 UNTS 0**
SIGNED: 10 Jul 69 FORCE: 10 Jul 69
REGISTERED: 19 Feb 70
ARTICLES: 0 LANGUAGE: French.
HEADNOTE: TECHNICAL COOPERATION
TOPIC: Tech Assistance
PARTIES:
Ethiopia
France

110319 Bilateral Protocol **0 UNTS 0**
SIGNED: 13 Oct 69 FORCE: 13 Oct 69
REGISTERED: 19 Feb 70
ARTICLES: 0 LANGUAGE: French. Russian.
HEADNOTE: RETURN BODIES FRENCH COMBA-TANTS
TOPIC: Other Military
PARTIES:
France
USSR (Soviet Union)

110320 Bilateral Treaty **0 UNTS 0**
SIGNED: 30 Apr 69 FORCE: 27 Dec 69
REGISTERED: 20 Feb 70
ARTICLES: 0 LANGUAGE: Mongolian. German. Russian.
HEADNOTE: LEGAL ASSISTANCE
TOPIC: Admin Cooperation
PARTIES:
Germany, East
Mongolia

110321 Bilateral Agreement **0 UNTS 0**
SIGNED: 17 Jul 69 FORCE: 2 Feb 70
REGISTERED: 20 Feb 70
ARTICLES: 0 LANGUAGE: Finnish. English.
HEADNOTE: DOUBLE TAXATION
TOPIC: Taxation
PARTIES:
Finland
UK Great Britain

110322 Multilateral Agreement **0 UNTS 0**
SIGNED: 25 Oct 67 FORCE: 7 Aug 69
REGISTERED: 25 Feb 70
ARTICLES: 0 LANGUAGE: French. English.
HEADNOTE: EDUCATION NURSES
TOPIC: Scientific Project
PARTIES:
Denmark SIGNED: 25 Oct 67 FORCE: 7 Aug 69
Malta SIGNED: 25 Oct 67 RATIFIED: 1 May 69 FORCE: 7 Aug 69
UK Great Britain SIGNED: 21 Dec 67 FORCE: 7 Aug 69

110323 Bilateral Protocol **0 UNTS 0**
SIGNED: 6 Nov 69 FORCE: 1 Jan 70
REGISTERED: 25 Feb 70
ARTICLES: 0 LANGUAGE: German.
HEADNOTE: TAXATION ROAD TRAFFIC
TOPIC: Taxation
PARTIES:
Austria
Liechtenstein

110324 Bilateral Agreement **0 UNTS 0**
SIGNED: 6 Feb 65 FORCE: 17 Sep 65
REGISTERED: 24 Mar 70 USA (United States)
ARTICLES: 0
HEADNOTE: INVESTMENT GUARANTEE

TOPIC: Direct Aid
PARTIES:
  Brazil
  USA (United States)

110325　　Bilateral Convention　**0 UNTS 0**
SIGNED: 28 Jul 67　　　　FORCE: 11 Aug 68
REGISTERED: 24 Mar 70 USA (United States)
ARTICLES: 0
HEADNOTE: TAXES INCOME PROPERTY
TOPIC: Taxation
PARTIES:
  France
  USA (United States)

110326　　Bilateral Agreement　**0 UNTS 0**
SIGNED: 10 May 68　　　　FORCE: 10 May 68
REGISTERED: 24 Mar 70 USA (United States)
ARTICLES: 0
HEADNOTE: AGRI COMMOD
TOPIC: US Agri Commod Aid
PARTIES:
  Dominican Republic
  USA (United States)

110327　　Bilateral Agreement　**0 UNTS 0**
SIGNED: 21 Jun 68　　　　FORCE: 21 Jun 58
REGISTERED: 24 Mar 70 USA (United States)
ARTICLES: 0
HEADNOTE: AGRI COMMOD
TOPIC: US Agri Commod Aid
PARTIES:
  Ceylon (Sri Lanka)
  USA (United States)

110328　　Bilateral Instrument　**0 UNTS 0**
SIGNED: 24 Jun 68　　　　FORCE: 24 Jun 68
REGISTERED: 4 Mar 70 USA (United States)
ARTICLES: 0
HEADNOTE: SCIENTIFIC TECHNICAL COOPER-
ATION WATER
TOPIC: Scientific Project
PARTIES:
  Italy
  USA (United States)

110329　　Bilateral Exchange　**0 UNTS 0**
SIGNED: 16 Oct 68　　　　FORCE: 1 Dec 68
REGISTERED: 4 Mar 70 USA (United States)
ARTICLES: 0
HEADNOTE: AMATEUR RADIO
TOPIC: Gen Communications
PARTIES:
  Monaco
  USA (United States)

110330　　Bilateral Exchange　**0 UNTS 0**
SIGNED: 17 Apr 69　　　　FORCE: 17 Apr 69
REGISTERED: 4 Mar 70 USA (United States)
ARTICLES: 0
HEADNOTE: PILOT TRAINING AIRCRAFT
TOPIC: General Military
PARTIES:
  Indonesia
  USA (United States)

110331　　Bilateral Agreement　**0 UNTS 0**
SIGNED: 18 Apr 69　　　　FORCE: 7 Jul 69
REGISTERED: 4 Mar 70 USA (United States)
ARTICLES: 0
HEADNOTE: TRUST TERRITORY PACIFIC IS-
LANDS
TOPIC: Territory Boundary
PARTIES:
  Japan
  USA (United States)

110332　　Bilateral Exchange　**0 UNTS 0**
SIGNED: 18 Jun 69　　　　FORCE: 18 Jun 69
REGISTERED: 4 Mar 70 USA (United States)
ARTICLES: 0
HEADNOTE: DEPLOYMENT US SHIPS MALTA
TOPIC: Specific Property
PARTIES:
  Malta
  USA (United States)

110333　　Bilateral Agreement　**0 UNTS 0**
SIGNED: 7 Jun 69　　　　FORCE: 7 Jun 69
REGISTERED: 4 Mar 70 USA (United States)
ARTICLES: 0
HEADNOTE: AGRI COMMOD
TOPIC: US Agri Commod Aid
PARTIES:
  Paraguay
  USA (United States)

110334　　Bilateral Exchange　**0 UNTS 0**
SIGNED: 18 Jun 69　　　　FORCE: 18 Jun 69
REGISTERED: 4 Mar 70 USA (United States)
ARTICLES: 0
HEADNOTE: EXTENSION LOANS US VESSELS
TOPIC: Milit Installation
PARTIES:
  Taiwan
  USA (United States)

110335　　Bilateral Agreement　**0 UNTS 0**
SIGNED: 12 Jun 69　　　　FORCE: 12 Jun 69
REGISTERED: 4 Mar 70 USA (United States)
ARTICLES: 0
HEADNOTE: FISHERIES MIDDLE ATLANTIC
OCEAN
TOPIC: Specific Resources
PARTIES:
  Poland
  USA (United States)

110336　　Bilateral Agreement　**0 UNTS 0**
SIGNED: 25 Jun 69　　　　FORCE: 25 Jul 69
REGISTERED: 4 Mar 70 USA (United States)
ARTICLES: 0
HEADNOTE: CIVIL USES ATOMIC ENERGY
TOPIC: Atomic Energy
PARTIES:
  Argentina
  USA (United States)

110337　　Bilateral Agreement　**0 UNTS 0**
SIGNED: 3 Jul 69　　　　FORCE: 19 Jul 69
REGISTERED: 4 Mar 70 USA (United States)
ARTICLES: 0
HEADNOTE: CIVIL USES ATOMIC ENERGY
TOPIC: Atomic Energy
PARTIES:
  Portugal
  USA (United States)

110338　　Bilateral Agreement　**0 UNTS 0**
SIGNED: 11 Jul 69　　　　FORCE: 11 Jul 69
REGISTERED: 4 Mar 70 USA (United States)
ARTICLES: 0
HEADNOTE: AGRI COMMOD
TOPIC: US Agri Commod Aid
PARTIES:
  Tunisia
  USA (United States)

110339　　Bilateral Exchange　**0 UNTS 0**
SIGNED: 21 Jul 69　　　　FORCE: 21 Jul 69
REGISTERED: 4 Mar 70 USA (United States)
ARTICLES: 0
HEADNOTE: PEACE CORPS
TOPIC: Non-ILO Labor
PARTIES:
  Trinidad/Tobago
  USA (United States)

110340　　Bilateral Agreement　**0 UNTS 0**
SIGNED: 22 Jul 69　　　　FORCE: 22 Jul 69
REGISTERED: 4 Mar 70 USA (United States)
ARTICLES: 0
HEADNOTE: INVESTMENT GUARANTY
TOPIC: Loans and Credits
PARTIES:
  USA (United States)
  Western Samoa

110341　　Bilateral Exchange　**0 UNTS 0**
SIGNED: 31 Jul 69　　　　FORCE: 31 Jul 69
REGISTERED: 4 Mar 70 USA (United States)
ARTICLES: 0

HEADNOTE: PILOTAGE GREAT LAKES ST. LAW-
RENCE
TOPIC: Water Transport
PARTIES:
  Canada
  USA (United States)

110342　　Bilateral Exchange　**0 UNTS 0**
SIGNED: 31 Jul 69　　　　FORCE: 31 Jul 69
REGISTERED: 4 Mar 70 USA (United States)
ARTICLES: 0
HEADNOTE: SPACE ACTIVITIES
TOPIC: Scientific Project
PARTIES:
  Japan
  USA (United States)

110343　　Bilateral Instrument　**0 UNTS 0**
SIGNED: 3 Aug 69　　　　FORCE: 3 Aug 69
REGISTERED: 4 Mar 70 USA (United States)
ARTICLES: 0
HEADNOTE: ESTABLISH LIBRARIES
TOPIC: Education
PARTIES:
  Romania
  USA (United States)

110344　　Bilateral Treaty　**0 UNTS 0**
SIGNED: 26 Apr 68　　　　FORCE: 30 Apr 69
REGISTERED: 6 Mar 70 Czechoslovakia
ARTICLES: 0
HEADNOTE: FRIENDSHIP COOPERATION MU-
TUAL ASSISTANCE
TOPIC: General Amity
PARTIES:
  Bulgaria
  Czechoslovakia

110345　　Multilateral Convention　**0 UNTS 0**
SIGNED: 20 Apr 59　　　　FORCE: 22 Sep 69
REGISTERED: 6 Mar 70 Council of Europe
ARTICLES: 0
HEADNOTE: INSURANCE MOTOR VEHICLES
TOPIC: Land Transport
PARTIES:
  Denmark　SIGNED:　20 Apr 59　RATIFIED:
    24 Jun 69 FORCE: 22 Sep 69
  Germany, West SIGNED: 20 Apr 59 RATIFIED:
    5 Jan 66 FORCE: 22 Sep 69
  Greece　SIGNED:　20 Apr 59　RATIFIED:
    29 May 61 FORCE: 22 Sep 69
  Norway　SIGNED:　20 Apr 59　RATIFIED:
    19 Sep 63 FORCE: 22 Sep 69
  Sweden　SIGNED:　20 Apr 59　RATIFIED:
    26 Jun 69 FORCE: 24 Sep 69

110346　　Multilateral Convention　**0 UNTS 0**
SIGNED: 7 Jun 68　　　　FORCE: 17 Dec 69
REGISTERED: 6 Mar 70 Council of Europe
ARTICLES: 0
HEADNOTE: FOREIGN LAW
TOPIC: Admin Cooperation
PARTIES:
  Cyprus SIGNED: 7 Jun 68 RATIFIED: 16 Apr 69
    FORCE: 17 Dec 69
  Iceland SIGNED: 7 Jun 68 RATIFIED: 2 Oct 69
    FORCE: 3 Jan 70
  Malta SIGNED: 7 Jun 68 RATIFIED: 22 Jan 69
    FORCE: 17 Dec 69
  Norway SIGNED: 7 Jun 68 RATIFIED: 30 Oct 69
    FORCE: 1 Feb 70
  Sweden SIGNED: 7 Jun 68 RATIFIED: 30 Oct 69
    FORCE: 1 Feb 70
  UK Great Britain SIGNED: 7 Jun 68 RATIFIED:
    16 Sep 69 FORCE: 17 Dec 69

110347　　Bilateral Agreement　**0 UNTS 0**
SIGNED: 21 Sep 68　　　　FORCE: 15 May 69
REGISTERED: 6 Mar 70 Czechoslovakia
ARTICLES: 0
HEADNOTE: ROAD TRANSPORT
TOPIC: Land Transport
PARTIES:
  Czechoslovakia
  France

110348 Bilateral Agreement **0 UNTS 0**
SIGNED: 23 Jan 70 FORCE: 23 Jan 70
REGISTERED: 6 Mar 70 ILO (Labor Org)
ARTICLES: 0
HEADNOTE: ESTABLISH ORGANIZATION MANILA
TOPIC: IGO Establishment
PARTIES:
 Philippines
 ILO (Labor Org)

110349 Bilateral Exchange **0 UNTS 0**
SIGNED: 22 Apr 63 FORCE: 22 Apr 63
REGISTERED: 11 Mar 70 France
ARTICLES: 0
HEADNOTE: PROFESSIONAL AVIATION SCHOOL
TOPIC: Education
PARTIES:
 Algeria
 France

110350 Bilateral Agreement **0 UNTS 0**
SIGNED: 16 Dec 44 FORCE: 1 Jan 65
REGISTERED: 11 Mar 70 France
ARTICLES: 0
HEADNOTE: RETIREMENT
TOPIC: Non-ILO Labor
PARTIES:
 Algeria
 France

110351 Bilateral Protocol **0 UNTS 0**
SIGNED: 8 Jul 67 FORCE: 1 Jul 67
REGISTERED: 11 Mar 70 France
ARTICLES: 0
HEADNOTE: SCHOOL ENGINEERS CAPE MATIFOU
TOPIC: Education
PARTIES:
 Algeria
 France

110352 Bilateral Agreement **0 UNTS 0**
SIGNED: 30 Jan 68 FORCE: 2 Jul 68
REGISTERED: 11 Mar 70 Denmark
ARTICLES: 0
HEADNOTE: INVESTMENTS
TOPIC: General Economic
PARTIES:
 Denmark
 Indonesia

110353 Bilateral Agreement **0 UNTS 0**
SIGNED: 20 Nov 69 FORCE: 20 Nov 69
REGISTERED: 11 Mar 70 Denmark
ARTICLES: 0
HEADNOTE: LOAN
TOPIC: Loans and Credits
PARTIES:
 Cambodia
 Denmark

110354 Bilateral Agreement **0 UNTS 0**
SIGNED: 26 Aug 68 FORCE: 1 Nov 69
REGISTERED: 12 Mar 70 Austria
ARTICLES: 0
HEADNOTE: SUPPLEMENT 1954 HAGUE CON-
VENTION CIVIL PROCEDURE
TOPIC: Admin Cooperation
PARTIES:
 Austria
 Switzerland

110355 Multilateral Convention **0 UNTS 0**
SIGNED: 28 Jun 67 FORCE: 10 Mar 70
REGISTERED: 16 Mar 70 ILO (Labor Org)
ARTICLES: 0
HEADNOTE: NO. 127 MAXIMUM WEIGHT CAR-
RIED PER WORKER
TOPIC: ILO Labor
PARTIES:
 Algeria SIGNED: 28 Jun 67 RATIFIED:
 12 Jun 69 FORCE: 12 Jun 70
 Taiwan SIGNED: 28 Jun 67 RATIFIED: 2 Feb 69
 FORCE: 2 Feb 70
 Ecuador SIGNED: 28 Jun 67 RATIFIED:
 10 Mar 69 FORCE: 10 Mar 70
 Spain SIGNED: 28 Jun 67 RATIFIED: 7 Jun 69
 FORCE: 7 Jun 70

Thailand SIGNED: 28 Jun 67 RATIFIED:
26 Feb 69 FORCE: 10 Mar 70

110356 Bilateral Instrument **0 UNTS 0**
SIGNED: 17 Nov 67 FORCE: 16 Mar 70
REGISTERED: 16 Mar 70 Netherlands
ARTICLES: 0
HEADNOTE: LEGAL PROCEEDINGS
TOPIC: Admin Cooperation
PARTIES:
 Netherlands
 UK Great Britain

110357 Bilateral Agreement **0 UNTS 0**
SIGNED: 26 Jun 69 FORCE: 28 Aug 69
REGISTERED: 16 Mar 70 IBRD (World Bank)
ARTICLES: 0
HEADNOTE: LOAN NINTH PAKISTAN
TOPIC: IBRD Project
PARTIES:
 Pakistan
 IBRD (World Bank)

110358 Bilateral Agreement **0 UNTS 0**
SIGNED: 1 Oct 69 FORCE: 1 Jan 69
REGISTERED: 16 Mar 70 Finland
ARTICLES: 0
HEADNOTE: ABOLITION VISAS
TOPIC: Visas
PARTIES:
 Finland
 Hungary

110359 Bilateral Instrument **0 UNTS 0**
SIGNED: 14 Jan 70
REGISTERED: 16 Mar 70 United Nations
ARTICLES: 0
HEADNOTE: ACCEPT ICJ JURISDICTION
TOPIC: ICJ Option Clause
PARTIES:
 Botswana

110360 Bilateral Agreement **0 UNTS 0**
SIGNED: 16 Mar 70 FORCE: 16 Mar 70
REGISTERED: 16 Mar 70 United Nations
ARTICLES: 0
HEADNOTE: HUMAN RIGHTS
TOPIC: Humanitarian
PARTIES:
 United Nations
 Yugoslavia

110361 Bilateral Agreement **0 UNTS 0**
SIGNED: 25 Feb 70 FORCE: 16 May 58
REGISTERED: 17 Mar 70 USSR (Soviet Union)
ARTICLES: 0
HEADNOTE: ECONOMIC TECHNICAL COOPER-
ATION
TOPIC: General Economic
PARTIES:
 Ceylon (Sri Lanka)
 USSR (Soviet Union)

110362 Bilateral Agreement **0 UNTS 0**
SIGNED: 17 Aug 59 FORCE: 30 Sep 59
REGISTERED: 17 Mar 70 USSR (Soviet Union)
ARTICLES: 0
HEADNOTE: ATOMIC ENERGY
TOPIC: Atomic Energy
PARTIES:
 Iraq
 USSR (Soviet Union)

110363 Bilateral Convention **0 UNTS 0**
SIGNED: 8 Dec 66 FORCE: 19 Sep 69
REGISTERED: 17 Mar 70 USSR (Soviet Union)
ARTICLES: 0
HEADNOTE: CONSULAR
TOPIC: Consul/Citizenship
PARTIES:
 France
 USSR (Soviet Union)

110364 Bilateral Agreement **0 UNTS 0**
SIGNED: 21 Jan 69 FORCE: 16 Sep 69

REGISTERED: 17 Mar 70 USSR (Soviet Union)
ARTICLES: 0
HEADNOTE: TRADE
TOPIC: General Trade
PARTIES:
 Jordan
 USSR (Soviet Union)

110365 Bilateral Agreement **0 UNTS 0**
SIGNED: 10 Jul 63 FORCE: 8 Feb 64
REGISTERED: 18 Mar 70 France
ARTICLES: 0
HEADNOTE: DEFENSE
TOPIC: General Military
PARTIES:
 France
 Togo

110366 Bilateral Convention **0 UNTS 0**
SIGNED: 10 Jul 63 FORCE: 8 Feb 64
REGISTERED: 18 Mar 70 France
ARTICLES: 0
HEADNOTE: DIPLOMATIC
TOPIC: Consul/Citizenship
PARTIES:
 France
 Togo

110367 Bilateral Convention **0 UNTS 0**
SIGNED: 10 Jul 63 FORCE: 8 Feb 64
REGISTERED: 18 Mar 70 France
ARTICLES: 0
HEADNOTE: JUDICIARY
TOPIC: Admin Cooperation
PARTIES:
 France
 Togo

110368 Bilateral Agreement **0 UNTS 0**
SIGNED: 10 Jul 63 FORCE: 8 Feb 64
REGISTERED: 18 Mar 70 France
ARTICLES: 0
HEADNOTE: CULTURE
TOPIC: Culture
PARTIES:
 France
 Togo

110369 Bilateral Agreement **0 UNTS 0**
SIGNED: 10 Jul 63 FORCE: 8 Feb 64
REGISTERED: 18 Mar 70 France
ARTICLES: 0
HEADNOTE: TECHNICAL COOPERATION
TOPIC: Tech Assistance
PARTIES:
 France
 Togo

110370 Bilateral Convention **0 UNTS 0**
SIGNED: 10 Jul 63 FORCE: 8 Feb 64
REGISTERED: 18 Mar 70 France
ARTICLES: 0
HEADNOTE: ESTABLISHMENT
TOPIC: Admin Cooperation
PARTIES:
 France
 Togo

110371 Bilateral Agreement **0 UNTS 0**
SIGNED: 10 Jul 63 FORCE: 8 Feb 64
REGISTERED: 18 Mar 70 France
ARTICLES: 0
HEADNOTE: COOPERATION ECONOMIC
TOPIC: General Economic
PARTIES:
 France
 Togo

110372 Bilateral Convention **0 UNTS 0**
SIGNED: 10 Jul 63 FORCE: 8 Feb 64
REGISTERED: 18 Mar 70 France
ARTICLES: 0
HEADNOTE: COOPERATION TREASURY SER-
VICES
TOPIC: Finance

PARTIES:
France
Togo

110373 Bilateral Protocol **0 UNTS 0**
SIGNED: 30 Apr 68 FORCE: 23 Dec 68
REGISTERED: 18 Mar 70 France
ARTICLES: 0
HEADNOTE: REAL PROPERTY
TOPIC: Territory Boundary
PARTIES:
France
Togo

110374 Bilateral Convention **0 UNTS 0**
SIGNED: 11 Jul 64 FORCE: 1 Jun 66
REGISTERED: 18 Mar 70 France
ARTICLES: 0
HEADNOTE: TWO BRIDGES BIDASSOA
TOPIC: Specific Property
PARTIES:
France
Spain

110375 Bilateral Convention **0 UNTS 0**
SIGNED: 29 Dec 65 FORCE: 29 Dec 68
REGISTERED: 18 Mar 70 Israel
ARTICLES: 0
HEADNOTE: SCIENTIFIC TECHNICAL COOPER-
ATION
TOPIC: Scientific Project
PARTIES:
Chile
Israel

110376 Bilateral Convention **0 UNTS 0**
SIGNED: 19 Jun 66 FORCE: 13 Feb 70
REGISTERED: 18 Mar 70 Israel
ARTICLES: 0
HEADNOTE: TECHNICAL COOPERATION
TOPIC: Culture
PARTIES:
Israel
Venezuela

110377 Multilateral Exchange **0 UNTS 0**
SIGNED: 17 Apr 67 FORCE: 17 Apr 67
REGISTERED: 18 Mar 70 Israel
ARTICLES: 0
HEADNOTE: COOPERATION CONSULAR
TOPIC: Consul/Citizenship
PARTIES:
Denmark SIGNED: 17 Apr 67 FORCE: 17 Apr 67
Finland SIGNED: 17 Apr 67 FORCE: 17 Apr 67
Iceland SIGNED: 17 Apr 67 FORCE: 17 Apr 67
Israel SIGNED: 17 Apr 67 FORCE: 17 Apr 67
Norway SIGNED: 17 Apr 67 FORCE: 17 Apr 67
Sweden SIGNED: 17 Apr 67 FORCE: 17 Apr 67

110378 Bilateral Agreement **0 UNTS 0**
SIGNED: 11 Oct 68 FORCE: 7 Sep 69
REGISTERED: 18 Mar 70 Israel
ARTICLES: 0
HEADNOTE: CULTURE
TOPIC: Culture
PARTIES:
Israel
Uganda

110379 Bilateral Exchange **0 UNTS 0**
SIGNED: 31 Dec 68 FORCE: 1 Apr 69
REGISTERED: 18 Mar 70 Israel
ARTICLES: 0
HEADNOTE: VISAS
TOPIC: Visas
PARTIES:
Israel
Trinidad/Tobago

110380 Bilateral Agreement **0 UNTS 0**
SIGNED: 10 Mar 67 FORCE: 19 Dec 69
REGISTERED: 18 Mar 70 Israel
ARTICLES: 0
HEADNOTE: EXTRADITION
TOPIC: Extradition

PARTIES:
Canada
Israel

110381 Bilateral Exchange **0 UNTS 0**
SIGNED: 3 Mar 69 FORCE: 3 Mar 69
REGISTERED: 18 Mar 70 Israel
ARTICLES: 0
HEADNOTE: DOUBLE TAX SHIP AIRCRAFT
TOPIC: Taxation
PARTIES:
Israel
Uruguay

110382 Bilateral Agreement **0 UNTS 0**
SIGNED: 20 Jan 69 FORCE: 20 Jan 69
REGISTERED: 18 Mar 70 Israel
ARTICLES: 0
HEADNOTE: COOPERATION TOURISM
TOPIC: Visas
PARTIES:
Greece
Israel

110383 Bilateral Exchange **0 UNTS 0**
SIGNED: 26 Feb 69 FORCE: 28 Mar 69
REGISTERED: 18 Mar 70 Israel
ARTICLES: 0
HEADNOTE: VISAS
TOPIC: Visas
PARTIES:
Greece
Israel

110384 Bilateral Exchange **0 UNTS 0**
SIGNED: 31 Mar 69 FORCE: 31 Mar 69
REGISTERED: 18 Mar 70 Israel
ARTICLES: 0
HEADNOTE: CIVIL STATUS ACTS WITHOUT FEES
TOPIC: Admin Cooperation
PARTIES:
Germany, West
Israel

110385 Bilateral Exchange **0 UNTS 0**
SIGNED: 15 May 69 FORCE: 13 Aug 69
REGISTERED: 18 Mar 70 Israel
ARTICLES: 0
HEADNOTE: VISAS
TOPIC: Visas
PARTIES:
Israel
Mauritius

110386 Bilateral Convention **0 UNTS 0**
SIGNED: 10 Jun 69 FORCE: 26 Feb 70
REGISTERED: 18 Mar 70 Israel
ARTICLES: 0
HEADNOTE: CULTURE
TOPIC: Culture
PARTIES:
Israel
UK Great Britain

110387 Bilateral Exchange **0 UNTS 0**
SIGNED: 18 Jun 69 FORCE: 18 Sep 69
REGISTERED: 18 Mar 70 Israel
ARTICLES: 0
HEADNOTE: VISAS
TOPIC: Visas
PARTIES:
Barbados
Israel

110388 Bilateral Agreement **0 UNTS 0**
SIGNED: 28 Nov 69 FORCE: 28 Dec 69
REGISTERED: 18 Mar 70 Israel
ARTICLES: 0
HEADNOTE: VISAS
TOPIC: Visas
PARTIES:
France
Israel

110389 Bilateral Exchange **0 UNTS 0**
SIGNED: 10 Dec 69 FORCE: 1 Jan 70
REGISTERED: 18 Mar 70 Israel
ARTICLES: 0
HEADNOTE: VISAS
TOPIC: Visas
PARTIES:
Israel
Philippines

110390 Bilateral Exchange **0 UNTS 0**
SIGNED: 21 Jan 70 FORCE: 1 Mar 70
REGISTERED: 18 Mar 70 Israel
ARTICLES: 0
HEADNOTE: VISAS
TOPIC: Visas
PARTIES:
Israel
Lesotho

110391 Bilateral Exchange **0 UNTS 0**
SIGNED: 4 Jul 69 FORCE: 24 Dec 69
REGISTERED: 19 Mar 70 Netherlands
ARTICLES: 0
HEADNOTE: PREK THNOT POWER IRRIGATION
TOPIC: Non-IBRD Project
PARTIES:
Cambodia
Netherlands

110392 Bilateral Treaty **0 UNTS 0**
SIGNED: 16 Aug 68 FORCE: 7 May 69
REGISTERED: 23 Mar 70 Czechoslovakia
ARTICLES: 0
HEADNOTE: FRIENDSHIP COOPERATION ASSIS-
TANCE
TOPIC: General Amity
PARTIES:
Czechoslovakia
Romania

110393 Bilateral Agreement **0 UNTS 0**
SIGNED: 22 Oct 69 FORCE: 22 Oct 69
REGISTERED: 23 Mar 70 Denmark
ARTICLES: 0
HEADNOTE: LOAN
TOPIC: Loans and Credits
PARTIES:
Denmark
Indonesia

110394 Bilateral Agreement **0 UNTS 0**
SIGNED: 27 Oct 69 FORCE: 27 Oct 69
REGISTERED: 23 Mar 70 Denmark
ARTICLES: 0
HEADNOTE: AIR SERVICES
TOPIC: Air Transport
PARTIES:
Barbados
Denmark

110395 Bilateral Agreement **0 UNTS 0**
SIGNED: 2 Nov 69 FORCE: 2 Nov 69
REGISTERED: 23 Mar 70 Denmark
ARTICLES: 0
HEADNOTE: AIR SERVICES
TOPIC: Air Transport
PARTIES:
Denmark
Trinidad/Tobago

110396 Bilateral Agreement **0 UNTS 0**
SIGNED: 4 Dec 69 FORCE: 4 Dec 69
REGISTERED: 23 Mar 70 Denmark
ARTICLES: 0
HEADNOTE: LOAN
TOPIC: Loans and Credits
PARTIES:
Denmark
Korea, South

110397 Bilateral Agreement **0 UNTS 0**
SIGNED: 25 Mar 70 FORCE: 25 Mar 70
REGISTERED: 25 Mar 70 United Nations
ARTICLES: 0
HEADNOTE: UN DEVELOPMENT PROGRAM

TOPIC: Tech Assistance
PARTIES:
  Gambia
  UN Special Fund

110398   Bilateral Agreement   **0 UNTS 0**
SIGNED: 25 Sep 69   FORCE: 17 Feb 70
REGISTERED: 26 Mar 70 Finland
ARTICLES: 0
HEADNOTE: ECONOMIC INDUSTRIAL COOPER-
  ATION
TOPIC: General Economic
PARTIES:
  Finland
  Romania

110399   Bilateral Agreement   **0 UNTS 0**
SIGNED: 30 Mar 70   FORCE: 30 Mar 70
REGISTERED: 30 Mar 70 United Nations
ARTICLES: 0
HEADNOTE: ECONOMIC SOCIAL RIGHTS
TOPIC: Humanitarian
PARTIES:
  United Nations
  Zambia

110400   Bilateral Instrument   **0 UNTS 0**
SIGNED: 14 Jun 61   FORCE: 14 Jun 61
REGISTERED: 2 Apr 70 USA (United States)
ARTICLES: 0
HEADNOTE: AMERICAN READING ROOMS
TOPIC: Admin Cooperation
PARTIES:
  USA (United States)
  Yugoslavia

110401   Bilateral Agreement   **0 UNTS 0**
SIGNED: 25 Jul 68   FORCE: 25 Jul 68
REGISTERED: 2 Apr 70 USA (United States)
ARTICLES: 0
HEADNOTE: CULTURAL EXCHANGE
TOPIC: Culture
PARTIES:
  Saudi Arabia
  USA (United States)

110402   Bilateral Exchange   **0 UNTS 0**
SIGNED: 26 Nov 68   FORCE: 26 Nov 68
REGISTERED: 2 Apr 70 USA (United States)
ARTICLES: 0
HEADNOTE: EDUCATIONAL SCIENTIFIC EX-
  CHANGES
TOPIC: Education
PARTIES:
  Romania
  USA (United States)

110403   Bilateral Exchange   **0 UNTS 0**
SIGNED: 24 Apr 69   FORCE: 4 Sep 69
REGISTERED: 2 Apr 70 USA (United States)
ARTICLES: 0
HEADNOTE: CUSTOMS REGULATIONS MILITARY
  FORCES
TOPIC: Customs
PARTIES:
  Philippines
  USA (United States)

110404   Bilateral Exchange   **0 UNTS 0**
SIGNED: 10 Jun 69   FORCE: 10 Jun 69
REGISTERED: 2 Apr 70 USA (United States)
ARTICLES: 0
HEADNOTE: EXTRADITION PROLONGATION
TOPIC: Extradition
PARTIES:
  Singapore
  USA (United States)

110405   Bilateral Exchange   **0 UNTS 0**
SIGNED: 22 Aug 69   FORCE: 22 Aug 69
REGISTERED: 2 Apr 70 USA (United States)
ARTICLES: 0
HEADNOTE: TAICHUNG FOREIGN SERVICE
  SCHOOL
TOPIC: Education

PARTIES:
  Taiwan
  USA (United States)

110406   Bilateral Exchange   **0 UNTS 0**
SIGNED: 29 Aug 69   FORCE: 29 Aug 69
REGISTERED: 2 Apr 70 USA (United States)
ARTICLES: 0
HEADNOTE: COTTON TEXTILES
TOPIC: General Trade
PARTIES:
  Czechoslovakia
  USA (United States)

110407   Bilateral Exchange   **0 UNTS 0**
SIGNED: 3 Sep 69   FORCE: 3 Sep 69
REGISTERED: 2 Apr 70 USA (United States)
ARTICLES: 0
HEADNOTE: FUNDS MILITARY PERSONNEL
TOPIC: Milit Assistance
PARTIES:
  New Zealand
  USA (United States)

110408   Bilateral Exchange   **0 UNTS 0**
SIGNED: 5 Sep 69   FORCE: 5 Sep 69
REGISTERED: 2 Apr 70 USA (United States)
ARTICLES: 0
HEADNOTE: EDUCATION SPECIAL FUND
TOPIC: Education
PARTIES:
  Philippines
  USA (United States)

110409   Bilateral Exchange   **0 UNTS 0**
SIGNED: 13 Jan 69   FORCE: 3 Nov 69
REGISTERED: 2 Apr 70 Austria
ARTICLES: 0
HEADNOTE: PROLONGATION LEGAL PROCEED-
  INGS CONVENTION
TOPIC: Admin Cooperation
PARTIES:
  Austria
  Singapore

110410   Bilateral Agreement   **0 UNTS 0**
SIGNED: 1 May 67   FORCE: 27 Mar 68
REGISTERED: 3 Apr 70 Dominican Republic
ARTICLES: 0
HEADNOTE: SOCIAL COOPERATION
TOPIC: Admin Cooperation
PARTIES:
  Dominican Republic
  Spain

110411   Bilateral Agreement   **0 UNTS 0**
SIGNED: 15 Mar 68   FORCE: 22 Jan 69
REGISTERED: 3 Apr 70 Dominican Republic
ARTICLES: 0
HEADNOTE: DOUBLE NATIONALITY
TOPIC: Consul/Citizenship
PARTIES:
  Dominican Republic
  Spain

110412   Bilateral Agreement   **0 UNTS 0**
SIGNED: 9 Sep 67   FORCE: 9 Sep 68
REGISTERED: 3 Apr 70 Dominican Republic
ARTICLES: 0
HEADNOTE: CULTURE
TOPIC: Culture
PARTIES:
  Argentina
  Dominican Republic

110413   Bilateral Agreement   **0 UNTS 0**
SIGNED: 9 Oct 67   FORCE: 14 Mar 69
REGISTERED: 3 Apr 70 Dominican Republic
ARTICLES: 0
HEADNOTE: CULTURE
TOPIC: Culture
PARTIES:
  Costa Rica
  Dominican Republic

110414   Bilateral Agreement   **0 UNTS 0**
SIGNED: 6 Apr 70   FORCE: 6 Apr 70
REGISTERED: 6 Apr 70 United Nations
ARTICLES: 0
HEADNOTE: UNICEF ACTIVITIES
TOPIC: IGO Operations
PARTIES:
  Maldive Islands
  UNICEF (Children)

110415   Bilateral Instrument   **0 UNTS 0**
SIGNED: 7 Apr 70
REGISTERED: 7 Apr 70 United Nations
ARTICLES: 0
HEADNOTE: ACCEPTANCE ICJ JURISDICTION
TOPIC: ICJ Option Clause
PARTIES:
  Canada

110416   Multilateral Convention   **0 UNTS 0**
SIGNED: 1 May 55   FORCE: 14 Jun 57
REGISTERED: 7 Apr 70 France
ARTICLES: 0
HEADNOTE: STANDARDIZATION WINES ANALY-
  SIS
TOPIC: Admin Cooperation
PARTIES:
  Argentina   SIGNED: 1 May 55   RATIFIED:
    24 Jan 68 FORCE: 24 Jul 68
  Austria SIGNED: 1 May 55 RATIFIED: 15 Jan 57
    FORCE: 15 Jul 57
  Chile SIGNED: 1 May 55 RATIFIED: 28 May 57
    FORCE: 28 Nov 57
  France SIGNED: 1 May 55 RATIFIED: 30 Oct 56
    FORCE: 14 Jun 57
  Germany, West SIGNED: 1 May 55 RATIFIED:
    24 Jul 59 FORCE: 24 Jan 60
  Greece SIGNED: 1 May 55 RATIFIED: 14 Dec 56
    FORCE: 14 Jun 57
  Italy SIGNED: 1 May 55 RATIFIED: 8 Mar 57
    FORCE: 8 Sep 57
  Morocco   SIGNED: 1 May 55   RATIFIED:
    14 Nov 57 FORCE: 14 May 58
  Portugal   SIGNED: 1 May 55   RATIFIED:
    31 Oct 56 FORCE: 14 Jun 57
  South Africa SIGNED: 1 May 55 RATIFIED:
    15 Feb 68 FORCE: 15 Aug 68
  Spain SIGNED: 1 May 55 RATIFIED: 6 Mar 56
    FORCE: 14 Jun 57
  Turkey SIGNED: 1 May 55 RATIFIED: 14 Nov 56
    FORCE: 14 Jun 57
  Yugoslavia   SIGNED: 1 May 55   RATIFIED:
    21 May 58 FORCE: 21 Nov 58

110417   Bilateral Agreement   **0 UNTS 0**
SIGNED: 16 May 66   FORCE: 8 Feb 67
REGISTERED: 8 Apr 70 Bulgaria
ARTICLES: 0
HEADNOTE: LEGAL ASSISTANCE
TOPIC: Admin Cooperation
PARTIES:
  Bulgaria
  Hungary

110418   Multilateral Convention   **0 UNTS 0**
SIGNED: 1 Jul 57   FORCE: 17 Sep 60
REGISTERED: 10 Apr 70 France
ARTICLES: 0
HEADNOTE: ESTABLISH SERICULTURE COMMIS-
  SION
TOPIC: Culture
PARTIES:
  France RATIFIED: 23 Nov 61 FORCE: 23 Nov 61
  India RATIFIED: 11 Sep 59 FORCE: 17 Sep 60
  Japan RATIFIED: 27 Mar 61 FORCE: 27 Mar 61
  Madagascar   RATIFIED: 2 Oct 61   FORCE:
    2 Oct 61
  Romania RATIFIED: 3 Apr 59 FORCE: 17 Sep 60
  Spain RATIFIED: 18 Aug 60 FORCE: 17 Sep 60
  Tunisia RATIFIED: 1 Apr 68 FORCE: 1 Apr 68
  Yugoslavia   RATIFIED: 24 Dec 58   FORCE:
    17 Sep 60

110419   Bilateral Agreement   **0 UNTS 0**
SIGNED: 14 Feb 68   FORCE: 27 Jan 70
REGISTERED: 13 Apr 70 Netherlands
ARTICLES: 0
HEADNOTE: CULTURE
TOPIC: Culture

261

PARTIES:
 Hungary
 Netherlands

110420   Bilateral Agreement   **0 UNTS 0**
SIGNED: 30 May 68   FORCE: 18 Jan 69
REGISTERED: 15 Apr 70 Singapore
ARTICLES: 0
HEADNOTE: TRADE
TOPIC: General Trade
PARTIES:
 Singapore
 United Arab Rep

110421   Bilateral Convention   **0 UNTS 0**
SIGNED: 21 Jul 67   FORCE: 26 Dec 69
REGISTERED: 21 Apr 70 UK Great Britain
ARTICLES: 0
HEADNOTE: HEALTH SERVICES
TOPIC: Sanitation
PARTIES:
 Poland
 UK Great Britain

110422   Bilateral Convention   **0 UNTS 0**
SIGNED: 22 May 68   FORCE: 29 Oct 68
REGISTERED: 21 Apr 70 UK Great Britain
ARTICLES: 0
HEADNOTE: DOUBLE TAXATION FISCAL EVA-
 SION
TOPIC: Taxation
PARTIES:
 France
 UK Great Britain

110423   Bilateral Agreement   **0 UNTS 0**
SIGNED: 28 May 69   FORCE: 4 Nov 69
REGISTERED: 21 Apr 70 UK Great Britain
ARTICLES: 0
HEADNOTE: TAXATION ROAD VEHICLES
TOPIC: Taxation
PARTIES:
 France
 UK Great Britain

110424   Bilateral Agreement   **0 UNTS 0**
SIGNED: 9 Aug 69   FORCE: 9 Aug 69
REGISTERED: 21 Apr 70 UK Great Britain
ARTICLES: 0
HEADNOTE: AIR SERVICES
TOPIC: Air Transport
PARTIES:
 Jordan
 UK Great Britain

110425   Bilateral Exchange   **0 UNTS 0**
SIGNED: 23 Aug 69   FORCE: 23 Aug 69
REGISTERED: 21 Apr 70 UK Great Britain
ARTICLES: 0
HEADNOTE: DEVELOPMENT LOAN
TOPIC: Loans and Credits
PARTIES:
 Sudan
 UK Great Britain

110426   Bilateral Agreement   **0 UNTS 0**
SIGNED: 6 Oct 69   FORCE: 6 Oct 69
REGISTERED: 21 Apr 70 UK Great Britain
ARTICLES: 0
HEADNOTE: SOCIAL INSURANCE
TOPIC: Non-ILO Labor
PARTIES:
 Cyprus
 UK Great Britain

110427   Bilateral Exchange   **0 UNTS 0**
SIGNED: 13 Oct 69   FORCE: 13 Oct 69
REGISTERED: 21 Apr 70 UK Great Britain
ARTICLES: 0
HEADNOTE: DEVELOPMENT LOAN
TOPIC: Loans and Credits
PARTIES:
 Jordan
 UK Great Britain

110428   Bilateral Exchange   **0 UNTS 0**
SIGNED: 18 Nov 69   FORCE: 18 Dec 69
REGISTERED: 21 Apr 70 UK Great Britain
ARTICLES: 0
HEADNOTE: ABOLITION VISAS
TOPIC: Visas
PARTIES:
 Korea, South
 UK Great Britain

110429   Bilateral Exchange   **0 UNTS 0**
SIGNED: 18 Jun 69   FORCE: 30 Jan 70
REGISTERED: 21 Apr 70 Netherlands
ARTICLES: 0
HEADNOTE: DOUBLE TAXATION FISCAL EVA-
 SION
TOPIC: Taxation
PARTIES:
 Malawi
 Netherlands

110430   Bilateral Agreement   **0 UNTS 0**
SIGNED: 6 Apr 70   FORCE: 6 Apr 70
REGISTERED: 21 Apr 70 ILO (Labor Org)
ARTICLES: 0
HEADNOTE: ESTABLISH ILO OFFICE
TOPIC: IGO Operations
PARTIES:
 Argentina
 ILO (Labor Org)

110431   Bilateral Agreement   **0 UNTS 0**
SIGNED: 11 Jul 69   FORCE: 24 Jan 70
REGISTERED: 22 Apr 70 USA (United States)
ARTICLES: 0
HEADNOTE: ATOMIC ENERGY COOPERATION
TOPIC: Atomic Energy
PARTIES:
 Austria
 USA (United States)

110432   Bilateral Protocol   **0 UNTS 0**
SIGNED: 29 Jan 63   FORCE: 7 Feb 70
REGISTERED: 30 Apr 70 Belgium
ARTICLES: 0
HEADNOTE: SUPPLY IN PERIOD OF NEED
TOPIC: Direct Aid
PARTIES:
 Belgium
 Luxembourg

110433   Bilateral Treaty   **0 UNTS 0**
SIGNED: 25 Feb 66   FORCE: 10 Sep 69
REGISTERED: 30 Apr 70 Taiwan
ARTICLES: 0
HEADNOTE: AMITY
TOPIC: Admin Cooperation
PARTIES:
 Taiwan
 Haiti

110434   Bilateral Treaty   **0 UNTS 0**
SIGNED: 29 Jul 66   FORCE: 15 Jul 69
REGISTERED: 30 Apr 70 Taiwan
ARTICLES: 0
HEADNOTE: FRIENDSHIP
TOPIC: Admin Cooperation
PARTIES:
 Bolivia
 Taiwan

110435   Bilateral Treaty   **0 UNTS 0**
SIGNED: 7 Jun 68   FORCE: 21 Feb 69
REGISTERED: 30 Apr 70 Taiwan
ARTICLES: 0
HEADNOTE: AMITY
TOPIC: General Amity
PARTIES:
 Taiwan
 Paraguay

110436   Bilateral Convention   **0 UNTS 0**
SIGNED: 22 Jan 69   FORCE: 16 Jan 70
REGISTERED: 30 Apr 70 UK Great Britain
ARTICLES: 0
HEADNOTE: DOUBLE TAXATION FISCAL EVA-
 SION
TOPIC: Taxation
PARTIES:
 Norway
 UK Great Britain

110437   Bilateral Agreement   **0 UNTS 0**
SIGNED: 3 Feb 69   FORCE: 1 Jan 70
REGISTERED: 30 Apr 70 UK Great Britain
ARTICLES: 0
HEADNOTE: GOODS ROAD TRANSPORT
TOPIC: Land Transport
PARTIES:
 UK Great Britain
 Yugoslavia

110438   Bilateral Agreement   **0 UNTS 0**
SIGNED: 1 May 69   FORCE: 5 Feb 70
REGISTERED: 30 Apr 70 UK Great Britain
ARTICLES: 0
HEADNOTE: TAXATION ROAD VEHICLES
TOPIC: Taxation
PARTIES:
 Netherlands
 UK Great Britain

110439   Bilateral Agreement   **0 UNTS 0**
SIGNED: 19 Jun 69   FORCE: 1 Jan 70
REGISTERED: 30 Apr 70 UK Great Britain
ARTICLES: 0
HEADNOTE: SOCIAL SECURITY
TOPIC: Non-ILO Labor
PARTIES:
 New Zealand
 UK Great Britain

110440   Bilateral Exchange   **0 UNTS 0**
SIGNED: 22 Oct 69   FORCE: 22 Oct 69
REGISTERED: 30 Apr 70 UK Great Britain
ARTICLES: 0
HEADNOTE: DEVELOPMENT LOAN
TOPIC: Loans and Credits
PARTIES:
 Indonesia
 UK Great Britain

110441   Bilateral Exchange   **0 UNTS 0**
SIGNED: 14 Nov 69   FORCE: 14 Nov 69
REGISTERED: 30 Apr 70 UK Great Britain
ARTICLES: 0
HEADNOTE: DEVELOPMENT LOAN
TOPIC: Loans and Credits
PARTIES:
 Turkey
 UK Great Britain

110442   Bilateral Exchange   **0 UNTS 0**
SIGNED: 19 Dec 69   FORCE: 19 Dec 69
REGISTERED: 30 Apr 70 UK Great Britain
ARTICLES: 0
HEADNOTE: UK SPECIAL PROJECT
TOPIC: Scientific Project
PARTIES:
 Eur Space Research
 UK Great Britain

110443   Bilateral Exchange   **0 UNTS 0**
SIGNED: 28 Aug 67   FORCE: 28 Aug 67
REGISTERED: 1 May 70 USA (United States)
ARTICLES: 0
HEADNOTE: ESTABLISH COMMERCIAL SECTION
 CZECH EMBASSY
TOPIC: Consul/Citizenship
PARTIES:
 Czechoslovakia
 USA (United States)

110444   Bilateral Exchange   **0 UNTS 0**
SIGNED: 11 Dec 67   FORCE: 2 Oct 69
REGISTERED: 1 May 70 USA (United States)
ARTICLES: 0
HEADNOTE: AMATEUR RADIO OPERATORS
TOPIC: Gen Communications

PARTIES:
Guatemala
USA (United States)

110445 Bilateral Agreement **0 UNTS 0**
SIGNED: 22 Nov 68 FORCE: 24 Oct 69
REGISTERED: 1 May 70 USA (United States)
ARTICLES: 0
HEADNOTE: INVESTMENT GUARANTEES
TOPIC: Finance
PARTIES:
Costa Rica
USA (United States)

110446 Bilateral Instrument **0 UNTS 0**
SIGNED: 3 Jul 69 FORCE: 3 Jul 69
REGISTERED: 1 May 70 USA (United States)
ARTICLES: 0
HEADNOTE: AGRI COMMOD
TOPIC: US Agri Commod Aid
PARTIES:
Pakistan
USA (United States)

110447 Bilateral Exchange **0 UNTS 0**
SIGNED: 19 Sep 69 FORCE: 19 Sep 69
REGISTERED: 1 May 70 USA (United States)
ARTICLES: 0
HEADNOTE: ESTABLISH COMMERCIAL SECTION
HUNGARIAN EMBASSY
TOPIC: Consul/Citizenship
PARTIES:
Hungary
USA (United States)

110448 Bilateral Agreement **0 UNTS 0**
SIGNED: 2 Oct 69 FORCE: 2 Oct 69
REGISTERED: 1 May 70 USA (United States)
ARTICLES: 0
HEADNOTE: AIR TRANSPORT
TOPIC: Air Transport
PARTIES:
Jamaica
USA (United States)

110449 Bilateral Instrument **0 UNTS 0**
SIGNED: 13 Oct 69 FORCE: 13 Oct 69
REGISTERED: 1 May 70 USA (United States)
ARTICLES: 0
HEADNOTE: AGRI COMMOD
TOPIC: US Agri Commod Aid
PARTIES:
India
USA (United States)

110450 Bilateral Agreement **0 UNTS 0**
SIGNED: 21 Oct 69 FORCE: 21 Oct 69
REGISTERED: 1 May 70 USA (United States)
ARTICLES: 0
HEADNOTE: AGRI COMMOD
TOPIC: US Agri Commod Aid
PARTIES:
Congo (Zaire)
USA (United States)

110451 Bilateral Instrument **0 UNTS 0**
SIGNED: 29 Oct 69 FORCE: 29 Oct 69
REGISTERED: 1 May 70 USA (United States)
ARTICLES: 0
HEADNOTE: AGRI COMMOD
TOPIC: US Agri Commod Aid
PARTIES:
USA (United States)
Vietnam, South

110452 Bilateral Instrument **0 UNTS 0**
SIGNED: 3 Nov 69 FORCE: 3 Nov 69
REGISTERED: 1 May 70 USA (United States)
ARTICLES: 0
HEADNOTE: AGRI COMMOD
TOPIC: US Agri Commod Aid
PARTIES:
Turkey
USA (United States)

110453 Bilateral Instrument **0 UNTS 0**
SIGNED: 17 Nov 69 FORCE: 17 Nov 69
REGISTERED: 1 May 70 USA (United States)
ARTICLES: 0
HEADNOTE: AGRI COMMOD
TOPIC: US Agri Commod Aid
PARTIES:
Indonesia
USA (United States)

110454 Bilateral Exchange **0 UNTS 0**
SIGNED: 27 Nov 69 FORCE: 27 Nov 69
REGISTERED: 1 May 70 USA (United States)
ARTICLES: 0
HEADNOTE: MEAT TRADE
TOPIC: Commodity Trade
PARTIES:
Honduras
USA (United States)

110455 Multilateral Instrument **0 UNTS 0**
SIGNED: 30 Nov 67 FORCE: 1 Jul 68
REGISTERED: 1 May 70 USA (United States)
ARTICLES: 0
HEADNOTE: INTERNATIONAL GRAINS ARRANGE-
MENT
TOPIC: Commodity Trade
PARTIES:
Multilateral

110456 Bilateral Exchange **0 UNTS 0**
SIGNED: 24 Nov 69 FORCE: 24 Nov 69
REGISTERED: 1 May 70 Denmark
ARTICLES: 0
HEADNOTE: WHEAT GRANT
TOPIC: Direct Aid
PARTIES:
Denmark
United Arab Rep

110457 Bilateral Agreement **0 UNTS 0**
SIGNED: 14 Mar 70 FORCE: 14 Mar 70
REGISTERED: 1 May 70 United Nations
ARTICLES: 0
HEADNOTE: OPERATIONAL ASSISTANCE
TOPIC: IGO Operations
PARTIES:
State/IGO Group
Dahomey

110458 Bilateral Agreement **0 UNTS 0**
SIGNED: 20 Mar 70 FORCE: 20 Mar 70
REGISTERED: 1 May 70 Thailand
ARTICLES: 0
HEADNOTE: TRADE
TOPIC: General Trade
PARTIES:
Romania
Thailand

110459 Bilateral Agreement **0 UNTS 0**
SIGNED: 4 May 70 FORCE: 4 May 70
REGISTERED: 4 May 70 United Nations
ARTICLES: 0
HEADNOTE: WOMEN IN ECONOMIC LIFE SEMI-
NAR
TOPIC: Education
PARTIES:
United Nations
USSR (Soviet Union)

110460 Bilateral Exchange **0 UNTS 0**
SIGNED: 24 Oct 69 FORCE: 24 Oct 69
REGISTERED: 5 May 70 France
ARTICLES: 0
HEADNOTE: PHOTO OBSERVATION SPACE OB-
JECTS
TOPIC: Scientific Project
PARTIES:
France
USSR (Soviet Union)

110461 Bilateral Agreement **0 UNTS 0**
SIGNED: 29 Oct 69 FORCE: 2 Feb 70
REGISTERED: 5 May 70 France
ARTICLES: 0

HEADNOTE: CULTURAL SCIENTIFIC TECHNICAL
COOPERATION
TOPIC: Culture
PARTIES:
Cyprus
France

110462 Multilateral Agreement **0 UNTS 0**
SIGNED: 13 Feb 69 FORCE: 2 Apr 70
REGISTERED: 7 May 70 Switzerland
ARTICLES: 0
HEADNOTE: ESTABLISH EUROPEAN MOLECULAR
BIOLOGY CONFERENCE
TOPIC: Education
PARTIES:
Multilateral

110463 Bilateral Agreement **0 UNTS 0**
SIGNED: 18 Oct 69 FORCE: 1 May 70
REGISTERED: 11 May 70 Finland
ARTICLES: 0
HEADNOTE: ROAD TRANSPORT
TOPIC: Land Transport
PARTIES:
Finland
Poland

110464 Bilateral Agreement **0 UNTS 0**
SIGNED: 5 Jul 57 FORCE: 22 Jan 66
REGISTERED: 12 May 70 ICAO (Civil Aviat)
ARTICLES: 0
HEADNOTE: AIR TRANSPORT
TOPIC: Air Transport
PARTIES:
Germany, West
Turkey

110465 Bilateral Agreement **0 UNTS 0**
SIGNED: 1 Jul 61 FORCE: 14 Jan 66
REGISTERED: 12 May 70 ICAO (Civil Aviat)
ARTICLES: 0
HEADNOTE: COMMERCIAL AIR SERVICES
TOPIC: Air Transport
PARTIES:
Germany, West
Iran

110466 Bilateral Agreement **0 UNTS 0**
SIGNED: 30 Apr 62 FORCE: 2 Sep 64
REGISTERED: 12 May 70 ICAO (Civil Aviat)
ARTICLES: 0
HEADNOTE: AIR TRANSPORT
TOPIC: Air Transport
PARTIES:
Germany, West
Peru

110467 Bilateral Agreement **0 UNTS 0**
SIGNED: 29 Oct 64 FORCE: 22 Jun 67
REGISTERED: 12 May 70 ICAO (Civil Aviat)
ARTICLES: 0
HEADNOTE: AIR TRANSPORT
TOPIC: Air Transport
PARTIES:
Germany, West
Senegal

110468 Bilateral Agreement **0 UNTS 0**
SIGNED: 18 Oct 66 FORCE: 5 Sep 67
REGISTERED: 12 May 70 ICAO (Civil Aviat)
ARTICLES: 0
HEADNOTE: AIR TRANSPORT
TOPIC: Air Transport
PARTIES:
Niger
Tunisia

110469 Bilateral Agreement **0 UNTS 0**
SIGNED: 3 Feb 69 FORCE: 5 Feb 70
REGISTERED: 12 May 70 ICAO (Civil Aviat)
ARTICLES: 0
HEADNOTE: AIR TRANSPORT
TOPIC: Air Transport
PARTIES:
Congo (Zaire)
Netherlands

110470   Bilateral Agreement   **0 UNTS 0**
SIGNED: 20 Mar 69   FORCE: 20 Mar 69
REGISTERED: 12 May 70 ICAO (Civil Aviat)
ARTICLES: 0
HEADNOTE: AIR TRANSPORT
TOPIC: Air Transport
PARTIES:
   Canada
   Czechoslovakia

110471   Bilateral Agreement   **0 UNTS 0**
SIGNED: 26 Mar 69   FORCE: 25 Apr 69
REGISTERED: 12 May 70 ICAO (Civil Aviat)
ARTICLES: 0
HEADNOTE: AIR TRANSPORT
TOPIC: Air Transport
PARTIES:
   Austria
   South Africa

110472   Bilateral Agreement   **0 UNTS 0**
SIGNED: 18 Apr 69   FORCE: 7 Nov 69
REGISTERED: 12 May 70 ICAO (Civil Aviat)
ARTICLES: 0
HEADNOTE: COMMERCIAL AIR SERVICES
TOPIC: Air Transport
PARTIES:
   Cyprus
   Netherlands

110473   Bilateral Agreement   **0 UNTS 0**
SIGNED: 24 Mar 60   FORCE: 24 Mar 60
REGISTERED: 13 May 70 France
ARTICLES: 0
HEADNOTE: SETTLEMENT QUESTION OWNER-
SHIP
TOPIC: Claims and Debts
PARTIES:
   France
   Vietnam, South

110474   Bilateral Convention   **0 UNTS 0**
SIGNED: 2 Aug 68   FORCE: 19 Feb 68
REGISTERED: 13 May 70 France
ARTICLES: 0
HEADNOTE: CARTOGRAPHIC COOPERATION
TOPIC: Scientific Project
PARTIES:
   Algeria
   France

110475   Bilateral Treaty   **0 UNTS 0**
SIGNED: 7 Dec 67   FORCE: 18 Mar 70
REGISTERED: 14 May 70 Austria
ARTICLES: 0
HEADNOTE: SETTLEMENT ECONOMIC QUES-
TIONS FRONTIER WATERS
TOPIC: Water Transport
PARTIES:
   Austria
   Czechoslovakia

110476   Multilateral Convention   **0 UNTS 0**
SIGNED: 15 May 52   FORCE: 13 Jul 55
REGISTERED: 15 May 70 France
ARTICLES: 0
HEADNOTE: AFRICAN MIGRATORY LOCUST CON-
VENTION
TOPIC: Sanitation
PARTIES:
   Belgium   SIGNED: 15 May 52   RATIFIED:
   13 Jul 55 FORCE: 13 Jul 55
   France   SIGNED: 15 May 52   RATIFIED:
   23 Jun 53 FORCE: 13 Jul 55
   UK Great Britain SIGNED: 15 May 52 RATIFIED:
   21 May 53 FORCE: 13 Jul 55

110477   Bilateral Agreement   **0 UNTS 0**
SIGNED: 1 Oct 68   FORCE: 1 Oct 68
REGISTERED: 15 May 70 France
ARTICLES: 0
HEADNOTE: NATIONAL AGRICULTURE CENTRE
TOPIC: Education
PARTIES:
   Algeria
   France

110478   Bilateral Exchange   **0 UNTS 0**
SIGNED: 27 Nov 69   FORCE: 27 Nov 69
REGISTERED: 15 May 70 France
ARTICLES: 0
HEADNOTE: ASSISTANCE AGRICULTURE TECH-
NICIANS
TOPIC: Tech Assistance
PARTIES:
   Algeria
   France

110479   Bilateral Agreement   **0 UNTS 0**
SIGNED: 10 Nov 69   FORCE: 10 Nov 69
REGISTERED: 15 May 70 Australia
ARTICLES: 0
HEADNOTE: ESTABLISH DEFENSE SPACE COM-
MUNICATIONS STATIONS
TOPIC: General Military
PARTIES:
   Australia
   USA (United States)

110480   Bilateral Agreement   **0 UNTS 0**
SIGNED: 5 Jun 69   FORCE: 22 Oct 69
REGISTERED: 18 May 70 IBRD (World Bank)
ARTICLES: 0
HEADNOTE: HIGHWAY LOAN
TOPIC: IBRD Project
PARTIES:
   IBRD (World Bank)
   Yugoslavia

110481   Bilateral Agreement   **0 UNTS 0**
SIGNED: 1 Oct 69   FORCE: 26 Mar 70
REGISTERED: 18 May 70 Finland
ARTICLES: 0
HEADNOTE: ECONOMIC INDUSTRIAL TECHNICAL
COOPERATION
TOPIC: General Economic
PARTIES:
   Finland
   Hungary

110482   Bilateral Agreement   **0 UNTS 0**
SIGNED: 10 May 68   FORCE: 31 Dec 68
REGISTERED: 20 May 70 Denmark
ARTICLES: 0
HEADNOTE: LOAN
TOPIC: Loans and Credits
PARTIES:
   Colombia
   Denmark

110483   Bilateral Agreement   **0 UNTS 0**
SIGNED: 28 Jul 69   FORCE: 19 Jan 70
REGISTERED: 21 May 70 IBRD (World Bank)
ARTICLES: 0
HEADNOTE: POWER PROJECT LOAN GUARANTEE
TOPIC: IBRD Project
PARTIES:
   Ceylon (Sri Lanka)
   IBRD (World Bank)

110484   Bilateral Agreement   **0 UNTS 0**
SIGNED: 18 Jul 69   FORCE: 9 Oct 69
REGISTERED: 22 May 70 IBRD (World Bank)
ARTICLES: 0
HEADNOTE: FINANCE CORP LOAN GUARANTEE
TOPIC: IBRD Project
PARTIES:
   Ceylon (Sri Lanka)
   IBRD (World Bank)

110485   Multilateral Treaty   **0 UNTS 0**
SIGNED: 1 Jul 68   FORCE: 5 Mar 70
REGISTERED: 25 May 70 USSR (Soviet Union)
ARTICLES: 0
HEADNOTE: NUCLEAR WEAPONS NON-PROLIF-
ERATION
TOPIC: Peace/Disarmament
PARTIES:
   Afghanistan   RATIFIED: 5 Mar 70   FORCE:
   5 Mar 70
   Austria RATIFIED: 27 Jun 69 FORCE: 5 Mar 70
   Botswana   RATIFIED: 28 Apr 69   FORCE:
   5 Mar 70
   Bulgaria RATIFIED: 3 Nov 69 FORCE: 5 Mar 70

Cameroon RATIFIED: 8 Jan 69 FORCE: 5 Mar 70
Canada RATIFIED: 8 Jan 69 FORCE: 5 Mar 70
Taiwan RATIFIED: 27 Jan 70 FORCE: 5 Mar 70
Costa Rica RATIFIED: 3 Mar 70 FORCE: 5 Mar 70
Cyprus RATIFIED: 10 Feb 70 FORCE: 5 Mar 70
Czechoslovakia   RATIFIED: 22 Jul 69   FORCE:
   5 Mar 70
Denmark RATIFIED: 3 Jan 69 FORCE: 5 Mar 70
Ecuador RATIFIED: 7 Mar 69 FORCE: 5 Mar 70
Ethiopia RATIFIED: 5 Mar 70 FORCE: 5 Mar 70
Finland RATIFIED: 5 Feb 69 FORCE: 5 Mar 70
Germany, East RATIFIED: 31 Oct 69 FORCE:
   5 Mar 70
Ghana RATIFIED: 4 May 70 FORCE: 5 Mar 70
Greece RATIFIED: 11 Mar 70 FORCE: 5 Mar 70
Hungary RATIFIED: 27 May 69 FORCE: 5 Mar 70
Iceland RATIFIED: 18 Jul 69 FORCE: 5 Mar 70
Iran RATIFIED: 5 Mar 70 FORCE: 5 Mar 70
Iraq RATIFIED: 29 Oct 69 FORCE: 5 Mar 70
Ireland RATIFIED: 4 Jul 68 FORCE: 5 Mar 70
Jamaica RATIFIED: 5 Mar 70 FORCE: 5 Mar 70
Jordan RATIFIED: 11 Feb 70 FORCE: 5 Mar 70
Laos RATIFIED: 5 Mar 70 FORCE: 5 Mar 70
Lesotho RATIFIED: 20 May 70 FORCE: 5 Mar 70
Liberia RATIFIED: 5 Mar 70 FORCE: 5 Mar 70
Malaysia RATIFIED: 5 Mar 70 FORCE: 5 Mar 70
Maldive Islands   RATIFIED: 7 Apr 70   FORCE:
   5 Mar 70
Mali RATIFIED: 10 Mar 70 FORCE: 5 Mar 70
Malta RATIFIED: 6 Feb 70 FORCE: 5 Mar 70
Mauritius RATIFIED: 25 Apr 69 FORCE: 5 Mar 70
Mexico RATIFIED: 21 Jan 69 FORCE: 5 Mar 70
Mongolia   RATIFIED: 14 May 69   FORCE:
   5 Mar 70
Nepal RATIFIED: 3 Feb 70 FORCE: 5 Mar 70
New Zealand   RATIFIED: 10 Sep 69   FORCE:
   5 Mar 70
Nigeria RATIFIED: 14 Oct 68 FORCE: 5 Mar 70
Norway RATIFIED: 5 Feb 69 FORCE: 5 Mar 70
Paraguay RATIFIED: 5 Mar 70 FORCE: 5 Mar 70
Peru RATIFIED: 3 Mar 70 FORCE: 5 Mar 70
Poland RATIFIED: 12 Jun 69 FORCE: 5 Mar 70
Romania RATIFIED: 4 Feb 70 FORCE: 5 Mar 70
Somalia RATIFIED: 5 Mar 70 FORCE: 5 Mar 70
Swaziland   RATIFIED: 11 Dec 69   FORCE:
   5 Mar 70
Sweden RATIFIED: 9 Jan 70 FORCE: 5 Mar 70
Syria RATIFIED: 24 Sep 69 FORCE: 5 Mar 70
Togo RATIFIED: 26 Feb 70 FORCE: 5 Mar 70
Tunisia RATIFIED: 26 Feb 70 FORCE: 5 Mar 70
UK Great Britain RATIFIED: 27 Nov 68 FORCE:
   5 Mar 70
USA (United States) RATIFIED: 5 Mar 70 FORCE:
   5 Mar 70
Upper Volta   RATIFIED: 3 Mar 70   FORCE:
   5 Mar 70
USSR (Soviet Union) RATIFIED: 5 Mar 70 FORCE:
   5 Mar 70
Yugoslavia   RATIFIED: 5 Mar 70   FORCE:
   5 Mar 70

110486   Bilateral Instrument   **0 UNTS 0**
SIGNED: 21 Jan 69   FORCE: 15 Jul 69
REGISTERED: 25 May 70 IDA (Devel Assoc)
ARTICLES: 0
HEADNOTE: NEW BRITAIN SMALLHOLDER DE-
VELOPMENT PROJECT
TOPIC: Non-IBRD Project
PARTIES:
   Australia
   IDA (Devel Assoc)

110487   Bilateral Agreement   **0 UNTS 0**
SIGNED: 10 Jul 69   FORCE: 20 Oct 69
REGISTERED: 25 May 70 IBRD (World Bank)
ARTICLES: 0
HEADNOTE: POWER PROJECT LOAN GUARANTEE
TOPIC: IBRD Project
PARTIES:
   Costa Rica
   IBRD (World Bank)

110488   Bilateral Agreement   **0 UNTS 0**
SIGNED: 10 Jul 69   FORCE: 20 Oct 69
REGISTERED: 25 May 70 IBRD (World Bank)
ARTICLES: 0
HEADNOTE: TELECOMMUNICATIONS LOAN
GUARANTEE
TOPIC: IBRD Project

PARTIES:
  Costa Rica
  IBRD (World Bank)

110489   Bilateral Agreement   **0 UNTS 0**
SIGNED: 17 Jul 69   FORCE: 1 Jan 70
REGISTERED: 25 May 70 IBRD (World Bank)
ARTICLES: 0
HEADNOTE: LIVESTOCK DEVELOPMENT LOAN
TOPIC: IBRD Project
PARTIES:
  IBRD (World Bank)
  Spain

110490   Bilateral Agreement   **0 UNTS 0**
SIGNED: 18 Aug 69   FORCE: 10 Oct 69
REGISTERED: 25 May 70 IBRD (World Bank)
ARTICLES: 0
HEADNOTE: IRRIGATION LOAN
TOPIC: IBRD Project
PARTIES:
  Philippines
  IBRD (World Bank)

110491   Bilateral Agreement   **0 UNTS 0**
SIGNED: 8 Feb 58   FORCE: 8 Feb 58
REGISTERED: 27 May 70 USSR (Soviet Union)
ARTICLES: 0
HEADNOTE: PAYMENTS
TOPIC: Finance
PARTIES:
  Ceylon (Sri Lanka)
  USSR (Soviet Union)

110492   Bilateral Agreement   **0 UNTS 0**
SIGNED: 15 Jul 53   FORCE: 15 Jul 53
REGISTERED: 27 May 70 USSR (Soviet Union)
ARTICLES: 0
HEADNOTE: TRADE
TOPIC: General Trade
PARTIES:
  France
  USSR (Soviet Union)

110493   Bilateral Agreement   **0 UNTS 0**
SIGNED: 2 Apr 60   FORCE: 10 Apr 60
REGISTERED: 27 May 70 USSR (Soviet Union)
ARTICLES: 0
HEADNOTE: PAYMENT
TOPIC: Finance
PARTIES:
  France
  USSR (Soviet Union)

110494   Bilateral Agreement   **0 UNTS 0**
SIGNED: 11 Jul 59   FORCE: 11 Jul 59
REGISTERED: 27 May 70 USSR (Soviet Union)
ARTICLES: 0
HEADNOTE: TRADE
TOPIC: General Trade
PARTIES:
  Ethiopia
  USSR (Soviet Union)

110495   Bilateral Agreement   **0 UNTS 0**
SIGNED: 12 Jun 61   FORCE: 12 Jun 61
REGISTERED: 27 May 70 USSR (Soviet Union)
ARTICLES: 0
HEADNOTE: TRADE
TOPIC: General Trade
PARTIES:
  Togo
  USSR (Soviet Union)

110496   Bilateral Protocol   **0 UNTS 0**
SIGNED: 14 Jun 61   FORCE: 14 Jun 61
REGISTERED: 27 May 70 USSR (Soviet Union)
ARTICLES: 0
HEADNOTE: TRADE REPRESENTATION STATUS
TOPIC: General Trade
PARTIES:
  Togo
  USSR (Soviet Union)

110497   Bilateral Agreement   **0 UNTS 0**
SIGNED: 14 Jul 67   FORCE: 17 Mar 70
REGISTERED: 27 May 70 USSR (Soviet Union)
ARTICLES: 0
HEADNOTE: CULTURAL COOPERATION
TOPIC: Culture
PARTIES:
  Netherlands
  USSR (Soviet Union)

110498   Bilateral Agreement   **0 UNTS 0**
SIGNED: 27 Jun 68   FORCE: 27 Jun 68
REGISTERED: 27 May 70 USA (United States)
ARTICLES: 0
HEADNOTE: INVESTMENT GUARANTEES
TOPIC: Finance
PARTIES:
  UK Great Britain
  USA (United States)

110499   Bilateral Agreement   **0 UNTS 0**
SIGNED: 9 Aug 68   FORCE: 9 Aug 68
REGISTERED: 27 May 70 USA (United States)
ARTICLES: 0
HEADNOTE: INVESTMENT GUARANTEE
TOPIC: Finance
PARTIES:
  UK Great Britain
  USA (United States)

110500   Bilateral Agreement   **0 UNTS 0**
SIGNED: 27 Jun 69   FORCE: 26 Sep 69
REGISTERED: 29 May 70 IBRD (World Bank)
ARTICLES: 0
HEADNOTE: FINANCE COMPANIES LOAN
TOPIC: IBRD Project
PARTIES:
  Colombia
  IBRD (World Bank)

110501   Bilateral Agreement   **0 UNTS 0**
SIGNED: 29 May 70   FORCE: 29 May 70
REGISTERED: 1 Jun 70 United Nations
ARTICLES: 0
HEADNOTE: TECHNICAL ASSISTANCE
TOPIC: Tech Assistance
PARTIES:
  State/IGO Group
  Zambia

110502   Bilateral Agreement   **0 UNTS 0**
SIGNED: 29 May 70   FORCE: 29 May 70
REGISTERED: 1 Jun 70 United Nations
ARTICLES: 0
HEADNOTE: OPERATIONAL ASSISTANCE
TOPIC: Tech Assistance
PARTIES:
  State/IGO Group
  Zambia

110503   Bilateral Exchange   **0 UNTS 0**
SIGNED: 25 Sep 67   FORCE: 25 Sep 67
REGISTERED: 2 Jun 70 USA (United States)
ARTICLES: 0
HEADNOTE: EXPORT PETROLEUM
TOPIC: Commodity Trade
PARTIES:
  Canada
  USA (United States)

110504   Bilateral Exchange   **0 UNTS 0**
SIGNED: 20 Aug 68   FORCE: 18 Jul 69
REGISTERED: 2 Jun 70 USA (United States)
ARTICLES: 0
HEADNOTE: RE-ACTIVATE RAWINSONDE STA-
TION
TOPIC: Scientific Project
PARTIES:
  Ecuador
  USA (United States)

110506   Bilateral Exchange   **0 UNTS 0**
SIGNED: 11 Sep 69   FORCE: 11 Sep 69
REGISTERED: 2 Jun 70 USA (United States)
ARTICLES: 0

HEADNOTE: COOPERATION SATELLITE RE-
SEARCH
TOPIC: Scientific Project
PARTIES:
  Italy
  USA (United States)

110507   Bilateral Exchange   **0 UNTS 0**
SIGNED: 1 Oct 69   FORCE: 1 Oct 69
REGISTERED: 2 Jun 70 USA (United States)
ARTICLES: 0
HEADNOTE: COTTON TEXTILES
TOPIC: Commodity Trade
PARTIES:
  Costa Rica
  USA (United States)

110508   Bilateral Agreement   **0 UNTS 0**
SIGNED: 3 Oct 69   FORCE: 3 Oct 69
REGISTERED: 2 Jun 70 USA (United States)
ARTICLES: 0
HEADNOTE: AGRI COMMOD
TOPIC: US Agri Commod Aid
PARTIES:
  Pakistan
  USA (United States)

110509   Bilateral Agreement   **0 UNTS 0**
SIGNED: 10 Jan 70   FORCE: 10 Jan 70
REGISTERED: 2 Jun 70 USA (United States)
ARTICLES: 0
HEADNOTE: AGRI COMMOD
TOPIC: US Agri Commod Aid
PARTIES:
  Pakistan
  USA (United States)

110510   Bilateral Agreement   **0 UNTS 0**
SIGNED: 18 Dec 69   FORCE: 18 Dec 69
REGISTERED: 2 Jun 70 USA (United States)
ARTICLES: 0
HEADNOTE: AGRI COMMOD
TOPIC: US Agri Commod Aid
PARTIES:
  Tunisia
  USA (United States)

110511   Bilateral Agreement   **0 UNTS 0**
SIGNED: 22 Aug 58   FORCE: 22 Aug 58
REGISTERED: 2 Jun 70 France
ARTICLES: 0
HEADNOTE: GENERAL AGREEMENT (SIC)
TOPIC: General Amity
PARTIES:
  France
  United Arab Rep

110512   Bilateral Convention   **0 UNTS 0**
SIGNED: 28 Jul 66   FORCE: 1 Sep 67
REGISTERED: 2 Jun 70 France
ARTICLES: 0
HEADNOTE: ASSETS FRENCH CITIZENS
TOPIC: Visas
PARTIES:
  France
  United Arab Rep

110513   Bilateral Convention   **0 UNTS 0**
SIGNED: 28 Mar 68   FORCE: 16 Apr 70
REGISTERED: 2 Jun 70 Belgium
ARTICLES: 0
HEADNOTE: DOUBLE TAXATION
TOPIC: Taxation
PARTIES:
  Belgium
  Japan

110514   Bilateral Agreement   **0 UNTS 0**
SIGNED: 30 Jun 69   FORCE: 10 Oct 69
REGISTERED: 2 Jun 70 IBRD (World Bank)
ARTICLES: 0
HEADNOTE: GURI POWERHOUSE
TOPIC: IGO Operations
PARTIES:
  IBRD (World Bank)
  Venezuela

110515　　Bilateral Agreement　　**0 UNTS 0**
SIGNED: 4 Jun 65　　　　　FORCE: 16 Jul 65
REGISTERED: 3 Jun 70 Bulgaria
ARTICLES: 0
HEADNOTE: ABOLITION VISAS
TOPIC: Visas
PARTIES:
　Bulgaria
　Czechoslovakia

110516　　Bilateral Instrument　　**0 UNTS 0**
SIGNED: 23 Aug 68　　　　FORCE: 23 Aug 68
REGISTERED: 4 Jun 70 IAEA (Atom Energy)
ARTICLES: 0
HEADNOTE: TRANSFER URANIUM
TOPIC: Atomic Energy
PARTIES:
　IAEA (Atom Energy)
　USA (United States)

110517　　Bilateral Agreement　　**0 UNTS 0**
SIGNED: 13 Oct 69　　　　FORCE: 13 Oct 69
REGISTERED: 4 Jun 70 IAEA (Atom Energy)
ARTICLES: 0
HEADNOTE: SAFEGUARDS REACTOR FACILITY
TOPIC: Atomic Energy
PARTIES:
　Taiwan
　IAEA (Atom Energy)

110518　　Multilateral Agreement　　**0 UNTS 0**
SIGNED: 17 Oct 69　　　　FORCE: 17 Oct 69
REGISTERED: 4 Jun 70 IAEA (Atom Energy)
ARTICLES: 0
HEADNOTE: APPLICATION SAFEGUARDS
TOPIC: Atomic Energy
PARTIES:
　Canada SIGNED: 17 Oct 69 FORCE: 17 Oct 69
　Pakistan SIGNED: 17 Oct 69 FORCE: 17 Oct 69
　IAEA (Atom Energy) SIGNED: 17 Oct 69 FORCE:
　　17 Oct 69

110519　　Multilateral Instrument　　**0 UNTS 0**
SIGNED: 27 Nov 69　　　　FORCE: 27 Nov 69
REGISTERED: 4 Jun 70 IAEA (Atom Energy)
ARTICLES: 0
HEADNOTE: TRANSFER URANIUM
TOPIC: Atomic Energy
PARTIES:
　Finland SIGNED: 27 Nov 69 FORCE: 27 Nov 69
　IAEA (Atom Energy) SIGNED: 27 Nov 69 FORCE:
　　27 Nov 69
　USA (United States) SIGNED: 27 Nov 69 FORCE:
　　27 Nov 69

110520　　Multilateral Instrument　　**0 UNTS 0**
SIGNED: 19 Dec 69　　　　FORCE: 19 Dec 69
REGISTERED: 4 Jun 70 IAEA (Atom Energy)
ARTICLES: 0
HEADNOTE: LEASE URANIUM
TOPIC: Atomic Energy
PARTIES:
　Chile SIGNED: 19 Dec 69 FORCE: 19 Dec 69
　IAEA (Atom Energy) SIGNED: 19 Dec 69 FORCE:
　　19 Dec 69
　USA (United States) SIGNED: 19 Dec 69 FORCE:
　　19 Dec 69

110521　　Bilateral Agreement　　**0 UNTS 0**
SIGNED: 19 Dec 69　　　　FORCE: 19 Dec 69
REGISTERED: 4 Jun 70 IAEA (Atom Energy)
ARTICLES: 0
HEADNOTE: ESTABLISH REACTOR
TOPIC: Atomic Energy
PARTIES:
　Chile
　IAEA (Atom Energy)

110522　　Multilateral Instrument　　**0 UNTS 0**
SIGNED: 19 Dec 69　　　　FORCE: 19 Dec 69
REGISTERED: 4 Jun 70 IAEA (Atom Energy)
ARTICLES: 0
HEADNOTE: TRANSFER URANIUM
TOPIC: Atomic Energy
PARTIES:
　Indonesia　SIGNED:　19 Dec 69　FORCE:
　　19 Dec 69

IAEA (Atom Energy) SIGNED: 19 Dec 69 FORCE:
　19 Dec 69
USA (United States) SIGNED: 19 Dec 69 FORCE:
　19 Dec 69

110523　　Bilateral Agreement　　**0 UNTS 0**
SIGNED: 19 Dec 69　　　　FORCE: 19 Dec 69
REGISTERED: 4 Jun 70 IAEA (Atom Energy)
ARTICLES: 0
HEADNOTE: ASSIST REACTOR
TOPIC: Atomic Energy
PARTIES:
　Indonesia
　IAEA (Atom Energy)

110524　　Bilateral Agreement　　**0 UNTS 0**
SIGNED: 19 Dec 69　　　　FORCE: 18 Jan 70
REGISTERED: 4 Jun 70 IAEA (Atom Energy)
ARTICLES: 0
HEADNOTE: DEVELOPMENT ASSISTANCE COOP-
　ERATION
TOPIC: Atomic Energy
PARTIES:
　IAEA (Atom Energy)
　Sweden

110525　　Bilateral Agreement　　**0 UNTS 0**
SIGNED: 20 Oct 69　　　　FORCE: 20 Oct 69
REGISTERED: 5 Jun 70 Denmark
ARTICLES: 0
HEADNOTE: INDUSTRIAL COOPERATION
TOPIC: Scientific Project
PARTIES:
　Denmark
　Hungary

110526　　Multilateral Agreement　　**0 UNTS 0**
SIGNED: 3 Dec 69　　　　FORCE: 1 Jan 70
REGISTERED: 5 Jun 70 Netherlands
ARTICLES: 0
HEADNOTE: ABOLITION VISAS
TOPIC: Visas
PARTIES:
　Belgium SIGNED: 3 Dec 69 FORCE: 1 Jan 70
　Luxembourg　SIGNED:　3 Dec 69　FORCE:
　　1 Jan 70
　Malawi SIGNED: 3 Dec 69 FORCE: 1 Jan 70
　Netherlands SIGNED: 3 Dec 69 FORCE: 1 Jan 70

110527　　Bilateral Convention　　**0 UNTS 0**
SIGNED: 21 May 64　　　　FORCE: 2 Oct 69
REGISTERED: 8 Jun 70 France
ARTICLES: 0
HEADNOTE: FRONTIER HIGHWAY CONTROLS
TOPIC: Territory Boundary
PARTIES:
　France
　Luxembourg

110528　　Bilateral Agreement　　**0 UNTS 0**
SIGNED: 11 Jan 65　　　　FORCE: 1 Apr 65
REGISTERED: 8 Jun 70 France
ARTICLES: 0
HEADNOTE: CULTURAL
TOPIC: Culture
PARTIES:
　France
　Romania

110529　　Bilateral Convention　　**0 UNTS 0**
SIGNED: 3 Apr 68　　　　FORCE: 2 Aug 69
REGISTERED: 8 Jun 70 France
ARTICLES: 0
HEADNOTE: DEPOSITS & CONSIGNMENTS
TOPIC: General Economic
PARTIES:
　France
　Gabon

110530　　Bilateral Agreement　　**0 UNTS 0**
SIGNED: 15 Jan 69　　　　FORCE: 1 Aug 69
REGISTERED: 8 Jun 70 France
ARTICLES: 0
HEADNOTE: ECONOMIC TECHNICAL COOPER-
　ATION
TOPIC: Scientific Project

PARTIES:
　France
　Yugoslavia

110531　　Bilateral Convention　　**0 UNTS 0**
SIGNED: 12 Mar 69　　　　FORCE: 1 Aug 69
REGISTERED: 8 Jun 70 France
ARTICLES: 0
HEADNOTE: PHYTOSANITARY CONTROL
TOPIC: Sanitation
PARTIES:
　France
　Romania

110532　　Bilateral Exchange　　**0 UNTS 0**
SIGNED: 3 Apr 69　　　　FORCE: 3 Apr 69
REGISTERED: 8 Jun 70 France
ARTICLES: 0
HEADNOTE: ST. PIERRE QUARANTINE STATION
TOPIC: Sanitation
PARTIES:
　Canada
　France

110533　　Bilateral Agreement　　**0 UNTS 0**
SIGNED: 25 Jun 69　　　　FORCE: 25 Jun 69
REGISTERED: 8 Jun 70 France
ARTICLES: 0
HEADNOTE: FRENCH LIBRARY
TOPIC: Culture
PARTIES:
　France
　Romania

110534　　Bilateral Agreement　　**0 UNTS 0**
SIGNED: 7 Oct 69　　　　FORCE: 7 Oct 69
REGISTERED: 8 Jun 70 France
ARTICLES: 0
HEADNOTE: MILITARY PERSONNEL COOPER-
　ATION
TOPIC: Milit Assistance
PARTIES:
　Burundi
　France

110535　　Bilateral Convention　　**0 UNTS 0**
SIGNED: 16 Feb 70　　　　FORCE: 1 Apr 70
REGISTERED: 8 Jun 70 France
ARTICLES: 0
HEADNOTE: MOVEMENT PERSONS
TOPIC: Visas
PARTIES:
　France
　Niger

110536　　Bilateral Convention　　**0 UNTS 0**
SIGNED: 21 Feb 70　　　　FORCE: 1 Apr 70
REGISTERED: 8 Jun 70 France
ARTICLES: 0
HEADNOTE: MOVEMENT PERSONS
TOPIC: Visas
PARTIES:
　France
　Ivory Coast

110537　　Bilateral Convention　　**0 UNTS 0**
SIGNED: 25 Feb 70　　　　FORCE: 1 Apr 70
REGISTERED: 8 Jun 70 France
ARTICLES: 0
HEADNOTE: MOVEMENT PERSONS
TOPIC: Visas
PARTIES:
　France
　Togo

110538　　Bilateral Agreement　　**0 UNTS 0**
SIGNED: 17 Feb 67　　　　FORCE: 15 Mar 69
REGISTERED: 9 Jun 70 Bulgaria
ARTICLES: 0
HEADNOTE: AIR SERVICES
TOPIC: Air Transport
PARTIES:
　Bulgaria
　Lebanon

110539   Bilateral Agreement   **0 UNTS 0**
SIGNED: 10 Feb 70   FORCE: 10 Feb 70
REGISTERED: 10 Jun 70 Belgium
ARTICLES: 0
HEADNOTE: TRANSPORT ROAD GOODS
TOPIC: Land Transport
PARTIES:
   Austria
   Belgium

110540   Bilateral Convention   **0 UNTS 0**
SIGNED: 29 Aug 67   FORCE: 17 Mar 70
REGISTERED: 12 Jun 70 Belgium
ARTICLES: 0
HEADNOTE: DOUBLE TAXATION
TOPIC: Taxation
PARTIES:
   Belgium
   UK Great Britain

110541   Bilateral Agreement   **0 UNTS 0**
SIGNED: 30 Sep 69   FORCE: 30 Sep 69
REGISTERED: 12 Jun 70 Denmark
ARTICLES: 0
HEADNOTE: ASSIST SPEECH-HEARING INSTI-
TUTE
TOPIC: Non-IBRD Project
PARTIES:
   Denmark
   India

110542   Bilateral Agreement   **0 UNTS 0**
SIGNED: 6 Mar 70   FORCE: 6 Mar 70
REGISTERED: 12 Jun 70 Denmark
ARTICLES: 0
HEADNOTE: GOVERNMENT LOAN
TOPIC: Finance
PARTIES:
   Denmark
   Turkey

110543   Bilateral Agreement   **0 UNTS 0**
SIGNED: 21 May 70   FORCE: 21 May 70
REGISTERED: 12 Jun 70 ILO (Labor Org)
ARTICLES: 0
HEADNOTE: ILO OFFICE DJAKARTA
TOPIC: IGO Establishment
PARTIES:
   Indonesia
   ILO (Labor Org)

110544   Bilateral Agreement   **0 UNTS 0**
SIGNED: 13 Nov 67   FORCE: 22 May 69
REGISTERED: 15 Jun 70 IBRD (World Bank)
ARTICLES: 0
HEADNOTE: LOAN HIGHWAY
TOPIC: IBRD Project
PARTIES:
   Morocco
   IBRD (World Bank)

110545   Bilateral Agreement   **0 UNTS 0**
SIGNED: 13 Nov 69   FORCE: 22 May 70
REGISTERED: 15 Jun 70 IDA (Devel Assoc)
ARTICLES: 0
HEADNOTE: CREDIT HIGHWAY
TOPIC: Non-IBRD Project
PARTIES:
   Morocco
   IDA (Devel Assoc)

110546   Bilateral Agreement   **0 UNTS 0**
SIGNED: 20 Nov 69   FORCE: 5 May 70
REGISTERED: 15 Jun 70 IBRD (World Bank)
ARTICLES: 0
HEADNOTE: LOAN SECOND EDUCATION
TOPIC: Loans and Credits
PARTIES:
   IBRD (World Bank)
   Zambia

110547   Bilateral Agreement   **0 UNTS 0**
SIGNED: 19 Dec 69   FORCE: 27 Feb 70
REGISTERED: 15 Jun 70 IBRD (World Bank)
ARTICLES: 0

HEADNOTE: GUARANTEE SECOND TELECOM-
MUNICATIONS
TOPIC: Loans and Credits
PARTIES:
   IBRD (World Bank)
   Singapore

110548   Bilateral Agreement   **0 UNTS 0**
SIGNED: 24 Dec 69   FORCE: 15 May 70
REGISTERED: 15 Jun 70 IBRD (World Bank)
ARTICLES: 0
HEADNOTE: GUARANTEE FINANCE
TOPIC: Non-IBRD Project
PARTIES:
   IBRD (World Bank)
   Tunisia

110549   Bilateral Agreement   **0 UNTS 0**
SIGNED: 30 Jan 70   FORCE: 15 May 70
REGISTERED: 15 Jun 70 IBRD (World Bank)
ARTICLES: 0
HEADNOTE: GUARANTEE INDUSTRIAL
PROJECTS 1970
TOPIC: Non-IBRD Project
PARTIES:
   IBRD (World Bank)
   Yugoslavia

110550   Bilateral Agreement   **0 UNTS 0**
SIGNED: 14 Nov 69   FORCE: 22 Apr 70
REGISTERED: 16 Jun 70 Finland
ARTICLES: 0
HEADNOTE: ECONOMIC TECHNICAL COOPER-
ATION
TOPIC: Scientific Project
PARTIES:
   Bulgaria
   Finland

110551   Bilateral Exchange   **0 UNTS 0**
SIGNED: 26 Mar 70   FORCE: 26 Mar 70
REGISTERED: 16 Jun 70 Belgium
ARTICLES: 0
HEADNOTE: ECONOMIC COMMODITIES COOPER-
ATION COMMISSION
TOPIC: Scientific Project
PARTIES:
   Belgium
   India

110552   Bilateral Convention   **0 UNTS 0**
SIGNED: 24 May 68   FORCE: 27 May 70
REGISTERED: 17 Jun 70 Belgium
ARTICLES: 0
HEADNOTE: DOUBLE TAXATION
TOPIC: Taxation
PARTIES:
   Belgium
   Greece

110553   Bilateral Agreement   **0 UNTS 0**
SIGNED: 10 Dec 65   FORCE: 10 Dec 65
REGISTERED: 22 Jun 70 Denmark
ARTICLES: 0
HEADNOTE: TRADE
TOPIC: General Trade
PARTIES:
   Denmark
   Madagascar

110554   Bilateral Agreement   **0 UNTS 0**
SIGNED: 23 Nov 66   FORCE: 23 Nov 66
REGISTERED: 22 Jun 70 Denmark
ARTICLES: 0
HEADNOTE: TRADE
TOPIC: General Trade
PARTIES:
   Denmark
   Ivory Coast

110555   Bilateral Exchange   **0 UNTS 0**
SIGNED: 6 Feb 69   FORCE: 8 Mar 69
REGISTERED: 22 Jun 70 France
ARTICLES: 0
HEADNOTE: FILM COPRODUCTION
TOPIC: Culture

PARTIES:
   Brazil
   France

110556   Bilateral Agreement   **0 UNTS 0**
SIGNED: 27 Mar 69   FORCE: 1 May 69
REGISTERED: 22 Jun 70 France
ARTICLES: 0
HEADNOTE: ROAD TRANSPORT
TOPIC: Land Transport
PARTIES:
   Bulgaria
   France

110557   Bilateral Agreement   **0 UNTS 0**
SIGNED: 25 Oct 69   FORCE: 23 Mar 70
REGISTERED: 22 Jun 70 Belgium
ARTICLES: 0
HEADNOTE: TOURISM COOPERATION
TOPIC: Visas
PARTIES:
   Belgium
   Romania

110558   Bilateral Exchange   **0 UNTS 0**
SIGNED: 27 Jan 70   FORCE: 27 Jan 70
REGISTERED: 22 Jun 70 Denmark
ARTICLES: 0
HEADNOTE: MILK TECHNOLOGY INSTITUTE
TOPIC: Non-IBRD Project
PARTIES:
   Chile
   Denmark

110559   Bilateral Agreement   **0 UNTS 0**
SIGNED: 27 Jun 69   FORCE: 11 Dec 69
REGISTERED: 23 Jun 70 IBRD (World Bank)
ARTICLES: 0
HEADNOTE: LOAN THIRD CUKUROVA POWER
TOPIC: IBRD Project
PARTIES:
   IBRD (World Bank)
   Turkey

110560   Bilateral Treaty   **0 UNTS 0**
SIGNED: 6 May 70   FORCE: 9 Jun 70
REGISTERED: 23 Jun 70 Czechoslovakia
ARTICLES: 0
HEADNOTE: FRIENDSHIP COOPERATION MU-
TUAL ASSISTANCE
TOPIC: General Amity
PARTIES:
   Czechoslovakia
   USSR (Soviet Union)

110561   Bilateral Agreement   **0 UNTS 0**
SIGNED: 25 Nov 69   FORCE: 28 Mar 70
REGISTERED: 24 Jun 70 Singapore
ARTICLES: 0
HEADNOTE: ECONOMIC COOPERATION
TOPIC: General Economic
PARTIES:
   Cambodia
   Singapore

110562   Bilateral Agreement   **0 UNTS 0**
SIGNED: 24 Jun 70   FORCE: 24 Jun 70
REGISTERED: 24 Jun 70 United Nations
ARTICLES: 0
HEADNOTE: UNICEF ACTIVITIES
TOPIC: IGO Operations
PARTIES:
   Kenya
   UNICEF (Children)

110563   Bilateral Agreement   **0 UNTS 0**
SIGNED: 12 Nov 69   FORCE: 10 Apr 70
REGISTERED: 26 Jun 70 Thailand
ARTICLES: 0
HEADNOTE: TRADE
TOPIC: General Trade
PARTIES:
   Iran
   Thailand

110564   Bilateral Agreement   **0 UNTS 0**
SIGNED: 12 Jan 70   FORCE: 12 Jan 70
REGISTERED: 26 Jun 70 Mexico
ARTICLES: 0
HEADNOTE: AGENCY HEADQUARTERS
TOPIC: IGO Establishment
PARTIES:
  Lat Am Nuclear Arm
  Mexico

110565   Bilateral Convention   **0 UNTS 0**
SIGNED: 22 Jan 65   FORCE: 25 May 69
REGISTERED: 30 Jun 70 Belgium
ARTICLES: 0
HEADNOTE: SCIENTIFIC TECHNICAL COOPER-
ATION
TOPIC: Tech Assistance
PARTIES:
  Belgium
  Peru

110566   Bilateral Agreement   **0 UNTS 0**
SIGNED: 24 May 69   FORCE: 21 May 70
REGISTERED: 30 Jun 70 United Arab Rep
ARTICLES: 0
HEADNOTE: SHIPPING
TOPIC: Water Transport
PARTIES:
  Bulgaria
  United Arab Rep

110567   Bilateral Agreement   **0 UNTS 0**
SIGNED: 13 Jun 69   FORCE: 3 Dec 69
REGISTERED: 1 Jul 20 IBRD (World Bank)
ARTICLES: 0
HEADNOTE: GUARANTEE PALM OIL PROCESSING
TOPIC: IBRD Project
PARTIES:
  Ivory Coast
  IBRD (World Bank)

110568   Bilateral Agreement   **0 UNTS 0**
SIGNED: 13 Jun 69   FORCE: 3 Dec 69
REGISTERED: 1 Jul 20 IBRD (World Bank)
ARTICLES: 0
HEADNOTE: GUARANTEE INDUSTRIAL OIL PALM
TOPIC: IBRD Project
PARTIES:
  Ivory Coast
  IBRD (World Bank)

110569   Bilateral Agreement   **0 UNTS 0**
SIGNED: 13 Jun 69   FORCE: 3 Dec 69
REGISTERED: 1 Jul 20 IBRD (World Bank)
ARTICLES: 0
HEADNOTE: GUARANTEE OIL PALM COCONUT
TOPIC: IBRD Project
PARTIES:
  Ivory Coast
  IBRD (World Bank)

110570   Bilateral Agreement   **0 UNTS 0**
SIGNED: 20 Jun 69   FORCE: 10 Dec 69
REGISTERED: 1 Jul 20 IDA (Devel Assoc)
ARTICLES: 0
HEADNOTE: CREDIT NORTH SUMATRA AGRICUL-
TURE
TOPIC: Non-IBRD Project
PARTIES:
  Indonesia
  IDA (Devel Assoc)

110571   Bilateral Agreement   **0 UNTS 0**
SIGNED: 20 Jun 69   FORCE: 2 Oct 69
REGISTERED: 1 Jul 20 IDA (Devel Assoc)
ARTICLES: 0
HEADNOTE: CREDIT HIGHWAY
TOPIC: Non-IBRD Project
PARTIES:
  Indonesia
  IDA (Devel Assoc)

110572   Bilateral Agreement   **0 UNTS 0**
SIGNED: 26 Jun 69   FORCE: 3 Dec 69
REGISTERED: 1 Jul 20 IDA (Devel Assoc)
ARTICLES: 0

HEADNOTE: CREDIT HIGHWAY MAINTENANCE
TOPIC: Non-IBRD Project
PARTIES:
  Mauritius
  IDA (Devel Assoc)

110573   Bilateral Agreement   **0 UNTS 0**
SIGNED: 28 Aug 69   FORCE: 4 Dec 69
REGISTERED: 1 Jul 20 IDA (Devel Assoc)
ARTICLES: 0
HEADNOTE: CREDIT ACCRA/TEMA WATER SUP-
PLY
TOPIC: Non-IBRD Project
PARTIES:
  Ghana
  IDA (Devel Assoc)

110574   Bilateral Agreement   **0 UNTS 0**
SIGNED: 24 Sep 69   FORCE: 4 Nov 69
REGISTERED: 1 Jul 70 IDA (Devel Assoc)
ARTICLES: 0
HEADNOTE: CREDIT TENTH RAILWAY
TOPIC: Non-IBRD Project
PARTIES:
  India
  IDA (Devel Assoc)

110575   Bilateral Agreement   **0 UNTS 0**
SIGNED: 15 Mar 68   FORCE: 16 May 69
REGISTERED: 1 Jul 70 Japan
ARTICLES: 0
HEADNOTE: CULTURE
TOPIC: Culture
PARTIES:
  Japan
  Yugoslavia

110576   Bilateral Agreement   **0 UNTS 0**
SIGNED: 3 Sep 68   FORCE: 6 Aug 69
REGISTERED: 1 Jul 70 Japan
ARTICLES: 0
HEADNOTE: DOUBLE TAX FISCAL EVASION
TOPIC: Taxation
PARTIES:
  Japan
  United Arab Rep

110577   Bilateral Agreement   **0 UNTS 0**
SIGNED: 21 Mar 69   FORCE: 1 Aug 69
REGISTERED: 1 Jul 70 Japan
ARTICLES: 0
HEADNOTE: PREK THNOT POWER
TOPIC: Non-IBRD Project
PARTIES:
  Cambodia
  Japan

110578   Bilateral Exchange   **0 UNTS 0**
SIGNED: 28 Apr 69   FORCE: 28 Apr 69
REGISTERED: 1 Jul 70 Denmark
ARTICLES: 0
HEADNOTE: CONVEY NORWEGIAN HOUSES
GREENLAND
TOPIC: Admin Cooperation
PARTIES:
  Denmark
  Norway

110579   Multilateral Agreement   **0 UNTS 0**
SIGNED: 4 May 70   FORCE: 4 Jun 70
REGISTERED: 1 Jul 70 Belgium
ARTICLES: 0
HEADNOTE: ABOLITION PASSPORT VISA FEES
TOPIC: Visas
PARTIES:
  Belgium SIGNED: 4 May 70 FORCE: 4 Jun 70
  Iran SIGNED: 4 May 70 FORCE: 4 Jun 70
  Luxembourg SIGNED: 4 May 70 FORCE:
    4 Jun 70
  Netherlands SIGNED: 4 May 70 FORCE:
    4 Jun 70

110580   Bilateral Agreement   **0 UNTS 0**
SIGNED: 23 Sep 69   FORCE: 29 Apr 70
REGISTERED: 6 Jul 70 IDA (Devel Assoc)
ARTICLES: 0

HEADNOTE: CREDIT EDUCATION
TOPIC: Non-IBRD Project
PARTIES:
  Cameroon
  IDA (Devel Assoc)

110581   Bilateral Agreement   **0 UNTS 0**
SIGNED: 10 Nov 69   FORCE: 26 Feb 70
REGISTERED: 6 Jul 70 IDA (Devel Assoc)
ARTICLES: 0
HEADNOTE: CREDIT TELECOMMUNICATIONS
TOPIC: Non-IBRD Project
PARTIES:
  Nepal
  IDA (Devel Assoc)

110582   Bilateral Agreement   **0 UNTS 0**
SIGNED: 13 Nov 69   FORCE: 5 Feb 70
REGISTERED: 6 Jul 70 IDA (Devel Assoc)
ARTICLES: 0
HEADNOTE: CREDIT DRAINAGE
TOPIC: Non-IBRD Project
PARTIES:
  Ceylon (Sri Lanka)
  IDA (Devel Assoc)

110583   Bilateral Agreement   **0 UNTS 0**
SIGNED: 26 Nov 69   FORCE: 28 Apr 70
REGISTERED: 6 Jul 70 IDA (Devel Assoc)
ARTICLES: 0
HEADNOTE: CREDIT WOLAMO AGRICULTURE
TOPIC: Non-IBRD Project
PARTIES:
  Ethiopia
  IDA (Devel Assoc)

110584   Bilateral Agreement   **0 UNTS 0**
SIGNED: 1 Apr 68   FORCE: 6 Oct 69
REGISTERED: 8 Jul 70 Turkey
ARTICLES: 0
HEADNOTE: TRANSPORT GOODS PASSENGERS
TOPIC: Land Transport
PARTIES:
  Jordan
  Turkey

110585   Bilateral Agreement   **0 UNTS 0**
SIGNED: 25 Sep 68   FORCE: 4 Oct 69
REGISTERED: 8 Jul 70 Turkey
ARTICLES: 0
HEADNOTE: TRANSIT
TOPIC: Land Transport
PARTIES:
  Iraq
  Turkey

110586   Multilateral Agreement   **0 UNTS 0**
SIGNED: 7 Feb 69   FORCE: 21 Dec 69
REGISTERED: 8 Jul 70 USA (United States)
ARTICLES: 0
HEADNOTE: STATUS OF FORCES NATO HEAD-
QUARTERS
TOPIC: Status of Forces
PARTIES:
  Belgium SIGNED: 7 Feb 69 RATIFIED: 30 Dec 69
    FORCE: 29 Jan 70
  Canada SIGNED: 7 Feb 69 RATIFIED: 31 Dec 69
    FORCE: 30 Jan 70
  Germany, West SIGNED: 7 Feb 69 RATIFIED:
    21 Nov 69 FORCE: 21 Dec 69
  Netherlands SIGNED: 7 Feb 69 RATIFIED:
    21 Nov 69 FORCE: 21 Dec 69
  UK Great Britain SIGNED: 7 Feb 69 RATIFIED:
    21 Nov 69 FORCE: 21 Dec 69
  USA (United States) SIGNED: 7 Feb 69 RATI-
    FIED: 7 Oct 69 FORCE: 21 Dec 69

110587   Multilateral Agreement   **0 UNTS 0**
SIGNED: 7 Feb 69   FORCE: 21 Dec 69
REGISTERED: 8 Jul 70 USA (United States)
ARTICLES: 0
HEADNOTE: ACCOMMODATION NATO HEAD-
QUARTERS
TOPIC: Status of Forces
PARTIES:
  Germany, West SIGNED: 7 Feb 69 RATIFIED:
    21 Nov 69 FORCE: 21 Dec 69

UK Great Britain SIGNED: 7 Feb 69 RATIFIED:
   21 Nov 69 FORCE: 21 Dec 69
USA (United States) SIGNED: 7 Feb 69 RATI-
   FIED: 21 Nov 69 FORCE: 21 Dec 69

110588   Bilateral Agreement   **0 UNTS 0**
SIGNED: 9 Jun 69   FORCE: 28 Aug 69
REGISTERED: 8 Jul 70 IDA (Devel Assoc)
ARTICLES: 0
HEADNOTE: CREDIT TECHNICAL ASSISTANCE
TOPIC: Non-IBRD Project
PARTIES:
   Congo (Zaire)
   IDA (Devel Assoc)

110589   Bilateral Agreement   **0 UNTS 0**
SIGNED: 29 Sep 69   FORCE: 1 Dec 69
REGISTERED: 8 Jul 70 IDA (Devel Assoc)
ARTICLES: 0
HEADNOTE: CREDIT SECOND ROAD
TOPIC: Non-IBRD Project
PARTIES:
   IDA (Devel Assoc)
   Uganda

110590   Bilateral Convention   **0 UNTS 0**
SIGNED: 20 Feb 69   FORCE: 30 Sep 69
REGISTERED: 9 Jul 70 India
ARTICLES: 0
HEADNOTE: DOUBLE TAX INCOME
TOPIC: Taxation
PARTIES:
   India
   United Arab Rep

110591   Bilateral Agreement   **0 UNTS 0**
SIGNED: 25 Sep 69   FORCE: 21 Jan 70
REGISTERED: 9 Jul 70 IDA (Devel Assoc)
ARTICLES: 0
HEADNOTE: CREDIT FISHERIES
TOPIC: Non-IBRD Project
PARTIES:
   Ghana
   IDA (Devel Assoc)

110592   Bilateral Agreement   **0 UNTS 0**
SIGNED: 17 Jul 70   FORCE: 17 Jul 70
REGISTERED: 17 Jul 70 United Nations
ARTICLES: 0
HEADNOTE: STANDARD OPERATIONAL ASSIS-
   TANCE
TOPIC: IGO Operations
PARTIES:
   State/IGO Group
   New Zealand

110593   Bilateral Agreement   **0 UNTS 0**
SIGNED: 17 Jul 70   FORCE: 17 Jul 70
REGISTERED: 17 Jul 70 United Nations
ARTICLES: 0
HEADNOTE: STANDARD TECHNICAL ASSIS-
   TANCE
TOPIC: Tech Assistance
PARTIES:
   State/IGO Group
   New Zealand

110594   Bilateral Agreement   **0 UNTS 0**
SIGNED: 4 Dec 67   FORCE: 26 Jun 70
REGISTERED: 22 Jul 70 Belgium
ARTICLES: 0
HEADNOTE: DOUBLE TAX SEA AIR TRANSPORT
TOPIC: Taxation
PARTIES:
   Belgium
   Ireland

110595   Bilateral Agreement   **0 UNTS 0**
SIGNED: 6 Sep 68   FORCE: 8 Jan 69
REGISTERED: 22 Jul 70 IBRD (World Bank)
ARTICLES: 0
HEADNOTE: LOAN MECHANIZED FARMING
TOPIC: IBRD Project
PARTIES:
   IBRD (World Bank)
   Sudan

110596   Bilateral Agreement   **0 UNTS 0**
SIGNED: 18 Sep 68   FORCE: 1 Dec 69
REGISTERED: 22 Jul 70 IBRD (World Bank)
ARTICLES: 0
HEADNOTE: LOAN BOKE
TOPIC: IBRD Project
PARTIES:
   Guinea
   IBRD (World Bank)

110597   Bilateral Agreement   **0 UNTS 0**
SIGNED: 14 Nov 68   FORCE: 19 Mar 69
REGISTERED: 22 Jul 70 IBRD (World Bank)
ARTICLES: 0
HEADNOTE: GUARANTEE THIRD BNDE PROJECT
TOPIC: IBRD Project
PARTIES:
   Morocco
   IBRD (World Bank)

110598   Bilateral Agreement   **0 UNTS 0**
SIGNED: 29 Nov 68   FORCE: 29 Apr 69
REGISTERED: 22 Jul 70 IBRD (World Bank)
ARTICLES: 0
HEADNOTE: GUARANTEE SECOND PORT
TOPIC: IBRD Project
PARTIES:
   IBRD (World Bank)
   Tunisia

110599   Bilateral Agreement   **0 UNTS 0**
SIGNED: 28 Mar 69   FORCE: 1 Feb 70
REGISTERED: 23 Jul 70 UK Great Britain
ARTICLES: 0
HEADNOTE: GOODS CARRIED BY ROAD
TOPIC: Land Transport
PARTIES:
   France
   UK Great Britain

110600   Bilateral Exchange   **0 UNTS 0**
SIGNED: 15 Nov 69   FORCE: 15 Nov 69
REGISTERED: 23 Jul 70 UK Great Britain
ARTICLES: 0
HEADNOTE: DEVELOPMENT LOAN
TOPIC: Loans and Credits
PARTIES:
   Ecuador
   UK Great Britain

110601   Bilateral Agreement   **0 UNTS 0**
SIGNED: 20 Oct 67   FORCE: 22 Aug 69
REGISTERED: 24 Jul 70 Austria
ARTICLES: 0
HEADNOTE: JUDICIAL ASSISTANCE
TOPIC: Admin Cooperation
PARTIES:
   Austria
   Bulgaria

110602   Bilateral Convention   **0 UNTS 0**
SIGNED: 30 Oct 67   FORCE: 17 Dec 69
REGISTERED: 27 Jul 70 Norway
ARTICLES: 0
HEADNOTE: DOUBLE TAX INCOME CAPITAL
TOPIC: Taxation
PARTIES:
   Brazil
   Norway

110603   Multilateral Instrument   **0 UNTS 0**
SIGNED: 12 Jan 70   FORCE: 14 May 70
REGISTERED: 27 Jul 70 GATT (Tariff/Trade)
ARTICLES: 0
HEADNOTE: DAIRY PRODUCTS
TOPIC: Commodity Trade
PARTIES:
   Australia
   Belgium
   Canada
   Denmark
   France
   Germany, West
   Italy
   Japan
   Netherlands
   New Zealand

EEC (Econ Commnty)
South Africa
UK Great Britain

110604   Bilateral Agreement   **0 UNTS 0**
SIGNED: 7 Jul 68   FORCE: 8 Jan 70
REGISTERED: 28 Jul 70 Netherlands
ARTICLES: 0
HEADNOTE: CULTURE
TOPIC: Culture
PARTIES:
   Indonesia
   Netherlands

110605   Bilateral Convention   **0 UNTS 0**
SIGNED: 11 Feb 69   FORCE: 12 May 70
REGISTERED: 28 Jul 70 Netherlands
ARTICLES: 0
HEADNOTE: DOUBLE TAX INCOME CAPITAL
TOPIC: Taxation
PARTIES:
   Ireland
   Netherlands

110606   Bilateral Agreement   **0 UNTS 0**
SIGNED: 13 Jun 69   FORCE: 24 May 70
REGISTERED: 28 Jul 70 Finland
ARTICLES: 0
HEADNOTE: FISHERIES & SEALERY
TOPIC: Specific Resources
PARTIES:
   Finland
   USSR (Soviet Union)

110607   Bilateral Convention   **0 UNTS 0**
SIGNED: 9 Jul 70   FORCE: 9 Jul 70
REGISTERED: 28 Jul 70 Belgium
ARTICLES: 0
HEADNOTE: DOUBLE TAX INCOME AVIATION
TOPIC: Taxation
PARTIES:
   Belgium
   Iceland

110608   Multilateral Agreement   **0 UNTS 0**
SIGNED: 29 Jul 70   FORCE: 29 Jul 70
REGISTERED: 29 Jul 70 United Nations
ARTICLES: 0
HEADNOTE: CADRE UNIT EARTHQUAKE HELP
TOPIC: Tech Assistance
PARTIES:
   Peru
   United Nations
   Sweden

110609   Bilateral Agreement   **0 UNTS 0**
SIGNED: 28 Jul 65   FORCE: 28 Jul 65
REGISTERED: 31 Jul 70 France
ARTICLES: 0
HEADNOTE: ALGERIAN PETROLEUM INSTITUTE
TOPIC: Tech Assistance
PARTIES:
   Algeria
   France

110610   Bilateral Agreement   **0 UNTS 0**
SIGNED: 29 Jul 65   FORCE: 30 Dec 65
REGISTERED: 31 Jul 70 France
ARTICLES: 0
HEADNOTE: INDUSTRIAL DEVELOPMENT AL-
   GERIA
TOPIC: Non-IBRD Project
PARTIES:
   Algeria
   France

110611   Bilateral Agreement   **0 UNTS 0**
SIGNED: 19 Mar 70   FORCE: 17 Jun 70
REGISTERED: 31 Jul 70 Finland
ARTICLES: 0
HEADNOTE: AIR SERVICES
TOPIC: Air Transport
PARTIES:
   Bulgaria
   Finland

110612   Multilateral Protocol   **0 UNTS 0**
SIGNED: 24 Sep 68   FORCE: 24 Oct 68
REGISTERED: 3 Aug 70
ARTICLES: 0
HEADNOTE: AUTHENTIC TRILINGUAL TEXT ICAO
TOPIC: Air Transport
PARTIES:
  Australia
  Belgium
  Bulgaria
  Cameroon
  Canada
  Chad
  Colombia
  Costa Rica
  France
  Gabon
  Germany, West
  Hungary
  India
  Ireland
  Ivory Coast
  Jordan
  Lebanon
  Madagascar
  Malawi
  Mali
  Mauritania
  Mexico
  Netherlands
  Nigeria
  Niger
  Panama
  Romania
  Saudi Arabia
  Switzerland
  Tanzania
  Togo
  Turkey
  United Arab Rep
  UK Great Britain
  Upper Volta
  Yemen

110613   Bilateral Instrument   **0 UNTS 0**
SIGNED: 23 Dec 69   FORCE: 23 Dec 69
REGISTERED: 3 Aug 70 USA (United States)
ARTICLES: 0
HEADNOTE: AGRI COMMOD
TOPIC: Commodity Trade
PARTIES:
  USA (United States)
  Vietnam, South

110614   Bilateral Instrument   **0 UNTS 0**
SIGNED: 25 Mar 70   FORCE: 25 Mar 70
REGISTERED: 3 Aug 70 USA (United States)
ARTICLES: 0
HEADNOTE: AGRI COMMOD
TOPIC: Commodity Trade
PARTIES:
  USA (United States)
  Vietnam, South

110615   Bilateral Exchange   **0 UNTS 0**
SIGNED: 29 Dec 69   FORCE: 29 Dec 69
REGISTERED: 3 Aug 70 USA (United States)
ARTICLES: 0
HEADNOTE: MEASURING EQUIPMENT PLAI-
SANCE
TOPIC: Scientific Project
PARTIES:
  Mauritius
  USA (United States)

110616   Bilateral Agreement   **0 UNTS 0**
SIGNED: 16 Jan 70   FORCE: 16 Jan 70
REGISTERED: 3 Aug 70 USA (United States)
ARTICLES: 0
HEADNOTE: NAVAL MEDICAL RESEARCH UNIT
TOPIC: Scientific Project
PARTIES:
  Indonesia
  USA (United States)

110617   Bilateral Exchange   **0 UNTS 0**
SIGNED: 29 Jan 70   FORCE: 29 Jan 70
REGISTERED: 3 Aug 70 USA (United States)
ARTICLES: 0

HEADNOTE: MEAT IMPORT
TOPIC: General Trade
PARTIES:
  New Zealand
  USA (United States)

110618   Bilateral Exchange   **0 UNTS 0**
SIGNED: 30 Jan 70   FORCE: 30 Jan 70
REGISTERED: 3 Aug 70 USA (United States)
ARTICLES: 0
HEADNOTE: MEAT IMPORT
TOPIC: General Trade
PARTIES:
  Australia
  USA (United States)

110619   Bilateral Exchange   **0 UNTS 0**
SIGNED: 30 Jan 70   FORCE: 30 Jan 70
REGISTERED: 3 Aug 70 USA (United States)
ARTICLES: 0
HEADNOTE: MEAT IMPORT
TOPIC: General Trade
PARTIES:
  Ireland
  USA (United States)

110620   Bilateral Agreement   **0 UNTS 0**
SIGNED: 2 Feb 70   FORCE: 2 Feb 70
REGISTERED: 3 Aug 70 USA (United States)
ARTICLES: 0
HEADNOTE: AIR TRANSPORT
TOPIC: Air Transport
PARTIES:
  Malaysia
  USA (United States)

110621   Bilateral Agreement   **0 UNTS 0**
SIGNED: 3 Feb 70   FORCE: 3 Mar 70
REGISTERED: 3 Aug 70 USA (United States)
ARTICLES: 0
HEADNOTE: CULTURE
TOPIC: Education
PARTIES:
  New Zealand
  USA (United States)

110623   Multilateral Exchange   **0 UNTS 0**
SIGNED: 24 Feb 70   FORCE: 24 Feb 70
REGISTERED: 3 Aug 70 USA (United States)
ARTICLES: 0
HEADNOTE: PINETREE RADAR HOPEDALE LABRA-
DOR
TOPIC: Non-IBRD Project
PARTIES:
  Burundi
  Canada
  USA (United States)

110624   Bilateral Exchange   **0 UNTS 0**
SIGNED: 26 Feb 70   FORCE: 26 Feb 70
REGISTERED: 3 Aug 70 USA (United States)
ARTICLES: 0
HEADNOTE: SAFEGUARD CLASSIFIED INFORMA-
TION
TOPIC: Admin Cooperation
PARTIES:
  Norway
  USA (United States)

110625   Bilateral Exchange   **0 UNTS 0**
SIGNED: 3 Mar 70   FORCE: 3 Mar 70
REGISTERED: 3 Aug 70 USA (United States)
ARTICLES: 0
HEADNOTE: TRANSFER ADMINISTRATIVE
RIGHTS
TOPIC: Recognition
PARTIES:
  Japan
  USA (United States)

110626   Bilateral Exchange   **0 UNTS 0**
SIGNED: 4 Mar 70   FORCE: 4 Mar 70
REGISTERED: 3 Aug 70 USA (United States)
ARTICLES: 0
HEADNOTE: MEAT IMPORT
TOPIC: Commodity Trade

PARTIES:
  Panama
  USA (United States)

110627   Bilateral Exchange   **0 UNTS 0**
SIGNED: 6 Mar 70   FORCE: 6 Mar 70
REGISTERED: 3 Aug 70 USA (United States)
ARTICLES: 0
HEADNOTE: MEAT IMPORT
TOPIC: Commodity Trade
PARTIES:
  Costa Rica
  USA (United States)

110628   Bilateral Instrument   **0 UNTS 0**
SIGNED: 16 Mar 70   FORCE: 16 Mar 70
REGISTERED: 3 Aug 70 USA (United States)
ARTICLES: 0
HEADNOTE: AGRI COMMOD
TOPIC: US Agri Commod Aid
PARTIES:
  Turkey
  USA (United States)

110629   Bilateral Exchange   **0 UNTS 0**
SIGNED: 20 Mar 70   FORCE: 20 Mar 70
REGISTERED: 3 Aug 70 USA (United States)
ARTICLES: 0
HEADNOTE: MEAT IMPORT
TOPIC: Commodity Trade
PARTIES:
  Mexico
  USA (United States)

110630   Bilateral Exchange   **0 UNTS 0**
SIGNED: 20 Mar 70   FORCE: 20 Mar 70
REGISTERED: 3 Aug 70 USA (United States)
ARTICLES: 0
HEADNOTE: IMPORTED AIRCRAFT
TOPIC: Air Transport
PARTIES:
  New Zealand
  USA (United States)

110631   Bilateral Agreement   **0 UNTS 0**
SIGNED: 20 Mar 70   FORCE: 20 Mar 70
REGISTERED: 3 Aug 70 USA (United States)
ARTICLES: 0
HEADNOTE: AGRI COMMOD
TOPIC: US Agri Commod Aid
PARTIES:
  Korea, South
  USA (United States)

110632   Bilateral Agreement   **0 UNTS 0**
SIGNED: 31 Mar 70   FORCE: 31 Mar 70
REGISTERED: 3 Aug 70 USA (United States)
ARTICLES: 0
HEADNOTE: AGRI COMMOD
TOPIC: US Agri Commod Aid
PARTIES:
  Dominican Republic
  USA (United States)

110633   Bilateral Agreement   **0 UNTS 0**
SIGNED: 22 Oct 69   FORCE: 21 Dec 69
REGISTERED: 4 Aug 70 France
ARTICLES: 0
HEADNOTE: TONNAGE MERCHANT SHIPS
TOPIC: Water Transport
PARTIES:
  France
  Pakistan

110634   Bilateral Treaty   **0 UNTS 0**
SIGNED: 13 Nov 60   FORCE: 27 Jan 61
REGISTERED: 5 Aug 70 France
ARTICLES: 0
HEADNOTE: COOPERATION
TOPIC: General Amity
PARTIES:
  Cameroon
  France

110635   Bilateral Convention   **0 UNTS 0**
SIGNED: 13 Nov 60   FORCE: 27 Jan 61
REGISTERED: 5 Aug 70 France
ARTICLES: 0
HEADNOTE: CONSULAR
TOPIC: Consul/Citizenship
PARTIES:
  Cameroon
  France

110636   Bilateral Convention   **0 UNTS 0**
SIGNED: 13 Nov 60   FORCE: 27 Jan 61
REGISTERED: 5 Aug 70 France
ARTICLES: 0
HEADNOTE: CULTURE
TOPIC: Culture
PARTIES:
  Cameroon
  France

110637   Bilateral Convention   **0 UNTS 0**
SIGNED: 13 Nov 60   FORCE: 27 Jan 61
REGISTERED: 5 Aug 70 France
ARTICLES: 0
HEADNOTE: JUDICIAL
TOPIC: Admin Cooperation
PARTIES:
  Cameroon
  France

110638   Bilateral Agreement   **0 UNTS 0**
SIGNED: 13 Nov 60   FORCE: 27 Jan 61
REGISTERED: 5 Aug 70 France
ARTICLES: 0
HEADNOTE: COOPERATION ECONOMIC MAT-
  TERS
TOPIC: General Economic
PARTIES:
  Cameroon
  France

110639   Bilateral Convention   **0 UNTS 0**
SIGNED: 13 Nov 60   FORCE: 27 Jan 61
REGISTERED: 5 Aug 70 France
ARTICLES: 0
HEADNOTE: TREASURY
TOPIC: General Economic
PARTIES:
  Cameroon
  France

110640   Bilateral Agreement   **0 UNTS 0**
SIGNED: 13 Nov 60   FORCE: 27 Jan 61
REGISTERED: 5 Aug 70 France
ARTICLES: 0
HEADNOTE: TECHNICAL MILITARY ASSISTANCE
TOPIC: Military Mission
PARTIES:
  Cameroon
  France

110641   Bilateral Convention   **0 UNTS 0**
SIGNED: 13 Nov 60   FORCE: 27 Jan 61
REGISTERED: 5 Aug 70 France
ARTICLES: 0
HEADNOTE: STATUS FRENCH MILITARY MIS-
  SION
TOPIC: Military Mission
PARTIES:
  Cameroon
  France

110642   Bilateral Agreement   **0 UNTS 0**
SIGNED: 13 Nov 60   FORCE: 27 Jan 61
REGISTERED: 5 Aug 70 France
ARTICLES: 0
HEADNOTE: CIVIL AVIATION METEOROLOGIC
  BASES
TOPIC: Air Transport
PARTIES:
  Cameroon
  France

110643   Bilateral Agreement   **0 UNTS 0**
SIGNED: 13 Nov 60   FORCE: 27 Jan 61
REGISTERED: 5 Aug 70 France

ARTICLES: 0
HEADNOTE: TECHNICAL COOPERATION PERSON-
  NEL
TOPIC: Admin Cooperation
PARTIES:
  Cameroon
  France

110644   Bilateral Convention   **0 UNTS 0**
SIGNED: 27 Aug 66   FORCE: 13 Jan 67
REGISTERED: 5 Aug 70 France
ARTICLES: 0
HEADNOTE: CULTURE
TOPIC: Culture
PARTIES:
  Ethiopia
  France

110645   Bilateral Agreement   **0 UNTS 0**
SIGNED: 27 Aug 66   FORCE: 13 Jan 67
REGISTERED: 5 Aug 70 France
ARTICLES: 0
HEADNOTE: CULTURE TECHNICAL COOPER-
  ATION
TOPIC: Culture
PARTIES:
  Ethiopia
  France

110646   Bilateral Exchange   **0 UNTS 0**
SIGNED: 27 Aug 66   FORCE: 13 Jan 67
REGISTERED: 5 Aug 70 France
ARTICLES: 0
HEADNOTE: FRANCO-ETHIOPIAN LYCEE
TOPIC: Culture
PARTIES:
  Ethiopia
  France

110647   Bilateral Exchange   **0 UNTS 0**
SIGNED: 28 Mar 69   FORCE: 28 Mar 69
REGISTERED: 5 Aug 70 France
ARTICLES: 0
HEADNOTE: MINISTRY OF EDUCATION
TOPIC: Education
PARTIES:
  Ethiopia
  France

110648   Bilateral Agreement   **0 UNTS 0**
SIGNED: 4 Jun 69   FORCE: 6 Oct 69
REGISTERED: 11 Aug 70 IBRD (World Bank)
ARTICLES: 0
HEADNOTE: LOAN HIGHWAY ENGINEERING
TOPIC: IBRD Project
PARTIES:
  IBRD (World Bank)
  Tunisia

110649   Bilateral Agreement   **0 UNTS 0**
SIGNED: 26 Jun 69   FORCE: 10 Jun 70
REGISTERED: 11 Aug 70 IBRD (World Bank)
ARTICLES: 0
HEADNOTE: CREDIT HIGHWAY MAINTENANCE
TOPIC: IBRD Project
PARTIES:
  Afghanistan
  IBRD (World Bank)

110650   Bilateral Agreement   **0 UNTS 0**
SIGNED: 29 Oct 69   FORCE: 1 Jun 70
REGISTERED: 11 Aug 70 IDA (Devel Assoc)
ARTICLES: 0
HEADNOTE: CREDIT ELECTRICITY DISTRIBUTION
TOPIC: Non-IBRD Project
PARTIES:
  Indonesia
  IDA (Devel Assoc)

110651   Bilateral Agreement   **0 UNTS 0**
SIGNED: 15 Dec 69   FORCE: 16 Mar 70
REGISTERED: 11 Aug 70 IDA (Devel Assoc)
ARTICLES: 0
HEADNOTE: CREDIT DACCA S. W. IRRIGATION
TOPIC: Non-IBRD Project

PARTIES:
  Indonesia
  IDA (Devel Assoc)

110652   Bilateral Agreement   **0 UNTS 0**
SIGNED: 13 Jan 70   FORCE: 18 Jun 70
REGISTERED: 11 Aug 70 IDA (Devel Assoc)
ARTICLES: 0
HEADNOTE: CREDIT SECOND BENI LIVESTOCK
TOPIC: Non-IBRD Project
PARTIES:
  Bolivia
  IDA (Devel Assoc)

110653   Bilateral Agreement   **0 UNTS 0**
SIGNED: 20 Jan 70   FORCE: 29 Jun 70
REGISTERED: 11 Aug 70 IDA (Devel Assoc)
ARTICLES: 0
HEADNOTE: CREDIT SECOND LIVESTOCK
TOPIC: Non-IBRD Project
PARTIES:
  Ecuador
  IDA (Devel Assoc)

110654   Bilateral Instrument   **0 UNTS 0**
SIGNED: 30 Jan 70   FORCE: 3 Jun 70
REGISTERED: 11 Aug 70 IDA (Devel Assoc)
ARTICLES: 0
HEADNOTE: AGRICULTURE CREDIT PAPUA NEW
  GUINEA
TOPIC: Non-IBRD Project
PARTIES:
  Australia
  IDA (Devel Assoc)

110655   Bilateral Agreement   **0 UNTS 0**
SIGNED: 11 Feb 70   FORCE: 20 Apr 70
REGISTERED: 11 Aug 70 IDA (Devel Assoc)
ARTICLES: 0
HEADNOTE: CREDIT MALAWI POWER
TOPIC: Non-IBRD Project
PARTIES:
  Malawi
  IDA (Devel Assoc)

110656   Bilateral Agreement   **0 UNTS 0**
SIGNED: 11 Feb 70   FORCE: 25 Jun 70
REGISTERED: 11 Aug 70 IDA (Devel Assoc)
ARTICLES: 0
HEADNOTE: CREDIT INDUSTRIAL DEVELOPMENT
  BANK
TOPIC: Non-IBRD Project
PARTIES:
  Pakistan
  IDA (Devel Assoc)

110657   Bilateral Agreement   **0 UNTS 0**
SIGNED: 24 Apr 70   FORCE: 27 May 70
REGISTERED: 11 Aug 70 IDA (Devel Assoc)
ARTICLES: 0
HEADNOTE: CREDIT SIXTH INDUSTRIAL IM-
  PORTS
TOPIC: Non-IBRD Project
PARTIES:
  India
  IDA (Devel Assoc)

110658   Bilateral Agreement   **0 UNTS 0**
SIGNED: 22 May 70   FORCE: 30 Jun 70
REGISTERED: 11 Aug 70 IDA (Devel Assoc)
ARTICLES: 0
HEADNOTE: CREDIT SECOND TELECOMMUNICA-
  TIONS
TOPIC: Non-IBRD Project
PARTIES:
  Pakistan
  IDA (Devel Assoc)

110659   Bilateral Agreement   **0 UNTS 0**
SIGNED: 28 May 70   FORCE: 10 Jun 70
REGISTERED: 11 Aug 70 IDA (Devel Assoc)
ARTICLES: 0
HEADNOTE: CREDIT DEVELOPMENT FINANCE
  COMPANY
TOPIC: Non-IBRD Project

PARTIES:
Congo (Zaire)
IDA (Devel Assoc)

110660 Bilateral Agreement **0 UNTS 0**
SIGNED: 12 Feb 70 FORCE: 20 May 70
REGISTERED: 11 Aug 70 Australia
ARTICLES: 0
HEADNOTE: RESIDENCE EMPLOYMENT YUGO-
SLAVS
TOPIC: Non-ILO Labor
PARTIES:
Australia
Yugoslavia

110661 Bilateral Exchange **0 UNTS 0**
SIGNED: 22 May 70 FORCE: 22 May 70
REGISTERED: 11 Aug 70 Australia
ARTICLES: 0
HEADNOTE: LAUNCHING THREE AEROBEE ROCK-
ETS
TOPIC: General Military
PARTIES:
Australia
USA (United States)

110662 Bilateral Exchange **0 UNTS 0**
SIGNED: 18 May 67 FORCE: 18 May 63
REGISTERED: 14 Aug 70 France
ARTICLES: 0
HEADNOTE: URBANIZATION
TOPIC: Culture
PARTIES:
France
Monaco

110663 Bilateral Exchange **0 UNTS 0**
SIGNED: 23 Jan 70 FORCE: 23 Jan 70
REGISTERED: 14 Aug 70 France
ARTICLES: 0
HEADNOTE: URBANIZATION
TOPIC: Culture
PARTIES:
France
Monaco

110664 Bilateral Exchange **0 UNTS 0**
SIGNED: 23 Jan 70 FORCE: 9 Feb 70
REGISTERED: 14 Aug 70 France
ARTICLES: 0
HEADNOTE: PROFESSION OF ARCHITECTURE
TOPIC: Education
PARTIES:
France
Monaco

110665 Bilateral Convention **0 UNTS 0**
SIGNED: 17 Dec 65 FORCE: 3 May 69
REGISTERED: 14 Aug 70 France
ARTICLES: 0
HEADNOTE: SOCIAL SECURITY
TOPIC: Non-ILO Labor
PARTIES:
France
Tunisia

110666 Bilateral Exchange **0 UNTS 0**
SIGNED: 20 Mar 70 FORCE: 20 Mar 70
REGISTERED: 14 Aug 70 France
ARTICLES: 0
HEADNOTE: AUTOMOBILE INSURANCE FUNDS
TOPIC: Finance
PARTIES:
France
Tunisia

110667 Bilateral Agreement **0 UNTS 0**
SIGNED: 14 Mar 67 FORCE: 2 May 70
REGISTERED: 14 Aug 70 France
ARTICLES: 0
HEADNOTE: PRIVILEGES IMMUNITIES CANCER
CENTER
TOPIC: IGO Operations
PARTIES:
France
WHO (World Health)

110668 Bilateral Exchange **0 UNTS 0**
SIGNED: 30 Nov 67 FORCE: 30 Nov 67
REGISTERED: 14 Aug 70 France
ARTICLES: 0
HEADNOTE: STATUS FRENCH SCHOOL
TOPIC: Education
PARTIES:
Costa Rica
France

110669 Bilateral Exchange **0 UNTS 0**
SIGNED: 23 Sep 69 FORCE: 23 Sep 69
REGISTERED: 14 Aug 70 France
ARTICLES: 0
HEADNOTE: STATUS FRENCH SCHOOL
TOPIC: Education
PARTIES:
Costa Rica
France

110670 Bilateral Convention **0 UNTS 0**
SIGNED: 3 Feb 69 FORCE: 3 Feb 69
REGISTERED: 14 Aug 70 France
ARTICLES: 0
HEADNOTE: SCIENTIFIC RESEARCH
TOPIC: Scientific Project
PARTIES:
France
Togo

110671 Bilateral Agreement **0 UNTS 0**
SIGNED: 10 Oct 69 FORCE: 16 Dec 69
REGISTERED: 18 Aug 70 IBRD (World Bank)
ARTICLES: 0
HEADNOTE: LOAN THIRD HIGHWAY
TOPIC: IBRD Project
PARTIES:
Kenya
IBRD (World Bank)

110672 Bilateral Agreement **0 UNTS 0**
SIGNED: 6 Nov 69 FORCE: 31 Jul 70
REGISTERED: 18 Aug 70 IBRD (World Bank)
ARTICLES: 0
HEADNOTE: LOAN HIGHWAY REHABILITATION
TOPIC: IBRD Project
PARTIES:
Nigeria
IBRD (World Bank)

110673 Bilateral Agreement **0 UNTS 0**
SIGNED: 7 Nov 69 FORCE: 13 Jul 69
REGISTERED: 18 Aug 70 IBRD (World Bank)
ARTICLES: 0
HEADNOTE: LOAN FOREST PLANTATIONS
TOPIC: IBRD Project
PARTIES:
Kenya
IBRD (World Bank)

110674 Bilateral Agreement **0 UNTS 0**
SIGNED: 13 Nov 69 FORCE: 8 Jun 70
REGISTERED: 18 Aug 70 IBRD (World Bank)
ARTICLES: 0
HEADNOTE: LOAN RHARB-SEBOU IRRIGATION
TOPIC: IBRD Project
PARTIES:
Morocco
IBRD (World Bank)

110675 Bilateral Agreement **0 UNTS 0**
SIGNED: 14 Nov 69 FORCE: 9 Feb 70
REGISTERED: 18 Aug 70 IBRD (World Bank)
ARTICLES: 0
HEADNOTE: GUARANTEE BUENOS AIRES POWER
TOPIC: IBRD Project
PARTIES:
Argentina
IBRD (World Bank)

110676 Bilateral Agreement **0 UNTS 0**
SIGNED: 24 Dec 69 FORCE: 31 Mar 70
REGISTERED: 18 Aug 70 IBRD (World Bank)
ARTICLES: 0
HEADNOTE: GUARANTEE THIRD POWER
TOPIC: IBRD Project

PARTIES:
Cyprus
IBRD (World Bank)

110677 Bilateral Agreement **0 UNTS 0**
SIGNED: 10 Feb 70 FORCE: 17 Apr 70
REGISTERED: 18 Aug 70 IBRD (World Bank)
ARTICLES: 0
HEADNOTE: GUARANTEE FIRST EGAT POWER
TOPIC: IBRD Project
PARTIES:
IBRD (World Bank)
Thailand

110678 Bilateral Agreement **0 UNTS 0**
SIGNED: 25 Feb 70 FORCE: 28 May 70
REGISTERED: 18 Aug 70 IBRD (World Bank)
ARTICLES: 0
HEADNOTE: GUARANTEE DBS PROJECT
TOPIC: IBRD Project
PARTIES:
IBRD (World Bank)
Singapore

110679 Bilateral Agreement **0 UNTS 0**
SIGNED: 6 Mar 70 FORCE: 8 Jun 70
REGISTERED: 18 Aug 70 IBRD (World Bank)
ARTICLES: 0
HEADNOTE: GUARANTEE FOURTH BNDE
PROJECT
TOPIC: IBRD Project
PARTIES:
Morocco
IBRD (World Bank)

110680 Bilateral Agreement **0 UNTS 0**
SIGNED: 16 Mar 70 FORCE: 28 Jul 70
REGISTERED: 18 Aug 70 IBRD (World Bank)
ARTICLES: 0
HEADNOTE: GUARANTEE SECOND POWER
TOPIC: IBRD Project
PARTIES:
Panama
IBRD (World Bank)

110681 Bilateral Agreement **0 UNTS 0**
SIGNED: 27 Mar 70 FORCE: 16 Jul 70
REGISTERED: 18 Aug 70 IBRD (World Bank)
ARTICLES: 0
HEADNOTE: LOAN HIGHWAY
TOPIC: IBRD Project
PARTIES:
Cameroon
IBRD (World Bank)

110682 Bilateral Agreement **0 UNTS 0**
SIGNED: 27 Mar 70 FORCE: 16 Jul 70
REGISTERED: 18 Aug 70 IDA (Devel Assoc)
ARTICLES: 0
HEADNOTE: CREDIT HIGHWAY
TOPIC: Non-IBRD Project
PARTIES:
Cameroon
IDA (Devel Assoc)

110683 Bilateral Agreement **0 UNTS 0**
SIGNED: 2 Apr 70 FORCE: 17 Jun 70
REGISTERED: 18 Aug 70 IBRD (World Bank)
ARTICLES: 0
HEADNOTE: LOAN SIQUIRRES-LIMON HIGHWAY
TOPIC: IBRD Project
PARTIES:
Costa Rica
IBRD (World Bank)

110684 Bilateral Agreement **0 UNTS 0**
SIGNED: 20 May 70 FORCE: 5 Aug 70
REGISTERED: 18 Aug 70 IDA (Devel Assoc)
ARTICLES: 0
HEADNOTE: CREDIT SECOND EDUCATION
TOPIC: Non-IBRD Project
PARTIES:
Kenya
IDA (Devel Assoc)

110685   Bilateral Agreement   **0 UNTS 0**
SIGNED: 4 Jun 70   FORCE: 15 Jun 70
REGISTERED: 18 Aug 70 IBRD (World Bank)
ARTICLES: 0
HEADNOTE: GUARANTEE POWER EXPANSION
TOPIC: IBRD Project
PARTIES:
  Liberia
  IBRD (World Bank)

110686   Bilateral Agreement   **0 UNTS 0**
SIGNED: 10 Jun 70   FORCE: 30 Jul 70
REGISTERED: 18 Aug 70 IDA (Devel Assoc)
ARTICLES: 0
HEADNOTE: CREDIT KARACHI PORT
TOPIC: Non-IBRD Project
PARTIES:
  Pakistan
  IDA (Devel Assoc)

110687   Multilateral Agreement   **0 UNTS 0**
SIGNED: 22 Aug 67   FORCE: 20 Nov 69
REGISTERED: 20 Aug 70 Netherlands
ARTICLES: 0
HEADNOTE: LONG-TERM TRADE
TOPIC: General Trade
PARTIES:
  Belgium
  Luxembourg
  Netherlands
  Poland

110688   Bilateral Agreement   **0 UNTS 0**
SIGNED: 16 May 70   FORCE: 7 Jul 70
REGISTERED: 21 Aug 70 IBRD (World Bank)
ARTICLES: 0
HEADNOTE: GUARANTEE FOURTH ODC PROJECT
TOPIC: IBRD Project
PARTIES:
  Taiwan
  IBRD (World Bank)

110689   Bilateral Agreement   **0 UNTS 0**
SIGNED: 10 Dec 69   FORCE: 26 Feb 70
REGISTERED: 24 Aug 70 IBRD (World Bank)
ARTICLES: 0
HEADNOTE: GUARANTEE NICKEL
TOPIC: IBRD Project
PARTIES:
  Dominican Republic
  IBRD (World Bank)

110690   Bilateral Agreement   **0 UNTS 0**
SIGNED: 30 Jun 69   FORCE: 30 Jun 69
REGISTERED: 1 Sep 70 USA (United States)
ARTICLES: 0
HEADNOTE: AGRI COMMOD
TOPIC: US Agri Commod Aid
PARTIES:
  Ecuador
  USA (United States)

110691   Bilateral Exchange   **0 UNTS 0**
SIGNED: 9 Mar 70   FORCE: 9 Mar 70
REGISTERED: 1 Sep 70 USA (United States)
ARTICLES: 0
HEADNOTE: MEAT IMPORTS
TOPIC: Commodity Trade
PARTIES:
  Dominican Republic
  USA (United States)

110692   Bilateral Agreement   **0 UNTS 0**
SIGNED: 24 Mar 70   FORCE: 24 Mar 70
REGISTERED: 1 Sep 70 USA (United States)
ARTICLES: 0
HEADNOTE: AGRI COMMOD
TOPIC: US Agri Commod Aid
PARTIES:
  Philippines
  USA (United States)

110693   Bilateral Exchange   **0 UNTS 0**
SIGNED: 25 Mar 70   FORCE: 26 Feb 70
REGISTERED: 1 Sep 70 USA (United States)
ARTICLES: 0

HEADNOTE: SPACE VEHICLE TRACKING
TOPIC: Gen Communications
PARTIES:
  Australia
  USA (United States)

110694   Bilateral Exchange   **0 UNTS 0**
SIGNED: 23 Apr 70   FORCE: 23 Apr 70
REGISTERED: 1 Sep 70 USA (United States)
ARTICLES: 0
HEADNOTE: DEPLOYMENT USS SHENANDOAH
TOPIC: Military Mission
PARTIES:
  Malta
  USA (United States)

110695   Bilateral Exchange   **0 UNTS 0**
SIGNED: 1 May 70   FORCE: 1 May 70
REGISTERED: 1 Sep 70 USA (United States)
ARTICLES: 0
HEADNOTE: ABOLISH ADVISORY COMMISSION
  RYUKYU
TOPIC: Admin Cooperation
PARTIES:
  Japan
  USA (United States)

110696   Bilateral Agreement   **0 UNTS 0**
SIGNED: 7 May 70   FORCE: 7 May 70
REGISTERED: 1 Sep 70 USA (United States)
ARTICLES: 0
HEADNOTE: FOURTH SUPPLEMENT AGRI COM-
  MOD
TOPIC: US Agri Commod Aid
PARTIES:
  Israel
  USA (United States)

110697   Bilateral Agreement   **0 UNTS 0**
SIGNED: 16 Feb 70   FORCE: 16 Feb 70
REGISTERED: 1 Sep 70 Denmark
ARTICLES: 0
HEADNOTE: TECHNICAL COOPERATION
TOPIC: Tech Assistance
PARTIES:
  Denmark
  India

110698   Bilateral Agreement   **0 UNTS 0**
SIGNED: 6 Apr 68   FORCE: 9 Jun 69
REGISTERED: 2 Sep 70 UK Great Britain
ARTICLES: 0
HEADNOTE: DOUBLE TAX INCOME
TOPIC: Taxation
PARTIES:
  UK Great Britain
  Zambia

110699   Bilateral Exchange   **0 UNTS 0**
SIGNED: 6 Jan 70   FORCE: 6 Jan 70
REGISTERED: 2 Sep 70 UK Great Britain
ARTICLES: 0
HEADNOTE: LESOTHO STERLING RESERVES
TOPIC: Finance
PARTIES:
  Lesotho
  UK Great Britain

110700   Bilateral Protocol   **0 UNTS 0**
SIGNED: 17 Aug 48   FORCE: 17 Aug 48
REGISTERED: 3 Sep 70 France
ARTICLES: 0
HEADNOTE: STATUS EMPLOYED PERSONS
TOPIC: Non-ILO Labor
PARTIES:
  France
  Poland

110701   Bilateral Protocol   **0 UNTS 0**
SIGNED: 25 May 61   FORCE: 1 Oct 61
REGISTERED: 3 Sep 70 France
ARTICLES: 0
HEADNOTE: STATUS WORKERS INSURANCE
TOPIC: Non-ILO Labor

PARTIES:
  France
  Poland

110702   Bilateral Protocol   **0 UNTS 0**
SIGNED: 28 Apr 66   FORCE: 1 Nov 66
REGISTERED: 3 Sep 70 France
ARTICLES: 0
HEADNOTE: OLD-AGE ALLOWANCE NON-
  EMPLOYED
TOPIC: Non-ILO Labor
PARTIES:
  France
  Poland

110703   Bilateral Exchange   **0 UNTS 0**
SIGNED: 9 Jun 54   FORCE: 1 May 54
REGISTERED: 3 Sep 70 France
ARTICLES: 0
HEADNOTE: EXEMPTION FRONTIER AGRICUL-
  TURISTS
TOPIC: Visas
PARTIES:
  Belgium
  France

110704   Bilateral Convention   **0 UNTS 0**
SIGNED: 27 Jun 57   FORCE: 11 Mar 59
REGISTERED: 3 Sep 70 France
ARTICLES: 0
HEADNOTE: SOCIAL SECURITY
TOPIC: Non-ILO Labor
PARTIES:
  France
  Spain

110705   Bilateral Agreement   **0 UNTS 0**
SIGNED: 8 Jul 63   FORCE: 1 Oct 63
REGISTERED: 3 Sep 70 France
ARTICLES: 0
HEADNOTE: DEPENDENCY ALLOWANCE
TOPIC: Non-ILO Labor
PARTIES:
  France
  Spain

110706   Bilateral Agreement   **0 UNTS 0**
SIGNED: 29 Aug 64   FORCE: 1 Jan 65
REGISTERED: 3 Sep 70 France
ARTICLES: 0
HEADNOTE: DEPENDENCY ALLOWANCE SEA-
  SONAL
TOPIC: Non-ILO Labor
PARTIES:
  France
  Spain

110707   Bilateral Agreement   **0 UNTS 0**
SIGNED: 7 Feb 69   FORCE: 6 Nov 69
REGISTERED: 3 Sep 70 France
ARTICLES: 0
HEADNOTE: CULTURAL SCIENTIFIC TECHNICAL
  COOPERATION
TOPIC: Culture
PARTIES:
  France
  Spain

110708   Bilateral Convention   **0 UNTS 0**
SIGNED: 9 Apr 69   FORCE: 1 Aug 70
REGISTERED: 3 Sep 70 France
ARTICLES: 0
HEADNOTE: JUDICIAL AID CRIMINAL MATTERS
TOPIC: Admin Cooperation
PARTIES:
  France
  Spain

110709   Bilateral Convention   **0 UNTS 0**
SIGNED: 9 Apr 69   FORCE: 1 Aug 70
REGISTERED: 3 Sep 70 France
ARTICLES: 0
HEADNOTE: NATIONAL SERVICE DUAL NATION-
  ALITY
TOPIC: Milit Servic/Citiz

PARTIES:
France
Spain

110710 Bilateral Convention **0 UNTS 0**
SIGNED: 28 May 69   FORCE: 29 Mar 60
REGISTERED: 3 Sep 70 France
ARTICLES: 0
HEADNOTE: JUDICIAL DECISIONS DOCUMENTS
TOPIC: Admin Cooperation
PARTIES:
France
Spain

110711 Bilateral Agreement **0 UNTS 0**
SIGNED: 28 Jul 69   FORCE: 3 Jun 70
REGISTERED: 3 Sep 70 France
ARTICLES: 0
HEADNOTE: SICKNESS INSURANCE SEASONAL
TOPIC: Non-ILO Labor
PARTIES:
France
Spain

110712 Bilateral Convention **0 UNTS 0**
SIGNED: 5 Oct 57   FORCE: 5 Oct 57
REGISTERED: 3 Sep 70 France
ARTICLES: 0
HEADNOTE: JUDICIAL MATTERS
TOPIC: Admin Cooperation
PARTIES:
France
Morocco

110713 Bilateral Convention **0 UNTS 0**
SIGNED: 5 Oct 57   FORCE: 16 Dec 59
REGISTERED: 3 Sep 70 France
ARTICLES: 0
HEADNOTE: JUDICIAL ASSISTANCE EXTRADI-
TION
TOPIC: Admin Cooperation
PARTIES:
France
Morocco

110714 Bilateral Convention **0 UNTS 0**
SIGNED: 18 Apr 58   FORCE: 1 Nov 60
REGISTERED: 3 Sep 70 France
ARTICLES: 0
HEADNOTE: JOINT BORDER CONTROL STATIONS
TOPIC: General Transport
PARTIES:
France
Germany, West

110715 Bilateral Agreement **0 UNTS 0**
SIGNED: 8 Mar 60   FORCE: 7 May 61
REGISTERED: 3 Sep 70 France
ARTICLES: 0
HEADNOTE: MARKS OF ORIGIN
TOPIC: Patents/Copyrights
PARTIES:
France
Germany, West

110716 Bilateral Convention **0 UNTS 0**
SIGNED: 28 Sep 60   FORCE: 8 Jul 61
REGISTERED: 3 Sep 70 France
ARTICLES: 0
HEADNOTE: JOINT ROAD CHECKS
TOPIC: General Transport
PARTIES:
France
Switzerland

110717 Bilateral Treaty **0 UNTS 0**
SIGNED: 24 Apr 61   FORCE: 4 Sep 61
REGISTERED: 3 Sep 70 France
ARTICLES: 0
HEADNOTE: COOPERATION
TOPIC: Admin Cooperation
PARTIES:
France
Ivory Coast

110718 Bilateral Agreement **0 UNTS 0**
SIGNED: 24 Apr 61   FORCE: 4 Sep 61
REGISTERED: 3 Sep 70 France
HEADNOTE: CULTURAL COOPERATION
TOPIC: Culture
PARTIES:
France
Ivory Coast

110719 Bilateral Convention **0 UNTS 0**
SIGNED: 18 May 63   FORCE: 1 Sep 63
REGISTERED: 3 Sep 70 France
ARTICLES: 0
HEADNOTE: INSURANCE
TOPIC: Non-ILO Labor
PARTIES:
France
Monaco

110720 Bilateral Exchange **0 UNTS 0**
SIGNED: 26 Sep 68   FORCE: 12 Dec 68
REGISTERED: 3 Sep 70 France
ARTICLES: 0
HEADNOTE: INSURANCE & CAPITALIZATION
TOPIC: Non-ILO Labor
PARTIES:
France
Monaco

110721 Bilateral Agreement **0 UNTS 0**
SIGNED: 16 Apr 70   FORCE: 16 Jun 70
REGISTERED: 3 Sep 70 France
ARTICLES: 0
HEADNOTE: RELIEF & CIVIL DEFENSE
TOPIC: Admin Cooperation
PARTIES:
France
Monaco

110722 Bilateral Convention **0 UNTS 0**
SIGNED: 24 Jun 64   FORCE: 4 Oct 69
REGISTERED: 3 Sep 70 France
ARTICLES: 0
HEADNOTE: ESTABLISHMENT & NAVIGATION
TOPIC: Consul/Citizenship
PARTIES:
France
Iran

110723 Bilateral Instrument **0 UNTS 0**
SIGNED: 31 Jul 64   FORCE: 31 Jul 64
REGISTERED: 3 Sep 70 France
ARTICLES: 0
HEADNOTE: SCIENTIFIC TECHNICAL COOPER-
ATION
TOPIC: Education
PARTIES:
France
Romania

110724 Bilateral Convention **0 UNTS 0**
SIGNED: 18 May 68   FORCE: 16 Jul 70
REGISTERED: 3 Sep 70 France
ARTICLES: 0
HEADNOTE: CONSULAR
TOPIC: Consul/Citizenship
PARTIES:
France
Romania

110725 Bilateral Agreement **0 UNTS 0**
SIGNED: 17 Jan 69   FORCE: 28 Mar 69
REGISTERED: 3 Sep 70 France
ARTICLES: 0
HEADNOTE: JOINT COOPERATION COMMISSION
TOPIC: Admin Cooperation
PARTIES:
France
Romania

110726 Bilateral Protocol **0 UNTS 0**
SIGNED: 26 Sep 64   FORCE: 26 Sep 64
REGISTERED: 3 Sep 70 France
ARTICLES: 0

HEADNOTE: CULTURAL SCIENTIFIC TECHNICAL
EXCHANGES
TOPIC: Culture
PARTIES:
Czechoslovakia
France

110727 Bilateral Agreement **0 UNTS 0**
SIGNED: 29 Jun 65   FORCE: 14 Jan 66
REGISTERED: 3 Sep 70 France
ARTICLES: 0
HEADNOTE: SCIENTIFIC TECHNICAL COOPER-
ATION
TOPIC: Scientific Project
PARTIES:
Czechoslovakia
France

110728 Bilateral Agreement **0 UNTS 0**
SIGNED: 1 Aug 66   FORCE: 1 Aug 66
REGISTERED: 3 Sep 70 France
ARTICLES: 0
HEADNOTE: FILM COPRODUCTION
TOPIC: Mass Media
PARTIES:
France
Italy

110729 Bilateral Exchange **0 UNTS 0**
SIGNED: 16 Feb 70   FORCE: 16 Feb 70
REGISTERED: 3 Sep 70 France
ARTICLES: 0
HEADNOTE: FILM COPRODUCTION
TOPIC: Mass Media
PARTIES:
France
Italy

110730 Bilateral Agreement **0 UNTS 0**
SIGNED: 20 Mar 68   FORCE: 1 Sep 70
REGISTERED: 3 Sep 70 France
ARTICLES: 0
HEADNOTE: SOCIAL SECURITY SEAMEN
TOPIC: Non-ILO Labor
PARTIES:
France
Tunisia

110731 Bilateral Agreement **0 UNTS 0**
SIGNED: 10 Jul 68   FORCE: 18 Apr 69
REGISTERED: 3 Sep 70 France
ARTICLES: 0
HEADNOTE: ECONOMIC INDUSTRIAL COOPER-
ATION
TOPIC: General Economic
PARTIES:
Bulgaria
France

110732 Bilateral Convention **0 UNTS 0**
SIGNED: 22 Jul 68   FORCE: 1 Apr 70
REGISTERED: 3 Sep 70 France
ARTICLES: 0
HEADNOTE: CONSULAR
TOPIC: Consul/Citizenship
PARTIES:
Bulgaria
France

110733 Bilateral Agreement **0 UNTS 0**
SIGNED: 9 Jan 69   FORCE: 27 Mar 69
REGISTERED: 3 Sep 70 France
ARTICLES: 0
HEADNOTE: MEDICAL COOPERATION
TOPIC: Health/Educ/Welfare
PARTIES:
France
USSR (Soviet Union)

110734 Bilateral Exchange **0 UNTS 0**
SIGNED: 24 Mar 69   FORCE: 1 May 69
REGISTERED: 3 Sep 70 France
ARTICLES: 0
HEADNOTE: VISA ABOLITION
TOPIC: Visas

PARTIES:
France
Malta

110735 Bilateral Convention **0 UNTS 0**
SIGNED: 26 Mar 69 FORCE: 20 Mar 70
REGISTERED: 3 Sep 70 France
ARTICLES: 0
HEADNOTE: DOUBLE TAX INCOME
TOPIC: Taxation
PARTIES:
France
India

110736 Bilateral Agreement **0 UNTS 0**
SIGNED: 3 Apr 69 FORCE: 3 Apr 69
REGISTERED: 3 Sep 70 France
ARTICLES: 0
HEADNOTE: PEACEFUL USE ATOMIC ENERGY
TOPIC: Atomic Energy
PARTIES:
France
Indonesia

110737 Bilateral Agreement **0 UNTS 0**
SIGNED: 20 Sep 69 FORCE: 23 Apr 70
REGISTERED: 3 Sep 70 France
ARTICLES: 0
HEADNOTE: CULTURAL TECHNICAL COOPER-
ATION
TOPIC: Culture
PARTIES:
France
Indonesia

110738 Bilateral Agreement **0 UNTS 0**
SIGNED: 9 Apr 69 FORCE: 1 Jul 69
REGISTERED: 3 Sep 70 France
ARTICLES: 0
HEADNOTE: ROAD TRANSPORT
TOPIC: Land Transport
PARTIES:
France
Greece

110739 Bilateral Agreement **0 UNTS 0**
SIGNED: 24 Apr 69 FORCE: 15 Dec 69
REGISTERED: 3 Sep 70 France
ARTICLES: 0
HEADNOTE: CULTURAL COOPERATION
TOPIC: Culture
PARTIES:
France
Iraq

110740 Bilateral Agreement **0 UNTS 0**
SIGNED: 19 Jun 69 FORCE: 31 Dec 69
REGISTERED: 3 Sep 70 France
ARTICLES: 0
HEADNOTE: TECHNICAL COOPERATION
TOPIC: Tech Assistance
PARTIES:
France
Iraq

110741 Bilateral Agreement **0 UNTS 0**
SIGNED: 30 May 69 FORCE: 5 Jan 70
REGISTERED: 3 Sep 70 France
ARTICLES: 0
HEADNOTE: CULTURAL TECHNICAL COOPER-
ATION
TOPIC: Culture
PARTIES:
Costa Rica
France

110742 Bilateral Agreement **0 UNTS 0**
SIGNED: 18 Sep 69 FORCE: 30 Dec 69
REGISTERED: 3 Sep 70 France
ARTICLES: 0
HEADNOTE: CULTURAL TECHNICAL COOPER-
ATION
TOPIC: Culture
PARTIES:
France
Kuwait

110743 Bilateral Agreement **0 UNTS 0**
SIGNED: 22 Dec 69 FORCE: 13 May 70
REGISTERED: 3 Sep 70 France
ARTICLES: 0
HEADNOTE: CULTURAL TECHNICAL COOPER-
ATION
TOPIC: Culture
PARTIES:
France
Sudan

110744 Bilateral Agreement **0 UNTS 0**
SIGNED: 21 May 70 FORCE: 1 Jul 70
REGISTERED: 3 Sep 70 France
ARTICLES: 0
HEADNOTE: VISA ABOLITION
TOPIC: Visas
PARTIES:
France
Philippines

110745 Bilateral Agreement **0 UNTS 0**
SIGNED: 30 May 70 FORCE: 1 Jul 70
REGISTERED: 3 Sep 70 France
ARTICLES: 0
HEADNOTE: MOVEMENT OF PERSONS
TOPIC: Visas
PARTIES:
France
Upper Volta

110746 Bilateral Convention **0 UNTS 0**
SIGNED: 13 Sep 66 FORCE: 1 Jul 70
REGISTERED: 3 Sep 70 Netherlands
ARTICLES: 0
HEADNOTE: SOCIAL SECURITY
TOPIC: Non-ILO Labor
PARTIES:
Greece
Netherlands

110747 Bilateral Agreement **0 UNTS 0**
SIGNED: 28 Dec 67 FORCE: 27 Jul 70
REGISTERED: 3 Sep 70 Netherlands
ARTICLES: 0
HEADNOTE: SOCIAL STUDIES COLLEGE CAPE
COAST
TOPIC: Education
PARTIES:
Ghana
Netherlands

110748 Bilateral Exchange **0 UNTS 0**
SIGNED: 13 Feb 68 FORCE: 13 Feb 68
REGISTERED: 3 Sep 70 Netherlands
ARTICLES: 0
HEADNOTE: DUTCH VOLUNTEERS
TOPIC: Non-ILO Labor
PARTIES:
Netherlands
Philippines

110749 Bilateral Exchange **0 UNTS 0**
SIGNED: 31 Mar 69 FORCE: 31 Mar 69
REGISTERED: 3 Sep 70 Netherlands
ARTICLES: 0
HEADNOTE: DUTCH VOLUNTEERS
TOPIC: Non-ILO Labor
PARTIES:
Bolivia
Netherlands

110750 Bilateral Agreement **0 UNTS 0**
SIGNED: 23 Jul 69 FORCE: 23 Jul 69
REGISTERED: 3 Sep 70 Netherlands
ARTICLES: 0
HEADNOTE: ANIMAL HUSBANDRY NAIVASHA
TOPIC: Sanitation
PARTIES:
Kenya
Netherlands

110751 Bilateral Agreement **0 UNTS 0**
SIGNED: 21 Jan 69 FORCE: 24 Jul 70
REGISTERED: 4 Sep 70 Netherlands
ARTICLES: 0

HEADNOTE: SOCIAL SECURITY
TOPIC: Non-ILO Labor
PARTIES:
Germany, West
Netherlands

110752 Bilateral Agreement **0 UNTS 0**
SIGNED: 8 Jan 70 FORCE: 8 Jan 70
REGISTERED: 15 Sep 70 Netherlands
ARTICLES: 0
HEADNOTE: ANIMAL HUSBANDRY TRAINING
TOPIC: Sanitation
PARTIES:
Kenya
Netherlands

110753 Bilateral Agreement **0 UNTS 0**
SIGNED: 8 Nov 67 FORCE: 8 Nov 67
REGISTERED: 15 Sep 70 Netherlands
ARTICLES: 0
HEADNOTE: FAMILY PLANNING
TOPIC: Scientific Project
PARTIES:
Netherlands
Pakistan

110754 Bilateral Agreement **0 UNTS 0**
SIGNED: 6 Feb 68 FORCE: 6 Feb 68
REGISTERED: 15 Sep 70 Netherlands
ARTICLES: 0
HEADNOTE: NUTRITION INSTITUTE
TOPIC: Scientific Project
PARTIES:
India
Netherlands

110755 Multilateral Agreement **0 UNTS 0**
SIGNED: 12 Dec 69 FORCE: 9 Mar 70
REGISTERED: 17 Sep 70 Denmark
ARTICLES: 0
HEADNOTE: INDUSTRIALIZATION FUND FOR ICE-
LAND
TOPIC: General Economic
PARTIES:
Denmark
Finland
Iceland
Norway
Sweden

110756 Bilateral Exchange **0 UNTS 0**
SIGNED: 2 Mar 70 FORCE: 1 May 70
REGISTERED: 17 Sep 70 UK Great Britain
ARTICLES: 0
HEADNOTE: DRIVING LICENSES
TOPIC: Land Transport
PARTIES:
Greece
UK Great Britain

110757 Bilateral Exchange **0 UNTS 0**
SIGNED: 13 Mar 70 FORCE: 13 Mar 70
REGISTERED: 17 Sep 70 UK Great Britain
ARTICLES: 0
HEADNOTE: INTEREST-FREE LOAN
TOPIC: Finance
PARTIES:
Indonesia
UK Great Britain

110758 Bilateral Exchange **0 UNTS 0**
SIGNED: 24 Mar 70 FORCE: 24 Mar 70
REGISTERED: 17 Sep 70 UK Great Britain
ARTICLES: 0
HEADNOTE: FOREIGN EXCHANGE OPERATIONS
FUND
TOPIC: Loans and Credits
PARTIES:
Laos
UK Great Britain

110759 Bilateral Agreement **0 UNTS 0**
SIGNED: 25 Mar 70 FORCE: 25 Mar 70
REGISTERED: 17 Sep 70 UK Great Britain
ARTICLES: 0
HEADNOTE: AIR SERVICES

TOPIC: Air Transport
PARTIES:
Jamaica
UK Great Britain

110760   Multilateral Agreement   **0 UNTS 0**
SIGNED: 9 Jul 63   FORCE: 16 Sep 63
REGISTERED: 21 Sep 70 UK Great Britain
ARTICLES: 0
HEADNOTE: AGREEMENT RE MALAYSIA
TOPIC: Admin Cooperation
PARTIES:
Malaya
North Borneo
Sarawak
Singapore
UK Great Britain

110761   Bilateral Agreement   **0 UNTS 0**
SIGNED: 11 Sep 63   FORCE: 16 Sep 63
REGISTERED: 21 Sep 70 UK Great Britain
ARTICLES: 0
HEADNOTE: SUPPLEMENTARY   AGREEMENT
   MALAYSIA
TOPIC: Admin Cooperation
PARTIES:
Fed of Malaya
UK Great Britain

110762   Bilateral Agreement   **0 UNTS 0**
SIGNED: 25 May 65   FORCE: 8 Aug 70
REGISTERED: 21 Sep 70 Belgium
ARTICLES: 0
HEADNOTE: ADMISSION TO MEDICAL PRACTICE
TOPIC: Non-ILO Labor
PARTIES:
Belgium
South Africa

110763   Bilateral Agreement   **0 UNTS 0**
SIGNED: 27 May 69   FORCE: 27 May 69
REGISTERED: 21 Sep 70 Denmark
ARTICLES: 0
HEADNOTE: TEACHERS COLLEGE IRINGA
TOPIC: Education
PARTIES:
Denmark
Tanzania

110764   Multilateral Convention   **0 UNTS 0**
SIGNED: 3 May 67   FORCE: 22 Sep 70
REGISTERED: 22 Sep 70 Monaco
ARTICLES: 0
HEADNOTE: INTERNATIONAL   HYDROGRAPHIC
   ORGANIZATION
TOPIC: IGO Operations
PARTIES:
Argentina
Australia
Brazil
Canada
Taiwan
Cuba
Finland
France
Iceland
India
Indonesia
Iran
Monaco
New Zealand
Pakistan
Portugal
South Africa
United Arab Rep
UK Great Britain
USA (United States)
Yugoslavia

110765   Bilateral Agreement   **0 UNTS 0**
SIGNED: 18 Nov 69   FORCE: 18 Nov 69
REGISTERED: 22 Sep 70 Denmark
ARTICLES: 0
HEADNOTE: TECHNICAL COOPERATION DAIRY
   FARMING
TOPIC: Admin Cooperation

PARTIES:
Denmark
Thailand

110766   Bilateral Agreement   **0 UNTS 0**
SIGNED: 18 Nov 69   FORCE: 18 Nov 69
REGISTERED: 22 Sep 70 Denmark
ARTICLES: 0
HEADNOTE: TEAK
TOPIC: Culture
PARTIES:
Denmark
Thailand

110767   Bilateral Agreement   **0 UNTS 0**
SIGNED: 8 Apr 70   FORCE: 7 Jul 70
REGISTERED: 23 Sep 70 Finland
ARTICLES: 0
HEADNOTE: CIVIL USE ATOMIC ENERGY
TOPIC: Atomic Energy
PARTIES:
Finland
USA (United States)

110768   Multilateral Agreement   **0 UNTS 0**
SIGNED: 26 Sep 70   FORCE: 26 Sep 70
REGISTERED: 26 Sep 70 United Nations
ARTICLES: 0
HEADNOTE: STANDARD OPERATIONAL ASSIS-
   TANCE
TOPIC: IGO Operations
PARTIES:
Barbados
FAO (Food Agri)
IDA (Devel Assoc)
ILO (Labor Org)
IMCO (Maritime Org)
ITU (Telecommun)
UNESCO (Educ/Cult)
United Nations
WHO (World Health)
WMO (Meteorology)

110769   Bilateral Agreement   **0 UNTS 0**
SIGNED: 11 Apr 62   FORCE: 11 Jul 62
REGISTERED: 28 Sep 70 Denmark
ARTICLES: 0
HEADNOTE: TRADE
TOPIC: General Trade
PARTIES:
Denmark
Senegal

110770   Bilateral Agreement   **0 UNTS 0**
SIGNED: 8 Oct 62   FORCE: 8 Oct 62
REGISTERED: 28 Sep 70 Denmark
ARTICLES: 0
HEADNOTE: TRADE
TOPIC: General Trade
PARTIES:
Cameroon
Denmark

110771   Bilateral Convention   **0 UNTS 0**
SIGNED: 7 Mar 69   FORCE: 7 Mar 69
REGISTERED: 28 Sep 70 Denmark
ARTICLES: 0
HEADNOTE: DOUBLE TAX INCOME
TOPIC: Taxation
PARTIES:
Denmark
Singapore

110772   Bilateral Agreement   **0 UNTS 0**
SIGNED: 10 Jun 69   FORCE: 10 Jun 69
REGISTERED: 28 Sep 70 Denmark
ARTICLES: 0
HEADNOTE: DANISH STATE LOAN
TOPIC: Loans and Credits
PARTIES:
Denmark
Tunisia

110773   Bilateral Agreement   **0 UNTS 0**
SIGNED: 18 Mar 70   FORCE: 18 Mar 70
REGISTERED: 30 Sep 70 Belgium

ARTICLES: 0
HEADNOTE: ECONOMIC TECHNICAL COOPER-
   ATION
TOPIC: General Economic
PARTIES:
Algeria
Benelux Econ Union

110774   Bilateral Agreement   **0 UNTS 0**
SIGNED: 10 Feb 70   FORCE: 10 Feb 70
REGISTERED: 6 Oct 70 USA (United States)
ARTICLES: 0
HEADNOTE: SCIENTIFIC & OTHER EXCHANGES
TOPIC: Scientific Project
PARTIES:
USA (United States)
USSR (Soviet Union)

110775   Bilateral Agreement   **0 UNTS 0**
SIGNED: 17 Apr 70   FORCE: 17 Apr 70
REGISTERED: 6 Oct 70 USA (United States)
ARTICLES: 0
HEADNOTE: AGRI COMMOD
TOPIC: General Trade
PARTIES:
USA (United States)
Uruguay

110776   Bilateral Exchange   **0 UNTS 0**
SIGNED: 23 Apr 70   FORCE: 23 Apr 70
REGISTERED: 6 Oct 70 USA (United States)
ARTICLES: 0
HEADNOTE: TOURISM
TOPIC: Visas
PARTIES:
Peru
USA (United States)

110778   Bilateral Exchange   **0 UNTS 0**
SIGNED: 30 Apr 70   FORCE: 30 Apr 70
REGISTERED: 6 Oct 70 USA (United States)
ARTICLES: 0
HEADNOTE: MEAT IMPORTS
TOPIC: General Trade
PARTIES:
Honduras
USA (United States)

110779   Bilateral Exchange   **0 UNTS 0**
SIGNED: 5 May 70   FORCE: 5 May 70
REGISTERED: 6 Oct 70 USA (United States)
ARTICLES: 0
HEADNOTE: MILITARY COOPERATION TECHNI-
   CAL SCIENTIFIC
TOPIC: General Military
PARTIES:
Argentina
USA (United States)

110780   Bilateral Exchange   **0 UNTS 0**
SIGNED: 6 May 70   FORCE: 6 May 70
REGISTERED: 6 Oct 70 USA (United States)
ARTICLES: 0
HEADNOTE: COTTON TEXTILES TRADE
TOPIC: Commodity Trade
PARTIES:
Pakistan
USA (United States)

110781   Bilateral Exchange   **0 UNTS 0**
SIGNED: 11 May 70   FORCE: 11 May 70
REGISTERED: 6 Oct 70 USA (United States)
ARTICLES: 0
HEADNOTE: INVESTMENT GUARANTEES
TOPIC: Finance
PARTIES:
Mauritius
USA (United States)

110782   Bilateral Agreement   **0 UNTS 0**
SIGNED: 22 Jun 70   FORCE: 22 Jun 70
REGISTERED: 6 Oct 70 USA (United States)
ARTICLES: 0
HEADNOTE: AGRI COMMOD
TOPIC: Commodity Trade

PARTIES:
Ghana
USA (United States)

110783   Bilateral Exchange   **0 UNTS 0**
SIGNED: 24 Jun 70   FORCE: 24 Jun 70
REGISTERED: 6 Oct 70 USA (United States)
ARTICLES: 0
HEADNOTE: AIR TRANSPORT
TOPIC: Air Transport
PARTIES:
Iceland
USA (United States)

110784   Bilateral Agreement   **0 UNTS 0**
SIGNED: 17 Jul 70   FORCE: 17 Jul 70
REGISTERED: 8 Oct 70 Denmark
ARTICLES: 0
HEADNOTE: ECONOMIC TECHNICAL SCIENTIFIC
COOPERATION
TOPIC: Scientific Project
PARTIES:
Denmark
USSR (Soviet Union)

110785   Bilateral Agreement   **0 UNTS 0**
SIGNED: 12 Jun 67   FORCE: 1 Jun 70
REGISTERED: 12 Oct 70 UK Great Britain
ARTICLES: 0
HEADNOTE: ROAD TRANSPORT
TOPIC: Land Transport
PARTIES:
UK Great Britain
USA (United States)

110786   Bilateral Exchange   **0 UNTS 0**
SIGNED: 13 Apr 70   FORCE: 13 Apr 70
REGISTERED: 12 Oct 70 UK Great Britain
ARTICLES: 0
HEADNOTE: INTEREST-FREE LOAN
TOPIC: Finance
PARTIES:
Indonesia
UK Great Britain

110787   Bilateral Agreement   **0 UNTS 0**
SIGNED: 27 Apr 70   FORCE: 27 Apr 70
REGISTERED: 12 Oct 70 UK Great Britain
ARTICLES: 0
HEADNOTE: LONG-TERM TRADE
TOPIC: General Trade
PARTIES:
Bulgaria
UK Great Britain

110788   Bilateral Agreement   **0 UNTS 0**
SIGNED: 28 May 70   FORCE: 28 May 70
REGISTERED: 12 Oct 70 UK Great Britain
ARTICLES: 0
HEADNOTE: AIR SERVICES
TOPIC: Air Transport
PARTIES:
Bulgaria
UK Great Britain

110789   Bilateral Instrument   **0 UNTS 0**
SIGNED: 10 Oct 70   FORCE: 13 Oct 70
REGISTERED: 13 Oct 70 UK Great Britain
ARTICLES: 0
HEADNOTE: ACCEPTANCE UN CHARTER
TOPIC: UN Charter
PARTIES:
Fiji Islands

110790   Bilateral Agreement   **0 UNTS 0**
SIGNED: 30 Oct 70   FORCE: 13 Oct 70
REGISTERED: 13 Oct 70 United Nations
ARTICLES: 0
HEADNOTE: STANDARD TECHNICAL ASSIS-
TANCE
TOPIC: Tech Assistance
PARTIES:
State/IGO Group
Fiji Islands

110791   Bilateral Agreement   **0 UNTS 0**
SIGNED: 13 Oct 70   FORCE: 13 Oct 70
REGISTERED: 13 Oct 70 United Nations
ARTICLES: 0
HEADNOTE: STANDARD OPERATIONAL ASSIS-
TANCE
TOPIC: General Aid
PARTIES:
State/IGO Group
Fiji Islands

110792   Bilateral Agreement   **0 UNTS 0**
SIGNED: 13 Oct 70   FORCE: 13 Oct 70
REGISTERED: 13 Oct 70 United Nations
ARTICLES: 0
HEADNOTE: SPECIAL FUND ASSISTANCE
TOPIC: IGO Operations
PARTIES:
Fiji Islands
UN Special Fund

110793   Multilateral Protocol   **0 UNTS 0**
SIGNED: 13 Apr 70   FORCE: 12 Jun 70
REGISTERED: 14 Oct 70 Luxembourg
ARTICLES: 0
HEADNOTE: ESTABLISHMENT   EUROPEAN
SCHOOLS
TOPIC: Education
PARTIES:
France
Germany, West
Italy
Luxembourg
Netherlands

110794   Bilateral Agreement   **0 UNTS 0**
SIGNED: 11 Jul 68   FORCE: 11 Jul 68
REGISTERED: 11 Jul 70 Denmark
ARTICLES: 0
HEADNOTE: TECHNICAL COOPERATION
TOPIC: Tech Assistance
PARTIES:
Denmark
Zambia

110795   Bilateral Agreement   **0 UNTS 0**
SIGNED: 19 Jun 70   FORCE: 19 Jun 70
REGISTERED: 21 Oct 70 Denmark
ARTICLES: 0
HEADNOTE: DANISH LOAN
TOPIC: Finance
PARTIES:
Bolivia
Denmark

110796   Bilateral Agreement   **0 UNTS 0**
SIGNED: 22 Oct 70   FORCE: 22 Oct 70
REGISTERED: 22 Oct 70 United Nations
ARTICLES: 0
HEADNOTE: OPERATIONAL ASSISTANCE
TOPIC: Tech Assistance
PARTIES:
State/IGO Group
El Salvador

110797   Bilateral Agreement   **0 UNTS 0**
SIGNED: 22 Oct 70   FORCE: 22 Oct 70
REGISTERED: 22 Oct 70 United Nations
ARTICLES: 0
HEADNOTE: UNICEF ACTIVITIES
TOPIC: IGO Operations
PARTIES:
Afghanistan
UNICEF (Children)

110798   Bilateral Agreement   **0 UNTS 0**
SIGNED: 15 Oct 68   FORCE: 5 Sep 70
REGISTERED: 23 Oct 70 Finland
ARTICLES: 0
HEADNOTE: PEACEFUL USE ATOMIC ENERGY
TOPIC: Atomic Energy
PARTIES:
Finland
Sweden

110799   Bilateral Exchange   **0 UNTS 0**
SIGNED: 6 May 69   FORCE: 6 May 69
REGISTERED: 23 Oct 70 USA (United States)
ARTICLES: 0
HEADNOTE: INVESTMENT GUARANTEES
TOPIC: Finance
PARTIES:
Burundi
USA (United States)

110800   Bilateral Exchange   **0 UNTS 0**
SIGNED: 29 Jan 70   FORCE: 29 Jan 70
REGISTERED: 23 Oct 70 USA (United States)
ARTICLES: 0
HEADNOTE: N.E. FOREST FIRE PROTECTION
TOPIC: Specific Resources
PARTIES:
Canada
USA (United States)

110801   Bilateral Exchange   **0 UNTS 0**
SIGNED: 5 Sep 68   FORCE: 20 Jul 70
REGISTERED: 26 Oct 70 France
ARTICLES: 0
HEADNOTE: DOUBLE TAX AVIATION
TOPIC: Taxation
PARTIES:
France
United Arab Rep

110802   Bilateral Agreement   **0 UNTS 0**
SIGNED: 27 Mar 70   FORCE: 9 Jul 70
REGISTERED: 26 Oct 70 France
ARTICLES: 0
HEADNOTE: DOUBLE TAX AVIATION
TOPIC: Taxation
PARTIES:
Australia
France

110803   Bilateral Agreement   **0 UNTS 0**
SIGNED: 5 Mar 70   FORCE: 1 Sep 70
REGISTERED: 26 Oct 70 France
ARTICLES: 0
HEADNOTE: SEASON WORKERS
TOPIC: Non-ILO Labor
PARTIES:
France
Yugoslavia

110804   Bilateral Agreement   **0 UNTS 0**
SIGNED: 9 Mar 70   FORCE: 11 Jun 70
REGISTERED: 26 Oct 70 Netherlands
ARTICLES: 0
HEADNOTE: YUGOSLAV WORKERS
TOPIC: Non-ILO Labor
PARTIES:
Netherlands
Yugoslavia

110805   Multilateral Agreement   **0 UNTS 0**
SIGNED: 28 Apr 70   FORCE: 1 Jun 70
REGISTERED: 26 Oct 70 Netherlands
ARTICLES: 0
HEADNOTE: VISA ABOLITION
TOPIC: Visas
PARTIES:
Belgium
Korea, South
Luxembourg
Netherlands

110806   Bilateral Treaty   **0 UNTS 0**
SIGNED: 9 Jan 63   FORCE: 12 Aug 70
REGISTERED: 27 Oct 70 UK Great Britain
ARTICLES: 0
HEADNOTE: EXTRADITION
TOPIC: Extradition
PARTIES:
Austria
UK Great Britain

110807   Bilateral Agreement   **0 UNTS 0**
SIGNED: 19 Sep 69   FORCE: 26 Jun 70
REGISTERED: 27 Oct 70 UK Great Britain
ARTICLES: 0

HEADNOTE: GOODS CARRIAGE BY ROAD
TOPIC: Land Transport
PARTIES:
 Netherlands
 UK Great Britain

110808 Bilateral Agreement **0 UNTS 0**
SIGNED: 6 Apr 70 FORCE: 26 Jun 70
REGISTERED: 27 Oct 70 UK Great Britain
ARTICLES: 0
HEADNOTE: DOUBLE TAX INCOME
TOPIC: Taxation
PARTIES:
 Botswana
 UK Great Britain

110809 Bilateral Exchange **0 UNTS 0**
SIGNED: 19 May 70 FORCE: 19 May 70
REGISTERED: 27 Oct 70 UK Great Britain
ARTICLES: 0
HEADNOTE: CONSULAR CUSTOMS PRIVILEGES
TOPIC: Consul/Citizenship
PARTIES:
 France
 UK Great Britain

110810 Multilateral Agreement **0 UNTS 0**
SIGNED: 25 Apr 65 FORCE: 23 Jul 70
REGISTERED: 29 Oct 70 Belgium
ARTICLES: 0
HEADNOTE: COMPENSATION FOR BELGO-LUX-
 EMBOURG INTERESTS
TOPIC: Finance
PARTIES:
 Belgium
 Bulgaria
 Luxembourg

110811 Bilateral Agreement **0 UNTS 0**
SIGNED: 7 Feb 68 FORCE: 23 Jul 70
REGISTERED: 29 Oct 70 Belgium
ARTICLES: 0
HEADNOTE: IMPLEMENTATION COMPENSATION
TOPIC: Finance
PARTIES:
 Belgium
 Luxembourg

110812 Bilateral Exchange **0 UNTS 0**
SIGNED: 25 Feb 70 FORCE: 25 Feb 70
REGISTERED: 3 Nov 70 USA (United States)
ARTICLES: 0
HEADNOTE: MEAT IMPORTS
TOPIC: General Trade
PARTIES:
 Nicaragua
 USA (United States)

110813 Bilateral Instrument **0 UNTS 0**
SIGNED: 10 Apr 70 FORCE: 10 Apr 70
REGISTERED: 3 Nov 70 USA (United States)
ARTICLES: 0
HEADNOTE: AGRI COMMOD
TOPIC: Commodity Trade
PARTIES:
 Indonesia
 USA (United States)

110814 Bilateral Exchange **0 UNTS 0**
SIGNED: 20 Jun 70 FORCE: 20 Jun 70
REGISTERED: 3 Nov 70 USA (United States)
ARTICLES: 0
HEADNOTE: SATELLITE LAUNCHING
TOPIC: Scientific Project
PARTIES:
 Italy
 USA (United States)

110815 Bilateral Exchange **0 UNTS 0**
SIGNED: 23 Jun 70 FORCE: 23 Jun 70
REGISTERED: 3 Nov 70 USA (United States)
ARTICLES: 0
HEADNOTE: BORDER AREA DEVELOPMENT
TOPIC: Direct Aid

PARTIES:
 Mexico
 USA (United States)

110816 Bilateral Exchange **0 UNTS 0**
SIGNED: 24 Jun 70 FORCE: 24 Jun 70
REGISTERED: 3 Nov 70 USA (United States)
ARTICLES: 0
HEADNOTE: PEACE CORPS
TOPIC: Non-ILO Labor
PARTIES:
 Malta
 USA (United States)

110817 Bilateral Exchange **0 UNTS 0**
SIGNED: 25 Jun 70 FORCE: 25 Jun 70
REGISTERED: 3 Nov 70 USA (United States)
ARTICLES: 0
HEADNOTE: RADAR STATIONS AIRCRAFT
TOPIC: Scientific Project
PARTIES:
 Canada
 USA (United States)

110818 Bilateral Convention **0 UNTS 0**
SIGNED: 21 Apr 69 FORCE: 3 Aug 70
REGISTERED: 4 Nov 70 Finland
ARTICLES: 0
HEADNOTE: DOUBLE TAX INCOME CAPITAL
TOPIC: Taxation
PARTIES:
 Finland
 Ireland

110819 Bilateral Protocol **0 UNTS 0**
SIGNED: 7 Sep 62 FORCE: 7 Sep 62
REGISTERED: 5 Nov 70 France
ARTICLES: 0
HEADNOTE: INSTITUTES OF LEARNING
TOPIC: Education
PARTIES:
 Algeria
 France

110820 Bilateral Protocol **0 UNTS 0**
SIGNED: 11 Jun 63 FORCE: 11 Jun 63
REGISTERED: 5 Nov 70 France
ARTICLES: 0
HEADNOTE: INSTITUTES OF LEARNING
TOPIC: Education
PARTIES:
 Algeria
 France

110821 Bilateral Protocol **0 UNTS 0**
SIGNED: 16 Mar 68 FORCE: 16 Mar 68
REGISTERED: 5 Nov 70 France
ARTICLES: 0
HEADNOTE: SCIENTIFIC COOPERATION
TOPIC: Scientific Project
PARTIES:
 Algeria
 France

110822 Bilateral Agreement **0 UNTS 0**
SIGNED: 25 Sep 67 FORCE: 17 Mar 69
REGISTERED: 5 Nov 70 France
ARTICLES: 0
HEADNOTE: TRADE
TOPIC: General Trade
PARTIES:
 France
 Iraq

110823 Multilateral Convention **0 UNTS 0**
SIGNED: 26 Nov 68 FORCE: 11 Nov 70
REGISTERED: 11 Nov 70 United Nations
ARTICLES: 0
HEADNOTE: STATUTORY LIMITATIONS WAR
 CRIMES
TOPIC: Humanitarian
PARTIES:
 Bulgaria
 Byelorussia
 Czechoslovakia
 Hungary

 Mongolia
 Poland
 Romania
 Ukrainian SSR
 USSR (Soviet Union)
 Yugoslavia

110824 Bilateral Agreement **0 UNTS 0**
SIGNED: 7 Oct 70 FORCE: 7 Oct 70
REGISTERED: 17 Nov 70 Thailand
ARTICLES: 0
HEADNOTE: TECHNICAL COOPERATION MAE
 MOH LIGNITE
TOPIC: General Economic
PARTIES:
 Switzerland
 Thailand

110825 Bilateral Agreement **0 UNTS 0**
SIGNED: 9 Jan 69 FORCE: 25 Aug 69
REGISTERED: 23 Nov 70 IBRD (World Bank)
ARTICLES: 0
HEADNOTE: LOAN SECOND ROAD MAINTE-
 NANCE
TOPIC: IBRD Project
PARTIES:
 Paraguay
 IBRD (World Bank)

110826 Bilateral Agreement **0 UNTS 0**
SIGNED: 16 Feb 70 FORCE: 31 Aug 70
REGISTERED: 23 Nov 70 IBRD (World Bank)
ARTICLES: 0
HEADNOTE: GUARANTEE N.E. INDUSTRIAL
 CREDIT
TOPIC: IBRD Project
PARTIES:
 Brazil
 IBRD (World Bank)

110827 Bilateral Agreement **0 UNTS 0**
SIGNED: 23 Apr 70 FORCE: 2 Sep 70
REGISTERED: 23 Nov 70 IBRD (World Bank)
ARTICLES: 0
HEADNOTE: GUARANTEE SECOND VOCATIONAL
 TRAINING
TOPIC: IBRD Project
PARTIES:
 Chile
 IBRD (World Bank)

110828 Bilateral Agreement **0 UNTS 0**
SIGNED: 20 May 70 FORCE: 15 Oct 70
REGISTERED: 23 Nov 70 IBRD (World Bank)
ARTICLES: 0
HEADNOTE: LOAN JENGKA FORESTRY
TOPIC: IBRD Project
PARTIES:
 Malaysia
 IBRD (World Bank)

110829 Bilateral Agreement **0 UNTS 0**
SIGNED: 20 May 70 FORCE: 20 Aug 70
REGISTERED: 23 Nov 70 IBRD (World Bank)
ARTICLES: 0
HEADNOTE: LOAN SECOND JENGKA TRIANGLE
 LAND
TOPIC: IBRD Project
PARTIES:
 Malaysia
 IBRD (World Bank)

110830 Bilateral Agreement **0 UNTS 0**
SIGNED: 3 Jun 70 FORCE: 31 Aug 70
REGISTERED: 23 Nov 70 IBRD (World Bank)
ARTICLES: 0
HEADNOTE: GUARANTEE EIGHTH INDUSTRIAL
 CREDIT
TOPIC: IBRD Project
PARTIES:
 India
 IBRD (World Bank)

110831 Bilateral Agreement **0 UNTS 0**
SIGNED: 15 Jun 70 FORCE: 25 Aug 70
REGISTERED: 23 Nov 70 IBRD (World Bank)

ARTICLES: 0
HEADNOTE: GUARANTEE THIRD INDUSTRIAL FI-
NANCE
TOPIC: IBRD Project
PARTIES:
Israel
IBRD (World Bank)

110832   Bilateral Agreement   **0 UNTS 0**
SIGNED: 26 Jun 70   FORCE: 18 Sep 70
REGISTERED: 23 Nov 70 IBRD (World Bank)
ARTICLES: 0
HEADNOTE: LOAN TRANSPORT REHABILITATION
TOPIC: IBRD Project
PARTIES:
Nigeria
IBRD (World Bank)

110833   Bilateral Agreement   **0 UNTS 0**
SIGNED: 29 Jun 70   FORCE: 28 Sep 70
REGISTERED: 23 Nov 70 IBRD (World Bank)
ARTICLES: 0
HEADNOTE: GUARANTEE THIRD SUI NORTHERN
GAS
TOPIC: IBRD Project
PARTIES:
Pakistan
IBRD (World Bank)

110834   Bilateral Agreement   **0 UNTS 0**
SIGNED: 7 Aug 70   FORCE: 7 Aug 70
REGISTERED: 23 Nov 70 Belgium
ARTICLES: 0
HEADNOTE: CIVIL STATUS RECORDS
TOPIC: Admin Cooperation
PARTIES:
Belgium
Rwanda

110835   Multilateral Protocol   **0 UNTS 0**
SIGNED: 1 Jun 68   FORCE: 8 Nov 68
REGISTERED: 24 Nov 70 OAS (Am States)
ARTICLES: 0
HEADNOTE: EMERGENCY PROVISIONS OCAS
TREATY
TOPIC: General Trade
PARTIES:
Costa Rica
El Salvador
Guatemala
Honduras
Nicaragua

110836   Bilateral Agreement   **0 UNTS 0**
SIGNED: 15 Dec 67   FORCE: 16 Apr 69
REGISTERED: 25 Nov 70 Bulgaria
ARTICLES: 0
HEADNOTE: GOODS PASSENGERS ROAD TRANS-
PORT
TOPIC: Land Transport
PARTIES:
Bulgaria
Turkey

110837   Bilateral Agreement   **0 UNTS 0**
SIGNED: 22 Apr 69   FORCE: 12 Jul 69
REGISTERED: 25 Nov 70 Bulgaria
ARTICLES: 0
HEADNOTE: TOURISM
TOPIC: Visas
PARTIES:
Bulgaria
Hungary

110838   Bilateral Agreement   **0 UNTS 0**
SIGNED: 15 Apr 69   FORCE: 23 Jul 69
REGISTERED: 25 Nov 70 Bulgaria
ARTICLES: 0
HEADNOTE: COMMUNICATIONS
TOPIC: Gen Communications
PARTIES:
Bulgaria
Germany, East

110839   Bilateral Agreement   **0 UNTS 0**
SIGNED: 29 Apr 69   FORCE: 29 Apr 69

REGISTERED: 25 Nov 70 Bulgaria
ARTICLES: 0
HEADNOTE: MARITIME NAVIGATION
TOPIC: Water Transport
PARTIES:
Bulgaria
Tunisia

110840   Bilateral Agreement   **0 UNTS 0**
SIGNED: 11 Sep 70   FORCE: 11 Sep 70
REGISTERED: 27 Nov 70 Denmark
ARTICLES: 0
HEADNOTE: MILITARY INFORMATION & MATE-
RIAL
TOPIC: General Military
PARTIES:
Denmark
Sweden

110841   Bilateral Agreement   **0 UNTS 0**
SIGNED: 29 Aug 70   FORCE: 29 Sep 70
REGISTERED: 30 Nov 70 Finland
ARTICLES: 0
HEADNOTE: TECHNICAL COOPERATION
TOPIC: Tech Assistance
PARTIES:
Finland
Zambia

200001   Multilateral Agreement   **1 UNTS 97**
SIGNED: 19 Jul 46   FORCE: 19 Jul 46
REGISTERED: 14 Dec 46 United Nations
ARTICLES: 10 LANGUAGE: English.
HEADNOTE: FIFTH SESSION UNRRA COUNCIL
TOPIC: IGO Operations
CONCEPTS: Funding procedures. Finances and
payments. Headquarters and facilities. Confer-
ences. UN administrative tribunal.
INTL ORGS: International Court of Justice. Special
Commission.
PARTIES:
League of Nations SIGNED: 19 Jul 46
UNRRA (Relief) SIGNED: 19 Jul 46
United Nations SIGNED: 19 Jul 46

200002   Bilateral Agreement   **1 UNTS 109**
SIGNED: 19 Jul 46   FORCE: 19 Jul 46
REGISTERED: 14 Dec 46 United Nations
ARTICLES: 10 LANGUAGE: English. French.
HEADNOTE: TRANSFER ASSETS
TOPIC: Specific Property
CONCEPTS: Treaty implementation. General prop-
erty. Use of facilities. Assets transfer. Facilities
and property.
INTL ORGS: Permanent Court of Arbitration. Inter-
national Labour Organization.
PARTIES:
League of Nations
United Nations

200003   Bilateral Instrument   **1 UNTS 119**
SIGNED: 31 Jul 46   FORCE: 31 Jul 46
REGISTERED: 14 Dec 46 United Nations
ARTICLES: 11 LANGUAGE: English.
HEADNOTE: GIVING EFFECT TRANSFER ASSETS
TOPIC: Specific Property
CONCEPTS: General cooperation. Private con-
tracts. Use of facilities. Indemnities and reim-
bursements. Assets transfer. Materials, equip-
ment and services. Facilities and property.
TREATY REF: 1UNTS109.
PARTIES:
League of Nations
United Nations

200004   Bilateral Protocol   **1 UNTS 131**
SIGNED: 1 Aug 46   FORCE: 1 Aug 46
REGISTERED: 14 Dec 46 United Nations
ARTICLES: 1 LANGUAGE: French.
HEADNOTE: EXECUTION TRANSFER ASSETS
TOPIC: Specific Property
CONCEPTS: Assets transfer. Facilities and prop-
erty.
TREATY REF: 1UNTS109.
PARTIES:
League of Nations
United Nations

200005   Bilateral Protocol   **1 UNTS 135**
SIGNED: 1 Aug 46   FORCE: 1 Aug 46
REGISTERED: 14 Dec 46 United Nations
ARTICLES: 1 LANGUAGE: French.
HEADNOTE: TRANSFER SERVICES
TOPIC: Specific Property
CONCEPTS: Assets transfer. Facilities and prop-
erty.
TREATY REF: 1UNTS109.
PARTIES:
League of Nations
United Nations

200006   Multilateral Protocol   **1 UNTS 139**
SIGNED: 28 Aug 46   FORCE: 28 Aug 46
REGISTERED: 14 Dec 46 United Nations
ARTICLES: 7 LANGUAGE: English.
HEADNOTE: PROTOCOL
TOPIC: IGO Operations
CONCEPTS: Default remedies. Annex or appendix
reference. Conferences. UN administrative tribu-
nal.
PARTIES:
League of Nations SIGNED: 28 Aug 46
UNRRA (Relief) SIGNED: 28 Aug 46
United Nations SIGNED: 28 Aug 46

200007   Bilateral Agreement   **1 UNTS 153**
SIGNED: 1 Jul 46   FORCE: 1 Jul 46
REGISTERED: 14 Dec 46 United Nations
ARTICLES: 14 LANGUAGE: English. French.
HEADNOTE: AGREEMENT ON SITE
TOPIC: Specific Property
CONCEPTS: General property. Use of facilities. Ar-
bitration. Procedure. Indemnities and reimburse-
ments. Materials, equipment and services. Bases
and facilities. Facilities and property.
INTL ORGS: International Court of Justice. Arbitra-
tion Commission.
PARTIES:
United Nations
Switzerland

200008   Bilateral Instrument   **1 UNTS 163**
SIGNED: 1 Jul 46   FORCE: 1 Jul 46
REGISTERED: 14 Dec 46 United Nations
ARTICLES: 9 LANGUAGE: English. French.
HEADNOTE: PRIVILEGES & IMMUNITIES
TOPIC: IGO Status/Immunit
CONCEPTS: Non-visa travel documents. Diplo-
matic privileges. Diplomatic missions. Inviolabil-
ity. Privileges and immunities. Property. Juridical
personality. Procedure. Existing tribunals. Cus-
toms exemptions. IGO status. Special status.
Status of experts.
INTL ORGS: International Court of Justice.
PROCEDURE: Amendment. Denunciation.
PARTIES:
United Nations
Switzerland
                    ANNEX
509 UNTS 308.   Switzerland.   Amendment
11 Apr 63. Force 11 Apr 63.
509 UNTS 308.   United   Nations.   Amendment
5 Apr 63. Force 11 Apr 63.

200009   Bilateral Protocol   **1 UNTS 183**
SIGNED: 19 Dec 46   FORCE: 14 Dec 46
REGISTERED: 19 Dec 46 United Nations
ARTICLES: 1 LANGUAGE: English. French.
HEADNOTE: ENTRY INTO FORCE PROTOCOL
TOPIC: IGO Operations
CONCEPTS: Treaty implementation. Annex or ap-
pendix reference. Exchange of information and
documents. Labor statistics. Accounting proce-
dures. Funding procedures. Headquarters and
facilities. Liaison with other IGO's. Inter-agency
agreements. Recognition of specialized agency.
PROCEDURE: Amendment.
PARTIES:
ILO (Labor Org)
United Nations

200010   Bilateral Protocol   **1 UNTS 207**
SIGNED: 3 Feb 47   FORCE: 14 Dec 46
REGISTERED: 3 Feb 47 United Nations
ARTICLES: 1 LANGUAGE: English. French.
HEADNOTE: ENTRY INTO FORCE PROTOCOL
TOPIC: IGO Operations

CONCEPTS: Treaty implementation. Personnel. Existing tribunals. Labor statistics. Accounting procedures. Funding procedures. General technical assistance. Liaison with other IGO's. Status of experts. Assistance to United Nations. UN administrative tribunal. Inter-agency agreements. Recognition of specialized agency. UN recommendations.
INTL ORGS: International Court of Justice.
PROCEDURE: Amendment.
PARTIES:
  FAO (Food Agri)
  United Nations
ANNEX
21 UNTS 338. FAO (Food Agri). Supplementation 21 Jul 48. Force 11 Dec 48.
21 UNTS 338. United Nations. Supplementation 14 Jul 48. Force 11 Dec 48.

200011   Bilateral Protocol   **1 UNTS 233**
SIGNED: 3 Feb 47   FORCE: 14 Dec 46
REGISTERED: 3 Feb 47 United Nations
ARTICLES: 1 LANGUAGE: English. French.
HEADNOTE: ENTRY INTO FORCE PROTOCOL
TOPIC: IGO Operations
CONCEPTS: Treaty implementation. Exchange of information and documents. Personnel. Existing tribunals. Labor statistics. Accounting procedures. Funding procedures. General technical assistance. Admission. Liaison with other IGO's. Assistance to United Nations. UN administrative tribunal. Inter-agency agreements. Recognition of specialized agency. UN recommendations.
INTL ORGS: International Court of Justice.
PROCEDURE: Amendment.
PARTIES:
  UNESCO (Educ/Cult)
  United Nations
ANNEX
21 UNTS 341. United Nations. Supplementation 24 Jun 48. Force 11 Dec 48.
21 UNTS 341. UNESCO (Educ/Cult). Supplementation 10 Jul 48. Force 11 Dec 48.

200012   Bilateral Agreement   **2 UNTS 209**
SIGNED: 2 Nov 39   FORCE: 15 Oct 39
REGISTERED: 8 Apr 47 UK Great Britain
ARTICLES: 6 LANGUAGE: English. French.
HEADNOTE: RADIOTELEGRAPHIC COMMUNICATION
TOPIC: Telecommunications
CONCEPTS: Accounting procedures. Non-interest rates and fees. Radio-telephone-telegraphic communications.
INTL ORGS: International Telecommunication Union.
TREATY REF: 151LTS191.
PROCEDURE: Denunciation.
PARTIES:
  Anglo-Egypt Sudan
  Fr Equatorial Afri

200013   Bilateral Exchange   **2 UNTS 215**
SIGNED: 22 Mar 40   FORCE: 22 Mar 40
REGISTERED: 8 Apr 47 UK Great Britain
ARTICLES: 2 LANGUAGE: English.
HEADNOTE: EXTENSION
TOPIC: General Economic
CONCEPTS: Annex type material.
TREATY REF: 188LTS333; 197LTS400; 200LTS558.
PARTIES:
  Thailand
  UK Great Britain

200014   Bilateral Exchange   **2 UNTS 221**
SIGNED: 16 Dec 43   FORCE: 16 Dec 43
REGISTERED: 8 Apr 47 UK Great Britain
ARTICLES: 2 LANGUAGE: English. Spanish.
HEADNOTE: RENEWAL COMMERCIAL MODUS VIVENDI
TOPIC: General Trade
CONCEPTS: Previous treaty extension.
TREATY REF: 128LTS417; 142LTS381; 160LTS401; 164LTS390.
PARTIES:
  El Salvador
  UK Great Britain

200015   Bilateral Exchange   **2 UNTS 227**
SIGNED: 23 Mar 44   FORCE: 23 Mar 44
REGISTERED: 8 Apr 47 UK Great Britain
ARTICLES: 4 LANGUAGE: English. French.
HEADNOTE: SETTLEMENT CLAIMS
TOPIC: Specif Claim/Waive
CONCEPTS: Payment schedules. Lump sum settlements. Specific claims or waivers.
INTL ORGS: Arbitration Commission.
PARTIES:
  Turkey
  UK Great Britain

200016   Bilateral Exchange   **2 UNTS 235**
SIGNED: 27 May 44   FORCE: 27 May 44
REGISTERED: 8 Apr 47 UK Great Britain
ARTICLES: 2 LANGUAGE: English. Portuguese.
HEADNOTE: SERVICE BRAZILIANS IN BRITISH ARMY
TOPIC: Milit Servic/Citiz
CONCEPTS: Military service and citizenship. Foreign nationals. Service in foreign army.
PROCEDURE: Duration.
PARTIES:
  Brazil
  UK Great Britain
ANNEX
67 UNTS 356. UK Great Britain. Prolongation 13 Jun 45. Force 4 Jul 45.
67 UNTS 356. Brazil. Prolongation 4 Jul 45. Force 4 Jul 45.
67 UNTS 358. UK Great Britain. Supplementation 9 Oct 45. Force 12 Oct 45.
67 UNTS 358. Brazil. Supplementation 12 Oct 45. Force 12 Oct 45.

200017   Bilateral Exchange   **2 UNTS 243**
SIGNED: 1 Jul 44   FORCE: 1 Jul 44
REGISTERED: 8 Apr 47 UK Great Britain
ARTICLES: 2 LANGUAGE: English. Spanish.
HEADNOTE: TEMPORARY COMMERCIAL AGREEMENT
TOPIC: General Trade
CONCEPTS: Exceptions and exemptions. Most favored nation clause.
TREATY REF: 128LTS439.
PROCEDURE: Duration.
PARTIES:
  Chile
  UK Great Britain

200018   Bilateral Agreement   **2 UNTS 251**
SIGNED: 14 Jun 40   FORCE: 14 Jun 40
REGISTERED: 25 Apr 47 Netherlands
ARTICLES: 13 LANGUAGE: English.
HEADNOTE: FINANCE
TOPIC: Finance
CONCEPTS: Definition of terms. Territorial application. General cooperation. Export quotas. Import quotas. Bonds. Balance of payments. Currency. Monetary and gold transfers. Currency deposits. Investments. Exchange rates and regulations. Interest rates. Payment schedules. Local currency.
PROCEDURE: Duration.
PARTIES:
  Netherlands
  UK Great Britain

200019   Bilateral Agreement   **2 UNTS 263**
SIGNED: 14 Jun 40   FORCE: 14 Jun 40
REGISTERED: 25 Apr 47 Netherlands
ARTICLES: 13 LANGUAGE: French.
HEADNOTE: FINANCE
TOPIC: Finance
CONCEPTS: Definition of terms. General cooperation. Responsibility and liability. Accounting procedures. Banking. Bonds. Balance of payments. Currency deposits. Exchange rates and regulations. Financial programs. Interest rates. Payment schedules.
PROCEDURE: Duration.
PARTIES:
  France
  Netherlands

200020   Bilateral Agreement   **2 UNTS 275**
SIGNED: 25 Jul 40   FORCE: 25 Jul 40
REGISTERED: 25 Apr 47 Netherlands
ARTICLES: 8 LANGUAGE: English.

HEADNOTE: FINANCE
TOPIC: Finance
CONCEPTS: Territorial application. General cooperation. Banking. Balance of payments. Exchange rates and regulations.
PARTIES:
  Netherlands
  UK Great Britain

200021   Multilateral Convention   **2 UNTS 281**
SIGNED: 21 Oct 43   FORCE: 21 Oct 43
REGISTERED: 25 Apr 47 Netherlands
ARTICLES: 17 LANGUAGE: Dutch. French.
HEADNOTE: MONETARY RELATIONS PAYMENTS
TOPIC: Finance
CONCEPTS: Definition of terms. Detailed regulations. Territorial application. Accounting procedures. Balance of payments. Currency. Monetary and gold transfers. Exchange rates and regulations. Interest rates. Payment schedules.
PROCEDURE: Accession. Ratification. Termination.
PARTIES:
  Belgium SIGNED: 21 Oct 43 FORCE: 21 Oct 43
  Luxembourg SIGNED: 21 Oct 43 FORCE: 21 Oct 43
  Netherlands SIGNED: 21 Oct 43 FORCE: 21 Oct 43

200022   Multilateral Agreement   **2 UNTS 299**
SIGNED: 20 Mar 45   FORCE: 11 Oct 45
REGISTERED: 25 Apr 47 Netherlands
ARTICLES: 5 LANGUAGE: French.
HEADNOTE: ECONOMIC AGREEMENT
TOPIC: General Economic
CONCEPTS: General trade.
INTL ORGS: Special Commission.
PROCEDURE: Denunciation. Ratification.
PARTIES:
  Belgium SIGNED: 20 Mar 45 FORCE: 11 Oct 45
  France SIGNED: 20 Mar 45 FORCE: 11 Oct 45
  Luxembourg SIGNED: 20 Mar 45 FORCE: 11 Oct 45
  Netherlands SIGNED: 20 Mar 45 FORCE: 11 Oct 45

200023   Bilateral Treaty   **2 UNTS 307**
SIGNED: 29 May 45   FORCE: 5 Dec 45
REGISTERED: 25 Apr 47 Netherlands
ARTICLES: 9 LANGUAGE: English.
HEADNOTE: RELINQUISHMENT EXTRATERRITORIAL RIGHTS CHINA
TOPIC: Privil/Immunities
CONCEPTS: Definition of terms. Previous treaty replacement. General consular functions. Privileges and immunities. Conformity with municipal law. General cooperation. General property. Title and deeds. Abolition of diplomatic quarters. Abolition of extraterritorial rights. Fees and exemptions. National treatment.
TREATY REF: 7SEP1901 NETHERLANDS-CHINA FINAL PROTOCOL.
PROCEDURE: Future Procedures Contemplated. Ratification.
PARTIES:
  Taiwan
  Netherlands

200024   Bilateral Agreement   **2 UNTS 325**
SIGNED: 7 Sep 45   FORCE: 7 Sep 45
REGISTERED: 25 Apr 47 Netherlands
ARTICLES: 12 LANGUAGE: English.
HEADNOTE: FINANCE
TOPIC: Finance
CONCEPTS: Conditions. Definition of terms. Detailed regulations. Territorial application. General cooperation. Accounting procedures. Banking. Balance of payments. Monetary and gold transfers. Investments. Exchange rates and regulations. Payment schedules.
TREATY REF: 2UNTS251; 2UNTS275.
PROCEDURE: Amendment. Termination.
PARTIES:
  Netherlands
  UK Great Britain

200025   Bilateral Treaty   **3 UNTS 313**
SIGNED: 3 Feb 44   FORCE: 8 Nov 45
REGISTERED: 20 May 47 USA (United States)

ARTICLES: 28 LANGUAGE: English. Spanish.
HEADNOTE: UTILIZATION WATERS COLORADO TIJUANA RIVERS
TOPIC: Specific Resources
CONCEPTS: Definition of terms. Privileges and immunities. Procedure. Indemnities and reimbursements. Claims and settlements. Delivery schedules. Customs exemptions. Hydro-electric power. Decisions. Status of experts. Facilities and property. Frontier waterways. Regulation of natural resources.
INTL ORGS: Special Commission.
PROCEDURE: Ratification.
PARTIES:
Mexico
USA (United States)

200028   Bilateral Exchange   **5 UNTS 65**
SIGNED: 13 Jun 39   FORCE: 1 Jan 39
REGISTERED: 12 Jun 47 Netherlands
ARTICLES: 2 LANGUAGE: English.
HEADNOTE: SANITARY CONTROL
TOPIC: Sanitation
CONCEPTS: Change of circumstances. Treaty implementation. Sanitation. Accounting procedures. Currency. Interest rates. Terms of loan.
TREATY REF: 57LTS41.
PROCEDURE: Ratification. Termination.
PARTIES:
Netherlands
UK Great Britain

200029   Bilateral Exchange   **5 UNTS 71**
SIGNED: 15 Mar 40   FORCE: 15 Mar 40
REGISTERED: 23 Jun 47 UK Great Britain
ARTICLES: 2 LANGUAGE: English. Portuguese.
HEADNOTE: DEMARCATE BOUNDARY-LINE
TOPIC: Territory Boundary
CONCEPTS: Annex or appendix reference. Markers and definitions.
TREATY REF: 92LTS311; 101LTS401; 177LTS127.
PARTIES:
Brazil
UK Great Britain

200030   Bilateral Exchange   **5 UNTS 205**
SIGNED: 10 Mar 44   FORCE: 10 Mar 44
REGISTERED: 23 Jun 47 UK Great Britain
ARTICLES: 2 LANGUAGE: English.
HEADNOTE: US COPYRIGHT LAWS
TOPIC: Patents/Copyrights
CONCEPTS: Domestic legislation. Laws and formalities. Post-war adjustment.
PARTIES:
UK Great Britain
USA (United States)
ANNEX
100 UNTS 310. UK Great Britain. Termination 26 Jul 50. Force 29 Dec 50.
100 UNTS 310. USA (United States). Termination 26 Jul 50. Force 29 Dec 50.

200031   Bilateral Agreement   **5 UNTS 227**
SIGNED: 5 Oct 44   FORCE: 5 Oct 44
REGISTERED: 23 Jun 47 UK Great Britain
ARTICLES: 12 LANGUAGE: English.
HEADNOTE: FINANCE
TOPIC: Finance
CONCEPTS: Definition of terms. Detailed regulations. Territorial application. General cooperation. Sanitation. Accounting procedures. Banking. Balance of payments. Monetary and gold transfers. Exchange rates and regulations. Internal finance. Payment schedules. Local currency.
TREATY REF: UKTS NO.1 (1941) CMD.6248.
PROCEDURE: Amendment. Termination.
PARTIES:
Belgium
UK Great Britain

200032   Bilateral Agreement   **5 UNTS 241**
SIGNED: 6 Mar 45   FORCE: 1 Jan 45
REGISTERED: 23 Jun 47 UK Great Britain
ARTICLES: 10 LANGUAGE: English.
HEADNOTE: FINANCE
TOPIC: Finance
CONCEPTS: Definition of terms. General cooperation. Accounting procedures. Banking. Balance

of payments. Currency. Monetary and gold transfers. Payment schedules. Local currency.
PROCEDURE: Amendment. Termination.
PARTIES:
Sweden
UK Great Britain

200033   Bilateral Agreement   **5 UNTS 251**
SIGNED: 16 Aug 45   FORCE: 20 Aug 45
REGISTERED: 23 Jun 47 UK Great Britain
ARTICLES: 10 LANGUAGE: English.
HEADNOTE: FINANCE
TOPIC: Finance
CONCEPTS: Definition of terms. Territorial application. Treaty implementation. General cooperation. Accounting procedures. Banking. Balance of payments. Monetary and gold transfers. Investments. Exchange rates and regulations. Payment schedules.
PROCEDURE: Amendment. Termination.
PARTIES:
Denmark
UK Great Britain

200034   Bilateral Agreement   **5 UNTS 263**
SIGNED: 1 Jul 45   FORCE: 1 Jun 46
REGISTERED: 23 Jun 47 UK Great Britain
ARTICLES: 35 LANGUAGE: English. Portuguese.
HEADNOTE: EXCHANGE PARCELS PARCEL POST
TOPIC: Postal Service
CONCEPTS: Compensation. Fees and exemptions. Lump sum settlements. Customs duties. Postal services. Regulations. Insured letters and boxes. Conveyance in transit. Parcel post. Rates and charges.
PROCEDURE: Duration. Termination.
PARTIES:
Portugal
UK Great Britain

200035   Multilateral Agreement   **5 UNTS 327**
SIGNED: 27 Sep 45   FORCE: 27 Sep 45
REGISTERED: 23 Jun 47 UK Great Britain
ARTICLES: 14 LANGUAGE: English. French. Russian.
HEADNOTE: ESTABLISH EUROPEAN CENTRAL INLAND TRANSPORTATION ORGANIZATION
TOPIC: IGO Establishment
CONCEPTS: IGO reference. Land transport. Commercial road vehicles. Railway border crossing. Railways. International organizations. IGO constitution. Establishment. Headquarters and facilities.
INTL ORGS: United Nations.
PARTIES:
Belgium SIGNED: 27 Sep 45 FORCE: 27 Sep 45
Czechoslovakia SIGNED: 27 Sep 45 FORCE: 27 Sep 45
Denmark SIGNED: 27 Sep 45 FORCE: 27 Sep 45
France SIGNED: 27 Sep 45 FORCE: 27 Sep 45
Greece SIGNED: 27 Sep 45 FORCE: 27 Sep 45
Luxembourg SIGNED: 27 Sep 45 FORCE: 27 Sep 45
Netherlands SIGNED: 27 Sep 45 FORCE: 27 Sep 45
Norway SIGNED: 27 Sep 45
Poland SIGNED: 27 Sep 45 FORCE: 27 Sep 45
UK Great Britain SIGNED: 27 Sep 45 FORCE: 27 Sep 45
USA (United States) SIGNED: 27 Sep 45 FORCE: 27 Sep 45
USSR (Soviet Union) SIGNED: 27 Sep 45 FORCE: 27 Sep 45
Yugoslavia SIGNED: 27 Sep 45 FORCE: 27 Sep 45

200036   Bilateral Protocol   **5 UNTS 389**
SIGNED: 27 Jun 47   FORCE: 27 Jun 47
REGISTERED: 10 Jul 47 United Nations
ARTICLES: 4 LANGUAGE: English.
HEADNOTE: TRANSFER OF FUND
TOPIC: Specific Property
CONCEPTS: Annex or appendix reference. Assets transfer. Facilities and property.
INTL ORGS: World Health Organization.
PARTIES:
League of Nations
United Nations

200037   Bilateral Protocol   **5 UNTS 395**
SIGNED: 27 Jun 47   FORCE: 27 Jun 47
REGISTERED: 10 Jul 47 United Nations
ARTICLES: 5 LANGUAGE: English.
HEADNOTE: TRANSFER ADMINISTRATION FOUNDATION
TOPIC: Specific Property
CONCEPTS: Annex or appendix reference. Assets transfer. Facilities and property.
INTL ORGS: World Health Organization.
PARTIES:
League of Nations
United Nations

200038   Multilateral Protocol   **5 UNTS 401**
SIGNED: 10 Jul 47   FORCE: 10 Jul 47
REGISTERED: 25 Jul 47 United Nations
ARTICLES: 1 LANGUAGE: English.
HEADNOTE: ADDITIONAL PROTOCOL
TOPIC: Specific Property
CONCEPTS: Annex type material. Facilities and property.
TREATY REF: 1UNTS139.
PARTIES:
League of Nations SIGNED: 10 Jul 47 FORCE: 10 Jul 47
UNRRA (Relief) SIGNED: 10 Jul 47 FORCE: 10 Jul 47
United Nations SIGNED: 10 Jul 47 FORCE: 10 Jul 47

200039   Bilateral Convention   **6 UNTS 359**
SIGNED: 16 Apr 45   FORCE: 25 Jul 46
REGISTERED: 7 Aug 47 UK Great Britain
ARTICLES: 11 LANGUAGE: English.
HEADNOTE: AVOIDANCE DOUBLE TAXATION PREVENTION FISCAL EVASION
TOPIC: Taxation
CONCEPTS: Conformity with municipal law. Exchange of information and documents. Non-interest rates and fees. Taxation. Death duties. Tax credits. General.
PROCEDURE: Duration. Ratification. Termination.
PARTIES:
UK Great Britain
USA (United States)

200040   Bilateral Agreement   **6 UNTS 377**
SIGNED: 7 May 42   FORCE: 7 May 42
REGISTERED: 11 Aug 47 USA (United States)
ARTICLES: 3 LANGUAGE: English. Portuguese.
HEADNOTE: NAVAL MISSION
TOPIC: Military Mission
CONCEPTS: Use of facilities. Compensation. Indemnities and reimbursements. Exchange rates and regulations. Tax exemptions. Customs duties. Customs exemptions. Military assistance. Military training. Security of information. Air-force-army-navy personnel ratio. Ranks and privileges. Conditions for assistance missions. Third country military personnel. Status of forces.
PROCEDURE: Denunciation. Duration. Renewal or Revival. Termination.
PARTIES:
Brazil
USA (United States)

200041   Bilateral Exchange   **6 UNTS 397**
SIGNED: 16 Dec 44   FORCE: 1 Jan 45
REGISTERED: 11 Aug 47 USA (United States)
ARTICLES: 2 LANGUAGE: English.
HEADNOTE: AIR TRANSPORT SERVICES
TOPIC: Air Transport
CONCEPTS: Exceptions and exemptions. Annex or appendix reference. Conformity with municipal law. Licenses and permits. Fees and exemptions. Most favored nation clause. Customs exemptions. Competency certificate. Routes and logistics. Navigational conditions. Permit designation. Air transport. Airport facilities. Airworthiness certificates. Conditions of airlines operating permission. Overflights and technical stops. Operating authorizations and regulations. Licenses and certificates of nationality.
INTL ORGS: International Civil Aviation Organization.
TREATY REF: 144LTS153.
PROCEDURE: Amendment. Registration. Termination.

PARTIES:
Sweden
USA (United States)

200042 Bilateral Exchange **6 UNTS 409**
SIGNED: 30 Jul 45   FORCE: 30 Jul 45
REGISTERED: 11 Aug 47 USA (United States)
ARTICLES: 2 LANGUAGE: English. Spanish.
HEADNOTE: COMMERCIAL RELATIONS
TOPIC: General Trade
CONCEPTS: Annex or appendix reference. Reciprocity in trade. Customs declarations.
INTL ORGS: United Nations.
TREATY REF: 204LTS381; 190LTS9.
PROCEDURE: Denunciation. Duration. Future Procedures Contemplated.
PARTIES:
Chile
USA (United States)

200043 Bilateral Exchange **7 UNTS 345**
SIGNED: 26 May 43   FORCE: 26 May 43
REGISTERED: 14 Aug 47 USA (United States)
ARTICLES: 2 LANGUAGE: English.
HEADNOTE: WAIVER CLAIMS ARISING RESULT COLLISIONS VESSELS WAR
TOPIC: Privil/Immunities
CONCEPTS: Time limit. Indemnities and reimbursements. Claims and settlements. Collision.
PROCEDURE: Termination.
PARTIES:
Canada
USA (United States)
ANNEX
21 UNTS 344. USA (United States). Implementation 3 Sep 43. Force 11 Nov 43.
21 UNTS 344.   Canada.   Implementation 11 Nov 43. Force 11 Nov 43.

200044 Multilateral Instrument **8 UNTS 237**
SIGNED: 22 Apr 42   FORCE: 27 Jun 42
REGISTERED: 19 Sep 47 UK Great Britain
ARTICLES: 8 LANGUAGE: English. Spanish.
HEADNOTE: PRODUCTION MARKETING WHEAT
TOPIC: Commodity Trade
CONCEPTS: Negotiation. Non-interest rates and fees. Commodity trade. Conferences.
PARTIES:
Argentina   SIGNED: 22 Apr 42   RATIFIED: 24 Jun 42 FORCE: 27 Jun 42
Australia   SIGNED: 22 Apr 42   RATIFIED: 24 Jun 42 FORCE: 27 Jun 42
Canada   SIGNED: 22 Apr 42   RATIFIED: 20 May 42 FORCE: 27 Jun 42
UK Great Britain SIGNED: 22 Apr 42 RATIFIED: 18 May 42 FORCE: 27 Jun 42
USA (United States) SIGNED: 22 Apr 42 RATIFIED: 27 Jun 42 FORCE: 27 Jun 42

200045 Bilateral Protocol **8 UNTS 315**
SIGNED: 1 Oct 47   FORCE: 13 May 47
REGISTERED: 1 Oct 47 United Nations
ARTICLES: 1 LANGUAGE: English. French.
HEADNOTE: INTERNATIONAL CIVIL AVIATION
TOPIC: IGO Operations
CONCEPTS: Annex type material.
TREATY REF: UN CHARTER.
PARTIES:
ICAO (Civil Aviat)
United Nations
ANNEX
21 UNTS 347. ICAO (Civil Aviat). Supplementation 31 May 48. Force 11 Dec 48.
21 UNTS 347. United Nations. Supplementation 10 May 48. Force 11 Dec 48.

200046 Bilateral Agreement **8 UNTS 345**
SIGNED: 4 Sep 41   FORCE: 4 Sep 41
REGISTERED: 16 Oct 47 USA (United States)
ARTICLES: 29 LANGUAGE: English. Spanish.
HEADNOTE: MILITARY AVIATION MISSION
TOPIC: Military Mission
CONCEPTS: Definition of terms. Use of facilities. Compensation. Indemnities and reimbursements. Exchange rates and regulations. Expense sharing formulae. Tax exemptions. Customs exemptions. Military assistance. Military training. Security of information. Airforce-army-navy personnel ratio. Ranks and privileges. Conditions for assistance missions. Third country military personnel. Status of forces.
PROCEDURE: Denunciation. Duration. Renewal or Revival. Termination.
PARTIES:

Bolivia
USA (United States)
ANNEX
8 UNTS 388. USA (United States). Extension and Amendment 12 Sep 47.

200047 Bilateral Agreement **8 UNTS 365**
SIGNED: 29 May 42   FORCE: 29 May 42
REGISTERED: 16 Oct 47 USA (United States)
ARTICLES: 29 LANGUAGE: English. Spanish.
HEADNOTE: MILITARY MISSION
TOPIC: Military Mission
CONCEPTS: Definition of terms. Use of facilities. Compensation. Indemnities and reimbursements. Exchange rates and regulations. Expense sharing formulae. Tax exemptions. Customs exemptions. Military assistance. Military training. Security of information. Airforce-army-navy personnel ratio. Ranks and privileges. Conditions for assistance missions. Third country military personnel. Status of forces.
PROCEDURE: Denunciation. Duration. Renewal or Revival. Termination.
PARTIES:
Colombia
USA (United States)

200048 Bilateral Agreement **9 UNTS 289**
SIGNED: 7 Jul 42   FORCE: 7 Jul 42
REGISTERED: 16 Oct 47 USA (United States)
ARTICLES: 27 LANGUAGE: English. Spanish.
HEADNOTE: US ARMY OFFICER ADVISOR
TOPIC: Military Mission
CONCEPTS: Definition of terms. Use of facilities. Compensation. Indemnities and reimbursements. Exchange rates and regulations. Expense sharing formulae. Tax exemptions. Customs exemptions. Military assistance. Security of information. Airforce-army-navy personnel ratio. Ranks and privileges. Conditions for assistance missions. Third country military personnel. Status of forces.
PROCEDURE: Denunciation. Duration. Renewal or Revival. Termination.
PARTIES:
Panama
USA (United States)
ANNEX
460 UNTS 360. USA (United States). Prolongation 26 Mar 62. Force 6 Jul 62.
460 UNTS 360. Panama. Prolongation 6 Jul 62. Force 6 Jul 62.
460 UNTS 362. USA (United States). Amendment 20 Sep 62. Force 8 Oct 62.
460 UNTS 362. Panama. Amendment 20 Sep 62. Force 8 Oct 62.

200049 Bilateral Agreement **9 UNTS 309**
SIGNED: 11 Aug 42   FORCE: 11 Aug 42
REGISTERED: 16 Oct 47 USA (United States)
ARTICLES: 29 LANGUAGE: English. Spanish.
HEADNOTE: MILITARY MISSION
TOPIC: Military Mission
CONCEPTS: Definition of terms. Use of facilities. Compensation. Indemnities and reimbursements. Exchange rates and regulations. Expense sharing formulae. Customs exemptions. Military assistance. Military training. Security of information. Airforce-army-navy personnel ratio. Ranks and privileges. Conditions for assistance missions. Third country military personnel. Status of forces.
PROCEDURE: Denunciation. Duration. Renewal or Revival. Termination.
PARTIES:
Bolivia
USA (United States)
ANNEX
9 UNTS 408.   USA   (United   States).   Other 12 Sep 47.

200050 Bilateral Exchange **9 UNTS 331**
SIGNED: 14 Apr 43   FORCE: 14 Apr 43
REGISTERED: 16 Oct 47 USA (United States)
ARTICLES: 3 LANGUAGE: English.
HEADNOTE: AMENDING EXTENDING MILITARY AVIATION MISSION AGREEMENT
TOPIC: Military Mission
CONCEPTS: Annex type material. Previous treaty extension. Military assistance missions.
TREATY REF: 203LTS29.
PARTIES:
Chile
USA (United States)

ANNEX
9 UNTS 409.   USA   (United   States).   Other 12 Sep 47.
9 UNTS 409.   USA   (United   States).   Other 12 Sep 47.

200051 Bilateral Agreement **9 UNTS 341**
SIGNED: 21 May 43   FORCE: 21 May 43
REGISTERED: 16 Oct 47 USA (United States)
ARTICLES: 21 LANGUAGE: English. Spanish.
HEADNOTE: DETAIL OF US ARMY OFFICER
TOPIC: Military Mission
CONCEPTS: Military assistance missions. Airforce-army-navy personnel ratio. Ranks and privileges. Conditions for assistance missions. Third country military personnel.
PARTIES:
El Salvador
USA (United States)
ANNEX
9 UNTS 410.   USA   (United   States).   Other 12 Sep 47.
152 UNTS 360. USA (United States). Prolongation 27 Apr 49. Force 21 May 49.
152 UNTS 360.   El   Salvador.   Prolongation 20 Jun 49. Force 21 May 49.
152 UNTS 360. USA (United States). Prolongation 21 Nov 50. Force 21 May 50.
152 UNTS 360.   El   Salvador.   Prolongation 15 Dec 50. Force 21 May 50.
152 UNTS 360. USA (United States). Prolongation 19 Jun 51. Force 21 May 51.
152 UNTS 360.   El   Salvador.   Prolongation 18 Jul 51. Force 21 May 51.
152 UNTS 360. USA (United States). Prolongation 3 Jul 52. Force 21 May 52.
152 UNTS 360.   El   Salvador.   Prolongation 16 Jul 52. Force 21 May 52.

200052 Bilateral Exchange **9 UNTS 363**
SIGNED: 2 Sep 43   FORCE: 2 Sep 43
REGISTERED: 16 Oct 47 USA (United States)
ARTICLES: 4 LANGUAGE: English.
HEADNOTE: RENEWING AMENDING AGREEMENT MILITARY AVIATION INSTRUCTIONS
TOPIC: Military Mission
CONCEPTS: Annex type material. Previous treaty extension. Military assistance missions.
TREATY REF: 203LTS57.
PARTIES:
Argentina
USA (United States)
ANNEX
9 UNTS 412.   USA   (United   States).   Other 12 Sep 47.
141 UNTS 406.   Argentina.   Prolongation 20 Sep 48. Force 29 Jun 48.
141 UNTS 406. USA (United States). Prolongation 2 Mar 51. Force 29 Jun 50.
141 UNTS 406. USA (United States). Prolongation 11 Aug 48. Force 29 Jun 48.
141 UNTS 406.   Argentina.   Prolongation 25 Nov 49. Force 29 Jun 49.
141 UNTS 406. USA (United States). Prolongation 10 Nov 49. Force 29 Jun 49.
141 UNTS 406.   Argentina.   Prolongation 27 Mar 51. Force 29 Jun 50.

200053 Bilateral Treaty **9 UNTS 373**
SIGNED: 27 Sep 45   FORCE: 11 Apr 46
REGISTERED: 24 Oct 47 United Arab Rep
ARTICLES: 4 LANGUAGE: Arabic.
HEADNOTE: FRIENDSHIP
TOPIC: General Amity
CONCEPTS: Diplomatic relations establishment. Privileges and immunities. Defense and security.
PROCEDURE: Denunciation. Duration. Future Procedures Contemplated. Ratification.
PARTIES:
United Arab Rep
Yemen

200054 Bilateral Agreement **9 UNTS 381**
SIGNED: 19 Jul 41   FORCE: 19 Jul 41
REGISTERED: 31 Oct 47 UK Great Britain
ARTICLES: 4 LANGUAGE: Arabic. English.
HEADNOTE: HAIFA - BAGHDAD ROAD
TOPIC: Territory Boundary
CONCEPTS: Indemnities and reimbursements. Roads and highways. Frontier crossing points.
TREATY REF: UKTS NO.7 (1930) CMD.3488.
PARTIES:
Jordan
UK Great Britain

ANNEX
93 UNTS 388. UK Great Britain. Termination
  29 Dec 49. Force 29 Dec 49.
93 UNTS 388. Transjordan. Termination
  29 Dec 49. Force 29 Dec 49.

200055   Bilateral Agreement   **9 UNTS 389**
SIGNED: 19 Jul 41   FORCE: 19 Jul 41
REGISTERED: 31 Oct 47 UK Great Britain
ARTICLES: 2 LANGUAGE: Arabic. English.
HEADNOTE: EXTRADITION OFFENDERS
TOPIC: Extradition
CONCEPTS: Extradition, deportation and repatria-
  tion. Extradition requests. Extraditable offenses.
  Location of crime. Refusal of extradition. Pre-
  treaty crimes. Limits of prosecution. General co-
  operation.
PROCEDURE: Amendment. Duration. Ratification.
  Termination.
PARTIES:
  Jordan
  UK Great Britain

200056   Bilateral Agreement   **10 UNTS 99**
SIGNED: 20 Apr 42   FORCE: 1 May 43
REGISTERED: 31 Oct 47 UK Great Britain
ARTICLES: 9 LANGUAGE: Arabic. English.
HEADNOTE: EXTRADITION
TOPIC: Extradition
CONCEPTS: Extradition, deportation and repatria-
  tion. Extraditable offenses. Special factors. Lim-
  its of prosecution.
PROCEDURE: Duration. Ratification.
PARTIES:
  Saudi Arabia
  UK Great Britain

200057   Bilateral Agreement   **10 UNTS 117**
SIGNED: 20 Apr 42   FORCE: 1 May 43
REGISTERED: 31 Oct 47 UK Great Britain
ARTICLES: 12 LANGUAGE: Arabic. English.
HEADNOTE: FRIENDSHIP NEIGHBORLY RELA-
  TIONS
TOPIC: General Amity
CONCEPTS: Friendship and amity. Border traffic
  and migration. Exchange of information and doc-
  uments. Procedure. Frontier peoples and person-
  nel.
PROCEDURE: Amendment. Ratification. Termina-
  tion.
PARTIES:
  Saudi Arabia
  UK Great Britain

200058   Bilateral Agreement   **10 UNTS 151**
SIGNED: 20 Apr 42   FORCE: 1 May 43
REGISTERED: 31 Oct 47 UK Great Britain
ARTICLES: 10 LANGUAGE: Arabic. English.
HEADNOTE: TRADE
TOPIC: General Trade
CONCEPTS: Definition of terms. Border traffic and
  migration. Passports non-diplomatic. Proxy di-
  plomacy. Informational records. Investigation of
  violations. Routes and logistics. Goods in transit.
  Transport of goods. Water transport.
PROCEDURE: Amendment. Duration. Ratification.
  Termination.
PARTIES:
  Saudi Arabia
  UK Great Britain

200059   Bilateral Exchange   **10 UNTS 165**
SIGNED: 31 Oct 43   FORCE: 31 Oct 43
REGISTERED: 31 Oct 47 UK Great Britain
ARTICLES: 2 LANGUAGE: Arabic. English.
HEADNOTE: PROLONGING 1927 TREATY JEDDA
TOPIC: General Amity
CONCEPTS: Detailed regulations.
TREATY REF: 71LTS131; 177LTS394.
PROCEDURE: Amendment. Termination.
PARTIES:
  Saudi Arabia
  UK Great Britain

200060   Bilateral Agreement   **10 UNTS 171**
SIGNED: 23 Sep 44   FORCE: 25 Aug 46
REGISTERED: 31 Oct 47 UK Great Britain
ARTICLES: 23 LANGUAGE: English. Russian.
HEADNOTE: ESTABLISHMENT DIRECT RADIO-
  TELEPHONE SERVICE
TOPIC: Telecommunications

CONCEPTS: Accounting procedures. Interest
  rates. Payment schedules. Non-interest rates and
  fees. Radio-telephone-telegraphic communica-
  tions. Conformity with IGO decisions.
TREATY REF: 151LTS5.
PROCEDURE: Amendment. Denunciation. Termi-
  nation.
PARTIES:
  UK Great Britain
  USSR (Soviet Union)

200061   Bilateral Treaty   **10 UNTS 193**
SIGNED: 16 Aug 45   FORCE: 5 Feb 46
REGISTERED: 4 Nov 47 Poland
ARTICLES: 4 LANGUAGE: Polish. Russian.
HEADNOTE: POLISH-SOVIET STATE FRONTIER
TOPIC: Territory Boundary
CONCEPTS: Markers and definitions.
INTL ORGS: Special Commission.
PROCEDURE: Ratification.
PARTIES:
  Poland
  USSR (Soviet Union)

200062   Bilateral Agreement   **10 UNTS 203**
SIGNED: 7 Aug 45   FORCE: 23 Nov 45
REGISTERED: 5 Nov 47 Denmark
ARTICLES: 6 LANGUAGE: Danish. Norwegian.
HEADNOTE: PROPERTY ETC. TRANSFER TWO
  TELEPHONE CABLES
TOPIC: Telecommunications
CONCEPTS: Facilities and equipment. Cable.
PARTIES:
  Denmark
  Norway

200063   Bilateral Exchange   **10 UNTS 213**
SIGNED: 16 Dec 44   FORCE: 29 Sep 45
REGISTERED: 17 Nov 47 Denmark
ARTICLES: 10 LANGUAGE: English.
HEADNOTE: AIR TRANSPORT SERVICES
TOPIC: Air Transport
CONCEPTS: Exceptions and exemptions. Annex or
  appendix reference. Conformity with municipal
  law. Licenses and permits. Recognition of legal
  documents. Use of facilities. Fees and exemptions. Most favored nation clause. National treatment. Customs exemptions. Competency certificate. Routes and logistics. Navigational conditions. Permit designation. Air transport. Airport
  facilities. Airworthiness certificates. Conditions
  of airlines operating permission. Overflights and
  technical stops. Operating authorizations and
  regulations. Licenses and certificates of nationality.
INTL ORGS: International Civil Aviation Organization.
TREATY REF: 3UNTS301; 149LTS493.
PROCEDURE: Amendment. Future Procedures
  Contemplated. Registration. Termination.
PARTIES:
  Denmark
  USA (United States)

200064   Bilateral Exchange   **10 UNTS 227**
SIGNED: 18 Jun 41   FORCE: 18 Jun 41
REGISTERED: 21 Nov 47 Taiwan
ARTICLES: 2 LANGUAGE: Chinese. English.
HEADNOTE: DEMARCATION BOUNDARY
TOPIC: Territory Boundary
CONCEPTS: Markers and definitions. Raw materi-
  als.
TREATY REF: 163LTS177; 89BFSP25.
PARTIES:
  Taiwan
  UK Great Britain

200065   Bilateral Treaty   **10 UNTS 243**
SIGNED: 12 Nov 42   FORCE: 18 Dec 43
REGISTERED: 21 Nov 47 Taiwan
ARTICLES: 10 LANGUAGE: Chinese. English.
  Spanish.
HEADNOTE: AMITY
TOPIC: General Amity
CONCEPTS: Treaty interpretation. Friendship and
  amity. Alien status. Consular relations establish-
  ment. Diplomatic relations establishment. Privi-
  leges and immunities.

PROCEDURE: Future Procedures Contemplated.
  Ratification.
PARTIES:
  Taiwan
  Cuba

200066   Bilateral Treaty   **10 UNTS 261**
SIGNED: 11 Jan 43   FORCE: 20 May 43
REGISTERED: 21 Nov 47 Taiwan
ARTICLES: 8 LANGUAGE: Chinese. English.
HEADNOTE: RELINQUISHMENT   EXTRATER-
  RITORIAL RIGHTS CHINA REGULATION RE-
  LATED MATTERS
TOPIC: Privil/Immunities
CONCEPTS: Previous treaty replacement. General
  consular functions. General cooperation. Gen-
  eral property. Abolition of diplomatic quarters.
  Abolition of extraterritorial rights.
PROCEDURE: Future Procedures Contemplated.
  Ratification.
PARTIES:
  Taiwan
  USA (United States)

200067   Bilateral Treaty   **10 UNTS 285**
SIGNED: 11 May 40   FORCE: 29 Dec 41
REGISTERED: 21 Nov 47 Taiwan
ARTICLES: 8 LANGUAGE: Chinese. English. Span-
  ish.
HEADNOTE: AMITY
TOPIC: General Amity
CONCEPTS: Treaty interpretation. Friendship and
  amity. Alien status. Consular relations establish-
  ment. Diplomatic relations establishment.
PROCEDURE: Future Procedures Contemplated.
  Ratification.
PARTIES:
  Taiwan
  Dominican Republic

200068   Bilateral Treaty   **10 UNTS 300**
SIGNED: 14 Aug 45   FORCE: 24 Aug 45
REGISTERED: 21 Nov 47 Taiwan
ARTICLES: 8 LANGUAGE: Chinese. Russian.
HEADNOTE: FRIENDSHIP ALLIANCE
TOPIC: General Amity
CONCEPTS: Non-prejudice to third party. Non-
  prejudice to UN charter. Economic assistance.
  Defense and security. Rearmament restrictions
  and controls.
PROCEDURE: Denunciation. Duration. Ratification.
PARTIES:
  Taiwan
  USSR (Soviet Union)
                    ANNEX
161 UNTS 374. Taiwan. Force 23 Feb 53.

200069   Bilateral Agreement   **11 UNTS 397**
SIGNED: 29 Aug 45   FORCE: 29 Aug 45
REGISTERED: 4 Dec 47 UK Great Britain
ARTICLES: 5 LANGUAGE: English. French.
HEADNOTE: INDUSTRIAL LITERARY ARTISTIC
  PROPERTY
TOPIC: Patents/Copyrights
CONCEPTS: Conformity with municipal law. Li-
  censes and permits. Post-war adjustment. Rec-
  ognition.
TREATY   REF: 192LTS17;   204LTS469;
  205LTS218.
PARTIES:
  France
  UK Great Britain

200070   Bilateral Treaty   **12 UNTS 391**
SIGNED: 21 Apr 45   FORCE: 21 Apr 45
REGISTERED: 23 Jan 48 Poland
ARTICLES: 8 LANGUAGE: Polish. Russian.
HEADNOTE: FRIENDSHIP MUTUAL ASSISTANCE
  & POST-WAR COOPERATION
TOPIC: General Military
CONCEPTS: General relations and amity. Friend-
  ship and amity. Peaceful relations. General mili-
  tary. Defense and security.
PROCEDURE: Denunciation. Duration.
PARTIES:
  Poland
  USSR (Soviet Union)
                    ANNEX
638 UNTS 338. USSR (Soviet Union). Termination
  21 Apr 65.
638 UNTS 338. Poland. Termination 21 Apr 65.

200071   Bilateral Exchange   **12 UNTS 405**
SIGNED: 1 Jul 41   FORCE: 1 Jul 41
REGISTERED: 30 Jan 48 USA (United States)
ARTICLES: 2 LANGUAGE: English.
HEADNOTE: DEFENSE ICELAND
TOPIC: Milit Assistance
CONCEPTS: Conditions. Guarantees and safe-
guards. Friendship and amity. Recognition. Ma-
terials, equipment and services. Defense and se-
curity. Military assistance. Jurisdiction.
PROCEDURE: Future Procedures Contemplated.
PARTIES:
Iceland
USA (United States)

200072   Bilateral Exchange   **13 UNTS 101**
SIGNED: 16 Jul 42   FORCE: 16 Jul 42
REGISTERED: 3 Mar 48 USA (United States)
ARTICLES: 2 LANGUAGE: English. Spanish.
HEADNOTE: COOPERATIVE HEALTH SANITATION
PROGRAM
TOPIC: Sanitation
CONCEPTS: Conditions. Personnel. Specialists ex-
change. Disease control. Public health. Sanita-
tion. Vocational training. Research and develop-
ment. Expense sharing formulae. Funding proce-
dures. Specific technical assistance. Grants.
PARTIES:
Bolivia
USA (United States)
ANNEX
136 UNTS 395. Bolivia. Prolongation 8 Aug 44.
Force 8 Aug 44.
136 UNTS 395. USA (United States). Prolongation
1 Aug 44. Force 8 Aug 44.

200073   Bilateral Agreement   **13 UNTS 109**
SIGNED: 3 Sep 42   FORCE: 3 Sep 42
REGISTERED: 3 Mar 48 USA (United States)
ARTICLES: 6 LANGUAGE: English. Portuguese.
HEADNOTE: DEVELOPMENT FOOD STUFFS PRO-
DUCTION
TOPIC: Non-IBRD Project
CONCEPTS: Inspection and observation. Establish-
ment of commission. Financial programs. Agri-
culture. Materials, equipment and services.
Plans and standards. Non-bank projects.
INTL ORGS: Special Commission.
PROCEDURE: Duration.
PARTIES:
Brazil
USA (United States)

200074   Bilateral Exchange   **13 UNTS 125**
SIGNED: 30 Sep 42   FORCE: 18 Jul 42
REGISTERED: 3 Mar 48 USA (United States)
ARTICLES: 2 LANGUAGE: English.
HEADNOTE: SERVICE NATIONALS ARMED
FORCES
TOPIC: Milit Servic/Citiz
CONCEPTS: Exchange of information and docu-
ments. Foreign nationals. Service in foreign
army.
PARTIES:
Australia
USA (United States)

200075   Bilateral Exchange   **13 UNTS 139**
SIGNED: 30 Sep 42   FORCE: 2 Jul 42
REGISTERED: 3 Mar 48 USA (United States)
ARTICLES: 2 LANGUAGE: English.
HEADNOTE: SERVICE NATIONALS ARMED
FORCES
TOPIC: Milit Servic/Citiz
CONCEPTS: Exchange of information and docu-
ments. Foreign nationals. Service in foreign
army.
PARTIES:
New Zealand
USA (United States)

200076   Bilateral Exchange   **13 UNTS 151**
SIGNED: 30 Sep 42   FORCE: 8 Jul 42
REGISTERED: 3 Mar 48 USA (United States)
ARTICLES: 2 LANGUAGE: English.
HEADNOTE: SERVICE NATIONALS ARMED
FORCES
TOPIC: Milit Servic/Citiz
CONCEPTS: Exchange of information and docu-

ments. Foreign nationals. Service in foreign
army.
PARTIES:
Netherlands
USA (United States)

200077   Bilateral Exchange   **13 UNTS 169**
SIGNED: 30 Sep 42   FORCE: 30 Apr 42
REGISTERED: 3 Mar 48 USA (United States)
ARTICLES: 2 LANGUAGE: English.
HEADNOTE: SERVICE NATIONALS ARMED
FORCES
TOPIC: Milit Servic/Citiz
CONCEPTS: Exchange of information and docu-
ments. Foreign nationals. Service in foreign
army.
PARTIES:
UK Great Britain
USA (United States)

200078   Bilateral Exchange   **13 UNTS 185**
SIGNED: 30 Sep 42   FORCE: 27 May 42
REGISTERED: 3 Mar 48 USA (United States)
ARTICLES: 2 LANGUAGE: English.
HEADNOTE: FOREIGN NATIONALS & MILITARY
SERVICE
TOPIC: Milit Servic/Citiz
CONCEPTS: Military service and citizenship. For-
eign nationals. Service in foreign army.
PARTIES:
India
USA (United States)

200079   Bilateral Exchange   **13 UNTS 199**
SIGNED: 30 Mar 42   FORCE: 18 May 42
REGISTERED: 3 Mar 48 USA (United States)
ARTICLES: 2 LANGUAGE: English.
HEADNOTE: SERVICE NATIONALS ARMED
FORCES
TOPIC: Milit Servic/Citiz
CONCEPTS: Military service and citizenship. For-
eign nationals. Service in foreign army.
PARTIES:
USA (United States)
Yugoslavia

200080   Bilateral Exchange   **13 UNTS 211**
SIGNED: 16 Oct 42   FORCE: 4 Aug 42
REGISTERED: 3 Mar 48 USA (United States)
ARTICLES: 2 LANGUAGE: English.
HEADNOTE: SERVICE NATIONALS ARMED
FORCES
TOPIC: Milit Servic/Citiz
CONCEPTS: Exchange of information and docu-
ments. Foreign nationals. Service in foreign
army.
PARTIES:
Belgium
USA (United States)

200081   Bilateral Agreement   **13 UNTS 231**
SIGNED: 23 Dec 42   FORCE: 30 Jan 43
REGISTERED: 3 Mar 48 USA (United States)
ARTICLES: 18 LANGUAGE: English. Spanish.
HEADNOTE: COMMERCE TRADE
TOPIC: Finance
CONCEPTS: Detailed regulations. Exceptions and
exemptions. Territorial application. Treaty imple-
mentation. Annex or appendix reference. Stan-
dardization. General cooperation. Exchange of
information and documents. Public information.
Investigation of violations. Procedure. Export
quotas. Import quotas. Trade procedures. Cur-
rency. Payment schedules. Non-interest rates
and fees. Transportation costs. Quotas. Most fa-
vored nation clause. General. Customs duties.
Customs declarations. General transportation.
PROCEDURE: Amendment. Termination.
PARTIES:
Mexico
USA (United States)

200082   Bilateral Exchange   **13 UNTS 335**
SIGNED: 16 Jan 43   FORCE: 24 Dec 42
REGISTERED: 3 Mar 48 USA (United States)
ARTICLES: 2 LANGUAGE: English.
HEADNOTE: SERVICE NATIONALS ARMED
FORCES

TOPIC: Milit Servic/Citiz
CONCEPTS: Exchange of information and docu-
ments. Foreign nationals. Service in foreign
army.
PARTIES:
Norway
USA (United States)

200083   Bilateral Agreement   **13 UNTS 399**
SIGNED: 25 Jan 43   FORCE: 25 Jan 43
REGISTERED: 3 Mar 48 USA (United States)
ARTICLES: 30 LANGUAGE: English. Spanish.
HEADNOTE: NAVAL MISSION
TOPIC: Military Mission
CONCEPTS: Definition of terms. Use of facilities.
Compensation. Indemnities and reimburse-
ments. Exchange rates and regulations. Expense
sharing formulae. Tax exemptions. Customs ex-
emptions. Military assistance. Military training.
Security of information. Airforce-army-navy per-
sonnel ratio. Ranks and privileges. Conditions
for assistance missions. Third country military
personnel. Status of forces.
PROCEDURE: Denunciation. Duration. Renewal or
Revival. Termination.
PARTIES:
Dominican Republic
USA (United States)

200084   Bilateral Exchange   **13 UNTS 371**
SIGNED: 30 Jan 43   FORCE: 30 Jan 43
REGISTERED: 3 Mar 48 USA (United States)
ARTICLES: 2 LANGUAGE: English.
HEADNOTE: PROVISIONS AID ARMED FORCES
TOPIC: Milit Assistance
CONCEPTS: Exceptions and exemptions. Annex
type material. General cooperation. Materials,
equipment and services. Defense and security.
Lease of military property. Military assistance.
Raw materials.
TREATY REF: 204UNTS381.
PROCEDURE: Future Procedures Contemplated.
PARTIES:
Belgium
USA (United States)

200085   Bilateral Exchange   **13 UNTS 379**
SIGNED: 1 Feb 43   FORCE: 11 Jan 43
REGISTERED: 3 Mar 48 USA (United States)
ARTICLES: 2 LANGUAGE: English. Spanish.
HEADNOTE: SERVICE NATIONALS ARMED
FORCES
TOPIC: Milit Servic/Citiz
CONCEPTS: Exchange of information and docu-
ments. Foreign nationals. Service in foreign
army.
PARTIES:
Cuba
USA (United States)

200086   Bilateral Exchange   **13 UNTS 395**
SIGNED: 25 Feb 43   FORCE: 27 Jan 43
REGISTERED: 3 Mar 48 USA (United States)
ARTICLES: 2 LANGUAGE: English.
HEADNOTE: SERVICE NATIONALS ARMED
FORCES
TOPIC: Milit Servic/Citiz
CONCEPTS: Exchange of information and docu-
ments. Foreign nationals. Service in foreign
army.
PARTIES:
Poland
USA (United States)

200087   Bilateral Exchange   **13 UNTS 411**
SIGNED: 4 Mar 43   FORCE: 4 Mar 43
REGISTERED: 3 Mar 48 USA (United States)
ARTICLES: 2 LANGUAGE: English.
HEADNOTE: CONINUING ARRANGEMENT AIR
TRANSPORT SERVICES
TOPIC: Air Transport
CONCEPTS: Change of circumstances. Annex type
material. Previous treaty extension. Routes and
logistics. Air transport.
TREATY REF: 203LTS219; 199LTS367.
PROCEDURE: Duration. Future Procedures Con-
templated. Termination.

PARTIES:
Canada
USA (United States)

200088 Bilateral Exchange **13 UNTS 419**
SIGNED: 25 Mar 43 FORCE: 25 Mar 43
REGISTERED: 3 Mar 48 USA (United States)
ARTICLES: 2 LANGUAGE: English. Spanish.
HEADNOTE: EXTENDING AGREEMENT US ARMY
OFFICER
TOPIC: Military Mission
CONCEPTS: Annex type material. Previous treaty
extension. Military assistance missions.
PARTIES:
El Salvador
USA (United States)

200089 Multilateral Agreement **13 UNTS 427**
SIGNED: 26 Mar 43 FORCE: 26 Mar 43
REGISTERED: 3 Mar 48 USA (United States)
ARTICLES: 14 LANGUAGE: English.
HEADNOTE: ESTABLISHMENT RESERVE INDUS-
TRIAL DIAMONDS
TOPIC: Specif Goods/Equip
CONCEPTS: Annex or appendix reference. Ex-
change of information and documents. Negotia-
tion. Indemnities and reimbursements. Monetary
and gold transfers. Assets transfer. Raw materi-
als.
PROCEDURE: Termination.
PARTIES:
Canada SIGNED: 26 Mar 46 FORCE: 26 Mar 43
UK Great Britain SIGNED: 26 Mar 46 FORCE:
26 Mar 43
USA (United States) SIGNED: 26 Mar 46 FORCE:
26 Mar 43

200090 Bilateral Exchange **13 UNTS 463**
SIGNED: 3 Apr 43 FORCE: 3 Apr 43
REGISTERED: 3 Mar 48 USA (United States)
ARTICLES: 2 LANGUAGE: English. Spanish.
HEADNOTE: COOPERATIVE RUBBER INVESTIGA-
TIONS
TOPIC: Specif Goods/Equip
CONCEPTS: Annex type material. Research coop-
eration.
TREATY REF: USA'EXEC. AGREE. SERIES
222;STAT1368;1.
PARTIES:
Costa Rica
USA (United States)
ANNEX
28 UNTS 452. USA (United States). Prolongation
21 Jun 43. Force 1 Jul 43.
28 UNTS 452. Costa Rica. Prolongation 1 Jul 43.
Force 1 Jul 43.

200091 Bilateral Treaty **14 UNTS 335**
SIGNED: 16 Mar 42 FORCE: 20 Feb 43
REGISTERED: 5 Apr 48 Taiwan
ARTICLES: 4 LANGUAGE: English.
HEADNOTE: AMITY
TOPIC: General Amity
CONCEPTS: Friendship and amity. Diplomatic rela-
tions establishment. Privileges and immunities.
PROCEDURE: Future Procedures Contemplated.
Ratification.
PARTIES:
Taiwan
Iraq

200092 Bilateral Agreement **14 UNTS 343**
SIGNED: 2 Jun 42 FORCE: 2 Jun 42
REGISTERED: 5 Apr 48 Taiwan
ARTICLES: 8 LANGUAGE: English.
HEADNOTE: MUTUAL AID PROSECUTION WAR
AGAINST AGGRESSION
TOPIC: Milit Assistance
CONCEPTS: General cooperation. Title and deeds.
General economics. General trade. Recognition.
Materials, equipment and services. Defense and
security. Lease of military property. Military as-
sistance. Lend lease. Return of equipment and
recapture. Restrictions on transfer.
TREATY REF: 204LTS381.
PROCEDURE: Duration. Future Procedures Con-
templated.

200093 Bilateral Exchange **14 UNTS 353**
SIGNED: 21 May 43 FORCE: 21 May 43
REGISTERED: 5 Apr 48 Taiwan
ARTICLES: 2 LANGUAGE: Chinese. English.
HEADNOTE: JURISDICTION CRIMINAL DEFENSES
TOPIC: Status of Forces
CONCEPTS: Investigation of violations. Jurisdic-
tion. Status of forces.
PROCEDURE: Duration.
PARTIES:
Taiwan
USA (United States)

200094 Bilateral Treaty **14 UNTS 365**
SIGNED: 20 Aug 43 FORCE: 9 May 45
REGISTERED: 5 Apr 48 Taiwan
ARTICLES: 6 LANGUAGE: Chinese. English. Por-
tuguese.
HEADNOTE: AMITY
TOPIC: General Amity
CONCEPTS: Treaty interpretation. Friendship and
amity. Alien status. Privileges and immunities.
Conformity with municipal law.
TREATY REF: 2'12DEMARTENS549;.
PROCEDURE: Future Procedures Contemplated.
Ratification.
PARTIES:
Brazil
Taiwan

200095 Bilateral Treaty **14 UNTS 376**
SIGNED: 20 Oct 43 FORCE: 1 Jun 45
REGISTERED: 5 Apr 48 Taiwan
ARTICLES: 14 LANGUAGE: Chinese. French.
HEADNOTE: ABOLITION EXTRATERRITORIAL
RIGHTS CHINA
TOPIC: Privil/Immunities
CONCEPTS: Exceptions and exemptions. Previous
treaty replacement. General consular functions.
Expropriation. General property. Abolition of
treaty ports. Abolition of diplomatic quarters.
Abolition of extraterritorial rights. National treat-
ment. Inland and territorial waters.
TREATY REF: 3'23DEMARTENS360; 2'23DEMAR-
TENS94;.
PROCEDURE: Future Procedures Contemplated.
Ratification.
PARTIES:
Belgium
Taiwan

200096 Bilateral Agreement **14 UNTS 397**
SIGNED: 22 Mar 44 FORCE: 22 Mar 44
REGISTERED: 5 Apr 48 Taiwan
ARTICLES: 11 LANGUAGE: English.
HEADNOTE: CANADIAN WAR SUPPLIES CHINA
TOPIC: Milit Assistance
CONCEPTS: General cooperation. General trade.
Accounting procedures. Domestic obligation.
Materials, equipment and services. Merchant
vessels. Defense and security. Lease of military
property. Military assistance. Lend lease. Return
of equipment and recapture. Restrictions on
transfer.
PROCEDURE: Duration. Future Procedures Con-
templated.
PARTIES:
Canada
Taiwan

200097 Bilateral Treaty **14 UNTS 408**
SIGNED: 14 Apr 44 FORCE: 3 Apr 45
REGISTERED: 5 Apr 48 Taiwan
ARTICLES: 4 LANGUAGE: Chinese. English.
HEADNOTE: RELINQUISHMENT EXTRATER-
RITORIAL RIGHTS CHINA
TOPIC: Privil/Immunities
CONCEPTS: Definition of terms. Annex or appen-
dix reference. General consular functions. Privi-
leges and immunities. General property. Aboli-
tion of extraterritorial rights. Fees and exemp-
tions. Most favored nation clause. National
treatment.
PROCEDURE: Future Procedures Contemplated.
Ratification.

PARTIES:
Taiwan
USA (United States)

200098 Bilateral Treaty **14 UNTS 427**
SIGNED: 5 May 44 FORCE: 15 Jun 45
REGISTERED: 5 Apr 48 Taiwan
ARTICLES: 10 LANGUAGE: Chinese. Spanish.
HEADNOTE: FRIENDSHIP
TOPIC: General Amity
CONCEPTS: Friendship and amity. Alien status.
Consular relations establishment. Diplomatic re-
lations resumption. Human rights. Privileges and
immunities.
PROCEDURE: Future Procedures Contemplated.
Ratification.
PARTIES:
Taiwan
Costa Rica

200099 Bilateral Treaty **14 UNTS 441**
SIGNED: 1 Aug 44 FORCE: 26 Feb 46
REGISTERED: 5 Apr 48 Taiwan
ARTICLES: 10 LANGUAGE: Chinese. English.
Spanish.
HEADNOTE: AMITY
TOPIC: General Amity
CONCEPTS: Treaty interpretation. Friendship and
amity. Alien status. Consular relations establish-
ment. Diplomatic relations establishment. Privi-
leges and immunities. Arbitration.
PROCEDURE: Ratification.
PARTIES:
Taiwan
Mexico

200100 Bilateral Exchange **14 UNTS 455**
SIGNED: 7 Jul 45 FORCE: 7 Jul 45
REGISTERED: 5 Apr 48 Taiwan
ARTICLES: 9 LANGUAGE: Chinese. English.
HEADNOTE: JURISDICTION MEMBERS RESPEC-
TIVE FORCES
TOPIC: Status of Forces
CONCEPTS: Annex or appendix reference. Juris-
diction. Status of forces.
PROCEDURE: Termination.
PARTIES:
Taiwan
UK Great Britain

200101 Bilateral Convention **14 UNTS 477**
SIGNED: 18 Aug 45 FORCE: 18 Aug 45
REGISTERED: 5 Apr 48 Taiwan
ARTICLES: 7 LANGUAGE: Chinese. French.
HEADNOTE: RETURN LEASED TERRITORY
TOPIC: Territory Boundary
CONCEPTS: Annex or appendix reference. Previ-
ous treaty renunciation. Conformity with munici-
pal law. Title and deeds. Changes of territory.
TREATY REF: SINO-FRENCH CONVENTION OF
16NOV1899.
PARTIES:
Taiwan
France

200102 Multilateral Convention **15 UNTS 295**
SIGNED: 7 Dec 44 FORCE: 4 Apr 47
REGISTERED: 19 Apr 48 USA (United States)
ARTICLES: 96 LANGUAGE: English.
HEADNOTE: INTERNATIONAL CIVIL AVIATION
TOPIC: IGO Establishment
CONCEPTS: Customs duties. Airport facilities. Air-
port equipment. Airworthiness certificates. Con-
ditions of airlines operating permission. Overf-
lights and technical stops. Operating authoriza-
tions and regulations. Licenses and certificates
of nationality. Subsidiary organ.
INTL ORGS: International Civil Aviation Organiza-
tion. United Nations.
PARTIES:
Afghanistan SIGNED: 7 Dec 44 RATIFIED:
4 Apr 47 FORCE: 4 May 47
Argentina RATIFIED: 4 Jun 46 FORCE: 4 Apr 47
Australia SIGNED: 7 Dec 44 RATIFIED: 1 Mar 47
FORCE: 4 Apr 47

Belgium SIGNED: 8 Apr 45 RATIFIED: 5 May 47
FORCE: 4 Jun 47
Bolivia SIGNED: 7 Dec 44 RATIFIED: 4 Apr 47
FORCE: 4 May 47
Brazil SIGNED: 29 May 45 RATIFIED: 8 Jul 46
FORCE: 4 Apr 47
Canada SIGNED: 7 Dec 44 RATIFIED: 13 Feb 46
FORCE: 4 Apr 47
Chile SIGNED: 7 Dec 44 RATIFIED: 11 Mar 47
FORCE: 10 Apr 47
Taiwan SIGNED: 7 Dec 44 RATIFIED: 20 Feb 46
FORCE: 4 Apr 47
Colombia SIGNED: 31 Oct 47 RATIFIED:
31 Oct 47 FORCE: 30 Nov 47
Costa Rica SIGNED: 10 Mar 45
Cuba SIGNED: 20 Apr 45
Czechoslovakia SIGNED: 18 Apr 45 RATIFIED:
1 Mar 47 FORCE: 4 Apr 47
Denmark SIGNED: 7 Dec 44 RATIFIED:
28 Feb 47 FORCE: 4 Apr 47
Dominican Republic SIGNED: 7 Dec 44 RATI-
FIED: 25 Jan 46 FORCE: 4 Apr 47
Ecuador SIGNED: 7 Dec 44
United Arab Rep SIGNED: 7 Dec 44 RATIFIED:
13 Mar 47 FORCE: 12 Apr 47
El Salvador SIGNED: 9 May 45 RATIFIED:
11 Jun 47 FORCE: 11 Jul 47
Ethiopia SIGNED: 10 Feb 47 RATIFIED: 1 Mar 47
FORCE: 4 Apr 47
France SIGNED: 7 Dec 44 RATIFIED: 25 Mar 47
FORCE: 24 Apr 47
Greece SIGNED: 7 Dec 44 RATIFIED: 13 Mar 47
FORCE: 12 Apr 47
Guatemala SIGNED: 30 Jan 45 RATIFIED:
28 Apr 47 FORCE: 28 May 47
Haiti SIGNED: 7 Dec 44 FORCE: 24 Apr 47
Honduras SIGNED: 7 Dec 44
Iceland SIGNED: 7 Dec 44 RATIFIED: 21 Mar 47
FORCE: 20 Apr 57
India SIGNED: 7 Dec 44 RATIFIED: 1 Mar 47
FORCE: 4 Apr 47
Iran SIGNED: 7 Dec 44
Iraq SIGNED: 7 Dec 44 RATIFIED: 2 Jun 47
FORCE: 2 Jul 47
Ireland SIGNED: 7 Dec 44 RATIFIED: 31 Oct 46
FORCE: 4 Apr 47
Italy RATIFIED: 31 Oct 47 FORCE: 30 Nov 47
Lebanon SIGNED: 7 Dec 44
Liberia SIGNED: 7 Dec 44 RATIFIED: 11 Feb 47
FORCE: 4 Apr 47
Luxembourg SIGNED: 9 Jul 45
Mexico SIGNED: 7 Dec 44 RATIFIED: 25 Jun 46
FORCE: 4 Apr 47
Netherlands SIGNED: 7 Dec 44 RATIFIED:
26 Mar 47 FORCE: 25 Apr 47
New Zealand SIGNED: 7 Dec 44 RATIFIED:
7 Mar 47 FORCE: 6 Apr 47
Nicaragua SIGNED: 7 Dec 44 RATIFIED:
28 Dec 45 FORCE: 4 Apr 47
Norway SIGNED: 30 Jan 45 RATIFIED: 5 May 47
FORCE: 4 Jun 47
Pakistan RATIFIED: 6 Nov 47 FORCE: 6 Dec 47
Panama SIGNED: 7 Dec 44
Paraguay SIGNED: 27 Jul 45 RATIFIED:
21 Jan 46 FORCE: 4 Apr 47
Peru SIGNED: 27 Jul 45 RATIFIED: 1 Mar 47
FORCE: 4 Apr 47
Poland SIGNED: 7 Dec 44 RATIFIED: 6 Apr 45
FORCE: 4 Apr 47
Portugal SIGNED: 7 Dec 44 RATIFIED:
27 Feb 47 FORCE: 4 Apr 47
South Africa SIGNED: 7 Dec 44 RATIFIED:
1 Mar 47 FORCE: 4 Apr 47
Spain SIGNED: 7 Dec 44 RATIFIED: 5 Mar 47
FORCE: 4 Apr 47
Sweden SIGNED: 7 Dec 44 RATIFIED: 7 Nov 46
FORCE: 4 Apr 47
Switzerland SIGNED: 6 Jul 45 RATIFIED:
6 Feb 47 FORCE: 4 Apr 47
Syria SIGNED: 7 Dec 44
Thailand SIGNED: 7 Dec 44 RATIFIED: 4 Apr 47
FORCE: 4 May 47
Transjordan RATIFIED: 18 Mar 47 FORCE:
17 Apr 47
Turkey SIGNED: 7 Dec 44 RATIFIED: 20 Dec 45
FORCE: 4 Apr 47
UK Great Britain SIGNED: 7 Dec 44 RATIFIED:
1 Mar 47 FORCE: 4 Apr 47
USA (United States) SIGNED: 7 Dec 44 RATI-
FIED: 9 Aug 46 FORCE: 4 Apr 47
Uruguay SIGNED: 7 Dec 44
ANNEX
32 UNTS 402. Finland. Adherence 30 Mar 49.
Force 29 Apr 49.

33 UNTS 352. Cuba. Ratification 11 May 49.
Force 10 Jun 49.
33 UNTS 352. Israel. Adherence 24 May 49.
Force 23 Jun 49.
44 UNTS 346. Lebanon. Ratification 19 Sep 49.
Force 19 Oct 49.
51 UNTS 336. Syria. Ratification 21 Dec 49.
Force 20 Jan 50.
139 UNTS 469. Guatemala. Denunciation
13 Jun 52. Force 13 Jun 53.
178 UNTS 418. Korea, South. Adherence
11 Nov 52. Force 11 Dec 52.
178 UNTS 418. Libya. Adherence 29 Jan 53.
Force 28 Feb 53.
178 UNTS 418. Honduras. Ratification 7 May 53.
Force 6 Jun 53.
178 UNTS 418. Guatemala. Withdrawal
8 Dec 52.
199 UNTS 362. Taiwan. Ratification 2 Dec 53.
Force 1 Jan 54.
199 UNTS 362. Uruguay. Ratification 14 Jan 54.
Force 13 Feb 54.
199 UNTS 362. Yugoslavia. Signature 6 Jan 54.
199 UNTS 362. Taiwan. Denunciation
31 May 50. Force 31 May 51.
199 UNTS 362. Japan. Adherence 8 Sep 53.
Force 8 Oct 53.
252 UNTS 410. Laos. Adherence 13 Jun 55.
Force 13 Jul 55.
252 UNTS 410. Sudan. Adherence 29 Jun 56.
Force 29 Jul 56.
252 UNTS 410. Ecuador. Ratification 20 Aug 54.
Force 19 Sep 54.
252 UNTS 410. Vietnam. Adherence 19 Oct 54.
Force 18 Nov 54.
252 UNTS 410. Germany, West. Adherence
9 May 56. Force 8 Jun 56.
252 UNTS 410. Cambodia. Adherence 16 Jan 56.
Force 15 Feb 56.
324 UNTS 340. Ghana. Adherence 9 May 57.
Force 8 Jun 57.
324 UNTS 340. Costa Rica. Ratification 1 May 58.
Force 31 May 58.
324 UNTS 340. Tunisia. Adherence 18 Nov 57.
Force 18 Dec 57.
324 UNTS 340. Fed of Malaya. Adherence
7 Apr 58. Force 7 May 58.
324 UNTS 340. Morocco. Adherence 13 Nov 56.
Force 13 Dec 56.
355 UNTS 418. Guinea. Adherence 27 Mar 59.
Force 26 Apr 59.
409 UNTS 370. Mali. Adherence 8 Nov 60. Force
8 Dec 60.
409 UNTS 370. Cyprus. Adherence 17 Jan 61.
Force 16 Feb 61.
409 UNTS 370. Niger. Adherence 29 May 61.
Force 28 Jun 61.
409 UNTS 370. Central Afri Rep. Adherence
28 Jun 61. Force 28 Jul 61.
409 UNTS 370. Yugoslavia. Ratification
9 Mar 61. Force 8 Apr 60.
409 UNTS 370. Panama. Qualified Adherence
18 Jan 60. Force 17 Feb 60.
409 UNTS 370. Kuwait. Adherence 18 May 60.
Force 17 Jun 60.
409 UNTS 370. Nepal. Adherence 29 Jun 60.
Force 29 Jul 60.
409 UNTS 370. Ivory Coast. Adherence
31 Oct 60. Force 30 Nov 60.
409 UNTS 370. Senegal. Adherence 11 Nov 60.
Force 11 Dec 60.
409 UNTS 370. Congo (Zaire). Adherence
27 Jul 61. Force 26 Aug 61.
409 UNTS 370. Cameroon. Adherence
15 Jan 60. Force 14 Feb 60.
409 UNTS 370. Nigeria. Adherence 14 Nov 60.
Force 14 Dec 60.
409 UNTS 370. Dahomey. Adherence 29 May 61.
Force 28 Jun 61.
472 UNTS 402. Sierra Leone. Adherence
22 Nov 61. Force 22 Dec 61.
472 UNTS 402. Mauritania. Adherence
13 Jan 62. Force 12 Feb 62.
472 UNTS 402. Gabon. Adherence 18 Jan 62.
Force 17 Feb 62.
472 UNTS 402. Saudi Arabia. Qualified Adherence 19 Feb 62. Force 21 Mar 62.
472 UNTS 402. Upper Volta. Adherence
21 Mar 62. Force 20 Apr 62.
472 UNTS 402. Madagascar. Adherence
14 Apr 62. Force 14 May 62.
472 UNTS 402. Tanganyika. Adherence
23 Apr 62. Force 23 May 62.

472 UNTS 402. Congo (Brazzaville). Adherence
26 Apr 62. Force 26 May 62.
472 UNTS 402. Chad. Adherence 3 Jul 62. Force
2 Aug 62.
472 UNTS 402. Trinidad/Tobago. Adherence
14 Mar 63. Force 13 Apr 63.
472 UNTS 402. Jamaica. Adherence 26 Mar 63.
Force 25 Apr 63.
472 UNTS 402. Algeria. Adherence 7 May 63.
Force 6 Jun 63.
604 UNTS 394. Indonesia. Adherence 27 Apr 50.
Force 27 May 50.
604 UNTS 394. Malawi. Adherence 11 Sep 64.
Force 11 Oct 64.
604 UNTS 394. Romania. Adherence 30 Apr 65.
Force 30 May 65.
604 UNTS 394. Singapore. Adherence
20 May 66. Force 19 Jun 66.
604 UNTS 394. Guyana. Adherence 3 Feb 67.
Force 5 Mar 67.
604 UNTS 394. Barbados. Adherence 21 Mar 67.
Force 20 Apr 67.
604 UNTS 394. Uganda. Adherence 10 Apr 67.
Force 10 May 67.
604 UNTS 394. Bulgaria. Adherence 8 Jun 67.
Force 8 Jul 67.
604 UNTS 394. Iran. Ratification 19 Apr 50.
Force 19 May 50.

200103 Bilateral Agreement **15 UNTS 377**
SIGNED: 11 Mar 46 FORCE: 11 Mar 46
REGISTERED: 27 May 48 ILO (Labor Org)
ARTICLES: 31 LANGUAGE: French
HEADNOTE: LEGAL STATUS
TOPIC: IGO Status/Immunit
CONCEPTS: Annex or appendix reference. Diplo-
matic privileges. Diplomatic missions. Inviolabil-
ity. Property. Diplomatic correspondence. Juridi-
cal personality. IGO status. Status of experts.
INTL ORGS: League of Nations. Special Commis-
sion.
PARTIES:
ILO (Labor Org)
Switzerland

200104 Bilateral Exchange **15 UNTS 413**
SIGNED: 28 Mar 44 FORCE: 28 Mar 44
REGISTERED: 21 Jun 48 USA (United States)
ARTICLES: 3 LANGUAGE: English.
HEADNOTE: CLAIMS DAMAGES
TOPIC: Status of Forces
CONCEPTS: Annex or appendix reference. Gen-
eral cooperation. Responsibility and liability. In-
vestigation of violations. Indemnities and reim-
bursements. Claims and settlements. Jurisdic-
tion.
PARTIES:
UK Great Britain
USA (United States)

200105 Bilateral Exchange **16 UNTS 241**
SIGNED: 11 Apr 45 FORCE: 11 Apr 45
REGISTERED: 21 Jun 48 USA (United States)
ARTICLES: 2 LANGUAGE: English.
HEADNOTE: AIR TRANSPORT SERVICES
TOPIC: Air Transport
CONCEPTS: Annex or appendix reference. Annex
type material. Fees and exemptions. Passenger
transport. Routes and logistics. Transport of
goods. Air transport. Airport facilities.
TREATY REF: US'EXEC. AGREE. SERIES 463;
59STAT1464;.
PARTIES:
Iceland
USA (United States)

200106 Multilateral Convention **16 UNTS 247**
SIGNED: 15 Dec 44 FORCE: 15 Jan 45
REGISTERED: 23 Jun 48 USA (United States)
ARTICLES: 24 LANGUAGE: English. French.
HEADNOTE: SANITARY CONVENTION AERIAL
SANITATION
TOPIC: Sanitation
CONCEPTS: Change of circumstances. Condi-
tions. Treaty implementation. Treaty interpreta-
tion. General cooperation. Border control. Dis-
ease control. Public health. Insect control. Sani-
tation. Research results. Air transport. UN
administrative tribunal.

INTL ORGS: United Nations Relief and Rehabilitation Administration.
TREATY REF: 161LTS65; 16UNTS179.
PROCEDURE: Accession. Duration. Ratification.
PARTIES:
  Australia RATIFIED: 3 Apr 45 FORCE: 3 Apr 45
  Belgium Belgian Colonies RATIFIED: 25 Jan 46 FORCE: 25 Jan 46
  Belgium Ruanda-Urundi RATIFIED: 25 Jan 46 FORCE: 25 Jan 46
  Belgium RATIFIED: 25 Jan 46 FORCE: 25 Jan 46
  Bolivia SIGNED: 15 Jan 45
  Canada SIGNED: 15 Jan 45 RATIFIED: 20 Nov 45 FORCE: 20 Nov 45
  Taiwan SIGNED: 11 Jan 45 FORCE: 15 Jan 45
  Cuba SIGNED: 15 Jan 45
  Dominican Republic SIGNED: 15 Jan 45 RATIFIED: 20 May 46 FORCE: 20 May 46
  Ecuador SIGNED: 15 Jan 45 FORCE: 15 Jan 45
  United Arab Rep SIGNED: 15 Jan 45
  France SIGNED: 5 Jan 45 FORCE: 15 Jan 45
  Greece SIGNED: 15 Jan 45 FORCE: 15 Jan 45
  Haiti SIGNED: 15 Jan 45 FORCE: 15 Jan 45
  Honduras SIGNED: 15 Jan 45 FORCE: 15 Jan 45
  India RATIFIED: 28 Aug 47 FORCE: 28 Aug 47
  Italy RATIFIED: 30 Apr 46 FORCE: 30 Apr 46
  Luxembourg SIGNED: 15 Jan 45 FORCE: 15 Jan 45
  Netherlands RATIFIED: 22 May 45 FORCE: 22 May 45
  New Zealand RATIFIED: 22 May 45 FORCE: 22 May 45
  New Zealand Western Samoa RATIFIED: 22 May 45 FORCE: 22 May 45
  Nicaragua SIGNED: 15 Jan 45 FORCE: 15 Jan 45
  Peru SIGNED: 15 Jan 45 FORCE: 15 Jan 45
  Poland SIGNED: 5 Jan 45 FORCE: 15 Jan 45
  South Africa SIGNED: 13 Jan 45 FORCE: 15 Jan 45
  Syria RATIFIED: 31 Oct 46 FORCE: 31 Oct 46
  UK Great Britain Aden RATIFIED: 25 Sep 45 FORCE: 25 Sep 45
  UK Great Britain Barbados RATIFIED: 29 Nov 45 FORCE: 29 Nov 45
  UK Great Britain Basutoland RATIFIED: 21 Feb 45 FORCE: 21 Feb 45
  UK Great Britain Bechuanaland RATIFIED: 21 Feb 45 FORCE: 21 Feb 45
  UK Great Britain British Guiana RATIFIED: 25 Feb 46 FORCE: 25 Feb 46
  UK Great Britain British Honduras RATIFIED: 29 Nov 45 FORCE: 29 Nov 45
  UK Great Britain Brit Solomon Is RATIFIED: 24 Feb 45 FORCE: 24 Feb 45
  UK Great Britain Cyprus RATIFIED: 24 Feb 45 FORCE: 24 Feb 45
  UK Great Britain Falkland Islands RATIFIED: 24 Feb 45 FORCE: 24 Feb 45
  UK Great Britain Fiji Islands RATIFIED: 24 Feb 45 FORCE: 24 Feb 45
  UK Great Britain Fed Rhod/Nyasaland RATIFIED: 25 Sep 45 FORCE: 25 Sep 45
  UK Great Britain Gambia RATIFIED: 25 Feb 46 FORCE: 25 Feb 46
  UK Great Britain Gilbert Islands RATIFIED: 24 Feb 45 FORCE: 24 Feb 45
  UK Great Britain Gilbert Islands RATIFIED: 25 Feb 46 FORCE: 25 Feb 46
  UK Great Britain Gold Coast RATIFIED: 24 Feb 45 FORCE: 24 Feb 45
  UK Great Britain Hong Kong RATIFIED: 7 Jan 47 FORCE: 7 Jan 47
  UK Great Britain Jamaica RATIFIED: 6 Jun 46 FORCE: 6 Jun 46
  UK Great Britain Kenya RATIFIED: 24 Feb 45 FORCE: 24 Feb 45
  UK Great Britain Leeward Islands RATIFIED: 29 Nov 45 FORCE: 29 Nov 45
  UK Great Britain Malayan Union RATIFIED: 17 Nov 47 FORCE: 17 Nov 47
  UK Great Britain Mauritius RATIFIED: 24 Feb 45 FORCE: 24 Feb 45
  UK Great Britain Newfoundland RATIFIED: 24 Feb 45 FORCE: 24 Feb 45
  UK Great Britain Nigeria RATIFIED: 24 Feb 45 FORCE: 24 Feb 45
  UK Great Britain Northern Rhodesia RATIFIED: 24 Feb 45 FORCE: 24 Feb 45
  UK Great Britain Palestine RATIFIED: 24 Feb 45 FORCE: 24 Feb 45
  UK Great Britain SIGNED: 5 Jan 45 FORCE: 15 Jan 45

  UK Great Britain Sierra Leone RATIFIED: 24 Feb 45 FORCE: 24 Feb 45
  UK Great Britain Singapore RATIFIED: 17 Nov 47 FORCE: 17 Nov 47
  UK Great Britain Southern Rhodesia RATIFIED: 24 Feb 45 FORCE: 24 Feb 45
  UK Great Britain Swaziland RATIFIED: 21 Feb 45 FORCE: 21 Feb 45
  UK Great Britain Tanganyika RATIFIED: 29 Nov 45 FORCE: 29 Nov 45
  UK Great Britain Transjordan RATIFIED: 21 Feb 45 FORCE: 21 Feb 45
  UK Great Britain Trinidad RATIFIED: 29 Nov 45 FORCE: 29 Nov 45
  UK Great Britain Uganda RATIFIED: 21 Feb 45 FORCE: 21 Feb 45
  UK Great Britain Windward Islands RATIFIED: 6 Jun 46 FORCE: 6 Jun 46
  UK Great Britain Zanzibar RATIFIED: 21 Feb 45 FORCE: 21 Feb 45
  USA (United States) SIGNED: 5 Jan 45 RATIFIED: 29 May 45 FORCE: 29 May 45

200107 Bilateral Agreement **16 UNTS 311**
SIGNED: 23 Oct 45 FORCE: 23 Oct 45
REGISTERED: 23 Jun 48 Norway
ARTICLES: 13 LANGUAGE: French.
HEADNOTE: PAYMENT SETTLEMENT
TOPIC: Finance
CONCEPTS: Exceptions and exemptions. Accounting procedures. Banking. Balance of payments. Currency. Monetary and gold transfers. Exchange rates and regulations. Financial programs. Internal finance. Payment schedules. Local currency.
PROCEDURE: Denunciation.
PARTIES:
  Belgium
  Norway

ANNEX
109 UNTS 325. Belgium. Denunciation 9 Jul 51. Force 8 Jan 52.

200108 Bilateral Protocol **16 UNTS 325**
SIGNED: 15 Apr 48 FORCE: 15 Nov 47
REGISTERED: 1 Jul 48 United Nations
ARTICLES: 1 LANGUAGE: English. French.
HEADNOTE: SOCKEYE SALMON FISHERIES
TOPIC: IGO Operations
CONCEPTS: Annex or appendix reference. Inspection and observation. Financial programs. Payment schedules. Fisheries and fishing.
INTL ORGS: International Court of Justice.
PARTIES:
  IMF (Fund)
  United Nations

200109 Bilateral Protocol **16 UNTS 341**
SIGNED: 15 Apr 48 FORCE: 15 Apr 48
REGISTERED: 1 Jul 48 United Nations
ARTICLES: 1 LANGUAGE: English. French.
HEADNOTE: IMPLEMENTING PROTOCOL
TOPIC: IGO Operations
CONCEPTS: Annex type material.
INTL ORGS: International Monetary Fund.
TREATY REF: UN CHARTER.
PARTIES:
  IBRD (World Bank)
  United Nations

200110 Multilateral Convention **17 UNTS 305**
SIGNED: 15 Dec 44 FORCE: 15 Jan 45
REGISTERED: 26 Jul 48 USA (United States)
ARTICLES: 27 LANGUAGE: English. French.
HEADNOTE: INTERNATIONAL SANITARY CONVENTION
TOPIC: Sanitation
CONCEPTS: Change of circumstances. Conditions. Definition of terms. Treaty implementation. Treaty interpretation. General cooperation. Border control. Disease control. Public health. Sanitation. Research results. UN administrative tribunal.
INTL ORGS: United Nations Relief and Rehabilitation Administration.
TREATY REF: 78LTS229; 17UNTS3.
PROCEDURE: Accession. Duration. Ratification.
PARTIES:
  Australia RATIFIED: 3 Apr 45 FORCE: 3 Apr 45
  Belgium RATIFIED: 25 Jan 46 FORCE: 25 Jan 46
  Belgium Belgian Colonies RATIFIED: 25 Jan 46 FORCE: 25 Jan 46

  Belgium Ruanda-Urundi RATIFIED: 25 Jan 46 FORCE: 25 Jan 46
  Canada SIGNED: 15 Jan 45 RATIFIED: 20 Nov 45 FORCE: 20 Nov 45
  Taiwan SIGNED: 11 Jan 45 FORCE: 15 Jan 45
  Cuba SIGNED: 15 Jan 45
  Czechoslovakia SIGNED: 15 Jan 45 RATIFIED: 30 Apr 46 FORCE: 30 Apr 46
  Denmark RATIFIED: 23 Aug 46 FORCE: 23 Aug 46
  Dominican Republic SIGNED: 15 Jan 45 RATIFIED: 20 May 46 FORCE: 20 May 46
  Ecuador SIGNED: 15 Jan 45 FORCE: 15 Jan 45
  United Arab Rep SIGNED: 15 Jan 45
  France SIGNED: 5 Jan 45 FORCE: 15 Jan 45
  Greece SIGNED: 15 Jan 45 FORCE: 15 Jan 45
  Haiti SIGNED: 15 Jan 45 FORCE: 15 Jan 45
  Honduras SIGNED: 15 Jan 45 FORCE: 15 Jan 45
  India RATIFIED: 28 Aug 47 FORCE: 28 Aug 47
  Italy RATIFIED: 30 Apr 46 FORCE: 30 Apr 46
  Luxembourg SIGNED: 15 Jan 45 FORCE: 15 Jan 45
  Netherlands RATIFIED: 22 May 45 FORCE: 22 May 45
  New Zealand RATIFIED: 22 May 45 FORCE: 22 May 45
  New Zealand Western Samoa RATIFIED: 22 May 45 FORCE: 22 May 45
  Nicaragua SIGNED: 15 Jan 45 FORCE: 15 Jan 45
  Peru SIGNED: 15 Jan 45
  Poland SIGNED: 5 Jan 45 FORCE: 15 Jan 45
  South Africa SIGNED: 13 Jan 45 FORCE: 15 Jan 45
  UK Great Britain Aden RATIFIED: 25 Sep 45 FORCE: 25 Sep 45
  UK Great Britain Barbados RATIFIED: 29 Nov 45 FORCE: 29 Nov 45
  UK Great Britain Basutoland RATIFIED: 25 Sep 45 FORCE: 25 Sep 45
  UK Great Britain Bechuanaland RATIFIED: 25 Sep 45 FORCE: 25 Sep 45
  UK Great Britain British Guiana RATIFIED: 25 Feb 46 FORCE: 25 Feb 46
  UK Great Britain British Honduras RATIFIED: 29 Nov 45 FORCE: 29 Nov 45
  UK Great Britain Brit Solomon Is RATIFIED: 21 Feb 45 FORCE: 21 Feb 45
  UK Great Britain Ceylon (Sri Lanka) RATIFIED: 21 Feb 45 FORCE: 21 Feb 45
  UK Great Britain Cyprus RATIFIED: 21 Feb 45 FORCE: 21 Feb 45
  UK Great Britain Falkland Islands RATIFIED: 21 Feb 45 FORCE: 21 Feb 45
  UK Great Britain Fiji Islands RATIFIED: 21 Feb 45 FORCE: 21 Feb 45
  UK Great Britain Fed Rhod/Nyasaland RATIFIED: 21 Feb 45 FORCE: 21 Feb 45
  UK Great Britain Gambia RATIFIED: 21 Feb 45 FORCE: 21 Feb 45
  UK Great Britain Gilbert Islands RATIFIED: 21 Feb 45 FORCE: 21 Feb 45
  UK Great Britain Gold Coast RATIFIED: 21 Feb 45 FORCE: 21 Feb 45
  UK Great Britain Hong Kong RATIFIED: 5 Jan 45 FORCE: 7 Jan 47
  UK Great Britain Jamaica RATIFIED: 6 Jun 46 FORCE: 6 Jun 46
  UK Great Britain Kenya RATIFIED: 21 Feb 45 FORCE: 21 Feb 45
  UK Great Britain Leeward Islands RATIFIED: 29 Nov 45 FORCE: 29 Nov 45
  UK Great Britain Malayan Union RATIFIED: 17 Nov 47 FORCE: 17 Nov 47
  UK Great Britain Mauritius RATIFIED: 25 Sep 45 FORCE: 25 Sep 45
  UK Great Britain Newfoundland RATIFIED: 21 Feb 45 FORCE: 21 Feb 45
  UK Great Britain Nigeria RATIFIED: 21 Feb 45 FORCE: 21 Feb 45
  UK Great Britain SIGNED: 5 Jan 45 FORCE: 15 Jan 45
  UK Great Britain Northern Rhodesia RATIFIED: 21 Feb 45 FORCE: 21 Feb 45
  UK Great Britain Palestine RATIFIED: 21 Feb 45 FORCE: 21 Feb 45
  UK Great Britain Seychelles RATIFIED: 25 Sep 45 FORCE: 25 Sep 45
  UK Great Britain Sierra Leone RATIFIED: 21 Feb 45 FORCE: 21 Feb 45
  UK Great Britain Singapore RATIFIED: 17 Nov 47 FORCE: 17 Nov 47
  UK Great Britain St. Helena RATIFIED: 21 Feb 45 FORCE: 21 Feb 45

UK Great Britain Swaziland RATIFIED: 25 Sep 45 FORCE: 25 Sep 45
UK Great Britain Tanganyika RATIFIED: 21 Feb 45 FORCE: 21 Feb 45
UK Great Britain Transjordan RATIFIED: 21 Feb 45 FORCE: 21 Feb 45
UK Great Britain Trinidad RATIFIED: 29 Nov 45 FORCE: 29 Nov 45
UK Great Britain Uganda RATIFIED: 21 Feb 45 FORCE: 21 Feb 45
UK Great Britain Windward Islands RATIFIED: 29 Nov 45 FORCE: 29 Nov 45
UK Great Britain Zanzibar RATIFIED: 21 Feb 45 FORCE: 21 Feb 45
USA (United States) SIGNED: 5 Jan 45 RATIFIED: 29 May 45 FORCE: 29 May 45

200111 Bilateral Agreement **18 UNTS 335**
SIGNED: 11 Sep 47 FORCE: 11 Sep 47
REGISTERED: 20 Aug 48 ILO (Labor Org)
ARTICLES: 11 LANGUAGE: English. French.
HEADNOTE: AGREEMENT
TOPIC: IGO Operations
CONCEPTS: Representation. Treaty implementation. Exchange of information and documents. Personnel. Labor statistics. Fees and exemptions. Liaison with other IGO's. Inter-agency agreements. Mutual consultation.
INTL ORGS: United Nations.
PROCEDURE: Amendment. Registration. Termination.
PARTIES:
FAO (Food Agri)
ILO (Labor Org)

200112 Bilateral Agreement **18 UNTS 345**
SIGNED: 23 Aug 48 FORCE: 15 Dec 47
REGISTERED: 23 Aug 48 ILO (Labor Org)
ARTICLES: 11 LANGUAGE: English. French.
HEADNOTE: AGREEMENT
TOPIC: IGO Operations
CONCEPTS: Representation. Treaty implementation. Exchange of information and documents. Personnel. Labor statistics. Funding procedures. Inter-agency agreements.
INTL ORGS: United Nations.
PROCEDURE: Amendment. Registration. Termination.
PARTIES:
FAO (Food Agri)
UNESCO (Educ/Cult)

200113 Bilateral Agreement **18 UNTS 357**
SIGNED: 21 Jan 44 FORCE: 21 Jun 44
REGISTERED: 8 Sep 48 Australia
ARTICLES: 44 LANGUAGE: English.
HEADNOTE: AGREEMENT
TOPIC: General Amity
CONCEPTS: Border traffic and migration. General cooperation. Exchange of information and documents. Expropriation. Establishment of commission. Assistance. Money orders and postal checks. Joint defense. Defense and security. Occupation regime. Subsidiary organ. Conferences.
INTL ORGS: United Nations Relief and Rehabilitation Administration. United Nations.
PROCEDURE: Ratification.
PARTIES:
Australia
New Zealand

200114 Bilateral Agreement **19 UNTS 187**
SIGNED: 4 May 46 FORCE: 17 May 46
REGISTERED: 1 Nov 48 ILO (Labor Org)
ARTICLES: 3 LANGUAGE: French.
HEADNOTE: TRANSFER LEAGUE OF NATIONS PROPERTY TO ILO
TOPIC: IGO Operations
CONCEPTS: General property. Headquarters and facilities.
PARTIES:
League of Nations
ILO (Labor Org)

200115 Bilateral Agreement **19 UNTS 193**
SIGNED: 15 Nov 47 FORCE: 10 Jul 48
REGISTERED: 12 Nov 48 United Nations
ARTICLES: 22 LANGUAGE: English. French.

HEADNOTE: ENTRY INTO FORCE 1947 AGREEMENT
TOPIC: IGO Operations
CONCEPTS: Representation. Treaty implementation. Annex or appendix reference. Non-visa travel documents. Exchange of information and documents. Personnel. Labor statistics. Accounting procedures. Funding procedures. General technical assistance. Regional offices. Headquarters and facilities. Assistance to United Nations. Inter-agency agreements. Recognition of specialized agency. UN recommendations.
INTL ORGS: United Nations Relief and Rehabilitation Administration.
PROCEDURE: Amendment.
PARTIES:
United Nations
WHO (World Health)

200116 Bilateral Agreement **19 UNTS 219**
SIGNED: 15 Nov 47 FORCE: 1 Jul 48
REGISTERED: 15 Nov 48 United Nations
ARTICLES: 16 LANGUAGE: English. French.
HEADNOTE: ENTRY INTO FORCE 1947 AGREEMENT
TOPIC: IGO Operations
CONCEPTS: Representation. Treaty implementation. Annex or appendix reference. Exchange of information and documents. Personnel. Labor statistics. Accounting procedures. Funding procedures. General technical assistance. Assistance to United Nations. Inter-agency agreements. Recognition of specialized agency. UN recommendations.
PROCEDURE: Amendment.
PARTIES:
United Nations
UPU (Postal Union)
ANNEX
43 UNTS 344. United Nations. Supplementation 27 Jul 49. Force 22 Oct 49.
43 UNTS 344. UPU (Postal Union). Supplementation 13 Jul 49. Force 22 Oct 49.

200117 Bilateral Agreement **19 UNTS 235**
SIGNED: 13 Mar 45 FORCE: 13 Mar 45
REGISTERED: 16 Nov 48 Belgium
ARTICLES: 10 LANGUAGE: French.
HEADNOTE: REPATRIATION DISPLACED NATIONALS
TOPIC: Refugees
CONCEPTS: Protection of nationals. Humanitarian matters. Foreign nationals.
PROCEDURE: Denunciation.
PARTIES:
Belgium
USSR (Soviet Union)

200118 Bilateral Agreement **19 UNTS 243**
SIGNED: 14 May 45 FORCE: 14 May 45
REGISTERED: 16 Nov 48 Belgium
ARTICLES: 12 LANGUAGE: French.
HEADNOTE: REPATRIATION DISPLACED NATIONALS
TOPIC: Refugees
CONCEPTS: Repatriation mission. Repatriation of nationals. General cooperation. National treatment.
INTL ORGS: United Nations Relief and Rehabilitation Administration.
PROCEDURE: Denunciation. Duration. Renewal or Revival.
PARTIES:
Belgium
Luxembourg

200119 Bilateral Agreement **19 UNTS 251**
SIGNED: 16 May 45 FORCE: 16 May 45
REGISTERED: 16 Nov 48 Belgium
ARTICLES: 12 LANGUAGE: French.
HEADNOTE: REPATRIATION DISPLACED NATIONALS
TOPIC: Refugees
CONCEPTS: Repatriation mission. Repatriation of nationals. General cooperation. National treatment.
INTL ORGS: United Nations Relief and Rehabilitation Administration.
PROCEDURE: Denunciation. Duration. Renewal or Revival.

PARTIES:
Belgium
Czechoslovakia

200120 Bilateral Agreement **19 UNTS 259**
SIGNED: 2 Jan 45 FORCE: 2 Jan 45
REGISTERED: 26 Nov 48 Belgium
ARTICLES: 13 LANGUAGE: Dutch. English.
HEADNOTE: REPATRIATION DISPLACED NATIONALS
TOPIC: Refugees
CONCEPTS: Repatriation mission. Repatriation of nationals. National treatment.
INTL ORGS: United Nations Relief and Rehabilitation Administration.
PROCEDURE: Denunciation. Duration. Renewal or Revival.
PARTIES:
Belgium
Netherlands

200121 Bilateral Agreement **19 UNTS 269**
SIGNED: 10 Jul 48 FORCE: 10 Jul 48
REGISTERED: 30 Nov 48 ILO (Labor Org)
ARTICLES: 11 LANGUAGE: English. French.
HEADNOTE: AGREEMENT
TOPIC: IGO Operations
CONCEPTS: Representation. Treaty implementation. Exchange of information and documents. Personnel. Labor statistics. Investments. Inter-agency agreements.
PROCEDURE: Amendment. Registration. Termination.
PARTIES:
ILO (Labor Org)
WHO (World Health)

200122 Bilateral Agreement **20 UNTS 297**
SIGNED: 30 Mar 45 FORCE: 30 Mar 45
REGISTERED: 7 Dec 48 Belgium
ARTICLES: 9 LANGUAGE: French.
HEADNOTE: NAVIGATION BELGIAN FRENCH INLAND WATERWAYS
TOPIC: Water Transport
CONCEPTS: Exceptions and exemptions. Resident permits. Non-visa travel documents. Nationality and citizenship. Licenses and permits. Fees and exemptions. Navigational conditions. Operating authorizations and regulations. Inland and territorial waters.
PROCEDURE: Denunciation. Duration.
PARTIES:
Belgium
France

200123 Bilateral Exchange **21 UNTS 189**
SIGNED: 24 Oct 42 FORCE: 24 Oct 42
REGISTERED: 10 Dec 48 USA (United States)
ARTICLES: 7 LANGUAGE: English. Spanish.
HEADNOTE: FISHERIES MISSION
TOPIC: Non-IBRD Project
CONCEPTS: Wages and salaries. Research cooperation. Materials, equipment and services. Non-bank projects. Ocean resources.
PARTIES:
Mexico
USA (United States)

200124 Bilateral Exchange **21 UNTS 215**
SIGNED: 5 May 42 FORCE: 5 May 42
REGISTERED: 10 Dec 48 USA (United States)
ARTICLES: 2 LANGUAGE: English. Spanish.
HEADNOTE: HEALTH SANITATION PROGRAM
TOPIC: Sanitation
CONCEPTS: Non-diplomatic delegations. General cooperation. General property. Programs. Specialists exchange. Disease control. Public health. Sanitation. Vocational training. Research and development. Expense sharing formulae. Funding procedures. Specific technical assistance. Grants.
PROCEDURE: Ratification.
PARTIES:
El Salvador
USA (United States)

200125 Bilateral Exchange **21 UNTS 225**
SIGNED: 18 Feb 43 FORCE: 18 Feb 43

REGISTERED: 10 Dec 48 USA (United States)
ARTICLES: 2 LANGUAGE: English. Spanish.
HEADNOTE: HEALTH SANITATION PROGRAM
TOPIC: Sanitation
CONCEPTS: General cooperation. General property. Private contracts. Establishment of commission. Programs. Public health. Sanitation. Research and development. Accounting procedures. Expense sharing formulae. Financial programs. Funding procedures. Grants. Defense and security.
PROCEDURE: Ratification.
PARTIES:
USA (United States)
Venezuela
ANNEX
106 UNTS 328. Venezuela. Extension and Amendment 28 Jun 44. Force 28 Jun 44.
106 UNTS 328. USA (United States). Extension and Amendment 28 Jun 44. Force 28 Jun 44.

200126   Bilateral Exchange   **21 UNTS 237**
SIGNED: 10 Apr 43   FORCE: 10 Apr 43
REGISTERED: 10 Dec 48 USA (United States)
ARTICLES: 2 LANGUAGE: English.
HEADNOTE: ACCESS ALASKA HIGHWAY
TOPIC: Territory Boundary
CONCEPTS: Customs exemptions. Frontier crossing points.
TREATY REF: USA'EXEC. AGREE. SERIES 246; 56STAT1458;.
PARTIES:
Canada
USA (United States)

200127   Bilateral Exchange   **21 UNTS 245**
SIGNED: 26 Apr 43   FORCE: 26 Apr 43
REGISTERED: 10 Dec 48 USA (United States)
ARTICLES: 2 LANGUAGE: English. Spanish.
HEADNOTE: TEMPORARY MIGRATION MEXICAN WORKERS
TOPIC: Non-ILO Labor
CONCEPTS: Definition of terms. General provisions. Private contracts. Public health. Wages and salaries. Non-ILO labor relations. Family allowances. Migrant worker. Accounting procedures. Bonds. Transportation costs. Foreign nationals.
TREATY REF: USA-EAS 278; 56STAT1759.
PROCEDURE: Denunciation.
PARTIES:
Mexico
USA (United States)

200128   Bilateral Exchange   **21 UNTS 269**
SIGNED: 7 Jun 43   FORCE: 7 Jun 43
REGISTERED: 10 Dec 48 USA (United States)
ARTICLES: 2 LANGUAGE: English. Spanish.
HEADNOTE: CONSTRUCTION HIGHWAY
TOPIC: Specific Property
CONCEPTS: Expense sharing formulae. Special projects. Roads and highways. Defense and security. Facilities and property.
PARTIES:
Panama
USA (United States)

200129   Bilateral Exchange   **21 UNTS 277**
SIGNED: 10 Jun 43   FORCE: 10 Jun 43
REGISTERED: 10 Dec 48 USA (United States)
ARTICLES: 2 LANGUAGE: English. Spanish.
HEADNOTE: PURCHASE SURPLUS DOMINICAN FOOD PRODUCTS
TOPIC: Specific Resources
CONCEPTS: Annex or appendix reference. Purchase authorization. Surplus commodities.
PARTIES:
Dominican Republic
USA (United States)

200130   Bilateral Exchange   **21 UNTS 295**
SIGNED: 19 Oct 43   FORCE: 19 Oct 43
REGISTERED: 10 Dec 48 USA (United States)
ARTICLES: 2 LANGUAGE: English. Spanish.
HEADNOTE: WORKMENS COMPENSATION
TOPIC: Non-ILO Labor
CONCEPTS: General cooperation. Domestic legislation. Use of facilities. Old age and invalidity insurance. Non-ILO labor relations. Sickness and invalidity insurance.
PARTIES:
Dominican Republic
USA (United States)

200131   Bilateral Agreement   **21 UNTS 305**
SIGNED: 10 Dec 43   FORCE: 10 Dec 43
REGISTERED: 10 Dec 48 USA (United States)
ARTICLES: 28 LANGUAGE: English. Spanish.
HEADNOTE: MILITARY MISSION
TOPIC: Military Mission
CONCEPTS: Use of facilities. Compensation. Indemnities and reimbursements. Expense sharing formulae. Tax exemptions. Customs exemptions. Military assistance. Military training. Security of information. Airforce-army-navy personnel ratio. Ranks and privileges. Conditions for assistance missions. Status of forces.
PROCEDURE: Denunciation. Duration. Renewal or Revival. Termination.
PARTIES:
Paraguay
USA (United States)
ANNEX
141 UNTS 407. USA (United States). Prolongation 25 Oct 47. Force 10 Dec 47.
141 UNTS 407. Paraguay. Prolongation 20 Nov 47. Force 10 Dec 47.

200132   Bilateral Agreement   **21 UNTS 325**
SIGNED: 30 Mar 45   FORCE: 30 Mar 45
REGISTERED: 16 Dec 48 Belgium
ARTICLES: 7 LANGUAGE: French.
HEADNOTE: PASSENGER TRAFFIC
TOPIC: Visas
CONCEPTS: Detailed regulations. Border traffic and migration. Visas.
PROCEDURE: Denunciation.
PARTIES:
Belgium
France

200133   Bilateral Agreement   **23 UNTS 215**
SIGNED: 21 May 45   FORCE: 21 May 45
REGISTERED: 5 Jan 49 Belgium
ARTICLES: 10 LANGUAGE: French.
HEADNOTE: MINOR FRONTIER TRAFFIC
TOPIC: Visas
CONCEPTS: Time limit. Border traffic and migration. Frontier permits. Markers and definitions. Frontier peoples and personnel.
TREATY REF: 21UNTS325;   162LTS437; 19UNTS95.
PROCEDURE: Denunciation.
PARTIES:
Belgium
France

200134   Bilateral Exchange   **23 UNTS 275**
SIGNED: 10 Nov 41   FORCE: 10 Nov 41
REGISTERED: 6 Jan 49 USA (United States)
ARTICLES: 2 LANGUAGE: English.
HEADNOTE: TEMPORARY RAISING LEVEL LAKE ST. FRANCIS
TOPIC: Specific Resources
CONCEPTS: Previous treaties adherence. Hydroelectric power. Regulation of natural resources.
TREATY REF: USA TREATY SERIES 548.
PARTIES:
Canada
USA (United States)
ANNEX
105 UNTS 306. Canada. Prolongation 5 Oct 43. Force 9 Oct 43.
105 UNTS 306. USA (United States). Prolongation 9 Oct 43. Force 9 Oct 43.
105 UNTS 310. Canada. Prolongation 31 Aug 44. Force 7 Sep 44.
105 UNTS 310. USA (United States). Prolongation 7 Sep 44. Force 7 Sep 44.

200135   Bilateral Exchange   **23 UNTS 285**
SIGNED: 16 Jan 42   FORCE: 16 Jan 42
REGISTERED: 6 Jan 49 USA (United States)
ARTICLES: 2 LANGUAGE: English.
HEADNOTE: CONSTRUCTION INTER-AMERICAN HIGHWAY COSTA RICA
TOPIC: Land Transport

CONCEPTS: Treaty implementation. Conformity with municipal law. General cooperation. Expense sharing formulae. Materials, equipment and services. Loan and credit. Terms of loan. Roads and highways.
PARTIES:
Costa Rica
USA (United States)

200136   Bilateral Exchange   **23 UNTS 293**
SIGNED: 13 Feb 42   FORCE: 13 Feb 42
REGISTERED: 6 Jan 49 USA (United States)
ARTICLES: 2 LANGUAGE: English. Spanish.
HEADNOTE: CONSTRUCTION INTER-AMERICAN HIGHWAY EL SALVADOR
TOPIC: Land Transport
CONCEPTS: Treaty implementation. Friendship and amity. Conformity with municipal law. General cooperation. Expense sharing formulae. Loan and credit. Roads and highways.
PARTIES:
El Salvador
USA (United States)

200137   Bilateral Agreement   **23 UNTS 302**
SIGNED: 31 Mar 42   FORCE: 31 Mar 42
REGISTERED: 6 Jan 49 USA (United States)
ARTICLES: 2 LANGUAGE: English.
HEADNOTE: DEFENSE AREAS
TOPIC: General Military
CONCEPTS: Definition of terms. Friendship and amity. Privileges and immunities. Customs exemptions. Operating authorizations and regulations. Defense and security. Military assistance. Procurement and logistics. Status of forces. Bases and facilities.
PROCEDURE: Duration.
PARTIES:
Liberia
USA (United States)

200138   Bilateral Exchange   **24 UNTS 145**
SIGNED: 8 Apr 42   FORCE: 8 Apr 42
REGISTERED: 6 Jan 49 USA (United States)
ARTICLES: 2 LANGUAGE: English.
HEADNOTE: CONSTRUCTION INTER-AMERICAN HIGHWAY NICARAGUA
TOPIC: Land Transport
CONCEPTS: Treaty implementation. Friendship and amity. Conformity with municipal law. General cooperation. Expense sharing formulae. Materials, equipment and services. Loan and credit. Routes and logistics. Roads and highways.
PARTIES:
Nicaragua
USA (United States)

200139   Bilateral Exchange   **24 UNTS 153**
SIGNED: 24 Aug 42   FORCE: 24 Aug 42
REGISTERED: 6 Jan 49 USA (United States)
ARTICLES: 2 LANGUAGE: English.
HEADNOTE: SCHOLARSHIP PROGRAM
TOPIC: Education
CONCEPTS: Detailed regulations. Exchange. Professorships. Scholarships and grants. Vocational training. Financial programs. Funding procedures.
PARTIES:
Peru
USA (United States)

200140   Bilateral Exchange   **24 UNTS 163**
SIGNED: 17 Aug 42   FORCE: 17 Aug 42
REGISTERED: 6 Jan 49 USA (United States)
ARTICLES: 2 LANGUAGE: English.
HEADNOTE: EXCHANGE OFFICAL PUBLICATIONS
TOPIC: Admin Cooperation
CONCEPTS: Annex or appendix reference. Exchange of official publications. Operating agencies. Indemnities and reimbursements.
PARTIES:
Iceland
USA (United States)

200141   Bilateral Exchange   **24 UNTS 177**
SIGNED: 3 Sep 42   FORCE: 3 Sep 42
REGISTERED: 6 Jan 49 USA (United States)
ARTICLES: 2 LANGUAGE: English.

HEADNOTE: PROVISIONS RECIPROCAL AID
TOPIC: Milit Assistance
CONCEPTS: Exceptions and exemptions. General cooperation. Accounting procedures. Materials, equipment and services. Defense and security. Lease of military property. Military assistance. Lend lease.
PROCEDURE: Future Procedures Contemplated.
PARTIES:
France
USA (United States)

200142 Bilateral Exchange **24 UNTS 185**
SIGNED: 3 Sep 42 FORCE: 3 Sep 42
REGISTERED: 6 Jan 49 USA (United States)
ARTICLES: 2 LANGUAGE: English.
HEADNOTE: PROVISIONS RECIPROCAL AID
TOPIC: Milit Assistance
CONCEPTS: Exceptions and exemptions. General cooperation. Accounting procedures. Materials, equipment and services. Defense and security. Lease of military property. Military assistance. Lend lease.
TREATY REF: 204LTS381; 204LTS289.
PROCEDURE: Future Procedures Contemplated.
PARTIES:
New Zealand
USA (United States)

200143 Bilateral Exchange **24 UNTS 195**
SIGNED: 3 Sep 42 FORCE: 3 Sep 42
REGISTERED: 6 Jan 49 USA (United States)
ARTICLES: 2 LANGUAGE: English.
HEADNOTE: PROVISIONS AID PROSECUTION WAR
TOPIC: Milit Assistance
CONCEPTS: Exceptions and exemptions. General cooperation. Accounting procedures. Materials, equipment and services. Defense and security. Lease of military property. Military assistance. Lend lease.
TREATY REF: 204LTS381; 204LTS389.
PROCEDURE: Future Procedures Contemplated.
PARTIES:
Australia
USA (United States)

200144 Bilateral Agreement **24 UNTS 205**
SIGNED: 30 Sep 42 FORCE: 30 Sep 42
REGISTERED: 6 Jan 49 USA (United States)
ARTICLES: 2 LANGUAGE: English. French.
HEADNOTE: SUPPLEMENTARY HAITIAN FINANCES
TOPIC: Other Ad Hoc
CONCEPTS: Annex type material. Payment schedules. Loan and credit. Control of internal finance.
TREATY REF: USA'EXEC.AGREE.SERIES 224; 55STAT1385;.
PARTIES:
Haiti
USA (United States)
ANNEX
105 UNTS 314. USA (United States). Extension and Amendment 28 Aug 43. Force 28 Aug 43.
105 UNTS 314. Haiti. Extension and Amendment 28 Aug 43. Force 28 Aug 43.
105 UNTS 316. USA (United States). Extension and Amendment 9 Nov 44. Force 9 Nov 44.
105 UNTS 316. Haiti. Extension and Amendment 9 Nov 44. Force 9 Nov 44.

200145 Bilateral Exchange **24 UNTS 209**
SIGNED: 26 Oct 42 FORCE: 26 Oct 42
REGISTERED: 6 Jan 49 USA (United States)
ARTICLES: 2 LANGUAGE: English. Spanish.
HEADNOTE: CONSTRUCTION INTER-AMERICAN HIGHWAY HONDURAS
TOPIC: Land Transport
CONCEPTS: Treaty implementation. Friendship and amity. Conformity with municipal law. General cooperation. Private contracts. Expense sharing formulae. Loan and credit. Terms of loan. Roads and highways.
PARTIES:
Honduras
USA (United States)

200146 Bilateral Exchange **24 UNTS 217**
SIGNED: 4 Nov 42 FORCE: 4 Nov 42

REGISTERED: 6 Jan 49 USA (United States)
ARTICLES: 2 LANGUAGE: English.
HEADNOTE: WORKMENS COMPENSATION UNEMPLOYMENT
TOPIC: Non-ILO Labor
CONCEPTS: Holidays and rest periods. Old age and invalidity insurance. Safety standards. Wages and salaries. Non-ILO labor relations. Sickness and invalidity insurance. Unemployment. Tax exemptions.
PARTIES:
Canada
USA (United States)

200147 Bilateral Exchange **24 UNTS 227**
SIGNED: 5 Nov 42 FORCE: 5 Nov 42
REGISTERED: 6 Jan 49 USA (United States)
ARTICLES: 2 LANGUAGE: English. Spanish.
HEADNOTE: EXTENDING ASSIGNMENT US NAVAL MISSION
TOPIC: Military Mission
CONCEPTS: Annex type material. Previous treaty extension. Military assistance missions.
TREATY REF: 196LTS157.
PARTIES:
Colombia
USA (United States)
ANNEX
28 UNTS 459. USA (United States). Prolongation 7 Aug 43. Force 7 Aug 43.
28 UNTS 459. Colombia. Prolongation 23 Jul 43. Force 7 Aug 43.
106 UNTS 336. USA (United States). Prolongation 18 Jul 44. Force 18 Jul 44.
106 UNTS 336. Colombia. Prolongation 26 Jun 44. Force 18 Jul 44.

200148 Bilateral Exchange **24 UNTS 233**
SIGNED: 14 Nov 42 FORCE: 14 Nov 42
REGISTERED: 6 Jan 49 USA (United States)
ARTICLES: 2 LANGUAGE: English. Spanish.
HEADNOTE: WAIVER TARIFF PREFERENCES
TOPIC: Customs
CONCEPTS: Tariffs. Most favored nation clause.
TREATY REF: USA'TREATY SERIES 700;.
PARTIES:
Dominican Republic
USA (United States)

200149 Bilateral Exchange **24 UNTS 241**
SIGNED: 24 Nov 42 FORCE: 24 Nov 42
REGISTERED: 6 Jan 49 USA (United States)
ARTICLES: 2 LANGUAGE: English. Spanish.
HEADNOTE: EXTENSION PRIOR AGREEMENT
TOPIC: Military Mission
CONCEPTS: Previous treaty extension. Personnel. Military assistance.
TREATY REF: 13UNTS419.
PARTIES:
El Salvador
USA (United States)

200150 Multilateral Agreement **24 UNTS 247**
SIGNED: 4 Dec 42 FORCE: 4 Dec 42
REGISTERED: 6 Jan 49 USA (United States)
ARTICLES: 2 LANGUAGE: English. Persian.
HEADNOTE: FOOD SUPPLY
TOPIC: Direct Aid
CONCEPTS: Assistance. Agricultural commodities.
PARTIES:
Iran SIGNED: 4 Dec 42 FORCE: 4 Dec 42
UK Great Britain SIGNED: 4 Dec 42 FORCE: 4 Dec 42
USA (United States) SIGNED: 4 Dec 42 FORCE: 4 Dec 42

200151 Bilateral Exchange **24 UNTS 257**
SIGNED: 10 Dec 42 FORCE: 10 Dec 42
REGISTERED: 6 Jan 49 USA (United States)
ARTICLES: 2 LANGUAGE: English. Spanish.
HEADNOTE: EXCHANGE OFFICIAL PUBLICATIONS
TOPIC: Admin Cooperation
CONCEPTS: Annex or appendix reference. Exchange of official publications. Operating agencies. Indemnities and reimbursements.
PARTIES:
Dominican Republic
USA (United States)

200152 Bilateral Exchange **24 UNTS 273**
SIGNED: 22 Jan 45 FORCE: 22 Jan 45
REGISTERED: 19 Jan 49 USA (United States)
ARTICLES: 2 LANGUAGE: English. Spanish.
HEADNOTE: COOPERATION EDUCATIONAL PROGRAM
TOPIC: Education
CONCEPTS: General cooperation. Personnel. General property. Specialists exchange. Exchange. Accounting procedures. Currency. Expense sharing formulae. Fees and exemptions. Funding procedures. Tax exemptions. Customs exemptions.
PROCEDURE: Duration.
PARTIES:
Ecuador
USA (United States)

200153 Bilateral Agreement **26 UNTS 299**
SIGNED: 7 Feb 49 FORCE: 18 Nov 48
REGISTERED: 7 Feb 49 United Nations
ARTICLES: 22 LANGUAGE: English. French.
HEADNOTE: AGREEMENT & PROTOCOL
TOPIC: IGO Operations
CONCEPTS: Representation. Treaty implementation. Annex or appendix reference. Non-visa travel documents. Exchange of information and documents. Personnel. Existing tribunals. Labor statistics. Accounting procedures. Funding procedures. General technical assistance. Regional offices. Inter-agency agreements. Passports diplomatic. Recognition of specialized agency. UN recommendations.
INTL ORGS: International Court of Justice. United Nations.
PROCEDURE: Amendment.
PARTIES:
IRO (Refugee Org)
United Nations

200154 Bilateral Instrument **26 UNTS 323**
SIGNED: 17 Feb 49 FORCE: 17 Feb 49
REGISTERED: 17 Feb 49 United Nations
ARTICLES: 9 LANGUAGE: English. French.
HEADNOTE: TREATY DEPOSIT & REGISTRATION PROCEDURE
TOPIC: IGO Operations
CONCEPTS: Annex type material. Recognition of specialized agency.
PROCEDURE: Ratification. Registration.
PARTIES:
ILO (Labor Org)
United Nations

200155 Bilateral Agreement **26 UNTS 331**
SIGNED: 12 Jan 49 FORCE: 21 Aug 48
REGISTERED: 29 Mar 49 WHO (World Health)
ARTICLES: 30 LANGUAGE: French.
HEADNOTE: LEGAL STATUS
TOPIC: IGO Status/Immunit
CONCEPTS: Non-visa travel documents. Diplomatic privileges. Diplomatic missions. Inviolability. Privileges and immunities. Property. Diplomatic correspondence. Juridical personality. Procedure. Special tribunals. IGO status. Special status. Status of experts.
INTL ORGS: International Court of Justice. Arbitration Commission.
PROCEDURE: Amendment.
PARTIES:
WHO (World Health)
Switzerland

200156 Bilateral Exchange **26 UNTS 363**
SIGNED: 19 Dec 42 FORCE: 30 May 44
REGISTERED: 1 Apr 49 USA (United States)
ARTICLES: 2 LANGUAGE: English.
HEADNOTE: PROVISIONAL AGREEMENT FUR SEALS
TOPIC: Commodity Trade
CONCEPTS: Treaty interpretation. Licenses and permits. Incorporation of treaty provisions into national law. Quotas. Ports and pilotage. Ocean resources. Wildlife.
PROCEDURE: Duration. Termination.
PARTIES:
Canada
USA (United States)

200157 Bilateral Exchange **26 UNTS 379**
SIGNED: 24 Feb 42 FORCE: 24 Feb 42

REGISTERED: 1 Apr 49 USA (United States)
ARTICLES: 2 LANGUAGE: English. Spanish.
HEADNOTE: HEALTH SANITATION PROGRAM
TOPIC: Sanitation
CONCEPTS: Time limit. General cooperation. General property. Programs. Specialists exchange. Public health. Sanitation. Research and development. Expense sharing formulae. Financial programs. Specific technical assistance. Grants.
PARTIES:
Ecuador
USA (United States)

200158 Bilateral Agreement **27 UNTS 349**
SIGNED: 27 Sep 48 FORCE: 24 Sep 48
REGISTERED: 1 Apr 49 United Nations
ARTICLES: 5 LANGUAGE: English.
HEADNOTE: TRANSFER UNRRA ASSETS & ACTIVITIES
TOPIC: IGO Operations
CONCEPTS: Annex or appendix reference. Inviolability. Privileges and immunities. Exchange of official publications. Labor statistics. Accounting procedures. Funding procedures.
INTL ORGS: United Nations Children's Fund.
PARTIES:
UNRRA (Relief)
United Nations

200159 Bilateral Exchange **28 UNTS 341**
SIGNED: 30 Apr 43 FORCE: 30 Apr 43
REGISTERED: 14 Apr 49 USA (United States)
ARTICLES: 2 LANGUAGE: English.
HEADNOTE: APPORTIONING SUPPLIES AFRICAN ASBESTOS
TOPIC: Specific Resources
CONCEPTS: Annex or appendix reference. Import quotas. Conservation of specific resources.
PARTIES:
UK Great Britain
USA (United States)

200160 Bilateral Exchange **28 UNTS 359**
SIGNED: 14 May 43 FORCE: 14 May 43
REGISTERED: 14 Apr 49 USA (United States)
ARTICLES: 2 LANGUAGE: English. Spanish.
HEADNOTE: FOODSTUFFS PRODUCTION
TOPIC: Non-IBRD Project
CONCEPTS: Inspection and observation. Wages and salaries. Financial programs. Funding procedures. Customs exemptions. Assistance. Plans and standards. Non-bank projects.
PROCEDURE: Duration.
PARTIES:
USA (United States)
Venezuela

200161 Bilateral Exchange **28 UNTS 377**
SIGNED: 19 May 43 FORCE: 19 May 43
REGISTERED: 14 Apr 49 USA (United States)
ARTICLES: 2 LANGUAGE: English. Spanish.
HEADNOTE: INTER-AMERICAN HIGHWAY
TOPIC: Land Transport
CONCEPTS: Friendship and amity. Conformity with municipal law. General cooperation. Inspection and observation. Negotiation. Expense sharing formulae. Internal finance. Roads and highways.
PARTIES:
Guatemala
USA (United States)

200162 Bilateral Exchange **28 UNTS 385**
SIGNED: 24 May 43 FORCE: 30 Apr 43
REGISTERED: 14 Apr 49 USA (United States)
ARTICLES: 3 LANGUAGE: English. Portuguese.
HEADNOTE: SERVICE ARMED FORCES
TOPIC: Status of Forces
CONCEPTS: Foreign nationals. Service in foreign army.
PARTIES:
Brazil
USA (United States)

200163 Bilateral Exchange **28 UNTS 397**
SIGNED: 14 Jun 43 FORCE: 14 Jun 43
REGISTERED: 14 Apr 49 USA (United States)
ARTICLES: 2 LANGUAGE: English.

HEADNOTE: PRINCIPLES PROVISION AID ARMED FORCES US
TOPIC: General Military
CONCEPTS: Exceptions and exemptions. Annex type material. Defense and security. Military assistance. Lend lease.
INTL ORGS: United Nations.
TREATY REF: USA'EAS 259; 56STAT1554; 204LTS381;.
PROCEDURE: Future Procedures Contemplated.
PARTIES:
Netherlands
USA (United States)

200164 Bilateral Exchange **28 UNTS 407**
SIGNED: 1 Jul 43 FORCE: 1 Jul 43
REGISTERED: 14 Apr 49 USA (United States)
ARTICLES: 2 LANGUAGE: English. Spanish.
HEADNOTE: HEALTH SANITATION PROGRAM
TOPIC: Sanitation
CONCEPTS: General cooperation. General property. Programs. Specialists exchange. Public health. Sanitation. Migrant worker. Research and development. Expense sharing formulae. Funding procedures. Specific technical assistance. Grants.
PROCEDURE: Ratification.
PARTIES:
Mexico
USA (United States)
ANNEX
160 UNTS 418. USA (United States). Prolongation 8 Dec 43. Force 8 Dec 43.
160 UNTS 418. Mexico. Prolongation 8 Dec 43. Force 8 Dec 43.

200165 Bilateral Exchange **28 UNTS 419**
SIGNED: 7 Jul 43 FORCE: 7 Jul 43
REGISTERED: 14 Apr 49 USA (United States)
ARTICLES: 2 LANGUAGE: English. Spanish.
HEADNOTE: HEALTH SANITATION PROGRAM
TOPIC: Sanitation
CONCEPTS: Conformity with municipal law. General property. Programs. Specialists exchange. Public health. Sanitation. Research and development. Expense sharing formulae. Funding procedures. Specific technical assistance. Defense and security.
PROCEDURE: Ratification.
PARTIES:
Dominican Republic
USA (United States)

200166 Bilateral Agreement **28 UNTS 431**
SIGNED: 17 Jul 43 FORCE: 17 Jul 43
REGISTERED: 14 Apr 49 USA (United States)
ARTICLES: 29 LANGUAGE: English. Spanish.
HEADNOTE: MILITARY OFFICER DIRECTOR POLYTECHNIC SCHOOL
TOPIC: Military Mission
CONCEPTS: Definition of terms. Use of facilities. Compensation. Indemnities and reimbursements. Exchange rates and regulations. Expense sharing formulae. Tax exemptions. Customs exemptions. Military assistance. Military training. Security of information. Airforce-army-navy personnel ratio. Ranks and privileges. Conditions for assistance missions. Third country military personnel. Status of forces.
PROCEDURE: Denunciation. Duration. Renewal or Revival. Termination.
PARTIES:
Guatemala
USA (United States)
ANNEX
109 UNTS 326. Guatemala. Prolongation 5 Jan 44. Force 17 Jan 44.
109 UNTS 326. USA (United States). Prolongation 17 Jan 44. Force 17 Jan 44.

200167 Bilateral Exchange **29 UNTS 289**
SIGNED: 19 Jul 43 FORCE: 19 Jul 43
REGISTERED: 14 Apr 49 USA (United States)
ARTICLES: 2 LANGUAGE: English.
HEADNOTE: ALASKA HIGHWAY OFFICIAL NAME
TOPIC: Land Transport
CONCEPTS: General cooperation. Roads and highways.
PARTIES:
Canada
USA (United States)

200168 Bilateral Exchange **29 UNTS 295**
SIGNED: 9 Aug 43 FORCE: 9 Aug 43

REGISTERED: 14 Apr 49 USA (United States)
ARTICLES: 2 LANGUAGE: English.
HEADNOTE: TAXATION DEFENSE PROJECTS
TOPIC: Milit Installation
CONCEPTS: Court procedures. Indemnities and reimbursements. General. Tax exemptions. Bases and facilities.
PARTIES:
Canada
USA (United States)

200169 Bilateral Agreement **29 UNTS 303**
SIGNED: 9 Aug 43 FORCE: 9 Aug 43
REGISTERED: 14 Apr 49 USA (United States)
ARTICLES: 8 LANGUAGE: English.
HEADNOTE: MUTUAL AID
TOPIC: Milit Installation
CONCEPTS: General cooperation. Recognition. Defense and security. Military assistance. Return of equipment and recapture. Restrictions on transfer.
PARTIES:
Ethiopia
USA (United States)

200170 Bilateral Agreement **29 UNTS 317**
SIGNED: 27 Sep 43 FORCE: 19 Nov 43
REGISTERED: 14 Apr 49 USA (United States)
ARTICLES: 18 LANGUAGE: English. Icelandic.
HEADNOTE: TRADE AGREEMENT
TOPIC: General Trade
CONCEPTS: Detailed regulations. Exceptions and exemptions. Territorial application. General provisions. Annex or appendix reference. General cooperation. Exchange of information and documents. Licenses and permits. Public information. Procedure. Trade procedures. Reciprocity in financial treatment. Payment schedules. Quotas. Most favored nation clause. Customs duties.
PROCEDURE: Duration. Ratification. Termination.
PARTIES:
Iceland
USA (United States)

200171 Bilateral Agreement **29 UNTS 349**
SIGNED: 13 Sep 43 FORCE: 13 Sep 43
REGISTERED: 14 Apr 49 USA (United States)
ARTICLES: 28 LANGUAGE: English. Spanish.
HEADNOTE: MILITARY OFFICER TECHNICAL DIRECTOR MILITARY COLLEGE
TOPIC: Military Mission
CONCEPTS: Definition of terms. Use of facilities. Compensation. Indemnities and reimbursements. Exchange rates and regulations. Expense sharing formulae. Customs exemptions. Military assistance. Military training. Security of information. Airforce-army-navy personnel ratio. Ranks and privileges. Conditions for assistance missions. Third country military personnel. Status of forces.
PROCEDURE: Denunciation. Duration. Renewal or Revival. Termination.
PARTIES:
Ecuador
USA (United States)

200172 Bilateral Exchange **29 UNTS 369**
SIGNED: 21 Oct 43 FORCE: 29 Sep 43
REGISTERED: 14 Apr 49 USA (United States)
ARTICLES: 4 LANGUAGE: English.
HEADNOTE: SERVICE FOREIGN NATIONALS ARMED FORCES
TOPIC: Milit Servic/Citiz
CONCEPTS: Exchange of information and documents. Foreign nationals. Service in foreign army.
PARTIES:
Czechoslovakia
USA (United States)

200173 Bilateral Exchange **29 UNTS 383**
SIGNED: 25 Oct 43 FORCE: 25 Oct 43
REGISTERED: 14 Apr 49 USA (United States)
ARTICLES: 2 LANGUAGE: English.
HEADNOTE: EXTENDING AGREEMENT US MILITARY OFFICER
TOPIC: Military Mission
CONCEPTS: Annex type material. Previous treaty extension. Military assistance missions.

PARTIES:
Nicaragua
USA (United States)

200174 Bilateral Agreement **29 UNTS 391**
SIGNED: 27 Oct 43   FORCE: 27 Oct 43
REGISTERED: 14 Apr 49 USA (United States)
ARTICLES: 28 LANGUAGE: English. Spanish.
HEADNOTE: MILITARY AVIATION MISSION
TOPIC: Military Mission
CONCEPTS: Definition of terms. Use of facilities.
Compensation. Indemnities and reimburse-
ments. Exchange rates and regulations. Expense
sharing formulae. Tax exemptions. Military assis-
tance. Military training. Security of information.
Airforce-army-navy personnel ratio. Ranks and
privileges. Conditions for assistance missions.
Third country military personnel. Status of
forces.
PROCEDURE: Denunciation. Duration. Renewal or
Revival. Termination.
PARTIES:
Paraguay
USA (United States)
                    ANNEX
141 UNTS 408. USA (United States). Prolongation
25 Oct 47. Force 27 Oct 47.
141 UNTS 408.   Paraguay.   Prolongation
20 Nov 47. Force 27 Oct 47.

200175 Bilateral Agreement **30 UNTS 315**
SIGNED: 26 Apr 49   FORCE: 1 Jan 49
REGISTERED: 1 May 49 United Nations
ARTICLES: 19 LANGUAGE: English. French.
HEADNOTE: AGREEMENT & PROTOCOL
TOPIC: IGO Operations
CONCEPTS: Representation. Treaty implementa-
tion. Annex or appendix reference. Non-visa
travel documents. Diplomatic correspondence.
Exchange of information and documents. Per-
sonnel. Existing tribunals. Labor statistics. Ac-
counting procedures. Funding procedures. Gen-
eral technical assistance. Assistance to United
Nations. Inter-agency agreements. Recognition
of specialized agency. UN recommendations.
PROCEDURE: Amendment.
PARTIES:
ITU (Telecommun)
United Nations

200176 Bilateral Agreement **31 UNTS 451**
SIGNED: 27 Nov 43   FORCE: 27 Nov 43
REGISTERED: 28 Jun 49 USA (United States)
ARTICLES: 30 LANGUAGE: English. Persian.
HEADNOTE: MILITARY MISSION
TOPIC: Military Mission
CONCEPTS: Definition of terms. Conformity with
municipal law. Use of facilities. Compensation.
Indemnities and reimbursements. Exchange
rates and regulations. Expense sharing formulae.
Tax exemptions. Customs exemptions. Military
assistance. Military training. Security of informa-
tion. Airforce-army-navy personnel ratio. Ranks
and privileges. Conditions for assistance mis-
sions. Third country military personnel. Status of
forces.
PROCEDURE: Denunciation. Duration. Renewal or
Revival. Termination.
PARTIES:
Iran
USA (United States)

200177 Bilateral Treaty **32 UNTS 381**
SIGNED: 26 Jul 39   FORCE: 27 Nov 48
REGISTERED: 7 Jul 49 Netherlands
ARTICLES: 4 LANGUAGE: French.
HEADNOTE: FRIENDSHIP
TOPIC: General Amity
CONCEPTS: Friendship and amity. Diplomatic rela-
tions establishment.
PROCEDURE: Future Procedures Contemplated.
Ratification.
PARTIES:
Afghanistan
Netherlands

200178 Bilateral Agreement **32 UNTS 387**
SIGNED: 24 May 49   FORCE: 1 Jul 49
REGISTERED: 23 Jul 49 WHO (World Health)

ARTICLES: 11 LANGUAGE: English. French.
HEADNOTE: INTEGRATION PAN AMERICAN SANI-
TATION ORGANIZATION INTO WHO
TOPIC: Sanitation
CONCEPTS: Conditions. Definition of terms.
Treaty implementation. Treaty interpretation. Ac-
counting procedures. Financial programs. Fund-
ing procedures. Admission. Special status.
PROCEDURE: Ratification. Termination.
PARTIES:
Pan Am Health Org
WHO (World Health)

200179 Bilateral Agreement **34 UNTS 361**
SIGNED: 24 Jul 42   FORCE: 24 Jul 42
REGISTERED: 26 Aug 49 USA (United States)
ARTICLES: 8 LANGUAGE: English.
HEADNOTE: PRINCIPLES APPLYING MUTUAL AID
PROSECUTION WAR
TOPIC: Milit Assistance
CONCEPTS: General cooperation. General eco-
nomics. Reexport of goods, etc.. Recognition.
Materials, equipment and services. Defense and
security. Military assistance. Return of equip-
ment and recapture.
TREATY REF: 204LTS381.
PROCEDURE: Duration. Future Procedures Con-
templated.
PARTIES:
USA (United States)
Yugoslavia

200180 Bilateral Exchange **34 UNTS 371**
SIGNED: 29 May 45   FORCE: 29 May 45
REGISTERED: 26 Aug 49 USA (United States)
ARTICLES: 2 LANGUAGE: English.
HEADNOTE: PROBLEMS MARINE TRANSPORTA-
TION LITIGATION
TOPIC: Water Transport
CONCEPTS: Definition of terms. Exceptions and
exemptions. Claims and settlements. Transport
of goods. Water transport. Merchant vessels.
Shipwreck and salvage.
PROCEDURE: Termination.
PARTIES:
Norway
USA (United States)

200181 Bilateral Exchange **41 UNTS 265**
SIGNED: 28 Apr 45   FORCE: 18 Apr 45
REGISTERED: 19 Sep 49 Belgium
ARTICLES: 2 LANGUAGE: French.
HEADNOTE: FREEDOM MOVEMENT PERSONS
TOPIC: Visas
CONCEPTS: Border traffic and migration. Non-visa
travel documents.
PARTIES:
Belgium
Luxembourg

200182 Bilateral Agreement **43 UNTS 315**
SIGNED: 9 Feb 49   FORCE: 29 Nov 48
REGISTERED: 11 Oct 49 UNESCO (Educ/Cult)
ARTICLES: 11 LANGUAGE: English. French.
HEADNOTE: AGREEMENT
TOPIC: IGO Operations
CONCEPTS: Representation. Treaty implementa-
tion. Exchange of information and documents.
Personnel. Labor statistics. Funding procedures.
Mutual consultation.
INTL ORGS: United Nations. Special Commission.
PROCEDURE: Amendment. Registration. Termina-
tion.
PARTIES:
FAO (Food Agri)
UNESCO (Educ/Cult)

200183 Bilateral Agreement **43 UNTS 327**
SIGNED: 14 Sep 49   FORCE: 14 Sep 49
REGISTERED: 27 Oct 49 United Nations
ARTICLES: 6 LANGUAGE: French.
HEADNOTE: SUPPLY OFFICAL STAMPS
TOPIC: IGO Operations
CONCEPTS: Postal services. International orga-
nizations.
PARTIES:
United Nations
Switzerland

200184 Bilateral Agreement **44 UNTS 323**
SIGNED: 15 Jul 48   FORCE: 17 Jul 48
REGISTERED: 25 Nov 49 WHO (World Health)
ARTICLES: 13 LANGUAGE: English. French.
HEADNOTE: AGREEMENT
TOPIC: IGO Operations
CONCEPTS: Treaty implementation. Annex or ap-
pendix reference. Exchange of information and
documents. Personnel. Labor statistics. Funding
procedures. Regional offices. Mutual consulta-
tion.
INTL ORGS: United Nations. Special Commission.
PROCEDURE: Amendment. Registration. Termina-
tion.
PARTIES:
UNESCO (Educ/Cult)
WHO (World Health)

200185 Bilateral Agreement **45 UNTS 283**
SIGNED: 1 Mar 45   FORCE: 1 Mar 45
REGISTERED: 19 Dec 49 Canada
ARTICLES: 7 LANGUAGE: English.
HEADNOTE: FINANCE
TOPIC: Finance
CONCEPTS: Detailed regulations. General cooper-
ation. General trade. Accounting procedures.
Banking. Bonds. Currency. Monetary and gold
transfers. Exchange rates and regulations. Inter-
est rates. Payment schedules. Local currency.
Debts. Debt settlement. Loan and credit. Pur-
chase authorization. Loan repayment. Terms of
loan.
PARTIES:
Canada
Czechoslovakia

200186 Bilateral Agreement **45 UNTS 297**
SIGNED: 25 Jun 45   FORCE: 25 Jun 45
REGISTERED: 19 Dec 49 Canada
ARTICLES: 10 LANGUAGE: English.
HEADNOTE: FINANCE
TOPIC: Finance
CONCEPTS: Detailed regulations. General trade.
Accounting procedures. Banking. Bonds. Cur-
rency. Monetary and gold transfers. Exchange
rates and regulations. Interest rates. Payment
schedules. Local currency. Debts. Debt settle-
ment. Loan and credit. Credit provisions. Pur-
chase authorization. Terms of loan.
PARTIES:
Canada
Norway

200187 Multilateral Protocol **45 UNTS 311**
SIGNED: 8 Oct 44   FORCE: 8 Oct 44
REGISTERED: 20 Dec 49 Canada
ARTICLES: 1 LANGUAGE: English. Russian.
HEADNOTE: PROTOCOL ARMISTICE AGREEMENT
TOPIC: Reparations
CONCEPTS: Compensation. Payment schedules.
Lump sum settlements. War claims and repara-
tions.
PARTIES:
Canada SIGNED: 8 Oct 44 FORCE: 8 Oct 44
UK Great Britain SIGNED: 8 Oct 44 FORCE:
8 Oct 44
USSR (Soviet Union) SIGNED: 8 Oct 44 FORCE:
8 Oct 44

200188 Bilateral Agreement **46 UNTS 327**
SIGNED: 10 Feb 50   FORCE: 15 Feb 50
REGISTERED: 15 Feb 50 United Nations
ARTICLES: 20 LANGUAGE: English. French.
HEADNOTE: WHO HEADQUARTERS GENEVA
TOPIC: IGO Operations
CONCEPTS: Annex or appendix reference. Privi-
leges and immunities. Arbitration. Funding pro-
cedures. Headquarters and facilities.
INTL ORGS: International Court of Justice. Interna-
tional Labour Organization. Arbitration Commis-
sion.
PARTIES:
United Nations
WHO (World Health)

200189 Bilateral Agreement **47 UNTS 319**
SIGNED: 20 May 48   FORCE: 1 Feb 48
REGISTERED: 1 Mar 50 United Nations
ARTICLES: 6 LANGUAGE: English.

HEADNOTE: CAMPAIGN UN APPEAL CHILDREN
TOPIC: Humanitarian
CONCEPTS: Definition of terms. Detailed regulations. Annex or appendix reference. Conformity with municipal law. General cooperation. Inspection and observation. Juridical personality. General property. Establishment of commission. Humanitarian matters. Accounting procedures. Expense sharing formulae. Tax exemptions. Assistance to United Nations. UN recommendations.
PARTIES:
Finland
United Nations

200190   Bilateral Agreement   47 UNTS 337
SIGNED: 7 Oct 48   FORCE: 10 Jun 48
REGISTERED: 1 Mar 50 United Nations
ARTICLES: 6 LANGUAGE: English.
HEADNOTE: CAMPAIGN UN APPEAL CHILDREN
TOPIC: Humanitarian
CONCEPTS: Definition of terms. Detailed regulations. Annex or appendix reference. Conformity with municipal law. General cooperation. Inspection and observation. Juridical personality. General property. Establishment of commission. Humanitarian matters. Accounting procedures. Expense sharing formulae. Tax exemptions. Assistance to United Nations. UN recommendations.
PARTIES:
United Nations
San Marino

200191   Bilateral Exchange   51 UNTS 233
SIGNED: 3 Aug 45   FORCE: 3 Aug 45
REGISTERED: 4 Apr 50 USA (United States)
ARTICLES: 2 LANGUAGE: English. French.
HEADNOTE: AIR TRANSPORT SERVICES
TOPIC: Air Transport
CONCEPTS: Exceptions and exemptions. Annex or appendix reference. Conformity with municipal law. Licenses and permits. Use of facilities. Fees and exemptions. Most favored nation clause. National treatment. Customs exemptions. Competency certificate. Routes and logistics. Navigational conditions. Permit designation. Air transport. Airport facilities. Conditions of airlines operating permission. Operating authorizations and regulations. Licenses and certificates of nationality.
TREATY REF: INTERNAT. CIVIL.AVIA.CONF.,- CHICAGO 7DEC44.
PROCEDURE: Registration. Termination.
PARTIES:
Switzerland
USA (United States)

200192   Bilateral Agreement   51 UNTS 245
SIGNED: 25 Feb 38   FORCE: 15 Sep 38
REGISTERED: 17 Apr 50 Brazil
ARTICLES: 11 LANGUAGE: Portuguese. Spanish.
HEADNOTE: EXPORTATION USE BOLIVIAN PETROLEUM
TOPIC: Specific Resources
CONCEPTS: Previous treaties adherence. Establishment of commission. Export quotas. Financial programs. Interest rates. Payment schedules. Natural resources. Transport of goods. Facilities and property. Regulation of natural resources.
INTL ORGS: Special Commission.
PROCEDURE: Ratification.
PARTIES:
Bolivia
Brazil

200193   Bilateral Agreement   51 UNTS 271
SIGNED: 27 Dec 27   FORCE: 9 Jul 41
REGISTERED: 1 May 50 Brazil
ARTICLES: 4 LANGUAGE: Portuguese. Spanish.
HEADNOTE: SUPPLEMENTARY FRONTIER AGREEMENT
TOPIC: Territory Boundary
CONCEPTS: Previous treaty amendment. Markers and definitions.
TREATY REF: 2'32DEMARTENS397;.
PROCEDURE: Ratification.

PARTIES:
Argentina
Brazil

200194   Bilateral Agreement   51 UNTS 281
SIGNED: 23 Jan 40   FORCE: 8 Apr 41
REGISTERED: 1 May 50 Brazil
ARTICLES: 4 LANGUAGE: Portuguese. Spanish.
HEADNOTE: LEGALIZATION CARGO MANIFESTS
TOPIC: Admin Cooperation
CONCEPTS: Consular functions in shipping. Tariffs. Fees and exemptions. Customs duties.
PROCEDURE: Denunciation.
PARTIES:
Argentina
Brazil

200195   Bilateral Treaty   51 UNTS 291
SIGNED: 30 Mar 40   FORCE: 9 Jan 41
REGISTERED: 1 May 50 Brazil
ARTICLES: 25 LANGUAGE: Portuguese. Spanish.
HEADNOTE: PACIFIC SETTLEMENT DISPUTES
TOPIC: Dispute Settlement
CONCEPTS: Time limit. Previous treaty replacement. Exchange of information and documents. Establishment of commission. Arbitration. Procedure. Domestic jurisdiction. Existing tribunals. Conciliation. Advisory opinions.
INTL ORGS: Permanent Court of International Justice. Arbitration Commission. Conciliation Commission.
TREATY REF: 54LTS435; 3'6DEMARTENS20;.
PROCEDURE: Duration. Ratification.
PARTIES:
Brazil
Venezuela

200196   Bilateral Agreement   54 UNTS 235
SIGNED: 14 Jun 41   FORCE: 1 Oct 41
REGISTERED: 5 May 50 Brazil
ARTICLES: 7 LANGUAGE: Portuguese. Spanish.
HEADNOTE: CULTURAL EXCHANGES
TOPIC: Culture
CONCEPTS: Tourism. Alien status. Recognition of degrees. Exchange. Teacher and student exchange. Professorships. Scholarships and grants. Vocational training. Exchange. Scientific exchange. Accounting procedures.
PROCEDURE: Denunciation. Ratification.
PARTIES:
Brazil
Paraguay

200197   Bilateral Agreement   54 UNTS 249
SIGNED: 14 Jun 41   FORCE: 1 Oct 41
REGISTERED: 5 May 50 Brazil
ARTICLES: 4 LANGUAGE: Portuguese. Spanish.
HEADNOTE: EXCHANGE BOOKS PUBLICATIONS
TOPIC: Culture
CONCEPTS: Friendship and amity. Exchange of official publications. Exchange of information and documents. Scientific exchange. Publications exchange.
TREATY REF: 24LTS213.
PROCEDURE: Denunciation. Ratification.
PARTIES:
Brazil
Paraguay

200198   Bilateral Agreement   54 UNTS 259
SIGNED: 14 Jun 41   FORCE: 1 Oct 41
REGISTERED: 5 May 50 Brazil
ARTICLES: 4 LANGUAGE: Portuguese. Spanish.
HEADNOTE: ESTABLISHMENT BONDED WAREHOUSE
TOPIC: Specific Property
CONCEPTS: Conformity with municipal law. Use of facilities. Trade agencies. Customs duties. Special projects. Facilities and property.
PROCEDURE: Denunciation. Ratification.
PARTIES:
Brazil
Paraguay

200199   Bilateral Agreement   54 UNTS 269
SIGNED: 14 Apr 41   FORCE: 1 Oct 41
REGISTERED: 5 May 50 Brazil
ARTICLES: 4 LANGUAGE: Portuguese. Spanish.

HEADNOTE: PURCHASE BREEDING STOCK
TOPIC: Commodity Trade
CONCEPTS: Banking. Interest rates. Payment schedules. Commodity trade. Loan and credit. Credit provisions.
PROCEDURE: Denunciation. Duration. Ratification. Renewal or Revival.
PARTIES:
Brazil
Paraguay

200200   Bilateral Agreement   54 UNTS 279
SIGNED: 14 Jun 41   FORCE: 1 Oct 41
REGISTERED: 5 May 50 Brazil
ARTICLES: 3 LANGUAGE: Portuguese. Spanish.
HEADNOTE: EXCHANGE EXPERTS
TOPIC: Admin Cooperation
CONCEPTS: General cooperation.
PROCEDURE: Denunciation. Ratification.
PARTIES:
Brazil
Paraguay

200201   Bilateral Agreement   54 UNTS 289
SIGNED: 14 Jun 41   FORCE: 1 Oct 41
REGISTERED: 5 May 50 Brazil
ARTICLES: 10 LANGUAGE: Portuguese. Spanish.
HEADNOTE: CONSTRUCTION OPERATION CONCEPCION-PEDRO JUAN CABALLERO RAILWAY
TOPIC: Land Transport
CONCEPTS: Exceptions and exemptions. Time limit. Responsibility and liability. Compensation. Fees and exemptions. Funding procedures. Payment schedules. Non-interest rates and fees. Assets. Tax exemptions. Customs exemptions. Routes and logistics. Railways.
PROCEDURE: Ratification.
PARTIES:
Brazil
Paraguay

200202   Bilateral Agreement   54 UNTS 303
SIGNED: 14 Jun 41   FORCE: 1 Oct 41
REGISTERED: 5 May 50 Brazil
ARTICLES: 5 LANGUAGE: Portuguese. Spanish.
HEADNOTE: JOINT COMMISSION ON PARAGUAY RIVER
TOPIC: IGO Establishment
CONCEPTS: Denial of admission. Merchant vessels. Inland and territorial waters. Subsidiary organ.
INTL ORGS: Special Commission.
PROCEDURE: Ratification.
PARTIES:
Brazil
Paraguay

200203   Bilateral Agreement   54 UNTS 313
SIGNED: 14 Jun 41   FORCE: 2 Aug 41
REGISTERED: 5 May 50 Brazil
ARTICLES: 3 LANGUAGE: Portuguese. Spanish.
HEADNOTE: GRANTING RECIPROCAL BANK CREDITS
TOPIC: Finance
CONCEPTS: Conformity with municipal law. Banking. Loan and credit. Purchase authorization.
PROCEDURE: Ratification.
PARTIES:
Brazil
Paraguay

200204   Bilateral Agreement   54 UNTS 323
SIGNED: 14 Jun 41   FORCE: 2 Aug 41
REGISTERED: 5 May 50 Brazil
ARTICLES: 3 LANGUAGE: Portuguese. Spanish.
HEADNOTE: COMMISSION TREATY COMMERCE & NAVIGATION
TOPIC: IGO Establishment
CONCEPTS: Establishment of commission. Subsidiary organ.
INTL ORGS: Special Commission.
PROCEDURE: Future Procedures Contemplated.
PARTIES:
Brazil
Paraguay

200205   Bilateral Treaty   54 UNTS 333
SIGNED: 25 Feb 38   FORCE: 26 Jul 42

REGISTERED: 16 May 50 Brazil
ARTICLES: 20 LANGUAGE: Portuguese. Spanish.
HEADNOTE: EXTRADITION
TOPIC: Extradition
CONCEPTS: Time limit. Previous treaty replacement. Nationality and citizenship. Extradition, deportation and repatriation. Extradition requests. Extraditable offenses. Location of crime. Refusal of extradition. Concurrent requests. Provisional detainment. Extradition postponement. Conformity with municipal law. Indemnities and reimbursements. Conveyance in transit.
PROCEDURE: Denunciation. Ratification.
PARTIES:
Bolivia
Brazil

200206   Bilateral Agreement   54 UNTS 359
SIGNED: 8 Jan 42   FORCE: 24 Dec 42
REGISTERED: 16 May 50 Brazil
ARTICLES: 4 LANGUAGE: Portuguese. Spanish.
HEADNOTE: LEGALIZATION CARGO MANIFESTS
TOPIC: Admin Cooperation
CONCEPTS: Consular functions in shipping. Tariffs. Fees and exemptions. Customs duties.
PARTIES:
Brazil
Uruguay

200207   Bilateral Exchange   54 UNTS 369
SIGNED: 18 May 42   FORCE: 1 Jul 42
REGISTERED: 16 May 50 Brazil
ARTICLES: 2 LANGUAGE: Portuguese. Spanish.
HEADNOTE: TELEGRAPHIC COMMUNICATIONS
TOPIC: Telecommunications
CONCEPTS: Previous treaty replacement. Conformity with municipal law. Non-interest rates and fees. Radio-telephone-telegraphic communications.
TREATY REF: MONTEVIDEO 1899.
PROCEDURE: Denunciation. Duration.
PARTIES:
Brazil
Uruguay

200208   Bilateral Agreement   65 UNTS 163
SIGNED: 20 Nov 47   FORCE: 20 Nov 47
REGISTERED: 1 Jun 50 United Nations
ARTICLES: 9 LANGUAGE: French.
HEADNOTE: UNICEF ACTIVITIES
TOPIC: IGO Operations
CONCEPTS: Privileges and immunities. Personnel. Existing tribunals. Labor statistics. Funding procedures. Materials, equipment and services. Assistance to United Nations.
INTL ORGS: United Nations.
PROCEDURE: Duration.
PARTIES:
Albania
UNICEF (Children)

200209   Bilateral Agreement   65 UNTS 171
SIGNED: 25 Mar 50   FORCE: 18 Feb 50
REGISTERED: 1 Jun 50 United Nations
ARTICLES: 8 LANGUAGE: English.
HEADNOTE: UNICEF ACTIVITIES
TOPIC: IGO Operations
CONCEPTS: Subsidiary organ. Headquarters and facilities. Extension of functions. IGO status. Status of experts.
INTL ORGS: United Nations.
TREATY REF: UN CHARTER.
PROCEDURE: Duration.
PARTIES:
Korea, South
UNICEF (Children)

200210   Bilateral Agreement   65 UNTS 183
SIGNED: 30 Apr 42   FORCE: 3 May 42
REGISTERED: 6 Jun 50 Brazil
ARTICLES: 10 LANGUAGE: Portuguese.
HEADNOTE: APPLICATION DOMESTIC POSTAL TARIFFS
TOPIC: Postal Service
CONCEPTS: Conformity with municipal law. Customs exemptions. Postal services. Conveyance in transit. Rates and charges.
INTL ORGS: Universal Postal Union.
TREATY REF: 202LTS50.

PROCEDURE: Denunciation. Duration.
PARTIES:
Brazil
Portugal

200211   Bilateral Exchange   65 UNTS 191
SIGNED: 8 Oct 42   FORCE: 1 Nov 42
REGISTERED: 6 Jun 50 Brazil
ARTICLES: 2 LANGUAGE: Portuguese. Spanish.
HEADNOTE: TELEGRAPHIC COMMUNICATIONS
TOPIC: Telecommunications
CONCEPTS: Previous treaty replacement. Conformity with municipal law. Non-interest rates and fees. Telegrams. Radio-telephone-telegraphic communications.' Conformity with IGO decisions.
INTL ORGS: International Telecommunication Union.
TREATY REF: BRAZIL-PARAGUAY 1927.
PROCEDURE: Denunciation. Duration.
PARTIES:
Brazil
Paraguay

200212   Bilateral Agreement   65 UNTS 203
SIGNED: 22 Oct 42   FORCE: 18 Feb 44
REGISTERED: 6 Jun 50 Brazil
ARTICLES: 10 LANGUAGE: Portuguese. Spanish.
HEADNOTE: CULTURAL EXCHANGES
TOPIC: Culture
CONCEPTS: Friendship and amity. Alien status. Exchange of official publications. Dispute settlement. Recognition of degrees. Teacher and student exchange. Exchange. Artists. Scientific exchange. Fees and exemptions. Publications exchange.
TREATY REF: 188LTS125.
PROCEDURE: Denunciation. Ratification.
PARTIES:
Brazil
Venezuela

200213   Bilateral Agreement   65 UNTS 217
SIGNED: 9 Dec 42   FORCE: 17 Jun 48
REGISTERED: 6 Jun 50 Brazil
ARTICLES: 10 LANGUAGE: Portuguese. Spanish.
HEADNOTE: CULTURAL AGREEMENT
TOPIC: Culture
CONCEPTS: Friendship and amity. Standardization. Conformity with municipal law. Specialists exchange. Recognition of degrees. Teacher and student exchange. Scholarships and grants. Exchange. General cultural cooperation. Scientific exchange. Fees and exemptions.
PROCEDURE: Denunciation. Duration. Ratification.
PARTIES:
Brazil
Dominican Republic

200214   Multilateral Exchange   65 UNTS 231
SIGNED: 21 Dec 43   FORCE: 21 Dec 43
REGISTERED: 6 Jun 50 Brazil
ARTICLES: 4 LANGUAGE: Portuguese. English.
HEADNOTE: RICE AGREEMENT
TOPIC: Commodity Trade
CONCEPTS: Export quotas. Trade procedures. Delivery guarantees.
PARTIES:
Brazil SIGNED: 21 Dec 43 FORCE: 21 Dec 43
UK Great Britain SIGNED: 21 Dec 43 FORCE: 21 Dec 43
USA (United States) SIGNED: 21 Dec 43 FORCE: 21 Dec 43

200215   Bilateral Exchange   65 UNTS 265
SIGNED: 24 May 44   FORCE: 24 May 44
REGISTERED: 6 Jun 50 Brazil
ARTICLES: 2 LANGUAGE: Portuguese. English.
HEADNOTE: CULTURAL AGREEMENT
TOPIC: Culture
CONCEPTS: Exchange of information and documents. Exchange. General cultural cooperation. Scientific exchange. Publications exchange. Mass media exchange.
PARTIES:
Brazil
Canada

200216   Bilateral Agreement   65 UNTS 271
SIGNED: 29 Sep 44   FORCE: 24 Sep 44
REGISTERED: 6 Jun 50 Brazil
ARTICLES: 26 LANGUAGE: Portuguese. English.
HEADNOTE: TECHNICAL ADVISOR TO MERCHANT MARINE COMMISSION
TOPIC: Military Mission
CONCEPTS: Definition of terms. Use of facilities. Compensation. Indemnities and reimbursements. Exchange rates and regulations. Expense sharing formulae. Tax exemptions. Customs exemptions. Naval vessels. Airforce-army-navy personnel ratio. Conditions for assistance missions. Third country military personnel. Status of forces.
PROCEDURE: Denunciation. Duration. Renewal or Revival. Termination.
PARTIES:
Brazil
USA (United States)

200217   Bilateral Exchange   65 UNTS 289
SIGNED: 22 Nov 44   FORCE: 22 Nov 44
REGISTERED: 6 Jun 50 Brazil
ARTICLES: 2 LANGUAGE: Portuguese. Spanish.
HEADNOTE: EXCHANGE SUPPLIES STONE
TOPIC: Specif Goods/Equip
CONCEPTS: Customs exemptions. Roads and highways. Specific goods and equipment.
PARTIES:
Brazil
Uruguay

200218   Bilateral Exchange   65 UNTS 305
SIGNED: 16 Dec 44   FORCE: 16 Dec 44
REGISTERED: 6 Jun 50 Brazil
ARTICLES: 2 LANGUAGE: Portuguese. Spanish.
HEADNOTE: EXCHANGE DIPLOMATIC CORRESPONDENCE AIRMAIL
TOPIC: Admin Cooperation
CONCEPTS: Previous treaty extension. Diplomatic correspondence.
PARTIES:
Brazil
Uruguay

200219   Bilateral Exchange   66 UNTS 307
SIGNED: 10 Nov 42   FORCE: 10 Nov 42
REGISTERED: 14 Jun 50 USA (United States)
ARTICLES: 3 LANGUAGE: English. Spanish.
HEADNOTE: WEATHER STATION MEXICO
TOPIC: Scientific Project
CONCEPTS: Research cooperation. Meteorology. General technical assistance. Special projects.
PARTIES:
Mexico
USA (United States)

200220   Bilateral Exchange   66 UNTS 331
SIGNED: 14 Jun 43   FORCE: 14 Jun 43
REGISTERED: 6 Jul 50 USA (United States)
ARTICLES: 2 LANGUAGE: English. Spanish.
HEADNOTE: WEATHER STATIONS MEXICO
TOPIC: Scientific Project
CONCEPTS: Vocational training. Research and scientific projects. Research cooperation. Meteorology. Research and development. Expense sharing formulae. Domestic obligation. Materials, equipment and services.
PARTIES:
Mexico
USA (United States)

200221   Multilateral Exchange   67 UNTS 221
SIGNED: 2 Aug 44   FORCE: 2 Aug 44
REGISTERED: 6 Jul 50 USA (United States)
ARTICLES: 2 LANGUAGE: English. Spanish.
HEADNOTE: WEATHER STATION
TOPIC: Scientific Project
CONCEPTS: Exchange of information and documents. Personnel. General property. Technical and commercial staff. Specialists exchange. Research and scientific projects. Research cooperation. Meteorology. Research and development. Expense sharing formulae. Domestic obligation. Materials, equipment and services. Facilities and equipment.
PROCEDURE: Duration. Renewal or Revival. Termination.

PARTIES:
Afghanistan
Albania
Argentina
Australia
Austria
Belgium
Bolivia
Brazil
Bulgaria
Byelorussia
Canada
Chile
Taiwan
Colombia
Costa Rica
Cuba
Czechoslovakia
Denmark
Dominican Republic
Ecuador
United Arab Rep
El Salvador
Ethiopia
Finland
France
Greece
Guatemala
Haiti
Honduras
Hungary
Iceland
India
Iran
Iraq
Ireland
Italy
Lebanon
Liberia
Luxembourg
Mexico
Netherlands
New Zealand
Nicaragua
Norway
Panama
Paraguay
Peru
Philippines
Poland
Portugal
Romania
Saudi Arabia
Siam
South Africa
Sweden
Switzerland
Syria
Transjordan
Turkey
UK Great Britain
USA (United States)
Ukrainian SSR
Uruguay
USSR (Soviet Union)
Venezuela
Yemen
Yugoslavia

200222 Multilateral Agreement **67 UNTS 231**
SIGNED: 27 Mar 41   FORCE: 27 Mar 41
REGISTERED: 11 Jul 50 USA (United States)
ARTICLES: 21 LANGUAGE: English. Spanish.
HEADNOTE: MILITARY OFFICER DIRECTOR MILI-
TARY SCHOOL
TOPIC: Military Mission
CONCEPTS: Annex or appendix reference. Use of
facilities. Compensation. Indemnities and reim-
bursements. Exchange rates and regulations. Ex-
pense sharing formulae. Tax exemptions. Cus-
toms exemptions. Military assistance. Military
training. Security of information. Airforce-army-
navy personnel ratio. Ranks and privileges. Con-
ditions for assistance missions. Third country
military personnel. Status of forces.
PROCEDURE: Duration. Renewal or Revival. Termination.
PARTIES:
Belgium
Brazil
Bulgaria
Czechoslovakia
Denmark

Dominican Republic
El Salvador
Finland
France
Greece
Hungary
Ireland
Italy
Lebanon
Liechtenstein
Luxembourg
Morocco
Netherlands
New Zealand
Norway
Poland
Portugal
Romania
South Africa
Spain
Sweden
Switzerland
Syria
Tunisia
Turkey
UK Great Britain
USA (United States)

200223 Bilateral Instrument **67 UNTS 253**
SIGNED: 16 May 44   FORCE: 16 May 44
REGISTERED: 11 Jul 50 USA (United States)
ARTICLES: 16 LANGUAGE: English.
HEADNOTE: ARRANGEMENTS NORWEGIAN CiViL
ADMINISTRATION AFTER LIBERATION
TOPIC: Privil/Immunities
CONCEPTS: General cooperation. Personnel. Gen-
eral property. Domestic obligation. General mili-
tary. Jurisdiction. Service in foreign army.
PARTIES:
Norway
USA (United States)

200224 Bilateral Agreement **67 UNTS 263**
SIGNED: 17 Oct 41   FORCE: 16 Apr 43
REGISTERED: 12 Jul 50 Brazil
ARTICLES: 10 LANGUAGE: English. Portuguese.
HEADNOTE: TRADE
TOPIC: General Trade
CONCEPTS: Exceptions and exemptions. Proce-
dure. Import quotas. Reciprocity in trade. Trade
procedures. Quotas. Most favored nation clause.
Equitable taxes.
PROCEDURE: Duration. Ratification. Termination.
PARTIES:
Brazil
Canada

200225 Bilateral Agreement **67 UNTS 279**
SIGNED: 18 Nov 41   FORCE: 7 Dec 43
REGISTERED: 12 Jul 50 Brazil
ARTICLES: 8 LANGUAGE: Portuguese. Spanish.
HEADNOTE: CULTURAL AGREEMENT
TOPIC: Culture
CONCEPTS: Friendship and amity. Exchange.
Teacher and student exchange. Professorships.
Scholarships and grants. Vocational training. Ex-
change. Artists. Scientific exchange. Accounting
procedures. Publications exchange. Mass media
exchange.
PROCEDURE: Denunciation. Ratification.
PARTIES:
Brazil
Chile

200226 Bilateral Agreement **67 UNTS 293**
SIGNED: 9 Apr 45   FORCE: 26 Dec 45
REGISTERED: 12 Jul 50 Brazil
ARTICLES: 4 LANGUAGE: Portuguese. Spanish.
HEADNOTE: EXCHANGE BOOKS PUBLICATIONS
TOPIC: Culture
CONCEPTS: Exchange of official publications. In-
stitute establishment. Vocational training. Ex-
change. General cultural cooperation. Artists.
Scientific exchange. Publications exchange.
TREATY REF: 24LTS213.
PROCEDURE: Denunciation. Ratification.
PARTIES:
Brazil
Dominican Republic

200227 Bilateral Agreement **67 UNTS 303**
SIGNED: 11 Aug 44   FORCE: 19 Sep 46
REGISTERED: 12 Jul 50 Brazil
ARTICLES: 11 LANGUAGE: Portuguese. Spanish.
HEADNOTE: CONSTRUCTION OPERATION CON-
CEPCION-PEDRO JUAN CABALLERO RAILWAY
TOPIC: Land Transport
CONCEPTS: Exceptions and exemptions. Time
limit. Previous treaty replacement. Expropriation.
Private contracts. Establishment of commission.
Compensation. Payment schedules. Non-interest
rates and fees. Tax exemptions. Customs exemp-
tions. Routes and logistics. Railways. Facilities
and property.
TREATY REF: 54UNTS289.
PROCEDURE: Ratification.
PARTIES:
Brazil
Paraguay

200228 Bilateral Agreement **67 UNTS 321**
SIGNED: 12 Oct 44   FORCE: 25 Oct 44
REGISTERED: 12 Jul 50 Brazil
ARTICLES: 7 LANGUAGE: English. Portuguese.
HEADNOTE: MIXED COMMISSION FOR UNRRA
TOPIC: IGO Establishment
CONCEPTS: Private contracts. Establishment of
trade relations. Accounting procedures. Funding
procedures. Establishment. Internal structure.
INTL ORGS: Special Commission.
PARTIES:
Brazil
UNRRA (Relief)

200229 Bilateral Agreement **68 UNTS 175**
SIGNED: 11 Feb 45   FORCE: 11 Feb 45
REGISTERED: 18 Jul 50 USA (United States)
ARTICLES: 9 LANGUAGE: English. Russian.
HEADNOTE: PRISONERS WAR LIBERATED CIVIL-
IANS
TOPIC: Other Military
CONCEPTS: Treaty implementation. Repatriation
of nationals. Compensation. Prisoners of war.
PARTIES:
USA (United States)
USSR (Soviet Union)

200230 Multilateral Instrument **68 UNTS 189**
SIGNED: 5 Jun 45   FORCE: 5 Jun 45
REGISTERED: 25 Jul 50 USA (United States)
ARTICLES: 15 LANGUAGE: English. French. Rus-
sian.
HEADNOTE: DECLARATION DEFEAT GERMANY
TOPIC: Milit Occupation
CONCEPTS: Informational records. Use of facili-
ties. Investigation of violations. Prisoners of war.
Naval vessels. Armistice and peace. Disarma-
ment and demilitarization. Industrial controls.
Control and occupation machinery.
PARTIES:
France SIGNED: 5 Jun 45 FORCE: 5 Jun 45
UK Great Britain SIGNED: 5 Jun 45 FORCE:
5 Jun 45

200231 Bilateral Instrument **68 UNTS 213**
SIGNED: 7 Jun 50   FORCE: 26 Jul 50
REGISTERED: 31 Jul 50 United Nations
ARTICLES: 15 LANGUAGE: English. French.
HEADNOTE: ILO ISSUE LAISSEZ-PASSER UN
VISAS
TOPIC: Visas
CONCEPTS: Detailed regulations. Non-visa travel
documents. Privileges and immunities. Juridical
personality.
PROCEDURE: Amendment. Denunciation. Re-
newal or Revival.
PARTIES:
ILO (Labor Org)
United Nations

200232 Bilateral Agreement **68 UNTS 223**
SIGNED: 23 Aug 47   FORCE: 23 Aug 47
REGISTERED: 1 Aug 50 United Nations
ARTICLES: 9 LANGUAGE: French.
HEADNOTE: UNICEF ACTIVITIES
TOPIC: IGO Operations
CONCEPTS: Tax exemptions. Subsidiary organ. Ex-
tension of functions. IGO status. Special status.
Status of experts.

INTL ORGS: United Nations.
PROCEDURE: Duration.
PARTIES:
　Bulgaria
　UNICEF (Children)
　　　　　ANNEX
559 UNTS 390. UNICEF (Children). Force
　10 Mar 66.
559 UNTS 390. Bulgaria. Force 10 Mar 66.

200233　Bilateral Agreement　**68 UNTS 224**
SIGNED: 23 Aug 47　　　　FORCE: 23 Aug 47
REGISTERED: 1 Aug 50 United Nations
ARTICLES: 9 LANGUAGE: English.
HEADNOTE: UNICEF ACTIVITIES
TOPIC: IGO Operations
CONCEPTS: Tax exemptions. Subsidiary organ. Extension of functions. IGO status. Special status. Status of experts.
INTL ORGS: United Nations.
PROCEDURE: Duration.
PARTIES:
　Finland
　UNICEF (Children)
　　　　　ANNEX
202 UNTS 386. UNICEF (Children). Supplementation 19 Nov 54. Force 3 Dec 54.
202 UNTS 386. Finland. Supplementation 3 Dec 54. Force 3 Dec 54.

200234　Bilateral Agreement　**68 UNTS 226**
SIGNED: 28 Aug 47　　　　FORCE: 28 Aug 47
REGISTERED: 1 Aug 50 United Nations
ARTICLES: 9 LANGUAGE: English. French.
HEADNOTE: UNICEF ACTIVITIES
TOPIC: IGO Operations
CONCEPTS: Tax exemptions. Subsidiary organ. Extension of functions. IGO status. Special status. Status of experts.
INTL ORGS: United Nations.
PROCEDURE: Duration.
PARTIES:
　Hungary
　UNICEF (Children)

200235　Bilateral Agreement　**68 UNTS 228**
SIGNED: 28 Aug 47　　　　FORCE: 28 Aug 47
REGISTERED: 1 Aug 50 United Nations
ARTICLES: 9 LANGUAGE: English.
HEADNOTE: UNICEF ACTIVITIES
TOPIC: IGO Operations
CONCEPTS: Tax exemptions. Subsidiary organ. Extension of functions. IGO status. Special status. Status of experts.
INTL ORGS: United Nations.
PROCEDURE: Duration.
PARTIES:
　Romania
　UNICEF (Children)

200236　Bilateral Agreement　**68 UNTS 240**
SIGNED: 6 Nov 47　　　　FORCE: 1 Sep 47
REGISTERED: 1 Aug 50 United Nations
ARTICLES: 9 LANGUAGE: English. Italian.
HEADNOTE: UNICEF ACTIVITIES
TOPIC: IGO Operations
CONCEPTS: Tax exemptions. Subsidiary organ. Extension of functions. IGO status. Special status. Status of experts.
INTL ORGS: United Nations.
PROCEDURE: Duration.
PARTIES:
　Italy
　UNICEF (Children)

200237　Bilateral Agreement　**68 UNTS 252**
SIGNED: 7 Nov 47　　　　FORCE: 7 Nov 47
REGISTERED: 1 Aug 50 United Nations
ARTICLES: 9 LANGUAGE: English. French.
HEADNOTE: UNICEF ACTIVITIES
TOPIC: IGO Operations
CONCEPTS: Tax exemptions. Subsidiary organ. Extension of functions. IGO status. Special status. Status of experts.
INTL ORGS: United Nations.
PROCEDURE: Duration.
PARTIES:
　Austria
　UNICEF (Children)

　　　　　ANNEX
208 UNTS 392. UNICEF (Children). Supplementation 11 Jan 55. Force 3 Mar 55.
208 UNTS 392. Austria. Supplementation 3 Mar 55. Force 3 Mar 55.

200238　Bilateral Agreement　**68 UNTS 254**
SIGNED: 6 Apr 50　　　　FORCE: 27 Dec 49
REGISTERED: 1 Aug 50 United Nations
ARTICLES: 9 LANGUAGE: English.
HEADNOTE: UNICEF ACTIVITIES
TOPIC: IGO Operations
CONCEPTS: Tax exemptions. Subsidiary organ. Extension of functions. IGO status. Special status. Status of experts.
INTL ORGS: United Nations.
PROCEDURE: Duration.
PARTIES:
　Indonesia
　UNICEF (Children)

200239　Bilateral Agreement　**68 UNTS 256**
SIGNED: 7 Jun 50　　　　FORCE: 7 Jun 50
REGISTERED: 1 Aug 50 United Nations
ARTICLES: 9 LANGUAGE: English.
HEADNOTE: UNICEF ACTIVITIES
TOPIC: IGO Operations
CONCEPTS: Tax exemptions. Subsidiary organ. Extension of functions. IGO status. Special status. Status of experts.
INTL ORGS: United Nations.
PARTIES:
　Ceylon (Sri Lanka)
　UNICEF (Children)

200240　Bilateral Agreement　**70 UNTS 223**
SIGNED: 7 Jun 50　　　　FORCE: 26 Jul 50
REGISTERED: 14 Aug 50 ILO (Labor Org)
ARTICLES: 7 LANGUAGE: English. French. Spanish.
HEADNOTE: AGREEMENT
TOPIC: IGO Operations
CONCEPTS: Representation. Exchange of information and documents. Labor statistics. Mutual consultation.
PROCEDURE: Amendment. Denunciation.
PARTIES:
　ILO (Labor Org)
　OAS (Am States)

200241　Multilateral Instrument　**70 UNTS 237**
SIGNED: 22 Mar 45　　　　FORCE: 10 May 45
REGISTERED: 29 Aug 50 United Arab Rep
ARTICLES: 20 LANGUAGE: Arabic.
HEADNOTE: PACT LEAGUE ARAB STATES
TOPIC: General Amity
CONCEPTS: Inviolability. Standardization. Arbitration. Mediation and good offices. Procedure. General health, education, culture, welfare and labor. Exchange. General economics. General transportation. General communications. General military. Decisions. Subsidiary organ. Establishment. Procedure. Conferences.
INTL ORGS: Arab League.
PROCEDURE: Future Procedures Contemplated. Ratification.
PARTIES:
　United Arab Rep SIGNED: 22 Mar 45 RATIFIED: 12 Apr 45 FORCE: 10 May 45
　Iraq SIGNED: 22 Mar 45 RATIFIED: 25 Apr 45 FORCE: 10 May 45
　Lebanon SIGNED: 22 Mar 45 RATIFIED: 16 May 45 FORCE: 1 Jun 45
　Saudi Arabia SIGNED: 22 Mar 45 RATIFIED: 16 Apr 45 FORCE: 10 May 45
　Syria SIGNED: 22 Mar 45 RATIFIED: 19 May 45 FORCE: 4 Jun 45
　Transjordan SIGNED: 22 Mar 45 RATIFIED: 10 May 45 FORCE: 10 May 45
　Yemen SIGNED: 5 May 45 RATIFIED: 9 Feb 46 FORCE: 24 Feb 45

200242　Bilateral Agreement　**73 UNTS 223**
SIGNED: 24 May 44　　　　FORCE: 20 Oct 49
REGISTERED: 5 Oct 50 Ecuador
ARTICLES: 12 LANGUAGE: Portuguese. Spanish.
HEADNOTE: CULTURAL AGREEMENT
TOPIC: Culture
CONCEPTS: Annex or appendix reference. Friendship and amity. Standardization. Recognition of degrees. Exchange. Teacher and student exchange. Professorships. Scholarships and grants. Vocational training. Exchange. Artists. Scientific exchange. Accounting procedures. Fees and exemptions. Publications exchange.
PROCEDURE: Denunciation. Ratification.
PARTIES:
　Brazil
　Ecuador

200243　Bilateral Exchange　**73 UNTS 237**
SIGNED: 14 Aug 45　　　　FORCE: 1 Jan 46
REGISTERED: 9 Oct 50 USA (United States)
ARTICLES: 2 LANGUAGE: English. French.
HEADNOTE: EXCHANGE OFFICIAL PUBLICATIONS
TOPIC: Admin Cooperation
CONCEPTS: Exchange of official publications. Operating agencies.
PARTIES:
　France
　USA (United States)

200244　Bilateral Agreement　**76 UNTS 171**
SIGNED: 17 Jul 48　　　　FORCE: 13 Dec 48
REGISTERED: 21 Nov 50 WHO (World Health)
ARTICLES: 14 LANGUAGE: English. French.
HEADNOTE: AGREEMENT
TOPIC: IGO Operations
CONCEPTS: Representation. Treaty implementation. Exchange of information and documents. Personnel. Labor statistics. Funding procedures. Regional offices. Inter-agency agreements. Mutual consultation.
INTL ORGS: United Nations.
PROCEDURE: Amendment. Registration. Renewal or Revival.
PARTIES:
　FAO (Food Agri)
　WHO (World Health)

200245　Bilateral Instrument　**76 UNTS 183**
SIGNED: 25 Sep 43　　　　FORCE: 25 Sep 43
REGISTERED: 19 Dec 50 USA (United States)
ARTICLES: 5 LANGUAGE: English. French.
HEADNOTE: RECIPROCAL AID
TOPIC: Direct Aid
CONCEPTS: Conformity with municipal law. General cooperation. Informational records. Accounting procedures. Indemnities and reimbursements. Funding procedures. Payment schedules. Local currency. Commodities and services. General aid. Materials, equipment and services. Procurement. Military assistance. Return of equipment and recapture.
PARTIES:
　France
　USA (United States)

200246　Bilateral Agreement　**76 UNTS 193**
SIGNED: 20 Feb 45　　　　FORCE: 28 Feb 45
REGISTERED: 19 Dec 50 USA (United States)
ARTICLES: 8 LANGUAGE: English.
HEADNOTE: MUTUAL AID WAR AGAINST AGGRESSION
TOPIC: Direct Aid
CONCEPTS: Annex or appendix reference. Conformity with municipal law. Payment schedules. Domestic obligation. Materials, equipment and services. Defense and security. Military assistance. Return of equipment and recapture. Security of information. Exchange of defense information. Restrictions on transfer.
TREATY REF: 204LTS381.
PROCEDURE: Duration. Future Procedures Contemplated.
PARTIES:
　France
　USA (United States)

200247　Bilateral Exchange　**76 UNTS 213**
SIGNED: 28 Feb 45　　　　FORCE: 28 Feb 45
REGISTERED: 19 Dec 50 USA (United States)
ARTICLES: 2 LANGUAGE: English.
HEADNOTE: AID TO US ARMED FORCES
TOPIC: IGO Status/Immunit
CONCEPTS: Treaty interpretation. Accounting procedures. Currency. Claims and settlements. Eco-

nomic assistance. Materials, equipment and services. Defense and security. Military assistance. Exchange of defense information.
TREATY REF: 204LTS381.
PARTIES:
France
USA (United States)

200248 Bilateral Agreement **76 UNTS 223**
SIGNED: 20 Feb 45 FORCE: 28 Feb 45
REGISTERED: 19 Dec 50 USA (United States)
ARTICLES: 6 LANGUAGE: English.
HEADNOTE: SUPPLIES SERVICES
TOPIC: IGO Status/Immunit
CONCEPTS: Annex or appendix reference. Conformity with municipal law. Materials, equipment and services. Payment for war supplies. Military assistance. Surplus war property.
TREATY REF: 204LTS381.
PARTIES:
France
USA (United States)

200249 Bilateral Treaty **79 UNTS 257**
SIGNED: 12 Apr 39 FORCE: 4 Apr 50
REGISTERED: 16 Jan 51 Netherlands
ARTICLES: 6 LANGUAGE: Arabic. Dutch.
HEADNOTE: TREATY TO RENEW FRIENDSHIP
TOPIC: General Amity
CONCEPTS: General relations and amity. Friendship and amity.
PARTIES:
Netherlands
Yemen

200250 Bilateral Agreement **80 UNTS 283**
SIGNED: 29 Jun 44 FORCE: 29 Jun 44
REGISTERED: 10 Feb 51 USA (United States)
ARTICLES: 30 LANGUAGE: English. Spanish.
HEADNOTE: MILITARY MISSION
TOPIC: Military Mission
CONCEPTS: Definition of terms. Use of facilities. Compensation. Indemnities and reimbursements. Exchange rates and regulations. Expense sharing formulae. Tax exemptions. Customs exemptions. Military assistance. Military training. Security of information. Airforce-army-navy personnel ratio. Ranks and privileges. Conditions for assistance missions. Third country military personnel. Status of forces.
PROCEDURE: Denunciation. Duration. Renewal or Revival. Termination.
PARTIES:
Ecuador
USA (United States)

200251 Multilateral Agreement **82 UNTS 279**
SIGNED: 8 Aug 45 FORCE: 8 Aug 45
REGISTERED: 15 Mar 51 UK Great Britain
ARTICLES: 7 LANGUAGE: English. French. Russian.
HEADNOTE: PROSECUTION PUNISHMENT MAJOR WAR CRIMINALS EUROPEAN AXIS
TOPIC: General Military
CONCEPTS: Definition of terms. Detailed regulations. General provisions. Annex or appendix reference. Location of crime. Investigation of violations. Establishment of commission.
INTL ORGS: Allied Military Occupation.
PROCEDURE: Accession. Duration. Termination.
PARTIES:
Australia RATIFIED: 5 Oct 45 FORCE: 5 Oct 45
Belgium RATIFIED: 5 Oct 45 FORCE: 5 Oct 45
Czechoslovakia RATIFIED: 26 Sep 45 FORCE: 26 Sep 45
Denmark RATIFIED: 10 Sep 45 FORCE: 10 Sep 45
Ethiopia RATIFIED: 9 Oct 45 FORCE: 9 Sep 45
France SIGNED: 8 Aug 45 FORCE: 8 Aug 45
Greece RATIFIED: 10 Sep 45 FORCE: 10 Sep 45
Haiti RATIFIED: 3 Nov 45 FORCE: 3 Nov 45
Honduras RATIFIED: 17 Oct 45 FORCE: 17 Oct 45
India RATIFIED: 22 Dec 45 FORCE: 22 Dec 45
Luxembourg RATIFIED: 1 Nov 45 FORCE: 1 Nov 45
Netherlands RATIFIED: 25 Sep 45 FORCE: 25 Sep 45
New Zealand RATIFIED: 19 Nov 45 FORCE: 19 Nov 45
Norway RATIFIED: 20 Oct 45 FORCE: 20 Oct 45
Panama RATIFIED: 17 Oct 45 FORCE: 17 Oct 45
Paraguay RATIFIED: 14 Nov 45 FORCE: 14 Nov 45
Poland RATIFIED: 25 Sep 45 FORCE: 25 Sep 45
UK Great Britain SIGNED: 8 Aug 45 FORCE: 8 Aug 45
USA (United States) SIGNED: 8 Aug 45 FORCE: 8 Aug 45
Uruguay RATIFIED: 11 Dec 45 FORCE: 11 Dec 45
USSR (Soviet Union) SIGNED: 8 Aug 45 FORCE: 8 Aug 45
Venezuela RATIFIED: 17 Nov 45 FORCE: 17 Nov 45
Yugoslavia RATIFIED: 29 Sep 45 FORCE: 29 Sep 45

200252 Multilateral Agreement **84 UNTS 389**
SIGNED: 7 Dec 44 FORCE: 30 Jan 45
REGISTERED: 30 Mar 51 USA (United States)
ARTICLES: 6 LANGUAGE: English.
HEADNOTE: INTERNATIONAL AIR SERVICES TRANSIT
TOPIC: Air Transport
CONCEPTS: Definition of terms. Exceptions and exemptions. Remedies. Use of facilities. Procedure. Negotiation. Fees and exemptions. Routes and logistics. Permit designation. Airport facilities. Conditions of airlines operating permission. Overflights and technical stops. Operating authorizations and regulations. Decisions. Procedure.
INTL ORGS: International Civil Aviation Organization.
TREATY REF: 15UNTS295.
PROCEDURE: Accession. Denunciation.
PARTIES:
Afghanistan SIGNED: 7 Dec 44 RATIFIED: 17 May 45 FORCE: 17 May 45
Argentina RATIFIED: 4 Jun 46 FORCE: 4 Jun 46
Australia SIGNED: 4 Jul 45 RATIFIED: 28 Aug 45 FORCE: 28 Aug 45
Belgium SIGNED: 29 Apr 45 RATIFIED: 19 Jul 45 FORCE: 19 Jul 45
Bolivia SIGNED: 7 Dec 44 RATIFIED: 4 Apr 47 FORCE: 4 Apr 47
Canada SIGNED: 10 Feb 45 RATIFIED: 10 Feb 45 FORCE: 10 Feb 45
Chile SIGNED: 7 Dec 44
Costa Rica SIGNED: 10 Mar 45
Cuba SIGNED: 20 Apr 45 RATIFIED: 20 Jun 47 FORCE: 20 Jun 47
Czechoslovakia SIGNED: 18 Apr 45 RATIFIED: 18 Apr 45 FORCE: 18 Apr 45
Denmark SIGNED: 7 Dec 44 RATIFIED: 1 Dec 48 FORCE: 1 Dec 48
Ecuador SIGNED: 7 Dec 44
United Arab Rep SIGNED: 7 Dec 44 RATIFIED: 13 Mar 47 FORCE: 13 Mar 47
El Salvador SIGNED: 9 May 45 RATIFIED: 1 Jun 45 FORCE: 1 Jun 45
Ethiopia SIGNED: 22 Mar 45 RATIFIED: 22 Mar 45 FORCE: 22 Mar 45
France SIGNED: 7 Dec 44 RATIFIED: 24 Jun 48 FORCE: 24 Jun 48
Greece SIGNED: 7 Dec 44 RATIFIED: 21 Sep 45 FORCE: 21 Sep 45
Guatemala SIGNED: 30 Jan 45 RATIFIED: 28 Apr 47 FORCE: 28 Apr 47
Haiti SIGNED: 7 Dec 44
Honduras SIGNED: 7 Dec 44 RATIFIED: 13 Nov 45 FORCE: 13 Nov 45
Iceland SIGNED: 4 Apr 45 RATIFIED: 21 Mar 47 FORCE: 21 Mar 47
India SIGNED: 7 Dec 44 RATIFIED: 2 May 45 FORCE: 2 May 45
Iran SIGNED: 7 Dec 44 RATIFIED: 19 Apr 50 FORCE: 19 Apr 50
Iraq SIGNED: 7 Dec 44 RATIFIED: 15 Jun 45 FORCE: 15 Jun 45
Jordan RATIFIED: 18 Mar 47 FORCE: 18 Mar 47
Lebanon SIGNED: 7 Dec 44
Liberia SIGNED: 7 Dec 44 RATIFIED: 19 Mar 45 FORCE: 19 Mar 45
Luxembourg SIGNED: 9 Jul 45 RATIFIED: 28 Apr 48 FORCE: 28 Apr 48
Mexico SIGNED: 7 Dec 44 RATIFIED: 25 Jun 46 FORCE: 25 Jun 46
Netherlands SIGNED: 7 Dec 44 RATIFIED: 12 Jan 45 FORCE: 30 Jan 45
New Zealand SIGNED: 7 Dec 44 RATIFIED: 19 Apr 45 FORCE: 19 Apr 45
Nicaragua SIGNED: 7 Dec 44 RATIFIED: 28 Apr 45 FORCE: 28 Apr 45
Norway SIGNED: 30 Jan 45 RATIFIED: 30 Jan 45 FORCE: 30 Jan 45
Pakistan RATIFIED: 15 Aug 47 FORCE: 15 Aug 47
Paraguay SIGNED: 27 Jul 47 RATIFIED: 27 Jul 47 FORCE: 27 Jul 47
Philippines SIGNED: 7 Dec 44 RATIFIED: 22 Mar 46 FORCE: 22 Mar 46
Poland SIGNED: 7 Dec 44 RATIFIED: 6 Apr 45 FORCE: 6 Apr 45
South Africa SIGNED: 4 Jun 45 RATIFIED: 30 Nov 45 FORCE: 30 Nov 45
Spain SIGNED: 7 Dec 44 RATIFIED: 30 Jul 45 FORCE: 30 Jul 45
Sweden SIGNED: 7 Dec 44 RATIFIED: 19 Nov 45 FORCE: 19 Nov 45
Switzerland SIGNED: 6 Jul 45 RATIFIED: 6 Jul 45 FORCE: 6 Jul 45
Syria SIGNED: 6 Jul 45
Thailand SIGNED: 7 Dec 44 RATIFIED: 6 Mar 47 FORCE: 6 Mar 47
Turkey SIGNED: 7 Dec 44 RATIFIED: 6 Jun 45 FORCE: 6 Jun 45
UK Great Britain SIGNED: 7 Dec 44 RATIFIED: 31 May 45 FORCE: 31 May 45
USA (United States) SIGNED: 7 Dec 44 RATIFIED: 8 Feb 45 FORCE: 8 Feb 45
Uruguay SIGNED: 7 Dec 44
Venezuela SIGNED: 7 Dec 44 RATIFIED: 28 Mar 46 FORCE: 28 Mar 46
ANNEX
139 UNTS 469. Guatemala. Denunciation 13 Jun 52. Force 13 Jun 53.
178 UNTS 419. Guatemala. Withdrawal 8 Dec 52.
199 UNTS 363. Japan. Acceptance 20 Oct 53.
260 UNTS 462. Germany, West. Acceptance 9 May 56. Force 8 Jun 56.
260 UNTS 462. Israel. Acceptance 16 Jun 54.
355 UNTS 419. Portugal. Acceptance 1 Sep 59.
355 UNTS 419. Poland. Acceptance 17 Mar 59.
409 UNTS 372. Cameroon. Acceptance 30 Mar 60.
409 UNTS 372. Kuwait. Acceptance 18 May 60.
409 UNTS 372. Senegal. Acceptance 8 Mar 61.
409 UNTS 372. Korea, South. Acceptance 22 Jun 60.
409 UNTS 372. Nigeria. Acceptance 25 Jan 61.
409 UNTS 372. Ivory Coast. Acceptance 20 Mar 61.
409 UNTS 372. Fed of Malaya. Succession 31 Dec 59.
417 UNTS 354. Cyprus. Acceptance 12 Oct 61.
472 UNTS 404. Tunisia. Acceptance 26 Apr 62.
472 UNTS 404. Dahomey. Acceptance 23 Apr 63.
472 UNTS 404. Madagascar. Acceptance 14 Apr 62.
472 UNTS 404. Niger. Succession 16 Mar 62.
472 UNTS 404. Trinidad/Tobago. Acceptance 14 Mar 63.

200253 Bilateral Convention **88 UNTS 365**
SIGNED: 28 Mar 40 FORCE: 9 Nov 48
REGISTERED: 1 May 51 USA (United States)
ARTICLES: 13 LANGUAGE: English.
HEADNOTE: DISPOSITION CLAIMS
TOPIC: Specif Claim/Waive
CONCEPTS: Detailed regulations. Arbitration. Procedure. Existing tribunals. Competence of tribunal. Indemnities and reimbursements. Expense sharing formulae. Claims and settlements. Specific claims or waivers.
PROCEDURE: Ratification.
PARTIES:
Norway
USA (United States)

200254 Bilateral Treaty **88 UNTS 379**
SIGNED: 25 Feb 38 FORCE: 15 Sep 38
REGISTERED: 16 May 51 Brazil
ARTICLES: 14 LANGUAGE: Portuguese. Spanish.
HEADNOTE: RAILWAY COMMUNICATIONS
TOPIC: Land Transport
CONCEPTS: Previous treaty amendment. General cooperation. Use of facilities. Indemnities and reimbursements. Funding procedures. Interest rates. Payment schedules. Tax exemptions. Customs exemptions. Routes and logistics. Ports and pilotage. Railways.

INTL ORGS: Special Commission.
TREATY REF: 3'3DEMARTENS62;.
PROCEDURE: Ratification.
PARTIES:
  Bolivia
  Brazil

200255   Bilateral Agreement   **88 UNTS 401**
SIGNED: 14 Jun 41   FORCE: 2 Aug 41
REGISTERED: 16 May 51 Brazil
ARTICLES: 3 LANGUAGE: Portuguese. Spanish.
HEADNOTE: FRONTIER TRAFFIC
TOPIC: Visas
CONCEPTS: Border traffic and migration. Establishment of trade relations. Markers and definitions.
PROCEDURE: Denunciation. Ratification.
PARTIES:
  Brazil
  Paraguay

200256   Bilateral Exchange   **89 UNTS 273**
SIGNED: 13 May 45   FORCE: 13 May 25
REGISTERED: 1 Jun 51 USA (United States)
ARTICLES: 2 LANGUAGE: English. Spanish.
HEADNOTE: RECIPROCAL WAIVER NON-IMMIGRANT PASSPORT VISA FEES
TOPIC: Visas
CONCEPTS: Definition of terms. Fees and exemptions.
PARTIES:
  Panama
  USA (United States)

200257   Multilateral Exchange   **89 UNTS 279**
SIGNED: 19 Apr 44   FORCE: 19 Apr 44
REGISTERED: 1 Jun 51 USA (United States)
ARTICLES: 2 LANGUAGE: English. Spanish.
HEADNOTE: ANTHROPOLOGICAL RESEARCH
TOPIC: Scientific Project
CONCEPTS: General cooperation. Personnel. Technical and commercial staff. Vocational training. Research and scientific projects. Anthropology and archeology. Research results. Indemnities and reimbursements. Domestic obligation.
PROCEDURE: Duration. Renewal or Revival. Termination.
PARTIES:
  Australia
  Belgium
  Canada
  Taiwan
  Dominican Republic
  Ecuador
  France
  Greece
  Haiti
  Honduras
  India
  Italy
  Luxembourg
  Mexico
  New Zealand
  Nicaragua
  Philippines
  Poland
  South Africa
  Syria
  UK Great Britain
  USA (United States)

200258   Bilateral Exchange   **89 UNTS 291**
SIGNED: 4 Apr 44   FORCE: 4 Aug 44
REGISTERED: 1 Jun 51 USA (United States)
ARTICLES: 2 LANGUAGE: English. Spanish.
HEADNOTE: ANTHROPOLOGICAL RESEARCH
TOPIC: Scientific Project
CONCEPTS: General cooperation. Vocational training. Research and scientific projects. Anthropology and archeology. Research results. Domestic obligation.
PROCEDURE: Future Procedures Contemplated.
PARTIES:
  Peru
  USA (United States)

200259   Bilateral Exchange   **89 UNTS 301**
SIGNED: 29 Oct 42   FORCE: 29 Oct 42

REGISTERED: 3 Jun 51 USA (United States)
ARTICLES: 2 LANGUAGE: English. Spanish.
HEADNOTE: AGRICULTURAL EXPERIMENT STATION
TOPIC: Scientific Project
CONCEPTS: Public information. Technical and commercial staff. Research and scientific projects. Research cooperation. Research results. Research and development. Indemnities and reimbursements. Tax exemptions. Domestic obligation. Agriculture. Materials, equipment and services.
PROCEDURE: Duration. Renewal or Revival. Termination.
PARTIES:
  Ecuador
  USA (United States)

200260   Bilateral Protocol   **89 UNTS 317**
SIGNED: 21 Apr 42   FORCE: 21 Apr 42
REGISTERED: 3 Jun 51 USA (United States)
ARTICLES: 7 LANGUAGE: English.
HEADNOTE: AGRICULTURAL EXPERIMENT STATION
TOPIC: Scientific Project
CONCEPTS: Personnel. Public information. Technical and commercial staff. Wages and salaries. Research and scientific projects. Research cooperation. Research results. Research and development. Indemnities and reimbursements. Tax exemptions. Domestic obligation. Agriculture. Materials, equipment and services.
INTL ORGS: Special Commission.
PARTIES:
  Peru
  USA (United States)

200261   Bilateral Exchange   **89 UNTS 327**
SIGNED: 15 Jun 45   FORCE: 15 Jun 45
REGISTERED: 3 Jun 51 USA (United States)
ARTICLES: 2 LANGUAGE: English.
HEADNOTE: USE DISPOSAL CAPTURED VESSELS
TOPIC: Reparations
CONCEPTS: Annex or appendix reference. Naval vessels. Return of equipment and recapture. Surplus war property.
PARTIES:
  UK Great Britain
  USA (United States)

200262   Bilateral Exchange   **89 UNTS 345**
SIGNED: 2 Dec 44   FORCE: 2 Dec 44
REGISTERED: 5 Jun 51 USA (United States)
ARTICLES: 4 LANGUAGE: English. Spanish.
HEADNOTE: AIR TRANSPORT SERVICES
TOPIC: Air Transport
CONCEPTS: Exceptions and exemptions. Conformity with municipal law. General cooperation. Exchange of information and documents. Licenses and permits. Personnel. Recognition of legal documents. Use of facilities. Investigation of violations. Most favored nation clause. Customs exemptions. Competency certificate. Passenger transport. Routes and logistics. Permit designation. Transport of goods. Air transport. Airport facilities. Airworthiness certificates. Conditions of airlines operating permission. Operating authorizations and regulations.
PROCEDURE: Amendment. Termination. Application to Non-self-governing Territories.
PARTIES:
  Spain
  USA (United States)

200263   Bilateral Agreement   **90 UNTS 257**
SIGNED: 11 Jul 42   FORCE: 11 Jul 42
REGISTERED: 8 Jun 51 USA (United States)
ARTICLES: 8 LANGUAGE: English.
HEADNOTE: MUTUAL AID
TOPIC: Milit Assistance
CONCEPTS: Peaceful relations. Conformity with municipal law. Recognition. Materials, equipment and services. Defense and security. Military assistance. Return of equipment and recapture. Exchange of defense information. Restrictions on transfer.
TREATY REF: 204LTS381.
PROCEDURE: Future Procedures Contemplated.

PARTIES:
  Czechoslovakia
  USA (United States)

200264   Bilateral Exchange   **90 UNTS 267**
SIGNED: 17 Apr 45   FORCE: 17 Apr 45
REGISTERED: 8 Jun 51 USA (United States)
ARTICLES: 2 LANGUAGE: English.
HEADNOTE: ALL FORMS MUTUAL AID FINANCED CASH PAYMENTS
TOPIC: Direct Aid
CONCEPTS: Annex or appendix reference. Responsibility and liability. Payment schedules. Procurement. Defense and security. Military assistance.
PARTIES:
  South Africa
  USA (United States)

200265   Bilateral Exchange   **90 UNTS 275**
SIGNED: 17 Apr 45   FORCE: 17 Apr 45
REGISTERED: 8 Jun 51 USA (United States)
ARTICLES: 2 LANGUAGE: English.
HEADNOTE: POST WAR ECONOMIC SETTLEMENTS
TOPIC: Reparations
CONCEPTS: Economic assistance. Reconversion to normalcy.
TREATY REF: 204LTS381.
PROCEDURE: Future Procedures Contemplated.
PARTIES:
  South Africa
  USA (United States)

200266   Bilateral Exchange   **90 UNTS 283**
SIGNED: 16 May 44   FORCE: 16 May 44
REGISTERED: 12 Jun 51 UK Great Britain
ARTICLES: 2 LANGUAGE: English.
HEADNOTE: CIVIL ADMINISTRATION JURISDICTION BELGIAN TERRITORY LIBERATED ALLIES
TOPIC: Admin Cooperation
CONCEPTS: Annex or appendix reference.
PARTIES:
  Belgium
  UK Great Britain

200267   Bilateral Protocol   **90 UNTS 295**
SIGNED: 22 Aug 44   FORCE: 22 Aug 44
REGISTERED: 12 Jun 51 UK Great Britain
ARTICLES: 14 LANGUAGE: English.
HEADNOTE: MUTUAL AID
TOPIC: Direct Aid
CONCEPTS: Previous treaty replacement. General cooperation. Legal protection and assistance. Indemnities and reimbursements. Exchange rates and regulations. Funding procedures. Local currency. Procurement. Military assistance. Return of equipment and recapture.
TREATY REF: 90UNTS283.
PROCEDURE: Duration. Future Procedures Contemplated.
PARTIES:
  Belgium
  UK Great Britain

200268   Bilateral Exchange   **90 UNTS 307**
SIGNED: 25 Jun 45   FORCE: 25 Jun 45
REGISTERED: 12 Jun 51 UK Great Britain
ARTICLES: 2 LANGUAGE: English. French.
HEADNOTE: CLAIMS AGREEMENT
TOPIC: Reparations
CONCEPTS: Annex or appendix reference. War claims and reparations. Post-war claims settlement.
PARTIES:
  Belgium
  UK Great Britain

200269   Bilateral Agreement   **91 UNTS 341**
SIGNED: 16 Aug 41   FORCE: 16 Aug 41
REGISTERED: 18 Jun 51 UK Great Britain
ARTICLES: 8 LANGUAGE: English. Russian.
HEADNOTE: PAYMENTS
TOPIC: Finance
CONCEPTS: Detailed regulations. General cooperation. General trade. Accounting procedures. Banking. Balance of payments. Currency. Monetary and gold transfers. Exchange rates and regu-

lations. Interest rates. Payment schedules. Non-interest rates and fees. Transportation costs. Debt settlement. Delivery guarantees. Transport of goods.
PARTIES:
UK Great Britain
USSR (Soviet Union)

200270   Bilateral Exchange   **91 UNTS 355**
SIGNED: 22 Jun 42   FORCE: 22 Jun 42
REGISTERED: 18 Jun 51 UK Great Britain
ARTICLES: 2 LANGUAGE: English. Russian.
HEADNOTE: FINANCE
TOPIC: Finance
CONCEPTS: Transportation costs. Transport of goods. Merchant vessels.
PARTIES:
UK Great Britain
USSR (Soviet Union)

200271   Multilateral Treaty   **93 UNTS 279**
SIGNED: 29 Jan 42   FORCE: 29 Jan 42
REGISTERED: 10 Jul 51 UK Great Britain
ARTICLES: 9 LANGUAGE: English. Persian. Russian.
HEADNOTE: TREATY ALLIANCE
TOPIC: General Military
CONCEPTS: Definition of terms. Treaty implementation. Annex or appendix reference. Peaceful relations. General cooperation. Use of facilities. Joint defense. Defense and security. Military assistance. Status of military forces. Withdrawal of forces. Status of forces.
PROCEDURE: Future Procedures Contemplated.
PARTIES:
Iran SIGNED: 29 Jan 42 FORCE: 29 Jan 42
UK Great Britain SIGNED: 29 Jan 42 FORCE: 29 Jan 42
USSR (Soviet Union) SIGNED: 29 Jan 42 FORCE: 29 Jan 42

200272   Bilateral Agreement   **93 UNTS 303**
SIGNED: 19 Dec 44   FORCE: 19 Dec 44
REGISTERED: 11 Jul 51 UK Great Britain
ARTICLES: 13 LANGUAGE: Amharic. English.
HEADNOTE: REGULATION MUTUAL RELATIONS
TOPIC: General Amity
CONCEPTS: Diplomatic relations establishment. Provisional detainment. Standardization. Free passage and transit. Competence of tribunal. Air transport. Railways. Advice lists and orders. General military. Defense and security. Military assistance. Withdrawal of forces.
INTL ORGS: United Nations.
TREATY REF: AGREEMENT&MILITARY CONVENTION 31JAN42.
PROCEDURE: Duration. Termination.
PARTIES:
Ethiopia
UK Great Britain

200273   Multilateral Agreement   **97 UNTS 291**
SIGNED: 27 Jul 51   FORCE: 27 Jul 51
REGISTERED: 27 Jul 51 United Nations
ARTICLES: 5 LANGUAGE: English. French.
HEADNOTE: TECHNICAL ASSISTANCE TRUST TERRITORY
TOPIC: Tech Assistance
CONCEPTS: Detailed regulations. Treaty implementation. Annex or appendix reference. Privileges and immunities. General cooperation. Title and deeds. Professorships. Vocational training. Expense sharing formulae. Local currency. Domestic obligation. General technical assistance. Materials, equipment and services. IGO status. Conformity with IGO decisions. Trusteeship.
INTL ORGS: United Nations.
TREATY REF: 76UNTS132; 1UNTS15,263; 33UNTS261.
PROCEDURE: Amendment. Termination.
PARTIES:
Italy SIGNED: 27 Jul 51 FORCE: 27 Jul 51
FAO (Food Agri) SIGNED: 27 Jul 51 FORCE: 27 Jul 51
ICAO (Civil Aviat) SIGNED: 27 Jul 51 FORCE: 27 Jul 51
ILO (Labor Org) SIGNED: 27 Jul 51 FORCE: 27 Jul 51
UNESCO (Educ/Cult) SIGNED: 27 Jul 51 FORCE: 27 Jul 51

United Nations SIGNED: 27 Jul 51 FORCE: 27 Jul 51
WHO (World Health) SIGNED: 27 Jul 51 FORCE: 27 Jul 51

200274   Bilateral Agreement   **98 UNTS 227**
SIGNED: 27 Mar 45   FORCE: 1 Mar 45
REGISTERED: 15 Aug 51 UK Great Britain
ARTICLES: 8 LANGUAGE: English. French.
HEADNOTE: FINANCE
TOPIC: Finance
CONCEPTS: Detailed regulations. General provisions. Annex or appendix reference. Previous treaty replacement. General cooperation. Exchange of information and documents. Accounting procedures. Banking. Balance of payments. Currency. Monetary and gold transfers. Exchange rates and regulations. Interest rates. Payment schedules. Claims and settlements. Debt settlement. Assistance. Loan and credit. Purchase authorization. Loan repayment. Mutual consultation. Transport of goods. Surplus war property. War claims and reparations.
TREATY REF: FINANCIAL AGREEMENTS 12DEC39 AND 8FEB44.
PROCEDURE: Duration. Duration. Future Procedures Contemplated.
PARTIES:
France
UK Great Britain

200275   Bilateral Agreement   **98 UNTS 249**
SIGNED: 31 Aug 45   FORCE: 31 Aug 45
REGISTERED: 15 Aug 51 UK Great Britain
ARTICLES: 11 LANGUAGE: English. French.
HEADNOTE: INTERNATIONAL ADMINISTRATION OF TANGIER
TOPIC: IGO Establishment
CONCEPTS: Annex type material. Previous treaty extension. Re-establishment. Funding procedures. Military assistance. Conditions for assistance missions. Withdrawal of forces. Withdrawal of occupation. Establishment. Internal structure.
INTL ORGS: Committee of Control of the International Zone of Tangier.
TREATY REF: MOROCCO NO.1 (1945) CMD.6678.
PROCEDURE: Ratification.
PARTIES:
France
UK Great Britain

200276   Bilateral Exchange   **99 UNTS 223**
SIGNED: 27 Jun 42   FORCE: 29 Jun 42
REGISTERED: 21 Aug 51 USA (United States)
ARTICLES: 2 LANGUAGE: English.
HEADNOTE: EXTENDING FUEL SUPPLY
TOPIC: Other Military
CONCEPTS: Private contracts. Use of facilities. Tax exemptions. Materials, equipment and services. Natural resources. General military.
INTL ORGS: United States-Canadian Defense Organization.
PARTIES:
Canada
USA (United States)

200277   Bilateral Exchange   **99 UNTS 233**
SIGNED: 15 Aug 42   FORCE: 15 Aug 42
REGISTERED: 21 Aug 51 USA (United States)
ARTICLES: 2 LANGUAGE: English.
HEADNOTE: ESTABLISHMENT OIL SUPPLY LINE
TOPIC: Other Military
CONCEPTS: Annex type material. Private contracts. Use of facilities. Natural resources. General military.
INTL ORGS: United States-Canadian Defense Organization.
TREATY REF: 99UNTS223.
PARTIES:
Canada
USA (United States)

200278   Bilateral Exchange   **99 UNTS 241**
SIGNED: 28 Dec 42   FORCE: 13 Jan 43
REGISTERED: 21 Aug 51 USA (United States)
ARTICLES: 2 LANGUAGE: English.
HEADNOTE: DRILLING EXPLORATORY OIL WELLS
TOPIC: Other Military
CONCEPTS: Annex type material. Exchange of in-

formation and documents. Natural resources. General military.
TREATY REF: 99UNTS223.
PARTIES:
Canada
USA (United States)

200279   Bilateral Exchange   **99 UNTS 249**
SIGNED: 13 Mar 43   FORCE: 13 Mar 43
REGISTERED: 21 Aug 51 USA (United States)
ARTICLES: 3 LANGUAGE: English.
HEADNOTE: DRILLING EXPLORATORY OIL WELLS
TOPIC: Other Military
CONCEPTS: Annex type material. Natural resources. General military.
TREATY REF: 99UNTS223.
PARTIES:
Canada
USA (United States)

200280   Bilateral Exchange   **99 UNTS 259**
SIGNED: 7 Jun 44   FORCE: 7 Jun 44
REGISTERED: 21 Aug 51 USA (United States)
ARTICLES: 2 LANGUAGE: English.
HEADNOTE: REVISIONS CANAL PROJECT
TOPIC: Specific Property
CONCEPTS: General property. Use of facilities. Surplus property. Facilities and property.
TREATY REF: 99UNTS223.
PARTIES:
Canada
USA (United States)

200281   Bilateral Exchange   **99 UNTS 273**
SIGNED: 26 Feb 45   FORCE: 26 Feb 45
REGISTERED: 21 Aug 51 USA (United States)
ARTICLES: 2 LANGUAGE: English.
HEADNOTE: VALUATION FACILITIES
TOPIC: Other Military
CONCEPTS: Use of facilities. Natural resources. General military.
TREATY REF: 99UNTS223.
PROCEDURE: Future Procedures Contemplated.
PARTIES:
Canada
USA (United States)

200282   Bilateral Exchange   **99 UNTS 281**
SIGNED: 6 Sep 45   FORCE: 6 Sep 45
REGISTERED: 21 Aug 51 USA (United States)
ARTICLES: 2 LANGUAGE: English.
HEADNOTE: RIGHTS RESPECT CRUDE OIL FACILITIES
TOPIC: Other Military
CONCEPTS: General property. Use of facilities. Natural resources. General military.
TREATY REF: 99UNTS223.
PARTIES:
Canada
USA (United States)

200283   Bilateral Exchange   **99 UNTS 287**
SIGNED: 27 Oct 42   FORCE: 27 Oct 42
REGISTERED: 21 Aug 51 USA (United States)
ARTICLES: 2 LANGUAGE: English.
HEADNOTE: AGRICULTURAL EXPERIMENT STATION
TOPIC: Scientific Project
CONCEPTS: Personnel. Use of facilities. Wages and salaries. Research and scientific projects. Research results. Research and development. Expense sharing formulae. Death duties. Domestic obligation. Agriculture. Special projects. Materials, equipment and services.
INTL ORGS: Special Commission.
PROCEDURE: Duration. Termination.
PARTIES:
Nicaragua
USA (United States)

200284   Bilateral Convention   **99 UNTS 301**
SIGNED: 29 May 39   FORCE: 3 Nov 49
REGISTERED: 23 Aug 51 UK Great Britain
ARTICLES: 5 LANGUAGE: English. French.
HEADNOTE: EXCHANGE OFFICIAL PUBLICATIONS
TOPIC: Extradition
CONCEPTS: Exchange of official publications. Op-

erating agencies. Indemnities and reimbursements.
TREATY REF: 69LTS127; 117LTS335.
PARTIES:
Luxembourg
UK Great Britain

200285   Bilateral Agreement   **100 UNTS 223**
SIGNED: 26 Jun 51   FORCE: 26 Jun 51
REGISTERED: 23 Aug 51 ILO (Labor Org)
ARTICLES: 5 LANGUAGE: French.
HEADNOTE: TECHNICAL ASSISTANCE
TOPIC: Tech Assistance
CONCEPTS: Treaty implementation. Privileges and immunities. General cooperation. Exchange of information and documents. Personnel. Title and deeds. Arbitration. Procedure. Scholarships and grants. Vocational training. Exchange rates and regulations. Expense sharing formulae. Local currency. Domestic obligation. General technical assistance. Materials, equipment and services. IGO status. Conformity with IGO decisions.
INTL ORGS: United Nations.
TREATY REF: 76UNTS132; 33UNTS261.
PROCEDURE: Amendment. Termination.
PARTIES:
ILO (Labor Org)
Vietnam, South

200286   Bilateral Agreement   **100 UNTS 235**
SIGNED: 6 Apr 51   FORCE: 6 Apr 51
REGISTERED: 30 Aug 51 ILO (Labor Org)
ARTICLES: 5 LANGUAGE: English.
HEADNOTE: TECHNICAL ASSISTANCE
TOPIC: Tech Assistance
CONCEPTS: Treaty implementation. Privileges and immunities. General cooperation. Exchange of information and documents. Personnel. Title and deeds. Arbitration. Procedure. Scholarships and grants. Vocational training. Exchange rates and regulations. Expense sharing formulae. Local currency. Domestic obligation. General technical assistance. Materials, equipment and services. IGO status. Conformity with IGO decisions.
INTL ORGS: United Nations.
TREATY REF: 76UNTS132; 33UNTS261.
PROCEDURE: Amendment. Termination.
PARTIES:
Ceylon (Sri Lanka)
ILO (Labor Org)

200287   Bilateral Agreement   **100 UNTS 247**
SIGNED: 29 Mar 51   FORCE: 26 Mar 51
REGISTERED: 30 Aug 51 ILO (Labor Org)
ARTICLES: 5 LANGUAGE: English.
HEADNOTE: TECHNICAL ASSISTANCE
TOPIC: Tech Assistance
CONCEPTS: Treaty implementation. Privileges and immunities. General cooperation. Exchange of information and documents. Personnel. Title and deeds. Arbitration. Procedure. Scholarships and grants. Vocational training. Exchange rates and regulations. Expense sharing formulae. Local currency. Domestic obligation. General technical assistance. Materials, equipment and services. IGO status. Conformity with IGO decisions.
INTL ORGS: United Nations.
TREATY REF: 76UNTS132; 33UNTS261.
PROCEDURE: Amendment. Termination.
PARTIES:
Jordan
ILO (Labor Org)

200288   Bilateral Exchange   **100 UNTS 259**
SIGNED: 20 May 43   FORCE: 20 May 43
REGISTERED: 7 Sep 51 USA (United States)
ARTICLES: 13 LANGUAGE: English. Spanish.
HEADNOTE: FOOD PRODUCTION SERVICE
TOPIC: Non-IBRD Project
CONCEPTS: Previous treaty amendment. Personnel. Establishment of commission. Wages and salaries. Financial programs. Assets transfer. Customs duties. Plans and standards.
PARTIES:
Peru
USA (United States)

200289   Bilateral Exchange   **101 UNTS 125**
SIGNED: 5 Jun 41   FORCE: 5 Jun 41

REGISTERED: 13 Sep 51 USA (United States)
ARTICLES: 2 LANGUAGE: English. French.
HEADNOTE: EXCHANGE OFFICIAL PUBLICATIONS
TOPIC: Admin Cooperation
CONCEPTS: Exchange of official publications. Operating agencies. Indemnities and reimbursements.
PARTIES:
Haiti
USA (United States)

200290   Bilateral Exchange   **101 UNTS 137**
SIGNED: 31 Jan 42   FORCE: 31 Jan 42
REGISTERED: 13 Sep 51 USA (United States)
ARTICLES: 2 LANGUAGE: English. Spanish.
HEADNOTE: EXCHANGE OFFICIAL PUBLICATIONS
TOPIC: Admin Cooperation
CONCEPTS: Exchange of official publications. Operating agencies. Indemnities and reimbursements.
PARTIES:
Bolivia
USA (United States)

200291   Bilateral Exchange   **101 UNTS 157**
SIGNED: 7 Mar 42   FORCE: 7 Mar 42
REGISTERED: 13 Sep 51 USA (United States)
ARTICLES: 2 LANGUAGE: English. Spanish.
HEADNOTE: EXCHANGE OFFICIAL PUBLICATIONS
TOPIC: Admin Cooperation
CONCEPTS: Exchange of official publications. Operating agencies. Indemnities and reimbursements.
PARTIES:
Panama
USA (United States)

200292   Bilateral Exchange   **101 UNTS 173**
SIGNED: 28 Nov 42   FORCE: 28 Nov 42
REGISTERED: 13 Sep 51 USA (United States)
ARTICLES: 2 LANGUAGE: English. Spanish.
HEADNOTE: EXCHANGE OFFICIAL PUBLICATIONS
TOPIC: Admin Cooperation
CONCEPTS: Exchange of official publications. Operating agencies. Indemnities and reimbursements.
PARTIES:
Paraguay
USA (United States)

200293   Bilateral Exchange   **101 UNTS 189**
SIGNED: 21 Aug 43   FORCE: 21 Aug 43
REGISTERED: 13 Sep 51 USA (United States)
ARTICLES: 2 LANGUAGE: English. Persian.
HEADNOTE: EXCHANGE OFFICIAL PUBLICATIONS
TOPIC: Admin Cooperation
CONCEPTS: Exchange of official publications. Operating agencies. Indemnities and reimbursements.
PARTIES:
Iran
USA (United States)

200294   Bilateral Exchange   **101 UNTS 205**
SIGNED: 18 Mar 42   FORCE: 18 Mar 42
REGISTERED: 13 Sep 51 USA (United States)
ARTICLES: 2 LANGUAGE: English.
HEADNOTE: CONSTRUCTION MAINTENANCE HIGHWAY ALASKA
TOPIC: Land Transport
CONCEPTS: Time limit. Treaty implementation. Border traffic and migration. Repatriation of nationals. Private contracts. Responsibility and liability. Title and deeds. Fees and exemptions. Tax exemptions. Customs exemptions. Routes and logistics. Airport facilities. Roads and highways. Military installations and equipment.
INTL ORGS: United States-Canadian Defense Organization.
PARTIES:
Canada
USA (United States)

200295   Bilateral Exchange   **101 UNTS 215**
SIGNED: 9 May 42   FORCE: 9 May 42
REGISTERED: 13 Sep 51 USA (United States)
ARTICLES: 2 LANGUAGE: English.
HEADNOTE: SOUTHERN TERMINUS ALASKA HIGHWAY
TOPIC: Land Transport
CONCEPTS: Annex type material. Roads and highways.
INTL ORGS: United States-Canadian Defense Organization.
TREATY REF: 101UNTS205.
PARTIES:
Canada
USA (United States)

200296   Bilateral Exchange   **101 UNTS 221**
SIGNED: 10 Sep 42   FORCE: 10 Sep 42
REGISTERED: 13 Sep 51 USA (United States)
ARTICLES: 2 LANGUAGE: English.
HEADNOTE: FLIGHT STRIPS ALONG ALASKA HIGHWAY
TOPIC: Land Transport
CONCEPTS: Annex type material. Air transport. Roads and highways.
TREATY REF: 101UNTS205.
PARTIES:
Canada
USA (United States)

200297   Bilateral Exchange   **101 UNTS 227**
SIGNED: 7 Dec 42   FORCE: 7 Dec 42
REGISTERED: 13 Sep 51 USA (United States)
ARTICLES: 2 LANGUAGE: English.
HEADNOTE: HAINES-CHAMPAGNE SECTION ALASKA HIGHWAY
TOPIC: Land Transport
CONCEPTS: Annex type material. Routes and logistics. Roads and highways. Military installations and equipment.
TREATY REF: 101UNTS205.
PARTIES:
Canada
USA (United States)

200298   Bilateral Exchange   **101 UNTS 233**
SIGNED: 9 Nov 42   FORCE: 9 Nov 42
REGISTERED: 13 Sep 51 USA (United States)
ARTICLES: 3 LANGUAGE: English.
HEADNOTE: IMPORTATION PRIVILEGES
TOPIC: General Trade
CONCEPTS: Export quotas. Customs duties. Customs exemptions. Temporary importation.
PARTIES:
Canada
USA (United States)

200299   Bilateral Exchange   **101 UNTS 243**
SIGNED: 23 Feb 43   FORCE: 23 Feb 43
REGISTERED: 13 Sep 51 USA (United States)
ARTICLES: 2 LANGUAGE: English.
HEADNOTE: OPERATION MAINTENANCE WHITE PASS YUKON RAILWAY
TOPIC: Land Transport
CONCEPTS: Time limit. Treaty implementation. Conformity with municipal law. Exchange of information and documents. Personnel. Accounting procedures. General. Railways.
PARTIES:
Canada
USA (United States)

200300   Bilateral Exchange   **101 UNTS 257**
SIGNED: 27 Jan 43   FORCE: 27 Jan 43
REGISTERED: 13 Sep 51 USA (United States)
ARTICLES: 4 LANGUAGE: English.
HEADNOTE: POST-WAR DISPOSITION DEFENSE INSTALLATIONS FACILITIES
TOPIC: Milit Installation
CONCEPTS: Annex or appendix reference. Surplus war property. Bases and facilities.
INTL ORGS: United States-Canadian Defense Organization.
PARTIES:
Canada
USA (United States)

200301 Bilateral Exchange **101 UNTS 273**
SIGNED: 27 Jun 44 FORCE: 27 Jun 44
REGISTERED: 13 Sep 51 USA (United States)
ARTICLES: 2 LANGUAGE: English.
HEADNOTE: PAYMENT DEFENSE INSTALLA-
TIONS
TOPIC: Milit Installation
CONCEPTS: Military installations and equipment.
Bases and facilities.
INTL ORGS: United States-Canadian Defense Or-
ganization.
PARTIES:
Canada
USA (United States)

200302 Bilateral Exchange **102 UNTS 195**
SIGNED: 14 Mar 42 FORCE: 14 Mar 42
REGISTERED: 16 Sep 51 USA (United States)
ARTICLES: 2 LANGUAGE: English.
HEADNOTE: HEALTH SANITATION PROGRAM
TOPIC: Sanitation
CONCEPTS: General property. Programs. Special-
ists exchange. Disease control. Public health.
Sanitation. Research and development. Expense
sharing formulae. Financial programs. Specific
technical assistance. Grants.
TREATY REF: USA'EAS 371 3MAR42;.
PARTIES:
Brazil
USA (United States)

200303 Bilateral Agreement **102 UNTS 203**
SIGNED: 17 Jul 42 FORCE: 8 Sep 42
REGISTERED: 16 Sep 51 USA (United States)
ARTICLES: 12 LANGUAGE: English. Portuguese.
HEADNOTE: HEALTH SANITATION PROGRAM
TOPIC: Sanitation
CONCEPTS: Annex type material. Personnel. Pro-
grams. Disease control. Public health. Sanita-
tion. Research and development. Accounting
procedures. Fees and exemptions. Tax exemp-
tions. Specific technical assistance. Credit provi-
sions. Subsidiary organ.
TREATY REF: 102UNTS195.
PROCEDURE: Duration.
PARTIES:
Brazil
USA (United States)

200304 Bilateral Instrument **102 UNTS 217**
SIGNED: 10 Feb 43 FORCE: 10 Feb 43
REGISTERED: 16 Sep 51 USA (United States)
ARTICLES: 4 LANGUAGE: English. Portuguese.
HEADNOTE: HEALTH SANITATION PROGRAM
TOPIC: Sanitation
CONCEPTS: Annex type material. Previous treaty
extension. Programs. Disease control. Public
health. Sanitation. Expense sharing formulae. Fi-
nancial programs. Funding procedures. Special
projects.
TREATY REF: 102UNTS203.
PROCEDURE: Renewal or Revival.
PARTIES:
Brazil
USA (United States)

200305 Bilateral Agreement **102 UNTS 227**
SIGNED: 25 Nov 43 FORCE: 25 Nov 43
REGISTERED: 16 Sep 51 USA (United States)
ARTICLES: 21 LANGUAGE: English. Portuguese.
HEADNOTE: HEALTH SANITATION PROGRAM
TOPIC: Sanitation
CONCEPTS: Previous treaty extension. Domestic
legislation. Personnel. General property. Pro-
grams. Public health. Sanitation. Research and
development. Accounting procedures. Balance
of payments. Expense sharing formulae. Fees
and exemptions. Tax exemptions. Customs ex-
emptions. Specific technical assistance.
PROCEDURE: Duration.
PARTIES:
Brazil
USA (United States)

200306 Bilateral Exchange **102 UNTS 269**
SIGNED: 2 Aug 41 FORCE: 6 Aug 41
REGISTERED: 20 Sep 51 USA (United States)
ARTICLES: 4 LANGUAGE: English.
HEADNOTE: COMMERCE

TOPIC: General Trade
CONCEPTS: Previous treaty extension.
TREATY REF: 182LTS.
PROCEDURE: Duration.
PARTIES:
USA (United States)
USSR (Soviet Union)
ANNEX
139 UNTS 470. USA (United States). Force
23 Dec 51.
139 UNTS 470. USSR (Soviet Union). Force
23 Dec 51.

200307 Bilateral Agreement **102 UNTS 279**
SIGNED: 31 May 51 FORCE: 31 May 51
REGISTERED: 20 Sep 51 WHO (World Health)
ARTICLES: 14 LANGUAGE: English. French.
HEADNOTE: TECHNICAL ADVISORY ASSISTANCE
OTHER SERVICES
TOPIC: Tech Assistance
CONCEPTS: Change of circumstances. Exceptions
and reservations. Treaty implementation. Annex
or appendix reference. Privileges and immuni-
ties. General cooperation. Exchange of informa-
tion and documents. Personnel. Arbitration. Pro-
cedure. Negotiation. Competence of tribunal. Fi-
nancial programs. Claims and settlements. Tax
exemptions. Customs exemptions. Domestic ob-
ligation. General technical assistance. Special
projects. Materials, equipment and services. IGO
status.
INTL ORGS: International Court of Justice.
TREATY REF: 33UNTS261.
PROCEDURE: Amendment. Termination.
PARTIES:
Cambodia
WHO (World Health)

200308 Multilateral Agreement **102 UNTS 291**
SIGNED: 18 Jul 51 FORCE: 18 Jul 51
REGISTERED: 20 Sep 51 WHO (World Health)
ARTICLES: 7 LANGUAGE: English.
HEADNOTE: SOUTHEAST ASIA TRAINING CEN-
TER
TOPIC: Direct Aid
CONCEPTS: Time limit. Informational records. Per-
sonnel. Exchange. Institute establishment. Do-
mestic obligation. General technical assistance.
Materials, equipment and services. Internal
structure.
INTL ORGS: United Nations.
PARTIES:
Ceylon (Sri Lanka) SIGNED: 26 Jun 51 FORCE:
18 Jul 51
United Nations SIGNED: 18 Jul 51 FORCE:
18 Jul 51
WHO (World Health) SIGNED: 2 Jul 51 FORCE:
18 Jul 51

200309 Bilateral Agreement **102 UNTS 309**
SIGNED: 17 Feb 50 FORCE: 17 Feb 50
REGISTERED: 20 Sep 51 WHO (World Health)
ARTICLES: 11 LANGUAGE: English.
HEADNOTE: SERVICES
TOPIC: Direct Aid
CONCEPTS: Treaty implementation. Privileges and
immunities. Personnel. Use of facilities. Arbitra-
tion. Procedure. Negotiation. Indemnities and re-
imbursements. Currency deposits. Expense shar-
ing formulae. Tax exemptions. Customs exemp-
tions. General technical assistance. Materials,
equipment and services. IGO status. Conformity
with IGO decisions.
TREATY REF: 14UNTS185; 33UNTS261.
PROCEDURE: Amendment. Termination.
PARTIES:
Ceylon (Sri Lanka)
WHO (World Health)

200310 Bilateral Agreement **103 UNTS 129**
SIGNED: 23 Sep 50 FORCE: 29 Sep 50
REGISTERED: 20 Sep 51 WHO (World Health)
ARTICLES: 5 LANGUAGE: English.
HEADNOTE: MEDICAL PROGRAM PALESTINE REF-
UGEES
TOPIC: Sanitation
CONCEPTS: Definition of terms. Personnel. Pro-
grams. Public health. WHO used as agency. Ex-
pense sharing formulae. Financial programs.

Funding procedures. Materials, equipment and
services. General transportation.
INTL ORGS: United Nations.
PROCEDURE: Duration.
PARTIES:
UN Relief Palestin
WHO (World Health)
ANNEX
134 UNTS 396. UN Relief Palestin. Prolongation
23 Jun 52. Force 23 Jun 52.
134 UNTS 396. WHO (World Health). Prolongation 30 Jun 52. Force 30 Jun 52.
219 UNTS 387. WHO (World Health). Prolongation 10 Aug 55. Force 23 Aug 55.
219 UNTS 387. UNRRA (Relief). Prolongation
23 Aug 55. Force 23 Aug 55.

200311 Bilateral Agreement **103 UNTS 141**
SIGNED: 13 Sep 41 FORCE: 13 Sep 41
REGISTERED: 20 Sep 51 USA (United States)
ARTICLES: 11 LANGUAGE: English. French.
HEADNOTE: HAITIAN FINANCES
TOPIC: Other Ad Hoc
CONCEPTS: Previous treaty replacement. Operat-
ing agencies. Arbitration. Negotiation. Account-
ing procedures. Banking. Currency deposits.
Debts. Control of internal finance.
TREATY REF: 146LTS305.
PROCEDURE: Termination.
PARTIES:
Haiti
USA (United States)

200312 Bilateral Exchange **103 UNTS 163**
SIGNED: 28 Mar 41 FORCE: 28 Mar 41
REGISTERED: 20 Sep 51 USA (United States)
ARTICLES: 3 LANGUAGE: English. Spanish.
HEADNOTE: DOUBLE INCOME TAX SHIPPING
PROFITS
TOPIC: Taxation
CONCEPTS: Conformity with municipal law. Do-
mestic legislation. Taxation. Tax exemptions.
Merchant vessels.
PARTIES:
Panama
USA (United States)

200313 Bilateral Exchange **103 UNTS 173**
SIGNED: 18 Jun 41 FORCE: 16 Jun 41
REGISTERED: 20 Sep 51 USA (United States)
ARTICLES: 2 LANGUAGE: English. Spanish.
HEADNOTE: COOPERATIVE RUBBER INVESTIGA-
TIONS
TOPIC: Specific Resources
CONCEPTS: Research cooperation. Funding pro-
cedures. Materials, equipment and services.
Plans and standards. Raw materials.
PROCEDURE: Duration. Termination.
PARTIES:
Costa Rica
USA (United States)

200314 Bilateral Exchange **103 UNTS 193**
SIGNED: 27 Nov 41 FORCE: 27 Nov 41
REGISTERED: 20 Sep 51 USA (United States)
ARTICLES: 4 LANGUAGE: English.
HEADNOTE: TEMPORARY DIVERSION WATERS
TOPIC: Specific Resources
CONCEPTS: Domestic legislation. Hydro-electric
power. Regulation of natural resources.
INTL ORGS: Special Commission.
TREATY REF: 204LTS199; 203LTS267.
PARTIES:
Canada
USA (United States)

200315 Bilateral Exchange **103 UNTS 205**
SIGNED: 27 Jun 41 FORCE: 17 Jun 41
REGISTERED: 20 Sep 51 USA (United States)
ARTICLES: 3 LANGUAGE: English.
HEADNOTE: ECONOMIC COOPERATION
TOPIC: IGO Establishment
CONCEPTS: Exchange of information and docu-
ments. Economic assistance. Equipment and
supplies. Establishment.
INTL ORGS: Special Commission.
PARTIES:
Canada
USA (United States)

200316 Bilateral Agreement **103 UNTS 219**
SIGNED: 7 May 42 FORCE: 29 Jul 42
REGISTERED: 20 Sep 51 USA (United States)
ARTICLES: 16 LANGUAGE: English. Spanish.
HEADNOTE: TRADE
TOPIC: General Trade
CONCEPTS: Detailed regulations. Exceptions and exemptions. Territorial application. Annex or appendix reference. General cooperation. Exchange of information and documents. Public information. Private contracts. Procedure. Export quotas. Import quotas. Reciprocity in trade. Trade agencies. Trade procedures. Payment schedules. Quotas. Most favored nation clause. General. Customs duties. Customs exemptions. Temporary importation. Materials, equipment and services.
PROCEDURE: Duration. Termination.
PARTIES:
 Peru
 USA (United States)

200317 Bilateral Agreement **103 UNTS 267**
SIGNED: 1 Jul 42 FORCE: 1 Jul 42
REGISTERED: 20 Sep 51 USA (United States)
ARTICLES: 8 LANGUAGE: English.
HEADNOTE: MUTUAL AID
TOPIC: Milit Assistance
CONCEPTS: Peaceful relations. Conformity with municipal law. Recognition. Materials, equipment and services. Defense and security. Military assistance. Return of equipment and recapture. Exchange of defense information. Restrictions on transfer.
TREATY REF: 204LTS381.
PROCEDURE: Future Procedures Contemplated.
PARTIES:
 Poland
 USA (United States)

200318 Bilateral Agreement **103 UNTS 277**
SIGNED: 8 Jul 42 FORCE: 8 Jul 42
REGISTERED: 20 Sep 51 USA (United States)
ARTICLES: 8 LANGUAGE: English.
HEADNOTE: MUTUAL AID
TOPIC: Milit Assistance
CONCEPTS: Previous treaty replacement. Peaceful relations. Conformity with municipal law. Recognition. Materials, equipment and services. Defense and security. Military assistance. Return of equipment and recapture. Exchange of defense information. Restrictions on transfer.
TREATY REF: 204LTS381.
PROCEDURE: Future Procedures Contemplated.
PARTIES:
 Netherlands
 USA (United States)

200319 Bilateral Agreement **103 UNTS 289**
SIGNED: 10 Jul 42 FORCE: 10 Jul 42
REGISTERED: 20 Sep 51 USA (United States)
ARTICLES: 8 LANGUAGE: English.
HEADNOTE: MUTUAL AID
TOPIC: Milit Assistance
CONCEPTS: Peaceful relations. Conformity with municipal law. Recognition. Materials, equipment and services. Defense and security. Military assistance. Return of equipment and recapture. Exchange of defense information. Restrictions on transfer.
TREATY REF: 204LTS381.
PARTIES:
 Greece
 USA (United States)

200320 Bilateral Exchange **103 UNTS 299**
SIGNED: 21 Jul 42 FORCE: 21 Jul 42
REGISTERED: 20 Sep 51 USA (United States)
ARTICLES: 3 LANGUAGE: English.
HEADNOTE: EXTENDING AGREEMENT US ARMY OFFICER
TOPIC: Military Mission
CONCEPTS: Annex type material. Previous treaty extension. Military assistance missions.
PARTIES:
 Guatemala
 USA (United States)

200321 Bilateral Exchange **103 UNTS 307**
SIGNED: 15 Apr 41 FORCE: 15 Apr 42
REGISTERED: 20 Sep 51 USA (United States)
ARTICLES: 2 LANGUAGE: English. Spanish.
HEADNOTE: WAIVER NON-IMMIGRANT PASSPORT VISA FEES
TOPIC: Visas
CONCEPTS: Passports non-diplomatic. Visas.
PARTIES:
 Argentina
 USA (United States)

200322 Bilateral Exchange **104 UNTS 323**
SIGNED: 21 Sep 51 FORCE: 21 Sep 51
REGISTERED: 21 Sep 51 United Nations
ARTICLES: 2 LANGUAGE: English.
HEADNOTE: PRIVILEGES & IMMUNITIES
TOPIC: IGO Status/Immunit
CONCEPTS: Non-visa travel documents. Diplomatic privileges. Privileges and immunities. Property. Diplomatic correspondence. Juridical personality. Procedure. Existing tribunals. Regional offices. IGO status. Status of experts. Inviolability.
TREATY REF: 1UNTS15.
PARTIES:
 Korea, South
 United Nations

200323 Bilateral Exchange **104 UNTS 335**
SIGNED: 10 Oct 45 FORCE: 10 Oct 45
REGISTERED: 4 Oct 51 Norway
ARTICLES: 2 LANGUAGE: Danish. Norwegian.
HEADNOTE: ABOLITION OF VISAS
TOPIC: Visas
CONCEPTS: Visa abolition. Denial of admission. Frontier permits.
PROCEDURE: Duration. Renewal or Revival.
PARTIES:
 Denmark
 Norway

200324 Bilateral Exchange **105 UNTS 91**
SIGNED: 3 Mar 42 FORCE: 3 Mar 42
REGISTERED: 9 Oct 51 USA (United States)
ARTICLES: 2 LANGUAGE: English. Portuguese.
HEADNOTE: ECONOMIC COOPERATION INCREASE RUBBER PRODUCTION
TOPIC: Tech Assistance
CONCEPTS: Treaty implementation. Sanitation. Export quotas. Funding procedures. Special projects. Economic assistance. Raw materials.
TREATY REF: 105UNTS99.
PARTIES:
 Brazil
 USA (United States)

200325 Bilateral Exchange **105 UNTS 99**
SIGNED: 3 Mar 42 FORCE: 3 Mar 42
REGISTERED: 9 Oct 51 USA (United States)
ARTICLES: 2 LANGUAGE: English. Portuguese.
HEADNOTE: ECONOMIC COOPERATION MOBILIZATION PRODUCTIVE RESOURCES
TOPIC: Tech Assistance
CONCEPTS: Conditions. General cooperation. Personnel. Financial programs. General technical assistance. Economic assistance. Materials, equipment and services. Loan and credit. Raw materials.
PARTIES:
 Brazil
 USA (United States)

200326 Bilateral Exchange **105 UNTS 109**
SIGNED: 23 Oct 42 FORCE: 23 Oct 42
REGISTERED: 9 Oct 51 USA (United States)
ARTICLES: 2 LANGUAGE: English. Spanish.
HEADNOTE: HEALTH AND SANITATION PROGRAM
TOPIC: Sanitation
CONCEPTS: Personnel. General property. Programs. Specialists exchange. Disease control. Public health. Sanitation. Vocational training. Research and development. Specific technical assistance. Technical cooperation. Materials, equipment and services. Grants.
PARTIES:
 Colombia
 USA (United States)

ANNEX
166 UNTS 382. USA (United States). Prolongation 24 Jan 44. Force 12 Feb 44.
166 UNTS 382. Colombia. Prolongation 12 Feb 44. Force 12 Feb 44.

200327 Bilateral Exchange **105 UNTS 119**
SIGNED: 29 Apr 43 FORCE: 29 Apr 43
REGISTERED: 9 Oct 51 USA (United States)
ARTICLES: 2 LANGUAGE: English. Spanish.
HEADNOTE: RECRUITMENT UNSKILLED LABOR
TOPIC: Non-ILO Labor
CONCEPTS: Definition of terms. General provisions. Responsibility and liability. Anti-discrimination. Employment regulations. Safety standards. Wages and salaries. Non-ILO labor relations. Family allowances. Migrant worker. Accounting procedures. Bonds. Transportation costs. National treatment. Foreign nationals.
TREATY REF: USA'EAS 278; 56STAT.1759;.
PARTIES:
 Mexico
 USA (United States)

200328 Bilateral Exchange **105 UNTS 141**
SIGNED: 22 May 42 FORCE: 22 May 42
REGISTERED: 9 Oct 51 USA (United States)
ARTICLES: 6 LANGUAGE: English. Spanish.
HEADNOTE: HEALTH & SANITATION PROGRAM
TOPIC: Sanitation
CONCEPTS: Domestic legislation. General property. Programs. Specialists exchange. Public health. Sanitation. Vocational training. Research and development. Expense sharing formulae. Financial programs. Specific technical assistance.
PARTIES:
 Nicaragua
 USA (United States)

200329 Bilateral Agreement **105 UNTS 159**
SIGNED: 16 Jun 42 FORCE: 16 Jun 42
REGISTERED: 9 Oct 51 USA (United States)
ARTICLES: 8 LANGUAGE: English.
HEADNOTE: MUTUAL AID
TOPIC: Milit Assistance
CONCEPTS: Peaceful relations. Conformity with municipal law. Recognition. Materials, equipment and services. Defense and security. Military assistance. Return of equipment and recapture. Exchange of defense information. Restrictions on transfer.
TREATY REF: 204LTS381.
PROCEDURE: Future Procedures Contemplated.
PARTIES:
 Belgium
 USA (United States)

200330 Bilateral Exchange **105 UNTS 169**
SIGNED: 20 Mar 42 FORCE: 20 Mar 42
REGISTERED: 9 Oct 51 USA (United States)
ARTICLES: 2 LANGUAGE: English.
HEADNOTE: TRANSFER CITIZENS BETWEEN ARMED FORCES
TOPIC: Milit Servic/Citiz
CONCEPTS: Exchange of information and documents. Establishment of commission. Dual nationality. Certificates of service. Foreign nationals. Service in foreign army.
PARTIES:
 Canada
 USA (United States)

200331 Bilateral Exchange **105 UNTS 179**
SIGNED: 8 Apr 42 FORCE: 8 Apr 42
REGISTERED: 9 Oct 51 USA (United States)
ARTICLES: 3 LANGUAGE: English.
HEADNOTE: APPLICATION SELECTIVE TRAINING SERVICE ACT
TOPIC: Milit Servic/Citiz
CONCEPTS: Exchange of information and documents. Dual nationality. Certificates of service. Foreign nationals. Service in foreign army.
PARTIES:
 Canada
 USA (United States)

200332 Bilateral Exchange **105 UNTS 195**
SIGNED: 2 Mar 42 FORCE: 2 Mar 42
REGISTERED: 9 Oct 51 USA (United States)
ARTICLES: 2 LANGUAGE: English. Spanish.
HEADNOTE: AMENDING TRADE AGREEMENT
TOPIC: General Trade
CONCEPTS: Exceptions and exemptions. Treaty interpretation. Annex type material. Exchange rates and regulations.
TREATY REF: 193LTS85.
PARTIES:
Ecuador
USA (United States)

200333 Bilateral Exchange **105 UNTS 205**
SIGNED: 31 May 43 FORCE: 15 May 43
REGISTERED: 9 Oct 51 USA (United States)
ARTICLES: 3 LANGUAGE: English. Spanish.
HEADNOTE: SERVICE NATIONALS ARMED FORCES
TOPIC: Milit Servic/Citiz
CONCEPTS: Exchange of information and documents. Foreign nationals. Service in foreign army.
PARTIES:
El Salvador
USA (United States)

200334 Bilateral Exchange **105 UNTS 219**
SIGNED: 30 Mar 42 FORCE: 30 Mar 42
REGISTERED: 9 Oct 51 USA (United States)
ARTICLES: 2 LANGUAGE: English.
HEADNOTE: REPATRIATION & HOSPITALIZATION PRISONERS
TOPIC: Humanitarian
CONCEPTS: Treaty implementation. Repatriation of nationals. Exchange of information and documents. Informational records. Public health. Humanitarian matters. Prisoners of war.
TREATY REF: 117LTS405; 118LTS343; 122LTS367; 117LTS303.
PARTIES:
Germany, West
USA (United States)

200335 Bilateral Exchange **105 UNTS 227**
SIGNED: 16 Mar 43 FORCE: 2 Mar 43
REGISTERED: 9 Oct 51 USA (United States)
ARTICLES: 4 LANGUAGE: English.
HEADNOTE: SERVICE NATIONALS ARMED FORCES
TOPIC: Milit Servic/Citiz
CONCEPTS: Exchange of information and documents. Foreign nationals. Service in foreign army.
PARTIES:
Greece
USA (United States)

200336 Bilateral Exchange **105 UNTS 238**
SIGNED: 19 Feb 42 FORCE: 19 Feb 42
REGISTERED: 9 Oct 51 USA (United States)
ARTICLES: 7 LANGUAGE: English. French.
HEADNOTE: WAIVER CERTAIN TARIFF PREFERENCES
TOPIC: Customs
CONCEPTS: Tariffs. Most favored nation clause. Customs duties.
TREATY REF: TREATY OF COMMERCE AUG.26,1941.
PARTIES:
Haiti
USA (United States)

200337 Bilateral Exchange **105 UNTS 259**
SIGNED: 22 Jan 43 FORCE: 22 Jan 43
REGISTERED: 9 Oct 51 USA (United States)
ARTICLES: 2 LANGUAGE: English. Spanish.
HEADNOTE: SERVICE NATIONALS ARMED FORCES
TOPIC: Milit Servic/Citiz
CONCEPTS: National treatment. Foreign nationals. Service in foreign army.
PROCEDURE: Duration.
PARTIES:
Mexico
USA (United States)

200338 Bilateral Exchange **105 UNTS 269**
SIGNED: 31 Oct 42 FORCE: 31 Oct 42
REGISTERED: 9 Oct 51 USA (United States)
ARTICLES: 5 LANGUAGE: English.
HEADNOTE: SERVICE NATIONALS ARMED FORCES
TOPIC: Milit Servic/Citiz
CONCEPTS: Exchange of information and documents. Foreign nationals. Service in foreign army.
PARTIES:
South Africa
USA (United States)

200339 Bilateral Agreement **105 UNTS 285**
SIGNED: 18 Apr 42 FORCE: 11 Jun 42
REGISTERED: 9 Oct 51 USA (United States)
ARTICLES: 7 LANGUAGE: English.
HEADNOTE: MUTUAL AID
TOPIC: Milit Assistance
CONCEPTS: Peaceful relations. Conformity with municipal law. Recognition. Materials, equipment and services. Defense and security. Military assistance. Return of equipment and recapture. Exchange of defense information. Restrictions on transfer.
TREATY REF: 20JLTS381.
PROCEDURE: Future Procedures Contemplated.
PARTIES:
USA (United States)
USSR (Soviet Union)

200340 Bilateral Agreement **106 UNTS 155**
SIGNED: 8 Apr 43 FORCE: 28 Jun 44
REGISTERED: 19 Oct 51 USA (United States)
ARTICLES: 15 LANGUAGE: English. Persian.
HEADNOTE: COMMERCE RECIPROCAL CONCESSIONS ADVANTAGES
TOPIC: General Trade
CONCEPTS: Exceptions and exemptions. Territorial application. Treaty implementation. Annex or appendix reference. General cooperation. Licenses and permits. Procedure. Reciprocity in trade. Reexport of goods, etc.. Trade procedures. Payment schedules. Most favored nation clause. Equitable taxes. Customs duties.
PROCEDURE: Duration. Ratification. Termination.
PARTIES:
Iran
USA (United States)

200341 Bilateral Agreement **106 UNTS 199**
SIGNED: 31 Dec 43 FORCE: 31 Dec 43
REGISTERED: 19 Oct 51 USA (United States)
ARTICLES: 9 LANGUAGE: English.
HEADNOTE: CONSTRUCTION PORT WORKS
TOPIC: Non-IBRD Project
CONCEPTS: General property. Private contracts. Financial programs. Payment schedules. Claims and settlements. Tax exemptions. General technical assistance. Irrigation. Natural resources. Defense and security. Bases and facilities.
INTL ORGS: Special Commission.
PARTIES:
Liberia
USA (United States)

200342 Bilateral Exchange **106 UNTS 213**
SIGNED: 13 Apr 44 FORCE: 23 Mar 44
REGISTERED: 19 Oct 51 USA (United States)
ARTICLES: 2 LANGUAGE: English. Spanish.
HEADNOTE: EXCHANGE OFFICIAL PUBLICATIONS
TOPIC: Admin Cooperation
CONCEPTS: Exchange of official publications. Operating agencies. Indemnities and reimbursements.
PARTIES:
Guatemala
USA (United States)

200343 Bilateral Exchange **106 UNTS 237**
SIGNED: 10 May 44 FORCE: 10 May 44
REGISTERED: 19 Oct 51 USA (United States)
ARTICLES: 2 LANGUAGE: English.
HEADNOTE: PRIZES TAKEN NAVAL FORCES
TOPIC: Reparations
CONCEPTS: Conformity with municipal law. Exchange of information and documents. Claims and settlements. Naval vessels.
PARTIES:
Australia
USA (United States)

200344 Bilateral Exchange **106 UNTS 247**
SIGNED: 29 Feb 44 FORCE: 29 Feb 44
REGISTERED: 19 Oct 51 USA (United States)
ARTICLES: 2 LANGUAGE: Afghan. English.
HEADNOTE: EXCHANGE OFFICIAL PUBLICATIONS
TOPIC: Admin Cooperation
CONCEPTS: Exchange of official publications. Operating agencies. Indemnities and reimbursements.
PARTIES:
Afghanistan
USA (United States)

200345 Bilateral Exchange **106 UNTS 265**
SIGNED: 29 Sep 43 FORCE: 29 Sep 43
REGISTERED: 19 Oct 51 USA (United States)
ARTICLES: 2 LANGUAGE: English. Spanish.
HEADNOTE: SETTLEMENT CLAIMS AMERICAN OIL INTERESTS
TOPIC: Claims and Debts
CONCEPTS: Expropriation. Currency. Interest rates. Payment schedules. Claims and settlements. Lump sum settlements. Specific claims or waivers.
PARTIES:
Mexico
USA (United States)

200346 Bilateral Exchange **106 UNTS 275**
SIGNED: 27 Jan 44 FORCE: 27 Jan 44
REGISTERED: 19 Oct 51 USA (United States)
ARTICLES: 2 LANGUAGE: English. Spanish.
HEADNOTE: MEXICAN AMERICAN AGRICULTURAL COMMISSION
TOPIC: IGO Establishment
CONCEPTS: Funding procedures. Specific technical assistance. Technical education. Establishment.
INTL ORGS: Special Commission.
PARTIES:
Mexico
USA (United States)

200347 Bilateral Instrument **106 UNTS 285**
SIGNED: 15 Jul 44 FORCE: 15 Jul 44
REGISTERED: 19 Oct 51 USA (United States)
ARTICLES: 6 LANGUAGE: English. Spanish.
HEADNOTE: AGRICULTURAL EXPERIMENT STATION
TOPIC: Scientific Project
CONCEPTS: Personnel. Use of facilities. Research and scientific projects. Research cooperation. Research results. Research and development. Expense sharing formulae. Tax exemptions. Domestic obligation. Agriculture. Materials, equipment and services.
INTL ORGS: Special Commission.
PROCEDURE: Duration. Termination.
PARTIES:
Guatemala
USA (United States)

200348 Bilateral Exchange **106 UNTS 311**
SIGNED: 1 Nov 43 FORCE: 1 Nov 43
REGISTERED: 19 Oct 51 Uruguay
ARTICLES: 2 LANGUAGE: English. Spanish.
HEADNOTE: HEALTH SANITATION PROGRAM
TOPIC: Sanitation
CONCEPTS: General cooperation. General property. Programs. Specialists exchange. Public health. Sanitation. Vocational training. Research and development. Expense sharing formulae. Specific technical assistance. Grants.
PARTIES:
USA (United States)
Uruguay

200349 Bilateral Exchange **106 UNTS 319**
SIGNED: 7 Apr 42 FORCE: 7 Apr 42
REGISTERED: 19 Oct 51 USA (United States)
ARTICLES: 2 LANGUAGE: English. French.

HEADNOTE: HEALTH SANITATION PROGRAM
TOPIC: Sanitation
CONCEPTS: Personnel. General property. Programs. Specialists exchange. Public health. Narcotic drugs. Research and development. Reciprocity in financial treatment. Specific technical assistance. Grants.
PARTIES:
Haiti
USA (United States)
ANNEX
136 UNTS 402. Haiti. Prolongation 12 Jul 44. Force 12 Jul 44.
136 UNTS 402. USA (United States). Prolongation 29 Jun 44. Force 12 Jul 44.

200350 Bilateral Exchange **107 UNTS 43**
SIGNED: 13 Jun 44   FORCE: 13 Jun 44
REGISTERED: 19 Oct 51 USA (United States)
ARTICLES: 3 LANGUAGE: English.
HEADNOTE: SERVICE ARMED FORCES
TOPIC: Status of Forces
CONCEPTS: Foreign nationals. Service in foreign army.
PARTIES:
Taiwan
USA (United States)

200351 Bilateral Exchange **107 UNTS 55**
SIGNED: 2 Mar 43   FORCE: 2 Mar 43
REGISTERED: 19 Oct 51 USA (United States)
ARTICLES: 2 LANGUAGE: English. Spanish.
HEADNOTE: HEALTH SANITATION PROGRAM
TOPIC: Sanitation
CONCEPTS: General cooperation. Personnel. General property. Programs. Specialists exchange. Disease control. Public health. Sanitation. Research and development. Expense sharing formulae. Specific technical assistance. Grants.
PARTIES:
Panama
USA (United States)

200352 Bilateral Agreement **107 UNTS 63**
SIGNED: 21 Sep 51   FORCE: 21 Sep 51
REGISTERED: 22 Oct 51 WHO (World Health)
ARTICLES: 15 LANGUAGE: English. French.
HEADNOTE: TECHNICAL ADVISORY ASSISTANCE
TOPIC: Tech Assistance
CONCEPTS: Change of circumstances. Treaty implementation. Annex or appendix reference. Privileges and immunities. General cooperation. Personnel. Public information. Responsibility and liability. Arbitration. Procedure. Negotiation. Competence of tribunal. Financial programs. Tax exemptions. Customs exemptions. Special projects. Materials, equipment and services. IGO status.
INTL ORGS: International Court of Justice. United Nations.
TREATY REF: 33UNTS261.
PROCEDURE: Amendment. Termination.
PARTIES:
WHO (World Health)
Vietnam, South

200353 Bilateral Exchange **109 UNTS 111**
SIGNED: 16 Oct 42   FORCE: 10 Oct 42
REGISTERED: 9 Nov 51 USA (United States)
ARTICLES: 4 LANGUAGE: English.
HEADNOTE: JURISDICTION OVER CRIMINAL OFFENSES US ARMED FORCES IN INDIA
TOPIC: Status of Forces
CONCEPTS: Status of forces.
PARTIES:
India
USA (United States)

200354 Bilateral Exchange **109 UNTS 127**
SIGNED: 3 Nov 42   FORCE: 3 Nov 42
REGISTERED: 9 Nov 51 USA (United States)
ARTICLES: 2 LANGUAGE: English.
HEADNOTE: JURISDICTION OVER PRIZES
TOPIC: Admin Cooperation
CONCEPTS: Prizes and arbitral awards. Establishment of commission.
PARTIES:
UK Great Britain
USA (United States)

200355 Bilateral Exchange **109 UNTS 135**
SIGNED: 13 Aug 43   FORCE: 13 Aug 43
REGISTERED: 9 Nov 51 USA (United States)
ARTICLES: 2 LANGUAGE: English.
HEADNOTE: JURISDICTION OVER PRIZES
TOPIC: Admin Cooperation
CONCEPTS: Prizes and arbitral awards.
PARTIES:
Canada
USA (United States)

200356 Bilateral Exchange **109 UNTS 149**
SIGNED: 4 Aug 43   FORCE: 4 Aug 43
REGISTERED: 9 Nov 51 USA (United States)
ARTICLES: 4 LANGUAGE: English.
HEADNOTE: OFFENSES US FORCES CONGO
TOPIC: Status of Forces
CONCEPTS: Status of forces.
PARTIES:
Belgium
USA (United States)

200357 Bilateral Exchange **109 UNTS 165**
SIGNED: 31 Mar 44   FORCE: 31 Mar 44
REGISTERED: 9 Nov 51 USA (United States)
ARTICLES: 4 LANGUAGE: English.
HEADNOTE: AMENDING EXTENDING NAVAL MISSION
TOPIC: Military Mission
CONCEPTS: Annex type material. Previous treaty extension. Military assistance missions.
PARTIES:
Peru
USA (United States)

200358 Bilateral Agreement **109 UNTS 171**
SIGNED: 13 Jan 44   FORCE: 13 Jan 44
REGISTERED: 9 Nov 51 USA (United States)
ARTICLES: 5 LANGUAGE: English. Spanish.
HEADNOTE: MILITARY AVIATION MISSION
TOPIC: Military Mission
CONCEPTS: Definition of terms. Use of facilities. Compensation. Indemnities and reimbursements. Exchange rates and regulations. Expense sharing formulae. Tax exemptions. Customs exemptions. Military assistance. Military training. Security of information. Airforce-army-navy personnel ratio. Ranks and privileges. Conditions for assistance missions. Third country military personnel. Status of forces.
TREATY REF: 109UNTS25.
PROCEDURE: Denunciation. Duration. Renewal or Revival. Termination.
PARTIES:
USA (United States)
Venezuela

200359 Bilateral Exchange **109 UNTS 191**
SIGNED: 3 Mar 44   FORCE: 3 Mar 44
REGISTERED: 9 Nov 51 USA (United States)
ARTICLES: 2 LANGUAGE: English.
HEADNOTE: STUDY INTERNATIONAL JOINT COMMISSION
TOPIC: Specific Resources
CONCEPTS: Inspection and observation. Regulation of natural resources.
INTL ORGS: Special Commission.
TREATY REF: 3'4DEMARTENS208;.
PARTIES:
Canada
USA (United States)

200360 Bilateral Exchange **109 UNTS 199**
SIGNED: 17 Jan 44   FORCE: 17 Jan 44
REGISTERED: 9 Nov 51 USA (United States)
ARTICLES: 3 LANGUAGE: English.
HEADNOTE: CONSTRUCTION OPERATION RADIO BROADCASTING STATIONS
TOPIC: Mass Media
CONCEPTS: Conformity with municipal law. Commercial and public radio. Bands and frequency allocation. Radio-telephone-telegraphic communications.
PARTIES:
Canada
USA (United States)

200361 Bilateral Exchange **109 UNTS 211**
SIGNED: 2 May 44   FORCE: 2 May 44
REGISTERED: 9 Nov 51 USA (United States)
ARTICLES: 5 LANGUAGE: English.
HEADNOTE: EXTENDING AMENDING AGREEMENT NAVAL AVIATION MISSION
TOPIC: Military Mission
CONCEPTS: Annex type material. Previous treaty extension. Military assistance missions.
PARTIES:
Peru
USA (United States)

200362 Bilateral Exchange **109 UNTS 223**
SIGNED: 16 Feb 44   FORCE: 16 Feb 44
REGISTERED: 9 Nov 51 USA (United States)
ARTICLES: 2 LANGUAGE: Arabic. English.
HEADNOTE: EXCHANGE OFFICIAL PUBLICATIONS
TOPIC: Admin Cooperation
CONCEPTS: Exchange of official publications. Operating agencies. Indemnities and reimbursements.
PARTIES:
Iraq
USA (United States)

200363 Bilateral Exchange **109 UNTS 251**
SIGNED: 11 Feb 44   FORCE: 11 Feb 44
REGISTERED: 9 Nov 51 USA (United States)
ARTICLES: 2 LANGUAGE: English. Spanish.
HEADNOTE: PURCHASE EXPORTABLE FOOD SURPLUSES
TOPIC: Milit Assistance
CONCEPTS: Definition of terms. Detailed regulations. Export quotas. Commodity trade. Delivery guarantees. Delivery schedules. Quotas. Agricultural commodities.
TREATY REF: 21UNTS277.
PARTIES:
Dominican Republic
USA (United States)

200364 Bilateral Exchange **109 UNTS 279**
SIGNED: 22 Apr 44   FORCE: 22 Apr 44
REGISTERED: 9 Nov 51 USA (United States)
ARTICLES: 2 LANGUAGE: English.
HEADNOTE: TARIFF DUTIES
TOPIC: Customs
CONCEPTS: Tariffs. Customs duties.
TREATY REF: 202LTS129.
PARTIES:
Turkey
USA (United States)

200365 Bilateral Exchange **109 UNTS 287**
SIGNED: 12 Feb 44   FORCE: 27 Jan 44
REGISTERED: 9 Nov 51 USA (United States)
ARTICLES: 3 LANGUAGE: English. Spanish.
HEADNOTE: SERVICE NATIONALS ARMED FORCES
TOPIC: Milit Servic/Citiz
CONCEPTS: Exchange of information and documents. Foreign nationals. Service in foreign army.
PARTIES:
Colombia
USA (United States)

200366 Bilateral Agreement **109 UNTS 297**
SIGNED: 19 Sep 51   FORCE: 19 Sep 51
REGISTERED: 12 Nov 51 WHO (World Health)
ARTICLES: 7 LANGUAGE: English. Korean.
HEADNOTE: HEALTH PROJECTS KOREA
TOPIC: Sanitation
CONCEPTS: Definition of terms. Privileges and immunities. Personnel. General property. Programs. Arbitration. Specialists exchange. Public health. WHO used as agency. Scholarships and grants. Vocational training. Research and development. Indemnities and reimbursements. Expense sharing formulae. Specific technical assistance. Materials, equipment and services.
INTL ORGS: United Nations.
TREATY REF: 14UNTS185; OFF.REC.WHO N.28 P.68; 76UNTS132.
PROCEDURE: Amendment. Termination.

PARTIES:
Korea, South
WHO (World Health)

200367 Bilateral Agreement **110 UNTS 297**
SIGNED: 3 Apr 51 FORCE: 13 Apr 51
REGISTERED: 26 Nov 51 WHO (World Health)
ARTICLES: 14 LANGUAGE: Arabic. English. .
HEADNOTE: TECHNICAL ADVISORY ASSISTANCE
TOPIC: Tech Assistance
CONCEPTS: Change of circumstances. Treaty im-
plementation. Treaty interpretation. Annex or ap-
pendix reference. Privileges and immunities.
General cooperation. Personnel. Public informa-
tion. Arbitration. Procedure. Negotiation. Com-
petence of tribunal. Financial programs. Claims
and settlements. Tax exemptions. Customs ex-
emptions. Special projects. Materials, equip-
ment and services. IGO status.
INTL ORGS: International Court of Justice.
TREATY REF: 33UNTS261; 71UNTS381.
PROCEDURE: Amendment. Termination.
PARTIES:
Jordan
WHO (World Health)

200368 Bilateral Agreement **117 UNTS 173**
SIGNED: 13 Dec 40 FORCE: 14 Aug 41
REGISTERED: 6 Dec 51 USA (United States)
ARTICLES: 6 LANGUAGE: English.
HEADNOTE: FOX FUR SKINS TRADE
TOPIC: General Trade
CONCEPTS: Detailed regulations. Previous treaty
replacement. Informational records. General
trade. Commodity trade. Quotas.
TREATY REF: 191LTS91.
PROCEDURE: Duration. Ratification. Termination.
PARTIES:
Canada
USA (United States)

200369 Bilateral Exchange **117 UNTS 185**
SIGNED: 19 Feb 42 FORCE: 19 Feb 42
REGISTERED: 6 Dec 51 USA (United States)
ARTICLES: 2 LANGUAGE: English. Spanish.
HEADNOTE: EXTENDING MILITARY MISSION
TOPIC: Military Mission
CONCEPTS: Annex type material. Previous treaty
extension. Military assistance missions.
PARTIES:
Colombia
USA (United States)

200370 Bilateral Agreement **117 UNTS 191**
SIGNED: 23 May 41 FORCE: 23 May 41
REGISTERED: 6 Dec 51 USA (United States)
ARTICLES: 5 LANGUAGE: English. French.
HEADNOTE: MILITARY MISSION
TOPIC: Military Mission
CONCEPTS: Definition of terms. Use of facilities.
Compensation. Indemnities and reimburse-
ments. Exchange rates and regulations. Expense
sharing formulae. Tax exemptions. Customs ex-
emptions. Military assistance. Military training.
Security of information. Airforce-army-navy per-
sonnel ratio. Ranks and privileges. Conditions
for assistance missions. Third country military
personnel. Status of forces.
PROCEDURE: Denunciation. Duration. Renewal or
Revival. Termination.
PARTIES:
Haiti
USA (United States)

200371 Bilateral Agreement **117 UNTS 205**
SIGNED: 28 Feb 41 FORCE: 28 Feb 41
REGISTERED: 6 Dec 51 USA (United States)
ARTICLES: 3 LANGUAGE: English. Spanish.
HEADNOTE: PLANTATION RUBBER INVESTIGA-
TIONS
TOPIC: Specific Resources
CONCEPTS: Inspection and observation. Research
and development. Funding procedures. Customs
exemptions. Materials, equipment and services.
Raw materials.
PARTIES:
Honduras
USA (United States)

200372 Bilateral Exchange **117 UNTS 227**
SIGNED: 15 Jan 42 FORCE: 15 Jan 42
REGISTERED: 6 Dec 51 USA (United States)
ARTICLES: 2 LANGUAGE: English.
HEADNOTE: EXCHANGE OFFICIAL PUBLICA-
TIONS
TOPIC: Admin Cooperation
CONCEPTS: Exchange of official publications. Op-
erating agencies. Indemnities and reimburse-
ments.
PARTIES:
Liberia
USA (United States)

200373 Bilateral Agreement **117 UNTS 242**
SIGNED: 8 Jun 43 FORCE: 8 Jun 43
REGISTERED: 6 Dec 51 USA (United States)
ARTICLES: 8 LANGUAGE: English.
HEADNOTE: MUTUAL AID
TOPIC: Milit Assistance
CONCEPTS: Annex or appendix reference. Peace-
ful relations. Conformity with municipal law. Rec-
ognition. Economic assistance. Defense and se-
curity. Military assistance. Return of equipment
and recapture. Exchange of defense information.
Restrictions on transfer.
PROCEDURE: Future Procedures Contemplated.
PARTIES:
Liberia
USA (United States)

200374 Bilateral Agreement **117 UNTS 253**
SIGNED: 11 Jan 41 FORCE: 11 Jan 41
REGISTERED: 6 Dec 51 USA (United States)
ARTICLES: 1 LANGUAGE: English. Spanish.
HEADNOTE: PLANTATION RUBBER INVESTIGA-
TIONS
TOPIC: Specific Resources
CONCEPTS: Research cooperation. Raw materials.
PROCEDURE: Duration. Termination.
PARTIES:
Nicaragua
USA (United States)

200375 Bilateral Agreement **117 UNTS 266**
SIGNED: 11 Mar 42 FORCE: 14 Feb 42
REGISTERED: 6 Dec 51 USA (United States)
ARTICLES: 29 LANGUAGE: English. Spanish.
HEADNOTE: MILITARY OFFICER ASSISTANT AD-
VISOR
TOPIC: Military Mission
CONCEPTS: Definition of terms. Use of facilities.
Compensation. Indemnities and reimburse-
ments. Exchange rates and regulations. Expense
sharing formulae. Tax exemptions. Customs ex-
emptions. Military assistance. Military training.
Security of information. Airforce-army-navy per-
sonnel ratio. Ranks and privileges. Conditions
for assistance missions. Third country military
personnel. Status of forces.
PROCEDURE: Denunciation. Duration. Renewal or
Revival. Termination.
PARTIES:
Peru
USA (United States)

200376 Bilateral Exchange **117 UNTS 285**
SIGNED: 20 Dec 43 FORCE: 20 Dec 43
REGISTERED: 6 Dec 51 USA (United States)
ARTICLES: 2 LANGUAGE: English.
HEADNOTE: RENEWAL MILITARY ADVISOR
AGREEMENT
TOPIC: Military Mission
CONCEPTS: Annex type material. Previous treaty
extension. Military assistance missions.
PARTIES:
Peru
USA (United States)

200377 Bilateral Agreement **117 UNTS 291**
SIGNED: 10 Jul 44 FORCE: 10 Jul 44
REGISTERED: 6 Dec 51 USA (United States)
ARTICLES: 30 LANGUAGE: English. Spanish.
HEADNOTE: MILITARY MISSION
TOPIC: Military Mission
CONCEPTS: Definition of terms. Use of facilities.
Compensation. Indemnities and reimburse-
ments. Exchange rates and regulations. Expense
sharing formulae. Tax exemptions. Customs ex-

emptions. Military assistance. Military training.
Security of information. Airforce-army-navy personnel ratio. Ranks and privileges. Conditions
for assistance missions. Third country military
personnel. Status of forces.
PARTIES:
Peru
USA (United States)
ANNEX
141 UNTS 409. USA (United States). Prolongation
9 Jul 48. Force 10 Jul 48.
141 UNTS 409. Peru. Prolongation 23 Aug 48.
Force 10 Jul 48.

200378 Bilateral Exchange **117 UNTS 311**
SIGNED: 27 Jul 42 FORCE: 27 Jul 42
REGISTERED: 6 Dec 51 USA (United States)
ARTICLES: 2 LANGUAGE: English.
HEADNOTE: JURISDICTION CRIMINAL OFFENSES
COMMITTED BY ARMED FORCES
TOPIC: Status of Forces
CONCEPTS: Jurisdiction.
TREATY REF: 204LTS15.
PARTIES:
UK Great Britain
USA (United States)

200379 Bilateral Agreement **117 UNTS 323**
SIGNED: 11 Apr 41 FORCE: 11 Apr 41
REGISTERED: 17 Dec 51 USA (United States)
ARTICLES: 10 LANGUAGE: English. Spanish.
HEADNOTE: PLANTATION RUBBER INVESTIGA-
TIONS
TOPIC: Non-IBRD Project
CONCEPTS: General technical assistance. Agricul-
ture. Assistance.
PARTIES:
Mexico
USA (United States)

200380 Bilateral Exchange **117 UNTS 355**
SIGNED: 24 Jan 51 FORCE: 24 Jan 51
REGISTERED: 27 Dec 51 ILO (Labor Org)
ARTICLES: 2 LANGUAGE: English.
HEADNOTE: TECHNICAL ASSISTANCE HANDI-
CRAFTS
TOPIC: Tech Assistance
CONCEPTS: Annex or appendix reference. Privi-
leges and immunities. General cooperation. Per-
sonnel. Public information. Expense sharing for-
mulae. Local currency. Domestic obligation.
Special projects. Conformity with IGO decisions.
INTL ORGS: United Nations.
TREATY REF: 76UNTS132; 33UNTS261.
PARTIES:
Ceylon (Sri Lanka)
ILO (Labor Org)

200381 Multilateral Agreement **118 UNTS 255**
SIGNED: 2 Dec 50 FORCE: 8 Jan 52
REGISTERED: 8 Jan 52 United Nations
ARTICLES: 25 LANGUAGE: English. French.
HEADNOTE: TRUSTEESHIP AGREEMENT
TOPIC: Trusteeship
CONCEPTS: Procedure. Trusteeship. Basic free-
doms. Administering authority. Disposition of
territory. Definition of territory. Socio-economic
development. Respect for local customs. Internal
travel.
INTL ORGS: International Court of Justice. United
Nations. Special Commission.
TREATY REF: 49UNTS; 50UNTS; 1UNTS15; ETC..
PARTIES:
United Nations

200382 Bilateral Agreement **118 UNTS 281**
SIGNED: 21 Jan 52 FORCE: 21 Jan 52
REGISTERED: 21 Jan 52 United Nations
ARTICLES: 5 LANGUAGE: English. French.
HEADNOTE: TECHNICAL ASSISTANCE
TOPIC: Tech Assistance
CONCEPTS: Definition of terms. Treaty implementation. Annex or appendix reference. Privileges
and immunities. General cooperation. Title and
deeds. Scholarships and grants. Vocational
training. Research and scientific projects. Expense sharing formulae. Local currency. Domestic obligation. General technical assistance. Ma-

terials, equipment and services. IGO status. Conformity with IGO decisions.
INTL ORGS: United Nations Educational, Scientific and Cultural Organization.
TREATY REF: 76UNTS132; 1UNTS15,263; 1UNTS14.
PROCEDURE: Amendment. Registration. Termination.
PARTIES:
Ceylon (Sri Lanka)
United Nations

200383 Multilateral Agreement **118 UNTS 290**
SIGNED: 24 Dec 51   FORCE: 24 Dec 51
REGISTERED: 21 Jan 52 United Nations
ARTICLES: 5 LANGUAGE: Arabic. English.
HEADNOTE: TECHNICAL ASSISTANCE
TOPIC: Tech Assistance
CONCEPTS: Definition of terms. Treaty implementation. Privileges and immunities. General cooperation. Title and deeds. Scholarships and grants. Vocational training. Research and scientific projects. Expense sharing formulae. Local currency. Domestic obligation. General technical assistance. Materials, equipment and services. IGO status. Conformity with IGO decisions.
INTL ORGS: United Nations Educational, Scientific and Cultural Organization.
TREATY REF: 76UNTS132; 1UNTS15,263; 33UNTS261.
PROCEDURE: Amendment. Termination.
PARTIES:
Libya SIGNED: 24 Dec 51 FORCE: 24 Dec 51
FAO (Food Agri) SIGNED: 24 Dec 51 FORCE: 24 Dec 51
ICAO (Civil Aviat) SIGNED: 24 Dec 51 FORCE: 24 Dec 51
ILO (Labor Org) SIGNED: 24 Dec 51 FORCE: 24 Dec 51
UNESCO (Educ/Cult) SIGNED: 24 Dec 51 FORCE: 24 Dec 51
United Nations SIGNED: 24 Dec 51 FORCE: 24 Dec 51
WHO (World Health) SIGNED: 24 Dec 51 FORCE: 24 Dec 51
ANNEX
519 UNTS 404. Libya. Force 28 Jun 64.
519 UNTS 404. United Nations. Force 28 Jun 64.

200384 Bilateral Agreement **119 UNTS 193**
SIGNED: 14 Oct 41   FORCE: 2 Jan 43
REGISTERED: 24 Jan 52 USA (United States)
ARTICLES: 27 LANGUAGE: English. Spanish.
HEADNOTE: TRADE
TOPIC: General Trade
CONCEPTS: Exceptions and exemptions. Territorial application. Establishment of commission. Procedure. Special tribunals. Export quotas. Import quotas. Customs exemptions.
INTL ORGS: Special Commission.
PROCEDURE: Duration. Ratification. Termination.
PARTIES:
Argentina
USA (United States)

200385 Bilateral Exchange **119 UNTS 285**
SIGNED: 29 May 40   FORCE: 29 May 40
REGISTERED: 24 Jan 52 USA (United States)
ARTICLES: 2 LANGUAGE: English.
HEADNOTE: VISITS UNIFORM MEMBERS DEFENSE FORCES
TOPIC: Status of Forces
CONCEPTS: Change of circumstances. Border traffic and migration. Non-visa travel documents. Conditions for assistance missions. Status of military forces.
PARTIES:
Canada
USA (United States)

200386 Bilateral Exchange **119 UNTS 295**
SIGNED: 12 Mar 42   FORCE: 12 Apr 42
REGISTERED: 24 Jan 52 USA (United States)
ARTICLES: 2 LANGUAGE: English.
HEADNOTE: UNEMPLOYMENT INSURANCE
TOPIC: Non-ILO Labor
CONCEPTS: Annex or appendix reference. Conformity with municipal law. Non-ILO labor relations. Unemployment.

PARTIES:
Canada
USA (United States)

200387 Bilateral Exchange **119 UNTS 305**
SIGNED: 30 Nov 42   FORCE: 30 Nov 42
REGISTERED: 24 Jan 52 USA (United States)
ARTICLES: 2 LANGUAGE: English.
HEADNOTE: POST-WAR ECONOMIC SETTLEMENTS
TOPIC: Reparations
CONCEPTS: Economic assistance. Reconversion to normalcy.
PARTIES:
Canada
USA (United States)

200388 Bilateral Agreement **119 UNTS 313**
SIGNED: 23 Dec 41   FORCE: 5 Jan 42
REGISTERED: 24 Jan 52 USA (United States)
ARTICLES: 9 LANGUAGE: English. Spanish.
HEADNOTE: SUPPLEMENT AMENDING TRADE AGREEMENT
TOPIC: General Trade
CONCEPTS: Annex type material.
TREATY REF: 153LTS369; 202LTS71.
PARTIES:
Cuba
USA (United States)

200389 Bilateral Exchange **120 UNTS 161**
SIGNED: 27 Nov 41   FORCE: 27 Nov 41
REGISTERED: 24 Jan 52 USA (United States)
ARTICLES: 2 LANGUAGE: English. Spanish.
HEADNOTE: EXCHANGE OFFICIAL PUBLICATIONS
TOPIC: Admin Cooperation
CONCEPTS: Exchange of official publications. Operating agencies. Indemnities and reimbursements.
PARTIES:
El Salvador
USA (United States)

200390 Bilateral Agreement **120 UNTS 171**
SIGNED: 19 Oct 42   FORCE: 19 Oct 42
REGISTERED: 24 Jan 52 USA (United States)
ARTICLES: 1 LANGUAGE: English. French.
HEADNOTE: EXCHANGE CERTAIN LANDS
TOPIC: Territory Boundary
CONCEPTS: Changes of territory.
PARTIES:
Haiti
USA (United States)

200391 Bilateral Exchange **120 UNTS 177**
SIGNED: 21 Sep 42   FORCE: 21 Sep 42
REGISTERED: 24 Jan 52 USA (United States)
ARTICLES: 2 LANGUAGE: English.
HEADNOTE: HAITIAN FINANCES
TOPIC: Other Ad Hoc
CONCEPTS: Credit provisions. Control of internal finance.
TREATY REF: 103UNTS141.
PARTIES:
Haiti
USA (United States)

200392 Bilateral Exchange **120 UNTS 183**
SIGNED: 18 Nov 42   FORCE: 18 Nov 42
REGISTERED: 24 Jan 52 USA (United States)
ARTICLES: 2 LANGUAGE: English. Spanish.
HEADNOTE: REHABILITATION CERTAIN NATIONALIZED RAILWAYS
TOPIC: Claims and Debts
CONCEPTS: Time limit. Specialists exchange. General trade. Export quotas. Special projects. Transport of goods. Land transport. Railways. Raw materials.
PARTIES:
Mexico
USA (United States)

200393 Bilateral Agreement **120 UNTS 211**
SIGNED: 21 Jul 42   FORCE: 1 Jan 43
REGISTERED: 24 Jan 52 USA (United States)
ARTICLES: 18 LANGUAGE: English. Spanish.

HEADNOTE: TRADE
TOPIC: General Trade
CONCEPTS: Detailed regulations. Annex or appendix reference. Informational records. Licenses and permits. Public information. Private contracts. Establishment of trade relations. Export quotas. Import quotas. Free trade. Reciprocity in trade. Payment schedules. Quotas. Most favored nation clause. National treatment. Customs duties. Customs declarations.
INTL ORGS: Special Commission.
PARTIES:
USA (United States)
Uruguay

200394 Bilateral Agreement **120 UNTS 277**
SIGNED: 20 Aug 51   FORCE: 20 Aug 51
REGISTERED: 1 Feb 52 United Nations
ARTICLES: 11 LANGUAGE: Arabic. English.
HEADNOTE: AGREEMENT
TOPIC: Refugees
CONCEPTS: Personnel. Use of facilities. Indemnities and reimbursements. Exchange rates and regulations. Funding procedures. Tax exemptions. IGO status.
PARTIES:
Jordan
UN Relief Palestin
ANNEX
136 UNTS 408. UN Relief Palestin. Amendment 19 Jun 52. Force 19 Jun 52.
136 UNTS 408. Jordan. Amendment 19 Jun 52. Force 19 Jun 52.

200395 Bilateral Exchange **121 UNTS 123**
SIGNED: 28 Jan 43   FORCE: 28 Jan 43
REGISTERED: 13 Feb 52 USA (United States)
ARTICLES: 2 LANGUAGE: English.
HEADNOTE: JURISDICTION OVER PRIZES
TOPIC: Admin Cooperation
CONCEPTS: Prizes and arbitral awards. Establishment of commission.
PARTIES:
New Zealand
USA (United States)

200396 Bilateral Agreement **121 UNTS 133**
SIGNED: 21 Feb 45   FORCE: 21 Feb 45
REGISTERED: 13 Feb 52 USA (United States)
ARTICLES: 30 LANGUAGE: English. Spanish.
HEADNOTE: MILITARY AVIATION MISSION
TOPIC: Military Mission
CONCEPTS: Definition of terms. Use of facilities. Compensation. Indemnities and reimbursements. Exchange rates and regulations. Expense sharing formulae. Tax exemptions. Customs exemptions. Military assistance. Military training. Security of information. Airforce-army-navy personnel ratio. Ranks and privileges. Conditions for assistance missions. Third country military personnel. Status of forces.
PROCEDURE: Denunciation. Duration. Renewal or Revival. Termination.
PARTIES:
Guatemala
USA (United States)

200397 Bilateral Exchange **121 UNTS 153**
SIGNED: 8 Jan 45   FORCE: 8 Jan 45
REGISTERED: 13 Feb 52 USA (United States)
ARTICLES: 2 LANGUAGE: English. French.
HEADNOTE: PLANTATION RUBBER INVESTIGATIONS
TOPIC: Specific Resources
CONCEPTS: Research cooperation. Funding procedures. Materials, equipment and services. Raw materials.
PROCEDURE: Amendment. Duration.
PARTIES:
Haiti
USA (United States)

200398 Bilateral Agreement **121 UNTS 165**
SIGNED: 23 Feb 45   FORCE: 23 Feb 45
REGISTERED: 13 Feb 52 USA (United States)
ARTICLES: 9 LANGUAGE: English. French. Turkish.
HEADNOTE: PRINCIPLES APPLYING AID
TOPIC: Direct Aid
CONCEPTS: Annex or appendix reference. Confor-

mity with municipal law. General aid. Materials, equipment and services. Access to materials. Military assistance. Return of equipment and recapture. Security of information. Exchange of defense information.
TREATY REF: 104UNTS381.
PROCEDURE: Duration. Future Procedures Contemplated.
PARTIES:
Turkey
USA (United States)

200399   Bilateral Agreement   **121 UNTS 185**
SIGNED: 21 May 45   FORCE: 21 May 45
REGISTERED: 13 Feb 52 USA (United States)
ARTICLES: 28 LANGUAGE: English. Spanish.
HEADNOTE: MILITARY MISSION
TOPIC: Military Mission
CONCEPTS: Definition of terms. Use of facilities. Compensation. Indemnities and reimbursements. Exchange rates and regulations. Expense sharing formulae. Tax exemptions. Customs exemptions. Military assistance. Military training. Security of information. Airforce-army-navy personnel ratio. Ranks and privileges. Conditions for assistance missions. Third country military personnel. Status of forces.
PARTIES:
Guatemala
USA (United States)

200400   Bilateral Agreement   **121 UNTS 205**
SIGNED: 8 Mar 45   FORCE: 8 Mar 45
REGISTERED: 13 Feb 52 USA (United States)
ARTICLES: 6 LANGUAGE: English.
HEADNOTE: WAIVER CLAIMS MARINE TRANSPORT INTEGRATION
TOPIC: Claims and Debts
CONCEPTS: Claims and settlements. Navigational conditions. Transport of goods. Water transport. Merchant vessels. Shipwreck and salvage.
PROCEDURE: Termination.
PARTIES:
Australia
USA (United States)

200401   Bilateral Agreement   **121 UNTS 219**
SIGNED: 24 May 45   FORCE: 24 May 45
REGISTERED: 13 Feb 52 USA (United States)
ARTICLES: 31 LANGUAGE: English. Spanish.
HEADNOTE: NAVAL MISSION
TOPIC: Military Mission
CONCEPTS: Definition of terms. Use of facilities. Compensation. Indemnities and reimbursements. Exchange rates and regulations. Expense sharing formulae. Tax exemptions. Customs exemptions. Military assistance. Military training. Security of information. Airforce-army-navy personnel ratio. Ranks and privileges. Conditions for assistance missions. Third country military personnel. Status of forces.
PROCEDURE: Denunciation. Duration. Renewal or Revival. Termination.
PARTIES:
Chile
USA (United States)

200402   Bilateral Agreement   **121 UNTS 239**
SIGNED: 31 Jul 45   FORCE: 31 Jul 45
REGISTERED: 13 Feb 52 USA (United States)
ARTICLES: 8 LANGUAGE: English.
HEADNOTE: AID DEFENSE
TOPIC: Milit Assistance
CONCEPTS: Peaceful relations. Conformity with municipal law. Recognition. Materials, equipment and services. Defense and security. Military assistance. Return of equipment and recapture. Exchange of defense information. Restrictions on transfer.
INTL ORGS: North Atlantic Treaty Organization. United Nations.
TREATY REF: 204LTS381.
PROCEDURE: Future Procedures Contemplated.
PARTIES:
Iraq
USA (United States)

200403   Bilateral Exchange   **121 UNTS 255**
SIGNED: 4 Feb 52   FORCE: 4 Jan 45

REGISTERED: 13 Feb 52 USA (United States)
ARTICLES: 2 LANGUAGE: English.
HEADNOTE: FELLOWSHIP PROGRAM
TOPIC: Education
CONCEPTS: Conditions. Standardization. Personnel. Exchange. Teacher and student exchange. Professorships. Scholarships and grants. Vocational training. Indemnities and reimbursements.
TREATY REF: 24UNTS153.
PARTIES:
Peru
USA (United States)

200404   Bilateral Exchange   **121 UNTS 265**
SIGNED: 5 Apr 45   FORCE: 5 Apr 45
REGISTERED: 13 Feb 52 USA (United States)
ARTICLES: 2 LANGUAGE: English. Spanish.
HEADNOTE: SERVICE NATIONALS ARMED FORCES
TOPIC: Milit Servic/Citiz
CONCEPTS: Exchange of information and documents. Foreign nationals. Service in foreign army.
PARTIES:
Ecuador
USA (United States)

200405   Bilateral Exchange   **121 UNTS 273**
SIGNED: 11 May 45   FORCE: 11 May 45
REGISTERED: 13 Feb 52 USA (United States)
ARTICLES: 2 LANGUAGE: English. Spanish.
HEADNOTE: SERVICE NATIONALS ARMED FORCES
TOPIC: Milit Servic/Citiz
CONCEPTS: Exchange of information and documents. Foreign nationals. Service in foreign army.
PARTIES:
USA (United States)
Venezuela

200406   Bilateral Exchange   **121 UNTS 283**
SIGNED: 12 Jun 45   FORCE: 12 Jun 45
REGISTERED: 13 Feb 52 USA (United States)
ARTICLES: 2 LANGUAGE: English. Spanish.
HEADNOTE: SERVICE NATIONALS ARMED FORCES
TOPIC: Milit Servic/Citiz
CONCEPTS: Exchange of information and documents. Foreign nationals. Service in foreign army.
PARTIES:
Peru
USA (United States)

200407   Bilateral Exchange   **121 UNTS 291**
SIGNED: 11 Jun 45   FORCE: 11 Jun 45
REGISTERED: 13 Feb 52 USA (United States)
ARTICLES: 2 LANGUAGE: English. Spanish.
HEADNOTE: SERVICE NATIONALS ARMED FORCES
TOPIC: Milit Servic/Citiz
CONCEPTS: Exchange of information and documents. Foreign nationals. Service in foreign army.
PARTIES:
Chile
USA (United States)

200408   Bilateral Exchange   **121 UNTS 299**
SIGNED: 5 Aug 44   FORCE: 5 Aug 44
REGISTERED: 13 Feb 52 USA (United States)
ARTICLES: 2 LANGUAGE: English.
HEADNOTE: SALMON FISHERIES
TOPIC: Specific Resources
CONCEPTS: Special projects. Fish, wildlife, and natural resources.
INTL ORGS: Pacific Salmon Commission.
TREATY REF: 184LTS305.
PARTIES:
Canada
USA (United States)

200409   Bilateral Exchange   **122 UNTS 261**
SIGNED: 17 Feb 45   FORCE: 17 Feb 45
REGISTERED: 5 Mar 52 USA (United States)
ARTICLES: 2 LANGUAGE: English.
HEADNOTE: AIR TRANSPORT SERVICES

TOPIC: Air Transport
CONCEPTS: Detailed regulations. Exceptions and exemptions. Annex or appendix reference. Previous treaty replacement. Conformity with municipal law. Use of facilities. Quarantine. Fees and exemptions. Most favored nation clause. National treatment. Customs duties. Customs exemptions. Routes and logistics. Navigational conditions. Air transport. Airport facilities. Airworthiness certificates. Overflights and technical stops. Operating authorizations and regulations. Postal services.
INTL ORGS: International Civil Aviation Organization.
TREATY REF: 15UNTS295;   199LTS367; 203LTS219; 13UNTS411; ETC..
PARTIES:
Canada
USA (United States)

200410   Bilateral Exchange   **122 UNTS 277**
SIGNED: 2 Dec 42   FORCE: 2 Dec 42
REGISTERED: 5 Mar 52 USA (United States)
ARTICLES: 2 LANGUAGE: English. Spanish.
HEADNOTE: AGRICULTURAL EXPERIMENT STATION
TOPIC: Scientific Project
CONCEPTS: Personnel. Technical and commercial staff. Vocational training. Research and scientific projects. Research cooperation. Research results. Research and development. Expense sharing formulae. Tax exemptions. Domestic obligation. Agriculture. Publications exchange.
TREATY REF: 15UNTS295.
PROCEDURE: Duration. Renewal or Revival. Termination.
PARTIES:
El Salvador
USA (United States)

200411   Bilateral Exchange   **122 UNTS 293**
SIGNED: 27 Jan 45   FORCE: 27 Jan 45
REGISTERED: 5 Mar 52 USA (United States)
ARTICLES: 2 LANGUAGE: English.
HEADNOTE: RELATING TO AIR TRANSPORT SERVICES
TOPIC: Air Transport
CONCEPTS: Exceptions and exemptions. Annex or appendix reference. Conformity with municipal law. Domestic legislation. Licenses and permits. Recognition of legal documents. Use of facilities. Fees and exemptions. Most favored nation clause. National treatment. Customs exemptions. Competency certificate. Routes and logistics. Navigational conditions. Permit designation. Air transport. Airport facilities. Airworthiness certificates. Conditions of airlines operating permission. Operating authorizations and regulations. Licenses and certificates of nationality.
INTL ORGS: International Civil Aviation Organization.
PROCEDURE: Amendment. Registration. Termination.
PARTIES:
Iceland
USA (United States)

200412   Bilateral Exchange   **122 UNTS 305**
SIGNED: 3 Feb 45   FORCE: 3 Feb 45
REGISTERED: 5 Mar 52 USA (United States)
ARTICLES: 2 LANGUAGE: English.
HEADNOTE: RELATING TO AIR TRANSPORT SERVICES
TOPIC: Air Transport
CONCEPTS: Exceptions and exemptions. Annex or appendix reference. Non-prejudice to third party. Conformity with municipal law. Domestic legislation. Licenses and permits. Recognition of legal documents. Use of facilities. Fees and exemptions. Most favored nation clause. National treatment. Customs exemptions. Competency certificate. Routes and logistics. Navigational conditions. Permit designation. Air transport. Airport facilities. Airworthiness certificates. Conditions of airlines operating permission. Operating authorizations and regulations. Licenses and certificates of nationality.
INTL ORGS: International Civil Aviation Organization.
TREATY REF: 15UNTS295.

PROCEDURE: Registration. Termination.
PARTIES:
Ireland
USA (United States)

200413 Bilateral Exchange **122 UNTS 319**
SIGNED: 6 Oct 45　　　　FORCE: 6 Oct 45
REGISTERED: 5 Mar 52 USA (United States)
ARTICLES: 2 LANGUAGE: English.
HEADNOTE: RELATING TO AIR TRANSPORT SERVICES
TOPIC: Air Transport
CONCEPTS: Exceptions and exemptions. Annex or appendix reference. Conformity with municipal law. Licenses and permits. Recognition of legal documents. Use of facilities. Fees and exemptions. Most favored nation clause. National treatment. Customs exemptions. Competency certificate. Routes and logistics. Navigational conditions. Permit designation. Air transport. Airport facilities. Airworthiness certificates. Conditions of airlines operating permission. Operating authorizations and regulations. Licenses and certificates of nationality.
INTL ORGS: International Civil Aviation Organization.
TREATY REF: 15UNTS295.
PROCEDURE: Amendment. Registration. Termination.
PARTIES:
Norway
USA (United States)

200414 Multilateral Agreement **123 UNTS 223**
SIGNED: 28 Oct 44　　　　FORCE: 28 Oct 44
REGISTERED: 5 Mar 52 USA (United States)
ARTICLES: 19 LANGUAGE: Bulgarian. English. Russian.
HEADNOTE: ARMISTICE
TOPIC: Peace/Disarmament
CONCEPTS: Annex or appendix reference. Repatriation of nationals. Nazi organizations. General property. Use of facilities. Investigation of violations. Establishment of commission. Archives and objects. Claims and settlements. Prisoners of war. Surplus war property. Procurement and logistics. Withdrawal of forces. Armistice and peace. Disarmament and demilitarization.
INTL ORGS: Allied Military Occupation.
PARTIES:
Bulgaria SIGNED: 28 Oct 44 FORCE: 28 Oct 44
UK Great Britain SIGNED: 28 Oct 44 FORCE: 28 Oct 44
USA (United States) SIGNED: 28 Oct 44 FORCE: 28 Oct 44
USSR (Soviet Union) SIGNED: 28 Oct 44 FORCE: 28 Oct 44

200415 Bilateral Agreement **103 UNTS 245**
SIGNED: 10 Apr 51　　　　FORCE: 20 Dec 51
REGISTERED: 11 Mar 52 United Nations
ARTICLES: 18 LANGUAGE: English. French.
HEADNOTE: AGREEMENT & PROTOCOL
TOPIC: IGO Status/Immunit
CONCEPTS: Representation. Treaty implementation. Exchange of information and documents. Personnel. Labor statistics. Accounting procedures. Funding procedures. General technical assistance. Headquarters and facilities. Assistance to United Nations. Inter-agency agreements. Recognition of specialized agency.
INTL ORGS: International Court of Justice.
PROCEDURE: Amendment.
PARTIES:
United Nations
WMO (Meteorology)

200416 Bilateral Exchange **124 UNTS 139**
SIGNED: 29 Mar 43　　　　FORCE: 29 Mar 43
REGISTERED: 20 Mar 52 USA (United States)
ARTICLES: 2 LANGUAGE: English. Spanish.
HEADNOTE: PROTECTION STRATEGIC MATERIALS
TOPIC: Milit Installation
CONCEPTS: Use of facilities. Indemnities and reimbursements. Tax exemptions. Customs exemptions. Materials, equipment and services. Defense and security. Surplus war property. Bases and facilities. Raw materials.
PROCEDURE: Termination.

PARTIES:
Colombia
USA (United States)

200417 Bilateral Exchange **124 UNTS 155**
SIGNED: 29 May 44　　　　FORCE: 29 May 44
REGISTERED: 20 Mar 52 USA (United States)
ARTICLES: 2 LANGUAGE: English. Spanish.
HEADNOTE: MIGRATION AGRICULTURAL WORKERS
TOPIC: Non-ILO Labor
CONCEPTS: General provisions. Friendship and amity. Resident permits. Private contracts. Public health. Employment regulations. Safety standards. Wages and salaries. Non-ILO labor relations. Sickness and invalidity insurance. Migrant worker. Transportation costs. National treatment.
PROCEDURE: Duration. Renewal or Revival.
PARTIES:
Costa Rica
USA (United States)

200418 Bilateral Agreement **124 UNTS 179**
SIGNED: 21 Nov 41　　　　FORCE: 21 Nov 41
REGISTERED: 20 Mar 52 USA (United States)
ARTICLES: 4 LANGUAGE: English.
HEADNOTE: LEND-LEASE AID
TOPIC: Milit Assistance
CONCEPTS: Exceptions and exemptions. Conformity with municipal law. Accounting procedures. Recognition. Payment for war supplies. Lend lease. Restrictions on transfer.
PARTIES:
Iceland
USA (United States)

200419 Bilateral Exchange **124 UNTS 187**
SIGNED: 8 Sep 44　　　　FORCE: 8 Sep 44
REGISTERED: 20 Mar 52 USA (United States)
ARTICLES: 2 LANGUAGE: English.
HEADNOTE: RECOGNITION INDEPENDENCE LEBANON RIGHTS US NATIONALS
TOPIC: Recognition
CONCEPTS: Recognition. Alien status.
TREATY REF: 3DEMARTENS15'283;.
PARTIES:
Lebanon
USA (United States)

200420 Bilateral Exchange **124 UNTS 195**
SIGNED: 23 Mar 40　　　　FORCE: 23 Mar 40
REGISTERED: 20 Mar 52 USA (United States)
ARTICLES: 2 LANGUAGE: English. Spanish.
HEADNOTE: CONSTRUCTION HIGHWAY BETWEEN CHORRERA & RIO ITATO IN PANAMA
TOPIC: Land Transport
CONCEPTS: General cooperation. Exchange of information and documents. Domestic legislation. Personnel. Private contracts. Responsibility and liability. Use of facilities. Indemnities and reimbursements. Fees and exemptions. Financial programs. Tax exemptions. Customs exemptions. Special projects. Materials, equipment and services. Routes and logistics. Railways. Military installations and equipment.
PARTIES:
Panama
USA (United States)

200421 Bilateral Exchange **124 UNTS 209**
SIGNED: 6 Sep 40　　　　FORCE: 6 Sep 40
REGISTERED: 20 Mar 52 USA (United States)
ARTICLES: 2 LANGUAGE: English. Spanish.
HEADNOTE: AGREEMENT SUPPLEMENTING CONVENTION CONSTRUCTION TRANS-ISTHMIAN HIGHWAY
TOPIC: Land Transport
CONCEPTS: Conformity with municipal law. Exchange of information and documents. Domestic legislation. Personnel. Responsibility and liability. Use of facilities. Fees and exemptions. Financial programs. Tax exemptions. Customs exemptions. Materials, equipment and services. Routes and logistics. Roads and highways. Military installations and equipment.
TREATY REF: 200LTS205.

PARTIES:
Panama
USA (United States)

200422 Bilateral Exchange **124 UNTS 221**
SIGNED: 18 May 42　　　　FORCE: 18 May 42
REGISTERED: 20 Mar 52 USA (United States)
ARTICLES: 2 LANGUAGE: English. Spanish.
HEADNOTE: GENERAL RELATIONS
TOPIC: General Amity
CONCEPTS: General cooperation. Expropriation. Title and deeds. Use of facilities. Migrant worker. General trade. Non-interest rates and fees. Debts. Hydro-electric power. Tonnage. Railways. Railways. Roads and highways.
TREATY REF: 431UTS33'2234; 200LTS17; 124UNTS25;.
PARTIES:
Panama
USA (United States)

200423 Bilateral Exchange **124 UNTS 243**
SIGNED: 22 May 42　　　　FORCE: 22 May 42
REGISTERED: 20 Mar 52 USA (United States)
ARTICLES: 2 LANGUAGE: English.
HEADNOTE: HEALTH SANITATION PROGRAM
TOPIC: Sanitation
CONCEPTS: General cooperation. Personnel. General property. Specialists exchange. Public health. Sanitation. Commissions and foundations. Vocational training. Research and development. Expense sharing formulae. Financial programs. Assistance. Grants.
PARTIES:
Paraguay
USA (United States)

200424 Bilateral Exchange **124 UNTS 251**
SIGNED: 8 Sep 44　　　　FORCE: 8 Sep 44
REGISTERED: 20 Mar 52 USA (United States)
ARTICLES: 2 LANGUAGE: English.
HEADNOTE: RECOGNITION INDEPENDENCE SYRIA RIGHTS US NATIONALS
TOPIC: Recognition
CONCEPTS: Recognition. Alien status.
PARTIES:
Syria
USA (United States)

200425 Bilateral Agreement **124 UNTS 259**
SIGNED: 30 Jan 52　　　　FORCE: 30 Jan 52
REGISTERED: 24 Mar 52 WHO (World Health)
ARTICLES: 6 LANGUAGE: English. French.
HEADNOTE: TECHNICAL ASSISTANCE
TOPIC: Tech Assistance
CONCEPTS: Definition of terms. Treaty implementation. Privileges and immunities. General cooperation. Personnel. Title and deeds. Exchange. Scholarships and grants. Vocational training. Research and development. Expense sharing formulae. Local currency. Domestic obligation. General technical assistance. Materials, equipment and services. IGO status. Conformity with IGO decisions.
INTL ORGS: International Civil Aviation Organization.
TREATY REF: 76UNTS132; 33UNTS261.
PROCEDURE: Amendment. Termination.
PARTIES:
WHO (World Health)
Spain

200426 Bilateral Convention **124 UNTS 271**
SIGNED: 4 Mar 42　　　　FORCE: 15 Jun 42
REGISTERED: 26 Mar 52 USA (United States)
ARTICLES: 22 LANGUAGE: English.
HEADNOTE: DOUBLE TAXATION PREVENTION FISCAL EVASION INCOME TAXES
TOPIC: Taxation
CONCEPTS: Conformity with municipal law. Exchange of official publications. Responsibility and liability. Teacher and student exchange. Assets. Claims and settlements. Taxation. Tax credits. General. Tax exemptions. Air transport. Merchant vessels.
TREATY REF: 920UTS50'1399; 95LTS09;.
PROCEDURE: Duration. Ratification. Termination.

PARTIES:
Canada
USA (United States)

200427 Bilateral Convention **124 UNTS 297**
SIGNED: 8 Jun 44   FORCE: 6 Feb 45
REGISTERED: 26 Mar 52 USA (United States)
ARTICLES: 14 LANGUAGE: English.
HEADNOTE: DOUBLE TAXATION FISCAL EVA-
SION ESTATE TAXES SUCCESSION DUTIES
TOPIC: Taxation
CONCEPTS: Definition of terms. Conformity with
municipal law. Exchange of official publications.
Immovable property. Negotiation. Claims and
settlements. Taxation. Death duties. General.
PROCEDURE: Duration. Ratification. Termination.
PARTIES:
Canada
USA (United States)

200428 Bilateral Instrument **125 UNTS 239**
SIGNED: 9 Sep 40   FORCE: 6 Jul 43
REGISTERED: 26 Mar 52 USA (United States)
ARTICLES: 13 LANGUAGE: English. Spanish.
HEADNOTE: SUPPLEMENTARY CONVENTION EX-
TRADITION
TOPIC: Extradition
CONCEPTS: Annex type material. Extradition, de-
portation and repatriation. Court procedures. Ex-
tradition requests. Extraditable offenses. Loca-
tion of crime. Refusal of extradition. Concurrent
requests.
PROCEDURE: Ratification.
PARTIES:
Colombia
USA (United States)

200429 Bilateral Convention **125 UNTS 259**
SIGNED: 25 Jul 39   FORCE: 1 Jan 45
REGISTERED: 26 Mar 52 USA (United States)
ARTICLES: 27 LANGUAGE: English. French.
HEADNOTE: AVOIDANCE DOUBLE TAXATION
TOPIC: Taxation
CONCEPTS: Taxation. Tax credits. Equitable taxes.
General. Tax exemptions.
TREATY REF: 114LTS413.
PROCEDURE: Ratification.
PARTIES:
France
USA (United States)

200430 Bilateral Convention **125 UNTS 287**
SIGNED: 19 Nov 41   FORCE: 2 Apr 42
REGISTERED: 26 Mar 52 USA (United States)
ARTICLES: 6 LANGUAGE: English. Spanish.
HEADNOTE: FINAL ADJUSTMENT UNSETTLED
CLAIMS
TOPIC: Claims and Debts
CONCEPTS: Detailed regulations. Time limit. Previ-
ous treaty replacement. Arbitration. Procedure.
Bonds. Interest rates. Claims and settlements.
Lump sum settlements. Loan repayment.
INTL ORGS: Claims Commission.
TREATY REF: UTS678'43'1730; 68LTS459;
149LTS49;.
PARTIES:
Mexico
USA (United States)

200431 Bilateral Convention **125 UNTS 301**
SIGNED: 12 Aug 42   FORCE: 1 Jul 43
REGISTERED: 26 Mar 52 USA (United States)
ARTICLES: 14 LANGUAGE: English. Spanish.
HEADNOTE: CONSULAR CONVENTION
TOPIC: Consul/Citizenship
CONCEPTS: General consular functions. Diplo-
matic privileges. Consular relations establish-
ment. Inviolability. Privileges and immunities.
Most favored nation clause. Foreign nationals.
PROCEDURE: Amendment. Ratification. Termina-
tion.
PARTIES:
Mexico
USA (United States)

200432 Bilateral Exchange **125 UNTS 345**
SIGNED: 23 Mar 44   FORCE: 23 Mar 44
REGISTERED: 26 Mar 52 USA (United States)

ARTICLES: 2 LANGUAGE: English.
HEADNOTE: SETTLEMENT CLAIMS
TOPIC: Claims and Debts
CONCEPTS: Detailed regulations. Claims and set-
tlements. Road rules. Jurisdiction. Status of
forces.
PARTIES:
Canada
USA (United States)

200433 Bilateral Exchange **125 UNTS 353**
SIGNED: 15 May 45   FORCE: 15 May 45
REGISTERED: 26 Mar 52 USA (United States)
ARTICLES: 2 LANGUAGE: English.
HEADNOTE: COOPERATION TRANSITION FROM
WAR PEACE
TOPIC: Peace/Disarmament
CONCEPTS: General cooperation. Defense and se-
curity. Surplus war property. Reconversion to
normalcy.
PARTIES:
Canada
USA (United States)

200434 Multilateral Agreement **126 UNTS 319**
SIGNED: 18 Feb 52   FORCE: 18 Feb 52
REGISTERED: 28 Mar 52 United Nations
ARTICLES: 4 LANGUAGE: English.
HEADNOTE: TECHNICAL ASSISTANCE
TOPIC: Tech Assistance
CONCEPTS: Privileges and immunities. General
cooperation. Scholarships and grants. Expense
sharing formulae. Domestic obligation. General
technical assistance. Special projects. Head-
quarters and facilities. Conformity with IGO deci-
sions.
TREATY REF: 76UNTS132; 1UNTS15'261;
33UNTS261;7.
PROCEDURE: Amendment. Termination.
PARTIES:
Ceylon (Sri Lanka) SIGNED: 18 Feb 52 FORCE:
18 Feb 52
FAO (Food Agri) SIGNED: 18 Feb 52 FORCE:
18 Feb 52
ICAO (Civil Aviat) SIGNED: 18 Feb 52 FORCE:
18 Feb 52
ILO (Labor Org) SIGNED: 18 Feb 52 FORCE:
18 Feb 52
UNESCO (Educ/Cult) SIGNED: 18 Feb 52
FORCE: 18 Feb 52
United Nations SIGNED: 18 Feb 52 FORCE:
18 Feb 52
WHO (World Health) SIGNED: 18 Feb 52 FORCE:
18 Feb 52

200435 Bilateral Agreement **126 UNTS 331**
SIGNED: 23 Nov 51   FORCE: 23 Nov 51
REGISTERED: 1 Apr 52 ILO (Labor Org)
ARTICLES: 12 LANGUAGE: English. French.
HEADNOTE: AGREEMENT
TOPIC: IGO Operations
CONCEPTS: Treaty implementation. Exchange of
information and documents. Labor statistics.
Funding procedures. General technical assis-
tance. Regional offices. Mutual consultation.
INTL ORGS: United Nations.
PROCEDURE: Amendment. Duration.
PARTIES:
Council of Europe
ILO (Labor Org)

200436 Bilateral Agreement **128 UNTS 269**
SIGNED: 7 Mar 52   FORCE: 7 Mar 52
REGISTERED: 5 May 52 WHO (World Health)
ARTICLES: 6 LANGUAGE: English.
HEADNOTE: PROVISIONAL BASIC AGREEMENT
TECHNICAL ASSISTANCE
TOPIC: Tech Assistance
CONCEPTS: Treaty implementation. Privileges and
immunities. General cooperation. Personnel. Ti-
tle and deeds. Exchange. Vocational training. Re-
search and development. Expense sharing for-
mulae. Local currency. Domestic obligation.
General technical assistance. Materials, equip-
ment and services.
INTL ORGS: United Nations.
TREATY REF: 76UNTS132.
PROCEDURE: Amendment. Termination.

PARTIES:
Finland
WHO (World Health)

200437 Bilateral Agreement **128 UNTS 281**
SIGNED: 4 Mar 52   FORCE: 4 Mar 52
REGISTERED: 5 May 52 WHO (World Health)
ARTICLES: 4 LANGUAGE: English.
HEADNOTE: PROVISION MEDICAL STORE MAN-
AGEMENT CONSULATANT
TOPIC: Direct Aid
CONCEPTS: Privileges and immunities. General
technical assistance. Assistance. Special
projects.
TREATY REF: 33UNTS261; ETC..
PROCEDURE: Amendment. Termination.
PARTIES:
Ceylon (Sri Lanka)
WHO (World Health)

200438 Bilateral Agreement **131 UNTS 295**
SIGNED: 10 Jan 52   FORCE: 10 Jan 52
REGISTERED: 10 Jun 52 WHO (World Health)
ARTICLES: 6 LANGUAGE: English.
HEADNOTE: TECHNICAL ADVISORY ASSISTANCE
TOPIC: Tech Assistance
CONCEPTS: Treaty implementation. Privileges and
immunities. General cooperation. Personnel. Ti-
tle and deeds. Arbitration. Procedure. Scholar-
ships and grants. Vocational training. Expense
sharing formulae. General technical assistance.
Special projects. Materials, equipment and ser-
vices. IGO status. Conformity with IGO decisions.
INTL ORGS: United Nations.
TREATY REF: 14UNTS185; 76UNTS132;
33UNTS261.
PROCEDURE: Amendment. Termination.
PARTIES:
Austria
WHO (World Health)

200439 Bilateral Exchange **132 UNTS 343**
SIGNED: 8 Apr 42   FORCE: 18 Apr 42
REGISTERED: 14 Jun 52 USA (United States)
ARTICLES: 2 LANGUAGE: English. Spanish.
HEADNOTE: CONSTRUCTION DEFENSE HIGH-
WAYS
TOPIC: Milit Installation
CONCEPTS: Roads and highways. Defense and se-
curity. Bases and facilities.
TREATY REF: 24UNTS145.
PARTIES:
Nicaragua
USA (United States)

200440 Bilateral Agreement **132 UNTS 355**
SIGNED: 16 May 44   FORCE: 16 May 44
REGISTERED: 14 Jun 52 USA (United States)
ARTICLES: 16 LANGUAGE: Dutch. English.
HEADNOTE: ADMINISTRATION JURISDICTION
NETHERLANDS TERRITORY
TOPIC: Milit Occupation
CONCEPTS: Status of military forces. Procurement
and logistics. Withdrawal of forces. Status of
forces.
PARTIES:
Netherlands
USA (United States)

200441 Bilateral Agreement **133 UNTS 287**
SIGNED: 5 Apr 52   FORCE: 15 Apr 52
REGISTERED: 16 Jun 52 United Nations
ARTICLES: 10 LANGUAGE: Arabic. English.
HEADNOTE: ACTIVITIES UNICEF
TOPIC: Direct Aid
CONCEPTS: Treaty implementation. Privileges and
immunities. General cooperation. Exchange of
information and documents. Informational
records. Inspection and observation. Public in-
formation. Use of facilities. Procedure. Existing
tribunals. Export quotas. Financial programs. Tax
exemptions. Commodities and services. Assis-
tance. General aid. Procurement. Distribution.
IGO status.
INTL ORGS: United Nations.
PARTIES:
Libya
UNICEF (Children)

ANNEX
214 UNTS 386. UNICEF (Children). Supplementation 30 Apr 55. Force 30 Apr 55.
214 UNTS 386. Libya. Supplementation 30 Apr 55. Force 30 Apr 55.

200442 Bilateral Agreement **134 UNTS 341**
SIGNED: 26 Mar 52   FORCE: 2 Apr 52
REGISTERED: 21 Jul 52 WHO (World Health)
ARTICLES: 4 LANGUAGE: English.
HEADNOTE: OPERATION VISITING TEAM WHO MEDICAL SCIENTISTS
TOPIC: Sanitation
CONCEPTS: Definition of terms. Privileges and immunities. Non-diplomatic delegations. General cooperation. Personnel. Responsibility and liability. Public health. WHO used as agency. Exchange. Indemnities and reimbursements. Expense sharing formulae.
TREATY REF: 33UNTS261.
PROCEDURE: Amendment. Duration.
PARTIES:
Ceylon (Sri Lanka)
WHO (World Health)

200443 Bilateral Agreement **135 UNTS 305**
SIGNED: 25 Jul 52   FORCE: 25 Jul 52
REGISTERED: 25 Jul 52 United Nations
ARTICLES: 11 LANGUAGE: English.
HEADNOTE: PRIVILEGES & IMMUNITIES
TOPIC: IGO Status/Immunit
CONCEPTS: Non-visa travel documents. Diplomatic correspondence. Procedure. Existing tribunals. IGO status. Special status. Status of experts.
INTL ORGS: International Court of Justice. United Nations Commission for Korean Reconstruction.
TREATY REF: 15UNTS263.
PROCEDURE: Duration.
PARTIES:
Japan
United Nations
ANNEX
460 UNTS 372. Japan. Termination 18 Apr 63. Force 18 Oct 63.

200444 Bilateral Exchange **135 UNTS 315**
SIGNED: 16 Sep 44   FORCE: 16 Sep 44
REGISTERED: 1 Aug 52 USA (United States)
ARTICLES: 2 LANGUAGE: English. Spanish.
HEADNOTE: COOPERATIVE EDUCATIONAL PROGRAM
TOPIC: Education
CONCEPTS: Privileges and immunities. Exchange. Currency. Funding procedures. Tax exemptions. Customs exemptions.
TREATY REF: 135UNTS104; TAIS 2073.
PARTIES:
Guatemala
USA (United States)

200445 Bilateral Exchange **135 UNTS 323**
SIGNED: 16 Jun 52   FORCE: 16 Jun 52
REGISTERED: 15 Aug 52 WHO (World Health)
ARTICLES: 2 LANGUAGE: English.
HEADNOTE: INTERNATIONAL LABORATORY EXPERTS
TOPIC: Direct Aid
CONCEPTS: Personnel. Public health. Assets transfer. Domestic obligation. General technical assistance. Materials, equipment and services.
INTL ORGS: United Nations Palestine Refugees Relief and Works Agency.
PARTIES:
Jordan
WHO (World Health)

200446 Bilateral Agreement **136 UNTS 341**
SIGNED: 28 Apr 56   FORCE: 28 Apr 52
REGISTERED: 18 Aug 52 United Nations
ARTICLES: 10 LANGUAGE: French.
HEADNOTE: ACTIVITIES UNICEF
TOPIC: Direct Aid
CONCEPTS: Treaty implementation. Privileges and immunities. General cooperation. Exchange of information and documents. Informational records. Inspection and observation. Public information. Use of facilities. Procedure. Existing tribunals. Export quotas. Financial programs. Tax exemptions. Customs exemptions. Commodities and services. Assistance. General aid. Distribution. IGO status.
INTL ORGS: United Nations.
TREATY REF: 1UNTS15.
PROCEDURE: Duration. Ratification.
PARTIES:
Cambodia
UNICEF (Children)

200447 Bilateral Exchange **136 UNTS 353**
SIGNED: 11 May 42   FORCE: 11 May 42
REGISTERED: 3 Sep 52 USA (United States)
ARTICLES: 2 LANGUAGE: English. Spanish.
HEADNOTE: HEALTH SANITATION
TOPIC: Sanitation
CONCEPTS: Personnel. General property. Specialists exchange. Public health. Funding procedures. Domestic obligation. Materials, equipment and services.
PARTIES:
Peru
USA (United States)

200448 Bilateral Agreement **137 UNTS 267**
SIGNED: 29 Mar 51   FORCE: 29 Mar 51
REGISTERED: 16 Sep 52 United Nations
ARTICLES: 5 LANGUAGE: English. French.
HEADNOTE: TECHNICAL ASSISTANCE
TOPIC: Tech Assistance
CONCEPTS: Definition of terms. Treaty implementation. Annex or appendix reference. Privileges and immunities. General cooperation. Personnel. Title and deeds. Scholarships and grants. Vocational training. Research and scientific projects. Expense sharing formulae. Local currency. Domestic obligation. General technical assistance. Materials, equipment and services. IGO status. Conformity with IGO decisions.
INTL ORGS: International Civil Aviation Organization. International Labour Organization. United Nations Educational, Scientific and Cultural Organization. World Health Organization.
TREATY REF: 6UNTS132; 1UNTS15,263; 33UNTS261.
PROCEDURE: Amendment. Termination.
PARTIES:
Jordan
United Nations

200449 Bilateral Exchange **138 UNTS 247**
SIGNED: 25 Aug 44   FORCE: 25 Aug 44
REGISTERED: 25 Sep 52 USA (United States)
ARTICLES: 4 LANGUAGE: English. French.
HEADNOTE: CIVIL ADMINISTRATION JURISDICTION LIBERATED TERRITORY
TOPIC: Milit Occupation
CONCEPTS: Annex or appendix reference. Democratic institutions. Transition period. Post-war reconstruction. Joint defense. Control and occupation machinery.
PARTIES:
France
USA (United States)

200450 Bilateral Exchange **138 UNTS 271**
SIGNED: 12 Apr 44   FORCE: 12 Apr 44
REGISTERED: 30 Sep 52 USA (United States)
ARTICLES: 2 LANGUAGE: English. Spanish.
HEADNOTE: COOPERATIVE EDUCATIONAL PROGRAM
TOPIC: Education
CONCEPTS: General cooperation. Personnel. Specialists exchange. Exchange. Currency. Expense sharing formulae. Financial programs. Funding procedures.
PROCEDURE: Duration. Future Procedures Contemplated.
PARTIES:
Honduras
USA (United States)

200451 Bilateral Exchange **138 UNTS 282**
SIGNED: 13 Oct 42   FORCE: 13 Oct 42
REGISTERED: 30 Sep 52 USA (United States)
ARTICLES: 2 LANGUAGE: English. Spanish.
HEADNOTE: RELATING RUBBER DEVELOPMENT
TOPIC: Commodity Trade

CONCEPTS: General cooperation. General trade. Trade agencies. Commodity trade.
PROCEDURE: Duration. Renewal or Revival. Termination.
PARTIES:
USA (United States)
Venezuela

200452 Multilateral Agreement **139 UNTS 159**
SIGNED: 28 Nov 40   FORCE: 16 Apr 41
REGISTERED: 1 Oct 52 USA (United States)
ARTICLES: 26 LANGUAGE: English. French. Portuguese. Spanish.
HEADNOTE: INTER-AMERICAN COFFEE AGREEMENT
TOPIC: Commodity Trade
CONCEPTS: Definition of terms. Detailed regulations. Time limit. Exchange of information and documents. Procedure. Trade agencies. Commodity trade. Quotas. Loan and credit.
INTL ORGS: Inter-American Coffee Board. Organization of American States.
PROCEDURE: Amendment. Termination.
PARTIES:
Brazil SIGNED: 28 Nov 40 FORCE: 16 Apr 61
Colombia SIGNED: 28 Nov 40 FORCE: 16 Apr 61
Costa Rica SIGNED: 28 Nov 40 FORCE: 16 Apr 61
Cuba SIGNED: 28 Nov 40 FORCE: 31 Dec 41
Dominican Republic SIGNED: 28 Nov 40 FORCE: 1 May 41
Ecuador SIGNED: 28 Nov 40 FORCE: 30 Apr 41
El Salvador SIGNED: 28 Nov 40 FORCE: 16 Apr 61
Guatemala SIGNED: 28 Nov 40 FORCE: 16 Apr 61
Haiti SIGNED: 28 Nov 40 FORCE: 16 Apr 61
Honduras SIGNED: 28 Nov 40 FORCE: 16 Apr 61
Mexico SIGNED: 28 Nov 40 FORCE: 16 Apr 61
Nicaragua SIGNED: 28 Nov 40 FORCE: 14 May 41
Peru SIGNED: 28 Nov 40 FORCE: 16 Apr 61
USA (United States) SIGNED: 28 Nov 40 FORCE: 16 Apr 61
Venezuela SIGNED: 28 Nov 40 FORCE: 15 Aug 41

200453 Bilateral Exchange **139 UNTS 227**
SIGNED: 9 May 45   FORCE: 9 May 45
REGISTERED: 2 Oct 52 USA (United States)
ARTICLES: 2 LANGUAGE: English. Spanish.
HEADNOTE: FUEL & VEGETABLE OILS
TOPIC: Commodity Trade
CONCEPTS: Definition of terms. Detailed regulations. Time limit. General cooperation. Export quotas. Import quotas. Trade agencies. Currency. Payment schedules. Non-interest rates and fees. Transportation costs. Commodity trade. Quotas. General transportation. Transport of goods.
PARTIES:
Argentina
USA (United States)

200454 Bilateral Agreement **139 UNTS 253**
SIGNED: 17 Apr 45   FORCE: 17 Apr 45
REGISTERED: 2 Oct 52 USA (United States)
ARTICLES: 6 LANGUAGE: English.
HEADNOTE: AGREEMENT UNDER LEND-LEASE ACT
TOPIC: Milit Assistance
CONCEPTS: Exceptions and exemptions. Annex or appendix reference. Conformity with municipal law. Indemnities and reimbursements. Materials, equipment and services. Surplus property. Payment for war supplies. Lend lease.
TREATY REF: 204LTS381.
PROCEDURE: Future Procedures Contemplated.
PARTIES:
Belgium
USA (United States)

200455 Bilateral Exchange **139 UNTS 179**
SIGNED: 19 Apr 45   FORCE: 17 Apr 45
REGISTERED: 2 Oct 52 USA (United States)
ARTICLES: 4 LANGUAGE: English.
HEADNOTE: PROVISION AID ARMED FORCES
TOPIC: Milit Installation

CONCEPTS: Treaty implementation. Previous treaty replacement. Accounting procedures. Local currency. Domestic obligation. Materials, equipment and services. Security of information. Exchange of defense information.
INTL ORGS: United Nations.
TREATY REF: 204LTS381.
PARTIES:
  Belgium
  USA (United States)

200456 Bilateral Exchange **139 UNTS 295**
SIGNED: 11 May 43   FORCE: 11 May 43
REGISTERED: 2 Oct 52 USA (United States)
ARTICLES: 2 LANGUAGE: English. Spanish.
HEADNOTE: HEALTH SANITATION PROGRAM
TOPIC: Sanitation
CONCEPTS: General cooperation. Personnel. General property. Specialists exchange. Public health. Sanitation. Expense sharing formulae. Financial programs. Assistance. Specific technical assistance. Grants. Defense and security.
PARTIES:
  Chile
  USA (United States)

200457 Bilateral Exchange **139 UNTS 303**
SIGNED: 17 Apr 45   FORCE: 17 Apr 45
REGISTERED: 2 Oct 52 USA (United States)
ARTICLES: 2 LANGUAGE: English. Spanish.
HEADNOTE: WAIVER CERTAIN TARIFF PREFERENCES
TOPIC: Customs
CONCEPTS: Tariffs. Most favored nation clause. Customs exemptions.
TREATY REF: 170LTS293.
PARTIES:
  Colombia
  USA (United States)

200458 Bilateral Exchange **139 UNTS 311**
SIGNED: 24 Aug 45   FORCE: 24 Aug 45
REGISTERED: 2 Oct 52 USA (United States)
ARTICLES: 2 LANGUAGE: English. French.
HEADNOTE: RECIPROCAL CUSTOMS PRIVILEGES CONSULAR OFFICERS & CLERKS
TOPIC: Visas
CONCEPTS: Diplomatic privileges.
PARTIES:
  Haiti
  USA (United States)

200459 Bilateral Exchange **139 UNTS 319**
SIGNED: 30 Apr 45   FORCE: 30 Apr 45
REGISTERED: 2 Oct 52 USA (United States)
ARTICLES: 8 LANGUAGE: English.
HEADNOTE: AID ARMED FORCES
TOPIC: Milit Installation
CONCEPTS: Previous treaty replacement. Local currency. Materials, equipment and services. Military assistance. Equipment and supplies.
INTL ORGS: United Nations.
TREATY REF: 103UNTS277.
PARTIES:
  Netherlands
  USA (United States)

200460 Bilateral Agreement **139 UNTS 341**
SIGNED: 30 Apr 45   FORCE: 30 Apr 45
REGISTERED: 2 Oct 52 USA (United States)
ARTICLES: 6 LANGUAGE: English.
HEADNOTE: AGREEMENT UNDER LEND-LEASE
TOPIC: Milit Assistance
CONCEPTS: Exceptions and exemptions. Annex or appendix reference. Conformity with municipal law. Indemnities and reimbursements. Materials,

equipment and services. Surplus property. Payment for war supplies. Lend lease.
TREATY REF: 204LTS381; 103UNTS.
PROCEDURE: Future Procedures Contemplated.
PARTIES:
  Netherlands
  USA (United States)

200461 Bilateral Exchange **139 UNTS 361**
SIGNED: 28 Aug 42   FORCE: 28 Aug 42
REGISTERED: 2 Oct 52 USA (United States)
ARTICLES: 2 LANGUAGE: English.
HEADNOTE: REGULATION MILITARY RELATIONS
TOPIC: Other Military
CONCEPTS: Title and deeds. Use of facilities. National treatment. Materials, equipment and services. Joint defense. Defense and security. Payment for war supplies. Military assistance. Jurisdiction. Withdrawal of forces. Status of forces.
PROCEDURE: Amendment. Termination.
PARTIES:
  Norway
  USA (United States)

200462 Bilateral Exchange **139 UNTS 367**
SIGNED: 14 Nov 44   FORCE: 14 Nov 44
REGISTERED: 2 Oct 52 USA (United States)
ARTICLES: 2 LANGUAGE: English. Spanish.
HEADNOTE: COOPERATIVE EDUCATIONAL PROGRAM
TOPIC: Education
CONCEPTS: Exchange. Conferences.
PROCEDURE: Future Procedures Contemplated.
PARTIES:
  Panama
  USA (United States)

200463 Bilateral Exchange **139 UNTS 373**
SIGNED: 24 Sep 43   FORCE: 24 Sep 43
REGISTERED: 2 Oct 52 USA (United States)
ARTICLES: 2 LANGUAGE: English.
HEADNOTE: JURISDICTION OVER PRIZES
TOPIC: Admin Cooperation
CONCEPTS: Prizes and arbitral awards. Establishment of commission.
PARTIES:
  UK Great Britain
  USA (United States)

200464 Multilateral Agreement **139 UNTS 381**
SIGNED: 9 Jun 45   FORCE: 9 Jun 45
REGISTERED: 2 Oct 52 USA (United States)
ARTICLES: 7 LANGUAGE: English.
HEADNOTE: PROVISIONAL ADMINISTRATION VENEZIA GIULIA
TOPIC: Milit Occupation
CONCEPTS: General military. Status of military forces. Jurisdiction. Control and occupation machinery.
INTL ORGS: Allied Military Occupation.
PARTIES:
  UK Great Britain SIGNED: 9 Jun 45 FORCE: 9 Jun 45
  USA (United States) SIGNED: 9 Jun 45 FORCE: 9 Jun 45
  Yugoslavia SIGNED: 9 Jun 45 FORCE: 9 Jun 45

200465 Multilateral Instrument **139 UNTS 387**
SIGNED: 2 Sep 45   FORCE: 2 Sep 45
REGISTERED: 2 Oct 52 United Nations
ARTICLES: 1 LANGUAGE: English.
HEADNOTE: INSTRUMENT SURRENDER
TOPIC: Peace/Disarmament
CONCEPTS: Repatriation of nationals. Prisoners of war. Armistice and peace. Control and occupation machinery.

INTL ORGS: Allied Military Occupation.
PARTIES:
  Australia SIGNED: 2 Sep 45 FORCE: 2 Sep 45
  Canada SIGNED: 2 Sep 45 FORCE: 2 Sep 45
  China SIGNED: 2 Sep 45 FORCE: 2 Sep 45
  France SIGNED: 2 Sep 45 FORCE: 2 Sep 45
  Japan SIGNED: 2 Sep 45 FORCE: 2 Sep 45
  Netherlands SIGNED: 2 Sep 45 FORCE: 2 Sep 45
  New Zealand SIGNED: 2 Sep 45 FORCE: 2 Sep 45
  UK Great Britain SIGNED: 2 Sep 45 FORCE: 2 Sep 45
  USA (United States) SIGNED: 2 Sep 45 FORCE: 2 Sep 45
  USSR (Soviet Union) SIGNED: 2 Sep 45 FORCE: 2 Sep 45

200466 Bilateral Agreement **139 UNTS 395**
SIGNED: 12 Oct 50   FORCE: 12 Oct 50
REGISTERED: 2 Oct 52 United Nations
ARTICLES: 11 LANGUAGE: English. French.
HEADNOTE: ADMIT ILO INTO UN JOINT STAFF PENSION FUND
TOPIC: IGO Operations
CONCEPTS: Default remedies. Exchange of information and documents. Holidays and rest periods. Accounting procedures. Conformity with IGO decisions. Assistance to United Nations. Recognition of specialized agency.
PARTIES:
  ILO (Labor Org)
  United Nations
                ANNEX
214 UNTS 388. United Nations. Implementation 24 Aug 55.
214 UNTS 388. ILO (Labor Org). Implementation 24 Aug 55. Force 24 Aug 55.
565 UNTS 328. ILO (Labor Org). Amendment 14 Jun 66. Force 14 Jun 66.
565 UNTS 328. United Nations. Amendment 30 May 66. Force 14 Jun 66.

200467 Bilateral Agreement **139 UNTS 407**
SIGNED: 2 Aug 50   FORCE: 9 Aug 50
REGISTERED: 2 Oct 52 United Nations
ARTICLES: 9 LANGUAGE: English. French.
HEADNOTE: ADMIT FAO INTO UN JOINT STAFF PENSION FUND
TOPIC: IGO Operations
CONCEPTS: Default remedies. Exchange of information and documents. Holidays and rest periods. Accounting procedures. Conformity with IGO decisions. Assistance to United Nations. Recognition of specialized agency.
INTL ORGS: United Nations.
PARTIES:
  FAO (Food Agri)
  United Nations
                ANNEX
219 UNTS 388. FAO (Food Agri). Implementation 29 Sep 55. Force 29 Sep 55.
219 UNTS 388. United Nations. Implementation 29 Sep 55. Force 29 Sep 55.

200468 Bilateral Agreement **139 UNTS 417**
SIGNED: 7 Mar 51   FORCE: 7 Mar 51
REGISTERED: 2 Oct 52 United Nations
ARTICLES: 10 LANGUAGE: English. French.
HEADNOTE: ADMIT UNESCO INTO UN JOINT STAFF PENSION FUND
TOPIC: IGO Operations
CONCEPTS: Default remedies. Exchange of information and documents. Holidays and rest periods. Accounting procedures. Conformity with IGO decisions. Assistance to United Nations. Recognition of specialized agency.
INTL ORGS: United Nations.
PARTIES:
  UNESCO (Educ/Cult)
  United Nations
                ANNEX
219 UNTS 392. United Nations. Implementation 23 Sep 55. Force 23 Sep 55.

219 UNTS 392. UNESCO (Educ/Cult). Implementation 23 Sep 55. Force 23 Sep 55.

200469 Bilateral Agreement **139 UNTS 429**
SIGNED: 28 Feb 51　　　　FORCE: 28 Feb 51
REGISTERED: 2 Oct 52 United Nations
ARTICLES: 8 LANGUAGE: English. French. Spanish.
HEADNOTE: ADMIT ICAO INTO UN JOINT STAFF PENSION FUND
TOPIC: IGO Operations
CONCEPTS: Default remedies. Exchange of information and documents. Holidays and rest periods. Accounting procedures. Conformity with IGO decisions. Assistance to United Nations. Recognition of specialized agency.
INTL ORGS: United Nations.
PARTIES:
　ICAO (Civil Aviat)
　United Nations
　　　　ANNEX
219 UNTS 396. ICAO (Civil Aviat). Implementation 7 Oct 55. Force 7 Oct 55.
219 UNTS 396. United Nations. Implementation 7 Oct 55. Force 7 Oct 55.
399 UNTS 306. United Nations. Amendment 28 Jun 60. Force 15 Jul 60.
399 UNTS 306. ICAO (Civil Aviat). Amendment 24 Jun 60. Force 15 Jul 60.

200470 Bilateral Agreement **139 UNTS 445**
SIGNED: 20 Apr 50　　　　FORCE: 20 Apr 50
REGISTERED: 2 Oct 52 United Nations
ARTICLES: 10 LANGUAGE: English. French.
HEADNOTE: ADMISSION WHO TO UN JOINT STAFF PENSION FUND
TOPIC: IGO Operations
CONCEPTS: Old age insurance. Liaison with other IGO's. Internal structure.
PARTIES:
　United Nations
　WHO (World Health)
　　　　ANNEX
394 UNTS 334. WHO (World Health). Amendment 27 Mar 61. Force 8 Apr 61.
394 UNTS 334. United Nations. Amendment 8 Apr 61. Force 8 Apr 61.

200471 Multilateral Agreement **140 UNTS 397**
SIGNED: 20 Jan 45　　　　FORCE: 20 Jan 45
REGISTERED: 8 Oct 52 USA (United States)
ARTICLES: 20 LANGUAGE: English. Hungarian. Russian.
HEADNOTE: ARMISTICE
TOPIC: Peace/Disarmament
CONCEPTS: Annex or appendix reference. Previous treaty renunciation. Repatriation of nationals. Nazi organizations. Human rights. Investigation of violations. Establishment of commission. Archives and objects. Compensation. Currency. Lump sum settlements. Prisoners of war. Rearmament restrictions and controls. Military assistance. Surplus war property. Procurement and logistics. Armistice and peace. Reparations and restrictions. Post-war claims settlement. Disarmament and demilitarization.
INTL ORGS: Allied Military Occupation. United Nations.
PARTIES:
　Hungary SIGNED: 20 Jan 45 FORCE: 20 Jan 40
　UK Great Britain SIGNED: 20 Jan 45 FORCE: 20 Jan 40
　USA (United States) SIGNED: 20 Jan 45 FORCE: 20 Jan 40
　USSR (Soviet Union) SIGNED: 20 Jan 45 FORCE: 20 Jan 40

200472 Bilateral Agreement **141 UNTS 341**
SIGNED: 21 Aug 52　　　　FORCE: 21 Aug 52
REGISTERED: 21 Oct 52 WHO (World Health)

ARTICLES: 4 LANGUAGE: English.
HEADNOTE: OPERATION PROJECT ASSIST PUBLIC HEALTH LABORATORY
TOPIC: Direct Aid
CONCEPTS: Privileges and immunities. General cooperation. Personnel. Use of facilities. Public health. Scholarships and grants. Expense sharing formulae. Tax exemptions. Domestic obligation. Materials, equipment and services. IGO status.
INTL ORGS: United Nations Palestine Refugees Relief and Works Agency.
TREATY REF: 110UNTS297.
PROCEDURE: Amendment. Duration. Renewal or Revival. Termination.
PARTIES:
　Jordan
　WHO (World Health)

200473 Bilateral Agreement **147 UNTS 109**
SIGNED: 10 May 43　　　　FORCE: 1 Feb 45
REGISTERED: 29 Oct 52 USA (United States)
ARTICLES: 34 LANGUAGE: English.
HEADNOTE: PARCEL POST
TOPIC: Postal Service
CONCEPTS: Detailed regulations. Conformity with municipal law. Domestic legislation. Payment schedules. Customs duties. Postal services. Regulations. Insured letters and boxes. Parcel post. Rates and charges.
INTL ORGS: Universal Postal Union.
TREATY REF: UNIV.POST.CONV..
PROCEDURE: Denunciation. Duration. Ratification.
PARTIES:
　UK Great Britain
　USA (United States)

200474 Bilateral Exchange **148 UNTS 367**
SIGNED: 19 Nov 41　　　　FORCE: 19 Nov 41
REGISTERED: 30 Oct 52 USA (United States)
ARTICLES: 2 LANGUAGE: English. Spanish.
HEADNOTE: COMPENSATION OIL INDUSTRY NATIONALIZATION
TOPIC: Claims and Debts
CONCEPTS: Exceptions and exemptions. Time limit. Exchange of official publications. Exchange of information and documents. Negotiation. Specialists exchange. Accounting procedures. Currency. Interest rates. Local currency. Assessment procedures. Specific claims or waivers.
INTL ORGS: Claims Commission.
PARTIES:
　Mexico
　USA (United States)

200475 Bilateral Exchange **148 UNTS 379**
SIGNED: 4 Aug 42　　　　FORCE: 4 Aug 42
REGISTERED: 3 Nov 52 USA (United States)
ARTICLES: 2 LANGUAGE: English. Spanish.
HEADNOTE: EMPLOYMENT AGRICULTURAL WORKERS
TOPIC: Non-ILO Labor
CONCEPTS: Annex type material. Conformity with municipal law. Non-ILO labor relations. Migrant worker.
PARTIES:
　Mexico
　USA (United States)

200476 Bilateral Exchange **149 UNTS 332**
SIGNED: 10 Jun 39　　　　FORCE: 10 Jun 39
REGISTERED: 6 Nov 52 USA (United States)
ARTICLES: 2 LANGUAGE: English.
HEADNOTE: NAVAL VESSELS GREAT LAKES
TOPIC: Milit Assistance
CONCEPTS: Friendship and amity. Peaceful relations. General cooperation. Naval vessels. Exchange of defense information.
PARTIES:

Canada
USA (United States)

200477 Bilateral Exchange **149 UNTS 361**
SIGNED: 13 Oct 45　　　　FORCE: 13 Oct 45
REGISTERED: 28 Nov 52 USA (United States)
ARTICLES: 2 LANGUAGE: English. Spanish.
HEADNOTE: COOPERATIVE PROGRAM EDUCATION
TOPIC: Education
CONCEPTS: Definition of terms. Friendship and amity. Alien status. Privileges and immunities. Conformity with municipal law. Exchange of information and documents. Inspection and observation. Personnel. General property. Private contracts. Specialists exchange. Exchange. Commissions and foundations. Teacher and student exchange. Scholarships and grants. Vocational training. Research and development. Accounting procedures. Exchange rates and regulations. Expense sharing formulae. Fees and exemptions. Financial programs. Funding procedures. Tax exemptions. Customs exemptions. Materials, equipment and services. Aid missions.
PARTIES:
　Dominican Republic
　USA (United States)

200478 Bilateral Exchange **149 UNTS 379**
SIGNED: 9 Jun 45　　　　FORCE: 9 Jun 45
REGISTERED: 28 Nov 52 USA (United States)
ARTICLES: 2 LANGUAGE: English. Spanish.
HEADNOTE: COOPERATIVE EDUCATIONAL PROGRAM
TOPIC: Education
CONCEPTS: General cooperation. Exchange. Research and development. Expense sharing formulae. Funding procedures.
PARTIES:
　El Salvador
　USA (United States)

200479 Bilateral Exchange **150 UNTS 317**
SIGNED: 15 Apr 44　　　　FORCE: 15 Apr 44
REGISTERED: 28 Nov 52 USA (United States)
ARTICLES: 2 LANGUAGE: English. Spanish.
HEADNOTE: COOPERATIVE EDUCATIONAL PROGRAM
TOPIC: Education
CONCEPTS: Annex or appendix reference. Alien status. Conformity with municipal law. Inspection and observation. Personnel. General property. Private contracts. Specialists exchange. Exchange. Commissions and foundations. Professorships. Scholarships and grants. Research and development. Accounting procedures. Currency. Expense sharing formulae. Financial programs. Funding procedures. Tax exemptions.
PROCEDURE: Amendment. Duration.
PARTIES:
　Peru
　USA (United States)

200480 Bilateral Agreement **156 UNTS 289**
SIGNED: 1 Aug 49　　　　FORCE: 12 Sep 49
REGISTERED: 13 Jan 53 IBRD (World Bank)
ARTICLES: 9 LANGUAGE: English.
HEADNOTE: GUARANTEE AGREEMENT
TOPIC: IBRD Project
CONCEPTS: Annex or appendix reference. Conformity with municipal law. Informational records. Inspection and observation. Arbitration. Procedure. Bonds. Currency. Fees and exemptions. Tax exemptions. Loan regulations. Loan guarantee. Guarantor non-interference.
INTL ORGS: Arbitration Commission.
TREATY REF: 2UNTS134.
PARTIES:
　Finland
　IBRD (World Bank)

200481 Bilateral Agreement **156 UNTS 355**
SIGNED: 17 Oct 49 FORCE: 16 Dec 49
REGISTERED: 13 Jan 53 IBRD (World Bank)
ARTICLES: 18 LANGUAGE: English.
HEADNOTE: LOAN AGREEMENT
TOPIC: IBRD Project
CONCEPTS: Default remedies. Definition of terms.
Annex or appendix reference. Conformity with
municipal law. Exchange of information and doc-
uments. Informational records. Inspection and
observation. Procedure. Reexport of goods, etc..
Accounting procedures. Bonds. Currency. Fees
and exemptions. Interest rates. Tax exemptions.
Domestic obligation. Loan repayment. Loan reg-
ulations. Loan guarantee. Guarantor non-inter-
ference.
INTL ORGS: Arbitration Commission.
TREATY REF: 2UNTS134.
PROCEDURE: Termination.
PARTIES:
Finland
IBRD (World Bank)

200482 Bilateral Agreement **159 UNTS 383**
SIGNED: 10 Oct 51 FORCE: 4 Sep 52
REGISTERED: 9 Feb 53 IBRD (World Bank)
ARTICLES: 6 LANGUAGE: English.
HEADNOTE: GUARANTEE AGREEMENT
TOPIC: IBRD Project
CONCEPTS: Annex or appendix reference. Ex-
change of information and documents. Informa-
tional records. Inspection and observation. Fees
and exemptions. Tax exemptions. Domestic obli-
gation. Loan regulations. Loan guarantee. Guar-
antor non-interference.
PARTIES:
Italy
IBRD (World Bank)

200483 Bilateral Agreement **159 UNTS 408**
SIGNED: 30 Apr 52 FORCE: 12 Aug 52
REGISTERED: 11 Feb 53 IBRD (World Bank)
ARTICLES: 5 LANGUAGE: English.
HEADNOTE: GUARANTEE AGREEMENT
TOPIC: IBRD Project
CONCEPTS: Annex or appendix reference. Ex-
change of information and documents. Informa-
tional records. Inspection and observation. Fees
and exemptions. Tax exemptions. Domestic obli-
gation. Loan regulations. Loan guarantee. Guar-
antor non-interference.
PARTIES:
Finland
IBRD (World Bank)

200484 Multilateral Agreement **160 UNTS 359**
SIGNED: 9 Jul 45 FORCE: 24 Jul 45
REGISTERED: 12 Feb 53 USA (United States)
ARTICLES: 7 LANGUAGE: English. French. Rus-
sian.
HEADNOTE: ZONES OCCUPATION
TOPIC: Milit Occupation
CONCEPTS: Establishment of commission. Occu-
pation regime. Control and occupation ma-
chinery. Markers and definitions.
INTL ORGS: Allied Military Occupation.
PARTIES:
France SIGNED: 9 Jul 45 FORCE: 24 Jul 45
UK Great Britain SIGNED: 9 Jul 45 FORCE:
24 Jul 45
USA (United States) SIGNED: 9 Jul 45 FORCE:
24 Jul 45
USSR (Soviet Union) SIGNED: 9 Jul 45 FORCE:
24 Jul 45

200485 Multilateral Convention **161 UNTS 193**
SIGNED: 12 Oct 40 FORCE: 30 Apr 42
REGISTERED: 3 Mar 53 USA (United States)
ARTICLES: 12 LANGUAGE: English. French. Por-
tuguese. Spanish.

HEADNOTE: NATURE PROTECTION WILD LIFE
PRESERVATION
TOPIC: Specific Resources
CONCEPTS: Definition of terms. Annex or appen-
dix reference. Previous treaties adherence. Ex-
change of information and documents. Export
quotas. Import quotas. Wildlife.
INTL ORGS: Organization of American States.
PROCEDURE: Denunciation. Ratification.
PARTIES:
Argentina RATIFIED: 27 Jun 46 FORCE:
27 Sep 46
Bolivia SIGNED: 12 Oct 40
Brazil SIGNED: 27 Dec 40
Chile SIGNED: 22 Jan 41
Colombia SIGNED: 17 Jan 41
Costa Rica SIGNED: 24 Oct 40
Cuba SIGNED: 12 Oct 40
Dominican Republic SIGNED: 12 Oct 40 RATI-
FIED: 3 Mar 42 FORCE: 3 Jun 42
Ecuador SIGNED: 12 Oct 40 RATIFIED:
20 Oct 44 FORCE: 20 Jan 45
El Salvador SIGNED: 12 Oct 40 RATIFIED:
2 Dec 41 FORCE: 30 Apr 42
Guatemala RATIFIED: 14 Aug 41 FORCE:
30 Apr 42
Haiti RATIFIED: 31 Jan 42 FORCE: 30 Apr 42
Mexico SIGNED: 20 Nov 40 RATIFIED:
27 Mar 42 FORCE: 27 Jun 42
Nicaragua SIGNED: 12 Oct 40 RATIFIED:
22 May 46 FORCE: 22 Aug 46
Peru SIGNED: 12 Oct 40 RATIFIED: 22 Nov 46
FORCE: 22 Feb 47
USA (United States) SIGNED: 12 Oct 40 RATI-
FIED: 28 Apr 41 FORCE: 30 Apr 4
Uruguay SIGNED: 9 Dec 40
Venezuela SIGNED: 12 Oct 40 RATIFIED:
3 Nov 41 FORCE: 30 Apr 42

200486 Multilateral Protocol **161 UNTS 217**
SIGNED: 25 Jun 36 FORCE: 10 Jul 41
REGISTERED: 3 Mar 53 USA (United States)
ARTICLES: 1 LANGUAGE: English. French. Por-
tuguese. Spanish.
HEADNOTE: JURIDICIAL PERSONALITY FOREIGN
COMPANIES
TOPIC: Privil/Immunities
CONCEPTS: Juridical personality. Establishment
of commission.
INTL ORGS: Organization of American States.
PARTIES:
Chile SIGNED: 25 Jun 36
Dominican Republic SIGNED: 7 Nov 39
Ecuador SIGNED: 22 Jul 36
El Salvador SIGNED: 22 Jul 36
Nicaragua SIGNED: 22 Jul 36
Peru SIGNED: 22 Jul 36
USA (United States) SIGNED: 23 Jun 39 RATI-
FIED: 10 Jul 41 FORCE: 10 Jul 41
Venezuela SIGNED: 30 Jun 36 RATIFIED:
23 Sep 37 FORCE: 10 Jul 41

200487 Multilateral Protocol **161 UNTS 229**
SIGNED: 17 Feb 40 FORCE: 6 Feb 41
REGISTERED: 3 Mar 53 USA (United States)
ARTICLES: 13 LANGUAGE: English. French. Por-
tuguese. Spanish.
HEADNOTE: UNIFORMITY POWERS OF ATTOR-
NEY UTILIZED ABROAD
TOPIC: Privil/Immunities
CONCEPTS: Detailed regulations. Establishment
of commission.
INTL ORGS: Organization of American States.
PROCEDURE: Termination.
PARTIES:
Bolivia SIGNED: 26 Sep 40
Brazil SIGNED: 6 Sep 40 RATIFIED: 6 Feb 41
FORCE: 6 Feb 41
Colombia SIGNED: 25 May 40 RATIFIED:
10 Jun 43 FORCE: 10 Jun 43
El Salvador SIGNED: 21 May 40 RATIFIED:
6 Feb 41 FORCE: 6 Feb 41
Nicaragua SIGNED: 27 May 40
Panama SIGNED: 10 Apr 40
USA (United States) SIGNED: 3 Oct 41 RATI-
FIED: 16 Apr 42 FORCE: 16 Apr 42
Venezuela SIGNED: 20 Feb 40 RATIFIED:
3 Nov 41 FORCE: 3 Nov 41

200488 Multilateral Convention **161 UNTS 253**
SIGNED: 30 Jul 40 FORCE: 8 Jan 42
REGISTERED: 3 Mar 53 USA (United States)
ARTICLES: 19 LANGUAGE: English. French. Por-
tuguese. Spanish.
HEADNOTE: PROVISIONAL ADMINISTRATION EU-
ROPEAN COLONIES & POSSESSIONS AMERICA
TOPIC: Admin Cooperation
CONCEPTS: Time limit. Democratic institutions.
Human rights. Conformity with municipal law.
Informational records. Post-colonial administra-
tion. Procedure. Education. Indemnities and re-
imbursements. Subsidiary organ.
INTL ORGS: Inter-American Territory Committee.
Organization of American States.
TREATY REF: US EXEC.AGREE.SERIES 199;
54STAT2491.
PROCEDURE: Ratification.
PARTIES:
Argentina SIGNED: 30 Jul 40 RATIFIED:
1 Oct 41 FORCE: 8 Jan 42
Bolivia SIGNED: 30 Jul 40
Brazil SIGNED: 30 Jul 40 RATIFIED: 14 Jan 41
FORCE: 8 Jan 42
Chile SIGNED: 30 Jul 40
Colombia SIGNED: 30 Jul 40 RATIFIED:
5 Nov 41 FORCE: 8 Jan 42
Costa Rica SIGNED: 30 Jul 40 RATIFIED:
17 Dec 40 FORCE: 8 Jan 42
Cuba SIGNED: 30 Jul 40
Dominican Republic SIGNED: 30 Jul 40 RATI-
FIED: 28 Nov 40 FORCE: 8 Jan 42
Ecuador SIGNED: 30 Jul 40 RATIFIED:
27 Dec 41 FORCE: 8 Jan 42
El Salvador SIGNED: 30 Jul 40 RATIFIED:
9 Jul 41 FORCE: 8 Jan 42
Guatemala SIGNED: 30 Jul 40 RATIFIED:
14 Aug 41 FORCE: 8 Jan 42
Haiti SIGNED: 30 Jul 40 RATIFIED: 13 Aug 41
FORCE: 8 Jan 42
Honduras SIGNED: 30 Jul 40 RATIFIED:
8 Jan 42 FORCE: 8 Jan 42
Mexico SIGNED: 30 Jul 40 RATIFIED: 21 Mar 42
FORCE: 21 Mar 42
Nicaragua SIGNED: 30 Jul 40 RATIFIED:
12 May 42 FORCE: 12 May 42
Panama SIGNED: 30 Jul 40 RATIFIED:
13 May 41 FORCE: 8 Jan 42
Paraguay SIGNED: 30 Jul 40
Peru SIGNED: 30 Jul 40 RATIFIED: 4 Apr 41
FORCE: 8 Jan 42
USA (United States) SIGNED: 30 Jul 40 RATI-
FIED: 24 Oct 40 FORCE: 8 Jan 42
Uruguay SIGNED: 30 Jul 40 RATIFIED:
26 Mar 42 FORCE: 26 Mar 42
Venezuela SIGNED: 30 Jul 40 RATIFIED:
22 Oct 41 FORCE: 8 Jan 42

200489 Multilateral Convention **161 UNTS 281**
SIGNED: 15 Jan 44 FORCE: 30 Nov 44
REGISTERED: 3 Mar 53 USA (United States)
ARTICLES: 16 LANGUAGE: English. French. Portuguese. Spanish.
HEADNOTE: INTER-AMERICAN INSTITUTE AGRI-
CULTURAL SCIENCES
TOPIC: IGO Establishment
CONCEPTS: Detailed regulations. General provisions. Treaty interpretation. General property.
Privileges and immunities. Conformity with municipal law. General cooperation. Juridical personality. Establishment of commission. Research
cooperation. Accounting procedures. Expense
sharing formulae. Fees and exemptions. Funding
procedures. Transportation costs. Tax exemptions. Customs exemptions. Agriculture. Special
projects. Specific technical assistance. Postal
services. Regulations. Subsidiary organ. Establishment. Regional offices. Headquarters and facilities. Internal structure. IGO status.
INTL ORGS: Inter-American Institute of Agricultural Sciences. Organization of American States.
PROCEDURE: Denunciation. Ratification.
PARTIES:
Bolivia SIGNED: 12 Jul 44
Chile SIGNED: 13 May 44
Colombia SIGNED: 23 Jul 48
Costa Rica SIGNED: 15 Jan 44 RATIFIED:
14 Aug 44 FORCE: 30 Nov 44
Cuba SIGNED: 20 Jan 44
Dominican Republic SIGNED: 28 Jan 44 RATI-
FIED: 8 Jan 45 FORCE: 8 Feb 45

Ecuador SIGNED: 20 Jan 44
El Salvador SIGNED: 8 Feb 44 RATIFIED: 31 May 44 FORCE: 30 Nov 44
Guatemala SIGNED: 16 Mar 44 RATIFIED: 6 Jul 44 FORCE: 30 Nov 44
Haiti RATIFIED: 19 Jun 51 FORCE: 19 Jul 51
Honduras SIGNED: 28 Jan 44 RATIFIED: 19 Mar 45 FORCE: 19 Apr 45
Mexico SIGNED: 19 Nov 46 RATIFIED: 26 May 47 FORCE: 26 Jun 47
Nicaragua SIGNED: 15 Jan 44 RATIFIED: 31 Aug 44 FORCE: 30 Nov 44
Panama SIGNED: 15 Jan 44 RATIFIED: 24 Jan 47 FORCE: 24 Feb 47
USA (United States) SIGNED: 15 Jan 44 RATIFIED: 4 Jul 44 FORCE: 30 Nov 44
Uruguay SIGNED: 17 Apr 44
Venezuela SIGNED: 10 Oct 44 RATIFIED: 6 Mar 46 FORCE: 6 Apr 46

200490 Bilateral Agreement **161 UNTS 315**
SIGNED: 21 Nov 52 FORCE: 21 Nov 52
REGISTERED: 3 Mar 52 WHO (World Health)
ARTICLES: 4 LANGUAGE: English.
HEADNOTE: MEDICO-LEGAL CONSULTANT
TOPIC: Sanitation
CONCEPTS: Definition of terms. Friendship and amity. Privileges and immunities. Free passage and transit. Personnel. Responsibility and liability. Sanitation. WHO used as agency. Exchange. Indemnities and reimbursements. Expense sharing formulae. Assistance. Specific technical assistance. Materials, equipment and services.
TREATY REF: 33UNTS261.
PROCEDURE: Amendment. Termination.
PARTIES:
Ceylon (Sri Lanka)
WHO (World Health)

200491 Bilateral Agreement **161 UNTS 323**
SIGNED: 15 Aug 52 FORCE: 15 Aug 52
REGISTERED: 11 Mar 53 United Nations
ARTICLES: 10 LANGUAGE: French.
HEADNOTE: ACTIVITIES UNICEF
TOPIC: Direct Aid
CONCEPTS: Treaty implementation. Privileges and immunities. General cooperation. Exchange of information and documents. Informational records. Inspection and observation. Public information. Procedure. Existing tribunals. Export quotas. Indemnities and reimbursements. Tax exemptions. Customs exemptions. Domestic obligation. Assistance. General aid. IGO status.
INTL ORGS: United Nations.
TREATY REF: 1UNTS15.
PROCEDURE: Duration. Ratification.
PARTIES:
Laos
UNICEF (Children)

200492 Bilateral Agreement **161 UNTS 335**
SIGNED: 29 Aug 52 FORCE: 29 Aug 52
REGISTERED: 11 Mar 53 United Nations
ARTICLES: 10 LANGUAGE: French.
HEADNOTE: ACTIVITIES UNICEF
TOPIC: Direct Aid
CONCEPTS: Treaty implementation. Privileges and immunities. General cooperation. Exchange of information and documents. Informational records. Inspection and observation. Public information. Procedure. Negotiation. Export quotas. Indemnities and reimbursements. Financial programs. Local currency. Tax exemptions. Customs exemptions. Commodities and services. Assistance. General aid. Distribution. IGO status.
INTL ORGS: United Nations.
TREATY REF: 1UNTS15.
PROCEDURE: Duration.
PARTIES:
UNICEF (Children)
Vietnam, South
ANNEX
251 UNTS 428. UNICEF (Children). Supplementa-

tion 30 Aug 56. Force 5 Oct 56.
251 UNTS 428. Vietnam. Supplementation 5 Oct 56. Force 5 Oct 56.

200493 Bilateral Agreement **161 UNTS 347**
SIGNED: 2 Mar 53 FORCE: 2 Mar 53
REGISTERED: 13 Mar 53 United Nations
ARTICLES: 6 LANGUAGE: English.
HEADNOTE: TECHNICAL ASSISTANCE
TOPIC: Tech Assistance
CONCEPTS: Treaty implementation. Privileges and immunities. General cooperation. Exchange of information and documents. Personnel. Title and deeds. Exchange. Scholarships and grants. Vocational training. Research and development. Expense sharing formulae. Local currency. Domestic obligation. General technical assistance. Materials, equipment and services. IGO status. Conformity with IGO decisions.
TREATY REF: 76UNTS132; 1UNTS15,263.
PROCEDURE: Amendment. Termination.
PARTIES:
Nepal
United Nations

200494 Bilateral Exchange **162 UNTS 315**
SIGNED: 7 Sep 44 FORCE: 7 Sep 44
REGISTERED: 20 Mar 53 USA (United States)
ARTICLES: 2 LANGUAGE: English. Spanish.
HEADNOTE: COOPERATION EDUCATION PROGRAM
TOPIC: Education
CONCEPTS: Annex or appendix reference. Friendship and amity. Privileges and immunities. Conformity with municipal law. Exchange. Vocational training. Accounting procedures. Expense sharing formulae. Financial programs. Funding procedures. Tax exemptions. Customs exemptions. Special projects.
TREATY REF: 12UNTS131; 12UNTS136.
PROCEDURE: Duration. Future Procedures Contemplated.
PARTIES:
Bolivia
USA (United States)

200495 Bilateral Agreement **165 UNTS 317**
SIGNED: 30 Mar 53 FORCE: 30 Mar 53
REGISTERED: 28 May 53 United Nations
ARTICLES: 6 LANGUAGE: Arabic. English.
HEADNOTE: PRELIMANARY AGREEMENT
TOPIC: Direct Aid
CONCEPTS: Treaty implementation. Assistance. General cooperation. Domestic legislation. Financial programs. Domestic obligation. General aid. Economic assistance.
INTL ORGS: United Nations.
PARTIES:
Jordan
UN Relief Palestin
ANNEX
190 UNTS 388. UN Relief Palestin. Amendment 30 Dec 53. Force 30 Dec 53.
190 UNTS 388. Jordan. Amendment 30 Dec 53. Force 30 Dec 53.
219 UNTS 400. Jordan. Prolongation 29 Jun 54. Force 6 Jul 54.
219 UNTS 400. Jordan. Prolongation 3 Aug 55. Force 6 Sep 55.
219 UNTS 400. UNRRA (Relief). Prolongation 6 Jul 54. Force 6 Jul 54.
219 UNTS 400. UNRRA (Relief). Prolongation 6 Sep 55. Force 6 Sep 55.

200496 Bilateral Treaty **166 UNTS 323**
SIGNED: 9 Jan 31 FORCE: 31 Aug 49
REGISTERED: 8 Jun 53 Greece
ARTICLES: 6 LANGUAGE: French.
HEADNOTE: FRIENDSHIP
TOPIC: General Amity

CONCEPTS: Treaty interpretation. Friendship and amity. Consular relations establishment. Diplomatic relations establishment. Arbitration. Special tribunals. Most favored nation clause.
INTL ORGS: International Court of Justice. Arbitration Commission.
PROCEDURE: Ratification.
PARTIES:
Greece
Iran

200497 Bilateral Convention **166 UNTS 331**
SIGNED: 9 Jan 31 FORCE: 13 Sep 49
REGISTERED: 8 Jun 53 Greece
ARTICLES: 18 LANGUAGE: French.
HEADNOTE: RESIDENCE TRADE & NAVIGATION
TOPIC: General Amity
CONCEPTS: General consular functions. National treatment. Customs duties. Ports and pilotage. Shipwreck and salvage. Military service and citizenship. Foreign nationals.
TREATY REF: 7LTS11; 28LTS151; ETC..
PROCEDURE: Denunciation. Duration. Ratification.
PARTIES:
Greece
Iran

200498 Bilateral Exchange **166 UNTS 351**
SIGNED: 8 May 42 FORCE: 8 May 42
REGISTERED: 12 Jun 53 USA (United States)
ARTICLES: 2 LANGUAGE: English. Spanish.
HEADNOTE: HEALTH SANITATION PROGRAM
TOPIC: Sanitation
CONCEPTS: Conditions. Annex or appendix reference. Personnel. General property. Specialists exchange. Disease control. Public health. Sanitation. Research and development. Indemnities and reimbursements. Expense sharing formulae. Financial programs. Funding procedures. Assistance. Special projects. Grants.
TREATY REF: DEPT.STATE.BULL. 7FEB42;P.117; TAIS 1557'19;.
PROCEDURE: Termination.
PARTIES:
Honduras
USA (United States)

200499 Bilateral Agreement **167 UNTS 249**
SIGNED: 24 Jun 53 FORCE: 24 Jun 53
REGISTERED: 24 Jun 53 United Nations
ARTICLES: 6 LANGUAGE: English.
HEADNOTE: TECHNICAL ASSISTANCE
TOPIC: Tech Assistance
CONCEPTS: Privileges and immunities. General cooperation. Exchange of information and documents. Personnel. Expense sharing formulae. Local currency. Domestic obligation. General technical assistance. Special projects. Conformity with IGO decisions.
TREATY REF: 76UNTS132; 135UNTS305.
PROCEDURE: Amendment. Termination.
PARTIES:
Japan
United Nations

200500 Bilateral Agreement **168 UNTS 309**
SIGNED: 24 Jun 53 FORCE: 8 Jul 53
REGISTERED: 8 Jul 53 United Nations
ARTICLES: 6 LANGUAGE: French.
HEADNOTE: TECHNICAL ASSISTANCE
TOPIC: Tech Assistance
CONCEPTS: Treaty implementation. Privileges and immunities. General cooperation. Exchange of information and documents. Personnel. Title and deeds. Exchange. Scholarships and grants. Vocational training. Research and development. Expense sharing formulae. Local currency. Domestic obligation. General technical assistance. Materials, equipment and services. IGO status. Conformity with IGO decisions.

TREATY REF: 76UNTS132; 1UNTS15,263.
PROCEDURE: Amendment. Termination.
PARTIES:
Cambodia
United Nations
ANNEX
251 UNTS 430. United Nations. Force 5 Oct 56.
251 UNTS 430. Cambodia. Force 5 Oct 56.

200501 Multilateral Agreement **171 UNTS 345**
SIGNED: 7 Dec 44   FORCE: 6 Jun 45
REGISTERED: 28 Jul 53 USA (United States)
ARTICLES: 17 LANGUAGE: English.
HEADNOTE: INTERNATIONAL CIVIL AVIATION
TOPIC: Air Transport
CONCEPTS: Conditions. Definition of terms. Detailed regulations. Guarantees and safeguards. Remedies. Time limit. Treaty implementation. Standardization. General cooperation. Exchange of official publications. Exchange of information and documents. Informational records. Juridical personality. Domestic legislation. Licenses and permits. Investigation of violations. Arbitration. Procedure. Special tribunals. Competence of tribunal. Quarantine. Disease control. Meteorology. Accounting procedures. Fees and exemptions. Funding procedures. Customs duties. Competency certificate. Registration certificate. Navigational conditions. Navigational equipment. Air transport. Airport facilities. Airworthiness certificates. Conditions of airlines operating permission. Operating authorizations and regulations. Admission. Establishment. Procedure. Headquarters and facilities. IGO operations.
INTL ORGS: International Civil Aviation Organization.
TREATY REF: 15UNTS295; 84UNTS289.
PROCEDURE: Duration. Application to Non-self-governing Territories. Accession. Termination.
PARTIES:
Afghanistan SIGNED: 7 Dec 44 RATIFIED: 6 Jun 45 FORCE: 6 Jun 45
Australia SIGNED: 7 Dec 44 RATIFIED: 6 Jun 45 FORCE: 6 Jun 45
Belgium SIGNED: 9 Apr 45 RATIFIED: 6 Jun 45 FORCE: 6 Jun 45
Bolivia SIGNED: 7 Dec 44 RATIFIED: 17 May 46 FORCE: 17 May 46
Brazil SIGNED: 29 May 45 RATIFIED: 6 Jun 45 FORCE: 6 Jun 45
Canada SIGNED: 7 Dec 44 RATIFIED: 6 Jun 45 FORCE: 6 Jun 45
Chile SIGNED: 7 Dec 44 RATIFIED: 6 Jun 45 FORCE: 6 Jun 45
Taiwan SIGNED: 7 Dec 44 RATIFIED: 6 Jun 45 FORCE: 6 Jun 45
Colombia SIGNED: 24 May 45 RATIFIED: 6 Jun 45 FORCE: 6 Jun 45
Costa Rica SIGNED: 10 Mar 45
Cuba SIGNED: 20 Apr 45 RATIFIED: 20 Jun 47 FORCE: 20 Jun 47
Czechoslovakia SIGNED: 18 Apr 45 RATIFIED: 6 Jun 45 FORCE: 6 Jun 45
Denmark SIGNED: 7 Dec 44 RATIFIED: 13 Nov 45 FORCE: 13 Nov 45
Dominican Republic SIGNED: 7 Dec 44 RATIFIED: 25 Jan 46 FORCE: 25 Jan 46
Ecuador SIGNED: 7 Dec 44
United Arab Rep SIGNED: 7 Dec 44 RATIFIED: 6 Jun 45 FORCE: 6 Jun 45
El Salvador SIGNED: 9 May 45 RATIFIED: 6 Jun 45 FORCE: 6 Jun 45
Ethiopia SIGNED: 22 Mar 45 RATIFIED: 6 Jun 45 FORCE: 6 Jun 45
France SIGNED: 7 Dec 44 RATIFIED: 6 Jun 45 FORCE: 6 Jun 45
Greece SIGNED: 7 Dec 44 RATIFIED: 21 Sep 45 FORCE: 21 Sep 45
Guatemala SIGNED: 30 Jan 45 RATIFIED: 28 Apr 47 FORCE: 28 Apr 47
Haiti SIGNED: 7 Dec 44 RATIFIED: 6 Jun 45 FORCE: 6 Jun 45
Honduras SIGNED: 7 Dec 44 RATIFIED: 13 Nov 45 FORCE: 13 Nov 45
Iceland SIGNED: 7 Dec 44 RATIFIED: 6 Jun 45 FORCE: 6 Jun 45
India SIGNED: 7 Dec 44 RATIFIED: 6 Jun 45 FORCE: 6 Jun 45
Iran SIGNED: 7 Dec 44 RATIFIED: 30 Dec 46 FORCE: 30 Dec 46
Iraq SIGNED: 7 Dec 44 RATIFIED: 6 Jun 45 FORCE: 6 Jun 45
Ireland SIGNED: 7 Dec 44 RATIFIED: 6 Jun 45 FORCE: 6 Jun 45
Jordan RATIFIED: 18 Mar 47 FORCE: 18 Mar 47
Lebanon SIGNED: 7 Dec 44 RATIFIED: 6 Jun 45 FORCE: 6 Jun 45
Liberia SIGNED: 7 Dec 44 RATIFIED: 6 Jun 45 FORCE: 6 Jun 45
Luxembourg SIGNED: 9 Jul 45 RATIFIED: 9 Jul 45 FORCE: 9 Jul 45
Mexico SIGNED: 7 Dec 44 RATIFIED: 6 Jun 45 FORCE: 6 Jun 45
Netherlands SIGNED: 7 Dec 44 RATIFIED: 6 Jun 45 FORCE: 6 Jun 45
New Zealand SIGNED: 7 Dec 44 RATIFIED: 6 Jun 45 FORCE: 6 Jun 45
Nicaragua SIGNED: 7 Dec 44 RATIFIED: 28 Dec 45 FORCE: 28 Dec 45
Norway SIGNED: 30 Jan 45 RATIFIED: 28 Dec 45 FORCE: 28 Dec 45
Panama SIGNED: 14 May 45
Paraguay SIGNED: 27 Jul 45 RATIFIED: 27 Jul 45 FORCE: 27 Jul 45
Peru SIGNED: 7 Dec 44 RATIFIED: 6 Jun 45 FORCE: 6 Jun 45
Philippines SIGNED: 7 Dec 44 RATIFIED: 22 Mar 46 FORCE: 22 Mar 46
Poland SIGNED: 7 Dec 44 RATIFIED: 6 Jun 45 FORCE: 6 Jun 45
Portugal SIGNED: 7 Dec 44 RATIFIED: 6 Jun 45 FORCE: 6 Jun 45
South Africa SIGNED: 4 Jun 45 RATIFIED: 30 Nov 45 FORCE: 30 Nov 45
Spain SIGNED: 7 Dec 44 RATIFIED: 30 Jul 45 FORCE: 30 Jul 45
Sweden SIGNED: 7 Dec 45 RATIFIED: 9 Jul 45 FORCE: 9 Jul 45
Switzerland SIGNED: 7 Dec 45 RATIFIED: 6 Jul 45 FORCE: 6 Jul 45
Syria SIGNED: 7 Dec 45 RATIFIED: 6 Jul 45 FORCE: 6 Jul 45
Thailand SIGNED: 7 Dec 44 RATIFIED: 6 Mar 47 FORCE: 6 Mar 47
Turkey SIGNED: 7 Dec 45 RATIFIED: 6 Jun 45 FORCE: 6 Jun 45
UK Great Britain SIGNED: 7 Dec 44 RATIFIED: 6 Jun 45 FORCE: 6 Jun 45
USA (United States) SIGNED: 7 Dec 44 FORCE: 6 Jun 45
Uruguay SIGNED: 7 Dec 44
Venezuela SIGNED: 7 Dec 44 RATIFIED: 28 Mar 46 FORCE: 28 Mar 46

200502 Multilateral Agreement **171 UNTS 387**
SIGNED: 7 Dec 44   FORCE: 17 May 45
REGISTERED: 28 Jul 53 USA (United States)
ARTICLES: 8 LANGUAGE: English.
HEADNOTE: INTERNATIONAL AIR TRANSPORT
TOPIC: Air Transport
CONCEPTS: Exceptions and exemptions. Remedies. Previous treaty replacement. Use of facilities. Procedure. Negotiation. Fees and exemptions. National treatment. Routes and logistics. Air transport. Airport facilities. Conditions of airlines operating permission. Overflights and technical stops. Operating authorizations and regulations.
INTL ORGS: Special Commission.
TREATY REF: 171UNTS345; 15UNTS295.
PROCEDURE: Accession. Denunciation.
PARTIES:
Afghanistan SIGNED: 7 Dec 44 RATIFIED: 17 May 45 FORCE: 17 May 45
Bolivia SIGNED: 7 Dec 44 RATIFIED: 4 Apr 47 FORCE: 4 Apr 47
Taiwan SIGNED: 7 Dec 44 RATIFIED: 6 Jun 45 FORCE: 6 Jun 45
Costa Rica SIGNED: 10 Mar 45
Cuba SIGNED: 20 Apr 45
Denmark SIGNED: 7 Dec 44
Dominican Republic SIGNED: 7 Dec 44 RATIFIED: 25 Jan 46 FORCE: 25 Jan 46
Ecuador SIGNED: 7 Dec 44
El Salvador SIGNED: 9 May 45 RATIFIED: 1 Jun 45 FORCE: 1 Jun 45
Ethiopia SIGNED: 22 Mar 45 RATIFIED: 22 Mar 45 FORCE: 22 Mar 45

Guatemala SIGNED: 30 Jun 45
Haiti SIGNED: 7 Dec 44
Honduras SIGNED: 7 Dec 44 RATIFIED: 13 Nov 45
Iceland SIGNED: 4 Apr 45
Iran SIGNED: 13 Aug 46
Lebanon SIGNED: 7 Dec 44
Liberia SIGNED: 7 Dec 44 RATIFIED: 19 Mar 45 FORCE: 19 Mar 45
Mexico SIGNED: 7 Dec 44
Netherlands SIGNED: 7 Dec 44 RATIFIED: 8 Feb 45 FORCE: 8 Feb 45
Nicaragua SIGNED: 7 Dec 44 RATIFIED: 28 Dec 45 FORCE: 28 Dec 45
Paraguay SIGNED: 27 Jul 45 RATIFIED: 27 Jul 45 FORCE: 27 Jul 45
Peru SIGNED: 7 Dec 44
Sweden SIGNED: 7 Dec 44 RATIFIED: 19 Nov 45 FORCE: 19 Nov 45
Syria SIGNED: 6 Jul 45
Thailand SIGNED: 7 Dec 44 RATIFIED: 6 Mar 47 FORCE: 6 Mar 47
Turkey SIGNED: 7 Dec 44 RATIFIED: 6 Jun 45 FORCE: 6 Jun 45
USA (United States) SIGNED: 7 Dec 44 RATIFIED: 8 Feb 45 FORCE: 8 Feb 45
Uruguay SIGNED: 7 Dec 44
Venezuela SIGNED: 7 Dec 44 RATIFIED: 28 Mar 46 FORCE: 28 Mar 46
ANNEX
178 UNTS 420. Thailand. Denunciation 18 Mar 53. Force 18 Mar 54.
260 UNTS 463. Venezuela. Denunciation 3 Jun 54. Force 3 Jun 55.

200503 Bilateral Agreement **173 UNTS 353**
SIGNED: 8 Jul 52   FORCE: 12 May 53
REGISTERED: 2 Sep 53 United Nations
ARTICLES: 10 LANGUAGE: English.
HEADNOTE: ACIVITIES UNICEF
TOPIC: Direct Aid
CONCEPTS: Treaty implementation. Annex or appendix reference. Privileges and immunities. General cooperation. Exchange of information and documents. Informational records. Inspection and observation. Public information. Procedure. Existing tribunals. Export quotas. Indemnities and reimbursements. Local currency. Tax exemptions. Customs exemptions. Commodities and services. Assistance. General aid. Procurement. IGO status.
INTL ORGS: United Nations.
TREATY REF: 1UNTS15.
PROCEDURE: Duration.
PARTIES:
Jordan
UNICEF (Children)

200504 Bilateral Agreement **178 UNTS 361**
SIGNED: 27 Mar 53   FORCE: 27 Mar 53
REGISTERED: 30 Oct 53 United Nations
ARTICLES: 8 LANGUAGE: English. French.
HEADNOTE: ADMIT WMO INTO UN JOINT STAFF PENSION FUND
TOPIC: IGO Operations
CONCEPTS: Default remedies. Holidays and rest periods. Accounting procedures. Conformity with IGO decisions.
INTL ORGS: United Nations.
PARTIES:
United Nations
WMO (Meteorology)
ANNEX
429 UNTS 310. United Nations. Implementation 17 Oct 56. Force 6 Jun 57.
429 UNTS 310. WMO (Meteorology). Implementation 22 Nov 56. Force 6 Jun 57.

200505 Bilateral Agreement **178 UNTS 371**
SIGNED: 4 Sep 52   FORCE: 4 Sep 52
REGISTERED: 30 Oct 53 ILO (Labor Org)
ARTICLES: 6 LANGUAGE: French.
HEADNOTE: TECHNICAL ASSISTANCE
TOPIC: Tech Assistance

CONCEPTS: Definition of terms. Treaty implemen-
tation. Privileges and immunities. General coop-
eration. Recognition and enforcement of legal
decisions. Personnel. Title and deeds. Exchange.
Scholarships and grants. Vocational training. Re-
search and development. Expense sharing for-
mulae. Local currency. Domestic obligation.
General technical assistance. Materials, equip-
ment and services. IGO status. Conformity with
IGO decisions.
INTL ORGS: United Nations.
TREATY REF: 76UNTS132; 33UNTS261.
PROCEDURE: Amendment. Termination.
PARTIES:
　Italy
　ILO (Labor Org)

200506　Bilateral Agreement　**182 UNTS 201**
SIGNED: 31 Dec 52　　　　FORCE: 12 Jan 53
REGISTERED: 10 Dec 53 ILO (Labor Org)
ARTICLES: 5 LANGUAGE: English.
HEADNOTE: TECHNICAL ASSISTANCE
TOPIC: Tech Assistance
CONCEPTS: Treaty implementation. Privileges and
immunities. General cooperation. Exchange of
information and documents. Personnel. Title and
deeds. Arbitration. Procedure. Scholarships and
grants. Vocational training. Exchange rates and
regulations. Expense sharing formulae. Domes-
tic obligation. General technical assistance. Ma-
terials, equipment and services. Conformity with
IGO decisions.
INTL ORGS: United Nations.
TREATY REF: 76UNTS132; 33UNTS261.
PROCEDURE: Amendment. Termination.
PARTIES:
　ILO (Labor Org)
　UN Relief Palestin

200507　Bilateral Agreement　**183 UNTS 297**
SIGNED: 21 Nov 53　　　　FORCE: 21 Nov 53
REGISTERED: 30 Dec 53 United Nations
ARTICLES: 2 LANGUAGE: English.
HEADNOTE: ACTIVITIES UNICEF
TOPIC: Direct Aid
CONCEPTS: Treaty implementation. Privileges and
immunities. General cooperation. Exchange of
information and documents. Informational
records. Inspection and observation. Public in-
formation. Procedure. Existing tribunals. Export
quotas. Tax exemptions. Customs exemptions.
Commodities and services. Assistance. General
aid. Distribution. IGO status.
INTL ORGS: United Nations.
TREATY REF: 135UNTS305.
PROCEDURE: Duration.
PARTIES:
　Japan
　UNICEF (Children)

200508　Bilateral Exchange　**183 UNTS 311**
SIGNED: 28 Nov 44　　　　FORCE: 28 Nov 44
REGISTERED: 31 Dec 53 USA (United States)
ARTICLES: 2 LANGUAGE: English. Portuguese.
HEADNOTE: EXPULSION JAPANESE POR-
TUGUESE TIMOR
TOPIC: Milit Assistance
CONCEPTS: Detailed regulations. Exceptions and
exemptions. Guarantees and safeguards. Time
limit. Annex or appendix reference. Customs ex-
emptions. Defense and security. Bases and facili-
ties.
PROCEDURE: Future Procedures Contemplated.
PARTIES:
　Portugal
　USA (United States)

200509　Bilateral Exchange　**183 UNTS 329**
SIGNED: 11 Oct 45　　　　FORCE: 11 Oct 45
REGISTERED: 4 Jan 54 Greece

ARTICLES: 2 LANGUAGE: English.
HEADNOTE: USE DISPOSAL CAPTURED VESSELS
TOPIC: Reparations
CONCEPTS: Annex or appendix reference. Naval
vessels. Post-war claims settlement.
PARTIES:
　Greece
　UK Great Britain

200510　Bilateral Agreement　**183 UNTS 337**
SIGNED: 23 Oct 45　　　　FORCE: 23 Oct 45
REGISTERED: 7 Jan 54 Belgium
ARTICLES: 1 LANGUAGE: French.
HEADNOTE: RELEASE ASSETS
TOPIC: Claims and Debts
CONCEPTS: Territorial application. Banking. As-
sets transfer. Enemy financial interests.
PARTIES:
　Belgium
　Norway

200511　Bilateral Agreement　**187 UNTS 271**
SIGNED: 15 Oct 53　　　　FORCE: 29 Dec 53
REGISTERED: 1 Mar 54 IBRD (World Bank)
ARTICLES: 5 LANGUAGE: English.
HEADNOTE: GUARANTEE AGREEMENT
TOPIC: IBRD Project
CONCEPTS: Definition of terms. Annex or appen-
dix reference. Exchange of information and doc-
uments. Informational records. Inspection and
observation. Fees and exemptions. Tax exemp-
tions. Domestic obligation. Terms of loan. Loan
regulations. Loan guarantee. Guarantor non-
interference.
PARTIES:
　Japan
　IBRD (World Bank)

200512　Bilateral Agreement　**187 UNTS 321**
SIGNED: 15 Oct 53　　　　FORCE: 29 Dec 53
REGISTERED: 1 Mar 54 IBRD (World Bank)
ARTICLES: 5 LANGUAGE: English.
HEADNOTE: GUARANTEE AGREEMENT
TOPIC: IBRD Project
CONCEPTS: Definition of terms. Annex or appen-
dix reference. Exchange of information and doc-
uments. Informational records. Inspection and
observation. Fees and exemptions. Tax exemp-
tions. Domestic obligation. Terms of loan. Loan
regulations. Loan guarantee. Guarantor non-
interference.
PARTIES:
　Japan
　IBRD (World Bank)

200513　Bilateral Agreement　**187 UNTS 367**
SIGNED: 15 Oct 53　　　　FORCE: 29 Dec 53
REGISTERED: 1 Mar 54 IBRD (World Bank)
ARTICLES: 5 LANGUAGE: English.
HEADNOTE: GUARANTEE AGREEMENT
TOPIC: IBRD Project
CONCEPTS: Definition of terms. Annex or appen-
dix reference. Exchange of information and doc-
uments. Informational records. Inspection and
observation. Bonds. Fees and exemptions. Tax
exemptions. Domestic obligation. Terms of loan.
Loan regulations. Loan guarantee. Guarantor
non-interference.
PARTIES:
　Japan
　IBRD (World Bank)

200514　Bilateral Agreement　**188 UNTS 345**
SIGNED: 24 Mar 54　　　　FORCE: 24 Mar 54
REGISTERED: 1 Apr 54 United Nations
ARTICLES: 6 LANGUAGE: French.

HEADNOTE: TECHNICAL ASSISTANCE AGREE-
MENT
TOPIC: Tech Assistance
CONCEPTS: Privileges and immunities. General
technical assistance. Assistance.
TREATY REF: 76UNTS132; 1UNTS15; ETC..
PROCEDURE: Amendment. Termination.
PARTIES:
　United Nations
　Vietnam, South
　　　　　　　ANNEX
247 UNTS 480.　United　Nations.　Abrogation
　8 Jun 56.
247 UNTS 480. Vietnam. Abrogation 8 Jun 56.

200515　Bilateral Agreement　**190 UNTS 357**
SIGNED: 7 May 54　　　　FORCE: 7 May 54
REGISTERED: 7 May 54 United Nations
ARTICLES: 10 LANGUAGE: Spanish.
HEADNOTE: ACTIVITIES UNICEF
TOPIC: Direct Aid
CONCEPTS: Treaty implementation. Privileges and
immunities. Exchange of information and docu-
ments. Informational records. Inspection and ob-
servation. Public information. Procedure. Exist-
ing tribunals. Export quotas. Indemnities and re-
imbursements.　Financial　programs.　Local
currency. Most favored nation clause. Tax ex-
emptions. Customs exemptions. Commodities
and services. Assistance. General aid. Distribution. IGO status.
INTL ORGS: United Nations.
PROCEDURE: Duration.
PARTIES:
　UNICEF (Children)
　Spain

200516　Bilateral Treaty　**191 UNTS 349**
SIGNED: 22 Oct 40　　　　FORCE: 6 Jun 41
REGISTERED: 11 Jun 54 Sweden
ARTICLES: 4 LANGUAGE: French.
HEADNOTE: FRIENDSHIP
TOPIC: General Amity
CONCEPTS: Friendship and amity. Diplomatic rela-
tions establishment.
PROCEDURE: Future Procedures Contemplated.
Ratification.
PARTIES:
　Afghanistan
　Sweden

200517　Bilateral Agreement　**198 UNTS 313**
SIGNED: 9 Jul 54　　　　FORCE: 31 Jul 54
REGISTERED: 12 Aug 54 IBRD (World Bank)
ARTICLES: 7 LANGUAGE: English.
HEADNOTE: LOAN AGREEMENT
TOPIC: IBRD Project
CONCEPTS: Default remedies. Definition of terms.
Annex or appendix reference. Exchange of infor-
mation and documents. Informational records.
Inspection and observation. Accounting proce-
dures. Bonds. Fees and exemptions. Interest
rates. Tax exemptions. Domestic obligation.
Terms of loan. Loan regulations. Loan guarantee.
Guarantor non-interference.
PARTIES:
　Ceylon (Sri Lanka)
　IBRD (World Bank)

200518　Bilateral Agreement　**198 UNTS 333**
SIGNED: 10 Mar 43　　　　FORCE: 1 Jun 43
REGISTERED: 12 Aug 54 Sweden
ARTICLES: 17 LANGUAGE: Swedish. Finnish.
HEADNOTE: ADMINISTRATIVE ASSISTANCE TAX-
ATION
TOPIC: Taxation
CONCEPTS: Conformity with municipal law. Gen-
eral cooperation. Exchange of official publica-
tions. Indemnities and reimbursements. Claims

and settlements. Assessment procedures. Taxation. General.
TREATY REF: 118LTS71.
PROCEDURE: Denunciation. Duration. Ratification.
PARTIES:
Finland
Sweden

200519 Bilateral Exchange **200 UNTS 219**
SIGNED: 13 Feb 45   FORCE: 13 Feb 45
REGISTERED: 30 Oct 54 USA (United States)
ARTICLES: 11 LANGUAGE: English.
HEADNOTE: FLIGHTS MILITARY AIRCRAFT
TOPIC: Status of Forces
CONCEPTS: Annex or appendix reference. Previous treaty replacement. Conformity with municipal law. General cooperation. Use of facilities. Airport facilities.
PROCEDURE: Termination.
PARTIES:
Canada
USA (United States)

200520 Multilateral Agreement **200 UNTS 235**
SIGNED: 1 Jun 54   FORCE: 18 Jun 54
REGISTERED: 30 Oct 54 United Nations
ARTICLES: 6 LANGUAGE: French.
HEADNOTE: TECHNICAL ASSISTANCE
TOPIC: Tech Assistance
CONCEPTS: Definition of terms. Privileges and immunities. General cooperation. Exchange of information and documents. Personnel. Responsibility and liability. Title and deeds. Use of facilities. Exchange. Scholarships and grants. Vocational training. Research and development. Exchange rates and regulations. Expense sharing formulae. Local currency. Claims and settlements. Domestic obligation. General technical assistance. Materials, equipment and services. IGO status. Conformity with IGO decisions.
TREATY   REF: 76UNTS132;   1UNTS15;
1UNTS263; 33UNTS261.
PROCEDURE: Amendment. Termination.
PARTIES:
Laos SIGNED: 1 Jun 54 FORCE: 18 Jun 54
FAO (Food Agri) SIGNED: 18 Jun 54 FORCE: 18 Jun 54
ICAO (Civil Aviat) SIGNED: 18 Jun 54 FORCE: 18 Jun 54
ILO (Labor Org) SIGNED: 18 Jun 54 FORCE: 18 Jun 54
UNESCO (Educ/Cult) SIGNED: 18 Jun 54 FORCE: 18 Jun 54
United Nations SIGNED: 18 Jun 54 FORCE: 18 Jun 54
WHO (World Health) SIGNED: 18 Jun 54 FORCE: 18 Jun 54
ANNEX
353 UNTS 376. ILO (Labor Org). Amendment 4 Feb 60. Force 4 Feb 60.
353 UNTS 376. FAO (Food Agri). Amendment 4 Feb 60. Force 4 Feb 60.
353 UNTS 376. United Nations. Amendment 4 Feb 60. Force 4 Feb 60.
353 UNTS 376. UNESCO (Educ/Cult). Amendment 4 Feb 60. Force 4 Feb 60.
353 UNTS 376. WHO (World Health). Amendment 4 Feb 60. Force 4 Feb 60.
353 UNTS 376. ICAO (Civil Aviat). Amendment 4 Feb 60. Force 4 Feb 60.
353 UNTS 376. Laos. Amendment 4 Feb 60. Force 4 Feb 60.

200521 Bilateral Agreement **204 UNTS 301**
SIGNED: 26 Nov 52   FORCE: 26 Nov 52
REGISTERED: 11 Feb 55 WHO (World Health)
ARTICLES: 6 LANGUAGE: English.
HEADNOTE: HEALTH PROJECTS
TOPIC: Tech Assistance
CONCEPTS: Treaty implementation. Annex type material. Privileges and immunities. General cooperation. Personnel. Title and deeds. Arbitration. Procedure. Public health. Scholarships and grants. Vocational training. Research and scien-

tific projects. Expense sharing formulae. Domestic obligation. General technical assistance. Assistance. Materials, equipment and services. IGO status.
TREATY   REF: 76UNTS132;   14UNTS185;
33UNTS261.
PROCEDURE: Amendment. Termination.
PARTIES:
Japan
WHO (World Health)

200522 Bilateral Agreement **204 UNTS 311**
SIGNED: 13 May 54   FORCE: 13 May 54
REGISTERED: 11 Feb 55 WHO (World Health)
ARTICLES: 6 LANGUAGE: English.
HEADNOTE: TECHNICAL ADVISORY ASSISTANCE
TOPIC: Tech Assistance
CONCEPTS: Treaty implementation. Privileges and immunities. General cooperation. Exchange of information and documents. Personnel. Responsibility and liability. Title and deeds. Use of facilities. Exchange. Scholarships and grants. Vocational training. Research and development. Exchange rates and regulations. Expense sharing formulae. Local currency. Domestic obligation. General technical assistance. Special projects. Materials, equipment and services. IGO status. Conformity with IGO decisions.
TREATY REF: 76UNTS; 33UNTS261.
PROCEDURE: Amendment. Termination.
PARTIES:
Nepal
WHO (World Health)

200523 Multilateral Agreement **204 UNTS 323**
SIGNED: 16 Dec 54   FORCE: 16 Dec 54
REGISTERED: 17 Feb 55 United Nations
ARTICLES: 6 LANGUAGE: English.
HEADNOTE: TECHNICAL ASSISTANCE
TOPIC: Tech Assistance
CONCEPTS: Previous treaty replacement. Use of facilities. Exchange rates and regulations. Conformity with IGO decisions.
PARTIES:
Ceylon (Sri Lanka) SIGNED: 16 Dec 54 FORCE: 16 Dec 54
FAO (Food Agri) SIGNED: 16 Dec 54 FORCE: 16 Dec 54
ICAO (Civil Aviat) SIGNED: 16 Dec 54 FORCE: 16 Dec 54
ILO (Labor Org) SIGNED: 16 Dec 54 FORCE: 16 Dec 54
UNESCO (Educ/Cult) SIGNED: 16 Dec 54 FORCE: 16 Dec 54
United Nations SIGNED: 16 Dec 54 FORCE: 16 Dec 54
WHO (World Health) SIGNED: 16 Dec 54 FORCE: 16 Dec 54

200524 Bilateral Agreement **211 UNTS 277**
SIGNED: 10 Mar 55   FORCE: 10 Mar 55
REGISTERED: 6 Jun 55 WMO (Meteorology)
ARTICLES: 29 LANGUAGE: French.
HEADNOTE: METEOROLOGICAL & SWITZERLAND
TOPIC: IGO Status/Immunit
CONCEPTS: Non-visa travel documents. Diplomatic privileges. Diplomatic missions. Inviolability. Privileges and immunities. Property. Diplomatic correspondence. Juridical personality. Procedure. Existing tribunals. Status of experts.
INTL ORGS: International Court of Justice. United Nations. Arbitration Commission.
PROCEDURE: Amendment.
PARTIES:
WMO (Meteorology)
Switzerland

200525 Bilateral Agreement **211 UNTS 305**
SIGNED: 24 Mar 55   FORCE: 27 May 55
REGISTERED: 10 Jun 55 IBRD (World Bank)
ARTICLES: 8 LANGUAGE: English.
HEADNOTE: GUARANTEE AGREEMENT
TOPIC: IBRD Project
CONCEPTS: Definition of terms. Annex or appendix reference. Exchange of information and documents. Informational records. Inspection and observation. Bonds. Fees and exemptions. Tax

exemptions. Domestic obligation. Terms of loan. Loan regulations. Loan guarantee. Guarantor non-interference.
PARTIES:
Finland
IBRD (World Bank)

200526 Multilateral Agreement **212 UNTS 263**
SIGNED: 14 Jun 55   FORCE: 14 Jun 55
REGISTERED: 13 Jul 55 United Nations
ARTICLES: 6 LANGUAGE: English. Arabic.
HEADNOTE: TECHNICAL ASSISTANCE
TOPIC: Tech Assistance
CONCEPTS: Definition of terms. Previous treaty replacement. Privileges and immunities. General cooperation. Exchange of information and documents. Personnel. Responsibility and liability. Title and deeds. Use of facilities. Exchange. Scholarships and grants. Vocational training. Research and development. Exchange rates and regulations. Expense sharing formulae. Local currency. Domestic obligation. General technical assistance. Materials, equipment and services. IGO status. Conformity with IGO decisions.
TREATY   REF: 76UNTS132;   1UNTS15;
1UNTS263; 33UNTS261; 137UNTS26.
PROCEDURE: Amendment. Termination.
PARTIES:
Jordan SIGNED: 14 Jun 55 FORCE: 14 Jun 55
ICAO (Civil Aviat) SIGNED: 14 Jun 55 FORCE: 14 Jun 55
ILO (Labor Org) SIGNED: 14 Jun 55 FORCE: 14 Jun 55
ITU (Telecommun) SIGNED: 14 Jun 55 FORCE: 14 Jun 55
UNESCO (Educ/Cult) SIGNED: 14 Jun 55 FORCE: 14 Jun 55
United Nations SIGNED: 14 Jun 55 FORCE: 14 Jun 55
WHO (World Health) SIGNED: 14 Jun 55 FORCE: 14 Jun 55
WMO (Meteorology) SIGNED: 14 Jun 55 FORCE: 14 Jun 55

200527 Bilateral Agreement **214 UNTS 341**
SIGNED: 19 Aug 43   FORCE: 19 Aug 43
REGISTERED: 12 Sep 55 USA (United States)
ARTICLES: 1 LANGUAGE: English.
HEADNOTE: COLLABORATION ATOMIC RESEARCH
TOPIC: Atomic Energy
CONCEPTS: General cooperation. Exchange of information and documents. Research results. Scientific exchange. General. Nuclear materials. Defense and security. Security of information. Subsidiary organ.
INTL ORGS: Special Commission.
PARTIES:
UK Great Britain
USA (United States)

200528 Bilateral Agreement **216 UNTS 305**
SIGNED: 8 Nov 54   FORCE: 8 Jun 55
REGISTERED: 21 Sep 55 IBRD (World Bank)
ARTICLES: 5 LANGUAGE: English.
HEADNOTE: GUARANTEE AGREEMENT
TOPIC: IBRD Project
CONCEPTS: Definition of terms. Annex or appendix reference. Exchange of information and documents. Informational records. Inspection and observation. Bonds. Fees and exemptions. Tax exemptions. Domestic obligation. Terms of loan. Loan regulations. Loan guarantee. Guarantor non-interference.
PARTIES:
Austria
IBRD (World Bank)

200529 Bilateral Agreement **216 UNTS 347**
SIGNED: 29 Jun 51   FORCE: 12 Oct 51
REGISTERED: 22 Sep 55 IBRD (World Bank)
ARTICLES: 9 LANGUAGE: English. French.
HEADNOTE: LEGAL STATUS IBRD
TOPIC: IGO Status/Immunit
CONCEPTS: Juridical personality. Jurisdiction. Procedure. General. IGO status. Special status. Status of experts.
INTL ORGS: International Court of Justice. Arbitration Commission.

TREATY REF: 2UNTS134; 19UNTS300;
141UNTS356; ETC..
PROCEDURE: Denunciation.
PARTIES:
IBRD (World Bank)
Switzerland

200530 Bilateral Agreement **219 UNTS 305**
SIGNED: 5 Jul 55   FORCE: 13 Aug 55
REGISTERED: 10 Oct 55 WHO (World Health)
ARTICLES: 6 LANGUAGE: English. Arabic.
HEADNOTE: TECHNICAL ADVISORY ASSISTANCE
TOPIC: Tech Assistance
CONCEPTS: General technical assistance. Assis-
tance. Materials, equipment and services. Status
of experts.
INTL ORGS: United Nations.
TREATY REF: 33UNTS261; 43UNTS342;
46UNTS355; ETC.
PARTIES:
Libya
WHO (World Health)

200531 Bilateral Agreement **221 UNTS 375**
SIGNED: 14 Jun 55   FORCE: 9 Nov 55
REGISTERED: 15 Nov 55 IBRD (World Bank)
ARTICLES: 5 LANGUAGE: English.
HEADNOTE: GUARANTEE AGREEMENT
TOPIC: IBRD Project
CONCEPTS: Definition of terms. Annex or appen-
dix reference. Exchange of information and doc-
uments. Informational records. Inspection and
observation. Accounting procedures. Fees and
exemptions. Tax exemptions. Domestic obliga-
tion. Terms of loan. Loan regulations. Loan guar-
antee. Guarantor non-interference.
PARTIES:
Austria
IBRD (World Bank)

200532 Multilateral Protocol **227 UNTS 279**
SIGNED: 12 Sep 44   FORCE: 6 Feb 45
REGISTERED: 13 Feb 56 USA (United States)
ARTICLES: 6 LANGUAGE: English. Russian.
HEADNOTE: ZONES OCCUPATION GERMANY
TOPIC: Milit Occupation
CONCEPTS: Annex or appendix reference. Estab-
lishment of commission. Control and occupation
machinery. Markers and definitions.
INTL ORGS: Allied Military Occupation.
PARTIES:
UK Great Britain SIGNED: 12 Sep 44 RATIFIED:
5 Dec 44 FORCE: 6 Feb 45
USA (United States) SIGNED: 12 Sep 44 RATI-
FIED: 2 Feb 45 FORCE: 6 Feb 45
USSR (Soviet Union) SIGNED: 12 Sep 44 RATI-
FIED: 6 Feb 45 FORCE: 6 Feb 45

200533 Multilateral Agreement **227 UNTS 297**
SIGNED: 26 Jul 45   FORCE: 13 Aug 45
REGISTERED: 13 Feb 56 USA (United States)
ARTICLES: 11 LANGUAGE: English. French. Rus-
sian.
HEADNOTE: AMENDMENTS PROTOCOL ZONES
OCCUPATION GERMANY
TOPIC: Milit Occupation
CONCEPTS: Annex or appendix reference. Annex
type material. Occupation regime. Markers and
definitions.
INTL ORGS: Allied Military Occupation.
PARTIES:
France SIGNED: 26 Jul 45 RATIFIED: 7 Aug 45
FORCE: 13 Aug 45
UK Great Britain SIGNED: 26 Jul 45 RATIFIED:
2 Aug 45 FORCE: 13 Aug 45
USA (United States) SIGNED: 26 Jul 45 RATI-
FIED: 29 Jul 45 FORCE: 13 Aug 45
USSR (Soviet Union) SIGNED: 26 Jul 45 RATI-
FIED: 13 Aug 45 FORCE: 13 Aug 45

200534 Bilateral Agreement **230 UNTS 379**
SIGNED: 25 Oct 55   FORCE: 16 Feb 56
REGISTERED: 2 Feb 56 IBRD (World Bank)
ARTICLES: 5 LANGUAGE: English.
HEADNOTE: GUARANTEE AGREEMENT
TOPIC: IBRD Project
CONCEPTS: Definition of terms. Annex or appen-
dix reference. Exchange of information and doc-
uments. Informational records. Inspection and
observation. Bonds. Fees and exemptions. Tax
exemptions. Domestic obligation. Terms of loan.
Loan regulations. Loan guarantee. Guarantor
non-interference.
PARTIES:
Japan
IBRD (World Bank)

200535 Bilateral Exchange **231 UNTS 317**
SIGNED: 2 Oct 44   FORCE: 2 Oct 44
REGISTERED: 28 Mar 56 Netherlands
ARTICLES: 6 LANGUAGE: English.
HEADNOTE: PROPERTY
TOPIC: Claims and Debts
CONCEPTS: Annex or appendix reference. Gen-
eral property.
INTL ORGS: Special Commission.
PARTIES:
Netherlands
UK Great Britain

200536 Bilateral Exchange **234 UNTS 277**
SIGNED: 31 Jan 35   FORCE: 31 Jan 55
REGISTERED: 17 Apr 56 USA (United States)
ARTICLES: 2 LANGUAGE: English. Spanish.
HEADNOTE: RECIPROCAL FREE IMPORTATION
PRIVILEGES CONSULAR OFFICERS
TOPIC: Consul/Citizenship
CONCEPTS: Diplomatic privileges.
PARTIES:
Panama
USA (United States)

200537 Bilateral Exchange **234 UNTS 283**
SIGNED: 16 May 32   FORCE: 16 May 32
REGISTERED: 23 Apr 56 USA (United States)
ARTICLES: 2 LANGUAGE: English. Spanish.
HEADNOTE: FREE ENTRY PRIVILEGES FOREIGN
SERVICE PERSONNEL
TOPIC: Consul/Citizenship
CONCEPTS: Diplomatic privileges.
PARTIES:
Cuba
USA (United States)

200538 Bilateral Agreement **235 UNTS 346**
SIGNED: 17 Sep 45   FORCE: 17 Sep 45
REGISTERED: 25 Apr 56 USA (United States)
ARTICLES: 1 LANGUAGE: English. Russian.
HEADNOTE: BOUNDARY CHANGES OCCUPATION
ZONES
TOPIC: Milit Occupation
CONCEPTS: Annex or appendix reference. Annex
type material. Control and occupation ma-
chinery. Markers and definitions.
PARTIES:
USA (United States)
USSR (Soviet Union)

200539 Multilateral Agreement **236 UNTS 359**
SIGNED: 14 Nov 44   FORCE: 6 Feb 45
REGISTERED: 26 Apr 56 USA (United States)
ARTICLES: 11 LANGUAGE: English. Russian.
HEADNOTE: CONTROL MACHINERY
TOPIC: Milit Occupation
CONCEPTS: Detailed regulations. General cooper-
ation. Exchange of information and documents.
Establishment of commission. Control and occu-
pation machinery.
INTL ORGS: Allied Military Occupation.
PROCEDURE: Future Procedures Contemplated.
PARTIES:
UK Great Britain SIGNED: 14 Nov 44 RATIFIED:
5 Dec 44 FORCE: 6 Feb 45
USA (United States) SIGNED: 14 Nov 44 RATI-
FIED: 24 Jan 45 FORCE: 6 Feb 45
USSR (Soviet Union) SIGNED: 14 Nov 44 RATI-
FIED: 6 Feb 45 FORCE: 6 Feb 45
ANNEX
236 UNTS 400. USSR (Soviet Union). Amend-
ment 25 May 45. Force 25 May 45.
236 UNTS 400. UK Great Britain. Amendment
17 May 45. Force 25 May 45.
236 UNTS 400. USA (United States). Amendment
14 May 45. Force 25 May 45.
236 UNTS 400. France. Amendment 18 May 45.
Force 25 May 45.

200540 Bilateral Agreement **241 UNTS 475**
SIGNED: 10 Jul 42   FORCE: 10 Jul 42
REGISTERED: 16 May 56 Netherlands
ARTICLES: 1 LANGUAGE: Dutch. Russian.
HEADNOTE: CONSULAR MATTERS
TOPIC: Consul/Citizenship
CONCEPTS: Diplomatic and consular relations.
PARTIES:
Netherlands
USSR (Soviet Union)

200541 Multilateral Agreement **247 UNTS 366**
SIGNED: 8 Jun 56   FORCE: 8 Jun 56
REGISTERED: 19 Jul 56 United Nations
ARTICLES: 6 LANGUAGE: French.
HEADNOTE: TECHNICAL ASSISTANCE
TOPIC: Tech Assistance
CONCEPTS: Definition of terms. Previous treaty replacement. Privileges and immunities. General
cooperation. Exchange of information and documents. Personnel. Responsibility and liability. Title and deeds. Use of facilities. Exchange. Scholarships and grants. Vocational training. Research and development. Exchange rates and
regulations. Expense sharing formulae. Domestic obligation. General technical assistance. Materials, equipment and services. IGO status. Conformity with IGO decisions.
TREATY REF: 76UNTS132; 188UNTS345;
1UNTS15,263; ETC..
PROCEDURE: Amendment. Termination.
PARTIES:
FAO (Food Agri) SIGNED: 28 May 56 FORCE:
8 Jun 56
ICAO (Civil Aviat) SIGNED: 28 May 56 FORCE:
8 Jun 56
ILO (Labor Org) SIGNED: 28 May 56 FORCE:
8 Jun 56
ITU (Telecommun) SIGNED: 28 May 56 FORCE:
8 Jun 56
UNESCO (Educ/Cult) SIGNED: 28 May 56
FORCE: 8 Jun 56
United Nations SIGNED: 28 May 56 FORCE:
8 Jun 56
WHO (World Health) SIGNED: 28 May 56
FORCE: 8 Jun 56
WMO (Meteorology) SIGNED: 28 May 56
FORCE: 8 Jun 56
Vietnam SIGNED: 8 Jun 56 FORCE: 8 Jun 56
ANNEX
551 UNTS 354. UNTAB (Tech Assis). Amendment
18 Mar 65. Force 2 Dec 65.
551 UNTS 354. Vietnam, South. Amendment
2 Dec 65. Force 2 Dec 65.

200542 Bilateral Agreement **248 UNTS 307**
SIGNED: 7 Aug 56   FORCE: 22 Aug 56
REGISTERED: 22 Aug 56 United Nations
ARTICLES: 11 LANGUAGE: English.
HEADNOTE: ACTIVITIES UNICEF
TOPIC: Direct Aid
CONCEPTS: Treaty implementation. Privileges and
immunities. General cooperation. Exchange of
information and documents. Informational
records. Inspection and observation. Public in-
formation. Procedure. Existing tribunals. Export
quotas. Tax exemptions. Customs exemptions.
Commodities and services. Assistance. General
aid. Distribution. IGO status.
INTL ORGS: United Nations.
TREATY REF: 1UNTS15.
PROCEDURE: Duration.
PARTIES:
UNICEF (Children)
Sudan
ANNEX
337 UNTS 443. Sudan. Amendment 14 May 58.

200543 Bilateral Agreement **248 UNTS 321**
SIGNED: 21 Feb 56   FORCE: 10 May 56
REGISTERED: 22 Aug 56 IBRD (World Bank)
ARTICLES: 5 LANGUAGE: English.
HEADNOTE: GUARANTEE AGREEMENT
TOPIC: IBRD Project
CONCEPTS: Definition of terms. Annex or appen-
dix reference. Exchange of information and doc-
uments. Informational records. Inspection and
observation. Bonds. Fees and exemptions. Tax
exemptions. Domestic obligation. Terms of loan.
Loan regulations. Loan guarantee. Guarantor
non-interference.

PARTIES:
Japan
IBRD (World Bank)

200544 Bilateral Agreement **249 UNTS 405**
SIGNED: 11 Jun 55   FORCE: 3 May 55
REGISTERED: 8 Sep 56 Switzerland
ARTICLES: 31 LANGUAGE: English. French.
HEADNOTE: SWITZERLAND & EUROPEAN NU-
CLEAR RESEARCH
TOPIC: IGO Status/Immunit
CONCEPTS: Annex or appendix reference. Diplo-
matic privileges. Diplomatic missions. Inviolabil-
ity. Privileges and immunities. Property. Diplo-
matic correspondence. Exchange of official pub-
lications. Juridical personality. Procedure.
Special tribunals. Special status. Status of ex-
perts.
INTL ORGS: International Court of Justice.
PROCEDURE: Amendment.
PARTIES:
CERN (Nuc Resrch)
Switzerland

200545 Bilateral Convention **253 UNTS 285**
SIGNED: 12 May 33   FORCE: 10 Nov 36
REGISTERED: 20 Nov 56 Canada
ARTICLES: 22 LANGUAGE: English. French.
HEADNOTE: RIGHTS NATIONALS COMMERCIAL
SHIPPING MATTER
TOPIC: Admin Cooperation
CONCEPTS: Alien status. Consular relations estab-
lishment. Conformity with municipal law. Legal
protection and assistance. General property.
Procedure. Existing tribunals. Tariffs. Fees and
exemptions. Most favored nation clause. Tax ex-
emptions. Transport of goods. Inland and territo-
rial waters. Ports and pilotage. Foreign nationals.
INTL ORGS: Permanent Court of International Jus-
tice.
PROCEDURE: Ratification. Termination.
PARTIES:
Canada
France

200546 Bilateral Agreement **265 UNTS 312**
SIGNED: 20 Feb 57   FORCE: 20 Feb 57
REGISTERED: 18 Apr 57 United Nations
ARTICLES: 4 LANGUAGE: English. French.
HEADNOTE: RELATIONSHIP AGREEMENT
TOPIC: IGO Operations
CONCEPTS: Conformity with IGO decisions. Inter-
agency agreements.
INTL ORGS: International Finance Corporation.
TREATY REF: 16UNTS346.
PARTIES:
IBRD (World Bank)
United Nations

200547 Bilateral Agreement **278 UNTS 151**
SIGNED: 15 Oct 45   FORCE: 15 Oct 45
REGISTERED: 18 Oct 57 USA (United States)
ARTICLES: 7 LANGUAGE: English.
HEADNOTE: DISPOSITION LEND-LEASE SUP-
PLIES
TOPIC: Milit Assistance
CONCEPTS: Annex or appendix reference. Confor-
mity with municipal law. Inspection and observa-
tion. Reexport of goods, etc.. Currency. Payment
schedules. Claims and settlements. Delivery
schedules. Lend lease. Surplus war property.
PARTIES:
USA (United States)
USSR (Soviet Union)
ANNEX
315 UNTS 249. USA (United States).
315 UNTS 249. USSR (Soviet Union).

200548 Bilateral Agreement **281 UNTS 369**
SIGNED: 23 Oct 57   FORCE: 14 Nov 57
REGISTERED: 14 Nov 57 United Nations
ARTICLES: 24 LANGUAGE: English.
HEADNOTE: RADIOACTIVITY SEA RESEARCH
TOPIC: IGO Operations
CONCEPTS: Definition of terms. Annex or appen-
dix reference. Privileges and immunities. Person-
nel. General property. Existing tribunals. Public
health. Scholarships and grants. Research re-
sults. Nuclear research. Research and develop-

ment. Expense sharing formulae. Domestic obli-
gation. Economic assistance. IGO obligations.
INTL ORGS: International Court of Justice.
PROCEDURE: Duration. Renewal or Revival.
PARTIES:
IAEA (Atom Energy)
United Nations
ANNEX
338 UNTS 406. United Nations. Implementation
10 Aug 59.
338 UNTS 406. IAEA (Atom Energy). Implementa-
tion 19 Jun 59.

200549 Bilateral Agreement **302 UNTS 343**
SIGNED: 26 May 58   FORCE: 26 May 58
REGISTERED: 30 May 58 ILO (Labor Org)
ARTICLES: 6 LANGUAGE: English.
HEADNOTE: ADMINISTRATION COOPERATION
TOPIC: IGO Operations
CONCEPTS: Representation. General cooperation.
Exchange of information and documents. ILO
conventions. Administrative cooperation.
INTL ORGS: United Nations.
TREATY REF: 15UNTS40.
PROCEDURE: Amendment. Denunciation.
PARTIES:
Arab League
ILO (Labor Org)

200550 Multilateral Agreement **306 UNTS 236**
SIGNED: 19 Jun 58   FORCE: 19 Jun 58
REGISTERED: 16 Jul 58 United Nations
ARTICLES: 6 LANGUAGE: English.
HEADNOTE: TECHNICAL ASSISTANCE
TOPIC: Tech Assistance
CONCEPTS: Definition of terms. Annex or appendix reference. Previous treaty replacement. Privileges and immunities. General cooperation. Ex-
change of information and documents. Person-
nel. Responsibility and liability. Title and deeds.
Use of facilities. Exchange. Scholarships and
grants. Vocational training. Research and development. Exchange rates and regulations. Expense sharing formulae. Local currency. Domestic obligation. General technical assistance. Materials, equipment and services. IGO status.
TREATY REF: 76UNTS132; 1UNTS15;
33UNTS261.
PROCEDURE: Amendment. Termination.
PARTIES:
Korea, South SIGNED: 19 Jun 58 FORCE:
19 Jun 58
FAO (Food Agri) SIGNED: 19 Jun 58 FORCE:
19 Jun 58
ICAO (Civil Aviat) SIGNED: 19 Jun 58 FORCE:
19 Jun 58
ILO (Labor Org) SIGNED: 19 Jun 58 FORCE:
19 Jun 58
ITU (Telecommun) SIGNED: 19 Jun 58 FORCE:
19 Jun 58
UNESCO (Educ/Cult) SIGNED: 19 Jun 58
FORCE: 19 Jun 58
United Nations SIGNED: 19 Jun 58 FORCE:
19 Jun 58
WHO (World Health) SIGNED: 19 Jun 58 FORCE:
19 Jun 58
WMO (Meteorology) SIGNED: 19 Jun 58 FORCE:
19 Jun 58
ANNEX
472 UNTS 406. UNTAB (Tech Assis). Amendment
4 Apr 63. Force 18 May 63.
472 UNTS 406. Korea, South. Amendment
18 May 63. Force 18 May 63.

200551 Bilateral Agreement **312 UNTS 387**
SIGNED: 7 Jul 58   FORCE: 7 Jul 58
REGISTERED: 19 Sep 58 ILO (Labor Org)
ARTICLES: 14 LANGUAGE: French.
HEADNOTE: LIAISON
TOPIC: IGO Operations
CONCEPTS: Treaty implementation. Exchange of
information and documents. General technical
assistance. Inter-agency agreements.
INTL ORGS: United Nations.
PARTIES:
EEC (Econ Commnty)
ILO (Labor Org)

200552 Bilateral Agreement **313 UNTS 323**
SIGNED: 22 Sep 58   FORCE: 29 Sep 58

REGISTERED: 29 Sep 58 United Nations
ARTICLES: 10 LANGUAGE: English. French.
HEADNOTE: ADMIT IAEA INTO UN JOINT STAFF
PENSION FUND
TOPIC: IGO Operations
CONCEPTS: Default remedies. Standardization.
Holidays and rest periods. Conformity with IGO
decisions.
PARTIES:
IAEA (Atom Energy)
United Nations
ANNEX
480 UNTS 484. United Nations. Implementation
4 Oct 63. Force 18 Oct 63.
480 UNTS 484. IAEA (Atom Energy). Implementa-
tion 18 Oct 63. Force 18 Oct 63.

200553 Bilateral Agreement **324 UNTS 273**
SIGNED: 13 Jan 59   FORCE: 13 Jan 59
REGISTERED: 1 Mar 59 United Nations
ARTICLES: 19 LANGUAGE: English. French.
HEADNOTE: RELATIONSHIP AGREEMENT
TOPIC: IGO Operations
CONCEPTS: Treaty implementation. Annex or ap-
pendix reference. Exchange of information and
documents. Personnel. Existing tribunals. Labor
statistics. Accounting procedures. Funding pro-
cedures. General technical assistance. Confor-
mity with IGO decisions. Assistance to United
Nations. Inter-agency agreements. Recognition
of specialized agency.
INTL ORGS: International Court of Justice. United
Nations.
PROCEDURE: Amendment.
PARTIES:
IMCO (Maritime Org)
United Nations

200554 Bilateral Agreement **327 UNTS 309**
SIGNED: 16 Jan 59   FORCE: 16 Jan 59
REGISTERED: 24 Apr 59 ILO (Labor Org)
ARTICLES: 11 LANGUAGE: English. French.
HEADNOTE: AGREEMENT
TOPIC: IGO Operations
CONCEPTS: Representation. Treaty implementa-
tion. Exchange of information and documents.
Personnel. Labor statistics. Investments. Mutual
consultation.
INTL ORGS: United Nations.
PROCEDURE: Amendment. Registration. Termina-
tion.
PARTIES:
ILO (Labor Org)
IMCO (Maritime Org)

200555 Bilateral Agreement **328 UNTS 273**
SIGNED: 8 May 59   FORCE: 21 Nov 58
REGISTERED: 14 Jun 59 ILO (Labor Org)
ARTICLES: 13 LANGUAGE: English. French.
HEADNOTE: AGREEMENT
TOPIC: IGO Operations
CONCEPTS: Treaty implementation. Annex or ap-
pendix reference. Exchange of information and
documents. Labor statistics. Funding proce-
dures. General technical assistance. Mutual con-
sultation.
TREATY REF: 281UNTS369; 1UNTS186;
15UNTS41.
PROCEDURE: Amendment.
PARTIES:
IAEA (Atom Energy)
ILO (Labor Org)

200556 Bilateral Agreement **336 UNTS 317**
SIGNED: 23 Jun 59   FORCE: 30 Jun 59
REGISTERED: 30 Jun 59 United Nations
ARTICLES: 10 LANGUAGE: English. French.
HEADNOTE: ADMIT IMCO INTO UN JOINT STAFF
PENSION FUND
TOPIC: IGO Operations
CONCEPTS: Exchange of information and docu-
ments. Accounting procedures. Funding proce-
dures. Recognition of specialized agency.
PARTIES:
IMCO (Maritime Org)
United Nations

200557   Bilateral Agreement   **337 UNTS 361**
SIGNED: 3 Jun 59   FORCE: 3 Jun 59
REGISTERED: 15 Jul 59 United Nations
ARTICLES: 6 LANGUAGE: French.
HEADNOTE: OPERATIONAL & EXECUTIVE PER-
SONNEL
TOPIC: IGO Status/Immunit
CONCEPTS: Annex or appendix reference. Diplo-
matic missions. Privileges and immunities. Pro-
cedure. General technical assistance. Special
status.
INTL ORGS: Permanent Court of Arbitration. Arbi-
tration Commission.
PROCEDURE: Amendment. Termination.
PARTIES:
 United Nations
 Vietnam, South
                    ANNEX
616 UNTS 588. USA (United States). Termination
 28 Nov 62.
616 UNTS 588. Vietnam, South. Termination
 28 Nov 62.

200558   Bilateral Agreement   **339 UNTS 373**
SIGNED: 1 Oct 58   FORCE: 1 Oct 58
REGISTERED: 24 Aug 59 IAEA (Atom Energy)
ARTICLES: 13 LANGUAGE: English. French.
HEADNOTE: AGREEMENT
TOPIC: IGO Operations
CONCEPTS: Representation. Treaty implementa-
tion. Exchange of information and documents.
Personnel. Labor statistics. Funding procedures.
General technical assistance. Mutual consulta-
tion.
INTL ORGS: United Nations.
PROCEDURE: Amendment. Termination.
PARTIES:
 IAEA (Atom Energy)
 UNESCO (Educ/Cult)

200559   Bilateral Agreement   **339 UNTS 387**
SIGNED: 28 May 59   FORCE: 28 May 59
REGISTERED: 24 Aug 59 IAEA (Atom Energy)
ARTICLES: 13 LANGUAGE: English. French.
HEADNOTE: AGREEMENT
TOPIC: IGO Operations
CONCEPTS: Administrative cooperation. General
cooperation. Exchange of information and docu-
ments. Programs. General technical assistance.
Liaison with other IGO's. Inter-agency agree-
ments. Mutual consultation.
INTL ORGS: United Nations.
TREATY   REF: 14UNTS185;   15UNTS447;
 16UNTS364; ETC..
PROCEDURE: Amendment. Termination.
PARTIES:
 IAEA (Atom Energy)
 WHO (World Health)

200560   Bilateral Agreement   **340 UNTS 311**
SIGNED: 17 Sep 56   FORCE: 21 Dec 56
REGISTERED: 28 Aug 59 IBRD (World Bank)
ARTICLES: 10 LANGUAGE: English. French.
HEADNOTE: LOAN
TOPIC: Loans and Credits
CONCEPTS: Negotiation. Interest rates. Local cur-
rency. Loan repayment. Terms of loan. World
Bank projects.
INTL ORGS: International Court of Justice. Arbitra-
tion Commission.
PARTIES:
 IBRD (World Bank)
 Switzerland
                    ANNEX
413 UNTS 400. Switzerland. Supplementation
 18 Oct 60. Force 18 Oct 60.
413 UNTS 400. IBRD (World Bank). Supplementa-
tion 18 Oct 60. Force 18 Oct 60.

200561   Bilateral Agreement   **341 UNTS 341**
SIGNED: 12 Aug 59   FORCE: 12 Aug 59
REGISTERED: 18 Sep 59 WMO (Meteorology)
ARTICLES: 13 LANGUAGE: English. French.
HEADNOTE: AGREEMENT
TOPIC: IGO Operations
CONCEPTS: Representation. Exchange of informa-
tion and documents. Labor statistics. Funding
procedures. General technical assistance. Mu-
tual consultation.
INTL ORGS: United Nations.

PROCEDURE: Amendment. Termination.
PARTIES:
 IAEA (Atom Energy)
 WMO (Meteorology)

200562   Bilateral Agreement   **341 UNTS 353**
SIGNED: 28 Sep 59   FORCE: 28 Sep 59
REGISTERED: 28 Sep 59 United Nations
ARTICLES: 12 LANGUAGE: English. French.
HEADNOTE: EXECUTION UNSF PROJECTS
TOPIC: IGO Operations
CONCEPTS: Privileges and immunities. Exchange
of information and documents. Juridical person-
ality. Accounting procedures. Currency. Ex-
change rates and regulations. Funding proce-
dures. Inter-agency agreements.
INTL ORGS: United Nations.
PROCEDURE: Amendment. Termination.
PARTIES:
 FAO (Food Agri)
 UN Special Fund

200563   Bilateral Agreement   **343 UNTS 325**
SIGNED: 12 Oct 59   FORCE: 12 Oct 59
REGISTERED: 12 Oct 59 United Nations
ARTICLES: 12 LANGUAGE: English. French.
HEADNOTE: EXECUTION UNSF PROJECTS
TOPIC: IGO Operations
CONCEPTS: Privileges and immunities. Exchange
of information and documents. Juridical person-
ality. Accounting procedures. Currency. Ex-
change rates and regulations. Funding proce-
dures. Inter-agency agreements.
INTL ORGS: United Nations.
TREATY REF: 341UNTS.
PROCEDURE: Amendment.
PARTIES:
 ILO (Labor Org)
 UN Special Fund

200564   Bilateral Agreement   **345 UNTS 311**
SIGNED: 17 Nov 59   FORCE: 17 Nov 59
REGISTERED: 17 Nov 59 United Nations
ARTICLES: 12 LANGUAGE: English.
HEADNOTE: EXECUTION UNSF PROJECTS
TOPIC: IGO Operations
CONCEPTS: Privileges and immunities. Exchange
of information and documents. Juridical person-
ality. Accounting procedures. Currency. Ex-
change rates and regulations. Funding proce-
dures. Inter-agency agreements.
INTL ORGS: International Atomic Energy Agency.
United Nations.
TREATY REF: 341UNTS.
PROCEDURE: Termination.
PARTIES:
 UN Special Fund
 WMO (Meteorology)

200565   Bilateral Agreement   **346 UNTS 289**
SIGNED: 6 Nov 59   FORCE: 11 Dec 59
REGISTERED: 11 Dec 59 United Nations
ARTICLES: 11 LANGUAGE: English.
HEADNOTE: ESTABLISHMENT MAINTENANCE UN
MEMORIAL CEMETARY
TOPIC: Other Military
CONCEPTS: Treaty implementation. Annex or ap-
pendix reference. Privileges and immunities. Ti-
tle and deeds. Arbitration. Procedure. Sanitation.
Compensation. Tax exemptions. Customs ex-
emptions. Responsibility for war dead. Upkeep
of war graves. Establishment of war cemeteries.
INTL ORGS: International Court of Justice. Arbitra-
tion Commission.
PARTIES:
 Korea, South
 United Nations

200566   Bilateral Agreement   **348 UNTS 331**
SIGNED: 14 Jan 60   FORCE: 14 Jan 60
REGISTERED: 14 Jan 60 United Nations
ARTICLES: 12 LANGUAGE: English. French.
HEADNOTE: ADMIT ITU INTO UN JOINT STAFF
PENSION FUND
TOPIC: IGO Operations
CONCEPTS: Default remedies. Holidays and rest
periods. Labor statistics. Social security. Fund-
ing procedures.

PARTIES:
 ITU (Telecommun)
 United Nations

200567   Bilateral Agreement   **357 UNTS 311**
SIGNED: 29 Apr 60   FORCE: 29 Apr 60
REGISTERED: 29 Apr 60 United Nations
ARTICLES: 10 LANGUAGE: English. French.
HEADNOTE: ASSISTANCE
TOPIC: Direct Aid
CONCEPTS: Detailed regulations. Treaty imple-
mentation. Annex or appendix reference. Visas.
Privileges and immunities. Exchange of informa-
tion and documents. Informational records. In-
spection and observation. Operating agencies.
Personnel. Public information. Responsibility
and liability. Title and deeds. Use of facilities.
Arbitration. Procedure. Negotiation. Import
quotas. Exchange rates and regulations. Ex-
pense sharing formulae. Financial programs.
Claims and settlements. Tax exemptions. Do-
mestic obligation. General technical assistance.
Economic assistance. Materials, equipment and
services. IGO status.
INTL ORGS: International Atomic Energy Agency.
International Court of Justice. United Nations.
TREATY   REF: 1UNTS15;   33UNTS261;
 374UNTS137.
PROCEDURE: Amendment. Termination.
PARTIES:
 UN Special Fund
 Vietnam, South

200568   Bilateral Agreement   **359 UNTS 375**
SIGNED: 25 May 60   FORCE: 25 May 60
REGISTERED: 25 May 60 United Nations
ARTICLES: 12 LANGUAGE: English. French.
HEADNOTE: EXECUTION UNSF PROJECTS
TOPIC: IGO Operations
CONCEPTS: Privileges and immunities. Exchange
of information and documents. Juridical person-
ality. Accounting procedures. Currency. Ex-
change rates and regulations. Funding proce-
dures. Inter-agency agreements.
INTL ORGS: United Nations.
PROCEDURE: Amendment. Termination.
PARTIES:
 UN Special Fund
 WHO (World Health)

200569   Bilateral Agreement   **360 UNTS 367**
SIGNED: 21 Apr 60   FORCE: 5 May 60
REGISTERED: 10 Jun 60 United Nations
ARTICLES: 12 LANGUAGE: English.
HEADNOTE: EXECUTION UNSF PROJECTS
TOPIC: IGO Operations
CONCEPTS: Privileges and immunities. Exchange
of information and documents. Juridical person-
ality. Accounting procedures. Currency. Ex-
change rates and regulations. Funding proce-
dures. Special status.
INTL ORGS: International Atomic Energy Agency.
United Nations.
TREATY REF: 341UNTS366.
PROCEDURE: Amendment. Termination.
PARTIES:
 ICAO (Civil Aviat)
 UN Special Fund

200570   Bilateral Agreement   **361 UNTS 193**
SIGNED: 1 Oct 59   FORCE: 1 Oct 59
REGISTERED. 13 Jun 60 IAEA (Atom Energy)
ARTICLES: 13 LANGUAGE: English. French. Span-
ish.
HEADNOTE: AGREEMENT
TOPIC: IGO Operations
CONCEPTS: Representation. Treaty implementa-
tion. Exchange of information and documents.
Personnel. Labor statistics. Funding procedures.
General technical assistance. Mutual consulta-
tion.
INTL ORGS: United Nations.
PROCEDURE: Amendment. Termination.
PARTIES:
 IAEA (Atom Energy)
 ICAO (Civil Aviat)

200571   Bilateral Agreement   **361 UNTS 211**
SIGNED: 1 Oct 58   FORCE: 18 Nov 59

REGISTERED: 13 Jun 60 IAEA (Atom Energy)
ARTICLES: 13 LANGUAGE: English. French.
HEADNOTE: AGREEMENT & PROTOCOL
TOPIC: IGO Operations
CONCEPTS: Representation. Treaty implementa-
tion. Exchange of information and documents.
Personnel. Labor statistics. Funding procedures.
General technical assistance. Mutual consulta-
tion.
INTL ORGS: Food and Agricultural Organization of
the United Nations. United Nations.
PROCEDURE: Amendment.
PARTIES:
FAO (Food Agri)
IAEA (Atom Energy)

200572 Bilateral Agreement **363 UNTS 367**
SIGNED: 29 Sep 54   FORCE: 5 Dec 59
REGISTERED: 29 Jun 60 United Nations
ARTICLES: 12 LANGUAGE: English. French.
HEADNOTE: EXECUTION UNSF PROJECTS
TOPIC: IGO Operations
CONCEPTS: Privileges and immunities. Exchange
of information and documents. Accounting pro-
cedures. Currency. Exchange rates and regula-
tions. Funding procedures. Mutual consultation.
INTL ORGS: United Nations.
PROCEDURE: Amendment. Termination.
PARTIES:
UNESCO (Educ/Cult)
UN Special Fund

200573 Bilateral Agreement **368 UNTS 329**
SIGNED: 13 Jul 60   FORCE: 13 Jul 60
REGISTERED: 13 Jul 60 United Nations
ARTICLES: 12 LANGUAGE: English. French.
HEADNOTE: EXECUTION UNSF PROJECTS
TOPIC: IGO Operations
CONCEPTS: Privileges and immunities. Exchange
of information and documents. Accounting pro-
cedures. Currency. Exchange rates and regula-
tions. Funding procedures. Interagency re-
quests.
INTL ORGS: International Atomic Energy Agency.
United Nations.
PROCEDURE: Amendment. Termination.
PARTIES:
ITU (Telecommun)
UN Special Fund

200574 Bilateral Agreement **369 UNTS 401**
SIGNED: 8 Jun 60   FORCE: 8 Jun 60
REGISTERED: 15 Jul 60 United Nations
ARTICLES: 10 LANGUAGE: English. French.
HEADNOTE: SPECIAL FUND ASSISTANCE
TOPIC: Tech Assistance
CONCEPTS: Privileges and immunities. Procedure.
Aid and development. Economic assistance.
Credit provisions.
INTL ORGS: International Atomic Energy Agency.
International Court of Justice. United Nations.
TREATY REF: 1UNTS15; 4UNTS461; 5UNTS413;
ETC..
PROCEDURE: Termination.
PARTIES:
UN Special Fund
Togo

200575 Bilateral Agreement **369 UNTS 419**
SIGNED: 29 Jun 60   FORCE: 29 Jun 60
REGISTERED: 18 Jul 60 United Nations
ARTICLES: 10 LANGUAGE: English. Arabic.
HEADNOTE: ASSISTANCE
TOPIC: Tech Assistance
CONCEPTS: Detailed regulations. Visas. Privileges
and immunities. Licenses and permits. General
property. Arbitration. Procedure. Negotiation.
Import quotas. Reexport of goods, etc.. Ex-
change rates and regulations. Fees and exemp-
tions. Tax exemptions. Customs exemptions.
IGO status.
INTL ORGS: International Atomic Energy Agency.
International Court of Justice. United Nations.
PARTIES:
Kuwait
UN Special Fund

200576 Bilateral Agreement **373 UNTS 327**
SIGNED: 23 Aug 60   FORCE: 23 Aug 60

REGISTERED: 23 Aug 60 United Nations
ARTICLES: 11 LANGUAGE: French.
HEADNOTE: FINANCIAL ASSISTANCE
TOPIC: Direct Aid
CONCEPTS: General cooperation. Exchange of in-
formation and documents. Import quotas. Ac-
counting procedures. Currency. Exchange rates
and regulations. Financial programs. Funding
procedures. Local currency. Assets. General aid.
Use restrictions.
PROCEDURE: Registration.
PARTIES:
Congo (Zaire)
United Nations

200577 Bilateral Agreement **384 UNTS 303**
SIGNED: 5 Jan 61   FORCE: 5 Jan 61
REGISTERED: 5 Jan 61 United Nations
ARTICLES: 8 LANGUAGE: English.
HEADNOTE: TRANSFER PENSION RIGHTS
TOPIC: IGO Operations
CONCEPTS: Definition of terms. Holidays and rest
periods. Labor statistics. Old age insurance.
Sickness and invalidity insurance.
PROCEDURE: Amendment.
PARTIES:
IBRD (World Bank)
United Nations

200578 Bilateral Agreement **384 UNTS 315**
SIGNED: 22 Dec 60   FORCE: 30 Dec 60
REGISTERED: 5 Jan 61 United Nations
ARTICLES: 7 LANGUAGE: English.
HEADNOTE: TRANSFER PENSION RIGHTS
TOPIC: IGO Operations
CONCEPTS: Definition of terms. Holidays and rest
periods. Labor statistics. Old age insurance.
Sickness and invalidity insurance.
PARTIES:
IMF (Fund)
United Nations

200579 Bilateral Instrument **389 UNTS 291**
SIGNED: 8 Dec 60   FORCE: 2 Dec 60
REGISTERED: 5 Mar 61 ILO (Labor Org)
ARTICLES: 8 LANGUAGE: French.
HEADNOTE: INTERNATIONAL VOCATIONAL
TRAINING CENTER
TOPIC: IGO Operations
CONCEPTS: Annex or appendix reference. Ex-
change of information and documents. Subsid-
iary organ.
PROCEDURE: Amendment.
PARTIES:
Council of Europe
ILO (Labor Org)

200580 Bilateral Convention **390 UNTS 323**
SIGNED: 26 Jan 61   FORCE: 28 Feb 61
REGISTERED: 13 Mar 61 ILO (Labor Org)
ARTICLES: 7 LANGUAGE: French.
HEADNOTE: COOPERATION
TOPIC: IGO Operations
CONCEPTS: Representation. Labor statistics. Gen-
eral technical assistance. Mutual consultation.
PARTIES:
Euratom
ILO (Labor Org)

200581 Bilateral Agreement **391 UNTS 295**
SIGNED: 31 Oct 60   FORCE: 31 Oct 60
REGISTERED: 20 Mar 61 United Nations
ARTICLES: 6 LANGUAGE: English. Arabic.
HEADNOTE: PROVISION OPERATIONAL EXECU-
TIVE PERSONNEL
TOPIC: Tech Assistance
CONCEPTS: Exceptions and exemptions. Treaty
implementation. Treaty interpretation. Annex or
appendix reference. Privileges and immunities.
General cooperation. Exchange of information
and documents. Personnel. Responsibility and li-
ability. Arbitration. Procedure. Compensation. In-
demnities and reimbursements. Expense sharing
formulae. Domestic obligation. Special projects.
Status of experts.
INTL ORGS: Permanent Court of Arbitration.
PARTIES:
Kuwait
United Nations

200582 Bilateral Agreement **394 UNTS 221**
SIGNED: 10 Apr 61   FORCE: 27 Mar 61
REGISTERED: 16 Apr 61 United Nations
ARTICLES: 3 LANGUAGE: English. French.
HEADNOTE: BOARD OF GOVERNORS AGREE-
MENT
TOPIC: IGO Operations
CONCEPTS: Subsidiary organ. Liaison with other
IGO's. IGO status.
INTL ORGS: International Bank for Reconstruction
and Development. United Nations Special Fund.
Special Commission.
TREATY REF: 16UNTS346.
PARTIES:
IDA (Devel Assoc)
United Nations

200583 Bilateral Agreement **394 UNTS 231**
SIGNED: 21 Apr 61   FORCE: 21 Apr 61
REGISTERED: 21 Apr 61 United Nations
ARTICLES: 10 LANGUAGE: English.
HEADNOTE: ASSISTANCE
TOPIC: Direct Aid
CONCEPTS: Detailed regulations. Treaty imple-
mentation. Visas. Privileges and immunities. Ex-
change of information and documents. Informa-
tional records. Inspection and observation. Oper-
ating agencies. Personnel. Public information.
Responsibility and liability. Title and deeds. Use
of facilities. Arbitration. Procedure. Negotiation.
Import quotas. Attachment of funds. Exchange
rates and regulations. Expense sharing formulae.
Financial programs. Domestic obligation. Gen-
eral technical assistance. Economic assistance.
Materials, equipment and services. IGO status.
INTL ORGS: Universal Postal Union. Arbitration
Commission.
TREATY REF: 1UNTS15; 33UNTS261;
374UNTS147.
PROCEDURE: Amendment. Termination.
PARTIES:
Korea, South
UN Special Fund

200584 Multilateral Agreement **396 UNTS 255**
SIGNED: 8 Mar 61   FORCE: 10 Mar 61
REGISTERED: 8 May 61 IAEA (Atom Energy)
ARTICLES: 13 LANGUAGE: English. French.
HEADNOTE: RESEARCH EFFECTS SEA RADIOAC-
TIVITY
TOPIC: Scientific Project
CONCEPTS: Privileges and immunities. Arbitra-
tion. Procedure. Research and scientific
projects. Research cooperation. Research re-
sults. Scientific exchange. Research and devel-
opment.
INTL ORGS: International Court of Justice. United
Nations. Special Commission.
TREATY REF: 276UNTS3; 296UNTS359;
312UNTS427; ETC.
PARTIES:
Monaco SIGNED: 10 Mar 61 FORCE: 10 Mar 61
Oceania SIGNED: 8 Mar 61 FORCE: 10 Mar 61
IAEA (Atom Energy) SIGNED: 10 Mar 61 FORCE:
10 Mar 61
                    ANNEX
490 UNTS 482. IAEA (Atom Energy). Prolongation
31 Dec 63. Force 31 Dec 63.
490 UNTS 482.   Monaco.   Prolongation
26 Dec 63. Force 31 Dec 63.
490 UNTS 482.   Oceania.   Prolongation
18 Dec 63. Force 31 Dec 63.

200585 Bilateral Agreement **396 UNTS 273**
SIGNED: 24 Nov 60   FORCE: 30 Sep 60
REGISTERED: 8 May 61 IAEA (Atom Energy)
ARTICLES: 11 LANGUAGE: English. French.
HEADNOTE: ORGANIZATION FOR EUROPEAN
ECONOMIC COOPERATION AGREEMENT
TOPIC: IGO Operations
CONCEPTS: Treaty implementation. IGO refer-
ence. Administrative cooperation. Exchange of
information and documents. Liaison with other
IGO's.
INTL ORGS: International Atomic Energy Agency.
United Nations.
TREATY REF: 281UNTS369; 338UNTS406.
PROCEDURE: Duration. Termination.
PARTIES:
IAEA (Atom Energy)
OECD (Econ Coop)

200586 Bilateral Agreement **396 UNTS 285**
SIGNED: 22 Dec 60   FORCE: 21 Dec 60
REGISTERED: 8 May 61 IAEA (Atom Energy)
ARTICLES: 11 LANGUAGE: English. Spanish.
HEADNOTE: IAEA & INTER-AMERICAN NUCLEAR
   ENERGY COMMISSION
TOPIC: IGO Operations
CONCEPTS: Representation. Treaty implementa-
   tion. Exchange of information and documents.
   Funding procedures. General technical assis-
   tance. Mutual consultation.
INTL ORGS: United Nations.
PROCEDURE: Amendment. Termination.
PARTIES:
   Inter-Am Nuc Energ
   IAEA (Atom Energy)

200587 Bilateral Agreement **396 UNTS 301**
SIGNED: 17 Apr 61   FORCE: 3 May 61
REGISTERED: 19 May 61 WHO (World Health)
ARTICLES: 6 LANGUAGE: French.
HEADNOTE: TECHNICAL ADVISORY ASSISTANCE
TOPIC: Tech Assistance
CONCEPTS: Definition of terms. Privileges and im-
   munities. General cooperation. Exchange of in-
   formation and documents. Personnel. Responsi-
   bility and liability. Title and deeds. Exchange.
   Scholarships and grants. Vocational training. Re-
   search and development. Expense sharing for-
   mulae. Local currency. Domestic obligation.
   Special projects. Materials, equipment and ser-
   vices. IGO status. Conformity with IGO decisions.
INTL ORGS: United Nations.
TREATY REF: 33UNTS261.
PROCEDURE: Amendment. Termination.
PARTIES:
   Mauritania
   WHO (World Health)

200588 Bilateral Agreement **397 UNTS 315**
SIGNED: 16 Mar 61   FORCE: 25 Apr 61
REGISTERED: 6 Jun 61 WHO (World Health)
ARTICLES: 6 LANGUAGE: English.
HEADNOTE: TECHNICAL ADVISORY ASSISTANCE
TOPIC: Tech Assistance
CONCEPTS: Definition of terms. Privileges and im-
   munities. General cooperation. Exchange of in-
   formation and documents. Personnel. Responsi-
   bility and liability. Title and deeds. Exchange.
   Scholarships and grants. Vocational training. Re-
   search and development. Expense sharing for-
   mulae. Local currency. Domestic obligation.
   Special projects. Materials, equipment and ser-
   vices. IGO status. Conformity with IGO decisions.
INTL ORGS: United Nations.
TREATY REF: 33UNTS261.
PROCEDURE: Amendment. Termination.
PARTIES:
   Kuwait
   WHO (World Health)

200589 Bilateral Agreement **406 UNTS 269**
SIGNED: 20 Jan 61   FORCE: 24 Jun 61
REGISTERED: 8 Sep 61 WHO (World Health)
ARTICLES: 6 LANGUAGE: English.
HEADNOTE: TECHNICAL ADVISORY ASSISTANCE
TOPIC: Tech Assistance
CONCEPTS: Definition of terms. Privileges and im-
   munities. General cooperation. Exchange of in-
   formation and documents. Personnel. Responsi-
   bility and liability. Title and deeds. Exchange.
   Scholarships and grants. Vocational training. Re-
   search and development. Expense sharing for-
   mulae. Local currency. Domestic obligation.
   Special projects. Materials, equipment and ser-
   vices. IGO status. Conformity with IGO decisions.
TREATY REF: 33UNTS261.
PROCEDURE: Amendment. Termination.
PARTIES:
   Korea, South
   WHO (World Health)

200590 Bilateral Agreement **409 UNTS 290**
SIGNED: 25 Jul 59   FORCE: 25 Jul 59
REGISTERED: 29 Sep 61 ILO (Labor Org)
ARTICLES: 7 LANGUAGE: English. French.
HEADNOTE: AGREEMENT
TOPIC: IGO Operations
CONCEPTS: Representation. Exchange of informa-
   tion and documents. Labor statistics. Subsidiary
   organ. Mutual consultation.

INTL ORGS: United Nations.
PARTIES:
   Subsahara Tech Com
   ILO (Labor Org)

200591 Bilateral Agreement **412 UNTS 273**
SIGNED: 16 Jul 53   FORCE: 16 Jul 53
REGISTERED: 30 Oct 61 ILO (Labor Org)
ARTICLES: 14 LANGUAGE: English. French.
HEADNOTE: COOPERATION
TOPIC: IGO Operations
CONCEPTS: Exchange of information and docu-
   ments. Labor statistics. Funding procedures.
   General technical assistance. Mutual consulta-
   tion.
PARTIES:
   ECSC (Coal/Steel)
   ILO (Labor Org)

200592 Bilateral Agreement **415 UNTS 396**
SIGNED: 11 Oct 61   FORCE: 20 Oct 61
REGISTERED: 29 Nov 61 IBRD (World Bank)
ARTICLES: 10 LANGUAGE: English. French.
HEADNOTE: AGREEMENT CONCERNING LOAN
TOPIC: IBRD Project
CONCEPTS: Treaty interpretation. Arbitration. Pro-
   cedure. Accounting procedures. Currency. Inter-
   est rates. Loan regulations.
PARTIES:
   IBRD (World Bank)
   Switzerland

200593 Bilateral Agreement **415 UNTS 408**
SIGNED: 29 Nov 61   FORCE: 29 Nov 61
REGISTERED: 29 Nov 61 United Nations
ARTICLES: 12 LANGUAGE: English.
HEADNOTE: EXECUTING AGENCY AGREEMENT
TOPIC: IGO Operations
CONCEPTS: Privileges and immunities. Exchange
   of information and documents. Accounting pro-
   cedures. Currency. Exchange rates and regula-
   tions. Funding procedures. Special status.
INTL ORGS: United Nations.
PROCEDURE: Amendment. Termination.
PARTIES:
   IAEA (Atom Energy)
   UN Special Fund

200594 Multilateral Agreement **422 UNTS 288**
SIGNED: 13 Feb 62   FORCE: 13 Feb 62
REGISTERED: 13 Feb 62 United Nations
ARTICLES: 6 LANGUAGE: English. Arabic.
HEADNOTE: TECHNICAL ASSISTANCE
TOPIC: Tech Assistance
CONCEPTS: Definition of terms. Treaty interpreta-
   tion. Privileges and immunities. General cooper-
   ation. Exchange of information and documents.
   Personnel. Responsibility and liability. Title and
   deeds. Use of facilities. Exchange. Scholarships
   and grants. Vocational training. Research and
   development. Exchange rates and regulations.
   Expense sharing formulae. Local currency. Do-
   mestic obligation. General technical assistance.
   Materials, equipment and services. IGO status.
   Conformity with IGO decisions.
TREATY REF: 76UNTS132; 1UNTS15;
   33UNTS261; 374UNTS147.
PARTIES:
   Kuwait SIGNED: 13 Feb 62 FORCE: 13 Feb 62
   FAO (Food Agri) SIGNED: 13 Feb 62 FORCE:
      13 Feb 62
   IAEA (Atom Energy) SIGNED: 13 Feb 62 FORCE:
      13 Feb 62
   ICAO (Civil Aviat) SIGNED: 13 Feb 62 FORCE:
      13 Feb 62
   ILO (Labor Org) SIGNED: 13 Feb 62 FORCE:
      13 Feb 62
   ITU (Telecommun) SIGNED: 13 Feb 62 FORCE:
      13 Feb 62
   UNESCO (Educ/Cult) SIGNED: 13 Feb 62
      FORCE: 13 Feb 62
   United Nations SIGNED: 13 Feb 62 FORCE:
      13 Feb 62
   WHO (World Health) SIGNED: 13 Feb 62 FORCE:
      13 Feb 62
   WMO (Meteorology) SIGNED: 13 Feb 62 FORCE:
      13 Feb 62
                     ANNEX
646 UNTS 422. UPU (Postal Union). Accession
   30 Sep 68. Force 30 Sep 68.

646 UNTS 422. IMCO (Maritime Org). Accession
   30 Sep 68. Force 30 Sep 68.
646 UNTS 422. UNIDO (Industrial). Accession
   30 Sep 68. Force 30 Sep 68.

200595 Bilateral Agreement **425 UNTS 281**
SIGNED: 13 Apr 61   FORCE: 5 Oct 61
REGISTERED: 9 Apr 62 IAEA (Atom Energy)
ARTICLES: 13 LANGUAGE: English. French.
HEADNOTE: INTER-GOVERNMENTAL MARITIME
   CONSULTATIVE ORGANIZATION AGREEMENT
TOPIC: IGO Operations
CONCEPTS: Administrative cooperation. Ex-
   change of information and documents. Exten-
   sion of functions. Liaison with other IGO's.
INTL ORGS: United Nations.
TREATY REF: 276UNTS3; 293UNTS359;
   312UNTS427; ETC.
PROCEDURE: Amendment. Termination.
PARTIES:
   IAEA (Atom Energy)
   IMCO (Maritime Org)

200596 Multilateral Agreement **429 UNTS 230**
SIGNED: 20 Jan 62   FORCE: 20 Jan 62
REGISTERED: 4 Jun 62 United Nations
ARTICLES: 6 LANGUAGE: English.
HEADNOTE: TECHNICAL ASSISTANCE
TOPIC: Tech Assistance
CONCEPTS: Definition of terms. Privileges and im-
   munities. General cooperation. Exchange of in-
   formation and documents. Personnel. Responsi-
   bility and liability. Title and deeds. Use of facili-
   ties. Exchange. Scholarships and grants.
   Vocational training. Research and development.
   Exchange rates and regulations. Expense shar-
   ing formulae. Local currency. Domestic obliga-
   tion. General technical assistance. Materials,
   equipment and services. IGO status. Conformity
   with IGO decisions.
INTL ORGS: United Nations Technical Assistance
   Board.
TREATY REF: 76UNTS132; 1UNTS15;
   33UNTS261.
PROCEDURE: Amendment. Termination.
PARTIES:
   FAO (Food Agri) SIGNED: 20 Jan 62 FORCE:
      20 Jan 62
   IAEA (Atom Energy) SIGNED: 20 Jan 62 FORCE:
      20 Jan 62
   ICAO (Civil Aviat) SIGNED: 20 Jan 62 FORCE:
      20 Jan 62
   ILO (Labor Org) SIGNED: 20 Jan 62 FORCE:
      20 Jan 62
   ITU (Telecommun) SIGNED: 20 Jan 62 FORCE:
      20 Jan 62
   UNESCO (Educ/Cult) SIGNED: 20 Jan 62 FORCE:
      20 Jan 62
   United Nations SIGNED: 20 Jan 62 FORCE:
      20 Jan 62
   WHO (World Health) SIGNED: 20 Jan 62 FORCE:
      20 Jan 62
   WMO (Meteorology) SIGNED: 20 Jan 62 FORCE:
      20 Jan 62
   Western Samoa SIGNED: 20 Jan 62 FORCE:
      20 Jan 62
                     ANNEX
646 UNTS 424. UPU (Postal Union). Accession
   20 Sep 68. Force 20 Sep 68.
646 UNTS 424. IMCO (Maritime Org). Accession
   20 Sep 68. Force 20 Sep 68.
646 UNTS 424. UNIDO (Industrial). Accession
   20 Sep 68. Force 20 Sep 68.

200597 Bilateral Exchange **434 UNTS 249**
SIGNED: 28 Jun 62   FORCE: 28 Jun 62
REGISTERED: 24 Jul 62 United Nations
ARTICLES: 2 LANGUAGE: English.
HEADNOTE: ARRANGE UN TECHNICAL CONFER-
   ENCE ON WORLD MAP
TOPIC: IGO Operations
CONCEPTS: Non-visa travel documents. Diplo-
   matic missions. Privileges and immunities. Per-
   sonnel. Funding procedures. Domestic obliga-
   tion. Subsidiary organ. Special status. Status of
   experts.
TREATY REF: 1UNTS15.
PARTIES:
   Germany, West
   United Nations

200598 Bilateral Agreement **437 UNTS 317**
SIGNED: 14 Aug 62 FORCE: 14 Aug 62
REGISTERED: 20 Sep 62 WHO (World Health)
ARTICLES: 6 LANGUAGE: English.
HEADNOTE: TECHNICAL ADVISORY ASSISTANCE
TOPIC: Tech Assistance
CONCEPTS: Definition of terms. Privileges and immunities. General cooperation. Exchange of information and documents. Personnel. Responsibility and liability. Title and deeds. Exchange. Scholarships and grants. Vocational training. Research and development. Expense sharing formulae. Local currency. Domestic obligation. Special projects. Materials, equipment and services. IGO status. Conformity with IGO decisions.
TREATY REF: 33UNTS261.
PROCEDURE: Amendment. Termination.
PARTIES:
WHO (World Health)
Western Samoa

200599 Bilateral Agreement **443 UNTS 297**
SIGNED: 5 Nov 62 FORCE: 5 Nov 62
REGISTERED: 5 Nov 62 United Nations
ARTICLES: 6 LANGUAGE: English.
HEADNOTE: PROVISION OPERATIONAL EXECUTIVE ADMINISTRATIVE PERSONNEL
TOPIC: Tech Assistance
CONCEPTS: Treaty implementation. Annex or appendix reference. Privileges and immunities. Personnel. Responsibility and liability. Arbitration. Procedure. Negotiation. Vocational training. Compensation. Expense sharing formulae. Tax exemptions. Customs exemptions. Domestic obligation. Special projects. Status of experts. Conformity with IGO decisions.
INTL ORGS: Permanent Court of Arbitration. Arbitration Commission.
PROCEDURE: Amendment. Termination.
PARTIES:
United Nations
Western Samoa

200600 Bilateral Agreement **453 UNTS 333**
SIGNED: 20 Feb 63 FORCE: 20 Feb 63
REGISTERED: 20 Feb 63 United Nations
ARTICLES: 6 LANGUAGE: English.
HEADNOTE: BOAT ENGINE MAINTENANCE TRAINING COURSE
TOPIC: Tech Assistance
CONCEPTS: Detailed regulations. Exchange of information and documents. Use of facilities. Expense sharing formulae. Domestic obligation. Special projects. Industry.
PROCEDURE: Amendment. Termination.
PARTIES:
United Nations
South Pacific Com

200601 Bilateral Agreement **467 UNTS 463**
SIGNED: 5 Jun 63 FORCE: 5 Jun 63
REGISTERED: 5 Jun 63 United Nations
ARTICLES: 10 LANGUAGE: English.
HEADNOTE: ASSISTANCE
TOPIC: Direct Aid
CONCEPTS: Detailed regulations. Treaty implementation. Visas. Privileges and immunities. Exchange of information and documents. Informational records. Inspection and observation. Operating agencies. Personnel. Public information. Responsibility and liability. Title and deeds. Use of facilities. Arbitration. Procedure. Negotiation. Import quotas. Attachment of funds. Exchange rates and regulations. Expense sharing formulae. Financial programs. Domestic obligation. General technical assistance. Economic assistance. Materials, equipment and services. IGO status.
INTL ORGS: International Atomic Energy Agency. International Court of Justice. United Nations. Arbitration Commission.
TREATY REF: 33UNTS261; 374UNTS147.
PROCEDURE: Amendment. Termination.
PARTIES:
UN Special Fund
Western Samoa

200602 Bilateral Agreement **467 UNTS 482**
SIGNED: 30 May 63 FORCE: 30 May 63
REGISTERED: 6 Jun 63 ILO (Labor Org)
ARTICLES: 6 LANGUAGE: French.

HEADNOTE: AGREEMENT
TOPIC: IGO Operations
CONCEPTS: Representation. Exchange of information and documents. General technical assistance. Mutual consultation.
INTL ORGS: United Nations.
TREATY REF: 15UNTS40.
PROCEDURE: Amendment. Denunciation.
PARTIES:
Afromalagasy Org
ILO (Labor Org)

200603 Bilateral Agreement **468 UNTS 387**
SIGNED: 17 Aug 62 FORCE: 6 Nov 62
REGISTERED: 11 Jun 63 IDA (Devel Assoc)
ARTICLES: 6 LANGUAGE: English.
HEADNOTE: DEVELOPMENT CREDIT RAILROAD
TOPIC: Non-IBRD Project
CONCEPTS: Change of circumstances. Definition of terms. Detailed regulations. Exchange of information and documents. Informational records. Accounting procedures. Interest rates. Tax exemptions. Credit provisions. Loan repayment. Terms of loan. Plans and standards. IDA development project.
PARTIES:
Korea, South
IDA (Devel Assoc)

200604 Bilateral Agreement **470 UNTS 361**
SIGNED: 24 Jan 63 FORCE: 28 Feb 63
REGISTERED: 1 Jul 63 United Nations
ARTICLES: 6 LANGUAGE: English.
HEADNOTE: BOAT ENGINE MAINTENANCE TRAINING COURSE
TOPIC: Tech Assistance
CONCEPTS: Detailed regulations. Exchange of information and documents. Personnel. Responsibility and liability. Use of facilities. Institute establishment. Vocational training. Expense sharing formulae. Commodities and services. Domestic obligation. Merchant vessels. Conformity with IGO decisions.
PROCEDURE: Amendment. Termination.
PARTIES:
United Nations
South Pacific Com

200605 Bilateral Agreement **489 UNTS 357**
SIGNED: 11 Feb 64 FORCE: 1 Dec 63
REGISTERED: 20 Feb 64 United Nations
ARTICLES: 4 LANGUAGE: English. French.
HEADNOTE: EXTEND COMPETENCE EMPLOY CONTRACTS & APPOINT TERMS
TOPIC: IGO Operations
CONCEPTS: Right to organize. Funding procedures. Inter-agency agreements.
INTL ORGS: United Nations Administrative Tribunal.
PARTIES:
IMCO (Maritime Org)
United Nations

200606 Bilateral Agreement **501 UNTS 285**
SIGNED: 6 Feb 64 FORCE: 6 Feb 64
REGISTERED: 26 Jun 64 IAEA (Atom Energy)
ARTICLES: 11 LANGUAGE: English. French.
HEADNOTE: AGREEMENT
TOPIC: IGO Operations
CONCEPTS: Treaty implementation. Annex or appendix reference. Exchange of information and documents. Funding procedures. General technical assistance. Inter-agency agreements. Mutual consultation.
INTL ORGS: United Nations.
PROCEDURE: Amendment. Termination.
PARTIES:
Subsahara Tech Com
IAEA (Atom Energy)

200607 Bilateral Treaty **504 UNTS 299**
SIGNED: 29 Jun 45 FORCE: 30 Jan 46
REGISTERED: 6 Aug 64 Czechoslovakia
ARTICLES: 2 LANGUAGE: Slovak. Russian. Ukrainian.
HEADNOTE: TRANS-CARPATHIAN UKRAINE BORDERS
TOPIC: Territory Boundary

CONCEPTS: Claims and settlements. Lump sum settlements. Boundaries of territory. Markers and definitions. Frontier peoples and personnel.
PARTIES:
Czechoslovakia
USSR (Soviet Union)

200608 Multilateral Agreement **514 UNTS 220**
SIGNED: 24 Oct 64 FORCE: 24 Oct 64
REGISTERED: 24 Oct 64 United Nations
ARTICLES: 6 LANGUAGE: English.
HEADNOTE: TECHNICAL ASSISTANCE
TOPIC: Tech Assistance
CONCEPTS: Privileges and immunities. General cooperation. Exchange of information and documents. Personnel. Responsibility and liability. Title and deeds. Use of facilities. Exchange. Scholarships and grants. Vocational training. Research and development. Exchange rates and regulations. Expense sharing formulae. Local currency. Domestic obligation. General technical assistance. Materials, equipment and services. IGO status. Conformity with IGO decisions.
TREATY REF: 76UNTS132; 1UNTS15; 33UNTS261; 374UNTS147.
PROCEDURE: Amendment. Termination.
PARTIES:
Malawi SIGNED: 24 Oct 64 FORCE: 24 Oct 64
FAO (Food Agri) SIGNED: 24 Oct 64 FORCE: 24 Oct 64
IAEA (Atom Energy) SIGNED: 24 Oct 64 FORCE: 24 Oct 64
ICAO (Civil Aviat) SIGNED: 24 Oct 64 FORCE: 24 Oct 64
ILO (Labor Org) SIGNED: 24 Oct 64 FORCE: 24 Oct 64
ITU (Telecommun) SIGNED: 24 Oct 64 FORCE: 24 Oct 64
UNESCO (Educ/Cult) SIGNED: 24 Oct 64 FORCE: 24 Oct 64
United Nations SIGNED: 24 Oct 64 FORCE: 24 Oct 64
UPU (Postal Union) SIGNED: 24 Oct 64 FORCE: 24 Oct 64
WHO (World Health) SIGNED: 24 Oct 64 FORCE: 24 Oct 64
WMO (Meteorology) SIGNED: 24 Oct 64 FORCE: 24 Oct 64

200609 Bilateral Agreement **514 UNTS 235**
SIGNED: 24 Oct 64 FORCE: 24 Oct 64
REGISTERED: 24 Oct 64 United Nations
ARTICLES: 10 LANGUAGE: English.
HEADNOTE: ASSISTANCE FROM SPECIAL FUND
TOPIC: Direct Aid
CONCEPTS: Diplomatic missions. Privileges and immunities. Exchange of information and documents. Arbitration. Procedure. Domestic obligation. General technical assistance.
INTL ORGS: International Atomic Energy Agency. International Court of Justice. United Nations. Arbitration Commission.
PROCEDURE: Amendment. Termination.
PARTIES:
Malawi
UN Special Fund

200610 Bilateral Agreement **516 UNTS 367**
SIGNED: 27 Oct 64 FORCE: 27 Oct 64
REGISTERED: 19 Nov 64 ILO (Labor Org)
ARTICLES: 6 LANGUAGE: English.
HEADNOTE: ILO ASIAN PRODUCTIVITY ORGANIZATION
TOPIC: IGO Operations
CONCEPTS: Representation. General cooperation. Exchange of information and documents. Public information. Vocational training. Research and development. General technical assistance. Economic assistance. Socio-economic development.
TREATY REF: 15UNTS40; 422UNTS101.
PROCEDURE: Amendment. Denunciation.
PARTIES:
Asian Productivity
ILO (Labor Org)

200611 Multilateral Agreement **537 UNTS 348**
SIGNED: 2 Jun 65 FORCE: 2 Jun 65
REGISTERED: 2 Jun 65 United Nations
ARTICLES: 6 LANGUAGE: English.

HEADNOTE: TECHNICAL ASSISTANCE
TOPIC: Tech Assistance
CONCEPTS: Definition of terms. Privileges and immunities. General cooperation. Exchange of information and documents. Personnel. Responsibility and liability. Title and deeds. Use of facilities. Exchange. Scholarships and grants.
Vocational training. Research and development.
Exchange rates and regulations. Expense sharing formulae. Local currency. Domestic obligation. General technical assistance. Materials,
equipment and services. IGO status. Conformity
with IGO decisions.
TREATY REF: 76UNTS132; 1UNTS15;
33UNTS261; 274UNTS147.
PROCEDURE: Amendment. Termination.
PARTIES:
Gambia SIGNED: 2 Jun 65 FORCE: 2 Jun 65
FAO (Food Agri) SIGNED: 2 Jun 65 FORCE:
2 Jun 65
IAEA (Atom Energy) SIGNED: 2 Jun 65 FORCE:
2 Jun 65
ICAO (Civil Aviat) SIGNED: 2 Jun 65 FORCE:
2 Jun 65
ILO (Labor Org) SIGNED: 2 Jun 65 FORCE:
2 Jun 65
IMCO (Maritime Org) SIGNED: 2 Jun 65 FORCE:
2 Jun 65
ITU (Telecommun) SIGNED: 2 Jun 65 FORCE:
2 Jun 65
UNESCO (Educ/Cult) SIGNED: 2 Jun 65 FORCE:
2 Jun 65
United Nations SIGNED: 2 Jun 65 FORCE:
2 Jun 65
UPU (Postal Union) SIGNED: 2 Jun 65 FORCE:
2 Jun 65
WHO (World Health) SIGNED: 2 Jun 65 FORCE:
2 Jun 65
WMO (Meteorology) SIGNED: 2 Jun 65 FORCE:
2 Jun 65
ANNEX
645 UNTS 394. UPU (Postal Union). Force
9 Sep 68.
645 UNTS 394. Gambia. Force 9 Sep 68.
645 UNTS 394. ITU (Telecommun). Force
9 Sep 68.
645 UNTS 394. WMO (Meteorology). Force
9 Sep 68.
645 UNTS 394. ICAO (Civil Aviat). Force 9 Sep 68.
645 UNTS 394. WHO (World Health). Force
9 Sep 68.
645 UNTS 394. IAEA (Atom Energy). Force
9 Sep 68.
645 UNTS 394. IMCO (Maritime Org). Force
9 Sep 68.

200612 Bilateral Exchange **538 UNTS 321**
SIGNED: 9 Jun 65 FORCE: 9 Jun 65
REGISTERED: 9 Jun 65 United Nations
ARTICLES: 2 LANGUAGE: English.
HEADNOTE: COOPERATION
TOPIC: IGO Operations
CONCEPTS: General provisions. Diplomatic rela-
tions establishment. General cooperation. Ex-
change of official publications. Exchange of in-
formation and documents. General technical as-
sistance.
PARTIES:
Gambia
UN Special Fund

200613 Multilateral Instrument **541 UNTS 271**
SIGNED: 26 May 64 FORCE: 26 May 64
REGISTERED: 10 Aug 65 IBRD (World Bank)
ARTICLES: 6 LANGUAGE: English.
HEADNOTE: HIGHWAY PROJECT
TOPIC: IBRD Project
CONCEPTS: Annex or appendix reference. Gen-
eral cooperation. Exchange of information and
documents. Informational records. Accounting
procedures. Indemnities and reimbursements.
Expense sharing formulae. Financial programs.
Materials, equipment and services. Terms of
loan. Roads and highways.
PARTIES:
Ecuador SIGNED: 26 May 64 FORCE: 26 May 64
Inter-Am Devel Bnk SIGNED: 26 May 64 FORCE:
26 May 64
AID (Int Devel) SIGNED: 26 May 64 FORCE:
26 May 64
IBRD (World Bank) SIGNED: 26 May 64 FORCE:
26 May 64

IDA (Devel Assoc) SIGNED: 26 May 64 FORCE:
26 May 64

200614 Bilateral Agreement **548 UNTS 315**
SIGNED: 15 Nov 65 FORCE: 15 Nov 65
REGISTERED: 15 Nov 65 United Nations
ARTICLES: 7 LANGUAGE: English. French.
HEADNOTE: COOPERATION
TOPIC: IGO Operations
CONCEPTS: Representation. Exchange of official
publications. Exchange of information and docu-
ments. Inter-agency agreements. Interagency re-
quests. Paragraph 2, Article 36.
INTL ORGS: United Nations.
PROCEDURE: Amendment.
PARTIES:
OAU (Afri Unity)
United Nations

200615 Bilateral Agreement **550 UNTS 365**
SIGNED: 17 Dec 65 FORCE: 17 Dec 65
REGISTERED: 17 Dec 65 United Nations
ARTICLES: 8 LANGUAGE: French.
HEADNOTE: INTERNATIONAL LAW COMMISSION
TOPIC: IGO Operations
CONCEPTS: Diplomatic missions. Privileges and
immunities. Personnel. Funding procedures.
Subsidiary organ.
TREATY REF: 1UNTS15.
PARTIES:
Monaco
United Nations

200616 Bilateral Agreement **550 UNTS 375**
SIGNED: 27 Nov 65 FORCE: 27 Nov 65
REGISTERED: 20 Dec 65 United Nations
ARTICLES: 6 LANGUAGE: English.
HEADNOTE: ESTABLISHMENT STATISTICAL
TRAINING CENTER
TOPIC: Health/Educ/Welfare
CONCEPTS: General cooperation. Commissions
and foundations. Teacher and student ex-
change. Professorships. Institute establishment.
Scholarships and grants. Vocational training. Re-
search and development. Special projects. Spe-
cific technical assistance.
PROCEDURE: Amendment. Duration. Termination.
PARTIES:
East Afri Service
United Nations

200617 Bilateral Agreement **550 UNTS 389**
SIGNED: 25 Nov 65 FORCE: 25 Nov 65
REGISTERED: 20 Dec 65 ILO (Labor Org)
ARTICLES: 6 LANGUAGE: English. French.
HEADNOTE: COOPERATION AGREEMENT
TOPIC: General Amity
CONCEPTS: Administrative cooperation. Ex-
change of information and documents. Exten-
sion of functions. Liaison with other IGO's.
TREATY REF: 15UNTS40; 191UNTS143;
466UNTS323; ETC.
PROCEDURE: Amendment.
PARTIES:
ILO (Labor Org)
OAU (Afri Unity)

200618 Multilateral Instrument **561 UNTS 333**
SIGNED: 22 Jul 65 FORCE: 22 Jul 65
REGISTERED: 28 Apr 66 IBRD (World Bank)
ARTICLES: 7 LANGUAGE: English.
HEADNOTE: NORTH ROAD PROJECT
TOPIC: IBRD Project
CONCEPTS: Annex or appendix reference. Gen-
eral cooperation. Exchange of information and
documents. Informational records. Inspection
and observation. Currency. Financial programs.
Loan regulations. Roads and highways.
INTL ORGS: International Development Associa-
tion.
TREATY REF: 561UNTS255.
PARTIES:
Honduras RATIFIED: 22 Jul 65 FORCE: 22 Jul 65
Inter-Am Devel Bnk SIGNED: 22 Jul 65 FORCE:
22 Jul 65
IBRD (World Bank) SIGNED: 22 Jul 65 FORCE:
22 Jul 65
IDA (Devel Assoc) SIGNED: 22 Jul 65 FORCE:
22 Jul 65

200619 Bilateral Agreement **563 UNTS 327**
SIGNED: 2 Jul 65 FORCE: 2 Jul 65
REGISTERED: 26 May 66 ILO (Labor Org)
ARTICLES: 7 LANGUAGE: Spanish.
HEADNOTE: AGREEMENT
TOPIC: IGO Operations
CONCEPTS: Representation. Treaty implementa-
tion. General cooperation. Exchange of informa-
tion and documents. Juridical personality. Gen-
eral technical assistance. Economic assistance.
Socio-economic development.
PROCEDURE: Amendment. Future Procedures
Contemplated.
PARTIES:
ILO (Labor Org)
LAFTA (Free Trade)

200620 Bilateral Agreement **563 UNTS 341**
SIGNED: 26 Jul 65 FORCE: 26 Jul 65
REGISTERED: 26 May 66 ILO (Labor Org)
ARTICLES: 7 LANGUAGE: Spanish.
HEADNOTE: AGREEMENT
TOPIC: IGO Operations
CONCEPTS: Representation. Treaty implementa-
tion. Exchange of information and documents.
General technical assistance. Inter-agency
agreements. Mutual consultation.
PROCEDURE: Amendment.
PARTIES:
ILO (Labor Org)
Org Ctrl Am States

200621 Bilateral Exchange **564 UNTS 193**
SIGNED: 3 Jun 66 FORCE: 3 Jun 66
REGISTERED: 3 Jun 66 United Nations
ARTICLES: 2 LANGUAGE: French.
HEADNOTE: CLAIMS SETTLEMENT
TOPIC: Claims and Debts
CONCEPTS: Detailed regulations. Privileges and
immunities. General cooperation. Responsibility
and liability. Claims and settlements. Assess-
ment procedures.
PARTIES:
United Nations
Switzerland

200622 Bilateral Exchange **564 UNTS 201**
SIGNED: 11 Jun 66 FORCE: 11 Jun 66
REGISTERED: 11 Jun 66 United Nations
ARTICLES: 2 LANGUAGE: English.
HEADNOTE: SPECIAL FUND PROJECTS
TOPIC: Non-IBRD Project
CONCEPTS: Non-bank projects.
PARTIES:
Guyana
UN Special Fund

200623 Bilateral Agreement **568 UNTS 327**
SIGNED: 29 Sep 65 FORCE: 20 Apr 66
REGISTERED: 21 Jul 66 IBRD (World Bank)
ARTICLES: 7 LANGUAGE: English.
HEADNOTE: LOAN RAILWAYS HARBORS
TOPIC: IBRD Project
CONCEPTS: Default remedies. Definition of terms.
Annex or appendix reference. Exchange of infor-
mation and documents. Informational records.
Inspection and observation. Accounting proce-
dures. Bonds. Fees and exemptions. Interest
rates. Tax exemptions. Domestic obligation.
Terms of loan. Loan regulations. Loan guarantee.
Guarantor non-interference. Water transport.
Railways.
PARTIES:
East Afri Service
IBRD (World Bank)

200624 Multilateral Exchange **571 UNTS 298**
SIGNED: 22 Aug 66 FORCE: 22 Aug 66
REGISTERED: 22 Aug 66 United Nations
ARTICLES: 2 LANGUAGE: English.
HEADNOTE: TECHNICAL ASSISTANCE
TOPIC: Tech Assistance
CONCEPTS: Previous treaty extension. General
technical assistance.
TREATY REF: 366UNTS310.

PARTIES:
Guyana SIGNED: 22 Aug 66 FORCE: 22 Aug 66
FAO (Food Agri) SIGNED: 7 Jun 66 FORCE: 22 Aug 66
IAEA (Atom Energy) SIGNED: 7 Jun 66 FORCE: 22 Aug 66
ICAO (Civil Aviat) SIGNED: 7 Jun 66 FORCE: 22 Aug 66
ILO (Labor Org) SIGNED: 7 Jun 66 FORCE: 22 Aug 66
ITU (Telecommun) SIGNED: 7 Jun 66 FORCE: 22 Aug 66
UNESCO (Educ/Cult) SIGNED: 7 Jun 66 FORCE: 22 Aug 66
United Nations SIGNED: 7 Jun 66 FORCE: 22 Aug 66
UPU (Postal Union) SIGNED: 7 Jun 66 FORCE: 22 Aug 66
WHO (World Health) SIGNED: 7 Jun 66 FORCE: 22 Aug 66
WMO (Meteorology) SIGNED: 7 Jun 66 FORCE: 22 Aug 66

200625 Bilateral Exchange **571 UNTS 305**
SIGNED: 22 Aug 66 FORCE: 22 Aug 66
REGISTERED: 22 Aug 66 United Nations
ARTICLES: 2 LANGUAGE: English.
HEADNOTE: APPLICATION OF UK-GUYANA AGREEMENT
TOPIC: IGO Operations
CONCEPTS: General cooperation. IGO operations.
TREATY REF: 469UNTS145.
PARTIES:
Guyana
United Nations

200626 Bilateral Agreement **573 UNTS 259**
SIGNED: 21 Sep 66 FORCE: 21 Sep 66
REGISTERED: 21 Sep 66 United Nations
ARTICLES: 12 LANGUAGE: French.
HEADNOTE: PROJECTS OF SPECIAL FUND
TOPIC: Non-IBRD Project
CONCEPTS: Annex or appendix reference. Privileges and immunities. Exchange of information and documents. Informational records. Operating agencies. Accounting procedures. Currency. Payment schedules. Non-bank projects.
PARTIES:
UN Special Fund
UPU (Postal Union)

200627 Bilateral Agreement **575 UNTS 238**
SIGNED: 11 Jul 66 FORCE: 1 Dec 65
REGISTERED: 7 Oct 66 IMCO (Maritime Org)
ARTICLES: 13 LANGUAGE: English. French.
HEADNOTE: COOPERATION
TOPIC: IGO Operations
CONCEPTS: Representation. Treaty implementation. General cooperation. Exchange of information and documents. Informational records. Specialists exchange. Labor statistics. Financial programs. General technical assistance. Inter-agency agreements. Mutual consultation.
INTL ORGS: United Nations.
TREATY REF: 289UNTS3.
PROCEDURE: Amendment. Termination.
PARTIES:
FAO (Food Agri)
IMCO (Maritime Org)

200628 Bilateral Agreement **586 UNTS 225**
SIGNED: 28 Oct 66 FORCE: 28 Oct 66
REGISTERED: 30 Dec 66 IBRD (World Bank)
ARTICLES: 4 LANGUAGE: English.
HEADNOTE: LOAN (INTERNATIONAL FINANCE CORPORATION LOAN)
TOPIC: Loans and Credits
CONCEPTS: Definition of terms. Annex or appendix reference. Accounting procedures. Currency. Exchange rates and regulations. Interest rates. Payment schedules. Purchase authorizations. Liens. Loan and credit. Loan repayment. Terms of loan. World Bank projects. Plans and standards.
PROCEDURE: Termination.
PARTIES:
IBRD (World Bank)
IFC (Finance Corp)

ANNEX
613 UNTS 430. IBRD (World Bank). Amendment 30 Oct 67. Force 30 Oct 67.
613 UNTS 430. IFC (Finance Corp). Amendment 30 Oct 67. Force 30 Oct 67.

200629 Bilateral Agreement **599 UNTS 335**
SIGNED: 17 Feb 67 FORCE: 12 May 67
REGISTERED: 26 Jun 67 IBRD (World Bank)
ARTICLES: 7 LANGUAGE: English.
HEADNOTE: LOAN
TOPIC: IBRD Project
CONCEPTS: Definition of terms. Annex or appendix reference. Exchange of information and documents. Informational records. Investigation of violations. Accounting procedures. Bonds. Interest rates. Debts. Liens. General. Withdrawal conditions. Credit provisions. Loan repayment. Terms of loan. Loan regulations.
PARTIES:
East Afri Service
IBRD (World Bank)

200630 Multilateral Exchange **613 UNTS 385**
SIGNED: 5 Nov 58 FORCE: 10 Nov 58
REGISTERED: 1 Dec 67 United Nations
ARTICLES: 2 LANGUAGE: English.
HEADNOTE: EXCHANGE INFORMATION DOCUMENTATION
TOPIC: Admin Cooperation
CONCEPTS: Exchange of information and documents.
PARTIES:
Other Party Combin
United Nations

200631 Multilateral Exchange **613 UNTS 391**
SIGNED: 22 Apr 59 FORCE: 16 May 59
REGISTERED: 1 Dec 67 United Nations
ARTICLES: 2 LANGUAGE: English.
HEADNOTE: EXCHANGE INFORAMTION DOCUMENTATION
TOPIC: Admin Cooperation
CONCEPTS: Exchange of information and documents.
PARTIES:
Other Party Combin
United Nations

200633 Multilateral Instrument **617 UNTS 347**
SIGNED: 24 Apr 64 FORCE: 24 Apr 64
REGISTERED: 17 Jan 68 IBRD (World Bank)
ARTICLES: 4 LANGUAGE: English.
HEADNOTE: CAMEROONS DEVELOPMENT CORPORATION
TOPIC: Loans and Credits
PARTIES:
Cmte Industr Devel SIGNED: 24 Apr 64 FORCE: 24 Apr 64
IBRD (World Bank) SIGNED: 24 Apr 64 FORCE: 24 Apr 64
IDA (Devel Assoc) SIGNED: 24 Apr 64 FORCE: 24 Apr 64

200634 Multilateral Instrument **617 UNTS 352**
SIGNED: 23 May 67 FORCE: 23 May 67
REGISTERED: 17 Jan 68 IBRD (World Bank)
ARTICLES: 2 LANGUAGE: French.
HEADNOTE: CAMEROONS DEVELOPMENT CORPORATION
TOPIC: Loans and Credits
PARTIES:
EEC (Econ Commnty) SIGNED: 23 May 67 FORCE: 23 May 67
AID (Int Devel) SIGNED: 23 May 67 FORCE: 23 May 67
IBRD (World Bank) SIGNED: 23 May 67 FORCE: 23 May 67
IDA (Devel Assoc) SIGNED: 23 May 67 FORCE: 23 May 67

200635 Bilateral Instrument **619 UNTS 321**
SIGNED: 3 Jan 67 FORCE: 3 Jan 67
REGISTERED: 23 Jan 68 IBRD (World Bank)
ARTICLES: 3 LANGUAGE: French.
HEADNOTE: CONGO POTASSIUM COMPANY
TOPIC: Direct Aid

200636 Bilateral Agreement **630 UNTS 379**
SIGNED: 16 Oct 67 FORCE: 16 Oct 67
REGISTERED: 13 Feb 68 IAEA (Atom Energy)
ARTICLES: 10 LANGUAGE: French.
HEADNOTE: ASSISTANCE REACTOR
TOPIC: Atomic Energy
CONCEPTS: Definition of terms. Annex or appendix reference. Exchange of information and documents. Inspection and observation. Procedure. Negotiation. Nuclear materials.

200637 Bilateral Agreement **636 UNTS 353**
SIGNED: 13 May 68 FORCE: 13 May 68
REGISTERED: 13 May 68 United Nations
ARTICLES: 1 LANGUAGE: French.
HEADNOTE: VOLUNTARY CONTRIBUTION UNIDO
TOPIC: IGO Operations
CONCEPTS: Assistance to United Nations.

200638 Bilateral Agreement **639 UNTS 263**
SIGNED: 31 Jan 68 FORCE: 28 Feb 68
REGISTERED: 5 Jul 68 IBRD (World Bank)
ARTICLES: 5 LANGUAGE: English.
HEADNOTE: GUARANTEE
TOPIC: IBRD Project
CONCEPTS: Annex or appendix reference. Bonds. Loan regulations. Loan guarantee. Guarantor non-interference.

200639 Bilateral Agreement **639 UNTS 303**
SIGNED: 18 Dec 67 FORCE: 13 Mar 68
REGISTERED: 5 Jul 68 IDA (Devel Assoc)
ARTICLES: 7 LANGUAGE: English.
HEADNOTE: DEVELOPMENT CREDIT
TOPIC: Non-IBRD Project
CONCEPTS: Definition of terms. Detailed regulations. Remedies. Annex or appendix reference. Use restrictions. Loan and credit. Credit provisions.

200640 Bilateral Agreement **640 UNTS 305**
SIGNED: 16 Jul 68 FORCE: 16 Jul 68
REGISTERED: 16 Jul 68 United Nations
ARTICLES: 12 LANGUAGE: English.
HEADNOTE: EXECUTION PROJECTS
TOPIC: Non-IBRD Project
CONCEPTS: General provisions. Annex or appendix reference. General cooperation. Exchange of information and documents. Accounting procedures. Indemnities and reimbursements. Currency. Exchange rates and regulations. Payment schedules. Assistance.
PROCEDURE: Amendment. Termination.

200641 Bilateral Agreement **0 UNTS 0**
SIGNED: 9 Oct 68 FORCE: 9 Oct 68
REGISTERED: 9 Oct 68 United Nations
ARTICLES: 0
HEADNOTE: SPECIAL FUND SECTOR PROJECTS
TOPIC: Non-IBRD Project

200642 Bilateral Agreement **0 UNTS 0**
SIGNED: 29 Nov 68 FORCE: 1 Jan 69
REGISTERED: 28 Jan 69 UNESCO (Educ/Cult)
ARTICLES: 0
HEADNOTE: TRANSFER ASSETS FUNCTIONS
TOPIC: IGO Operations

200643 Bilateral Agreement **0 UNTS 0**
SIGNED: 24 Dec 68 FORCE: 24 Dec 68
REGISTERED: 28 Jan 69 UNESCO (Educ/Cult)
ARTICLES: 0
HEADNOTE: TRANSFER ASSETS RESPONSIBILITIES
TOPIC: IGO Operations

200644 Bilateral Agreement **0 UNTS 0**
SIGNED: 12 Jun 68 FORCE: 13 Sep 68
REGISTERED: 14 Feb 69 IBRD (World Bank)
ARTICLES: 0
HEADNOTE: RIO LINDO HYDROELECTRIC
TOPIC: IBRD Project

200645 Bilateral Agreement **0 UNTS 0**
SIGNED: 20 Aug 32 FORCE: 2 Jan 33

REGISTERED: 3 Mar 69 Ireland
ARTICLES: 0
HEADNOTE: TRADE
TOPIC: General Trade

200646 Bilateral Agreement **0 UNTS 0**
SIGNED: 26 Mar 69 FORCE: 26 Mar 69
REGISTERED: 28 Apr 69 IAEA (Atom Energy)
ARTICLES: 0
HEADNOTE: COOPERATION
TOPIC: Atomic Energy
CONCEPTS: Exchange of information and docu-
ments. Exchange. Scientific exchange. Peaceful
use. Subsidiary organ. Liaison with other IGO's.
TREATY REF: 281UNTS363.
PROCEDURE: Amendment. Denunciation.

200647 Bilateral Agreement **0 UNTS 0**
SIGNED: 24 Jul 68 FORCE: 8 Oct 68
REGISTERED: 25 Jun 69 IDA (Devel Assoc)
ARTICLES: 0
HEADNOTE: DEVELOP CREDIT TECHNICAL ASSIS-
TANCE
TOPIC: Non-IBRD Project

200648 Bilateral Agreement **0 UNTS 0**
SIGNED: 26 Jun 67 FORCE: 16 Apr 68
REGISTERED: 25 Sep 69 IDA (Devel Assoc)
ARTICLES: 0
HEADNOTE: LOAN 52 MILLION SWISS FRANCS
TOPIC: Loans and Credits

200649 Bilateral Agreement **0 UNTS 0**
SIGNED: 11 Dec 68 FORCE: 1 Oct 69
REGISTERED: 1 Oct 69 United Nations
ARTICLES: 0
HEADNOTE: POSTAL
TOPIC: Postal Service

200650 Bilateral Agreement **0 UNTS 0**
SIGNED: 21 May 69 FORCE: 21 May 69
REGISTERED: 13 Oct 69 IAEA (Atom Energy)
ARTICLES: 0
HEADNOTE: STUDIES SEA RADIOACTIVITY
TOPIC: Scientific Project

200651 Bilateral Agreement **0 UNTS 0**
SIGNED: 24 Sep 69 FORCE: 24 Sep 69
REGISTERED: 4 Nov 69 WHO (World Health)
ARTICLES: 0
HEADNOTE: AGREEMENT (SIC)
TOPIC: IGO Operations

200653 Bilateral Agreement **0 UNTS 0**
SIGNED: 23 Dec 69 FORCE: 23 Dec 69
REGISTERED: 12 Mar 70 IBRD (World Bank)
ARTICLES: 0
HEADNOTE: LOAN
TOPIC: IBRD Project

200654 Bilateral Agreement **0 UNTS 0**
SIGNED: 15 Jul 69 FORCE: 1 Jan 70

REGISTERED: 4 Jun 70 IAEA (Atom Energy)
ARTICLES: 0
HEADNOTE: TRIESTE THEORETICAL PHYSICS
CENTER
TOPIC: IGO Operations

200655 Bilateral Agreement **0 UNTS 0**
SIGNED: 23 May 69 FORCE: 25 May 70
REGISTERED: 15 Jun 70 IBRD (World Bank)
ARTICLES: 0
HEADNOTE: GUARANTEE PYONGTAEK-KUM-
GANG IRRIGATION
TOPIC: Loans and Credits

200656 Bilateral Agreement **0 UNTS 0**
SIGNED: 30 Jul 70 FORCE: 30 Jul 70
REGISTERED: 30 Jul 70 United Nations
ARTICLES: 0
HEADNOTE: STANDARD OPERATIONAL ASSIS-
TANCE
TOPIC: IGO Operations

200657 Bilateral Agreement **0 UNTS 0**
SIGNED: 4 Jun 69 FORCE: 25 May 70
REGISTERED: 11 Aug 70 IDA (Devel Assoc)
ARTICLES: 0
HEADNOTE: CREDIT EDUCATION
TOPIC: Non-IBRD Project

National Treaty Collections

403001 Bilateral Exchange **60 ABGB 215**
SIGNED: 17 Jun 60
HEADNOTE: VISAS
TOPIC: Visas
PARTIES:
  Argentina
  Austria

403002 Bilateral Agreement **67 ABGB 152**
SIGNED: 22 Mar 67
HEADNOTE: AIR SERVICES
TOPIC: Air Transport
PARTIES:
  Australia
  Austria

403003 Bilateral Agreement **58 ABGB 197**
SIGNED: 25 Mar 57
HEADNOTE: SALT MINES BAVARIA
TOPIC: Specific Resources
PARTIES:
  Austria
  Germany, West

403004 Bilateral Agreement **63 ABGB 296**
SIGNED: 12 Sep 63
HEADNOTE: BAVARIA BORDER CATTLE GRAZING
TOPIC: Visas
PARTIES:
  Austria
  Germany, West

403005 Bilateral Agreement **70 ABGB 70**
SIGNED: 10 Feb 70
HEADNOTE: BORDER TRANSPORT GOODS
TOPIC: Land Transport
PARTIES:
  Austria
  Belgium

403006 Bilateral Exchange **60 ABGB 216**
SIGNED: 3 Aug 60
HEADNOTE: VISAS
TOPIC: Visas
PARTIES:
  Austria
  Bolivia

403007 Bilateral Exchange **57 ABGB 46**
SIGNED: 4 Jul 56
HEADNOTE: TRADE & PAYMENTS
TOPIC: General Economic
PARTIES:
  Austria
  Brazil

403008 Bilateral Exchange **57 ABGB 47**
SIGNED: 4 Jul 56
HEADNOTE: FINANCE & INVESTMENTS
TOPIC: Finance
PARTIES:
  Austria
  Brazil

403009 Bilateral Exchange **67 ABGB 332**
SIGNED: 7 Dec 59
HEADNOTE: VISAS
TOPIC: Visas
PARTIES:
  Austria
  Brazil

403010 Bilateral Agreement **56 ABGB 140**
SIGNED: 10 Mar 55
HEADNOTE: DANUBE NAVIGATION
TOPIC: Water Transport
PARTIES:
  Austria
  Bulgaria

403011 Bilateral Agreement **68 ABGB 23**
SIGNED: 27 Oct 67
HEADNOTE: CUSTOMS
TOPIC: Customs
PARTIES:
  Austria
  Bulgaria

403012 Bilateral Agreement **68 ABGB 404**
SIGNED: 9 May 68
HEADNOTE: CUSTOMS
TOPIC: Customs
PARTIES:
  Austria
  Bulgaria

403013 Bilateral Agreement **72 ABGB 86**
SIGNED: 27 May 68
HEADNOTE: SCIENTIFIC COOPERATION
TOPIC: Scientific Project
PARTIES:
  Austria
  Bulgaria

403014 Bilateral Agreement **70 ABGB 204**
SIGNED: 17 Apr 70
HEADNOTE: CULTURAL
TOPIC: Culture
PARTIES:
  Austria
  Bulgaria

403015 Bilateral Agreement **70 ABGB 279**
SIGNED: 8 Jul 70
HEADNOTE: ROAD TRANSPORT PERSONS
TOPIC: Land Transport
PARTIES:
  Austria
  Bulgaria

403016 Bilateral Agreement **71 ABGB 442**
SIGNED: 13 Oct 71
HEADNOTE: PAYMENTS
TOPIC: Finance
PARTIES:
  Austria
  Bulgaria

403017 Bilateral Agreement **72 ABGB 113**
SIGNED: 22 Feb 72
HEADNOTE: TOURISM PROMOTION
TOPIC: Admin Cooperation
PARTIES:
  Austria
  Bulgaria

403018 Bilateral Agreement **69 ABGB 324**
SIGNED: 11 May 67
HEADNOTE: EXTRADITION
TOPIC: Extradition
PARTIES:
  Austria
  Canada

403019 Bilateral Agreement **55 ABGB 173**
SIGNED: 25 Oct 54
HEADNOTE: VISAS
TOPIC: Visas
PARTIES:
  Austria
  Chile

403020 Bilateral Agreement **68 ABGB 344**
SIGNED: 15 Jul 68
HEADNOTE: VISAS
TOPIC: Visas
PARTIES:
  Austria
  Costa Rica

403021 Bilateral Agreement **69 ABGB 357**
SIGNED: 17 Sep 69
HEADNOTE: TELECOMMUNICATIONS
TOPIC: Telecommunications
PARTIES:
  Austria
  Costa Rica

403022   Bilateral Agreement   **56 ABGB 74**
SIGNED: 29 Oct 48
HEADNOTE: WATER TRANSPORT
TOPIC: Water Transport
PARTIES:
  Austria
  Czechoslovakia

403023   Bilateral Agreement   **61 ABGB 222**
SIGNED: 17 Jan 61
HEADNOTE: ADMIN COOPERATION CUSTOMS
TOPIC: Customs
PARTIES:
  Austria
  Czechoslovakia

403024   Bilateral Agreement   **62 ABGB 319**
SIGNED: 1 Mar 62
HEADNOTE: AIR TRANSPORT
TOPIC: Air Transport
PARTIES:
  Austria
  Czechoslovakia

403025   Bilateral Agreement   **67 ABGB 348**
SIGNED: 3 Jan 67
HEADNOTE: RAILROAD BORDER PROCEDURE
TOPIC: Visas
PARTIES:
  Austria
  Czechoslovakia

403026   Bilateral Agreement   **67 ABGB 299**
SIGNED: 30 Jun 67
HEADNOTE: CUSTOMS
TOPIC: Customs
PARTIES:
  Austria
  Czechoslovakia

403027   Bilateral Agreement   **70 ABGB 106**
SIGNED: 7 Dec 67
HEADNOTE: USE BORDER WATERS
TOPIC: Specific Resources
PARTIES:
  Austria
  Czechoslovakia

403028   Bilateral Agreement   **70 ABGB 129**
SIGNED: 2 Jul 69
HEADNOTE: TRADE
TOPIC: General Trade
PARTIES:
  Austria
  Czechoslovakia

403029   Bilateral Protocol   **71 ABGB 84**
SIGNED: 16 Dec 70
HEADNOTE: CUSTOMS
TOPIC: Customs
PARTIES:
  Austria
  Czechoslovakia

403030   Bilateral Protocol   **72 ABGB 24**
SIGNED: 12 Sep 71
HEADNOTE: ECONOMIC COOPERATION
TOPIC: General Economic
PARTIES:
  Austria
  Czechoslovakia

403031   Bilateral Agreement   **71 ABGB 496**
SIGNED: 22 Oct 71
HEADNOTE: PAYMENTS
TOPIC: Finance
PARTIES:
  Austria
  Czechoslovakia

403032   Bilateral Exchange   **55 ABGB 192**
SIGNED: 27 Mar 54
HEADNOTE: VISAS
TOPIC: Visas

PARTIES:
  Austria
  Denmark

403033   Bilateral Exchange   **68 ABGB 109**
SIGNED: 21 Feb 68
HEADNOTE: VISAS
TOPIC: Visas
PARTIES:
  Austria
  Dominican Republic

403034   Bilateral Exchange   **68 ABGB 108**
SIGNED: 7 Feb 68
HEADNOTE: VISAS
TOPIC: Visas
PARTIES:
  Austria
  Ecuador

403035   Bilateral Agreement   **71 ABGB 121**
SIGNED: 28 Mar 69
HEADNOTE: TRADE
TOPIC: General Trade
PARTIES:
  Austria
  Ecuador

403041   Bilateral Agreement   **70 ABGB 128**
SIGNED: 26 Jun 69
HEADNOTE: TRADE
TOPIC: General Trade
PARTIES:
  Austria
  EEC (Econ Commnty)

403042   Bilateral Exchange   **71 ABGB 156**
SIGNED: 4 Nov 70
HEADNOTE: WINE
TOPIC: Commodity Trade
PARTIES:
  Austria
  EEC (Econ Commnty)

403043   Bilateral Exchange   **71 ABGB 157**
SIGNED: 4 Nov 70
HEADNOTE: WINE
TOPIC: Commodity Trade
PARTIES:
  Austria
  EEC (Econ Commnty)

403044   Bilateral Treaty   **72 ABGB 56**
SIGNED: 31 Mar 71
HEADNOTE: AIR TRANSPORT
TOPIC: Air Transport
PARTIES:
  Austria
  Eurocontrol

403045   Bilateral Exchange   **56 ABGB 47**
SIGNED: 5 Nov 54
HEADNOTE: CHANGE VISA RULES
TOPIC: Visas
PARTIES:
  Austria
  Finland

403046   Bilateral Agreement   **65 ABGB 117**
SIGNED: 23 Jul 64
HEADNOTE: EXEMPT DIVIDEND & INTEREST
TOPIC: Taxation
PARTIES:
  Austria
  Finland

403047   Bilateral Agreement   **69 ABGB 3**
SIGNED: 9 Dec 65
HEADNOTE: DIPLOMA EQUIVALENCE
TOPIC: Admin Cooperation
PARTIES:
  Austria
  Finland

403048   Bilateral Agreement   **69 ABGB 257**
SIGNED: 4 Jun 69
HEADNOTE: AIR TRANSPORT
TOPIC: Air Transport
PARTIES:
  Austria
  Finland

403049   Bilateral Protocol   **72 ABGB 110**
SIGNED: 21 Sep 70
HEADNOTE: DOUBLE TAXATION
TOPIC: Taxation
PARTIES:
  Austria
  Finland

403050   Bilateral Agreement   **55 ABGB 208**
SIGNED: 31 Aug 55
HEADNOTE: EXCHANGE MIGRANT LABOR
TOPIC: Non-ILO Labor
PARTIES:
  Austria
  France

403054   Bilateral Agreement   **64 ABGB 324**
SIGNED: 14 Oct 64
HEADNOTE: GOODS TRAFFIC ON ROADS
TOPIC: Land Transport
PARTIES:
  Austria
  France

403055   Bilateral Agreement   **69 ABGB 335**
SIGNED: 4 Jul 69
HEADNOTE: GOODS TRAFFIC ON ROADS
TOPIC: Land Transport
PARTIES:
  Austria
  France

403056   Bilateral Protocol   **72 ABGB 147**
SIGNED: 30 Oct 70
HEADNOTE: DOUBLE TAXATION
TOPIC: Taxation
PARTIES:
  Austria
  France

403057   Bilateral Agreement   **71 ABGB 325**
SIGNED: 5 Jul 71
HEADNOTE: AMATEUR RADIO
TOPIC: Telecommunications
PARTIES:
  Austria
  France

403058   Bilateral Agreement   **55 ABGB 248**
SIGNED: 31 Oct 53
HEADNOTE: SOCIAL SECURITY
TOPIC: Non-ILO Labor
PARTIES:
  Austria
  Germany, West

403059   Bilateral Agreement   **54 ABGB 250**
SIGNED: 11 Jul 53
HEADNOTE: SOCIAL SECURITY
TOPIC: Non-ILO Labor
PARTIES:
  Austria
  Germany, West

403060   Bilateral Agreement   **53 ABGB 10**
SIGNED: 23 Nov 51
HEADNOTE: SOCIAL SECURITY
TOPIC: Non-ILO Labor
PARTIES:
  Austria
  Germany, West

403061   Bilateral Agreement   **55 ABGB 74**
SIGNED: 31 Oct 53
HEADNOTE: SOCIAL SECURITY
TOPIC: Non-ILO Labor

PARTIES:
Austria
Germany, West

403062   Bilateral Agreement   55 ABGB 247
SIGNED: 6 Apr 54
HEADNOTE: VISA ABOLITION
TOPIC: Visas
PARTIES:
Austria
Germany, West

403063   Bilateral Agreement   57 ABGB 245
SIGNED: 14 Sep 54
HEADNOTE: JUDICIAL COOPERATION
TOPIC: Admin Cooperation
PARTIES:
Austria
Germany, West

403064   Bilateral Agreement   57 ABGB 192
SIGNED: 31 May 57
HEADNOTE: PASSPORT ABOLITION
TOPIC: Visas
PARTIES:
Austria
Germany, West

403065   Bilateral Agreement   57 ABGB 198
SIGNED: 9 Jul 57
HEADNOTE: BORDER ARRESTS
TOPIC: Admin Cooperation
PARTIES:
Austria
Germany, West

403066   Bilateral Agreement   68 ABGB 409
SIGNED: 23 Oct 68
HEADNOTE: EASING CUSTOMS
TOPIC: Customs
PARTIES:
Austria
Germany, West

403067   Bilateral Agreement   68 ABGB 410
SIGNED: 23 Oct 68
HEADNOTE: EASING CUSTOMS
TOPIC: Customs
PARTIES:
Austria
Germany, West

403068   Bilateral Agreement   69 ABGB 259
SIGNED: 25 Oct 68
HEADNOTE: YOUTH WELFARE
TOPIC: Health/Educ/Welfare
PARTIES:
Austria
Germany, West

403069   Bilateral Treaty   70 ABGB 210
SIGNED: 7 Feb 69
HEADNOTE: DISABLED VETERANS
TOPIC: Health/Educ/Welfare
PARTIES:
Austria
Germany, West

403070   Bilateral Exchange   70 ABGB 340
SIGNED: 31 Mar 69
HEADNOTE: EASING PLANT IMPORTS
TOPIC: Admin Cooperation
PARTIES:
Austria
Germany, West

403071   Bilateral Agreement   70 ABGB 130
SIGNED: 11 Mar 70
HEADNOTE: EASING BORDER PROCEDURES
TOPIC: Visas
PARTIES:
Austria
Germany, West

403072   Bilateral Agreement   70 ABGB 285
SIGNED: 6 Jul 70
HEADNOTE: EASING BORDER PROCEDURES
TOPIC: Visas
PARTIES:
Austria
Germany, West

403073   Bilateral Agreement   71 ABGB 97
SIGNED: 25 Jan 71
HEADNOTE: EASING BORDER PROCEDURES
TOPIC: Visas
PARTIES:
Austria
Germany, West

403074   Bilateral Agreement   71 ABGB 98
SIGNED: 25 Jan 71
HEADNOTE: EASING BORDER PROCEDURES
TOPIC: Visas
PARTIES:
Austria
Germany, West

403075   Bilateral Agreement   71 ABGB 99
SIGNED: 25 Jan 71
HEADNOTE: EASING BORDER PROCEDURES
TOPIC: Visas
PARTIES:
Austria
Germany, West

403076   Bilateral Agreement   71 ABGB 100
SIGNED: 25 Jan 71
HEADNOTE: EASING BORDER PROCEDURES
TOPIC: Visas
PARTIES:
Austria
Germany, West

403077   Bilateral Agreement   71 ABGB 101
SIGNED: 25 Jan 71
HEADNOTE: EASING BORDER PROCEDURES
TOPIC: Visas
PARTIES:
Austria
Germany, West

403078   Bilateral Agreement   71 ABGB 102
SIGNED: 25 Jan 71
HEADNOTE: EASING BORDER PROCEDURES
TOPIC: Visas
PARTIES:
Austria
Germany, West

403079   Bilateral Agreement   72 ABGB 308
SIGNED: 5 Jul 72
HEADNOTE: EASING BORDER PROCEDURES
TOPIC: Visas
PARTIES:
Austria
Germany, West

403080   Bilateral Agreement   72 ABGB 309
SIGNED: 5 Jul 72
HEADNOTE: EASING BORDER PROCEDURES
TOPIC: Visas
PARTIES:
Austria
Germany, West

403081   Bilateral Agreement   72 ABGB 310
SIGNED: 5 Jul 72
HEADNOTE: EASING BORDER PROCEDURES
TOPIC: Visas
PARTIES:
Austria
Germany, West

403082   Bilateral Agreement   72 ABGB 311
SIGNED: 5 Jul 72
HEADNOTE: EASING BORDER PROCEDURES
TOPIC: Visas

PARTIES:
Austria
Germany, West

403083   Bilateral Agreement   72 ABGB 312
SIGNED: 5 Jul 72
HEADNOTE: EASING BORDER PROCEDURES
TOPIC: Visas
PARTIES:
Austria
Germany, West

403084   Bilateral Agreement   53 ABGB 158
SIGNED: 12 Aug 53
HEADNOTE: VISA ABOLITION
TOPIC: Visas
PARTIES:
Austria
Greece

403085   Bilateral Treaty   71 ABGB 2
SIGNED: 6 Dec 65
HEADNOTE: CIVIL & COMMERCIAL LAW
TOPIC: Admin Cooperation
PARTIES:
Austria
Greece

403086   Bilateral Agreement   71 ABGB 83
SIGNED: 4 Mar 70
HEADNOTE: BUS TRAFFIC
TOPIC: Land Transport
PARTIES:
Austria
Greece

403087   Bilateral Agreement   72 ABGB 39
SIGNED: 22 Sep 70
HEADNOTE: DOUBLE TAXATION
TOPIC: Taxation
PARTIES:
Austria
Greece

403088   Bilateral Agreement   55 ABGB 195
SIGNED: 18 May 55
HEADNOTE: DANUBE NAVIGATION
TOPIC: Water Transport
PARTIES:
Austria
Hungary

403089   Bilateral Agreement   60 ABGB 76
SIGNED: 17 Jul 59
HEADNOTE: AIR TRANSPORT
TOPIC: Air Transport
PARTIES:
Austria
Hungary

403090   Bilateral Agreement   71 ABGB 403
SIGNED: 5 May 71
HEADNOTE: AIR TRANSPORT
TOPIC: Air Transport
PARTIES:
Austria
Hungary

403091   Bilateral Agreement   61 ABGB 42
SIGNED: 17 Jan 61
HEADNOTE: TRUCKED GOODS
TOPIC: Customs
PARTIES:
Austria
Hungary

403092   Bilateral Agreement   67 ABGB 293
SIGNED: 31 Oct 67
HEADNOTE: FINANCIAL QUESTIONS
TOPIC: Claims and Debts
PARTIES:
Austria
Hungary

403093   Bilateral Protocol   **68 ABGB 293**
SIGNED: 8 Jun 68
HEADNOTE: GOODS TRAFFIC TAXES
TOPIC: Customs
PARTIES:
  Austria
  Hungary

403094   Bilateral Agreement   **69 ABGB 261**
SIGNED: 27 Nov 68
HEADNOTE: CUSTOMS PREFERENCES
TOPIC: Customs
PARTIES:
  Austria
  Hungary

403095   Bilateral Agreement   **69 ABGB 167**
SIGNED: 29 Apr 69
HEADNOTE: OFFICIAL PASSPORTS
TOPIC: Visas
PARTIES:
  Austria
  Hungary

403096   Bilateral Agreement   **72 ABGB 111**
SIGNED: 28 May 69
HEADNOTE: SCIENTIFIC & TECHNICAL COOPER-
ATION
TOPIC: Health/Educ/Welfare
PARTIES:
  Austria
  Hungary

403097   Bilateral Agreement   **71 ABGB 203**
SIGNED: 28 Apr 71
HEADNOTE: PASSPORT & CUSTOMS
TOPIC: Visas
PARTIES:
  Austria
  Hungary

403098   Bilateral Agreement   **71 ABGB 252**
SIGNED: 17 May 71
HEADNOTE: SOJOURN DANUBE SAILORS
TOPIC: Visas
PARTIES:
  Austria
  Hungary

403099   Bilateral Agreement   **71 ABGB 421**
SIGNED: 28 Oct 71
HEADNOTE: PAYMENTS
TOPIC: Finance
PARTIES:
  Austria
  Hungary

403100   Bilateral Exchange   **68 ABGB 326**
SIGNED: 10 Jul 68
HEADNOTE: KLAGENFURT CEMETERY
TOPIC: Other Military
PARTIES:
  Austria
  India

403101   Bilateral Agreement   **71 ABGB 152**
SIGNED: 1 Apr 71
HEADNOTE: CONFERENCE ARRANGEMENTS
TOPIC: IGO Operations
PARTIES:
  Austria
  ICAO (Civil Aviat)

403102   Bilateral Agreement   **71 ABGB 270**
SIGNED: 21 Nov 70
HEADNOTE: AIR TRANSPORT
TOPIC: Air Transport
PARTIES:
  Austria
  Iraq

403103   Bilateral Treaty   **66 ABGB 45**
SIGNED: 9 Sep 59
HEADNOTE: FRIENDSHIP & ESTABLISHMENT

TOPIC: General Amity
PARTIES:
  Austria
  Iran

403104   Bilateral Protocol   **70 ABGB 111**
SIGNED: 5 Mar 70
HEADNOTE: SUPPLEMENT 9 SEP 59 AMITY
TOPIC: General Amity
PARTIES:
  Austria
  Iran

403105   Bilateral Agreement   **70 ABGB 428**
SIGNED: 10 Dec 70
HEADNOTE: VISA ABOLITION
TOPIC: Visas
PARTIES:
  Austria
  Ireland

403106   Bilateral Exchange   **59 ABGB 162**
SIGNED: 17 Jan 56
HEADNOTE: FIRST AIR RIGHT
TOPIC: Air Transport
PARTIES:
  Austria
  Israel

403107   Bilateral Agreement   **63 ABGB 260**
SIGNED: 22 Aug 63
HEADNOTE: AIR TRANSPORT
TOPIC: Air Transport
PARTIES:
  Austria
  Israel

403108   Bilateral Treaty   **68 ABGB 349**
SIGNED: 6 Jun 66
HEADNOTE: JUDICIAL COOPERATION CIVIL LAW
TOPIC: Admin Cooperation
PARTIES:
  Austria
  Israel

403109   Bilateral Agreement   **68 ABGB 348**
SIGNED: 6 Jun 66
HEADNOTE: JUDICIAL COOPERATION CRIMINAL
LAW
TOPIC: Admin Cooperation
PARTIES:
  Austria
  Israel

403110   Bilateral Agreement   **68 ABGB 438**
SIGNED: 22 Nov 68
HEADNOTE: VISA ABOLITION
TOPIC: Visas
PARTIES:
  Austria
  Israel

403111   Bilateral Agreement   **71 ABGB 85**
SIGNED: 29 Jan 70
HEADNOTE: DOUBLE TAXATION
TOPIC: Taxation
PARTIES:
  Austria
  Israel

403112   Bilateral Agreement   **50 ABGB 220**
SIGNED: 4 Oct 50
HEADNOTE: OPTANTS ASSETS TRANSFER
TOPIC: Finance
PARTIES:
  Austria
  Italy

403113   Bilateral Agreement   **51 ABGB 253**
SIGNED: 2 Aug 51
HEADNOTE: BORDER TRAFFIC
TOPIC: Visas

PARTIES:
  Austria
  Italy

403114   Bilateral Agreement   **53 ABGB 130**
SIGNED: 1 Feb 52
HEADNOTE: TRADEMARKS
TOPIC: Patents/Copyrights
PARTIES:
  Austria
  Italy

403115   Bilateral Agreement   **54 ABGB 270**
SIGNED: 14 Mar 52
HEADNOTE: CULTURE
TOPIC: Culture
PARTIES:
  Austria
  Italy

403116   Bilateral Exchange   **56 ABGB 87**
SIGNED: 14 Mar 52
HEADNOTE: RECOGNIZE ACADEMIC DEGREES
TOPIC: Admin Cooperation
PARTIES:
  Austria
  Italy

403117   Bilateral Exchange   **56 ABGB 42**
SIGNED: 5 Feb 55
HEADNOTE: TIMBER GROWTH
TOPIC: Specific Resources
PARTIES:
  Austria
  Italy

403118   Bilateral Treaty   **72 ABGB 15**
SIGNED: 21 Apr 67
HEADNOTE: CIVIL STATUS
TOPIC: Admin Cooperation
PARTIES:
  Austria
  Italy

403119   Bilateral Agreement   **68 ABGB 197**
SIGNED: 24 Apr 68
HEADNOTE: FILMS
TOPIC: Culture
PARTIES:
  Austria
  Italy

403120   Bilateral Agreement   **70 ABGB 306**
SIGNED: 25 Aug 70
HEADNOTE: VISA ABOLITION
TOPIC: Visas
PARTIES:
  Austria
  Jamaica

403121   Bilateral Agreement   **70 ABGB 242**
SIGNED: 29 Jun 70
HEADNOTE: VISA ABOLITION
TOPIC: Visas
PARTIES:
  Austria
  Korea, South

403122   Bilateral Agreement   **71 ABGB 398**
SIGNED: 1 Sep 71
HEADNOTE: TRADE
TOPIC: General Trade
PARTIES:
  Austria
  Korea, South

403123   Bilateral Treaty   **56 ABGB 213**
SIGNED: 1 Apr 55
HEADNOTE: JUDICIAL COOPERATION
TOPIC: Admin Cooperation
PARTIES:
  Austria
  Liechtenstein

403124   Bilateral Treaty   56 ABGB 212
SIGNED: 1 Apr 55
HEADNOTE: JUDICIAL COOPERATION
TOPIC: Admin Cooperation
PARTIES:
  Austria
  Liechtenstein

403125   Bilateral Treaty   68 ABGB 99
SIGNED: 1 Jun 66
HEADNOTE: JUDICIAL COOPERATION
TOPIC: Admin Cooperation
PARTIES:
  Austria
  Liechtenstein

403126   Bilateral Agreement   56 ABGB 214
SIGNED: 7 Dec 55
HEADNOTE: DOUBLE TAXATION
TOPIC: Taxation
PARTIES:
  Austria
  Liechtenstein

403128   Bilateral Treaty   60 ABGB 228
SIGNED: 17 Mar 60
HEADNOTE: BORDER DEFINITION
TOPIC: Territory Boundary
PARTIES:
  Austria
  Liechtenstein

403129   Bilateral Protocol   65 ABGB 11
SIGNED: 2 Sep 63
HEADNOTE: BORDER PROCEDURES
TOPIC: Visas
PARTIES:
  Austria
  Liechtenstein

403130   Bilateral Agreement   68 ABGB 21
SIGNED: 24 Oct 67
HEADNOTE: BORDER PROCEDURES
TOPIC: Visas
PARTIES:
  Austria
  Liechtenstein

403131   Bilateral Agreement   69 ABGB 72
SIGNED: 26 Sep 68
HEADNOTE: SOCIAL SECURITY
TOPIC: Non-ILO Labor
PARTIES:
  Austria
  Liechtenstein

403132   Bilateral Agreement   69 ABGB 73
SIGNED: 30 Oct 68
HEADNOTE: SOCIAL SECURITY
TOPIC: Non-ILO Labor
PARTIES:
  Austria
  Liechtenstein

403133   Bilateral Agreement   71 ABGB 24
SIGNED: 5 Nov 69
HEADNOTE: DOUBLE TAXATION
TOPIC: Taxation
PARTIES:
  Austria
  Liechtenstein

403134   Bilateral Protocol   69 ABGB 479
SIGNED: 6 Nov 69
HEADNOTE: ROAD TRAFFIC TAXES
TOPIC: Taxation
PARTIES:
  Austria
  Liechtenstein

403135   Bilateral Agreement   71 ABGB 493
SIGNED: 12 Oct 71
HEADNOTE: TAXES
TOPIC: Taxation

PARTIES:
  Austria
  Liechtenstein

403136   Bilateral Exchange   59 ABGB 27
SIGNED: 12 Sep 58
HEADNOTE: EXCHANGE MIGRANT WORKERS
TOPIC: Non-ILO Labor
PARTIES:
  Austria
  Luxembourg

403137   Bilateral Agreement   64 ABGB 143
SIGNED: 10 Apr 64
HEADNOTE: DOUBLE TAXATION
TOPIC: Taxation
PARTIES:
  Austria
  Luxembourg

403138   Bilateral Agreement   71 ABGB 404
SIGNED: 16 Jul 71
HEADNOTE: BUS TRAFFIC
TOPIC: Land Transport
PARTIES:
  Austria
  Luxembourg

403139   Bilateral Agreement   59 ABGB 44
SIGNED: 6 Jun 58
HEADNOTE: VISA ABOLITION
TOPIC: Visas
PARTIES:
  Austria
  Mexico

403140   Bilateral Agreement   55 ABGB 215
SIGNED: 4 Jun 54
HEADNOTE: VISA ABOLITION
TOPIC: Visas
PARTIES:
  Austria
  Monaco

403141   Bilateral Agreement   58 ABGB 63
SIGNED: 26 Jul 57
HEADNOTE: RAILROAD RATES
TOPIC: Land Transport
PARTIES:
  Austria
  ECSC (Coal/Steel)

403142   Bilateral Agreement   52 ABGB 26
SIGNED: 24 May 51
HEADNOTE: VISA ABOLITION
TOPIC: Visas
PARTIES:
  Austria
  Netherlands

403143   Bilateral Agreement   70 ABGB 86
SIGNED: 2 Feb 70
HEADNOTE: COMMERCIAL TRAFFIC
TOPIC: Land Transport
PARTIES:
  Austria
  Netherlands

403144   Bilateral Agreement   71 ABGB 191
SIGNED: 1 Sep 70
HEADNOTE: DOUBLE TAXATION
TOPIC: Taxation
PARTIES:
  Austria
  Netherlands

403145   Bilateral Agreement   60 ABGB 205
SIGNED: 25 Feb 60
HEADNOTE: DOUBLE TAXATION
TOPIC: Taxation
PARTIES:
  Austria
  Norway

403146   Bilateral Protocol   71 ABGB 414
SIGNED: 16 Dec 70
HEADNOTE: DOUBLE TAXATION
TOPIC: Taxation
PARTIES:
  Austria
  Norway

403147   Bilateral Agreement   71 ABGB 297
SIGNED: 6 Jul 70
HEADNOTE: DOUBLE TAXATION
TOPIC: Taxation
PARTIES:
  Austria
  Pakistan

403148   Bilateral Agreement   71 ABGB 296
SIGNED: 28 May 71
HEADNOTE: AIR TRANSPORT
TOPIC: Air Transport
PARTIES:
  Austria
  Pakistan

403149   Bilateral Agreement   69 ABGB 92
SIGNED: 17 Jan 69
HEADNOTE: VISA ABOLITION
TOPIC: Visas
PARTIES:
  Austria
  Paraguay

403150   Bilateral Exchange   59 ABGB 242
SIGNED: 25 Jul 59
HEADNOTE: VISA ABOLITION
TOPIC: Visas
PARTIES:
  Austria
  Peru

403151   Bilateral Agreement   63 ABGB 294
SIGNED: 21 Jun 63
HEADNOTE: AIR TRANSPORT
TOPIC: Air Transport
PARTIES:
  Austria
  Poland

403152   Bilateral Agreement   68 ABGB 123
SIGNED: 5 Feb 68
HEADNOTE: ROAD TRAFFIC TAXES
TOPIC: Taxation
PARTIES:
  Austria
  Poland

403153   Bilateral Agreement   70 ABGB 278
SIGNED: 9 Jun 70
HEADNOTE: ROAD TRAFFIC TAXES
TOPIC: General Amity
PARTIES:
  Austria
  Poland

403154   Bilateral Agreement   71 ABGB 495
SIGNED: 9 Sep 71
HEADNOTE: TRADE & PAYMENTS
TOPIC: General Economic
PARTIES:
  Austria
  Poland

403155   Bilateral Agreement   55 ABGB 175
SIGNED: 14 Dec 54
HEADNOTE: VISA ABOLITION
TOPIC: Visas
PARTIES:
  Austria
  Portugal

403156   Bilateral Agreement   72 ABGB 85
SIGNED: 29 Dec 70
HEADNOTE: DOUBLE TAXATION
TOPIC: Taxation

PARTIES:
Austria
Portugal

403157   Bilateral Agreement   **65 ABGB 34**
SIGNED: 18 Dec 64
HEADNOTE: DISEASE CONTROL
TOPIC: Sanitation
PARTIES:
Austria
Romania

403158   Bilateral Agreement   **69 ABGB 39**
SIGNED: 17 Dec 68
HEADNOTE: VISA ABOLITION
TOPIC: Visas
PARTIES:
Austria
Romania

403159   Bilateral Agreement   **70 ABGB 328**
SIGNED: 24 Sep 70
HEADNOTE: LONG-TERM TRADE
TOPIC: General Trade
PARTIES:
Austria
Romania

403160   Bilateral Agreement   **70 ABGB 338**
SIGNED: 2 Oct 70
HEADNOTE: ROAD TRAFFIC TAXES
TOPIC: Customs
PARTIES:
Austria
Romania

403161   Bilateral Agreement   **60 ABGB 189**
SIGNED: 21 Jun 60
HEADNOTE: VISA ABOLITION
TOPIC: Visas
PARTIES:
Austria
El Salvador

403162   Bilateral Exchange   **64 ABGB 34**
SIGNED: 3 Oct 63
HEADNOTE: VISA ABOLITION
TOPIC: Visas
PARTIES:
Austria
El Salvador

403163   Bilateral Agreement   **72 ABGB 259**
SIGNED: 30 May 72
HEADNOTE: VISA ABOLITION
TOPIC: Visas
PARTIES:
Austria
San Marino

403164   Bilateral Exchange   **69 ABGB 435**
SIGNED: 13 Jan 69
HEADNOTE: JUDICIAL COOPERATION
TOPIC: Admin Cooperation
PARTIES:
Austria
Singapore

403165   Bilateral Exchange   **56 ABGB 241**
SIGNED: 9 Nov 56
HEADNOTE: DIPLOMATS VISAS
TOPIC: Visas
PARTIES:
Austria
Spain

403166   Bilateral Exchange   **59 ABGB 223**
SIGNED: 10 Jun 59
HEADNOTE: VISA ABOLITION
TOPIC: Visas
PARTIES:
Austria
Spain

403167   Bilateral Exchange   **61 ABGB 256**
SIGNED: 4 Aug 59
HEADNOTE: PROTECT LITERARY & ARTISTIC
WORKS
TOPIC: Culture
PARTIES:
Austria
Spain

403168   Bilateral Agreement   **66 ABGB 9**
SIGNED: 14 Oct 64
HEADNOTE: SOCIAL SECURITY
TOPIC: Non-ILO Labor
PARTIES:
Austria
Spain

403169   Bilateral Agreement   **70 ABGB 358**
SIGNED: 23 Oct 69
HEADNOTE: SOCIAL SECURITY
TOPIC: Non-ILO Labor
PARTIES:
Austria
Spain

403170   Bilateral Agreement   **70 ABGB 87**
SIGNED: 9 Feb 70
HEADNOTE: FILMS
TOPIC: Culture
PARTIES:
Austria
Spain

403171   Bilateral Agreement   **70 ABGB 358**
SIGNED: 14 May 70
HEADNOTE: SOCIAL SECURITY
TOPIC: Non-ILO Labor
PARTIES:
Austria
Spain

403172   Bilateral Exchange   **72 ABGB 249**
SIGNED: 14 Mar 72
HEADNOTE: CERTIFICATES OF ORIGIN
TOPIC: Admin Cooperation
PARTIES:
Austria
Spain

403173   Bilateral Exchange   **55 ABGB 193**
SIGNED: 9 Apr 54
HEADNOTE: VISA ABOLITION
TOPIC: Visas
PARTIES:
Austria
Sweden

403174   Bilateral Exchange   **59 ABGB 30**
SIGNED: 18 Jun 58
HEADNOTE: VISA ABOLITION
TOPIC: Visas
PARTIES:
Austria
Sweden

403175   Bilateral Agreement   **60 ABGB 143**
SIGNED: 22 Feb 60
HEADNOTE: DOUBLE TAXATION
TOPIC: Taxation
PARTIES:
Austria
Sweden

403176   Bilateral Agreement   **63 ABGB 212**
SIGNED: 21 Nov 62
HEADNOTE: DOUBLE TAXATION
TOPIC: Taxation
PARTIES:
Austria
Sweden

403177   Bilateral Protocol   **70 ABGB 34**
SIGNED: 6 Apr 70
HEADNOTE: DOUBLE TAXATION

TOPIC: Taxation
PARTIES:
Austria
Sweden

403178   Bilateral Agreement   **72 ABGB 298**
SIGNED: 14 Mar 72
HEADNOTE: DOUBLE TAXATION
TOPIC: Taxation
PARTIES:
Austria
Sweden

403179   Bilateral Agreement   **51 ABGB 232**
SIGNED: 15 Jul 50
HEADNOTE: SOCIAL SECURITY
TOPIC: Non-ILO Labor
PARTIES:
Austria
Switzerland

403180   Bilateral Agreement   **66 ABGB 41**
SIGNED: 20 Feb 65
HEADNOTE: SOCIAL SECURITY
TOPIC: Non-ILO Labor
PARTIES:
Austria
Switzerland

403181   Bilateral Agreement   **54 ABGB 164**
SIGNED: 9 Dec 53
HEADNOTE: CIVIL STATUS
TOPIC: Admin Cooperation
PARTIES:
Austria
Switzerland

403182   Bilateral Exchange   **59 ABGB 196**
SIGNED: 6 Apr 59
HEADNOTE: DOUBLE TAXATION
TOPIC: Taxation
PARTIES:
Austria
Switzerland

403183   Bilateral Exchange   **67 ABGB 355**
SIGNED: 29 Dec 66
HEADNOTE: DOUBLE TAXATION
TOPIC: Taxation
PARTIES:
Austria
Switzerland

403184   Bilateral Agreement   **55 ABGB 42**
SIGNED: 13 Jul 54
HEADNOTE: PAYMENTS
TOPIC: Finance
PARTIES:
Austria
Switzerland

403185   Bilateral Exchange   **57 ABGB 159**
SIGNED: 1 Jun 57
HEADNOTE: PASSPORTS
TOPIC: Visas
PARTIES:
Austria
Switzerland

403186   Bilateral Agreement   **57 ABGB 268**
SIGNED: 22 Jul 57
HEADNOTE: ARLBERG ROUTE EXPANSION
TOPIC: Land Transport
PARTIES:
Austria
Switzerland

403187   Bilateral Agreement   **59 ABGB 123**
SIGNED: 22 Dec 58
HEADNOTE: VEHICULAR BORDER TRAFFIC
TOPIC: Land Transport
PARTIES:
Austria
Switzerland

403188 Bilateral Exchange **68 ABGB 84**
SIGNED: 29 Dec 67
HEADNOTE: RECOGNITION OF JUDGEMENTS
TOPIC: Admin Cooperation
PARTIES:
Austria
Switzerland

403189 Bilateral Agreement **62 ABGB 320**
SIGNED: 26 Apr 62
HEADNOTE: JUDICIAL COOPERATION
TOPIC: Admin Cooperation
PARTIES:
Austria
Switzerland

403190 Bilateral Agreement **66 ABGB 41**
SIGNED: 20 Feb 65
HEADNOTE: SOCIAL SECURITY
TOPIC: Non-ILO Labor
PARTIES:
Austria
Switzerland

403191 Bilateral Exchange **67 ABGB 333**
SIGNED: 23 Aug 67
HEADNOTE: COOPERATION IN GIVING DEVELOP-
MENT AID
TOPIC: Tech Assistance
PARTIES:
Austria
Switzerland

403192 Bilateral Agreement **68 ABGB 21**
SIGNED: 24 Oct 67
HEADNOTE: BORDER PROCEDURE IN TRAINS
TOPIC: Visas
PARTIES:
Austria
Switzerland

403193 Bilateral Agreement **69 ABGB 4**
SIGNED: 15 Nov 67
HEADNOTE: SOCIAL SECURITY
TOPIC: Non-ILO Labor
PARTIES:
Austria
Switzerland

403194 Bilateral Agreement **69 ABGB 5**
SIGNED: 1 Oct 68
HEADNOTE: SOCIAL SECURITY
TOPIC: Non-ILO Labor
PARTIES:
Austria
Switzerland

403195 Bilateral Agreement **66 ABGB 135**
SIGNED: 25 Apr 66
HEADNOTE: LEGAL STATUS AUSTRIAN EXPERTS
TOPIC: Admin Cooperation
PARTIES:
Austria
Thailand

403196 Bilateral Exchange **65 ABGB 255**
SIGNED: 28 Jun 65
HEADNOTE: REPATRIATION CITIZENS
TOPIC: Admin Cooperation
PARTIES:
Austria
Tunisia

403197 Bilateral Exchange **65 ABGB 254**
SIGNED: 28 Jun 65
HEADNOTE: VISA ABOLITION
TOPIC: Visas
PARTIES:
Austria
Tunisia

403198 Bilateral Agreement **67 ABGB 251**
SIGNED: 17 Oct 66
HEADNOTE: AIR TRANSPORT
TOPIC: Air Transport
PARTIES:
Austria
Tunisia

403199 Bilateral Instrument **49 ABGB 234**
SIGNED: 8 Aug 49
HEADNOTE: NAVIGATION & CUSTOMS
TOPIC: Mostfavored Nation
PARTIES:
Austria
Turkey

403200 Bilateral Agreement **55 ABGB 194**
SIGNED: 7 Apr 54
HEADNOTE: VISA ABOLITION
TOPIC: Visas
PARTIES:
Austria
Turkey

403201 Bilateral Agreement **69 ABGB 338**
SIGNED: 12 Oct 66
HEADNOTE: SOCIAL SECURITY
TOPIC: Non-ILO Labor
PARTIES:
Austria
Turkey

403202 Bilateral Agreement **68 ABGB 280**
SIGNED: 8 Feb 68
HEADNOTE: ROAD TRAFFIC TAXES
TOPIC: Customs
PARTIES:
Austria
Turkey

403203 Bilateral Agreement **70 ABGB 274**
SIGNED: 7 Nov 69
HEADNOTE: ROAD TRANSPORT
TOPIC: Land Transport
PARTIES:
Austria
Turkey

403204 Bilateral Agreement **63 ABGB 337**
SIGNED: 4 Nov 63
HEADNOTE: EUROPEAN CENTER SOCIAL
SCIENCES
TOPIC: IGO Establishment
PARTIES:
Austria
UNESCO (Educ/Cult)

403205 Bilateral Agreement **46 ABGB 116**
SIGNED: 5 Apr 46
HEADNOTE: RECONSTRUCTION AID
TOPIC: Direct Aid
PARTIES:
Austria
UNRRA (Relief)

403206 Bilateral Exchange **63 ABGB 223**
SIGNED: 6 Jul 61
HEADNOTE: VISA ABOLITION
TOPIC: Visas
PARTIES:
Austria
Uruguay

403207 Bilateral Treaty **60 ABGB 195**
SIGNED: 23 Jun 60
HEADNOTE: MONETARY ASSETS
TOPIC: Claims and Debts
PARTIES:
Austria
Vatican/Holy See

403208 Bilateral Treaty **70 ABGB 107**
SIGNED: 29 Sep 69
HEADNOTE: MONETARY ASSETS
TOPIC: Claims and Debts

PARTIES:
Austria
Vatican/Holy See

403209 Bilateral Treaty **60 ABGB 196**
SIGNED: 23 Jun 60
HEADNOTE: BURGENLAND DIOCESE
TOPIC: Admin Cooperation
PARTIES:
Austria
Vatican/Holy See

403210 Bilateral Treaty **62 ABGB 273**
SIGNED: 9 Jul 62
HEADNOTE: SCHOOLS
TOPIC: Education
PARTIES:
Austria
Vatican/Holy See

403211 Bilateral Treaty **64 ABGB 227**
SIGNED: 7 Jul 64
HEADNOTE: TIROL & VORARLBERG DIOCESE
TOPIC: Admin Cooperation
PARTIES:
Austria
Vatican/Holy See

403212 Bilateral Treaty **68 ABGB 417**
SIGNED: 7 Oct 68
HEADNOTE: FELDKIRCH DIOCESE
TOPIC: Admin Cooperation
PARTIES:
Austria
Vatican/Holy See

403213 Bilateral Agreement **54 ABGB 259**
SIGNED: 31 May 54
HEADNOTE: LOAN
TOPIC: Claims and Debts
PARTIES:
Austria
UK Great Britain

403214 Bilateral Agreement **67 ABGB 119**
SIGNED: 1 Mar 67
HEADNOTE: AIR ROUTES
TOPIC: Air Transport
PARTIES:
Austria
UK Great Britain

403215 Bilateral Protocol **70 ABGB 169**
SIGNED: 15 Jan 69
HEADNOTE: EXTRADITION
TOPIC: Extradition
PARTIES:
Austria
UK Great Britain

403216 Bilateral Exchange **67 ABGB 192**
SIGNED: 9 Mar 67
HEADNOTE: KLAGENFURT CEMETERY
TOPIC: Other Military
PARTIES:
Austria
UK Great Britain

403217 Bilateral Agreement **69 ABGB 260**
SIGNED: 9 Jun 69
HEADNOTE: VISA ABOLITION
TOPIC: Visas
PARTIES:
Austria
UK Great Britain

403218 Bilateral Agreement **70 ABGB 39**
SIGNED: 29 May 69
HEADNOTE: ROAD GOODS TRAFFIC
TOPIC: Land Transport
PARTIES:
Austria
UK Great Britain

403219   Bilateral Exchange   **70 ABGB 167**
SIGNED: 27 May 70
HEADNOTE: GROUP PASSPORT VISA ABOLITION
TOPIC: Visas
PARTIES:
  Austria
  UK Great Britain

403220   Bilateral Exchange   **71 ABGB 278**
SIGNED: 12 Jul 71
HEADNOTE: VISA ABOLITION
TOPIC: Visas
PARTIES:
  Austria
  UK Great Britain

403221   Bilateral Agreement   **56 ABGB 86**
SIGNED: 17 Oct 55
HEADNOTE: PAYMENTS
TOPIC: Finance
PARTIES:
  Austria
  USSR (Soviet Union)

403222   Bilateral Agreement   **68 ABGB 295**
SIGNED: 2 Jul 68
HEADNOTE: AIR TRANSPORT
TOPIC: Air Transport
PARTIES:
  Austria
  USSR (Soviet Union)

403223   Bilateral Agreement   **70 ABGB 109**
SIGNED: 15 Jan 70
HEADNOTE: NON-VISA FLIGHTS
TOPIC: Air Transport
PARTIES:
  Austria
  USSR (Soviet Union)

403224   Bilateral Agreement   **72 ABGB 112**
SIGNED: 11 Mar 70
HEADNOTE: CIVIL PROCEDURE
TOPIC: Admin Cooperation
PARTIES:
  Austria
  USSR (Soviet Union)

403225   Bilateral Agreement   **70 ABGB 317**
SIGNED: 5 Aug 70
HEADNOTE: TRADE & PAYMENTS
TOPIC: General Economic
PARTIES:
  Austria
  USSR (Soviet Union)

403226   Bilateral Agreement   **60 ABGB 232**
SIGNED: 18 Mar 60
HEADNOTE: LOCAL BORDER TRAFFIC
TOPIC: Visas
PARTIES:
  Austria
  Yugoslavia

403227   Bilateral Agreement   **63 ABGB 244**
SIGNED: 18 Jul 63
HEADNOTE: LOCAL BORDER TRAFFIC
TOPIC: Visas
PARTIES:
  Austria
  Yugoslavia

403228   Bilateral Agreement   **64 ABGB 325**
SIGNED: 27 Nov 64
HEADNOTE: LOCAL BORDER TRAFFIC
TOPIC: Visas
PARTIES:
  Austria
  Yugoslavia

403229   Bilateral Agreement   **55 ABGB 199**
SIGNED: 2 Nov 54
HEADNOTE: TRADEMARKS
TOPIC: Patents/Copyrights

PARTIES:
  Austria
  Yugoslavia

403230   Bilateral Agreement   **56 ABGB 118**
SIGNED: 10 Nov 54
HEADNOTE: DANUBE NAVIGATION
TOPIC: Water Transport
PARTIES:
  Austria
  Yugoslavia

403231   Bilateral Agreement   **56 ABGB 119**
SIGNED: 16 Dec 54
HEADNOTE: BORDER DEFINITION
TOPIC: Territory Boundary
PARTIES:
  Austria
  Yugoslavia

403232   Bilateral Agreement   **55 ABGB 224**
SIGNED: 16 Dec 54
HEADNOTE: JUDICIAL COOPERATION
TOPIC: Admin Cooperation
PARTIES:
  Austria
  Yugoslavia

403233   Bilateral Agreement   **58 ABGB 144**
SIGNED: 19 Mar 58
HEADNOTE: BORDER DEFINITION
TOPIC: Territory Boundary
PARTIES:
  Austria
  Yugoslavia

403234   Bilateral Agreement   **59 ABGB 163**
SIGNED: 14 Mar 59
HEADNOTE: RECOGNITION SEAMEN PAPERS
TOPIC: Admin Cooperation
PARTIES:
  Austria
  Yugoslavia

403235   Bilateral Agreement   **61 ABGB 115**
SIGNED: 18 Mar 60
HEADNOTE: JUDICIAL COOPERATION
TOPIC: Admin Cooperation
PARTIES:
  Austria
  Yugoslavia

403236   Bilateral Agreement   **61 ABGB 223**
SIGNED: 23 Mar 61
HEADNOTE: ROAD TRAFFIC
TOPIC: Land Transport
PARTIES:
  Austria
  Yugoslavia

403237   Bilateral Agreement   **62 ABGB 310**
SIGNED: 10 Oct 61
HEADNOTE: JUDICIAL COOPERATION
TOPIC: Admin Cooperation
PARTIES:
  Austria
  Yugoslavia

403238   Bilateral Treaty   **66 ABGB 229**
SIGNED: 8 Apr 64
HEADNOTE: BORDER DEFINITION
TOPIC: Territory Boundary
PARTIES:
  Austria
  Yugoslavia

403239   Bilateral Agreement   **66 ABGB 239**
SIGNED: 28 Sep 65
HEADNOTE: GOODS LOCAL BORDER TRAFFIC
TOPIC: Customs
PARTIES:
  Austria
  Yugoslavia

403240   Bilateral Agreement   **66 ABGB 23**
SIGNED: 28 Jun 65
HEADNOTE: LOCAL BORDER TRAFFIC
TOPIC: Visas
PARTIES:
  Austria
  Yugoslavia

403241   Bilateral Agreement   **66 ABGB 290**
SIGNED: 17 Dec 65
HEADNOTE: SOCIAL SECURITY
TOPIC: Non-ILO Labor
PARTIES:
  Austria
  Yugoslavia

403242   Bilateral Agreement   **70 ABGB 82**
SIGNED: 5 Mar 69
HEADNOTE: BORDER PROCEDURE IN TRAINS
TOPIC: Visas
PARTIES:
  Austria
  Yugoslavia

403243   Bilateral Exchange   **67 ABGB 177**
SIGNED: 26 Apr 67
HEADNOTE: ACCESS ST. PANKRATZEN CHURCH
TOPIC: Visas
PARTIES:
  Austria
  Yugoslavia

403244   Bilateral Agreement   **68 ABGB 173**
SIGNED: 28 Apr 67
HEADNOTE: RAILROAD BORDER CROSSING
TOPIC: Visas
PARTIES:
  Austria
  Yugoslavia

403245   Bilateral Agreement   **68 ABGB 379**
SIGNED: 28 Jul 67
HEADNOTE: LOCAL BORDER TRAFFIC
TOPIC: Visas
PARTIES:
  Austria
  Yugoslavia

403246   Bilateral Agreement   **68 ABGB 400**
SIGNED: 22 Apr 68
HEADNOTE: GOODS LOCAL BORDER TRAFFIC
TOPIC: Customs
PARTIES:
  Austria
  Yugoslavia

403247   Bilateral Agreement   **68 ABGB 345**
SIGNED: 12 Jul 68
HEADNOTE: ACCESS WINTER SPORTS AREAS
TOPIC: Visas
PARTIES:
  Austria
  Yugoslavia

403248   Bilateral Agreement   **70 ABGB 141**
SIGNED: 3 Apr 70
HEADNOTE: ACCESS WINTER SPORTS AREAS
TOPIC: Visas
PARTIES:
  Austria
  Yugoslavia

403249   Bilateral Agreement   **68 ABGB 377**
SIGNED: 24 Sep 68
HEADNOTE: ROAD TRAFFIC CONFERENCE
TOPIC: IGO Operations
PARTIES:
  Austria
  United Nations

403250   Bilateral Agreement   **70 ABGB 390**
SIGNED: 30 Apr 69
HEADNOTE: UNTS 11084
TOPIC: Taxation

PARTIES:
Austria
UK Great Britain

403251 Bilateral Agreement **68 ABGB 378**
SIGNED: 18 Mar 60
HEADNOTE: CONSULAR UNTS 10915
TOPIC: Consul/Citizenship
PARTIES:
Austria
Yugoslavia

403252 Bilateral Agreement **70 ABGB 318**
SIGNED: 22 Sep 70
HEADNOTE: UNTS 10853
TOPIC: IGO Operations
PARTIES:
Austria
United Nations

403253 Bilateral Agreement **71 ABGB 424**
SIGNED: 15 Dec 70
HEADNOTE: SOCIAL SECURITY UNTS 11492
TOPIC: Non-ILO Labor
PARTIES:
Austria
United Nations

403254 Bilateral Agreement **54 ABGB 235**
SIGNED: 1 Feb 52
HEADNOTE: CERTIFICATE OF ORIGIN
TOPIC: Admin Cooperation
PARTIES:
Austria
Italy

403255 Bilateral Agreement **60 ABGB 265**
SIGNED: 18 Mar 60
HEADNOTE: PLANT PROTECTION COOPERATION
TOPIC: Admin Cooperation
PARTIES:
Austria
Yugoslavia

410002 Bilateral Agreement **50 CCJC 2**
SIGNED: 7 Feb 50
HEADNOTE: PARCEL & MAIL EXCHANGE
TOPIC: Gen Communications
PARTIES:
China People's Rep
USSR (Soviet Union)

410003 Bilateral Treaty **50 CCJC 4**
SIGNED: 14 Feb 50
HEADNOTE: FRIENDSHIP, ALLIANCE, COOPER-
ATION
TOPIC: General Amity
PARTIES:
China People's Rep
USSR (Soviet Union)

410004 Bilateral Agreement **50 CCJC 5**
SIGNED: 14 Feb 50
HEADNOTE: CHANGCHUN RAILWAY JOINT AD-
MINISTRATION
TOPIC: Consul/Citizenship
PARTIES:
China People's Rep
USSR (Soviet Union)

410005 Bilateral Agreement **50 CCJC 6**
SIGNED: 14 Feb 50
HEADNOTE: CREDIT FROM USSR
TOPIC: Loans and Credits
PARTIES:
China People's Rep
USSR (Soviet Union)

410009 Bilateral Agreement **50 CCJC 13**
SIGNED: 27 Mar 50
HEADNOTE: JOINT STOCK METALS COMPANY
TOPIC: Specif Goods/Equip

PARTIES:
China People's Rep
USSR (Soviet Union)

410010 Bilateral Agreement **50 CCJC 14**
SIGNED: 27 Mar 50
HEADNOTE: JOINT STOCK PETROLEUM COM-
PANY
TOPIC: Specif Goods/Equip
PARTIES:
China People's Rep
USSR (Soviet Union)

410011 Bilateral Agreement **50 CCJC 15**
SIGNED: 27 Mar 50
HEADNOTE: JOINT STOCK AVIATION COMPANY
TOPIC: Specif Goods/Equip
PARTIES:
China People's Rep
USSR (Soviet Union)

410012 Bilateral Agreement **50 CCJC 16**
SIGNED: 27 Mar 50
HEADNOTE: WORK CONDITIONS USSR EXPERTS
TOPIC: Non-ILO Labor
PARTIES:
China People's Rep
USSR (Soviet Union)

410013 Bilateral Agreement **50 CCJC 17**
SIGNED: 19 Apr 50
HEADNOTE: TRADE
TOPIC: General Trade
PARTIES:
China People's Rep
USSR (Soviet Union)

410014 Bilateral Protocol **50 CCJC 18**
SIGNED: 19 Apr 50
HEADNOTE: TRADE 1950
TOPIC: General Trade
PARTIES:
China People's Rep
USSR (Soviet Union)

410015 Bilateral Protocol **50 CCJC 20**
SIGNED: 19 Apr 50
HEADNOTE: INDUSTRIAL AID 1950-52
TOPIC: General Aid
PARTIES:
China People's Rep
USSR (Soviet Union)

410017 Bilateral Agreement **50 CCJC 22**
SIGNED: 14 Jun 50
HEADNOTE: TRADE 1950
TOPIC: General Trade
PARTIES:
China People's Rep
Czechoslovakia

410020 Bilateral Agreement **50 CCJC 25**
SIGNED: 18 Aug 50
HEADNOTE: BARTER
TOPIC: General Trade
PARTIES:
China People's Rep
Korea, North

410021 Bilateral Agreement **50 CCJC 26**
SIGNED: 28 Aug 50
HEADNOTE: USSR TRANSFER JAPANESE PROP-
ERTY
TOPIC: Specific Property
PARTIES:
China People's Rep
USSR (Soviet Union)

410022 Bilateral Agreement **50 CCJC 27**
SIGNED: 10 Oct 50
HEADNOTE: TRADE AND PAYMENTS 1951
TOPIC: General Economic

PARTIES:
China People's Rep
Germany, East

410024 Bilateral Agreement **51 CCJC 1**
SIGNED: 2 Jan 51
HEADNOTE: BORDER RIVERS ADMINISTRATION
TOPIC: Water Transport
PARTIES:
China People's Rep
USSR (Soviet Union)

410026 Bilateral Agreement **51 CCJC 3**
SIGNED: 22 Jan 51
HEADNOTE: TRADE & PAYMENTS 1951
TOPIC: General Economic
PARTIES:
China People's Rep
Hungary

410027 Bilateral Agreement **51 CCJC 4**
SIGNED: 29 Jan 51
HEADNOTE: TRADE & PAYMENTS 1951
TOPIC: General Economic
PARTIES:
China People's Rep
Poland

410028 Bilateral Agreement **51 CCJC 5**
SIGNED: 29 Jan 51
HEADNOTE: TELECOMMUNICATIONS
TOPIC: Telecommunications
PARTIES:
China People's Rep
Poland

410029 Bilateral Agreement **51 CCJC 6**
SIGNED: 29 Jan 51
HEADNOTE: MAIL AND PARCEL EXCHANGE
TOPIC: Postal Service
PARTIES:
China People's Rep
Poland

410030 Bilateral Agreement **51 CCJC 7**
SIGNED: 29 Jan 51
HEADNOTE: NAVIGATION & SHIPPING
TOPIC: Water Transport
PARTIES:
China People's Rep
Poland

410033 Bilateral Agreement **51 CCJC 12**
SIGNED: 3 Apr 51
HEADNOTE: CULTURAL COOPERATION
TOPIC: Culture
PARTIES:
China People's Rep
Poland

410038 Bilateral Protocol **51 CCJC 17**
SIGNED: 15 Jun 51
HEADNOTE: TRADE 1951
TOPIC: General Trade
PARTIES:
China People's Rep
USSR (Soviet Union)

410040 Bilateral Agreement **51 CCJC 19**
SIGNED: 21 Jun 51
HEADNOTE: TRADE 1951
TOPIC: General Trade
PARTIES:
China People's Rep
Czechoslovakia

410041 Bilateral Agreement **51 CCJC 21**
SIGNED: 12 Jul 51
HEADNOTE: CULTURAL COOPERATION
TOPIC: Culture
PARTIES:
China People's Rep
Hungary

410043　　Bilateral Agreement　　**51 CCJC 23**
SIGNED: 9 Oct 51
HEADNOTE: CULTURAL COOPERATION
TOPIC: Culture
PARTIES:
　China People's Rep
　Germany, East

410044　　Bilateral Agreement　　**51 CCJC 24**
SIGNED: 12 Oct 51
HEADNOTE: POSTAL SERVICES
TOPIC: Postal Service
PARTIES:
　China People's Rep
　Germany, East

410045　　Bilateral Agreement　　**51 CCJC 25**
SIGNED: 21 Oct 51
HEADNOTE: TELECOMMUNICATIONS
TOPIC: Telecommunications
PARTIES:
　China People's Rep
　Germany, East

410046　　Bilateral Agreement　　**51 CCJC 26**
SIGNED: 6 Dec 51
HEADNOTE: USSR TRAINING CPR TECHNICIANS
TOPIC: Tech Assistance
PARTIES:
　China People's Rep
　USSR (Soviet Union)

410047　　Bilateral Agreement　　**51 CCJC 27**
SIGNED: 12 Dec 51
HEADNOTE: CULTURAL COOPERATION
TOPIC: Culture
PARTIES:
　China People's Rep
　Romania

410050　　Bilateral Protocol　　**52 CCJC 5**
SIGNED: 12 Apr 52
HEADNOTE: EXCHANGE OF GOODS 1952
TOPIC: General Trade
PARTIES:
　China People's Rep
　USSR (Soviet Union)

410062　　Bilateral Agreement　　**52 CCJC 17**
SIGNED: 6 May 52
HEADNOTE: POSTAL SERVICES
TOPIC: Postal Service
PARTIES:
　China People's Rep
　Czechoslovakia

410063　　Bilateral Agreement　　**52 CCJC 18**
SIGNED: 6 May 52
HEADNOTE: TELECOMMUNICATIONS
TOPIC: Telecommunications
PARTIES:
　China People's Rep
　Czechoslovakia

410064　　Bilateral Agreement　　**52 CCJC 19**
SIGNED: 6 May 52
HEADNOTE: SCIENTIFIC & TECHNICAL COOPER-
ATION
TOPIC: Scientific Project
PARTIES:
　China People's Rep
　Czechoslovakia

410065　　Bilateral Agreement　　**52 CCJC 20**
SIGNED: 24 May 52
HEADNOTE: CULTURAL COOPERATION
TOPIC: Culture
PARTIES:
　China People's Rep
　Czechoslovakia

410068　　Bilateral Agreement　　**52 CCJC 23**
SIGNED: 28 May 52
HEADNOTE: TRADE & PAYMENTS 1952

TOPIC: General Economic
PARTIES:
　China People's Rep
　Germany, East

410070　　Bilateral Agreement　　**52 CCJC 35**
SIGNED: 14 Jul 52
HEADNOTE: CULTURAL COOPERATION
TOPIC: Culture
PARTIES:
　Bulgaria
　China People's Rep

410071　　Bilateral Agreement　　**52 CCJC 40**
SIGNED: 21 Jul 52
HEADNOTE: TRADE & PAYMENTS 1952
TOPIC: General Economic
PARTIES:
　Bulgaria
　China People's Rep

410072　　Bilateral Agreement　　**52 CCJC 42**
SIGNED: 30 Jul 52
HEADNOTE: TRADE & PAYMENTS 1952
TOPIC: General Economic
PARTIES:
　China People's Rep
　Romania

410073　　Bilateral Agreement　　**52 CCJC 45**
SIGNED: 9 Aug 52
HEADNOTE: SOVIET COLLEGE FOR CHINESE
TOPIC: Education
PARTIES:
　China People's Rep
　USSR (Soviet Union)

410076　　Bilateral Exchange　　**52 CCJC 49**
SIGNED: 15 Sep 52
HEADNOTE: EXTEND JOINT USE PORT ARTHUR
TOPIC: Milit Installation
PARTIES:
　China People's Rep
　USSR (Soviet Union)

410078　　Bilateral Agreement　　**52 CCJC 54**
SIGNED: 4 Oct 52
HEADNOTE: ECONOMIC & CULTURAL COOPER-
ATION 1952-62
TOPIC: Health/Educ/Welfare
PARTIES:
　China People's Rep
　Mongolia

410079　　Bilateral Agreement　　**52 CCJC 55**
SIGNED: 4 Oct 52
HEADNOTE: TRADE
TOPIC: General Trade
PARTIES:
　Ceylon (Sri Lanka)
　China People's Rep

410084　　Bilateral Agreement　　**52 CCJC 60**
SIGNED: 3 Dec 52
HEADNOTE: TRADE AND PAYMENTS 1953
TOPIC: General Economic
PARTIES:
　Bulgaria
　China People's Rep

410085　　Bilateral Agreement　　**52 CCJC 62**
SIGNED: 18 Dec 52
HEADNOTE: RICE & RUBBER EXCHANGE 1953-57
TOPIC: Commodity Trade
PARTIES:
　Ceylon (Sri Lanka)
　China People's Rep

410086　　Bilateral Agreement　　**53 CCJC 1**
SIGNED: 9 Jan 53
HEADNOTE: SCIENTIFIC & TECHNICAL COOPER-
ATION
TOPIC: Scientific Project

PARTIES:
　China People's Rep
　Romania

410087　　Bilateral Agreement　　**53 CCJC 2**
SIGNED: 16 Jan 53
HEADNOTE: POSTAL SERVICES
TOPIC: Postal Service
PARTIES:
　China People's Rep
　Mongolia

410088　　Bilateral Agreement　　**53 CCJC 3**
SIGNED: 16 Jan 53
HEADNOTE: TELECOMMUNICATIONS
TOPIC: Telecommunications
PARTIES:
　China People's Rep
　Mongolia

410089　　Bilateral Agreement　　**53 CCJC 4**
SIGNED: 19 Jan 53
HEADNOTE: TRADE & PAYMENTS 1953
TOPIC: General Trade
PARTIES:
　China People's Rep
　Romania

410094　　Bilateral Agreement　　**53 CCJC 11**
SIGNED: 14 Mar 53
HEADNOTE: COTTON SALE TO PRC
TOPIC: Commodity Trade
PARTIES:
　China People's Rep
　Pakistan

410095　　Bilateral Protocol　　**53 CCJC 13**
SIGNED: 21 Mar 53
HEADNOTE: GOODS TURNOVER 1953
TOPIC: General Trade
PARTIES:
　China People's Rep
　USSR (Soviet Union)

410098　　Bilateral Agreement　　**53 CCJC 17**
SIGNED: 30 Mar 53
HEADNOTE: TRADE & PAYMENTS 1953
TOPIC: General Economic
PARTIES:
　China People's Rep
　Hungary

410099　　Bilateral Agreement　　**53 CCJC 20**
SIGNED: 30 Apr 53
HEADNOTE: TRADE & PAYMENTS 1953
TOPIC: General Economic
PARTIES:
　China People's Rep
　Germany, East

410100　　Bilateral Agreement　　**53 CCJC 22**
SIGNED: 7 May 53
HEADNOTE: TRADE & PAYMENTS 1953
TOPIC: General Trade
PARTIES:
　China People's Rep
　Czechoslovakia

410101　　Bilateral Agreement　　**53 CCJC 24**
SIGNED: 7 May 53
HEADNOTE: RADIO BROADCAST COOP
TOPIC: Telecommunications
PARTIES:
　China People's Rep
　Czechoslovakia

410103　　Bilateral Agreement　　**53 CCJC 27**
SIGNED: 25 May 53
HEADNOTE: GOODS TURNOVER & PAYMENTS
1953
TOPIC: General Economic
PARTIES:
　China People's Rep
　Poland

410104   Bilateral Agreement   **53 CCJC 29**
SIGNED:
HEADNOTE: ECONOMIC & TECHNICAL AID
TOPIC: Direct Aid
PARTIES:
  China People's Rep
  USSR (Soviet Union)

410105   Bilateral Agreement   **53 CCJC 30**
SIGNED: 5 Jun 53
HEADNOTE: TRADE 1953-54
TOPIC: General Trade
PARTIES:
  China People's Rep
  Finland

410106   Bilateral Agreement   **53 CCJC 32**
SIGNED: 5 Jun 53
HEADNOTE: PAYMENTS
TOPIC: Finance
PARTIES:
  China People's Rep
  Finland

410107   Bilateral Agreement   **53 CCJC 33**
SIGNED: 5 Jun 53
HEADNOTE: BARTER
TOPIC: General Trade
PARTIES:
  China People's Rep
  France

410111   Bilateral Instrument   **53 CCJC 39**
SIGNED: 6 Jul 53
HEADNOTE: TRADE
TOPIC: General Trade
PARTIES:
  China People's Rep
  UK Great Britain

410112   Bilateral Agreement   **53 CCJC 40**
SIGNED: 16 Jul 53
HEADNOTE: POSTAL SERVICES
TOPIC: Postal Service
PARTIES:
  China People's Rep
  Hungary

410113   Bilateral Agreement   **53 CCJC 41**
SIGNED: 16 Jul 53
HEADNOTE: TELECOMMUNICATIONS
TOPIC: Telecommunications
PARTIES:
  China People's Rep
  Hungary

410114   Bilateral Agreement   **53 CCJC 48**
SIGNED: 18 Aug 53
HEADNOTE: INSECT & CROP DISEASE CONTROL
TOPIC: Sanitation
PARTIES:
  China People's Rep
  Czechoslovakia

410116   Bilateral Protocol   **53 CCJC 51**
SIGNED: 25 Aug 53
HEADNOTE: BORDER AREA TRADE
TOPIC: General Trade
PARTIES:
  China People's Rep
  Vietnam, North

410118   Bilateral Exchange   **53 CCJC 54**
SIGNED: 20 Sep 53
HEADNOTE: PEARL RIVER DELTA INCIDENT
TOPIC: Reparations
PARTIES:
  China People's Rep
  UK Great Britain

410119   Bilateral Agreement   **53 CCJC 56**
SIGNED: 3 Oct 53
HEADNOTE: SCIENTIFIC & TECHNICAL COOPER-
  ATION

TOPIC: Scientific Project
PARTIES:
  China People's Rep
  Hungary

410120   Bilateral Agreement   **53 CCJC 57**
SIGNED: 15 Oct 53
HEADNOTE: RADIO BROADCAST COOPERATION
TOPIC: Mass Media
PARTIES:
  China People's Rep
  Hungary

410121   Bilateral Agreement   **53 CCJC 58**
SIGNED: 15 Oct 53
HEADNOTE: RADIO BROADCAST COOPERATION
TOPIC: Mass Media
PARTIES:
  China People's Rep
  Poland

410122   Bilateral Agreement   **53 CCJC 59**
SIGNED: 15 Oct 53
HEADNOTE: RADIO BROADCAST COOPERATION
TOPIC: Mass Media
PARTIES:
  China People's Rep
  Romania

410123   Bilateral Agreement   **53 CCJC 60**
SIGNED: 15 Oct 53
HEADNOTE: RADIO BROADCAST COOPERATION
TOPIC: Mass Media
PARTIES:
  Bulgaria
  China People's Rep

410125   Bilateral Agreement   **53 CCJC 63**
SIGNED: 30 Oct 53
HEADNOTE: TECHNOLOGICAL COOPERATION
TOPIC: Scientific Project
PARTIES:
  China People's Rep
  Germany, East

410126   Bilateral Agreement   **53 CCJC 66**
SIGNED: 23 Nov 53
HEADNOTE: ECONOMIC & CULTURAL COOPER-
  ATION
TOPIC: Health/Educ/Welfare
PARTIES:
  China People's Rep
  Korea, North

410127   Bilateral Instrument   **53 CCJC 67**
SIGNED: 28 Nov 53
HEADNOTE: CULTURAL COOPERATION 1954
TOPIC: Culture
PARTIES:
  China People's Rep
  Germany, East

410128   Bilateral Agreement   **53 CCJC 68**
SIGNED: 30 Nov 53
HEADNOTE: TRADE 1953-65
TOPIC: General Trade
PARTIES:
  China People's Rep
  Indonesia

410133   Bilateral Agreement   **54 CCJC 5**
SIGNED: 19 Feb 54
HEADNOTE: GOODS TURNOVER & PAYMENTS
  1954
TOPIC: General Economic
PARTIES:
  China People's Rep
  Poland

410135   Bilateral Agreement   **54 CCJC 8**
SIGNED: 25 Mar 54
HEADNOTE: TRADE & PAYMENTS 1954
TOPIC: General Economic

PARTIES:
  Bulgaria
  China People's Rep

410137   Bilateral Agreement   **54 CCJC 11**
SIGNED: 30 Mar 54
HEADNOTE: PARCEL POST
TOPIC: Postal Service
PARTIES:
  China People's Rep
  Korea, North

410138   Bilateral Agreement   **54 CCJC 12**
SIGNED: 30 Mar 54
HEADNOTE: TRADE & PAYMENTS 1954
TOPIC: General Economic
PARTIES:
  China People's Rep
  Germany, East

410139   Bilateral Protocol   **54 CCJC 14**
SIGNED: 7 Apr 54
HEADNOTE: TRADE & PAYMENTS 1954
TOPIC: General Economic
PARTIES:
  China People's Rep
  Mongolia

410140   Bilateral Agreement   **54 CCJC 16**
SIGNED: 19 Apr 54
HEADNOTE: TRADE & PAYMENTS 1954
TOPIC: General Economic
PARTIES:
  China People's Rep
  Romania

410141   Bilateral Agreement   **54 CCJC 18**
SIGNED: 22 Apr 54
HEADNOTE: TRADE 1954-57
TOPIC: General Trade
PARTIES:
  Burma
  China People's Rep

410142   Bilateral Exchange   **54 CCJC 19**
SIGNED: 22 Apr 54
HEADNOTE: TRADE BALANCE PRINCIPLES
TOPIC: Finance
PARTIES:
  Burma
  China People's Rep

410143   Bilateral Agreement   **54 CCJC 20**
SIGNED: 27 Apr 54
HEADNOTE: TRADE & PAYMENTS
TOPIC: General Economic
PARTIES:
  China People's Rep
  Czechoslovakia

410144   Bilateral Agreement   **54 CCJC 22**
SIGNED: 29 Apr 54
HEADNOTE: GENERAL RELATIONS & TRADE
TOPIC: General Economic
PARTIES:
  China People's Rep
  India

410145   Bilateral Exchange   **54 CCJC 23**
SIGNED: 29 Apr 54
HEADNOTE: INDIA WITHDRAWAL FROM TIBET
TOPIC: Specif Claim/Waive
PARTIES:
  China People's Rep
  India

410155   Bilateral Agreement   **54 CCJC 35**
SIGNED: 10 Jun 54
HEADNOTE: RADIO BROADCAST COOPERATION
TOPIC: Mass Media
PARTIES:
  China People's Rep
  Germany, East

410156   Bilateral Instrument   **54 CCJC 36**
SIGNED: 17 Jun 54
HEADNOTE: TRADE CONDITIONS
TOPIC: General Trade
PARTIES:
  China People's Rep
  Finland

410157   Bilateral Agreement   **54 CCJC 37**
SIGNED: 21 Jun 54
HEADNOTE: TRADE 1954-55
TOPIC: General Trade
PARTIES:
  China People's Rep
  Finland

410158   Bilateral Protocol   **54 CCJC 38**
SIGNED: 23 Jun 54
HEADNOTE: SCIENTIFIC & TECHNICAL COOPER-
  ATION
TOPIC: Scientific Project
PARTIES:
  China People's Rep
  Germany, East

410159   Bilateral Protocol   **54 CCJC 41**
SIGNED: 30 Jun 54
HEADNOTE: TRADE CONDITIONS
TOPIC: General Trade
PARTIES:
  China People's Rep
  Korea, North

410161   Bilateral Protocol   **54 CCJC 44**
SIGNED: 7 Jul 54
HEADNOTE: BORDER TRADING
TOPIC: General Trade
PARTIES:
  China People's Rep
  Vietnam, North

410164   Bilateral Agreement   **54 CCJC 47**
SIGNED: 20 Jul 54
HEADNOTE: SCIENTIFIC & TECHNICAL COOPER-
  ATION
TOPIC: Scientific Project
PARTIES:
  China People's Rep
  Poland

410166   Bilateral Agreement   **54 CCJC 51**
SIGNED: 21 Aug 54
HEADNOTE: RADIO BROADCAST COOPERATION
TOPIC: Mass Media
PARTIES:
  China People's Rep
  USSR (Soviet Union)

410168   Bilateral Protocol   **54 CCJC 54**
SIGNED: 1 Sep 54
HEADNOTE: TRADE
TOPIC: General Trade
PARTIES:
  China People's Rep
  Indonesia

410169   Bilateral Agreement   **54 CCJC 55**
SIGNED: 1 Sep 54
HEADNOTE: PAYMENTS
TOPIC: Finance
PARTIES:
  China People's Rep
  Indonesia

410174   Bilateral Agreement   **54 CCJC 65**
SIGNED: 12 Oct 54
HEADNOTE: SCIENTIFIC & TECHNICAL COOPER-
  ATION
TOPIC: Scientific Project
PARTIES:
  China People's Rep
  USSR (Soviet Union)

410177   Bilateral Agreement   **54 CCJC 70**
SIGNED: 14 Oct 54
HEADNOTE: SCIENTIFIC & TECHNICAL COOPER-
  ATION
TOPIC: Scientific Project
PARTIES:
  Albania
  China People's Rep

410178   Bilateral Agreement   **54 CCJC 71**
SIGNED: 14 Oct 54
HEADNOTE: CULTURAL COOPERATION
TOPIC: Culture
PARTIES:
  Albania
  China People's Rep

410179   Bilateral Agreement   **54 CCJC 72**
SIGNED: 14 Oct 54
HEADNOTE: TRADE 1954-56
TOPIC: General Trade
PARTIES:
  China People's Rep
  India

410180   Bilateral Exchange   **54 CCJC 73**
SIGNED: 14 Oct 54
HEADNOTE: TRANSIT PRC GOODS IN INDIA
TOPIC: Privil/Immunities
PARTIES:
  China People's Rep
  India

410181   Bilateral Exchange   **54 CCJC 74**
SIGNED: 14 Oct 54
HEADNOTE: TRADE PROCEDURE NEGOTIATIONS
TOPIC: General Trade
PARTIES:
  China People's Rep
  India

410184   Bilateral Protocol   **54 CCJC 77**
SIGNED: 3 Nov 54
HEADNOTE: BURMESE RICE EXCHANGE 1954-55
TOPIC: Commodity Trade
PARTIES:
  Burma
  China People's Rep

410186   Bilateral Agreement   **54 CCJC 79**
SIGNED: 3 Dec 54
HEADNOTE: TRADE & PAYMENTS 1955
TOPIC: General Economic
PARTIES:
  Albania
  China People's Rep

410187   Bilateral Agreement   **54 CCJC 80**
SIGNED: 3 Dec 54
HEADNOTE: LONG TERM CREDIT TO ALBANIA
TOPIC: Loans and Credits
PARTIES:
  Albania
  China People's Rep

410190   Bilateral Protocol   **54 CCJC 85**
SIGNED: 16 Dec 54
HEADNOTE: MUTUAL GOODS SUPPLY 1955
TOPIC: General Trade
PARTIES:
  China People's Rep
  Mongolia

410191   Bilateral Agreement   **54 CCJC 86**
SIGNED: 24 Dec 54
HEADNOTE: POSTAL SERVICES
TOPIC: Postal Service
PARTIES:
  China People's Rep
  Vietnam, North

410192   Bilateral Agreement   **54 CCJC 88**
SIGNED: 24 Dec 54
HEADNOTE: TELECOMMUNICATIONS

TOPIC: Telecommunications
PARTIES:
  China People's Rep
  Vietnam, North

410194   Bilateral Protocol   **54 CCJC 90**
SIGNED: 24 Dec 54
HEADNOTE: PRC AID TO RESTORE RAIL LINK
TOPIC: Direct Aid
PARTIES:
  China People's Rep
  Vietnam, North

410199   Bilateral Protocol   **54 CCJC 95**
SIGNED: 27 Dec 54
HEADNOTE: EDUCATIONAL EXCHANGE
TOPIC: Education
PARTIES:
  China People's Rep
  Germany, East

410200   Bilateral Agreement   **54 CCJC 96**
SIGNED: 28 Dec 54
HEADNOTE: INSECT & CROP DISEASE CONTROL
TOPIC: Sanitation
PARTIES:
  China People's Rep
  Hungary

410202   Bilateral Agreement   **54 CCJC 99**
SIGNED: 30 Dec 54
HEADNOTE: REGULAR AIR SERVICES
TOPIC: Air Transport
PARTIES:
  China People's Rep
  USSR (Soviet Union)

410210   Bilateral Agreement   **55 CCJC 3**
SIGNED: 20 Jan 55
HEADNOTE: TRADE & PAYMENTS 1955
TOPIC: General Economic
PARTIES:
  China People's Rep
  Romania

410212   Bilateral Agreement   **55 CCJC 6**
SIGNED: 27 Jan 55
HEADNOTE: TRADE & PAYMENTS 1955
TOPIC: General Economic
PARTIES:
  Bulgaria
  China People's Rep

410215   Bilateral Protocol   **55 CCJC 10**
SIGNED: 12 Feb 55
HEADNOTE: GOODS DELIVERY CONDITIONS
TOPIC: General Trade
PARTIES:
  China People's Rep
  USSR (Soviet Union)

410221   Bilateral Agreement   **55 CCJC 16**
SIGNED: 21 Mar 55
HEADNOTE: GOODS TURNOVER & PAYMENTS
  1955
TOPIC: General Economic
PARTIES:
  China People's Rep
  Poland

410222   Bilateral Agreement   **55 CCJC 18**
SIGNED: 23 Mar 55
HEADNOTE: SCIENTIFIC & TECHNICAL COOPER-
  ATION
TOPIC: Scientific Project
PARTIES:
  Bulgaria
  China People's Rep

410223   Bilateral Protocol   **55 CCJC 20**
SIGNED: 1 Apr 55
HEADNOTE: INDIA TRANSFER TIBET ASSETS
TOPIC: Specific Property

PARTIES:
China People's Rep
India

410224   Bilateral Agreement   55 CCJC 21
SIGNED: 6 Apr 55
HEADNOTE: TRADE & PAYMENTS 1955
TOPIC: General Economic
PARTIES:
China People's Rep
Czechoslovakia

410225   Bilateral Protocol   55 CCJC 22
SIGNED: 6 Apr 55
HEADNOTE: GOODS DELIVERY CONDITIONS
TOPIC: General Trade
PARTIES:
China People's Rep
Czechoslovakia

410226   Bilateral Agreement   55 CCJC 24
SIGNED: 15 Apr 55
HEADNOTE: YELLOW & E. CHINA SEA FISHING
TOPIC: Specific Resources
PARTIES:
China People's Rep
Japan

410227   Bilateral Exchange   55 CCJC 25
SIGNED: 15 Apr 55
HEADNOTE: NO FISHING AREAS
TOPIC: Territory Boundary
PARTIES:
China People's Rep
Japan

410228   Bilateral Exchange   55 CCJC 26
SIGNED: 15 Apr 55
HEADNOTE: FISHING DISPUTE AVOIDANCE
TOPIC: Specif Claim/Waive
PARTIES:
China People's Rep
Japan

410230   Bilateral Treaty   55 CCJC 28
SIGNED: 22 Apr 55
HEADNOTE: DUAL NATIONALITY
TOPIC: Consul/Citizenship
PARTIES:
China People's Rep
Indonesia

410231   Bilateral Agreement   55 CCJC 30
SIGNED: 24 Apr 55
HEADNOTE: TRADE & PAYMENTS 1955
TOPIC: General Economic
PARTIES:
China People's Rep
Germany, East

410232   Bilateral Agreement   55 CCJC 32
SIGNED: 26 Apr 55
HEADNOTE: TRADE & PAYMENTS 1955
TOPIC: General Economic
PARTIES:
China People's Rep
Hungary

410234   Bilateral Agreement   55 CCJC 36
SIGNED: 4 May 55
HEADNOTE: TRADE 1955
TOPIC: General Trade
PARTIES:
China People's Rep
Japan

410235   Bilateral Agreement   55 CCJC 38
SIGNED: 25 May 55
HEADNOTE: THROUGH RAILWAY TRAFFIC
TOPIC: Land Transport
PARTIES:
China People's Rep
Vietnam, North

410239   Bilateral Exchange   55 CCJC 45
SIGNED: 24 Jun 55
HEADNOTE: EXTABLISH CONSULAR RELATIONS
TOPIC: Consul/Citizenship
PARTIES:
China People's Rep
Sweden

410240   Bilateral Protocol   55 CCJC 47
SIGNED: 7 Jul 55
HEADNOTE: CULTURAL COOPERATION
TOPIC: Culture
PARTIES:
China People's Rep
Vietnam, North

410241   Bilateral Protocol   55 CCJC 48
SIGNED: 7 Jul 55
HEADNOTE: BORDER TRADING COMPANIES
TOPIC: General Trade
PARTIES:
China People's Rep
Vietnam, North

410242   Bilateral Protocol   55 CCJC 49
SIGNED: 7 Jul 55
HEADNOTE: SMALL-SCALE BORDER TRADE
TOPIC: General Trade
PARTIES:
China People's Rep
Vietnam, North

410243   Bilateral Agreement   55 CCJC 50
SIGNED: 11 Jul 55
HEADNOTE: INSECT & CROP DISEASE CONTROL
TOPIC: Sanitation
PARTIES:
Bulgaria
China People's Rep

410246   Bilateral Agreement   55 CCJC 53
SIGNED: 30 Jul 55
HEADNOTE: POSTAL & TELECOMMUNICATIONS
TOPIC: Gen Communications
PARTIES:
China People's Rep
Romania

410247   Bilateral Agreement   55 CCJC 54
SIGNED: 8 Aug 55
HEADNOTE: TRADE 1955-56
TOPIC: General Trade
PARTIES:
China People's Rep
Finland

410249   Bilateral Agreement   55 CCJC 56
SIGNED: 16 Aug 55
HEADNOTE: INSECT & CROP DISEASE CONTROL
TOPIC: Sanitation
PARTIES:
China People's Rep
USSR (Soviet Union)

410250   Bilateral Protocol   55 CCJC 57
SIGNED: 20 Aug 55
HEADNOTE: SCIENTIFIC & TECHNICAL COOPER-
ATION
TOPIC: Scientific Project
PARTIES:
China People's Rep
Germany, East

410251   Bilateral Agreement   55 CCJC 58
SIGNED: 22 Aug 55
HEADNOTE: TRADE 1955-58
TOPIC: General Trade
PARTIES:
China People's Rep
United Arab Rep

410252   Bilateral Protocol   55 CCJC 59
SIGNED: 22 Aug 55
HEADNOTE: TRADE 1955-56

TOPIC: General Trade
PARTIES:
China People's Rep
United Arab Rep

410255   Bilateral Instrument   55 CCJC 63
SIGNED: 10 Sep 55
HEADNOTE: REPATRIATION OF CITIZENS
TOPIC: Extradition
PARTIES:
China People's Rep
USA (United States)

410256   Bilateral Agreement   55 CCJC 64
SIGNED: 14 Sep 55
HEADNOTE: POSTAL & TELECOMMUNICATIONS
TOPIC: Gen Communications
PARTIES:
Bulgaria
China People's Rep

410257   Bilateral Instrument   55 CCJC 65
SIGNED: 16 Sep 55
HEADNOTE: TRADE DELIVERIES 1955
TOPIC: General Trade
PARTIES:
China People's Rep
Germany, East

410258   Bilateral Agreement   55 CCJC 66
SIGNED: 28 Sep 55
HEADNOTE: RADIO BROADCAST COOPERATION
TOPIC: Mass Media
PARTIES:
Albania
China People's Rep

410260   Bilateral Agreement   55 CCJC 68
SIGNED: 12 Oct 55
HEADNOTE: RUBBER PRICE INCREASE
TOPIC: Commodity Trade
PARTIES:
Ceylon (Sri Lanka)
China People's Rep

410265   Bilateral Agreement   55 CCJC 77
SIGNED: 8 Nov 55
HEADNOTE: AIR TRANSPORT
TOPIC: Air Transport
PARTIES:
Burma
China People's Rep

410266   Bilateral Protocol   55 CCJC 78
SIGNED: 8 Nov 55
HEADNOTE: AIR TRANSPORT
TOPIC: Air Transport
PARTIES:
Burma
China People's Rep

410267   Bilateral Exchange   55 CCJC 79
SIGNED: 8 Nov 55
HEADNOTE: PILOT NATIONALITIES
TOPIC: Consul/Citizenship
PARTIES:
Burma
China People's Rep

410269   Bilateral Agreement   55 CCJC 81
SIGNED: 11 Nov 55
HEADNOTE: TRADE & PAYMENTS 1956
TOPIC: General Economic
PARTIES:
China People's Rep
Czechoslovakia

410271   Bilateral Agreement   55 CCJC 84
SIGNED: 20 Nov 55
HEADNOTE: TRADE & PAYMENTS 1956
TOPIC: General Economic
PARTIES:
China People's Rep
Germany, East

410275   Bilateral Agreement   **55 CCJC 90**
SIGNED: 27 Nov 55
HEADNOTE: CULTURAL EXCHANGE LIAISONS
TOPIC: Culture
PARTIES:
  China People's Rep
  Japan

410277   Bilateral Agreement   **55 CCJC 92**
SIGNED: 30 Nov 55
HEADNOTE: TRADE
TOPIC: General Trade
PARTIES:
  China People's Rep
  Syria

410278   Bilateral Agreement   **55 CCJC 93**
SIGNED: 30 Nov 55
HEADNOTE: PAYMENTS
TOPIC: Finance
PARTIES:
  China People's Rep
  Syria

410279   Bilateral Protocol   **55 CCJC 94**
SIGNED: 3 Dec 55
HEADNOTE: SCIENTIFIC & TECHNICAL COOPER-
ATION
TOPIC: Scientific Project
PARTIES:
  China People's Rep
  Czechoslovakia

410282   Bilateral Agreement   **55 CCJC 98**
SIGNED: 21 Dec 55
HEADNOTE: RADIO BROADCAST COOPERATION
TOPIC: Mass Media
PARTIES:
  China People's Rep
  Mongolia

410283   Bilateral Agreement   **55 CCJC 99**
SIGNED: 21 Dec 55
HEADNOTE: GOODS TURNOVER & PAYMENTS
1956
TOPIC: General Trade
PARTIES:
  China People's Rep
  Poland

410284   Bilateral Treaty   **55 CCJC 102**
SIGNED: 25 Dec 55
HEADNOTE: FRIENDSHIP & COOPERATION
TOPIC: General Amity
PARTIES:
  China People's Rep
  Germany, East

410285   Bilateral Agreement   **55 CCJC 103**
SIGNED: 25 Dec 55
HEADNOTE: CULTURAL COOPERATION
TOPIC: Culture
PARTIES:
  China People's Rep
  Germany, East

410286   Bilateral Agreement   **55 CCJC 104**
SIGNED: 25 Dec 55
HEADNOTE: INSECT & CROP DISEASE CONTROL
TOPIC: Sanitation
PARTIES:
  China People's Rep
  Germany, East

410287   Bilateral Protocol   **55 CCJC 105**
SIGNED: 27 Dec 55
HEADNOTE: GOODS EXCHANGE 1956
TOPIC: General Trade
PARTIES:
  China People's Rep
  USSR (Soviet Union)

410288   Bilateral Protocol   **55 CCJC 107**
SIGNED: 29 Dec 55

HEADNOTE: EXCHANGE BURMESE RICE 1955-56
TOPIC: Commodity Trade
PARTIES:
  Burma
  China People's Rep

410291   Bilateral Agreement   **55 CCJC 110**
SIGNED: 31 Dec 55
HEADNOTE: TRADE
TOPIC: General Trade
PARTIES:
  China People's Rep
  Lebanon

410292   Bilateral Exchange   **55 CCJC 111**
SIGNED: 31 Dec 55
HEADNOTE: PRC TRADE MISSION IN BEIRUT
TOPIC: General Trade
PARTIES:
  China People's Rep
  Lebanon

410293   Bilateral Exchange   **55 CCJC 112**
SIGNED: 31 Dec 55
HEADNOTE: TRADE WITH THIRD COUNTRIES
TOPIC: General Trade
PARTIES:
  China People's Rep
  Lebanon

410295   Bilateral Agreement   **56 CCJC 2**
SIGNED: 3 Jan 56
HEADNOTE: TRADE & PAYMENTS 1956
TOPIC: General Economic
PARTIES:
  China People's Rep
  Romania

410299   Bilateral Protocol   **56 CCJC 10**
SIGNED: 14 Jan 56
HEADNOTE: RIVER LUMBER TRANSPORT
TOPIC: Specific Resources
PARTIES:
  China People's Rep
  Korea, North

410302   Bilateral Agreement   **56 CCJC 13**
SIGNED: 21 Jan 56
HEADNOTE: TRADE & PAYMENTS 1956
TOPIC: General Economic
PARTIES:
  Bulgaria
  China People's Rep

410303   Bilateral Agreement   **56 CCJC 15**
SIGNED: 27 Jan 56
HEADNOTE: TRADE & PAYMENTS 1956
TOPIC: General Economic
PARTIES:
  China People's Rep
  Hungary

410307   Bilateral Protocol   **56 CCJC 20**
SIGNED: 7 Feb 56
HEADNOTE: MUTUAL GOODS SUPPLY 1956
TOPIC: General Trade
PARTIES:
  China People's Rep
  Mongolia

410309   Bilateral Agreement   **56 CCJC 23**
SIGNED: 14 Feb 56
HEADNOTE: POSTAL SERVICES
TOPIC: Postal Service
PARTIES:
  China People's Rep
  Yugoslavia

410310   Bilateral Agreement   **56 CCJC 24**
SIGNED: 14 Feb 56
HEADNOTE: TELECOMMUNICATIONS
TOPIC: Telecommunications

PARTIES:
  China People's Rep
  Yugoslavia

410311   Bilateral Agreement   **56 CCJC 25**
SIGNED: 17 Feb 56
HEADNOTE: TRADE
TOPIC: General Trade
PARTIES:
  China People's Rep
  Yugoslavia

410312   Bilateral Exchange   **56 CCJC 26**
SIGNED: 17 Feb 56
HEADNOTE: DISPUTE SETTLEMENTS
TOPIC: Dispute Settlement
PARTIES:
  China People's Rep
  Yugoslavia

410313   Bilateral Agreement   **56 CCJC 27**
SIGNED: 17 Feb 56
HEADNOTE: PAYMENTS
TOPIC: Finance
PARTIES:
  China People's Rep
  Yugoslavia

410314   Bilateral Exchange   **56 CCJC 28**
SIGNED: 17 Feb 56
HEADNOTE: DISPUTE SETTLEMENTS
TOPIC: Dispute Settlement
PARTIES:
  China People's Rep
  Yugoslavia

410315   Bilateral Agreement   **56 CCJC 29**
SIGNED: 17 Feb 56
HEADNOTE: SCIENTIFIC & TECHNICAL COOPER-
ATION
TOPIC: Scientific Project
PARTIES:
  China People's Rep
  Yugoslavia

410316   Bilateral Exchange   **56 CCJC 30**
SIGNED: 17 Feb 56
HEADNOTE: DISPUTE SETTLEMENTS 17 FEB 56
TOPIC: Dispute Settlement
PARTIES:
  China People's Rep
  Yugoslavia

410317   Bilateral Protocol   **56 CCJC 33**
SIGNED: 19 Feb 56
HEADNOTE: PAYMENTS PROCEDURES
TOPIC: Finance
PARTIES:
  China People's Rep
  France

410318   Bilateral Protocol   **56 CCJC 34**
SIGNED: 19 Feb 56
HEADNOTE: PAYMENTS
TOPIC: Finance
PARTIES:
  China People's Rep
  France

410319   Bilateral Exchange   **56 CCJC 35**
SIGNED: 24 Feb 56
HEADNOTE: POST & TELEGRAPH SERVICES
TOPIC: Gen Communications
PARTIES:
  China People's Rep
  Poland

410320   Bilateral Protocol   **56 CCJC 36**
SIGNED: 25 Feb 56
HEADNOTE: POST & TELECOMMUNICATION CO-
OPERATION
TOPIC: Gen Communications

PARTIES:
China People's Rep
Poland

410321   Bilateral Agreement   56 CCJC 37
SIGNED: 25 Feb 56
HEADNOTE: PARCEL POST
TOPIC: Postal Service
PARTIES:
China People's Rep
Mongolia

410324   Bilateral Protocol   56 CCJC 40
SIGNED: 13 Mar 56
HEADNOTE: TRADE & PAYMENTS 1956
TOPIC: General Economic
PARTIES:
Albania
China People's Rep

410325   Bilateral Instrument   56 CCJC 41
SIGNED: 19 Mar 56
HEADNOTE: PRC COAL TO PAKISTAN
TOPIC: Direct Aid
PARTIES:
China People's Rep
Pakistan

410326   Bilateral Exchange   56 CCJC 44
SIGNED: 31 Mar 56
HEADNOTE: MOST FAVORED NATION
TOPIC: Mostfavored Nation
PARTIES:
China People's Rep
Finland

410327   Bilateral Agreement   56 CCJC 45
SIGNED: 5 Apr 56
HEADNOTE: CIVIL AIR TRANSPORT
TOPIC: Air Transport
PARTIES:
China People's Rep
Vietnam, North

410330   Bilateral Exchange   56 CCJC 50
SIGNED: 12 Apr 56
HEADNOTE: DEVELOP TRADE RELATIONS
TOPIC: General Trade
PARTIES:
China People's Rep
Sudan

410331   Bilateral Agreement   56 CCJC 51
SIGNED: 15 Apr 56
HEADNOTE: CULTURAL COOPERATION
TOPIC: Culture
PARTIES:
China People's Rep
United Arab Rep

410332   Bilateral Protocol   56 CCJC 53
SIGNED: 23 Apr 56
HEADNOTE: SCIENTIFIC & TECHNICAL COOPER-
ATION
TOPIC: Scientific Project
PARTIES:
China People's Rep
Poland

410333   Bilateral Agreement   56 CCJC 54
SIGNED: 24 Apr 56
HEADNOTE: TRADE
TOPIC: General Trade
PARTIES:
Cambodia
China People's Rep

410334   Bilateral Agreement   56 CCJC 55
SIGNED: 24 Apr 56
HEADNOTE: PAYMENTS
TOPIC: General Trade
PARTIES:
Cambodia
China People's Rep

410337   Bilateral Instrument   56 CCJC 66
SIGNED: 20 May 56
HEADNOTE: PRC COAL TO PAKISTAN
TOPIC: Culture
PARTIES:
China People's Rep
United Arab Rep

410338   Bilateral Protocol   56 CCJC 67
SIGNED: 22 May 56
HEADNOTE: GOODS DELIVERIES 1956
TOPIC: General Trade
PARTIES:
China People's Rep
Germany, East

410339   Bilateral Instrument   56 CCJC 68
SIGNED: 30 May 56
HEADNOTE: CULTURAL COOPERATION 1956
TOPIC: Culture
PARTIES:
China People's Rep
Korea, North

410340   Bilateral Exchange   56 CCJC 69
SIGNED: 1 Jun 56
HEADNOTE: TRADEMARK REGISTRATION
TOPIC: Patents/Copyrights
PARTIES:
China People's Rep
UK Great Britain

410341   Bilateral Agreement   56 CCJC 71
SIGNED: 12 Jun 56
HEADNOTE: CULTURAL COOPERATION
TOPIC: Culture
PARTIES:
China People's Rep
Syria

410342   Bilateral Instrument   56 CCJC 72
SIGNED: 12 Jun 56
HEADNOTE: CULTURAL COOPERATION 1956-57
TOPIC: Culture
PARTIES:
China People's Rep
Syria

410343   Bilateral Exchange   56 CCJC 73
SIGNED: 14 Jun 56
HEADNOTE: COMMODITY DELIVERIES
TOPIC: General Trade
PARTIES:
China People's Rep
USSR (Soviet Union)

410344   Bilateral Protocol   56 CCJC 74
SIGNED: 18 Jun 56
HEADNOTE: GOODS DELIVERY CONDITIONS
TOPIC: General Trade
PARTIES:
China People's Rep
Vietnam, North

410345   Bilateral Agreement   56 CCJC 76
SIGNED: 21 Jun 56
HEADNOTE: 800 MILLION RIALS AID 1956-57
TOPIC: Direct Aid
PARTIES:
Cambodia
China People's Rep

410349   Bilateral Agreement   56 CCJC 84
SIGNED: 5 Jul 56
HEADNOTE: CULTURAL COOPERATION
TOPIC: Culture
PARTIES:
China People's Rep
USSR (Soviet Union)

410351   Bilateral Agreement   56 CCJC 86
SIGNED: 14 Jul 56
HEADNOTE: EXCHANGE STUDENTS
TOPIC: Education

PARTIES:
China People's Rep
Poland

410355   Bilateral Agreement   56 CCJC 91
SIGNED: 31 Jul 56
HEADNOTE: TRADE 1956-57
TOPIC: General Trade
PARTIES:
China People's Rep
Finland

410356   Bilateral Agreement   56 CCJC 92
SIGNED: 13 Aug 56
HEADNOTE: RADIO BROADCAST COOPERATION
TOPIC: Mass Media
PARTIES:
China People's Rep
Korea, North

410359   Bilateral Agreement   56 CCJC 96
SIGNED: 29 Aug 56
HEADNOTE: ECONOMIC & TECHNICAL AID
TOPIC: Direct Aid
PARTIES:
China People's Rep
Mongolia

410360   Bilateral Protocol   56 CCJC 97
SIGNED: 2 Sep 56
HEADNOTE: CONSERVATION TUMEN RIVER
TOPIC: Specific Resources
PARTIES:
China People's Rep
Korea, North

410362   Bilateral Protocol   56 CCJC 99
SIGNED: 13 Sep 56
HEADNOTE: TRADE PROMOTION
TOPIC: General Trade
PARTIES:
Austria
China People's Rep

410365   Bilateral Agreement   56 CCJC 104
SIGNED: 20 Sep 56
HEADNOTE: FRIENDSHIP & COOPERATION
TOPIC: General Amity
PARTIES:
China People's Rep
Nepal

410366   Bilateral Exchange   56 CCJC 105
SIGNED: 20 Sep 56
HEADNOTE: TRADE NATIONALITY MILITARY
TOPIC: Consul/Citizenship
PARTIES:
China People's Rep
Nepal

410367   Bilateral Exchange   56 CCJC 106
SIGNED: 20 Sep 56
HEADNOTE: EXCHANGE ENVOYS
TOPIC: Consul/Citizenship
PARTIES:
China People's Rep
Nepal

410368   Bilateral Agreement   56 CCJC 111
SIGNED: 7 Oct 56
HEADNOTE: 60 MILLION RUPEES AID
TOPIC: Direct Aid
PARTIES:
China People's Rep
Nepal

410369   Bilateral Exchange   56 CCJC 112
SIGNED: 7 Oct 56
HEADNOTE: PAYMENTS OF 7 OCT 56 AID
TOPIC: Finance
PARTIES:
China People's Rep
Nepal

410370　　Bilateral Exchange　　**56 CCJC 113**
SIGNED: 7 Oct 56
HEADNOTE: FOREIGN EXCHANGE FACILITIES
TOPIC: Finance
PARTIES:
　China People's Rep
　Nepal

410371　　Bilateral Protocol　　**56 CCJC 117**
SIGNED: 22 Oct 56
HEADNOTE: TRADE 1956-57
TOPIC: General Trade
PARTIES:
　China People's Rep
　United Arab Rep

410372　　Bilateral Agreement　　**56 CCJC 118**
SIGNED: 22 Oct 56
HEADNOTE: PAYMENTS
TOPIC: Finance
PARTIES:
　China People's Rep
　United Arab Rep

410377　　Bilateral Agreement　　**56 CCJC 126**
SIGNED: 3 Nov 56
HEADNOTE: TRADE
TOPIC: General Trade
PARTIES:
　China People's Rep
　Indonesia

410378　　Bilateral Exchange　　**56 CCJC 128**
SIGNED: 3 Nov 56
HEADNOTE: DEBT PAYMENT IN GOODS
TOPIC: Finance
PARTIES:
　China People's Rep
　Indonesia

410379　　Bilateral Exchange　　**56 CCJC 129**
SIGNED: 3 Nov 56
HEADNOTE: ECONOMIC & TECHNICAL COOPER-
ATION
TOPIC: Direct Aid
PARTIES:
　China People's Rep
　Indonesia

410383　　Bilateral Agreement　　**49 CCJC 1**
SIGNED: 25 Dec 49
HEADNOTE: POSTAL SERVICES
TOPIC: Postal Service
PARTIES:
　China People's Rep
　Korea, North

410384　　Bilateral Agreement　　**49 CCJC 3**
SIGNED: 25 Dec 49
HEADNOTE: ESTABLISH TELECOMMUNICA-
TIONS
TOPIC: Telecommunications
PARTIES:
　China People's Rep
　Korea, North

410385　　Bilateral Agreement　　**49 CCJC 4**
SIGNED: 25 Dec 49
HEADNOTE: ESTABLISH TELEPHONE SERVICE
TOPIC: Telecommunications
PARTIES:
　China People's Rep
　Korea, North

410386　　Bilateral Agreement　　**50 CCJC 1**
SIGNED: 7 Feb 50
HEADNOTE: TELEPHONE & TELEGRAPH COMMU-
NICATIONS
TOPIC: Gen Communications
PARTIES:
　China People's Rep
　USSR (Soviet Union)

410388　　Bilateral Agreement　　**56 CCJC 139**
SIGNED: 20 Dec 56
HEADNOTE: MARITIME TRANSPORT
TOPIC: Water Transport
PARTIES:
　China People's Rep
　Vietnam, North

410390　　Bilateral Protocol　　**56 CCJC 141**
SIGNED: 22 Dec 56
HEADNOTE: TRADE 1957
TOPIC: General Trade
PARTIES:
　China People's Rep
　Mongolia

410391　　Bilateral Protocol　　**56 CCJC 143**
SIGNED: 24 Dec 56
HEADNOTE: SCIENTIFIC & TECHNICAL COOPER-
ATION
TOPIC: Scientific Project
PARTIES:
　China People's Rep
　USSR (Soviet Union)

410392　　Bilateral Instrument　　**56 CCJC 146**
SIGNED: 29 Dec 56
HEADNOTE: PRC FOR CEYLONESE RUBBER
TOPIC: Commodity Trade
PARTIES:
　Ceylon (Sri Lanka)
　China People's Rep

410393　　Bilateral Protocol　　**57 CCJC 1**
SIGNED: 4 Jan 57
HEADNOTE: TRADE 1957
TOPIC: General Trade
PARTIES:
　China People's Rep
　Yugoslavia

410394　　Bilateral Exchange　　**57 CCJC 2**
SIGNED: 4 Jan 57
HEADNOTE: AIR TRANSPORT & MARINE INSUR-
ANCE
TOPIC: General Transport
PARTIES:
　China People's Rep
　Yugoslavia

410398　　Bilateral Agreement　　**57 CCJC 13**
SIGNED: 28 Jan 57
HEADNOTE: TRADE & PAYMENTS 1957
TOPIC: General Economic
PARTIES:
　Bulgaria
　China People's Rep

410399　　Bilateral Protocol　　**57 CCJC 17**
SIGNED: 15 Feb 57
HEADNOTE: POSTAL & PAYMENTS 1957
TOPIC: Gen Communications
PARTIES:
　China People's Rep
　USSR (Soviet Union)

410404　　Bilateral Agreement　　**57 CCJC 22**
SIGNED: 6 Mar 57
HEADNOTE: TRADE & PAYMENTS
TOPIC: General Economic
PARTIES:
　China People's Rep
　Czechoslovakia

410405　　Bilateral Exchange　　**57 CCJC 23**
SIGNED: 14 Apr 57
HEADNOTE: TRADEMARK REGISTRATION
TOPIC: Patents/Copyrights
PARTIES:
　China People's Rep
　Switzerland

410407　　Bilateral Protocol　　**57 CCJC 25**
SIGNED: 8 Mar 57

HEADNOTE: TRADE & PAYMENTS 1957
TOPIC: General Economic
PARTIES:
　Albania
　China People's Rep

410409　　Bilateral Treaty　　**57 CCJC 29**
SIGNED: 27 Mar 57
HEADNOTE: FRIENDSHIP & COOPERATION
TOPIC: General Amity
PARTIES:
　China People's Rep
　Czechoslovakia

410410　　Bilateral Agreement　　**57 CCJC 30**
SIGNED: 27 Mar 57
HEADNOTE: CULTURAL COOPERATION
TOPIC: Culture
PARTIES:
　China People's Rep
　Czechoslovakia

410411　　Bilateral Agreement　　**57 CCJC 31**
SIGNED: 27 Mar 57
HEADNOTE: PUBLIC HEALTH COOPERATION
TOPIC: Sanitation
PARTIES:
　China People's Rep
　Czechoslovakia

410414　　Bilateral Agreement　　**57 CCJC 34**
SIGNED: 1 Apr 57
HEADNOTE: GOODS TURNOVER & PAYMENTS
1957
TOPIC: General Trade
PARTIES:
　China People's Rep
　Poland

410415　　Bilateral Agreement　　**57 CCJC 36**
SIGNED: 5 Apr 57
HEADNOTE: TRADE & PAYMENTS 1957
TOPIC: General Economic
PARTIES:
　China People's Rep
　Germany, East

410416　　Bilateral Exchange　　**57 CCJC 38**
SIGNED: 8 Apr 57
HEADNOTE: TRADEMARK REGISTRATION
TOPIC: Patents/Copyrights
PARTIES:
　China People's Rep
　Sweden

410417　　Bilateral Protocol　　**57 CCJC 39**
SIGNED: 10 Apr 57
HEADNOTE: GOODS DELIVERY CONDITIONS
TOPIC: General Trade
PARTIES:
　China People's Rep
　USSR (Soviet Union)

410418　　Bilateral Agreement　　**57 CCJC 40**
SIGNED: 10 Apr 57
HEADNOTE: INSECT & CROP DISEASE CONTROL
TOPIC: Sanitation
PARTIES:
　China People's Rep
　Korea, North

410422　　Bilateral Agreement　　**57 CCJC 46**
SIGNED: 19 Apr 57
HEADNOTE: TRADE & PAYMENTS 1957
TOPIC: General Economic
PARTIES:
　China People's Rep
　Romania

410425　　Bilateral Agreement　　**57 CCJC 54**
SIGNED: 31 May 57
HEADNOTE: POSTAL & TELECOMMUNICATIONS
TOPIC: Gen Communications

PARTIES:
Albania
China People's Rep

410427   Bilateral Agreement   **57 CCJC 59**
SIGNED: 7 Jun 57
HEADNOTE: EXTEND 1944 POSTAL AGREEMENT
TOPIC: Postal Service
PARTIES:
China People's Rep
Korea, North

410428   Bilateral Agreement   **57 CCJC 60**
SIGNED: 7 Jun 57
HEADNOTE: EXTEND 1949 TELECOMMUNICA-
TIONS AGREEMENT
TOPIC: Telecommunications
PARTIES:
China People's Rep
Korea, North

410429   Bilateral Agreement   **57 CCJC 62**
SIGNED: 7 Jun 57
HEADNOTE: CULTURAL COOPERATION
TOPIC: Culture
PARTIES:
China People's Rep
Yugoslavia

410431   Bilateral Instrument   **58 CCJC 64**
SIGNED: 3 Jun 58
HEADNOTE: PRC COAL FOR PAKISTAN COTTON
TOPIC: Commodity Trade
PARTIES:
China People's Rep
Pakistan

410432   Bilateral Agreement   **57 CCJC 65**
SIGNED: 8 Jun 57
HEADNOTE: TRADE & PAYMENTS 1957
TOPIC: General Economic
PARTIES:
China People's Rep
Hungary

410434   Bilateral Agreement   **57 CCJC 69**
SIGNED: 3 Jul 57
HEADNOTE: REVISES 30 NOV 55 TRADE & PAY-
MENTS
TOPIC: General Trade
PARTIES:
China People's Rep
Syria

410437   Bilateral Agreement   **57 CCJC 72**
SIGNED: 28 Jul 57
HEADNOTE: TRADE & PAYMENTS 1957-59
TOPIC: General Economic
PARTIES:
Afghanistan
China People's Rep

410438   Bilateral Agreement   **57 CCJC 73**
SIGNED: 31 Jul 57
HEADNOTE: TRADE & PAYMENTS 1957
TOPIC: General Economic
PARTIES:
China People's Rep
Vietnam, North

410440   Bilateral Protocol   **57 CCJC 75**
SIGNED: 31 Jul 57
HEADNOTE: BORDER TRADING
TOPIC: General Trade
PARTIES:
China People's Rep
Vietnam, North

410444   Bilateral Agreement   **57 CCJC 83**
SIGNED: 19 Sep 57
HEADNOTE: TRADE & PAYMENTS 1958-62
TOPIC: General Economic

PARTIES:
Ceylon (Sri Lanka)
China People's Rep

410445   Bilateral Exchange   **57 CCJC 84**
SIGNED: 19 Sep 57
HEADNOTE: IMPORT CONTROL REGULATIONS
TOPIC: Customs
PARTIES:
Ceylon (Sri Lanka)
China People's Rep

410446   Bilateral Exchange   **57 CCJC 85**
SIGNED: 19 Sep 57
HEADNOTE: TRADE WITH THIRD COUNTRIES
TOPIC: General Trade
PARTIES:
Ceylon (Sri Lanka)
China People's Rep

410447   Bilateral Protocol   **57 CCJC 86**
SIGNED: 19 Sep 57
HEADNOTE: GOODS EXCHANGE 1958
TOPIC: General Trade
PARTIES:
Ceylon (Sri Lanka)
China People's Rep

410448   Bilateral Agreement   **57 CCJC 87**
SIGNED: 19 Sep 57
HEADNOTE: PRC ECONOMIC AID
TOPIC: Direct Aid
PARTIES:
Ceylon (Sri Lanka)
China People's Rep

410450   Bilateral Agreement   **57 CCJC 90**
SIGNED: 27 Sep 57
HEADNOTE: TRADE
TOPIC: General Trade
PARTIES:
China People's Rep
Germany, West

410451   Bilateral Exchange   **57 CCJC 91**
SIGNED: 27 Sep 57
HEADNOTE: APPLY 27 SEP 57 TRADE AGREE-
MENT
TOPIC: General Trade
PARTIES:
China People's Rep
Germany, West

410452   Bilateral Exchange   **57 CCJC 92**
SIGNED: 27 Sep 57
HEADNOTE: ARBITRATING 27 SEP 57 AGREE-
MENT
TOPIC: Dispute Settlement
PARTIES:
China People's Rep
Germany, West

410457   Bilateral Protocol   **57 CCJC 102**
SIGNED: 29 Oct 57
HEADNOTE: PUBLIC HEALTH WORK COOPER-
ATION
TOPIC: Sanitation
PARTIES:
China People's Rep
Poland

410458   Bilateral Instrument   **57 CCJC 103**
SIGNED: 1 Nov 57
HEADNOTE: SCIENTIFIC & TECHNICAL COOPER-
ATION
TOPIC: Scientific Project
PARTIES:
China People's Rep
Yugoslavia

410459   Bilateral Agreement   **57 CCJC 104**
SIGNED: 1 Nov 57
HEADNOTE: POSTAL SERVICES
TOPIC: Postal Service

PARTIES:
Burma
China People's Rep

410460   Bilateral Agreement   **57 CCJC 105**
SIGNED: 1 Nov 57
HEADNOTE: PARCEL POST
TOPIC: Postal Service
PARTIES:
Burma
China People's Rep

410462   Bilateral Agreement   **57 CCJC 108**
SIGNED: 8 Nov 57
HEADNOTE: TRADE
TOPIC: General Trade
PARTIES:
China People's Rep
Sweden

410465   Bilateral Agreement   **57 CCJC 111**
SIGNED: 1 Dec 57
HEADNOTE: TRADE & PAYMENTS
TOPIC: General Economic
PARTIES:
China People's Rep
Denmark

410466   Bilateral Exchange   **57 CCJC 112**
SIGNED: 1 Dec 57
HEADNOTE: MOST FAVORED NATION
TOPIC: Mostfavored Nation
PARTIES:
China People's Rep
Denmark

410468   Bilateral Protocol   **57 CCJC 114**
SIGNED: 11 Dec 57
HEADNOTE: SCIENCE ACADEMY COOPERATION
TOPIC: Scientific Project
PARTIES:
China People's Rep
USSR (Soviet Union)

410471   Bilateral Agreement   **57 CCJC 118**
SIGNED: 16 Dec 57
HEADNOTE: PUBLIC HEALTH WORK COOPER-
ATION
TOPIC: Sanitation
PARTIES:
China People's Rep
Germany, East

410472   Bilateral Agreement   **57 CCJC 119**
SIGNED: 18 Dec 57
HEADNOTE: TRADE 1957-58
TOPIC: General Trade
PARTIES:
China People's Rep
Finland

410473   Bilateral Agreement   **57 CCJC 120**
SIGNED: 21 Dec 57
HEADNOTE: BORDER WATERS NAVIGATION
TOPIC: Water Transport
PARTIES:
China People's Rep
USSR (Soviet Union)

410474   Bilateral Protocol   **57 CCJC 122**
SIGNED: 21 Dec 57
HEADNOTE: TRADE 1958
TOPIC: General Trade
PARTIES:
China People's Rep
United Arab Rep

410475   Bilateral Protocol   **57 CCJC 125**
SIGNED: 27 Dec 57
HEADNOTE: SCIENTIFIC & TECHNICAL COOPER-
ATION
TOPIC: Scientific Project

PARTIES:
China People's Rep
Yugoslavia

410479 Bilateral Agreement **57 CCJC 129**
SIGNED: 31 Dec 57
HEADNOTE: SCIENTIFIC & TECHNICAL COOPER-
ATION
TOPIC: Scientific Project
PARTIES:
China People's Rep
Korea, North

410480 Bilateral Agreement **57 CCJC 130**
SIGNED: 31 Dec 57
HEADNOTE: HYDROLOGICAL WORK COOPER-
ATION
TOPIC: Scientific Project
PARTIES:
China People's Rep
Korea, North

410481 Bilateral Treaty **58 CCJC 3**
SIGNED: 12 Jan 58
HEADNOTE: FRIENDSHIP
TOPIC: General Amity
PARTIES:
China People's Rep
Yemen

410482 Bilateral Treaty **58 CCJC 4**
SIGNED: 12 Jan 58
HEADNOTE: COMMERCE
TOPIC: General Trade
PARTIES:
China People's Rep
Yemen

410483 Bilateral Agreement **58 CCJC 5**
SIGNED: 12 Jan 58
HEADNOTE: SCIENTIFIC & CULTURAL COOPER-
ATION
TOPIC: Health/Educ/Welfare
PARTIES:
China People's Rep
Yemen

410484 Bilateral Agreement **58 CCJC 6**
SIGNED: 17 Jan 58
HEADNOTE: AIR COMMUNICATIONS
TOPIC: Air Transport
PARTIES:
China People's Rep
Mongolia

410488 Bilateral Protocol **58 CCJC 10**
SIGNED: 21 Jan 58
HEADNOTE: TRADE 1958
TOPIC: General Trade
PARTIES:
China People's Rep
Korea, North

410490 Bilateral Protocol **58 CCJC 13**
SIGNED: 24 Jan 58
HEADNOTE: AIR TRANSPORT & SERVICES
TOPIC: Air Transport
PARTIES:
China People's Rep
Mongolia

410491 Bilateral Protocol **58 CCJC 14**
SIGNED: 28 Jan 58
HEADNOTE: TRADE 1958
TOPIC: General Trade
PARTIES:
China People's Rep
Mongolia

410492 Bilateral Agreement **58 CCJC 15**
SIGNED: 31 Jan 58
HEADNOTE: TELECOMMUNICATIONS
TOPIC: Telecommunications

PARTIES:
Burma
China People's Rep

410494 Bilateral Agreement **58 CCJC 19**
SIGNED: 21 Feb 58
HEADNOTE: CULTURAL COOPERATION
TOPIC: Culture
PARTIES:
China People's Rep
Mongolia

410496 Bilateral Agreement **58 CCJC 21**
SIGNED: 21 Feb 58
HEADNOTE: TRADE
TOPIC: General Trade
PARTIES:
Burma
China People's Rep

410499 Bilateral Agreement **58 CCJC 24**
SIGNED: 5 Mar 58
HEADNOTE: TRADE
TOPIC: General Trade
PARTIES:
China People's Rep
Japan

410500 Bilateral Protocol **58 CCJC 25**
SIGNED: 12 Mar 58
HEADNOTE: TRADE & PAYMENTS 1958
TOPIC: General Economic
PARTIES:
Albania
China People's Rep

410501 Bilateral Protocol **58 CCJC 27**
SIGNED: 13 Mar 58
HEADNOTE: TRADE & PAYMENTS 1958
TOPIC: General Economic
PARTIES:
Bulgaria
China People's Rep

410502 Bilateral Agreement **58 CCJC 28**
SIGNED: 15 Mar 58
HEADNOTE: RADIO BROADCAST COOPERATION
TOPIC: Mass Media
PARTIES:
China People's Rep
Vietnam, North

410504 Bilateral Agreement **58 CCJC 30**
SIGNED: 21 Mar 58
HEADNOTE: TRADE & PAYMENTS 1958
TOPIC: General Economic
PARTIES:
China People's Rep
Hungary

410506 Bilateral Agreement **58 CCJC 34**
SIGNED: 27 Mar 58
HEADNOTE: NONCOMMERCIAL PAYMENTS
TOPIC: Finance
PARTIES:
China People's Rep
Germany, East

410507 Bilateral Instrument **58 CCJC 35**
SIGNED: 29 Mar 58
HEADNOTE: CULTURAL COOPERATION 1958
TOPIC: Culture
PARTIES:
China People's Rep
Yugoslavia

410508 Bilateral Agreement **58 CCJC 36**
SIGNED: 30 Mar 58
HEADNOTE: TRADE & PAYMENTS 1958
TOPIC: General Economic
PARTIES:
China People's Rep
Romania

410509 Bilateral Agreement **58 CCJC 38**
SIGNED: 31 Mar 58
HEADNOTE: TRADE & PAYMENTS 1958
TOPIC: General Economic
PARTIES:
China People's Rep
Vietnam, North

410514 Bilateral Agreement **58 CCJC 47**
SIGNED: 7 Apr 58
HEADNOTE: GOODS TURNOVER & PAYMENTS
TOPIC: General Trade
PARTIES:
China People's Rep
Poland

410515 Bilateral Exchange **58 CCJC 49**
SIGNED: 12 Apr 58
HEADNOTE: TRADEMARK REGISTRATION
TOPIC: Patents/Copyrights
PARTIES:
China People's Rep
Denmark

410517 Bilateral Agreement **58 CCJC 51**
SIGNED: 16 Apr 58
HEADNOTE: TRADE & PAYMENTS 1958
TOPIC: General Economic
PARTIES:
China People's Rep
Czechoslovakia

410520 Bilateral Treaty **58 CCJC 56**
SIGNED: 23 Apr 58
HEADNOTE: COMMERCE & NAVIGATION
TOPIC: General Trade
PARTIES:
China People's Rep
USSR (Soviet Union)

410521 Bilateral Protocol **58 CCJC 57**
SIGNED: 23 Apr 58
HEADNOTE: TRADE 1958
TOPIC: General Trade
PARTIES:
China People's Rep
USSR (Soviet Union)

410522 Bilateral Agreement **58 CCJC 58**
SIGNED: 23 Apr 58
HEADNOTE: TRADE & PAYMENTS 1958
TOPIC: General Economic
PARTIES:
China People's Rep
Germany, East

410526 Bilateral Agreement **58 CCJC 62**
SIGNED: 17 May 58
HEADNOTE: SCIENCE ACADEMY COOPERATION
TOPIC: Scientific Project
PARTIES:
China People's Rep
Hungary

410527 Bilateral Agreement **58 CCJC 65**
SIGNED: 4 Jun 58
HEADNOTE: TRADE & PAYMENTS
TOPIC: General Economic
PARTIES:
China People's Rep
Norway

410538 Bilateral Agreement **58 CCJC 81**
SIGNED: 25 Aug 58
HEADNOTE: POSTAL SERVICES
TOPIC: Postal Service
PARTIES:
China People's Rep
United Arab Rep

410540 Bilateral Exchange **58 CCJC 83**
SIGNED: 17 Sep 58
HEADNOTE: PRC FLOOD RELIEF LOAN
TOPIC: Loans and Credits

PARTIES:
Ceylon (Sri Lanka)
China People's Rep

410541   Bilateral Agreement   **58 CCJC 84**
SIGNED: 25 Sep 58
HEADNOTE: GOODS EXCHANGE 1959
TOPIC: General Trade
PARTIES:
China People's Rep
Tunisia

410545   Bilateral Protocol   **58 CCJC 88**
SIGNED: 27 Sep 58
HEADNOTE: PRC AID YALU RIVER POWERPLANT
TOPIC: Specif Goods/Equip
PARTIES:
China People's Rep
Korea, North

410546   Bilateral Exchange   **58 CCJC 89**
SIGNED: 4 Oct 58
HEADNOTE: MOST FAVORED NATION
TOPIC: Mostfavored Nation
PARTIES:
China People's Rep
Pakistan

410554   Bilateral Protocol   **58 CCJC 99**
SIGNED: 19 Nov 58
HEADNOTE: GOODS EXCHANGE 1959
TOPIC: General Trade
PARTIES:
China People's Rep
Korea, North

410556   Bilateral Protocol   **58 CCJC 102**
SIGNED: 8 Dec 58
HEADNOTE: BORDER RAILWAYS
TOPIC: Land Transport
PARTIES:
China People's Rep
Vietnam, North

410557   Bilateral Agreement   **58 CCJC 104**
SIGNED: 15 Dec 58
HEADNOTE: TRADE 1959-61
TOPIC: General Trade
PARTIES:
China People's Rep
United Arab Rep

410558   Bilateral Agreement   **58 CCJC 105**
SIGNED: 15 Dec 58
HEADNOTE: PAYMENTS
TOPIC: Finance
PARTIES:
China People's Rep
United Arab Rep

410559   Bilateral Protocol   **58 CCJC 106**
SIGNED: 15 Dec 58
HEADNOTE: TRADE 1959
TOPIC: General Trade
PARTIES:
China People's Rep
United Arab Rep

410561   Bilateral Protocol   **58 CCJC 108**
SIGNED: 18 Dec 58
HEADNOTE: TRADE & PAYMENTS 1959
TOPIC: General Economic
PARTIES:
Bulgaria
China People's Rep

410566   Bilateral Agreement   **59 CCJC 2**
SIGNED: 3 Jan 59
HEADNOTE: TRADE & PAYMENTS
TOPIC: General Economic
PARTIES:
China People's Rep
Iraq

410567   Bilateral Exchange   **59 CCJC 3**
SIGNED: 3 Jan 59
HEADNOTE: TRADE WITH THIRD COUNTRIES
TOPIC: General Trade
PARTIES:
China People's Rep
Iraq

410570   Bilateral Agreement   **59 CCJC 6**
SIGNED: 16 Jan 59
HEADNOTE: TRADE 1961-65
TOPIC: General Trade
PARTIES:
Albania
China People's Rep

410571   Bilateral Agreement   **59 CCJC 7**
SIGNED: 16 Jan 59
HEADNOTE: TRADE 1961-65
TOPIC: Loans and Credits
PARTIES:
Albania
China People's Rep

410572   Bilateral Protocol   **59 CCJC 8**
SIGNED: 16 Jan 59
HEADNOTE: TRADE AND PAYMENTS 1959
TOPIC: General Economic
PARTIES:
Albania
China People's Rep

410573   Bilateral Agreement   **59 CCJC 11**
SIGNED: 16 Jan 59
HEADNOTE: CULTURAL COOPERATION 1959-64
TOPIC: Culture
PARTIES:
China People's Rep
Vietnam, North

410579   Bilateral Treaty   **59 CCJC 19**
SIGNED: 27 Jan 59
HEADNOTE: CONSULAR
TOPIC: Consul/Citizenship
PARTIES:
China People's Rep
Germany, East

410581   Bilateral Protocol   **59 CCJC 21**
SIGNED: 30 Jan 59
HEADNOTE: MUTUAL GOODS SUPPLY 1959
TOPIC: General Trade
PARTIES:
China People's Rep
Mongolia

410582   Bilateral Agreement   **59 CCJC 22**
SIGNED: 5 Feb 59
HEADNOTE: TRADE & PAYMENTS 1959
TOPIC: General Economic
PARTIES:
China People's Rep
Germany, East

410583   Bilateral Agreement   **59 CCJC 24**
SIGNED: 7 Feb 59
HEADNOTE: USSR ECONOMIC & TECHNICAL AID 1959-67
TOPIC: Direct Aid
PARTIES:
China People's Rep
USSR (Soviet Union)

410585   Bilateral Protocol   **59 CCJC 26**
SIGNED: 14 Feb 59
HEADNOTE: GOODS DELIVERY 1959
TOPIC: General Trade
PARTIES:
China People's Rep
Poland

410587   Bilateral Agreement   **59 CCJC 28**
SIGNED: 18 Feb 59
HEADNOTE: TRADE & PAYMENTS 1959

TOPIC: General Economic
PARTIES:
China People's Rep
Vietnam, North

410589   Bilateral Agreement   **59 CCJC 34**
SIGNED: 18 Feb 59
HEADNOTE: AIR TRANSPORT
TOPIC: Air Transport
PARTIES:
China People's Rep
Korea, North

410592   Bilateral Agreement   **59 CCJC 38**
SIGNED: 21 Feb 59
HEADNOTE: CULTURAL COOPERATION
TOPIC: Culture
PARTIES:
China People's Rep
Korea, North

410595   Bilateral Agreement   **59 CCJC 41**
SIGNED: 3 Mar 59
HEADNOTE: SCIENTIFIC COOPERATION 1959-61
TOPIC: Scientific Project
PARTIES:
China People's Rep
Czechoslovakia

410597   Bilateral Agreement   **59 CCJC 43**
SIGNED: 6 Mar 59
HEADNOTE: GOODS TURNOVER & PAYMENTS 1959
TOPIC: General Trade
PARTIES:
China People's Rep
Poland

410601   Bilateral Agreement   **59 CCJC 48**
SIGNED: 12 Mar 59
HEADNOTE: TRADE & PAYMENTS 1959
TOPIC: General Economic
PARTIES:
China People's Rep
Czechoslovakia

410602   Bilateral Agreement   **59 CCJC 49**
SIGNED: 17 Mar 59
HEADNOTE: TRADE & PAYMENTS 1959
TOPIC: General Economic
PARTIES:
China People's Rep
Hungary

410603   Bilateral Agreement   **59 CCJC 51**
SIGNED: 17 Mar 59
HEADNOTE: SCIENCE ACADEMY COOPERATION
TOPIC: Scientific Project
PARTIES:
China People's Rep
Germany, East

410605   Bilateral Protocol   **59 CCJC 53**
SIGNED: 18 Mar 59
HEADNOTE: TRADE 1959
TOPIC: General Trade
PARTIES:
China People's Rep
Yugoslavia

410607   Bilateral Protocol   **59 CCJC 55**
SIGNED: 22 Mar 59
HEADNOTE: TRADE & PAYMENTS 1959
TOPIC: General Economic
PARTIES:
China People's Rep
Romania

410608   Bilateral Agreement   **59 CCJC 57**
SIGNED: 26 Mar 59
HEADNOTE: AIR TRANSPORT
TOPIC: Air Transport

PARTIES:
 Ceylon (Sri Lanka)
 China People's Rep

410610   Bilateral Agreement   **59 CCJC 61**
SIGNED: 4 Apr 59
HEADNOTE: CULTURAL COOPERATION
TOPIC: Culture
PARTIES:
 China People's Rep
 Iraq

410611   Bilateral Agreement   **59 CCJC 62**
SIGNED: 6 Apr 59
HEADNOTE: RADIO BROADCAST COOPERATION
TOPIC: Mass Media
PARTIES:
 China People's Rep
 Hungary

410613   Bilateral Agreement   **59 CCJC 64**
SIGNED: 13 Apr 59
HEADNOTE: SCIENCE ACADEMY COOPERATION
TOPIC: Scientific Project
PARTIES:
 China People's Rep
 Romania

410615   Bilateral Agreement   **59 CCJC 66**
SIGNED: 15 Apr 59
HEADNOTE: RADIO & TV BROADCAST COOPER-
 ATION
TOPIC: Mass Media
PARTIES:
 China People's Rep
 Poland

410617   Bilateral Agreement   **59 CCJC 69**
SIGNED: 23 Apr 59
HEADNOTE: SCIENCE ACADEMY COOPERATION
TOPIC: Scientific Project
PARTIES:
 Bulgaria
 China People's Rep

410618   Bilateral Agreement   **59 CCJC 70**
SIGNED: 25 Apr 59
HEADNOTE: RADIO & TV BROADCAST COOPER-
 ATION
TOPIC: Mass Media
PARTIES:
 China People's Rep
 Germany, East

410619   Bilateral Protocol   **59 CCJC 71**
SIGNED: 25 Apr 59
HEADNOTE: TV COOPERATION
TOPIC: Mass Media
PARTIES:
 China People's Rep
 Germany, East

410620   Bilateral Agreement   **59 CCJC 73**
SIGNED: 30 Apr 59
HEADNOTE: RADIO & TV BROADCAST COOPER-
 ATION
TOPIC: Mass Media
PARTIES:
 China People's Rep
 Czechoslovakia

410621   Bilateral Treaty   **59 CCJC 75**
SIGNED: 6 May 59
HEADNOTE: FRIENDSHIP & COOPERATION
TOPIC: General Amity
PARTIES:
 China People's Rep
 Hungary

410622   Bilateral Agreement   **59 CCJC 76**
SIGNED: 15 May 59
HEADNOTE: TRADE 1958-59
TOPIC: General Trade

PARTIES:
 China People's Rep
 Finland

410625   Bilateral Instrument   **59 CCJC 81**
SIGNED: 1 Jun 59
HEADNOTE: SCIENCE ACADEMY COOPERATION
 1959
TOPIC: Scientific Project
PARTIES:
 China People's Rep
 USSR (Soviet Union)

410626   Bilateral Protocol   **59 CCJC 83**
SIGNED: 13 Jun 59
HEADNOTE: TRADE 1959
TOPIC: General Trade
PARTIES:
 Ceylon (Sri Lanka)
 China People's Rep

410627   Bilateral Instrument   **59 CCJC 84**
SIGNED: 13 Jun 59
HEADNOTE: PRC RICE FOR CEYLONESE RUBBER
TOPIC: Commodity Trade
PARTIES:
 Ceylon (Sri Lanka)
 China People's Rep

410628   Bilateral Agreement   **59 CCJC 85**
SIGNED: 20 Jun 59
HEADNOTE: CURRENCY EXCHANGE & NONCOM-
 MERCIAL PAYMENTS
TOPIC: Finance
PARTIES:
 China People's Rep
 Vietnam, North

410629   Bilateral Treaty   **59 CCJC 86**
SIGNED: 23 Jun 59
HEADNOTE: CONSULAR
TOPIC: Consul/Citizenship
PARTIES:
 China People's Rep
 USSR (Soviet Union)

410630   Bilateral Protocol   **59 CCJC 87**
SIGNED: 27 Jun 59
HEADNOTE: JOINT SURVEY TONKIN GULF
TOPIC: Scientific Project
PARTIES:
 China People's Rep
 Vietnam, North

410632   Bilateral Agreement   **59 CCJC 89**
SIGNED: 11 Jul 59
HEADNOTE: RADIO BROADCAST COOPERATION
TOPIC: Mass Media
PARTIES:
 Albania
 China People's Rep

410633   Bilateral Agreement   **59 CCJC 90**
SIGNED: 6 Aug 59
HEADNOTE: RADIO & TV BROADCAST COOPER-
 ATION
TOPIC: Mass Media
PARTIES:
 Bulgaria
 China People's Rep

410637   Bilateral Agreement   **29 CCJC 595**
SIGNED: 7 Oct 59
HEADNOTE: CULTURAL COOPERATION
TOPIC: Culture
PARTIES:
 China People's Rep
 Guinea

410645   Bilateral Exchange   **59 CCJC 104**
SIGNED: 21 Nov 59
HEADNOTE: RECIPROCAL TARIFF CONCESSIONS
TOPIC: Customs

PARTIES:
 Cambodia
 China People's Rep

410650   Bilateral Agreement   **59 CCJC 111**
SIGNED: 16 Dec 59
HEADNOTE: TRADE 1959-60
TOPIC: General Trade
PARTIES:
 China People's Rep
 Finland

410656   Bilateral Treaty   **60 CCJC 2**
SIGNED: 18 Jan 60
HEADNOTE: COMMERCE & NAVIGATION
TOPIC: General Amity
PARTIES:
 China People's Rep
 Germany, East

410658   Bilateral Treaty   **60 CCJC 7**
SIGNED: 28 Jan 60
HEADNOTE: FRIENDSHIP & NON-AGGRESSION
TOPIC: General Amity
PARTIES:
 Burma
 China People's Rep

410659   Bilateral Agreement   **60 CCJC 8**
SIGNED: 28 Jan 60
HEADNOTE: BOUNDARY
TOPIC: Territory Boundary
PARTIES:
 Burma
 China People's Rep

410660   Bilateral Agreement   **60 CCJC 9**
SIGNED: 29 Jan 60
HEADNOTE: CONSERVE & PROTECT FORESTS
TOPIC: Specific Resources
PARTIES:
 China People's Rep
 USSR (Soviet Union)

410661   Bilateral Protocol   **60 CCJC 10**
SIGNED: 2 Feb 60
HEADNOTE: TRADE & PAYMENTS 1960
TOPIC: General Economic
PARTIES:
 China People's Rep
 Czechoslovakia

410673   Bilateral Protocol   **60 CCJC 23**
SIGNED: 23 Feb 60
HEADNOTE: TRADE 1960
TOPIC: General Trade
PARTIES:
 China People's Rep
 Mongolia

410677   Bilateral Agreement   **60 CCJC 29**
SIGNED: 28 Feb 60
HEADNOTE: TRADE & PAYMENTS 1960
TOPIC: General Economic
PARTIES:
 China People's Rep
 Hungary

410678   Bilateral Protocol   **60 CCJC 31**
SIGNED: 29 Feb 60
HEADNOTE: TRADE 1960
TOPIC: General Trade
PARTIES:
 China People's Rep
 Korea, North

410682   Bilateral Protocol   **60 CCJC 36**
SIGNED: 7 Mar 60
HEADNOTE: TRADE & PAYMENTS 1960
TOPIC: General Economic
PARTIES:
 China People's Rep
 Vietnam, North

410685   Bilateral Protocol   **60 CCJC 39**
SIGNED: 15 Mar 60
HEADNOTE: TRADE & PAYMENTS
TOPIC: General Economic
PARTIES:
  China People's Rep
  Romania

410686   Bilateral Protocol   **60 CCJC 41**
SIGNED: 15 Mar 60
HEADNOTE: TRADE & PAYMENTS 1960
TOPIC: General Economic
PARTIES:
  Albania
  China People's Rep

410689   Bilateral Protocol   **60 CCJC 45**
SIGNED: 15 Mar 60
HEADNOTE: TRADE 1960
TOPIC: General Trade
PARTIES:
  Bulgaria
  China People's Rep

410690   Bilateral Agreement   **60 CCJC 47**
SIGNED: 21 Mar 60
HEADNOTE: BOUNDARY
TOPIC: Territory Boundary
PARTIES:
  China People's Rep
  Nepal

410691   Bilateral Agreement   **60 CCJC 48**
SIGNED: 21 Mar 60
HEADNOTE: ECONOMIC AID
TOPIC: Direct Aid
PARTIES:
  China People's Rep
  Nepal

410692   Bilateral Protocol   **60 CCJC 49**
SIGNED: 23 Mar 60
HEADNOTE: TRADE 1960
TOPIC: General Trade
PARTIES:
  China People's Rep
  Germany, East

410694   Bilateral Protocol   **60 CCJC 52**
SIGNED: 25 Mar 60
HEADNOTE: TRADE 1960
TOPIC: General Trade
PARTIES:
  China People's Rep
  Yugoslavia

410698   Bilateral Treaty   **60 CCJC 58**
SIGNED: 28 Apr 60
HEADNOTE: PEACE & FRIENDSHIP
TOPIC: General Amity
PARTIES:
  China People's Rep
  Nepal

410699   Bilateral Agreement   **60 CCJC 60**
SIGNED: 6 May 60
HEADNOTE: RADIO BROADCAST COOPERATION
TOPIC: Mass Media
PARTIES:
  China People's Rep
  Mongolia

410700   Bilateral Treaty   **60 CCJC 61**
SIGNED: 7 May 60
HEADNOTE: CONSULAR
TOPIC: Consul/Citizenship
PARTIES:
  China People's Rep
  Czechoslovakia

410702   Bilateral Agreement   **60 CCJC 66**
SIGNED: 23 May 60
HEADNOTE: BORDER RIVER NAVIGATION
TOPIC: Water Transport

PARTIES:
  China People's Rep
  Korea, North

410705   Bilateral Treaty   **60 CCJC 72**
SIGNED: 31 May 60
HEADNOTE: FRIENDSHIP & MUTUAL ASSIS-
TANCE
TOPIC: General Amity
PARTIES:
  China People's Rep
  Mongolia

410707   Bilateral Agreement   **60 CCJC 74**
SIGNED: 31 May 60
HEADNOTE: SCIENTIFIC & TECHNICAL COOPER-
ATION
TOPIC: Tech Assistance
PARTIES:
  China People's Rep
  Mongolia

410712   Bilateral Agreement   **60 CCJC 81**
SIGNED: 23 Jul 60
HEADNOTE: TRADE & PAYMENTS
TOPIC: General Economic
PARTIES:
  China People's Rep
  Cuba

410713   Bilateral Agreement   **60 CCJC 82**
SIGNED: 23 Jul 60
HEADNOTE: SCIENTIFIC & TECHNICAL COOPER-
ATION
TOPIC: Tech Assistance
PARTIES:
  China People's Rep
  Cuba

410714   Bilateral Agreement   **60 CCJC 83**
SIGNED: 23 Jul 60
HEADNOTE: CULTURAL COOPERATION
TOPIC: Culture
PARTIES:
  China People's Rep
  Cuba

410716   Bilateral Treaty   **60 CCJC 88**
SIGNED: 26 Aug 60
HEADNOTE: FRIENDSHIP & NON-AGGRESSION
TOPIC: General Amity
PARTIES:
  Afghanistan
  China People's Rep

410717   Bilateral Treaty   **60 CCJC 93**
SIGNED: 13 Sep 60
HEADNOTE: FRIENDSHIP
TOPIC: General Amity
PARTIES:
  China People's Rep
  Guinea

410718   Bilateral Agreement   **60 CCJC 94**
SIGNED: 13 Sep 60
HEADNOTE: ECONOMIC & TECHNICAL AID
TOPIC: Direct Aid
PARTIES:
  China People's Rep
  Guinea

410719   Bilateral Agreement   **60 CCJC 95**
SIGNED: 13 Sep 60
HEADNOTE: TRADE & PAYMENTS
TOPIC: General Trade
PARTIES:
  China People's Rep
  Guinea

410721   Bilateral Treaty   **60 CCJC 98**
SIGNED: 1 Oct 60
HEADNOTE: BOUNDARY
TOPIC: Territory Boundary

PARTIES:
  Burma
  China People's Rep

410722   Bilateral Exchange   **60 CCJC 99**
SIGNED: 1 Oct 60
HEADNOTE: CULTIVATE & REGULATE BORDERS
TOPIC: Territory Boundary
PARTIES:
  Burma
  China People's Rep

410735   Bilateral Agreement   **60 CCJC 118**
SIGNED: 28 Nov 60
HEADNOTE: SCIENTIFIC & TECHNICAL COOPER-
ATION
TOPIC: Scientific Project
PARTIES:
  China People's Rep
  Vietnam, North

410737   Bilateral Agreement   **60 CCJC 122**
SIGNED: 30 Nov 60
HEADNOTE: 240 MILLION RUBLES PRC LOAN
TOPIC: Direct Aid
PARTIES:
  China People's Rep
  Cuba

410741   Bilateral Treaty   **60 CCJC 129**
SIGNED: 19 Dec 60
HEADNOTE: FRIENDSHIP & NON-AGGRESSION
TOPIC: General Amity
PARTIES:
  Cambodia
  China People's Rep

410745   Bilateral Agreement   **61 CCJC 2**
SIGNED: 9 Jan 61
HEADNOTE: ECONOMIC & TECHNICAL COOPER-
ATION
TOPIC: Direct Aid
PARTIES:
  Burma
  China People's Rep

410746   Bilateral Agreement   **61 CCJC 3**
SIGNED: 9 Jan 61
HEADNOTE: PAYMENTS
TOPIC: Finance
PARTIES:
  Burma
  China People's Rep

410749   Bilateral Agreement   **61 CCJC 6**
SIGNED: 27 Jan 61
HEADNOTE: TRADE IN 1961-66
TOPIC: General Trade
PARTIES:
  Burma
  China People's Rep

410753   Bilateral Protocol   **61 CCJC 12**
SIGNED: 31 Jan 61
HEADNOTE: CARGO TRANSIT
TOPIC: Land Transport
PARTIES:
  China People's Rep
  Vietnam, North

410754   Bilateral Treaty   **61 CCJC 16**
SIGNED: 2 Feb 61
HEADNOTE: COMMERCE & NAVIGATION
TOPIC: General Amity
PARTIES:
  Albania
  China People's Rep

410755   Bilateral Protocol   **61 CCJC 17**
SIGNED: 2 Feb 61
HEADNOTE: TRADE & PAYMENTS 1961
TOPIC: General Trade

PARTIES:
Albania
China People's Rep

410756 Bilateral Agreement **61 CCJC 18**
SIGNED: 2 Feb 61
HEADNOTE: PRC LOAN
TOPIC: Loans and Credits
PARTIES:
Albania
China People's Rep

410758 Bilateral Protocol **61 CCJC 23**
SIGNED: 5 Feb 61
HEADNOTE: TRADE 1961
TOPIC: General Trade
PARTIES:
China People's Rep
United Arab Rep

410761 Bilateral Agreement **61 CCJC 27**
SIGNED: 28 Feb 61
HEADNOTE: TRADE & PAYMENTS
TOPIC: General Trade
PARTIES:
China People's Rep
Mali

410764 Bilateral Exchange **61 CCJC 32**
SIGNED: 8 Mar 61
HEADNOTE: FAMILY FINANCE MATTERS
TOPIC: Finance
PARTIES:
China People's Rep
Cuba

410766 Bilateral Protocol **61 CCJC 34**
SIGNED: 8 Mar 61
HEADNOTE: TRADE & PAYMENTS 1961
TOPIC: General Trade
PARTIES:
Bulgaria
China People's Rep

410770 Bilateral Agreement **61 CCJC 38**
SIGNED: 20 Mar 61
HEADNOTE: CURRENCY MOVEMENTS & EX-
CHANGE
TOPIC: Finance
PARTIES:
China People's Rep
USSR (Soviet Union)

410774 Bilateral Treaty **61 CCJC 43**
SIGNED: 1 Apr 61
HEADNOTE: FRIENDSHIP
TOPIC: General Amity
PARTIES:
China People's Rep
Indonesia

410775 Bilateral Agreement **61 CCJC 44**
SIGNED: 1 Apr 61
HEADNOTE: CULTURAL COOPERATION
TOPIC: Culture
PARTIES:
China People's Rep
Indonesia

410776 Bilateral Exchange **61 CCJC 45**
SIGNED: 4 Apr 61
HEADNOTE: VISA FEE EXEMPTION
TOPIC: Visas
PARTIES:
China People's Rep
Norway

410777 Bilateral Protocol **61 CCJC 47**
SIGNED: 4 Apr 61
HEADNOTE: TRADE 1961
TOPIC: General Trade
PARTIES:
Ceylon (Sri Lanka)
China People's Rep

410784 Bilateral Agreement **61 CCJC 55**
SIGNED: 11 Apr 61
HEADNOTE: TRADE 1960-61
TOPIC: General Trade
PARTIES:
China People's Rep
Finland

410792 Bilateral Treaty **61 CCJC 69**
SIGNED: 26 Apr 61
HEADNOTE: COMMERCE
TOPIC: General Amity
PARTIES:
China People's Rep
Mongolia

410793 Bilateral Protocol **61 CCJC 70**
SIGNED: 26 Apr 61
HEADNOTE: TRADE 1961
TOPIC: General Trade
PARTIES:
China People's Rep
Mongolia

410796 Bilateral Agreement **61 CCJC 75**
SIGNED: 15 May 61
HEADNOTE: CURRENCY MOVEMENTS & EX-
CHANGE
TOPIC: Finance
PARTIES:
China People's Rep
Poland

410797 Bilateral Protocol **61 CCJC 76**
SIGNED: 15 May 61
HEADNOTE: TRADE & PAYMENTS 1961
TOPIC: General Economic
PARTIES:
China People's Rep
Germany, East

410799 Bilateral Agreement **61 CCJC 79**
SIGNED: 25 May 61
HEADNOTE: RADIO & TV BROADCAST COOPER-
ATION
TOPIC: Mass Media
PARTIES:
China People's Rep
USSR (Soviet Union)

410801 Bilateral Agreement **61 CCJC 84**
SIGNED: 15 Jun 61
HEADNOTE: CURRENCY MOVEMENTS & EX-
CHANGE
TOPIC: Finance
PARTIES:
China People's Rep
Germany, East

410803 Bilateral Agreement **61 CCJC 87**
SIGNED: 19 Jun 61
HEADNOTE: SCIENTIFIC & TECHNICAL COOPER-
ATION
TOPIC: Scientific Project
PARTIES:
China People's Rep
USSR (Soviet Union)

410804 Bilateral Protocol **61 CCJC 88**
SIGNED: 21 Jun 61
HEADNOTE: SCIENCE ACADEMY COOPERATION
TOPIC: Scientific Project
PARTIES:
China People's Rep
USSR (Soviet Union)

410807 Bilateral Protocol **61 CCJC 93**
SIGNED: 7 Jul 61
HEADNOTE: TRADE & PAYMENTS 1961
TOPIC: General Economic
PARTIES:
China People's Rep
Romania

410808 Bilateral Protocol **61 CCJC 95**
SIGNED: 10 Jul 61
HEADNOTE: GOODS DELIVERY CONDITIONS
TOPIC: General Trade
PARTIES:
China People's Rep
Poland

410809 Bilateral Treaty **61 CCJC 96**
SIGNED: 11 Jul 61
HEADNOTE: FRIENDSHIP, COOPERATION & AS-
SISTANCE
TOPIC: General Amity
PARTIES:
China People's Rep
Korea, North

410812 Bilateral Agreement **61 CCJC 100**
SIGNED: 15 Jul 61
HEADNOTE: CURRENCY MOVEMENTS & EX-
CHANGE
TOPIC: Finance
PARTIES:
China People's Rep
Hungary

410813 Bilateral Protocol **61 CCJC 102**
SIGNED: 15 Jul 61
HEADNOTE: TRADE & PAYMENTS 1961
TOPIC: General Economic
PARTIES:
China People's Rep
Hungary

410814 Bilateral Protocol **61 CCJC 103**
SIGNED: 15 Jul 61
HEADNOTE: TRADE 1961
TOPIC: General Trade
PARTIES:
China People's Rep
Yugoslavia

410817 Bilateral Treaty **61 CCJC 108**
SIGNED: 18 Aug 61
HEADNOTE: FRIENDSHIP
TOPIC: General Amity
PARTIES:
China People's Rep
Ghana

410818 Bilateral Agreement **61 CCJC 109**
SIGNED: 18 Aug 61
HEADNOTE: ECONOMIC & TECHNICAL COOPER-
ATION
TOPIC: General Aid
PARTIES:
China People's Rep
Ghana

410819 Bilateral Agreement **61 CCJC 110**
SIGNED: 18 Aug 61
HEADNOTE: TRADE & PAYMENTS
TOPIC: Milit Assistance
PARTIES:
China People's Rep
Ghana

410820 Bilateral Agreement **61 CCJC 111**
SIGNED: 18 Aug 61
HEADNOTE: CULTURAL COOPERATION
TOPIC: Culture
PARTIES:
China People's Rep
Ghana

410830 Bilateral Agreement **61 CCJC 125**
SIGNED: 22 Sep 61
HEADNOTE: ECONOMIC & TECHNICAL COOPER-
ATION
TOPIC: General Aid
PARTIES:
China People's Rep
Mali

410831   Bilateral Exchange   **61 CCJC 126**
SIGNED: 23 Sep 61
HEADNOTE: RECIPROCAL TAX EXEMPTIONS
TOPIC: Taxation
PARTIES:
  China People's Rep
  Denmark

410832   Bilateral Treaty   **61 CCJC 128**
SIGNED: 5 Oct 61
HEADNOTE: BOUNDARY
TOPIC: Territory Boundary
PARTIES:
  China People's Rep
  Nepal

410836   Bilateral Protocol   **61 CCJC 132**
SIGNED: 7 Oct 61
HEADNOTE: TRADE 1962
TOPIC: General Trade
PARTIES:
  Ceylon (Sri Lanka)
  China People's Rep

410837   Bilateral Agreement   **61 CCJC 134**
SIGNED: 11 Oct 61
HEADNOTE: ECONOMIC & TECHNICAL COOPER-
ATION
TOPIC: General Aid
PARTIES:
  China People's Rep
  Indonesia

410838   Bilateral Protocol   **61 CCJC 135**
SIGNED: 13 Oct 61
HEADNOTE: BOUNDARY DEMARCATION
TOPIC: Territory Boundary
PARTIES:
  Burma
  China People's Rep

410839   Bilateral Agreement   **61 CCJC 138**
SIGNED: 15 Oct 61
HEADNOTE: TIBET-NEPAL HIGHWAY AID
TOPIC: Non-IBRD Project
PARTIES:
  China People's Rep
  Nepal

410840   Bilateral Agreement   **61 CCJC 140**
SIGNED: 18 Oct 61
HEADNOTE: EXTENDS 25 MAY 60 AGREEMENT
TOPIC: General Trade
PARTIES:
  China People's Rep
  Iraq

410841   Bilateral Protocol   **61 CCJC 141**
SIGNED: 20 Oct 61
HEADNOTE: TRADE & PAYMENTS 1961-62
TOPIC: General Trade
PARTIES:
  China People's Rep
  Czechoslovakia

410842   Bilateral Agreement   **61 CCJC 143**
SIGNED: 21 Oct 61
HEADNOTE: TELECOMMUNICATIONS
TOPIC: Telecommunications
PARTIES:
  China People's Rep
  Cuba

410843   Bilateral Agreement   **61 CCJC 144**
SIGNED: 21 Oct 61
HEADNOTE: POSTAL SERVICES
TOPIC: Postal Service
PARTIES:
  China People's Rep
  Cuba

410844   Bilateral Agreement   **61 CCJC 145**
SIGNED: 27 Oct 61
HEADNOTE: PAYMENTS

TOPIC: Finance
PARTIES:
  China People's Rep
  Morocco

410854   Bilateral Protocol   **62 CCJC 1**
SIGNED: 8 Jan 62
HEADNOTE: TRADE 1962
TOPIC: General Trade
PARTIES:
  China People's Rep
  Korea, North

410864   Bilateral Agreement   **62 CCJC 15**
SIGNED: 27 Jan 62
HEADNOTE: RADIO & TV BROADCAST COOPER-
ATION
TOPIC: Mass Media
PARTIES:
  China People's Rep
  Cuba

410867   Bilateral Exchange   **62 CCJC 18**
SIGNED: 7 Feb 62
HEADNOTE: SHIP PAPERS RECOGNITION
TOPIC: Admin Cooperation
PARTIES:
  Ceylon (Sri Lanka)
  China People's Rep

410869   Bilateral Protocol   **62 CCJC 20**
SIGNED: 25 Feb 62
HEADNOTE: TRADE 1962
TOPIC: General Trade
PARTIES:
  China People's Rep
  Mongolia

410871   Bilateral Agreement   **62 CCJC 22**
SIGNED: 7 Mar 62
HEADNOTE: CURRENCY MOVEMENTS & EX-
CHANGE
TOPIC: Finance
PARTIES:
  China People's Rep
  Czechoslovakia

410873   Bilateral Agreement   **62 CCJC 24**
SIGNED: 17 Mar 62
HEADNOTE: TRADE
TOPIC: General Trade
PARTIES:
  China People's Rep
  United Arab Rep

410874   Bilateral Agreement   **62 CCJC 25**
SIGNED: 17 Mar 62
HEADNOTE: PAYMENTS
TOPIC: Finance
PARTIES:
  China People's Rep
  United Arab Rep

410875   Bilateral Protocol   **62 CCJC 26**
SIGNED: 17 Mar 62
HEADNOTE: TRADE 1962
TOPIC: General Trade
PARTIES:
  China People's Rep
  United Arab Rep

410878   Bilateral Agreement   **62 CCJC 30**
SIGNED: 29 Mar 62
HEADNOTE: TRADE 1961-62
TOPIC: General Trade
PARTIES:
  China People's Rep
  Finland

410879   Bilateral Protocol   **62 CCJC 31**
SIGNED: 30 Mar 62
HEADNOTE: TRADE & PAYMENTS 1962
TOPIC: General Economic

PARTIES:
  Bulgaria
  China People's Rep

410880   Bilateral Agreement   **62 CCJC 33**
SIGNED: 30 Mar 62
HEADNOTE: TRADE & PAYMENTS 1962
TOPIC: General Economic
PARTIES:
  China People's Rep
  Hungary

410891   Bilateral Agreement   **62 CCJC 49**
SIGNED: 23 May 62
HEADNOTE: TRADE
TOPIC: General Trade
PARTIES:
  China People's Rep
  Sudan

410892   Bilateral Exchange   **62 CCJC 50**
SIGNED: 23 May 62
HEADNOTE: SHIPS PAPERS RECOGNITION
TOPIC: Admin Cooperation
PARTIES:
  Cambodia
  China People's Rep

410893   Bilateral Protocol   **62 CCJC 52**
SIGNED: 29 May 62
HEADNOTE: TRADE & PAYMENTS 1962
TOPIC: General Economic
PARTIES:
  China People's Rep
  Romania

410898   Bilateral Protocol   **62 CCJC 60**
SIGNED: 28 Jun 62
HEADNOTE: TRADE 1962
TOPIC: General Trade
PARTIES:
  China People's Rep
  Yugoslavia

410901   Bilateral Protocol   **62 CCJC 64**
SIGNED: 17 Jul 62
HEADNOTE: TRADE & PAYMENTS 1962
TOPIC: General Economic
PARTIES:
  China People's Rep
  Czechoslovakia

410910   Bilateral Protocol   **62 CCJC 77**
SIGNED: 4 Aug 62
HEADNOTE: TRADE & PAYMENTS 1962
TOPIC: General Economic
PARTIES:
  China People's Rep
  Germany, East

410911   Bilateral Exchange   **62 CCJC 79**
SIGNED: 14 Aug 62
HEADNOTE: BORDER FARMING REGULATION
TOPIC: Consul/Citizenship
PARTIES:
  China People's Rep
  Nepal

410918   Bilateral Agreement   **62 CCJC 90**
SIGNED: 30 Sep 62
HEADNOTE: SCIENCE ACADEMY COOPERATION
1962-66
TOPIC: Scientific Project
PARTIES:
  China People's Rep
  Czechoslovakia

410919   Bilateral Agreement   **62 CCJC 93**
SIGNED: 3 Oct 62
HEADNOTE: TRADE & PAYMENTS 1962-67
TOPIC: General Economic
PARTIES:
  Ceylon (Sri Lanka)
  China People's Rep

410920 Bilateral Agreement **62 CCJC 94**
SIGNED: 3 Oct 62
HEADNOTE: ECONOMIC & TECHNICAL COOPER-
ATION
TOPIC: Direct Aid
PARTIES:
Ceylon (Sri Lanka)
China People's Rep

410921 Bilateral Protocol **62 CCJC 95**
SIGNED: 3 Oct 62
HEADNOTE: TRADE 1963
TOPIC: General Trade
PARTIES:
Ceylon (Sri Lanka)
China People's Rep

410924 Bilateral Agreement **62 CCJC 98**
SIGNED: 1 Nov 62
HEADNOTE: RADIO & TV BROADCAST COOPER-
ATION
TOPIC: Scientific Project
PARTIES:
China People's Rep
Indonesia

410925 Bilateral Treaty **62 CCJC 100**
SIGNED: 5 Nov 62
HEADNOTE: COMMERCE & NAVIGATION
TOPIC: General Amity
PARTIES:
China People's Rep
Korea, North

410928 Bilateral Instrument **62 CCJC 103**
SIGNED: 9 Nov 62
HEADNOTE: TRADE EXPANSION 1963-67
TOPIC: General Trade
PARTIES:
China People's Rep
Japan

410931 Bilateral Treaty **62 CCJC 108**
SIGNED: 5 Dec 62
HEADNOTE: COMMERCE & NAVIGATION
TOPIC: General Amity
PARTIES:
China People's Rep
Vietnam, North

410932 Bilateral Protocol **62 CCJC 109**
SIGNED: 5 Dec 62
HEADNOTE: TRADE & PAYMENTS 1963
TOPIC: General Economic
PARTIES:
China People's Rep
Vietnam, North

410935 Bilateral Agreement **62 CCJC 114**
SIGNED: 13 Dec 62
HEADNOTE: CULTURAL COOPERATION
TOPIC: Culture
PARTIES:
China People's Rep
Tanganyika

410938 Bilateral Treaty **62 CCJC 117**
SIGNED: 26 Dec 62
HEADNOTE: BOUNDARY
TOPIC: Territory Boundary
PARTIES:
China People's Rep
Mongolia

410939 Bilateral Protocol **62 CCJC 118**
SIGNED: 27 Dec 62
HEADNOTE: TRADE
TOPIC: General Trade
PARTIES:
China People's Rep
Japan

410942 Bilateral Agreement **63 CCJC 2**
SIGNED: 5 Jan 63

HEADNOTE: TELECOMMUNICATIONS
TOPIC: Telecommunications
PARTIES:
China People's Rep
United Arab Rep

410943 Bilateral Agreement **63 CCJC 6**
SIGNED: 10 Jan 63
HEADNOTE: CULTURAL COOPERATION
TOPIC: Culture
PARTIES:
China People's Rep
Somalia

410947 Bilateral Protocol **63 CCJC 10**
SIGNED: 20 Jan 63
HEADNOTE: BOUNDARY DEMARCATION
TOPIC: Territory Boundary
PARTIES:
China People's Rep
Nepal

410948 Bilateral Agreement **63 CCJC 14**
SIGNED: 18 Feb 63
HEADNOTE: INSECT & CROP DISEASE CONTROL
TOPIC: Sanitation
PARTIES:
Albania
China People's Rep

410949 Bilateral Agreement **63 CCJC 15**
SIGNED: 21 Feb 63
HEADNOTE: TRADE
TOPIC: General Trade
PARTIES:
China People's Rep
Syria

410950 Bilateral Agreement **63 CCJC 16**
SIGNED: 21 Feb 63
HEADNOTE: PAYMENTS
TOPIC: Finance
PARTIES:
China People's Rep
Syria

410951 Bilateral Agreement **63 CCJC 17**
SIGNED: 21 Feb 63
HEADNOTE: ECONOMIC & TECHNICAL COOPER-
ATION
TOPIC: Direct Aid
PARTIES:
China People's Rep
Syria

410957 Bilateral Agreement **63 CCJC 28**
SIGNED: 2 Mar 63
HEADNOTE: BORDER REGULATION
TOPIC: Territory Boundary
PARTIES:
China People's Rep
Pakistan

410959 Bilateral Agreement **63 CCJC 31**
SIGNED: 5 Mar 63
HEADNOTE: TRADE & PAYMENTS 1963
TOPIC: General Economic
PARTIES:
Bulgaria
China People's Rep

410961 Bilateral Protocol **63 CCJC 34**
SIGNED: 18 Mar 63
HEADNOTE: TRADE 1963
TOPIC: General Trade
PARTIES:
China People's Rep
Mongolia

410963 Bilateral Agreement **63 CCJC 36**
SIGNED: 26 Mar 63
HEADNOTE: MARITIME TRANSPORT
TOPIC: Water Transport

PARTIES:
China People's Rep
Ghana

410966 Bilateral Agreement **63 CCJC 39**
SIGNED: 30 Mar 63
HEADNOTE: TRADE
TOPIC: General Trade
PARTIES:
China People's Rep
Morocco

410967 Bilateral Agreement **63 CCJC 40**
SIGNED: 8 Apr 63
HEADNOTE: TRADE & PAYMENTS 1963
TOPIC: General Economic
PARTIES:
China People's Rep
Romania

410968 Bilateral Agreement **63 CCJC 42**
SIGNED: 10 Apr 63
HEADNOTE: TRADE & PAYMENTS 1963
TOPIC: General Economic
PARTIES:
China People's Rep
Hungary

410969 Bilateral Agreement **63 CCJC 44**
SIGNED: 19 Apr 63
HEADNOTE: TRADE & PAYMENTS 1963
TOPIC: General Economic
PARTIES:
China People's Rep
Czechoslovakia

410976 Bilateral Agreement **63 CCJC 58**
SIGNED: 15 May 63
HEADNOTE: CULTURAL COOPERATION
TOPIC: Culture
PARTIES:
China People's Rep
Mali

410979 Bilateral Agreement **63 CCJC 61**
SIGNED: 15 May 63
HEADNOTE: TRADE & PAYMENTS 1963
TOPIC: General Economic
PARTIES:
China People's Rep
Somalia

410983 Bilateral Agreement **63 CCJC 68**
SIGNED: 29 May 63
HEADNOTE: TRADE 1963
TOPIC: General Trade
PARTIES:
China People's Rep
Finland

410984 Bilateral Instrument **63 CCJC 70**
SIGNED: 7 Jun 63
HEADNOTE: CULTURAL COOPERATION 1963
TOPIC: Culture
PARTIES:
China People's Rep
Germany, East

410985 Bilateral Agreement **63 CCJC 71**
SIGNED: 8 Jun 63
HEADNOTE: SCIENTIFIC & TECHNICAL COOPER-
ATION
TOPIC: Scientific Project
PARTIES:
China People's Rep
Romania

410987 Bilateral Agreement **63 CCJC 76**
SIGNED: 18 Jun 63
HEADNOTE: CULTURAL COOPERATION
TOPIC: Culture
PARTIES:
China People's Rep
Norway

410991　　Bilateral Agreement　　**63 CCJC 80**
SIGNED: 22 Jun 63
HEADNOTE: TRADE & PAYMENTS 1963
TOPIC: General Economic
PARTIES:
　China People's Rep
　Germany, East

410992　　Bilateral Agreement　　**63 CCJC 83**
SIGNED: 25 Jun 63
HEADNOTE: SCIENCE ACADEMY COOPERATION
TOPIC: Scientific Project
PARTIES:
　China People's Rep
　Cuba

410994　　Bilateral Agreement　　**63 CCJC 86**
SIGNED: 6 Jul 63
HEADNOTE: SCIENCE ACADEMY COOPERATION
TOPIC: Scientific Project
PARTIES:
　China People's Rep
　Romania

410995　　Bilateral Protocol　　**63 CCJC 88**
SIGNED: 14 Jul 63
HEADNOTE: TRADE 1963-64
TOPIC: General Trade
PARTIES:
　China People's Rep
　United Arab Rep

410999　　Bilateral Agreement　　**63 CCJC 92**
SIGNED: 25 Jul 63
HEADNOTE: MARITIME TRANSPORT
TOPIC: Water Transport
PARTIES:
　Ceylon (Sri Lanka)
　China People's Rep

411004　　Bilateral Exchange　　**63 CCJC 100**
SIGNED: 28 Aug 63
HEADNOTE: SHIP PAPERS RECOGNITION
TOPIC: Admin Cooperation
PARTIES:
　Burma
　China People's Rep

411005　　Bilateral Agreement　　**63 CCJC 101**
SIGNED: 29 Aug 63
HEADNOTE: AIR TRANSPORT
TOPIC: Air Transport
PARTIES:
　China People's Rep
　Pakistan

411007　　Bilateral Agreement　　**63 CCJC 103**
SIGNED: 31 Aug 63
HEADNOTE: RADIO BROADCAST COOPERATION
TOPIC: Mass Media
PARTIES:
　China People's Rep
　Mali

411009　　Bilateral Agreement　　**63 CCJC 106**
SIGNED: 11 Sep 63
HEADNOTE: CULTURAL COOPERATION
TOPIC: Culture
PARTIES:
　Algeria
　China People's Rep

411015　　Bilateral Protocol　　**63 CCJC 114**
SIGNED: 10 Oct 63
HEADNOTE: TRADE 1964
TOPIC: General Trade
PARTIES:
　Ceylon (Sri Lanka)
　China People's Rep

411017　　Bilateral Instrument　　**63 CCJC 116**
SIGNED: 11 Oct 63
HEADNOTE: LONG-TERM LOAN TO ALGERIA
TOPIC: Loans and Credits

PARTIES:
　Algeria
　China People's Rep

411019　　Bilateral Protocol　　**63 CCJC 118**
SIGNED: 14 Oct 63
HEADNOTE: TRADE 1964
TOPIC: General Trade
PARTIES:
　China People's Rep
　Korea, North

411025　　Bilateral Agreement　　**63 CCJC 126**
SIGNED: 28 Oct 63
HEADNOTE: TRADE 1964
TOPIC: General Trade
PARTIES:
　China People's Rep
　Finland

411027　　Bilateral Protocol　　**63 CCJC 128**
SIGNED: 5 Nov 63
HEADNOTE: TRADE 1963-64
TOPIC: General Trade
PARTIES:
　China People's Rep
　Yugoslavia

411028　　Bilateral Agreement　　**63 CCJC 129**
SIGNED: 9 Nov 63
HEADNOTE: YELLOW & E. CHINA SEA FISHING
TOPIC: Specific Resources
PARTIES:
　China People's Rep
　Japan

411029　　Bilateral Exchange　　**63 CCJC 130**
SIGNED: 9 Nov 63
HEADNOTE: NO FISHING MILITARY ZONES
TOPIC: General Ad Hoc
PARTIES:
　China People's Rep
　Japan

411030　　Bilateral Exchange　　**63 CCJC 131**
SIGNED: 9 Nov 63
HEADNOTE: PREVENT YELLOW SEA FISH DIS-
PUTE
TOPIC: Dispute Settlement
PARTIES:
　China People's Rep
　Japan

411032　　Bilateral Agreement　　**63 CCJC 135**
SIGNED: 20 Nov 63
HEADNOTE: CURRENCY MOVEMENTS & EX-
CHANGE
TOPIC: Finance
PARTIES:
　China People's Rep
　Czechoslovakia

411033　　Bilateral Treaty　　**63 CCJC 136**
SIGNED: 22 Nov 63
HEADNOTE: BOUNDARY
TOPIC: Territory Boundary
PARTIES:
　Afghanistan
　China People's Rep

411034　　Bilateral Agreement　　**63 CCJC 138**
SIGNED: 25 Nov 63
HEADNOTE: AIR TRANSPORT
TOPIC: Air Transport
PARTIES:
　Cambodia
　China People's Rep

411037　　Bilateral Protocol　　**63 CCJC 141**
SIGNED: 26 Nov 63
HEADNOTE: CIVIL AVIATION SERVICES
TOPIC: Air Transport

PARTIES:
　Cambodia
　China People's Rep

411039　　Bilateral Protocol　　**63 CCJC 144**
SIGNED: 6 Dec 63
HEADNOTE: TRADE & PAYMENTS 1964
TOPIC: General Economic
PARTIES:
　Albania
　China People's Rep

411041　　Bilateral Agreement　　**63 CCJC 151**
SIGNED: 27 Dec 63
HEADNOTE: TRADE & PAYMENTS 1964
TOPIC: General Economic
PARTIES:
　China People's Rep
　Romania

411042　　Bilateral Protocol　　**65 CCJC 136**
SIGNED: 6 Nov 65
HEADNOTE: TRADE 1965-66
TOPIC: General Trade
PARTIES:
　Afghanistan
　China People's Rep

411044　　Bilateral Protocol　　**65 CCJC 39**
SIGNED: 24 Mar 65
HEADNOTE: BOUNDARY DEMARCATION
TOPIC: Territory Boundary
PARTIES:
　Afghanistan
　China People's Rep

411045　　Bilateral Agreement　　**65 CCJC 40**
SIGNED: 24 Mar 65
HEADNOTE: ECONOMIC & TECHNICAL COOPER-
ATION
TOPIC: Direct Aid
PARTIES:
　Afghanistan
　China People's Rep

411046　　Bilateral Agreement　　**65 CCJC 41**
SIGNED: 24 Mar 65
HEADNOTE: CULTURAL COOPERATION
TOPIC: Culture
PARTIES:
　Afghanistan
　China People's Rep

411047　　Bilateral Instrument　　**66 CCJC 37**
SIGNED: 24 May 66
HEADNOTE: CULTURAL COOPERATION 1966
TOPIC: Culture
PARTIES:
　Afghanistan
　China People's Rep

411048　　Bilateral Protocol　　**66 CCJC 73**
SIGNED: 29 Jul 66
HEADNOTE: ECONOMIC & TECHNICAL COOPER-
ATION
TOPIC: General Economic
PARTIES:
　Afghanistan
　China People's Rep

411049　　Bilateral Protocol　　**66 CCJC 105**
SIGNED: 28 Dec 66
HEADNOTE: TRADE 1966-67
TOPIC: General Trade
PARTIES:
　Afghanistan
　China People's Rep

411050　　Bilateral Agreement　　**64 CCJC 3**
SIGNED: 2 Jan 64
HEADNOTE: PUBLIC HEALTH WORK COOPER-
ATION
TOPIC: Sanitation

PARTIES:
Albania
China People's Rep

411051   Bilateral Agreement   **64 CCJC 34**
SIGNED: 5 Mar 64
HEADNOTE: AGRICULTURAL COOPERATION
TOPIC: Health/Educ/Welfare
PARTIES:
Albania
China People's Rep

411052   Bilateral Instrument   **65 CCJC 72**
SIGNED: 3 Jun 65
HEADNOTE: CULTURAL COOPERATION 1965
TOPIC: Culture
PARTIES:
Algeria
China People's Rep

411053   Bilateral Agreement   **65 CCJC 75**
SIGNED: 8 Jun 65
HEADNOTE: PRC LOAN TO ALBANIA
TOPIC: Loans and Credits
PARTIES:
Albania
China People's Rep

411054   Bilateral Agreement   **65 CCJC 76**
SIGNED: 8 Jun 65
HEADNOTE: TRADE & PAYMENTS 1966-70
TOPIC: General Economic
PARTIES:
Albania
China People's Rep

411055   Bilateral Protocol   **65 CCJC 77**
SIGNED: 8 Jun 65
HEADNOTE: ECONOMIC COOPERATION
TOPIC: General Economic
PARTIES:
Albania
China People's Rep

411056   Bilateral Protocol   **65 CCJC 131**
SIGNED: 6 Oct 65
HEADNOTE: SCIENTIFIC & TECHNICAL COOPER-
ATION
TOPIC: Tech Assistance
PARTIES:
Albania
China People's Rep

411057   Bilateral Protocol   **66 CCJC 27**
SIGNED: 4 May 66
HEADNOTE: SHIPPING
TOPIC: Water Transport
PARTIES:
Albania
China People's Rep

411060   Bilateral Agreement   **64 CCJC 48**
SIGNED: 14 Apr 64
HEADNOTE: RADIO & TV BROADCAST COOPER-
ATION
TOPIC: Mass Media
PARTIES:
Algeria
China People's Rep

411063   Bilateral Agreement   **64 CCJC 118**
SIGNED: 19 Sep 64
HEADNOTE: TRADE
TOPIC: General Trade
PARTIES:
Algeria
China People's Rep

411064   Bilateral Agreement   **64 CCJC 119**
SIGNED: 19 Sep 64
HEADNOTE: PAYMENTS
TOPIC: Finance

PARTIES:
Algeria
China People's Rep

411068   Bilateral Agreement   **64 CCJC 187**
SIGNED: 25 Dec 64
HEADNOTE: SCIENTIFIC & TECHNICAL COOPER-
ATION
TOPIC: Scientific Project
PARTIES:
Algeria
China People's Rep

411069   Bilateral Instrument   **65 CCJC 6**
SIGNED: 14 Jan 65
HEADNOTE: FILM PURCHASE FROM PRC
TOPIC: Commodity Trade
PARTIES:
Algeria
China People's Rep

411070   Bilateral Instrument   **65 CCJC 26**
SIGNED: 12 Mar 65
HEADNOTE: CULTURAL COOPERATION 1965-66
TOPIC: Culture
PARTIES:
Albania
China People's Rep

411071   Bilateral Protocol   **65 CCJC 34**
SIGNED: 22 Mar 65
HEADNOTE: SHIPPING
TOPIC: General Transport
PARTIES:
Albania
China People's Rep

411072   Bilateral Protocol   **65 CCJC 140**
SIGNED: 12 Nov 65
HEADNOTE: TRADE & PAYMENTS 1965
TOPIC: General Trade
PARTIES:
Albania
China People's Rep

411073   Bilateral Instrument   **66 CCJC 38**
SIGNED: 24 May 66
HEADNOTE: SCIENCE ACADEMY COOPERATION
1966-67
TOPIC: Scientific Project
PARTIES:
Albania
China People's Rep

411074   Bilateral Agreement   **66 CCJC 86**
SIGNED: 20 Oct 66
HEADNOTE: PRC OIL INDUSTRY LOAN
TOPIC: Loans and Credits
PARTIES:
Albania
China People's Rep

411075   Bilateral Protocol   **66 CCJC 96**
SIGNED: 21 Nov 66
HEADNOTE: TRADE & PAYMENTS 1967
TOPIC: General Economic
PARTIES:
Albania
China People's Rep

411076   Bilateral Protocol   **66 CCJC 102**
SIGNED: 30 Nov 66
HEADNOTE: SCIENTIFIC & TECHNICAL COOPER-
ATION
TOPIC: Tech Assistance
PARTIES:
Albania
China People's Rep

411077   Bilateral Instrument   **67 CCJC 14**
SIGNED: 24 Apr 67
HEADNOTE: CULTURAL COOPERATION 1967-68
TOPIC: Culture

PARTIES:
Albania
China People's Rep

411078   Bilateral Protocol   **67 CCJC 22**
SIGNED: 28 May 67
HEADNOTE: SHIPPING
TOPIC: Water Transport
PARTIES:
Albania
China People's Rep

411079   Bilateral Agreement   **67 CCJC 23**
SIGNED: 23 Jun 67
HEADNOTE: ECONOMIC & TECHNICAL COOPER-
ATION
TOPIC: Direct Aid
PARTIES:
Albania
China People's Rep

411080   Bilateral Agreement   **64 CCJC 175**
SIGNED: 7 Dec 64
HEADNOTE: PROMOTE ECONOMIC RELATIONS
TOPIC: General Economic
PARTIES:
Austria
China People's Rep

411081   Bilateral Protocol   **65 CCJC 137**
SIGNED: 9 Nov 65
HEADNOTE: SCIENTIFIC & TECHNICAL COOPER-
ATION
TOPIC: Scientific Project
PARTIES:
Bulgaria
China People's Rep

411082   Bilateral Instrument   **66 CCJC 62**
SIGNED: 1 Jul 66
HEADNOTE: CULTURAL COOPERATION 1966
TOPIC: Culture
PARTIES:
Bulgaria
China People's Rep

411084   Bilateral Agreement   **64 CCJC 46**
SIGNED: 14 Apr 64
HEADNOTE: TRADE & PAYMENTS 1964
TOPIC: General Economic
PARTIES:
Bulgaria
China People's Rep

411086   Bilateral Agreement   **64 CCJC 148**
SIGNED: 22 Oct 64
HEADNOTE: TRADE & PAYMENTS
TOPIC: General Economic
PARTIES:
Burundi
China People's Rep

411088   Bilateral Agreement   **64 CCJC 180**
SIGNED: 12 Dec 64
HEADNOTE: TRADE & PAYMENTS 1965
TOPIC: General Economic
PARTIES:
Bulgaria
China People's Rep

411089   Bilateral Protocol   **65 CCJC 9**
SIGNED: 26 Jan 65
HEADNOTE: BURMESE RICE SALE 1965
TOPIC: Commodity Trade
PARTIES:
Burma
China People's Rep

411090   Bilateral Instrument   **65 CCJC 65**
SIGNED: 13 May 65
HEADNOTE: CULTURAL COOPERATION 1965
TOPIC: Culture

PARTIES:
Bulgaria
China People's Rep

411091   Bilateral Agreement   **66 CCJC 7**
SIGNED: 16 Mar 66
HEADNOTE: TRADE & PAYMENTS 1966
TOPIC: General Economic
PARTIES:
Bulgaria
China People's Rep

411092   Bilateral Agreement   **67 CCJC 3**
SIGNED: 31 Jan 67
HEADNOTE: TRADE & PAYMENTS 1967
TOPIC: General Economic
PARTIES:
Bulgaria
China People's Rep

411093   Bilateral Protocol   **67 CCJC 9**
SIGNED: 27 Feb 67
HEADNOTE: SCIENTIFIC & TECHNICAL COOPER-
ATION
TOPIC: Scientific Project
PARTIES:
Bulgaria
China People's Rep

411095   Bilateral Treaty   **64 CCJC 135**
SIGNED: 2 Oct 64
HEADNOTE: FRIENDSHIP
TOPIC: General Amity
PARTIES:
China People's Rep
Congo (Brazzaville)

411096   Bilateral Agreement   **64 CCJC 136**
SIGNED: 2 Oct 64
HEADNOTE: MARITIME TRANSPORT
TOPIC: Water Transport
PARTIES:
China People's Rep
Congo (Brazzaville)

411100   Bilateral Protocol   **65 CCJC 14**
SIGNED: 6 Feb 65
HEADNOTE: ECONOMIC & TECHNICAL COOPER-
ATION
TOPIC: Direct Aid
PARTIES:
China People's Rep
Congo (Brazzaville)

411101   Bilateral Agreement   **65 CCJC 53**
SIGNED: 8 Apr 65
HEADNOTE: TRADE & PAYMENTS 1965
TOPIC: General Economic
PARTIES:
China People's Rep
Czechoslovakia

411102   Bilateral Protocol   **65 CCJC 147**
SIGNED: 1 Dec 65
HEADNOTE: PRC RICE FOR CEYLONESE RUBBER
TOPIC: Commodity Trade
PARTIES:
Ceylon (Sri Lanka)
China People's Rep

411103   Bilateral Agreement   **66 CCJC 3**
SIGNED: 4 Feb 66
HEADNOTE: TRADE & PAYMENTS 1966
TOPIC: General Economic
PARTIES:
China People's Rep
Czechoslovakia

411104   Bilateral Agreement   **66 CCJC 67**
SIGNED: 6 Jul 66
HEADNOTE: SCIENTIFIC & TECHNICAL COOPER-
ATION
TOPIC: Tech Assistance

PARTIES:
China People's Rep
Cuba

411106   Bilateral Protocol   **64 CCJC 9**
SIGNED: 15 Jan 64
HEADNOTE: TRADE & PAYMENTS 1964
TOPIC: General Economic
PARTIES:
China People's Rep
Cuba

411113   Bilateral Agreement   **64 CCJC 100**
SIGNED: 23 Jul 64
HEADNOTE: TRADE & PAYMENTS
TOPIC: General Economic
PARTIES:
China People's Rep
Congo (Brazzaville)

411114   Bilateral Protocol   **64 CCJC 108**
SIGNED: 11 Aug 64
HEADNOTE: ECONOMIC COOPERATION
TOPIC: General Economic
PARTIES:
China People's Rep
Cuba

411116   Bilateral Agreement   **64 CCJC 128**
SIGNED: 29 Sep 64
HEADNOTE: ECONOMIC & TECHNICAL COOPER-
ATION
TOPIC: Direct Aid
PARTIES:
China People's Rep
Central Afri Rep

411117   Bilateral Agreement   **64 CCJC 129**
SIGNED: 29 Sep 64
HEADNOTE: CULTURAL COOPERATION
TOPIC: Culture
PARTIES:
China People's Rep
Central Afri Rep

411118   Bilateral Agreement   **64 CCJC 130**
SIGNED: 29 Sep 64
HEADNOTE: TRADE & PAYMENTS
TOPIC: General Economic
PARTIES:
China People's Rep
Central Afri Rep

411119   Bilateral Protocol   **64 CCJC 150**
SIGNED: 24 Oct 64
HEADNOTE: TRADE 1965
TOPIC: General Trade
PARTIES:
Ceylon (Sri Lanka)
China People's Rep

411124   Bilateral Agreement   **64 CCJC 189**
SIGNED: 31 Dec 64
HEADNOTE: TRADE 1965-70
TOPIC: General Trade
PARTIES:
China People's Rep
Cuba

411125   Bilateral Protocol   **65 CCJC 7**
SIGNED: 14 Jan 65
HEADNOTE: ECONOMIC & TECHNICAL COOPER-
ATION
TOPIC: Direct Aid
PARTIES:
China People's Rep
Central Afri Rep

411126   Bilateral Exchange   **65 CCJC 27**
SIGNED: 15 Mar 65
HEADNOTE: PRC AID FOR CEYLON BUILDINGS
TOPIC: Direct Aid

PARTIES:
Ceylon (Sri Lanka)
China People's Rep

411127   Bilateral Agreement   **65 CCJC 35**
SIGNED: 22 Mar 65
HEADNOTE: SCIENTIFIC & CULTURAL COOP
TOPIC: Health/Educ/Welfare
PARTIES:
Cambodia
China People's Rep

411128   Bilateral Instrument   **65 CCJC 42**
SIGNED: 24 Mar 65
HEADNOTE: SCIENCE ACADEMY COOPERATION
1964-65
TOPIC: Scientific Project
PARTIES:
China People's Rep
Czechoslovakia

411129   Bilateral Agreement   **65 CCJC 64**
SIGNED: 12 May 65
HEADNOTE: NEWS SERVICE EXCHANGES
TOPIC: Mass Media
PARTIES:
China People's Rep
Congo (Brazzaville)

411130   Bilateral Protocol   **65 CCJC 68**
SIGNED: 21 May 65
HEADNOTE: SCIENTIFIC & TECHNICAL COOPER-
ATION 1965
TOPIC: Tech Assistance
PARTIES:
China People's Rep
Cuba

411131   Bilateral Protocol   **65 CCJC 83**
SIGNED: 13 Jun 65
HEADNOTE: ECONOMIC & TECHNICAL COOPER-
ATION
TOPIC: Direct Aid
PARTIES:
China People's Rep
Congo (Brazzaville)

411132   Bilateral Instrument   **65 CCJC 84**
SIGNED: 18 Jun 65
HEADNOTE: CULTURAL COOPERATION 1965
TOPIC: Culture
PARTIES:
China People's Rep
Czechoslovakia

411133   Bilateral Protocol   **65 CCJC 91**
SIGNED: 13 Jul 65
HEADNOTE: ROLLING STOCK TO CEYLON
TOPIC: Direct Aid
PARTIES:
Ceylon (Sri Lanka)
China People's Rep

411134   Bilateral Instrument   **65 CCJC 106**
SIGNED: 13 Aug 65
HEADNOTE: CULTURAL COOPERATION 1965
TOPIC: Culture
PARTIES:
China People's Rep
Congo (Brazzaville)

411135   Bilateral Agreement   **65 CCJC 119**
SIGNED: 16 Sep 65
HEADNOTE: NEWS AGENCY COOPERATION
TOPIC: Mass Media
PARTIES:
Cambodia
China People's Rep

411136   Bilateral Protocol   **65 CCJC 132**
SIGNED: 12 Oct 65
HEADNOTE: COMMODITY TRADE 1966
TOPIC: General Trade

PARTIES:
Ceylon (Sri Lanka)
China People's Rep

411137   Bilateral Protocol   **65 CCJC 133**
SIGNED: 26 Oct 65
HEADNOTE: SCIENTIFIC & TECHNICAL COOPER-
ATION
TOPIC: Scientific Project
PARTIES:
China People's Rep
Czechoslovakia

411138   Bilateral Instrument   **65 CCJC 160**
SIGNED: 23 Dec 65
HEADNOTE: SCIENCE ACADEMY COOPERATION
1966-67
TOPIC: Scientific Project
PARTIES:
China People's Rep
Czechoslovakia

411139   Bilateral Protocol   **65 CCJC 161**
SIGNED: 29 Dec 65
HEADNOTE: CULTURAL COOPERATION 1966-67
TOPIC: Culture
PARTIES:
China People's Rep
Cuba

411140   Bilateral Instrument   **66 CCJC 12**
SIGNED: 31 Mar 66
HEADNOTE: CULTURAL & SCIENTIFIC COOPER-
ATION 1966
TOPIC: Health/Educ/Welfare
PARTIES:
Cambodia
China People's Rep

411141   Bilateral Instrument   **66 CCJC 16**
SIGNED: 14 Apr 66
HEADNOTE: CULTURAL COOPERATION 1966
TOPIC: Culture
PARTIES:
China People's Rep
Congo (Brazzaville)

411142   Bilateral Agreement   **66 CCJC 22**
SIGNED: 29 Apr 66
HEADNOTE: ECONOMIC & CULTURAL COOPER-
ATION
TOPIC: General Economic
PARTIES:
Cambodia
China People's Rep

411143   Bilateral Instrument   **66 CCJC 32**
SIGNED: 11 May 66
HEADNOTE: CULTURAL COOPERATION 1966
TOPIC: Culture
PARTIES:
China People's Rep
Czechoslovakia

411144   Bilateral Protocol   **66 CCJC 39**
SIGNED: 26 May 66
HEADNOTE: TRADE 1966
TOPIC: General Trade
PARTIES:
China People's Rep
Cuba

411145   Bilateral Instrument   **66 CCJC 40**
SIGNED: 27 May 66
HEADNOTE: SCIENCE ACADEMY COOPERATION
1966-67
TOPIC: Scientific Project
PARTIES:
China People's Rep
Cuba

411146   Bilateral Protocol   **66 CCJC 90**
SIGNED: 28 Oct 66

HEADNOTE: SCIENTIFIC & TECHNICAL COOPER-
ATION
TOPIC: Scientific Project
PARTIES:
China People's Rep
Czechoslovakia

411147   Bilateral Protocol   **66 CCJC 100**
SIGNED: 29 Nov 66
HEADNOTE: TRADE 1967
TOPIC: General Trade
PARTIES:
Ceylon (Sri Lanka)
China People's Rep

411148   Bilateral Instrument   **66 CCJC 101**
SIGNED: 29 Nov 66
HEADNOTE: RICE & RUBBER TRADE 1967
TOPIC: Commodity Trade
PARTIES:
Ceylon (Sri Lanka)
China People's Rep

411149   Bilateral Protocol   **67 CCJC 11**
SIGNED: 21 Mar 67
HEADNOTE: TRADE 1967
TOPIC: General Trade
PARTIES:
China People's Rep
Cuba

411150   Bilateral Instrument   **65 CCJC 126**
SIGNED: 1 Oct 65
HEADNOTE: CULTURAL EXCHANGE 1965-66
TOPIC: Culture
PARTIES:
China People's Rep
France

411151   Bilateral Agreement   **66 CCJC 43**
SIGNED: 1 Jun 66
HEADNOTE: AIR COMMUNICATIONS
TOPIC: Air Transport
PARTIES:
China People's Rep
France

411152   Bilateral Agreement   **65 CCJC 43**
SIGNED: 24 Mar 65
HEADNOTE: TRADE 1965
TOPIC: General Trade
PARTIES:
China People's Rep
Finland

411153   Bilateral Agreement   **65 CCJC 145**
SIGNED: 23 Nov 65
HEADNOTE: TRADE 1966
TOPIC: General Trade
PARTIES:
China People's Rep
Finland

411154   Bilateral Protocol   **66 CCJC 71**
SIGNED: 25 Jul 66
HEADNOTE: CIVIL AVIATION TECHNICAL COOP-
ERATION
TOPIC: Air Transport
PARTIES:
China People's Rep
France

411155   Bilateral Exchange   **67 CCJC 2**
SIGNED: 26 Jan 67
HEADNOTE: TRADEMARK REGISTRATION
TOPIC: Patents/Copyrights
PARTIES:
China People's Rep
Finland

411156   Bilateral Agreement   **67 CCJC 16**
SIGNED: 25 Apr 67
HEADNOTE: TRADE 1967
TOPIC: General Trade

PARTIES:
China People's Rep
Finland

411157   Bilateral Protocol   **64 CCJC 4**
SIGNED: 7 Jan 64
HEADNOTE: TRADE 1964
TOPIC: General Trade
PARTIES:
China People's Rep
Guinea

411158   Bilateral Protocol   **64 CCJC 24**
SIGNED: 5 Feb 64
HEADNOTE: TRADE 1964
TOPIC: General Trade
PARTIES:
China People's Rep
Ghana

411160   Bilateral Agreement   **64 CCJC 106**
SIGNED: 1 Aug 64
HEADNOTE: TRADE & PAYMENTS 1964
TOPIC: General Economic
PARTIES:
China People's Rep
Germany, East

411161   Bilateral Agreement   **64 CCJC 107**
SIGNED: 5 Aug 64
HEADNOTE: RADIO BROADCAST COOPERATION
TOPIC: Mass Media
PARTIES:
China People's Rep
Guinea

411163   Bilateral Protocol   **64 CCJC 174**
SIGNED: 3 Dec 64
HEADNOTE: TRADE 1965
TOPIC: General Trade
PARTIES:
China People's Rep
Ghana

411164   Bilateral Instrument   **65 CCJC 59**
SIGNED: 3 May 65
HEADNOTE: CULTURAL COOPERATION 1965
TOPIC: Culture
PARTIES:
China People's Rep
Germany, East

411165   Bilateral Instrument   **65 CCJC 74**
SIGNED: 5 Jun 65
HEADNOTE: CULTURAL COOPERATION 1965
TOPIC: Culture
PARTIES:
China People's Rep
Guinea

411166   Bilateral Protocol   **65 CCJC 154**
SIGNED: 5 Aug 65
HEADNOTE: PRC MILITARY EXPERTS TO GHANA
TOPIC: Milit Assistance
PARTIES:
China People's Rep
Ghana

411167   Bilateral Instrument   **65 CCJC 127**
SIGNED: 2 Oct 65
HEADNOTE: NEWSREEL & FILM EXCHANGES
TOPIC: Culture
PARTIES:
China People's Rep
Guinea

411168   Bilateral Protocol   **66 CCJC 2**
SIGNED: 1 Feb 66
HEADNOTE: TRADE 1966
TOPIC: General Trade
PARTIES:
China People's Rep
Guinea

411169   Bilateral Agreement   **66 CCJC 46**
SIGNED: 2 Jun 66
HEADNOTE: NEWS AGENCY EXCHANGE
TOPIC: Scientific Project
PARTIES:
   China People's Rep
   Guinea

411170   Bilateral Protocol   **66 CCJC 65**
SIGNED: 4 Jul 66
HEADNOTE: SCIENTIFIC & TECHNICAL COOPER-
   ATION
TOPIC: Scientific Project
PARTIES:
   China People's Rep
   Germany, East

411179   Bilateral Agreement   **65 CCJC 20**
SIGNED: 19 Feb 65
HEADNOTE: TRADE & PAYMENTS 1965
TOPIC: General Economic
PARTIES:
   China People's Rep
   Germany, East

411180   Bilateral Agreement   **65 CCJC 67**
SIGNED: 19 May 65
HEADNOTE: SCIENCE ACADEMY COOPERATION
TOPIC: Scientific Project
PARTIES:
   China People's Rep
   Ghana

411181   Bilateral Agreement   **65 CCJC 94**
SIGNED: 15 Jul 65
HEADNOTE: STUDENT EXCHANGE & RESEARCH
TOPIC: Education
PARTIES:
   China People's Rep
   Germany, East

411182   Bilateral Agreement   **65 CCJC 114**
SIGNED: 14 Sep 65
HEADNOTE: POSTAL SERVICES
TOPIC: Postal Service
PARTIES:
   China People's Rep
   Guinea

411183   Bilateral Agreement   **65 CCJC 115**
SIGNED: 14 Sep 65
HEADNOTE: ESTABLISH   TELECOMMUNICA-
   TIONS
TOPIC: Telecommunications
PARTIES:
   China People's Rep
   Guinea

411184   Bilateral Protocol   **65 CCJC 146**
SIGNED: 22 Nov 65
HEADNOTE: SCIENTIFIC & TECHNICAL COOPER-
   ATION
TOPIC: Scientific Project
PARTIES:
   China People's Rep
   Germany, East

411185   Bilateral Agreement   **66 CCJC 10**
SIGNED: 25 Mar 66
HEADNOTE: TRADE & PAYMENTS 1966
TOPIC: General Economic
PARTIES:
   China People's Rep
   Germany, East

411186   Bilateral Instrument   **66 CCJC 24**
SIGNED: 30 Apr 66
HEADNOTE: CULTURAL COOPERATION 1966
TOPIC: Culture
PARTIES:
   China People's Rep
   Guinea

411187   Bilateral Instrument   **66 CCJC 70**
SIGNED: 22 Jul 66
HEADNOTE: CULTURAL COOPERATION 1966
TOPIC: Culture
PARTIES:
   China People's Rep
   Germany, East

411188   Bilateral Agreement   **66 CCJC 92**
SIGNED: 16 Nov 66
HEADNOTE: ECONOMIC & TECHNICAL COOPER-
   ATION
TOPIC: General Economic
PARTIES:
   China People's Rep
   Guinea

411189   Bilateral Protocol   **66 CCJC 93**
SIGNED: 16 Nov 66
HEADNOTE: ECONOMIC & TECHNICAL AID
TOPIC: Direct Aid
PARTIES:
   China People's Rep
   Guinea

411190   Bilateral Agreement   **·66 CCJC 94**
SIGNED: 16 Nov 66
HEADNOTE: PRC COMMERCIAL LOAN
TOPIC: Loans and Credits
PARTIES:
   China People's Rep
   Guinea

411191   Bilateral Protocol   **66 CCJC 95**
SIGNED: 16 Nov 66
HEADNOTE: TRADE 1967
TOPIC: General Trade
PARTIES:
   China People's Rep
   Guinea

411192   Bilateral Agreement   **67 CCJC 13**
SIGNED: 14 Apr 67
HEADNOTE: TRADE & PAYMENTS 1967
TOPIC: General Economic
PARTIES:
   China People's Rep
   Germany, East

411193   Bilateral Instrument   **65 CCJC 73**
SIGNED: 5 Jun 65
HEADNOTE: CULTURAL COOPERATION 1965
TOPIC: Culture
PARTIES:
   China People's Rep
   Hungary

411194   Bilateral Protocol   **66 CCJC 76**
SIGNED: 9 Aug 66
HEADNOTE: SCIENTIFIC & TECHNICAL COOPER-
   ATION
TOPIC: Scientific Project
PARTIES:
   China People's Rep
   Hungary

411195   Bilateral Agreement   **64 CCJC 20**
SIGNED: 31 Jan 64
HEADNOTE: RADIO & TV BROADCAST COOPER-
   ATION
TOPIC: Mass Media
PARTIES:
   China People's Rep
   Hungary

411197   Bilateral Agreement   **64 CCJC 42**
SIGNED: 28 Mar 64
HEADNOTE: TRADE & PAYMENTS 1964
TOPIC: General Economic
PARTIES:
   China People's Rep
   Hungary

411198   Bilateral Agreement   **65 CCJC 46**
SIGNED: 26 Mar 65
HEADNOTE: TRADE & PAYMENTS 1965
TOPIC: General Economic
PARTIES:
   China People's Rep
   Hungary

411199   Bilateral Protocol   **65 CCJC 71**
SIGNED: 28 May 65
HEADNOTE: SCIENTIFIC & TECHNICAL COOPER-
   ATION
TOPIC: Scientific Project
PARTIES:
   China People's Rep
   Hungary

411200   Bilateral Agreement   **66 CCJC 5**
SIGNED: 20 Feb 66
HEADNOTE: TRADE & PAYMENTS 1966
TOPIC: General Economic
PARTIES:
   China People's Rep
   Hungary

411201   Bilateral Instrument   **66 CCJC 69**
SIGNED: 20 Jul 66
HEADNOTE: CULTURAL COOPERATION 1966
TOPIC: Culture
PARTIES:
   China People's Rep
   Hungary

411202   Bilateral Agreement   **67 CCJC 25**
SIGNED: 22 Jun 67
HEADNOTE: TRADE & PAYMENTS 1967
TOPIC: General Economic
PARTIES:
   China People's Rep
   Hungary

411203   Bilateral Agreement   **64 CCJC 161**
SIGNED: 6 Nov 64
HEADNOTE: AIR COMMUNICATIONS
TOPIC: Air Transport
PARTIES:
   China People's Rep
   Indonesia

411204   Bilateral Instrument   **66 CCJC 48**
SIGNED: 4 Jun 66
HEADNOTE: CULTURAL COOPERATION 1966-67
TOPIC: Culture
PARTIES:
   China People's Rep
   Iraq

411205   Bilateral Protocol   **66 CCJC 49**
SIGNED: 4 Jun 66
HEADNOTE: RADIO & TV BROADCAST COOPER-
   ATION
TOPIC: Mass Media
PARTIES:
   China People's Rep
   Iraq

411207   Bilateral Agreement   **64 CCJC 123**
SIGNED: 23 Sep 64
HEADNOTE: TRADE
TOPIC: General Trade
PARTIES:
   China People's Rep
   Iraq

411209   Bilateral Agreement   **65 CCJC 4**
SIGNED: 12 Jan 65
HEADNOTE: TOURIST COOPERATION
TOPIC: Visas
PARTIES:
   China People's Rep
   Indonesia

411210   Bilateral Agreement   **65 CCJC 11**
SIGNED: 28 Jan 65

HEADNOTE: ECONOMIC & TECHNICAL COOPER-
ATION
TOPIC: Direct Aid
PARTIES:
  China People's Rep
  Indonesia

411211   Bilateral Agreement   **65 CCJC 12**
SIGNED: 28 Jan 65
HEADNOTE: CREDIT
TOPIC: Loans and Credits
PARTIES:
  China People's Rep
  Indonesia

411212   Bilateral Agreement   **65 CCJC 28**
SIGNED: 16 Mar 65
HEADNOTE: SCIENTIFIC & TECHNICAL COOPER-
ATION
TOPIC: Tech Assistance
PARTIES:
  China People's Rep
  Indonesia

411213   Bilateral Instrument   **65 CCJC 100**
SIGNED: 24 Jul 65
HEADNOTE: MARITIME TRANSPORT
TOPIC: Water Transport
PARTIES:
  China People's Rep
  Indonesia

411214   Bilateral Protocol   **65 CCJC 117**
SIGNED: 14 Sep 65
HEADNOTE: NEWLY EMERGING FORCES HALL
TOPIC: Non-IBRD Project
PARTIES:
  China People's Rep
  Indonesia

411215   Bilateral Agreement   **65 CCJC 122**
SIGNED: 30 Sep 65
HEADNOTE: ECONOMIC & TECHNICAL COOPER-
ATION
TOPIC: Direct Aid
PARTIES:
  China People's Rep
  Indonesia

411216   Bilateral Agreement   **65 CCJC 123**
SIGNED: 30 Sep 65
HEADNOTE: TRADE
TOPIC: General Trade
PARTIES:
  China People's Rep
  Indonesia

411217   Bilateral Agreement   **65 CCJC 124**
SIGNED: 30 Sep 65
HEADNOTE: PAYMENTS
TOPIC: Finance
PARTIES:
  China People's Rep
  Indonesia

411218   Bilateral Agreement   **65 CCJC 104**
SIGNED: 5 Aug 65
HEADNOTE: FARMING TECHNICAL EXCHANGE
TOPIC: Specific Resources
PARTIES:
  China People's Rep
  Japan

411219   Bilateral Agreement   **65 CCJC 156**
SIGNED: 17 Dec 65
HEADNOTE: YELLOW & E. CHINA SEA FISHING
TOPIC: Specific Resources
PARTIES:
  China People's Rep
  Japan

411221   Bilateral Protocol   **65 CCJC 135**
SIGNED: 1 Nov 65

HEADNOTE: SCIENTIFIC & TECHNICAL COOPER-
ATION
TOPIC: Scientific Project
PARTIES:
  China People's Rep
  Korea, North

411222   Bilateral Agreement   **65 CCJC 138**
SIGNED: 9 Nov 65
HEADNOTE: PUBLIC HEALTH WORK COOPER-
ATION
TOPIC: Sanitation
PARTIES:
  China People's Rep
  Korea, North

411223   Bilateral Instrument   **65 CCJC 150**
SIGNED: 2 Dec 65
HEADNOTE: RIVER NAVIGATION
TOPIC: Water Transport
PARTIES:
  China People's Rep
  Korea, North

411224   Bilateral Agreement   **66 CCJC 44**
SIGNED: 1 Jun 66
HEADNOTE: ANIMAL DISEASE CONTROL
TOPIC: Sanitation
PARTIES:
  China People's Rep
  Korea, North

411225   Bilateral Protocol   **66 CCJC 66**
SIGNED: 5 Jul 66
HEADNOTE: SCIENTIFIC & TECHNICAL COOPER-
ATION
TOPIC: Tech Assistance
PARTIES:
  China People's Rep
  Korea, North

411226   Bilateral Protocol   **66 CCJC 103**
SIGNED: 3 Dec 66
HEADNOTE: TRADE 1967
TOPIC: General Trade
PARTIES:
  China People's Rep
  Korea, North

411229   Bilateral Agreement   **64 CCJC 64**
SIGNED: 10 May 64
HEADNOTE: ECONOMIC & TECHNICAL COOPER-
ATION
TOPIC: Direct Aid
PARTIES:
  China People's Rep
  Kenya

411232   Bilateral Protocol   **64 CCJC 126**
SIGNED: 24 Sep 64
HEADNOTE: TRADE 1965
TOPIC: General Trade
PARTIES:
  China People's Rep
  Korea, North

411237   Bilateral Agreement   **64 CCJC 188**
SIGNED: 27 Dec 64
HEADNOTE: RADIO & TV BROADCAST COOPER-
ATION
TOPIC: Mass Media
PARTIES:
  China People's Rep
  Korea, North

411238   Bilateral Instrument   **65 CCJC 85**
SIGNED: 18 Jun 65
HEADNOTE: FILM PURCHASES & EXHIBITIONS
TOPIC: Commodity Trade
PARTIES:
  China People's Rep
  Korea, North

411239   Bilateral Instrument   **65 CCJC 102**
SIGNED: 30 Jul 65
HEADNOTE: SCIENCE ACADEMY COOPERATION
1965
TOPIC: Culture
PARTIES:
  China People's Rep
  Korea, North

411240   Bilateral Protocol   **65 CCJC 144**
SIGNED: 18 Nov 65
HEADNOTE: BORDER RAILWAY
TOPIC: Land Transport
PARTIES:
  China People's Rep
  Korea, North

411241   Bilateral Protocol   **65 CCJC 154**
SIGNED: 14 Dec 65
HEADNOTE: TRADE 1966
TOPIC: General Trade
PARTIES:
  China People's Rep
  Korea, North

411242   Bilateral Instrument   **66 CCJC 6**
SIGNED: 25 Feb 66
HEADNOTE: CULTURAL COOPERATION 1966-67
TOPIC: Culture
PARTIES:
  China People's Rep
  Korea, North

411243   Bilateral Instrument   **66 CCJC 74**
SIGNED: 30 Jul 66
HEADNOTE: SCIENCE ACADEMY COOPERATION
1966-67
TOPIC: Direct Aid
PARTIES:
  China People's Rep
  Korea, North

411244   Bilateral Agreement   **66 CCJC 106**
SIGNED: 30 Dec 66
HEADNOTE: RADIO & TV BROADCAST COOPER-
ATION
TOPIC: Mass Media
PARTIES:
  China People's Rep
  Korea, North

411246   Bilateral Treaty   **64 CCJC 157**
SIGNED: 3 Nov 64
HEADNOTE: FRIENDSHIP
TOPIC: General Amity
PARTIES:
  China People's Rep
  Mali

411249   Bilateral Instrument   **65 CCJC 80**
SIGNED: 9 Jun 65
HEADNOTE: CULTURAL COOPERATION 1965
TOPIC: Culture
PARTIES:
  China People's Rep
  Mongolia

411250   Bilateral Agreement   **66 CCJC 51**
SIGNED: 9 Jun 66
HEADNOTE: PRC LOANS TO MALI
TOPIC: Loans and Credits
PARTIES:
  China People's Rep
  Mali

411252   Bilateral Protocol   **64 CCJC 13**
SIGNED: 20 Jan 64
HEADNOTE: TRADE 1964
TOPIC: General Trade
PARTIES:
  China People's Rep
  Mongolia

411255   Bilateral Protocol   **64 CCJC 90**
SIGNED: 30 Jun 64
HEADNOTE: BOUNDARY DEMARCATION
TOPIC: Territory Boundary
PARTIES:
  China People's Rep
  Mongolia

411257   Bilateral Protocol   **65 CCJC 30**
SIGNED: 17 Mar 65
HEADNOTE: PRC AID SEGOU TEXTILE COMBINE
TOPIC: Direct Aid
PARTIES:
  China People's Rep
  Mali

411258   Bilateral Protocol   **65 CCJC 38**
SIGNED: 24 Mar 65
HEADNOTE: TRADE 1965
TOPIC: General Trade
PARTIES:
  China People's Rep
  Mongolia

411259   Bilateral Instrument   **65 CCJC 54**
SIGNED: 17 Apr 65
HEADNOTE: CULTURAL COOPERATION 1965
TOPIC: Culture
PARTIES:
  China People's Rep
  Mali

411260   Bilateral Instrument   **65 CCJC 95**
SIGNED: 15 Jul 65
HEADNOTE: PRC AID MALI TEXTILE PLANT
TOPIC: Specific Property
PARTIES:
  China People's Rep
  Mali

411261   Bilateral Protocol   **66 CCJC 11**
SIGNED: 28 Mar 66
HEADNOTE: TRADE 1966
TOPIC: General Trade
PARTIES:
  China People's Rep
  Mongolia

411262   Bilateral Instrument   **66 CCJC 33**
SIGNED: 13 May 66
HEADNOTE: CULTURAL COOPERATION 1966
TOPIC: Culture
PARTIES:
  China People's Rep
  Mali

411263   Bilateral Protocol   **66 CCJC 42**
SIGNED: 30 May 66
HEADNOTE: SCIENTIFIC & TECHNICAL COOPER-
ATION
TOPIC: Tech Assistance
PARTIES:
  China People's Rep
  Mongolia

411264   Bilateral Instrument   **66 CCJC 77**
SIGNED: 13 Aug 66
HEADNOTE: PRC TECHNICAL AID
TOPIC: Tech Assistance
PARTIES:
  China People's Rep
  Malagasy

411265   Bilateral Instrument   **66 CCJC 82**
SIGNED: 29 Sep 66
HEADNOTE: CULTURAL COOPERATION 1966
TOPIC: Culture
PARTIES:
  China People's Rep
  Mongolia

411266   Bilateral Agreement   **67 CCJC 5**
SIGNED: 16 Feb 67
HEADNOTE: TRADE

TOPIC: General Trade
PARTIES:
  China People's Rep
  Mauritania

411267   Bilateral Agreement   **67 CCJC 6**
SIGNED: 16 Feb 67
HEADNOTE: ECONOMIC & TECHNICAL COOPER-
ATION
TOPIC: Direct Aid
PARTIES:
  China People's Rep
  Mauritania

411268   Bilateral Agreement   **67 CCJC 7**
SIGNED: 16 Feb 67
HEADNOTE: CULTURAL COOPERATION
TOPIC: Culture
PARTIES:
  China People's Rep
  Mauritania

411269   Bilateral Agreement   **67 CCJC 30**
SIGNED: 14 Aug 67
HEADNOTE: PRC AID TO MALI
TOPIC: Direct Aid
PARTIES:
  China People's Rep
  Mali

411272   Bilateral Instrument   **65 CCJC 111**
SIGNED: 3 Sep 65
HEADNOTE: CULTURAL COOPERATION 1965
TOPIC: Culture
PARTIES:
  China People's Rep
  Nepal

411273   Bilateral Agreement   **66 CCJC 26**
SIGNED: 2 May 66
HEADNOTE: TIBET-NEPAL TRADE
TOPIC: General Trade
PARTIES:
  China People's Rep
  Nepal

411276   Bilateral Agreement   **64 CCJC 147**
SIGNED: 11 Oct 64
HEADNOTE: CULTURAL COOPERATION
TOPIC: Culture
PARTIES:
  China People's Rep
  Nepal

411277   Bilateral Agreement   **65 CCJC 8**
SIGNED: 21 Jan 65
HEADNOTE: DIRECT POSTAL EXCHANGE
TOPIC: Postal Service
PARTIES:
  China People's Rep
  Nepal

411278   Bilateral Protocol   **65 CCJC 109**
SIGNED: 29 Aug 65
HEADNOTE: PRC AID NEPAL HIGHWAY
TOPIC: Non-IBRD Project
PARTIES:
  China People's Rep
  Nepal

411279   Bilateral Instrument   **66 CCJC 23**
SIGNED: 30 Apr 66
HEADNOTE: CULTURAL EXCHANGE 1966-67
TOPIC: Culture
PARTIES:
  China People's Rep
  Norway

411280   Bilateral Exchange   **66 CCJC 85**
SIGNED: 18 Oct 66
HEADNOTE: PRC ECONOMIC AID
TOPIC: Direct Aid

PARTIES:
  China People's Rep
  Nepal

411281   Bilateral Agreement   **66 CCJC 104**
SIGNED: 21 Dec 66
HEADNOTE: ECONOMIC & TECHNICAL COOPER-
ATION
TOPIC: Direct Aid
PARTIES:
  China People's Rep
  Nepal

411282   Bilateral Instrument   **67 CCJC 10**
SIGNED: 14 Mar 67
HEADNOTE: PRC RICE TO NEPAL
TOPIC: Direct Aid
PARTIES:
  China People's Rep
  Nepal

411283   Bilateral Protocol   **67 CCJC 20**
SIGNED: 25 May 67
HEADNOTE: PRC AID NEPAL POWER STATION
TOPIC: Non-IBRD Project
PARTIES:
  China People's Rep
  Nepal

411284   Bilateral Agreement   **67 CCJC 21**
SIGNED: 28 May 67
HEADNOTE: PRC AID KODA HIGHWAY
TOPIC: Non-IBRD Project
PARTIES:
  China People's Rep
  Nepal

411287   Bilateral Instrument   **65 CCJC 62**
SIGNED: 5 May 65
HEADNOTE: CULTURAL COOPERATION 1965
TOPIC: Culture
PARTIES:
  China People's Rep
  Poland

411288   Bilateral Agreement   **65 CCJC 134**
SIGNED: 1 Nov 65
HEADNOTE: PRC ECONOMIC AID
TOPIC: Direct Aid
PARTIES:
  China People's Rep
  Pakistan

411289   Bilateral Instrument   **66 CCJC 45**
SIGNED: 1 Jun 66
HEADNOTE: CULTURAL COOPERATION 1966-67
TOPIC: Culture
PARTIES:
  China People's Rep
  Pakistan

411290   Bilateral Agreement   **66 CCJC 64**
SIGNED: 4 Jul 66
HEADNOTE: BARTER
TOPIC: General Trade
PARTIES:
  China People's Rep
  Pakistan

411295   Bilateral Agreement   **65 CCJC 19**
SIGNED: 18 Feb 65
HEADNOTE: PRC LOAN & TECHNICAL AID
TOPIC: Direct Aid
PARTIES:
  China People's Rep
  Pakistan

411296   Bilateral Agreement   **65 CCJC 29**
SIGNED: 16 Mar 65
HEADNOTE: TRADE & PAYMENTS 1965
TOPIC: General Economic
PARTIES:
  China People's Rep
  Poland

411297　Bilateral Protocol　**65 CCJC 44**
SIGNED: 26 Mar 65
HEADNOTE: BORDER DEMARCATION & CONTROL
TOPIC: Territory Boundary
PARTIES:
　China People's Rep
　Pakistan

411298　Bilateral Agreement　**65 CCJC 45**
SIGNED: 26 Mar 65
HEADNOTE: CULTURAL COOPERATION
TOPIC: Culture
PARTIES:
　China People's Rep
　Pakistan

411299　Bilateral Protocol　**65 CCJC 56**
SIGNED: 26 Apr 65
HEADNOTE: SCIENTIFIC & TECHNICAL COOPER-
　ATION
TOPIC: Scientific Project
PARTIES:
　China People's Rep
　Poland

411300　Bilateral Instrument　**65 CCJC 155**
SIGNED: 15 Dec 65
HEADNOTE: SCIENCE ACADEMY COOPERATION
　1965-66
TOPIC: Scientific Project
PARTIES:
　China People's Rep
　Poland

411301　Bilateral Agreement　**66 CCJC 9**
SIGNED: 22 Mar 66
HEADNOTE: TRADE & PAYMENTS 1966
TOPIC: General Economic
PARTIES:
　China People's Rep
　Poland

411302　Bilateral Protocol　**66 CCJC 54**
SIGNED: 20 Jun 66
HEADNOTE: SCIENTIFIC & TECHNICAL COOPER-
　ATION
TOPIC: Scientific Project
PARTIES:
　China People's Rep
　Poland

411303　Bilateral Protocol　**66 CCJC 56**
SIGNED: 23 Jun 66
HEADNOTE: INDUSTRIAL PLANT AID BY PRC
TOPIC: Direct Aid
PARTIES:
　China People's Rep
　Pakistan

411304　Bilateral Instrument　**66 CCJC 57**
SIGNED: 24 Jun 66
HEADNOTE: CULTURAL COOPERATION 1966
TOPIC: Culture
PARTIES:
　China People's Rep
　Poland

411305　Bilateral Agreement　**66 CCJC 87**
SIGNED: 21 Oct 66
HEADNOTE: MARITIME TRANSPORT
TOPIC: Water Transport
PARTIES:
　China People's Rep
　Pakistan

411306　Bilateral Instrument　**67 CCJC 1**
SIGNED: 17 Jan 67
HEADNOTE: PRC SUPPLY OF GRAIN
TOPIC: Direct Aid
PARTIES:
　China People's Rep
　Pakistan

411307　Bilateral Agreement　**67 CCJC 26**
SIGNED: 30 Jun 67
HEADNOTE: TRADE & PAYMENTS 1967
TOPIC: General Economic
PARTIES:
　China People's Rep
　Poland

411308　Bilateral Instrument　**67 CCJC 34**
SIGNED: 14 Sep 67
HEADNOTE: CULTURAL COOPERATION 1967-68
TOPIC: Culture
PARTIES:
　China People's Rep
　Pakistan

411310　Bilateral Agreement　**64 CCJC 140**
SIGNED: 3 Oct 64
HEADNOTE: RADIO & TV BROADCAST COOPER-
　ATION
TOPIC: Mass Media
PARTIES:
　China People's Rep
　Romania

411312　Bilateral Instrument　**65 CCJC 149**
SIGNED: 1 Dec 65
HEADNOTE: SCIENCE ACADEMY COOPERATION
　1965-66
TOPIC: Scientific Project
PARTIES:
　China People's Rep
　Romania

411314　Bilateral Protocol　**65 CCJC 66**
SIGNED: 15 May 65
HEADNOTE: SCIENTIFIC & TECHNICAL COOPER-
　ATION
TOPIC: Scientific Project
PARTIES:
　China People's Rep
　Romania

411315　Bilateral Agreement　**65 CCJC 70**
SIGNED: 27 May 65
HEADNOTE: CULTURAL COOPERATION
TOPIC: Culture
PARTIES:
　China People's Rep
　Romania

411316　Bilateral Agreement　**65 CCJC 159**
SIGNED: 21 Dec 65
HEADNOTE: BARTER & PAYMENTS 1966
TOPIC: General Trade
PARTIES:
　China People's Rep
　Romania

411317　Bilateral Instrument　**66 CCJC 4**
SIGNED: 11 Feb 66
HEADNOTE: CULTURAL COOPERATION 1966-67
TOPIC: Culture
PARTIES:
　China People's Rep
　Romania

411318　Bilateral Protocol　**66 CCJC 75**
SIGNED: 31 Jul 66
HEADNOTE: SCIENTIFIC & TECHNICAL COOPER-
　ATION
TOPIC: Scientific Project
PARTIES:
　China People's Rep
　Romania

411319　Bilateral Agreement　**67 CCJC 4**
SIGNED: 14 Feb 67
HEADNOTE: TRADE & PAYMENTS 1967
TOPIC: General Economic
PARTIES:
　China People's Rep
　Romania

411322　Bilateral Protocol　**65 CCJC 130**
SIGNED: 6 Oct 65
HEADNOTE: RADIO & TV BROADCAST COOPER-
　ATION
TOPIC: Mass Media
PARTIES:
　China People's Rep
　Syria

411323　Bilateral Agreement　**65 CCJC 31**
SIGNED: 18 Mar 65
HEADNOTE: CULTURAL COOPERATION
TOPIC: Culture
PARTIES:
　China People's Rep
　Syria

411324　Bilateral Instrument　**65 CCJC 107**
SIGNED: 17 Aug 65
HEADNOTE: CULTURAL COOPERATION 1965
TOPIC: Culture
PARTIES:
　China People's Rep
　Somalia

411325　Bilateral Instrument　**66 CCJC 19**
SIGNED: 20 Apr 66
HEADNOTE: CULTURAL COOPERATION 1966-67
TOPIC: Culture
PARTIES:
　China People's Rep
　Syria

411326　Bilateral Instrument　**66 CCJC 53**
SIGNED: 11 Jun 66
HEADNOTE: CULTURAL COOPERATION 1966
TOPIC: Culture
PARTIES:
　China People's Rep
　Somalia

411327　Bilateral Protocol　**66 CCJC 72**
SIGNED: 27 Jul 66
HEADNOTE: TRADE 1967
TOPIC: General Trade
PARTIES:
　China People's Rep
　Sudan

411328　Bilateral Exchange　**66 CCJC 88**
SIGNED: 23 Oct 66
HEADNOTE: WORK CONDITIONS PRC EXPERT
TOPIC: Non-ILO Labor
PARTIES:
　China People's Rep
　Somalia

411329　Bilateral Exchange　**67 CCJC 12**
SIGNED: 13 Apr 67
HEADNOTE: PRC AID SYRIAN COTTON MILL
TOPIC: Tech Assistance
PARTIES:
　China People's Rep
　Syria

411330　Bilateral Instrument　**67 CCJC 32**
SIGNED: 19 Aug 67
HEADNOTE: CULTURAL COOPERATION 1967-68
TOPIC: Culture
PARTIES:
　China People's Rep
　Somalia

411331　Bilateral Protocol　**65 CCJC 2**
SIGNED: 5 Jan 65
HEADNOTE: ECONOMIC & TECHNICAL COOPER-
　ATION
TOPIC: Direct Aid
PARTIES:
　China People's Rep
　Tanzania

411332　Bilateral Exchange　**65 CCJC 3**
SIGNED: 5 Jan 65

HEADNOTE: PRC TECHNICIANS TO TANZANIA
TOPIC: Tech Assistance
PARTIES:
  China People's Rep
  Tanzania

411333   Bilateral Instrument   66 CCJC 29
SIGNED: 7 May 66
HEADNOTE: CULTURAL COOPERATION 1966
TOPIC: Culture
PARTIES:
  China People's Rep
  Tanzania

411334   Bilateral Agreement   66 CCJC 50
SIGNED: 8 Jun 66
HEADNOTE: ECONOMIC COOPERATION
TOPIC: General Economic
PARTIES:
  China People's Rep
  Tanzania

411335   Bilateral Agreement   64 CCJC 85
SIGNED: 16 Jun 64
HEADNOTE: ECONOMIC & TECHNICAL COOPER-
ATION
TOPIC: Direct Aid
PARTIES:
  China People's Rep
  Tanzania

411336   Bilateral Agreement   65 CCJC 15
SIGNED: 10 Feb 65
HEADNOTE: TRADE
TOPIC: General Trade
PARTIES:
  China People's Rep
  Tanzania

411337   Bilateral Protocol   65 CCJC 16
SIGNED: 10 Feb 65
HEADNOTE: TRADE 1965-69
TOPIC: General Trade
PARTIES:
  China People's Rep
  Tanzania

411338   Bilateral Treaty   65 CCJC 21
SIGNED: 20 Feb 65
HEADNOTE: FRIENDSHIP
TOPIC: General Amity
PARTIES:
  China People's Rep
  Tanzania

411339   Bilateral Instrument   66 CCJC 21
SIGNED: 22 Apr 66
HEADNOTE: ESTABLISH JOINT STOCK MARITIME
COMPANY
TOPIC: Water Transport
PARTIES:
  China People's Rep
  Tanzania

411340   Bilateral Instrument   66 CCJC 83
SIGNED: 10 Oct 66
HEADNOTE: PRC AID TANZANIA TEXTILE MILL
TOPIC: Direct Aid
PARTIES:
  China People's Rep
  Tanzania

411341   Bilateral Agreement   65 CCJC 58
SIGNED: 2 May 65
HEADNOTE: AIR SERVICES
TOPIC: Air Transport
PARTIES:
  China People's Rep
  United Arab Rep

411342   Bilateral Agreement   66 CCJC 14
SIGNED: 4 Apr 66
HEADNOTE: CIVIL AIR TRANSPORT
TOPIC: Air Transport

PARTIES:
  China People's Rep
  USSR (Soviet Union)

411343   Bilateral Protocol   66 CCJC 28
SIGNED: 4 May 66
HEADNOTE: TRADE 1966
TOPIC: General Trade
PARTIES:
  China People's Rep
  United Arab Rep

411344   Bilateral Instrument   66 CCJC 30
SIGNED: 7 May 66
HEADNOTE: CULTURAL COOPERATION 1966-67
TOPIC: Culture
PARTIES:
  China People's Rep
  United Arab Rep

411345   Bilateral Protocol   66 CCJC 91
SIGNED: 6 Nov 66
HEADNOTE: SCIENTIFIC & TECHNICAL COOPER-
ATION
TOPIC: Scientific Project
PARTIES:
  China People's Rep
  USSR (Soviet Union)

411350   Bilateral Agreement   64 CCJC 184
SIGNED: 22 Dec 64
HEADNOTE: ECONOMIC & TECHNICAL COOPER-
ATION
TOPIC: Direct Aid
PARTIES:
  China People's Rep
  United Arab Rep

411351   Bilateral Protocol   64 CCJC 186
SIGNED: 22 Dec 64
HEADNOTE: TRADE 1965
TOPIC: General Trade
PARTIES:
  China People's Rep
  United Arab Rep

411352   Bilateral Agreement   65 CCJC 5
SIGNED: 13 Jan 65
HEADNOTE: SCIENTIFIC & TECHNICAL COOPER-
ATION
TOPIC: Tech Assistance
PARTIES:
  China People's Rep
  United Arab Rep

411353   Bilateral Agreement   65 CCJC 55
SIGNED: 21 Apr 65
HEADNOTE: ECONOMIC & TECHNICAL COOPER-
ATION
TOPIC: Direct Aid
PARTIES:
  China People's Rep
  Uganda

411354   Bilateral Protocol   65 CCJC 57
SIGNED: 29 Apr 65
HEADNOTE: TRADE 1965
TOPIC: General Trade
PARTIES:
  China People's Rep
  USSR (Soviet Union)

411355   Bilateral Instrument   65 CCJC 69
SIGNED: 25 May 65
HEADNOTE: CULTURAL COOPERATION 1965
TOPIC: Culture
PARTIES:
  China People's Rep
  USSR (Soviet Union)

411356   Bilateral Protocol   65 CCJC 82
SIGNED: 12 Jun 65
HEADNOTE: SCIENTIFIC & TECHNICAL COOPER-
ATION

TOPIC: Scientific Project
PARTIES:
  China People's Rep
  USSR (Soviet Union)

411357   Bilateral Instrument   65 CCJC 143
SIGNED: 18 Nov 65
HEADNOTE: SCIENCE ACADEMY COOPERATION
1965-66
TOPIC: Scientific Project
PARTIES:
  China People's Rep
  USSR (Soviet Union)

411358   Bilateral Protocol   66 CCJC 18
SIGNED: 19 Apr 66
HEADNOTE: TRADE 1966
TOPIC: General Trade
PARTIES:
  China People's Rep
  USSR (Soviet Union)

411359   Bilateral Instrument   66 CCJC 59
SIGNED: 27 Jun 66
HEADNOTE: CULTURAL COOPERATION 1966
TOPIC: Culture
PARTIES:
  China People's Rep
  USSR (Soviet Union)

411360   Bilateral Protocol   67 CCJC 19
SIGNED: 25 May 67
HEADNOTE: TRADE 1967
TOPIC: General Trade
PARTIES:
  China People's Rep
  United Arab Rep

411361   Bilateral Protocol   67 CCJC 27
SIGNED: 27 Jul 67
HEADNOTE: TRADE 1967
TOPIC: General Trade
PARTIES:
  China People's Rep
  USSR (Soviet Union)

411363   Bilateral Protocol   64 CCJC 36
SIGNED: 9 Mar 64
HEADNOTE: BORDER RAILWAYS
TOPIC: Land Transport
PARTIES:
  China People's Rep
  Vietnam, North

411364   Bilateral Protocol   65 CCJC 151
SIGNED: 3 Dec 65
HEADNOTE: SCIENTIFIC & TECHNICAL COOPER-
ATION
TOPIC: Tech Assistance
PARTIES:
  China People's Rep
  Vietnam, North

411365   Bilateral Agreement   65 CCJC 152
SIGNED: 5 Dec 65
HEADNOTE: PRC LOAN
TOPIC: Loans and Credits
PARTIES:
  China People's Rep
  Vietnam, North

411366   Bilateral Protocol   65 CCJC 153
SIGNED: 5 Dec 65
HEADNOTE: TRADE & PAYMENTS 1966
TOPIC: General Trade
PARTIES:
  China People's Rep
  Vietnam, North

411367   Bilateral Agreement   66 CCJC 63
SIGNED: 2 Jul 66
HEADNOTE: PRC AGRICULTURAL AID
TOPIC: Direct Aid

PARTIES:
China People's Rep
Vietnam, North

411368   Bilateral Protocol   67 CCJC 28
SIGNED: 3 Aug 67
HEADNOTE: SCIENTIFIC & TECHNICAL COOPER-
ATION
TOPIC: Direct Aid
PARTIES:
China People's Rep
Vietnam, North

411369   Bilateral Agreement   67 CCJC 29
SIGNED: 5 Aug 67
HEADNOTE: ECONOMIC & TECHNICAL AID
TOPIC: Direct Aid
PARTIES:
China People's Rep
Vietnam, North

411370   Bilateral Agreement   64 CCJC 102
SIGNED: 29 Jul 64
HEADNOTE: POSTAL SERVICES
TOPIC: Postal Service
PARTIES:
China People's Rep
Vietnam, North

411371   Bilateral Agreement   64 CCJC 103
SIGNED: 29 Jul 64
HEADNOTE: TELECOMMUNICATIONS
TOPIC: Telecommunications
PARTIES:
China People's Rep
Vietnam, North

411372   Bilateral Agreement   64 CCJC 105
SIGNED: 31 Jul 64
HEADNOTE: PUBLIC HEALTH WORK COOPER-
ATION
TOPIC: Sanitation
PARTIES:
China People's Rep
Vietnam, North

411374   Bilateral Protocol   64 CCJC 116
SIGNED: 12 Sep 64
HEADNOTE: CIVIL AVIATION
TOPIC: Air Transport
PARTIES:
China People's Rep
Vietnam, North

411376   Bilateral Instrument   65 CCJC 86
SIGNED: 19 Jun 65
HEADNOTE: CULTURAL COOPERATION 1965
TOPIC: Culture
PARTIES:
China People's Rep
Vietnam, North

411377   Bilateral Agreement   65 CCJC 90
SIGNED: 13 Jul 65
HEADNOTE: ECONOMIC & TECHNICAL AID
TOPIC: Direct Aid
PARTIES:
China People's Rep
Vietnam, North

411378   Bilateral Instrument   65 CCJC 118
SIGNED: 16 Sep 65
HEADNOTE: PUBLIC HEALTH WORK COOPER-
ATION 1966
TOPIC: Sanitation
PARTIES:
China People's Rep
Vietnam, North

411379   Bilateral Instrument   65 CCJC 142
SIGNED: 13 Nov 65
HEADNOTE: SCIENCE ACADEMY COOPERATION
1965
TOPIC: Scientific Project

PARTIES:
China People's Rep
Vietnam, North

411380   Bilateral Protocol   66 CCJC 8
SIGNED: 21 Mar 66
HEADNOTE: BORDER RAILWAY
TOPIC: Land Transport
PARTIES:
China People's Rep
Vietnam, North

411381   Bilateral Protocol   66 CCJC 20
SIGNED: 22 Apr 66
HEADNOTE: SCIENTIFIC & TECHNICAL COOPER-
ATION
TOPIC: Tech Assistance
PARTIES:
China People's Rep
Vietnam, North

411382   Bilateral Instrument   66 CCJC 41
SIGNED: 28 May 66
HEADNOTE: CULTURAL COOPERATION 1966
TOPIC: Culture
PARTIES:
China People's Rep
Vietnam, North

411383   Bilateral Instrument   66 CCJC 78
SIGNED: 21 Aug 66
HEADNOTE: SCIENCE ACADEMY COOPERATION
1966-67
TOPIC: Scientific Project
PARTIES:
China People's Rep
Vietnam, North

411384   Bilateral Agreement   66 CCJC 81
SIGNED: 29 Aug 66
HEADNOTE: ECONOMIC & TECHNICAL AID
TOPIC: Direct Aid
PARTIES:
China People's Rep
Vietnam, North

411385   Bilateral Instrument   66 CCJC 84
SIGNED: 12 Oct 66
HEADNOTE: PUBLIC HEALTH WORK COOPER-
ATION 1967
TOPIC: Sanitation
PARTIES:
China People's Rep
Vietnam, North

411386   Bilateral Agreement   66 CCJC 99
SIGNED: 23 Nov 66
HEADNOTE: TRADE & PAYMENTS 1967
TOPIC: General Economic
PARTIES:
China People's Rep
Vietnam, North

411387   Bilateral Instrument   67 CCJC 15
SIGNED: 25 Apr 67
HEADNOTE: CULTURAL COOPERATION 1967
TOPIC: Culture
PARTIES:
China People's Rep
Vietnam, North

411388   Bilateral Treaty   64 CCJC 78
SIGNED: 9 Jun 64
HEADNOTE: FRIENDSHIP
TOPIC: General Amity
PARTIES:
China People's Rep
Yemen

411390   Bilateral Agreement   64 CCJC 80
SIGNED: 9 Jun 64
HEADNOTE: CULTURAL COOPERATION
TOPIC: Culture

PARTIES:
China People's Rep
Yemen

411391   Bilateral Instrument   65 CCJC 60
SIGNED: 3 May 65
HEADNOTE: CULTURAL COOPERATION 1965
TOPIC: Culture
PARTIES:
China People's Rep
Yemen

411392   Bilateral Protocol   64 CCJC 82
SIGNED: 11 Jun 64
HEADNOTE: TRADE 1964
TOPIC: General Trade
PARTIES:
China People's Rep
Yugoslavia

411393   Bilateral Protocol   65 CCJC 37
SIGNED: 23 Mar 65
HEADNOTE: PRC AID SANAA TEXTILE FACTORY
TOPIC: Direct Aid
PARTIES:
China People's Rep
Yemen

411394   Bilateral Protocol   65 CCJC 63
SIGNED: 11 May 65
HEADNOTE: TRADE 1965
TOPIC: General Trade
PARTIES:
China People's Rep
Yugoslavia

411395   Bilateral Instrument   66 CCJC 36
SIGNED: 23 May 66
HEADNOTE: CULTURAL COOPERATION 1966-67
TOPIC: Culture
PARTIES:
China People's Rep
Yemen

411396   Bilateral Protocol   66 CCJC 52
SIGNED: 10 Jun 66
HEADNOTE: TRADE 1966
TOPIC: General Trade
PARTIES:
China People's Rep
Yugoslavia

411397   Bilateral Agreement   66 CCJC 80
SIGNED: 22 Aug 66
HEADNOTE: CULTURAL COOPERATION
TOPIC: Culture
PARTIES:
China People's Rep
Zambia

411398   Bilateral Agreement   67 CCJC 18
SIGNED: 28 Apr 67
HEADNOTE: TRADE
TOPIC: General Trade
PARTIES:
China People's Rep
Zambia

413001   Bilateral Convention   0 CTRC 43
SIGNED: 27 Mar 46
HEADNOTE: CULTURAL
TOPIC: Culture
PARTIES:
Brazil
Taiwan

413002   Bilateral Exchange   0 CTRC 160
SIGNED: 14 Dec 46
HEADNOTE: INDOCHINA AIR SERVICE
TOPIC: Air Transport
PARTIES:
Taiwan
France

413003   Bilateral Agreement   0 CTRC 174
SIGNED: 12 May 54
HEADNOTE: TRADE
TOPIC: General Trade
PARTIES:
 Taiwan
 France

413004   Bilateral Agreement   0 CTRC 178
SIGNED: 12 May 54
HEADNOTE: PAYMENT
TOPIC: Finance
PARTIES:
 Taiwan
 France

413005   Bilateral Agreement   0 CTRC 186
SIGNED: 21 Oct 55
HEADNOTE: RADIO COMMUNICATIONS
TOPIC: Telecommunications
PARTIES:
 Taiwan
 France

413006   Bilateral Exchange   0 CTRC 10
SIGNED: 24 May 58
HEADNOTE: INVENTIONS & TRADEMARKS
TOPIC: Patents/Copyrights
PARTIES:
 Taiwan
 France

413007   Bilateral Agreement   0 CTRC 202
SIGNED: 30 Nov 57
HEADNOTE: TRADE
TOPIC: General Trade
PARTIES:
 Taiwan
 Greece

413008   Bilateral Convention   0 CTRC 210
SIGNED: 14 Aug 57
HEADNOTE: CULTURAL
TOPIC: Culture
PARTIES:
 Taiwan
 Iraq

413009   Bilateral Treaty   0 CTRC 222
SIGNED: 22 Apr 49
HEADNOTE: AMITY
TOPIC: General Amity
PARTIES:
 Taiwan
 Italy

413010   Bilateral Exchange   0 CTRC 227
SIGNED: 25 Aug 49
HEADNOTE: TRADE
TOPIC: General Trade
PARTIES:
 Taiwan
 Italy

413011   Bilateral Exchange   0 CTRC 229
SIGNED: 2 Feb 57
HEADNOTE: TRADE
TOPIC: General Trade
PARTIES:
 Taiwan
 Italy

413012   Bilateral Instrument   0 CTRC 263
SIGNED: 13 Jun 53
HEADNOTE: TRADE & PAYMENTS
TOPIC: General Economic
PARTIES:
 Taiwan
 Japan

413013   Bilateral Exchange   0 CTRC 281
SIGNED: 15 Mar 55
HEADNOTE: AIR AGREEMENT
TOPIC: Air Transport

PARTIES:
 Taiwan
 Japan

413014   Bilateral Agreement   0 CTRC 33
SIGNED: 3 Mar 61
HEADNOTE: TRADE
TOPIC: General Trade
PARTIES:
 Taiwan
 Korea, South

413015   Bilateral Agreement   0 CTRC 305
SIGNED: 6 Apr 57
HEADNOTE: TRADE
TOPIC: General Trade
PARTIES:
 Taiwan
 Lebanon

413016   Bilateral Agreement   0 CTRC 317
SIGNED: 27 May 57
HEADNOTE: TRADE
TOPIC: General Trade
PARTIES:
 Taiwan
 Morocco

413017   Bilateral Agreement   0 CTRC 63
SIGNED: 28 May 47
HEADNOTE: AMENDS 1946 AID AGREEMENT
TOPIC: Direct Aid
PARTIES:
 Canada
 Taiwan

413018   Bilateral Exchange   0 CTRC 165
SIGNED: 28 Jun 47
HEADNOTE: ANNEX INDOCHINA AIR SERVICE
TOPIC: Air Transport
PARTIES:
 Taiwan
 France

413019   Bilateral Exchange   0 CTRC 169
SIGNED: 10 May 48
HEADNOTE: ANNEX INDOCHINA AIR SERVICE
TOPIC: Air Transport
PARTIES:
 Taiwan
 France

413020   Bilateral Exchange   0 CTRC 172
SIGNED: 30 Apr 49
HEADNOTE: ANNEX INDOCHINA AIR SERVICE
TOPIC: Air Transport
PARTIES:
 Taiwan
 France

413021   Bilateral Exchange   0 CTRC 183
SIGNED: 15 Apr 55
HEADNOTE: REVISION 12 MAY 54 AGREEMENT
TOPIC: General Economic
PARTIES:
 Taiwan
 France

413022   Bilateral Exchange   0 CTRC 26
SIGNED: 18 May 60
HEADNOTE: AMENDS 15 MAR 55 AGREEMENT
TOPIC: Air Transport
PARTIES:
 Taiwan
 Japan

413023   Bilateral Exchange   0 CTRC 415
SIGNED: 4 Mar 48
HEADNOTE: FINANCIAL
TOPIC: Finance
PARTIES:
 Taiwan
 Portugal

413024   Bilateral Exchange   0 CTRC 419
SIGNED: 20 May 48
HEADNOTE: ANTI-SMUGGLING
TOPIC: Customs
PARTIES:
 Taiwan
 Portugal

413025   Bilateral Convention   0 CTRC 439
SIGNED: 7 Feb 57
HEADNOTE: CULTURAL
TOPIC: Culture
PARTIES:
 Taiwan
 Spain

413026   Bilateral Treaty   0 CTRC 448
SIGNED: 5 Apr 45
HEADNOTE: RELINQUISH EXTRATERRITORIAL RIGHTS
TOPIC: Privil/Immunities
PARTIES:
 Taiwan
 Sweden

413027   Bilateral Exchange   0 CTRC 46
SIGNED: 9 Mar 60
HEADNOTE: AMENDS 29 SEP 51 AGREEMENT
TOPIC: Air Transport
PARTIES:
 Taiwan
 Thailand

413028   Bilateral Agreement   0 CTRC 645
SIGNED: 18 Oct 48
HEADNOTE: AMENDS 1948 CUSTOMS
TOPIC: Customs
PARTIES:
 Taiwan
 UK Great Britain

413029   Bilateral Exchange   0 CTRC 719
SIGNED: 29 Apr 47
HEADNOTE: AMENDS 1946 SURPLUS PROPERTY
TOPIC: Milit Assistance
PARTIES:
 Taiwan
 USA (United States)

413030   Bilateral Exchange   0 CTRC 747
SIGNED: 10 Nov 47
HEADNOTE: EDUCATIONAL EXCHANGE
TOPIC: Education
PARTIES:
 Taiwan
 USA (United States)

413031   Bilateral Exchange   0 CTRC 753
SIGNED: 30 Apr 48
HEADNOTE: CHINA AID ACT 1948
TOPIC: Direct Aid
PARTIES:
 Taiwan
 USA (United States)

413032   Bilateral Exchange   0 CTRC 767
SIGNED: 3 Jul 48
HEADNOTE: MOST FAVORED NATION
TOPIC: Mostfavored Nation
PARTIES:
 Taiwan
 USA (United States)

413033   Bilateral Exchange   0 CTRC 770
SIGNED: 27 Mar 49
HEADNOTE: AMENDS 1948 AID ACT
TOPIC: Direct Aid
PARTIES:
 Taiwan
 USA (United States)

413034   Bilateral Exchange   0 CTRC 772
SIGNED: 26 Jan 50
HEADNOTE: AMENDS 1948 AID ACT

TOPIC: Direct Aid
PARTIES:
Taiwan
USA (United States)

413035   Bilateral Exchange   0 CTRC 783
SIGNED: 27 Jun 49
HEADNOTE: MODIFIES JCCR ESTABLISHMENT
TOPIC: Tech Assistance
PARTIES:
Taiwan
USA (United States)

413036   Bilateral Agreement   0 CTRC 790
SIGNED: 27 Jan 49
HEADNOTE: AMENDS 1946 BULK SALES
TOPIC: Direct Aid
PARTIES:
Taiwan
USA (United States)

413037   Bilateral Exchange   0 CTRC 792
SIGNED: 19 Dec 50
HEADNOTE: AMENDS 1946 AIR TRANSPORT
TOPIC: Air Transport
PARTIES:
Taiwan
USA (United States)

413038   Bilateral Exchange   0 CTRC 807
SIGNED: 12 Dec 52
HEADNOTE: AMENDS 1948 RELIEF PACKAGE
TOPIC: Direct Aid
PARTIES:
Taiwan
USA (United States)

413039   Bilateral Exchange   0 CTRC 809
SIGNED: 1 Nov 52
HEADNOTE: MAAG PERSONNEL TREATMENT
TOPIC: Admin Cooperation
PARTIES:
Taiwan
USA (United States)

413040   Bilateral Agreement   0 CTRC 815
SIGNED: 4 Feb 53
HEADNOTE: ORIGIN CERTIFICATES
TOPIC: Patents/Copyrights
PARTIES:
Taiwan
USA (United States)

413041   Bilateral Exchange   0 CTRC 823
SIGNED: 26 Oct 54
HEADNOTE: AMENDS 1948 RELIEF PACKAGE
TOPIC: Direct Aid
PARTIES:
Taiwan
USA (United States)

413042   Bilateral Exchange   0 CTRC 827
SIGNED: 15 Apr 55
HEADNOTE: AMENDS 1946 AIR TRANSPORT
TOPIC: Air Transport
PARTIES:
Taiwan
USA (United States)

413043   Bilateral Agreement   0 CTRC 868
SIGNED: 14 Sep 56
HEADNOTE: LOAN
TOPIC: Loans and Credits
PARTIES:
Taiwan
USA (United States)

413044   Bilateral Exchange   0 CTRC 874
SIGNED: 27 Dec 56
HEADNOTE: US MEDICAL CENTER TAIPEI
TOPIC: Admin Cooperation
PARTIES:
Taiwan
USA (United States)

413045   Bilateral Exchange   0 CTRC 877
SIGNED: 3 May 57
HEADNOTE: REVISE 1952 INVESTMENT GUAR-
ANTEE
TOPIC: Claims and Debts
PARTIES:
Taiwan
USA (United States)

413046   Bilateral Agreement   0 CTRC 880
SIGNED: 28 Jun 57
HEADNOTE: LOAN
TOPIC: Loans and Credits
PARTIES:
Taiwan
USA (United States)

413047   Bilateral Exchange   0 CTRC 885
SIGNED: 30 Nov 57
HEADNOTE: AMENDS EDUCATIONAL EXCHANGE
TOPIC: Culture
PARTIES:
Taiwan
USA (United States)

414048   Bilateral Exchange   0 CTCY 447
SIGNED: 24 Apr 52
HEADNOTE: TRADE RELATIONS
TOPIC: General Trade
PARTIES:
Taiwan
Japan

414049   Bilateral Instrument   0 CTCY 447
SIGNED: 13 Jun 53
HEADNOTE: PAYMENTS
TOPIC: Finance
PARTIES:
Taiwan
Japan

415001   Bilateral Agreement   61 FRRT 40
SIGNED: 6 Jan 59
HEADNOTE: ECONOMIC & TECHNICAL COOPER-
ATION
TOPIC: General Aid
PARTIES:
Afghanistan
France

415002   Bilateral Agreement   62 FRRT 4
SIGNED: 15 May 61
HEADNOTE: AIR TRANSPORT
TOPIC: Air Transport
PARTIES:
Afghanistan
France

415004   Bilateral Treaty   65 FRRT 41
SIGNED: 14 Dec 63
HEADNOTE: COMMERCE & NAVIGATION
TOPIC: General Amity
PARTIES:
Albania
France

415007   Bilateral Convention   62 FRRT 27
SIGNED: 28 Aug 62
HEADNOTE: JOINT OIL DEVELOPMENT
TOPIC: Specific Resources
PARTIES:
Algeria
France

415008   Bilateral Protocol   62 FRRT 30
SIGNED: 24 Sep 62
HEADNOTE: TECHNICAL COOPERATION
TOPIC: Tech Assistance
PARTIES:
Algeria
France

415009   Bilateral Protocol   63 FRRT 8
SIGNED: 17 Dec 62

HEADNOTE: PUBLIC UTILITIES TECHNICAL AID
TOPIC: Tech Assistance
PARTIES:
Algeria
France

415010   Bilateral Protocol   63 FRRT 13
SIGNED: 31 Dec 62
HEADNOTE: FINANCIAL TECHNICAL AID
TOPIC: Tech Assistance
PARTIES:
Algeria
France

415011   Bilateral Convention   63 FRRT 11
SIGNED: 16 Jan 63
HEADNOTE: CAPITAL AID
TOPIC: Direct Aid
PARTIES:
Algeria
France

415012   Bilateral Instrument   63 FRRT 17
SIGNED: 19 Jan 63
HEADNOTE: FINANCIAL RELATIONS
TOPIC: Finance
PARTIES:
Algeria
France

415013   Bilateral Protocol   63 FRRT 12
SIGNED: 23 Jan 63
HEADNOTE: RADIO & TV COOPERATION
TOPIC: Mass Media
PARTIES:
Algeria
France

415014   Bilateral Protocol   64 FRRT 20
SIGNED: 19 Apr 63
HEADNOTE: FRENCH MEDICAL MISSION
TOPIC: Tech Assistance
PARTIES:
Algeria
France

415015   Bilateral Protocol   64 FRRT 21
SIGNED: 11 Jun 63
HEADNOTE: TECHNICAL AID
TOPIC: Tech Assistance
PARTIES:
Algeria
France

415016   Bilateral Protocol   64 FRRT 24
SIGNED: 23 Oct 63
HEADNOTE: CULTURAL & TECHNICAL COOPER-
ATION
TOPIC: Health/Educ/Welfare
PARTIES:
Algeria
France

415017   Bilateral Convention   65 FRRT 72
SIGNED: 27 Aug 64
HEADNOTE: EXTRADITION
TOPIC: Extradition
PARTIES:
Algeria
France

415018   Bilateral Agreement   65 FRRT 4
SIGNED: 16 Dec 64
HEADNOTE: EXTRADITION
TOPIC: Extradition
PARTIES:
Algeria
France

415019   Bilateral Convention   65 FRRT 50
SIGNED: 19 Jan 65
HEADNOTE: SOCIAL SECURITY
TOPIC: Non-ILO Labor

PARTIES:
Algeria
France

415021   Bilateral Agreement   **65 FRRT 107**
SIGNED: 28 Jul 65
HEADNOTE: ALGERIAN PETROLEUM INSTITUTE
TOPIC: Non-IBRD Project
PARTIES:
Algeria
France

415022   Bilateral Agreement   **65 FRRT 106**
SIGNED: 29 Jul 65
HEADNOTE: OIL INDUSTRY DEVELOPMENT
TOPIC: Specific Resources
PARTIES:
Algeria
France

415023   Bilateral Convention   **66 FRRT 34**
SIGNED: 8 Apr 66
HEADNOTE: CULTURAL & TECHNICAL COOPER-
ATION
TOPIC: Health/Educ/Welfare
PARTIES:
Algeria
France

415041   Bilateral Agreement   **62 FRRT 23**
SIGNED: 27 Apr 62
HEADNOTE: APPLIES 18 APR 58 BORDER CON-
VENTION
TOPIC: Admin Cooperation
PARTIES:
France
Germany, West

415043   Bilateral Agreement   **63 FRRT 69**
SIGNED: 13 Aug 63
HEADNOTE: MODIFIES 18 APR 58 BORDER CON-
VENTION
TOPIC: Admin Cooperation
PARTIES:
France
Germany, West

415045   Bilateral Agreement   **65 FRRT 79**
SIGNED: 22 Mar 65
HEADNOTE: MOTION PICTURE COOPERATION
TOPIC: Culture
PARTIES:
France
Germany, West

415046   Bilateral Agreement   **66 FRRT 24**
SIGNED: 27 Jun 66
HEADNOTE: MODIFIES 22 MAR 65
TOPIC: Culture
PARTIES:
France
Germany, West

415047   Bilateral Agreement   **58 FRRT 28**
SIGNED: 22 Aug 58
HEADNOTE: FINANCIAL TRANSFERS
TOPIC: Finance
PARTIES:
France
Germany, West

415048   Bilateral Agreement   **64 FRRT 73**
SIGNED: 5 Nov 64
HEADNOTE: GUARANTEE FRENCH PROPERTY
TOPIC: Claims and Debts
PARTIES:
France
United Arab Rep

415051   Bilateral Agreement   **65 FRRT 21**
SIGNED: 7 Jul 63
HEADNOTE: CULTURAL & TECHNICAL COOPER-
ATION
TOPIC: Health/Educ/Welfare

PARTIES:
France
Saudi Arabia

415054   Bilateral Agreement   **65 FRRT 44**
SIGNED: 17 Jan 63
HEADNOTE: MOTION PICTURE COOPERATION
TOPIC: Culture
PARTIES:
Argentina
France

415056   Bilateral Agreement   **60 FRRT 19**
SIGNED: 26 Jun 58
HEADNOTE: TREATIES IN FORCE
TOPIC: Admin Cooperation
PARTIES:
Austria
France

415057   Bilateral Agreement   **60 FRRT 21**
SIGNED: 1 Oct 59
HEADNOTE: PATENTS ROYALTIES
TOPIC: Patents/Copyrights
PARTIES:
Austria
France

415058   Bilateral Agreement   **65 FRRT 43**
SIGNED: 19 Jul 63
HEADNOTE: MOTION PICTURE COOPERATION
TOPIC: Culture
PARTIES:
Austria
France

415059   Bilateral Agreement   **64 FRRT 46**
SIGNED: 5 May 64
HEADNOTE: COPYRIGHT EXTENSION
TOPIC: Patents/Copyrights
PARTIES:
Austria
France

415062   Bilateral Treaty   **59 FRRT 39**
SIGNED: 6 Sep 57
HEADNOTE: DEVELOP BORDER COAL MINES
TOPIC: Specific Resources
PARTIES:
Belgium
France

415064   Bilateral Agreement   **60 FRRT 20**
SIGNED: 31 May 58
HEADNOTE: PATENTS FEE EXEMPTION
TOPIC: Patents/Copyrights
PARTIES:
Belgium
France

415066   Bilateral Agreement   **65 FRRT 34**
SIGNED: 20 Sep 62
HEADNOTE: MOTION PICTURE COOPERATION
TOPIC: Culture
PARTIES:
Belgium
France

415067   Bilateral Convention   **64 FRRT 61**
SIGNED: 12 Oct 62
HEADNOTE: MILITARY SERVICE
TOPIC: Milit Servic/Citiz
PARTIES:
Belgium
France

415076   Bilateral Agreement   **60 FRRT 58**
SIGNED: 6 Dec 48
HEADNOTE: CULTURAL
TOPIC: Culture
PARTIES:
Brazil
France

415079   Bilateral Agreement   **66 FRRT 10**
SIGNED: 26 Oct 65
HEADNOTE: CREDIT REPAYMENT
TOPIC: Finance
PARTIES:
Brazil
France

415086   Bilateral Agreement   **59 FRRT 4**
SIGNED: 28 Jul 55
HEADNOTE: FINANCIAL SETTLEMENT
TOPIC: Finance
PARTIES:
Bulgaria
France

415087   Bilateral Agreement   **65 FRRT 81**
SIGNED: 4 Aug 65
HEADNOTE: AIR TRANSPORT
TOPIC: Air Transport
PARTIES:
Bulgaria
France

415093   Bilateral Agreement   **65 FRRT 18**
SIGNED: 11 Feb 63
HEADNOTE: CULTURAL & TECHNICAL COOPER-
ATION
TOPIC: Health/Educ/Welfare
PARTIES:
Burundi
France

415095   Bilateral Protocol   **59 FRRT 7**
SIGNED: 29 Aug 53
HEADNOTE: RECOGNITION
TOPIC: Recognition
PARTIES:
Cambodia
France

415096   Bilateral Convention   **59 FRRT 7**
SIGNED: 9 Sep 53
HEADNOTE: JUDICIAL MATTERS
TOPIC: Admin Cooperation
PARTIES:
Cambodia
France

415097   Bilateral Agreement   **64 FRRT 14**
SIGNED: 15 Jan 64
HEADNOTE: AIR TRANSPORT
TOPIC: Air Transport
PARTIES:
Cambodia
France

415099   Bilateral Treaty   **61 FRRT 29**
SIGNED: 13 Nov 60
HEADNOTE: GENERAL RELATIONS
TOPIC: General Amity
PARTIES:
Cameroon
France

415100   Bilateral Agreement   **63 FRRT 53**
SIGNED: 16 Jan 63
HEADNOTE: HIGHER EDUCATION COOPERATION
TOPIC: Education
PARTIES:
Cameroon
France

415101   Bilateral Agreement   **63 FRRT 15**
SIGNED: 16 Jan 63
HEADNOTE: CUSTOMS AGREEMENT
TOPIC: Customs
PARTIES:
Cameroon
France

415102   Bilateral Convention   **65 FRRT 48**
SIGNED: 5 May 63
HEADNOTE: RADIO BROADCAST COOPERATION

TOPIC: Mass Media
PARTIES:
  Cameroon
  France

415103   Bilateral Convention   **64 FRRT 71**
SIGNED: 10 Aug 63
HEADNOTE: PROPERTY TRANSFER
TOPIC: Specific Property
PARTIES:
  Cameroon
  France

415105   Bilateral Agreement   **65 FRRT 37**
SIGNED: 15 Jan 64
HEADNOTE: CANADIAN TRAINEES IN FRANCE
TOPIC: Education
PARTIES:
  Canada
  France

415106   Bilateral Agreement   **65 FRRT 40**
SIGNED: 27 Feb 65
HEADNOTE: QUEBEC EDUCATIONAL EXCHANGE
TOPIC: Education
PARTIES:
  Canada
  France

415110   Bilateral Agreement   **60 FRRT 50**
SIGNED: 12 Jul 60
HEADNOTE: RECOGNITION
TOPIC: Recognition
PARTIES:
  Central Afri Rep
  France

415111   Bilateral Agreement   **60 FRRT 76**
SIGNED: 13 Aug 60
HEADNOTE: COMMUNAUTE PARTICIPATION
TOPIC: General Amity
PARTIES:
  Central Afri Rep
  France

415112   Bilateral Protocol   **63 FRRT 19**
SIGNED: 26 Aug 61
HEADNOTE: TRANSFER PROPERTY
TOPIC: Specific Property
PARTIES:
  Central Afri Rep
  France

415113   Bilateral Protocol   **63 FRRT 43**
SIGNED: 27 Mar 63
HEADNOTE: CUSTOMS AGREEMENT
TOPIC: Customs
PARTIES:
  Central Afri Rep
  France

415115   Bilateral Agreement   **60 FRRT 61**
SIGNED: 23 Nov 55
HEADNOTE: CULTURAL
TOPIC: Culture
PARTIES:
  Chile
  France

415116   Bilateral Agreement   **65 FRRT 17**
SIGNED: 14 Sep 62
HEADNOTE: SCIENTIFIC & TECHNICAL COOPER-
ATION
TOPIC: Tech Assistance
PARTIES:
  Chile
  France

415117   Bilateral Agreement   **66 FRRT 23**
SIGNED: 1 Jun 66
HEADNOTE: AIR COMMUNICATIONS
TOPIC: Air Transport

PARTIES:
  China People's Rep
  France

415119   Bilateral Convention   **62 FRRT 16**
SIGNED: 28 Apr 53
HEADNOTE: COPYRIGHT PROTECTION
TOPIC: Patents/Copyrights
PARTIES:
  Colombia
  France

415120   Bilateral Agreement   **65 FRRT 19**
SIGNED: 18 Sep 63
HEADNOTE: SCIENTIFIC & TECHNICAL COOPER-
ATION
TOPIC: Tech Assistance
PARTIES:
  Colombia
  France

415121   Bilateral Agreement   **60 FRRT 50**
SIGNED: 12 Jul 60
HEADNOTE: RECOGNITION
TOPIC: Recognition
PARTIES:
  Congo (Brazzaville)
  France

415122   Bilateral Agreement   **60 FRRT 76**
SIGNED: 15 Aug 60
HEADNOTE: MUTUAL DEFENSE & MILITARY AID
TOPIC: General Military
PARTIES:
  Congo (Brazzaville)
  France

415123   Bilateral Agreement   **63 FRRT 25**
SIGNED: 2 May 62
HEADNOTE: AIR TRANSPORT
TOPIC: Air Transport
PARTIES:
  Congo (Brazzaville)
  France

415124   Bilateral Agreement   **65 FRRT 9**
SIGNED: 18 May 62
HEADNOTE: JUDICIAL COOPERATION
TOPIC: Admin Cooperation
PARTIES:
  Congo (Brazzaville)
  France

415125   Bilateral Protocol   **63 FRRT 43**
SIGNED: 27 Mar 63
HEADNOTE: CUSTOMS AGREEMENT
TOPIC: Customs
PARTIES:
  Congo (Brazzaville)
  France

415130   Bilateral Agreement   **61 FRRT 11**
SIGNED: 1 Feb 61
HEADNOTE: TRADEMARKS
TOPIC: Patents/Copyrights
PARTIES:
  France
  Korea, South

415131   Bilateral Agreement   **64 FRRT 2**
SIGNED: 26 Apr 63
HEADNOTE: PATENTS ON INVENTIONS
TOPIC: Patents/Copyrights
PARTIES:
  France
  Korea, South

415135   Bilateral Treaty   **55 FRRT 9002**
SIGNED: 2 Jun 55
HEADNOTE: AMITY
TOPIC: General Amity
PARTIES:
  Costa Rica
  France

415136   Bilateral Agreement   **65 FRRT 32**
SIGNED: 18 Jun 64
HEADNOTE: TELECOMMUNICATIONS COOPER-
ATION
TOPIC: Telecommunications
PARTIES:
  Costa Rica
  France

415138   Bilateral Agreement   **60 FRRT 52**
SIGNED: 11 Jul 60
HEADNOTE: RECOGNITION
TOPIC: Recognition
PARTIES:
  France
  Ivory Coast

415139   Bilateral Treaty   **62 FRRT 8**
SIGNED: 24 Apr 61
HEADNOTE: TREATY OF COOPERATION
TOPIC: General Amity
PARTIES:
  France
  Ivory Coast

415140   Bilateral Protocol   **62 FRRT 37**
SIGNED: 26 Oct 61
HEADNOTE: CUSTOMS AGREEMENT
TOPIC: Customs
PARTIES:
  France
  Ivory Coast

415145   Bilateral Agreement   **60 FRRT 52**
SIGNED: 11 Jul 60
HEADNOTE: RECOGNITION
TOPIC: Recognition
PARTIES:
  Dahomey
  France

415146   Bilateral Treaty   **62 FRRT 8**
SIGNED: 24 Apr 61
HEADNOTE: TREATY OF COOPERATION
TOPIC: General Amity
PARTIES:
  Dahomey
  France

415147   Bilateral Protocol   **63 FRRT 30**
SIGNED: 28 Mar 62
HEADNOTE: PREFERENTIAL CUSTOMS COOPER-
ATION
TOPIC: Customs
PARTIES:
  Dahomey
  France

415148   Bilateral Convention   **62 FRRT 38**
SIGNED: 10 Apr 62
HEADNOTE: TRANSFER ASSETS
TOPIC: Claims and Debts
PARTIES:
  Dahomey
  France

415149   Bilateral Agreement   **64 FRRT 13**
SIGNED: 9 Dec 63
HEADNOTE: AIR TRANSPORT
TOPIC: Air Transport
PARTIES:
  Dahomey
  France

415150   Bilateral Convention   **67 FRRT 905**
SIGNED: 21 Oct 65
HEADNOTE: FISCAL CONVENTION
TOPIC: Finance
PARTIES:
  Dahomey
  France

415151   Bilateral Convention   **58 FRRT 27**
SIGNED: 8 Feb 57

HEADNOTE: INCOME TAX & DOUBLE TAXATION
TOPIC: Taxation
PARTIES:
  Denmark
  France

415155   Bilateral Agreement   59 FRRT 42
SIGNED: 20 Mar 59
HEADNOTE: COMMERCE
TOPIC: General Trade
PARTIES:
  Ecuador
  France

415156   Bilateral Agreement   65 FRRT 16
SIGNED: 13 Apr 59
HEADNOTE: TECHNICAL AID
TOPIC: Tech Assistance
PARTIES:
  Ecuador
  France

415157   Bilateral Convention   64 FRRT 38
SIGNED: 3 Feb 64
HEADNOTE: AIR TRANSPORT
TOPIC: Air Transport
PARTIES:
  Ecuador
  France

415158   Bilateral Agreement   65 FRRT 89
SIGNED: 2 Sep 65
HEADNOTE: VISA ABOLITION & TRAVEL
TOPIC: Visas
PARTIES:
  Ecuador
  France

415163   Bilateral Agreement   61 FRRT 42
SIGNED: 15 Jun 61
HEADNOTE: REGULATION OF SAILOR TRAFFIC
TOPIC: Admin Cooperation
PARTIES:
  France
  Spain

415164   Bilateral Convention   63 FRRT 68
SIGNED: 30 May 62
HEADNOTE: CUSTOMS ENFORCEMENT COOPER-
ATION
TOPIC: Customs
PARTIES:
  France
  Spain

415165   Bilateral Agreement   66 FRRT 17
SIGNED: 17 Jul 62
HEADNOTE: MOTION PICTURES
TOPIC: Culture
PARTIES:
  France
  Spain

415166   Bilateral Agreement   64 FRRT 48
SIGNED: 23 May 64
HEADNOTE: COMMERCE
TOPIC: General Trade
PARTIES:
  France
  Spain

415168   Bilateral Convention   66 FRRT 16
SIGNED: 7 Jul 65
HEADNOTE: BORDER REGULATION
TOPIC: Admin Cooperation
PARTIES:
  France
  Spain

415179   Bilateral Exchange   62 FRRT 12
SIGNED: 10 Jul 59
HEADNOTE: MILITARY PATENTS
TOPIC: Patents/Copyrights

PARTIES:
  France
  USA (United States)

415180   Bilateral Convention   68 FRRT 7
SIGNED: 18 Jul 66
HEADNOTE: CONSULAR CONVENTION
TOPIC: Consul/Citizenship
PARTIES:
  France
  USA (United States)

415183   Bilateral Treaty   60 FRRT 30
SIGNED: 12 Nov 59
HEADNOTE: DJIBOUTI-ADDIS-ABABA RAILWAY
TOPIC: Land Transport
PARTIES:
  Ethiopia
  France

415189   Bilateral Convention   59 FRRT 28
SIGNED: 25 Aug 58
HEADNOTE: DOUBLE TAXATION & INCOME TAX
TOPIC: Taxation
PARTIES:
  Finland
  France

415190   Bilateral Convention   59 FRRT 28
SIGNED: 25 Aug 58
HEADNOTE: DOUBLE TAXATION & TAX EVASION
TOPIC: Taxation
PARTIES:
  Finland
  France

415191   Bilateral Agreement   60 FRRT 51
SIGNED: 15 Jul 60
HEADNOTE: RECOGNITION
TOPIC: Recognition
PARTIES:
  France
  Gabon

415192   Bilateral Agreement   60 FRRT 77
SIGNED: 17 Aug 60
HEADNOTE: PARTICIPATE FRENCH COMMUNITY
TOPIC: General Amity
PARTIES:
  France
  Gabon

415193   Bilateral Protocol   63 FRRT 20
SIGNED: 6 Jun 61
HEADNOTE: TRANSFER PROPERTIES
TOPIC: Specific Property
PARTIES:
  France
  Gabon

415194   Bilateral Protocol   62 FRRT 39
SIGNED: 28 Sep 62
HEADNOTE: RECIPROCAL CUSTOMS PRIVILEGES
TOPIC: Customs
PARTIES:
  France
  Gabon

415195   Bilateral Convention   65 FRRT 26
SIGNED: 23 Jul 63
HEADNOTE: JUDICIAL COOPERATION & EXTRA-
DITION
TOPIC: Admin Cooperation
PARTIES:
  France
  Gabon

415196   Bilateral Agreement   64 FRRT 9
SIGNED: 2 Dec 63
HEADNOTE: AIR TRANSPORT
TOPIC: Air Transport
PARTIES:
  France
  Gabon

415200   Bilateral Agreement   65 FRRT 92
SIGNED: 3 Jun 64
HEADNOTE: TUNNEL UNDER LA MANCHE
TOPIC: General Ad Hoc
PARTIES:
  France
  UK Great Britain

415201   Bilateral Agreement   65 FRRT 105
SIGNED: 19 Nov 65
HEADNOTE: MIGRANT WORKER REGULATION
TOPIC: Non-ILO Labor
PARTIES:
  France
  UK Great Britain

415204   Bilateral Convention   59 FRRT 14
SIGNED: 19 Apr 58
HEADNOTE: SOCIAL SECURITY
TOPIC: Non-ILO Labor
PARTIES:
  France
  Greece

415207   Bilateral Agreement   60 FRRT 82
SIGNED: 26 Sep 50
HEADNOTE: CULTURAL
TOPIC: Culture
PARTIES:
  France
  Guatemala

415208   Bilateral Convention   62 FRRT 17
SIGNED: 29 Jul 61
HEADNOTE: CULTURAL
TOPIC: Culture
PARTIES:
  France
  Guinea

415209   Bilateral Agreement   63 FRRT 59
SIGNED: 21 Mar 62
HEADNOTE: AIR TRANSPORT
TOPIC: Air Transport
PARTIES:
  France
  Guinea

415210   Bilateral Agreement   63 FRRT 61
SIGNED: 22 May 63
HEADNOTE: TECHNICAL AID
TOPIC: Tech Assistance
PARTIES:
  France
  Guinea

415211   Bilateral Agreement   63 FRRT 62
SIGNED: 22 May 63
HEADNOTE: COMMERCE
TOPIC: General Trade
PARTIES:
  France
  Guinea

415214   Bilateral Agreement   60 FRRT 52
SIGNED: 11 Jul 60
HEADNOTE: RECOGNITION
TOPIC: Recognition
PARTIES:
  France
  Upper Volta

415215   Bilateral Treaty   62 FRRT 8
SIGNED: 24 Apr 61
HEADNOTE: TREATY OF COOPERATION
TOPIC: General Amity
PARTIES:
  France
  Upper Volta

415216   Bilateral Protocol   62 FRRT 42
SIGNED: 31 Mar 62
HEADNOTE: RECIPROCAL CUSTOMS PRIVILEGES
TOPIC: Customs

PARTIES:
France
Upper Volta

415217　Bilateral Agreement　**63 FRRT 2**
SIGNED: 29 May 62
HEADNOTE: AIR TRANSPORT
TOPIC: Air Transport
PARTIES:
France
Upper Volta

415219　Bilateral Convention　**60 FRRT 29**
SIGNED: 15 Aug 55
HEADNOTE: ESTABLISHMENT
TOPIC: Consul/Citizenship
PARTIES:
France
Honduras

415222　Bilateral Agreement　**60 FRRT 63**
SIGNED: 2 May 60
HEADNOTE: AIR TRANSPORT
TOPIC: Air Transport
PARTIES:
France
Hungary

415223　Bilateral Agreement　**65 FRRT 68**
SIGNED: 14 May 65
HEADNOTE: FRENCH PROPERTY CLAIMS
TOPIC: Claims and Debts
PARTIES:
France
Hungary

415229　Bilateral Agreement　**62 FRRT 33**
SIGNED: 21 Oct 54
HEADNOTE: FRENCH PROPERTY
TOPIC: Specific Property
PARTIES:
France
India

415230　Bilateral Treaty　**62 FRRT 33**
SIGNED: 28 May 56
HEADNOTE: TRANSFER FRENCH HOLDINGS
TOPIC: Specific Property
PARTIES:
France
India

415231　Bilateral Agreement　**66 FRRT 32**
SIGNED: 7 Jun 66
HEADNOTE: CULTURAL & SCIENTIFIC & TECHNI-
CAL COOPERATION
TOPIC: Health/Educ/Welfare
PARTIES:
France
India

415238　Bilateral Agreement　**86 FRRT 5009**
SIGNED: 21 Apr 60
HEADNOTE: AIR TRANSPORT
TOPIC: Air Transport
PARTIES:
France
Iran

415241　Bilateral Agreement　**66 FRRT 14**
SIGNED: 3 Feb 66
HEADNOTE: SHORT-TERM VISA ABOLITION
TOPIC: Visas
PARTIES:
France
Iran

415246　Bilateral Convention　**60 FRRT 15**
SIGNED: 6 Apr 56
HEADNOTE: BORDER REGULATION
TOPIC: Admin Cooperation
PARTIES:
France
Italy

415249　Bilateral Agreement　**65 FRRT 71**
SIGNED: 16 Jul 65
HEADNOTE: JOINT CHECKPOINT
TOPIC: Visas
PARTIES:
France
Italy

415251　Bilateral Agreement　**66 FRRT 30**
SIGNED: 3 Jun 66
HEADNOTE: TOURIST BORDER CROSSINGS
TOPIC: Visas
PARTIES:
France
Italy

415252　Bilateral Agreement　**66 FRRT 40**
SIGNED: 1 Aug 66
HEADNOTE: MOTION PICTURE COPRODUCTION
TOPIC: Culture
PARTIES:
France
Italy

415255　Bilateral Convention　**65 FRRT 75**
SIGNED: 27 Nov 64
HEADNOTE: DOUBLE TAXATION AVOIDANCE
TOPIC: Taxation
PARTIES:
France
Japan

415256　Bilateral Agreement　**65 FRRT 86**
SIGNED: 16 Jun 65
HEADNOTE: CULTURAL & TECHNICAL COOPER-
ATION
TOPIC: Health/Educ/Welfare
PARTIES:
France
Jordan

415259　Bilateral Convention　**59 FRRT 7**
SIGNED: 22 Oct 53
HEADNOTE: JUDICIAL CONVENTION
TOPIC: Admin Cooperation
PARTIES:
France
Laos

415260　Bilateral Convention　**60 FRRT 22**
SIGNED: 16 Nov 56
HEADNOTE: JUDICIAL COOPERATION
TOPIC: Admin Cooperation
PARTIES:
France
Laos

415261　Bilateral Convention　**64 FRRT 6**
SIGNED: 24 Jul 62
HEADNOTE: INCOME & ESTATE & DOUBLE TAXA-
TION
TOPIC: Taxation
PARTIES:
France
Lebanon

415269　Bilateral Exchange　**60 FRRT 45**
SIGNED: 23 Jul 56
HEADNOTE: JUDICIAL COOPERATION
TOPIC: Admin Cooperation
PARTIES:
France
Luxembourg

415270　Bilateral Convention　**60 FRRT 18**
SIGNED: 1 Apr 58
HEADNOTE: CAPITAL & INCOME & DOUBLE TAX-
ATION
TOPIC: Taxation
PARTIES:
France
Luxembourg

415272　Bilateral Agreement　**63 FRRT 9**
SIGNED: 10 Dec 62
HEADNOTE: FIRE & RESCUE SERVICE COOPER-
ATION
TOPIC: Humanitarian
PARTIES:
France
Luxembourg

415278　Bilateral Agreement　**60 FRRT 38**
SIGNED: 2 Apr 60
HEADNOTE: RECOGNITION
TOPIC: Recognition
PARTIES:
France
Malagasy

415279　Bilateral Agreement　**60 FRRT 46**
SIGNED: 27 Jun 60
HEADNOTE: COMMUNAUTE PARTICIPATION
TOPIC: General Amity
PARTIES:
France
Malagasy

415280　Bilateral Protocol　**63 FRRT 21**
SIGNED: 18 Oct 61
HEADNOTE: TRANSFER PROPERTIES
TOPIC: Specific Property
PARTIES:
France
Malagasy

415281　Bilateral Protocol　**62 FRRT 40**
SIGNED: 23 May 62
HEADNOTE: CUSTOMS PRIVILEGES
TOPIC: Customs
PARTIES:
France
Malagasy

415282　Bilateral Convention　**65 FRRT 69**
SIGNED: 29 Sep 62
HEADNOTE: DOUBLE TAXATION & FISCAL COOP-
ERATION
TOPIC: General Economic
PARTIES:
France
Malagasy

415283　Bilateral Convention　**65 FRRT 83**
SIGNED: 25 Apr 63
HEADNOTE: CONSULAR CONVENTION
TOPIC: Consul/Citizenship
PARTIES:
France
Malagasy

415284　Bilateral Convention　**63 FRRT 81**
SIGNED: 6 Jul 63
HEADNOTE: TRANSFER ASSETS
TOPIC: Claims and Debts
PARTIES:
France
Malagasy

415285　Bilateral Exchange　**64 FRRT 69**
SIGNED: 19 Jun 64
HEADNOTE: MOVEMENT OF SEAMEN
TOPIC: Visas
PARTIES:
France
Malagasy

415288　Bilateral Convention　**63 FRRT 27**
SIGNED: 22 Aug 61
HEADNOTE: TRANSFER ASSETS
TOPIC: Claims and Debts
PARTIES:
France
Mali

415289　Bilateral Agreement　**64 FRRT 49**
SIGNED: 9 Mar 62

HEADNOTE: AMITY & COOPERATION
TOPIC: General Amity
PARTIES:
 France
 Mali

415290   Bilateral Convention   63 FRRT 42
SIGNED: 8 Mar 63
HEADNOTE: TRAVEL REGULATIONS
TOPIC: Visas
PARTIES:
 France
 Mali

415293   Bilateral Agreement   68 FRRT 60
SIGNED: 14 Feb 68
HEADNOTE: CULTURAL
TOPIC: Culture
PARTIES:
 France
 Malta

415294   Bilateral Agreement   69 FRRT 50
SIGNED: 27 Mar 69
HEADNOTE: SHORT-TERM VISA ABOLITION
TOPIC: Visas
PARTIES:
 France
 Malta

415295   Bilateral Convention   60 FRRT 11
SIGNED: 6 Feb 57
HEADNOTE: TECHNICAL & ADMINISTRATIVE CO-
 OPERATION
TOPIC: Admin Cooperation
PARTIES:
 France
 Morocco

415296   Bilateral Convention   60 FRRT 4
SIGNED: 5 Oct 57
HEADNOTE: JUDICIAL COOPERATION
TOPIC: Admin Cooperation
PARTIES:
 France
 Morocco

415297   Bilateral Agreement   60 FRRT 40
SIGNED: 14 May 60
HEADNOTE: COTTON RESEARCH TECHNICAL AID
TOPIC: Non-IBRD Project
PARTIES:
 France
 Morocco

415298   Bilateral Convention   60 FRRT 80
SIGNED: 20 Sep 60
HEADNOTE: SAVINGS PROGRAM
TOPIC: Health/Educ/Welfare
PARTIES:
 France
 Morocco

415299   Bilateral Agreement   61 FRRT 52
SIGNED: 10 Mar 61
HEADNOTE: AIR TRANSPORT
TOPIC: Air Transport
PARTIES:
 France
 Morocco

415300   Bilateral Agreement   61 FRRT 38
SIGNED: 21 Jun 61
HEADNOTE: TARIFFS
TOPIC: Customs
PARTIES:
 France
 Morocco

415311   Bilateral Agreement   60 FRRT 75
SIGNED: 19 Oct 60
HEADNOTE: RECOGNITION
TOPIC: Recognition

PARTIES:
 France
 Mauritania

415312   Bilateral Treaty   62 FRRT 9
SIGNED: 19 Jun 61
HEADNOTE: TREATY OF COOPERATION
TOPIC: General Amity
PARTIES:
 France
 Mauritania

415313   Bilateral Protocol   63 FRRT 72
SIGNED: 10 May 63
HEADNOTE: TRANSFER PROPERTIES
TOPIC: Specific Property
PARTIES:
 France
 Mauritania

415314   Bilateral Convention   65 FRRT 99
SIGNED: 29 May 63
HEADNOTE: FINANCIAL AID
TOPIC: Direct Aid
PARTIES:
 France
 Mauritania

415315   Bilateral Convention   64 FRRT 8
SIGNED: 15 Jul 63
HEADNOTE: TRAVEL REGULATIONS
TOPIC: Visas
PARTIES:
 France
 Mauritania

415316   Bilateral Agreement   64 FRRT 10
SIGNED: 24 Oct 63
HEADNOTE: AIR TRANSPORT
TOPIC: Air Transport
PARTIES:
 France
 Mauritania

415318   Bilateral Protocol   65 FRRT 91
SIGNED: 16 Nov 64
HEADNOTE: PROFESSIONAL TRAINING
TOPIC: Education
PARTIES:
 France
 Mauritania

415324   Bilateral Agreement   63 FRRT 13
SIGNED: 22 Apr 65
HEADNOTE: TECHNICAL & SCIENTIFIC COOPER-
 ATION
TOPIC: Tech Assistance
PARTIES:
 France
 Mexico

415333   Bilateral Convention   63 FRRT 66
SIGNED: 18 May 63
HEADNOTE: FISCAL CONVENTION
TOPIC: Finance
PARTIES:
 France
 Monaco

415334   Bilateral Agreement   63 FRRT 77
SIGNED: 15 Oct 63
HEADNOTE: SHIPMENT OF CORPSES
TOPIC: Admin Cooperation
PARTIES:
 France
 Monaco

415335   Bilateral Agreement   64 FRRT 66
SIGNED: 31 Aug 64
HEADNOTE: TRAVEL PERMITS
TOPIC: Visas
PARTIES:
 France
 Monaco

415339   Bilateral Agreement   60 FRRT 52
SIGNED: 11 Jul 60
HEADNOTE: RECOGNITION
TOPIC: Recognition
PARTIES:
 France
 Niger

415340   Bilateral Treaty   62 FRRT 8
SIGNED: 24 Apr 61
HEADNOTE: GENERAL COOPERATION
TOPIC: General Amity
PARTIES:
 France
 Niger

415341   Bilateral Agreement   63 FRRT 1
SIGNED: 28 May 62
HEADNOTE: AIR TRANSPORT
TOPIC: Air Transport
PARTIES:
 France
 Niger

415342   Bilateral Protocol   63 FRRT 28
SIGNED: 29 Nov 62
HEADNOTE: CUSTOMS PRIVILEGES
TOPIC: Customs
PARTIES:
 France
 Niger

415343   Bilateral Convention   66 FRRT 48
SIGNED: 1 Jun 65
HEADNOTE: FISCAL CONVENTION
TOPIC: Finance
PARTIES:
 France
 Niger

415344   Bilateral Agreement   65 FRRT 90
SIGNED: 23 Sep 65
HEADNOTE: EXTRADITION
TOPIC: Extradition
PARTIES:
 France
 Niger

415348   Bilateral Agreement   65 FRRT 95
SIGNED: 28 Apr 64
HEADNOTE: AIR TRANSPORT
TOPIC: Air Transport
PARTIES:
 France
 Uganda

415352   Bilateral Convention   58 FRRT 19
SIGNED: 10 Jul 53
HEADNOTE: ESTABLISHMENT
TOPIC: Consul/Citizenship
PARTIES:
 France
 Panama

415353   Bilateral Agreement   58 FRRT 18
SIGNED: 11 Sep 56
HEADNOTE: TRADE
TOPIC: General Trade
PARTIES:
 France
 Paraguay

415354   Bilateral Agreement   63 FRRT 50
SIGNED: 5 Apr 63
HEADNOTE: TRAVEL REGULATIONS
TOPIC: Visas
PARTIES:
 France
 Paraguay

415355   Bilateral Agreement   65 FRRT 15
SIGNED: 10 Dec 63
HEADNOTE: CULTURAL & TECHNICAL COOPER-
 ATION

TOPIC: Health/Educ/Welfare
PARTIES:
  France
  Paraguay

415356   Bilateral Exchange   **63 FRRT 76**
SIGNED: 2 Dec 47
HEADNOTE: FINANCIAL
TOPIC: Finance
PARTIES:
  France
  Netherlands

415358   Bilateral Exchange   **63 FRRT 76**
SIGNED: 3 Jul 51
HEADNOTE: FINANCIAL
TOPIC: Finance
PARTIES:
  France
  Netherlands

415359   Bilateral Agreement   **61 FRRT 19**
SIGNED: 23 Apr 59
HEADNOTE: AIR TRANSPORT
TOPIC: Air Transport
PARTIES:
  France
  Peru

415362   Bilateral Agreement   **61 FRRT 20**
SIGNED: 25 Jun 60
HEADNOTE: AIR TRANSPORT
TOPIC: Air Transport
PARTIES:
  France
  Poland

415368   Bilateral Convention   **59 FRRT 16**
SIGNED: 16 Nov 57
HEADNOTE: SOCIAL SECURITY
TOPIC: Non-ILO Labor
PARTIES:
  France
  Portugal

415369   Bilateral Agreement   **59 FRRT 16**
SIGNED: 30 Oct 58
HEADNOTE: MIGRANT WORKERS
TOPIC: Non-ILO Labor
PARTIES:
  France
  Portugal

415370   Bilateral Agreement   **64 FRRT 12**
SIGNED: 31 Dec 63
HEADNOTE: MIGRANT WORKERS
TOPIC: Non-ILO Labor
PARTIES:
  France
  Portugal

415371   Bilateral Protocol   **64 FRRT 68**
SIGNED: 16 Oct 64
HEADNOTE: PROFESSIONAL TRAINING
TOPIC: Education
PARTIES:
  France
  Portugal

415372   Bilateral Agreement   **65 FRRT 25**
SIGNED: 26 Jan 65
HEADNOTE: MERCHANT SEAMEN REGULATION
TOPIC: Admin Cooperation
PARTIES:
  France
  Portugal

415375   Bilateral Instrument   **64 FRRT 64**
SIGNED: 31 Jul 64
HEADNOTE: SCIENTIFIC & TECHNICAL COOPER-
  ATION
TOPIC: Tech Assistance

PARTIES:
  France
  Romania

415376   Bilateral Agreement   **65 FRRT 46**
SIGNED: 11 Jan 65
HEADNOTE: CULTURE
TOPIC: Culture
PARTIES:
  France
  Romania

415378   Bilateral Agreement   **66 FRRT 38**
SIGNED: 22 Apr 66
HEADNOTE: MOTION PICTURE COOPERATION &
  EXCHANGE
TOPIC: Culture
PARTIES:
  France
  Romania

415381   Bilateral Agreement   **65 FRRT 20**
SIGNED: 4 Dec 62
HEADNOTE: CULTURAL & TECHNICAL COOPER-
  ATION
TOPIC: General Amity
PARTIES:
  France
  Rwanda

415384   Bilateral Agreement   **65 FRRT 58**
SIGNED: 21 May 65
HEADNOTE: MIGRANT LABOR FAMILY TREAT-
  MENT
TOPIC: Non-ILO Labor
PARTIES:
  France
  San Marino

415387   Bilateral Agreement   **65 FRRT 38**
SIGNED: 19 Feb 64
HEADNOTE: TELECOMMUNICATION
TOPIC: Telecommunications
PARTIES:
  El Salvador
  France

415388   Bilateral Agreement   **60 FRRT 47**
SIGNED: 22 Jun 60
HEADNOTE: COMMUNAUTE PARTICIPATION
TOPIC: General Amity
PARTIES:
  France
  Senegal

415389   Bilateral Exchange   **61 FRRT 22**
SIGNED: 19 Sep 60
HEADNOTE: VALIDITY MALI AGREEMENT 22 JUN
  60
TOPIC: Admin Cooperation
PARTIES:
  France
  Senegal

415390   Bilateral Agreement   **65 FRRT 28**
SIGNED: 14 Jun 62
HEADNOTE: JUDICIAL COOPERATION
TOPIC: Admin Cooperation
PARTIES:
  France
  Senegal

415391   Bilateral Convention   **63 FRRT 22**
SIGNED: 18 Sep 62
HEADNOTE: TRANSFER PROPERTIES
TOPIC: Specific Property
PARTIES:
  France
  Senegal

415392   Bilateral Protocol   **63 FRRT 55**
SIGNED: 13 Oct 62
HEADNOTE: CUSTOMS PRIVILEGES
TOPIC: Customs

PARTIES:
  France
  Senegal

415393   Bilateral Convention   **65 FRRT 51**
SIGNED: 16 Feb 63
HEADNOTE: CONSULAR CONVENTION
TOPIC: Consul/Citizenship
PARTIES:
  France
  Senegal

415394   Bilateral Convention   **65 FRRT 7**
SIGNED: 24 Apr 63
HEADNOTE: TRANSFER ASSETS
TOPIC: Claims and Debts
PARTIES:
  France
  Senegal

415395   Bilateral Convention   **64 FRRT 32**
SIGNED: 21 Jan 64
HEADNOTE: TRAVEL REGULATIONS
TOPIC: Visas
PARTIES:
  France
  Senegal

415396   Bilateral Protocol   **64 FRRT 25**
SIGNED: 21 Jan 64
HEADNOTE: PROFESSIONAL TRAINING
TOPIC: Education
PARTIES:
  France
  Senegal

415399   Bilateral Agreement   **65 FRRT 30**
SIGNED: 19 Oct 64
HEADNOTE: CULTURAL & TECHNICAL COOPER-
  ATION
TOPIC: Health/Educ/Welfare
PARTIES:
  France
  Sierra Leone

415402   Bilateral Agreement   **65 FRRT 103**
SIGNED: 13 Oct 65
HEADNOTE: MOTION PICTURE COOPERATION
TOPIC: Culture
PARTIES:
  France
  Sweden

415405   Bilateral Exchange   **66 FRRT 33**
SIGNED: 15 Jun 48
HEADNOTE: FISHING RIGHTS
TOPIC: Specific Resources
PARTIES:
  France
  Switzerland

415406   Bilateral Exchange   **58 FRRT 4**
SIGNED: 14 Oct 57
HEADNOTE: AIRLINE EMPLOYEE ID CARDS
TOPIC: Visas
PARTIES:
  France
  Switzerland

415407   Bilateral Agreement   **60 FRRT 41**
SIGNED: 12 Apr 60
HEADNOTE: REFUGEES
TOPIC: Refugees
PARTIES:
  France
  Switzerland

415408   Bilateral Agreement   **63 FRRT 34**
SIGNED: 28 Feb 63
HEADNOTE: JOINT CHECKPOINT
TOPIC: Visas
PARTIES:
  France
  Switzerland

415409   Bilateral Agreement   **63 FRRT 37**
SIGNED: 28 Feb 63
HEADNOTE: ANNEMASSE BORDER STATION
TOPIC: Visas
PARTIES:
  France
  Switzerland

415410   Bilateral Agreement   **63 FRRT 45**
SIGNED: 4 Apr 63
HEADNOTE: DIVERTED RIVER WATER RIGHTS
TOPIC: Claims and Debts
PARTIES:
  France
  Switzerland

415411   Bilateral Agreement   **63 FRRT 83**
SIGNED: 19 Sep 63
HEADNOTE: ACCOUNTING
TOPIC: Finance
PARTIES:
  France
  Switzerland

415412   Bilateral Agreement   **64 FRRT 42**
SIGNED: 27 May 64
HEADNOTE: MIGRANT WORKER REGULATIONS
TOPIC: Non-ILO Labor
PARTIES:
  France
  Switzerland

415413   Bilateral Agreement   **64 FRRT 63**
SIGNED: 28 Sep 64
HEADNOTE: GENEVA RAILWAY CHECKPOINT
TOPIC: Admin Cooperation
PARTIES:
  France
  Switzerland

415415   Bilateral Agreement   **65 FRRT 78**
SIGNED: 30 Jun 65
HEADNOTE: BORDER REGULATION
TOPIC: Admin Cooperation
PARTIES:
  France
  Switzerland

415416   Bilateral Agreement   **65 FRRT 80**
SIGNED: 24 Jul 65
HEADNOTE: NYON TRANSPORTATION ROUTE
TOPIC: General Transport
PARTIES:
  France
  Switzerland

415417   Bilateral Agreement   **65 FRRT 80**
SIGNED: 24 Jul 65
HEADNOTE: PFETTERHOUSE-BONEOL RAILWAY
TOPIC: Land Transport
PARTIES:
  France
  Switzerland

415425   Bilateral Agreement   **65 FRRT 97**
SIGNED: 28 Apr 64
HEADNOTE: AIR TRANSPORT
TOPIC: Air Transport
PARTIES:
  France
  Tanzania

415426   Bilateral Agreement   **60 FRRT 50**
SIGNED: 12 Jul 60
HEADNOTE: RECOGNITION
TOPIC: Recognition
PARTIES:
  Chad
  France

415427   Bilateral Agreement   **60 FRRT 76**
SIGNED: 11 Aug 60
HEADNOTE: COMMUNAUTE PARTICIPATION
TOPIC: General Amity

PARTIES:
  Chad
  France

415428   Bilateral Protocol   **63 FRRT 23**
SIGNED: 25 Oct 61
HEADNOTE: TRANSFER PROPERTIES
TOPIC: Specific Property
PARTIES:
  Chad
  France

415429   Bilateral Protocol   **63 FRRT 43**
SIGNED: 29 Mar 63
HEADNOTE: CUSTOMS PRIVILEGES
TOPIC: Customs
PARTIES:
  Chad
  France

415430   Bilateral Agreement   **63 FRRT 31**
SIGNED: 8 Jan 63
HEADNOTE: AIR TRANSPORT
TOPIC: Air Transport
PARTIES:
  Chad
  France

415431   Bilateral Convention   **64 FRRT 16**
SIGNED: 17 Aug 63
HEADNOTE: FINANCIAL AID
TOPIC: Direct Aid
PARTIES:
  Chad
  France

415440   Bilateral Agreement   **63 FRRT 51**
SIGNED: 2 Jun 50
HEADNOTE: FRENCH NATIONALIZED PROPERTY
TOPIC: Claims and Debts
PARTIES:
  Czechoslovakia
  France

415441   Bilateral Protocol   **64 FRRT 15**
SIGNED: 16 Jan 64
HEADNOTE: FINANCIAL DISPUTE SETTLEMENT
TOPIC: Dispute Settlement
PARTIES:
  Czechoslovakia
  France

415449   Bilateral Convention   **62 FRRT 41**
SIGNED: 9 Apr 62
HEADNOTE: FINANCIAL AID
TOPIC: Direct Aid
PARTIES:
  France
  Togo

415450   Bilateral Convention   **64 FRRT 39**
SIGNED: 10 Jul 63
HEADNOTE: DIPLOMATIC CONVENTION
TOPIC: General Amity
PARTIES:
  France
  Togo

415454   Bilateral Convention   **58 FRRT 8**
SIGNED: 9 Mar 57
HEADNOTE: JUDICIAL COOPERATION
TOPIC: General Amity
PARTIES:
  France
  Tunisia

415455   Bilateral Agreement   **60 FRRT 17**
SIGNED: 27 Oct 58
HEADNOTE: WATER TRANSPORT
TOPIC: Water Transport
PARTIES:
  France
  Tunisia

415456   Bilateral Protocol   **59 FRRT 47**
SIGNED: 15 Apr 59
HEADNOTE: CULTURAL & TECHNICAL COOPER-
  ATION
TOPIC: Health/Educ/Welfare
PARTIES:
  France
  Tunisia

415457   Bilateral Agreement   **65 FRRT 53**
SIGNED: 20 May 61
HEADNOTE: AIR TRANSPORT
TOPIC: Air Transport
PARTIES:
  France
  Tunisia

415458   Bilateral Convention   **63 FRRT 10**
SIGNED: 8 Jan 63
HEADNOTE: SAVINGS PROGRAM
TOPIC: Health/Educ/Welfare
PARTIES:
  France
  Tunisia

415459   Bilateral Agreement   **63 FRRT 32**
SIGNED: 31 Jan 63
HEADNOTE: CUSTOMS PRIVILEGES
TOPIC: Customs
PARTIES:
  France
  Tunisia

415460   Bilateral Protocol   **63 FRRT 70**
SIGNED: 9 Aug 63
HEADNOTE: PROFESSIONAL TRAINING
TOPIC: Education
PARTIES:
  France
  Tunisia

415461   Bilateral Convention   **65 FRRT 77**
SIGNED: 9 Aug 63
HEADNOTE: INVESTMENT GAURANTEES
TOPIC: Claims and Debts
PARTIES:
  France
  Tunisia

415462   Bilateral Agreement   **64 FRRT 30**
SIGNED: 29 Jan 64
HEADNOTE: TRAVEL REGULATIONS
TOPIC: Visas
PARTIES:
  France
  Tunisia

415463   Bilateral Agreement   **64 FRRT 26**
SIGNED: 29 Jan 64
HEADNOTE: TRAVEL REGULATIONS
TOPIC: Visas
PARTIES:
  France
  Tunisia

415464   Bilateral Convention   **66 FRRT 37**
SIGNED: 17 Dec 65
HEADNOTE: SOCIAL SECURITY
TOPIC: Non-ILO Labor
PARTIES:
  France
  Tunisia

415468   Bilateral Convention   **65 FRRT 57**
SIGNED: 8 Jan 65
HEADNOTE: LABOR CONVENTION
TOPIC: Non-ILO Labor
PARTIES:
  France
  Turkey

415469   Bilateral Agreement   **65 FRRT 52**
SIGNED: 23 Jul 56
HEADNOTE: MOTION PICTURE EXCHANGE

TOPIC: Culture
PARTIES:
  France
  USSR (Soviet Union)

415472   Bilateral Agreement   **65 FRRT 60**
SIGNED: 22 Mar 65
HEADNOTE: COLOR TV COOPERATION
TOPIC: Mass Media
PARTIES:
  France
  USSR (Soviet Union)

415478   Bilateral Agreement   **60 FRRT 43**
SIGNED: 9 May 60
HEADNOTE: FINANCIAL SETTLEMENT
TOPIC: Finance
PARTIES:
  France
  Uruguay

415480   Bilateral Convention   **59 FRRT 7**
SIGNED: 16 Sep 54
HEADNOTE: RECOGNITION
TOPIC: Recognition
PARTIES:
  France
  Vietnam, South

415481   Bilateral Convention   **59 FRRT 7**
SIGNED: 16 Aug 55
HEADNOTE: CITIZENSHIP
TOPIC: Consul/Citizenship
PARTIES:
  France
  Vietnam, South

415485   Bilateral Agreement   **59 FRRT 11**
SIGNED: 2 Aug 58
HEADNOTE: FRENCH ASSETS
TOPIC: Claims and Debts
PARTIES:
  France
  Yugoslavia

415486   Bilateral Agreement   **64 FRRT 31**
SIGNED: 12 Jul 63
HEADNOTE: NATIONALIZATION INDEMNITIES
TOPIC: Claims and Debts
PARTIES:
  France
  Yugoslavia

415488   Bilateral Agreement   **65 FRRT 31**
SIGNED: 19 Jun 64
HEADNOTE: CULTURE
TOPIC: Culture
PARTIES:
  France
  Yugoslavia

415489   Bilateral Agreement   **65 FRRT 88**
SIGNED: 17 Oct 64
HEADNOTE: INTERNATIONAL   TRANSPORT
ROUTES
TOPIC: General Transport
PARTIES:
  France
  Yugoslavia

415490   Bilateral Agreement   **65 FRRT 82**
SIGNED: 25 Jan 65
HEADNOTE: YUGOSLAV WORKERS IN FRANCE
TOPIC: Non-ILO Labor
PARTIES:
  France
  Yugoslavia

415498   Bilateral Agreement   **58 FRRT 32**
SIGNED: 9 Jun 58
HEADNOTE: SOCIAL SECURITY
TOPIC: Non-ILO Labor

PARTIES:
  France
  WEU (West Europe)

415499   Bilateral Agreement   **59 FRRT 40**
SIGNED: 5 Mar 59
HEADNOTE: SOCIAL SECURITY
TOPIC: Non-ILO Labor
PARTIES:
  France
  OECD (Econ Coop)

415500   Bilateral Agreement   **60 FRRT 34**
SIGNED: 21 Dec 59
HEADNOTE: SOCIAL SECURITY
TOPIC: Non-ILO Labor
PARTIES:
  Council of Europe
  France

415501   Bilateral Agreement   **65 FRRT 74**
SIGNED: 30 Jun 64
HEADNOTE: STATUS ON FRENCH TERRITORY
TOPIC: IGO Status/Immunit
PARTIES:
  France
  Eur Plant Protect

415502   Bilateral Agreement   **65 FRRT 76**
SIGNED: 1 Sep 64
HEADNOTE: STATUS ON FRENCH TERRITORY
TOPIC: IGO Status/Immunit
PARTIES:
  France
  Int Org Metrology

415503   Bilateral Agreement   **66 FRRT 35**
SIGNED: 20 Jan 65
HEADNOTE: STATUS ON FRENCH TERRITORY
TOPIC: IGO Status/Immunit
PARTIES:
  France
  Int Wine Office

415504   Bilateral Agreement   **66 FRRT 21**
SIGNED: 11 Mar 65
HEADNOTE: ROCKET ENGINE CONSTRUCTION
TOPIC: Scientific Project
PARTIES:
  France
  Eur Space Vehicle

415505   Bilateral Agreement   **66 FRRT 19**
SIGNED: 8 Oct 65
HEADNOTE: EMPLOYEE SOCIAL SECURITY
TOPIC: Non-ILO Labor
PARTIES:
  France
  Eur Space Research

415506   Bilateral Agreement   **66 FRRT 12**
SIGNED: 26 Jan 66
HEADNOTE: EMPLOYEE SOCIAL SECURITY
TOPIC: Non-ILO Labor
PARTIES:
  France
  OECD (Econ Coop)

415513   Bilateral Agreement   **66 FRRT 36**
SIGNED: 11 Jan 65
HEADNOTE: STATUS ON FRENCH TERRITORY
TOPIC: IGO Status/Immunit
PARTIES:
  Int Exhibit Bureau
  France

415515   Bilateral Agreement   **60 FRRT 2**
SIGNED: 17 Jun 52
HEADNOTE: CULTURE
TOPIC: Culture
PARTIES:
  France
  Turkey

416003   Bilateral Agreement   **67 FRJO 801**
SIGNED: 21 Aug 66
HEADNOTE: CULTURAL & TECHNICAL COOPER-
ATION
TOPIC: Health/Educ/Welfare
PARTIES:
  Afghanistan
  France

416006   Bilateral Instrument   **62 FRJO 2003**
SIGNED: 19 Mar 62
HEADNOTE: RECOGNITION
TOPIC: Recognition
PARTIES:
  Algeria
  France

416020   Bilateral Instrument   **65 FRJO 1905**
SIGNED: 19 Jan 65
HEADNOTE: SOCIAL SECURITY
TOPIC: Non-ILO Labor
PARTIES:
  Algeria
  France

416024   Bilateral Convention   **67 FRJO 3003**
SIGNED: 23 Dec 66
HEADNOTE: SAVINGS PROGRAM
TOPIC: Health/Educ/Welfare
PARTIES:
  Algeria
  France

416025   Bilateral Agreement   **67 FRJO 2809**
SIGNED: 26 Jun 67
HEADNOTE: STUDENT INSURANCE
TOPIC: Health/Educ/Welfare
PARTIES:
  Algeria
  France

416026   Bilateral Protocol   **69 FRJO 2006**
SIGNED: 8 Jul 67
HEADNOTE: ALGERIAN TECHNICAL SCHOOL
TOPIC: Non-IBRD Project
PARTIES:
  Algeria
  France

416027   Bilateral Agreement   **67 FRJO 2510**
SIGNED: 20 Jul 67
HEADNOTE: WATER TRANSPORT
TOPIC: Water Transport
PARTIES:
  Algeria
  France

416028   Bilateral Protocol   **69 FRJO 1101**
SIGNED: 26 Dec 67
HEADNOTE: AIR SAFETY
TOPIC: Air Transport
PARTIES:
  Algeria
  France

416029   Bilateral Protocol   **69 FRJO 2006**
SIGNED: 16 Mar 68
HEADNOTE: SCIENTIFIC COOPERATION
TOPIC: Tech Assistance
PARTIES:
  Algeria
  France

416030   Bilateral Exchange   **68 FRJO 1008**
SIGNED: 20 Jun 67
HEADNOTE: CIVILIAN GRAVE RELOCATION
TOPIC: General Ad Hoc
PARTIES:
  Algeria
  France

416031   Bilateral Agreement   **70 FRJO 1004**
SIGNED: 1 Oct 67
HEADNOTE: AGRICULTURAL INSTITUTE

TOPIC: Non-IBRD Project
PARTIES:
 Algeria
 France

416032 Bilateral Agreement **69 FRJO 2203**
SIGNED: 27 Dec 68
HEADNOTE: REGULATION MIGRANT WORKERS
TOPIC: Non-ILO Labor
PARTIES:
 Algeria
 France

416033 Bilateral Agreement **51 FRJO 706**
SIGNED: 10 Jul 50
HEADNOTE: INTERN EXCHANGE
TOPIC: Education
PARTIES:
 France
 Germany, West

416034 Bilateral Agreement **54 FRJO 1909**
SIGNED: 31 Aug 54
HEADNOTE: REVIVAL OLD TREATIES
TOPIC: Admin Cooperation
PARTIES:
 France
 Germany, West

416039 Bilateral Agreement **63 FRJO 33**
SIGNED: 27 Jul 61
HEADNOTE: CLAIMS ADJUSTMENT
TOPIC: Claims and Debts
PARTIES:
 France
 Germany, West

416040 Bilateral Agreement **62 FRJO 13**
SIGNED: 19 Jan 62
HEADNOTE: KEHL-STRASBOURG BORDER REGU-
LATION
TOPIC: Admin Cooperation
PARTIES:
 France
 Germany, West

416042 Bilateral Exchange **62 FRJO 2812**
SIGNED: 19 Dec 62
HEADNOTE: POSTAL RATES
TOPIC: Postal Service
PARTIES:
 France
 Germany, West

416044 Bilateral Agreement **69 FRJO 1810**
SIGNED: 25 Mar 65
HEADNOTE: EXCHANGE MILITARY UNITS
TOPIC: Status of Forces
PARTIES:
 France
 Germany, West

416049 Bilateral Convention **67 FRJO 810**
SIGNED: 28 Jul 66
HEADNOTE: INHERITANCE FRENCH RESIDENTS
TOPIC: Admin Cooperation
PARTIES:
 France
 United Arab Rep

416050 Bilateral Agreement **69 FRJO 3005**
SIGNED: 19 Mar 68
HEADNOTE: CULTURAL & SCIENTIFIC & TECHNI-
CAL COOPERATION
TOPIC: Health/Educ/Welfare
PARTIES:
 France
 United Arab Rep

416055 Bilateral Exchange **69 FRJO 1609**
SIGNED: 21 Mar 69
HEADNOTE: EOLE LAUNCHING FACILITIES
TOPIC: Scientific Project

PARTIES:
 Argentina
 France

416060 Bilateral Agreement **69 FRJO 1001**
SIGNED: 12 Mar 68
HEADNOTE: SCIENTIFIC & TECHNICAL COOPER-
ATION
TOPIC: Scientific Project
PARTIES:
 Austria
 France

416061 Bilateral Agreement **69 FRJO 2006**
SIGNED: 7 Jun 54
HEADNOTE: REGULATE FRONTIER AGRICULTURE
TOPIC: Admin Cooperation
PARTIES:
 Belgium
 France

416063 Bilateral Exchange **57 FRJO 1910**
SIGNED: 20 Sep 57
HEADNOTE: POSTAL RATES
TOPIC: Postal Service
PARTIES:
 Belgium
 France

416065 Bilateral Agreement **58 FRJO 1910**
SIGNED: 3 Sep 58
HEADNOTE: AUTO INSURANCE FUNDS
TOPIC: Health/Educ/Welfare
PARTIES:
 Belgium
 France

416068 Bilateral Agreement **64 FRJO 51**
SIGNED: 24 Mar 64
HEADNOTE: MIGRANT WORKERS SOCIAL SECU-
RITY
TOPIC: Non-ILO Labor
PARTIES:
 Belgium
 France

416069 Bilateral Agreement **67 FRJO 408**
SIGNED: 31 May 67
HEADNOTE: BORDER REGULATION
TOPIC: Admin Cooperation
PARTIES:
 Belgium
 France

416070 Bilateral Exchange **68 FRJO 1008**
SIGNED: 17 Oct 67
HEADNOTE: MODIFIES 20 SEP 62
TOPIC: Culture
PARTIES:
 Belgium
 France

416071 Bilateral Exchange **68 FRJO 2801**
SIGNED: 19 Dec 67
HEADNOTE: BORDER REGULATION
TOPIC: Admin Cooperation
PARTIES:
 Belgium
 France

416072 Bilateral Agreement **68 FRJO 2211**
SIGNED: 20 Sep 68
HEADNOTE: BORDER REGULATION
TOPIC: Admin Cooperation
PARTIES:
 Belgium
 France

416073 Bilateral Agreement **69 FRJO 2006**
SIGNED: 2 Dec 68
HEADNOTE: BORDER AGRICULTURE REGULA-
TION
TOPIC: Admin Cooperation

PARTIES:
 Belgium
 France

416074 Bilateral Agreement **69 FRJO 2009**
SIGNED: 6 Jun 69
HEADNOTE: BORDER CONTROL
TOPIC: Admin Cooperation
PARTIES:
 Belgium
 France

416075 Bilateral Agreement **68 FRJO 1606**
SIGNED: 26 May 66
HEADNOTE: CULTURAL & SCIENTIFIC & TECHNI-
CAL COOPERATION
TOPIC: Health/Educ/Welfare
PARTIES:
 Bolivia
 France

416078 Bilateral Agreement **69 FRJO 2005**
SIGNED: 22 Jan 63
HEADNOTE: FRENCH TECHNICIAN CONDITIONS
TOPIC: Tech Assistance
PARTIES:
 Brazil
 France

416080 Bilateral Agreement **67 FRJO 1105**
SIGNED: 29 Oct 65
HEADNOTE: AIR TRANSPORT
TOPIC: Air Transport
PARTIES:
 Brazil
 France

416081 Bilateral Agreement **69 FRJO 2704**
SIGNED: 16 Jan 67
HEADNOTE: SCIENTIFIC & TECHNICAL COOPER-
ATION
TOPIC: Tech Assistance
PARTIES:
 Brazil
 France

416082 Bilateral Agreement **69 FRJO 1903**
SIGNED: 20 Jun 68
HEADNOTE: TELEMETRY STATION CONSTRUC-
TION
TOPIC: Specific Property
PARTIES:
 Brazil
 France

416083 Bilateral Agreement **69 FRJO 506**
SIGNED: 6 Feb 69
HEADNOTE: MOTION PICTURE COOPERATION
TOPIC: Culture
PARTIES:
 Brazil
 France

416084 Bilateral Agreement **69 FRJO 1609**
SIGNED: 21 Mar 69
HEADNOTE: SPACE LAUNCH FACILITIES
TOPIC: Specific Property
PARTIES:
 Brazil
 France

416085 Bilateral Exchange **50 FRJO 1607**
SIGNED: 7 Mar 50
HEADNOTE: INDIGENTS ADMINISTRATIVE PRO-
CEDURES
TOPIC: Admin Cooperation
PARTIES:
 Bulgaria
 France

416088 Bilateral Agreement **67 FRJO 204**
SIGNED: 15 Oct 66
HEADNOTE: SCIENTIFIC & TECHNICAL COOPER-
ATION

TOPIC: Tech Assistance
PARTIES:
  Bulgaria
  France

416089   Bilateral Agreement   **67 FRJO 204**
SIGNED: 15 Oct 66
HEADNOTE: CULTURAL
TOPIC: Culture
PARTIES:
  Bulgaria
  France

416090   Bilateral Convention   **68 FRJO 1808**
SIGNED: 30 Jan 68
HEADNOTE: VETERINARY CONVENTION
TOPIC: Sanitation
PARTIES:
  Bulgaria
  France

416091   Bilateral Agreement   **69 FRJO 3007**
SIGNED: 10 Jul 68
HEADNOTE: ECONOMIC & INDUSTRIAL COOPER-
ATION
TOPIC: General Economic
PARTIES:
  Bulgaria
  France

416092   Bilateral Agreement   **69 FRJO 1906**
SIGNED: 27 Mar 69
HEADNOTE: WATER TRANSPORT
TOPIC: Water Transport
PARTIES:
  Bulgaria
  France

416094   Bilateral Treaty   **53 FRJO 1403**
SIGNED: 8 Nov 49
HEADNOTE: RECOGNITION
TOPIC: Recognition
PARTIES:
  Cambodia
  France

416098   Bilateral Agreement   **67 FRJO 2107**
SIGNED: 4 Jul 64
HEADNOTE: ECONOMIC & FINANCIAL COOPER-
ATION
TOPIC: General Aid
PARTIES:
  Cambodia
  France

416104   Bilateral Convention   **68 FRJO 2703**
SIGNED: 10 Jul 65
HEADNOTE: FINANCIAL MATTERS
TOPIC: Finance
PARTIES:
  Cameroon
  France

416107   Bilateral Agreement   **66 FRJO 1401**
SIGNED: 17 Nov 65
HEADNOTE: CULTURAL
TOPIC: Culture
PARTIES:
  Canada
  France

416108   Bilateral Agreement   **66 FRJO 1401**
SIGNED: 24 Nov 65
HEADNOTE: QUEBEC CULTURAL COOPERATION
TOPIC: Culture
PARTIES:
  Canada
  France

416109   Bilateral Agreement   **69 FRJO 2512**
SIGNED: 3 Apr 69
HEADNOTE: QUARANTINE STATION MIQUELON
TOPIC: Sanitation

PARTIES:
  Canada
  France

416114   Bilateral Agreement   **67 FRJO 1905**
SIGNED: 18 Jan 65
HEADNOTE: JUDICIAL COOPERATION
TOPIC: Admin Cooperation
PARTIES:
  Central Afri Rep
  France

416118   Bilateral Agreement   **68 FRJO 2801**
SIGNED: 22 Sep 66
HEADNOTE: MODIFIES 1 JUN 66
TOPIC: Air Transport
PARTIES:
  China People's Rep
  France

416126   Bilateral Convention   **66 FRJO 6051**
SIGNED: 9 Jun 66
HEADNOTE: FINANCIAL AID
TOPIC: Direct Aid
PARTIES:
  Congo (Brazzaville)
  France

416127   Bilateral Convention   **70 FRJO 307**
SIGNED: 13 Nov 67
HEADNOTE: FISCAL MATTERS
TOPIC: Finance
PARTIES:
  Congo (Brazzaville)
  France

416128   Bilateral Exchange   **67 FRJO 1511**
SIGNED: 17 Jul 63
HEADNOTE: BENEFITS FRENCH TECHNICIANS
TOPIC: Non-ILO Labor
PARTIES:
  Congo (Zaire)
  France

416129   Bilateral Agreement   **67 FRJO 1511**
SIGNED: 17 Dec 63
HEADNOTE: CULTURAL & TECHNICAL COOPER-
ATION
TOPIC: Health/Educ/Welfare
PARTIES:
  Congo (Zaire)
  France

416132   Bilateral Agreement   **68 FRJO 1909**
SIGNED: 28 Dec 65
HEADNOTE: CULTURAL & TECHNICAL COOPER-
ATION
TOPIC: Health/Educ/Welfare
PARTIES:
  France
  Korea, South

416133   Bilateral Agreement   **67 FRJO 1204**
SIGNED: 11 Feb 67
HEADNOTE: SHORT TERM VISA ABOLITION
TOPIC: Visas
PARTIES:
  France
  Korea, South

416134   Bilateral Treaty   **54 FRJO 1902**
SIGNED: 30 Apr 53
HEADNOTE: COMMERCE
TOPIC: General Trade
PARTIES:
  Costa Rica
  France

416137   Bilateral Exchange   **68 FRJO 206**
SIGNED: 30 Nov 67
HEADNOTE: SAN JOSE SECONDARY SCHOOL
TOPIC: Education

PARTIES:
  Costa Rica
  France

416141   Bilateral Convention   **69 FRJO 2201**
SIGNED: 6 Apr 66
HEADNOTE: FISCAL AGREEMENT
TOPIC: Finance
PARTIES:
  France
  Ivory Coast

416142   Bilateral Convention   **66 FRJO 2011**
SIGNED: 7 May 66
HEADNOTE: TRANSFER ASSETS
TOPIC: Claims and Debts
PARTIES:
  France
  Ivory Coast

416143   Bilateral Convention   **52 FRJO 2609**
SIGNED: 17 Jan 51
HEADNOTE: FRENCH PROPERTY IN CUBA
TOPIC: Claims and Debts
PARTIES:
  Cuba
  France

416144   Bilateral Convention   **46 FRJO 7041**
SIGNED: 16 Mar 67
HEADNOTE: NATIONALIZED PROPERTY CLAIMS
TOPIC: Claims and Debts
PARTIES:
  Cuba
  France

416159   Bilateral Agreement   **66 FRJO 2206**
SIGNED: 17 Feb 66
HEADNOTE: FRENCH TECHNICIAN PRIVILEGES
TOPIC: Tech Assistance
PARTIES:
  Ecuador
  France

416160   Bilateral Agreement   **66 FRJO 2011**
SIGNED: 5 Jul 66
HEADNOTE: CULTURAL
TOPIC: Culture
PARTIES:
  Ecuador
  France

416161   Bilateral Instrument   **55 FRJO 2408**
SIGNED: 13 May 55
HEADNOTE: CUSTOMS
TOPIC: Customs
PARTIES:
  France
  Spain

416162   Bilateral Agreement   **51 FRJO 1108**
SIGNED: 21 Jun 57
HEADNOTE: PATENTS & COPYRIGHTS
TOPIC: Patents/Copyrights
PARTIES:
  France
  Spain

416167   Bilateral Convention   **67 FRJO 2502**
SIGNED: 11 Jul 64
HEADNOTE: TWO BRIDGES OVER BIDASSOA
TOPIC: General Ad Hoc
PARTIES:
  France
  Spain

416169   Bilateral Agreement   **67 FRJO 408**
SIGNED: 22 Jul 66
HEADNOTE: FRENCH CUSTOMSHOUSE IN SPAIN
TOPIC: Admin Cooperation
PARTIES:
  France
  Spain

416170   Bilateral Agreement   **67 FRJO 408**
SIGNED: 20 Mar 67
HEADNOTE: FISHING REGULATION
TOPIC: Specific Resources
PARTIES:
  France
  Spain

416171   Bilateral Convention   **67 FRJO 1108**
SIGNED: 3 May 67
HEADNOTE: MOUNTAIN CLIMBER BORDER
  CROSS
TOPIC: Admin Cooperation
PARTIES:
  France
  Spain

416172   Bilateral Agreement   **67 FRJO 608**
SIGNED: 15 Jun 67
HEADNOTE: JOINT CHECKPOINT
TOPIC: Visas
PARTIES:
  France
  Spain

416173   Bilateral Agreement   **67 FRJO 608**
SIGNED: 20 Jun 67
HEADNOTE: JOINT CHECKPOINT
TOPIC: Visas
PARTIES:
  France
  Spain

416174   Bilateral Instrument   **70 FRJO 2503**
SIGNED: 15 Mar 68
HEADNOTE: FRONTIER PASTURE REGULATION
TOPIC: Admin Cooperation
PARTIES:
  France
  Spain

416175   Bilateral Exchange   **69 FRJO 1809**
SIGNED: 2 Aug 68
HEADNOTE: MIGRANT WORKER FAMILY RIGHTS
TOPIC: Non-ILO Labor
PART!ES:
  France
  Spain

416176   Bilateral Exchange   **69 FRJO 909**
SIGNED: 11 Mar 69
HEADNOTE: PAYS-QUINT PASTURES USE
TOPIC: Specific Resources
PARTIES:
  France
  Spain

416177   Bilateral Exchange   **76 FRJO 9070**
SIGNED: 30 May 69
HEADNOTE: JUNQUERA CUSTOMSHOUSE
TOPIC: Specific Resources
PARTIES:
  France
  Spain

416178   Bilateral Protocol   **64 FRJO 1010**
SIGNED: 17 Jun 69
HEADNOTE: BIDASSOA INERNATIONAL BRIDGE
TOPIC: General Ad Hoc
PARTIES:
  France
  Spain

416181   Bilateral Convention   **68 FRJO 1210**
SIGNED: 28 Jul 67
HEADNOTE: INCOME & ESTATE TAXATION
TOPIC: Taxation
PARTIES:
  France
  USA (United States)

416182   Bilateral Agreement   **69 FRJO 607**
SIGNED: 24 May 68
HEADNOTE: SOCIAL SECURITY

TOPIC: Non-ILO Labor
PARTIES:
  France
  USA (United States)

416184   Bilateral Agreement   **67 FRJO 3103**
SIGNED: 27 Aug 66
HEADNOTE: CULTURAL & SCIENTIFIC & TECHNI-
  CAL COOPERATION
TOPIC: Health/Educ/Welfare
PARTIES:
  Ethiopia
  France

416185   Bilateral Agreement   **67 FRJO 3103**
SIGNED: 27 Aug 66
HEADNOTE: GUEBRE-MARIAM SCHOOL STATUS
TOPIC: Education
PARTIES:
  Ethiopia
  France

416186   Bilateral Convention   **67 FRJO 3103**
SIGNED: 27 Aug 66
HEADNOTE: CULTURAL CONVENTION   .
TOPIC: Culture
PARTIES:
  Ethiopia
  France

416187   Bilateral Agreement   **69 FRJO 2412**
SIGNED: 28 Mar 69
HEADNOTE: EDUCATION & FINE-ARTS MISSION
TOPIC: Health/Educ/Welfare
PARTIES:
  Ethiopia
  France

416188   Bilateral Agreement   **50 FRJO 206**
SIGNED: 15 Apr 50
HEADNOTE: INTERN EXCHANGE
TOPIC: Education
PARTIES:
  Finland
  France

416197   Bilateral Convention   **69 FRJO 2404**
SIGNED: 21 Apr 66
HEADNOTE: FISCAL CONVENTION
TOPIC: Finance
PARTIES:
  France
  Gabon

416198   Bilateral Convention   **51 FRJO 2108**
SIGNED: 14 Dec 50
HEADNOTE: DOUBLE TAXATION & TAX EVASION
TOPIC: Taxation
PARTIES:
  France
  UK Great Britain

416199   Bilateral Convention   **51 FRJO 2010**
SIGNED: 30 Jan 51
HEADNOTE: FISHING REGULATIONS
TOPIC: Specific Resources
PARTIES:
  France
  UK Great Britain

416202   Bilateral Convention   **69 FRJO 2511**
SIGNED: 22 May 68
HEADNOTE: FISCAL
TOPIC: Finance
PARTIES:
  France
  UK Great Britain

416203   Bilateral Agreement   **69 FRJO 1001**
SIGNED: 13 Sep 68
HEADNOTE: MOTION PICTURE COPRODUCTION
TOPIC: Culture

PARTIES:
  France
  UK Great Britain

416205   Bilateral Agreement   **67 FRJO 1005**
SIGNED: 14 Dec 65
HEADNOTE: FRENCH CREDIT REGULATION
TOPIC: Loans and Credits
PARTIES:
  France
  Greece

416206   Bilateral Agreement   **69 FRJO 3007**
SIGNED: 9 Apr 69
HEADNOTE: LAND TRANSPORT
TOPIC: Land Transport
PARTIES:
  France
  Greece

416212   Bilateral Agreement   **52 FRJO 2404**
SIGNED: 8 Apr 52
HEADNOTE: ADMISSION OF INTERNS
TOPIC: Education
PARTIES:
  France
  Haiti

416213   Bilateral Agreement   **67 FRJO 1205**
SIGNED: 15 Jun 65
HEADNOTE: AIR TRANSPORT
TOPIC: Air Transport
PARTIES:
  France
  Haiti

416218   Bilateral Convention   **67 FRJO 106**
SIGNED: 11 Aug 65
HEADNOTE: FISCAL
TOPIC: Finance
PARTIES:
  France
  Upper Volta

416220   Bilateral Agreement   **69 FRJO 1101**
SIGNED: 13 Jan 68
HEADNOTE: CULTURAL & TECHNICAL COOPER-
  ATION
TOPIC: Health/Educ/Welfare
PARTIES:
  France
  Honduras

416221   Bilateral Agreement   **52 FRJO 2509**
SIGNED: 12 Jun 50
HEADNOTE: FRENCH PROPERTY CLAIMS
TOPIC: Claims and Debts
PARTIES:
  France
  Hungary

416225   Bilateral Convention   **67 FRJO 2210**
SIGNED: 28 Jul 66
HEADNOTE: CONSULAR CONVENTION
TOPIC: Consul/Citizenship
PARTIES:
  France
  Hungary

416226   Bilateral Agreement   **67 FRJO 201**
SIGNED: 28 Jul 66
HEADNOTE: SCIENTIFIC & TECHNICAL COOPER-
  ATION
TOPIC: Scientific Project
PARTIES:
  France
  Hungary

416227   Bilateral Agreement   **67 FRJO 204**
SIGNED: 28 Jul 66
HEADNOTE: CULTURAL
TOPIC: Culture

PARTIES:
France
Hungary

416228   Bilateral Agreement   **67 FRJO 3003**
SIGNED: 8 Oct 66
HEADNOTE: INTERNATIONAL LAND TRANSPORT
TOPIC: Land Transport
PARTIES:
France
Hungary

416232   Bilateral Agreement   **69 FRJO 709**
SIGNED: 31 Jul 67
HEADNOTE: AIR SERVICE
TOPIC: Air Transport
PARTIES:
France
India

416233   Bilateral Convention   **70 FRJO 2803**
SIGNED: 26 Mar 69
HEADNOTE: DOUBLE TAXATION AVOIDANCE
TOPIC: Taxation
PARTIES:
France
India

416234   Bilateral Agreement   **68 FRJO 3103**
SIGNED: 24 Nov 67
HEADNOTE: AIR TRANSPORT
TOPIC: Air Transport
PARTIES:
France
Indonesia

416235   Bilateral Agreement   **69 FRJO 2707**
SIGNED: 3 Apr 69
HEADNOTE: CIVIL ATOMIC DEVELOPMENT
TOPIC: Atomic Energy
PARTIES:
France
Indonesia

416236   Bilateral Agreement   **67 FRJO 1901**
SIGNED: 19 May 66
HEADNOTE: AIR TRANSPORT
TOPIC: Air Transport
PARTIES:
France
Iraq

416237   Bilateral Agreement   **69 FRJO 1408**
SIGNED: 25 Sep 67
HEADNOTE: COMMERCE
TOPIC: General Trade
PARTIES:
France
Iraq

416239   Bilateral Convention   **67 FRJO 3003**
SIGNED: 24 Jun 64
HEADNOTE: EXTRADITION
TOPIC: Extradition
PARTIES:
France
Iran

416240   Bilateral Convention   **69 FRJO 511**
SIGNED: 24 Jun 64
HEADNOTE: NAVIGATION
TOPIC: Water Transport
PARTIES:
France
Iran

416242   Bilateral Agreement   **69 FRJO 1304**
SIGNED: 27 Dec 67
HEADNOTE: SCIENTIFIC & TECHNICAL COOPER-
ATION
TOPIC: Tech Assistance
PARTIES:
France
Iran

416243   Bilateral Agreement   **68 FRJO 2402**
SIGNED: 4 Nov 67
HEADNOTE: CULTURAL
TOPIC: Culture
PARTIES:
France
Ireland

416245   Bilateral Agreement   **50 FRJO 702**
SIGNED: 9 Feb 48
HEADNOTE: ADMISSION OF INTERNS
TOPIC: Education
PARTIES:
France
Italy

416247   Bilateral Convention   **68 FRJO 1403**
SIGNED: 29 Oct 58
HEADNOTE: DOUBLE TAXATION & INCOME TAX
TOPIC: Taxation
PARTIES:
France
Italy

416248   Bilateral Convention   **69 FRJO 2704**
SIGNED: 28 Apr 64
HEADNOTE: ORIGIN LABELS
TOPIC: Patents/Copyrights
PARTIES:
France
Italy

416250   Bilateral Agreement   **67 FRJO 1108**
SIGNED: 1 Mar 66
HEADNOTE: MONT-BLANC TUNNEL COMMIS-
SION
TOPIC: Admin Cooperation
PARTIES:
France
Italy

416253   Bilateral Agreement   **69 FRJO 2810**
SIGNED: 24 Sep 68
HEADNOTE: VISA ABOLITION
TOPIC: Visas
PARTIES:
France
Jamaica

416254   Bilateral Agreement   **53 FRJO 610**
SIGNED: 12 May 53
HEADNOTE: CULTURAL
TOPIC: Culture
PARTIES:
France
Japan

416257   Bilateral Agreement   **66 FRJO 2606**
SIGNED: 30 Apr 66
HEADNOTE: AIR TRANSPORT
TOPIC: Air Transport
PARTIES:
France
Jordan

416258   Bilateral Agreement   **65 FRJO 2511**
SIGNED: 28 Jul 64
HEADNOTE: AIR TRANSPORT
TOPIC: Air Transport
PARTIES:
France
Kenya

416262   Bilateral Agreement   **68 FRJO 1904**
SIGNED: 13 Jan 66
HEADNOTE: AIR TRANSPORT
TOPIC: Air Transport
PARTIES:
France
Liberia

416263   Bilateral Treaty   **57 FRJO 704**
SIGNED: 10 Aug 55
HEADNOTE: AMITY & COOPERATION

TOPIC: General Amity
PARTIES:
France
Libya

416264   Bilateral Convention   **50 FRJO 1003**
SIGNED: 30 Mar 49
HEADNOTE: MILITARY SERVICE
TOPIC: Milit Servic/Citiz
PARTIES:
France
Luxembourg

416265   Bilateral Instrument   **49 FRJO 2510**
SIGNED: 27 Jun 49
HEADNOTE: ADMISSION OF INTERNS
TOPIC: Education
PARTIES:
France
Luxembourg

416266   Bilateral Convention   **50 FRJO 110**
SIGNED: 12 Nov 49
HEADNOTE: SOCIAL SECURITY
TOPIC: Non-ILO Labor
PARTIES:
France
Luxembourg

416267   Bilateral Convention   **55 FRJO 601**
SIGNED: 29 Apr 52
HEADNOTE: CUSTOMS CONTROL
TOPIC: Customs
PARTIES:
France
Luxembourg

416268   Bilateral Agreement   **55 FRJO 1603**
SIGNED: 8 Feb 54
HEADNOTE: CULTURAL
TOPIC: Culture
PARTIES:
France
Luxembourg

416271   Bilateral Exchange   **58 FRJO 2507**
SIGNED: 25 Jul 58
HEADNOTE: POSTAL RATES
TOPIC: Postal Service
PARTIES:
France
Luxembourg

416273   Bilateral Agreement   **68 FRJO 1101**
SIGNED: 16 Jul 63
HEADNOTE: BORDER RECTIFICATION
TOPIC: Territory Boundary
PARTIES:
France
Luxembourg

416274   Bilateral Protocol   **67 FRJO 2412**
SIGNED: 3 Jun 64
HEADNOTE: OLD-AGE INSURANCE
TOPIC: Non-ILO Labor
PARTIES:
France
Luxembourg

416275   Bilateral Agreement   **68 FRJO 1910**
SIGNED: 31 Aug 65
HEADNOTE: AUTO INSURANCE COVERAGE
TOPIC: Health/Educ/Welfare
PARTIES:
France
Luxembourg

416276   Bilateral Convention   **49 FRJO 1509**
SIGNED: 17 Apr 46
HEADNOTE: LUXEMBOURG RAILWAYS
TOPIC: Land Transport
PARTIES:
Belgium
France

416277   Bilateral Agreement   **67 FRJO 508**
SIGNED: 22 May 67
HEADNOTE: AIR TRANSPORT
TOPIC: Air Transport
PARTIES:
  France
  Malaysia

416286   Bilateral Convention   **68 FRJO 708**
SIGNED: 8 May 67
HEADNOTE: SOCIAL SECURITY
TOPIC: Non-ILO Labor
PARTIES:
  France
  Malagasy

416287   Bilateral Convention   **68 FRJO 2211**
SIGNED: 22 May 68
HEADNOTE: TV TECHNICAL AID
TOPIC: Tech Assistance
PARTIES:
  France
  Malagasy

416291   Bilateral Convention   **67 FRJO 3008**
SIGNED: 11 Mar 65
HEADNOTE: SOCIAL SECURITY
TOPIC: Non-ILO Labor
PARTIES:
  France
  Mali

416292   Bilateral Agreement   **67 FRJO 2706**
SIGNED: 15 Feb 67
HEADNOTE: FINANCIAL RELATIONS
TOPIC: Finance
PARTIES:
  France
  Mali

416309   Bilateral Convention   **67 FRJO 605**
SIGNED: 9 Jul 65
HEADNOTE: SOCIAL SECURITY
TOPIC: Non-ILO Labor
PARTIES:
  France
  Morocco

416317   Bilateral Convention   **66 FRJO 1901**
SIGNED: 7 Feb 64
HEADNOTE: CONSULAR CONVENTION
TOPIC: Consul/Citizenship
PARTIES:
  France
  Mauritania

416319   Bilateral Convention   **67 FRJO 1202**
SIGNED: 22 Jul 65
HEADNOTE: SOCIAL SECURITY
TOPIC: Non-ILO Labor
PARTIES:
  France
  Mauritania

416320   Bilateral Convention   **69 FRJO 2704**
SIGNED: 15 Nov 67
HEADNOTE: FISCAL CONVENTION
TOPIC: Finance
PARTIES:
  France
  Mauritania

416321   Bilateral Protocol   **68 FRJO 706**
SIGNED: 17 Feb 68
HEADNOTE: HISTORY, ARCHEOLOGY RESEARCH
TOPIC: Scientific Project
PARTIES:
  France
  Mauritania

416322   Bilateral Convention   **51 FRJO 1111**
SIGNED: 11 Dec 50
HEADNOTE: MUSICAL COPYRIGHTS
TOPIC: Patents/Copyrights

PARTIES:
  France
  Mexico

416323   Bilateral Agreement   **53 FRJO 2905**
SIGNED: 29 Nov 51
HEADNOTE: TRADE
TOPIC: General Trade
PARTIES:
  France
  Mexico

416325   Bilateral Convention   **45 FRJO 106**
SIGNED: 14 Apr 45
HEADNOTE: PRICE CONTROLS
TOPIC: Finance
PARTIES:
  France
  Monaco

416326   Bilateral Convention   **45 FRJO 106**
SIGNED: 14 Apr 45
HEADNOTE: EXCHANGE CONTROLS
TOPIC: Finance
PARTIES:
  France
  Monaco

416327   Bilateral Convention   **45 FRJO 106**
SIGNED: 14 Apr 45
HEADNOTE: ILLEGAL PROFITS
TOPIC: Admin Cooperation
PARTIES:
  France
  Monaco

416328   Bilateral Exchange   **60 FRJO 44**
SIGNED: 26 Oct 46
HEADNOTE: WAR DAMAGES
TOPIC: Reparations
PARTIES:
  France
  Monaco

416329   Bilateral Instrument   **47 FRJO 2106**
SIGNED: 16 Jun 47
HEADNOTE: IMMIGRATION & NATURALIZATION
TOPIC: Consul/Citizenship
PARTIES:
  France
  Monaco

416330   Bilateral Convention   **53 FRJO 1006**
SIGNED: 1 Apr 50
HEADNOTE: INHERITANCE & DOUBLE TAXATION
TOPIC: Taxation
PARTIES:
  France
  Monaco

416331   Bilateral Convention   **54 FRJO 2706**
SIGNED: 13 Sep 50
HEADNOTE: BANKRUPTCY & JUDGEMENT SALES
TOPIC: Claims and Debts
PARTIES:
  France
  Monaco

416332   Bilateral Agreement   **54 FRJO 508**
SIGNED: 13 Nov 52
HEADNOTE: MONACAN CREDITOR PRIVILEGES
TOPIC: Claims and Debts
PARTIES:
  France
  Monaco

416336   Bilateral Exchange   **70 FRJO 1601**
SIGNED: 26 Sep 68
HEADNOTE: INSURANCE & CAPITAL FORMATION
TOPIC: General Economic
PARTIES:
  France
  Monaco

416337   Bilateral Agreement   **68 FRJO 1010**
SIGNED: 31 Jan 68
HEADNOTE: CULTURAL
TOPIC: Culture
PARTIES:
  France
  Mongolia

416338   Bilateral Agreement   **68 FRJO 1105**
SIGNED: 22 Dec 66
HEADNOTE: CULTURAL & TECHNICAL COOPER-
  ATION
TOPIC: Health/Educ/Welfare
PARTIES:
  France
  Nicaragua

416345   Bilateral Convention   **68 FRJO 204**
SIGNED: 25 Feb 67
HEADNOTE: RADIO BROADCAST COOPERATION
TOPIC: Mass Media
PARTIES:
  France
  Niger

416347   Bilateral Agreement   **68 FRJO 103**
SIGNED: 9 Nov 67
HEADNOTE: AIR TRANSPORT
TOPIC: Air Transport
PARTIES:
  France
  New Zealand

416357   Bilateral Agreement   **50 FRJO 1002**
SIGNED: 2 Jun 48
HEADNOTE: ADMISSION OF INTERNS
TOPIC: Education
PARTIES:
  France
  Netherlands

416360   Bilateral Agreement   **51 FRJO 1111**
SIGNED: 19 Mar 48
HEADNOTE: NATIONALIZED PROPERTY
TOPIC: Claims and Debts
PARTIES:
  France
  Poland

416361   Bilateral Agreement   **57 FRJO 708**
SIGNED: 7 Sep 51
HEADNOTE: FRENCH ASSETS
TOPIC: Claims and Debts
PARTIES:
  France
  Poland

416364   Bilateral Agreement   **67 FRJO 404**
SIGNED: 20 May 66
HEADNOTE: SCIENTIFIC & TECHNICAL COOPER-
  ATION
TOPIC: Tech Assistance
PARTIES:
  France
  Poland

416365   Bilateral Agreement   **67 FRJO 204**
SIGNED: 20 May 66
HEADNOTE: CULTURE
TOPIC: Culture
PARTIES:
  France
  Poland

416366   Bilateral Convention   **69 FRJO 2202**
SIGNED: 5 Apr 67
HEADNOTE: ALIEN RIGHTS
TOPIC: Consul/Citizenship
PARTIES:
  France
  Poland

416367   Bilateral Agreement   **68 FRJO 308**
SIGNED: 3 Mar 68

HEADNOTE: TRAVEL & MERCHANDISE ROUTES
TOPIC: General Transport
PARTIES:
France
Poland

416373   Bilateral Agreement   **67 FRJO 2910**
SIGNED: 11 Sep 67
HEADNOTE: MIGRANT WORKERS
TOPIC: Non-ILO Labor
PARTIES:
France
Portugal

416374   Bilateral Agreement   **59 FRJO 1903**
SIGNED: 9 Feb 59
HEADNOTE: FINANCIAL SETTLEMENTS
TOPIC: Finance
PARTIES:
France
Romania

416379   Bilateral Convention   **67 FRJO 508**
SIGNED: 13 Feb 67
HEADNOTE: VETERINARY CONVENTION
TOPIC: Sanitation
PARTIES:
France
Romania

416380   Bilateral Convention   **69 FRJO 609**
SIGNED: 12 Mar 69
HEADNOTE: CROP DISEASE PREVENTION
TOPIC: Sanitation
PARTIES:
France
Romania

416382   Bilateral Convention   **51 FRJO 203**
SIGNED: 12 Jul 49
HEADNOTE: MIGRANT LABOR SOCIAL SECURITY
TOPIC: Non-ILO Labor
PARTIES:
France
San Marino

416383   Bilateral Convention   **56 FRJO 106**
SIGNED: 15 Jan 54
HEADNOTE: ESTABLISHMENT
TOPIC: Consul/Citizenship
PARTIES:
France
San Marino

416385   Bilateral Convention   **69 FRJO 1503**
SIGNED: 25 May 67
HEADNOTE: JUDICIAL COOPERATION
TOPIC: Admin Cooperation
PARTIES:
France
San Marino

416386   Bilateral Treaty   **54 FRJO 1902**
SIGNED: 23 Mar 53
HEADNOTE: TRADE
TOPIC: General Trade
PARTIES:
El Salvador
France

416397   Bilateral Protocol   **66 FRJO 1601**
SIGNED: 15 May 64
HEADNOTE: EDUCATIONAL COOPERATION
TOPIC: Education
PARTIES:
France
Senegal

416398   Bilateral Convention   **67 FRJO 3110**
SIGNED: 5 Mar 65
HEADNOTE: SOCIAL SECURITY
TOPIC: Non-ILO Labor

PARTIES:
France
Senegal

416400   Bilateral Agreement   **67 FRJO 1410**
SIGNED: 18 Jul 67
HEADNOTE: AIR TRANSPORT
TOPIC: Air Transport
PARTIES:
France
Sierra Leone

416401   Bilateral Agreement   **67 FRJO 1110**
SIGNED: 29 Jun 67
HEADNOTE: AIR TRANSPORT
TOPIC: Air Transport
PARTIES:
France
Singapore

416403   Bilateral Agreement   **69 FRJO 2702**
SIGNED: 16 Dec 68
HEADNOTE: INTERNATIONAL   TRANSPORT
    ROUTES
TOPIC: General Transport
PARTIES:
France
Sweden

416404   Bilateral Instrument   **47 FRJO 2905**
SIGNED: 29 Jun 46
HEADNOTE: WAR REFUGEES
TOPIC: Refugees
PARTIES:
France
Switzerland

416414   Bilateral Agreement   **67 FRJO 604**
SIGNED: 10 Mar 65
HEADNOTE: BORDER MAINTAINENCE
TOPIC: Admin Cooperation
PARTIES:
France
Switzerland

416418   Bilateral Agreement   **69 FRJO 1004**
SIGNED: 13 Sep 65
HEADNOTE: CERN STATUS FRENCH TERRITORY
TOPIC: IGO Status/Immunit
PARTIES:
France
Switzerland

416419   Bilateral Agreement   **66 FRJO 2406**
SIGNED: 12 May 66
HEADNOTE: MILITARY VISAS
TOPIC: Visas
PARTIES:
France
Switzerland

416420   Bilateral Convention   **67 FRJO 1010**
SIGNED: 9 Sep 66
HEADNOTE: DOUBLE TAXATION AVOIDANCE
TOPIC: Taxation
PARTIES:
France
Switzerland

416421   Bilateral Convention   **67 FRJO 1108**
SIGNED: 16 Jun 67
HEADNOTE: DELLE RAILWAY CHECKPOINT
TOPIC: Admin Cooperation
PARTIES:
France
Switzerland

416422   Bilateral Agreement   **67 FRJO 1108**
SIGNED: 19 Jul 67
HEADNOTE: VALLORBE RAILWAY CHECKPOINT
TOPIC: Admin Cooperation
PARTIES:
France
Switzerland

416423   Bilateral Agreement   **50 FRJO 1003**
SIGNED: 7 Feb 49
HEADNOTE: FINANCES
TOPIC: Finance
PARTIES:
France
Syria

416424   Bilateral Agreement   **67 FRJO 404**
SIGNED: 7 Jan 66
HEADNOTE: AIR TRANSPORT
TOPIC: Air Transport
PARTIES:
France
Syria

416432   Bilateral Convention   **68 FRJO 1112**
SIGNED: 19 May 64
HEADNOTE: CIVIL SERVICE EXAMINATION
TOPIC: Non-ILO Labor
PARTIES:
Chad
France

416434   Bilateral Agreement   **68 FRJO 1112**
SIGNED: 19 May 64
HEADNOTE: CULTURE
TOPIC: Culture
PARTIES:
Chad
France

416435   Bilateral Agreement   **68 FRJO 1112**
SIGNED: 19 May 64
HEADNOTE: MILITARY ASSISTANCE
TOPIC: Milit Assistance
PARTIES:
Chad
France

416436   Bilateral Agreement   **48 FRJO 1501**
SIGNED: 20 Nov 46
HEADNOTE: REPARATIONS
TOPIC: Reparations
PARTIES:
Czechoslovakia
France

416437   Bilateral Convention   **50 FRJO 0**
SIGNED: 1 Dec 47
HEADNOTE: PENSIONS TO WAR DISABLED
TOPIC: Reparations
PARTIES:
Czechoslovakia
France

416438   Bilateral Convention   **49 FRJO 2207**
SIGNED: 6 Aug 48
HEADNOTE: DOUBLE TAXATION AVOIDANCE
TOPIC: Taxation
PARTIES:
Czechoslovakia
France

416443   Bilateral Agreement   **66 FRJO 2502**
SIGNED: 29 Jun 65
HEADNOTE: SCIENTIFIC & TECHNICAL COOPER-
    ATION
TOPIC: Tech Assistance
PARTIES:
Czechoslovakia
France

416444   Bilateral Convention   **68 FRJO 1101**
SIGNED: 30 May 67
HEADNOTE: VETERINARY
TOPIC: Sanitation
PARTIES:
Czechoslovakia
France

416445   Bilateral Agreement   **68 FRJO 2109**
SIGNED: 26 Oct 67
HEADNOTE: CULTURE

TOPIC: Culture
PARTIES:
  Czechoslovakia
  France

416446   Bilateral Agreement   **68 FRJO 1709**
SIGNED: 3 Mar 68
HEADNOTE: MOTION PICTURE COOPERATION &
  EXCHANGE
TOPIC: Culture
PARTIES:
  Czechoslovakia
  France

416447   Bilateral Agreement   **69 FRJO 2006**
SIGNED: 21 Sep 68
HEADNOTE: INTERNATIONAL   TRANSPORT
  ROUTES
TOPIC: General Transport
PARTIES:
  Czechoslovakia
  France

416448   Bilateral Agreement   **47 FRJO 1503**
SIGNED: 17 Nov 46
HEADNOTE: GENERAL RELATIONS
TOPIC: Admin Cooperation
PARTIES:
  France
  Thailand

416451   Bilateral Protocol   **69 FRJO 2006**
SIGNED: 30 Apr 68
HEADNOTE: REAL ESTATE REGULATION
TOPIC: Claims and Debts
PARTIES:
  France
  Togo

416452   Bilateral Convention   **53 FRJO 2407**
SIGNED: 16 Apr 53
HEADNOTE: WEATHER SERVICE
TOPIC: Health/Educ/Welfare
PARTIES:
  France
  Tunisia

416453   Bilateral Convention   **55 FRJO 609**
SIGNED: 3 Jun 55
HEADNOTE: ADMINISTRATIVE & TECHNICAL CO-
  OPERATION
TOPIC: General Amity
PARTIES:
  France
  Tunisia

416465   Bilateral Protocol   **69 FRJO 110**
SIGNED: 17 Feb 69
HEADNOTE: CULTURE
TOPIC: Culture
PARTIES:
  France
  Tunisia

416466   Bilateral Protocol   **69 FRJO 2109**
SIGNED: 5 Jun 69
HEADNOTE: TECHNICAL COOPERATION
TOPIC: Tech Assistance
PARTIES:
  France
  Tunisia

416467   Bilateral Agreement   **47 FRJO 310**
SIGNED: 31 Aug 46
HEADNOTE: TRADE & PAYMENT
TOPIC: General Economic
PARTIES:
  France
  Turkey

416473   Bilateral Convention   **69 FRJO 1610**
SIGNED: 8 Dec 66
HEADNOTE: CONSULAR CONVENTION
TOPIC: Consul/Citizenship

PARTIES:
  France
  USSR (Soviet Union)

416474   Bilateral Agreement   **68 FRJO 2103**
SIGNED: 14 Mar 67
HEADNOTE: PATENT FINANCES
TOPIC: Patents/Copyrights
PARTIES:
  France
  USSR (Soviet Union)

416475   Bilateral Agreement   **67 FRJO 2709**
SIGNED: 20 Apr 67
HEADNOTE: WATER TRANSPORT
TOPIC: Water Transport
PARTIES:
  France
  USSR (Soviet Union)

416476   Bilateral Agreement   **68 FRJO 1603**
SIGNED: 8 Jul 67
HEADNOTE: MOTION PICTURE COOPERATION
TOPIC: Culture
PARTIES:
  France
  USSR (Soviet Union)

416477   Bilateral Agreement   **69 FRJO 3007**
SIGNED: 9 Jan 69
HEADNOTE: MEDICAL COOPERATION
TOPIC: Health/Educ/Welfare
PARTIES:
  France
  USSR (Soviet Union)

416482   Bilateral Agreement   **70 FRJO 2203**
SIGNED: 24 Mar 60
HEADNOTE: TRANSFER PROPERTIES
TOPIC: Specific Property
PARTIES:
  France
  Vietnam, South

416483   Bilateral Agreement   **51 FRJO 2404**
SIGNED: 5 Jan 50
HEADNOTE: SOCIAL SECURITY
TOPIC: Non-ILO Labor
PARTIES:
  France
  Yugoslavia

416484   Bilateral Agreement   **53 FRJO 3107**
SIGNED: 14 Apr 51
HEADNOTE: NATIONALIZATION INDEMNITIES
TOPIC: Claims and Debts
PARTIES:
  France
  Yugoslavia

416491   Bilateral Convention   **67 FRJO 102**
SIGNED: 8 Feb 66
HEADNOTE: VETERINARY
TOPIC: Sanitation
PARTIES:
  France
  Yugoslavia

416492   Bilateral Protocol   **67 FRJO 1802**
SIGNED: 8 Feb 66
HEADNOTE: STUDENT HEALTH CARE
TOPIC: Health/Educ/Welfare
PARTIES:
  France
  Yugoslavia

416493   Bilateral Agreement   **67 FRJO 504**
SIGNED: 27 Jun 66
HEADNOTE: SCIENTIFIC & TECHNICAL COOPER-
  ATION
TOPIC: Tech Assistance
PARTIES:
  France
  Yugoslavia

416494   Bilateral Agreement   **67 FRJO 410**
SIGNED: 23 Mar 67
HEADNOTE: AIR TRANSPORT
TOPIC: Air Transport
PARTIES:
  France
  Yugoslavia

416495   Bilateral Agreement   **69 FRJO 2811**
SIGNED: 15 Jan 69
HEADNOTE: ECONOMIC & INDUSTRIAL & TECH-
  NICAL COOPERATION
TOPIC: General Economic
PARTIES:
  France
  Yugoslavia

416496   Bilateral Agreement   **69 FRJO 2205**
SIGNED: 15 Jan 69
HEADNOTE: SHORT-TERM VISA ABOLITION
TOPIC: Visas
PARTIES:
  France
  Yugoslavia

416497   Bilateral Convention   **55 FRJO 1208**
SIGNED: 25 Jun 54
HEADNOTE: LEASE OF PLACE FONTENOY
TOPIC: Specific Property
PARTIES:
  France
  UNESCO (Educ/Cult)

416507   Bilateral Agreement   **67 FRJO 1903**
SIGNED: 19 Apr 66
HEADNOTE: STATUS ON FRENCH TERRITORY
TOPIC: IGO Status/Immunit
PARTIES:
  African Coffee Org
  France

416508   Bilateral Agreement   **67 FRJO 1203**
SIGNED: 5 Jul 66
HEADNOTE: STATUS ON FRENCH TERRITORY
TOPIC: IGO Status/Immunit
PARTIES:
  France
  Refrigeration Inst

416509   Bilateral Agreement   **67 FRJO 212**
SIGNED: 8 Feb 67
HEADNOTE: STATUS ON FRENCH TERRITORY
TOPIC: IGO Status/Immunit
PARTIES:
  African Insur Org
  France

416510   Bilateral Agreement   **69 FRJO 2204**
SIGNED: 14 Apr 67
HEADNOTE: STATUS ON FRENCH TERRITORY
TOPIC: IGO Status/Immunit
PARTIES:
  Afromalagasy Coffee
  France

416511   Bilateral Agreement   **68 FRJO 506**
SIGNED: 30 Nov 67
HEADNOTE: VOLUNTARY OLD-AGE INSURANCE
TOPIC: Non-ILO Labor
PARTIES:
  France
  WEU (West Europe)

416512   Bilateral Agreement   **69 FRJO 1903**
SIGNED: 11 Jun 68
HEADNOTE: FORTALEZZA TELEMETRY STATION
TOPIC: Specific Property
PARTIES:
  France
  Eur Space Vehicle

416514   Bilateral Agreement   **69 FRJO 1004**
SIGNED: 13 Sep 65
HEADNOTE: STATUS ON FRENCH TERRITORY

TOPIC: IGO Status/Immunit
PARTIES:
  France
  CERN (Nuc Resrch)

417005   Bilateral Agreement   **69 FRMD 2402**
SIGNED: 10 Feb 69
HEADNOTE: COMMERCE
TOPIC: General Trade
PARTIES:
  Albania
  France

417052   Bilateral Agreement   **57 FRMD 1112**
SIGNED: 25 Nov 57
HEADNOTE: PAYMENTS
TOPIC: Finance
PARTIES:
  Argentina
  France

417053   Bilateral Agreement   **57 FRMD 1112**
SIGNED: 25 Nov 57
HEADNOTE: COMMERCIAL
TOPIC: General Trade
PARTIES:
  Argentina
  France

417077   Bilateral Agreement   **56 FRMD 1009**
SIGNED: 23 Aug 56
HEADNOTE: TRADE & PAYMENTS
TOPIC: General Economic
PARTIES:
  Brazil
  France

417152   Bilateral Agreement   **59 FRMD 1706**
SIGNED: 29 May 59
HEADNOTE: COMMERCE
TOPIC: General Trade
PARTIES:
  Denmark
  France

417153   Bilateral Agreement   **66 FRMD 2076**
SIGNED: 14 Jun 66
HEADNOTE: TRADE REGULATION
TOPIC: General Trade
PARTIES:
  Denmark
  France

417154   Bilateral Agreement   **49 FRMD 2411**
SIGNED: 25 Oct 49
HEADNOTE: PAYMENTS
TOPIC: Finance
PARTIES:
  Ecuador
  France

417224   Bilateral Agreement   **66 FRMD 2602**
SIGNED: 15 Feb 66
HEADNOTE: COMMERCE
TOPIC: General Trade
PARTIES:
  France
  Hungary

417244   Bilateral Agreement   **53 FRMD 2307**
SIGNED: 10 Jul 53
HEADNOTE: COMMERCIAL & FINANCIAL
TOPIC: General Economic
PARTIES:
  France
  Israel

417310   Bilateral Agreement   **69 FRMD 3107**
SIGNED: 19 May 69
HEADNOTE: TRADE FOR 1969
TOPIC: General Trade
PARTIES:
  France
  Mauritius

417346   Bilateral Protocol   **60 FRMD 904**
SIGNED: 2 Apr 60
HEADNOTE: TRADE
TOPIC: General Trade
PARTIES:
  France
  Norway

417349   Bilateral Agreement   **58 FRMD 2202**
SIGNED: 17 Feb 58
HEADNOTE: TRADE
TOPIC: General Trade
PARTIES:
  France
  Pakistan

417350   Bilateral Agreement   **64 FRMD 67**
SIGNED: 27 Aug 64
HEADNOTE: TRAVEL REGULATIONS
TOPIC: Visas
PARTIES:
  France
  Pakistan

417351   Bilateral Convention   **69 FRMD 25**
SIGNED: 22 Jul 66
HEADNOTE: INCOME TAX & TAX EVASION
TOPIC: Taxation
PARTIES:
  France
  Pakistan

417363   Bilateral Agreement   **65 FRMD 611**
SIGNED: 22 Oct 65
HEADNOTE: TRADE
TOPIC: General Trade
PARTIES:
  France
  Poland

417377   Bilateral Agreement   **65 FRMD 1302**
SIGNED: 8 Feb 65
HEADNOTE: TRADE & PAYMENTS
TOPIC: General Economic
PARTIES:
  France
  Romania

417439   Bilateral Agreement   **48 FRMD 1908**
SIGNED: 6 Aug 48
HEADNOTE: FRENCH NATIONALIZED PROPERTY
TOPIC: Claims and Debts
PARTIES:
  Czechoslovakia
  France

417442   Bilateral Agreement   **65 FRMD 2807**
SIGNED: 29 Jun 65
HEADNOTE: LONG-TERM TRADE
TOPIC: General Trade
PARTIES:
  Czechoslovakia
  France

417470   Bilateral Agreement   **63 FRMD 1302**
SIGNED: 24 Jan 63
HEADNOTE: INSURANCE FINANCES
TOPIC: Finance
PARTIES:
  France
  USSR (Soviet Union)

417471   Bilateral Agreement   **64 FRMD 411**
SIGNED: 30 Oct 64
HEADNOTE: TRADE DELIVERIES 1965-69
TOPIC: General Trade
PARTIES:
  France
  USSR (Soviet Union)

417479   Bilateral Agreement   **50 FRMD 2408**
SIGNED: 26 Jul 50
HEADNOTE: COMMERCE & NAVIGATION
TOPIC: General Economic

PARTIES:
  France
  Venezuela

417487   Bilateral Agreement   **64 FRMD 102**
SIGNED: 25 Jan 64
HEADNOTE: TRADE
TOPIC: General Trade
PARTIES:
  France
  Yugoslavia

419001   Bilateral Agreement   **3 EGDA 621**
SIGNED: 10 Nov 55
HEADNOTE: LONG RANGE TRADE INCREASE
TOPIC: General Trade
PARTIES:
  United Arab Rep
  Germany, East

419002   Bilateral Agreement   **3 EGDA 624**
SIGNED: 12 Nov 55
HEADNOTE: ESTABLISH TRADE MISSIONS
TOPIC: Consul/Citizenship
PARTIES:
  United Arab Rep
  Germany, East

419003   Bilateral Protocol   **5 EGDA 278**
SIGNED: 6 Aug 56
HEADNOTE: RADIO COOPERATION
TOPIC: Mass Media
PARTIES:
  United Arab Rep
  Germany, East

419004   Bilateral Protocol   **5 EGDA 281**
SIGNED: 7 Sep 57
HEADNOTE: TRADE MISSIONS CERTAIN RIGHTS
TOPIC: Consul/Citizenship
PARTIES:
  United Arab Rep
  Germany, East

419005   Bilateral Protocol   **5 EGDA 280**
SIGNED: 7 Sep 57
HEADNOTE: TRADE & PAYMENTS
TOPIC: General Economic
PARTIES:
  United Arab Rep
  Germany, East

419006   Bilateral Agreement   **1 EGDA 474**
SIGNED: 27 Mar 51
HEADNOTE: TRADE 1951-55
TOPIC: General Trade
PARTIES:
  Albania
  Germany, East

419007   Bilateral Agreement   **4 EGDA 547**
SIGNED: 26 Feb 52
HEADNOTE: SCIENTIFIC & TECHNICAL COOPER-
ATION
TOPIC: Tech Assistance
PARTIES:
  Albania
  Germany, East

419008   Bilateral Agreement   **4 EGDA 548**
SIGNED: 31 Jul 53
HEADNOTE: CULTURAL COOPERATION
TOPIC: Culture
PARTIES:
  Albania
  Germany, East

419009   Bilateral Protocol   **1 EGDA 474**
SIGNED: 26 Oct 53
HEADNOTE: SCIENTIFIC & TECHNICAL COOPER-
ATION
TOPIC: Tech Assistance

PARTIES:
Albania
Germany, East

419010   Bilateral Instrument   **1 EGDA 478**
SIGNED: 5 Nov 53
HEADNOTE: RAISE MISSIONS TO LEGATIONS
TOPIC: Consul/Citizenship
PARTIES:
Albania
Germany, East

419011   Bilateral Instrument   **2 EGDA 477**
SIGNED: 28 Mar 55
HEADNOTE: RAISE LEGATIONS TO EMBASSIES
TOPIC: Consul/Citizenship
PARTIES:
Albania
Germany, East

419012   Bilateral Agreement   **3 EGDA 596**
SIGNED: 15 Feb 56
HEADNOTE: AGRICULTURE & LIGHT INDUSTRY
TOPIC: Tech Assistance
PARTIES:
Albania
Germany, East

419013   Bilateral Agreement   **5 EGDA 284**
SIGNED: 22 Feb 57
HEADNOTE: TECHNOLOGY & SCIENCE
TOPIC: Tech Assistance
PARTIES:
Albania
Germany, East

419014   Bilateral Agreement   **5 EGDA 285**
SIGNED: 5 Jun 57
HEADNOTE: MAIL & PARCELS
TOPIC: Postal Service
PARTIES:
Albania
Germany, East

419015   Bilateral Agreement   **5 EGDA 292**
SIGNED: 5 Jun 57
HEADNOTE: TELECOMMUNICATIONS
TOPIC: Telecommunications
PARTIES:
Albania
Germany, East

419016   Bilateral Agreement   **5 EGDA 302**
SIGNED: 17 Aug 57
HEADNOTE: PLANT DISEASES
TOPIC: Sanitation
PARTIES:
Albania
Germany, East

419017   Bilateral Treaty   **7 EGDA 275**
SIGNED: 11 Jan 59
HEADNOTE: CONSULAR
TOPIC: Consul/Citizenship
PARTIES:
Albania
Germany, East

419018   Bilateral Treaty   **7 EGDA 283**
SIGNED: 11 Jan 59
HEADNOTE: CIVIL & CRIMINAL LAW
TOPIC: Admin Cooperation
PARTIES:
Albania
Germany, East

419019   Bilateral Treaty   **7 EGDA 311**
SIGNED: 8 Oct 59
HEADNOTE: COMMERCE & NAVIGATION
TOPIC: General Economic
PARTIES:
Albania
Germany, East

419020   Bilateral Agreement   **8 EGDA 310**
SIGNED: 21 Jan 60
HEADNOTE: AIR TRANSPORT
TOPIC: Air Transport
PARTIES:
Albania
Germany, East

419021   Bilateral Agreement   **8 EGDA 316**
SIGNED: 25 Apr 60
HEADNOTE: LONG-RANGE PAYMENTS 1961-65
TOPIC: Finance
PARTIES:
Albania
Germany, East

419022   Bilateral Agreement   **9 EGDA 309**
SIGNED: 11 Jan 61
HEADNOTE: TRADE 1961-65
TOPIC: General Trade
PARTIES:
Albania
Germany, East

419023   Bilateral Agreement   **9 EGDA 310**
SIGNED: 13 Jan 61
HEADNOTE: FIVE YEAR HEALTH COOPERATION
TOPIC: Sanitation
PARTIES:
Albania
Germany, East

419031   Bilateral Agreement   **4 EGDA 459**
SIGNED: 19 Jun 50
HEADNOTE: SCIENTIFIC & TECHNICAL COOPER-
ATION
TOPIC: Health/Educ/Welfare
PARTIES:
Bulgaria
Germany, East

419032   Bilateral Protocol   **4 EGDA 462**
SIGNED: 25 Sep 50
HEADNOTE: NON-COMMERCIAL FINANCES
TOPIC: Finance
PARTIES:
Bulgaria
Germany, East

419033   Bilateral Agreement   **4 EGDA 465**
SIGNED: 25 Sep 50
HEADNOTE: CULTURE
TOPIC: Culture
PARTIES:
Bulgaria
Germany, East

419034   Bilateral Agreement   **4 EGDA 468**
SIGNED: 30 Jan 51
HEADNOTE: MAIL
TOPIC: Postal Service
PARTIES:
Bulgaria
Germany, East

419035   Bilateral Agreement   **4 EGDA 472**
SIGNED: 30 Jan 51
HEADNOTE: PARCELS
TOPIC: Postal Service
PARTIES:
Bulgaria
Germany, East

419036   Bilateral Agreement   **4 EGDA 477**
SIGNED: 30 Jan 51
HEADNOTE: TELECOMMUNICATIONS
TOPIC: Telecommunications
PARTIES:
Bulgaria
Germany, East

419037   Bilateral Agreement   **4 EGDA 482**
SIGNED: 15 May 53
HEADNOTE: RADIO

TOPIC: Mass Media
PARTIES:
Bulgaria
Germany, East

419038   Bilateral Agreement   **1 EGDA 467**
SIGNED: 17 Oct 53
HEADNOTE: CONSUMER GOODS
TOPIC: Commodity Trade
PARTIES:
Bulgaria
Germany, East

419039   Bilateral Instrument   **1 EGDA 468**
SIGNED: 23 Oct 53
HEADNOTE: RAISE MISSIONS TO EMBASSIES
TOPIC: Consul/Citizenship
PARTIES:
Bulgaria
Germany, East

419043   Bilateral Protocol   **2 EGDA 462**
SIGNED: 14 Apr 55
HEADNOTE: HEAVY INDUSTRY
TOPIC: General Economic
PARTIES:
Bulgaria
Germany, East

419044   Bilateral Agreement   **4 EGDA 486**
SIGNED: 29 Apr 55
HEADNOTE: PAYMENTS 1955-57
TOPIC: Finance
PARTIES:
Bulgaria
Germany, East

419045   Bilateral Protocol   **3 EGDA 545**
SIGNED: 26 May 55
HEADNOTE: MACHINE BUILDING
TOPIC: General Economic
PARTIES:
Bulgaria
Germany, East

419046   Bilateral Agreement   **4 EGDA 490**
SIGNED: 17 Jun 55
HEADNOTE: PLANT DISEASE
TOPIC: Sanitation
PARTIES:
Bulgaria
Germany, East

419047   Bilateral Agreement   **4 EGDA 495**
SIGNED: 30 Jul 55
HEADNOTE: AIR TRANSPORT
TOPIC: Air Transport
PARTIES:
Bulgaria
Germany, East

419048   Bilateral Agreement   **3 EGDA 546**
SIGNED: 22 Aug 55
HEADNOTE: INCREASE ECONOMIC COOPER-
ATION
TOPIC: General Economic
PARTIES:
Bulgaria
Germany, East

419051   Bilateral Agreement   **5 EGDA 311**
SIGNED: 5 Jul 56
HEADNOTE: VETERINARY
TOPIC: Sanitation
PARTIES:
Bulgaria
Germany, East

419052   Bilateral Agreement   **5 EGDA 790**
SIGNED: 10 Jan 57
HEADNOTE: INVENTIONS, MODELS, TRADE-
MARKS
TOPIC: Patents/Copyrights

PARTIES:
Bulgaria
Germany, East

419054 Bilateral Agreement **6 EGDA 216**
SIGNED: 10 Jan 58
HEADNOTE: PAYMENTS 1958-60
TOPIC: Finance
PARTIES:
Bulgaria
Germany, East

419055 Bilateral Treaty **6 EGDA 221**
SIGNED: 27 Jan 58
HEADNOTE: CIVIL & CRIMINAL LAW
TOPIC: Admin Cooperation
PARTIES:
Bulgaria
Germany, East

419056 Bilateral Agreement **6 EGDA 250**
SIGNED: 20 Feb 58
HEADNOTE: SOCIAL POLICY
TOPIC: Health/Educ/Welfare
PARTIES:
Bulgaria
Germany, East

419057 Bilateral Treaty **6 EGDA 270**
SIGNED: 18 Apr 58
HEADNOTE: CONSULAR
TOPIC: Consul/Citizenship
PARTIES:
Bulgaria
Germany, East

419058 Bilateral Agreement **6 EGDA 278**
SIGNED: 18 Apr 58
HEADNOTE: CULTURAL & ECONOMIC COOPER-
ATION
TOPIC: Health/Educ/Welfare
PARTIES:
Bulgaria
Germany, East

419059 Bilateral Agreement **6 EGDA 282**
SIGNED: 18 Apr 58
HEADNOTE: HEALTH
TOPIC: Sanitation
PARTIES:
Bulgaria
Germany, East

419060 Bilateral Agreement **6 EGDA 519**
SIGNED: 25 Sep 58
HEADNOTE: RAW MATERIALS & FRUIT 1959-65
TOPIC: Commodity Trade
PARTIES:
Bulgaria
Germany, East

419061 Bilateral Agreement **7 EGDA 319**
SIGNED: 20 Mar 59
HEADNOTE: INTENSIFIES ECONOMIC COOPER-
ATION & TRADE
TOPIC: General Economic
PARTIES:
Bulgaria
Germany, East

419062 Bilateral Treaty **7 EGDA 320**
SIGNED: 16 Jul 59
HEADNOTE: COMMERCE & NAVIGATION
TOPIC: General Economic
PARTIES:
Bulgaria
Germany, East

419063 Bilateral Agreement **8 EGDA 325**
SIGNED: 11 Apr 60
HEADNOTE: TRADE 1961-65
TOPIC: General Trade

PARTIES:
Bulgaria
Germany, East

419064 Bilateral Agreement **9 EGDA 319**
SIGNED: 10 Oct 61
HEADNOTE: STUDENT ADMISSION & EXCHANGE
TOPIC: Education
PARTIES:
Bulgaria
Germany, East

419065 Bilateral Agreement **9 EGDA 325**
SIGNED: 14 Dec 61
HEADNOTE: ECONOMIC & SCIENTIFIC & TECHNI-
CAL COOPERATION
TOPIC: General Economic
PARTIES:
Bulgaria
Germany, East

419066 Bilateral Agreement **10 EGDA 368**
SIGNED: 11 Sep 62
HEADNOTE: AMENDS AIR AGREEMENT 30 JUN
55
TOPIC: Air Transport
PARTIES:
Bulgaria
Germany, East

419067 Bilateral Protocol **11 EGDA 610**
SIGNED: 15 Jul 63
HEADNOTE: ON-JOB TRAINING IN GDR PLANTS
TOPIC: Tech Assistance
PARTIES:
Bulgaria
Germany, East

419075 Bilateral Agreement **9 EGDA 459**
SIGNED: 14 Mar 61
HEADNOTE: NAVIGATION
TOPIC: Water Transport
PARTIES:
Burma
Germany, East

419080 Bilateral Agreement **4 EGDA 73**
SIGNED: 9 Oct 51
HEADNOTE: CULTURE
TOPIC: Culture
PARTIES:
China People's Rep
Germany, East

419081 Bilateral Agreement **4 EGDA 73**
SIGNED: 12 Oct 51
HEADNOTE: MAIL
TOPIC: Postal Service
PARTIES:
China People's Rep
Germany, East

419082 Bilateral Agreement **4 EGDA 81**
SIGNED: 12 Oct 51
HEADNOTE: TELECOMMUNICATIONS
TOPIC: Telecommunications
PARTIES:
China People's Rep
Germany, East

419083 Bilateral Instrument **1 EGDA 327**
SIGNED: 5 Oct 53
HEADNOTE: RAISE MISSIONS TO EMBASSIES
TOPIC: Consul/Citizenship
PARTIES:
China People's Rep
Germany, East

419084 Bilateral Agreement **4 EGDA 85**
SIGNED: 30 Oct 53
HEADNOTE: SCIENTIFIC & TECHNICAL COOPER-
ATION
TOPIC: Health/Educ/Welfare

PARTIES:
China People's Rep
Germany, East

419085 Bilateral Agreement **4 EGDA 86**
SIGNED: 8 Jun 54
HEADNOTE: RADIO
TOPIC: Mass Media
PARTIES:
China People's Rep
Germany, East

419086 Bilateral Protocol **2 EGDA 368**
SIGNED: 23 Jun 54
HEADNOTE: SCIENTIFIC & TECHNICAL COOPER-
ATION
TOPIC: Health/Educ/Welfare
PARTIES:
China People's Rep
Germany, East

419087 Bilateral Protocol **2 EGDA 407**
SIGNED: 27 Dec 54
HEADNOTE: STUDENT EXCHANGE
TOPIC: Education
PARTIES:
China People's Rep
Germany, East

419089 Bilateral Treaty **4 EGDA 95**
SIGNED: 25 Dec 55
HEADNOTE: FRIENDSHIP & COOPERATION
TOPIC: General Amity
PARTIES:
China People's Rep
Germany, East

419090 Bilateral Agreement **4 EGDA 98**
SIGNED: 25 Dec 55
HEADNOTE: CULTURE
TOPIC: Culture
PARTIES:
China People's Rep
Germany, East

419091 Bilateral Agreement **4 EGDA 100**
SIGNED: 25 Dec 55
HEADNOTE: PLANT DISEASES
TOPIC: Sanitation
PARTIES:
China People's Rep
Germany, East

419092 Bilateral Protocol **5 EGDA 332**
SIGNED: 26 Sep 57
HEADNOTE: DELIVERY COMPLETE FACILITIES
TOPIC: Commodity Trade
PARTIES:
China People's Rep
Germany, East

419093 Bilateral Agreement **5 EGDA 333**
SIGNED: 16 Dec 57
HEADNOTE: HEALTH
TOPIC: Sanitation
PARTIES:
China People's Rep
Germany, East

419095 Bilateral Treaty **7 EGDA 335**
SIGNED: 27 Jan 59
HEADNOTE: CONSULAR
TOPIC: Consul/Citizenship
PARTIES:
China People's Rep
Germany, East

419096 Bilateral Treaty **8 EGDA 333**
SIGNED: 18 Jan 60
HEADNOTE: COMMERCE & NAVIGATION
TOPIC: General Economic
PARTIES:
China People's Rep
Germany, East

419097 Bilateral Protocol **12 EGDA 726**
SIGNED: 16 Jan 64
HEADNOTE: AMEND TECHNICAL AGREEMENT 30
 OCT 53
TOPIC: Health/Educ/Welfare
PARTIES:
 China People's Rep
 Germany, East

419099 Bilateral Agreement **1 EGDA 498**
SIGNED: 15 Oct 49
HEADNOTE: TRADE
TOPIC: General Trade
PARTIES:
 Finland
 Germany, East

419100 Bilateral Agreement **3 EGDA 646**
SIGNED: 25 Jan 56
HEADNOTE: LONG-TERM PAYMENTS
TOPIC: Finance
PARTIES:
 Finland
 Germany, East

419101 Bilateral Agreement **5 EGDA 790**
SIGNED: 10 Mar 57
HEADNOTE: IMPROVE COOPERATION IN AGRI-
 CULTURE
TOPIC: General Economic
PARTIES:
 Finland
 Germany, East

419102 Bilateral Agreement **7 EGDA 356**
SIGNED: 9 Feb 59
HEADNOTE: CLEARING ACCOUNTS
TOPIC: Finance
PARTIES:
 Finland
 Germany, East

419103 Bilateral Agreement **7 EGDA 357**
SIGNED: 25 Feb 59
HEADNOTE: PAYMENTS
TOPIC: Finance
PARTIES:
 Finland
 Germany, East

419105 Bilateral Agreement **7 EGDA 363**
SIGNED: 25 Feb 59
HEADNOTE: TRADE MISSIONS CONSUL STATUS
TOPIC: Consul/Citizenship
PARTIES:
 Germany, East
 Ghana

419106 Bilateral Exchange **9 EGDA 338**
SIGNED: 8 Jul 61
HEADNOTE: TRADE
TOPIC: General Trade
PARTIES:
 Germany, East
 Ghana

419107 Bilateral Agreement **9 EGDA 333**
SIGNED: 19 Oct 61
HEADNOTE: LONG-TERM TRADE 1962-67
TOPIC: General Trade
PARTIES:
 Germany, East
 Ghana

419108 Bilateral Agreement **9 EGDA 338**
SIGNED: 19 Oct 61
HEADNOTE: LONG-TERM PAYMENTS 1962-67
TOPIC: Finance
PARTIES:
 Germany, East
 Ghana

419109 Bilateral Agreement **9 EGDA 342**
SIGNED: 19 Oct 61

HEADNOTE: SCIENTIFIC & TECHNICAL COOPER-
ATION
TOPIC: Tech Assistance
PARTIES:
 Germany, East
 Ghana

419110 Bilateral Agreement **9 EGDA 344**
SIGNED: 19 Oct 61
HEADNOTE: CULTURE
TOPIC: Culture
PARTIES:
 Germany, East
 Ghana

419111 Bilateral Agreement **12 EGDA 740**
SIGNED: 14 May 64
HEADNOTE: JOB SKILLS OF GHANAIANS
TOPIC: Non-ILO Labor
PARTIES:
 Germany, East
 Ghana

419112 Bilateral Agreement **12 EGDA 746**
SIGNED: 14 May 64
HEADNOTE: STUDENT ADMISSION & EXCHANGE
TOPIC: Education
PARTIES:
 Germany, East
 Ghana

419114 Bilateral Agreement **6 EGDA 309**
SIGNED: 17 Nov 58
HEADNOTE: TRADE MISSIONS CONSUL STATUS
TOPIC: Consul/Citizenship
PARTIES:
 Germany, East
 Guinea

419115 Bilateral Agreement **6 EGDA 309**
SIGNED: 17 Nov 58
HEADNOTE: TRADE & PAYMENTS
TOPIC: General Economic
PARTIES:
 Germany, East
 Guinea

419116 Bilateral Agreement **6 EGDA 309**
SIGNED: 17 Nov 58
HEADNOTE: CULTURE
TOPIC: Culture
PARTIES:
 Germany, East
 Guinea

419117 Bilateral Agreement **7 EGDA 365**
SIGNED: 3 Mar 59
HEADNOTE: LONG-TERM TRADE
TOPIC: General Trade
PARTIES:
 Germany, East
 Guinea

419118 Bilateral Agreement **8 EGDA 345**
SIGNED: 10 Jan 60
HEADNOTE: TRADE & PAYMENTS 1960-65
TOPIC: General Economic
PARTIES:
 Germany, East
 Guinea

419119 Bilateral Protocol **11 EGDA 584**
SIGNED: 11 Feb 63
HEADNOTE: ECONOMIC RELATIONS
TOPIC: General Economic
PARTIES:
 Germany, East
 Guinea

419120 Bilateral Agreement **12 EGDA 759**
SIGNED: 29 May 64
HEADNOTE: JOB SKILLS OF GUINEANS
TOPIC: Non-ILO Labor

PARTIES:
 Germany, East
 Guinea

419121 Bilateral Agreement **12 EGDA 765**
SIGNED: 29 May 64
HEADNOTE: STUDENT ADMISSION & EXCHANGE
TOPIC: Education
PARTIES:
 Germany, East
 Guinea

419125 Bilateral Agreement **2 EGDA 521**
SIGNED: 16 Oct 54
HEADNOTE: TRADE & PAYMENTS
TOPIC: General Economic
PARTIES:
 Germany, East
 India

419126 Bilateral Agreement **2 EGDA 521**
SIGNED: 16 Oct 54
HEADNOTE: TECHNICAL AID
TOPIC: Tech Assistance
PARTIES:
 Germany, East
 India

419127 Bilateral Agreement **5 EGDA 342**
SIGNED: 8 Oct 56
HEADNOTE: LONG-TERM TRADE 1956-59
TOPIC: General Trade
PARTIES:
 Germany, East
 India

419128 Bilateral Agreement **7 EGDA 367**
SIGNED: 18 Dec 59
HEADNOTE: TRADE & PAYMENTS
TOPIC: General Economic
PARTIES:
 Germany, East
 India

419129 Bilateral Agreement **11 EGDA 388**
SIGNED: 23 Nov 63
HEADNOTE: JOINT NAVIGATION LINE
TOPIC: Water Transport
PARTIES:
 Germany, East
 India

419130 Bilateral Agreement **12 EGDA 1128**
SIGNED: 20 Feb 64
HEADNOTE: CULTURAL EXCHANGE
TOPIC: Culture
PARTIES:
 Germany, East
 India

419131 Bilateral Agreement **12 EGDA 771**
SIGNED: 12 Sep 64
HEADNOTE: TRADE & PAYMENTS 1965-67
TOPIC: General Economic
PARTIES:
 Germany, East
 India

419132 Bilateral Agreement **5 EGDA 344**
SIGNED: 12 Dec 56
HEADNOTE: TRADE
TOPIC: General Trade
PARTIES:
 Germany, East
 Indonesia

419133 Bilateral Agreement **9 EGDA 350**
SIGNED: 16 Feb 61
HEADNOTE: TRADE
TOPIC: General Trade
PARTIES:
 Germany, East
 Indonesia

419134   Bilateral Exchange   **9 EGDA 350**
SIGNED: 16 Feb 61
HEADNOTE: FAIRS & EXHIBITIONS
TOPIC: Health/Educ/Welfare
PARTIES:
  Germany, East
  Indonesia

419135   Bilateral Exchange   **9 EGDA 351**
SIGNED: 16 Feb 61
HEADNOTE: DELIVERY COMPLETE FACILITIES
TOPIC: Commodity Trade
PARTIES:
  Germany, East
  Indonesia

419136   Bilateral Exchange   **9 EGDA 351**
SIGNED: 16 Feb 61
HEADNOTE: MERCHANT MARINE
TOPIC: Water Transport
PARTIES:
  Germany, East
  Indonesia

419137   Bilateral Protocol   **6 EGDA 314**
SIGNED: 26 Oct 58
HEADNOTE: TRADE MISSIONS CONSUL STATUS
TOPIC: Consul/Citizenship
PARTIES:
  Germany, East
  Iraq

419138   Bilateral Agreement   **6 EGDA 314**
SIGNED: 26 Oct 58
HEADNOTE: TRADE
TOPIC: General Trade
PARTIES:
  Germany, East
  Iraq

419139   Bilateral Agreement   **7 EGDA 370**
SIGNED: 1 Apr 59
HEADNOTE: CULTURAL & SCIENTIFIC COOPER-
ATION
TOPIC: Health/Educ/Welfare
PARTIES:
  Germany, East
  Iraq

419140   Bilateral Agreement   **10 EGDA 384**
SIGNED: 24 May 62
HEADNOTE: CONSULATES GENERAL
TOPIC: Consul/Citizenship
PARTIES:
  Germany, East
  Iraq

419143   Bilateral Agreement   **11 EGDA 627**
SIGNED: 28 Oct 63
HEADNOTE: CONSULATES GENERAL
TOPIC: Consul/Citizenship
PARTIES:
  Germany, East
  Yemen

419144   Bilateral Agreement   **5 EGDA 348**
SIGNED: 10 Oct 57
HEADNOTE: DIPLOMATIC RELATIONS
TOPIC: Consul/Citizenship
PARTIES:
  Germany, East
  Yugoslavia

419145   Bilateral Agreement   **5 EGDA 352**
SIGNED: 19 Oct 57
HEADNOTE: TRADE
TOPIC: General Trade
PARTIES:
  Germany, East
  Yugoslavia

419146   Bilateral Agreement   **5 EGDA 352**
SIGNED: 19 Oct 57
HEADNOTE: PAYMENTS

TOPIC: Finance
PARTIES:
  Germany, East
  Yugoslavia

419147   Bilateral Agreement   **8 EGDA 354**
SIGNED: 6 Feb 60
HEADNOTE: AIR TRANSPORT
TOPIC: Air Transport
PARTIES:
  Germany, East
  Yugoslavia

419148   Bilateral Agreement   **8 EGDA 364**
SIGNED: 2 Dec 60
HEADNOTE: PRODUCTION & TECHNICAL COOP-
ERATION
TOPIC: General Economic
PARTIES:
  Germany, East
  Yugoslavia

419149   Bilateral Protocol   **9 EGDA 484**
SIGNED: 27 Jul 61
HEADNOTE: PRODUCTION & TECHNICAL COOP-
ERATION
TOPIC: General Economic
PARTIES:
  Germany, East
  Yugoslavia

419150   Bilateral Agreement   **11 EGDA 603**
SIGNED: 22 May 63
HEADNOTE: CERTAIN SETTLEMENTS
TOPIC: General Ad Hoc
PARTIES:
  Germany, East
  Yugoslavia

419152   Bilateral Protocol   **11 EGDA 620**
SIGNED: 28 Sep 63
HEADNOTE: INCREASE ECONOMIC & TECHNICAL
COOPERATION
TOPIC: General Economic
PARTIES:
  Germany, East
  Yugoslavia

419153   Bilateral Agreement   **11 EGDA 620**
SIGNED: 28 Sep 63
HEADNOTE: EARTHQUAKE RELIEF CREDIT
TOPIC: Humanitarian
PARTIES:
  Germany, East
  Yugoslavia

419154   Bilateral Agreement   **11 EGDA 395**
SIGNED: 19 Dec 63
HEADNOTE: PLANT DISEASES
TOPIC: Sanitation
PARTIES:
  Germany, East
  Yugoslavia

419155   Bilateral Treaty   **12 EGDA 792**
SIGNED: 12 Feb 64
HEADNOTE: CONSULAR
TOPIC: Consul/Citizenship
PARTIES:
  Germany, East
  Yugoslavia

419156   Bilateral Agreement   **12 EGDA 806**
SIGNED: 15 May 64
HEADNOTE: JOINT COMMITTEE ECONOMIC CO-
OPERATION
TOPIC: IGO Establishment
PARTIES:
  Germany, East
  Yugoslavia

419157   Bilateral Agreement   **12 EGDA 815**
SIGNED: 10 Jul 64
HEADNOTE: SCIENCE & EDUCATION & CULTURE

TOPIC: Health/Educ/Welfare
PARTIES:
  Germany, East
  Yugoslavia

419165   Bilateral Agreement   **8 EGDA 371**
SIGNED: 29 Aug 60
HEADNOTE: TRADE
TOPIC: General Trade
PARTIES:
  Cambodia
  Germany, East

419166   Bilateral Agreement   **8 EGDA 372**
SIGNED: 29 Aug 60
HEADNOTE: PAYMENTS
TOPIC: Finance
PARTIES:
  Cambodia
  Germany, East

419167   Bilateral Agreement   **8 EGDA 371**
SIGNED: 29 Aug 60
HEADNOTE: ECONOMIC & TECHNICAL COOPER-
ATION
TOPIC: Tech Assistance
PARTIES:
  Cambodia
  Germany, East

419168   Bilateral Agreement   **12 EGDA 826**
SIGNED: 2 Feb 64
HEADNOTE: CULTURAL & SCIENTIFIC COOPER-
ATION
TOPIC: Health/Educ/Welfare
PARTIES:
  Cambodia
  Germany, East

419171   Bilateral Agreement   **4 EGDA 505**
SIGNED: 30 Dec 54
HEADNOTE: NON-COMMERCIAL FINANCES
TOPIC: Finance
PARTIES:
  Germany, East
  Korea, North

419172   Bilateral Agreement   **4 EGDA 507**
SIGNED: 27 Jan 55
HEADNOTE: SCIENTIFIC & TECHNICAL COOPER-
ATION
TOPIC: Tech Assistance
PARTIES:
  Germany, East
  Korea, North

419173   Bilateral Agreement   **4 EGDA 508**
SIGNED: 1 Dec 55
HEADNOTE: MAIL & PARCELS
TOPIC: Postal Service
PARTIES:
  Germany, East
  Korea, North

419174   Bilateral Agreement   **4 EGDA 516**
SIGNED: 1 Dec 55
HEADNOTE: TELECOMMUNICATIONS
TOPIC: Telecommunications
PARTIES:
  Germany, East
  Korea, North

419175   Bilateral Agreement   **4 EGDA 532**
SIGNED: 12 Jun 56
HEADNOTE: CULTURAL & ECONOMIC COOPER-
ATION
TOPIC: Health/Educ/Welfare
PARTIES:
  Germany, East
  Korea, North

419176   Bilateral Agreement   **1 EGDA 534**
SIGNED: 12 Jun 56
HEADNOTE: RADIO

TOPIC: Mass Media
PARTIES:
  Germany, East
  Korea, North

419177   Bilateral Agreement   **5 EGDA 355**
SIGNED: 22 Feb 57
HEADNOTE: LONG-TERM TRADE 1958-61
TOPIC: General Trade
PARTIES:
  Germany, East
  Korea, North

419178   Bilateral Protocol   **5 EGDA 355**
SIGNED: 12 Mar 57
HEADNOTE: SCIENTIFIC & TECHNICAL COOPER-
  ATION
TOPIC: Tech Assistance
PARTIES:
  Germany, East
  Korea, North

419179   Bilateral Agreement   **6 EGDA 323**
SIGNED: 18 Apr 58
HEADNOTE: CULTURAL & SCIENTIFIC COOPER-
  ATION
TOPIC: Health/Educ/Welfare
PARTIES:
  Germany, East
  Korea, North

419180   Bilateral Agreement   **7 EGDA 384**
SIGNED: 7 Dec 59
HEADNOTE: STUDENT EXCHANGE
TOPIC: Education
PARTIES:
  Germany, East
  Korea, North

419181   Bilateral Treaty   **8 EGDA 381**
SIGNED: 3 Jun 60
HEADNOTE: CONSULAR
TOPIC: Consul/Citizenship
PARTIES:
  Germany, East
  Korea, North

419182   Bilateral Treaty   **10 EGDA 399**
SIGNED: 29 Dec 61
HEADNOTE: COMMERCE & NAVIGATION
TOPIC: General Economic
PARTIES:
  Germany, East
  Korea, North

419184   Bilateral Agreement   **8 EGDA 394**
SIGNED: 29 Feb 60
HEADNOTE: TRADE MISSIONS
TOPIC: Consul/Citizenship
PARTIES:
  Cuba
  Germany, East

419185   Bilateral Agreement   **8 EGDA 397**
SIGNED: 17 Dec 60
HEADNOTE: SCIENTIFIC & TECHNICAL COOPER-
  ATION
TOPIC: Tech Assistance
PARTIES:
  Cuba
  Germany, East

419186   Bilateral Agreement   **10 EGDA 407**
SIGNED: 4 Oct 62
HEADNOTE: RADIO & TV
TOPIC: Mass Media
PARTIES:
  Cuba
  Germany, East

419187   Bilateral Agreement   **11 EGDA 585**
SIGNED: 13 Feb 63
HEADNOTE: GENERAL DELIVERY CONDITIONS
TOPIC: General Trade

PARTIES:
  Cuba
  Germany, East

419188   Bilateral Protocol   **11 EGDA 414**
SIGNED: 11 May 63
HEADNOTE: AMENDS RADIO-TV 4 OCT 62
TOPIC: Mass Media
PARTIES:
  Cuba
  Germany, East

419189   Bilateral Agreement   **11 EGDA 615**
SIGNED: 3 Sep 63
HEADNOTE: LONG-TERM 10 MILLION PESOS
TOPIC: Loans and Credits
PARTIES:
  Cuba
  Germany, East

419190   Bilateral Agreement   **12 EGDA 837**
SIGNED: 26 Apr 64
HEADNOTE: ECONOMIC & SCIENTIFIC & TECHNI-
  CAL COOPERATION
TOPIC: General Aid
PARTIES:
  Cuba
  Germany, East

419191   Bilateral Agreement   **12 EGDA 1149**
SIGNED: 20 Jul 64
HEADNOTE: 84 MILLION DM CREDIT 1965-70
TOPIC: Loans and Credits
PARTIES:
  Cuba
  Germany, East

419192   Bilateral Agreement   **12 EGDA 841**
SIGNED: 5 Oct 64
HEADNOTE: HEALTH
TOPIC: Sanitation
PARTIES:
  Cuba
  Germany, East

419193   Bilateral Treaty   **12 EGDA 1166**
SIGNED: 29 Oct 64
HEADNOTE: SUGAR
TOPIC: Commodity Trade
PARTIES:
  Cuba
  Germany, East

419196   Bilateral Exchange   **11 EGDA 603**
SIGNED: 20 May 63
HEADNOTE: THREE-YEAR EXTENSION TRADE &
  PAYMENTS
TOPIC: General Economic
PARTIES:
  Germany, East
  Lebanon

419197   Bilateral Agreement   **9 EGDA 462**
SIGNED: 1 Apr 61
HEADNOTE: FUTURE TRADE MISSIONS
TOPIC: Consul/Citizenship
PARTIES:
  Germany, East
  Mali

419198   Bilateral Agreement   **9 EGDA 372**
SIGNED: 17 Apr 61
HEADNOTE: PAYMENTS
TOPIC: Finance
PARTIES:
  Germany, East
  Mali

419199   Bilateral Agreement   **11 EGDA 424**
SIGNED: 30 Sep 63
HEADNOTE: ON-JOB TRAINING IN GDR PLANTS
TOPIC: Tech Assistance

PARTIES:
  Germany, East
  Mali

419200   Bilateral Agreement   **12 EGDA 844**
SIGNED: 3 Jun 64
HEADNOTE: CULTURAL & SCIENTIFIC COOPER-
  ATION
TOPIC: Health/Educ/Welfare
PARTIES:
  Germany, East
  Mali

419201   Bilateral Agreement   **12 EGDA 849**
SIGNED: 3 Jun 64
HEADNOTE: STUDENT EXCHANGE
TOPIC: Education
PARTIES:
  Germany, East
  Mali

419207   Bilateral Agreement   **8 EGDA 401**
SIGNED: 8 Aug 60
HEADNOTE: PAYMENTS
TOPIC: Finance
PARTIES:
  Germany, East
  Morocco

419208   Bilateral Agreement   **12 EGDA 856**
SIGNED: 31 Jul 64
HEADNOTE: LONG-TERM TRADE
TOPIC: General Trade
PARTIES:
  Germany, East
  Morocco

419209   Bilateral Agreement   **12 EGDA 859**
SIGNED: 31 Jul 64
HEADNOTE: PAYMENTS
TOPIC: Finance
PARTIES:
  Germany, East
  Morocco

419211   Bilateral Instrument   **1 EGDA 482**
SIGNED: 16 Oct 53
HEADNOTE: RAISE MISSIONS TO LEGATIONS
TOPIC: Consul/Citizenship
PARTIES:
  Germany, East
  Mongolia

419212   Bilateral Agreement   **4 EGDA 559**
SIGNED: 18 Jul 55
HEADNOTE: RADIO
TOPIC: Mass Media
PARTIES:
  Germany, East
  Mongolia

419213   Bilateral Instrument   **3 EGDA 600**
SIGNED: 17 Oct 55
HEADNOTE: RAISE LEGATIONS TO EMBASSIES
TOPIC: Consul/Citizenship
PARTIES:
  Germany, East
  Mongolia

419214   Bilateral Agreement   **5 EGDA 363**
SIGNED: 22 Aug 57
HEADNOTE: CULTURAL & SCIENTIFIC COOPER-
  ATION
TOPIC: Health/Educ/Welfare
PARTIES:
  Germany, East
  Mongolia

419215   Bilateral Agreement   **5 EGDA 366**
SIGNED: 30 Oct 57
HEADNOTE: PAYMENTS 1957-60
TOPIC: Finance

PARTIES:
Germany, East
Mongolia

419216   Bilateral Agreement   **5 EGDA 370**
SIGNED: 6 Nov 57
HEADNOTE: TRADE 1958-60
TOPIC: General Trade
PARTIES:
Germany, East
Mongolia

419217   Bilateral Agreement   **6 EGDA 518**
SIGNED: 1 Jul 58
HEADNOTE: SOCIALIZED AGRICULTURE
TOPIC: Health/Educ/Welfare
PARTIES:
Germany, East
Mongolia

419218   Bilateral Agreement   **7 EGDA 399**
SIGNED: 11 Apr 59
HEADNOTE: SCIENTIFIC & TECHNICAL COOPER-
ATION
TOPIC: Tech Assistance
PARTIES:
Germany, East
Mongolia

419219   Bilateral Agreement   **7 EGDA 392**
SIGNED: 12 Jun 59
HEADNOTE: MAIL & PARCELS
TOPIC: Postal Service
PARTIES:
Germany, East
Mongolia

419220   Bilateral Agreement   **7 EGDA 399**
SIGNED: 12 Jun 59
HEADNOTE: TELECOMMUNICATIONS
TOPIC: Telecommunications
PARTIES:
Germany, East
Mongolia

419221   Bilateral Treaty   **11 EGDA 430**
SIGNED: 7 Jan 63
HEADNOTE: CONSULAR
TOPIC: Consul/Citizenship
PARTIES:
Germany, East
Mongolia

419222   Bilateral Protocol   **12 EGDA 1153**
SIGNED: 26 Aug 64
HEADNOTE: SCIENTIFIC & TECHNICAL COOPER-
ATION
TOPIC: Tech Assistance
PARTIES:
Germany, East
Mongolia

419227   Bilateral Instrument   **4 EGDA 113**
SIGNED: 6 Jun 50
HEADNOTE: MARKING ODER-NEISSE BORDER
TOPIC: Territory Boundary
PARTIES:
Germany, East
Poland

419228   Bilateral Protocol   **4 EGDA 115**
SIGNED: 6 Jun 50
HEADNOTE: FINANCES
TOPIC: Finance
PARTIES:
Germany, East
Poland

419229   Bilateral Agreement   **4 EGDA 114**
SIGNED: 6 Jun 50
HEADNOTE: ECONOMIC & TECHNICAL COOPER-
ATION
TOPIC: General Economic

PARTIES:
Germany, East
Poland

419230   Bilateral Protocol   **4 EGDA 118**
SIGNED: 6 Jun 50
HEADNOTE: CULTURAL COOPERATION
TOPIC: Culture
PARTIES:
Germany, East
Poland

419232   Bilateral Protocol   **4 EGDA 128**
SIGNED: 6 Jul 50
HEADNOTE: RADIOPHONE
TOPIC: Telecommunications
PARTIES:
Germany, East
Poland

419233   Bilateral Protocol   **4 EGDA 130**
SIGNED: 19 Jan 51
HEADNOTE: BORDER COMMISSION REPORT
TOPIC: Territory Boundary
PARTIES:
Germany, East
Poland

419234   Bilateral Agreement   **4 EGDA 137**
SIGNED: 3 Feb 51
HEADNOTE: MAIL
TOPIC: Postal Service
PARTIES:
Germany, East
Poland

419235   Bilateral Agreement   **4 EGDA 144**
SIGNED: 3 Feb 51
HEADNOTE: TELECOMMUNICATIONS
TOPIC: Telecommunications
PARTIES:
Germany, East
Poland

419236   Bilateral Agreement   **4 EGDA 153**
SIGNED: 18 Jan 52
HEADNOTE: PAYMENTS 1952-55
TOPIC: Finance
PARTIES:
Germany, East
Poland

419237   Bilateral Agreement   **1 EGDA 370**
SIGNED: 6 Oct 53
HEADNOTE: RAISE MISSIONS TO EMBASSIES
TOPIC: Consul/Citizenship
PARTIES:
Germany, East
Poland

419238   Bilateral Protocol   **4 EGDA 171**
SIGNED: 19 Dec 53
HEADNOTE: TRANSFER ART WORKS TO GDR
TOPIC: Culture
PARTIES:
Germany, East
Poland

419239   Bilateral Agreement   **4 EGDA 175**
SIGNED: 27 May 54
HEADNOTE: TRAFFIC ON INLAND WATERWAYS
TOPIC: Water Transport
PARTIES:
Germany, East
Poland

419240   Bilateral Agreement   **4 EGDA 193**
SIGNED: 27 May 54
HEADNOTE: TRANSPORT ON INLAND WATER-
WAYS
TOPIC: Water Transport
PARTIES:
Germany, East
Poland

419241   Bilateral Agreement   **2 EGDA 426**
SIGNED: 2 Aug 54
HEADNOTE: STETTIN HAFF FISHERIES
TOPIC: Specific Resources
PARTIES:
Germany, East
Poland

419242   Bilateral Agreement   **4 EGDA 204**
SIGNED: 5 Nov 54
HEADNOTE: RAILROAD BORDER
TOPIC: Land Transport
PARTIES:
Germany, East
Poland

419244   Bilateral Protocol   **2 EGDA 431**
SIGNED: 21 Feb 55
HEADNOTE: SCIENTIFIC & TECHNICAL COOPER-
ATION
TOPIC: General Economic
PARTIES:
Germany, East
Poland

419245   Bilateral Protocol   **3 EGDA 458**
SIGNED: 28 May 55
HEADNOTE: IMPROVING POSTAL COOPERATION
TOPIC: Postal Service
PARTIES:
Germany, East
Poland

419246   Bilateral Agreement   **4 EGDA 224**
SIGNED: 20 Jun 55
HEADNOTE: AIR TRANSPORT
TOPIC: Air Transport
PARTIES:
Germany, East
Poland

419247   Bilateral Agreement   **4 EGDA 230**
SIGNED: 9 Jul 55
HEADNOTE: VETERINARY
TOPIC: Sanitation
PARTIES:
Germany, East
Poland

419248   Bilateral Agreement   **4 EGDA 234**
SIGNED: 7 Oct 55
HEADNOTE: HEALTH
TOPIC: Sanitation
PARTIES:
Germany, East
Poland

419249   Bilateral Agreement   **4 EGDA 237**
SIGNED: 12 Jan 56
HEADNOTE: SAFETY AT SEA BALTIC FISHERY
TOPIC: Water Transport
PARTIES:
Germany, East
Poland

419250   Bilateral Agreement   **3 EGDA 504**
SIGNED: 27 Jan 56
HEADNOTE: LONG-TERM SCIENTIFIC COOPER-
ATION
TOPIC: Scientific Project
PARTIES:
Germany, East
Poland

419251   Bilateral Treaty   **3 EGDA 504**
SIGNED: 31 Jan 56
HEADNOTE: WATERWAYS
TOPIC: Water Transport
PARTIES:
Germany, East
Poland

419252   Bilateral Agreement   **5 EGDA 407**
SIGNED: 17 Apr 57

HEADNOTE: TUROW KONIN ADAMOW COAL
MINES
TOPIC: Specific Resources
PARTIES:
Germany, East
Poland

419253   Bilateral Agreement   **5 EGDA 433**
SIGNED: 5 Sep 57
HEADNOTE: CUSTOMS
TOPIC: Customs
PARTIES:
Germany, East
Poland

419254   Bilateral Agreement   **5 EGDA 438**
SIGNED: 17 Sep 57
HEADNOTE: PEACEFUL USE ATOMIC ENERGY
TOPIC: Atomic Energy
PARTIES:
Germany, East
Poland

419255   Bilateral Agreement   **5 EGDA 440**
SIGNED: 16 Nov 57
HEADNOTE: MACHINE INDUSTRY
TOPIC: General Economic
PARTIES:
Germany, East
Poland

419256   Bilateral Agreement   **5 EGDA 794**
SIGNED: 3 Dec 57
HEADNOTE: CONSTRUCTION INDUSTRY
TOPIC: General Economic
PARTIES:
Germany, East
Poland

419257   Bilateral Protocol   **6 EGDA 332**
SIGNED: 14 Mar 58
HEADNOTE: SCIENTIFIC & TECHNICAL COOPER-
ATION
TOPIC: Health/Educ/Welfare
PARTIES:
Germany, East
Poland

419258   Bilateral Agreement   **6 EGDA 332**
SIGNED: 24 Oct 58
HEADNOTE: DELIVERIES 1961-65
TOPIC: Commodity Trade
PARTIES:
Germany, East
Poland

419259   Bilateral Protocol   **6 EGDA 332**
SIGNED: 24 Oct 58
HEADNOTE: ECONOMIC COOPERATION 1961-65
TOPIC: General Economic
PARTIES:
Germany, East
Poland

419260   Bilateral Protocol   **7 EGDA 409**
SIGNED: 6 May 59
HEADNOTE: CULTURAL INFORMATION CENTERS
TOPIC: Culture
PARTIES:
Germany, East
Poland

419261   Bilateral Agreement   **7 EGDA 568**
SIGNED: 27 May 59
HEADNOTE: BORDER AREA CONSUMER GOODS
TOPIC: Commodity Trade
PARTIES:
Germany, East
Poland

419262   Bilateral Agreement   **7 EGDA 416**
SIGNED: 23 Sep 59
HEADNOTE: RAIL TRANSIT CERTAIN LINES
TOPIC: Visas

PARTIES:
Germany, East
Poland

419263   Bilateral Agreement   **7 EGDA 426**
SIGNED: 10 Nov 59
HEADNOTE: NEISSE WATER USE
TOPIC: Specific Resources
PARTIES:
Germany, East
Poland

419264   Bilateral Protocol   **8 EGDA 414**
SIGNED: 9 Jan 60
HEADNOTE: AMENDS 27 MAY 54 PROTOCOL
TOPIC: Water Transport
PARTIES:
Germany, East
Poland

419265   Bilateral Protocol   **8 EGDA 419**
SIGNED: 9 Jan 60
HEADNOTE: AMENDS 22 FEB 55 PROTOCOL
TOPIC: Water Transport
PARTIES:
Germany, East
Poland

419266   Bilateral Agreement   **8 EGDA 423**
SIGNED: 22 Apr 60
HEADNOTE: ECONOMIC & TECHNICAL COOPER-
ATION
TOPIC: General Economic
PARTIES:
Germany, East
Poland

419267   Bilateral Agreement   **9 EGDA 379**
SIGNED: 18 Jan 61
HEADNOTE: SOVIET OIL PIPELINE
TOPIC: Specific Property
PARTIES:
Germany, East
Poland

419268   Bilateral Protocol   **9 EGDA 469**
SIGNED: 13 May 61
HEADNOTE: ARCHIVE EXCHANGE
TOPIC: Admin Cooperation
PARTIES:
Germany, East
Poland

419269   Bilateral Agreement   **10 EGDA 575**
SIGNED: 9 May 62
HEADNOTE: NEW ROAD CHECKPOINT
TOPIC: Visas
PARTIES:
Germany, East
Poland

419270   Bilateral Agreement   **11 EGDA 589**
SIGNED: 17 Mar 63
HEADNOTE: 500 POLISH MINERS FOR GDR
TOPIC: Non-ILO Labor
PARTIES:
Germany, East
Poland

419271   Bilateral Exchange   **11 EGDA 416**
SIGNED: 30 Dec 63
HEADNOTE: AMENDS AGREEMENT 20 JUN 55
TOPIC: Air Transport
PARTIES:
Germany, East
Poland

419272   Bilateral Agreement   **12 EGDA 1144**
SIGNED: 7 Jun 64
HEADNOTE: VISA ABOLITION
TOPIC: Visas
PARTIES:
Germany, East
Poland

419279   Bilateral Agreement   **4 EGDA 419**
SIGNED: 22 Sep 50
HEADNOTE: SCIENTIFIC & TECHNICAL COOPER-
ATION
TOPIC: Scientific Project
PARTIES:
Germany, East
Romania

419280   Bilateral Protocol   **4 EGDA 420**
SIGNED: 22 Sep 50
HEADNOTE: NON-COMMERCIAL FINANCES
TOPIC: Finance
PARTIES:
Germany, East
Romania

419281   Bilateral Agreement   **4 EGDA 422**
SIGNED: 22 Sep 50
HEADNOTE: CULTURAL COOPERATION
TOPIC: Culture
PARTIES:
Germany, East
Romania

419282   Bilateral Treaty   **1 EGDA 453**
SIGNED: 6 Nov 50
HEADNOTE: TRADE
TOPIC: General Trade
PARTIES:
Germany, East
Romania

419283   Bilateral Agreement   **1 EGDA 454**
SIGNED: 23 Jan 52
HEADNOTE: TRADE 1952-55
TOPIC: General Trade
PARTIES:
Germany, East
Romania

419284   Bilateral Protocol   **1 EGDA 455**
SIGNED: 12 Sep 52
HEADNOTE: ECONOMIC COOPERATION
TOPIC: General Economic
PARTIES:
Germany, East
Romania

419285   Bilateral Agreement   **4 EGDA 425**
SIGNED: 31 Oct 52
HEADNOTE: MAIL & PARCEL
TOPIC: Postal Service
PARTIES:
Germany, East
Romania

419286   Bilateral Agreement   **4 EGDA 431**
SIGNED: 31 Oct 52
HEADNOTE: TELECOMMUNICATIONS
TOPIC: Telecommunications
PARTIES:
Germany, East
Romania

419287   Bilateral Instrument   **1 EGDA 457**
SIGNED: 17 Oct 53
HEADNOTE: RAISE MISSIONS TO EMBASSIES
TOPIC: Consul/Citizenship
PARTIES:
Germany, East
Romania

419288   Bilateral Agreement   **4 EGDA 437**
SIGNED: 21 Dec 53
HEADNOTE: RADIO
TOPIC: Mass Media
PARTIES:
Germany, East
Romania

419290   Bilateral Protocol   **3 EGDA 577**
SIGNED: 3 Jun 55

HEADNOTE: SCIENTIFIC & TECHNICAL COOPER-
ATION
TOPIC: Scientific Project
PARTIES:
  Germany, East
  Romania

419291   Bilateral Agreement   **4 EGDA 451**
SIGNED: 21 Dec 55
HEADNOTE: LONG-RANGE PAYMENTS
TOPIC: Finance
PARTIES:
  Germany, East
  Romania

419292   Bilateral Agreement   **5 EGDA 468**
SIGNED: 28 Apr 57
HEADNOTE: SOCIAL POLICY
TOPIC: Health/Educ/Welfare
PARTIES:
  Germany, East
  Romania

419293   Bilateral Agreement   **5 EGDA 479**
SIGNED: 28 Apr 57
HEADNOTE: HEALTH
TOPIC: Sanitation
PARTIES:
  Germany, East
  Romania

419294   Bilateral Protocol   **7 EGDA 432**
SIGNED: 16 Mar 59
HEADNOTE: ECONOMIC   COOPERATION   &
  1959-65 TRADE
TOPIC: General Economic
PARTIES:
  Germany, East
  Romania

419295   Bilateral Protocol   **7 EGDA 438**
SIGNED: 18 Mar 59
HEADNOTE: TELEVISION
TOPIC: Mass Media
PARTIES:
  Germany, East
  Romania

419296   Bilateral Agreement   **7 EGDA 443**
SIGNED: 12 Nov 59
HEADNOTE: PEACEFUL USE ATOMIC ENERGY
TOPIC: Atomic Energy
PARTIES:
  Germany, East
  Romania

419297   Bilateral Agreement   **9 EGDA 388**
SIGNED: 17 Feb 61
HEADNOTE: TRADE 1961-65
TOPIC: General Trade
PARTIES:
  Germany, East
  Romania

419298   Bilateral Agreement   **9 EGDA 389**
SIGNED: 2 Mar 61
HEADNOTE: SCIENTIFIC & TECHNICAL COOPER-
ATION
TOPIC: Scientific Project
PARTIES:
  Germany, East
  Romania

419300   Bilateral Agreement   **11 EGDA 605**
SIGNED: 12 Jun 63
HEADNOTE: EXCHANGE HOTEL EMPLOYEES
TOPIC: Non-ILO Labor
PARTIES:
  Germany, East
  Romania

419301   Bilateral Exchange   **11 EGDA 478**
SIGNED: 20 Nov 63
HEADNOTE: AMENDS AGREEMENT 28 JUL 55

TOPIC: Air Transport
PARTIES:
  Germany, East
  Romania

419302   Bilateral Agreement   **11 EGDA 638**
SIGNED: 19 Dec 63
HEADNOTE: ACADEMIES OF SCIENCE
TOPIC: Education
PARTIES:
  Germany, East
  Romania

419306   Bilateral Agreement   **12 EGDA 1139**
SIGNED: 17 May 64
HEADNOTE: AID & MUTUAL ASSISTANCE
TOPIC: General Aid
PARTIES:
  Germany, East
  Zanzibar

419307   Bilateral Agreement   **12 EGDA 1146**
SIGNED: 27 Jun 64
HEADNOTE: GDR AID IN PUBLIC HEALTH
TOPIC: Tech Assistance
PARTIES:
  Germany, East
  Zanzibar

419308   Bilateral Agreement   **3 EGDA 660**
SIGNED: 10 Jun 55
HEADNOTE: GOODS LISTS & CLEARING AC-
  COUNT
TOPIC: Finance
PARTIES:
  Germany, East
  Sudan

419310   Bilateral Agreement   **3 EGDA 668**
SIGNED: 7 Nov 55
HEADNOTE: ESTABLISH TRADE MISSIONS
TOPIC: Consul/Citizenship
PARTIES:
  Germany, East
  Syria

419311   Bilateral Agreement   **3 EGDA 668**
SIGNED: 27 Nov 55
HEADNOTE: TRADE & PAYMENTS
TOPIC: General Economic
PARTIES:
  Germany, East
  Syria

419312   Bilateral Agreement   **5 EGDA 485**
SIGNED: 8 Jul 56
HEADNOTE: CULTURAL COOPERATION
TOPIC: Culture
PARTIES:
  Germany, East
  Syria

419313   Bilateral Agreement   **5 EGDA 485**
SIGNED: 3 Sep 57
HEADNOTE: SYRIAN AGRICULTURAL PRODUCTS
TOPIC: General Trade
PARTIES:
  Germany, East
  Syria

419314   Bilateral Protocol   **6 EGDA 515**
SIGNED: 27 Jan 58
HEADNOTE: RADIO
TOPIC: Mass Media
PARTIES:
  Germany, East
  Syria

419325   Bilateral Agreement   **4 EGDA 248**
SIGNED: 23 Jun 50
HEADNOTE: SCIENTIFIC & TECHNICAL COOPER-
ATION
TOPIC: Scientific Project

PARTIES:
  Czechoslovakia
  Germany, East

419326   Bilateral Agreement   **1 EGDA 376**
SIGNED: 23 Jun 50
HEADNOTE: CREDIT
TOPIC: Finance
PARTIES:
  Czechoslovakia
  Germany, East

419327   Bilateral Protocol   **4 EGDA 250**
SIGNED: 23 Jun 50
HEADNOTE: NON-COMMERCIAL FINANCES
TOPIC: Finance
PARTIES:
  Czechoslovakia
  Germany, East

419328   Bilateral Protocol   **4 EGDA 252**
SIGNED: 23 Jun 50
HEADNOTE: CULTURAL COOPERATION
TOPIC: Culture
PARTIES:
  Czechoslovakia
  Germany, East

419329   Bilateral Agreement   **4 EGDA 255**
SIGNED: 12 Jul 50
HEADNOTE: PLANT PROTECTION
TOPIC: Sanitation
PARTIES:
  Czechoslovakia
  Germany, East

419330   Bilateral Agreement   **4 EGDA 259**
SIGNED: 25 Aug 50
HEADNOTE: MAIL
TOPIC: Postal Service
PARTIES:
  Czechoslovakia
  Germany, East

419331   Bilateral Agreement   **4 EGDA 263**
SIGNED: 25 Aug 50
HEADNOTE: PARCELS
TOPIC: Postal Service
PARTIES:
  Czechoslovakia
  Germany, East

419332   Bilateral Agreement   **4 EGDA 267**
SIGNED: 25 Aug 50
HEADNOTE: TELECOMMUNICATIONS
TOPIC: Telecommunications
PARTIES:
  Czechoslovakia
  Germany, East

419333   Bilateral Agreement   **4 EGDA 272**
SIGNED: 30 Dec 50
HEADNOTE: RAIL TRANSIT CERTAIN AREAS
TOPIC: Visas
PARTIES:
  Czechoslovakia
  Germany, East

419334   Bilateral Agreement   **1 EGDA 393**
SIGNED: 1 Dec 51
HEADNOTE: TRADE & PAYMENTS 1952-55
TOPIC: General Economic
PARTIES:
  Czechoslovakia
  Germany, East

419335   Bilateral Agreement   **4 EGDA 282**
SIGNED: 19 Feb 53
HEADNOTE: CULTURAL COOPERATION
TOPIC: Culture
PARTIES:
  Czechoslovakia
  Germany, East

419336   Bilateral Agreement   1 EGDA 421
SIGNED: 20 Mar 53
HEADNOTE: SUPPLEMENT TO 1 DEC 51
TOPIC: General Trade
PARTIES:
  Czechoslovakia
  Germany, East

419337   Bilateral Agreement   4 EGDA 288
SIGNED: 1 Apr 53
HEADNOTE: PAYMENTS 1953-55
TOPIC: Finance
PARTIES:
  Czechoslovakia
  Germany, East

419338   Bilateral Agreement   4 EGDA 194
SIGNED: 3 Oct 53
HEADNOTE: RAPID TRAIN BERLIN-PRAGUE
TOPIC: Land Transport
PARTIES:
  Czechoslovakia
  Germany, East

419339   Bilateral Agreement   1 EGDA 422
SIGNED: 13 Oct 53
HEADNOTE: RAISE MISSIONS TO EMBASSIES
TOPIC: Consul/Citizenship
PARTIES:
  Czechoslovakia
  Germany, East

419340   Bilateral Agreement   4 EGDA 302
SIGNED: 17 Feb 54
HEADNOTE: HEALTH
TOPIC: Sanitation
PARTIES:
  Czechoslovakia
  Germany, East

419341   Bilateral Protocol   2 EGDA 442
SIGNED: 21 Jul 54
HEADNOTE: LIGHT INDUSTRY
TOPIC: General Economic
PARTIES:
  Czechoslovakia
  Germany, East

419342   Bilateral Agreement   4 EGDA 308
SIGNED: 15 Oct 54
HEADNOTE: INLAND WATERWAYS
TOPIC: Water Transport
PARTIES:
  Czechoslovakia
  Germany, East

419343   Bilateral Agreement   4 EGDA 320
SIGNED: 28 Jan 55
HEADNOTE: RADIO
TOPIC: Mass Media
PARTIES:
  Czechoslovakia
  Germany, East

419344   Bilateral Protocol   4 EGDA 267
SIGNED: 31 Mar 55
HEADNOTE: SUPPLEMENT 25 AUG 50
TOPIC: Postal Service
PARTIES:
  Czechoslovakia
  Germany, East

419345   Bilateral Protocol   3 EGDA 511
SIGNED: 20 Jun 55
HEADNOTE: ENERGY
TOPIC: General Economic
PARTIES:
  Czechoslovakia
  Germany, East

419346   Bilateral Agreement   4 EGDA 325
SIGNED: 8 Aug 55
HEADNOTE: CIVIL AIR TRANSPORT
TOPIC: Air Transport

PARTIES:
  Czechoslovakia
  Germany, East

419347   Bilateral Agreement   4 EGDA 345
SIGNED: 14 Nov 55
HEADNOTE: BORDER RIVERS
TOPIC: Specific Resources
PARTIES:
  Czechoslovakia
  Germany, East

419348   Bilateral Agreement   3 EGDA 516
SIGNED: 23 Nov 55
HEADNOTE: SCIENTIFIC & TECHNICAL COOPER-
ATION
TOPIC: Scientific Project
PARTIES:
  Czechoslovakia
  Germany, East

419349   Bilateral Agreement   4 EGDA 359
SIGNED: 25 Apr 56
HEADNOTE: RAIL BORDER TRAFFIC
TOPIC: Land Transport
PARTIES:
  Czechoslovakia
  Germany, East

419350   Bilateral Protocol   4 EGDA 366
SIGNED: 4 May 56
HEADNOTE: CULTURAL INFORMATION CENTERS
TOPIC: Consul/Citizenship
PARTIES:
  Czechoslovakia
  Germany, East

419351   Bilateral Agreement   5 EGDA 486
SIGNED: 24 Aug 56
HEADNOTE: CUSTOMS COOPERATION
TOPIC: Customs
PARTIES:
  Czechoslovakia
  Germany, East

419352   Bilateral Agreement   5 EGDA 491
SIGNED: 31 Aug 56
HEADNOTE: PAYMENTS 1957-60
TOPIC: Finance
PARTIES:
  Czechoslovakia
  Germany, East

419353   Bilateral Agreement   5 EGDA 506
SIGNED: 11 Sep 56
HEADNOTE: CONSULATES GENERAL
TOPIC: Consul/Citizenship
PARTIES:
  Czechoslovakia
  Germany, East

419354   Bilateral Protocol   5 EGDA 507
SIGNED: 11 Sep 56
HEADNOTE: ECONOMIC COOPERATION
TOPIC: General Economic
PARTIES:
  Czechoslovakia
  Germany, East

419355   Bilateral Treaty   5 EGDA 511
SIGNED: 11 Sep 56
HEADNOTE: CIVIL & CRIMINAL LAW
TOPIC: Admin Cooperation
PARTIES:
  Czechoslovakia
  Germany, East

419356   Bilateral Agreement   5 EGDA 539
SIGNED: 11 Sep 56
HEADNOTE: SOCIAL POLICY
TOPIC: Health/Educ/Welfare
PARTIES:
  Czechoslovakia
  Germany, East

419357   Bilateral Protocol   5 EGDA 554
SIGNED: 21 Dec 56
HEADNOTE: SCIENTIFIC & TECHNICAL COOPER-
ATION
TOPIC: Scientific Project
PARTIES:
  Czechoslovakia
  Germany, East

419358   Bilateral Protocol   5 EGDA 557
SIGNED: 29 Jan 57
HEADNOTE: INTENSIFY CULTURAL COOPER-
ATION
TOPIC: Culture
PARTIES:
  Czechoslovakia
  Germany, East

419359   Bilateral Agreement   5 EGDA 580
SIGNED: 20 Dec 57
HEADNOTE: JOINT COMMITTEE ECONOMIC CO-
OPERATION
TOPIC: IGO Establishment
PARTIES:
  Czechoslovakia
  Germany, East

419360   Bilateral Agreement   7 EGDA 447
SIGNED: 29 Jan 59
HEADNOTE: ECONOMIC COOPERATION & TRADE
1961-65
TOPIC: General Economic
PARTIES:
  Czechoslovakia
  Germany, East

419361   Bilateral Agreement   7 EGDA 449
SIGNED: 12 Sep 59
HEADNOTE: DEVELOP GDR POTASSIUM
TOPIC: General Aid
PARTIES:
  Czechoslovakia
  Germany, East

419362   Bilateral Agreement   8 EGDA 438
SIGNED: 1 Jun 60
HEADNOTE: TRADE 1961-65
TOPIC: General Trade
PARTIES:
  Czechoslovakia
  Germany, East

419363   Bilateral Agreement   8 EGDA 452
SIGNED: 26 Nov 60
HEADNOTE: HELLENDORF POWER DAM
TOPIC: Specific Property
PARTIES:
  Czechoslovakia
  Germany, East

419364   Bilateral Agreement   8 EGDA 457
SIGNED: 15 Dec 60
HEADNOTE: LONG-TERM PAYMENTS
TOPIC: Finance
PARTIES:
  Czechoslovakia
  Germany, East

419365   Bilateral Agreement   9 EGDA 395
SIGNED: 9 Dec 61
HEADNOTE: RAUSCHENBACH POWER DAM
TOPIC: Specific Property
PARTIES:
  Czechoslovakia
  Germany, East

419367   Bilateral Exchange   11 EGDA 647
SIGNED: 27 Jun 63
HEADNOTE: INCREASE TOURISM
TOPIC: Health/Educ/Welfare
PARTIES:
  Czechoslovakia
  Germany, East

419368   Bilateral Exchange   **11 EGDA 501**
SIGNED: 9 Dec 63
HEADNOTE: AMENDS 8 AUG 55
TOPIC: Air Transport
PARTIES:
  Czechoslovakia
  Germany, East

419372   Bilateral Protocol   **9 EGDA 400**
SIGNED: 26 May 61
HEADNOTE: RADIO & TV
TOPIC: Mass Media
PARTIES:
  Germany, East
  Tunisia

419373   Bilateral Agreement   **10 EGDA 566**
SIGNED: 28 Feb 62
HEADNOTE: PAYMENTS
TOPIC: Finance
PARTIES:
  Germany, East
  Tunisia

419374   Bilateral Agreement   **12 EGDA 1171**
SIGNED: 27 Nov 64
HEADNOTE: TRADE 1965-68
TOPIC: General Trade
PARTIES:
  Germany, East
  Tunisia

419375   Bilateral Agreement   **12 EGDA 903**
SIGNED: 27 Nov 64
HEADNOTE: PAYMENTS 1965-68
TOPIC: Finance
PARTIES:
  Germany, East
  Tunisia

419376   Bilateral Exchange   **1 EGDA 329**
SIGNED: 19 Nov 49
HEADNOTE: SOVIET TRADE MISSION BERLIN
TOPIC: Consul/Citizenship
PARTIES:
  Germany, East
  USSR (Soviet Union)

419377   Bilateral Agreement   **1 EGDA 245**
SIGNED: 12 Apr 50
HEADNOTE: TRADE & PAYMENTS
TOPIC: General Economic
PARTIES:
  Germany, East
  USSR (Soviet Union)

419378   Bilateral Agreement   **4 EGDA 11**
SIGNED: 1 Jul 50
HEADNOTE: MAIL
TOPIC: Postal Service
PARTIES:
  Germany, East
  USSR (Soviet Union)

419379   Bilateral Agreement   **4 EGDA 16**
SIGNED: 1 Jul 50
HEADNOTE: PARCEL
TOPIC: Postal Service
PARTIES:
  Germany, East
  USSR (Soviet Union)

419380   Bilateral Agreement   **4 EGDA 27**
SIGNED: 1 Jul 50
HEADNOTE: TELECOMMUNICATIONS
TOPIC: Telecommunications
PARTIES:
  Germany, East
  USSR (Soviet Union)

419381   Bilateral Agreement   **1 EGDA 256**
SIGNED: 27 Sep 51
HEADNOTE: TRADE 1952-55
TOPIC: General Trade

PARTIES:
  Germany, East
  USSR (Soviet Union)

419382   Bilateral Agreement   **4 EGDA 33**
SIGNED: 27 Sep 51
HEADNOTE: SCIENTIFIC & TECHNICAL COOPER-
ATION
TOPIC: Scientific Project
PARTIES:
  Germany, East
  USSR (Soviet Union)

419383   Bilateral Agreement   **4 EGDA 428**
SIGNED: 12 May 52
HEADNOTE: GERMAN STUDENTS SOVIET UNI-
VERSITIES
TOPIC: Education
PARTIES:
  Germany, East
  USSR (Soviet Union)

419384   Bilateral Agreement   **4 EGDA 34**
SIGNED: 13 Jan 53
HEADNOTE: RADIO
TOPIC: Mass Media
PARTIES:
  Germany, East
  USSR (Soviet Union)

419385   Bilateral Agreement   **1 EGDA 273**
SIGNED: 20 Jul 53
HEADNOTE: SOVIET FOOD & RAW MATERIALS
TOPIC: Direct Aid
PARTIES:
  Germany, East
  USSR (Soviet Union)

419386   Bilateral Agreement   **1 EGDA 286**
SIGNED: 22 Aug 53
HEADNOTE: RAISE MISSIONS TO EMBASSIES
TOPIC: Consul/Citizenship
PARTIES:
  Germany, East
  USSR (Soviet Union)

419387   Bilateral Agreement   **1 EGDA 286**
SIGNED: 22 Aug 53
HEADNOTE: RELEASE GERMAN WAR PRISONERS
TOPIC: Other Military
PARTIES:
  Germany, East
  USSR (Soviet Union)

419388   Bilateral Protocol   **1 EGDA 299**
SIGNED: 31 Dec 53
HEADNOTE: TRANSFER 33 PLANTS TO GDR
TOPIC: Specif Goods/Equip
PARTIES:
  Germany, East
  USSR (Soviet Union)

419389   Bilateral Protocol   **4 EGDA 41**
SIGNED: 30 Apr 54
HEADNOTE: TRANSFER SOVIET FILMS TO GDR
TOPIC: Specif Goods/Equip
PARTIES:
  Germany, East
  USSR (Soviet Union)

419390   Bilateral Agreement   **2 EGDA 275**
SIGNED: 30 Sep 54
HEADNOTE: ESTABLISH CONSULATES
TOPIC: Consul/Citizenship
PARTIES:
  Germany, East
  USSR (Soviet Union)

419391   Bilateral Agreement   **4 EGDA 42**
SIGNED: 30 Sep 54
HEADNOTE: NON-COMMERCIAL FINANCES
TOPIC: Finance

PARTIES:
  Germany, East
  USSR (Soviet Union)

419392   Bilateral Agreement   **2 EGDA 337**
SIGNED: 27 Apr 55
HEADNOTE: USE AIRPORT SCHONEFELD
TOPIC: Specific Property
PARTIES:
  Germany, East
  USSR (Soviet Union)

419393   Bilateral Protocol   **3 EGDA 205**
SIGNED: 30 Jun 55
HEADNOTE: TRANSFER GERMAN ARCHIVES
TOPIC: Specif Goods/Equip
PARTIES:
  Germany, East
  USSR (Soviet Union)

419394   Bilateral Agreement   **2 EGDA 206**
SIGNED: 1 Jul 55
HEADNOTE: FILMS
TOPIC: Culture
PARTIES:
  Germany, East
  USSR (Soviet Union)

419395   Bilateral Protocol   **3 EGDA 242**
SIGNED: 3 Sep 55
HEADNOTE: SCIENTIFIC & TECHNICAL COOPER-
ATION
TOPIC: Scientific Project
PARTIES:
  Germany, East
  USSR (Soviet Union)

419397   Bilateral Agreement   **3 EGDA 327**
SIGNED: 18 Oct 55
HEADNOTE: ECONOMIC COOPERATION AIR
TRANSPORT
TOPIC: Air Transport
PARTIES:
  Germany, East
  USSR (Soviet Union)

419398   Bilateral Protocol   **4 EGDA 51**
SIGNED: 27 Nov 55
HEADNOTE: RETURN DRESDEN PAINTINGS
TOPIC: Specif Goods/Equip
PARTIES:
  Germany, East
  USSR (Soviet Union)

419399   Bilateral Agreement   **3 EGDA 353**
SIGNED: 23 Dec 55
HEADNOTE: GDR SUPPLIES SHIPS TO USSR
TOPIC: Commodity Trade
PARTIES:
  Germany, East
  USSR (Soviet Union)

419400   Bilateral Agreement   **4 EGDA 61**
SIGNED: 18 Jun 56
HEADNOTE: AIR TRANSPORT
TOPIC: Air Transport
PARTIES:
  Germany, East
  USSR (Soviet Union)

419401   Bilateral Instrument   **5 EGDA 645**
SIGNED: 17 Jul 56
HEADNOTE: REDUCE COST SOVIET TROOPS
TOPIC: Milit Occupation
PARTIES:
  Germany, East
  USSR (Soviet Union)

419402   Bilateral Agreement   **5 EGDA 686**
SIGNED: 26 Feb 57
HEADNOTE: OUTPUT JOINT WISMUT COMPANY
TOPIC: Specific Property

PARTIES:
  Germany, East
  USSR (Soviet Union)

419403   Bilateral Protocol   **5 EGDA 697**
SIGNED: 25 May 57
HEADNOTE: MACHINE INDUSTRY
TOPIC: General Economic
PARTIES:
  Germany, East
  USSR (Soviet Union)

419404   Bilateral Agreement   **5 EGDA 699**
SIGNED: 2 Aug 57
HEADNOTE: LEGAL STATUS SOVIET TROOPS
TOPIC: Status of Forces
PARTIES:
  Germany, East
  USSR (Soviet Union)

419405   Bilateral Treaty   **5 EGDA 730**
SIGNED: 27 Sep 57
HEADNOTE: TRADE & NAVIGATION
TOPIC: General Economic
PARTIES:
  Germany, East
  USSR (Soviet Union)

419406   Bilateral Agreement   **6 EGDA 429**
SIGNED: 21 Feb 58
HEADNOTE: TRANSFER SCHONEFELD AIRPORT
TOPIC: Specific Property
PARTIES:
  Germany, East
  USSR (Soviet Union)

419407   Bilateral Agreement   **6 EGDA 425**
SIGNED: 21 Feb 58
HEADNOTE: STUDENT EXCHANGE
TOPIC: Education
PARTIES:
  Germany, East
  USSR (Soviet Union)

419408   Bilateral Agreement   **6 EGDA 431**
SIGNED: 25 Feb 58
HEADNOTE: DEVELOP CHEMICAL INDUSTRY
TOPIC: General Economic
PARTIES:
  Germany, East
  USSR (Soviet Union)

419409   Bilateral Protocol   **6 EGDA 447**
SIGNED: 24 Jun 58
HEADNOTE: REDUCE COST SOVIET TROOPS
TOPIC: Milit Occupation
PARTIES:
  Germany, East
  USSR (Soviet Union)

419410   Bilateral Protocol   **6 EGDA 452**
SIGNED: 8 Sep 58
HEADNOTE: RETURN GERMAN ART WORKS
TOPIC: Specif Goods/Equip
PARTIES:
  Germany, East
  USSR (Soviet Union)

419411   Bilateral Agreement   **6 EGDA 457**
SIGNED: 21 Oct 58
HEADNOTE: HEALTH
TOPIC: Sanitation
PARTIES:
  Germany, East
  USSR (Soviet Union)

419412   Bilateral Agreement   **6 EGDA 521**
SIGNED: 22 Oct 58
HEADNOTE: OIL PROCESSING PLANT SCHWEDT
TOPIC: Tech Assistance
PARTIES:
  Germany, East
  USSR (Soviet Union)

419414   Bilateral Agreement   **7 EGDA 531**
SIGNED: 21 Nov 59
HEADNOTE: TRADE 1961-65
TOPIC: General Trade
PARTIES:
  Germany, East
  USSR (Soviet Union)

419415   Bilateral Protocol   **8 EGDA 538**
SIGNED: 1 Mar 60
HEADNOTE: EXPAND IRON WORKS STALIN-STADT
TOPIC: Tech Assistance
PARTIES:
  Germany, East
  USSR (Soviet Union)

419416   Bilateral Protocol   **8 EGDA 577**
SIGNED: 29 Jul 60
HEADNOTE: RETURN GERMAN ART WORKS
TOPIC: Specif Goods/Equip
PARTIES:
  Germany, East
  USSR (Soviet Union)

419417   Bilateral Protocol   **9 EGDA 418**
SIGNED: 30 May 61
HEADNOTE: DEVELOP ECONOMIC RELATIONS
TOPIC: General Economic
PARTIES:
  Germany, East
  USSR (Soviet Union)

419418   Bilateral Agreement   **9 EGDA 442**
SIGNED: 28 Dec 61
HEADNOTE: PEACEFUL USE ATOMIC ENERGY
TOPIC: Atomic Energy
PARTIES:
  Germany, East
  USSR (Soviet Union)

419419   Bilateral Agreement   **10 EGDA 504**
SIGNED: 5 Mar 62
HEADNOTE: 1.3 BILLION MARK CREDIT
TOPIC: Loans and Credits
PARTIES:
  Germany, East
  USSR (Soviet Union)

419420   Bilateral Protocol   **10 EGDA 574**
SIGNED: 3 May 62
HEADNOTE: SOVIET AID VARIOUS INDUSTRIES
TOPIC: Tech Assistance
PARTIES:
  Germany, East
  USSR (Soviet Union)

419421   Bilateral Protocol   **10 EGDA 521**
SIGNED: 8 Aug 62
HEADNOTE: SUPPLEMENT 27 SEP 51
TOPIC: Scientific Project
PARTIES:
  Germany, East
  USSR (Soviet Union)

419422   Bilateral Agreement   **11 EGDA 588**
SIGNED: 11 Mar 63
HEADNOTE: CONSUMER GOODS 5 MILLION RUBLE
TOPIC: Commodity Trade
PARTIES:
  Germany, East
  USSR (Soviet Union)

419423   Bilateral Protocol   **11 EGDA 611**
SIGNED: 18 Jul 63
HEADNOTE: IRON WORKS OST
TOPIC: Tech Assistance
PARTIES:
  Germany, East
  USSR (Soviet Union)

419424   Bilateral Protocol   **12 EGDA 1137**
SIGNED: 5 May 64

HEADNOTE: SOVIET AID VARIOUS INDUSTRIES
TOPIC: Tech Assistance
PARTIES:
  Germany, East
  USSR (Soviet Union)

419425   Bilateral Agreement   **12 EGDA 1077**
SIGNED: 1 Oct 64
HEADNOTE: CULTURAL & SCIENTIFIC COOPERATION
TOPIC: Health/Educ/Welfare
PARTIES:
  Germany, East
  USSR (Soviet Union)

419431   Bilateral Agreement   **1 EGDA 426**
SIGNED: 19 Oct 49
HEADNOTE: TRADE & PAYMENTS
TOPIC: General Economic
PARTIES:
  Germany, East
  Hungary

419432   Bilateral Agreement   **4 EGDA 378**
SIGNED: 24 Jun 50
HEADNOTE: SCIENTIFIC & TECHNICAL COOPERATION
TOPIC: Scientific Project
PARTIES:
  Germany, East
  Hungary

419433   Bilateral Protocol   **4 EGDA 380**
SIGNED: 24 Jun 50
HEADNOTE: NON-COMMERCIAL FINANCES
TOPIC: Finance
PARTIES:
  Germany, East
  Hungary

419434   Bilateral Agreement   **1 EGDA 428**
SIGNED: 24 Jun 50
HEADNOTE: TRADE OUTSIDE AGREEMENT
TOPIC: General Trade
PARTIES:
  Germany, East
  Hungary

419435   Bilateral Agreement   **4 EGDA 382**
SIGNED: 24 Jun 50
HEADNOTE: CULTURAL COOPERATION
TOPIC: Culture
PARTIES:
  Germany, East
  Hungary

419436   Bilateral Agreement   **4 EGDA 384**
SIGNED: 3 Mar 51
HEADNOTE: RADIO
TOPIC: Mass Media
PARTIES:
  Germany, East
  Hungary

419437   Bilateral Agreement   **1 EGDA 438**
SIGNED: 1 Aug 51
HEADNOTE: INSURANCE ACCOUNTS
TOPIC: Finance
PARTIES:
  Germany, East
  Hungary

419438   Bilateral Agreement   **1 EGDA 439**
SIGNED: 7 Mar 52
HEADNOTE: TRADE 1952-55
TOPIC: General Trade
PARTIES:
  Germany, East
  Hungary

419439   Bilateral Agreement   **4 EGDA 387**
SIGNED: 25 Mar 52
HEADNOTE: MAIL
TOPIC: Postal Service

PARTIES:
  Germany, East
  Hungary

419440   Bilateral Agreement   **4 EGDA 390**
SIGNED: 25 Mar 52
HEADNOTE: PARCEL
TOPIC: Postal Service
PARTIES:
  Germany, East
  Hungary

419441   Bilateral Agreement   **4 EGDA 394**
SIGNED: 26 Mar 52
HEADNOTE: TELECOMMUNICATIONS
TOPIC: Telecommunications
PARTIES:
  Germany, East
  Hungary

419442   Bilateral Instrument   **1 EGDA 446**
SIGNED: 17 Oct 53
HEADNOTE: RAISE MISSIONS TO EMBASSIES
TOPIC: Consul/Citizenship
PARTIES:
  Germany, East
  Hungary

419443   Bilateral Protocol   **2 EGDA 448**
SIGNED: 23 Oct 54
HEADNOTE: LIGHT INDUSTRY
TOPIC: General Economic
PARTIES:
  Germany, East
  Hungary

419444   Bilateral Agreement   **4 EGDA 405**
SIGNED: 23 Sep 55
HEADNOTE: RADIO & TV
TOPIC: Mass Media
PARTIES:
  Germany, East
  Hungary

419445   Bilateral Agreement   **3 EGDA 527**
SIGNED: 10 Nov 55
HEADNOTE: RELEASE GERMAN WAR PRISONERS
TOPIC: Other Military
PARTIES:
  Germany, East
  Hungary

419446   Bilateral Agreement   **4 EGDA 410**
SIGNED: 1 Dec 55
HEADNOTE: TELEVISION
TOPIC: Mass Media
PARTIES:
  Germany, East
  Hungary

419447   Bilateral Protocol   **3 EGDA 528**
SIGNED: 12 Dec 55
HEADNOTE: FOOD INDUSTRY
TOPIC: General Economic
PARTIES:
  Germany, East
  Hungary

419448   Bilateral Agreement   **3 EGDA 530**
SIGNED: 30 Jan 56
HEADNOTE: LIGHT INDUSTRY
TOPIC: General Economic
PARTIES:
  Germany, East
  Hungary

419449   Bilateral Agreement   **5 EGDA 582**
SIGNED: 6 Jul 56
HEADNOTE: TOURIST GROUP EXCHANGES
TOPIC: Health/Educ/Welfare
PARTIES:
  Germany, East
  Hungary

419450   Bilateral Agreement   **5 EGDA 583**
SIGNED: 5 Oct 56
HEADNOTE: PAYMENTS 1957-60
TOPIC: Finance
PARTIES:
  Germany, East
  Hungary

419451   Bilateral Agreement   **5 EGDA 792**
SIGNED: 29 Jun 57
HEADNOTE: INVENTIONS & TRADEMARKS
TOPIC: Patents/Copyrights
PARTIES:
  Germany, East
  Hungary

419452   Bilateral Protocol   **6 EGDA 422**
SIGNED: 14 Oct 58
HEADNOTE: TRADE 1961-65
TOPIC: General Trade
PARTIES:
  Germany, East
  Hungary

419453   Bilateral Agreement   **6 EGDA 422**
SIGNED: 14 Oct 58
HEADNOTE: JOINT PLANS INDUSTRIAL OUTPUT
TOPIC: General Economic
PARTIES:
  Germany, East
  Hungary

419454   Bilateral Agreement   **7 EGDA 490**
SIGNED: 19 Dec 59
HEADNOTE: CULTURAL & SCIENTIFIC COOPER-
ATION
TOPIC: Health/Educ/Welfare
PARTIES:
  Germany, East
  Hungary

419455   Bilateral Agreement   **8 EGDA 478**
SIGNED: 8 Apr 60
HEADNOTE: TRADE 1961-65
TOPIC: General Trade
PARTIES:
  Germany, East
  Hungary

419456   Bilateral Protocol   **8 EGDA 479**
SIGNED: 27 Apr 60
HEADNOTE: TRANSFER ESTERHAZY LIBRARY
TOPIC: Specif Goods/Equip
PARTIES:
  Germany, East
  Hungary

419457   Bilateral Agreement   **8 EGDA 480**
SIGNED: 9 Jul 60
HEADNOTE: RADIO & TV
TOPIC: Mass Media
PARTIES:
  Germany, East
  Hungary

419458   Bilateral Agreement   **9 EGDA 402**
SIGNED: 26 Apr 61
HEADNOTE: AGRICULTURAL COOPERATION
TOPIC: General Economic
PARTIES:
  Germany, East
  Hungary

419459   Bilateral Agreement   **10 EGDA 497**
SIGNED: 11 May 62
HEADNOTE: STUDENT EXCHANGE
TOPIC: Education
PARTIES:
  Germany, East
  Hungary

419460   Bilateral Agreement   **11 EGDA 648**
SIGNED: 5 Sep 63
HEADNOTE: EXCHANGE HOTEL EMPLOYEES

TOPIC: Non-ILO Labor
PARTIES:
  Germany, East
  Hungary

419461   Bilateral Agreement   **11 EGDA 619**
SIGNED: 18 Sep 63
HEADNOTE: VISA ABOLITION
TOPIC: Visas
PARTIES:
  Germany, East
  Hungary

419471   Bilateral Agreement   **6 EGDA 474**
SIGNED: 27 Mar 58
HEADNOTE: CERTAIN NAVIGATION MATTERS
TOPIC: Water Transport
PARTIES:
  Germany, East
  United Arab Rep

419472   Bilateral Agreement   **6 EGDA 484**
SIGNED: 29 Aug 58
HEADNOTE: ECONOMIC COOPERATION & LONG-
TERM CREDIT
TOPIC: General Aid
PARTIES:
  Germany, East
  United Arab Rep

419473   Bilateral Agreement   **6 EGDA 484**
SIGNED: 29 Aug 58
HEADNOTE: SCIENTIFIC & TECHNICAL COOPER-
ATION
TOPIC: Tech Assistance
PARTIES:
  Germany, East
  United Arab Rep

419474   Bilateral Treaty   **6 EGDA 521**
SIGNED: 27 Nov 58
HEADNOTE: GDR SUPPLIES COTTON FACTORY
TOPIC: Specific Property
PARTIES:
  Germany, East
  United Arab Rep

419475   Bilateral Agreement   **6 EGDA 485**
SIGNED: 13 Dec 58
HEADNOTE: PAYMENTS 1959-61
TOPIC: Finance
PARTIES:
  Germany, East
  United Arab Rep

419476   Bilateral Agreement   **8 EGDA 559**
SIGNED: 13 Dec 58
HEADNOTE: TRADE 1959-61
TOPIC: General Trade
PARTIES:
  Germany, East
  United Arab Rep

419477   Bilateral Agreement   **10 EGDA 547**
SIGNED: 2 Aug 62
HEADNOTE: RADIO & TV
TOPIC: Mass Media
PARTIES:
  Germany, East
  United Arab Rep

419478   Bilateral Agreement   **10 EGDA 620**
SIGNED: 16 Dec 62
HEADNOTE: LONG-TERM TRADE 1963-65
TOPIC: General Trade
PARTIES:
  Germany, East
  United Arab Rep

419485   Bilateral Treaty   **12 EGDA 1139**
SIGNED: 17 May 64
HEADNOTE: FRIENDHIP & MUTUAL ASSISTANCE
TOPIC: General Amity

PARTIES:
Germany, East
Tanzania

419486   Bilateral Agreement   **4 EGDA 567**
SIGNED: 14 Mar 56
HEADNOTE: SCIENTIFIC & TECHNICAL COOPER-
ATION
TOPIC: Tech Assistance
PARTIES:
Germany, East
Vietnam, North

419487   Bilateral Agreement   **3 EGDA 612**
SIGNED: 15 Jun 56
HEADNOTE: NON-COMMERCIAL FINANCES
TOPIC: Finance
PARTIES:
Germany, East
Vietnam, North

419488   Bilateral Agreement   **5 EGDA 780**
SIGNED: 31 Jul 57
HEADNOTE: CULTURAL COOPERATION
TOPIC: Culture
PARTIES:
Germany, East
Vietnam, North

419489   Bilateral Agreement   **6 EGDA 494**
SIGNED: 14 May 58
HEADNOTE: MAIL
TOPIC: Postal Service
PARTIES:
Germany, East
Vietnam, North

419490   Bilateral Agreement   **6 EGDA 505**
SIGNED: 14 May 58
HEADNOTE: TELECOMMUNICATIONS
TOPIC: Telecommunications
PARTIES:
Germany, East
Vietnam, North

419491   Bilateral Agreement   **7 EGDA 559**
SIGNED: 1 Dec 58
HEADNOTE: TRADE & PAYMENTS 1959-60
TOPIC: General Economic
PARTIES:
Germany, East
Vietnam, North

419492   Bilateral Treaty   **7 EGDA 541**
SIGNED: 7 Mar 59
HEADNOTE: COMMERCE & NAVIGATION
TOPIC: General Economic
PARTIES:
Germany, East
Vietnam, North

419493   Bilateral Treaty   **7 EGDA 547**
SIGNED: 9 Oct 59
HEADNOTE: CONSULAR
TOPIC: Consul/Citizenship
PARTIES:
Germany, East
Vietnam, North

419494   Bilateral Agreement   **9 EGDA 448**
SIGNED: 9 Feb 61
HEADNOTE: TRADE & PAYMENTS TO 1965
TOPIC: General Economic
PARTIES:
Germany, East
Vietnam, North

419498   Bilateral Agreement   **12 EGDA 1107**
SIGNED: 7 Nov 64
HEADNOTE: TRADE & PAYMENTS 1964-65
TOPIC: General Economic
PARTIES:
Cyprus
Germany, East

420024   Bilateral Agreement   **51 EGDZ 340**
SIGNED: 23 Jul 65
HEADNOTE: OCEAN NAVIGATION
TOPIC: Water Transport
PARTIES:
Albania
Germany, East

420025   Bilateral Agreement   **51 EGDZ 355**
SIGNED: 1 Mar 66
HEADNOTE: TRADE 1966-70
TOPIC: General Trade
PARTIES:
Albania
Germany, East

420026   Bilateral Agreement   **44 EGDZ 362**
SIGNED: 24 Jun 66
HEADNOTE: TRAINING ALGERIAN SPECIALISTS
TOPIC: Education
PARTIES:
Algeria
Germany, East

420027   Bilateral Agreement   **41 EGDZ 374**
SIGNED: 12 Dec 66
HEADNOTE: TRADE
TOPIC: General Trade
PARTIES:
Algeria
Germany, East

420028   Bilateral Agreement   **41 EGDZ 374**
SIGNED: 21 Dec 66
HEADNOTE: CULTURE
TOPIC: Culture
PARTIES:
Algeria
Germany, East

420029   Bilateral Agreement   **41 EGDZ 374**
SIGNED: 21 Dec 66
HEADNOTE: AIR TRANSPORT
TOPIC: Air Transport
PARTIES:
Algeria
Germany, East

420040   Bilateral Treaty   **58 EGDZ 172**
SIGNED: 4 Feb 55
HEADNOTE: TRAVELS
TOPIC: General Transport
PARTIES:
Bulgaria
Germany, East

420041   Bilateral Treaty   **58 EGDZ 172**
SIGNED: 5 Feb 55
HEADNOTE: FILM
TOPIC: Culture
PARTIES:
Bulgaria
Germany, East

420049   Bilateral Agreement   **58 EGDZ 172**
SIGNED: 22 Sep 55
HEADNOTE: BUILDING CEMENT PLANT
TOPIC: General Economic
PARTIES:
Bulgaria
Germany, East

420050   Bilateral Agreement   **58 EGDZ 172**
SIGNED: 17 Oct 55
HEADNOTE: CONSUMER GOODS
TOPIC: Commodity Trade
PARTIES:
Bulgaria
Germany, East

420053   Bilateral Protocol   **58 EGDZ 172**
SIGNED: 27 Apr 57
HEADNOTE: ECONOMIC COOPERATION IN AGRI-
CULTURE

TOPIC: General Economic
PARTIES:
Bulgaria
Germany, East

420068   Bilateral Agreement   **50 EGDZ 332**
SIGNED: 19 Mar 65
HEADNOTE: CULTURAL & SCIENTIFIC COOPER-
ATION
TOPIC: Health/Educ/Welfare
PARTIES:
Bulgaria
Germany, East

420069   Bilateral Agreement   **43 EGDZ 342**
SIGNED: 21 Aug 65
HEADNOTE: GDR CONSULATE IN WARNA
TOPIC: Consul/Citizenship
PARTIES:
Bulgaria
Germany, East

420070   Bilateral Agreement   **59 EGDZ 350**
SIGNED: 20 Dec 65
HEADNOTE: TRADE 1966-70
TOPIC: General Trade
PARTIES:
Bulgaria
Germany, East

420071   Bilateral Agreement   **34 EGDZ 370**
SIGNED: 15 Oct 66
HEADNOTE: PAYMENTS & CLEARING 1966-70
TOPIC: Finance
PARTIES:
Bulgaria
Germany, East

420072   Bilateral Agreement   **36 EGDZ 370**
SIGNED: 25 Oct 66
HEADNOTE: AUTOMOBILE TRAFFIC
TOPIC: Land Transport
PARTIES:
Bulgaria
Germany, East

420074   Bilateral Agreement   **45 EGDZ 255**
SIGNED: 26 Aug 60
HEADNOTE: ESTABLISH CONSULATES GENERAL
TOPIC: Consul/Citizenship
PARTIES:
Burma
Germany, East

420076   Bilateral Agreement   **51 EGDZ 351**
SIGNED: 8 Jan 66
HEADNOTE: ECONOMIC & SCIENTIFIC & TECHNI-
CAL COOPERATION
TOPIC: General Economic
PARTIES:
Burma
Germany, East

420077   Bilateral Agreement   **51 EGDZ 330**
SIGNED: 22 Feb 65
HEADNOTE: LONG-TERM ECONOMIC COOPER-
ATION
TOPIC: General Economic
PARTIES:
Ceylon (Sri Lanka)
Germany, East

420078   Bilateral Agreement   **34 EGDZ 373**
SIGNED: 5 Dec 66
HEADNOTE: ARTIST EXCHANGE
TOPIC: Culture
PARTIES:
Chile
Germany, East

420094   Bilateral Treaty   **18 EGDZ 198**
SIGNED: 9 Oct 58
HEADNOTE: PURCHASE & DISTRIBUTION FILMS
TOPIC: Commodity Trade

PARTIES:
China People's Rep
Germany, East

420098   Bilateral Agreement   **48 EGDZ 339**
SIGNED: 15 Jul 65
HEADNOTE: STUDENT EXCHANGE
TOPIC: Education
PARTIES:
China People's Rep
Germany, East

420104   Bilateral Agreement   **40 EGDZ 366**
SIGNED: 23 Aug 66
HEADNOTE: HEALTH
TOPIC: Sanitation
PARTIES:
Finland
Germany, East

420113   Bilateral Agreement   **51 EGDZ 340**
SIGNED: 24 Jul 65
HEADNOTE: SCIENTIFIC & TECHNICAL COOPER-
ATION
TOPIC: Tech Assistance
PARTIES:
Germany, East
Ghana

420122   Bilateral Agreement   **52 EGDZ 341**
SIGNED: 9 Aug 65
HEADNOTE: ECONOMIC COOPERATION
TOPIC: General Economic
PARTIES:
Germany, East
Guinea

420123   Bilateral Agreement   **51 EGDZ 349**
SIGNED: 10 Dec 65
HEADNOTE: TRADE & PAYMENTS
TOPIC: General Economic
PARTIES:
Germany, East
Guinea

420141   Bilateral Agreement   **36 EGDZ 370**
SIGNED: 22 Oct 66
HEADNOTE: AIR TRANSPORT
TOPIC: Air Transport
PARTIES:
Germany, East
Iraq

420151   Bilateral Protocol   **51 EGDZ 292**
SIGNED: 20 Jul 63
HEADNOTE: 7 PERCENT TRADE INCREASE
TOPIC: General Trade
PARTIES:
Germany, East
Yugoslavia

420158   Bilateral Agreement   **50 EGDZ 332**
SIGNED: 22 Mar 65
HEADNOTE: HEALTH
TOPIC: Sanitation
PARTIES:
Germany, East
Yugoslavia

420159   Bilateral Agreement   **44 EGDZ 342**
SIGNED: 31 Aug 65
HEADNOTE: VETERINARY
TOPIC: Sanitation
PARTIES:
Germany, East
Yugoslavia

420160   Bilateral Agreement   **47 EGDZ 358**
SIGNED: 22 Apr 66
HEADNOTE: MAIL & TELECOMMUNICATIONS
TOPIC: Gen Communications
PARTIES:
Germany, East
Yugoslavia

420161   Bilateral Treaty   **45 EGDZ 360**
SIGNED: 20 May 66
HEADNOTE: CIVIL & CRIMINAL LAW
TOPIC: Admin Cooperation
PARTIES:
Germany, East
Yugoslavia

420162   Bilateral Agreement   **34 EGDZ 368**
SIGNED: 18 Sep 66
HEADNOTE: ROAD TRAFFIC
TOPIC: Land Transport
PARTIES:
Germany, East
Yugoslavia

420163   Bilateral Agreement   **46 EGDZ 369**
SIGNED: 1 Oct 66
HEADNOTE: RAISE MISSIONS TO EMBASSIES
TOPIC: Consul/Citizenship
PARTIES:
Germany, East
Yugoslavia

420164   Bilateral Agreement   **42 EGDZ 385**
SIGNED: 3 Jun 67
HEADNOTE: RESEARCH COOPERATION
TOPIC: Scientific Project
PARTIES:
Germany, East
Yugoslavia

420169   Bilateral Protocol   **43 EGDZ 335**
SIGNED: 6 May 65
HEADNOTE: ECONOMIC COOPERATION
TOPIC: General Aid
PARTIES:
Congo (Brazzaville)
Germany, East

420183   Bilateral Agreement   **52 EGDZ 340**
SIGNED: 27 Jul 65
HEADNOTE: HEALTH
TOPIC: Sanitation
PARTIES:
Germany, East
Korea, North

420194   Bilateral Agreement   **49 EGDZ 332**
SIGNED: 15 Mar 65
HEADNOTE: HIGHER EDUCATION THROUGH
1970
TOPIC: Education
PARTIES:
Cuba
Germany, East

420195   Bilateral Agreement   **41 EGDZ 361**
SIGNED: 1 Jun 66
HEADNOTE: POST & TELECOMMUNICATIONS
TOPIC: Gen Communications
PARTIES:
Cuba
Germany, East

420202   Bilateral Treaty   **50 EGDZ 336**
SIGNED: 17 May 65
HEADNOTE: RADIO
TOPIC: Mass Media
PARTIES:
Germany, East
Mali

420203   Bilateral Agreement   **51 EGDZ 336**
SIGNED: 30 May 65
HEADNOTE: TECHNICAL ADVISERS
TOPIC: Tech Assistance
PARTIES:
Germany, East
Mali

420204   Bilateral Agreement   **44 EGDZ 347**
SIGNED: 12 Nov 65

HEADNOTE: SCIENTIFIC & TECHNICAL COOPER-
ATION
TOPIC: Tech Assistance
PARTIES:
Germany, East
Mali

420205   Bilateral Agreement   **42 EGDZ 361**
SIGNED: 8 Jun 66
HEADNOTE: AIR TRANSPORT
TOPIC: Air Transport
PARTIES:
Germany, East
Mali

420206   Bilateral Protocol   **34 EGDZ 368**
SIGNED: 17 Sep 66
HEADNOTE: NEWS SERVICES
TOPIC: Mass Media
PARTIES:
Germany, East
Mali

420223   Bilateral Agreement   **51 EGDZ 336**
SIGNED: 28 May 65
HEADNOTE: STUDENT EXCHANGE
TOPIC: Education
PARTIES:
Germany, East
Mongolia

420224   Bilateral Agreement   **52 EGDZ 341**
SIGNED: 11 Aug 65
HEADNOTE: HEALTH
TOPIC: Sanitation
PARTIES:
Germany, East
Mongolia

420225   Bilateral Agreement   **51 EGDZ 356**
SIGNED: 19 Mar 66
HEADNOTE: MONGOLIAN AGRICULTURE
TOPIC: Tech Assistance
PARTIES:
Germany, East
Mongolia

420273   Bilateral Agreement   **52 EGDZ 331**
SIGNED: 11 Mar 65
HEADNOTE: BORDER AREA WATER USE
TOPIC: Specific Resources
PARTIES:
Germany, East
Poland

420274   Bilateral Protocol   **44 EGDZ 335**
SIGNED: 12 May 65
HEADNOTE: RETURN ITEMS PRUSSIAN LIBRARY
TOPIC: Specific Property
PARTIES:
Germany, East
Poland

420275   Bilateral Agreement   **60 EGDZ 350**
SIGNED: 30 Dec 65
HEADNOTE: GOODS & SERVICES 1966-70
TOPIC: General Economic
PARTIES:
Germany, East
Poland

420276   Bilateral Protocol   **51 EGDZ 355**
SIGNED: 5 Mar 66
HEADNOTE: DELIVERY CHEMICAL PLANT
TOPIC: Commodity Trade
PARTIES:
Germany, East
Poland

420277   Bilateral Protocol   **48 EGDZ 383**
SIGNED: 5 May 67
HEADNOTE: RESEARCH & DEVELOPMENT 1970
TOPIC: Scientific Project

PARTIES:
Germany, East
Poland

420299   Bilateral Instrument   **51 EGDZ 278**
SIGNED: 18 Dec 62
HEADNOTE: STATUTE ECONOMIC COOPERATION
COMMISSION
TOPIC: IGO Establishment
PARTIES:
Germany, East
Romania

420303   Bilateral Agreement   **44 EGDZ 337**
SIGNED: 15 Jun 65
HEADNOTE: VISA ABOLITION
TOPIC: Visas
PARTIES:
Germany, East
Romania

420304   Bilateral Agreement   **40 EGDZ 352**
SIGNED: 22 Jan 66
HEADNOTE: DELIVERIES 1966-70
TOPIC: General Trade
PARTIES:
Germany, East
Romania

420305   Bilateral Agreement   **48 EGDZ 363**
SIGNED: 7 Jul 66
HEADNOTE: RADIO & TV
TOPIC: Mass Media
PARTIES:
Germany, East
Romania

420309   Bilateral Agreement   **46 EGDZ 364**
SIGNED: 3 Mar 60
HEADNOTE: ARCHEOLOGY RESEARCH
TOPIC: Scientific Project
PARTIES:
Germany, East
Sudan

420315   Bilateral Agreement   **43 EGDZ 337**
SIGNED: 6 Jun 65
HEADNOTE: AIR TRANSPORT
TOPIC: Air Transport
PARTIES:
Germany, East
Syria

420316   Bilateral Agreement   **51 EGDZ 341**
SIGNED: 2 Aug 65
HEADNOTE: LONG-RANGE TRADE
TOPIC: General Trade
PARTIES:
Germany, East
Syria

420317   Bilateral Agreement   **51 EGDZ 341**
SIGNED: 2 Aug 65
HEADNOTE: TECHNICAL-SCIENTIFIC RELATIONS
TOPIC: Tech Assistance
PARTIES:
Germany, East
Syria

420318   Bilateral Agreement   **51 EGDZ 341**
SIGNED: 2 Aug 65
HEADNOTE: LONG-TERM PAYMENTS
TOPIC: Finance
PARTIES:
Germany, East
Syria

420319   Bilateral Agreement   **51 EGDZ 341**
SIGNED: 2 Aug 65
HEADNOTE: NAVIGATION
TOPIC: Water Transport
PARTIES:
Germany, East
Syria

420320   Bilateral Agreement   **52 EGDZ 356**
SIGNED: 17 Oct 65
HEADNOTE: ECONOMIC & TECHNICAL COOPER-
ATION
TOPIC: General Economic
PARTIES:
Germany, East
Syria

420321   Bilateral Agreement   **47 EGDZ 358**
SIGNED: 23 Apr 66
HEADNOTE: RADIO & TV
TOPIC: Mass Media
PARTIES:
Germany, East
Syria

420322   Bilateral Agreement   **42 EGDZ 366**
SIGNED: 30 Aug 66
HEADNOTE: SPEED-UP ECONOMIC & TECHNICAL
COOPERATION
TOPIC: General Economic
PARTIES:
Germany, East
Syria

420323   Bilateral Agreement   **37 EGDZ 367**
SIGNED: 14 Sep 66
HEADNOTE: CULTURE
TOPIC: Culture
PARTIES:
Germany, East
Syria

420324   Bilateral Protocol   **37 EGDZ 370**
SIGNED: 30 Oct 66
HEADNOTE: FURTHER TECHNICAL COOPER-
ATION
TOPIC: Tech Assistance
PARTIES:
Germany, East
Syria

420366   Bilateral Protocol   **52 EGDZ 276**
SIGNED: 28 Nov 62
HEADNOTE: BORDER RIVERS
TOPIC: Specific Resources
PARTIES:
Czechoslovakia
Germany, East

420369   Bilateral Agreement   **59 EGDZ 350**
SIGNED: 21 Dec 65
HEADNOTE: TRADE 1966-70
TOPIC: General Trade
PARTIES:
Czechoslovakia
Germany, East

420370   Bilateral Agreement   **51 EGDZ 354**
SIGNED: 16 Feb 66
HEADNOTE: PAYMENTS 1966-70
TOPIC: Finance
PARTIES:
Czechoslovakia
Germany, East

420371   Bilateral Protocol   **45 EGDZ 364**
SIGNED: 20 Jul 66
HEADNOTE: DIRECT COOPERATION CHEMICAL
ADMINISTRATION
TOPIC: Admin Cooperation
PARTIES:
Czechoslovakia
Germany, East

420426   Bilateral Agreement   **48 EGDZ 339**
SIGNED: 14 Jul 65
HEADNOTE: GERMAN ATOMIC PLANTS
TOPIC: Atomic Energy
PARTIES:
Germany, East
USSR (Soviet Union)

420427   Bilateral Agreement   **61 EGDZ 349**
SIGNED: 3 Dec 65
HEADNOTE: TRADE 1966-70
TOPIC: General Trade
PARTIES:
Germany, East
USSR (Soviet Union)

420428   Bilateral Agreement   **51 EGDZ 356**
SIGNED: 16 Mar 66
HEADNOTE: JOINT ECONOMIC-TECHNICAL COM-
MISSION
TOPIC: IGO Establishment
PARTIES:
Germany, East
USSR (Soviet Union)

420429   Bilateral Agreement   **41 EGDZ 361**
SIGNED: 1 Jun 66
HEADNOTE: AUTOMOBILE TRAFFIC
TOPIC: Land Transport
PARTIES:
Germany, East
USSR (Soviet Union)

420430   Bilateral Agreement   **34 EGDZ 367**
SIGNED: 1 Sep 66
HEADNOTE: AIR TRANSPORT
TOPIC: Air Transport
PARTIES:
Germany, East
USSR (Soviet Union)

420462   Bilateral Protocol   **51 EGDZ 328**
SIGNED: 18 Jan 65
HEADNOTE: JOINT PLANS 1966-70
TOPIC: General Economic
PARTIES:
Germany, East
Hungary

420463   Bilateral Agreement   **52 EGDZ 349**
SIGNED: 15 Dec 65
HEADNOTE: TRADE 1966-70
TOPIC: General Trade
PARTIES:
Germany, East
Hungary

420464   Bilateral Protocol   **51 EGDZ 354**
SIGNED: 19 Feb 66
HEADNOTE: SCIENTIFIC & TECHNICAL COOPER-
ATION
TOPIC: Scientific Project
PARTIES:
Germany, East
Hungary

420465   Bilateral Agreement   **51 EGDZ 355**
SIGNED: 11 Mar 66
HEADNOTE: USE & LEASE EMBASSY GROUNDS
TOPIC: Specific Property
PARTIES:
Germany, East
Hungary

420466   Bilateral Agreement   **49 EGDZ 365**
SIGNED: 1 Aug 66
HEADNOTE: ROAD TRAFFIC
TOPIC: Land Transport
PARTIES:
Germany, East
Hungary

420467   Bilateral Agreement   **45 EGDZ 369**
SIGNED: 3 Oct 66
HEADNOTE: RADIO & TV
TOPIC: Mass Media
PARTIES:
Germany, East
Hungary

420468   Bilateral Agreement   **38 EGDZ 384**
SIGNED: 30 May 67

HEADNOTE: DIRECT COOPERATION MINING AD-
MINISTRATION
TOPIC: Admin Cooperation
PARTIES:
  Germany, East
  Hungary

420469   Bilateral Agreement   42 EGDZ 386
SIGNED: 24 Jun 67
HEADNOTE: DIRECT COOPERATION FOOD AD-
MINISTRATION
TOPIC: Admin Cooperation
PARTIES:
  Germany, East
  Hungary

420470   Bilateral Agreement   48 EGDZ 387
SIGNED: 7 Jul 67
HEADNOTE: CULTURAL & SCIENTIFIC COOPER-
ATION
TOPIC: Health/Educ/Welfare
PARTIES:
  Germany, East
  Hungary

420479   Bilateral Protocol   43 EGDZ 335
SIGNED: 6 May 65
HEADNOTE: QUALITY CONTROL LABS
TOPIC: Tech Assistance
PARTIES:
  Germany, East
  United Arab Rep

420480   Bilateral Agreement   52 EGDZ 329
SIGNED: 20 May 65
HEADNOTE: AIR TRANSPORT
TOPIC: Air Transport
PARTIES:
  Germany, East
  United Arab Rep

420481   Bilateral Protocol   52 EGDZ 353
SIGNED: 11 Feb 66
HEADNOTE: NAVIGATION
TOPIC: Water Transport
PARTIES:
  Germany, East
  United Arab Rep

420482   Bilateral Protocol   33 EGDZ 359
SIGNED: 3 May 66
HEADNOTE: CONSTRUCTION INDUSTRY
TOPIC: General Economic
PARTIES:
  Germany, East
  United Arab Rep

420483   Bilateral Protocol   33 EGDZ 359
SIGNED: 3 May 66
HEADNOTE: TEXTILE INDUSTRY
TOPIC: General Economic
PARTIES:
  Germany, East
  United Arab Rep

420484   Bilateral Agreement   49 EGDZ 365
SIGNED: 2 Aug 66
HEADNOTE: PUBLIC HEALTH
TOPIC: Sanitation
PARTIES:
  Germany, East
  United Arab Rep

420495   Bilateral Agreement   43 EGDZ 347
SIGNED: 4 Nov 65
HEADNOTE: 170 VIETNAM STUDENTS TO GDR
TOPIC: Education
PARTIES:
  Germany, East
  Vietnam, North

420496   Bilateral Agreement   46 EGDZ 369
SIGNED: 10 Oct 66
HEADNOTE: AID & LONG-TERM LOAN

TOPIC: Loans and Credits
PARTIES:
  Germany, East
  Vietnam, North

420497   Bilateral Protocol   46 EGDZ 369
SIGNED: 10 Oct 66
HEADNOTE: VIETNAM TRAINEES IN GDR
TOPIC: Education
PARTIES:
  Germany, East
  Vietnam, North

420499   Bilateral Agreement   52 EGDZ 353
SIGNED: 12 Feb 66
HEADNOTE: TRADE & PAYMENTS 1966-68
TOPIC: General Economic
PARTIES:
  Cyprus
  Germany, East

420500   Bilateral Agreement   50 EGDZ 365
SIGNED: 4 Aug 66
HEADNOTE: PUBLIC HEALTH
TOPIC: Sanitation
PARTIES:
  Cyprus
  Germany, East

421533   Bilateral Agreement   57 WGBB 581
SIGNED: 14 Sep 55
HEADNOTE: EASING CUSTOMS PROCEDURES
TOPIC: Customs
PARTIES:
  Austria
  Germany, West

424001   Bilateral Agreement   58 WBGA 83
SIGNED: 31 Jan 58
HEADNOTE: TRADE & PAYMENTS
TOPIC: General Economic
PARTIES:
  Afghanistan
  Germany, West

424004   Bilateral Agreement   65 WBGA 116
SIGNED: 3 Oct 64
HEADNOTE: FINANCE
TOPIC: Finance
PARTIES:
  Algeria
  Germany, West

424005   Bilateral Agreement   65 WBGA 100
SIGNED: 17 Dec 64
HEADNOTE: TECHNICAL COOPERATION
TOPIC: Tech Assistance
PARTIES:
  Algeria
  Germany, West

424006   Bilateral Protocol   51 WBGA 227
SIGNED: 26 Oct 51
HEADNOTE: TRADE & PAYMENTS
TOPIC: General Trade
PARTIES:
  Argentina
  Germany, West

424007   Bilateral Agreement   58 WBGA 6
SIGNED: 25 Nov 57
HEADNOTE: TRADE & PAYMENTS
TOPIC: General Trade
PARTIES:
  Argentina
  Germany, West

424009   Bilateral Agreement   69 WBGA 39
SIGNED: 4 Dec 68
HEADNOTE: CAPITAL AID
TOPIC: Loans and Credits
PARTIES:
  Argentina
  Germany, West

424011   Bilateral Agreement   70 WBGA 6
SIGNED: 23 Oct 69
HEADNOTE: CAPITAL AID LA PLATA VALLEY
TOPIC: Non-IBRD Project
PARTIES:
  Argentina
  Germany, West

424012   Bilateral Agreement   70 WBGA 82
SIGNED: 3 Feb 70
HEADNOTE: FINANCIAL AID
TOPIC: Loans and Credits
PARTIES:
  Argentina
  Germany, West

424016   Bilateral Agreement   68 WBGA 38
SIGNED: 21 Apr 64
HEADNOTE: TRADE AND PAYMENTS
TOPIC: General Economic
PARTIES:
  Ethiopia
  Germany, West

424017   Bilateral Protocol   68 WBGA 38
SIGNED: 21 Apr 64
HEADNOTE: WATER TRANSPORT
TOPIC: Water Transport
PARTIES:
  Ethiopia
  Germany, West

424018   Bilateral Protocol   68 WBGA 38
SIGNED: 21 Apr 64
HEADNOTE: AIR TRANSPORT
TOPIC: Air Transport
PARTIES:
  Ethiopia
  Germany, West

424021   Bilateral Agreement   54 WBGA 128
SIGNED: 28 May 54
HEADNOTE: GERMAN WAR GRAVES
TOPIC: Other Military
PARTIES:
  Belgium
  Germany, West

424028   Bilateral Agreement   60 WBGA 150
SIGNED: 1 Jun 60
HEADNOTE: RETURN OF DEPENDENTS
TOPIC: Admin Cooperation
PARTIES:
  Belgium
  Germany, West

424030   Bilateral Agreement   63 WBGA 48
SIGNED: 12 Jul 62
HEADNOTE: SOCIAL SECURITY
TOPIC: Non-ILO Labor
PARTIES:
  Belgium
  Germany, West

424031   Bilateral Agreement   63 WBGA 171
SIGNED: 1 Feb 63
HEADNOTE: MILITARY INVENTIONS
TOPIC: General Military
PARTIES:
  Belgium
  Germany, West

424032   Bilateral Agreement   64 WBGA 78
SIGNED: 30 Dec 63
HEADNOTE: INFORMATION ON MENTAL PA-
TIENTS
TOPIC: Admin Cooperation
PARTIES:
  Belgium
  Germany, West

424033   Bilateral Agreement   67 WBGA 236
SIGNED: 27 Jul 64
HEADNOTE: FILMS

TOPIC: Commodity Trade
PARTIES:
  Belgium
  Germany, West

424034   Bilateral Agreement   **65 WBGA 157**
SIGNED: 6 Oct 64
HEADNOTE: OLD-AGE BENEFITS
TOPIC: Non-ILO Labor
PARTIES:
  Belgium
  Germany, West

424042   Bilateral Agreement   **70 WBGA 85**
SIGNED: 4 May 70
HEADNOTE: NATO CLAIMS PROCEDURE
TOPIC: General Military
PARTIES:
  Belgium
  Germany, West

424043   Bilateral Protocol   **62 WBGA 161**
SIGNED: 12 Jul 62
HEADNOTE: ECONOMIC AID
TOPIC: Direct Aid
PARTIES:
  Burma
  Germany, West

424044   Bilateral Agreement   **68 WBGA 15**
SIGNED: 11 Nov 67
HEADNOTE: FINANCIAL AID
TOPIC: Loans and Credits
PARTIES:
  Burma
  Germany, West

424045   Bilateral Agreement   **70 WBGA 145**
SIGNED: 9 May 70
HEADNOTE: FINANCIAL AID
TOPIC: Loans and Credits
PARTIES:
  Burma
  Germany, West

424046   Bilateral Agreement   **70 WBGA 220**
SIGNED: 18 Sep 70
HEADNOTE: FINANCIAL AID
TOPIC: Loans and Credits
PARTIES:
  Burma
  Germany, West

424049   Bilateral Agreement   **69 WBGA 204**
SIGNED: 5 Aug 69
HEADNOTE: FINANCIAL AID
TOPIC: Loans and Credits
PARTIES:
  Bolivia
  Germany, West

424052   Bilateral Exchange   **50 WBGA 212**
SIGNED: 4 Sep 53
HEADNOTE: GERMAN INVESTMENT
TOPIC: Claims and Debts
PARTIES:
  Brazil
  Germany, West

424053   Bilateral Agreement   **55 WBGA 141**
SIGNED: 1 Jul 55
HEADNOTE: TRADE
TOPIC: General Trade
PARTIES:
  Brazil
  Germany, West

424054   Bilateral Exchange   **58 WBGA 91**
SIGNED: 15 May 57
HEADNOTE: INFORMATION ON CRIMINAL
  RECORDS
TOPIC: Admin Cooperation

PARTIES:
  Brazil
  Germany, West

424056   Bilateral Agreement   **64 WBGA 49**
SIGNED: 30 Nov 63
HEADNOTE: TECHNICAL COOPERATION
TOPIC: Tech Assistance
PARTIES:
  Brazil
  Germany, West

424058   Bilateral Protocol   **69 WBGA 106**
SIGNED: 9 Apr 69
HEADNOTE: FINANCIAL COOPERATION
TOPIC: Loans and Credits
PARTIES:
  Brazil
  Germany, West

424059   Bilateral Protocol   **69 WBGA 138**
SIGNED: 30 May 69
HEADNOTE: FINANCIAL COOPERATION
TOPIC: Loans and Credits
PARTIES:
  Brazil
  Germany, West

424060   Bilateral Agreement   **69 WBGA 2118**
SIGNED: 9 Jun 69
HEADNOTE: SCIENTIFIC RESEARCH
TOPIC: Scientific Project
PARTIES:
  Brazil
  Germany, West

424062   Bilateral Protocol   **70 WBGA 232**
SIGNED: 2 Oct 70
HEADNOTE: FINANCIAL COOPERATION
TOPIC: Loans and Credits
PARTIES:
  Brazil
  Germany, West

424063   Bilateral Protocol   **71 WBGA 109**
SIGNED: 23 Apr 71
HEADNOTE: FINANCIAL COOPERATION
TOPIC: Loans and Credits
PARTIES:
  Brazil
  Germany, West

424064   Bilateral Agreement   **64 WBGA 148**
SIGNED: 6 Mar 64
HEADNOTE: TRADE
TOPIC: General Trade
PARTIES:
  Bulgaria
  Germany, West

424066   Bilateral Agreement   **71 WBGA 69**
SIGNED: 12 Feb 71
HEADNOTE: TRADE
TOPIC: General Trade
PARTIES:
  Bulgaria
  Germany, West

424067   Bilateral Agreement   **65 WBGA 142**
SIGNED: 31 Mar 65
HEADNOTE: TECHNICAL COOPERATION
TOPIC: Tech Assistance
PARTIES:
  Burundi
  Germany, West

424068   Bilateral Agreement   **66 WBGA 88**
SIGNED: 23 Dec 65
HEADNOTE: FINANCIAL AID
TOPIC: Loans and Credits
PARTIES:
  Burundi
  Germany, West

424069   Bilateral Agreement   **69 WBGA 14**
SIGNED: 21 Nov 68
HEADNOTE: FINANCIAL AID
TOPIC: Loans and Credits
PARTIES:
  Burundi
  Germany, West

424073   Bilateral Agreement   **66 WBGA 160**
SIGNED: 30 Jun 66
HEADNOTE: FINANCIAL AID
TOPIC: Loans and Credits
PARTIES:
  Ceylon (Sri Lanka)
  Germany, West

424074   Bilateral Agreement   **66 WBGA 212**
SIGNED: 20 Aug 66
HEADNOTE: FINANCIAL AID
TOPIC: Loans and Credits
PARTIES:
  Ceylon (Sri Lanka)
  Germany, West

424075   Bilateral Agreement   **68 WBGA 15**
SIGNED: 30 Sep 67
HEADNOTE: FINANCIAL AID
TOPIC: Loans and Credits
PARTIES:
  Ceylon (Sri Lanka)
  Germany, West

424076   Bilateral Agreement   **68 WBGA 170**
SIGNED: 20 Jun 68
HEADNOTE: FINANCIAL AID
TOPIC: Loans and Credits
PARTIES:
  Ceylon (Sri Lanka)
  Germany, West

424077   Bilateral Agreement   **69 WBGA 199**
SIGNED: 3 Aug 69
HEADNOTE: FINANCIAL AID
TOPIC: Loans and Credits
PARTIES:
  Ceylon (Sri Lanka)
  Germany, West

424082   Bilateral Agreement   **56 WBGA 230**
SIGNED: 2 Nov 56
HEADNOTE: TRADE & PAYMENTS
TOPIC: General Economic
PARTIES:
  Chile
  Germany, West

424084   Bilateral Agreement   **62 WBGA 35**
SIGNED: 10 Nov 61
HEADNOTE: WELFARE
TOPIC: Admin Cooperation
PARTIES:
  Chile
  Germany, West

424085   Bilateral Agreement   **63 WBGA 13**
SIGNED: 13 Sep 62
HEADNOTE: INFORMATION ON NATURALIZA-
TION
TOPIC: Admin Cooperation
PARTIES:
  Chile
  Germany, West

424087   Bilateral Agreement   **70 WBGA 64**
SIGNED: 18 Oct 68
HEADNOTE: ECONOMIC & TECH COOPERATION
TOPIC: General Aid
PARTIES:
  Chile
  Germany, West

424088   Bilateral Agreement   **69 WBGA 146**
SIGNED: 18 Oct 68
HEADNOTE: CAPITAL AID

TOPIC: Loans and Credits
PARTIES:
  Chile
  Germany, West

424090   Bilateral Agreement   **66 WBGA 66**
SIGNED: 23 Jul 65
HEADNOTE: TECHNICAL COOPERATION
TOPIC: Tech Assistance
PARTIES:
  Costa Rica
  Germany, West

424091   Bilateral Agreement   **68 WBGA 185**
SIGNED: 19 Jul 68
HEADNOTE: CAPITAL AID
TOPIC: Loans and Credits
PARTIES:
  Costa Rica
  Germany, West

424092   Bilateral Agreement   **64 WBGA 196**
SIGNED: 19 Jun 61
HEADNOTE: ECONOMIC COOPERATION
TOPIC: General Economic
PARTIES:
  Dahomey
  Germany, West

424093   Bilateral Agreement   **61 WBGA 196**
SIGNED: 19 Jun 61
HEADNOTE: ECONOMIC & TECHNICAL COOPER-
ATION
TOPIC: General Economic
PARTIES:
  Dahomey
  Germany, West

424094   Bilateral Protocol   **61 WBGA 196**
SIGNED: 19 Jun 61
HEADNOTE: WATER TRANSPORT
TOPIC: Water Transport
PARTIES:
  Dahomey
  Germany, West

424095   Bilateral Agreement   **63 WBGA 192**
SIGNED: 15 Jul 63
HEADNOTE: CAPITAL AID
TOPIC: Loans and Credits
PARTIES:
  Dahomey
  Germany, West

424096   Bilateral Agreement   **70 WBGA 215**
SIGNED: 23 Jul 70
HEADNOTE: CAPITAL AID
TOPIC: Loans and Credits
PARTIES:
  Dahomey
  Germany, West

424097   Bilateral Agreement   **61 WBGA 58**
SIGNED: 15 Feb 52
HEADNOTE: PASSENGERS & GOODS
TOPIC: Land Transport
PARTIES:
  Denmark
  Germany, West

424100   Bilateral Agreement   **59 WBGA 37**
SIGNED: 22 Dec 58
HEADNOTE: GENERAL GOODS
TOPIC: General Trade
PARTIES:
  Denmark
  Germany, West

424108   Bilateral Agreement   **53 WBGA 192**
SIGNED: 1 Aug 53
HEADNOTE: TRADE
TOPIC: General Trade

PARTIES:
  Ecuador
  Germany, West

424109   Bilateral Agreement   **53 WBGA 192**
SIGNED: 1 Aug 53
HEADNOTE: PATENTS
TOPIC: Patents/Copyrights
PARTIES:
  Ecuador
  Germany, West

424110   Bilateral Agreement   **57 WBGA 193**
SIGNED: 13 May 54
HEADNOTE: VISAS
TOPIC: Visas
PARTIES:
  Ecuador
  Germany, West

424111   Bilateral Agreement   **58 WBGA 218**
SIGNED: 21 Jul 58
HEADNOTE: INFORMATION ON NATURALIZA-
TION
TOPIC: Admin Cooperation
PARTIES:
  Ecuador
  Germany, West

424112   Bilateral Agreement   **64 WBGA 41**
SIGNED: 8 Nov 63
HEADNOTE: CURRENCY CONVERTIBILITY
TOPIC: Finance
PARTIES:
  Ecuador
  Germany, West

424113   Bilateral Agreement   **65 WBGA 185**
SIGNED: 28 Jun 65
HEADNOTE: FINANCIAL AID
TOPIC: Loans and Credits
PARTIES:
  Ecuador
  Germany, West

424115   Bilateral Agreement   **67 WBGA 166**
SIGNED: 12 Jul 67
HEADNOTE: VISAS
TOPIC: Visas
PARTIES:
  Ecuador
  Germany, West

424116   Bilateral Agreement   **68 WBGA 148**
SIGNED: 10 Apr 68
HEADNOTE: PRIVILEGES GERMAN TEACHERS
TOPIC: Education
PARTIES:
  Ecuador
  Germany, West

424118   Bilateral Agreement   **69 WBGA 232**
SIGNED: 14 Aug 69
HEADNOTE: CAPITAL AID
TOPIC: Loans and Credits
PARTIES:
  Ecuador
  Germany, West

424119   Bilateral Agreement   **70 WBGA 135**
SIGNED: 24 Apr 70
HEADNOTE: CAPITAL AID
TOPIC: Loans and Credits
PARTIES:
  Ecuador
  Germany, West

424120   Bilateral Agreement   **62 WBGA 58**
SIGNED: 18 Dec 61
HEADNOTE: ECONOMIC RELATIONS
TOPIC: General Economic
PARTIES:
  Germany, West
  Ivory Coast

424121   Bilateral Agreement   **62 WBGA 58**
SIGNED: 18 Dec 61
HEADNOTE: ECONOMIC & TECHNICAL COOPER-
ATION
TOPIC: Direct Aid
PARTIES:
  Germany, West
  Ivory Coast

424122   Bilateral Protocol   **62 WBGA 58**
SIGNED: 18 Dec 61
HEADNOTE: WATER TRANSPORT
TOPIC: Water Transport
PARTIES:
  Germany, West
  Ivory Coast

424123   Bilateral Agreement   **63 WBGA 210**
SIGNED: 3 Sep 63
HEADNOTE: CAPITAL AID
TOPIC: Loans and Credits
PARTIES:
  Germany, West
  Ivory Coast

424124   Bilateral Treaty   **68 WBGA 61**
SIGNED: 27 Oct 66
HEADNOTE: INVESTMENT GAURANTEE
TOPIC: Claims and Debts
PARTIES:
  Germany, West
  Ivory Coast

424126   Bilateral Agreement   **68 WBGA 153**
SIGNED: 17 Jun 68
HEADNOTE: CAPITAL AID
TOPIC: Loans and Credits
PARTIES:
  Germany, West
  Ivory Coast

424127   Bilateral Agreement   **70 WBGA 145**
SIGNED: 5 May 70
HEADNOTE: CAPITAL AID
TOPIC: Loans and Credits
PARTIES:
  Germany, West
  Ivory Coast

424129   Bilateral Agreement   **64 WBGA 198**
SIGNED: 24 Sep 63
HEADNOTE: TECHNICAL COOPERATION
TOPIC: Tech Assistance
PARTIES:
  El Salvador
  Germany, West

424130   Bilateral Agreement   **67 WBGA 42**
SIGNED: 19 Sep 66
HEADNOTE: CAPITAL AID
TOPIC: Loans and Credits
PARTIES:
  El Salvador
  Germany, West

424131   Bilateral Agreement   **52 WBGA 81**
SIGNED: 16 Apr 52
HEADNOTE: COMMERCE & NAVIGATION
TOPIC: General Economic
PARTIES:
  Finland
  Germany, West

424132   Bilateral Agreement   **62 WBGA 217**
SIGNED: 25 Sep 62
HEADNOTE: PASSENGERS & GOODS
TOPIC: Land Transport
PARTIES:
  Finland
  Germany, West

424133   Bilateral Agreement   **70 WBGA 31**
SIGNED: 3 Dec 69
HEADNOTE: TRADE & PAYMENTS

TOPIC: General Economic
PARTIES:
  Finland
  Germany, West

424141   Bilateral Agreement   57 WBGA 225
SIGNED: 23 Oct 54
HEADNOTE: DEPORTATION
TOPIC: Extradition
PARTIES:
  France
  Germany, West

424143   Bilateral Agreement   58 WBGA 64
SIGNED: 23 Oct 54
HEADNOTE: WAR GRAVES
TOPIC: Other Military
PARTIES:
  France
  Germany, West

424144   Bilateral Agreement   55 WBGA 34
SIGNED: 27 Nov 54
HEADNOTE: WATER SERVICE EMPLOYEES
TOPIC: Visas
PARTIES:
  France
  Germany, West

424145   Bilateral Agreement   55 WBGA 41
SIGNED: 16 Dec 54
HEADNOTE: BORDER TRAFFIC
TOPIC: Visas
PARTIES:
  France
  Germany, West

424146   Bilateral Protocol   55 WBGA 159
SIGNED: 24 Jun 55
HEADNOTE: FILM INDUSTRY
TOPIC: Commodity Trade
PARTIES:
  France
  Germany, West

424150   Bilateral Agreement   58 WBGA 4
SIGNED: 8 Dec 56
HEADNOTE: PASSENGER TRAFFIC
TOPIC: Land Transport
PARTIES:
  France
  Germany, West

424151   Bilateral Agreement   57 WBGA 137
SIGNED: 14 Jan 57
HEADNOTE: ALSATIAN CANAL EMPLOYEES
TOPIC: Visas
PARTIES:
  France
  Germany, West

424158   Bilateral Agreement   61 WBGA 11
SIGNED: 27 Oct 59
HEADNOTE: SAILORS DOCUMENTS AS PASS-
  PORTS
TOPIC: Visas
PARTIES:
  France
  Germany, West

424159   Bilateral Agreement   60 WBGA 63
SIGNED: 22 Jan 60
HEADNOTE: BORDER ARRESTS
TOPIC: Extradition
PARTIES:
  France
  Germany, West

424184   Bilateral Agreement   66 WBGA 245
SIGNED: 13 Jun 61
HEADNOTE: GOODS CROSSING BORDER
TOPIC: Visas

PARTIES:
  France
  Germany, West

424185   Bilateral Agreement   63 WBGA 171
SIGNED: 28 Sep 61
HEADNOTE: SECRECY MILITARY INVENTIONS
TOPIC: General Military
PARTIES:
  France
  Germany, West

424188   Bilateral Agreement   63 WBGA 75
SIGNED: 12 Jul 62
HEADNOTE: SOCIAL SECURITY MIGRANT WORK-
  ERS
TOPIC: Non-ILO Labor
PARTIES:
  France
  Germany, West

424190   Bilateral Agreement   63 WBGA 231
SIGNED: 27 Jun 63
HEADNOTE: SOCIAL SECURITY
TOPIC: Non-ILO Labor
PARTIES:
  France
  Germany, West

424195   Bilateral Agreement   64 WBGA 238
SIGNED: 27 Feb 64
HEADNOTE: COMMISSION BORDER TRAFFIC
TOPIC: Visas
PARTIES:
  France
  Germany, West

424196   Bilateral Agreement   67 WBGA 10
SIGNED: 18 Jan 65
HEADNOTE: INFORMATION ON MENTAL PA-
  TIENTS
TOPIC: Admin Cooperation
PARTIES:
  France
  Germany, West

424197   Bilateral Agreement   65 WBGA 157
SIGNED: 16 Mar 65
HEADNOTE: CLAIMS OF RETIRED PERSONS
TOPIC: Non-ILO Labor
PARTIES:
  France
  Germany, West

424198   Bilateral Agreement   66 WBGA 192
SIGNED: 11 Jun 66
HEADNOTE: OIL STORAGE RESERVES
TOPIC: Admin Cooperation
PARTIES:
  France
  Germany, West

424199   Bilateral Agreement   66 WBGA 161
SIGNED: 19 Apr 66
HEADNOTE: GERMAN WAR GRAVES
TOPIC: Other Military
PARTIES:
  France
  Germany, West

424205   Bilateral Agreement   63 WBGA 58
SIGNED: 11 Jul 62
HEADNOTE: ECONOMIC RELATIONS
TOPIC: General Economic
PARTIES:
  Gabon
  Germany, West

424206   Bilateral Agreement   63 WBGA 58
SIGNED: 11 Jul 62
HEADNOTE: ECONOMIC & TECHNICAL COOPER-
  ATION
TOPIC: Direct Aid

PARTIES:
  Gabon
  Germany, West

424207   Bilateral Protocol   63 WBGA 58
SIGNED: 11 Jul 62
HEADNOTE: AIR & WATER TRANSPORT
TOPIC: General Transport
PARTIES:
  Gabon
  Germany, West

424208   Bilateral Agreement   64 WBGA 155
SIGNED: 31 Oct 63
HEADNOTE: CAPITAL AID
TOPIC: Loans and Credits
PARTIES:
  Gabon
  Germany, West

424209   Bilateral Agreement   67 WBGA 63
SIGNED: 10 Jan 67
HEADNOTE: CAPITAL AID
TOPIC: Loans and Credits
PARTIES:
  Gabon
  Germany, West

424210   Bilateral Agreement   69 WBGA 27
SIGNED: 27 Nov 68
HEADNOTE: CAPITAL AID
TOPIC: Loans and Credits
PARTIES:
  Gabon
  Germany, West

424212   Bilateral Agreement   70 WBGA 235
SIGNED: 5 Nov 70
HEADNOTE: CAPITAL AID
TOPIC: Loans and Credits
PARTIES:
  Gabon
  Germany, West

424213   Bilateral Agreement   68 WBGA 80
SIGNED: 2 Nov 67
HEADNOTE: VISAS
TOPIC: Visas
PARTIES:
  Gambia
  Germany, West

424214   Bilateral Agreement   60 WBGA 196
SIGNED: 21 Dec 59
HEADNOTE: ECONOMIC & TECHNICAL COOPER-
  ATION
TOPIC: Direct Aid
PARTIES:
  Germany, West
  Ghana

424215   Bilateral Agreement   60 WBGA 241
SIGNED: 21 Dec 59
HEADNOTE: TRADE
TOPIC: General Trade
PARTIES:
  Germany, West
  Ghana

424216   Bilateral Agreement   63 WBGA 131
SIGNED: 15 May 63
HEADNOTE: FINANCIAL AID
TOPIC: Loans and Credits
PARTIES:
  Germany, West
  Ghana

424217   Bilateral Protocol   63 WBGA 131
SIGNED: 15 May 63
HEADNOTE: NAVIGATION
TOPIC: Water Transport
PARTIES:
  Germany, West
  Ghana

424218   Bilateral Exchange   **63 WBGA 131**
SIGNED: 15 May 63
HEADNOTE: AIR TRANSPORT
TOPIC: Air Transport
PARTIES:
  Germany, West
  Ghana

424219   Bilateral Agreement   **66 WBGA 131**
SIGNED: 6 Apr 66
HEADNOTE: CAPITAL AID
TOPIC: Loans and Credits
PARTIES:
  Germany, West
  Ghana

424222   Bilateral Agreement   **67 WBGA 193**
SIGNED: 1 Sep 67
HEADNOTE: CAPITAL AID
TOPIC: Loans and Credits
PARTIES:
  Germany, West
  Ghana

424223   Bilateral Agreement   **68 WBGA 147**
SIGNED: 30 Mar 68
HEADNOTE: DEVELOPMENT VOLUNTEERS
TOPIC: Tech Assistance
PARTIES:
  Germany, West
  Ghana

424224   Bilateral Agreement   **68 WBGA 130**
SIGNED: 7 May 68
HEADNOTE: CAPITAL AID
TOPIC: Loans and Credits
PARTIES:
  Germany, West
  Ghana

424226   Bilateral Agreement   **69 WBGA 176**
SIGNED: 11 Jul 69
HEADNOTE: CAPITAL AID
TOPIC: Loans and Credits
PARTIES:
  Germany, West
  Ghana

424227   Bilateral Agreement   **71 WBGA 64**
SIGNED: 8 Dec 70
HEADNOTE: CAPITAL AID
TOPIC: Loans and Credits
PARTIES:
  Germany, West
  Ghana

424228   Bilateral Agreement   **53 WBGA 228**
SIGNED: 11 Nov 53
HEADNOTE: ECONOMIC COOPERATION
TOPIC: General Economic
PARTIES:
  Germany, West
  Greece

424229   Bilateral Protocol   **55 WBGA 203**
SIGNED: 21 Sep 55
HEADNOTE: TALKS 19-21 SEP 55
TOPIC: Admin Cooperation
PARTIES:
  Germany, West
  Greece

424231   Bilateral Agreement   **59 WBGA 3**
SIGNED: 27 Nov 58
HEADNOTE: ECONOMIC COOPERATION
TOPIC: General Economic
PARTIES:
  Germany, West
  Greece

424232   Bilateral Agreement   **60 WBGA 173**
SIGNED: 18 Feb 60
HEADNOTE: MIGRANT WORKERS
TOPIC: Non-ILO Labor

PARTIES:
  Germany, West
  Greece

424235   Bilateral Agreement   **61 WBGA 25**
SIGNED: 30 Mar 60
HEADNOTE: RECRUITING MIGRANT WORKERS
TOPIC: Non-ILO Labor
PARTIES:
  Germany, West
  Greece

424241   Bilateral Agreement   **67 WBGA 39**
SIGNED: 24 Apr 66
HEADNOTE: TECHNICAL COOPERATION
TOPIC: Tech Assistance
PARTIES:
  Germany, West
  Guatemala

424242   Bilateral Agreement   **59 WBGA 77**
SIGNED: 18 Mar 59
HEADNOTE: ECONOMIC & TECHNICAL COOPER-
ATION
TOPIC: Direct Aid
PARTIES:
  Germany, West
  Guinea

424243   Bilateral Instrument   **61 WBGA 160**
SIGNED: 9 Mar 61
HEADNOTE: NAVIGATION
TOPIC: Water Transport
PARTIES:
  Germany, West
  Guinea

424245   Bilateral Agreement   **62 WBGA 134**
SIGNED: 19 Apr 62
HEADNOTE: ECONOMIC RELATIONS
TOPIC: General Economic
PARTIES:
  Germany, West
  Guinea

424246   Bilateral Agreement   **62 WBGA 134**
SIGNED: 19 Apr 62
HEADNOTE: FINANCIAL AID
TOPIC: Loans and Credits
PARTIES:
  Germany, West
  Guinea

424247   Bilateral Protocol   **62 WBGA 134**
SIGNED: 19 Apr 62
HEADNOTE: AIR TRANSPORT
TOPIC: Air Transport
PARTIES:
  Germany, West
  Guinea

424248   Bilateral Protocol   **64 WBGA 195**
SIGNED: 10 Jul 64
HEADNOTE: FILM INDUSTRY
TOPIC: Commodity Trade
PARTIES:
  Germany, West
  Guinea

424249   Bilateral Agreement   **65 WBGA 136**
SIGNED: 3 Jun 65
HEADNOTE: CAPITAL AID
TOPIC: Loans and Credits
PARTIES:
  Germany, West
  Guinea

424250   Bilateral Agreement   **66 WBGA 33**
SIGNED: 18 Apr 64
HEADNOTE: TECHNICAL COOPERATION
TOPIC: Tech Assistance
PARTIES:
  Germany, West
  Honduras

424251   Bilateral Agreement   **52 WBGA 83**
SIGNED: 19 Mar 52
HEADNOTE: TRADE
TOPIC: General Trade
PARTIES:
  Germany, West
  India

424252   Bilateral Agreement   **55 WBGA 174**
SIGNED: 31 Mar 55
HEADNOTE: TRADE
TOPIC: General Trade
PARTIES:
  Germany, West
  India

424253   Bilateral Agreement   **68 WBGA 202**
SIGNED: 5 Mar 56
HEADNOTE: WAR GRAVES
TOPIC: Other Military
PARTIES:
  Germany, West
  India

424254   Bilateral Agreement   **58 WBGA 178**
SIGNED: 7 Aug 58
HEADNOTE: SCHOOL OF TECHNOLOGY
TOPIC: Education
PARTIES:
  Germany, West
  India

424257   Bilateral Agreement   **64 WBGA 235**
SIGNED: 15 Oct 64
HEADNOTE: INVESTMENT GUARANTEE
TOPIC: Claims and Debts
PARTIES:
  Germany, West
  India

424258   Bilateral Agreement   **66 WBGA 190**
SIGNED: 15 Jun 66
HEADNOTE: WATER TRANSPORT
TOPIC: Water Transport
PARTIES:
  Germany, West
  India

424261   Bilateral Agreement   **53 WBGA 163**
SIGNED: 22 Apr 53
HEADNOTE: TRADE
TOPIC: General Trade
PARTIES:
  Germany, West
  Indonesia

424262   Bilateral Agreement   **57 WBGA 228**
SIGNED: 29 Aug 57
HEADNOTE: ECONOMIC & TECHNICAL COOPER-
ATION
TOPIC: Direct Aid
PARTIES:
  Germany, West
  Indonesia

424263   Bilateral Agreement   **68 WBGA 139**
SIGNED: 17 May 68
HEADNOTE: CAPITAL AID
TOPIC: Loans and Credits
PARTIES:
  Germany, West
  Indonesia

424265   Bilateral Agreement   **69 WBGA 189**
SIGNED: 8 May 69
HEADNOTE: CAPITAL AID
TOPIC: Loans and Credits
PARTIES:
  Germany, West
  Indonesia

424266   Bilateral Agreement   **70 WBGA 28**
SIGNED: 23 Oct 69
HEADNOTE: CAPITAL AID

TOPIC: Loans and Credits
PARTIES:
  Germany, West
  Indonesia

424268   Bilateral Agreement   **70 WBGA 226**
SIGNED: 27 Aug 70
HEADNOTE: CAPITAL AID
TOPIC: Loans and Credits
PARTIES:
  Germany, West
  Indonesia

424270   Bilateral Agreement   **59 WBGA 93**
SIGNED: 7 Nov 58
HEADNOTE: INFORMATION ON ARRESTS
TOPIC: Admin Cooperation
PARTIES:
  Germany, West
  Iraq

424275   Bilateral Agreement   **68 WBGA 112**
SIGNED: 22 Apr 68
HEADNOTE: CAPITAL AID
TOPIC: Loans and Credits
PARTIES:
  Germany, West
  Iran

424276   Bilateral Agreement   **69 WBGA 216**
SIGNED: 8 Sep 68
HEADNOTE: CAPITAL AID
TOPIC: Loans and Credits
PARTIES:
  Germany, West
  Iran

424280   Bilateral Agreement   **54 WBGA 124**
SIGNED: 20 May 54
HEADNOTE: TRADE
TOPIC: General Trade
PARTIES:
  Germany, West
  Iceland

424281   Bilateral Agreement   **57 WBGA 192**
SIGNED: 14 Sep 56
HEADNOTE: VISAS
TOPIC: Visas
PARTIES:
  Germany, West
  Iceland

424282   Bilateral Agreement   **66 WBGA 111**
SIGNED: 12 May 66
HEADNOTE: ECONOMIC AID
TOPIC: Direct Aid
PARTIES:
  Germany, West
  Israel

424284   Bilateral Agreement   **69 WBGA 94**
SIGNED: 25 Feb 68
HEADNOTE: ADMINISTRATIVE EXPENSES REPA-
  RATIONS
TOPIC: Admin Cooperation
PARTIES:
  Germany, West
  Israel

424285   Bilateral Agreement   **68 WBGA 165**
SIGNED: 18 Jul 68
HEADNOTE: ECONOMIC AID
TOPIC: Direct Aid
PARTIES:
  Germany, West
  Israel

424288   Bilateral Agreement   **53 WBGA 134**
SIGNED: 5 May 53
HEADNOTE: MIGRANT WORKERS
TOPIC: Non-ILO Labor

PARTIES:
  Germany, West
  Italy

424291   Bilateral Protocol   **56 WBGA 17**
SIGNED: 18 Oct 55
HEADNOTE: FILM INDUSTRY
TOPIC: Commodity Trade
PARTIES:
  Germany, West
  Italy

424294   Bilateral Agreement   **64 WBGA 97**
SIGNED: 4 Jul 57
HEADNOTE: PASSENGERS & GOODS
TOPIC: General Transport
PARTIES:
  Germany, West
  Italy

424300   Bilateral Agreement   **63 WBGA 75**
SIGNED: 12 Jul 62
HEADNOTE: SOCIAL SECURITY MIGRANTS
TOPIC: Non-ILO Labor
PARTIES:
  Germany, West
  Italy

424301   Bilateral Agreement   **63 WBGA 231**
SIGNED: 27 Jun 63
HEADNOTE: SOCIAL SECURITY MIGRANTS
TOPIC: Non-ILO Labor
PARTIES:
  Germany, West
  Italy

424303   Bilateral Agreement   **65 WBGA 63**
SIGNED: 23 Feb 65
HEADNOTE: RECRUITING MIGRANT WORKERS
TOPIC: Non-ILO Labor
PARTIES:
  Germany, West
  Italy

424304   Bilateral Agreement   **67 WBGA 81**
SIGNED: 27 Jul 66
HEADNOTE: FILM INDUSTRY
TOPIC: Commodity Trade
PARTIES:
  Germany, West
  Italy

424309   Bilateral Agreement   **69 WBGA 197**
SIGNED: 17 Jul 69
HEADNOTE: OIL STORAGE RESERVES
TOPIC: Admin Cooperation
PARTIES:
  Germany, West
  Italy

424311   Bilateral Agreement   **70 WBGA 37**
SIGNED: 28 Nov 69
HEADNOTE: CAPITAL AID
TOPIC: Loans and Credits
PARTIES:
  Germany, West
  Yemen

424312   Bilateral Agreement   **70 WBGA 226**
SIGNED: 28 Sep 70
HEADNOTE: CAPITAL AID
TOPIC: Loans and Credits
PARTIES:
  Germany, West
  Yemen

424313   Bilateral Agreement   **71 WBGA 146**
SIGNED: 3 Jun 71
HEADNOTE: CAPITAL AID
TOPIC: Loans and Credits
PARTIES:
  Germany, West
  Yemen

424314   Bilateral Agreement   **67 WBGA 90**
SIGNED: 14 Mar 67
HEADNOTE: CAPITAL AID
TOPIC: Loans and Credits
PARTIES:
  Germany, West
  Jordan

424315   Bilateral Agreement   **68 WBGA 42**
SIGNED: 24 Oct 67
HEADNOTE: CAPITAL AID
TOPIC: Loans and Credits
PARTIES:
  Germany, West
  Jordan

424316   Bilateral Agreement   **68 WBGA 199**
SIGNED: 25 Jul 68
HEADNOTE: CAPITAL AID
TOPIC: Loans and Credits
PARTIES:
  Germany, West
  Jordan

424317   Bilateral Agreement   **70 WBGA 54**
SIGNED: 29 Jan 70
HEADNOTE: CAPITAL AID
TOPIC: Loans and Credits
PARTIES:
  Germany, West
  Jordan

424319   Bilateral Agreement   **52 WBGA 169**
SIGNED: 11 Jun 52
HEADNOTE: TRADE
TOPIC: General Trade
PARTIES:
  Germany, West
  Yugoslavia

424320   Bilateral Agreement   **55 WBGA 36**
SIGNED: 18 Dec 53
HEADNOTE: INFORMATION ON NATURALIZA-
  TION
TOPIC: Admin Cooperation
PARTIES:
  Germany, West
  Yugoslavia

424323   Bilateral Agreement   **57 WBGA 146**
SIGNED: 14 May 55
HEADNOTE: EXTRADITION
TOPIC: Extradition
PARTIES:
  Germany, West
  Yugoslavia

424326   Bilateral Protocol   **57 WBGA 9**
SIGNED: 10 Mar 56
HEADNOTE: ECONOMIC & FINANCES
TOPIC: General Economic
PARTIES:
  Germany, West
  Yugoslavia

424327   Bilateral Agreement   **57 WBGA 9**
SIGNED: 10 Mar 56
HEADNOTE: COMPENSATION CLAIMS
TOPIC: Claims and Debts
PARTIES:
  Germany, West
  Yugoslavia

424328   Bilateral Agreement   **57 WBGA 9**
SIGNED: 10 Mar 56
HEADNOTE: YUGOSLAV POSTWAR TRADE
  DEBTS
TOPIC: Specif Claim/Waive
PARTIES:
  Germany, West
  Yugoslavia

424330   Bilateral Agreement   **56 WBGA 160**
SIGNED: 17 Jul 56

HEADNOTE: PAYMENTS
TOPIC: Finance
PARTIES:
  Germany, West
  Yugoslavia

424331   Bilateral Agreement   **57 WBGA 183**
SIGNED: 19 Jul 57
HEADNOTE: FILM INDUSTRY
TOPIC: Commodity Trade
PARTIES:
  Germany, West
  Yugoslavia

424332   Bilateral Agreement   **64 WBGA 192**
SIGNED: 16 Jul 64
HEADNOTE: PASSENGERS & GOODS
TOPIC: Visas
PARTIES:
  Germany, West
  Yugoslavia

424333   Bilateral Exchange   **65 WBGA 17**
SIGNED: 16 Jul 64
HEADNOTE: ECONOMIC & TECHNICAL COOPER-
  ATION
TOPIC: Direct Aid
PARTIES:
  Germany, West
  Yugoslavia

424338   Bilateral Agreement   **69 WBGA 59**
SIGNED: 23 Oct 68
HEADNOTE: VISAS
TOPIC: Visas
PARTIES:
  Germany, West
  Yugoslavia

424339   Bilateral Agreement   **69 WBGA 145**
SIGNED: 10 Feb 69
HEADNOTE: COOPERATION INDUSTRY & TECH-
  NOLOGY
TOPIC: General Economic
PARTIES:
  Germany, West
  Yugoslavia

424342   Bilateral Agreement   **62 WBGA 126**
SIGNED: 8 Mar 62
HEADNOTE: TRADE
TOPIC: General Trade
PARTIES:
  Cameroon
  Germany, West

424343   Bilateral Protocol   **62 WBGA 126**
SIGNED: 8 Mar 62
HEADNOTE: WATER TRANSPORT
TOPIC: Water Transport
PARTIES:
  Cameroon
  Germany, West

424345   Bilateral Agreement   **62 WBGA 172**
SIGNED: 29 Jun 62
HEADNOTE: ECONOMIC & TECHNICAL COOPER-
  ATION
TOPIC: Direct Aid
PARTIES:
  Cameroon
  Germany, West

424346   Bilateral Agreement   **63 WBGA 115**
SIGNED: 3 May 63
HEADNOTE: CAPITAL AID
TOPIC: Loans and Credits
PARTIES:
  Cameroon
  Germany, West

424348   Bilateral Agreement   **68 WBGA 203**
SIGNED: 5 Mar 56
HEADNOTE: WAR GRAVES

TOPIC: Other Military
PARTIES:
  Cameroon
  Germany, West

424349   Bilateral Agreement   **58 WBGA 46**
SIGNED: 11 Dec 57
HEADNOTE: CIVIL USE ATOMIC ENERGY
TOPIC: Atomic Energy
PARTIES:
  Cameroon
  Germany, West

424351   Bilateral Agreement   **64 WBGA 195**
SIGNED: 28 Aug 64
HEADNOTE: MILITARY SCIENTIFIC INFORMATION
TOPIC: General Military
PARTIES:
  Cameroon
  Germany, West

424356   Bilateral Agreement   **66 WBGA 165**
SIGNED: 4 Dec 64
HEADNOTE: TRADE & ECONOMIC RELATIONS
TOPIC: General Economic
PARTIES:
  Germany, West
  Kenya

424357   Bilateral Agreement   **66 WBGA 165**
SIGNED: 4 Dec 64
HEADNOTE: TECHNICAL COOPERATION
TOPIC: Tech Assistance
PARTIES:
  Germany, West
  Kenya

424358   Bilateral Agreement   **66 WBGA 165**
SIGNED: 4 Dec 64
HEADNOTE: CAPITAL AID
TOPIC: Loans and Credits
PARTIES:
  Germany, West
  Kenya

424359   Bilateral Agreement   **67 WBGA 52**
SIGNED: 8 Dec 66
HEADNOTE: CAPITAL AID
TOPIC: Loans and Credits
PARTIES:
  Germany, West
  Kenya

424360   Bilateral Agreement   **68 WBGA 47**
SIGNED: 30 Nov 67
HEADNOTE: CAPITAL AID
TOPIC: Loans and Credits
PARTIES:
  Germany, West
  Kenya

424361   Bilateral Agreement   **68 WBGA 184**
SIGNED: 8 Aug 68
HEADNOTE: VISAS
TOPIC: Visas
PARTIES:
  Germany, West
  Kenya

424362   Bilateral Agreement   **69 WBGA 115**
SIGNED: 11 Apr 69
HEADNOTE: CAPITAL AID
TOPIC: Loans and Credits
PARTIES:
  Germany, West
  Kenya

424363   Bilateral Agreement   **70 WBGA 98**
SIGNED: 13 Mar 70
HEADNOTE: CAPITAL AID
TOPIC: Loans and Credits
PARTIES:
  Germany, West
  Kenya

424365   Bilateral Agreement   **70 WBGA 151**
SIGNED: 1 Jul 70
HEADNOTE: CAPITAL AID
TOPIC: Loans and Credits
PARTIES:
  Germany, West
  Kenya

424366   Bilateral Agreement   **71 WBGA 114**
SIGNED: 13 May 71
HEADNOTE: CAPITAL AID
TOPIC: Loans and Credits
PARTIES:
  Germany, West
  Kenya

424367   Bilateral Exchange   **54 WBGA 184**
SIGNED: 19 May 54
HEADNOTE: RETURN GERMAN PATENT RIGHTS
TOPIC: Patents/Copyrights
PARTIES:
  Colombia
  Germany, West

424368   Bilateral Agreement   **58 WBGA 49**
SIGNED: 9 Nov 57
HEADNOTE: TRADE
TOPIC: General Trade
PARTIES:
  Colombia
  Germany, West

424372   Bilateral Agreement   **65 WBGA 140**
SIGNED: 2 Mar 65
HEADNOTE: TECHNICAL COOPERATION
TOPIC: Tech Assistance
PARTIES:
  Colombia
  Germany, West

424374   Bilateral Agreement   **66 WBGA 238**
SIGNED: 11 Jun 65
HEADNOTE: CAPITAL AID
TOPIC: Loans and Credits
PARTIES:
  Colombia
  Germany, West

424377   Bilateral Agreement   **70 WBGA 74**
SIGNED: 27 Jan 70
HEADNOTE: CAPITAL AID
TOPIC: Loans and Credits
PARTIES:
  Colombia
  Germany, West

424378   Bilateral Agreement   **71 WBGA 58**
SIGNED: 10 Dec 70
HEADNOTE: CAPITAL AID
TOPIC: Loans and Credits
PARTIES:
  Colombia
  Germany, West

424379   Bilateral Agreement   **63 WBGA 59**
SIGNED: 30 Oct 62
HEADNOTE: ECONOMIC RELATIONS
TOPIC: General Economic
PARTIES:
  Congo (Brazzaville)
  Germany, West

424380   Bilateral Protocol   **63 WBGA 59**
SIGNED: 30 Oct 62
HEADNOTE: WATER & AIR TRANSPORT
TOPIC: General Transport
PARTIES:
  Congo (Brazzaville)
  Germany, West

424381   Bilateral Agreement   **63 WBGA 59**
SIGNED: 30 Oct 62
HEADNOTE: TECHNICAL COOPERATION
TOPIC: Tech Assistance

PARTIES:
Congo (Brazzaville)
Germany, West

424383   Bilateral Agreement   66 WBGA 4
SIGNED: 27 Oct 65
HEADNOTE: CAPITAL AID
TOPIC: Loans and Credits
PARTIES:
Congo (Brazzaville)
Germany, West

424384   Bilateral Agreement   65 WBGA 38
SIGNED: 23 Nov 64
HEADNOTE: CAPITAL AID
TOPIC: Loans and Credits
PARTIES:
Congo (Zaire)
Germany, West

424385   Bilateral Agreement   65 WBGA 170
SIGNED: 23 Jun 65
HEADNOTE: CAPITAL AID
TOPIC: Loans and Credits
PARTIES:
Congo (Zaire)
Germany, West

424386   Bilateral Agreement   67 WBGA 98
SIGNED: 7 Mar 67
HEADNOTE: CAPITAL AID
TOPIC: Loans and Credits
PARTIES:
Congo (Zaire)
Germany, West

424387   Bilateral Agreement   69 WBGA 84
SIGNED: 18 Mar 69
HEADNOTE: CAPITAL AID
TOPIC: Loans and Credits
PARTIES:
Congo (Zaire)
Germany, West

424389   Bilateral Agreement   62 WBGA 8
SIGNED: 22 Sep 61
HEADNOTE: ABOLITION VISA FEES
TOPIC: Visas
PARTIES:
Germany, West
Korea, South

424393   Bilateral Agreement   65 WBGA 29
SIGNED: 7 Dec 64
HEADNOTE: CAPITAL AID
TOPIC: Loans and Credits
PARTIES:
Germany, West
Korea, South

424394   Bilateral Agreement   65 WBGA 29
SIGNED: 8 Apr 65
HEADNOTE: TRADE
TOPIC: General Trade
PARTIES:
Germany, West
Korea, South

424396   Bilateral Agreement   70 WBGA 99
SIGNED: 18 Feb 70
HEADNOTE: TEMPORARY EMPLOYMENT KOREAN
MINERS
TOPIC: Non-ILO Labor
PARTIES:
Germany, West
Korea, South

424397   Bilateral Agreement   71 WBGA 142
SIGNED: 21 May 71
HEADNOTE: CAPITAL AID
TOPIC: Loans and Credits
PARTIES:
Germany, West
Korea, South

424405   Bilateral Exchange   57 WBGA 173
SIGNED: 12 Jun 56
HEADNOTE: CRIMINAL LAW
TOPIC: Admin Cooperation
PARTIES:
Germany, West
Lebanon

424408   Bilateral Agreement   60 WBGA 69
SIGNED: 17 Nov 59
HEADNOTE: ECONOMIC & TECHNICAL COOPER-
ATION
TOPIC: Direct Aid
PARTIES:
Germany, West
Liberia

424410   Bilateral Protocol   62 WBGA 46
SIGNED: 12 Dec 61
HEADNOTE: WATER & AIR TRANSPORT
TOPIC: General Transport
PARTIES:
Germany, West
Liberia

424411   Bilateral Agreement   62 WBGA 46
SIGNED: 12 Dec 61
HEADNOTE: FINANCIAL AID
TOPIC: Direct Aid
PARTIES:
Germany, West
Liberia

424412   Bilateral Agreement   67 WBGA 40
SIGNED: 5 Dec 66
HEADNOTE: CAPITAL AID
TOPIC: Loans and Credits
PARTIES:
Germany, West
Liberia

424414   Bilateral Agreement   61 WBGA 21
SIGNED: 8 Jul 60
HEADNOTE: ECONOMIC & TECHNICAL COOPER-
ATION
TOPIC: Direct Aid
PARTIES:
Germany, West
Libya

424416   Bilateral Agreement   59 WBGA 73
SIGNED: 29 May 58
HEADNOTE: CIVIL AND CRIMINAL LAW
TOPIC: Admin Cooperation
PARTIES:
Germany, West
Liechtenstein

424417   Bilateral Agreement   61 WBGA 173
SIGNED: 30 Apr 52
HEADNOTE: PASSENGERS & GOODS
TOPIC: General Transport
PARTIES:
Germany, West
Luxembourg

424418   Bilateral Agreement   63 WBGA 47
SIGNED: 9 Dec 53
HEADNOTE: REPATRIATION OF MINORS
TOPIC: Extradition
PARTIES:
Germany, West
Luxembourg

424419   Bilateral Agreement   51 WBGA 114
SIGNED: 25 Jul 56
HEADNOTE: VISAS ABOLITION
TOPIC: Visas
PARTIES:
Germany, West
Luxembourg

424420   Bilateral Agreement   60 WBGA 180
SIGNED: 13 May 57

HEADNOTE: INFORMATION ON ANIMAL EPIDEM-
ICS
TOPIC: Sanitation
PARTIES:
Germany, West
Luxembourg

424426   Bilateral Agreement   61 WBGA 141
SIGNED: 31 May 61
HEADNOTE: ALIEN POLICE
TOPIC: Consul/Citizenship
PARTIES:
Germany, West
Luxembourg

424427   Bilateral Agreement   62 WBGA 23
SIGNED: 31 May 61
HEADNOTE: INFORMATION ON MENTAL PA-
TIENTS
TOPIC: Admin Cooperation
PARTIES:
Germany, West
Luxembourg

424430   Bilateral Agreement   63 WBGA 75
SIGNED: 12 Jul 62
HEADNOTE: INSURANCE MIGRANT WORKERS
TOPIC: Non-ILO Labor
PARTIES:
Germany, West
Luxembourg

424432   Bilateral Agreement   63 WBGA 231
SIGNED: 27 Jun 63
HEADNOTE: INSURANCE MIGRANT WORKERS
TOPIC: Non-ILO Labor
PARTIES:
Germany, West
Luxembourg

424433   Bilateral Agreement   65 WBGA 157
SIGNED: 6 Oct 64
HEADNOTE: RETIREMENT BENEFITS
TOPIC: Non-ILO Labor
PARTIES:
Germany, West
Luxembourg

424435   Bilateral Agreement   66 WBGA 131
SIGNED: 17 May 66
HEADNOTE: DELIVERY AT BORDER
TOPIC: Extradition
PARTIES:
Germany, West
Luxembourg

424438   Bilateral Agreement   62 WBGA 153
SIGNED: 6 Jun 62
HEADNOTE: ECONOMIC RELATIONS
TOPIC: General Economic
PARTIES:
Germany, West
Malagasy

424439   Bilateral Agreement   62 WBGA 153
SIGNED: 6 Jun 62
HEADNOTE: ECONOMIC & TECHNICAL COOPER-
ATION
TOPIC: Direct Aid
PARTIES:
Germany, West
Malagasy

424440   Bilateral Protocol   62 WBGA 153
SIGNED: 6 Jun 62
HEADNOTE: WATER TRANSPORT
TOPIC: Water Transport
PARTIES:
Germany, West
Malagasy

424442   Bilateral Agreement   66 WBGA 151
SIGNED: 10 Mar 66
HEADNOTE: CAPITAL AID

TOPIC: Loans and Credits
PARTIES:
 Germany, West
 Malagasy

424443 Bilateral Agreement **68 WBGA 175**
SIGNED: 18 Jul 68
HEADNOTE: CAPITAL AID
TOPIC: Loans and Credits
PARTIES:
 Germany, West
 Malagasy

424445 Bilateral Agreement **65 WBGA 67**
SIGNED: 25 Sep 64
HEADNOTE: CAPITAL AID
TOPIC: Loans and Credits
PARTIES:
 Germany, West
 Malawi

424446 Bilateral Agreement **66 WBGA 188**
SIGNED: 8 Aug 66
HEADNOTE: CAPITAL AID
TOPIC: Loans and Credits
PARTIES:
 Germany, West
 Malawi

424447 Bilateral Agreement **68 WBGA 129**
SIGNED: 22 Apr 68
HEADNOTE: CAPITAL AID
TOPIC: Loans and Credits
PARTIES:
 Germany, West
 Malawi

424448 Bilateral Agreement **68 WBGA 215**
SIGNED: 4 Sep 68
HEADNOTE: CAPITAL AID
TOPIC: Loans and Credits
PARTIES:
 Germany, West
 Malawi

424449 Bilateral Agreement **70 WBGA 221**
SIGNED: 7 Oct 70
HEADNOTE: CAPITAL AID
TOPIC: Loans and Credits
PARTIES:
 Germany, West
 Malawi

424451 Bilateral Agreement **64 WBGA 13**
SIGNED: 9 Dec 63
HEADNOTE: CAPITAL AID
TOPIC: Loans and Credits
PARTIES:
 Germany, West
 Malaysia

424452 Bilateral Agreement **65 WBGA 242**
SIGNED: 8 Nov 65
HEADNOTE: CAPITAL AID
TOPIC: Loans and Credits
PARTIES:
 Germany, West
 Malaysia

424454 Bilateral Agreement **69 WBGA 99**
SIGNED: 18 Mar 69
HEADNOTE: CAPITAL AID
TOPIC: Loans and Credits
PARTIES:
 Germany, West
 Malaysia

424455 Bilateral Agreement **71 WBGA 82**
SIGNED: 11 Feb 71
HEADNOTE: CAPITAL AID
TOPIC: Loans and Credits
PARTIES:
 Germany, West
 Malaysia

424456 Bilateral Agreement **62 WBGA 75**
SIGNED: 14 Feb 62
HEADNOTE: CAPITAL AID
TOPIC: Loans and Credits
PARTIES:
 Germany, West
 Mali

424457 Bilateral Agreement **66 WBGA 124**
SIGNED: 6 May 66
HEADNOTE: CAPITAL AID
TOPIC: Loans and Credits
PARTIES:
 Germany, West
 Mali

424458 Bilateral Agreement **70 WBGA 15**
SIGNED: 21 Nov 69
HEADNOTE: CAPITAL AID
TOPIC: Loans and Credits
PARTIES:
 Germany, West
 Mali

424459 Bilateral Agreement **71 WBGA 86**
SIGNED: 13 Mar 71
HEADNOTE: CAPITAL AID
TOPIC: Loans and Credits
PARTIES:
 Germany, West
 Mali

424460 Bilateral Agreement **70 WBGA 8**
SIGNED: 6 Nov 69
HEADNOTE: VISAS
TOPIC: Visas
PARTIES:
 Barbados
 Germany, West

424461 Bilateral Agreement **64 WBGA 87**
SIGNED: 29 Feb 64
HEADNOTE: TRADE FIRST PROTOCOL
TOPIC: General Trade
PARTIES:
 Germany, West
 Malta

424462 Bilateral Agreement **68 WBGA 119**
SIGNED: 9 May 68
HEADNOTE: WATER TRANSPORT
TOPIC: Water Transport
PARTIES:
 Germany, West
 Malta

424464 Bilateral Agreement **61 WBGA 150**
SIGNED: 15 Apr 61
HEADNOTE: TRADE
TOPIC: General Trade
PARTIES:
 Germany, West
 Morocco

424467 Bilateral Agreement **66 WBGA 207**
SIGNED: 13 Sep 66
HEADNOTE: CAPITAL AID
TOPIC: Loans and Credits
PARTIES:
 Germany, West
 Morocco

424468 Bilateral Agreement **67 WBGA 49**
SIGNED: 24 Nov 66
HEADNOTE: FINANCIAL COOPERATION
TOPIC: Loans and Credits
PARTIES:
 Germany, West
 Morocco

424469 Bilateral Agreement **67 WBGA 49**
SIGNED: 24 Nov 66
HEADNOTE: WATER TRANSPORT
TOPIC: Water Transport

424456

PARTIES:
 Germany, West
 Morocco

424470 Bilateral Agreement **67 WBGA 49**
SIGNED: 24 Nov 66
HEADNOTE: ECONOMIC & TECHNICAL COOPER-
ATION
TOPIC: General Economic
PARTIES:
 Germany, West
 Morocco

424471 Bilateral Agreement **68 WBGA 154**
SIGNED: 22 Jun 68
HEADNOTE: FINANCIAL COOPERATION
TOPIC: Loans and Credits
PARTIES:
 Germany, West
 Morocco

424472 Bilateral Agreement **69 WBGA 165**
SIGNED: 19 Jun 69
HEADNOTE: FINANCIAL COOPERATION
TOPIC: Loans and Credits
PARTIES:
 Germany, West
 Morocco

424473 Bilateral Agreement **70 WBGA 165**
SIGNED: 2 Jul 70
HEADNOTE: FINANCIAL COOPERATION
TOPIC: Loans and Credits
PARTIES:
 Germany, West
 Morocco

424474 Bilateral Agreement **71 WBGA 151**
SIGNED: 10 Jun 71
HEADNOTE: FINANCIAL COOPERATION
TOPIC: Loans and Credits
PARTIES:
 Germany, West
 Morocco

424475 Bilateral Agreement **56 WBGA 91**
SIGNED: 2 Oct 67
HEADNOTE: CAPITAL AID
TOPIC: Loans and Credits
PARTIES:
 Germany, West
 Mauritania

424476 Bilateral Agreement **70 WBGA 84**
SIGNED: 20 Nov 69
HEADNOTE: VISAS
TOPIC: Visas
PARTIES:
 Germany, West
 Mauritius

424479 Bilateral Treaty **60 WBGA 101**
SIGNED: 19 Nov 59
HEADNOTE: VISA ABOLITION
TOPIC: Visas
PARTIES:
 Germany, West
 Mexico

424481 Bilateral Agreement **60 WBGA 85**
SIGNED: 14 May 59
HEADNOTE: VISA ABOLITION
TOPIC: Visas
PARTIES:
 Germany, West
 Monaco

424485 Bilateral Agreement **65 WBGA 169**
SIGNED: 8 Apr 65
HEADNOTE: TECHNICAL COOPERATION
TOPIC: Tech Assistance
PARTIES:
 Germany, West
 Nicaragua

424486   Bilateral Agreement   **69 WBGA 11**
SIGNED: 9 Oct 68
HEADNOTE: CAPITAL AID
TOPIC: Loans and Credits
PARTIES:
  Germany, West
  Nicaragua

424487   Bilateral Agreement   **64 WBGA 168**
SIGNED: 16 May 61
HEADNOTE: NATO PATENTS MILITARY INVEN-
TION
TOPIC: General Military
PARTIES:
  Germany, West
  Netherlands

424488   Bilateral Agreement   **63 WBGA 75**
SIGNED: 12 Jul 62
HEADNOTE: SOCIAL SECURITY MIGRANT WORK-
ERS
TOPIC: Non-ILO Labor
PARTIES:
  Germany, West
  Netherlands

424489   Bilateral Agreement   **63 WBGA 231**
SIGNED: 27 Jun 63
HEADNOTE: SOCIAL SECURITY MIGRANT WORK-
ERS
TOPIC: Non-ILO Labor
PARTIES:
  Germany, West
  Netherlands

424490   Bilateral Agreement   **64 WBGA 237**
SIGNED: 27 May 64
HEADNOTE: INSURANCE CLAIM WAIVERS
TOPIC: Non-ILO Labor
PARTIES:
  Germany, West
  Netherlands

424491   Bilateral Agreement   **65 WBGA 157**
SIGNED: 6 Oct 64
HEADNOTE: RETIREMENT BENEFITS
TOPIC: Non-ILO Labor
PARTIES:
  Germany, West
  Netherlands

424492   Bilateral Agreement   **65 WBGA 203**
SIGNED: 14 Sep 65
HEADNOTE: STATUS NATO FORCES SUPPLIES
TOPIC: Status of Forces
PARTIES:
  Germany, West
  Netherlands

424493   Bilateral Agreement   **68 WBGA 81**
SIGNED: 14 Mar 68
HEADNOTE: STATUS NATO FORCES SUPPLIES
TOPIC: Status of Forces
PARTIES:
  Germany, West
  Netherlands

424494   Bilateral Agreement   **68 WBGA 106**
SIGNED: 15 Mar 68
HEADNOTE: PROCEDURES LAND TRANSPORT
TOPIC: Admin Cooperation
PARTIES:
  Germany, West
  Netherlands

424502   Bilateral Agreement   **61 WBGA 195**
SIGNED: 14 Jun 61
HEADNOTE: ECONOMIC RELATIONS
TOPIC: General Economic
PARTIES:
  Germany, West
  Niger

424503   Bilateral Agreement   **61 WBGA 195**
SIGNED: 14 Jun 61
HEADNOTE: ECONOMIC & TECHNICAL COOPER-
ATION
TOPIC: Direct Aid
PARTIES:
  Germany, West
  Niger

424504   Bilateral Agreement   **65 WBGA 14**
SIGNED: 30 Jun 64
HEADNOTE: CAPITAL AID
TOPIC: Loans and Credits
PARTIES:
  Germany, West
  Niger

424506   Bilateral Agreement   **68 WBGA 108**
SIGNED: 18 Mar 68
HEADNOTE: CAPITAL AID
TOPIC: Loans and Credits
PARTIES:
  Germany, West
  Niger

424507   Bilateral Agreement   **69 WBGA 193**
SIGNED: 19 Jul 69
HEADNOTE: CAPITAL AID
TOPIC: Loans and Credits
PARTIES:
  Germany, West
  Niger

424508   Bilateral Agreement   **64 WBGA 5**
SIGNED: 25 Mar 63
HEADNOTE: TRADE
TOPIC: General Trade
PARTIES:
  Germany, West
  Nigeria

424509   Bilateral Agreement   **64 WBGA 5**
SIGNED: 25 Mar 63
HEADNOTE: FINANCIAL AID
TOPIC: Loans and Credits
PARTIES:
  Germany, West
  Nigeria

424510   Bilateral Agreement   **64 WBGA 5**
SIGNED: 25 Mar 63
HEADNOTE: TECHNICAL COOPERATION
TOPIC: Tech Assistance
PARTIES:
  Germany, West
  Nigeria

424511   Bilateral Protocol   **64 WBGA 5**
SIGNED: 25 Mar 63
HEADNOTE: WATER & AIR TRANSPORT
TOPIC: General Transport
PARTIES:
  Germany, West
  Nigeria

424512   Bilateral Agreement   **69 WBGA 193**
SIGNED: 31 Jul 69
HEADNOTE: CAPITAL AID
TOPIC: Loans and Credits
PARTIES:
  Germany, West
  Nigeria

424513   Bilateral Agreement   **71 WBGA 102**
SIGNED: 12 Feb 71
HEADNOTE: CAPITAL AID
TOPIC: Loans and Credits
PARTIES:
  Germany, West
  Nigeria

424514   Bilateral Agreement   **71 WBGA 115**
SIGNED: 13 May 71
HEADNOTE: CAPITAL AID

TOPIC: Loans and Credits
PARTIES:
  Germany, West
  Nigeria

424516   Bilateral Agreement   **61 WBGA 58**
SIGNED: 15 Feb 52
HEADNOTE: PASSENGERS & GOODS
TOPIC: Land Transport
PARTIES:
  Germany, West
  Norway

424521   Bilateral Agreement   **61 WBGA 193**
SIGNED: 8 Jun 61
HEADNOTE: ECONOMIC RELATIONS
TOPIC: General Economic
PARTIES:
  Germany, West
  Upper Volta

424522   Bilateral Agreement   **61 WBGA 193**
SIGNED: 8 Jun 61
HEADNOTE: ECONOMIC & TECHNICAL COOPER-
ATION
TOPIC: Direct Aid
PARTIES:
  Germany, West
  Upper Volta

424526   Bilateral Agreement   **59 WBGA 13**
SIGNED: 23 Nov 51
HEADNOTE: EASING EMPLOYMENT PROCEDURE
TOPIC: Non-ILO Labor
PARTIES:
  Austria
  Germany, West

424527   Bilateral Agreement   **54 WBGA 99**
SIGNED: 13 May 54
HEADNOTE: TRADE
TOPIC: General Trade
PARTIES:
  Austria
  Germany, West

424528   Bilateral Agreement   **55 WBGA 148**
SIGNED: 15 Sep 54
HEADNOTE: LOCAL BORDER TRAFFIC
TOPIC: Visas
PARTIES:
  Austria
  Germany, West

424532   Bilateral Agreement   **55 WBGA 103**
SIGNED: 10 May 55
HEADNOTE: EASING LOCAL TOURISM
TOPIC: Visas
PARTIES:
  Austria
  Germany, West

424543   Bilateral Agreement   **58 WBGA 228**
SIGNED: 10 Oct 58
HEADNOTE: INFORMATION ON CITIZENSHIP
TOPIC: Admin Cooperation
PARTIES:
  Austria
  Germany, West

424544   Bilateral Agreement   **59 WBGA 51**
SIGNED: 16 Jan 59
HEADNOTE: EMPLOYMENT JOINT POWER PLANT
TOPIC: Specific Property
PARTIES:
  Austria
  Germany, West

424548   Bilateral Agreement   **61 WBGA 169**
SIGNED: 19 Jul 61
HEADNOTE: BORDER DELIVERY PERSONS
TOPIC: Extradition

PARTIES:
Austria
Germany, West

424554   Bilateral Agreement   **66 WBGA 235**
SIGNED: 27 Sep 66
HEADNOTE: FILM INDUSTRY
TOPIC: Commodity Trade
PARTIES:
Austria
Germany, West

424563   Bilateral Agreement   **68 WBGA 203**
SIGNED: 5 Mar 56
HEADNOTE: WAR GRAVES
TOPIC: Other Military
PARTIES:
Germany, West
Pakistan

424564   Bilateral Agreement   **52 WBGA 132**
SIGNED: 9 Mar 57
HEADNOTE: TRADE
TOPIC: General Trade
PARTIES:
Germany, West
Pakistan

424567   Bilateral Agreement   **60 WBGA 169**
SIGNED: 9 Feb 60
HEADNOTE: INFORMATION ON NATURALIZA-
TION
TOPIC: Admin Cooperation
PARTIES:
Germany, West
Panama

424568   Bilateral Agreement   **65 WBGA 7**
SIGNED: 30 Sep 64
HEADNOTE: TECHNICAL COOPERATION
TOPIC: Tech Assistance
PARTIES:
Germany, West
Panama

424569   Bilateral Agreement   **67 WBGA 171**
SIGNED: 31 Jul 67
HEADNOTE: VISAS
TOPIC: Visas
PARTIES:
Germany, West
Panama

424571   Bilateral Agreement   **55 WBGA 187**
SIGNED: 25 Jul 55
HEADNOTE: TRADE
TOPIC: General Trade
PARTIES:
Germany, West
Paraguay

424572   Bilateral Agreement   **55 WBGA 187**
SIGNED: 25 Jul 55
HEADNOTE: PAYMENTS
TOPIC: Finance
PARTIES:
Germany, West
Paraguay

424574   Bilateral Agreement   **70 WBGA 41**
SIGNED: 11 Nov 69
HEADNOTE: CAPITAL AID
TOPIC: Loans and Credits
PARTIES:
Germany, West
Paraguay

424575   Bilateral Agreement   **71 WBGA 114**
SIGNED: 29 Apr 71
HEADNOTE: CAPITAL AID
TOPIC: Loans and Credits
PARTIES:
Germany, West
Paraguay

424577   Bilateral Agreement   **61 WBGA 200**
SIGNED: 20 Dec 56
HEADNOTE: INFORMATION ON NATURALIZA-
TION
TOPIC: Admin Cooperation
PARTIES:
Germany, West
Peru

424580   Bilateral Agreement   **69 WBGA 126**
SIGNED: 21 Jul 65
HEADNOTE: TECHNICAL COOPERATION
TOPIC: Tech Assistance
PARTIES:
Germany, West
Peru

424581   Bilateral Protocol   **64 WBGA 89**
SIGNED: 3 Mar 64
HEADNOTE: TALKS 10 FEB-3 MAR 64
TOPIC: Admin Cooperation
PARTIES:
Germany, West
Philippines

424582   Bilateral Agreement   **68 WBGA 135**
SIGNED: 30 Apr 68
HEADNOTE: VISAS
TOPIC: Visas
PARTIES:
Germany, West
Philippines

424583   Bilateral Agreement   **71 WBGA 158**
SIGNED: 27 May 71
HEADNOTE: CAPITAL AID
TOPIC: Loans and Credits
PARTIES:
Germany, West
Philippines

424584   Bilateral Protocol   **57 WBGA 1**
SIGNED: 16 Nov 56
HEADNOTE: TRADE & PAYMENTS
TOPIC: General Economic
PARTIES:
Germany, West
Poland

424585   Bilateral Protocol   **63 WBGA 64**
SIGNED: 7 Mar 63
HEADNOTE: COMMERCE & NAVIGATION
TOPIC: General Economic
PARTIES:
Germany, West
Poland

424586   Bilateral Agreement   **69 WBGA 191**
SIGNED: 11 Sep 69
HEADNOTE: PASSENGERS & GOODS
TOPIC: Land Transport
PARTIES:
Germany, West
Poland

424587   Bilateral Agreement   **70 WBGA 211**
SIGNED: 15 Oct 70
HEADNOTE: LONG-RANGE TRADE & ECONOMIC
COOPERATION
TOPIC: General Economic
PARTIES:
Germany, West
Poland

424588   Bilateral Agreement   **50 WBGA 164**
SIGNED: 24 Aug 50
HEADNOTE: COMMERCE & NAVIGATION
TOPIC: General Economic
PARTIES:
Germany, West
Portugal

424593   Bilateral Protocol   **59 WBGA 131**
SIGNED: 30 May 59

HEADNOTE: ECONOMIC COOPERATION
TOPIC: General Economic
PARTIES:
Germany, West
Portugal

424594   Bilateral Protocol   **61 WBGA 125**
SIGNED: 13 May 61
HEADNOTE: RESULTS ERHARD VISIT
TOPIC: Admin Cooperation
PARTIES:
Germany, West
Portugal

424595   Bilateral Agreement   **64 WBGA 104**
SIGNED: 17 Mar 64
HEADNOTE: RECRUITMENT MIGRANT WORKERS
TOPIC: Non-ILO Labor
PARTIES:
Germany, West
Portugal

424600   Bilateral Agreement   **64 WBGA 243**
SIGNED: 25 Apr 64
HEADNOTE: CAPITAL AID
TOPIC: Loans and Credits
PARTIES:
Germany, West
Rwanda

424601   Bilateral Agreement   **65 WBGA 90**
SIGNED: 16 Feb 65
HEADNOTE: TECHNICAL COOPERATION
TOPIC: Tech Assistance
PARTIES:
Germany, West
Rwanda

424603   Bilateral Agreement   **71 WBGA 112**
SIGNED: 8 Apr 71
HEADNOTE: CAPITAL AID
TOPIC: Loans and Credits
PARTIES:
Germany, West
Rwanda

424604   Bilateral Agreement   **64 WBGA 57**
SIGNED: 24 Dec 63
HEADNOTE: TRADE
TOPIC: General Trade
PARTIES:
Germany, West
Romania

424605   Bilateral Agreement   **69 WBGA 72**
SIGNED: 10 Jun 69
HEADNOTE: SCIENTIFIC & TECHNICAL COOPER-
ATION
TOPIC: Tech Assistance
PARTIES:
Germany, West
Romania

424607   Bilateral Agreement   **67 WBGA 51**
SIGNED: 10 Dec 66
HEADNOTE: ECONOMIC RELATIONS
TOPIC: General Economic
PARTIES:
Germany, West
Zambia

424608   Bilateral Agreement   **67 WBGA 51**
SIGNED: 10 Dec 66
HEADNOTE: CAPITAL AID
TOPIC: Loans and Credits
PARTIES:
Germany, West
Zambia

424609   Bilateral Agreement   **67 WBGA 51**
SIGNED: 10 Dec 66
HEADNOTE: TECHNICAL COOPERATION
TOPIC: Tech Assistance

PARTIES:
Germany, West
Zambia

424611   Bilateral Agreement   68 WBGA 147
SIGNED: 11 Apr 68
HEADNOTE: DEVELOPMENT VOLUNTEERS
TOPIC: Tech Assistance
PARTIES:
Germany, West
Zambia

424613   Bilateral Agreement   51 WBGA 23
SIGNED: 26 Jan 51
HEADNOTE: TRADE
TOPIC: General Trade
PARTIES:
Germany, West
Sweden

424618   Bilateral Agreement   66 WBGA 213
SIGNED: 21 Sep 66
HEADNOTE: WAR GRAVES
TOPIC: Other Military
PARTIES:
Germany, West
Sweden

424619   Bilateral Agreement   61 WBGA 194
SIGNED: 27 Jun 61
HEADNOTE: ECONOMIC & TECHNICAL COOPER-
ATION
TOPIC: Direct Aid
PARTIES:
Germany, West
Senegal

424620   Bilateral Exchange   61 WBGA 171
SIGNED: 27 Jun 61
HEADNOTE: WATER TRANSPORT
TOPIC: Water Transport
PARTIES:
Germany, West
Senegal

424623   Bilateral Agreement   68 WBGA 78
SIGNED: 13 Feb 68
HEADNOTE: CAPITAL AID
TOPIC: Loans and Credits
PARTIES:
Germany, West
Senegal

424625   Bilateral Agreement   69 WBGA 28
SIGNED: 20 Nov 68
HEADNOTE: CAPITAL AID
TOPIC: Loans and Credits
PARTIES:
Germany, West
Senegal

424627   Bilateral Agreement   70 WBGA 214
SIGNED: 28 Sep 70
HEADNOTE: CAPITAL AID
TOPIC: Loans and Credits
PARTIES:
Germany, West
Senegal

424628   Bilateral Agreement   63 WBGA 222
SIGNED: 13 Sep 63
HEADNOTE: ECONOMIC RELATIONS
TOPIC: General Economic
PARTIES:
Germany, West
Sierra Leone

424629   Bilateral Agreement   63 WBGA 222
SIGNED: 13 Sep 63
HEADNOTE: TECHNICAL COOPERATION
TOPIC: Tech Assistance
PARTIES:
Germany, West
Sierra Leone

424630   Bilateral Agreement   63 WBGA 222
SIGNED: 13 Sep 63
HEADNOTE: CAPITAL AID
TOPIC: Loans and Credits
PARTIES:
Germany, West
Sierra Leone

424631   Bilateral Protocol   63 WBGA 222
SIGNED: 13 Sep 63
HEADNOTE: WATER TRANSPORT
TOPIC: Water Transport
PARTIES:
Germany, West
Sierra Leone

424633   Bilateral Agreement   67 WBGA 214
SIGNED: 5 Sep 67
HEADNOTE: CAPITAL AID
TOPIC: Loans and Credits
PARTIES:
Germany, West
Sierra Leone

424634   Bilateral Agreement   71 WBGA 64
SIGNED: 15 Dec 70
HEADNOTE: CAPITAL AID
TOPIC: Loans and Credits
PARTIES:
Germany, West
Sierra Leone

424635   Bilateral Agreement   62 WBGA 113
SIGNED: 19 Jan 62
HEADNOTE: TRADE
TOPIC: General Trade
PARTIES:
Germany, West
Somalia

424636   Bilateral Agreement   62 WBGA 113
SIGNED: 19 Jan 62
HEADNOTE: ECONOMIC & TECHNICAL COOPER-
ATION
TOPIC: Direct Aid
PARTIES:
Germany, West
Somalia

424637   Bilateral Protocol   62 WBGA 113
SIGNED: 19 Jan 62
HEADNOTE: WATER & AIR TRANSPORT
TOPIC: General Transport
PARTIES:
Germany, West
Somalia

424638   Bilateral Agreement   62 WBGA 113
SIGNED: 19 Jan 62
HEADNOTE: FINANCIAL AID
TOPIC: Loans and Credits
PARTIES:
Germany, West
Somalia

424639   Bilateral Agreement   68 WBGA 77
SIGNED: 30 Nov 67
HEADNOTE: CAPITAL AID
TOPIC: Loans and Credits
PARTIES:
Germany, West
Somalia

424640   Bilateral Agreement   68 WBGA 149
SIGNED: 6 Jun 68
HEADNOTE: CAPITAL AID
TOPIC: Loans and Credits
PARTIES:
Germany, West
Somalia

424641   Bilateral Agreement   69 WBGA 157
SIGNED: 28 Nov 68
HEADNOTE: CAPITAL AID

TOPIC: Loans and Credits
PARTIES:
Germany, West
Somalia

424642   Bilateral Agreement   70 WBGA 48
SIGNED: 20 Jan 70
HEADNOTE: CAPITAL AID
TOPIC: Loans and Credits
PARTIES:
Germany, West
Somalia

424644   Bilateral Agreement   61 WBGA 12
SIGNED: 31 Dec 60
HEADNOTE: LONG-RANGE TRADE & PAYMENTS
TOPIC: General Economic
PARTIES:
Germany, West
USSR (Soviet Union)

424645   Bilateral Exchange   51 WBGA 216
SIGNED: 28 Aug 51
HEADNOTE: ECONOMIC NEGOTIATIONS
TOPIC: General Economic
PARTIES:
Germany, West
South Africa

424646   Bilateral Agreement   68 WBGA 205
SIGNED: 5 Mar 56
HEADNOTE: WAR GRAVES
TOPIC: Other Military
PARTIES:
Germany, West
South Africa

424649   Bilateral Agreement   64 WBGA 6
SIGNED: 7 Feb 63
HEADNOTE: TECHNICAL COOPERATION
TOPIC: Tech Assistance
PARTIES:
Germany, West
Sudan

424650   Bilateral Agreement   64 WBGA 79
SIGNED: 22 Aug 63
HEADNOTE: ECONOMIC & TECHNICAL COOPER-
ATION
TOPIC: Direct Aid
PARTIES:
Germany, West
Syria

424651   Bilateral Agreement   62 WBGA 225
SIGNED: 6 Sep 62
HEADNOTE: ECONOMIC RELATIONS
TOPIC: General Economic
PARTIES:
Germany, West
Tanzania

424652   Bilateral Agreement   62 WBGA 225
SIGNED: 6 Sep 62
HEADNOTE: TECHNICAL COOPERATION
TOPIC: Tech Assistance
PARTIES:
Germany, West
Tanzania

424653   Bilateral Agreement   62 WBGA 225
SIGNED: 11 Sep 62
HEADNOTE: CAPITAL AID
TOPIC: Loans and Credits
PARTIES:
Germany, West
Tanzania

424654   Bilateral Protocol   62 WBGA 225
SIGNED: 11 Sep 62
HEADNOTE: WATER TRANSPORT
TOPIC: Water Transport

PARTIES:
Germany, West
Tanzania

424656 Bilateral Agreement **71 WBGA 114**
SIGNED: 6 Feb 71
HEADNOTE: CAPITAL AID
TOPIC: Loans and Credits
PARTIES:
Germany, West
Tanzania

424658 Bilateral Agreement **68 WBGA 234**
SIGNED: 8 Oct 68
HEADNOTE: CAPITAL AID
TOPIC: Loans and Credits
PARTIES:
Germany, West
Thailand

424659 Bilateral Protocol **60 WBGA 237**
SIGNED: 20 Jul 60
HEADNOTE: WATER TRANSPORT
TOPIC: Water Transport
PARTIES:
Germany, West
Togo

424660 Bilateral Agreement **60 WBGA 243**
SIGNED: 20 Jul 60
HEADNOTE: ECONOMIC & TECHNICAL COOPER-
ATION
TOPIC: Direct Aid
PARTIES:
Germany, West
Togo

424662 Bilateral Agreement **63 WBGA 199**
SIGNED: 9 Jul 63
HEADNOTE: CAPITAL AID
TOPIC: Loans and Credits
PARTIES:
Germany, West
Togo

424663 Bilateral Agreement **66 WBGA 111**
SIGNED: 25 Mar 66
HEADNOTE: CAPITAL AID PROJECT SOKODE
TOPIC: Non-IBRD Project
PARTIES:
Germany, West
Togo

424664 Bilateral Agreement **67 WBGA 136**
SIGNED: 3 Feb 67
HEADNOTE: CAPITAL AID
TOPIC: Loans and Credits
PARTIES:
Germany, West
Togo

424665 Bilateral Agreement **67 WBGA 218**
SIGNED: 31 Jul 67
HEADNOTE: CAPITAL AID
TOPIC: Loans and Credits
PARTIES:
Germany, West
Togo

424666 Bilateral Agreement **68 WBGA 219**
SIGNED: 28 Aug 68
HEADNOTE: DEVELOPMENT VOLUNTEERS
TOPIC: Tech Assistance
PARTIES:
Germany, West
Togo

424667 Bilateral Agreement **70 WBGA 196**
SIGNED: 18 Jun 70
HEADNOTE: CAPITAL AID
TOPIC: Loans and Credits
PARTIES:
Germany, West
Togo

424668 Bilateral Agreement **71 WBGA 115**
SIGNED: 20 Mar 71
HEADNOTE: CAPITAL AID
TOPIC: Loans and Credits
PARTIES:
Germany, West
Togo

424669 Bilateral Agreement **71 WBGA 114**
SIGNED: 27 May 71
HEADNOTE: CAPITAL AID
TOPIC: Loans and Credits
PARTIES:
Germany, West
Togo

424670 Bilateral Agreement **63 WBGA 224**
SIGNED: 31 May 63
HEADNOTE: ECONOMIC RELATIONS
TOPIC: General Economic
PARTIES:
Chad
Germany, West

424671 Bilateral Agreement **63 WBGA 224**
SIGNED: 31 May 63
HEADNOTE: TECHNICAL COOPERATION
TOPIC: Tech Assistance
PARTIES:
Chad
Germany, West

424672 Bilateral Agreement **65 WBGA 135**
SIGNED: 7 May 65
HEADNOTE: CAPITAL AID
TOPIC: Loans and Credits
PARTIES:
Chad
Germany, West

424674 Bilateral Agreement **68 WBGA 152**
SIGNED: 10 Apr 68
HEADNOTE: CAPITAL AID
TOPIC: Loans and Credits
PARTIES:
Chad
Germany, West

424675 Bilateral Agreement **69 WBGA 143**
SIGNED: 18 Apr 69
HEADNOTE: CAPITAL AID
TOPIC: Loans and Credits
PARTIES:
Chad
Germany, West

424676 Bilateral Agreement **68 WBGA 61**
SIGNED: 3 Aug 67
HEADNOTE: TRADE & PAYMENTS
TOPIC: General Economic
PARTIES:
Czechoslovakia
Germany, West

424677 Bilateral Agreement **71 WBGA 1**
SIGNED: 17 Dec 70
HEADNOTE: LONG-RANGE COOPERATION
TOPIC: General Economic
PARTIES:
Czechoslovakia
Germany, West

424678 Bilateral Agreement **60 WBGA 107**
SIGNED: 29 Jan 60
HEADNOTE: TRADE
TOPIC: General Trade
PARTIES:
Germany, West
Tunisia

424680 Bilateral Agreement **64 WBGA 73**
SIGNED: 20 Dec 63
HEADNOTE: CAPITAL AID
TOPIC: Loans and Credits

PARTIES:
Germany, West
Tunisia

424681 Bilateral Agreement **65 WBGA 123**
SIGNED: 20 Apr 65
HEADNOTE: TECHNICAL COOPERATION
TOPIC: Tech Assistance
PARTIES:
Germany, West
Tunisia

424682 Bilateral Agreement **65 WBGA 182**
SIGNED: 14 Jul 65
HEADNOTE: CAPITAL AID
TOPIC: Loans and Credits
PARTIES:
Germany, West
Tunisia

424683 Bilateral Agreement **66 WBGA 57**
SIGNED: 18 Oct 65
HEADNOTE: RECRUITMENT MIGRANT WORKERS
TOPIC: Non-ILO Labor
PARTIES:
Germany, West
Tunisia

424684 Bilateral Agreement **66 WBGA 90**
SIGNED: 28 Mar 66
HEADNOTE: WAR GRAVES
TOPIC: Other Military
PARTIES:
Germany, West
Tunisia

424685 Bilateral Agreement **66 WBGA 148**
SIGNED: 3 Jun 66
HEADNOTE: CAPITAL AID
TOPIC: Loans and Credits
PARTIES:
Germany, West
Tunisia

424686 Bilateral Agreement **67 WBGA 66**
SIGNED: 19 Jul 66
HEADNOTE: WATER TRANSPORT
TOPIC: Water Transport
PARTIES:
Germany, West
Tunisia

424690 Bilateral Agreement **67 WBGA 128**
SIGNED: 2 Jun 67
HEADNOTE: FINANCIAL COOPERATION
TOPIC: Loans and Credits
PARTIES:
Germany, West
Tunisia

424691 Bilateral Agreement **68 WBGA 156**
SIGNED: 28 May 68
HEADNOTE: FINANCIAL COOPERATION
TOPIC: Loans and Credits
PARTIES:
Germany, West
Tunisia

424692 Bilateral Agreement **69 WBGA 144**
SIGNED: 24 Apr 69
HEADNOTE: FINANCIAL COOPERATION
TOPIC: Loans and Credits
PARTIES:
Germany, West
Tunisia

424694 Bilateral Agreement **70 WBGA 126**
SIGNED: 23 Apr 70
HEADNOTE: FINANCIAL COOPERATION
TOPIC: Finance
PARTIES:
Germany, West
Tunisia

424695   Bilateral Agreement   **70 WBGA 196**
SIGNED: 23 Apr 70
HEADNOTE: TECHNICAL COOPERATION
TOPIC: Tech Assistance
PARTIES:
  Germany, West
  Tunisia

424696   Bilateral Agreement   **71 WBGA 116**
SIGNED: 7 May 71
HEADNOTE: FINANCIAL COOPERATION
TOPIC: Finance
PARTIES:
  Germany, West
  Tunisia

424697   Bilateral Protocol   **66 WBGA 167**
SIGNED: 17 Mar 64
HEADNOTE: WATER TRANSPORT
TOPIC: Water Transport
PARTIES:
  Germany, West
  Uganda

424698   Bilateral Agreement   **67 WBGA 89**
SIGNED: 17 Mar 64
HEADNOTE: TRADE
TOPIC: General Trade
PARTIES:
  Germany, West
  Uganda

424699   Bilateral Agreement   **66 WBGA 167**
SIGNED: 20 Mar 64
HEADNOTE: CAPITAL AID
TOPIC: Loans and Credits
PARTIES:
  Germany, West
  Uganda

424700   Bilateral Agreement   **66 WBGA 167**
SIGNED: 20 Mar 64
HEADNOTE: TECHNICAL COOPERATION
TOPIC: Tech Assistance
PARTIES:
  Germany, West
  Uganda

424702   Bilateral Agreement   **68 WBGA 224**
SIGNED: 19 Oct 67
HEADNOTE: CAPITAL AID
TOPIC: Loans and Credits
PARTIES:
  Germany, West
  Uganda

424703   Bilateral Agreement   **69 WBGA 123**
SIGNED: 15 Jan 69
HEADNOTE: CAPITAL AID
TOPIC: Loans and Credits
PARTIES:
  Germany, West
  Uganda

424704   Bilateral Exchange   **57 WBGA 164**
SIGNED: 27 Jul 57
HEADNOTE: FILM INDUSTRY
TOPIC: Commodity Trade
PARTIES:
  Germany, West
  Hungary

424705   Bilateral Agreement   **64 WBGA 14**
SIGNED: 10 Nov 63
HEADNOTE: TRADE AND PAYMENTS
TOPIC: General Economic
PARTIES:
  Germany, West
  Hungary

424706   Bilateral Agreement   **70 WBGA 218**
SIGNED: 27 Oct 70
HEADNOTE: LONG-RANGE ECONOMIC COOPER-
  ATION

TOPIC: General Economic
PARTIES:
  Germany, West
  Hungary

424708   Bilateral Agreement   **53 WBGA 94**
SIGNED: 18 Apr 53
HEADNOTE: TRADE
TOPIC: General Trade
PARTIES:
  Germany, West
  Uruguay

424712   Bilateral Agreement   **56 WBGA 110**
SIGNED: 18 Feb 56
HEADNOTE: TRADE
TOPIC: General Trade
PARTIES:
  Germany, West
  United Arab Rep

424713   Bilateral Agreement   **57 WBGA 48**
SIGNED: 22 Feb 56
HEADNOTE: WAR GRAVES
TOPIC: Other Military
PARTIES:
  Germany, West
  United Arab Rep

424716   Bilateral Agreement   **67 WBGA 22**
SIGNED: 11 Jan 67
HEADNOTE: HONGKONG COTTON PRODUCTS
TOPIC: Commodity Trade
PARTIES:
  Germany, West
  UK Great Britain

424717   Bilateral Agreement   **67 WBGA 83**
SIGNED: 31 Mar 67
HEADNOTE: HONGKONG WOOL PRODUCTS
TOPIC: Commodity Trade
PARTIES:
  Germany, West
  UK Great Britain

424718   Bilateral Agreement   **67 WBGA 135**
SIGNED: 2 Jun 67
HEADNOTE: ROAD TRANSPORT GOODS
TOPIC: Land Transport
PARTIES:
  Germany, West
  UK Great Britain

424719   Bilateral Protocol   **67 WBGA 176**
SIGNED: 20 Jul 67
HEADNOTE: TRADE
TOPIC: General Trade
PARTIES:
  Germany, West
  UK Great Britain

424720   Bilateral Agreement   **64 WBGA 113**
SIGNED: 17 Mar 64
HEADNOTE: STATUS UNIVERSITY CAMPUSES
TOPIC: Education
PARTIES:
  Germany, West
  USA (United States)

424721   Bilateral Agreement   **66 WBGA 144**
SIGNED: 25 Mar 66
HEADNOTE: WIGS CERTIFICATE OF ORIGIN
TOPIC: Commodity Trade
PARTIES:
  Germany, West
  USA (United States)

424722   Bilateral Agreement   **68 WBGA 21**
SIGNED: 23 Dec 66
HEADNOTE: STATUS UNIVERSITY CAMPUSES
TOPIC: Education
PARTIES:
  Germany, West
  USA (United States)

424723   Bilateral Agreement   **67 WBGA 150**
SIGNED: 16 Mar 67
HEADNOTE: SILK CERTIFICATE OF ORIGIN
TOPIC: Commodity Trade
PARTIES:
  Germany, West
  USA (United States)

424724   Bilateral Agreement   **67 WBGA 213**
SIGNED: 24 Oct 67
HEADNOTE: CREDIT UNIONS US FORCES
TOPIC: Status of Forces
PARTIES:
  Germany, West
  USA (United States)

424725   Bilateral Agreement   **69 WBGA 156**
SIGNED: 24 Jun 69
HEADNOTE: STATUS UNITED SERVICE ORGA-
  NIZATION
TOPIC: Specific Property
PARTIES:
  Germany, West
  USA (United States)

424730   Bilateral Agreement   **63 WBGA 210**
SIGNED: 29 Dec 62
HEADNOTE: ECONOMIC RELATIONS
TOPIC: General Economic
PARTIES:
  Central Afri Rep
  Germany, West

424731   Bilateral Agreement   **63 WBGA 210**
SIGNED: 29 Dec 62
HEADNOTE: ECONOMIC & TECHNICAL COOPER-
  ATION
TOPIC: Direct Aid
PARTIES:
  Central Afri Rep
  Germany, West

424732   Bilateral Agreement   **64 WBGA 234**
SIGNED: 2 Oct 64
HEADNOTE: CAPITAL AID
TOPIC: Loans and Credits
PARTIES:
  Central Afri Rep
  Germany, West

424734   Bilateral Agreement   **67 WBGA 73**
SIGNED: 31 Jan 67
HEADNOTE: CAPITAL AID
TOPIC: Loans and Credits
PARTIES:
  Central Afri Rep
  Germany, West

424735   Bilateral Agreement   **69 WBGA 148**
SIGNED: 22 May 69
HEADNOTE: CAPITAL AID
TOPIC: Loans and Credits
PARTIES:
  Central Afri Rep
  Germany, West

424736   Bilateral Agreement   **62 WBGA 3**
SIGNED: 30 Oct 61
HEADNOTE: TRADE
TOPIC: General Trade
PARTIES:
  Cyprus
  Germany, West

424737   Bilateral Agreement   **62 WBGA 3**
SIGNED: 30 Oct 61
HEADNOTE: ECONOMIC COOPERATION
TOPIC: General Economic
PARTIES:
  Cyprus
  Germany, West

424738   Bilateral Agreement   **62 WBGA 3**
SIGNED: 30 Oct 61

HEADNOTE: TECHNICAL ASSISTANCE
TOPIC: Tech Assistance
PARTIES:
    Cyprus
    Germany, West

424739   Bilateral Agreement   **69 WBGA 2**
SIGNED: 30 May 67
HEADNOTE: DESSERT WINES
TOPIC: Commodity Trade
PARTIES:
    Cyprus
    Germany, West

424741   Bilateral Agreement   **70 WBGA 163**
SIGNED: 24 Jun 70
HEADNOTE: CAPITAL AID
TOPIC: Loans and Credits
PARTIES:
    Cyprus
    Germany, West

424745   Bilateral Agreement   **69 WBGA 207**
SIGNED: 6 May 69
HEADNOTE: SERVICES OF EXPERTS
TOPIC: IGO Operations
PARTIES:
    Germany, West
    UNESCO (Educ/Cult)

424749   Bilateral Agreement   **70 WBGA 149**
SIGNED: 22 Jul 70
HEADNOTE: CAPITAL AID
TOPIC: Loans and Credits
PARTIES:
    Central Am Bank
    Germany, West

424750   Bilateral Agreement   **60 WBGA 156**
SIGNED: 1 Jul 60
HEADNOTE: TRADE
TOPIC: General Trade
PARTIES:
    Germany, West
    Japan

424751   Bilateral Agreement   **68 WBGA 43**
SIGNED: 27 Dec 67
HEADNOTE: NAVIGATION
TOPIC: Water Transport
PARTIES:
    Germany, West
    Japan

424755   Bilateral Agreement   **55 WBGA 19**
SIGNED: 28 Dec 54
HEADNOTE: TRANSFER AT BORDER
TOPIC: Extradition
PARTIES:
    Germany, West
    Switzerland

424756   Bilateral Agreement   **55 WBGA 48**
SIGNED: 2 Feb 55
HEADNOTE: EXCHANGE INTERNS
TOPIC: Non-ILO Labor
PARTIES:
    Germany, West
    Switzerland

424757   Bilateral Agreement   **57 WBGA 107**
SIGNED: 21 Jul 56
HEADNOTE: BORDER TRAFFIC
TOPIC: Visas
PARTIES:
    Germany, West
    Switzerland

424763   Bilateral Agreement   **67 WBGA 165**
SIGNED: 25 May 66
HEADNOTE: FINANCING RHINE WORKS
TOPIC: Territory Boundary

PARTIES:
    Germany, West
    Switzerland

424765   Bilateral Agreement   **69 WBGA 142**
SIGNED: 26 Mar 69
HEADNOTE: CRIMINAL RECORD DELETION
TOPIC: Admin Cooperation
PARTIES:
    Germany, West
    Switzerland

424769   Bilateral Agreement   **52 WBGA 50**
SIGNED: 16 Feb 52
HEADNOTE: PAYMENTS
TOPIC: Finance
PARTIES:
    Germany, West
    Turkey

424770   Bilateral Agreement   **58 WBGA 336**
SIGNED: 8 May 57
HEADNOTE: CULTURE
TOPIC: Culture
PARTIES:
    Germany, West
    Turkey

424773   Bilateral Agreement   **68 WBGA 22**
SIGNED: 30 Sep 64
HEADNOTE: SUPPLEMENT AGREEMENT 30 OCT 61
TOPIC: Non-ILO Labor
PARTIES:
    Germany, West
    Turkey

424775   Bilateral Agreement   **62 WBGA 217**
SIGNED: 11 Sep 62
HEADNOTE: VISA FEE ABOLITION
TOPIC: Visas
PARTIES:
    Germany, West
    Turkey

424778   Bilateral Agreement   **69 WBGA 133**
SIGNED: 3 Jun 69
HEADNOTE: CAPITAL AID
TOPIC: Loans and Credits
PARTIES:
    Germany, West
    Turkey

424779   Bilateral Agreement   **70 WBGA 135**
SIGNED: 16 Jun 70
HEADNOTE: FINANCIAL AID
TOPIC: Loans and Credits
PARTIES:
    Germany, West
    Turkey

424780   Bilateral Agreement   **71 WBGA 242**
SIGNED: 3 Dec 71
HEADNOTE: FINANCIAL AID
TOPIC: Loans and Credits
PARTIES:
    Germany, West
    Turkey

424781   Bilateral Protocol   **64 WBGA 89**
SIGNED: 3 Mar 64
HEADNOTE: TALKS 10 FEB TO 3 MAR 64
TOPIC: General Amity
PARTIES:
    Germany, West
    Philippines

424782   Bilateral Agreement   **68 WBGA 135**
SIGNED: 30 Apr 68
HEADNOTE: VISAS
TOPIC: Visas
PARTIES:
    Germany, West
    Philippines

424783   Bilateral Agreement   **71 WBGA 158**
SIGNED: 27 May 71
HEADNOTE: CAPITAL AID
TOPIC: Loans and Credits
PARTIES:
    Germany, West
    Philippines

425002   Bilateral Agreement   **58 WGBB 83**
SIGNED: 31 Jan 58
HEADNOTE: ECONOMIC & TECHNICAL COOPER-ATION
TOPIC: Direct Aid
PARTIES:
    Afghanistan
    Germany, West

425003   Bilateral Agreement   **63 WGBB 1069**
SIGNED: 18 Apr 61
HEADNOTE: CULTURE
TOPIC: Culture
PARTIES:
    Afghanistan
    Germany, West

425008   Bilateral Agreement   **61 WGBB 1045**
SIGNED: 20 Sep 60
HEADNOTE: AIR TRANSPORT
TOPIC: Air Transport
PARTIES:
    Argentina
    Germany, West

425010   Bilateral Agreement   **70 WGBB 5**
SIGNED: 31 Mar 69
HEADNOTE: SCIENTIFIC & TECHNICAL COOPER-ATION
TOPIC: Scientific Project
PARTIES:
    Argentina
    Germany, West

425013   Bilateral Treaty   **71 WGBB 2655**
SIGNED: 21 May 71
HEADNOTE: ATOMIC SHIPS ARGENTINE WATERS
TOPIC: Water Transport
PARTIES:
    Argentina
    Germany, West

425014   Bilateral Agreement   **59 WGBB 1065**
SIGNED: 16 Apr 58
HEADNOTE: AIR TRANSPORT
TOPIC: Air Transport
PARTIES:
    Ethiopia
    Germany, West

425015   Bilateral Treaty   **65 WGBB 1521**
SIGNED: 21 Apr 64
HEADNOTE: COMPENSATION GERMAN PROP-ERTY
TOPIC: Claims and Debts
PARTIES:
    Ethiopia
    Germany, West

425019   Bilateral Agreement   **52 WGBB 437**
SIGNED: 1 Feb 52
HEADNOTE: PASSENGERS & COMMODITIES
TOPIC: Land Transport
PARTIES:
    Belgium
    Germany, West

425020   Bilateral Treaty   **53 WGBB 534**
SIGNED: 20 Mar 53
HEADNOTE: CUSTOMS
TOPIC: Customs
PARTIES:
    Belgium
    Germany, West

425022   Bilateral Agreement   **58 WGBB 190**
SIGNED: 15 May 56
HEADNOTE: ROAD & RAIL CHECKPOINTS
TOPIC: Visas
PARTIES:
  Belgium
  Germany, West

425023   Bilateral Exchange   **59 WGBB 409**
SIGNED: 9 Jul 57
HEADNOTE: MUTUAL AID ARTICLE 3 NATO
TOPIC: General Military
PARTIES:
  Belgium
  Germany, West

425024   Bilateral Agreement   **63 WGBB 404**
SIGNED: 7 Dec 57
HEADNOTE: SOCIAL SECURITY
TOPIC: Non-ILO Labor
PARTIES:
  Belgium
  Germany, West

425025   Bilateral Agreement   **64 WGBB 170**
SIGNED: 7 Dec 57
HEADNOTE: UNEMPLOYMENT
TOPIC: Non-ILO Labor
PARTIES:
  Belgium
  Germany, West

425026   Bilateral Agreement   **59 WGBB 1524**
SIGNED: 25 Apr 59
HEADNOTE: JUDICIAL COOPERATION
TOPIC: Admin Cooperation
PARTIES:
  Belgium
  Germany, West

425027   Bilateral Agreement   **61 WGBB 1183**
SIGNED: 3 Aug 59
HEADNOTE: JUDICIAL COOPERATION
TOPIC: Admin Cooperation
PARTIES:
  Belgium
  Germany, West

425029   Bilateral Treaty   **61 WGBB 2640**
SIGNED: 28 Sep 60
HEADNOTE: PAYMENTS TO NAZI VICTIMS
TOPIC: Specif Claim/Waive
PARTIES:
  Belgium
  Germany, West

425035   Bilateral Agreement   **66 WGBB 1508**
SIGNED: 17 Dec 64
HEADNOTE: TAX ON CARS IN TRANSIT
TOPIC: Taxation
PARTIES:
  Belgium
  Germany, West

425036   Bilateral Agreement   **67 WGBB 813**
SIGNED: 20 Jul 65
HEADNOTE: SOCIAL SECURITY
TOPIC: Non-ILO Labor
PARTIES:
  Belgium
  Germany, West

425037   Bilateral Agreement   **69 WGBB 17**
SIGNED: 11 Apr 67
HEADNOTE: DOUBLE TAXATION
TOPIC: Taxation
PARTIES:
  Belgium
  Germany, West

425038   Bilateral Agreement   **67 WGBB 2545**
SIGNED: 14 Apr 67
HEADNOTE: OFFICIAL DOCUMENTS
TOPIC: Admin Cooperation

PARTIES:
  Belgium
  Germany, West

425039   Bilateral Agreement   **71 WGBB 857**
SIGNED: 29 Jan 69
HEADNOTE: SOCIAL SECURITY
TOPIC: Non-ILO Labor
PARTIES:
  Belgium
  Germany, West

425040   Bilateral Agreement   **69 WGBB 1147**
SIGNED: 7 Mar 69
HEADNOTE: DRIVERS LICENCES
TOPIC: Admin Cooperation
PARTIES:
  Belgium
  Germany, West

425041   Bilateral Agreement   **70 WGBB 1205**
SIGNED: 24 Dec 69
HEADNOTE: POLLUTION BORDER RIVER
TOPIC: Specific Resources
PARTIES:
  Belgium
  Germany, West

425047   Bilateral Agreement   **70 WGBB 977**
SIGNED: 4 Aug 66
HEADNOTE: CULTURE
TOPIC: Culture
PARTIES:
  Bolivia
  Germany, West

425048   Bilateral Agreement   **70 WGBB 1197**
SIGNED: 15 Nov 68
HEADNOTE: AIR TRANSPORT
TOPIC: Air Transport
PARTIES:
  Bolivia
  Germany, West

425050   Bilateral Protocol   **51 WGBB 11**
SIGNED: 17 Aug 50
HEADNOTE: TRADE
TOPIC: General Trade
PARTIES:
  Brazil
  Germany, West

425051   Bilateral Agreement   **54 WGBB 533**
SIGNED: 4 Sep 53
HEADNOTE: PATENTS & COPYRIGHTS
TOPIC: Patents/Copyrights
PARTIES:
  Brazil
  Germany, West

425055   Bilateral Agreement   **59 WGBB 73**
SIGNED: 29 Aug 57
HEADNOTE: AIR TRANSPORT
TOPIC: Air Transport
PARTIES:
  Brazil
  Germany, West

425057   Bilateral Treaty   **65 WGBB 1565**
SIGNED: 30 Nov 63
HEADNOTE: PRIVILEGES & IMMUNITIES
TOPIC: Consul/Citizenship
PARTIES:
  Brazil
  Germany, West

425061   Bilateral Agreement   **71 WGBB 117**
SIGNED: 9 Jun 69
HEADNOTE: CULTURE
TOPIC: Culture
PARTIES:
  Brazil
  Germany, West

425065   Bilateral Agreement   **64 WGBB 781**
SIGNED: 7 Jul 64
HEADNOTE: TRADE
TOPIC: General Trade
PARTIES:
  Bulgaria
  Germany, West

425070   Bilateral Protocol   **55 WGBB 189**
SIGNED: 22 Nov 52
HEADNOTE: GENERAL TRADE
TOPIC: General Trade
PARTIES:
  Ceylon (Sri Lanka)
  Germany, West

425071   Bilateral Agreement   **64 WGBB 789**
SIGNED: 4 Jul 62
HEADNOTE: DOUBLE TAXATION
TOPIC: Taxation
PARTIES:
  Ceylon (Sri Lanka)
  Germany, West

425072   Bilateral Treaty   **66 WGBB 909**
SIGNED: 8 Nov 63
HEADNOTE: FINANCIAL AID
TOPIC: Loans and Credits
PARTIES:
  Ceylon (Sri Lanka)
  Germany, West

425078   Bilateral Treaty   **52 WGBB 325**
SIGNED: 2 Feb 51
HEADNOTE: TRADE
TOPIC: General Trade
PARTIES:
  Chile
  Germany, West

425079   Bilateral Agreement   **53 WGBB 292**
SIGNED: 6 Sep 52
HEADNOTE: DUTY-FREE SALTPETER
TOPIC: Customs
PARTIES:
  Chile
  Germany, West

425080   Bilateral Agreement   **54 WGBB 631**
SIGNED: 3 Nov 53
HEADNOTE: DUTY-FREE SALTPETER
TOPIC: Customs
PARTIES:
  Chile
  Germany, West

425081   Bilateral Agreement   **58 WGBB 108**
SIGNED: 29 Jun 56
HEADNOTE: DUTY-FREE SALTPETER
TOPIC: Customs
PARTIES:
  Chile
  Germany, West

425083   Bilateral Agreement   **59 WGBB 549**
SIGNED: 20 Nov 56
HEADNOTE: CULTURE
TOPIC: Culture
PARTIES:
  Chile
  Germany, West

425086   Bilateral Agreement   **65 WGBB 79**
SIGNED: 30 Mar 64
HEADNOTE: AIR TRAFFIC
TOPIC: Air Transport
PARTIES:
  Chile
  Germany, West

425089   Bilateral Agreement   **71 WGBB 106**
SIGNED: 28 Aug 70
HEADNOTE: RESEARCH AND TECHNOLOGY
TOPIC: Scientific Project

PARTIES:
  Chile
  Germany, West

425098   Bilateral Exchange   59 WGBB 409
SIGNED: 7 Jun 57
HEADNOTE: MUTUAL AID ARTICLE 3 NATO
TOPIC: General Military
PARTIES:
  Denmark
  Germany, West

425099   Bilateral Agreement   59 WGBB 1072
SIGNED: 29 May 58
HEADNOTE: FISHERY FLENSBURG SOUND
TOPIC: Specific Resources
PARTIES:
  Denmark
  Germany, West

425101   Bilateral Agreement   60 WGBB 2109
SIGNED: 1 Aug 59
HEADNOTE: UNEMPLOYMENT COMPENSATION
TOPIC: Non-ILO Labor
PARTIES:
  Denmark
  Germany, West

425102   Bilateral Treaty   60 WGBB 1333
SIGNED: 24 Aug 59
HEADNOTE: CLAIMS OF NAZI VICTIMS
TOPIC: Specif Claim/Waive
PARTIES:
  Denmark
  Germany, West

425103   Bilateral Agreement   63 WGBB 1311
SIGNED: 30 Jan 62
HEADNOTE: DOUBLE TAXATION
TOPIC: Taxation
PARTIES:
  Denmark
  Germany, West

425104   Bilateral Treaty   69 WGBB 937
SIGNED: 30 Mar 67
HEADNOTE: CUSTOMS DUTIES
TOPIC: Customs
PARTIES:
  Denmark
  Germany, West

425105   Bilateral Agreement   71 WGBB 1092
SIGNED: 11 Jun 71
HEADNOTE: DANISH TROOPS IN GERMANY
TOPIC: Status of Forces
PARTIES:
  Denmark
  Germany, West

425106   Bilateral Treaty   59 WGBB 1468
SIGNED: 23 Dec 57
HEADNOTE: GENERAL RELATIONS
TOPIC: General Amity
PARTIES:
  Dominican Republic
  Germany, West

425107   Bilateral Treaty   54 WGBB 712
SIGNED: 1 Aug 53
HEADNOTE: TRADE
TOPIC: General Trade
PARTIES:
  Ecuador
  Germany, West

425114   Bilateral Treaty   66 WGBB 825
SIGNED: 28 Jun 65
HEADNOTE: INVESTMENT GUARANTEE
TOPIC: Claims and Debts
PARTIES:
  Ecuador
  Germany, West

425117   Bilateral Agreement   70 WGBB 1025
SIGNED: 13 Mar 69
HEADNOTE: CULTURE
TOPIC: Culture
PARTIES:
  Ecuador
  Germany, West

425125   Bilateral Agreement   68 WGBB 167
SIGNED: 11 Jun 68
HEADNOTE: CAPITAL AID
TOPIC: Loans and Credits
PARTIES:
  Germany, West
  Ivory Coast

425128   Bilateral Agreement   54 WGBB 49
SIGNED: 31 Oct 52
HEADNOTE: MOST FAVORED NATION
TOPIC: Mostfavored Nation
PARTIES:
  El Salvador
  Germany, West

425134   Bilateral Agreement   51 WGBB 177
SIGNED: 10 Jul 50
HEADNOTE: SOCIAL SECURITY
TOPIC: Non-ILO Labor
PARTIES:
  France
  Germany, West

425135   Bilateral Agreement   51 WGBB 87
SIGNED: 10 Jul 50
HEADNOTE: BORDER TRAFFIC
TOPIC: Visas
PARTIES:
  France
  Germany, West

425136   Bilateral Agreement   51 WGBB 98
SIGNED: 10 Jul 50
HEADNOTE: MIGRANT LABOR
TOPIC: Non-ILO Labor
PARTIES:
  France
  Germany, West

425137   Bilateral Agreement   51 WGBB 69
SIGNED: 10 Jul 50
HEADNOTE: MIGRANT LABOR
TOPIC: Non-ILO Labor
PARTIES:
  France
  Germany, West

425138   Bilateral Treaty   53 WGBB 151
SIGNED: 19 Nov 51
HEADNOTE: EXTRADITION
TOPIC: Extradition
PARTIES:
  France
  Germany, West

425139   Bilateral Agreement   53 WGBB 508
SIGNED: 27 Feb 53
HEADNOTE: REPAY FRENCH POST-1945 AID
TOPIC: Specif Claim/Waive
PARTIES:
  France
  Germany, West

425140   Bilateral Agreement   55 WGBB 295
SIGNED: 23 Oct 54
HEADNOTE: SAAR STATUTE
TOPIC: Territory Boundary
PARTIES:
  France
  Germany, West

425142   Bilateral Agreement   55 WGBB 885
SIGNED: 23 Oct 54
HEADNOTE: CULTURE
TOPIC: Culture

PARTIES:
  France
  Germany, West

425147   Bilateral Treaty   56 WGBB 1587
SIGNED: 27 Oct 56
HEADNOTE: SAAR STATUTE
TOPIC: Territory Boundary
PARTIES:
  France
  Germany, West

425148   Bilateral Treaty   56 WGBB 1863
SIGNED: 27 Oct 56
HEADNOTE: BROADENING OF UPPER RHINE
TOPIC: Specific Resources
PARTIES:
  France
  Germany, West

425149   Bilateral Treaty   57 WGBB 1661
SIGNED: 27 Oct 56
HEADNOTE: ESTABLISHMENT & NAVIGATION
TOPIC: General Amity
PARTIES:
  France
  Germany, West

425152   Bilateral Exchange   59 WGBB 409
SIGNED: 7 Jun 57
HEADNOTE: MUTUAL AID ARTICLE 3 NATO
TOPIC: General Military
PARTIES:
  France
  Germany, West

425153   Bilateral Agreement   59 WGBB 189
SIGNED: 31 Mar 58
HEADNOTE: RESEARCH INSTITUTE ST. LOUIS
TOPIC: Specific Property
PARTIES:
  France
  Germany, West

425154   Bilateral Agreement   60 WGBB 1533
SIGNED: 18 Apr 58
HEADNOTE: BORDER RAIL CHECKPOINTS
TOPIC: Visas
PARTIES:
  France
  Germany, West

425155   Bilateral Exchange   59 WGBB 389
SIGNED: 30 Jun 59
HEADNOTE: LOCAL BORDER TRAFFIC
TOPIC: Visas
PARTIES:
  France
  Germany, West

425156   Bilateral Agreement   61 WGBB 397
SIGNED: 21 Jul 59
HEADNOTE: DOUBLE TAXATION
TOPIC: Taxation
PARTIES:
  France
  Germany, West

425157   Bilateral Agreement   61 WGBB 1183
SIGNED: 3 Aug 59
HEADNOTE: OFF-SHORE PURCHASES
TOPIC: Dispute Settlement
PARTIES:
  France
  Germany, West

425160   Bilateral Agreement   61 WGBB 22
SIGNED: 8 Mar 60
HEADNOTE: CERTIFICATES OF ORIGIN
TOPIC: Patents/Copyrights
PARTIES:
  France
  Germany, West

425181 Bilateral Agreement **60 WGBB 2325**
SIGNED: 22 Apr 60
HEADNOTE: JUDICIAL COOPERATION
TOPIC: Admin Cooperation
PARTIES:
 France
 Germany, West

425182 Bilateral Treaty **61 WGBB 1029**
SIGNED: 15 Jul 60
HEADNOTE: CLAIMS OF NAZI VICTIMS
TOPIC: Specif Claim/Waive
PARTIES:
 France
 Germany, West

425183 Bilateral Agreement **61 WGBB 1040**
SIGNED: 6 May 61
HEADNOTE: JUDICIAL COOPERATION
TOPIC: Admin Cooperation
PARTIES:
 France
 Germany, West

425186 Bilateral Agreement **62 WGBB 705**
SIGNED: 27 Nov 61
HEADNOTE: INFORMATION ON CRIMINAL
 RECORDS
TOPIC: Admin Cooperation
PARTIES:
 France
 Germany, West

425187 Bilateral Protocol **62 WGBB 1106**
SIGNED: 20 Dec 61
HEADNOTE: SAAR POLLUTION COMMISSION
TOPIC: IGO Establishment
PARTIES:
 France
 Germany, West

425189 Bilateral Treaty **63 WGBB 405**
SIGNED: 22 Jan 63
HEADNOTE: GENERAL RELATIONS
TOPIC: General Amity
PARTIES:
 France
 Germany, West

425191 Bilateral Agreement **63 WGBB 1612**
SIGNED: 5 Jul 63
HEADNOTE: YOUTH ORGANIZATIONS
TOPIC: Health/Educ/Welfare
PARTIES:
 France
 Germany, West

425192 Bilateral Agreement **65 WGBB 1287**
SIGNED: 20 Dec 63
HEADNOTE: SOCIAL SECURITY SAARLAND
TOPIC: Non-ILO Labor
PARTIES:
 France
 Germany, West

425193 Bilateral Agreement **64 WGBB 702**
SIGNED: 20 Dec 63
HEADNOTE: FAMILY ASSISTANCE
TOPIC: Non-ILO Labor
PARTIES:
 France
 Germany, West

425194 Bilateral Agreement **70 WGBB 1**
SIGNED: 15 Jan 64
HEADNOTE: OFFICIAL DOCUMENTS
TOPIC: Admin Cooperation
PARTIES:
 France
 Germany, West

425200 Bilateral Agreement **67 WGBB 2430**
SIGNED: 19 Jan 67
HEADNOTE: ATOMIC REACTOR

TOPIC: Atomic Energy
PARTIES:
 France
 Germany, West

425201 Bilateral Agreement **69 WGBB 84**
SIGNED: 6 Jun 67
HEADNOTE: COMMUNICATION SATELLITE
TOPIC: Telecommunications
PARTIES:
 France
 Germany, West

425202 Bilateral Treaty **70 WGBB 726**
SIGNED: 4 Jul 69
HEADNOTE: BROADENING RHINE
TOPIC: Specific Resources
PARTIES:
 France
 Germany, West

425203 Bilateral Agreement **70 WGBB 1317**
SIGNED: 3 Nov 69
HEADNOTE: TAX ON CARS IN TRANSIT
TOPIC: Taxation
PARTIES:
 France
 Germany, West

425204 Bilateral Agreement **71 WGBB 2434**
SIGNED: 2 Feb 71
HEADNOTE: JURISDICTION CERTAIN CRIMES
TOPIC: Admin Cooperation
PARTIES:
 France
 Germany, West

425211 Bilateral Treaty **70 WGBB 657**
SIGNED: 16 May 69
HEADNOTE: INVESTMENT GUARANTEE
TOPIC: Claims and Debts
PARTIES:
 Gabon
 Germany, West

425220 Bilateral Agreement **67 WGBB 1743**
SIGNED: 10 Jun 66
HEADNOTE: FUGITIVES FROM JUSTICE
TOPIC: Extradition
PARTIES:
 Germany, West
 Ghana

425221 Bilateral Treaty **68 WGBB 1251**
SIGNED: 19 May 67
HEADNOTE: CAPITAL AID
TOPIC: Loans and Credits
PARTIES:
 Germany, West
 Ghana

425225 Bilateral Agreement **69 WGBB 1553**
SIGNED: 6 Aug 68
HEADNOTE: AIR TRANSPORT
TOPIC: Air Transport
PARTIES:
 Germany, West
 Ghana

425230 Bilateral Agreement **57 WGBB 501**
SIGNED: 17 May 56
HEADNOTE: CULTURE
TOPIC: Culture
PARTIES:
 Germany, West
 Greece

425233 Bilateral Treaty **61 WGBB 1596**
SIGNED: 18 Mar 60
HEADNOTE: CLAIMS OF NAZI VICTIMS
TOPIC: Specif Claim/Waive
PARTIES:
 Germany, West
 Greece

425234 Bilateral Treaty **62 WGBB 1505**
SIGNED: 18 Mar 60
HEADNOTE: ESTABLISHMENT & NAVIGATION
TOPIC: General Economic
PARTIES:
 Germany, West
 Greece

425236 Bilateral Treaty **63 WGBB 216**
SIGNED: 27 Mar 61
HEADNOTE: INVESTMENT GUARANTEE
TOPIC: Claims and Debts
PARTIES:
 Germany, West
 Greece

425237 Bilateral Agreement **63 WGBB 678**
SIGNED: 25 Apr 61
HEADNOTE: SOCIAL SECURITY
TOPIC: Non-ILO Labor
PARTIES:
 Germany, West
 Greece

425238 Bilateral Agreement **62 WGBB 1109**
SIGNED: 31 May 61
HEADNOTE: UNEMPLOYMENT COMPENSATION
TOPIC: Non-ILO Labor
PARTIES:
 Germany, West
 Greece

425239 Bilateral Treaty **63 WGBB 109**
SIGNED: 4 Nov 61
HEADNOTE: JUDICIAL COOPERATION
TOPIC: Admin Cooperation
PARTIES:
 Germany, West
 Greece

425240 Bilateral Agreement **67 WGBB 852**
SIGNED: 18 Apr 66
HEADNOTE: DOUBLE TAXATION
TOPIC: Taxation
PARTIES:
 Germany, West
 Greece

425244 Bilateral Treaty **64 WGBB 145**
SIGNED: 19 Apr 62
HEADNOTE: INVESTMENT PROMOTION
TOPIC: Claims and Debts
PARTIES:
 Germany, West
 Guinea

425255 Bilateral Agreement **60 WGBB 1828**
SIGNED: 18 Mar 59
HEADNOTE: DOUBLE TAXATION
TOPIC: Taxation
PARTIES:
 Germany, West
 India

425256 Bilateral Agreement **64 WGBB 677**
SIGNED: 31 May 63
HEADNOTE: AIR TRANSPORT
TOPIC: Air Transport
PARTIES:
 Germany, West
 India

425259 Bilateral Agreement **69 WGBB 1012**
SIGNED: 24 Jul 68
HEADNOTE: DUTY-FREE GIFTS
TOPIC: Customs
PARTIES:
 Germany, West
 India

425260 Bilateral Agreement **69 WGBB 1713**
SIGNED: 20 Mar 69
HEADNOTE: CULTURE
TOPIC: Culture

PARTIES:
Germany, West
India

425264   Bilateral Treaty   **70 WGBB 492**
SIGNED: 8 Nov 68
HEADNOTE: CAPITAL AID
TOPIC: Loans and Credits
PARTIES:
Germany, West
Indonesia

425267   Bilateral Agreement   **71 WGBB 192**
SIGNED: 4 Dec 69
HEADNOTE: AIR TRANSPORT
TOPIC: Air Transport
PARTIES:
Germany, West
Indonesia

425269   Bilateral Agreement   **53 WGBB 543**
SIGNED: 7 Oct 51
HEADNOTE: TRADE
TOPIC: General Trade
PARTIES:
Germany, West
Iraq

425271   Bilateral Treaty   **56 WGBB 2091**
SIGNED: 4 Nov 54
HEADNOTE: ECONOMIC & TECHNICAL COOPER-
ATION
TOPIC: Direct Aid
PARTIES:
Germany, West
Iran

425272   Bilateral Agreement   **61 WGBB 105**
SIGNED: 22 Dec 59
HEADNOTE: END FORMER PAYMENTS SYSTEM
TOPIC: Admin Cooperation
PARTIES:
Germany, West
Iran

425273   Bilateral Agreement   **63 WGBB 1086**
SIGNED: 1 Jul 61
HEADNOTE: AIR TRANSPORT
TOPIC: Air Transport
PARTIES:
Germany, West
Iran

425274   Bilateral Treaty   **67 WGBB 2549**
SIGNED: 11 Nov 65
HEADNOTE: CAPITAL AID
TOPIC: Loans and Credits
PARTIES:
Germany, West
Iran

425277   Bilateral Agreement   **69 WGBB 2133**
SIGNED: 20 Dec 68
HEADNOTE: DOUBLE TAXATION
TOPIC: Taxation
PARTIES:
Germany, West
Iran

425278   Bilateral Protocol   **56 WGBB 899**
SIGNED: 19 Dec 50
HEADNOTE: PATENTS & TRADEMARKS
TOPIC: Patents/Copyrights
PARTIES:
Germany, West
Iceland

425279   Bilateral Treaty   **51 WGBB 153**
SIGNED: 19 Dec 50
HEADNOTE: PRELIMINARY COMMERCE NAVIGA-
TION
TOPIC: General Amity

PARTIES:
Germany, West
Iceland

425283   Bilateral Agreement   **67 WGBB 719**
SIGNED: 19 Sep 66
HEADNOTE: COOPERATION CUSTOMS FRAUDS
TOPIC: Admin Cooperation
PARTIES:
Germany, West
Israel

425286   Bilateral Agreement   **52 WGBB 975**
SIGNED: 30 Apr 52
HEADNOTE: TRADEMARKS
TOPIC: Patents/Copyrights
PARTIES:
Germany, West
Italy

425287   Bilateral Agreement   **54 WGBB 485**
SIGNED: 5 May 53
HEADNOTE: UNEMPLOYMENT INSURANCE
TOPIC: Non-ILO Labor
PARTIES:
Germany, West
Italy

425289   Bilateral Agreement   **56 WGBB 1883**
SIGNED: 12 Nov 53
HEADNOTE: PATENTS
TOPIC: Patents/Copyrights
PARTIES:
Germany, West
Italy

425290   Bilateral Agreement   **55 WGBB 108**
SIGNED: 20 Apr 54
HEADNOTE: LICENSING OF PHYSICIANS
TOPIC: Admin Cooperation
PARTIES:
Germany, West
Italy

425292   Bilateral Agreement   **57 WGBB 1277**
SIGNED: 22 Dec 55
HEADNOTE: WAR GRAVES
TOPIC: Other Military
PARTIES:
Germany, West
Italy

425293   Bilateral Agreement   **58 WGBB 77**
SIGNED: 8 Feb 56
HEADNOTE: CULTURE
TOPIC: Culture
PARTIES:
Germany, West
Italy

425295   Bilateral Treaty   **59 WGBB 949**
SIGNED: 21 Nov 57
HEADNOTE: GENERAL RELATIONS
TOPIC: General Amity
PARTIES:
Germany, West
Italy

425296   Bilateral Agreement   **60 WGBB 1961**
SIGNED: 17 Apr 59
HEADNOTE: STATUS NATO FORCES
TOPIC: Status of Forces
PARTIES:
Germany, West
Italy

425297   Bilateral Treaty   **63 WGBB 791**
SIGNED: 2 Jun 61
HEADNOTE: CLAIMS OF NAZI VICTIMS
TOPIC: Specif Claim/Waive
PARTIES:
Germany, West
Italy

425298   Bilateral Agreement   **63 WGBB 668**
SIGNED: 2 Jun 61
HEADNOTE: CERTAIN ASSETS AND PAYMENTS
TOPIC: Claims and Debts
PARTIES:
Germany, West
Italy

425299   Bilateral Exchange   **65 WGBB 843**
SIGNED: 12 Jul 61
HEADNOTE: PRIVILEGES CULTURAL INSTITUTES
TOPIC: Privil/Immunities
PARTIES:
Germany, West
Italy

425302   Bilateral Agreement   **65 WGBB 156**
SIGNED: 23 Jul 63
HEADNOTE: PATENTS & TRADEMARKS
TOPIC: Patents/Copyrights
PARTIES:
Germany, West
Italy

425305   Bilateral Exchange   **67 WGBB 1997**
SIGNED: 19 Oct 67
HEADNOTE: WARTIME PROPERTY CLAIMS
TOPIC: Specif Claim/Waive
PARTIES:
Germany, West
Italy

425307   Bilateral Exchange   **70 WGBB 723**
SIGNED: 17 Sep 68
HEADNOTE: DOUBLE TAXATION
TOPIC: Taxation
PARTIES:
Germany, West
Italy

425308   Bilateral Agreement   **70 WGBB 797**
SIGNED: 5 Nov 68
HEADNOTE: HEALTH INSURANCE
TOPIC: Non-ILO Labor
PARTIES:
Germany, West
Italy

425310   Bilateral Treaty   **54 WGBB 573**
SIGNED: 21 Apr 53
HEADNOTE: FRIENDSHIP & TRADE
TOPIC: General Amity
PARTIES:
Germany, West
Yemen

425318   Bilateral Agreement   **71 WGBB 1080**
SIGNED: 29 Jan 70
HEADNOTE: AIR TRANSPORT
TOPIC: Air Transport
PARTIES:
Germany, West
Jordan

425321   Bilateral Agreement   **59 WGBB 735**
SIGNED: 26 Jun 54
HEADNOTE: WATER TRANSPORT
TOPIC: Water Transport
PARTIES:
Germany, West
Yugoslavia

425322   Bilateral Agreement   **55 WGBB 89**
SIGNED: 21 Jul 54
HEADNOTE: PATENTS & TRADEMARKS
TOPIC: Patents/Copyrights
PARTIES:
Germany, West
Yugoslavia

425324   Bilateral Treaty   **58 WGBB 168**
SIGNED: 10 Mar 56
HEADNOTE: SOCIAL SECURITY CLAIMS
TOPIC: Non-ILO Labor

PARTIES:
Germany, West
Yugoslavia

425325   Bilateral Treaty   **56 WGBB 967**
SIGNED: 10 Mar 56
HEADNOTE: ECONOMIC COOPERATION
TOPIC: General Economic
PARTIES:
Germany, West
Yugoslavia

425329   Bilateral Agreement   **59 WGBB 735**
SIGNED: 17 Jul 56
HEADNOTE: CUSTOMS DANUBE NAVIGATION
TOPIC: Customs
PARTIES:
Germany, West
Yugoslavia

425333   Bilateral Agreement   **56 WGBB 9437**
SIGNED: 12 Oct 36
HEADNOTE: SOCIAL SECURITY
TOPIC: Non-ILO Labor
PARTIES:
Germany, West
Yugoslavia

425336   Bilateral Agreement   **69 WGBB 1473**
SIGNED: 12 Oct 36
HEADNOTE: UNEMPLOYMENT INSURANCE
TOPIC: Non-ILO Labor
PARTIES:
Germany, West
Yugoslavia

425337   Bilateral Agreement   **69 WGBB 1107**
SIGNED: 12 Oct 68
HEADNOTE: RECRUITMENT OF MIGRANT WORK-
ERS
TOPIC: Non-ILO Labor
PARTIES:
Germany, West
Yugoslavia

425340   Bilateral Agreement   **70 WGBB 1191**
SIGNED: 28 Jul 69
HEADNOTE: GERMAN INFORMATION CENTERS
YUGOSLAVIA
TOPIC: Consul/Citizenship
PARTIES:
Germany, West
Yugoslavia

425341   Bilateral Agreement   **70 WGBB 1375**
SIGNED: 28 Jul 69
HEADNOTE: CULTURE AND SCIENCE
TOPIC: Health/Educ/Welfare
PARTIES:
Germany, West
Yugoslavia

425344   Bilateral Treaty   **63 WGBB 911**
SIGNED: 29 Jun 62
HEADNOTE: INVESTMENT PROMOTION
TOPIC: Claims and Debts
PARTIES:
Cameroon
Germany, West

425347   Bilateral Agreement   **66 WGBB 109**
SIGNED: 22 Oct 64
HEADNOTE: AIR TRANSPORT
TOPIC: Air Transport
PARTIES:
Cameroon
Germany, West

425350   Bilateral Agreement   **61 WGBB 1183**
SIGNED: 3 Aug 59
HEADNOTE: NATO OFF-SHORE PURCHASES
TOPIC: General Military

PARTIES:
Cameroon
Germany, West

425352   Bilateral Agreement   **70 WGBB 97**
SIGNED: 8 Jul 69
HEADNOTE: CHURCHILL RESEARCH RANGE
TOPIC: Scientific Project
PARTIES:
Cameroon
Germany, West

425353   Bilateral Agreement   **70 WGBB 846**
SIGNED: 23 Oct 69
HEADNOTE: OFFICIAL DOCUMENTS
TOPIC: Admin Cooperation
PARTIES:
Cameroon
Germany, West

425354   Bilateral Agreement   **70 WGBB 253**
SIGNED: 19 Dec 69
HEADNOTE: INSURANCE LOCAL EMPLOYEES
TOPIC: Non-ILO Labor
PARTIES:
Cameroon
Germany, West

425355   Bilateral Treaty   **66 WGBB 899**
SIGNED: 4 Dec 64
HEADNOTE: INVESTMENT GUARANTEE
TOPIC: Claims and Debts
PARTIES:
Germany, West
Kenya

425364   Bilateral Agreement   **71 WGBB 924**
SIGNED: 20 Jun 70
HEADNOTE: CRIMINAL LAW
TOPIC: Admin Cooperation
PARTIES:
Germany, West
Kenya

425369   Bilateral Treaty   **61 WGBB 13**
SIGNED: 11 May 59
HEADNOTE: COPYRIGHT   ART   LITERATURE
SCIENCE
TOPIC: Patents/Copyrights
PARTIES:
Colombia
Germany, West

425370   Bilateral Agreement   **65 WGBB 1948**
SIGNED: 11 Oct 60
HEADNOTE: CULTURE
TOPIC: Culture
PARTIES:
Colombia
Germany, West

425371   Bilateral Agreement   **64 WGBB 257**
SIGNED: 4 Aug 62
HEADNOTE: GERMAN ASSETS
TOPIC: Claims and Debts
PARTIES:
Colombia
Germany, West

425373   Bilateral Treaty   **67 WGBB 1552**
SIGNED: 11 Jun 65
HEADNOTE: INVESTMENT GUARANTEE
TOPIC: Claims and Debts
PARTIES:
Colombia
Germany, West

425375   Bilateral Agreement   **67 WGBB 762**
SIGNED: 10 Sep 65
HEADNOTE: DOUBLE TAXATION
TOPIC: Taxation
PARTIES:
Colombia
Germany, West

425376   Bilateral Agreement   **70 WGBB 673**
SIGNED: 25 Nov 68
HEADNOTE: AIR TRANSPORT
TOPIC: Air Transport
PARTIES:
Colombia
Germany, West

425382   Bilateral Treaty   **67 WGBB 1733**
SIGNED: 13 Sep 65
HEADNOTE: INVESTMENT GUARANTEE
TOPIC: Claims and Debts
PARTIES:
Congo (Brazzaville)
Germany, West

425388   Bilateral Treaty   **70 WGBB 509**
SIGNED: 18 Mar 69
HEADNOTE: INVESTMENT GUARANTEE
TOPIC: Claims and Debts
PARTIES:
Congo (Zaire)
Germany, West

425390   Bilateral Agreement   **64 WGBB 143**
SIGNED: 16 Dec 63
HEADNOTE: TEMPORARY EMPLOYMENT KOREAN
MINERS
TOPIC: Non-ILO Labor
PARTIES:
Germany, West
Korea, South

425391   Bilateral Treaty   **66 WGBB 841**
SIGNED: 4 Feb 64
HEADNOTE: INVESTMENT GUARANTEE
TOPIC: Claims and Debts
PARTIES:
Germany, West
Korea, South

425395   Bilateral Protocol   **71 WGBB 1259**
SIGNED: 9 Apr 65
HEADNOTE: WATER TRANSPORT
TOPIC: Water Transport
PARTIES:
Germany, West
Korea, South

425398   Bilateral Agreement   **71 WGBB 927**
SIGNED: 2 Jun 71
HEADNOTE: TEMPORARY EMPLOYMENT KOREAN
MINERS
TOPIC: Non-ILO Labor
PARTIES:
Germany, West
Korea, South

425399   Bilateral Agreement   **52 WGBB 958**
SIGNED: 7 Jul 51
HEADNOTE: PROVISIONAL TRADE
TOPIC: General Trade
PARTIES:
Cuba
Germany, West

425400   Bilateral Treaty   **55 WGBB 1055**
SIGNED: 11 May 53
HEADNOTE: COMMERCE & NAVIGATION
TOPIC: General Economic
PARTIES:
Cuba
Germany, West

425401   Bilateral Agreement   **54 WGBB 1112**
SIGNED: 22 Mar 54
HEADNOTE: PATENTS & TRADEMARKS
TOPIC: Patents/Copyrights
PARTIES:
Cuba
Germany, West

425402   Bilateral Agreement   **61 WGBB 441**
SIGNED: 23 May 57

HEADNOTE: POSTAL PACKAGES
TOPIC: Postal Service
PARTIES:
  Cuba
  Germany, West

425403   Bilateral Agreement   **53 WGBB 540**
SIGNED: 16 Nov 51
HEADNOTE: MOST FAVORED NATION
TOPIC: Mostfavored Nation
PARTIES:
  Germany, West
  Lebanon

425404   Bilateral Agreement   **55 WGBB 897**
SIGNED: 8 Mar 55
HEADNOTE: TRADEMARKS
TOPIC: Patents/Copyrights
PARTIES:
  Germany, West
  Lebanon

425406   Bilateral Agreement   **62 WGBB 184**
SIGNED: 15 Mar 61
HEADNOTE: AIR TRANSPORT
TOPIC: Air Transport
PARTIES:
  Germany, West
  Lebanon

425407   Bilateral Agreement   **67 WGBB 1673**
SIGNED: 21 May 65
HEADNOTE: TRADE LEBANON EEC MEMBERS
TOPIC: General Economic
PARTIES:
  Germany, West
  Lebanon

425409   Bilateral Treaty   **67 WGBB 1537**
SIGNED: 12 Dec 61
HEADNOTE: INVESTMENT GUARANTEE
TOPIC: Claims and Debts
PARTIES:
  Germany, West
  Liberia

425413   Bilateral Treaty   **71 WGBB 953**
SIGNED: 27 May 70
HEADNOTE: ATOMIC SHIP OTTO HAHN
TOPIC: Specific Property
PARTIES:
  Germany, West
  Liberia

425415   Bilateral Agreement   **54 WGBB 522**
SIGNED: 30 Jan 53
HEADNOTE: CLAIMS
TOPIC: Claims and Debts
PARTIES:
  Germany, West
  Liechtenstein

425421   Bilateral Agreement   **60 WGBB 2305**
SIGNED: 1 Dec 57
HEADNOTE: MIGRANT WORKERS
TOPIC: Non-ILO Labor
PARTIES:
  Germany, West
  Luxembourg

425422   Bilateral Agreement   **59 WGBB 1269**
SIGNED: 28 Aug 58
HEADNOTE: DOUBLE TAXATION
TOPIC: Taxation
PARTIES:
  Germany, West
  Luxembourg

425423   Bilateral Treaty   **60 WGBB 2077**
SIGNED: 11 Jul 59
HEADNOTE: REPARATIONS,   INSURANCE,
  BOUNDARY
TOPIC: Admin Cooperation

PARTIES:
  Germany, West
  Luxembourg

425424   Bilateral Agreement   **63 WGBB 385**
SIGNED: 14 Feb 60
HEADNOTE: INSURANCE MIGRANT WORKERS
TOPIC: Non-ILO Labor
PARTIES:
  Germany, West
  Luxembourg

425425   Bilateral Agreement   **63 WGBB 397**
SIGNED: 14 Jul 60
HEADNOTE: SOCIAL SECURITY BORDER RESI-
  DENTS
TOPIC: Non-ILO Labor
PARTIES:
  Germany, West
  Luxembourg

425428   Bilateral Agreement   **62 WGBB 195**
SIGNED: 5 Jul 61
HEADNOTE: AIR TRANSPORT
TOPIC: Air Transport
PARTIES:
  Germany, West
  Luxembourg

425429   Bilateral Agreement   **63 WGBB 141**
SIGNED: 16 Feb 62
HEADNOTE: JOINT RAIL CHECKPOINTS
TOPIC: Visas
PARTIES:
  Germany, West
  Luxembourg

425431   Bilateral Agreement   **64 WGBB 193**
SIGNED: 7 Dec 62
HEADNOTE: AUTHENTICATION OF DOCUMENTS
TOPIC: Admin Cooperation
PARTIES:
  Germany, West
  Luxembourg

425434   Bilateral Agreement   **67 WGBB 909**
SIGNED: 9 Dec 65
HEADNOTE: EXPEDITING BORDER TRAFFIC
TOPIC: Visas
PARTIES:
  Germany, West
  Luxembourg

425436   Bilateral Agreement   **67 WGBB 1694**
SIGNED: 28 Feb 67
HEADNOTE: BENEFITS FOR NAZI VICTIMS
TOPIC: Specif Claim/Waive
PARTIES:
  Germany, West
  Luxembourg

425437   Bilateral Agreement   **71 WGBB 40**
SIGNED: 9 Dec 69
HEADNOTE: RETIREMENT BENEFITS
TOPIC: Non-ILO Labor
PARTIES:
  Germany, West
  Luxembourg

425441   Bilateral Treaty   **65 WGBB 369**
SIGNED: 21 Sep 62
HEADNOTE: INVESTMENT PROMOTION
TOPIC: Claims and Debts
PARTIES:
  Germany, West
  Malagasy

425444   Bilateral Treaty   **57 WGBB 284**
SIGNED: 30 Jul 56
HEADNOTE: CONSULAR
TOPIC: Consul/Citizenship
PARTIES:
  Germany, West
  Malawi

425450   Bilateral Agreement   **62 WGBB 1064**
SIGNED: 22 Dec 60
HEADNOTE: INVESTMENT GUARANTEE
TOPIC: Claims and Debts
PARTIES:
  Germany, West
  Malaysia

425453   Bilateral Agreement   **70 WGBB 681**
SIGNED: 23 Jul 68
HEADNOTE: AIR TRANSPORT
TOPIC: Air Transport
PARTIES:
  Germany, West
  Malaysia

425463   Bilateral Agreement   **59 WGBB 118**
SIGNED: 17 Jul 58
HEADNOTE: CRIMINAL LAW
TOPIC: Admin Cooperation
PARTIES:
  Germany, West
  Morocco

425465   Bilateral Treaty   **67 WGBB 1641**
SIGNED: 31 Aug 61
HEADNOTE: INVESTMENT PROMOTION
TOPIC: Claims and Debts
PARTIES:
  Germany, West
  Morocco

425466   Bilateral Agreement   **71 WGBB 1365**
SIGNED: 21 May 63
HEADNOTE: TEMPORARY EMPLOYMENT MOROC-
  CAN WORKERS
TOPIC: Non-ILO Labor
PARTIES:
  Germany, West
  Morocco

425477   Bilateral Treaty   **55 WGBB 903**
SIGNED: 4 Nov 54
HEADNOTE: COPYRIGHT IN MUSIC
TOPIC: Patents/Copyrights
PARTIES:
  Germany, West
  Mexico

425478   Bilateral Treaty   **57 WGBB 500**
SIGNED: 18 Dec 56
HEADNOTE: CRIMINAL LAW
TOPIC: Admin Cooperation
PARTIES:
  Germany, West
  Mexico

425480   Bilateral Treaty   **69 WGBB 193**
SIGNED: 8 Mar 67
HEADNOTE: AIR TRANSPORT
TOPIC: Air Transport
PARTIES:
  Germany, West
  Mexico

425482   Bilateral Treaty   **64 WGBB 1297**
SIGNED: 21 May 62
HEADNOTE: EXTRADITION
TOPIC: Extradition
PARTIES:
  Germany, West
  Monaco

425483   Bilateral Treaty   **64 WGBB 1297**
SIGNED: 21 May 62
HEADNOTE: CRIMINAL LAW
TOPIC: Admin Cooperation
PARTIES:
  Germany, West
  Monaco

425484   Bilateral Agreement   **68 WGBB 81**
SIGNED: 6 Oct 67
HEADNOTE: NEPAL RESEARCH CENTER

TOPIC: Scientific Project
PARTIES:
  Germany, West
  Nepal

425495   Bilateral Treaty   **69 WGBB 1121**
SIGNED: 28 Oct 68
HEADNOTE: ATOMIC SHIP OTTO HAHN
TOPIC: Specific Property
PARTIES:
  Germany, West
  Netherlands

425496   Bilateral Agreement   **69 WGBB 609**
SIGNED: 20 Dec 68
HEADNOTE: OFFICIAL DOCUMENTS
TOPIC: Admin Cooperation
PARTIES:
  Germany, West
  Netherlands

425497   Bilateral Treaty   **70 WGBB 277**
SIGNED: 21 Jan 69
HEADNOTE: SOCIAL SECURITY DUES
TOPIC: Non-ILO Labor
PARTIES:
  Germany, West
  Netherlands

425498   Bilateral Agreement   **71 WGBB 37**
SIGNED: 3 Sep 69
HEADNOTE: RETIREMENT BENEFITS
TOPIC: Non-ILO Labor
PARTIES:
  Germany, West
  Netherlands

425499   Bilateral Agreement   **70 WGBB 1056**
SIGNED: 22 Sep 70
HEADNOTE: GOODS BORDER TRAFFIC
TOPIC: Land Transport
PARTIES:
  Germany, West
  Netherlands

425500   Bilateral Agreement   **70 WGBB 1056**
SIGNED: 22 Sep 70
HEADNOTE: CEILING BORDER TRAFFIC
TOPIC: Land Transport
PARTIES:
  Germany, West
  Netherlands

425501   Bilateral Agreement   **71 WGBB 122**
SIGNED: 18 Dec 70
HEADNOTE: OIL STORAGE RESERVES
TOPIC: Specific Property
PARTIES:
  Germany, West
  Netherlands

425505   Bilateral Treaty   **65 WGBB 1402**
SIGNED: 29 Oct 64
HEADNOTE: INVESTMENT PROMOTION
TOPIC: Claims and Debts
PARTIES:
  Germany, West
  Niger

425520   Bilateral Agreement   **71 WGBB 1266**
SIGNED: 9 Sep 71
HEADNOTE: OFFICIAL DOCUMENTS
TOPIC: Admin Cooperation
PARTIES:
  Germany, West
  Norway

425523   Bilateral Agreement   **52 WGBB 317**
SIGNED: 21 Apr 51
HEADNOTE: SOCIAL SECURITY
TOPIC: Non-ILO Labor
PARTIES:
  Austria
  Germany, West

425524   Bilateral Agreement   **52 WGBB 612**
SIGNED: 19 May 51
HEADNOTE: UNEMPLOYMENT INSURANCE
TOPIC: Non-ILO Labor
PARTIES:
  Austria
  Germany, West

425525   Bilateral Agreement   **52 WGBB 609**
SIGNED: 23 Nov 51
HEADNOTE: MIGRANT WORKERS
TOPIC: Non-ILO Labor
PARTIES:
  Austria
  Germany, West

425529   Bilateral Agreement   **55 WGBB 749**
SIGNED: 4 Oct 54
HEADNOTE: DOUBLE TAX INCOME PROPERTY
TOPIC: Taxation
PARTIES:
  Austria
  Germany, West

425530   Bilateral Agreement   **55 WGBB 755**
SIGNED: 4 Oct 54
HEADNOTE: DOUBLE TAX INHERITANCE
TOPIC: Taxation
PARTIES:
  Austria
  Germany, West

425531   Bilateral Treaty   **55 WGBB 833**
SIGNED: 4 Oct 54
HEADNOTE: TAX LAW ADMINISTRATION
TOPIC: Admin Cooperation
PARTIES:
  Austria
  Germany, West

425534   Bilateral Agreement   **57 WGBB 585**
SIGNED: 14 Sep 55
HEADNOTE: ROAD TRANSIT CERTAIN BORDERS
TOPIC: Visas
PARTIES:
  Austria
  Germany, West

425535   Bilateral Agreement   **57 WGBB 589**
SIGNED: 14 Sep 55
HEADNOTE: RAIL TRANSIT CERTAIN BORDERS
TOPIC: Visas
PARTIES:
  Austria
  Germany, West

425536   Bilateral Agreement   **57 WGBB 592**
SIGNED: 14 Sep 55
HEADNOTE: PRIVILEGES OF OFFICIALS
TOPIC: Privil/Immunities
PARTIES:
  Austria
  Germany, West

425537   Bilateral Agreement   **57 WGBB 594**
SIGNED: 14 Sep 55
HEADNOTE: RAIL TRANSIT PRISONERS
TOPIC: Visas
PARTIES:
  Austria
  Germany, West

425538   Bilateral Agreement   **57 WGBB 596**
SIGNED: 14 Sep 55
HEADNOTE: LIABILITY OF OFFICIALS
TOPIC: Privil/Immunities
PARTIES:
  Austria
  Germany, West

425539   Bilateral Agreement   **57 WGBB 598**
SIGNED: 28 Oct 55
HEADNOTE: RAILROAD BORDER CROSSING
TOPIC: Visas

PARTIES:
  Austria
  Germany, West

425540   Bilateral Treaty   **58 WGBB 129**
SIGNED: 15 Jun 57
HEADNOTE: PROPERTY RIGHTS
TOPIC: Finance
PARTIES:
  Austria
  Germany, West

425541   Bilateral Treaty   **60 WGBB 1341**
SIGNED: 22 Sep 58
HEADNOTE: EXTRADITION
TOPIC: Extradition
PARTIES:
  Austria
  Germany, West

425542   Bilateral Treaty   **60 WGBB 1341**
SIGNED: 22 Sep 58
HEADNOTE: CRIMINAL LAW
TOPIC: Admin Cooperation
PARTIES:
  Austria
  Germany, West

425545   Bilateral Agreement   **59 WGBB 1523**
SIGNED: 6 Jun 59
HEADNOTE: SIMPLIFY 1954 HAGUE CONVEN-
TION
TOPIC: Admin Cooperation
PARTIES:
  Austria
  Germany, West

425546   Bilateral Treaty   **60 WGBB 1245**
SIGNED: 6 Jun 59
HEADNOTE: RECOGNITION COURT DECISIONS
TOPIC: Admin Cooperation
PARTIES:
  Austria
  Germany, West

425547   Bilateral Agreement   **62 WGBB 933**
SIGNED:
HEADNOTE: CUSTOMS DANUBE SHIPS
TOPIC: Customs
PARTIES:
  Austria
  Germany, West

425549   Bilateral Treaty   **62 WGBB 1041**
SIGNED: 27 Nov 61
HEADNOTE: REFUGEE CLAIMS
TOPIC: Refugees
PARTIES:
  Austria
  Germany, West

425550   Bilateral Treaty   **63 WGBB 1279**
SIGNED: 6 Sep 62
HEADNOTE: LOCAL BORDER TRAFFIC
TOPIC: Visas
PARTIES:
  Austria
  Germany, West

425551   Bilateral Treaty   **64 WGBB 220**
SIGNED: 7 May 63
HEADNOTE: DISABLED VETERANS BENEFITS
TOPIC: Health/Educ/Welfare
PARTIES:
  Austria
  Germany, West

425552   Bilateral Agreement   **66 WGBB 126**
SIGNED: 15 Mar 65
HEADNOTE: AIR TRANSPORT
TOPIC: Air Transport
PARTIES:
  Austria
  Germany, West

425553 Bilateral Agreement **69 WGBB 1**
SIGNED: 17 Jan 66
HEADNOTE: WELFARE, YOUTH CARE
TOPIC: Health/Educ/Welfare
PARTIES:
Austria
Germany, West

425555 Bilateral Treaty **67 WGBB 2318**
SIGNED: 17 Oct 66
HEADNOTE: STANDARDS & MEASURES
TOPIC: Admin Cooperation
PARTIES:
Austria
Germany, West

425556 Bilateral Agreement **69 WGBB 1233**
SIGNED: 22 Dec 66
HEADNOTE: SOCIAL SECURITY
TOPIC: Non-ILO Labor
PARTIES:
Austria
Germany, West

425557 Bilateral Treaty **70 WGBB 697**
SIGNED: 31 May 67
HEADNOTE: SPECIAL CASES DAMS & BRIDGES
TOPIC: Visas
PARTIES:
Austria
Germany, West

425558 Bilateral Exchange **68 WGBB 5**
SIGNED: 7 Aug 67
HEADNOTE: EXTENSION OF COPYRIGHTS
TOPIC: Patents/Copyrights
PARTIES:
Austria
Germany, West

425559 Bilateral Agreement **69 WGBB 1457**
SIGNED: 13 Nov 68
HEADNOTE: PASSENGER TRANSPORT
TOPIC: General Transport
PARTIES:
Austria
Germany, West

425560 Bilateral Agreement **70 WGBB 1370**
SIGNED: 18 Nov 69
HEADNOTE: TRANSIT CAR TAX
TOPIC: Taxation
PARTIES:
Austria
Germany, West

425561 Bilateral Treaty **71 WGBB 1001**
SIGNED: 11 Sep 70
HEADNOTE: CUSTOMS, TAXES, STATE TRADING
TOPIC: Admin Cooperation
PARTIES:
Austria
Germany, West

425562 Bilateral Agreement **50 WGBB 717**
SIGNED: 4 Mar 50
HEADNOTE: PROVISIONAL TRADE
TOPIC: General Trade
PARTIES:
Germany, West
Pakistan

425565 Bilateral Agreement **60 WGBB 1799**
SIGNED: 7 Aug 58
HEADNOTE: DOUBLE TAX INCOME
TOPIC: Taxation
PARTIES:
Germany, West
Pakistan

425566 Bilateral Agreement **63 WGBB 43**
SIGNED: 9 Nov 61
HEADNOTE: CULTURE
TOPIC: Culture

PARTIES:
Germany, West
Pakistan

425570 Bilateral Agreement **69 WGBB 1560**
SIGNED: 5 Jul 68
HEADNOTE: AIR TRANSPORT
TOPIC: Air Transport
PARTIES:
Germany, West
Panama

425573 Bilateral Agreement **57 WGBB 1273**
SIGNED: 30 Jul 55
HEADNOTE: MOST FAVOR NATION TRADEMARK
TOPIC: Mostfavored Nation
PARTIES:
Germany, West
Paraguay

425576 Bilateral Agreement **52 WGBB 333**
SIGNED: 20 Jul 51
HEADNOTE: TRADE
TOPIC: General Trade
PARTIES:
Germany, West
Peru

425578 Bilateral Agreement **63 WGBB 373**
SIGNED: 30 Apr 62
HEADNOTE: AIR TRANSPORT
TOPIC: Air Transport
PARTIES:
Germany, West
Peru

425579 Bilateral Agreement **66 WGBB 76**
SIGNED: 20 Nov 64
HEADNOTE: CULTURE
TOPIC: Culture
PARTIES:
Germany, West
Peru

425589 Bilateral Exchange **52 WGBB 505**
SIGNED: 26 Sep 51
HEADNOTE: CHANGE OF CUSTOMS DUTIES
TOPIC: Customs
PARTIES:
Germany, West
Portugal

425590 Bilateral Agreement **59 WGBB 264**
SIGNED: 3 Jun 58
HEADNOTE: GERMAN ASSETS
TOPIC: Claims and Debts
PARTIES:
Germany, West
Portugal

425591 Bilateral Agreement **59 WGBB 264**
SIGNED: 3 Apr 58
HEADNOTE: TRADEMARKS
TOPIC: Patents/Copyrights
PARTIES:
Germany, West
Portugal

425592 Bilateral Agreement **59 WGBB 264**
SIGNED: 3 Apr 58
HEADNOTE: END FORMER PAYMENTS PROCE-
DURE
TOPIC: Finance
PARTIES:
Germany, West
Portugal

425596 Bilateral Treaty **67 WGBB 2345**
SIGNED: 15 Jun 64
HEADNOTE: EXTRADITION & CRIMINAL LAW
TOPIC: Extradition
PARTIES:
Germany, West
Portugal

425597 Bilateral Agreement **68 WGBB 473**
SIGNED: 6 Nov 64
HEADNOTE: SOCIAL SECURITY
TOPIC: Non-ILO Labor
PARTIES:
Germany, West
Portugal

425598 Bilateral Agreement **67 WGBB 721**
SIGNED: 22 Oct 65
HEADNOTE: CULTURE
TOPIC: Culture
PARTIES:
Germany, West
Portugal

425602 Bilateral Treaty **68 WGBB 1260**
SIGNED: 18 May 67
HEADNOTE: INVESTMENT PROMOTION
TOPIC: Claims and Debts
PARTIES:
Germany, West
Rwanda

425606 Bilateral Agreement **70 WGBB 1217**
SIGNED: 12 Oct 70
HEADNOTE: PASSENGERS & GOODS
TOPIC: Land Transport
PARTIES:
Germany, West
Romania

425610 Bilateral Treaty **68 WGBB 33**
SIGNED: 10 Dec 66
HEADNOTE: INVESTMENT GUARANTEE
TOPIC: Claims and Debts
PARTIES:
Germany, West
Zambia

425612 Bilateral Agreement **69 WGBB 203**
SIGNED: 8 Oct 68
HEADNOTE: PASSENGER TRAFFIC
TOPIC: Visas
PARTIES:
Germany, West
San Marino

425614 Bilateral Agreement **51 WGBB 105**
SIGNED: 2 Feb 51
HEADNOTE: EXTENSION TRADEMARK DEAD-
LINES
TOPIC: Patents/Copyrights
PARTIES:
Germany, West
Sweden

425615 Bilateral Agreement **59 WGBB 401**
SIGNED: 29 Aug 58
HEADNOTE: EMBEZZLEMENT
TOPIC: Admin Cooperation
PARTIES:
Germany, West
Sweden

425616 Bilateral Agreement **60 WGBB 2299**
SIGNED: 7 Jun 60
HEADNOTE: THEFT & FORGERY
TOPIC: Admin Cooperation
PARTIES:
Germany, West
Sweden

425617 Bilateral Agreement **64 WGBB 1402**
SIGNED: 3 Aug 64
HEADNOTE: CLAIMS OF NAZI VICTIMS
TOPIC: Specif Claim/Waive
PARTIES:
Germany, West
Sweden

425621 Bilateral Treaty **65 WGBB 1391**
SIGNED: 24 Jan 64
HEADNOTE: INVESTMENT PROMOTION

TOPIC: Claims and Debts
PARTIES:
  Germany, West
  Senegal

425622   Bilateral Agreement   **66 WGBB 118**
SIGNED: 29 Oct 64
HEADNOTE: AIR TRANSPORT
TOPIC: Air Transport
PARTIES:
  Germany, West
  Senegal

425624   Bilateral Agreement   **70 WGBB 1224**
SIGNED: 23 Sep 68
HEADNOTE: CULTURE
TOPIC: Culture
PARTIES:
  Germany, West
  Senegal

425626   Bilateral Agreement   **71 WGBB 1309**
SIGNED: 17 Apr 69
HEADNOTE: CRIMINAL LAW
TOPIC: Admin Cooperation
PARTIES:
  Germany, West
  Senegal

425632   Bilateral Treaty   **66 WGBB 861**
SIGNED: 8 Apr 65
HEADNOTE: INVESTMENT GUARANTEE
TOPIC: Claims and Debts
PARTIES:
  Germany, West
  Sierra Leone

425643   Bilateral Agreement   **71 WGBB 184**
SIGNED: 15 Feb 69
HEADNOTE: AIR TRANSPORT
TOPIC: Air Transport
PARTIES:
  Germany, West
  Singapore

425647   Bilateral Agreement   **64 WGBB 13**
SIGNED: 11 Jun 62
HEADNOTE: CULTURE
TOPIC: Culture
PARTIES:
  Germany, West
  South Africa

425648   Bilateral Treaty   **66 WGBB 889**
SIGNED: 7 Feb 63
HEADNOTE: PROMOTION OF INVESTMENTS
TOPIC: Claims and Debts
PARTIES:
  Germany, West
  Sudan

425655   Bilateral Treaty   **66 WGBB 873**
SIGNED: 30 Jan 65
HEADNOTE: INVESTMENT GUARANTEE
TOPIC: Claims and Debts
PARTIES:
  Germany, West
  Tanzania

425657   Bilateral Agreement   **68 WGBB 589**
SIGNED: 10 Jul 67
HEADNOTE: DOUBLE TAX INCOME PROPERTY
TOPIC: Taxation
PARTIES:
  Germany, West
  Thailand

425661   Bilateral Treaty   **64 WGBB 154**
SIGNED: 16 May 61
HEADNOTE: INVESTMENT PROMOTION
TOPIC: Claims and Debts
PARTIES:
  Germany, West
  Togo

425673   Bilateral Treaty   **68 WGBB 221**
SIGNED: 11 Apr 67
HEADNOTE: INVESTMENT GUARANTEES
TOPIC: Claims and Debts
PARTIES:
  Chad
  Germany, West

425679   Bilateral Treaty   **65 WGBB 1377**
SIGNED: 20 Dec 63
HEADNOTE: INVESTMENT GUARANTEES
TOPIC: Claims and Debts
PARTIES:
  Germany, West
  Tunisia

425687   Bilateral Agreement   **67 WGBB 1210**
SIGNED: 19 Jul 66
HEADNOTE: CULTURE
TOPIC: Culture
PARTIES:
  Germany, West
  Tunisia

425688   Bilateral Treaty   **69 WGBB 889**
SIGNED: 19 Jul 66
HEADNOTE: COURT ORDERS & TRADE ARBITRA-
TION
TOPIC: Admin Cooperation
PARTIES:
  Germany, West
  Tunisia

425689   Bilateral Treaty   **69 WGBB 1157**
SIGNED: 19 Jul 66
HEADNOTE: EXTRADITION & CRIMINAL LAW
TOPIC: Extradition
PARTIES:
  Germany, West
  Tunisia

425693   Bilateral Agreement   **71 WGBB 177**
SIGNED: 26 May 69
HEADNOTE: AIR TRANSPORT
TOPIC: Air Transport
PARTIES:
  Germany, West
  Tunisia

425701   Bilateral Treaty   **68 WGBB 449**
SIGNED: 29 Nov 66
HEADNOTE: INVESTMENT GUARANTEES
TOPIC: Claims and Debts
PARTIES:
  Germany, West
  Uganda

425707   Bilateral Treaty   **54 WGBB 51**
SIGNED: 18 Apr 53
HEADNOTE: TRADE & MOST FAVORED NATION
TOPIC: General Trade
PARTIES:
  Germany, West
  Uruguay

425709   Bilateral Agreement   **59 WGBB 80**
SIGNED: 31 Aug 57
HEADNOTE: AIR TRANSPORT
TOPIC: Air Transport
PARTIES:
  Germany, West
  Uruguay

425710   Bilateral Agreement   **52 WGBB 525**
SIGNED: 21 Apr 51
HEADNOTE: TRADE
TOPIC: General Trade
PARTIES:
  Germany, West
  United Arab Rep

425711   Bilateral Agreement   **55 WGBB 857**
SIGNED: 31 Jul 54
HEADNOTE: CUSTOMS QUOTA COTTON YARN

TOPIC: Customs
PARTIES:
  Germany, West
  United Arab Rep

425714   Bilateral Agreement   **60 WGBB 2351**
SIGNED: 11 Nov 59
HEADNOTE: CULTURE
TOPIC: Culture
PARTIES:
  Germany, West
  United Arab Rep

425715   Bilateral Agreement   **61 WGBB 420**
SIGNED: 17 Nov 59
HEADNOTE: DOUBLE TAX INCOME
TOPIC: Taxation
PARTIES:
  Germany, West
  United Arab Rep

425726   Bilateral Agreement   **70 WGBB 2778**
SIGNED: 11 Sep 70
HEADNOTE: SOCIAL SECURITY LOCAL EM-
PLOYEES
TOPIC: Non-ILO Labor
PARTIES:
  Germany, West
  USA (United States)

425727   Bilateral Agreement   **71 WGBB 407**
SIGNED: 3 Dec 70
HEADNOTE: LOCAL CONSTRUCT US FORCES
TOPIC: Milit Installation
PARTIES:
  Germany, West
  USA (United States)

425728   Bilateral Agreement   **66 WGBB 322**
SIGNED: 28 Mar 66
HEADNOTE: HOSPITAL SHIP HELGOLAND
TOPIC: Specif Goods/Equip
PARTIES:
  Germany, West
  Vietnam, South

425729   Bilateral Agreement   **67 WGBB 2105**
SIGNED: 30 Mar 67
HEADNOTE: MALTESE AID SERVICE
TOPIC: Humanitarian
PARTIES:
  Germany, West
  Vietnam, South

425733   Bilateral Treaty   **67 WGBB 1657**
SIGNED: 23 Aug 65
HEADNOTE: INVESTMENT GUARANTEES
TOPIC: Claims and Debts
PARTIES:
  Central Afri Rep
  Germany, West

425740   Bilateral Agreement   **69 WGBB 981**
SIGNED: 18 Oct 67
HEADNOTE: AIR TRANSPORT
TOPIC: Air Transport
PARTIES:
  Cyprus
  Germany, West

425742   Bilateral Treaty   **66 WGBB 209**
SIGNED: 29 Nov 65
HEADNOTE: REPAYMENT OF REICHSMARK AS-
SETS
TOPIC: Claims and Debts
PARTIES:
  Germany, West
  Bank Int Settlement

425743   Bilateral Agreement   **70 WGBB 185**
SIGNED: 26 Jan 70
HEADNOTE: ELDO FACILITIES IN GERMANY
TOPIC: IGO Operations

PARTIES:
Germany, West
Eur Space Vehicle

425744　Bilateral Agreement　**69 WGBB 1997**
SIGNED: 13 Mar 67
HEADNOTE: INTERNATIONAL MILITARY HEAD-
QUARTERS
TOPIC: Military Mission
PARTIES:
Germany, West
NATO (North Atlan)

425747　Bilateral Agreement　**69 WGBB 92**
SIGNED: 8 Sep 67
HEADNOTE: EUROPEAN SPACE RESEARCH CEN-
TER
TOPIC: IGO Establishment
PARTIES:
Germany, West
Eur Space Research

425748　Bilateral Agreement　**71 WGBB 1153**
SIGNED: 8 Sep 70
HEADNOTE: AIR ROUTE FEES
TOPIC: Admin Cooperation
PARTIES:
Eurocontrol
Germany, West

425752　Bilateral Agreement　**51 WGBB 63**
SIGNED: 2 Nov 50
HEADNOTE: EXTENSION DEADLINES TRADE-
MARKS
TOPIC: Patents/Copyrights
PARTIES:
Germany, West
Switzerland

425753　Bilateral Agreement　**53 WGBB 703**
SIGNED: 26 Aug 52
HEADNOTE: FORMER REICH DEBTS
TOPIC: Claims and Debts
PARTIES:
Germany, West
Switzerland

425754　Bilateral Agreement　**53 WGBB 519**
SIGNED: 8 Oct 52
HEADNOTE: MARRIAGE DOCUMENTS
TOPIC: Admin Cooperation
PARTIES:
Germany, West
Switzerland

425758　Bilateral Agreement　**60 WGBB 941**
SIGNED: 21 Nov 58
HEADNOTE: GENERAL CUSTOMS
TOPIC: Customs
PARTIES:
Germany, West
Switzerland

425759　Bilateral Agreement　**65 WGBB 1293**
SIGNED: 25 Feb 64
HEADNOTE: SOCIAL SECURITY
TOPIC: Non-ILO Labor
PARTIES:
Germany, West
Switzerland

425760　Bilateral Treaty　**67 WGBB 2040**
SIGNED: 23 Nov 64
HEADNOTE: BORDER KONSTANZ NEUHAUSEN
TOPIC: Territory Boundary
PARTIES:
Germany, West
Switzerland

425761　Bilateral Treaty　**67 WGBB 2029**
SIGNED: 23 Nov 64
HEADNOTE: BUSINGEN WITHIN SWISS CUS-
TOMS
TOPIC: Territory Boundary

PARTIES:
Germany, West
Switzerland

425762　Bilateral Agreement　**67 WGBB 773**
SIGNED: 29 Apr 65
HEADNOTE: AIR RESCUE & RETURN
TOPIC: Humanitarian
PARTIES:
Germany, West
Switzerland

425764　Bilateral Treaty　**69 WGBB 138**
SIGNED: 7 Mar 67
HEADNOTE: MARKS OF ORIGIN
TOPIC: Patents/Copyrights
PARTIES:
Germany, West
Switzerland

425766　Bilateral Treaty　**71 WGBB 90**
SIGNED: 26 May 69
HEADNOTE: TRAFFIC ACCIDENT LIABILITY
TOPIC: Admin Cooperation
PARTIES:
Germany, West
Switzerland

425767　Bilateral Agreement　**70 WGBB 745**
SIGNED: 21 May 70
HEADNOTE: LOCAL BORDER TRAFFIC
TOPIC: Visas
PARTIES:
Germany, West
Switzerland

425768　Bilateral Protocol　**52 WGBB 616**
SIGNED: 16 Feb 52
HEADNOTE: CUSTOMS
TOPIC: Customs
PARTIES:
Germany, West
Turkey

425771　Bilateral Agreement　**62 WGBB 2376**
SIGNED: 5 Jul 57
HEADNOTE: AIR SERVICES
TOPIC: Air Transport
PARTIES:
Germany, West
Turkey

425772　Bilateral Agreement　**60 WGBB 2365**
SIGNED: 26 Jun 59
HEADNOTE: SUPPLEMENT AGREEMENT 11 MAY
59
TOPIC: Claims and Debts
PARTIES:
Germany, West
Turkey

425774　Bilateral Treaty　**65 WGBB 1193**
SIGNED: 20 Jun 62
HEADNOTE: INVESTMENT GUARANTEE
TOPIC: Loans and Credits
PARTIES:
Germany, West
Turkey

425776　Bilateral Agreement　**65 WGBB 1169**
SIGNED: 30 Apr 64
HEADNOTE: SOCIAL SECURITY
TOPIC: Health/Educ/Welfare
PARTIES:
Germany, West
Turkey

425777　Bilateral Agreement　**67 WGBB 1692**
SIGNED: 8 Dec 65
HEADNOTE: CRIMINAL LAW
TOPIC: Admin Cooperation
PARTIES:
Germany, West
Turkey

433001　Bilateral Protocol　**0 IRTB 1**
SIGNED: 30 Jun 48
HEADNOTE: BORDER DEMARCATION
TOPIC: Territory Boundary
PARTIES:
Afghanistan
Iran

433002　Bilateral Treaty　**0 IRTB 2**
SIGNED: 26 Jun 56
HEADNOTE: BORDER REGULATION
TOPIC: Admin Cooperation
PARTIES:
Afghanistan
Iran

433003　Bilateral Agreement　**0 IRTB 2**
SIGNED: 31 Oct 63
HEADNOTE: TRADE
TOPIC: General Trade
PARTIES:
Afghanistan
Iran

433004　Bilateral Agreement　**0 IRTB 2**
SIGNED: 31 Oct 63
HEADNOTE: PAYMENT
TOPIC: Finance
PARTIES:
Afghanistan
Iran

433005　Bilateral Agreement　**0 IRTB 2**
SIGNED: 1 Feb 62
HEADNOTE: TRANSPORT
TOPIC: General Transport
PARTIES:
Afghanistan
Iran

433006　Bilateral Agreement　**0 IRTB 2**
SIGNED: 2 Nov 63
HEADNOTE: TELECOMMUNICATIONS
TOPIC: Telecommunications
PARTIES:
Afghanistan
Iran

433007　Bilateral Protocol　**0 IRTB 3**
SIGNED: 11 Jan 69
HEADNOTE: TELECOMMUNICATIONS
TOPIC: Telecommunications
PARTIES:
Afghanistan
Iran

433008　Bilateral Exchange　**0 IRTB 3**
SIGNED: 31 Dec 63
HEADNOTE: AIR TRANSPORT TAX EXEMPTIONS
TOPIC: Taxation
PARTIES:
Afghanistan
Iran

433009　Bilateral Exchange　**0 IRTB 4**
SIGNED: 11 Oct 71
HEADNOTE: VISA ABOLITION
TOPIC: Visas
PARTIES:
Iran
South Africa

433010　Bilateral Agreement　**0 IRTB 5**
SIGNED: 8 Aug 68
HEADNOTE: CULTURAL
TOPIC: Culture
PARTIES:
Algeria
Iran

433011　Bilateral Exchange　**0 IRTB 7**
SIGNED: 7 Apr 57
HEADNOTE: AIR TRANSPORT TAX EXEMPTIONS
TOPIC: Taxation

PARTIES:
Germany, West
Iran

433012   Bilateral Exchange   0 IRTB 7
SIGNED: 4 May 68
HEADNOTE: MARITIME TAX EXEMPTIONS
TOPIC: Taxation
PARTIES:
Germany, West
Iran

433013   Bilateral Agreement   0 IRTB 8
SIGNED: 4 Feb 60
HEADNOTE: SHIRAZ AGRICULTURE INSTITUTE
TOPIC: Non-IBRD Project
PARTIES:
Germany, West
Iran

433014   Bilateral Agreement   0 IRTB 9
SIGNED: 16 Apr 60
HEADNOTE: CROP DISEASE RESEARCH CENTER
TOPIC: Non-IBRD Project
PARTIES:
Germany, West
Iran

433015   Bilateral Agreement   0 IRTB 9
SIGNED: 7 Nov 68
HEADNOTE: TECHNICAL COOPERATION
TOPIC: Tech Assistance
PARTIES:
Germany, West
Iran

433016   Bilateral Exchange   0 IRTB 9
SIGNED: 27 Nov 69
HEADNOTE: DEVELOP SUGAR-BEET MARVDASHT
TOPIC: Non-IBRD Project
PARTIES:
Germany, West
Iran

433017   Bilateral Agreement   0 IRTB 10
SIGNED: 24 Oct 68
HEADNOTE: TERRITORY DEMARCATION
TOPIC: Territory Boundary
PARTIES:
Iran
Saudi Arabia

433018   Bilateral Agreement   0 IRTB 10
SIGNED: 14 Nov 67
HEADNOTE: CULTURAL
TOPIC: Culture
PARTIES:
Iran
Saudi Arabia

433019   Bilateral Agreement   0 IRTB 11
SIGNED: 12 May 65
HEADNOTE: CULTURAL
TOPIC: Culture
PARTIES:
Argentina
Iran

433021   Bilateral Exchange   0 IRTB 14
SIGNED: 1 Sep 65
HEADNOTE: AIR TRANSPORT TAX EXEMPTIONS
TOPIC: Taxation
PARTIES:
Belgium
Iran

433022   Bilateral Agreement   0 IRTB 14
SIGNED: 19 Nov 64
HEADNOTE: VISA ABOLITION
TOPIC: Visas
PARTIES:
Belgium
Iran

433023   Bilateral Agreement   0 IRTB 14
SIGNED: 12 Mar 70
HEADNOTE: CULTURAL & ECONOMIC & TECHNI-
CAL COOPERATION
TOPIC: Health/Educ/Welfare
PARTIES:
Belgium
Iran

433024   Bilateral Agreement   0 IRTB 15
SIGNED: 22 Nov 57
HEADNOTE: CULTURAL
TOPIC: Culture
PARTIES:
Brazil
Iran

433025   Bilateral Agreement   0 IRTB 16
SIGNED: 26 Nov 67
HEADNOTE: CULTURAL
TOPIC: Culture
PARTIES:
Bulgaria
Iran

433026   Bilateral Agreement   0 IRTB 16
SIGNED: 9 Feb 67
HEADNOTE: TRADE
TOPIC: General Trade
PARTIES:
Bulgaria
Iran

433027   Bilateral Agreement   0 IRTB 16
SIGNED: 9 Feb 67
HEADNOTE: PAYMENTS
TOPIC: Finance
PARTIES:
Bulgaria
Iran

433028   Bilateral Agreement   0 IRTB 16
SIGNED: 9 Feb 67
HEADNOTE: ECONOMIC COOPERATION
TOPIC: General Economic
PARTIES:
Bulgaria
Iran

433029   Bilateral Treaty   0 IRTB 17
SIGNED: 5 May 69
HEADNOTE: GENERAL RELATIONS
TOPIC: General Amity
PARTIES:
Iran
Korea, South

433030   Bilateral Exchange   0 IRTB 19
SIGNED: 16 Sep 56
HEADNOTE: AIR TRANSPORT TAX EXEMPTIONS
TOPIC: Taxation
PARTIES:
Denmark
Iran

433031   Bilateral Agreement   0 IRTB 19
SIGNED: 23 Jun 67
HEADNOTE: ABOLITION OF VISAS
TOPIC: Visas
PARTIES:
Denmark
Iran

433032   Bilateral Agreement   0 IRTB 20
SIGNED: 9 Sep 58
HEADNOTE: CULTURAL
TOPIC: Culture
PARTIES:
United Arab Rep
Iran

433033   Bilateral Agreement   0 IRTB 21
SIGNED: 12 Mar 56
HEADNOTE: CULTURAL

TOPIC: Culture
PARTIES:
Iran
Spain

433034   Bilateral Agreement   0 IRTB 21
SIGNED: 20 Sep 67
HEADNOTE: ABOLITION OF VISAS
TOPIC: Visas
PARTIES:
Iran
Spain

433035   Bilateral Agreement   0 IRTB 23
SIGNED: 24 Apr 52
HEADNOTE: CONTINUE MILITARY AID
TOPIC: Milit Assistance
PARTIES:
Iran
USA (United States)

433036   Bilateral Agreement   0 IRTB 23
SIGNED: 31 Oct 57
HEADNOTE: MILITARY AID EQUIPMENT
TOPIC: Milit Installation
PARTIES:
Iran
USA (United States)

433037   Bilateral Agreement   0 IRTB 23
SIGNED: 16 Sep 62
HEADNOTE: PEACE CORPS IN IRAN
TOPIC: Tech Assistance
PARTIES:
Iran
USA (United States)

433038   Bilateral Exchange   0 IRTB 24
SIGNED: 5 Jan 52
HEADNOTE: DEVELOPMENT PROGRAMS
TOPIC: Direct Aid
PARTIES:
Iran
USA (United States)

433039   Bilateral Treaty   0 IRTB 28
SIGNED: 6 Jun 68
HEADNOTE: GENERAL RELATIONS
TOPIC: General Amity
PARTIES:
Ethiopia
Iran

433040   Bilateral Exchange   0 IRTB 29
SIGNED: 25 Apr 69
HEADNOTE: VISA ABOLITION
TOPIC: Visas
PARTIES:
Finland
Iran

433041   Bilateral Exchange   0 IRTB 30
SIGNED: 30 Aug 56
HEADNOTE: AIR TRANSPORT TAX EXEMPTION
TOPIC: Taxation
PARTIES:
France
Iran

433042   Bilateral Agreement   0 IRTB 31
SIGNED: 12 May 59
HEADNOTE: JOINT TEXTILE CENTER ISPHAHAN
TOPIC: General Trade
PARTIES:
France
Iran

433043   Bilateral Agreement   0 IRTB 34
SIGNED: 20 Nov 56
HEADNOTE: CULTURAL
TOPIC: Culture
PARTIES:
Greece
Iran

433044   Bilateral Agreement   0 IRTB 34
SIGNED: 6 Aug 69
HEADNOTE: ABOLITION OF VISAS
TOPIC: Visas
PARTIES:
   Greece
   Iran

433045   Bilateral Agreement   0 IRTB 35
SIGNED: 22 May 59
HEADNOTE: CULTURAL
TOPIC: Culture
PARTIES:
   Iran
   Netherlands

433046   Bilateral Agreement   0 IRTB 35
SIGNED: 31 Oct 49
HEADNOTE: AIR TRANSPORT
TOPIC: Air Transport
PARTIES:
   Iran
   Netherlands

433047   Bilateral Exchange   0 IRTB 35
SIGNED: 27 Jul 56
HEADNOTE: AIR TRANSPORT TAX EXEMPTIONS
TOPIC: Taxation
PARTIES:
   Iran
   Netherlands

433048   Bilateral Exchange   0 IRTB 36
SIGNED: 13 Jul 68
HEADNOTE: MARITIME TAX EXEMPTIONS
TOPIC: Taxation
PARTIES:
   Iran
   Netherlands

433049   Bilateral Exchange   0 IRTB 36
SIGNED: 19 Nov 64
HEADNOTE: VISA ABOLITION
TOPIC: Visas
PARTIES:
   Iran
   Netherlands

433050   Bilateral Exchange   0 IRTB 36
SIGNED: 6 Feb 58
HEADNOTE: CONSUL PROCEDURE FOR SHIP-
   WRECKS
TOPIC: Consul/Citizenship
PARTIES:
   Iran
   Netherlands

433051   Bilateral Agreement   0 IRTB 37
SIGNED: 24 May 68
HEADNOTE: CULTURAL
TOPIC: Culture
PARTIES:
   Hungary
   Iran

433052   Bilateral Agreement   0 IRTB 7
SIGNED: 21 May 69
HEADNOTE: LONG-TERM TRADE
TOPIC: General Trade
PARTIES:
   Hungary
   Iran

433053   Bilateral Agreement   0 IRTB 7
SIGNED: 21 May 69
HEADNOTE: LONG-TERM PAYMENTS
TOPIC: Finance
PARTIES:
   Hungary
   Iran

433054   Bilateral Agreement   0 IRTB 37
SIGNED: 10 May 65
HEADNOTE: ECONOMIC COOPERATION

TOPIC: General Economic
PARTIES:
   Hungary
   Iran

433055   Bilateral Agreement   0 IRTB 37
SIGNED: 10 Apr 68
HEADNOTE: ECONOMIC & TECHNICAL COOPER-
   ATION
TOPIC: General Economic
PARTIES:
   Hungary
   Iran

433056   Bilateral Agreement   0 IRTB 38
SIGNED: 1 Dec 56
HEADNOTE: CULTURAL
TOPIC: Culture
PARTIES:
   India
   Iran

433057   Bilateral Agreement   0 IRTB 38
SIGNED: 11 Mar 64
HEADNOTE: TRADE
TOPIC: General Trade
PARTIES:
   India
   Iran

433058   Bilateral Convention   0 IRTB 38
SIGNED: 14 Jul 54
HEADNOTE: LOCUST CONTROL
TOPIC: Sanitation
PARTIES:
   India
   Iran

433059   Bilateral Treaty   0 IRTB 39
SIGNED: 29 Dec 58
HEADNOTE: GENERAL RELATIONS
TOPIC: General Amity
PARTIES:
   Indonesia
   Iran

433060   Bilateral Agreement   0 IRTB 39
SIGNED: 27 Apr 71
HEADNOTE: CULTURAL
TOPIC: Culture
PARTIES:
   Indonesia
   Iran

433061   Bilateral Exchange   0 IRTB 40
SIGNED: 1 Jun 65
HEADNOTE: VISA TAX ABOLITION
TOPIC: Visas
PARTIES:
   Iran
   Iraq

433062   Bilateral Agreement   0 IRTB 43
SIGNED: 29 Nov 58
HEADNOTE: CULTURAL
TOPIC: Culture
PARTIES:
   Iran
   Italy

433063   Bilateral Agreement   0 IRTB 43
SIGNED: 28 Jun 69
HEADNOTE: ABOLITION VISAS
TOPIC: Visas
PARTIES:
   Iran
   Italy

433064   Bilateral Exchange   0 IRTB 43
SIGNED: 7 Oct 69
HEADNOTE: AIR TRANSPORT TAX EXEMPTIONS
TOPIC: Taxation

PARTIES:
   Iran
   Italy

433065   Bilateral Agreement   0 IRTB 44
SIGNED: 27 Sep 70
HEADNOTE: SCIENTIFIC & TECHNICAL COOPER-
   ATION
TOPIC: Scientific Project
PARTIES:
   Iran
   Italy

433066   Bilateral Exchange   0 IRTB 45
SIGNED: 11 Oct 60
HEADNOTE: ECONOMIC COOPERATION
TOPIC: General Economic
PARTIES:
   Iran
   Japan

433067   Bilateral Exchange   0 IRTB 46
SIGNED: 23 Jul 63
HEADNOTE: JUDICIAL COOPERATION
TOPIC: Admin Cooperation
PARTIES:
   Iran
   Japan

433068   Bilateral Exchange   0 IRTB 46
SIGNED: 17 Mar 70
HEADNOTE: AIR TRANSPORT TAX EXEMPTIONS
TOPIC: Taxation
PARTIES:
   Iran
   Japan

433069   Bilateral Agreement   0 IRTB 46
SIGNED: 16 Aug 70
HEADNOTE: TELECOMMUNICATIONS CENTER
TOPIC: Telecommunications
PARTIES:
   Iran
   Japan

433070   Bilateral Treaty   0 IRTB 47
SIGNED: 16 Nov 49
HEADNOTE: GENERAL RELATIONS
TOPIC: General Amity
PARTIES:
   Iran
   Jordan

433071   Bilateral Agreement   0 IRTB 47
SIGNED: 26 Apr 60
HEADNOTE: CULTURAL
TOPIC: Culture
PARTIES:
   Iran
   Jordan

433072   Bilateral Agreement   0 IRTB 47
SIGNED: 7 Jul 63
HEADNOTE: TRADE
TOPIC: General Trade
PARTIES:
   Iran
   Jordan

433073   Bilateral Exchange   0 IRTB 47
SIGNED: 10 Jul 71
HEADNOTE: AIR TRANSPORT TAX EXEMPTIONS
TOPIC: Taxation
PARTIES:
   Iran
   Jordan

433074   Bilateral Agreement   0 IRTB 48
SIGNED: 6 Nov 68
HEADNOTE: TRADE
TOPIC: General Trade
PARTIES:
   Iran
   Kuwait

433075   Bilateral Exchange   **0 IRTB 48**
SIGNED: 8 May 68
HEADNOTE: AIR TRANSPORT TAX EXEMPTIONS
TOPIC: Taxation
PARTIES:
  Iran
  Kuwait

433076   Bilateral Treaty   **0 IRTB 49**
SIGNED: 7 Oct 53
HEADNOTE: GENERAL RELATIONS
TOPIC: General Amity
PARTIES:
  Iran
  Lebanon

433077   Bilateral Agreement   **0 IRTB 49**
SIGNED: 17 Oct 56
HEADNOTE: CULTURAL
TOPIC: Culture
PARTIES:
  Iran
  Lebanon

433078   Bilateral Agreement   **0 IRTB 50**
SIGNED: 19 Nov 64
HEADNOTE: VISA ABOLITION
TOPIC: Visas
PARTIES:
  Iran
  Luxembourg

433079   Bilateral Agreement   **0 IRTB 54**
SIGNED: 6 Feb 58
HEADNOTE: FRONTIERS
TOPIC: Territory Boundary
PARTIES:
  Iran
  Pakistan

433080   Bilateral Treaty   **0 IRTB 54**
SIGNED: 20 Apr 59
HEADNOTE: EXTRADITION
TOPIC: Extradition
PARTIES:
  Iran
  Pakistan

433081   Bilateral Agreement   **0 IRTB 54**
SIGNED: 18 May 57
HEADNOTE: AIR TRANSPORT
TOPIC: Air Transport
PARTIES:
  Iran
  Pakistan

433082   Bilateral Exchange   **0 IRTB 54**
SIGNED: 1 Nov 71
HEADNOTE: FREE ENTRY MILITARY PLANES
TOPIC: Taxation
PARTIES:
  Iran
  Pakistan

433083   Bilateral Agreement   **0 IRTB 55**
SIGNED: 20 May 62
HEADNOTE: TRADE
TOPIC: General Trade
PARTIES:
  Iran
  Pakistan

433084   Bilateral Agreement   **0 IRTB 55**
SIGNED: 20 Mar 56
HEADNOTE: LOCUST CONTROL
TOPIC: Sanitation
PARTIES:
  Iran
  Pakistan

433085   Bilateral Agreement   **0 IRTB 55**
SIGNED: 14 Dec 60
HEADNOTE: INFECTIOUS DISEASE CONTROL
TOPIC: Sanitation

PARTIES:
  Iran
  Pakistan

433086   Bilateral Agreement   **0 IRTB 55**
SIGNED: 18 Oct 64
HEADNOTE: VISA ABOLITION
TOPIC: Visas
PARTIES:
  Iran
  Pakistan

433087   Bilateral Agreement   **0 IRTB 55**
SIGNED: 16 Feb 59
HEADNOTE: TRANSFER MIRJAVA-ZAHIDEN RAIL-
WAY
TOPIC: Specific Property
PARTIES:
  Iran
  Pakistan

433088   Bilateral Exchange   **0 IRTB 56**
SIGNED: 27 Jan 68
HEADNOTE: MARITIME TONNAGE CERTIFICATES
TOPIC: Admin Cooperation
PARTIES:
  Iran
  Pakistan

433090   Bilateral Agreement   **0 IRTB 57**
SIGNED: 16 Dec 69
HEADNOTE: LONG-TERM TRADE
TOPIC: General Trade
PARTIES:
  Iran
  Poland

433091   Bilateral Agreement   **0 IRTB 57**
SIGNED: 16 Dec 69
HEADNOTE: LONG-TERM PAYMENTS
TOPIC: Finance
PARTIES:
  Iran
  Poland

433092   Bilateral Agreement   **0 IRTB 57**
SIGNED: 13 Feb 64
HEADNOTE: ECONOMIC COOPERATION
TOPIC: General Economic
PARTIES:
  Iran
  Poland

433093   Bilateral Exchange   **0 IRTB 57**
SIGNED: 4 Oct 69
HEADNOTE: AIR TRANSPORT TAX EXEMPTIONS
TOPIC: Taxation
PARTIES:
  Iran
  Poland

433094   Bilateral Exchange   **0 IRTB 58**
SIGNED: 13 Aug 68
HEADNOTE: MARITIME TAX EXEMPTIONS
TOPIC: Taxation
PARTIES:
  Iran
  Poland

433095   Bilateral Agreement   **0 IRTB 59**
SIGNED: 20 Sep 69
HEADNOTE: TERRITORIAL BOUNDARIES
TOPIC: Territory Boundary
PARTIES:
  Iran
  Qatar

433096   Bilateral Agreement   **0 IRTB 60**
SIGNED: 15 Aug 67
HEADNOTE: CULTURAL
TOPIC: Culture
PARTIES:
  Iran
  Romania

433097   Bilateral Agreement   **0 IRTB 60**
SIGNED: 24 Jan 68
HEADNOTE: LONG-TERM TRADE
TOPIC: General Trade
PARTIES:
  Iran
  Romania

433098   Bilateral Agreement   **0 IRTB 60**
SIGNED: 24 Jan 68
HEADNOTE: LONG-TERM PAYMENTS
TOPIC: Finance
PARTIES:
  Iran
  Romania

433099   Bilateral Agreement   **0 IRTB 60**
SIGNED: 25 Oct 65
HEADNOTE: ECONOMIC & TECHNICAL COOPER-
ATION
TOPIC: General Economic
PARTIES:
  Iran
  Romania

433100   Bilateral Agreement   **0 IRTB 60**
SIGNED: 8 Aug 66
HEADNOTE: TRACTOR PLANT IN IRAN
TOPIC: Specific Property
PARTIES:
  Iran
  Romania

433101   Bilateral Exchange   **0 IRTB 63**
SIGNED: 16 Sep 56
HEADNOTE: AIR TRANSPORT TAX EXEMPTIONS
TOPIC: Taxation
PARTIES:
  Iran
  Sweden

433102   Bilateral Exchange   **0 IRTB 63**
SIGNED: 30 Oct 68
HEADNOTE: VISA ABOLITION
TOPIC: Visas
PARTIES:
  Iran
  Sweden

433103   Bilateral Agreement   **0 IRTB 65**
SIGNED: 20 Mar 66
HEADNOTE: INVESTMENT GUARANTEE
TOPIC: Claims and Debts
PARTIES:
  Iran
  Switzerland

433104   Bilateral Agreement   **0 IRTB 65**
SIGNED: 31 Dec 68
HEADNOTE: LIMITED VISA ABOLITION
TOPIC: Visas
PARTIES:
  Iran
  Switzerland

433105   Bilateral Agreement   **0 IRTB 66**
SIGNED: 26 May 67
HEADNOTE: CULTURAL
TOPIC: Culture
PARTIES:
  Czechoslovakia
  Iran

433106   Bilateral Agreement   **0 IRTB 66**
SIGNED: 29 Jan 66
HEADNOTE: ECONOMIC & TECHNICAL COOPER-
ATION
TOPIC: General Economic
PARTIES:
  Czechoslovakia
  Iran

433107   Bilateral Agreement   **0 IRTB 66**
SIGNED: 12 Mar 69

HEADNOTE: ECONOMIC & TECHNICAL COOPER-
ATION
TOPIC: General Economic
PARTIES:
  Czechoslovakia
  Iran

433108   Bilateral Agreement   **0 IRTB 66**
SIGNED: 12 Mar 69
HEADNOTE: LONG-TERM TRADE
TOPIC: General Trade
PARTIES:
  Czechoslovakia
  Iran

433109   Bilateral Agreement   **0 IRTB 67**
SIGNED: 12 Mar 69
HEADNOTE: LONG-TERM PAYMENTS
TOPIC: Finance
PARTIES:
  Czechoslovakia
  Iran

433110   Bilateral Agreement   **0 IRTB 68**
SIGNED: 12 Nov 69
HEADNOTE: TRADE
TOPIC: General Trade
PARTIES:
  Iran
  Thailand

433111   Bilateral Treaty   **0 IRTB 69**
SIGNED: 17 Apr 69
HEADNOTE: GENERAL RELATIONS
TOPIC: General Amity
PARTIES:
  Iran
  Tunisia

433112   Bilateral Agreement   **0 IRTB 69**
SIGNED: 17 Apr 69
HEADNOTE: CULTURAL
TOPIC: Culture
PARTIES:
  Iran
  Tunisia

433113   Bilateral Agreement   **0 IRTB 69**
SIGNED: 20 Jul 68
HEADNOTE: TRADE
TOPIC: General Trade
PARTIES:
  Iran
  Tunisia

433114   Bilateral Agreement   **0 IRTB 69**
SIGNED: 17 Apr 69
HEADNOTE: VISA ABOLITION
TOPIC: Visas
PARTIES:
  Iran
  Tunisia

433115   Bilateral Agreement   **0 IRTB 74**
SIGNED: 2 Dec 54
HEADNOTE: FRONTIER REGULATION & FINANCE
TOPIC: Admin Cooperation
PARTIES:
  Iran
  USSR (Soviet Union)

433116   Bilateral Protocol   **0 IRTB 74**
SIGNED: 7 May 70
HEADNOTE: BORDER REDEMARCATION
TOPIC: Territory Boundary
PARTIES:
  Iran
  USSR (Soviet Union)

433117   Bilateral Protocol   **0 IRTB 75**
SIGNED: 15 Oct 56
HEADNOTE: IRAN-TURKEY-USSR BORDERS
TOPIC: Territory Boundary

PARTIES:
  Iran
  USSR (Soviet Union)

433118   Bilateral Protocol   **0 IRTB 75**
SIGNED: 30 Jun 48
HEADNOTE: IRAN-AFGHAN-USSR BORDERS
TOPIC: Territory Boundary
PARTIES:
  Iran
  USSR (Soviet Union)

433119   Bilateral Protocol   **0 IRTB 78**
SIGNED: 13 Mar 67
HEADNOTE: IMPORT NON-INSPECTED ANIMALS
TOPIC: Sanitation
PARTIES:
  Iran
  USSR (Soviet Union)

433120   Bilateral Protocol   **0 IRTB 78**
SIGNED: 24 Dec 66
HEADNOTE: DISEASE CONTROL PROGRAM
TOPIC: Sanitation
PARTIES:
  Iran
  USSR (Soviet Union)

433121   Bilateral Exchange   **0 IRTB 79**
SIGNED: 17 Jan 66
HEADNOTE: CAPTURED AIR PHOTOS
TOPIC: Admin Cooperation
PARTIES:
  Iran
  USSR (Soviet Union)

433122   Bilateral Agreement   **0 IRTB 79**
SIGNED: 22 Aug 66
HEADNOTE: CULTURAL
TOPIC: Culture
PARTIES:
  Iran
  USSR (Soviet Union)

433123   Bilateral Agreement   **0 IRTB 79**
SIGNED: 17 Aug 64
HEADNOTE: AIR TRANSPORT
TOPIC: Air Transport
PARTIES:
  Iran
  USSR (Soviet Union)

433124   Bilateral Exchange   **0 IRTB 79**
SIGNED: 18 Jul 71
HEADNOTE: AIR TRANSPORT TAX EXEMPTIONS
TOPIC: Taxation
PARTIES:
  Iran
  USSR (Soviet Union)

433125   Bilateral Exchange   **0 IRTB 80**
SIGNED: 14 Jan 66
HEADNOTE: ABOLITION VISA TAX
TOPIC: Visas
PARTIES:
  Iran
  USSR (Soviet Union)

433126   Bilateral Agreement   **0 IRTB 80**
SIGNED: 30 Jul 70
HEADNOTE: FIVE YEAR TRADE
TOPIC: General Trade
PARTIES:
  Iran
  USSR (Soviet Union)

433127   Bilateral Agreement   **0 IRTB 80**
SIGNED: 20 Jun 64
HEADNOTE: PAYMENT
TOPIC: Finance
PARTIES:
  Iran
  USSR (Soviet Union)

433128   Bilateral Agreement   **0 IRTB 80**
SIGNED: 27 Jul 63
HEADNOTE: DAM, DREDGING, FISHERIES
TOPIC: Non-IBRD Project
PARTIES:
  Iran
  USSR (Soviet Union)

433129   Bilateral Agreement   **0 IRTB 81**
SIGNED: 13 Jan 66
HEADNOTE: STEEL & TOOL MAKING PLANT
TOPIC: Non-IBRD Project
PARTIES:
  Iran
  USSR (Soviet Union)

433130   Bilateral Agreement   **0 IRTB 81**
SIGNED: 13 Jan 66
HEADNOTE: TRADE IN GAS & MACHINERY
TOPIC: Commodity Trade
PARTIES:
  Iran
  USSR (Soviet Union)

433131   Bilateral Agreement   **0 IRTB 81**
SIGNED: 22 Jun 68
HEADNOTE: ECONOMIC & TECHNICAL COOPER-
ATION
TOPIC: General Economic
PARTIES:
  Iran
  USSR (Soviet Union)

433132   Bilateral Agreement   **0 IRTB 81**
SIGNED: 30 Jul 70
HEADNOTE: LONG-TERM TRADE
TOPIC: General Trade
PARTIES:
  Iran
  USSR (Soviet Union)

433133   Bilateral Agreement   **0 IRTB 81**
SIGNED: 25 Feb 71
HEADNOTE: SCIENTIFIC & TECHNICAL COOPER-
ATION
TOPIC: Scientific Project
PARTIES:
  Iran
  USSR (Soviet Union)

433134   Bilateral Protocol   **0 IRTB 82**
SIGNED: 30 Jul 70
HEADNOTE: JOINT STOCK TRANSPORT COM-
PANY
TOPIC: Specific Property
PARTIES:
  Iran
  USSR (Soviet Union)

433135   Bilateral Convention   **0 IRTB 83**
SIGNED: 5 Dec 63
HEADNOTE: CULTURAL & ECONOMIC & SCIEN-
TIFIC COOPERATION
TOPIC: Health/Educ/Welfare
PARTIES:
  Iran
  Yugoslavia

433136   Bilateral Agreement   **0 IRTB 83**
SIGNED: 24 Apr 66
HEADNOTE: ECONOMIC & TECHNICAL COOPER-
ATION
TOPIC: General Economic
PARTIES:
  Iran
  Yugoslavia

433137   Bilateral Agreement   **0 IRTB 83**
SIGNED: 16 Apr 70
HEADNOTE: VISA ABOLITION
TOPIC: Visas
PARTIES:
  Iran
  Yugoslavia

433138   Bilateral Agreement   0 IRTB 85
SIGNED: 14 Oct 63
HEADNOTE: TRADE
TOPIC: General Trade
PARTIES:
 Iran
 EEC (Econ Commnty)

433139   Bilateral Agreement   0 IRTB 86
SIGNED: 6 Oct 59
HEADNOTE: GRANT-IN-AID
TOPIC: Direct Aid
PARTIES:
 Iran
 UN Special Fund

433140   Bilateral Agreement   0 IRTB 86
SIGNED: 21 Nov 63
HEADNOTE: GRANT-IN-AID
TOPIC: Direct Aid
PARTIES:
 Iran
 UNICEF (Children)

433141   Bilateral Agreement   0 IRTB 86
SIGNED: 10 May 67
HEADNOTE: INSTALL EXPERIMENTAL REACTOR
TOPIC: Atomic Energy
PARTIES:
 Iran
 IAEA (Atom Energy)

433142   Bilateral Agreement   0 IRTB 87
SIGNED: 4 Mar 69
HEADNOTE: ATOMIC SECURITY MEASURES
TOPIC: Atomic Energy
PARTIES:
 Iran
 IAEA (Atom Energy)

433143   Bilateral Agreement   0 IRTB 87
SIGNED: 7 Jun 67
HEADNOTE: PROVIDE URANIUM FOR REACTOR
TOPIC: Atomic Energy
PARTIES:
 Iran
 IAEA (Atom Energy)

433144   Bilateral Agreement   0 IRTB 87
SIGNED: 16 Dec 68
HEADNOTE: ADULT LITERACY PROJECT
TOPIC: Non-IBRD Project
PARTIES:
 Iran
 UNESCO (Educ/Cult)

433145   Bilateral Agreement   0 IRTB 87
SIGNED: 7 Sep 55
HEADNOTE: TECHNICAL COOPERATION
TOPIC: Tech Assistance
PARTIES:
 Iran
 WHO (World Health)

435002   Bilateral Agreement   63 ITGU 9
SIGNED: 10 Dec 60
HEADNOTE: ECONOMIC & TECHNICAL COOPER-
ATION
TOPIC: Tech Assistance
PARTIES:
 Afghanistan
 Italy

435003   Bilateral Agreement   57 ITGU 263
SIGNED: 22 Jun 57
HEADNOTE: QUESTIONS ON 10 FEB 47 TREATY
TOPIC: Peace/Disarmament
PARTIES:
 Albania
 Italy

435006   Bilateral Exchange   58 ITGU 244
SIGNED: 11 Jun 58
HEADNOTE: MARITIME NAVIGATION

TOPIC: Water Transport
PARTIES:
 Albania
 Italy

435009   Bilateral Convention   57 ITGU 87
SIGNED: 12 Jan 55
HEADNOTE: JUDICIAL ASSISTANCE
TOPIC: Admin Cooperation
PARTIES:
 Algeria
 Italy

435010   Bilateral Agreement   67 ITGU 137
SIGNED: 3 Jun 65
HEADNOTE: AERIAL SERVICES
TOPIC: Air Transport
PARTIES:
 Algeria
 Italy

435013   Bilateral Agreement   48 ITGU 179
SIGNED: 18 Feb 48
HEADNOTE: AIR TRANSPORT
TOPIC: Air Transport
PARTIES:
 Argentina
 Italy

435014   Bilateral Exchange   52 ITGU 22
SIGNED: 12 Apr 49
HEADNOTE: NAVIGATION DOUBLE TAXATION
TOPIC: Taxation
PARTIES:
 Argentina
 Italy

435017   Bilateral Protocol   58 ITGU 120
SIGNED: 25 Nov 57
HEADNOTE: EMIGRANT PENSIONS
TOPIC: Health/Educ/Welfare
PARTIES:
 Argentina
 Italy

435021   Bilateral Exchange   63 ITGU 9
SIGNED: 1 Aug 60
HEADNOTE: INHERITANCE TAX
TOPIC: Taxation
PARTIES:
 Argentina
 Italy

435022   Bilateral Agreement   63 ITGU 86
SIGNED: 12 Apr 61
HEADNOTE: CULTURAL AGREEMENT
TOPIC: Culture
PARTIES:
 Argentina
 Italy

435023   Bilateral Convention   63 ITGU 8
SIGNED: 12 Apr 61
HEADNOTE: SOCIAL INSURANCES
TOPIC: Non-ILO Labor
PARTIES:
 Argentina
 Italy

435024   Bilateral Agreement   6 ITGU 6
SIGNED: 27 Jul 60
HEADNOTE: PERSONS & GOODS TRAFFIC
TOPIC: Land Transport
PARTIES:
 Italy
 Yugoslavia

435027   Bilateral Agreement   47 ITGU 295
SIGNED: 5 Sep 46
HEADNOTE: ALTO ADIGE
TOPIC: Peace/Disarmament
PARTIES:
 Austria
 Italy

435028   Bilateral Convention   50 ITGU 44
SIGNED: 9 Nov 48
HEADNOTE: RAILROAD REGULATIONS
TOPIC: Land Transport
PARTIES:
 Austria
 Italy

435029   Bilateral Convention   51 ITGU 71
SIGNED: 9 Nov 48
HEADNOTE: ROAD REGULATIONS
TOPIC: Land Transport
PARTIES:
 Austria
 Italy

435030   Bilateral Agreement   51 ITGU 201
SIGNED: 12 May 49
HEADNOTE: TRADE TRANSPORT REGULATIONS
TOPIC: General Trade
PARTIES:
 Austria
 Italy

435031   Bilateral Agreement   50 ITGU 137
SIGNED: 19 May 49
HEADNOTE: COMMERCIAL
TOPIC: General Trade
PARTIES:
 Austria
 Italy

435032   Bilateral Convention   54 ITGU 278
SIGNED: 30 Dec 50
HEADNOTE: SOCIAL INSURANCES
TOPIC: Non-ILO Labor
PARTIES:
 Austria
 Italy

435033   Bilateral Agreement   53 ITGU 78
SIGNED: 2 Aug 51
HEADNOTE: TRADE
TOPIC: General Trade
PARTIES:
 Austria
 Italy

435034   Bilateral Agreement   54 ITGU 143
SIGNED: 1 Feb 52
HEADNOTE: ORIGIN & TITLE OF PRODUCTS
TOPIC: Patents/Copyrights
PARTIES:
 Austria
 Italy

435035   Bilateral Agreement   54 ITGU 215
SIGNED: 14 Mar 53
HEADNOTE: CULTURAL RELATIONS
TOPIC: Culture
PARTIES:
 Austria
 Italy

435036   Bilateral Exchange   55 ITGU 75
SIGNED: 10 Jul 54
HEADNOTE: PUBLIC COURTS
TOPIC: Admin Cooperation
PARTIES:
 Austria
 Italy

435037   Bilateral Agreement   67 ITGU 3
SIGNED: 16 Jul 54
HEADNOTE: DOMESTIC SERVANTS UGOVIZZA
TOPIC: Admin Cooperation
PARTIES:
 Austria
 Italy

435039   Bilateral Agreement   65 ITGU 152
SIGNED: 24 Oct 63
HEADNOTE: MOTION PICTURES
TOPIC: Mass Media

PARTIES:
Austria
Italy

435041   Bilateral Agreement   50 ITGU 296
SIGNED: 20 Oct 50
HEADNOTE: MODIFIES 30 APR 48
TOPIC: Non-ILO Labor
PARTIES:
Belgium
Italy

435042   Bilateral Agreement   51 ITGU 45
SIGNED: 19 Jan 51
HEADNOTE: MODIFIES 30 APR 48
TOPIC: Non-ILO Labor
PARTIES:
Belgium
Italy

435043   Bilateral Agreement   51 ITGU 46
SIGNED: 19 Jan 51
HEADNOTE: MODIFIES 30 APR 48
TOPIC: Non-ILO Labor
PARTIES:
Belgium
Italy

435044   Bilateral Agreement   54 ITGU 244
SIGNED: 10 May 52
HEADNOTE: MODIFIES 30 APR 48
TOPIC: Non-ILO Labor
PARTIES:
Belgium
Italy

435045   Bilateral Convention   54 ITGU 185
SIGNED: 1 Aug 52
HEADNOTE: MODIFIES 30 APR 48
TOPIC: Non-ILO Labor
PARTIES:
Belgium
Italy

435046   Bilateral Agreement   53 ITGU 51
SIGNED: 24 Jan 52
HEADNOTE: PEACE TREATY (10 FEB 47)
TOPIC: Peace/Disarmament
PARTIES:
Belgium
Italy

435047   Bilateral Exchange   54 ITGU 123
SIGNED: 6 Aug 53
HEADNOTE: MODIFY AGREEMENT 29 SEPT 38
TOPIC: Non-ILO Labor
PARTIES:
Belgium
Italy

435048   Bilateral Agreement   58 ITGU 9
SIGNED: 9 Dec 57
HEADNOTE: MODIFIES 30 APR 48
TOPIC: Non-ILO Labor
PARTIES:
Belgium
Italy

435049   Bilateral Agreement   58 ITGU 19
SIGNED: 10 Dec 57
HEADNOTE: MODIFIES 30 APR 48
TOPIC: Non-ILO Labor
PARTIES:
Belgium
Italy

435052   Bilateral Exchange   66 ITGU 165
SIGNED: 23 Apr 65
HEADNOTE: CULTURAL INSTITUTE EXEMPTION
TOPIC: Privil/Immunities
PARTIES:
Belgium
Italy

435054   Bilateral Agreement   50 ITGU 195
SIGNED: 8 Oct 49
HEADNOTE: PEACE TREATY (10 FEB 47)
TOPIC: Peace/Disarmament
PARTIES:
Brazil
Italy

435056   Bilateral Exchange   51 ITGU 36
SIGNED: 5 Jul 50
HEADNOTE: ECONOMIC COOPERATION
TOPIC: General Economic
PARTIES:
Brazil
Italy

435057   Bilateral Agreement   51 ITGU 38
SIGNED: 5 Jul 50
HEADNOTE: TRADE & PAYMENT
TOPIC: General Economic
PARTIES:
Brazil
Italy

435058   Bilateral Agreement   52 ITGU 169
SIGNED: 25 Jan 51
HEADNOTE: AIR TRANSPORT
TOPIC: Air Transport
PARTIES:
Brazil
Italy

435059   Bilateral Agreement   62 ITGU 240
SIGNED: 4 Oct 57
HEADNOTE: COMMERCIAL
TOPIC: Taxation
PARTIES:
Brazil
Italy

435060   Bilateral Agreement   60 ITGU 215
SIGNED: 6 Sep 58
HEADNOTE: MILITARY SERVICE
TOPIC: Milit Servic/Citiz
PARTIES:
Brazil
Italy

435061   Bilateral Agreement   60 ITGU 96
SIGNED: 6 Sep 58
HEADNOTE: ATOMIC ENERGY
TOPIC: Atomic Energy
PARTIES:
Brazil
Italy

435062   Bilateral Agreement   62 ITGU 153
SIGNED: 6 Sep 58
HEADNOTE: CULTURE
TOPIC: Culture
PARTIES:
Brazil
Italy

435065   Bilateral Agreement   63 ITGU 109
SIGNED: 9 Dec 60
HEADNOTE: EMIGRATION
TOPIC: Health/Educ/Welfare
PARTIES:
Brazil
Italy

435068   Bilateral Protocol   52 ITGU 224
SIGNED: 19 Dec 50
HEADNOTE: CUSTOMS
TOPIC: Customs
PARTIES:
Bulgaria
Italy

435074   Bilateral Exchange   55 ITGU 53
SIGNED: 12 Feb 54
HEADNOTE: CULTURAL RELATIONS
TOPIC: Culture

PARTIES:
Canada
Italy

435075   Bilateral Agreement   62 ITGU 22
SIGNED: 2 Feb 60
HEADNOTE: AIR SERVICE
TOPIC: Air Transport
PARTIES:
Canada
Italy

435077   Bilateral Exchange   48 ITGU 167
SIGNED: 2 Jul 47
HEADNOTE: MOST FAVORED NATION
TOPIC: Mostfavored Nation
PARTIES:
Czechoslovakia
Italy

435078   Bilateral Agreement   58 ITGU 129
SIGNED: 5 May 58
HEADNOTE: PAYMENT
TOPIC: Finance
PARTIES:
Czechoslovakia
Italy

435092   Bilateral Instrument   53 ITGU 77
SIGNED: 19 Jun 52
HEADNOTE: COMMERCE
TOPIC: General Trade
PARTIES:
Colombia
Italy

435094   Bilateral Agreement   66 ITGU 211
SIGNED: 7 Dec 62
HEADNOTE: AERIAL AGREEMENT
TOPIC: Air Transport
PARTIES:
Congo (Zaire)
Italy

435098   Bilateral Instrument   54 ITGU 198
SIGNED: 20 Feb 53
HEADNOTE: COMMERCE
TOPIC: General Trade
PARTIES:
Costa Rica
Italy

435099   Bilateral Treaty   47 ITGU 300
SIGNED: 30 Jun 47
HEADNOTE: PEACE TREATY
TOPIC: Peace/Disarmament
PARTIES:
Cuba
Italy

435104   Bilateral Treaty   51 ITGU 15
SIGNED: 27 Sep 49
HEADNOTE: PEACE TREATY
TOPIC: Peace/Disarmament
PARTIES:
Dominican Republic
Italy

435105   Bilateral Agreement   55 ITGU 124
SIGNED: 18 Feb 54
HEADNOTE: COMMERCE
TOPIC: General Trade
PARTIES:
Dominican Republic
Italy

435107   Bilateral Agreement   55 ITGU 80
SIGNED: 7 Mar 52
HEADNOTE: EQUAL EDUCATION DEGREES
TOPIC: Education
PARTIES:
Ecuador
Italy

435110   Bilateral Agreement   **48 ITGU 38**
SIGNED: 29 Nov 47
HEADNOTE: MODIFIES 10 FEB 47
TOPIC: Peace/Disarmament
PARTIES:
France
Italy

435111   Bilateral Convention   **49 ITGU 157**
SIGNED: 31 Mar 48
HEADNOTE: SOCIAL SECURITY & PENSIONS
TOPIC: Non-ILO Labor
PARTIES:
France
Italy

435112   Bilateral Agreement   **49 ITGU 247**
SIGNED: 29 May 48
HEADNOTE: INDUSTRIAL PROPERTY
TOPIC: Patents/Copyrights
PARTIES:
France
Italy

435113   Bilateral Agreement   **49 ITGU 250**
SIGNED: 29 May 48
HEADNOTE: PRODUCT ORIGIN & TITLES
TOPIC: Patents/Copyrights
PARTIES:
France
Italy

435114   Bilateral Agreement   **53 ITGU 91**
SIGNED: 3 Feb 49
HEADNOTE: CIVIL AERONAUTICS
TOPIC: Air Transport
PARTIES:
France
Italy

435115   Bilateral Protocol   **50 ITGU 89**
SIGNED: 30 May 49
HEADNOTE: CHANGE PEACE TREATY (10 FEB 47)
TOPIC: Peace/Disarmament
PARTIES:
France
Italy

435116   Bilateral Exchange   **52 ITGU 124**
SIGNED: 26 Sep 49
HEADNOTE: TRADEMARKS & TITLE OF ORIGIN
TOPIC: Patents/Copyrights
PARTIES:
France
Italy

435117   Bilateral Agreement   **52 ITGU 213**
SIGNED: 4 Nov 49
HEADNOTE: CULTURE
TOPIC: Culture
PARTIES:
France
Italy

435118   Bilateral Agreement   **53 ITGU 296**
SIGNED: 7 Mar 50
HEADNOTE: MAIL, TELEPHONE, TELEGRAPH
TOPIC: Gen Communications
PARTIES:
France
Italy

435119   Bilateral Exchange   **52 ITGU 127**
SIGNED: 14 Mar 50
HEADNOTE: TITLE OF ORIGIN
TOPIC: Patents/Copyrights
PARTIES:
France
Italy

435121   Bilateral Exchange   **52 ITGU 203**
SIGNED: 20 Jun 50
HEADNOTE: CEMETERIES OF WAR
TOPIC: Other Military

PARTIES:
France
Italy

435122   Bilateral Agreement   **50 ITGU 240**
SIGNED: 4 Oct 50
HEADNOTE: AMENDS 31 MAR 48
TOPIC: Non-ILO Labor
PARTIES:
France
Italy

435123   Bilateral Convention   **52 ITGU 287**
SIGNED: 29 Jan 51
HEADNOTE: MODANE RAILWAY
TOPIC: Land Transport
PARTIES:
France
Italy

435124   Bilateral Convention   **52 ITGU 10**
SIGNED: 29 Jan 51
HEADNOTE: BORDER TRAFFIC
TOPIC: Visas
PARTIES:
France
Italy

435125   Bilateral Convention   **52 ITGU 24**
SIGNED: 29 Jan 51
HEADNOTE: ANIMAL BORDER REGULATION
TOPIC: Sanitation
PARTIES:
France
Italy

435126   Bilateral Exchange   **52 ITGU 68**
SIGNED: 2 Feb 51
HEADNOTE: ITALIAN GOODS IN TUNISIA
TOPIC: General Trade
PARTIES:
France
Italy

435127   Bilateral Agreement   **53 ITGU 22**
SIGNED: 21 Mar 51
HEADNOTE: EMIGRATION
TOPIC: Health/Educ/Welfare
PARTIES:
France
Italy

435128   Bilateral Agreement   **53 ITGU 22**
SIGNED: 21 Mar 51
HEADNOTE: SEASONAL LABOR MIGRATION
TOPIC: Non-ILO Labor
PARTIES:
France
Italy

435129   Bilateral Agreement   **53 ITGU 22**
SIGNED: 21 Mar 51
HEADNOTE: MIGRANT LABOR
TOPIC: Non-ILO Labor
PARTIES:
France
Italy

435132   Bilateral Exchange   **52 ITGU 127**
SIGNED: 5 Apr 52
HEADNOTE: CERTIFICATE OF ORIGIN
TOPIC: Patents/Copyrights
PARTIES:
France
Italy

435133   Bilateral Exchange   **53 ITGU 51**
SIGNED: 2 Dec 52
HEADNOTE: ITALIAN CLAIMS IN TUNISIA
TOPIC: Claims and Debts
PARTIES:
France
Italy

435137   Bilateral Exchange   **57 ITGU 137**
SIGNED: 8 Jan 55
HEADNOTE: MODIFIES 5 APR 52
TOPIC: Patents/Copyrights
PARTIES:
France
Italy

435138   Bilateral Exchange   **57 ITGU 68**
SIGNED: 8 Jan 55
HEADNOTE: MODIFIES 5 APR 52
TOPIC: Patents/Copyrights
PARTIES:
France
Italy

435139   Bilateral Convention   **58 ITGU 99**
SIGNED: 12 Jan 55
HEADNOTE: CONSULAR AGREEMENT
TOPIC: Consul/Citizenship
PARTIES:
France
Italy

435140   Bilateral Convention   **57 ITGU 87**
SIGNED: 12 Jan 55
HEADNOTE: JUDICIAL ASSISTANCE
TOPIC: Admin Cooperation
PARTIES:
France
Italy

435141   Bilateral Agreement   **56 ITGU 13**
SIGNED: 12 Jan 55
HEADNOTE: ELECTRICAL PLANT FUNCTIONING
TOPIC: Specific Resources
PARTIES:
France
Italy

435142   Bilateral Instrument   **57 ITGU 139**
SIGNED: 14 Feb 56
HEADNOTE: AMENDS 4 NOV 49
TOPIC: Culture
PARTIES:
France
Italy

435146   Bilateral Agreement   **58 ITGU 123**
SIGNED: 25 Jan 58
HEADNOTE: AMENDS 21 MAR 51
TOPIC: Non-ILO Labor
PARTIES:
France
Italy

435157   Bilateral Convention   **65 ITGU 181**
SIGNED: 11 Oct 63
HEADNOTE: ROAD CONTROLS
TOPIC: Land Transport
PARTIES:
France
Italy

435159   Bilateral Agreement   **65 ITGU 193**
SIGNED: 25 Mar 65
HEADNOTE: AMENDS 14 MAR 53
TOPIC: Land Transport
PARTIES:
France
Italy

435162   Bilateral Convention   **53 ITGU 90**
SIGNED: 26 Oct 51
HEADNOTE: SOCIAL SECURITY IN SAAR
TOPIC: Non-ILO Labor
PARTIES:
Germany, West
Italy

435178   Bilateral Agreement   **66 ITGU 214**
SIGNED: 20 Dec 64
HEADNOTE: WAR CLAIMS SETTLEMENT
TOPIC: Dispute Settlement

PARTIES:
Germany, West
Italy

435180 Bilateral Agreement **65 ITGU 193**
SIGNED: 20 Jun 63
HEADNOTE: AIR TRANSPORT
TOPIC: Air Transport
PARTIES:
Ghana
Italy

435182 Bilateral Agreement **55 ITGU 286**
SIGNED: 31 Jul 54
HEADNOTE: CULTURE
TOPIC: Culture
PARTIES:
Italy
Japan

435186 Bilateral Exchange **48 ITGU 168**
SIGNED: 16 Jan 47
HEADNOTE: ITALIAN LABOR FOR FOUNDRIES
TOPIC: Non-ILO Labor
PARTIES:
Italy
UK Great Britain

435192 Bilateral Exchange **63 ITGU 99**
SIGNED: 20 Apr 61
HEADNOTE: WAR GRAVES MAINTAINENCE
TOPIC: Other Military
PARTIES:
Italy
UK Great Britain

435194 Bilateral Convention **67 ITGU 230**
SIGNED: 15 Feb 66
HEADNOTE: DOUBLE TAXATION & TAX EVASION
TOPIC: Taxation
PARTIES:
Italy
UK Great Britain

435195 Bilateral Treaty **50 ITGU 265**
SIGNED: 5 Nov 48
HEADNOTE: COMMERCE & NAVIGATION
TOPIC: General Amity
PARTIES:
Greece
Italy

435196 Bilateral Convention **51 ITGU 205**
SIGNED: 5 Nov 48
HEADNOTE: JUDICIAL COOPERATION
TOPIC: Admin Cooperation
PARTIES:
Greece
Italy

435200 Bilateral Agreement **65 ITGU 280**
SIGNED: 30 Oct 62
HEADNOTE: AERIAL AGREEMENT
TOPIC: Air Transport
PARTIES:
Guinea
Italy

435204 Bilateral Treaty **47 ITGU 140**
SIGNED: 12 May 47
HEADNOTE: REESTABLISH PEACE
TOPIC: Peace/Disarmament
PARTIES:
Honduras
Italy

435206 Bilateral Exchange **66 ITGU 218**
SIGNED: 20 Aug 64
HEADNOTE: MODIFIES 17 MAR 57
TOPIC: General Amity
PARTIES:
India
Italy

435208 Bilateral Treaty **57 ITGU 149**
SIGNED: 26 Jan 55
HEADNOTE: COMMERCE AND NAVIGATION
TOPIC: General Trade
PARTIES:
Iran
Italy

435210 Bilateral Agreement **58 ITGU 39**
SIGNED: 29 Jan 58
HEADNOTE: ORIGIN CERTIFICATE & COMMERCE
TOPIC: General Economic
PARTIES:
Iran
Italy

435218 Bilateral Agreement **55 ITGU 17**
SIGNED: 5 Mar 54
HEADNOTE: COMMERCE
TOPIC: General Trade
PARTIES:
Israel
Italy

435219 Bilateral Agreement **56 ITGU 292**
SIGNED: 28 Jun 54
HEADNOTE: QUESTIONS IN SUSPENSION
TOPIC: Dispute Settlement
PARTIES:
Israel
Italy

435220 Bilateral Agreement **55 ITGU 73**
SIGNED: 23 Dec 50
HEADNOTE: PEACE TREATY OPTION QUESTIONS
TOPIC: Peace/Disarmament
PARTIES:
Italy
Yugoslavia

435221 Bilateral Agreement **55 ITGU 73**
SIGNED: 23 Dec 50
HEADNOTE: COPYRIGHT
TOPIC: Patents/Copyrights
PARTIES:
Italy
Yugoslavia

435222 Bilateral Agreement **52 ITGU 142**
SIGNED: 23 Dec 50
HEADNOTE: AIR TRANSPORT
TOPIC: Air Transport
PARTIES:
Italy
Yugoslavia

435223 Bilateral Exchange **58 ITGU 136**
SIGNED: 23 Dec 50
HEADNOTE: DIPLOMATIC PROPERTY IN ROME
TOPIC: Consul/Citizenship
PARTIES:
Italy
Yugoslavia

435229 Bilateral Agreement **57 ITGU 32**
SIGNED: 31 Mar 55
HEADNOTE: BORDER AREA
TOPIC: General Trade
PARTIES:
Italy
Yugoslavia

435230 Bilateral Agreement **57 ITGU 32**
SIGNED: 31 Mar 55
HEADNOTE: BORDER AREA
TOPIC: General Trade
PARTIES:
Italy
Yugoslavia

435231 Bilateral Agreement **58 ITGU 64**
SIGNED: 18 Jul 57
HEADNOTE: GORIZIA WATER SUPPLY
TOPIC: Specific Resources

PARTIES:
Italy
Yugoslavia

435232 Bilateral Convention **60 ITGU 210**
SIGNED: 14 Nov 57
HEADNOTE: SOCIAL INSURANCE
TOPIC: Non-ILO Labor
PARTIES:
Italy
Yugoslavia

435238 Bilateral Convention **62 ITGU 255**
SIGNED: 5 Oct 59
HEADNOTE: BORDER RAILROAD SERVICE
TOPIC: Land Transport
PARTIES:
Italy
Yugoslavia

435241 Bilateral Agreement **63 ITGU 30**
SIGNED: 3 Dec 60
HEADNOTE: CULTURE
TOPIC: Culture
PARTIES:
Italy
Yugoslavia

435242 Bilateral Convention **63 ITGU 15**
SIGNED: 3 Dec 60
HEADNOTE: CONSULAR
TOPIC: Consul/Citizenship
PARTIES:
Italy
Yugoslavia

435243 Bilateral Convention **62 ITGU 237**
SIGNED: 3 Dec 60
HEADNOTE: CIVIL & ADMINISTRATIVE LAW
TOPIC: Admin Cooperation
PARTIES:
Italy
Yugoslavia

435244 Bilateral Agreement **62 ITGU 80**
SIGNED: 15 Sep 61
HEADNOTE: RESITUTION CULTURAL GOODS
TOPIC: Culture
PARTIES:
Italy
Yugoslavia

435245 Bilateral Agreement **65 ITGU 192**
SIGNED: 31 Oct 62
HEADNOTE: BORDER TRAFFIC
TOPIC: Visas
PARTIES:
Italy
Yugoslavia

435252 Bilateral Agreement **67 ITGU 210**
SIGNED: 5 Nov 65
HEADNOTE: FISHING IN YUGOSLAV WATERS
TOPIC: Specific Resources
PARTIES:
Italy
Yugoslavia

435253 Bilateral Agreement **66 ITGU 244**
SIGNED: 10 Nov 65
HEADNOTE: INFORMATION INSTITUTES
TOPIC: Admin Cooperation
PARTIES:
Italy
Yugoslavia

435254 Bilateral Agreement **67 ITGU 169**
SIGNED: 10 Nov 65
HEADNOTE: SMUGGLING
TOPIC: Admin Cooperation
PARTIES:
Italy
Yugoslavia

435256   Bilateral Convention   **50 ITGU 187**
SIGNED: 15 Feb 49
HEADNOTE: JUDICIAL COOPERATION
TOPIC: Admin Cooperation
PARTIES:
  Italy
  Lebanon

435257   Bilateral Treaty   **51 ITGU 106**
SIGNED: 15 Feb 49
HEADNOTE: FRIENDSHIP, COMMERCE, NAVIGA-
  TION
TOPIC: General Amity
PARTIES:
  Italy
  Lebanon

435259   Bilateral Agreement   **57 ITGU 237**
SIGNED: 2 Oct 56
HEADNOTE: ECONOMIC COOPERATION
TOPIC: Tech Assistance
PARTIES:
  Italy
  Libya

435261   Bilateral Agreement   **49 ITGU 166**
SIGNED: 6 Apr 48
HEADNOTE: MIGRANT AGRICULTURAL LABOR
TOPIC: Non-ILO Labor
PARTIES:
  Italy
  Luxembourg

435262   Bilateral Convention   **54 ITGU 194**
SIGNED: 29 May 51
HEADNOTE: SOCIAL INSURANCE
TOPIC: Non-ILO Labor
PARTIES:
  Italy
  Luxembourg

435263   Bilateral Exchange   **55 ITGU 162**
SIGNED: 5 Jun 54
HEADNOTE: WORLD WAR II CLAIMS
TOPIC: Reparations
PARTIES:
  Italy
  Luxembourg

435265   Bilateral Agreement   **58 ITGU 121**
SIGNED: 3 May 56
HEADNOTE: CULTURE
TOPIC: Culture
PARTIES:
  Italy
  Luxembourg

435273   Bilateral Agreement   **52 ITGU 69**
SIGNED: 15 Sep 49
HEADNOTE: COMMERCE
TOPIC: General Trade
PARTIES:
  Italy
  Mexico

435280   Bilateral Exchange   **52 ITGU 226**
SIGNED: 4 Dec 51
HEADNOTE: WORLD WAR II CLAIMS
TOPIC: Reparations
PARTIES:
  Italy
  Monaco

435282   Bilateral Convention   **63 ITGU 122**
SIGNED: 11 Oct 61
HEADNOTE: SOCIAL INSURANCE
TOPIC: Non-ILO Labor
PARTIES:
  Italy
  Monaco

435284   Bilateral Agreement   **54 ITGU 107**
SIGNED: 20 Apr 53
HEADNOTE: COMMERCE

TOPIC: General Trade
PARTIES:
  Italy
  Norway

435286   Bilateral Agreement   **52 ITGU 207**
SIGNED: 5 Dec 51
HEADNOTE: CULTURE
TOPIC: Culture
PARTIES:
  Italy
  Netherlands

435291   Bilateral Exchange   **47 ITGU 127**
SIGNED: 29 Mar 47
HEADNOTE: PEACE
TOPIC: Peace/Disarmament
PARTIES:
  Italy
  Panama

435294   Bilateral Agreement   **61 ITGU 76**
SIGNED: 8 Jul 59
HEADNOTE: COMMERCE
TOPIC: General Trade
PARTIES:
  Italy
  Paraguay

435300   Bilateral Agreement   **63 ITGU 36**
SIGNED: 8 Apr 61
HEADNOTE: CULTURE
TOPIC: Culture
PARTIES:
  Italy
  Peru

435301   Bilateral Agreement   **50 ITGU 130**
SIGNED: 15 Jun 49
HEADNOTE: COMMERCE
TOPIC: General Trade
PARTIES:
  Italy
  Poland

435302   Bilateral Agreement   **58 ITGU 105**
SIGNED: 25 Feb 58
HEADNOTE: PAYMENT
TOPIC: Finance
PARTIES:
  Italy
  Poland

435303   Bilateral Protocol   **58 ITGU 105**
SIGNED: 25 Feb 58
HEADNOTE: TRADE COMMISSION
TOPIC: Admin Cooperation
PARTIES:
  Italy
  Poland

435311   Bilateral Convention   **62 ITGU 6**
SIGNED: 20 Dec 60
HEADNOTE: FINANCE
TOPIC: Finance
PARTIES:
  Italy
  San Marino

435313   Bilateral Agreement   **53 ITGU 67**
SIGNED: 25 May 50
HEADNOTE: AIR SERVICE
TOPIC: Air Transport
PARTIES:
  Italy
  United Arab Rep

435321   Bilateral Agreement   **66 ITGU 215**
SIGNED: 23 Mar 65
HEADNOTE: INDEMNITY ITALIAN INTERESTS
TOPIC: Claims and Debts
PARTIES:
  Italy
  United Arab Rep

435323   Bilateral Protocol   **52 ITGU 39**
SIGNED: 25 Nov 50
HEADNOTE: CUSTOMS
TOPIC: Customs
PARTIES:
  Italy
  Romania

435324   Bilateral Convention   **66 ITGU 290**
SIGNED: 14 Apr 65
HEADNOTE: VETERINARY
TOPIC: Sanitation
PARTIES:
  Italy
  Romania

435328   Bilateral Convention   **55 ITGU 45**
SIGNED: 20 Oct 53
HEADNOTE: TELEPHONE SERVICE
TOPIC: Telecommunications
PARTIES:
  Italy
  San Marino

435329   Bilateral Convention   **62 ITGU 6**
SIGNED: 20 Nov 58
HEADNOTE: ROAD IMPROVEMENT
TOPIC: Land Transport
PARTIES:
  Italy
  San Marino

435332   Bilateral Agreement   **62 ITGU 6**
SIGNED: 20 Dec 60
HEADNOTE: WAR DAMAGES
TOPIC: Reparations
PARTIES:
  Italy
  San Marino

435333   Bilateral Exchange   **66 ITGU 21**
SIGNED: 26 Oct 63
HEADNOTE: TOBACCO
TOPIC: Commodity Trade
PARTIES:
  Italy
  San Marino

435335   Bilateral Exchange   **47 ITGU 169**
SIGNED: 16 Apr 45
HEADNOTE: OSTIA AREA
TOPIC: Territory Boundary
PARTIES:
  Italy
  Vatican/Holy See

435337   Bilateral Agreement   **48 ITGU 190**
SIGNED: 31 Apr 47
HEADNOTE: EXTRATERRITORIAL ZONES
TOPIC: Territory Boundary
PARTIES:
  Italy
  Vatican/Holy See

435338   Bilateral Agreement   **50 ITGU 99**
SIGNED: 24 Apr 48
HEADNOTE: PAPAL VILLAS
TOPIC: Territory Boundary
PARTIES:
  Italy
  Vatican/Holy See

435339   Bilateral Agreement   **52 ITGU 150**
SIGNED: 8 Oct 51
HEADNOTE: VATICAN RADIOS
TOPIC: Telecommunications
PARTIES:
  Italy
  Vatican/Holy See

435340   Bilateral Convention   **64 ITGU 281**
SIGNED: 31 Jul 62
HEADNOTE: MONETARY
TOPIC: Finance

PARTIES:
Italy
Vatican/Holy See

435343   Bilateral Treaty   **62 ITGU 148**
SIGNED: 1 Jul 60
HEADNOTE: FRIENDSHIP
TOPIC: General Amity
PARTIES:
Italy
Somalia

435344   Bilateral Convention   **62 ITGU 148**
SIGNED: 1 Jul 60
HEADNOTE: CONSULAR CONVENTION
TOPIC: Consul/Citizenship
PARTIES:
Italy
Somalia

435345   Bilateral Agreement   **62 ITGU 148**
SIGNED: 1 Jul 60
HEADNOTE: TRADE & PAYMENTS
TOPIC: General Economic
PARTIES:
Italy
Somalia

435347   Bilateral Agreement   **62 ITGU 148**
SIGNED: 1 Jul 60
HEADNOTE: AIR SERVICE
TOPIC: Air Transport
PARTIES:
Italy
Somalia

435348   Bilateral Agreement   **63 ITGU 36**
SIGNED: 26 Apr 61
HEADNOTE: CULTURE
TOPIC: Culture
PARTIES:
Italy
Somalia

435352   Bilateral Agreement   **58 ITGU 237**
SIGNED: 8 May 58
HEADNOTE: PAYMENT
TOPIC: Finance
PARTIES:
Italy
Spain

435355   Bilateral Exchange   **66 ITGU 159**
SIGNED: 28 Jun 61
HEADNOTE: INHERITANCE TAX
TOPIC: Taxation
PARTIES:
Italy
Spain

435358   Bilateral Exchange   **65 ITGU 279**
SIGNED: 18 Aug 64
HEADNOTE: US MARRIAGES IN ITALY
TOPIC: Admin Cooperation
PARTIES:
Italy
USA (United States)

435361   Bilateral Agreement   **48 ITGU 27**
SIGNED: 19 Apr 47
HEADNOTE: MIGRANT LABOR
TOPIC: Non-ILO Labor
PARTIES:
Italy
Sweden

435362   Bilateral Exchange   **54 ITGU 144**
SIGNED: 17 Jun 52
HEADNOTE: INSTITUTE FINANCES
TOPIC: Finance
PARTIES:
Italy
Sweden

435367   Bilateral Exchange   **52 ITGU 29**
SIGNED: 24 Mar 50
HEADNOTE: SWISS SHIPS ITALIAN PORTS
TOPIC: Water Transport
PARTIES:
Italy
Switzerland

435368   Bilateral Agreement   **52 ITGU 57**
SIGNED: 21 Oct 50
HEADNOTE: COMMERCE
TOPIC: General Trade
PARTIES:
Italy
Switzerland

435372   Bilateral Convention   **53 ITGU 91**
SIGNED: 5 Apr 51
HEADNOTE: BORDER CHIASSO BRIDGE
TOPIC: Territory Boundary
PARTIES:
Italy
Switzerland

435376   Bilateral Protocol   **57 ITGU 159**
SIGNED: 1 Jun 56
HEADNOTE: TELEPHONE
TOPIC: Telecommunications
PARTIES:
Italy
Switzerland

435377   Bilateral Instrument   **58 ITGU 50**
SIGNED: 31 Oct 56
HEADNOTE: INHERITANCE
TOPIC: Taxation
PARTIES:
Italy
Switzerland

435382   Bilateral Protocol   **62 ITGU 312**
SIGNED: 22 Nov 58
HEADNOTE: LUMBER & FOREST PRODUCTS
TOPIC: Commodity Trade
PARTIES:
Italy
Switzerland

435385   Bilateral Convention   **62 ITGU 212**
SIGNED: 4 Mar 60
HEADNOTE: BRIDGE CONSTRUCTION
TOPIC: Land Transport
PARTIES:
Italy
Switzerland

435396   Bilateral Agreement   **65 ITGU 54**
SIGNED: 10 Aug 64
HEADNOTE: MIGRANT LABOR
TOPIC: Non-ILO Labor
PARTIES:
Italy
Switzerland

435398   Bilateral Agreement   **52 ITGU 206**
SIGNED: 5 Apr 51
HEADNOTE: RADIO LINK TRAPANI TUNISIA
TOPIC: Telecommunications
PARTIES:
Italy
Tunisia

435404   Bilateral Agreement   **52 ITGU 203**
SIGNED: 17 Jul 51
HEADNOTE: CULTURE
TOPIC: Culture
PARTIES:
Italy
Turkey

435406   Bilateral Agreement   **53 ITGU 27**
SIGNED: 24 Jan 52
HEADNOTE: COMMERCE
TOPIC: General Trade

PARTIES:
Italy
Turkey

435415   Bilateral Protocol   **52 ITGU 68**
SIGNED: 28 Mar 50
HEADNOTE: CUSTOMS
TOPIC: Customs
PARTIES:
Hungary
Italy

435416   Bilateral Agreement   **58 ITGU 19**
SIGNED: 17 Dec 57
HEADNOTE: PAYMENTS
TOPIC: Finance
PARTIES:
Hungary
Italy

435420   Bilateral Agreement   **50 ITGU 5**
SIGNED: 11 Dec 48
HEADNOTE: COMMERCE
TOPIC: General Trade
PARTIES:
Italy
USSR (Soviet Union)

435421   Bilateral Agreement   **58 ITGU 10**
SIGNED: 28 Dec 57
HEADNOTE: PAYMENT
TOPIC: Finance
PARTIES:
Italy
USSR (Soviet Union)

435425   Bilateral Protocol   **67 ITGU 231**
SIGNED: 22 Feb 65
HEADNOTE: AIR SERVICE
TOPIC: Air Transport
PARTIES:
Italy
USSR (Soviet Union)

435426   Bilateral Treaty   **48 ITGU 82**
SIGNED: 26 Feb 47
HEADNOTE: COMMERCE
TOPIC: General Trade
PARTIES:
Italy
Uruguay

435427   Bilateral Agreement   **65 ITGU 194**
SIGNED: 4 Jul 62
HEADNOTE: AIR TRANSPORT
TOPIC: Air Transport
PARTIES:
Italy
Venezuela

436001   Bilateral Instrument   **61 ITDI 347**
SIGNED: 30 Jan 59
HEADNOTE: CIVIL AVIATION
TOPIC: Air Transport
PARTIES:
Afghanistan
Italy

436004   Bilateral Exchange   **59 ITDI 216**
SIGNED: 22 Jun 57
HEADNOTE: ILLYRIA GUNBOAT
TOPIC: Admin Cooperation
PARTIES:
Albania
Italy

436005   Bilateral Exchange   **59 ITDI 216**
SIGNED: 22 Jun 57
HEADNOTE: ITALIAN DEAD
TOPIC: Other Military
PARTIES:
Albania
Italy

436007   Bilateral Exchange   63 ITDI 273
SIGNED: 21 Apr 62
HEADNOTE: AERIAL REGULATIONS
TOPIC: Air Transport
PARTIES:
  Albania
  Italy

436008   Bilateral Agreement   65 ITDI 115
SIGNED: 19 Dec 64
HEADNOTE: COMMERCE
TOPIC: General Trade
PARTIES:
  Albania
  Italy

436015   Bilateral Protocol   52 ITDI 223
SIGNED: 25 Jun 52
HEADNOTE: EMIGRATION & SETTLEMENT
TOPIC: Health/Educ/Welfare
PARTIES:
  Argentina
  Italy

436016   Bilateral Agreement   52 ITDI 225
SIGNED: 5 Dec 52
HEADNOTE: MOVIE PRODUCTION
TOPIC: Mass Media
PARTIES:
  Argentina
  Italy

436018   Bilateral Exchange   61 ITDI 245
SIGNED: 19 Nov 59
HEADNOTE: DIPLOMATIC VISAS
TOPIC: Visas
PARTIES:
  Argentina
  Italy

436019   Bilateral Exchange   62 ITDI 313
SIGNED: 21 Jan 60
HEADNOTE: CLARIFICATION OF 25 NOV 57
TOPIC: General Economic
PARTIES:
  Argentina
  Italy

436020   Bilateral Agreement   62 ITDI 314
SIGNED: 14 Jun 60
HEADNOTE: NUCLEAR ENERGY PEACEFUL USE
TOPIC: Atomic Energy
PARTIES:
  Argentina
  Italy

436024   Bilateral Agreement   62 ITDI 490
SIGNED: 12 Apr 61
HEADNOTE: SMALL BUSINESS LOANS
TOPIC: Loans and Credits
PARTIES:
  Argentina
  Italy

436040   Bilateral Exchange   66 ITDI 118
SIGNED: 2 Aug 65
HEADNOTE: AIR NAVIGATION
TOPIC: Air Transport
PARTIES:
  Austria
  Italy

436050   Bilateral Protocol   59 ITDI 245
SIGNED: 11 Dec 57
HEADNOTE: TREATMENT MIGRANT MINERS
TOPIC: Health/Educ/Welfare
PARTIES:
  Belgium
  Italy

436051   Bilateral Convention   65 ITDI 119
SIGNED: 21 Feb 64
HEADNOTE: OCCUPATIONAL DISEASES
TOPIC: Health/Educ/Welfare

PARTIES:
  Belgium
  Italy

436053   Bilateral Exchange   62 ITDI 317
SIGNED: 6 Dec 60
HEADNOTE: TOURIST VISAS
TOPIC: Visas
PARTIES:
  Bolivia
  Italy

436063   Bilateral Exchange   62 ITDI 319
SIGNED: 21 Apr 60
HEADNOTE: VISAS
TOPIC: Visas
PARTIES:
  Brazil
  Italy

436064   Bilateral Exchange   62 ITDI 468
SIGNED: 28 Nov 60
HEADNOTE: EMBASSY BUILDING
TOPIC: Consul/Citizenship
PARTIES:
  Brazil
  Italy

436066   Bilateral Exchange   64 ITDI 240
SIGNED: 6 Sep 63
HEADNOTE: COPYRIGHT LAW
TOPIC: Patents/Copyrights
PARTIES:
  Brazil
  Italy

436067   Bilateral Exchange   65 ITDI 120
SIGNED: 18 Apr 64
HEADNOTE: MOTION PICTURE
TOPIC: Mass Media
PARTIES:
  Brazil
  Italy

436069   Bilateral Agreement   64 ITDI 344
SIGNED: 30 May 63
HEADNOTE: SCIENTIFIC & TECHNICAL COOPER-
ATION
TOPIC: Tech Assistance
PARTIES:
  Bulgaria
  Italy

436070   Bilateral Agreement   66 ITDI 120
SIGNED: 10 Dec 65
HEADNOTE: COMMERCE
TOPIC: General Trade
PARTIES:
  Bulgaria
  Italy

436071   Bilateral Exchange   66 ITDI 121
SIGNED: 10 Dec 65
HEADNOTE: MERCHANT NAVIGATION
TOPIC: Water Transport
PARTIES:
  Bulgaria
  Italy

436072   Bilateral Exchange   53 ITDI 80
SIGNED: 30 May 50
HEADNOTE: CULTURE
TOPIC: Culture
PARTIES:
  Canada
  Italy

436076   Bilateral Agreement   64 ITDI 245
SIGNED: 18 Sep 63
HEADNOTE: AMENDS 18 DEC 61
TOPIC: Specific Resources
PARTIES:
  Canada
  Italy

436079   Bilateral Instrument   62 ITDI 470
SIGNED: 22 Sep 60
HEADNOTE: SUSPENDED FINANCE QUESTIONS
TOPIC: Finance
PARTIES:
  Czechoslovakia
  Italy

436080   Bilateral Exchange   63 ITDI 277
SIGNED: 2 Oct 62
HEADNOTE: TRADE MISSION
TOPIC: Admin Cooperation
PARTIES:
  Czechoslovakia
  Italy

436081   Bilateral Agreement   66 ITDI 123
SIGNED: 27 Mar 65
HEADNOTE: SCIENTIFIC & TECHNICAL COOPER-
ATION
TOPIC: Tech Assistance
PARTIES:
  Czechoslovakia
  Italy

436082   Bilateral Agreement   66 ITDI 124
SIGNED: 15 Jul 65
HEADNOTE: COMMERCE
TOPIC: General Trade
PARTIES:
  Czechoslovakia
  Italy

436083   Bilateral Agreement   63 ITDI 14
SIGNED: 1 Jun 59
HEADNOTE: AIR SERVICE
TOPIC: Air Transport
PARTIES:
  Ceylon (Sri Lanka)
  Italy

436084   Bilateral Agreement   65 ITDI 216
SIGNED: 4 Jun 64
HEADNOTE: ECONOMIC & TECHNICAL COOPER-
ATION
TOPIC: General Aid
PARTIES:
  Chad
  Italy

436087   Bilateral Agreement   62 ITDI 320
SIGNED: 2 Aug 60
HEADNOTE: ECONOMIC & TECHNICAL COOPER-
ATION
TOPIC: General Aid
PARTIES:
  Chile
  Italy

436088   Bilateral Agreement   66 ITDI 127
SIGNED: 30 Jun 65
HEADNOTE: CHILEAN COMMERCIAL DEBTS
TOPIC: Claims and Debts
PARTIES:
  Chile
  Italy

436089   Bilateral Exchange   66 ITDI 229
SIGNED: 30 Jun 65
HEADNOTE: SEA TRANSPORT
TOPIC: Water Transport
PARTIES:
  Chile
  Italy

436093   Bilateral Exchange   63 ITDI 279
SIGNED: 25 May 62
HEADNOTE: DIPLOMATIC VISAS
TOPIC: Visas
PARTIES:
  Colombia
  Italy

436095   Bilateral Exchange   62 ITDI 497
SIGNED: 7 Mar 61
HEADNOTE: PATENTS & TRADEMARKS
TOPIC: Patents/Copyrights
PARTIES:
   Italy
   Korea, South

436096   Bilateral Instrument   62 ITDI 577
SIGNED: 21 Nov 61
HEADNOTE: ECONOMIC
TOPIC: General Economic
PARTIES:
   Italy
   Korea, South

436101   Bilateral Exchange   65 ITDI 219
SIGNED: 18 May 64
HEADNOTE: COMMERCIAL CREDIT
TOPIC: Loans and Credits
PARTIES:
   Cuba
   Italy

436102   Bilateral Agreement   66 ITDI 175
SIGNED: 10 Mar 65
HEADNOTE: SCIENTIFIC & TECHNICAL COOPER-
ATION
TOPIC: Tech Assistance
PARTIES:
   Dahomey
   Italy

436103   Bilateral Exchange   64 ITDI 252
SIGNED: 18 Jul 63
HEADNOTE: ACADEMIC FINANCE PRIVILEGES
TOPIC: Privil/Immunities
PARTIES:
   Denmark
   Italy

436106   Bilateral Agreement   53 ITDI 410
SIGNED: 30 Mar 53
HEADNOTE: COMMERCE
TOPIC: General Trade
PARTIES:
   El Salvador
   Italy

436108   Bilateral Exchange   65 ITDI 127
SIGNED: 16 Apr 64
HEADNOTE: TOURIST VISAS
TOPIC: Visas
PARTIES:
   Ecuador
   Italy

436109   Bilateral Exchange   52 ITDI 295
SIGNED: 10 Apr 52
HEADNOTE: DIPLOMATIC PROPERTY
TOPIC: Consul/Citizenship
PARTIES:
   Finland
   Italy

436131   Bilateral Exchange   52 ITDI 336
SIGNED: 22 Mar 52
HEADNOTE: REGULATE MOVEMENT OF SEAMEN
TOPIC: Consul/Citizenship
PARTIES:
   France
   Italy

436134   Bilateral Exchange   53 ITDI 289
SIGNED: 29 Jul 53
HEADNOTE: ARTICLE OF PEACE TREATY
TOPIC: Peace/Disarmament
PARTIES:
   France
   Italy

436144   Bilateral Protocol   59 ITDI 264
SIGNED: 11 Jan 57
HEADNOTE: OLD-AGE & INVALID INDEMNITY

TOPIC: Non-ILO Labor
PARTIES:
   France
   Italy

436145   Bilateral Instrument   59 ITDI 264
SIGNED: 27 Feb 57
HEADNOTE: AMENDS 21 MAR 51
TOPIC: Non-ILO Labor
PARTIES:
   France
   Italy

436147   Bilateral Exchange   61 ITDI 264
SIGNED: 21 Oct 59
HEADNOTE: PATENTS & CONCESSION TAX
TOPIC: General Economic
PARTIES:
   France
   Italy

436151   Bilateral Agreement   62 ITDI 325
SIGNED: 6 Feb 60
HEADNOTE: MODIFIES 11 JAN 57
TOPIC: Non-ILO Labor
PARTIES:
   France
   Italy

436152   Bilateral Exchange   62 ITDI 325
SIGNED: 1 Jun 60
HEADNOTE: NAVAL VISIT PROCEDURES
TOPIC: General Military
PARTIES:
   France
   Italy

436153   Bilateral Convention   61 ITDI 213
SIGNED: 14 Sep 60
HEADNOTE: MONCENISIO POWER PLANT
TOPIC: General Ad Hoc
PARTIES:
   France
   Italy

436154   Bilateral Exchange   62 ITDI 506
SIGNED: 18 Dec 61
HEADNOTE: MODIFIES 4 NOV 49
TOPIC: Culture
PARTIES:
   France
   Italy

436155   Bilateral Protocol   64 ITDI 253
SIGNED: 17 Jul 63
HEADNOTE: OLD-AGE & INVALID INDEMNITY
TOPIC: Non-ILO Labor
PARTIES:
   France
   Italy

436156   Bilateral Exchange   64 ITDI 254
SIGNED: 17 Jul 63
HEADNOTE: MIGRANT LABOR
TOPIC: Non-ILO Labor
PARTIES:
   France
   Italy

436158   Bilateral Exchange   65 ITDI 128
SIGNED: 28 Apr 64
HEADNOTE: MONCENISIO BORDER
TOPIC: Territory Boundary
PARTIES:
   France
   Italy

436161   Bilateral Exchange   66 ITDI 131
SIGNED: 9 Dec 65
HEADNOTE: VISAS RULES
TOPIC: Visas
PARTIES:
   Gambia
   Italy

436177   Bilateral Exchange   65 ITDI 129
SIGNED: 27 Feb 64
HEADNOTE: HOUSING OF LABORERS
TOPIC: Non-ILO Labor
PARTIES:
   Germany, West
   Italy

436181   Bilateral Exchange   53 ITDI 336
SIGNED: 5 Dec 53
HEADNOTE: TREATMENT OF NAVY IN PORTS
TOPIC: General Military
PARTIES:
   Italy
   Japan

436183   Bilateral Exchange   64 ITDI 258
SIGNED: 15 Mar 63
HEADNOTE: DIPLOMATIC VISAS
TOPIC: Visas
PARTIES:
   Italy
   Japan

436184   Bilateral Exchange   64 ITDI 258
SIGNED: 25 Mar 63
HEADNOTE: AIR SERVICES
TOPIC: Air Transport
PARTIES:
   Italy
   Jordan

436185   Bilateral Instrument   66 ITDI 265
SIGNED: 23 May 65
HEADNOTE: WEEKLY FLIGHTS ROME-AMMAN
TOPIC: Air Transport
PARTIES:
   Italy
   Jordan

436190   Bilateral Exchange   60 ITDI 243
SIGNED: 9 Sep 58
HEADNOTE: PRIVATE INSURANCE
TOPIC: Non-ILO Labor
PARTIES:
   Italy
   UK Great Britain

436191   Bilateral Exchange   60 ITDI 245
SIGNED: 14 Oct 58
HEADNOTE: SOUND RECORDINGS PROTECTION
TOPIC: Patents/Copyrights
PARTIES:
   Italy
   UK Great Britain

436197   Bilateral Protocol   53 ITDI 374
SIGNED: 3 Dec 53
HEADNOTE: ECONOMIC COOPERATION
TOPIC: General Economic
PARTIES:
   Greece
   Italy

436198   Bilateral Exchange   62 ITDI 289
SIGNED: 20 Jun 62
HEADNOTE: CONCERNS 10 NOV 54 & 9 JUL 61
TOPIC: General Trade
PARTIES:
   Greece
   Italy

436199   Bilateral Exchange   66 ITDI 138
SIGNED: 26 Jun 65
HEADNOTE: FINANCE
TOPIC: Finance
PARTIES:
   Greece
   Italy

436201   Bilateral Agreement   65 ITDI 191
SIGNED: 20 Feb 64
HEADNOTE: ECONOMIC & TECHNICAL COOPER-
ATION

TOPIC: Tech Assistance
PARTIES:
  Guinea
  Italy

436202   Bilateral Agreement   65 ITDI 130
SIGNED: 20 Feb 64
HEADNOTE: GUARANTEE INVESTMENTS
TOPIC: Claims and Debts
PARTIES:
  Guinea
  Italy

436203   Bilateral Protocol   65 ITDI 131
SIGNED: 29 Oct 64
HEADNOTE: MERCHANT MARINE
TOPIC: Water Transport
PARTIES:
  Guinea
  Italy

436207   Bilateral Exchange   64 ITDI 260
SIGNED: 19 Apr 63
HEADNOTE: MILAN COMMERCE INFORMATION
  OFFICE
TOPIC: Admin Cooperation
PARTIES:
  Indonesia
  Italy

436211   Bilateral Exchange   60 ITDI 329
SIGNED: 7 May 58
HEADNOTE: CONCERNS 26 JAN 55
TOPIC: General Trade
PARTIES:
  Iran
  Italy

436213   Bilateral Exchange   61 ITDI 281
SIGNED: 25 Jul 59
HEADNOTE: VISAS
TOPIC: Visas
PARTIES:
  Iran
  Italy

436214   Bilateral Agreement   64 ITDI 261
SIGNED: 30 Sep 63
HEADNOTE: COMMERCE
TOPIC: General Trade
PARTIES:
  Iraq
  Italy

436215   Bilateral Agreement   64 ITDI 264
SIGNED: 30 Sep 63
HEADNOTE: ECONOMIC COOPERATION
TOPIC: Tech Assistance
PARTIES:
  Iraq
  Italy

436216   Bilateral Exchange   59 ITDI 320
SIGNED: 15 Nov 57
HEADNOTE: MODIFIES 27 NOV 47
TOPIC: Air Transport
PARTIES:
  Ireland
  Italy

436217   Bilateral Exchange   62 ITDI 327
SIGNED: 18 May 60
HEADNOTE: ENTRANCE INTO IRELAND
TOPIC: Visas
PARTIES:
  Ireland
  Italy

436234   Bilateral Agreement   59 ITDI 327
SIGNED: 3 Aug 57
HEADNOTE: PAYMENT
TOPIC: Finance

PARTIES:
  Italy
  Yugoslavia

436235   Bilateral Convention   60 ITDI 345
SIGNED: 13 Dec 58
HEADNOTE: MUGGIA WATER SUPPLY
TOPIC: Specific Resources
PARTIES:
  Italy
  Yugoslavia

436237   Bilateral Protocol   61 ITDI 284
SIGNED: 21 Apr 59
HEADNOTE: FREE ACCESS MOUNTAIN PEAKS
TOPIC: Visas
PARTIES:
  Italy
  Yugoslavia

436247   Bilateral Agreement   64 ITDI 321
SIGNED: 23 Dec 63
HEADNOTE: TOURIST
TOPIC: Visas
PARTIES:
  Italy
  Yugoslavia

436249   Bilateral Agreement   65 ITDI 194
SIGNED: 28 Nov 64
HEADNOTE: ECONOMIC COOPERATION
TOPIC: General Economic
PARTIES:
  Italy
  Yugoslavia

436250   Bilateral Exchange   65 ITDI 140
SIGNED: 28 Nov 64
HEADNOTE: ADRIATIC COAST TRADE
TOPIC: General Economic
PARTIES:
  Italy
  Yugoslavia

436258   Bilateral Protocol   62 ITDI 353
SIGNED: 13 Feb 60
HEADNOTE: AMENDS AGREEMENT 24 JAN 49
TOPIC: Air Transport
PARTIES:
  Italy
  Lebanon

436260   Bilateral Exchange   61 ITDI 272
SIGNED: 25 Jan 63
HEADNOTE: TRADE MISSION IN MILAN
TOPIC: General Trade
PARTIES:
  Italy
  Libya

436266   Bilateral Agreement   59 ITDI 347
SIGNED: 16 Jan 57
HEADNOTE: MIGRANT LABOR
TOPIC: Non-ILO Labor
PARTIES:
  Italy
  Luxembourg

436267   Bilateral Agreement   65 ITDI 195
SIGNED: 1 Jul 64
HEADNOTE: TRADE AND PAYMENTS
TOPIC: General Economic
PARTIES:
  Italy
  Malagasy

436268   Bilateral Agreement   65 ITDI 197
SIGNED: 1 Jul 64
HEADNOTE: ECONOMIC & TECHNICAL COOPER-
  ATION
TOPIC: Tech Assistance
PARTIES:
  Italy
  Malagasy

436269   Bilateral Agreement   65 ITDI 142
SIGNED: 3 Jun 64
HEADNOTE: ECONOMIC & TECHNICAL COOPER-
  ATION
TOPIC: Tech Assistance
PARTIES:
  Italy
  Mali

436270   Bilateral Exchange   62 ITDI 356
SIGNED: 25 Nov 60
HEADNOTE: VISAS
TOPIC: Visas
PARTIES:
  Italy
  Morocco

436271   Bilateral Agreement   62 ITDI 511
SIGNED: 28 Jan 61
HEADNOTE: COMMERCE
TOPIC: General Trade
PARTIES:
  Italy
  Morocco

436272   Bilateral Agreement   62 ITDI 513
SIGNED: 10 Feb 61
HEADNOTE: ECONOMIC & TECHNICAL COOPER-
  ATION
TOPIC: Tech Assistance
PARTIES:
  Italy
  Morocco

436274   Bilateral Exchange   66 ITDI 142
SIGNED: 30 Mar 65
HEADNOTE: LIVE ANIMALS & FROZEN MEAT
TOPIC: Commodity Trade
PARTIES:
  Italy
  Mexico

436275   Bilateral Exchange   66 ITDI 143
SIGNED: 7 Jun 65
HEADNOTE: TOURIST VISAS
TOPIC: Visas
PARTIES:
  Italy
  Mexico

436276   Bilateral Exchange   66 ITDI 144
SIGNED: 20 Jul 65
HEADNOTE: ECONOMIC COOPERATION COMMIT-
  TEE
TOPIC: IGO Establishment
PARTIES:
  Italy
  Mexico

436277   Bilateral Exchange   66 ITDI 146
SIGNED: 8 Dec 65
HEADNOTE: MEXICAN ELECTRIFICATION
TOPIC: Tech Assistance
PARTIES:
  Italy
  Mexico

436278   Bilateral Exchange   66 ITDI 147
SIGNED: 8 Dec 65
HEADNOTE: LABOR ELECTRIC PROJECT
TOPIC: Loans and Credits
PARTIES:
  Italy
  Mexico

436279   Bilateral Agreement   66 ITDI 210
SIGNED: 23 Dec 65
HEADNOTE: AIR TRANSPORT
TOPIC: Air Transport
PARTIES:
  Italy
  Mexico

436281   Bilateral Exchange   **60 ITDI 263**
SIGNED: 8 Apr 58
HEADNOTE: FOREIGN RESIDENTS
TOPIC: Visas
PARTIES:
  Italy
  Monaco

436283   Bilateral Agreement   **65 ITDI 131**
SIGNED: 2 Apr 64
HEADNOTE: PENSIONS
TOPIC: Non-ILO Labor
PARTIES:
  Italy
  Monaco

436288   Bilateral Exchange   **61 ITDI 288**
SIGNED: 22 Oct 59
HEADNOTE: FACILITATE TOURISM
TOPIC: Visas
PARTIES:
  Italy
  Netherlands

436290   Bilateral Agreement   **62 ITDI 516**
SIGNED: 10 Jan 61
HEADNOTE: COMMERCE
TOPIC: General Trade
PARTIES:
  Italy
  Pakistan

436293   Bilateral Exchange   **65 ITDI 155**
SIGNED: 6 Jan 64
HEADNOTE: DIPLOMATIC VISAS
TOPIC: Visas
PARTIES:
  Italy
  Panama

436295   Bilateral Agreement   **63 ITDI 293**
SIGNED: 8 Jul 59
HEADNOTE: PAYMENT
TOPIC: Finance
PARTIES:
  Italy
  Paraguay

436297   Bilateral Exchange   **62 ITDI 361**
SIGNED: 18 Feb 60
HEADNOTE: DIPLOMATIC VISAS
TOPIC: Visas
PARTIES:
  Italy
  Peru

436298   Bilateral Exchange   **62 ITDI 362**
SIGNED: 18 Feb 60
HEADNOTE: TRADE COMMISSION
TOPIC: Admin Cooperation
PARTIES:
  Italy
  Peru

436299   Bilateral Exchange   **62 ITDI 363**
SIGNED: 2 Sep 60
HEADNOTE: VISAS
TOPIC: Visas
PARTIES:
  Italy
  Peru

436304   Bilateral Protocol   **61 ITDI 382**
SIGNED: 3 Feb 59
HEADNOTE: FINANCES
TOPIC: Finance
PARTIES:
  Italy
  Poland

436305   Bilateral Agreement   **62 ITDI 437**
SIGNED: 27 Nov 60
HEADNOTE: SCIENTIFIC & TECHNICAL COOPER-
ATION

TOPIC: Tech Assistance
PARTIES:
  Italy
  Poland

436306   Bilateral Exchange   **62 ITDI 517**
SIGNED: 9 Dec 61
HEADNOTE: MIXED COMMISSION
TOPIC: Culture
PARTIES:
  Italy
  Poland

436307   Bilateral Exchange   **63 ITDI 294**
SIGNED: 8 Jun 62
HEADNOTE: TRADE MISSION MILAN
TOPIC: General Trade
PARTIES:
  Italy
  Poland

436308   Bilateral Exchange   **63 ITDI 295**
SIGNED: 29 Dec 62
HEADNOTE: EXEMPTION AIRCRAFT FUEL
TOPIC: Customs
PARTIES:
  Italy
  Poland

436309   Bilateral Agreement   **66 ITDI 150**
SIGNED: 25 Feb 65
HEADNOTE: COMMERCE
TOPIC: General Trade
PARTIES:
  Italy
  Poland

436310   Bilateral Agreement   **66 ITDI 154**
SIGNED: 14 Jul 65
HEADNOTE: INDUSTRIAL & TECHNICAL COOPER-
ATION
TOPIC: General Economic
PARTIES:
  Italy
  Poland

436311   Bilateral Exchange   **59 ITDI 369**
SIGNED: 4 Jan 57
HEADNOTE: VISAS
TOPIC: Visas
PARTIES:
  Italy
  Portugal

436314   Bilateral Agreement   **52 ITDI 291**
SIGNED: 17 Oct 52
HEADNOTE: WAR GRAVES
TOPIC: Other Military
PARTIES:
  Italy
  United Arab Rep

436315   Bilateral Agreement   **61 ITDI 342**
SIGNED: 8 Jan 59
HEADNOTE: CULTURE
TOPIC: Culture
PARTIES:
  Italy
  United Arab Rep

436316   Bilateral Exchange   **61 ITDI 289**
SIGNED: 8 Jan 59
HEADNOTE: CULTURAL INSTITUTES
TOPIC: Admin Cooperation
PARTIES:
  Italy
  United Arab Rep

436317   Bilateral Exchange   **61 ITDI 289**
SIGNED: 8 Jan 59
HEADNOTE: REPATRIATES ASSETS
TOPIC: Claims and Debts

PARTIES:
  Italy
  United Arab Rep

436318   Bilateral Protocol   **61 ITDI 291**
SIGNED: 29 Apr 59
HEADNOTE: COMMERCE
TOPIC: General Trade
PARTIES:
  Italy
  United Arab Rep

436319   Bilateral Protocol   **62 ITDI 518**
SIGNED: 19 Apr 61
HEADNOTE: FISHING
TOPIC: Specific Resources
PARTIES:
  Italy
  United Arab Rep

436320   Bilateral Exchange   **63 ITDI 380**
SIGNED: 13 Apr 62
HEADNOTE: REPATRIATES ASSETS
TOPIC: Claims and Debts
PARTIES:
  Italy
  United Arab Rep

436322   Bilateral Exchange   **66 ITDI 231**
SIGNED: 23 Mar 65
HEADNOTE: REPATRIATES FUNDS
TOPIC: Claims and Debts
PARTIES:
  Italy
  United Arab Rep

436341   Bilateral Agreement   **63 ITDI 347**
SIGNED: 2 Oct 62
HEADNOTE: ECONOMIC & TECHNICAL COOPER-
ATION
TOPIC: Tech Assistance
PARTIES:
  Italy
  Senegal

436342   Bilateral Exchange   **60 ITDI 265**
SIGNED: 28 May 58
HEADNOTE: MEDICAL LICENSES
TOPIC: Sanitation
PARTIES:
  Italy
  Syria

436346   Bilateral Exchange   **62 ITDI 366**
SIGNED: 1 Jul 60
HEADNOTE: ITALIAN REAL ESTATE SOMALIA
TOPIC: Admin Cooperation
PARTIES:
  Italy
  Somalia

436353   Bilateral Exchange   **60 ITDI 282**
SIGNED: 28 Aug 58
HEADNOTE: DIPLOMATIC BAGGAGE
TOPIC: Customs
PARTIES:
  Italy
  Spain

436354   Bilateral Agreement   **62 ITDI 370**
SIGNED: 28 Jun 60
HEADNOTE: COMMERCE
TOPIC: General Trade
PARTIES:
  Italy
  Spain

436357   Bilateral Exchange   **62 ITDI 376**
SIGNED: 4 Aug 60
HEADNOTE: AIR TRAFFIC STATUTE EXCHANGE
TOPIC: Admin Cooperation
PARTIES:
  Italy
  USA (United States)

436360 Bilateral Agreement 66 ITDI 243
SIGNED: 22 Jul 65
HEADNOTE: SCIENTIFIC & TECHNICAL COOPER-
ATION
TOPIC: Tech Assistance
PARTIES:
Italy
Sudan

436363 Bilateral Agreement 65 ITDI 161
SIGNED: 29 Oct 64
HEADNOTE: EXCHANGE INTERN LAWYERS
TOPIC: Non-ILO Labor
PARTIES:
Italy
Sweden

436378 Bilateral Agreement 59 ITDI 411
SIGNED: 1 Apr 57
HEADNOTE: RAILROAD LOAN SUBALP SOCIETY
TOPIC: Loans and Credits
PARTIES:
Italy
Switzerland

436383 Bilateral Exchange 60 ITDI 306
SIGNED: 10 Dec 58
HEADNOTE: CAMPIONE GAMBLING HOUSE
TOPIC: Admin Cooperation
PARTIES:
Italy
Switzerland

436384 Bilateral Exchange 61 ITDI 298
SIGNED: 10 Dec 59
HEADNOTE: SWISS SHIPS ITALIAN PORTS
TOPIC: Water Transport
PARTIES:
Italy
Switzerland

436390 Bilateral Exchange 63 ITDI 301
SIGNED: 16 Apr 62
HEADNOTE: MOUNTAIN PASS OPENING
TOPIC: Land Transport
PARTIES:
Italy
Switzerland

436391 Bilateral Exchange 63 ITDI 302
SIGNED: 14 Aug 62
HEADNOTE: ROAD TUNNEL FINANCES
TOPIC: Land Transport
PARTIES:
Italy
Switzerland

436392 Bilateral Exchange 63 ITDI 303
SIGNED: 16 Dec 62
HEADNOTE: ENLARGE INTERNATIONAL BRIDGE
TOPIC: General Ad Hoc
PARTIES:
Italy
Switzerland

436394 Bilateral Agreement 64 ITDI 283
SIGNED: 31 May 63
HEADNOTE: CUSTOMS OFFICE BERNARDO TUN-
NEL
TOPIC: Customs
PARTIES:
Italy
Switzerland

436397 Bilateral Agreement 66 ITDI 246
SIGNED: 4 Aug 65
HEADNOTE: ECONOMIC & TECHNICAL COOPER-
ATION
TOPIC: Tech Assistance
PARTIES:
Italy
Tanzania

436400 Bilateral Agreement 62 ITDI 530
SIGNED: 23 Nov 61
HEADNOTE: ECONOMIC & TECHNICAL COOPER-
ATION
TOPIC: Tech Assistance
PARTIES:
Italy
Tunisia

436401 Bilateral Exchange 63 ITDI 398
SIGNED: 26 Jul 62
HEADNOTE: FINANCIAL CREDIT
TOPIC: Loans and Credits
PARTIES:
Italy
Tunisia

436402 Bilateral Exchange 63 ITDI 399
SIGNED: 26 Jul 62
HEADNOTE: WORK PERMITS ITALIAN LABOR
TOPIC: Non-ILO Labor
PARTIES:
Italy
Tunisia

436403 Bilateral Exchange 63 ITDI 397
SIGNED: 26 Jul 62
HEADNOTE: REMITTANCES ITALIAN LABOR
TOPIC: Non-ILO Labor
PARTIES:
Italy
Tunisia

436405 Bilateral Exchange 52 ITDI 481
SIGNED: 22 Oct 51
HEADNOTE: VISAS
TOPIC: Visas
PARTIES:
Italy
Turkey

436408 Bilateral Agreement 60 ITDI 306
SIGNED: 29 Nov 58
HEADNOTE: FINANCIAL ASSISTANCE
TOPIC: Direct Aid
PARTIES:
Italy
Turkey

436409 Bilateral Agreement 61 ITDI 302
SIGNED: 10 Jun 59
HEADNOTE: ECONOMIC & TECHNICAL COOPER-
ATION
TOPIC: Tech Assistance
PARTIES:
Italy
Turkey

436411 Bilateral Agreement 66 ITDI 159
SIGNED: 23 Jan 65
HEADNOTE: FINANCE
TOPIC: Finance
PARTIES:
Italy
Turkey

436412 Bilateral Agreement 66 ITDI 161
SIGNED: 18 Sep 65
HEADNOTE: FINANCE
TOPIC: Finance
PARTIES:
Italy
Turkey

436413 Bilateral Agreement 66 ITDI 162
SIGNED: 18 Sep 65
HEADNOTE: THREE LOANS
TOPIC: Loans and Credits
PARTIES:
Italy
Turkey

436417 Bilateral Agreement 66 ITDI 247
SIGNED: 21 Sep 61

HEADNOTE: SCIENTIFIC & TECHNICAL COOPER-
ATION
TOPIC: General Economic
PARTIES:
Hungary
Italy

436418 Bilateral Agreement 66 ITDI 248
SIGNED: 1 Dec 65
HEADNOTE: INDUSTRIAL & TECHNICAL COOPER-
ATION
TOPIC: General Economic
PARTIES:
Italy
Turkey

436419 Bilateral Agreement 66 ITDI 163
SIGNED: 1 Dec 65
HEADNOTE: COMMERCIAL EXCHANGES
TOPIC: General Trade
PARTIES:
Italy
Turkey

436422 Bilateral Exchange 62 ITDI 382
SIGNED: 20 Jan 60
HEADNOTE: VISAS
TOPIC: Visas
PARTIES:
Italy
USSR (Soviet Union)

436423 Bilateral Exchange 62 ITDI 385
SIGNED: 30 Jun 60
HEADNOTE: TRADEMARKS
TOPIC: Patents/Copyrights
PARTIES:
Italy
USSR (Soviet Union)

436424 Bilateral Agreement 65 ITDI 165
SIGNED: 5 Feb 64
HEADNOTE: TRADE 1966-69
TOPIC: General Trade
PARTIES:
Italy
USSR (Soviet Union)

436429 Bilateral Agreement 61 ITDI 306
SIGNED: 5 Oct 59
HEADNOTE: TRADE & PAYMENTS
TOPIC: General Economic
PARTIES:
Italy
Yemen

436430 Bilateral Exchange 64 ITDI 288
SIGNED: 3 Oct 63
HEADNOTE: NON-DISCRIMINATION
TOPIC: Admin Cooperation
PARTIES:
Italy
Yemen

437011 Bilateral Agreement 61 ITMA 451
SIGNED: 16 Apr 47
HEADNOTE: EMIGRATION SANITATION
TOPIC: Sanitation
PARTIES:
Argentina
Italy

437012 Bilateral Agreement 1 ITMA 82
SIGNED: 26 Jan 48
HEADNOTE: EMIGRATION
TOPIC: Health/Educ/Welfare
PARTIES:
Argentina
Italy

437055 Bilateral Instrument 1 ITMA 365
SIGNED: 12 Oct 49
HEADNOTE: FRIENDSHIP COOPERATION
TOPIC: General Amity

PARTIES:
Brazil
Italy

437085   Bilateral Instrument   1 ITMA 525
SIGNED: 24 Mar 49
HEADNOTE: FRIENDSHIP & COOPERATION
TOPIC: General Amity
PARTIES:
Chile
Italy

437086   Bilateral Instrument   1 ITMA 526
SIGNED: 1 Dec 49
HEADNOTE: EMIGRATION
TOPIC: Health/Educ/Welfare
PARTIES:
Chile
Italy

437091   Bilateral Instrument   1 ITMA 551
SIGNED: 27 Aug 49
HEADNOTE: FRIENDSHIP & COOPERATION
TOPIC: General Amity
PARTIES:
Colombia
Italy

437100   Bilateral Instrument   1 ITMA 616
SIGNED: 19 Sep 49
HEADNOTE: FRIENDSHIP & COOPERATION
TOPIC: General Amity
PARTIES:
Cuba
Italy

437292   Bilateral Protocol   2 ITMA 442
SIGNED: 2 Sep 49
HEADNOTE: FRIENDSHIP & COLLABORATION
TOPIC: General Amity
PARTIES:
Italy
Panama

437296   Bilateral Protocol   2 ITMA 387
SIGNED: 21 Aug 49
HEADNOTE: FRIENDSHIP & COLLABORATION
TOPIC: General Amity
PARTIES:
Italy
Peru

437336   Bilateral Exchange   60 ITMA 422
SIGNED: 21 Aug 46
HEADNOTE: BISHOPS TRIAL OATH
TOPIC: Admin Cooperation
PARTIES:
Italy
Vatican/Holy See

439001   Bilateral Agreement   52 JHZ 12
SIGNED: 22 Nov 52
HEADNOTE: LOAN OF VESSELS
TOPIC: Milit Installation
PARTIES:
Japan
USA (United States)

439002   Bilateral Agreement   55 JHZ 9
SIGNED: 6 Sep 55
HEADNOTE: CULTURE
TOPIC: Culture
PARTIES:
Japan
Thailand

439003   Bilateral Agreement   67 JHZ 3
SIGNED: 21 Jan 66
HEADNOTE: AIR SERVICES
TOPIC: Air Transport
PARTIES:
Japan
USSR (Soviet Union)

439004   Bilateral Treaty   67 JHZ 8
SIGNED: 29 Jul 66
HEADNOTE: CONSULAR
TOPIC: Consul/Citizenship
PARTIES:
Japan
USSR (Soviet Union)

439005   Bilateral Convention   67 JHZ 12
SIGNED: 24 Jan 67
HEADNOTE: DOUBLE TAXES ON INCOME
TOPIC: Taxation
PARTIES:
Brazil
Japan

439006   Bilateral Agreement   67 JHZ 8
SIGNED: 14 Feb 67
HEADNOTE: AIR SERVICES
TOPIC: Air Transport
PARTIES:
Japan
Singapore

439007   Bilateral Agreement   67 JHZ 7
SIGNED: 14 Mar 67
HEADNOTE: OECD PRIVILEGES IN JAPAN
TOPIC: IGO Status/Immunit
PARTIES:
Japan
OECD (Econ Coop)

439008   Bilateral Agreement   67 JHZ 7
SIGNED: 5 Apr 67
HEADNOTE: APO PRIVILEGES IN JAPAN
TOPIC: IGO Status/Immunit
PARTIES:
Asian Productivity
Japan

439009   Bilateral Convention   68 JHZ 10
SIGNED: 11 May 67
HEADNOTE: DOUBLE TAX INCOME
TOPIC: Taxation
PARTIES:
Japan
Norway

439010   Bilateral Agreement   67 JHZ 8
SIGNED: 16 May 67
HEADNOTE: AIR SERVICES
TOPIC: Air Transport
PARTIES:
Japan
Korea, South

439011   Bilateral Exchange   68 JHZ 5
SIGNED: 30 Jun 67
HEADNOTE: CARS 1967 GATT PROTOCOL
TOPIC: General Trade
PARTIES:
Japan
EEC (Econ Commnty)

439012   Bilateral Agreement   68 JHZ 7
SIGNED: 12 Jul 67
HEADNOTE: FISHERIES
TOPIC: Specific Resources
PARTIES:
Japan
New Zealand

439013   Bilateral Agreement   68 JHZ 5
SIGNED: 21 Sep 67
HEADNOTE: REPARATIONS & CLAIMS
TOPIC: Reparations
PARTIES:
Japan
Singapore

439014   Bilateral Agreement   68 JHZ 5
SIGNED: 21 Sep 67
HEADNOTE: ECONOMIC COOPERATION
TOPIC: General Economic

PARTIES:
Japan
Malaysia

439015   Bilateral Convention   68 JHZ 9
SIGNED: 12 Dec 67
HEADNOTE: DOUBLE TAX INCOME
TOPIC: Taxation
PARTIES:
Ceylon (Sri Lanka)
Japan

439016   Bilateral Convention   68 JHZ 7
SIGNED: 3 Feb 68
HEADNOTE: DOUBLE TAX INCOME
TOPIC: Taxation
PARTIES:
Denmark
Japan

439017   Bilateral Agreement   68 JHZ 7
SIGNED: 26 Feb 68
HEADNOTE: CIVIL USE ATOMIC ENERGY
TOPIC: Atomic Energy
PARTIES:
Japan
USA (United States)

439018   Bilateral Agreement   68 JHZ 10
SIGNED: 6 Mar 68
HEADNOTE: CIVIL USE ATOMIC ENERGY
TOPIC: Atomic Energy
PARTIES:
Japan
UK Great Britain

439019   Bilateral Agreement   68 JHZ 6
SIGNED: 7 Mar 68
HEADNOTE: FISHERIES MEXICAN WATERS
TOPIC: Specific Resources
PARTIES:
Japan
Mexico

439020   Bilateral Agreement   69 JHZ 5
SIGNED: 15 Mar 68
HEADNOTE: CULTURE
TOPIC: Culture
PARTIES:
Japan
Yugoslavia

439021   Bilateral Convention   70 JHZ 4
SIGNED: 28 Mar 68
HEADNOTE: DOUBLE TAX INCOME
TOPIC: Taxation
PARTIES:
Belgium
Japan

439022   Bilateral Agreement   68 JHZ 6
SIGNED: 5 Apr 68
HEADNOTE: NONPO SHOTO & OTHER ISLANDS
TOPIC: Territory Boundary
PARTIES:
Japan
USA (United States)

439023   Bilateral Agreement   69 JHZ 8
SIGNED: 26 Jun 68
HEADNOTE: MONEY ORDERS
TOPIC: Postal Service
PARTIES:
Japan
Philippines

439024   Bilateral Convention   69 JHZ 8
SIGNED: 3 Sep 68
HEADNOTE: DOUBLE TAX INCOME
TOPIC: Taxation
PARTIES:
Japan
United Arab Rep

439025 Bilateral Agreement 69 JHZ 8
SIGNED: 27 Nov 68
HEADNOTE: FISHERIES
TOPIC: Specific Resources
PARTIES:
Australia
Japan

439026 Bilateral Convention 69 JHZ 12
SIGNED: 30 Jan 69
HEADNOTE: TRADE
TOPIC: General Trade
PARTIES:
Japan
Mexico

439027 Bilateral Convention 70 JHZ 12
SIGNED: 10 Feb 69
HEADNOTE: DOUBLE TAX INCOME
TOPIC: Taxation
PARTIES:
Japan
UK Great Britain

439028 Bilateral Agreement 70 JHZ 7
SIGNED: 20 Mar 69
HEADNOTE: DOUBLE TAX INCOME
TOPIC: Taxation
PARTIES:
Australia
Japan

439029 Bilateral Agreement 69 JHZ 7
SIGNED: 18 Apr 69
HEADNOTE: TRUST TERRITORIES PACIFIC IS-
LANDS
TOPIC: Territory Boundary
PARTIES:
Japan
USA (United States)

439030 Bilateral Agreement 69 JHZ 8
SIGNED: 1 Aug 69
HEADNOTE: IRRIGATION PREK THNOT
TOPIC: Non-IBRD Project
PARTIES:
Cambodia
Japan

439031 Bilateral Treaty 70 JHZ 7
SIGNED: 1 Sep 69
HEADNOTE: TRADE & NAVIGATION
TOPIC: General Economic
PARTIES:
Japan
Romania

439032 Bilateral Agreement 70 JHZ 5
SIGNED: 9 Sep 69
HEADNOTE: ASIAN STATISTICAL INSTITUTE
TOPIC: IGO Establishment
PARTIES:
Japan
IBRD (World Bank)

439033 Bilateral Agreement 70 JHZ 5
SIGNED: 20 Jan 70
HEADNOTE: AIR SERVICES
TOPIC: Air Transport
PARTIES:
Japan
Philippines

439034 Bilateral Agreement 70 JHZ 12
SIGNED: 30 Jan 70
HEADNOTE: DOUBLE TAX INCOME
TOPIC: Taxation
PARTIES:
Japan
Malaysia

439035 Bilateral Treaty 70 JHZ 8
SIGNED: 28 Feb 70
HEADNOTE: TRADE & NAVIGATION

TOPIC: General Economic
PARTIES:
Bulgaria
Japan

439036 Bilateral Convention 70 JHZ 10
SIGNED: 3 Mar 70
HEADNOTE: DOUBLE TAX INCOME
TOPIC: Taxation
PARTIES:
Japan
Korea, South

439037 Bilateral Convention 70 JHZ 10
SIGNED: 3 Mar 70
HEADNOTE: DOUBLE TAX INCOME
TOPIC: Taxation
PARTIES:
Japan
Netherlands

439038 Bilateral Treaty 67 JHZ 9
SIGNED: 20 Dec 61
HEADNOTE: FRIENDSHIP COMMERCE NAVIGA-
TION
TOPIC: General Amity
PARTIES:
Argentina
Japan

439191 Bilateral Agreement 71 JHZ 3
SIGNED: 2 Jun 67
HEADNOTE: AIR TRANSPORT SERVICES
TOPIC: Air Transport
PARTIES:
Japan
Lebanon

439261 Bilateral Agreement 71 JHZ 1
SIGNED: 19 Feb 70
HEADNOTE: DOUBLE TAXATION
TOPIC: Taxation
PARTIES:
Japan
Zambia

440064 Bilateral Instrument 57 JAIL 85
SIGNED: 4 Apr 51
HEADNOTE: PELAGIC FUR SEALING
TOPIC: Specific Resources
PARTIES:
Japan
USA (United States)

440065 Bilateral Exchange 57 JAIL 86
SIGNED: 23 Oct 53
HEADNOTE: WAIVERING FEES
TOPIC: Visas
PARTIES:
Japan
USA (United States)

440066 Bilateral Protocol 57 JAIL 86
SIGNED: 26 Oct 53
HEADNOTE: CRIMINAL JURISDICTION UN
FORCES
TOPIC: IGO Operations
PARTIES:
Japan
United Nations

440067 Bilateral Agreement 57 JAIL 86
SIGNED: 29 Oct 53
HEADNOTE: MONEY ORDERS
TOPIC: Postal Service
PARTIES:
Japan
USA (United States)

440068 Bilateral Agreement 57 JAIL 88
SIGNED: 21 Dec 56
HEADNOTE: REPARATIONS
TOPIC: General Military

PARTIES:
Japan
Spain

440069 Bilateral Agreement 68 JAIL 201
SIGNED: 22 Apr 66
HEADNOTE: DOUBLE TAX INCOME
TOPIC: Taxation
PARTIES:
Germany, West
Japan

440154 Bilateral Agreement 57 JAIL 78
SIGNED: 16 Dec 53
HEADNOTE: REPARATIONS SUNKEN VESSALS
TOPIC: Reparations
PARTIES:
Indonesia
Japan

440155 Bilateral Agreement 57 JAIL 78
SIGNED: 9 May 54
HEADNOTE: REPARATIONS
TOPIC: Reparations
PARTIES:
Japan
Philippines

440156 Bilateral Treaty 57 JAIL 80
SIGNED: 27 May 55
HEADNOTE: AMITY
TOPIC: General Amity
PARTIES:
Japan
Yemen

440161 Bilateral Agreement 57 JAIL 82
SIGNED: 4 Apr 56
HEADNOTE: TRADE
TOPIC: General Trade
PARTIES:
Japan
Pakistan

440162 Bilateral Agreement 57 JAIL 82
SIGNED: 9 Apr 56
HEADNOTE: TRADE
TOPIC: General Trade
PARTIES:
Japan
Thailand

440163 Bilateral Exchange 65 JAIL 233
SIGNED: 17 Mar 64
HEADNOTE: ESTABLISH DIPLOMATIC RELA-
TIONS
TOPIC: Consul/Citizenship
PARTIES:
Jamaica
Japan

440164 Bilateral Protocol 65 JAIL 234
SIGNED: 8 Apr 64
HEADNOTE: TRADE
TOPIC: General Trade
PARTIES:
Germany, West
Japan

440165 Bilateral Agreement 65 JAIL 235
SIGNED: 17 Jun 64
HEADNOTE: TRADE
TOPIC: General Trade
PARTIES:
Iraq
Japan

440188 Bilateral Exchange 68 JAIL 163
SIGNED: 19 May 67
HEADNOTE: CONSULATE ESTABLISHMENT
TOPIC: Consul/Citizenship
PARTIES:
Japan
USSR (Soviet Union)

440206   Bilateral Agreement   **68 JAIL 169**
SIGNED: 27 Dec 67
HEADNOTE: RECIPROCAL IMPORTS INCREASE
TOPIC: General Trade
PARTIES:
  Germany, West
  Japan

440207   Bilateral Exchange   **69 JAIL 169**
SIGNED: 12 Jan 68
HEADNOTE: YEN ASSISTANCE LOANS
TOPIC: Loans and Credits
PARTIES:
  Japan
  Thailand

440210   Bilateral Agreement   **69 JAIL 171**
SIGNED: 5 Mar 68
HEADNOTE: SOUTH ASIAN AGRICULTURAL CEN-
  TER
TOPIC: Education
PARTIES:
  India
  Japan

440228   Bilateral Exchange   **70 JAIL 190**
SIGNED: 10 Jan 69
HEADNOTE: TRADE
TOPIC: General Trade
PARTIES:
  Japan
  Norway

440236   Bilateral Protocol   **70 JAIL 191**
SIGNED: 14 Mar 69
HEADNOTE: TRADE
TOPIC: General Trade
PARTIES:
  Japan
  USSR (Soviet Union)

440238   Bilateral Agreement   **70 JAIL 191**
SIGNED: 27 Mar 69
HEADNOTE: EXPAND TOKYO SEISMOLOGY IN-
  STITUTE
TOPIC: IGO Operations
PARTIES:
  Japan
  UN Special Fund

441070   Bilateral Treaty   **0 JGJI 1000**
SIGNED: 9 Jun 52
HEADNOTE: PEACE
TOPIC: Peace/Disarmament
PARTIES:
  India
  Japan

441071   Bilateral Exchange   **0 JGJI 4507**
SIGNED: 8 Aug 52
HEADNOTE: DEATH NOTICES
TOPIC: Admin Cooperation
PARTIES:
  Germany, West
  Japan

441073   Bilateral Agreement   **0 JGJI 1172**
SIGNED: 8 May 53
HEADNOTE: INDUSTRIAL PROPERTY
TOPIC: Patents/Copyrights
PARTIES:
  Germany, West
  Japan

441076   Bilateral Agreement   **0 JGJI 1171**
SIGNED: 21 Oct 53
HEADNOTE: INDUSTRIAL PROPERTY
TOPIC: Patents/Copyrights
PARTIES:
  Denmark
  Japan

441077   Bilateral Agreement   **0 JGJI 1162**
SIGNED: 19 Feb 54

HEADNOTE: STATUS UN FORCES JAPAN
TOPIC: Status of Forces
PARTIES:
  Japan
  United Nations

441078   Bilateral Agreement   **0 JGJI 7**
SIGNED: 19 Feb 54
HEADNOTE: CLAIMS US & UN FORCES
TOPIC: Status of Forces
PARTIES:
  Japan
  United Nations

441079   Bilateral Agreement   **0 JGJI 1173**
SIGNED: 31 May 54
HEADNOTE: INDUSTRIAL PROPERTY
TOPIC: Patents/Copyrights
PARTIES:
  Denmark
  Japan

441080   Bilateral Exchange   **0 JGJI 4508**
SIGNED: 24 May 54
HEADNOTE: NATURALIZATION NOTICES
TOPIC: Admin Cooperation
PARTIES:
  Germany, West
  Japan

441082   Bilateral Agreement   **0 JGJI 1250**
SIGNED: 25 Oct 54
HEADNOTE: CULTURE
TOPIC: Culture
PARTIES:
  Japan
  Mexico

441085   Bilateral Exchange   **0 JGJI 1262**
SIGNED: 18 Jun 55
HEADNOTE: WAIVE VISAS & FEES
TOPIC: Visas
PARTIES:
  Germany, West
  Japan

441086   Bilateral Agreement   **0 JGJI 1287**
SIGNED: 21 Sep 55
HEADNOTE: COMMONWEALTH WAR CEMETERY
TOPIC: Other Military
PARTIES:
  Japan
  UK Great Britain

441087   Bilateral Exchange   **0 JGJI 1280**
SIGNED: 16 Nov 55
HEADNOTE: PERMANENT NEUTRALITY
TOPIC: Recognition
PARTIES:
  Austria
  Japan

441088   Bilateral Exchange   **0 JGJI 1263**
SIGNED: 18 Nov 55
HEADNOTE: ABOLITION VISAS
TOPIC: Visas
PARTIES:
  France
  Japan

441089   Bilateral Treaty   **0 JGJI 1301**
SIGNED: 9 Dec 55
HEADNOTE: FRIENDSHIP
TOPIC: General Amity
PARTIES:
  Cambodia
  Japan

441090   Bilateral Exchange   **0 JGJI 1291**
SIGNED: 9 May 56
HEADNOTE: ECONOMIC DEVELOPMENT
TOPIC: Direct Aid

PARTIES:
  Japan
  Philippines

441091   Bilateral Exchange   **0 JGJI 1302**
SIGNED: 10 May 56
HEADNOTE: ABOLITION VISAS
TOPIC: Visas
PARTIES:
  Greece
  Japan

441092   Bilateral Treaty   **0 JGJI 1314**
SIGNED: 14 May 56
HEADNOTE: HIGH SEAS FISHERIES
TOPIC: Specific Resources
PARTIES:
  Japan
  USSR (Soviet Union)

441093   Bilateral Agreement   **0 JGJI 1315**
SIGNED: 14 May 56
HEADNOTE: RESCUE PERSONS DISTRESS SEA
TOPIC: Humanitarian
PARTIES:
  Japan
  USSR (Soviet Union)

441094   Bilateral Exchange   **0 JGJI 1294**
SIGNED: 31 May 56
HEADNOTE: ABOLITION VISAS
TOPIC: Visas
PARTIES:
  Japan
  Tunisia

441095   Bilateral Exchange   **0 JGJI 1296**
SIGNED: 20 Jul 56
HEADNOTE: ABOLITION VISAS & FEES
TOPIC: Visas
PARTIES:
  Denmark
  Japan

441096   Bilateral Agreement   **0 JGJI 1299**
SIGNED: 2 Aug 56
HEADNOTE: MIGRATION
TOPIC: Health/Educ/Welfare
PARTIES:
  Bolivia
  Japan

441097   Bilateral Exchange   **0 JGJI 1303**
SIGNED: 8 Aug 56
HEADNOTE: ABOLITION VISAS
TOPIC: Visas
PARTIES:
  Japan
  Sweden

441099   Bilateral Exchange   **0 JGJI 1325**
SIGNED: 2 Nov 56
HEADNOTE: JAPANESE MINERS RUHR
TOPIC: Non-ILO Labor
PARTIES:
  Germany, West
  Japan

441100   Bilateral Agreement   **0 JGJI 1146**
SIGNED: 10 Dec 56
HEADNOTE: MONEY ORDERS
TOPIC: Postal Service
PARTIES:
  Japan
  USA (United States)

441101   Bilateral Agreement   **0 JGJI 1485**
SIGNED: 14 Dec 56
HEADNOTE: AIR SERVICES
TOPIC: Air Transport
PARTIES:
  Brazil
  Japan

441102   Bilateral Exchange   0 JGJI 1262
SIGNED: 26 Jul 57
HEADNOTE: ABOLITION VISAS
TOPIC: Visas
PARTIES:
  Germany, West
  Japan

441103   Bilateral Instrument   0 JGJI 1369
SIGNED: 31 Dec 57
HEADNOTE: KOREAN INTERNEES
TOPIC: Admin Cooperation
PARTIES:
  Japan
  Korea, South

441104   Bilateral Exchange   0 JGJI 1365
SIGNED: 20 Jan 58
HEADNOTE: ECONOMIC DEVELOPMENT LOAN
TOPIC: Loans and Credits
PARTIES:
  Indonesia
  Japan

441105   Bilateral Exchange   0 JGJI 9
SIGNED: 22 Jul 59
HEADNOTE: SHIP-BUILDING
TOPIC: Loans and Credits
PARTIES:
  Japan
  Paraguay

441106   Bilateral Exchange   0 JGJI 9
SIGNED: 7 Sep 59
HEADNOTE: SHIP-BUILDING
TOPIC: Loans and Credits
PARTIES:
  Japan
  Philippines

441107   Bilateral Agreement   0 JGJI 1413
SIGNED: 3 May 60
HEADNOTE: SEMINAR CRIMINAL LAW
TOPIC: IGO Operations
PARTIES:
  Japan
  United Nations

441108   Bilateral Agreement   0 JGJI 1445
SIGNED: 19 May 61
HEADNOTE: NUCLEAR MATERIAL LEASE
TOPIC: Atomic Energy
PARTIES:
  Japan
  USA (United States)

441109   Bilateral Exchange   0 JGJI 1460
SIGNED: 20 Dec 61
HEADNOTE: FRESH RUMINANTS & SWINE
TOPIC: Sanitation
PARTIES:
  Argentina
  Japan

441110   Bilateral Exchange   0 JGJI 1461
SIGNED: 20 Dec 61
HEADNOTE: ANIMAL PRODUCTS
TOPIC: Commodity Trade
PARTIES:
  Argentina
  Japan

441111   Bilateral Exchange   0 JGJI 1462
SIGNED: 20 Dec 61
HEADNOTE: CURED RUMINANTS & SWINE
TOPIC: Sanitation
PARTIES:
  Argentina
  Japan

441112   Bilateral Agreement   0 JGJI 1504
SIGNED: 20 Dec 61
HEADNOTE: MIGRATION
TOPIC: Health/Educ/Welfare

PARTIES:
  Argentina
  Japan

441113   Bilateral Exchange   0 JGJI 1477
SIGNED: 1 Aug 62
HEADNOTE: WAIVE VISAS & FEES
TOPIC: Visas
PARTIES:
  Japan
  Pakistan

441114   Bilateral Agreement   0 JGJI 1501
SIGNED: 24 Sep 62
HEADNOTE: ECONOMIC & TECHNICAL COOPER-
ATION
TOPIC: Direct Aid
PARTIES:
  Ghana
  Japan

441115   Bilateral Exchange   0 JGJI 1502
SIGNED: 21 Dec 62
HEADNOTE: INCOME AIR WATER NAVIGATION
TOPIC: Taxation
PARTIES:
  France
  Japan

441116   Bilateral Instrument   0 JGJI 1506
SIGNED: 23 May 63
HEADNOTE: TEXTILE TRAINING CENTER
TOPIC: Education
PARTIES:
  Ghana
  Japan

441117   Bilateral Agreement   0 JGJI 1527
SIGNED: 16 Nov 63
HEADNOTE: TELECOMMUNICATIONS RESEARCH
  WATER
TOPIC: Education
PARTIES:
  Japan
  Pakistan

441118   Bilateral Instrument   0 JGJI 1529
SIGNED: 14 Dec 63
HEADNOTE: SETTLE CERTAIN INDIAN CLAIMS
TOPIC: Claims and Debts
PARTIES:
  India
  Japan

441119   Bilateral Exchange   0 JGJI 1536
SIGNED: 27 Apr 64
HEADNOTE: INCOME AIR TRANSPORT
TOPIC: Taxation
PARTIES:
  Japan
  United Arab Rep

441120   Bilateral Exchange   0 JGJI 1548
SIGNED: 25 Jun 64
HEADNOTE: WAIVE VISA FEES
TOPIC: Visas
PARTIES:
  Japan
  Yugoslavia

441121   Bilateral Agreement   0 JGJI 1550
SIGNED: 30 Jul 64
HEADNOTE: TRAINING CENTER SMALL INDUS-
TRIES
TOPIC: Education
PARTIES:
  Japan
  Kenya

441122   Bilateral Exchange   0 JGJI 1558
SIGNED: 5 Sep 64
HEADNOTE: WAIVE VISAS & FEES
TOPIC: Visas

PARTIES:
  Canada
  Japan

441123   Bilateral Exchange   0 JGJI 1559
SIGNED: 5 Oct 64
HEADNOTE: INCOME AIR TRANSPORT
TOPIC: Taxation
PARTIES:
  Germany, West
  Japan

441124   Bilateral Agreement   0 JGJI 1563
SIGNED: 30 Oct 64
HEADNOTE: LEASE NUCLEAR MATERIAL
TOPIC: Atomic Energy
PARTIES:
  Japan
  USA (United States)

441125   Bilateral Agreement   0 JGJI 1564
SIGNED: 16 Nov 64
HEADNOTE: TRAINING CENTER ROAD CON-
STRUCTION
TOPIC: Education
PARTIES:
  Japan
  Thailand

441126   Bilateral Agreement   0 JGJI 1591
SIGNED: 24 Nov 64
HEADNOTE: TRADE
TOPIC: General Trade
PARTIES:
  Chad
  Japan

441127   Bilateral Agreement   0 JGJI 1567
SIGNED: 17 Dec 64
HEADNOTE: AGRICULTURE DEMONSTRATION
FARMS
TOPIC: Education
PARTIES:
  India
  Japan

441128   Bilateral Agreement   0 JGJI 1606
SIGNED: 26 Jan 65
HEADNOTE: MONEY ORDERS
TOPIC: Postal Service
PARTIES:
  India
  Japan

441129   Bilateral Agreement   0 JGJI 1614
SIGNED: 11 Feb 65
HEADNOTE: AIR SERVICES
TOPIC: Air Transport
PARTIES:
  Japan
  Malaysia

441130   Bilateral Instrument   0 JGJI 1585
SIGNED: 19 Feb 65
HEADNOTE: DEFERRED PAYMENTS
TOPIC: Finance
PARTIES:
  Brazil
  Japan

441131   Bilateral Instrument   0 JGJI 1622
SIGNED: 26 Feb 65
HEADNOTE: EXEMPTION VISAS
TOPIC: Visas
PARTIES:
  Japan
  USSR (Soviet Union)

441132   Bilateral Instrument   0 JGJI 1572
SIGNED: 16 Mar 65
HEADNOTE: VISAS
TOPIC: Visas

PARTIES:
Japan
Spain

441133   Bilateral Instrument   **0 JGJI 1587**
SIGNED: 26 Mar 65
HEADNOTE: DEFERRED PAYMENTS
TOPIC: Finance
PARTIES:
Brazil
Japan

441134   Bilateral Instrument   **0 JGJI 1588**
SIGNED: 2 Apr 65
HEADNOTE: OKINAWA ECONOMIC COMMITTEE
TOPIC: Admin Cooperation
PARTIES:
Japan
USA (United States)

441135   Bilateral Instrument   **0 JGJI 1589**
SIGNED: 7 Apr 65
HEADNOTE: MONEY ORDERS
TOPIC: Postal Service
PARTIES:
Japan
Laos

441136   Bilateral Instrument   **0 JGJI 1584**
SIGNED: 9 Apr 65
HEADNOTE: TRADE
TOPIC: General Trade
PARTIES:
Greece
Japan

441137   Bilateral Instrument   **0 JGJI 1598**
SIGNED: 30 Apr 65
HEADNOTE: TRADE
TOPIC: General Trade
PARTIES:
Austria
Japan

441138   Bilateral Instrument   **0 JGJI 1607**
SIGNED: 21 May 65
HEADNOTE: TRADE
TOPIC: General Trade
PARTIES:
Japan
Zambia

441139   Bilateral Instrument   **0 JGJI 1604**
SIGNED: 23 Jul 65
HEADNOTE: CIVIL USE ATOMIC ENERGY
TOPIC: Atomic Energy
PARTIES:
France
Japan

441140   Bilateral Instrument   **0 JGJI 1609**
SIGNED: 30 Aug 65
HEADNOTE: SALE NUCLEAR MATERIAL
TOPIC: Atomic Energy
PARTIES:
Japan
USA (United States)

441141   Bilateral Instrument   **0 JGJI 1610**
SIGNED: 31 Aug 65
HEADNOTE: DEFERRED PAYMENTS
TOPIC: Finance
PARTIES:
Chile
Japan

441142   Bilateral Instrument   **0 JGJI 1613**
SIGNED: 15 Oct 65
HEADNOTE: DEFERRED PAYMENTS
TOPIC: Finance
PARTIES:
Argentina
Japan

441143   Bilateral Instrument   **0 JGJI 1615**
SIGNED: 14 Dec 65
HEADNOTE: INFORMATION HIGH SPEED FURNACE
TOPIC: Admin Cooperation
PARTIES:
Japan
UK Great Britain

441144   Bilateral Exchange   **0 JGJI 1021**
SIGNED: 11 Jun 52
HEADNOTE: APPLY PART 19 AUG 11 TREATY
TOPIC: Admin Cooperation
PARTIES:
France
Japan

441145   Bilateral Agreement   **0 JGJI 1234**
SIGNED: 6 Jul 55
HEADNOTE: LOAN
TOPIC: Loans and Credits
PARTIES:
Export-Import Bank
Japan

441146   Bilateral Instrument   **0 JGJI 1254**
SIGNED: 18 Oct 55
HEADNOTE: IMPLEMENT REPARATIONS
TOPIC: Admin Cooperation
PARTIES:
Burma
Japan

441147   Bilateral Agreement   **0 JGJI 1300**
SIGNED: 10 Aug 56
HEADNOTE: LOAN
TOPIC: Loans and Credits
PARTIES:
Export-Import Bank
Japan

441148   Bilateral Exchange   **0 JGJI 1313**
SIGNED: 30 Nov 56
HEADNOTE: SALVAGE SUNKEN VESSELS
TOPIC: Reparations
PARTIES:
Japan
Philippines

441149   Bilateral Exchange   **0 JGJI 1401**
SIGNED: 16 May 59
HEADNOTE: ECONOMIC & TECHNICAL COOPERATION
TOPIC: General Economic
PARTIES:
Cambodia
Japan

441301   Bilateral Agreement   **61 JGJI 38**
SIGNED: 5 Aug 61
HEADNOTE: AIR BASE TRANSFER
TOPIC: Milit Installation
PARTIES:
Japan
Morocco

441302   Bilateral Convention   **62 JGJI 18**
SIGNED: 13 Feb 62
HEADNOTE: AGRICULTURE TECHNICAL AID
TOPIC: Tech Assistance
PARTIES:
Japan
Morocco

441303   Bilateral Instrument   **62 JGJI 19**
SIGNED: 17 Feb 62
HEADNOTE: MODIFIES 14 MAY 60
TOPIC: Non-IBRD Project
PARTIES:
Japan
Morocco

441304   Bilateral Convention   **62 JGJI 20**
SIGNED: 30 Mar 62

HEADNOTE: AGRICULTURE EDUCATION COOPERATION
TOPIC: Education
PARTIES:
Japan
Morocco

441305   Bilateral Convention   **63 JGJI 46**
SIGNED: 10 May 63
HEADNOTE: TRANSFER OF ASSETS
TOPIC: Claims and Debts
PARTIES:
Japan
Morocco

441306   Bilateral Convention   **65 JGJI 49**
SIGNED: 31 May 63
HEADNOTE: RADIO & TV COOPERATION
TOPIC: Mass Media
PARTIES:
Japan
Morocco

441307   Bilateral Convention   **63 JGJI 52**
SIGNED: 1 Jun 63
HEADNOTE: LABOR CONVENTION
TOPIC: Non-ILO Labor
PARTIES:
Japan
Morocco

441308   Bilateral Protocol   **63 JGJI 52**
SIGNED: 1 Jun 63
HEADNOTE: LABOR
TOPIC: Non-ILO Labor
PARTIES:
Japan
Morocco

442166   Bilateral Instrument   **66 JJS 229**
SIGNED: 7 Jan 66
HEADNOTE: COTTON YARNS
TOPIC: Commodity Trade
PARTIES:
Japan
Sierra Leone

442167   Bilateral Exchange   **66 JJS 201**
SIGNED: 29 Jan 66
HEADNOTE: MONEY ORDERS
TOPIC: Postal Service
PARTIES:
Japan
Laos

442168   Bilateral Exchange   **66 JJS 217**
SIGNED: 15 Feb 66
HEADNOTE: VOLUNTEERS
TOPIC: Direct Aid
PARTIES:
Japan
Philippines

442169   Bilateral Agreement   **66 JJS 257**
SIGNED: 22 Feb 66
HEADNOTE: TRADE
TOPIC: General Trade
PARTIES:
Japan
Spain

442170   Bilateral Agreement   **66 JJS 183**
SIGNED: 24 Mar 66
HEADNOTE: TRADE
TOPIC: General Trade
PARTIES:
Japan
Korea, South

442171   Bilateral Exchange   **66 JJS 177**
SIGNED: 31 Mar 66
HEADNOTE: VOLUNTEERS
TOPIC: Direct Aid

PARTIES:
Japan
Kenya

442172   Bilateral Exchange   **66 JJS 31**
SIGNED: 22 Jul 66
HEADNOTE: DOUBLE TAXATION
TOPIC: General Trade
PARTIES:
Benelux Econ Union
Japan

442173   Bilateral Exchange   **66 JJS 57**
SIGNED: 12 Aug 66
HEADNOTE: VOLUNTEERS
TOPIC: Direct Aid
PARTIES:
India
Japan

442174   Bilateral Instrument   **66 JJS 171**
SIGNED: 1 Sep 66
HEADNOTE: ABOLITION VISAS
TOPIC: Visas
PARTIES:
Ireland
Japan

442175   Bilateral Exchange   **66 JJS 89**
SIGNED: 9 Sep 66
HEADNOTE: YEN ASSISTANCE LOAN
TOPIC: Loans and Credits
PARTIES:
Ceylon (Sri Lanka)
Japan

442176   Bilateral Agreement   **66 JJS 221**
SIGNED: 29 Sep 66
HEADNOTE: TECHNICAL CENTER
TOPIC: Education
PARTIES:
Japan
Philippines

442177   Bilateral Exchange   **66 JJS 53**
SIGNED: 30 Sep 66
HEADNOTE: TECHNICAL COOPERATION
TOPIC: Tech Assistance
PARTIES:
Cambodia
Japan

442178   Bilateral Exchange   **68 JJS 39**
SIGNED: 7 Oct 66
HEADNOTE: FINANCIAL ASSISTANCE
TOPIC: Loans and Credits
PARTIES:
Brazil
Japan

442179   Bilateral Agreement   **66 JJS 247**
SIGNED: 15 Oct 66
HEADNOTE: TECHNICAL CENTER
TOPIC: Education
PARTIES:
Japan
Singapore

442180   Bilateral Exchange   **66 JJS 187**
SIGNED: 18 Oct 66
HEADNOTE: FISHING FLEETS
TOPIC: Specific Resources
PARTIES:
Japan
Korea, South

442181   Bilateral Exchange   **66 JJS 317**
SIGNED: 20 Oct 66
HEADNOTE: VOLUNTEERS
TOPIC: Direct Aid
PARTIES:
Japan
Tanzania

442182   Bilateral Exchange   **66 JJS 1**
SIGNED: 4 Nov 66
HEADNOTE: TRADE RELATIONS
TOPIC: General Trade
PARTIES:
Austria
Japan

442183   Bilateral Instrument   **66 JJS 153**
SIGNED: 15 Nov 66
HEADNOTE: ABOLITION VISAS
TOPIC: Visas
PARTIES:
Iceland
Japan

442184   Bilateral Exchange   **66 JJS 161**
SIGNED: 16 Dec 66
HEADNOTE: YEN ASSISTANCE LOAN
TOPIC: Loans and Credits
PARTIES:
India
Japan

442185   Bilateral Exchange   **67 JJS 201**
SIGNED: 13 Feb 67
HEADNOTE: TRADE
TOPIC: General Trade
PARTIES:
Greece
Japan

442186   Bilateral Exchange   **67 JJS 249**
SIGNED: 28 Apr 67
HEADNOTE: WATER RESOURCES
TOPIC: Scientific Project
PARTIES:
Japan
Korea, South

442187   Bilateral Exchange   **67 JJS 251**
SIGNED: 28 Apr 67
HEADNOTE: FISHING RESOURCES
TOPIC: Scientific Project
PARTIES:
Japan
Korea, South

442189   Bilateral Exchange   **67 JJS 193**
SIGNED: 22 May 67
HEADNOTE: TECHNICAL CENTER
TOPIC: Education
PARTIES:
Ghana
Japan

442190   Bilateral Agreement   **67 JJS 103**
SIGNED: 28 Mar 67
HEADNOTE: TRADE
TOPIC: General Trade
PARTIES:
Bulgaria
Japan

442192   Bilateral Exchange   **67 JJS 299**
SIGNED: 5 Jun 67
HEADNOTE: MONEY ORDERS
TOPIC: Postal Service
PARTIES:
Japan
Laos

442193   Bilateral Exchange   **67 JJS 229**
SIGNED: 9 Jun 67
HEADNOTE: YEN ASSISTANCE LOAN
TOPIC: Loans and Credits
PARTIES:
Indonesia
Japan

442194   Bilateral Exchange   **67 JJS 537**
SIGNED: 10 Jun 67
HEADNOTE: MEDICAL TREATMENT
TOPIC: Sanitation

PARTIES:
Japan
Vietnam, South

442195   Bilateral Exchange   **67 JJS 93**
SIGNED: 23 Jun 67
HEADNOTE: CUSTOMS EXEMPTIONS
TOPIC: Customs
PARTIES:
Brazil
Japan

442196   Bilateral Exchange   **67 JJS 207**
SIGNED: 14 Jul 67
HEADNOTE: YEN ASSISTANCE LOAN
TOPIC: Loans and Credits
PARTIES:
India
Japan

442197   Bilateral Agreement   **67 JJS 455**
SIGNED: 20 Jul 67
HEADNOTE: TECHNICAL COOPERATION
TOPIC: Scientific Project
PARTIES:
Japan
USSR (Soviet Union)

442198   Bilateral Exchange   **67 JJS 311**
SIGNED: 24 Jul 67
HEADNOTE: TECHNICAL COOPERATION
TOPIC: Tech Assistance
PARTIES:
Japan
Mexico

442199   Bilateral Agreement   **68 JJS 175**
SIGNED: 18 Aug 67
HEADNOTE: TRADE
TOPIC: General Trade
PARTIES:
Ethiopia
Japan

442200   Bilateral Exchange   **67 JJS 205**
SIGNED: 29 Aug 67
HEADNOTE: DEBT RELIEF MEASURES
TOPIC: Claims and Debts
PARTIES:
India
Japan

442201   Bilateral Exchange   **67 JJS 221**
SIGNED: 5 Sep 67
HEADNOTE: AID
TOPIC: Loans and Credits
PARTIES:
India
Japan

442202   Bilateral Exchange   **67 JJS 119**
SIGNED: 22 Sep 67
HEADNOTE: COMMODITY AID
TOPIC: Loans and Credits
PARTIES:
Ceylon (Sri Lanka)
Japan

442203   Bilateral Exchange   **67 JJS 325**
SIGNED: 11 Sep 67
HEADNOTE: VOLUNTEER
TOPIC: Direct Aid
PARTIES:
Japan
Morocco

442204   Bilateral Exchange   **67 JJS 291**
SIGNED: 25 Oct 67
HEADNOTE: TECHNICAL CENTER
TOPIC: Education
PARTIES:
Japan
Korea, South

442205   Bilateral Agreement   **67 JJS 243**
SIGNED: 10 Nov 67
HEADNOTE: SURPLUS GOODS SERVICES
TOPIC: General Aid
PARTIES:
  Indonesia
  Japan

442208   Bilateral Instrument   **68 JJS 421**
SIGNED: 15 Jan 68
HEADNOTE: ABOLITION VISAS
TOPIC: Visas
PARTIES:
  Japan
  San Marino

442209   Bilateral Exchange   **68 JJS 299**
SIGNED: 28 Feb 68
HEADNOTE: CREDIT LOANS
TOPIC: Loans and Credits
PARTIES:
  Japan
  Laos

442211   Bilateral Instrument   **68 JJS 3**
SIGNED: 15 Mar 68
HEADNOTE: ABOLITION VISAS
TOPIC: Visas
PARTIES:
  Bulgaria
  Japan

442212   Bilateral Protocol   **68 JJS 187**
SIGNED: 30 Mar 68
HEADNOTE: TRADE
TOPIC: General Trade
PARTIES:
  France
  Japan

442213   Bilateral Agreement   **68 JJS 247**
SIGNED: 29 May 68
HEADNOTE: TECHNICAL COOPERATION
TOPIC: Tech Assistance
PARTIES:
  Indonesia
  Japan

442214   Bilateral Agreement   **68 JJS 283**
SIGNED: 23 Jun 68
HEADNOTE: TRADE
TOPIC: General Trade
PARTIES:
  Iran
  Japan

442215   Bilateral Agreement   **68 JJS 445**
SIGNED: 28 Jun 68
HEADNOTE: VOCATIONAL TRAINING
TOPIC: Education
PARTIES:
  Japan
  Uganda

442216   Bilateral Exchange   **68 JJS 263**
SIGNED: 2 Jul 68
HEADNOTE: VERIFY LOAN
TOPIC: Loans and Credits
PARTIES:
  Indonesia
  Japan

442217   Bilateral Exchange   **68 JJS 165**
SIGNED: 26 Jul 68
HEADNOTE: VOLUNTEER
TOPIC: Direct Aid
PARTIES:
  El Salvador
  Japan

442218   Bilateral Exchange   **68 JJS 113**
SIGNED: 3 Sep 68
HEADNOTE: YEN ASSISTANCE LOAN
TOPIC: Loans and Credits

PARTIES:
  Ceylon (Sri Lanka)
  Japan

442219   Bilateral Instrument   **68 JJS 57**
SIGNED: 15 Oct 68
HEADNOTE: COMMERCIAL
TOPIC: General Economic
PARTIES:
  Central Afri Rep
  Japan

442220   Bilateral Exchange   **68 JJS 439**
SIGNED: 21 Oct 68
HEADNOTE: DOUBLE TAXATION
TOPIC: Taxation
PARTIES:
  Japan
  South Africa

442221   Bilateral Exchange   **68 JJS 49**
SIGNED: 2 Nov 68
HEADNOTE: DEVELOPMENT ASSISTANCE
TOPIC: Tech Assistance
PARTIES:
  Cambodia
  Japan

442222   Bilateral Agreement   **68 JJS 327**
SIGNED: 13 Nov 68
HEADNOTE: TRADE
TOPIC: General Trade
PARTIES:
  Japan
  Malta

442223   Bilateral Exchange   **68 JJS 417**
SIGNED: 29 Nov 68
HEADNOTE: TECHNICAL ASSISTANCE
TOPIC: Tech Assistance
PARTIES:
  Japan
  Philippines

442224   Bilateral Instrument   **68 JJS 293**
SIGNED: 3 Dec 68
HEADNOTE: TRADEMARKS
TOPIC: Patents/Copyrights
PARTIES:
  Japan
  Korea, South

442225   Bilateral Exchange   **68 JJS 1**
SIGNED: 24 Dec 68
HEADNOTE: TRADE
TOPIC: General Trade
PARTIES:
  Austria
  Japan

442226   Bilateral Exchange   **68 JJS 305**
SIGNED: 24 Dec 68
HEADNOTE: AGRICULTURAL GOODS
TOPIC: General Aid
PARTIES:
  Japan
  Laos

442227   Bilateral Exchange   **68 JJS 121**
SIGNED: 27 Dec 68
HEADNOTE: COMMERCIAL CREDIT
TOPIC: Loans and Credits
PARTIES:
  Ceylon (Sri Lanka)
  Japan

442229   Bilateral Instrument   **69 JJS 35**
SIGNED: 10 Jan 69
HEADNOTE: VISA FEES
TOPIC: Visas
PARTIES:
  Australia
  Japan

442230   Bilateral Exchange   **69 JJS 275**
SIGNED: 21 Jan 69
HEADNOTE: VOLUNTEERS
TOPIC: Direct Aid
PARTIES:
  Japan
  Kenya

442231   Bilateral Exchange   **69 JJS 561**
SIGNED: 22 Jan 69
HEADNOTE: ASSIST MIDDLE EAST REFUGEES
TOPIC: Direct Aid
PARTIES:
  Japan
  FAO (Food Agri)

442232   Bilateral Exchange   **69 JJS 211**
SIGNED: 14 Feb 69
HEADNOTE: YEN ASSISTANCE LOANS
TOPIC: Loans and Credits
PARTIES:
  India
  Japan

442233   Bilateral Exchange   **69 JJS 69**
SIGNED: 15 Feb 69
HEADNOTE: YEN ASSISTANCE LOANS
TOPIC: Loans and Credits
PARTIES:
  Burma
  Japan

442234   Bilateral Exchange   **69 JJS 357**
SIGNED: 21 Feb 69
HEADNOTE: YEN ASSISTANCE LOANS
TOPIC: Loans and Credits
PARTIES:
  Japan
  Philippines

442235   Bilateral Exchange   **69 JJS 397**
SIGNED: 7 Mar 69
HEADNOTE: AIR ROUTES
TOPIC: Air Transport
PARTIES:
  Japan
  USSR (Soviet Union)

442237   Bilateral Exchange   **69 JJS 75**
SIGNED: 21 Mar 69
HEADNOTE: YEN ASSISTANCE LOANS
TOPIC: Direct Aid
PARTIES:
  Cambodia
  Japan

442239   Bilateral Exchange   **69 JJS 287**
SIGNED: 1 Apr 69
HEADNOTE: TAX EXEMPTIONS
TOPIC: Taxation
PARTIES:
  Japan
  Korea, South

442240   Bilateral Exchange   **69 JJS 423**
SIGNED: 18 Apr 69
HEADNOTE: FISHERIES
TOPIC: Specific Resources
PARTIES:
  Japan
  USSR (Soviet Union)

442241   Bilateral Agreement   **69 JJS 367**
SIGNED: 17 Jun 69
HEADNOTE: PILOT FIRMS
TOPIC: Tech Assistance
PARTIES:
  Japan
  Philippines

442242   Bilateral Exchange   **69 JJS 317**
SIGNED: 19 Jun 69
HEADNOTE: DOUBLE TAXATION
TOPIC: Taxation

PARTIES:
Japan
Lebanon

442243   Bilateral Exchange   **69 JJS 183**
SIGNED: 24 Jun 69
HEADNOTE: COMMERCE
TOPIC: General Economic
PARTIES:
Greece
Japan

442244   Bilateral Exchange   **69 JJS 211**
SIGNED: 4 Jul 69
HEADNOTE: YEN ASSISTANCE LOAN
TOPIC: Direct Aid
PARTIES:
Indonesia
Japan

442245   Bilateral Agreement   **69 JJS 235**
SIGNED: 18 Jul 69
HEADNOTE: TECHNICAL ASSISTANCE
TOPIC: Tech Assistance
PARTIES:
Indonesia
Japan

442246   Bilateral Exchange   **69 JJS 341**
SIGNED: 25 Jul 69
HEADNOTE: DEBT REPAYMENT
TOPIC: Finance
PARTIES:
Japan
Pakistan

442247   Bilateral Agreement   **69 JJS 349**
SIGNED: 8 Aug 68
HEADNOTE: MONEY ORDERS
TOPIC: Postal Service
PARTIES:
Japan
Philippines

442248   Bilateral Agreement   **69 JJS 155**
SIGNED: 30 Sep 69
HEADNOTE: COTTON TEXTILES
TOPIC: Commodity Trade
PARTIES:
France
Japan

442249   Bilateral Exchange   **69 JJS 11**
SIGNED: 4 Oct 69
HEADNOTE: AGRICULTURAL ASSISTANCE
TOPIC: Direct Aid
PARTIES:
Afghanistan
Japan

442250   Bilateral Agreement   **69 JJS 45**
SIGNED: 22 Oct 69
HEADNOTE: COTTON TEXTILES
TOPIC: Commodity Trade
PARTIES:
Benelux Econ Union
Japan

442251   Bilateral Agreement   **69 JJS 169**
SIGNED: 22 Oct 69
HEADNOTE: COTTON GOODS
TOPIC: Commodity Trade
PARTIES:
Germany, West
Japan

442252   Bilateral Instrument   **69 JJS 133**
SIGNED: 22 Oct 69
HEADNOTE: ABOLITION VISAS
TOPIC: Visas
PARTIES:
Chile
Japan

442253   Bilateral Agreement   **69 JJS 259**
SIGNED: 22 Oct 69
HEADNOTE: COTTON TEXTILES
TOPIC: Commodity Trade
PARTIES:
Italy
Japan

442254   Bilateral Exchange   **69 JJS 117**
SIGNED: 24 Oct 69
HEADNOTE: YEN ASSISTANCE LOAN
TOPIC: Loans and Credits
PARTIES:
Ceylon (Sri Lanka)
Japan

442255   Bilateral Exchange   **69 JJS 391**
SIGNED: 30 Oct 69
HEADNOTE: VOLUNTEERS
TOPIC: Direct Aid
PARTIES:
Japan
Syria

442256   Bilateral Exchange   **69 JJS 125**
SIGNED: 2 Nov 69
HEADNOTE: AGRICULTURE ASSISTANCE
TOPIC: Direct Aid
PARTIES:
Ceylon (Sri Lanka)
Japan

442257   Bilateral Exchange   **69 JJS 3**
SIGNED: 27 Nov 68
HEADNOTE: FINANCIAL ASSISTANCE
TOPIC: Loans and Credits
PARTIES:
Afghanistan
Japan

442258   Bilateral Agreement   **69 JJS 145**
SIGNED: 5 Dec 69
HEADNOTE: VOCATIONAL TRAINING
TOPIC: Education
PARTIES:
Taiwan
Japan

442259   Bilateral Exchange   **69 JJS 303**
SIGNED: 5 Dec 69
HEADNOTE: YEN ASSISTANCE LOAN
TOPIC: Loans and Credits
PARTIES:
Japan
Laos

442260   Bilateral Exchange   **69 JJS 309**
SIGNED: 23 Dec 69
HEADNOTE: AGRICULTURE ASSISTANCE
TOPIC: Direct Aid
PARTIES:
Japan
Laos

444001   Bilateral Convention   **66 MEXD 1708**
SIGNED: 12 Apr 62
HEADNOTE: CULTURAL EXCHANGE
TOPIC: Culture
PARTIES:
Bolivia
Mexico

444002   Bilateral Convention   **65 MEXD 2306**
SIGNED: 20 Jan 60
HEADNOTE: CULTURAL EXCHANGE
TOPIC: Culture
PARTIES:
Brazil
Mexico

444003   Bilateral Convention   **71 MEXD 903**
SIGNED: 17 Oct 66
HEADNOTE: AIR TRANSPORT
TOPIC: Air Transport

PARTIES:
Brazil
Mexico

444004   Bilateral Convention   **64 MEXD 607**
SIGNED: 21 Dec 61
HEADNOTE: AIR TRANSPORT
TOPIC: Air Transport
PARTIES:
Canada
Mexico

444005   Bilateral Convention   **70 MEXD 2904**
SIGNED: 29 Apr 66
HEADNOTE: CULTURE
TOPIC: Culture
PARTIES:
Korea, South
Mexico

444006   Bilateral Convention   **70 MEXD 2904**
SIGNED: 12 Dec 66
HEADNOTE: TRADE
TOPIC: General Trade
PARTIES:
Korea, South
Mexico

444007   Bilateral Treaty   **50 MEXD 1810**
SIGNED: 4 Feb 46
HEADNOTE: TRADE
TOPIC: General Trade
PARTIES:
Costa Rica
Mexico

444008   Bilateral Convention   **67 MEXD 2511**
SIGNED: 19 Jan 66
HEADNOTE: TECHNICAL ASSISTANCE
TOPIC: Tech Assistance
PARTIES:
Costa Rica
Mexico

444009   Bilateral Convention   **67 MEXD 2511**
SIGNED: 19 Jan 66
HEADNOTE: CULTURE
TOPIC: Culture
PARTIES:
Costa Rica
Mexico

444010   Bilateral Convention   **70 MEXD 304**
SIGNED: 8 Sep 66
HEADNOTE: AIR TRANSPORT
TOPIC: Air Transport
PARTIES:
Costa Rica
Mexico

444011   Bilateral Convention   **71 MEXD 903**
SIGNED: 9 Aug 68
HEADNOTE: CULTURAL EXCHANGE
TOPIC: Culture
PARTIES:
Czechoslovakia
Mexico

444012   Bilateral Convention   **63 MEXD 3010**
SIGNED: 28 Jan 60
HEADNOTE: CULTURAL EXCHANGE
TOPIC: Culture
PARTIES:
Chile
Mexico

444013   Bilateral Convention   **55 MEXD 2608**
SIGNED: 12 Jul 54
HEADNOTE: PROTECTION INTELLECTUAL PROPERTY
TOPIC: Patents/Copyrights
PARTIES:
Denmark
Mexico

444014　Bilateral Convention　**71 MEXD 503**
SIGNED: 4 Feb 70
HEADNOTE: AIR TRANSPORT
TOPIC: Air Transport
PARTIES:
　Denmark
　Mexico

444015　Bilateral Convention　**52 MEXD 2810**
SIGNED: 10 Aug 48
HEADNOTE: CULTURAL RELATIONS
TOPIC: Culture
PARTIES:
　Ecuador
　Mexico

444016　Bilateral Treaty　**52 MEXD 605**
SIGNED: 14 Dec 50
HEADNOTE: TRADE
TOPIC: General Trade
PARTIES:
　El Salvador
　Mexico

444017　Bilateral Convention　**67 MEXD 1711**
SIGNED: 13 Jan 66
HEADNOTE: CULTURAL EXCHANGE
TOPIC: Culture
PARTIES:
　El Salvador
　Mexico

444018　Bilateral Convention　**68 MEXD 1403**
SIGNED: 23 Jun 66
HEADNOTE: TECHNICAL ASSISTANCE
TOPIC: Tech Assistance
PARTIES:
　El Salvador
　Mexico

444019　Bilateral Treaty　**46 MEXD 3003**
SIGNED: 8 Nov 45
HEADNOTE: WATER DISTRIBUTION
TOPIC: Specific Resources
PARTIES:
　Mexico
　USA (United States)

444020　Bilateral Agreement　**71 MEXD 2001**
SIGNED: 11 Dec 68
HEADNOTE: RADIO BANDS SUNRISE SUNSET
TOPIC: Telecommunications
PARTIES:
　Mexico
　USA (United States)

444021　Bilateral Treaty　**71 MEXD 906**
SIGNED: 17 Jul 70
HEADNOTE: RECOVERY STOLEN CULTURAL
GOODS
TOPIC: Admin Cooperation
PARTIES:
　Mexico
　USA (United States)

444022　Bilateral Treaty　**72 MEXD 1501**
SIGNED: 23 Nov 70
HEADNOTE: BRAVO & COLORADO RIVERS
TOPIC: Territory Boundary
PARTIES:
　Mexico
　USA (United States)

444023　Bilateral Convention　**65 MEXD 2901**
SIGNED: 12 Jun 63
HEADNOTE: TELECOMMUNICATIONS
TOPIC: Telecommunications
PARTIES:
　Guatemala
　Mexico

444024　Bilateral Convention　**67 MEXD 402**
SIGNED: 16 Dec 66
HEADNOTE: CULTURAL EXCHANGE

TOPIC: Culture
PARTIES:
　Guatemala
　Mexico

444025　Bilateral Treaty　**64 MEXD 3012**
SIGNED: 12 Apr 60
HEADNOTE: TRADE
TOPIC: General Trade
PARTIES:
　Greece
　Mexico

444026　Bilateral Convention　**68 MEXD 1902**
SIGNED: 27 Oct 66
HEADNOTE: TECHNICAL ASSISTANCE
TOPIC: Tech Assistance
PARTIES:
　Honduras
　Mexico

444027　Bilateral Convention　**70 MEXD 703**
SIGNED: 15 Jan 66
HEADNOTE: CULTURAL EXCHANGE
TOPIC: Culture
PARTIES:
　Honduras
　Mexico

444028　Bilateral Convention　**62 MEXD 1602**
SIGNED: 10 Nov 61
HEADNOTE: TRADE
TOPIC: General Trade
PARTIES:
　Indonesia
　Mexico

444029　Bilateral Convention　**68 MEXD 2510**
SIGNED: 11 Jul 66
HEADNOTE: TECHNICAL COOPERATION
TOPIC: Tech Assistance
PARTIES:
　Israel
　Mexico

444030　Bilateral Treaty　**52 MEXD 1502**
SIGNED: 26 Jul 50
HEADNOTE: CULTURE
TOPIC: Culture
PARTIES:
　Lebanon
　Mexico

444031　Bilateral Convention　**51 MEXD 1105**
SIGNED: 19 Nov 46
HEADNOTE: ESTABLISH RADIO COMMUNICA-
TION
TOPIC: Telecommunications
PARTIES:
　Mexico
　Nicaragua

444032　Bilateral Convention　**68 MEXD 510**
SIGNED: 17 Jan 66
HEADNOTE: MUTUAL TECHNICAL ASSISTANCE
TOPIC: Tech Assistance
PARTIES:
　Mexico
　Nicaragua

444033　Bilateral Convention　**68 MEXD 1005**
SIGNED: 17 Jan 66
HEADNOTE: CULTURAL EXCHANGE
TOPIC: Culture
PARTIES:
　Mexico
　Nicaragua

444034　Bilateral Convention　**71 MEXD 603**
SIGNED: 4 Feb 70
HEADNOTE: AIR TRANSPORT
TOPIC: Air Transport

PARTIES:
　Mexico
　Norway

444035　Bilateral Convention　**67 MEXD 807**
SIGNED: 20 Jan 66
HEADNOTE: CULTURAL EXCHANGE
TOPIC: Culture
PARTIES:
　Mexico
　Panama

444036　Bilateral Convention　**60 MEXD 907**
SIGNED: 13 Aug 58
HEADNOTE: CULTURAL EXCHANGE
TOPIC: Culture
PARTIES:
　Mexico
　Paraguay

444037　Bilateral Convention　**62 MEXD 3010**
SIGNED: 3 Feb 60
HEADNOTE: CULTURAL EXCHANGE & COOPER-
ATION
TOPIC: Culture
PARTIES:
　Mexico
　Peru

444038　Bilateral Convention　**64 MEXD 1408**
SIGNED: 8 Apr 60
HEADNOTE: CULTURAL EXCHANGE
TOPIC: Culture
PARTIES:
　Mexico
　United Arab Rep

444039　Bilateral Convention　**66 MEXD 1708**
SIGNED: 25 Oct 63
HEADNOTE: TRADE
TOPIC: General Trade
PARTIES:
　Mexico
　United Arab Rep

444040　Bilateral Convention　**71 MEXD 803**
SIGNED: 4 Feb 70
HEADNOTE: AIR TRANSPORT
TOPIC: Air Transport
PARTIES:
　Mexico
　Sweden

444041　Bilateral Convention　**68 MEXD 2702**
SIGNED: 2 Jun 66
HEADNOTE: AIR TRANSPORT
TOPIC: Air Transport
PARTIES:
　Mexico
　Switzerland

444042　Bilateral Convention　**70 MEXD 808**
SIGNED: 28 May 68
HEADNOTE: CULTURAL & SCIENTIFIC EXCHANGE
TOPIC: Health/Educ/Welfare
PARTIES:
　Mexico
　USSR (Soviet Union)

444043　Bilateral Convention　**48 MEXD 1011**
SIGNED: 25 Jul 46
HEADNOTE: CULTURAL EXCHANGE
TOPIC: Culture
PARTIES:
　Mexico
　Venezuela

444044　Bilateral Convention　**54 MEXD 2202**
SIGNED: 17 Mar 50
HEADNOTE: TRADE
TOPIC: General Trade
PARTIES:
　Mexico
　Yugoslavia

444045　Bilateral Convention　**66 MEXD 1607**
SIGNED: 26 Mar 60
HEADNOTE: CULTURAL EXCHANGE
TOPIC: Culture
PARTIES:
　Mexico
　Yugoslavia

444046　Bilateral Protocol　**67 MEXD 1711**
SIGNED: 3 Jul 63
HEADNOTE: ADDITION TO TRADE CONVENTION
TOPIC: General Trade
PARTIES:
　Mexico
　Yugoslavia

447001　Bilateral Agreement　**52 NET 139**
SIGNED: 3 May 46
TOPIC: General Trade
PARTIES:
　Denmark
　Netherlands

447002　Bilateral Agreement　**52 NET 25**
SIGNED: 3 Aug 46
TOPIC: Finance
PARTIES:
　Netherlands
　Yugoslavia

447003　Bilateral Agreement　**51 NET 162**
SIGNED: 15 Nov 46
TOPIC: Finance
PARTIES:
　Czechoslovakia
　Netherlands

447004　Bilateral Exchange　**52 NET 64**
SIGNED: 21 Mar 47
TOPIC: Visas
PARTIES:
　Netherlands
　UK Great Britain

447005　Bilateral Agreement　**51 NET 151**
SIGNED: 12 May 47
TOPIC: Air Transport
PARTIES:
　Netherlands
　Uruguay

447006　Bilateral Agreement　**51 NET 95**
SIGNED: 20 Dec 47
TOPIC: Finance
PARTIES:
　Hungary
　Netherlands

447007　Bilateral Agreement　**51 NET 91**
SIGNED: 30 Dec 47
TOPIC: General Trade
PARTIES:
　Netherlands
　Sweden

447008　Bilateral Agreement　**51 NET 49**
SIGNED: 24 Jun 48
TOPIC: General Trade
PARTIES:
　Czechoslovakia
　Netherlands

447009　Bilateral Agreement　**0 NET 0**
SIGNED: 2 Jul 48
TOPIC: General Economic
PARTIES:
　Netherlands
　USSR (Soviet Union)

447010　Bilateral Agreement　**51 NET 67**
SIGNED: 20 May 49
TOPIC: General Trade

PARTIES:
　Netherlands
　Poland

447011　Bilateral Agreement　**51 NET 163**
SIGNED: 7 Jul 49
TOPIC: General Trade
PARTIES:
　Czechoslovakia
　Netherlands

447012　Bilateral Agreement　**51 NET 40**
SIGNED: 3 Aug 49
TOPIC: General Trade
PARTIES:
　France
　Netherlands

447013　Bilateral Treaty　**51 NET 137**
SIGNED: 20 Sep 49
TOPIC: Reparations
PARTIES:
　Netherlands
　UK Great Britain

447014　Bilateral Instrument　**51 NET 4**
SIGNED: 14 Jul 50
TOPIC: Status of Forces
PARTIES:
　Indonesia
　Netherlands

447015　Bilateral Exchange　**51 NET 1**
SIGNED: 6 Oct 50
TOPIC: Finance
PARTIES:
　Netherlands
　USA (United States)

447016　Bilateral Agreement　**51 NET 15**
SIGNED: 25 Nov 50
TOPIC: Non-ILO Labor
PARTIES:
　Belgium
　Netherlands

447017　Bilateral Exchange　**51 NET 11**
SIGNED: 22 Dec 50
TOPIC: General Trade
PARTIES:
　Ireland
　Netherlands

447018　Bilateral Agreement　**51 NET 59**
SIGNED: 22 Mar 51
TOPIC: General Transport
PARTIES:
　Austria
　Netherlands

447019　Bilateral Agreement　**51 NET 60**
SIGNED: 22 Mar 51
TOPIC: Finance
PARTIES:
　Austria
　Netherlands

447020　Bilateral Agreement　**51 NET 50**
SIGNED: 13 Apr 51
TOPIC: General Trade
PARTIES:
　Japan
　Netherlands

447021　Bilateral Agreement　**51 NET 51**
SIGNED: 13 Apr 51
TOPIC: Finance
PARTIES:
　Japan
　Netherlands

447022　Bilateral Agreement　**51 NET 64**
SIGNED: 21 Apr 51
TOPIC: Non-ILO Labor
PARTIES:
　Belgium
　Netherlands

447023　Bilateral Agreement　**51 NET 97**
SIGNED: 19 May 51
TOPIC: Finance
PARTIES:
　Italy
　Netherlands

447024　Bilateral Exchange　**51 NET 88**
SIGNED: 24 May 51
TOPIC: Visas
PARTIES:
　Austria
　Netherlands

447025　Bilateral Agreement　**51 NET 83**
SIGNED: 30 May 51
TOPIC: General Trade
PARTIES:
　Finland
　Netherlands

447026　Bilateral Agreement　**51 NET 106**
SIGNED: 15 Jun 51
TOPIC: Claims and Debts
PARTIES:
　Belgium
　Netherlands

447027　Bilateral Agreement　**51 NET 98**
SIGNED: 28 Jun 51
TOPIC: Non-ILO Labor
PARTIES:
　Netherlands
　Norway

447028　Bilateral Agreement　**51 NET 119**
SIGNED: 29 Jun 51
TOPIC: General Trade
PARTIES:
　Germany, West
　Netherlands

447029　Bilateral Agreement　**51 NET 113**
SIGNED: 11 Jul 51
TOPIC: Non-ILO Labor
PARTIES:
　Finland
　Netherlands

447030　Bilateral Agreement　**51 NET 104**
SIGNED: 14 Aug 51
TOPIC: Finance
PARTIES:
　Greece
　Netherlands

447031　Bilateral Exchange　**52 NET 27**
SIGNED: 29 Oct 51
TOPIC: General Trade
PARTIES:
　Ireland
　Netherlands

447032　Bilateral Agreement　**54 NET 90**
SIGNED: 7 Feb 52
TOPIC: General Trade
PARTIES:
　France
　Netherlands

447033　Bilateral Agreement　**52 NET 67**
SIGNED: 5 Mar 52
TOPIC: Air Transport
PARTIES:
　Netherlands
　Paraguay

447034   Bilateral Exchange   **52 NET 97**
SIGNED: 22 Jul 52
TOPIC: Land Transport
PARTIES:
  Netherlands
  Switzerland

447035   Bilateral Exchange   **52 NET 106**
SIGNED: 24 Jul 52
TOPIC: Visas
PARTIES:
  Finland
  Netherlands

447036   Bilateral Agreement   **53 NET 37**
SIGNED: 8 Jan 53
TOPIC: General Trade
PARTIES:
  Netherlands
  Portugal

447037   Bilateral Exchange   **53 NET 135**
SIGNED: 12 Mar 53
TOPIC: Claims and Debts
PARTIES:
  Netherlands
  USA (United States)

447038   Bilateral Agreement   **53 NET 43**
SIGNED: 21 Mar 53
TOPIC: General Trade
PARTIES:
  United Arab Rep
  Netherlands

447039   Bilateral Agreement   **53 NET 44**
SIGNED: 21 Mar 53
TOPIC: Finance
PARTIES:
  United Arab Rep
  Netherlands

447040   Bilateral Agreement   **54 NET 25**
SIGNED: 28 May 53
TOPIC: General Trade
PARTIES:
  Netherlands
  Switzerland

447041   Bilateral Agreement   **53 NET 95**
SIGNED: 7 Aug 53
TOPIC: General Trade
PARTIES:
  Italy
  Netherlands

447042   Bilateral Exchange   **53 NET 84**
SIGNED: 26 Aug 53
TOPIC: Finance
PARTIES:
  Netherlands
  Switzerland

447043   Bilateral Agreement   **53 NET 134**
SIGNED: 8 Dec 53
TOPIC: General Trade
PARTIES:
  Netherlands
  Spain

447044   Bilateral Exchange   **54 NET 157**
SIGNED: 7 Jan 54
TOPIC: Air Transport
PARTIES:
  Libya
  Netherlands

447045   Bilateral Agreement   **54 NET 46**
SIGNED: 27 Jan 54
TOPIC: Non-ILO Labor
PARTIES:
  Belgium
  Netherlands

447046   Bilateral Agreement   **54 NET 175**
SIGNED: 6 May 54
TOPIC: General Economic
PARTIES:
  Argentina
  Netherlands

447047   Bilateral Treaty   **54 NET 92**
SIGNED: 8 Jun 54
TOPIC: Taxation
PARTIES:
  Indonesia
  Netherlands

447048   Bilateral Agreement   **54 NET 187**
SIGNED: 9 Jul 54
TOPIC: Claims and Debts
PARTIES:
  Netherlands
  Norway

447049   Bilateral Protocol   **54 NET 113**
SIGNED: 10 Aug 54
TOPIC: General Amity
PARTIES:
  Indonesia
  Netherlands

447050   Bilateral Treaty   **54 NET 153**
SIGNED: 10 Sep 54
TOPIC: Customs
PARTIES:
  Belgium
  Netherlands

447051   Bilateral Agreement   **55 NET 23**
SIGNED: 16 Oct 54
TOPIC: Air Transport
PARTIES:
  Iraq
  Netherlands

447052   Bilateral Agreement   **55 NET 26**
SIGNED: 24 Dec 54
TOPIC: Non-ILO Labor
PARTIES:
  Italy
  Netherlands

447053   Bilateral Agreement   **55 NET 95**
SIGNED: 18 Feb 55
TOPIC: Finance
PARTIES:
  Austria
  Netherlands

447054   Bilateral Agreement   **55 NET 62**
SIGNED: 1 Apr 55
TOPIC: General Trade
PARTIES:
  Hungary
  Netherlands

447055   Bilateral Agreement   **55 NET 91**
SIGNED: 29 Jun 55
TOPIC: Finance
PARTIES:
  Finland
  Netherlands

447056   Bilateral Protocol   **55 NET 140**
SIGNED: 26 Jul 55
TOPIC: General Economic
PARTIES:
  Netherlands
  Turkey

447057   Bilateral Agreement   **56 NET 18**
SIGNED: 29 Oct 55
TOPIC: General Trade
PARTIES:
  Netherlands
  Poland

447058   Bilateral Agreement   **56 NET 19**
SIGNED: 29 Oct 55
TOPIC: Finance
PARTIES:
  Netherlands
  Poland

447059   Bilateral Agreement   **56 NET 96**
SIGNED: 29 Nov 55
TOPIC: General Economic
PARTIES:
  Brazil
  Netherlands

451001   Bilateral Agreement   **2 NORT 475**
SIGNED: 18 Mar 48
HEADNOTE: AIR TRANSPORT
TOPIC: Air Transport
PARTIES:
  Argentina
  Norway

451002   Bilateral Exchange   **2 NORT 488**
SIGNED: 9 Nov 48
HEADNOTE: TRANSPORT TAX EXEMPTIONS
TOPIC: Taxation
PARTIES:
  Argentina
  Norway

451003   Bilateral Treaty   **3 NORT 826**
SIGNED: 10 Mar 61
HEADNOTE: AVOID DUAL MILITARY SERVICE
TOPIC: Milit Servic/Citiz
PARTIES:
  Argentina
  Norway

451004   Bilateral Exchange   **3 NORT 842**
SIGNED: 6 Sep 61
HEADNOTE: ABOLITION OF VISAS
TOPIC: Visas
PARTIES:
  Argentina
  Norway

451005   Bilateral Exchange   **3 NORT 999**
SIGNED: 4 Jan 68
HEADNOTE: MARITIME AFFAIRS
TOPIC: Water Transport
PARTIES:
  Australia
  Norway

451006   Bilateral Agreement   **3 NORT 0**
SIGNED: 28 May 57
HEADNOTE: GOODS EXCHANGE
TOPIC: General Trade
PARTIES:
  Belgium
  Norway

451007   Bilateral Agreement   **3 NORT 999**
SIGNED: 30 Jun 67
HEADNOTE: DOUBLE TAXATION
TOPIC: Taxation
PARTIES:
  Belgium
  Norway

451008   Bilateral Agreement   **3 NORT 838**
SIGNED: 19 Jul 61
HEADNOTE: ABOLITION OF VISAS
TOPIC: Visas
PARTIES:
  Bolivia
  Norway

451009   Bilateral Agreement   **2 NORT 583**
SIGNED: 27 May 52
HEADNOTE: DIPLOMATIC MAIL
TOPIC: Consul/Citizenship

PARTIES:
Brazil
Norway

451010   Bilateral Exchange   **3 NORT 705**
SIGNED: 19 Dec 56
HEADNOTE: COPYRIGHT EXTENSIONS
TOPIC: Patents/Copyrights
PARTIES:
Brazil
Norway

451011   Bilateral Exchange   **3 NORT 772**
SIGNED: 29 May 59
HEADNOTE: PARTIAL VISA ABOLITION
TOPIC: Visas
PARTIES:
Brazil
Norway

451012   Bilateral Agreement   **3 NORT 839**
SIGNED: 11 Aug 61
HEADNOTE: PAYMENTS
TOPIC: Finance
PARTIES:
Brazil
Norway

451013   Bilateral Agreement   **3 NORT 1005**
SIGNED: 20 Oct 67
HEADNOTE: DOUBLE TAXATION
TOPIC: Taxation
PARTIES:
Brazil
Norway

451014   Bilateral Agreement   **3 NORT 746**
SIGNED: 19 Jun 58
HEADNOTE: AIR TRANSPORT
TOPIC: Air Transport
PARTIES:
Bulgaria
Norway

451015   Bilateral Agreement   **3 NORT 1007**
SIGNED: 28 Oct 67
HEADNOTE: ABOLITION OF VISAS
TOPIC: Visas
PARTIES:
Bulgaria
Norway

451016   Bilateral Agreement   **3 NORT 0**
SIGNED: 15 Nov 68
HEADNOTE: COMMERCE
TOPIC: General Trade
PARTIES:
Bulgaria
Norway

451017   Bilateral Exchange   **2 NORT 637**
SIGNED: 6 Jul 54
HEADNOTE: LEGATION AUTOS CUSTOMS EX-
EMPTION
TOPIC: Privil/Immunities
PARTIES:
Canada
Norway

451018   Bilateral Exchange   **3 NORT 0**
SIGNED: 26 Apr 68
HEADNOTE: SEALING REGULATIONS
TOPIC: Specific Resources
PARTIES:
Canada
Norway

451019   Bilateral Exchange   **3 NORT 0**
SIGNED: 8 Oct 68
HEADNOTE: AMATEUR RADIO OPERATIONS
TOPIC: Gen Communications
PARTIES:
Canada
Norway

451020   Bilateral Agreement   **2 NORT 592**
SIGNED: 27 Oct 52
HEADNOTE: AIR TRANSPORT
TOPIC: Air Transport
PARTIES:
Chile
Norway

451021   Bilateral Agreement   **3 NORT 849**
SIGNED: 5 Feb 62
HEADNOTE: CHILE IMPORT DEBIT GUARANTEE
TOPIC: Claims and Debts
PARTIES:
Chile
Norway

451022   Bilateral Agreement   **3 NORT 742**
SIGNED: 4 Jun 58
HEADNOTE: PAYMENTS & TRADE
TOPIC: General Economic
PARTIES:
China People's Rep
Norway

451023   Bilateral Exchange   **3 NORT 829**
SIGNED: 4 Apr 61
HEADNOTE: VISA FEE ABOLITION
TOPIC: Visas
PARTIES:
China People's Rep
Norway

451024   Bilateral Agreement   **3 NORT 890**
SIGNED: 18 Jun 63
HEADNOTE: CULTURAL
TOPIC: Culture
PARTIES:
China People's Rep
Norway

451025   Bilateral Agreement   **3 NORT 1008**
SIGNED: 2 Dec 67
HEADNOTE: NORWAY EMBASSY COMPLEX
TOPIC: Consul/Citizenship
PARTIES:
China People's Rep
Norway

451026   Bilateral Exchange   **3 NORT 785**
SIGNED: 1 Oct 59
HEADNOTE: PARTIAL VISA ABOLITION
TOPIC: Visas
PARTIES:
Colombia
Norway

451027   Bilateral Instrument   **2 NORT 590**
SIGNED: 15 Oct 52
HEADNOTE: COMMERCE MODUS VIVENDI
TOPIC: General Trade
PARTIES:
Costa Rica
Norway

451028   Bilateral Instrument   **3 NORT 785**
SIGNED: 21 Oct 59
HEADNOTE: NORWAY VISA ABOLITION
TOPIC: Visas
PARTIES:
Costa Rica
Norway

451029   Bilateral Instrument   **3 NORT 785**
SIGNED: 6 Jan 60
HEADNOTE: ABOLISH COSTA RICA VISA FEE
TOPIC: Visas
PARTIES:
Costa Rica
Norway

451030   Bilateral Exchange   **2 NORT 599**
SIGNED: 6 Mar 53
HEADNOTE: ABOLITION OF VISAS
TOPIC: Visas

PARTIES:
Cuba
Norway

451031   Bilateral Treaty   **2 NORT 553**
SIGNED: 18 May 55
HEADNOTE: DOUBLE TAXATION
TOPIC: Taxation
PARTIES:
Cyprus
Norway

451032   Bilateral Exchange   **3 NORT 857**
SIGNED: 25 May 62
HEADNOTE: ABOLITION OF VISAS
TOPIC: Visas
PARTIES:
Cyprus
Norway

451033   Bilateral Protocol   **2 NORT 636**
SIGNED: 9 Jun 54
HEADNOTE: FINANCIAL CLAIMS SETTLEMENT
TOPIC: Claims and Debts
PARTIES:
Czechoslovakia
Norway

451034   Bilateral Agreement   **3 NORT 0**
SIGNED: 3 Dec 68
HEADNOTE: AIR TRANSPORT
TOPIC: Air Transport
PARTIES:
Czechoslovakia
Norway

451035   Bilateral Agreement   **3 NORT 0**
SIGNED: 3 Dec 68
HEADNOTE: COMMERCE
TOPIC: General Trade
PARTIES:
Czechoslovakia
Norway

451036   Bilateral Exchange   **3 NORT 752**
SIGNED: 31 Oct 58
HEADNOTE: KOREA MEDICAL STAFF TAX FREE
TOPIC: Privil/Immunities
PARTIES:
Denmark
Norway

451037   Bilateral Exchange   **3 NORT 863**
SIGNED: 5 Sep 62
HEADNOTE: SOUND BUS ACCESS
TOPIC: Water Transport
PARTIES:
Denmark
Norway

451038   Bilateral Exchange   **3 NORT 0**
SIGNED: 26 Apr 68
HEADNOTE: JUTLAND FISHERY
TOPIC: Specific Resources
PARTIES:
Denmark
Norway

451039   Bilateral Instrument   **3 NORT 786**
SIGNED: 27 Oct 59
HEADNOTE: NORWAY VISA ABOLITION
TOPIC: Visas
PARTIES:
Dominican Republic
Norway

451040   Bilateral Instrument   **3 NORT 786**
SIGNED: 28 Apr 60
HEADNOTE: VISA FEE ABOLITION
TOPIC: Visas
PARTIES:
Dominican Republic
Norway

451041   Bilateral Exchange   **2 NORT 548**
SIGNED: 15 Jan 51
HEADNOTE: COMMERCE MODUS VIVENDI
TOPIC: General Trade
PARTIES:
  Ecuador
  Norway

451042   Bilateral Exchange   **3 NORT 899**
SIGNED: 29 Jan 64
HEADNOTE: ABOLITION OF VISAS
TOPIC: Visas
PARTIES:
  Ecuador
  Norway

451043   Bilateral Agreement   **3 NORT 963**
SIGNED: 30 Apr 66
HEADNOTE: COMMERCE
TOPIC: General Trade
PARTIES:
  Ivory Coast
  Norway

451044   Bilateral Agreement   **3 NORT 967**
SIGNED: 7 Jun 66
HEADNOTE: AIR TRANSPORT
TOPIC: Air Transport
PARTIES:
  Ivory Coast
  Norway

451045   Bilateral Agreement   **3 NORT 968**
SIGNED: 7 Jun 66
HEADNOTE: ABOLITION OF VISAS
TOPIC: Visas
PARTIES:
  Ivory Coast
  Norway

451046   Bilateral Exchange   **3 NORT 1009**
SIGNED: 4 Dec 67
HEADNOTE: EMBASSY HOME BUILT DUTY FREE
TOPIC: Privil/Immunities
PARTIES:
  Ivory Coast
  Norway

451048   Bilateral Convention   **2 NORT 551**
SIGNED: 25 Apr 51
HEADNOTE: WATER TRANSFERS
TOPIC: Specific Resources
PARTIES:
  Finland
  Norway

451049   Bilateral Exchange   **2 NORT 578**
SIGNED: 16 Jan 52
HEADNOTE: FRONTIER INSPECTION 1950
TOPIC: General Ad Hoc
PARTIES:
  Finland
  Norway

451051   Bilateral Agreement   **2 NORT 623**
SIGNED: 29 Mar 54
HEADNOTE: DOUBLE INCOME TAXATION
TOPIC: Taxation
PARTIES:
  Finland
  Norway

451052   Bilateral Agreement   **2 NORT 624**
SIGNED: 29 Mar 54
HEADNOTE: DOUBLE DEATH DUTIES
TOPIC: Taxation
PARTIES:
  Finland
  Norway

451053   Bilateral Agreement   **2 NORT 625**
SIGNED: 29 Mar 54
HEADNOTE: TAX MATTERS ASSISTANCE
TOPIC: Taxation

PARTIES:
  Finland
  Norway

451055   Bilateral Exchange   **2 NORT 241**
SIGNED: 29 Jun 61
HEADNOTE: EXTRADITION
TOPIC: Extradition
PARTIES:
  Finland
  Norway

451056   Bilateral Agreement   **3 NORT 0**
SIGNED: 10 Dec 68
HEADNOTE: FRONTIER CUSTOMS
TOPIC: Customs
PARTIES:
  Finland
  Norway

451057   Bilateral Agreement   **2 NORT 572**
SIGNED: 6 Nov 51
HEADNOTE: ACCEPTANCE OF TRAINEES
TOPIC: Education
PARTIES:
  France
  Norway

451058   Bilateral Agreement   **2 NORT 607**
SIGNED: 22 Sep 53
HEADNOTE: DOUBLE TAXATION
TOPIC: Taxation
PARTIES:
  France
  Norway

451059   Bilateral Agreement   **2 NORT 611**
SIGNED: 4 Dec 53
HEADNOTE: CULTURAL
TOPIC: Culture
PARTIES:
  France
  Norway

451060   Bilateral Convention   **2 NORT 641**
SIGNED: 30 Sep 54
HEADNOTE: SOCIAL SECURITY
TOPIC: Non-ILO Labor
PARTIES:
  France
  Norway

451061   Bilateral Exchange   **3 NORT 699**
SIGNED: 20 Nov 56
HEADNOTE: COPYRIGHT EXTENSION
TOPIC: Patents/Copyrights
PARTIES:
  France
  Norway

451062   Bilateral Instrument   **3 NORT 886**
SIGNED: 24 May 63
HEADNOTE: IDENTITY CARD RECOGNITION
TOPIC: Visas
PARTIES:
  France
  Norway

451063   Bilateral Agreement   **2 NORT 553**
SIGNED: 18 May 55
HEADNOTE: DOUBLE TAXATION
TOPIC: Taxation
PARTIES:
  Gambia
  Norway

451064   Bilateral Exchange   **3 NORT 948**
SIGNED: 28 Oct 65
HEADNOTE: ABOLITION OF VISAS
TOPIC: Visas
PARTIES:
  Gambia
  Norway

451065   Bilateral Agreement   **3 NORT 0**
SIGNED: 29 Jun 68
HEADNOTE: FISHERMAN TRAINING CENTER
TOPIC: Tech Assistance
PARTIES:
  Ghana
  Norway

451066   Bilateral Agreement   **3 NORT 747**
SIGNED: 20 Jun 58
HEADNOTE: ABOLITION OF VISAS
TOPIC: Visas
PARTIES:
  Greece
  Norway

451067   Bilateral Instrument   **3 NORT 869**
SIGNED: 25 Oct 62
HEADNOTE: NORWAY VISA ABOLITION
TOPIC: Visas
PARTIES:
  Guatemala
  Norway

451068   Bilateral Instrument   **3 NORT 869**
SIGNED: 27 Apr 65
HEADNOTE: VISA FEE WAIVER
TOPIC: Visas
PARTIES:
  Guatemala
  Norway

451069   Bilateral Exchange   **3 NORT 869**
SIGNED: 29 Aug 67
HEADNOTE: VISA ABOLITION
TOPIC: Visas
PARTIES:
  Guatemala
  Norway

451070   Bilateral Exchange   **3 NORT 868**
SIGNED: 24 Oct 62
HEADNOTE: NORWAY VISA ABOLITION
TOPIC: Visas
PARTIES:
  Haiti
  Norway

451071   Bilateral Exchange   **3 NORT 873**
SIGNED: 29 Nov 62
HEADNOTE: ABOLITION OF VISAS
TOPIC: Visas
PARTIES:
  Honduras
  Norway

451072   Bilateral Agreement   **3 NORT 712**
SIGNED: 22 Feb 57
HEADNOTE: NATIONALIZATION CLAIMS
TOPIC: Claims and Debts
PARTIES:
  Hungary
  Norway

451073   Bilateral Agreement   **3 NORT 769**
SIGNED: 30 Apr 59
HEADNOTE: AIR TRANSPORT
TOPIC: Air Transport
PARTIES:
  Hungary
  Norway

451074   Bilateral Agreement   **3 NORT 883**
SIGNED: 9 May 63
HEADNOTE: PAYMENTS
TOPIC: Finance
PARTIES:
  Hungary
  Norway

451075   Bilateral Agreement   **3 NORT 981**
SIGNED: 9 Dec 66
HEADNOTE: COMMERCE
TOPIC: General Trade

PARTIES:
Hungary
Norway

451076   Bilateral Agreement   **2 NORT 664**
SIGNED: 17 Sep 55
HEADNOTE: TAX EXEMPTION
TOPIC: Taxation
PARTIES:
Iceland
Norway

451077   Bilateral Agreement   **3 NORT 959**
SIGNED: 30 Mar 66
HEADNOTE: TAX EVASION & DOUBLE TAX
TOPIC: Taxation
PARTIES:
Iceland
Norway

451078   Bilateral Exchange   **3 NORT 0**
SIGNED: 9 Sep 68
HEADNOTE: AMATEUR RADIO OPERATION
TOPIC: Gen Communications
PARTIES:
Iceland
Norway

451079   Bilateral Agreement   **3 NORT 992**
SIGNED: 17 Mar 67
HEADNOTE: FISHERIES DEVELOPMENT
TOPIC: Specific Resources
PARTIES:
India
Norway

451080   Bilateral Agreement   **3 NORT 0**
SIGNED: 16 Sep 68
HEADNOTE: DEVELOPMENT CREDIT
TOPIC: Loans and Credits
PARTIES:
India
Norway

451081   Bilateral Exchange   **3 NORT 0**
SIGNED: 14 Nov 68
HEADNOTE: WAIVER VISA FEE
TOPIC: Visas
PARTIES:
India
Norway

451082   Bilateral Agreement   **2 NORT 552**
SIGNED: 30 Apr 51
HEADNOTE: COMMERCE
TOPIC: General Trade
PARTIES:
Indonesia
Norway

451083   Bilateral Agreement   **2 NORT 621**
SIGNED: 22 Jun 54
HEADNOTE: PAYMENTS
TOPIC: Finance
PARTIES:
Indonesia
Norway

451084   Bilateral Agreement   **2 NORT 535**
SIGNED: 31 May 50
HEADNOTE: AIR TRANSPORT
TOPIC: Air Transport
PARTIES:
Iran
Norway

451085   Bilateral Exchange   **3 NORT 699**
SIGNED: 4 Nov 56
HEADNOTE: AIR TRANSPORT TAX EXEMPTION
TOPIC: Taxation
PARTIES:
Iran
Norway

451086   Bilateral Exchange   **3 NORT 958**
SIGNED: 10 Mar 66
HEADNOTE: NORWAY PEACE CORPS TERMS
TOPIC: Tech Assistance
PARTIES:
Iran
Norway

451087   Bilateral Exchange   **3 NORT 0**
SIGNED: 25 Jan 68
HEADNOTE: ABOLITION OF VISAS
TOPIC: Visas
PARTIES:
Iran
Norway

451088   Bilateral Agreement   **3 NORT 836**
SIGNED: 15 Jun 61
HEADNOTE: TRADE & PAYMENTS
TOPIC: General Economic
PARTIES:
Israel
Norway

451090   Bilateral Agreement   **3 NORT 961**
SIGNED: 29 Apr 66
HEADNOTE: CULTURAL INSTITUTES TAX FREE
TOPIC: Taxation
PARTIES:
Italy
Norway

451091   Bilateral Exchange   **3 NORT 692**
SIGNED: 22 Aug 56
HEADNOTE: ABOLITION OF VISAS
TOPIC: Visas
PARTIES:
Japan
Norway

451092   Bilateral Agreement   **3 NORT 997**
SIGNED: 11 May 67
HEADNOTE: DOUBLE TAXATION AVOIDANCE
TOPIC: Taxation
PARTIES:
Japan
Norway

451093   Bilateral Exchange   **2 NORT 558**
SIGNED: 31 May 51
HEADNOTE: NATIONALIZED NORWAY PROPERTY
TOPIC: Claims and Debts
PARTIES:
Norway
Yugoslavia

451094   Bilateral Agreement   **2 NORT 660**
SIGNED: 24 Jun 55
HEADNOTE: CULTURAL
TOPIC: Culture
PARTIES:
Norway
Yugoslavia

451095   Bilateral Agreement   **3 NORT 689**
SIGNED: 30 May 56
HEADNOTE: EXCHANGE OF GOODS
TOPIC: General Trade
PARTIES:
Norway
Yugoslavia

451096   Bilateral Exchange   **3 NORT 794**
SIGNED: 21 Dec 59
HEADNOTE: TONNAGE CERTIFICATES
TOPIC: General Trade
PARTIES:
Norway
Yugoslavia

451097   Bilateral Agreement   **3 NORT 909**
SIGNED: 6 May 64
HEADNOTE: ABOLITION OF VISAS
TOPIC: Visas

PARTIES:
Norway
Yugoslavia

451098   Bilateral Exchange   **3 NORT 970**
SIGNED: 18 May 66
HEADNOTE: COMMERCIAL TAX EXEMPTIONS
TOPIC: Taxation
PARTIES:
Norway
Yugoslavia

451099   Bilateral Agreement   **3 NORT 0**
SIGNED: 21 Aug 68
HEADNOTE: ECONOMIC & INDUSTRIAL & TECH-
NICAL COOPERATION
TOPIC: General Economic
PARTIES:
Norway
Yugoslavia

451100   Bilateral Agreement   **3 NORT 937**
SIGNED: 3 Apr 65
HEADNOTE: TECHNICAL COOPERATION
TOPIC: Tech Assistance
PARTIES:
Kenya
Norway

451101   Bilateral Exchange   **2 NORT 553**
SIGNED: 9 Jul 65
HEADNOTE: AVOID DOUBLE TAXATION
TOPIC: Taxation
PARTIES:
Kenya
Norway

451102   Bilateral Agreement   **3 NORT 973**
SIGNED: 28 Aug 66
HEADNOTE: NURSE SCHOOL IN KENYA
TOPIC: Tech Assistance
PARTIES:
Kenya
Norway

451103   Bilateral Exchange   **3 NORT 942**
SIGNED: 24 May 65
HEADNOTE: TRADEMARK PATENT PROTECTION
TOPIC: Patents/Copyrights
PARTIES:
Korea, South
Norway

451104   Bilateral Agreement   **3 NORT 674**
SIGNED: 2 Feb 56
HEADNOTE: AIR TRANSPORT
TOPIC: Air Transport
PARTIES:
Lebanon
Norway

451105   Bilateral Exchange   **3 NORT 0**
SIGNED: 10 Dec 68
HEADNOTE: COMMERCIAL TAX EXEMPTIONS
TOPIC: Taxation
PARTIES:
Lebanon
Norway

451106   Bilateral Instrument   **3 NORT 889**
SIGNED: 23 Dec 63
HEADNOTE: IDENTITY CARD RECOGNITION
TOPIC: Visas
PARTIES:
Liechtenstein
Norway

451107   Bilateral Agreement   **2 NORT 568**
SIGNED: 17 Sep 51
HEADNOTE: PAYMENT
TOPIC: Finance
PARTIES:
Luxembourg
Norway

451108 Bilateral Agreement **3 NORT 717**
SIGNED: 28 May 57
HEADNOTE: EXCHANGE OF GOODS
TOPIC: General Trade
PARTIES:
 Luxembourg
 Norway

451109 Bilateral Treaty **3 NORT 964**
SIGNED: 13 May 66
HEADNOTE: FRIENDSHIP & NAVIGATION
TOPIC: General Amity
PARTIES:
 Malagasy
 Norway

451110 Bilateral Agreement **3 NORT 965**
SIGNED: 13 May 66
HEADNOTE: INVESTMENT GUARANTEE TRADE
TOPIC: General Economic
PARTIES:
 Malagasy
 Norway

451111 Bilateral Exchange **2 NORT 553**
SIGNED: 12 Jul 65
HEADNOTE: DOUBLE TAXATION
TOPIC: Taxation
PARTIES:
 Malawi
 Norway

451112 Bilateral Exchange **3 NORT 962**
SIGNED: 30 Apr 66
HEADNOTE: ABOLITION OF VISAS
TOPIC: Visas
PARTIES:
 Malawi
 Norway

451113 Bilateral Agreement **3 NORT 812**
SIGNED: 19 Sep 60
HEADNOTE: ABOLITION OF VISAS
TOPIC: Visas
PARTIES:
 Malaysia
 Norway

451114 Bilateral Agreement **3 NORT 1005**
SIGNED: 19 Oct 67
HEADNOTE: AIR TRANSPORT
TOPIC: Air Transport
PARTIES:
 Malaysia
 Norway

451115 Bilateral Agreement **3 NORT 798**
SIGNED: 11 Feb 60
HEADNOTE: ABOLITION OF VISAS
TOPIC: Visas
PARTIES:
 Morocco
 Norway

451116 Bilateral Agreement **3 NORT 792**
SIGNED: 10 Dec 59
HEADNOTE: ABOLITION OF VISAS
TOPIC: Visas
PARTIES:
 Mexico
 Norway

451117 Bilateral Agreement **2 NORT 456**
SIGNED: 3 Jun 47
HEADNOTE: ABOLITION OF VISAS
TOPIC: Visas
PARTIES:
 Netherlands
 Norway

451118 Bilateral Agreement **2 NORT 562**
SIGNED: 28 Jun 51
HEADNOTE: ACCEPTANCE OF TRAINEES
TOPIC: Non-ILO Labor

PARTIES:
 Netherlands
 Norway

451119 Bilateral Agreement **3 NORT 717**
SIGNED: 28 May 57
HEADNOTE: EXCHANGE OF GOODS
TOPIC: General Trade
PARTIES:
 Netherlands
 Norway

451120 Bilateral Instrument **3 NORT 815**
SIGNED: 17 Oct 60
HEADNOTE: NORWAY VISA ABOLITION
TOPIC: Visas
PARTIES:
 Nicaragua
 Norway

451121 Bilateral Instrument **3 NORT 815**
SIGNED: 27 Mar 68
HEADNOTE: NICARAGUA VISA ABOLITION
TOPIC: Visas
PARTIES:
 Nicaragua
 Norway

451122 Bilateral Agreement **3 NORT 956**
SIGNED: 15 Feb 66
HEADNOTE: ABOLITION OF VISAS
TOPIC: Visas
PARTIES:
 Niger
 Norway

451123 Bilateral Agreement **2 NORT 553**
SIGNED: 18 May 55
HEADNOTE: DOUBLE TAXATION
TOPIC: Taxation
PARTIES:
 Nigeria
 Norway

451124 Bilateral Agreement **3 NORT 974**
SIGNED: 8 Sep 66
HEADNOTE: AIR TRANSPORT
TOPIC: Air Transport
PARTIES:
 Nigeria
 Norway

451125 Bilateral Agreement **2 NORT 555**
SIGNED: 22 May 51
HEADNOTE: COMMERCE
TOPIC: General Trade
PARTIES:
 Norway
 Pakistan

451126 Bilateral Exchange **3 NORT 775**
SIGNED: 16 Jun 59
HEADNOTE: PARTIAL VISA FEE ABOLITION
TOPIC: Visas
PARTIES:
 Norway
 Panama

451127 Bilateral Instrument **3 NORT 848**
SIGNED: 30 Jan 62
HEADNOTE: NORWAY VISA ABOLITION
TOPIC: Visas
PARTIES:
 Norway
 Panama

451128 Bilateral Exchange **3 NORT 880**
SIGNED: 21 Mar 63
HEADNOTE: ABOLITION OF VISAS
TOPIC: Visas
PARTIES:
 Norway
 Paraguay

451129 Bilateral Instrument **3 NORT 778**
SIGNED: 27 Jul 59
HEADNOTE: ABOLITION OF VISAS
TOPIC: Visas
PARTIES:
 Norway
 Peru

451130 Bilateral Agreement **2 NORT 671**
SIGNED: 23 Dec 55
HEADNOTE: FINANCIAL CLAIMS SETTLEMENT
TOPIC: Claims and Debts
PARTIES:
 Norway
 Poland

451131 Bilateral Agreement **3 NORT 928**
SIGNED: 30 Oct 64
HEADNOTE: PAYMENTS
TOPIC: Finance
PARTIES:
 Norway
 Poland

451132 Bilateral Agreement **3 NORT 1004**
SIGNED: 21 Sep 67
HEADNOTE: COMMERCE
TOPIC: General Trade
PARTIES:
 Norway
 Poland

451133 Bilateral Protocol **3 NORT 0**
SIGNED: 18 Oct 68
HEADNOTE: EXCHANGE OF GOODS
TOPIC: General Trade
PARTIES:
 Norway
 Poland

451134 Bilateral Exchange **3 NORT 751**
SIGNED: 24 Sep 58
HEADNOTE: ABOLITION OF VISAS
TOPIC: Visas
PARTIES:
 Norway
 Portugal

451135 Bilateral Agreement **3 NORT 1006**
SIGNED: 21 Oct 67
HEADNOTE: COMMERCE
TOPIC: General Trade
PARTIES:
 Norway
 Romania

451136 Bilateral Exchange **3 NORT 0**
SIGNED: 26 Nov 68
HEADNOTE: ABOLITION OF VISAS
TOPIC: Visas
PARTIES:
 Norway
 Romania

451137 Bilateral Agreement **3 NORT 0**
SIGNED: 29 Nov 68
HEADNOTE: ECONOMIC & INDUSTRIAL & TECH-
NICAL COOPERATION
TOPIC: General Economic
PARTIES:
 Norway
 Romania

451138 Bilateral Exchange **3 NORT 786**
SIGNED: 21 Oct 59
HEADNOTE: ABOLITION OF VISAS
TOPIC: Visas
PARTIES:
 El Salvador
 Norway

451139 Bilateral Treaty **2 NORT 553**
SIGNED: 2 May 51
HEADNOTE: DOUBLE TAXATION

TOPIC: Taxation
PARTIES:
  Norway
  Sierra Leone

451140   Bilateral Agreement   **3 NORT 975**
SIGNED: 9 Sep 66
HEADNOTE: TAX EVASION & DOUBLE TAX
TOPIC: Taxation
PARTIES:
  Norway
  Singapore

451141   Bilateral Agreement   **3 NORT 985**
SIGNED: 20 Dec 66
HEADNOTE: AIR TRANSPORT
TOPIC: Air Transport
PARTIES:
  Norway
  Singapore

451142   Bilateral Exchange   **3 NORT 0**
SIGNED: 28 Nov 68
HEADNOTE: ABOLITION OF VISAS
TOPIC: Visas
PARTIES:
  Norway
  Singapore

451143   Bilateral Exchange   **3 NORT 705**
SIGNED: 21 Dec 56
HEADNOTE: COPYRIGHT EXTENSION
TOPIC: Patents/Copyrights
PARTIES:
  Norway
  Spain

451144   Bilateral Exchange   **3 NORT 771**
SIGNED: 22 May 59
HEADNOTE: ABOLITION OF VISAS
TOPIC: Visas
PARTIES:
  Norway
  Spain

451145   Bilateral Exchange   **3 NORT 801**
SIGNED: 16 Mar 60
HEADNOTE: CLEARING ACCOUNT DEBITS
TOPIC: Claims and Debts
PARTIES:
  Norway
  Spain

451146   Bilateral Agreement   **3 NORT 805**
SIGNED: 17 May 60
HEADNOTE: EXCHANGE OF GOODS
TOPIC: General Trade
PARTIES:
  Norway
  Spain

451147   Bilateral Agreement   **3 NORT 941**
SIGNED: 5 May 65
HEADNOTE: AIR TRANSPORT
TOPIC: Air Transport
PARTIES:
  Norway
  Spain

451148   Bilateral Exchange   **3 NORT 943**
SIGNED: 3 Jun 65
HEADNOTE: LITERARY & ART PROTECTION
TOPIC: Patents/Copyrights
PARTIES:
  Norway
  Spain

451149   Bilateral Instrument   **2 NORT 430**
SIGNED: 11 Oct 45
HEADNOTE: DISPOSAL UN SHIPS
TOPIC: Milit Installation
PARTIES:
  Norway
  UK Great Britain

451150   Bilateral Exchange   **2 NORT 627**
SIGNED: 12 May 54
HEADNOTE: TONNAGE CERTIFICATES
TOPIC: General Trade
PARTIES:
  Norway
  UK Great Britain

451151   Bilateral Agreement   **3 NORT 991**
SIGNED: 6 Mar 67
HEADNOTE: PLACEMENT OF AU-PAIR GIRLS
TOPIC: Non-ILO Labor
PARTIES:
  Norway
  UK Great Britain

451152   Bilateral Instrument   **3 NORT 0**
SIGNED: 6 Nov 68
HEADNOTE: HONG KONG GARMENT EXPORTS
TOPIC: Commodity Trade
PARTIES:
  Norway
  UK Great Britain

451153   Bilateral Agreement   **3 NORT 765**
SIGNED: 5 Apr 59
HEADNOTE: AIR TRANSPORT
TOPIC: Air Transport
PARTIES:
  Norway
  Sudan

451154   Bilateral Agreement   **2 NORT 547**
SIGNED: 13 Jan 51
HEADNOTE: EXCHANGE OF GOODS
TOPIC: General Trade
PARTIES:
  Norway
  Switzerland

451155   Bilateral Exchange   **2 NORT 602**
SIGNED: 31 Mar 53
HEADNOTE: MILITARY SERVICE EXEMPTION
TOPIC: Milit Servic/Citiz
PARTIES:
  Norway
  Switzerland

451156   Bilateral Convention   **3 NORT 700**
SIGNED: 7 Dec 56
HEADNOTE: DOUBLE TAXATION
TOPIC: Taxation
PARTIES:
  Norway
  Switzerland

451157   Bilateral Convention   **3 NORT 701**
SIGNED: 7 Dec 56
HEADNOTE: DOUBLE TAXATION
TOPIC: Taxation
PARTIES:
  Norway
  Switzerland

451158   Bilateral Exchange   **3 NORT 761**
SIGNED: 29 Jan 59
HEADNOTE: ABOLITION OF VISAS
TOPIC: Visas
PARTIES:
  Norway
  Switzerland

451159   Bilateral Instrument   **3 NORT 889**
SIGNED: 25 May 63
HEADNOTE: IDENTITY CARD RECOGNITION
TOPIC: Visas
PARTIES:
  Norway
  Switzerland

451160   Bilateral Agreement   **2 NORT 530**
SIGNED: 24 Feb 50
HEADNOTE: SWISS CREDIT REPAYMENT
TOPIC: Claims and Debts

PARTIES:
  Norway
  Sweden

451161   Bilateral Agreement   **2 NORT 638**
SIGNED: 9 Jul 54
HEADNOTE: DEBT CONSOLIDATION
TOPIC: Claims and Debts
PARTIES:
  Norway
  Sweden

451162   Bilateral Agreement   **3 NORT 673**
SIGNED: 26 Jan 56
HEADNOTE: CONSTRUCT ROAD CONNECTION
TOPIC: General Ad Hoc
PARTIES:
  Norway
  Sweden

451163   Bilateral Agreement   **3 NORT 827**
SIGNED: 16 Mar 61
HEADNOTE: CUSTOMS FACILITIES RAFTING
TOPIC: Customs
PARTIES:
  Norway
  Sweden

451164   Bilateral Agreement   **3 NORT 891**
SIGNED: 28 Jun 63
HEADNOTE: REINDEER PASTURES
TOPIC: Specific Resources
PARTIES:
  Norway
  Sweden

451165   Bilateral Convention   **3 NORT 994**
SIGNED: 5 Apr 67
HEADNOTE: SKAGERAK FISHING AREAS
TOPIC: Specific Resources
PARTIES:
  Norway
  Sweden

451166   Bilateral Instrument   **3 NORT 994**
SIGNED: 5 Apr 67
HEADNOTE: SKAGERAK TERRITORIAL WATERS
TOPIC: Specific Resources
PARTIES:
  Norway
  Sweden

451167   Bilateral Agreement   **3 NORT 1012**
SIGNED: 14 Dec 67
HEADNOTE: CARTOGRAPHIC EXCHANGE
TOPIC: Admin Cooperation
PARTIES:
  Norway
  Sweden

451168   Bilateral Agreement   **3 NORT 0**
SIGNED: 24 Jul 68
HEADNOTE: DELIMIT CONTINENTAL SHELF
TOPIC: Territory Boundary
PARTIES:
  Norway
  Sweden

451169   Bilateral Agreement   **3 NORT 676**
SIGNED: 25 Feb 56
HEADNOTE: AIR TRANSPORT
TOPIC: Air Transport
PARTIES:
  Norway
  Syria

451170   Bilateral Exchange   **2 NORT 560**
SIGNED: 19 Jun 51
HEADNOTE: DOUBLE TAXATION
TOPIC: Taxation
PARTIES:
  Norway
  South Africa

451171 Bilateral Exchange **3 NORT 875**
SIGNED: 11 Dec 62
HEADNOTE: PARTIAL ABOLITION OF VISAS
TOPIC: Visas
PARTIES:
 Norway
 Thailand

451172 Bilateral Exchange **3 NORT 0**
SIGNED: 27 Sep 68
HEADNOTE: ABOLITION OF VISAS
TOPIC: Visas
PARTIES:
 Norway
 Trinidad/Tobago

451173 Bilateral Exchange **3 NORT 807**
SIGNED: 27 May 60
HEADNOTE: ABOLITION OF VISAS
TOPIC: Visas
PARTIES:
 Norway
 Tunisia

451174 Bilateral Convention **3 NORT 808**
SIGNED: 9 Jun 60
HEADNOTE: EXCHANGE OF GOODS
TOPIC: General Trade
PARTIES:
 Norway
 Tunisia

451175 Bilateral Exchange **2 NORT 588**
SIGNED: 23 Aug 52
HEADNOTE: ABOLITION OF VISAS
TOPIC: Visas
PARTIES:
 Norway
 Turkey

451176 Bilateral Exchange **2 NORT 715**
SIGNED: 24 Apr 57
HEADNOTE: TRADE RELATIONS
TOPIC: General Trade
PARTIES:
 Norway
 Turkey

451177 Bilateral Agreement **2 NORT 758**
SIGNED: 19 Dec 58
HEADNOTE: LOAN
TOPIC: Loans and Credits
PARTIES:
 Norway
 Turkey

451178 Bilateral Agreement **2 NORT 770**
SIGNED: 14 Jul 59
HEADNOTE: RELATIVE 11 MAY 59 MULTILAT-
ERAL
TOPIC: Claims and Debts
PARTIES:
 Norway
 Turkey

451179 Bilateral Agreement **2 NORT 931**
SIGNED: 23 Dec 64
HEADNOTE: DEVELOPMENT CREDIT
TOPIC: Loans and Credits
PARTIES:
 Norway
 Turkey

451180 Bilateral Agreement **2 NORT 953**
SIGNED: 24 Dec 64
HEADNOTE: DEVELOPMENT CREDIT
TOPIC: Loans and Credits
PARTIES:
 Norway
 Turkey

451181 Bilateral Agreement **3 NORT 987**
SIGNED: 27 Dec 66
HEADNOTE: CREDIT

TOPIC: Loans and Credits
PARTIES:
 Norway
 Turkey

451182 Bilateral Agreement **3 NORT 0**
SIGNED: 13 Jun 68
HEADNOTE: DEVELOPMENT CREDIT
TOPIC: Loans and Credits
PARTIES:
 Norway
 Turkey

451183 Bilateral Agreement **2 NORT 545**
SIGNED: 20 Dec 50
HEADNOTE: EXCHANGE OF GOODS
TOPIC: General Trade
PARTIES:
 Germany, West
 Norway

451184 Bilateral Agreement **2 NORT 618**
SIGNED: 30 Dec 53
HEADNOTE: CUSTOMS
TOPIC: Customs
PARTIES:
 Germany, West
 Norway

451185 Bilateral Exchange **2 NORT 633**
SIGNED: 25 May 54
HEADNOTE: NORWAY ABOLITION OF VISAS
TOPIC: Visas
PARTIES:
 Germany, West
 Norway

451186 Bilateral Exchange **2 NORT 639**
SIGNED: 27 Jul 54
HEADNOTE: LEGATION AUTO CUSTOMS
TOPIC: Privil/Immunities
PARTIES:
 Germany, West
 Norway

451187 Bilateral Agreement **3 NORT 688**
SIGNED: 29 May 56
HEADNOTE: CULTURAL
TOPIC: Culture
PARTIES:
 Germany, West
 Norway

451188 Bilateral Agreement **3 NORT 728**
SIGNED: 30 Oct 57
HEADNOTE: WEAPONS SPARE PARTS
TOPIC: Milit Installation
PARTIES:
 Germany, West
 Norway

451189 Bilateral Agreement **3 NORT 822**
SIGNED: 17 Dec 60
HEADNOTE: ARMED FORCES SUPPLIES
TOPIC: Milit Installation
PARTIES:
 Germany, West
 Norway

451190 Bilateral Agreement **3 NORT 887**
SIGNED: 24 May 63
HEADNOTE: IDENTITY CARD RECOGNITION
TOPIC: Visas
PARTIES:
 Germany, West
 Norway

451191 Bilateral Agreement **3 NORT 896**
SIGNED: 30 Nov 63
HEADNOTE: NAVAL VESSEL REPAIR
TOPIC: Milit Installation
PARTIES:
 Germany, West
 Norway

451192 Bilateral Exchange **3 NORT 923**
SIGNED: 4 Sep 64
HEADNOTE: CUSTOMS NATO SUPPLIES
TOPIC: Customs
PARTIES:
 Germany, West
 Norway

451193 Bilateral Exchange **3 NORT 946**
SIGNED: 6 Sep 65
HEADNOTE: MODIFIES 11 DEC 53 CONVENTION
TOPIC: General Aid
PARTIES:
 Germany, West
 Norway

451194 Bilateral Exchange **3 NORT 0**
SIGNED: 29 Oct 68
HEADNOTE: AMATEUR RADIO OPERATIONS
TOPIC: Gen Communications
PARTIES:
 Germany, West
 Norway

451195 Bilateral Exchange **3 NORT 940**
SIGNED: 4 May 65
HEADNOTE: ABOLITION OF VISAS
TOPIC: Visas
PARTIES:
 Norway
 Uganda

451196 Bilateral Exchange **3 NORT 900**
SIGNED: 23 Mar 64
HEADNOTE: NORWAY PEACE CORPS TERMS
TOPIC: Tech Assistance
PARTIES:
 Norway
 Uganda

451197 Bilateral Exchange **2 NORT 666**
SIGNED: 20 Oct 55
HEADNOTE: DIPLOMATIC MAIL SERVICE
TOPIC: Consul/Citizenship
PARTIES:
 Norway
 Uruguay

451198 Bilateral Exchange **3 NORT 824**
SIGNED: 24 Jan 61
HEADNOTE: PARTIAL ABOLITION OF VISAS
TOPIC: Visas
PARTIES:
 Norway
 Uruguay

451199 Bilateral Exchange **2 NORT 528**
SIGNED: 8 May 58
HEADNOTE: LOAN USS GARDINERS BAY
TOPIC: Milit Installation
PARTIES:
 Norway
 USA (United States)

451200 Bilateral Exchange **3 NORT 972**
SIGNED: 13 Jul 66
HEADNOTE: WORLD WAR II LICENSE DUES
TOPIC: Claims and Debts
PARTIES:
 Norway
 USA (United States)

451201 Bilateral Agreement **3 NORT 997**
SIGNED: 4 May 67
HEADNOTE: PEACEFUL USE ATOMIC ENERGY
TOPIC: Atomic Energy
PARTIES:
 Norway
 USA (United States)

451202 Bilateral Agreement **3 NORT 0**
SIGNED: 15 Jun 68
HEADNOTE: SEISMOLOGICAL RESEARCH
TOPIC: Scientific Project

PARTIES:
Norway
USA (United States)

451203   Bilateral Exchange   **3 NORT 0**
SIGNED: 26 Jun 68
HEADNOTE: SOCIAL SECURITY BENEFITS
TOPIC: Non-ILO Labor
PARTIES:
Norway
USA (United States)

451205   Bilateral Exchange   **2 NORT 478**
SIGNED: 21 May 48
HEADNOTE: ACCOUNT INTEREST RATES
TOPIC: Claims and Debts
PARTIES:
Norway
USSR (Soviet Union)

451206   Bilateral Exchange   **2 NORT 500**
SIGNED: 23 May 49
HEADNOTE: 1947 FRONTIER DOCUMENTS
TOPIC: Territory Boundary
PARTIES:
Norway
USSR (Soviet Union)

451209   Bilateral Agreement   **3 NORT 784**
SIGNED: 30 Sep 59
HEADNOTE: SOVIET REPUBLICS CLAIMS
TOPIC: Claims and Debts
PARTIES:
Norway
USSR (Soviet Union)

451210   Bilateral Exchange   **3 NORT 833**
SIGNED: 12 May 61
HEADNOTE: ABOLITION CONSULAR FEES
TOPIC: Consul/Citizenship
PARTIES:
Norway
USSR (Soviet Union)

451211   Bilateral Protocol   **3 NORT 897**
SIGNED: 24 Dec 63
HEADNOTE: POWER STATION LAND
TOPIC: Territory Boundary
PARTIES:
Norway
USSR (Soviet Union)

451212   Bilateral Exchange   **3 NORT 921**
SIGNED: 8 Aug 64
HEADNOTE: FRONTIER REDEMARCATION
TOPIC: Territory Boundary
PARTIES:
Norway
USSR (Soviet Union)

451213   Bilateral Agreement   **3 NORT 932**
SIGNED: 29 Jan 65
HEADNOTE: PAYMENTS
TOPIC: Finance
PARTIES:
Norway
USSR (Soviet Union)

451214   Bilateral Agreement   **3 NORT 934**
SIGNED: 6 Mar 65
HEADNOTE: EMBASSY CONSTRUCTION
TOPIC: Consul/Citizenship
PARTIES:
Norway
USSR (Soviet Union)

451215   Bilateral Protocol   **3 NORT 1013**
SIGNED: 18 Dec 67
HEADNOTE: FRONTIER REDEMARCATION
TOPIC: Territory Boundary
PARTIES:
Norway
USSR (Soviet Union)

451216   Bilateral Exchange   **3 NORT 0**
SIGNED: 9 Jul 68
HEADNOTE: CAPTURED VESSEL PROCEDURES
TOPIC: Admin Cooperation
PARTIES:
Norway
USSR (Soviet Union)

451217   Bilateral Exchange   **3 NORT 725**
SIGNED: 30 Jul 57
HEADNOTE: TONNAGE CERTIFICATES
TOPIC: General Trade
PARTIES:
Norway
Venezuela

451218   Bilateral Instrument   **3 NORT 790**
SIGNED: 1 Dec 59
HEADNOTE: NORWAY VISA ABOLITION
TOPIC: Visas
PARTIES:
Norway
Venezuela

451219   Bilateral Exchange   **2 NORT 553**
SIGNED: 21 Dec 63
HEADNOTE: DOUBLE TAXATION
TOPIC: Taxation
PARTIES:
Norway
Zambia

451220   Bilateral Agreement   **3 NORT 993**
SIGNED: 31 Mar 67
HEADNOTE: TECHNICAL COOPERATION
TOPIC: Tech Assistance
PARTIES:
Norway
Zambia

451221   Bilateral Agreement   **2 NORT 490**
SIGNED: 27 Nov 48
HEADNOTE: EXCHANGE OF GOODS
TOPIC: General Trade
PARTIES:
Austria
Norway

451222   Bilateral Exchange   **2 NORT 626**
SIGNED: 23 Apr 54
HEADNOTE: ABOLITION OF VISAS
TOPIC: Visas
PARTIES:
Austria
Norway

451223   Bilateral Agreement   **2 NORT 650**
SIGNED: 18 Mar 55
HEADNOTE: PAYMENTS
TOPIC: Finance
PARTIES:
Austria
Norway

451224   Bilateral Exchange   **3 NORT 701**
SIGNED: 12 Dec 56
HEADNOTE: EXTEND COPYRIGHT PROTECTION
TOPIC: Patents/Copyrights
PARTIES:
Austria
Norway

451225   Bilateral Exchange   **3 NORT 750**
SIGNED: 7 Jul 58
HEADNOTE: RECOGNITION DRIVING PERMITS
TOPIC: Admin Cooperation
PARTIES:
Austria
Norway

451226   Bilateral Instrument   **3 NORT 888**
SIGNED: 24 May 63
HEADNOTE: PERSONAL IDENTITY CARDS
TOPIC: Visas

PARTIES:
Austria
Norway

457001   Bilateral Convention   **47 PDZU 1044**
SIGNED: 19 Feb 47
HEADNOTE: SCIENTIFIC COOPERATION
TOPIC: Scientific Project
PARTIES:
France
Poland

457002   Bilateral Convention   **50 PDZU 93**
SIGNED: 4 Jul 47
HEADNOTE: ECONOMIC COOPERATION
TOPIC: General Economic
PARTIES:
Czechoslovakia
Poland

457003   Bilateral Agreement   **47 PDZU 293**
SIGNED: 22 Aug 47
HEADNOTE: AIR TRANSPORT
TOPIC: Air Transport
PARTIES:
Poland
Yugoslavia

457004   Bilateral Protocol   **49 PDZU 27**
SIGNED: 22 Apr 48
HEADNOTE: TRADE & PAYMENTS
TOPIC: Claims and Debts
PARTIES:
Poland
Sweden

457090   Bilateral Agreement   **64 PDZU 361**
SIGNED: 2 Nov 61
HEADNOTE: CULTURAL COOPERATION
TOPIC: Culture
PARTIES:
Mali
Poland

457109   Bilateral Agreement   **65 PDZU 393**
SIGNED: 17 Jan 64
HEADNOTE: CULTURAL COOPERATION
TOPIC: Culture
PARTIES:
Ghana
Poland

457114   Bilateral Agreement   **64 PDZU 71**
SIGNED: 22 Jul 64
HEADNOTE: CULTURAL COOPERATION
TOPIC: Culture
PARTIES:
Algeria
Poland

457118   Bilateral Agreement   **66 PDZU 395**
SIGNED: 5 Mar 65
HEADNOTE: CULTURAL COOPERATION
TOPIC: Culture
PARTIES:
Dahomey
Poland

457121   Bilateral Convention   **66 PDZU 135**
SIGNED: 17 May 65
HEADNOTE: DOUBLE NATIONALITY
TOPIC: Consul/Citizenship
PARTIES:
Czechoslovakia
Poland

457128   Bilateral Convention   **66 PDZU 279**
SIGNED: 10 Dec 65
HEADNOTE: PLANT PROTECTION
TOPIC: Sanitation
PARTIES:
Poland
Yugoslavia

457130   Bilateral Agreement   **67 PDZU 201**
SIGNED: 10 Mar 66
HEADNOTE: CULTURAL COOPERATION
TOPIC: Culture
PARTIES:
    Guinea
    Poland

457132   Bilateral Agreement   **67 PDZU 249**
SIGNED: 27 Apr 66
HEADNOTE: CULTURAL COOPERATION
TOPIC: Culture
PARTIES:
    Poland
    Tunisia

457137   Bilateral Agreement   **72 PDZU 373**
SIGNED: 25 Jun 66
HEADNOTE: CULTURAL COOPERATION
TOPIC: Culture
PARTIES:
    Afghanistan
    Poland

457138   Bilateral Agreement   **72 PDZU 237**
SIGNED: 23 Sep 65
HEADNOTE: BORDER CHECKPOINTS
TOPIC: Admin Cooperation
PARTIES:
    Czechoslovakia
    Poland

457139   Bilateral Convention   **71 PDZU 186**
SIGNED: 23 Feb 67
HEADNOTE: CONSULAR MATTERS
TOPIC: Consul/Citizenship
PARTIES:
    Poland
    UK Great Britain

457142   Bilateral Convention   **69 PDZU 29**
SIGNED: 5 Apr 67
HEADNOTE: JUDICIAL COOPERATION
TOPIC: Admin Cooperation
PARTIES:
    France
    Poland

457143   Bilateral Agreement   **72 PDZU 240**
SIGNED: 8 Apr 67
HEADNOTE: RAIL TRANSPORT
TOPIC: Land Transport
PARTIES:
    Czechoslovakia
    Poland

457145   Bilateral Convention   **70 PDZU 1**
SIGNED: 21 Jul 67
HEADNOTE: PUBLIC HEALTH
TOPIC: Sanitation
PARTIES:
    Poland
    UK Great Britain

457147   Bilateral Agreement   **68 PDZU 209**
SIGNED: 22 Aug 67
HEADNOTE: CULTURAL COOPERATION
TOPIC: Culture
PARTIES:
    Netherlands
    Poland

457150   Bilateral Agreement   **71 PDZU 117**
SIGNED: 2 Dec 67
HEADNOTE: LOCAL BORDER AREAS
TOPIC: Admin Cooperation
PARTIES:
    Czechoslovakia
    Poland

457156   Bilateral Agreement   **69 PDZU 73**
SIGNED: 13 May 68
HEADNOTE: CULTURAL COOPERATION
TOPIC: Culture

PARTIES:
    Iran
    Poland

457157   Bilateral Treaty   **68 PDZU 257**
SIGNED: 16 May 68
HEADNOTE: GENERAL FRIENDSHIP
TOPIC: General Amity
PARTIES:
    Hungary
    Poland

457160   Bilateral Agreement   **69 PDZU 217**
SIGNED: 29 Oct 67
HEADNOTE: CONTINENTAL SHELF
TOPIC: Territory Boundary
PARTIES:
    Germany, East
    Poland

457161   Bilateral Agreement   **70 PDZU 91**
SIGNED: 31 Oct 68
HEADNOTE: CULTURAL & SCIENTIFIC COOPER-
    ATION
TOPIC: Health/Educ/Welfare
PARTIES:
    Hungary
    Poland

457162   Bilateral Convention   **70 PDZU 13**
SIGNED: 6 Dec 68
HEADNOTE: PLANT PROTECTION & QUARANTINE
TOPIC: Sanitation
PARTIES:
    Bulgaria
    Poland

457163   Bilateral Agreement   **70 PDZU 96**
SIGNED: 15 May 69
HEADNOTE: INLAND WATER TRAFFIC
TOPIC: Water Transport
PARTIES:
    Germany, East
    Poland

457164   Bilateral Agreement   **70 PDZU 165**
SIGNED: 29 Aug 69
HEADNOTE: CONTINENTIAL SHELF
TOPIC: Territory Boundary
PARTIES:
    Poland
    USSR (Soviet Union)

457165   Bilateral Agreement   **70 PDZU 221**
SIGNED: 28 Oct 69
HEADNOTE: LOCAL BORDER AREAS
TOPIC: Admin Cooperation
PARTIES:
    Germany, East
    Poland

457166   Bilateral Convention   **71 PDZU 321**
SIGNED: 24 Jul 70
HEADNOTE: CULTURE SCIENCE TECHNOLOGY
TOPIC: Health/Educ/Welfare
PARTIES:
    Mexico
    Poland

457167   Bilateral Agreement   **71 PDZU 37**
SIGNED: 5 Oct 70
HEADNOTE: FISHING FACILITIES
TOPIC: Specific Property
PARTIES:
    Poland
    Sweden

457168   Bilateral Treaty   **71 PDZU 53**
SIGNED: 12 Nov 70
HEADNOTE: GENERAL FRIENDSHIP
TOPIC: General Amity
PARTIES:
    Poland
    Romania

457169   Bilateral Treaty   **72 PDZU 229**
SIGNED: 7 Dec 70
HEADNOTE: RECOGNITION   ODER-NEISSE
    BOUNDARY
TOPIC: Territory Boundary
PARTIES:
    Germany, West
    Poland

457170   Bilateral Agreement   **71 PDZU 213**
SIGNED: 14 Oct 70
HEADNOTE: CULTURE & SCIENCE
TOPIC: Health/Educ/Welfare
PARTIES:
    Poland
    USSR (Soviet Union)

457171   Bilateral Convention   **72 PDZU 125**
SIGNED: 27 May 71
HEADNOTE: CONSULAR MATTERS
TOPIC: Consul/Citizenship
PARTIES:
    Poland
    USSR (Soviet Union)

457172   Bilateral Agreement   **72 PDZU 33**
SIGNED: 1 Jun 71
HEADNOTE: FISHING FACILITIES
TOPIC: Specific Property
PARTIES:
    Denmark
    Poland

457173   Bilateral Convention   **72 PDZU 1**
SIGNED: 28 Jun 71
HEADNOTE: VISA ABOLITION
TOPIC: Visas
PARTIES:
    Poland
    Romania

457174   Bilateral Treaty   **72 PDZU 41**
SIGNED: 16 Jul 71
HEADNOTE: GENERAL COMMUNICATIONS
TOPIC: Gen Communications
PARTIES:
    Germany, East
    Poland

457175   Bilateral Agreement   **72 PDZU 321**
SIGNED: 14 Sep 71
HEADNOTE: JUDICIAL COOPERATION
TOPIC: Admin Cooperation
PARTIES:
    Mongolia
    Poland

457176   Bilateral Agreement   **72 PDZU 48**
SIGNED: 25 Nov 71
HEADNOTE: BORDER TRAFFIC CONTROL
TOPIC: Admin Cooperation
PARTIES:
    Germany, East
    Poland

457177   Bilateral Agreement   **71 PDZU 357**
SIGNED: 25 Nov 71
HEADNOTE: PASSPORT ABOLITION
TOPIC: Visas
PARTIES:
    Germany, East
    Poland

457178   Bilateral Convention   **72 PDZU 401**
SIGNED: 7 Feb 72
HEADNOTE: DOUBLE NATIONALITY
TOPIC: Consul/Citizenship
PARTIES:
    Bulgaria
    Poland

458006   Bilateral Exchange   **53 PZUM 59**
SIGNED: 24 Oct 52
HEADNOTE: TRADE & PAYMENTS

TOPIC: General Economic
PARTIES:
  Brazil
  Poland

458007   Bilateral Agreement   **53 PZUM 67**
SIGNED: 29 Oct 52
HEADNOTE: TRADE & FINANCE
TOPIC: General Economic
PARTIES:
  Argentina
  Poland

458008   Bilateral Agreement   **53 PZUM 77**
SIGNED: 20 Dec 52
HEADNOTE: ORAWA WATER DAM CONSTRUC-
TION
TOPIC: General Economic
PARTIES:
  Czechoslovakia
  Poland

458009   Bilateral Agreement   **53 PZUM 85**
SIGNED: 6 May 53
HEADNOTE: TRADE & PAYMENTS
TOPIC: General Economic
PARTIES:
  Indonesia
  Poland

458010   Bilateral Agreement   **53 PZUM 109**
SIGNED: 8 May 53
HEADNOTE: POLISH HOSPITAL FOR KOREA
TOPIC: Tech Assistance
PARTIES:
  Korea, North
  Poland

458011   Bilateral Exchange   **53 PZUM 113**
SIGNED: 6 Oct 53
HEADNOTE: RAISE MISSIONS TO EMBASSIES
TOPIC: Consul/Citizenship
PARTIES:
  Germany, East
  Poland

458012   Bilateral Agreement   **53 PZUM 115**
SIGNED: 15 Oct 53
HEADNOTE: RADIO BROADCAST COOPERATION
TOPIC: Mass Media
PARTIES:
  China People's Rep
  Poland

458013   Bilateral Agreement   **53 PZUM 117**
SIGNED: 19 Oct 53
HEADNOTE: POST & TELECOMMUNICATION
TOPIC: Gen Communications
PARTIES:
  Bulgaria
  Poland

458014   Bilateral Agreement   **54 PZUM 11**
SIGNED: 0 Feb 54
HEADNOTE: RADIO BROADCAST COOPERATION
TOPIC: Mass Media
PARTIES:
  Czechoslovakia
  Poland

458015   Bilateral Agreement   **54 PZUM 14**
SIGNED: 26 May 54
HEADNOTE: RADIO BROADCAST COOPERATION
TOPIC: Mass Media
PARTIES:
  Mongolia
  Poland

458016   Bilateral Agreement   **54 PZUM 16**
SIGNED: 27 May 54
HEADNOTE: INLAND WATER TRAFFIC
TOPIC: Water Transport

PARTIES:
  Germany, East
  Poland

458017   Bilateral Agreement   **54 PZUM 22**
SIGNED: 27 May 54
HEADNOTE: INLAND WATER TRANSPORT
TOPIC: Water Transport
PARTIES:
  Germany, East
  Poland

458018   Bilateral Agreement   **54 PZUM 34**
SIGNED: 29 May 54
HEADNOTE: POSTAL MATTERS
TOPIC: Postal Service
PARTIES:
  Czechoslovakia
  Poland

458019   Bilateral Agreement   **54 PZUM 50**
SIGNED: 20 Jul 54
HEADNOTE: SCIENTIFIC & TECHNICAL COOPER-
ATION
TOPIC: Scientific Project
PARTIES:
  China People's Rep
  Poland

458020   Bilateral Protocol   **54 PZUM 53**
SIGNED: 2 Aug 54
HEADNOTE: SZCZECIN HAFF FISHERIES
TOPIC: Specific Resources
PARTIES:
  Germany, East
  Poland

458021   Bilateral Agreement   **55 PZUM 9**
SIGNED: 18 Feb 55
HEADNOTE: ESTABLISH AIR SERVICES
TOPIC: Air Transport
PARTIES:
  Poland
  USSR (Soviet Union)

458022   Bilateral Agreement   **55 PZUM 13**
SIGNED: 20 Jun 55
HEADNOTE: AIR TRANSPORT
TOPIC: Air Transport
PARTIES:
  Germany, East
  Poland

458023   Bilateral Agreement   **55 PZUM 19**
SIGNED: 9 Jul 55
HEADNOTE: VETERINARY
TOPIC: Sanitation
PARTIES:
  Germany, East
  Poland

458024   Bilateral Agreement   **55 PZUM 23**
SIGNED: 6 Sep 55
HEADNOTE: LOCAL BORDER TRAFFIC
TOPIC: Visas
PARTIES:
  Czechoslovakia
  Poland

458025   Bilateral Protocol   **55 PZUM 27**
SIGNED: 23 Sep 55
HEADNOTE: BORDER DEMARCATION SECURITY
TOPIC: Territory Boundary
PARTIES:
  Czechoslovakia
  Poland

458026   Bilateral Instrument   **55 PZUM 33**
SIGNED: 30 Sep 55
HEADNOTE: SOCIAL SECURITY PAYMENTS
TOPIC: Non-ILO Labor
PARTIES:
  Czechoslovakia
  Poland

458027   Bilateral Agreement   **55 PZUM 41**
SIGNED: 7 Oct 55
HEADNOTE: PUBLIC HEALTH SERVICES
TOPIC: Sanitation
PARTIES:
  Germany, East
  Poland

458028   Bilateral Instrument   **55 PZUM 45**
SIGNED: 14 Nov 55
HEADNOTE: SCIENTIFIC & TECHNICAL COOPER-
ATION
TOPIC: Scientific Project
PARTIES:
  Poland
  Yugoslavia

458029   Bilateral Agreement   **55 PZUM 49**
SIGNED: 14 Nov 55
HEADNOTE: AIR TRANSPORT
TOPIC: Air Transport
PARTIES:
  Poland
  Yugoslavia

458030   Bilateral Agreement   **55 PZUM 67**
SIGNED: 30 Dec 55
HEADNOTE: TELECOMMUNICATION
TOPIC: Telecommunications
PARTIES:
  Korea, North
  Poland

458031   Bilateral Agreement   **55 PZUM 57**
SIGNED: 30 Dec 55
HEADNOTE: POSTAL MATTERS
TOPIC: Postal Service
PARTIES:
  Korea, North
  Poland

458032   Bilateral Agreement   **56 PZUM 11**
SIGNED: 12 Jan 56
HEADNOTE: SAFETY AT SEA IN BALTIC
TOPIC: Water Transport
PARTIES:
  Germany, East
  Poland

458033   Bilateral Protocol   **56 PZUM 25**
SIGNED: 13 Jan 56
HEADNOTE: INLAND WATER TRAFFIC
TOPIC: Water Transport
PARTIES:
  Czechoslovakia
  Poland

458034   Bilateral Protocol   **56 PZUM 30**
SIGNED: 13 Jan 56
HEADNOTE: RAIL TRANSPORT
TOPIC: Land Transport
PARTIES:
  Czechoslovakia
  Poland

458035   Bilateral Agreement   **56 PZUM 32**
SIGNED: 24 Jan 56
HEADNOTE: POSTAL MATTERS
TOPIC: Postal Service
PARTIES:
  Poland
  Vietnam, North

458036   Bilateral Agreement   **56 PZUM 50**
SIGNED: 24 Jan 56
HEADNOTE: TELECOMMUNICATION
TOPIC: Telecommunications
PARTIES:
  Poland
  Vietnam, North

458037   Bilateral Protocol   **56 PZUM 66**
SIGNED: 24 Jan 56
HEADNOTE: INCREASED COOPERATION

TOPIC: Gen Communications
PARTIES:
  Poland
  Vietnam, North

458038   Bilateral Instrument   **56 PZUM 70**
SIGNED: 1 Feb 56
HEADNOTE: PSKOW MUSEUM & LIBRARY
TOPIC: Specific Property
PARTIES:
  Poland
  USSR (Soviet Union)

458039   Bilateral Agreement   **56 PZUM 82**
SIGNED: 14 Feb 56
HEADNOTE: ESTABLISH AIR SERVICES
TOPIC: Air Transport
PARTIES:
  United Arab Rep
  Poland

458040   Bilateral Protocol   **56 PZUM 109**
SIGNED: 25 Feb 56
HEADNOTE: POST & TELECOMMUNICATION
TOPIC: Postal Service
PARTIES:
  China People's Rep
  Poland

458041   Bilateral Agreement   **56 PZUM 115**
SIGNED: 7 Mar 56
HEADNOTE: TELECOMMUNICATION
TOPIC: Telecommunications
PARTIES:
  Poland
  Yugoslavia

458042   Bilateral Agreement   **56 PZUM 121**
SIGNED: 7 Mar 56
HEADNOTE: POSTAL MATTERS
TOPIC: Postal Service
PARTIES:
  Poland
  Yugoslavia

458043   Bilateral Agreement   **56 PZUM 128**
SIGNED: 25 Apr 56
HEADNOTE: POSTAL MATTERS
TOPIC: Postal Service
PARTIES:
  Hungary
  Poland

458044   Bilateral Agreement   **56 PZUM 140**
SIGNED: 25 Apr 56
HEADNOTE: TELECOMMUNICATION
TOPIC: Telecommunications
PARTIES:
  Hungary
  Poland

458045   Bilateral Protocol   **56 PZUM 156**
SIGNED: 25 Apr 56
HEADNOTE: INCREASED COOPERATION
TOPIC: Gen Communications
PARTIES:
  Hungary
  Poland

458046   Bilateral Agreement   **56 PZUM 185**
SIGNED: 18 Jun 56
HEADNOTE: TELEPHONE
TOPIC: Telecommunications
PARTIES:
  Hungary
  Poland

458047   Bilateral Instrument   **56 PZUM 205**
SIGNED: 2 Oct 56
HEADNOTE: RETURN POLISH ART TREASURES
TOPIC: Specific Property
PARTIES:
  Poland
  USSR (Soviet Union)

458048   Bilateral Instrument   **57 PZUM 62**
SIGNED: 4 Apr 57
HEADNOTE: PEACEFUL USE ATOMIC ENERGY
TOPIC: Atomic Energy
PARTIES:
  Poland
  Yugoslavia

458049   Bilateral Instrument   **57 PZUM 67**
SIGNED: 17 Apr 57
HEADNOTE: SCIENTIFIC & TECHNICAL COOPER-
ATION
TOPIC: Scientific Project
PARTIES:
  Korea, North
  Poland

458050   Bilateral Treaty   **57 PZUM 69**
SIGNED: 7 May 57
HEADNOTE: JOINT COMMITTEE ECONOMIC CO-
OPERATION
TOPIC: General Economic
PARTIES:
  Czechoslovakia
  Poland

458051   Bilateral Agreement   **57 PZUM 74**
SIGNED: 8 Jul 57
HEADNOTE: AIR TRANSPORT
TOPIC: Air Transport
PARTIES:
  Albania
  Poland

458052   Bilateral Instrument   **56 PZUM 90**
SIGNED: 23 Aug 57
HEADNOTE: EDUCATIONAL EXCHANGE
TOPIC: Education
PARTIES:
  Poland
  USSR (Soviet Union)

458053   Bilateral Agreement   **57 PZUM 94**
SIGNED: 5 Sep 57
HEADNOTE: CUSTOMS COOPERATION
TOPIC: Customs
PARTIES:
  Germany, East
  Poland

458054   Bilateral Agreement   **57 PZUM 99**
SIGNED: 17 Sep 57
HEADNOTE: PEACEFUL USE ATOMIC ENERGY
TOPIC: Atomic Energy
PARTIES:
  Germany, East
  Poland

458055   Bilateral Instrument   **57 PZUM 102**
SIGNED: 20 Oct 57
HEADNOTE: HEALTH PROTECTION
TOPIC: Sanitation
PARTIES:
  Poland
  Yugoslavia

458056   Bilateral Instrument   **57 PZUM 114**
SIGNED: 12 Nov 56
HEADNOTE: INDUSTRIAL COOPERATION
TOPIC: General Economic
PARTIES:
  Poland
  Yugoslavia

458057   Bilateral Agreement   **57 PZUM 125**
SIGNED: 12 Dec 57
HEADNOTE: LEGAL STATUS IN POLAND
TOPIC: IGO Operations
PARTIES:
  Poland
  Org Rail Collabor

458058   Bilateral Agreement   **57 PZUM 130**
SIGNED: 17 Dec 57

HEADNOTE: SCIENTIFIC & TECHNICAL COOPER-
ATION
TOPIC: Tech Assistance
PARTIES:
  Cambodia
  Poland

458059   Bilateral Instrument   **58 PZUM 48**
SIGNED: 20 Feb 58
HEADNOTE: JOINT COMMITTEE ECONOMIC CO-
OPERATION
TOPIC: General Economic
PARTIES:
  Poland
  Yugoslavia

458060   Bilateral Protocol   **58 PZUM 61**
SIGNED: 27 Mar 58
HEADNOTE: CULTURAL INFORMATION CENTERS
TOPIC: Culture
PARTIES:
  Czechoslovakia
  Poland

458061   Bilateral Agreement   **58 PZUM 87**
SIGNED: 25 Oct 58
HEADNOTE: JOINT COMMITTEE ECONOMIC CO-
OPERATION
TOPIC: General Economic
PARTIES:
  Hungary
  Poland

458062   Bilateral Agreement   **58 PZUM 111**
SIGNED: 9 Dec 58
HEADNOTE: JOINT COMMITTEE ECONOMIC CO-
OPERATION
TOPIC: General Economic
PARTIES:
  Poland
  Romania

458063   Bilateral Exchange   **58 PZUM 122**
SIGNED: 30 Dec 58
HEADNOTE: DIPLOMATIC PRIVILEGES
TOPIC: Privil/Immunities
PARTIES:
  Australia
  Poland

458064   Bilateral Agreement   **58 PZUM 124**
SIGNED: 30 Dec 58
HEADNOTE: JOINT COMMITTEE ECONOMIC CO-
OPERATION
TOPIC: General Economic
PARTIES:
  Bulgaria
  Poland

458065   Bilateral Agreement   **59 PZUM 9**
SIGNED: 3 Jan 59
HEADNOTE: ECONOMIC, SCIENTIFIC & TECHNI-
CAL COOPERATION
TOPIC: General Economic
PARTIES:
  Iraq
  Poland

458066   Bilateral Agreement   **59 PZUM 60**
SIGNED: 8 Apr 59
HEADNOTE: VETERINARY
TOPIC: Sanitation
PARTIES:
  Czechoslovakia
  Poland

458067   Bilateral Protocol   **59 PZUM 64**
SIGNED: 8 May 59
HEADNOTE: CULTURAL INFORMATION CENTERS
TOPIC: Culture
PARTIES:
  Germany, East
  Poland

458068   Bilateral Agreement   **59 PZUM 78**
SIGNED: 20 Jun 59
HEADNOTE: CUSTOMS COOPERATION
TOPIC: Customs
PARTIES:
  Bulgaria
  Poland

458069   Bilateral Agreement   **59 PZUM 90**
SIGNED: 23 Sep 59
HEADNOTE: CERTAIN RAIL LINES
TOPIC: Land Transport
PARTIES:
  Germany, East
  Poland

458070   Bilateral Agreement   **59 PZUM 100**
SIGNED: 10 Nov 59
HEADNOTE: NEISSE RIVER WATER USE
TOPIC: Specific Resources
PARTIES:
  Germany, East
  Poland

458071   Bilateral Exchange   **59 PZUM 106**
SIGNED: 12 Nov 59
HEADNOTE: TAX EXEMPTIONS
TOPIC: Taxation
PARTIES:
  France
  Poland

458072   Bilateral Instrument   **60 PZUM 11**
SIGNED: 19 Feb 60
HEADNOTE: CUSTOMS COOPERATION
TOPIC: Customs
PARTIES:
  Poland
  USSR (Soviet Union)

458073   Bilateral Agreement   **60 PZUM 16**
SIGNED: 2 Apr 60
HEADNOTE: WITKA RIVER DAM CONSTRUCTION
TOPIC: General Economic
PARTIES:
  Czechoslovakia
  Poland

458074   Bilateral Agreement   **60 PZUM 20**
SIGNED: 22 Apr 60
HEADNOTE: ECONOMIC & TECHNICAL COOPER-
ATION
TOPIC: General Economic
PARTIES:
  Germany, East
  Poland

458075   Bilateral Agreement   **60 PZUM 53**
SIGNED: 25 Jun 60
HEADNOTE: AIR TRANSPORT
TOPIC: Air Transport
PARTIES:
  France
  Poland

458076   Bilateral Agreement   **60 PZUM 63**
SIGNED: 27 Jun 60
HEADNOTE: NAVIGATION
TOPIC: Water Transport
PARTIES:
  India
  Poland

458077   Bilateral Agreement   **60 PZUM 71**
SIGNED: 1 Jul 60
HEADNOTE: SCIENTIFIC & TECHNICAL COOPER-
ATION
TOPIC: Tech Assistance
PARTIES:
  Cuba
  Poland

458078   Bilateral Agreement   **60 PZUM 110**
SIGNED: 10 Sep 60

HEADNOTE: ECONOMIC, SCIENTIFIC & TECHNI-
CAL COOPERATION
TOPIC: General Economic
PARTIES:
  Czechoslovakia
  Poland

458079   Bilateral Agreement   **60 PZUM 116**
SIGNED: 19 Sep 60
HEADNOTE: ECONOMIC, SCIENTIFIC & TECHNI-
CAL COOPERATION
TOPIC: Tech Assistance
PARTIES:
  Afghanistan
  Poland

458080   Bilateral Agreement   **58 PZUM 132**
SIGNED: 27 Nov 60
HEADNOTE: SCIENTIFIC & TECHNICAL COOPER-
ATION
TOPIC: Scientific Project
PARTIES:
  Italy
  Poland

458081   Bilateral Agreement   **61 PZUM 88**
SIGNED: 28 Feb 61
HEADNOTE: SCIENTIFIC & TECHNICAL COOPER-
ATION
TOPIC: Tech Assistance
PARTIES:
  Mongolia
  Poland

458082   Bilateral Agreement   **61 PZUM 94**
SIGNED: 19 Apr 61
HEADNOTE: SCIENTIFIC & TECHNICAL COOPER-
ATION
TOPIC: Tech Assistance
PARTIES:
  Ghana
  Poland

458083   Bilateral Protocol   **61 PZUM 118**
SIGNED: 25 May 61
HEADNOTE: SOCIAL SECURITY
TOPIC: Non-ILO Labor
PARTIES:
  France
  Poland

458084   Bilateral Exchange   **61 PZUM 121**
SIGNED: 13 Jun 61
HEADNOTE: TAX EXEMPTIONS
TOPIC: Taxation
PARTIES:
  Poland
  Switzerland

458085   Bilateral Exchange   **61 PZUM 127**
SIGNED: 15 Jun 61
HEADNOTE: DIPLOMATS DRIVERS LICENSES
TOPIC: Consul/Citizenship
PARTIES:
  France
  Poland

458086   Bilateral Agreement   **61 PZUM 183**
SIGNED: 27 Jul 61
HEADNOTE: AIR TRANSPORT
TOPIC: Air Transport
PARTIES:
  Iraq
  Poland

458087   Bilateral Agreement   **61 PZUM 192**
SIGNED: 16 Sep 61
HEADNOTE: SCIENTIFIC & TECHNICAL COOPER-
ATION
TOPIC: Tech Assistance
PARTIES:
  Poland
  Tunisia

458088   Bilateral Instrument   **61 PZUM 209**
SIGNED: 4 Oct 61
HEADNOTE: ARCHIVE TRANSFER TO POLAND
TOPIC: Specific Property
PARTIES:
  Poland
  USSR (Soviet Union)

458089   Bilateral Agreement   **61 PZUM 211**
SIGNED: 10 Oct 61
HEADNOTE: SCIENTIFIC & TECHNICAL COOPER-
ATION
TOPIC: Tech Assistance
PARTIES:
  Indonesia
  Poland

458091   Bilateral Agreement   **61 PZUM 217**
SIGNED: 2 Nov 61
HEADNOTE: SCIENTIFIC & TECHNICAL COOPER-
ATION
TOPIC: Tech Assistance
PARTIES:
  Mali
  Poland

458092   Bilateral Agreement   **61 PZUM 229**
SIGNED: 9 Nov 61
HEADNOTE: TECHNICAL & CULTURAL COOPER-
ATION
TOPIC: Health/Educ/Welfare
PARTIES:
  Niger
  Poland

458093   Bilateral Exchange   **61 PZUM 266**
SIGNED: 9 Dec 61
HEADNOTE: ESTABLISH JOINT COMMISSION
TOPIC: Culture
PARTIES:
  Italy
  Poland

458094   Bilateral Agreement   **62 PZUM 48**
SIGNED: 18 Jun 62
HEADNOTE: CULTURAL COOPERATION
TOPIC: Culture
PARTIES:
  Poland
  Senegal

458095   Bilateral Agreement   **62 PZUM 51**
SIGNED: 18 Jun 62
HEADNOTE: ECONOMIC, SCIENTIFIC & TECHNI-
CAL COOPERATION
TOPIC: General Economic
PARTIES:
  Poland
  Senegal

458096   Bilateral Agreement   **62 PZUM 57**
SIGNED: 27 Jun 62
HEADNOTE: AIR TRANSPORT
TOPIC: Air Transport
PARTIES:
  Afghanistan
  Poland

458097   Bilateral Protocol   **62 PZUM 81**
SIGNED: 29 Sep 62
HEADNOTE: ARCHIVES & ART EXCHANGE
TOPIC: Specific Property
PARTIES:
  Czechoslovakia
  Poland

458098   Bilateral Agreement   **62 PZUM 93**
SIGNED: 12 Oct 62
HEADNOTE: RADIO & TV
TOPIC: Mass Media
PARTIES:
  Cuba
  Poland

458099   Bilateral Agreement   **62 PZUM 100**
SIGNED: 15 Oct 62
HEADNOTE: ECONOMIC & TECHNICAL COOPER-
    ATION
TOPIC: Tech Assistance
PARTIES:
  Morocco
  Poland

458100   Bilateral Agreement   **63 PZUM 11**
SIGNED: 26 Jan 63
HEADNOTE: ECONOMIC, SCIENTIFIC & TECHNI-
    CAL COOPERATION
TOPIC: Tech Assistance
PARTIES:
  Algeria
  Poland

458101   Bilateral Agreement   **63 PZUM 27**
SIGNED: 26 Apr 63
HEADNOTE: ECONOMIC & TECHNICAL COOPER-
    ATION
TOPIC: Tech Assistance
PARTIES:
  Cameroon
  Poland

458102   Bilateral Agreement   **63 PZUM 31**
SIGNED: 26 Apr 63
HEADNOTE: CULTURAL COOPERATION
TOPIC: Culture
PARTIES:
  Cameroon
  Poland

458103   Bilateral Agreement   **63 PZUM 34**
SIGNED: 27 Apr 63
HEADNOTE: RADIO
TOPIC: Mass Media
PARTIES:
  Czechoslovakia
  Poland

458104   Bilateral Agreement   **63 PZUM 39**
SIGNED: 27 Apr 63
HEADNOTE: TELEVISION
TOPIC: Mass Media
PARTIES:
  Czechoslovakia
  Poland

458105   Bilateral Agreement   **63 PZUM 61**
SIGNED: 17 Jun 63
HEADNOTE: FISHERIES TECHNOLOGY
TOPIC: Tech Assistance
PARTIES:
  Guinea
  Poland

458106   Bilateral Instrument   **63 PZUM 67**
SIGNED: 25 Oct 63
HEADNOTE: ROAD TRANSPORT
TOPIC: Land Transport
PARTIES:
  Austria
  Poland

458107   Bilateral Treaty   **66 PZUM 85**
SIGNED: 14 Nov 63
HEADNOTE: DAMAGES
TOPIC: Claims and Debts
PARTIES:
  Belgium
  Poland

458108   Bilateral Agreement   **63 PZUM 76**
SIGNED: 11 Dec 63
HEADNOTE: JUDICIAL COOPERATION
TOPIC: Admin Cooperation
PARTIES:
  Austria
  Poland

458110   Bilateral Agreement   **64 PZUM 16**
SIGNED: 14 Mar 64
HEADNOTE: VISA ABOLITION
TOPIC: Visas
PARTIES:
  Germany, East
  Poland

458111   Bilateral Agreement   **64 PZUM 20**
SIGNED: 18 Apr 64
HEADNOTE: VISA ABOLITION
TOPIC: Visas
PARTIES:
  Hungary
  Poland

458112   Bilateral Agreement   **64 PZUM 23**
SIGNED: 20 Apr 64
HEADNOTE: SCIENTIFIC & TECHNICAL COOPER-
    ATION
TOPIC: Tech Assistance
PARTIES:
  Kenya
  Poland

458113   Bilateral Agreement   **64 PZUM 29**
SIGNED: 30 Jun 64
HEADNOTE: INDUSTRIAL COOPERATION
TOPIC: General Economic
PARTIES:
  Poland
  Yugoslavia

458115   Bilateral Agreement   **64 PZUM 48**
SIGNED: 3 Oct 64
HEADNOTE: ROAD TRAFFIC
TOPIC: Land Transport
PARTIES:
  Bulgaria
  Poland

458116   Bilateral Agreement   **64 PZUM 63**
SIGNED: 26 Oct 64
HEADNOTE: SCIENTIFIC & TECHNICAL COOPER-
    ATION
TOPIC: Tech Assistance
PARTIES:
  United Arab Rep
  Poland

458117   Bilateral Agreement   **64 PZUM 9**
SIGNED: 6 Feb 65
HEADNOTE: AIR TRANSPORT
TOPIC: Air Transport
PARTIES:
  Algeria
  Poland

458119   Bilateral Agreement   **69 PZUM 213**
SIGNED: 25 Mar 65
HEADNOTE: CULTURAL COOPERATION
TOPIC: Culture
PARTIES:
  Italy
  Poland

458120   Bilateral Agreement   **65 PZUM 38**
SIGNED: 15 May 65
HEADNOTE: SCIENTIFIC & TECHNICAL COOPER-
    ATION
TOPIC: Tech Assistance
PARTIES:
  Poland
  Tanzania

458122   Bilateral Agreement   **65 PZUM 44**
SIGNED: 8 Jun 65
HEADNOTE: VISA ABOLITION & TOURISM
TOPIC: Visas
PARTIES:
  Bulgaria
  Poland

458123   Bilateral Agreement   **66 PZUM 33**
SIGNED: 18 Jun 65
HEADNOTE: SCIENTIFIC & TECHNICAL COOPER-
    ATION
TOPIC: Tech Assistance
PARTIES:
  Poland
  Syria

458124   Bilateral Agreement   **65 PZUM 50**
SIGNED: 14 Jul 65
HEADNOTE: ECONOMIC & TECHNICAL COOPER-
    ATION
TOPIC: General Economic
PARTIES:
  Italy
  Poland

458125   Bilateral Agreement   **65 PZUM 65**
SIGNED: 4 Nov 65
HEADNOTE: EDUCATIONAL EXCHANGE
TOPIC: Education
PARTIES:
  Germany, East
  Poland

458126   Bilateral Agreement   **65 PZUM 71**
SIGNED: 1 Dec 65
HEADNOTE: SCIENTIFIC & TECHNICAL COOPER-
    ATION
TOPIC: Tech Assistance
PARTIES:
  Ethiopia
  Poland

458127   Bilateral Agreement   **65 PZUM 77**
SIGNED: 7 Dec 65
HEADNOTE: PEACEFUL USE ATOMIC ENERGY
TOPIC: Atomic Energy
PARTIES:
  Belgium
  Poland

458129   Bilateral Treaty   **66 PZUM 25**
SIGNED: 19 Jan 66
HEADNOTE: REAL ESTATE PROPERTY
TOPIC: Finance
PARTIES:
  Poland
  Sweden

458131   Bilateral Protocol   **66 PZUM 14**
SIGNED: 7 Apr 66
HEADNOTE: CULTURAL INFORMATION CENTERS
TOPIC: Culture
PARTIES:
  Bulgaria
  Poland

458133   Bilateral Protocol   **66 PZUM 76**
SIGNED: 28 Apr 66
HEADNOTE: SOCIAL SECURITY
TOPIC: Non-ILO Labor
PARTIES:
  France
  Poland

458134   Bilateral Agreement   **66 PZUM 60**
SIGNED: 7 May 66
HEADNOTE: ROAD TRAFFIC
TOPIC: Land Transport
PARTIES:
  Poland
  USSR (Soviet Union)

458135   Bilateral Agreement   **66 PZUM 79**
SIGNED: 20 May 66
HEADNOTE: SCIENTIFIC & TECHNICAL COOPER-
    ATION
TOPIC: Scientific Project
PARTIES:
  France
  Poland

458136 Bilateral Agreement **66 PZUM 70**
SIGNED: 22 May 66
HEADNOTE: CULTURAL COOPERATION
TOPIC: Culture
PARTIES:
  France
  Poland

458140 Bilateral Exchange **67 PZUM 69**
SIGNED: 21 Mar 67
HEADNOTE: RECOGNITION OF DIPLOMAS
TOPIC: Admin Cooperation
PARTIES:
  Pakistan
  Poland

458144 Bilateral Instrument **67 PZUM 88**
SIGNED: 9 May 67
HEADNOTE: CUSTOMS COOPERATION
TOPIC: Customs
PARTIES:
  Poland
  Yugoslavia

458146 Bilateral Agreement **68 PZUM 26**
SIGNED: 22 Aug 67
HEADNOTE: INDUSTRIAL & TECHNICAL COOPER-
ATION
TOPIC: General Economic
PARTIES:
  Netherlands
  Poland

458148 Bilateral Agreement **68 PZUM 32**
SIGNED: 16 Sep 67
HEADNOTE: TOURISM
TOPIC: Admin Cooperation
PARTIES:
  Hungary
  Poland

458149 Bilateral Agreement **68 PZUM 35**
SIGNED: 10 Oct 67
HEADNOTE: SCIENTIFIC & TECHNICAL COOPER-
ATION
TOPIC: Scientific Project
PARTIES:
  Poland
  UK Great Britain

458151 Bilateral Convention **68 PZUM 42**
SIGNED: 29 Jan 68
HEADNOTE: VETERINARY
TOPIC: Land Transport
PARTIES:
  Poland
  Romania

458152 Bilateral Agreement **68 PZUM 52**
SIGNED: 29 Jan 68
HEADNOTE: ROAD TRANSPORT
TOPIC: Land Transport
PARTIES:
  Poland
  Romania

458153 Bilateral Agreement **68 PZUM 65**
SIGNED: 3 Mar 68
HEADNOTE: ROAD TRANSPORT
TOPIC: Land Transport
PARTIES:
  France
  Poland

458154 Bilateral Agreement **68 PZUM 71**
SIGNED: 4 Apr 68
HEADNOTE: ROAD TRANSPORT
TOPIC: Land Transport
PARTIES:
  Poland
  Sweden

458155 Bilateral Agreement **68 PZUM 77**
SIGNED: 24 Apr 68

HEADNOTE: AIR TRANSPORT
TOPIC: Air Transport
PARTIES:
  Poland
  USSR (Soviet Union)

458158 Bilateral Instrument **68 PZUM 88**
SIGNED: 25 May 68
HEADNOTE: OCEAN TRANSPORT
TOPIC: Water Transport
PARTIES:
  Brazil
  Poland

458159 Bilateral Agreement **68 PZUM 94**
SIGNED: 13 Jul 68
HEADNOTE: ROAD TRANSPORT
TOPIC: Land Transport
PARTIES:
  Italy
  Poland

460001 Bilateral Treaty **58 SPBO 2507**
SIGNED: 28 Oct 57
HEADNOTE: GENERAL RELATIONS
TOPIC: General Amity
PARTIES:
  Afghanistan
  Spain

460002 Bilateral Convention **53 SPBO 1616**
SIGNED: 25 Jan 52
HEADNOTE: EXCHANGE WORKERS
TOPIC: Non-ILO Labor
PARTIES:
  Germany, West
  Spain

460003 Bilateral Convention **56 SPBO 2503**
SIGNED: 10 Dec 54
HEADNOTE: CULTURE
TOPIC: Culture
PARTIES:
  Germany, West
  Spain

460004 Bilateral Agreement **56 SPBO 706**
SIGNED: 3 May 56
HEADNOTE: FILM EXCHANGE
TOPIC: Mass Media
PARTIES:
  Germany, West
  Spain

460005 Bilateral Agreement **56 SPBO 706**
SIGNED: 3 May 56
HEADNOTE: JOINT FILM PRODUCTION
TOPIC: Mass Media
PARTIES:
  Germany, West
  Spain

460006 Bilateral Agreement **55 SPBO 2106**
SIGNED: 16 May 55
HEADNOTE: TRADE
TOPIC: General Trade
PARTIES:
  Germany, West
  Spain

460007 Bilateral Agreement **55 SPBO 2106**
SIGNED: 16 May 55
HEADNOTE: PAYMENTS
TOPIC: Finance
PARTIES:
  Germany, West
  Spain

460008 Bilateral Instrument **56 SPBO 307**
SIGNED: 18 May 56
HEADNOTE: TRADE SUPPLEMENT
TOPIC: General Trade

PARTIES:
  Germany, West
  Spain

460009 Bilateral Instrument **56 SPBO 307**
SIGNED: 18 May 56
HEADNOTE: PAYMENTS SUPPLEMENT
TOPIC: Finance
PARTIES:
  Germany, West
  Spain

460010 Bilateral Exchange **57 SPBO 1007**
SIGNED: 27 May 57
HEADNOTE: TRADE
TOPIC: General Trade
PARTIES:
  Germany, West
  Spain

460011 Bilateral Exchange **59 SPBO 2606**
SIGNED: 8 Apr 58
HEADNOTE: WARTIME EXPROPRIATION
TOPIC: Claims and Debts
PARTIES:
  Germany, West
  Spain

460012 Bilateral Exchange **59 SPBO 2606**
SIGNED: 8 Apr 58
HEADNOTE: COMPATIBILITY AGREEMENTS
TOPIC: Finance
PARTIES:
  Germany, West
  Spain

460013 Bilateral Exchange **59 SPBO 2606**
SIGNED: 8 Apr 58
HEADNOTE: COMPATIBILITY AGREEMENTS
TOPIC: Finance
PARTIES:
  Germany, West
  Spain

460014 Bilateral Exchange **59 SPBO 2606**
SIGNED: 8 Apr 58
HEADNOTE: COMPATIBILITY AGREEMENTS
TOPIC: Specif Goods/Equip
PARTIES:
  Germany, West
  Spain

460015 Bilateral Exchange **59 SPBO 2606**
SIGNED: 8 Apr 58
HEADNOTE: NON-APPLICATION TO SAAR
TOPIC: Finance
PARTIES:
  Germany, West
  Spain

460016 Bilateral Convention **59 SPBO 2606**
SIGNED: 8 Apr 58
HEADNOTE: INDUSTRIAL PROPERTY
TOPIC: Patents/Copyrights
PARTIES:
  Germany, West
  Spain

460017 Bilateral Exchange **59 SPBO 2606**
SIGNED: 8 Apr 58
HEADNOTE: APPLIES ALL SPANISH TERRITORIES
TOPIC: Finance
PARTIES:
  Germany, West
  Spain

460018 Bilateral Protocol **59 SPBO 2606**
SIGNED: 8 Apr 58
HEADNOTE: CORPORATIONS
TOPIC: Finance
PARTIES:
  Germany, West
  Spain

460019   Bilateral Convention   **59 SPBO 2606**
SIGNED: 8 Apr 58
HEADNOTE: WARTIME MATTERS
TOPIC: Finance
PARTIES:
  Germany, West
  Spain

460020   Bilateral Convention   **59 SPBO 2606**
SIGNED: 8 Apr 58
HEADNOTE: INDUSTRIAL PROPERTY
TOPIC: Patents/Copyrights
PARTIES:
  Germany, West
  Spain

460021   Bilateral Convention   **61 SPBO 1110**
SIGNED: 29 Oct 59
HEADNOTE: SOCIAL SECURITY
TOPIC: Non-ILO Labor
PARTIES:
  Germany, West
  Spain

460022   Bilateral Agreement   **61 SPBO 1110**
SIGNED: 29 Oct 59
HEADNOTE: SOCIAL SECURITY
TOPIC: Non-ILO Labor
PARTIES:
  Germany, West
  Spain

460023   Bilateral Protocol   **61 SPBO 1110**
SIGNED: 29 Oct 59
HEADNOTE: SOCIAL SECURITY
TOPIC: Non-ILO Labor
PARTIES:
  Germany, West
  Spain

460024   Bilateral Agreement   **61 SPBO 2312**
SIGNED: 29 Oct 59
HEADNOTE: SOCIAL SECURITY
TOPIC: Non-ILO Labor
PARTIES:
  Germany, West
  Spain

460025   Bilateral Agreement   **60 SPBO 505**
SIGNED: 29 Mar 60
HEADNOTE: MIGRANT LABOR
TOPIC: Non-ILO Labor
PARTIES:
  Germany, West
  Spain

460026   Bilateral Protocol   **61 SPBO 710**
SIGNED: 24 Oct 60
HEADNOTE: SOCIAL SECURITY
TOPIC: Non-ILO Labor
PARTIES:
  Germany, West
  Spain

460027   Bilateral Convention   **61 SPBO 2905**
SIGNED: 9 May 61
HEADNOTE: ECONOMIC COOPERATION
TOPIC: General Economic
PARTIES:
  Germany, West
  Spain

460028   Bilateral Convention   **65 SPBO 706**
SIGNED: 29 May 62
HEADNOTE: WAR VICTIMS
TOPIC: Humanitarian
PARTIES:
  Germany, West
  Spain

460029   Bilateral Convention   **63 SPBO 2205**
SIGNED: 27 Apr 63
HEADNOTE: AGRICULTURAL EXPERIMENT
TOPIC: Scientific Project

PARTIES:
  Germany, West
  Spain

460030   Bilateral Convention   **65 SPBO 1907**
SIGNED: 15 May 64
HEADNOTE: SOCIAL SECURITY
TOPIC: Non-ILO Labor
PARTIES:
  Germany, West
  Spain

460031   Bilateral Convention   **47 SPBO 2004**
SIGNED: 1 Mar 47
HEADNOTE: AIR TRANSPORT
TOPIC: Air Transport
PARTIES:
  Argentina
  Spain

460032   Bilateral Convention   **48 SPBO 3110**
SIGNED: 18 Oct 48
HEADNOTE: MILITARY SERVICE
TOPIC: Milit Servic/Citiz
PARTIES:
  Argentina
  Spain

460033   Bilateral Convention   **48 SPBO 3110**
SIGNED: 18 Oct 48
HEADNOTE: EDUCATION
TOPIC: Culture
PARTIES:
  Argentina
  Spain

460034   Bilateral Convention   **48 SPBO 3110**
SIGNED: 18 Oct 48
HEADNOTE: MIGRATION
TOPIC: Health/Educ/Welfare
PARTIES:
  Argentina
  Spain

460035   Bilateral Convention   **48 SPBO 3110**
SIGNED: 18 Oct 48
HEADNOTE: BOOKS
TOPIC: Culture
PARTIES:
  Argentina
  Spain

460036   Bilateral Convention   **60 SPBO 508**
SIGNED: 8 Jul 60
HEADNOTE: MIGRATION
TOPIC: Health/Educ/Welfare
PARTIES:
  Argentina
  Spain

460037   Bilateral Agreement   **61 SPBO 2109**
SIGNED: 22 Apr 60
HEADNOTE: FILM PRODUCTION
TOPIC: Mass Media
PARTIES:
  Argentina
  Spain

460038   Bilateral Treaty   **62 SPBO 606**
SIGNED: 9 Jan 61
HEADNOTE: GENERAL RELATIONS
TOPIC: General Amity
PARTIES:
  Saudi Arabia
  Spain

460039   Bilateral Agreement   **56 SPBO 2404**
SIGNED: 21 Mar 56
HEADNOTE: TRADE
TOPIC: General Trade
PARTIES:
  Austria
  Spain

460040   Bilateral Agreement   **56 SPBO 2404**
SIGNED: 21 Mar 56
HEADNOTE: PAYMENTS
TOPIC: Finance
PARTIES:
  Austria
  Spain

460041   Bilateral Exchange   **57 SPBO 2004**
SIGNED: 28 Mar 57
HEADNOTE: TRADE EXTENSION
TOPIC: General Trade
PARTIES:
  Austria
  Spain

460042   Bilateral Convention   **62 SPBO 2910**
SIGNED: 19 Feb 62
HEADNOTE: AIR TRANSPORT
TOPIC: Air Transport
PARTIES:
  Austria
  Spain

460043   Bilateral Convention   **62 SPBO 606**
SIGNED: 2 May 62
HEADNOTE: MIGRANT LABOR
TOPIC: Non-ILO Labor
PARTIES:
  Austria
  Spain

460044   Bilateral Exchange   **55 SPBO 2302**
SIGNED: 27 Jan 55
HEADNOTE: TRADE & PAYMENTS EXTENSION
TOPIC: General Economic
PARTIES:
  Belgium
  Spain

460045   Bilateral Exchange   **55 SPBO 908**
SIGNED: 22 Jun 55
HEADNOTE: PAYMENTS EXTENSION
TOPIC: Finance
PARTIES:
  Belgium
  Spain

460046   Bilateral Exchange   **56 SPBO 803**
SIGNED: 30 Jan 56
HEADNOTE: TRADE & PAYMENTS EXTENSION
TOPIC: General Economic
PARTIES:
  Belgium
  Spain

460047   Bilateral Exchange   **56 SPBO 2405**
SIGNED: 25 Apr 56
HEADNOTE: PAYMENTS EXTENSION
TOPIC: Finance
PARTIES:
  Belgium
  Spain

460048   Bilateral Exchange   **56 SPBO 610**
SIGNED: 30 Jul 56
HEADNOTE: PAYMENTS EXTENSION
TOPIC: Finance
PARTIES:
  Belgium
  Spain

460049   Bilateral Agreement   **56 SPBO 3108**
SIGNED: 7 Aug 56
HEADNOTE: TRADE
TOPIC: General Trade
PARTIES:
  Belgium
  Spain

460050   Bilateral Instrument   **58 SPBO 2605**
SIGNED: 28 Nov 56
HEADNOTE: MIGRANT MINERS
TOPIC: Non-ILO Labor

PARTIES:
Belgium
Spain

460051   Bilateral Exchange   58 SPBO 2705
SIGNED: 28 Nov 56
HEADNOTE: MIGRANT LABOR
TOPIC: Non-ILO Labor
PARTIES:
Belgium
Spain

460052   Bilateral Exchange   58 SPBO 2705
SIGNED: 28 Nov 56
HEADNOTE: SOCIAL SECURITY
TOPIC: Non-ILO Labor
PARTIES:
Belgium
Spain

460053   Bilateral Exchange   57 SPBO 2208
SIGNED: 26 Jul 57
HEADNOTE: PAYMENTS EXTENSION
TOPIC: Finance
PARTIES:
Belgium
Spain

460054   Bilateral Agreement   58 SPBO 3005
SIGNED: 10 Sep 57
HEADNOTE: SOCIAL SECURITY
TOPIC: Non-ILO Labor
PARTIES:
Belgium
Spain

460055   Bilateral Convention   64 SPBO 1406
SIGNED: 12 Oct 61
HEADNOTE: DUAL NATIONALITY
TOPIC: Consul/Citizenship
PARTIES:
Bolivia
Spain

460056   Bilateral Exchange   55 SPBO 2201
SIGNED: 30 Dec 54
HEADNOTE: TRADE & PAYMENTS EXTENSION
TOPIC: General Economic
PARTIES:
Brazil
Spain

460057   Bilateral Exchange   57 SPBO 1810
SIGNED: 30 Sep 57
HEADNOTE: TRADE & PAYMENTS EXTENSION
TOPIC: General Economic
PARTIES:
Brazil
Spain

460058   Bilateral Convention   65 SPBO 907
SIGNED: 25 Jun 60
HEADNOTE: CULTURE
TOPIC: Culture
PARTIES:
Brazil
Spain

460059   Bilateral Agreement   64 SPBO 508
SIGNED: 27 Dec 60
HEADNOTE: MIGRATION
TOPIC: Health/Educ/Welfare
PARTIES:
Brazil
Spain

460060   Bilateral Exchange   64 SPBO 508
SIGNED: 27 Dec 60
HEADNOTE: MIGRANTS RIGHTS
TOPIC: Health/Educ/Welfare
PARTIES:
Brazil
Spain

460061   Bilateral Exchange   64 SPBO 508
SIGNED: 27 Dec 60
HEADNOTE: MIGRANTS CLAIMS
TOPIC: Health/Educ/Welfare
PARTIES:
Brazil
Spain

460062   Bilateral Agreement   65 SPBO 2505
SIGNED: 8 Sep 64
HEADNOTE: ATOMIC ENERGY
TOPIC: Atomic Energy
PARTIES:
Canada
Spain

460063   Bilateral Convention   56 SPBO 2310
SIGNED: 22 Jul 55
HEADNOTE: TRADE
TOPIC: General Trade
PARTIES:
Ceylon (Sri Lanka)
Spain

460064   Bilateral Convention   65 SPBO 1201
SIGNED: 1 Apr 53
HEADNOTE: CULTURE
TOPIC: Culture
PARTIES:
Colombia
Spain

460065   Bilateral Exchange   56 SPBO 1704
SIGNED: 10 Nov 55
HEADNOTE: HAM RADIO LICENCES
TOPIC: Telecommunications
PARTIES:
Colombia
Spain

460066   Bilateral Treaty   54 SPBO 303
SIGNED: 9 Jan 53
HEADNOTE: FRIENDSHIP
TOPIC: General Amity
PARTIES:
Costa Rica
Spain

460067   Bilateral Convention   65 SPBO 2506
SIGNED: 8 Jun 64
HEADNOTE: DUAL NATIONALITY
TOPIC: Consul/Citizenship
PARTIES:
Costa Rica
Spain

460068   Bilateral Convention   53 SPBO 2504
SIGNED: 19 Jun 51
HEADNOTE: AIR TRANSPORT
TOPIC: Air Transport
PARTIES:
Cuba
Spain

460069   Bilateral Treaty   54 SPBO 408
SIGNED: 18 Aug 53
HEADNOTE: TRADE & PAYMENTS
TOPIC: General Economic
PARTIES:
Cuba
Spain

460070   Bilateral Exchange   56 SPBO 1702
SIGNED: 6 Jul 54
HEADNOTE: TRADE & PAYMENTS MODIFICATION
TOPIC: General Economic
PARTIES:
Cuba
Spain

460071   Bilateral Exchange   55 SPBO 1508
SIGNED: 21 Jul 55
HEADNOTE: TRADE & PAYMENTS
TOPIC: General Economic

PARTIES:
Cuba
Spain

460072   Bilateral Exchange   56 SPBO 609
SIGNED: 14 Aug 56
HEADNOTE: TRADE & PAYMENTS EXTENSION
TOPIC: General Economic
PARTIES:
Cuba
Spain

460073   Bilateral Agreement   54 SPBO 1308
SIGNED: 9 Aug 50
HEADNOTE: TRADE & PAYMENTS
TOPIC: General Economic
PARTIES:
Chile
Spain

460074   Bilateral Convention   58 SPBO 1411
SIGNED: 24 May 58
HEADNOTE: DUAL NATIONALITY
TOPIC: Health/Educ/Welfare
PARTIES:
Chile
Spain

460075   Bilateral Exchange   58 SPBO 1411
SIGNED: 23 Jun 58
HEADNOTE: NATIONALITY
TOPIC: Health/Educ/Welfare
PARTIES:
Chile
Spain

460076   Bilateral Convention   65 SPBO 1911
SIGNED: 7 Jun 61
HEADNOTE: MIGRATION
TOPIC: Health/Educ/Welfare
PARTIES:
Chile
Spain

460077   Bilateral Exchange   56 SPBO 1512
SIGNED: 3 Dec 56
HEADNOTE: TRADE
TOPIC: General Trade
PARTIES:
Taiwan
Spain

460078   Bilateral Agreement   57 SPBO 1009
SIGNED: 1 Jul 57
HEADNOTE: TRADE
TOPIC: General Trade
PARTIES:
Denmark
Spain

460079   Bilateral Exchange   57 SPBO 1009
SIGNED: 15 Jul 57
HEADNOTE: TRADE
TOPIC: General Trade
PARTIES:
Denmark
Spain

460080   Bilateral Treaty   53 SPBO 309
SIGNED: 10 Nov 52
HEADNOTE: GENERAL RELATIONS
TOPIC: General Amity
PARTIES:
Dominican Republic
Spain

460081   Bilateral Convention   53 SPBO 112
SIGNED: 27 Jan 53
HEADNOTE: CULTURE
TOPIC: Culture
PARTIES:
Dominican Republic
Spain

460082   Bilateral Agreement   **54 SPBO 1808**
SIGNED: 14 Jan 54
HEADNOTE: TRADE
TOPIC: General Trade
PARTIES:
  Dominican Republic
  Spain

460083   Bilateral Convention   **57 SPBO 2901**
SIGNED: 1 Feb 56
HEADNOTE: MIGRATION
TOPIC: Health/Educ/Welfare
PARTIES:
  Dominican Republic
  Spain

460084   Bilateral Convention   **54 SPBO 3001**
SIGNED: 5 May 53
HEADNOTE: CULTURE
TOPIC: Culture
PARTIES:
  Ecuador
  Spain

460085   Bilateral Convention   **55 SPBO 1909**
SIGNED: 12 Jul 54
HEADNOTE: TRADE
TOPIC: General Trade
PARTIES:
  Ecuador
  Spain

460086   Bilateral Agreement   **55 SPBO 1909**
SIGNED: 12 Jul 54
HEADNOTE: PAYMENT
TOPIC: Finance
PARTIES:
  Ecuador
  Spain

460087   Bilateral Exchange   **55 SPBO 3009**
SIGNED: 9 Jun 55
HEADNOTE: TRADE & PAYMENTS LIST
TOPIC: General Economic
PARTIES:
  Ecuador
  Spain

460088   Bilateral Protocol   **56 SPBO 706**
SIGNED: 6 Dec 54
HEADNOTE: CULTURE
TOPIC: Culture
PARTIES:
  Ecuador
  Spain

460089   Bilateral Convention   **62 SPBO 2310**
SIGNED: 1 Apr 60
HEADNOTE: SOCIAL SECURITY
TOPIC: Non-ILO Labor
PARTIES:
  Ecuador
  Spain

460090   Bilateral Convention   **65 SPBO 1301**
SIGNED: 4 Mar 64
HEADNOTE: DUAL NATIONALITY
TOPIC: Consul/Citizenship
PARTIES:
  Ecuador
  Spain

460091   Bilateral Treaty   **52 SPBO 1611**
SIGNED: 19 Feb 52
HEADNOTE: GENERAL RELATIONS
TOPIC: General Amity
PARTIES:
  El Salvador
  Spain

460092   Bilateral Agreement   **53 SPBO 511**
SIGNED: 2 Dec 52
HEADNOTE: TRADE
TOPIC: General Trade

PARTIES:
  El Salvador
  Spain

460093   Bilateral Agreement   **53 SPBO 511**
SIGNED: 2 Dec 52
HEADNOTE: PAYMENT
TOPIC: Finance
PARTIES:
  El Salvador
  Spain

460094   Bilateral Treaty   **54 SPBO 508**
SIGNED: 6 Nov 53
HEADNOTE: CONSULAR
TOPIC: Consul/Citizenship
PARTIES:
  El Salvador
  Spain

460095   Bilateral Agreement   **53 SPBO 2006**
SIGNED: 26 Apr 52
HEADNOTE: CULTURE
TOPIC: Culture
PARTIES:
  Spain
  United Arab Rep

460096   Bilateral Treaty   **49 SPBO 1306**
SIGNED: 4 Mar 49
HEADNOTE: CULTURE
TOPIC: Culture
PARTIES:
  Philippines
  Spain

460097   Bilateral Treaty   **49 SPBO 1812**
SIGNED: 4 Mar 49
HEADNOTE: ACADEMIC TITLES
TOPIC: Culture
PARTIES:
  Philippines
  Spain

460098   Bilateral Convention   **54 SPBO 2101**
SIGNED: 6 Oct 51
HEADNOTE: COMMON POSTAL TERRITORY
TOPIC: Postal Service
PARTIES:
  Philippines
  Spain

460099   Bilateral Agreement   **56 SPBO 906**
SIGNED: 21 May 56
HEADNOTE: TRADE
TOPIC: General Trade
PARTIES:
  Finland
  Spain

460100   Bilateral Agreement   **56 SPBO 906**
SIGNED: 21 May 56
HEADNOTE: PAYMENT
TOPIC: Finance
PARTIES:
  Finland
  Spain

460101   Bilateral Exchange   **48 SPBO 1605**
SIGNED: 29 Apr 48
HEADNOTE: AIR TRANSPORT
TOPIC: Air Transport
PARTIES:
  France
  Spain

460102   Bilateral Instrument   **54 SPBO 1230**
SIGNED: 24 Sep 52
HEADNOTE: BORDER RIVERS & FISHERY
TOPIC: Territory Boundary
PARTIES:
  France
  Spain

460103   Bilateral Agreement   **55 SPBO 1508**
SIGNED: 15 May 53
HEADNOTE: BORDER POLICE
TOPIC: Admin Cooperation
PARTIES:
  France
  Spain

460104   Bilateral Agreement   **55 SPBO 1301**
SIGNED: 19 Nov 54
HEADNOTE: TRADE
TOPIC: General Trade
PARTIES:
  France
  Spain

460105   Bilateral Instrument   **55 SPBO 2101**
SIGNED: 17 Dec 54
HEADNOTE: FILMS
TOPIC: Mass Media
PARTIES:
  France
  Spain

460106   Bilateral Exchange   **55 SPBO 1503**
SIGNED: 17 Feb 55
HEADNOTE: AGRICULTURE
TOPIC: Specific Resources
PARTIES:
  France
  Spain

460107   Bilateral Instrument   **55 SPBO 304**
SIGNED: 15 Mar 55
HEADNOTE: FINAL ACT MIXED COMMISSION
TOPIC: General Trade
PARTIES:
  France
  Spain

460108   Bilateral Agreement   **55 SPBO 105**
SIGNED: 31 Mar 55
HEADNOTE: TRADE
TOPIC: General Trade
PARTIES:
  France
  Spain

460109   Bilateral Agreement   **55 SPBO 105**
SIGNED: 31 Mar 55
HEADNOTE: JOINT FILM PRODUCTION
TOPIC: Mass Media
PARTIES:
  France
  Spain

460110   Bilateral Agreement   **56 SPBO 202**
SIGNED: 25 Nov 55
HEADNOTE: TRADE
TOPIC: General Trade
PARTIES:
  France
  Spain

460111   Bilateral Instrument   **56 SPBO 2704**
SIGNED: 28 Mar 56
HEADNOTE: FINAL ACT MIXED COMMISSION
TOPIC: General Trade
PARTIES:
  France
  Spain

460112   Bilateral Agreement   **56 SPBO 2406**
SIGNED: 2 Jun 56
HEADNOTE: FILMS
TOPIC: Mass Media
PARTIES:
  France
  Spain

460113   Bilateral Agreement   **57 SPBO 301**
SIGNED: 1 Dec 56
HEADNOTE: TRADE
TOPIC: General Trade

PARTIES:
France
Spain

460114 Bilateral Instrument **57 SPBO 606**
SIGNED: 17 May 57
HEADNOTE: FINAL ACT MIXED COMMISSION
TOPIC: General Trade
PARTIES:
France
Spain

460115 Bilateral Exchange **58 SPBO 2203**
SIGNED: 25 Jun 57
HEADNOTE: INTELLECTUAL PROPERTY
TOPIC: Patents/Copyrights
PARTIES:
France
Spain

460116 Bilateral Convention **59 SPBO 3003**
SIGNED: 27 Jun 57
HEADNOTE: SOCIAL SECURITY
TOPIC: Non-ILO Labor
PARTIES:
France
Spain

460117 Bilateral Agreement **57 SPBO 1409**
SIGNED: 27 Jun 57
HEADNOTE: MIGRANT AGRICULTURAL LABOR
TOPIC: Non-ILO Labor
PARTIES:
France
Spain

460118 Bilateral Agreement **57 SPBO 1409**
SIGNED: 27 Jun 57
HEADNOTE: SOCIAL SECURITY
TOPIC: Non-ILO Labor
PARTIES:
France
Spain

460119 Bilateral Exchange **58 SPBO 301**
SIGNED: 19 Nov 57
HEADNOTE: TRADE AND PAYMENTS
TOPIC: General Economic
PARTIES:
France
Spain

460120 Bilateral Instrument **57 SPBO 3112**
SIGNED: 29 Nov 57
HEADNOTE: SOCIAL SECURITY FAMILY
CHARGES
TOPIC: Non-ILO Labor
PARTIES:
France
Spain

460121 Bilateral Agreement **58 SPBO 301**
SIGNED: 4 Dec 57
HEADNOTE: TRADE
TOPIC: General Trade
PARTIES:
France
Spain

460122 Bilateral Exchange **58 SPBO 1504**
SIGNED: 28 Mar 58
HEADNOTE: SOCIAL SECURITY FAMILY
CHARGES
TOPIC: Non-ILO Labor
PARTIES:
France
Spain

460123 Bilateral Exchange **58 SPBO 2204**
SIGNED: 28 Mar 58
HEADNOTE: SOCIAL SECURITY RETIRED AGRI-
CULTURAL LABOR
TOPIC: Non-ILO Labor

460124 Bilateral Instrument **58 SPBO 805**
SIGNED: 19 Apr 58
HEADNOTE: FINAL ACT MIXED COMMISSION
TOPIC: General Trade
PARTIES:
France
Spain

460125 Bilateral Convention **65 SPBO 202**
SIGNED: 14 Jul 59
HEADNOTE: FISHERY
TOPIC: Specific Resources
PARTIES:
France
Spain

460126 Bilateral Convention **60 SPBO 305**
SIGNED: 14 Jul 59
HEADNOTE: LIVESTOCK HYGIENE
TOPIC: Sanitation
PARTIES:
France
Spain

460127 Bilateral Convention **60 SPBO 404**
SIGNED: 14 Jul 59
HEADNOTE: FIRE PROTECTION
TOPIC: Health/Educ/Welfare
PARTIES:
France
Spain

460128 Bilateral Instrument **60 SPBO 404**
SIGNED: 14 Jul 59
HEADNOTE: TRANSIT LIVESTOCK
TOPIC: Visas
PARTIES:
France
Spain

460129 Bilateral Instrument **60 SPBO 2603**
SIGNED: 20 Oct 59
HEADNOTE: SOCIAL SECURITY SUPPLEMENT 27
JUN 57
TOPIC: Non-ILO Labor
PARTIES:
France
Spain

460130 Bilateral Exchange **60 SPBO 2007**
SIGNED: 11 Apr 60
HEADNOTE: SOCIAL SECURITY
TOPIC: Non-ILO Labor
PARTIES:
France
Spain

460131 Bilateral Agreement **61 SPBO 2802**
SIGNED: 25 Jan 61
HEADNOTE: SUPPLEMENT TREATY 2 NOV 32
TOPIC: Non-ILO Labor
PARTIES:
France
Spain

460132 Bilateral Agreement **62 SPBO 2103**
SIGNED: 25 Jan 61
HEADNOTE: SUPPLEMENT TREATY 2 NOV 32
TOPIC: Non-ILO Labor
PARTIES:
France
Spain

460133 Bilateral Exchange **61 SPBO 2505**
SIGNED: 17 Apr 61
HEADNOTE: BORDER POLICE AGREEMENT 15
MAY 53
TOPIC: Admin Cooperation

460134 Bilateral Convention **63 SPBO 1009**
SIGNED: 30 May 61
HEADNOTE: WORK AGAINST CUSTOMS FRAUD
TOPIC: Customs
PARTIES:
France
Spain

460135 Bilateral Instrument **62 SPBO 401**
SIGNED: 4 Oct 61
HEADNOTE: SOCIAL SECURITY AGREEMENT 27
JUN 57
TOPIC: Non-ILO Labor
PARTIES:
France
Spain

460136 Bilateral Exchange **62 SPBO 1902**
SIGNED: 14 Dec 61
HEADNOTE: SOCIAL SECURITY
TOPIC: Non-ILO Labor
PARTIES:
France
Spain

460137 Bilateral Instrument **62 SPBO 2002**
SIGNED: 14 Dec 61
HEADNOTE: SOCIAL SECURITY PROTOCOL 27
JUN 57
TOPIC: Non-ILO Labor
PARTIES:
France
Spain

460138 Bilateral Convention **62 SPBO 1911**
SIGNED: 30 Mar 62
HEADNOTE: BUILDING TRANS-PYRENEAN TUN-
NEL
TOPIC: General Transport
PARTIES:
France
Spain

460139 Bilateral Convention **62 SPBO 2311**
SIGNED: 30 Mar 62
HEADNOTE: BUILDING NEW BORDER BRIDGE
TOPIC: General Transport
PARTIES:
France
Spain

460140 Bilateral Agreement **62 SPBO 1711**
SIGNED: 30 Mar 62
HEADNOTE: BORDER POLICE
TOPIC: Admin Cooperation
PARTIES:
France
Spain

460141 Bilateral Instrument **62 SPBO 3107**
SIGNED: 12 Apr 62
HEADNOTE: SOCIAL SECURITY CONVENTION 27
JUN 57
TOPIC: Non-ILO Labor
PARTIES:
France
Spain

460142 Bilateral Exchange **63 SPBO 403**
SIGNED: 2 Nov 62
HEADNOTE: SOCIAL SECURITY CONVENTION 27
JUN 57
TOPIC: Non-ILO Labor
PARTIES:
France
Spain

460143 Bilateral Instrument **63 SPBO 202**
SIGNED: 23 Nov 62
HEADNOTE: SOCIAL SECURITY

TOPIC: Non-ILO Labor
PARTIES:
France
Spain

460144   Bilateral Convention   **64 SPBO 701**
SIGNED: 8 Jan 63
HEADNOTE: DOUBLE TAXATION
TOPIC: Taxation
PARTIES:
France
Spain

460145   Bilateral Agreement   **63 SPBO 1312**
SIGNED: 8 Jul 63
HEADNOTE: SOCIAL SECURITY
TOPIC: Non-ILO Labor
PARTIES:
France
Spain

460146   Bilateral Convention   **64 SPBO 108**
SIGNED: 29 Jul 63
HEADNOTE: USE OF GARONA RIVER
TOPIC: Specific Resources
PARTIES:
France
Spain

460147   Bilateral Instrument   **63 SPBO 1612**
SIGNED: 11 Oct 63
HEADNOTE: SOCIAL SECURITY
TOPIC: Non-ILO Labor
PARTIES:
France
Spain

460148   Bilateral Protocol   **64 SPBO 1403**
SIGNED: 15 Nov 63
HEADNOTE: 750 MILLION FRANCS CREDIT
TOPIC: Loans and Credits
PARTIES:
France
Spain

460149   Bilateral Agreement   **65 SPBO 1805**
SIGNED: 4 Jun 64
HEADNOTE: SPACE TRACKING STATION
TOPIC: Scientific Project
PARTIES:
France
Spain

460150   Bilateral Instrument   **65 SPBO 302**
SIGNED: 29 Aug 64
HEADNOTE: SOCIAL SECURITY
TOPIC: Non-ILO Labor
PARTIES:
France
Spain

460151   Bilateral Exchange   **64 SPBO 1509**
SIGNED: 3 Jul 64
HEADNOTE: WIDENING BORDER ZONE LABOR
TOPIC: Non-ILO Labor
PARTIES:
France
Spain

460152   Bilateral Agreement   **65 SPBO 1602**
SIGNED: 29 Aug 64
HEADNOTE: SOCIAL SECURITY
TOPIC: Non-ILO Labor
PARTIES:
France
Spain

460153   Bilateral Instrument   **64 SPBO 112**
SIGNED: 29 Aug 64
HEADNOTE: SOCIAL SECURITY
TOPIC: Non-ILO Labor
PARTIES:
France
Spain

460154   Bilateral Exchange   **65 SPBO 2906**
SIGNED: 1 Jun 65
HEADNOTE: BORDER ZONE LABOR
TOPIC: Non-ILO Labor
PARTIES:
France
Spain

460155   Bilateral Protocol   **56 SPBO 2701**
SIGNED: 1 Jun 55
HEADNOTE: SUPPLEMENT AGREEMENT 15 MAY
   54 MIXED COMMISSION
TOPIC: General Trade
PARTIES:
Greece
Spain

460156   Bilateral Exchange   **56 SPBO 1406**
SIGNED: 14 May 56
HEADNOTE: EXTEND LISTS AGREEMENT 1 JUNE
   55
TOPIC: General Trade
PARTIES:
Greece
Spain

460157   Bilateral Exchange   **57 SPBO 3005**
SIGNED: 8 May 57
HEADNOTE: EXTEND LISTS AGREEMENT 1 JUN
   55
TOPIC: General Trade
PARTIES:
Greece
Spain

460158   Bilateral Convention   **56 SPBO 2801**
SIGNED: 31 Dec 55
HEADNOTE: TRADE
TOPIC: General Trade
PARTIES:
Guatemala
Spain

460159   Bilateral Convention   **62 SPBO 1003**
SIGNED: 28 Jul 61
HEADNOTE: NATIONALITY
TOPIC: Consul/Citizenship
PARTIES:
Guatemala
Spain

460160   Bilateral Convention   **65 SPBO 2506**
SIGNED: 27 Apr 64
HEADNOTE: CULTURE
TOPIC: Culture
PARTIES:
Guatemala
Spain

460161   Bilateral Treaty   **63 SPBO 1105**
SIGNED: 12 Jun 57
HEADNOTE: CULTURAL EXCHANGE
TOPIC: Culture
PARTIES:
Honduras
Spain

460162   Bilateral Treaty   **57 SPBO 1912**
SIGNED: 12 Mar 56
HEADNOTE: GENERAL RELATIONS
TOPIC: General Amity
PARTIES:
Iran
Spain

460163   Bilateral Treaty   **55 SPBO 101**
SIGNED: 3 Sep 51
HEADNOTE: GENERAL RELATIONS
TOPIC: General Amity
PARTIES:
Iraq
Spain

460164   Bilateral Convention   **57 SPBO 1502**
SIGNED: 14 Feb 55
HEADNOTE: CULTURE
TOPIC: Culture
PARTIES:
Iraq
Spain

460165   Bilateral Exchange   **55 SPBO 401**
SIGNED: 21 Dec 54
HEADNOTE: EXTEND TRADE AGREEMENT 17 DEC
   49
TOPIC: General Trade
PARTIES:
Iceland
Spain

460166   Bilateral Exchange   **56 SPBO 2701**
SIGNED: 31 Dec 55
HEADNOTE: EXTEND TRADE AGREEMENT 17 DEC
   49
TOPIC: General Trade
PARTIES:
Iceland
Spain

460167   Bilateral Exchange   **57 SPBO 103**
SIGNED: 13 Feb 57
HEADNOTE: EXTEND TRADE AGREEMENT 17 DEC
   49
TOPIC: General Trade
PARTIES:
Iceland
Spain

460168   Bilateral Agreement   **47 SPBO 2008**
SIGNED: 20 Jun 47
HEADNOTE: VALIDITY AGREEMENTS 1940 &
   1942
TOPIC: General Trade
PARTIES:
Italy
Spain

460169   Bilateral Agreement   **55 SPBO 505**
SIGNED: 20 Apr 55
HEADNOTE: FILM PRODUCTION
TOPIC: Mass Media
PARTIES:
Italy
Spain

460170   Bilateral Protocol   **55 SPBO 2908**
SIGNED: 16 Jun 55
HEADNOTE: SUPPLEMENT AGREEMENT 26 MAR
   52
TOPIC: General Trade
PARTIES:
Italy
Spain

460171   Bilateral Protocol   **56 SPBO 3004**
SIGNED: 13 Apr 56
HEADNOTE: SUPPLEMENT AGREEMENT 26 MAR
   52
TOPIC: General Trade
PARTIES:
Italy
Spain

460172   Bilateral Agreement   **57 SPBO 102**
SIGNED: 16 Apr 56
HEADNOTE: FILMS
TOPIC: Mass Media
PARTIES:
Italy
Spain

460173   Bilateral Convention   **58 SPBO 1503**
SIGNED: 21 Jul 56
HEADNOTE: SOCIAL SECURITY
TOPIC: Non-ILO Labor
PARTIES:
Italy
Spain

460174　　Bilateral Instrument　　**59 SPBO 1601**
SIGNED: 25 Nov 57
HEADNOTE: SOCIAL SECURITY CONVENTION 21
　JUL 56
TOPIC: Non-ILO Labor
PARTIES:
　Italy
　Spain

460175　　Bilateral Exchange　　**58 SPBO 2605**
SIGNED: 28 Mar 58
HEADNOTE: SOCIAL SECURITY FAMILY LOANS
TOPIC: Non-ILO Labor
PARTIES:
　Italy
　Spain

460176　　Bilateral Protocol　　**56 SPBO 406**
SIGNED: 8 May 58
HEADNOTE: SUPPLEMENT AGREEMENT 26 MAR
　52
TOPIC: General Trade
PARTIES:
　Italy
　Spain

460177　　Bilateral Exchange　　**59 SPBO 904**
SIGNED: 14 Mar 59
HEADNOTE: MODIFY AGREEMENT 25 NOV 57
TOPIC: Non-ILO Labor
PARTIES:
　Italy
　Spain

460178　　Bilateral Protocol　　**56 SPBO 801**
SIGNED: 24 Dec 55
HEADNOTE: TRADE
TOPIC: General Trade
PARTIES:
　Japan
　Spain

460179　　Bilateral Treaty　　**51 SPBO 1710**
SIGNED: 7 Oct 50
HEADNOTE: GENERAL RELATIONS
TOPIC: General Amity
PARTIES:
　Jordan
　Spain

460180　　Bilateral Convention　　**49 SPBO 1812**
SIGNED: 7 Mar 49
HEADNOTE: CULTURE
TOPIC: Culture
PARTIES:
　Lebanon
　Spain

460181　　Bilateral Treaty　　**51 SPBO 607**
SIGNED: 6 May 50
HEADNOTE: GENERAL RELATIONS
TOPIC: General Amity
PARTIES:
　Lebanon
　Spain

460182　　Bilateral Treaty　　**53 SPBO 912**
SIGNED: 2 Apr 53
HEADNOTE: GENERAL RELATIONS
TOPIC: General Amity
PARTIES:
　Liberia
　Spain

460183　　Bilateral Treaty　　**56 SPBO 2603**
SIGNED: 26 May 54
HEADNOTE: TRADE
TOPIC: General Trade
PARTIES:
　Liberia
　Spain

460184　　Bilateral Convention　　**62 SPBO 2307**
SIGNED: 5 May 59

HEADNOTE: CULTURE
TOPIC: Culture
PARTIES:
　Libya
　Spain

460185　　Bilateral Convention　　**65 SPBO 2408**
SIGNED: 22 Jun 63
HEADNOTE: SOCIAL SECURITY
TOPIC: Non-ILO Labor
PARTIES:
　Luxembourg
　Spain

460186　　Bilateral Agreement　　**65 SPBO 1509**
SIGNED: 22 Jun 63
HEADNOTE: SOCIAL SECURITY ADMINISTRA-
　TION IMPLEMENT
TOPIC: Non-ILO Labor
PARTIES:
　Luxembourg
　Spain

460187　　Bilateral Instrument　　**57 SPBO 403**
SIGNED: 7 Apr 56
HEADNOTE: TERMINATING PROTECTORATE
TOPIC: Recognition
PARTIES:
　Morocco
　Spain

460188　　Bilateral Protocol　　**57 SPBO 403**
SIGNED: 7 Apr 56
HEADNOTE: TERMINATING PROTECTORATE
TOPIC: Recognition
PARTIES:
　Morocco
　Spain

460189　　Bilateral Exchange　　**57 SPBO 403**
SIGNED: 7 Apr 56
HEADNOTE: DIPLOMATIC　REPRESENTATION
　THIRD COUNTRIES
TOPIC: Recognition
PARTIES:
　Morocco
　Spain

460190　　Bilateral Convention　　**57 SPBO 403**
SIGNED: 11 Feb 57
HEADNOTE: GENERAL RELATIONS FOREIGN POL-
　ICY
TOPIC: General Amity
PARTIES:
　Morocco
　Spain

460191　　Bilateral Convention　　**57 SPBO 403**
SIGNED: 11 Feb 57
HEADNOTE: JUDICIAL COOPERATION
TOPIC: Admin Cooperation
PARTIES:
　Morocco
　Spain

460192　　Bilateral Instrument　　**57 SPBO 1706**
SIGNED: 4 Jun 57
HEADNOTE: RENUNCIATION CUSTOMS PRIVI-
　LEGES
TOPIC: General Trade
PARTIES:
　Morocco
　Spain

460193　　Bilateral Agreement　　**57 SPBO 709**
SIGNED: 7 Jul 57
HEADNOTE: PAYMENT
TOPIC: Finance
PARTIES:
　Morocco
　Spain

460194　　Bilateral Agreement　　**57 SPBO 709**
SIGNED: 7 Jul 57

HEADNOTE: WITHDRAW SPANISH CURRENCY
TOPIC: Finance
PARTIES:
　Morocco
　Spain

460195　　Bilateral Agreement　　**57 SPBO 709**
SIGNED: 7 Jul 57
HEADNOTE: TRADE
TOPIC: General Trade
PARTIES:
　Morocco
　Spain

460196　　Bilateral Exchange　　**57 SPBO 709**
SIGNED: 7 Jul 57
HEADNOTE: MAINTENANCE OF TRADE VOLUME
TOPIC: General Trade
PARTIES:
　Morocco
　Spain

460197　　Bilateral Exchange　　**57 SPBO 709**
SIGNED: 7 Jul 57
HEADNOTE: AGRICULTURAL PRODUCTS
TOPIC: Commodity Trade
PARTIES:
　Morocco
　Spain

460198　　Bilateral Exchange　　**57 SPBO 709**
SIGNED: 7 Jul 57
HEADNOTE: FISHERIES
TOPIC: Specific Resources
PARTIES:
　Morocco
　Spain

460199　　Bilateral Convention　　**58 SPBO 402**
SIGNED: 7 Jul 57
HEADNOTE: CULTURE
TOPIC: Culture
PARTIES:
　Morocco
　Spain

460200　　Bilateral Convention　　**58 SPBO 502**
SIGNED: 7 Jul 57
HEADNOTE: ADMINISTRATIVE & TECHNICAL CO-
　OPERATION
TOPIC: Tech Assistance
PARTIES:
　Morocco
　Spain

460201　　Bilateral Convention　　**62 SPBO 205**
SIGNED: 25 Jul 61
HEADNOTE: DUAL NATIONALITY
TOPIC: Consul/Citizenship
PARTIES:
　Nicaragua
　Spain

460202　　Bilateral Exchange　　**55 SPBO 2101**
SIGNED: 31 Dec 54
HEADNOTE: EXTEND AGREEMENT 5 MAR 54
TOPIC: General Trade
PARTIES:
　Norway
　Spain

460203　　Bilateral Agreement　　**55 SPBO 2607**
SIGNED: 25 Jun 55
HEADNOTE: TRADE
TOPIC: General Trade
PARTIES:
　Norway
　Spain

460204　　Bilateral Agreement　　**56 SPBO 808**
SIGNED: 17 Jul 56
HEADNOTE: TRADE
TOPIC: General Trade

PARTIES:
Norway
Spain

460205   Bilateral Exchange   56 SPBO 803
SIGNED: 21 Dec 56
HEADNOTE: INTELLECTUAL PROPERTY
TOPIC: Patents/Copyrights
PARTIES:
Norway
Spain

460206   Bilateral Exchange   57 SPBO 808
SIGNED: 22 Jul 57
HEADNOTE: EXTEND AGREEMENT 17 JUL 56
TOPIC: General Trade
PARTIES:
Norway
Spain

460207   Bilateral Agreement   46 SPBO 3010
SIGNED: 21 Oct 46
HEADNOTE: TRADE
TOPIC: General Trade
PARTIES:
Netherlands
Spain

460208   Bilateral Agreement   46 SPBO 3010
SIGNED: 21 Oct 46
HEADNOTE: PAYMENTS
TOPIC: Finance
PARTIES:
Netherlands
Spain

460209   Bilateral Exchange   48 SPBO 1108
SIGNED: 22 Oct 47
HEADNOTE: DENOUNCES CONVENTION 13 JUL 46
TOPIC: Air Transport
PARTIES:
Netherlands
Spain

460210   Bilateral Protocol   55 SPBO 2908
SIGNED: 12 Jul 55
HEADNOTE: SUPPLEMENT AGREEMENT 8 DEC 53
TOPIC: General Trade
PARTIES:
Netherlands
Spain

460211   Bilateral Protocol   55 SPBO 2908
SIGNED: 12 Jul 55
HEADNOTE: SUPPLEMENT AGREEMENT 17 SEP 46
TOPIC: Finance
PARTIES:
Netherlands
Spain

460212   Bilateral Agreement   64 SPBO 1306
SIGNED: 16 Apr 64
HEADNOTE: APPLICATION CONVENTION 17 DEC 62
TOPIC: Non-ILO Labor
PARTIES:
Netherlands
Spain

460213   Bilateral Treaty   59 SPBO 1706
SIGNED: 8 Jul 57
HEADNOTE: GENERAL RELATIONS
TOPIC: General Amity
PARTIES:
Pakistan
Spain

460214   Bilateral Treaty   54 SPBO 607
SIGNED: 18 Mar 53
HEADNOTE: GENERAL RELATIONS
TOPIC: General Amity

PARTIES:
Panama
Spain

460215   Bilateral Treaty   51 SPBO 908
SIGNED: 12 Oct 49
HEADNOTE: GENERAL RELATIONS
TOPIC: General Amity
PARTIES:
Paraguay
Spain

460216   Bilateral Agreement   52 SPBO 1211
SIGNED: 25 Aug 50
HEADNOTE: TRADE & PAYMENTS
TOPIC: General Economic
PARTIES:
Paraguay
Spain

460217   Bilateral Treaty   58 SPBO 2904
SIGNED: 26 Mar 57
HEADNOTE: CULTURAL EXCHANGE
TOPIC: Culture
PARTIES:
Paraguay
Spain

460218   Bilateral Convention   59 SPBO 1007
SIGNED: 11 Aug 58
HEADNOTE: PURCHASE OF SHIPS
TOPIC: Commodity Trade
PARTIES:
Paraguay
Spain

460219   Bilateral Convention   60 SPBO 1804
SIGNED: 25 Jun 59
HEADNOTE: SOCIAL SECURITY
TOPIC: Non-ILO Labor
PARTIES:
Paraguay
Spain

460220   Bilateral Convention   60 SPBO 1804
SIGNED: 25 Jun 59
HEADNOTE: FREE ZONE
TOPIC: General Trade
PARTIES:
Paraguay
Spain

460221   Bilateral Convention   60 SPBO 1804
SIGNED: 25 Jun 59
HEADNOTE: PURCHASE OF SHIPS
TOPIC: General Trade
PARTIES:
Paraguay
Spain

460222   Bilateral Convention   60 SPBO 1904
SIGNED: 25 Jun 59
HEADNOTE: DUAL NATIONALITY
TOPIC: Consul/Citizenship
PARTIES:
Paraguay
Spain

460223   Bilateral Convention   60 SPBO 1904
SIGNED: 25 Jun 59
HEADNOTE: NAVIGATIONAL FACILITIES
TOPIC: Water Transport
PARTIES:
Paraguay
Spain

460224   Bilateral Convention   65 SPBO 2207
SIGNED: 21 May 63
HEADNOTE: FACTORY SHIPS & DRY DOCK
TOPIC: Specif Goods/Equip
PARTIES:
Paraguay
Spain

460225   Bilateral Convention   65 SPBO 1108
SIGNED: 13 Nov 64
HEADNOTE: DRY DOCK & EQUIPMENT
TOPIC: Specif Goods/Equip
PARTIES:
Paraguay
Spain

460226   Bilateral Agreement   54 SPBO 1810
SIGNED: 23 May 53
HEADNOTE: TRADE
TOPIC: General Trade
PARTIES:
Peru
Spain

460227   Bilateral Convention   60 SPBO 1904
SIGNED: 16 May 59
HEADNOTE: DUAL NATIONALITY
TOPIC: Consul/Citizenship
PARTIES:
Peru
Spain

460228   Bilateral Convention   47 SPBO 1107
SIGNED: 31 Mar 47
HEADNOTE: CIVIL AIR SERVICES
TOPIC: Air Transport
PARTIES:
Portugal
Spain

460229   Bilateral Instrument   55 SPBO 2803
SIGNED: 21 Feb 55
HEADNOTE: FINAL ACT MIXED COMMISSION
TOPIC: General Economic
PARTIES:
Portugal
Spain

460230   Bilateral Agreement   57 SPBO 802
SIGNED: 28 Feb 56
HEADNOTE: VETERINARY HYGIENE
TOPIC: Sanitation
PARTIES:
Portugal
Spain

460231   Bilateral Convention   57 SPBO 209
SIGNED: 21 Jan 57
HEADNOTE: HELP AGAINST CUSTOMS FRAUDS
TOPIC: Customs
PARTIES:
Portugal
Spain

460232   Bilateral Agreement   61 SPBO 1107
SIGNED: 20 Oct 59
HEADNOTE: ANTI-MALARIA COOPERATION
TOPIC: Sanitation
PARTIES:
Portugal
Spain

460233   Bilateral Convention   60 SPBO 312
SIGNED: 17 Feb 60
HEADNOTE: LAND BORDER TRAFFIC
TOPIC: Customs
PARTIES:
Portugal
Spain

460234   Bilateral Convention   62 SPBO 1809
SIGNED: 20 Jan 62
HEADNOTE: SOCIAL SECURITY GENERAL
TOPIC: Non-ILO Labor
PARTIES:
Portugal
Spain

460235   Bilateral Protocol   63 SPBO 3010
SIGNED: 27 Feb 63
HEADNOTE: SOCIAL SECURITY IMPLEMENTA-
TION

TOPIC: Non-ILO Labor
PARTIES:
  Portugal
  Spain

460236 Bilateral Agreement **63 SPBO 3010**
SIGNED: 27 Aug 63
HEADNOTE: SOCIAL SECURITY IMPLEMENTA-
  TION
TOPIC: Non-ILO Labor
PARTIES:
  Portugal
  Spain

460237 Bilateral Exchange **47 SPBO 2004**
SIGNED: 30 Oct 44
HEADNOTE: AIR TRANSPORT
TOPIC: Air Transport
PARTIES:
  Spain
  UK Great Britain

460238 Bilateral Instrument **55 SPBO 301**
SIGNED: 21 Dec 54
HEADNOTE: FINAL ACT TRADE TALKS
TOPIC: General Trade
PARTIES:
  Spain
  UK Great Britain

460239 Bilateral Instrument **55 SPBO 608**
SIGNED: 1 Jul 55
HEADNOTE: FINAL ACT TRADE & PAYMENT
  TALKS
TOPIC: General Economic
PARTIES:
  Spain
  UK Great Britain

460240 Bilateral Instrument **57 SPBO 1601**
SIGNED: 21 Dec 56
HEADNOTE: GOODS APPROVED IN TRADE TALKS
TOPIC: General Trade
PARTIES:
  Spain
  UK Great Britain

460241 Bilateral Instrument **58 SPBO 803**
SIGNED: 19 Feb 58
HEADNOTE: LISTS OF GOODS
TOPIC: General Trade
PARTIES:
  Spain
  UK Great Britain

460242 Bilateral Treaty **53 SPBO 2401**
SIGNED: 18 Apr 52
HEADNOTE: GENERAL RELATIONS
TOPIC: General Amity
PARTIES:
  Spain
  Syria

460243 Bilateral Agreement **53 SPBO 2401**
SIGNED: 18 Apr 52
HEADNOTE: CULTURE
TOPIC: Culture
PARTIES:
  Spain
  Syria

460244 Bilateral Agreement **47 SPBO 1008**
SIGNED: 17 Jul 47
HEADNOTE: EXTEND AGREEMENT 26 JAN 46
TOPIC: General Trade
PARTIES:
  Spain
  Sweden

460245 Bilateral Protocol **55 SPBO 1108**
SIGNED: 11 Jun 55
HEADNOTE: TRADE & PAYMENTS
TOPIC: General Economic

PARTIES:
  Spain
  Sweden

460246 Bilateral Protocol **56 SPBO 705**
SIGNED: 11 Apr 56
HEADNOTE: TRADE & PAYMENTS
TOPIC: General Economic
PARTIES:
  Spain
  Sweden

460247 Bilateral Protocol **58 SPBO 1612**
SIGNED: 5 Nov 58
HEADNOTE: TRADE & PAYMENTS
TOPIC: General Economic
PARTIES:
  Spain
  Sweden

460248 Bilateral Convention **64 SPBO 1601**
SIGNED: 25 Apr 63
HEADNOTE: DOUBLE TAX & INHERITANCE
TOPIC: Taxation
PARTIES:
  Spain
  Sweden

460249 Bilateral Convention **64 SPBO 1801**
SIGNED: 25 Apr 63
HEADNOTE: DOUBLE TAX & ADMINISTRATIVE
  ASSISTANCE
TOPIC: Taxation
PARTIES:
  Spain
  Sweden

460250 Bilateral Exchange **47 SPBO 2004**
SIGNED: 17 Jul 46
HEADNOTE: PROVISIONAL AGREEMENT
TOPIC: Air Transport
PARTIES:
  Spain
  Switzerland

460251 Bilateral Agreement **55 SPBO 1001**
SIGNED: 27 Nov 54
HEADNOTE: TRADE & PAYMENTS
TOPIC: General Economic
PARTIES:
  Spain
  Switzerland

460252 Bilateral Convention **60 SPBO 1406**
SIGNED: 21 Sep 59
HEADNOTE: SOCIAL SECURITY
TOPIC: Non-ILO Labor
PARTIES:
  Spain
  Switzerland

460253 Bilateral Agreement **60 SPBO 2707**
SIGNED: 25 Jan 60
HEADNOTE: SOCIAL SECURITY CONVENTION 21
  SEP 59
TOPIC: Non-ILO Labor
PARTIES:
  Spain
  Switzerland

460254 Bilateral Agreement **61 SPBO 912**
SIGNED: 2 Mar 61
HEADNOTE: WORKERS CONTRACTS FOR SWIT-
  ZERLAND
TOPIC: Non-ILO Labor
PARTIES:
  Spain
  Switzerland

460255 Bilateral Agreement **63 SPBO 1109**
SIGNED: 23 Jan 63
HEADNOTE: ROAD TRANSPORT
TOPIC: Land Transport

PARTIES:
  Spain
  Switzerland

460256 Bilateral Agreement **65 SPBO 1201**
SIGNED: 27 Nov 63
HEADNOTE: AIR TRANSPORT TAX
TOPIC: Taxation
PARTIES:
  Spain
  Switzerland

460257 Bilateral Agreement **58 SPBO 908**
SIGNED: 28 Mar 56
HEADNOTE: CULTURE
TOPIC: Culture
PARTIES:
  Spain
  Turkey

460258 Bilateral Treaty **61 SPBO 803**
SIGNED: 16 Apr 59
HEADNOTE: GENERAL RELATIONS
TOPIC: General Amity
PARTIES:
  Spain
  Turkey

460259 Bilateral Agreement **57 SPBO 2502**
SIGNED: 24 Feb 54
HEADNOTE: PAYMENTS
TOPIC: Finance
PARTIES:
  Spain
  Uruguay

460260 Bilateral Convention **57 SPBO 2502**
SIGNED: 24 Feb 54
HEADNOTE: TRADE
TOPIC: General Trade
PARTIES:
  Spain
  Uruguay

460261 Bilateral Treaty **57 SPBO 2502**
SIGNED: 24 Feb 54
HEADNOTE: MOST FAVORED NATION
TOPIC: General Trade
PARTIES:
  Spain
  Uruguay

460262 Bilateral Exchange **55 SPBO 1902**
SIGNED: 24 Jan 55
HEADNOTE: EXTEND MODUS VIVENDI 22 OCT 54
TOPIC: Customs
PARTIES:
  Spain
  Uruguay

460263 Bilateral Exchange **55 SPBO 1508**
SIGNED: 25 Jun 55
HEADNOTE: TRANSITIONAL CUSTOMS REGIME
TOPIC: General Trade
PARTIES:
  Spain
  Uruguay

460264 Bilateral Exchange **56 SPBO 1003**
SIGNED: 21 Jan 56
HEADNOTE: EXTEND TRANSITIONAL CUSTOMS
  REGIME
TOPIC: General Trade
PARTIES:
  Spain
  Uruguay

460265 Bilateral Exchange **56 SPBO 2310**
SIGNED: 9 Aug 56
HEADNOTE: EXTEND TRANSITIONAL CUSTOMS
  REGIME
TOPIC: General Trade

PARTIES:
Spain
Uruguay

460266 Bilateral Treaty **55 SPBO 1505**
SIGNED: 19 May 52
HEADNOTE: GENERAL RELATIONS
TOPIC: General Amity
PARTIES:
Spain
Yemen

460267 Bilateral Agreement **53 SPBO 1911**
SIGNED: 7 Jun 41
HEADNOTE: REPRESENTATION
TOPIC: Admin Cooperation
PARTIES:
Spain
Vatican/Holy See

460268 Bilateral Convention **53 SPBO 1911**
SIGNED: 16 Jul 46
HEADNOTE: NON-RELIGIOUS BENEFITS
TOPIC: Non-ILO Labor
PARTIES:
Spain
Vatican/Holy See

460270 Bilateral Convention **50 SPBO 1811**
SIGNED: 5 Aug 50
HEADNOTE: RELIGIOUS SERVICE ARMED FORCES
TOPIC: Admin Cooperation
PARTIES:
Spain
Vatican/Holy See

460271 Bilateral Instrument **53 SPBO 1910**
SIGNED: 27 Aug 53
HEADNOTE: GENERAL RELATIONS
TOPIC: General Amity
PARTIES:
Spain
Vatican/Holy See

460272 Bilateral Exchange **57 SPBO 1207**
SIGNED: 6 Jul 57
HEADNOTE: PRIESTS BEFORE STATE COURTS
TOPIC: Admin Cooperation
PARTIES:
Spain
Vatican/Holy See

460273 Bilateral Convention **62 SPBO 2007**
SIGNED: 5 Apr 62
HEADNOTE: NONRELIGIOUS STUDIES CATHOLIC
SCHOOLS
TOPIC: Education
PARTIES:
Spain
Vatican/Holy See

460274 Bilateral Agreement **58 SPBO 1207**
SIGNED: 10 Jan 58
HEADNOTE: ASSOCIATION OF SPAIN WITH OEEC
TOPIC: IGO Operations
PARTIES:
OECD (Econ Coop)
Spain

460276 Bilateral Agreement **59 SPBO 3003**
SIGNED: 27 Jun 57
HEADNOTE: SOCIAL SECURITY BORDER WORK-
ERS
TOPIC: Non-ILO Labor
PARTIES:
France
Spain

460277 Bilateral Exchange **59 SPBO 1104**
SIGNED: 27 Jun 57
HEADNOTE: SOCIAL SECURITY PROOF OF CITI-
ZENSHIP
TOPIC: Non-ILO Labor

PARTIES:
France
Spain

460278 Bilateral Instrument **58 SPBO 2405**
SIGNED: 10 May 58
HEADNOTE: FINAL ACT 1958 TALKS
TOPIC: General Trade
PARTIES:
Finland
Spain

460279 Bilateral Instrument **57 SPBO 2007**
SIGNED: 25 May 57
HEADNOTE: MAY 1957 TALKS
TOPIC: General Trade
PARTIES:
Finland
Spain

460280 Bilateral Exchange **65 SPBO 611**
SIGNED: 1 Oct 65
HEADNOTE: SPACE TRACKING STATION
TOPIC: Scientific Project
PARTIES:
Spain
USA (United States)

461001 Bilateral Exchange **45 SOFM 65**
SIGNED: 12 Apr 45
HEADNOTE: AIR ROUTES
TOPIC: Air Transport
PARTIES:
Canada
Sweden

461002 Bilateral Agreement **45 SOFM 67**
SIGNED: 20 Apr 45
HEADNOTE: AIR TRAFFIC
TOPIC: Air Transport
PARTIES:
Iceland
Sweden

461003 Bilateral Exchange **45 SOFM 69**
SIGNED: 16 Aug 45
HEADNOTE: TEMPORARY AIR TRAFFIC
TOPIC: Air Transport
PARTIES:
France
Sweden

461004 Bilateral Exchange **45 SOFM 70**
SIGNED: 24 Aug 45
HEADNOTE: TEMPORARY AIR TRAFFIC
TOPIC: Air Transport
PARTIES:
Poland
Sweden

461005 Bilateral Agreement **45 SOFM 71**
SIGNED: 15 Nov 45
HEADNOTE: TEMPORARY AIR TRAFFIC
TOPIC: Air Transport
PARTIES:
Czechoslovakia
Sweden

461006 Bilateral Agreement **45 SOFM 95**
SIGNED: 7 Apr 45
HEADNOTE: COMMERCE
TOPIC: General Trade
PARTIES:
Iceland
Sweden

461007 Bilateral Agreement **45 SOFM 99**
SIGNED: 30 May 45
HEADNOTE: COMMERCE
TOPIC: General Trade
PARTIES:
Belgium
Sweden

461008 Bilateral Agreement **45 SOFM 100**
SIGNED: 30 May 45
HEADNOTE: PAYMENTS
TOPIC: Finance
PARTIES:
Belgium
Sweden

461009 Bilateral Exchange **45 SOFM 105**
SIGNED: 21 Jun 45
HEADNOTE: GOODS EXCHANGE
TOPIC: General Trade
PARTIES:
France
Sweden

461010 Bilateral Agreement **45 SOFM 107**
SIGNED: 21 Jun 45
HEADNOTE: PAYMENTS
TOPIC: Finance
PARTIES:
France
Sweden

461011 Bilateral Agreement **45 SOFM 115**
SIGNED: 9 Jul 45
HEADNOTE: REGULATING GOODS EXCHANGE
TOPIC: General Trade
PARTIES:
Poland
Sweden

461012 Bilateral Exchange **45 SOFM 119**
SIGNED: 31 Jul 45
HEADNOTE: TRADE
TOPIC: General Trade
PARTIES:
Argentina
Sweden

461013 Bilateral Exchange **45 SOFM 124**
SIGNED: 17 Aug 45
HEADNOTE: EXCHANGE GOODS
TOPIC: General Trade
PARTIES:
Finland
Sweden

461014 Bilateral Agreement **45 SOFM 125**
SIGNED: 20 Aug 45
HEADNOTE: TRADE & PAYMENTS
TOPIC: General Economic
PARTIES:
Poland
Sweden

461015 Bilateral Agreement **45 SOFM 137**
SIGNED: 17 Nov 45
HEADNOTE: EXCHANGE GOODS
TOPIC: General Trade
PARTIES:
Czechoslovakia
Sweden

461016 Bilateral Agreement **45 SOFM 138**
SIGNED: 17 Nov 45
HEADNOTE: PAYMENTS
TOPIC: Finance
PARTIES:
Czechoslovakia
Sweden

461017 Bilateral Agreement **45 SOFM 143**
SIGNED: 24 Nov 45
HEADNOTE: TRADE
TOPIC: General Trade
PARTIES:
Italy
Sweden

461018 Bilateral Agreement **45 SOFM 146**
SIGNED: 24 Nov 45
HEADNOTE: PAYMENTS
TOPIC: Finance

PARTIES:
Italy
Sweden

461019 Bilateral Agreement **45 SOFM 151**
SIGNED: 30 Nov 45
HEADNOTE: TRADE
TOPIC: General Trade
PARTIES:
Netherlands
Sweden

461020 Bilateral Exchange **46 SOFM 169**
SIGNED: 26 Jan 46
HEADNOTE: TRADE & PAYMENTS
TOPIC: General Economic
PARTIES:
Spain
Sweden

461021 Bilateral Protocol **46 SOFM 183**
SIGNED: 16 Feb 46
HEADNOTE: TRADE & PAYMENTS
TOPIC: General Economic
PARTIES:
Poland
Sweden

461022 Bilateral Agreement **45 SOFM 191**
SIGNED: 24 Apr 46
HEADNOTE: TRADE
TOPIC: General Trade
PARTIES:
Sweden
Turkey

461023 Bilateral Agreement **46 SOFM 192**
SIGNED: 24 Apr 46
HEADNOTE: PAYMENTS
TOPIC: Finance
PARTIES:
Sweden
Turkey

461024 Bilateral Agreement **46 SOFM 197**
SIGNED: 18 May 46
HEADNOTE: TRADE
TOPIC: General Trade
PARTIES:
Iceland
Sweden

461025 Bilateral Exchange **46 SOFM 199**
SIGNED: 23 Jun 46
HEADNOTE: TRADE
TOPIC: General Trade
PARTIES:
Italy
Sweden

461026 Bilateral Protocol **46 SOFM 201**
SIGNED: 28 Jun 46
HEADNOTE: TRADE
TOPIC: General Trade
PARTIES:
France
Sweden

461027 Bilateral Protocol **46 SOFM 203**
SIGNED: 28 Jun 46
HEADNOTE: PAYMENTS
TOPIC: Finance
PARTIES:
France
Sweden

461028 Bilateral Instrument **46 SOFM 204**
SIGNED: 29 Jun 46
HEADNOTE: TRADE
TOPIC: General Trade
PARTIES:
Netherlands
Sweden

461029 Bilateral Agreement **46 SOFM 247**
SIGNED: 26 Jul 46
HEADNOTE: TRADE
TOPIC: General Trade
PARTIES:
Hungary
Sweden

461030 Bilateral Agreement **46 SOFM 250**
SIGNED: 26 Jul 46
HEADNOTE: PAYMENTS
TOPIC: Finance
PARTIES:
Hungary
Sweden

461031 Bilateral Protocol **46 SOFM 253**
SIGNED: 29 Jul 46
HEADNOTE: TRADE
TOPIC: General Trade
PARTIES:
Czechoslovakia
Sweden

461032 Bilateral Protocol **46 SOFM 255**
SIGNED: 29 Jul 46
HEADNOTE: PAYMENTS
TOPIC: Finance
PARTIES:
Czechoslovakia
Sweden

461033 Bilateral Exchange **46 SOFM 257**
SIGNED: 3 Oct 46
HEADNOTE: TRADE
TOPIC: General Trade
PARTIES:
Spain
Sweden

461034 Bilateral Agreement **46 SOFM 307**
SIGNED: 22 Nov 46
HEADNOTE: CERTAIN FISHERIES
TOPIC: Specific Resources
PARTIES:
Norway
Sweden

461035 Bilateral Protocol **46 SOFM 311**
SIGNED: 26 Oct 46
HEADNOTE: TRADE & PAYMENTS
TOPIC: General Economic
PARTIES:
Poland
Sweden

461036 Bilateral Exchange **46 SOFM 313**
SIGNED: 23 Oct 45
HEADNOTE: VALIDITY EARLIER AGREEMENTS
TOPIC: Admin Cooperation
PARTIES:
Czechoslovakia
Sweden

461037 Bilateral Agreement **47 SOFM 1**
SIGNED: 23 Dec 46
HEADNOTE: TRADE
TOPIC: General Trade
PARTIES:
Netherlands
Sweden

461038 Bilateral Agreement **47 SOFM 23**
SIGNED: 30 Dec 46
HEADNOTE: TRADE
TOPIC: General Trade
PARTIES:
Belgium
Sweden

461039 Bilateral Agreement **47 SOFM 137**
SIGNED: 18 Mar 47
HEADNOTE: PAYMENTS
TOPIC: Finance

PARTIES:
Poland
Sweden

461040 Bilateral Agreement **47 SOFM 161**
SIGNED: 12 Apr 47
HEADNOTE: TRADE
TOPIC: General Trade
PARTIES:
Sweden
Yugoslavia

461041 Bilateral Protocol **47 SOFM 181**
SIGNED: 12 Apr 47
HEADNOTE: PAYMENTS
TOPIC: Finance
PARTIES:
Sweden
Yugoslavia

461045 Bilateral Protocol **47 SOFM 455**
SIGNED: 31 Oct 47
HEADNOTE: TRADE
TOPIC: General Trade
PARTIES:
France
Sweden

461046 Bilateral Protocol **47 SOFM 480**
SIGNED: 31 Oct 47
HEADNOTE: PAYMENTS
TOPIC: Finance
PARTIES:
France
Sweden

461047 Bilateral Protocol **47 SOFM 480**
SIGNED: 19 Oct 47
HEADNOTE: TRADE
TOPIC: General Trade
PARTIES:
Iceland
Sweden

461048 Bilateral Protocol **47 SOFM 485**
SIGNED: 30 Oct 47
HEADNOTE: TRADE
TOPIC: General Trade
PARTIES:
Czechoslovakia
Sweden

461049 Bilateral Agreement **47 SOFM 494**
SIGNED: 30 Oct 47
HEADNOTE: PAYMENTS
TOPIC: Finance
PARTIES:
Czechoslovakia
Sweden

461050 Bilateral Agreement **47 SOFM 499**
SIGNED: 22 Sep 47
HEADNOTE: TRADE
TOPIC: General Trade
PARTIES:
Bulgaria
Sweden

461051 Bilateral Protocol **47 SOFM 508**
SIGNED: 22 Sep 47
HEADNOTE: PAYMENTS
TOPIC: Finance
PARTIES:
Bulgaria
Sweden

461052 Bilateral Exchange **47 SOFM 511**
SIGNED: 5 Aug 47
HEADNOTE: TRADE
TOPIC: General Trade
PARTIES:
Norway
Sweden

461053 Bilateral Protocol 47 SOFM 511
SIGNED: 31 Dec 47
HEADNOTE: TRADE
TOPIC: General Trade
PARTIES:
 Sweden
 USSR (Soviet Union)

461054 Bilateral Protocol 47 SOFM 513
SIGNED: 14 Nov 47
HEADNOTE: TRADE
TOPIC: General Trade
PARTIES:
 Denmark
 Sweden

461055 Bilateral Exchange 47 SOFM 571
SIGNED: 10 Mar 47
HEADNOTE: TRADE
TOPIC: General Trade
PARTIES:
 Czechoslovakia
 Sweden

461056 Bilateral Exchange 47 SOFM 572
SIGNED: 15 Mar 47
HEADNOTE: CZECH NATIONALIZATIONS
TOPIC: Claims and Debts
PARTIES:
 Czechoslovakia
 Sweden

461057 Bilateral Exchange 47 SOFM 573
SIGNED: 12 Dec 46
HEADNOTE: TRADE
TOPIC: General Trade
PARTIES:
 Denmark
 Sweden

461058 Bilateral Protocol 47 SOFM 575
SIGNED: 28 Nov 47
HEADNOTE: TRADE
TOPIC: General Trade
PARTIES:
 Hungary
 Sweden

461059 Bilateral Agreement 47 SOFM 583
SIGNED: 30 Dec 47
HEADNOTE: TRADE
TOPIC: General Trade
PARTIES:
 Netherlands
 Sweden

461060 Bilateral Agreement 47 SOFM 631
SIGNED: 22 Dec 47
HEADNOTE: HEALTH INSURANCE
TOPIC: Non-ILO Labor
PARTIES:
 Norway
 Sweden

461061 Bilateral Agreement 47 SOFM 635
SIGNED: 23 Dec 47
HEADNOTE: HEALTH INSURANCE
TOPIC: Non-ILO Labor
PARTIES:
 Denmark
 Sweden

461062 Bilateral Agreement 47 SOFM 651
SIGNED: 5 Oct 47
HEADNOTE: PAYMENTS
TOPIC: Finance
PARTIES:
 Germany, West
 Sweden

461070 Bilateral Exchange 47 SOFM 667
SIGNED: 17 Jul 47
HEADNOTE: TRADE & PAYMENTS
TOPIC: General Economic

PARTIES:
 Spain
 Sweden

461071 Bilateral Protocol 49 SOFM 1
SIGNED: 8 Feb 49
HEADNOTE: TRADE
TOPIC: General Trade
PARTIES:
 Denmark
 Sweden

461072 Bilateral Exchange 49 SOFM 13
SIGNED: 24 Jan 49
HEADNOTE: TRADE
TOPIC: General Trade
PARTIES:
 Germany, East
 Sweden

461073 Bilateral Protocol 49 SOFM 63
SIGNED: 1 Feb 49
HEADNOTE: TRADE
TOPIC: General Trade
PARTIES:
 Czechoslovakia
 Sweden

461074 Bilateral Protocol 49 SOFM 76
SIGNED: 1 Feb 49
HEADNOTE: PAYMENTS
TOPIC: Finance
PARTIES:
 Czechoslovakia
 Sweden

461075 Bilateral Protocol 49 SOFM 84
SIGNED: 14 Jan 49
HEADNOTE: PAYMENTS
TOPIC: Finance
PARTIES:
 Germany, West
 Sweden

461076 Bilateral Agreement 49 SOFM 87
SIGNED: 14 Feb 49
HEADNOTE: PAYMENTS
TOPIC: Finance
PARTIES:
 Belgium
 Sweden

461077 Bilateral Agreement 49 SOFM 97
SIGNED: 3 Mar 49
HEADNOTE: TRADE
TOPIC: General Trade
PARTIES:
 France
 Sweden

461078 Bilateral Protocol 49 SOFM 137
SIGNED: 18 Mar 49
HEADNOTE: TRADE
TOPIC: General Trade
PARTIES:
 Finland
 Sweden

461079 Bilateral Protocol 49 SOFM 145
SIGNED: 2 Apr 49
HEADNOTE: TRADE
TOPIC: General Trade
PARTIES:
 Sweden
 USSR (Soviet Union)

461080 Bilateral Exchange 49 SOFM 155
SIGNED: 19 Jan 49
HEADNOTE: TRADE
TOPIC: General Trade
PARTIES:
 Hungary
 Sweden

461081 Bilateral Protocol 49 SOFM 157
SIGNED: 21 May 49
HEADNOTE: TRADE
TOPIC: General Trade
PARTIES:
 Sweden
 Yugoslavia

461082 Bilateral Agreement 49 SOFM 251
SIGNED: 19 Jul 49
HEADNOTE: TRADE & PAYMENTS
TOPIC: General Economic
PARTIES:
 Germany, East
 Sweden

461083 Bilateral Agreement 49 SOFM 301
SIGNED: 13 Jun 49
HEADNOTE: PAYMENTS
TOPIC: Finance
PARTIES:
 Sweden
 Uruguay

461084 Bilateral Exchange 49 SOFM 307
SIGNED: 17 Jun 49
HEADNOTE: FISH TRADE
TOPIC: Commodity Trade
PARTIES:
 Denmark
 Sweden

461085 Bilateral Instrument 49 SOFM 311
SIGNED: 27 Jun 49
HEADNOTE: TRADE
TOPIC: General Trade
PARTIES:
 Sweden
 USA (United States)

461086 Bilateral Exchange 49 SOFM 391
SIGNED: 7 Apr 49
HEADNOTE: TRADE
TOPIC: General Trade
PARTIES:
 Netherlands
 Sweden

461087 Bilateral Agreement 49 SOFM 457
SIGNED: 25 May 49
HEADNOTE: PAYMENTS
TOPIC: Finance
PARTIES:
 Germany, West
 Sweden

461088 Bilateral Exchange 49 SOFM 484
SIGNED: 30 Jun 49
HEADNOTE: TRADE
TOPIC: General Trade
PARTIES:
 France
 Sweden

461089 Bilateral Protocol 49 SOFM 497
SIGNED: 15 Jul 49
HEADNOTE: TRADE
TOPIC: General Trade
PARTIES:
 Iceland
 Sweden

461090 Bilateral Exchange 49 SOFM 519
SIGNED: 11 Oct 49
HEADNOTE: TRADE
TOPIC: General Trade
PARTIES:
 Bulgaria
 Sweden

461091 Bilateral Agreement 49 SOFM 529
SIGNED: 18 Oct 49
HEADNOTE: PAYMENTS
TOPIC: Finance

PARTIES:
Poland
Sweden

461092   Bilateral Protocol   49 SOFM 549
SIGNED: 3 Nov 49
HEADNOTE: TRADE & PAYMENTS
TOPIC: General Economic
PARTIES:
Poland
Sweden

461093   Bilateral Protocol   49 SOFM 561
SIGNED: 30 Nov 49
HEADNOTE: TRADE
TOPIC: General Trade
PARTIES:
Hungary
Sweden

461094   Bilateral Agreement   49 SOFM 571
SIGNED: 23 Nov 48
HEADNOTE: TRADE & PAYMENTS
TOPIC: General Economic
PARTIES:
Argentina
Sweden

461095   Bilateral Exchange   49 SOFM 584
SIGNED: 17 Dec 49
HEADNOTE: TRADE
TOPIC: General Trade
PARTIES:
France
Sweden

461096   Bilateral Exchange   49 SOFM 625
SIGNED: 19 Dec 49
HEADNOTE: TRADE
TOPIC: General Trade
PARTIES:
Netherlands
Sweden

461097   Bilateral Agreement   49 SOFM 767
SIGNED: 31 Oct 49
HEADNOTE: AIR TRAFFIC
TOPIC: Air Transport
PARTIES:
Iran
Sweden

461098   Bilateral Exchange   50 SOFM 1
SIGNED: 2 Jan 50
HEADNOTE: TRADE
TOPIC: General Trade
PARTIES:
Sweden
Yugoslavia

461099   Bilateral Exchange   50 SOFM 43
SIGNED: 24 Feb 50
HEADNOTE: TRADE
TOPIC: General Trade
PARTIES:
India
Sweden

461100   Bilateral Protocol   50 SOFM 59
SIGNED: 2 Mar 50
HEADNOTE: TRADE
TOPIC: General Trade
PARTIES:
Austria
Sweden

461101   Bilateral Exchange   50 SOFM 69
SIGNED: 18 Apr 50
HEADNOTE: TRADE
TOPIC: General Trade
PARTIES:
Italy
Sweden

461102   Bilateral Protocol   50 SOFM 89
SIGNED: 8 Mar 50
HEADNOTE: TRADE
TOPIC: General Trade
PARTIES:
Denmark
Sweden

461103   Bilateral Exchange   50 SOFM 93
SIGNED: 8 Mar 50
HEADNOTE: PAYMENTS
TOPIC: Finance
PARTIES:
Denmark
Sweden

461104   Bilateral Protocol   50 SOFM 95
SIGNED: 30 Mar 50
HEADNOTE: TRADE
TOPIC: General Trade
PARTIES:
Czechoslovakia
Sweden

461105   Bilateral Protocol   50 SOFM 116
SIGNED: 30 Mar 50
HEADNOTE: PAYMENTS
TOPIC: Finance
PARTIES:
Czechoslovakia
Sweden

461106   Bilateral Protocol   50 SOFM 118
SIGNED: 31 Mar 50
HEADNOTE: TRADE
TOPIC: General Trade
PARTIES:
Iceland
Sweden

461107   Bilateral Agreement   50 SOFM 153
SIGNED: 1 Apr 50
HEADNOTE: TRADE
TOPIC: General Trade
PARTIES:
Japan
Sweden

461108   Bilateral Agreement   50 SOFM 165
SIGNED: 1 Apr 50
HEADNOTE: PAYMENTS
TOPIC: Finance
PARTIES:
Japan
Sweden

461109   Bilateral Instrument   50 SOFM 169
SIGNED: 1 Apr 50
HEADNOTE: TRADE & PAYMENTS
TOPIC: General Economic
PARTIES:
Finland
Sweden

461110   Bilateral Exchange   50 SOFM 178
SIGNED: 1 Jul 50
HEADNOTE: TRADE
TOPIC: General Trade
PARTIES:
India
Sweden

461111   Bilateral Protocol   50 SOFM 181
SIGNED: 4 Sep 50
HEADNOTE: TRADE
TOPIC: General Trade
PARTIES:
Germany, West
Sweden

461112   Bilateral Agreement   50 SOFM 196
SIGNED: 4 Sep 50
HEADNOTE: PAYMENTS
TOPIC: Finance

PARTIES:
Germany, West
Sweden

461113   Bilateral Exchange   50 SOFM 781
SIGNED: 18 Apr 50
HEADNOTE: TRADE
TOPIC: General Trade
PARTIES:
Netherlands
Sweden

461114   Bilateral Agreement   50 SOFM 817
SIGNED: 15 Nov 49
HEADNOTE: TRADE
TOPIC: General Trade
PARTIES:
Italy
Sweden

461115   Bilateral Agreement   50 SOFM 840
SIGNED: 15 Nov 49
HEADNOTE: PAYMENTS
TOPIC: Finance
PARTIES:
Italy
Sweden

461116   Bilateral Agreement   50 SOFM 849
SIGNED: 17 Nov 49
HEADNOTE: SWEDISH ASSETS
TOPIC: Claims and Debts
PARTIES:
Finland
Sweden

461117   Bilateral Agreement   50 SOFM 853
SIGNED: 3 Jun 50
HEADNOTE: TRADE
TOPIC: General Trade
PARTIES:
Sweden
Switzerland

461118   Bilateral Agreement   50 SOFM 900
SIGNED: 29 Dec 50
HEADNOTE: PAYMENTS
TOPIC: Finance
PARTIES:
Belgium
Sweden

461119   Bilateral Agreement   50 SOFM 921
SIGNED: 16 Nov 49
HEADNOTE: POLISH NATIONALIZATIONS
TOPIC: Claims and Debts
PARTIES:
Poland
Sweden

461120   Bilateral Exchange   50 SOFM 931
SIGNED: 18 May 50
HEADNOTE: TRADE
TOPIC: General Trade
PARTIES:
Portugal
Sweden

461121   Bilateral Agreement   50 SOFM 933
SIGNED: 18 May 50
HEADNOTE: PAYMENTS
TOPIC: Finance
PARTIES:
Portugal
Sweden

461122   Bilateral Exchange   50 SOFM 943
SIGNED: 16 Aug 50
HEADNOTE: FISH TRADE
TOPIC: Commodity Trade
PARTIES:
Denmark
Sweden

461123   Bilateral Protocol   **50 SOFM 945**
SIGNED: 19 Aug 50
HEADNOTE: TRADE & PAYMENTS
TOPIC: General Economic
PARTIES:
  Sweden
  Yugoslavia

461124   Bilateral Exchange   **50 SOFM 981**
SIGNED: 31 Oct 50
HEADNOTE: TRADE
TOPIC: General Trade
PARTIES:
  France
  Sweden

461125   Bilateral Exchange   **50 SOFM 1017**
SIGNED: 2 Dec 50
HEADNOTE: TRADE
TOPIC: General Trade
PARTIES:
  Italy
  Sweden

461126   Bilateral Agreement   **50 SOFM 1036**
SIGNED: 6 Dec 50
HEADNOTE: PAYMENTS
TOPIC: Finance
PARTIES:
  Italy
  Sweden

461127   Bilateral Exchange   **50 SOFM 1045**
SIGNED: 8 Dec 50
HEADNOTE: TRADE
TOPIC: General Trade
PARTIES:
  Greece
  Sweden

461128   Bilateral Protocol   **50 SOFM 1056**
SIGNED: 8 Dec 50
HEADNOTE: PAYMENTS
TOPIC: Finance
PARTIES:
  Greece
  Sweden

461129   Bilateral Exchange   **50 SOFM 1061**
SIGNED: 2 Dec 50
HEADNOTE: APPRENTICE EXCHANGE
TOPIC: Non-ILO Labor
PARTIES:
  France
  Sweden

461130   Bilateral Protocol   **50 SOFM 1065**
SIGNED: 19 Dec 50
HEADNOTE: TRADE
TOPIC: General Trade
PARTIES:
  Norway
  Sweden

461131   Bilateral Exchange   **50 SOFM 1075**
SIGNED: 22 Sep 50
HEADNOTE: TRADE
TOPIC: General Trade
PARTIES:
  Australia
  Sweden

461132   Bilateral Exchange   **51 SOFM 1**
SIGNED: 11 Jan 51
HEADNOTE: TRADE & PAYMENTS
TOPIC: General Economic
PARTIES:
  Sweden
  Switzerland

461133   Bilateral Protocol   **51 SOFM 18**
SIGNED: 24 Jan 51
HEADNOTE: TRADE & PAYMENTS
TOPIC: General Economic

PARTIES:
  Spain
  Sweden

461134   Bilateral Protocol   **51 SOFM 94**
SIGNED: 10 Feb 51
HEADNOTE: TRADE
TOPIC: General Trade
PARTIES:
  Denmark
  Sweden

461135   Bilateral Agreement   **51 SOFM 104**
SIGNED: 10 Feb 51
HEADNOTE: PAYMENTS
TOPIC: Finance
PARTIES:
  Denmark
  Sweden

461136   Bilateral Protocol   **51 SOFM 109**
SIGNED: 16 Mar 51
HEADNOTE: TRADE & PAYMENTS
TOPIC: General Economic
PARTIES:
  Finland
  Sweden

461137   Bilateral Exchange   **51 SOFM 123**
SIGNED: 28 Feb 51
HEADNOTE: TRADE
TOPIC: General Trade
PARTIES:
  India
  Sweden

461138   Bilateral Protocol   **51 SOFM 125**
SIGNED: 16 Mar 51
HEADNOTE: TRADE
TOPIC: General Trade
PARTIES:
  Czechoslovakia
  Sweden

461139   Bilateral Agreement   **51 SOFM 145**
SIGNED: 31 Mar 51
HEADNOTE: NATIONALIZATIONS
TOPIC: Claims and Debts
PARTIES:
  Hungary
  Sweden

461140   Bilateral Agreement   **51 SOFM 193**
SIGNED: 5 Apr 51
HEADNOTE: TRADE
TOPIC: General Trade
PARTIES:
  Indonesia
  Sweden

461141   Bilateral Exchange   **51 SOFM 203**
SIGNED: 11 Apr 51
HEADNOTE: TRADE
TOPIC: General Trade
PARTIES:
  France
  Sweden

461142   Bilateral Protocol   **51 SOFM 211**
SIGNED: 12 Apr 51
HEADNOTE: TRADE
TOPIC: General Trade
PARTIES:
  Iceland
  Sweden

461143   Bilateral Exchange   **51 SOFM 243**
SIGNED: 23 May 51
HEADNOTE: TRADE
TOPIC: General Trade
PARTIES:
  Austria
  Sweden

461144   Bilateral Exchange   **51 SOFM 251**
SIGNED: 23 May 51
HEADNOTE: PAYMENTS
TOPIC: Finance
PARTIES:
  Austria
  Sweden

461145   Bilateral Exchange   **51 SOFM 253**
SIGNED: 29 May 51
HEADNOTE: TRADE
TOPIC: General Trade
PARTIES:
  Netherlands
  Sweden

461146   Bilateral Agreement   **51 SOFM 277**
SIGNED: 20 Jun 51
HEADNOTE: TRADE
TOPIC: General Trade
PARTIES:
  Sweden
  Switzerland

461147   Bilateral Agreement   **51 SOFM 296**
SIGNED: 20 Jun 51
HEADNOTE: PAYMENTS
TOPIC: Finance
PARTIES:
  Sweden
  Switzerland

461148   Bilateral Protocol   **51 SOFM 307**
SIGNED: 10 Jul 51
HEADNOTE: TRADE
TOPIC: General Trade
PARTIES:
  Spain
  Sweden

461149   Bilateral Exchange   **51 SOFM 343**
SIGNED: 17 Jul 51
HEADNOTE: TRADE
TOPIC: General Trade
PARTIES:
  Greece
  Sweden

461150   Bilateral Protocol   **51 SOFM 401**
SIGNED: 29 Oct 51
HEADNOTE: TRADE
TOPIC: General Trade
PARTIES:
  Sweden
  Yugoslavia

461151   Bilateral Exchange   **51 SOFM 411**
SIGNED: 16 Nov 51
HEADNOTE: TRADE
TOPIC: General Trade
PARTIES:
  France
  Sweden

461152   Bilateral Protocol   **51 SOFM 447**
SIGNED: 7 Dec 51
HEADNOTE: TRADE
TOPIC: General Trade
PARTIES:
  Norway
  Sweden

461153   Bilateral Agreement   **51 SOFM 461**
SIGNED: 3 Dec 51
HEADNOTE: PAYMENTS
TOPIC: Finance
PARTIES:
  Poland
  Sweden

461154   Bilateral Agreement   **51 SOFM 477**
SIGNED: 18 Oct 51
HEADNOTE: AIR ROUTES
TOPIC: Air Transport

PARTIES:
Sweden
Switzerland

461155   Bilateral Agreement   **51 SOFM 567**
SIGNED: 19 Feb 51
HEADNOTE: PAYMENTS
TOPIC: Finance
PARTIES:
Norway
Sweden

461156   Bilateral Exchange   **51 SOFM 623**
SIGNED: 13 Nov 51
HEADNOTE: DIPLOMATIC REPRESENTATION
TOPIC: Consul/Citizenship
PARTIES:
Japan
Sweden

461157   Bilateral Protocol   **52 SOFM 83**
SIGNED: 14 Mar 52
HEADNOTE: TRADE
TOPIC: General Trade
PARTIES:
Czechoslovakia
Sweden

461158   Bilateral Exchange   **52 SOFM 103**
SIGNED: 18 Jan 52
HEADNOTE: TRADE
TOPIC: General Trade
PARTIES:
Italy
Sweden

461159   Bilateral Agreement   **52 SOFM 127**
SIGNED: 5 Mar 52
HEADNOTE: TRADE
TOPIC: General Trade
PARTIES:
Japan
Sweden

461160   Bilateral Agreement   **52 SOFM 142**
SIGNED: 5 Mar 52
HEADNOTE: PAYMENTS
TOPIC: Finance
PARTIES:
Japan
Sweden

461161   Bilateral Exchange   **52 SOFM 167**
SIGNED: 31 Mar 52
HEADNOTE: TRADE
TOPIC: General Trade
PARTIES:
Netherlands
Sweden

461162   Bilateral Protocol   **52 SOFM 191**
SIGNED: 31 Mar 52
HEADNOTE: TRADE
TOPIC: General Trade
PARTIES:
Iceland
Sweden

461163   Bilateral Protocol   **52 SOFM 193**
SIGNED: 13 Dec 51
HEADNOTE: TRADE
TOPIC: General Trade
PARTIES:
Portugal
Sweden

461164   Bilateral Protocol   **52 SOFM 203**
SIGNED: 9 Apr 52
HEADNOTE: TRADE
TOPIC: General Trade
PARTIES:
Finland
Sweden

461165   Bilateral Exchange   **52 SOFM 231**
SIGNED: 28 Apr 52
HEADNOTE: AIR TRAFFIC
TOPIC: Air Transport
PARTIES:
Japan
Sweden

461166   Bilateral Agreement   **52 SOFM 235**
SIGNED: 29 Apr 52
HEADNOTE: TRADE
TOPIC: General Trade
PARTIES:
Austria
Sweden

461167   Bilateral Exchange   **52 SOFM 265**
SIGNED: 1 Jul 52
HEADNOTE: TRADE
TOPIC: General Trade
PARTIES:
Indonesia
Sweden

461168   Bilateral Exchange   **52 SOFM 289**
SIGNED: 2 Jul 52
HEADNOTE: TRADE
TOPIC: General Trade
PARTIES:
Sweden
Switzerland

461169   Bilateral Protocol   **52 SOFM 303**
SIGNED: 14 Jul 52
HEADNOTE: TRADE & PAYMENTS
TOPIC: General Economic
PARTIES:
Spain
Sweden

461170   Bilateral Exchange   **52 SOFM 468**
SIGNED: 23 Jun 52
HEADNOTE: SCANDINAVIAN AIRLINES
TOPIC: Air Transport
PARTIES:
Sweden
UK Great Britain

461171   Bilateral Agreement   **52 SOFM 483**
SIGNED: 28 Aug 51
HEADNOTE: AIR TRANSPORT
TOPIC: Air Transport
PARTIES:
Iraq
Sweden

461172   Bilateral Exchange   **52 SOFM 491**
SIGNED: 8 Sep 52
HEADNOTE: TRADE
TOPIC: General Trade
PARTIES:
Greece
Sweden

461173   Bilateral Exchange   **52 SOFM 506**
SIGNED: 8 Sep 52
HEADNOTE: PAYMENTS
TOPIC: Finance
PARTIES:
Greece
Sweden

461174   Bilateral Exchange   **52 SOFM 529**
SIGNED: 18 Oct 52
HEADNOTE: TRADE
TOPIC: General Trade
PARTIES:
Poland
Sweden

461175   Bilateral Protocol   **52 SOFM 535**
SIGNED: 22 Nov 52
HEADNOTE: TRADE
TOPIC: General Trade

PARTIES:
Norway
Sweden

461176   Bilateral Exchange   **52 SOFM 541**
SIGNED: 26 Nov 52
HEADNOTE: AIR TRAFFIC
TOPIC: Air Transport
PARTIES:
South Africa
Sweden

461177   Bilateral Exchange   **52 SOFM 545**
SIGNED: 29 Nov 52
HEADNOTE: TRADE
TOPIC: General Trade
PARTIES:
France
Sweden

461178   Bilateral Protocol   **52 SOFM 569**
SIGNED: 20 Dec 52
HEADNOTE: TRADE
TOPIC: General Trade
PARTIES:
Sweden
Yugoslavia

461179   Bilateral Agreement   **52 SOFM 893**
SIGNED: 10 Nov 52
HEADNOTE: JOINT WEATHER OBSERVATION
TOPIC: Scientific Project
PARTIES:
Norway
Sweden

461180   Bilateral Exchange   **53 SOFM 1**
SIGNED: 27 Jan 53
HEADNOTE: TRADE
TOPIC: General Trade
PARTIES:
Colombia
Sweden

461181   Bilateral Protocol   **53 SOFM 5**
SIGNED: 11 Feb 53
HEADNOTE: TRADE
TOPIC: General Trade
PARTIES:
Denmark
Sweden

461182   Bilateral Exchange   **53 SOFM 81**
SIGNED: 10 Apr 53
HEADNOTE: TRADE
TOPIC: General Trade
PARTIES:
Netherlands
Sweden

461183   Bilateral Exchange   **53 SOFM 577**
SIGNED: 24 Apr 53
HEADNOTE: TRADE
TOPIC: General Trade
PARTIES:
France
Sweden

461184   Bilateral Exchange   **53 SOFM 699**
SIGNED: 1 Jun 53
HEADNOTE: TRADE
TOPIC: General Trade
PARTIES:
Austria
Sweden

461185   Bilateral Exchange   **53 SOFM 708**
SIGNED: 5 Jun 53
HEADNOTE: TRADE
TOPIC: General Trade
PARTIES:
Sweden
Switzerland

461186   Bilateral Protocol   **53 SOFM 733**
SIGNED: 3 Jul 53
HEADNOTE: TRADE
TOPIC: General Trade
PARTIES:
   Iceland
   Sweden

461188   Bilateral Exchange   **53 SOFM 1023**
SIGNED: 7 Nov 53
HEADNOTE: TRADE
TOPIC: General Trade
PARTIES:
   France
   Sweden

461189   Bilateral Protocol   **53 SOFM 1047**
SIGNED: 16 Nov 53
HEADNOTE: TRADE
TOPIC: General Trade
PARTIES:
   Norway
   Sweden

461190   Bilateral Protocol   **53 SOFM 1049**
SIGNED: 17 Nov 53
HEADNOTE: TRADE & PAYMENTS
TOPIC: General Economic
PARTIES:
   Hungary
   Sweden

461191   Bilateral Exchange   **53 SOFM 1057**
SIGNED: 20 Nov 53
HEADNOTE: TRADE
TOPIC: General Trade
PARTIES:
   Belgium
   Sweden

461192   Bilateral Exchange   **53 SOFM 1063**
SIGNED: 27 Nov 53
HEADNOTE: TRADE
TOPIC: General Trade
PARTIES:
   Italy
   Sweden

461193   Bilateral Exchange   **53 SOFM 1067**
SIGNED: 30 Jun 53
HEADNOTE: TRADE
TOPIC: General Trade
PARTIES:
   India
   Sweden

461194   Bilateral Exchange   **53 SOFM 1099**
SIGNED: 25 May 53
HEADNOTE: TRADE
TOPIC: General Trade
PARTIES:
   Australia
   Sweden

461195   Bilateral Exchange   **53 SOFM 1155**
SIGNED: 6 May 53
HEADNOTE: TRADE
TOPIC: General Trade
PARTIES:
   Japan
   Sweden

461197   Bilateral Protocol   **53 SOFM 1013**
SIGNED: 16 Oct 53
HEADNOTE: TRADE
TOPIC: General Trade
PARTIES:
   Sweden
   Yugoslavia

462001   Bilateral Convention   **64 SWRO 1272**
SIGNED: 23 Aug 63
HEADNOTE: BOUNDARY LAKE GENEVA
TOPIC: Territory Boundary

PARTIES:
   France
   Switzerland

462002   Bilateral Convention   **57 SWRO 884**
SIGNED: 25 Feb 53
HEADNOTE: BOUNDARY LAKE GENEVA
TOPIC: Territory Boundary
PARTIES:
   France
   Switzerland

462003   Bilateral Convention   **60 SWRO 1550**
SIGNED: 3 Dec 59
HEADNOTE: RECTIFY BOUNDARY HERMANCE
TOPIC: Territory Boundary
PARTIES:
   France
   Switzerland

462004   Bilateral Convention   **58 SWRO 135**
SIGNED: 25 Apr 56
HEADNOTE: GENEVA AIRPORT
TOPIC: Specific Property
PARTIES:
   France
   Switzerland

462005   Bilateral Convention   **63 SWRO 143**
SIGNED: 15 Jan 59
HEADNOTE: MILITARY CITIZENSHIP
TOPIC: Milit Servic/Citiz
PARTIES:
   Colombia
   Switzerland

462006   Bilateral Convention   **59 SWRO 223**
SIGNED: 1 Aug 58
HEADNOTE: MILITARY CITIZENSHIP
TOPIC: Milit Servic/Citiz
PARTIES:
   France
   Switzerland

462007   Bilateral Agreement   **55 SWRO 25**
SIGNED: 25 Oct 54
HEADNOTE: BORDER ARRESTS
TOPIC: Extradition
PARTIES:
   Germany, West
   Switzerland

462008   Bilateral Agreement   **55 SWRO 315**
SIGNED: 2 Feb 55
HEADNOTE: EXCHANGE OF INTERNS
TOPIC: Non-ILO Labor
PARTIES:
   Germany, West
   Switzerland

462009   Bilateral Agreement   **55 SWRO 61**
SIGNED: 5 Jan 55
HEADNOTE: BORDER ARRESTS
TOPIC: Extradition
PARTIES:
   Austria
   Switzerland

462010   Bilateral Agreement   **51 SWRO 639**
SIGNED: 14 Sep 50
HEADNOTE: ESTABLISHMENT
TOPIC: Admin Cooperation
PARTIES:
   Austria
   Switzerland

462011   Bilateral Convention   **48 SWRO 204**
SIGNED: 30 Apr 47
HEADNOTE: CUSTOMS
TOPIC: Customs
PARTIES:
   Austria
   Switzerland

462012   Bilateral Agreement   **56 SWRO 663**
SIGNED: 19 Mar 56
HEADNOTE: EXCHANGE OF INTERNS
TOPIC: Non-ILO Labor
PARTIES:
   Austria
   Switzerland

462013   Bilateral Agreement   **51 SWRO 642**
SIGNED: 14 Sep 50
HEADNOTE: VISA ABOLITION
TOPIC: Visas
PARTIES:
   Austria
   Switzerland

462017   Bilateral Convention   **51 SWRO 1019**
SIGNED: 27 Apr 48
HEADNOTE: PROFESSIONAL LABOR
TOPIC: Non-ILO Labor
PARTIES:
   France
   Switzerland

462019   Bilateral Instrument   **48 SWRO 818**
SIGNED: 22 Jun 48
HEADNOTE: MIGRANT LABOR
TOPIC: Non-ILO Labor
PARTIES:
   Italy
   Switzerland

462020   Bilateral Instrument   **57 SWRO 44**
SIGNED: 22 Dec 56
HEADNOTE: SPECIAL TAX
TOPIC: Taxation
PARTIES:
   Italy
   Switzerland

462023   Bilateral Agreement   **60 SWRO 617**
SIGNED: 6 Jun 56
HEADNOTE: SIMPLIFY EXCHANGE CIVIL STATUS
TOPIC: Admin Cooperation
PARTIES:
   Germany, West
   Switzerland

462024   Bilateral Agreement   **62 SWRO 1659**
SIGNED: 6 Apr 62
HEADNOTE: SIMPLIFY EXCHANGE CIVIL STATUS
TOPIC: Admin Cooperation
PARTIES:
   Austria
   Switzerland

462025   Bilateral Agreement   **57 SWRO 821**
SIGNED: 6 Dec 55
HEADNOTE: RHINE POWER PLANT
TOPIC: Admin Cooperation
PARTIES:
   Germany, West
   Switzerland

462026   Bilateral Agreement   **53 SWRO 413**
SIGNED: 19 Jul 52
HEADNOTE: INDUSTRIAL PROPERTY
TOPIC: Claims and Debts
PARTIES:
   Germany, West
   Switzerland

462027   Bilateral Agreement   **54 SWRO 530**
SIGNED: 25 Jun 53
HEADNOTE: INDUSTRIAL PROPERTY
TOPIC: Claims and Debts
PARTIES:
   Japan
   Switzerland

462028   Bilateral Exchange   **64 SWRO 276**
SIGNED: 30 Jan 64
HEADNOTE: CONTINUE VALID BRITISH TREATY
TOPIC: Admin Cooperation

PARTIES:
Switzerland
Tanganyika

462029   Bilateral Convention   **62 SWRO 270**
SIGNED: 16 Dec 60
HEADNOTE: JUDICIAL COOPERATION
TOPIC: Admin Cooperation
PARTIES:
Austria
Switzerland

462030   Bilateral Agreement   **52 SWRO 529**
SIGNED: 17 May 52
HEADNOTE: CORPSES
TOPIC: Admin Cooperation
PARTIES:
Austria
Switzerland

462031   Bilateral Agreement   **51 SWRO 644**
SIGNED: 14 May 51
HEADNOTE: CORPSES
TOPIC: Admin Cooperation
PARTIES:
Italy
Switzerland

462032   Bilateral Convention   **64 SWRO 1255**
SIGNED: 23 Aug 63
HEADNOTE: HYDRO POWER
TOPIC: Specific Property
PARTIES:
France
Switzerland

462033   Bilateral Convention   **60 SWRO 1548**
SIGNED: 3 Dec 59
HEADNOTE: FLOOD CONTROL
TOPIC: Specific Resources
PARTIES:
France
Switzerland

462034   Bilateral Convention   **60 SWRO 1552**
SIGNED: 3 Dec 59
HEADNOTE: FLOOD CONTROL
TOPIC: Specific Resources
PARTIES:
France
Switzerland

462035   Bilateral Treaty   **55 SWRO 741**
SIGNED: 10 Apr 54
HEADNOTE: FLOOD CONTROL
TOPIC: Specific Resources
PARTIES:
Austria
Switzerland

462036   Bilateral Convention   **59 SWRO 432**
SIGNED: 27 May 57
HEADNOTE: HYDRO POWER
TOPIC: Specific Resources
PARTIES:
Italy
Switzerland

462037   Bilateral Agreement   **55 SWRO 611**
SIGNED: 18 Jun 49
HEADNOTE: HYDRO POWER
TOPIC: Specific Property
PARTIES:
Italy
Switzerland

462039   Bilateral Convention   **63 SWRO 961**
SIGNED: 16 Nov 62
HEADNOTE: LAKE POLLUTION
TOPIC: Specific Resources
PARTIES:
France
Switzerland

462040   Bilateral Agreement   **58 SWRO 724**
SIGNED: 6 Mar 58
HEADNOTE: ATOMIC ENERGY
TOPIC: Atomic Energy
PARTIES:
Canada
Switzerland

462041   Bilateral Exchange   **56 SWRO 655**
SIGNED: 7 Nov 55
HEADNOTE: TAXATION
TOPIC: Taxation
PARTIES:
South Africa
Switzerland

462042   Bilateral Exchange   **50 SWRO 584**
SIGNED: 13 Jan 50
HEADNOTE: TAXATION
TOPIC: Taxation
PARTIES:
Argentina
Switzerland

462043   Bilateral Convention   **54 SWRO 1109**
SIGNED: 12 Nov 53
HEADNOTE: TAXATION
TOPIC: Taxation
PARTIES:
Austria
Switzerland

462044   Bilateral Instrument   **54 SWRO 1125**
SIGNED: 8 Apr 54
HEADNOTE: TAX CAPITAL
TOPIC: Taxation
PARTIES:
Austria
Switzerland

462045   Bilateral Exchange   **56 SWRO 1087**
SIGNED: 22 Jun 56
HEADNOTE: TAX NAVIGATION
TOPIC: Taxation
PARTIES:
Brazil
Switzerland

462046   Bilateral Exchange   **59 SWRO 639**
SIGNED: 29 Jun 59
HEADNOTE: TAX NAVIGATION
TOPIC: Taxation
PARTIES:
Congo (Zaire)
Switzerland

462047   Bilateral Agreement   **64 SWRO 953**
SIGNED: 27 Nov 63
HEADNOTE: TAX AIR TRANSPORT
TOPIC: Taxation
PARTIES:
Spain
Switzerland

462048   Bilateral Instrument   **57 SWRO 756**
SIGNED: 17 Jun 57
HEADNOTE: TAX CAPITAL
TOPIC: Taxation
PARTIES:
Finland
Switzerland

462049   Bilateral Convention   **55 SWRO 115**
SIGNED: 31 Dec 53
HEADNOTE: TAXATION
TOPIC: Taxation
PARTIES:
France
Switzerland

462050   Bilateral Instrument   **55 SWRO 138**
SIGNED: 31 Dec 53
HEADNOTE: RETAIN TAX
TOPIC: Taxation

PARTIES:
France
Switzerland

462051   Bilateral Convention   **55 SWRO 132**
SIGNED: 31 Dec 53
HEADNOTE: INHERITANCE TAX
TOPIC: Taxation
PARTIES:
France
Switzerland

462052   Bilateral Exchange   **64 SWRO 426**
SIGNED: 6 Dec 63
HEADNOTE: TAX NAVIGATION
TOPIC: Taxation
PARTIES:
Ghana
Switzerland

462053   Bilateral Instrument   **49 SWRO 135**
SIGNED: 2 Feb 48
HEADNOTE: EFFECT EARLIER TREATY
TOPIC: Taxation
PARTIES:
Hungary
Switzerland

462054   Bilateral Agreement   **58 SWRO 795**
SIGNED: 28 Aug 58
HEADNOTE: TAX AIR TRANSPORT
TOPIC: Taxation
PARTIES:
India
Switzerland

462055   Bilateral Exchange   **57 SWRO 213**
SIGNED: 7 Feb 57
HEADNOTE: TAX AIR TRANSPORT
TOPIC: Taxation
PARTIES:
Iran
Switzerland

462056   Bilateral Convention   **61 SWRO 413**
SIGNED: 31 Jul 58
HEADNOTE: DOUBLE TAX TRANSPORT
TOPIC: Taxation
PARTIES:
Italy
Switzerland

462057   Bilateral Exchange   **57 SWRO 846**
SIGNED: 11 Sep 57
HEADNOTE: TAX WATER & AIR TRANSPORT
TOPIC: Taxation
PARTIES:
Lebanon
Switzerland

462058   Bilateral Convention   **57 SWRO 715**
SIGNED: 7 Dec 56
HEADNOTE: DOUBLE TAXATION
TOPIC: Taxation
PARTIES:
Norway
Switzerland

462059   Bilateral Convention   **57 SWRO 728**
SIGNED: 7 Dec 56
HEADNOTE: INHERITANCE TAX
TOPIC: Taxation
PARTIES:
Norway
Switzerland

462060   Bilateral Instrument   **57 SWRO 733**
SIGNED: 3 Jul 57
HEADNOTE: CAPITAL TAX
TOPIC: Taxation
PARTIES:
Norway
Switzerland

462061 Bilateral Convention **60 SWRO 1058**
SIGNED: 30 Dec 59
HEADNOTE: DOUBLE TAXATION
TOPIC: Taxation
PARTIES:
Pakistan
Switzerland

462062 Bilateral Exchange **61 SWRO 570**
SIGNED: 13 Jun 61
HEADNOTE: TAX WATER & AIR TRANSPORT
TOPIC: Taxation
PARTIES:
Poland
Switzerland

462063 Bilateral Exchange **60 SWRO 538**
SIGNED: 26 Apr 60
HEADNOTE: TAX AIR TRANSPORT
TOPIC: Taxation
PARTIES:
Czechoslovakia
Switzerland

462064 Bilateral Agreement **63 SWRO 724**
SIGNED: 15 Dec 61
HEADNOTE: EXEMPT TEACHING MATTERS
TOPIC: Customs
PARTIES:
Italy
Switzerland

462065 Bilateral Convention **60 SWRO 1639**
SIGNED: 5 Feb 58
HEADNOTE: BORDER TRAFFIC
TOPIC: Land Transport
PARTIES:
Germany, West
Switzerland

462066 Bilateral Convention **60 SWRO 1671**
SIGNED: 5 Feb 58
HEADNOTE: RIGHT OF TRANSIT
TOPIC: Land Transport
PARTIES:
Germany, West
Switzerland

462067 Bilateral Convention **53 SWRO 4**
SIGNED: 25 Jan 52
HEADNOTE: LOCAL BORDER TRAFFIC
TOPIC: Land Transport
PARTIES:
Germany, West
Switzerland

462068 Bilateral Convention **48 SWRO 183**
SIGNED: 30 Apr 47
HEADNOTE: BORDER TRAFFIC
TOPIC: Land Transport
PARTIES:
Austria
Switzerland

462069 Bilateral Convention **50 SWRO 781**
SIGNED: 30 May 50
HEADNOTE: LOCAL BORDER TRAFFIC
TOPIC: Land Transport
PARTIES:
Austria
Switzerland

462070 Bilateral Exchange **62 SWRO 1657**
SIGNED: 17 Sep 62
HEADNOTE: BORDER TIMBER
TOPIC: Customs
PARTIES:
France
Switzerland

462072 Bilateral Convention **64 SWRO 387**
SIGNED: 1 Jun 61
HEADNOTE: VEHICLE CHECKPOINT
TOPIC: Customs

PARTIES:
Germany, West
Switzerland

462073 Bilateral Convention **48 SWRO 197**
SIGNED: 30 Apr 47
HEADNOTE: CUSTOMS GATES
TOPIC: Customs
PARTIES:
Austria
Switzerland

462074 Bilateral Convention **61 SWRO 574**
SIGNED: 28 Sep 60
HEADNOTE: ROAD CHECKPOINT
TOPIC: Customs
PARTIES:
France
Switzerland

462075 Bilateral Convention **63 SWRO 711**
SIGNED: 11 Mar 61
HEADNOTE: ROAD CHECKPOINT
TOPIC: Customs
PARTIES:
Italy
Switzerland

462076 Bilateral Agreement **57 SWRO 906**
SIGNED: 22 Jul 57
HEADNOTE: RAILROAD FINANCE
TOPIC: Land Transport
PARTIES:
Austria
Switzerland

462077 Bilateral Agreement **54 SWRO 1148**
SIGNED: 11 May 54
HEADNOTE: RAILROAD ELECTRIFICATION
TOPIC: Land Transport
PARTIES:
France
Switzerland

462078 Bilateral Agreement **58 SWRO 781**
SIGNED: 10 May 58
HEADNOTE: NAVIGATION
TOPIC: Water Transport
PARTIES:
Portugal
Switzerland

462079 Bilateral Agreement **54 SWRO 449**
SIGNED: 17 Dec 53
HEADNOTE: COMMERCIAL ROAD TRANSPORT
TOPIC: Land Transport
PARTIES:
Germany, West
Switzerland

462080 Bilateral Agreement **59 SWRO 329**
SIGNED: 22 Oct 58
HEADNOTE: ROAD TRAFFIC
TOPIC: Land Transport
PARTIES:
Austria
Switzerland

462081 Bilateral Exchange **63 SWRO 797**
SIGNED: 14 Aug 63
HEADNOTE: ROAD TRAFFIC
TOPIC: Land Transport
PARTIES:
Denmark
Switzerland

462083 Bilateral Agreement **52 SWRO 623**
SIGNED: 20 Nov 51
HEADNOTE: TRANSPORT OF GOODS & PERSONS
TOPIC: Land Transport
PARTIES:
France
Switzerland

462084 Bilateral Exchange **58 SWRO 1087**
SIGNED: 16 Oct 58
HEADNOTE: ACCIDENT LIABILITY
TOPIC: Land Transport
PARTIES:
France
Switzerland

462085 Bilateral Agreement **52 SWRO 603**
SIGNED: 20 May 52
HEADNOTE: TRANSPORT OF PERSONS
TOPIC: Land Transport
PARTIES:
Netherlands
Switzerland

462086 Bilateral Agreement **62 SWRO 1359**
SIGNED: 29 Mar 62
HEADNOTE: ROAD TRANSPORT
TOPIC: Land Transport
PARTIES:
Switzerland
Yugoslavia

462087 Bilateral Convention **58 SWRO 135**
SIGNED: 25 Apr 56
HEADNOTE: GENEVA AIRPORT
TOPIC: Specific Property
PARTIES:
France
Switzerland

462088 Bilateral Convention **50 SWRO 1334**
SIGNED: 4 Jul 49
HEADNOTE: BALE AIRPORT
TOPIC: Specific Property
PARTIES:
France
Switzerland

462089 Bilateral Agreement **63 SWRO 874**
SIGNED: 27 Sep 61
HEADNOTE: AIR TRANSPORT
TOPIC: Air Transport
PARTIES:
Afghanistan
Switzerland

462090 Bilateral Agreement **61 SWRO 907**
SIGNED: 19 Oct 59
HEADNOTE: AIR TRANSPORT
TOPIC: Air Transport
PARTIES:
South Africa
Switzerland

462091 Bilateral Agreement **51 SWRO 573**
SIGNED: 5 Apr 50
HEADNOTE: AIR TRANSPORT
TOPIC: Air Transport
PARTIES:
Switzerland
UK Great Britain

462092 Bilateral Convention **51 SWRO 937**
SIGNED: 24 Oct 50
HEADNOTE: SOCIAL SECURITY
TOPIC: Non-ILO Labor
PARTIES:
Germany, West
Switzerland

462093 Bilateral Convention **51 SWRO 787**
SIGNED: 15 Jul 50
HEADNOTE: SOCIAL SECURITY
TOPIC: Non-ILO Labor
PARTIES:
Austria
Switzerland

462094 Bilateral Convention **55 SWRO 290**
SIGNED: 21 May 54
HEADNOTE: SOCIAL SECURITY
TOPIC: Non-ILO Labor

PARTIES:
Denmark
Switzerland

462096   Bilateral Convention   50 SWRO 1164
SIGNED: 9 Jul 49
HEADNOTE: OLD-AGE INSURANCE
TOPIC: Non-ILO Labor
PARTIES:
France
Switzerland

462097   Bilateral Convention   54 SWRO 250
SIGNED: 17 Oct 51
HEADNOTE: SOCIAL SECURITY
TOPIC: Non-ILO Labor
PARTIES:
Italy
Switzerland

462098   Bilateral Convention   64 SWRO 730
SIGNED: 14 Dec 62
HEADNOTE: SOCIAL SECURITY
TOPIC: Non-ILO Labor
PARTIES:
Italy
Switzerland

462099   Bilateral Convention   57 SWRO 282
SIGNED: 14 Nov 55
HEADNOTE: SOCIAL SECURITY
TOPIC: Non-ILO Labor
PARTIES:
Luxembourg
Switzerland

462100   Bilateral Convention   64 SWRO 157
SIGNED: 8 Jun 62
HEADNOTE: SOCIAL SECURITY
TOPIC: Non-ILO Labor
PARTIES:
Switzerland
Yugoslavia

462101   Bilateral Convention   61 SWRO 24
SIGNED: 16 Apr 59
HEADNOTE: FAMILY ALLOWANCE
TOPIC: Non-ILO Labor
PARTIES:
France
Switzerland

462102   Bilateral Convention   62 SWRO 1016
SIGNED: 24 Sep 58
HEADNOTE: FAMILY ALLOWANCE
TOPIC: Non-ILO Labor
PARTIES:
France
Switzerland

462103   Bilateral Convention   53 SWRO 423
SIGNED: 14 Jul 52
HEADNOTE: INDIGENT AID
TOPIC: Non-ILO Labor
PARTIES:
Germany, West
Switzerland

462104   Bilateral Convention   48 SWRO 192
SIGNED: 30 Apr 47
HEADNOTE: EPIZOOTICS
TOPIC: Sanitation
PARTIES:
Austria
Switzerland

462105   Bilateral Convention   59 SWRO 369
SIGNED: 1 Nov 57
HEADNOTE: RHINE FISHERIES
TOPIC: Specific Resources
PARTIES:
Germany, West
Switzerland

462106   Bilateral Agreement   58 SWRO 49
SIGNED: 4 Dec 57
HEADNOTE: FISHERIES
TOPIC: Specific Resources
PARTIES:
France
Switzerland

462107   Bilateral Exchange   62 SWRO 77
SIGNED: 24 Nov 61
HEADNOTE: SWISS BANK CREDIT
TOPIC: Loans and Credits
PARTIES:
Chile
Switzerland

462108   Bilateral Agreement   64 SWRO 67
SIGNED: 2 Dec 61
HEADNOTE: INVESTMENT CAPITAL
TOPIC: Finance
PARTIES:
Switzerland
Tunisia

462109   Bilateral Agreement   64 SWRO 70
SIGNED: 2 Dec 61
HEADNOTE: SCIENTIFIC & TECHNICAL COOPER-
ATION
TOPIC: Tech Assistance
PARTIES:
Switzerland
Tunisia

462110   Bilateral Agreement   62 SWRO 99
SIGNED: 24 Apr 61
HEADNOTE: 22 MILLION FRANCS LOAN
TOPIC: Loans and Credits
PARTIES:
Switzerland
Yugoslavia

462112   Bilateral Agreement   54 SWRO 1291
SIGNED: 2 Dec 54
HEADNOTE: COMMERCE
TOPIC: General Trade
PARTIES:
Germany, West
Switzerland

462113   Bilateral Agreement   57 SWRO 399
SIGNED: 16 Jul 56
HEADNOTE: GERMAN CLEARING
TOPIC: Finance
PARTIES:
Germany, West
Switzerland

462114   Bilateral Agreement   52 SWRO 367
SIGNED: 20 Dec 51
HEADNOTE: CUSTOMS
TOPIC: Customs
PARTIES:
Germany, West
Switzerland

462115   Bilateral Agreement   53 SWRO 119
SIGNED: 26 Aug 52
HEADNOTE: GERMAN ASSETS
TOPIC: Claims and Debts
PARTIES:
Germany, West
Switzerland

462116   Bilateral Agreement   53 SWRO 134
SIGNED: 26 Aug 52
HEADNOTE: EQUALIZATION OF CHARGES
TOPIC: Finance
PARTIES:
Germany, West
Switzerland

462117   Bilateral Agreement   53 SWRO 936
SIGNED: 11 Jul 53
HEADNOTE: POWER STATION DEBT

TOPIC: Claims and Debts
PARTIES:
Germany, West
Switzerland

462118   Bilateral Agreement   54 SWRO 3
SIGNED: 27 Feb 53
HEADNOTE: GERMAN DEBTS
TOPIC: Claims and Debts
PARTIES:
Germany, West
Switzerland

462120   Bilateral Agreement   58 SWRO 38
SIGNED: 25 Nov 57
HEADNOTE: TRADE AND PAYMENTS
TOPIC: General Economic
PARTIES:
Argentina
Switzerland

462121   Bilateral Agreement   58 SWRO 239
SIGNED: 16 Dec 57
HEADNOTE: PRE-1945 DEBTS
TOPIC: Claims and Debts
PARTIES:
Austria
Switzerland

462122   Bilateral Agreement   54 SWRO 1005
SIGNED: 15 Sep 54
HEADNOTE: TRADE & PAYMENTS
TOPIC: General Economic
PARTIES:
Austria
Switzerland

462123   Bilateral Agreement   54 SWRO 1171
SIGNED: 26 Nov 54
HEADNOTE: TRADE & PAYMENTS
TOPIC: General Economic
PARTIES:
Bulgaria
Switzerland

462124   Bilateral Agreement   64 SWRO 400
SIGNED: 28 Jan 63
HEADNOTE: TRADE & INVESTMENT
TOPIC: General Economic
PARTIES:
Cameroon
Switzerland

462125   Bilateral Agreement   55 SWRO 705
SIGNED: 17 Jun 55
HEADNOTE: TRADE
TOPIC: General Trade
PARTIES:
Chile
Switzerland

462126   Bilateral Agreement   64 SWRO 635
SIGNED: 18 Oct 62
HEADNOTE: TRADE & INVESTMENT
TOPIC: General Economic
PARTIES:
Congo (Brazzaville)
Switzerland

462127   Bilateral Agreement   63 SWRO 53
SIGNED: 26 Jun 62
HEADNOTE: TRADE & INVESTMENT
TOPIC: General Economic
PARTIES:
Ivory Coast
Switzerland

462128   Bilateral Agreement   54 SWRO 537
SIGNED: 30 Mar 54
HEADNOTE: TRADE
TOPIC: General Trade
PARTIES:
Cuba
Switzerland

462129 Bilateral Agreement **50 SWRO 329**
SIGNED: 6 Apr 50
HEADNOTE: PAYMENTS
TOPIC: Finance
PARTIES:
  Switzerland
  United Arab Rep

462130 Bilateral Agreement **59 SWRO 194**
SIGNED: 8 Oct 57
HEADNOTE: TRADE
TOPIC: General Trade
PARTIES:
  Ecuador
  Switzerland

462131 Bilateral Exchange **59 SWRO 2095**
SIGNED: 21 Nov 59
HEADNOTE: TRADE
TOPIC: General Trade
PARTIES:
  Spain
  Switzerland

462132 Bilateral Agreement **60 SWRO 457**
SIGNED: 2 Apr 60
HEADNOTE: TRADE
TOPIC: General Trade
PARTIES:
  Spain
  Switzerland

462133 Bilateral Agreement **55 SWRO 579**
SIGNED: 8 Jun 55
HEADNOTE: SUPPLEMENT TRADE
TOPIC: General Trade
PARTIES:
  Switzerland
  USA (United States)

462134 Bilateral Agreement **55 SWRO 1014**
SIGNED: 15 Oct 55
HEADNOTE: PAYMENT
TOPIC: Finance
PARTIES:
  Finland
  Switzerland

462135 Bilateral Agreement **55 SWRO 1017**
SIGNED: 15 Oct 55
HEADNOTE: TRADE
TOPIC: General Trade
PARTIES:
  Finland
  Switzerland

462136 Bilateral Agreement **55 SWRO 1092**
SIGNED: 29 Oct 55
HEADNOTE: TRADE
TOPIC: General Trade
PARTIES:
  France
  Switzerland

462137 Bilateral Agreement **55 SWRO 407**
SIGNED: 1 Apr 55
HEADNOTE: TRADE
TOPIC: General Trade
PARTIES:
  Guatemala
  Switzerland

462138 Bilateral Agreement **63 SWRO 732**
SIGNED: 26 Apr 62
HEADNOTE: TRADE & INVESTMENT
TOPIC: General Economic
PARTIES:
  Guinea
  Switzerland

462139 Bilateral Agreement **50 SWRO 612**
SIGNED: 27 Jun 50
HEADNOTE: TRADE & PAYMENTS
TOPIC: General Economic

PARTIES:
  Hungary
  Switzerland

462140 Bilateral Agreement **60 SWRO 1678**
SIGNED: 30 Jul 60
HEADNOTE: TRANSFER CREDIT
TOPIC: Finance
PARTIES:
  India
  Switzerland

462141 Bilateral Agreement **55 SWRO 64**
SIGNED: 30 Dec 54
HEADNOTE: TRADE
TOPIC: General Trade
PARTIES:
  Indonesia
  Switzerland

462142 Bilateral Exchange **64 SWRO 87**
SIGNED: 1 Feb 64
HEADNOTE: ECONOMIC RELATIONS
TOPIC: General Economic
PARTIES:
  Iran
  Switzerland

462143 Bilateral Instrument **56 SWRO 1281**
SIGNED: 14 Sep 56
HEADNOTE: TRADE
TOPIC: General Trade
PARTIES:
  Israel
  Switzerland

462144 Bilateral Agreement **62 SWRO 189**
SIGNED: 25 Apr 61
HEADNOTE: WINE IMPORTS
TOPIC: Commodity Trade
PARTIES:
  Italy
  Switzerland

462146 Bilateral Instrument **58 SWRO 271**
SIGNED: 29 Aug 57
HEADNOTE: MOST FAVORED NATION
TOPIC: Mostfavored Nation
PARTIES:
  Morocco
  Switzerland

462147 Bilateral Agreement **50 SWRO 915**
SIGNED: 2 Sep 50
HEADNOTE: TRADE
TOPIC: General Trade
PARTIES:
  Mexico
  Switzerland

462148 Bilateral Agreement **63 SWRO 46**
SIGNED: 28 Mar 62
HEADNOTE: TRADE & INVESTMENT
TOPIC: General Economic
PARTIES:
  Niger
  Switzerland

462149 Bilateral Agreement **57 SWRO 521**
SIGNED: 21 Jun 57
HEADNOTE: TRADE
TOPIC: General Trade
PARTIES:
  Netherlands
  Switzerland

462150 Bilateral Agreement **55 SWRO 287**
SIGNED: 20 Jul 53
HEADNOTE: TRADE
TOPIC: General Trade
PARTIES:
  Peru
  Switzerland

462151 Bilateral Agreement **49 SWRO 832**
SIGNED: 25 Jun 49
HEADNOTE: TRADE & PAYMENTS
TOPIC: General Economic
PARTIES:
  Poland
  Switzerland

462152 Bilateral Instrument **62 SWRO 257**
SIGNED: 22 Feb 62
HEADNOTE: AGRICULTURAL PRODUCTS
TOPIC: Commodity Trade
PARTIES:
  Portugal
  Switzerland

462153 Bilateral Agreement **51 SWRO 827**
SIGNED: 3 Aug 51
HEADNOTE: TRADE & PAYMENTS
TOPIC: General Economic
PARTIES:
  Romania
  Switzerland

462154 Bilateral Agreement **54 SWRO 687**
SIGNED: 11 Feb 54
HEADNOTE: TRADE
TOPIC: General Trade
PARTIES:
  El Salvador
  Switzerland

462155 Bilateral Agreement **64 SWRO 718**
SIGNED: 16 Aug 62
HEADNOTE: TRADE & INVESTMENT
TOPIC: General Economic
PARTIES:
  Senegal
  Switzerland

462156 Bilateral Agreement **51 SWRO 619**
SIGNED: 20 Jun 51
HEADNOTE: TRADE
TOPIC: General Trade
PARTIES:
  Sweden
  Switzerland

462157 Bilateral Treaty **54 SWRO 745**
SIGNED: 24 Nov 53
HEADNOTE: TRADE
TOPIC: General Trade
PARTIES:
  Czechoslovakia
  Switzerland

462158 Bilateral Agreement **50 SWRO 15**
SIGNED: 22 Dec 49
HEADNOTE: TRADE & PAYMENTS
TOPIC: General Economic
PARTIES:
  Czechoslovakia
  Switzerland

462159 Bilateral Instrument **58 SWRO 260**
SIGNED: 26 Oct 57
HEADNOTE: MOST FAVORED NATION
TOPIC: Mostfavored Nation
PARTIES:
  Switzerland
  Tunisia

462160 Bilateral Agreement **62 SWRO 1517**
SIGNED: 2 Dec 61
HEADNOTE: TRADE
TOPIC: General Trade
PARTIES:
  Switzerland
  Tunisia

462161 Bilateral Instrument **63 SWRO 1073**
SIGNED: 15 Nov 63
HEADNOTE: INSURANCE
TOPIC: Claims and Debts

PARTIES:
  Switzerland
  Tunisia

462162   Bilateral Agreement   **57 SWRO 521**
SIGNED: 21 Jun 57
HEADNOTE: TRADE
TOPIC: General Trade
PARTIES:
  Belgium
  Switzerland

462163   Bilateral Instrument   **55 SWRO 729**
SIGNED: 11 Jul 55
HEADNOTE: TRADE
TOPIC: General Trade
PARTIES:
  Switzerland
  Venezuela

462164   Bilateral Treaty   **48 SWRO 986**
SIGNED: 27 Sep 48
HEADNOTE: TRADE
TOPIC: General Trade
PARTIES:
  Switzerland
  Yugoslavia

462165   Bilateral Agreement   **48 SWRO 990**
SIGNED: 27 Sep 48
HEADNOTE: TRADE & PAYMENTS
TOPIC: General Economic
PARTIES:
  Switzerland
  Yugoslavia

462166   Bilateral Agreement   **60 SWRO 475**
SIGNED: 23 Oct 59
HEADNOTE: CERTAIN SWISS FINANCES
TOPIC: Claims and Debts
PARTIES:
  Switzerland
  Yugoslavia

462167   Bilateral Agreement   **62 SWRO 1311**
SIGNED: 29 Jun 61
HEADNOTE: PERSECUTION VICTIMS
TOPIC: Claims and Debts
PARTIES:
  Germany, West
  Switzerland

462168   Bilateral Convention   **49 SWRO 1953**
SIGNED: 21 Nov 49
HEADNOTE: COMPENSATION FOR NATIONALIZA-
TION
TOPIC: Claims and Debts
PARTIES:
  France
  Switzerland

462169   Bilateral Agreement   **50 SWRO 736**
SIGNED: 19 Jul 50
HEADNOTE: INDEMNIFY SWISS INTERESTS
TOPIC: Claims and Debts
PARTIES:
  Hungary
  Switzerland

462170   Bilateral Instrument   **55 SWRO 357**
SIGNED: 21 Jan 55
HEADNOTE: CERTAIN SWISS CLAIMS
TOPIC: Claims and Debts
PARTIES:
  Japan
  Switzerland

462171   Bilateral Agreement   **49 SWRO 839**
SIGNED: 25 Jun 49
HEADNOTE: INDEMNIFY SWISS INTERESTS
TOPIC: Claims and Debts
PARTIES:
  Poland
  Switzerland

462172   Bilateral Agreement   **48 SWRO 995**
SIGNED: 27 Sep 48
HEADNOTE: INDEMNIFY SWISS INTERESTS
TOPIC: Claims and Debts
PARTIES:
  Switzerland
  Yugoslavia

462173   Bilateral Convention   **60 SWRO 1554**
SIGNED: 3 Dec 59
HEADNOTE: FIX BORDER NEUCHATEL DOUBS
TOPIC: Territory Boundary
PARTIES:
  France
  Switzerland

462174   Bilateral Convention   **60 SWRO 1546**
SIGNED: 25 Feb 53
HEADNOTE: MODIFY BORDER BERNE SOLEURE
TOPIC: Territory Boundary
PARTIES:
  France
  Switzerland

462175   Bilateral Convention   **60 SWRO 1555**
SIGNED: 3 Dec 59
HEADNOTE: FIX BORDER BALEVILLE HAUTRHIN
TOPIC: Territory Boundary
PARTIES:
  France
  Switzerland

462176   Bilateral Convention   **55 SWRO 626**
SIGNED: 25 Nov 52
HEADNOTE: FIX BORDER VAL DI LEI
TOPIC: Territory Boundary
PARTIES:
  Italy
  Switzerland

462177   Bilateral Convention   **53 SWRO 403**
SIGNED: 5 Apr 51
HEADNOTE: FIX BORDER ROGGIA MOLINARA
TOPIC: Territory Boundary
PARTIES:
  Italy
  Switzerland

462178   Bilateral Convention   **53 SWRO 409**
SIGNED: 5 Apr 51
HEADNOTE: FIX BORDER PONTE CHIASSO
TOPIC: Territory Boundary
PARTIES:
  Italy
  Switzerland

462179   Bilateral Convention   **63 SWRO 520**
SIGNED: 16 May 61
HEADNOTE: FIX BORDER STRAITS OF LAVENA
TOPIC: Territory Boundary
PARTIES:
  Italy
  Switzerland

462180   Bilateral Convention   **55 SWRO 557**
SIGNED: 4 Jul 52
HEADNOTE: FIX BORDER KRIEGALPPASS
TOPIC: Territory Boundary
PARTIES:
  Italy
  Switzerland

462181   Bilateral Convention   **56 SWRO 143**
SIGNED: 7 May 55
HEADNOTE: FIX BORDER RHINE
TOPIC: Territory Boundary
PARTIES:
  Liechtenstein
  Switzerland

462182   Bilateral Agreement   **64 SWRO 851**
SIGNED: 24 Sep 64
HEADNOTE: QUOTA EXPENSES CUSTOMS AD-
MINISTRATION

TOPIC: Customs
PARTIES:
  Liechtenstein
  Switzerland

462183   Bilateral Agreement   **64 SWRO 1**
SIGNED: 6 Nov 63
HEADNOTE: STATUS OF CITIZENS
TOPIC: Consul/Citizenship
PARTIES:
  Liechtenstein
  Switzerland

462184   Bilateral Agreement   **64 SWRO 5**
SIGNED: 6 Nov 63
HEADNOTE: STATUS OF ALIENS
TOPIC: Consul/Citizenship
PARTIES:
  Liechtenstein
  Switzerland

462185   Bilateral Agreement   **64 SWRO 849**
SIGNED: 24 Sep 64
HEADNOTE: QUOTA EXPENSES FEDERAL TAX
TOPIC: Customs
PARTIES:
  Liechtenstein
  Switzerland

462186   Bilateral Convention   **55 SWRO 537**
SIGNED: 10 Dec 54
HEADNOTE: OLD-AGE INSURANCE
TOPIC: Non-ILO Labor
PARTIES:
  Liechtenstein
  Switzerland

462187   Bilateral Instrument   **56 SWRO 1210**
SIGNED: 15 Nov 46
HEADNOTE: LEGAL STATUS OF BUREAU
TOPIC: IGO Status/Immunit
PARTIES:
  Int Bureau Educ
  Switzerland

462188   Bilateral Agreement   **56 SWRO 1367**
SIGNED: 28 Sep 56
HEADNOTE: LEGAL STATUS OF OFFICE
TOPIC: IGO Status/Immunit
PARTIES:
  Int Rail Transport
  Switzerland

462189   Bilateral Exchange   **56 SWRO 1194**
SIGNED: 22 Apr 48
HEADNOTE: LEGAL STATUS OF UNION
TOPIC: IGO Status/Immunit
PARTIES:
  UPU (Postal Union)
  Switzerland

462190   Bilateral Exchange   **56 SWRO 1196**
SIGNED: 25 Feb 48
HEADNOTE: LEGAL STATUS OF UNION
TOPIC: IGO Status/Immunit
PARTIES:
  ITU (Telecommun)
  Switzerland

462191   Bilateral Instrument   **56 SWRO 1273**
SIGNED: 9 Jul 56
HEADNOTE: RADIO COMMUNICATION
TOPIC: Telecommunications
PARTIES:
  United Nations
  Switzerland

462192   Bilateral Exchange   **56 SWRO 1213**
SIGNED: 3 May 54
HEADNOTE: LEGAL STATUS OF COMMITTEE
TOPIC: IGO Status/Immunit
PARTIES:
  Intgov Eur Migrat
  Switzerland

462193   Bilateral Agreement   **61 SWRO 763**
SIGNED: 10 Aug 61
HEADNOTE: LEGAL STATUS OF ASSOCIATION
TOPIC: IGO Status/Immunit
PARTIES:
   EFTA (Free Trade)
   Switzerland

463015   Bilateral Treaty   **11 SWRS 615**
SIGNED: 1 Aug 46
HEADNOTE: LABOR
TOPIC: Non-ILO Labor
PARTIES:
   France
   Switzerland

463016   Bilateral Agreement   **11 SWRS 621**
SIGNED: 1 Aug 46
HEADNOTE: AGRICULTURAL LABOR
TOPIC: Non-ILO Labor
PARTIES:
   France
   Switzerland

463018   Bilateral Agreement   **11 SWRS 623**
SIGNED: 1 Aug 46
HEADNOTE: ADMISSION OF INTERNS
TOPIC: Non-ILO Labor
PARTIES:
   France
   Switzerland

463021   Bilateral Exchange   **11 SWRS 673**
SIGNED: 3 Dec 45
HEADNOTE: RECOGNITION
TOPIC: Recognition
PARTIES:
   Lebanon
   Switzerland

463022   Bilateral Exchange   **11 SWRS 708**
SIGNED: 3 Dec 45
HEADNOTE: RECOGNITION
TOPIC: Recognition
PARTIES:
   Switzerland
   Syria

463071   Bilateral Agreement   **12 SWRS 656**
SIGNED: 1 Aug 46
HEADNOTE: BORDER TRAFFIC
TOPIC: Customs
PARTIES:
   France
   Switzerland

463111   Bilateral Agreement   **14 SWRS 351**
SIGNED: 22 Nov 46
HEADNOTE: FROZEN SWISS ASSETS
TOPIC: Claims and Debts
PARTIES:
   Switzerland
   USA (United States)

463145   Bilateral Agreement   **14 SWRS 526**
SIGNED: 9 Jul 47
HEADNOTE: INSURANCE
TOPIC: Health/Educ/Welfare
PARTIES:
   Italy
   Switzerland

465001   Bilateral Agreement   **1 PTS 243**
SIGNED: 4 Aug 46
HEADNOTE: ABACA FIBER
TOPIC: General Trade
PARTIES:
   Philippines
   USA (United States)

465002   Bilateral Agreement   **1 PTS 251**
SIGNED: 8 Aug 46
HEADNOTE: COCONUT OIL
TOPIC: General Trade

PARTIES:
   Philippines
   USA (United States)

465003   Bilateral Agreement   **1 PTS 255**
SIGNED: 22 Aug 46
HEADNOTE: ENEMY PROPERTY
TOPIC: Reparations
PARTIES:
   Philippines
   USA (United States)

465004   Bilateral Agreement   **1 PTS 271**
SIGNED: 4 Oct 46
HEADNOTE: RADIO STATION KZFM
TOPIC: Specif Goods/Equip
PARTIES:
   Philippines
   USA (United States)

465005   Bilateral Agreement   **1 PTS 319**
SIGNED: 26 Oct 46
HEADNOTE: INTERIM TRADE
TOPIC: General Trade
PARTIES:
   Philippines
   Switzerland

465006   Bilateral Treaty   **1 PTS 321**
SIGNED: 16 Nov 46
HEADNOTE: CONCILIATION
TOPIC: Dispute Settlement
PARTIES:
   Philippines
   USA (United States)

465007   Bilateral Agreement   **1 PTS 393**
SIGNED: 1 Apr 46
HEADNOTE: TRANSFER PENDISAAN COMPANY
STOCK
TOPIC: Specific Property
PARTIES:
   Philippines
   USA (United States)

465008   Bilateral Treaty   **1 PTS 427**
SIGNED: 26 Jun 47
HEADNOTE: GENERAL RELATIONS
TOPIC: General Amity
PARTIES:
   France
   Philippines

465009   Bilateral Agreement   **1 PTS 435**
SIGNED: 4 Sep 47
HEADNOTE: RADIO FACILITIES
TOPIC: Gen Communications
PARTIES:
   Philippines
   USA (United States)

465010   Bilateral Convention   **1 PTS 445**
SIGNED: 30 Sep 47
HEADNOTE: MAIL
TOPIC: Postal Service
PARTIES:
   Philippines
   USA (United States)

465011   Bilateral Exchange   **1 PTS 519**
SIGNED: 12 Oct 47
HEADNOTE: TRANSFER CORREGIDOR ISLANDS
TOPIC: Territory Boundary
PARTIES:
   Philippines
   USA (United States)

465012   Bilateral Exchange   **1 PTS 639**
SIGNED: 19 Dec 47
HEADNOTE: TRANSFER QUARANTINE STATION
TOPIC: Territory Boundary
PARTIES:
   Philippines
   USA (United States)

465013   Bilateral Exchange   **1 PTS 645**
SIGNED: 24 Dec 47
HEADNOTE: TRANSFER NICHOLS FIELD
TOPIC: Territory Boundary
PARTIES:
   Philippines
   USA (United States)

465014   Bilateral Treaty   **1 PTS 695**
SIGNED: 24 Mar 48
HEADNOTE: GENERAL RELATIONS
TOPIC: General Amity
PARTIES:
   Ecuador
   Philippines

465015   Bilateral Exchange   **1 PTS 705**
SIGNED: 20 Apr 48
HEADNOTE: TRANSFER TURTLE & MANGSEE
TOPIC: Territory Boundary
PARTIES:
   Philippines
   UK Great Britain

465016   Bilateral Agreement   **2 PTS 93**
SIGNED: 22 Dec 48
HEADNOTE: ARBITRATION & CONCILIATION
TOPIC: Dispute Settlement
PARTIES:
   Philippines
   Spain

465019   Bilateral Exchange   **2 PTS 145**
SIGNED: 24 May 49
HEADNOTE: DIPLOMATIC PROPERTY
TOPIC: Consul/Citizenship
PARTIES:
   Philippines
   UK Great Britain

465020   Bilateral Treaty   **2 PTS 155**
SIGNED: 13 Jun 49
HEADNOTE: GENERAL RELATIONS
TOPIC: General Amity
PARTIES:
   Philippines
   Turkey

465021   Bilateral Agreement   **2 PTS 517**
SIGNED: 20 Dec 49
HEADNOTE: MILITARY SCRIP
TOPIC: Finance
PARTIES:
   Philippines
   USA (United States)

465022   Bilateral Agreement   **2 PTS 555**
SIGNED: 18 May 50
HEADNOTE: TRADE & PAYMENTS
TOPIC: General Economic
PARTIES:
   Philippines
   SCAP Japan

465023   Bilateral Treaty   **2 PTS 605**
SIGNED: 3 Jan 51
HEADNOTE: GENERAL RELATIONS
TOPIC: General Amity
PARTIES:
   Pakistan
   Philippines

465024   Bilateral Exchange   **2 PTS 609**
SIGNED: 23 Jan 51
HEADNOTE: EXCHANGE PUBLICATIONS
TOPIC: Admin Cooperation
PARTIES:
   Philippines
   UK Great Britain

465025   Bilateral Instrument   **2 PTS 613**
SIGNED: 3 Mar 51
HEADNOTE: TRADE PLAN
TOPIC: General Trade

PARTIES:
  Philippines
  SCAP Japan

465026   Bilateral Agreement   2 PTS 615
SIGNED: 12 Mar 51
HEADNOTE: TRADE PLAN
TOPIC: General Trade
PARTIES:
  Philippines
  SCAP Japan

465027   Bilateral Treaty   2 PTS 689
SIGNED: 21 Jun 51
HEADNOTE: GENERAL RELATIONS
TOPIC: General Amity
PARTIES:
  Indonesia
  Philippines

465029   Bilateral Agreement   2 PTS 783
SIGNED: 19 Mar 52
HEADNOTE: FINANCES
TOPIC: Finance
PARTIES:
  Philippines
  SCAP Japan

465030   Bilateral Treaty   3 PTS 3
SIGNED: 3 Sep 52
HEADNOTE: GENERAL RELATIONS
TOPIC: General Amity
PARTIES:
  Cuba
  Philippines

465031   Bilateral Exchange   3 PTS 63
SIGNED: 24 Jan 53
HEADNOTE: SUNKEN VESSELS SURVEY
TOPIC: Water Transport
PARTIES:
  Japan
  Philippines

465032   Bilateral Agreement   3 PTS 85
SIGNED: 12 Mar 53
HEADNOTE: INTERIM REPARATIONS SUNKEN
  VESSELS
TOPIC: Reparations
PARTIES:
  Japan
  Philippines

465033   Bilateral Agreement   3 PTS 175
SIGNED: 16 Jul 53
HEADNOTE: HYGIENE INSTITUTE PLANS
TOPIC: Tech Assistance
PARTIES:
  Philippines
  WHO (World Health)

465034   Bilateral Treaty   3 PTS 399
SIGNED: 18 Jan 55
HEADNOTE: GENERAL RELATIONS
TOPIC: General Amity
PARTIES:
  United Arab Rep
  Philippines

465035   Bilateral Instrument   3 PTS 417
SIGNED: 25 Apr 55
HEADNOTE: TRADE RELATIONS
TOPIC: General Trade
PARTIES:
  Germany, West
  Philippines

465036   Bilateral Exchange   3 PTS 529
SIGNED: 8 Dec 55
HEADNOTE: GOODS EXCHANGE
TOPIC: General Trade
PARTIES:
  Japan
  Philippines

465037   Bilateral Agreement   3 PTS 699
SIGNED: 7 Jan 58
HEADNOTE: DEVELOPMENT TRADE RELATIONS
TOPIC: General Trade
PARTIES:
  Japan
  Philippines

465038   Bilateral Exchange   3 PTS 715
SIGNED: 14 Apr 58
HEADNOTE: SCHEDULE OF ROUTES AMEND-
  MENT
TOPIC: Air Transport
PARTIES:
  Philippines
  UK Great Britain

465039   Bilateral Instrument   3 PTS 761
SIGNED: 5 Aug 58
HEADNOTE: DETAILED POSTAL REGULATIONS
TOPIC: Postal Service
PARTIES:
  Taiwan
  Philippines

465040   Bilateral Exchange   3 PTS 827
SIGNED: 21 Apr 59
HEADNOTE: ABOLITION VISAS
TOPIC: Visas
PARTIES:
  Denmark
  Philippines

465041   Bilateral Treaty   3 PTS 829
SIGNED: 26 Apr 59
HEADNOTE: GENERAL RELATIONS
TOPIC: General Amity
PARTIES:
  Philippines
  Vietnam, South

465042   Bilateral Instrument   4 PTS 11
SIGNED: 12 Oct 59
HEADNOTE: COMBAT USE OF BASES
TOPIC: General Military
PARTIES:
  Philippines
  USA (United States)

465043   Bilateral Instrument   4 PTS 25
SIGNED: 18 Dec 59
HEADNOTE: DEPORTEES
TOPIC: Consul/Citizenship
PARTIES:
  Taiwan
  Philippines

465044   Bilateral Agreement   4 PTS 349
SIGNED: 27 Jul 60
HEADNOTE: LAW ENFORCEMENT
TOPIC: Admin Cooperation
PARTIES:
  Indonesia
  Philippines

465045   Bilateral Agreement   4 PTS 371
SIGNED: 6 Dec 60
HEADNOTE: GRANT DEVELOPMENT RIGHTS
TOPIC: Other Economic
PARTIES:
  Philippines
  USA (United States)

465046   Bilateral Treaty   4 PTS 383
SIGNED: 9 Dec 60
HEADNOTE: FRIENDSHIP COMMERCE NAVGA-
  TION
TOPIC: General Amity
PARTIES:
  Japan
  Philippines

465047   Bilateral Agreement   4 PTS 425
SIGNED: 30 Jan 61

HEADNOTE: NAVY COORDINATION
TOPIC: General Military
PARTIES:
  Indonesia
  Philippines

465048   Bilateral Agreement   4 PTS 551
SIGNED: 3 May 62
HEADNOTE: CULTURE
TOPIC: Culture
PARTIES:
  Philippines
  United Arab Rep

465049   Bilateral Agreement   4 PTS 639
SIGNED: 5 Feb 63
HEADNOTE: TECHNICAL COOPERATION
TOPIC: Tech Assistance
PARTIES:
  Germany, West
  Philippines

465050   Bilateral Agreement   4 PTS 739
SIGNED: 27 May 63
HEADNOTE: TRADE PROMOTION
TOPIC: General Trade
PARTIES:
  Indonesia
  Philippines

465051   Bilateral Agreement   4 PTS 747
SIGNED: 27 May 63
HEADNOTE: COCONUT COMMISSION
TOPIC: Admin Cooperation
PARTIES:
  Indonesia
  Philippines

465052   Bilateral Agreement   4 PTS 749
SIGNED: 27 May 63
HEADNOTE: SCIENTIFIC & TECHNICAL COOPER-
  ATION
TOPIC: Tech Assistance
PARTIES:
  Indonesia
  Philippines

465053   Bilateral Instrument   4 PTS 753
SIGNED: 27 May 63
HEADNOTE: ECONOMIC COOPERATION
TOPIC: General Economic
PARTIES:
  Indonesia
  Philippines

465054   Bilateral Agreement   4 PTS 761
SIGNED: 25 Jul 63
HEADNOTE: NAVAL LIAISON
TOPIC: General Military
PARTIES:
  Indonesia
  Philippines

465055   Bilateral Agreement   4 PTS 791
SIGNED: 15 Aug 63
HEADNOTE: PEACE CORPS
TOPIC: Tech Assistance
PARTIES:
  Philippines
  USA (United States)

465056   Bilateral Exchange   4 PTS 811
SIGNED: 8 Oct 63
HEADNOTE: SOCIAL SECURITY AGENCY EM-
  PLOYEES
TOPIC: Non-ILO Labor
PARTIES:
  Philippines
  USA (United States)

465057   Bilateral Agreement   4 PTS 831
SIGNED: 28 Feb 64
HEADNOTE: GENERAL TRADE
TOPIC: General Trade

PARTIES:
Germany, West
Philippines

465058   Bilateral Agreement   **4 PTS 835**
SIGNED: 29 Feb 64
HEADNOTE: FINANCIAL ASSISTANCE
TOPIC: Direct Aid
PARTIES:
Germany, West
Philippines

465059   Bilateral Instrument   **4 PTS 839**
SIGNED: 3 Mar 64
HEADNOTE: IMMIGRATION & VISA MATTERS
TOPIC: Visas
PARTIES:
Germany, West
Philippines

465060   Bilateral Agreement   **4 PTS 841**
SIGNED: 3 Mar 64
HEADNOTE: MARITIME TRANSPORT
TOPIC: Water Transport
PARTIES:
Germany, West
Philippines

465061   Bilateral Treaty   **4 PTS 843**
SIGNED: 3 Mar 64
HEADNOTE: PROMOTION INVESTMENT
TOPIC: General Economic
PARTIES:
Germany, West
Philippines

465062   Bilateral Instrument   **4 PTS 855**
SIGNED: 19 Mar 64
HEADNOTE: ESTABLISH SEA COMMUNICATIONS
COMMISSION
TOPIC: IGO Establishment
PARTIES:
Indonesia
Philippines

465063   Bilateral Instrument   **4 PTS 859**
SIGNED: 19 Mar 64
HEADNOTE: PROMOTION SEA COMMUNICATION
TOPIC: Gen Communications
PARTIES:
Indonesia
Philippines

465064   Bilateral Convention   **4 PTS 879**
SIGNED: 5 Oct 64
HEADNOTE: PREVENTION DOUBLE TAXATION
TOPIC: Taxation
PARTIES:
Philippines
USA (United States)

465065   Bilateral Exchange   **4 PTS 919**
SIGNED: 10 Sep 65
HEADNOTE: BROADCAST FACILITIES
TOPIC: Gen Communications
PARTIES:
Philippines
USA (United States)

465066   Bilateral Exchange   **4 PTS 925**
SIGNED: 10 Mar 65
HEADNOTE: SOCIAL SECURITY
TOPIC: Non-ILO Labor
PARTIES:
Philippines
USA (United States)

465067   Bilateral Exchange   **4 PTS 973**
SIGNED: 5 Oct 65
HEADNOTE: COTTON TEXTILES
TOPIC: General Trade
PARTIES:
Philippines
USA (United States)

465068   Bilateral Exchange   **4 PTS 1037**
SIGNED: 16 Dec 65
HEADNOTE: SOLDIERS REST PROGRAM
TOPIC: General Military
PARTIES:
Philippines
USA (United States)

465069   Bilateral Exchange   **4 PTS 1041**
SIGNED: 20 Dec 65
HEADNOTE: DOCUMENT EXCHANGE
TOPIC: Admin Cooperation
PARTIES:
Philippines
USA (United States)

465070   Bilateral Exchange   **4 PTS 1051**
SIGNED: 29 Dec 65
HEADNOTE: MOTOR VEHICLE TAX
TOPIC: Taxation
PARTIES:
Philippines
USA (United States)

465071   Bilateral Instrument   **2 PTS 553**
SIGNED: 20 Apr 50
HEADNOTE: SURPLUS PROPERTY
TOPIC: Specif Goods/Equip
PARTIES:
Philippines
USA (United States)

465072   Bilateral Agreement   **2 PTS 775**
SIGNED: 1 Mar 52
HEADNOTE: CLAY POTTERY PROJECT
TOPIC: Tech Assistance
PARTIES:
Philippines
UNTAB (Tech Assis)

465073   Bilateral Agreement   **2 PTS 785**
SIGNED: 3 Apr 52
HEADNOTE: LOGGING CENTER
TOPIC: Tech Assistance
PARTIES:
Philippines
FAO (Food Agri)

465074   Bilateral Agreement   **2 PTS 789**
SIGNED: 24 Apr 52
HEADNOTE: MARBLE & CEMENT INDUSTRY
TOPIC: Tech Assistance
PARTIES:
Philippines
UNTAB (Tech Assis)

465075   Bilateral Agreement   **3 PTS 36**
SIGNED: 30 Oct 52
HEADNOTE: FORESTRY EXPERTS
TOPIC: Tech Assistance
PARTIES:
Philippines
FAO (Food Agri)

465076   Bilateral Agreement   **3 PTS 41**
SIGNED: 5 Nov 52
HEADNOTE: COOPERATIVES EXPERT
TOPIC: Tech Assistance
PARTIES:
Philippines
UNTAB (Tech Assis)

465077   Bilateral Agreement   **3 PTS 45**
SIGNED: 5 Nov 52
HEADNOTE: STORE MANAGEMENT
TOPIC: Tech Assistance
PARTIES:
Philippines
UNTAB (Tech Assis)

465078   Bilateral Agreement   **3 PTS 49**
SIGNED: 14 Nov 52
HEADNOTE: RICE PRODUCTION IMPROVEMENT
TOPIC: Tech Assistance

PARTIES:
Philippines
FAO (Food Agri)

465079   Bilateral Agreement   **3 PTS 137**
SIGNED: 19 Jun 53
HEADNOTE: AIR SERVICES EXPERTS
TOPIC: Tech Assistance
PARTIES:
Philippines
UNTAB (Tech Assis)

465080   Bilateral Agreement   **3 PTS 161**
SIGNED: 25 Jun 53
HEADNOTE: IRON & STEEL EXPERTS
TOPIC: Tech Assistance
PARTIES:
Philippines
UNTAB (Tech Assis)

465081   Bilateral Agreement   **3 PTS 165**
SIGNED: 25 Jun 53
HEADNOTE: FORESTRY EXPERT
TOPIC: Tech Assistance
PARTIES:
Philippines
FAO (Food Agri)

465082   Bilateral Agreement   **3 PTS 175**
SIGNED: 16 Jul 53
HEADNOTE: HYGIENE INSTITUTE ASSISTANCE
TOPIC: Tech Assistance
PARTIES:
Philippines
WHO (World Health)

465083   Bilateral Agreement   **3 PTS 187**
SIGNED: 6 Aug 53
HEADNOTE: LABOR INSPECTION
TOPIC: Tech Assistance
PARTIES:
Philippines
UNTAB (Tech Assis)

465084   Bilateral Agreement   **3 PTS 191**
SIGNED: 6 Aug 53
HEADNOTE: CHILD WELFARE EXPERT
TOPIC: Tech Assistance
PARTIES:
Philippines
UNTAB (Tech Assis)

465085   Bilateral Instrument   **3 PTS 661**
SIGNED: 4 May 57
HEADNOTE: HUMAN RIGHTS EXPERT
TOPIC: Tech Assistance
PARTIES:
Philippines
UNTAB (Tech Assis)

465086   Bilateral Agreement   **3 PTS 749**
SIGNED: 23 Jul 58
HEADNOTE: STATISTICAL PROGRAM
TOPIC: Tech Assistance
PARTIES:
Philippines
UNTAB (Tech Assis)

466001   Bilateral Treaty   **52 TURG 605**
SIGNED: 28 Nov 51
HEADNOTE: GENERAL RELATIONS
TOPIC: General Amity
PARTIES:
Dominican Republic
Turkey

466004   Bilateral Treaty   **53 TURG 2107**
SIGNED: 9 Oct 52
HEADNOTE: GENERAL RELATIONS
TOPIC: General Amity
PARTIES:
Turkey
Yemen

466005   Bilateral Agreement   **64 TURG 1202**
SIGNED: 12 Sep 63
HEADNOTE: ASSOCIATION
TOPIC: Other Economic
PARTIES:
    EEC (Econ Commnty)
    Turkey

466006   Bilateral Exchange   **52 TURG 305**
SIGNED: 16 Feb 52
HEADNOTE: EXTRADITION
TOPIC: Extradition
PARTIES:
    Germany, West
    Turkey

466007   Bilateral Exchange   **48 TURG 702**
SIGNED: 7 Dec 46
HEADNOTE: CITIZENSHIP OPTION
TOPIC: Consul/Citizenship
PARTIES:
    Lebanon
    Turkey

466008   Bilateral Exchange   **57 TURG 1309**
SIGNED: 28 Jan 57
HEADNOTE: CITIZENSHIP OPTION
TOPIC: Consul/Citizenship
PARTIES:
    Lebanon
    Turkey

466010   Bilateral Exchange   **56 TURG 2710**
SIGNED: 19 Oct 56
HEADNOTE: ADDITIONAL TO VISA ABOLITION
TOPIC: Visas
PARTIES:
    Austria
    Turkey

466012   Bilateral Agreement   **59 TURG 1006**
SIGNED: 29 Sep 54
HEADNOTE: VISA
TOPIC: Visas
PARTIES:
    Finland
    Turkey

466015   Bilateral Exchange   **55 TURG 1402**
SIGNED: 10 Feb 55
HEADNOTE: ABOLITION VISAS
TOPIC: Visas
PARTIES:
    Greece
    Turkey

466017   Bilateral Agreement   **64 TURG 2912**
SIGNED: 8 Oct 64
HEADNOTE: ABOLITION VISAS
TOPIC: Visas
PARTIES:
    Iran
    Turkey

466023   Bilateral Exchange   **59 TURG 1006**
SIGNED: 24 Apr 59
HEADNOTE: SCANDINAVIAN VISAS
TOPIC: Visas
PARTIES:
    Norway
    Turkey

466024   Bilateral Exchange   **55 TURG 1912**
SIGNED: 12 Dec 55
HEADNOTE: ABOLITION VISAS
TOPIC: Visas
PARTIES:
    Pakistan
    Turkey

466027   Bilateral Exchange   **60 TURG 2106**
SIGNED: 1 Jun 60
HEADNOTE: AMENDMENT
TOPIC: Visas

PARTIES:
    Sweden
    Turkey

466028   Bilateral Exchange   **53 TURG 202**
SIGNED: 16 Feb 52
HEADNOTE: TRADE & PAYMENTS
TOPIC: General Trade
PARTIES:
    Germany, West
    Turkey

466029   Bilateral Exchange   **50 TURG 1002**
SIGNED: 14 Nov 49
HEADNOTE: APPLY MOST FAVORED NATION
    CLAUSE TO SHIPS
TOPIC: Mostfavored Nation
PARTIES:
    Germany, West
    Turkey

466030   Bilateral Protocol   **50 TURG 1803**
SIGNED: 5 Jan 50
HEADNOTE: REGULATION PROPERTY INTERESTS
TOPIC: General Economic
PARTIES:
    Turkey
    Yugoslavia

466031   Bilateral Agreement   **57 TURG 1309**
SIGNED: 13 Jul 56
HEADNOTE: NATIONALIZED PROPERTY
TOPIC: Claims and Debts
PARTIES:
    Turkey
    Yugoslavia

466032   Bilateral Exchange   **58 TURG 2602**
SIGNED: 6 Apr 57
HEADNOTE: LEGAL CONVENTIONS REVIVAL
TOPIC: Admin Cooperation
PARTIES:
    Austria
    Turkey

466033   Bilateral Exchange   **52 TURG 1602**
SIGNED: 16 Feb 52
HEADNOTE: LEGAL CONVENTIONS REVIVAL
TOPIC: Admin Cooperation
PARTIES:
    Germany, West
    Turkey

466034   Bilateral Agreement   **64 TURG 601**
SIGNED: 7 Nov 59
HEADNOTE: CULTURE
TOPIC: Culture
PARTIES:
    Afghanistan
    Turkey

466036   Bilateral Agreement   **58 TURG 1505**
SIGNED: 7 May 58
HEADNOTE: CULTURE
TOPIC: Culture
PARTIES:
    Germany, West
    Turkey

466037   Bilateral Agreement   **64 TURG 601**
SIGNED: 2 Jan 59
HEADNOTE: CULTURE
TOPIC: Culture
PARTIES:
    Iran
    Turkey

466039   Bilateral Agreement   **59 TURG 206**
SIGNED: 9 Feb 58
HEADNOTE: CULTURE
TOPIC: Culture
PARTIES:
    Libya
    Turkey

466040   Bilateral Agreement   **61 TURG 509**
SIGNED: 7 Feb 61
HEADNOTE: SALE OF NATURAL URANIUM
TOPIC: Atomic Energy
PARTIES:
    Turkey
    USA (United States)

466041   Bilateral Convention   **61 TURG 504**
SIGNED: 22 Sep 60
HEADNOTE: VETERINARY
TOPIC: Sanitation
PARTIES:
    Turkey
    Yugoslavia

466043   Bilateral Convention   **54 TURG 2203**
SIGNED: 6 Aug 53
HEADNOTE: STORAGE METHOD SWEET WINE
TOPIC: Commodity Trade
PARTIES:
    Germany, West
    Turkey

466044   Bilateral Exchange   **48 TURG 2906**
SIGNED: 25 Mar 48
HEADNOTE: TRADE & PAYMENTS
TOPIC: General Economic
PARTIES:
    Belgium
    Turkey

466045   Bilateral Agreement   **50 TURG 3001**
SIGNED: 2 Dec 48
HEADNOTE: TRADE & PAYMENTS
TOPIC: General Economic
PARTIES:
    Belgium
    Turkey

466046   Bilateral Protocol   **58 TURG 2903**
SIGNED: 15 Apr 55
HEADNOTE: TRADE & PAYMENTS
TOPIC: General Economic
PARTIES:
    Belgium
    Turkey

466047   Bilateral Agreement   **56 TURG 202**
SIGNED: 23 Feb 55
HEADNOTE: TRADE & PAYMENTS
TOPIC: General Economic
PARTIES:
    Bulgaria
    Turkey

466048   Bilateral Exchange   **46 TURG 2112**
SIGNED: 7 Jun 46
HEADNOTE: BARTER 9 MILLION POUNDS
TOPIC: General Trade
PARTIES:
    Bulgaria
    Turkey

466049   Bilateral Agreement   **47 TURG 2802**
SIGNED: 5 Dec 46
HEADNOTE: TRADE & PAYMENTS
TOPIC: General Economic
PARTIES:
    Bulgaria
    Turkey

466050   Bilateral Agreement   **50 TURG 1001**
SIGNED: 7 Sep 49
HEADNOTE: TRADE & PAYMENTS
TOPIC: General Economic
PARTIES:
    Bulgaria
    Turkey

466052   Bilateral Agreement   **46 TURG 2312**
SIGNED: 15 May 46
HEADNOTE: TRADE & PAYMENTS
TOPIC: General Economic

PARTIES:
Finland
Turkey

466053   Bilateral Agreement   **49 TURG 1902**
SIGNED: 12 Jun 48
HEADNOTE: PAYMENTS
TOPIC: Finance
PARTIES:
Finland
Turkey

466054   Bilateral Agreement   **49 TURG 1902**
SIGNED: 12 Jun 48
HEADNOTE: TRADE
TOPIC: General Trade
PARTIES:
Finland
Turkey

466055   Bilateral Protocol   **55 TURG 702**
SIGNED: 27 Oct 53
HEADNOTE: COMMERCIAL MATTERS
TOPIC: General Trade
PARTIES:
Finland
Turkey

466056   Bilateral Agreement   **60 TURG 1908**
SIGNED: 13 May 60
HEADNOTE: TRADE
TOPIC: General Trade
PARTIES:
Finland
Turkey

466057   Bilateral Agreement   **60 TURG 1908**
SIGNED: 13 May 60
HEADNOTE: PAYMENTS
TOPIC: Finance
PARTIES:
Finland
Turkey

466060   Bilateral Convention   **48 TURG 2302**
SIGNED: 21 Oct 46
HEADNOTE: COMMERCE
TOPIC: General Trade
PARTIES:
France
Turkey

466062   Bilateral Agreement   **55 TURG 3105**
SIGNED: 19 Jan 54
HEADNOTE: ORDER OF EQUIPMENT
TOPIC: Commodity Trade
PARTIES:
France
Turkey

466063   Bilateral Protocol   **58 TURG 407**
SIGNED: 6 Apr 57
HEADNOTE: ECONOMIC & FINANCIAL
TOPIC: General Economic
PARTIES:
France
Turkey

466064   Bilateral Exchange   **61 TURG 1109**
SIGNED: 8 Apr 61
HEADNOTE: TURKISH QUOTA IMPORTS
TOPIC: Commodity Trade
PARTIES:
France
Turkey

466065   Bilateral Agreement   **49 TURG 1902**
SIGNED: 19 Apr 48
HEADNOTE: TRADE
TOPIC: General Trade
PARTIES:
Germany, West
Turkey

466066   Bilateral Agreement   **49 TURG 2812**
SIGNED: 15 Jan 49
HEADNOTE: TRADE & PAYMENTS
TOPIC: General Economic
PARTIES:
Germany, West
Turkey

466067   Bilateral Agreement   **52 TURG 305**
SIGNED: 16 Feb 52
HEADNOTE: TRADE & PAYMENTS
TOPIC: General Economic
PARTIES:
Germany, West
Turkey

466068   Bilateral Agreement   **49 TURG 2812**
SIGNED: 12 May 49
HEADNOTE: TRADE & PAYMENTS
TOPIC: General Economic
PARTIES:
Hungary
Turkey

466069   Bilateral Agreement   **54 TURG 2203**
SIGNED: 4 Jun 53
HEADNOTE: TRADE
TOPIC: General Trade
PARTIES:
India
Turkey

466070   Bilateral Agreement   **64 TURG 2909**
SIGNED: 14 Sep 59
HEADNOTE: TRADE
TOPIC: General Trade
PARTIES:
Indonesia
Turkey

466071   Bilateral Agreement   **51 TURG 1512**
SIGNED: 25 Dec 49
HEADNOTE: PAYMENTS
TOPIC: Finance
PARTIES:
Iran
Turkey

466072   Bilateral Protocol   **57 TURG 2506**
SIGNED: 13 Oct 56
HEADNOTE: TRADE & PAYMENTS
TOPIC: General Economic
PARTIES:
Iran
Turkey

466073   Bilateral Agreement   **47 TURG 109**
SIGNED: 12 Apr 47
HEADNOTE: TRADE & PAYMENTS
TOPIC: General Economic
PARTIES:
Italy
Turkey

466074   Bilateral Agreement   **50 TURG 301**
SIGNED: 10 Nov 48
HEADNOTE: TRADE & PAYMENTS
TOPIC: General Economic
PARTIES:
Italy
Turkey

466076   Bilateral Exchange   **56 TURG 409**
SIGNED: 10 Apr 55
HEADNOTE: LONG-TERM WHEAT SALES
TOPIC: Commodity Trade
PARTIES:
Italy
Turkey

466077   Bilateral Exchange   **58 TURG 407**
SIGNED: 15 Apr 57
HEADNOTE: TRADE FOR 1956-57
TOPIC: General Trade

PARTIES:
Italy
Turkey

466078   Bilateral Agreement   **56 TURG 301**
SIGNED: 8 Feb 55
HEADNOTE: TRADE & PAYMENTS
TOPIC: General Economic
PARTIES:
Japan
Turkey

466079   Bilateral Agreement   **50 TURG 1901**
SIGNED: 6 Sep 49
HEADNOTE: TRADE & PAYMENTS
TOPIC: General Economic
PARTIES:
Netherlands
Turkey

466081   Bilateral Agreement   **49 TURG 1802**
SIGNED: 18 Jul 48
HEADNOTE: TRADE & PAYMENTS
TOPIC: General Economic
PARTIES:
Poland
Turkey

466082   Bilateral Agreement   **49 TURG 1802**
SIGNED: 18 Jul 49
HEADNOTE: TRADE & PAYMENTS
TOPIC: General Economic
PARTIES:
Poland
Turkey

466083   Bilateral Protocol   **55 TURG 204**
SIGNED: 4 Dec 53
HEADNOTE: WHEAT
TOPIC: Commodity Trade
PARTIES:
Poland
Turkey

466084   Bilateral Agreement   **55 TURG 1602**
SIGNED: 5 Apr 54
HEADNOTE: TRADE & PAYMENTS
TOPIC: General Economic
PARTIES:
Romania
Turkey

466085   Bilateral Exchange   **48 TURG 902**
SIGNED: 8 Sep 47
HEADNOTE: PAYMENTS
TOPIC: Finance
PARTIES:
Spain
Turkey

466086   Bilateral Agreement   **52 TURG 2805**
SIGNED: 19 Jun 51
HEADNOTE: TRADE & PAYMENTS
TOPIC: General Economic
PARTIES:
Spain
Turkey

466087   Bilateral Exchange   **55 TURG 204**
SIGNED: 23 Jan 54
HEADNOTE: WHEAT SALE TO SPAIN
TOPIC: Commodity Trade
PARTIES:
Spain
Turkey

466088   Bilateral Agreement   **46 TURG 2312**
SIGNED: 24 Apr 46
HEADNOTE: TRADE & PAYMENTS
TOPIC: General Economic
PARTIES:
Sweden
Turkey

466089   Bilateral Agreement   **49 TURG 1902**
SIGNED: 7 Jun 48
HEADNOTE: TRADE & PAYMENTS
TOPIC: General Economic
PARTIES:
  Sweden
  Turkey

466090   Bilateral Agreement   **46 TURG 2301**
SIGNED: 12 Sep 45
HEADNOTE: TRADE & PAYMENTS
TOPIC: General Economic
PARTIES:
  Switzerland
  Turkey

466091   Bilateral Agreement   **50 TURG 403**
SIGNED: 23 Jul 49
HEADNOTE: WHEAT SALE TO SYRIA
TOPIC: Commodity Trade
PARTIES:
  Syria
  Turkey

466092   Bilateral Agreement   **57 TURG 701**
SIGNED: 3 Mar 56
HEADNOTE: MODUS VIVENDI AND TRADE
TOPIC: General Trade
PARTIES:
  Syria
  Turkey

466093   Bilateral Exchange   **59 TURG 606**
SIGNED: 17 Apr 58
HEADNOTE: MOST FAVORED NATION
TOPIC: Mostfavored Nation
PARTIES:
  Tunisia
  Turkey

466094   Bilateral Agreement   **55 TURG 204**
SIGNED: 15 Aug 53
HEADNOTE: TRADE & PAYMENTS
TOPIC: General Economic
PARTIES:
  Turkey
  United Arab Rep

466095   Bilateral Agreement   **46 TURG 2301**
SIGNED: 4 May 45
HEADNOTE: TRADE & PAYMENTS
TOPIC: General Economic
PARTIES:
  Turkey
  UK Great Britain

466096   Bilateral Agreement   **48 TURG 2302**
SIGNED: 18 Sep 47
HEADNOTE: TRADE,   PAYMENTS,   MODUS
  VIVENDI
TOPIC: General Economic
PARTIES:
  Turkey
  Yugoslavia

466097   Bilateral Agreement   **50 TURG 2503**
SIGNED: 5 Jan 50
HEADNOTE: TRADE & PAYMENTS
TOPIC: General Economic
PARTIES:
  Turkey
  Yugoslavia

466098   Bilateral Protocol   **55 TURG 1602**
SIGNED: 10 Apr 54
HEADNOTE: TRADE
TOPIC: General Trade
PARTIES:
  Turkey
  Yugoslavia

466099   Bilateral Protocol   **51 TURG 1512**
SIGNED: 25 Dec 49
HEADNOTE: CUSTOMS

TOPIC: Customs
PARTIES:
  Iran
  Turkey

466100   Bilateral Protocol   **56 TURG 404**
SIGNED: 9 Oct 54
HEADNOTE: ECONOMIC & TECHNICAL COOPER-
  ATION
TOPIC: General Aid
PARTIES:
  Austria
  Turkey

466101   Bilateral Agreement   **64 TURG 903**
SIGNED: 30 Dec 63
HEADNOTE: FINANCIAL AID
TOPIC: Direct Aid
PARTIES:
  Austria
  Turkey

466102   Bilateral Agreement   **64 TURG 909**
SIGNED: 28 Nov 58
HEADNOTE: LOAN
TOPIC: Loans and Credits
PARTIES:
  Belgium
  Turkey

466103   Bilateral Agreement   **64 TURG 909**
SIGNED: 17 Dec 58
HEADNOTE: FINANCIAL AID
TOPIC: Direct Aid
PARTIES:
  Denmark
  Turkey

466104   Bilateral Agreement   **54 TURG 1003**
SIGNED: 18 Jan 54
HEADNOTE: PAYMENT
TOPIC: Claims and Debts
PARTIES:
  France
  Turkey

466106   Bilateral Agreement   **64 TURG 909**
SIGNED: 27 Nov 58
HEADNOTE: FINANCIAL AID
TOPIC: Direct Aid
PARTIES:
  Germany, West
  Turkey

466107   Bilateral Agreement   **60 TURG 2208**
SIGNED: 19 Apr 60
HEADNOTE: FINANCIAL AID
TOPIC: Direct Aid
PARTIES:
  Germany, West
  Turkey

466108   Bilateral Agreement   **61 TURG 1907**
SIGNED: 6 Jun 61
HEADNOTE: CREDIT
TOPIC: Loans and Credits
PARTIES:
  Germany, West
  Turkey

466109   Bilateral Agreement   **56 TURG 202**
SIGNED: 29 Jan 55
HEADNOTE: ECONOMIC & TECHNICAL COOPER-
  ATION
TOPIC: General Aid
PARTIES:
  Italy
  Turkey

466111   Bilateral Agreement   **63 TURG 609**
SIGNED: 21 Jun 63
HEADNOTE: FINANCES
TOPIC: General Economic

PARTIES:
  Italy
  Turkey

466113   Bilateral Agreement   **64 TURG 909**
SIGNED: 18 Dec 58
HEADNOTE: FINANCIAL AID
TOPIC: Direct Aid
PARTIES:
  Portugal
  Turkey

466114   Bilateral Agreement   **64 TURG 909**
SIGNED: 17 Dec 58
HEADNOTE: FINANCIAL AID
TOPIC: Direct Aid
PARTIES:
  Sweden
  Turkey

466115   Bilateral Agreement   **64 TURG 909**
SIGNED: 22 Dec 58
HEADNOTE: FINANCIAL AID
TOPIC: Direct Aid
PARTIES:
  Switzerland
  Turkey

466116   Bilateral Agreement   **63 TURG 2109**
SIGNED: 1 May 63
HEADNOTE: CREDIT
TOPIC: Loans and Credits
PARTIES:
  Turkey
  UK Great Britain

466117   Bilateral Agreement   **46 TURG 1005**
SIGNED: 27 Feb 46
HEADNOTE: CREDIT
TOPIC: Loans and Credits
PARTIES:
  Turkey
  USA (United States)

466118   Bilateral Agreement   **50 TURG 3003**
SIGNED: 21 Jan 50
HEADNOTE: TECHNICAL ASSISTANCE FUNDS
TOPIC: Direct Aid
PARTIES:
  Turkey
  USA (United States)

466119   Bilateral Agreement   **58 TURG 1004**
SIGNED: 12 Sep 57
HEADNOTE: JOINT PROJECT BAGHDAD PACT
TOPIC: Direct Aid
PARTIES:
  Turkey
  USA (United States)

466120   Bilateral Agreement   **61 TURG 2207**
SIGNED: 20 Aug 59
HEADNOTE: MINE EXPLORATION GUARANTEE
TOPIC: Claims and Debts
PARTIES:
  Turkey
  USA (United States)

466121   Bilateral Agreement   **61 TURG 2207**
SIGNED: 29 Aug 59
HEADNOTE: COAL MINE GUARANTEE
TOPIC: Claims and Debts
PARTIES:
  Turkey
  USA (United States)

466122   Bilateral Agreement   **61 TURG 2407**
SIGNED: 31 Dec 60
HEADNOTE: RAILWAY EXTENSION
TOPIC: Loans and Credits
PARTIES:
  Turkey
  USA (United States)

466123   Bilateral Agreement   **61 TURG 1707**
SIGNED: 9 Jan 61
HEADNOTE: IRON & STEEL PRODUCTION
TOPIC: General Economic
PARTIES:
  Turkey
  USA (United States)

466124   Bilateral Agreement   **61 TURG 2407**
SIGNED: 21 Jan 61
HEADNOTE: ELECTRIC POWER DEVELOPMENT
TOPIC: Loans and Credits
PARTIES:
  Turkey
  USA (United States)

466125   Bilateral Agreement   **63 TURG 106**
SIGNED: 8 Feb 62
HEADNOTE: LOAN
TOPIC: Loans and Credits
PARTIES:
  Turkey
  USA (United States)

466126   Bilateral Agreement   **63 TURG 106**
SIGNED: 29 Mar 62
HEADNOTE: LOAN
TOPIC: Loans and Credits
PARTIES:
  Turkey
  USA (United States)

466127   Bilateral Agreement   **63 TURG 106**
SIGNED: 23 Jul 62
HEADNOTE: LOAN
TOPIC: Loans and Credits
PARTIES:
  Turkey
  USA (United States)

466128   Bilateral Agreement   **63 TURG 404**
SIGNED: 23 Nov 62
HEADNOTE: LOAN
TOPIC: Loans and Credits
PARTIES:
  Turkey
  USA (United States)

466129   Bilateral Agreement   **63 TURG 504**
SIGNED: 7 Dec 62
HEADNOTE: LOAN
TOPIC: Loans and Credits
PARTIES:
  Turkey
  USA (United States)

466130   Bilateral Agreement   **65 TURG 1506**
SIGNED: 13 May 63
HEADNOTE: CREDIT
TOPIC: Loans and Credits
PARTIES:
  Turkey
  USA (United States)

466131   Bilateral Agreement   **63 TURG 2809**
SIGNED: 15 Jul 63
HEADNOTE: A.I.D. LOAN
TOPIC: Loans and Credits
PARTIES:
  Turkey
  USA (United States)

466132   Bilateral Agreement   **63 TURG 2509**
SIGNED: 11 Sep 63
HEADNOTE: LOAN
TOPIC: Loans and Credits
PARTIES:
  Turkey
  USA (United States)

466133   Bilateral Agreement   **64 TURG 904**
SIGNED: 15 Oct 63
HEADNOTE: LOAN
TOPIC: Loans and Credits

PARTIES:
  Turkey
  USA (United States)

466134   Bilateral Agreement   **51 TURG 407**
SIGNED: 14 Apr 51
HEADNOTE: FAO TECHNICAL ASSISTANCE
TOPIC: Tech Assistance
PARTIES:
  FAO (Food Agri)
  Turkey

466135   Bilateral Agreement   **52 TURG 1306**
SIGNED: 21 Mar 52
HEADNOTE: LABOR ACTIVITIES CENTER
TOPIC: Tech Assistance
PARTIES:
  ILO (Labor Org)
  Turkey

466136   Bilateral Agreement   **51 TURG 1512**
SIGNED: 25 Dec 49
HEADNOTE: GROWTH OF VOLUME TRANSPORT
TOPIC: General Transport
PARTIES:
  Iran
  Turkey

466137   Bilateral Agreement   **51 TURG 1512**
SIGNED: 20 Mar 51
HEADNOTE: AIR SERVICE ESTABLISHMENT
TOPIC: Air Transport
PARTIES:
  Iran
  Turkey

466138   Bilateral Agreement   **49 TURG 1712**
SIGNED: 12 Feb 46
HEADNOTE: AIR TRANSPORT
TOPIC: Air Transport
PARTIES:
  Syria
  Turkey

466139   Bilateral Protocol   **0 TURG 217**
SIGNED: 8 Nov 55
HEADNOTE: SARISU KARASU WATER USE
TOPIC: Water Transport
PARTIES:
  Iran
  Turkey

466140   Bilateral Agreement   **50 TURG 1001**
SIGNED: 18 Dec 48
HEADNOTE: TRADE AND PAYMENTS
TOPIC: General Economic
PARTIES:
  Germany, West
  Turkey

468001   Bilateral Agreement   **0 SUST 231**
SIGNED: 13 Apr 47
HEADNOTE: COMMUNICATION ESTABLISHMENT
TOPIC: Telecommunications
PARTIES:
  Afghanistan
  USSR (Soviet Union)

468002   Bilateral Agreement   **0 SUST 276**
SIGNED: 17 Jul 50
HEADNOTE: TRADE & PAYMENTS
TOPIC: General Economic
PARTIES:
  Afghanistan
  USSR (Soviet Union)

468003   Bilateral Agreement   **0 SUST 306**
SIGNED: 27 Jan 54
HEADNOTE: CREDIT
TOPIC: Loans and Credits
PARTIES:
  Afghanistan
  USSR (Soviet Union)

468005   Bilateral Instrument   **0 SUST 347**
SIGNED: 28 Jan 56
HEADNOTE: 100 MILLION LONG-TERM CREDIT
TOPIC: Loans and Credits
PARTIES:
  Afghanistan
  USSR (Soviet Union)

468006   Bilateral Agreement   **0 SUST 351**
SIGNED: 24 Mar 56
HEADNOTE: ESTABLISH AIR TRANSPORT
TOPIC: Air Transport
PARTIES:
  Afghanistan
  USSR (Soviet Union)

468007   Bilateral Instrument   **0 SUST 235**
SIGNED: 26 Jul 47
HEADNOTE: ECONOMIC & CULTURAL
TOPIC: General Economic
PARTIES:
  Albania
  USSR (Soviet Union)

468008   Bilateral Instrument   **0 SUST 258**
SIGNED: 10 Apr 49
HEADNOTE: ECONOMIC RELATIONS
TOPIC: General Economic
PARTIES:
  Albania
  USSR (Soviet Union)

468009   Bilateral Agreement   **0 SUST 275**
SIGNED: 27 Jun 50
HEADNOTE: RADIO BROADCASTING
TOPIC: Mass Media
PARTIES:
  Albania
  USSR (Soviet Union)

468010   Bilateral Agreement   **0 SUST 280**
SIGNED: 17 Feb 51
HEADNOTE: INDUSTRIAL EQUIPMENT CREDIT
TOPIC: Loans and Credits
PARTIES:
  Albania
  USSR (Soviet Union)

468011   Bilateral Agreement   **0 SUST 286**
SIGNED: 19 Apr 52
HEADNOTE: TECHNICAL COOPERATION
TOPIC: Tech Assistance
PARTIES:
  Albania
  USSR (Soviet Union)

468012   Bilateral Agreement   **0 SUST 288**
SIGNED: 5 Jul 52
HEADNOTE: ALBANIANS IN SOVIET COLLEGES
TOPIC: Education
PARTIES:
  Albania
  USSR (Soviet Union)

468013   Bilateral Convention   **0 SUST 334**
SIGNED: 27 Aug 55
HEADNOTE: AGRICULTURAL DISEASES
TOPIC: Sanitation
PARTIES:
  Albania
  USSR (Soviet Union)

468014   Bilateral Instrument   **0 SUST 381**
SIGNED: 17 Apr 57
HEADNOTE: GENERAL RELATIONS
TOPIC: General Amity
PARTIES:
  Albania
  USSR (Soviet Union)

468017   Bilateral Instrument   **0 SUST 392**
SIGNED: 22 Nov 57
HEADNOTE: ECONOMIC & TECHNICAL AID
TOPIC: General Aid

PARTIES:
Albania
USSR (Soviet Union)

468018   Bilateral Exchange   0 SUST 212
SIGNED: 5 Jun 46
HEADNOTE: GENERAL RELATIONS
TOPIC: General Amity
PARTIES:
Argentina
USSR (Soviet Union)

468019   Bilateral Exchange   0 SUST 316
SIGNED: 3 Jun 54
HEADNOTE: MOTION PICTURE EXCHANGE
TOPIC: Culture
PARTIES:
Argentina
USSR (Soviet Union)

468020   Bilateral Protocol   0 SUST 328
SIGNED: 19 May 55
HEADNOTE: TRADE
TOPIC: General Trade
PARTIES:
Argentina
USSR (Soviet Union)

468021   Bilateral Exchange   0 SUST 234
SIGNED: 15 Jul 47
HEADNOTE: MISSIONS TO EMBASSIES
TOPIC: Consul/Citizenship
PARTIES:
Australia
USSR (Soviet Union)

468022   Bilateral Exchange   0 SUST 212
SIGNED: 27 Nov 45
HEADNOTE: JUDICIAL INSTRUCTIONS
TOPIC: Admin Cooperation
PARTIES:
Belgium
USSR (Soviet Union)

468023   Bilateral Instrument   0 SUST 371
SIGNED: 2 Nov 56
HEADNOTE: GENERAL RELATIONS
TOPIC: General Amity
PARTIES:
Belgium
USSR (Soviet Union)

468024   Bilateral Agreement   0 SUST 244
SIGNED: 18 Feb 48
HEADNOTE: COMMERCIAL CONVENTION
TOPIC: General Trade
PARTIES:
Belgium
USSR (Soviet Union)

468025   Bilateral Agreement   0 SUST 245
SIGNED: 18 Feb 48
HEADNOTE: PAYMENTS
TOPIC: Finance
PARTIES:
Belgium
USSR (Soviet Union)

468026   Bilateral Protocol   0 SUST 278
SIGNED: 14 Nov 50
HEADNOTE: TRADE
TOPIC: General Trade
PARTIES:
Belgium
USSR (Soviet Union)

468027   Bilateral Exchange   0 SUST 437
SIGNED: 2 Apr 45
HEADNOTE: ESTABLISH DIPLOMATIC RELA-
TIONS
TOPIC: Consul/Citizenship
PARTIES:
Brazil
USSR (Soviet Union)

468028   Bilateral Agreement   0 SUST 175
SIGNED: 14 Mar 45
HEADNOTE: TRADE
TOPIC: General Trade
PARTIES:
Bulgaria
USSR (Soviet Union)

468029   Bilateral Treaty   0 SUST 226
SIGNED: 10 Feb 47
HEADNOTE: PEACE TREATY
TOPIC: Peace/Disarmament
PARTIES:
Bulgaria
USSR (Soviet Union)

468030   Bilateral Agreement   0 SUST 233
SIGNED: 5 Jul 47
HEADNOTE: TRADE & PAYMENTS
TOPIC: General Economic
PARTIES:
Bulgaria
USSR (Soviet Union)

468031   Bilateral Agreement   0 SUST 241
SIGNED: 17 Dec 47
HEADNOTE: POST & TELEGRAPH
TOPIC: Gen Communications
PARTIES:
Bulgaria
USSR (Soviet Union)

468032   Bilateral Agreement   0 SUST 241
SIGNED: 17 Dec 47
HEADNOTE: PARCEL POST
TOPIC: Postal Service
PARTIES:
Bulgaria
USSR (Soviet Union)

468035   Bilateral Agreement   0 SUST 251
SIGNED: 9 Aug 48
HEADNOTE: 65 MILLION CREDIT
TOPIC: Loans and Credits
PARTIES:
Bulgaria
USSR (Soviet Union)

468036   Bilateral Agreement   0 SUST 271
SIGNED: 18 Feb 50
HEADNOTE: TECHNICAL COOPERATION
TOPIC: Tech Assistance
PARTIES:
Bulgaria
USSR (Soviet Union)

468037   Bilateral Exchange   0 SUST 274
SIGNED: 24 May 50
HEADNOTE: JUDICIAL COOPERATION
TOPIC: Admin Cooperation
PARTIES:
Bulgaria
USSR (Soviet Union)

468039   Bilateral Agreement   0 SUST 281
SIGNED: 10 Apr 51
HEADNOTE: FISHERIES RESEARCH
TOPIC: Scientific Project
PARTIES:
Bulgaria
USSR (Soviet Union)

468040   Bilateral Agreement   0 SUST 285
SIGNED: 7 Mar 51
HEADNOTE: BULGARS IN SOVIET COLLEGES
TOPIC: Education
PARTIES:
Bulgaria
USSR (Soviet Union)

468041   Bilateral Agreement   0 SUST 317
SIGNED: 9 Oct 54
HEADNOTE: SALE SOVIET INDUSTRIAL STOCK
TOPIC: Specific Property

PARTIES:
Bulgaria
USSR (Soviet Union)

468042   Bilateral Agreement   0 SUST 342
SIGNED: 26 Nov 55
HEADNOTE: SALE SOVIET INDUSTRIAL STOCK
TOPIC: Specific Property
PARTIES:
Bulgaria
USSR (Soviet Union)

468043   Bilateral Agreement   0 SUST 348
SIGNED: 3 Feb 56
HEADNOTE: FINANCIAL & TECHNICAL AID
TOPIC: General Aid
PARTIES:
Bulgaria
USSR (Soviet Union)

468045   Bilateral Agreement   0 SUST 378
SIGNED: 20 Feb 57
HEADNOTE: TRADE & FINANCIAL
TOPIC: General Economic
PARTIES:
Bulgaria
USSR (Soviet Union)

468046   Bilateral Agreement   0 SUST 391
SIGNED: 19 Nov 57
HEADNOTE: 1960-70 TRADE
TOPIC: General Trade
PARTIES:
Bulgaria
USSR (Soviet Union)

468049   Bilateral Instrument   0 SUST 215
SIGNED: 16 Jul 46
HEADNOTE: SOVIET CLAIMS GERMAN ASSETS
TOPIC: Claims and Debts
PARTIES:
Austria
USSR (Soviet Union)

468050   Bilateral Exchange   0 SUST 200
SIGNED: 24 Oct 45
HEADNOTE: RESUME DIPLOMATIC RELATIONS
TOPIC: Consul/Citizenship
PARTIES:
Austria
USSR (Soviet Union)

468051   Bilateral Agreement   0 SUST 297
SIGNED: 17 Jul 53
HEADNOTE: POWER PLANT ASSETS TRANSFER
TOPIC: Specif Goods/Equip
PARTIES:
Austria
USSR (Soviet Union)

468052   Bilateral Exchange   0 SUST 298
SIGNED: 30 Jul 53
HEADNOTE: OCCUPATION COSTS
TOPIC: Milit Occupation
PARTIES:
Austria
USSR (Soviet Union)

468053   Bilateral Instrument   0 SUST 325
SIGNED: 15 Apr 55
HEADNOTE: OCCUPATION CONCLUSION
TOPIC: General Ad Hoc
PARTIES:
Austria
USSR (Soviet Union)

468054   Bilateral Treaty   0 SUST 328
SIGNED: 15 May 55
HEADNOTE: AUSTRIAN INDEPENDENCE
TOPIC: Recognition
PARTIES:
Austria
USSR (Soviet Union)

468055   Bilateral Protocol   0 SUST 335
SIGNED: 31 Aug 55
HEADNOTE: TRANSFER SOVIET ASSETS
TOPIC: Specific Property
PARTIES:
 Austria
 USSR (Soviet Union)

468058   Bilateral Exchange   0 SUST 444
SIGNED: 6 Dec 55
HEADNOTE: AUSTRIAN NEUTRALITY
TOPIC: General Amity
PARTIES:
 Austria
 USSR (Soviet Union)

468059   Bilateral Agreement   0 SUST 345
SIGNED: 28 Dec 55
HEADNOTE: PARCEL POST
TOPIC: Postal Service
PARTIES:
 Austria
 USSR (Soviet Union)

468060   Bilateral Instrument   0 SUST 382
SIGNED: 27 Apr 57
HEADNOTE: GENERAL RELATIONS
TOPIC: General Amity
PARTIES:
 Austria
 USSR (Soviet Union)

468061   Bilateral Exchange   0 SUST 245
SIGNED: 18 Feb 48
HEADNOTE: ESTABLISH RELATIONS
TOPIC: Consul/Citizenship
PARTIES:
 Burma
 USSR (Soviet Union)

468062   Bilateral Agreement   0 SUST 331
SIGNED: 1 Jul 55
HEADNOTE: COMMERCIAL
TOPIC: General Trade
PARTIES:
 Burma
 USSR (Soviet Union)

468063   Bilateral Instrument   0 SUST 352
SIGNED: 1 Apr 56
HEADNOTE: COMMODITY EXCHANGE
TOPIC: Commodity Trade
PARTIES:
 Burma
 USSR (Soviet Union)

468064   Bilateral Instrument   0 SUST 363
SIGNED: 7 Jul 56
HEADNOTE: HOSPITAL IN PHNOM-PENH
TOPIC: Direct Aid
PARTIES:
 Cambodia
 USSR (Soviet Union)

468065   Bilateral Agreement   0 SUST 384
SIGNED: 31 May 57
HEADNOTE: TRADE
TOPIC: General Trade
PARTIES:
 Cambodia
 USSR (Soviet Union)

468066   Bilateral Agreement   0 SUST 384
SIGNED: 31 May 57
HEADNOTE: CULTURAL & SCIENTIFIC COOPER-
 ATION
TOPIC: Health/Educ/Welfare
PARTIES:
 Cambodia
 USSR (Soviet Union)

468067   Bilateral Agreement   0 SUST 384
SIGNED: 31 May 57
HEADNOTE: PAYMENTS

TOPIC: Finance
PARTIES:
 Cambodia
 USSR (Soviet Union)

468068   Bilateral Exchange   0 SUST 263
SIGNED: 2 Oct 49
HEADNOTE: ESTABLISH RELATIONS
TOPIC: Consul/Citizenship
PARTIES:
 China People's Rep
 USSR (Soviet Union)

468069   Bilateral Agreement   0 SUST 268
SIGNED: 7 Feb 50
HEADNOTE: MAIL & PARCEL POST
TOPIC: Postal Service
PARTIES:
 China People's Rep
 USSR (Soviet Union)

468070   Bilateral Agreement   0 SUST 268
SIGNED: 7 Feb 50
HEADNOTE: TELEPHONE & TELEGRAPH
TOPIC: Telecommunications
PARTIES:
 China People's Rep
 USSR (Soviet Union)

468071   Bilateral Exchange   0 SUST 270
SIGNED: 14 Feb 50
HEADNOTE: INDUSTRIAL PROPERTY TRANSFER
TOPIC: Specific Property
PARTIES:
 China People's Rep
 USSR (Soviet Union)

468072   Bilateral Exchange   0 SUST 270
SIGNED: 14 Feb 50
HEADNOTE: MILITARY COMPOUND TRANSFER
TOPIC: Milit Installation
PARTIES:
 China People's Rep
 USSR (Soviet Union)

468073   Bilateral Agreement   0 SUST 272
SIGNED: 27 Mar 50
HEADNOTE: JOINT STOCK OIL COMPANY
TOPIC: Specific Property
PARTIES:
 China People's Rep
 USSR (Soviet Union)

468074   Bilateral Agreement   0 SUST 272
SIGNED: 27 Mar 50
HEADNOTE: JOINT STOCK METALS COMPANY
TOPIC: Specific Property
PARTIES:
 China People's Rep
 USSR (Soviet Union)

468075   Bilateral Agreement   0 SUST 272
SIGNED: 27 Mar 50
HEADNOTE: JOINT STOCK AVIATION COMPANY
TOPIC: Specific Property
PARTIES:
 China People's Rep
 USSR (Soviet Union)

468076   Bilateral Agreement   0 SUST 272
SIGNED: 27 Mar 50
HEADNOTE: TREATMENT SOVIET INSTRUCTORS
TOPIC: Privil/Immunities
PARTIES:
 China People's Rep
 USSR (Soviet Union)

468077   Bilateral Agreement   0 SUST 273
SIGNED: 19 Apr 50
HEADNOTE: TRADE
TOPIC: General Trade
PARTIES:
 China People's Rep
 USSR (Soviet Union)

468078   Bilateral Agreement   0 SUST 278
SIGNED: 25 Oct 50
HEADNOTE: TREATMENT SOVIET INSTRUCTORS
TOPIC: Privil/Immunities
PARTIES:
 China People's Rep
 USSR (Soviet Union)

468079   Bilateral Agreement   0 SUST 279
SIGNED: 2 Jan 51
HEADNOTE: BORDER RIVER NAVIGATION
TOPIC: Water Transport
PARTIES:
 China People's Rep
 USSR (Soviet Union)

468080   Bilateral Agreement   0 SUST 280
SIGNED: 14 Mar 51
HEADNOTE: RAIL TRANSPORT LINKS
TOPIC: Land Transport
PARTIES:
 China People's Rep
 USSR (Soviet Union)

468081   Bilateral Agreement   0 SUST 282
SIGNED: 28 Jul 51
HEADNOTE: JOINT STOCK SHIPBUILDING COM-
 PANY
TOPIC: Specific Property
PARTIES:
 China People's Rep
 USSR (Soviet Union)

468082   Bilateral Agreement   0 SUST 283
SIGNED: 6 Dec 51
HEADNOTE: TRAINING CHINESE TECHNICIANS
TOPIC: Education
PARTIES:
 China People's Rep
 USSR (Soviet Union)

468083   Bilateral Agreement   0 SUST 289
SIGNED: 9 Aug 52
HEADNOTE: TRAINING CHINESE TECHNICIANS
TOPIC: Education
PARTIES:
 China People's Rep
 USSR (Soviet Union)

468084   Bilateral Instrument   0 SUST 290
SIGNED: 15 Sep 52
HEADNOTE: TRANSFER CHANGCHUN RAILWAY
TOPIC: Specific Property
PARTIES:
 China People's Rep
 USSR (Soviet Union)

468085   Bilateral Agreement   0 SUST 294
SIGNED: 21 Mar 53
HEADNOTE: POWER STATION CONSTRUCTION
TOPIC: Direct Aid
PARTIES:
 China People's Rep
 USSR (Soviet Union)

468086   Bilateral Agreement   0 SUST 315
SIGNED: 21 Aug 54
HEADNOTE: RADIO BROADCAST COOPERATION
TOPIC: Mass Media
PARTIES:
 China People's Rep
 USSR (Soviet Union)

468087   Bilateral Instrument   0 SUST 317
SIGNED: 12 Oct 54
HEADNOTE: TRANSFER SOVIET JOINT STOCK
TOPIC: Specific Property
PARTIES:
 China People's Rep
 USSR (Soviet Union)

468088   Bilateral Agreement   0 SUST 318
SIGNED: 12 Oct 54

HEADNOTE: CULTURAL & SCIENTIFIC COOPER-
ATION
TOPIC: Health/Educ/Welfare
PARTIES:
  China People's Rep
  USSR (Soviet Union)

468089   Bilateral Instrument   0 SUST 318
SIGNED: 12 Oct 54
HEADNOTE: LANCHOW TO ALMA-ATA RAILWAY
TOPIC: General Ad Hoc
PARTIES:
  China People's Rep
  USSR (Soviet Union)

468090   Bilateral Agreement   0 SUST 318
SIGNED: 12 Oct 54
HEADNOTE: 520 MILLION RUBLES
TOPIC: Loans and Credits
PARTIES:
  China People's Rep
  USSR (Soviet Union)

468091   Bilateral Protocol   0 SUST 318
SIGNED: 12 Oct 54
HEADNOTE: TECHNICAL AID
TOPIC: Tech Assistance
PARTIES:
  China People's Rep
  USSR (Soviet Union)

468092   Bilateral Agreement   0 SUST 321
SIGNED: 30 Dec 54
HEADNOTE: ESTABLISH AIR COMMUNICATIONS
TOPIC: Air Transport
PARTIES:
  China People's Rep
  USSR (Soviet Union)

468093   Bilateral Convention   0 SUST 334
SIGNED: 16 Aug 55
HEADNOTE: COMBAT AGRICULTURAL DISEASES
TOPIC: Sanitation
PARTIES:
  China People's Rep
  USSR (Soviet Union)

468094   Bilateral Agreement   0 SUST 353
SIGNED: 7 Apr 56
HEADNOTE: 2.5 BILLION RUBLES SOVIET AID
TOPIC: Direct Aid
PARTIES:
  China People's Rep
  USSR (Soviet Union)

468095   Bilateral Agreement   0 SUST 353
SIGNED: 7 Apr 56
HEADNOTE: LANCHOW TO AKTOGAI RAILWAY
TOPIC: Direct Aid
PARTIES:
  China People's Rep
  USSR (Soviet Union)

468096   Bilateral Agreement   0 SUST 366
SIGNED: 18 Aug 56
HEADNOTE: EXPLORATION AMUR RIVER BASIN
TOPIC: Scientific Project
PARTIES:
  China People's Rep
  USSR (Soviet Union)

468099   Bilateral Agreement   0 SUST 200
SIGNED: 22 Oct 45
HEADNOTE: ESTABLISH MAIL & TELEGRAPH
TOPIC: Postal Service
PARTIES:
  Czechoslovakia
  USSR (Soviet Union)

468100   Bilateral Agreement   0 SUST 210
SIGNED: 12 Apr 46
HEADNOTE: TRADE
TOPIC: General Trade

PARTIES:
  Czechoslovakia
  USSR (Soviet Union)

468101   Bilateral Protocol   0 SUST 210
SIGNED: 12 Apr 46
HEADNOTE: PRE-WAR CLAIMS
TOPIC: Claims and Debts
PARTIES:
  Czechoslovakia
  USSR (Soviet Union)

468102   Bilateral Agreement   0 SUST 214
SIGNED: 10 Jul 46
HEADNOTE: CHOICE OF CITIZENSHIP
TOPIC: Consul/Citizenship
PARTIES:
  Czechoslovakia
  USSR (Soviet Union)

468103   Bilateral Instrument   0 SUST 234
SIGNED: 12 Jul 47
HEADNOTE: TRADE 1948-54
TOPIC: General Trade
PARTIES:
  Czechoslovakia
  USSR (Soviet Union)

468104   Bilateral Agreement   0 SUST 240
SIGNED: 11 Dec 47
HEADNOTE: SCIENTIFIC & TECHNICAL COOPER-
ATION
TOPIC: Scientific Project
PARTIES:
  Czechoslovakia
  USSR (Soviet Union)

468105   Bilateral Agreement   0 SUST 244
SIGNED: 9 Feb 48
HEADNOTE: TRADE DELIVERIES
TOPIC: General Trade
PARTIES:
  Czechoslovakia
  USSR (Soviet Union)

468106   Bilateral Instrument   0 SUST 255
SIGNED: 15 Dec 48
HEADNOTE: ECONOMIC RELATIONS
TOPIC: General Economic
PARTIES:
  Czechoslovakia
  USSR (Soviet Union)

468107   Bilateral Agreement   0 SUST 278
SIGNED: 3 Nov 50
HEADNOTE: FIVE YEAR ECONOMIC PLAN
TOPIC: General Economic
PARTIES:
  Czechoslovakia
  USSR (Soviet Union)

468108   Bilateral Agreement   0 SUST 282
SIGNED: 8 Aug 51
HEADNOTE: PARCEL POST
TOPIC: Postal Service
PARTIES:
  Czechoslovakia
  USSR (Soviet Union)

468109   Bilateral Agreement   0 SUST 286
SIGNED: 11 Apr 52
HEADNOTE: SOVIET COLLEGE FOR CZECHS
TOPIC: Education
PARTIES:
  Czechoslovakia
  USSR (Soviet Union)

468110   Bilateral Agreement   0 SUST 326
SIGNED: 23 Apr 55
HEADNOTE: ATOMIC ENERGY DEVELOPMENT
TOPIC: Atomic Energy
PARTIES:
  Czechoslovakia
  USSR (Soviet Union)

468111   Bilateral Agreement   0 SUST 376
SIGNED: 14 Jan 57
HEADNOTE: TRADE 1957
TOPIC: General Trade
PARTIES:
  Czechoslovakia
  USSR (Soviet Union)

468112   Bilateral Agreement   0 SUST 385
SIGNED: 6 Jul 57
HEADNOTE: UKRAINE INCORPORATION CLAIMS
TOPIC: Claims and Debts
PARTIES:
  Czechoslovakia
  USSR (Soviet Union)

468115   Bilateral Exchange   0 SUST 178
SIGNED: 16 May 45
HEADNOTE: RESUME DIPLOMATIC RELATIONS
TOPIC: Consul/Citizenship
PARTIES:
  Denmark
  USSR (Soviet Union)

468116   Bilateral Agreement   0 SUST 214
SIGNED: 8 Jul 46
HEADNOTE: TRADE & COMMERCE
TOPIC: General Trade
PARTIES:
  Denmark
  USSR (Soviet Union)

468117   Bilateral Agreement   0 SUST 217
SIGNED: 8 Aug 46
HEADNOTE: ESTABLISH TELEGRAPH COMMUNI-
CATION
TOPIC: Telecommunications
PARTIES:
  Denmark
  USSR (Soviet Union)

468118   Bilateral Protocol   0 SUST 217
SIGNED: 17 Aug 46
HEADNOTE: ARBITRATION METHODS
TOPIC: Dispute Settlement
PARTIES:
  Denmark
  USSR (Soviet Union)

468119   Bilateral Agreement   0 SUST 336
SIGNED: 17 Sep 55
HEADNOTE: CHANGE MISSIONS TO EMBASSIES
TOPIC: Consul/Citizenship
PARTIES:
  Denmark
  USSR (Soviet Union)

468120   Bilateral Agreement   0 SUST 350
SIGNED: 6 Mar 56
HEADNOTE: LIFESAVING IN BALTIC SEA
TOPIC: Health/Educ/Welfare
PARTIES:
  Denmark
  USSR (Soviet Union)

468121   Bilateral Exchange   0 SUST 174
SIGNED: 8 Mar 45
HEADNOTE: ESTABLISH DIPLOMATIC RELA-
TIONS
TOPIC: Consul/Citizenship
PARTIES:
  Dominican Republic
  USSR (Soviet Union)

468122   Bilateral Exchange   0 SUST 180
SIGNED: 16 Jun 45
HEADNOTE: ESTABLISH DIPLOMATIC RELA-
TIONS
TOPIC: Consul/Citizenship
PARTIES:
  Ecuador
  USSR (Soviet Union)

468123 Bilateral Protocol **0 SUST 246**
SIGNED: 3 Mar 48
HEADNOTE: MOST FAVORED NATION
TOPIC: Mostfavored Nation
PARTIES:
  United Arab Rep
  USSR (Soviet Union)

468124 Bilateral Agreement **0 SUST 299**
SIGNED: 18 Aug 53
HEADNOTE: PAYMENTS
TOPIC: Finance
PARTIES:
  United Arab Rep
  USSR (Soviet Union)

468125 Bilateral Agreement **0 SUST 308**
SIGNED: 23 Mar 54
HEADNOTE: CHANGE MISSIONS TO EMBASSIES
TOPIC: Consul/Citizenship
PARTIES:
  United Arab Rep
  USSR (Soviet Union)

468126 Bilateral Agreement **0 SUST 309**
SIGNED: 27 Mar 54
HEADNOTE: TRADE
TOPIC: General Trade
PARTIES:
  United Arab Rep
  USSR (Soviet Union)

468127 Bilateral Exchange **0 SUST 309**
SIGNED: 27 Mar 54
HEADNOTE: TRADE SHIPMENTS TRANSPORT
TOPIC: General Trade
PARTIES:
  United Arab Rep
  USSR (Soviet Union)

468128 Bilateral Exchange **0 SUST 309**
SIGNED: 27 Mar 54
HEADNOTE: TRADE AGENT EMPLOYMENT
TOPIC: Non-ILO Labor
PARTIES:
  United Arab Rep
  USSR (Soviet Union)

468129 Bilateral Agreement **0 SUST 363**
SIGNED: 12 Jul 56
HEADNOTE: PEACEFUL ATOMIC DEVELOPMENT
TOPIC: Atomic Energy
PARTIES:
  United Arab Rep
  USSR (Soviet Union)

468130 Bilateral Agreement **0 SUST 391**
SIGNED: 19 Oct 57
HEADNOTE: CULTURAL COOPERATION
TOPIC: Culture
PARTIES:
  United Arab Rep
  USSR (Soviet Union)

468131 Bilateral Instrument **0 SUST 357**
SIGNED: 2 Jun 56
HEADNOTE: CHANGE MISSIONS TO EMBASSIES
TOPIC: Consul/Citizenship
PARTIES:
  Ethiopia
  USSR (Soviet Union)

468132 Bilateral Agreement **0 SUST 170**
SIGNED: 31 Jan 45
HEADNOTE: TRADE
TOPIC: General Trade
PARTIES:
  Finland
  USSR (Soviet Union)

468133 Bilateral Protocol **0 SUST 200**
SIGNED: 26 Oct 45
HEADNOTE: PECHENGA BOUNDARY
TOPIC: Territory Boundary

PARTIES:
  Finland
  USSR (Soviet Union)

468134 Bilateral Agreement **0 SUST 211**
SIGNED: 30 Apr 46
HEADNOTE: POSER STATION SITE
TOPIC: Specific Property
PARTIES:
  Finland
  USSR (Soviet Union)

468135 Bilateral Agreement **0 SUST 217**
SIGNED: 19 Aug 46
HEADNOTE: TELEGRAPH & TELEPHONE
TOPIC: Telecommunications
PARTIES:
  Finland
  USSR (Soviet Union)

468136 Bilateral Agreement **0 SUST 222**
SIGNED: 5 Dec 46
HEADNOTE: TRADE & PAYMENTS
TOPIC: General Economic
PARTIES:
  Finland
  USSR (Soviet Union)

468137 Bilateral Agreement **0 SUST 217**
SIGNED: 19 Aug 46
HEADNOTE: POSTAL EXCHANGE
TOPIC: Postal Service
PARTIES:
  Finland
  USSR (Soviet Union)

468138 Bilateral Agreement **0 SUST 225**
SIGNED: 3 Feb 47
HEADNOTE: TRANSFER FORMER GERMAN
FUNDS
TOPIC: Finance
PARTIES:
  Finland
  USSR (Soviet Union)

468139 Bilateral Protocol **0 SUST 225**
SIGNED: 3 Feb 47
HEADNOTE: JOINT STOCK FIBER COMPANY
TOPIC: Specific Property
PARTIES:
  Finland
  USSR (Soviet Union)

468140 Bilateral Protocol **0 SUST 226**
SIGNED: 3 Feb 47
HEADNOTE: JOINT STOCK METALS COMPANY
TOPIC: Specific Property
PARTIES:
  Finland
  USSR (Soviet Union)

468141 Bilateral Agreement **0 SUST 231**
SIGNED: 24 Apr 47
HEADNOTE: REGULATION OF LAKE INARI
TOPIC: Specific Resources
PARTIES:
  Finland
  USSR (Soviet Union)

468142 Bilateral Agreement **0 SUST 232**
SIGNED: 24 May 47
HEADNOTE: NAVAL BASE RAIL RIGHT-OF-WAY
TOPIC: Specific Property
PARTIES:
  Finland
  USSR (Soviet Union)

468143 Bilateral Protocol **0 SUST 239**
SIGNED: 7 Dec 47
HEADNOTE: BORDER DEMARCATION
TOPIC: Territory Boundary
PARTIES:
  Finland
  USSR (Soviet Union)

468144 Bilateral Agreement **0 SUST 242**
SIGNED: 19 Dec 47
HEADNOTE: RAIL TRANSPORT
TOPIC: Land Transport
PARTIES:
  Finland
  USSR (Soviet Union)

468145 Bilateral Exchange **0 SUST 246**
SIGNED: 16 Mar 48
HEADNOTE: RENEWAL PRE-WAR TREATIES
TOPIC: Admin Cooperation
PARTIES:
  Finland
  USSR (Soviet Union)

468146 Bilateral Convention **0 SUST 249**
SIGNED: 19 Jun 48
HEADNOTE: DISPUTE SETTLEMENT METHODS
TOPIC: Dispute Settlement
PARTIES:
  Finland
  USSR (Soviet Union)

468147 Bilateral Agreement **0 SUST 275**
SIGNED: 13 Jun 50
HEADNOTE: TRADE 1951-55
TOPIC: General Trade
PARTIES:
  Finland
  USSR (Soviet Union)

468148 Bilateral Protocol **0 SUST 311**
SIGNED: 29 Apr 54
HEADNOTE: MODIFIES 24 APR 47 AGREEMENT
TOPIC: Specific Resources
PARTIES:
  Finland
  USSR (Soviet Union)

468150 Bilateral Treaty **0 SUST 181**
SIGNED: 29 Jun 45
HEADNOTE: REPATRIATION OF CITIZENS
TOPIC: Refugees
PARTIES:
  France
  USSR (Soviet Union)

468151 Bilateral Agreement **0 SUST 205**
SIGNED: 29 Dec 45
HEADNOTE: COMMERCIAL
TOPIC: General Trade
PARTIES:
  France
  USSR (Soviet Union)

468155 Bilateral Agreement **0 SUST 313**
SIGNED: 29 Jun 54
HEADNOTE: AIR TRANSPORT
TOPIC: Air Transport
PARTIES:
  France
  USSR (Soviet Union)

468156 Bilateral Protocol **0 SUST 351**
SIGNED: 31 Mar 56
HEADNOTE: TRADE
TOPIC: General Trade
PARTIES:
  France
  USSR (Soviet Union)

468157 Bilateral Instrument **0 SUST 355**
SIGNED: 31 Mar 56
HEADNOTE: TRADE
TOPIC: Culture
PARTIES:
  France
  USSR (Soviet Union)

468158 Bilateral Agreement **0 SUST 377**
SIGNED: 11 Feb 57
HEADNOTE: TRADE 1957-59
TOPIC: General Trade

PARTIES:
France
USSR (Soviet Union)

468159   Bilateral Exchange   0 SUST 334
SIGNED: 13 Sep 55
HEADNOTE: ESTABLISH DIPLOMATIC RELA-
TIONS
TOPIC: Consul/Citizenship
PARTIES:
Germany, West
USSR (Soviet Union)

468160   Bilateral Exchange   0 SUST 274
SIGNED: 15 May 50
HEADNOTE: REPARATIONS REDUCTION
TOPIC: Reparations
PARTIES:
Germany, East
USSR (Soviet Union)

468161   Bilateral Instrument   0 SUST 274
SIGNED: 19 May 50
HEADNOTE: TRANSFER APPROPRIATED PLANTS
TOPIC: Claims and Debts
PARTIES:
Germany, East
USSR (Soviet Union)

468162   Bilateral Agreement   0 SUST 327
SIGNED: 28 Apr 55
HEADNOTE: ATOMIC ENERGY DEVELOPMENT
TOPIC: Atomic Energy
PARTIES:
Germany, East
USSR (Soviet Union)

468163   Bilateral Protocol   0 SUST 334
SIGNED: 25 Aug 55
HEADNOTE: RETURN ART TREASURES
TOPIC: Claims and Debts
PARTIES:
Germany, East
USSR (Soviet Union)

468164   Bilateral Exchange   0 SUST 338
SIGNED: 20 Sep 55
HEADNOTE: GERMAN PATROL DUTIES
TOPIC: Admin Cooperation
PARTIES:
Germany, East
USSR (Soviet Union)

468165   Bilateral Agreement   0 SUST 369
SIGNED: 12 Oct 56
HEADNOTE: MASS MEDIA COOPERATION
TOPIC: Mass Media
PARTIES:
Germany, East
USSR (Soviet Union)

468166   Bilateral Protocol   0 SUST 369
SIGNED: 12 Oct 56
HEADNOTE: TELEVISION COOPERATION
TOPIC: Mass Media
PARTIES:
Germany, East
USSR (Soviet Union)

68169   Bilateral Agreement   0 SUST 395
IGNED: 27 Dec 57
EADNOTE: CLAIMS SETTLEMENT METHODS
TOPIC: Admin Cooperation
PARTIES:
Germany, East
USSR (Soviet Union)

468170   Bilateral Agreement   0 SUST 298
SIGNED: 28 Jul 53
HEADNOTE: TRADE & PAYMENTS
TOPIC: General Economic
PARTIES:
Greece
USSR (Soviet Union)

468171   Bilateral Exchange   0 SUST 176
SIGNED: 19 Apr 45
HEADNOTE: BEGIN DIPLOMATIC RELATIONS
TOPIC: Consul/Citizenship
PARTIES:
Guatemala
USSR (Soviet Union)

468172   Bilateral Agreement   0 SUST 180
SIGNED: 15 Jun 45
HEADNOTE: REPARATIONS PAYMENTS
TOPIC: Reparations
PARTIES:
Hungary
USSR (Soviet Union)

468173   Bilateral Agreement   0 SUST 98
SIGNED: 25 Sep 45
HEADNOTE: RENEW DIPLOMATIC RELATIONS
TOPIC: Consul/Citizenship
PARTIES:
Hungary
USSR (Soviet Union)

468174   Bilateral Agreement   0 SUST 208
SIGNED: 29 Mar 46
HEADNOTE: JOINT STOCK AVIATION COMPANY
TOPIC: Specific Property
PARTIES:
Hungary
USSR (Soviet Union)

468175   Bilateral Agreement   0 SUST 208
SIGNED: 29 Mar 46
HEADNOTE: JOINT STOCK NAVIGATION COM-
PANY
TOPIC: Specific Property
PARTIES:
Hungary
USSR (Soviet Union)

468176   Bilateral Agreement   0 SUST 209
SIGNED: 8 Apr 46
HEADNOTE: JOINT STOCK OIL COMPANY
TOPIC: Specific Property
PARTIES:
Hungary
USSR (Soviet Union)

468177   Bilateral Agreement   0 SUST 209
SIGNED: 8 Apr 46
HEADNOTE: JOINT STOCK ALUMINUM COM-
PANY
TOPIC: Specific Property
PARTIES:
Hungary
USSR (Soviet Union)

468178   Bilateral Treaty   0 SUST 227
SIGNED: 10 Feb 47
HEADNOTE: PEACE
TOPIC: Peace/Disarmament
PARTIES:
Hungary
USSR (Soviet Union)

468179   Bilateral Agreement   0 SUST 234
SIGNED: 15 Jul 47
HEADNOTE: TRADE & PAYMENTS
TOPIC: General Economic
PARTIES:
Hungary
USSR (Soviet Union)

468180   Bilateral Agreement   0 SUST 236
SIGNED: 22 Sep 47
HEADNOTE: POSTAL & TELEGRAPH SERVICE
TOPIC: Gen Communications
PARTIES:
Hungary
USSR (Soviet Union)

468181   Bilateral Agreement   0 SUST 237
SIGNED: 1 Oct 47

468   HEADNOTE: PARCEL POST
TOPIC: Postal Service
PARTIES:
Hungary
USSR (Soviet Union)

468182   Bilateral Instrument   0 SUST 239
SIGNED: 9 Dec 47
HEADNOTE: ECONOMIC MATTERS
TOPIC: General Economic
PARTIES:
Hungary
USSR (Soviet Union)

468184   Bilateral Agreement   0 SUST 438
SIGNED: 1 Mar 48
HEADNOTE: MISSIONS TO EMBASSIES
TOPIC: Consul/Citizenship
PARTIES:
Hungary
USSR (Soviet Union)

468185   Bilateral Exchange   0 SUST 249
SIGNED: 7 Jun 48
HEADNOTE: REPARATIONS REDUCTION
TOPIC: Reparations
PARTIES:
Hungary
USSR (Soviet Union)

468186   Bilateral Protocol   0 SUST 253
SIGNED: 2 Oct 48
HEADNOTE: AMENDS 15 JUL 47 AGREEMENT
TOPIC: General Economic
PARTIES:
Hungary
USSR (Soviet Union)

468187   Bilateral Agreement   0 SUST 261
SIGNED: 26 Jul 49
HEADNOTE: SCIENTIFIC & TECHNICAL COOPER-
ATION
TOPIC: Scientific Project
PARTIES:
Hungary
USSR (Soviet Union)

468188   Bilateral Protocol   0 SUST 261
SIGNED: 30 Jul 49
HEADNOTE: BORDER REDEMARCATION
TOPIC: Territory Boundary
PARTIES:
Hungary
USSR (Soviet Union)

468189   Bilateral Treaty   0 SUST 271
SIGNED: 24 Feb 50
HEADNOTE: BORDER REGULATION
TOPIC: Admin Cooperation
PARTIES:
Hungary
USSR (Soviet Union)

468190   Bilateral Convention   0 SUST 271
SIGNED: 24 Feb 50
HEADNOTE: SETTLING BORDER DISPUTES
TOPIC: Admin Cooperation
PARTIES:
Hungary
USSR (Soviet Union)

468191   Bilateral Agreement   0 SUST 273
SIGNED: 12 Apr 50
HEADNOTE: RADIO BROADCAST COOPERATION
TOPIC: Mass Media
PARTIES:
Hungary
USSR (Soviet Union)

468192   Bilateral Convention   0 SUST 274
SIGNED: 9 Jun 50
HEADNOTE: FLOOD CONTROL
TOPIC: Specific Resources

PARTIES:
Hungary
USSR (Soviet Union)

468193   Bilateral Agreement   **0 SUST 284**
SIGNED: 23 Jan 52
HEADNOTE: TRADE 1952-55
TOPIC: General Trade
PARTIES:
Hungary
USSR (Soviet Union)

468194   Bilateral Agreement   **0 SUST 284**
SIGNED: 20 Jan 52
HEADNOTE: EQUIPMENT & TECHNICAL AID
TOPIC: General Aid
PARTIES:
Hungary
USSR (Soviet Union)

468195   Bilateral Agreement   **0 SUST 284**
SIGNED: 19 May 52
HEADNOTE: TRAINING HUNGARIAN STUDENTS
TOPIC: Education
PARTIES:
Hungary
USSR (Soviet Union)

468196   Bilateral Agreement   **0 SUST 291**
SIGNED: 30 Sep 52
HEADNOTE: TRANSFER SOVIET ENTERPRISES
TOPIC: Specific Property
PARTIES:
Hungary
USSR (Soviet Union)

468197   Bilateral Agreement   **0 SUST 319**
SIGNED: 6 Nov 54
HEADNOTE: SALE SOVIET JOINT STOCK
TOPIC: Finance
PARTIES:
Hungary
USSR (Soviet Union)

468198   Bilateral Agreement   **0 SUST 330**
SIGNED: 13 Jun 55
HEADNOTE: CIVIL ATOMIC ENERGY AID
TOPIC: Atomic Energy
PARTIES:
Hungary
USSR (Soviet Union)

468199   Bilateral Protocol   **0 SUST 385**
SIGNED: 14 Jun 56
HEADNOTE: SUPPLEMENTS 12 APR 50
TOPIC: Mass Media
PARTIES:
Hungary
USSR (Soviet Union)

468200   Bilateral Instrument   **0 SUST 368**
SIGNED: 5 Oct 56
HEADNOTE: 100 MILLION RUBLE LOAN
TOPIC: Loans and Credits
PARTIES:
Hungary
USSR (Soviet Union)

468201   Bilateral Agreement   **0 SUST 383**
SIGNED: 27 May 57
HEADNOTE: STATUS OF FORCES IN HUNGARY
TOPIC: Status of Forces
PARTIES:
Hungary
USSR (Soviet Union)

468204   Bilateral Agreement   **0 SUST 394**
SIGNED: 18 Dec 57
HEADNOTE: ECONOMIC & TECHNICAL AID
TOPIC: General Aid
PARTIES:
Hungary
USSR (Soviet Union)

468205   Bilateral Agreement   **0 SUST 298**
SIGNED: 1 Aug 53
HEADNOTE: TRADE & PAYMENTS
TOPIC: General Economic
PARTIES:
Iceland
USSR (Soviet Union)

468206   Bilateral Exchange   **0 SUST 307**
SIGNED: 5 Feb 54
HEADNOTE: REVISE 1 AUG 53 AGREEMENT
TOPIC: General Economic
PARTIES:
Iceland
USSR (Soviet Union)

468207   Bilateral Exchange   **0 SUST 338**
SIGNED: 23 Sep 55
HEADNOTE: REVISE 1 AUG 53 AGREEMENT
TOPIC: General Economic
PARTIES:
Iceland
USSR (Soviet Union)

468208   Bilateral Agreement   **0 SUST 343**
SIGNED: 3 Dec 55
HEADNOTE: MISSIONS TO EMBASSIES
TOPIC: Consul/Citizenship
PARTIES:
Iceland
USSR (Soviet Union)

468209   Bilateral Exchange   **0 SUST 231**
SIGNED: 7 Apr 47
HEADNOTE: ESTABLISH DIPLOMATIC RELA-
TIONS
TOPIC: Consul/Citizenship
PARTIES:
India
USSR (Soviet Union)

468211   Bilateral Exchange   **0 SUST 304**
SIGNED: 2 Dec 53
HEADNOTE: SOVIET TRADE MISSION
TOPIC: General Trade
PARTIES:
India
USSR (Soviet Union)

468212   Bilateral Agreement   **0 SUST 322**
SIGNED: 24 Jan 55
HEADNOTE: LOAN FOR METALS PLANT
TOPIC: Non-IBRD Project
PARTIES:
India
USSR (Soviet Union)

468213   Bilateral Instrument   **0 SUST 330**
SIGNED: 22 Jun 55
HEADNOTE: GENERAL RELATIONS
TOPIC: General Amity
PARTIES:
India
USSR (Soviet Union)

468214   Bilateral Agreement   **0 SUST 345**
SIGNED: 23 Dec 55
HEADNOTE: SALE TWENTY DRILL RIGS
TOPIC: Specif Goods/Equip
PARTIES:
India
USSR (Soviet Union)

468215   Bilateral Agreement   **0 SUST 352**
SIGNED: 6 Apr 56
HEADNOTE: ESTABLISH SHIPPING SERVICE
TOPIC: Water Transport
PARTIES:
India
USSR (Soviet Union)

468216   Bilateral Agreement   **0 SUST 356**
SIGNED: 21 May 56
HEADNOTE: SALE OIL DRILLING RIGS

TOPIC: Specif Goods/Equip
PARTIES:
India
USSR (Soviet Union)

468217   Bilateral Agreement   **0 SUST 391**
SIGNED: 9 Nov 57
HEADNOTE: LOAN & COMMERCIAL COOPER-
ATION
TOPIC: General Economic
PARTIES:
India
USSR (Soviet Union)

468218   Bilateral Exchange   **0 SUST 248**
SIGNED: 22 May 48
HEADNOTE: ESTABLISH CONSULAR RELATIONS
TOPIC: Consul/Citizenship
PARTIES:
Indonesia
USSR (Soviet Union)

468219   Bilateral Exchange   **0 SUST 268**
SIGNED: 3 Feb 50
HEADNOTE: ESTABLISH DIPLOMATIC RELA-
TIONS
TOPIC: Consul/Citizenship
PARTIES:
Indonesia
USSR (Soviet Union)

468220   Bilateral Exchange   **0 SUST 304**
SIGNED: 17 Dec 53
HEADNOTE: MOSCOW, DJAKARTA EMBASSIES
TOPIC: Consul/Citizenship
PARTIES:
Indonesia
USSR (Soviet Union)

468221   Bilateral Agreement   **0 SUST 366**
SIGNED: 18 Aug 56
HEADNOTE: COMMERCIAL AGREEMENT
TOPIC: General Economic
PARTIES:
Indonesia
USSR (Soviet Union)

468222   Bilateral Agreement   **0 SUST 367**
SIGNED: 12 Jun 56
HEADNOTE: MOST FAVORED NATION
TOPIC: Mostfavored Nation
PARTIES:
Indonesia
USSR (Soviet Union)

468223   Bilateral Agreement   **0 SUST 368**
SIGNED: 15 Sep 56
HEADNOTE: LOAN & TECHNICAL AID
TOPIC: General Aid
PARTIES:
Indonesia
USSR (Soviet Union)

468224   Bilateral Protocol   **0 SUST 199**
SIGNED: 3 Oct 45
HEADNOTE: PREVENTION CROP DISEASES
TOPIC: Sanitation
PARTIES:
Iran
USSR (Soviet Union)

468225   Bilateral Exchange   **0 SUST 2**
SIGNED: 4 Nov 50
HEADNOTE: RENEW 25 MAR 40 AGREEMENTS
TOPIC: General Trade
PARTIES:
Iran
USSR (Soviet Union)

468227   Bilateral Exchange   **0 SUST 3**
SIGNED: 2 Dec 54
HEADNOTE: PAYMENT
TOPIC: Finance

PARTIES:
Iran
USSR (Soviet Union)

468228   Bilateral Exchange   0 SUST 320
SIGNED: 2 Dec 54
HEADNOTE: BORDER RECTIFICATION
TOPIC: Territory Boundary
PARTIES:
Iran
USSR (Soviet Union)

468229   Bilateral Agreement   0 SUST 323
SIGNED: 15 Feb 55
HEADNOTE: WHEAT SALE
TOPIC: Commodity Trade
PARTIES:
Iran
USSR (Soviet Union)

468230   Bilateral Agreement   0 SUST 329
SIGNED: 9 Jun 55
HEADNOTE: PEHLEVI PORT LAND LEASE
TOPIC: Specific Property
PARTIES:
Iran
USSR (Soviet Union)

468231   Bilateral Instrument   0 SUST 381
SIGNED: 11 Apr 57
HEADNOTE: BORDER REDEMARCATION
TOPIC: Territory Boundary
PARTIES:
Iran
USSR (Soviet Union)

468232   Bilateral Exchange   0 SUST 381
SIGNED: 16 Apr 57
HEADNOTE: TRADE LISTS
TOPIC: General Trade
PARTIES:
Iran
USSR (Soviet Union)

468233   Bilateral Agreement   0 SUST 382
SIGNED: 27 Apr 57
HEADNOTE: GOODS TRANSIT
TOPIC: General Trade
PARTIES:
Iran
USSR (Soviet Union)

468235   Bilateral Agreement   0 SUST 387
SIGNED: 11 Aug 57
HEADNOTE: ARAX & ARTEK RIVER USE
TOPIC: Specific Resources
PARTIES:
Iran
USSR (Soviet Union)

468236   Bilateral Exchange   0 SUST 248
SIGNED: 18 May 48
HEADNOTE: RECOGNITION
TOPIC: Recognition
PARTIES:
Israel
USSR (Soviet Union)

468237   Bilateral Exchange   0 SUST 248
SIGNED: 26 May 48
HEADNOTE: ESTABLISH DIPLOMATIC MISSION
TOPIC: Consul/Citizenship
PARTIES:
Israel
USSR (Soviet Union)

468238   Bilateral Exchange   0 SUST 297
SIGNED: 15 Jul 53
HEADNOTE: RENEW DIPLOMATIC RELATIONS
TOPIC: Consul/Citizenship
PARTIES:
Israel
USSR (Soviet Union)

468239   Bilateral Exchange   0 SUST 312
SIGNED: 13 May 54
HEADNOTE: MISSIONS TO EMBASSIES
TOPIC: Consul/Citizenship
PARTIES:
Israel
USSR (Soviet Union)

468240   Bilateral Treaty   0 SUST 255
SIGNED: 11 Dec 48
HEADNOTE: REPARATIONS
TOPIC: Reparations
PARTIES:
Italy
USSR (Soviet Union)

468241   Bilateral Agreement   0 SUST 255
SIGNED: 11 Dec 48
HEADNOTE: PAYMENTS
TOPIC: Finance
PARTIES:
Italy
USSR (Soviet Union)

468242   Bilateral Agreement   0 SUST 224
SIGNED: 19 Aug 46
HEADNOTE: REPATRIATION WAR PRISONERS
TOPIC: Refugees
PARTIES:
Japan
USSR (Soviet Union)

468243   Bilateral Instrument   0 SUST 380
SIGNED: 6 Apr 57
HEADNOTE: NORTHWEST PACIFIC FISHING
TOPIC: Specific Resources
PARTIES:
Japan
USSR (Soviet Union)

468245   Bilateral Agreement   0 SUST 392
SIGNED: 6 Dec 57
HEADNOTE: TRADE & PAYMENTS
TOPIC: General Economic
PARTIES:
Japan
USSR (Soviet Union)

468246   Bilateral Exchange   0 SUST 253
SIGNED: 18 Sep 48
HEADNOTE: WITHDRAWAL OF FORCES
TOPIC: Milit Occupation
PARTIES:
Korea, North
USSR (Soviet Union)

468247   Bilateral Exchange   0 SUST 253
SIGNED: 12 Oct 48
HEADNOTE: DIPLOMATIC & TRADE RELATIONS
TOPIC: General Amity
PARTIES:
Korea, North
USSR (Soviet Union)

468248   Bilateral Instrument   0 SUST 257
SIGNED: 17 Mar 49
HEADNOTE: ECONOMIC RELATIONS
TOPIC: General Economic
PARTIES:
Korea, North
USSR (Soviet Union)

468249   Bilateral Agreement   0 SUST 287
SIGNED: 6 May 52
HEADNOTE: KOREANS IN SOVIET COLLEGES
TOPIC: Education
PARTIES:
Korea, North
USSR (Soviet Union)

468250   Bilateral Instrument   0 SUST 302
SIGNED: 19 Jun 53
HEADNOTE: AID
TOPIC: Direct Aid

PARTIES:
Korea, North
USSR (Soviet Union)

468251   Bilateral Agreement   0 SUST 321
SIGNED: 28 Dec 54
HEADNOTE: MAIL & POST EXCHANGE
TOPIC: Postal Service
PARTIES:
Korea, North
USSR (Soviet Union)

468252   Bilateral Agreement   0 SUST 321
SIGNED: 28 Dec 54
HEADNOTE: TELEGRAPH & TELEPHONE COMMU-
NICATIONS
TOPIC: Telecommunications
PARTIES:
Korea, North
USSR (Soviet Union)

468253   Bilateral Instrument   0 SUST 329
SIGNED: 31 May 55
HEADNOTE: JOINT STOCK TRANSFER
TOPIC: Finance
PARTIES:
Korea, North
USSR (Soviet Union)

468254   Bilateral Agreement   0 SUST 335
SIGNED: 31 Aug 55
HEADNOTE: JOINT STOCK TRANSFER
TOPIC: Finance
PARTIES:
Korea, North
USSR (Soviet Union)

468255   Bilateral Convention   0 SUST 342
SIGNED: 30 Nov 55
HEADNOTE: PREVENTION CROP DISEASES
TOPIC: Sanitation
PARTIES:
Korea, North
USSR (Soviet Union)

468256   Bilateral Agreement   0 SUST 343
SIGNED: 9 Dec 55
HEADNOTE: AIR TRANSPORT
TOPIC: Air Transport
PARTIES:
Korea, North
USSR (Soviet Union)

468257   Bilateral Instrument   0 SUST 363
SIGNED: 12 Jul 56
HEADNOTE: AID
TOPIC: Direct Aid
PARTIES:
Korea, North
USSR (Soviet Union)

468258   Bilateral Instrument   0 SUST 382
SIGNED: 25 Apr 57
HEADNOTE: TRANSFER MEDICAL FACILITIES
TOPIC: Specific Property
PARTIES:
Korea, North
USSR (Soviet Union)

468259   Bilateral Agreement   0 SUST 387
SIGNED: 14 Aug 57
HEADNOTE: TECHNICAL AID
TOPIC: Tech Assistance
PARTIES:
Korea, North
USSR (Soviet Union)

468260   Bilateral Protocol   0 SUST 387
SIGNED: 14 Aug 57
HEADNOTE: EXPAND FERTILIZER PRODUCTION
TOPIC: Non-IBRD Project
PARTIES:
Korea, North
USSR (Soviet Union)

468261   Bilateral Agreement   0 SUST 390
SIGNED: 11 Oct 57
HEADNOTE: EDUCATIONAL EXCHANGE
TOPIC: Education
PARTIES:
   Korea, North
   USSR (Soviet Union)

468262   Bilateral Convention   0 SUST 390
SIGNED: 14 Oct 57
HEADNOTE: BORDER REGULATION
TOPIC: Admin Cooperation
PARTIES:
   Korea, North
   USSR (Soviet Union)

468266   Bilateral Agreement   0 SUST 439
SIGNED: 24 Feb 49
HEADNOTE: OIL RESERVES & PROSPECTING
TOPIC: Specific Resources
PARTIES:
   Mongolia
   USSR (Soviet Union)

468267   Bilateral Agreement   0 SUST 439
SIGNED: 12 Mar 49
HEADNOTE: JOINT STOCK MINING COMPANY
TOPIC: Specific Property
PARTIES:
   Mongolia
   USSR (Soviet Union)

468268   Bilateral Agreement   0 SUST 260
SIGNED: 6 Jun 49
HEADNOTE: JOINT STOCK RAILROAD COMPANY
TOPIC: Specific Property
PARTIES:
   Mongolia
   USSR (Soviet Union)

468269   Bilateral Agreement   0 SUST 439
SIGNED: 6 Jun 49
HEADNOTE: RAILWAY CONSTRUCTION LOAN
TOPIC: Loans and Credits
PARTIES:
   Mongolia
   USSR (Soviet Union)

468270   Bilateral Agreement   0 SUST 265
SIGNED: 9 Dec 49
HEADNOTE: TRADE 1950-54
TOPIC: General Trade
PARTIES:
   Mongolia
   USSR (Soviet Union)

468271   Bilateral Protocol   0 SUST 439
SIGNED: 1 Nov 50
HEADNOTE: SUPPLEMENTS 6 JUN 49
TOPIC: Specific Property
PARTIES:
   Mongolia
   USSR (Soviet Union)

468272   Bilateral Agreement   0 SUST 440
SIGNED: 21 Dec 51
HEADNOTE: PAYMENT SOVIET SPECIALISTS
TOPIC: Non-ILO Labor
PARTIES:
   Mongolia
   USSR (Soviet Union)

468273   Bilateral Agreement   0 SUST 440
SIGNED: 29 Dec 51
HEADNOTE: TRADE DELIVERY CONDITIONS
TOPIC: General Trade
PARTIES:
   Mongolia
   USSR (Soviet Union)

468274   Bilateral Protocol   0 SUST 440
SIGNED: 13 Jun 52
HEADNOTE: TECHNICAL AID
TOPIC: Tech Assistance

PARTIES:
   Mongolia
   USSR (Soviet Union)

468275   Bilateral Protocol   0 SUST 441
SIGNED: 8 Apr 53
HEADNOTE: SUPPLEMENTS 15 SEP 52
TOPIC: Specific Property
PARTIES:
   Mongolia
   USSR (Soviet Union)

468277   Bilateral Agreement   0 SUST 286
SIGNED: 30 Apr 52
HEADNOTE: MONGOLS IN SOVIET COLLEGES
TOPIC: Education
PARTIES:
   Mongolia
   USSR (Soviet Union)

468278   Bilateral Agreement   0 SUST 301
SIGNED: 11 Sep 53
HEADNOTE: RADIO BROADCAST COOPERATION
TOPIC: Mass Media
PARTIES:
   Mongolia
   USSR (Soviet Union)

468279   Bilateral Agreement   0 SUST 319
SIGNED: 19 Nov 54
HEADNOTE: TRADE 1955-57
TOPIC: General Trade
PARTIES:
   Mongolia
   USSR (Soviet Union)

468280   Bilateral Agreement   0 SUST 443
SIGNED: 12 Aug 55
HEADNOTE: LOAN & TECHNICAL AID
TOPIC: General Aid
PARTIES:
   Mongolia
   USSR (Soviet Union)

468281   Bilateral Protocol   0 SUST 340
SIGNED: 17 Oct 55
HEADNOTE: RAIL COMMUNICATIONS
TOPIC: Land Transport
PARTIES:
   Mongolia
   USSR (Soviet Union)

468282   Bilateral Agreement   0 SUST 373
SIGNED: 1 Dec 56
HEADNOTE: AIR COMMUNICATIONS
TOPIC: Air Transport
PARTIES:
   Mongolia
   USSR (Soviet Union)

468283   Bilateral Protocol   0 SUST 381
SIGNED: 16 Apr 57
HEADNOTE: SUPPLEMENTS 6 JUN 49
TOPIC: Specific Property
PARTIES:
   Mongolia
   USSR (Soviet Union)

468284   Bilateral Agreement   0 SUST 381
SIGNED: 22 Apr 57
HEADNOTE: AIR TRANSPORT
TOPIC: Air Transport
PARTIES:
   Mongolia
   USSR (Soviet Union)

468285   Bilateral Agreement   0 SUST 382
SIGNED: 20 Apr 57
HEADNOTE: AIR TRANSPORT TECHNICAL COOP-
   ERATION
TOPIC: Air Transport
PARTIES:
   Mongolia
   USSR (Soviet Union)

468286   Bilateral Protocol   0 SUST 393
SIGNED: 16 Dec 57
HEADNOTE: CULTURAL & SCIENTIFIC COOPER-
   ATION
TOPIC: Health/Educ/Welfare
PARTIES:
   Mongolia
   USSR (Soviet Union)

468287   Bilateral Treaty   0 SUST 394
SIGNED: 17 Dec 57
HEADNOTE: TREATY OF COMMERCE
TOPIC: General Trade
PARTIES:
   Mongolia
   USSR (Soviet Union)

468288   Bilateral Agreement   0 SUST 394
SIGNED: 17 Dec 57
HEADNOTE: TRADE 1958-60
TOPIC: General Trade
PARTIES:
   Mongolia
   USSR (Soviet Union)

468289   Bilateral Protocol   0 SUST 381
SIGNED: 18 Apr 57
HEADNOTE: TRADE
TOPIC: General Trade
PARTIES:
   Morocco
   USSR (Soviet Union)

468291   Bilateral Protocol   0 SUST 359
SIGNED: 27 Jun 56
HEADNOTE: TRADE
TOPIC: General Trade
PARTIES:
   Netherlands
   USSR (Soviet Union)

468292   Bilateral Agreement   0 SUST 228
SIGNED: 11 Feb 47
HEADNOTE: TELEGRAPH & TELEPHONE COMMU-
   NICATIONS
TOPIC: Telecommunications
PARTIES:
   Norway
   USSR (Soviet Union)

468293   Bilateral Agreement   0 SUST 229
SIGNED: 11 Feb 47
HEADNOTE: PARCEL POST
TOPIC: Postal Service
PARTIES:
   Norway
   USSR (Soviet Union)

468294   Bilateral Agreement   0 SUST 441
SIGNED: 2 Jul 53
HEADNOTE: WAR GRAVES CARE
TOPIC: Other Military
PARTIES:
   Norway
   USSR (Soviet Union)

468295   Bilateral Protocol   0 SUST 341
SIGNED: 15 Nov 55
HEADNOTE: TRADE 1956-58
TOPIC: General Trade
PARTIES:
   Norway
   USSR (Soviet Union)

468298   Bilateral Protocol   0 SUST 384
SIGNED: 7 Jun 57
HEADNOTE: DEVELOP PASVIK-ELV RIVER
TOPIC: Specific Resources
PARTIES:
   Norway
   USSR (Soviet Union)

468299   Bilateral Protocol   0 SUST 386
SIGNED: 1 Aug 57

HEADNOTE: SEA BOUNDARY DEMARCATION
TOPIC: Territory Boundary
PARTIES:
 Norway
 USSR (Soviet Union)

468301 Bilateral Instrument **0 SUST 392**
SIGNED: 29 Nov 57
HEADNOTE: VRANGER FJORD BOUNDARY
TOPIC: Territory Boundary
PARTIES:
 Norway
 USSR (Soviet Union)

468303 Bilateral Exchange **0 SUST 248**
SIGNED: 1 May 48
HEADNOTE: ESTABLISH DIPLOMATIC RELA-
TIONS
TOPIC: Consul/Citizenship
PARTIES:
 Pakistan
 USSR (Soviet Union)

468304 Bilateral Agreement **0 SUST 359**
SIGNED: 27 Jun 56
HEADNOTE: TRADE
TOPIC: General Trade
PARTIES:
 Pakistan
 USSR (Soviet Union)

468305 Bilateral Exchange **0 SUST 169**
SIGNED: 5 Jan 45
HEADNOTE: ESTABLISH DIPLOMATIC RELA-
TIONS
TOPIC: Consul/Citizenship
PARTIES:
 Poland
 USSR (Soviet Union)

468306 Bilateral Agreement **0 SUST 182**
SIGNED: 6 Jul 45
HEADNOTE: CITIZENSHIP DETERMINATION
TOPIC: Consul/Citizenship
PARTIES:
 Poland
 USSR (Soviet Union)

468307 Bilateral Treaty **0 SUST 182**
SIGNED: 7 Jul 45
HEADNOTE: COMMERCE & NAVIGATION
TOPIC: General Trade
PARTIES:
 Poland
 USSR (Soviet Union)

468308 Bilateral Agreement **0 SUST 183**
SIGNED: 11 Jul 45
HEADNOTE: RAILWAY MANAGEMNT TRANSFER
TOPIC: Admin Cooperation
PARTIES:
 Poland
 USSR (Soviet Union)

468309 Bilateral Agreement **0 SUST 193**
SIGNED: 16 Aug 45
HEADNOTE: REPARATIONS
TOPIC: Reparations
PARTIES:
 Poland
 USSR (Soviet Union)

468310 Bilateral Agreement **0 SUST 201**
SIGNED: 23 Nov 45
HEADNOTE: ESTABLISH RAIL COMMUNICATION
TOPIC: Land Transport
PARTIES:
 Poland
 USSR (Soviet Union)

468311 Bilateral Agreement **0 SUST 206**
SIGNED: 8 Feb 46
HEADNOTE: GRAIN ON CREDIT
TOPIC: Loans and Credits

PARTIES:
 Poland
 USSR (Soviet Union)

468312 Bilateral Agreement **0 SUST 207**
SIGNED: 20 Mar 46
HEADNOTE: POSTAL & TELEGRAPH
TOPIC: Gen Communications
PARTIES:
 Poland
 USSR (Soviet Union)

468313 Bilateral Agreement **0 SUST 210**
SIGNED: 12 Apr 46
HEADNOTE: TRADE
TOPIC: General Trade
PARTIES:
 Poland
 USSR (Soviet Union)

468314 Bilateral Agreement **0 SUST 230**
SIGNED: 5 Mar 47
HEADNOTE: LOAN
TOPIC: Loans and Credits
PARTIES:
 Poland
 USSR (Soviet Union)

468315 Bilateral Agreement **0 SUST 230**
SIGNED: 5 Mar 47
HEADNOTE: FINANCIAL SETTLEMENTS
TOPIC: Finance
PARTIES:
 Poland
 USSR (Soviet Union)

468316 Bilateral Agreement **0 SUST 230**
SIGNED: 5 Mar 47
HEADNOTE: COAL DELIVERIES
TOPIC: Commodity Trade
PARTIES:
 Poland
 USSR (Soviet Union)

468317 Bilateral Agreement **0 SUST 230**
SIGNED: 5 Mar 47
HEADNOTE: ROLLING STOCK TRANSFER
TOPIC: Specif Goods/Equip
PARTIES:
 Poland
 USSR (Soviet Union)

468318 Bilateral Agreement **0 SUST 230**
SIGNED: 5 Mar 47
HEADNOTE: SCIENTIFIC COLLABORATION
TOPIC: Tech Assistance
PARTIES:
 Poland
 USSR (Soviet Union)

468319 Bilateral Agreement **0 SUST 230**
SIGNED: 5 Mar 47
HEADNOTE: MILITARY EQUIPMENT ON CREDIT
TOPIC: Milit Assistance
PARTIES:
 Poland
 USSR (Soviet Union)

468320 Bilateral Protocol **0 SUST 232**
SIGNED: 6 May 47
HEADNOTE: REPATRIATION
TOPIC: Refugees
PARTIES:
 Poland
 USSR (Soviet Union)

468321 Bilateral Protocol **0 SUST 232**
SIGNED: 30 Apr 47
HEADNOTE: BORDER DEMARCATION
TOPIC: Territory Boundary
PARTIES:
 Poland
 USSR (Soviet Union)

468322 Bilateral Agreement **0 SUST 235**
SIGNED: 4 Aug 47
HEADNOTE: TRADE
TOPIC: General Trade
PARTIES:
 Poland
 USSR (Soviet Union)

468323 Bilateral Agreement **0 SUST 237**
SIGNED: 1 Oct 47
HEADNOTE: PARCEL POST
TOPIC: Postal Service
PARTIES:
 Poland
 USSR (Soviet Union)

468324 Bilateral Agreement **0 SUST 243**
SIGNED: 26 Jan 48
HEADNOTE: TRADE 1948-52
TOPIC: General Trade
PARTIES:
 Poland
 USSR (Soviet Union)

468325 Bilateral Agreement **0 SUST 244**
SIGNED: 26 Jan 48
HEADNOTE: GOODS ON CREDIT
TOPIC: Loans and Credits
PARTIES:
 Poland
 USSR (Soviet Union)

468327 Bilateral Agreement **0 SUST 263**
SIGNED: 22 Oct 49
HEADNOTE: RADIO BROADCAST COOPERATION
TOPIC: Mass Media
PARTIES:
 Poland
 USSR (Soviet Union)

468328 Bilateral Agreement **0 SUST 275**
SIGNED: 29 Jun 50
HEADNOTE: TRADE 1953-58
TOPIC: General Trade
PARTIES:
 Poland
 USSR (Soviet Union)

468329 Bilateral Agreement **0 SUST 275**
SIGNED: 29 Jun 50
HEADNOTE: EQUIPMENT ON CREDIT 1951-58
TOPIC: Loans and Credits
PARTIES:
 Poland
 USSR (Soviet Union)

468332 Bilateral Agreement **0 SUST 285**
SIGNED: 29 Feb 52
HEADNOTE: TRADE DELIVERY CONDITIONS
TOPIC: General Trade
PARTIES:
 Poland
 USSR (Soviet Union)

468333 Bilateral Agreement **0 SUST 285**
SIGNED: 5 Apr 52
HEADNOTE: WARSAW CULTURE PALACE
TOPIC: Culture
PARTIES:
 Poland
 USSR (Soviet Union)

468334 Bilateral Agreement **0 SUST 287**
SIGNED: 19 May 52
HEADNOTE: POLES IN SOVIET COLLEGES
TOPIC: Education
PARTIES:
 Poland
 USSR (Soviet Union)

468335 Bilateral Protocol **0 SUST 301**
SIGNED: 5 Sep 53
HEADNOTE: SUPPLEMENTS 22 OCT 49
TOPIC: Mass Media

PARTIES:
Poland
USSR (Soviet Union)

468336   Bilateral Agreement   **0 SUST 323**
SIGNED: 18 Feb 55
HEADNOTE: ESTABLISH AIR SERVICE
TOPIC: Air Transport
PARTIES:
Poland
USSR (Soviet Union)

468337   Bilateral Agreement   **0 SUST 326**
SIGNED: 23 Apr 55
HEADNOTE: PEACEFUL ATOMIC ENERGY AID
TOPIC: Atomic Energy
PARTIES:
Poland
USSR (Soviet Union)

468338   Bilateral Protocol   **0 SUST 349**
SIGNED: 7 Feb 56
HEADNOTE: MEDIA COOPERATION EXPANSION
TOPIC: Mass Media
PARTIES:
Poland
USSR (Soviet Union)

468339   Bilateral Agreement   **0 SUST 368**
SIGNED: 18 Sep 56
HEADNOTE: CREDIT
TOPIC: Loans and Credits
PARTIES:
Poland
USSR (Soviet Union)

468340   Bilateral Agreement   **0 SUST 379**
SIGNED: 27 Mar 57
HEADNOTE: EDUCATIONAL EXCHANGE
TOPIC: Education
PARTIES:
Poland
USSR (Soviet Union)

468341   Bilateral Agreement   **0 SUST 388**
SIGNED: 23 May 57
HEADNOTE: EDUCATIONAL EXCHANGE
TOPIC: Education
PARTIES:
Poland
USSR (Soviet Union)

468344   Bilateral Agreement   **0 SUST 169**
SIGNED: 16 Jan 45
HEADNOTE: 300 MILLION REPARATIONS
TOPIC: Reparations
PARTIES:
Romania
USSR (Soviet Union)

468345   Bilateral Exchange   **0 SUST 174**
SIGNED: 9 Mar 45
HEADNOTE: ROMANIAN TRANSYLVANIA ADMIN-
ISTRATION
TOPIC: Admin Cooperation
PARTIES:
Romania
USSR (Soviet Union)

468346   Bilateral Agreement   **0 SUST 178**
SIGNED: 8 May 45
HEADNOTE: TRADE
TOPIC: General Trade
PARTIES:
Romania
USSR (Soviet Union)

468347   Bilateral Protocol   **0 SUST 178**
SIGNED: 8 May 45
HEADNOTE: LIQUIDATE USSR BANK ACCOUNTS
TOPIC: Finance
PARTIES:
Romania
USSR (Soviet Union)

468348   Bilateral Agreement   **0 SUST 183**
SIGNED: 17 Jul 45
HEADNOTE: JOINT STOCK OIL COMPANY
TOPIC: Specific Property
PARTIES:
Romania
USSR (Soviet Union)

468349   Bilateral Agreement   **0 SUST 183**
SIGNED: 19 Jul 45
HEADNOTE: JOINT STOCK NAVIGATION CO.
TOPIC: Specific Property
PARTIES:
Romania
USSR (Soviet Union)

468350   Bilateral Exchange   **0 SUST 188**
SIGNED: 6 Aug 45
HEADNOTE: RENEW DIPLOMATIC RELATIONS
TOPIC: Consul/Citizenship
PARTIES:
Romania
USSR (Soviet Union)

468351   Bilateral Agreement   **0 SUST 189**
SIGNED: 8 Aug 45
HEADNOTE: JOINT STOCK AVIATION COMPANY
TOPIC: Specific Property
PARTIES:
Romania
USSR (Soviet Union)

468352   Bilateral Agreement   **0 SUST 193**
SIGNED: 15 Aug 45
HEADNOTE: JOINT STOCK BANK
TOPIC: Specific Property
PARTIES:
Romania
USSR (Soviet Union)

468353   Bilateral Exchange   **0 SUST 194**
SIGNED: 20 Aug 45
HEADNOTE: CHANGE MISSIONS TO EMBASSIES
TOPIC: Consul/Citizenship
PARTIES:
Romania
USSR (Soviet Union)

468354   Bilateral Agreement   **0 SUST 197**
SIGNED: 13 Sep 45
HEADNOTE: GRAIN PURCHASES
TOPIC: Commodity Trade
PARTIES:
Romania
USSR (Soviet Union)

468355   Bilateral Agreement   **0 SUST 197**
SIGNED: 13 Sep 45
HEADNOTE: REPARATIONS ALTERATIONS
TOPIC: Reparations
PARTIES:
Romania
USSR (Soviet Union)

468356   Bilateral Agreement   **0 SUST 197**
SIGNED: 13 Sep 45
HEADNOTE: REPARATIONS ALTERATIONS
TOPIC: Reparations
PARTIES:
Romania
USSR (Soviet Union)

468357   Bilateral Agreement   **0 SUST 197**
SIGNED: 13 Sep 45
HEADNOTE: REPARATIONS ALTERATIONS
TOPIC: Reparations
PARTIES:
Romania
USSR (Soviet Union)

468358   Bilateral Agreement   **0 SUST 197**
SIGNED: 13 Sep 45
HEADNOTE: RAILROAD FACILITIES & ADMINIS-
TRATION

TOPIC: Land Transport
PARTIES:
Romania
USSR (Soviet Union)

468359   Bilateral Agreement   **0 SUST 197**
SIGNED: 13 Sep 45
HEADNOTE: REPATRIATION OF CITIZENS
TOPIC: Refugees
PARTIES:
Romania
USSR (Soviet Union)

468360   Bilateral Agreement   **0 SUST 198**
SIGNED: 13 Sep 45
HEADNOTE: CULTURAL & EDUCATIONAL COOP-
ERATION
TOPIC: Health/Educ/Welfare
PARTIES:
Romania
USSR (Soviet Union)

468361   Bilateral Agreement   **0 SUST 206**
SIGNED: 15 Feb 46
HEADNOTE: PAYMENTS
TOPIC: Finance
PARTIES:
Romania
USSR (Soviet Union)

468362   Bilateral Protocol   **0 SUST 206**
SIGNED: 15 Feb 46
HEADNOTE: MOST FAVORED NATION
TOPIC: Mostfavored Nation
PARTIES:
Romania
USSR (Soviet Union)

468363   Bilateral Agreement   **0 SUST 208**
SIGNED: 20 Mar 46
HEADNOTE: JOINT STOCK LUMBER COMPANY
TOPIC: Specific Property
PARTIES:
Romania
USSR (Soviet Union)

468364   Bilateral Agreement   **0 SUST 210**
SIGNED: 15 Apr 46
HEADNOTE: REPARATIONS PAYMENT EXTEN-
SION
TOPIC: Reparations
PARTIES:
Romania
USSR (Soviet Union)

468365   Bilateral Agreement   **0 SUST 229**
SIGNED: 20 Feb 47
HEADNOTE: TRADE & PAYMENTS
TOPIC: General Economic
PARTIES:
Romania
USSR (Soviet Union)

468366   Bilateral Agreement   **0 SUST 232**
SIGNED: 12 Jun 47
HEADNOTE: RAIL COMMUNICATION
TOPIC: Land Transport
PARTIES:
Romania
USSR (Soviet Union)

468367   Bilateral Protocol   **0 SUST 244**
SIGNED: 4 Feb 48
HEADNOTE: BORDER DEMARCATION
TOPIC: Territory Boundary
PARTIES:
Romania
USSR (Soviet Union)

468368   Bilateral Agreement   **0 SUST 245**
SIGNED: 18 Feb 48
HEADNOTE: TRADE & PAYMENTS
TOPIC: General Economic

PARTIES:
Romania
USSR (Soviet Union)

468369   Bilateral Exchange   0 SUST 249
SIGNED: 7 Jun 48
HEADNOTE: REPARATIONS REDUCTION
TOPIC: Reparations
PARTIES:
Romania
USSR (Soviet Union)

468370   Bilateral Agreement   0 SUST 252
SIGNED: 20 Aug 48
HEADNOTE: POSTAL, TELECOMMUNICATION
TOPIC: Gen Communications
PARTIES:
Romania
USSR (Soviet Union)

468371   Bilateral Agreement   0 SUST 252
SIGNED: 20 Aug 48
HEADNOTE: PARCEL POST
TOPIC: Postal Service
PARTIES:
Romania
USSR (Soviet Union)

468372   Bilateral Agreement   0 SUST 257
SIGNED: 24 Jan 49
HEADNOTE: TECHNICAL AID
TOPIC: Tech Assistance
PARTIES:
Romania
USSR (Soviet Union)

468373   Bilateral Agreement   0 SUST 257
SIGNED: 24 Jan 49
HEADNOTE: TRADE & PAYMENTS
TOPIC: General Economic
PARTIES:
Romania
USSR (Soviet Union)

468374   Bilateral Agreement   0 SUST 258
SIGNED: 27 Apr 49
HEADNOTE: RADIO BROADCAST COOPERATION
TOPIC: Mass Media
PARTIES:
Romania
USSR (Soviet Union)

468375   Bilateral Protocol   0 SUST 263
SIGNED: 27 Apr 49
HEADNOTE: BORDER DEMARCATION
TOPIC: Territory Boundary
PARTIES:
Romania
USSR (Soviet Union)

468376   Bilateral Treaty   0 SUST 264
SIGNED: 25 Nov 49
HEADNOTE: BORDER REGULATION
TOPIC: Admin Cooperation
PARTIES:
Romania
USSR (Soviet Union)

468377   Bilateral Convention   0 SUST 264
SIGNED: 25 Nov 49
HEADNOTE: BORDER DISPUTE SETTLEMENT
TOPIC: Dispute Settlement
PARTIES:
Romania
USSR (Soviet Union)

468378   Bilateral Agreement   0 SUST 270
SIGNED: 17 Feb 50
HEADNOTE: SCIENTIFIC COOPERATION
TOPIC: Scientific Project
PARTIES:
Romania
USSR (Soviet Union)

468379   Bilateral Agreement   0 SUST 270
SIGNED: 17 Feb 50
HEADNOTE: TRADE & PAYMENTS
TOPIC: General Economic
PARTIES:
Romania
USSR (Soviet Union)

468380   Bilateral Agreement   0 SUST 280
SIGNED: 15 Mar 51
HEADNOTE: TRADE & PAYMENTS
TOPIC: General Economic
PARTIES:
Romania
USSR (Soviet Union)

468381   Bilateral Agreement   0 SUST 282
SIGNED: 24 Aug 51
HEADNOTE: TECHNICAL & INDUSTRIAL AID
TOPIC: General Aid
PARTIES:
Romania
USSR (Soviet Union)

468382   Bilateral Agreement   0 SUST 285
SIGNED: 20 Mar 52
HEADNOTE: ROMANIANS IN USSR COLLEGES
TOPIC: Education
PARTIES:
Romania
USSR (Soviet Union)

468383   Bilateral Convention   0 SUST 292
SIGNED: 25 Dec 52
HEADNOTE: PRUT RIVER FLOOD CONTROL
TOPIC: Specific Resources
PARTIES:
Romania
USSR (Soviet Union)

468384   Bilateral Protocol   0 SUST 299
SIGNED: 17 Aug 53
HEADNOTE: SUPPLEMENTS 27 APR 49
TOPIC: Mass Media
PARTIES:
Romania
USSR (Soviet Union)

468385   Bilateral Exchange   0 SUST 304
SIGNED: 5 Dec 53
HEADNOTE: FACILITIES TO MAINTAIN DANUBE
TOPIC: Specific Property
PARTIES:
Romania
USSR (Soviet Union)

468386   Bilateral Agreement   0 SUST 304
SIGNED: 5 Dec 53
HEADNOTE: DANUBE RIVER MAINTAINENCE
TOPIC: Admin Cooperation
PARTIES:
Romania
USSR (Soviet Union)

468387   Bilateral Agreement   0 SUST 309
SIGNED: 31 Mar 54
HEADNOTE: JOINT STOCK TRANSFERS
TOPIC: Finance
PARTIES:
Romania
USSR (Soviet Union)

468388   Bilateral Agreement   0 SUST 310
SIGNED: 31 Mar 54
HEADNOTE: CREDIT AGREEMENT
TOPIC: Loans and Credits
PARTIES:
Romania
USSR (Soviet Union)

468389   Bilateral Agreement   0 SUST 323
SIGNED: 25 Jan 55
HEADNOTE: ESTABLISH AIR COMMUNICATION
TOPIC: Air Transport

PARTIES:
Romania
USSR (Soviet Union)

468390   Bilateral Agreement   0 SUST 326
SIGNED: 22 Apr 55
HEADNOTE: CIVIL ATOMIC DEVELOPMENT AID
TOPIC: Atomic Energy
PARTIES:
Romania
USSR (Soviet Union)

468391   Bilateral Agreement   0 SUST 344
SIGNED: 13 Dec 55
HEADNOTE: OIL JOINT STOCK SALE
TOPIC: Finance
PARTIES:
Romania
USSR (Soviet Union)

468392   Bilateral Agreement   0 SUST 346
SIGNED: 3 Jan 56
HEADNOTE: CIVIL AIR TECHNICAL COOPERATION
TOPIC: Air Transport
PARTIES:
Romania
USSR (Soviet Union)

468393   Bilateral Protocol   0 SUST 353
SIGNED: 14 Apr 56
HEADNOTE: COMMUNICATIONS EXPANSION
TOPIC: Gen Communications
PARTIES:
Romania
USSR (Soviet Union)

468394   Bilateral Agreement   0 SUST 364
SIGNED: 21 Jul 56
HEADNOTE: SHIPBUILDING FOR USSR 1957-60
TOPIC: Commodity Trade
PARTIES:
Romania
USSR (Soviet Union)

468395   Bilateral Agreement   0 SUST 370
SIGNED: 22 Oct 56
HEADNOTE: URANIUM JOINT STOCK TRANSFER
TOPIC: Finance
PARTIES:
Romania
USSR (Soviet Union)

468396   Bilateral Protocol   0 SUST 373
SIGNED: 3 Dec 56
HEADNOTE: 370 MILLION RUBLE LOAN
TOPIC: Loans and Credits
PARTIES:
Romania
USSR (Soviet Union)

468397   Bilateral Agreement   0 SUST 379
SIGNED: 4 Mar 57
HEADNOTE: TRADE
TOPIC: General Trade
PARTIES:
Romania
USSR (Soviet Union)

468398   Bilateral Protocol   0 SUST 385
SIGNED: 18 Jun 57
HEADNOTE: FACILITIES TO MAINTAIN DANUBE
TOPIC: Specific Property
PARTIES:
Romania
USSR (Soviet Union)

468399   Bilateral Protocol   0 SUST 386
SIGNED: 18 Jul 57
HEADNOTE: MODIFIES 5 DEC 53 ON DANUBE
TOPIC: Admin Cooperation
PARTIES:
Romania
USSR (Soviet Union)

468400   Bilateral Agreement   0 SUST 386
SIGNED: 1 Aug 57
HEADNOTE: REGULATION BORDER WATERWAYS
TOPIC: Admin Cooperation
PARTIES:
  Romania
  USSR (Soviet Union)

468404   Bilateral Protocol   0 SUST 218
SIGNED: 7 Oct 46
HEADNOTE: MODIFIES 7 SEP 40
TOPIC: General Trade
PARTIES:
  Sweden
  USSR (Soviet Union)

468405   Bilateral Agreement   0 SUST 218
SIGNED: 7 Oct 46
HEADNOTE: BILLION CROWN CREDIT TO USSR
TOPIC: Loans and Credits
PARTIES:
  Sweden
  USSR (Soviet Union)

468406   Bilateral Exchange   0 SUST 219
SIGNED: 7 Oct 46
HEADNOTE: TRADE INCREASE
TOPIC: General Trade
PARTIES:
  Sweden
  USSR (Soviet Union)

468407   Bilateral Agreement   0 SUST 219
SIGNED: 7 Oct 46
HEADNOTE: SETTLEMENT WAR CLAIMS
TOPIC: Claims and Debts
PARTIES:
  Sweden
  USSR (Soviet Union)

468408   Bilateral Agreement   0 SUST 220
SIGNED: 25 Oct 46
HEADNOTE: ESTABLISH AIR COMMUNICATIONS
TOPIC: Air Transport
PARTIES:
  Sweden
  USSR (Soviet Union)

468409   Bilateral Protocol   0 SUST 220
SIGNED: 25 Oct 46
HEADNOTE: FINLAND AIR FACILITIES USE
TOPIC: Air Transport
PARTIES:
  Sweden
  USSR (Soviet Union)

468410   Bilateral Agreement   0 SUST 221
SIGNED: 5 Nov 46
HEADNOTE: PARCEL POST
TOPIC: Postal Service
PARTIES:
  Sweden
  USSR (Soviet Union)

468411   Bilateral Agreement   0 SUST 225
SIGNED: 30 Jan 47
HEADNOTE: TRADE DELIVERY CONDITIONS
TOPIC: General Trade
PARTIES:
  Sweden
  USSR (Soviet Union)

468412   Bilateral Protocol   0 SUST 306
SIGNED: 23 Jan 54
HEADNOTE: MODIFIES 25 OCT 46
TOPIC: Air Transport
PARTIES:
  Sweden
  USSR (Soviet Union)

468413   Bilateral Exchange   0 SUST 207
SIGNED: 18 Mar 46
HEADNOTE: RENEW DIPLOMATIC RELATIONS
TOPIC: Consul/Citizenship

PARTIES:
  Switzerland
  USSR (Soviet Union)

468414   Bilateral Agreement   0 SUST 246
SIGNED: 17 Mar 48
HEADNOTE: TRADE
TOPIC: General Trade
PARTIES:
  Switzerland
  USSR (Soviet Union)

468415   Bilateral Convention   0 SUST 351
SIGNED: 7 Jan 56
HEADNOTE: DIPLOMATIC MISSIONS EXCHANGE
TOPIC: Consul/Citizenship
PARTIES:
  Sudan
  USSR (Soviet Union)

468416   Bilateral Agreement   0 SUST 444
SIGNED: 19 Nov 55
HEADNOTE: CHANGE MISSIONS TO EMBASSIES
TOPIC: Consul/Citizenship
PARTIES:
  Syria
  USSR (Soviet Union)

468417   Bilateral Agreement   0 SUST 385
SIGNED: 29 Jun 57
HEADNOTE: ESTABLISH RADIO COMMUNICA-
TION
TOPIC: Telecommunications
PARTIES:
  Syria
  USSR (Soviet Union)

468418   Bilateral Agreement   0 SUST 391
SIGNED: 28 Oct 57
HEADNOTE: ECONOMIC & TECHNICAL COOPER-
ATION
TOPIC: General Aid
PARTIES:
  Syria
  USSR (Soviet Union)

468419   Bilateral Agreement   0 SUST 394
SIGNED: 19 Dec 57
HEADNOTE: TRADE
TOPIC: General Trade
PARTIES:
  Syria
  USSR (Soviet Union)

468420   Bilateral Exchange   0 SUST 225
SIGNED: 31 Dec 46
HEADNOTE: RENEW DIPLOMATIC RELATIONS
TOPIC: Consul/Citizenship
PARTIES:
  Thailand
  USSR (Soviet Union)

468421   Bilateral Instrument   0 SUST 355
SIGNED: 20 May 56
HEADNOTE: CHANGE MISSIONS TO EMBASSIES
TOPIC: Consul/Citizenship
PARTIES:
  Thailand
  USSR (Soviet Union)

468422   Bilateral Exchange   0 SUST 298
SIGNED: 18 Jul 53
HEADNOTE: MONTREUX STRAITS DISPUTE
TOPIC: Dispute Settlement
PARTIES:
  Turkey
  USSR (Soviet Union)

468423   Bilateral Agreement   0 SUST 301
SIGNED: 15 Sep 53
HEADNOTE: IGDIR PLAIN IRRIGATION
TOPIC: Specific Resources

PARTIES:
  Turkey
  USSR (Soviet Union)

468424   Bilateral Agreement   0 SUST 173
SIGNED: 11 Feb 45
HEADNOTE: REPATRIATION
TOPIC: Refugees
PARTIES:
  UK Great Britain
  USSR (Soviet Union)

468425   Bilateral Exchange   0 SUST 173
SIGNED: 11 Feb 45
HEADNOTE: STATUS OF SOVIETS IN UK
TOPIC: Refugees
PARTIES:
  UK Great Britain
  USSR (Soviet Union)

468426   Bilateral Agreement   0 SUST 173
SIGNED: 11 Feb 45
HEADNOTE: UK OCCUPIED AREA REFUGEES
TOPIC: Refugees
PARTIES:
  UK Great Britain
  USSR (Soviet Union)

468427   Bilateral Exchange   0 SUST 174
SIGNED: 11 Feb 45
HEADNOTE: MODIFIES REFUGEE AGREEMENTS
TOPIC: Refugees
PARTIES:
  UK Great Britain
  USSR (Soviet Union)

468428   Bilateral Exchange   0 SUST 199
SIGNED: 2 Oct 45
HEADNOTE: SOVIET WITHDRAWAL FROM IRAN
TOPIC: Milit Occupation
PARTIES:
  UK Great Britain
  USSR (Soviet Union)

468429   Bilateral Exchange   0 SUST 214
SIGNED: 9 Jul 46
HEADNOTE: MODIFIES 23 SEP 44
TOPIC: Telecommunications
PARTIES:
  UK Great Britain
  USSR (Soviet Union)

468430   Bilateral Exchange   0 SUST 293
SIGNED: 19 Mar 53
HEADNOTE: BRITONS INTERNED IN KOREA
TOPIC: Refugees
PARTIES:
  UK Great Britain
  USSR (Soviet Union)

468432   Bilateral Instrument   0 SUST 206
SIGNED: 5 Feb 46
HEADNOTE: JOINT KOREAN STUDY COMMIS-
SION
TOPIC: General Ad Hoc
PARTIES:
  USA (United States)
  USSR (Soviet Union)

468433   Bilateral Instrument   0 SUST 210
SIGNED: 18 Apr 46
HEADNOTE: KOREAN POLITICAL REFORM
TOPIC: General Ad Hoc
PARTIES:
  USA (United States)
  USSR (Soviet Union)

468434   Bilateral Exchange   0 SUST 210
SIGNED: 23 Apr 46
HEADNOTE: AMERIKA MAGAZINE CIRCULATION
TOPIC: Culture
PARTIES:
  USA (United States)
  USSR (Soviet Union)

468435   Bilateral Exchange   **0 SUST 218**
SIGNED: 19 Aug 46
HEADNOTE: REVISE 20 JUL 36
TOPIC: Admin Cooperation
PARTIES:
  USA (United States)
  USSR (Soviet Union)

468436   Bilateral Agreement   **0 SUST 438**
SIGNED: 15 Apr 47
HEADNOTE: LEND-LEASE
TOPIC: General Aid
PARTIES:
  USA (United States)
  USSR (Soviet Union)

468437   Bilateral Agreement   **0 SUST 232**
SIGNED: 16 Jun 47
HEADNOTE: LENINGRAD CONSULATE OPENING
TOPIC: Consul/Citizenship
PARTIES:
  USA (United States)
  USSR (Soviet Union)

468438   Bilateral Exchange   **0 SUST 305**
SIGNED: 26 Dec 53
HEADNOTE: RETURN LEND-LEASE VESSELS
TOPIC: Specif Goods/Equip
PARTIES:
  USA (United States)
  USSR (Soviet Union)

468439   Bilateral Exchange   **0 SUST 344**
SIGNED: 16 Dec 55
HEADNOTE: RECIPROCAL MAGAZINE DISTRIBU-
TION
TOPIC: Culture
PARTIES:
  USA (United States)
  USSR (Soviet Union)

468440   Bilateral Exchange   **0 SUST 363**
SIGNED: 9 Jul 56
HEADNOTE: LEND-LEASE VESSELS DESTROYED
TOPIC: Specif Goods/Equip
PARTIES:
  USA (United States)
  USSR (Soviet Union)

468441   Bilateral Exchange   **0 SUST 371**
SIGNED: 29 Dec 56
HEADNOTE: EMBASSY STAFF IMMUNITY
TOPIC: Privil/Immunities
PARTIES:
  USA (United States)
  USSR (Soviet Union)

468442   Bilateral Agreement   **0 SUST 315**
SIGNED: 28 Jul 54
HEADNOTE: PAYMENTS
TOPIC: Finance
PARTIES:
  Uruguay
  USSR (Soviet Union)

468443   Bilateral Treaty   **0 SUST 366**
SIGNED: 11 Aug 56
HEADNOTE: COMMERCE & NAVIGATION
TOPIC: General Trade
PARTIES:
  Uruguay
  USSR (Soviet Union)

468444   Bilateral Agreement   **0 SUST 366**
SIGNED: 11 Aug 56
HEADNOTE: TRADE & PAYMENTS
TOPIC: General Economic
PARTIES:
  Uruguay
  USSR (Soviet Union)

468445   Bilateral Exchange   **0 SUST 175**
SIGNED: 14 Mar 45

HEADNOTE: ESTABLISH DIPLOMATIC RELA-
TIONS
TOPIC: Consul/Citizenship
PARTIES:
  USSR (Soviet Union)
  Venezuela

468446   Bilateral Exchange   **0 SUST 268**
SIGNED: 30 Jan 50
HEADNOTE: ESTABLISH DIPLOMATIC RELA-
TIONS
TOPIC: Consul/Citizenship
PARTIES:
  USSR (Soviet Union)
  Vietnam, North

468447   Bilateral Agreement   **0 SUST 331**
SIGNED: 8 Jul 55
HEADNOTE: TRADE
TOPIC: General Trade
PARTIES:
  USSR (Soviet Union)
  Vietnam, North

468448   Bilateral Exchange   **0 SUST 331**
SIGNED: 8 Jul 55
HEADNOTE: SOVIET TRADE MISSION
TOPIC: General Trade
PARTIES:
  USSR (Soviet Union)
  Vietnam, North

468449   Bilateral Agreement   **0 SUST 333**
SIGNED: 18 Jul 55
HEADNOTE: 400 MILLION RUBLES AID
TOPIC: Direct Aid
PARTIES:
  USSR (Soviet Union)
  Vietnam, North

468450   Bilateral Agreement   **0 SUST 333**
SIGNED: 18 Jul 55
HEADNOTE: TRADE
TOPIC: General Trade
PARTIES:
  USSR (Soviet Union)
  Vietnam, North

468451   Bilateral Agreement   **0 SUST 445**
SIGNED: 1 Dec 56
HEADNOTE: SOVIET CREDIT
TOPIC: Loans and Credits
PARTIES:
  USSR (Soviet Union)
  Vietnam, North

468452   Bilateral Agreement   **0 SUST 379**
SIGNED: 11 Mar 57
HEADNOTE: NON-COMMERCIAL PAYMENTS
TOPIC: Finance
PARTIES:
  USSR (Soviet Union)
  Vietnam, North

468453   Bilateral Instrument   **0 SUST 380**
SIGNED: 8 Apr 57
HEADNOTE: GOODS DELIVERY CONDITIONS
TOPIC: General Trade
PARTIES:
  USSR (Soviet Union)
  Vietnam, North

468454   Bilateral Instrument   **0 SUST 395**
SIGNED: 25 Dec 57
HEADNOTE: CULTURAL COLLABORATION
TOPIC: Culture
PARTIES:
  USSR (Soviet Union)
  Vietnam, North

468455   Bilateral Agreement   **0 SUST 395**
SIGNED: 26 Dec 57
HEADNOTE: ESTABLISH TELECOMMUNICA-
TIONS

TOPIC: Telecommunications
PARTIES:
  USSR (Soviet Union)
  Vietnam, North

468456   Bilateral Agreement   **0 SUST 395**
SIGNED: 26 Dec 57
HEADNOTE: ESTABLISH POSTAL SERVICE
TOPIC: Postal Service
PARTIES:
  USSR (Soviet Union)
  Vietnam, North

468457   Bilateral Agreement   **0 SUST 350**
SIGNED: 8 Mar 56
HEADNOTE: TRADE
TOPIC: General Trade
PARTIES:
  USSR (Soviet Union)
  Yemen

468458   Bilateral Agreement   **0 SUST 363**
SIGNED: 11 Jul 56
HEADNOTE: ECONOMIC COLLABORATION
TOPIC: General Economic
PARTIES:
  USSR (Soviet Union)
  Yemen

468459   Bilateral Treaty   **0 SUST 175**
SIGNED: 11 Apr 45
HEADNOTE: FRIENDSHIP & ASSISTANCE
TOPIC: General Amity
PARTIES:
  USSR (Soviet Union)
  Yugoslavia

468460   Bilateral Agreement   **0 SUST 175**
SIGNED: 13 Apr 45
HEADNOTE: TRADE
TOPIC: General Trade
PARTIES:
  USSR (Soviet Union)
  Yugoslavia

468461   Bilateral Agreement   **0 SUST 213**
SIGNED: 8 Jun 46
HEADNOTE: TRADE
TOPIC: General Trade
PARTIES:
  USSR (Soviet Union)
  Yugoslavia

468462   Bilateral Agreement   **0 SUST 234**
SIGNED: 5 Jul 47
HEADNOTE: TRADE & PAYMENTS
TOPIC: General Economic
PARTIES:
  USSR (Soviet Union)
  Yugoslavia

468463   Bilateral Agreement   **0 SUST 234**
SIGNED: 5 Jul 47
HEADNOTE: NON-COMMERCIAL PAYMENTS
TOPIC: Finance
PARTIES:
  USSR (Soviet Union)
  Yugoslavia

468464   Bilateral Agreement   **0 SUST 296**
SIGNED: 14 Jun 53
HEADNOTE: RESUME DIPLOMATIC RELATIONS
TOPIC: Consul/Citizenship
PARTIES:
  USSR (Soviet Union)
  Yugoslavia

468465   Bilateral Agreement   **0 SUST 316**
SIGNED: 1 Oct 54
HEADNOTE: BARTER AGREEMENT
TOPIC: General Trade
PARTIES:
  USSR (Soviet Union)
  Yugoslavia

468466   Bilateral Agreement   **0 SUST 322**
SIGNED: 5 Jan 55
HEADNOTE: COMMERCIAL AGREEMENT
TOPIC: General Trade
PARTIES:
  USSR (Soviet Union)
  Yugoslavia

468467   Bilateral Exchange   **0 SUST 322**
SIGNED: 10 Jan 55
HEADNOTE: CIVIL FLIGHTS OVER AUSTRIA
TOPIC: Air Transport
PARTIES:
  USSR (Soviet Union)
  Yugoslavia

468468   Bilateral Exchange   **0 SUST 322**
SIGNED: 10 Jan 55
HEADNOTE: SOVIET-YUGOSLAVIA FLIGHTS
TOPIC: Air Transport
PARTIES:
  USSR (Soviet Union)
  Yugoslavia

468469   Bilateral Exchange   **0 SUST 334**
SIGNED: 30 Jul 55
HEADNOTE: SUPPLEMENTS 1 JAN 55
TOPIC: General Trade
PARTIES:
  USSR (Soviet Union)
  Yugoslavia

468470   Bilateral Agreement   **0 SUST 338**
SIGNED: 27 Sep 55
HEADNOTE: POST & TELEGRAPH
TOPIC: Gen Communications
PARTIES:
  USSR (Soviet Union)
  Yugoslavia

468471   Bilateral Agreement   **0 SUST 339**
SIGNED: 27 Sep 55
HEADNOTE: PARCEL POST
TOPIC: Postal Service
PARTIES:
  USSR (Soviet Union)
  Yugoslavia

468472   Bilateral Exchange   **0 SUST 340**
SIGNED: 12 Nov 55
HEADNOTE: SOVIET BOOKS TO YUGOSLAVIA
TOPIC: Culture
PARTIES:
  USSR (Soviet Union)
  Yugoslavia

468474   Bilateral Agreement   **0 SUST 347**
SIGNED: 12 Jan 56
HEADNOTE: INDUSTRIAL DEVELOPMENT AID
TOPIC: Direct Aid
PARTIES:
  USSR (Soviet Union)
  Yugoslavia

468475   Bilateral Agreement   **0 SUST 348**
SIGNED: 28 Jan 56
HEADNOTE: CIVIL ATOMIC DEVELOPMENT
TOPIC: Atomic Energy
PARTIES:
  USSR (Soviet Union)
  Yugoslavia

468477   Bilateral Agreement   **0 SUST 350**
SIGNED: 3 Mar 56
HEADNOTE: DANUBE STEAMSHIP SERVICE CO-
  OPERATION
TOPIC: Water Transport
PARTIES:
  USSR (Soviet Union)
  Yugoslavia

468478   Bilateral Agreement   **0 SUST 351**
SIGNED: 9 Mar 56
HEADNOTE: INSURANCE

TOPIC: Claims and Debts
PARTIES:
  USSR (Soviet Union)
  Yugoslavia

468479   Bilateral Exchange   **0 SUST 358**
SIGNED: 20 Jun 56
HEADNOTE: INFORMATION SERVICE REGULARI-
  ZATION
TOPIC: Admin Cooperation
PARTIES:
  USSR (Soviet Union)
  Yugoslavia

468480   Bilateral Protocol   **0 SUST 377**
SIGNED: 9 Feb 57
HEADNOTE: NUCLEAR PHYSICS COOPERATION
TOPIC: Scientific Project
PARTIES:
  USSR (Soviet Union)
  Yugoslavia

468481   Bilateral Agreement   **0 SUST 381**
SIGNED: 10 Apr 57
HEADNOTE: TRADE 1958-60
TOPIC: General Trade
PARTIES:
  USSR (Soviet Union)
  Yugoslavia

468482   Bilateral Exchange   **0 SUST 386**
SIGNED: 10 Jul 57
HEADNOTE: RADIO & TELEVISION COOP
TOPIC: Mass Media
PARTIES:
  USSR (Soviet Union)
  Yugoslavia

468483   Bilateral Protocol   **0 SUST 386**
SIGNED: 29 Jul 57
HEADNOTE: DEVELOP ALUMINUM INDUSTRY
TOPIC: Direct Aid
PARTIES:
  USSR (Soviet Union)
  Yugoslavia

469074   Bilateral Agreement   **0 SUGG 304**
SIGNED: 17 Oct 69
HEADNOTE: AGRI COMMOD
TOPIC: US Agri Commod Aid
PARTIES:
  USA (United States)
  Vietnam, South

469484   Bilateral Agreement   **7 SUGG 101**
SIGNED: 13 Jan 58
HEADNOTE: TRADE 1958-60
TOPIC: General Trade
PARTIES:
  Hungary
  USSR (Soviet Union)

469485   Bilateral Agreement   **7 SUGG 102**
SIGNED: 14 Jan 58
HEADNOTE: ESTABLISH DIPLOMATIC RELA-
TIONS
TOPIC: Consul/Citizenship
PARTIES:
  Ghana
  USSR (Soviet Union)

469486   Bilateral Agreement   **7 SUGG 102**
SIGNED: 18 Jan 58
HEADNOTE: BORDER REGULATION
TOPIC: Admin Cooperation
PARTIES:
  Afghanistan
  USSR (Soviet Union)

469487   Bilateral Protocol   **7 SUGG 102**
SIGNED: 18 Jan 58
HEADNOTE: CLAIMS FROM INCORPORATION
TOPIC: Claims and Debts

PARTIES:
  Bulgaria
  USSR (Soviet Union)

469488   Bilateral Agreement   **7 SUGG 102**
SIGNED: 18 Jan 58
HEADNOTE: SCIENTIFIC COLLABORATION
TOPIC: Scientific Project
PARTIES:
  China People's Rep
  USSR (Soviet Union)

469489   Bilateral Agreement   **7 SUGG 103**
SIGNED: 20 Jan 58
HEADNOTE: RAIL COMMUNICATIONS
TOPIC: Land Transport
PARTIES:
  Iran
  USSR (Soviet Union)

469492   Bilateral Agreement   **7 SUGG 103**
SIGNED: 22 Jan 58
HEADNOTE: CIVIL ATOMIC DEVELOPMENT
TOPIC: Atomic Energy
PARTIES:
  Poland
  USSR (Soviet Union)

469493   Bilateral Agreement   **7 SUGG 103**
SIGNED: 29 Jan 58
HEADNOTE: ECONOMIC & TECHNICAL AID
TOPIC: General Aid
PARTIES:
  United Arab Rep
  USSR (Soviet Union)

469494   Bilateral Agreement   **7 SUGG 104**
SIGNED: 4 Feb 58
HEADNOTE: TRADE 1958-60
TOPIC: General Trade
PARTIES:
  Poland
  USSR (Soviet Union)

469495   Bilateral Agreement   **7 SUGG 105**
SIGNED: 5 Feb 58
HEADNOTE: TECHNICIAN EXCHANGE
TOPIC: Scientific Project
PARTIES:
  Poland
  USSR (Soviet Union)

469496   Bilateral Agreement   **7 SUGG 105**
SIGNED: 8 Feb 58
HEADNOTE: TRADE
TOPIC: General Trade
PARTIES:
  Ceylon (Sri Lanka)
  USSR (Soviet Union)

469497   Bilateral Agreement   **7 SUGG 105**
SIGNED: 15 Feb 58
HEADNOTE: TRADE
TOPIC: General Trade
PARTIES:
  Albania
  USSR (Soviet Union)

469499   Bilateral Agreement   **7 SUGG 107**
SIGNED: 5 Mar 58
HEADNOTE: GERI-RUD RIVER USE
TOPIC: Specific Resources
PARTIES:
  Iran
  USSR (Soviet Union)

469500   Bilateral Protocol   **7 SUGG 107**
SIGNED: 7 Mar 58
HEADNOTE: CLAIMS FROM INCORPORATION
TOPIC: Claims and Debts
PARTIES:
  Romania
  USSR (Soviet Union)

469501 Bilateral Agreement 7 SUGG 108
SIGNED: 27 Mar 58
HEADNOTE: EMBASSY CONSTRUCTION
TOPIC: Specific Property
PARTIES:
Sweden
USSR (Soviet Union)

469502 Bilateral Agreement 7 SUGG 108
SIGNED: 1 Apr 58
HEADNOTE: CUSTOMS COOPERATION
TOPIC: Customs
PARTIES:
Czechoslovakia
USSR (Soviet Union)

469503 Bilateral Instrument 7 SUGG 109
SIGNED: 10 Apr 58
HEADNOTE: CULTURAL COLLABORATION
TOPIC: Culture
PARTIES:
United Arab Rep
USSR (Soviet Union)

469504 Bilateral Agreement 7 SUGG 110
SIGNED: 15 Apr 58
HEADNOTE: TRADE
TOPIC: General Trade
PARTIES:
Iran
USSR (Soviet Union)

469505 Bilateral Agreement 7 SUGG 110
SIGNED: 19 Apr 58
HEADNOTE: TRADE
TOPIC: General Trade
PARTIES:
Morocco
USSR (Soviet Union)

469506 Bilateral Agreement 7 SUGG 110
SIGNED: 19 Apr 58
HEADNOTE: PAYMENTS
TOPIC: Finance
PARTIES:
Morocco
USSR (Soviet Union)

469507 Bilateral Agreement 7 SUGG 111
SIGNED: 26 Apr 58
HEADNOTE: VESSEL DELIVERY 1961-65
TOPIC: Commodity Trade
PARTIES:
Bulgaria
USSR (Soviet Union)

469508 Bilateral Protocol 7 SUGG 111
SIGNED: 26 Apr 58
HEADNOTE: EQUIPMENT DELIVERIES
TOPIC: General Trade
PARTIES:
Bulgaria
USSR (Soviet Union)

469509 Bilateral Protocol 7 SUGG 112
SIGNED: 11 May 58
HEADNOTE: CIVIL ATOMIC DEVELOPMENT
TOPIC: Atomic Energy
PARTIES:
Hungary
USSR (Soviet Union)

469510 Bilateral Protocol 7 SUGG 112
SIGNED: 11 May 58
HEADNOTE: TRADE 1959-65 & ECONOMIC COOP-
ERATION
TOPIC: General Economic
PARTIES:
Korea, North
USSR (Soviet Union)

469511 Bilateral Protocol 7 SUGG 112
SIGNED: 22 May 58
HEADNOTE: CULTURAL COLLABORATION

TOPIC: Culture
PARTIES:
Poland
USSR (Soviet Union)

469512 Bilateral Agreement 7 SUGG 113
SIGNED: 3 Jun 58
HEADNOTE: ESTABLISH STEAMSHIP COMMUNI-
CATION
TOPIC: Water Transport
PARTIES:
Japan
USSR (Soviet Union)

469513 Bilateral Protocol 7 SUGG 114
SIGNED: 14 Jun 58
HEADNOTE: MARITIME TRANSPORT COOPER-
ATION
TOPIC: Water Transport
PARTIES:
Poland
USSR (Soviet Union)

469514 Bilateral Agreement 7 SUGG 114
SIGNED: 18 Jun 58
HEADNOTE: TROOP STATUS IN POLAND
TOPIC: Status of Forces
PARTIES:
Poland
USSR (Soviet Union)

469515 Bilateral Protocol 7 SUGG 114
SIGNED: 25 Jun 58
HEADNOTE: AMU-DARIA RIVER USE
TOPIC: Specific Resources
PARTIES:
Afghanistan
USSR (Soviet Union)

469516 Bilateral Agreement 7 SUGG 114
SIGNED: 26 Jun 58
HEADNOTE: SOVIET WHEAT-FINNISH BUTTER
TOPIC: Commodity Trade
PARTIES:
Finland
USSR (Soviet Union)

469517 Bilateral Protocol 7 SUGG 115
SIGNED: 30 Jun 58
HEADNOTE: CLAIMS FROM INCORPORATION
TOPIC: Claims and Debts
PARTIES:
Czechoslovakia
USSR (Soviet Union)

469518 Bilateral Exchange 7 SUGG 115
SIGNED: 3 Jul 58
HEADNOTE: BORDER REDEMARCATION
TOPIC: Territory Boundary
PARTIES:
Iran
USSR (Soviet Union)

469519 Bilateral Exchange 7 SUGG 116
SIGNED: 16 Jul 58
HEADNOTE: EXTEND FISHING ZONE
TOPIC: Specific Resources
PARTIES:
Iceland
USSR (Soviet Union)

469520 Bilateral Exchange 7 SUGG 116
SIGNED: 8 Jul 58
HEADNOTE: ESTABLISH DIPLOMATIC RELA-
TIONS
TOPIC: Consul/Citizenship
PARTIES:
Iraq
USSR (Soviet Union)

469521 Bilateral Agreement 7 SUGG 116
SIGNED: 19 Jul 58
HEADNOTE: SOVIET TECHNICAL AID
TOPIC: Tech Assistance

PARTIES:
Bulgaria
USSR (Soviet Union)

469522 Bilateral Agreement 7 SUGG 118
SIGNED: 8 Aug 58
HEADNOTE: SOVIET TECHNICAL AID
TOPIC: Tech Assistance
PARTIES:
China People's Rep
USSR (Soviet Union)

469523 Bilateral Agreement 7 SUGG 118
SIGNED: 18 Aug 58
HEADNOTE: 50 MILLION KRONUR LOAN
TOPIC: Loans and Credits
PARTIES:
Iceland
USSR (Soviet Union)

469524 Bilateral Exchange 7 SUGG 118
SIGNED: 10 Aug 58
HEADNOTE: MODIFIES 15 JUL 56
TOPIC: General Trade
PARTIES:
United Arab Rep
USSR (Soviet Union)

469525 Bilateral Exchange 7 SUGG 120
SIGNED: 4 Sep 58
HEADNOTE: AMBASSADOR EXCHANGE
TOPIC: Consul/Citizenship
PARTIES:
Morocco
USSR (Soviet Union)

469526 Bilateral Agreement 7 SUGG 120
SIGNED: 5 Sep 58
HEADNOTE: TECHNICIAN EXCHANGE
TOPIC: Scientific Project
PARTIES:
Czechoslovakia
USSR (Soviet Union)

469527 Bilateral Agreement 7 SUGG 120
SIGNED: 5 Sep 58
HEADNOTE: TECHNICIAN EXCHANGE
TOPIC: Scientific Project
PARTIES:
Czechoslovakia
USSR (Soviet Union)

469528 Bilateral Instrument 7 SUGG 120
SIGNED: 10 Sep 58
HEADNOTE: BORDER DEMARCATION
TOPIC: Territory Boundary
PARTIES:
Poland
USSR (Soviet Union)

469529 Bilateral Protocol 7 SUGG 121
SIGNED: 10 Sep 58
HEADNOTE: CULTURAL EXHIBIT EXCHANGE
TOPIC: Culture
PARTIES:
USA (United States)
USSR (Soviet Union)

469530 Bilateral Agreement 7 SUGG 121
SIGNED: 11 Sep 58
HEADNOTE: ESTABLISH AIR COMMUNICATION
TOPIC: Air Transport
PARTIES:
United Arab Rep
USSR (Soviet Union)

469531 Bilateral Protocol 7 SUGG 121
SIGNED: 12 Sep 58
HEADNOTE: PHNOM-PENH HOSPITAL AID
TOPIC: Non-IBRD Project
PARTIES:
Cambodia
USSR (Soviet Union)

469532   Bilateral Agreement   **7 SUGG 121**
SIGNED: 2 Oct 58
HEADNOTE: TRADE
TOPIC: General Trade
PARTIES:
  Poland
  USSR (Soviet Union)

469533   Bilateral Exchange   **7 SUGG 121**
SIGNED: 4 Oct 58
HEADNOTE: ESTABLISH DIPLOMATIC RELA-
TIONS
TOPIC: Consul/Citizenship
PARTIES:
  Guinea
  USSR (Soviet Union)

469534   Bilateral Protocol   **7 SUGG 122**
SIGNED: 9 Oct 58
HEADNOTE: MOTION PICTURE EXCHANGE
TOPIC: Mass Media
PARTIES:
  USA (United States)
  USSR (Soviet Union)

469535   Bilateral Agreement   **7 SUGG 122**
SIGNED: 14 Oct 58
HEADNOTE: CHEMICAL EQUIPMENT DELIVERIES
TOPIC: Commodity Trade
PARTIES:
  Czechoslovakia
  USSR (Soviet Union)

469536   Bilateral Instrument   **7 SUGG 122**
SIGNED: 20 Oct 58
HEADNOTE: CULTURAL EXCHANGE
TOPIC: Culture
PARTIES:
  Norway
  USSR (Soviet Union)

469537   Bilateral Agreement   **7 SUGG 122**
SIGNED: 27 Oct 58
HEADNOTE: OIL EQUIPMENT ON CREDIT
TOPIC: Loans and Credits
PARTIES:
  Argentina
  USSR (Soviet Union)

469538   Bilateral Agreement   **7 SUGG 124**
SIGNED: 5 Nov 58
HEADNOTE: EQUIPMENT, LOANS, AID
TOPIC: General Aid
PARTIES:
  Hungary
  USSR (Soviet Union)

469539   Bilateral Agreement   **7 SUGG 125**
SIGNED: 5 Nov 58
HEADNOTE: TECHNICAL AID
TOPIC: Tech Assistance
PARTIES:
  Hungary
  USSR (Soviet Union)

469540   Bilateral Agreement   **7 SUGG 125**
SIGNED: 14 Nov 58
HEADNOTE: TRADE 1960-62
TOPIC: General Trade
PARTIES:
  France
  USSR (Soviet Union)

469541   Bilateral Protocol   **7 SUGG 125**
SIGNED: 14 Nov 58
HEADNOTE: 5 YEAR EXTENSION 03 SEP 51
TOPIC: General Trade
PARTIES:
  France
  USSR (Soviet Union)

469542   Bilateral Agreement   **7 SUGG 126**
SIGNED: 16 Nov 58
HEADNOTE: 5 YEAR TRADE AGREEMENT

TOPIC: General Trade
PARTIES:
  India
  USSR (Soviet Union)

469543   Bilateral Agreement   **7 SUGG 126**
SIGNED: 19 Nov 58
HEADNOTE: GOODS ON CREDIT
TOPIC: Loans and Credits
PARTIES:
  Mongolia
  USSR (Soviet Union)

469544   Bilateral Agreement   **7 SUGG 128**
SIGNED: 12 Dec 58
HEADNOTE: TECHNICAL & CAPITAL AID
TOPIC: General Aid
PARTIES:
  India
  USSR (Soviet Union)

469545   Bilateral Agreement   **7 SUGG 129**
SIGNED: 22 Dec 58
HEADNOTE: TECHNICIAN EXCHANGE
TOPIC: Scientific Project
PARTIES:
  Germany, East
  USSR (Soviet Union)

469546   Bilateral Agreement   **7 SUGG 130**
SIGNED: 26 Dec 58
HEADNOTE: OIL PLANT CONSTRUCTION AID
TOPIC: Non-IBRD Project
PARTIES:
  Bulgaria
  USSR (Soviet Union)

469547   Bilateral Agreement   **7 SUGG 130**
SIGNED: 26 Dec 58
HEADNOTE: OIL SURVEYING AID
TOPIC: Non-IBRD Project
PARTIES:
  Bulgaria
  USSR (Soviet Union)

469548   Bilateral Agreement   **7 SUGG 131**
SIGNED: 29 Dec 58
HEADNOTE: CULTURAL & SCIENTIFIC EXHIBIT
EXCHANGE
TOPIC: Culture
PARTIES:
  USA (United States)
  USSR (Soviet Union)

469549   Bilateral Protocol   **8 SUGG 132**
SIGNED: 3 Jan 59
HEADNOTE: ECONOMIC & TECHNICAL AID
TOPIC: General Aid
PARTIES:
  Indonesia
  USSR (Soviet Union)

469550   Bilateral Protocol   **8 SUGG 133**
SIGNED: 7 Jan 59
HEADNOTE: ROLLING MILL CONSTRUCTION AID
TOPIC: Non-IBRD Project
PARTIES:
  Czechoslovakia
  USSR (Soviet Union)

469551   Bilateral Exchange   **8 SUGG 133**
SIGNED: 15 Jan 59
HEADNOTE: DIPLOMATIC MAIL PROCEDURES
TOPIC: Consul/Citizenship
PARTIES:
  Canada
  USSR (Soviet Union)

469552   Bilateral Protocol   **8 SUGG 134**
SIGNED: 17 Jan 59
HEADNOTE: TRADE
TOPIC: General Trade

PARTIES:
  Czechoslovakia
  USSR (Soviet Union)

469553   Bilateral Agreement   **8 SUGG 134**
SIGNED: 18 Jan 59
HEADNOTE: ALEXANDRIA SHIPYARD AID
TOPIC: Non-IBRD Project
PARTIES:
  United Arab Rep
  USSR (Soviet Union)

469554   Bilateral Agreement   **8 SUGG 135**
SIGNED: 28 Jan 59
HEADNOTE: TECHNICIAN EXCHANGE
TOPIC: Scientific Project
PARTIES:
  Hungary
  USSR (Soviet Union)

469555   Bilateral Agreement   **8 SUGG 136**
SIGNED: 2 Feb 59
HEADNOTE: TRADE 1959
TOPIC: General Trade
PARTIES:
  Romania
  USSR (Soviet Union)

469556   Bilateral Agreement   **8 SUGG 136**
SIGNED: 4 Feb 59
HEADNOTE: RADIO-TELEPHONE COMMUNICA-
TION
TOPIC: Telecommunications
PARTIES:
  Afghanistan
  USSR (Soviet Union)

469557   Bilateral Agreement   **8 SUGG 136**
SIGNED: 6 Feb 59
HEADNOTE: TRADE EXPANSION
TOPIC: General Trade
PARTIES:
  Albania
  USSR (Soviet Union)

469558   Bilateral Agreement   **8 SUGG 136**
SIGNED: 7 Feb 59
HEADNOTE: TECHNICAL AID 1959-67
TOPIC: Tech Assistance
PARTIES:
  China People's Rep
  USSR (Soviet Union)

469559   Bilateral Agreement   **8 SUGG 136**
SIGNED: 10 Feb 59
HEADNOTE: TECHNICAL, FINANCIAL, CAPITAL
AID
TOPIC: General Aid
PARTIES:
  Mongolia
  USSR (Soviet Union)

469560   Bilateral Agreement   **8 SUGG 137**
SIGNED: 13 Feb 59
HEADNOTE: TRADE & PAYMENTS
TOPIC: General Economic
PARTIES:
  Guinea
  USSR (Soviet Union)

469561   Bilateral Agreement   **8 SUGG 138**
SIGNED: 3 Mar 59
HEADNOTE: TECHNICAL AID
TOPIC: Tech Assistance
PARTIES:
  Poland
  USSR (Soviet Union)

469562   Bilateral Agreement   **8 SUGG 138**
SIGNED: 3 Mar 59
HEADNOTE: CULTURAL EXCHANGE
TOPIC: Culture

PARTIES:
UK Great Britain
USSR (Soviet Union)

469563   Bilateral Agreement   8 SUGG 139
SIGNED: 7 Mar 59
HEADNOTE: TECHNICAL AID
TOPIC: Tech Assistance
PARTIES:
USSR (Soviet Union)
Vietnam, North

469564   Bilateral Agreement   8 SUGG 139
SIGNED: 13 Mar 59
HEADNOTE: RENEW DIPLOMATIC RELATIONS
TOPIC: Consul/Citizenship
PARTIES:
Australia
USSR (Soviet Union)

469565   Bilateral Agreement   8 SUGG 140
SIGNED: 16 Mar 59
HEADNOTE: TRADE
TOPIC: General Trade
PARTIES:
Sudan
USSR (Soviet Union)

469566   Bilateral Agreement   8 SUGG 140
SIGNED: 17 Mar 59
HEADNOTE: TECHNICAL AID
TOPIC: Tech Assistance
PARTIES:
Korea, North
USSR (Soviet Union)

469567   Bilateral Protocol   8 SUGG 141
SIGNED: 20 Mar 59
HEADNOTE: TECHNICAL AID
TOPIC: Tech Assistance
PARTIES:
Romania
USSR (Soviet Union)

469568   Bilateral Agreement   8 SUGG 141
SIGNED: 25 Mar 59
HEADNOTE: TECHNICAL EXCHANGE
TOPIC: Scientific Project
PARTIES:
Germany, West
USSR (Soviet Union)

469569   Bilateral Instrument   8 SUGG 141
SIGNED: 28 Mar 59
HEADNOTE: CULTURAL, EDUCATIONAL, TECHNI-
CAL EXCHANGE
TOPIC: Health/Educ/Welfare
PARTIES:
UK Great Britain
USSR (Soviet Union)

469570   Bilateral Protocol   8 SUGG 141
SIGNED: 3 Apr 59
HEADNOTE: ECONOMIC COOPERATION 1961-65
TOPIC: General Economic
PARTIES:
Albania
USSR (Soviet Union)

469571   Bilateral Agreement   8 SUGG 141
SIGNED: 3 Apr 59
HEADNOTE: COMMUNICATIONS LINE AID
TOPIC: Non-IBRD Project
PARTIES:
Poland
USSR (Soviet Union)

469572   Bilateral Agreement   8 SUGG 142
SIGNED: 16 Apr 59
HEADNOTE: PERFORMING ARTS EXCHANGE
TOPIC: Culture
PARTIES:
USA (United States)
USSR (Soviet Union)

469573   Bilateral Agreement   8 SUGG 143
SIGNED: 24 Apr 59
HEADNOTE: ECONOMIC & TECHNICAL AID
TOPIC: General Aid
PARTIES:
Nepal
USSR (Soviet Union)

469574   Bilateral Agreement   8 SUGG 143
SIGNED: 24 Apr 59
HEADNOTE: KATMANDU HOSPITAL AID
TOPIC: Non-IBRD Project
PARTIES:
Nepal
USSR (Soviet Union)

469575   Bilateral Instrument   8 SUGG 145
SIGNED: 13 May 59
HEADNOTE: FISHERIES REGULATION
TOPIC: Specific Resources
PARTIES:
Japan
USSR (Soviet Union)

469576   Bilateral Agreement   8 SUGG 145
SIGNED: 28 May 59
HEADNOTE: ECONOMIC & TECHNICAL IAD
TOPIC: General Aid
PARTIES:
Afghanistan
USSR (Soviet Union)

469577   Bilateral Agreement   8 SUGG 146
SIGNED: 29 May 59
HEADNOTE: FINANCIAL & TECHNICAL AID
TOPIC: General Aid
PARTIES:
India
USSR (Soviet Union)

469578   Bilateral Agreement   8 SUGG 146
SIGNED: 30 May 59
HEADNOTE: PAYMENTS
TOPIC: Finance
PARTIES:
Denmark
USSR (Soviet Union)

469579   Bilateral Agreement   8 SUGG 146
SIGNED: 30 May 59
HEADNOTE: CULTURAL, SCIENTIFIC, TECHNICAL
EXCHANGE
TOPIC: Health/Educ/Welfare
PARTIES:
Germany, West
USSR (Soviet Union)

469580   Bilateral Protocol   8 SUGG 147
SIGNED: 5 Jun 59
HEADNOTE: METALS COMBINE EXPANSION AID
TOPIC: Non-IBRD Project
PARTIES:
Poland
USSR (Soviet Union)

469581   Bilateral Agreement   8 SUGG 147
SIGNED: 6 Jun 59
HEADNOTE: AIRLINE SERVICING
TOPIC: Air Transport
PARTIES:
Austria
USSR (Soviet Union)

469582   Bilateral Exchange   8 SUGG 147
SIGNED: 10 Jun 59
HEADNOTE: COMMERCIAL RELATIONS
TOPIC: General Trade
PARTIES:
Ghana
USSR (Soviet Union)

469583   Bilateral Agreement   8 SUGG 147
SIGNED: 23 Jun 59

HEADNOTE: MADRAS THERMAL POWER STA-
TION
TOPIC: Non-IBRD Project
PARTIES:
India
USSR (Soviet Union)

469584   Bilateral Agreement   8 SUGG 148
SIGNED: 3 Jul 59
HEADNOTE: TIRANA CULTURAL PALACE
TOPIC: Culture
PARTIES:
Albania
USSR (Soviet Union)

469585   Bilateral Agreement   8 SUGG 148
SIGNED: 3 Jul 59
HEADNOTE: TECHNICAL AID
TOPIC: Tech Assistance
PARTIES:
Albania
USSR (Soviet Union)

469586   Bilateral Agreement   8 SUGG 148
SIGNED: 3 Jul 59
HEADNOTE: RADIO CENTER AID
TOPIC: Non-IBRD Project
PARTIES:
Albania
USSR (Soviet Union)

469587   Bilateral Agreement   8 SUGG 148
SIGNED: 3 Jul 59
HEADNOTE: GEOLOGICAL SURVEY AID
TOPIC: Non-IBRD Project
PARTIES:
Albania
USSR (Soviet Union)

469588   Bilateral Agreement   8 SUGG 149
SIGNED: 11 Jul 59
HEADNOTE: TRADE
TOPIC: General Trade
PARTIES:
Ethiopia
USSR (Soviet Union)

469589   Bilateral Exchange   8 SUGG 149
SIGNED: 12 Jul 59
HEADNOTE: CAPITAL & FINANCIAL AID
TOPIC: General Aid
PARTIES:
Ethiopia
USSR (Soviet Union)

469590   Bilateral Exchange   8 SUGG 149
SIGNED: 12 Jul 59
HEADNOTE: CULTURAL EXCHANGE 1959-61
TOPIC: Culture
PARTIES:
Ethiopia
USSR (Soviet Union)

469591   Bilateral Agreement   8 SUGG 149
SIGNED: 18 Jul 59
HEADNOTE: BRIDGE CONSTRUCTION AID
TOPIC: Non-IBRD Project
PARTIES:
Afghanistan
USSR (Soviet Union)

469592   Bilateral Exchange   8 SUGG 150
SIGNED: 23 Jul 59
HEADNOTE: TECHNICAL AID
TOPIC: Tech Assistance
PARTIES:
India
USSR (Soviet Union)

469593   Bilateral Protocol   8 SUGG 150
SIGNED: 28 Jul 59
HEADNOTE: 12.5 MILLION LOAN STADIUM
TOPIC: Loans and Credits

PARTIES:
Indonesia
USSR (Soviet Union)

469594   Bilateral Protocol   **8 SUGG 150**
SIGNED: 28 Jul 59
HEADNOTE: 5M LOAN AMBON TECHNICAL
    SCHOOL
TOPIC: Loans and Credits
PARTIES:
Indonesia
USSR (Soviet Union)

469595   Bilateral Exchange   **8 SUGG 150**
SIGNED: 31 Jul 59
HEADNOTE: SOVIET TRADE MISSION
TOPIC: General Trade
PARTIES:
Morocco
USSR (Soviet Union)

469596   Bilateral Agreement   **8 SUGG 151**
SIGNED: 7 Aug 59
HEADNOTE: INCREASE 1961-65 TRADE
TOPIC: General Trade
PARTIES:
Hungary
USSR (Soviet Union)

469597   Bilateral Agreement   **8 SUGG 151**
SIGNED: 7 Aug 59
HEADNOTE: SOVIET TECHNICAL AID
TOPIC: Tech Assistance
PARTIES:
Hungary
USSR (Soviet Union)

469598   Bilateral Instrument   **8 SUGG 152**
SIGNED: 14 Aug 59
HEADNOTE: CONDITIONS FOR TECHNICAL AID
TOPIC: Tech Assistance
PARTIES:
Indonesia
USSR (Soviet Union)

469599   Bilateral Agreement   **8 SUGG 152**
SIGNED: 17 Aug 59
HEADNOTE: CIVIL ATOMIC DEVELOPMENT AID
TOPIC: Atomic Energy
PARTIES:
Iraq
USSR (Soviet Union)

469600   Bilateral Protocol   **8 SUGG 152**
SIGNED: 24 Aug 59
HEADNOTE: ECONOMIC & TECHNICAL AID
TOPIC: General Aid
PARTIES:
Guinea
USSR (Soviet Union)

469601   Bilateral Agreement   **8 SUGG 152**
SIGNED: 24 Aug 59
HEADNOTE: 140M RUBLES LONG TERM LOAN
TOPIC: Loans and Credits
PARTIES:
Guinea
USSR (Soviet Union)

469602   Bilateral Agreement   **8 SUGG 153**
SIGNED: 7 Sep 59
HEADNOTE: CIVIL ATOMIC DEVELOPMENT
TOPIC: Atomic Energy
PARTIES:
Korea, North
USSR (Soviet Union)

469603   Bilateral Agreement   **8 SUGG 153**
SIGNED: 12 Sep 59
HEADNOTE: 1.5 BILLION RUBLES CREDIT
TOPIC: Loans and Credits
PARTIES:
India
USSR (Soviet Union)

469604   Bilateral Agreement   **8 SUGG 154**
SIGNED: 28 Sep 59
HEADNOTE: OIL REFINERY AID
TOPIC: Non-IBRD Project
PARTIES:
India
USSR (Soviet Union)

469605   Bilateral Instrument   **8 SUGG 155**
SIGNED: 18 Oct 59
HEADNOTE: WORLD WAR II PRISONERS & REF-
    UGEES
TOPIC: Refugees
PARTIES:
Italy
USSR (Soviet Union)

469606   Bilateral Agreement   **8 SUGG 155**
SIGNED: 22 Oct 59
HEADNOTE: TRADE 1961-65
TOPIC: General Trade
PARTIES:
Finland
USSR (Soviet Union)

469607   Bilateral Agreement   **8 SUGG 156**
SIGNED: 4 Nov 59
HEADNOTE: TRADE 1961-65
TOPIC: General Trade
PARTIES:
Bulgaria
USSR (Soviet Union)

469608   Bilateral Agreement   **8 SUGG 156**
SIGNED: 4 Nov 59
HEADNOTE: TECHNICAL AID FOR POWER
    PLANTS
TOPIC: Tech Assistance
PARTIES:
Bulgaria
USSR (Soviet Union)

469609   Bilateral Agreement   **8 SUGG 157**
SIGNED: 6 Nov 59
HEADNOTE: TRADE FOR 1960
TOPIC: General Trade
PARTIES:
Netherlands
USSR (Soviet Union)

469610   Bilateral Agreement   **8 SUGG 158**
SIGNED: 20 Nov 59
HEADNOTE: JAPANESE INDUSTRIAL EXHIBIT
TOPIC: General Trade
PARTIES:
Japan
USSR (Soviet Union)

469611   Bilateral Agreement   **8 SUGG 159**
SIGNED: 26 Nov 59
HEADNOTE: CULTURAL COLLABORATION
TOPIC: Culture
PARTIES:
Guinea
USSR (Soviet Union)

469612   Bilateral Agreement   **8 SUGG 159**
SIGNED: 1 Dec 59
HEADNOTE: INDUSTRIAL TECHNICAL AID
TOPIC: Tech Assistance
PARTIES:
Romania
USSR (Soviet Union)

469613   Bilateral Protocol   **8 SUGG 160**
SIGNED: 1 Dec 59
HEADNOTE: AGRICULTURAL TECHNICAL AID
TOPIC: Tech Assistance
PARTIES:
USSR (Soviet Union)
Yemen

469614   Bilateral Agreement   **8 SUGG 160**
SIGNED: 2 Dec 59

HEADNOTE: CHEMICAL TECHNICAL AID
TOPIC: Tech Assistance
PARTIES:
Romania
USSR (Soviet Union)

469615   Bilateral Agreement   **8 SUGG 160**
SIGNED: 9 Dec 59
HEADNOTE: TRADE & PAYMENTS
TOPIC: General Economic
PARTIES:
Brazil
USSR (Soviet Union)

469616   Bilateral Instrument   **8 SUGG 162**
SIGNED: 16 Dec 59
HEADNOTE: CONDITIONS FOR TECHNICAL AID
TOPIC: Tech Assistance
PARTIES:
Iraq
USSR (Soviet Union)

469617   Bilateral Agreement   **8 SUGG 163**
SIGNED: 22 Dec 59
HEADNOTE: CREDIT TO 500 MILLION RUBLES
TOPIC: Loans and Credits
PARTIES:
Finland
USSR (Soviet Union)

469618   Bilateral Protocol   **8 SUGG 163**
SIGNED: 22 Dec 59
HEADNOTE: INDUSTRIAL EXHIBIT EXCHANGES
TOPIC: General Trade
PARTIES:
UK Great Britain
USSR (Soviet Union)

469619   Bilateral Exchange   **8 SUGG 163**
SIGNED: 22 Dec 59
HEADNOTE: LEND-LEASE SETTLEMENT
TOPIC: Claims and Debts
PARTIES:
USA (United States)
USSR (Soviet Union)

469620   Bilateral Agreement   **8 SUGG 164**
SIGNED: 27 Dec 59
HEADNOTE: INDUSTRIAL TECHNICAL AID
TOPIC: Tech Assistance
PARTIES:
Iraq
USSR (Soviet Union)

469621   Bilateral Exchange   **9 SUGG 121**
SIGNED: 17 Jan 60
HEADNOTE: ASWAN DAM FINANCIAL AID
TOPIC: Non-IBRD Project
PARTIES:
United Arab Rep
USSR (Soviet Union)

469622   Bilateral Agreement   **9 SUGG 121**
SIGNED: 16 Jan 60
HEADNOTE: TRADE & PAYMENTS
TOPIC: General Trade
PARTIES:
Tunisia
USSR (Soviet Union)

469623   Bilateral Agreement   **9 SUGG 121**
SIGNED: 19 Jan 60
HEADNOTE: TECHNICAL & FINANCIAL AID
TOPIC: General Aid
PARTIES:
Afghanistan
USSR (Soviet Union)

469624   Bilateral Exchange   **9 SUGG 22**
SIGNED: 20 Jan 60
HEADNOTE: TECHNICAL AID
TOPIC: Tech Assistance

PARTIES:
Bulgaria
USSR (Soviet Union)

PARTIES:
Guinea
USSR (Soviet Union)

PARTIES:
Iraq
USSR (Soviet Union)

469625   Bilateral Agreement   **9 SUGG 122**
SIGNED: 20 Jan 60
HEADNOTE: TRADE
TOPIC: General Trade
PARTIES:
Czechoslovakia
USSR (Soviet Union)

469635   Bilateral Instrument   **9 SUGG 128**
SIGNED: 1 Mar 60
HEADNOTE: CONDITIONS FOR TECHNICAL AID
TOPIC: Tech Assistance
PARTIES:
Guinea
USSR (Soviet Union)

469645   Bilateral Protocol   **9 SUGG 131**
SIGNED: 25 Mar 60
HEADNOTE: INDUSTRIAL TECHNICAL AID
TOPIC: Tech Assistance
PARTIES:
Ethiopia
USSR (Soviet Union)

469626   Bilateral Agreement   **9 SUGG 122**
SIGNED: 25 Jan 60
HEADNOTE: TRADE
TOPIC: General Trade
PARTIES:
Albania
USSR (Soviet Union)

469636   Bilateral Agreement   **9 SUGG 128**
SIGNED: 2 Mar 60
HEADNOTE: TRADE & PAYMENTS
TOPIC: General Trade
PARTIES:
Japan
USSR (Soviet Union)

469646   Bilateral Exchange   **9 SUGG 131**
SIGNED: 28 Mar 60
HEADNOTE: CAPITAL AID
TOPIC: Direct Aid
PARTIES:
Mongolia
USSR (Soviet Union)

469627   Bilateral Agreement   **9 SUGG 124**
SIGNED: 9 Feb 60
HEADNOTE: EASING VISA REQUIREMENTS
TOPIC: Visas
PARTIES:
Italy
USSR (Soviet Union)

469637   Bilateral Exchange   **9 SUGG 128**
SIGNED: 2 Mar 60
HEADNOTE: BARTER AGREEMENTS
TOPIC: General Trade
PARTIES:
Japan
USSR (Soviet Union)

469647   Bilateral Agreement   **9 SUGG 132**
SIGNED: 31 Mar 60
HEADNOTE: SLOVAKIA METALLURGIC COMBINE
TOPIC: Non-IBRD Project
PARTIES:
Czechoslovakia
USSR (Soviet Union)

469628   Bilateral Agreement   **9 SUGG 124**
SIGNED: 11 Feb 60
HEADNOTE: ECONOMIC & TECHNICAL AID
1960-65
TOPIC: General Aid
PARTIES:
Mongolia
USSR (Soviet Union)

469638   Bilateral Agreement   **9 SUGG 129**
SIGNED: 4 Mar 60
HEADNOTE: CULTURAL COOPERATION
TOPIC: Culture
PARTIES:
Afghanistan
USSR (Soviet Union)

469648   Bilateral Agreement   **9 SUGG 132**
SIGNED: 1 Apr 60
HEADNOTE: PAYMENT TERMS
TOPIC: Finance
PARTIES:
Poland
USSR (Soviet Union)

469629   Bilateral Agreement   **9 SUGG 124**
SIGNED: 11 Feb 60
HEADNOTE: HOUSING ECONOMIC & TECHNICAL
AID
TOPIC: General Aid
PARTIES:
Mongolia
USSR (Soviet Union)

469639   Bilateral Agreement   **9 SUGG 129**
SIGNED: 7 Mar 60
HEADNOTE: HIGH-VOLTAGE LINE CONSTRUC-
TION AID
TOPIC: Tech Assistance
PARTIES:
Czechoslovakia
USSR (Soviet Union)

469649   Bilateral Agreement   **9 SUGG 132**
SIGNED: 2 Apr 60
HEADNOTE: PAYMENT TERMS
TOPIC: Finance
PARTIES:
France
USSR (Soviet Union)

469630   Bilateral Agreement   **9 SUGG 125**
SIGNED: 12 Feb 60
HEADNOTE: AMENDS 12 SEP 59
TOPIC: General Aid
PARTIES:
India
USSR (Soviet Union)

469640   Bilateral Agreement   **9 SUGG 129**
SIGNED: 8 Mar 60
HEADNOTE: TECHNICAL SCHOOL IN BAHAR-
DARE
TOPIC: Non-IBRD Project
PARTIES:
Ethiopia
USSR (Soviet Union)

469650   Bilateral Exchange   **9 SUGG 133**
SIGNED: 4 Apr 60
HEADNOTE: SOHNA AQUEDUCT AID
TOPIC: Non-IBRD Project
PARTIES:
USSR (Soviet Union)
Yemen

469631   Bilateral Exchange   **9 SUGG 126**
SIGNED: 18 Feb 60
HEADNOTE: TECHNICIAN TRAINING
TOPIC: Education
PARTIES:
Afghanistan
USSR (Soviet Union)

469641   Bilateral Agreement   **9 SUGG 129**
SIGNED: 10 Mar 60
HEADNOTE: TRADE 1961-65
TOPIC: General Trade
PARTIES:
Poland
USSR (Soviet Union)

469651   Bilateral Agreement   **9 SUGG 134**
SIGNED: 28 Apr 60
HEADNOTE: TRADE 1961-65
TOPIC: General Trade
PARTIES:
Czechoslovakia
USSR (Soviet Union)

469632   Bilateral Exchange   **9 SUGG 126**
SIGNED: 20 Feb 60
HEADNOTE: PROVISIONAL TRADE MISSION
TOPIC: General Trade
PARTIES:
Cuba
USSR (Soviet Union)

469642   Bilateral Agreement   **9 SUGG 130**
SIGNED: 10 Mar 60
HEADNOTE: INDUSTRIAL TECHNICAL AID
TOPIC: Tech Assistance
PARTIES:
Poland
USSR (Soviet Union)

469652   Bilateral Agreement   **9 SUGG 134**
SIGNED: 1 May 60
HEADNOTE: ESTABLISH DIPLOMATIC RELATION
TOPIC: Consul/Citizenship
PARTIES:
Togo
USSR (Soviet Union)

469633   Bilateral Protocol   **9 SUGG 127**
SIGNED: 1 Mar 60
HEADNOTE: TECHNICAL AID 1960-63
TOPIC: Tech Assistance
PARTIES:
Guinea
USSR (Soviet Union)

469643   Bilateral Exchange   **9 SUGG 130**
SIGNED: 14 Mar 60
HEADNOTE: TRADE MISSION TO MADRAS
TOPIC: General Trade
PARTIES:
India
USSR (Soviet Union)

469653   Bilateral Exchange   **9 SUGG 134**
SIGNED: 4 May 60
HEADNOTE: MODIFIES 17 JAN 57
TOPIC: Direct Aid
PARTIES:
Burma
USSR (Soviet Union)

469634   Bilateral Exchange   **9 SUGG 128**
SIGNED: 1 Mar 60
HEADNOTE: CAPITAL AID
TOPIC: Direct Aid

469644   Bilateral Exchange   **9 SUGG 131**
SIGNED: 20 Mar 60
HEADNOTE: SAND QUARRY & SURVEY AID
TOPIC: Non-IBRD Project

469654   Bilateral Agreement   **9 SUGG 134**
SIGNED: 4 May 60
HEADNOTE: EXCHANGE AMBASSADORS
TOPIC: Consul/Citizenship
PARTIES:
Tunisia
USSR (Soviet Union)

469655   Bilateral Agreement   **9 SUGG 135**
SIGNED: 6 May 60
HEADNOTE: TRADE 1961-65
TOPIC: General Trade
PARTIES:
 Hungary
 USSR (Soviet Union)

469656   Bilateral Agreement   **9 SUGG 135**
SIGNED: 8 May 60
HEADNOTE: RENEW DIPLOMATIC RELATIONS
TOPIC: Consul/Citizenship
PARTIES:
 Cuba
 USSR (Soviet Union)

469657   Bilateral Protocol   **9 SUGG 135**
SIGNED: 10 May 60
HEADNOTE: CAPITAL AID
TOPIC: Direct Aid
PARTIES:
 Cambodia
 USSR (Soviet Union)

469658   Bilateral Protocol   **9 SUGG 165**
SIGNED: 10 May 60
HEADNOTE: MEDICAL AID
TOPIC: Direct Aid
PARTIES:
 Cambodia
 USSR (Soviet Union)

469659   Bilateral Exchange   **9 SUGG 135**
SIGNED: 12 May 60
HEADNOTE: OIL INDUSTRY TECHNICAL AID
TOPIC: Tech Assistance
PARTIES:
 Czechoslovakia
 USSR (Soviet Union)

469660   Bilateral Exchange   **9 SUGG 136**
SIGNED: 17 May 60
HEADNOTE: DEVALUED ICELAND PAYMENTS
TOPIC: Finance
PARTIES:
 Iceland
 USSR (Soviet Union)

469661   Bilateral Instrument   **9 SUGG 136**
SIGNED: 18 May 60
HEADNOTE: NW PACIFIC FISHING REGULATION
TOPIC: Specific Resources
PARTIES:
 Japan
 USSR (Soviet Union)

469662   Bilateral Protocol   **9 SUGG 136**
SIGNED: 25 May 60
HEADNOTE: QIZIL-QALA PORT DEVELOPMENT
TOPIC: Non-IBRD Project
PARTIES:
 Afghanistan
 USSR (Soviet Union)

469663   Bilateral Protocol   **9 SUGG 137**
SIGNED: 27 May 60
HEADNOTE: SUPPLEMENTS 27 OCT 58
TOPIC: Loans and Credits
PARTIES:
 Argentina
 USSR (Soviet Union)

469664   Bilateral Agreement   **9 SUGG 138**
SIGNED: 14 Jun 60
HEADNOTE: EQUIPMENT ON LONG TERM CREDIT
TOPIC: Loans and Credits
PARTIES:
 USSR (Soviet Union)
 Vietnam, North

469665   Bilateral Agreement   **9 SUGG 138**
SIGNED: 16 Jun 60
HEADNOTE: TECHNICAL AID
TOPIC: Tech Assistance

PARTIES:
 India
 USSR (Soviet Union)

469666   Bilateral Agreement   **9 SUGG 139**
SIGNED: 18 Jun 60
HEADNOTE: SOVIET OIL PRODUCTS
TOPIC: General Trade
PARTIES:
 Cuba
 USSR (Soviet Union)

469667   Bilateral Agreement   **9 SUGG 139**
SIGNED: 18 Jun 60
HEADNOTE: PAYMENTS
TOPIC: Finance
PARTIES:
 Cuba
 USSR (Soviet Union)

469668   Bilateral Protocol   **9 SUGG 140**
SIGNED: 25 Jun 60
HEADNOTE: SOVIET AID PLANNING HODEIDA
TOPIC: Tech Assistance
PARTIES:
 USSR (Soviet Union)
 Yemen

469669   Bilateral Exchange   **9 SUGG 140**
SIGNED: 28 Jun 60
HEADNOTE: SOVIET TELEVISION CENTER AID
TOPIC: Tech Assistance
PARTIES:
 Bulgaria
 USSR (Soviet Union)

469670   Bilateral Agreement   **9 SUGG 141**
SIGNED: 1 Jul 60
HEADNOTE: CIVIL ATOMIC DEVELOPMENT AID
TOPIC: Atomic Energy
PARTIES:
 Indonesia
 USSR (Soviet Union)

469671   Bilateral Agreement   **9 SUGG 141**
SIGNED: 7 Jul 60
HEADNOTE: ESTABLISH DIPLOMATIC RELA-
TIONS
TOPIC: Consul/Citizenship
PARTIES:
 Congo (Zaire)
 USSR (Soviet Union)

469672   Bilateral Agreement   **9 SUGG 141**
SIGNED: 9 Jul 60
HEADNOTE: TRADE 1961-63
TOPIC: General Trade
PARTIES:
 Indonesia
 USSR (Soviet Union)

469673   Bilateral Exchange   **9 SUGG 142**
SIGNED: 9 Jul 60
HEADNOTE: SOVIET TECHNICAL AID
TOPIC: Tech Assistance
PARTIES:
 Indonesia
 USSR (Soviet Union)

469674   Bilateral Protocol   **9 SUGG 142**
SIGNED: 11 Jul 60
HEADNOTE: FILM STUDIO TECHNICAL AID
TOPIC: Tech Assistance
PARTIES:
 Korea, North
 USSR (Soviet Union)

469675   Bilateral Agreement   **9 SUGG 142**
SIGNED: 12 Jul 60
HEADNOTE: SOVIET NATIONAL EXHIBIT PARIS
TOPIC: Culture
PARTIES:
 France
 USSR (Soviet Union)

469676   Bilateral Exchange   **9 SUGG 142**
SIGNED: 19 Jul 60
HEADNOTE: REINFORCED CONCRETE TECHNICAL
 AID
TOPIC: Tech Assistance
PARTIES:
 Albania
 USSR (Soviet Union)

469677   Bilateral Convention   **9 SUGG 142**
SIGNED: 21 Jul 60
HEADNOTE: CONSULAR CONVENTION
TOPIC: Consul/Citizenship
PARTIES:
 USSR (Soviet Union)
 Yugoslavia

469678   Bilateral Exchange   **9 SUGG 143**
SIGNED: 22 Jul 60
HEADNOTE: SOVIET TECHNICAL AID
TOPIC: Tech Assistance
PARTIES:
 Bulgaria
 USSR (Soviet Union)

469680   Bilateral Exchange   **9 SUGG 143**
SIGNED: 2 Aug 60
HEADNOTE: SOVIET TECHNICAL AID
TOPIC: Tech Assistance
PARTIES:
 USSR (Soviet Union)
 Vietnam, North

469681   Bilateral Exchange   **9 SUGG 144**
SIGNED: 11 Aug 60
HEADNOTE: SOVIET TECHNICAL AID
TOPIC: Tech Assistance
PARTIES:
 United Arab Rep
 USSR (Soviet Union)

469682   Bilateral Agreement   **9 SUGG 144**
SIGNED: 12 Aug 60
HEADNOTE: TRADE
TOPIC: General Trade
PARTIES:
 Afghanistan
 USSR (Soviet Union)

469683   Bilateral Exchange   **9 SUGG 144**
SIGNED: 12 Aug 60
HEADNOTE: SOVIET HYDROELECTRIC TECHNI-
CAL AID
TOPIC: Tech Assistance
PARTIES:
 Nepal
 USSR (Soviet Union)

469684   Bilateral Agreement   **9 SUGG 144**
SIGNED: 18 Aug 60
HEADNOTE: INCREASES 16 MAR 59 LOAN
TOPIC: Loans and Credits
PARTIES:
 Iraq
 USSR (Soviet Union)

469685   Bilateral Exchange   **9 SUGG 145**
SIGNED: 22 Aug 60
HEADNOTE: COTTON TECHNICIAN EXCHANGE
TOPIC: Education
PARTIES:
 India
 USSR (Soviet Union)

469686   Bilateral Agreement   **9 SUGG 145**
SIGNED: 25 Aug 60
HEADNOTE: CULTURAL COOPERATION
TOPIC: Culture
PARTIES:
 Ghana
 USSR (Soviet Union)

469687   Bilateral Exchange   **9 SUGG 145**
SIGNED: 26 Aug 60

HEADNOTE: ECONOMIC & TECHNICAL AID IN
FISHING
TOPIC: General Aid
PARTIES:
  USSR (Soviet Union)
  Vietnam, North

469688   Bilateral Exchange   **9 SUGG 146**
SIGNED: 30 Aug 60
HEADNOTE: TECHNICIAN TRAINING
TOPIC: Education
PARTIES:
  Germany, East
  USSR (Soviet Union)

469689   Bilateral Exchange   **9 SUGG 146**
SIGNED: 31 Aug 60
HEADNOTE: SOVIET HYDROELECTRIC TECHNI-
CAL AID
TOPIC: Tech Assistance
PARTIES:
  Albania
  USSR (Soviet Union)

469690   Bilateral Exchange   **9 SUGG 146**
SIGNED: 31 Aug 60
HEADNOTE: SOVIET SURVEYING TECHNICAL AID
TOPIC: Tech Assistance
PARTIES:
  Korea, North
  USSR (Soviet Union)

469691   Bilateral Agreement   **9 SUGG 147**
SIGNED: 8 Sep 60
HEADNOTE: TRADE 1961-65
TOPIC: General Trade
PARTIES:
  Guinea
  USSR (Soviet Union)

469692   Bilateral Agreement   **9 SUGG 147**
SIGNED: 9 Sep 60
HEADNOTE: ECONOMIC & TECHNICAL AID
TOPIC: General Aid
PARTIES:
  Mongolia
  USSR (Soviet Union)

469693   Bilateral Exchange   **9 SUGG 148**
SIGNED: 13 Sep 60
HEADNOTE: TECHNICAL AID WARSAW SEWER
CONSTRUCTION
TOPIC: Tech Assistance
PARTIES:
  Poland
  USSR (Soviet Union)

469694   Bilateral Protocol   **9 SUGG 148**
SIGNED: 13 Sep 60
HEADNOTE: THERMO-ELECTRIC TECHNICAL AID
TOPIC: Tech Assistance
PARTIES:
  Poland
  USSR (Soviet Union)

469695   Bilateral Protocol   **9 SUGG 148**
SIGNED: 27 Sep 60
HEADNOTE: OIL SURVEYING TECHNICAL AID
TOPIC: Tech Assistance
PARTIES:
  Germany, East
  USSR (Soviet Union)

469696   Bilateral Exchange   **9 SUGG 148**
SIGNED: 27 Sep 60
HEADNOTE: ELECTRIFICATION TECHNICAL AID
TOPIC: Tech Assistance
PARTIES:
  Mongolia
  USSR (Soviet Union)

469697   Bilateral Exchange   **9 SUGG 148**
SIGNED: 27 Sep 60
HEADNOTE: GENERAL TECHNICAL AID

TOPIC: Tech Assistance
PARTIES:
  Mongolia
  USSR (Soviet Union)

469698   Bilateral Agreement   **9 SUGG 148**
SIGNED: 29 Sep 60
HEADNOTE: NATURAL GAS DELIVERIES
TOPIC: Commodity Trade
PARTIES:
  Poland
  USSR (Soviet Union)

469699   Bilateral Exchange   **9 SUGG 148**
SIGNED: 30 Sep 60
HEADNOTE: COAL MINING TECHNICAL AID
TOPIC: Tech Assistance
PARTIES:
  USSR (Soviet Union)
  Vietnam, North

469700   Bilateral Exchange   **9 SUGG 148**
SIGNED: 30 Sep 60
HEADNOTE: TECHNICAL AID HEATING PYON-
GYANG
TOPIC: Tech Assistance
PARTIES:
  Korea, North
  USSR (Soviet Union)

469701   Bilateral Exchange   **9 SUGG 149**
SIGNED: 11 Sep 60
HEADNOTE: ESTABLISH DIPLOMATIC RELA-
TIONS
TOPIC: Consul/Citizenship
PARTIES:
  Somalia
  USSR (Soviet Union)

469702   Bilateral Agreement   **9 SUGG 149**
SIGNED: 7 Oct 60
HEADNOTE: ESTABLISH DIPLOMATIC RELA-
TIONS
TOPIC: Consul/Citizenship
PARTIES:
  Laos
  USSR (Soviet Union)

469703   Bilateral Exchange   **9 SUGG 149**
SIGNED: 8 Oct 60
HEADNOTE: TECHNICAL AID FOR DAMS
TOPIC: Tech Assistance
PARTIES:
  Bulgaria
  USSR (Soviet Union)

469704   Bilateral Agreement   **9 SUGG 149**
SIGNED: 8 Oct 60
HEADNOTE: EDUCATIONAL EXCHANGES
TOPIC: Education
PARTIES:
  Mongolia
  USSR (Soviet Union)

469705   Bilateral Protocol   **9 SUGG 149**
SIGNED: 13 Oct 60
HEADNOTE: LOAN REPAYMENT RELEASE
TOPIC: Finance
PARTIES:
  Korea, North
  USSR (Soviet Union)

469706   Bilateral Agreement   **9 SUGG 150**
SIGNED: 14 Oct 60
HEADNOTE: HOSPITAL & POLYCLINIC CON-
STRUCTION
TOPIC: Non-IBRD Project
PARTIES:
  Indonesia
  USSR (Soviet Union)

469707   Bilateral Agreement   **9 SUGG 151**
SIGNED: 11 Nov 60
HEADNOTE: TRADE 1961-65

TOPIC: General Trade
PARTIES:
  Romania
  USSR (Soviet Union)

469708   Bilateral Exchange   **9 SUGG 151**
SIGNED: 13 Nov 60
HEADNOTE: LAPIS-LAZULI MINING TECH AID
TOPIC: Tech Assistance
PARTIES:
  Afghanistan
  USSR (Soviet Union)

469709   Bilateral Agreement   **9 SUGG 151**
SIGNED: 13 Nov 60
HEADNOTE: ESTABLISH DIPLOMATIC RELA-
TIONS
TOPIC: Consul/Citizenship
PARTIES:
  Cyprus
  USSR (Soviet Union)

469710   Bilateral Agreement   **9 SUGG 151**
SIGNED: 11 Nov 60
HEADNOTE: TECHNICAL AID 1961-68
TOPIC: Tech Assistance
PARTIES:
  Romania
  USSR (Soviet Union)

469711   Bilateral Exchange   **9 SUGG 151**
SIGNED: 14 Nov 60
HEADNOTE: TECHNICAL AID
TOPIC: Tech Assistance
PARTIES:
  Mongolia
  USSR (Soviet Union)

469712   Bilateral Agreement   **9 SUGG 151**
SIGNED: 15 Nov 60
HEADNOTE: 14 SOVIET MILITARY JETS
TOPIC: Milit Assistance
PARTIES:
  Morocco
  USSR (Soviet Union)

469713   Bilateral Agreement   **9 SUGG 152**
SIGNED: 16 Nov 60
HEADNOTE: TECHNICAL AID
TOPIC: Tech Assistance
PARTIES:
  Cuba
  USSR (Soviet Union)

469714   Bilateral Agreement   **9 SUGG 152**
SIGNED: 16 Nov 60
HEADNOTE: USSR TRAINING FOR CUBAN TECH-
NICIANS
TOPIC: Education
PARTIES:
  Cuba
  USSR (Soviet Union)

469715   Bilateral Agreement   **9 SUGG 152**
SIGNED: 24 Nov 60
HEADNOTE: CUSTOMS
TOPIC: Customs
PARTIES:
  Finland
  USSR (Soviet Union)

469716   Bilateral Exchange   **9 SUGG 152**
SIGNED: 29 Nov 60
HEADNOTE: TECHNICAL AID
TOPIC: Tech Assistance
PARTIES:
  Bulgaria
  USSR (Soviet Union)

469717   Bilateral Exchange   **9 SUGG 153**
SIGNED: 30 Nov 60
HEADNOTE: TECHNICAL & CAPITAL FARMING
AID
TOPIC: General Aid

PARTIES:
Bulgaria
USSR (Soviet Union)

469718 Bilateral Exchange **9 SUGG 153**
SIGNED: 30 Nov 60
HEADNOTE: MINING TECHNICAL AID
TOPIC: Tech Assistance
PARTIES:
Bulgaria
USSR (Soviet Union)

469720 Bilateral Agreement **9 SUGG 154**
SIGNED: 8 Jul 60
HEADNOTE: INDUSTRY & AGRICULTURE LOANS
TOPIC: Loans and Credits
PARTIES:
United Arab Rep
USSR (Soviet Union)

469721 Bilateral Agreement **9 SUGG 154**
SIGNED: 7 Dec 60
HEADNOTE: ESTABLISH DIPLOMATIC RELA-
TIONS
TOPIC: Consul/Citizenship
PARTIES:
Central Afri Rep
USSR (Soviet Union)

469722 Bilateral Agreement **9 SUGG 154**
SIGNED: 13 Dec 60
HEADNOTE: TRADE 1961-65
TOPIC: General Trade
PARTIES:
Austria
USSR (Soviet Union)

469723 Bilateral Agreement **9 SUGG 155**
SIGNED: 19 Dec 60
HEADNOTE: CAPITAL & TECHNICAL AID
TOPIC: General Aid
PARTIES:
Cuba
USSR (Soviet Union)

469724 Bilateral Agreement **9 SUGG 155**
SIGNED: 19 Dec 60
HEADNOTE: USSR TRAINING FOR CUBANS
TOPIC: Education
PARTIES:
Cuba
USSR (Soviet Union)

469725 Bilateral Agreement **9 SUGG 156**
SIGNED: 20 Dec 60
HEADNOTE: TRADE 1961-65
TOPIC: General Trade
PARTIES:
Mongolia
USSR (Soviet Union)

469726 Bilateral Agreement **9 SUGG 157**
SIGNED: 23 Dec 60
HEADNOTE: ECONOMIC & TECHNICAL AID
TOPIC: General Aid
PARTIES:
USSR (Soviet Union)
Vietnam, North

469727 Bilateral Agreement **9 SUGG 157**
SIGNED: 23 Dec 60
HEADNOTE: TRADE 1961-65
TOPIC: General Trade
PARTIES:
USSR (Soviet Union)
Vietnam, North

469728 Bilateral Agreement **9 SUGG 158**
SIGNED: 24 Dec 60
HEADNOTE: TECHNICAL AID 1961
TOPIC: Tech Assistance
PARTIES:
Korea, North
USSR (Soviet Union)

469729 Bilateral Agreement **9 SUGG 158**
SIGNED: 24 Dec 60
HEADNOTE: TRADE 1961-65
TOPIC: General Trade
PARTIES:
Korea, North
USSR (Soviet Union)

469730 Bilateral Agreement **9 SUGG 158**
SIGNED: 31 Dec 60
HEADNOTE: 650 MILLION RUBLE LOAN
TOPIC: Loans and Credits
PARTIES:
Bulgaria
USSR (Soviet Union)

469731 Bilateral Protocol **9 SUGG 159**
SIGNED: 31 Dec 60
HEADNOTE: EXTENDS 25 APR 58
TOPIC: General Economic
PARTIES:
Germany, East
USSR (Soviet Union)

469732 Bilateral Agreement **10 SUGG 117**
SIGNED: 4 Jan 61
HEADNOTE: TRADE & PAYMENTS
TOPIC: General Economic
PARTIES:
Albania
USSR (Soviet Union)

469733 Bilateral Agreement **10 SUGG 117**
SIGNED: 4 Jan 61
HEADNOTE: CULTURAL & SCIENTIFIC COOPER-
ATION
TOPIC: Health/Educ/Welfare
PARTIES:
Poland
USSR (Soviet Union)

469734 Bilateral Agreement **10 SUGG 117**
SIGNED: 6 Jan 61
HEADNOTE: SALE SOVIET MILITARY GOODS
TOPIC: Milit Assistance
PARTIES:
Indonesia
USSR (Soviet Union)

469735 Bilateral Exchange **10 SUGG 117**
SIGNED: 7 Jan 61
HEADNOTE: CORN PROCESSING PLANT AID
TOPIC: Direct Aid
PARTIES:
Poland
USSR (Soviet Union)

469736 Bilateral Agreement **10 SUGG 118**
SIGNED: 1 Dec 60
HEADNOTE: CHANGE MISSIONS TO EMBASSIES
TOPIC: Consul/Citizenship
PARTIES:
Luxembourg
USSR (Soviet Union)

469737 Bilateral Protocol **10 SUGG 118**
SIGNED: 18 Jan 61
HEADNOTE: TRADE 1962-65 EXPANDED
TOPIC: General Trade
PARTIES:
Bulgaria
USSR (Soviet Union)

469738 Bilateral Exchange **10 SUGG 119**
SIGNED: 27 Jan 61
HEADNOTE: FISHING EQUIPMENT TRANSFER
TOPIC: Direct Aid
PARTIES:
USSR (Soviet Union)
Vietnam, North

469739 Bilateral Agreement **10 SUGG 120**
SIGNED: 1 Feb 61
HEADNOTE: DELIVERY OF AIRLINERS

TOPIC: Specif Goods/Equip
PARTIES:
Ghana
USSR (Soviet Union)

469740 Bilateral Protocol **10 SUGG 120**
SIGNED: 3 Feb 61
HEADNOTE: HELSINKI-LENINGRAD CABLE
TOPIC: Specific Property
PARTIES:
Finland
USSR (Soviet Union)

469741 Bilateral Treaty **10 SUGG 121**
SIGNED: 15 Feb 61
HEADNOTE: BORDER REGULATION
TOPIC: Admin Cooperation
PARTIES:
Poland
USSR (Soviet Union)

469742 Bilateral Exchange **10 SUGG 122**
SIGNED: 18 Feb 61
HEADNOTE: METALLURGY TECHNICAL AID
TOPIC: Tech Assistance
PARTIES:
Bulgaria
USSR (Soviet Union)

469743 Bilateral Protocol **10 SUGG 122**
SIGNED: 21 Feb 61
HEADNOTE: SCIENTIFIC & TECHNICAL COOPER-
ATION
TOPIC: Scientific Project
PARTIES:
Czechoslovakia
USSR (Soviet Union)

469744 Bilateral Agreement **10 SUGG 122**
SIGNED: 21 Feb 61
HEADNOTE: CAPITAL & TECHNICAL AID
TOPIC: General Aid
PARTIES:
India
USSR (Soviet Union)

469745 Bilateral Protocol **10 SUGG 123**
SIGNED: 24 Feb 61
HEADNOTE: CAPITAL & TECHNICAL AID
TOPIC: General Aid
PARTIES:
Indonesia
USSR (Soviet Union)

469746 Bilateral Protocol **10 SUGG 123**
SIGNED: 25 Feb 61
HEADNOTE: FILM STUDIO EXPANSION AID
TOPIC: Non-IBRD Project
PARTIES:
Mongolia
USSR (Soviet Union)

469747 Bilateral Treaty **10 SUGG 123**
SIGNED: 27 Feb 61
HEADNOTE: BORDER REGULATION
TOPIC: Admin Cooperation
PARTIES:
Romania
USSR (Soviet Union)

469748 Bilateral Agreement **10 SUGG 124**
SIGNED: 28 Feb 61
HEADNOTE: CIVIL ATOMIC DEVELOPMENT
TOPIC: Atomic Energy
PARTIES:
Ghana
USSR (Soviet Union)

469749 Bilateral Agreement **10 SUGG 124**
SIGNED: 4 Mar 61
HEADNOTE: TECHNICAL & CAPITAL AID
TOPIC: General Aid

PARTIES:
Pakistan
USSR (Soviet Union)

469750   Bilateral Exchange   **10 SUGG 124**
SIGNED: 6 Mar 61
HEADNOTE: FISHING TECHNICAL AID
TOPIC: Tech Assistance
PARTIES:
USSR (Soviet Union)
Vietnam, North

469751   Bilateral Protocol   **10 SUGG 124**
SIGNED: 9 Mar 61
HEADNOTE: AERIAL SURVEY TECHNICAL AID
TOPIC: Tech Assistance
PARTIES:
USSR (Soviet Union)
Vietnam, North

469752   Bilateral Agreement   **10 SUGG 125**
SIGNED: 18 Mar 61
HEADNOTE: TECHNICAL & FINANCIAL AID
TOPIC: General Aid
PARTIES:
Mali
USSR (Soviet Union)

469753   Bilateral Agreement   **10 SUGG 125**
SIGNED: 18 Mar 61
HEADNOTE: TRADE
TOPIC: General Trade
PARTIES:
Mali
USSR (Soviet Union)

469754   Bilateral Agreement   **10 SUGG 125**
SIGNED: 18 Mar 61
HEADNOTE: CULTURAL COOPERATION
TOPIC: Culture
PARTIES:
Mali
USSR (Soviet Union)

469755   Bilateral Protocol   **10 SUGG 126**
SIGNED: 28 Mar 61
HEADNOTE: CHEMICAL TECHNICAL AID
TOPIC: Tech Assistance
PARTIES:
Romania
USSR (Soviet Union)

469756   Bilateral Agreement   **10 SUGG 126**
SIGNED: 30 Mar 61
HEADNOTE: TRADE 1961-65
TOPIC: General Trade
PARTIES:
USSR (Soviet Union)
Yugoslavia

469757   Bilateral Exchange   **10 SUGG 127**
SIGNED: 1 Apr 61
HEADNOTE: IMPORT DUTY REDUCTIONS
TOPIC: Customs
PARTIES:
Finland
USSR (Soviet Union)

469758   Bilateral Exchange   **10 SUGG 127**
SIGNED: 6 Apr 61
HEADNOTE: METALLURGY TECHNICAL AID
TOPIC: Tech Assistance
PARTIES:
Finland
USSR (Soviet Union)

469759   Bilateral Agreement   **10 SUGG 127**
SIGNED: 3 Apr 61
HEADNOTE: EXCHANGE EMBASSIES
TOPIC: Consul/Citizenship
PARTIES:
Nigeria
USSR (Soviet Union)

469760   Bilateral Agreement   **10 SUGG 127**
SIGNED: 7 Apr 61
HEADNOTE: POSTPONE REPAYMENT 1960 DEBTS
TOPIC: Finance
PARTIES:
China People's Rep
USSR (Soviet Union)

469761   Bilateral Protocol   **10 SUGG 127**
SIGNED: 7 Apr 61
HEADNOTE: 500,000 TONS SUGAR AID
TOPIC: Direct Aid
PARTIES:
China People's Rep
USSR (Soviet Union)

469762   Bilateral Agreement   **10 SUGG 128**
SIGNED: 13 Apr 61
HEADNOTE: ADDITIONAL AID 1961-65
TOPIC: Direct Aid
PARTIES:
Mongolia
USSR (Soviet Union)

469763   Bilateral Exchange   **10 SUGG 128**
SIGNED: 21 Apr 61
HEADNOTE: SEKERKA POWER PLANT AID
TOPIC: Non-IBRD Project
PARTIES:
Poland
USSR (Soviet Union)

469764   Bilateral Agreement   **10 SUGG 129**
SIGNED: 25 Apr 61
HEADNOTE: CULTURAL & SCIENTIFIC COOPER-ATION
TOPIC: Health/Educ/Welfare
PARTIES:
Iceland
USSR (Soviet Union)

469765   Bilateral Exchange   **10 SUGG 130**
SIGNED: 29 Apr 61
HEADNOTE: HOTEL CONSTRUCTION AID
TOPIC: Non-IBRD Project
PARTIES:
Guinea
USSR (Soviet Union)

469766   Bilateral Agreement   **10 SUGG 130**
SIGNED: 19 May 61
HEADNOTE: CAPITAL AID
TOPIC: Direct Aid
PARTIES:
Poland
USSR (Soviet Union)

469767   Bilateral Agreement   **10 SUGG 130**
SIGNED: 19 May 61
HEADNOTE: TECHNICAL AID
TOPIC: Tech Assistance
PARTIES:
Poland
USSR (Soviet Union)

469768   Bilateral Agreement   **10 SUGG 131**
SIGNED: 19 May 61
HEADNOTE: PEACEFUL USE OF ATOMIC ENERGY
TOPIC: Atomic Energy
PARTIES:
UK Great Britain
USSR (Soviet Union)

469769   Bilateral Protocol   **10 SUGG 131**
SIGNED: 27 May 61
HEADNOTE: AMENDS 1959 TRADE PAYMENT AGREEMENT
TOPIC: Loans and Credits
PARTIES:
Brazil
USSR (Soviet Union)

469770   Bilateral Protocol   **10 SUGG 131**
SIGNED: 27 May 61
HEADNOTE: ESTABLISH TRADE DELEGATIONS
TOPIC: General Trade
PARTIES:
Brazil
USSR (Soviet Union)

469771   Bilateral Exchange   **10 SUGG 131**
SIGNED: 27 May 61
HEADNOTE: SOVIET TRADE-INDUSTRY EXHIBIT
TOPIC: General Trade
PARTIES:
Brazil
USSR (Soviet Union)

469772   Bilateral Exchange   **10 SUGG 132**
SIGNED: 29 May 61
HEADNOTE: TECHNICAL & CAPITAL AID
TOPIC: General Aid
PARTIES:
Guinea
USSR (Soviet Union)

469773   Bilateral Agreement   **10 SUGG 132**
SIGNED: 1 Jun 61
HEADNOTE: NICKEL INDUSTRY TECHNICAL AID
TOPIC: Tech Assistance
PARTIES:
Cuba
USSR (Soviet Union)

469774   Bilateral Agreement   **10 SUGG 134**
SIGNED: 4 Jun 61
HEADNOTE: AKHMEDI SEAPORT AID
TOPIC: Non-IBRD Project
PARTIES:
USSR (Soviet Union)
Yemen

469775   Bilateral Agreement   **10 SUGG 134**
SIGNED: 7 Jun 61
HEADNOTE: TRADE 1962-65
TOPIC: General Trade
PARTIES:
Italy
USSR (Soviet Union)

469776   Bilateral Exchange   **10 SUGG 134**
SIGNED: 8 Jun 61
HEADNOTE: LUMBER SPECIALIST ASSIGN-MENTS
TOPIC: Tech Assistance
PARTIES:
Mongolia
USSR (Soviet Union)

469777   Bilateral Agreement   **10 SUGG 135**
SIGNED: 12 Jun 61
HEADNOTE: HOUSING TECHNICAL AID
TOPIC: Tech Assistance
PARTIES:
Ghana
USSR (Soviet Union)

469778   Bilateral Agreement   **10 SUGG 136**
SIGNED: 19 Jun 61
HEADNOTE: ECONOMIC COOPERATION
TOPIC: General Economic
PARTIES:
China People's Rep
USSR (Soviet Union)

469779   Bilateral Agreement   **10 SUGG 136**
SIGNED: 19 Jun 61
HEADNOTE: SCIENTIFIC & TECHNICAL COOPER-ATION
TOPIC: Scientific Project
PARTIES:
China People's Rep
USSR (Soviet Union)

469780   Bilateral Exchange   **10 SUGG 136**
SIGNED: 22 Jun 61

HEADNOTE: MODEL 2800 LATHE PLANNING
TOPIC: Non-IBRD Project
PARTIES:
 Poland
 USSR (Soviet Union)

469781   Bilateral Agreement   **10 SUGG 136**
SIGNED: 24 Jun 61
HEADNOTE: TECHNICAL INSTITUTE IN PHNOM-
PENH
TOPIC: Non-IBRD Project
PARTIES:
 Cambodia
 USSR (Soviet Union)

469782   Bilateral Exchange   **10 SUGG 136**
SIGNED: 28 Jun 61
HEADNOTE: PASKOV COAL MINE CONSTRUC-
TION
TOPIC: Non-IBRD Project
PARTIES:
 Czechoslovakia
 USSR (Soviet Union)

469783   Bilateral Agreement   **10 SUGG 137**
SIGNED: 30 Jun 61
HEADNOTE: DELIVERY TO USSR OF 15 VESSELS
TOPIC: Specif Goods/Equip
PARTIES:
 Poland
 USSR (Soviet Union)

469784   Bilateral Agreement   **10 SUGG 137**
SIGNED: 6 Jul 61
HEADNOTE: ECONOMIC & TECHNICAL AID
TOPIC: General Aid
PARTIES:
 Korea, North
 USSR (Soviet Union)

469785   Bilateral Protocol   **10 SUGG 136**
SIGNED: 20 Jun 61
HEADNOTE: CHEMICAL INDUSTRY AID
TOPIC: General Aid
PARTIES:
 Hungary
 USSR (Soviet Union)

469786   Bilateral Agreement   **10 SUGG 137**
SIGNED: 6 Jul 61
HEADNOTE: CHEMICAL INDUSTRY AID 1962-65
TOPIC: General Aid
PARTIES:
 Korea, North
 USSR (Soviet Union)

469787   Bilateral Agreement   **10 SUGG 137**
SIGNED: 7 Jul 61
HEADNOTE: ATOMIC ENERGY UTILIZATION
TOPIC: Atomic Energy
PARTIES:
 Poland
 USSR (Soviet Union)

469788   Bilateral Exchange   **10 SUGG 138**
SIGNED: 17 Jul 61
HEADNOTE: RESOURCE USE SPECIALISTS
TOPIC: Tech Assistance
PARTIES:
 Mongolia
 USSR (Soviet Union)

469789   Bilateral Protocol   **10 SUGG 138**
SIGNED: 20 Jul 61
HEADNOTE: JOINT CONSTRUCTION POWER LINE
TOPIC: Non-IBRD Project
PARTIES:
 Poland
 USSR (Soviet Union)

469790   Bilateral Protocol   **10 SUGG 139**
SIGNED: 22 Jul 61
HEADNOTE: RESOURCE USE SPECIALISTS
TOPIC: Tech Assistance

PARTIES:
 Mongolia
 USSR (Soviet Union)

469791   Bilateral Agreement   **10 SUGG 139**
SIGNED: 24 Jul 61
HEADNOTE: TRADE PAYMENTS
TOPIC: Finance
PARTIES:
 Ghana
 USSR (Soviet Union)

469792   Bilateral Protocol   **10 SUGG 140**
SIGNED: 1 Aug 61
HEADNOTE: MODIFIES 6 MAY 60
TOPIC: General Trade
PARTIES:
 Hungary
 USSR (Soviet Union)

469793   Bilateral Exchange   **10 SUGG 140**
SIGNED: 21 Aug 61
HEADNOTE: METALS CONCENTRATES TESTS
TOPIC: Non-IBRD Project
PARTIES:
 Czechoslovakia
 USSR (Soviet Union)

469794   Bilateral Agreement   **10 SUGG 142**
SIGNED: 21 Sep 61
HEADNOTE: ITALY TO CONSTRUCT 6 TANKERS
TOPIC: Specif Goods/Equip
PARTIES:
 Italy
 USSR (Soviet Union)

469795   Bilateral Agreement   **10 SUGG 142**
SIGNED: 29 Sep 61
HEADNOTE: TECHNICAL AID
TOPIC: Tech Assistance
PARTIES:
 Bulgaria
 USSR (Soviet Union)

469796   Bilateral Treaty   **10 SUGG 142**
SIGNED: 3 Oct 61
HEADNOTE: BORDER REGULATION
TOPIC: Admin Cooperation
PARTIES:
 Hungary
 USSR (Soviet Union)

469797   Bilateral Agreement   **10 SUGG 143**
SIGNED: 6 Oct 61
HEADNOTE: CIVIL ATOMIC DEVELOPMENT
TOPIC: Atomic Energy
PARTIES:
 India
 USSR (Soviet Union)

469798   Bilateral Exchange   **10 SUGG 143**
SIGNED: 7 Oct 61
HEADNOTE: ESTABLISH DIPLOMATIC RELA-
TIONS
TOPIC: Consul/Citizenship
PARTIES:
 Syria
 USSR (Soviet Union)

469799   Bilateral Agreement   **10 SUGG 143**
SIGNED: 11 Oct 61
HEADNOTE: TEACHING INSTITUTE TECHNICAL
AID
TOPIC: Tech Assistance
PARTIES:
 Cuba
 USSR (Soviet Union)

469800   Bilateral Agreement   **10 SUGG 143**
SIGNED: 16 Oct 61
HEADNOTE: CAPITAL, TECHNICAL, FINANCIAL
AID
TOPIC: General Aid

PARTIES:
 Afghanistan
 USSR (Soviet Union)

469801   Bilateral Agreement   **10 SUGG 143**
SIGNED: 1 Nov 61
HEADNOTE: TRADE 1962-64
TOPIC: General Trade
PARTIES:
 Sudan
 USSR (Soviet Union)

469802   Bilateral Agreement   **10 SUGG 144**
SIGNED: 4 Nov 61
HEADNOTE: PAYMENTS
TOPIC: Finance
PARTIES:
 Ghana
 USSR (Soviet Union)

469803   Bilateral Protocol   **10 SUGG 144**
SIGNED: 4 Nov 61
HEADNOTE: COCOA-BEAN PURCHASES
TOPIC: Commodity Trade
PARTIES:
 Ghana
 USSR (Soviet Union)

469804   Bilateral Protocol   **10 SUGG 145**
SIGNED: 10 Nov 61
HEADNOTE: METALLURGY TECHNICAL
TOPIC: Tech Assistance
PARTIES:
 Germany, East
 USSR (Soviet Union)

469805   Bilateral Agreement   **10 SUGG 145**
SIGNED: 21 Nov 61
HEADNOTE: CAPITAL AID
TOPIC: Direct Aid
PARTIES:
 Sudan
 USSR (Soviet Union)

469806   Bilateral Exchange   **10 SUGG 145**
SIGNED: 23 Nov 61
HEADNOTE: RENEW DIPLOMATIC RELATIONS
TOPIC: Consul/Citizenship
PARTIES:
 Brazil
 USSR (Soviet Union)

469807   Bilateral Protocol   **10 SUGG 145**
SIGNED: 1 Dec 61
HEADNOTE: EXPAND TECHNICAL AID
TOPIC: Tech Assistance
PARTIES:
 Romania
 USSR (Soviet Union)

469808   Bilateral Protocol   **10 SUGG 145**
SIGNED: 3 Dec 61
HEADNOTE: CIVIL ATOMIC DEVELOPMENT
TOPIC: Atomic Energy
PARTIES:
 Poland
 USSR (Soviet Union)

469809   Bilateral Protocol   **10 SUGG 146**
SIGNED: 13 Dec 61
HEADNOTE: CAPITAL & TECHNICAL AID
TOPIC: General Aid
PARTIES:
 Poland
 USSR (Soviet Union)

469811   Bilateral Exchange   **10 SUGG 147**
SIGNED: 21 Dec 61
HEADNOTE: CORN PROCESSING PLANT AID
TOPIC: Non-IBRD Project
PARTIES:
 Czechoslovakia
 USSR (Soviet Union)

469812   Bilateral Agreement   **10 SUGG 147**
SIGNED: 21 Dec 61
HEADNOTE: COMMUNICATIONS COOPERATION
TOPIC: Gen Communications
PARTIES:
  Indonesia
  USSR (Soviet Union)

469813   Bilateral Agreement   **10 SUGG 147**
SIGNED: 22 Dec 61
HEADNOTE: TRADE & PAYMENTS
TOPIC: General Economic
PARTIES:
  Cyprus
  USSR (Soviet Union)

469814   Bilateral Protocol   **10 SUGG 148**
SIGNED: 23 Dec 61
HEADNOTE: ARDZHESH HYDROELECTRIC PLANT
TOPIC: Non-IBRD Project
PARTIES:
  Romania
  USSR (Soviet Union)

469815   Bilateral Instrument   **11 SUGG 130**
SIGNED: 1 Jan 62
HEADNOTE: RECOGNITION
TOPIC: Recognition
PARTIES:
  USSR (Soviet Union)
  Western Samoa

469816   Bilateral Protocol   **11 SUGG 130**
SIGNED: 13 Jan 62
HEADNOTE: TRADE 1962-66
TOPIC: General Trade
PARTIES:
  Afghanistan
  USSR (Soviet Union)

469817   Bilateral Agreement   **11 SUGG 130**
SIGNED: 16 Jan 62
HEADNOTE: ESTABLISH AIR COMMUNICATIONS
TOPIC: Air Transport
PARTIES:
  Guinea
  USSR (Soviet Union)

469818   Bilateral Protocol   **11 SUGG 131**
SIGNED: 2 Feb 62
HEADNOTE: TRADE 1962-64
TOPIC: General Trade
PARTIES:
  Sweden
  USSR (Soviet Union)

469819   Bilateral Protocol   **11 SUGG 131**
SIGNED: 6 Feb 62
HEADNOTE: FINANCIAL & CAPITAL AID
TOPIC: Direct Aid
PARTIES:
  Nepal
  USSR (Soviet Union)

469820   Bilateral Agreement   **11 SUGG 132**
SIGNED: 12 Feb 62
HEADNOTE: TECHNICAL & CAPITAL AID
TOPIC: General Aid
PARTIES:
  India
  USSR (Soviet Union)

469821   Bilateral Protocol   **11 SUGG 133**
SIGNED: 19 Feb 62
HEADNOTE: CAPITAL AID
TOPIC: Direct Aid
PARTIES:
  Burma
  USSR (Soviet Union)

469822   Bilateral Agreement   **11 SUGG 133**
SIGNED: 22 Feb 62
HEADNOTE: TRADE 1962-64
TOPIC: General Trade

PARTIES:
  Ceylon (Sri Lanka)
  USSR (Soviet Union)

469823   Bilateral Exchange   **11 SUGG 133**
SIGNED: 22 Feb 62
HEADNOTE: FISHING CONCESSIONS
TOPIC: Specific Resources
PARTIES:
  Norway
  USSR (Soviet Union)

469824   Bilateral Protocol   **11 SUGG 134**
SIGNED: 26 Feb 62
HEADNOTE: CAPITAL & TECHNICAL AID
TOPIC: General Aid
PARTIES:
  Guinea
  USSR (Soviet Union)

469825   Bilateral Agreement   **11 SUGG 135**
SIGNED: 14 Mar 62
HEADNOTE: TRADE 1962-64
TOPIC: General Trade
PARTIES:
  Tunisia
  USSR (Soviet Union)

469826   Bilateral Exchange   **11 SUGG 135**
SIGNED: 14 Mar 62
HEADNOTE: MOST FAVORED NATION
TOPIC: Mostfavored Nation
PARTIES:
  Tunisia
  USSR (Soviet Union)

469827   Bilateral Agreement   **11 SUGG 135**
SIGNED: 14 Mar 62
HEADNOTE: PAYMENTS
TOPIC: Finance
PARTIES:
  Tunisia
  USSR (Soviet Union)

469828   Bilateral Exchange   **11 SUGG 136**
SIGNED: 23 Mar 62
HEADNOTE: RECOGNIZE   PROVISIONAL
  GOVERNMENT
TOPIC: Recognition
PARTIES:
  Algeria
  USSR (Soviet Union)

469829   Bilateral Protocol   **11 SUGG 136**
SIGNED: 27 Mar 62
HEADNOTE: TECHNICAL & CAPITAL AID
TOPIC: General Aid
PARTIES:
  Somalia
  USSR (Soviet Union)

469830   Bilateral Agreement   **11 SUGG 136**
SIGNED: 27 Mar 62
HEADNOTE: DIRECT AID
TOPIC: Direct Aid
PARTIES:
  Somalia
  USSR (Soviet Union)

469831   Bilateral Agreement   **11 SUGG 136**
SIGNED: 28 Mar 62
HEADNOTE: ESTABLISH AIR SERVICE
TOPIC: Air Transport
PARTIES:
  Morocco
  USSR (Soviet Union)

469832   Bilateral Agreement   **11 SUGG 137**
SIGNED: 11 Apr 62
HEADNOTE: URBAN PLANNING & CONSTRUC-
  TION AID
TOPIC: Tech Assistance
PARTIES:
  Afghanistan
  USSR (Soviet Union)

469833   Bilateral Agreement   **11 SUGG 138**
SIGNED: 17 Apr 62
HEADNOTE: CIVIL ATOMIC DEVELOPMENT
TOPIC: Atomic Energy
PARTIES:
  Czechoslovakia
  USSR (Soviet Union)

469834   Bilateral Agreement   **11 SUGG 138**
SIGNED: 19 Apr 62
HEADNOTE: CIVIL ATOMIC DEVELOPMENT
TOPIC: Atomic Energy
PARTIES:
  Romania
  USSR (Soviet Union)

469835   Bilateral Agreement   **11 SUGG 139**
SIGNED: 25 Apr 62
HEADNOTE: TRADE 1962-64
TOPIC: General Trade
PARTIES:
  Greece
  USSR (Soviet Union)

469836   Bilateral Agreement   **11 SUGG 139**
SIGNED: 8 May 62
HEADNOTE: CHEMICAL INDUSTRY AID
TOPIC: Direct Aid
PARTIES:
  Cuba
  USSR (Soviet Union)

469837   Bilateral Agreement   **11 SUGG 139**
SIGNED: 8 May 62
HEADNOTE: CAPITAL AID
TOPIC: Direct Aid
PARTIES:
  Indonesia
  USSR (Soviet Union)

469838   Bilateral Protocol   **11 SUGG 140**
SIGNED: 14 May 62
HEADNOTE: SUPPLEMENTARY TRADE
TOPIC: General Trade
PARTIES:
  Cuba
  USSR (Soviet Union)

469839   Bilateral Protocol   **11 SUGG 140**
SIGNED: 17 May 62
HEADNOTE: TECHNICAL & CAPITAL AID
TOPIC: General Aid
PARTIES:
  Afghanistan
  USSR (Soviet Union)

469840   Bilateral Agreement   **11 SUGG 141**
SIGNED: 4 Jun 62
HEADNOTE: ESTABLISH DIPLOMATIC RELA-
  TIONS
TOPIC: Consul/Citizenship
PARTIES:
  Dahomey
  USSR (Soviet Union)

469841   Bilateral Protocol   **11 SUGG 143**
SIGNED: 12 Jun 62
HEADNOTE: MODIFIES 25 FEB 58
TOPIC: General Aid
PARTIES:
  Ceylon (Sri Lanka)
  USSR (Soviet Union)

469842   Bilateral Agreement   **11 SUGG 143**
SIGNED: 14 Jun 62
HEADNOTE: TRADE
TOPIC: General Trade
PARTIES:
  Senegal
  USSR (Soviet Union)

469843   Bilateral Agreement   **11 SUGG 143**
SIGNED: 14 Jun 62

HEADNOTE: ECONOMIC & TECHNICAL COOPER-
ATION
TOPIC: General Aid
PARTIES:
Senegal
USSR (Soviet Union)

469844   Bilateral Agreement   **11 SUGG 144**
SIGNED: 20 Jun 62
HEADNOTE: SUPPLEMENTARY TRADE
TOPIC: General Trade
PARTIES:
Bulgaria
USSR (Soviet Union)

469845   Bilateral Protocol   **11 SUGG 144**
SIGNED: 20 Jun 62
HEADNOTE: BULGARIAN SHIP DELIVERIES
TOPIC: Commodity Trade
PARTIES:
Bulgaria
USSR (Soviet Union)

469846   Bilateral Exchange   **11 SUGG 144**
SIGNED: 23 Jun 62
HEADNOTE: REPAYMENT SOVIET CREDITS
TOPIC: Finance
PARTIES:
United Arab Rep
USSR (Soviet Union)

469847   Bilateral Exchange   **11 SUGG 145**
SIGNED: 23 Jun 62
HEADNOTE: TRADE PRIVILEGES
TOPIC: General Trade
PARTIES:
United Arab Rep
USSR (Soviet Union)

469848   Bilateral Instrument   **11 SUGG 145**
SIGNED: 30 Jun 62
HEADNOTE: RECOGNITION
TOPIC: Recognition
PARTIES:
Burundi
USSR (Soviet Union)

469849   Bilateral Instrument   **11 SUGG 145**
SIGNED: 30 Jun 62
HEADNOTE: RECOGNITION
TOPIC: Recognition
PARTIES:
Rwanda
USSR (Soviet Union)

469850   Bilateral Agreement   **11 SUGG 147**
SIGNED: 17 Jul 62
HEADNOTE: MOSCOW-HAVANA AIR SERVICE
TOPIC: Air Transport
PARTIES:
Cuba
USSR (Soviet Union)

469852   Bilateral Agreement   **11 SUGG 149**
SIGNED: 4 Aug 62
HEADNOTE: CUBAN TECHNICIAN TRAINING
TOPIC: Education
PARTIES:
Cuba
USSR (Soviet Union)

469853   Bilateral Instrument   **11 SUGG 149**
SIGNED: 5 Aug 62
HEADNOTE: RECOGNITION
TOPIC: Recognition
PARTIES:
Jamaica
USSR (Soviet Union)

469854   Bilateral Protocol   **11 SUGG 149**
SIGNED: 9 Aug 62
HEADNOTE: EXTENDS 25 FEB 58
TOPIC: General Aid

PARTIES:
Ceylon (Sri Lanka)
USSR (Soviet Union)

469855   Bilateral Exchange   **11 SUGG 149**
SIGNED: 9 Aug 62
HEADNOTE: TRADE
TOPIC: General Trade
PARTIES:
Iran
USSR (Soviet Union)

469856   Bilateral Agreement   **11 SUGG 150**
SIGNED: 29 Aug 62
HEADNOTE: ASSAB OIL REFINERY AID
TOPIC: Non-IBRD Project
PARTIES:
Ethiopia
USSR (Soviet Union)

469857   Bilateral Protocol   **11 SUGG 150**
SIGNED: 30 Aug 62
HEADNOTE: BURMA IRRIGATION SYSTEM
TOPIC: Non-IBRD Project
PARTIES:
Burma
USSR (Soviet Union)

469858   Bilateral Protocol   **11 SUGG 150**
SIGNED: 30 Aug 62
HEADNOTE: AUTO REPAIR WORKS
TOPIC: Non-IBRD Project
PARTIES:
Cuba
USSR (Soviet Union)

469859   Bilateral Instrument   **11 SUGG 150**
SIGNED: 30 Aug 62
HEADNOTE: RECOGNITION
TOPIC: Recognition
PARTIES:
Trinidad/Tobago
USSR (Soviet Union)

469860   Bilateral Agreement   **11 SUGG 152**
SIGNED: 15 Sep 62
HEADNOTE: ECONOMIC & TECHNICAL AID
TOPIC: General Aid
PARTIES:
USSR (Soviet Union)
Vietnam, North

469861   Bilateral Agreement   **11 SUGG 153**
SIGNED: 22 Sep 62
HEADNOTE: COTTON PLANTING PROJECT
TOPIC: Non-IBRD Project
PARTIES:
Ceylon (Sri Lanka)
USSR (Soviet Union)

469862   Bilateral Agreement   **11 SUGG 153**
SIGNED: 24 Sep 62
HEADNOTE: TRADE
TOPIC: General Trade
PARTIES:
Cameroon
USSR (Soviet Union)

469863   Bilateral Exchange   **11 SUGG 153**
SIGNED: 24 Sep 62
HEADNOTE: SOVIET TRADE MISSION
TOPIC: General Trade
PARTIES:
Cameroon
USSR (Soviet Union)

469864   Bilateral Agreement   **11 SUGG 153**
SIGNED: 25 Sep 62
HEADNOTE: FISHING REGULATION COOPER-
ATION
TOPIC: Specific Resources
PARTIES:
Cuba
USSR (Soviet Union)

469865   Bilateral Agreement   **11 SUGG 153**
SIGNED: 25 Sep 62
HEADNOTE: FISHING PORT CONSTRUCTION
TOPIC: Non-IBRD Project
PARTIES:
Cuba
USSR (Soviet Union)

469866   Bilateral Instrument   **11 SUGG 154**
SIGNED: 1 Oct 62
HEADNOTE: ESTABLISH DIPLOMATIC RELA-
TIONS
TOPIC: Consul/Citizenship
PARTIES:
Burundi
USSR (Soviet Union)

469867   Bilateral Exchange   **11 SUGG 155**
SIGNED: 4 Oct 62
HEADNOTE: RECOGNIZE YEMENI ARAB REPUBLIC
TOPIC: Recognition
PARTIES:
USSR (Soviet Union)
Yemen

469868   Bilateral Instrument   **11 SUGG 155**
SIGNED: 8 Oct 62
HEADNOTE: RECOGNITION
TOPIC: Recognition
PARTIES:
Uganda
USSR (Soviet Union)

469869   Bilateral Instrument   **11 SUGG 156**
SIGNED: 13 Oct 62
HEADNOTE: ESTABLISH DIPLOMATIC RELA-
TIONS
TOPIC: Consul/Citizenship
PARTIES:
Uganda
USSR (Soviet Union)

469870   Bilateral Agreement   **11 SUGG 156**
SIGNED: 20 Oct 62
HEADNOTE: ESTABLISH AIR SERVICE
TOPIC: Air Transport
PARTIES:
Sudan
USSR (Soviet Union)

469871   Bilateral Exchange   **11 SUGG 156**
SIGNED: 30 Oct 62
HEADNOTE: SPACE EXPLORATION COOPER-
ATION
TOPIC: Scientific Project
PARTIES:
USA (United States)
USSR (Soviet Union)

469872   Bilateral Agreement   **11 SUGG 156**
SIGNED: 14 Nov 62
HEADNOTE: ESTABLISH SHIP LINES
TOPIC: Water Transport
PARTIES:
Ceylon (Sri Lanka)
USSR (Soviet Union)

469873   Bilateral Agreement   **11 SUGG 157**
SIGNED: 15 Nov 62
HEADNOTE: ALUMINUM TRADE
TOPIC: General Trade
PARTIES:
Hungary
USSR (Soviet Union)

469874   Bilateral Protocol   **11 SUGG 157**
SIGNED: 17 Nov 62
HEADNOTE: TRADE 1962-65
TOPIC: General Trade
PARTIES:
Hungary
USSR (Soviet Union)

469875   Bilateral Protocol   **11 SUGG 157**
SIGNED: 20 Nov 62
HEADNOTE: SHIPPING LINES IMPROVEMENT
TOPIC: Water Transport
PARTIES:
    India
    USSR (Soviet Union)

469876   Bilateral Agreement   **11 SUGG 158**
SIGNED: 1 Dec 62
HEADNOTE: HOSPITAL AND RADIO STATION
TOPIC: Direct Aid
PARTIES:
    Laos
    USSR (Soviet Union)

469877   Bilateral Protocol   **11 SUGG 159**
SIGNED: 19 Dec 62
HEADNOTE: TRADE 1963-65
TOPIC: General Trade
PARTIES:
    Iceland
    USSR (Soviet Union)

469878   Bilateral Agreement   **11 SUGG 160**
SIGNED: 20 Dec 62
HEADNOTE: SOCIAL SECURITY COOPERATION
TOPIC: Non-ILO Labor
PARTIES:
    Hungary
    USSR (Soviet Union)

469879   Bilateral Agreement   **11 SUGG 160**
SIGNED: 25 Dec 62
HEADNOTE: RADIO & TELEVISION BROADCAST
TOPIC: Mass Media
PARTIES:
    Bulgaria
    USSR (Soviet Union)

469880   Bilateral Agreement   **16 SUGG 61**
SIGNED: 31 Mar 45
HEADNOTE: DIVISION WAR BOOTY
TOPIC: Claims and Debts
PARTIES:
    Czechoslovakia
    USSR (Soviet Union)

469881   Bilateral Agreement   **16 SUGG 62**
SIGNED: 31 Mar 45
HEADNOTE: DIVISION OF MILITARY EXPENSES
TOPIC: General Military
PARTIES:
    Czechoslovakia
    USSR (Soviet Union)

469882   Bilateral Agreement   **16 SUGG 62**
SIGNED: 14 Apr 45
HEADNOTE: EQUIPMENT TRANSFERS
TOPIC: Milit Installation
PARTIES:
    Czechoslovakia
    USSR (Soviet Union)

469883   Bilateral Exchange   **16 SUGG 62**
SIGNED: 24 Oct 45
HEADNOTE: SOVIET TRADE MISSION
TOPIC: General Trade
PARTIES:
    Netherlands
    USSR (Soviet Union)

469884   Bilateral Protocol   **16 SUGG 63**
SIGNED: 17 Aug 46
HEADNOTE: ACCOUNTS SETTLEMENT
TOPIC: Finance
PARTIES:
    Denmark
    USSR (Soviet Union)

469885   Bilateral Protocol   **16 SUGG 64**
SIGNED: 30 Jun 48
HEADNOTE: PAYMENTS
TOPIC: Finance

PARTIES:
    Belgium
    USSR (Soviet Union)

469886   Bilateral Agreement   **16 SUGG 64**
SIGNED: 28 Jul 48
HEADNOTE: 50 PERCENT REPARATIONS REDUC-
    TION
TOPIC: Reparations
PARTIES:
    Finland
    USSR (Soviet Union)

469887   Bilateral Convention   **16 SUGG 64**
SIGNED: 1 Nov 48
HEADNOTE: JOINT STOCK CORPORATIONS
TOPIC: Specific Property
PARTIES:
    Romania
    USSR (Soviet Union)

469888   Bilateral Convention   **16 SUGG 64**
SIGNED: 20 Feb 49
HEADNOTE: JOINT STOCK CORPORATION SOV-
    ROMGAZ
TOPIC: Specific Property
PARTIES:
    Romania
    USSR (Soviet Union)

469889   Bilateral Agreement   **16 SUGG 65**
SIGNED: 24 Feb 49
HEADNOTE: RIVER NAVIGATION
TOPIC: Water Transport
PARTIES:
    Mongolia
    USSR (Soviet Union)

469890   Bilateral Convention   **16 SUGG 65**
SIGNED: 4 Jul 49
HEADNOTE: JOINT STOCK CORPORATIONS
TOPIC: Specific Property
PARTIES:
    Romania
    USSR (Soviet Union)

469891   Bilateral Convention   **16 SUGG 65**
SIGNED: 4 Aug 49
HEADNOTE: JOINT STOCK CORPORATION SOV-
    ROMSTRAKJ
TOPIC: Specific Property
PARTIES:
    Romania
    USSR (Soviet Union)

469892   Bilateral Agreement   **16 SUGG 65**
SIGNED: 3 Nov 49
HEADNOTE: RADIO BROADCAST COOPERATION
TOPIC: Mass Media
PARTIES:
    Czechoslovakia
    USSR (Soviet Union)

469893   Bilateral Exchange   **16 SUGG 65**
SIGNED: 30 Nov 49
HEADNOTE: DEVALUATION NORWEGIAN KRONE
TOPIC: Finance
PARTIES:
    Norway
    USSR (Soviet Union)

469894   Bilateral Exchange   **16 SUGG 66**
SIGNED: 2 Dec 49
HEADNOTE: BELGIAN FRANC GOLD CHANGE
TOPIC: Finance
PARTIES:
    Belgium
    USSR (Soviet Union)

469895   Bilateral Exchange   **16 SUGG 66**
SIGNED: 9 Aug 50
HEADNOTE: BORDER REGULATION
TOPIC: Admin Cooperation

PARTIES:
    Iran
    USSR (Soviet Union)

469896   Bilateral Treaty   **16 SUGG 66**
SIGNED: 16 Jun 51
HEADNOTE: MAINTAIN ULAN-BATOR RAILWAY
TOPIC: Specific Property
PARTIES:
    Mongolia
    USSR (Soviet Union)

469897   Bilateral Convention   **16 SUGG 66**
SIGNED: 15 Aug 52
HEADNOTE: JOINT STOCK CORPORATIONS
TOPIC: Specific Property
PARTIES:
    Romania
    USSR (Soviet Union)

469898   Bilateral Protocol   **16 SUGG 66**
SIGNED: 20 Aug 52
HEADNOTE: AMENDS 7 JUL 36
TOPIC: Air Transport
PARTIES:
    Mongolia
    USSR (Soviet Union)

469899   Bilateral Agreement   **16 SUGG 67**
SIGNED: 15 Sep 52
HEADNOTE: MONGOL-CHINESE RAILWAY
TOPIC: Specific Property
PARTIES:
    Mongolia
    USSR (Soviet Union)

469900   Bilateral Exchange   **16 SUGG 67**
SIGNED: 18 Aug 53
HEADNOTE: RE-EXPORT EGYPTIAN GOODS
TOPIC: General Trade
PARTIES:
    United Arab Rep
    USSR (Soviet Union)

469901   Bilateral Agreement   **16 SUGG 67**
SIGNED: 27 Aug 53
HEADNOTE: TRAINING MONGOL TECHNICIANS
TOPIC: Education
PARTIES:
    Mongolia
    USSR (Soviet Union)

469902   Bilateral Agreement   **16 SUGG 67**
SIGNED: 28 Nov 53
HEADNOTE: SOVIET CREDIT
TOPIC: Loans and Credits
PARTIES:
    Mongolia
    USSR (Soviet Union)

469903   Bilateral Protocol   **16 SUGG 68**
SIGNED: 31 Dec 53
HEADNOTE: TRANSFER BANK INTERESTS
TOPIC: Specific Property
PARTIES:
    Mongolia
    USSR (Soviet Union)

469904   Bilateral Protocol   **16 SUGG 68**
SIGNED: 12 Feb 55
HEADNOTE: TRADE DELIVERY CONDITIONS
TOPIC: General Trade
PARTIES:
    China People's Rep
    USSR (Soviet Union)

469905   Bilateral Convention   **16 SUGG 68**
SIGNED: 28 Apr 55
HEADNOTE: REGULATE LATORICA & UZH RIVER
TOPIC: Specific Resources
PARTIES:
    Czechoslovakia
    USSR (Soviet Union)

469906   Bilateral Agreement   **16 SUGG 68**
SIGNED: 24 Jun 55
HEADNOTE: PARCEL POST
TOPIC: Postal Service
PARTIES:
   Canada
   USSR (Soviet Union)

469907   Bilateral Protocol   **16 SUGG 68**
SIGNED: 21 Jul 55
HEADNOTE: CULTURE PALACE GIFT TRANSFER
TOPIC: Direct Aid
PARTIES:
   Poland
   USSR (Soviet Union)

469908   Bilateral Exchange   **16 SUGG 69**
SIGNED: 18 Aug 55
HEADNOTE: CHANGE MISSIONS TO EMBASSIES
TOPIC: Consul/Citizenship
PARTIES:
   Denmark
   USSR (Soviet Union)

469909   Bilateral Agreement   **16 SUGG 69**
SIGNED: 27 Aug 55
HEADNOTE: USSR EDUCATION FOR VIETNAMESE
TOPIC: Education
PARTIES:
   USSR (Soviet Union)
   Vietnam, North

469910   Bilateral Exchange   **16 SUGG 69**
SIGNED: 4 Sep 55
HEADNOTE: ESTABLISH DIPLOMATIC RELA-
TIONS
TOPIC: Consul/Citizenship
PARTIES:
   Libya
   USSR (Soviet Union)

469911   Bilateral Exchange   **16 SUGG 70**
SIGNED: 27 Dec 55
HEADNOTE: REVISES 12 FEB 55
TOPIC: General Trade
PARTIES:
   China People's Rep
   USSR (Soviet Union)

469912   Bilateral Exchange   **16 SUGG 70**
SIGNED: 29 Feb 56
HEADNOTE: ESTABLISH CONSULAR RELATIONS
TOPIC: Consul/Citizenship
PARTIES:
   San Marino
   USSR (Soviet Union)

469913   Bilateral Agreement   **16 SUGG 70**
SIGNED: 23 Apr 56
HEADNOTE: RAILWAY LINE TRANSFER
TOPIC: Specific Property
PARTIES:
   Mongolia
   USSR (Soviet Union)

469914   Bilateral Agreement   **16 SUGG 70**
SIGNED: 23 Apr 56
HEADNOTE: RESIDENTIAL TECHNICAL AID
TOPIC: Tech Assistance
PARTIES:
   Mongolia
   USSR (Soviet Union)

469915   Bilateral Exchange   **16 SUGG 70**
SIGNED: 13 May 56
HEADNOTE: ESTABLISH DIPLOMATIC RELA-
TIONS
TOPIC: Consul/Citizenship
PARTIES:
   Cambodia
   USSR (Soviet Union)

469916   Bilateral Exchange   **16 SUGG 71**
SIGNED: 17 May 56

HEADNOTE: CHANGE MISSIONS TO EMBASSIES
TOPIC: Consul/Citizenship
PARTIES:
   Thailand
   USSR (Soviet Union)

469917   Bilateral Exchange   **16 SUGG 71**
SIGNED: 18 May 56
HEADNOTE: CHANGE MISSIONS TO EMBASSIES
TOPIC: Consul/Citizenship
PARTIES:
   Ethiopia
   USSR (Soviet Union)

469918   Bilateral Exchange   **16 SUGG 71**
SIGNED: 14 Jun 56
HEADNOTE: COMMODITY DELIVERIES
TOPIC: Commodity Trade
PARTIES:
   China People's Rep
   USSR (Soviet Union)

469919   Bilateral Exchange   **16 SUGG 71**
SIGNED: 27 Jun 56
HEADNOTE: SOVIET TRADE MISSION
TOPIC: General Trade
PARTIES:
   Pakistan
   USSR (Soviet Union)

469920   Bilateral Exchange   **16 SUGG 71**
SIGNED: 27 Jun 56
HEADNOTE: PAYMENT
TOPIC: Finance
PARTIES:
   Pakistan
   USSR (Soviet Union)

469921   Bilateral Exchange   **16 SUGG 72**
SIGNED: 9 Jul 56
HEADNOTE: ESTABLISH DIPLOMATIC RELA-
TIONS
TOPIC: Consul/Citizenship
PARTIES:
   Nepal
   USSR (Soviet Union)

469922   Bilateral Exchange   **16 SUGG 72**
SIGNED: 11 Jul 56
HEADNOTE: RECOGNITION
TOPIC: Recognition
PARTIES:
   Tunisia
   USSR (Soviet Union)

469923   Bilateral Agreement   **16 SUGG 72**
SIGNED: 4 Aug 56
HEADNOTE: 300 MILLION RUBLES AID
TOPIC: Direct Aid
PARTIES:
   Korea, North
   USSR (Soviet Union)

469924   Bilateral Exchange   **16 SUGG 72**
SIGNED: 12 Aug 56
HEADNOTE: SOVIET TRADE MISSION
TOPIC: General Trade
PARTIES:
   Indonesia
   USSR (Soviet Union)

469925   Bilateral Instrument   **16 SUGG 73**
SIGNED: 27 Aug 56
HEADNOTE: ARCHIVES TRANSFER
TOPIC: Specif Goods/Equip
PARTIES:
   USSR (Soviet Union)
   Yugoslavia

469926   Bilateral Exchange   **16 SUGG 73**
SIGNED: 6 Sep 56
HEADNOTE: BLACK SEA RESCUE COOPERATION
TOPIC: Humanitarian

PARTIES:
   Greece
   USSR (Soviet Union)

469927   Bilateral Instrument   **16 SUGG 73**
SIGNED: 18 Sep 56
HEADNOTE: ARCHIVES TRANSFER
TOPIC: Specif Goods/Equip
PARTIES:
   China People's Rep
   USSR (Soviet Union)

469928   Bilateral Exchange   **16 SUGG 73**
SIGNED: 24 Sep 56
HEADNOTE: FISHING REGULATION
TOPIC: Specific Resources
PARTIES:
   Romania
   USSR (Soviet Union)

469929   Bilateral Agreement   **16 SUGG 74**
SIGNED: 19 Oct 56
HEADNOTE: HYDROMETEOROLOGY COOPER-
ATION
TOPIC: Scientific Project
PARTIES:
   Mongolia
   USSR (Soviet Union)

469930   Bilateral Agreement   **16 SUGG 74**
SIGNED: 22 Nov 56
HEADNOTE: RADIO BROADCAST COOPERATION
TOPIC: Mass Media
PARTIES:
   Bulgaria
   USSR (Soviet Union)

469931   Bilateral Exchange   **16 SUGG 74**
SIGNED: 6 Dec 56
HEADNOTE: ESTABLISH DIPLOMATIC RELA-
TIONS
TOPIC: Consul/Citizenship
PARTIES:
   Ceylon (Sri Lanka)
   USSR (Soviet Union)

469932   Bilateral Agreement   **16 SUGG 118**
SIGNED: 25 Jan 57
HEADNOTE: RADIO BROADCAST COOPERATION
TOPIC: Mass Media
PARTIES:
   Czechoslovakia
   USSR (Soviet Union)

469933   Bilateral Instrument   **16 SUGG 119**
SIGNED: 1 Mar 57
HEADNOTE: ARCHIVES TRANSFER
TOPIC: Specif Goods/Equip
PARTIES:
   Czechoslovakia
   USSR (Soviet Union)

469934   Bilateral Agreement   **16 SUGG 119**
SIGNED: 14 Mar 57
HEADNOTE: RADIO BROADCAST COOPERATION
TOPIC: Mass Media
PARTIES:
   Romania
   USSR (Soviet Union)

469935   Bilateral Protocol   **16 SUGG 119**
SIGNED: 27 Mar 57
HEADNOTE: PEKING HOSPITAL TRANSFER
TOPIC: Specific Property
PARTIES:
   China People's Rep
   USSR (Soviet Union)

469936   Bilateral Instrument   **16 SUGG 119**
SIGNED: 4 Apr 57
HEADNOTE: ARCHIVES TRANSFER
TOPIC: Specif Goods/Equip

PARTIES:
Germany, East
USSR (Soviet Union)

469937   Bilateral Agreement   16 SUGG 120
SIGNED: 20 Apr 57
HEADNOTE: RADIO BROADCAST COOPERATION
TOPIC: Mass Media
PARTIES:
Korea, North
USSR (Soviet Union)

469938   Bilateral Agreement   16 SUGG 120
SIGNED: 6 May 57
HEADNOTE: COMMODITY TRADE
TOPIC: Commodity Trade
PARTIES:
Romania
USSR (Soviet Union)

469939   Bilateral Protocol   16 SUGG 120
SIGNED: 14 May 57
HEADNOTE: BORDER REGULATION
TOPIC: Admin Cooperation
PARTIES:
Iran
USSR (Soviet Union)

469940   Bilateral Agreement   16 SUGG 120
SIGNED: 15 May 57
HEADNOTE: METALS COMPANY USSR STOCK
  SALE
TOPIC: Specific Property
PARTIES:
Mongolia
USSR (Soviet Union)

469941   Bilateral Agreement   16 SUGG 120
SIGNED: 15 May 57
HEADNOTE: FREE TRANS USSR TRUST SHARES
TOPIC: Direct Aid
PARTIES:
Mongolia
USSR (Soviet Union)

469942   Bilateral Agreement   16 SUGG 121
SIGNED: 15 Jun 57
HEADNOTE: RADIO BROADCAST COOPERATION
TOPIC: Mass Media
PARTIES:
Hungary
USSR (Soviet Union)

469943   Bilateral Agreement   16 SUGG 121
SIGNED: 22 Jun 57
HEADNOTE: RADIO BROADCAST COOPERATION
TOPIC: Mass Media
PARTIES:
Poland
USSR (Soviet Union)

469944   Bilateral Agreement   16 SUGG 121
SIGNED: 31 Jul 57
HEADNOTE: SUPPLEMENTS 25 DEC 52
TOPIC: Specific Resources
PARTIES:
Romania
USSR (Soviet Union)

469945   Bilateral Exchange   16 SUGG 121
SIGNED: 5 Aug 57
HEADNOTE: JUDICIAL COOPERATION
TOPIC: Admin Cooperation
PARTIES:
Germany, West
USSR (Soviet Union)

469946   Bilateral Exchange   16 SUGG 121
SIGNED: 30 Sep 57
HEADNOTE: RICE SHIPMENT TO USSR
TOPIC: Specif Goods/Equip
PARTIES:
Burma
USSR (Soviet Union)

469947   Bilateral Agreement   16 SUGG 122
SIGNED: 15 Oct 57
HEADNOTE: ATOMIC DEFENSE COOPERATION
TOPIC: Atomic Energy
PARTIES:
China People's Rep
USSR (Soviet Union)

469948   Bilateral Agreement   16 SUGG 122
SIGNED: 26 Oct 57
HEADNOTE: RADIO BROADCAST COOPERATION
TOPIC: Mass Media
PARTIES:
Albania
USSR (Soviet Union)

469949   Bilateral Exchange   16 SUGG 122
SIGNED: 6 Dec 57
HEADNOTE: ESTABLISH REGULAR SHIPPING
TOPIC: Water Transport
PARTIES:
Japan
USSR (Soviet Union)

469950   Bilateral Agreement   16 SUGG 123
SIGNED: 19 Dec 57
HEADNOTE: CONDITIONS FOR TECHNICAL AID
TOPIC: Tech Assistance
PARTIES:
Romania
USSR (Soviet Union)

469951   Bilateral Agreement   16 SUGG 123
SIGNED: 19 Dec 57
HEADNOTE: TECH INSTRUCTION CONDITIONS
TOPIC: Education
PARTIES:
Romania
USSR (Soviet Union)

469953   Bilateral Agreement   16 SUGG 124
SIGNED: 28 Dec 57
HEADNOTE: TECHNICAL AID CONDITIONS
TOPIC: Tech Assistance
PARTIES:
China People's Rep
USSR (Soviet Union)

469954   Bilateral Agreement   16 SUGG 124
SIGNED: 28 Dec 57
HEADNOTE: TECHNICAL INSTRUCTION CONDI-
  TIONS
TOPIC: Education
PARTIES:
China People's Rep
USSR (Soviet Union)

469955   Bilateral Exchange   16 SUGG 124
SIGNED: 8 Feb 58
HEADNOTE: TRADE CONDITIONS
TOPIC: General Trade
PARTIES:
Ceylon (Sri Lanka)
USSR (Soviet Union)

469956   Bilateral Exchange   16 SUGG 124
SIGNED: 13 Mar 58
HEADNOTE: DIPLOMATIC MAIL PROCEDURES
TOPIC: Consul/Citizenship
PARTIES:
Iceland
USSR (Soviet Union)

469957   Bilateral Agreement   16 SUGG 124
SIGNED: 11 Apr 58
HEADNOTE: TECHNICAL AID CONDITIONS
TOPIC: Tech Assistance
PARTIES:
Mongolia
USSR (Soviet Union)

469958   Bilateral Agreement   16 SUGG 125
SIGNED: 11 Apr 58

HEADNOTE: TECHNICAL INSTRUCTION CONDI-
  TIONS
TOPIC: Education
PARTIES:
Mongolia
USSR (Soviet Union)

469959   Bilateral Exchange   16 SUGG 125
SIGNED: 23 Jun 58
HEADNOTE: SOVIET TRADE MISSION STAFF
TOPIC: General Trade
PARTIES:
Japan
USSR (Soviet Union)

469960   Bilateral Agreement   16 SUGG 125
SIGNED: 21 Jul 58
HEADNOTE: CUSTOMS COOPERATION
TOPIC: Customs
PARTIES:
Hungary
USSR (Soviet Union)

469961   Bilateral Agreement   16 SUGG 125
SIGNED: 21 Oct 58
HEADNOTE: PUBLIC HEALTH SERVICE COOP
TOPIC: Sanitation
PARTIES:
Germany, East
USSR (Soviet Union)

469962   Bilateral Exchange   16 SUGG 125
SIGNED: 16 Nov 58
HEADNOTE: TRADE EXPANSION
TOPIC: General Trade
PARTIES:
India
USSR (Soviet Union)

469963   Bilateral Protocol   16 SUGG 126
SIGNED: 17 Jan 59
HEADNOTE: TRADE
TOPIC: General Trade
PARTIES:
China People's Rep
USSR (Soviet Union)

469964   Bilateral Agreement   16 SUGG 126
SIGNED: 17 Apr 59
HEADNOTE: PUBLIC HEALTH SERVICE COOP
TOPIC: Sanitation
PARTIES:
Hungary
USSR (Soviet Union)

469965   Bilateral Agreement   16 SUGG 126
SIGNED: 28 Jul 59
HEADNOTE: COMMUNICATIONS TECHNICAL AID
TOPIC: Tech Assistance
PARTIES:
Mongolia
USSR (Soviet Union)

469966   Bilateral Agreement   16 SUGG 126
SIGNED: 15 Oct 59
HEADNOTE: SUPPLEMENTS 25 DEC 52
TOPIC: Specific Resources
PARTIES:
Romania
USSR (Soviet Union)

469967   Bilateral Protocol   16 SUGG 126
SIGNED: 9 Dec 59
HEADNOTE: TECHNICAL & ECONOMIC AID
TOPIC: General Aid
PARTIES:
Mongolia
USSR (Soviet Union)

469968   Bilateral Exchange   16 SUGG 127
SIGNED: 23 Dec 59
HEADNOTE: VISA TAX ABOLITION
TOPIC: Visas

PARTIES:
 Canada
 USSR (Soviet Union)

469969   Bilateral Exchange   **16 SUGG 127**
SIGNED: 20 Jan 60
HEADNOTE: VISA ISSUANCE
TOPIC: Visas
PARTIES:
 Italy
 USSR (Soviet Union)

469970   Bilateral Agreement   **16 SUGG 127**
SIGNED: 29 Jan 60
HEADNOTE: FOREST FIRE PREVENTION
TOPIC: Specific Resources
PARTIES:
 China People's Rep
 USSR (Soviet Union)

469971   Bilateral Agreement   **16 SUGG 127**
SIGNED: 19 Feb 60
HEADNOTE: CUSTOMS COOPERATION
TOPIC: Customs
PARTIES:
 Poland
 USSR (Soviet Union)

469972   Bilateral Exchange   **16 SUGG 127**
SIGNED: 25 Feb 60
HEADNOTE: VISA TAX ABOLITION
TOPIC: Visas
PARTIES:
 Italy
 USSR (Soviet Union)

469973   Bilateral Exchange   **16 SUGG 127**
SIGNED: 14 Mar 60
HEADNOTE: CONSULAR ACT TAX ABOLITION
TOPIC: Consul/Citizenship
PARTIES:
 Iceland
 USSR (Soviet Union)

469974   Bilateral Exchange   **16 SUGG 127**
SIGNED: 21 Mar 60
HEADNOTE: VISA TAX ABOLITION
TOPIC: Visas
PARTIES:
 United Arab Rep
 USSR (Soviet Union)

469975   Bilateral Exchange   **16 SUGG 127**
SIGNED: 10 May 60
HEADNOTE: INCOME TAXATION
TOPIC: Taxation
PARTIES:
 Denmark
 USSR (Soviet Union)

469976   Bilateral Agreement   **16 SUGG 128**
SIGNED: 28 May 60
HEADNOTE: ABOLISH VACCINATION CERTIFI-
CATE
TOPIC: Visas
PARTIES:
 China People's Rep
 USSR (Soviet Union)

469977   Bilateral Agreement   **16 SUGG 128**
SIGNED: 16 Jun 60
HEADNOTE: RADIO BROADCAST COOPERATION
TOPIC: Mass Media
PARTIES:
 Hungary
 USSR (Soviet Union)

469978   Bilateral Exchange   **16 SUGG 128**
SIGNED: 7 Jul 60
HEADNOTE: RECOGNITION
TOPIC: Recognition
PARTIES:
 Congo (Zaire)
 USSR (Soviet Union)

469979   Bilateral Exchange   **16 SUGG 128**
SIGNED: 20 Jul 60
HEADNOTE: CONSULAR ACT TAX ABOLITION
TOPIC: Consul/Citizenship
PARTIES:
 Denmark
 USSR (Soviet Union)

469980   Bilateral Exchange   **16 SUGG 128**
SIGNED: 17 Aug 60
HEADNOTE: DIPLOMATIC MAIL PROCEDURES
TOPIC: Consul/Citizenship
PARTIES:
 Guinea
 USSR (Soviet Union)

469981   Bilateral Exchange   **16 SUGG 128**
SIGNED: 18 Aug 60
HEADNOTE: RECOGNITION
TOPIC: Recognition
PARTIES:
 Cyprus
 USSR (Soviet Union)

469982   Bilateral Agreement   **16 SUGG 129**
SIGNED: 22 Sep 60
HEADNOTE: EDUCATIONAL EXCHANGE
TOPIC: Education
PARTIES:
 Bulgaria
 USSR (Soviet Union)

469983   Bilateral Agreement   **16 SUGG 129**
SIGNED: 3 Oct 60
HEADNOTE: EDUCATIONAL EXCHANGE
TOPIC: Education
PARTIES:
 Mongolia
 USSR (Soviet Union)

469984   Bilateral Exchange   **16 SUGG 129**
SIGNED: 14 Oct 60
HEADNOTE: RECOGNITION
TOPIC: Recognition
PARTIES:
 Mali
 USSR (Soviet Union)

469985   Bilateral Agreement   **16 SUGG 129**
SIGNED: 4 Nov 60
HEADNOTE: EDUCTIONAL EXCHANGE
TOPIC: Education
PARTIES:
 Hungary
 USSR (Soviet Union)

469986   Bilateral Agreement   **16 SUGG 129**
SIGNED: 8 Dec 60
HEADNOTE: EDUCTIONAL EXCHANGE
TOPIC: Education
PARTIES:
 Romania
 USSR (Soviet Union)

469987   Bilateral Agreement   **16 SUGG 130**
SIGNED: 22 Dec 60
HEADNOTE: CUSTOMS COOPERATION
TOPIC: Customs
PARTIES:
 Romania
 USSR (Soviet Union)

469988   Bilateral Exchange   **16 SUGG 130**
SIGNED: 10 Jan 61
HEADNOTE: DIPLOMATIC MAIL PROCUDURES
TOPIC: Consul/Citizenship
PARTIES:
 Tunisia
 USSR (Soviet Union)

469989   Bilateral Exchange   **16 SUGG 130**
SIGNED: 12 Jan 61
HEADNOTE: RECOGNITION
TOPIC: Recognition

PARTIES:
 Nigeria
 USSR (Soviet Union)

469990   Bilateral Exchange   **16 SUGG 130**
SIGNED: 23 Jan 61
HEADNOTE: PARCEL POST
TOPIC: Postal Service
PARTIES:
 Greece
 USSR (Soviet Union)

469991   Bilateral Agreement   **16 SUGG 130**
SIGNED: 15 Feb 61
HEADNOTE: EDUCATIONAL EXCHANGE
TOPIC: Education
PARTIES:
 Korea, North
 USSR (Soviet Union)

469992   Bilateral Exchange   **16 SUGG 131**
SIGNED: 22 Mar 61
HEADNOTE: DIPLOMATIC MAIL PROCEDURES
TOPIC: Consul/Citizenship
PARTIES:
 Iraq
 USSR (Soviet Union)

469993   Bilateral Exchange   **16 SUGG 131**
SIGNED: 17 May 61
HEADNOTE: DIPLOMATIC MAIL PROCEDURES
TOPIC: Consul/Citizenship
PARTIES:
 Mali
 USSR (Soviet Union)

469994   Bilateral Agreement   **16 SUGG 131**
SIGNED: 19 Jun 61
HEADNOTE: CONDITIONS TECHNICAL AID
TOPIC: Tech Assistance
PARTIES:
 China People's Rep
 USSR (Soviet Union)

469995   Bilateral Exchange   **16 SUGG 131**
SIGNED: 19 Jun 61
HEADNOTE: RESCINDS 12 OCT 54 & 18 JAN 58
TOPIC: General Aid
PARTIES:
 China People's Rep
 USSR (Soviet Union)

469996   Bilateral Protocol   **16 SUGG 131**
SIGNED: 2 Jul 61
HEADNOTE: SOVIET TRADE MISSION
TOPIC: General Trade
PARTIES:
 Ghana
 USSR (Soviet Union)

469997   Bilateral Exchange   **16 SUGG 132**
SIGNED: 10 Dec 61
HEADNOTE: RECOGNITION
TOPIC: Recognition
PARTIES:
 Tanganyika
 USSR (Soviet Union)

469998   Bilateral Agreement   **16 SUGG 132**
SIGNED: 17 Jan 62
HEADNOTE: USSR TECHNICAL SCHOOL INDONE-
SIANS
TOPIC: Education
PARTIES:
 Indonesia
 USSR (Soviet Union)

469999   Bilateral Exchange   **16 SUGG 132**
SIGNED: 18 Jan 62
HEADNOTE: RECOGNITION
TOPIC: Recognition
PARTIES:
 Sierra Leone
 USSR (Soviet Union)

470001 Bilateral Exchange **16 SUGG 132**
SIGNED: 1 Feb 62
HEADNOTE: ASWAN SOVIET CONSULATE
TOPIC: Consul/Citizenship
PARTIES:
  United Arab Rep
  USSR (Soviet Union)

470002 Bilateral Exchange **16 SUGG 132**
SIGNED: 28 Feb 62
HEADNOTE: DIPLOMATIC MAIL PROCEDURES
TOPIC: Consul/Citizenship
PARTIES:
  Syria
  USSR (Soviet Union)

470003 Bilateral Exchange **16 SUGG 132**
SIGNED: 10 Mar 62
HEADNOTE: DIPLOMATIC MAIL PROCEDURES
TOPIC: Consul/Citizenship
PARTIES:
  India
  USSR (Soviet Union)

470004 Bilateral Agreement **16 SUGG 132**
SIGNED: 20 Mar 62
HEADNOTE: ESTABLISH AIR SERVICE
TOPIC: Air Transport
PARTIES:
  Mali
  USSR (Soviet Union)

470005 Bilateral Exchange **16 SUGG 132**
SIGNED: 27 Mar 62
HEADNOTE: VISA TAX ABOLITION
TOPIC: Visas
PARTIES:
  New Zealand
  USSR (Soviet Union)

470006 Bilateral Exchange **16 SUGG 133**
SIGNED: 31 Mar 62
HEADNOTE: ENFORCING FISHING REGULATIONS
TOPIC: Admin Cooperation
PARTIES:
  Japan
  USSR (Soviet Union)

470007 Bilateral Exchange **16 SUGG 133**
SIGNED: 19 May 62
HEADNOTE: SURABAJA CONSULATE-GENERAL
TOPIC: Consul/Citizenship
PARTIES:
  Indonesia
  USSR (Soviet Union)

470008 Bilateral Agreement **16 SUGG 133**
SIGNED: 14 Jun 62
HEADNOTE: ESTABLISH DIPLOMATIC RELA-
TIONS
TOPIC: Consul/Citizenship
PARTIES:
  Senegal
  USSR (Soviet Union)

470009 Bilateral Exchange **16 SUGG 133**
SIGNED: 27 Jul 62
HEADNOTE: DIPLOMATIC MAIL PROCEDURES
TOPIC: Consul/Citizenship
PARTIES:
  Ghana
  USSR (Soviet Union)

470010 Bilateral Protocol **16 SUGG 134**
SIGNED: 3 Aug 62
HEADNOTE: FISHING TECHNICAL AID
TOPIC: Tech Assistance
PARTIES:
  Cuba
  USSR (Soviet Union)

470011 Bilateral Exchange **16 SUGG 134**
SIGNED: 26 Sep 62
HEADNOTE: FISHERIES COOPERATION

TOPIC: Specific Resources
PARTIES:
  Cuba
  USSR (Soviet Union)

470012 Bilateral Agreement **16 SUGG 134**
SIGNED: 10 Nov 62
HEADNOTE: RADIO BROADCAST COOPERATION
TOPIC: Mass Media
PARTIES:
  Indonesia
  USSR (Soviet Union)

470013 Bilateral Agreement **16 SUGG 134**
SIGNED: 5 Dec 62
HEADNOTE: EDUCATIONAL MATERIALS IMPORT
TOPIC: Education
PARTIES:
  Indonesia
  USSR (Soviet Union)

471014 Bilateral Exchange **0 SUST 176**
SIGNED: 18 Apr 45
HEADNOTE: ESTABLISH DIPLOMATIC RELA-
TIONS
TOPIC: Consul/Citizenship
PARTIES:
  Bolivia
  USSR (Soviet Union)

471015 Bilateral Instrument **0 SUST 176**
SIGNED: 29 Apr 45
HEADNOTE: RECOGNITION PROVISIONAL GOV-
ERNMENT
TOPIC: Recognition
PARTIES:
  Austria
  USSR (Soviet Union)

471016 Bilateral Agreement **0 SUST 177**
SIGNED: 8 May 45
HEADNOTE: TRADE
TOPIC: General Trade
PARTIES:
  Finland
  USSR (Soviet Union)

471017 Bilateral Exchange **0 SUST 188**
SIGNED: 6 Aug 45
HEADNOTE: RENEW DIPLOMATIC RELATIONS
TOPIC: Consul/Citizenship
PARTIES:
  Finland
  USSR (Soviet Union)

471018 Bilateral Exchange **0 SUST 193**
SIGNED: 16 Aug 45
HEADNOTE: RENEW DIPLOMATIC RELATIONS
TOPIC: Consul/Citizenship
PARTIES:
  Bulgaria
  USSR (Soviet Union)

471019 Bilateral Exchange **0 SUST 201**
SIGNED: 10 Nov 45
HEADNOTE: ESTABLISH DIPLOMATIC RELA-
TIONS
TOPIC: Consul/Citizenship
PARTIES:
  Albania
  USSR (Soviet Union)

471020 Bilateral Agreement **0 SUST 205**
SIGNED: 31 Dec 45
HEADNOTE: REDUCE & EXTEND REPARATIONS
TOPIC: Reparations
PARTIES:
  Finland
  USSR (Soviet Union)

471021 Bilateral Agreement **0 SUST 209**
SIGNED: 6 Apr 46
HEADNOTE: GRAIN DELIVERY TO USSR
TOPIC: Commodity Trade

PARTIES:
  France
  USSR (Soviet Union)

471022 Bilateral Agreement **0 SUST 236**
SIGNED: 23 Aug 47
HEADNOTE: EQUIPMENT ON CREDIT
TOPIC: Loans and Credits
PARTIES:
  Bulgaria
  USSR (Soviet Union)

471023 Bilateral Agreement **0 SUST 240**
SIGNED: 11 Dec 47
HEADNOTE: SHORT-TERM CREDIT
TOPIC: Loans and Credits
PARTIES:
  Czechoslovakia
  USSR (Soviet Union)

471024 Bilateral Agreement **0 SUST 240**
SIGNED: 11 Dec 47
HEADNOTE: TRADE & PAYMENTS
TOPIC: General Economic
PARTIES:
  Czechoslovakia
  USSR (Soviet Union)

471025 Bilateral Agreement **0 SUST 247**
SIGNED: 1 Apr 48
HEADNOTE: TRADE FOR 1948
TOPIC: General Trade
PARTIES:
  Bulgaria
  USSR (Soviet Union)

471026 Bilateral Agreement **0 SUST 252**
SIGNED: 3 Sep 48
HEADNOTE: TRADE
TOPIC: General Trade
PARTIES:
  Albania
  USSR (Soviet Union)

471027 Bilateral Agreement **0 SUST 252**
SIGNED: 3 Sep 48
HEADNOTE: TRADE CREDIT
TOPIC: Loans and Credits
PARTIES:
  Albania
  USSR (Soviet Union)

471028 Bilateral Agreement **0 SUST 255**
SIGNED: 11 Dec 48
HEADNOTE: TRADE
TOPIC: General Trade
PARTIES:
  Italy
  USSR (Soviet Union)

471029 Bilateral Agreement **0 SUST 256**
SIGNED: 17 Dec 48
HEADNOTE: TRADE FOR 1949
TOPIC: General Trade
PARTIES:
  Finland
  USSR (Soviet Union)

471030 Bilateral Agreement **0 SUST 135**
SIGNED: 12 Jun 61
HEADNOTE: TRADE
TOPIC: General Trade
PARTIES:
  Togo
  USSR (Soviet Union)

486001 Bilateral Exchange **13 UST 948**
SIGNED: 9 Feb 62
HEADNOTE: GATT COMPENSATORY CONCES-
SION
TOPIC: General Trade
PARTIES:
  Japan
  USA (United States)

486002   Bilateral Exchange   **16 UST 657**
SIGNED: 2 Apr 65
HEADNOTE: FUNCTIONS RYUKYU COMMITTEE
TOPIC: IGO Operations
PARTIES:
 Japan
 USA (United States)

486004   Bilateral Exchange   **18 UST 1309**
SIGNED: 9 May 67
HEADNOTE: FISHERIES US COAST
TOPIC: Specific Resources
PARTIES:
 Japan
 USA (United States)

486005   Bilateral Exchange   **18 UST 1678**
SIGNED: 8 Aug 67
HEADNOTE: RETURN 7 LOAN VESSELS
TOPIC: Milit Assistance
PARTIES:
 Japan
 USA (United States)

486006   Bilateral Exchange   **18 UST 2804**
SIGNED: 13 Dec 67
HEADNOTE: HAWK & NIKE PRODUCTION
TOPIC: Milit Assistance
PARTIES:
 Japan
 USA (United States)

486007   Bilateral Exchange   **19 UST 4419**
SIGNED: 12 Jan 68
HEADNOTE: COTTON TEXTILES
TOPIC: Commodity Trade
PARTIES:
 Japan
 USA (United States)

486009   Bilateral Exchange   **19 UST 6011**
SIGNED: 2 Sep 68
HEADNOTE: SATELLITE TRACKING OKINAWA
TOPIC: Scientific Project
PARTIES:
 Japan
 USA (United States)

486011   Bilateral Exchange   **20 UST 545**
SIGNED: 4 Apr 69
HEADNOTE: F-43J AIRCRAFT PRODUCTION
TOPIC: Milit Installation
PARTIES:
 Japan
 USA (United States)

486012   Bilateral Exchange   **20 UST 2720**
SIGNED: 31 Jul 69
HEADNOTE: PEACEFUL SPACE USE COOPER-
ATION
TOPIC: Scientific Project
PARTIES:
 Japan
 USA (United States)

486013   Bilateral Exchange   **21 UST 473**
SIGNED: 3 Mar 70
HEADNOTE: PREPAR COMMISSION OKINAWA
TOPIC: IGO Operations
PARTIES:
 Japan
 USA (United States)

486014   Bilateral Exchange   **21 UST 1167**
SIGNED: 1 May 70
HEADNOTE: ABOLITION RYUKYU COMMITTEE
TOPIC: IGO Operations
PARTIES:
 Japan
 USA (United States)

487003   Bilateral Exchange   **0 TIAS 6170**
SIGNED: 19 Sep 66
HEADNOTE: SATELLITE OBSERVATION KANOYA

TOPIC: Scientific Project
PARTIES:
 Japan
 USA (United States)

487008   Bilateral Exchange   **0 TIAS 6442**
SIGNED: 19 Jan 68
HEADNOTE: ADVISORY COMMITTEE RYUKYU
TOPIC: Military Mission
PARTIES:
 Japan
 USA (United States)

487010   Bilateral Exchange   **0 TIAS 6600**
SIGNED: 23 Dec 68
HEADNOTE: SALMON FISHING US COAST
TOPIC: Specific Resources
PARTIES:
 Japan
 USA (United States)

487015   Bilateral Exchange   **0 TIAS 7019**
SIGNED: 11 Dec 70
HEADNOTE: CRAB EASTERN BERING SEA
TOPIC: Specific Resources
PARTIES:
 Japan
 USA (United States)

487016   Bilateral Exchange   **0 TIAS 7020**
SIGNED: 11 Dec 70
HEADNOTE: FISHERIES US COAST
TOPIC: Specific Resources
PARTIES:
 Japan
 USA (United States)

487017   Bilateral Exchange   **0 TIAS 7021**
SIGNED: 11 Dec 70
HEADNOTE: SALMON FISHING US COAST
TOPIC: Specific Resources
PARTIES:
 Japan
 USA (United States)

496001   Bilateral Convention   **0 VKNG 9**
SIGNED: 30 May 50
HEADNOTE: HANOI UNIVERSITY SCHOOL
TOPIC: Education
PARTIES:
 France
 Vietnam, South

496002   Bilateral Convention   **0 VKNG 10**
SIGNED: 15 Jun 50
HEADNOTE: ARCHIVE & LIBRARY SERVICE
TOPIC: Education
PARTIES:
 France
 Vietnam, South

496003   Bilateral Convention   **0 VKNG 11**
SIGNED: 16 Jun 50
HEADNOTE: MERCHANT MARINE
TOPIC: Water Transport
PARTIES:
 France
 Vietnam, South

496004   Bilateral Exchange   **0 VKNG 13**
SIGNED: 17 Jun 50
HEADNOTE: MIXED ADMINISTRATIVE TRIBUNAL
TOPIC: IGO Establishment
PARTIES:
 France
 Vietnam, South

496005   Bilateral Convention   **0 VKNG 25**
SIGNED: 12 Mar 51
HEADNOTE: PROPERTY HANOI SCHOOL SYSTEM
TOPIC: Specific Property
PARTIES:
 France
 Vietnam, South

496006   Bilateral Convention   **0 VKNG 41**
SIGNED: 8 Feb 52
HEADNOTE: PASTEUR INSTITUTE HANOI
TOPIC: Education
PARTIES:
 France
 Vietnam, South

496007   Bilateral Convention   **0 VKNG 45**
SIGNED: 26 May 52
HEADNOTE: RAIL LINES TRANSFER
TOPIC: Land Transport
PARTIES:
 France
 Vietnam, South

496008   Bilateral Convention   **0 VKNG 47**
SIGNED: 7 Jun 52
HEADNOTE: OCEANOGRAPHIC INSTITUTE NHA
TRANG
TOPIC: Education
PARTIES:
 France
 Vietnam, South

496009   Bilateral Agreement   **0 VKNG 48**
SIGNED: 12 Jun 52
HEADNOTE: PROCEDURE APPLICATION PEACE
TREATY
TOPIC: Dispute Settlement
PARTIES:
 Japan
 Vietnam, South

496010   Bilateral Agreement   **0 VKNG 52**
SIGNED: 28 Jan 53
HEADNOTE: BASIC AGREEMENT
TOPIC: Tech Assistance
PARTIES:
 FAO (Food Agri)
 Vietnam, South

496011   Bilateral Protocol   **0 VKNG 53**
SIGNED: 9 May 53
HEADNOTE: TRANSFER MILITARY TASKS
TOPIC: General Military
PARTIES:
 France
 Vietnam, South

496012   Bilateral Instrument   **0 VKNG 56**
SIGNED: 29 May 53
HEADNOTE: BELGO-LUXEMBOURG TRADE
TOPIC: General Trade
PARTIES:
 Belgium
 Vietnam, South

496013   Bilateral Convention   **0 VKNG 59**
SIGNED: 9 Jul 53
HEADNOTE: HANOI GENERAL LIBRARY
TOPIC: Education
PARTIES:
 France
 Vietnam, South

496014   Bilateral Convention   **0 VKNG 62**
SIGNED: 19 Oct 53
HEADNOTE: FRENCH RAIL ADMINISTRATIVE SER-
VICE
TOPIC: Admin Cooperation
PARTIES:
 France
 Vietnam, South

496015   Bilateral Agreement   **0 VKNG 63**
SIGNED: 14 Nov 53
HEADNOTE: TRADE
TOPIC: General Trade
PARTIES:
 Italy
 Vietnam, South

496016   Bilateral Agreement   **0 VKNG 64**
SIGNED: 14 Nov 53
HEADNOTE: TRADE
TOPIC: General Trade
PARTIES:
  Netherlands
  Vietnam, South

496017   Bilateral Agreement   **0 VKNG 66**
SIGNED: 10 Dec 53
HEADNOTE: TRADE
TOPIC: General Trade
PARTIES:
  Germany, West
  Vietnam, South

496018   Bilateral Protocol   **0 VKNG 67**
SIGNED: 5 Apr 54
HEADNOTE: FRENCH ISSUE VIETNAM PASS-
  PORTS
TOPIC: Admin Cooperation
PARTIES:
  France
  Vietnam, South

496019   Bilateral Treaty   **0 VKNG 68**
SIGNED: 4 Jun 54
HEADNOTE: VIETNAM INDEPENDENCE & ASSOCI-
  ATION
TOPIC: General Amity
PARTIES:
  France
  Vietnam, South

496020   Bilateral Agreement   **0 VKNG 72**
SIGNED: 20 Jul 54
HEADNOTE: GENEVA ACCORDS INDOCHINA
TOPIC: Peace/Disarmament
PARTIES:
  France
  Vietnam, South

496021   Bilateral Agreement   **0 VKNG 74**
SIGNED: 20 Aug 54
HEADNOTE: PRIVATE RELIEF AGENCIES
TOPIC: Humanitarian
PARTIES:
  USA (United States)
  Vietnam, South

496022   Bilateral Agreement   **0 VKNG 81**
SIGNED: 4 Oct 54
HEADNOTE: EXCHANGE OFFICIAL PUBLICA-
  TIONS
TOPIC: Admin Cooperation
PARTIES:
  Australia
  Vietnam, South

496023   Bilateral Convention   **0 VKNG 85**
SIGNED: 29 Dec 54
HEADNOTE: SAIGON PORT USE
TOPIC: Water Transport
PARTIES:
  Cambodia
  Vietnam, South

496024   Bilateral Convention   **0 VKNG 85**
SIGNED: 30 Dec 54
HEADNOTE: TRADE & PAYMENTS
TOPIC: General Economic
PARTIES:
  France
  Vietnam, South

496025   Bilateral Convention   **0 VKNG 85**
SIGNED: 30 Dec 54
HEADNOTE: PAYMENT FRENCH MILITARY COSTS
TOPIC: Status of Forces
PARTIES:
  France
  Vietnam, South

496026   Bilateral Convention   **0 VKNG 85**
SIGNED: 29 Dec 54
HEADNOTE: SAIGON PORT USE
TOPIC: Water Transport
PARTIES:
  Laos
  Vietnam, South

496027   Bilateral Protocol   **0 VKNG 91**
SIGNED: 11 May 55
HEADNOTE: HANOI UNIVERSITY TRANSFER
TOPIC: Education
PARTIES:
  France
  Vietnam, South

496028   Bilateral Convention   **0 VKNG 92**
SIGNED: 15 May 55
HEADNOTE: MILITARY RAIL TARIFF
TOPIC: Status of Forces
PARTIES:
  France
  Vietnam, South

496029   Bilateral Protocol   **0 VKNG 94**
SIGNED: 13 Jun 55
HEADNOTE: TRANSFER NHATRANG AIRBASE
TOPIC: Milit Installation
PARTIES:
  France
  Vietnam, South

496030   Bilateral Protocol   **0 VKNG 95**
SIGNED: 20 Jun 55
HEADNOTE: HUE & NHA TRANG AIRPORTS
TOPIC: Air Transport
PARTIES:
  France
  Vietnam, South

496031   Bilateral Convention   **0 VKNG 98**
SIGNED: 17 Aug 55
HEADNOTE: FRENCH & VIETNAMESE TREASU-
  RIES
TOPIC: Finance
PARTIES:
  France
  Vietnam, South

496032   Bilateral Agreement   **0 VKNG 100**
SIGNED: 22 Aug 55
HEADNOTE: PAYMENTS
TOPIC: Finance
PARTIES:
  Cambodia
  Vietnam, South

496033   Bilateral Exchange   **0 VKNG 104**
SIGNED: 5 Apr 56
HEADNOTE: RADIO PROGRAMS
TOPIC: Mass Media
PARTIES:
  France
  Vietnam, South

496034   Bilateral Protocol   **0 VKNG 109**
SIGNED: 14 Jul 56
HEADNOTE: LIAISON INTERNATIONAL CONTROL
  COMMISSION
TOPIC: Consul/Citizenship
PARTIES:
  France
  Vietnam, South

496035   Bilateral Protocol   **0 VKNG 110**
SIGNED: 28 Jul 56
HEADNOTE: TRANSFER TOURANE AIRPORT
TOPIC: Air Transport
PARTIES:
  France
  Vietnam, South

496036   Bilateral Agreement   **0 VKNG 122**
SIGNED: 15 Aug 57

HEADNOTE: CERTIFICATE ORIGIN EXPORT TO US
TOPIC: Admin Cooperation
PARTIES:
  USA (United States)
  Vietnam, South

496037   Bilateral Convention   **0 VKNG 130**
SIGNED: 10 Sep 58
HEADNOTE: PURCHASE FRENCH-OWNED RICE
TOPIC: Finance
PARTIES:
  France
  Vietnam, South

496038   Bilateral Agreement   **0 VKNG 131**
SIGNED: 12 Sep 58
HEADNOTE: METEOROLOGICAL SERVICES
TOPIC: Admin Cooperation
PARTIES:
  Laos
  Vietnam, South

496039   Bilateral Exchange   **0 VKNG 135**
SIGNED: 9 Mar 59
HEADNOTE: PALUDISME PROJECT
TOPIC: Sanitation
PARTIES:
  WHO (World Health)
  Vietnam, South

496040   Bilateral Agreement   **0 VKNG 141**
SIGNED: 27 May 59
HEADNOTE: TECHNICAL APPRENTICESHIP
TOPIC: Education
PARTIES:
  Germany, West
  Vietnam, South

496041   Bilateral Convention   **0 VKNG 143**
SIGNED: 11 Jun 59
HEADNOTE: GENERAL RELATIONS
TOPIC: General Amity
PARTIES:
  Laos
  Vietnam, South

496042   Bilateral Agreement   **0 VKNG 146**
SIGNED: 18 Sep 59
HEADNOTE: COMMODITY AID
TOPIC: Direct Aid
PARTIES:
  Canada
  Vietnam, South

496043   Bilateral Convention   **0 VKNG 151**
SIGNED: 29 Sep 59
HEADNOTE: AGRICULTURAL STUDY MY-PHUOC
TOPIC: Scientific Project
PARTIES:
  France
  Vietnam, South

496044   Bilateral Protocol   **0 VKNG 153**
SIGNED: 14 Nov 59
HEADNOTE: ECONOMIC & FINANCIAL COOPER-
  ATION
TOPIC: General Economic
PARTIES:
  France
  Vietnam, South

496045   Bilateral Agreement   **0 VKNG 153**
SIGNED: 24 Mar 60
HEADNOTE: ECONOMIC & FINANCIAL COOPER-
  ATION
TOPIC: General Economic
PARTIES:
  France
  Vietnam, South

496046   Bilateral Agreement   **0 VKNG 154**
SIGNED: 29 Apr 60
HEADNOTE: ASSISTANCE
TOPIC: Direct Aid

PARTIES:
UN Special Fund
Vietnam, South

496047   Bilateral Agreement   **0 VKNG 159**
SIGNED: 28 Jan 61
HEADNOTE: PEACEFUL USE ATOMIC ENERGY
TOPIC: Atomic Energy
PARTIES:
France
Vietnam, South

496048   Bilateral Exchange   **0 VKNG 160**
SIGNED: 11 Feb 61
HEADNOTE: BOOKS & FILMS FOR VIETNAM
TOPIC: Culture
PARTIES:
France
Vietnam, South

496049   Bilateral Agreement   **0 VKNG 168**
SIGNED: 28 May 62
HEADNOTE: AGRI COMMOD
TOPIC: US Agri Commod Aid
PARTIES:
USA (United States)
Vietnam, South

496050   Bilateral Convention   **0 VKNG 170**
SIGNED: 10 Aug 61
HEADNOTE: COTTON EXPERIMENT
TOPIC: Tech Assistance
PARTIES:
France
Vietnam, South

496051   Bilateral Exchange   **0 VKNG 171**
SIGNED: 10 Aug 61
HEADNOTE: COTTON PILOT PROJECT
TOPIC: Tech Assistance
PARTIES:
Germany, West
Vietnam, South

496052   Bilateral Exchange   **0 VKNG 172**
SIGNED: 25 Sep 61
HEADNOTE: $100,000 FLOUR COLOMBO PLAN
TOPIC: Direct Aid
PARTIES:
Canada
Vietnam, South

496053   Bilateral Instrument   **0 VKNG 178**
SIGNED: 19 Aug 63
HEADNOTE: LEASE NUCLEAR MATERIAL
TOPIC: Atomic Energy
PARTIES:
USA (United States)
Vietnam, South

496054   Bilateral Exchange   **0 VKNG 184**
SIGNED: 22 Nov 62
HEADNOTE: STUDENT SOCIAL SECURITY
TOPIC: Education
PARTIES:
France
Vietnam, South

496055   Bilateral Agreement   **0 VKNG 187**
SIGNED: 19 Dec 62
HEADNOTE: TRADE
TOPIC: General Trade
PARTIES:
Korea, South
Vietnam, South

496056   Bilateral Convention   **0 VKNG 190**
SIGNED: 15 May 63
HEADNOTE: FRENCH RAIL ADMINISTRATIVE SER-
VICE
TOPIC: Admin Cooperation
PARTIES:
France
Vietnam, South

496057   Bilateral Exchange   **0 VKNG 191**
SIGNED: 22 May 63
HEADNOTE: TRANSFER FAR EAST SCHOOL
TOPIC: Specific Property
PARTIES:
France
Vietnam, South

496058   Bilateral Agreement   **0 VKNG 192**
SIGNED: 19 Jul 63
HEADNOTE: FINANCIAL & TECHNICAL AID
TOPIC: Direct Aid
PARTIES:
Germany, West
Vietnam, South

496059   Bilateral Agreement   **0 VKNG 194**
SIGNED: 4 Dec 63
HEADNOTE: 15 MILLION MARKS CREDIT
TOPIC: Loans and Credits
PARTIES:
Germany, West
Vietnam, South

496060   Bilateral Exchange   **0 VKNG 208**
SIGNED: 11 Jan 65
HEADNOTE: CONTROL BORDER WATERS
TOPIC: Specific Resources
PARTIES:
Japan
Vietnam, South

496061   Bilateral Agreement   **0 VKNG 216**
SIGNED: 24 Apr 65
HEADNOTE: CONTROL TERRITORAL WATERS
TOPIC: Specific Resources
PARTIES:
USA (United States)
Vietnam, South

496062   Bilateral Agreement   **0 VKNG 235**
SIGNED: 10 May 66
HEADNOTE: TRADE
TOPIC: General Trade
PARTIES:
Tunisia
Vietnam, South

496063   Bilateral Agreement   **0 VKNG 237**
SIGNED: 28 Jun 66
HEADNOTE: FINANCIAL AID
TOPIC: Direct Aid
PARTIES:
Germany, West
Vietnam, South

496064   Bilateral Agreement   **0 VKNG 238**
SIGNED: 19 Aug 66
HEADNOTE: AIR SERVICES
TOPIC: Air Transport
PARTIES:
Taiwan
Vietnam, South

496065   Bilateral Agreement   **0 VKNG 240**
SIGNED: 16 Jan 67
HEADNOTE: CLAIMS
TOPIC: Claims and Debts
PARTIES:
Korea, South
Vietnam, South

496066   Bilateral Agreement   **0 VKNG 241**
SIGNED: 16 Jan 67
HEADNOTE: AIR SERVICES
TOPIC: Air Transport
PARTIES:
Korea, South
Vietnam, South

496067   Bilateral Agreement   **0 VKNG 244**
SIGNED: 13 Mar 67
HEADNOTE: AGRI COMMOD
TOPIC: US Agri Commod Aid

PARTIES:
USA (United States)
Vietnam, South

496068   Bilateral Agreement   **0 VKNG 246**
SIGNED: 3 May 67
HEADNOTE: VIETNAM TAX US GOVERNMENT EM-
PLOYEES
TOPIC: Taxation
PARTIES:
USA (United States)
Vietnam, South

496069   Bilateral Agreement   **0 VKNG 251**
SIGNED: 29 Jun 67
HEADNOTE: SAIGON POWER COMPANY GRANT
TOPIC: Direct Aid
PARTIES:
USA (United States)
Vietnam, South

496070   Bilateral Exchange   **0 VKNG 252**
SIGNED: 18 Sep 67
HEADNOTE: REPATRIATE VIETNAM REFUGEES
TOPIC: Refugees
PARTIES:
Thailand
Vietnam, South

496071   Bilateral Agreement   **0 VKNG 255**
SIGNED: 4 Oct 67
HEADNOTE: BONDED WAREHOUSE SALES
TOPIC: Finance
PARTIES:
Korea, South
Vietnam, South

496072   Bilateral Exchange   **0 VKNG 278**
SIGNED: 27 Nov 68
HEADNOTE: TRAFFIC RIGHTS CATHAY AIRWAYS
TOPIC: Air Transport
PARTIES:
UK Great Britain
Vietnam, South

496073   Bilateral Agreement   **0 VKNG 281**
SIGNED: 9 Nov 68
HEADNOTE: US PROPERTY IN VIETNAM UNITS
TOPIC: Status of Forces
PARTIES:
USA (United States)
Vietnam, South

496075   Bilateral Exchange   **0 VKNG 311**
SIGNED: 20 Jan 70
HEADNOTE: RICE PURCHASE IN US
TOPIC: Commodity Trade
PARTIES:
USA (United States)
Vietnam, South

496076   Bilateral Agreement   **0 VKNG 312**
SIGNED: 13 Jan 70
HEADNOTE: AIR SERVICES
TOPIC: Air Transport
PARTIES:
Thailand
Vietnam, South

496077   Bilateral Exchange   **0 VKNG 314**
SIGNED: 12 Feb 70
HEADNOTE: INVESTMENT GUARANTEE
TOPIC: Claims and Debts
PARTIES:
USA (United States)
Vietnam, South

496078   Bilateral Agreement   **0 VKNG 315**
SIGNED: 17 Feb 70
HEADNOTE: AGRI COMMOD
TOPIC: US Agri Commod Aid
PARTIES:
USA (United States)
Vietnam, South

496079   Bilateral Agreement   0 VKNG 316
SIGNED: 7 Mar 70
HEADNOTE: AGRICULTURAL FACULTY CAN-THO
  UNIVERSITY
TOPIC: Tech Assistance
PARTIES:
  Japan
  Vietnam, South

496080   Bilateral Agreement   0 VKNG 319
SIGNED: 15 Dec 66
HEADNOTE: AGRI COMMOD
TOPIC: US Agri Commod Aid
PARTIES:
  USA (United States)
  Vietnam, South

496081   Bilateral Exchange   0 VKNG 323
SIGNED: 31 Oct 64
HEADNOTE: KOREAN ASSISTANCE
TOPIC: Milit Assistance
PARTIES:
  Korea, South
  Vietnam, South

496082   Bilateral Exchange   0 VKNG 326
SIGNED: 20 May 70
HEADNOTE: HOUSING FOR REFUGEES
TOPIC: Refugees
PARTIES:
  Japan
  Vietnam, South

496083   Bilateral Agreement   0 VKNG 327
SIGNED: 15 May 70
HEADNOTE: AGRI COMMOD
TOPIC: US Agri Commod Aid
PARTIES:
  USA (United States)
  Vietnam, South

496084   Bilateral Agreement   0 VKNG 332
SIGNED: 27 May 70
HEADNOTE: ESTABLISH DIPLOMATIC RELA-
  TIONS
TOPIC: Consul/Citizenship
PARTIES:
  Cambodia
  Vietnam, South

496085   Bilateral Agreement   0 VKNG 333
SIGNED: 27 May 70
HEADNOTE: ECONOMIC & FINANCIAL COOPER-
  ATION
TOPIC: General Economic
PARTIES:
  Cambodia
  Vietnam, South

496086   Bilateral Agreement   0 VKNG 334
SIGNED: 27 May 70
HEADNOTE: VIETNAM NATIONALS IN CAMBODIA
TOPIC: Consul/Citizenship
PARTIES:
  Cambodia
  Vietnam, South

496087   Bilateral Agreement   0 VKNG 337
SIGNED: 4 Jun 70
HEADNOTE: ECONOMIC & TECHNICAL COOPER-
  ATION
TOPIC: General Economic
PARTIES:
  Korea, South
  Vietnam, South

496088   Bilateral Exchange   0 VKNG 339
SIGNED: 9 Jun 70
HEADNOTE: 1967 INTERNATIONAL GRAINS AR-
  RANGEMENT
TOPIC: Direct Aid
PARTIES:
  Japan
  Vietnam, South

496089   Bilateral Exchange   0 VKNG 351
SIGNED: 20 Jul 70
HEADNOTE: AIR SERVICES & RIGHTS
TOPIC: Air Transport
PARTIES:
  UK Great Britain
  Vietnam, South

496090   Bilateral Exchange   0 VKNG 361
SIGNED: 17 Oct 70
HEADNOTE: RESTORE DANHIM POWER STATION
TOPIC: Direct Aid
PARTIES:
  Japan
  Vietnam, South

496091   Bilateral Agreement   0 VKNG 366
SIGNED: 16 Dec 70
HEADNOTE: DIESEL PLANT PROJECT SAIGON
TOPIC: Direct Aid
PARTIES:
  Japan
  Vietnam, South

496092   Bilateral Agreement   0 VKNG 368
SIGNED: 10 Dec 70
HEADNOTE: AIR SERVICES
TOPIC: Air Transport
PARTIES:
  Malaysia
  Vietnam, South

496093   Bilateral Agreement   0 VKNG 370
SIGNED: 22 Jan 71
HEADNOTE: MULTIPLE MUTUAL RELATIONS
TOPIC: General Amity
PARTIES:
  Cambodia
  Vietnam, South

496094   Bilateral Agreement   0 VKNG 377
SIGNED: 30 Mar 71
HEADNOTE: PRIVILEGES JAPANESE OTCA
TOPIC: Privil/Immunities
PARTIES:
  Japan
  Vietnam, South

496095   Bilateral Agreement   0 VKNG 381
SIGNED: 16 Dec 70

HEADNOTE: FISHERIES PROJECT
TOPIC: Loans and Credits
PARTIES:
  Asian Devel Bank
  Vietnam, South

496096   Bilateral Agreement   0 VKNG 382
SIGNED: 4 Jun 71
HEADNOTE: CUSTOMS FRAUDS
TOPIC: Customs
PARTIES:
  Cambodia
  Vietnam, South

496097   Bilateral Agreement   0 VKNG 383
SIGNED: 4 Jun 71
HEADNOTE: BORDER TRANSIT
TOPIC: Visas
PARTIES:
  Cambodia
  Vietnam, South

496098   Bilateral Agreement   0 VKNG 384
SIGNED: 4 Jun 70
HEADNOTE: ECONOMIC & TECHNICAL COOPER-
  ATION
TOPIC: General Economic
PARTIES:
  Korea, South
  Vietnam, South

496099   Bilateral Agreement   0 VKNG 387
SIGNED: 2 Jul 71
HEADNOTE: ESTAB DIPLOMATIC RELATIONS
TOPIC: Consul/Citizenship
PARTIES:
  Chad
  Vietnam, South

496100   Bilateral Exchange   0 VKNG 389
SIGNED: 18 Sep 71
HEADNOTE: CANTHO   THERMAL   POWER
  PROJECT
TOPIC: Direct Aid
PARTIES:
  Japan
  Vietnam, South

496101   Bilateral Exchange   0 VKNG 391
SIGNED: 2 Oct 71
HEADNOTE: ADDITION TO DANHIM PROJECT
TOPIC: Direct Aid
PARTIES:
  Japan
  Vietnam, South

496102   Bilateral Exchange   0 VKNG 394
SIGNED: 27 Nov 71
HEADNOTE: BIEN-HOA ORPHANS CENTER
TOPIC: Direct Aid
PARTIES:
  Japan
  Vietnam, South

496103   Bilateral Exchange   0 VKNG 397
SIGNED: 24 Dec 71
HEADNOTE: EQUIPMENT CHO-RAY HOSPITAL
TOPIC: Direct Aid
PARTIES:
  Japan
  Vietnam, South